TEXAS ALMANAC

2022–2023

Texas State Historical Association   71st Edition

TEXAS ALMANAC
2022–2023

MANAGING EDITOR
Rosie Hatch

ASSOCIATE EDITOR
Rachel Kaelin

ASSISTANT EDITOR
John Willis

COVER DESIGN
Joel Phillips

PAINTING ON COVER
Michele Newton

ISBN (hardcover) 978-1-62511-066-4
ISBN (flexbound) 978-1-62511-067-1
ISBN (ebook) 978-1-62511-068-8

Library of Congress ISSN: 2378-2188 (Print)
Library of Congress ISSN: 2378-2234 (Digital)

Copyright © 2022

TEXAS STATE HISTORICAL ASSOCIATION

The University of Texas at Austin
3001 Lake Austin Blvd., Suite 3.116, Austin, TX 78703; (512) 471-2600
TSHAonline.org and LegacyofTexas.com

Printed in Dallas, Texas, by Taylor Specialty Books
Bound in San Antonio by Universal Bindery
For permission requests, contact **Rosie.Hatch@TSHAonline.org**.

Distributed by Texas A&M University Press and the Texas Book Consortium
4354 TAMU, College Station, Texas, 77843-4354

Order hardcover or flexbound editions at **(800) 826-8911**
or online at www.tamupress.com

TexasAlmanac.com

PREFACE

Welcome to the *Texas Almanac 2022–2023*. I hope the past two years have treated you kindly.

We've got three terrific new features this year. You'll find the first one, "Texas Wildlife," on page 75. Dr. Travis LaDuc and Dr. Drew Davis expand on our usual list of mammals with descriptions and lists of many of the fishes, reptiles, amphibians, and birds you'll see in Texas. The second feature is "African American Texans" by Dr. Merline Pitre on page 536. It covers the long history of Black Texans and their many contributions to our culture.

Our last feature was a late addition to the book, but one we couldn't ignore. "COVID-19 Pandemic in Texas 2020–2021" by Dr. Ana Martinez-Catsum will give you the details of how the virus hit our state and the impact it had on our economy, society, and politics. There's also a table that compares our current pandemic to the last one: the Spanish influenza that hit the world hard in 1918. Read all about it, starting on page 563.

Thanks as always to everyone at the TSHA, the board of directors, our members, and my amazing team: Rachel Kaelin and John Willis.

I hope you enjoy the book!

Rosie Hatch
Managing Editor, Texas Almanac

126th TSHA Annual Meeting
February 24-26, 2022
AT&T Hotel and Conference Center in Austin, Tx

The largest gathering of its kind for the Texas history community. Join us for three days of sessions on the latest research in the field. Enjoy networking, events, and professional development that will expand your knowledge, energize you, and help you to deepen your connections with the state's extraordinary past.

FOR MORE INFORMATION: https://am.tsha.events

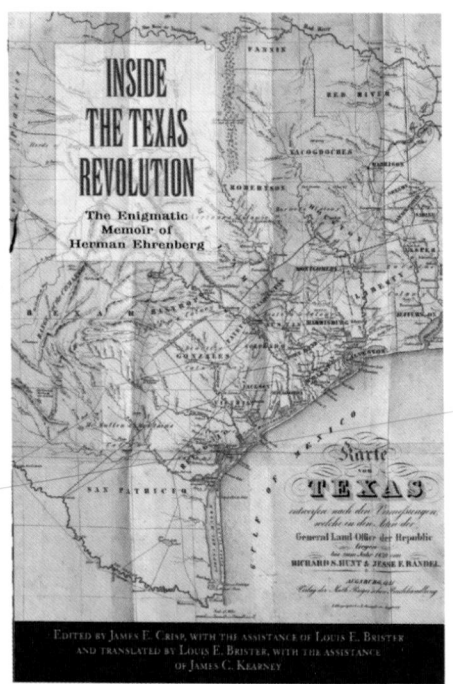

Patrick Cox

*P*ublished by the Texas State Historical Association (TSHA), the *Texas Almanac* is a wealth of information on the state's people, culture, history, landmarks, government, business, science, education, and much more. Since 1857, the *Texas Almanac* has served as an invaluable, engaging, and popular publication. A full history of the *Texas Almanac* and many early editions can be found in the *Handbook of Texas Online*; www.tshaonline.org.

TSHA focuses our efforts on two important areas: historical publications and education programs. TSHA is the oldest learned society in our state. Organized in Austin on March 2, 1897, the founders of TSHA brought lay and professional historians together to document and celebrate our state's multifaceted history.

Today, TSHA follows the path laid out by its founders, sharing our rich Texas history with stories of events and people from all walks of life. People and organizations across the state, nation, and globe rely on TSHA for accurate and substantive information. The *Texas Almanac*, the *Southwestern Historical Quarterly*, the *Handbook of Texas* and all TSHA's publications follow the tenets, methods and practices advocated by the professional historical community.

Importantly, we are involved with educators and students throughout the state who are enthusiastically engaged in these initiatives: Texas History Day, Texas History Challenge, Teaching Texas, Junior Historians of Texas, and the Walter Prescott Webb Historical Society.

I have many vintage volumes of the *Texas Almanac* in my personal library. Combined with the modern editions, this historic publication provides a wealth of information about Texas and how we have evolved over the years. On behalf of the TSHA members and staff, we invite everyone to know more about this special place we call Texas.

We proudly present the latest edition of the *Texas Almanac 2022-2023*.

Patrick Cox, Ph.D.
Texas State Historical Association President, 2021–2022

TSHA
Texas State Historical Association
An Independent Nonprofit Since 1897

Organized in Austin on March 2, 1897, the Texas State Historical Association is the oldest learned society in the state. Its mission is to "foster the appreciation, understanding, and teaching of the rich and unique history of Texas and, by example and through programs and activities, encourage and promote research, preservation, and publication of historical material affecting the state of Texas." The association's publications include the *Southwestern Historical Quarterly*, more than 150 scholarly books, the *Texas Almanac*, and the well-known *Handbook of Texas Online*. The online Handbook, the nation's preeminent state history encyclopedia, attracts 400,000 visitors per month from more than 200 countries and territories around the world. Through its varied education programs, the Association directly serves more than 50,000 elementary through college-aged students each year, while indirectly reaching an additional 86,000 through its teacher training opportunities.

TSHA Board of Directors, 2021–2022

Officers

Patrick Cox
Wimberley . . . . President

R. Lance Lolley
Austin. . . . . First Vice President and Treasurer

Nancy Baker Jones
Austin. . . . . Second Vice President

Sean P. Cunningham
Lubbock . . . . (2020–2023) Secretary

Mary Margaret McAllen
San Antonio . . . . Past President

Emilio Zamora
Austin. . . . . Past President

Board Members

H. Scott Caven Jr.
Houston . . . .(2019–2022)

Stephanie Cole
Arlington . . . .(2021–2024)

Carlos R. Hamilton, Jr.
Houston . . . .(2021–2024)

Kent R. Hance
Austin . . . .(2019–2022)

Larry Ketchersid
Austin . . . .(2021–2024)

Andrew J. Torget
Denton . . . .(2019–2022)

Alan Tully
Austin . . . .(2019–2022)

Joan Marshall
Galveston . . . .(2020–2023)

W.W. Whit Jones III
Corpus Christi. . . . .(2020–2023)

Ricardo Romo
San Antonio . . . .(2020–2023)

Stephanie Cole
Arlington. . . . .(2021–2024)

George Diaz
McAllen . . . .(2021–2022)

Larry Ketchersid
Austin. . . . .(2021–2024)

Gene Preuss
Houston . . . .(2021–2024)

Bernadette Pruitt
Huntsville . . . .(2021–2024)

Ken Wise
Humble. . . . .(2021–2024)

Heather Wooten
Houston . . . . Chief Executive Officer

Walter L. Buenger
Bryan . . . . .Chief Historian, Honorary Life Board Member

J. P. Bryan
Houston . . . . Honorary Life Board Member

John W. Crain
Dallas. . . . . Honorary Life Board Member

Stephen C. Cook
Houston . . . . Honorary Life Board Member

*G*reetings,

As the 48th Governor of the great state of Texas, it is my honor to welcome you to the 2022-2023 edition of the *Texas Almanac*, the premier reference for everything Texas.

Texas is the Lone Star State for a reason: We stand apart as a model for the nation. Jobs are growing here, businesses are growing here, and families are growing here. In fact, Texas is growing faster than the nation, and more than eight in 10 who are born here stay here.

Now the 9th-largest economy when compared to the nations of the world, the Texas of today was built on the bold ideas of those who came before us. Men and women who dared to

GREG ABBOTT
Governor of Texas

explore the vast new frontier pulled themselves up by their own bootstraps and made a living from the bounty of the land. They innovated, invested, and persevered. And they built an even bigger Texas of tomorrow for the generations yet to come.

I invite you to explore the pages that follow to learn more about the rich and storied history of the Lone Star State and its people, government, economics, natural resources, holidays, diverse cultures, education, recreation, the arts and so much more. Texas is big, and each of our 254 counties has something unique to offer – as do the featured articles in this edition.

If you're not in Texas right now, we invite you to come visit for a while. We're making history every day.

First Lady Cecilia Abbott joins me in thanking the Texas State Historical Association for their dedication to sharing the history and blessings of Texas and for producing this invaluable Almanac preserving the past and present for the future of this great state.

Greg Abbott
Governor of Texas

*P*eople from all over the world envy Texas; our natural beauty, bustling economy, vibrant culture and rich history are second to none.

The Texas story is one of liberty, perseverance and determination to succeed, and our independence was bought with the blood of our forefathers. Texas history is filled with stories of settlers, immigrants, native peoples, freedmen, outlaws and carpetbaggers, forging their own way forward. Each Texan has contributed to building a better Texas for all of posterity.

DAN PATRICK
Lt. Governor of Texas

Our commitment to God-given freedoms, liberty and the right to self-determination has presented generations of Texans the opportunity to prosper.

The *Texas Almanac* remains a premier resource to learn about Texas' beautiful history and culture that make our state the light of the United States and the world. Please join me in honoring it as you learn about the greatest state that God ever made: Texas.

Dan Patrick
Lt. Governor of Texas

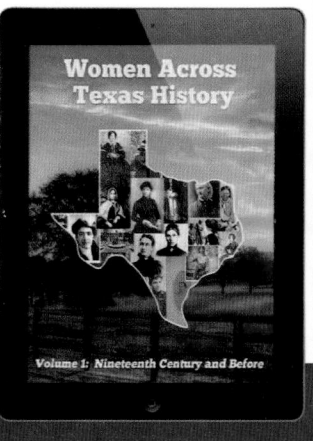
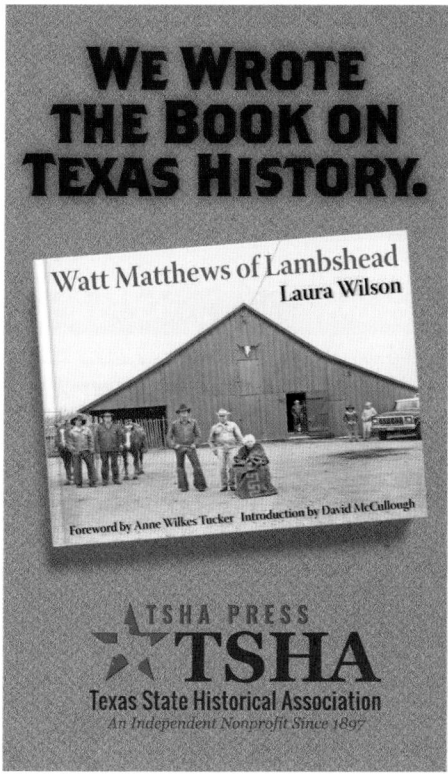

TABLE OF CONTENTS

INDEX OF TABLES

HEALTH & SCIENCE

EDUCATION

BUSINESS

TRANSPORTATION

AGRICULTURE

A common slider taking in some sun. Photo by Shiva Shenoy, CC by 2.0/Flickr

INDEX OF MAPS

TEXAS

The Lone Star State

This section offers a demographic and geographic profile of the second-largest, second-most-populous state in the United States. Check the **Table of Contents** and the **Index** for more-detailed information about each subject.

GOVERNMENT

Capital: Austin
Government: Bicameral Legislature
28th State to enter the Union: Dec. 29, 1845
Present Constitution adopted: 1876
State Senators: 31
State Representatives: 150
Legislative sessions are held for a maximum of 140 days, every 2 years

State motto: Friendship (1930)
Origin of name: Texas, or Tejas, was the Spanish pronunciation of a Caddo Indian word meaning "friends" or "allies."

BUSINESS

Per Capita Personal Income (2019) $52,813
Per Capita Consumption (2019) $40,552
    Top spending categories:
                Housing and utilities $6,885
                Health care $6,279

Non-Farm Employment (2020) 12,087,300
Employment by industry:
    Trade, transportation, utilities. 2,418,300
    Government .1,887,400
    Goods producing 1,808,300
    Professional and business services 1,730,200
    Education and health services 1,667,200
    Leisure and hospitality 1,168,800
    Manufacturing 873,400
    Construction .743,600

(Per capita income/consumption: U.S. Bureau of Economic Analysis. Employment: Texas Workforce Commission.)

POPULATION

Population, 2019 . . . . **28,995,881**
Population, 2010 U.S. Census 25,145,561
Population increase, 2010–2019. . . . . 15.3%
Population, 2000 U.S. Census 20,851,820
Population increase, 2000–2019 . . . . 39.1%

Ethnicity, 2019

Group	Percent
White, NH	41.5%
Hispanic	39.5%
Black	11.9%
Asian	4.9%
Other	2.2%

Ten Largest Cities

Houston (Harris Co.) 2,325,489
San Antonio (Bexar Co.) 1,555,370
Dallas (Dallas Co.) .1,358,328
Austin (Travis Co.) 993,129
Fort Worth (Tarrant Co.) 899,597
El Paso (El Paso Co.). 687,690
Arlington (Tarrant Co.) 391,443
Corpus Christi (Nueces Co.) 328,390
Plano (Collin Co.) 291,791
Laredo (Webb Co.). 267,001

Number of counties 254
Largest by pop: Harris Co.. 4,713,325
Smallest by pop: Loving Co. 169

Number of incorporated cities. **1,229**
Number of cities of 100,000 pop. or more 41
Number of cities of 50,000 pop. or more 68
Number of cities of 10,000 pop. or more 239

(Texas Demographic Center estimates for Jan. 1, 2019.)

NATURAL ENVIRONMENT

Area (total) . . . . 268,596 sq. miles
. . . . (171,901,440 acres)

Land Area . . . . 261,232 sq. miles
. . . . (167,188,480 acres)

Water Area . . . . 7,365 sq. miles
. . . .(4,713,600 acres)

Geographic Center:
About 15 miles northeast of Brady in northern McCulloch County.

Highest Point:
Guadalupe Peak (8,749 ft.) in Culberson County in far West Texas.

Lowest Point:
Gulf of Mexico (sea level).

Normal Average Annual Precipitation Range:
From 60.57 inches at Jasper County in far East Texas to 9.43 inches at El Paso, in far West Texas.

Record Highest Temperature:
Seymour, Baylor Co., ...Aug. 12, 1936, 120°F
Monahans, Ward Co.,. . . . . .June 28, 1994, 120°F

Record Lowest Temperature:
Tulia, Swisher Co., ...Feb. 12, 1899, -23°F
Seminole, Gaines Co.,. . . . . .Feb. 8, 1933, -23°F

PRINCIPAL PRODUCTS

Manufactures: Chemicals and allied products, petroleum and coal products, food and kindred products, transportation equipment.

Farm Products: Cattle, cotton, vegetables, fruits, nursery and greenhouse, dairy products.

Minerals: Petroleum, natural gas, and natural gas liquids.

Finance (as of 12/31/2018):
Number of banks 409
Total deposits $328,907,699,000
Number of savings & loan associations. 5
Total deposits $73,570,292,000
Number of savings banks 24
Total deposits $17,635,204,000
(Banks: Federal Reserve Bank of Dallas; savings and loans and savings banks: Texas Dept. of Savings and Mortgage Lending.)

Agriculture (2019):
Total cash receipts. . . . . $21.25 billion
Animals & products . . . . $14.36 billion
All Crops . . . . $6.89 billion
Total exports . . . . $6.30 billion
Land in farms in acres, ...130.0 million
(U.S. Department of Agriculture, National Agricultural Statistics Service Farm Numbers.)

The Texas State Fair. Photo by Nicholas Henderson, CC by 2.0/Flickr

Texas' Rank Among the States

GDP by State, FYE 2020

	State	In Millions
1.	California	$3,091,871.5
2.	**Texas**	**$1,759,734.4**
3.	New York	$1,699,044.7
4.	Florida	$1,095,888.2
5.	Illinois	$863,516.7
6.	Pennsylvania	$780,176.1
7.	Ohio	$675,037.3
8.	Georgia	$619,240.0
9.	New Jersey	$619,061.1
10.	Washington	$618,704.9

United States: $20,936,558.0

Number of Births, 2019

	State	Total
1.	California	446,479
2.	**Texas**	**377,599**
3.	New York	221,539
4.	Florida	220,002
5.	Illinois	140,128
6.	Ohio	134,461
7.	Pennsylvania	134,230
8.	Georgia	126,371
9.	North Carolina	118,725
10.	Michigan	107,886

United States: 3,747,540

Crude Oil Production, April 2021

	State	1,000's of Barrels
1.	**Texas**	**4,741**
2.	New Mexico	1,222
3.	North Dakota	1,061
4.	Alaska	443
5.	Colorado	408
6.	Oklahoma	400
7.	California	362
8.	Wyoming	228
9.	Louisiana	97
10.	Utah	90

Energy Consumption, 2019

	State	Million BTU, per capita
1.	Wyoming	932
2.	Louisiana	922
3.	North Dakota	875
4.	Alaska	839
5.	Iowa	517
6.	**Texas**	**491**
7.	Nebraska	466
8.	West Virginia	461
9.	South Dakota	453
10.	Oklahoma	432

Agriculture, All Commodities, 2019

	State	Income
1.	California	$49,938,076
2.	Iowa	$27,487,829
3.	Nebraska	$21,436,242
4.	**Texas**	**$21,249,024**
5.	Minnesota	$16,632,782
6.	Illinois	$16,318,156
7.	Kansas	$16,301,222
8.	Wisconsin	$11,246,602
9.	North Carolina	$10,603,108
10.	Indiana	$10,587,053

Energy Production, 2019

	State	Percent of Total
1.	**Texas**	**23.1%**
2.	Pennsylvania	9.5%
3.	Wyoming	7.0%
4.	Oklahoma	5.2%
5.	West Virginia	5.1%
6.	North Dakota	4.6%
7.	New Mexico	4.3%
8.	Louisiana	3.9%
9.	Colorado	3.8%
10.	Ohio	3.6%

Sources for these tables are: the Bureau of Economic Analysis, U.S. Census Bureau, U.S. Dept. of Agriculture, and the U.S. Energy Information Administration.

FLAGS OF TEXAS

United States
1845–Present

Spain
1519–1821

France
1685–1690

Republic
Republic: 1836–1845; State: 1845–Present

Mexico
1821–1836

Confederate States of America
1861–1865

Texas is called the **Lone Star State** because of its state flag with a single star. The state flag was also the **flag of the Republic of Texas**.

The following information about historic Texas flags, the current flag, and other Texas symbols is from the **Texas State Library & Archives** in Austin. More information is at:

www.tsl.texas.gov/ref/abouttx/index.html#flags

Six Flags of Texas

Six different flags have flown over Texas during eight changes of sovereignty. The accepted sequence of these flags follows:

Spanish: 1519–1821
French: 1685–1690
Mexican: 1821–1836
Republic of Texas: 1836–1845
Confederate States of America: 1861–1865
United States: 1845 to the present.

Evolution of the Lone Star Flag

The Convention at Washington-on-the-Brazos in March 1836 allegedly adopted a flag for the Republic that was designed by **Lorenzo de Zavala**. The design of de Zavala's flag is unknown, but the convention journals state that a "Rainbow and star of five points above the western horizon; and a star of six points sinking below" was added to de Zavala's flag.

There was a suggestion the letters "T E X A S" be placed around the star in the flag, but there is no evidence that the Convention ever approved a final flag design. Probably because of the hasty dispersion of the Convention and the loss of part of the Convention notes, nothing further was done with the Convention's proposals for a national flag.

A **so-called "Zavala flag"** is sometimes flown in Texas today that consists of a blue field with a white five-pointed star in the center and the letters "T E X A S" between the star points, but there is no historical evidence to support this flag's design.

The **first official flag of the Republic,** known as the **National Standard of Texas** or **David G. Burnet's flag,** was adopted by the Texas Congress and approved by President Sam Houston on Dec. 10, 1836. The design "**shall be an azure ground with a large golden star central.**"

The Lone Star Flag

On Jan. 25, 1839, President Mirabeau B. Lamar approved the adoption by Congress of a new national flag. This flag consisted of "a blue perpendicular stripe of the width of one third of the whole length of the flag, with a white star of five points in the centre thereof, and two horizontal stripes of equal breadth, the upper stripe white, the lower red, of the length of two thirds of the length of the whole flag." This is the **Lone Star Flag,** which later became the state flag.

Although Senator William H. Wharton proposed the adoption of the Lone Star Flag in 1838, no one knows who actually designed the flag. The legislature in 1879 inadvertently repealed the law establishing the state flag, but the legislature adopted a new law in 1933 that legally re-established the flag's design.

The red, white, and blue of the state flag stand, respectively, for bravery, purity, and loyalty. The proper **finial** for use with the state flag is either **a star or a spearhead.** Texas is one of only two states that has a flag that formerly served as the flag of an independent nation. The other is Hawaii.

Displaying the State Flag

The Texas Flag Code was first adopted in 1933 and completely revised in 1993. Laws governing display of the state flag are found in sections 3100.002 through 3100.152 of the Texas Government Code: **www.tsl.state.tx.us/ref/abouttx/flagcode.html**.

Here is a summary of those rules:

★ The Texas flag should be **displayed on state and national holidays** and on special occasions of historical significance, and it should be displayed at every school on regular school days. **When flown out of doors,** the Texas flag should not be flown earlier than sunrise nor later than sunset unless properly illuminated. It should not be left out in inclement weather unless a weather-proof flag is used. It should be flown with the white stripe uppermost **except in case of distress.**

★ No flag other than the United States flag should be placed above or, if on the same level, to the state flag's right (observer's left). The state flag should be underneath the national flag when the two are flown from the same halyard. **When flown from adjacent flagpoles,** the national flag and the state flag should be of approximately the same size and on flagpoles of equal height; the national flag should be on the flag's own right (observer's left).

★ If the state flag is displayed with the flag of another U.S. state, a nation other than the United States, or an international organization, the state flag should be, from an observer's perspective, to the left of the other flag on a separate flagpole or flagstaff, and the state flag should not be above the other flag on the same flagpole or flagstaff or on a taller flagpole or flagstaff. If the state flag

and the U.S. flag are **displayed from crossed flagstaffs,** the state flag should be, from an observer's perspective, to the right of the U.S. flag and the state flag's flagstaff should be behind the U.S. flag's flagstaff.

★ When the flag is displayed horizontally, the white stripe should be above the red stripe and, from an observer's perspective, to the right of the blue stripe. **When the flag is displayed vertically,** the blue stripe should be uppermost and the white stripe should be to the state flag's right (observer's left).

★ If the state and national flags are both **carried in a procession,** the national flag should be on the marching right and state flag should be on the national flag's left (observer's right).

★ **On Memorial Day,** the state flag should be displayed at half-staff until noon and then completely raised. **On Peace Officers Memorial Day** (May 15), the state flag should be displayed at half-staff all day, unless that day is also Armed Forces Day.

★ The state flag should not touch anything beneath it or be dipped to any person or thing except the U.S. flag. Advertising should not be fastened to a flagpole, flagstaff, or halyard on which the state flag is displayed.

★ If a state flag is no longer used or useful as an emblem for display, it should be destroyed, preferably by burning. A **flag retirement ceremony** is set out in the Texas Government Code mentioned earlier.

Honor the Texas flag;
I pledge allegiance
to thee, Texas,
one state under God,
one and indivisible.

Pledge to the Texas Flag

A pledge to the Texas flag was adopted in 1933 by the 43rd Legislature. It contained a phrase, "Flag of 1836," which inadvertently referred to the **David G. Burnet flag** instead of the Lone Star Flag adopted in 1839. In 2007, the 80th Legislature changed the pledge to its current form:

A person reciting the pledge to the state flag should face the flag, place the right hand over the heart, and remove any easily removable hat.

The pledge to the Texas flag may be recited at all public and private meetings at which the Pledge of Allegiance to the national flag is recited and at state historical events and celebrations.

The pledge to the Texas flag should be recited after the pledge of allegiance to the United States flag, if both are recited. ☆

TEXAS STATE SYMBOLS

State Song

The state song of Texas is "Texas, Our Texas." The music was written by the late William J. Marsh (who died Feb. 1, 1971, in Fort Worth at age 90), and the words by Marsh and Gladys Yoakum Wright, also of Fort Worth. It was the winner of a state song contest sponsored by the 41st Legislature and was adopted in 1929. The wording has been changed once: Shortly after Alaska became a state in January 1959, the word "Largest" in the third line was changed by Mr. Marsh to "Boldest." The text follows:

TEXAS, OUR TEXAS

Texas, our Texas! All hail the mighty State!
Texas, our Texas! So wonderful, so great!
Boldest and grandest, Withstanding ev'ry test;
O Empire wide and glorious, You stand supremely blest.

CHORUS
God bless you Texas!
And keep you brave and strong,
That you may grow in power and worth,
Thro'out the ages long.

REFRAIN
Texas, O Texas! Your freeborn single star,
Sends out its radiance to nations near and far.
Emblem of freedom! It sets our hearts aglow,
With thoughts of San Jacinto and glorious Alamo.
Texas, dear Texas! From tyrant grip now free,
Shines forth in splendor your star of destiny!
Mother of heroes! We come your children true,
Proclaiming our allegiance, our faith, our love for you.

State Motto

The state motto is "Friendship." The word Texas, or Tejas, was the Spanish pronunciation of a Caddo Indian word meaning "friends" or "allies." It was designated by the 41st Legislature in 1930.

State Citizenship Designation

The people of Texas usually call themselves Texans. However, Texian was generally used in the early period of the state's history.

State Seal

The design of the obverse (front) of the State Seal consists of "a star of five points encircled by olive and live oak branches, and the words, 'The State of Texas.'" (State Constitution, Art. IV, Sec. 19.) This design is a slight modification of the Great Seal of the Republic of Texas, adopted by the Congress of the Republic, Dec. 10, 1836, and readopted with modifications in 1839.

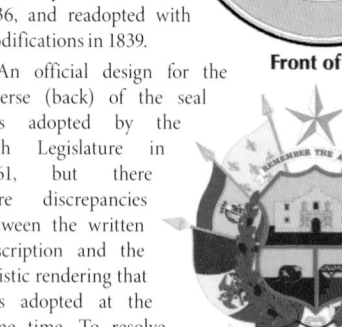

Front of Seal

An official design for the reverse (back) of the seal was adopted by the 57th Legislature in 1961, but there were discrepancies between the written description and the artistic rendering that was adopted at the same time. To resolve the problems, the 72nd Legislature in 1991 adopted an official design.

Back of Seal

The 73rd Legislature in 1993 finally adopted the reverse by law. The current description is in the Texas Government Code, section 3101.001:

"(b) The reverse side of the state seal contains a shield displaying a depiction of:

(1) the Alamo; (2) the cannon of the Battle of Gonzales; and (3) Vince's Bridge.

(c) The shield on the reverse side of the state seal is encircled by:

(1) live oak and olive branches; and (2) the unfurled flags of: (A) the Kingdom of France; (B) the Kingdom of Spain; (C) the United Mexican States; (D) the Republic of Texas; (E) the Confederate States of America; and (F) the United States of America.

(d) Above the shield is emblazoned the motto, 'REMEMBER THE ALAMO,' and beneath are the words, 'TEXAS ONE AND INDIVISIBLE.'

(e) A white five-pointed star hangs over the shield, centered between the flags."

Texas State Symbols

State Bird: The mockingbird (*Mimus polyglottos*) is the state bird of Texas, adopted by the 40th Legislature of 1927 at the request of the Texas Federation of Women's Clubs.

State Flower: The state flower of Texas is the bluebonnet, also called buffalo clover, wolf flower, and el conejo (the rabbit). The bluebonnet was adopted as the state flower, at the request of the Society of Colonial Dames in Texas, by the 27th Legislature in 1901. The original resolution made Lupinus subcarnosus the state flower, but a resolution by the 62nd Legislature in 1971 provided legal status as the state flower of Texas for "Lupinus Texensis and any other variety of bluebonnet."

State Tree: The pecan tree (*Carya illinoinensis*) was adopted as the state tree of Texas by the 36th Legislature in 1919. The sentiment that led to its adoption probably grew out of the request of Gov. James Stephen Hogg that a pecan tree be planted at his grave.

Other State Symbols

(In 2001, the Texas Legislature placed restrictions on the adoption of future symbols by requiring that a joint resolution to designate a symbol must specify the item's historical or cultural significance to the state.)

State Air Force: The Commemorative Air Force (formerly known as the Confederate Air Force), based in Midland at Midland International Airport, was proclaimed the state air force of Texas by the 71st Legislature in 1989.

State Amphibian: The Texas toad was named the state amphibian by the 81st Legislature in 2009.

State Aquarium: The Texas State Aquarium in Corpus Christi was designated the state aquarium of Texas by the 69th Legislature in 1985.

State Bison Herd: The bison herd at Caprock Canyons State Park was named the official Texas State Bison Herd by the 82nd Legislature in 2011.

State Bluebonnet City: The city of Ennis in Ellis County was designated the state bluebonnet city by the 75th Legislature in 1997.

State Bluebonnet Festival: The Chappell Hill Bluebonnet Festival, held in April, was named state bluebonnet festival by the 75th Legislature in 1997.

State Bluebonnet Trail: The city of Ennis was proclaimed the official state bluebonnet trail by the 75th Legislature in 1997.

State Bread: Pan de campo, translated "camp bread" and often called cowboy bread, was named the state bread by the 79th Legislature in 2005. It is a simple baking-powder bread that was a staple of early Texans and often baked in a Dutch oven.

State Cobbler: Peach cobbler was named the state cobbler of Texas by the 83rd Legislature in 2013.

State Cooking Implement: The cast iron Dutch oven was named the cooking implement of Texas by the 79th Legislature in 2005.

State Crustacean: Texas Gulf Shrimp was designated the state crustacean by the 84th Legislature in 2015.

State Dinosaur: *Paluxysaurus jonesi* was proclaimed the state dinosaur by the 81st Legislature in 2009, after it was discovered that the previous state dinosaur, the Brachiosaur Sauropod, Pleurocoelus, (75th Legislature in 1997) had been a misidentification.

State Dish: Chili was proclaimed the Texas state dish by the 65th Legislature in 1977.

State Dog Breed: The Blue Lacy was designated the state dog breed by the 79th Legislature in 2005. The Blue Lacy is a herding and hunting breed descended from greyhound, scent-hound, and coyote stock and developed by the Lacy brothers, who left Kentucky and settled near Marble Falls in 1858.

State Domino Game: 42 was named the state domino game by the 82nd Legislature in 2011.

State Epic Poem: "The Legend of Old Stone Ranch," written by John Worth Cloud, was named the epic poem of Texas by the 61st Legislature in 1969. The work is a 400-page history of the Albany–Fort Griffin area written in verse form.

State Fiber and Fabric: Cotton was designated the state fiber and fabric of Texas by the 75th Legislature in 1997.

State Fish: The Guadalupe bass, a member of the genus *Micropterus* within the sunfish family, was named the state fish of Texas by the 71st Legislature in 1989. It is one of a group of fish collectively known as black bass.

State Flower Song: "Bluebonnets," written by Julia D. Booth and Lora C. Crockett, was named the state flower song by the 43rd Legislature in 1933.

State Folk Dance: The square dance was designated the state folk dance by the 72nd Legislature in 1991.

State Footwear: The cowboy boot was named the state footwear by the 80th Legislature in 2007.

State Fruit: Texas red grapefruit was designated the state fruit by the 73rd Legislature in 1993.

This Colt Walker pistol was donated to the Metropolitan Museum of Art by John E. Parsons in 1958. Public Domain/Wikimedia Commons.

State Gem: Texas blue topaz, the state gem of Texas, is found in the Llano uplift area in Central Texas, especially west to northwest of Mason. It was designated by the 61st Legislature in 1969.

State Gemstone Cut: The Lone Star Cut was named the state gemstone cut by the 65th Legislature in 1977.

State Grass: Sideoats grama (Bouteloua curtipendula), a native grass found on many different Texas soils, was designated the state grass of Texas by the 62nd Legislature in 1971.

State Handgun: The 1847 Colt Walker pistol was named the state handgun by the 87th Legislature in 2021.

State Hashtags: #Texas (state), #TexasToDo (tourism), and #txlege (legislature) were all proclaimed state hashtags by the 84th Legislature in 2015.

State Hat: The cowboy hat was named the state hat of Texas by the 84th Legislature in 2015.

State Health Nut: The pecan was designated the state health nut by the 77th Legislature in 2001.

State Horse: The American Quarter Horse was named state horse by the 81st Legislature in 2009.

State Insect: The Monarch butterfly (Danaus plexippus) was designated the state insect by the 74th Legislature in 1995.

State Knife: The 87th Legislature designated the Bowie knife our official state knife in 2021.

State Longhorn Herd: The longhorn herd at Fort Griffin State Historic Site was named the state longhorn herd by the 61st Legislature in 1969.

State Mammals: The state mammals were all designated by the 74th Legislature in 1995:

- **Flying:** Mexican free-tailed bat (Tadarida brasiliensis);
- **Large:** Longhorn (Bos Texanus);

- **Small:** Armadillo (Dasypus novemcinctus).

State Maritime Museum: The Texas Maritime Museum in Rockport was named the state maritime museum by the 70th Legislature in 1987.

State Mushroom: The Texas Star Mushroom (*Chorioactis geaster*) was recognized as the official state mushroom by the 87th Legislature in 2021.

State Music: Western swing was named the state's official music by the 82nd Legislature in 2011.

State Musical Instrument: The guitar was designated the state musical instrument by the 75th Legislature in 1997.

State Native Pepper: The chiltepin (Capsicum annuum var. glabriusculum) was named the native pepper of Texas by the 75th Legislature in 1997.

State Native Shrub: Texas purple sage (Leucophyllum frutescens) was designated the state native shrub by the 79th Legislature in 2005.

State Nickname: "The Lone Star State" was designated the state nickname of Texas by the 84th Legislature in 2015.

State Pastries: Both the sopaipilla and strudel were named the state pastries of Texas by the 78th Legislature in 2003.

State Pepper: The jalapeño pepper (Capsicum annuum) was designated the state pepper by the 74th Legislature in 1995.

The Texas Star mushroom, also known as the Devil's Cigar mushroom, first resembles a dark cigar before splitting and unfurling into rays while releasing spores. Photo by Tim Jones, CC 3.0/Wikipedia Commons.

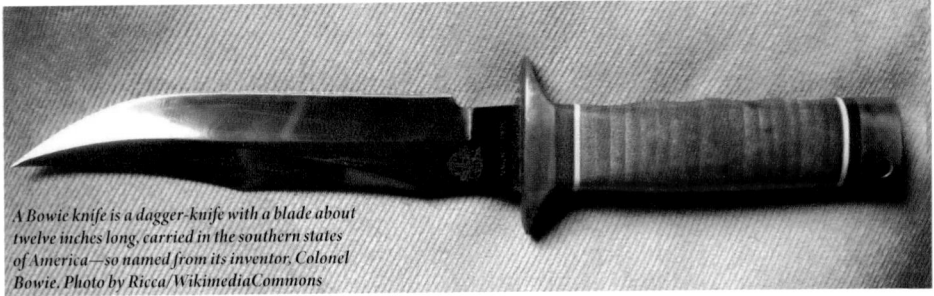

A Bowie knife is a dagger-knife with a blade about twelve inches long, carried in the southern states of America—so named from its inventor, Colonel Bowie. Photo by Ricca/WikimediaCommons

State Pie: Pecan pie was named the state pie by the 83rd Legislature in 2013.

State Plant: The prickly pear cactus (*Genus Opuntia*) was named the state plant by the 74th Legislature in 1995.

State Plays: There are four official state plays that were designated by the 66th Legislature in 1979:

1. **The Lone Star**

2. **Texas**

3. **Beyond the Sundown**

4. **Fandangle**

State Pollinator: The Western Honey Bee (*Apis mellifera*) was designated the official pollinator of Texas by the 84th Legislature in 2015.

State Precious Metal: Silver was named the official precious metal by the 80th Legislature in 2007.

State Railroad: The Texas State Railroad was designated the state railroad by the 78th Legislature in 2003. It is a steam-powered tourist excursion train that runs between the towns of Rusk and Palestine.

State Reptile: The Texas horned lizard (*Phrynosoma cornutum*) was named the state reptile by the 73rd Legislature in 1993.

State Rodeo Drill Team: Ghostriders were named the official rodeo drill team of Texas by the 80th Legislature in 2007.

State Saltwater Fish: Red Drum (*Sciaenops ocellatus*) was named the state's saltwater fish by the 82nd Legislature in 2011.

State Sea Turtle: Kemp's Ridley Sea Turtle was named the state sea turtle of Texas by the 83rd Legislature in 2013.

State Seashell: The lightning whelk (*Busycon perversum pulleyi*) was named the state seashell by the 70th Legislature in 1987. One of the few shells that open on the left side, the lightning whelk is named for its colored stripes and is found only on the Gulf Coast.

State Ship: The battleship USS Texas was designated the state ship by the 74th Legislature in 1995. The USS Texas was launched on May 18, 1912, from Newport News, Virginia, and commissioned on March 12, 1914. In 1919, it became the first U.S. battleship to launch an aircraft, and in 1939, it received the first commercial radar in the U.S. Navy. In 1940, the Texas was designated flagship of the U.S. Atlantic Fleet and was the last of the battleships to participate in both World Wars I and II. It was decommissioned on April 21, 1948, and is a National Historic Landmark and a National Mechanical Engineering Landmark. It is docked along the Houston Ship Channel.

State Shrub: The crape myrtle (*Lagerstroemia indica*) was designated the official state shrub by the 75th Legislature in 1997.

State Snack: Tortilla chips and salsa was named the state snack by the 78th Legislature in 2003.

State Sport: Rodeo was named the state sport of Texas by the 75th Legislature in 1997.

State Squash: Pumpkin was designated the state squash of Texas by the 83rd Legislature in 2013.

State Stone: Petrified palmwood, found in Texas principally near the Gulf Coast, was designated the state stone by the 61st Legislature in 1969.

State Tall Ship: The Elissa was named the state tall ship by the 79th Legislature in 2005. The 1877 ship makes its home at the Texas Seaport Museum at the port of Galveston.

State Tartan: The Texas Bluebonnet Tartan was named the official state tartan by the 71st Texas Legislature in 1989.

State 10K: The Texas Roundup 10K was named the official state 10K by the 79th Legislature in 2005 to encourage Texans to exercise and incorporate physical activity into their daily lives.

State Tie: The bolo tie was designated the state tie by the 80th Legislature in 2007.

State Vegetable: The Texas sweet onion was designated the state vegetable by the 75th Legislature in 1997.

State Vehicle: The chuck wagon was named the state vehicle by the 79th Legislature in 2005. Texas rancher Charles Goodnight is credited with inventing the chuck wagon to carry food and supplies for the cowboys on trail drives.

State Waterlily: The Nymphaea "Texas Dawn" was named the state waterlily by the 82nd Legislature in 2011. ☆

Explore Texas History

Texas State Historical Association
HANDBOOK OF TEXAS

The *Texas Almanac* has long published feature articles about various aspects of Texas history, all of which are still available on our website, **TexasAlmanac.com**. In recent years, many of those articles were edited and combined to create a single article, "A Brief Sketch of Texas History," which was featured in several editions of the book. That article served its purpose, but a brief look has obvious limitations. After all, the history of Texas is anything but brief.

For this edition we are calling upon our colleagues at the *Handbook of Texas* to present an introductory selection of entries you can read online to learn about the history of Texas. Every entry offers a piece of the fabric of Texas past and present, and just as originally envisioned, the goal of those who write, revise, and edit entries remains ensuring that the *Handbook* is accurate, inclusive, accessible, and reflective of current scholarly standards.

Consider this list a starting point in your further study of Texas history, and explore our chronological overview entries and a few examples of our entries on cities and regions, specific topics, and biographies of deceased individuals. Dig in to these interesting samples of Texas history, and then go on to discover more at the *Handbook of Texas Online,*

https://www.tshaonline.org/handbook.

Chronological Overview

Prehistory: www.tshaonline.org/handbook/entries/prehistory

Spanish Texas: www.tshaonline.org/handbook/entries/spanish-texas

Texas in the Age of Mexican Independence:: www.tshaonline.org/handbook/entries/texas-in-the-age-of-mexican-independence

Mexican Texas: www.tshaonline.org/handbook/entries/mexican-texas

Texas Revolution: tshaonline.org/handbook/online/articles/qdt01

Republic of Texas: www.tshaonline.org/handbook/entries/texas-revolution

Antebellum Texas: www.tshaonline.org/handbook/entries/antebellum-texas

Civil War: www.tshaonline.org/handbook/entries/civil-war

Reconstruction: www.tshaonline.org/handbook/entries/reconstruction

Late-Nineteenth Century Texas: www.tshaonline.org/handbook/entries/late-nineteenth-century-texas

Progressive Era: www.tshaonline.org/handbook/entries/progressive-era

Texas in the 1920s: www.tshaonline.org/handbook/entries/texas-in-the-1920s

Great Depression: www.tshaonline.org/handbook/entries/great-depression

World War II: www.tshaonline.org/handbook/entries/world-war-ii

Texas Post World War II: www.tshaonline.org/handbook/entries/texas-post-world-war-ii

Biographical

Athanase de Mézières: www.tshaonline.org/handbook/entries/mezieres-athanase-de

Sam Houston: www.tshaonline.org/handbook/entries/houston-sam

Stephen F. Austin: www.tshaonline.org/handbook/entries/austin-stephen-fuller

Mary Eleanor Brackenridge: www.tshaonline.org/handbook/entries/brackenridge-mary-eleanor

Lyndon B. Johnson: www.tshaonline.org/handbook/entries/johnson-lyndon-baines

Minnie Fisher Cunningham: www.tshaonline.org/handbook/entries/cunningham-minnie-fisher

Jesse H. Jones: www.tshaonline.org/handbook/entries/jones-jesse-holman

Ernie Banks: www.tshaonline.org/handbook/entries/banks-ernest-ernie-mr-cub

José Francisco Ruiz: www.tshaonline.org/handbook/entries/ruiz-jose-francisco

Barbara Jordan: www.tshaonline.org/handbook/entries/jordan-barbara-charline

George T. Ruby: www.tshaonline.org/handbook/entries/ruby-george-thompson

Jovita Idar: www.tshaonline.org/handbook/entries/idar-jovita

Lady Bird Johnson: www.tshaonline.org/handbook/entries/johnson-claudia-alta-taylor-lady-bird

Henry B. González: www.tshaonline.org/handbook/entries/gonzalez-henry-barbosa

Katherine Stinson: www.tshaonline.org/handbook/entries/stinson-katherine

Babe Didrikson Zaharias: www.tshaonline.org/handbook/entries/zaharias-mildred-ella-didrikson-babe

Topical

Spanish Missions: www.tshaonline.org/handbook/entries/spanish-missions

Slavery: www.tshaonline.org/handbook/entries/slavery

Battle of the Alamo: www.tshaonline.org/handbook/entries/alamo-battle-of-the

Civil Rights in Texas: www.tshaonline.org/handbook/entries/civil-rights

Music: www.tshaonline.org/handbook/entries/music

Woman Suffrage: www.tshaonline.org/handbook/entries/woman-suffrage

Germans: www.tshaonline.org/handbook/entries/germans

African Americans: www.tshaonline.org/handbook/entries/african-americans

Anglo American Colonization: www.tshaonline.org/handbook/entries/anglo-american-colonization

LULAC: www.tshaonline.org/handbook/entries/league-of-united-latin-american-citizens

Kerrville Folk Festival: www.tshaonline.org/handbook/entries/kerrville-folk-festival

Surface Water: www.tshaonline.org/handbook/entries/surface-water

Comanche: www.tshaonline.org/handbook/entries/comanche-indians

People's Party: www.tshaonline.org/handbook/entries/peoples-party

Houston Astros: www.tshaonline.org/handbook/entries/houston-astros

San Antonio Spurs: www.tshaonline.org/handbook/entries/san-antonio-spurs

Witte Museum: www.tshaonline.org/handbook/entries/witte-museum

Railroads: www.tshaonline.org/handbook/entries/railroads

Vietnamese: www.tshaonline.org/handbook/entries/vietnamese

Mexican Americans: www.tshaonline.org/handbook/entries/mexican-americans

Segregation: www.tshaonline.org/handbook/entries/segregation

Porvenir Massacre: www.tshaonline.org/handbook/entries/porvenir-massacre

Armadillo: www.tshaonline.org/handbook/entries/armadillo

Visual Arts: www.tshaonline.org/handbook/entries/visual-arts

Cities and Regions

Dallas: www.tshaonline.org/handbook/entries/dallas-tx

Fort Worth: www.tshaonline.org/handbook/entries/fort-worth-tx

Houston: www.tshaonline.org/handbook/entries/houston-tx

Panhandle: www.tshaonline.org/handbook/entries/panhandle

Trans-Pecos: www.tshaonline.org/handbook/entries/trans-pecos

Hill Country: www.tshaonline.org/handbook/entries/hill-country

El Paso: www.tshaonline.org/handbook/entries/el-paso-tx

Austin: www.tshaonline.org/handbook/entries/austin-tx-travis-

San Antonio: www.tshaonline.org/handbook/entries/san-antonio-tx

Rio Grande Valley: www.tshaonline.org/handbook/entries/rio-grande-valley

East Texas: www.tshaonline.org/handbook/entries/east-texas

Permian Basin: www.tshaonline.org/handbook/entries/permian-basin

The *Handbook of Texas* is a collaborative scholarly project of the Texas State Historical Association (TSHA) that began in 1939 under the direction of Professor Walter Prescott Webb at the University of Texas at Austin to create, "the most useful book that has ever been published in Texas."

- FREE and Accessible on computers, phones, and tablets
- Nearly 27,000 entries by 6,000+ authors
- 10 million page views annually
- 4.5 million users annually

Lady Bird Johnson at the groundbreaking of the wildflower center that bears her name. Photo by Frank Wolfe/Wikimedia Commons

Environment

PHYSICAL REGIONS, GEOLOGY, SOILS

AQUIFERS, RIVERS, LAKES, ESTUARIES

PLANT LIFE, FORESTS, GRASSLANDS

TEXAS WILDLIFE: FISH, AMPHIBIANS, REPTILES, BIRDS, MAMMALS

The Red-tailed Hawk (Buteo jamaicensis) is found statewide, often seen soaring or perched on telephone poles and fence posts. Photo by Jill D. Miller.

The Physical State of Texas

The Area of Texas

Texas occupies about 7 percent of the total water and land area of the United States. Second in size among the states, Texas has a land and water area of 268,596 square miles, as compared with Alaska's 665,384 square miles, according to the United States Bureau of the Census. California, the third-largest state, has 163,695 square miles. Texas is as large as all of New England, New York, Delaware, Pennsylvania, Ohio, and Virginia combined.

The state's total area consists of 261,232 square miles of land and 7,365 square miles of water.

Length and Breadth

The longest straight-line distance in a general north-south direction is 801 miles from the northwest corner of the Panhandle to the extreme southern tip of Texas on the Rio Grande southeast of Brownsville. The greatest east-west distance is 773 miles from the extreme eastward bend in the Sabine River in Newton County to the extreme western bulge of the Rio Grande just northwest of El Paso.

Texas' Boundary Lines

The boundary of Texas by segments, including only larger river bends and only the great arc of the coastline, is as follows:

Boundary	Length (miles)
Rio Grande	889.0
Coastline	367.0
Sabine River, Lake, and Pass	180.0
Sabine River to Red River	106.5
Red River	480.0
East Panhandle line	133.6
North Panhandle line	167.0
West Panhandle line	310.2
Along 32nd parallel	209.0
TOTAL	**2,842.3**

Following the smaller meanderings of the rivers and the tidewater coastline, the following are the boundary measurements:

Boundary	Length (miles)
Rio Grande	1,254.0
Coastline (tidewater)	624.0
Sabine River, Lake, and Pass	292.0
Sabine River to Red River	106.5
Red River	726.0
East Panhandle line	133.6
North Panhandle line	167.0
West Panhandle line	310.2
Along 32nd parallel	209.0
TOTAL	**3,822.3**

Latitude and Longitude

The extremes of latitude and longitude in Texas are as follows:

★ From 25° 50' North latitude at the extreme southern turn of the Rio Grande on the south line of Cameron County to 36° 30' North latitude along the north line of the Panhandle, and

★ From 93° 31' West longitude at the extreme eastern point of the Sabine River on the east line of Newton County to 106° 38' West longitude at the extreme westward point of the Rio Grande on the western edge of El Paso.

Named Mountain Peaks in Texas Above 8,000 Feet

The highest point in the state is Guadalupe Peak at 8,749 feet above sea level. Its twin, El Capitan, stands at 8,085 feet and also is located in Culberson County near the New Mexico state line. Both are in Guadalupe Mountains National Park, which includes the scenic McKittrick Canyon.

The elevations used on this page are from various sources, including the U.S. Geological Survey, the National Park Service, and the Texas Department of Transportation. The named peaks above 8,000 feet and the counties in which they are located are listed below.

Name	County	Height (Ft.)
Guadalupe Peak	Culberson	8,749
Bush Mountain	Culberson	8,631
Shumard Peak	Culberson	8,615
Bartlett Peak	Culberson	8,508
Mount Livermore (Baldy Peak)	Jeff Davis	8,378
Hunter Peak (Pine Top Mtn.)	Culberson	8,368
El Capitan	Culberson	8,085

Elevation Highs and Lows

Highest Town: Fort Davis in Jeff Davis County is the highest town of any size in Texas at 5,050 feet above sea level, and the county has the highest average elevation.

Highest Highway: The highest state highway point also is in Jeff Davis County at McDonald Observatory on Mount Locke, where the road reaches 6,781 feet above sea level, as determined by the Texas Department of Transportation.

Highest Railway: The highest railway point is Paisano Pass, 14 miles east of Marfa in Presidio County, which is 5,074 above sea level.

Lowest Point: Sea level is the lowest elevation determined in Texas, and it can be found in all the coastal counties. No point in the state has been found by the geological survey to be below sea level. ☆

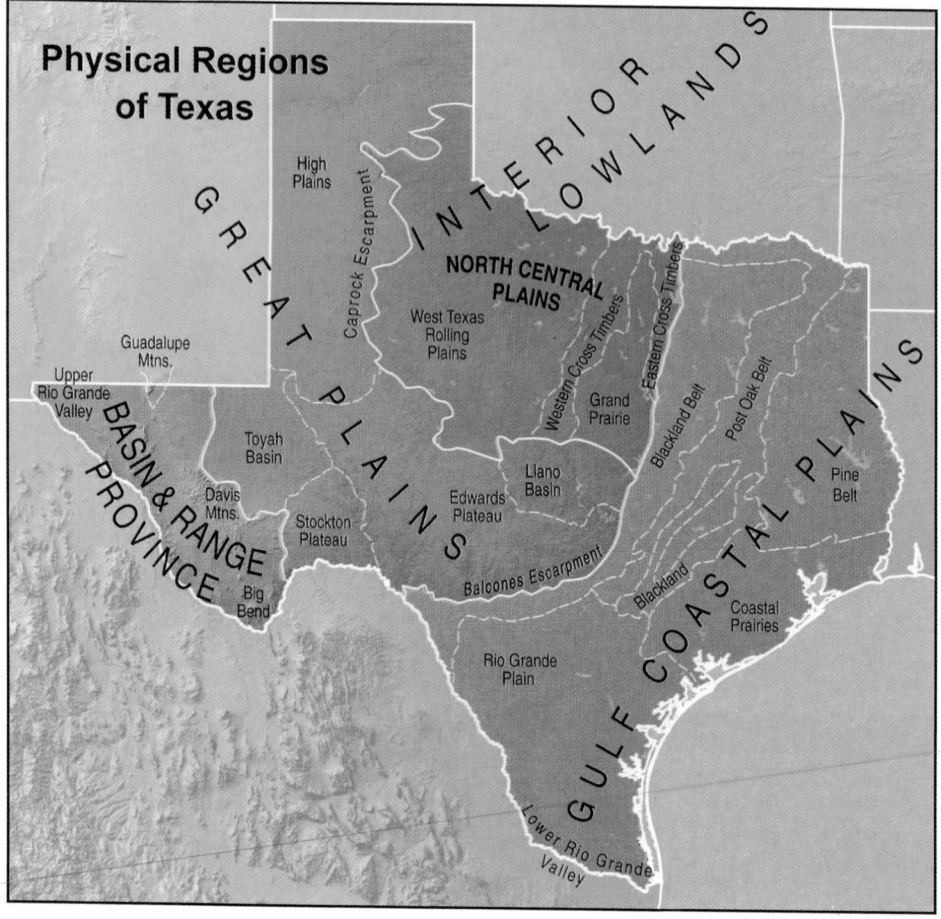

Physical Regions

This section was reviewed by Dr. David R. Butler, Texas State University System Regents' Professor of Geography

The principal physical regions of Texas are usually listed as follows:

I. Gulf Coastal Plains

Texas' Gulf Coastal Plains are the western extension of the coastal plain extending from the Atlantic Ocean to beyond the Rio Grande. Its characteristic rolling to hilly surface covered with a heavy growth of pine and hardwoods extends into East Texas. In the increasingly arid west, however, its forests become secondary in nature, consisting largely of post oaks and, farther west, prairies and brushlands.

The interior limit of the Gulf Coastal Plains in Texas is the line of the Balcones Fault and Escarpment. This geologic fault or shearing of underground strata extends eastward from a point on the Rio Grande near Del Rio. It extends to the northwestern part of Bexar County, where it turns northeastward and extends through Comal, Hays, and Travis counties, intersecting the Colorado River immediately north of Austin. The fault line is a single, definite geologic feature, accompanied by a line of southward- and eastward-facing hills.

The resemblance of the hills to balconies when viewed from the plain below accounts for the Spanish name for this area: balcones.

North of Waco, features of the fault zone are sufficiently inconspicuous that the interior boundary of the Coastal Plain follows the traditional geologic contact between upper and lower Cretaceous rocks. This contact is along the eastern edge of the Eastern Cross Timbers.

This fault line is usually accepted as the boundary between lowland and upland Texas. Below the fault line, the surface is characteristically coastal plains. Above the Balcones Fault, the surface is characteristically interior rolling plains.

A. Pine Belt or "Piney Woods"

The Pine Belt, called the "Piney Woods," extends 75 to 125 miles into Texas from the east. From north to south, it extends from the Red River to within about 25 miles of the Gulf Coast. Interspersed among the pines are hardwood timbers, usually in valleys of rivers and creeks. This area is the source of practically all of Texas' commercial timber production (see Texas Forest Resources, page 115). It was settled early in Texas' history and is one of the oldest farming areas in the state.

This area's soils and climate are adaptable to the production of a variety of fruit and vegetable crops. Cattle raising is widespread, along with the development of pastures planted to improved grasses. Lumber production is the principal industry. There is a large iron-and-steel industry near Daingerfield in Morris County based on nearby iron deposits. Iron deposits are also worked in Rusk and one or two other counties.

A great oil field discovered in Gregg, Rusk, and Smith counties in 1931 has done more than anything else to contribute to the economic growth of the area. This area has a variety of clays, lignite, and other minerals as potentials for development.

B. Post Oak Belt

The main Post Oak Belt of Texas is wedged between the Pine Belt on the east, Blacklands on the west, and the Coastal Prairies on the south, covering a considerable area in East-Central Texas. The principal industry is diversified farming and livestock raising.

It is spotty in character, with some insular areas of blackland soil and some that closely resemble those of the Pine Belt. There is a small, isolated area of loblolly pines in Bastrop, Caldwell, Fayette, and Lee counties known as the "Lost Pines," the westernmost southern pines in the United States. The Post Oak Belt has lignite, commercial clays, and some other minerals.

C. Blackland Belt

The Blackland Belt stretches from the Rio Grande to the Red River, lying just below the line of the Balcones Fault and varying in width from 15 to 70 miles. It is narrowest below the segment of the Balcones Fault from the Rio Grande to Bexar County and gradually widens as it runs northeast to the Red River.

Its rolling prairie, easily turned by the plow, developed rapidly as a farming area until the 1930s and was the principal cotton-producing area of Texas. Now, however, other Texas areas that are irrigated and mechanized lead in farming.

Because of the early growth, the Blackland Belt is still the most thickly populated area in the state and contains within it and along its border more of the state's large and middle-sized cities than any other area. Primarily because of this concentration of population, this belt has the most diversified manufacturing industry of the state.

D. Coastal Prairies

The Texas Coastal Prairies extend westward along the coast from the Sabine River, reaching inland 30 to 60 miles. Between the Sabine and Galveston Bay, the line of demarcation between the prairies and the Pine Belt forests to the north is very distinct. The Coastal Prairies extend along the Gulf of Mexico from the Sabine to the Lower Rio Grande Valley.

The eastern half is covered with a heavy growth of grass; the western half, which is more arid, is covered with short grass and, in some places, with small timber and brush. The soil is heavy clay. Grass supports the densest cattle population in Texas, and cattle ranching is the principal agricultural industry. Rice is a major crop, grown under irrigation from wells and rivers. Cotton, grain sorghum, and truck crops also are grown.

Coastal Prairie areas have seen the greatest industrial development in Texas history since World War II. Chief concentration has been from Orange and Beaumont to Houston, and much of the development has been in petrochemicals and the aerospace industry.

Corpus Christi, in the Coastal Bend, and Brownsville, in the Lower Rio Grande Valley, have seaports and agricultural and industrial sections. Cotton, grain, vegetables, and citrus fruits are the principal crops. Cattle production is significant, with the famed King Ranch and other large ranches located here.

E. Lower Rio Grande Valley

The deep alluvial soils and distinctive economy cause the Lower Rio Grande Valley to be classified as a subregion of the Gulf Coastal Plains. "The Valley," as it is called locally, is Texas' greatest citrus and winter vegetable growing region because of the normal absence of freezing weather and the rich delta soils of the Rio Grande. Despite occasional damaging freezes, the Lower Valley ranks high among the nation's fruit and truck-farming regions. Much of the acreage is irrigated, although dry-land farming also is practiced.

F. Rio Grande Plain

This area may be roughly defined as lying south of San Antonio between the Rio Grande and the Gulf Coast. The Rio Grande Plain shows characteristics of both the Gulf Coastal Plains and the North Mexico Plains because there is similarity of topography, climate, and plant life all the way from the Balcones Escarpment in Texas to the Sierra Madre Oriental in Mexico, which runs past Monterrey about 160 miles south of Laredo.

The Rio Grande Plain is partly prairie, but much of it is covered with a dense growth of prickly pear, mesquite, dwarf oak, catclaw, guajillo, huisache, blackbrush, cenizo, and other cactus and wild shrubs. It is devoted primarily to raising cattle, sheep, and goats. The Texas Angora goat and mohair industry centers in this area and on the Edwards Plateau, which borders it on the north. San Antonio and Laredo are its chief commercial centers, with San Antonio dominating trade.

There is some farming, and the Winter Garden, centering in Dimmit and Zavala counties north of Laredo, is irrigated from wells and streams to produce vegetables in late winter and early spring. Primarily, however, the central and western part of the Rio Grande Plain is devoted to livestock raising.

The rainfall is less than 25 inches annually, and the hot summers cause heavy evaporation, so that cultivation without irrigation is limited.

Over a large area in the central and western parts of the Rio Grande Plain, the growth of small oaks, mesquite, prickly pear (Opuntia) cactus, and a variety of wild shrubs is very dense, and it is often called the Brush Country. It is also referred to as the chaparral and the monte, from a Spanish word that can mean dense brush.)

II. Interior Lowlands

North Central Plains

The North Central Plains of Texas are a southwestern extension into Texas of the interior, or central, lowlands that extend northward to the Canadian border, paralleling the Great Plains to the West. The North Central Plains of Texas extend from the Blackland Belt on the east to the Caprock Escarpment on the west. From north to south, they extend from the Red River to the Colorado River.

A. West Texas Rolling Plains

The West Texas Rolling Plains, approximately the western two-thirds of the North Central Plains in Texas, rise from east to west in altitude from about 750 feet to 2,000 feet at the base of the Caprock Escarpment. Annual rainfall ranges from about 30 inches on the east to 20 inches on the west. In general, as one progresses westward in Texas, the precipitation not only declines but also becomes more variable from year to year. Temperature varies rather widely between summer's heat and winter's cold.

This area still has a large cattle-raising industry with many of the state's largest ranches. However, there is much level, cultivable land.

B. Grand Prairie

Near the eastern edge of the North Central Plains is the Grand Prairie, extending south from the Red River in an irregular band through Cooke, Montague, Wise, Denton, Tarrant, Parker, Hood, Johnson, Bosque, Coryell, and some adjacent counties.

It is a limestone-based area, usually treeless except along the numerous streams, and adapted primarily to raising livestock and growing staple crops. Sometimes called the Fort Worth Prairie, it has an agricultural economy and largely rural population, with no large cities, except Fort Worth on its eastern boundary.

C. Eastern and Western Cross Timbers

Hanging over the top of the Grand Prairie and dropping down on each side are the Eastern and Western Cross Timbers. The two southward-extending bands are connected by a narrow strip along the Red River.

The Eastern Cross Timbers extend southward from the Red River through eastern Denton County and along the boundary between Dallas and Tarrant counties. It then stretches through Johnson County to the Brazos River and into Hill County.

The much larger Western Cross Timbers extend from the Red River south through Clay, Montague, Jack, Wise, Parker, Palo Pinto, Hood, Erath, Eastland, Comanche, Brown, and Mills counties to the Colorado River, where they meet the Llano Basin.

Their soils are adapted to fruit and vegetable crops, which reach considerable commercial production in some areas in Parker, Erath, Eastland, and Comanche counties.

III. Great Plains

A. High Plains

The Great Plains, which lie to the east of the base of the Rocky Mountains, extend into northwestern Texas. This area, commonly known as the High Plains, is a vast, flat, high plain covered with thick layers of alluvial material. It is also known as the Staked Plains or Llano Estacado.

Historians differ as to the origin of this name. Some say it came from the fact that the explorer Coronado's expedition used stakes to mark its route across the trackless sea of grass so that it would be guided on its return trip. Others think that the estacado refers to the palisaded appearance of the Caprock in many places, especially the west-facing escarpment in New Mexico.

The Caprock Escarpment is the dividing line between the High Plains and the lower West Texas Rolling Plains. Like the Balcones Escarpment, the Caprock Escarpment is a striking physical feature, rising abruptly 200 feet, 500 feet, and in some places almost 1,000 feet above the plains. Unlike the Balcones Escarpment, the Caprock was caused by surface erosion.

Where rivers issue from the eastern face of the Caprock, there frequently are notable canyons, such as Palo Duro Canyon on the Prairie Dog Town Fork of the Red River, Blanco Canyon on the White River, as well as the breaks along the Canadian River as it crosses the Panhandle north of Amarillo.

Along the eastern edge of the Panhandle, there is a gradual descent of the land's surface from high to low plains; but at the Red River, the Caprock Escarpment becomes a striking surface feature.

It continues as an east-facing wall south through Briscoe, Floyd, Motley, Dickens, Crosby, Garza, and Borden counties, gradually decreasing in elevation. South of Borden County, the escarpment is less obvious, and the boundary between the High Plains and the Edwards Plateau occurs where the alluvial cover of the High Plains disappears.

Stretching over the largest level plain of its kind in the United States, the High Plains rise gradually from about 2,700 feet on the east to more than 4,000 in spots along the New Mexico border.

Chiefly because of climate and the resultant agriculture, subdivisions are called the North Plains and South Plains. The North Plains, from Hale County north, has primarily wheat and grain sorghum farming, but with significant ranching and petroleum developments. Amarillo is the largest city, with Plainview on the south and Borger on the north as important commercial centers.

The South Plains, also a leading grain sorghum region, leads Texas in cotton production. Lubbock is the principal city, and Lubbock County is one of the state's largest cotton producers. Irrigation from underground reservoirs, centered around Lubbock and Plainview, waters much of the crop acreage.

B. Edwards Plateau

Geographers usually consider that the Great Plains at the foot of the Rocky Mountains actually continue southward from the High Plains of Texas to the Rio Grande and the Balcones Escarpment. This southern and lower extension of the Great Plains in Texas is known as the Edwards Plateau.

It lies between the Rio Grande and the Colorado River. Its southeastern border is the Balcones Escarpment from the Rio Grande at Del Rio eastward to San Antonio and thence

A view of Palo Duro Canyon from the sky. Palo Duro Canyon is part of the Caprock Escarpment, and the second largest canyon in the U.S. Photo by Ken Lund, CC by 2.0/Flickr

to Austin on the Colorado River. Its upper boundary is the Pecos River, though the Stockton Plateau is geologically and topographically classed with the Edwards Plateau.

The Edwards Plateau varies from about 750 feet high at its southern and eastern borders to about 2,700 feet in places. Almost the entire surface is a thin, limestone-based soil covered with a medium to thick growth of cedar, small oak, and mesquite and a varying growth of prickly pear. Grass for cattle, weeds for sheep, and tree foliage for the browsing goats support three industries — cattle, goat, and sheep raising — upon which the area's economy depends. It is the nation's leading Angora goat and mohair producing region and one of the nation's leading sheep and wool areas. A few crops are grown.

Hill Country

The Hill Country is a popular name for the eastern portion of the Edwards Plateau south of the Llano Basin. Its notable large springs include Barton Springs at Austin, San Marcos Springs at San Marcos, Comal Springs at New Braunfels, several springs at San Antonio, and a number of others.

The Hill Country is characterized by rugged hills with relatively steep slopes and thin soils overlying limestone bedrock. High gradient streams combine with these steep hillslopes and occasionally heavy precipitation to produce an area with a significant flash-flood hazard.

C. Toyah Basin

To the northwest of the Edwards and Stockton plateaus is the Toyah Basin, a broad, flat remnant of an old sea floor that occupied the region as recently as Quaternary time.

Located in the Pecos River Valley, this region, in relatively recent time, has become important for many agricultural products as a result of irrigation. Additional economic activity is afforded by local oil fields.

D. Llano Basin

The Llano Basin lies at the junction of the Colorado and Llano rivers in Burnet and Llano counties. Earlier, this was known as the "Central Mineral Region" because of evidence there of a large number of minerals.

On the Colorado River in this area, a succession of dams impounds two large and five small reservoirs. Uppermost is Lake Buchanan, one of the large reservoirs, between Burnet and Llano counties. Below it in the western part of Travis County is Lake Travis.

Between these two large reservoirs are three smaller ones, Inks, Lyndon B. Johnson (formerly Granite Shoals), and Marble Falls reservoirs, used primarily to produce electric power from the overflow from Lake Buchanan. Lake Austin is along the western part of the city of Austin. Still another small lake, Lady Bird Lake (formerly Town Lake), is formed by a low-water dam in Austin.

The recreational area around these lakes has been called the Highland Lakes Country. This is an interesting area with Precambrian and Paleozoic rocks found on the surface. Granitic domes, exemplified by Enchanted Rock north of Fredericksburg, form the core of this area of ancient rocks.

IV. Basin and Range Province

The Basin and Range Province, with its center in Nevada, surrounds the Colorado Plateau on the west and south and enters far West Texas from southern New Mexico on the east. It consists of broad interior drainage basins interspersed with scattered fault-block mountain ranges.

Although this is the only part of Texas regarded as mountainous, these should not be confused with the Rocky

Mountains. Of all the independent ranges in West Texas, only the Davis Mountains resemble the Rockies, and there is much debate about this.

Texas west of the Edwards Plateau, bounded on the north by New Mexico and on the south by the Rio Grande, is distinctive in its physical and economic conditions. Traversed from north to south by fault-block mountains, it contains all of Texas' true mountains and also is very interesting geologically.

A. Guadalupe Mountains

Highest of the Trans-Pecos Mountains is the Guadalupe Range, which enters Texas from New Mexico. It abruptly ends about 20 miles south of the boundary line, where Guadalupe Peak, (8,749 feet, highest in Texas) and El Capitan (8,085 feet) are situated. El Capitan, because of perspective, appears to the observer on the plain below to be higher than Guadalupe.

Lying just west of the Guadalupe Range and extending to the Hueco Mountains a short distance east of El Paso is the Diablo Plateau or basin. It has no drainage outlet to the sea. The runoff from the scant rain that falls on its surface drains into a series of salt lakes that lie just west of the Guadalupe Mountains. These lakes are dry during periods of low rainfall, exposing bottoms of solid salt; for years they were a source of commercial salt. West of the Hueco Mountains are the Franklin Mountains in El Paso, with the Hueco Bolson (a down-dropped area approximately 4,000 feet above sea level) separating the two fault-block ranges.

B. Davis Mountains

The Davis Mountains are principally in Jeff Davis County. The highest peak, Mount Livermore (8,378 feet),

is one of the highest in Texas; there are several others more than 7,000 feet high. These mountains intercept the moisture-bearing winds and receive more precipitation than elsewhere in the Trans-Pecos, so they have more vegetation than the other Trans-Pecos mountains. Noteworthy are the San Solomon Springs at the northern base of these mountains.

C. Big Bend

South of the Davis Mountains lies the Big Bend country, so called because it is encompassed on three sides by a great southward swing of the Rio Grande. It is a mountainous country of scant rainfall and sparse population. Its principal mountains, the Chisos, rise to 7,825 feet in Mount Emory.

Along the Rio Grande are the Santa Elena, Mariscal, and Boquillas canyons with rim elevations of 3,500 to 3,775 feet. They are among the noteworthy canyons of the North American continent.

Because of its remarkable topography and plant and animal life, the southern part of this region along the Rio Grande is home to Big Bend National Park, with headquarters in the Chisos Basin, a deep valley in the Chisos Mountains. It is a favorite recreation area.

D. Upper Rio Grande Valley

The Upper Rio Grande Valley, or El Paso Valley, is a narrow strip of irrigated land running down the river from El Paso for a distance of 75 miles or more.

In this area are the historic towns and missions of Ysleta, Socorro, and San Elizario, some of the oldest in Texas. Cotton is the chief product of this valley, much of it the long-staple variety. This limited area has a dense urban and rural population, in marked contrast to the territory surrounding it. ☆

Hikers enjoying a vista in the Guadalupe Mountains. Photo by Jonathan Cutrer/jcutrer.com

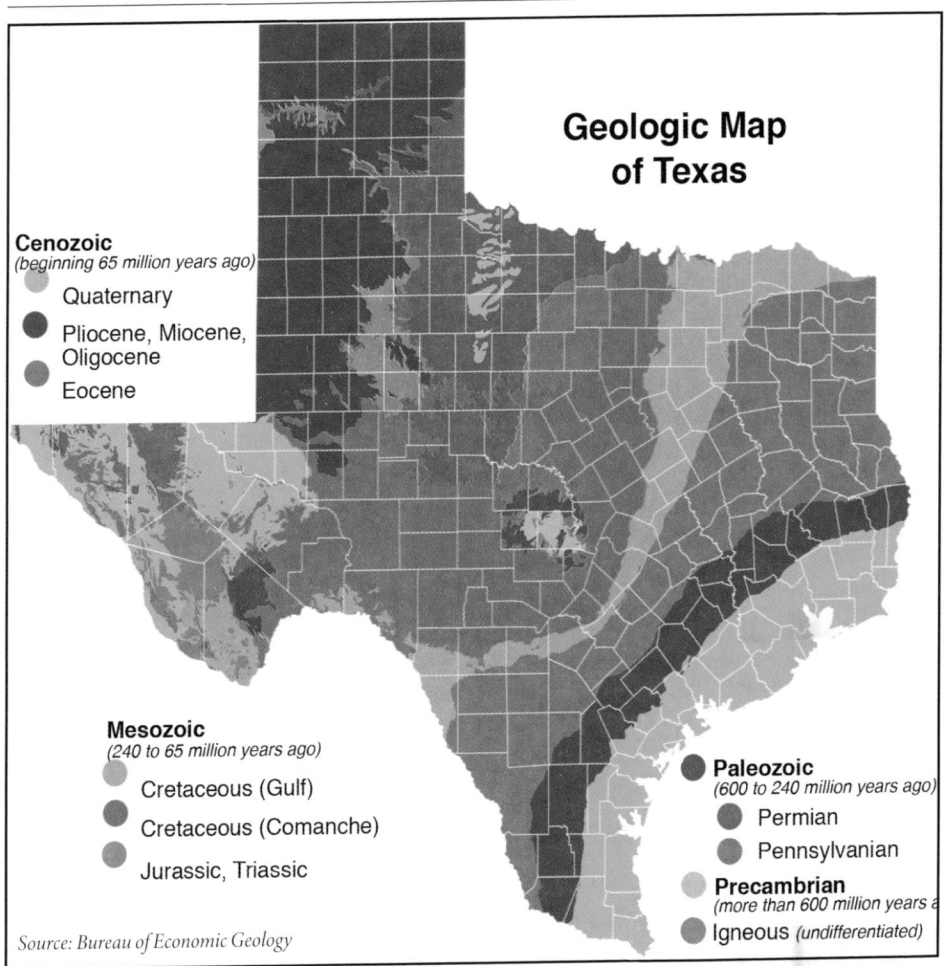

Geologic Map of Texas

Cenozoic
(beginning 65 million years ago)
- Quaternary
- Pliocene, Miocene, Oligocene
- Eocene

Mesozoic
(240 to 65 million years ago)
- Cretaceous (Gulf)
- Cretaceous (Comanche)
- Jurassic, Triassic

Paleozoic
(600 to 240 million years ago)
- Permian
- Pennsylvanian

Precambrian
(more than 600 million years a...)
- Igneous *(undifferentiated)*

Source: Bureau of Economic Geology

Geology of Texas

Source: Bureau of Economic Geology, The University of Texas at Austin; www.beg.utexas.edu

Mountains, seas, coastal plains, rocky plateaus, high plains, forests — all of this physiographic variety in Texas is controlled by the varied rocks and structures that underlie and crop out across the state. The fascinating geologic history of Texas is recorded in the rocks — both those exposed at the surface and those penetrated by holes drilled in search of oil and natural gas.

The rocks reveal a dynamic, ever-changing earth: ancient mountains, seas, volcanoes, earthquake belts, rivers, hurricanes, and winds. Today, the volcanoes and great earthquake belts are no longer active, but rivers and streams, wind and rain, and the slow, inexorable alterations of rocks at or near the surface continue to change the face of Texas.

The geologic history of Texas, as documented by the rocks, began more than a billion years ago. Its legacy is the mineral wealth and varied land forms of modern Texas.

Geologic Time Travel

The story preserved in rocks requires an understanding of the origin of strata and how they have been deformed.

Stratigraphy is the study of the composition, sequence, and origin of rocks: what rocks are made of, how they were formed, and the order in which the layers were formed.

Structural geology reveals the architecture of rocks: the locations of the mountains, volcanoes, sedimentary basins, and earthquake belts.

The map above shows where rocks of various geologic ages are visible on the surface of Texas today. History concerns events through time, but geologic time is such a grandiose concept, most find it difficult to comprehend. So geologists have **named the various chapters of earth history.**

Precambrian Eon

Precambrian rocks, more than 600 million years old, are exposed at the surface in the Llano Uplift of Central Texas and in scattered outcrops in West Texas, around and north of Van Horn and near El Paso.

These rocks, some more than a billion years old, include complexly deformed rocks that were originally formed by cooling from a liquid state, as well as rocks that were altered from pre-existing rocks.

Precambrian rocks, often called the "basement complex," are thought to form the foundation of continental masses. They underlie all of Texas. The outcrop in Central Texas is only the exposed part of the Texas Craton, which is primarily buried by younger rocks. (A craton is a stable, almost immovable portion of the earth's crust that forms the nuclear mass of a continent.)

Paleozoic Era

During the early part of the Paleozoic Era (approximately 600 million to 350 million years ago), **broad, relatively shallow seas repeatedly inundated the Texas Craton and much of North and West Texas.** The evidence for these events is found exposed around the Llano Uplift and in far West Texas near Van Horn and El Paso, and also in the subsurface throughout most of West and North Texas.

The evidence includes early Paleozoic rocks, sandstones, shales, and limestones, similar to sediments that form in seas today, and the fossils of animals, similar to modern crustaceans: the brachiopods, clams, snails, and related organisms that live in modern marine environments.

By late Paleozoic (approximately 350 million to 240 million years ago), the Texas Craton was bordered on the east and south by a long, deep marine basin called the Ouachita Trough. Sediments slowly accumulated in this trough until late in the Paleozoic Era.

Plate-tectonic theory postulates that the collision of the North American Plate (upon which the Texas Craton is located) with the European and African–South American plates uplifted the thick sediments that had accumulated in the trough **to form the Ouachita Mountains**.

At that time, the Ouachitas extended across Texas. Today, the Texas portion of the old mountain range is mostly buried by younger rocks. Ancient remnants can be seen in the Marathon Basin of West Texas due to uplift and erosion of younger sediments.

The public can see the remains of this once-majestic Ouachita Mountain range at Post Park, just south of Marathon in Brewster County. Other remnants at the surface are exposed in southeastern Oklahoma and southwestern Arkansas.

During the **Pennsylvanian** Period, however, the Ouachita Mountains bordered the eastern margin of shallow inland seas that covered most of West Texas. Rivers flowed westward from the mountains to the seas bringing sediment to form deltas along an ever-changing coastline.

The sediments were then reworked by the waves and currents of the inland sea. Today, these fluvial, delta, and shallow marine deposits compose the late Paleozoic rocks that crop out and underlie the surface of North-Central Texas.

Broad marine shelves divided the West Texas seas into several sub-basins, or deeper areas, that received more sediments than accumulated on the limestone shelves. Limestone reefs rimmed the deeper basins. **Today, these limestone reefs are important oil reservoirs in West Texas.**

These seas gradually withdrew from Texas, and by the late **Permian** Period, all that was left in West Texas were shallow basins and wide tidal flats in which salt, gypsum, and red muds accumulated in a hot, arid land. Strata deposited during the Permian Period are exposed today along the edge of the Panhandle, as far east as Wichita Falls and south to Concho County, and in the Trans-Pecos.

Mesozoic Era

Approximately 240 million years ago, the major geologic events in Texas shifted from West Texas to East and Southeast Texas. The European and African–South American plates, which had collided with the North American plate to form the Ouachita Mountains, began to separate from North America.

A series of faulted basins, or rifts, extending from Mexico to Nova Scotia were formed. These rifted basins received sediments from adjacent uplifts. As Europe and the southern continents continued to drift away from North America, **the Texas basins were eventually buried beneath thick deposits of marine salt within the newly formed East Texas and Gulf Coast basins.**

Jurassic and Cretaceous rocks in East and Southeast Texas document a sequence of broad limestone shelves at the edge of the developing Gulf of Mexico. From time to time, the shelves were buried beneath deltaic sandstones and shales, which built the northwestern margin of the widening Gulf of Mexico to the south and southeast.

As the underlying salt was buried more deeply by dense sediments, the salt became unstable and moved toward areas of least pressure. As the salt moved, it arched or pierced overlying sediments forming, in some cases, columns known as "salt domes." In some cases, these salt domes moved to the surface; others remain beneath a sedimentary overburden. This mobile salt formed numerous structures that would later serve to trap oil and natural gas.

By the early **Cretaceous** (approximately 140 million years ago), the shallow Mesozoic seas covered a large part of Texas, eventually extending west to the Trans-Pecos area and north almost to present-day state boundaries.

Today, the **limestone deposited in those seas is exposed in the walls of the magnificent canyons of the Rio Grande in the Big Bend National Park area** and in the canyons and headwaters of streams that drain the Edwards Plateau, as well as in Central Texas from San Antonio to Dallas.

Animals of many types lived in the shallow Mesozoic seas, tidal pools, and coastal swamps. Today, these lower Cretaceous rocks are some of the most fossiliferous in the state. **Tracks of dinosaurs occur in several places,** and remains of terrestrial, aquatic, and flying reptiles have been collected from Cretaceous rocks in many areas.

During most of the late Cretaceous, much of Texas lay beneath marine waters that were deeper than those of the early Cretaceous seas, except where rivers, deltas, and shallow marine shelves existed.

River delta and strandline sandstones are the reservoir rocks for the most prolific oil field in Texas. When discovered in 1930, this East Texas oil field contained recoverable reserves estimated at 5.6 billion barrels.

The chalky rock that we now call the "Austin Chalk" was deposited when the Texas seas became deeper. Today, the chalk and other Upper Cretaceous rocks crop out in a wide band that extends from near Eagle Pass on the Rio Grande, east to San Antonio, north to Dallas, and east to the Texarkana area. The Austin Chalk and other upper Cretaceous rocks dip southeastward beneath the East Texas and Gulf Coast basins.

The late Cretaceous was the time of the last major seaway across Texas, because mountains were forming in the western United States that influenced areas as far away as Texas.

A chain of volcanoes formed beneath the late Cretaceous seas in an area roughly parallel to and south and east of the old, buried Ouachita Mountains. The eruptions of these volcanoes were primarily on the sea floor and great clouds of steam and ash likely accompanied them.

Between eruptions, invertebrate marine animals built reefs on the shallow volcanic cones. Pilot Knob, located southeast of Austin, is one of these old volcanoes that is now exposed at the surface.

Cenozoic Era

At the dawn of the Cenozoic Era, approximately 65 million years ago, deltas fed by rivers were in the northern and northwestern margins of the East Texas Basin. These streams flowed eastward, draining areas to the north and west. Although there were minor incursions of the seas, the Cenozoic rocks principally document extensive seaward building by broad deltas, marshy lagoons, sandy barrier islands, and embayments.

Thick vegetation covered the levees and areas between streams. Coastal plains were taking shape under the same processes still at work today.

The Mesozoic marine salt became buried by thick sediments in the coastal plain area. The salt began to form ridges and domes in the Houston and Rio Grande areas. The heavy load of sand, silt, and mud deposited by the deltas eventually caused some areas of the coast to subside and form large fault systems, essentially parallel to the coast.

Many of these coastal faults moved slowly and probably generated little earthquake activity. However, movement along the Balcones and Luling-Mexia-Talco zones, a complex system of faults along the western and northern edge of the basins, likely generated large earthquakes millions of years ago.

Predecessors of modern animals roamed the Texas Cenozoic coastal plains and woodlands. Bones and teeth of horses, camels, sloths, giant armadillos, mammoths, mastodons, bats, rats, large cats, and other modern or extinct mammals have been excavated from coastal plain deposits.

Vegetation in the area included varieties of plants and trees both similar and dissimilar to modern ones. Fossil palmwood, the Texas "state stone," is found in sediments of early Cenozoic age.

The Cenozoic Era in Trans-Pecos Texas was entirely different. There, extensive volcanic eruptions formed great calderas and produced copious lava flows. These eruptions ejected great clouds of volcanic ash and rock particles into the air — many times the amount of material ejected by the 1980 eruption of Mount St. Helens.

Photo by April Andreas

Want to Visit the Late Cenozoic Era?

Check out the **Waco Mammoth National Monument**. The park was opened in 2015 around the site where, in 1978, Paul Barron and Eddie Bufkin discovered large bones sticking out of a ravine.

Researchers found the remains of 19 mammoths, "an unidentified animal associated with a juvenile sabertooth cat", and other animals that had been buried there by floods some 65,000 years ago.

Visit **www.nps.gov/waco/index.htm** for more information. (And read more on page 165 of this book.)

Ash from the eruptions drifted eastward and is found in many of the sand-and-siltstones of the Gulf Coastal Plains. Lava flowed over older Paleozoic and Mesozoic rocks, and igneous intrusions melted their way upward into crustal rocks. These volcanic and intrusive igneous rocks are well exposed in arid areas of the Trans-Pecos today.

In the Texas Panhandle, streams originating in the recently elevated southern Rocky Mountains brought floods of gravel and sand into Texas. As the braided streams crisscrossed the area, they formed great alluvial fans.

These fans, which were deposited on the older Paleozoic and Mesozoic rocks, occur from northwestern Texas into Nebraska. Between 1 million and 2 million years ago, the streams of the Panhandle were isolated from their Rocky Mountain source, and the eastern edge of this sheet of alluvial material began to retreat westward, forming the Caprock of the modern High Plains.

Late in the Cenozoic Era, a great Ice Age descended on the northern North American continent. For more than 2 million years, there were successive advances and retreats of the thick sheets of glacial ice. Four periods of extensive glaciation were separated by warmer interglacial periods. Although the glaciers never reached as far south as Texas, the state's climate and sea level underwent major changes with each period of glacial advance and retreat.

Sea level during times of glacial advance was 300 to 450 feet lower than during the warmer interglacial periods because so much sea water was captured in the ice sheets. The climate was both more humid and cooler than today, and the major Texas rivers carried more water and more sand and gravel to the sea. These deposits underlie the outer 50 miles or more of the Gulf Coastal Plain.

Approximately 3,000 years ago, sea level reached its modern position. The rivers, deltas, lagoons, beaches, and barrier islands that we know as coastal Texas today have formed since that time. ☆

Soils of Texas

Source: Natural Resources Conservation Service, U.S. Department of Agriculture, www.tx.nrcs.usda.gov

One of Texas' most important natural resources is its soil. Texas soils are complex because of the wide diversity of climate, vegetation, geology, and landscape. More than 1,300 different kinds of soil are recognized in Texas. Each has a specific set of properties that affect its use.

Soils information that was once available only through paper maps or books is now easily accessed online through the Web Soil Survey, found here: **http://websoilsurvey.nrcs.usda.gov.**

As the state's population continues to move from rural to urban areas, the Web Soil Survey is a tool landowners can use to make land-use and management decisions. This free tool allows landowners to analyze soil data and maps. It is used by farmers and ranchers to find information about soil properties and qualities to optimize agricultural production.

The soil survey is also used by homeowners and commercial builders looking for information on the suitability or the limitations of a building site.

For more information, contact the Natural Resources Conservation Service at 101 S. Main, Temple 76501-7602; (254) 742-9800; or visit www.tx.nrcs.usda.gov; find the "Topic" menu and choose the "Soils" option.

Major Soil Areas

Texas can be divided into **21 Major Land Resource Areas** that have similar or related soils, vegetation, topography, climate, and land uses. Following are brief descriptions of these 21 areas:

Trans-Pecos Soils

The 18.7 million acres of the Trans-Pecos, mostly west of the Pecos River, are diverse plains and valleys intermixed with mountains. Surface drainage is slow to rapid. This arid region is used mainly as rangeland. A small amount of irrigated cropland lies on the more fertile soils along the Rio Grande and the Pecos River. Vineyards are a more recent use of these soils, as is the disposal of large volumes of municipal wastes.

Upland soils are mostly well-drained, light reddish-brown to brown clay loams, clays, and sands. Some have a large amount of gypsum or other salts. Many areas have shallow soils and rock outcrops, and sizable areas have deep sands.

Bottomland soils are deep, well-drained, dark grayish-brown to reddish-brown silt loams, loams, clay loams, and clays. The lack of soil moisture and wind erosion are the major soil-management problems. Only irrigated crops can be grown on these soils, and most areas lack an adequate source of good water.

Upper Pecos, Canadian Valleys and Plains Soils

The Upper Pecos, Canadian Valleys, and Plains area occupies a little over a half-million acres and is in the northwest part of Texas near the Texas–New Mexico border. It is characterized by broad rolling plains and tablelands broken by drainageways and tributaries of the Canadian River. It includes the Canadian Breaks, which are rough, steep lands

below the adjacent High Plains. The average annual precipitation is about 15 inches, but it fluctuates widely from year to year. Surface drainage is slow to rapid.

The soils are well drained and alkaline. The mostly reddish-brown clay loams and sandy loams were formed mostly in material weathered from sandstone and shale. Depths range from shallow to very deep.

The area is used mainly as rangeland and wildlife habitat. Native vegetation is mid- to short-grass prairie species, such as hairy grama, sideoats grama, little bluestem, alkali sacaton, vine-mesquite, and galleta in the plains and tablelands. Juniper and mesquite grow on the relatively higher breaks. Soil management problems include low soil moisture and brush control.

High Plains Soils

The High Plains area comprises a vast high plateau of more than 19.4 million acres in northwestern Texas. It lies in the southern part of the Great Plains province that includes large, similar areas in Oklahoma and New Mexico. The flat, nearly level treeless plain has few streams to cause local relief. However, several major rivers originate in the High Plains or cross the area. The largest is the Canadian River, which has cut a deep valley across the Panhandle section.

Playas, small intermittent lakes scattered through the area, lie up to 20 feet below the surrounding plains. A 1965 survey counted more than 19,000 playas in 44 counties occupying some 340,000 acres. Most runoff from rainfall is collected in the playas, but only 10 to 40% of this water percolates back to the Ogallala Aquifer. The aquifer is virtually the exclusive water source in this area.

Upland soils are mostly well-drained, deep, neutral to alkaline clay loams and sandy loams in shades of brown or red. Sandy soils are in the southern part. Many soils have large amounts of lime at various depths and some are shallow over caliche. Soils of bottomlands are minor in extent.

The area is used mostly for cropland, but significant areas of rangeland are in the southwestern and extreme northern parts. Millions of cattle populate the many large feedlots in the area. The soils are moderately productive, and the flat surface encourages irrigation and mechanization. Limited soil moisture, constant danger of wind erosion, and irrigation water management are the major soil-management problems, but the region is Texas' leading producer of three important crops: cotton, grain sorghums, and wheat.

Rolling Plains Soils

The Rolling Plains include 21.7 million acres east of the High Plains in northwestern Texas. The area lies west of the North Central Prairies and extends from the edge of the Edwards Plateau in Tom Green County northward into Oklahoma. The landscape is nearly level to strongly rolling, and surface drainage is moderate to rapid. Outcrops of red beds, geologic materials, and associated reddish soils have led some scientists to use the name "Red Plains." Limestone underlies the soils in the southeastern part. The eastern part contains large areas of badlands (dry terrain with extensive erosion).

Upland soils are mostly deep, pale-brown through reddish-brown to dark grayish-brown, neutral to alkaline sandy loams, clay loams, and clays; some are deep sands.

Many soils have a large amount of lime in the lower part, and a few others are saline; some are shallow and stony. Bottomland soils are mostly reddish-brown and sandy to clayey; some are saline.

This area is used mostly for rangeland, but cotton, grain sorghums, and wheat are important crops. The major soil-management problems are brush control, wind erosion, low fertility, and lack of soil moisture. Salt spots are a concern in some areas.

North Central Prairie Soils

The North Central Prairie occupies about 7 million acres in North Central Texas. Adjacent to this area on the north is the rather small area (less than 1 million acres) called Rolling Red Prairies, which extends into Oklahoma and is included here because the soils and land use are similar.

This area lies between the Western Cross Timbers and the Rolling Plains. It is predominantly grassland intermixed with small wooded areas. The landscape is undulating with slow to rapid surface drainage.

Upland soils are mostly deep, well-drained, brown or reddish-brown, slightly acid loams over neutral to alkaline, clayey subsoils. Some soils are shallow or moderately deep to shale. Bottomland soils are mostly well-drained, dark-brown or gray loams and clays.

This area is used mostly as rangeland, but wheat, grain sorghums, and other crops are grown on the better soils. Brush control, wind and water erosion, and limited soil moisture are the major management concerns.

Edwards Plateau Soils

The 22.7 million acres of the Edwards Plateau are in South Central Texas east of the Trans-Pecos and west of the Blackland Prairie. Uplands are nearly level to undulating except near large stream valleys, where the landscape is hilly with deep canyons and steep slopes. There are many cedar brakes in this area. Surface drainage is rapid.

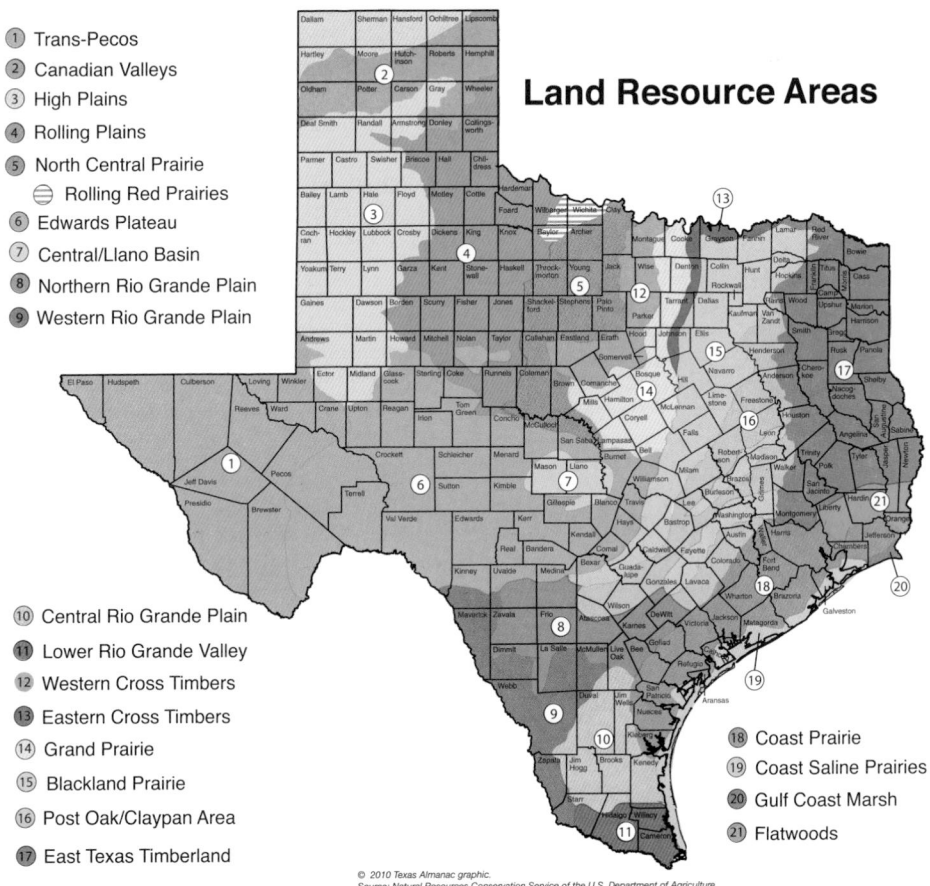

① Trans-Pecos
② Canadian Valleys
③ High Plains
④ Rolling Plains
⑤ North Central Prairie
  ⊜ Rolling Red Prairies
⑥ Edwards Plateau
⑦ Central/Llano Basin
⑧ Northern Rio Grande Plain
⑨ Western Rio Grande Plain

⑩ Central Rio Grande Plain
⑪ Lower Rio Grande Valley
⑫ Western Cross Timbers
⑬ Eastern Cross Timbers
⑭ Grand Prairie
⑮ Blackland Prairie
⑯ Post Oak/Claypan Area
⑰ East Texas Timberland

⑱ Coast Prairie
⑲ Coast Saline Prairies
⑳ Gulf Coast Marsh
㉑ Flatwoods

Land Resource Areas

© 2010 Texas Almanac graphic.
Source: Natural Resources Conservation Service of the U.S. Department of Agriculture.

The map above shows the land resource areas of Texas, as defined by the Natural Resources Conservation Service at the U.S. Department of Agriculture. A land resource area is defined as "a geographic area, usually several thousand acres in extent, that is characterized by a particular pattern of soils, climate, water resources, land uses, and type of farming."

Mesquite trees and prickly pear cacti are common in most parts of the state, and are often cleared from pastureland as part of regular land management. Photo by USDA NRCS Texas/Flickr.

Upland soils are mostly shallow, stony, or gravelly, dark alkaline clays and clay loams underlain by limestone. Lighter-colored soils are on steep sideslopes and deep, less-stony soils are in the valleys. Bottomland soils are mostly deep, dark-gray or brown, alkaline loams and clays.

Raising beef cattle is the main enterprise in this region, but it is also the center of Texas' and the nation's mohair and wool production. The area is a major deer habitat, and hunting leases produce income. Cropland is mostly in the valleys on the deeper soils and is used mainly for growing forage crops and hay. The major soil-management concerns are brush control, large stones, low fertility, excess lime, and limited soil moisture.

Central or Llano Basin Soils

The Central Basin, also known as the Llano Basin, occupies a relatively small area in Central Texas. It includes parts or all of Llano, Mason, Gillespie, and adjoining counties. The total area is about 1.6 million acres of undulating to hilly landscape.

Upland soils are mostly shallow, reddish-brown to brown, mostly gravelly and stony, neutral to slightly acid sandy loams over granite, limestone, gneiss, and schist bedrock. Large boulders are on the soil surface in some areas. Deeper, less stony sandy-loam soils are in the valleys. Bottomland soils are minor areas of deep, dark-gray or brown loams and clays.

Ranching is the main enterprise, with some farms producing peaches, grain sorghum, and wheat. The area provides excellent deer habitat, and hunting leases are a major source of income. Brush control, large stones, and limited soil moisture are soil-management concerns.

Northern Rio Grande Plain Soils

The Northern Rio Grande Plain comprises about 6.3 million acres in South Texas extending from Uvalde to Beeville. The landscape is nearly level to rolling, mostly brush-covered plains with slow to rapid surface drainage.

The major upland soils are deep, reddish-brown or dark grayish-brown, neutral to alkaline loams and clays. Bottomland soils are mostly dark-colored loams.

The area is mostly rangeland with significant areas of cropland. Grain sorghums, cotton, corn, and small grains are the major crops. Crops are irrigated in the western part, especially in the Winter Garden area, where vegetables such as spinach, carrots, and cabbage are grown. Much of the area is good deer and dove habitat; hunting leases are a major source of income. Brush control, soil fertility, and irrigation-water management are the major soil-management concerns.

Western Rio Grande Plain Soils

The Western Rio Grande Plain comprises about 5.3 million acres in an area of southwestern Texas from Del Rio to Rio Grande City. The landscape is nearly level to undulating except near the Rio Grande where it is hilly. Surface drainage is slow to rapid.

The major soils are mostly deep, brown or gray alkaline clays and loams. Some are saline.

Most of the soils are used for rangeland. Irrigated grain sorghums and vegetables are grown along the Rio Grande. Hunting leases are a major source of income. Brush control and limited soil moisture are the major soil-management problems.

Central Rio Grande Plain Soils

The Central Rio Grande Plain comprises about 5.9 million acres in an area of South Texas from Live Oak County to Hidalgo County. It includes the South Texas Sand Sheet, an area of deep, sandy soils and active sand dunes. The landscape is nearly level to gently undulating. Surface drainage is slow to rapid. Upland soils are mostly deep, light-colored, neutral to alkaline sands and loams. Many are saline or sodic. Bottomland soils are of minor extent.

Most of the area is used for raising beef cattle. A few areas, mostly in the northeast part, are used for growing grain sorghums, cotton, and small grains. Hunting leases are a major source of income. Brush control is the major soil-management problem on rangeland; wind erosion and limited soil moisture are major concerns on cropland.

Lower Rio Grande Valley Soils

The Lower Rio Grande Valley comprises about 2.1 million acres in extreme southern Texas. The landscape is level to gently sloping with slow surface drainage.

Upland soils are mostly deep, grayish-brown, neutral to alkaline loams; coastal areas are mostly gray, silty clay loam and silty clay; some are saline. Bottomland soils are minor in extent.

Most of the soils are used for growing irrigated vegetables and citrus, along with cotton, grain sorghums, and sugar cane. Some areas are used for growing beef cattle. Irrigation water management and wind erosion are the major soil-management problems on cropland; brush control is the major problem on rangeland.

Western Cross Timbers Soils

The Western Cross Timbers area comprises about 2.6 million acres. It includes the wooded section west of the Grand Prairie and extends from the Red River southward to the north edge of Brown County. The landscape is undulating and is dissected by many drainageways including the Brazos and Red rivers. Surface drainage is rapid.

Upland soils are mostly deep, grayish-brown, slightly acid loams with loamy and clayey subsoils. Bottomland soils along the major rivers are deep, reddish-brown, neutral to alkaline silt loams and clays.

The area is used mostly for grazing beef and dairy cattle on native range and improved pastures. Crops are peanuts, grain sorghums, small grains, peaches, pecans, and vegetables. The major soil-management problem on grazing lands is brush control. Waste management on dairy farms is a more recent concern. Wind and water erosion are the major problems on cropland.

Eastern Cross Timbers Soils

The Eastern Cross Timbers area comprises about 1 million acres in a long narrow strip of wooded land that separates the northern parts of the Blackland Prairie and Grand Prairie and extends from the Red River southward to Hill County. The landscape is gently undulating to rolling and is dissected by many streams, including the Red and Trinity rivers. Sandstone-capped hills are prominent in some areas. Surface runoff is moderate to rapid.

The upland soils are mostly deep, light-colored, slightly acid sandy loams and loamy sands with reddish loamy or clayey subsoils. Bottomland soils are reddish-brown to dark gray, slightly acid to alkaline loams or gray clays.

Grassland consisting of native range and improved pastures is the major land use. Peanuts, grain sorghums, small grains, peaches, pecans, and vegetables are grown in some areas. Brush control, water erosion, and low fertility are the major soil concerns in management.

Grand Prairie Soils

The Grand Prairie comprises about 6.3 million acres in North Central Texas. It extends from the Red River to about the Colorado River. It lies between the Eastern and Western Cross Timbers in the northern part and just west of the Blackland Prairie in the southern part. The landscape is undulating to hilly and is dissected by many streams including the Red, Trinity, and Brazos rivers. Surface drainage is rapid.

Upland soils are mostly dark-gray, alkaline clays; some are shallow over limestone and some are stony. Some areas have light-colored loamy soils over chalky limestone. Bottomland soils along the Red and Brazos rivers are reddish silt loams and clays. Other bottomlands have dark-gray loams and clays.

Land use is a mixture of rangeland, pastureland, and cropland. The area is mainly used for growing beef cattle. Some small grain, grain sorghums, corn, and hay are grown. Brush control and water erosion are the major management concerns.

Blackland Prairie Soils

The Blackland Prairies consist of about 12.6 million acres of east-central Texas extending southwesterly from the Red River to Bexar County. There are smaller areas to the south-east. The landscape is undulating with few scattered wooded areas that are mostly in the bottomlands. Surface drainage is moderate to rapid.

Both upland and bottomland soils are deep, dark-gray to black alkaline clays. Some soils in the western part are shallow to moderately deep over chalk. Some soils on the eastern edge are neutral to slightly acid, grayish clays and loams over mottled clay subsoils (sometimes called graylands).

Blackland soils are known as "cracking clays" because of the large, deep cracks that form in dry weather. This high shrink-swell property can cause serious damage to foundations, highways, and other structures and is a safety hazard in pits and trenches.

Land use is divided about equally between cropland and grassland. Cotton, grain sorghums, corn, wheat, oats, and hay are grown. Grassland is mostly improved pastures, with native range on the shallower and steeper soils. Water erosion, cotton root rot, soil tilth, and brush control are the major management problems.

Claypan Area Soils

The Claypan Area consists of about 6.1 million acres in east-central Texas just east of the Blackland Prairie. The landscape is a gently undulating to rolling, moderately dissected woodland also known as the Post Oak Belt or Post Oak Savannah. Surface drainage is moderate.

Upland soils commonly have a thin, light-colored, acid sandy loam surface layer over dense, mottled red, yellow, and gray claypan subsoils. Some deep, sandy soils with less clayey subsoils exist. Bottomlands are deep, highly fertile, reddish-brown to dark-gray loamy to clayey soils.

Land use is mainly rangeland. Some areas are in improved pastures. Most cropland is in bottomlands that are protected from flooding. Major crops are cotton, grain sorghums, corn, hay, and forage crops, most of which are irrigated. Brush control on rangeland and irrigation water management on cropland are the major soil-management problems. Water erosion is a serious problem on the highly erosive claypan soils, especially where they are overgrazed.

East Texas Timberland Soils

The East Texas Timberlands area comprises about 16.1 million acres of the forested eastern part of the state. The land is gently undulating to hilly and well dissected by many streams. Surface drainage is moderate to rapid.

This area has many kinds of upland soils but most are deep, light-colored, acid sands and loams over loamy and clayey subsoils. Deep sands are in scattered areas, and red clays are in areas of "redlands." Bottomland soils are mostly brown to dark-gray, acid loams and some clays.

The land is used mostly for growing commercial pine timber and for woodland grazing. Improved pastures are scattered throughout and are used for grazing beef and dairy cattle and for hay production. Some commercial hardwoods are in the bottomlands. Woodland management problems include seedling survival, invasion of hardwoods in pine stands, effects of logging on water quality, and control of the southern pine beetle. Lime and fertilizers are necessary for productive cropland and pastures.

Coast Prairie Soils

The Coast Prairie includes about 8.7 million acres near the Gulf Coast. It ranges from 30 miles to 80 miles in width and parallels the coast from the Sabine River in Orange County in Southeast Texas to Baffin Bay in Kleberg County in South Texas. The landscape is level to gently undulating with slow surface drainage.

Upland soils are mostly deep, dark-gray, neutral to slightly acid clay loams and clays. Lighter-colored and more-sandy soils are in a strip on the northwestern edge. Some soils in the southern part are alkaline; some are saline and sodic. Bottomland soils are mostly deep, dark-colored clays and loams along small streams but are greatly varied along the rivers.

Land use is mainly grazing lands and cropland. Some hardwood timber is in the bottomlands. Many areas are also managed for wetland wildlife habitat. The nearly level topography and productive soils encourage farming. Rice, grain sorghums, cotton, corn, and hay are the main crops. Brush management on grasslands and removal of excess water on cropland are the major management concerns.

Coast Saline Prairies Soils

The Coast Saline Prairies area includes about 3.2 million acres along a narrow strip of wet lowlands adjacent to the coast; it includes the barrier islands that extend from Mexico to Louisiana. The surface is at or only a few feet above sea level with many areas of salt-water marsh. Surface drainage is very slow.

The soils are mostly deep, dark-colored clays and loams; many are saline and sodic. Light-colored sandy soils are on the barrier islands. The water table is at or near the surface of most soils.

Cattle grazing is the chief economic use of the various salt-tolerant cordgrasses and sedges. Many areas are managed for wetland wildlife. Recreation is popular on the barrier islands. Providing fresh water and access to grazing areas are the major management concerns.

Gulf Coast Marsh Soils

This 150,000-acre area lies in the extreme southeastern corner of Texas. The area can be subdivided into four parts: freshwater, intermediate, brackish, and saline (saltwater) marsh. The degree of salinity of this system grades landward from saltwater marshes along the coast to freshwater marshes inland. Surface drainage is very slow.

This area contains many lakes, bayous, tidal channels, and man-made canals. About one-half of the marsh is fresh; one-half is salty. Most of it is susceptible to flooding either by fresh water drained from lands adjacent to the marsh or by saltwater from the Gulf of Mexico.

Most of the soils are poorly drained, continuously saturated, soft, and can carry little weight. In general, the organic soils have a thick layer of dark gray, relatively undecomposed organic material over a gray, clayey subsoil. The mineral soils have a surface of dark gray, highly decomposed organic material over a gray, clayey subsoil.

Most of the almost treeless and uninhabited area is in marsh vegetation, such as grasses, sedges, and rushes. It is used mainly for wildlife habitat. Part of the fertile and productive estuarine complex supports marine life of the Gulf of Mexico. It also provides wintering ground for waterfowl and habitat for many fur-bearing animals and alligators. A significant acreage is firm enough to support livestock and is used for winter grazing of cattle. The major management problems are providing fresh water and access to grazing areas.

Flatwoods Soils

The Flatwoods area includes about 2.5 million acres of woodland in humid Southeast Texas just north of the Coast Prairie and extending into Louisiana. The landscape is level to gently undulating. Surface drainage is slow.

Upland soils are mostly deep, light-colored, acid loams with gray, loamy, or clayey subsoils. Bottomland soils are deep, dark-colored, acid clays and loams. The water table is near the surface at least part of the year.

The land is mainly used for forest, although cattle are grazed in some areas. Woodland management problems include seedling survival, invasion of hardwoods in pine stands, effects of logging on water quality, and control of the southern pine beetle. ☆

A footbridge over the Concho River. Photo by Jonathan Cutrer, jcutrer.com.

Texas Water Resources

Contributed by Dr. Andrew Sansom, leading conservationist and executive director of the Meadows Center for Water and the Environment.

Water shortage is the **most serious** natural resource issue facing Texas today.

Here, as elsewhere in the world, the struggle over the uses to which water should be put — and who has the right to decide on those uses — is **intense and escalating**, particularly as the cyclical occurrence of severe flooding and drought increase. The bottom line is that Texas' population is going to double in the next fifty years (for more about this, see our feature article on page 373) and if all the water rights we have issued in our major rivers since Texas was a colony of Spain were fully exercised, many of them would be dry today. Thus, **many of our most iconic rivers**, which are vital to both our economy and the environment, **are at risk**.

Due in part to increasing stress on our rivers and lakes in Texas, we are also increasingly dependent on groundwater from the State's diverse major and minor aquifers. Unfortunately, **we do not recognize in law or policy the hydrologic linkage of our groundwater resources to surface water** — this failure will complicate sound water management of both in the future.

Texas' sensational system of bays and estuaries are arguably the finest such system of any state in the union. These coastal systems provide billions of dollars of economic benefit to the State and constitute some of the most prolific marine ecosystems in the world. What is less understood is that this spectacular natural resource is entirely dependent on continued supplies of freshwater flowing down our rivers and streams to mix with saltwater to **create the unique conditions vital to the existence of so many species of fish and wildlife**. Despite the enormous economic and environmental benefits we receive from these freshwater inflows, we have done a very inadequate job of insuring their continuation.

Historically, we have been reluctant to make difficult choices and decisions relating to water but when faced with crisis we have reacted. Following the drought of the 1950's, which we formally consider the worst on record, we built over 200 major reservoirs for flood control, water supply, and hydropower and they have served us well. However, since the 1970's there has been a dramatic decline in reservoir construction, due to a number of reasons.

More and more communities are creating underground reservoirs in a process called aquifer storage and retrieval, which captures water in times of high flows and stores it to avoid evaporation. We also have millions of acre feet of **brackish groundwater** in Texas **which has been largely untapped** and is less saline than water from the Gulf and closer to the consumer, making it less costly to produce and deliver.

But will that be enough to ensure our future? Despite much progress in water conservation, particularly in cities like San Antonio and El Paso, we still waste far too much water. **It is likely that the key to having a healthy water supply in the future will be increased efficiency.**

Our rivers and streams, our bays, estuaries, and our aquifers not only help define us as a state but are essential components of the one resource that no plant and animal can live without: water. We must do everything we can to make sure it is there for our economy, our environment, and our children. ☆

Major Aquifers of Texas

Sources: Texas Water Development Board, www.twdb.texas.gov; U.S. Geological Survey, https://www.usgs.gov/centers/tx-water

Aquifers are water-bearing rock formations beneath the earth's surface. Texas has a wealth of fresh to slightly saline groundwater in **nine major and 22 minor aquifers** that underlie more than 81 percent of the state.

Each year, groundwater provides approximately 60 percent of the water used in the state. Annual water use ranged from 14.23 million acre-feet in 2016 to 18.18 million acre-feet in 2011. The median annual water use between the years 2007 and 2016 was 14.6 million acre-feet.

Groundwater is an important resource to every industry in Texas, from farming, ranching, and manufacturing to energy exploration and refining.

Groundwater also provides water for municipal and environmental needs. Approximately 55 percent of the groundwater produced in 2016 was used for agriculture (mostly for irrigation). About half of this amount is used in the Panhandle region of the state. In 2016, groundwater supplied approximately 31 percent of the state's municipal water needs.

For more information about the aquifers of Texas and groundwater management, watch these videos created by the Texas Water Development Board:

www.twdb.texas.gov/groundwater/video/index.asp

Ogallala

The Ogallala Aquifer underlies most of the Texas Panhandle. It is the southernmost extension of the largest aquifer (High Plains Aquifer) in North America. The Ogallala Formation of late Miocene to early Pliocene age consists of heterogeneous sequences of coarse-grained sand and gravel in the lower part, grading upward into clay, silt, and fine sand.

The formation reaches a maximum thickness of 800 feet, and its freshwater saturated thickness averages 95 feet. In Texas, the Panhandle is the most extensive region irrigated with groundwater. About 95 percent of the water pumped from the Ogallala Aquifer is used for irrigation.

Extensive pumping that exceeds the amount of recharge has resulted in consistently declining water levels throughout much of the aquifer. Water conservation measures promoted by agricultural and municipal users have slowed the rate of decline, and water levels have risen in a few areas. Several agencies are investigating playa recharge and agricultural reuse projects in the aquifer area.

Gulf Coast

The Gulf Coast Aquifer system forms a broad belt parallel to the Texas coastline, extending through 54 counties from the Rio Grande northeastward to the Louisiana border. The aquifer system is composed of Quaternary- and Tertiary-age layers including the Catahoula, Oakville, Fleming, Goliad, Willis, Lissie, Bentley, Montgomery, and Beaumont formations.

The Gulf Coast Aquifer system has been divided into three major water-producing components referred to as the Chicot, Evangeline, and Jasper aquifers. These aquifers are composed of discontinuous layers of sand, silt, clay, and gravel.

The maximum total sand thickness of the Gulf Coast Aquifer system ranges from 700 feet in the south to 1,300 feet in the north. Freshwater saturated thickness averages 1,000 feet. The Gulf Coast Aquifer system is used primarily for municipal, industrial, and agricultural purposes.

Water quality is generally good in the central and northeastern parts of the aquifer but deteriorates to the southwest. Years of heavy pumping have caused significant water-level declines in portions of the aquifer. Some of these declines have resulted in land subsidence, particularly in the Houston-Galveston area.

Edwards Balcones Fault Zone

The Edwards Balcones Fault Zone (BFZ) Aquifer forms a narrow belt extending through the south-central part of the state from a groundwater divide in Kinney County through the San Antonio area northeastward to the Leon River in Bell County. A groundwater divide in Hays County hydrologically separates the aquifer into the San Antonio and Austin regions.

The aquifer is highly permeable, with water occurring in fractures, honeycomb-like zones (or intergranular pores), and solution channels that characterize the Edwards and associated limestone formations of Cretaceous age. Because the aquifer is highly permeable, water levels and spring flows respond quickly to rainfall, drought, and pumping. Aquifer thickness ranges from 200 to 600 feet, and freshwater saturated thickness averages 560 feet in the southern part of the aquifer.

Water from the Edwards BFZ is used primarily for municipal, irrigation, and recreational purposes. The City of San Antonio meets the majority of its water needs with Edwards BFZ water. The aquifer also feeds several well-known recreational springs and underlies some of Texas's most environmentally sensitive areas.

In 1993, the Texas Legislature created the Edwards Aquifer Authority (EAA) to regulate pumping from the aquifer to benefit all users within EAA's jurisdiction. The Barton Springs/Edwards Aquifer Conservation District and the Kinney County Groundwater Conservation District also provide aquifer management in the areas of the aquifer that are not within the EAA boundaries.

The EAA has an active outreach program used to educate the public on water conservation. It also operates several active groundwater recharge sites. The San Antonio River Authority also has a number of flood-control structures that effectively recharge the aquifer.

Carrizo-Wilcox

The Carrizo-Wilcox Aquifer extends from south of the Rio Grande in Mexico through Texas northeastward into Arkansas and Louisiana in a wide band parallel to and northwest of the Gulf Coast Aquifer.

The aquifer consists of the Tertiary-age Wilcox Group and overlying Carrizo Sand Formation of the Claiborne Group. The aquifer is composed of a hydrologically connected system of sand locally interbedded with clay, silt, lignite, and gravel. Although the Carrizo-Wilcox Aquifer reaches 3,000 feet in thickness, the freshwater saturated thickness of the sands averages 670 feet.

Throughout most of its extent in Texas, the aquifer yields fresh to slightly saline water. A little more than half of the water pumped from the aquifer is used for irrigation; the remaining amount pumped is used for municipal, industrial, domestic, and livestock purposes.

Recently, the Carrizo-Wilcox Aquifer has been considered as an alternative water supply for growing central Texas communities that have traditionally used the Edwards BFZ Aquifer to meet municipal needs.

Trinity

The Trinity Aquifer consists of Cretaceous-age Trinity Group formations that extend from the Red River in North Texas southward to the Hill Country of Central Texas. It is composed of several smaller aquifers contained within the Trinity Group. Depending on where they occur in the state, they are referred to as the Antlers, Glen Rose, Paluxy, Twin Mountains, Travis Peak, Hensell, and Hosston aquifers.

These aquifers consist of limestones, sands, clays, gravels, and conglomerates. Their combined freshwater saturated thickness averages about 600 feet in North Texas, and about 1,900 feet in Central Texas. The aquifer discharges to many small springs, with most flowing less than 10 cubic feet per second.

The Trinity Aquifer is primarily used to meet municipal water demands, but also provides water for irrigation, livestock, and other domestic purposes. Extensive development of the Trinity Aquifer in the Dallas–Fort Worth and Waco areas has resulted in water-level declines of 350 feet to more than 1,000 feet, though these declines have slowed with more reliance on surface water and reductions in groundwater pumping.

Edwards-Trinity Plateau

The Edwards-Trinity Plateau Aquifer extends from the Hill Country of Central Texas westward and southwestward to the Trans-Pecos region, covering much of the southwestern part of the state. The aquifer consists of early Cretaceous limestone and dolomites of the Edwards Group and sands of the Trinity Group. Although the maximum saturated thickness of the aquifer is greater than 800 feet, freshwater saturated thickness averages 433 feet.

The aquifer lies beneath the Edwards Plateau. Near the plateau's edge, along the northern, eastern, and southern

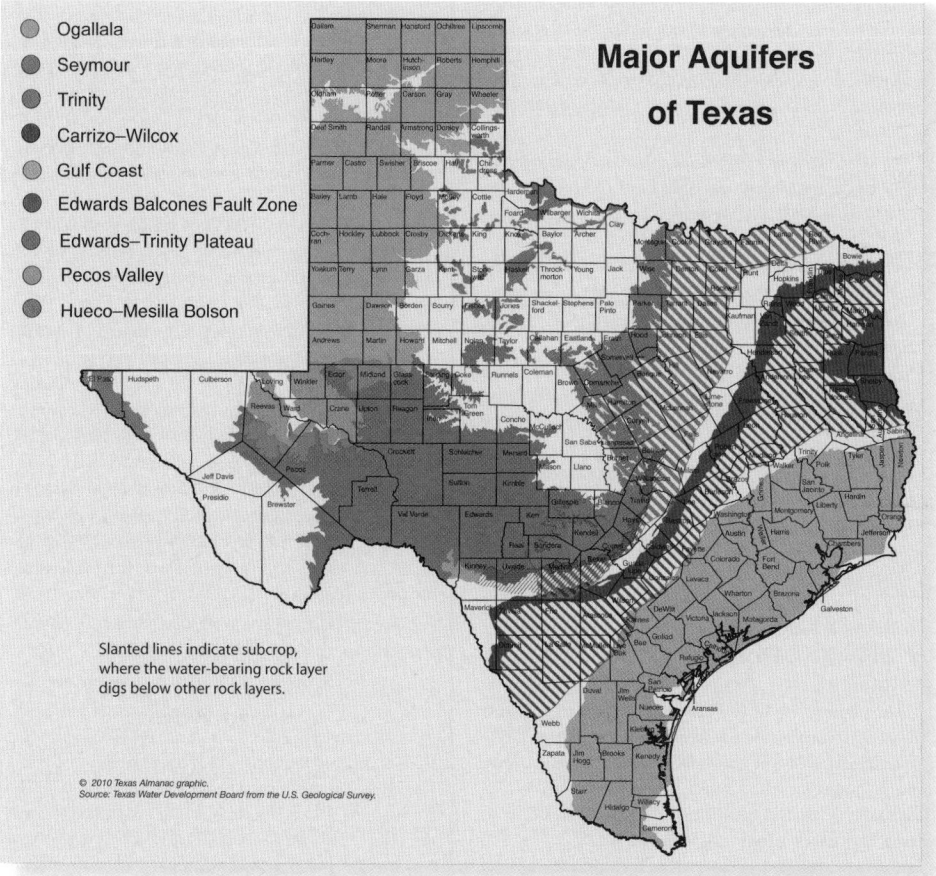

Ogallala
Seymour
Trinity
Carrizo–Wilcox
Gulf Coast
Edwards Balcones Fault Zone
Edwards–Trinity Plateau
Pecos Valley
Hueco–Mesilla Bolson

Major Aquifers of Texas

Slanted lines indicate subcrop, where the water-bearing rock layer digs below other rock layers.

© 2010 Texas Almanac graphic.
Source: Texas Water Development Board from the U.S. Geological Survey.

margins of the aquifer, groundwater flows towards streams, where water discharges from springs. Irrigation, mainly in the northwestern portion of the region, accounts for more than two-thirds of aquifer use.

Seymour

The Seymour Aquifer extends across north-central Texas. It consists of Quaternary-age, alluvial sediments unconformably overlying Permian-age rocks. Water is contained within isolated patches of discontinuous beds of poorly sorted gravel, conglomerate, sand, and silty clay. These deposits may reach 360 feet in thickness, but most of the Seymour is less than 100 feet thick.

About 90 percent of the water pumped from the Seymour is used for irrigation. Water quality generally ranges from fresh to slightly saline; however, some areas have moderately to very saline water quality. Nitrate concentrations occur above primary drinking water standards throughout much of the aquifer.

Hueco-Mesilla Bolsons

The Hueco-Mesilla Bolsons Aquifer is located in El Paso and Hudspeth counties in far West Texas. The aquifer consists of Tertiary and Quaternary basin-fill deposits of silt, sand, gravel, and clay that extend northward into New Mexico and westward into Mexico in two basins. The Hueco Bolson, located on the eastern side of the Franklin Mountains, has a maximum thickness of 9,000 feet and is an important source of drinking water for both El Paso and Juárez, Mexico. The Mesilla Bolson, located on the western side of the Franklin Mountains, has a maximum thickness of 2,000 feet.

Historical large-scale groundwater withdrawals, especially for the municipal uses of El Paso and Juárez, have caused major water-level declines. This pumping has also caused a deterioration of the chemical quality of the groundwater in the aquifer, according to El Paso Water Utilities and the United States Geological Survey.

Nearly 90 percent of the water pumped from the aquifer in the Texas extent of the bolsons is used for public supply. The City of El Paso has reduced its use of groundwater from the Hueco Bolson since 1989, and observation wells indicate that water levels have stabilized from a previously declining trend. El Paso and Fort Bliss also have built the world's largest inland desalination plant in El Paso County, which uses brackish groundwater from the Hueco Bolson.

Pecos Valley

The Pecos Valley Aquifer is located in the upper Pecos River Valley of West Texas. This aquifer, formerly called the Cenozoic Pecos Alluvium, consists of up to 1,500 feet of Tertiary and Quaternary alluvial fill and windblown deposits.

The aquifer occupies two hydrologically separate basins: the Pecos Trough in the west and the Monument Draw Trough in the east. The alluvial fill reaches 1,500 feet thick, and freshwater saturated thickness averages about 250 feet. Naturally occurring arsenic and radionuclides occur in excess of primary drinking water standards.

More than 80 percent of groundwater pumped from the aquifer is used for irrigation, and the remainder is withdrawn for industrial, power supply, and municipal uses. Water-level declines in excess of 200 feet have occurred in Reeves and Pecos counties but have slowed since the mid-1970s as irrigation pumping has decreased. Declines continue in Ward County due to increased municipal and industrial pumping. ☆

Water Regulation in Texas

In Texas, water law historically has been different for surface water and groundwater. **Surface water belongs to the state** and, except for limited amounts of water for household and on-farm livestock use, requires a permit for use.

The **Texas Commission on Environmental Quality (TCEQ)** is responsible for permitting and adjudicating surface water rights. The TCEQ is the primary regulator of surface water and polices contamination and pollution of both surface and groundwater.

In general, groundwater is considered the private property of the surface landowner by "rule of capture," meaning the landowner may pump as much water as he wishes from beneath his land for any beneficial use and that does not harm neighboring property.

This right may be limited only by groundwater conservation districts, which are the state's preferred method of groundwater management and provide for the conservation, preservation, protection, recharging, and prevention of waste of groundwater resources within their jurisdictions.

As of August 2021, there are 98 **groundwater conservation districts** in Texas, covering nearly 70 percent of the state. In addition, two subsidence districts cover Harris, Galveston, and Fort Bend counties. Subsidence districts regulate groundwater production to prevent land subsidence: the gradual caving in or sinking of an area of land.

The **Texas Water Development Board (TWDB)** collects data on water quality and availability within the state, plans for future supply and use, and administers the state's funds for grants and loans to finance future water development and supply. See the current members of the TWDB on page 481.

On July 7, 2021, the TWDB voted to adopt the 2022 State Water Plan. It outlines water conservation strategies for meeting projected water supply needs in 2070. The board has also adopted 16 regional water plans focusing on specific parts of the state.

You can see an interactive version of the current state water plan here:

2022.texasstatewaterplan.org/statewide

In addition, Texas has a Water Conservation Advisory Council, created in 2007. The council provides reports to the Texas Legislature to make recommendations about funding for water-related programs and suggest legislation to extend the lives of our water resources. Learn more at:

savetexaswater.org

Diners sit along the San Antonio River Walk. Photo by Pedro Szekely, CC by 2.0/Flickr.

Major Rivers of Texas

Sources: Texas Water Development Board, www.twdb.texas.gov; U.S. Geological Survey, https://www.usgs.gov/centers/tx-water

There are 11,247 named Texas streams identified in the U.S. Geological Survey Geographic Names Information System. Their combined length is about 80,000 miles, and they drain 263,513 square miles within Texas. Fourteen major rivers are described in this section, starting with the southernmost and moving northward.

Rio Grande

The Pueblo Indians called this river P'osoge, which means the "river of great water." In 1582, Antonio de Espejo of Nueva Vizcaya, Mexico, followed the course of the Río Conchos to its confluence with a great river, which he named Río del Norte (River of the North). The name Rio Grande was first used, apparently by the explorer Juan de Oñate, who arrived on its banks near present-day El Paso in 1598.

Thereafter the names were often consolidated as Río Grande del Norte. It was shown also on early Spanish maps as Río San Buenaventura and Río Ganapetuán. In its lower course, it early acquired the name Río Bravo, which is its name on most Mexican maps. At times it has also been known as Río Turbio, probably because of its muddy appearance during its frequent rises. Some people erroneously call this watercourse the Rio Grande River.

This river forms the boundary of Texas and the international U.S.-Mexican border for 889 or 1,254 river miles, depending upon method of measurement. (See Texas Boundary Lines, page 27.)

The U.S. Geological Survey figure for the total length from its headwaters to its mouth on the Gulf of Mexico is 1,900 miles.

According to the USGS, the Rio Grande is tied with the St. Lawrence River (also 1,900 miles) as the fourth-longest North American river, exceeded only by the Missouri-Mississippi, Mackenzie-Peace, and Yukon rivers. Since all of these except the Missouri-Mississippi are partly in Canada, the Rio Grande is the second-longest river entirely within or bordering the United States. It is Texas' longest river.

The snow-fed flow of the Rio Grande is used for irrigation in Colorado below the San Juan Mountains, where the river rises at the Continental Divide. Turning south, it flows through a canyon in northern New Mexico and again irrigates a broad valley of central New Mexico. Southern

Average Annual Flow		
	River	Acre-Feet*
1.	Brazos	6,074,000
2.	Sabine	5,864,000
3.	Trinity	5,727,000
4.	Neches	4,323,000
5.	Red	3,464,000
6.	Colorado	1,904,000

* One acre-foot equals 325,851 gallons of water.
Source: Texas Water Development Board, 2017 State Water Plan.

Lengths Of Major Rivers		
	River	Length (Miles)
1.	Rio Grande	1,900
2.	Red	1,290
3.	Brazos	1,280
4.	Pecos	926
5.	Canadian	906
6.	Colorado	865

Source: U.S. Geological Survey, 2008.

New Mexico impounds Rio Grande waters in Elephant Butte Reservoir for irrigation of the valley above and below El Paso.

The valley near El Paso is thought to be the oldest irrigated area in Texas because Indians were irrigating crops here when Spanish explorers arrived in the early 1500s.

From source to mouth, the Rio Grande drops 12,000 feet to sea level as a mountain torrent, desert stream, and meandering coastal river. Along its banks and in its valley, Europeans established some of their first North American settlements. Here are situated three of the oldest towns in Texas: Ysleta, Socorro, and San Elizario.

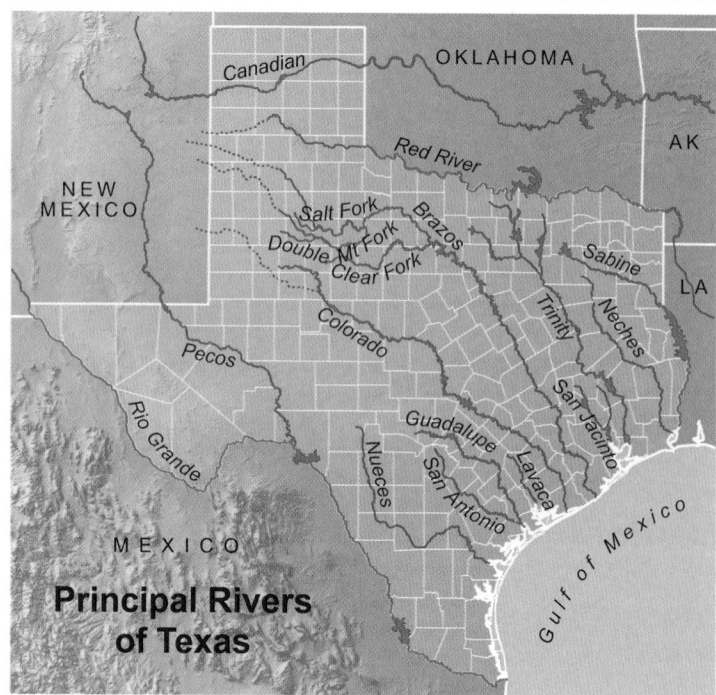

Principal Rivers of Texas

Because of the extensive irrigation, the Rio Grande virtually ends at the lower end of the El Paso valley, except in seasons of above-normal flow.

The river starts again as a perennially flowing stream where the Río Conchos of Mexico flows into it at Presidio-Ojinaga. Through the Big Bend, the Rio Grande flows through three successive canyons, the Santa Elena, the Mariscal, and the Boquillas. The Santa Elena has a river bed elevation of 2,145 feet and a canyon-rim elevation of 3,661. Corresponding figures for Mariscal are 1,925 and 3,625, and for Boquillas, 1,850 and 3,490. The river here flows for about 100 miles around the base of the Chisos Mountains as the southern boundary of Big Bend National Park.

Below the Big Bend, the Rio Grande gradually emerges from mountains onto the Coastal Plains. A 191.2-mile strip on the U.S. side from Big Bend National Park downstream to the Terrell–Val Verde county line has federal designation as the Rio Grande Wild and Scenic River.

At the confluence of the Rio Grande and Devils River, the United States and Mexico have built Amistad Dam, to impound 3,275,532 acre-feet of water, of which Texas' share is 56.2 percent. Falcon Reservoir, also an international project in Zapata and Starr counties, impounds 2,646,813 acre-feet of water, of which Texas' share in Zapata and Starr counties is 58.6 percent.

The Rio Grande, where it joins the Gulf of Mexico, has created a fertile delta called the Lower Rio Grande Valley, a major vegetable- and fruit-growing area. The river drains 49,387 square miles of Texas and has an average annual flow of 1,064,613 acre-feet.

Principal tributaries flowing from the Texas side are the Pecos and Devils rivers. On the Mexican side are Río Conchos, Río Salado, and Río San Juan. About three-fourths of the water running into the Rio Grande below El Paso comes from the Mexican side.

Pecos River

The Pecos, one of the major tributaries of the Rio Grande, rises on the western slope of the Santa Fe Mountains in the Sangre de Cristo Range of northern New Mexico. It enters Texas as the boundary between Loving and Reeves counties and flows 350 miles southeast as the boundary for several other counties, entering Val Verde County at its northwestern corner and angles across that county to its mouth on the Rio Grande, northwest of Del Rio.

According to the Handbook of Texas, the origins of the river's several names began with Antonio de Espejo, who called the river the Río de las Vacas ("river of the cows") because of the number of buffalo in the vicinity. Gaspar Castaño de Sosa, who followed the Pecos northward, called it the Río Salado because of its salty taste, which caused it to be shunned by men and animals alike.

It is believed that the name "Pecos" first appears in Juan de Oñate's reports concerning the Indian pueblo of Cicuye, now known as the Pecos Pueblo in New Mexico, and is of unknown origin.

Through most of its 926-mile-long course from its headwaters, the Pecos River parallels the Rio Grande. The total drainage area of the Pecos in New Mexico and Texas is about 44,000 square miles. Most of its tributaries flow from the west; these include the Delaware River and Toyah Creek.

The topography of the river valley in Texas ranges from semi-arid irrigated farmlands, desert with sparse vegetation, and, in the lowermost reaches of the river, deep canyons.

Nueces River

The Nueces River rises in two forks in Edwards and Real counties and flows 315 miles to Nueces Bay on the Gulf near Corpus Christi. Draining 16,700 square miles, it is a beautiful, spring-fed stream flowing through canyons until it issues from the Balcones Escarpment onto the Coastal Plains in northern Uvalde County.

Alonso de León, in 1689, gave it its name. Nueces, plural of nuez, means nuts in Spanish. (More than a century earlier, Cabeza de Vaca had referred to a Río de las Nueces in this region, but that is now thought to have been the Guadalupe.)

The original Indian name for this river seems to have been Chotilapacquen. Crossing Texas in 1691, Terán de los Ríos named the river San Diego.

The Nueces was the boundary line between the Spanish provinces of Texas and Nuevo Santander. After the Texas Revolution of 1836, both Texas and Mexico claimed the territory between the Nueces and the Rio Grande, a dispute that was settled in 1848 by the Treaty of Guadalupe Hidalgo, which fixed the international boundary at the Rio Grande.

Average runoff of the Nueces is about 539,700 acre-feet a year. Principal water supply projects are Lake Corpus Christi and Choke Canyon Reservoir. Principal tributaries of the Nueces are the Frio and the Atascosa rivers. The river terminates in Nueces and Corpus Christi bays along the Coastal Bend.

San Antonio River

The San Antonio River has at its source large springs within and near the city limits of San Antonio. It flows 180 miles across the Coastal Plains to a junction with the Guadalupe River to enter San Antonio Bay along the Gulf Coast. Its channel through San Antonio has been developed into a parkway known as the River Walk.

Its principal tributaries are the Medina River and Cibolo Creek, both spring-fed streams, and this, with its own spring origin, gives it remarkably clear water and makes it one of the steadiest of Texas rivers. Including the Medina River headwaters, it is 238 miles in length.

The river was first named the León by Alonso de León in 1689; the name was not for himself, but he called it "lion" because its channel was filled with a rampaging flood.

Because of its limited and arid drainage area (4,180 square miles) the average runoff of the San Antonio River is relatively small, about 562,700 acre-feet annually.

Guadalupe River

The Guadalupe rises in its North and South forks in western Kerr County. A spring-fed stream, it flows eastward through the Hill Country until it issues from the Balcones Escarpment near New Braunfels. It then crosses the Coastal Plains to San Antonio Bay. Its total length is 409 miles, and its drainage area is 5,953 square miles. Its principal tributaries are the Comal, which joins it at New Braunfels; the San Marcos, another spring-fed stream, which joins it in Gonzales County; and the San Antonio, which joins it just above its mouth on San Antonio Bay.

There has been power development on the Guadalupe near Gonzales and Cuero for many years, and there is also power generation at Canyon Lake. Because of its springs and its considerable drainage area, the Guadalupe has an average annual runoff of more than 1.42 million acre-feet.

The name Guadalupe is derived from Nuestra Señora de Guadalupe, the name given the stream by Alonso de León.

Lavaca River

The Lavaca rises in extreme southwestern Fayette County and flows 117 miles to terminate in Lavaca Bay. Without a spring-fed water source and with only a small watershed, including that of its principal tributary, the Navidad, its flow is intermittent. Runoff averages about 277,000 acre-feet yearly.

The Spanish called it the Lavaca (the cow) because of the numerous bison found near it. It is the principal stream flowing to the Texas Coast between the Guadalupe and the Colorado, and drains 2,309 square miles. The principal lake on the Navidad is Lake Texana.

Colorado River

The Colorado River rises in east-central Dawson County and flows 600 miles to Matagorda Bay. Its drainage area, which extends into New Mexico, is 42,318 square miles. The U.S. Geological Survey puts is total length from source at 865 miles.

Its average annual runoff reaches a volume of 1.9 million acre-feet near the coast. Its name is a Spanish word meaning "reddish." There is evidence that Spanish explorers originally named the muddy Brazos "Colorado," but Spanish mapmakers later transposed the two names.

The river flows through a rolling, mostly prairie terrain to the vicinity of San Saba County, where it enters the rugged Hill Country and Llano Basin. It passes through a picturesque series of canyons until it issues from the Balcones Escarpment at Austin and flows across the Coastal Plains.

In the Hill Country, a remarkable series of reservoirs has been built to provide hydoelectric power, flood control, and water supply. The largest of these are Lake Buchanan in Burnet and Llano counties and Lake Travis in Travis County. Between the two in Burnet County are three smaller reservoirs: Inks, Lyndon B. Johnson (formerly Granite Shoals), and Marble Falls. Below Lake Travis is the older Lake Austin, largely filled with silt, whose dam is used to produce power from waters flowing down from the lakes above. Lady Bird Lake (formerly Town Lake) is in the city of Austin. This entire area is known as the Highland Lakes Country.

As early as the 1820s, Anglo-Americans settled on the banks of the lower Colorado, and in 1839, the Capital Commission of the Republic of Texas chose the picturesque area where the river flows from the Balcones Escarpment as the site of a new capital of the Republic — now Austin, capital of the state.

The early colonists encouraged navigation along the lower channel with some success. However, a natural log raft that formed 10 miles from the Gulf blocked river traffic after 1839, although shallow-draught vessels occasionally ventured as far upstream as Austin.

Conservation and utilization of the waters of the Colorado are under the jurisdiction of two agencies created

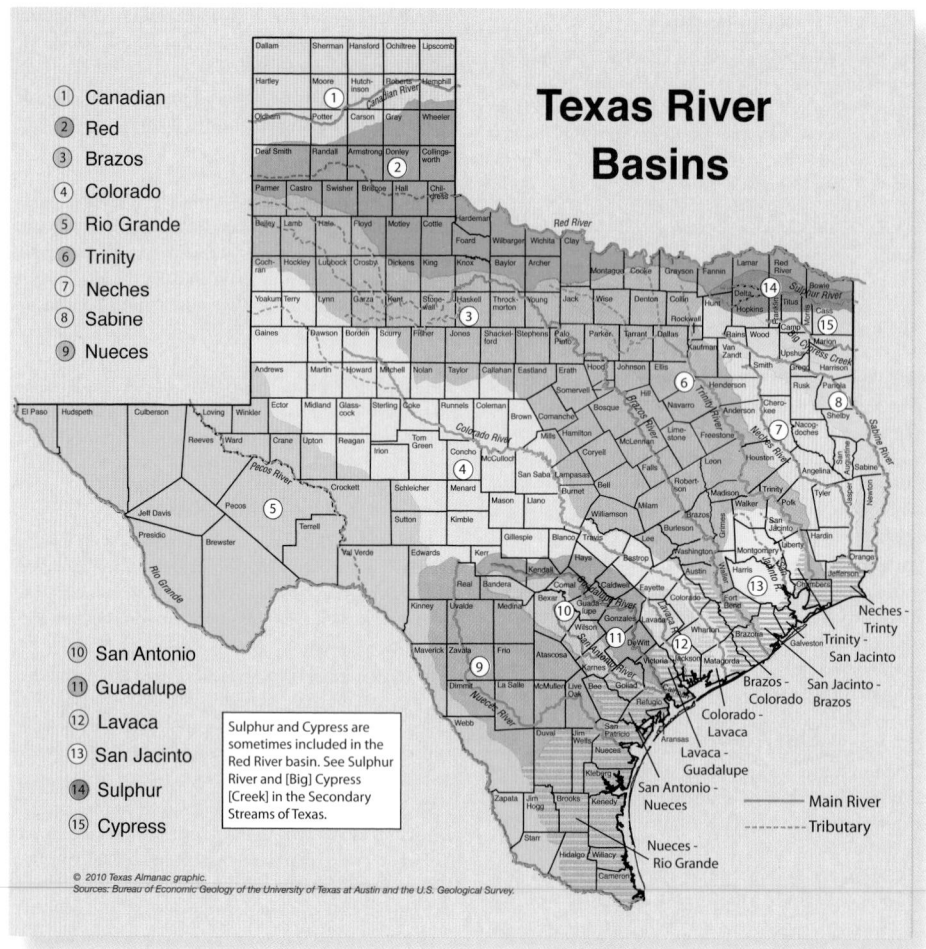

Texas River Basins

1. Canadian
2. Red
3. Brazos
4. Colorado
5. Rio Grande
6. Trinity
7. Neches
8. Sabine
9. Nueces
10. San Antonio
11. Guadalupe
12. Lavaca
13. San Jacinto
14. Sulphur
15. Cypress

Sulphur and Cypress are sometimes included in the Red River basin. See Sulphur River and [Big] Cypress [Creek] in the Secondary Streams of Texas.

Neches - Trinty
Trinity - San Jacinto
Brazos - San Jacinto
San Jacinto - Brazos
Brazos - Colorado
Colorado - Lavaca
Lavaca - Guadalupe
San Antonio - Nueces
Nueces - Rio Grande

—— Main River
------ Tributary

© 2010 Texas Almanac graphic.
Sources: Bureau of Economic Geology of the University of Texas at Austin and the U.S. Geological Survey.

by the Legislature — the Lower and Upper Colorado River authorities.

The principal tributaries of the Colorado River are the several prongs of the Concho River on its upper course, Pecan Bayou (farthest west "bayou" in the United States), and the Llano, San Saba, and Pedernales rivers. All except Pecan Bayou flow into the Colorado from the Edwards Plateau and are spring-fed, perennially flowing rivers. In the numerous mussels found along these streams, pearls occasionally have been found. On early Spanish maps, the Middle Concho was called Río de las Perlas.

Brazos River

The Brazos River proper is considered to begin where the Double Mountain and Salt Forks flow together in northeastern Stonewall County; it then flows 840 miles across Texas. The U.S. Geological Survey puts the total length from the New Mexico source of its longest upper prong at 1,280 miles.

With a drainage area of about 42,865 square miles, it is the second-largest river basin in Texas, after the Rio Grande. It flows directly into the Gulf southwest of Freeport in Brazoria County. Its average annual flow approaches 6.1 million acrefeet, the largest volume of any river in the state.

The Brazos' third upper fork is the Clear Fork, which joins the main stream in Young County, just above Possum Kingdom Lake. The Brazos crosses most of the main physiographic regions of Texas: High Plains, West Texas Rolling Plains, Western Cross Timbers, Grand Prairie, and Gulf Coastal Plains.

The original name of this river was Brazos de Dios, meaning "Arms of God." There are several legends as to why. One story is that the Coronado expedition, wandering on the trackless Llano Estacado, exhausted its water and was threatened with death from thirst. Arriving at the bank of the river, they gave it the name "Brazos de Dios" in thankfulness. Another legend is that a ship exhausted its water supply, and its crew was saved when they found the mouth of the Brazos. Still another story is that miners on the San Saba were forced by drought to seek water near present-day Waco and in gratitude called it Brazos de Dios.

Much early Anglo-American colonization of Texas took place in the Brazos Valley. Along its channel were San Felipe de Austin, capital of Austin's colony;

Washington-on-the-Brazos, where Texans declared independence from Mexico; and other historic settlements. There was some navigation of the lower channel of the Brazos in this period. Near its mouth, it intersects the Gulf Intracoastal Waterway, which provides connection with commerce throughout Texas and the Gulf Coast.

Most of the Brazos Valley lies within the boundaries of the Brazos River Authority, which conducts a multipurpose program for development. A large reservoir on the main channel of the Brazos is Lake Whitney (554,203 acre-feet capacity), where it is the boundary line between Hill and Bosque counties. Lake Waco on the Bosque and Belton Lake on the Leon are among the principal reservoirs on its tributaries. In addition to its three upper forks, other chief tributaries are the Paluxy, Little, and Navasota rivers.

San Jacinto River

The San Jacinto is a short river with a drainage basin of 3,936 square miles and an average annual runoff of about 1.36 million acre-feet. It is formed by the junction of its East and West forks in northeastern Harris County and runs to the Gulf through Galveston Bay. Its total length, including the East Fork, is about 85 miles.

Lake Conroe is on the West Fork, and Lake Houston is at the junction of the West Fork and the East Fork. The Houston Ship Channel runs through the lower course of the San Jacinto and its tributary, Buffalo Bayou, connecting the Port of Houston to the Gulf.

There are two stories concerning the origin of its name. One is that when early explorers discovered it, its channel was choked with hyacinth ("jacinto" is the Spanish word for hyacinth). The other is that it was discovered on Aug. 17, St. Hyacinth's Day.

The Battle of San Jacinto was fought on the bank of this river on April 21, 1836, when Texas won its independence from Mexico. San Jacinto Battleground State Historic Site and monument commemorate the battle.

Trinity River

The Trinity rises in its East Fork, Elm Fork, West Fork, and Clear Fork in Grayson, Montague, Archer, and Parker counties, respectively. The main stream begins with the junction of the Elm and West forks at Dallas. Its length is 550 miles, and its drainage area is 17,913 square miles. Because of moderate to heavy rainfall over its drainage area, it has an average annual flow of 5.7 million acre-feet near its mouth on Trinity Bay in the Galveston Bay system.

The Trinity derives its name from the Spanish "Trinidad." Alonso de León named it La Santísima Trinidad (the Most Holy Trinity).

Navigation was developed along its lower course with several riverport towns, such as Sebastopol in Trinity County. For many years, there has been a basin-wide movement for navigation, conservation, and utilization of its water. The Trinity River Authority is a state agency and the Trinity Improvement Association is a publicly supported nonprofit organization that has advocated its development.

The Trinity has in its valley more large cities, greater population, and more industrial development than any other river basin in Texas. On the Coastal Plains, there is large use of its waters for rice irrigation. Large reservoirs on the Elm Fork are Lewisville Lake and Ray Roberts Lake. There are four reservoirs above Fort Worth: Lake Worth, Eagle Mountain Lake, and Lake Bridgeport on the West Fork and Benbrook Lake on the Clear Fork.

Lake Lavon in southeast Collin County and Lake Ray Hubbard in Collin, Dallas, Kaufman, and Rockwall counties are on the East Fork. Lake Livingston is in Polk, San Jacinto, Trinity, and Walker counties.Two other reservoirs in the Trinity basin below the Dallas–Fort Worth area are Cedar Creek Reservoir and Richland-Chambers Reservoir.

Neches River

The Neches rises in Van Zandt County in East Texas and flows 416 miles to Sabine Lake near Port Arthur. It has a drainage area of 9,937 square miles. Abundant rainfall over its entire basin gives it an average annual flow near the Gulf of about 4.3 million acre-feet a year. The river takes its name from the Neches Indians, who the early Spanish explorers found living along its banks. Principal tributary of the Neches, and comparable with the Neches in length and flow above their confluence, is the Angelina River, so named for Angelina (Little Angel), a Hainai Indian girl who converted to Christianity and played an important role in the early development of this region.

Both the Neches and the Angelina run most of their courses in the Piney Woods, and there was much settlement along them as early as the 1820s.

Sam Rayburn Reservoir, near Jasper on the Angelina River, was completed and dedicated in 1965. With a storage capacity of 2.88 million acre-feet, it is the fourth-largest reservoir in Texas. Reservoirs located on the Neches River include Lake Palestine in the upper basin and B. A. Steinhagen Lake located at the junction of the Neches and the Angelina rivers.

Sabine River

The Sabine River is formed by three forks rising in Collin and Hunt counties. From its sources to its mouth on Sabine Lake, it flows approximately 360 miles and drains 7,570 square miles.

Sabine comes from the Spanish word for cypress, as does the name of the Sabinal River, which flows into the Frio River in Southwest Texas. The Sabine has an average annual flow volume of 5.8 million acre-feet.

Throughout most of Texas history, the lower Sabine has been the eastern Texas boundary line, although for a while there was doubt as to whether the Sabine or the Arroyo Hondo, east of the Sabine in Louisiana, was the boundary. For a number of years, the outlaw-infested neutral ground lay between them. There was also a boundary dispute in which it was alleged that the Neches River was really the Sabine and, therefore, the boundary.

Travelers over the part of the Camino Real known as the Old San Antonio Road crossed the Sabine at the Gaines Ferry in Sabine County, and there were crossings for the Atascosito Road and other travel and trade routes of that day.

Toledo Bend Reservoir is the largest lake lying wholly or partly in Texas. The reservoir impounds 4.47 million acre-feet of water on the Sabine River in Newton, Panola, Sabine, and Shelby counties. It is the 16th-largest reservoir (in capacity by volume) in the United States. This is a joint project of Texas and Louisiana, through the Sabine River Authority.

Red River

The Red River, with a length of 1,290 miles from its headwaters, is exceeded in length only by the Rio Grande among rivers associated with Texas. Its original source is water in Curry County, New Mexico, near the Texas boundary, forming a definite channel as it crosses Deaf Smith County, Texas, in tributaries that flow into the Prairie Dog Town Fork of the Red River. These waters carve the spectacular Palo Duro Canyon of the High Plains before the Red River leaves the Caprock Escarpment, flowing eastward.

Where the Red River crosses the 100th meridian at the bottom of the Panhandle, the river becomes the Texas-Oklahoma boundary and is soon joined by Buck Creek to form the main channel, according to the U.S. Geological Survey. Its length in Texas is 695 miles, before it flows into Arkansas, where it swings south to flow through Louisiana.

The Red River, which drains 24,297 square miles in Texas, is a part of the Mississippi drainage basin, and at one time it emptied all of its water into the Mississippi. In recent years, however, part of its water, especially at flood stage, has flowed to the Gulf via the Atchafalaya River in Louisiana.

The Red River takes its name from the red color of the water. This caused every explorer who came to its banks to call it "red" regardless of the language he spoke — Río Rojo or Río Roxo in Spanish, Rivière Rouge in French. At an early date, the river became the axis for French advance from Louisiana northwestward as far as present-day Montague County. There was consistent early navigation of the river from its mouth on the Mississippi to Shreveport, above which navigation was blocked by a natural log raft.

A number of important gateways into Texas from the north were established along the stream, such as Pecan Point and Jonesborough in Red River County, Colbert's Ferry and Preston in Grayson County, and later, Doan's Store Crossing in Wilbarger County. The river was a menace to the early traveler because of both its variable current and its quicksands, which brought disaster to many a trail-herd cow, as well as ox team and covered wagon.

The largest water conservation project on the Red River is Lake Texoma, with a conservation storage capacity of 2.5 million acre-feet.

The Red River's high content of salt and other minerals limits the usefulness of its water along its upper reaches. Ten salt springs and tributaries in Texas and Oklahoma contribute most of these minerals.

The uppermost tributaries of the Red River in Texas are Tierra Blanca Creek, which rises in Curry County, N.M., and flows easterly across Deaf Smith and Randall counties to meet Palo Duro Creek and form the Prairie Dog Town Fork a few miles east of Canyon.

Other principal tributaries in Texas are the Pease and the Wichita in North Central Texas and the Sulphur in Northeast Texas, which flows through Wright Patman Lake, then into the Red River after it has crossed the boundary line into Arkansas.

The last major tributary in Northeast Texas is the Cypress Creek system, which flows into Louisiana before joining with the Red River. Major reservoirs in this basin are Lake O' The Pines and Caddo Lake.

From Oklahoma, the principal tributary is the Washita, which has its headwaters in Roberts County, Texas. The Ouachita, a river with the same pronunciation though spelled differently, is the principal tributary to the Red River's lower course in Arkansas.

The Red River boundary dispute, a long-standing feud between Oklahoma and Texas, was finally settled in 2000 when the boundary was set at the vegetation line on the south bank, except for Lake Texoma, where the boundary was set within the channel of the lake.

Canadian River

The Canadian River heads near Raton Pass in northern New Mexico near the Colorado boundary line and flows into Texas on the west line of Oldham County. It crosses the Texas Panhandle into Oklahoma and there flows into the Arkansas River, a total distance of 906 miles. It drains 12,865 square miles in Texas, and much of its 213-mile course across the Panhandle is in a deep gorge.

A tributary, the North Canadian River, dips briefly into the Texas Panhandle in Sherman County before it joins the main channel in Oklahoma.

One of several theories as to how the Canadian got its name is that some early explorers thought it flowed into Canada. Lake Meredith, formed by Sanford Dam, provides water for several Panhandle cities.

Because of the deep gorge and the quicksand that occurs in many places, the Canadian River has been a particularly difficult stream to bridge. It is known, especially in its lower course in Oklahoma, as outstanding among the streams of the country for the great amount of quicksand in its channel. ☆

The Hunt Crossing Dam across the Guadalupe River.
Photo by Jonathan Cutrer, jcutrer.com.

Secondary Streams of Texas

In addition to the principal rivers, Texas has many other streams of various size. The following list gives a few of these streams as designated by the U.S. Geological Survey, with additional information from the new Handbook of Texas and previous Texas Almanacs.

Alamito Creek: Formed by confluence of North, South forks 3 mi. N Marfa in Presidio County. Flows SE 82 mi. to Rio Grande 5 mi. S Presidio.

Angelina River: Rises in central Rusk County; flows SE 120 mi. through Cherokee, Nacogdoches, Angelina, San Augustine counties into Sam Rayburn Reservoir, then into Jasper County to the Neches River 12 mi. west of Jasper. A meandering stream through forested country.

Aransas River: Formed 2 mi. N Skidmore in SC Bee County by union of Poesta and Aransas creeks; flows SE 40 mi. forming boundary between San Patricio and Refugio counties; then briefly into Aransas County where it empties into Copano Bay.

Atascosa River: Formed NW Atascosa County by confluence of North, West prongs, flows SE 92 mi. through Atascosa and Live Oak counties into Frio River 2 mi. NW Three Rivers.

Attoyac Bayou: Rises 2.8 mi. NE Mount Enterprise in SE Rusk County; flows SE 67 mi. through Shelby, San Augustine and Nacogdoches counties into Angelina River at Sam Rayburn Reservoir.

Barton Creek: Rises NE of Henly in NW Hays County; flows E 40 mi. through Travis County to Colorado River at Lady Bird Lake in Austin.

Beals Creek: Formed by confluence of Sulphur Springs and Mustang draws 4 mi. W Big Spring SW Howard County; flows E 55 mi. into Mitchell County to mouth on Colorado River.

Big Cypress Creek: Forms in SE Hopkins County E of Pickton; flows SE 60 mi. to mouth on Big Cypress Bayou 3 mi. E Jefferson in Marion County and just before the bayou flows into Caddo Lake. The creek forms the boundary lines between Camp and Titus, Camp and Morris, and Morris and Upshur counties. It passes through Lake Cypress Springs, Lake Bob Sandlin, and Lake O' The Pines, and is part of the Red River drainage basin.

Blackwater Draw: Rises in Curry County, N.M.; flows into Texas in extreme NW Bailey County; flows SE through Lamb, Hale, and Lubbock counties to junction with Yellow House Draw to form North Fork of the Double Mountain Fork Brazos River. Length, 100 mi.

Blanco Creek: Rises near the intersection of Bee, Goliad and Karnes county lines in extreme S Karnes County; flows SE 45 mi. forming boundary of Bee and Goliad counties. Joins Medio Creek in Refugio County to form Mission River.

Blanco Creek: Rises E of Concan in Uvalde County; flows S 44 mi. to Frio River.

Blanco River: Rises W Lindendale in NE Kendall County; flows SE 64 mi. through Blanco and Hays counties; joins San Marcos River, a tributary of the Guadalupe; fed by many springs.

Bosque River: Flows from Lake Waco in McLennan County 5 mi. into Brazos River.

Bosque River, North: Formed at Stephenville by the union of North, South forks in Erath County; flows generally SE 96 mi. through Hamilton, Bosque and McLennan counties into Lake Waco.

Bosque River, South: Rises near Coryell-McLennan county line; flows NE 24 mi. into Lake Waco.

Brady Creek: Rises 14 mi. SW Eden in SW Concho County; flows 90 mi. through McCulloch and San Saba counties into San Saba River 10 mi. SW of Richland Springs.

Brazos River, Clear Fork: Rises 8 mi. E Snyder in Scurry County; flows NE 180 mi. through Fisher, Jones, Haskell, Throckmorton, Shackelford and Stephens counties into Brazos River in S Young County; drainage area 5,728 sq. mi.

Brazos River, Double Mountain Fork: Rises 12 mi. SE Tahoka, Lynn County; flows E 175 mi. through Garza, Kent, Fisher and Haskell counties to confluence with Salt Fork of the Brazos, north of Old Glory in Stonewall County.

Brazos River, North Fork: DOUBLE MOUNTAIN FORK: Formed by union of Yellow House and Blackwater draws in Lubbock; flows SE 75 miles through Crosby, Garza and Kent counties to junction with Double Mountain Fork Brazos River.

Brazos River, Salt Fork: Rises in SE Crosby County; flows 150 mi. through Garza and Kent counties to confluence

Boykin Creek runs through Angelina National Forest. Photo by William L. Farr, CC by SA 4.0/Flickr.

with Double Mountain Fork in NE Stonewall County to form the main stream of Brazos River.

Buck Creek: Also called Spiller Creek. Rises SE Donley County; flows SE 49 mi. through Collingsworth and Childress counties to Texas-Oklahoma boundary; then 3 mi. through Oklahoma to junction with Prairie Dog Town Fork of Red River NW Hardeman County to form main stream of the Red River.

Buffalo Bayou: Rises in extreme N Fort Bend County; flows E 46 mi. through Houston into San Jacinto River in Harris County. Part of Houston Ship Channel.

California Creek: Rises 10 mi. NE Roby in Fisher County; flows NE 70 mi. through Jones County into Paint Creek in E Haskell County.

Caney Creek: Rises near Wharton in Wharton County; flows 75 mi. through Matagorda County into east end of Matagorda Bay. Centuries ago, the current Caney Creek channel was the channel for the Colorado River.

Capote/Wildhorse Draw: Rises N of Van Horn in Culberson County; runs 86 mi. S through Jeff Davis County to SW of Marfa in Presidio County. One of a number of streams in this area with no outlet to the sea.

Cedar Bayou: Rises 11 mi. NW Liberty in Liberty County; flows 46 mi. S as boundary between Harris County and Liberty and Chambers counties, and into Trinity Bay.

Chambers Creek: Formed SW Waxahachie in Ellis County by union North, South forks; flows SE 45 mi. through Navarro County into Richland Creek at Richland-Chambers Reservoir.

Cibolo Creek: Rises 7 mi. W Boerne in Kendall County; flows SE through Bexar, Comal, Guadalupe and Wilson counties into San Antonio River in Karnes County; 96 mi. in length. Spring-fed, perennially flowing stream.

Coleto Creek: Formed SW of Mission Valley in NW Victoria County by union of Twelve Mile and Fifteen Mile creeks forming boundary between Victoria and Goliad counties. From Coleto Creek Reservoir flows to Guadalupe River in Victoria County.

Comal River: Rises in Comal Springs in City of New Braunfels and flows SE about 2.5 miles to Guadalupe River. Shortest river in Texas by name.

Concho River: Formed at San Angelo by conjunction North, South Concho rivers; flows E 24 mi. through Tom Green County, then 29 mi. through Concho County into Colorado River 12 m. NE Paint Rock. Drainage basin, including North and South Concho, 6,613 sq. mi. A spring-fed stream.

Concho River, Middle: Rises SW Sterling County; flows S, then E 66 mi. through Tom Green panhandle, Irion and Reagan counties into South Concho River at Lake Nasworthy near Tankersley in Tom Green County.

Concho River, North: Rises in S Howard County; flows 137 mi. through Glasscock, Sterling and Coke counties to confluence with South Concho to form Concho River in Tom Green County. Drainage basin, 1,510 sq. mi.

Concho River, South: Rises in C Schleicher County; flows N through Lake Nasworthy to confluence with North Concho River in Tom Green County; length, 41 mi.; drainage basin area 3,866 sq. mi. Perennial flow from springs.

Cowleech Fork Sabine River: Rises 2 mi. NW Celeste NW Hunt County; flows SE 40 mi. to Lake Tawakoni.

Deep Creek: Rises SE Baird, Callahan County; flows N 55 mi. into Hubbard Creek in Shackelford County near McCatherine Mountain.

Deep Creek: Rises 4 mi. N Fluvanna NW Scurry County; flows SSE 70 mi. to mouth on Colorado River in extreme N Mitchell County.

Delaware River: Rises eastern slope Delaware Mountains in N Culberson County; flows in NE course; crosses

Texas-New Mexico state line and enters Pecos River; length, 50 mi.

Devils River: Formed SW Sutton County by union Dry Devils River and Granger Draw; flows SE 95 mi. through Val Verde County into Rio Grande at Amistad Reservoir. Spring-fed, perennially flowing stream throughout most of its course.

Elm Creek: Rises 3 mi. SE Nolan in Nolan County; flows NE 60 mi., passes through Lake Abilene, Buffalo Gap and Abilene in Taylor County and through Lake Fort Phantom Hill into Clear Fork Brazos River near Nugent, SE Jones County.

Frio River: Formed at Leakey in Real County by union of West and East Frio rivers; flows S 190 mi. through Uvalde, Medina, Frio, La Salle, McMullen counties (Choke Canyon Reservoir); joins Nueces River S of Three Rivers in Live Oak County. Drainage area, 7,310 sq. mi. Fed by springs in northern part, where it flows through picturesque canyon.

Greens Bayou: Rises 9 mi. W Aldine, C Harris County; flows ESE into Houston Ship Channel; 42 mi. long.

Hondo Creek: Rises 7.5 mi. NW Tarpley C Bandera County; flows SSE 67 mi. through Medina and Frio counties to Frio River 5 mi. NW Pearsall.

Howard Draw: Rises at Crockett-Reagan county line; flows SSW 45 mi. through Val Verde County to Pecos River near Pandale.

Hubbard Creek: Rises 3 mi. NW Baird N Callahan County; flows NE 62 mi. through Shackelford County; then into Stephens County (Hubbard Creek Reservoir) and joins Clear Fork of the Brazos River 10 mi. NW Breckenridge.

James River: Rises SE Kimble County; flows NE 37 mi. to join Llano River in Mason County.

Jim Ned Creek: Rises 10 mi. NW Tuscola SC Taylor County; flows SE 71 mi. through Callahan and Coleman counties to Brown County to join Pecan Bayou, a tributary of Colorado River.

Johnson Draw: Rises NE Crockett County; runs SSE 66 miles to mouth on Devils River in Val Verde County.

Lampasas River: Rises NW Mills County; flows SE 100 miles through Hamilton, Lampasas, Burnet and Bell counties (Stillhouse Hollow Lake); unites with Leon River to form Little River.

Leon River: Formed by confluence North, Middle and South Forks in NC Eastland County; flows SE 185 mi. through Comanche, Hamilton and Coryell counties to junction with Lampasas River to form Little River in Bell County.

Leona River: Rises N Uvalde in central Uvalde County; flows SE 83 mi. through Zavala County into Frio River in Frio County.

Limpia Creek: Heads in the Davis Mountains on the NE slope of Mount Livermore in Jeff Davis County and flows 52 mi. E, NE and E through Limpia Canyon to disappear at the head of Barrilla Draw in Pecos County.

Part of course through Limpia Canyon noted for its scenic beauty.

Little Brazos River: Rises 5 mi. SW Thornton, SW Limestone County; flows 72 mi. SE through Falls and Robertson counties into Brazos River in Brazos County.

Little River: Formed central Bell County by union Leon, Lampasas rivers; flows 75 mi. SE through Milam County into Brazos River.

Llano River: Formed C Kimble County by union North, South Llano rivers; flows E 100 mi. through Mason, Llano counties to Colorado River. Drainage area, including North, South Llano rivers, 4,460 sq. mi. A spring-fed stream of the Edwards Plateau, known for scenic beauty.

Llano River, North: Rises C Sutton County; flows E 40 mi. to union with South Llano River at Junction in Kimble County.

Llano River, South: Rises in NC Edwards County; flows 55 mi. NE to confluence with North Llano River at Junction in Kimble County.

Los Olmos Creek: Rises central Duval County; flows SE 71 mi. through Jim Wells and Brooks counties; forms boundary between Kenedy and Kleberg counties; into Baffin Bay.

Madera Canyon: Rises N slope Mount Livermore, Jeff Davis County, at altitude of 7,500 ft.; flows 40 mi. NE to join Aguja Creek at Reeves County line to form Toyah Creek, tributary through Pecos River to Rio Grande. Intermittent stream. Noteworthy for its beauty.

Medina River: Rises in North, West prongs in W Bandera County; flows SE 116 mi. through Medina and Bexar counties to San Antonio River. A spring-fed stream. Scenically beautiful along upper course.

Medio Creek: Rises S Karnes County; flows SE 2 mi. through Karnes County, then 7 mi. along boundary Karnes and Bee counties, then SE 37 mi. through Bee County, SE 7 mi. through Refugio County to junction with Blanco Creek to form Mission River.

Mission River: Formed by confluence of Blanco and Medio creeks in C Refugio County; flows SE 24 mi. to mouth on Mission Bay, an inlet of Copano Bay.

Mulberry Creek: Rises NW Armstrong County at Fairview; flows SE 58 mi. through Donley and Briscoe counties into Prairie Dog Town Fork Red River in NW Hall County.

Navasota River: Rises SE Hill County; flows SE 125 mi. through Limestone County and along boundary Leon, Madison, Robertson, Brazos and Grimes counties to Brazos River near Navasota.

Navidad River: Forms at juncture of East and West Navidad rivers in NE Lavaca County; flows 74 mi. through Lavaca and Jackson counties into Lake Texana near Ganado; then joins Lavaca River.

Nolan River: Rises in NW Johnson County; flows S 30 mi. through Lake Pat Cleburne and into Hill County, where it empties into Brazos River at Lake Whitney.

Onion Creek: Rises 1 mi. W of Hays-Blanco county line SE Blanco County; flows SE 37 mi. through N Hays County; then 22 mi. through S Travis County into Colorado River near Garfield.

Paint Creek: Rises in extreme NW Jones County near Tuxedo; flows NE, then SE 53 mi. through SE corner of Stonewall County; then across S Haskell County (Lake Stamford) and into W Throckmorton County to mouth on Clear Fork Brazos River.

Palo Blanco Creek: Rises SE Hebbronville in N Jim Hogg County; flows SE 59 mi. through Duval and Brooks, where it passes through Laguna Salada; then into NW Kenedy County.

Palo Duro Creek: Rises in W Deaf Smith County; flows E 45 mi. into C Randall County to junction with Tierra Blanca Creek near Canyon to form the Prairie Dog Town Fork of the Red River. Lends its name to the notable canyon.

Paluxy River: Formed in E Erath County by convergence of North and South branches at Bluff Dale; flows SE 29 mi. through Hood and Somervell counties to mouth on Brazos River. Dinosaur Valley State Park at a large bend of the river in Somervell County is site of 100-million-year-old dinosaur tracks.

Pease River: Formed by union of North and Middle Pease rivers in NE Cottle County; flows E 100 mi. through Hardeman, Foard and Wilbarger counties into Red River 8 mi. NE of Vernon.

Pease River, Middle: Rises 8 mi. NW Matador in WC Motley County; flows E 63 miles into North Pease River to form the Pease River in NE Cottle County.

Pease River, North: Rises 9 mi. SE Cedar Hill in E Floyd County; flows E 60 mi. through Motley, Hall and Cottle counties. Joins Middle Pease to form Pease River.

Pease River, South: Also called Tongue River. Rises 11 mi. SW Roaring Springs in SW Motley County; flows ENE 40 mi. to mouth on Middle Pease River in W Cottle County.

Pecan Bayou: Formed by union of South, North prongs in SC Callahan County; flows SE 90 mi. through Coleman, Brown (Lake Brownwood) and Mills counties into Colorado River SW Goldthwaite. Westernmost bayou.

Pedernales River: Rises NE corner of Kerr County; flows E 106 mi. through Kimble, Gillespie, Blanco, Hays and Travis counties into Colorado River at Lake Travis. Spring-fed; a beautiful stream.

Pine Island Bayou: Rises near Rye, NE Liberty County; flows 76 mi. SE through Hardin and Jefferson counties into Neches River.

Red River, Prairie Dog Town Fork: Formed by union of Palo Duro and Tierra Blanca creeks in Randall County; flows E 160 mi. through Armstrong, Briscoe, Hall, and Childress counties to junction with Buck Creek to form Red River in NW corner of Hardeman County. Palo Duro Canyon is along course of this stream as it descends from Great Plains.

Red River, North Fork: Rises W Gray County; flows SE 180 mi. through Wheeler County into Oklahoma to junction with the Red River NE Vernon in Wilbarger County.

Red River, Salt Fork: Rises N Armstrong County; flows SE 155 mi. through Donley and Collingsworth counties and into Oklahoma. It joins the Red River opposite the northernmost point of Wilbarger County.

Richland Creek: Rises 3.5 mi. E Itasca N Hill County; flows E 50 mi. through Ellis and Navarro counties, through Navarro Mills Lake and Richland-Chambers Reservoir; then into the Trinity River in Freestone County.

Running Water Draw: Rises 24 mi. WNW Clovis, N.M.; flows ESE into Texas in C Parmer County; then through Castro, Lamb, Hale and Floyd counties to join Callahan Draw 8 mi. W Floydada at head of White River, a tributary of the Brazos River.

Sabana River: Rises at Callahan-Eastland county line; flows SE 50 mi. through Comanche County into Leon River at Proctor Lake.

Sabinal River: Rises 7 mi. N Vanderpool in NW Bandera County; flows S 60 mi. to junction with Frio River in SE Uvalde County. The West Sabinal River, which rises in Real County, joins the main stream at the Bandera-Uvalde county line.

San Bernard River: Rises 1 mi. S New Ulm in W Austin County; flows SE, forming boundary Austin and Colorado counties, 31 mi.; Austin and Wharton counties, 8 mi.; Wharton and Fort Bend counties, 28 mi.; approaches Gulf of Mexico in Brazoria County. Total length, 120 mi. (For more than 100 years locals have reported hearing the wail of a violin from the river. The mystery has never been solved, although some say the musical sounds are caused by escaping gas. The phenomenon has caused the stream to be called the Singing River: Handbook of Texas.)

San Gabriel River: Formed at Georgetown in C Williamson County by union of North and South forks; flows NE 50 mi. into Milam County to join Little River. Originally called San Xavier River.

San Jacinto River, East: Rises E Walker County; flows SE and S 69 mi. through San Jacinto, Liberty, Montgomery and Harris counties into Lake Houston and San Jacinto River.

San Jacinto River, West: Rises E Grimes County NE Shiro; flows SE 90 mi. through Walker County; into Lake Conroe in Montgomery County; then through Montgomery County to Lake Houston in Harris County.

San Marcos River: Formed near N limits City of San Marcos, Hays County, by several large springs, although watershed extends about 10 mi. NE of springs; Blanco River joins the San Marcos River 4 mi. downstream; flows SE 59 mi. as boundary between Guadalupe and Caldwell counties; then through Gonzales County to join Guadalupe River 2 mi. W Gonzales.

Sandy Creek: Rises SW Colorado County; flows SSE 42 mi. through Lavaca, Wharton and Jackson counties into Lake Texana.

San Saba River: Formed W Fort McKavett at Schleicher-Menard county line by union of North Valley and Middle Valley prongs; flows NE 140 mi. through Menard, Mason, McCulloch and San Saba counties into Colorado River 8 mi. NE San Saba. One of the picturesque streams of the Edwards Plateau.

Spring Creek: Rises NE Waller County near Fields Store; flows E 64 mi. forming boundary between Waller and Harris counties, and Montgomery and Harris counties to junction with West Fork San Jacinto River and Lake Houston.

Sulphur River: Formed E Delta County by junction North, South branches; flows E 183 miles forming boundary between Franklin and Red River counties; Titus and Red River counties; Morris and Red River and Bowie counties; then between Bowie and Cass counties, where it flows into Wright Patman Lake; continues on into Red River in S Miller County, Ark.

Sulphur River, North: Rises 1 mi. SW Gober S Fannin County; flows SE, E 54 mi. as boundary between Delta and Lamar counties and to union with South Sulphur River to form Sulphur River.

Sulphur River, South: Rises N Leonard S Fannin County; flows ESE 50 mi. through Hunt County; then as boundary between Hopkins and Delta counties (through Cooper Lake) to union with North Sulphur to form Sulphur River.

Sulphur Springs Draw: Rises in E Lea County, N.M.; enters Texas W Yoakum County at Bronco; flows SE 100 mi. through Terry, Gaines, Dawson, Martin, and Howard counties to confluence with Mustang Creek to form Beals Creek, a tributary of Colorado River.

Sweetwater Creek: Rises 2 mi. W Maryneal, C Nolan County; flows NE 45 mi. through Fisher and Jones counties into Clear Fork Brazos River.

Terlingua Creek: Rises WC Brewster County; flows S 83 mi. into Rio Grande just E Santa Elena Canyon.

Tierra Blanca Creek: Rises N Curry County, N.M.; flows E across Texas state line in SW Deaf Smith County and 75 mi. through Deaf Smith, Parmer and Randall counties to junction with Palo Duro Creek where it forms Prairie Dog Town Fork Red River.

Toyah Creek: Forms near boundary Jeff Davis-Reeves counties; flows NE 50 mi. into Pecos River NC Reeves County.

Trinity River, Clear Fork: Rises NW Poolville in NW Parker County; flows SE 56 mi. through Tarrant County into West Fork Trinity River at Fort Worth.

Trinity River, East Fork: Rises 1.5 mi. NW Dorchester in SC Grayson County; flows S 85 mi. through Collin County (Lake Lavon and Lake Ray Hubbard); then Rockwall and Dallas counties into Trinity River in SE Kaufman County.

Trinity River, Elm Fork: Rises 1 mi. NW Saint Jo in E Montague County; flows 85 mi. SE through Cooke, Denton counties (Ray Roberts Lake and Lewisville Lake) to junction with West Fork to form Trinity River proper at Irving in WC Dallas County.

Trinity River, West Fork: Rises in SC Archer County; flows SE 145 mi. through Jack, Wise (Lake Bridgeport) and Tarrant (Eagle Mountain Lake and Lake Worth) counties to conjunction with Elm Fork to form Trinity River proper in WC Dallas County.

Tule Creek: Formed in Swisher County by union of North, Middle and South Tule draws; flows E 40 mi. through Mackenzie Reservoir and Briscoe County into Prairie Dog Town Fork Red River. Remarkably beautiful Tule Canyon along lower course.

Turkey Creek: Rises near Turkey Mountain EC Kinney County; flows SE 54 mi. through Uvalde, Zavala, Dimmit counties to Nueces River.

Washita River: Rises SE Roberts County; flows E 35 mi. through Hemphill County to Oklahoma state line, then SE to Red River at Lake Texoma. Total length, 295 mi.

West Caney Creek: Rises 1 mi. SW Normangee in SW Leon County; flows SW 11 mi. through NW Madison County to junction with Navasota River on Brazos county line. The historic Old San Antonio Road, a thoroughfare for early Spanish and French explorers, crossed the headwaters of the stream.

White River: Formed 8 mi. W Floydada in WC Floyd County by union of Running Water and Callahan draws; flows SE 62 mi. through Blanco Canyon and White River Lake in Crosby County; then through Garza and Kent counties into Salt Fork Brazos River; principal tributary to Salt Fork.

Wichita River: Formed NE Knox County by union North, South Wichita rivers; flows NE 90 mi. through Baylor (Lake Kemp and Lake Diversion), Archer, Wichita and Clay counties to Red River N Byers.

Wichita River, Little: Formed in C Archer County by union of its North, Middle and South forks; flows NE 62 mi. through Clay County (Lake Arrowhead) into Red River.

Wichita River, North: Rises 6 mi. E East Afton in NE Dickens County; flows E through King, Cottle, Foard counties; then as boundary for Foard and Knox counties; then briefly into Baylor County to junction with South Wichita River to form Wichita River proper NE Vera in Knox County. Length, 100 mi.

Wichita River, South: Rises 10 mi. E Dickens in EC Dickens County; flows E 85 mi. through King and Knox counties to junction with North Wichita to form Wichita River.

Yellow House Draw: Rises in SE Bailey County; flows SE 80 mi. through Cochran, Hockley and Lubbock counties to confluence with Blackwater Draw at Lubbock to form the North Fork of Double Mountain Fork Brazos River. ☆

Fishermen on Cooper Lake. Photo by Texas Parks and Wildlife/Flickr

Artificial Lakes and Reservoirs

Sources: U.S. Geological Survey; Texas Water Development Board; New Handbook of Texas; Texas Parks & Wildlife; U.S. Army Corps of Engineers; various river basin authorities; reservoir websites.

The large increase in the number of reservoirs in Texas during the past half-century has greatly improved water conservation and supplies.

As late as 1917, Texas had only four major reservoirs with a total storage capacity of 288,340 acre-feet. (One acre-foot is the amount of water necessary to cover an acre of surface area with water one foot deep, about 325,851 gallons of water.) Most of this capacity was in Medina Lake in southwest Texas, with 254,000 acre-feet capacity, created by a dam completed in May 1913.

By January 2012, Texas had 188 major water supply reservoirs (those with a normal capacity of 5,000 acre-feet or larger) and 21 major non-water supply reservoirs (those that do not have a water supply function). The 188 water supply reservoirs have a total conservation surface area of 1.67 million acres and an original conservation storage capacity of 35 million acre-feet (only Texas' share is counted in border reservoirs). The 21 non-water supply reservoirs have a total normal surface area of 62,079 acres and an original normal storage capacity of 760,000 acre-feet.

According to the U.S. Census Bureau's Master Address File (last updated August 2010), Texas has 5,616 square miles of inland water, ranking it first in the 48 contiguous states, followed by Florida, with 5,027 sq. mi. The only state with more inland water is Alaska, with 19,304 sq. mi.

There are 6,976 reservoirs in Texas with a normal storage capacity of 10 acre-feet or larger.

Natural Lakes in Texas

There are many natural lakes in Texas, though none is of great size. The largest designated natural lake touching the border of Texas is **Sabine Lake**, into which the Sabine and Neches rivers discharge. It is more properly called the **Sabine-Neches Estuary** of the Gulf of Mexico. (Find more information about this estuary on page 64.)

Also near the coast, in Calhoun County, is **Green Lake**, which has about 10,000 acre-feet of storage capacity. It is one of the state's largest natural freshwater lakes.

Caddo Lake, on the Texas-Louisiana border, was a natural lake originally, but its present capacity and surface area are largely due to dams built to raise the surface of the original body of water.

Natural Dam Lake, in Howard County, has a similar history to Caddo Lake.

In East Texas, there are many small natural lakes formed by "horse-shoe" bends that have been eliminated from the main channel of a river. There are also a number of these "horse-shoe" lakes along the Rio Grande in the Lower Valley, where they are called resacas.

On the South Plains and west of San Angelo there are lakes, such as **Big Lake** in Reagan County, that are usually dry.

List of Lakes and Reservoirs

The table that begins below lists the lakes and reservoirs in Texas that have **more than 5,000 acre-feet of storage capacity**. Some industrial cooling reservoirs are not included in this table.

The surface area listed in the table is the **area at conservation elevation** as calculated by the Texas Water Development Board (TWDB). Because sediment deposition constantly changes reservoir volumes over time, storage capacity figures are from the most recent surveys available.

Various methods of computing capacity area are used, and detailed information may be obtained from the TWDB, from the U.S. Army Corps of Engineers, or from local sources. Boundary reservoir capacities include water

designated for Texas and non-Texas water. Texas' share will be included in the description.

Information is in the following order: (1) Name of lake or reservoir; (2) year of first impounding of water; (3) county or counties in which it is located; (4) river or creek on which it is located; (5) location with respect to some city or town; (6) purpose of reservoir; (7) owner of reservoir.

Some of these items, when not listed, are not available. For the larger lakes and reservoirs, the dam impounding water to form the lake bears the same name, unless otherwise indicated. The years in the table refer to first impounding of water. Double years refer to later, larger dams.

Lakes and Reservoirs, Date of Origin	Surface Area (acres)	Storage Capacity (acre-ft.)
Abilene, L.: (1919) Taylor Co.; Elm Cr.; 6 mi. NW Tuscola; (M-In.-R); City of Abilene	588	7,900
Addicks Reservoir: (1948) Harris Co.; South Mayde Cr.; 1 mi. E of Addicks; (FC only); USAE; Addicks only has water during times of flood and is dry most of the year	16,780	202,128
Alan Henry, L.: (1993) Garza Co.; Double Mountain Fork Brazos River; 10 mi. E Justiceburg; (M-In.-Ir.); City of Lubbock	2,395	96,207
Alcoa L.: (1952) Milam Co.; Sandy Cr.; 7 mi. SW Rockdale; (In.-R); Alcoa Aluminum (also called Sandow L.)	914	15,650
Amistad Reservoir, International: (1969) Val Verde Co.; Rio Grande; an international project of the U.S. and Mexico; 12 mi. NW Del Rio; (C-R Ir.-P-FC); International Boundary and Water Commission (Texas' share of conservation capacity is 56.2 percent.) (Formerly Diablo Reservoir)	65,597	3,275,532
Amon G. Carter, L.: (1961) Montague Co.; Big Sandy Cr.; 6 mi. S Bowie; (M-In.); City of Bowie	1,524	19,266
Anahuac, L.: (1936, 1954) Chambers Co.; Turtle Bayou; near Anahuac; (Ir.-In.-Mi.); Chambers-Liberty Counties Navigation District. (also called Turtle Bayou Reservoir)	5,035	33,348
Anzalduas Channel Dam: Hidalgo Co.; Rio Grande; 11 mi. upstream from Hidalgo; (Ir.-FC); United States and Mexico	1,472	13,910
Aquilla L.: (1983) Hill Co.; Aquilla Cr.; 10.2 mi. W of Hillsboro; (FC-M-Ir.-R); USAE–Brazos R. Auth.	3,119	43,243
Arlington, L.: (1957) Tarrant Co.; Village Cr.; 7 mi. W Arlington; (M-In.); City of Arlington	1,908	40,188
Arrowhead, L.: (1966) Clay-Archer counties.; Little Wichita R.; 13 mi. SE Wichita Falls; (M); City of Wichita Falls	14,372	230,359
Athens, L.: (1962) Henderson Co.; 8 mi. E Athens; (M-FC-R); Athens Municipal Water Authority (formerly Flat Creek Reservoir)	1,799	29,503
Austin, L.: (1893, 1915, 1939) Travis Co.; Colorado R.; W Austin city limits; (M-In.-P); City of Austin, leased to LCRA (Imp. by Tom Miller Dam) (In 1893, the first dam was completed. It broke in 1900. In 1915, a second dam was partially built but not completed. In 1939, the present Tom Miller Dam was completed.)	1,589	23,972
Ballinger L.: (1947) Runnels Co.; Valley Creek; 5 mi. W Ballinger; (M); City of Ballinger (also known as Lake Moonen)	500	8,215
Balmorhea L.: (1917) Reeves Co.; Sandia Cr.; 3 mi. SE Balmorhea; (Ir.-R); Reeves Co. WID No. 1	573	6,350
Bardwell L.: (1965) Ellis Co.; Waxahachie Cr.; 3 mi. SE Bardwell; (FC-C-R); USAE	3,138	46,122
Barker Reservoir: (1945) Harris Co.; above Buffalo Bayou; (FC only); USAE; Barker only has water during times of flood and is dry most of the year	17,225	206,860
B. A. Steinhagen L.: (1951) Tyler-Jasper counties; Neches R.; 1/2 mi. N Town Bluff; (FC-R-C); USAE; (also called Town Bluff Reservoir and Dam B. Reservoir); (Imp. by Town Bluff Dam)	10,421	66,961
Bastrop, L.: (1964) Bastrop Co.; Spicer Cr.; 3 mi. NE Bastrop; (In.-R); LCRA	906	16,590
Baylor L.: (1950) Childress Co.; 10 mi. NW Childress; (M-R); City of Childress (also called Baylor Creek Reservoir)	610	9,220
Belton L.: (1954) Bell-Coryell counties; Leon R.; 3 mi. N. Belton; (M-FC-R); USAE–Brazos R. Auth.	12,135	435,225
Benbrook L.: (1952) Tarrant Co.; Clear Fk. Trinity R.; 10 mi. SW Fort Worth; (FC-R); USAE	3,635	85,648
Bivins L.: (1927) Randall Co.; Palo Duro Cr.; 8 mi. NW Canyon; (M); Amarillo; City of Amarillo (also called Amarillo City Lake)	379	5,122
Bob Sandlin, L.: (1977) Titus-Wood-Camp-Franklin counties; Big Cypress Cr.; 5 mi. SW Mount Pleasant; (In.-M-R); Titus Co. FWSD No. 1 (Imp. by Fort Sherman Dam)	8,888	203,148

Abbreviations used in this table: L., lake; R., river; Co., county; Cr., creek; (C) conservation; (FC) flood control; (R) recreation; (P) power; (M) municipal; (D) domestic; (Ir.) irrigation; (In.) industry; (Mi.) mining, including oil production; (FH) fish hatchery; USAE, United States Army Corps of Engineers; WC&ID, Water Control and Improvement District; WID, Water Improvement District; USBR, United States Bureau of Reclamation; Auth., Authority; LCRA, Lower Colorado River Authority; TPWD, Texas Parks & Wildlife Dept.; USDA, United States Department of Agriculture; Imp., impounded.

Lakes and Reservoirs, Date of Origin	Surface Area (acres)	Storage Capacity (acre-ft.)
Bonham, L.: (1969) Fannin Co.; Timber Cr.; 5 mi. NE Bonham; (M); Bonham Municipal Water Auth.	1,056	11,027
Brady Creek Reservoir: (1963) McCulloch Co.; Brady Cr.; 3 mi. W Brady; (M-In.-R); City of Brady	2,020	30,430
Brandy Branch Reservoir: (1983) Harrison Co.; Brandy Br.; 10 mi. SW Marshall; (In.); AEP-Southwestern Electric Power Co.	1,242	29,513
Brazoria Reservoir: (1954) Brazoria Co.; off-channel reservoir; 1 mi. NE Brazoria; (In.); Dow Chemical Co.	1,865	21,970
Bridgeport, L.: (1932) Wise-Jack counties; W. Fk. of Trinity R.; 4 mi. W Bridgeport; (M-FC-R); Tarrant Regional Water District	11,712	366,236
Brownwood, L.: (1933) Brown Co.; Pecan Bayou; 8 mi. N Brownwood; (M-R); Brown Co. WID No. 1	6,460	128,839
Bryan Utilities L.: (1977) Brazos Co.; unnamed stream; 6 mi. NW Bryan; (In.); City of Bryan (also called Lake Bryan)	818	14,163
Buchanan, L.: (1937) Burnet-Llano-San Saba counties; Colorado R.; 13 mi. W Burnet; (M-FC-R-P); LCRA	21,618	860,607
Buffalo L.: (1938) Randall Co.; Tierra Blanca Cr.; 2 mi. S. Umbarger; (C-FC); U.S. Fish and Wildlife Service; Imp. by Umbarger Dam; See Buffalo Lake entry in Wildlife Refuge section for more info. Buffalo Lake is dry most of the year.	1,900	18,150
Caddo L.: (1873, 1914, 1971) Harrison-Marion counties, Texas, and Caddo Parish, La.; Cypress Bayou; 29 mi. NE Marshall; (C-R-M); Northeast Texas Municipal Water District; An original natural lake, whose surface and capacity were increased by construction of dams.	26,138	129,000
Calaveras L.: (1969) Bexar Co.; Calaveras Cr.; 15 mi. SE San Antonio; (In.-R); CPS Energy of San Antonio	3,624	63,200
Camp Creek L.: (1949) Robertson Co.; 13 mi. E Franklin; (R); Camp Creek Water Co.	750	8,550
Canyon L.: (1964) Comal Co.; Guadalupe R.; 12 mi. NW New Braunfels; (M-R-P-FC); Guadalupe-Blanco R. Authority & USAE	8,308	378,781
Casa Blanca, L.: (1951) Webb Co.; Chacon Cr.; 3 mi. NE Laredo; (R); Webb Co.; (Imp. by Country Club Dam)	1,680	20,000
Cedar Creek Reservoir: (1965) Henderson-Kaufman counties; Cedar Cr.; 3 mi. NE Trinidad; (M-R);Tarrant Regional Water District; (also called Lake Joe B. Hogsett)	32,796	644,686
Champion Creek Reservoir: (1959) Mitchell Co.; 7 mi. S. Colorado City; (M-In.); City of Colorado City	1,196	41,580
Cherokee, L.: (1948) Gregg-Rusk counties; Cherokee Bayou; 12 mi. SE Longview; (M-In.-R); Cherokee Water Co.	3,889	40,094
Choke Canyon Reservoir: (1982) Live Oak-McMullen counties; Frio R.; 4 mi. W Three Rivers; (M-In.-R-FC); City of Corpus Christi-USBR	17,660	662,820
Cisco, L.: (1923) Eastland Co.; Sandy Cr.; 4 mi. N. Cisco; (M); City of Cisco (Imp. by Williamson Dam)	985	29,003
Clyde, L.: (1970) Callahan Co.; N. Prong Pecan Bayou; 6 mi. S. Clyde; (M-R); City of Clyde and USDA Soil Conservation Service	449	5,748
Coffee Mill L.: (1939, 1967) Fannin Co.; Coffee Mill Cr.; 12 mi. NW Honey Grove; (R); U.S. Forest Service	650	8,000
Coleman L.: (1966) Coleman Co.; Jim Ned Cr.; 14 mi. N. Coleman; (M-In.); City of Coleman	1,811	38,094
Coleto Creek Reservoir: (1980) Goliad–Victoria counties; Coleto Cr.; 12 mi. SW Victoria; (In); Guadalupe-Blanco River Auth.	3,100	31,040
Colorado City, L.: (1949) Mitchell Co.; Morgan Cr.; 4 mi. SW Colorado City; (M-In.-P); TXU	1,612	30,758
Conroe, L.: (1973) Montgomery-Walker counties; W. Fork San Jacinto R.; 7 mi. NW Conroe; (M-In.); San Jacinto River Authority, City of Houston and Texas Water Development Board	19,590	410,988
Cooper, L./Olney: (1935) Archer Co.; Mesquite Crk; 8 mi. E Megargel; (M-R); City of Olney; (see L. Olney)	446	6,650
Cooper L.: (1991) Delta-Hopkins counties; Sulphur R.; 3 mi.SE Cooper; (FC-M-R); USAE; (also called Jim Chapman Lake)	17,958	260,332
Corpus Christi, L.: (1930) Live Oak-San Patricio-Jim Wells counties; Nueces R.; 4 mi. SW Mathis; (M-R); City of Corpus Christi (Imp. by Wesley E. Seale Dam)	18,700	256,062
Cox Creek Reservoir: Calhoun Co.; Cox Creek; 2 mi. E Point Comfort; (In); Alcoa Alumninum; (Also called Raw Water Lake and Recycle Lake)	541	5,034
Crook, L.: (1923) Lamar Co.; Pine Cr.; 5 Mi. N. Paris; (M); City of Paris	1,051	9,195
Cypress Springs, L.: (1970) Franklin Co.; Big Cypress Cr.; 8 mi. SE Mount Vernon; (In-M); Franklin Co. Water Development and Texas Water Development Board (formerly Franklin Co. L.); (Imp. by Franklin Co. Dam)	3,252	66,756
Daniel, L.: (1948) Stephens Co.; Gunsolus Cr.; 7 mi. S Breckenridge; (M-In.); City of Breckenridge; (Imp. by Gunsolus Creek Dam)	924	9,515
Davis, L.: Knox Co.; Double Dutchman Cr.; 5 mi. SE Benjamin; (Ir); League Ranch	585	5,454
Delta Lake Res. Units 1 and 2: (1939) Hidalgo Co.; Rio Grande (off channel); 4 mi. N. Monte Alto; (Ir.); Hidalgo-Willacy counties WC&ID No. 1 (formerly Monte Alto Reservoir)	2,371	14,000

Abbreviations used in this table: L., lake; R., river; Co., county; Cr., creek; (C) conservation; (FC) flood control; (R) recreation; (P) power; (M) municipal; (D) domestic; (Ir.) irrigation; (In.) industry; (Mi.) mining, including oil production; (FH) fish hatchery; USAE, United States Army Corps of Engineers; WC&ID, Water Control and Improvement District; WID, Water Improvement District; USBR, United States Bureau of Reclamation; Auth., Authority; LCRA, Lower Colorado River Authority; TPWD, Texas Parks & Wildlife Dept.; USDA, United States Department of Agriculture; Imp., impounded.

Lakes and Reservoirs, Date of Origin	Surface Area (acres)	Storage Capacity (acre-ft.)
Diversion, L.: (1924) Archer-Baylor counties; Wichita R.; 14 mi. W Holliday; (M-In.); City of Wichita Falls and Wichita Co. WID No. 2	3,397	35,324
Dunlap, L.: (1928) Guadalupe Co.; Guadalupe R.; 9 mi. NW Seguin; (P); Guadalupe-Blanco R. Auth.; (Imp. by TP-1 Dam)	410	5,900
Eagle L.: (1900) Colorado Co.; Colorado R. (off channel); in Eagle Lake; (Ir.); Lakeside Irrigation Co.	1,200	9,600
Eagle Mountain L.: (1934) Tarrant-Wise counties; West Fork Trinity R.; 14 mi. NW Fort Worth; (M-In.-Ir.); Tarrant Regional Water District	8,666	179,880
Eagle Nest L.: (1951) Brazoria Co.; off-channel Brazos R.; 12 mi. WNW Angleton; (Ir.); T.M. Smith, et al. (also called Manor Lake)	N/A	18,000
Eastman Lakes: 8 lakes; Harrison Co.; Sabine R. basin; NW of Longview; Texas Eastman Co.	N/A	8,135
Electra, L.: (1950) Wilbarger Co.; Camp Cr. and Beaver Cr.; 7 mi. SW Electra; (In.-M); City of Electra	731	5,626
Ellison Creek Reservoir: (1943) Morris Co.; Ellison Cr.; 8 mi. S. Daingerfield; (P-In.); Lone Star Steel	1,516	24,700
E. V. Spence Reservoir: (1969) Coke Co.; Colorado R.; 2 mi. W. Robert Lee; (M-In.-Mi); Colorado R. Municipal Water District; (Imp. by Robert Lee Dam)	6,372	517,272
Fairfield L.: (1970) Freestone Co.; Big Brown Cr.; 11 mi. NE Fairfield; (In.); TXU; (formerly Big Brown Creek Reservoir)	2,159	44,169
Falcon International Reservoir: (1954) Starr-Zapata counties; Rio Grande; (International U.S.-Mexico); 3 mi. W Falcon Heights; (M-In.-Ir.-FC-P-R); International Boundary and Water Commission; (Texas' share of total conservation capacity is 58.6 percent)	85,195	2,646,765
Fayette County Reservoir: (1978) Fayette Co.; Cedar Cr.; 8.5 mi. E. La Grange; (P-R); LCRA (also called Cedar Creek Reservoir)	2,400	71,400
Forest Grove Reservoir: (1982) Henderson Co.; Caney Cr.; 7 mi. NW Athens; (In.); TXU, Agent	1,502	20,038
Fort Phantom Hill, L.: (1938) Jones Co.; Elm Cr.; 5 mi. S. Nugent; (M-R); City of Abilene	4,213	70,030
Georgetown, L.: (1980) Williamson Co.; N. Fk. San Gabriel R.; 3.5 mi. W Georgetown; (FC-M-In.); USAE	1,287	36,823
Gibbons Creek Reservoir: (1981) Grimes Co.; Gibbons Cr.; 9.5 mi NW Anderson; (In.); Texas Municipal Power Agency	2,576	27,603
Gilmer Reservoir: (2001) Upshur Co.; Kelsey Creek; 15 mi. N of Longview; 4 mi. W of Gilmer; (M); City of Gilmer	895	12,720
Gladewater, L.: (1952) Upshur Co.; Glade Cr.; in Gladewater; (M-R); City of Gladewater	481	4,637
Gonzales, L.: (1931) Gonzales Co.; Guadalupe R.; 4.5 mi. SE Belmont; (P); Guadalupe-Blanco R. Auth.(also called H-4 Reservoir)	696	6,500
Graham, L.: (1929) Young Co.; Flint and Salt creeks; 2 mi. NW Graham; (M-In.); City of Graham	2,436	45,288
Granbury, L.: (1969) Hood Co.; Brazos R.; 8 mi. SE Granbury; (M-In.-Ir.-P); Brazos River Authority (Imp. by DeCordova Bend Dam)	8,139	132,949
Granger, L.: (1980) Williamson Co.; San Gabriel R.; 10 mi. NE Taylor; (FC-M-In.); USAE (formerly Laneport L.)	4,159	51,822
Grapevine L.: (1952) Tarrant-Denton counties; Denton Cr.; 2 mi. NE Grapevine; (M-FC-In.-R.); USAE	6,978	164,703
Greenbelt L.: (1967) Donley Co.; Salt Fork of Red R.; 5 mi. N Clarendon; (M-In.); Greenbelt Municipal and Industrial Water Auth.	668	59,968
Greenville City Lakes: 6 lakes; Hunt Co.; Cowleech Fork, Sabine R.; 2 mi. Greenville; (M-Other); City of Greenville	N/A	6,864
Halbert, L.: (1921) Navarro Co.; Elm Cr.; 4 mi. SE Corsicana; (M-In-R); City of Corsicana	549	6,033
Hawkins, L.: (1962) Wood Co.; Little Sandy Cr.; 3 mi. NW Hawkins; (FC-R); Wood County; (Imp. by Wood Co. Dam No. 3)	776	11,690
Holbrook, L.: (1962) Wood Co.; Keys Cr.; 4 mi. NW Mineola; (FC-R); Wood County; (Imp. by Wood Co. Dam No. 2)	653	7,790
Hords Creek L.: (1948) Coleman Co.; Hords Cr.; 5 mi. NW Valera; (M-FC); City of Coleman and USAE	364	8,443
Houston, L.: (1954) Harris Co.; San Jacinto R.; 4 mi. N Sheldon; (M-In.-Ir.-Mi.-R); City of Houston	10,023	120,686
Houston County L.: (1966) Houston Co.; Little Elkhart Cr.; 10 mi. NW Crockett; (M-In.); Houston Co. WC&ID No. 1	1,330	17,113
Hubbard Creek Reservoir: (1962) Stephens Co.; 6 mi. NW Breckenridge; (M-In.-Mi.); West Central Texas Municipal Water Authority	15,687	313,174
Hubert H. Moss L.: (1960) Cooke Co.; Fish Cr.; 10 mi. NW Gainesville; (M-In.); City of Gainesville	1,121	24,058
Imperial Reservoir: (1912) Reeves-Pecos counties; Pecos R.; 35 mi. N Fort Stockton; (Ir.); Pecos County WC&ID No. 2	1,530	6,000
Inks L.: (1938) Burnet-Llano counties; Colorado R.; 12 mi. W Burnet; (M-Ir.-Mi.-P); LCRA	757	13,962

Abbreviations used in this table: L., lake; R., river; Co., county; Cr., creek; (C) conservation; (FC) flood control; (R) recreation; (P) power; (M) municipal; (D) domestic; (Ir.) irrigation; (In.) industry; (Mi.) mining, including oil production; (FH) fish hatchery; USAE, United States Army Corps of Engineers; WC&ID, Water Control and Improvement District; WID, Water Improvement District; USBR, United States Bureau of Reclamation; Auth., Authority; LCRA, Lower Colorado River Authority; TPWD, Texas Parks & Wildlife Dept.; USDA, United States Department of Agriculture; Imp., impounded.

The Austin skyline over Lady Bird Lake. Photo by Jonathan Cutrer, jcutrer.com.

Lakes and Reservoirs, Date of Origin	Surface Area (acres)	Storage Capacity (acre-ft.)
Jacksonville, L.: (1959) Cherokee Co.; Gum Cr.; 5 mi. SW Jacksonville; (M-R); City of Jacksonville; (Imp. by Buckner Dam)	1,164	25,670
J. B. Thomas, L.: (1952) Scurry-Borden counties; Colorado R.; 16 mi. SW Snyder; (M- In.-R); Colorado River Municipal Water District; (Imp. by Colorado R. Dam)	4,060	199,931
J. D. Murphree Wildlife Management Area Impoundments: Jefferson Co.; off-channel reservoirs between Big Hill and Taylor bayous; at Port Acres; (FH-R); TPWD (formerly Big Hill Reservoir)	6,881	32,000
Joe Pool L.: (1986) Dallas-Tarrant-Ellis counties; Mountain Cr.; 14 mi. SW Dallas; (FC-M-R); USAE–Trinity River Auth. (formerly Lakeview Lake)	7,470	175,358
Johnson Creek Reservoir: (1961) Marion Co.; 13 mi. NW Jefferson; (In.); AEP-Southwestern Electric Power Co.	650	10,100
Kemp, L.: (1923) Baylor Co.; Wichita R.; 6 mi. N Mabelle; (M-P-Ir.); City of Wichita Falls; Wichita Co. WID 2	15,357	245,307
Kickapoo, L.: (1945) Archer Co.; N. Fk. Little Wichita R.; 10 mi. NW Archer City; (M); City of Wichita Falls	5,861	86,345
Kiowa, L.: (1967) Cooke Co.; Indian Cr.; 8 mi. SE Gainesville; (R); Lake Kiowa, Inc.	560	7,000
Kirby, L.: (1928) Taylor Co.; Cedar Cr.; 5 mi. S. Abilene; (M); City of Abilene	740	7,620
Kurth, L.: (1950) Angelina Co.; off-channel reservoir; 8 mi. N Lufkin; (In.); Abitibi Consolidated Industries	726	14,769
Lady Bird L.: (1960) Travis Co.; Colorado R.; within Austin city limits; (R); City of Austin (formerly Town Lake)	468	6,409
Lake Creek L.: (1952) McLennan Co.; Manos Cr.; 4 mi. SW Riesel; (In.); TXU	550	8,400
Lake Fork Reservoir: (1980) Wood-Rains counties; Lake Fork Cr.; 5 mi. W Quitman; (M-In.); Sabine River Authority	26,889	605,061
Lake O' the Pines: (1959) Marion-Upshur-Morris counties; Cypress Cr.; 9 mi. W Jefferson; (FC-C-R-In.-M); USAE; (Imp. by Ferrell's Bridge Dam)	17,638	241,363
Lavon, L.: (1953) Collin Co.; East Fk. Trinity R.; 2 mi. W Lavon; (M-FC-In.); USAE	20,650	406,388
Leon, Lake: (1954) Eastland Co.; Leon R.; 7 mi. S Ranger; (M-In.); Eastland Co. Water Supply District	1,738	27,762
Lewis Creek Reservoir: (1969) Montgomery Co.; Lewis Cr.; 10 mi. NW Conroe; (In.); Entergy	1,010	16,400
Lewisville L.: (1929, 1954) Denton Co.; Elm Fork of Trinity R.; 2 mi. NE Lewisville; (M-FC-In.-R); USAE; (also called Lake Dallas and Garza-Little Elm)	27,175	563,228
Limestone, L.: (1978) Leon-Limestone-Robertson counties; Navasota R.; 7 mi. NW Marquez; (M-In.-Ir.); Brazos River Authority	12,486	203,780

Abbreviations used in this table: L., lake; R., river; Co., county; Cr., creek; (C) conservation; (FC) flood control; (R) recreation; (P) power; (M) municipal; (D) domestic; (Ir.) irrigation; (In.) industry; (Mi.) mining, including oil production; (FH) fish hatchery; USAE, United States Army Corps of Engineers; WC&ID, Water Control and Improvement District; WID, Water Improvement District; USBR, United States Bureau of Reclamation; Auth., Authority; LCRA, Lower Colorado River Authority; TPWD, Texas Parks & Wildlife Dept.; USDA, United States Department of Agriculture; Imp., impounded.

Lakes and Reservoirs, Date of Origin	Surface Area (acres)	Storage Capacity (acre-ft.)
Livingston, L.: (1969) Polk-San Jacinto-Trinity-Walker counties; Trinity R.; 6 mi. SW Livingston; (M-In.-Ir.); City of Houston and Trinity River Authority	83,730	1,785,348
Loma Alta Lake: (1963) Cameron Co.; off-channel Rio Grande; 8 mi. NE Brownsville; (M-In.); Brownsville Navigation District	2,490	26,500
Lost Creek Reservoir: (1990) Jack Co.; Lost Cr.; 4 mi. NE Jacksboro; (M); City of Jacksboro	413	11,950
Lyndon B. Johnson, L.: (1951) Burnet-Llano counties; Colorado R.; 5 mi. SW Marble Falls; (P); LCRA; (Imp. by Alvin Wirtz Dam); (formerly Granite Shoals L.)	6,110	115,249
Mackenzie Reservoir: (1974) Briscoe Co.; Tule Cr.; 9 mi. NW Silverton; (M); Mackenzie Mun. Water Auth.	253	46,450
Marble Falls, L.: (1951) Burnet Co.; Colorado R.; 1.25 mi. SE Marble Falls; (P); LCRA; (Imp. by Max Starcke Dam)	347	6,901
Martin Creek L.: (1974) Rusk-Panola counties; Martin Cr.; 17 mi. NE Henderson; (P); TXU.	4,954	75,726
Medina L.: (1913) Medina-Bandera counties; Medina R.; 8 mi. W Rio Medina; (Ir.); Bexar-Medina-Atascosa Co. WID No. 1	6,059	254,823
Meredith, L.: (1965) Moore-Potter-Hutchinson counties; Canadian R.; 10 mi. NW Borger; (M-In.-FC-R); cooperative project for municipal water supply by Amarillo, Lubbock and other High Plains cities. Canadian R. Municipal Water Authority–USBR; (Imp. by Sanford Dam); Governed by the Canadian R. Compact (1950), Lake Meredith can only hold 500,000 acre-ft. before it must release water to flow to Oklahoma.	7,097	500,000
Millers Creek Reservoir: (1990) Baylor-Throckmorton counties.; Millers Cr.; 9 mi. SE Goree; (M); North Central Texas Municipal Water Auth. and Texas Water Development Board	2,212	26,768
Mineral Wells, L.: (1920) Parker Co.; Rock Cr.; 4 mi. E Mineral Wells; (M); Palo Pinto Co. Municipal Water District No. 1	473	5,273
Mitchell County Reservoir: (1993) Mitchell Co.; branch of Beals Creek; (Mi.-In.); Colorado River Municipal Water District	1,463	27,266
Monticello Reservoir: (1972) Titus Co.; Blundell Cr.; 2.5 mi. E. Monticello; (In.); TXU	1,795	34,740
Mountain Creek L.: (1937) Dallas Co.; Mountain Cr.; 4 mi. SE Grand Prairie; (In.); TXU.	2,710	22,840
Murvaul, L.: (1958) Panola Co.; Murvaul Bayou; 10 mi. W Carthage; (M-In.-R); Panola Co. Fresh Water Supply District No. 1	3,507	38,285
Mustang Lake East/West: Brazoria Co.; Mustang Bayou; 6 mi. S Alvin; (Ir.-In.-R); Chocolate Bayou Land & Water Co.	N/A	6,451
Nacogdoches, L.: (1976) Nacogdoches Co.; Bayou Loco Cr.; 10 mi. W Nacogdoches; (M); City of Nacogdoches	2,180	39,522
Naconiche, L.: (2009) Nacogdoches Co.; Naconishe Cr. and Telesco Cr.; 14 mi. NE Nacogdoches; (R); Nacogdoches Co.	692	15,031
Nasworthy, L.: (1930) Tom Green Co.; S Concho R.; 6 mi. SW San Angelo; (M-In.-Ir); City of San Angelo	1,249	9,615
Natural Dam L.: (1957, 1989) Howard Co.; Sulphur Springs Draw; 8 mi. W Big Spring; An original natural lake, whose surface and capacity were increased by construction of dams; (FC); Wilkinson Ranch & Colorado River Municipal Water District. Natural Dam Lake only has water during times of flood and is dry most of the year	2,272	54,560
Navarro Mills L.: (1963) Navarro-Hill counties; Richland Cr.; 16 mi. SW Corsicana; (M-FC); USAE	4,736	49,827
Nocona, L.: (1960) Montague Co.; 8 mi. NE Nocona; (M-In.-Mi.); North Montague County Water Supply District (also known as Farmers Creek Reservoir)	1,362	21,444
North Fork Buffalo Creek Reservoir: (1964) Wichita Co.; 5 mi. NW Iowa Park; (M); Wichita Co. WC&ID No.3	1,489	15,400
North L.: (1957) Dallas Co.; S. Fork Grapevine Cr.; 2 mi. SE Coppell; (In.); TXU	800	9,400
Oak Creek Reservoir: (1952) Coke Co.; 5 mi. SE Blackwell; (M-In.); City of Sweetwater	2,389	39,210
O. C. Fisher L.: (1952) Tom Green Co.; N Concho R.; 3 mi. NW San Angelo; (M-FC-C- Ir.-R-In.-Mi.); USAE; Upper Colorado River Auth. (formerly San Angelo L.)	1,265	119,445
O. H. Ivie Reservoir: (1990) Coleman-Concho-Runnels counties; 24 mi. SE Ballinger; (M-In.), Colorado R. Municipal Water District (formerly Stacy Reservoir)	19,149	554,340
Olney, L./Cooper: (1935) Archer Co.; Mesquite Crk; 8 mi. E Megargel; (M-R); City of Olney; (see L. Cooper)	432	4,546
Palestine, L.: (1962) Anderson-Cherokee-Henderson-Smith counties; Neches R.; 4 mi. E Frankston; (M-In.-R); Upper Neches R. Municipal Water Auth.; (Imp. by Blackburn Crossing Dam)	23,112	367,303
Palo Duro Reservoir: (1991) Hansford Co.; Palo Duro Cr.; 12 mi. N Spearman; (M-R); Palo Duro River Auth.	2,407	61,066
Palo Pinto, L.: (1964) Palo Pinto Co.; 15 mi. SW Mineral Wells; (M-In.); Palo Pinto Co. Municipal Water District 1	2,173	26,766

Abbreviations used in this table: L., lake; R., river; Co., county; Cr., creek; (C) conservation; (FC) flood control; (R) recreation; (P) power; (M) municipal; (D) domestic; (Ir.) irrigation; (In.) industry; (Mi.) mining, including oil production; (FH) fish hatchery; USAE, United States Army Corps of Engineers; WC&ID, Water Control and Improvement District; WID, Water Improvement District; USBR, United States Bureau of Reclamation; Auth., Authority; LCRA, Lower Colorado River Authority; TPWD, Texas Parks & Wildlife Dept.; USDA, United States Department of Agriculture; Imp., impounded.

Lakes and Reservoirs, Date of Origin	Surface Area (acres)	Storage Capacity (acre-ft.)
Pat Cleburne, L.: (1964) Johnson Co.; Nolan R.; 4 mi. S. Cleburne; (M-FC-In.-Ir.); City of Cleburne	1,568	26,008
Pat Mayse L.: (1967) Lamar Co.; Sanders Cr.; 2 mi. SW Arthur City; (M-In.-FC); USAE	5,638	113,683
Pinkston Reservoir: (1976) Shelby Co.; Sandy Cr.; 12.5 mi. SW Center; (M); City of Center; (formerly Sandy Creek Reservoir)	523	7,380
Possum Kingdom L.: (1941) Palo Pinto-Young-Stephens-Jack counties; Brazos R.; 11 mi. SW Graford; (M-In.-Ir.-Mi.-P-R); Brazos R. Auth.; (Imp. by Morris Sheppard Dam)	17,970	538,139
Proctor L.: (1963) Comanche Co.; Leon R.; 9 mi. NE Comanche; (M-In.-Ir.-FC); USAE–Brazos River Auth.	4,715	54,762
Quitman, L.: (1962) Wood Co.; Dry Cr.; 4 mi. N Quitman; (FC-R); Wood County; (Imp. by Wood Co. Dam No.1)	814	7,440
Randell L.: (1909) Grayson Co.; Shawnee Cr.; 4 mi. NW Denison; (M); City of Denison	311	5,900
Ray Hubbard, L.: (1968) Collin-Dallas-Kaufman-Rockwall counties; (formerly Forney Reservoir); E. Fork of Trinity R.; 15 mi. E Dallas; (M); City of Dallas	20,739	439,559
Ray Roberts, L.: (1987) Denton-Cooke-Grayson counties; Elm Fk. Trinity R.; 11 mi. NE Denton; (FC-M-D); City of Denton, Dallas, USAE; (also known as Aubrey Reservoir)	28,612	788,167
Red Bluff Reservoir: (1937) Loving-Reeves counties, Texas; and Eddy Co., N.M.; Pecos R.; 5 mi. N Orla; (Ir.-P); Red Bluff Water Power Control District	7,495	151,110
Red Draw Reservoir: (1985) Howard Co.; Red Draw; 5 mi. E Bi Spring; (Mi.-In.); Colorado River Municipal Water District	374	8,538
Richland-Chambers Reservoir: (1987) Freestone-Navarro counties; Richland Cr.; 20 mi. SE Corsicana; (M); Tarrant Regional Water District.	43,384	1,087,839
Rita Blanca, L.: (1940) Hartley Co.; Rita Blanca Cr.; 2 mi. S Dalhart; (R) City of Dalhart	524	12,050
River Crest L.: (1953) Red River Co.; off-channel reservoir; 7 mi. SE Bogata; (In.); TXU	555	7,000
Sam Rayburn Reservoir: (1965) Jasper-Angelina-Sabine-Nacogdoches-San Augustine counties; Angelina R.; (FC-P-M-In.-Ir.-R); USAE; (formerly McGee Bend Reservoir)	112,590	2,857,077
San Bernard Reservoirs #1, #2, #3: Brazoria Co.; Off-Channel San Bernard R.; 3 mi. N Sweeney; (In.); ConocoPhillips	N/A	8,610
Santa Rosa L.: (1929) Wilbarger Co.; Beaver Cr.; 15 mi. S Vernon; (Mi.); W. T. Waggoner Estate	1,500	11,570
Sheldon Reservoir: (1943) Harris Co.; Carpenters Bayou; 2 mi. SW Sheldon; (R-FH); TPWD	1,244	4,224
Smithers L.: (1957) Fort Bend Co.; Dry Creek; 10 mi. SE Richmond; (In.); Texas Genco	2,480	18,700
Somerville L.: (1967) Burleson-Washington-Lee counties; Yegua Cr.; 2 mi. S Somerville; (M-In.-Ir.- FC); USAE–Brazos River Authority	10,928	147,104
South Texas Project Reservoir: (1983) Matagorda Co.; off-channel Colorado R.; 16 mi. S Bay City; (In.); STP Nuclear Operating Co.	7,000	202,600
Squaw Creek Reservoir: (1983) Somervell-Hood counties; Squaw Cr.; 4.5 mi. N Glen Rose; (In.); TXU	3,163	151,250
Stamford, L.: (1953) Haskell Co.; Paint Cr.; 10 mi. SE Haskell; (M-In.); City of Stamford	5,316	51,570
Stillhouse Hollow L.: (1968) Bell Co.; Lampasas R.; 5 mi. SW Belton; (M-In.-Ir.-FC); USAE–Brazos River Authority; (also called Lampasas Reservoir)	6,484	227,825
Striker Creek Reservoir: (1957) Rusk-Cherokee counties; Striker Cr.; 18 mi. SW Henderson; (M-In.); Angelina-Nacogdoches WC&ID No. 1	1,920	16,934
Sulphur Springs, L.: (1950) Hopkins Co.; White Oak Cr.; 2 mi. N Sulphur Springs; (M); Sulphur Springs Water District; (formerly called White Oak Creek Reservoir)	1,340	17,747
Sulphur Springs Draw Reservoir: (1992) Martin Co.; Sulphur Springs Draw; 12 mi. NE Stanton; (FC); Colorado River Municipal Water District	970	7,997
Sweetwater, L.: (1930) Nolan Co.; Bitter Creek; 6 mi. SE Sweetwater (M-R); City of Sweetwater	652	12,267
Tawakoni, L.: (1960) Rains-Van Zandt-Hunt counties; Sabine R.; 9 mi. NE Wills Point; (M-In.-Ir-R); Sabine River Authority; (Imp. by Iron Bridge Dam)	37,325	871,695
Terrell City L.: (1955) Kaufman Co.; Muddy Cedar Cr.; 6 mi. E Terrell; (M-R); City of Terrell	849	8,594
Texana, L.: (1980) Jackson Co.; Navidad R. and Sandy Cr.; 6.8 mi. SE Edna; (M-Ir); USBR, Lavaca-Navidad R. Auth., Texas Water Dev. Bd.; (formerly Palmetto Bend Reservoir)	9,154	159,566
Texoma, L.: (1943) Grayson-Cooke counties, Texas; Bryan-Marshall-Love counties, Okla.; (Imp. by Denison Dam) on Red R. below confluence of Red and Washita rivers; (P-FC-C-R); USAE; Texas and Oklahoma each have the right to 50 percent of capacity	71,975	2,516,226
Toledo Bend Reservoir: (1967) Newton-Panola-Sabine-Shelby counties; Sabine R.; 14 mi. NE Burkeville; (M-In.-Ir.-PR); Sabine River Authority; Texas and Louisiana each have rights to 50 percent capacity	178,553	4,472,900
Tradinghouse Creek Reservoir: (1968) McLennan Co.; Tradinghouse Cr.; 9 mi. E Waco; (In.); TXU	2,010	35,124
Travis, L.: (1942) Travis-Burnet counties; Colorado R.; 13 mi. NW Austin; (M-In.-Ir.- Mi.-P-FC-R); LCRA; (Imp. by Mansfield Dam)	19,533	1,113,348

Abbreviations used in this table: L., lake; R., river; Co., county; Cr., creek; (C) conservation; (FC) flood control; (R) recreation; (P) power; (M) municipal; (D) domestic; (Ir.) irrigation; (In.) industry; (Mi.) mining, including oil production; (FH) fish hatchery; USAE, United States Army Corps of Engineers; WC&ID, Water Control and Improvement District; WID, Water Improvement District; USBR, United States Bureau of Reclamation; Auth., Authority; LCRA, Lower Colorado River Authority; TPWD, Texas Parks & Wildlife Dept.; USDA, United States Department of Agriculture; Imp., impounded.

A boat ramp at O.H. Ivie Reservoir. Photo by Jonathan Cutrer, jcutrer.com.

Lakes and Reservoirs, Date of Origin	Surface Area (acres)	Storage Capacity (acre-ft.)
Trinidad L.: (1923) Henderson Co.; off-channel reservoir Trinity R.; 2 mi. S. Trinidad; (P); TXU	690	6,200
Truscott Brine L.: (1987) Knox Co.; Bluff Cr.; 26 mi. NNW Knox City; (Chlorine Control); Red River Auth.	3,146	111,147
Twin Buttes Reservoir: (1963) Tom Green Co.; Concho R.; 8 mi. SW San Angelo; (M-In. -FC-Ir.-R.); City of San Angelo, USBR, Tom Green Co. WC&ID No. 1	6,320	182,454
Twin Oaks Reservoir: (1982) Robertson Co.; Duck Cr.; 12 mi. N. Franklin; (In); TXU	2,330	30,319
Tyler, L. /Lake Tyler East: (1949/1967) Smith Co.; Prairie and Mud creeks.; 12 mi. SE Tyler; (M-In); City of Tyler; (Imp. by Whitehouse and Mud Creek dams)	4,714	72,073
Upper Nueces L.: (1926, 1948) Zavala Co.; Nueces R.; 6 mi. N Crystal City; (Ir.); Zavala-Dimmit Co. WID No. 1	316	5,200
Valley Acres Reservoir: (1956) Hidalgo Co.; off-channel Rio Grande; 7 mi. N Mercedes; (Ir-M-FC); Valley Acres Water District.	325	1,950
Valley L.: (1961) Fannin-Grayson counties; 2.5 mi. N Savoy; (P); TXU; (formerly Brushy Creek Reservoir)	1,080	16,400
Victor Braunig LAKE: (1962) Bexar Co.; Arroyo Seco; 15 mi. SE San Antonio; (In.-R); CPS Energy of San Antonio	1,350	26,500
Waco, L.: (1929) McLennan Co.; Bosque R.; 2 mi. W Waco; (M-FC-C-R); City of Waco, USAE, Brazos River Authority	8,161	189,418
Walter E. Long, L.: (1967) Travis Co.; Decker Cr.; 9 mi. E Austin; (M-In.-R); City of Austin; (formerly Decker Lake)	1,269	33,940
Waxahachie, L.: (1956) Ellis Co.; S Prong Waxahachie Cr.; 4 mi. SE Waxahachie; (M-In); Ellis County WC&ID No. 1; (Imp. by S. Prong Dam)	656	10,780
Weatherford, L.: (1956) Parker Co.; Clear Fork Trinity River; 7 mi. E Weatherford; (M-In.); City of Weatherford	1,083	17,812
Welsh Reservoir: (1976) Titus Co.; Swauano Cr.; 11 mi. SE Mount Pleasant; (R-In.); AEP- Southwestern Electric Power Co.; (formerly Swauano Creek Reservoir)	1,269	18,431
White River L.: (1963) Crosby Co.; 16 mi. SE Crosbyton; (M-In.-Mi.); White River Municipal Water District	653	29,880
White Rock L.: (1911) Dallas Co.; White Rock Cr.; within NE Dallas city limits; (R); City of Dallas	1,088	9,004
Whitney, L.: (1951) Hill-Bosque-Johnson counties; Brazos R.; 5.5 mi. SW Whitney; (FC-P); USAE	21,442	553,344
Wichita, L.: (1901) Wichita Co.; Holliday Cr.; 6 mi. SW Wichita Falls; (M-P-R); City of Wichita Falls	2,200	14,000
William Harris Reservoir: (1947) Brazoria Co.; off-channel between Brazos R. and Oyster Cr.; 8 mi. NW Angleton; (In.); Dow Chemical Co.	1,663	9,200
Winnsboro, L.: (1962) Wood Co.; Big Sandy Cr.; 6 mi. SW Winnsboro; (FC-R); Wood County; (Imp. by Wood Co. Dam No. 4)	806	8,100
Winters, L.: (1983) Runnels Co.; Elm Cr.; 4.5 mi. E Winters; (M); City of Winters (also known as Elm Creek Lake and New Lake Winters)	638	7,779
Worth, L.: (1914) Tarrant Co.; West Fork of Trinity R.; in NW Fort Worth; (M); City of Fort Worth	3,377	33,495
Wright Patman L.: (1957) Bowie-Cass-Morris-Titus-Red River counties; Sulphur R.; 8 mi. SW Texarkana; (FC-M); USAE; (formerly Lake Texarkana)	18,247	97,927
Abbreviations used in this table: L., lake; R., river; Co., county; Cr., creek; (C) conservation; (FC) flood control; (R) recreation; (P) power; (M) municipal; (D) domestic; (Ir.) irrigation; (In.) industry; (Mi.) mining, including oil production; (FH) fish hatchery; USAE, United States Army Corps of Engineers; WC&ID, Water Control and Improvement District; WID, Water Improvement District; USBR, United States Bureau of Reclamation; Auth., Authority; LCRA, Lower Colorado River Authority; TPWD, Texas Parks & Wildlife Dept.; USDA, United States Department of Agriculture; Imp., impounded.		

Estuaries and Bays on the Texas Coast

Source: Texas Water Development Board; www.twdb.texas.gov

Texas has 367 miles of coastline along which 11 major river basins and eight coastal basins terminate, bringing fresh water from rivers, streams, and surface runoff to the coast to mix with the Gulf of Mexico seawater. These unique zones, known as estuaries, are a significant feature of the Texas coast.

Texas has seven major estuaries, which are formed by a complex of individual bays separated from the Gulf by barrier islands, and five minor, riverine estuaries, which occur near the mouths of major rivers that flow directly into the Gulf.

Texas estuaries range from the nearly fresh-water Sabine-Neches, which borders Louisiana, to the frequently hypersaline Laguna Madre along the southern coast.

Most Texas bays are shallow, ranging in average depth from two feet to ten feet.

Although each estuary differs in size and hydrological and ecological characteristics, together they support a diverse array of species that serve as the raw materials for a variety of economic activities associated with commercial and recreational fishing, hunting, and birding.

In addition, estuaries provide many other ecological services, such as:

- Water filtration and nutrient regulation through nutrient cycling
- Storm surge protection
- Shoreline stabilization through trapping sediments that support the growth of wetlands

The major estuaries, in order from east to west, include:

Sabine-Neches Estuary (Sabine Lake)

The Sabine-Neches Estuary, commonly known as Sabine Lake, is located along the Texas-Louisiana border and is the smallest of Texas' seven major estuaries with an area of 45,320 acres.

This estuary receives around 14 million acre-feet of fresh water inflow per year from the Sabine and Neches rivers and surrounding coastal watersheds, making it the freshest estuary along the Texas coast. Average bay salinity is eight parts per thousand.

The Sabine-Neches Waterway and Gulf Intracoastal Waterway are important shipping channels in this system.

The estuary is connected to the Gulf by Sabine Pass and lies within Orange and Jefferson counties on the Texas side.

Trinity-San Jacinto Estuary (Galveston Bay)

The Trinity-San Jacinto Estuary, also known as Galveston Bay, is located on the upper Texas coast. It is the largest estuary in Texas, with an area of 345,280 acres, and is the seventh largest in the United States.

Key features include Trinity Bay, Galveston Bay, East Bay, West Bay, and connections with the Gulf at Bolivar Roads, San Luis Pass, and Rollover Pass.

The Houston Ship Channel and the Gulf Intracoastal Waterway are notable man-made features of the system.

This estuary receives on average 11 million acre-feet of fresh water inflow annually from the Trinity and San Jacinto rivers and surrounding coastal watersheds. It is bounded by Bolivar Peninsula and Galveston Island and lies within Chambers, Harris, Galveston, and Brazoria counties.

Colorado-Lavaca Estuary (Matagorda Bay System)

The Colorado-Lavaca Estuary, or Matagorda Bay system, is located along the mid-Texas coast and covers an area of 244,490 acres. The estuary is bounded by Matagorda Island and consists of Matagorda Bay, Lavaca Bay, and several smaller bays, including Carancahua Bay, Tres Palacios Bay, Keller Bay, Cox Bay, and Turtle Bay.

Other key features include Pass Cavallo, the Matagorda Ship Channel, and the Gulf Intracoastal Waterway.

The estuary averages 3.5 million acre-feet of fresh water inflow annually from the Colorado, Lavaca, and Tres Palacios rivers and surrounding coastal watersheds. It is bordered by Matagorda, Jackson, Victoria, and Calhoun counties.

Guadalupe Estuary

The Guadalupe Estuary is located on the mid-Texas coast and covers 148,703 acres. The estuary includes San Antonio Bay, Mission Lake, Hynes Bay, Espiritu Santo Bay, and Mesquite Bay.

This estuary is largely protected from the Gulf by Matagorda Island and typically does not have a direct connection to the Gulf except through Cedar Bayou.

The other closest connection with the Gulf is through Pass Cavallo to the northeast in the Colorado-Lavaca Estuary.

The Guadalupe Estuary typically receives an average of 2.5 million acre-feet of fresh water inflow per year from the Guadalupe and San Antonio rivers and from surrounding coastal watersheds. The estuary lies adjacent to Calhoun, Aransas, and Refugio counties.

Mission-Aransas Estuary

The Mission-Aransas Estuary, located in the Coastal Bend, covers 111,780 acres and consists of Aransas Bay, Copano Bay, and several smaller bays, including Saint Charles Bay, Mission Bay, and Redfish Bay.

The estuary has a direct connection to the Gulf through Aransas Pass but is largely protected by a barrier island, San Jose Island.

Typically, the estuary receives 490,000 acre-feet of freshwater inflow per year from the Aransas and Mission rivers and surrounding coastal basins. The estuary is bordered by Aransas, Refugio, and San Patricio counties.

Nueces Estuary

The Nueces Estuary, located in the Coastal Bend, consists of Nueces Bay, Corpus Christi Bay, and Oso Bay. It spans 106,990 acres and is separated from the Gulf by Mustang Island, except for a direct connection through Aransas Pass.

The Corpus Christi Ship Channel and the Gulf Intracoastal Waterway are notable man-made features of the system.

This estuary typically receives 587,000 acre-feet of fresh water inflow per year from the Nueces River, Oso Creek, and surrounding coastal watersheds. The estuary is bordered by San Patricio and Nueces counties.

Laguna Madre Estuary

The Laguna Madre Estuary is the southernmost major estuary in Texas and extends almost to the Texas-Mexico border.

The Laguna Madre is a unique hypersaline lagoon with an average salinity between 32 and 38 parts per thousand. It is the only hypersaline estuary in the nation and one of only a handful that exist worldwide.

The estuary spans 280,910 acres but is divided by a coastal land mass known as Saltillo Flats, though more commonly referred to as the Landcut, and separated from the Gulf by Padre Island.

The Upper Laguna Madre has one major bay, Baffin Bay, and is hydrologically connected to the Nueces Estuary on its northern end and to the Gulf via the Packery Channel.

San Fernando Creek is the principal source of fresh-water inflow to this arid estuary, where freshwater inflows typically are 326,000 acre-feet per year.

The Lower Laguna Madre has one major bay, South Bay, and is connected to the Gulf via the Port Mansfield Channel and Brazos-Santiago Pass.

The Arroyo Colorado and surrounding coastal watersheds are principal sources of freshwater inflow to the Lower Laguna Madre, providing on average 425,000 acre-feet of inflows per year.

The estuary is bordered by Nueces, Kleberg, Kenedy, Willacy, and Cameron counties.

Minor Estuaries and Bays

Christmas Bay

Southwest of Galveston Bay, this system includes both Bastrop Bay and Drum Bay, and it is protected from the Gulf of Mexico by Follet's Island. It has two connections to the gulf, through Cold Pass and San Luis Pass.

It receives fresh water from runoff and through Bastrop Bayou.

Brazos River Estuary

The Brazos River Estuary, located on the upper Texas coast, is a riverine estuary that flows directly into the Gulf rather than into a system of bays. The estuarine portion of the river occurs near the mouth where tidal water from the Gulf mixes with river water.

Typically, this estuary receives 6.3 million acre-feet of fresh water inflow per year. It is located in Brazoria county.

San Bernard Estuary

The San Bernard Estuary is a minor estuary located along the mid-Texas coast, covering an area of 3,760 acres.

While the San Bernard River flows directly into the Gulf, creating a riverine estuary, neighboring Cowtrap Lake and Cedar Lake are small bays that connect with the Gulf through small tidal inlets.

On average, this estuary receives 683,753 acre-feet of fresh water inflow per year from the San Bernard River and surrounding coastal watersheds. It is located in Brazoria and Matagorda counties.

East Matagorda Bay

East Matagorda Bay is a small bay covering an area of 37,810 acres and is separated from the larger estuary by the Colorado River delta. There are no direct sources of river inflow into this bay, which receives an average of 536,165 acre-feet of fresh water per year from runoff of surrounding coastal watershed.

Rio Grande Estuary

The Rio Grande Estuary forms a natural border between the United States and Mexico and is a riverine estuary, which flows directly into the Gulf with no associated bay system.

The estuarine portion of the river occurs where tides from the Gulf mix with fresh water from the river. Annual average inflow from the Rio Grande is 370,722 acre-feet per year. The estuary is bordered by Cameron County on the north, and Mexico on the south. ☆

Water Conservation Tips

- Check all faucets, pipes, and toilets for leaks.
- Install water-saving showerheads and ultra-low-flush toilets.
- Take shorter showers.
- Never use the toilet as a wastebasket.
- Turn off the water while brushing teeth or shaving.
- Wash full loads of clothes.
- Fully load the dishwasher.
- Rinse dishes and vegetables in a full sink or pot of water and not under running water.
- Defrost frozen food in the refrigerator and not under running water.
- Do not over-water landscaping.
- Water the lawn or garden early in the morning or late in evening.
- Adjust sprinklers so they do not water the sidewalk or street.
- Do not water on cool, rainy, or windy days.
- Equip all hoses with shut-off nozzles.
- Use drip irrigation systems.
- Plant drought-tolerant or low-water-use plants and grasses.
- Place mulch around plants to reduce evaporation and discourage weeds.

Texas Plant Life

Source: This article was updated for the Texas Almanac by Stephan L. Hatch, Director, S.M. Tracy Herbarium and professor, Department of Ecosystem Science and Management, Texas A&M University

The types of plants found in Texas vary widely from one region to the next. This is due to the amount and frequency of rainfall, diversity of soils, and the number of frost-free days. From the forests of East Texas to the deserts of West Texas, from the grassy plains of North Texas to the semi-arid brushlands of South Texas, plant species change continuously.

More than 100 million acres of Texas are devoted to grazing, both for domestic and wild animals. This is the largest single use of land in the state. More than 80 percent of the acreage is devoted to range in the Edwards Plateau, Cross Timbers and Prairies, South Texas Plains, and Trans-Pecos Mountains and Basins.

Sideoats grama, which occurs on more different soils in Texas than any other native grass, was officially designated as the state grass of Texas by the Texas Legislature in 1971.

The 10 principal plant life areas of Texas, starting in the east, are:

1. Piney Woods

Most of this area of some 16 million acres ranges from about 50 to 700 feet above sea level and receives 40 to 56 inches of rain yearly. Many rivers, creeks, and bayous drain the region. Nearly all of Texas' commercial timber comes from this area. There are three native species of pine, the principal timber: longleaf, shortleaf, and loblolly. An introduced species, the slash pine, also is widely grown. Hardwoods include oaks, elm, hickory, magnolia, sweet and black gum, tupelo, and others.

The area is interspersed with native and improved grasslands. Cattle are the primary grazing animals. Deer and quail are abundant in properly managed habitats. Primary forage plants, under proper grazing management, include species of bluestems, rosettegrass, panicums, paspalums, blackseed needlegrass, Canada and Virginia wildryes, purpletop, broadleaf and spike woodoats, switchcane, lovegrasses, indiangrass, and numerous legume species.

Highly disturbed areas have understory and overstory of undesirable woody plants that suppress growth of pine and desirable grasses. The primary forage grasses have been reduced, and the grasslands have been invaded by threeawns, annual grasses, weeds, broomsedge bluestem, red lovegrass, and shrubby woody species.

2. Gulf Prairies and Marshes

The Gulf Prairies and Marshes cover approximately 10 million acres. There are two subunits: (a) the marsh and salt grasses immediately at tidewater, and (b) a little farther inland, a strip of bluestems and tall grasses, with some gramas in the western part. Many of these grasses make excellent grazing.

Oaks, elm, and other hardwoods grow to some extent, especially along streams, and the area has some post oak and brushy extensions along its borders. Much of the Gulf Prairies is fertile farmland, and the area is well suited for cattle.

Principal grasses of the Gulf Prairies are tall bunchgrasses, including big bluestem, little bluestem, seacoast bluestem, indiangrass, eastern gamagrass, Texas wintergrass, switchgrass, and gulf cordgrass. Saltgrass occurs on moist saline sites.

Heavy grazing has changed the native vegetation in many cases so the predominant grasses are the less desirable broomsedge bluestem, smutgrass, threeawns, tumblegrass, and many other less desirable grasses. Other plants that have invaded the productive grasslands include oak underbrush, Macartney rose, huisache, mesquite, prickly pear, ragweed, bitter sneezeweed, broomweed, and others.

Vegetation of the Gulf Marshes consists primarily of sedges, bullrush, flat-sedges, beakrush and other rushes, smooth cordgrass, marshhay cordgrass, marshmillet, and maidencane. The marshes are grazed best during winter.

3. Post Oak Savannah

This secondary forest area, also called the Post Oak Belt, covers some 7 million acres. It is immediately west of the primary forest region, with less annual rainfall and a little higher elevation. Principal trees are post oak, blackjack oak, and elm. Pecans, walnuts, and other kinds of water-demanding trees grow along streams. The southwestern extension of this belt is often poorly defined, with large areas of prairie.

The upland soils are sandy and sandy loam, while the bottomlands are sandy loams and clays.

The original vegetation consisted mainly of little bluestem, big bluestem, indiangrass, switchgrass, purpletop, silver bluestem, Texas wintergrass, woodoats, narrowleaf, post oak, and blackjack oak. The area is still largely native or improved grasslands, with small farms located throughout. Intensive grazing has contributed to dense stands of a woody understory of yaupon, greenbriar, and oak brush.

Mesquite has become a serious problem. Good forage plants have been replaced by such plants as split-beard bluestem, red lovegrass, broomsedge bluestem, broomweed, bullnettle, and western ragweed.

4. Blackland Prairies

This area of about 12 million acres, while called a "prairie," has much timber along the streams, including a variety of oaks, pecan, elm, bois d'arc, and mesquite. In its native state, it was largely a grassy plain — the first native grassland in the westward extension of the Southern Forest Region.

Most of this fertile area has been cultivated, and only small acreages of grassland remain in original vegetation. In heavily grazed pastures, the tall bunchgrass has been replaced by buffalograss, Texas grama, and other less productive grasses. Mesquite, lotebush, and other woody plants have invaded the grasslands.

The original grass vegetation includes big and little bluestem, indiangrass, switchgrass, sideoats grama, hairy grama, tall dropseed, Texas wintergrass, and buffalograss. Non-grass vegetation is largely legumes and composites.

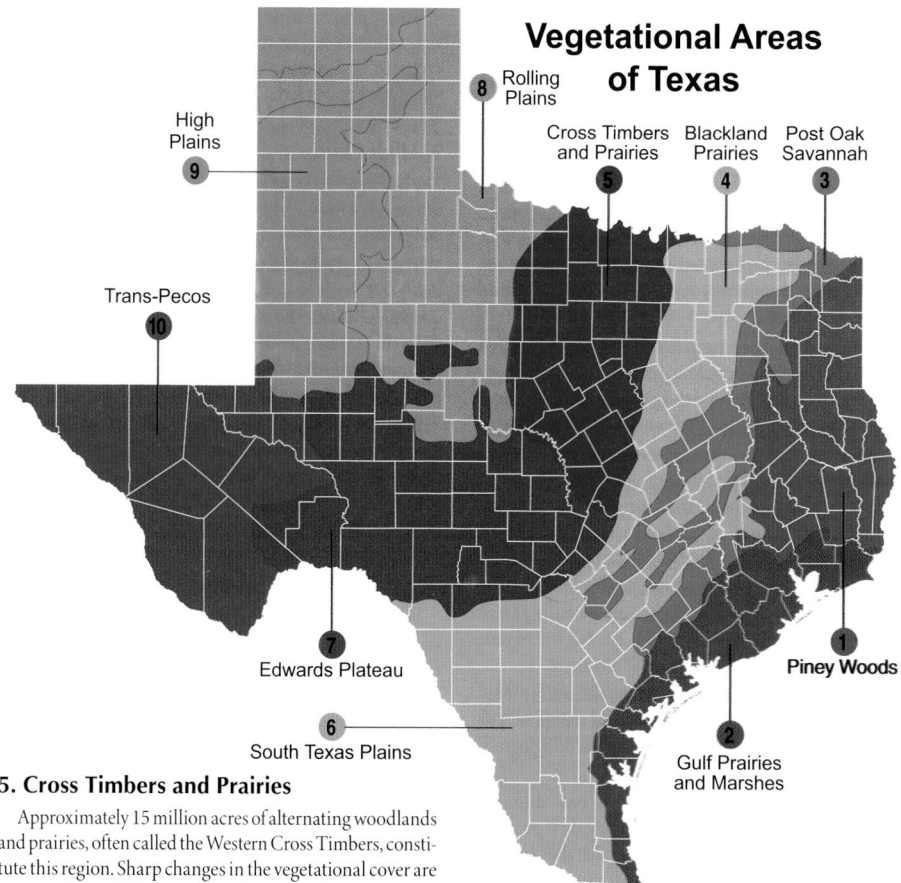

Vegetational Areas of Texas

8 Rolling Plains

High Plains 9

Cross Timbers and Prairies 5

Blackland Prairies 4

Post Oak Savannah 3

Trans-Pecos 10

Edwards Plateau 7

South Texas Plains 6

Piney Woods 1

Gulf Prairies and Marshes 2

5. Cross Timbers and Prairies

Approximately 15 million acres of alternating woodlands and prairies, often called the Western Cross Timbers, constitute this region. Sharp changes in the vegetational cover are associated with different soils and topography, but the grass composition is rather uniform.

The prairie grasses are big bluestem, little bluestem, indiangrass, switchgrass, Canada wildrye, sideoats grama, hairy grama, tall grama, tall dropseed, Texas wintergrass, blue grama, and buffalograss.

On Cross Timbers soils, the vegetation is composed of big bluestem, little bluestem, hooded windmillgrass, sand lovegrass, indiangrass, switchgrass, and many species of legumes. The woody vegetation includes shinnery, blackjack, post, and live oaks.

The entire area has been invaded heavily by woody brush plants of oaks, mesquite, juniper, and other unpalatable plants that furnish little forage for livestock.

6. South Texas Plains

South of San Antonio, between the coast and the Rio Grande, are some 21 million acres of subtropical dryland vegetation, consisting of small trees, shrubs, cactus, weeds, and grasses. The area is noteworthy for extensive brushlands and is known as the Brush Country, or the Spanish equivalents of chaparral or monte. Principal plants are mesquite, small live oak, post oak, prickly pear (Opuntia) cactus, catclaw, blackbrush, whitebrush, guajillo, huisache, cenizo, and others that often grow very densely.

The original vegetation was mainly perennial warm-season bunchgrasses in savannahs of post oak, live oak, and mesquite. Other brush species form dense thickets on the ridges and along streams. Long-continued grazing has contributed to the dense cover of brush. Most of the desirable grasses have only persisted under the protection of brush and cacti.

There are distinct differences in the original plant communities on various soils. Dominant grasses on the sandy loam soils are seacoast bluestem, bristlegrass, paspalum, windmillgrass, silver bluestem, big sandbur, and tanglehead. Dominant grasses on the clay and clay loams are silver bluestem, Arizona cottontop, buffalograss, common curlymesquite, bristlegrass, pappusgrass, gramas, plains lovegrass, Texas cupgrass, vinemesquite, other panicums, and Texas wintergrass.

Low saline areas are characterized by gulf cordgrass, saltgrass, alkali sacaton, and switchgrass. In the post oak and live oak savannahs, the grasses are mainly seacoast bluestem, indiangrass, switchgrass, crinkleawn, paspalums, and panicums. Today much of the area has been reseeded to buffelgrass.

acres, respectively). This is a diverse forest, with both hardwoods (including white oak, red oak, hickory, chestnut oak, cherry-bark oak, sweetgum, nutall oak, and willow) and pines (loblolly and shortleaf). In the northern part of Davy Crockett NF you'll find the Big Slough Wilderness Area (3,639 acres). The forest also contains the Alabama Creek Wildlife Management Area, 14,500 acres.

Sabine National Forest (161,087 acres) is another wide ranging forest that touches 5 different counties, Sabine (95,195 acres), Shelby (59,897), San Augustine (4,184), Newton (1,754), and Jasper (57), and even forms part of the border between Texas and Louisiana. The forest contains both hardwoods (American beech, southern red oak) and pines (loblolly, shortleaf, and longleaf). The Toledo Bend Reservoir runs along the eastern edge of much of the forest, including the Indian Mounds Wilderness Area (12,369 acres) near the middle.

Sam Houston National Forest (163,257 acres) is about 50 miles north of Houston, with parts found in San Jacinto (60,970 acres), Walker (55,115), and Montgomery (47,172) counties. It contains a variety of pines and hardwoods, and features redbuds and dogwoods, which are said to create a spectacular show of flowers in mid-February (redbud) and March (dogwood). Part of the forest stretches around the northern end of Lake Conroe, including the Little Lake Creek Wilderness (3,855 acres). Big Creek Scenic Area is near the eastern-most part of the forest.

National Grasslands

The national grasslands were originally submarginal Dust Bowl project lands, purchased by the federal government primarily under the Bankhead-Jones Farm Tenant Act (1937). Today they are well covered with grasses and native shrubs.

The national grasslands cover 117,077 acres in six Texas counties. Two of these grasslands extend into Oklahoma, as well.

Lyndon B. Johnson National Grassland (20,102 acres) and Caddo National Grassland (17,630 acres) are located northeast and northwest of DFW, with a district ranger office at Decatur.These grasslands provide grazing land for cattle, but also habitat for native wildlife, including white-tailed deer, bobcats, red foxes, and several game birds. Lyndon B. Johnson NG is found mostly in Wise county (20,042 acres). The remaining 60 acres are in Montague county. Caddo NG is only in Fannin county. The Bois d' Arc unit of Caddo contains Lake Fannin, Coffee Mill Lake, and Lake Crockett, which are popular for fishing.

Black Kettle National Grassland (31,264 acres) and McClellan Creek National Grassland (1,402 acres) are both administered by the Cibola National Forest & National Grasslands in Albuquerque, New Mexico. Black Kettle NG lies mostly in Oklahoma, with a mere 577 acres in Texas' Hemphill county; McClellan Creek NG is found near Pampa, TX (in Gray county) and includes the Lake McClellan Recreation area. Both grasslands have active oil and gas wells installed, and lie within the Anadarko Basin.

Rita Blanca National Grassland (117,077 acres) is also managed by Cibola National Forest & National Grasslands,

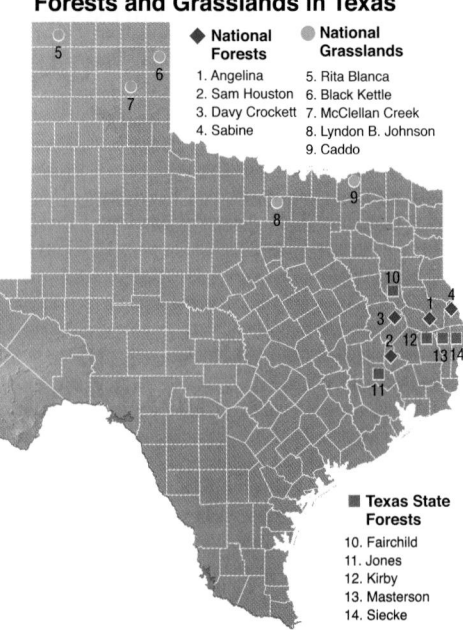

Forests and Grasslands in Texas

◆ National Forests
1. Angelina
2. Sam Houston
3. Davy Crockett
4. Sabine

● National Grasslands
5. Rita Blanca
6. Black Kettle
7. McClellan Creek
8. Lyndon B. Johnson
9. Caddo

■ Texas State Forests
10. Fairchild
11. Jones
12. Kirby
13. Masterson
14. Siecke

in Albuqueuque. These grasslands also stretch across the Texas border, from Dallam county (77,366 acres) into Oklahoma (15,653).

State Forests

Texas has **five state forests**, all of which are used primarily for demonstration and research. They are all game sanctuaries with no firearms or hunting allowed.

Recreational opportunities, such as horseback riding, hiking, bird watching, and picnicking, are available in all but the Masterson Forest.

I.D. Fairchild State Forest: Texas' largest forest is located west of Rusk in Cherokee County. This forest was transferred from the state prison system in 1925. Additional land was obtained in 1963 from the Texas State Hospitals and Special Schools for a total acreage of 2,740.

W. Goodrich Jones State Forest: Located south of Conroe in Montgomery County, it comprises 1,733 acres. It was purchased in 1926 and named for the founder of the Texas Forestry Association.

John Henry Kirby Memorial State Forest: This 600-acre forest in Tyler County was donated by lumberman John Henry Kirby in 1929, as well as later donors. Revenue from this forest is given to the Association of Former Students of Texas A&M University for student-loan purposes.

Paul N. Masterson Memorial Forest: Mrs. Leonora O'Neal Masterson of Beaumont donated this 519 acres in Jasper County in 1984 in honor of her husband, who was a tree farmer and an active member of the Texas Forestry Association.

E.O. Siecke State Forest: The first state forest, it was purchased by the state in 1924. It contains 1,722 acres of pine land in Newton County. An additional 100 acres was obtained by a 99-year lease in 1946. ☆

Angelina National Forest in East Texas. Photo by William L. Farr, CC by SA 4.0/Wikimedia Commons.

Texas Forest Resources

Source: Texas A&M Forest Service, Texas A&M University System; http://tfsweb.tamu.edu.

Forests resources in Texas are abundant and diverse. Forest land covers roughly 38 percent of the state's land area. According to the Forest Inventory and Analysis (FIA), there are over 63 million acres of forests and woodlands in Texas.

The principal forest region in Texas is called the **East Texas Piney Woods**, due to the abundance of pine-hardwood in the region. The 43-county region forms the western edge of the southern pine region, extending from Bowie and Red River counties in Northeast Texas to Jefferson, Harris, and Waller counties in Southeast Texas. The counties contain 12.0 million acres of forestland and 9.4 million acres of non-forest land.

Family forest ownership (non-industrial, private) in East Texas accounts for 6.0 million acres (50%). Forest industry owns 4.6 million acres (3.7%). The rest of the timberland in the east is owned by national forests (580,000 acres; 5%) and other public entities (427,000, 4%).

Forest Types

Five major forest types are found in the East Texas Piney Woods. Two are pine-forest types: loblolly-shortleaf and longleaf-slash. These are dominated by the four species of southern yellow pine. In these forests, the various pine trees make up at least 50 percent of the trees. Loblolly-shortleaf forest is the predominate forest type in the area.

Oak-hickory is the next most common forest type. These are upland hardwood forests in which oaks or hickories make up at least 50 percent of the trees, and pine species are less than 25 percent. Oak-pine is a mixed-forest type in which more than 50 percent of the trees are hardwoods, but pines make up 25–49 percent of the trees.

Bottomland hardwood forests can include a variety of trees, including oak, gum, cypress, elm, and ash, and are commonly found along creeks, river bottoms, swamps, and other wet areas.

Other forest types found in East Texas include small acreages of mesquite, exotic hardwoods, red cedar, and unproductive lands that are considered forested but do not meet stocking requirements.

Forest Types in East Texas	
Forest Type Group	**Area**
Loblolly-shortleaf pine	5.5 million acres (46%)
Oak-hickory	2.6 million acres (22%)
Bottomland hardwood	2.2 million acres (19%)
Oak-pine	1.3 million acres (11%)
Longleaf-slash	0.1 million acres (1%)

Southern pine plantations, established by tree planting and usually managed intensively to maximize timber production, are an important source of wood fiber. Texas forests include 3.2 million acres of pine plantations, 63 percent of which are on industrially managed land, 34 percent on non-industrial private land, and 3 percent on public land. Genetically superior tree seedlings are usually planted to improve survival and growth.

Growth and Removals

Keeping track of growth and removals on timberland is extremely important as a measure of sustainability. On average, timberland annual net growth in East Texas is about 590.8 cubic feet. Removals of live trees in East Texas timberland is estimated to average 561.3 million cubic feet. Softwood represents 73 percent of that total. Annual growth exceeds removals by an average of 29.5 million cubic feet.

The 2019 Timber Harvest

Total volume of growing stock removed in 2019 was 542.9 million cubic feet, a 4.5 percent increase over the 519.7 million cubic feet removed the year before. The 2019 figure is comprised of 462.2 milion cubic feet of pine and 80.8 million cubic feet of hardwood.

Industrial roundwood harvest in Texas in 2019, utilized in the manufacture of wood products, totaled 484.8 million cubic feet for pine and 81.3 million cubic feet for hardwood. The combined harvest of 566.2 million cubic feet was an increase of 4.8 percent over 2018. Top producing counties included Cass, Cherokee, Newton, Polk, and San Augustine.

Total Harvest Value

Stumpage value of the East Texas timber harvest in 2019 was $331.2 million, a 19.1-percent increase from 2018. The delivered value of timber was up 10.2 percent to $695.4 million. Pine timber accounted for 86 percent of the total stumpage value.

Compared with 2018, the harvest of sawlogs for production of lumber increased 1.4 percent in 2018 to 1.1 billion board feet. The pine sawlog cut totaled 1.0 billion board feet, and the hardwood sawlog harvest was 73.1 million board feet. Angelina, Cherokee, Jasper Newton, and Polk counties were the top producers of sawlogs.

Timber cut for the production of structural panels, including both plywood and OSB (oriented strand board) and hardwood veneer, totaled 169.2 million cubic feet, a 15.4 percent increase from the prior year. Cherokee, Harrison, Houston, Polk, and Trinity counties were the top producers of veneer and panel roundwood.

Harvest of timber for manufacture of pulp and paper products increased 0.3 percent from 2018 to 2019 to 2.6 million cords. Cass, Hardin, Jasper, Newton and San Augustine counties were the top producers of pulpwood.

Other roundwood harvest, including posts, poles, and pilings, totaled 3.9 million cubic feet in 2019.

Import–Export Trends

Texas was a net importer of timber products in 2019. Total imports from other states was 109.4 million cubic feet, while the total export was 52.4 million cubic feet. Texas mills utilized 90.7 percent of the timber harvested in the state in 2017. The remainder was processed mainly by mills in Arkansas, Louisiana, and Oklahoma.

Production of Forest Products

Lumber: Texas sawmill production of 1.5 billion board feet of lumber in 2019 represents a decrease of 3.5 percent from 2018. Production of pine lumber decreased 2.7 percent to 1.4 billion board feet in 2019, and hardwood lumber production decreased 16.1 percent to 76.0 million board feet.

Structural Panel Products: Production of structural panels, including plywood and OSB, increased 14.3 percent to 3.1 billion square feet in 2019.

Paper Products: Production of pulp and paperboard products (includes fiberboard, paperboard, market pulp and miscellaneous products) totaled 2.4 million tons in 2019, down 9.6 percent from the previous year. There has not been any major paper production in Texas since 2003.

Treated Wood: There was a 13.4 percent decrease in the volume of wood processed by Texas wood treaters in 2019 from 2018. The total volume treated in 2019 was 33.7 million cubic feet. Among major treated products, lumber accounted for 58.5 percent of the total volume; crossties accounted for 12.5 percent; utility poles and pilings accounted for 11.3 percent.

Primary Mill Residue: Total mill residue, including chips, sawdust, shavings, and bark in primary mills, such as sawmills, panel mills, and chip mills, was 5.7 million tons in 2019. Pine residue was 88 percent of the total and the rest was from hardwood. Mill residue was a combination of chips (48.9 percent), bark (31.7 percent), sawdust (13.3 percent), and shavings (6.1 percent).

Issues Facing Texas Forests

Reforestation

A total of 75,983 acres were planted during the winter 2018 and spring 2019 planting season. Industrial landowners planted 37,667 acres, a decrease of 49.7 percent from the previous season.

Family forest owners planted 37,744 acres, and public landowners planted 572 acres. Family forest owners received $3.3 million in cost-share assistance for reforestation through federal cost-share programs.

Texas Industrial Roundwood Products 2005–2019				
Lumber* (thousand board feet)		Paper Products (short tons)	Structural Panel (thousand square feet*)	
Pine	Hardwood	Paperboard	Pine	
Year				
2005	1,733,314	230,090	2,512,262	3,249,558
2006	1,676,461	240,214	2,781,865	2,935,637
2007	1,550,716	180,713	2,788,308	2,503,941
2008	1,406,103	213,191	2,329,347	2,204,544
2009	1,237,801	171,514	2,007,054	1,958,794
2010	1,188,294	139,389	2,089,521	1,881,763
2011	1,308,427	154,593	2,029,405	1,915,605
2012	1,291,578	118,823	2,081,521	2,049,084
2013	1,385,043	140,427	2,168,403	2,017,406
2014	1,444,203	104,089	2,213,026	2,348,023
2015	1,410,472	107,029	2,106,412	2,444,464
2016	1,357,409	88,001	2,317,537	2,729,569
2017	1,399,502	79,090	2,384,711	2,443,043
2018	1,451,042	90,568	1,541,610	2,303,996
2019	1,411,440	76,026	1,487,466	3,106,076
* Includes tie volumes.			* 3/8-inch basis	
Sources: Annual Harvest Trends reports by Texas A&M Forest Service				

The column headers row "Year | Pine | Hardwood | Paperboard | Pine" applies to the rows below.

Texas Primary Mill Residue, 2019*

Residue Type	Pine	Hardwood	Total
Chips[1]	2,555,737	143,038	2,698,775
Sawdust	643,846	87,221	731,067
Shavings	319,412	16,827	336,238
Bark[2]	1,561,114	417,194	1,978,308
Total	5,080,108	664,280	5,744,388

* Primary mills include sawmills, structural panel mills, and chip mills.
[1] Does not include chips produced in chip mills.
[2] Includes bark from sawmills, panel mills, and chip mills.
Source: Harvest Trends 2019, *Texas A&M Forest Service*

Total Industrial Timber Production and Value by County in Texas, 2019

County	Pine	Hardwood	Total	Stumpage Value	Total Value
	– – – – cubic feet – – – –			– – thousand dollars – –	
Anderson	8,093,193	1,046,588	9,139,781	5,799	11,704
Angelina	20,961,922	2,691,691	23,653,613	16,947	32,252
Bowie	9,021,627	2,730,855	11,752,482	6,912	14,553
Camp	1,100,898	46,844	1,147,742	733	1,467
Cass	29,839,327	9,858,130	39,697,457	21,850	47,578
Chambers	182,203	2,348	184,551	71	186
Cherokee	26,299,155	5,373,447	31,672,602	21,331	41,952
Franklin	18,641	67,268	85,909	85	148
Gregg	1,004,104	527,603	1,531,707	1,151	2,181
Grimes	746,830	2,348	749,178	671	1,159
Hardin	19,297,500	1,960,332	21,257,832	10,807	24,316
Harris	1,685,565	153,211	1,838,776	1,691	2,908
Harrison	19,252,202	2,439,665	21,691,867	13,668	27,622
Henderson	1,093,361	288,720	1,382,081	935	1,835
Houston	16,723,679	204,902	16,928,581	9,353	20,057
Jasper	28,834,773	1,694,974	30,529,747	15,971	35,311
Jefferson	195,889	3,628	199,517	170	300
Leon	879,481	1,858,591	2,738,072	1,426	3,272
Liberty	10,552,899	3,899,135	14,452,034	9,070	18,572
Madison	63,096	0	63,096	60	101
Marion	7,463,596	746,854	8,210,450	4,052	9,254
Montgomery	4,160,922	213,161	4,374,083	3,124	5,945
Morris	1,288,661	757,371	2,046,032	1,145	2,490
Nacogdoches	22,165,332	2,909,835	25,075,167	15,625	31,763
Newton	42,348,936	1,687,853	44,036,789	23,336	51,187
Orange	426,522	76,988	503,510	309	634
Panola	14,125,761	1,483,546	15,609,307	9,348	19,340
Polk	40,547,445	1,751,405	42,298,850	25,474	52,483
Red River	7,013,180	3,433,757	10,446,937	5,533	12,361
Rusk	17,682,723	2,718,349	20,401,072	14,306	27,579
Sabine	16,932,598	2,195,200	19,127,798	10,234	22,425
San Augustine	18,752,325	14,147,868	32,900,193	16,569	38,137
San Jacinto	7,057,158	134,185	7,191,343	5,031	9,640
Shelby	16,819,312	2,512,634	19,331,946	11,779	24,203
Smith	4,422,030	3,147,871	7,569,901	3,963	8,929
Titus	132,621	182,502	315,123	321	548
Trinity	22,234,058	410,378	22,644,436	13,113	27,492
Tyler	23,932,092	1,540,267	25,472,359	14,282	30,522
Upshur	7,969,784	2,865,425	10,835,209	5,688	12,710
Van Zandt	285,190	800	285,990	173	354
Walker	7,716,037	226,133	7,942,170	4,651	9,693
Waller	685,221	2,348	687,569	629	1,078
Wood	3,904,479	1,765,601	5,670,080	2,459	6,111
Other Counties	933,943	1,567,875	2,501,818	1,324	3,014
Total Production	**484,846,271**	**81,328,486**	**566,174,757**	**$ 331,169**	**$ 695,367**

Source: Harvest Trends 2019, *Texas A&M Forest Service*

Beyond the Piney Woods: Texas' Other Tree Regions

In addition to the 12 million acres of timberland in East Texas, there are an additional 51.1 million acres of land in the remainder of Texas that are considered forestland. These forests consist of mesquite woodlands, oak-hickory forests, juniper woodlands, and other western forest types. These forests do not have the commercial timber value of the East Texas Piney Woods but are environmentally important with benefits of wildlife habitat, improved water quality, recreation, and aesthetics.

- **Post Oak Belt**: The Post Oak Belt forms a band of wooded savannah mixed with pasture and cropland immediately west of the Piney Woods. It extends from Lamar and Red River counties southwest as far as Bee and Atascosa counties. Predominant species include post oak, blackjack oak, and elm. An interesting area called the "Lost Pines" forms an isolated island of southern-pine forest in Bastrop, Caldwell, Fayette, and Lee counties just a few miles southeast of Austin.

- **Eastern and Western Cross Timbers:** The Eastern and Western Cross Timbers cover an area of about 3 million acres in North-Central Texas. The term "cross timbers" originated with the early settlers who, in their travels from east to west, crossed alternating patches of oak forest and prairies and so affixed the name "cross timbers" to these forests.

- **Cedar Brakes:** Farther south in the Edwards Plateau region are the cedar brakes, which extend over 3.7 million acres. Cedar, live oak, and mesquite dominate these steep slopes and rolling hills. Mesquite is harvested for cooking wood, knick-knacks, and woodworking. Live oak in this region is declining because of the oak wilt disease.

- **Mountain Forests:** The mountain forests of the Trans-Pecos region, including Jeff Davis County and the Big Bend, are rugged and picturesque. Several western tree species, including piñon pine, ponderosa pine, southwestern white pine, and even Douglas fir are found there, along with aspen and several species of oak.

- **Coastal Forests:** The coastal forests of the southern Gulf Coast are characterized by a mix of brush and short, scrubby trees. Common species include mesquite, live oak, and acacia. Some of these scrub forests are particularly important as migratory bird habitat.

Do you have forests in your region of Texas? Go explore!

Wildfires

Once a primarily rural concern, wildfires are now a threat statewide. Texas has seen significant fire seasons since 1996, some of which threatened or burned through small towns and cities and destroyed homes. The December 2020 Forest Action Plan, published by Texas A&M Forest Service, cites three factors that are intensifying the threat: population growth, changing land use, and increasing drought frequency.

Information on state wildfire response, wildfire risk assessments, fire department assistance programs, and how homeowners and communities can reduce their wildfire risk is online at: (http://tfsweb.tamu.edu and http://ticc.tamu.edu).

Sustainability

Although East Texas forests have provided jobs and economic growth for more than a century, the resource is coming under increasing pressure with changes in management and use of the piney woods. The forests are being impacted by residential development, ownership changes and parcelization, and population growth.

The woodlands in Central and West Texas are facing similar pressures, along with additional challenges such as wildfires, invasive plants, oak wilt, and other pests.

It will require partnerships and cooperation to protect these resources so that the high quality of life in these regions can continue.

Urban Forest Sustainability

An estimated 86 percent of Texans live in urban areas, making urban trees and forests important. Trees reduce urban heat island effect with shade and evaporative cooling; purify the air by absorbing pollutants, slowing chemical reactions that produce harmful ozone, and filter dust; reduce storm water runoff, and soil erosion; buffer against noise, glare, and strong winds; and provide habitat for urban wildlife.

Texas has seen an increase of 4 million residents since 2010, resulting in rapid urbanization in some areas. That in turn has increased the pressure on the sustainability of trees and forests in urban areas.

Water Resource Protection

Did you know that almost half of Texas' freshwater resources originate on forests? Covering about one-third of the state's land area, those forests and woodlands are integral to keeping a stable supply of clean drinking water for Texans. When those lands are cleared for other uses, our water supply is adversely affected.

Learn more about our state's water resources on page 41. ☆

TEXAS WILDLIFE

By Drew R. Davis and Travis J. LaDuc

The wide variation in soils, climate, and vegetation in Texas has resulted in a rich diversity of animal life. There are over 1,600 species of vertebrates (animals with backbones) found in Texas, categorized into five groups or classes: fishes, amphibians, reptiles, birds, and mammals. A summary of each class is listed, followed by annotated lists of the species diversity in each of the five groups.

These annotated lists are not intended to be exhaustive, but rather to provide a review of both the common and uncommon species in our state. Those marked by an asterisk (*) are non-native species.

For more information about Texas wildlife, we recommend the following references: The Fishes of Texas database (fishesoftexas.org); the *Texas Natural History Guide* series for reptiles and amphibians (2005–2020, University of Texas Press); *The Texas Ornithological Society Handbook of Texas Birds*, 2nd edition (2014, Texas A&M University Press), *The Mammals of Texas*, 3rd edition (2016, University of Texas Press and https://www.depts.ttu.edu/nsrl/mammals-of-texas-online-edition); and David Schmidly's *Texas Natural History: A Century of Change* (2002, Texas Tech University Press).

There are, of course, numerous other regional print and online guides. We encourage you to visit online citizen science platforms such as iNaturalist.org, eBird.org, and HerpMapper.org to learn more about the natural world around you as well and contribute your observations. Go explore!

Phrynosoma cornutum (aka Texas Horned Lizard, or Horny Toad) taking in the sun. Photo by Travis LaDuc.

Fishes

Fishes are a large group of gilled aquatic vertebrates, which include jawless fish, cartilaginous fish, and bony fish. Jawless fish include both hagfish and lampreys, the latter of which only two species are known from Texas. Cartilaginous fish are a class of fish that have skeletons primarily composed of cartilage (rather than bone) and include sharks, skates, and rays.

The final group, the bony fish, is the most diverse and abundant class of fish and is named due to their skeletons being primarily composed of bone (rather than cartilage). Over 34,000 species of bony fish are recognized and include species that range widely in size, shape, and behaviors, making them the most diverse group of vertebrates.

Despite there being over 560 species of fish from 117 different families in freshwater and marine environments in Texas, fishes are only the second most diverse group of vertebrates in Texas, after birds. In addition to native species, many non-native species of fish have become established in Texas.

Fish are all aquatic, gilled animals that lack limbs with digits. Like amphibians and reptiles, most fish are cold-blooded (or ectothermic), meaning that their body temperatures vary as environmental temperatures change and they cannot self-regulate their temperature. Most fish are covered in scales, which help protect them from predators and pathogens and can help serve as camouflage, but some species like catfish and eels lack scales altogether.

Fish are an important source of food for humans worldwide. Species of carp, anchovy, pollock, tilapia, salmon, and tuna all top lists of commercially important fishes.

Recreational fishing has been recognized as an important economic activity for the state. Popular freshwater sport fishes include Largemouth Bass, several species of sunfish,

The Rio Grande Cichlid is the only species of cichlid that is native to the United States. Photo by Clinton & Charles Robertson, CC by SA 4.0.

crappie, Blue Catfish, Channel Catfish, Flathead Catfish, Striped Bass, and Rainbow Trout. Popular saltwater sport fish include Red Drum, Black Drum, Spotted Sea Trout, flounder, mackerel, Sheepshead, and Red Snapper. (Read more about fishing in the state on page 175.)

Amphibians

Amphibians include frogs, toads, salamanders, newts, and caecilians. Approximately 8,100 amphibian species are found worldwide, and new species are described each year. Texas is home to 70 native species of amphibians, comprising 13 different families and two orders. These species include frogs, toads, salamanders, and newts, but no caecilians. Texas is also home to one introduced species, the Greenhouse Frog.

Amphibians lack claws, although arboreal frogs often have toe pads that assist in climbing and burrowing toads may have spades on the hind feet for digging. Amphibians typically have moist, smooth skin, although species like toads have dry, warty skin. The skin of aquatic frogs is highly permeable to allow gas exchange in aquatic environments. Toads have parotid glands just behind the head. These glands release a toxin to deter predators by irritating their mouths.

All amphibians play important roles in ecosystems. Frogs and toads are primarily herbivorous as larvae and carnivorous as adults, eating insects and other invertebrate pests. Larval salamanders are known to consume mosquito larvae. Further, amphibians

You'll find Squirrel Tree frogs in East Texas and along the coast. Photo by Dr. Drew R. Davis

are an essential food source for many animals and help to move nutrients from aquatic habitats into upland, terrestrial food webs.

Most of the amphibian diversity in Texas is in the eastern and central regions. A large number of aquatic blind and spring salamanders occur in springs and karst environments along the Edwards Plateau, many of which are only found in a handful of localities and are classified as threatened or endangered. Outside of blind salamanders and spring salamanders and a few other species, most other species of salamanders occur in the eastern third of Texas.

Despite fewer species of amphibians occurring in South Texas, several species that do occur there exist nowhere else

in the United States and occupy very limited distributions, such as the Mexican Burrowing Toad, Mexican Treefrog (featured on this year's cover), and Mexican White-lipped Frog.

Several of our native amphibians have been accidentally spread and introduced to areas of Texas where they do not naturally occur. For example, the Rio Grande Chirping Frog was widely introduced across the state due to the horticultural trade, and the Green Treefrog became established at Big Bend National Park due to individuals likely hitchhiking on RVs or other camping equipment from areas where this species is native.

Reptiles

The order Reptilia consists of over 1,200 genera and 11,000 species and includes lizards, snakes, turtles, and crocodilians. Texas is home to 153 native species of reptiles and ten introduced species: Florida Red-bellied Cooter, Bent-toed Gecko, Common House Gecko, Indo-Pacific House Gecko, Tropical House Gecko, Sri Lankan Spotted House Gecko, Mediterranean Gecko, Mexican Spiny-tailed Iguana, Brown Anole, and the Brahminy Blindsnake.

Unlike amphibians, all reptiles have skin that is covered in scales. These scales serve as protection, but also help to prevent water loss, allowing reptiles to tolerate more arid habitats than amphibians.

Most species of reptiles lay eggs, but some species will give birth to live young, such as rattlesnakes. For egg-laying species, young develop in hard or leathery-shelled eggs, which are often laid in a nest and abandoned by the female.

The sex of many juveniles that are developing in eggs is often determined by the temperature at which the eggs develop, and for species like turtles, warmer temperatures produce higher proportions of female individuals. Species that give birth to live young are better able to regulate the temperature at which offspring develop and can avoid predation of unguarded nests.

Most reptiles have a well-developed sense of smell and use their tongue to collect chemical compounds from the air and move the compounds to the Jacobson's organ. This chemosensory organ is located on the roof of the mouth and provides sensory feedback for detecting airborne chemicals.

Reptiles also have relatively good vision. Snakes often detect movement with their eyes, and visual cues help them locate prey or attract mates.

Like amphibians, reptiles play an important role in nature as part of the food chain. Within Texas, the highest reptile diversity is located in South and West Texas. The Chihuahuan Desert of West Texas is home to most of the diversity of venomous snakes found in the state, including six species of rattlesnakes. Species like the Pond Slider, Texas Spiny Lizard, and Coachwhip are found across almost the entire state, while species like the Rough-footed Mud Turtle, Reticulate Banded Gecko, and Speckled Racer have extremely limited occurrences in the state.

Anolis carolinensis, or Green Anole. Photo by Drew R. Davis.

Most of the introduced species of reptiles cannot tolerate harsh winter temperatures, and as such many of these species are only known in South Texas due to its milder winters. For several introduced species, individuals are only known from few populations, but species like the Brown Anole and Mediterranean Gecko have been documented from large regions across the state.

Birds

The order Aves consists of over 2,000 genera and over 10,000 species. Texas is home to 639 species of birds, including purposefully introduced species (e.g., House Sparrow, European Starling) and accidental releases (e.g., Monk Parakeet), as well as recent introductions or range

expansions (e.g., Cattle Egret, Red-crowned Parrot). Because many species migrate long distances flying between spring breeding grounds and overwintering sites, some individuals find themselves off-course and are recorded as accidental visitors in our state each year.

All birds in Texas can fly, though modes of flight can range from soaring to actively flapping to preferring not to fly unless threatened. All birds have feathers that provide lightweight insulation and an increased surface area to help generate power and lift, as well as aerodynamics for flight. Bright colors and feather patterns are frequently seen in those species where there may be limited resources and/or mating occurs between a single male and multiple females.

Birds are well-known for their vocalizations, which are unique to each species. Calls include courtship songs, alarm calls, and threat displays. Both males and females will vocalize, but the males typically have elaborate songs

A male Peregrine Falcon. Photo by Roy W. Lowe, CC by 2.0/Flickr.

used to attract mates. Song attractiveness may be enhanced by behavioral displays in some species that include bright colorations and elaborate dances or flight patterns. Some bird species will form single pair bonds (some for life), while other species may breed with more than one partner.

All birds lay eggs; some species may construct elaborate nests from vegetation or build nests in cavities, while some species like Killdeer and nighthawks lay camouflaged eggs directly on the ground. A few species are nest parasites, laying eggs in the nests of other species.

When chicks hatch, they may be altricial (naked, helpless, blind; e.g., songbirds), semi-precocial (downy, dependent, eyes open; e.g., gulls), or precocial (downy, independent, eyes open; e.g., ducklings).

Bird diets vary from scavenging and eating carrion to hunting small and medium-sized vertebrates; other diet items can include invertebrates from grasshoppers to spiders, snails to worms, and many other bird species eat a variety of

seeds, fruit, and even nectar. Birds also serve as important diet items for many species.

The areas of highest bird diversity in Texas are South Texas and along the Gulf Coast, particularly during spring migration. Species like the Northern Mockingbird and Red-tailed Hawk are found across almost the entire state, while species like the Altamira Oriole and Colima Warbler have extremely limited occurrences in the state. Some species, like the Greater Prairie Chicken and the Whooping Crane, only exist in Texas because of active federal and state management programs.

Several species are game species (e.g., doves, ducks, geese, quail, Sandhill Crane, Wild Turkey) harvested annually by permit holders. Many introduced bird species have proven to be resilient generalists and have spread statewide; the persistence and establishment of additional introduced bird species have yet to be documented (e.g., Red-vented Bulbul, Nutmeg Mannikin, and Orange Bishop, all observed in Harris County).

Mammals

Mammals, with a few notable exceptions (the egg-laying monotremes: four species of echidna and the Platypus), are a large group of vertebrates with hair that give birth to live young. There are over 6,400 species worldwide (~1,200 genera), including species-rich groups like rodents, bats, and shrews.

A total of 145 species of native terrestrial mammals occur in Texas, a number exceeded in the United States only by California and New Mexico. Also, 28 species of marine mammals have been reported from the Texas coast or are expected to occur there. A single species of marsupial, the Virginia Opossum, is found in the state.

Mammals are found in every ecoregion across the state, with species diversity highest in the Trans-Pecos. Mammals occupy many different habitats, such as species that live almost

entirely underground (moles and gophers), are primarily aquatic (American Beaver, Nutria, River Otter), or can fly (bats) or glide (Flying Squirrel).

A badger and a skunk having a confrontation. Photo by Jill D. Miller.

Recreational hunting is an important economic activity for the state, with the breeding and hunting of deer impacting the Texas economy by over $1 billion each year. Game animals include White-tailed Deer, Mule Deer, Pronghorn, Javelina, and squirrels. There are also 18 exotics or non-native species that have been introduced by man either accidentally (e.g., Japanese Macaque, House Mouse, Black Rat, Norway Rat) or intentionally (e.g., Nutria, Red Fox, Feral Pig, Axis Deer, Fallow Deer, Sika Deer, Nilgai, Greater Kudu, Eastern Thomson's Gazelle, Sable Antelope, Scimitar-horned Oryx, Common Eland, Aoudad, Blackbuck) and have become established.

Threats and Successes

The distribution and abundance of Texas wildlife have changed dramatically over the last 100 years. While a few native species have increased their numbers and expanded their ranges during this period (e.g., White-tailed Deer, Coyote, White-winged Dove), these species are the exceptions. Many species have declined and face continued threats across their shrinking distributions in Texas.

In general, these threats are not focused on individual species, but are widespread risks to ecoregions as a whole, impacting both plant and animal communities. Habitat loss is the primary threat and can include land lost to urbanization and agriculture. The development of land for resource extraction activities contributes to habitat loss and fragmentation. Some technologies, such as wind turbines, have led to the direct mortality of some groups of animals (e.g., birds and bats).

The loss of riparian habitats is often linked to the reallocation or reprioritization of water resources. The suppression of wildfire across many habitats has removed the natural cycle of vegetative change important for maintaining species diversity. Modifications to rainfall patterns and temperatures due to climate change affect the distribution of plant and animal communities as well as the timing of processes and behaviors (e.g., dates for plants to flower and birds to begin migration).

The introduction of invasive grasses (e.g., King Ranch Bluestem, Bufflegrass), aquatic plants (e.g., Hydrilla, Giant Reed), trees (e.g., Chinaberry, Tamarisk), and animals (e.g., Red Imported Fire Ant, Zebra Mussel) has allowed non-native species to outcompete and replace populations of native species across the state. Historical instances of overhunting led to the demise of native Bighorn Sheep, Bison, and Elk; predator control efforts removed the Jaguar and Gray Wolf from the state as well.

All hope is not lost; success stories do exist. Focused conservation efforts have removed species such as the Black-capped Vireo, Concho Watersnake, and American Alligator from the Federal Threatened and Endangered Species List. However, many species still require thoughtful and intensive management plans at local, state, and federal levels to help them remain a part of our state's natural heritage.

To learn more about threats to Texas wildlife and what steps you can do to help conserve native species and their habitats, visit the websites of Texas Parks and Wildlife Department (tpwd.texas.gov), U.S. Fish and Wildlife Service (fws.gov/offices), Natural Resources Conservation Center (nrcs.usda.gov), the Texas Master Naturalist Program (txmn.tamu.edu), private conservation groups like The Nature Conservancy (nature.org/texas), Texas Conservation Alliance (tcatexas.org), and Texas Land Conservancy (texaslandconservancy.org), and species- or location-specific conservation groups, like Audubon Texas (tx.audubon.org) and the Coastal Bend Bays and Estuaries Program (cbbep.org). ☆

Meet the Authors

Drew R. Davis

Drew is an Associate Research Scientist at the University of Texas Rio Grande Valley in Brownsville where he studies several threatened species of amphibians and reptiles, including the Black-spotted Newt and Rio Grande Cooter. Much of his current research involves using novel survey methods to generate occurrence and distribution data in order to better conserve imperiled species and their habitats. He received a Ph.D. from the University of South Dakota, an M.S. from Texas State University, and a B.S. from the University of Texas at Austin. His past research has utilized field-based and laboratory studies to better understand how natural and anthropogenic stressors affect the behavior and physiology of amphibians and reptiles.

Travis J. LaDuc

Travis, a native of Tucson, Arizona, has been interested in reptiles since a young age, with a particular affinity for snakes. He received degrees from the University of Arizona, The University of Texas at El Paso, and the University of Texas at Austin. As the Curator of Herpetology at the Biodiversity Center at the University of Texas at Austin, his job includes working with the preserved collection of 115,000 amphibian and reptile specimens, teaching natural history field courses, and continuing his own research program. His research focuses on the biodiversity and natural history of Texas reptiles and amphibians, with current projects centered on the Spot-tailed Earless Lizard and the Yellow Mud Turtle.

The scalloped hammerhead is one of the sharks found in Texas coastal waters. Photo by Barry Peters; CC by 2.0.

Fishes

amberjack: see jack

American sole: see flatfish

anchovy: Three species of anchovy occur in Texas, including the Striped Anchovy (*Anchoa hepsetus*) and Bay Anchovy (*Anchoa mitchilli*). All anchovies occur along the Texas Gulf Coast, inhabiting bays and estuaries and reaching lengths up to 4". These fish are somewhat translucent, with a silver head and broad lateral streak, and a large, rounded head.

barracuda: Three species of barracuda are known from Texas, including the Great Barracuda (*Sphyraena barracuda*), Northern Sennet (*Sphyraena borealis*), and the Guaguanche (*Sphyraena guachancho*). Barracudas are large, predatory fishes that occur in marine waters along the Texas coast, and have large jaws with fang-like teeth, and two dorsal fins that are widely separated.

bass: see sunfish or sea bass

bowfin: The Bowfin (*Amia calva*) can be found across East Texas. These fish have a long, robust body, a conical head, short barbels, a single long dorsal fin, a large bony gular plate, and are patterned with dark reticulations.

buffalo: see sucker

bullhead: see catfish

butterfly ray: see ray

carp: see cyprinid

carpsucker: see sucker

catfish: Two families of native catfish are known in Texas. North American catfish consist of at least 11 freshwater species, including the Yellow Bullhead (*Ameiurus natalis*), Channel Catfish (*Ictalurus punctatus*), and Tadpole Madtom (*Noturus gyrinus*). Most species have relatively widespread distributions across the state and vary in their body size and shape, but all species have four pairs of barbels (whiskers). Additionally, three species of blind, aquifer-dwelling species are part of this group: the Toothless Blindcat (*Trogloglanis pattersoni*), Widemouth Blindcat (*Satan eurystomus*), and Mexican Blindcat (*Prietella phreatophila*), which was only discovered in 2016. The second group, sea catfish, is marine, and only two species are known: Hardhead Catfish (*Ariopsis felis*) and Gafftopsail Catfish (*Bagre marinus*). Sea catfish are large fish that lack scales, typically are gray in coloration, and have two or three pairs of barbels. A third, non-native family of catfish called suckermouth armored catfish have been introduced in Texas from Central and South America, and are covered in tough, bony plates, and have a sucker-like mouth.

chub: see cyprinid

cichlid: One native species of cichlid, the Rio Grande Cichlid (*Herichthys cyanoguttatus*) can be found in South Texas but has been introduced throughout central Texas. The Rio Grande Cichlid typically has gray background coloration covered in small cream or turquoise-colored spots. Additional species of non-native cichlids also occur in Texas, such as the Blue Tilapia* (*Oreochromis aureus*).

combtooth blenny: Six species of combtooth blennies are known to occur along the Texas coast, including the Molly Miller (*Scartella cristata*) and the Featherduster Blenny (*Hypleurochilus multifilis*). Combtooth blennies have large heads, large eyes, fleshy flaps called cirri between the eyes, compressed and elongated bodies, long and continuous dorsal fins, and rounded caudal fins.

cownose ray: see ray

crappie: see sunfish

croaker: see drum

cusk-eel: see eel

cutlassfish: One species, the Atlantic Cutlassfish (*Trichiurus lepturus*) occurs along the Texas coast. These elongated silver fish have a thin, tapering tail, and a large mouth with fang-like teeth.

cyprinid: This group of fishes is the most diverse in Texas, with over 75 recognized species. This group includes species such as the Central Stoneroller (*Campostoma anomalum*), Blacktail Shiner (*Cyprinella venusta*), Common Carp (*Cyprinus carpio*), Shoal Chub (*Macrhybopsis hyostoma*), and Bullhead Minnow (*Pimephales vigilax*). These fish vary greatly in size and specific habitats used, but all occupy freshwater habitats.

damselfish: Four species of damselfish occur in marine habitats off the Texas coast, including the Sergeant Major (*Abudefduf saxatilis*). The Sergeant Major has a deep, laterally compressed body that is silvery-blue and five dark vertical bars.

darter: see perch

dolphinfish: The Dolphinfish (*Coryphaena hippurus*) is an elongate, laterally compressed marine fish that has is often metallic blue or green in coloration. Their dorsal fin is long, extending from the head to its deeply forked tail.

drum: Eighteen species of drum occur along the Texas Gulf Coast, many of which are popular sport fish, and include Red Drum (*Sciaenops ocellatus*), Black Drum (*Pogonias cromis*), Freshwater Drum (*Aplodinotus grunniens*), Spotted Seatrout (*Cynoscion nebulosus*), and Atlantic Croaker (*Micropogonias undulatus*). These fish vary greatly in their shape, but all can be relatively large fish, and all have a deep notch separating the dorsal fin into two parts. The Red Drum is the state saltwater fish.

eel: At least six different families of eels are known to occur in marine habitats along the Texas coast. There are seven species of cusk-eel, including the Crested Cusk-eel (*Ophidion josephi*). Cusk-eels have long dorsal and anal fins and their pelvic fins are modified into barbel-like structures occurring below the mouth. There are seven species of snake eels, including the Speckled Worm Eel (*Myrophis punctatus*) and Shrimp Eel (*Ophichthus gomesii*). Snake eels have long, snake-like bodies and often bury among sand or mud substrates. Additional eels, like the Conger Eel (*Conger oceanicus*), Ridged Eel (*Neoconger mucronatus*), Blackedge Moray (*Gymnothorax nigromarginatus*), and Freckled Pikeconger (*Hoplunnis macrura*) also occur along the Texas coast, but are less abundant. In addition to marine species, one native species of freshwater eel occurs in Texas, the American Eel (*Anguilla rostrata*). This eel has small scales embedded in the skin giving it a smooth appearance, a long snake-like body, and a single continuous dorsal, caudal, and anal fin.

flatfish: Four families of flatfish inhabit coastal waters. Flatfish are flat, laterally compressed fishes, with two eyes on one side of their head, and often bury down into the mud. Flatfish consist of American soles, lefteye flounders, sand flounders, and tonguefish. American soles, including the Lined Sole (*Achirus lineatus*), Fringed Sole (*Gymnachirus texae*), and Hogchoker (*Trinectes maculatus*), have eyes on their right side, fleshy lips, and a distinct caudal fin. Lefteye flounders, including the Twospot Flounder (*Bothus robinsi*), have an oval-shaped, flattened body with eyes on their left side and elongated dorsal and anal fins that are separate from the caudal fin. There are at least 14 different species of sand flounders, including the Southern Flounder (*Paralichthys lethostigma*) and Bay Whiff (*Citharichthys spilopterus*), which are football-shaped, have eyes on the left side of their body, and have both a distinct snout and tail. Tonguefish, such as the Blackcheek Tonguefish (*Symphurus plagiusa*), can be distinguished from other flatfish by having a single continuous dorsal, caudal, and anal fin.

flounder: see flatfish

frogfish: Three species of frogfish occur along the Texas coast, including the Sargassumfish (*Histrio histrio*). The Sargassumfish has a short, rounded body with many fleshy extensions, that aid in its camouflage among sargassum (marine algae), and angled limb-like pectoral fins.

gar: Four species of gars are native to Texas, including the Alligator Gar (*Atractosteus spatula*), Spotted Gar (*Lepisosteus oculatus*), Longnose Gar (*Lepisosteus osseus*), and Shortnose Gar (*Lepisosteus platostomus*). All gars have elongated, cylindrical bodies, elongate slender snouts, and bony scales. The Alligator Gar can reach lengths up to 9' and up to 275 pounds.

goby: Fourteen species of gobies are found along the Texas coast, including the Naked Goby (*Gobiosoma bosc*) and Darter Goby (*Ctenogobius boleosoma*). Gobies are small, elongated, bottom-dwelling fishes that have rounded heads with eyes that are positioned close together and on top of the head. Additionally, gobies have pelvic fins that are fused together to form a suctioning disk. Gobies are the most diverse group of marine fishes.

grinnel: see bowfin

grouper: see sea bass

grunt: Six species of grunts occur in marine habitats along the Texas coast, including the Pigfish (*Orthopristis chrysoptera*), Tomtate (*Haemulon aurolineatum*), and Barred Grunt (*Conodon nobilis*). Grunts are variable in appearance, but all are moderately-sized fishes with mouths that have thick lips. The pharyngeal teeth in these species make a grunting noise when rubbed together, which is how this group was named.

halfbeak: Two species occur along the Texas coast, including the False Silverstripe Halfbeak (*Hyporhamphus meeki*). These unusual-looking fish have round, elongated bodies with a very short upper jaw and an elongated, needle-like lower jaw.

hammerhead shark: see shark

herring: Ten species of herrings are found in both marine and freshwater habitats in Texas. Four of the more common species include the Gizzard Shad (*Dorosoma cepedianum*), Threadfin Shad (*Dorosoma petenense*), Gulf Menhaden (*Brevoortia patronus*), and Skipjack Herring (*Alosa chrysochloris*). These silvery fish are important as food for many other fishes and can reach lengths up to 2'. Herrings are variable in their body shape and typically have forked caudal fins.

hind: see sea bass

jack: Twenty species of jacks have been recorded along the Texas Gulf Coast, including the Greater Amberjack (*Seriola dumerili*), Crevalle Jack (*Caranx hippos*), and Florida Pompano (*Trachinotus carolinus*). Jacks vary widely in their shape and size but are generally large fish that form schools and are important for commercial fisheries. All jacks have a narrow base of the tail and a deeply forked tail.

killifish: see topminnow

kingfish: see drum

lamprey: Both the Chestnut Lamprey (*Ichthyomyzon castaneus*) and Southern Brook Lamprey (*Ichthyomyzon gagei*) occur in streams and rivers in East Texas. These eel-like fish have a characteristic circular disk-like mouth. The Chestnut Lamprey parasitizes fish as an adult, but adult Southern Brook Lamprey do not feed and rely on previously accumulated energy stores from its filter-feeding larval stage.

lefteye flounder: see flatfish

livebearer: There are at least 17 species of livebearers in Texas, including the Western Mosquitofish (*Gambusia affinis*) and Sailfin Molly (*Poecilia latipinna*). These small freshwater fish are widespread across most of Texas and species like the Western Mosquitofish have been widely introduced around the world. As the name suggests, all Texas species are live-bearing, and males have a modified anal fin called a gonopodium.

lizardfish: Three species of marine lizardfish occur along the Texas coast, including the Inshore Lizardfish (*Synodus foetens*). Lizardfish have elongated cylindrical bodies, large mouths with needle-like teeth, and a large eye.

mackerel: Five species of mackerels are known from the Texas Gulf Coast, with the most abundant being the Spanish Mackerel (*Scomberomorus maculatus*) and King Mackerel (*Scomberomorus cavalla*). Mackerels have elongated, laterally compressed bodies, with a pointed snout. A defining characteristic of these fish is that there is a series of small fins behind both the dorsal and anal fin.

madtom: see catfish

menhaden: see herring

minnow: see cyprinid

mojarra: Nine species of mojarra occur in coastal waters along Texas, including the Spotfin Mojarra (*Eucinostomus argenteus*). Mojarras are silvery fish that are 8–12" in length, with arched backs, deeply forked tails, and a downward-facing mouth to accommodate feeding on bottom-dwelling organisms.

molly: see livebearer

mosquitofish: see livebearer

mullet: Four species of mullet occur in Texas, including the Striped Mullet (*Mugil cephalus*) and White Mullet (*Mugil curema*). Most mullets are marine, but individuals can also be found in freshwater rivers much further inland. Mullets

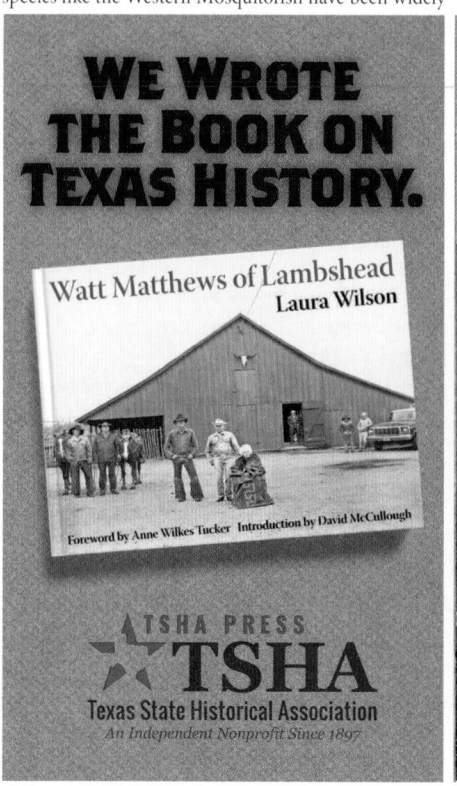

are silvery in appearance and have an elongated, cylindrical body, a flat head, and a large eye relative to their head size.

needlefish: Four species of needlefish occur along the Texas coast, including the Atlantic Needlefish (*Strongylura marina*), which on occasion move up rivers into freshwater habitats. All needlefish have an elongated, round body with their upper and lower jaws extended into long, narrow beaks that are filled with small teeth.

New World silverside: Five species of New World silversides occur in Texas, including the Brook Silverside (*Labidesthes sicculus*), Rough Silverside (*Membras martinica*), Inland Silverside (*Menidia beryllina*), Texas Silverside (*Menidia clarkhubbsi*), and Tidewater Silverside (*Menidia peninsulae*). Silversides are long slender fish, often with translucent bodies and a silver streak running down the sides of the body. Most species are freshwater, but some also are found in brackish waters.

perch: Over 25 species of perch can be found in freshwater habitats in Texas, including the Plains Orangethroat Darter (*Etheostoma pulchellum*) and the Dusky Darter (*Percina sciera*). These fish are often found in riverine systems and often rest on the substrates or woody debris on the bottom of these habitats. All perch have a dorsal fin that is split into two large lobes or has a narrow connection, and some species have bright colors, especially in breeding males. They get their name due to their darting movements through the water.

pickerel: see pike

pike: Two species of pike, the Redfin Pickerel (*Esox americanus*) and Chain Pickerel (*Esox niger*), occur in East Texas. The much more widespread and larger Redfin Pickerel has a long, cylindrical body, with a broad, short, flat snout, and a body coloration that is often green with dark wavy vertical bars and a vertical stripe through the eye. The Chain Pickerel is similar in appearance but is considerably larger than the Redfin Pickerel.

pipefish: This group of seven species includes the Gulf Pipefish (*Syngnathus scovelli*) and the Lined Seahorse (*Hippocampus erectus*). Pipefish have elongate bodies covered in armored plates or spines and tubular snouts, and males possess a brood pouch where they store fertilized eggs from the female until they hatch.

pirate perch: One species of Pirate Perch (*Aphredoderus sayanus*) can be found throughout freshwater habitats in East Texas. Pirate Perch superficially resemble sunfishes but are often quite dark in body coloration with black speckles on a light underside.

pompano: see jack

porcupinefish: see puffer

porgy: Six species of porgies are known from marine habitats in Texas, including the Pinfish (*Lagodon rhomboides*) and Sheepshead (*Archosargus probatocephalus*). Porgies have laterally compressed, deep bodies and most have teeth that are flattened for grinding.

puffer: Two families of puffers are known from marine habitats along the Texas coastline: puffers and porcupinefish. Puffers, including the Least Putter (*Sphoeroides parvus*), have elongated, globular-shaped bodies covered in small spines (*sometimes unnoticeable*), loose skin on the underside, a

beaklike mouth with two teeth in the upper and lower jaw. Porcupinefish, such as the Striped Burrfish (*Chilomycterus schoepfii*), have globular bodies covered in short spines and a beaklike mouth with one upper and lower tooth. Both families can swallow water to expand their bodies when threatened.

pupfish: Six species of pupfish are native to Texas, including the federally endangered Leon Springs Pupfish (*Cyprinodon bovinus*) and Comanche Springs Pupfish (*Cyprinodon elegans*) and the state threatened Conchos Pupfish (*Cyprinodon eximius*), Pecos Pupfish (*Cyprinodon pecosensis*), and Red River Pupfish (*Cyprinodon rubrofluviatilis*). Several of these imperiled species have extremely limited distributions or have suffered widespread declines. Unlike the other species of pupfish, the Sheepshead Minnow (*Cyprinodon variegatus*) remains common and has a widespread distribution across coastal Texas and the Rio Grande drainage, and has been widely introduced into freshwater habitats in Texas.

pygmy sunfish: The Banded Pygmy Sunfish (*Elassoma zonatum*) occurs in freshwater habitats in East Texas. These small (<2" long) fish have a shallow body shape, are laterally compressed, have 9–12 dark bands, and are covered in small dark spots.

ray: Two families of rays occur in shallow estuaries and lagoons along the Texas coast. Butterfly rays, such as the Smooth Butterfly Ray (*Gymnura micrura*), are diamond-shaped and have a short tail with dark lines on it that lacks a dorsal spine. The other family is cownose rays, which is represented by a single species, the Cownose Ray (*Rhinoptera bonasus*). Cownose Rays reach 2–3' in width, are brown on top and white underneath, have a long tail with a venomous barb and get their name from their squared, indented snout and wide-set eyes.

redfish: see drum

redhorse: see sucker

remora: Four species occur in Texas, including the Remora (*Remora remora*) and the Sharksucker (*Echeneis naucrates*). These marine fish have heavily modified dorsal fins that form an oval-shaped sucker-like organ that allows them to attach to larger marine animals like whales, sea turtles, and sharks.

sand flounder: see flatfish

sardine: see herring

scorpionfish: Six species of scorpionfish, including the Spotted Scorpionfish (*Scorpaena plumieri*), can be found along the Texas coast. Scorpionfish are large, robust fish with large heads and venomous spines.

sea bass: This group of fish are popular saltwater sport fishes and include hind and grouper. At least 25 species occur along the Texas coast, including the Rock Sea Bass (*Centropristis philadelphica*) and Warsaw Grouper (*Epinephelus nigritus*). Species in this diverse group range in size and shape, but many species are brightly colored, have robust bodies, and large teeth.

seahorse: see pipefish

searobin: Nine species of searobins, including the Bighead Searobin (*Prionotus tribulus*), occur along the Gulf Coast of Texas. All searobins have a large, bony head that has numerous spines and ridges and modified pectoral fins that allow the fish to "walk" along the substrate.

seatrout: see drum

shad: see herring

shark: Sharks include both the requiem and hammerhead sharks, with 13 species found in marine habitats along the Texas coast. Species include the Atlantic Sharpnose Shark (*Rhizoprionodon terraenovae*), which is relatively small, only reaching lengths up to 4', has a poinfed snout, and is typically gray in coloration with lighter undersides. The Scalloped Hammerhead (*Sphyrna lewini*) and the Bonnethead (*Sphyrna tiburo*) are easily differentiated from other sharks by their flattened heads that resemble a hammer or shovel and eyes on the outer edges.

shiner: see cyprinid

skate: The Roundel Skate (*Raja texana*) occurs along the Texas coastline and can be differentiated from other skates by a dark rounded spot on each pectoral wing. In addition, Roundel Skates have a slightly pointed snout, two dorsal fins at the base of the tail, and lack a serrated spine on their tails.

sleepers: Four species of sleepers can be found in Texas, including the Fat Sleeper (*Dormitator maculatus*), Spinycheek Sleeper (*Eleotris pisonis*), Emerald Sleeper (*Erotelis smaragdus*), and Bigmouth Sleeper (*Gobiomorus dormitor*). All species occur along the Texas Gulf Coast and use both freshwater and brackish habitats. Of these four species, the most abundant appears to be the Fat Sleeper, which has a small, rounded body, two distinct dorsal fins, and black lines along the sides of its face.

snake eel: see eel

snapper: Ten species of snappers are known from Texas, including the Red Snapper (*Lutjanus campechanus*) and Gray Snapper (*Lutjanus griseus*), and all are popular sport and commercial fish. Snappers are diverse in their size, pattern, and coloration, but are generally oblong, heavy-bodied, and have pointed snouts with large teeth.

snook: Two species of snook, the Smallscale Fat Snook (*Centropomus parallelus*) and the Common Snook (*Centropomus undecimalis*), occur in coastal waters along South Texas. Snook reach 2–4' in length, have elongate, laterally compressed bodies covered in silvery scales, and a thin dark line running down the length of the body.

stargazer: Stargazers are marine fish that have eyes on the top of their heads and upward-pointing mouths. Species like the Southern Stargazer (*Astroscopus y-graecum*) typically bury in the mud and ambush prey as they pass overhead.

stingray: Four species of whiptail stingrays occur in Texas, and the most common is the Atlantic Stingray (*Dasyatis sabina*). The Atlantic Stingray has a pointed snout and a long, whip-like tail with a serrated spine.

stoneroller: see cyprinid

sucker: At least 16 species of suckers can be found across Texas, including the River Carpsucker (*Carpiodes carpio*), Smallmouth Buffalo (*Ictiobus bubalus*), Spotted Sucker (*Minytrema melanops*), and the Gray Redhorse (*Moxostoma congestum*). All suckers have their mouth located on the underside of their head, have thick, fleshy lips, and primarily inhabit freshwater river systems.

suckermouth armored catfish: see catfish

sunfish: This group (sometimes also called "perch") includes bass and crappie, all of which are popular freshwater sport fishes. Eighteen species are known from Texas, including the Bluegill (*Lepomis macrochirus*), Green Sunfish (*Lepomis cyanellus*), Longear Sunfish (*Lepomis megalotis*), Largemouth Bass (*Micropterus salmoides*), and White Crappie (*Pomoxis annularis*). Most sunfish species are deep-bodied and laterally compressed, with a series of vertical bars. Crappie are similar in shape to sunfish, but reach larger sizes. Basses are more elongated and with spotting or a large dark stripe down the sides. The Guadalupe Bass (*Micropterus treculii*) is the state fish of Texas.

tarpon: The Tarpon (*Megalops atlanticus*) is a large marine fish that is present along the Gulf Coast of Texas. It can reach lengths of up to 8' in length and weigh more than 350 pounds. The mouth is turned upwards, the last ray of the dorsal fin is elongated, the caudal fin is deeply forked, and it is covered in shiny silver scales.

temperate bass: There are three species of temperate basses in Texas: the native White Bass (*Morone chrysops*) and Yellow Bass (*Morone mississippiensis*) and the non-native Striped Bass* (*Morone saxatilis*). Temperate basses are somewhat deep-bodied, laterally compressed, and have a pointed snout. Species are typically white or silver in appearance with 6–10 dark stripes running the length of the body.

tenpounder: One species, the Ladyfish (*Elops saurus*), occurs along the Texas coastline in bays and estuarine habitats. The Ladyfish has a long, rounded body, silvery scales, a deeply forked caudal fin, and can be up 2–3' in length.

tetra: The Mexican Tetra (*Astyanax mexicanus*) is a small (<4" long) freshwater fish found throughout flowing river systems in south, central and West Texas, and has an oblong, laterally compressed body shape. It is silver in body coloration but has a small black band at the base of the caudal fin. Adult males will have red coloration on the anal fins.

threadfin: The Atlantic Threadfin (*Polydactylus octonemus*) is a marine fish occurring along the Texas coastline and reaches lengths up to 12". These fish have two, widely separated dorsal fins, a deeply forked caudal fin, and 8 soft and flexible pectoral filaments giving it its name.

tilapia: see cichlid

toadfish: Two species of toadfish occur in marine habitats along the Texas coast and include the Gulf Toadfish (*Opsanus beta*) and the Atlantic Midshipman (*Porichthys plectrodon*). Both species are ambush predators that wait among muddy substrates. They are scaleless and have numerous barbels or skin flaps that help provide camouflage.

tonguefish: see flatfish

topminnow: Thirteen species of freshwater topminnows occur in Texas, including the Blackstripe Topminnow (*Fundulus notatus*) and Plains Killifish (*Fundulus zebrinus*). Topminnows can be found throughout the state, are up to approximately 4" in length, and can be variable in their patterning, with some species having a single horizontal strip down the body, while others have numerous vertical bands.

wahoo: see mackerel

The black spotted newt in South Texas is on the state endangered list. Photo by Clinton J. Guadiana.

Amphibians

amphiuma: There is one species of amphiuma found in Texas, the Three-toed Amphiuma (*Amphiuma tridactylum*). These aquatic salamanders look similar to sirens in that they are elongate and eel-like, but lack external gills, and have four small, frail limbs (sirens have external gills and lack hindlimbs). In aquatic environments, amphiumas can be voracious predators, consuming a wide variety of prey items.

barking frog: The Barking Frog (*Craugastor augusti*) is a secretive species found on the Edwards Plateau in rocky outcrops, though they are also known to inhabit mammal burrows. This species gets its name from the bark-like call it makes. Juveniles have a gray background coloration with numerous black spots covering the body and a light band across the midsection of the body. As adults, this light band darks and becomes less noticeable. Like some other species of frogs, Barking Frogs have skin secretions that can be noxious which serve as an anti-predator defense.

blind salamander: Five species of blind salamanders occur in Texas, all occurring along the Edwards Plateau and Balcones Faultline in central Texas. These five species include the Texas Blind Salamander (*Eurycea rathbuni*), Blanco Blind Salamander (*Eurycea robusta*), Comal Blind Salamander (*Eurycea tridentifera*), Valdina Farms Salamander (*Eurycea troglodytes*), and Austin Blind Salamander (*Eurycea waterlooensis*). Like the closely related spring salamanders, these species are fully aquatic but have reduced or absent vision, as these species occur in aquifers, spring outflows, or within karst habitats where there is little visible light. Several species, such as the Texas Blind Salamander, have lost skin pigmentation and appear white, with elongated limbs.

bullfrog: The American Bullfrog (*Rana catesbeiana*) occurs statewide and is the largest species of frog in North America, having a body length up to 7", and is capable of jumping 3–6'. This large frog lives in large, permanent lakes and wetlands and breeds throughout the summer on warm, humid nights. This species has been widely introduced around the world where it is often farmed for human consumption.

burrowing toad: The Mexican Burrowing Toad (*Rhinophrynus dorsalis*) is an odd-looking, secretive frog that only occurs in extreme South Texas. These frogs are dark gray with small white spots with a red or orange line running down their back. Mexican Burrowing Toads spend the majority of their lives underground and only emerge after heavy rains, often associated with hurricanes or tropical storms. The larval development of Mexican Burrowing Toads is extremely rapid, as the ponds they frequently use dry quickly after filling up after rains.

chirping frog: Texas is home to three species of native chirping frog and one introduced species. The Spotted Chirping Frog (*Eleutherodactylus guttilatus*) can be found in montane regions of West Texas such as Big Bend and the Cliff Chirping Frog (*Eleutherodactylus marnockii*) can be found in the Edwards Plateau. The third native species is the Rio Grande Chirping Frog (*Eleutherodactylus cystignathoides*) which is native to the Rio Grande Valley in South Texas but has great spread throughout much of central and East Texas through the horticultural trade. The non-native Greenhouse Frog* (*Eleutherodactylus planirostris*), originally from the Caribbean Islands, has established populations in Houston, Corpus Christi, and South Padre Island. All chirping frogs are small, mostly leaf-litter-dwelling frogs that get their name from the sound of their call. Additionally, all chirping frogs have direct development, meaning that there is no aquatic swimming tadpole stage and small juvenile frogs hatch from eggs.

chorus frog: Four species of chorus frog occur in Texas. Chorus frogs are closely related to treefrogs and have expanded toe pads on the ends of their digits that allow them to climb up vegetation. The Spotted Chorus Frog (*Pseudacris clarkii*) has a gray background color with irregular green markings and ranges from the panhandle South through central and North Texas into South Texas. Both the Spring Peeper (*Pseudacris crucifer*) and the Cajun Chorus Frog (*Pseudacris fouquettei*) occur in wooded habitats in East Texas. The Strecker's Chorus Frog (*Pseudacris streckeri*) occurs throughout central, east, and North Texas. Most chorus frogs are considerably smaller than treefrogs, except the Strecker's Chorus Frog. Chorus frogs primarily use temporary wetlands that fill up after heavy rains for reproduction. Despite their small size, their call can be surprisingly loud.

congo eel: see amphiuma

cricket frog: The Blanchard's Cricket Frog (*Acris blanchardi*) occurs throughout much of Texas except the western panhandle, far West Texas, and South Texas. This small frog is variable in its appearance and can range from grey to green to brown in background coloration with darker markings that can be black, green, or rust-colored. Typically, a dark-colored triangle occurs between the eyes on the top of the head. Blanchard's Cricket Frogs occur along flowing and non-flowing aquatic habitats. Though closely related to treefrogs and chorus frogs, this species has diminished toe pads resulting in more terrestrial behaviors.

dusky salamander: One species of dusky salamander, Spotted Dusky Salamander (*Desmognathus conanti*) has a limited distribution in East Texas. Apparent declines in this species have occurred throughout much of their historic range in the state.

dwarf salamander: One species of dwarf salamander occurs in Texas, the Western Dwarf Salamander (*Eurycea paludicola*). This small, slender species of salamander can be found among leaf litter and logs on forest floors in East Texas. Until recently, this species was part of a single species that ranged from East Texas along the Gulf Coast to North Carolina, that has since been separated into four separate species.

greenhouse frog: see chirping frog

leopard frog: Four species of leopard frogs occur in Texas: the Plains Leopard Frog (*Rana blairi*), Rio Grande Leopard Frog (*Rana berlandieri*), Southern Leopard Frog (*Rana sphenocephala*), and Northern Leopard Frog (*Rana pipiens*). All four species look similar to one another and are olive-green to brown in coloration, with dark spots and dorsolateral stripes from the eye to the hindlimb. These large frogs use permanent water bodies and rivers and have powerful hindlimbs that allow them to jump large distances.

mole salamander: Six species of mole salamanders are found in Texas, including the Spotted Salamander (*Ambystoma maculatum*), Eastern Tiger Salamander (*Ambystoma tigrinum*), Western Tiger Salamander (*Ambystoma mavortium*), Marbled Salamander (*Ambystoma opacum*), Small-mouthed Salamander (*Ambystoma texanum*), and Mole Salamander (*Ambystoma talpoideum*). All species are found throughout East Texas, except the Western Tiger Salamander, which occurs in south, west, and North Texas. All species are largely terrestrial and spend much of their time in upland habitats after breeding in wetland habitats. As aquatic larvae, these salamanders are sometimes colloquially called waterdogs or mudpuppies.

mudpuppy: see waterdog

narrow-mouthed toad: Two species of narrow-mouthed toads are found in Texas. The Eastern Narrow-mouthed Toad (*Gastrophryne carolinensis*) is restricted to eastern and coastal Texas, the Western Narrow-mouthed Toad (*Gastrophryne olivacea*) occurs throughout much of the state. The Eastern Narrow-mouth Toad is small (>1.5" in length) and is typically brown or gray in coloration with dark flecks and a heavily mottled underside. The Western Narrow-mouthed Toad is similar in size but is typically light gray with small black flecks and an unpatterned underside. Both species spend a large amount of time underground and use ephemeral habitats that fill up after rains for breeding.

newt: Two species of newts occur in Texas: the Eastern Newt (*Notophthalmus viridescens*) and the Black-spotted Newt (*Notophthalmus meridionalis*). The Eastern Newt occurs throughout East Texas and parts of coastal Texas while the Black-spotted Newt is restricted to South Texas, where it experienced widespread population declines in recent decades. As a result, the Black-spotted Newt is listed as state-threatened and is a proposed species for federal protection. The Eastern Newt is known to have a terrestrial immature stage called an eft, which is typically bright orange with orange spots outlined in black. As efts mature into adults, they often return to aquatic habitats.

sheep frog: The Sheep Frog (*Hypopachus variolosus*) is closely related to narrow-mouthed toads and is restricted to South Texas. The Sheep Frog is larger than narrow-mouthed toads (2" in length), has a brown background coloration, gray sides with irregular black markings, and a yellow or orange thin stripe down the middle of the back. This species is typically active only after rains where it uses temporary wetlands for reproduction.

siren: Sirens are elongate, slender aquatic salamanders that have external gills behind the head, reduced forelimbs, and no hindlimbs. One species of siren, the Lesser Siren (*Siren intermedia*) is native to Texas and occurs from South Texas up the Gulf Coast and throughout East Texas. These salamanders are sometimes confused as eels due to their body shape and can bury down into the mud at the bottom of wetlands as they dry for prolonged periods and wait for these habitats to fill again after rains.

slimy salamander: The Western Slimy Salamander (*Plethodon albagula*) occurs along the Edwards Plateau and Balcones Faultline in central Texas. These salamanders are black with white speckling along their bodies and can be found under rocks and logs in moist areas in the winter and early spring. As it becomes warm and dry, these salamanders often move deeper underground. Western Slimy Salamanders can secrete a white, sticky substance if disturbed which deters would-be predators.

spadefoot: Spadefoots are toad-like amphibians, which have elliptical (vertical) pupils, smooth skin, and large keratinized spades on their hind feet. Four species occur in Texas: Couch's Spadefoot (*Scaphiopus couchii*), Hurter's Spadefoot (*Scaphiopus hurterii*), Plains Spadefoot (*Spea bombifrons*), and the New Mexico Spadefoot (*Spea multiplicata*). All species spend large amounts of time underground and emerge on warm, wet, rainy nights to forage and reproduce. Like some other species of amphibians, spadefoots are often considered explosive breeders, as reproduction often takes place over a few days following heavy rains when breeding sites (temporary pools) form. Like the Barking Frog and toads, spadefoots can secrete a noxious substance from their skin that is irritating to the eyes and skin of potential predators.

spring peeper: see chorus frog

spring salamander: Eight species of spring salamanders occur in central Texas, all occurring in spring outflows and associated stream runs. Most of these species occur in a limited number of localities and have very small ranges. These species include the Salado Salamander (*Eurycea chisholmensis*), Cascade Caverns Salamander (*Eurycea latitans*), San Marcos Salamander (*Eurycea nana*), Georgetown Salamander (*Eurycea naufragia*), Texas Salamander (*Eurycea neotenes*), Fern Bank Salamander (*Eurycea pterophila*), Barton Springs Salamander (*Eurycea sosorum*), and Jollyville Plateau Salamander (*Eurycea tonkawae*). Most species are federally and state-protected due to their limited occurrence in Texas and the threats these species face.

tiger salamander: see mole salamander

treefrog: Six species of treefrogs occur in Texas. The Canyon Treefrog (*Hyla arenicolor*) occurs in rocky, montane habitats in West Texas, and the Squirrel Treefrog (*Hyla squirella*) is restricted to the Texas coast and parts of East Texas. The Green Treefrog (*Hyla cinerea*) occurs throughout East and coastal Texas, West to the Edwards Plateau, and South towards Corpus Christi and an introduced population is present in Big Bend National Park. Two additional species of treefrogs, the Cope's Gray Treefrog (*Hyla chrysoscelis*) and the Gray Treefrog (*Hyla versicolor*) are indistinguishable from one another and only able to be differentiated by the number of chromosomes they have and by their call. Both Cope's Gray Treefrogs and Gray Treefrogs overlap in much of their range throughout east, central, and North Texas. The Mexican Treefrog (*Smilisca baudinii*) is restricted to South Texas and is listed as threatened by TPWD. All treefrogs have expanded toe pads on the tips of their digits which allow them to climb well. Treefrogs are primarily arboreal and can be found near permanent aquatic habitats during the spring breeding season.

true frog: True frogs are a group of large frogs which also include leopard frogs and bullfrogs. Species of true frogs that occur in Texas include the Pickerel Frog (*Rana palustris*) and Green Frog (*Rana clamitans*), which both have relatively large distributions throughout East Texas. The Pickerel Frog looks similar to leopard frogs but has squarish blotches instead of round blotches and yellow or orange coloration on the inside of its hind legs. Despite their name, Green Frogs can also be tan or bronze in coloration and can look similar to American Bullfrogs. These two species can be differentiated by looking at the dorsolateral fold (a fold of skin occurring from behind the eye). In Green Frogs, the dorsolateral fold extends to the hind limb, but in American Bullfrogs, the dorsolateral fold curves around the tympanum (eardrum) and never reaches the hind limb. Both the Pig Frog (*Rana grylio*) and Crawfish Frog (*Rana areolata*) also occur in East Texas but have a much more limited distribution in the state.

true toad: Ten species of toads occur throughout Texas, all varying in size, distribution, and preferred habitats. The largest toad that occurs in Texas is the Mesoamerican Cane Toad (*Rhinella horribilis*) that occurs in extreme South Texas, which can exceed 7" in length. The smallest toad in Texas is the Green Toad (*Anaxyrus debilis*), rarely exceeding 2" in length, which is found across much of the state except East Texas. All other species of toads are similar in size. Likely the rarest toad in Texas is the Houston Toad (*Anaxyrus houstonensis*). The Houston Toad only occurs in a handful of counties in the east-central portion of the state, has suffered widespread population declines, and is both federally- and state-protected. Two of the most widespread and abundant toads in Texas are the Texas Toad (*Anaxyrus speciosus*), which occurs throughout much of Texas except the eastern portion of the state and is also the state amphibian, and the Gulf Coast Toad (*Incilius nebulifer*), which occurs throughout south, central, and East Texas. The American Toad (*Anaxyrus americanus*) occurs in the extreme northeast corner of the state and is similar in appearance to the Fowler's Toad (*Anaxyrus fowleri*), which occupies a larger distribution throughout East Texas. The Great Plains Toad (*Anaxyrus cognatus*) primarily occurs in the Texas panhandle and the Trans-Pecos region. Widespread across west, north, and central Texas, the Red-spotted Toad (*Anaxyrus punctatus*) can be found in rocky, limestone habitats. The Woodhouse's Toad (*Anaxyrus woodhousii*) historically ranged from the Texas panhandle down the Gulf Coast but has experienced declines across much of its range in central Texas. Despite these declines, there remain areas where populations are still robust. Toads typically have dry, warty skin, bony ridges on the top of their head, and large poison glands called parotoid glands behind their eyes. These parotoid glands can secrete noxious compounds which are distasteful and irritating to potential predators.

waterdog: These salamanders are also occasionally called mudpuppy and one species occurs in Texas: the Gulf Coast Waterdog (*Necturus beyeri*). The Gulf Coast Waterdog occurs in small creek systems in the Big Thicket of East Texas. This species is fully aquatic, has four limbs, and bushy external gills on the sides of its head.

white-lipped frog: The Mexican White-lipped Frog (*Leptodactylus fragilis*) barely makes it into Texas along the Rio Grande in extreme South Texas. In Texas, this species is rare and can only be found after rains, but it is much more common throughout Central America. These frogs appear similar to other true frogs in body shape but have rougher skin, a more pointed snout, and a prominent white stripe along the upper lip. The Mexican White-lipped Frog has a unique nesting habitat unlike other species of frogs in Texas. During reproduction, a foam nest is created from skin secretions and surrounds the eggs. This foam nest helps to prevent the eggs from drying out until the eggs hatch and tadpoles emerge.

The Rio Grande Cooter is found in the Rio Grande and Pecos rivers of West Texas. Photo by Drew R. Davis.

Reptiles

alligator: The American Alligator (*Alligator mississippiensis*) is the largest reptile in North America and is found across the eastern third of Texas.

alligator lizard: The Texas Alligator Lizard (*Gerrhonotus infernalis*) can be found on rocky hillsides and wooded canyons in central and West Texas. With a long and somewhat prehensile tail, this species can measure over 17" in total length.

anole: The Green Anole (*Anolis carolinensis*) is a frequent visitor seen on fences and trees in the eastern two-thirds of Texas. Sometimes called chameleons because of their ability to change color between brown and green, but they are not related to true chameleons. The Brown Anole* (*Anolis sagrei*) is found along the coast from Brownsville to Galveston and is displacing the native Green Anole in parts of its range.

black-headed snake: Four species of black-headed snakes in Texas reach lengths of 6–8 inches, and a fifth species that lives in West Texas, the Trans-Pecos Black-headed Snake (*Tantilla cucullata*), can grow to 2' in length. The Flat-headed Snake (*Tantilla gracilis*) has a salmon-colored belly and lives in the eastern half of the state. The Plains Black-headed Snake (*Tantilla nigriceps*) is found in West and South Texas as well as the Panhandle.

blindsnake: see threadsnake

box turtle: Box turtles have a domed shell with a single hinge on the underside that allows the turtles to completely withdraw their limbs and head into the shell when threatened. These turtles have a generalist diet, consuming worms, insects, and vegetation. The Eastern Box Turtle (*Terrapene carolina*) is primarily found in eastern Texas, while the Ornate Box Turtle (*Terrapene ornata*) is found across most of the remainder of the state.

brownsnake: The Dekay's Brownsnake (*Storeria dekayi*) is one of several small (6–8") snakes found under rocks and logs in both urban backyards and rural settings. Other small snakes that are similar include the Rough Earthsnake (*Haldea striatula*), Smooth Earthsnake (*Virginia valeriae*), Lined Snake (*Tropidoclonion lineatum*), and Western Groundsnake (*Sonora semiannulata*). This group of snakes feeds on a variety of invertebrates, from worms and slugs to centipedes, scorpions, and spiders. Most are brown or tan, though Dekay's Brownsnakes and Lined Snakes are striped, and Western Groundsnakes may be either striped or banded.

bullsnake: see gophersnake

chicken snake: see ratsnake

chicken turtle: The Chicken Turtle (*Deirochelys reticularia*) is an uncommon species of turtle found in East Texas that looks similar to some sliders in shape and size. This turtle was once widely consumed, and its name refers to the taste of its meat.

coachwhip: see whipsnake

collared lizard: The Eastern Collared Lizard (*Crotaphytus collaris*), or Mountain Boomer, is found in rocky areas of central, north, and West Texas. This species has a dark collar around its neck with overall green body color. The Reticulate Collared Lizard (*Crotaphytus reticulatus*) is mostly brown or gray with a network of light lines and dark spots on its back. This species is found in South Texas from Maverick to Hidalgo counties.

cooter: Cooters are large, aquatic turtles that inhabit river systems throughout Texas. Four species of cooters are found in Texas, including one non-native species. The River Cooter (*Pseudemys concinna*) is found throughout East Texas, the Texas Cooter (*Pseudemys texana*) is found throughout central Texas, and the Rio Grande Cooter (*Pseudemys gorzugi*) is found in the Rio Grande and Pecos Rivers of West Texas. The Florida Red-bellied Cooter* (*Pseudemys nelsoni*) is not native to Texas and has been introduced to the headwaters of the San Marcos River and Houston.

copperhead: VENOMOUS. The Copperhead (*Agkistrodon contortrix*) is found in most of the state, except South Texas and the Panhandle. Its copper-colored body with rusty orange or grayish bands help camouflage the snake in leaf litter. They feed on small mammals and insects, particularly, freshly-molted cicadas in the summer.

coralsnake: VENOMOUS. The Texas Coralsnake (*Micrurus tener*) is a common species across south, central, and East Texas. It is infrequently seen because it spends the majority of its life underground, and it feeds almost exclusively on other snakes. Because of variability in color intensity and pattern in Texas Coralsnakes, the commonly used rhyme "red next to yellow, kill a fellow; red next to black, venom lack" is not a reliable method to distinguish venomous coralsnakes from look-a-likes, such as the non-venomous Milksnake (*Lampropeltis triangulum*).

cottonmouth: VENOMOUS. The Cottonmouth (*Agkistrodon piscivorus*), or Water Moccasin, is more commonly encountered in East Texas though populations persist as far West as San Angelo and Junction. Not an aggressive animal, however, it will vigorously defend itself against would-be predators. Defensive behavior includes vibrating its tail and gaping open its mouth, showing off the white lining.

earless lizard: All five species of earless lizards have ears, but they have skin covering the ear opening. The largest species, the Greater Earless Lizard (*Cophosaurus texanus*) is a conspicuous and fast-moving species identified by the black-and-white bands on the bottom of its tail. The Common Lesser Earless Lizard (*Holbrookia maculata*) is found across the west, north, and central portions of Texas. The Keeled Earless Lizard (*Holbrookia propinqua*) is restricted to the sand sheets and dunes of South Texas. The Plateau Earless Lizard (*Holbrookia lacerata*) is found patchily across central Texas, South of the Colorado River and East of the Pecos River. The Tamaulipan Spot-tailed Lizard (*Holbrookia subcaudalis*) is restricted to populations near Del Rio and Kingsville.

earthsnake: see brownsnake

gartersnake: Four species occur in the state, primarily feeding on amphibians and fish, but also earthworms. All species have light-colored lines running the length of their dark-colored bodies. The Checkered Gartersnake (*Thamnophis marcianus*) is found everywhere except East Texas. The Black-necked Gartersnake (*Thamnophis cyrtopsis*), found in central and West Texas, is one of the most beautiful snakes in the state with a brilliant orange stripe. Both the Plains Gartersnake (*Thamnophis radix*) and Common Gartersnake (*Thamnophis sirtalis*), though widely found across the north-central and eastern portions of the United States, only have limited ranges in Texas.

gecko: The Texas Banded Gecko (*Coleonyx brevis*) is the smaller of the two native geckos in the state and is found in West and South Texas. The Reticulate Banded Gecko (*Coleonyx reticulatus*) is native to the Big Bend. Six species of geckos have been introduced to Texas. The Mediterranean Gecko* (*Hemidactylus turcicus*) first arrived in Brownsville in the 1950s and is now found as far North as Lubbock and the Red River. Other species like the Tropical House Gecko* (*Hemidactylus mabouia*) and the Sri Lankan Spotted Gecko* (*Hemidactylus parvimaculatus*) are recent arrivals to the state.

glass lizard: The legless Slender Glass Lizard (*Ophisaurus attenuatus*) is restricted to sandy habitats across the eastern half of the state. This species has eyelids and ear openings, distinguishing them from snakes. They can be seen among the coastal dunes on Mustang Island and Padre Island National Seashore where they feed on insects and small vertebrates.

gophersnake: The Gophersnake (*Pituophis catenifer*), sometimes called Bullsnake, can grow to be the longest snake in the U.S., reaching over 9' in length. Found across the western three-quarters of the state, this non-venomous species may hiss and vibrate its tail when threatened. The related Louisiana Pinesnake (*Pituophis ruthveni*) is a federally-listed species historically found in longleaf pine-oak sandhills habitats in East Texas.

greensnake: The Rough Greensnake (*Opheodrys aestivus*) feeds on spiders and insects, growing to 2' in length in the eastern third of Texas. The Smooth Greensnake (*Opheodrys vernalis*) is thought to be extirpated from the state and is only known from six specimens collected in the 1960s and 1970s.

groundsnake: see brownsnake

hog-nosed snake: Hog-nosed snakes are known for their defensive displays towards predators, ending with the snake playing dead. The Eastern Hog-nosed Snake (*Heterodon platirhinos*) prefers to eat toads and is found in the eastern half of the state. The Plains Hog-nosed Snake (*Heterodon nasicus*) is more commonly found in sandy and gravely habitats in West Texas and the Panhandle.

horned lizard: The Texas Horned Lizard (*Phrynosoma cornutum*), or Horny Toad, is the state reptile. Originally found across the majority of the state, it is now restricted to pockets in west, south, and North Texas due to habitat loss and the introduction of invasive grasses and insects. The Greater Short-horned Lizard (*Phrynosoma hernandesi*) is found at higher elevations in the Davis, Guadalupe, and Hueco mountains. The Round-tailed Horned Lizard (*Phrynosoma modestum*) is found mostly in West Texas and the Panhandle and blends into its arid habitats as a rock mimic.

horny toad: see horned lizard

iguana: The Mexican Spiny-tailed Iguana* (*Ctenosaura pectinata*) is the only species of iguana found in the state. It was introduced in Brownsville in the 1960s but has not expanded its range outside of Cameron County.

indigo snake: Famed for their ability to eat rattlesnakes, the Central American Indigo Snake (*Drymarchon melanurus*) also eats a variety of mammals, birds, turtles, amphibians, and other snakes. Found in South Texas, this heavy-bodied snake is colored dark black and can grow over 8' long.

kingsnake: The Prairie Kingsnake (*Lampropeltis calligaster*) is found in the grasslands and woodlands of East Texas, with some populations in the Panhandle and South Texas. The Gray-banded Kingsnake (*Lampropeltis alterna*) lives in the drier regions of West Texas and is prized by collectors for its beautiful banding patterns of orange or dark grey. The Common Kingsnake (*Lampropeltis getula*) is found throughout the state, though its pattern is more speckled in East Texas and more dark-blotched in West Texas.

lined snake: see brownsnake

loggerhead: see snapping turtle

map turtle: Map turtles, sometimes called sawback turtles, are characterized by a keeled ridge down the middle of the shell and numerous yellow lines on their head and limbs and inhabit river systems across the state. The Texas Map Turtle (*Graptemys versa*) is found in the Colorado and Concho rivers and the Cagle's Map Turtle (*Graptemys caglei*) is restricted to the Guadalupe River. Both the False Map Turtle (*Graptemys pseudogeographica*) and the Ouachita Map Turtle (*Graptemys ouachitensis*) are found in river systems in East and North Texas.

milksnake: The Milksnake (*Lampropeltis triangulum*) is a close relative of the kingsnakes. Its bright red, black, and yellow colors help confuse would-be predators that might instead think this snake to be the venomous Texas Coralsnake (*Micrurus tener*). Because of variability in color intensity and pattern in Texas coralsnakes, the commonly used rhyme "red next to yellow, kill a fellow; red next to black, venom lack" is not a reliable method to distinguish coralsnakes from look-a-likes, such as the Milksnake, the Scarletsnake (*Cemophora coccinea*), the Texas Scarletsnake (*Cemophora lineri*), or the Long-nosed Snake (*Rhinocheilus lecontei*).

moccasin: see cottonmouth

mountain boomer: see collared lizard

mudsnake: The Red-bellied Mudsnake (*Farancia abacura*) is a boldly patterned snake, with dark glossy scales on its back with a bright red belly. It will defend itself when captured by pressing the hard and pointed tip of its tail into the attacker's skin. Occasionally, this species is called a Hoop Snake because of the false myth that it can roll down a hill like a wheel with its tail in its mouth!

mud turtle: Three species of mud turtles are found in Texas, all of which are small (4–6" shell length), secretive species rarely encountered. The Yellow Mud Turtle (*Kinosternon flavescens*) is found throughout most of Texas, except the Piney Woods, and spend a large amount of time in rodent burrows on land, waiting for rains to move into temporary wetlands. The Rough-footed Mud Turtle (*Kinosternon hirtipes*) can only be found in the Alamito Creek drainage of West Texas. The Eastern Mud Turtle (*Kinosternon subrubrum*) occurs across East Texas, often in slow-moving water bodies, including bayous and flooded forests.

musk turtle: These turtles are similar in appearance and ecology to mud turtles, with only two species known in the state. Like mud turtles, musk turtles can discharge a foul-smelling substance from specialized glands on their undersides to deter predators. The Razor-backed Musk Turtle (*Sternotherus carinatus*) gets its name from its shell having small, raised ridges along the midline, and is restricted to aquatic habitats in East Texas. The Eastern Musk Turtle (*Sternotherus odoratus*) is more widespread across eastern and central Texas and has a smooth top of its shell.

painted turtle: Two species of painted turtles can be found in Texas, both extremely uncommon and limited in their range. The Southern Painted Turtle (*Chrysemys dorsalis*) can be found in extreme northeast Texas and only a few records of the Painted Turtle (*Chrysemys picta*) are known from along the Red River and in far West Texas.

pinesnake: see gophersnake

racer: Often a dull green and around 3' in length, the North American Racer (*Coluber constrictor*) is found across the majority of the state, typically in open areas with large amounts of undergrowth. Racers feed on small mammals, birds, reptiles, amphibians, and insects. In East Texas, North American Racers can be brown or tan with some populations being steel-blue or olive intermixed with light white or yellow scales (buttermilk phase).

racerunner: see whiptail lizard

ratsnake: Five species of ratsnake occur in Texas. The Western Ratsnake (*Pantherophis obsoletus*), also Chicken Snake, is frequently encountered in the eastern half of the state. It can reach lengths over 5' and spends much of its time in trees, eating squirrels, birds, and bird eggs. The Baird's Ratsnake (*Pantherophis bairdi*) is found only in the Trans-Pecos. This species changes its pattern from blotches (juvenile) to stripes (adult). A mostly gray snake with dark brown blotches, the Great Plains Ratsnake (*Pantherophis emoryi*) is found across most of the state. The Trans-Pecos Ratsnake (*Bogertophis subocularis*) is found in rocky areas of West Texas where it eats mammals, including bats.

rattlesnake: VENOMOUS. Rattlesnakes are seen in every habitat in Texas, with 11 species represented in the state. The largest, the Western Diamond-backed Rattlesnake (*Crotalus atrox*), can reach lengths over 7' and is found everywhere except far East Texas. The Timber Rattlesnake (*Crotalus horridus*) is a heavy-bodied snake found in the hardwood bottomlands of East and North Texas. The Rock Rattlesnake (*Crotalus lepidus*) can reach 2.5' in length and is restricted to the Trans-Pecos. The smallest rattlesnake species in Texas, the Pygmy Rattlesnake (*Sistrurus miliarius*) is found in East Texas, rarely growing longer than 20".

ribbonsnake: The Western Ribbonsnake (*Thamnophis proximus*) is found almost everywhere in the state, except West Texas. It has a series of three stripes down its olive-colored back and is closely related to the gartersnakes.

sea turtle: Five species of sea turtles can be found in saltwater habitats along the Texas coastline. The largest of all sea turtles, the Leatherback Sea Turtle (*Dermochelys coriacea*), has a shell length that exceeds 7' in length and can weigh almost a ton. The Kemp's Ridley Sea Turtle (*Lepidochelys* *kempii*) is among the rarest and smallest of the sea turtles, which primarily nest along South Padre Island and into coastal Mexico and is designated as the state sea turtle. Other sea turtles include the Green Sea Turtle (*Chelonia mydas*), Hawksbill Sea Turtle (*Eretmochelys imbricata*), and Loggerhead Sea Turtle (*Caretta caretta*). All species of sea turtle are federally- and state-protected and any observed nesting or stranded along the coastline should be reported to appropriate individuals, such as TPWD.

skink: Eight species of skinks in Texas, all with smooth and shiny scales. The smallest species is the Ground Skink (*Scincella lateralis*) is often seen scurrying off dirt paths or sidewalks to hide from predators across the eastern three-quarters of Texas. The largest species is the Great Plains Skink (*Plestiodon obsoletus*) and is found in the western half of the state. This species can measure over 1' in total length.

slider: Two species of sliders are found in Texas. One species, the Pond Slider (*Trachemys scripta*) is among the most common turtle found throughout Texas, occurring in most aquatic habitats. The second species, the Mexican Plateau Slider (*Trachemys gaigeae*) only occurs in the Rio Grande of West Texas.

snapping turtle: Snapping turtles are among the largest freshwater turtles in North America and have a generalist diet, consuming almost anything in the water it encounters, including carrion. Two species of snapping turtles are found in Texas. The Snapping Turtle (*Chelydra serpentina*) is found throughout the central and eastern regions while the Alligator Snapping Turtle (*Macrochelys temminckii*) is restricted to East Texas.

softshell: Softshells get their name from the reduced bony elements in their shell, which gives them a leathery, flexible shell, unlike most other turtles. Having this modified shape gives the turtles the ability to be extremely agile and fast swimmers. These species also have a snorkel-like snout and long necks that allow individuals to raise their heads up and breathe while they are submerged in the sandy bottoms of rivers and streams. Two species of softshells occur in Texas, including the Smooth Softshell (*Apalone mutica*) that is uncommon throughout parts of northern, central, and eastern Texas, and the Spiny Softshell (*Apalone spinifera*) that is much more abundant in suitable habitats across most of Texas.

spiny lizard: Over 10 species of spiny lizards are found in Texas, so-called 'spiny' because of their large, keeled scales that give them a rough appearance. The Crevice Spiny Lizard (*Sceloporus poinsettii*) is unique among Texas spiny lizards as it does not lay eggs but instead gives birth to live young. The Texas Spiny Lizard (*Sceloporus olivaceus*), or Rusty Lizard, prefers to spend their time in trees, often on the opposite side of the trunk from any observers! The Dunes Sagebrush Lizard (*Sceloporus arenicolus*) is restricted to the shinnery-oak dunes of West Texas near Kermit and Andrews. The Rose-bellied Lizard (*Sceloporus variabilis*) is found in rocky and drier environments in South Texas. The Tree Lizard (*Urosaurus ornatus*) is found on trees and rocks

from El Paso to central Texas. The Side-blotched Lizard (*Uta stansburiana*) is found in the western deserts and southern portions of the Panhandle.

terrapin: The Diamond-backed Terrapin (*Malaclemys terrapin*) inhabits brackish waters along the Texas coast from the Louisiana border to Corpus Christi. Throughout the 1800s, this turtle was widely consumed, and population declines were widespread.

threadsnake: The three native species of threadsnakes can initially look like earthworms; however, their tiny tongues and scaled bodies give them away as snakes. Threadsnakes feed on ant and termite larvae. The Texas Threadsnake (*Rena dulcis*) is found in the middle third of Texas; two other species, the New Mexico Threadsnake (*Rena dissecta*) and Western Threadsnake (*Rena humilis*), are found in West Texas. The Brahminy Blindsnake* (*Indotyphlops braminus*) has been introduced to Texas as it hitchhikes around the world, hiding in the soil of plants in the nursery trade.

tortoise: One species of tortoise occurs in Texas, the Berlandier's Tortoise (*Gopherus berlandieri*). This tortoise occurs throughout South Texas and into Mexico and has a domed shell and elephant-like feet. Unlike most other turtles, tortoises spend the majority of their time on land foraging on vegetation.

watersnake: Seven species are known in the state and all are non-venomous. Often, these species are confused with the venomous Cottonmouth (*Agkistrodon piscivorous*). The Diamond-backed Watersnake (*Nerodia rhombifer*), is the largest in the state, often reaching 4', and is found in the eastern two-thirds of Texas. The Plain-bellied Watersnake (*Nerodia erythrogaster*) feeds on amphibians and fish. Both the Brazos River Watersnake (*Nerodia harteri*) and Concho Watersnake (*Nerodia paucimaculata*) are found only in Texas (endemic species).

whipsnake: Whipsnakes are long and slender snakes with large eyes that hunt almost exclusively during the day. The Coachwhip (*Masticophis flagellum*) is found across the entire state and can be found with a variety of body colors: brown, tan, black, and red. Schott's Whipsnake (*Masticophis schotti*) is found in the thornscrub of South Texas and the Striped Whipsnake (*Masticophis taeniatus*) is found in the drier regions of central and West Texas.

whiptail lizard: There are 10 species of whiptail lizards found across the state, with the majority of species found in West Texas. Two species are widely distributed in Texas, except portions of West Texas: the Six-lined Racerunner (*Aspidoscelis sexlineata*), which has six light stripes across its dark back, and the Common Spotted Whiptail (*Aspidoscelis gularis*), which also has light stripes but with additional small light spots between the stripes and across its dark back. The Laredo Striped Whiptail (*Aspidoscelis laredoensis*) is the only species restricted to South Texas, found along the Rio Grande from Val Verde to Cameron counties. The Chihuahuan Spotted Whiptail (*Aspidoscelis exsanguis*) is an all-female species and can reproduce without fertilization from males.

Lucifer Hummingbird (*Calothorax lucifer*) can be found in the Christmas and Chisos mountains in the Big Bend during the summer; the Green-breasted Mango (*Anthracothorax prevostii*) has been seen sporadically in the Lower Rio Grande Valley, primarily in the fall.

jay: Seven species are recorded from Texas. The Blue Jay (*Cyanocitta cristata*) is the most wide-ranging species, inhabiting rural and urban areas across the state, except West Texas. Eating insects and large amounts of nuts and fruit, this species will also hoard surplus food. The spectacular and distinctive Green Jay (*Cyanocorax yncas*) has slowly been expanding its South Texas range northward towards San Antonio. The Brown Jay (*Psilorhinus morio*) is known only from Starr and Zapata counties.

kestrel: see falcon.

killdeer: The Killdeer (*Charadrius vociferus*) is a type of plover found throughout Texas, often seen along open fields and grassy lots. They lay their eggs directly on the ground, camouflaged among rocks and pebbles. Well-known for their distraction displays leading predators away from their nests, they will often pretend to have a broken wing.

kingbird: see flycatcher.

kingfisher: Three resident species in Texas. They hover and dive into the water to catch fish. The Belted Kingfisher (*Megaceryle alcyon*) is found throughout the state. Both the Ringed Kingfisher (*Megaceryle torquata*) and the Green Kingfisher (*Chloroceryle americana*) are restricted to central and South Texas.

kiskadee: see flycatcher.

kite: Kites are small raptors that feed insects and small vertebrates, but some species, like the Hook-billed Kite (*Chondrohierax uncinatus*) specialize in snails. Kites can catch and eat insects while in flight or can hover, then swoop down to grab prey off the ground. The Mississippi Kite Actiniaa mississippiensis) can be seen across the state; the White-tailed Kite (*Elanus leucurus*), and the Swallow-tailed Kite (*Elanoides forficatus*) are found in Eastt Texas and along the coast.

meadowlark: Meadowlarks are conspicuous birds found perched on fences along open prairie or grassy habitats. The call of the Western Meadowlark (*Sturnella neglecta*) is a bit more complex than that of the Eastern Meadowlark (*Sternella magna*), but subtle differences in their markings can make the species difficult to tell apart without the aid of their calls.

mockingbird: The Northern Mockingbird (*Mimus polyglottos*) is the state bird of Texas. Known for mimicking songs of other birds to attract mates and intimidate other males; unmated males will sing at night in the spring. Both males and females may vigorously attack would-be predators to defend their eggs and young.

nighthawk: These are nocturnal birds, with large mouths edged with large bristles that act as flytraps, feed at night to catch flying insects. They are also called goatsuckers. They do not build nests, but instead lay camouflaged eggs on bare ground. The Common Nighthawk (*Chordeiles minor*) is seen across the state, whereas the Common Pauraque (*Nyctidromus albicollis*) is restricted to South Texas.

oriole: Orioles are somewhat conspicuous with their bright yellow, orange, or rusty red colors, particularly the males in spring breeding plumage. Nine species reported in the state. The Orchard Oriole (*Icterus spurius*) can be a common resident in East Texas. The Altamira Oriole (*Icterus gularis*) is an orange and black species found only along the Rio Grande in extreme South Texas. The Scott's Oriole (*Icterus parisorum*) is a yellow and black species found across the drier Trans-Pecos region.

osprey: The Osprey (*Pandion haliaetus*) feeds on fish, hovering above the water before plunging in feet first to grab its prey. When flying, they are sometimes confused with gulls, but their sharply hooked beak and dark eye stripe help in their identification.

owl: Seventeen species are observed in the state. With large eyes, incredible hearing, and wings adapted to maintain silence in flight, owls are amazing nocturnal predators. More frequently seen owls include the Barn Owl (*Tyto alba*), Great Horned Owl (*Bufo virginianus*), Eastern Screech Owl (*Megascops asio*), Burrowing Owl (*Athene cunicularia*), and Barred Owl (*Strix varia*). In the summer, the small Elf Owl (*Micrathene whitneyi*) can be seen in West Texas.

parakeet: Following several accidental and at least one intentional introduction, the Monk Parakeet* (*Myiopsitta monachus*), or Quaker Parakeet*, is established in several urban areas from Dallas to Austin, San Antonio to Kingsville. The presence of another species found in South Texas along the Rio Grande, the Green Parakeet (*Aratinga holochlora*), may be linked to habitat loss further South in its native range of Mexico.

parrot: A single species, the Red-crowned Parrot (*Amazona viridigenalis*) is found in Texas, common in the metropolitan areas of Cameron, Hidalgo, and Starr counties along the lower Rio Grande border.

pelican: The Brown Pelican (*Pelecanus occidentalis*) is a resident along the Texas coast and may range inland up to 150 miles. The White Pelican (*Pelecanus erythrorhynchos*) is a common winter resident in the eastern half of the state.

phoebe: see flycatcher.

pigeon: see dove.

plover: see shorebird.

prairie chicken: Both the Greater Prairie-chicken (*Tympanuchus cupido*) and the Lesser Prairie-chicken (*Tympanuchus pallidicinctus*) are famed for their elaborate courtship displays: the males gather in tall-grass prairie clearings to dance in a competition for females. The males inflate their large orange neck pouches with air, then force air out with a "boom" that can be heard for over half a mile.

purple martin: see swallow.

quail: The Northern Bobwhite (*Colinus virginianus*) is the most widespread quail species in Texas, found across all but West Texas. The Gambel's Quail (*Callipepla gambelii*) and the Montezuma Quail (*Cyrtonyx montezumae*) are restricted to the Trans-Pecos; the Scaled Quail (*Callipepla squamata*), or Blue Quail, is found in the Panhandle as well as West and South Texas. All but the Montezuma Quail are legal game species in the state.

rail: Found in both freshwater and brackish marshes, rails are typically heard rather than seen. The Sora (*Porzana* carolina) may be the most conspicuous of the rails, hunting along the open margins in search of seeds and insects. Other species, like the Yellow Rail (*Coturnicops noveboracensis*) and Black Rail (*Laterallus jamaicensis*) are elusive winter migrants to brackish marshes along the coast.

raven: The Common Raven (*Corvus corax*) is a large black bird found in central and West Texas; the Chihuahuan Raven (*Corvus cryptoleucus*) is slightly smaller in size but with a wider distribution in the Panhandle and both West and South Texas. The larger body size, stouter bill, and longer wings distinguish ravens from the crow. Ravens are omnivorous, eating vertebrates, insects, seeds, and fruit.

roadrunner: The Greater Roadrunner (*Geococcyx californicus*) is found across the state, though uncommon in East Texas. They feed on a variety of prey, including insects, spiders, small mammals, small birds, lizards, and snakes, including rattlesnakes, but will also eat fruit and seeds. Other names include Paisano and Chaparral Cock.

robin: The American Robin (*Turdus migratorius*) is known across the state as either a winter visitor (west and South Texas) or as a summer resident (north, central, and East Texas), although its summer range in Texas continues to expand. With its red breast and brown or black back, this species can form large flocks that feed on insects and fruit.

sandpiper: see shorebird.

shorebird: A large group of wading birds commonly found along the water's edge, whether ocean or freshwater. Shorebirds' long bills are used to probe moist sand and sediment for invertebrates and featherless legs adapted for wading. The Willet (*Tringa semipalmata*) breeds along the Gulf Coast, identified by its black-and-white wing pattern visible during flight. The Spotted Sandpiper (*Actitis macularius*) can be identified by the exaggerated bobbing of its longish tail when walking. The Mountain Plover (*Charadrius montanus*) is a summer resident in open grasslands of the northern Panhandle with some populations wintering in central and South Texas. The secretive and solitary Wilson's Snipe (*Callinago delicata*), the focus of many invented hunts, is an actual game bird found along grassy marshes and meadows.

shrike: The Loggerhead Shrike (*Lanius ludovicianus*), or Butcher Bird, is known for impaling its prey (insects and small vertebrates) on barbed wire fences or sharp-thorned plants. The food items are eaten quickly or saved for future use. Its gray, black, and white body makes this species look similar to a Northern Mockingbird, but its black eye mask and sharp, hooked bill instead help identify it as a shrike.

snipe: see shorebird.

sparrow: Many of the 30 species of sparrows found in Texas are small brown or gray birds that may be difficult to identify from one another. Identification relies on noting the presence (or absence), number, and color of stripes on their head and bars on their wings. The Chipping Sparrow (*Spizella passerina*) can be found throughout the state, breeding in pockets of the west, central, and East Texas. The Black-throated Sparrow (*Amphispiza bilineata*) is a common

A pair of Scaled Quail. Photo by Jill D. Miller.

species in drier habitats of central, west, and South Texas. The Seaside Sparrow (*Ammodramus maritimus*) is restricted to coastal marshes on the coast. The White-collared Seedeater (*Sporophila torqueola*) is restricted to habitat along the Rio Grande from Val Verde to Starr counties. The ubiquitous House Sparrow* (*Passer domesticus*), distantly related to the New World sparrows, was intentionally released in Galveston in 1867 and spread throughout the state by 1905.

starling: The European Starling* (*Sturnus vulgaris*) was first introduced to North America in New York in 1890. It reached East Texas by 1925 and El Paso in 1939. This aggressive species will often take over cavities and nest boxes, often out-competing native species such as bluebirds and Purple Martins. A visually striking bird in its breeding plumage with a brilliant yellow bill and iridescent black feathers.

swallow: Nine species of small, swift fliers that feed on insects while in flight are found in Texas. The arrival of the first Purple Martin (*Progne subis*) is a harbinger of spring; fall migratory roosts can number in the hundreds of thousands. The Cliff Swallow (*Poetrochelidon pyrrhonota*) has a short, squared tail and builds mud nests in groups on cliffs or bridges. The Barn Swallow (*Hirundo rustica*) has a longer, forked tail and builds small mud nests under the eaves of buildings.

swift: With their long wings and slender bodies, swifts have been called "flying cigars." They are fast fliers, catching and feeding on insects in flight. The Chimney Swift (*Chaetura pelagica*) uses hollow trees and crevices for nesting sites, using saliva to glue together a nest of twigs on the inside of the structure. This species has gained its name because it can utilize man-made structures such as abandoned buildings, silos, and chimneys for nesting sites.

tern: Related to gulls, terns can be found along the coast and inland near lakes and marshes. Terns form large breeding colonies to provide protection in numbers, more experienced adults occupying the center of the colony. The Caspian Tern (*Hydroprogne caspia*) is the largest species in the world. The Royal Tern (*Thalasseus maximus*) and the Sandwich Tern (*Thalasseus sanvicensis*) are restricted to coastal habitats; the Forester's Tern (*Sterna forsteri*) is common along the coast and inland lakes.

thrush: Related to bluebirds and the robin, thrushes are medium-sized birds with melodious calls. Many species are secretive winter migrants, their inconspicuous brown coloration helping hide them in woody brush. The Hermit Thrush (*Catharus guttatus*) is a common winter visitor across the state, with a breeding population in the Davis Mountains. The Wood Thrush (*Hylocichla mustelina*) is a summer resident of East Texas.

titmouse: Titmice in Texas are conspicuous and talkative birds with a noticeable tuft or crest on their head. Often in mixed-species flocks with chickadees and small woodpeckers. The Tufted Titmouse (*Baeolophus bicolor*) is found in the eastern third of the state; the Black-crested Titmouse (*Baeolophus atricristatus*), with a prominent black patch on its crest, is found in the western two-thirds of the state.

turkey: The Wild Turkey (*Maleagris gallopavo*) has a patchwork distribution across Texas, commonly seen in the middle third of state, but in more isolated pockets in West and East Texas. Males with conspicuous display to attract females: they will strut and gobble, while extending their wings, tail and body feathers. Turkeys often roost in trees at night.

vireo: see flycatcher.

vulture: With their long wings, both species of vultures are experts at soaring, generally only flapping their wings when they take off from feeding or roosting. Featherless heads and curved bills are adaptations to feeding on carrion. The Black Vulture (*Coragyps atratus*) has a black head and white wing-tips when viewed from below; the Turkey Vulture (*Cathartes aura*) has a red head and two-toned (black and white) wings from below: black on the leading edge, gray or white on the trailing edge. Turkey Vultures use both sight and smell to find food, Black Vultures rely more on sight.

warbler: Almost 50 species of warblers, more properly called "wood-warblers," are known from Texas. Many are migrants passing through, while others are breeding summer residents. Many bird watchers anxiously await the last two weeks of April for the peak of spring migration, when birds return from their winter locations in spectacular full breeding plumage. If birds flying from the Yucatan across the Gulf of Mexico encounter strong winds or storms, they will be exhausted from their non-stop flight and "fallout" once they finally reach land. The Golden-cheeked Warbler (*Setophaga chrysoparia*) breeds only in the steep, wooded canyons of central Texas. The population of Colima Warblers (*Oreothlypis crissalis*) found in the Chisos Mountains (Big Bend) is the only U.S. population. The Tropical Parula (*Setophaga pitiayumi*) is a large warbler found in South Texas. The Yellow-rumped Warbler (*Setophaga coronata*) is a common winter visitor to most of Texas.

waxwing: A conspicuous winter visitor, the Cedar Waxwing (*Bombycilla cedrorum*) moves around in large flocks feeding on berries and fruits. It has a black mask, head crest, and a row of feathers on the wings are tipped with a bright red waxy substance.

woodpecker: Over a dozen species of woodpeckers occur in Texas, all with sharp, stout bills used to probe wood for insects or used to excavate cavities to nest. At 16" long, the Pileated Woodpecker (*Dryocopus pileatus*) is the largest species in Texas and is found in East Texas; at just under 7", the Downy Woodpecker (*Picoides pubescens*) is one of the smallest and is found across all but West and South Texas. The Acorn Woodpecker (*Melanerpes formicivorus*) is known for storing (and defending) large amounts of acorns wedged into small holes in dead limbs and trees.

wren: Wrens are small brown birds that can be quite vocal when advertising for mates or in defense of their nests. Many species have a white eye-stripe and often hold their tails up at an angle over their backs and are insectivorous. The Carolina Wren (*Thyrothorus ludovicianus*), House Wren (*Troglodytes aedon*), and the Bewick's Wren (*Thryomanes bewickii*) build nests in cavities, often close to human dwellings. The slowly cascading call of the Canyon Wren (*Catherpes mexicanus*) is often heard in rocky areas of West and central Texas.

Mule Deer are commonly found in the Panhandle and Trans-Pecos regions of the state. Photo by Jill D. Miller.

Mammals

armadillo: The Nine-banded Armadillo (*Dasypus novemcinctus*) is one of Texas' most iconic mammals and is the state small mammal. It is found in most of the state except the western Trans-Pecos. It is now common as far North and East as Kansas and Mississippi.

badger: The American Badger (*Taxidea taxus*) is most common in parts of West and South Texas and is occasionally spotted in the eastern part of the state. It is a fierce fighter and is valuable in helping control the rodent population.

bat: Thirty-two species of these winged mammals have been found in Texas, more than in any other state in the United States. Of these, 27 species are known residents, though they are seldom seen by the casual observer. The Mexican Free-tailed Bat (*Tadarida brasiliensis*) and the Cave Myotis (*Myotis velifer*) constitute most of the cave-dwelling bats of central and West Texas. They have some economic value for their deposits of nitrogen-rich guano. Some commercial guano has been produced from Beaver Creek Cavern (Burnet County) and James River Bat Cave (Mason County), and from large deposits in other caves, including Bandera Bat Cave (Bandera County), Blowout Cave (Blanco County), and Devil's Sinkhole (Edwards County). The largest concentration of bats in the world is found at Bracken Cave in Comal County, which is thought to hold between 20 and 40 million bats. The Big Brown Bat (*Eptesicus fuscus*), the Eastern Red Bat (*Lasiurus borealis*), and the Evening Bat (*Nycticeius humeralis*) are found in East and southeast Texas. The Evening Bat and Big Brown Bat are forest and woodland dwelling mammals. The rarer species of Texas bats have been found along the Rio Grande and in the Trans-Pecos.

Bats can be observed at dusk near a water source, and many species may also be found foraging on insects attracted to streetlights. Everywhere bats occur, they are the main predators of night-flying insects, including mosquitoes and many crop pests. The state flying mammal of Texas is the Mexican Free-tailed Bat.

bear: The American Black Bear (*Ursus americanus*), formerly common throughout most of the state, is now surviving in remnant populations in mountainous areas of the Trans-Pecos from Big Bend to Del Rio.

beaver: The American Beaver (*Castor canadensis*) is found over most of the state except for the Llano Estacado and parts of the Trans-Pecos.

bighorn: see sheep

bison: The largest of native terrestrial wild mammals of North America, the American Bison (*Bos bison*), commonly called buffalo, was formerly found in the western two-thirds of the state. Today, it is extirpated or confined on ranches. Deliberate slaughter of this majestic animal for hides and to eliminate the Plains Indians' main food source reached a peak about 1877–1878, and the American Bison was almost eradicated by 1885. Estimates of the number of buffalo killed vary, but as many as 200,000 hides were sold in Fort Worth at a single two-day sale. Except for the interest of the late Col. Charles Goodnight and a few other foresighted men, the American Bison might be extinct.

buffalo: see bison

cat: The Jaguar (*Felis onca*) is probably now extinct in Texas (last recorded in 1948 near Kingsville), along with the Jaguarundi (*Puma yagouaroundi*) and Margay (*Felis wiedii*). The Bobcat (*Lynx rufus*) is found throughout the state in large numbers. The Mountain Lion (*Felis concolor*), also known as the cougar or puma, was once found statewide and is now found in the mountainous areas of the Trans-Pecos and the dense Rio Grande brushland. The Ocelot (*Felis pardalis*) is now restricted to extreme South Texas. The last documented report of a Jaguarundi, was reported from Brownsville in 1986, although unverified reports continue to be described along the length of the Rio Grande. The Margay was last reported before 1852 near Eagle Pass.

chipmunk: The Gray-footed Chipmunk (*Tamias canipes*) is found at high altitudes in the Guadalupe and Sierra Diablo ranges of the Trans-Pecos. See also ground squirrel, with which the chipmunk is often confused in public reference.

coati: The White-nosed coati (*Nasua narica*), a relative of the raccoon, historically ranged from Brownsville to the Big Bend, but today its distribution is mostly restricted to the Trans-Pecos and it is listed as a threatened species in the state. It inhabits woodland areas and feeds both on the ground and in trees. In Texas, the Whit-nosed Coati is most commonly seen in Big Bend National Park.

coyote: The Coyote (*Canis latrans*) exists in great numbers in Texas, including in and around urban areas. While a significant predator of Texas livestock, it is also a valuable predator in the balance of nature, providing a layer of protection to crops and range lands by its control of rodents and rabbits. In terms of economic importance, it is second only to the raccoon in being the most important fur-bearing animal in the state.

deer: The White-tailed Deer (*Odocoileus virginianus*), found throughout the state in brushy or wooded areas, is the most important Texas game animal. Its numbers in Texas are estimated at more than 3 million. The Mule Deer (*Odocoileus heminous*) is found principally in the Trans-Pecos and Panhandle areas and has increased in number in recent years. In Texas, the only native species of Elk (*Cervus canadensis merriami*) was found in the southern Guadalupe Mountains and became extinct about the turn of the 20th century. A separate subspecies of Elk (*Cervus c. canadensis*) was introduced into the same area from South Dakota around 1928. There are currently several herds totaling several thousand individuals. Several exotic deer species have been introduced, mostly for hunting purposes. The Axis Deer* (*Axis axis*) is the most numerous of the exotics. Native to India, it is found mostly in central and South Texas, both free-ranging and confined on ranches. Blackbuck* (*Antilope cervicapra*), also native to India, is the second-most numerous exotic deer in the state and is found on ranches in 86 counties. Fallow Deer* (*Dama dama*), native to the Mediterranean, have been introduced to 93 counties, while the Nilgai* (*Boselaphus tragocamelus*), native of India and Pakistan, is found mostly in Kenedy, Willacy, and Cameron counties. The Sika Deer* (*Cervus nippon*), native of southern Siberia, Japan, and China, has been introduced in 77 counties in central and South Texas.

dolphin: The Atlantic Spotted Dolphin (*Stenella frontalis*) is rather small, long snouted, and spotted; it is purplish gray, appearing blackish at a distance, usually with numerous small white or gray spots on its sides and back. In the Gulf of Mexico, this dolphin is second in abundance only to the Common Bottlenose Dolphin. The Common Bottlenose Dolphin (*Tursiops truncatus*) is stout and short-beaked with sloping forehead, projecting lower jaw, and high dorsal fin. Other species, such as the Clymene Dolphin, Pantropical Spotted Dolphin, Risso's Dolphin, Rough-toothed Dolphin, Spinner Dolphin, and Striped Dolphin are unusual and known in Texas only through strandings along gulf beaches.

ferret: The Black-footed Ferret (*Mustela nigripes*) was formerly found widely ranging through the West Texas country where its main prey, the prairie dog, was formerly plentiful. Related to the mink and weasel, it is now considered extinct in Texas.

fox: The Common Gray Fox (*Urocyon cinereoargenteus*) is found throughout most of the state, primarily in the woods of East Texas, in broken parts of the Edwards Plateau, and in the rough country at the foot of the High Plains. The Swift Fox (*Vulpes velox*) is found in the western third of the state. A second species of Kit Fox (*Vulpes macrotis*) is found in the Trans-Pecos and is fairly numerous in some localities. The Red Fox* (*Vulpes vulpes*), which ranges across central Texas, was introduced for sport.

gopher: Eleven species of pocket gopher occur in Texas. The Botta's Pocket Gopher (*Thomomys bottae*) is found from the Trans-Pecos eastward across the Edwards Plateau. The Plains Pocket Gopher (*Geomys bursarius*) is found from Midland and Tom Green counties East and North to McLennan, Dallas, and Grayson counties. The Desert Pocket Gopher (*Geomys arenarius*) is found only in the Trans-Pecos, while the Yellow-faced Pocket Gopher (*Cratogeomys castanops*) is found in the western third of the state, with occasional sightings along the Rio Grande in Maverick and Cameron counties. The Texas Pocket Gopher (*Geomys personatus*) is found in South Texas from San Patricio County to Val Verde County. Attwater's Pocket Gopher (*Geomys attwateri*) and Baird's Pocket Gopher (*Geomys breviceps*) are both found generally in south-central and coastal Texas from the Brazos River to the San Antonio River and South to Matagorda and San Patricio counties. Jones' Pocket Gopher (*Geomys knoxjonesi*) is found only in far West Texas, while the Llano Pocket Gopher (*Geomys texensis*) is found only in two isolated areas of the Hill Country. Hall's Pocket Gopher (*Geomys jugossicularis*) is restricted to Dallam and Hartley counties in the far northwest Panhandle and Strecker's Pocket Gopher (*Geomys streckeri*) is found only in Dimmit and Zavala counties in South Texas.

ground squirrel: Five species of ground squirrel live in Texas, mostly in the western part of the state. The Rock Squirrel (*Otopermophilus variegatus*) is found throughout the Edwards Plateau and Trans-Pecos. The Rio Grande Ground Squirrel (*Ictidomys parvidens*) occurs throughout much of South Texas, the Trans-Pecos, and almost to the Red River just East of the Panhandle. The Spotted Ground Squirrel (*Xermospermophilus spilosoma*) is found generally in the western half of the state. The Thirteen-lined Ground Squirrel (*Ictidomys tridecemlineatus*) is found in a narrow strip from Dallas and Tarrant counties to the gulf. The Texas Antelope Squirrel (*Ammospermophilus interpres*) is found along the Rio Grande from El Paso to Val Verde County.

hog: Feral Hogs (*Sus scrofa*) are found in almost every county in Texas but especially in areas of the Rio Grande and Coastal Plains, as well as in the woods of East Texas. They are descendants of escaped domestic hogs or of European wild hogs that were imported for sport. Their rooting habits can extensively destroy vegetation and soil and their ever-expanding populations threaten many native mammal populations through competition and disease.

javelina: The Javelina or Collared Peccary (*Pecari tajacu*) is found in brushy semidesert areas where Prickly Pear, a favorite food, is found. The Javelina was hunted commercially for its hide until 1939. They are harmless to livestock and to people, though they can defend themselves ferociously when attacked by hunting dogs.

mink: The American Mink (*Vison vison*) is found in the eastern half of the state, always near streams, lakes, or other water sources. Although it is an economically important fur-bearing animal in the eastern United States, it ranked only 13th in both numbers and economic value to trappers in Texas in 2001–2002 trapping season.

mole: The Eastern Mole (*Scalopus aquaticus*) is found in the eastern two-thirds of Texas. Moles cannot see and spend most of their life in underground burrows they excavate for themselves or usurp from other mammals, such as pocket gophers. The burrowing of moles can damage lawns, row crops, and the greens of golf courses. Benefits, however, are aerating soil and eating larval insects that destroy roots of grass and crops.

muskrat: The Common Muskrat (*Ondatra zibethicus*) occurs in aquatic habitats in the northern and southeastern parts of the state as well as along the Pecos River in West Texas. Although the muskrat was once economically valuable for its fur, its numbers have declined, mostly because of the loss of habitat.

nutria: The Nutria* (*Myocastor coypus*) is an introduced species of rodent originally native to South America. It is found primarily in the eastern two-thirds of the state, but they have expanded their range into the Big Bend region. The fur is not highly valued and, because Nutrias are in competition with muskrats, their spread is discouraged. They have been used widely in Texas as a cure-all for ponds choked with vegetation, with spotty results.

opossum: A marsupial, the Virginia Opossum (*Didelphis virginiana*) is found in nearly all parts of the state. The opossum has economic value for its pelt, and its meat is considered a delicacy by some.

otter: Northern River Otters (*Lontra canadensis*) are found in the eastern third of the state. This species has probably been extirpated from the Panhandle and some north-central locations but over the past 20 years, it has been expanding its range back into remaining suitable habitat in East and South Texas.

peccary: see javelina

pig: see hog

porcupine: The North American Porcupine (*Erethizon dorsatum*) is found from the western half of the state east to Bosque County. It is adapted to a variety of habitats and, in recent years, has expanded into South Texas. Porcupines are expert at climbing trees but are as much at home in rocks as on the ground or in trees. They have a relatively long lifespan; one marked female lived more than 10 years under natural conditions.

prairie dog: Until recent years, probably no sight was so universal in West Texas as the Black-tailed Prairie Dog (*Cynomys ludovicianus*). Naturalists estimated its population in the hundreds of millions, and prairie dog towns often covered many acres with thickly spaced burrows. However, this species has been replaced by livestock and cultivated crops across most of its range, a loss of over 98% of the original population in the state. It is being propagated in several public zoos, notably in the prairie dog town in Mackenzie Park at Lubbock. It has been honored in Texas by the naming of the Prairie Dog Town Fork of the Red River, in one segment of which is located the beautiful Palo Duro Canyon.

pronghorn: The Pronghorn (*Antilocapra americana*) formerly was found in the western two-thirds of the state. It is currently found only in limited areas from the Panhandle to the Trans-Pecos. Despite management efforts, its numbers have been decreasing in recent years.

rabbit: The Black-tailed Jackrabbit (*Lepus californicus*) is found throughout Texas except the Big Thicket area of East Texas. It breeds rapidly, and its long hind legs make it one of the world's faster-running animals. The Eastern Cottontail (*Sylvilagus floridanus*) is found mostly in the eastern three-quarters of the state. The Desert Cottontail (*Sylvilagus audubonii*) is found in the western half of the state, usually on the open range. The Swamp Rabbit (*Sylvilagus aquaticus*) is found in East Texas and the coastal area. The Davis Mountains Cottontail (*Sylvilagus robustus*) is restricted to Jeff Davis County.

raccoon: The Northern Raccoon (*Procyon lotor*) is found throughout Texas, especially in woodlands and near water. It is strictly nocturnal. A raccoon makes its den in a large hollow tree or hollow log, in which it spends the daylight hours sleeping and in which it also rears its young. In western areas, dens usually are in crevices of rocky bluffs.

rats, mice, and voles: There are 40 to 50 species of rats, mice, and voles in Texas of varying characteristics, habitats, and economic destructiveness. The Norway Rat* (*Rattus norvegicus*) and the Roof Rat* (*Rattus rattus*), both non-native species, are probably the most common and most destructive. They also are instrumental in the transmission of several dread diseases, including bubonic plague and typhus. Populations of the Common House Mouse* (*Mus musculus*) are estimated in the hundreds of millions annually. The Mogollon Vole (*Microtus mogollonensis*) is found only in the higher elevations of Guadalupe Mountains National Park. With its long tail tipped with a white tuft of fur, the state-threatened Texas Kangaroo Rat (*Dipodomys elator*) is restricted to less than a dozen Texas counties near the Red River.

ringtail: The Ringtail (*Bassariscus astutus*) is a cat-sized carnivore resembling a small fox with a long raccoon-like tail. It found statewide but is rare in the extreme South Texas and the Panhandle. Ringtails are nocturnal and live in a variety of habitats, preferring rocky areas, such as rock piles, stone fences, and canyon walls.

Texas Wildlife Management Areas

Source: Texas Parks and Wildlife Department; http://tpwd. texas.gov/huntwild/hunt/wma/

Texas Parks and Wildlife Department is responsible for managing 47 wildlife management areas (WMAs) in the state totaling more than 710,000 acres. Every vegetational area in the state has at least one WMA, with the exception of the Cross Timbers and Prairies area, in north central Texas. (See page 69 for more information about the Vegetational Areas of Texas.)

Wildlife management areas are used principally for hunting, but many are also used for research, fishing, wildlife viewing, hiking, camping, bicycling, and horseback riding, when those activities are compatible with the primary goals

for which the WMA was established. See the table below for activities available in Texas' WMAs.

Access to WMAs at times designated for public use is provided through various permits, depending on the activity.

A Limited Public Use Permit ($12) allows access for such activities as birdwatching, hiking, camping, or picnicking.

On most WMAs, restrooms and drinking water are not provided, but **check with the TPWD about facilities before visiting a WMA**.

For further information, contact the Texas Parks and Wildlife Department, 4200 Smith School Rd., Austin 78744; or call 1-800-792-1112 and choose menu #5, selection #1. ☆

Texas Wildlife Management Areas

Name (Acreage)	County	Hunting	Fishing	Camping	Wildlife Viewing	Hiking	Driving	Bicycling	Equestrian	Comments
Alabama Creek (14,561)	Trinity	★	★	★	★	★	★	★	★	In Davy Crockett NF
Alazan Bayou (2,063)	Nacogdoches	★	★	★	★				★	
Angelina-Neches/Dam B (12,636)	Jasper/Tyler	★	★	★	★	★		★		
Atkinson Island (150)	Harris		★		★					Boat access only
Bannister (25,695)	San Augustine	★	★	★	★	★		★	★	In Angelina NF
Big Lake Bottom (3,894)	Anderson	★	★		★					
Black Gap (103,000)	Brewster	★	★	★	★	★	★	★	★	NW of Big Bend NP
Caddo Lake (8,124)	Marion/Harrison	★	★	★	★				★	
Caddo Nat. Grasslands (16,140)	Fannin	★	★	★	★	★		★	★	Separated into two units
Candy Cain Abshier (207)	Chambers				★					Excellent birding spring and fall
Cedar Creek Islands (160)	Henderson		★		★					Wildlife viewing from boat or bank of reservoir only
Chaparral (15,200)	La Salle/Dimmit	★		★	★	★	★	★		
Cooper (14,480)	Delta/Hopkins	★	★		★	★		★		Camping: Cooper Lake SP
D.R. Wintermann (246)	Wharton				★					Restricted access; bird refuge
East Texas Conservation Center (223)	Jasper									By appointment only
Elephant Mountain (23,147)	Brewster	★		★	★	★	★			
Gene Howe (5,886)	Hemphill	★	★	★	★	★		★	★	Riding March–August only
Gene Howe: W.A. "Pat" Murphy (889)	Hemphill	★	★		★	★				
Guadalupe Delta (7,411)	Calhoun/Refugio	★	★		★	★		★		Freshwater marsh
Gus Engeling (10,958)	Anderson	★	★	★	★	★	★	★	★	
J.D. Murphree (24,498)	Jefferson	★	★		★					Access by boat only
James E. Daughtrey (34,000)	Live Oak/McMullen	★			★					Primitive camping requires special permit
Justin Hurst (15,612)	Brazoria	★	★		★	★		★		On Texas Coastal Birding Trail
Keechi Creek (1,500)	Leon	★								
Kerr (6,493)	Kerr	★	★		★		★	★		On Guadalupe River
Las Palomas: Anacua (222)	Cameron	★			★					
Las Palomas: Lower Rio Grande Valley (3,311)	Cameron/Hidalgo	★			★	★				Also Presidio County
Lower Neches (7,998)	Orange	★	★		★	★				Coastal marsh
M.O. Neasloney (100)	Gonzales				★	★				Primarily for school groups
Mad Island (7,200)	Matagorda	★			★					Reservations needed for wildlife tours
Mason Mountain (5,300)	Mason	★								Restricted access
Matador (28,183)	Cottle	★	★	★	★	★	★		★	Primitive camping; tours
Matagorda Island (56,688)	Calhoun	★	★	★	★	★		★		
Moore Plantation (26,772)	Sabine/Jasper	★	★	★	★	★		★	★	In Sabine National Forest
Muse (1,972)	Brown	★			★					
Nannie M. Stringfellow (3,666)	Brazoria	★			★					Open for special hunts only

National Wildlife Refuges in Texas

Source: U.S. Fish and Wildlife Service, U.S. Department of the Interior.

Texas has more than 470,000 acres in 17 national wildlife refuges. Their descriptions, with date of acquisition in parentheses, follow.

Included in this acreage are two conservation easement refuges, which may be visited at different times of the year for bird watching and wildlife viewing, as well as hunting and fishing. Write or call before visiting to check on facilities and days and hours of operation. On the web: **www.fws. gov/southwest/**.

Anahuac (1963): The more than 37,000 acres of this refuge are located along the upper Gulf Coast in Chambers County. Fresh and saltwater marshes and miles of beautiful, sweeping coastal prairie provide wintering habitat for large flocks of waterfowl, including geese, 27 species of ducks, and six species of rails. Roseate spoonbills, great and snowy egrets, and white-faced ibis are among the other birds frequenting the refuge. Other species include alligator, muskrat, and bobcat. Fishing, bird watching, auto tours, and hunting are available. Office: Box 278, Anahuac 77514; (409) 267-3337.

Aransas (1937): This refuge complex comprises 115,000 acres including Blackjack Peninsula, Matagorda Island, and three satellite units in Aransas and Refugio counties. Besides providing wintering grounds for the largest wild flock of endangered whooping cranes, the refuge is home to more than 390 species of waterfowl and other migratory birds. Refuge Tour Loop is open daily, sunrise to sunset. Claude F. Lard Visitor Center is open daily, 6:45 a.m. to 7:30 p.m. Other

facilities include a 40-foot observation tower and walking trails. Office: Box 100, Austwell 77950; (361) 349-1181.

Attwater Prairie Chicken (1972): Established in Colorado County to preserve habitat for the endangered Attwater's prairie chicken (a ground-dwelling grouse), the refuge comprises 10,528 acres of native tallgrass prairie, sandy knolls, and wooded areas. A 5-mile auto tour loop is available year-round. There are two hiking trails — the Sycamore and the Pipit trails — that traverse the prairie, potholes, and riparian areas. The auto tour loop can also serve as a hiking trail. Refuge open sunrise to sunset. Office: Box 519, Eagle Lake 77434; (979) 234-3021.

Balcones Canyonlands (1992): This 25,000-acre refuge is located in Burnet, Travis, and Williamson counties northwest of Austin. It was established to protect the nesting habitat of two endangered birds: black-capped vireo and golden-cheeked warbler. The Shin Oak Observation Deck is open almost year around (excluding a few weekends in the fall). Hunting available. Open Monday–Friday, 8:00 a.m.–4:30 p.m Office: 24518 FM-1431, Marble Falls, 78654; (512) 339-9432.

Big Boggy (1983): This refuge occupies 5,000 acres of coastal prairie and salt marsh along East Matagorda Bay for the benefit of wintering waterfowl. The refuge is only open to waterfowl hunting in season. Office: 6801 County Road 306, Brazoria, 77422; (979) 964-4011.

Brazoria (1966): The 43,388 acres of this refuge, located along the Gulf Coast in Brazoria County, serve as haven for wintering waterfowl and a wide variety of other migratory birds. The refuge also supports many marsh and water birds, from

Texas Wildlife Management Areas Name (Acreage)	County	Hunting	Fishing	Camping	Wildlife Viewing	Hiking	Driving	Bicycling	Equestrian	Comments
Nature Center (82)	Smith				★	★				Primarily for school groups
North Toldeo Bend (3,650)	Shelby	★	★	★	★	★			★	
Old Sabine Bottom (5,158)	Smith	★	★	★	★	★		★	★	
Pat Mayse (8,925)	Lamar	★	★	★	★	★			★	
Playa Lakes: Armstrong (160)	Castro				★					Registration req., must stay on the roads
Playa Lakes: Dimmitt (422)	Cottle	★								Limited access
Playa Lakes: Taylor Lakes (530)	Donley	★			★	★				
Powderhorn (15,069)	Calhoun	★			★					Birding tours in Spring
Redhead Pond (37)	Nueces				★					Freshwater wetland; part of Great Texas Birding Trail
Richland Creek (13,783)	Freestone/Navarro	★	★	★	★	★		★	★	
Roger R. Fawcett (5,459)	Palo Pinto	★	★							Restricted access
Sam Houston National Forest (161,508)	San Jacinto/Walker	★	★	★	★	★	★	★	★	Also Montgomery County
Sierra Diablo (11,624)	Hudspeth/ Culberson	★								Restricted access
Tawakoni (2,335)	Hunt/Van Zandt	★	★	★	★	★			★	Primitive camping
Tony Houseman (3,985)	Orange	★	★	★	★	★				Canoeing
Welder Flats (1,480)	Calhoun		★		★					Boat access only
White Oak Creek (25,777)	Bowie/Cass/Morris/ Titus	★	★		★	★			★	Camp in Atlanta and Daingerfield SPs
Yoakum Dunes (14,037)	Cochran/Terry/ Yoakum	*In development, not yet open to the public. Commissioned and authorized in 2014, this site will preserve the breeding and nesting habitats of the lesser prairie-chicken, as well as many other native wildlife, including quail, mule deer, and Texas horned lizards.*								

roseate spoonbills and great blue herons to white-faced ibis and sandhill cranes. Brazoria Refuge is within the Freeport Christmas Bird Count circle, which frequently achieves the highest number of species seen in a 24-hour period. Open daily sunrise to sunset. Hunting and fishing also available. Office: 24907 FM 2004, Angleton, 77515; (979) 922-1037.

Buffalo Lake (1958): Comprising 7,664 acres in the Central Flyway in Randall County in the Panhandle, this refuge contains some of the best remaining shortgrass prairie in the United States. Buffalo Lake is now dry; a marsh area is artificially maintained for the numerous birds, reptiles, and mammals. Available activities include picnicking, auto tour, birding, photography, and hiking. Office: Box 179, Umbarger 79091; (806) 499-3382.

Caddo Lake (2000): Established on portions of the 8,5000-acre Longhorn Army Ammunition Plant in Harrison County, this refuge contains a mature flooded bald cypress forest, with some trees nearly 400 years old. The wetlands support a diverse plant community. The bottomland hardwood forest ecosystem provides essential habitat for migratory and resident wildlife. The wetlands of Caddo Lake are important to migratory birds within the Central Flyway. The area supports one of the highest breeding populations of wood ducks and prothonotary warblers. Bird watching, hunting, equestrian use, auto tour, hiking, and biking are available. Office: (903) 679-9144.

Hagerman (1946): Hagerman National Wildlife Refuge lies on the Big Mineral arm of Lake Texoma in Grayson County. The 4,500 acres of marsh and water and 6,900 acres of upland and farmland provide a feeding and resting place for migrating waterfowl. Bird watching, fishing, and hunting are available. Office: 6465 Refuge Road, Sherman, 75092-5817; (903) 786-2826.

Laguna Atascosa: (1946): This refuge is the southernmost waterfowl refuge in the Central Flyway and contains more than 45,000 acres fronting on the Laguna Madre in the Lower Rio Grande Valley in Cameron and Willacy counties. Open lagoons, coastal prairies, salt flats, and brushlands support a wide diversity of wildlife. The United States' largest concentration of redhead ducks winters here, along with many other species of waterfowl and shorebirds. White-tailed deer, javelina, and armadillo can be found, along with endangered ocelot. Bird watching and nature study are popular; auto-tour roads and nature trails are available. Camping and fishing are permitted within Adolph Thomae Jr. County Park. Hunting also available. Office: 22817 Ocelot Road, Los Fresnos, 78566; (956) 748-3607.

Lower Rio Grande Valley (1979): Part of the 180,000 acre South Texas Refuge Complex, this refuge lies within Cameron, Hidalgo, Starr, and Willacy counties. It comprises more than 100 separate tracts of land, some fallow farm fields connecting healthy habitat that can become travel corridors for wildlife. The refuge includes 11 different habitat types, including sabal palm forest, tidal flats, coastal brushland, mid-delta thorn forest, woodland potholes and basins, upland thorn scrub, flood forest, barretal, riparian woodland, and Chihuahuan thorn forest. Nearly 500 species of birds and over 300 butterfly species have been found there, as well as four of the five cats that occur within the United States: jaguarundi, ocelot, bobcat, and mountain lion. Seasonal hunting and canoe tours are available. Office: 3325 Green Jay Road, Alamo, 78516; (956) 784-7500.

McFaddin (1980): This refuge's 55,000 acres in Jefferson and Chambers counties are of great importance to wintering populations of migratory waterfowl. One of the densest populations of alligators in Texas is found here. Activities on the refuge include wildlife observation, hunting, fishing, and crabbing. Seven boat ramps provide access to inland lakes and waterways; limited roadways. Open daily from sunrise until sunset. Office: Box 358, Sabine Pass, 77655; (409) 971-2909.

Muleshoe (1935): Oldest of the national refuges in Texas, Muleshoe provides winter habitat for waterfowl and the continent's largest wintering population of sandhill cranes. Comprising 5,809 acres in the High Plains of Bailey County, the refuge contains playa lakes, marsh areas, caliche outcroppings, and native grasslands. A nature trail, campground, and picnic area are available. Office: Box 549, Muleshoe 79347; (806) 946-3341.

Neches River (2013): Anderson and Cherokee counties. It was established to protect wintering and nesting habitat for migratory birds of the Central Flyway and the bottomland hardwoods for their diverse biological value. Office: 262 West Highway 79, Jacksonville 75766; (956) 245-9426.

San Bernard (1968): Located in Brazoria and Matagorda counties on the Gulf Coast near Freeport, this refuge's 27,414 acres attract migrating waterfowl, including thousands of white-fronted and Canada geese and several duck species, which spend the winter on the refuge. Habitats, consisting of coastal prairies, salt-mud flats, and saltwater and freshwater ponds and potholes, also attract yellow rails, roseate spoonbills, reddish egrets, and American bitterns. Visitors enjoy auto and hiking trails, photography, bird watching, fishing, and waterfowl hunting in season. Office: 6801 County Road 306, Brazoria, 77422; (979) 964-4011.

Santa Ana (1943): Santa Ana is located on the north bank of the Rio Grande in Hidalgo County. Santa Ana's 2,088 acres of subtropical forest and native brushland are at an ecological crossroads of subtropical, Gulf Coast, Great Plains, and Chihuahuan desert habitats. Santa Ana attracts birders from across the United States who can view many species of Mexican birds as they reach the northern edge of their ranges in South Texas. Also found at Santa Ana are ocelot and jaguarundi, endangered members of the cat family. Visitors enjoy a tram or auto drive, bicycling and hiking trails, and a tower overlook. Office: 3325 Green Jay Road, Alamo, 78516; (956) 784-7500.

Texas Point (1980): Texas Point's 8,900 acres are located in Jefferson County on the upper Gulf Coast, 12 miles east of McFaddin NWR, where they serve a large wintering population of waterfowl and migratory birds. The endangered southern bald eagle and peregrine falcon may occasionally be seen during peak fall and spring migrations. Alligators are commonly observed during the spring, summer, and fall months. Activities include wildlife observation, hunting, fishing, and crabbing. Access to the refuge is by boat and on foot only. Open daily from sunrise until sunset. Office: Box 358, Sabine Pass, 77655; (409) 971-2909.

Trinity River (1994): Established to protect remnant bottomland hardwood forests and associated wetlands, this refuge, located in northern Liberty County off State Highway 787 about 15 miles east of Cleveland, provides habitat for wintering, migrating, and breeding waterfowl and a variety of other wetland-dependent wildlife. A tract south of Liberty includes Champion Lake. Office: Box 10015, Liberty 77575; (936) 336-9786. ☆

Weather

HIGHLIGHTS & SUMMARIES, 2029 & 2020

TEMPERATURES, PRECIPITATION

TORNADOS, DROUGHTS

DESTRUCTIVE WEATHER

RECORDS BY COUNTY

A thunderstorm rolls over the Lubbock/Shallowater skyline April 2016 in Hockley County. Photo by Ashley K. Saed/www.livingtreedesignsphoto.com.

Weather

All temperatures are given in Fahrenheit. CDT stands for "Central Daylight Time."

Sources: Unless otherwise noted, this information is provided by Texas State Climatologist John W. Nielsen-Gammon and graduate research assistants Christopher Larson and Hayden Dove at Texas A&M University. Monthly summaries are supplemented by the National Centers for Environmental Information, State of the Climate: National Climate Report.

Weather Highlights 2019

March 12–13, 2019: An intense, slow-moving storm system brought showers and thunderstorms into western Texas. As moisture content improved, the storms organized into an intense line of thunderstorms. These storms produced gusty winds; some became severe and produced a brief EF-1 tornado near Anton. Widespread rain totals ranged from 0.75 to 1.25 inches, with some areas receiving almost 1.5 inches. The storms produced straight-line winds up to 72 mph. Near O'Donnell, the wind damaged large buildings, flipped a semitruck, and knocked over trees and power lines.

March 22, 2019: A strong upper-level low moved across the Four Corners region, gradually shifting from east to northeast throughout the day. Mid-level lift and convergence along a weak moisture gradient supported the development of thunderstorms. Hail from the sizes of quarters to baseballs was reported. Two tornadoes were confirmed, one near Wilco and one near Cactus.

March 24, 2019: The storm system explained above continued moving across the southern Plains, bringing large hail to the Dallas area. Grapefruit-size hail was reported near McKinney.

April 7, 2019: In April, an unusually severe storm system brought gusty winds and three reported tornadoes to the coastal regions of Texas. Baseball-size hail was reported near Grapeland. An EF-1 tornado touched down in Pasadena,

Climatic Data Regions of Texas

causing moderate damage to power lines and ripping the back wall off a vacant business. Strong winds up to 70 mph also caused considerable damage around Houston. Downed power lines caused more than 175,000 homes to lose power.

April 17, 2019: A cold front came through the Texas Panhandle and stalled as a low-pressure system moved into the area from New Mexico. These two components enhanced the already high instability in the region. Severe storms soon developed, producing one to two inches of hail and

	Average Temperatures 2019											Precipitation in Inches 2019										
	High Plains	Low Plains	North Central	East Texas	Trans-Pecos	Edwards Plateau	South Central	Upper Coast	South Texas	Lower Valley		High Plains	Low Plains	North Central	East Texas	Trans-Pecos	Edwards Plateau	South Central	Upper Coast	South Texas	Lower Valley
Jan.	40.4	43.6	45.3	47.4	46.5	48.4	52.6	53.7	55.1	60.1		0.14	0.44	1.79	4.69	0.23	0.64	2.42	4.29	0.81	1.22
Feb.	42.4	46.4	50.1	53.1	52	53.5	58.1	59.8	61	65.3		0.24	0.17	1.29	3.12	0.08	0.27	1.1	2.72	0.29	0.42
Mar.	47.5	50.8	53.7	56.2	56.5	56.7	61.2	62.1	65.1	67.6		1.45	1.4	1.81	2.08	0.46	0.88	0.53	0.75	0.68	2.42
April	59.3	62.9	64.2	64.6	65.4	65.9	68.5	68.6	70.8	73.5		1.78	4.41	5.93	6.56	1.07	3.32	4.10	2.67	1.95	1.13
May	64.7	69.1	72.1	74.4	71.6	72.6	77.4	78.1	80.3	82.9		4	5.71	8.05	9.87	1.23	4.16	4.69	7.60	2.81	1.52
June	74.5	77.4	78.3	78.7	78.8	79.1	82.4	82.4	85.8	86.5		2.46	3.18	5.21	7.42	1.94	4.22	4.7	9.35	2.45	7.26
July	80.4	83	82.7	81.7	82.4	82.5	84.6	84.2	86.7	86.7		1.71	1.04	0.99	2.02	1.36	0.85	1.08	2.15	0.61	1.09
Aug.	82.5	86.5	86.2	85	85.1	86.5	87.8	86.1	89.4	89.5		1.58	1.03	2.04	2.05	1	1	0.53	3.55	0.64	0.94
Sep.	76.9	81.3	83.3	82.1	78.6	82	84.7	83.7	85.2	84.6		2.53	2.69	0.92	3.46	2.18	0.71	1.63	11.06	1.97	3.65
Oct.	55.1	61	64.5	66.5	64.3	66.4	71.4	72.3	75	77.4		2.53	0.48	3.49	6.06	0.82	1.35	3.44	5.32	2.21	2.44
Nov.	45.5	48.8	52	53.5	53.6	53.9	58.4	59.8	61.3	66.1		1.23	2.16	2.20	1.22	1.11	0.95	1.41	1.84	0.81	1.81
Dec.	43.3	47.2	49.3	51.5	49	51.6	56.2	57.6	59.2	63.6		0.76	0.59	0.96	1.59	0.69	0.68	0.91	1.13	0.71	0.65
Ann.	59.4	63.2	65.1	66.2	65.3	66.6	70.3	70.7	72.9	75.3		20.41	23.30	34.68	50.14	12.17	19.03	26.54	52.43	15.94	24.55

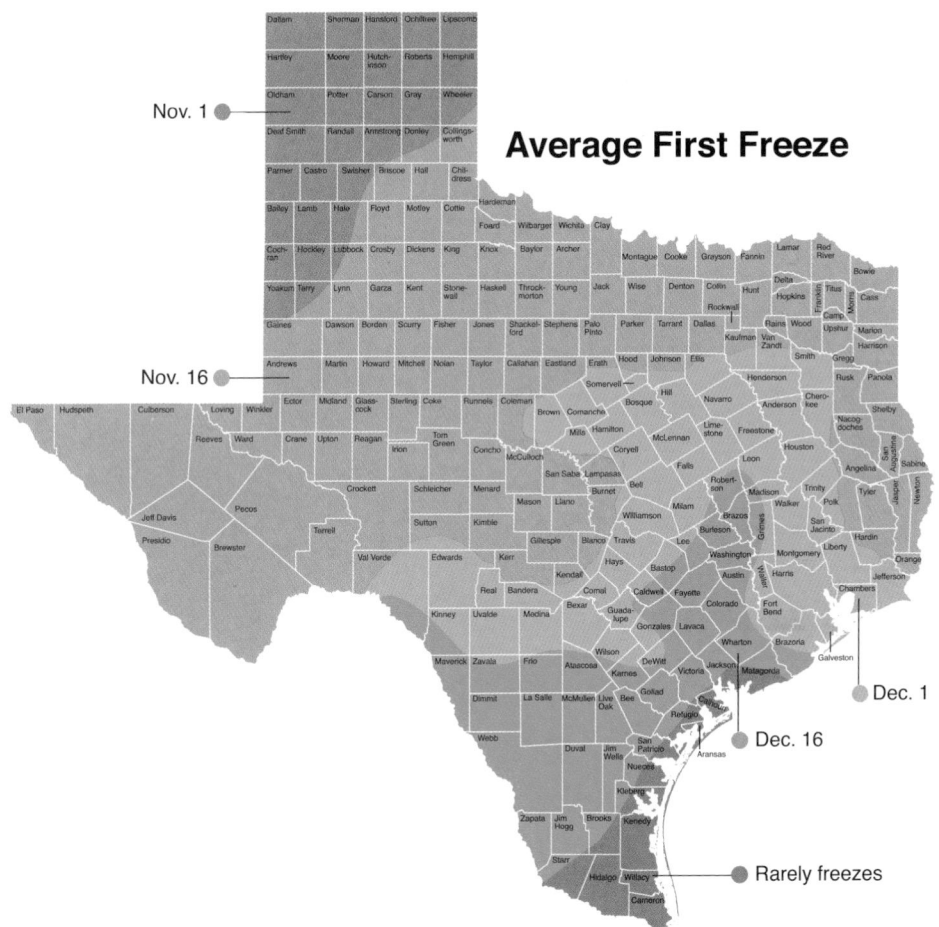

Average First Freeze

Nov. 1

Nov. 16

Dec. 1

Dec. 16

Rarely freezes

numerous small rope tornadoes, with four confirmed to have touched down.

April 24, 2019: Strong storms moved from central to southeast Texas, bringing locally heavy rain, hail up to 1.75 inches, and an EF-2 tornado to Bryan. The tornado damaged one house and four commercial buildings and warehouses, injuring one person inside the warehouse.

May 5, 2019: Persistent southwesterly flow aloft, upper-level disturbances, and plenty of moisture and instability east of a dryline passing through the Panhandle brought multiple rounds of severe weather to northwest Texas. May 5 was a particularly active day: an EF-2 tornado caused damage near Tahoka and was on the ground for 17 miles. There were no injuries or deaths, but high winds caused damage to several homes, buildings, trees, and power poles. Tennis ball-size hail was also reported with this storm. This same supercell also dropped torrential rain in Lynn County—as much as two inches—inundating some roads.

May 7, 2019: Moisture advected from the Gulf of Mexico and an upper-level low moved into the Four Corners region, bringing surface low pressure to New Mexico and severe weather conditions for the Panhandle. Hail up to the size

2019 Weather Extremes

Lowest Temp.: Lipscomb, Lipscomb Co., February 7 . . . . −1°
Highest Temp.: Rio Grande Village, Brewster Co., August 27. . . . .116°
24-Hour Precip.: Beaumont, Jefferson Co., September 19 . . . . . 19.80″
Monthly Precip.: Roman Forest, Montgomery Co., September . . . 33.47″
Least Annual Precip.: El Paso, El Paso Co. . . . . 6.92″
Greatest Annual Precip.: Beaumont, Jefferson Co . . . . 93.67″

of baseballs fell near Lake Meredith and Fritch. Wind shear increased throughout the afternoon, allowing the storms to drop seven tornadoes around the Panhandle, all rated EF-0, with the longest path being 11.6 miles. In southeast Texas, heavy rains battered the Houston area, with as much as ten inches of rainfall in some areas. In Sugar Land, more than seven inches of rain fell in four hours, causing major flash flooding in the city. Some children had to spend the night at their school as buses couldn't drive in the flooded roadways.

May 23, 2019: An upper-level low had set itself up over southern Nevada with a frontal boundary settled across the Panhandle. Significant wind shear and instability increased in magnitude as moisture was advected into the region. Severe thunderstorms quickly popped up in the Panhandle,

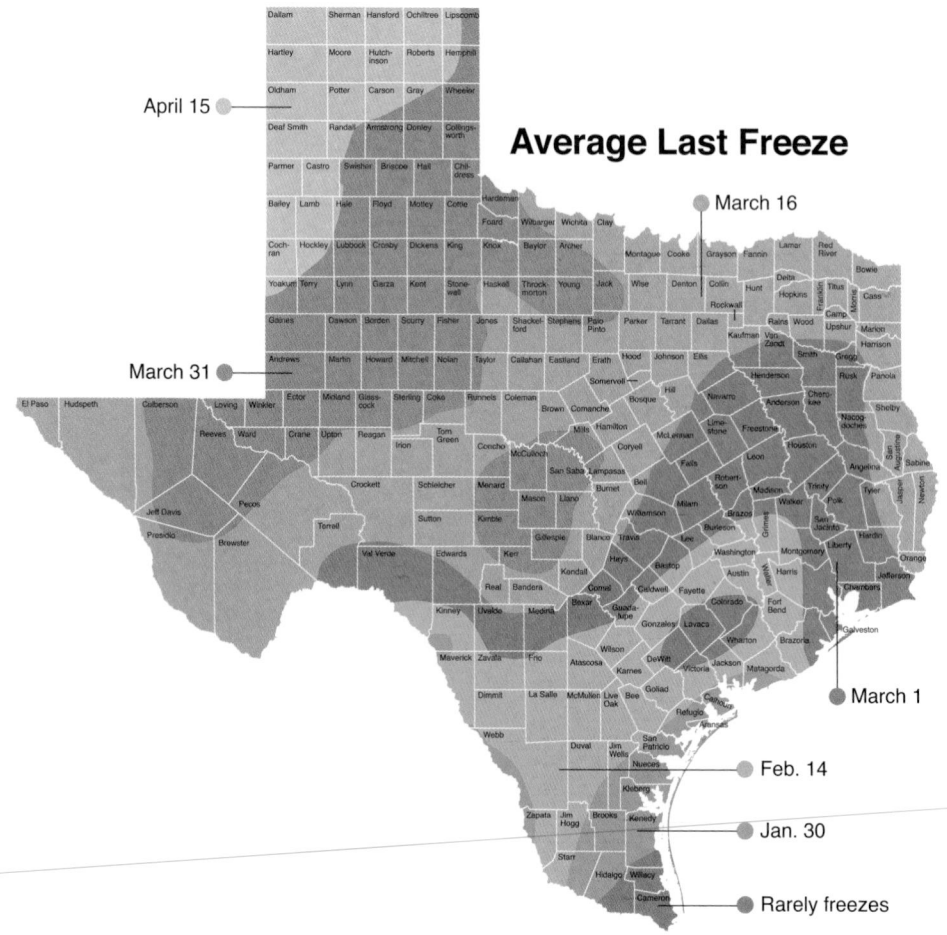

Average Last Freeze

April 15

March 16

March 31

March 1

Feb. 14

Jan. 30

Rarely freezes

producing baseball-size hail and tornadoes. Two tornadoes were very large, reaching over a half-mile wide at some point, both in Lipscomb County. These were both rated EF-2. These tornadoes only destroyed a single home and damaged trees and power lines. Four more tornadoes were reported in the Panhandle, all EF-1 or less.

June 18, 2019: An upper-level disturbance and weak frontal boundary initiated storm development in the Texas Panhandle. This event produced hail larger than baseballs, strong winds, a few funnels, and an EF-0 tornado near Pampa.

June 24, 2019: A returning warm front brought strong instability to the Panhandle, fueling intense thunderstorms. Softball-size hail fell near Wilson and Slaton, strong winds blew over a wind turbine near Petersburg, and 2.08 inches of rain fell near Lubbock, causing street flooding.

Monthly Summaries 2019

Texas experienced mostly above-normal temperatures in **January.** Parts of southern and eastern Texas experienced temperatures two to four degrees below normal. Parts of western, southern, central, and eastern Texas experienced temperatures zero to two degrees below normal. Parts of western, southern, central, eastern, and northern Texas experienced temperatures two to four degrees above normal. Parts of northern and eastern Texas experienced

temperatures four to six degrees above normal. The average temperature in Texas during January was 47 degrees. Parts of southwestern, western, northwestern, and northern Texas received 50 percent or less of normal precipitation. Far southern, eastern, and northeastern Texas received 150 percent or more of normal precipitation. Texas received 1.47 inches of precipitation in January.

Some parts of northern Texas experienced temperatures three to six degrees below normal in **February.** Other parts of northern Texas experienced temperatures zero to three degrees below normal. Western, central, and eastern Texas experienced temperatures three to six degrees above normal. The average temperature for February in Texas was 51.9 degrees. Parts of northern, western, southern, central, and eastern Texas received 50 percent or less of normal precipitation. Other parts of northern, central, southern, and western Texas received 25 percent or less of normal precipitation. Parts of northern and western Texas received five percent or less of normal precipitation. Texas received 0.88 inches of precipitation in February.

During **March,** parts of central, north-central, and western Texas experienced temperatures four to six degrees below normal. Parts of southern, central, western, eastern, and northern Texas experienced temperatures two to four degrees below normal. In extreme western Texas, there were temperatures zero to four degrees above normal. Texas

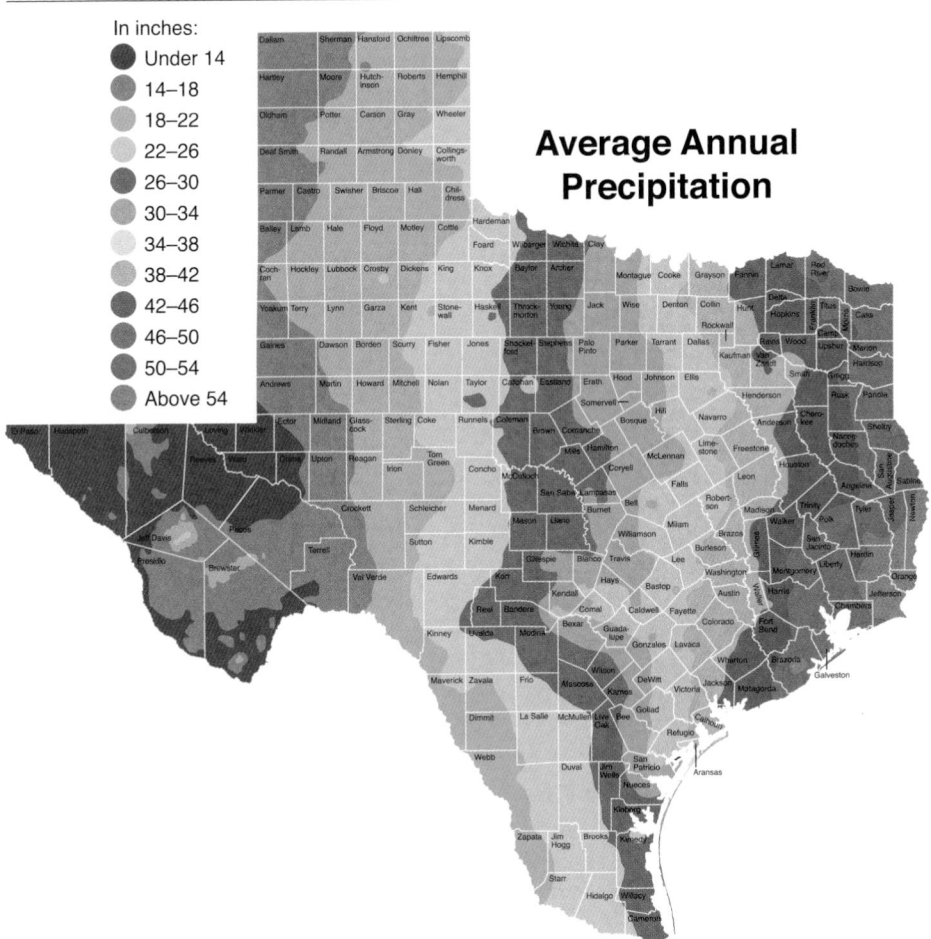

In inches:
- Under 14
- 14–18
- 18–22
- 22–26
- 26–30
- 30–34
- 34–38
- 38–42
- 42–46
- 46–50
- 50–54
- Above 54

Average Annual Precipitation

experienced an average temperature of 56 degrees. Eastern, central, southern, and western Texas received 50 percent or less of normal precipitation. Parts of south-central and extreme western Texas received five percent or less of normal precipitation. In northern, extreme western, and extreme southern Texas, 110 percent or more of normal precipitation fell. Texas received 1.13 inches of precipitation in March.

Parts of southern and eastern Texas experienced temperatures two to three degrees below normal in **April.** Parts of southern, eastern, and central Texas experienced temperatures one to two degrees below normal. Parts of western and northern Texas experienced temperatures one to two degrees above normal. Parts of far western Texas experienced temperatures two to three degrees above normal. The average temperature in Texas was 64.1 degrees. Far northern, far western, and southeastern Texas received 25 percent or less of normal precipitation. Parts of western, central, southern, northern, and eastern Texas received 150 percent or more of normal precipitation. Parts of western, central, northern, and eastern Texas received 200 percent or more of normal precipitation. Parts of western and central Texas received as much as 300 percent or more of normal precipitation. Texas received 3.52 inches of precipitation during April.

In **May,** parts of northern Texas experienced temperatures four to six degrees below normal. Parts of western

and northern Texas experienced temperatures two to four degrees below normal. Parts of southern and eastern Texas experienced temperatures two to four degrees above normal. The average temperature experienced in Texas was 72.5 degrees. Parts of western and southern Texas received 50 percent or less of normal precipitation. Parts of southern and western Texas received 25 percent or less of normal precipitation. Parts of central, southern, northern, and eastern Texas received 150 percent or more of normal precipitation. Parts of central, northern, and eastern Texas received 200 percent or more of normal precipitation. Parts of eastern Texas received 300 percent or more of normal precipitation. Texas received 5.08 inches of precipitation in May.

Parts of northern, central, and southwestern Texas experienced temperatures two to three degrees below normal in **June.** Parts of northern, central, western, and eastern Texas experienced temperatures one to two degrees below normal. Parts of central, southern, and southeastern Texas experienced temperatures one to two degrees above normal. The average temperature in Texas was 78.9 degrees. Parts of western and southern Texas received 25 percent or less of normal precipitation. Parts of southwestern, southern, northern, and eastern Texas received 150 percent or more of normal precipitation. Parts of southwestern, southern, south-eastern, and eastern Texas received 200 percent or more of

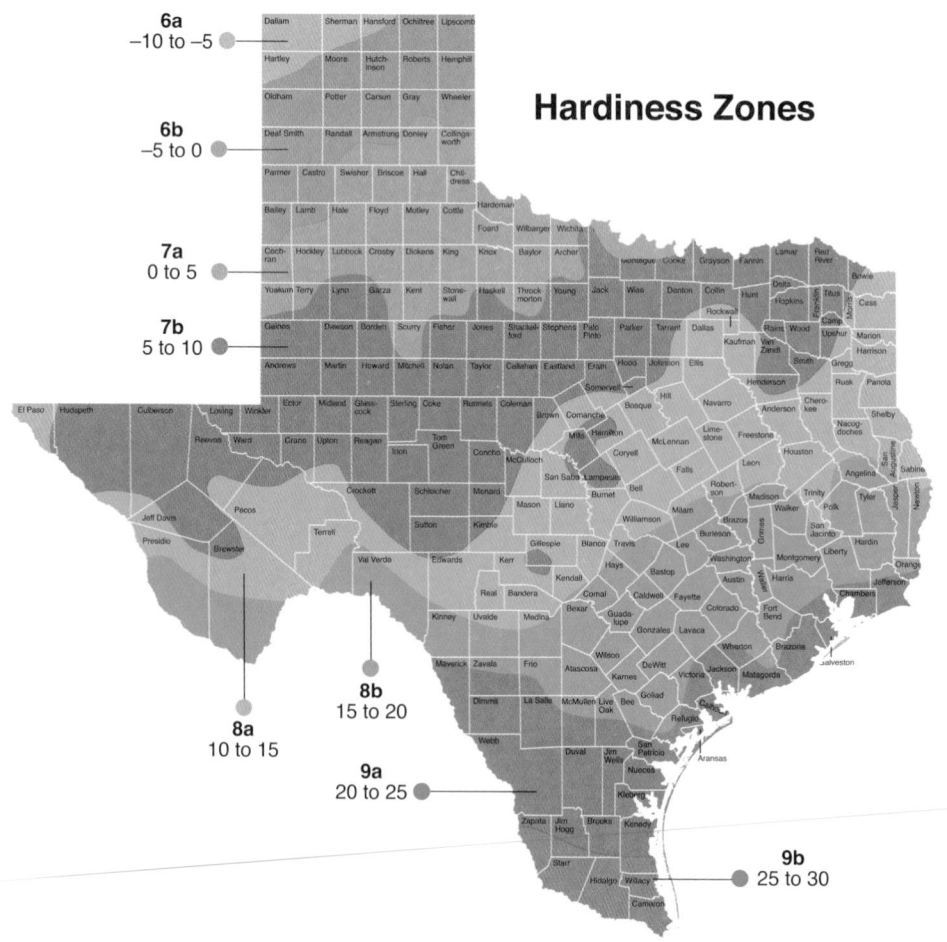

Hardiness Zones

6a
−10 to −5

6b
−5 to 0

7a
0 to 5

7b
5 to 10

8a
10 to 15

8b
15 to 20

9a
20 to 25

9b
25 to 30

normal precipitation. Texas received 4.01 inches of precipitation during June.

In **July,** parts of north-central and eastern Texas experienced temperatures one to two degrees below normal, while some isolated parts experienced temperatures two to three degrees below normal. Parts of northern, western, southern, and southeastern Texas experienced temperatures one to two degrees above normal. Parts of southern and western Texas experienced temperatures two to three degrees above normal. Parts of far western Texas experienced temperatures three to five degrees above normal. Texas experienced an average of 82.8 degrees. Parts of central, eastern, and western Texas received 50 percent or less of normal precipitation. Parts of central, western, southern, and eastern Texas received 25 percent or less of normal precipitation. Parts of southern and central Texas received five percent or less of normal precipitation. Texas received 1.27 inches of precipitation in July.

Most of Texas experienced temperatures two to four degrees above normal during **August.** Parts of northern and western Texas experienced temperatures four to six degrees above normal. Parts of far western Texas experienced

2020 Weather Extremes	
Lowest Temp.: Big Spring McMahon-Wrinkle Airport, Howard Co., February 6	0°
Highest Temp.: Turkey, Hall Co., July 15	117°
24-hour Precip.: Santa Rosa, Hidalgo Co., July 28	15.49"
Monthly Precip.: Houston, Harris Co., September	15.89"
Least Annual Precip.: Kermit, Winkler Co.	3.65"
Greatest Annual Precip.: Douglasville, Cass Co.	74.16"

temperatures six to eight degrees above normal. The average temperature in Texas during August was 86 degrees. Parts of northern, western, southern, central, and eastern Texas received 50 percent or less of normal precipitation. Parts of northern, western, and southern Texas received 25 percent or less of normal precipitation. Parts of southern and western Texas received five percent or less of normal precipitation. Parts of northeastern Texas received 150 percent or more of normal precipitation. Parts of northeastern Texas received 200 percent or more of normal precipitation. Texas received 1.35 inches of precipitation during August.

In **September,** Texas experienced above-normal temperatures, putting this month in the top-three warmest Septembers on record. Parts of southeastern, southern, and western Texas experienced temperatures four to six degrees above normal. Parts of northern, eastern, central, and southern Texas experienced temperatures six to eight degrees above normal. Parts of central, northern, and eastern Texas experienced temperatures eight to ten degrees above normal. The average temperature during September in Texas was 81.4 degrees. Parts of central, eastern, and northern Texas received 50 percent or less of normal precipitation. Parts of central, eastern, and southwestern Texas received 25 percent or less of normal precipitation. Parts of central and eastern Texas received five percent or less of normal precipitation. Parts of northern, western, and southeastern Texas received 150 percent or more of normal precipitation. Parts of southeastern Texas received 200 percent or more of normal precipitation. Parts of southeastern Texas received 300 percent or more of normal precipitation, due in part to Tropical Storm Imelda. Texas received 2.48 inches of precipitation in September.

Parts of northern Texas experienced temperatures zero to eight degrees below normal in **October.** Parts of southern Texas experienced temperatures two to four degrees above normal. The average temperature in Texas during this month was 65.6 degrees. Parts of northern, western, central, and southern Texas received 50 percent or less of normal precipitation. Parts of north-central, southern, and western Texas received 25 percent or less of normal precipitation. Parts of north-central and western Texas received 5 percent or less of normal precipitation. Parts of northern and eastern Texas received 150 percent or more of normal precipitation. Parts of northern Texas received 200 percent or more of normal precipitation. Other parts of northern Texas received 300 percent or more of normal precipitation. Texas received 2.56 inches of precipitation during October.

In **November,** parts of central, eastern, and southern Texas experienced temperatures four to six degrees below normal. Most of Texas experienced temperatures two to four degrees below normal. Parts of western Texas experienced temperatures zero to two degrees above normal. Texas experienced an average temperature of 53.2 degrees during this month. Parts of eastern, central, and southern Texas received 50 percent or less of normal precipitation. Other parts of eastern, central, and southern Texas received 25 percent or less of normal precipitation. Parts of north-central, western, and southern Texas received 150 percent or

more of normal precipitation. Other parts of north-central, western, and southern Texas received 200 percent or more of normal precipitation. Texas received 1.33 inches of precipitation in November.

Parts of eastern, southern, and western Texas experienced temperatures zero to two degrees above normal during **December.** Parts of eastern, central, southern, western, and northern Texas experienced temperatures two to four degrees above normal. Parts of western, southwestern, central, eastern, and northern Texas experienced temperatures four to six degrees above normal. Parts of northern Texas experienced temperatures six to eight degrees above normal. The average temperature during this month in Texas was 50.6 degrees. Parts of eastern, northern, western, central, and southern Texas received 50 percent or less of normal precipitation. Parts of northern, eastern, western, and southern Texas received 25 percent or less of normal precipitation. Parts of western and southwestern Texas received five percent or less of normal precipitation. Parts of southern, western, and northern Texas received 150 percent or more of normal precipitation. Parts of southern and western Texas received 200 percent or more of normal precipitation. Texas received 0.85 inches of precipitation during December.

Weather Highlights 2020

April 11–14, 2020: Severe storms developed in the western Panhandle as a result of Gulf moisture, a dryline, and an upper-level disturbance. Hail as large as golf balls was reported near Aspermont. Aspermont also received 1.43 inches of rain on the 11th. A cold front then advected in from the north, bringing temperatures to the 20s for most of the Panhandle. Another storm system then developed across the region and brought snow. Friona accumulated the most snow, with five inches reported.

May 7–13, 2020: Strong instability and moderate wind shear led to strong storms in the Panhandle region, producing large hail and heavy rainfall. Hail up to the size of baseballs was reported. The next few days, an upper-level disturbance combining with increasing moisture brought strong storms back to the region. Hail up to the size of golf balls was reported on May 11. Strong winds caused damage around Woodrow and New Home. Rainfall amounts measured around half an inch to an inch throughout the region that day. On the 13th,

	Average Temperatures 2020											Precipitation in Inches 2020									
	High Plains	Low Plains	North Central	East Texas	Trans-Pecos	Edwards Plateau	South Central	Upper Coast	South Texas	Lower Valley		High Plains	Low Plains	North Central	East Texas	Trans-Pecos	Edwards Plateau	South Central	Upper Coast	South Texas	Lower Valley
Jan.	42.1	46.9	49.7	51.4	48.3	51.7	57.7	58.4	60.9	66.1		0.56	1.55	2.95	4.79	0.46	1.65	2	4.37	0.57	0.46
Feb.	40.3	44.4	48.4	51.2	48.5	50.2	55.6	57.1	59.1	63.5		0.63	1.51	3.51	5.31	0.64	1.61	1.21	1.29	0.33	0.11
Mar.	54.2	58.4	62.3	65.2	61.1	64.1	69.9	70.8	72.8	76.2		2.08	3.63	6.44	5.37	1.21	3.24	2.07	1.01	1.18	0.47
April	57.9	61.1	62.9	64.6	66.5	66.2	69.7	70.5	73.8	78.6		0.27	0.54	2.20	5.37	0.06	1.61	3.03	3.40	2.04	0.96
May	70.1	73.3	72.8	72.3	76.1	75.7	77.5	77	80.3	81.7		0.79	2.76	5.47	5.28	0.70	3.44	6.09	5.84	4.55	4.81
June	78.8	80.6	79.9	79.5	81.6	80.9	81.6	81.6	83.1	83.6		1.21	2.22	3.07	2.88	0.79	0.92	2.80	5.30	2.35	5.17
July	83.1	86.4	85.2	83.3	85.3	86.2	86.5	85	87.2	86.9		2.22	1.84	2.13	4.22	0.72	0.95	1.88	5.38	2.24	6.62
Aug.	81.1	84.7	84.8	83	84.6	85.5	86.3	85.3	86.5	86.1		1.08	1.19	1.51	3.37	0.19	0.69	1.29	2.10	1.07	0.67
Sep.	68.6	71.7	73.4	75.8	72.5	73.9	78.3	80.3	79.8	81.4		0.88	3.68	7.05	6.72	1.31	3.96	5.40	7.08	3.75	4.44
Oct.	58.4	61.7	64.1	66	66	67.4	71.5	71.9	73.8	76.4		1.07	1.34	1.72	1.95	0.03	0.25	0.51	1.83	0.63	0.66
Nov.	52.9	57.2	59.4	60.7	59.7	61.4	66.3	66.9	69.4	73.2		0.27	0.66	0.98	1.81	0.01	0.45	1.76	4.04	0.98	0.32
Dec.	40.4	45.2	47.9	49.8	45.5	49.1	54.7	55.6	57.2	61.7		0.30	0.74	2.26	5.65	0.57	0.97	2.02	5.34	0.66	0.85
Ann.	60.7	64.3	65.9	66.9	66.3	67.7	71.3	71.7	73.7	76.3		11.36	21.66	39.29	52.72	6.69	19.74	30.06	46.98	20.35	25.54

Winter Storm Uri left a frozen landscape behind in Orient on February 15, 2021. Photo by Jonathan Cutrer, jcutrer.com.

similar weather conditions reoccurred, bringing ping pong ball-size hail, strong winds, and heavy rainfall.

May 20, 2020: A dryline moved into the western Panhandle region, combining with warm temperatures, significant moisture, strong instability, and moderate wind shear, thus bringing large hail. Tennis ball-size hail was reported near Post and baseball-size hail was reported near Lubbock. The hail destroyed many plants, vehicles, and roofs. Rainfall of 0.42 inches fell in Lubbock while 0.96 inches of rain fell in Childress.

May 23, 2020: Increasing moisture, warm temperatures, and instability in the Panhandle region produced severe thunderstorms. One supercell in Garza County remained stationary for a few hours and dropped large hail, heavy rain, and a couple of tornadoes. Other storms produced baseball-size hail, strong winds, and heavy rain. Three to five inches fell in a couple of hours in Garza County, with 6.6 inches measured in Graham. Flash flooding occurred in the area near the Brazos River.

June 18, 2020: Severe storms in Hidalgo County produced straight-line winds up to 70 mph that ripped the roofs off of nine homes, flipped three vehicles, and damaged three dozen trees. Hail up to 1.75 inches was also reported.

June 19, 2020: A cold front moved south of the Panhandle region, stalled, and lifted northward, developing strong storms. Storms near Amarillo produced three to five inches of rain over three rounds of thunderstorms. A brief landspout was also reported near Groom.

June 22, 2020: An upper-level disturbance, along with abundant moisture and instability, brought severe storms to the Panhandle region. Hail with a diameter of 2.5 inches was reported near Cactus, 1.5 to 3 inches of rain fell near Dumas and caused flash flooding, 3.25-inch hail was reported near Vega, a brief EF-0 tornado occurred near Dawn, and strong winds flipped over multiple semitrucks near Vega.

August 13–14, 2020: Record heat was measured in Lubbock, where the temperature hit 107 degrees on the 13th and 14th. Record high minimum temperatures were also reached, dropping to only 75 and 80 degrees. Childress recorded a high of 109 degrees, while Paducah, Guthrie, and Aspermont reached 112 degrees, although none of these were new records.

August 16, 2020: Warm temperatures and mid-level moisture in the Panhandle region generated strong storms. Strong winds up to 86 mph and heavy rain battered the region. A record daily rainfall of 2.38 inches fell in Childress.

December 30, 2020: Severe storms swept across north Texas, bringing an EF-0 tornado to Corsicana. The tornado damaged roofs and 13 manufactured homes, and several trees were downed. Wind speeds were estimated to have peaked at 85 mph. There were no deaths or injuries.

Monthly Summaries 2020

Texas experienced above-normal temperatures in **January.** Parts of western Texas experienced temperatures zero to two degrees above normal. Parts of northern, western, and eastern Texas experienced temperatures two to four degrees above normal. Parts of northern, central, southern, and eastern Texas experienced temperatures four to six degrees above normal. Parts of southern and southeastern Texas experienced temperatures six to eight degrees above normal. The average temperature in Texas during January was 50.8 degrees. Precipitation in January was also mostly above normal in Texas. Parts of southern, northern, and western Texas received 50 percent or less of normal precipitation. Parts of southern and western Texas received 25 percent or less of normal precipitation. Parts of far southern and far western Texas received two percent or less of normal precipitation. Parts of central, northern, and eastern Texas received 150 percent or more of normal precipitation. Parts of central and eastern Texas received 200 percent or more of normal precipitation. Parts of northern Texas received 400 percent or more of normal precipitation. Texas received 1.89 inches of precipitation in January.

Texas experienced varied temperatures across the state in **February.** Parts of northern and western Texas experienced temperatures two to four degrees below normal. Parts of northern, western, central, southern, and eastern Texas experienced temperatures zero to two degrees below normal. Parts of eastern and southern Texas experienced temperatures zero to two degrees above normal. Parts of eastern Texas experienced temperatures two to four degrees above normal. The average temperature in Texas during February was 49.4 degrees. Precipitation was mostly above normal in February in Texas. Parts of northern, western, and southern Texas received 50 percent or less of normal precipitation. Parts of southern Texas received 25 percent or less of normal precipitation. Parts of southern Texas received two percent or less of normal precipitation. Parts of western, central, and eastern Texas received 150 percent or more of normal precipitation. Parts of eastern Texas received 200 percent or more of normal precipitation. Texas received 1.83 inches of precipitation in February.

Texas experienced above normal temperatures during **March.** Parts of northern and western Texas experienced temperatures two to four degrees above normal. Parts of northern, central, eastern, and western Texas experienced temperatures four to six degrees above normal. Parts of eastern, central, and southern Texas experienced temperatures six to eight degrees above normal. Parts of eastern and southern Texas experienced temperatures eight to ten degrees above normal. The average temperature in Texas in March was 63.2 degrees. Parts of northern, southern, southeastern, and eastern Texas received 50 percent or less of normal precipitation. Parts of coastal Texas received 25 percent or less of normal precipitation. Other parts of coastal Texas received two percent or less of normal precipitation. Parts of northern, central, eastern, and western Texas received 150 percent or more of normal precipitation. Parts of central, eastern, and western Texas received 200 percent or more of normal precipitation. Parts of western Texas received 400 percent or

more of normal precipitation. Texas received 3.12 inches of precipitation in March.

Temperatures were mostly below normal across Texas in **April.** Parts of north-central Texas experienced temperatures two to four degrees below normal. Parts of central, eastern, and northern Texas experienced temperatures zero to two degrees below normal. Parts of northern, western, southern, and southeastern Texas experienced temperatures zero to two degrees above normal. Parts of western and southern Texas experienced temperatures two to four degrees above normal. The average temperature in Texas during April was 65.0 degrees. Parts of north-central, southern, and western Texas received 50 percent or less of normal precipitation. Parts of northern, western, and southern Texas received 25 percent or less of normal precipitation. Parts of western and southern Texas received 5 percent or less of normal precipitation. Parts of southern and eastern Texas received 150 percent or more of normal precipitation. Parts of eastern Texas received 200 percent or more of normal precipitation. Texas received 1.78 inches of precipitation in April.

Temperatures during **May** were above normal in Texas. Parts of eastern Texas experienced temperatures zero to two degrees below normal. Parts of southern, southeastern, central, western, and northern Texas experienced temperatures zero to two degrees above normal. Parts of northern and western Texas experienced temperatures two to four degrees above normal. The average temperature in Texas was 74.4 degrees. Precipitation varied across Texas in May. Parts of northern and western Texas received 25 percent or less of normal precipitation. Other parts of western Texas received five percent or less of normal precipitation. Parts of southern, north-central, and eastern Texas received 150 percent or more of normal precipitation. Parts of southern Texas received 200 percent or more of normal precipitation. Other parts of southern Texas received 300 percent or more of normal precipitation. Texas received 3.5 inches of precipitation in May.

Temperatures during **June** were mostly below normal across Texas. Parts of southern Texas experienced temperatures one to two degrees below normal. Parts of eastern and southern Texas experienced temperatures zero to one degrees below normal. Parts of eastern and central Texas experienced temperatures zero to one degrees above

Flowers freeze after Winter Storm Uri on February 11, 2021. Photo by Thomas Park/ Unsplash (CC).

normal. Parts of northern and western Texas experienced temperatures one to two degrees above normal. Other parts of northern and western Texas experienced temperatures two to three degrees above normal. Parts of northern Texas experienced temperatures four to five degrees above normal. Texas experienced an average temperature of 80.6 degrees in June. Precipitation varied across Texas. Parts of northern, western, central, and eastern Texas received 50 percent or less of normal precipitation. Parts of northern, central, and western Texas received 25 percent or less of normal precipitation. Parts of western and central Texas received five percent or less of normal precipitation. Parts of southern Texas received 150 percent or more of normal precipitation. Parts of southern Texas received 200 percent or more of normal precipitation. Texas received 2.16 inches of precipitation during June.

Temperatures were primarily above normal across Texas in **July.** Parts of eastern Texas experienced temperatures zero to two degrees below normal. Parts of eastern and southern Texas experienced temperatures zero to two degrees above normal. Parts of central, northern, and western Texas experienced temperatures two to four degrees above normal. Other parts of northern, central, and western Texas experienced temperatures four to six degrees above normal. Parts of western Texas experienced temperatures six to eight degrees above normal. Texas experienced an average temperature of 85.1 degrees during July. Precipitation varied across Texas. Parts of northern, southern, central, and western Texas received 50 percent or less of normal precipitation. Parts of northern, central, and western Texas received 25 percent or less of normal precipitation. Parts of western Texas received five percent or less of normal precipitation. Parts of eastern and southern Texas received 150 percent or more of normal precipitation. Parts of eastern and southern Texas received 200 percent or more of normal precipitation. Other parts of eastern and southern Texas received 300 percent or more of normal precipitation. Texas received 2.22 inches of precipitation in July.

Temperatures varied across Texas during **August.** Parts of northeastern Texas experienced temperatures two to four degrees below normal. Parts of southern and eastern Texas experienced temperatures zero to two degrees below normal. Parts of northern, eastern, and southern Texas experienced temperatures zero to two degrees above normal. Parts of southeastern, central, northern, and western Texas experienced temperatures two to four degrees above normal. Parts of central, northern, and western Texas experienced temperatures four to six degrees above normal. Parts of western Texas experienced temperatures six to eight degrees above normal. The average temperature during August in Texas was 84.3 degrees. Precipitation also varied across Texas. Parts of northern, eastern, central, southern, and western Texas received 50 percent or less of normal precipitation. Parts of northern, central, southern, and western Texas received 25 percent or less of normal precipitation. Parts of eastern and northeastern Texas received 150 percent or more of normal precipitation. Other parts of eastern and northeastern Texas received 200 percent or more of normal precipitation. Texas received 1.25 inches of precipitation during August.

Temperatures were mainly below normal across Texas during **September.** Parts of northern, central, western, and eastern Texas experienced temperatures two to four degrees below normal. A large portion of Texas experienced temperatures zero to two degrees below normal. Parts of eastern and southern Texas experienced temperatures zero to two

degrees above normal. Parts of southeastern Texas experienced temperatures two to four degrees above normal. The average temperature during September in Texas was 74.1 degrees. Precipitation varied across Texas. Parts of northern and western Texas received 25 percent or less of normal precipitation. Parts of northern and western Texas received 50 percent or less of normal precipitation. Parts of western Texas received two percent or less of normal precipitation. Parts of central, eastern, and southern Texas received 150 percent or more of normal precipitation. Parts of central and eastern Texas received 200 percent or more of normal precipitation. Texas received 3.97 inches of precipitation during September.

Temperatures during **October** in Texas were mainly above normal. Parts of northern, north-central, and northeastern Texas experienced temperatures two to four degrees below normal. Parts of northern, eastern, and southern Texas experienced temperatures zero to two degrees below normal. Parts of western, southern, and eastern Texas experienced temperatures zero to two degrees above normal. Parts of western Texas experienced temperatures two to four degrees above normal. Texas experienced an average of 65.9 degrees during October. Precipitation during October varied across Texas. Parts of northern, central, eastern, western, and southern Texas received 50 percent or less of normal precipitation. Parts of eastern, central, western, and southern Texas received 25 percent or less of normal precipitation. Parts of western and southern Texas received two percent or less of normal precipitation. Parts of northern Texas received 150 percent or more of normal precipitation. Texas received 0.96 inches of precipitation in October.

Temperatures during **November** were above normal in Texas. Parts of eastern and central Texas experienced temperatures two to four degrees above normal. Parts of northern, western, southern, southeastern, and eastern Texas experienced temperatures four to six degrees above normal. Parts of central, southern, and western Texas experienced temperatures six to eight degrees above normal. Texas experienced an average temperature of 60.5 degrees during November. Precipitation during November in Texas was mainly below normal. Parts of northern, eastern, central, southern, and western Texas received 50 percent or less of normal precipitation. Parts of northern, eastern, southern, and western Texas received 25 percent or less of normal precipitation. Parts of western and southern Texas received five percent or less of normal precipitation. Parts of southern Texas received 110 percent or more of normal precipitation. Texas received 0.90 inches of precipitation in November.

Temperatures during **December** varied in Texas. Parts of western Texas experienced temperatures zero to two degrees below normal. Parts of northern, central, western, southern, and eastern Texas experienced temperatures zero to two degrees above normal. Parts of northern, central, and southern Texas experienced temperatures two to four degrees above normal. The average temperature in Texas in December was 48.3 degrees. Precipitation also varied across Texas. Parts of northern, central, western, and southern Texas received 50 percent or less of normal precipitation. Parts of northern and western Texas received five percent or less of normal precipitation. Parts of eastern and western Texas received 130 percent or more of normal precipitation. Other parts of eastern and western Texas received 150 percent or more of normal precipitation. Parts of western Texas received 200 percent or more of normal precipitation. Texas received 1.76 inches of precipitation in December.☆

Meteorological Data

Source: National Climatic Data Center. Additional data for these locations are listed by county in the table of Texas Climatological Normals for 1981–2010 and Extreme Weather Records by County, beginning on page 126.

| City | Temperature | | Precipitation | | | | | Relative Humidity | | Wind | | | Sun |
	No. Days Max. 100° and Above	No. Days Min. 32° and Below	Maximum in 24 Hours	Month & Year	Snowfall (Mean Annual)	Max. Snowfall in 24 Hours	Month & Year	6:00 a.m., CT	Noon, CT	Speed, MPH (Mean Annual)	Highest MPH	Month & Year	Percent Possible Sunshine
Abilene	90	48	6.70	9/1961	3.7	9.3	4/1996	75	50	10.9	55	4/1998	70
Amarillo	61	108	7.25	7/2010	17.2	20.6	3/1934	75	46	12.8	68	6/2008	74
Austin	111	12	15.00	9/1931	1.0	9.7	11/1937	84	57	7.0	52	5/1997	60
Brownsville	123	1	12.19	9/1967	0.0	**	3/1993	90	61	10.4	51	7/2008	59
Corpus Christi	106	4	11.52	6/2006	0.2	2.3	12/2004	90	62	11.7	56	5/1999	60
Dallas-Fort Worth	95	29	5.91	10/1959	1.2	12.1	1/1964	82	56	10.5	73	8/1959	61
Del Rio	131	15	17.03	8/1998	0.9	8.6	1/1985	73	65	8.8	60	8/1970	84
El Paso	99	44	6.50	7/1881	6.9	16.8	12/1987	58	35	8.1	64	1/1996	84
Galveston	30	5	13.91	10/1901	0.2	15.4	2/1895	91	64	11.0	*100	9/1900	62
Houston †	102	10	11.02	6/2001	0.1	2.0	1/1973	90	60	7.5	51	8/1983	59
Lubbock	78	84	7.80	9/2008	8.2	16.3	1/1983	75	46	12.0	70	3/1952	72
Midland-Odessa	101	58	5.99	7/1961	5.1	10.6	1/2012	74	43	10.9	67	2/1960	74
Port Arthur-Beaumont	80	9	17.16	9/1980	0.0	4.4	2/1960	91	64	8.6	105	8/2005	58
San Angelo	102	46	6.25	9/1980	2.4	7.4	1/1978	80	49	9.7	75	4/1969	70
San Antonio	111	15	13.35	10/1998	0.7	13.2	1/1985	84	56	8.2	51	6/2010	60
Victoria	107	11	9.87	4/1991	0.1	2.1	1/1985	91	60	9.5	99	7/1963	49
Waco	104	31	7.98	12/1997	1.2	7.0	1/1949	86	57	10.1	69	6/1961	59
Wichita Falls	98	59	6.22	9/1980	4.2	9.7	3/1989	82	52	11.2	69	6/2002	60
Shreveport, LA §	88	32	10.76	5/2008	1.0	5.6	1/1982	89	59	7.3	63	5/2000	64

*100 mph recorded at 6:15 p.m., Sept. 8, 1900, just before the anemometer blew away. Maximum velocity was estimated to be 120 mph from the northeast between 7:30 p.m. and 8:30 p.m.
†The official Houston station was moved from near downtown to Intercontinental Airport, 12 miles north of the old station.
§Shreveport is included because it is near the boundary line and its data can be considered representative of Texas' east border.
**Trace is an amount too small to measure.

Storms rumble over the plains outside Smyer on May 11, 2020. Photo by Ashley K. Saed/www.livingtreedesignsphoto.com.

Texas Droughts

Drought is difficult to define, and there is no universally accepted definition. The most commonly used drought definitions are based on meteorological, agricultural, hydrological, and socioeconomic effects.

Meteorological drought is often defined as a period when precipitation is diminished in duration and/or intensity. The commonly used definition of meteorological drought is an interval of time, generally on the order of months or years, during which the moisture supply at a given place consistently falls below the climatically appropriate moisture supply.

Agricultural drought occurs when there is inadequate soil moisture to meet the needs of a particular crop at a particular time. Agricultural drought usually occurs after or during meteorological drought but before hydrological drought and can also affect livestock and other dryland agricultural operations.

Hydrological drought refers to deficiencies in surface and subsurface water supplies. It is measured as streamflow and as lake, reservoir, and groundwater levels. There is usually a delay between lack of rain and less measurable water in streams, lakes, and reservoirs. Therefore, hydrological measurements tend to lag other drought indicators.

Socioeconomic drought occurs when physical water shortages start to affect the health, well-being, and quality of life of the people, or when the drought starts to affect the supply and demand of an economic product.

The table on this page uses the **Palmer drought severity index (PDSI)**, the index preferred by the Texas State Climatologist's Office, the National Weather Service, and NOAA. It was developed by meteorologist Wayne Palmer, who first published this method in 1965.

The PDSI is based on a **supply-and-demand model of soil moisture** that factors in temperature, the amount of moisture in the soil, evapotranspiration, and recharge rates. It is most effective in determining long-term drought. Years were included in the table if at least one climate division had a PDSI of -4 or below, and the past 10 years, even when no periods of drought occurred. ☆

Source: Texas State Climatologist and the New Mexico Drought Planning Team

PDSI Table Indicators

Moderate drought, PDSI between –2 and –4

Severe drought, PDSI between –4 and –6

Extreme drought, PDSI below –6

Palmer Drought Severity Index

	High Plains	Low Rolling Plains	North Central	East Texas	Trans–Pecos	Edwards Plateau	South Central	Upper Coast	South Texas	Lower Valley
Frequency	27	28	27	25	28	28	26	26	25	25
1901	-2.01	-2.55	-4.58	-2.39	-2.28	-3.14	-3.84	-2.78	-3.21	-5.05
1902	-2.54	-3.73	-5.64	-3.23	-3.23	-4.05	-4.99	-3.45	-4.97	-5.70
1910	-3.47	-3.89	-5.04	-3.99	-4.21	-4.48	-3.63	-2.51	-3.26	-3.43
1911	-3.69	-4.10	-5.97	-5.02	-4.02	-4.03	-4.21	-4.31	-4.39	-3.03
1916	-2.60	-2.79	-2.49	-3.23	-3.53	-2.37	-4.19	-3.26	-4.71	-4.51
1917	-3.90	-4.66	-4.53	-4.90	-4.58	-4.88	-6.00	-6.03	-4.56	-3.91
1918	-3.88	-5.97	-6.11	-6.42	-3.75	-5.61	-6.13	-7.00	-4.50	-4.09
1925	-2.96	-3.26	-6.41	-6.20	-3.09	-3.95	-6.09	-5.20	-3.79	-2.51
1934	-4.66	-4.42	-4.84	-3.55	-4.88	-4.51	-2.82	-2.27	-1.54	-1.33
1935	-4.57	-3.83	-0.58	0.19	-4.68	-3.99	0.66	-0.39	0.10	-1.76
1951	-1.65	-3.36	-4.26	-3.84	-4.15	-4.66	-4.64	-4.37	-3.91	-4.10
1952	-4.23	-5.38	-5.53	-3.72	-4.28	-5.10	-4.53	-4.47	-4.45	-3.71
1953	-5.33	-5.41	-3.12	-1.27	-5.67	-4.64	-2.58	-2.21	-5.26	-4.45
1954	-4.46	-4.24	-4.29	-4.27	-4.59	-5.09	-4.87	-3.89	-3.59	-3.38
1955	-4.13	-3.76	-3.81	-3.18	-3.35	-4.78	-4.95	-3.75	-4.59	-3.60
1956	-5.62	-6.25	-6.82	-5.09	-5.47	-6.16	-6.68	-5.72	-4.77	-3.81
1957	-4.94	-5.02	-5.08	-4.92	-4.85	-5.10	-5.82	-5.64	-4.29	-4.12
1963	-2.38	-2.91	-3.95	-3.77	-2.07	-4.29	-4.80	-4.15	-3.71	-3.57
1967	-3.31	-3.42	-4.61	-3.34	-2.55	-4.12	-4.73	-2.99	-3.62	-2.44
1971	-3.33	-4.18	-4.41	-3.11	-2.80	-3.46	-5.01	-3.28	-3.68	-2.70
1974	-4.43	-4.20	-2.44	1.60	-3.44	-3.09	1.26	1.95	-1.29	-1.97
1996	-3.83	-3.57	-4.28	-3.63	-3.76	-3.88	-4.51	-2.59	-3.64	-3.04
2000	-3.88	-3.97	-3.76	-4.34	-4.93	-4.78	-4.39	-5.17	-4.12	-3.73
2006	-4.58	-4.80	-4.93	-4.16	-3.72	-4.14	-5.23	-4.32	-4.73	-4.77
2009	-2.24	-2.97	-3.88	-2.43	-2.35	-3.82	-6.36	-4.23	-5.19	-4.09
2010	-1.13	-1.20	-1.27	-3.67	-2.08	-2.02	-1.49	-1.19	-1.59	-1.68
2011	-6.98	-6.99	-5.99	-6.86	-6.52	-6.39	-6.21	-5.70	-5.45	-4.87
2012	-5.12	-4.75	-3.70	-4.36	-4.93	-3.75	-4.37	-4.72	-4.17	-4.69
2013	-4.16	-4.26	-3.43	-2.94	-3.02	-3.40	-4.47	-3.47	-4.33	-4.94
2014	-3.45	-3.29	-2.56	-1.34	-2.85	-2.93	-3.29	-2.49	-2.72	-1.23
2015	0.69	0.39	0.38	0.84	1.74	0.33	0.41	-0.59	-1.14	-0.56
2016	1.30	2.57	2.85	-2.04	-1.15	1.98	-0.47	-1.63	-1.50	-2.86
2017	-1.15	-1.43	-1.31	-2.40	-1.82	-1.47	-1.72	0.59	-1.97	-3.72
2018	-3.84	-4.35	-3.30	-2.16	-3.18	-3.67	-2.31	0.79	-2.72	-4.09
2020	-3.57	-0.58	1.41	1.63	-4.94	-3.17	-3.74	-0.40	-3.05	-3.22

Normal Annual Rainfall in Inches by Texas Climatic Region

Listed below is the normal annual rainfall in inches for three 30-year periods in each geographical region (see map, p. 106).

Region	HP	LRP	NC	ET	TP	EP	SC	UC	ST	LV
1961–1990	18.88	23.77	33.99	45.67	13.01	24.00	34.49	47.63	23.47	25.31
1971–2000	19.64	24.51	35.23	48.08	13.19	24.73	36.21	50.31	24.08	25.43
1981–2010	20.02	24.85	36.17	48.21	13.16	24.86	35.54	51.14	24.17	24.67

Texas Is Tornado Capital

Source: The Office of the State Climatologist.

An average of 130 tornadoes touch Texas soil each year. The annual total varies considerably, and certain areas are struck more often than others. Tornadoes occur with greatest frequency in the Red River Valley.

Tornadoes may occur in any month and at any hour of the day, but they occur with greatest frequency during the late spring and early summer months, and between the hours of 4:00 p.m. and 8:00 p.m. In the period 1951–2020, 63 percent of all Texas tornadoes occurred within the three-month period of April, May, and June, with almost one-third of the total tornadoes occurring in May.

More tornadoes have been recorded in Texas than in any other state, which is partly due to the state's size. Between 1951–2020, 9,166 funnel clouds are known to have reached the ground, thus becoming tornadoes. Texas ranks 11th among the 50 states in the density of tornadoes, experiencing an annual average of 4.85 tornadoes per 10,000 square miles.

The greatest outbreak of tornadoes on record in Texas was associated with Hurricane Beulah in September 1967. Within a five-day period (Sept. 19–23) 115 known tornadoes, all in Texas, were spawned by this great hurricane. Sixty-seven occurred on Sept. 20, a Texas record for a single day.

In May 2015, there were 130 tornadoes, which is a Texas record for a single month. The greatest number of tornadoes in Texas in a single year was 248, which was also in 2015. The second-highest number in a single year was in 1967, when 232 tornadoes occurred in Texas.

On average, May has the highest number of tornadoes with 40. January has the lowest average number of tornadoes with 3.

The accompanying table, compiled by the National Climatic Data Center, Environmental Data Service, and the National Oceanic and Atmospheric Administration, lists tornado occurrences in Texas, by months, for the period 1951–2020. Additional years are available at texasalmanac.org.☆

Tornadoes by Year and Month

Year	Jan.	Feb.	March	April	May	June	July	Aug.	Sept.	Oct.	Nov.	Dec.	TOTAL
1951-56	0	9	19	49	93	61	16	16	8	16	3	7	297
1957	0	1	21	69	33	5	0	3	2	6	5	0	145
1958-66	8	16	61	107	224	201	66	59	41	29	33	4	849
1967	0	2	11	17	34	22	10	5	124	2	0	5	232
1968-72	4	25	38	89	205	91	41	68	35	61	23	42	722
1973	14	1	29	25	21	24	4	8	5	3	9	4	147
1974	2	1	8	19	18	26	3	9	6	22	2	0	116
1975	5	2	9	12	50	18	10	3	3	3	1	1	117
1976	1	1	8	53	63	11	16	6	13	4	0	0	176
1977	0	0	3	34	50	4	5	5	12	0	6	4	123
1978	0	0	0	34	65	10	13	6	6	1	2	0	137
1979	1	2	24	33	39	14	12	10	4	15	3	0	157
1980	0	2	7	26	44	21	2	34	10	5	0	2	153
1981	0	7	7	9	71	26	5	20	5	23	3	0	176
1982	0	0	6	27	123	36	4	0	3	0	3	1	203
1983	5	7	24	1	62	35	4	22	5	0	7	14	186
1984	0	13	9	18	19	19	0	4	1	5	2	5	95
1985	0	0	5	41	28	5	3	1	1	3	1	2	90
1986	0	12	4	21	50	24	3	5	4	7	1	0	131
1987	1	1	7	0	54	19	11	3	8	0	16	4	124
1988	0	0	0	11	7	7	6	2	42	4	10	0	89
1989	3	0	5	3	70	63	0	6	3	6	1	0	160
1990	3	3	4	56	62	20	5	2	3	0	0	0	158
1991	20	5	2	39	72	36	1	2	3	8	4	0	192
1992	0	5	13	22	43	66	4	4	4	7	21	0	189
1993	1	4	5	17	39	4	4	0	12	23	8	0	117
1994	0	1	1	48	88	2	1	4	3	9	8	0	165
1995	6	0	13	36	66	75	11	3	2	1	0	10	223
1996	7	1	2	21	33	9	3	8	33	8	4	1	130
1997	0	6	7	31	59	50	2	2	1	16	3	0	177
1998	24	15	4	9	11	6	3	5	3	28	1	0	109
1999	22	0	22	23	70	26	3	8	0	0	0	4	178
2000	0	7	49	33	23	8	3	0	0	10	20	1	154
2001	0	0	4	12	36	12	0	7	15	24	27	5	142
2002	0	0	44	25	61	5	1	4	13	8	0	22	183
2003	0	0	4	31	50	29	6	1	4	12	29	0	166
2004	1	1	27	25	29	34	1	5	0	4	55	2	184
2005	0	0	6	7	27	46	15	4	2	0	0	2	109
2006	0	1	4	20	43	7	3	3	0	9	0	27	117
2007	2	1	56	61	43	21	8	4	14	2	1	3	216
2008	0	3	15	48	33	9	5	1	2	3	1	3	123
2009	0	5	4	48	18	32	2	4	1	4	1	12	131
2010	10	0	0	19	34	23	3	1	12	10	0	0	112
2011	1	1	3	57	20	6	1	4	1	2	8	0	104
2012	22	3	9	36	31	3	0	1	2	3	0	5	115
2013	1	16	0	8	41	3	0	6	0	6	0	3	84
2014	0	0	0	6	15	15	5	0	0	2	0	3	46
2015	0	0	0	48	130	3	0	0	2	20	23	22	248
2016	0	1	14	33	43	4	1	1	5	0	0	0	102
2017	22	17	36	29	43	3	3	25	1	1	0	3	183
2018	5	0	9	4	6	3	3	2	1	22	1	2	58
2019	0	0	12	39	104	13	1	0	2	13	0	0	184
2020	14	0	18	17	24	3	8	2	1	0	2	3	92
Total	205	198	692	1,606	2,820	1,318	340	408	483	470	348	228	9,116
Avg.	3	3	10	23	40	19	5	6	7	7	5	3	130
Max	24	20	56	69	130	75	19	34	124	28	55	27	248

Extreme Weather Records in Texas

Sources: Office of the State Climatologist and the National Weather Service, Dallas–Fort Worth.

Temperature			
Lowest	-23°F	Tulia	Feb. 12, 1899
	-23°F	Seminole	Feb. 8, 1933
Highest	120°F	Seymour	Aug. 12, 1936
	120°F	Monahans	June 28, 1994
Coldest Winter	41.3°F average		1898–1899
Hottest Summer	86.8°F average		2011

Wind Velocity		
Highest sustained wind		
145 mph SE	Matagorda	Sept. 11, 1961
145 mph NE	Port Lavaca	Sept. 11, 1961
Highest peak gust		
180 mph SW	Aransas Pass	Aug. 3, 1970
180 mph WSW	Robstown	Aug. 3, 1970

These winds occurred during Hurricane Carla in 1961 and
Hurricane Celia in 1970.

Tornadoes		

*Since 1950, there have been six tornadoes of the F-5
category, that is, with winds between 261–318 mph.*

Waco	McLennan County	May 11, 1953
Wichita Falls	Wichita County	April 3, 1964
Lubbock	Lubbock County	May 11, 1970
Valley Mills	McLennan County	May 6, 1973
Brownwood	Brown County	April 19, 1976
Jarrell	Williamson County	May 27, 1997

Rainfall			
Wettest year statewide		2015	41.23 in.
Driest year statewide		1917	14.06 in.
Most annual	Bridge City	2017	109.42 in.
Least annual	Terlingua	2011	1.30 in.
Most in 24 hours†	Alvin	July 25–26, 1979	43.00 in.
Most in 18 hours	Thrall	Sept. 9, 1921	36.40 in.

†Unofficial estimate of rainfall during Tropical Storm Claudette.
Greatest 24-hour rainfall at an official site occurred at Albany,
Shackelford County, on Aug. 4, 1978: 29.05 inches.

Hail		
Hailstones six inches or greater, since 1950		
7.50 in.	Young County	April 14, 1965
7.05 in.	Burleson County	Dec. 17, 1995
7.00 in.	Winkler County	May 31, 1960
6.42 in.	Medina County	April 28, 2021
6.00 in.	Ward County	May 10, 1991
6.00 in.	Moore County	June 12, 2010

Snowfall			
65.0 in.	Season	Romero*	1923–1924
61.0 in.	Month	Vega	Feb. 1956
61.0 in.	Single storm	Vega	Feb. 1–8, 1956
26.0 in.	24 hours	Cleburne	Dec. 21–22, 1929
24.2 in	Annual avg.	Vega, Oldham County	

*Romero was in southwestern Hartley County.

A thunderstorm rolls over the Texas prairie. Photo by Raychel Sanner/Unsplash (CC).

Hurricane Hanna hits the southern coast of Texas on July 25, 2020. Photo by International Space Station, courtesy of NASA Johnson Space Center/Flickr (CC).

Significant and Destructive Weather

This list of significant weather events in Texas since 1980 was compiled from ESSA–Weather Bureau information, previous Texas Almanacs, the Handbook of Texas, The Dallas Morning News, and the Office of the State Climatologist. For historical significant weather dating back to 1766, see texasalmanac.com!

2020

March 18, 2020: Tornadoes, North Central & High Plains. Severe storms rolled through North Texas and brought a couple of significant tornadoes. Eight were confirmed, with two as strong as EF-2. An EF-1 tornado was confirmed in Graham, and there was widespread damage throughout the area, including damaged buildings, downed power lines, and uprooted trees. Two EF-2 tornadoes, with winds estimated up to 135 mph, were confirmed near Abilene, where several wind turbines were damaged, a small home was destroyed, and at least 75 vehicles were tossed around the area. Hail as large as 2.25 inches was also reported. There were no injuries.

April 22, 2020: Tornado, Upper Coast. A line of severe storms moved through southeastern Texas, bringing an EF-3 tornado in Onalaska and hail up to two inches in diameter. The tornado had peak winds of 140 mph and was on the ground for 32 miles. Many homes were destroyed and trees were uprooted. Thirty-three people were injured and three were killed.

May 22, 2020: Hail, North Central. Strong instability and moisture brought severe storms through far northern Texas, producing significant hail in Burkburnett. The largest hail reported had a diameter of 5.33 inches. Widespread damage in the area was also reported.

July 25–27, 2020: Hurricane, Lower Valley. Hurricane Hanna, the 2020 Atlantic season's first hurricane, made landfall near Padre Island on July 25th. Winds at this time were around 90 mph with gusts over 100 mph. Eight to 15 inches of rain fell throughout the Valley, 250,000 people lost power, hundreds of homes were damaged, tens of thousands of tree limbs were blown down, hundreds of trees were uprooted, and there was an estimated $366 million in damage.

September 21–23, 2020: Tropical Storm, South Central. Tropical Storm Beta formed on the 18th in the Gulf of Mexico, slowed considerably, and moved towards the Texas coast. Beta made landfall at Matagorda Bay on the 21st and weakened significantly shortly after. Torrential rainfall caused major flooding in streets, highways, and interstates in Houston, as rainfall surpassed nine inches, forcing road closures. There was one death. Total damage from Beta was estimated at $225 million.

November 24, 2020: Tornado, North Central. Severe storms moved through North Texas, bringing heavy rain and an EF-2 tornado to Arlington. The tornado had wind speeds estimated at 115 mph, stayed on the ground for 5.04 miles, and had a width of 150 yards. Buildings were destroyed, power lines were downed, roads were impassable because of debris, and five people were injured.

2019

April 13, 2019: Tornadoes, East Texas. A large, upper-level storm system moved across the southern Plains states. Severe thunderstorms impacted southeast Texas, producing two EF-3 tornadoes. One of the EF-3 tornadoes hit Franklin with peak winds estimated at 140 mph, injuring 14 people and damaging upwards of 20 buildings. Mobile homes were damaged, cars were overturned, and power lines were downed; about 4,000 people lost power. The other EF-3 tornado touched down near Weches, killing the occupant of a double-wide trailer.

May 20, 2019: Tornadoes/Hail, High Plains. All the ingredients were present for a severe weather outbreak. NWS offices called for a strong chance of long-track, destructive tornadoes, and schools and businesses closed in preparation. Although the outbreak wasn't as significant as expected, tornadoes and hail pummeled northwest Texas. There were seven tornado reports that day, with the strongest being an EF-3 near West Odessa. Hail 5.5 inches in diameter was reported near Wellington, and now holds a record for one of the largest hailstones to fall in the state.

June 9, 2019: Strong Winds, North-Central. Severe thunderstorms moved through northern Texas, bringing heavy rain and strong winds to the Dallas area. Wind damage to power lines caused 350,000 to lose power and collapsed a large construction crane on an apartment building in downtown Dallas. The wind was

worth $4 million. Three injuries were reported; other property losses were around $1 million.

April 6, 2011: Wildfire, Swenson. A wildfire near Swenson was spawned during critical fire conditions due to a cutting torch. The fire burned for 15 days, burning 122,500 acres of grass and ranchland; damage, $2.54 million.

April 9, 2011: Wildfire, West Texas. Dry conditions near the Pecos River spawned two fires near Midland and Marfa. The former burned 16,500 acres and 34 homes, causing 500 evacuations; the latter was caused by an electrical problem and burned 314,444 acres, 41 homes, and hundreds of cattle and utility poles. Total property damage was estimated at $7.7 million.

April 9–13, 2011: Wildfire, Possum Kingdom Lake. Drought and high winds helped spark a massive fire complex that burned for 16 days, destroying 167 homes, 126 other buildings, and 90 percent of Possum Kingdom State Park — about 126,734 acres total. Damage was $120 million, not including the estimated $11 million needed to combat the fire, nor the loss of cattle.

April 15, 2011: Wildfire, Cisco. Dry conditions caused several wildfires in North Texas. The largest was near Cisco, burning around 2,000 acres and destroying five homes. The fires burned 18,000 acres, costing $1.01 million.

April 17, 2011: Wildfire, Oak Hill. Dry conditions and human negligence combined to cause a wildfire in Travis County. Although it covered only 100 acres, it destroyed 11 homes and damage estimates reached $2 million.

April 19, 2011: Hail, North Texas. A series of supercells brought widespread hail ranging from 0.75 inches to 3.5 inches over the course of the 5-hour storm. Damage was around $1 million.

April 25–26, 2011: Supercells, East Texas. An upper level trough brought severe storms to East Texas for two days. On the 25th, 3 tornadoes touched down in Cherokee and Angelina counties, including two EF-1s; moderate hail was seen and downburst winds of 90-plus mph were reported. The next day, 10 tornadoes were reported, two of which were EF-1s near Ben Wheeler and Groesbeck, causing injuries. Total damage, $2.718 million.

May 1, 2011: Thunderstorm Wind, Clyde. Isolated thunderstorms popped up in the Big Country, bringing hail and strong winds. In Clyde, straight-line winds were reported in excess of 100 mph; damage, $2 million.

May 11, 2011: Thunderstorm Wind, Interstate-20 Corridor. Scattered thunderstorms from Killeen to Burns caused strong winds, hail, flash flooding, and an EF-0 tornado near Lake Kiowa; damage, $1 million.

June 18, 2011: Thunderstorm Wind, Meunster. Thunderstorms followed by a strong microburst in the early evening and straight-line winds greater than 80 mph caused widespread damage in excess of $1.36 million.

June 20–21, 2011: Thunderstorm Wind, East Texas. Severe thunderstorms culminated in strong downburst winds, hail, and an EF-0 tornado. Winds greater than 80 mph occurred in Nacogdoches and San Augustine, a tornado in Shelby County, and moderate hail; damage, $1.04 million.

June 28, 2011: Thunderstorm Wind, Titus County. Thunderstorms with 65 mph winds caused widespread damage at a cost of $1.6 million.

Aug. 11, 2011: Flash Flood, Lubbock. Scattered thunderstorms brought heavy rain, wind, and hail to the Lubbock area. Some area received 1–4 inches of rain in an hour, causing high water damage to homes and vehicles. Farm and weather equipment in Dimmit were damaged by 90 mph winds. Total damage, $1.175 million.

September–October 2011: Wildfires, Bastrop County. Three separate fires that began Sept. 4 merged into a single blaze east of the city of Bastrop and became known as the Bastrop County Complex fire. The fire destroyed 1,691 homes and much of Bastrop State Park was burned. Declared the most destructive wildfire in Texas history, it was finally extinguished on Oct. 29.

Oct. 9, 2011: Tornado, San Antonio. An EF-1 tornado with winds up to 90–100 mph tore apart roofs, utility poles, and vehicles; damage, $1 million.

2010

June 9, 2010: Flash Flood. New Braunfels. Storms produced rains in excess of 11 inches, which caused the Guadalupe River to rise over 20 feet in just two hours. Campers, vehicles, boats, homes, and businesses suffered extensive damages along the riverbanks. The flash flood resulted in one death; damage, more than $10 million.

July 2, 2010: Tornado. Hebbronville. An EF-1 tornado that developed following Hurricane Alex caused considerable damage in Hebbronville. Over half of the town's population lost power, and the tornado was reported to be as wide as a football field. Estimated damage, $1.5 million.

July 4, 2010: Flood. Terry, Lubbock, Garza, and Lynn Counties. A series of thunderstorms erupted in the early morning of the Fourth of July over the west South Texas Plains. Local flooding caused roadway closures and damage to more 100 vehicles. More than 300 homes and businesses were affected; economic losses were around $16.5 million.

July 8, 2010: Flood. Starr County. Another storm that formed in the aftermath of Hurricane Alex, dumped an estimated 50 inches or more of rain on the lower Rio Grande Valley over 10 days leading up to the 8th. Falcon Reservoir rose during days of rain and finally spilled over on the 8th. The Rio Grande was nearly 2 miles wide at some points. Estimated damage was around $37 million.

Oct. 24, 2010: Tornado. Rice, Navarro County. An intense EF-2 tornado struck with maximum winds of 135 mph. Vehicles were overturned on Interstate 45 and 11 train cars were derailed when the tornado hit the tracks. The football, baseball, and softball fields of the local high school were damaged; the intermediate school lost the gymnasium roof and suffered a caved-in wall; damage was $1 million.

2009

Jan. 19, 2009: Wildfire. Hidalgo County. Aided by strong gusts, low humidity, lack of rain, and warm temperatures, a wildfire spread across 2,560 acres in Hidalgo County and consumed four buildings at Moore Air Force Base. Damage at the base was $10 million.

March 30, 2009: Hail. Northeast Tarrant County. A strong line of severe storms dumped ping-pong- to baseball-sized hail on numerous cities in northeast Tarrant County. Much of the damage was to automobiles; overall damage was $95 million.

April 11, 2009: Hail. Midland. Up to golf-ball-sized hail caused tremendous damage to homes and vehicles during a severe storm, with an estimated $160 million in roof damage. A woman was pelted in the stomach by a hailstone that broke through the window in her dining room.

May 2, 2009: Thunderstorm Wind. Irving. The National Weather Service determined that a microburst caused the Dallas Cowboys' bubble practice facility to collapse from winds estimated at 70 mph. Twelve people were injured, including one coach who was paralyzed from the waist down. The damage was estimated at $5 million.

June 11, 2009: Thunderstorm Wind. Burnet. A peak wind of 67 mph was measured at the Burnet Airport and numerous planes were flipped or blown across the tarmac. Damage in the city was $5 million.

Sept. 16, 2009: Hail. El Paso. A series of supercell storms produced golf-ball- to tennis-ball-sized hail and the most costly hailstorm in recorded history for the El Paso area. Estimated damage was $150 million.

Dec. 23, 2009: Tornado. Lufkin. An EF-3 tornado touched down in Lufkin, damaging structures, homes, and vehicles. The twister and heavy rains caused damage estimated at $10 million.

2008

March 31, 2008: Hail. Northeast Texas. Severe thunderstorms developed across the Red River valley, many producing large hail that damaged car windows, skylights, and roofs in Texarkana and elsewhere in Bowie County. Damage was estimated at $120 million.

April 10, 2008: Tornadoes. Johnson County. A lone supercell thunderstorm evolved in the afternoon of the 9th, producing tornadoes and large hail. A tornado touched down near Happy Hill and traveled northeast 3 miles to Pleasant Point, where it dissipated. The F-1 tornado, with maximum wind speeds of 90–95 mph, destroyed three homes and damaged more than 30 homes and other buildings. Damage was $25 million.

May 14, 2008: Hail. Austin. A severe thunderstorm southwest of Austin moved northeast across downtown, causing extensive damage from winds and large hail. Large trees and branches were knocked down, and baseball-sized hail and 70–80 mph winds blew out windows in apartments and office buildings, including the State Capitol. Total damage was estimated at $50 million.

August 18, 2008: Floods. Wichita Falls. An unseasonably strong upper-level storm system moved over North Texas, and several waves of heavy thunderstorms caused heavy rain and widespread flooding in the Iowa Park, Burkburnett, and Wichita Falls areas. In Wichita Falls, at least 118 homes were flooded, 19 of which were destroyed, and residents were evacuated by boat. Burkburnett and Iowa Park were isolated for a few hours because of street flooding. Damage was estimated at $25 million, and Gov. Rick Perry declared Wichita County a disaster area.

Sept. 12, 2008: Hurricane Ike. Galveston. The eye of the hurricane moved ashore near the Galveston with central pressure of 951.6 millibars and maximum sustained winds around 110 mph, which made Hurricane Ike a strong category-2 storm. There were 12 deaths directly related to Ike (11 occurring in Galveston County from drowning due to storm surge) and at least another 25 fatalities either due to carbon monoxide poisoning from generators, accidents while clearing debris, or house fires from candles. Storm tide and storm surge caused the majority of property damage at the coast. Damage in Harris, Chambers, Galveston, Liberty, Polk, Matagorda, Brazoria, Fort Bend, San Jacinto, and Montgomery counties totaled $14 billion.

2007

March 29, 2007: Floods. Corsicana. Flash flooding along Interstate 45 submerged two cars in Navarro County, north of Corsicana, and 2 feet of water was reported on I-45 and Texas 31, east of town; damage to businesses, roads, and bridges, $19 million.

April 13, 2007: Hail. Colleyville. Teacup-size hail was reported as strong storms developed in Tarrant County. Hail damage to 5,500 cars and 3,500 homes and businesses was estimated at $10 million.

April 24, 2007: Tornado. Eagle Pass. A large tornado crossed the Rio Grande from Mexico around 6 p.m., striking Rosita Valley, near Eagle Pass. Ten deaths were reported, including a family of five in a mobile home. Golf-ball-sized hail and the tornado struck Rosita Valley Elementary School, leaving only the interior walls standing. Damage indicated wind speeds near 140 mph and an F-3 level, with a path 1/4-mile wide and 4 miles long. The tornado also destroyed 59 manufactured homes and 57 houses. Total damage was estimated at $80 million.

June 17–18, 2007: Floods. North Texas. Torrential rain fell as an upper-level low lingered for several days. In Tarrant County, one person drowned after her rescue boat capsized. Hundreds of people were rescued from high water. In Grayson County, a woman died in floodwaters as she drove under an overpass, and another death occurred in a flooded truck. Three people in Cooke County died when a mobile home was carried away by floodwaters. Damage was estimated at $30 million in Tarrant County, $20 million in Grayson County, and $28 million in Cooke County.

June 27, 2007: Floods. Marble Falls. Two lines of thunderstorms produced 10–19 inches of rain in southern Burnet County. Hardest hit was Marble Falls, where two young men died in the early morning when their jeep was swept into high water east of town. Damage to more than 315 homes and businesses was $130 million.

Sept. 13, 2007: Hurricane Humberto. Jefferson County. The hurricane made landfall around 1 a.m. in rural southwestern Jefferson County near McFaddin National Wildlife Refuge. Minimum pressure was around 985 millibars, with maximum winds at 90 mph. Flash flooding occurred in urban areas between Beaumont and Orange, as 11 inches of rain fell. Coastal storm tides

were 3–5 feet, with the highest storm surge occurring at Texas Point. Humberto caused one death, 12 injuries, and $25 million in damage.

2006

Jan. 1, 2006: Wildfires. North Texas. Several wildfires exploded across North Texas due to low humidity, strong winds, and the ongoing drought. Fires were reported in Montague, Eastland, and Palo Pinto counties. Five injuries were reported, as well as $10.8 million in property damage.

March 12–18, 2006: Wildfires. Borger. A wildfire now known as the Borger wildfire started four miles southwest of Borger, Hutchinson County. It killed seven people and burned 479,500 acres and 28 structures; total property damage, $49.9 million; crop damage, $45.4 million. A second wildfire known as the Interstate-40 wildfire burned 427,696 acres. The Texas Forest Service named the two wildfires the East Amarillo Complex. In all, 12 people were killed; total property damage, $49.9 million; crop damage, $45.4 million.

March 19, 2006: Tornado. Uvalde. An F-2 tornado moved through the Uvalde area causing $1.5 million in property damage. It was the strongest tornado in South-Central Texas since Oct. 12, 2001.

April 11–13, 2006: Wildfire. Canadian. A wildfire 10 miles north of Canadian, Hemphill County, injured two; burned 18,000 acres; and destroyed $90 million of crops.

April 18, 2006: Hail. Gillespie County. Hailstones as large as 2.5 inches in diameter destroyed windows in homes and car windshields between Harper and Doss in Gillespie County. The hail also damaged 70 percent of the area's peach crop, an estimated loss of $5 million.

April 20, 2006: Hail. San Marcos. Hailstones as large as 4.25 inches in diameter (grapefruit-size) were reported south of San Marcos, damaging 10,000 vehicles on the road and another 7,000 vehicles at homes; total damage was estimated at $100 million.

May 4, 2006: Hail. Snyder. Lime-to-baseball-size hail fell across Snyder in Scurry County for at least 15 minutes. The hail was blown sideways at times by 60-to-70-mph winds. Total damage was estimated at $15 million.

May 5, 2006: Tornado. Waco. A tornado with peak intensity estimated at low F-2 caused damage of $3 million.

May 9, 2006: Tornado. Childress. An F-2 tornado caused significant damage along a 1-1/2-mile path through the north side of Childress in the evening. An instrument at Childress High School measured a wind gust of 109 mph. Property damage was estimated at $5.7 million.

Aug. 1, 2006: Thunderstorms. El Paso. Storms in a saturated atmosphere repeatedly developed and moved over the northwest third of El Paso County, concentrating near the Franklin Mountains. Rainfall reports varied from 4–6 inches within 15 hours, with an isolated report of about 8 inches on the western slope of the mountain range. Four days of heavy rains, combined with the mountains' terrain, led to excessive runoff and flooding not seen on such a large scale in the El Paso area in more than 100 years. Property damage was estimated at $180 million.

2005

March 25, 2005: Hail. Austin. In the evening, the most destructive hailstorm in 10 years struck the greater Austin area. The storm knocked out power to 5,000 homes in northwest Austin. Hail 2 inches in diameter was reported near the Travis County Exposition Center. Total damage was estimated at $100 million.

May 2005–December 2006: Drought. North-Central Texas. In May, portions of the area were upgraded from moderate to severe drought. By month's end, the drought had made significant agricultural and hydrological impacts on the region. In November, many Central Texas counties were added to the drought. The Texas Cooperative Extension estimated statewide drought losses at $4.1 billion, $1.9 billion in North Texas alone.

June 9, 2005: Tornado. Petersburg. An F-3 tornado affected an area from Petersburg in southeast Hale County to portions of

Texas Climatological Normals for 1981–2010 and Extreme Weather Records by County through 2020

Explanations and Sources

Data in this table are provided by the Office of the Texas State Climatologist, Texas A&M University, College Station, Texas.

The Climatological Normals include Mean Maximum July Temperature, Mean Minimum January Temperature, Average Freeze Dates, Growing Season, and Mean Precipitation. They are calculated every 10 years and are based on the previous 30-year period, which is 1981–2010. Data in italics are from the period 1971–2000.

Data for counties where a weather station has not been maintained long enough to establish a reliable mean are interpolated from isoline charts prepared from mean values from stations with long-established records.

Mean Maximum for July is computed from the sum of the daily maxima. Mean Minimum for January is computed from the sum of the daily minima.

Extreme Weather Records include Record High Temperature, Record Low Temperature, and Record Rainfall; they are compiled yearly and are current through 2018.

The far left column lists Texas' 254 counties and identifies the town or landmark nearest to the National Weather Service station used to calculate Climatological Normals. If that weather station is outside the county, the town or landmark is in italics. Extreme Weather Records may have occurred at any weather station in that county and are identified only for Record Rainfall.

An asterisk (*) preceding an Extreme Weather Record means it also occurred on a previous date.

County, Town or Landmark Closest to Station for Normals	Temperature								Average Freeze Dates			
	Mean Max. July	No. At or Above 100°	Mean Min. January	No. At or Below 32°	Record Highest	Record High Date	Record Lowest	Record Low Date	Last in Spring		First in Fall	
	F.	Days	F.	Days	F.	M-D-Y	F.	M-D-Y	Mo.	Day	Mo.	Day
Anderson, Palestine	92.8	4	36.9	38	114	7-26-1954	−6	2-12-1899	Mar.	24	Nov.	12
Andrews, Andrews	95.2	15	33.0	59	113	6-27-1994	−1	2-2-1985	Mar.	31	Nov.	10
Angelina, County Airport	92.4	5	39.4	28	*110	8-19-1909	−2	2-2-1951	Mar.	10	Nov.	20
Aransas, Rockport	91.6	0	48.3	4	107	9-5-2000	9	12-23-1989	Feb.	6	Dec.	20
Archer, Archer City	95.5	22	32.6	57	114	6-28-1980	*−10	12-23-1989	Mar.	27	Nov.	8
Armstrong, Claude	91.2	3	26.0	108	*108	6-28-1980	−16	2-13-1905	Apr.	16	Oct.	24
Atascosa, Pleasanton	96.0	15	42.1	19	*113	8-22-1917	−1	1-31-1949	Feb.	27	Nov.	29
Austin, Sealy	94.0	7	43.5	13	*111	9-4-2000	0	12-23-1989	Feb.	22	Dec.	5
Bailey, Muleshoe NWR	91.6	9	22.1	123	*112	6-28-1994	−21	2-8-1933	Apr.	20	Oct.	23
Bandera, Medina	93.9	4	37.0	44	*110	7-9-1939	*−5	2-2-1951	Mar.	24	Nov.	13
Bastrop, Elgin	94.3	13	41.0	18	*111	9-5-2000	−3	12-23-1989	Mar.	5	Nov.	28
Baylor, Seymour	95.5	24	29.7	69	120	8-12-1936	−14	1-4-1947	Mar.	28	Nov.	7
Bee, Beeville	93.8	7	45.5	9	114	6-22-1990	5	2-12-1899	Feb.	18	Dec.	10
Bell, Stillhouse Hollow Dam	94.1	13	37.7	33	*112	8-11-1947	−5	12-23-1989	Mar.	10	Nov.	27
Bexar, San Antonio Intl. Airport	94.4	8	42.8	14	*113	8-28-2011	*0	1-31-1949	Mar.	1	Dec.	1
Blanco, Blanco	92.4	5	37.2	44	110	9-6-2000	*−6	1-31-1949	Mar.	22	Nov.	13
Borden, Gail	92.6	15	33.7	56	116	6-27-1994	−1	12-23-1989	Mar.	24	Nov.	12
Bosque, Lake Whitney Dam	94.1	20	36.3	43	113	9-5-2000	*−3	12-23-1989	Mar.	13	Nov.	18
Bowie, Texarkana	92.0	7	35.2	46	*112	8-5-2011	−9	2-12-1899	Mar.	16	Nov.	19
Brazoria, Angleton	91.1	0	48.3	4	109	9-4-2000	6	2-12-1899	Feb.	6	Dec.	17
Brazos, College Station	94.7	12	43.1	16	112	9-4-2000	−3	1-31-1949	Feb.	26	Dec.	2
Brewster, Alpine	90.9	2	32.5	56	*117	6-17-1992	*−6	1-12-1962	Apr.	4	Nov.	2
Briscoe, Silverton	90.6	4	25.2	111	112	07-15-2020	−10	12-25-2004	Apr.	13	Oct.	27
Brooks, Falfurrias	97.2	28	45.3	10	116	7-13-2016	9	1-12-1962	Feb.	23	Dec.	5
Brown, Brownwood	95.4	18	33.9	55	113	7-19-1925	−6	12-23-1989	Mar.	29	Nov.	7
Burleson, Somerville Dam	95.9	13	36.8	37	114	9-5-2000	3	12-23-1989	Mar.	8	Nov.	24
Burnet, Burnet Muni. Airport	94.1	6	39.7	26	*114	7-11-1917	*−4	12-23-1989	Mar.	6	Nov.	24
Caldwell, Luling	96.2	13	41.2	29	111	8-28-2011	−3	1-31-1949	Mar.	9	Nov.	23
Calhoun, Port O'Connor	88.8	1	48.6	4	*109	8-29-2011	9	12-23-1989	Jan.	29	Dec.	22
Callahan, Putnam	94.0	15	33.6	53	*110	5-28-2011	−8	12-23-1989	Mar.	31	Nov.	8
Cameron, Brownsville	95.1	1	54.9	1	108	8-18-1915	12	2-13-1899	Dec.	25	Jan.	24
Camp, Daingerfield	91.4	9	36.8	34	111	8-3-2011	*10	12-9-2005	Mar.	8	Nov.	23
Carson, Panhandle	91.3	7	25.2	122	112	6-27-2011	*−10	1-12-1963	Apr.	22	Oct.	19

Table Highlights

Record Highs in 2011

Thirty-five new record highs were set in 2011 from the Gulf Coast to West Texas and the Panhandle. The highest records were 118 degrees set in Knox County on June 20 and in Cottle county on June 27. That year began a severe drought that lasted through part of 2015. This period is now considered a "drought of record" by some water suppliers.

The years 1951–1957, however, are still considered the drought of record for other officials and agencies. On a statewide basis, the most intense drought, as measured by the Palmer Drought Severity Index, was in 2011; but the most severe drought, as measured by combined intensity and duration, was 1951–1957.

Rain Records in 2015

Eleven rainfall records were set in 2015, including six records during Oct. 24–25. Most records were set in Central and East Texas and ranged from 9.5 inches in Mineola in Wood County to 18.95 inches in Corsicana in Navarro County.

Rain Records in 2017

Twenty one rainfall records were set in 2017, 17 of which occurred between August 26 and August 30, during Hurricane Harvey. Six counties recorded more than 20 inches of rain: Galveston, Harris, Jefferson, Lavaca, Liberty, and Orange. The highest rainfall total, 26.03 inches, fell on Port Arthur in Jefferson County.

Rain Records in 2018

Eight rain records were set in 2018. Six of those occurred in the months of September (the third wettest month in Texas history) and October (the second wettest month in Texas history).

Combined, September–October 2018 are the wettest consecutive months ever. ☆

| Growing Season | Mean Precipitation | | | | | | | | | | | | | Record Rainfall | | |
| | January | February | March | April | May | June | July | August | September | October | November | December | Annual | Location | Highest Daily Total | |
Days	In.	In.	In.	In.	In.	In.	In.	In.	In.	In.	In.	In.	In.		In.	M-D-Y
234	3.66	3.90	3.89	3.29	4.21	4.97	2.65	3.31	3.21	5.07	4.24	4.20	46.60	Palestine	9.10	8-14-1991
240	0.56	0.69	0.86	0.66	1.63	2.03	1.83	1.65	1.85	1.58	0.71	0.69	14.74	Andrews	7.60	7-2-1914
247	4.18	3.87	3.78	3.05	4.64	4.68	3.05	3.34	4.08	4.83	5.01	4.44	48.95	Lufkin	10.65	10-17-1994
328	2.42	2.20	2.40	1.76	3.10	3.17	3.46	2.57	5.08	4.22	3.02	1.78	35.18	Aransas NWR	14.25	11-1-1974
231	1.36	2.07	2.24	2.53	4.09	3.81	1.92	2.61	2.62	3.81	1.82	1.84	30.72	Olney	8.45	5-15-1989
195	0.72	0.56	1.39	1.40	2.29	3.16	2.84	2.91	1.92	1.66	0.80	0.71	20.36	Claude	6.42	5-16-1951
274	1.94	1.95	2.19	2.06	4.05	4.19	2.78	2.36	3.22	3.03	2.43	1.87	32.07	Rossville	9.09	9-15-1919
276	3.25	2.72	2.84	3.56	4.57	3.62	2.65	3.56	3.91	4.84	4.51	2.89	42.92	San Felipe	12.25	4-18-2016
177	0.54	0.48	0.86	0.81	2.32	2.50	2.18	2.88	2.50	1.73	0.71	0.73	18.24	Muleshoe	5.25	5-16-1951
244	2.00	1.92	3.28	2.37	4.74	4.17	3.96	2.14	3.58	4.36	2.61	2.24	37.37	Vanderpool	11.53	8-1-1978
264	2.41	2.30	2.81	2.13	4.29	4.03	2.00	2.05	2.74	4.07	3.13	2.47	34.43	Smithville	16.05	6-30-1940
222	1.21	1.89	1.94	1.95	4.11	4.00	2.38	2.76	2.91	2.71	1.66	1.43	28.95	Lake Kemp	6.25	9-1-1986
299	1.96	1.74	2.28	2.55	2.88	3.86	3.39	2.30	3.74	3.45	2.14	1.68	31.97	Chase Field	11.55	7-16-1990
251	2.13	2.59	3.19	2.59	4.51	4.23	1.93	2.25	3.70	3.97	2.94	2.75	36.78	Killeen	11.43	9-8-2010
277	1.76	1.79	2.31	2.10	4.01	4.14	2.74	2.09	3.03	4.11	2.28	1.91	32.27	San Antonio	14.33	10-18-1998
236	2.11	2.04	2.92	2.29	4.16	4.23	2.41	1.90	3.33	4.26	2.88	2.34	34.87	Hye	20.70	9-11-1952
226	0.66	0.77	1.06	1.44	2.68	2.62	1.73	2.30	2.32	1.78	0.97	0.73	19.06	Gail	10.79	9-20-2014
243	2.16	2.42	3.50	2.81	4.16	4.58	1.76	2.04	3.28	3.98	2.75	2.75	36.19	Kopperl	11.87	6-23-2014
249	3.90	4.32	4.65	4.16	5.13	4.79	3.78	2.17	3.59	5.25	4.99	5.23	51.96	New Boston	8.15	5-10-2009
338	4.12	2.79	3.08	2.80	3.30	4.91	4.68	4.02	6.73	4.81	4.83	3.50	49.57	Alvin	25.75	7-26-1979
278	3.24	2.85	3.17	2.66	4.33	4.45	2.14	2.68	3.18	4.91	3.22	3.23	40.06	College Station	13.39	10-16-1994
216	0.54	0.57	0.46	0.60	1.48	2.62	2.74	2.93	2.60	1.40	0.47	0.59	17.00	O2 Ranch	7.80	8-6-1920
197	0.72	0.82	1.32	1.60	2.86	4.15	2.34	2.78	2.18	1.87	0.92	0.85	22.41	Quitaque	8.58	6-1-1957
285	1.13	1.53	1.14	1.46	3.10	2.85	3.08	2.49	4.07	3.23	1.12	1.27	26.47	Falfurrias	10.00	9-20-1967
233	1.35	2.38	2.68	2.31	3.75	4.49	2.01	2.24	2.93	3.07	1.68	1.54	30.43	Winchell	8.20	9-23-1955
238	2.98	2.91	3.05	2.73	3.96	4.35	1.89	2.50	3.19	4.47	3.53	3.11	38.67	Somerville Dam	15.25	10-17-1994
262	1.84	2.03	2.98	2.15	4.03	4.25	2.04	1.82	3.10	3.40	2.76	2.01	32.41	Marble Falls	11.00	9-10-1921
263	2.30	2.30	2.56	2.66	4.30	4.28	2.04	2.14	3.34	4.56	2.89	2.56	35.93	Lockhart	13.38	10-18-1998
323	3.90	1.88	2.09	1.39	2.94	3.87	5.32	1.84	3.47	3.13	2.52	3.58	35.93	Point Comfort	14.65	6-26-1960
225	1.10	1.78	2.35	1.77	3.32	4.01	2.12	2.05	2.58	3.06	1.93	1.35	27.42	Baird	10.29	8-3-1978
365	1.27	1.08	1.23	1.54	2.64	2.57	2.04	2.44	5.92	3.74	1.82	1.15	27.44	San Benito	12.67	9-5-1933
259	3.24	3.85	4.55	3.56	4.75	4.16	3.29	2.72	3.22	4.58	4.45	4.42	46.79	Pittsburg	8.11	4-27-1958
196	0.61	0.61	1.35	1.68	2.74	3.53	2.57	2.94	2.19	1.87	0.93	0.76	21.78	Panhandle	8.05	5-16-1951

County, Town or Landmark Closest to Station for Normals	Mean Max. July	No. At or Above 100°	Mean Min. January	No. At or Below 32°	Record Highest	Record High Date	Record Lowest	Record Low Date	Last in Spring		First in Fall	
	F.	Days	F.	Days	F.	M-D-Y	F.	M-D-Y	Mo.	Day	Mo.	Day
Cass, Wright Patman Dam	90.9	4	37.1	44	*111	8-5-2011	–1	12-23-1989	Mar.	5	Nov.	21
Castro, Dimmitt	90.6	4	23.5	131	111	7-4-1983	–11	12-25-2004	Apr.	23	Oct.	20
Chambers, Anahuac	90.3	1	44.8	11	106	7-9-1939	8	12-23-1989	Feb.	15	Dec.	7
Cherokee, Rusk	89.8	3	39.2	27	*111	8-20-1925	*–5	2-13-1899	Mar.	11	Nov.	24
Childress, Childress	94.3	20	28.8	76	*117	6-26-2011	–13	1-17-1930	Apr.	1	Nov.	7
Clay, Henrietta	94.7	23	30.8	70	*116	8-7-1951	*–8	12-24-1989	Mar.	27	Nov.	9
Cochran, Morton	92.2	6	25.8	102	111	6-26-2011	–12	1-13-1963	Apr.	8	Oct.	31
Coke, Robert Lee	94.4	27	31.9	63	114	5-25-2000	–2	12-24-1989	Mar.	31	Nov.	6
Coleman, Coleman	95.4	20	36.4	42	114	8-3-1943	–9	12-23-1989	Mar.	19	Nov.	17
Collin, McKinney	93.1	3	35.5	45	115	8-4-2001	–11	12-23-1989	Mar.	28	Nov.	7
Collingsworth, Wellington	96.9	30	29.7	79	117	6-26-2011	–6	12-23-1989	Apr.	1	Nov.	5
Colorado, Columbus	95.7	15	40.7	30	116	9-4-2000	*4	12-24-1989	Feb.	25	Dec.	2
Comal, Canyon Dam	93.6	4	41.6	18	*112	8-4-2011	*2	12-23-1989	Mar.	1	Dec.	3
Comanche, Proctor Reservoir	95.1	19	36.2	56	113	8-3-2000	–8	12-23-1989	Mar.	20	Nov.	14
Concho, Paint Rock	95.1	17	32.1	61	*111	5-29-2011	–8	2-2-1985	Apr.	1	Nov.	5
Cooke, Gainesville	92.1	14	33.8	50	114	8-10-1936	–12	2-12-1899	Mar.	20	Nov.	17
Coryell, Gatesville	94.1	8	37.1	43	*112	9-5-2000	–6	1-31-1949	Mar.	29	Nov.	6
Cottle, Paducah	95.5	31	29.0	71	*118	6-27-2011	*–7	12-24-1989	Mar.	27	Nov.	8
Crane, Crane	95.1	7	33.6	49	115	6-27-1994	–6	2-2-1985	Mar.	24	Nov.	11
Crockett, Ozona	93.7	8	31.9	67	113	8-3-2015	–8	2-2-1951	Mar.	29	Nov.	7
Crosby, Crosbyton	91.5	8	27.6	89	113	6-28-1994	–14	2-12-1899	Apr.	4	Nov.	3
Culberson, Van Horn	93.1	8	31.6	70	112	6-25-1969	–14	2-3-2011	Mar.	31	Nov.	7
Dallam, Dalhart (6 mi. SW)	91.6	2	22.4	131	110	6-26-2011	–21	1-4-1959	Apr.	28	Oct.	12
Dallas, Dallas Love Field	95.5	17	39.9	23	115	8-18-1909	–10	2-12-1899	Mar.	4	Nov.	30
Dawson, Lamesa	93.3	10	27.6	93	114	6-28-1994	–12	2-8-1933	Apr.	3	Nov.	5
Deaf Smith, Hereford	91.1	4	23.9	118	111	6-8-1910	–17	2-1-1951	Apr.	14	Oct.	26
Delta, Cooper Dam	92.5		36.1	45	110		–1		Mar.	25	Nov.	13
Denton, Denton	94.3	15	35.9	38	*113	7-25-1954	–3	1-31-1949	Mar.	19	Nov.	17
DeWitt, Cuero	96.4	20	43.7	21	114	8-29-2011	2	1-31-1949	Mar.	13	Nov.	18
Dickens, Spur	93.5	17	28.0	89	117	6-28-1994	*–17	2-8-1933	Apr.	4	Nov.	4
Dimmit, Carrizo Springs	98.9	40	39.4	25	*114	6-11-1942	8	12-24-1989	Feb.	22	Dec.	3
Donley, Clarendon	92.8	17	25.3	105	117	8-12-1936	*–13	1-19-1984	Apr.	10	Oct.	26
Duval, Freer	96.8	32	45.5	9	116	6-15-1998	*12	1-24-1963	Feb.	13	Dec.	8
Eastland, Eastland	94.4	13	31.6	68	*115	8-11-1936	–8	12-24-1989	Mar.	31	Nov.	5
Ector, Penwell	93.6	20	33.9	44	116	6-28-1994	–12	2-2-1985	Mar.	31	Nov.	7
Edwards, Rocksprings	90.1	1	38.8	31	110	6-9-1988	0	12-22-1929	Mar.	16	Nov.	22
Ellis, Waxahachie	92.5	7	33.3	59	115	8-18-1909	–9	2-12-1899	Mar.	19	Nov.	17
El Paso, El Paso Intl. Airport	93.5	14	35.8	33	*115	8-18-2002	*–13	2-5-2011	Mar.	17	Nov.	14
Erath, Stephenville	96.0	11	32.9	54	114	8-11-1936	–9	2-12-1899	Mar.	27	Nov.	11
Falls, Marlin	93.6	8	35.3	38	*112	8-11-1969	*–7	1-31-1949	Mar.	16	Nov.	15
Fannin, Bonham	92.1	6	34.5	55	115	8-10-1936	–5	1-19-1930	Mar.	26	Nov.	8
Fayette, La Grange	95.4	15	41.8	19	111	8-23-1917	3	12-23-1989	Mar.	8	Nov.	23
Fisher, Rotan	94.4	13	35.4	55	116	6-27-1994	–12	2-12-1899	Mar.	30	Nov.	8
Floyd, Floydada	91.0	7	26.8	97	111	6-28-1994	–9	1-13-1963	Apr.	5	Nov.	3
Foard, Truscott	95.6	29	31.0	66	114		–7		Mar.	28	Nov.	9
Fort Bend, Sugar Land	93.4	7	45.3	7	*108	8-27-2011	8	12-23-1989	Feb.	6	Dec.	16
Franklin, Mount Vernon	93.0	6	36.0	41	112	8-3-2011	*–5	12-23-1989	Mar.	24	Nov.	12
Freestone, Fairfield	92.5	9	37.9	32	*110	9-4-2000	–2	12-23-1989	Mar.	19	Nov.	17
Frio, Dilley	96.7	27	43.4	10	113	9-6-2000	7	12-23-1989	Feb.	18	Dec.	6
Gaines, Seminole	93.4	11	29.1	82	114	6-28-1994	*–23	2-8-1933	Mar.	31	Nov.	7
Galveston, Galveston	89.4	0	49.9	3	106	9-4-2000	7	2-12-1899	Feb.	3	Dec.	28
Garza, Lake Alan Henry	93.6	9	31.6	65	116	6-28-1994	–1	12-22-1989	Mar.	28	Nov.	11
Gillespie, Fredericksburg	92.6	4	36.2	42	*109	9-5-2000	–5	1-31-1949	Mar.	26	Nov.	4
Glasscock, Garden City	93.7	6	30.6	73	114	6-27-1994	*–3	12-22-1989	Mar.	31	Nov.	5
Goliad, Goliad	94.1	7	45.0	13	*112	6-14-1998	7	1-12-1962	Mar.	2	Nov.	26

Growing Season	Mean Precipitation													Record Rainfall Highest Daily Total		
Days	January In.	February In.	March In.	April In.	May In.	June In.	July In.	August In.	September In.	October In.	November In.	December In.	Annual In.	Location	In.	M-D-Y
261	3.75	4.04	4.52	3.79	4.74	4.58	3.29	2.53	3.14	4.92	4.87	5.00	49.17	Linden	8.45	3-28-1989
182	0.62	0.56	1.04	1.05	2.83	3.72	2.21	3.21	2.59	1.86	0.75	0.78	21.22	Hart	5.17	6-11-1965
302	4.47	3.21	3.40	3.59	5.20	6.50	5.45	5.09	6.39	5.06	4.21	4.54	57.11	Anahuac	15.87	8-28-1945
263	4.08	4.35	4.44	3.34	4.36	4.73	3.25	3.07	3.55	5.27	4.57	4.53	49.54	Jacksonville	11.00	11-22-1940
217	0.85	1.16	1.74	2.28	3.95	4.33	2.23	2.50	3.21	2.04	1.18	0.96	26.43	Childress Airport	5.32	10-20-1983
221	1.56	2.17	2.70	2.74	4.57	4.28	1.89	2.59	2.73	3.31	2.01	2.13	32.68	Henrietta	6.07	6-23-1959
199	0.64	0.67	1.11	0.89	2.09	2.50	2.55	2.57	2.35	1.78	0.92	0.86	18.93	Morton	4.69	7-7-1960
226	0.88	1.35	1.41	1.55	2.94	3.11	1.51	2.52	2.55	2.76	1.21	0.96	22.75	Robert Lee	8.40	10-13-1957
249	1.11	2.07	2.45	1.92	3.62	4.43	1.99	2.38	2.57	3.00	1.85	1.35	28.74	Burkett	9.47	7-5-2002
241	2.63	3.17	4.06	3.69	5.72	4.48	2.43	1.90	3.03	4.31	3.85	3.05	42.32	Gunter	11.03	5-13-1982
215	0.79	0.73	1.44	1.86	3.02	3.45	2.25	1.86	2.32	2.45	1.18	0.91	22.26	Wellington	9.50	10-3-1986
255	3.57	2.88	3.18	3.12	4.77	4.98	3.24	2.87	3.06	4.68	4.42	3.16	43.93	New Ulm	12.13	4-18-2016
276	2.24	2.10	2.91	2.48	4.20	5.14	2.93	2.24	3.39	4.30	3.22	2.29	37.44	New Braunfels	18.35	10-18-1998
249	1.38	2.23	2.70	2.42	4.36	4.90	1.89	2.46	3.02	3.27	2.13	1.62	32.38	Comanche	8.86	8-19-2004
222	1.00	1.64	1.92	1.33	3.26	3.92	1.98	2.13	2.31	2.68	1.60	1.19	24.96	Paint Rock	8.25	9-9-1980
242	1.96	2.70	3.63	3.87	5.34	5.69	2.58	2.39	4.02	4.64	2.98	2.90	42.70	Gainesville	10.07	7-2-1903
236	0.00	0.00	0.00	0.00	0.00	0.00	0.00	0.00	0.00	0.00	0.00	0.00	0.00	Gatesville	8.67	9-8-2010
223	0.88	1.09	1.58	2.17	3.47	4.05	1.96	2.05	2.73	2.38	1.47	1.11	24.94	Paducah	7.00	6-2-1991
243	0.77	0.69	0.59	0.87	1.47	1.79	1.60	2.17	2.11	1.89	0.81	0.84	15.60	Crane	5.55	8-11-1986
227	0.93	1.04	1.63	1.74	2.20	2.04	1.39	1.97	2.00	2.36	0.90	0.66	18.86	Ozona (22 mi. SE)	8.02	8-18-2007
213	0.82	0.99	1.41	2.05	2.75	3.17	2.36	2.52	2.99	2.22	1.10	0.96	23.34	Crosbyton	5.78	6-30-1913
234	0.45	0.49	0.20	0.32	0.53	1.22	2.37	2.15	1.50	1.31	0.49	0.55	11.58	Pine Springs	9.42	9-12-2014
181	0.52	0.40	1.17	1.08	2.24	2.30	2.79	2.85	1.65	1.47	0.58	0.54	17.59	Bunker Hill	5.25	7-11-1959
272	2.06	2.59	3.49	3.07	4.92	4.11	2.21	1.87	2.84	4.79	2.88	2.74	37.57	Joe Pool Lake	12.05	7-29-2004
212	0.58	0.86	1.11	0.90	2.30	2.96	1.83	1.73	3.19	1.93	0.93	0.82	19.14	Lamesa	6.24	10-10-1985
189	0.72	0.56	1.27	1.01	2.03	3.53	2.17	3.43	2.07	1.68	0.74	0.84	20.05	Hereford	*5.30	8-3-1976
241	3.00	3.61	4.37	3.41	5.11	4.11	3.29	2.46	2.92	4.06	4.35	4.11	44.80	Cooper	8.46	5-13-1982
251	2.06	2.81	3.23	3.25	5.11	3.59	2.39	2.14	3.09	4.96	2.90	2.56	38.09	Isle Du Bois SP	13.00	5-13-1982
270	2.23	1.88	2.64	3.05	4.02	4.58	2.93	2.41	3.33	3.60	2.80	2.20	35.67	Cuero	12.40	6-30-1940
209	0.78	0.95	1.26	1.87	2.95	3.40	2.11	2.52	2.26	2.50	1.15	1.00	22.75	Pitchfork Ranch	7.60	9-18-1996
265	1.10	1.12	1.16	1.59	2.82	2.06	1.96	1.53	2.42	2.12	1.12	0.77	19.77	Carrizo Springs	11.48	10-14-2013
194	0.76	0.81	1.48	2.27	3.31	3.53	2.13	3.02	2.54	2.20	1.02	0.95	24.02	Clarendon	9.25	5-4-2001
304	1.43	1.56	2.26	2.08	3.16	3.68	2.24	2.11	2.49	2.47	1.47	1.04	25.99	Benavides	9.60	9-12-1971
222	1.17	2.05	2.57	1.98	3.45	4.21	1.77	2.43	2.56	3.44	1.74	1.65	29.02	Eastland	7.00	10-13-1957
243	0.53	0.64	0.68	0.65	1.79	1.22	1.55	1.70	1.82	1.63	0.65	0.59	13.45	Pleasant Farms	4.57	8-01-2017
258	0.99	1.16	1.80	1.97	3.37	3.22	2.07	2.74	2.83	3.62	1.58	1.21	26.56	Carta Valley	10.75	8-24-1998
230	0.50	0.54	0.38	0.35	0.47	0.98	2.52	2.46	1.53	1.03	0.52	0.76	12.04	Waxahachie	10.80	9-19-1958
245	2.27	2.93	3.84	3.34	3.99	4.12	2.66	2.34	3.05	4.45	3.03	3.10	39.12	El Paso	6.50	7-9-1881
226	1.45	2.25	2.86	2.52	4.39	4.01	1.56	2.38	3.02	3.11	2.09	1.90	31.54	Huckabay	10.21	4-26-1990
234	2.63	2.78	3.52	2.72	4.76	3.91	2.07	2.57	2.77	4.25	3.15	3.33	38.46	Marlin	11.90	7-31-1903
242	2.69	3.60	4.37	3.87	5.57	5.30	3.15	2.17	3.41	5.06	3.37	3.57	46.13	Bonham	13.30	7-3-1903
267	3.07	3.08	2.99	2.58	4.25	4.16	2.48	2.57	3.61	4.91	3.55	3.21	40.46	La Grange	14.69	8-27-2017
243	0.89	1.59	1.70	1.96	3.68	2.93	2.22	2.44	2.71	2.19	1.33	1.12	24.76	Rotan	6.85	8-13-1972
208	0.61	0.75	1.28	1.65	2.82	3.96	2.11	2.23	2.82	1.73	0.82	0.82	21.60	Floydada	7.75	9-12-2008
227	1.12	1.52	1.78	2.19	4.33	3.63	2.08	2.15	2.85	2.85	1.63	1.10	27.23	Crowell	8.25	9-19-1965
305	3.55	3.07	3.43	3.36	4.30	5.65	3.97	4.43	5.10	5.28	4.84	3.37	50.35	Katy	16.43	8-28-2017
245	2.77	3.62	4.47	3.34	5.13	4.61	3.68	2.43	3.25	5.22	4.57	4.33	47.42	Winfield	10.44	9-15-1913
243	2.96	3.64	3.84	3.12	5.14	4.29	2.08	2.58	3.02	4.37	4.30	3.78	43.12	Fairfield	7.90	1-29-1999
296	1.36	1.33	1.85	1.86	2.85	2.92	2.71	2.01	2.46	3.00	1.46	1.13	24.94	Derby	12.80	5-16-1980
219	0.71	0.84	0.98	0.96	2.46	2.37	2.51	1.85	2.47	1.48	0.91	0.82	18.36	Loop	6.35	10-19-1983
348	3.69	2.99	2.85	2.19	3.01	4.83	3.85	3.35	5.36	4.15	3.42	3.36	43.05	Bacliff	21.62	8-27-2017
225	0.72	1.15	1.34	1.57	2.29	3.00	2.40	2.30	2.16	2.12	1.07	0.77	20.89	Polar	9.00	9-25-1955
235	1.60	2.01	2.45	2.34	3.90	3.80	2.40	2.20	2.91	3.71	2.20	2.01	31.53	Gold	13.80	9-10-1952
215	0.87	0.92	1.18	1.17	2.31	1.82	1.53	1.97	2.48	1.68	0.94	0.70	17.57	Garden City	8.75	7-7-1945
280	2.41	1.98	2.44	2.52	4.06	4.14	3.71	2.94	4.26	3.85	2.56	1.91	36.78	Goliad	12.15	7-16-1990

County, Town or Landmark Closest to Station for Normals	Mean Max. July F.	No. At or Above 100° Days	Mean Min. January F.	No. At or Below 32° Days	Record Highest F.	Record High Date M-D-Y	Record Lowest F.	Record Low Date M-D-Y	Last in Spring Mo.	Day	First in Fall Mo.	Day
Gonzales, Gonzales	93.9	10	41.8	19	*114	8-10-1962	1	1-31-1949	Feb.	28	Dec.	1
Gray, Pampa	90.8	5	24.5	110	113	6-27-2011	−12	1-11-1962	Apr.	14	Oct.	27
Grayson, Sherman	91.1	5	35.7	43	113	8-10-1936	−3	12-23-1989	Mar.	17	Nov.	19
Gregg, Longview	92.7	6	36.1	44	113	8-10-1936	−7	2-12-1899	Mar.	17	Nov.	18
Grimes, Washington St. Park	94.1	17	40.3	31	108	8-11-1969	14	1-7-1970	Mar.	14	Nov.	19
Guadalupe, New Braunfels	92.8	3	39.1	32	112	9-5-2000	0	1-30-1949	Mar.	9	Nov.	25
Hale, Plainview	91.2	4	27.5	92	112	6-27-2011	−8	2-8-1933	Apr.	5	Nov.	1
Hall, Memphis	94.3	21	27.0	89	*117	8-3-1944	−11	1-18-1930	Apr.	1	Nov.	4
Hamilton, Hico	93.6	9	33.2	54	113	8-11-1936	−11	1-31-1949	Mar.	31	Nov.	6
Hansford, Spearman	94.2	19	26.2	102	111	8-13-1936	−22	1-4-1959	Apr.	11	Oct.	28
Hardeman, Quanah	94.9	20	28.3	78	*119	6-27-1994	−15	12-23-1989	Apr.	3	Nov.	1
Hardin, Evadale	92.1		41.3	24	110	9-1-2000	15	12-22-2000	Mar.	31	Nov.	14
Harris, Houston Hobby Airport	92.5	1	48.1	4	111	9-4-2000	5	1-18-1930	Feb.	3	Dec.	20
Harrison, Marshall	92.8	5	34.9	39	*112	8-18-1909	*−9	2-12-1899	Mar.	11	Nov.	22
Hartley, Channing	90.2	5	22.8	121	110	9-7-1907	*−20	2-8-1933	Apr.	17	Oct.	24
Haskell, Haskell	93.8	15	30.8	63	115	6-27-1994	*−6	12-23-1989	Mar.	28	Nov.	9
Hays, Dripping Springs	93.5	6	40.8	29	111	9-5-2000	−2	1-31-1949	Mar.	19	Nov.	17
Hemphill, Canadian	92.3	10	19.1	136	*112	6-26-1994	−14	1-5-1942	Apr.	16	Oct.	20
Henderson, Athens	93.1	5	36.5	41	*109	9-5-2000	−6	2-2-1985	Mar.	19	Nov.	14
Hidalgo, McAllen Intl. Airport	98.5	26	54.6	1	113	6-16-1998	10	1-12-1962	Jan.	13	Dec.	31
Hill, Hillsboro	94.9	10	35.9	37	113	7-10-1917	−6	12-23-1989	Mar.	23	Nov.	13
Hockley, Levelland	91.4	7	26.7	98	115	6-28-1994	−16	1-13-1963	Apr.	4	Nov.	3
Hood, Cresson	94.7		33.1	58	*111	8-10-1947	−6	1-31-1949	Mar.	26	Nov.	13
Hopkins, Sulphur Springs	93.0	5	36.0	49	*115	8-10-1969	−10	2-12-1899	Mar.	21	Nov.	13
Houston, Crockett	93.6	9	38.0	31	114	8-18-1909	0	2-1-1951	Mar.	9	Nov.	24
Howard, Big Spring	94.8	14	32.9	54	114	6-28-1994	−7	1-11-1962	Mar.	22	Nov.	16
Hudspeth, Sierra Blanca	93.1	7	31.6	70	115	6-28-1994	−10	2-2-1985	Apr.	12	Oct.	29
Hunt, Greenville	96.0	23	35.3	50	116	8-10-1936	*−4	1-18-1930	Mar.	19	Nov.	18
Hutchinson, Borger	93.7	12	27.6	93	116	7-11-2020	−19	1-8-1912	Apr.	13	Oct.	27
Irion, Cope Ranch	95.3	15	29.8	79	*108	6-9-1985	4	2-1-1985	Apr.	8	Oct.	31
Jack, Jacksboro	94.2	13	31.8	56	*113	8-29-2011	−8	12-22-1989	Mar.	25	Nov.	9
Jackson, Point Comfort	91.0	0	47.7	5	107	7-27-1954	8	1-31-1949	Feb.	8	Dec.	16
Jasper, Sam Rayburn Dam	93.2	2	42.9	30	109	9-5-2000	*2	2-2-1951	Mar.	6	Nov.	27
Jeff Davis, Fort Davis	90.2	1	32.4	72	*108	6-27-1994	*−10	1-11-1962	Apr.	8	Oct.	30
Jefferson, Port Arthur / Airport	92.2	1	45.8	8	*108	8-31-2000	4	2-12-1899	Feb.	16	Dec.	8
Jim Hogg, Hebbronville	98.5	25	47.9	8	118	7-9-2009	12	12-23-1989	Feb.	14	Dec.	12
Jim Wells, Alice	96.7	18	49.5	4	*114	7-6-1997	11	12-25-1989	Feb.	5	Dec.	17
Johnson, Cleburne	93.5	15	35.3	41	114	9-2-1939	−6	12-23-1989	Mar.	24	Nov.	11
Jones, Anson	94.5	23	31.2	56	118	6-28-1994	*−12	12-23-1989	Mar.	27	Nov.	11
Karnes, Karnes City	95.2	14	44.2	11	112	7-27-1954	6	2-12-1899	Feb.	24	Dec.	5
Kaufman, Kaufman	93.0	11	35.2	46	113	8-10-1936	−3	12-23-1989	Mar.	20	Nov.	16
Kendall, Boerne	92.1	4	38.4	40	112	8-23-1925	−4	1-31-1949	Mar.	20	Nov.	14
Kenedy, Port Mansfield	97.2	0	45.3	10	110	6-16-1963	14	1-13-1975	Jan.	22	Dec.	30
Kent, Jayton	95.1	16	29.4	82	116	6-28-1994	−6	2-3-1985	Apr.	1	Nov.	6
Kerr, Kerrville	91.0	5	35.8	46	110	7-27-1954	−7	1-31-1949	Mar.	29	Nov.	8
Kimble, Junction / Co. Airport	94.5	12	35.5	52	112	8-2-2011	−11	12-22-1929	Mar.	25	Nov.	7
King, Guthrie	96.2	23	28.8	87	119	6-28-1994	−10	12-23-1989	Apr.	2	Nov.	4
Kinney, Brackettville	93.2	17	37.9	31	111	6-10-1988	4	1-12-1962	Mar.	6	Nov.	27
Kleberg, Kingsville Air Station	95.7	8	48.4	5	115	6-15-1998	10	12-24-1989	Feb.	5	Dec.	13
Knox, Munday	95.8	21	33.1	56	*118	6-20-2011	−11	1-4-1947	Mar.	27	Nov.	9
Lamar, Paris	98.3	20	41.1	25	115	8-10-1936	−13	2-12-1899	Mar.	18	Nov.	17
Lamb, Littlefield	94.4	6	35.4	46	112	6-28-1994	*−14	1-13-1963	Apr.	8	Oct.	31
Lampasas, Lampasas	91.4	17	24.3	109	*112	7-11-1917	−12	1-31-1949	Mar.	22	Nov.	15
La Salle, Fowlerton	94.9	33	35.5	55	*116	9-8-1893	9	1-12-1962	Mar.	3	Nov.	26
Lavaca, Hallettsville	95.7	4	46.4	13	112	8-29-2011	5	12-23-1989	Mar.	2	Nov.	30

Growing Season	Mean Precipitation													Record Rainfall Highest Daily Total		
	January	February	March	April	May	June	July	August	September	October	November	December	Annual	Location		M-D-Y
Days	In.	In.	In.	In.	In.	In.	In.	In.	In.	In.	In.	In.	In.	Location	In.	M-D-Y
272	2.39	2.15	2.44	2.51	4.23	4.17	2.23	2.27	3.07	3.92	2.99	2.54	34.91	Gonzales	16.31	8-31-1981
194	0.70	0.69	1.64	2.04	2.98	3.65	2.71	2.77	2.12	1.95	1.06	0.88	23.19	McLean	7.60	4-3-1997
250	2.47	2.94	3.92	3.55	5.32	5.00	2.62	2.06	3.59	5.29	3.70	3.14	43.60	Van Alstyne	9.30	9-22-2018
244	3.69	4.26	4.28	3.73	4.79	4.44	2.95	2.87	3.46	4.46	4.47	4.69	48.09	Longview	12.03	3-9-2012
259	3.54	2.83	3.52	2.80	3.90	4.76	2.37	2.79	3.36	4.63	3.80	3.38	41.68	Richards	11.98	10-16-1994
253	1.95	1.98	2.58	2.03	3.95	4.78	2.93	2.11	3.04	3.80	2.46	2.36	33.97	Kingsbury	9.25	10-9-2002
209	0.72	0.63	1.16	1.64	2.80	3.20	2.42	2.25	2.17	1.74	0.92	0.80	20.45	Plainview	7.00	7-8-1960
215	0.69	0.94	1.47	2.05	3.07	3.32	2.05	2.56	2.49	1.89	1.12	0.94	22.59	Memphis	8.80	6-7-1960
229	2.00	2.58	3.16	2.63	4.91	4.86	1.97	2.48	3.02	3.44	2.20	2.03	35.28	Hamilton	8.20	10-4-1959
209	0.47	0.63	1.62	1.68	2.50	3.89	2.69	2.62	1.97	1.55	0.83	0.74	21.19	Gruver	9.72	6-13-2010
210	1.00	1.19	1.90	2.13	3.29	3.95	2.42	2.79	2.83	2.56	1.64	1.15	26.85	Quanah	8.03	8-2-1995
281	4.87	4.38	3.30	3.86	4.80	6.63	5.32	4.65	5.02	5.79	6.37	6.07	61.06	Kountze	15.50	8-30-2017
330	3.87	3.21	3.20	3.25	4.75	7.10	4.66	5.06	5.21	5.99	4.32	4.03	54.65	Houston-South	20.84	8-27-2017
233	3.72	4.33	4.49	3.64	4.85	5.18	3.49	2.61	3.32	4.93	4.58	5.04	50.18	Harleton	10.50	3-29-1989
190	2.70	0.61	1.58	0.80	1.91	2.02	2.64	3.85	1.68	1.52	0.79	0.92	21.02	Romero	8.27	5-17-1914
225	1.04	1.75	1.80	2.20	3.43	3.95	1.92	2.20	2.63	2.54	1.48	1.46	26.40	Haskell	14.29	8-4-1978
242	2.36	2.24	3.00	2.20	4.13	5.02	2.09	1.76	3.08	4.08	3.17	2.61	35.74	San Marcos	15.78	10-17-1998
170	0.56	0.74	1.79	1.76	2.91	3.92	2.35	2.68	1.84	1.77	1.02	0.91	22.25	Canadian	7.00	6-8-2008
242	2.98	3.87	4.04	3.21	4.77	4.35	2.11	2.37	2.56	4.96	3.74	3.98	42.94	Payne Springs	11.28	10-25-2015
365	1.05	1.11	1.03	1.34	2.25	2.58	2.00	2.21	4.47	2.08	0.89	1.19	22.20	Santa Rosa	15.49	7-28-2020
235	2.39	2.92	3.78	2.95	4.37	4.34	1.59	2.10	3.03	4.53	2.84	3.09	37.93	Aquilla	11.49	10-24-2015
205	0.72	0.68	1.02	1.02	2.48	2.84	2.17	2.63	2.74	1.68	0.99	0.87	19.84	Ropesville	5.06	9-12-2008
228	0.00	0.00	0.00	0.00	0.00	0.00	0.00	0.00	0.00	0.00	0.00	0.00	0.00	Cresson	11.08	6-4-2000
245	3.07	3.66	4.41	3.83	4.79	4.36	3.38	2.44	2.99	5.39	4.54	4.32	47.18	Cumby	8.64	4-11-2017
251	3.77	3.62	3.66	3.16	4.41	4.64	3.02	3.03	3.02	4.76	4.09	4.00	45.18	Crockett	9.11	6-8-2001
239	0.71	0.90	1.02	1.36	2.41	2.69	1.64	2.55	2.65	1.88	1.09	0.60	19.50	Ackerly	6.40	6-9-1993
234	0.45	0.49	0.20	0.32	0.53	1.22	2.37	2.15	1.50	1.31	0.49	0.55	11.58	Dell City	7.10	9-12-2013
244	2.75	3.44	4.22	3.48	5.52	4.18	3.16	1.88	3.34	5.09	4.01	3.58	44.65	Commerce	12.00	8-13-2017
198	0.71	0.69	1.54	1.79	2.68	3.28	2.68	3.56	2.09	1.94	1.03	0.86	22.85	Borger	6.27	9-22-2004
202	0.79	1.04	1.08	1.14	2.19	2.78	1.76	2.22	2.58	2.06	0.90	0.95	19.50	Mertzon	8.35	8-12-1971
225	1.31	2.19	2.82	2.67	4.80	4.19	1.91	1.54	3.36	3.86	2.29	1.98	32.92	Antelope	11.18	5-16-1989
321	3.06	2.46	3.10	2.30	4.27	4.72	4.06	2.66	4.42	4.78	3.93	2.63	42.39	Maurbro	14.80	6-26-1960
280	5.27	4.70	4.95	3.94	4.50	6.18	3.89	4.01	4.29	5.54	6.33	6.15	59.75	Evadale	14.52	9-18-1963
209	0.48	0.51	0.46	0.67	1.50	2.46	3.26	3.28	2.23	1.45	0.52	0.65	17.47	Jasper	8.05	3-29-2018
301	5.26	3.58	3.53	3.21	5.23	7.09	5.95	5.38	5.97	5.58	4.40	5.29	60.47	Port Arthur Reg AP	26.03	8-29-2017
320	1.25	1.45	1.19	1.46	3.10	2.57	2.67	1.69	3.30	2.36	1.35	1.40	23.79	Kaffie Ranch	21.02	9-12-1971
337	0.00	0.00	0.00	0.00	0.00	0.00	0.00	0.00	0.00	0.00	0.00	0.00	0.00	Alice Intl. Airport	13.21	9-13-1951
240	2.24	2.59	3.64	2.91	4.85	4.27	2.10	2.59	3.15	3.89	2.80	2.58	37.61	Lillian	9.30	5-17-1989
221	1.12	1.55	1.69	2.10	3.32	3.66	2.32	2.42	2.35	2.66	1.51	1.36	26.06	Stamford	8.22	8-4-1978
300	1.63	1.68	2.20	2.20	3.03	3.47	2.97	2.35	3.06	3.33	2.30	1.92	30.14	Cibolo Creek	13.75	9-21-1967
243	2.85	3.03	3.89	2.68	4.50	3.51	2.20	2.50	2.83	5.07	3.56	3.30	39.92	Crandall	10.22	4-19-1976
243	2.08	2.39	2.95	2.26	4.64	4.63	3.27	2.73	3.41	4.38	3.12	2.24	38.10	Kendalia	12.32	5-24-2015
285	1.13	1.53	1.14	1.46	3.10	2.85	3.08	2.49	4.07	3.23	1.12	1.27	26.47	Sarita	9.30	10-12-1973
220	0.96	1.22	1.42	1.83	3.39	3.46	2.40	2.21	2.25	2.36	1.17	0.84	23.51	Jayton	*6.50	7-29-2004
226	1.58	1.81	2.48	2.10	4.00	3.97	2.82	1.69	3.65	3.66	2.43	1.86	32.05	Lynxhaven Ranch	15.20	8-2-1978
229	0.86	1.57	2.41	2.12	3.29	3.61	1.95	2.34	2.76	2.96	1.89	1.22	26.98	Junction	8.56	10-08-2018
213	1.03	1.42	1.53	2.06	3.42	3.66	2.27	2.69	2.58	2.50	1.30	1.07	25.53	Guthrie	8.85	7-4-1986
255	0.73	0.92	1.61	1.56	3.16	2.81	1.92	2.52	3.15	2.88	1.29	1.01	23.56	Fort Clark	18.00	6-15-1899
314	1.55	1.79	1.45	1.64	3.59	3.49	2.46	2.67	5.15	3.39	1.75	1.45	30.38	Ricardo	11.30	6-21-1924
232	1.12	1.67	2.08	2.11	3.49	4.16	1.83	2.24	2.48	2.72	1.33	1.20	26.43	Munday	8.00	6-14-1930
266	1.15	1.16	1.85	1.96	2.95	2.75	2.61	1.83	2.96	2.76	1.44	1.28	24.70	Arthur City	10.50	5-12-1920
247	2.70	3.28	4.44	3.41	5.56	4.17	3.68	2.22	3.84	5.10	4.68	3.99	47.07	Olton	6.30	6-4-1985
192	0.65	0.63	1.08	1.10	2.05	3.08	2.30	2.53	2.20	1.55	0.86	0.84	18.87	Lometa	9.50	10-4-1959
238	1.88	2.23	2.79	2.25	4.20	3.96	2.05	2.28	2.62	3.49	2.31	2.17	32.23	Fowlerton	12.80	9-9-2002
297	3.01	2.50	2.72	3.14	4.66	4.73	2.81	2.80	3.87	4.44	3.74	2.64	41.06	Halletsville	20.60	8-27-2017

County, Town or Landmark Closest to Station for Normals	Mean Max. July	No. At or Above 100°	Mean Min. January	No. At or Below 32°	Record Highest	Record High Date	Record Lowest	Record Low Date	Last in Spring		First in Fall	
	F.	Days	F.	Days	F.	M-D-Y	F.	M-D-Y	Mo.	Day	Mo.	Day
Lee, Lexington	94.2	7	40.5	27	111	9-6-2000	*2	12-23-1989	Mar.	7	Nov.	24
Leon, Centerville	93.1	7	36.9	46	113	8-18-1909	0	2-1-1951	Mar.	21	Nov.	16
Liberty, Liberty	92.9	1	43.0	14	112	8-9-1962	5	12-24-1989	Feb.	24	Dec.	4
Limestone, Mexia	94.6	10	38.0	34	112	8-18-1909	–5	12-23-1989	Mar.	10	Nov.	24
Lipscomb, Lipscomb	92.3	16	19.1	136	*114	6-27-2011	–19	1-19-1984	Apr.	23	Oct.	14
Live Oak, Choke Canyon Dam	95.0	20	44.7	9	112	9-6-2000	11	12-26-1983	Feb.	17	Dec.	9
Llano, Llano	95.3	34	35.9	50	115	7-14-1933	–7	12-22-1929	Mar.	24	Nov.	10
Loving, Red Bluff Dam	97.7	52	31.5	69	*112	7-30-1944	0	1-5-1947	Mar.	29	Nov.	9
Lubbock, Lubbock	92.4	7	28.7	84	114	6-27-1994	–17	2-8-1933	Apr.	4	Nov.	2
Lynn, Tahoka	92.2	6	29.8	80	111	6-28-1994	–15	2-8-1933	Apr.	1	Nov.	8
Madison, Madisonville	94.1	9	38.4	35	112	9-5-2000	*–2	1-31-1949	Mar.	17	Nov.	14
Marion, Jefferson	93.0	6	35.5	55	*112	8-5-2011	*–5	12-23-1989	Mar.	21	Nov.	10
Martin, Lenorah	94.8		32.7	54	109		*–8		Apr.	5	Nov.	6
Mason, Mason	94.6	4	35.6	51	110	7-13-2020	*3	2-2-1985	Mar.	27	Nov.	10
Matagorda, Bay City	90.2	1	45.0	7	109	9-4-2000	7	12-23-1989	Feb.	10	Dec.	18
Maverick, Eagle Pass	97.4	42	41.0	13	*115	7-25-1944	2	2-12-1899	Feb.	14	Dec.	8
McCulloch, Brady	92.3	11	37.0	43	110	6-29-1980	*–2	1-18-1930	Mar.	26	Nov.	11
McLennan, Waco Reg. Airport	95.5	17	37.9	34	*114	7-23-2018	*–7	1-31-1949	Mar.	13	Nov.	21
McMullen, Tilden	97.2	26	45.3	12	119	7-2-1910	5	12-22-1989	Feb.	16	Dec.	6
Medina, Hondo Muni. Airport	96.1	12	40.7	25	*112	9-5-2000	4	2-1-1949	Mar.	6	Nov.	24
Menard, Menard	93.8	6	31.2	64	114	5-29-1927	–6	1-9-1879	Apr.	9	Oct.	30
Midland, Midland	95.2	15	34.3	58	*116	6-27-1994	*–12	1-11-1962	Mar.	29	Nov.	10
Milam, Cameron	93.1	0	41.0	28	114	7-10-1917	–7	1-17-1930	Mar.	25	Nov.	10
Mills, Goldthwaite	91.8	2	35.3	37	110	8-6-1964	–7	12-23-1989	Mar.	21	Nov.	13
Mitchell, Lake Colorado City	93.1	12	32.7	57	115	6-30-1907	*–7	1-4-1947	Mar.	25	Nov.	15
Montague, Bowie	92.0	9	32.0	64	115	6-28-1980	–12	2-12-1899	Mar.	30	Nov.	9
Montgomery, Conroe	94.4	5	43.8	17	113	9-4-2000	2	2-12-1899	Feb.	28	Dec.	1
Moore, Dumas	90.5	5	23.1	124	*109	6-28-1980	–18	1-5-1959	Apr.	17	Oct.	24
Morris, Daingerfield	91.4	9	36.8	34	112	8-4-1998	4	1-10-1962	Mar.	8	Nov.	23
Motley, Matador	91.9	13	29.6	72	116	6-28-1994	*–5	12-23-1989	Apr.	1	Nov.	7
Nacogdoches, Nacogdoches	91.7	7	37.9	41	*113	9-3-2000	–4	1-18-1930	Mar.	19	Nov.	16
Navarro, Corsicana	93.5	10	36.8	38	*113	7-26-1954	–7	2-12-1899	Mar.	13	Nov.	21
Newton, Toledo Bend Dam	92.9	4	39.0	39	110	6-5-2011	4	1-19-1930	Mar.	14	Nov.	20
Nolan, Roscoe	93.1	11	32.7	57	113	6-27-1994	–11	1-5-1947	Apr.	2	Nov.	6
Nueces, Corpus Christi	93.4	2	49.9	4	113	8-31-1983	*7	2-12-1899	Feb.	2	Dec.	19
Ochiltree, Perryton	93.2	9	24.9	131	*113	6-10-1981	–17	1-7-1988	Apr.	25	Oct.	18
Oldham, Vega	89.4	3	22.1	128	110	7-27-1982	*–17	2-1-1951	Apr.	22	Oct.	19
Orange, Orange	89.4	1	42.1	19	107	9-1-2000	10	12-25-1989	Feb.	28	Nov.	26
Palo Pinto, Mineral Wells	94.6	16	34.8	48	115	8-14-1999	–8	12-23-1989	Mar.	23	Nov.	11
Panola, Carthage	91.6	5	37.9	39	109	9-5-2000	1	12-24-1989	Mar.	14	Nov.	19
Parker, Weatherford	93.1	8	33.7	61	119	6-26-1980	*–11	2-12-1899	Mar.	31	Nov.	5
Parmer, Friona	90.2	3	23.7	118	109	6-19-2017	–15	1-13-1963	Apr.	20	Oct.	23
Pecos, Fort Stockton	94.4	15	37.3	40	117	6-29-1994	–7	1-3-1911	Mar.	17	Nov.	18
Polk, Livingston	93.9	5	41.7	36	116	8-3-2016	*3	12-24-1989	Mar.	4	Nov.	26
Potter, Amarillo	91.2	5	26.0	108	111	6-26-2011	–16	2-12-1899	Apr.	15	Oct.	24
Presidio, Presidio	101.4	73	36.4	25	*117	6-18-1960	–2	1-5-1972	Feb.	27	Nov.	28
Rains, Emory	90.6	4	34.4	54	112	9-5-2000	–5	12-25-1989	Mar.	25	Nov.	10
Randall, Canyon	91.4	4	23.7	107	*109	6-27-2011	–14	2-1-1951	Apr.	16	Oct.	22
Reagan, Big Lake	94.0	9	35.1	56	115	6-28-1994	–9	2-2-1985	Mar.	27	Nov.	10
Real, Camp Wood	93.3	5	36.7	48	*109	9-6-2000	0	11-29-1976	Mar.	22	Nov.	12
Red River, DeKalb	92.1	7	33.3	49	115	8-10-1936	*–7	1-18-1930	Mar.	27	Nov.	7
Reeves, Balmorhea	93.8	15	32.1	65	118	6-29-1968	–14	1-11-1962	Mar.	29	Nov.	10
Refugio, Refugio	93.3	2	46.2	11	112	9-5-2000	8	1-12-1962	Feb.	24	Dec.	5
Roberts, Miami	90.5	7	23.3	116	114	6-11-1917	–15	1-5-1942	Apr.	16	Oct.	21
Robertson, Franklin	94.3	12	41.3	24	112	9-4-2000	–1	12-23-1989	Mar.	8	Nov.	22
Rockwall, Lavon Dam	91.3	10	36.1	44	*109	7-25-1954	4	2-2-1951	Mar.	10	Nov.	24

| Growing Season | Mean Precipitation | | | | | | | | | | | | Record Rainfall Highest Daily Total | | |
Days	January In.	February In.	March In.	April In.	May In.	June In.	July In.	August In.	September In.	October In.	November In.	December In.	Annual In.	Location	In.	M-D-Y
262	2.58	2.43	2.84	2.05	4.20	3.74	2.11	2.17	2.98	5.04	3.52	2.95	36.61	Fedor	13.00	10-17-1994
239	3.16	3.45	3.82	2.73	4.61	4.18	2.49	2.65	2.79	4.96	3.80	3.65	42.29	Buffalo	9.19	10-14-1957
286	4.42	4.18	3.90	3.88	5.58	7.35	5.20	4.24	5.49	6.51	5.25	5.25	61.25	Dayton	25.00	8-27-2017
251	2.46	3.34	3.82	2.91	4.39	3.92	1.93	2.35	3.46	4.35	3.64	3.77	40.34	Mexia	8.63	2-4-1986
170	0.56	0.74	1.79	1.76	2.91	3.92	2.35	2.68	1.84	1.77	1.02	0.91	22.25	Booker	7.76	6-9-1997
302	1.45	1.47	1.88	2.16	2.62	3.16	3.38	1.53	3.07	2.45	1.70	1.49	26.36	Whitsett	15.69	9-22-1967
235	1.43	1.83	2.51	1.92	3.64	3.57	2.00	1.55	2.21	2.97	2.22	1.85	27.70	Moss Ranch	13.53	9-11-1952
239	0.53	0.53	0.48	0.56	1.45	1.98	2.17	2.06	1.96	1.26	0.59	0.63	14.20	Mentone	3.79	9-24-1955
210	0.65	0.75	1.10	1.41	2.30	3.04	1.91	1.91	2.51	1.93	0.85	0.76	19.12	Lubbock	7.81	9-12-2008
220	0.76	0.85	1.07	1.44	2.82	3.16	2.63	2.25	2.28	2.07	1.00	0.88	21.21	Tahoka	9.10	5-5-2015
240	3.86	3.28	3.26	2.82	4.49	4.10	3.84	2.91	3.42	4.84	4.38	3.92	45.12	Madisonville	8.89	10-16-2018
236	3.96	4.45	4.48	3.50	4.61	5.17	2.88	2.25	3.43	5.01	4.51	4.71	48.96	Jefferson	9.10	4-26-1921
226	0.67	0.58	0.69	0.71	2.00	1.56	1.50	2.14	1.99	1.52	0.90	0.54	14.80	Tarzan	6.54	9-20-2014
241	1.13	1.97	2.30	2.16	3.58	4.31	2.47	1.95	2.73	3.12	2.08	1.39	29.19	Mason	7.80	10-16-2018
290	3.86	2.69	3.07	2.98	4.45	5.30	4.78	3.75	5.11	5.06	4.25	3.59	48.89	Matagorda	12.20	5-7-1951
287	0.90	0.96	1.01	1.88	2.55	2.73	2.08	1.46	3.11	2.07	0.95	0.71	20.41	Eagle Pass	15.60	6-29-1936
244	1.18	1.81	2.24	1.94	3.61	3.40	2.23	2.21	2.83	2.75	1.84	1.56	27.60	Brady	9.13	7-8-2015
245	2.12	2.63	3.15	2.69	4.30	3.43	1.79	2.05	3.06	3.90	2.82	2.75	34.69	McGregor	13.08	6-16-1964
299	1.11	1.30	1.64	2.05	3.15	3.24	1.74	1.95	3.16	2.11	1.24	1.30	23.99	Calliham	12.00	4-17-2010
263	1.38	1.49	2.13	1.98	3.38	3.49	2.09	1.67	2.60	3.31	1.58	1.14	26.24	Natalia	11.47	9-27-1973
204	1.17	1.52	2.01	1.47	2.97	3.17	1.86	1.90	2.10	2.43	1.56	1.16	23.32	Callan	7.67	10-10-1961
239	0.56	0.71	0.60	0.65	1.74	1.80	1.82	1.84	1.86	1.73	0.69	0.60	14.60	Midland	7.20	5-9-1968
261	2.29	2.66	2.74	2.53	4.94	3.69	2.17	2.15	3.44	4.14	3.33	2.89	36.97	Cameron	12.45	9-10-1921
234	1.43	2.34	2.57	2.15	3.87	4.79	1.89	2.16	2.60	3.15	2.05	1.61	30.61	Goldthwaite	7.20	10-5-1969
223	0.98	1.21	1.23	1.62	2.86	3.38	2.17	2.16	2.38	2.45	0.93	1.05	22.42	Colorado City	8.65	4-6-1900
228	1.45	2.44	3.08	2.99	5.00	4.34	1.98	2.07	3.41	4.02	2.21	2.07	35.06	Bonita	12.47	4-30-2009
285	3.85	3.47	3.25	2.91	4.94	5.26	3.07	3.61	3.75	5.73	5.09	3.84	48.77	Roman Forest	18.88	2019-9-19
183	0.62	0.52	1.26	1.28	2.17	2.41	2.43	2.89	1.87	1.37	0.73	0.82	18.37	Sunray	4.49	10-16-1968
259	3.24	3.85	4.55	3.56	4.75	4.16	3.29	2.72	3.22	4.58	4.45	4.42	46.79	Daingerfield	7.50	7-28-2009
213	0.80	0.90	1.49	1.92	2.91	3.67	2.19	2.44	2.90	2.15	1.14	0.92	23.43	Flomot	7.08	7-9-1994
248	4.13	4.42	4.20	3.73	4.38	4.42	3.01	3.25	3.64	4.70	4.56	4.84	49.28	Nacogdoches	14.22	6-28-1902
246	2.64	3.39	3.91	3.02	4.70	3.52	2.25	2.14	2.96	4.50	3.30	3.45	39.78	Corsicana	18.95	10-24-2015
253	4.74	4.94	4.47	3.57	4.62	5.50	4.00	3.11	3.38	5.07	5.53	5.99	54.92	Deweyville	20.60	9-18-1963
223	0.98	1.21	1.23	1.62	2.86	3.38	2.17	2.16	2.38	2.45	0.93	1.05	22.42	Roscoe	8.28	9-9-1980
331	1.54	1.93	1.89	1.84	3.07	3.36	2.79	2.92	4.98	3.64	1.97	1.83	31.76	Port Aransas	13.89	8-22-1999
197	0.47	0.62	1.75	1.82	2.96	3.32	3.12	2.63	1.86	1.83	0.88	0.84	22.10	Perryton	7.11	5-17-1989
182	0.63	0.60	1.36	1.44	2.28	3.58	2.75	3.37	1.99	1.63	0.72	0.79	21.14	Vega	6.07	5-16-1951
273	5.40	4.63	3.67	3.50	5.45	7.32	5.77	5.69	6.23	6.04	4.99	5.52	64.21	Bridge City	23.82	8-30-2017
231	1.45	2.14	3.19	2.38	3.95	4.16	1.99	2.24	2.82	3.73	2.16	1.84	32.05	Gordon	8.20	5-8-1997
255	4.38	4.46	4.22	3.78	4.53	4.73	3.31	2.92	3.64	5.15	4.94	5.37	51.43	Carthage	9.25	4-14-1991
230	1.57	2.82	3.27	2.54	4.59	4.56	2.14	2.07	3.10	4.00	2.95	2.16	35.77	Weatherford	8.57	8-20-2016
182	0.72	0.63	1.20	1.03	2.20	2.65	2.48	3.33	2.40	1.81	0.83	0.86	20.14	Bovina	4.73	7-21-1918
254	0.61	0.59	0.53	0.84	1.40	2.23	1.75	2.29	2.08	1.76	0.53	0.54	15.15	Bakersfield	7.10	4-30-2007
269	4.24	3.92	3.87	3.26	4.88	5.70	3.56	3.34	4.06	4.85	5.15	4.70	51.53	Corrigan	14.69	10-17-1994
195	0.72	0.56	1.39	1.40	2.29	3.16	2.84	2.91	1.92	1.66	0.80	0.71	20.36	Amarillo	5.89	10-08-2018
275	0.51	0.47	0.22	0.28	0.65	1.27	1.66	1.73	1.20	0.94	0.34	0.39	9.66	Bunton Rch	5.50	8-23-1944
238	2.87	3.82	4.60	3.30	4.91	4.20	2.99	2.22	2.97	4.87	3.95	3.77	44.47	Lake Tawakoni	10.05	10-25-2015
192	0.60	0.48	1.12	1.10	2.55	3.33	2.24	3.43	2.13	1.81	0.76	0.60	20.15	Canyon	7.87	8-29-1968
238	0.95	1.11	1.29	1.48	2.19	2.14	2.77	1.96	2.00	1.69	0.91	0.80	19.29	Big Lake	5.87	8-15-2005
248	1.21	1.30	1.96	1.99	2.91	3.40	2.35	2.41	3.22	3.14	2.14	1.35	27.38	Leakey	11.95	9-26-2016
225	3.54	4.19	5.19	4.17	5.67	4.35	4.10	2.70	3.60	6.01	5.33	5.26	54.11	Avery	9.29	12-28-2015
228	0.58	0.00	0.00	0.00	0.00	0.00	0.00	0.00	0.00	0.00	0.00	0.00	0.58	Red Bluff Dam	7.24	6-19-1984
283	2.15	2.39	3.01	2.27	3.17	3.52	3.64	3.15	4.39	4.31	2.82	2.07	36.89	Austwell	15.96	8-26-2017
192	0.91	0.76	2.04	1.97	3.42	3.36	2.33	2.65	2.30	2.30	1.02	1.02	24.08	Miami	5.58	10-10-1985
277	2.92	2.99	3.22	2.58	4.54	3.52	1.84	2.90	3.08	4.71	3.57	3.63	39.50	Bremond	8.49	8-19-2008
254	2.45	2.97	3.67	3.44	5.17	4.47	2.02	1.85	3.17	4.55	3.55	3.22	40.53	Rockwall	7.08	9-22-2018

County, Town or Landmark Closest to Station for Normals	Mean Max. July F.	No. At or Above 100° Days	Mean Min. January F.	No. At or Below 32° Days	Record Highest F.	Record High Date M-D-Y	Record Lowest F.	Record Low Date M-D-Y	Last in Spring Mo.	Day	First in Fall Mo.	Day
Runnels, Ballinger	94.2	11	33.1	52	116	6-30-1907	–6	1-31-1949	Mar.	25	Nov.	10
Rusk, Henderson	93.0	6	37.3	41	*111	9-2-2000	*–1	12-23-1989	Mar.	19	Nov.	18
Sabine, Toledo Bend Dam	92.9	4	39.0	39	114	8-9-1947	6	2-2-1951	Mar.	14	Nov.	20
San Augustine, Broaddus	92.7		37.0	37	112	8-18-1909	7	1-17-2018	Mar.	19	Nov.	12
San Jacinto, Coldspring	94.4	6	43.8	17	110	8-2-1998	3	12-24-1989	Mar.	8	Nov.	27
San Patricio, Sinton	92.8	4	46.9	7	111	9-6-2000	10	12-23-1989	Feb.	9	Dec.	13
San Saba, San Saba	94.1	16	34.8	51	113	8-30-2020	–1	12-23-1989	Mar.	13	Nov.	18
Schleicher, Fort McKavett	92.1	8	34.0	56	*107	6-26-1972	–7	2-2-1985	Mar.	29	Nov.	6
Scurry, Snyder	94.1	10	30.5	71	115	8-12-1936	–11	2-2-1985	Mar.	30	Nov.	10
Shackelford, Albany	93.4	16	33.3	57	115	6-27-1972	–8	1-4-1947	Apr.	1	Nov.	6
Shelby, Center	92.9	10	37.3	42	112	9-2-2000	0	2-2-1951	Mar.	16	Nov.	16
Sherman, Stratford	91.3	4	22.0	137	108	6-24-1953	–20	2-9-1933	Apr.	25	Oct.	17
Smith, Tyler	92.2	4	40.3	29	*110	8-3-2011	–8	2-12-1899	Mar.	14	Nov.	19
Somervell, Glen Rose	94.7	24	33.4	63	115	8-19-1984	–15	12-23-1989	Apr.	8	Oct.	22
Starr, Rio Grande City	98.9	44	47.2	6	*116	6-14-1998	7	2-13-1899	Jan.	30	Dec.	19
Stephens, Breckenridge	94.5	19	30.4	70	114	8-12-1936	–7	12-22-1989	Mar.	29	Nov.	9
Sterling, Sterling City	92.5	8	31.5	72	112	6-27-1994	–13	2-2-1985	Apr.	4	Nov.	2
Stonewall, Aspermont	95.2	29	31.0	73	117	6-28-1994	–10	12-23-1989	Mar.	30	Nov.	8
Sutton, Sonora	95.0	10	32.6	70	109	6-28-1980	–8	2-2-1951	Apr.	4	Nov.	3
Swisher, Tulia	89.7	6	24.2	119	111	6-27-2011	*–23	2-12-1899	Apr.	16	Oct.	23
Tarrant, Benbrook Dam	95.8	16	35.4	43	115	8-18-1909	*–12	2-12-1899	Mar.	16	Nov.	18
Taylor, Abilene Reg. Airport	95.1	10	35.5	48	*111	8-3-1943	–9	1-4-1947	Mar.	24	Nov.	12
Terrell, Sanderson	94.2	7	34.1	49	120	6-14-2008	1	12-22-1989	Mar.	18	Nov.	11
Terry, Brownfield	92.8	7	28.1	89	111	6-28-1994	–8	1-14-1963	Apr.	1	Nov.	6
Throckmorton, Throckmorton	95.2	22	31.4	71	119	8-30-1947	–11	12-23-1989	Mar.	31	Nov.	7
Titus, Mount Pleasant	92.3	6	33.9	61	109	8-5-2011	–12	2-2-1951	Mar.	28	Nov.	7
Tom Green, San Angelo	96.1	15	35.4	49	113	6-30-1907	–6	1-18-1930	Mar.	26	Nov.	11
Travis, Austin-Camp Mabry	95.9	16	43.7	12	112	9-5-2000	*–5	1-31-1949	Feb.	19	Dec.	6
Trinity, Groveton	94.9	5	40.3	26	111	9-4-2000	1	12-23-1989	Mar.	19	Nov.	14
Tyler, Town Bluff Dam	90.6	2	39.9	28	*111	9-4-2000	*2	1-31-1949	Mar.	9	Nov.	24
Upshur, Gilmer	91.1	7	34.0	54	114	8-10-1936	*–4	12-24-1989	Mar.	31	Nov.	7
Upton, McCamey	95.9	18	34.7	46	*113	6-27-1994	*–2	1-11-1962	Mar.	20	Nov.	14
Uvalde, Uvalde	96.1	23	40.7	25	114	6-9-1910	*6	2-3-1951	Mar.	1	Nov.	28
Val Verde, Del Rio Intl. Airport	97.9	25	42.6	12	*114	7-30-1995	*2	2-3-1985	Feb.	19	Dec.	4
Van Zandt, Wills Point	93.2	10	36.7	41	115	8-18-1909	–2	12-24-1989	Mar.	16	Nov.	21
Victoria, Victoria Reg. Airport	94.1	4	45.5	9	*111	9-5-2000	*9	1-18-1930	Feb.	22	Dec.	6
Walker, Huntsville	91.3	4	41.0	17	110	9-4-2000	*–2	2-12-1899	Feb.	28	Dec.	3
Waller, Sealy	94.0	7	43.5	13	107	8-12-1969	13	1-30-1966	Feb.	22	Dec.	5
Ward, Monahans	97.3	33	28.8	74	120	6-28-1994	–9	1-11-1962	Mar.	31	Nov.	7
Washington, Brenham	93.2	8	41.3	18	113	9-5-2000	–2	1-19-1930	Mar.	2	Dec.	1
Webb, Laredo	100.1	54	48.8	5	116	6-17-1998	5	2-12-1899	Feb.	3	Dec.	14
Wharton, Pierce	94.5	2	44.5	11	112	9-5-2000	3	2-12-1899	Feb.	21	Dec.	8
Wheeler, Shamrock	91.9	11	25.3	97	117	7-12-2011	*–13	1-19-1984	Apr.	6	Oct.	29
Wichita, Wichita Falls Airport	95.3	25	31.8	59	117	6-28-1980	–15	1-4-1947	Mar.	28	Nov.	10
Wilbarger, Lake Kemp	95.4	26	30.2	71	119	8-3-1943	–9	12-23-1989	Mar.	21	Nov.	14
Willacy, Raymondville	96.8	18	49.9	3	109	6-6-1916	14	1-13-1962	Jan.	31	Dec.	22
Williamson, Taylor	94.9	9	38.1	28	113	7-11-1917	*–5	1-31-1949	Mar.	7	Nov.	24
Wilson, Floresville	95.7	15	40.9	27	*114	7-6-1984	5	1-21-1985	Mar.	12	Nov.	22
Winkler, County Airport	97.1	32	31.5	65	117	6-27-1994	*–14	1-11-1962	Mar.	31	Nov.	5
Wise, Bridgeport	94.1	13	32.8	61	*115	6-29-1980	*–8	12-23-1989	Apr.	2	Nov.	5
Wood, Mineola	91.9	8	35.3	52	114	6-18-1996	1	12-30-1983	Mar.	29	Nov.	8
Yoakum, Plains	91.9	7	26.2	99	113	6-27-1994	–12	2-1-1951	Apr.	6	Nov.	2
Young, Olney	95.4	22	31.8	56	*120	6-3-1998	–8	12-23-1989	Apr.	1	Nov.	6
Zapata, Zapata	98.5	39	48.6	4	116	6-16-1998	13	1-4-1911	Jan.	27	Dec.	23
Zavala, Crystal City	97.6	29	45.9	8	115	9-5-2000	6	1-12-1962	Feb.	13	Dec.	7

Growing Season	Mean Precipitation												Record Rainfall Highest Daily Total		
	January	February	March	April	May	June	July	August	September	October	November	December	Annual	Location	Highest Daily Total	M-D-Y
Days	In.	In.	In.	In.	In.	In.	In.	In.	In.	In.	In.	In.	In.	Location	In.	M-D-Y
233	0.99	0.00	0.00	0.00	0.00	0.00	0.00	0.00	0.00	0.00	0.00	0.00	0.99	Wingate	7.68	6-19-1982
247	3.68	4.22	4.40	3.65	4.70	5.22	3.06	2.86	3.48	4.78	4.78	4.47	49.36	Henderson	11.05	3-29-1989
253	4.74	4.94	4.47	3.57	4.62	5.50	4.00	3.11	3.38	5.07	5.53	5.99	54.92	Hemphill	11.70	3-10-2018
240	4.47	4.96	4.50	3.69	5.25	5.32	3.39	3.59	4.07	4.87	5.02	5.44	54.57	San Augustine	10.60	8-18-1915
285	3.85	3.47	3.25	2.91	4.94	5.26	3.07	3.61	3.75	5.73	5.09	3.84	48.77	Oakhurst	16.50	8-28-2017
324	1.75	2.15	2.25	1.85	3.26	3.28	3.52	2.36	5.29	4.75	2.27	1.55	34.28	Welder Wildlife	14.40	9-13-1974
239	1.38	1.97	2.60	2.11	3.62	4.55	1.99	2.47	2.51	3.03	2.04	1.71	29.98	San Saba	11.20	10-5-1969
234	0.86	1.51	1.68	1.54	2.90	3.06	2.06	2.34	2.01	2.83	1.50	0.92	23.21	D. Wilson Ranch	9.51	7-16-1990
227	0.82	1.14	1.55	1.74	2.96	3.37	2.22	2.28	2.28	2.22	1.06	1.04	22.68	Knapp	5.93	5-15-1980
225	1.12	1.92	2.35	2.47	3.64	4.07	2.11	2.01	2.40	3.00	1.70	1.57	28.36	Albany	29.05	8-4-1978
248	4.45	4.95	4.60	4.16	4.47	5.30	3.31	3.52	3.65	5.32	5.04	5.43	54.20	Neuville	10.20	10-30-1941
181	0.54	0.45	1.27	1.26	2.41	2.37	2.25	2.75	1.74	1.35	0.70	0.68	17.77	Stratford	5.60	8-17-1992
257	3.42	4.12	4.19	3.10	4.41	5.15	2.75	2.66	3.05	4.91	4.38	4.49	46.63	Eads	8.24	6-7-1943
225	1.71	2.26	2.95	2.58	4.28	4.09	1.56	2.57	2.88	3.15	2.18	1.97	32.18	Glen Rose	10.73	6-22-2014
321	1.00	1.25	0.89	1.14	2.22	3.07	2.26	1.89	4.46	2.48	1.14	0.85	22.65	Rio Grande City	12.51	9-22-1967
213	1.44	1.89	2.58	2.12	4.01	4.09	2.23	2.36	2.65	3.48	1.56	1.57	29.98	Breckenridge	15.70	10-13-1981
219	0.89	1.12	1.21	1.33	2.59	2.37	1.72	2.57	2.48	2.20	0.98	1.00	20.46	Case Ranch	6.79	9-21-1972
223	1.00	1.36	1.64	1.88	3.22	3.56	1.86	2.75	2.10	2.16	1.14	1.10	23.77	Aspermont	6.92	4-28-1930
221	0.97	1.31	1.57	1.71	2.60	2.59	1.92	2.62	2.96	2.54	1.30	0.94	23.03	Humble Pump Stn	8.60	7-11-1988
189	0.77	0.75	1.38	1.54	2.79	3.32	2.26	2.91	2.13	1.95	0.95	0.82	21.57	Tulia	6.01	10-21-1918
245	1.90	2.42	3.33	2.86	4.69	3.98	1.91	2.16	3.26	3.98	2.66	2.35	35.50	Arlington	9.70	5-17-1949
236	1.02	1.36	1.74	1.64	3.18	3.56	1.87	2.59	2.24	2.98	1.41	1.23	24.82	Lawn	9.19	8-4-1978
243	0.55	0.65	0.65	0.73	1.68	2.25	2.04	1.60	1.70	1.74	0.63	0.50	14.72	Dryden	6.30	9-23-1990
215	0.68	0.75	1.03	1.18	2.75	3.01	2.41	1.95	2.38	1.77	0.90	0.77	19.58	Brownfield	7.85	9-21-1936
223	1.20	1.93	2.26	2.18	4.49	3.99	2.22	2.12	2.71	3.38	1.70	1.60	29.78	Throckmorton	6.53	8-4-1978
230	3.17	4.12	4.30	3.49	5.54	4.63	3.51	2.21	3.03	5.09	4.19	4.42	47.70	Mount Pleasant	8.06	11-5-1994
232	0.93	1.35	1.50	1.42	2.82	2.59	1.20	2.26	2.46	2.73	1.14	0.85	21.25	Mathis Field	11.75	9-15-1936
291	2.22	2.02	2.76	2.09	4.44	4.33	1.88	2.35	2.99	3.88	2.96	2.40	34.32	Hill's Ranch	16.02	9-10-1921
267	3.90	3.71	3.96	2.82	4.81	5.23	3.16	3.20	3.81	5.57	4.90	4.24	49.31	Groveton	12.10	10-17-1994
258	4.57	4.58	4.12	3.89	4.94	5.97	3.85	3.90	4.66	4.85	5.29	5.56	56.18	Spurger	11.50	8-30-2017
229	3.46	4.16	4.37	3.38	4.55	3.90	3.08	2.79	3.40	4.98	4.31	4.46	46.84	Gilmer	7.88	4-23-1966
247	0.68	0.64	0.48	1.02	1.31	2.11	1.32	2.14	1.85	2.23	0.70	0.66	15.14	McCamey	9.13	10-4-1986
263	1.38	1.49	2.13	1.98	3.38	3.49	2.09	1.67	2.60	3.31	1.58	1.14	26.24	Montell	20.05	6-29-1913
293	0.72	0.88	1.14	1.65	2.81	2.35	1.78	2.18	2.20	2.23	0.93	0.65	19.52	Del Rio Intl. AP	17.03	8-23-1998
252	3.18	3.58	4.30	3.01	4.73	4.47	2.19	2.25	3.23	4.96	4.41	3.84	44.15	S. County Line	11.55	10-24-2015
291	2.52	2.08	2.77	2.82	5.19	4.46	4.18	2.85	4.16	4.64	3.24	2.31	41.22	Inez	10.45	8-26-2017
272	4.25	3.33	3.70	3.26	4.45	5.45	2.80	3.67	4.16	4.68	5.19	4.14	49.08	Huntsville	14.75	8-28-2017
276	3.25	2.72	2.84	3.56	4.57	3.62	2.65	3.56	3.91	4.84	4.51	2.89	42.92	Brookshire	16.75	8-28-2017
216	0.58	0.70	0.59	0.64	1.44	1.37	1.94	1.68	2.16	1.66	0.60	0.79	14.15	Grandfalls	5.87	9-4-1986
273	3.46	3.09	3.42	2.89	4.66	4.88	2.56	2.93	4.46	5.09	4.28	3.42	45.14	Brenham	21.46	5-27-2016
329	0.90	0.94	1.12	1.42	2.49	2.23	2.01	1.88	2.93	2.21	1.19	0.88	20.20	Laredo	9.70	5-10-1972
287	3.16	2.68	3.52	2.92	4.52	4.70	4.67	4.30	4.75	4.98	5.20	3.47	48.87	New Gulf	14.00	6-26-1960
202	0.76	0.88	1.96	2.13	3.56	3.99	2.25	2.45	2.59	2.27	1.35	0.97	25.16	Shamrock	8.24	6-4-1995
228	1.14	1.75	2.20	2.61	3.79	4.15	1.59	2.50	2.81	3.11	1.65	1.62	28.92	Wichita V. Farm	8.00	8-15-1971
225	1.17	1.40	2.21	2.25	3.34	4.24	2.09	2.43	3.15	2.79	1.66	1.21	27.94	Vernon	14.82	8-2-1995
340	1.14	1.55	1.24	1.46	3.03	2.31	2.27	2.31	5.51	3.12	0.99	1.15	26.08	Port Mansfield	14.50	7-26-2020
259	2.18	2.54	3.12	2.73	4.38	4.66	2.07	2.19	3.75	4.19	3.00	2.51	37.32	Taylor	16.11	9-10-1921
261	1.59	1.76	2.01	2.14	3.39	3.05	2.48	2.11	3.08	3.36	2.20	1.90	29.07	Falls City	8.83	9-15-1968
222	0.43	0.56	0.75	0.59	1.62	1.60	1.99	1.49	1.35	1.56	0.59	0.56	13.09	NE of Kermit	3.80	9-20-2014
222	1.55	2.38	3.09	2.88	5.23	4.22	2.04	1.98	3.06	4.01	2.20	2.07	34.71	Boyd	9.15	10-31-1981
235	3.07	3.74	3.99	3.41	4.24	3.86	2.40	1.88	2.94	4.86	4.17	4.46	43.02	Mineola	9.50	10-24-2015
200	0.46	0.70	0.90	0.82	1.89	2.78	2.58	2.32	2.63	1.35	0.84	0.93	18.20	Plains	6.11	7-5-1960
222	1.40	1.86	2.56	2.70	5.00	4.03	2.41	1.98	2.43	3.56	1.89	1.64	31.46	Olney	8.74	7-28-2004
341	0.95	0.99	0.80	1.33	2.50	2.11	2.71	1.50	3.53	1.38	1.22	0.75	19.77	Zapata	6.10	4-14-1966
307	1.06	1.06	1.43	1.52	2.15	2.54	2.25	1.54	2.08	2.08	1.11	0.76	19.58	Crystal City	13.88	10-14-2013

Astronomical Calendar

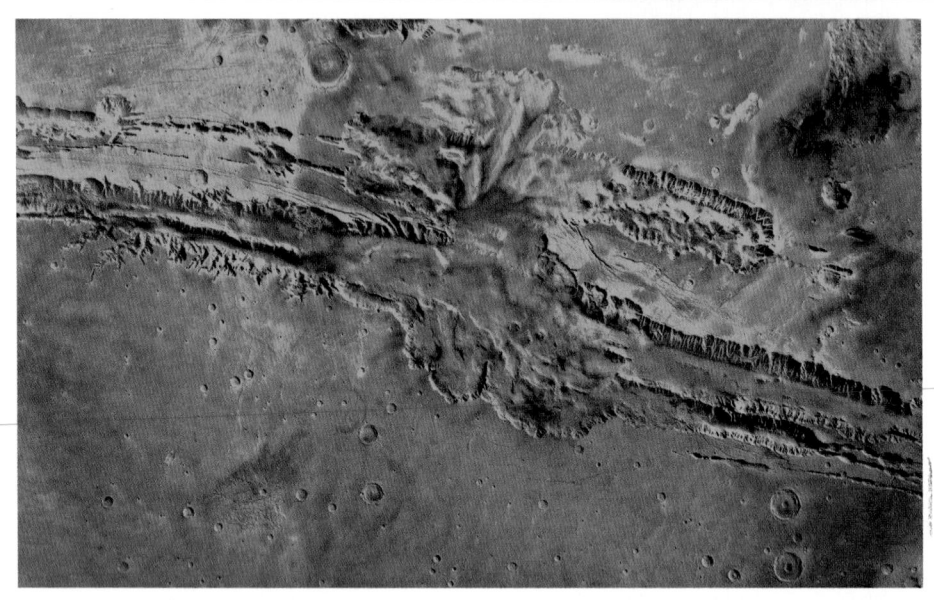

MORNING AND EVENING STARS

SEASONS, ECLIPSES, METEOR SHOWERS

CHRONOLOGIAL ERAS AND CYCLES

CALENDARS FOR 2022 AND 2023

One small section of the Valles Marineris canyon system that runs along the Martian equator. Photo courtesy of NASA/JPL-Caltech.

Astronomical Calendars for 2022 & 2023

Sources: McDonald Observatory; U.S. Naval Observatory's website (https://aa.usno.navy.mil/index.php) and publications, Astronomical Phenomena For The Year 2022 and Astronomical Phenomena For The Year 2023; In-The-Sky.org

The Year 2022

The year 2022 CE comprises the latter part of the 246th and the beginning of the 247th year of the independence of the United States of America. All dates in this book are given in terms of the Gregorian calendar.

The Seasons

Spring begins on Sunday, March 20, at 10:33 a.m. (CDT)

Summer begins on Tuesday, June 21, at 4:13 a.m. (CDT)

Autumn begins on Thursday, Sept. 22, at 8:03 p.m. (CDT)

Winter begins on Wednesday, Dec. 21, at 3:48 p.m. (CST)

Chronological Eras, 2022		
Era	**Year**	**Begins**
Julian	6735	Jan. 14
Byzantine	7531	Sept. 14
Jewish (A.M.)*	5783	Sept. 25
Chinese (rén yín)	—	Feb. 1
Roman (A.U.C.)	2775	Jan. 14
Nabonassar	2771	April 18
Japanese	2682	Jan. 1
Seleucidæ (Grecian)	2334	Sept. 14 or Oct. 14
Saka (Indian)	1944	March 21
Diocletian (Coptic)	1739	Sept. 11
Islamic (Hegira)*	1444	Aug. 19
*Year begins at sunset.		

Chronological Cycles, 2022			
Dominical Letter	B	Golden Number (Lunar Cycle)	IX
Epact	27		
Roman Indiction	15	Solar Cycle	15

Morning & Evening Stars, 2022	
Morning Stars	
Venus ♀	January 15 through September 15
Mars ♂	January 1 through December 8
Jupiter ♃	March 19 through September 26
Saturn ♄	February 22 through August 14
Evening Stars	
Venus ♀	Jan. 1–Jan. 3; Dec. 3–Dec. 8
Mars ♂	December 8 through December 31
Jupiter ♃	Jan. 1–Feb. 20; Sept. 26–Dec. 31
Saturn ♄	Jan. 1–Jan. 19; Aug. 14–Dec. 31

Eclipses 2022

April 30: Solar, partial. Visible in S.E Pacific Ocean, Antarctic Peninsula, Ellsworth Land, and S. South America.

May 16: Lunar, total. Visible in most of Africa, W. Europe, Iceland, Americas except N.W. part, Polynesia except W. part.

Oct. 25: Solar, partial. Visible in Iceland, Europe, N.E. Africa, Middle East, W. Asia, India, W. China.

Nov. 8: Lunar, total. Visible in N.W. South America, North America, Pacific Ocean, Australasia, S.E. Asia, Japan, China, E. Russia.

The Year 2023

The year 2023 CE comprises the latter part of the 247th and the beginning of the 248th year of the independence of the United States of America.

The Seasons

Spring begins on Monday, March 20, at 4:24 p.m. (CDT)

Summer begins on Wednesday, June 21, at 9:57 a.m. (CDT)

Autumn begins on Friday, Sept. 22, at 1:50 a.m. (CDT)

Winter begins on Thursday, Dec. 21, at 9:27 p.m. (CST)

Chronological Eras, 2023		
Era	**Year**	**Begins**
Julian	6736	Jan. 14
Byzantine	7532	Sept. 14
Jewish (A.M.)*	5784	Sept. 6
Chinese (gui mao)	—	Jan. 22
Roman (A.U.C.)	2776	Jan. 14
Nabonassar	2772	April 18
Japanese	2683	Jan. 1
Seleucidæ (Grecian)	2335	Sept. 14 or Oct. 14
Saka (Indian)	1945	March 22
Diocletian (Coptic)	1740	Sept. 12
Islamic (Hegira)*	1445	July 18
*Year begins at sunset.		

Chronological Cycles, 2023			
Dominical Letter	A	Golden Number (Lunar Cycle)	X
Epact	8		
Roman Indiction	1	Solar Cycle	16

Morning & Evening Stars, 2023	
Morning Stars	
Venus ♀	August 18 through December 31
Jupiter ♃	April 26 through November 3
Saturn ♄	March 6 through August 27
Evening Stars	
Venus ♀	January 1 through August 8
Mars ♂	January 1 through September 30
Jupiter ♃	Jan. 1–March 29, Nov. 3–Dec. 31
Saturn ♄	Jan. 1–Jan. 30, Aug. 27–Dec. 31

Eclipses 2023

April 20: Solar, annular-total. Visible to Southern Indian Ocean, parts of Antarctica, most of Australasia, Indonesia, Philippines, most of Oceania, Western Pacific Ocean.

May 5: Lunar, penumbral. Visible to Antarctica, Oceania, Australasia, Asia, Europe (except British Isles and Norway), Africa, S. Georgia, and S. Sandwich Island.

Texas Times

See text for explanation of how to calculate sunrise, sunset, moonrise and moonset

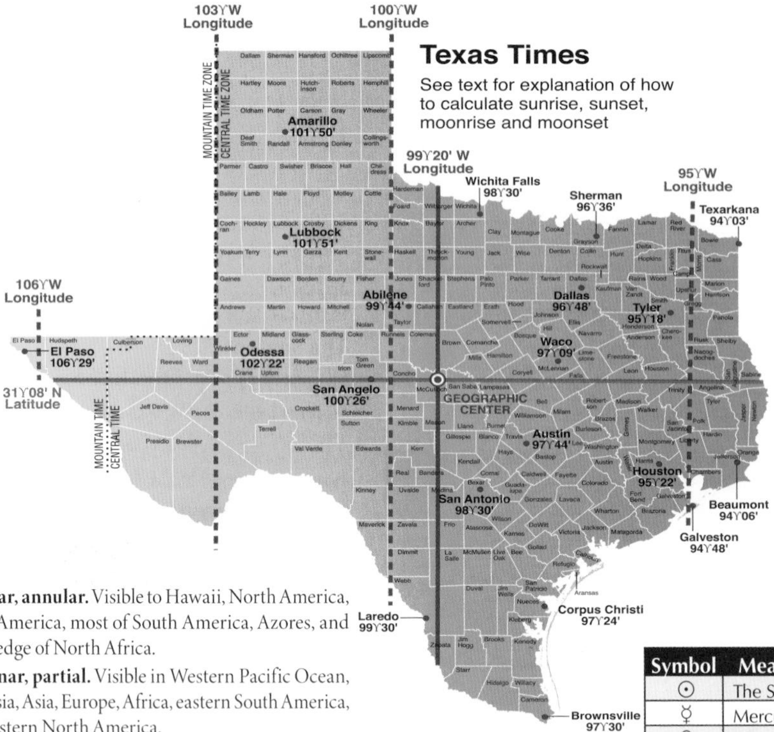

Oct. 14: Solar, annular. Visible to Hawaii, North America, Central America, most of South America, Azores, and western edge of North Africa.

Oct. 28: Lunar, partial. Visible in Western Pacific Ocean, Australasia, Asia, Europe, Africa, eastern South America, north-eastern North America.

An Explanation of Texas Time

Times listed here are **Central Standard Time**, except for the period from 2:00 a.m. on the second Sunday in March until 2:00 a.m. on the first Sunday in November, when **Daylight Saving Time**, which is one hour later than Central Standard Time, is in effect.

All of Texas is in the Central Time Zone, except El Paso and Hudspeth counties and the northwest corner of Culberson County, which observe **Mountain Time**. Mountain Time is one hour earlier than Central Time.

All times are calculated for the intersection of 99° 20' west longitude and 31° 08' north latitude, which is **closest to the town of Mercury and** about 15 miles northeast of Brady, McCulloch County. This point is the **approximate geographical center of the state.**

How to Adjust Rise & Set Times

To adjust the time of sunrise or sunset, moonrise or moonset for any point in Texas, apply the following rules:

- For each degree of longitude that the place lies **west** of the 99th meridian, **add four minutes** to the times given in the calendar.
- For each degree of longitude the place lies **east** of the 99th meridian, **subtract four minutes**.

At times there will be considerable variation for distances north and south of the line of 31° 08' north latitude, but this formula will give sufficiently close results.

The map above shows the intersection for which all times given in this chapter are calculated, with some major cities and longitudes to aid in calculating times.

Astronomical Calendars

The calendars on the following pages feature phenomena and planetary configurations of the heavens for 2022 and 2023 in the center columns. The table to the right is a key to those symbols. You'll find find additional keys below the calendars.

Symbol	Meaning
☉	The Sun
☿	Mercury
♀	Venus
●	The Earth
☾	The Moon
♂	Mars
♃	Jupiter
♄	Saturn
⛢	Uranus
♆	Neptune
☌	conjunction
☍	opposition

Aspects: Conjunction & Opposition

☌ This symbol, appearing between symbols for heavenly bodies, means they are "in conjunction," that is, having the same longitude in the sky and appearing near each other. For example, ♀ ☌ ☾ means Venus is north or south of the moon by a few degrees. Conjunctions listed in this calendar are separated by 10 degrees or less. Inferior and superior conjuctions mean an inner planet, Venus or Mercury, is in line with the Sun, either between the Earth and the Sun (inferior) or on the opposite side of the Sun (superior).

☍ This symbol means that the heavenly body listed is in "opposition" to the Sun, or that they differ by 180 degrees of longitude.

Common Astronomical Terms

Aphelion: Point at which a planet's orbit is farthest from the sun.

Perihelion: Point at which a planet's orbit is nearest the sun.

Apogee: Point of the moon's orbit farthest from the earth.

Perigee: Point of the moon's orbit nearest the earth.

2022

Times are **Central Standard Time**, except from **Sunday, March 13 to Sunday, Nov. 6**, during which **Daylight Saving Time** is observed. **Boldface times for moonrise and moonset indicate p.m**. Times are figured for the point **31° 08' N 99° 20' W**, the approximate geographical center of the state. **See page 138 for explanation of how to get the approximate time at any other Texas point.**

1st Month — January 2022 — 31 Days

Moon Phases — New Moon Jan. 2, 12:33 pm; First Qtr. Jan 9, 12:11 pm; Full Moon Jan. 17, 5:48 pm; Last Qtr. Jan. 25, 7:41 am; New Moon Jan 31, 11:46 pm

Day of Year	Day of Month	Day of Week	Planetary Configurations and Phenomena	Sunrise	Sunset	Moon-rise	Moon-set
1	1	Sat	☾ at perigee (5 pm)	7:35	5:46	6:30	**4:40**
2	2	Sun	New ☾	7:36	5:46	7:40	**5:46**
3	3	Mon	☿ ☌ ☾ (7 pm)	7:36	5:47	8:42	**6:57**
4	4	Tue	● at perihelion (1 am)	7:36	5:48	9:35	**8:09**
5	5	Wed	♃ ☌ ☾ (6 pm)	7:36	5:49	10:19	**9:17**
6	6	Thu		7:36	5:50	10:56	**10:22**
7	7	Fri	☿ gr. elongation E (5 am)	7:36	5:50	11:29	**11:22**
8	8	Sat	♀ in inferior ☌ (7 pm)	7:36	5:51	11:58	
9	9	Sun	First qtr. ☾	7:36	5:52	**12:27**	12:20
10	10	Mon		7:36	5:53	**12:55**	1:17
11	11	Tue	⛢ ☌ ☾ (5 am)	7:36	5:54	**1:25**	2:12
12	12	Wed		7:36	5:55	**1:57**	3:08
13	13	Thu	☿ stationary (7 pm)	7:36	5:55	**2:33**	4:04
14	14	Fri	☾ at apogee (3 am)	7:36	5:56	**3:14**	5:00
15	15	Sat		7:36	5:57	**4:00**	5:55
16	16	Sun		7:36	5:58	**4:51**	6:48
17	17	Mon	Full ☾	7:35	5:59	**5:46**	7:36
18	18	Tue		7:35	6:00	**6:45**	8:20
19	19	Wed		7:35	6:01	**7:44**	9:00
20	20	Thu		7:35	6:02	**8:43**	9:35
21	21	Fri		7:34	6:02	**9:42**	10:07
22	22	Sat		7:34	6:03	**10:42**	10:37
23	23	Sun	☿ in inferior ☌ (4 am)	7:33	6:04	**11:42**	11:07
24	24	Mon		7:33	6:05		11:38
25	25	Tue	Last qtr. ☾	7:33	6:06	12:44	**12:11**
26	26	Wed		7:32	6:07	1:50	**12:48**
27	27	Thu		7:32	6:08	2:58	**1:32**
28	28	Fri		7:31	6:09	4:08	**2:23**
29	29	Sat	♀ ♂ ☌ ☾	7:31	6:10	5:18	**3:23**
30	30	Sun	☿ ☌ ☾ (6 pm)	7:30	6:11	6:23	**4:31**
31	31	Mon	New ☾	7:29	6:11	7:20	**5:42**

2nd Month — February 2022 — 28 Days

Moon Phases — First Qtr. Feb. 8, 6:50 am; Full Moon Feb. 16, 10:56 am; Last Qtr. Feb. 23, 4:32 pm

Day of Year	Day of Month	Day of Week	Planetary Configurations and Phenomena	Sunrise	Sunset	Moon-rise	Moon-set
32	1	Tue		7:29	6:12	8:08	**6:53**
33	2	Wed	♃ ☌ ☾ (3 pm)	7:28	6:13	8:49	**8:01**
34	3	Thu	☿ stationary (4 pm)	7:28	6:14	9:24	**9:05**
35	4	Fri	♄ ☌ ☉ (1 pm)	7:27	6:15	9:56	**10:06**
36	5	Sat		7:26	6:16	10:26	**11:05**
37	6	Sun		7:25	6:17	10:54	
38	7	Mon	⛢ ☌ ☾ (2 pm)	7:25	6:18	11:24	12:02
39	8	Tue	First qtr. ☾	7:24	6:18	11:56	12:59
40	9	Wed		7:23	6:19	**12:31**	1:56
41	10	Thu	☾ at apogee (9 pm)	7:22	6:20	**1:10**	2:52
42	11	Fri		7:21	6:21	**1:54**	3:48
43	12	Sat	♀ gr. illumination (4 pm)	7:21	6:22	**2:43**	4:41
44	13	Sun		7:20	6:23	**3:37**	5:31
45	14	Mon		7:19	6:24	**4:35**	6:17
46	15	Tue		7:18	6:24	**5:35**	6:58
47	16	Wed	Full ☾	7:17	6:25	**6:35**	7:35
48	17	Thu		7:16	6:26	**7:35**	8:08
49	18	Fri		7:15	6:27	**8:35**	8:40
50	19	Sat		7:14	6:28	**9:36**	9:10
51	20	Sun		7:13	6:28	**10:38**	9:40
52	21	Mon		7:12	6:29	**11:42**	10:12
53	22	Tue		7:11	6:30		10:48
54	23	Wed	Last qtr. ☾	7:10	6:31	12:49	11:28
55	24	Thu		7:09	6:31	1:57	**12:16**
56	25	Fri		7:08	6:32	3:05	**1:11**
57	26	Sat	☾ at perigee (4 pm)	7:07	6:33	4:10	**2:14**
58	27	Sun	♀ ♂ ☌ ☾	7:06	6:34	5:08	**3:22**
59	28	Mon	☿ ♄ ☌ ☾	7:04	6:35	5:59	**4:32**

3rd Month — March 2022 — 31 Days

Moon Phases — New Moon Mar. 2, 11:35 am; First Qtr. Mar. 10, 4:45 am; Full Moon Mar. 18, 2:18 am; Last Qtr. Mar. 25, 12:37 am

Day of Year	Day of Month	Day of Week	Planetary Configurations and Phenomena	Sunrise	Sunset	Moon-rise	Moon-set
60	1	Tue		7:03	6:35	6:42	**5:40**
61	2	Wed	New ☾; ☿ ☌ ♄ (7 am)	7:02	6:36	7:19	**6:46**
62	3	Thu		7:01	6:37	7:52	**7:49**
63	4	Fri		7:00	6:37	8:23	**8:49**
64	5	Sat	♃ ☌ ☉ (8 am)	6:59	6:38	8:52	**9:48**
65	6	Sun		6:58	6:39	9:22	**10:46**
66	7	Mon	⛢ ☌ ☾ (12 am)	6:56	6:40	9:53	**11:44**
67	8	Tue		6:55	6:40	10:27	
68	9	Wed		6:54	6:41	11:04	12:42
69	10	Thu	First qtr. ☾ at apogee	6:53	6:42	11:46	1:38
70	11	Fri		6:52	6:42	**12:34**	2:33
71	12	Sat	♀ ☌ ♂ (8 am)	6:50	6:43	**1:26**	3:24
72	13	Sun	**DST begins (2 am)**	7:49	7:44	**3:22**	5:11
73	14	Mon		7:48	7:44	**4:21**	5:54
74	15	Tue		7:47	7:45	**5:22**	6:32
75	16	Wed		7:45	7:46	**6:22**	7:07
76	17	Thu		7:44	7:46	**7:24**	7:39
77	18	Fri	Full ☾	7:43	7:47	**8:26**	8:10
78	19	Sat		7:42	7:48	**9:29**	8:41
79	20	Sun	Equinox (10:33 am)	7:41	7:48	**10:34**	9:13
80	21	Mon		7:39	7:49	**11:41**	9:48
81	22	Tue		7:38	7:50		10:27
82	23	Wed	☾ at perigee (7 pm)	7:37	7:50	12:50	11:13
83	24	Thu		7:36	7:51	1:59	**12:05**
84	25	Fri	Last qtr. ☾	7:34	7:52	3:04	**1:06**
85	26	Sat		7:33	7:52	4:04	**2:11**
86	27	Sun	♂ ☌ ☾ (10 pm)	7:32	7:53	4:55	**3:19**
87	28	Mon	♀ ♄ ☌ ☾ (6 am)	7:31	7:54	5:40	**4:27**
88	29	Tue	♀ ☌ ♄ (8 am)	7:29	7:54	6:18	**5:32**
89	30	Wed	♃ ♆ ☌ ☾	7:28	7:55	6:51	**6:34**
90	31	Thu		7:27	7:56	7:22	**7:35**

Astronomical Calendar for 2022

4th Month — April 2022 — 30 Days

Moon Phases — New Moon Apr. 1, 1:24 am; First Qtr. Apr. 9, 1:48 am; Full Moon Apr 16, 1:55 pm; Last Qtr. Apr 23, 6:56 am; New Moon Apr. 30, 3:28 pm

Day of Year	Day of Month	Day of Week	Planetary Configurations and Phenomena	Sunrise	Sunset	Moon-rise	Moon-set
91	1	Fri	New ☾	7:26	7:56	7:51	**8:34**
92	2	Sat	☿ in superior ☌ (6 pm)	7:24	7:57	8:20	**9:33**
93	3	Sun	⛢ ☌ ☾ (12 pm)	7:23	7:57	8:51	**10:31**
94	4	Mon	♂ ☌ ♄ (5 pm)	7:22	7:58	9:23	**11:30**
95	5	Tue		7:21	7:59	9:59	
96	6	Wed		7:19	7:59	10:40	12:27
97	7	Thu	☾ at apogee (2 pm)	7:18	8:00	11:25	1:23
98	8	Fri		7:17	8:01	**12:15**	2:16
99	9	Sat	First qtr. ☾	7:16	8:01	**1:10**	3:05
100	10	Sun		7:15	8:02	**2:07**	3:49
101	11	Mon		7:13	8:03	**3:06**	4:29
102	12	Tue	♃ ☌ ♆ (3 pm)	7:12	8:03	**4:06**	5:04
103	13	Wed		7:11	8:04	**5:07**	5:37
104	14	Thu		7:10	8:05	**6:09**	6:08
105	15	Fri		7:09	8:05	**7:12**	6:39
106	16	Sat	Full ☾	7:08	8:06	**8:17**	7:10
107	17	Sun		7:07	8:07	**9:26**	7:44
108	18	Mon		7:05	8:07	**10:37**	8:23
109	19	Tue	☾ at perigee (10 am)	7:04	8:08	**11:48**	9:07
110	20	Wed		7:03	8:09		9:59
111	21	Thu		7:02	8:09	12:57	10:58
112	22	Fri		7:01	8:10	2:00	**12:03**
113	23	Sat	Last qtr. ☾	7:00	8:11	2:54	**1:11**
114	24	Sun	♄ ☌ ☾ (4 pm)	6:59	8:11	3:40	**2:19**
115	25	Mon	♂ ☌ ☾ (5 pm)	6:58	8:12	4:19	**3:24**
116	26	Tue	♀ ♆ ☌ ☾ (9 pm)	6:57	8:13	4:53	**4:26**
117	27	Wed	♃ ☌ ☾; ♀ ☌ ♆	6:56	8:13	5:24	**5:26**
118	28	Thu		6:55	8:14	5:53	**6:25**
119	29	Fri	☿ gr. elongation E (3 am)	6:54	8:15	6:21	**7:23**
120	30	Sat	New ☾; ⊙ eclipse (5 pm)	6:53	8:15	6:51	**8:21**

5th Month — May 2022 — 31 Days

Moon Phases — First Qtr. May 8, 7:21 pm; Full Moon May 15, 11:14 pm; Last Qtr. May 22, 1:43 pm; New Moon May 30, 6:30 am

Day of Year	Day of Month	Day of Week	Planetary Configurations and Phenomena	Sunrise	Sunset	Moon-rise	Moon-set
121	1	Sun	☿ ☌ ☾ (9 am)	6:52	8:16	7:22	**9:19**
122	2	Mon		6:51	8:17	7:57	**10:17**
123	3	Tue		6:50	8:17	8:35	**11:14**
124	4	Wed		6:50	8:18	9:19	
125	5	Thu	☾ at apogee (8 am)	6:49	8:19	10:07	12:09
126	6	Fri		6:48	8:19	11:00	12:59
127	7	Sat		6:47	8:20	11:56	1:45
128	8	Sun	First qtr. ☾	6:46	8:21	**12:54**	2:26
129	9	Mon		6:45	8:22	**1:52**	3:02
130	10	Tue	☿ stationary (6 pm)	6:45	8:22	**2:51**	3:35
131	11	Wed		6:44	8:23	**3:51**	4:06
132	12	Thu		6:43	8:24	**4:53**	4:36
133	13	Fri		6:43	8:24	**5:56**	5:06
134	14	Sat		6:42	8:25	**7:03**	5:39
135	15	Sun	Full ☾; eclipse (11 pm)	6:41	8:26	**8:14**	6:15
136	16	Mon		6:41	8:26	**9:27**	6:57
137	17	Tue	☾ at perigee (10 am)	6:40	8:27	**10:40**	7:47
138	18	Wed		6:39	8:28	**11:49**	8:45
139	19	Thu		6:39	8:28		9:51
140	20	Fri		6:38	8:29	12:48	11:00
141	21	Sat	☿ in inferior ☌ (2 pm)	6:38	8:30	1:39	**12:10**
142	22	Sun	♄ ☌ last qtr. ☾ (12 am)	6:37	8:30	2:21	**1:17**
143	23	Mon		6:37	8:31	2:56	**2:20**
144	24	Tue	♂ ♃ ♆ ☌ ☾	6:36	8:31	3:28	**3:21**
145	25	Wed		6:36	8:32	3:57	**4:19**
146	26	Thu	♀ ☌ ☾ (10 pm)	6:36	8:33	4:25	**5:17**
147	27	Fri		6:35	8:33	4:54	**6:14**
148	28	Sat	⛢ ☌ ☾; ♂ ☌ ♃	6:35	8:34	5:24	**7:11**
149	29	Sun		6:34	8:34	5:57	**8:09**
150	30	Mon	New ☾	6:34	8:35	6:34	**9:07**
151	31	Tue		6:34	8:36	7:15	**10:02**

6th Month — June 2022 — 30 Days

Moon Phases — First Qtr. Jun. 8, 7:21; Full Moon Jun. 14, 6:52 am; Last Qtr. Jun. 20, 10:11; New Moon Jun. 28, 9:52 pm

Day of Year	Day of Month	Day of Week	Planetary Configurations and Phenomena	Sunrise	Sunset	Moon-rise	Moon-set
152	1	Wed	☾ at apogee (8 pm)	6:34	8:36	8:02	**10:54**
153	2	Thu	☿ stationary (7 pm)	6:33	8:37	8:53	**11:41**
154	3	Fri		6:33	8:37	9:48	
155	4	Sat		6:33	8:38	10:45	12:24
156	5	Sun	♄ stationary (9 am)	6:33	8:38	11:42	1:01
157	6	Mon		6:33	8:39	**12:40**	1:35
158	7	Tue	First qtr. ☾	6:33	8:39	**1:38**	2:06
159	8	Wed		6:33	8:40	**2:37**	2:35
160	9	Thu		6:32	8:40	**3:38**	3:04
161	10	Fri		6:32	8:40	**4:41**	3:34
162	11	Sat	♀ ☌ ⛢ (8 am)	6:32	8:41	**5:49**	4:08
163	12	Sun		6:32	8:41	**7:01**	4:46
164	13	Mon		6:32	8:42	**8:15**	5:32
165	14	Tue	Full ☾ at perigee (6 pm)	6:33	8:42	**9:27**	6:26
166	15	Wed		6:33	8:42	**10:33**	7:30
167	16	Thu	☿ gr. elongation W (10 am)	6:33	8:43	**11:30**	8:40
168	17	Fri		6:33	8:43		9:53
169	18	Sat	♄ ☌ ☾ (7 am)	6:33	8:43	12:17	11:04
170	19	Sun		6:33	8:43	12:56	**12:11**
171	20	Mon	Last qtr. ☾	6:33	8:44	1:30	**1:14**
172	21	Tue	Solstice (4:14 am)	6:34	8:44	2:00	**2:14**
173	22	Wed	♂ ☌ ☾ (1 pm)	6:34	8:44	2:28	**3:12**
174	23	Thu	☿ ☌ Aldebaran (9 am)	6:34	8:44	2:57	**4:09**
175	24	Fri	⛢ ☌ ☾ (5 pm)	6:34	8:44	3:26	**5:06**
176	25	Sat		6:35	8:45	3:58	**6:04**
177	26	Sun	♀ ☌ ☾ (3 am)	6:35	8:45	4:34	**7:01**
178	27	Mon	☿ ☌ ☾ (3 am)	6:35	8:45	5:14	**7:57**
179	28	Tue	New ☾	6:36	8:45	5:59	**8:50**
180	29	Wed	☾ at apogee (1 am)	6:36	8:45	6:49	**9:39**
181	30	Thu		6:36	8:45	7:43	**10:23**

⊙ The Sun ● The Earth ☾ The Moon ☿ Mercury ♀ Venus ♂ Mars ♃ Jupiter ♄ Saturn ♆ Neptune ⛢ Uranus ☌ = in conjunction ☍ = opposition to the ⊙

Astronomical Calendar for 2022

7th Month — July 2022 — 31 Days

Moon Phases — First Qtr. Jul. 6, 9:14 pm; Full Moon Jul. 13, 1:38 pm; Last Qtr. Jul 20, 9:19 am; New Moon Jul. 28, 12:55 pm

Day of Year	Day of Month	Day of Week	Planetary Configurations and Phenomena	Sunrise	Sunset	Moon-rise	Moon-set
182	1	Fri	♀ ☌ Aldebaran (7 pm)	6:37	8:45	8:39	**11:02**
183	2	Sat		6:37	8:45	9:36	**11:36**
184	3	Sun		6:38	8:45	10:34	
185	4	Mon	● aphelion (2 am)	6:38	8:45	11:31	12:07
186	5	Tue		6:38	8:44	**12:28**	12:36
187	6	Wed	First qtr. ☾	6:39	8:44	**1:26**	1:05
188	7	Thu		6:39	8:44	**2:27**	1:34
189	8	Fri		6:40	8:44	**3:30**	2:04
190	9	Sat		6:40	8:44	**4:38**	2:39
191	10	Sun		6:41	8:44	**5:49**	3:20
192	11	Mon		6:41	8:43	**7:02**	4:09
193	12	Tue		6:42	8:43	**8:12**	5:07
194	13	Wed	Full ☾ at perigee (4 am)	6:42	8:43	**9:13**	6:15
195	14	Thu		6:43	8:42	**10:06**	7:28
196	15	Fri	♄ ☌ ☾ (3 pm)	6:44	8:42	**10:50**	8:42
197	16	Sat	☿ in superior ☌ (3 pm)	6:44	8:42	**11:27**	9:53
198	17	Sun	♆ ☌ ☾ (8 pm)	6:45	8:41	**11:59**	11:00
199	18	Mon	♃ ☌ ☾ (8 pm)	6:45	8:41		**12:03**
200	19	Tue	Pluto ☍ (9 pm)	6:46	8:40	12:29	**1:03**
201	20	Wed	Last qtr. ☾	6:46	8:40	12:59	**2:02**
202	21	Thu	♂ ☌ ☾ (12 pm)	6:47	8:39	1:28	**3:00**
203	22	Fri	♅ ☌ ☾ (1 am)	6:48	8:39	2:00	**3:58**
204	23	Sat		6:48	8:38	2:34	**4:55**
205	24	Sun		6:49	8:38	3:13	**5:52**
206	25	Mon		6:50	8:37	3:56	**6:46**
207	26	Tue	♀ ☌ ☾ (9 am)	6:50	8:36	4:44	**7:36**
208	27	Wed		6:51	8:36	5:37	**8:22**
209	28	Thu	New ☾	6:51	8:35	6:33	**9:02**
210	29	Fri	♃ stationary (7 am)	6:52	8:34	7:31	**9:38**
211	30	Sat		6:53	8:34	8:29	**10:10**
212	31	Sun		6:53	8:33	9:26	**10:40**

8th Month — August 2022 — 31 Days

Moon Phases — First Qtr. Aug. 5, 6:07 am; Full Moon Aug. 11, 8:36 pm; Last Qtr. Aug. 18, 11:36 pm; New Moon Aug. 27, 3:17 am

Day of Year	Day of Month	Day of Week	Planetary Configurations and Phenomena	Sunrise	Sunset	Moon-rise	Moon-set
213	1	Mon	♂ ☌ ♅ (4 am)	6:54	8:32	10:23	**11:08**
214	2	Tue		6:55	8:31	11:20	**11:36**
215	3	Wed		6:55	8:30	**12:19**	
216	4	Thu	☿ ☌ Regulus (12 am)	6:56	8:30	**1:20**	12:05
217	5	Fri	First qtr. ☾	6:56	8:29	**2:24**	12:37
218	6	Sat		6:57	8:28	**3:32**	1:14
219	7	Sun	♀ ☌ Pollux (5 am)	6:58	8:27	**4:42**	1:58
220	8	Mon		6:58	8:26	**5:51**	2:50
221	9	Tue		6:59	8:25	**6:55**	3:52
222	10	Wed	☾ at perigee (12 pm)	7:00	8:24	**7:52**	5:02
223	11	Thu	♄ ☌ Full ☾ (11 pm)	7:00	8:23	**8:40**	6:16
224	12	Fri		7:01	8:22	**9:20**	7:29
225	13	Sat		7:02	8:21	**9:55**	8:39
226	14	Sun	♆ ☌ ☾ (5 am); ♄ ☍ (12 pm)	7:02	8:20	**10:27**	9:46
227	15	Mon	♃ ☌ ☾ (5 am)	7:03	8:19	**10:57**	10:49
228	16	Tue		7:03	8:18	**11:27**	11:50
229	17	Wed		7:04	8:17	**11:59**	**12:50**
230	18	Thu	Last qtr. ☾	7:05	8:16		**1:49**
231	19	Fri	♂ ☌ ☾ (7 am)	7:05	8:15	12:32	**2:48**
232	20	Sat		7:06	8:14	1:10	**3:45**
233	21	Sun		7:06	8:13	1:52	**4:40**
234	22	Mon	☾ at apogee (5 pm)	7:07	8:12	2:39	**5:32**
235	23	Tue		7:08	8:11	3:31	**6:19**
236	24	Wed		7:08	8:10	4:26	**7:01**
237	25	Thu	♀ ☌ ☾ (4 pm)	7:09	8:08	5:23	**7:39**
238	26	Fri		7:09	8:07	6:22	**8:12**
239	27	Sat	New ☾; ☿ gr. elongation E	7:10	8:06	7:20	**8:42**
240	28	Sun		7:11	8:05	8:17	**9:11**
241	29	Mon	☿ ☌ ☾ (6 am)	7:11	8:04	9:15	**9:39**
242	30	Tue		7:12	8:02	10:14	**10:08**
243	31	Wed		7:12	8:01	11:14	**10:39**

9th Month — September 2022 — 30 Days

Moon Phases — First Qtr. Sep 3, 1:08 pm; Full Moon Sep. 10, 4:59 am; Last Qtr. Sep. 17, 4:52 pm; New Moon Sep. 25, 4:55 pm

Day of Year	Day of Month	Day of Week	Planetary Configurations and Phenomena	Sunrise	Sunset	Moon-rise	Moon-set
244	1	Thu		7:13	8:00	**12:17**	**11:14**
245	2	Fri		7:14	7:59	**1:23**	**11:54**
246	3	Sat	First qtr. ☾	7:14	7:58	**2:31**	
247	4	Sun	☿ ☌ Regulus (8 pm)	7:15	7:56	**3:38**	12:42
248	5	Mon		7:15	7:55	**4:43**	1:39
249	6	Tue		7:16	7:54	**5:41**	2:44
250	7	Wed	☾ at perigee (1 pm)	7:17	7:53	**6:31**	3:54
251	8	Thu	♄ ☌ ☾ (6 am)	7:17	7:51	**7:13**	5:06
252	9	Fri	☿ stationary (3 pm)	7:18	7:50	**7:50**	6:17
253	10	Sat	Full ☾	7:18	7:49	**8:23**	7:25
254	11	Sun	♃ ☌ ☾ (10 am)	7:19	7:47	**8:54**	8:30
255	12	Mon		7:19	7:46	**9:24**	9:33
256	13	Tue		7:20	7:45	**9:56**	10:35
257	14	Wed	♅ ☌ ☾ (6 pm)	7:21	7:44	**10:29**	11:36
258	15	Thu		7:21	7:42	**11:05**	**12:36**
259	16	Fri	♆ ☍ (5 pm); ♂ ☌ ☾ (9 pm)	7:22	7:41	**11:46**	**1:35**
260	17	Sat	Last qtr. ☾	7:22	7:40		**2:32**
261	18	Sun		7:23	7:38	12:32	**3:26**
262	19	Mon	☾ at apogee (12 pm)	7:23	7:37	1:22	**4:15**
263	20	Tue		7:24	7:36	2:16	**4:59**
264	21	Wed		7:25	7:35	3:13	**5:37**
265	22	Thu	Equinox (8:04 pm)	7:25	7:33	4:11	**6:12**
266	23	Fri	☿ in inferior ☌ (2 am)	7:26	7:32	5:10	**6:43**
267	24	Sat		7:26	7:31	6:08	**7:13**
268	25	Sun	New ☾	7:27	7:29	7:06	**7:41**
269	26	Mon	♃ ☍ (3 pm)	7:28	7:28	8:06	**8:10**
270	27	Tue		7:28	7:27	9:07	**8:41**
271	28	Wed		7:29	7:26	10:10	**9:14**
272	29	Thu		7:29	7:24	11:16	**9:53**
273	30	Fri		7:30	7:23	12:23	**10:39**

Bright stars: Aldebaran, Antares, Spica, Pollux, Regulus. **Minor planets or asteroids:** Pluto, Ceres, Pallas, Juno, Vesta. ☌ = in conjunction by 10° or < ☍ = opposition to the ☉

Astronomical Calendar for 2022

10th Month — October 2022 — 31 Days

Moon Phases — First Qtr. Oct. 2, 7:14 pm; Full Moon Oct. 9, 3:55 pm; Last Qtr. Oct. 17, 12:15 pm; New Moon Oct. 25, 5:49 am

Day of			Planetary Configurations and Phenomena	Hour of			
Year	Month	Week		Sunrise	Sunset	Moon-rise	Moon-set
274	1	Sat	☿ stationary (10 am)	7:31	7:22	**1:31**	11:32
275	2	Sun	First qtr. ☾	7:31	7:21	**2:36**	
276	3	Mon		7:32	7:19	**3:35**	12:34
277	4	Tue	☾ at perigee (12 pm)	7:32	7:18	**4:26**	1:41
278	5	Wed	♄ ☌ ☾ (11 am)	7:33	7:17	**5:10**	2:51
279	6	Thu		7:34	7:16	**5:48**	4:01
280	7	Fri	♆ ☌ ☾ (10 pm)	7:34	7:14	**6:21**	5:08
281	8	Sat	♃ ☌ ☾ (1 pm)	7:35	7:13	**6:52**	6:13
282	9	Sun	Full ☾	7:36	7:12	**7:22**	7:16
283	10	Mon		7:36	7:11	**7:53**	8:18
284	11	Tue		7:37	7:10	**8:25**	9:20
285	12	Wed	⛢ ☌ ☾ (2 am)	7:38	7:08	**9:00**	10:21
286	13	Thu		7:38	7:07	**9:40**	11:22
287	14	Fri		7:39	7:06	**10:24**	**12:21**
288	15	Sat	♂ ☌ ☾ (12 am)	7:40	7:05	**11:12**	**1:17**
289	16	Sun		7:40	7:04		**2:08**
290	17	Mon	Last qtr. ☾ at apogee	7:41	7:03	12:05	**2:54**
291	18	Tue		7:42	7:02	1:01	**3:35**
292	19	Wed		7:42	7:01	1:59	**4:10**
293	20	Thu		7:43	7:00	2:57	**4:43**
294	21	Fri		7:44	6:58	3:55	**5:13**
295	22	Sat	♀ in superior ☌ (4 pm)	7:45	6:57	4:53	**5:41**
296	23	Sun	♄ stationary (4 am)	7:45	6:56	5:52	**6:10**
297	24	Mon		7:46	6:55	6:53	**6:40**
298	25	Tue	New ☾; ☉ eclipse (6 am)	7:47	6:54	7:56	**7:13**
299	26	Wed		7:48	6:53	9:02	**7:50**
300	27	Thu		7:48	6:53	10:12	**8:34**
301	28	Fri		7:49	6:52	11:22	**9:27**
302	29	Sat	☾ at perigee (10 am)	7:50	6:51	**12:30**	**10:27**
303	30	Sun	♂ stationary (6 am)	7:51	6:50	**1:31**	**11:33**
304	31	Mon		7:52	6:49	**2:25**	

11th Month — November 2022 — 30 Days

Moon Phases — First Qtr. Nov. 1, 1:37 am; Full Moon Nov. 8, 6:02 am; Last Qtr. Nov. 16, 7:27 am; New Moon Nov. 23, 4:57 pm; First Qtr. Nov. 30, 8:37 am

Day of			Planetary Configurations and Phenomena	Hour of			
Year	Month	Week		Sunrise	Sunset	Moon-rise	Moon-set
305	1	Tue	♄ ☌ first qtr. ☾ (4 pm)	7:52	6:48	**3:10**	12:43
306	2	Wed		7:53	6:47	**3:49**	1:51
307	3	Thu	Juno ☌ ☾ (3 am)	7:54	6:46	**4:22**	2:58
308	4	Fri	♃ ♆ ☌ ☾	7:55	6:46	**4:53**	4:02
309	5	Sat		7:56	6:45	**5:23**	5:04
310	6	Sun	**DST ends (2 am)**	6:56	5:44	**4:52**	5:05
311	7	Mon		6:57	5:43	**5:23**	6:06
312	8	Tue	Full ☾; eclipse (5 am)	6:58	5:43	**5:57**	7:07
313	9	Wed	⛢ ☍ (2 am)	6:59	5:42	**6:34**	8:08
314	10	Thu		7:00	5:41	**7:16**	9:08
315	11	Fri	♂ ☌ ☾ (8 am)	7:01	5:41	**8:04**	10:06
316	12	Sat		7:01	5:40	**8:55**	11:00
317	13	Sun		7:02	5:40	**9:50**	11:48
318	14	Mon	☾ at apogee (1 am)	7:03	5:39	**10:47**	**12:31**
319	15	Tue		7:04	5:39	**11:44**	**1:08**
320	16	Wed	Last qtr. ☾	7:05	5:38		**1:41**
321	17	Thu		7:06	5:38	12:41	**2:12**
322	18	Fri		7:07	5:37	1:38	**2:40**
323	19	Sat		7:07	5:37	2:36	**3:08**
324	20	Sun		7:08	5:36	3:35	**3:37**
325	21	Mon		7:09	5:36	4:37	**4:08**
326	22	Tue		7:10	5:36	5:42	**4:43**
327	23	Wed	New ☾	7:11	5:35	6:51	**5:25**
328	24	Thu	♃ stationary (7 am)	7:12	5:35	8:03	**6:15**
329	25	Fri	☾ at perigee (8 pm)	7:13	5:35	9:14	**7:14**
330	26	Sat		7:13	5:35	10:21	**8:21**
331	27	Sun		7:14	5:35	11:20	**9:32**
332	28	Mon	♄ ☌ ☾ (11 pm)	7:15	5:34	**12:09**	**10:43**
333	29	Tue		7:16	5:34	**12:50**	**11:51**
334	30	Wed	Juno ☌ first qtr. ☾	7:17	5:34	**1:25**	

12th Month — December 2022 — 31 Days

Moon Phases — Full Moon Dec. 7, 10:08 pm; Last Qtr. Dec. 16, 2:56 am; New Moon Dec. 23, 4:17 am; First Qtr. Dec. 29, 7:21 pm

Day of			Planetary Configurations and Phenomena	Hour of			
Year	Month	Week		Sunrise	Sunset	Moon-rise	Moon-set
335	1	Thu.	♃ ♆ ☌ ☾	7:18	5:34	**1:56**	12:56
336	2	Fri		7:18	5:34	**2:26**	1:58
337	3	Sat		7:19	5:34	**2:55**	2:58
338	4	Sun	♆ stationary (4 am)	7:20	5:34	**3:24**	3:58
339	5	Mon	⛢ ☌ ☾ (12 pm)	7:21	5:34	**3:56**	4:58
340	6	Tue		7:22	5:34	**4:32**	5:58
341	7	Wed	♂ ☌ full ☾ (10 pm)	7:22	5:34	**5:12**	6:58
342	8	Thu	♂ ☍ (12 am)	7:23	5:34	**5:57**	7:56
343	9	Fri		7:24	5:35	**6:48**	8:52
344	10	Sat		7:24	5:35	**7:42**	9:42
345	11	Sun	☾ at apogee (6 pm)	7:25	5:35	**8:38**	10:27
346	12	Mon		7:26	5:35	**9:35**	11:06
347	13	Tue		7:27	5:36	**10:31**	11:41
348	14	Wed		7:27	5:36	**11:27**	**12:12**
349	15	Thu		7:28	5:36		**12:40**
350	16	Fri	Last qtr. ☾	7:28	5:37	12:23	**1:07**
351	17	Sat		7:29	5:37	1:20	**1:35**
352	18	Sun		7:30	5:37	2:18	**2:04**
353	19	Mon		7:30	5:38	3:20	**2:36**
354	20	Tue		7:31	5:38	4:26	**3:14**
355	21	Wed	Solstice (3:48 pm)	7:31	5:39	5:36	**3:59**
356	22	Thu		7:32	5:39	6:49	**4:54**
357	23	Fri	New ☾	7:32	5:40	8:00	**5:59**
358	24	Sat	☿ ♀ ☌ ☾ at perigee	7:33	5:40	9:05	**7:11**
359	25	Sun		7:33	5:41	10:00	**8:25**
360	26	Mon	♄ ☌ ☾ (10 am)	7:33	5:42	10:46	**9:38**
361	27	Tue		7:34	5:42	11:25	**10:46**
362	28	Wed	♆ ☌ ☾; ☿ stationary	7:34	5:43	11:58	**11:51**
363	29	Thu	☿ ☌ ♀; ♄ ☌ first qtr. ☾	7:35	5:43	**12:29**	
364	30	Fri		7:35	5:44	**12:58**	12:52
365	31	Sat		7:35	5:45	**1:27**	1:53

☉ The Sun ● The Earth ☾ The Moon ☿ Mercury ♀ Venus ♂ Mars ♃ Jupiter ♄ Saturn ♆ Neptune ⛢ Uranus ☌ = in conjunction ☍ = opposition to the ☉

2023

Times are **Central Standard Time**, except from **Sunday, March 12 to Sunday, Nov. 5**, during which **Daylight Saving Time** is observed. **Boldface times for moonrise and moonset indicate p.m.** Times are figured for the point **31° 08' N 99° 20' W**, the approximate geographical center of the state. **See page 138 for explanation of how to get the approximate time at any other Texas point.**

1st Month — January 2023 — 31 Days

Moon Phases — Full Moon Jan. 6, 5:08 pm; Last Qtr. Jan. 14, 8:10 pm; New Moon Jan. 21, 2:53 pm; First Qtr. Jan. 28, 9:19 am

Day of Year	Day of Month	Day of Week	Planetary Configurations and Phenomena	Sunrise	Sunset	Moonrise	Moonset
1	1	Sun	♅ ☌ ☾ (4 pm)	7:35	5:46	**1:58**	2:52
2	2	Mon		7:36	5:46	**2:32**	3:52
3	3	Tue	♂ ☌ ☾ (2 pm)	7:36	5:47	**3:11**	4:51
4	4	Wed	● at perihelion (10 am)	7:36	5:48	**3:54**	5:50
5	5	Thu		7:36	5:49	**4:42**	6:46
6	6	Fri	Full ☾	7:36	5:49	**5:35**	7:38
7	7	Sat	☿ in inferior ☌ (7 am)	7:36	5:50	**6:31**	8:24
8	8	Sun	☾ at apogee (3 am)	7:36	5:51	**7:28**	9:05
9	9	Mon		7:36	5:52	**8:24**	9:41
10	10	Tue		7:36	5:53	**9:20**	10:13
11	11	Wed		7:36	5:53	**10:16**	10:42
12	12	Thu	♂ stationary (2 pm)	7:36	5:54	**11:11**	11:09
13	13	Fri		7:36	5:55		11:35
14	14	Sat	Last qtr. ☾	7:36	5:56	12:07	**12:03**
15	15	Sun		7:36	5:57	1:06	**12:32**
16	16	Mon		7:36	5:58	2:07	**1:06**
17	17	Tue		7:35	5:59	3:13	**1:46**
18	18	Wed	☿ stationary (6 am)	7:35	6:00	4:23	**2:35**
19	19	Thu		7:35	6:00	5:34	**3:34**
20	20	Fri	☿ ☌ ☾ (2 am)	7:35	6:01	6:42	**4:42**
21	21	Sat	New ☾ at perigee (3 pm)	7:34	6:02	7:42	**5:57**
22	22	Sun	♀ ☌ ♄ (2 pm)	7:34	6:03	8:34	**7:13**
23	23	Mon	♀ ♄ ☌ ☾ (2 am)	7:34	6:04	9:17	**8:26**
24	24	Tue		7:33	6:05	9:54	**9:35**
25	25	Wed	♄ ♆ ☌ ☾	7:33	6:06	10:27	**10:40**
26	26	Thu		7:32	6:07	10:58	**11:43**
27	27	Fri		7:32	6:08	11:28	
28	28	Sat	First qtr. ☾	7:31	6:09	11:59	12:45
29	29	Sun		7:31	6:09	**12:33**	1:45
30	30	Mon	♂ ☌ ☾ (10 pm)	7:30	6:10	**1:10**	2:45
31	31	Tue		7:30	6:11	**1:52**	3:44

2nd Month — February 2023 — 28 Days

Moon Phases — Full Moon Feb. 5, 12:29 pm; Last Qtr. Feb. 13, 10:01 am; New Moon Feb 20, 1:06 am; First Qtr. Feb 27, 2:06 am

Day of Year	Day of Month	Day of Week	Planetary Configurations and Phenomena	Sunrise	Sunset	Moonrise	Moonset
32	1	Wed		7:29	6:12	**2:38**	4:41
33	2	Thu		7:28	6:13	**3:30**	5:34
34	3	Fri		7:28	6:14	**4:25**	6:22
35	4	Sat	☾ at apogee (3 am)	7:27	6:15	**5:22**	7:05
36	5	Sun	♂ ☌ Aldebaran; full ☾	7:26	6:16	**6:19**	7:42
37	6	Mon		7:26	6:17	**7:15**	8:15
38	7	Tue		7:25	6:17	**8:11**	8:45
39	8	Wed		7:24	6:18	**9:06**	9:12
40	9	Thu		7:23	6:19	**10:02**	9:39
41	10	Fri		7:22	6:20	**10:58**	10:05
42	11	Sat		7:22	6:21	**11:58**	10:33
43	12	Sun		7:21	6:22		11:05
44	13	Mon	Last qtr. ☾	7:20	6:22	1:00	11:41
45	14	Tue		7:19	6:23	2:06	**12:24**
46	15	Wed	♀ ☌ ♆ (6 am)	7:18	6:24	3:14	**1:16**
47	16	Thu	♄ ☌ ☉ (11 am)	7:17	6:25	4:21	**2:18**
48	17	Fri		7:16	6:26	5:24	**3:28**
49	18	Sat	☿ ☌ ☾ (3 pm)	7:15	6:27	6:19	**4:43**
50	19	Sun	☾ at perigee (3 am)	7:14	6:27	7:06	**5:58**
51	20	Mon	New ☾	7:13	6:28	7:46	**7:10**
52	21	Tue	♆ ☌ ☾ (12 pm)	7:12	6:29	8:22	**8:19**
53	22	Wed	♀ ♃ ☌ ☾	7:11	6:30	8:54	**9:25**
54	23	Thu		7:10	6:31	9:25	**10:30**
55	24	Fri		7:09	6:31	9:57	**11:33**
56	25	Sat	♅ ☌ ☾ (7 am)	7:08	6:32	10:30	
57	26	Sun		7:07	6:33	11:07	12:35
58	27	Mon	♂ ☌ first qtr. ☾ (11 pm)	7:06	6:34	11:48	1:36
59	28	Tue		7:05	6:34	**12:33**	2:35

3rd Month — March 2023 — 31 Days

Moon Phases — Full Moon Mar. 7, 6:40 am; Last Qtr. Mar. 14, 9:08 pm; New Moon Mar. 21, 12:23 pm; First Qtr. Mar. 28, 9:32 pm

Day of Year	Day of Month	Day of Week	Planetary Configurations and Phenomena	Sunrise	Sunset	Moonrise	Moonset
60	1	Wed		7:04	6:35	**1:24**	3:30
61	2	Thu	♀ ☌ ♃ (5 am)	7:03	6:36	**2:18**	4:20
62	3	Fri	☾ at apogee (12 pm)	7:01	6:37	**3:14**	5:04
63	4	Sat		7:00	6:37	**4:11**	5:43
64	5	Sun		6:59	6:38	**5:08**	6:17
65	6	Mon		6:58	6:39	**6:05**	6:47
66	7	Tue	Full ☾	6:57	6:39	**7:01**	7:15
67	8	Wed		6:56	6:40	**7:57**	7:42
68	9	Thu		6:54	6:41	**8:53**	8:09
69	10	Fri		6:53	6:41	**9:52**	8:36
70	11	Sat		6:52	6:42	**10:54**	9:07
71	12	Sun	**DST begins (2 am)**	7:51	7:43		10:41
72	13	Mon		7:49	7:44	12:58	11:21
73	14	Tue	Last qtr. ☾	7:48	7:44	2:04	**12:08**
74	15	Wed	♆ ☌ ☉ (7 pm)	7:47	7:45	3:10	**1:05**
75	16	Thu		7:46	7:46	4:13	**2:10**
76	17	Fri	☿ in superior ☌ (6 am)	7:45	7:46	5:09	**3:21**
77	18	Sat		7:43	7:47	5:57	**4:34**
78	19	Sun	♄ ☌ ☾ at perigee (10 am)	7:42	7:48	6:39	**5:45**
79	20	Mon	Equinox (4:24 pm)	7:41	7:48	7:16	**6:55**
80	21	Tue	New ☾	7:40	7:49	7:49	**8:03**
81	22	Wed	♃ ☌ ☾ (3 pm)	7:38	7:50	8:21	**9:09**
82	23	Thu		7:37	7:50	8:52	**10:14**
83	24	Fri	♀ ♅ ☌ ☾	7:36	7:51	9:25	**11:18**
84	25	Sat		7:35	7:52	10:01	
85	26	Sun		7:33	7:52	10:41	12:22
86	27	Mon		7:32	7:53	11:26	1:24
87	28	Tue	♂ ☌ first qtr. ☾; ☿ ☌ ♃	7:31	7:53	**12:15**	2:21
88	29	Wed		7:30	7:54	**1:09**	3:14
89	30	Thu		7:28	7:55	**2:05**	4:01
90	31	Fri	♀ ☌ ♅; ☾ at apogee	7:27	7:55	**3:02**	4:42

Astronomical Calendar for 2023

4th Month — April 2023 — 30 Days

Moon Phases — Full Moon Apr. 5, 11:35 pm; Last Qtr. Apr. 13, 4:11 am; New Moon Apr. 19, 11:13 pm; First Qtr. Apr. 27, 4:20 pm

Day of Year	Day of Month	Day of Week	Planetary Configurations and Phenomena	Sunrise	Sunset	Moonrise	Moonset
91	1	Sat		7:26	7:56	**3:59**	5:17
92	2	Sun		7:25	7:57	**4:56**	5:49
93	3	Mon		7:23	7:57	**5:52**	6:18
94	4	Tue		7:22	7:58	**6:48**	6:45
95	5	Wed	Full ☾	7:21	7:59	**7:45**	7:11
96	6	Thu		7:20	7:59	**8:44**	7:39
97	7	Fri		7:18	8:00	**9:46**	8:08
98	8	Sat		7:17	8:01	**10:50**	8:41
99	9	Sun		7:16	8:01	**11:57**	9:20
100	10	Mon		7:15	8:02		10:05
101	11	Tue	☿ gr. elongation E (5 pm)	7:14	8:03	1:04	10:59
102	12	Wed		7:13	8:03	2:07	**12:01**
103	13	Thu	Last qtr. ☾	7:11	8:04	3:04	**1:09**
104	14	Fri		7:10	8:04	3:54	**2:20**
105	15	Sat	♄ ☌ ☾ at perigee (10 pm)	7:09	8:05	4:37	**3:30**
106	16	Sun		7:08	8:06	5:14	**4:38**
107	17	Mon	♆ ☌ ☾ (12 pm)	7:07	8:06	5:47	**5:44**
108	18	Tue		7:06	8:07	6:18	**6:50**
109	19	Wed	New ☾; ☉ eclipse	7:05	8:08	6:49	**7:54**
110	20	Thu		7:04	8:08	7:21	**8:59**
111	21	Fri	⛢ ☌ ☾; ☿ stationary	7:02	8:09	7:55	**10:04**
112	22	Sat		7:01	8:10	8:34	**11:08**
113	23	Sun	♀ ☌ ☾ (8 am)	7:00	8:10	9:17	
114	24	Mon		6:59	8:11	10:05	12:09
115	25	Tue	♂ ☌ ☾ (9 pm)	6:58	8:12	10:58	1:05
116	26	Wed		6:57	8:13	11:54	1:55
117	27	Thu	First qtr. ☾	6:56	8:13	**12:51**	2:38
118	28	Fri	☾ at apogee (2 am)	6:55	8:14	**1:48**	3:16
119	29	Sat		6:54	8:15	**2:45**	3:49
120	30	Sun		6:53	8:15	**3:41**	4:18

5th Month — May 2023 — 31 Days

Moon Phases — Full Moon May 5, 12:34 pm; Last Qtr. May 12, 9:28 am; New Moon May 19, 10:53 am; First Qtr. May 27 10:22 am

Day of Year	Day of Month	Day of Week	Planetary Configurations and Phenomena	Sunrise	Sunset	Moonrise	Moonset
121	1	Mon	☿ in inferior ☌ (6 pm)	6:52	8:16	**4:37**	4:46
122	2	Tue		6:52	8:17	**5:33**	5:12
123	3	Wed		6:51	8:17	**6:32**	5:39
124	4	Thu		6:50	8:18	**7:33**	6:08
125	5	Fri	Full ☾; eclipse	6:49	8:19	**8:37**	6:40
126	6	Sat		6:48	8:19	**9:45**	7:17
127	7	Sun		6:47	8:20	**10:54**	8:01
128	8	Mon		6:46	8:21		8:53
129	9	Tue	⛢ ☌ ☉ (3 pm)	6:46	8:21	12:00	9:54
130	10	Wed	♂ ☌ Pollux (3 pm)	6:45	8:22	1:00	11:01
131	11	Thu	☾ at perigee (12 am)	6:44	8:23	1:53	**12:11**
132	12	Fri	Last qtr. ☾	6:43	8:23	2:37	**1:21**
133	13	Sat	♄ ☌ ☾ (8 am)	6:43	8:24	3:15	**2:29**
134	14	Sun	☿ stationary; ♆ ☌ ☾	6:42	8:25	3:48	**3:34**
135	15	Mon		6:41	8:25	4:19	**4:38**
136	16	Tue		6:41	8:26	4:49	**5:41**
137	17	Wed	☿ ♃ ☌ ☾	6:40	8:27	5:20	**6:44**
138	18	Thu		6:40	8:27	5:53	**7:48**
139	19	Fri	New ☾	6:39	8:28	6:29	**8:52**
140	20	Sat		6:38	8:29	7:10	**9:55**
141	21	Sun		6:38	8:29	7:56	**10:53**
142	22	Mon		6:37	8:30	8:47	**11:46**
143	23	Tue	♀ ☌ ☾ (7 am)	6:37	8:31	9:42	
144	24	Wed	♂ ☌ ☾ (1 pm)	6:36	8:31	10:40	12:33
145	25	Thu	☾ at apogee (9 pm)	6:36	8:32	11:37	1:13
146	26	Fri		6:36	8:32	**12:34**	1:48
147	27	Sat	First qtr. ☾	6:35	8:33	**1:30**	2:18
148	28	Sun		6:35	8:34	**2:25**	2:46
149	29	Mon	☿ gr. elongation W (1 am)	6:35	8:34	**3:20**	3:13
150	30	Tue	♀ ☌ Pollux (11 am)	6:34	8:35	**4:17**	3:39
151	31	Wed		6:34	8:35	**5:16**	4:07

6th Month — June 2023 — 30 Days

Moon Phases — Full Moon Jun. 3, 10:42 pm; Last Qtr. Jun. 10, 2:31 pm; New Moon Jun 17, 11:37 pm; First Qtr. Jun. 26, 2:50 am

Day of Year	Day of Month	Day of Week	Planetary Configurations and Phenomena	Sunrise	Sunset	Moonrise	Moonset
152	1	Thu		6:34	8:36	**6:19**	4:37
153	2	Fri		6:33	8:36	**7:26**	5:11
154	3	Sat	Full ☾	6:33	8:37	**8:36**	5:52
155	4	Sun	☿ ☌ ⛢ (12 am)	6:33	8:38	**9:45**	6:42
156	5	Mon		6:33	8:38	**10:50**	7:41
157	6	Tue	☾ at perigee (6 pm)	6:33	8:39	**11:47**	8:48
158	7	Wed		6:33	8:39		10:00
159	8	Thu		6:33	8:39	12:35	11:12
160	9	Fri	♄ ☌ ☾ (3 pm)	6:32	8:40	1:16	**12:21**
161	10	Sat	Last qtr. ☾	6:32	8:40	1:51	**1:28**
162	11	Sun	♆ ☌ ☾ (3 am)	6:32	8:41	2:22	**2:32**
163	12	Mon		6:32	8:41	2:52	**3:34**
164	13	Tue		6:32	8:42	3:22	**4:36**
165	14	Wed	♃ ☌ ☾ (2 am)	6:33	8:42	3:53	**5:39**
166	15	Thu	⛢ ☌ ☾ (5 am)	6:33	8:42	4:28	**6:42**
167	16	Fri	☿ ☌ ☾ (4 pm)	6:33	8:43	5:06	**7:44**
168	17	Sat	New ☾	6:33	8:43	5:50	**8:44**
169	18	Sun	♄ stationary	6:33	8:43	6:39	**9:39**
170	19	Mon		6:33	8:43	7:33	**10:28**
171	20	Tue		6:33	8:44	8:30	**11:10**
172	21	Wed	Solstice (9:58 am); ♀ ☌ ☾	6:34	8:44	9:28	**11:47**
173	22	Thu	♂ ☌ ☾ at apogee	6:34	8:44	10:25	
174	23	Fri		6:34	8:44	11:21	12:19
175	24	Sat		6:34	8:44	**12:15**	12:47
176	25	Sun		6:35	8:44	**1:10**	1:14
177	26	Mon	First qtr. ☾	6:35	8:45	**2:05**	1:39
178	27	Tue		6:35	8:45	**3:02**	2:06
179	28	Wed		6:35	8:45	**4:02**	2:34
180	29	Thu		6:36	8:45	**5:06**	3:06
181	30	Fri		6:36	8:45	**6:13**	3:43

☉ The Sun ● The Earth ☾ The Moon ☿ Mercury ♀ Venus ♂ Mars ♃ Jupiter ♄ Saturn ♆ Neptune ⛢ Uranus ☌ = in conjunction ☍ = opposition to the ☉

Astronomical Calendar for 2023

7th Month — July 2023 — 31 Days

Moon Phases — Full Moon Jul. 3, 6:39 am; Last Qtr. Jul. 9, 8:48 pm; New Moon Jul. 17, 1:32 pm; First Qtr. Jul. 25, 5:07 pm

Day of Year	Day of Month	Day of Week	Planetary Configurations and Phenomena	Hour of Sunrise	Hour of Sunset	Hour of Moon-rise	Hour of Moon-set
182	1	Sat	☿ in superior ☌ (12 am)	6:37	8:45	**7:23**	4:28
183	2	Sun		6:37	8:45	**8:32**	5:23
184	3	Mon	Full ☾	6:37	8:45	**9:34**	6:28
185	4	Tue	☾ at perigee	6:38	8:45	**10:27**	7:40
186	5	Wed		6:38	8:44	**11:12**	8:54
187	6	Thu	● at aphelion (3 pm)	6:39	8:44	**11:50**	10:07
188	7	Fri	♀ gr. illumination (3 pm)	6:39	8:44		11:17
189	8	Sat	♆ ☌ ☾ (9 am)	6:40	8:44	12:24	**12:24**
190	9	Sun	Last qtr. ☾	6:40	8:44	12:55	**1:28**
191	10	Mon	♂ ☌ Regulus (3 am)	6:41	8:44	1:25	**2:30**
192	11	Tue	♃ ☌ ☾ (4 pm)	6:41	8:43	1:56	**3:33**
193	12	Wed	⛢ ☌ ☾ (1 pm)	6:42	8:43	2:29	**4:35**
194	13	Thu		6:42	8:43	3:06	**5:37**
195	14	Fri		6:43	8:42	3:47	**6:37**
196	15	Sat		6:43	8:42	4:35	**7:33**
197	16	Sun		6:44	8:42	5:27	**8:24**
198	17	Mon	New ☾	6:45	8:41	6:22	**9:08**
199	18	Tue		6:45	8:41	7:20	**9:46**
200	19	Wed	☿ ☌ ☾ (4 am)	6:46	8:40	8:17	**10:20**
201	20	Thu	♀ ☌ ☾ at apogee	6:46	8:40	9:14	**10:49**
202	21	Fri	Pluto ☍ (11 pm)	6:47	8:39	10:09	**11:16**
203	22	Sat		6:48	8:39	11:03	**11:42**
204	23	Sun		6:48	8:38	11:57	
205	24	Mon		6:49	8:38	**12:52**	12:07
206	25	Tue	First qtr. ☾	6:49	8:37	**1:49**	12:34
207	26	Wed	☿ ☌ ♀ (8 am)	6:50	8:36	**2:50**	1:03
208	27	Thu		6:51	8:36	**3:54**	1:37
209	28	Fri	☿ ☌ Regulus (8 pm)	6:51	8:35	**5:02**	2:17
210	29	Sat		6:52	8:34	**6:10**	3:06
211	30	Sun		6:53	8:34	**7:15**	4:05
212	31	Mon		6:53	8:33	**8:13**	5:14

8th Month — August 2023 — 31 Days

Moon Phases —Full Moon Aug. 1, 1:32 pm; Last Qtr. Aug. 8, 5:28 am; New Moon Aug. 16, 4:38 am; First Qtr. Aug. 24, 4:57 am; Full Moon Aug. 30, 8:36 pm

Day of Year	Day of Month	Day of Week	Planetary Configurations and Phenomena	Hour of Sunrise	Hour of Sunset	Hour of Moon-rise	Hour of Moon-set
213	1	Tue	Full ☾	6:54	8:32	**9:02**	6:28
214	2	Wed	☾ at perigee (1 am)	6:54	8:31	**9:44**	7:44
215	3	Thu	♄ ☌ ☾ (5 am)	6:55	8:31	**10:21**	8:58
216	4	Fri	♆ ☌ ☾ (5 pm)	6:56	8:30	**10:54**	10:08
217	5	Sat		6:56	8:29	**11:25**	11:15
218	6	Sun		6:57	8:28	**11:56**	**12:21**
219	7	Mon		6:58	8:27		**1:25**
220	8	Tue	♃ ⛢ ☌ last qtr. ☾	6:58	8:26	12:29	**2:28**
221	9	Wed	☿ gr. elongation E (9 pm)	6:59	8:25	1:05	**3:31**
222	10	Thu		6:59	8:25	1:46	**4:32**
223	11	Fri		7:00	8:24	2:31	**5:30**
224	12	Sat		7:01	8:23	3:22	**6:22**
225	13	Sun	♀ in inferior ☌ (6 am)	7:01	8:22	4:17	**7:07**
226	14	Mon		7:02	8:21	5:14	**7:47**
227	15	Tue		7:03	8:20	6:11	**8:22**
228	16	Wed	New ☾ at apogee (7 am)	7:03	8:19	7:08	**8:52**
229	17	Thu		7:04	8:18	8:04	**9:20**
230	18	Fri	☿ ♂ Pallas ☌ ☾	7:04	8:16	8:58	**9:45**
231	19	Sat		7:05	8:15	9:52	**10:11**
232	20	Sun		7:06	8:14	10:46	**10:36**
233	21	Mon		7:06	8:13	11:42	**11:04**
234	22	Tue		7:07	8:12	**12:40**	**11:35**
235	23	Wed	☿ stationary (12 am)	7:08	8:11	**1:42**	
236	24	Thu	Antares ☌ first qtr. ☾	7:08	8:10	**2:46**	12:12
237	25	Fri		7:09	8:09	**3:52**	12:55
238	26	Sat		7:09	8:08	**4:57**	1:48
239	27	Sun	♄ ☍ (3 am)	7:10	8:06	**5:57**	2:51
240	28	Mon	⛢ stationary (10 pm)	7:11	8:05	**6:50**	4:01
241	29	Tue		7:11	8:04	**7:35**	5:16
242	30	Wed	♄ ☌ full ☾ at perigee	7:12	8:03	**8:14**	6:31
243	31	Thu		7:12	8:02	**8:49**	7:44

9th Month — September 2023 — 30 Days

Moon Phases — Last Qtr. Sep. 6, 5:21 pm; New Moon Sep. 14, 8:40 pm; First Qtr. Sep. 22, 2:32 pm; Full Moon Sep. 29, 4:58 am

Day of Year	Day of Month	Day of Week	Planetary Configurations and Phenomena	Hour of Sunrise	Hour of Sunset	Hour of Moon-rise	Hour of Moon-set
244	1	Fri	♆ ☌ ☾ (2 am)	7:13	8:00	**9:21**	8:54
245	2	Sat	♀ stationary (11 pm)	7:13	7:59	**9:53**	10:02
246	3	Sun		7:14	7:58	**10:27**	11:09
247	4	Mon	♃ stationary ☌ ☾ (4 pm)	7:15	7:57	**11:03**	**12:16**
248	5	Tue	⛢ ☌ ☾ (4 am)	7:15	7:55	**11:42**	**1:21**
249	6	Wed	Last qtr. ☾	7:16	7:54		**2:24**
250	7	Thu		7:16	7:53	12:27	**3:24**
251	8	Fri		7:17	7:52	1:17	**4:18**
252	9	Sat		7:18	7:50	2:11	**5:06**
253	10	Sun		7:18	7:49	3:08	**5:48**
254	11	Mon	♀ ☌ ☾ (8 am)	7:19	7:48	4:05	**6:24**
255	12	Tue	☾ at apogee (11 am)	7:19	7:46	5:02	**6:55**
256	13	Wed		7:20	7:45	5:58	**7:23**
257	14	Thu	☿ stationary; new ☾	7:20	7:44	6:53	**7:50**
258	15	Fri		7:21	7:43	7:47	**8:15**
259	16	Sat	♂ ☌ ☾ (2 pm)	7:22	7:41	8:42	**8:40**
260	17	Sun		7:22	7:40	9:37	**9:07**
261	18	Mon		7:23	7:39	10:35	**9:37**
262	19	Tue	♀ gr. illumination (2 am)	7:23	7:37	11:35	**10:11**
263	20	Wed		7:24	7:36	**12:38**	**10:52**
264	21	Thu	Antares ☌ ☾ (3 am)	7:24	7:35	**1:42**	**11:40**
265	22	Fri	First qtr. ☾	7:25	7:34	**2:46**	
266	23	Sat	Equinox (1:50 am)	7:26	7:32	**3:46**	12:37
267	24	Sun		7:26	7:31	**4:40**	1:42
268	25	Mon		7:27	7:30	**5:26**	2:53
269	26	Tue	♄ ☌ ☾ (8 pm)	7:27	7:28	**6:07**	4:06
270	27	Wed	☾ at perigee (8 pm)	7:28	7:27	**6:43**	5:18
271	28	Thu	♆ ☌ ☾ (12 pm)	7:29	7:26	**7:16**	6:29
272	29	Fri	Full ☾	7:29	7:25	**7:48**	7:39
273	30	Sat		7:30	7:23	**8:21**	8:47

Bright stars: Aldebaran, Antares, Spica, Pollux, Regulus. **Minor planets or asteroids:** Pluto, Ceres, Pallas, Juno, Vesta ☌ = in conjunction by 10° or < ☍ = opposition to the ⊙

Astronomical Calendar for 2023

10th Month — October 2023 — 31 Days

Moon Phases —Last Qtr. Oct. 6, 8:48 am; New Moon Oct. 14, 12:55 pm; First Qtr. Oct. 21, 10:29 pm; Full Moon Oct. 28, 3:24 pm

Day of Year	Day of Month	Day of Week	Planetary Configurations and Phenomena	Sunrise	Sunset	Moon-rise	Moon-set
274	1	Sun	♃ ☌ ☾ (10 pm)	7:30	7:22	**8:57**	9:55
275	2	Mon	⛢ ☌ ☾ (12 pm)	7:31	7:21	**9:36**	11:03
276	3	Tue		7:32	7:20	**10:19**	**12:10**
277	4	Wed		7:32	7:18	**11:08**	**1:13**
278	5	Thu		7:33	7:17		**2:11**
279	6	Fri	Last qtr. ☾	7:34	7:16	12:02	**3:02**
280	7	Sat		7:34	7:15	12:59	**3:47**
281	8	Sun		7:35	7:13	1:57	**4:24**
282	9	Mon		7:35	7:12	2:54	**4:57**
283	10	Tue	♀ ☌ ☾ at apogee	7:36	7:11	3:51	**5:26**
284	11	Wed		7:37	7:10	4:46	**5:53**
285	12	Thu		7:37	7:09	5:41	**6:19**
286	13	Fri		7:38	7:08	6:35	**6:44**
287	14	Sat	New ☾; ☉ eclipse (12:36 pm)	7:39	7:06	7:31	**7:11**
288	15	Sun		7:40	7:05	8:28	**7:40**
289	16	Mon		7:40	7:04	9:28	**8:13**
290	17	Tue		7:41	7:03	10:31	**8:51**
291	18	Wed	Antares ☌ ☾ (9 am)	7:42	7:02	11:36	**9:37**
292	19	Thu		7:42	7:01	**12:40**	**10:31**
293	20	Fri	☿ in superior ☌ (1 am)	7:43	7:00	**1:40**	**11:33**
294	21	Sat	First qtr. ☾	7:44	6:59	**2:35**	
295	22	Sun		7:45	6:58	**3:22**	12:41
296	23	Mon	♀ gr. elongation W (6 pm)	7:45	6:57	**4:04**	1:51
297	24	Tue	♄ ☌ ☾ (3 am)	7:46	6:56	**4:40**	3:01
298	25	Wed	♆ ☌ ☾ at perigee (9 pm)	7:47	6:55	**5:13**	4:10
299	26	Thu		7:47	6:54	**5:44**	5:17
300	27	Fri		7:48	6:53	**6:16**	6:25
301	28	Sat	Full ☾; eclipse (3 pm)	7:49	6:52	**6:50**	7:32
302	29	Sun	♃ ☌ ☾ (3 am)	7:50	6:51	**7:27**	8:41
303	30	Mon		7:51	6:50	**8:09**	9:49
304	31	Tue		7:51	6:49	**8:57**	10:55

11th Month — November 2023 — 30 Days

Moon Phases — Last Qtr. Nov. 5, 2:37 am; New Moon Nov. 13, 3:27 am; First Qtr. Nov. 20, 4:50 am; Full Moon Nov. 27, 3:16 am

Day of Year	Day of Month	Day of Week	Planetary Configurations and Phenomena	Sunrise	Sunset	Moon-rise	Moon-set
305	1	Wed		7:52	6:48	**9:50**	11:58
306	2	Thu		7:53	6:47	**10:47**	**12:53**
307	3	Fri	♃ ☍ (12 am)	7:54	6:47	**11:46**	**1:41**
308	4	Sat	♄ stationary (12 pm)	7:55	6:46		**2:22**
309	5	Sun	**DST ends (2 am)**; last qtr. ☾	6:55	5:45	12:44	**1:57**
310	6	Mon	☾ at apogee (4 pm)	6:56	5:44	12:41	**2:27**
311	7	Tue		6:57	5:44	1:37	**2:55**
312	8	Wed		6:58	5:43	2:31	**3:21**
313	9	Thu	♀ ☌ ☾ (3 am)	6:59	5:42	3:26	**3:46**
314	10	Fri		7:00	5:42	4:21	**4:12**
315	11	Sat		7:00	5:41	5:18	**4:40**
316	12	Sun		7:01	5:40	6:17	**5:12**
317	13	Mon	New ☾; ⛢ ☍ (11 am)	7:02	5:40	7:20	**5:49**
318	14	Tue	Antares ☌ ☾ (2 pm)	7:03	5:39	8:26	**6:33**
319	15	Wed		7:04	5:39	9:31	**7:26**
320	16	Thu	☿ ☌ Antares (12 pm)	7:05	5:38	10:34	**8:26**
321	17	Fri		7:06	5:38	11:32	**9:33**
322	18	Sat	♂ ☌ ☉ (12 am)	7:06	5:37	**12:21**	**10:42**
323	19	Sun		7:07	5:37	**1:04**	**11:51**
324	20	Mon	♄ ☌ first qtr. ☾ (8 am)	7:08	5:36	**1:41**	
325	21	Tue	☾ at perigee (3 pm)	7:09	5:36	**2:13**	12:59
326	22	Wed	♆ ☌ ☾ (2 am)	7:10	5:36	**2:44**	2:05
327	23	Thu		7:11	5:36	**3:15**	3:10
328	24	Fri		7:12	5:35	**3:47**	4:15
329	25	Sat	♃ ☌ ☾ (5 am)	7:12	5:35	**4:22**	5:22
330	26	Sun	⛢ ☌ ☾ (3 am)	7:13	5:35	**5:01**	6:29
331	27	Mon	Full ☾	7:14	5:35	**5:46**	7:36
332	28	Tue	♀ ☌ Spica (3 am)	7:15	5:34	**6:37**	8:41
333	29	Wed		7:16	5:34	**7:33**	9:40
334	30	Thu		7:17	5:34	**8:32**	10:32

12th Month — December 2023 — 31 Days

Moon Phases — Last Qtr. Dec. 4, 11:49 pm; New Moon Dec. 12, 5:32 pm; First Qtr. Dec. 19, 12:39 pm; Full Moon Dec. 26, 6:33 pm

Day of Year	Day of Month	Day of Week	Planetary Configurations and Phenomena	Sunrise	Sunset	Moon-rise	Moon-set
335	1	Fri		7:17	5:34	**9:31**	11:17
336	2	Sat		7:18	5:34	**10:30**	11:54
337	3	Sun		7:19	5:34	**11:26**	**12:27**
338	4	Mon	☿ gr. elong. E (8 am); Last qtr. ☾	7:20	5:34		**12:55**
339	5	Tue		7:21	5:34	12:21	**1:22**
340	6	Wed	♆ stationary (6 pm)	7:21	5:34	1:15	**1:47**
341	7	Thu		7:22	5:34	2:09	**2:12**
342	8	Fri		7:23	5:34	3:05	**2:39**
343	9	Sat	♀ ☌ ☾ (11 am)	7:24	5:35	4:03	**3:09**
344	10	Sun		7:24	5:35	5:04	**3:44**
345	11	Mon		7:25	5:35	6:09	**4:25**
346	12	Tue	New ☾; ☿ stationary	7:26	5:35	7:16	**5:15**
347	13	Wed	☿ ☌ ☾ (11 pm)	7:26	5:36	8:22	**6:14**
348	14	Thu		7:27	5:36	9:23	**7:21**
349	15	Fri		7:28	5:36	10:17	**8:32**
350	16	Sat	☾ at perigee (1 pm)	7:28	5:37	11:03	**9:43**
351	17	Sun	♄ ☌ ☾ (4 pm)	7:29	5:37	11:42	**10:52**
352	18	Mon		7:30	5:37	**12:16**	**11:58**
353	19	Tue	First qtr. ☾	7:30	5:38	**12:47**	
354	20	Wed		7:31	5:38	**1:17**	1:03
355	21	Thu	Solstice (9:27 pm)	7:31	5:39	**1:48**	2:07
356	22	Fri	♃ ☌ ☾; ☿ in inferior ☌	7:32	5:39	**2:21**	3:11
357	23	Sat	⛢ ☌ ☾ (9 am)	7:32	5:40	**2:57**	4:17
358	24	Sun		7:33	5:40	**3:39**	5:22
359	25	Mon		7:33	5:41	**4:27**	6:27
360	26	Tue	Full ☾	7:33	5:41	**5:21**	7:28
361	27	Wed		7:34	5:42	**6:19**	8:23
362	28	Thu		7:34	5:43	**7:19**	9:10
363	29	Fri		7:34	5:43	**8:18**	9:51
364	30	Sat		7:35	5:44	**9:16**	10:25
365	31	Sun	♃ stationary (9 am)	7:35	5:45	**10:11**	10:55

☉ The Sun ● The Earth ☾ The Moon ☿ Mercury ♀ Venus ♂ Mars ♃ Jupiter ♄ Saturn ♆ Neptune ⛢ Uranus ☌ = in conjunction ☍ = opposition to the ☉

Recreation

STATE PARKS & HISTORIC SITES

STATE FORESTS

NATIONAL PARKS & LANDMARKS

BIRDING

FAIRS & FESTIVALS

HUNTING & FISHING

People enjoying the day at South Padre Island.
Photo by Vince Smith, CC by 2.0/Flickr

Cedar Hill State Park, an urban park on 1,826 acres ten miles southwest of Dallas via US 67 and FM 1382 on Joe Pool Lake, was acquired by long-term lease from the Army Corp of Engineers in 1982. Camping mostly in wooded areas. Fishing from two lighted jetties and a perch pond for children. Swimming, boating, bicycling, birdwatching and picnicking. Vegetation includes several sections of tall-grass prairie. Penn Farm Agricultural History Center includes reconstructed buildings of the 19th-century Penn Farm and exhibits; self-guided tours.

Choke Canyon State Park consists of two units, South Shore and Calliham, located on 26,000-acre Choke Canyon Reservoir. Park acquired in 1981 in a 50-year agreement among Bureau of Reclamation, City of Corpus Christi and Nueces River Authority. Thickets of mesquite and blackbrush acacia predominate, supporting populations of javelina, coyote, skunk and alligator, as well as the crested caracara. The 385-acre South Shore Unit is located 3.5 miles west of Three Rivers on TX 72 in Live Oak County; the 1,100-acre Calliham Unit is located 12 miles west of Three Rivers, on TX 72, in McMullen County. Both units offer camping, picnicking, boating, fishing, lake swimming, and baseball and volleyball areas. The Calliham Unit also has a hiking trail, wildlife educational center, screened shelters, rentable gym and kitchen. Sports complex includes swimming pool and tennis, volleyball, shuffleboard and basketball courts. Across dam from South Shore is North Shore Equestrian and Camping Area; 18 miles of horseback riding trails.

Cleburne State Park is a 528-acre park located 10 miles southwest of Cleburne via US 67 and PR 21 in Johnson County with 116-acre spring-fed lake; acquired from the City of Cleburne and private owners in 1935 and 1936. Oak, elm, mesquite, cedar and redbud cover white rocky hills. Bluebonnets in spring. Activities include camping, picnicking, hiking, bicycling, canoeing, swimming, boating, fishing. Nearby are Fossil Rim Wildlife Center and dinosaur tracks in Paluxy River at Dinosaur Valley State Park.

Colorado Bend State Park, a 5,328.3-acre facility, is 28 miles west of Lampasas in Lampasas and San Saba counties. Access is from Lampasas to Bend on FM 580 west, then follow signs (access road subject to flooding). Park site was purchased partly in 1984, with balance acquired in 1987. Primitive camping, fishing, swimming, hiking, biking and picnicking; guided tours to Gorman Falls; crawling cave tours require reservations. Rare and endangered species here include golden-cheeked warbler, black-capped vireo and bald eagle.

Confederate Reunion Grounds State Historic Site, located in Limestone County on the Navasota River, is 77.1 acres in size. Acquired 1983 by deed from Joseph E. Johnston Camp No. 94 CSA. Entrance is 6 miles south of Mexia on TX 14, then 2.5 miles west on FM 2705. Historic buildings, two scenic footbridges span creek; hiking trail. Nearby are Fort Parker State Park and Old Fort Parker.

Cooper Lake State Park comprises 3,026 acres and just three miles southeast of Cooper in Delta and Hopkins counties. The park was acquired in 1991 from Army Corps of Engineers. Two units, Doctors Creek and South Sulphur, adjoin 19,300-surface-acre Cooper Lake. Fishing, boating, camping, picnicking, swimming. Screened shelters and cabins South Sulphur offers equestrian camping and horseback riding trails.

Hikers at sunset in Choke Canyon State Park. Photo by Stuart Seeger, CC by 2.0/Flickr.

Copper Breaks State Park, 12 miles south of Quanah on TX 6 in Hardeman County, was acquired by purchase from private owner in 1970. Park features rugged scenic beauty on 1,898.8 acres, two lakes, grass-covered mesas and juniper breaks. Nearby medicine mounds were important ceremonial sites of Comanche Indians. Nearby Pease River was site of 1860 battle in which Cynthia Ann Parker was recovered from Comanches. Part of state longhorn herd lives at park. Abundant wildlife. Nature, hiking and equestrian trails; natural and historical exhibits; summer programs; horseback riding; camping, equestrian camping.

Daingerfield State Park, off TX 49 and PR 17 southeast of Daingerfield in Morris County, is a 550.9-acre recreational area that includes an 80-surface-acre lake; deeded in 1935 by private owners. This area is center of iron industry in Texas; nearby is Lone Star Steel Co. In spring, dogwood, redbuds and wisteria bloom; in fall, brilliant foliage of sweetgum, oaks and maples contrast with dark green pines. Campsites, lodge and cabins.

Davis Mountains State Park is 2,709 acres in Jeff Davis County, four miles northwest of Fort Davis via TX 118 and PR 3. The scenic area was deeded in 1933-1937 by private owners. First European, Antonio de Espejo, came to area in 1583. Extremes of altitude produce both plains grasslands and piñon-juniper-oak woodlands. Montezuma quail, rare in Texas, visit park. Scenic drives, camping and hiking. Indian Lodge, built by the Civilian Conservation Corps during the early 1930s, has 39 rooms, restaurant and swimming pool (reservations: 432-426-3254). Four-mile hiking trail leads to Fort Davis National Historic Site. Other nearby points of interest include McDonald Observatory and 74-mile scenic loop through Davis Mountains. Nearby are scenic Limpia, Madera, Musquiz and Keesey canyons; Camino del Rio; ghost town of Shafter; Big Bend National Park; Big Bend Ranch State Park; Fort Davis National Historic Site; and Fort Leaton State Historic Site.

Devils River State Natural Area comprises 37,000 acres in Val Verde County, 22 miles off US 277, about 65 miles north of Del Rio on graded road. It is an ecological and archaeological crossroads. Ecologically, it is in a transitional area between the Edwards Plateau, the Trans-Pecos desert and the South Texas brush country. Archaeological studies suggest occupation and use by cultures from both east and west. Camping, hiking, and mountain biking. All camping, facility stays, canyon, and pictograph-site tours are by reservation only. Dolan Falls is nearby and is accessible only through The Nature Conservancy of Texas.

Devil's Sinkhole State Natural Area, comprising 1,859.7 acres about six miles northeast of Rocksprings on US 377 in Edwards County, is a vertical cavern. The sinkhole, discovered by Anglo settlers in 1867, is a registered National Natural Landmark; it was purchased in 1985 from private owners. The cavern opening is about 40 by 60 feet, with a vertical drop of about 140 feet. Access by prearranged tour with Devil's Sinkhole Society (830-683-BATS). Bats can be viewed in summer leaving cave at dusk; no access to cave itself. Contact Kickapoo Cavern State Park to arrange a tour.

Dinosaur Valley State Park, located off US 67 four miles west of Glen Rose in Somervell County, is a 1,524.72-acre scenic park. Land was acquired from private owners in 1968. Features dinosaur tracks in bed of Paluxy River and two full-scale dinosaur models, originally created for New York World's Fair in 1964–65, on display. Part of state longhorn herd is in park. Camping, picnicking, hiking, mountain biking, swimming, fishing. The riverbed featuring the dinosaur tracks was designated a national landmark in 1968. See page 154 for more.

Eisenhower Birthplace State Historic Site is six acres off US 75 at 609 S. Lamar, Denison, Grayson County. The property was acquired in 1958 from the Eisenhower Birthplace Foundation. Restoration of home of President Dwight Eisenhower includes furnishings of period and some personal effects of Gen. Eisenhower. Guided tour; call for schedule. Park open daily, except Christmas Day and New Year's Day; call for hours. Town of Denison established on Butterfield Overland Mail Route in 1858.

Eisenhower State Park, 423.1 acres five miles northwest of Denison via US 75 to TX 91N to FM 1310 on the shores of Lake Texoma in Grayson County, was acquired by an Army lease in 1954. Named for the 34th U.S. president, Dwight D. Eisenhower. First Anglo settlers came to area in 1835; Fort Johnson was established in area in 1840; Colbert's Ferry established on Red River in 1853 and operated until 1931. Areas of tall-grass prairie exist. Hiking, camping, picnicking, fishing, swimming.

Enchanted Rock State Natural Area is 1,643.5 acres on Big Sandy Creek 18 miles north of Fredericksburg on FM 965 on the line between Gillespie and Llano counties. Acquired in 1978 by The Nature Conservancy of Texas; state acquired from TNCT in 1984. Enchanted Rock is huge pink granite boulder rising 425 feet above ground and covering 640 acres. It is second-largest batholith (underground rock formation uncovered by erosion) in the United States. Indians believed ghost fires flickered at top and were awed by weird creaking and groaning, which geologists say resulted from rock's heating and expanding by day, cooling and contracting at night. Enchanted Rock is a National Natural Landmark and is on the National Register of Historic Places. Activities include hiking, geological study, camping, rock climbing and star gazing.

Estero Llano Grande State Park, part of the World Birding Center network, is a 176-acre wetlands refuge 3.2 miles southeast of Weslaco off FM 1015. Birds seen here include waders, shorebirds and migrating waterfowl, as well as coastal species such as Roseate spoonbill and Ibis. Rare spottings include red-crowned parrots and green parakeets. Opened daily. Guided tours offered.

Fairfield Lake State Park is 1,460 acres adjacent to Lake Fairfield, six miles northeast of the city of Fairfield off FM 2570 and FM 3285 in Freestone County. It was leased from Texas Utilities in 1971-72. Surrounding woods offer sanctuary for many species of birds and wildlife. Camping, hiking, backpacking, nature study, water-related activities available. Extensive schedule of tours, seminars and other activities.

Parks text continues on page 154.

Falcon State Park is 572.6 acres located 15 miles north of Roma off US 83 and FM 2098 at southern end of Falcon Reservoir in Starr and Zapata counties. Park leased from International Boundary and Water Commission in 1949. Gently rolling hills covered by mesquite, huisache, wild olive, ebony, cactus. Excellent birding and fishing. Camping and water activities also. Nearby are Mexico, Fort Ringgold in Rio Grande City and historic city of Roma. Bentsen-Rio Grande Valley State Park is 65 miles away.

Fannin Battleground State Historic Site, nine miles east of Goliad in Goliad County off US 59 to PR 27. The 13.6-acre park site was acquired by the state in 1914; transferred to TPW by legislative enactment in 1965. At this site on March 20, 1836, Col. James Fannin surrendered to Mexican Gen. José Urrea after Battle of Coleto; 342 massacred and 28 escaped near what is now Goliad SP.

Fanthorp Inn State Historic Site includes a historic double-pen cedar-log dogtrot house and 1.4 acres in Anderson, county seat of Grimes County, south of TX 90. Acquired by purchase in 1977 from a Fanthorp descendant and opened to the public in 1987. Inn records report visits from many prominent civic and military leaders, including Sam Houston, Anson Jones, and generals Ulysses S. Grant, Robert E. Lee and Stonewall Jackson. Originally built in 1834, it has been restored to its 1850 use as a family home and travelers' hotel. Tours available Friday, Saturday, Sunday. Call TPW for stagecoach-ride schedule. No dining or overnight facilities.

Fort Boggy State Park is 1,847 acres of wooded, rolling hills in Leon County near Boggy Creek, about four miles south of Centerville on TX 75. Land donated to TPWD in 1985 by Eileen Crain Sullivan. Area once home to Keechi and Kickapoo tribes. Log fort was built by settlers in 1840s; first settlement north of the Old San Antonio Road and between the Navasota and Trinity rivers. Swimming beach, fishing, picnicking, nature trails for hiking and mountain biking. Fifteen-acre lake open to small craft. Open-air group pavilion overlooking lake can be reserved ($50 per day). Nearby attractions include Rusk/Palestine, Fort Parker, and Texas State Railroad state parks, and Old Fort Parker Historic Site. Open Wed.–Sun. for day use only; entrance fee. For reservations, call 512-389-8900.

Fort Griffin State Historic Site is 506.2 acres 15 miles north of Albany off US 283 in Shackelford County. The state was deeded the land by the county in 1935. Portion of state longhorn herd resides in park. On bluff overlooking townsite of Fort Griffin and Clear Fork of Brazos River valley are partially restored ruins of Old Fort Griffin, restored bakery, replicas of enlisted men's huts. Fort constructed in 1867, deactivated 1881. Camping, equestrian camping, hiking. Nearby are Albany with restored courthouse square, Abilene and Possum Kingdom state parks. Albany annually holds "Fandangle" musical show in commemoration of frontier times.

Fort Lancaster State Historic Site, 81.6-acres located about eight miles east of Sheffield on TX 290 in Crockett County. Acquired in 1968 by deed from Crockett County; Henry Meadows donated 41 acres in 1975. Fort Lancaster established Aug. 20, 1855, to guard San Antonio-El Paso Road and protect movement of supplies and immigrants from Indian hostilities. Site of part of Camel Corps experiment. Fort abandoned March 19, 1861, after Texas seceded from Union. Exhibits on history, natural history and archaeology; nature trail, picnicking. Open daily; day use only.

Fort Leaton State Historic Site, four miles southeast of Presidio in Presidio County on FM 170, was acquired in 1967 from private owners. Consists of 23.4 acres, 5 of which are on site of trading post. In 1848, Ben Leaton built fortified adobe trading post known as Fort Leaton near present Presidio. Ben Leaton died in 1851. Guided tours; exhibits trace history, natural history and archaeological history of area. Serves as western entrance to Big Bend Ranch State Park. Day use only.

Fort McKavett State Historic Site, 79.5 acres acquired from 1967 through the mid-1970s from Fort McKavett Restoration, Inc., Menard County and private individuals, is located 23 miles west of Menard off US 190 and FM 864. Originally called Camp San Saba, the fort was built by War Department in 1852 to protect frontier settlers and travelers on Upper El Paso Road from Indians. Camp later renamed for Capt. Henry McKavett, killed at Battle of Monterrey, Sept. 21, 1846. Fort abandoned March 1859; reoccupied April 1868. A Buffalo Soldier post. Abandoned again June 30, 1883. Once called by Gen. Wm. T. Sherman, "the prettiest post in Texas." More than 25 restored buildings, ruins of many others. Interpretive exhibits. Day use only.

Fort Parker State Park includes 1,458.8 acres, including 758.78 land acres and 700-acre lake between Mexia and Groesbeck off TX 14 in Limestone County. Named for the former private fort built near present park in 1836, the site was acquired from private owners and the City of Mexia 1935-1937. Camping, fishing, swimming, canoeing, picnicking. Nearby is Old Fort Parker Historic Site, which is operated by the City of Groesbeck.

Fort Richardson State Park, Historic Site, and Lost Creek Reservoir Trailway, located one-half mile south of Jacksboro off US 281 in Jack County, contains 454 acres. Acquired in 1968 from City of Jacksboro. Fort founded in 1867, northernmost of line of federal forts established after Civil War for protection from Indians; originally named Fort Jacksboro. In April 1867, fort was moved to its present location from 20 miles farther south; on Nov. 19, 1867, made permanent post at Jacksboro and named for Israel Richardson, who was fatally wounded at Battle of Antietam. Expeditions sent from Fort Richardson arrested Indians responsible for Warren Wagon Train Massacre in 1871 and fought Comanches in Palo Duro Canyon. Fort abandoned in May 1878. Park contains seven restored buildings and two replicas. Interpretive center, picnicking, camping, fishing; ten-mile trailway.

Franklin Mountains State Park, created by an act of the legislature in 1979 to protect the mountain range as a wilderness preserve and acquired by TPW in 1981, comprises 24,247.56 acres, all within El Paso city limits. Largest urban park in the nation. It includes virtually an entire Chihuahuan Desert mountain range, with an elevation of 7,192 feet at the summit. The park is habitat for

A Ringed Kingfisher at Estero Llano Grande State Park. This park is a popular site for birders and other wildlife photographers. Photo by Andy Reago and Chrissy McClarren, CC by 2.0/Flickr

many Chihuahuan Desert plants including sotol, lechuguilla, ocotillo, cholla and barrel cactus, and such animals as mule deer, fox and an occasional cougar. Camping, mountain biking, nature study, hiking, picnicking, rock-climbing. Wyler Aerial Tramway, an aerial cable-car tramway on 195 acres of rugged mountain on east side of Franklin Mountains. Purchase tickets at tramway station on McKinley Ave. Check with park for fees and hours; 915-566-6622. Other area attractions include Hueco Tanks State Historic Site and Magoffin Home State Historic Site.

French Legation State Historic Site was built in 1841 as a private home for Alphones Dubois, French chargé d'affaires to the Republic of Texas. In 1848 it was purchased by Dr. Joseph W. Robertson, who lived there with his large family and nine enslaved workers. Daughter Lillie Robertson lived in the house her entire life. The state acquired the house after her death, and appointed the Daughters of the Republic as custodian. In 2017, HB 3810 transferred the French Legation to the THC. The site is currently closed for restoration.

Fulton Mansion State Historic Site in Fulton is 3.5 miles north of Rockport off TX Business 35 on South Fulton Beach Rd. in Aransas County. The 2.3 acre-property was acquired by purchase from private owner in 1976. Three-story wooden structure, built in 1874-1877, was home of George W. Fulton, prominent in South Texas for economic and commercial influence; mansion derives significance from its innovative construction and Victorian design. Call ahead for days and hours of guided tours; open Wednesday–Sunday; 800-792-1112.

Galveston Island State Park, on the west end of Galveston Island on FM 3005, is a 2,013.1-acre site acquired in 1969

from private owners. Camping, birding, nature study, swimming, bicycling and fishing amid **sand dunes and grassland**. Musical productions in amphitheater during summer.

Garner State Park is 1,419.8 acres of recreational facilities on US 83 on the Frio River in Uvalde County 9 miles south of Leakey. Named for John Nance Garner, U.S. Vice President, 1933-1941, the park was deeded in 1934-36 by private owners. Camping, hiking, picnicking, river recreation, miniature golf, biking, boat rentals. Cabins available. Nearby is John Nance "Cactus Jack" Garner Museum in Uvalde. Nearby also are ruins of historic Mission Nuestra Señora de la Candelaria del Cañon, founded in 1749; Camp Sabinal (a U.S. Cavalry post and later Texas Ranger camp) established 1856; Fort Inge, established 1849.

Goliad State Park and Mission Espíritu Santo Historic Site are 188.3 acres one-fourth mile south of Goliad on US 183 and 77A, along the San Antonio River in Goliad County. The land was deeded to the state in 1931 by the City and County of Goliad; transferred to TPW 1949. Nearby are the sites of several battles in the Texas fight for independence from Mexico. The park includes a replica of Mission Nuestra Señora del Espíritu Santo de Zúñiga, originally established 1722 and settled at its present site in 1749. At Goliad State Park are camping, picnicking, historical exhibits, nature trail. (See also Fannin Battleground State Historic Site.)

Goose Island State Park, 321.4 acres 10 miles northeast of Rockport on TX 35 and PR 13 on St. Charles and Aransas bays in Aransas County, was deeded by private owners in 1931-1935 plus an additional seven acres donated in the early 1990s by Sun Oil Co. Located here is "Big Tree"

Tall trees at Huntsville State Park. Photo by Roy Luck, CC by 2.0/Flickr.

estimated to be a 1,000-year-old live oak. Fishing, picnicking and camping, plus excellent birding; no swimming. Rare and endangered whooping cranes can be viewed during winter just across St. Charles Bay in Aransas National Wildlife Refuge.

Government Canyon State Natural Area is an 8,622-acre area in Bexar County, northwest of San Antonio, 3.5 miles northwest of Loop 1604 and FM 471, then 1.6 miles north on Galm Road. Day use only. No camping. Open Friday–Monday. Trees such as mounatin laurel, Ashe juniper, Mexican buckeye and Escarpment black cherry.

Guadalupe River State Park comprises 1,938.7 acres on cypress-shaded Guadalupe River in Kendall and Comal counties, 13 miles east of Boerne on TX 46. Acquired by deed from private owners in 1974. Park has four miles of river frontage with several white-water rapids and is located in a stretch of Guadalupe River noted for canoeing, tubing. Picnicking, camping, hiking, nature study. Trees include sycamore, elm, basswood, pecan, walnut, persimmon, willow and hackberry (see also Honey Creek State Natural Area).

Hill Country State Natural Area in Bandera and Medina counties, 9 miles west of Bandera on FM 1077. The 5,369.8-acre site acquired by gift from Merrick Bar-O-Ranch and purchased in 1976. Park is located in typical Texas Hill Country on West Verde Creek and contains several spring-fed streams. Primitive and equestrian camping, hiking, horseback riding, mountain biking, fishing. Group lodge.

Hueco Tanks State Park and Historic Site, located 32 miles northeast of El Paso in El Paso County on FM 2775 just north of US 62-180, was obtained from the county in 1969, with additional 121 acres purchased in 1970. Featured in this 860.3-acre park are large natural rock basins that provided water for archaic hunters, Plains Indians, Butterfield Overland Mail coach horses and passengers, and other travelers in this arid region. In park are Indian pictographs, old ranch house and relocated ruins of stage station. Rock climbing, picnicking, camping, hiking. Wildlife includes gray fox, bobcat, prairie falcons, golden eagles. Visitation is limited. Pictograph tours are by advanced request. Call 1-800-792-112, (Option 3).

Huntsville State Park is 2,083.2-acre recreational area off IH 45 and PR 40 six miles south of Huntsville in Walker County, acquired by deeds from private owners in 1937. Heavily wooded park adjoins Sam Houston National Forest and encloses Lake Raven. Hiking, camping, fishing, biking, paddle boats, canoeing. At nearby Huntsville are Sam Houston's old homestead (Steamboat House), containing some of his personal effects, and his grave. Approximately 50 miles away is Alabama-Coushatta Indian Reservation in Polk County.

Inks Lake State Park is 1,201 acres of recreational facilities along Inks Lake, 9 miles west of Burnet on the Colorado River off TX 29 on PR 4 in Burnet County. Acquired by deeds from the Lower Colorado River Authority and private owners in 1940. Camping, hiking, fishing, swimming, boating, golf. Deer, turkey and other wildlife abundant. Nearby are Longhorn Cavern State Park, LBJ Ranch, LBJ State Historic Site, Pedernales Falls State Park and Enchanted Rock State Natural Area. Granite Mountain quarry at nearby Marble Falls furnished red granite for Texas state capitol. Buchanan Dam, considered the largest multi-arch dam in the nation, located 4 miles from park.

Kickapoo Cavern State Park is located about 22 miles north of Brackettville on RM 674 on the Kinney/Edwards county line in the southern Edwards Plateau. The park (6,368.4 acres) contains 20 known caves, two of which are large enough to be significant: Kickapoo Cavern, about 1/4 mile in length, has impressive formations, and Stuart Bat Cave (formally Green Cave), slightly shorter, supports a nursery colony of Mexican freetail bats in summer. Public observations of bat flights are available with an entrance permit. Birds include rare species such as black-capped vireo, varied bunting and Montezuma quail. Reptiles and amphibians include barking frog, mottled rock rattlesnake and Texas alligator lizard. Open Friday–Monday. Cavern tours on Saturday by reservation. Group lodge; primitive camping; hiking and mountain-biking trails.

Lake Arrowhead State Park consists of 524 acres in Clay County, about 14 miles south of Wichita Falls on US 281 to FM 1954, then 8 miles to park. Acquired in 1970 from the City of Wichita Falls. Lake Arrowhead is a reservoir on the Little Wichita River with 106 miles of shoreline. The land surrounding the lake is generally semiarid, gently rolling prairie, much of which has been invaded by mesquite in recent decades. Fishing, camping, lake swimming, picnicking, horseback-riding area.

Lake Bob Sandlin State Park, on the wooded shoreline of 9,400-acre Lake Bob Sandlin, is located 12 miles southwest of Mount Pleasant off FM 21 in Titus County. Activities in the 639.8-acre park include picnicking, camping, mountain biking, hiking, swimming, fishing and boating. Oak, hickory, dogwood, redbud, maple and pine produce spectacular fall color. Eagles can sometimes be spotted in winter months.

Lake Brownwood State Park in Brown County is 537.5 acres acquired from Brown County Water Improvement District No. 1 in 1934. Park reached from TX 279 to PR 15, 16 miles northwest of Brownwood on Lake Brownwood near geographical center of Texas. Water sports, hiking, camping. Cabins available.

Lake Casa Blanca International State Park, located one mile east of Laredo off US 59 on Loop 20, was formerly operated by the City of Laredo and Webb County and was acquired by TPW in 1990. Park includes 371 acres on Lake Casa Blanca. Recreation hall can be reserved. Camping, picnicking, fishing, ball fields, playgrounds, amphitheater, and tennis courts. County-operated golf course nearby.

Lake Colorado City State Park, 500 acres leased for 99 years from a utility company. It is located in Mitchell County 11 miles southwest of Colorado City off IH 20 on FM 2836. Water sports, picnicking, camping, hiking. Part of state longhorn herd can be seen in park.

Lake Corpus Christi State Park, a 14,112-acre park in San Patricio, Jim Wells and Live Oak counties. Located 35 miles northwest of Corpus Christi and four miles southwest of Mathis off TX 359 and Park Road 25. Was leased from City of Corpus Christi in 1934. Camping, picnicking, birding, water sports. Nearby are Padre Island National Seashore; Mustang Island, Choke Canyon, Goliad and Goose Island state parks; Aransas National Wildlife Refuge, and Fulton Mansion State Historic Site.

Lake Livingston State Park, in Polk County, about one mile southwest of Livingston on FM 3126 and PR 65, contains 635.5 acres along Lake Livingston. Acquired by

deed from private landowners in 1971. Near ghost town of Swartwout, steamboat landing on Trinity River in 1830s and 1850s. Camping, picnicking, swimming pool, fishing, mountain biking and stables.

Lake Mineral Wells State Park and Trailway, located four miles east of Mineral Wells on US 180 in Parker County, consists of 3,282.5 acres encompassing Lake Mineral Wells. In 1975, the City of Mineral Wells donated 1,095 land acres and the lake to TPW; the federal government transferred additional land from Fort Wolters army post. Popular for rock-climbing/rappelling. Swimming, fishing, boating, camping; the 20-mile Lake Mineral Wells State Trailway avaiable for hiking, bicycling, equestrian use.

Lake Somerville State Park, northwest of Brenham in Lee and Burleson counties, was leased from the federal government in 1969. Birch Creek Unit (2,365 acres reached from TX 60 and PR 57) and Nails Creek Unit (3,155 acres reached from US 290 and FM 180), are connected by a 13-mile trailway system, with equestrian and primitive camp sites, rest benches, shelters and drinking water. Also camping, birding, picnicking, volleyball and water sports. Somerville Wildlife Management Area, 3,180 acres is nearby.

Lake Tawakoni State Park is a 376.3-acre park in Hunt County along the shore of its namesake reservoir. It was acquired in 1984 through a 50-year lease agreement with the Sabine River Authority and opened in 2001. Includes a swimming beach, half-mile trail, picnic sites, boat ramp and campsites. A 40-acre tallgrass prairie managed in the post-oak woodlands. The park is reached from IH 20 on TX 47 north to FM 2475 about 20 miles past Wills Point.

Lake Whitney State Park is 1,280.7 acres along the east shore of Lake Whitney west of Hillsboro via TX 22 and FM 1244 in Hill County. Acquired in 1954 by a Department of the Army lease. Located near ruins of Towash, early Texas settlement inundated by the lake. Towash Village named for chief of Hainai Indians. Park noted for bluebonnets in spring. Camping, hiking, birding, picnicking, water activities.

Landmark Inn State Historic Site, 4.7 acres in Castroville, Medina County, about 15 miles west of San Antonio, was acquired through donation by Miss Ruth Lawler in 1974. Castroville, settled in the 1840s by Alsatian farmers, is called Little Alsace of Texas. Landmark Inn built about 1844 as residence and store for Cesar Monod, mayor of Castroville 1851-1864. Special workshops, tours and events held at inn; grounds may be rented for receptions, family reunions and weddings. Overnight lodging; all rooms air-conditioned and nonsmoking.

Levi Jordan Plantation State Historic Site was a sugar and cotton plantation, established in the 1850s. The site is currently under development and is not open to the public.

Lipantitlan State Historic Site is five acres, found nine miles east of Orange Grove in Nueces County off Texas 359, FM 624 and FM 70. The property was deeded by private owners in 1937. Fort constructed here in 1833 by Mexican government fell to Texas forces in 1835. Only facilities are picnic tables. Lake Corpus Christi State Park is nearby.

Lockhart State Park is 263.7 acres, found four miles south of Lockhart via US 183, FM 20 and PR 10 in Caldwell County. The land was deeded by private owners between 1934 and 1937. Camping, picnicking, hiking, fishing, 9-hole golf course. After Comanche raid at Linnville, the Battle of Plum Creek (1840) was fought in area.

Longhorn Cavern State Park, off US 281 and PR 4 about six miles west and six miles south of Burnet in Burnet County, is 645.62 acres dedicated as a natural landmark in 1971. It was acquired in 1932-1937 from private owners. The cave has been used as a shelter since prehistoric times. Among legends about the cave is that the outlaw Sam Bass hid stolen money there. Confederates made gunpowder in the cave during the Civil War. Nature trail; guided tours of cave; picnicking, hiking. Cavern operated by concession agreement. Inks Lake State Park and Lyndon B. Johnson Ranch located nearby.

Lost Maples State Natural Area consists of 2,174.2 scenic acres on the Sabinal River in Bandera and Real counties, five miles north of Vanderpool on FM 187. Acquired by purchase from private owners in 1973-1974. Outstanding example of Edwards Plateau flora and fauna, features isolated stand of uncommon Uvalde bigtooth maple. Rare golden-cheeked warbler, black-capped vireo and green kingfisher nest and feed in park. Fall foliage can be spectacular (late Oct. through early Nov.). Hiking trails, camping, fishing, picnicking, birding.

Lyndon B. Johnson State Park & Historic Site, off US 290 in Gillespie County 14 miles west of Johnson City near Stonewall, contains 717.9 acres. Acquired in 1965 with private donations. Home of Lyndon B. Johnson located north bank of Pedernales River across Ranch Road 1 from park; portion of official Texas longhorn herd maintained at park. Wildlife exhibit includes turkey, deer and bison. Living-history demonstrations at restored Sauer-Beckmann house. Reconstruction of Johnson birthplace is open to public. Historic structures, swimming pool, tennis courts, baseball field, picnicking. Day use only. Nearby is family cemetery where former president and relatives are buried. In Johnson City is boyhood home of President Johnson. (See National Parks.)

Magoffin Home State Historic Site, in El Paso, is a 19-room territorial-style adobe on a 1.5-acre site. Purchased by the state and City of El Paso in 1976, it is operated by TPW. Home was built in 1875 by El Pasoan Joseph Magoffin. Furnished with original family artifacts. Guided tours; call for schedule. Day use only.

Martin Creek Lake State Park, 286.9 acres, is located four miles south of Tatum off TX 43 and CR 2183 in Rusk County. It was deeded to the TPW by Texas Utilities in 1976. Water activities; also cabins, camping, picnicking. Roadbed of Trammel's Trace, old Indian trail that became major route for settlers moving to Texas from Arkansas, can be seen. Hardwood and pine forest shelters abundant wildlife including swamp rabbits, gophers, nutria and numerous species of land birds and waterfowl. Annual

perch fishing contest for children ages 4–12 the first Saturday in September.

Martin Dies Jr. State Park is 705 acres in Jasper and Tyler counties on the B. A. Steinhagen Reservoir between Woodville and Jasper via US 190. Land leased for 50 years from Corps of Engineers in 1964. Located at edge of Big Thicket. Plant and animal life varied and abundant. Winter bald eagle census conducted at nearby Sam Rayburn Reservoir Camping, hiking, mountain biking, water activities. Wildscape herb garden. Park is about 30 miles from Alabama and Coushatta Indian Reservation.

McKinney Falls State Park is 744.4 acres, located about 13 miles southeast of the state Capitol in Austin, off US 183. Acquired in 1970 by gift from private owners. Named for Thomas F. McKinney, one of Stephen F. Austin's first 300 colonists, who built his home here in the mid-1800s on Onion Creek. Ruins of his homestead can be viewed. Swimming, hiking, biking, camping, picnicking, fishing, guided tours.

Meridian State Park in Bosque County is a 505.4-acre park. The heavily wooded land, on TX 22 three miles southwest of Meridian, was acquired from private owners in 1933-1935. Texas-Santa Fe expedition of 1841 passed through Bosque County near present site of park on Bee Creek. Endangered golden-cheeked warbler nests here. Camping, picnicking, hiking, fishing, lake swimming, birding, bicycling.

Mission Dolores State Historic Site was once a Spanish mission built in 1721 just 20 miles west of the Texas-Louisiana border. There are no longer any above ground remains of the mission. Visitors can camp, view the museum and explore its rich history.

Mission Rosario State Historic Site is located four miles west of Goliad on US 59. It contains the ruins of Nuestra Señora del Rosario mission, established 1754.

Mission Tejas State Park is a 363.5-acre park in Houston County. Situated 12 miles west of Alto via TX 21 and PR 44, the park was acquired from the Texas Forest Service in 1957. In the park is a representation of Mission San Francisco de los Tejas, the first mission in East Texas (1690). It was abandoned, then re-established 1716; abandoned again 1719; re-established again 1721; abandoned for last time in 1730 when the mission was moved to San Antonio. Also in park is restored Rice Family Log Home, built about 1828. Camping, hiking, fishing, picnicking.

Monahans Sandhills State Park consists of 3,840 acres of sand dunes, some up to 70 feet high, in Ward and Winkler counties 5 miles northeast of Monahans on IH 20 to PR 41. Land leased by state from private foundation until 2056. Dunes used as meeting place by raiding Indians. Camping, hiking, picnicking, sand-surfing. Scheduled tours. Odessa meteor crater is nearby, as is Balmorhea State Park.

Monument Hill State Historic Site and Kreische Brewery State Historic Site are operated as one park unit. Monument Hill consists of 40.4 acres one mile south of La Grange on US 77 to Spur Road 92 in Fayette County. Monument and tomb area acquired by state in 1907; additional acreage acquired from the Archdiocese of San Antonio in 1956. Brewery and home purchased from private owners in 1977. Monument is dedicated to Capt. Nicholas Dawson and his men, who fought at Salado Creek in 1842, in Mexican Gen. Adrián Woll's invasion of Texas, and to the men of the "black bean lottery" (1843) of the Mier Expedition. Remains were brought to Monument Hill for reburial in 1848. Kreische Complex, on 36 acres, is linked to Monument Hill through interpretive trail. Kreische Brewery State Historic Site includes the brewery and stone-and-wood house built between 1850–1855 on Colorado River. One of first commercial breweries in state, it closed in 1884. Smokehouse and barn also in complex. Guided tours of brewery and house; call for schedule. Also picknicking, nature study.

Mother Neff State Park was the first official state park in Texas. It originated with six acres donated by Mrs. I. E. Neff, mother of Pat M. Neff, governor of Texas from 1921 to 1925. Gov. Neff and Frank Smith donated remainder in 1934. The park, located eight miles west of Moody on FM 107 and TX 236, now contains 259 acres along the Leon River in Coryell County. Heavily wooded. Camping, picnicking, fishing, hiking.

Mustang Island State Park, 3,954 acres on Gulf of Mexico in Nueces County, 14 miles south of Port Aransas on TX 361, was acquired from private owners in 1972. Mustang Island is a barrier island with a complicated ecosystem, dependent upon the sand dune. The foundation plants of the dunes are sea oats, beach panic grass and soilbind morning glory. Beach camping, picknicking; sun, sand and water activities. Excellent birding. Padre Island National Seashore 14 miles south.

National Museum of the Pacific War and Admiral Nimitz State Historic Site is on seven acres in downtown Fredericksburg. First established as a state agency in 1969 by Texas Legislature; transferred to TPW in 1981. George Bush Gallery opened in 1999. Named for Adm. Chester W. Nimitz of World War II fame, it includes the Pacific War Museum in the Nimitz Steamboat Hotel; the Japanese Garden of Peace, donated by the people of Japan; the History Walk of the Pacific War, featuring planes, boats and other equipment from World War II; and other special exhibits. Nearby is Kerrville State Park.

Old Tunnel State Park sits on 16.1 acres of land, making it the smallest state park in Texas. Located at 10619 Old San Antonio Road, 13.6 miles south of Fredericksburg, the park is great for wildlife-viewing opportunites. The abandoned railroad tunnel provides a home to over 3 million Mexican free-tailed bats and 3,000 cave myotis from May to October, and the park provides nightly bat viewing access. An upper viewing area, open seven days a week, is limited to 250 visitors. Thursday through Sunday, a secondary viewing area opens. Call (866) 978-2287 for viewing time information. The park also has a half-mile trail open year-round for bird-watching or for a short hike.

Palmetto State Park, a scenic park of 270.3 acres, is eight miles southeast of Luling on US 183 and PR 11 along the San Marcos River in Gonzales County. Land deeded in 1934-1936 by private owners and City of Gonzales. Named for tropical dwarf palmetto found there. Diverse plant and animal life; excellent birding. Also picnicking, fishing, hiking, pedal boats, swimming. Nearby Gonzales and Ottine important in early Texas history. Gonzales settled 1825 as center of Green DeWitt's colonies.

Palo Duro Canyon State Park consists of 16,402 acres found 12 miles east of Canyon on TX 217 in Armstrong and Randall counties. The land was deeded by private owners in 1933 and is the scene of the annual summer production of the musical drama, "Texas." Spectacular one-million-year-old scenic canyon exposes rocks spanning about 200 million years of geological time. Coronado may have visited canyon in 1541. Canyon officially discovered by Capt. R. B. Marcy in 1852. Scene of decisive battle in 1874 between Comanche and Kiowa Indians and U.S. Army troops under Gen. Ranald Mackenzie. Also scene of ranching enterprise started by Charles Goodnight in 1876. Part of state longhorn herd is kept here. Camping, mountain biking, scenic drives, horseback and hiking trails, horse rentals.

Pedernales Falls State Park, 5,211.7 acres in Blanco County about nine miles east of Johnson City on FM 2766 along Pedernales River, was acquired from private owners in 1970. Typical Edwards Plateau terrain, with live oaks, deer, turkey and stone hills. Camping, picnicking, hiking, swimming, tubing. Falls main scenic attraction.

Port Isabel Lighthouse State Historic Site consists of 0.9 acres in Port Isabel, Cameron County. Acquired by purchase from private owners in 1950, site includes lighthouse constructed in 1852; visitors can climb to top. Park is near sites of Civil War battle of Palmito Ranch (1865), and Mexican War battles of Palo Alto and Resaca de la Palma (1846). Operated by City of Port Isabel.

Monahans Sandhills State Park near Odessa. Photo by Plum Pine, CC by 2.0/Flickr.

Possum Kingdom State Park, west of Mineral Wells via US 180 and PR 33 in Palo Pinto County, is 1,529 acres adjacent to Possum Kingdom Lake, in Palo Pinto Mountains and Brazos River Valley. Rugged canyons home to deer, other wildlife. Acquired from the Brazos River Authority in 1940. Camping, picnicking, swimming, fishing, boating. Cabins available.

Purtis Creek State Park is 1,582 acres in Henderson and Van Zandt counties 3.5 miles north of Eustace on FM 316. Acquired in 1977 from private owners. Fishing, camping, hiking, picnicking, paddle boats and canoes.

Ray Roberts Lake State Park (Isle du Bois Unit) consists of 2,263 acres on the south side of Ray Roberts Lake on FM 455 in Denton County. Johnson Branch Unit contains 1,514 acres on north side of the lake in Denton and Cooke counties, seven miles east of IH 30 on FM 3002. There are also six satellite parks. Land acquired in 1984 by lease from Department of the Army. Abundant and varied plant and animal life. Fishing, camping, picnicking, swimming, hiking, biking; tours of 19th-century farm buildings at Johnson Branch. Includes Lantana Ridge Lodge on the east side of the lake. It is a full-service lodging facility with restaurant.

Resaca de la Palma State Park, part of the World Birding Center network, is 1,700 semi-tropical acres off US 281, four miles west of Brownsville in Cameron County. Park grounds are open seven days a week year-round from sunrise to sunset. Birding and natural history tours offered. Colorful Neotropical and Neartic migrant birds have been seen.

Sabine Pass Battleground State Historic Site in Jefferson County 1.5 miles south of Sabine Pass on Dick Dowling Road, contains 57.6 acres acquired from Kountze and Couch Trust in 1972. Lt. Richard W. Dowling, with small Confederate force, repelled an attempted 1863 invasion of Texas by Union gunboats. Monument, World War II ammunition bunkers. Fishing, picnicking, camping.

Sam Bell Maxey House State Historic Site, at the corner of South Church and Washington streets in Paris, Lamar County, was donated by City of Paris in 1976. Consists of 0.4 acres with 1868 Victorian Italianate-style frame house, plus outbuildings. Most of furnishings accumulated by Maxey family. Maxey served in Mexican and Civil wars and was two-term U.S. Senator. House is on the National Register of Historic Places. Open for tours Friday through Sunday.

Sam Rayburn House State Historic Site preserves personal belongings, original furniture, and photos just as they were when Sam Rayburn lived here. Visitors can explore the home and grounds to the once powerful and influential Texas politician.

San Angelo State Park, on O.C. Fisher Reservoir adjacent to the city of San Angelo in Tom Green County, contains 7,677 acres of land, most of which will remain undeveloped. Leased from U.S. Corps of Engineers in 1995. Access is from US 87 or US 67, then FM 2288. Highly diversified plant and animal life. Activities include boating, water activities, hiking, mountain biking, horseback riding, camping, picnicking. Part of state longhorn herd in park. Nearby is Fort Concho.

San Felipe de Austin State Historic Site was once the location of Stephen F. Austin's headquarters for his colony in Mexican Texas. Visitors are able to walk the grounds of the former political and economic center of American immigration to Texas before its fall in the war of Texas independence.

San Jacinto Battleground State Historic Site and Battleship Texas State Historic Site are located 20 miles east of downtown Houston off TX 225 east to TX 134 to PR 1836 in east Harris County. The park is 1,200 acres with a 570-foot-tall monument erected in 1936-1939 in honor of Texans who defeated Mexican Gen. Antonio López de Santa Anna on April 21, 1836, to win Texas' independence from Mexico. The park is original site of Texans' camp acquired in 1883. Subsequent acquisitions made in 1897, 1899 and 1985. Park transferred to TPW in 1965. Park registered as National Historic Landmark. Elevator ride to observation tower near top of monument; museum. Monument known as tallest free-standing concrete structure in the world at the time it was erected. Interpretive trail around battleground. Adjacent to park is the *U.S.S. Texas*, commissioned in 1914. The battleship, the only survivor of the dreadnought class and the only surviving veteran of two world wars, was donated to people of Texas by U.S. Navy. Ship was moored in the Houston Ship Channel at the San Jacinto Battleground on San Jacinto Day, 1948. Extensive repairs were done 1988-1990. Some renovation is on-going, but ship is open for tours. Ship closed Christmas Eve and Christmas Day.

Sea Rim State Park in Jefferson County, 20 miles south of Port Arthur, off TX 87, contains 4,141 acres of marshland and 5.2 miles of Gulf beach shoreline, acquired from private owners in 1972. It is prime wintering area for waterfowl. Wetlands also shelter such wildlife as river otter, nutria, alligator, mink, muskrat. Camping, fishing, swimming; wildlife observation; nature trail; boating. Airboat tours of marsh. Near McFaddin National Wildlife Refuge.

Sebastopol House State Historic Site at 704 Zorn Street in Seguin, Guadalupe County, was acquired by purchase in 1976 from Seguin Conservation Society; approximately 2.2 acres. Built about 1856 by Col. Joshua W. Young of limecrete, concrete made from local gravel and lime, the Greek Revival-style house, which was restored to its 1880 appearance by the TPW, is on National Register of Historic Places. Tours available Friday and Sunday. Also of interest in the area is historic Seguin, founded 1838.

Seminole Canyon State Historic Site in Val Verde County, nine miles west of Comstock off US 90, contains 2,17 acres; acquired by purchase from private owners 1973-1977. Fate Bell Shelter in canyon contains several important prehistoric Indian pictographs. Historic interpretive center. Tours of rock-art sites Wednesday-Sunday; also hiking, mountain biking, camping.

Sheldon Lake State Park and Environmental Learning Center, 2,800 acres in Harris County on Garrett Road two miles east of Beltway 8. Acquired by purchase in

Texas Lakes

Bodies of water with a normal capacity of 5,000 acre-feet or larger. *Italicized* reservoirs are usually dry.

● PANHANDLE PLAINS
1. Palo Duro Reservoir
2. Lake Rita Blanca
3. Lake Meredith
4. Bivins Lake
5. *Buffalo Lake*
6. Mackenzie Reservoir
7. Greenbelt Lake
8. Baylor Lake
9. White River Lake
10. Lake Alan Henry
11. Lake J.B. Thomas
12. Sulphur Springs Draw Reservoir
13. *Natural Dam Lake*
14. Red Draw Reservoir
15. Lake Colorado City
16. Champion Creek Reservoir
17. Mitchell County Reservoir
18. Lake Sweetwater
19. E.V. Spence Reservoir
20. Oak Creek Reservoir
21. O.C. Fisher Lake
22. Twin Buttes Reservoir
23. Lake Nasworthy
24. Ballinger Lake
25. O.H. Ivie Reservoir
26. Hords Creek Lake
27. Lake Winters
28. Lake Abilene
29. Lake Coleman
30. Lake Brownwood
31. Lake Clyde
32. Lake Kirby
33. Lake Fort Phantom Hill
34. Lake Stamford
35. Lake Davis
36. Truscott Brine Lake
37. Santa Rosa Lake
38. Lake Electra
39. Lake Kemp
40. Lake Diversion
41. Lake Kickapoo
42. North Fork Buffalo Creek Reservoir
43. Lake Wichita
44. Lake Arrowhead
45. Millers Creek Reservoir
46. Lake Cooper/Olney
47. Lake Graham
48. Lost Creek Reservoir
49. Possum Kingdom Lake
50. Hubbard Creek Reservoir
51. Lake Daniel
52. Lake Cisco
53. Lake Palo Pinto
54. Lake Leon
55. Proctor Lake

● BIG BEND
56. Red Bluff Reservoir
57. Balmorhea Lake
58. Imperial Reservoir
59. Amistad International Reservoir

● HILL COUNTRY
60. Brady Creek Reservoir
61. Lake Buchanan
62. Inks Lake
63. Lake Lyndon B. Johnson
64. Lake Marble Falls
65. Lake Travis
66. Lake Austin
67. Lady Bird Lake
68. Lake Walter E. Long
69. Lake Georgetown
70. Granger Lake
71. Canyon Lake
72. Medina Lake

● PRAIRIES AND LAKES
73. Lake Nocona
74. Hubert H. Moss Lake
75. Lake Texoma
76. Randell Lake
77. Valley Lake
78. Lake Bonham
79. Coffee Mill Lake
80. Pat Mayse Lake
81. Lake Crook
82. River Crest Lake
83. Cooper Lake
84. Lake Sulphur Springs
85. Lake Cypress Springs
86. Greenville City Lakes
87. Lake Tawakoni
88. Terrell City Lake
89. Lake Lavon
90. Lake Ray Hubbard
91. Lake Kiowa
92. Lake Ray Roberts
93. Lewisville Lake
94. Grapevine Lake
95. North Lake
96. White Rock Lake
97. Mountain Creek Lake
98. Joe Pool Lake
99. Lake Arlington
100. Lake Worth
101. Eagle Mountain Lake
102. Lake Weatherford
103. Lake Amon G. Carter
104. Lake Bridgeport
105. Lake Mineral Wells
106. Benbrook Lake
107. Lake Granbury
108. Squaw Creek Reservoir
109. Lake Pat Cleburne
110. Lake Waxahachie
111. Bardwell Lake
112. Cedar Creek Reservoir
113. Forest Grove Reservoir
114. Lake Athens
115. Trinidad Lake
116. Lake Halbert
117. Richland-Chambers Reservoir
118. Fairfield Lake
119. Navarro Mills Lake
120. Aquilla Lake
121. Lake Whitney
122. Lake Waco
123. Tradinghouse Creek Reservoir
124. Lake Creek Lake
125. Belton Lake
126. Stillhouse Hollow Lake
127. Alcoa Lake
128. Lake Limestone
129. Twin Oaks Reservoir
130. Camp Creek Lake
131. Lake Bryan
132. Gibbons Creek Reservoir
133. Somerville Lake
134. Lake Bastrop
135. Fayette County Reservoir
136. Lake Dunlap
137. Lake Gonzales
138. Eagle Lake

● PINEYWOODS
139. Wright Patman Lake
140. Monticello Reservoir
141. Lake Winnsboro
142. Lake Bob Sandlin
143. Welsh Reservoir
144. Ellison Creek Reservoir
145. Lake O' the Pines
146. Johnson Creek Reservoir
147. Caddo Lake
148. Lake Fork Reservoir
149. Lake Quitman
150. Lake Holbrook
151. Lake Hawkins
152. Gilmer Reservoir
153. Lake Gladewater
154. Eastman Lakes
155. Brandy Branch Reservoir
156. Lake Cherokee
157. Martin Creek Lake
158. Murvaul Lake

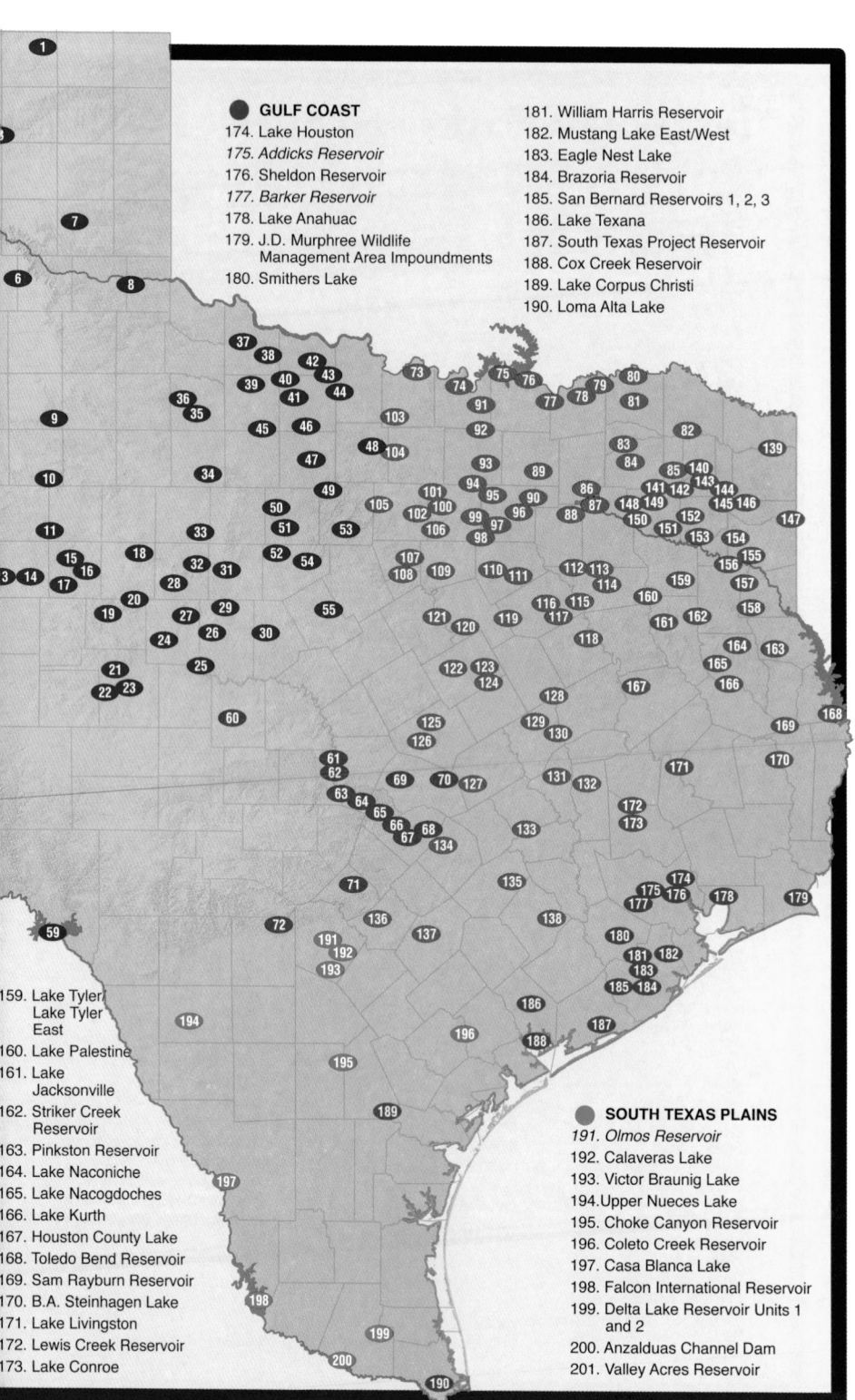

GULF COAST

174. Lake Houston
175. *Addicks Reservoir*
176. Sheldon Reservoir
177. *Barker Reservoir*
178. Lake Anahuac
179. J.D. Murphree Wildlife
     Management Area Impoundments
180. Smithers Lake

181. William Harris Reservoir
182. Mustang Lake East/West
183. Eagle Nest Lake
184. Brazoria Reservoir
185. San Bernard Reservoirs 1, 2, 3
186. Lake Texana
187. South Texas Project Reservoir
188. Cox Creek Reservoir
189. Lake Corpus Christi
190. Loma Alta Lake

159. Lake Tyler/
     Lake Tyler
     East
160. Lake Palestine
161. Lake
     Jacksonville
162. Striker Creek
     Reservoir
163. Pinkston Reservoir
164. Lake Naconiche
165. Lake Nacogdoches
166. Lake Kurth
167. Houston County Lake
168. Toledo Bend Reservoir
169. Sam Rayburn Reservoir
170. B.A. Steinhagen Lake
171. Lake Livingston
172. Lewis Creek Reservoir
173. Lake Conroe

SOUTH TEXAS PLAINS

191. *Olmos Reservoir*
192. Calaveras Lake
193. Victor Braunig Lake
194. Upper Nueces Lake
195. Choke Canyon Reservoir
196. Coleto Creek Reservoir
197. Casa Blanca Lake
198. Falcon International Reservoir
199. Delta Lake Reservoir Units 1
     and 2
200. Anzalduas Channel Dam
201. Valley Acres Reservoir

Sebastopol House State Historic Site in Seguin. Photo by Larry D. Moore, CC by SA 3.0./Wikimedia Commons.

1952 from the City of Houston. Freshwater marsh habitat. Activities include nature study, birding, fishing. Wildscape gardens of native plants.

South Llano River State Park, five miles south of Junction in Kimble County off US 377, is a 524-acre site donated to the TPW by a private owner in 1977. Wooded bottomland along the winding South Llano River is the largest and oldest winter roosting site for the Rio Grande turkey in Central Texas. Roosting area closed to visitors October-March. Other animals include wood ducks, javelina, fox, beaver, bobcat and armadillo. Camping, picnicking, tubing, swimming and fishing, hiking, mountain biking.

Starr Family Home State Historic Site, 3.1 acres at 407 W. Travis in Marshall, Harrison County. Greek Revival-style mansion, Maplecroft, built 1870-1871, was home to four generations of Starr family, powerful and economically influential Texans. Two other family homes also in park. Acquired by gift in 1976; additional land donated in 1982. Maplecroft is on National Register of Historic Places. Tours Friday–Sunday or by appointment. Special events during year.

Stephen F. Austin State Park is 663.3 acres along the Brazos River in San Felipe, Austin County, named for the "Father of Texas." The area was deeded by the San Felipe de Austin Corporation and the San Felipe Park Association in 1940. Site of township of San Felipe was seat of government where conventions of 1832 and 1833 and Consultation of 1835 held. These led to Texas Declaration of Independence. San Felipe was home of Stephen F. Austin and other famous early Texans; home of Texas' first Anglo newspaper (the Texas Gazette) founded in 1829; postal system of Texas originated here. Area called "Cradle of Texas Liberty." Museum. Camping, picnicking, golf, fishing, hiking.

Tyler State Park is 985.5 acres found two miles north of IH 20 on FM 14 north of Tyler in Smith County. Includes

64-acre lake. The land was deeded by private owners in 1934–1935. Heavily wooded. Camping, hiking, fishing, boating, lake swimming. Nearby Tyler called Rose Capital of Nation, with Tyler Rose Garden and annual Tyler Rose Festival. Also in Tyler are Caldwell Children's Zoo and Goodman Museum.

Varner-Hogg Plantation State Historic Site is 66 acres in Brazoria County, two miles north of West Columbia on FM 2852. Land originally owned by Martin Varner, a member of Stephen F. Austin's "Old Three Hundred" colony; later was home of Texas governor James Stephen Hogg. Property was deeded to the state in 1957 by Miss Ima Hogg, Gov. Hogg's daughter. First rum distillery in Texas established in 1829 by Varner. Mansion tours Tuesday through Saturday. Also picnicking, fishing.

Village Creek State Park, comprising 1,004 heavily forested acres, is located in Lumberton, Hardin County, ten miles north of Beaumont off US 69 and FM 3513. Purchased in 1979 from private owner, the park contains abundant flora and fauna typical of the Big Thicket area. The 200 species of birds found here include wood ducks, egrets and herons. Activities include fishing, camping, canoeing, swimming, hiking and picnicking. Nearby is the Big Thicket National Preserve.

Walter Umphrey State Park is operated by Jefferson County on the south end of Pleasure Island off TX 82. For RV site reservations, contact SGS Causeway Bait & Tackle, 409-985-4811.

Washington-on-the-Brazos State Historic Site consists of 293.1 acres found seven miles southwest of Navasota in Washington County on TX 105 and FM 1155. Land acquired by deed from private owners in 1916, 1976 and 1996. Park includes the site of the signing on March 2, 1836, of the Texas Declaration of Independence from Mexico, as well as the site of the later signing of the Constitution of the Republic of Texas. In 1842 and 1845, the land included the capitol of the Republic. Star of the Republic Museum. Activities include picnicking and birding. Barrington Living History Farm is the home of Anson Jones, the last president of the Republic of Texas. Activities are guided by entries that Jones made in his daybook while living there. For more information: call 916-878-2214 or email office@wheretexasbecametexas.org.

Zaragoza Birthplace State Historic Site is located across the river from Goliad SP. Gen. Ignacio Zaragoza was the Mexican national hero who led troops in the fight for Mexican independence against the French at historic Battle of Puebla on May 5, 1862. The nearby Zaragoza statue was donated by the people of Puebla, Mexico. Also found nearby is Presidio la Bahía, which was originally constructed in 1721 near Matagorda Bay and moved to the present site in 1749. Adjacent is a memorial monument, marking the common burial site of Col. Fannin and his men, victims of Goliad massacre (1836).

Recreation in State Forests

All Texas State Forests are game sanctuaries with no firearms or hunting allowed. For general information about the Texas State Forests, see page 70 in the Environment chapter.

I.D. Fairchild State Forest

Located in Cherokee County, recreation includes hiking, horseback riding, picnicking, wildlife viewing and biking. Special attractions are a historical fire tower site with plaque, Red Cockaded Woodpecker Management Area and a pond with picnic area. Forest management demonstration sites throughout the forest. There are no restroom facilities in this forest.

Open year-round during daylight hours. Obtain information and maps at the Jacksonville District Office, 1015 SE Looop 456 or call (903) 586-7545 weekdays.

W. Goodrich Jones State Forest

Recreational opportunities in this forest, located in Montgomery County, include bird watching, hiking, horseback riding, picnicking, wildlife viewing and biking.

Special attractions include Sweetleaf Nature Trail with State Champion Sweetleaf Tree, Red Cockaded Woodpecker Management Area, two small lakes with limited fishing and picnicking. Forest management demonstration sites throughout the forest.

Open year-round during daylight hours. Information, maps, permits and restrooms available at the Conroe District Office on FM 1488, 1.5 miles west of I-45. Call (936) 273-2261 for information.

John Henry Kirby Memorial State Forest

Located in Tyler County, forest resource educational opportunities at this forest include demonstrations and nature study. Group education tours available by appointment. Recreational opportunities include hiking, picnicking, bird and wildlife watching. Special attractions are forest management demonstration sites, small picnic area and John Henry Kirby Monument.

Open year-round to foot traffic during daylight hours. Contact the district office prior to entry. Special arrangements are needed for vehicle access. Information and maps

can be obtained at the Olive District Office on Hwy. 69 north of Kountze or by calling (409) 246-2484 weekdays. No restroom facilities are available in this forest.

Masterson State Forest

All use of this forest in Jasper County is by reservation only. Group resource education tours are available by appointment. No public facilities are available. Information and maps can be obtained at the Kirbyville District Office, FM 82, 4.5 miles southeast of Kirbyville; call weekdays at (409) 423-2890.

E.O. Siecke State Forest

Recreational opportunities in this Newton County forest include hiking, bird watching, nature study, horseback riding, picnicking and wildlife viewing.

Special attractions are a historic fire tower, the oldest slash pine stand in Texas and a trout creek. Forest management demonstration sites throughout.

Open year-round during daylight hours. Limited access by vehicle. Information, maps and restrooms are available at the Kirbyville District Office, located at the state forest on FM 82, 4.5 miles southeast of Kirbyville. Call (409) 423-2890 weekdays for information. ☆

Recreational Facilities, Corps of Engineers Lakes, 2021

Reservoir	Swim Beaches	Boat Ramps	Picnic Sites	Camp Sites	Group Camping	Rental Cabins
Aquilla		★				
Bardwell	★	★	★	★	★	
Belton	★	★	★	★	★	★
Benbrook	★	★	★	★	★	★
Buffalo Bayou	★		★	★		★
Canyon	★	★	★	★	★	★
Cooper	★	★	★	★	★	★
Georgetown	★	★	★	★	★	
Granger	★	★	★	★	★	
Grapevine	★	★	★	★	★	★
Hords Creek	★	★	★	★	★	
Joe Pool	★	★	★	★		★
Lake O' the Pines	★	★	★	★	★	
Lavon	★	★	★	★	★	
Lewisville	★	★	★	★		★
Navarro Mills	★	★	★	★		
O.C. Fisher		★	★	★		
Pat Mayse		★	★	★		★
Proctor	★	★	★	★	★	
Ray Roberts	★	★	★	★	★	
Sam Rayburn	★	★	★	★	★	★
Somerville	★	★	★	★	★	★
Stillhouse Hollow	★	★	★	★		
Texoma	★	★	★	★	★	★
Town Bluff	★	★	★	★		
Waco	★	★	★	★	★	★
Wallisville		★	★			
Whitney	★	★	★	★	★	★
Wright Patman	★	★	★	★	★	

Source: U.S. Army Corps of Engineers

National Parks, Historic Sites, Recreation Areas

Source: U.S. Dept of Interior, https://www.nps.gov/state/tx/index.htm

Below is a list of facilities and activities that can be enjoyed at Texas' two national parks, a national seashore, a biological preserve, a marine sanctuary, and several historic sites, memorials, and recreation areas in Texas. Most are under supervision of the **U.S. Department of Interior**. Recreational opportunities in the state and national forests and national grasslands in Texas are under the jurisdiction of the **U.S. Department of Agriculture**.

Alibates Flint Quarries National Monument consists of 1,371 acres in Potter County. For more than 10,000 years, pre-Columbian Indians dug agatized limestone from the quarries to make projectile points, knives, scrapers and other tools. The area is presently undeveloped. You may visit the flint quarries on guided walking tours with a park ranger. Tours are at 10:00 a.m. and 2:00 p.m. from Memorial Day to Labor Day. Off-season tours can be arranged by writing to Lake Meredith National Recreation Area, Box 1460, Fritch 79036, or by calling 806-857-3151.

Amistad National Recreation Area is located on the U.S. side of Amistad Reservoir, an international reservoir on the Texas-Mexico border. The 57,292-acre park's attractions include boating, water skiing, swimming, fishing, camping and archaeological sites. If lake level is normal, visitors can see 4000-year-old prehistoric pictographs in Panther and Parida caves, which are accessible only by boat. Check with park before visiting. The area is one of the densest concentrations of Archaic rock art in North America — more than 300 sites. Commercial campgrounds, motels and restaurants nearby. Marinas located at Diablo East and Rough Canyon. Open year round. NPS Administration, 4121 Hwy. 90 W, Del Rio 78840; 830-775-7491.

Big Bend National Park, established in 1944, has spectacular mountain and desert scenery and a variety of unusual geological structures. It is the nation's largest protected area of Chihuahuan Desert. Located in the great bend of the Rio Grande, the 801,000-acre park, which is part of the international boundary between the United States and Mexico, was designated a U.S. Biosphere Reserve in 1976. Hiking, birding and float trips are popular. Numerous campsites are located in park, and the Chisos Mountain Lodge has accommodations for approximately 345 guests. Write for reservations to National Park Concessions, Inc., Big Bend National Park, Texas 79834; 915-477-2291; www.chisosmountainslodge.com. Park open year round; facilities most crowded during spring break. PO Box 129, Big Bend National Park 79834; 915-477-2251.

Big Thicket National Preserve, established in 1974, consists of 15 separate units totalling 97,000 acres of diverse flora and fauna, often nicknamed the "biological crossroads of North America." The preserve, which includes parts of seven East Texas counties, has been designated an "International Biosphere Reserve" by the United Nations Educational, Scientific and Cultural Organization (UNESCO). The preserve includes four different ecological systems: Southeastern swamps, Eastern forests, Central Plains and Southwestern deserts. The visitor information station is located on FM 420, seven miles north of Kountze; phone 409-951-6725. Open daily from 9 a.m. to 5 p.m. Naturalist activities are available by reservation only; reservations are made through the station. Eight trails, ranging in length from one-half mile to 18 miles, visit a variety of forest communities. The two shortest trails are handicapped accessible. Trails are open year round, but flooding may occur after heavy rains. Horses permitted on the Big Sandy Horse Trail only. Boating and canoeing are popular on preserve corridor units. Park headquarters are at 3785 Milam, Beaumont 77701; 409-246-2337.

Chamizal National Memorial, established in 1963 and opened to the public in 1973, stands as a monument to Mexican-American friendship and goodwill. The memorial, on 52 acres in El Paso, commemorates the peaceful settlement on Aug. 29, 1963, of a 99-year-old boundary dispute between the United States and Mexico. Chamizal uses the visual and performing arts as a medium of interchange, helping people better understand not only other cultures but their own, as well. It hosts a variety of programs throughout the year, including: the fall Chamizal Festival musical event; the Siglo de Oro drama festival (early March); the Oñate Historical Festival celebrating the First Thanksgiving (April); and Music Under the Stars (Sundays, June-August). The park has a 1.8-mile walking trail and picnic areas. Phone: 915-532-7273.

El Camino Real de los Tejas was designated a National Historic Trail in 2004. It traces the "royal road" from Mexico to the Red River Valley, established when the area was under Spanish rule. The full route stretched over 2,500 miles, down to Mexico City, and connected to Spanish missions and posts along the way to Los Adaes, the first capital of the Texas province. Today's trail travels many roads, the longest straight route being TX 21 to Hwy 6 in Louisiana, connecting parks, historic sites, and museums along the way. The website, **https://www. nps.gov/elte/index.htm**, has tools to help you plan your trip, and photos and videos to learn more about travelers in the past.

El Camino Real De Tierra Adentro became a National Historic Trail in 2000. This royal road brought travelers from Mexico City through what is now El Paso and north into New Mexico, ending near Santa Fe, which was one of the capitals of New Mexico under Spanish rule. This path takes travelers to historic sites and museums along Interstate 25. Learn more and plan your trip at **https:// www.nps.gov/elca/index.htm**.

Flower Garden Banks National Marine Sanctuary was named after the brightly colored sponges, plants, and other marine life found in the area. The reefs were discovered by snapper and grouper fishermen in the early 1900s. Situated 70–115 miles offshore, the sanctuary is only accessible by boat, so divers interested in visiting

Flower Garden Banks National Marine Sanctuary is home to many varieties of coral and other marine life. Photo by NOAA

can book dive charters that depart from numerous Texas ports, including: Galveston, Freeport, Sabine Pass, and Surfside. The sanctuary protects three separate areas: East Flower Garden Bank and West Flower Garden Bank were designed as a sanctuary under the National Marine Sanctuary Act in 1992, and the algal-sponge communities of Stetson Bank were added to the sanctuary in 1996. Exceptional underwater visibility allows divers to experience spectacular sights, such as giant coral heads, schools of fish, eagle and manta rays, and even majestic whale sharks during summer visits to the area. The banks of the sanctuary include more than a dozen moored dive sites, with typical dive profiles of 70–130 feet. Several ports that offer dive trips are also home to commercial fishing charters for anglers wanting to fish the Flower Garden and Stetson banks. Snappers, jacks, barracuda, and wahoo are just a few of the fish commonly caught by sportfishing enthusiasts. On the web: flowergarden.noaa.gov.

Fort Davis National Historic Site in Jeff Davis County was a key post in the West Texas defense system, guarding immigrants and tradesmen on the San Antonio-El Paso road from 1854 to 1891. At one time, Fort Davis was manned by black troops, called "Buffalo Soldiers" (because of their curly hair) who fought with great distinction in the Indian Wars. Henry O. Flipper, the first black graduate of West Point, served at Fort Davis in the early 1880s. The 474-acre historic site is located on the north edge of the town of Fort Davis in the Davis Mountains, the second-highest mountain range in the state. The site includes a museum, an auditorium with daily audio-visual programs, restored and refurnished buildings, picnic area and hiking trails. Open year round except Christmas Day. PO Box 1379, Fort Davis 79734; 915-426-3224.

Guadalupe Mountains National Park, established in 1972, includes 86,416 acres in Hudspeth and Culberson counties. The Park contains one of the most extensive fossil reefs on record. Deep canyons cut through this reef and provide a rare opportunity for geological study. Special points of interest are McKittrick Canyon, a fragile riparian environment, and Guadalupe Peak, the highest in Texas. Camping, hiking on 80 miles of trails, Frijole Ranch Museum, summer amphitheater programs. Orientation, free information and natural history exhibits available at Visitor Center. Open year round. Lodging at Van Horn, Texas, and White's City or Carlsbad, NM. HC 60, Box 400, Salt Flat 79847; 915-828-3251.

Lake Meredith National Recreation Area, 30 miles northeast of Amarillo, centers on a reservoir on the Canadian River, in Moore, Hutchinson and Potter counties. The 50,000-acre recreational area is popular for water-based activities. Boat ramps, picnic areas, unimproved campsites. Commercial lodging and trailer hookups available in nearby towns. Open year round. PO Box 1460, Fritch 79036; 806-857-3151.

Lyndon B. Johnson National Historic Park includes two separate districts 14 miles apart. The Johnson City District comprises the boyhood home of the 36th President of United States and the Johnson Settlement, where his grandparents resided during the late 1800s. The LBJ Ranch District can be visited only by taking the National Park Service bus tour starting at the LBJ State Historic Site. The tour includes the reconstructed LBJ Birthplace, old school, family cemetery, show barn and a view of the Texas White House. Site in Blanco and Gillespie counties was established in 1969, and contains 1,570 acres, 674 of which are federal. Open year round except Thanksgiving, Christmas Day, and New Year's Day. No camping on site; commercial campgrounds, motels in area. PO Box 329, Johnson City 78636; 830-868-7128.

Padre Island National Seashore consists of a 67.5-mile stretch of a barrier island along the Gulf Coast; noted for white-sand beaches, excellent fishing and abundant bird and marine life. Contains 133,000 acres in Kleberg, Willacy and Kenedy counties. Open year round. One paved campground (fee charged) located north of Malaquite Beach; unpaved (primitive) campground area south on beach. Five miles of beach are accessible by regular vehicles; 55 miles are accessible only by 4x4 vehicles. Off-road vehicles prohibited. Camping permitted in two designated areas. Commercial lodging available on the island outside the National Seashore boundaries. PO Box 181300, Corpus Christi 78480; 361-949-8068.

Palo Alto Battlefield National Historic Park preserves the site of the first major battle in the Mexican-American War. Fought on May 8, 1846, near Brownsville, it is recognized for the innovative use of light or "flying" artillery. Participating in the battle were three future presidents: General Zachary Taylor and Ulysses S. Grant on the U.S. side, and Gen. Mariano Arista on the Mexican. Historical markers are located at the junction of Farm-to-Market roads 1847 and 511. Access to the 3,400-acre site is currently limited. Exhibits at the visitors center interpret the battle as well as the causes and consequences of the war. Phone 956-541-2785.

Rio Grande Wild and Scenic River is a 196-mile strip on the U.S. shore of the Rio Grande in the Chihuahuan Desert, beginning in Big Bend National Park and continuing downstream to the Terrell-Val Verde County line. There are federal facilities in Big Bend National Park only. Contact Big Bend National Park for more information.

San Antonio Missions National Historical Park preserves four Spanish Colonial Missions — Concepción, San José, San Juan and Espada — as well as the Espada dam and aqueduct, which are two of the best-preserved remains in the United States of the Spanish Colonial irrigation system, and Rancho de las Cabras, the colonial ranch of Mission Espada. All were crucial elements to Spanish settlement on the Texas frontier. When Franciscan attempts to establish a chain of missions in East Texas in the late 1600s failed, the Spanish Crown ordered three missions transferred to the San Antonio River valley in 1731. The missions are located within the city limits of San Antonio, while Rancho de las Cabras is located 25 miles south in Wilson County near Floresville. The four missions, which are still in use as active parishes, are open to the public from 9 a.m. to 5 p.m. daily except Thanksgiving, Christmas and New Year's. Public roadways connect the sites; a hike-bike trail is being developed. The visitor center for the mission complex is at San José. For more information, write to 2202 Roosevelt Ave., San Antonio 78210; 210-932-1001.

Waco Mammoth National Monument was designated in 2015 and is the newest Texas unit of the National Park System. This paleontological site represents the nation's only recorded discovery of a nursery herd of Columbian mammoths. Visitors can view "in situ" fossils including female mammoths, a bull mammoth, and a camel that lived approximately 67,000 years ago. The park is managed in partnership by the National Park Service, the City of Waco, and Baylor University. Welcome Center located at 6220 Steinbeck Bend Road. It is open Tuesday through Saturday, except Thanksgiving, Christmas Day, and New Year's Day. ☆

National Forests

For general information about the National Forests and National Grasslands, see page 69 in the Environment chapter.

An estimated three million people visit the National Forests in Texas for recreation annually. These visitors use established recreation areas primarily for hiking, picnicking, swimming, fishing, camping, boating and nature enjoyment. In the following list of some of these areas, Forest Service Road is abbreviated FSR:

Angelina National Forest

Boykin Springs, 14 miles southeast of Zavalla, has a 6-acre lake and facilities for hiking, swimming, picnicking, fishing, and camping. Bouton Lake, 14 miles southeast of Zavalla off Texas 63 and FSR 303, has a 9-acre natural lake with primitive facilities for camping, picnicking, and fishing.

Caney Creek on Sam Rayburn Reservoir, ten miles southeast of Zavalla off FM 2743, offers fishing, boating, and camping. Sandy Creek, 15.5 miles east of Zavalla on Sam Rayburn, offers fishing, boating, and camping.

The Sawmill Hiking Trail is 2.5 miles long and winds from Aldridge Sawmill trail head to Boykin Springs Recreation Area.

Davy Crockett National Forest

Ratcliff Lake, 25 miles west of Lufkin on TX 7, is a 45-acre lake with facilities for picnicking, hiking, swimming, boating, fishing, and camping. There is also an amphitheater.

The 20-mile-long 4C National Recreation Trail connects Ratcliff Recreation Area to the Neches Bluff overlook. The Piney Creek Horse Trail is 54 miles long and can be entered

The hacienda at Quinta Mazatlan, near McAllen. Photo by Alan Schmierer.

Birding in Texas

World Birding Center

The World Birding Center comprises nine birding education centers and observation sites in the Lower Rio Grande Valley designed to protect wildlife habitat and offer visitors a view of more than 500 species of birds. The center has partnered with the Texas Parks and Wildlife Department, the U.S. Fish and Wildlife Service and nine communities to turn 10,000 acres back into natural areas for birds, butterflies and other wildlife.

This area in Cameron, Hidalgo and Starr counties is a natural migratory path for millions of birds that move between the Americas. The nine WBC sites listed here are situated along the border with Mexico. Learn more at **http://www.theworldbirdingcenter.com/**.

Bentsen–Rio Grande Valley State Park

This is the World Birding Center Headquarters and comprises the 760-acre Bentsen-RGV State Park and 1,700 acres of adjoining federal refuge land near Mission.

The site offers: daily tram service; four nature trails ranging in length from one quarter mile to two miles; 2-story high Hawk Observation Tower with a 210-foot-long handicapped access ramp; 2 observation decks; 2 accessible bird blinds; primitive camping sites (by reservation); rest areas; picnic sites with tables; exhibit hall; park store; coffee bar; meeting room (available for rental); catering kitchen; bike rentals (1 and 2 seat bikes). Access within the park is by foot, bike and tram only; (956) 585-1107.

Hours: 6 a.m. to 10 p.m., seven days a week.

Edinburg Scenic Wetlands

This 40-acre wetlands in Edinburg is an oasis for water-loving birds, butterflies and other wildlife. The site is currently offering:walking trails, nature tours and classes; (956) 381-9922.

Hours: 8 a.m.–5 p.m., Monday through Wednesday; 8 a.m.–6 p.m., Thursday through Saturday. Closed Sunday.

Estero Llano Grande State Park

This 176-acre refuge in Weslaco attracts a wide array of South Texas wildlife with its varied landscape of shallow lake, woodlands and thorn forest; (956) 565-3919.

Hours: 8 a.m.–5 p.m., Monday through Friday; 8 a.m.–7:30 p.m., Saturday and Sunday through August.

Harlingen Arroyo Colorado

This site in Harlingen is connected by an arroyo waterway, as well as hike-and-bike trails meandering through the city, Hugh Ramsey Nature Park to the east and the Harlingen Thicket to the west; (956) 427-8873.

Hours: Office, 8 a.m.–5:00 p.m., Monday through Friday. Nature trails are open seven days a week, sunrise to sunset.

Old Hidalgo Pumphouse

Visitors to this museum in Hidalgo on the Rio Grande can learn about the steam-driven irrigation pumps that transformed Hidalgo County into a year-round farming area. The museum's grounds feature hummingbird gardens, walking trails and historic tours; (956) 843-8686.

Hours: 10 a.m.–5 p.m., Monday through Friday; 1 p.m.–5 p.m., Sunday. Closed Saturday.

Quinta Mazatlan

This 1930s country estate in McAllen is a historic Spanish Revival adobe hacienda surrounded by lush tropical landscaping and native woodland. It is also an urban oasis, where quiet trails wind through more than 15 acres of birding habitat; (956) 688-3370.

Hours: 8 a.m.–5 p.m., Tuesday through Saturday. Open until sunset on Thursdays. Closed Mondays and holidays.

Resaca de la Palma State Park

More than 1,700 acres of newly opened wilderness near Brownsville, this site comprises the largest tract of native habitat in the World Birding Center network. The park offers birding tours and natural history tours. Admission is by appointment and reservation only; (956) 565-3919.

Roma Bluffs

History and nature meet on scenic bluffs above the Rio Grande, where the World Birding Center in Roma is located on the old plaza of a once-thriving steamboat port. Part of a national historic district, the WBC Roma Bluffs includes a riverside nature area of three acres in Starr County. The site offers: walking trails, canoe trips, birding tours, natural history tours and classes; (956) 849-4930.

Hours: 8 a.m.–4 p.m. Tuesday through Saturday, although trails are open seven days a week and are free to the public.

South Padre Island Birding and Nature Center

At the southern tip of the world's longest barrier island, South Padre Island Birding and Nature Center is a slender thread of land between the shallow Laguna Madre and the Gulf of Mexico. This site offers: a nature trail boardwalk and birding tours; 1-800-SOPADRE. Hours: 9 a.m.–5 p.m., seven days a week.

A Tropical Parula found at Quinta Mazatlan. Photo by Alan Schmierer

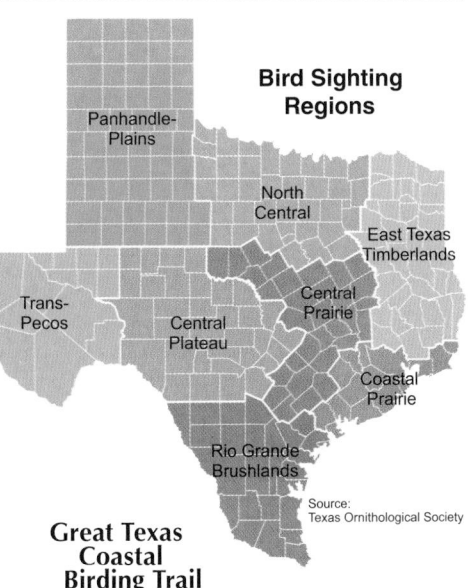

Bird Sighting Regions

Panhandle-Plains

North Central

East Texas Timberlands

Trans-Pecos

Central Plateau

Central Prairie

Coastal Prairie

Rio Grande Brushlands

Source: Texas Ornithological Society

Great Texas Coastal Birding Trail

This trail winds its way through 43 Texas counties along the entire Texas coastal region. The trail was completed in April 2000 and is divided into upper, central, and lower coastal regions. It includes 308 wildlife-viewing sites and such amenities as boardwalks, parking pullouts, kiosks, observation platforms, and landscaping to attract native wildlife.

Color-coded maps are available, and signs mark each site. Trail maps contain information about the birds and habitats likely to be found at each site, the best season to visit, and food and lodging.

For information, contact: Nature Tourism Coordinator, Texas Parks and Wildlife Department, 4200 Smith School Road, Austin, TX 78744; (512) 389-4396.

On the web: **http://tpwd.texas.gov/huntwild/wildlife/wildlife-trails/coastal.**

I-20 Wildlife Preserve and Jenna Welch Nature Study Center

The I-20 Wildlife Preserve is an 87-acre urban playa lake in its natural state in southwest Midland that opened in 2013. It was maintained for many years by the Midland Naturalists and other volunteers, including Jenna Welch, a birding enthusiast and a member of the group. It comprises 3.4 miles of hiking trails, including 1.5 miles of ADA-accessible trails, seven bird observation blinds, four teaching platforms, the 24-foot tall Hawk Observation Platform, and the Merritt Pavilion.

Jenna Welch Nature Study Center operates an educational outreach program to local schools and area colleges and universities. Land was acquired to build a facility to house the nature study center.

The preserve, at 2201 S. Midland Dr., Midland, TX 79701, is open to the public daily from dawn until dusk. For more information, call (432) 853-9453. On the web: **www.i20wildlifepreserve.org.** ☆

The carnival at the San Angelo Rodeo. Photo by Jonathan Cutrer, jcutrer.com.

Denton: North Texas State Fair & Rodeo; August; 2217 N. Carroll Blvd., 76201; www.ntfair.com. Since 1929. info@ntfair.com. (940) 391-3452.

Edna: Jackson County Youth Fair; October; 284 Brackenridge Parkway, 77957; www.jcyf.org. Since 1949.

Ennis: National Polka Festival; May; PO Box 1177, 75120-1237; www.nationalpolkafestival.com. ennis4u@swbell.net.

Fairfield: Freestone County Fair; June; www.freestone-countyfairandrodeo.com.

Flatonia: Czhilispiel; October (4th full wknd.); PO Box 610, 78941; www.flatoniachamber.com. Since 1973. flatonia-cofc@sbcglobal.net. (361) 865-3920.

Fort Worth: Pioneer Days; September; 131 E. Exchange Ave., Ste 100B, 76106; www.fortworthstockyards.org.

Fort Worth: Southwestern Exposition & Livestock Show; January-February; PO Box 150, 76101; www.fwssr.com. Since 1896. contact@fwssr.com. (817) 877-2400.

Fredericksburg: Food and Wine Fest; October (4th Sat.); 703 North Llano Street, 78624; www.fbgfoodandwine-fest.com. Since 1990. creativemarketing1975@gmail.com. (830) 997-8515.

Fredericksburg: Night in Old Fredericksburg; July; 302 E. Austin, 78624; www.gillespiefair.net. Since 1963. info@gillespiefair.com. (830) 997-2359.

Fredericksburg: Oktoberfest; October (1st wknd.); PO Box 222, 78624; www.oktoberfestinfbg.com. Since 1980. creativemarketing1975@gmail.com. (830) 997-4810.

Freer: Freer Rattlesnake Roundup; May; PO Box 717, 78357; www.therattlesnakeroundup.com. Since 1966. freercofc@yahoo.com. (361) 394-6891.

Galveston: Dickens on The Strand; December; 502 20th St., 77550; www.dickensonthestrand.org. Since 1973.

Galveston: Galveston Historic Homes Tour; May; 502 20th St., 77550-2014; www.galvestonhistory.org. Since 1974.

Gilmer: East Texas Yamboree; October; PO Box 854, 75644; www.yamboree.com. Since 1937. gilmerareachamber@gmail.com. (903) 843-2413.

Glen Flora: Wharton County Youth Fair; April; PO Box 167, 77443; www.whartoncountyyouthfair.org. Since 1976. wcyf@whartoncountyyouthfair.org. (979) 677-3350.

Graham: Art Splash on the Square; May.

Graham: Red, White & You Parade & Festivities; July; 608 Elm St.; 76450; www.visitgrahamtexas.com. (940) 549-0401.

Granbury: Annual July 4th Celebration; July; 116 W. Bridge St., 76048; www.granburychamber.com.

Granbury: Harvest Moon Festival; October; PO Box 2011 201 E. Pearl St., 76048; www.granburysquare.com. Since 1977. granburyhgma@gmail.com. (682) 936-4550.

Grand Prairie: National Championship Pow-Wow; September; 2602 Mayfield Rd, 75052; www.tradersvillage.com. Since 1963. dfwinfo@tradersvillage.com. (972) 647-2331.

Grapevine: GrapeFest; September; 636 S. Main St., 76051; www.grapevinetexasusa.com. Since 1986. (800) 457-6338

Greenville: Hunt County Fair; June; PO Box 1403, 75403; www.huntcountyfair.com. Since 1970. info@huntcountyfair.net. (903) 454.1503.

Groesbeck: Limestone County Fair; March–April; PO Box 965, 76642. limestonefair.org.

Hallettsville: Hallettsville Kolache Fest; September; PO Box 313, 77964; www.hallettsville.com. Since 1995.

Helotes: Helotes Cornyval; May (1st wknd.); PO Box 376, 78023; www.cornyval.com. Since 1967. cornyval@sbcglobal.net. (210) 695-2103.

Hempstead: Waller County Fair; September–October; PO Box 911, 77445. www.wallercountyfair.com. Since 1946. (979) 826-2825.

Hico: Hico Old Settler Reunion; July; PO Box 93, 76457; www.hico-tx.com. Since 1887.

Hidalgo: BorderFest; March; PO Box 722; 78557; www.hidalgoborderfest.com.

Hondo: Medina County Fair; September (3rd wknd.); PO Box 4, 78861; www.medinacountyfair.net. Since 1980. havefun@medinacountyfair.net. (830) 426-5406.

Houston: Houston Livestock Show and Rodeo; March; PO Box 20070, 77225; www.rodeohouston.com. questions@rodeohouston.com. (832) 667-1134

Hughes Springs: Wildflower Trails of Texas; April; PO Box 805, 75656; www.hughesspringstxusa.com Since 1970. (903) 639-7519

Huntsville: Walker County Fair & Rodeo; March–April; PO Box 1817, 77342; www.walkercountyfair.com. Since 1979. wcfa@walkercountyfair.com. (936) 291-8763

Ingram: The Official Texas State Arts & Crafts Fair; September; PO Box 489, 78025; txartsandcraftsfair.com. wgcash@hcaf.com. (830) 367-5121.

Jefferson: Historical Pilgrimage and Spring Festival; May (1st wknd.); PO Box 301, 75657-0301; www.jeffersonpilgrimage.com. Since 1947.

Johnson City: Blanco County Fair; August; PO Box 1257, 78636; www.bcfra.org. info@bcfra.org.

Kenedy: Bluebonnet Days; April; 205 South 2nd St., 78119. kenedychamber.org. (830) 583-3223.

Kerrville: Kerr County Fair; October; PO Box 290842, 78029; www.kerrcountyfair.com. Since 1980. kcfa@kerrcountyfair.com. (830) 257-6833.

Kerrville: Kerrville Folk Festival; May–June; PO Box 291466, 78029; www.kerrvillefolkfestival.com. Since 1972. info@kerrville-music.com. (830) 257-3600.

Killeen: Take 190 WestArts Festival; 3601 S. WS Young Dr., 76542; www.take190west.com. info@take190west.com. (254) 501-3888

LaGrange: Fayette County Fair; September; PO Box 544, 78945; www.fayettecountyfairnet. Since 1926. info@fayettecountyfair.org. (979) 968-3911.

Laredo: Border Olympics; January–March; PO Box 450037, 78044; borderolympics.net. Since 1947.

Laredo: Laredo International Fair & Expo; March; PO Box 1770, 78043; www.laredofair.com. Since 1963. laredofair.net@att.net. (956) 722-9948

Laredo: Washington's Birthday Celebration; January–February; 1819 E. Hillside Rd., 78041; www.wbcalaredo.com. Since 1898. wbca@wbcalaredo.org. (956) 722-0589

Longview: Gregg County Fair & Exposition; September; 1511 Judson Rd., Ste. F, 75601; www.greggcountyfair.com. Since 1951. ayohe3184@gmail.com. (903) 753-4478.

Lubbock: 4th on Broadway Festival; July; PO Box 1643, 79408; www.broadwayfestivals.com. Since 1991. (806) 749.2929.

Lubbock: Lights on Broadway Celebration; December; PO Box 1643, 79408; www.broadwayfestivals.com.

Lubbock: Panhandle-South Plains Fair; September; PO Box 208, 79408; www.southplainsfair.com. Since 1914. info@southplainsfair.com. (806) 763-2833.

Lufkin: Texas Forest Festival; September; 1200 Ellen Trout Dr., 75904; www.texasforestfestival.com. (936) 634.6644.

Luling: Luling Watermelon Thump; June (last full wknd); PO Box 710, 78648; www.watermelonthump.com. Since 1953.

McKinney: Texas Scottish Festival & Highland Games; May; 1705 West University Drive, Suite 108 - 110, 75069; www.texasscots.com. Since 1986. postmaster@texasscottishfestival.com. (469) 424.1930

Marshall: Fire Ant Festival; October; PO Box 520, 75671; www.marshalltexas.com. Since 1984.

Marshall: Stagecoach Days Festival; May; PO Box 520, 75671; www.marshalltexas.com. Since 1973.

Marshall: Wonderland of Lights; November–December; PO Box 520, 75671; www.marshalltxchamber.com.

Mercedes: Rio Grande Valley Livestock Show; March; 1000 N. Texas; www.rgvls.com. Since 1940. info@rgvls.com. (956) 565-2456.

Mesquite: Mesquite Championship Rodeo; April–September (each Fri. & Sat.); 1818 Rodeo Dr, 75149-3800; www.mesquiterodeo.com. Since 1957. info@ mesquiterodeo.com. (972) 285-8777.

Monahans: Butterfield-Overland Stage Coach and Wagon Festival; July; 401 S. Dwight Ave., 79756; www.monahans.org. Since 1994. chamber@monahans.org.

Mount Pleasant: Titus County Fair; September; PO Box 1232, 75456; www.tituscountyfair.com. Since 1975. info@tituscountyfair.com.

Nacogdoches: Piney Woods Fair; October; 3805 NW Stallings Dr., 75964; www.nacexpo.net. Since 1978. nacexpo@co.nacogdoches.tx.us. (936) 564-0849.

Nederland: Nederland Heritage Festival; March; PO Box 1176, 77627; www.nederlandhf.org. Since 1973. (409) 724-2269.

New Braunfels: Comal County Fair; September; PO Box 310223, 78131; www.comalcountyfair.org. Since 1894. ccfa.nbtx@sbcglobal.net. (830) 625.1505.

New Braunfels: Wurstfest; October–November; PO Box 310309, 78131; www.wurstfest.com. info@ wurstfest.com. (830) 625-9167.

Odessa: Permian Basin Fair & Expo; September; 218 W. 46th St., 79764; www.pbfair.com.

Palestine: Dogwood Trails Festival; March–April; PO Box 2828, 75802-2828; www.visitpalestine.com.

Paris: Red River Valley Fair; August–September; 570 E. Center St., 75460; www.paristx-rrvfair.com. Since 1911. rrvfair@suddenlinkmail.com. (903) 785-7971.

Pasadena: Pasadena Livestock Show & Rodeo; September–October; 7601 Red Bluff Rd., 77507-1035; www.pasadenarodeo.com. contactus@ pasadenarodeo.com. (281) 487-0240.

Port Aransas: Whooping Crane Festival; February (last weekend); 403 West Cotter, 78373; www.whoopingcranefestival.org. Since 1996. (361) 749-5919.

Port Arthur: cavOILcade; October; PO Box 2336, 77643; www.cavoilcade.portarthur.com. Since 1953. cavoilcade@portarthur.com. (409) 983-1009.

Port Lavaca: Calhoun County Fair; October (3rd wknd.); PO Box 42, 77979; http://www.calcofair.com Since 1963. calcofair77979@gmail.com. (361) 250-0930.

Poteet: Poteet Strawberry Festival; April; PO Box 227, 78065; www.strawberryfestival.com. Since 1948. info@strawberryfestival.com. (830) 742-8144.

Refugio: Refugio County Fair & Rodeo & Livestock Show; March; PO Box 88, 78377. Since 1961.

Rio Grande City: Starr County Fair; March (1st full wknd.); PO Box 841, 78582; www.starrcountyfair.com. Since 1961. starrcountyfair@aol.com. (956) 488-0122.

Rosenberg: Fort Bend County Fair; September–October; PO Box 428, 77471; www.fortbendcountyfair.com. Since 1937. info@fbcfa.org. (281) 342-6171.

Salado: Salado Scottish Games and Competitions; November (2nd wknd); 423 S. Main St.; www.saladomuseum.org. office@saladomuseum.org. (254) 947-5232.

San Angelo: San Angelo Stock Show & Rodeo; February; 200 W 43rd St., 76903; www.sanangelorodeo.com. Since 1932. (325)653-7785.

San Antonio: Fiesta San Antonio; April; 2611 Broadway St.; 78215; www.fiesta-sa.org. Since 1891. info@fiesta-sa.org. (210) 227-5191.

San Antonio: Texas Folklife Festival; June; 801 E. Cesar E. Chavez Blvd., 78205; www.texasfolklifefestival.org. Since 1972. itcweb@utsa.edu. (210) 458-2300.

Sanderson: Cinco de Mayo Celebration; May; PO Box 598, 79848; www.sandersonchamber.com. sandersonchamber@yahoo.com. (432) 345-3331.

Sanderson: 4th of July Celebration; July; PO Box 598, 79848; www.sandersonchamber.com. Since 1908. sandersonchamber@yahoo.com. (432) 345-3331.

Sanderson: Pachanga!; November; July; PO Box 598, 79848; www.sandersonchamber.com. Since 2001. sandersonchamber@yahoo.com. (432) 345-3331.

Santa Fe: Galveston County Fair & Rodeo; April; PO Box 889, 77510; www.galvestoncountyfair.com. (409) 986-6010

Schulenburg: Schulenburg Festival; August (1st full wknd.); PO Box 115; 78956; www.schulenburgfestival.com. Since 1976.

Shamrock: St. Patrick's Day Celebration; March; 207 N. Main St., 79079. www.shamrocktexas.net. Since 1947. shamrockedc@gmail.com. (806) 256-2516.

Stamford: Texas Cowboy Reunion; July; PO Box 928, 79553; www.texascowboyreunion.com. Since 1933. tcrrodeo@gmail.com

Sulphur Springs: Hopkins County Fall Festival; September; 125 S. Davis St., 75482. www.sulphurspringstx.org. hopkinscountyfallfestival@gmail. (903) 243-1925.

Sweetwater: Rattlesnake Roundup; March; PO Box 416, 79556; www.rattlesnakeroundup.net. Since 1958.

Terlingua: Terlingua International Chili Championship; November; PO Box 39, 79852; www.casichili.net. Since 1947.

Texarkana: Four States Fair; September; 3700 E. 50th St., Texarkana AR, 75504; www.fourstatesfair.com. (870) 773-2941.

Todd Mission: Texas Renaissance Festival; October–November (8 weekends); 21778 FM 1774, 77363; www.texrenfest.com. Since 1975. info@texasrenfest.com. (800) 458-3435.

Tyler: East Texas State Fair; September; 2112 W. Front St., 75702; www.etstatefair.com. Since 1914. info@etstatefair.com. (903) 597-2501.

Tyler: Texas Rose Festival; Ocober (3rd wknd.); PO Box 8224, 75711; www.texasrosefestival.com. Since 1933. (903) 597-3130.

Waco: Heart O' Texas Fair & Rodeo; October; 4601 Bosque Blvd.; 76710; www.hotfair.com. Since 1954. (254) 776-1660.

Waxahachie: Gingerbread Trail Tour of Homes; June (1st full wknd); PO Box 706, 75168; www.-rootsweb.com/~txecm/ginger. Since 1969.

Waxahachie: Scarborough Renaissance Festival; April–May; PO Box 538, 75168; www.srfestival.com. Since 1980. (972) 938-3247.

Weatherford: Parker County Peach Festival; July (2nd Sat.); PO Box 310, 76086; www.parkercountypeachfestival.org. Since 1985. info@weatherford-chamber.com. (817) 596-3801.

Weatherford: Christmas on the Square; December; PO Box 310, 76086; www.weatherford-chamber.com. Since 1988.

West: Westfest; September (Labor Day wknd.); PO Box 65, 76691; www.westfest.com. Since 1976. (254) 826-5058

Winnsboro: Autumn Trails Festival; October (every wknd.); PO Box 464, 75494; www.winnsboroautumntrails.com. winnsboroautumntrails@gmail.com. (903) 342-1958.

Woodville: Tyler County Dogwood Festival; March–April; PO Box 2151, 75979-2151; www.tylercountydogwoodfestival.org. Since 1944. dogwood_festival@yahoo.com. (409) 283-2632.

Yorktown: Yorktown's Annual Western Days Celebration; October (3rd full wknd.); PO Box 488, 78164; www.yorktowntx.com. Since 1959. westerndays@yorktowntx.com. (361)564.2611. ☆

A kayak angler caught this Guadalupe Bass as part of the Habitat and Angler Access Program with Texas Parks and Wildlife. Photo by Texas Parks and Wildlife.

Hunting and Fishing

Source: Texas Parks and Wildlife Department; http://tpwd.texas.gov

The popularity of hunting and fishing in Texas cannot be denied. Just ask the Texas Parks and Wildlife Department — which should probably be the place you start, because that's where you can find all of the current hunting and fishing regulations for the state.

According to the 2018 State of Texas Annual Cash Report, public hunting, fishing and other participation fees (including sales of hunting and fishing licenses) brought in revenues of $106,511,841.49 in 2017 and $103,447,864.28 in 2018.

Hunting Licenses

A **hunting license** is required of Texas residents and non-residents who hunt any legal bird or animal. Hunting licenses and endorsements are valid during the period Sept. 1 through the following Aug. 31 of each year, except licenses issued for a specific number of days or time periods.

A hunting license (except the non-resident special hunting license and non-resident 5-day special hunting license) is valid for taking all legal species of wildlife in Texas including deer, turkey, javelina, antelope, aoudad (sheep), alligator, and all small game and migratory game birds. Endorsement and tag requirements apply.

A trapper's license is required for all persons to hunt, shoot, or take for sale those species classified as fur-bearing animals or their pelts.

In addition to a valid hunting license:

- An **Archery Endorsement** is required to hunt deer or turkey during Archery-Only open season.
- An **Upland Game Bird Endorsement** is required to hunt turkey, pheasant, quail, or chachalaca. Non-residents

who purchase the non-resident spring turkey license are exempt from this endorsement requirement.

- A **Migratory Game Bird Endorsement** and **HIP (Harvest Information Program) Certification** is required to hunt any migratory game birds, including waterfowl, coot, rail, gallinule, snipe, dove, sandhill crane, and woodcock.
- A valid **Federal Duck Stamp** is required of waterfowl hunters age 16 or older.

On the web, information from TPWD on hunting can be found at:**tpwd.texas.gov/huntwild/hunt/**

Hunting and Fishing Licenses Sold	
2019	**Volume**
Hunting Licenses	477,399
Fishing Licenses	1,276,384
Combined Licenses	614,877
TOTALS	**2,368,660**
2020*	**Volume**
Hunting Licenses	465,331
Fishing Licenses	1,539,576
Combined Licenses	624,196
TOTALS	**2,629,103**

* Volumes for 2020 are estimated.
Source: 2022–23 Legislative Appropriation Request, TPWD

Game Harvest Estimates

The TPWD conducts random surveys of hunters every year to create estimates of hunter and harvest trends in two categories: small game (23 species total, birds and small mammals), and big game (white-tailed deer, mule deer, and javelina). They collect data not just on what animals were hunted, but also where, and how. You can learn about the methodology and see the full results of these surveys on the web at: **https://tpwd.texas.gov/publications/huntwild/hunt**

2019–2020 Wildlife Game Harvest

Game	Hunters	Harvest Estimates
Dove, combined*	292,346	6,881,986
Duck	82,134	1,085,509
Gallinule	0	0
Goose	11,994	51,891
Pheasant	9,329	20,065
Quail, combined**	39,669	383,829
Rabbit	35,209	168,156
Rail	491	4,339
Snipe	1,948	4,424
Squirrel	44,870	333,094
Teal	23,584	212,392
Turkey (fall and spring)	57,844	27,979
Woodcock	1,144	2,354
White-tailed Deer	791,619	846,330
Mule Deer	36,250	15,201
Javalina	40,632	35,505

*Dove, combined includes the following species: Eurasian, mourning, white-tipped, and white-winged.
**Quail, combined includes the following species: bobwhite and scaled.

Source: TPWD Game Harvest Surveys

Fishing Licenses

All fishing licenses and endorsements are valid only from Sept. 1 through the following Aug. 31, except licenses issued for a specific number of days or time periods. If you own any valid freshwater fishing package, you will be able to purchase a saltwater stamp and also fish saltwater.

If you own any valid saltwater fishing package, you will be able to purchase a freshwater stamp and also fish freshwater. An all-water fishing package is available that enables anglers to fish both fresh- and saltwater.

Detailed information concerning licenses, endorsements, seasons, and regulations can be obtained from Texas Parks and Wildlife Department, 4200 Smith School Road, Austin 78744, (800) 792-1112 or (512) 389-4820; or on the web at: **tpwd.texas.gov/business/licenses**

Freshwater Fishing

Freshwater fishing in Texas is an activity enjoyed by an estimated 1.21 million recreational anglers. In 2015, these anglers contributed an economic output of approximately $96 million to the Texas economy.

Among the 268 species of freshwater fish in Texas, the most popular fish for recreational fishing are: **largemouth bass, catfish, crappie, and striped, white, and hybrid striped bass**.

Texas anglers can fish in approximately 1,100 public reservoirs and about 191,000 miles of rivers and streams, together totaling 1.7 million acres.

The Texas Parks and Wildlife Department operates field stations, fish hatcheries, and research facilities to support the conservation and management of fishery resources. The hatcheries operated by TPWD raise largemouth and smallmouth bass, as well as catfish, striped and hybrid striped bass, and sunfish.

TPWD has continued its programs of stocking fish in public waters to increase angling opportunities. Many conservation-minded anglers who desire continued quality fishing practice catch-and-release fishing.

Texas Freshwater Fisheries Center

The Texas Freshwater Fisheries Center in Athens, about 75 miles southeast of Dallas, is an $18-million hatchery and educational center, where visitors can learn about underwater life.

The interactive Visitors Center includes aquarium displays of fish in their natural environment. Visitors get an "eye-to-eye" view of three authentically designed Texas freshwater habitats: a Hill Country stream, an East Texas pond, and a reservoir. A marsh exhibit features live American alligators.

A casting pond stocked with rainbow trout in the winter and catfish year-around provides a place for visitors to learn how to bait a hook, cast a line, and land a fish. The center has conference facilities and hosts groups by appointment.

The Texas Freshwater Fisheries Center is open Tuesday through Saturday, 9 a.m. to 4 p.m., and Sunday, 1 p.m. to 4 p.m. It is closed on Monday. Admission is charged. The center is located 4.5 miles east of Athens on FM 2495 at Lake Athens. Address: 5550 FM 2495, Athens 75752, or call (903) 676-2277. For more information, visit: **https://tpwd.texas.gov/spdest/visitorcenters/tffc/.**

Saltwater Fishing

According to the most recent report available, Texas has about 672,000 saltwater anglers (16 years old and older) who spend an estimated $1.1 billion annually on fishing-related expenditures. In 2013, anglers harvested 1.74 million fish from both Texas bays and the Gulf of Mexico off Texas.

The most popular saltwater sport fish in Texas bays are **spotted seatrout, sand seatrout, Atlantic croaker, red drum, southern flounder, black drum, sheepshead, and gafftopsail catfish**.

Offshore, some of the fish that anglers target are **red snapper, king mackerel, Spanish mackerel, dolphinfish, cobia, tarpon, and yellowfin tuna.** ☆

Learn more about the fish found in Texas in our expanded wildlife section, starting on page 75.

For information about commercial fishing, see page 621 in the Business chapter.

Sports

HIGH SCHOOL CHAMPIONS

COLLEGE CHAMPIONS

PROFESSIONAL SPORTS TEAMS

HALL OF FAME & OLYMPIC MEDALISTS

Westlake Chaparrals face off against the Steele Knights at the UIL quarterfinals for high school football at Kelly Reeves Athletic Complex in 'Round Rock on January 2, 2021. Photo by Ralph Arvesen/Flickr (CC)

Liberty Hill Panthers face the Rouse Raiders in the 5A Division II regional semifinals at Kelly Reeves Athletic Complex in Round Rock, Texas, on December 26, 2020. Photographer/Photo by Ralph Arvesen/Flickr (CC).

Texas Sports and the COVID-19 Pandemic

Reporting by A.J. Smuskiewicz

The COVID-19 pandemic, caused by the SARS-CoV-2 coronavirus, had a major impact on sports in Texas through 2020 and 2021. Texas, under the leadership of Republican governor Greg Abbott, maintained looser restrictions on sports, schools, and other public gatherings compared with most other states, and lifted those restrictions sooner.

Many public health experts disagreed with Governor Abbott's policies, maintaining that they would worsen the crisis. [1] Abbott defended his efforts to "reopen Texas," citing the importance of school activities to the social and emotional health of students, as well as the economic and social importance of sports and other businesses. He also argued that the state maintained sufficient safety protocols to keep the spread of the virus under control. [2]

Pandemic-Related Closings

As the pandemic spread in early 2020, most professional, amateur, and school sports throughout the United States were shut down, closed to in-person spectators, or otherwise altered to slow the spread of the virus. In Texas, most school sports were shut down by the schools themselves in early 2020. [3] If school games were played, no fans were allowed. [4] For the first time ever, the high school football season was delayed in fall 2020. [5] Many professional sports, including baseball and football, played shortened preseasons and seasons in 2020 throughout the nation, including in Texas, with few or no fans allowed in attendance. [6]

Reopenings Begin

Texas sports were reopened to fans ahead of those in most other states. By the summer of 2020, some fans began to be allowed into sporting events, from high school through professional. [7]

By late 2020 to early 2021, most high school sports, even those played indoors, were being played in Texas. [3] To mitigate risks, students wore face masks while sitting on the bench. If not participating in the game, they used hand sanitizer, and the playing ball was frequently sanitized. [3, 8] Student athletes were tested multiple times each week for the virus. [9] Spectators, if allowed to attend the game, were required to wear masks. [3] As high school football was being played throughout Texas in January 2021, Brandon Smith, coach of the Prosper High School team, reflected the famous

Texas love of the game when he said, "It's Friday night in Texas. It's what we do." [8]

Fan attendance at sporting events generally remained limited from late 2020 to early 2021. The state initially limited attendance at university games for football, basketball, and other sports to 25% capacity in 2020; this figure was later raised to 50%. [4, 9] Despite the 50% maximum capacity, most universities chose to keep the 25% limit through early 2021. [4, 10]

Moves to Texas

In late 2020, some university teams from other states played their home games in Texas to escape their own states' restrictions banning "nonessential businesses." [9] Such teams included the University of New Mexico men's and women's basketball teams.

In February 2021, the National Collegiate Athletic Association (NCAA) announced that all games of the current season's women's Division I national tournament would be held in Texas—in San Antonio, Austin, and San Marcos. [11] The games had originally been scheduled for San Antonio; Austin; Albany, New York; Cincinnati, Ohio; and Spokane, Washington. The latter three cities maintained tougher restrictions on sports than those in Texas. The consolidation of the tournament in the San Antonio area made it easy to manage the event in terms of hotel accommodations and other safety considerations. In the 2020 season, the NCAA cancelled both the women's and the men's tournaments because of the pandemic. All of the 2021 men's games were scheduled for Indiana, which also had looser restrictions than most other states.

The USA Olympic wrestling team announced in February 2021 that it would relocate its team trials to Texas. The usual location was in Pennsylvania, where pandemic restrictions prevented the trials. [12]

"Reopen Texas 100%"

In March 2021, Governor Abbott issued a number of executive orders to reopen businesses and other activities back to normal levels in Texas. [2, 4, 13] He said, "It's time to reopen Texas 100%," [4] adding that this move was possible because of "advancements of vaccines and antibody therapeutic drugs." [13] Businesses in the state could operate at full capacity with "no COVID-19-related operating limits."

[2, 7] His orders ended the mask-wearing mandate and the crowd-capacity limits at sporting events. [14]

Despite Abbott's orders, individual leagues and teams could each set their own policies. For example, Mark Cuban, owner of the Dallas Mavericks National Basketball Association franchise, said that the team's mask mandate and other COVID-related safety protocols would remain in place. [4]

On April 5, 2021, the season home opener for the Texas Rangers Major League Baseball team had a full-capacity crowd at the new 40,518-seat Globe Life Field in Arlington, Texas. It was the largest crowd at any sporting event in the United States since the start of the pandemic. [7, 14] The stadium had opened in 2020, but no fans had been allowed at the regular-season games. [7] The 2020 National League Championship Series and the World Series had both been played there, but at only 28% capacity. [7] For the 2021 opening day, fans were encouraged to wear masks at their seats and to practice social distancing at concession stands and on concourses. Among the fans in attendance was former President George W. Bush, who had once been an owner of the Rangers. [14]

Allowing the sell-out crowd at the Rangers game was criticized by some public health authorities and Democrat politicians, including President Joe Biden, who said that it was "not responsible." [15] Texas officials responded by pointing out

that the number of COVID-19 infections was declining in Texas, while numbers were still increasing in much of the rest of the country. [14] They argued that these figures showed that the pandemic policies in Texas were working.

Evaluation of Impact

As of June 2021, about 40% of Texans had been fully vaccinated against the coronavirus that causes COVID-19. [16] The vaccines allowed the public to advance further to normal conditions regarding sports and other public events. As 2021 progressed, an increasing number of universities allowed full-capacity crowds at sporting events. [10]

While Texas sports returned to normal in 2021, many teams evaluated the financial impact of the pandemic. In May 2021, Ross Bjork, athletic director at Texas A&M University, announced that the university's athletics programs had lost $48 million as a result of the pandemic-related restrictions. [17, 18]

Officials at the University of Texas had previously announced that revenue from its athletics programs had declined more than $23 million in the 2019-2020 fiscal year compared with 2018-2019. [19] The university expected to have a much more profitable 2021 for its athletics department, especially with the unveiling of a stadium expansion and renovation that included additional premium seating and amenities. [19]

References

1. Beauvais, Sally, Lexi Churchill, Kiah Collier, Vianna Davilla, and Ren Larson. Gov. Greg Abbott is limiting enforcement of COVID-19 orders, but many cities already took a lax approach. The Texas Tribune. May 14, 2020. https://www.texastribune.org/2020/05/14/texas-coronavirus-enforcement/

2. Opening the state of Texas. Texas Health and Human Services. Updated June 8, 2021. https://www.dshs.state.tx.us/coronavirus/opentexas.aspx

3. Taboada, Melissa B. Texas school sports moved indoors for the winter. So did the coronavirus. The Texas Tribune. January 4, 2021. https://www.texastribune.org/2021/01/04/texas-high-school-sports-coronavirus-pandemic/

4. Schnitker, Andrew. What does Gov. Abbott's mandate mean for Texas Longhorns sports? KXAN. March 3, 2021. https://www.kxan.com/sports/what-does-gov-abbotts-mandate-mean-for-texas-longhorns-sports/

5. Marquez, RJ, and Valerie Gomez. COVID-19 pandemic puts Texas high school football, fall sports in jeopardy. KSAT. July 31, 2020. https://www.ksat.com/news/local/2020/07/31/covid-19-pandemic-puts-texas-high-school-football-fall-sports-in-jeopardy/

6. Walker, Andrew. NFL cancels all 2020 preseason games. Colts.com. July 27, 2020. https://www.colts.com/news/preseason-canceled-roger-goodell-2020-covid-19

7. Hawkins, Stephen. MLB's Rangers in line to be first team back to full capacity. AP News. March 10, 2021. https://apnews.com/article/mlb-baseball-coronavirus-pandemic-greg-abbott-texas-rangers-dcd4d8bf0c62904f8c392522304b1bf6

8. Jackson, Austin. Inside the battle between COVID-19 & the 2020 Texas high school football season. Local Profile. January 18, 2021. https://localprofile.com/2021/01/18/hospitals-are-filling-covid-19-lingers-but-for-better-or-worse-texas-high-school-football-finds-a-way/

9. Rosenzweig-Ziff, Dan. Fleeing their home state's strict restrictions on sports, New Mexico basketball teams seek refuge in two of Texas' worst hot spots. The Texas Tribune. November 19, 2020. https://www.texastribune.org/2020/11/19/new-mexico-basketball-texas-lubbock-coronavirus/

10. Straka, Dean. Report: Sarkisian calls for Texas fans to mirror intensity from NCAA Super Regional at home football games. 247 Sports. June 17, 2021. https://247sports.com/

LongFormArticle/The-best-of-the-best-Highest-ranked-recruits-on-each-MaxPreps-Top-25-team-166682367/

11. Blinder, Alan. N.C.A.A. women's basketball tournament will be held in Texas. The New York Times. February 5, 2021. https://www.nytimes.com/2021/02/05/sports/ncaa-basketball/ncaa-womens-basketball-tournament-texas.html

12. Radnofsky, Louise, and Rachel Bachman. Moving sports events to Texas was easy, maybe too easy. The Wall Street Journal. March 14, 2021. https://www.wsj.com/articles/texas-mask-rules-sports-events-11615685393

13. Governor Abbott lifts mask mandate, opens Texas 100 percent [press release]. Office of the Texas Governor. March 2, 2021. https://gov.texas.gov/news/post/governor-abbott-lifts-mask-mandate-opens-texas-100-percent

14. Boren, Cindy. Here's what the largest crowd at a U.S. sports event since the pandemic looked like. The Washington Post. April 6, 2021. https://www.washingtonpost.com/sports/2021/04/06/texas-rangers-sports-crowd-coronavirus/

15. Scribner, Herb. The Texas Rangers have no crowd limit for opening day. President Joe Biden says that's 'not responsible'. Deseret News. April 1, 2021. https://www.deseret.com/sports/2021/4/1/22362180/texas-rangers-no-crowd-limit-opening-day-president-joe-biden

16. Texas coronavirus vaccination progress. USA Facts. Updated June 2021. https://usafacts.org/visualizations/covid-vaccine-tracker-states/state/texas

17. Paterik, Brice. AD Ross Bjork says Texas A&M athletics suffered $48 million loss due to COVID-19 pandemic. The Dallas Morning News. May 23, 2021. https://www.dallasnews.com/sports/texas-am-aggies/2021/05/23/texas-am-athletic-director-ross-bjork-says-aggies-athletics-suffered-48-million-loss-due-to-covid-19-pandemic/

18. Zwerneman, Brent. Texas A&M lost $48 million between department, 12th Man Foundation during pandemic, say AD. Houston Chronicle. May 23, 2021. https://www.houstonchronicle.com/texas-sports-nation/college/article/A-M-AD-84-million-in-losses-between-department-16196627.php

19. Davis, Brian. Texas athletics generates $200.7 million in revenue, $22.1 million profit in 2019-20 fiscal year. Hook'Em. January 29, 2021. https://www.hookem.com/story/sports/football/2021/01/29/texas-football-longhorns-turn-22-1-million-profit-2020/4301655001/

The Llano Yellow Jackets play against the Hallettsville Brahmas in the UIL 3A Division I varsity high school football semifinals at Birkelbach Field in Georgetown, Texas, on December 10, 2020. Photo by Ralph Arvesen/ Flickr (CC)..

STATE: High School Championships

The University Interscholastic League (UIL), which governs literary and athletic competition among public schools in Texas, was organized in 1910 as a division of the University of Texas extension service.

Initially, it sponsored forensic competition. By 1920, the UIL organized the structure of the high school football game in response to the growing popularity of the sport in Texas.

The Texas Association of Private and Parochial Schools (TAPPS) is the largest group of private schools in the state

with more than 225 member institutions. The interscholastic competition began in 1978 and was significantly expanded when the Texas Christian Interscholastic League ceased to exist in 2000 and many of those schools moved into TAPPS.

The Southwest Preparatory Conference (SPC), established in 1952, is an athletic conference of certain private schools in Oklahoma and Texas.

Listed are state champions and the game scores.

Sources: The University Interscholastic League at uil.utexas.edu; the Texas Association of Private and Parochial Schools.

Football

Year	Division	Champion	Runner Up
UIL 2020	1A Division I	Sterling City 68	May 22
	1A Division II	Balmorhea 74	Richland Springs 38
	2A Division I	Shiner 42	Post 20
	2A Division II	Windthorst 22	Mart 21
	3A Division I	Tuscola Jim Ned 29	Hallettsville 28
	3A Division II	Canadian 35	Franklin 34
	4A Division I	Argyle 49	Lindale 21
	4A Division II	Carthage 70	Gilmer 14
	5A Division I	Denton Ryan 59	Cedar Park 14
	5A Division II	Aledo 56	Crosby 21
	6A Division I	Austin Westlake 52	Southlake Carroll 34
	6A Division II	Katy 51	Cedar Hill 14
TAPPS 2020	Division I	Dallas Parish Episcopal 42	Fort Worth Nolan Catholic 28
	Division II	Austin Regents 26	Dallas Christian 20
	Division III	Colleyville Covenant 40	Houston Cypress Christian 30
	Division IV	Shiner St. Paul 63	Waco Reicher Catholic 13

Year	Division	Champion	Runner Up
UIL 2019	1A Division I	Blum 58	McLean 52
	1A Division II	Richland Springs 62	Matador Motley County 16
	2A Division I	Refugio 28	Post 7
	2A Division II	Mart 25	Hamlin 20
	3A Division I	Grandview 42	Pottsboro 35
	3A Division II	Gunter 43	Omaha Pewitt 22
	4A Division I	Carthage 42	Waco La Vega 28
	4A Division II	Texarkana Pleasant Grove 35	Wimberley 21
	5A Division I	Alvin Shadow Creek 28	Denton Ryan 22
	5A Division II	Aledo 45	Fort Bend Marshall 42
	6A Division I	Galena Park North Shore 31	Duncanville 17
	6A Division II	Austin Westlake 24	Denton Guyer 0
TAPPS 2019	Division I	Dallas Parish Episcopal 42	Plano John Paul II 14
	Division II	Cedar Hill Trinity 48	Austin Regents 19
	Division III	Boerne Geneva 49	Lubbock Christian 21
	Division IV	Shiner St. Paul 20	Hallettsville Sacred Heart 16
SPC 2019	3A Division	Fort Worth Country Day 41	The Woodlands John Cooper 0
	4A Division	Bellaire Episcopal 42	Houston Kinkaid 21

Volleyball

Year	Division	Champion	Runner Up
UIL 2020	1A	Neches 3	Blum 0
	2A	Iola 3	Crawford 1
	3A	Bushland 3	Goliad 0
	4A	Decatur 3	Wimberley 0
	5A	Lucas Lovejoy 3	Lamar Fulshear 0
	6A	Katy Seven Lakes 3	Klein 1
TAPPS 2020	1A	Wichita Falls Christ Academy 3	San Antonio The Atonement 0
	2A	Red Oak Ovilla Christian 3	Bulverde Bracken Christian 0
	3A	New Braunfels Christian 3	Midland Classical 0
	4A	Houston Northland Christian 3	Fort Worth Lake Country Christian 1
	5A	Victoria St. Joseph 3	Carrollton Prince of Peace 0
	6A	Argyle Liberty Christian 3	Houston St. Agnes 2
UIL 2019	1A	Neches 3	Round Top-Carmine 0
	2A	Crawford 3	Jewett Leon 0
	3A	Vanderbilt Industrial 3	Van Alstyne 0
	4A	Lamar Fulshear 3	Hereford 0
	5A	Lucas Lovejoy 3	Canyon Randall 0
	6A	Northwest Nelson 3	Plano West 2
TAPPS 2019	1A	Wichita Falls Notre Dame 3	San Antonio Legacy Christian 0
	2A	Red Oak Ovilla Christian 3	Austin Waldorf 0
	3A	New Braunfels Christian 3	Round Rock Christian 0
	4A	Lubbock Trinity Christian 3	Boerne Geneva School 1
	5A	Carrollton Prince of Peace 3	San Antonio Christian 0
	6A	Houston St. Agnes 3	Plano Prestonwood Christian 2

Boys Basketball

Year	Division	Champion	Runner Up
UIL 2021	1A	Texline 54	Slidell 53
	2A	Clarendon 64	Grapeland 60
	3A	San Antonio Cole 77	Tatum 60
	4A	Argyle 49	Huffman Hargrave 30
	5A	Beaumont United 71 (OT)	Dallas Kimball 70
	6A	Duncanville 66	Austin Westlake 53
TAPPS 2021	1A	Cypress Covenant 50	Irving Faustina Academy 37
	2A	Houston Grace Christian 59	Lubbock Kingdom Prep 48
	3A	Huntsville Alpha Omega 31	Midland Classical 26
	4A	Houston Westbury Christian 97	Lubbock Trinity 93
	5A	The Woodlands Christian 60	Fort Worth Christian 47
	6A	San Antonio Antonian 73	Dallas Bishop Lynch 57
UIL 2020	Canceled due to COVID-19 pandemic.		
TAPPS 2020	1A	Longview Trinity School of Texas 50	Houston Robert M. Beren 33
	2A	Huntsville Alpha Omega 43	Lubbock All Saints Episcopal 38
	3A	Dallas Yavneh 50	Tomball Rosehill Christian 35
	4A	The Woodlands Christian 68	Colleyville Covenant Christian 50
	5A	Frisco Legacy Christian 62	Houston Westbury Christian 59
	6A	Plano John Paul II 51	San Antonio Antonian College Prep 48
UIL 2019	1A	Slidell 49	Jayton 36
	2A	Shelbyville 67	Gruver 48
	3A	Dallas Madison 49	Brock 48
	4A	Oak Cliff Faith Family Academy 53	Liberty Hill 51
	5A	Mansfield Timberview 77	San Antonio Wagner 64
	6A	Duncanville 73	Klein Forest 69
TAPPS 2019	1A	Baytown Christian 63	Dallas Tyler Street 39
	2A	Bryan Allen Academy 68	Abilene Christian 47
	3A	Kerrville Our Lady of the Hills 50	Midland Classical 47
	4A	Arlington Grace Prep 58	The Woodlands Christian 54
	5A	Frisco Legacy Christian 66	Houston Lutheran South 51
	6A	San Antonio Antonian 70	Plano Prestonwood Christian 67

Girls Basketball

Year	Division	Champion	Runner Up
UIL 2021	1A	Dodd City 30	Nazareth 21
	2A	Lipan 44	Martin's Mill 39
	3A	Brownfield 68 (OT)	Fairfield 64
	4A	Canyon 56	Hardin-Jefferson 55
	5A	Cedar Park 46	Frisco Liberty 39
	6A	DeSoto 53	S. Grand Prairie 37

Year	Division	Champion	Runner Up
TAPPS 2021	1A	San Angelo Cornerstone Christian 35	Wichita Falls Christ Academy 27
	2A	Lubbock Southcrest Christian 58	Shiner St. Paul 33
	3A	Houston Lutheran High North 62	McKinney Cornerstone 34
	4A	Lubbock Christian 75	The Woodlands Legacy Prep 39
	5A	Fort Worth Southwest 54	Houston Second Baptist 40
	6A	Dallas Bishop Lynch 56	Houston The Village 46
UIL 2020	1A	Nazareth 44	Lipan 31
	2A	Gruver 42	Muenster 39
	3A	Shallowater 61	Woodville 43
	4A	Fairfield 40	Argyle 39 (OT)
	5A	Frisco Liberty 35	SA Veterans Memorial 26
	6A	Duncanville 63	Cypress Creek 47
TAPPS 2020	1A	San Antonio Legacy Christian 58	Lubbock Kingdom Preparatory Academy 32
	2A	Lubbock Southcrest Christian 46	Austin Waldorf 28
	3A	Midland Classical 72	Beaumont Legacy Christian 37
	4A	Lubbock Trinity Christian 50	Austin Texas School for the Deaf 25
	5A	Fort Worth Southwest Christian 73	Houston Second Baptist 63
	6A	Houston The Village 75	Plano Prestonwood Christian 48
UIL 2019	1A	Nazareth 54	Dodd City 33
	2A	Martins Mill 60	Grapeland 56
	3A	Chapel Hill (Tyler) 55	Woodville 46
	4A	Argyle 49	Hardin-Jefferson 41
	5A	Amarillo 47	Frisco Liberty 42
	6A	Converse Judson 49	DeSoto 46
TAPPS 2019	1A	San Antonio Legacy Christian 50	Wichita Falls Notre Dame 39
	2A	Lubbock Southcrest Christian 41	Shiner St. Paul 34
	3A	Midland Classical 72	Beaumont Legacy Christian 47
	4A	Lubbock Trinity Christian 72	Houston Lutheran North 34
	5A	Cedar Hill Trinity Christian 76	San Antonio Christian 33
	6A	Dallas Bishop Lynch 81	Houston Village 62

Boys Soccer

Year	Division	Champion	Runner Up
UIL 2021	4A	Boerne 3	Fort Worth Diamond Hill-Jarvis 1
	5A	Frisco Wakeland 3	Humble Kingwood Park 2
	6A	San Antonio LEE 2	Rockwall Heath 0
TAPPS 2021	Fall 2020	Dallas International 2	San Antonio Lutheran 0
	Division I	Monsignor Kelly Catholic 2	Plano John Paul II 1
	Division II	San Antonio TMI Episcopal 5	Frisco Legacy 0
	Division III	Dallas Covenant 1	Schertz John Paul II 0
UIL 2020	Canceled due to COVID-19 pandemic.		

For track, tennis, and other high school sports champions, see page 589 in the Education section.

Year	Division	Champion	Runner Up
TAPPS 2020	Fall 2019	Dallas International 2	Brownsville First Baptist 1
	Division I	San Antonio Central Catholic 2	El Paso Cathedral 1
	Division II	San Antonio TMI Episcopal 3	Bullard Brook Hill 2
	Division III	Houston St. Thomas Episcopal 1	Dallas Covenant 0
UIL 2019	4A	San Elizario 1	Midlothian Heritage 0 (OT)
	5A	El Paso Bel Air 2	Frisco Wakeland 1
	6A	Flower Mound 1	San Antonio Lee 0 (SO 4-1)
TAPPS 2019	Fall 2018	Nacogdoches Regents 2	Pflugerville Concordia 1
	Division III	Dallas Covenant 2	Houston St. Thomas Episcopal 1
	Division II	San Antonio TMI Episcopal 3	Carrollton Prince of Peace 2
	Division I	San Antonio Central Catholic 4	Dallas Bishop Lynch 0

Girls Soccer

Year	Division	Champion	Runner Up
UIL 2021	4A	Midlothian Heritage 6	Corpus Christi Calallen 0
	5A	Dripping Springs 2	Frisco Wakeland 1
	6A	Lewisville Flower Mound 2	Austin Vandegrift 1
TAPPS 2021	Division I	Ursuline Academy 5	St. Agnes 0
	Division II	Grapevine Faith 7	St. Michael's 1
	Division III	Dallas Covenant 3	Schertz John Paul II 1
UIL 2020	Canceled due to COVID-19 pandemic.		
TAPPS 2020	Division I	Houston St. Agnes 6	Fort Worth Nolan Catholic 0
	Division II	Grapevine Faith Christian 2	San Antonio Christian 0
	Division III	Schertz John Paul II 4	Dallas Covenant 1
UIL 2019	4A	Stephenville 2	Liberty Hill 0
	5A	Highland Park (Dallas) 2	Mansfield Legacy 0
	6A	Southlake Carroll 5	Katy Tompkins 0
TAPPS 2019	Division III	Houston St. Thomas Episcopal 6	Austin Veritas 0
	Division II	Grapevine Faith 7	Houston Second Baptist 0
	Division I	Dallas Bishop Lynch 1	Houston St. Agnes 0

Baseball

Year	Division	Champion	Runner Up
UIL 2021	1A	Fayetteville 6	Kennard 4
	2A	New Deal 7	Garrison 2
	3A	Malakoff 8	Corpus Christi London 7
	4A	Texarkana Pleasant Grove 2	Rusk 1
	5A	Mont Belvieu Barbers Hill 2	Hallsville 1
	6A	Rockwall Heath 4	Keller 3
TAPPS 2021	Division I	Midland Christian 1	Concordia Lutheran 0
	Division II	Lutheran South Academy 16	Southwest Christian 0
	Division III	Bay Area Christian 3	Lubbock Trinity Christian 1
	Division IV	Midland Classical 5	Rosehill Christian 4
	Division V	Weatherford Christian 14	Sacred Heart Hallettsville 2

Year	Division	Champion	Runner Up
UIL 2020	Canceled due to COVID-19 pandemic.		
TAPPS 2020	Canceled due to COVID-19 pandemic.		
UIL 2019	1A	D'Hanis 4	New Home 0
	2A	Dallardsville Big Sandy 7	Linden-Kildare 1
	3A	Wall 2	Blanco 1
	4A	Argyle 6	Sweeny 3
	5A	Colleyville Heritage 14	Georgetown 2 (6 innings)
	6A	Southlake Carroll 17	Ft. Bend Ridge Point 0 (5 innings)
TAPPS 2019	Division V	Weatherford Christian 7	Brazosport Christian 6
	Division IV	Amarillo San Jacinto Christian 5	New Braunfels Chrisitan 3
	Division III	Houston Northland Christian 3	Willow Park Trinity Christian 2
	Division II	Houston Lutheran South 11	Fort Worth Christian 1
	Division I	Argyle Liberty Christian 3	Fort Worth All Saints Episcopal 5

Softball

Year	Division	Champion	Runner Up
UIL 2021	1A	Dodd City 8	D'Hanis 4
	2A	Stamford 5	Crawford 4
	3A	Rains 11	Diboll 5
	4A	Liberty 10	Calallen 3
	5A	Mont Belvieu Barbers Hill 4	Aledo 1
	6A	Deer Park 1	Converse Judson 0
TAPPS 2021	Division I	John Paul II Plano 4	Antonian College Prep 2
	Division II	Second Baptist 13	Faith Christian Grapevine 0
	Division III	Holy Cross of San Antonio 10	Bay Area Christian 0
	Division IV	Sacred Heart Hallettsville 13	Temple Christian 3
UIL 2020	Canceled due to COVID-19 pandemic.		
TAPPS 2020	Canceled due to COVID-19 pandemic.		
UIL 2019	1A	D'Hanis 9	Chireno 7
	2A	Crawford 8	Thorndale 7 (8 innings)
	3A	Rains 6	Hallettsville 2
	4A	Huffman Hargrave 12	Anna 0 (6 innings)
	5A	Angleton 8	Calallen 1
	6A	Katy 8	Klein Collins 2
TAPPS 2019	Division IV	Shiner St. Paul 15	Round Rock Concordia 0
	Division III	Waco Reicher 10	The Woodlands Christian 2
	Division II	Houston Lutheran South 6	Bullard Brook Hill 2
	Division I	Houston St. Agnes 3	Dallas Bishop Lynch 2

American Athletic Conference Champions

The 2013-14 season was the first for the AAC after the breakup of the Big East Conference. Texas schools in the AAC are:

- Southern Methodist University
- University of Houston

Other schools in the conference are the University of Memphis, University of Cincinnati, University of Central Florida, East Carolina University, Temple University, University of South Florida, Tulane University, University of Tulsa, the University of Connecticut, and Wichita State University.

Football

Year	Season	Championship	College Football Playoff
2020	Cincinnati, Tulsa	Cincinnati	Neither AAC Texas team entered the College Football Playoff.
2019	East: Cincinnati West: Memphis	Memphis	Neither AAC Texas team entered the College Football Playoff.
2018	East: UCF West: Memphis	UCF	Neither AAC Texas team entered the College Football Playoff.

Men's Basketball

Year	Season	Tournament	Postseason
2021	Wichita State	Houston	Houston lost to Baylor 78-59 in Elite Eight.
2020	Cincinnati, Houston, Tulsa	Canceled	Canceled due to COVID-19 pandemic.
2019	Houston	Cincinnati	Houston lost to Kentucky 62-58 in Sweet Sixteen.

Women's Basketball

Year	Season	Tournament	Postseason
2021	South Florida	South Florida	Houston beat Arizona State 50-48 in the Women's National Invitational Tournament Fort Worth Region Consolation Final.
2020	University of Connecticut	University of Connecticut	Canceled due to COVID-19 pandemic.
2019	University of Connecticut	University of Connecticut	Neither AAC Texas team entered the NCAA Division I Championship nor Women's National Invitational Tournament.

Baseball

Year	Season	Championship	NCAA Division I Baseball Tournament
2021	East Carolina	South Florida	Neither AAC Texas team advanced to the NCAA Division I Baseball Tournament.
2020	Alabama, University of Mississippi, Florida	Canceled	Canceled due to COVID-19 pandemic.
2019	East Carolina	Cincinnati	Neither AAC Texas team advanced to the NCAA Division I Baseball Tournament.

Softball

Year	Season	Championship	NCAA Division I Softball Tournament
2021	Wichita State	Wichita State	Neither AAC Texas team advanced to the NCAA Division I Softball Tournament.
2020	Florida	Canceled	Canceled due to COVID-19 pandemic.
2019	South Florida	Championship canceled; no champion declared	Houston lost to Texas 7-0 in NCAA Division I Softball Championship's Austin Regional Final.

C-USA Champions

Texas schools in the West Division of Conference USA in 2021 were:

- Rice University
- University of Texas at San Antonio
- University of Texas at El Paso
- University of North Texas

Rice and UTEP joined in 2005. In 2013, the University of North Texas and the University of Texas at San Antonio joined the conference. The University of Houston joined in 1996 and left in 2013.

Other teams in the West Division of Conference USA are University of Alabama-Birmingham, Louisiana Tech University, and University of Southern Mississippi.

Teams in the East Division include Florida Atlantic University, Florida International University, Marshall University, Middle Tennessee State University, University of North Carolina at Charlotte, Old Dominion University (in Virginia), and Western Kentucky University.

Football

Year	Season	Championship	College Football Playoff
2020	East: Marshall West: UAB	UAB	No C-USA Texas teams advanced to the College Football Playoff.
2019	East: Florida Atlantic West: UAB	Florida Atlantic	No C-USA Texas teams advanced to the College Football Playoff.

Men's Basketball

Year	Season	Tournament	Postseason
2021	East: WKU West: Louisiana Tech	North Texas	North Texas lost to Villanova 84-61 in second round.
2020	North Texas	Canceled	Canceled due to COVID-19 pandemic.

Women's Basketball

Year	Season	Tournament	Postseason
2021	East: Middle Tennessee West: Rice	Middle Tennessee	Rice beat University of Mississippi 71-58 in Women's National Invitation Tournament championship game.
2020	Rice	Canceled	Canceled due to COVID-19 pandemic.

Baseball

Year	Season	Championship	NCAA Division I Baseball Tournament
2021	East: Charlotte West: LA Tech	Old Dominion	No C-USA Texas teams advanced to the postseason.
2020	Old Dominion, Southern Miss	Canceled	Canceled due to COVID-19 pandemic.

Softball

Year	Season	Championship	NCAA Division I Softball Tournament
2021	East: Charlotte West: North Texas	University of Texas-San Antonio	No C-USA Texas teams advanced to the postseason.
2020	Canceled	Canceled	Canceled due to COVID-19 pandemic.

Did you know

More than one team from a conference can advance to the NCAA tournament.

Sometimes, if a team just misses an NCAA play-off berth, they might be chosen for an invitational tournament. The two most prominent are in basketball: the National Invitational Tournament (NIT, for men's teams), and the Women's National Invitational Tournament (WNIT).

Southwestern Athletic Conference Champions

Texas schools in the Western Division of the Southwestern Athletic Conference in 2019 were:

- Prairie View A&M University
- Texas Southern University

The Prairie View A&M Panthers have been in the conference since its founding in 1920 and the Texas Southern Tigers joined the conference in 1954. Other teams in the SWAC Western Division are Grambling State University (Louisiana), Southern University (Louisiana), and University of Arkansas at Pine Bluff.

Schools in the Eastern Division are Jackson State University (in Mississippi), Mississippi Valley State University, Alcorn State University (in Mississippi), Alabama State University, and Alabama A&M University.

SWAC schools opt to play the Celebration Bowl as opposed to the NCAA Division I Football Championships.

Football

Year	Season	Championship	Celebration Bowl
Spring 2021	East: Alabama A&M West: University of Arkansas-Pine Bluff	Alabama A&M	Not applicable.
2020	Canceled	Canceled	Canceled due to COVID-19 pandemic.
2019	East: Alcorn State West: Southern (Louisiana)	Alcorn State	North Carolina A&T 64, Alcorn State 44

Men's Basketball

Year	Season	Tournament	Postseason
2021	Prairie View A&M, Jackson State	Texas Southern	Texas Southern lost to Michigan 82-66 in first round.
2020	Prairie View A&M	Canceled	Canceled due to COVID-19 pandemic.
2019	Prairie View A&M	Prairie View A&M	• Prairie View A&M lost to 82-76 in the First Four of the NCAA Division I Basketball Championship. • Texas Southern lost to Green Bay 87-86 OT in the semifinals at the CollegeInsider.com Postseason Tournament.

Women's Basketball

Year	Season	Tournament	Postseason
2021	Jackson State	Jackson State	Jackson State lost to Baylor 101-52 in first round.
2020	Jackson State	Canceled	Canceled due to COVID-19 pandemic.
2019	Jackson State	Southern (Louisiana)	Prairie View A&M lost to Texas Christian University 72-41 in the first round of the Women's National Invitational Tournament.

Baseball

Year	Season	Championship	NCAA Division I Baseball Tournament
2021	East: Jackson State West: Prairie View	Texas Southern	Texas Southern lost to Fairfield 6-2 in Austin Regional of the NCAA Division I Baseball Tournament.
2020	Canceled	Canceled	Canceled due to COVID-19 pandemic.
2019	East: Alabama West: Southern (Louisiana)	Southern (Louisiana)	Neither SWAC Texas team advanced to the NCAA Division I Baseball Tournament.

Softball

Year	Season	Championship	NCAA Division I Softball Tournament
2021	East: Jackson State West: Texas Southern	Alabama State	No SWAC Texas team advanced to the postseason.
2020	Canceled	Canceled	Canceled due to COVID-19 pandemic.

Sun Belt Conference Champions

In 2013, Texas State University and the University of Texas at Arlington joined the Sun Belt Conference.

Other schools in the conference are the University of Louisiana-Monroe, the University of Louisiana-Lafayette, the University of Arkansas-Little Rock, Arkansas State University, Coastal Carolina University (South Carolina), Troy University (Alabama), the University of South Alabama, Middle Tennessee State University, Appalachian State University (in North Carolina), Georgia Southern University, and Georgia State University.

Football

Year	Season	Championship	College Football Playoff
2020	East: Coastal Carolina West: Louisiana-Lafayette	Coastal Carolina, Louisiana-Lafayette	No SBC teams advanced to the College Football Playoff.
2019	East: App State West: Louisiana-Lafayette	Appalachian State	No SBC teams advanced to the College Football Playoff.
2018	East: Appalachian State West: Louisiana-Lafayette	Appalachian State	No SBC teams advanced to the College Football Playoff.

Men's Basketball

Year	Season	Tournament	Postseason
2021	East: Georgia State West: Texas State	Appalachian State	No SBC Texas teams advanced to the postseason.
2020	Little Rock	Canceled	Canceled due to COVID-19 pandemic.
2019	Georgia State	Georgia State	Texas State lost to Florida International University 87-81 in the first round of the CollegeInsider.com Postseason Tournament.

Women's Basketball

Year	Season	Tournament	Postseason
2021	East: Troy West: Louisiana-Lafayette	Troy	No SBC Texas teams advanced to the postseason.
2020	Troy	Canceled	Canceled due to COVID-19 pandemic.
2019	Little Rock, University of Texas-Arlington	Little Rock	University of Texas-Arlington lost to Texas Christian University 71-54 in the second round of the Women's National Invitational Tournament.

Baseball

Year	Season	Championship	NCAA Division I Baseball Tournament
2021	East: South Alabama West: Louisiana-Lafayette	South Alabama	No SBC Texas teams advanced to the postseason.
2020	Canceled	Canceled	Canceled due to COVID-19 pandemic.
2019	East: Georgia Southern West: Texas State	Coastal Carolina	Neither SBC Texas team advanced to the postseason.

Softball

Year	Season	Championship	Postseason
2021	Louisiana-Lafayette	Louisiana-Lafayette	Texas State lost to University of Texas 6-0 at Austin in the Austin Regional of the NCAA Division I Softball Tournament.
2020	Canceled	Canceled	Canceled due to COVID-19 pandemic.
2019	Louisiana-Lafayette	Louisiana-Lafayette	University of Texas-Arlington beat Iowa State 4-3 to win the Postseason National Invitational Softball Championship.

Southland Conference Champions

Texas schools in the Southland Conference in 2019:

- Abilene Christian University
- Houston Baptist University
- Texas A&M University–Corpus Christi
- Stephen F. Austin State University
- Sam Houston State University

- Lamar University
- University of the Incarnate Word

Other schools are Central Arkansas University, McNeese State University, the University of New Orleans, Nicholls State University, Northwestern State University, and Southeastern Louisiana University.

McNeese, Nicholls, and Northwestern are all in Louisiana

Football

Year	Season	NCAA Division I Football Championship
2020	Sam Houston	Sam Houston beat South Dakota State 23-21 to win Football Championship.
2019	Central Arkansas	Central Arkansas lost to Illinois State 24-14 in Football Championship first round.
2018	Nicholls, Incarnate Word	Incarnate Word lost to Montana State 35-14 in Football Championship first round.

Men's Basketball

Year	Season	Tournament	Postseason
2021	Nicholls	Abilene Christian	Abilene Christian loses to UCLA 67-47 in second round.
2020	Stephen F. Austin	Canceled	Canceled due to COVID-19 pandemic.
2019	Sam Houston	Abilene Christian	• Abilene Christian lost to Kentucky 75-44 in NCAA Division I Basketball Championship first round. • Sam Houston lost to Texas Christian University 82-69 in National Invitation Tournament first round.

Women's Basketball

Year	Season	Tournament	Postseason
2021	Stephen F. Austin	Stephen F. Austin	Stephen F. Austin loses to Georgia Tech 54-52 in first round.
2020	Texas A&M-Corpus Christi	Canceled	Canceled due to COVID-19 pandemic.
2019	Lamar	Abilene Christian	• Abilene Christian lost to Baylor 95-38 in NCAA Division 1 Basketball Championship first round. • Stephen F. Austin lost to University of Texas-Arlington 60-54 in Women's National Invitation Tournament first round. • Lamar lost to South Alabama 73-71 in Women's National Invitation Tournament first round.

Baseball

Year	Season	Championship	NCAA Division I Baseball Tournament
2021	Abilene Christian	McNeese	McNeese lost to Texas Christian University 12-4 in Fort Worth Regional of the NCAA Division I Baseball Tournament.
2020	Canceled	Canceled	Canceled due to COVID-19 pandemic.
2019	Sam Houston	McNeese	McNeese lost to Ohio State 9-8 in single-elimination game in NCAA Division I Baseball Nashville Regional.

Softball

Year	Season	Championship	Postseason
2021	Stephen F. Austin	McNeese	McNeese lost to LSU 10-2 in Baton Rouge Regional.
2020	Canceled	Canceled	Canceled due to COVID-19 pandemic.
2019	Sam Houston	Sam Houston	• Sam Houston lost to University of Texas-Austin 3-0 in NCAA Division I Softball Austin Regional. • Stephen F. Austin lost to McNeese 3-1 in Postseason National Invitational Softball Championship, Stephen F. Austin Regional.

NCAA Division II

Lone Star Conference Champions

The Lone Star Conference, founded in 1931, has long been the athletic conference for Texas schools in the NCAA second tier of schools, Division II.

Texas schools in the conference in 2021 were:

- Angelo State University
- Dallas Baptist University
- Lubbock Christian University
- Midwestern State University
- St. Mary's University
- St. Edward's University
- Tarleton State University

- Texas A&M International University
- Texas A&M University—Commerce
- Texas A&M University—Kingsville
- Texas Woman's University
- West Texas A&M University
- University of Texas at Tyler
- University of Texas of the Permian Basin

Other teams in the conference are Cameron University (Oklahoma), Eastern New Mexico State University, Oklahoma Christian University, Rogers State University (in Oklahoma), University of Arkansas-Fort Smith, and Western New Mexico University.

Football

Year	Season	NCAA Division II Football Championship
2020	Canceled	Canceled due to the COVID-19 pandemic.
2019	Tarleton	No Lone Star Conference teams advanced to the Division II FCS.

Men's Basketball

Year	Season	Tournament	NCAA Division II Championship
2021	Lubbock Christian	West Texas A&M	• West Texas A&M loses to Northwest Missouri State 80-54 in national championship game. • Lubbock Christian lost to West Texas A&M 101-92 in third round. • Dallas Baptist lost to West Texas A&M 82-65 in second round.
2020	West Texas A&M	Canceled	Canceled due to COVID-19 pandemic.

Women's Basketball

Year	Season	Tournament	NCAA Division II Championship
2021	Lubbock Christian	Lubbock Christian	• Lubbock Christian beat Drury 69-59 to win national championship. • Texas A&M-Commerce lost to Southwestern Oklahoma 97-79 in regional.
2020	Lubbock Christian	Canceled	Canceled due to COVID-19 pandemic.

Baseball

Year	Season	Championship	NCAA Division II Baseball Tournament
2021	West Texas A&M	Angelo State	• Angelo State lost to Wingate 8-7 in semifinals. • West Texas A&M lost to Angelo State 10-2 in regional.
2020	Canceled	Canceled	Canceled due to COVID-19 pandemic.

Softball

Year	Season	Championship	NCAA Division II Softball Tournament
2021	UT Tyler	West Texas A&M	• West Texas A&M beat Biola 4-1 to win national championship. • Texas A&M Commerce lost to West Texas A&M 4-0 in regional championship. • Texas A&M-Kingsville lost to West Texas A&M 9-1 in regional second round. • Angelo State lost to A&M Kingsville 7-3 in regional first round.
2020	Canceled	Canceled	Canceled due to COVID-19 pandemic.

Texas A&M football players cheer teammates December 27, 2019, at the Texas Bowl. Photo by Jackson Lavarnway/Flickr (CC).

Football Bowl Games

Following are the college football bowl games involving Texas schools, as well as bowl and national championship games held in the state.

2020-2021

Bowl	Winner	Opponent	Date, Place
Myrtle Beach Bowl	Appalachian St. 56	North Texas 28	Dec. 21, Conway, Brooks Stadium
New Mexico Bowl	Hawaii 28	Houston 14	Dec. 24, Frisco, Toyota Stadium
First Responder Bowl	Louisiana-Lafayette 31	University of Texas-San Antonio 24	Dec. 26, Dallas, Gerald J. Ford St.
Alamo Bowl	Texas 55	Colorado 23	Dec. 29, San Antonio, Alamodome
Cotton Bowl	Oklahoma 55	Florida 20	Dec. 30, Arlington, AT&T Stadium
Armed Forces Bowl	Mississippi St. 28	Tulsa 26	Dec. 31, Ft. Worth, Amon Carter St.
Rose Bowl	Alabama 31	Notre Dame 14	Jan. 1, Arlington, AT&T Stadium
Orange Bowl	Texas A&M 41	North Carolina 27	Jan. 2, Miami, Hard Rock Stadium

2019-2020

Bowl	Winner	Opponent	Date, Place
Frisco Bowl	Kent State 51	Utah State 41	Dec. 21, Frisco, Toyota Stadium
Boca Raton Bowl	FAU 52	SMU 28	Dec. 21, Boca Raton, FAU Stadium
Texas Bowl	Texas A&M 24	Oklahoma State 21	Dec. 27, Houston, NRG Stadium
First Responder Bowl	W. Kentucky 23	W. Michigan 20	Dec. 30, Dallas, Gerald J. Ford Sta.
Sun Bowl	Arizona St. 20	Florida St. 14	Dec. 31, El Paso, Sun Bowl
Alamo Bowl	Texas 38	Utah 10	Dec. 31, San Antonio, Alamodome
Sugar Bowl	Georgia 26	Baylor 14	Jan. 1, New Orleans, Superdome
Armed Forces Bowl	Tulane 30	S. Mississippi 13	Jan. 4, Fort Worth, Amon G. Carter

Major Professional Sports

Major League Baseball

Houston Astros (American League West)

Year	Win	Loss	%	Finish
2013	51	111	.315	5th in division.
2014	70	92	.432	4th in division.
2015	86	76	.531	2nd in division; lost division series to Kansas City Royals 3-2.
2016	84	78	.519	3rd in division.
*2017	101	61	.623	**World Series champions**; defeated LA Dodgers 4-3.
2018	103	59	.636	1st in division; lost ALCS to Boston Red Sox 4-1.
2019	107	55	.660	1st in division; lost to Washington Nationals in World Series, 4-3.
**2020	29	31	.483	2nd in division.

*Astros used cameras to steal signals during 2018 and 2019 seasons, notably the 2017 postseason.
**COVID-19 pandemic-shortened season

Texas Rangers (American League West)

Year	Win	Loss	%	Finish
2013	91	72	.562	2nd in division.
2014	67	95	.414	5th in division.
2015	88	74	.543	1st in division; lost division series to Toronto Blue Jays 3-2.
2016	95	67	.586	1st in division; lost division series to Toronto Blue Jays 3-0.
2017	78	84	.481	Tied for 3rd in division.
2018	67	95	.414	5th in division.
2019	78	84	.481	3rd in division.
2020	22	38	.414	5th in division.

National Football League (NFL)

Houston Texans (AFC South)

Year	Win	Loss	Finish
2013	2	14	4th in division.
2014	9	7	2nd in division.
2015	9	7	1st in division; lost wild-card round to Kansas City Chiefs 30-0.
2016	9	7	1st in division; lost division playoff to New England Patriots 34-16.
2017	4	12	4th in division.
2018	11	5	1st in division; lost wild-card playoff to Indianapolis Colts 21-7.
2019	10	6	1st in division; lost divisional round to Kansas City Chiefs 51-31.
2020	4	12	3rd in division.

Dallas Cowboys (NFC East)

Year	Win	Loss	Finish
2013	8	8	2nd in division.
2014	12	4	1st in division; lost divisional playoff to Green Bay Packers 26-21.
2015	4	12	4th in division.
2016	13	3	1st in division; lost divisional playoff to Green Bay Packers 34-31.
2017	9	7	2nd in division.
2018	10	6	2nd in division; lost divisional playoff to Los Angeles Rams 30-22.
2019	8	8	2nd in division.
2020	6	10	3rd in division.

Major League Soccer (MLS)

Austin FC (Western Conference)

On January 15, 2019, Major League Soccer announced the addition of its 27th member, the Austin Football Club. A new stadium, dubbed Q2 Stadium, was built at McKalla Place in north Austin specifically to house the team.

Austin FC is the first major professional sports team to play in the Texas capital; prior to 2021, Austin was the largest city in the United States without any kind of major league presence.

Austin FC's first eight games were played on the road. The inaugural match was played on April 17, 2021, against the Los Angeles FC, where Austin FC lost 2-0. The first win was also on the road, this against the Colorado Rapids, 3-1, on April 24, 2021. Diego Fagundez scored the team's first official goal during this match.

The first home match was played on June 19, 2021, to a scoreless draw, and the first home win was on July 1, 2021,

against the Portland Timbers, 4-1. Jon Gallagher scored Q2 Stadium's inaugural goal during the Timbers match.

> ### Choosing a Logo
>
> Austin FC's logo features four intertwined live oaks, their roots representing the four cardinal directions. This represents the four quarters of Austin: north, south, east, and west. It was designed by a local studio known as "The Butler Bros." Following the theme of "growth," the team's rallying cry is, "Grow the legend."

Sources: Major League Soccer, Austin FC, Forbes, Austin Statesman.

FC Dallas (Western Conference)

Year	Win	Loss	Draw	Finish
2013	11	12	11	8th in conference
2014	16	12	6	4th in conference; lost semifinals to Seattle Sounders
2015	18	10	6	1st in conference; lost finals to Portland Timbers 5-3
2016	17	8	9	1st in conference; lost semifinals to Seattle Sounders 4-2
2017	11	10	13	7th in conference
2018	16	9	9	4th in conference; lost knockout round to Portland Timbers 2-1
2019	13	12	9	7th in conference; lost round one to Seattle Sounders 4-3
2020	9	6	7	6th in conference; lost semifinals to Seattle Sounders 1-0

Houston Dynamo (Western Conference)

Year	Win	Loss	Draw	Finish
				Eastern Conference
2013	14	11	9	4th in conference; lost final to Kansas City 2-1
2014	11	17	6	8th in conference
				Western Conference
2015	11	14	9	8th in conference
2016	7	14	13	8th in conference
2017	13	10	11	4th in conference
2018	10	16	8	9th in conference
2019	12	18	4	10th in conference
2020	23	4	10	12th in conference

National Women's Soccer League (NWSL)

Houston Dash

Year	Win	Loss	Draw	Finish
2016	6	10	4	8th in league
2017	7	14	3	8th in league
2018	9	10	5	6th in league
2019	7	12	5	7th in league
2020	3	1	0	Season cancelled due to COVID-19 pandemic.

Texas Sports Hall of Fame

The Texas Sports Hall of Fame was organized in 1951 by the Texas Sports Writers Association. Each year the honorees are inducted into the Hall of Fame at a gala dinner.

The second such fete in 1952 was headlined by, "That filmland athlete, Ronald Reagan, and his actress wife, Nancy Davis," according to *The Dallas Morning News* on June 9, 1952.

The hall was originally in Grand Prairie in the Dallas-Fort Worth area. The Hall of Fame was closed in 1986 for financial reasons, but in 1991 it was reopened in Waco. In addition to memorabilia, the new location also houses archives.

Under the current selection process, dues-paying members of the Texas Sports Hall of Fame can nominate any number of individuals. (Anyone can become a member.)

The selection committee, chaired by Dave Campbell, founder of *Texas Football Magazine*, reviews all nominees and creates the "Official Voting Membership" ballot.

Ballots are then mailed to the voting membership, former Texas Sports Hall of Fame inductees, and the media selection committee.

The results of the balloting are announced in the autumn with the induction banquet following in the winter.

The hall of fame website is at tshof.org.

Year	Inductee	Sport	Texas connection, career
2020	Adrian Beltre	Baseball	Texas Ranger baseman; 4-time All-Star, 5-time Golden Glove
	Paul Cass	Tennis	Developed State Team Tournament; coached winning teams
	Michelle Carter	Track and Field	US record-holder in shot with throw of 67'8" in 2016 Olympics
	Clint Dempsey	Soccer	Scored in 3 World Cups; 5th-fastest score in Cup history
	Robert Griffin III	Football	Led Baylor to 10-3 record; Heisman winner; AP Player of Year
	Shane Lechler	Football	Houston Texan punter; records for career punting average
	Chuck Sanchelli	Tennis	Founder, volunteer, and member of multiple tennis programs
	Francie Larrieu Smith	Track & Field	Olympian; established 36 US records, 12 world bests
	Kathy Vick	Tennis	Ranked first in Texas in singles, doubles consistently, ages 40-60
	Teresa Weatherspoon	Basketball	Led LA Tech to title, 1988; won gold medal in 1988 Olympics
	Carol Weyman	Tennis	Founded circuit for junior players, "Road to Little Mo Nationals"
2019	Maureen Connolly-Brinker	Tennis	Dallas, 9 Grand Slam singles titles 1950s
	Tony Franklin	Football	Big Spring, FW Arlington Heights, A&M, NFL kicker 1979–88
	Andre Johnson	Football	Wide receiver 14 years mostly with Houston Texans
	Nancy Liebermann	Basketball	First woman coach of men's professionals, for Texas Legends
	Loyd Phillips	Football	Longview, 1967–69 Chicago Bears, Outland Trophy
	Greg Swindell	Baseball	Houston Sharpstown High, UT, MLB pitcher 1986–2002
	Jason Witten	Football	All-Pro tight end, Dallas Cowboys 2003–17
2018	Johnny Bailey	Football	Running back, Houston Yates, Texas A&I, NFL 1990-95
	Nell Fortner	Basketball	New Braunfels, UT, Olympics 2000, coach 1983-2012
	Pete Fredenburg	Football	Player SWT 1966-70, coach Mary Hardin-Baylor 1998–present
	Gary Kubiak	Football	QB Houston St. Pius, A&M 1983, coach Texans, Broncos
	Cathy Self-Morgan	Basketball	Jourdanton, coach Duncanville, 8 girls state champs 2003–19
	Gerald Myers	Basketball	Borger, player, coach, AD, Houston Baptist, Texas Tech – 2011
	Michael Young	Baseball	All-star infielder, Texas Rangers 2000-12
	Vince Young	Football	Houston Madison, QB UT national champs 2005, NFL
	Jill Sterkel	Swimming	UT 1980–83, Olympic medalist 1976, 1980, 1984

Go to **texasalmanac.com/topics/sports/texas-sports-hall-fame** for a complete list of inductees beginning with 1951.

Year	Inductee	Sport	Texas connection, career
2017	Rita Buck-Crockett	Volleyball	San Antonio, U of H All-American 1977, Olympics 1980, 1984
	Dave Elmendorf	Football/Baseball	Houston, All-American at A&M 1970, LA Rams
	Pat Henry	Track	Blinn 1988–2004, A&M coach 2007–11, 35 team national titles
	Flo Hyman	Volleyball	U of H All-American 1970s, Olympics 1984
	Nastia Liukin	Gymnastics	Parker, 5 medals at Olympics 2008
	Eric Metcalf	Football/Track	UT 1980s All-American, NFL
	Wade Phillips	Football	Orange, U of H, coach Cowboys, Houston Oilers, Texans
	Darren Woodson	Football	Cowboys tackle 1992–2004
2016	Fred Akers	Football	Coach, Edinburg, Lubbock 1960s, UT 1977–86
	Larry Allen	Football	Dallas Cowboys All-Pro lineman 1994–2005
	Trevor Brazile	Rodeo	Amarillo, 13-time cowboy world champion 2006–15
	T.J. Ford	Basketball	Houston Willowridge, UT All-American, NBA 2003–12
	Ken Gray	Football	San Saba, Howard Payne, Cardinals, Oilers lineman 1958–70
	Jacob Green	Football	Pasadena, A&M, Seattle, 49ers lineman 1980–92
	Andy Pettitte	Baseball	Deer Park, Yankees, Astros pitcher 1995–2013
	"Smokey" Joe Williams	Baseball	Seguin, San Antonio, Negro Leagues pitcher 1907–32
2015	Zelmo Beaty	Basketball	Hillister, Woodville, Prairie View A&M, NBA-ABA 1962–75
	Gil Brandt	Football	Dallas Cowboys personnel executive 1960–88
	Ty Detmer	Football	Laredo, SA Southwest quarterback, 1990 Heisman at BYU
	Cliff Harris	Football	Dallas Cowboys safety 1970–79
	Richard Quick	Swimming	Highland Park, SMU, UT coach, Olympics coach 1984–2004
	Nolan Richardson	Basketball	El Paso, Texas Western 1961–64, Western Texas coach
	Everson Walls	Football	Richardson Berkner, Cowboys defensive back 1981–89
	Jeremy Wariner	Track	Arlington Lamar, Baylor, Olympic medalist 2004–08
2014*	Doug English	Football	Dallas Adams, UT tackle, Detroit Lions 1975–85
	Larry Johnson	Basketball	Dallas Skyline, Odessa College, UNLV, NBA 1991–2001
	Charlie Krueger	Football	Caldwell, A&M All-American under Bear Bryant, 49ers 1959–73
	Dat Nguyen	Football	Rockport-Fulton, A&M linebacker 1995-98, Dallas 1999–2005
	Pudge Rodriguez	Baseball	Texas Ranger starting in 1991, All-Star catcher 14 times
	Thurman Thomas	Football	Houston, Oklahoma State, NFL running back 1988–2000
	Sanya Richards-Ross	Track	Austin, UT track, Olympic medalist 2004, 2008, 2012
	Don Trull	Football	All-American quarterback Baylor 1960s, AFL-NFL 1963–74
2012*	Drew Brees	Football	Austin Westlake quarterback 1993–96, New Orleans Saints
	Walt Garrison	Football	Lewisville, fullback Dallas Cowboys 1966–74
	Eddie Mathews	Baseball	Texarkana, Boston/Milwaukee/Atlanta Braves 1952–66
	Bobby Moegle	Baseball	Winningest high school coach, Lubbock Monterey 1960–99
	Shaquille O'Neal	Basketball	San Antonio Cole, 19 years NBA, Lakers, Heat
	Cat Osterman	Softball	Houston, Cypress Springs, UT pitcher, Olympics
	Ricky Williams	Football	UT running back 1995–98, Heisman, NFL 1999–2011

*Designation changed in 2013 from year the inductees were selected to the year the award was presented.

Sources: Texas Sports Hall of Fame, The Handbook of Texas, The Dallas Morning News and other sources.

Texas Olympic Medalists

This is a list of athletes with Texas connections who have won medals in the Olympics including the 2016 games in Rio de Janeiro. This list includes those born here or have lived in Texas, as well as U.S. team members who spent their collegiate careers at Texas universities.

Information included is: the athlete's name, the sport and the year, as well as the types of medals (G-Gold, S-Silver, B-Bronze).

If the athlete won more than one of the same kind of medal in any one year, the number is noted before the letter

code; i.e., 2G indicates that the athlete won two gold medals in the games that year.

The symbol (†) following the medal code indicates that the athlete participated in preliminary contests only; the medal was awarded because of membership on a winning team.

Years in which the athlete participated but did not win a medal are not included. Track indicates all track and field events except those noted separately.

More results can be seen at tshaonline.org.

Source: United States Olympic Committee.

Olympian	Sport	Year	Medal
Abdallah, Nia Nicole	Taekwondo	2004	S
Adams, Rachel	Volleyball	2016	B
Allen, Chad	Baseball	1996	B
Armstrong, Lance	*Cycling*	*2000*	*B**
Arnette, Jay Hoyland	Basketball	1960	G
Austin, Charles	Track	1996	G
Baker, Walter Thane	Track	1956	G,S,B
		1952	S
Baptiste, Kirk	Track	1984	S
Barr, Beth	Swimming	1988	S
Bassham, Lanny Robert	Shooting	1976	G
		1972	S
Bates, Michael D.	Track	1992	B
Beck, Robert Lee	Pentathlon	1960	2B
Beckie, Janine	Soccer	2016	B
Bedforth, B.J.	Swimming	2000	G
Berens, Ricky	Swimming	2012	G, S
		2008	G
Berube, Ryan Thomas	Swimming	1996	G
Biles, Simone	Gymnastics	2016	4G, B
Boudia, David	Diving	2016	S, B
		2012	G, B
Brew, Derrick K.	Track	2004	G, B
Brown, Earlene Dennis	Track	1960	B
Browning, David (Skippy)	Diving	1952	G
Buckner, William Quinn	Basketball	1976	G
Buford-Bailey, Tonja	Track	1996	B
Burrell, Leroy Russel	Track	1992	G
Butler, Jimmy	Basketball	2016	G
Carey, Rick	Swimming	1984	3G
Carlisle, Daniel T.	Shooting	1984	B
Carter, Michael D.	Shotput	1984	S
Carter, Michelle	Shotput	2016	G

Olympian	Sport	Year	Medal
Catchings, Tamika	Basketball	2016	G
		2012	G
Clay, Bryan E.	Decathlon	2008	G
		2004	S
Clement, Kerron	Track	2016	G
Cline, Nancy Lieberman	Basketball	1976	S
Cohen, Tiffany	Swimming	1984	G
Conger, Jack	Swimming	2016	G
Corbelli, Laurie Flachmeier	Volleyball	1984	S
Cotton, John	Baseball	2000	G
Crocker, Ian	Swimming	2008	G
		2004	G,S,B
		2000	G
Cross-Battle, Tara	Volleyball	1992	B
Crouser, Ryan	Shotput	2016	G
Davis, Clarissa G.	Basketball	1992	B
Davis, Jack Wells	Track	1956	S
		1952	S
Davis, Josh C.	Swimming	2000	2S
		1996	3G
Davis, W.F. (Buddy)	High Jump	1952	G
DeLoach, Joseph N. Jr.	Track	1988	G
Dersch, Hans	Swimming	1992	G
Didrikson, Mildred (Babe)	Track	1932	2G, S
Donie, Scott R.	Diving	1992	S
Drexler, Clyde	Basketball	1992	G
Dumais, Troy	Diving	2012	B
Durant, Kevin	Basketball	2016	G
		2012	G
Dusing, Nate	Swimming	2004	B
		2000	S
Eller, Glenn	Shooting	2008	G
Ethridge, Mary (Kamie)	Basketball	1988	G
Farmer-Patrick, Sandra	Track	1992	S
Feigen, Jimmy	Swimming	2016	G
		2012	S†

* In January 2013, the International Olympic Committee disqualified Lance Armstrong from the 2000 events he competed in after he was found to have used drugs to enhance his performance.

Olympian	Sport	Year	Medal
Fields, Connor	Cycling	2016	G
Finn-Burrell, Michelle Bonae	Track	1992	G
Foerster, Paul	Sailing	1992	S
		2000	S
		2004	G
Forbes, James Ricardo	Basketball	1972	S
Ford, Gilbert (Gib)	Basketball	1956	G
Foreman, George	Boxing	1968	G
Fortenberry, Joe Cephis	Basketball	1936	G
Francis, Phyllis	Track	2016	G
Galloway, Jackie	Taekwondo	2016	B
Garrison, Zina	Tennis	1988	G, B
George, Chris	Baseball	2000	G
Gjertson, Doug	Swimming	1992	G, B
		1988	G
Glenesk, Dean William	Pentathlon	1984	S
Goldblatt, Scott	Swimming	2004	G
		2000	B
Gonzáles, Paul G. Jr.	Boxing	1984	G
Gordon, Chris-Ann	Track	2016	S
Griner, Brittney	Basketball	2016	G
Guidry, Carlette D.	Track	1996	G†
		1992	G
Haas, Townley	Swimming	2016	G
Hall, Gary Jr.	Swimming	2004	G, B
		2000	2G,S,B
		1996	2G, 2S
Hamm, Mia	Soccer	2004	G
		2000	S
		1996	G
Hannan, Tommy	Swimming	2000	G
Hansen, Brendan	Swimming	2012	G, B
		2008	G
		2004	G,S,B
Hansen, Fred Morgan	Track	1964	G
Hardee, Trey	Track	2012	S
Harkrider, Kiplan P.	Baseball	1996	B
Hartwell, Erin Wesley	Cycling	1996	S
		1992	B
Hays, Todd	Bobsled	2002	S
Heath, Michael Steward	Swimming	1984	2G, S
Hedgepeth, Whitney L.	Swimming	1996	G, 2S
Hedrick, Chad	Speed Skating	2010	S,B
		2006	G,S,B
Heidenreich, Jerry	Swimming	1972	2G,S,B
Henry, James Edward	Diving	1968	B

Olympian	Sport	Year	Medal
Hill, Denean E.	Track	1992	S
		1988	S
		1984	G
Hill, Grant Henry	Basketball	1996	G
Homfeld, Conrad E.	Equestrian	1984	G, S
Hooker, Destinee	Volleyball	2012	S
Hooper, Darrow	Shotput	1952	S
Horton, Jonathan	Gymnastics	2008	S
Howard, Sherri Francis	Track	1988	S
		1984	G
Jackson, Lucious Brown	Basketball	1964	G
Jacobs, Chris	Swimming	1988	2G, S
Johnson, Michael	Track	2000	2G
		1996	2G
		1992	G
Johnson, Rafer L.	Decathlon	1960	G
		1956	S
Jones, John Wesley (Lam)	Track	1976	G
Jordan, DeAndre	Basketball	2016	G
Jordan, Shaun	Swimming	1992	G
		1988	G
Juarez, Ricardo Rocky	Boxing	2000	S
Julich, Robert William	Cycling	2004	B
Keeler, Kathryn Elliott	Rowing	1984	G
Kern, Douglas James	Sailing	1992	S
Kiefer, Adolph	Swimming	1936	G
Kimmons, Trell	Track	2012	S
King, Judith Brown	Track	1984	S
Kleine, Megan	Swimming	1992	G†
Knight, Bianca	Track	2012	G
Kocian, Madison	Gymnastics	2016	G, S
Kolius, John Waldrip	Sailing	1976	S
Lane, Colleen	Swimming	2004	S
Langkop, Dorothy Franey	Speed Skating	1932	B
Leetch, Brian Joseph	Ice Hockey	2002	S
Lewis, F. (Carl) Carlton	Track	1996	G
		1992	2G
		1988	2G, S
		1984	4G
Lienhard, William Barner	Basketball	1952	G
Lipinski, Tara K.	Figure Skating	1998	G
Liukin, Nastia	Gymnastics	2008	G,3S,B
Lloyd, Andrea	Basketball	1988	G
Losey, Robert G. (Greg)	Pentathlon	1984	S
Lopez, Diana	Taekwondo	2008	B
Lopez, Mark	Taekwondo	2008	S

Counties

This bridge, where State Highway 53 bridge crosses Leon River in Bell County, is on the National Register of Historic Places. Photo by Larry D. Moore, CC by 3/Wikimedia Commons

Counties of Texas

These pages describe Texas' 254 counties and hundreds of towns. Descriptions are based on reports from chambers of commerce, the Texas AgriLife Extension agents, federal and state agencies, the Handbook of Texas, and other sources. Consult the index for other county information.

County maps are based on those of the Texas Department of Transportation and are copyrighted, 2019, as are the entire contents.

Physical Features: Descriptions are from U.S. Geological Survey and local sources.

Economy: From information provided by local chambers of commerce and county extension agents.

History: From Texas statutes, Fulmore's History and Geography of Texas as Told in County Names, WPA Historical Records Survey, Texas Centennial Commission Report, and the Handbook of Texas.

Race/Ethnicity: Percentage estimates from the 2017 American Community Survey conducted by the U.S. Bureau of the Census. "Anglo" refers to non-Hispanic whites; "Asian" refers to persons having origins in the Far East, Southeast Asia, or the Indian subcontinent. "Other" includes those of American Indian origin, Pacific Islanders, and those who identify with two or more races. People may choose to report more than one race to indicate their racial mixture, such as "American Indian" and "White." People who identify their origin as Hispanic may be of any race. Thus, the totals may add up to more than 100 percent.

Vital Statistics: From the Texas Department of State Health Services Annual Report 2015, the most recent report available.

Recreation: From information provided by local chambers of commerce and county extension agents. Attempts were made to note activities unique to the area or that point to ethnic or cultural heritage.

Minerals: From county extension agents.

Agriculture: Condensed from information provided to the Texas Almanac by county extension agents in 2019. Market value (total cash receipts) of agricultural products sold is from the Census of Agriculture of the U.S. Department of Agriculture that was conducted in 2017, the most recent report available.

Cities: Towns listed include the county seat, incorporated cities, and towns with post offices, as well as certain census designated places (CDP). Population figures for incorporated towns and CDPs are estimates for July 1, 2019, from the Texas Demographic Center. Population estimates for other towns are from local officials received through a Texas Almanac survey. When figures for small portions of major cities are given, they are in brackets, such as **part [46,885] of Dallas** in Collin County.

Sources Of Data Lists

Population (of county): The county population estimate of July 1, 2019, U.S. Census Bureau. The line following gives the percentage of increase or decrease from the 2010 U.S. census count.

Area: Total area in square miles, including water surfaces, as determined in the 2010 U.S. census.

Land Area: The land area in square miles as determined by the U.S. Census Bureau in 2010.

Altitude (ft.): Principally from U.S. Geological Survey topographic maps, including revisions available in 2008. Not all of the surface of Texas has been precisely surveyed for elevation; in some cases data are from the Texas Railroad Commission or the Texas Department of Transportation.

Climate: Provided by the National Oceanic and Atmospheric Administration state climatologist, College Station. Data are revised at 10-year intervals to cover the previous three decades. Listed are the latest compilations, as of Feb. 1, 2013, and pertain to a particular site within the county (usually the county seat). The data include: Rainfall (annual mean in inches); Temperature (in degrees Fahrenheit); January mean minimum and July mean maximum.

Workforce/Wages: Prepared by the Texas Workforce Commission, Austin, in cooperation with the Bureau of Labor Statistics of the U.S. Department of Labor. The data are computed from reports by all establishments subject to the Texas Unemployment Compensation Act.

(Agricultural employers are subject to the act if they employ as many as three workers for 20 weeks or pay cash wages of $6,250 in a quarter. Employers who pay $1,000 in wages in a quarter for domestic services are subject also. Still not mandatorily covered are self-employed, unpaid family workers, and those employed by churches and some small nonprofit organizations.)

The work/wage data include (state total, lowest county and highest county included here):

Civ. Labor: Civilian labor force as of April 1, 2021. Texas, 14,043,919; Kenedy County, 175; Harris County, 2,280,347.

Unemployed: The unemployment rate (percentage of workforce) as of April 1, 2021. Texas, 6.3; Loving County, 1.3; Starr County, 17.7.

Wages: Total Wages paid in the fourth quarter of 2020. Texas, $205,148,778,233; King County, $2,218,449; Harris County, $43,242,163,732.

Per Capita Income: Per capita personal income for 2019, as reported by the U.S. Bureau of Economic Analysis. Texas, $52,813; Hudspeth County, $23,569; Midland County, $130,983.

Property Values: Appraised gross market value of real and personal property from the Comptroller's Property Tax Assistance Division 2020 report.

Retail Sales: Figures for 2020 as reported to the state Comptroller of Public Accounts.

Anderson County

Physical Features: Forested, hilly East Texas county, slopes to Trinity and Neches rivers; Lake Palestine; sandy, clay, black soils; pines, hardwoods.

Economy: Manufacturing, distribution, agribusiness, tourism; hunting and fishing leases; prison units.

History: Comanche, Waco, other tribes. Anglo-American settlers arrived in the 1830s. Antebellum slaveholding area. County created and organized from Houston County in 1846; named for K.L. Anderson, last vice president of the Republic of Texas.

Race/Ethnicity: Anglo, 57.8%; Black, 21.2%; Hispanic, 18.1%; Asian, 0.5%; Other, 2.3%.

Vital Statistics, annual: Births, 636; deaths, 655; marriages, 352; divorces, 102.

Recreation: Fishing and hunting, streams, lakes; dogwood trails; national wildlife refuge; historic sites; Texas State Railroad depot, park; museums.

Minerals: Oil and gas.

Agriculture: Beef cattle, hay, truck vegetables, melons, pecans, peaches. Market value $92.9 million. Timber sold.

PALESTINE (19,115) county seat; medical services, education, transportation; clothing, metal, wood products; scientific balloon station; historic bakery; library;

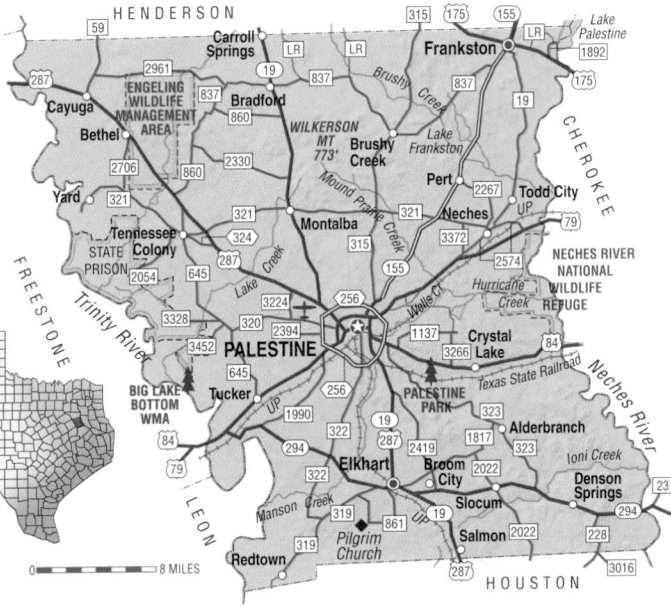

vocational-technical facilities; hospital; UT-Tyler extension, community college; Museum of East Texas Culture; hot pepper festival in October.

Other towns include: **Cayuga** (137); **Elkhart** (1,299); **Frankston** (1,216), tourism, packaging industry, oil and gas, commuters to Tyler; depot museum, Square Fair in October; **Montalba** (110); **Neches** (175); and **Tennessee Colony** (300) site of state prisons.

Population.	**59,025**
Change from 2010 (%).	1.0
Area (sq. mi.)	1,078.0
Land Area (sq. mi.).	1,062.6
Altitude (ft.)	174–773
Rainfall (in.).	46.6
Jan. mean min (°F)	34.5
July mean max (°F).	92.3
Civ. Labor	22,818
Unemployed (%).	5.4
Wages	$255,017,241
Per Capita Income	$36,027
Prop. Value	$4,623,249,054
Retail Sales	$558,575,224

Railroad Abbreviations

AAT . . . . Austin Area Terminal Railroad	RC . . . . . . Rusk County Rural Rail Transportation District
AGC. . . . . .Alamo Gulf Coast Railway	RSS. . . . . Rockdale, Sandow & Southern Railroad
ATK . . . . AMTRAK	RVSC . . . . Rio Valley Switching
ANR. . . . . .Angelina & Neches River Railroad	SAW. . . . . South Plains Switching LTD
ATCX . . . . .Austin & Texas Central Railroad	SRN . . . . . . Sabine River & Northern Railroad Company
BLR . . . . .Blacklands Railroad	SSC. . . . . Southern Switching (Lone Star Railroad)
BNSF . . . . .BNSF Railroad	SW. . . . . Southwestern Shortline Railroad
BOP. . . . . Border Pacific Railroad	TCT . . . . .Texas City Terminal Railway
BRG . . . . Brownsville & Rio Grande Int'l Railroad	TIBR. . . . . Timber Rock Railroad
CMC. . . . . CMC Railroad	TM. . . . . The Texas Mexican Railway Company
DART . . . . .Dallas Area Rapid Transit	TN . . . . Texas & Northern Railway
DGNO . . . . . . .Dallas, Garland & Northeastern Railroad	TNER . . . . Texas Northeastern Railroad
FWWR . . . . Fort Worth & Western Railroad/Tarantula	TNMR . . . . .Texas & New Mexico Railroad
GCSR . . . . . . Gulf, Colorado & San Saba RailwayCorp.	TNW . . . . Texas North Western Railway
GRR . . . . Georgetown Railroad	TP. . . . . Texas Pacifico Transportation
GVSR . . . . Galveston Railroad	TSE . . . . Texas South-Eastern Railroad Company
KCS . . . . Kansas City Southern Railway	TXGN. . . . . .Texas, Gonzales & Northern Railway
KRR . . . . Kiamichi Railroad Company	TXR . . . . Texas Rock Crusher Railway
MCSA. . . . . Moscow, Camden & San Augustine RR	TSSR. . . . . .Texas State Railroad
PCN . . . . Point Comfort & Northern Railroad	UP . . . . Union Pacific Railroad Company
PNR . . . . .Panhandle Northern Railroad Company	WTJR . . . . .Wichita, Tillman & Jackson Railway
PTRA . . . . .Port Terminal Railroad Association	WTLR. . . . . .West Texas & Lubbock Railroad
PVS . . . . Pecos Valley Southern Railway	

Andrews County

Physical Features: South Plains, drain to playas; grass, mesquite, shin oak; red clay, sandy soils.

Economy: Natural resources/mining; manufacturing; construction; government/services; agribusiness.

History: Apache, Comanche area until U.S. Army campaigns of 1875. Ranching developed around 1900. Oil boom in 1940s. County created 1876 from Bexar Territory; organized 1910; named for Texas Revolutionary soldier Richard Andrews.

Race/Ethnicity: Anglo, 35.1%; Black, 1.1%; Hispanic, 62.1%; Asian, 0.4%; Other, 1.1%.

Vital Statistics, annual: Births, 323; deaths, 137; marriages, 119; divorces, 67.

Recreation: Prairie dog town, wetlands, bird viewing; museum; camper facilities; Fall Fiesta in September.

Minerals: Oil and gas.

Agriculture: Beef, cotton, sorghums, grains, corn, hay; significant irrigation. Market value $10.6 million.

ANDREWS (14,704) county seat; trade center, amphitheatre, hospital.

Other towns include, **McKinney Acres** (1,079).

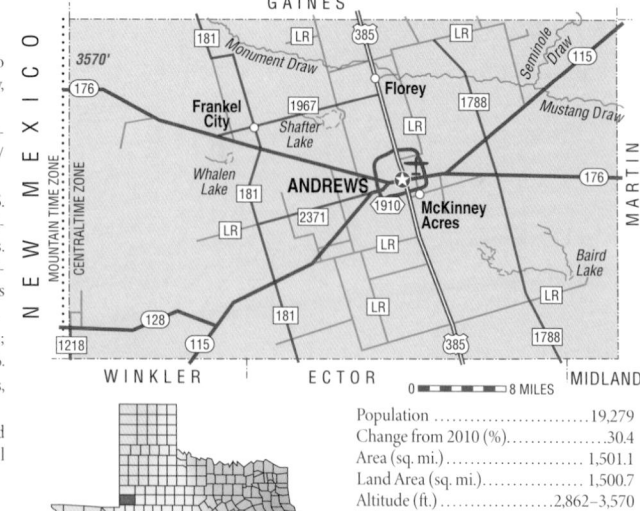

Population	19,279
Change from 2010 (%)	30.4
Area (sq. mi.)	1,501.1
Land Area (sq. mi.)	1,500.7
Altitude (ft.)	2,862–3,570
Rainfall (in.)	14.7
Jan. mean min (°F)	30.7
July mean max (°F)	94.8
Civ. Labor	8,703
Unemployed (%)	6.7
Wages	$122,230,195
Per Capita Income	$51,769
Prop. Value	$5,717,766,952
Retail Sales	$205,278,799

Physical Features: Rolling, hilly East Texas county; black, red, gray soils; Angelina National Forest.

Economy: Timber; manufacturers of iron and steel castings, truck trailers, mobile homes; government/services; wood and paper products.

History: Caddoan area. First land deed to Vicente Micheli 1801. Anglo-American setters arrived in 1820s. County created and organized in 1846 from Nacogdoches County; named for legendary Indian maiden Angelina.

Race/Ethnicity: Anglo, 59.7%; Black, 15%; Hispanic, 22.6%; Asian, 1%; Other, 1.6%.

Vital Statistics, annual: Births, 1,215; deaths, 871; marriages, 672; divorces, 327.

Recreation: Sam Rayburn Reservoir; national, state forests, parks; locomotive exhibit; Forest Festival; bike ride in fall.

Minerals: Limited output of natural gas and oil.

Agriculture: Poultry, beef, horticulture, limited fruits and vegetables. Market value $61.4 million. A leading timber-producing county.

LUFKIN (36,423) county seat; manufacturing; Angelina College; hospitals; U.S., Texas Forest centers; zoo; Expo Center and

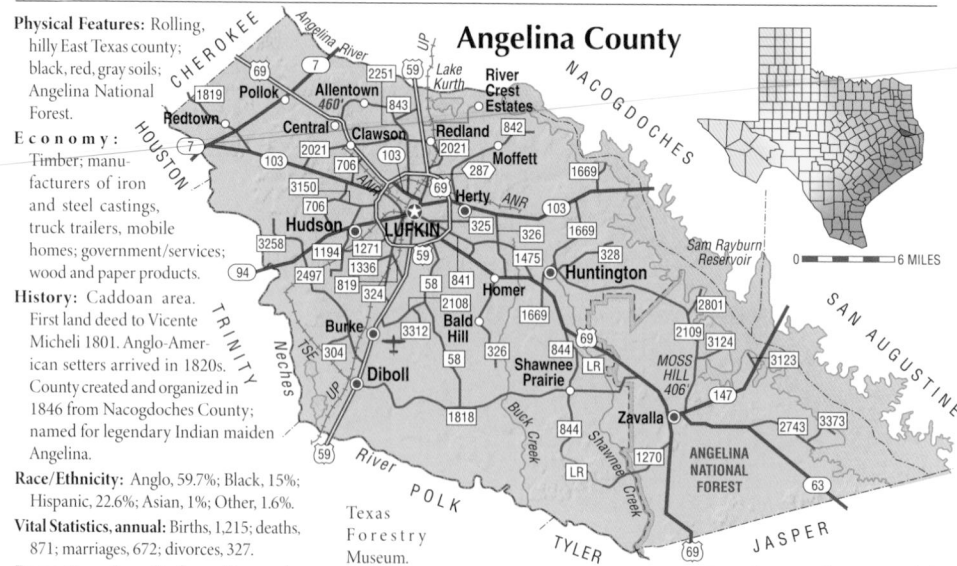

Angelina County

Texas Forestry Museum.

Other towns include: **Burke** (727); **Diboll** (5,279); **Hudson** (4,979); **Huntington** (2,149); **Pollok** (400); **Redland** (1,118); **Zavalla** (730).

For explanation of sources, symbols and abbreviations, see p. 204, and foldout map.

Altitude (ft.)	102–460
Rainfall (in.)	49.0
Jan. mean min (°F)	38.3
July mean max (°F)	93.3
Civ. Labor	35,055
Unemployed (%)	7.2
Wages	$397,384,176
Per Capita Income	$39,644
Prop. Value	$6,508,462,256
Retail Sales	$1,356,419,538

Population	90,989
Change from 2010 (%)	4.9
Area (sq. mi.)	864.7
Land Area (sq. mi.)	797.8

The Aransas National Wildlife Refuge, which spans through Aransas, Refugio, and Calhoun counties, sees a lot of Whooping Cranes in the wintertime. Photo by Klaus Nigge, CC 2/Wikimedia Commons

Aransas County

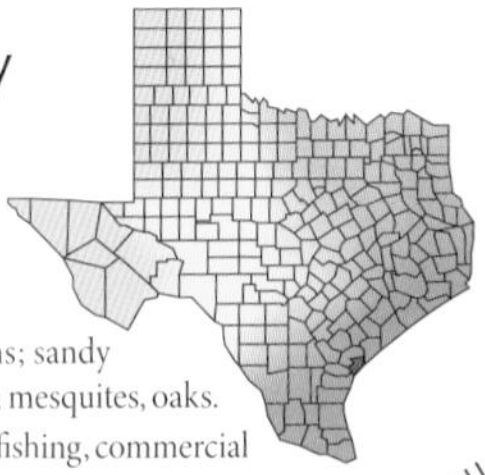

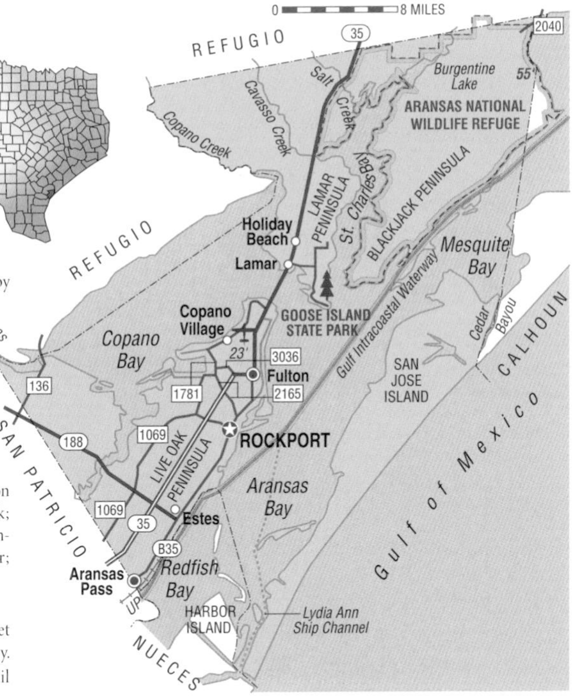

Physical Features: Coastal plains; sandy loam, coastal clays; bays, inlets; mesquites, oaks.

Economy: Tourism, recreational fishing, commercial shrimping, hunting.

History: Karankawa, Coahuiltecan area. Settlement by Irish and Mexicans began in 1829. County created and organized in 1871 from Refugio County; named for Rio Nuestra Señora de Aranzazu, derived from a Spanish palace.

Race/Ethnicity: Anglo, 65.6%; Black, 1%; Hispanic, 29.6%; Asian, 1.7%; Other, 1.9%.

Vital Statistics, annual: Births, 276; deaths, 360; marriages, 256; divorces, 100.

Recreation: Sport fishing, waterfowl hunting; Fulton Mansion; state marine lab; Goose Island State Park; Texas Maritime Museum; bird sanctuaries (a nationally known birding hotspot); Rockport art center; Hummer Bird festival in September.

Minerals: Oil and gas, also oystershell and sand.

Agriculture: Cotton, hay, cow-calf operations. Market value $1.9 million. Fishing, hunting; redfish hatchery.

ROCKPORT (10,449) county seat; tourism, retail trade, health care, construction/real estate; Festival of Wines Memorial Day weekend.

Fulton (1,437) tourism, retail trade, oyster and shrimp harvesting, museums, Oysterfest in March; **Holiday Beach** (507); and **Lamar** (618).

Also, part [808] of **Aransas Pass**.

Population......................... **23,710**	July mean max (°F)....................91.5
Change from 2010 (%)..................2.4	Civ. Labor............................. 9,167
Area (sq. mi.)........................ 528.0	Unemployed (%)........................7.9
Land Area (sq. mi.)................... 252.1	Wages $57,195,777
Altitude (ft.)...................sea level–55	Per Capita Income $51,614
Rainfall (in.)...........................34.6	Prop. Value $4,237,577,962
Jan. mean min (°F)...................47.9	Retail Sales.................. $303,206,949

Archer County

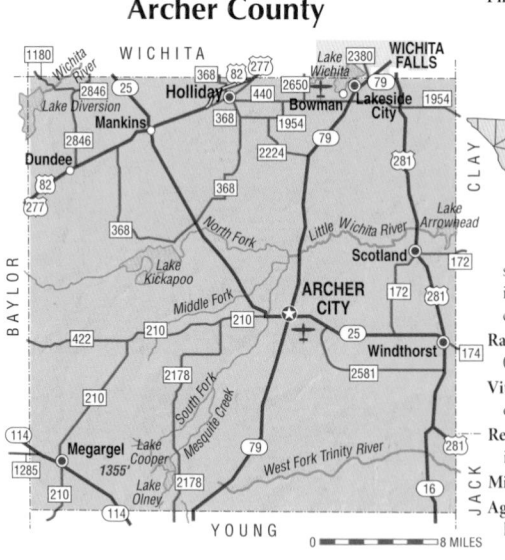

Physical Features: Northwestern county, rolling to hilly, drained by Wichita, Trinity River forks; Lake Kickapoo, Lake Diversion, Lake Wichita, Lake Arrowhead, Lake Cooper and Lake Olney; black, red loams, sandy soils; mesquites, post oaks.

Economy: Cattle, milk production, oil, hunting leases. Part of Wichita Falls metropolitan area.

History: Caddo, Comanche, Kiowas and other tribes in the area until 1875; Anglo-American settlement developed soon afterward. County created from Fannin Land District in 1858; organized in 1880. Named for Dr. B.T. Archer, Republic commissioner to United States.

Race/Ethnicity: Anglo, 85.7%; Black, 0.6%; Hispanic, 10.4%; Asian, 0.2%; Other, 2.8%.

Vital Statistics, annual: Births, 78; deaths, 91; marriages, 33; divorces, 42.

Recreation: Hunting of deer, turkey, dove, feral hog, coyote; fishing in area lakes, rodeo in June.

Minerals: Oil and natural gas.

Agriculture: Cow/calf, stocker cattle, dairy, wheat, hay, silage and horses. Market value $72.4 million.

Population......................... **9,228**	July mean max (°F).....................96.5
Change from 2010 (%)..................1.9	Civ. Labor.............................3,922
Area (sq. mi.)........................925.4	Unemployed (%)........................4.3
Land Area (sq. mi.)..................903.1	Wages........................$16,359,449
Altitude (ft.).....................900–1,355	Per Capita Income................$52,335
Rainfall (in.)..........................30.7	Prop. Value................$2,043,858,534
Jan. mean min (°F)....................29.0	Retail Sales....................$50,170,110

ARCHER CITY (1,920) county seat; cattle, oil field service center; museum; book center; Royal Theatre productions; some manufacturing.

Other towns include: **Holliday** (1,774) Mayfest in spring; **Lakeside City** (1,047); **Megargel** (196); **Scotland** (512); **Windthorst** (395), biannual German sausage festival (also in Scotland).

For explanation of sources, symbols and abbreviations, see p. 204, and foldout map.

Armstrong County

Physical Features: Partly on High Plains, broken by Palo Duro Canyon. Chocolate loam, gray soils.

Economy: Agribusiness, tourism, commuting to Amarillo.

History: Apache tribal area, then Comanche territory until U.S. Army campaigns of 1874-75. Anglo-Americans began ranching soon afterward. County created from Bexar District, 1876; organized in 1890; name honors pioneer Texas family.

Race/Ethnicity: Anglo, 90.7%; Black, 0.5%; Hispanic, 6.6%; Asian, 0%; Other, 2%.

Vital Statistics, annual: Births, 21; deaths, 38; marriages, 11; divorces, 3.

Recreation: Palo Duro Canyon State Park; Goodnight Ranch Home.

Minerals: Sand, gravel.

Agriculture: Stocker cattle, cow-calf operations; wheat, sorghum, cotton and hay; some irrigation. Market value $49.3 million.

CLAUDE (1,210) county seat; farm, ranch supplies; glass company; medical center; Caprock Roundup in July.

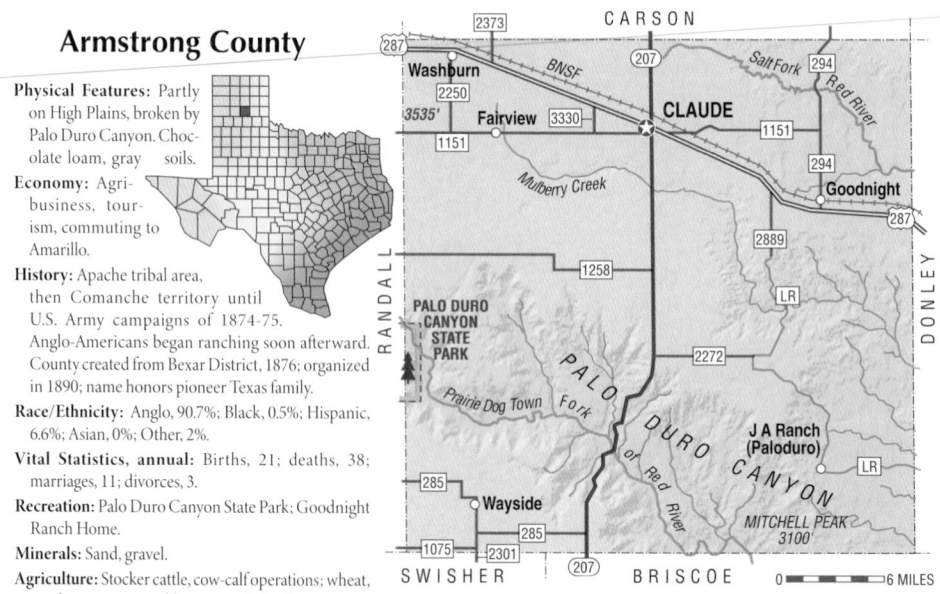

Population....................... **2,001**	July mean max (°F)....................90.6
Change from 2010 (%)..................5.3	Civ. Labor..............................943
Area (sq. mi.)........................913.8	Unemployed (%)........................3.8
Land Area (sq. mi.)..................909.1	Wages.........................$4,710,368
Altitude (ft.)..................2,300–3,535	Per Capita Income................$53,422
Rainfall (in.)..........................22.3	Prop. Value.................$835,057,181
Jan. mean min (°F)....................22.4	Retail Sales...................$15,735,412

Atascosa County

Physical Features: On grassy prairie south of San Antonio, drained by Atascosa River, tributaries; mesquites, other brush.

Economy: Coal plant, oil, commuters to San Antonio.

History: Coahuiltecan tribal area; later Apaches and Comanches. Families from Mexico established ranches in mid-1700s. Anglo-Americans arrived in 1840s. County created from Bexar District in 1856 and organized the same year. Atascosa means boggy in Spanish.

Race/Ethnicity: Anglo, 33.1%; Black, 0.5%; Hispanic, 64.9%; Asian, 0.2%; Other, 1%.

Vital Statistics, annual: Births, 689; deaths, 408; marriages, 329; divorces, 100.

Recreation: Quail, deer hunting; museums; river park; theater group.

Minerals: Lignite, oil, gas.

Agriculture: Beef cattle, peanuts, vegetable farming. Some 25,000 acres irrigated. Market value $74.3 million.

JOURDANTON (4,522) county seat; coal mining; hospital; park, walking trail; chili cookoff in May, Czech Day in July.

PLEASANTON (10,912) farming, oil-field drilling, health services; cowboy homecoming in August, Longhorn museum; hospital.

Other towns include: **Campbellton** (350); **Charlotte** (1,865); **Christine** (439); **Leming** (1,028); **Lytle** (3,069) greenhouse, peanuts processed; **Peggy** (22); **Poteet** (3,554) government/services, library, strawberry festival in April.

Population...........................**50,898**	July mean max...........................95.4
Change from 2010 (%)................13.3	Civ. Labor............................22,206
Area (sq. mi.).......................1,221.5	Unemployed (%).......................6.6
Land Area (sq. mi.)................1,219.5	Wages.......................$163,005,213
Altitude (ft.)......................180–784	Per Capita Income................$37,644
Rainfall (in.)..........................32.1	Prop. Value...............$6,487,746,450
Jan. mean min (°F)....................39.3	Retail Sales.................$670,593,391

Palo Duro Canyon takes up a lot of the land in Armstrong County. It is the second largest canyon in the United States. Photo by Peter Fitzgerald, CC 3/Wikimedia Commons

Austin County

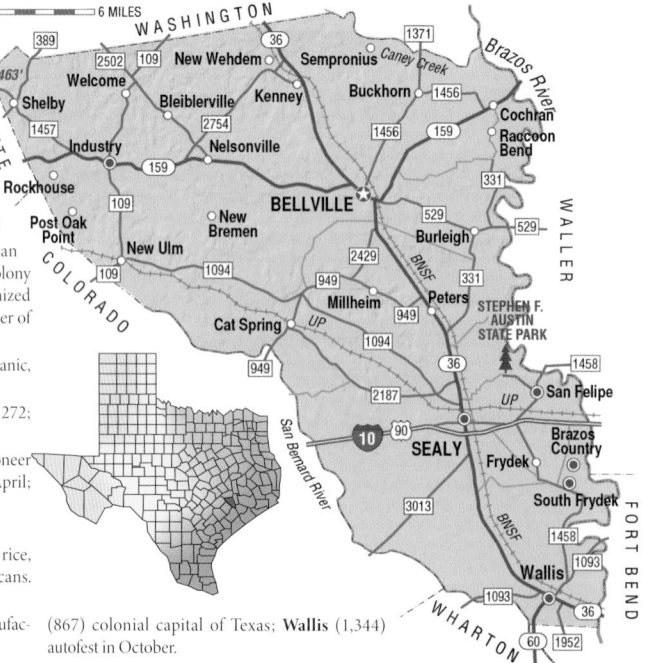

Physical Features: Level to hilly, drained by San Bernard, Brazos rivers; black prairie to sandy upland soils.

Economy: Agribusiness; tourism, government/services; metal, other manufacturing; commuting to Houston.

History: Tonkawa Indian tribal area; reduced by diseases. Birthplace of Anglo-American colonization, 1821, and German mother colony at Industry, 1831. County created and organized in 1837; named for Stephen F. Austin, father of Texas.

Race/Ethnicity: Anglo, 61%; Black, 9%; Hispanic, 27.5%; Asian, 0.4%; Other, 1.8%.

Vital Statistics, annual: Births, 347; deaths, 272; marriages, 182; divorces, 125.

Recreation: Fishing, hunting; state park, Pioneer Trail; Bellville Country Livin' festival in April; Lone Star Raceway Park.

Minerals: Oil and natural gas.

Agriculture: Beef production and hay. Also rice, corn, sorghum, nursery crops, grapes, pecans. Market value $33.1 million.

BELLVILLE (4,602) county seat; varied manufacturing; hospital; oil.

SEALY (6,805) oil-field and military vehicle manufacturing, varied industries; Blinn College branch; polka fest in March.

Other towns include: **Bleiblerville** (125); **Brazos Country** (488); **Cat Spring** (200); **Frydek** (900) Grotto celebration in April; **Industry** (331); **Kenney** (957); **New Ulm** (974) retail, art festival in April; **San Felipe** (867) colonial capital of Texas; **Wallis** (1,344) autofest in October.

Population.......................32,067	July mean max (°F)....................93.2
Change from 2010 (%)..................12.8	Civ. Labor.............................13,820
Area (sq. mi.)..........................656.4	Unemployed (%).........................5.9
Land Area (sq. mi.)....................646.5	Wages.......................$162,535,288
Altitude (ft.).........................70–463	Per Capita Income...............$51,118
Rainfall (in.)..........................41.8	Prop. Value................$6,961,592,737
Jan. mean min (°F).....................39.7	Retail Sales..................$370,248,025

Bailey County

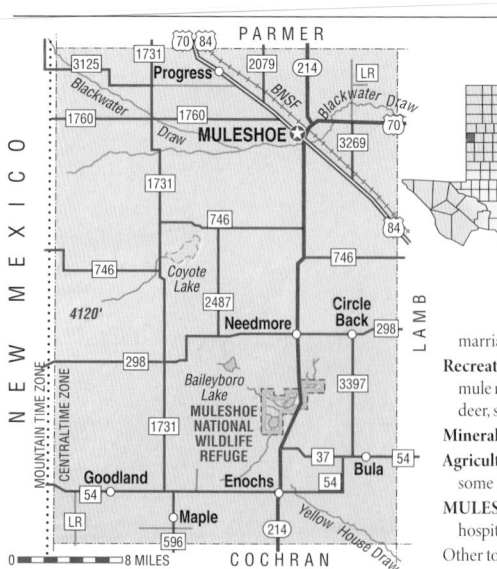

Physical Features: High Plains county, sandy loam soils; mesquite brush; drains to draws forming upper watershed of Brazos River, playas.

Economy: Farm supply manufacturing; electric generating plant; food-processing plants.

History: Settlement began after 1900. County created from Bexar District 1876, organized 1917. Named for Alamo hero Peter J. Bailey.

Race/Ethnicity: Anglo, 31.2%; Black, 0.8%; Hispanic, 65.4%; Asian, 0.3%; Other, 2%.

Vital Statistics, annual: Births, 137; deaths, 50; marriages, 58; divorces, 13..

Recreation: Muleshoe National Wildlife Refuge; "Old Pete," the national mule memorial; historical building park; museum; motorcycle rally; mule deer, sandhill crane, pheasant hunting.

Minerals: Insignificant.

Agriculture: Feedlot, dairy cattle; cotton, wheat, sorghum, corn, vegetables; some 50,000 acres irrigated. Market value $357.0 million.

MULESHOE (5,159) county seat; agribusiness center; feed-corn milling; hospital; livestock show.

Other towns include: **Enochs** (80); **Maple** (40).

Population.......................7,113	Rainfall (in.)..........................18.4	Wages.......................$29,271,987
Change from 2010 (%)..................-0.7	Jan. mean min (°F)....................19.4	Per Capita Income...............$44,665
Area (sq. mi.)..........................827.5	July mean max (°F)....................92.0	Prop. Value................$682,599,141
Land Area (sq. mi.)....................826.8	Civ. Labor.............................2,499	Retail Sales..................$57,568,612
Altitude (ft.)...................3,660–4,120	Unemployed (%)........................4.6	

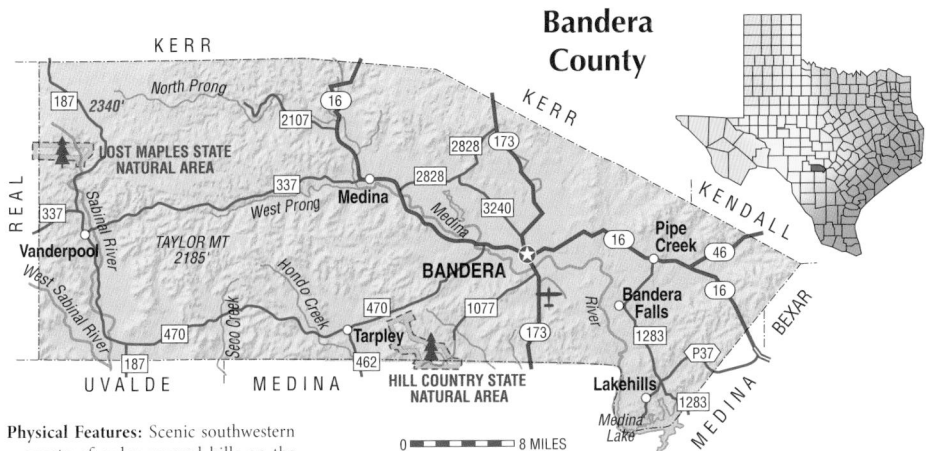

Bandera County

Physical Features: Scenic southwestern county of cedar-covered hills on the Edwards Plateau; Medina, Sabinal Rivers; limestone, sandy soils; species of oaks, walnuts, native cherry and Uvalde maple.

Economy: Tourism, hunting, fishing, ranching supplies, forest products.

History: Apache tribal area, then Comanche territory. White settlement began in the early 1850s, including Mormons and Poles. County created, organized from Bexar, Uvalde counties in 1856; named for Bandera (flag) Mountains.

Race/Ethnicity: Anglo, 77.1%; Black, 0.4%; Hispanic, 19.8%; Asian, 0.2%; Other, 2.2%.

Vital Statistics, annual: Births, 154; deaths, 221; marriages, 131; divorces, 94.

Recreation: RV parks; resort ranches; Lost Maples and Hill Country State Natural Areas; rodeo, parade on Memorial Day weekend; Medina Lake.

Minerals: Not significant.

Agriculture: Beef cattle, sheep, goats, horses, deer (first in numbers in captivity), apples. Market value $6.9 million. Hunting and nature tourism important.

BANDERA (941) county seat; tourism, ranching, service industries; historic sites, Frontier Times Museum.

Other towns include: **Medina** (850) apple growing; **Pipe Creek** (130); **Tarpley** (30); **Vanderpool** (20). Also, the community of **Lakehills** (5,912) on Medina Lake, Cajun Fest in September, and **Lake Medina Shores** (1,375)

Population	23,129
Change from 2010 (%)	12.9
Area (sq. mi.)	797.6
Land Area (sq. mi.)	791.0
Altitude (ft.)	1,064–2,340
Rainfall (in.)	37.4
Jan. mean min (°F)	34.5
July mean max (°F)	93.0
Civ. Labor	10,111
Unemployed (%)	4.9
Wages	$37,734,338
Per Capita Income	$44,925
Prop. Value	$4,391,467,607
Retail Sales	$134,100,585

For explanation of sources, symbols and abbreviations, see p. 204, and foldout map.

The city hall in Muleshoe, county seat of Bailey County. Photo by Larry D. Moore, CC 4/Wikipedia Commons

Bastrop County

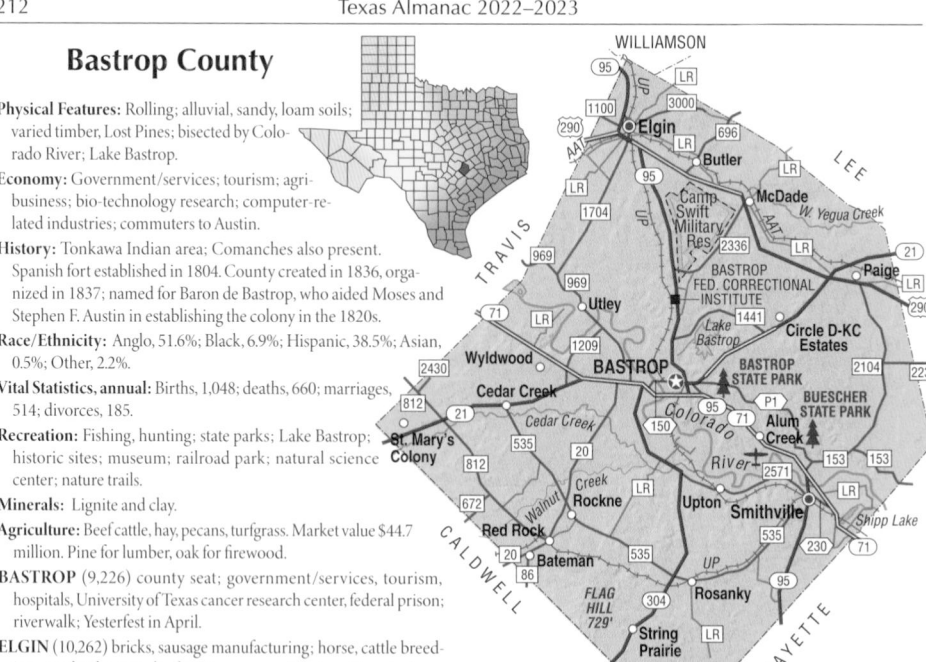

Physical Features: Rolling; alluvial, sandy, loam soils; varied timber, Lost Pines; bisected by Colorado River; Lake Bastrop.

Economy: Government/services; tourism; agribusiness; bio-technology research; computer-related industries; commuters to Austin.

History: Tonkawa Indian area; Comanches also present. Spanish fort established in 1804. County created in 1836, organized in 1837; named for Baron de Bastrop, who aided Moses and Stephen F. Austin in establishing the colony in the 1820s.

Race/Ethnicity: Anglo, 51.6%; Black, 6.9%; Hispanic, 38.5%; Asian, 0.5%; Other, 2.2%.

Vital Statistics, annual: Births, 1,048; deaths, 660; marriages, 514; divorces, 185.

Recreation: Fishing, hunting; state parks; Lake Bastrop; historic sites; museum; railroad park; natural science center; nature trails.

Minerals: Lignite and clay.

Agriculture: Beef cattle, hay, pecans, turfgrass. Market value $44.7 million. Pine for lumber, oak for firewood.

BASTROP (9,226) county seat; government/services, tourism, hospitals, University of Texas cancer research center, federal prison; riverwalk; Yesterfest in April.

ELGIN (10,262) bricks, sausage manufacturing; horse, cattle breeding; medical research; depot museum; Western Days in June, Hogeye festival in October.

Smithville (4,461) government/services, hospital, railroad; parks, hike & bike trails, museums; jamboree on weekend after Easter, Reel Film Expo in May.

Other towns: Cedar Creek (145); **Circle D-KC Estates** (2,730); **McDade** (746) watermelon festival in July; **Paige** (275); **Red Rock** (40); **Rosanky** (210) automotive museum; **Wyldwood** (2,756). Also, **Camp Swift** (7,908).

Population	89,564
Change from 2010 (%)	20.8
Area (sq. mi.)	895.6
Land Area (sq. mi.)	888.2
Altitude (ft.)	300–729
Rainfall (in.)	37.6
Jan. mean min (°F)	37.6
July mean max (°F)	95.4
Civ. Labor	43,750
Unemployed (%)	4.8
Wages	$217,283,698
Per Capita Income	$38,289
Prop. Value	$11,472,929,435
Retail Sales	$1,394,732,326

A member of AmeriCorps pauses to pose for a picture. The group cleaned up a community garden in Beeville on MLK Jr. Day in 2021. Photo by AmeriCorps, PD/Wikimedia Commons

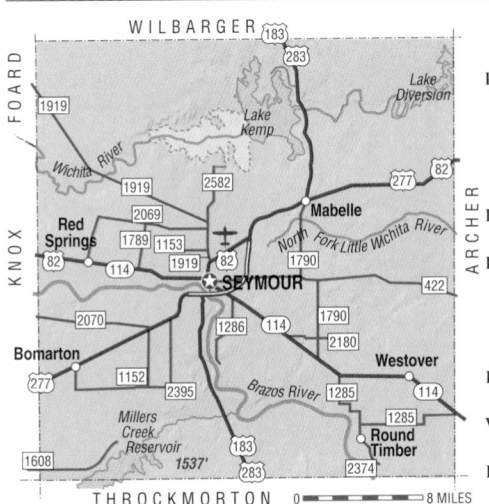

Baylor County

Physical Features: Northwest county; level to hilly; drains to Brazos, Wichita rivers; Lake Kemp, Lake Diversion, Millers Creek Reservoir; sandy, loam, red soils; grassy, mesquites, cedars.

Economy: Agribusiness; retail/service; health services.

History: Comanches, with Wichitas and other tribes also in the area; U.S. Army removed tribes in 1874-75. Anglo-Americans settled in the 1870s. County created from Fannin County in 1858; organized in 1879. Named for H.W. Baylor, Texas Ranger surgeon.

Race/Ethnicity: Anglo, 82.1%; Black, 1.8%; Hispanic, 13.2%; Asian, 0.1%; Other, 2.6%.

Vital Statistics, annual: Births, 41; deaths, 61; marriages, 19; divorces, 7.

Recreation: Lakes; hunting; settlers reunion, rodeo, go-cart races in July.

Population	3,751
Change from 2010 (%)	0.7
Area (sq. mi.)	901.1
Land Area (sq. mi.)	867.5
Altitude (ft.)	1,053–1,537
Rainfall (in.)	29.0
Jan. mean min (°F)	28.1
July mean max (°F)	96.5
Civ. Labor	1,811
Unemployed (%)	3.4
Wages	$15,593,175
Per Capita Income	$46,615
Prop. Value	$1,148,838,793
Retail Sales	$29,607,145

Minerals: Oil, gas produced.

Agriculture: Wheat, cattle, cow-calf operations, grain sorghum, cotton, hay. Market value $53.7 million.

SEYMOUR (2,740) county seat; agribusiness; hospital; dove hunters' breakfast in September.

Bee County

Physical Features: South Coastal Plain, level to rolling; black clay, sandy, loam soils; brushy.

Economy: Agriculture, government/services; hunting leases; oil and gas business.

History: Karankawa, Apache, Pawnee territory. First Spanish land grant, 1789. Irish settlers arrived 1826-29. County created from Karnes, Live Oak, Goliad, Refugio, San Patricio, 1857; organized 1858; named for Barnard Bee Sr., secretary of state and diplomat for the Republic.

Race/Ethnicity: Anglo, 30.4%; Black, 8%; Hispanic, 59.9%; Asian, 0.4%; Other, 1%.

Vital Statistics, annual: Births, 412; deaths, 271; marriages, 167; divorces, 61.

Recreation: Hunting, birding, camping; historical sites, antiques; rodeo/roping events.

Minerals: Oil, gas produced.

Agriculture: Beef cattle, corn, cotton and grain sorghum. Market value $37.7 million. Hunting leases.

BEEVILLE (13,554) county seat; aircraft maintenance, waste-bind manufacturing, retail center; Coastal Bend College; hospital; art museum; Diez y Seis festival in September.

Other towns and places include: **Blueberry Hill** (863); **Mineral** (65); **Normanna** (112); **Pawnee** (155); **Pettus** (559); **Skidmore** (932); **Tuleta** (306); **Tynan** (283).

Population	33,471
Change from 2010 (%)	5.1
Area (sq. mi.)	880.3
Land Area (sq. mi.)	880.2
Altitude (ft.)	39–540
Rainfall (in.)	32.0
Jan. mean min (°F)	43.7
July mean max (°F)	93.9
Civ. Labor	9,486
Unemployed (%)	9.4
Wages	$81,842,152
Per Capita Income	$29,792
Prop. Value	$3,564,090,581
Retail Sales	$333,098,236

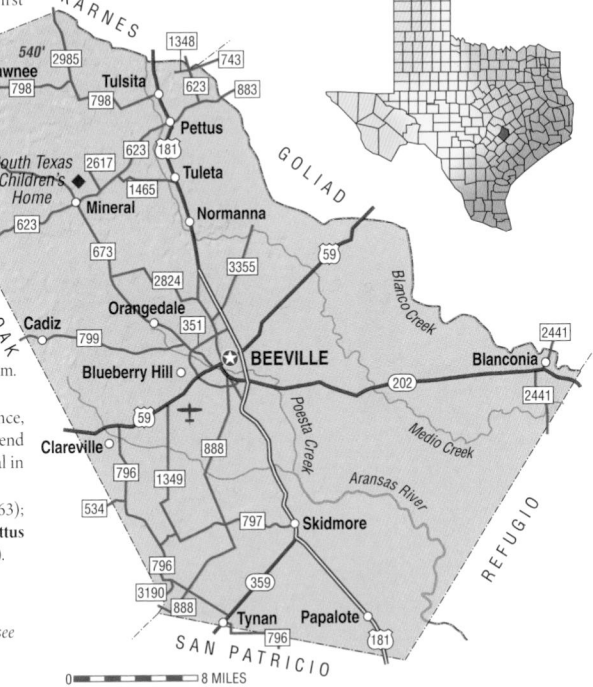

For explanation of sources, symbols and abbreviations, see p. 204, and foldout map.

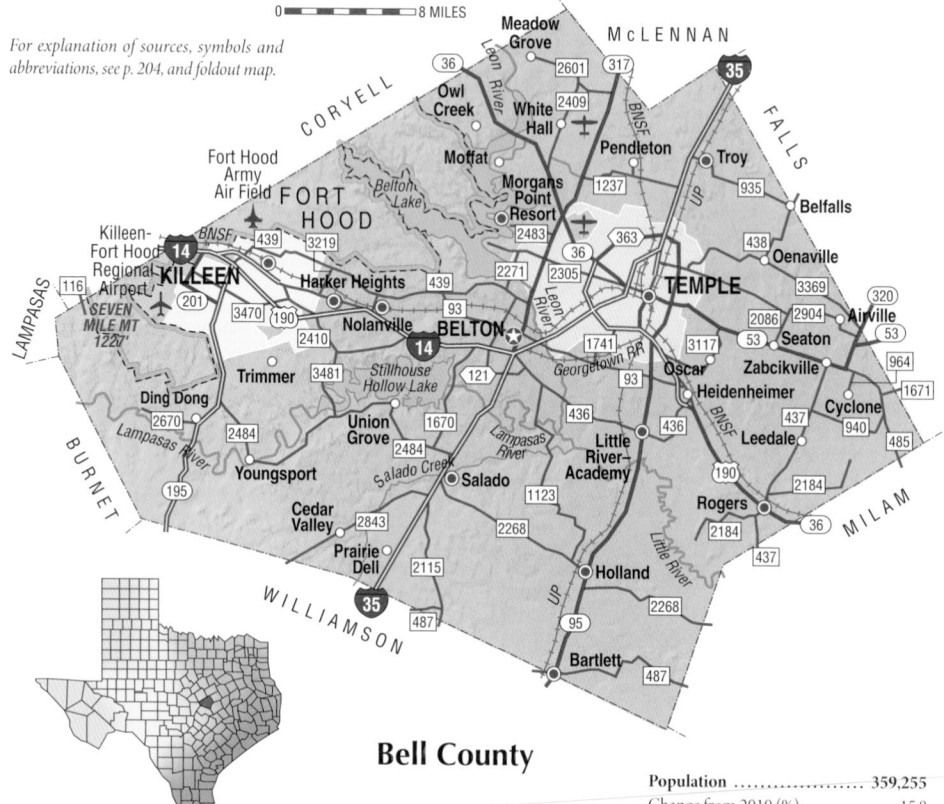

For explanation of sources, symbols and abbreviations, see p. 204, and foldout map.

Bell County

Physical Features: Central Texas Blackland, level to hilly; black to light soils in west; mixed timber; Belton Lake, Stillhouse Hollow Lake.

Economy: Fort Hood; manufacturing includes computers, plastic goods, furniture, clothing; agribusiness; distribution center; tourism.

History: Tonkawas, Lipan Apaches; reduced by disease and advancing frontier by 1840s. Comanches raided into 1870s.

Settled in 1830s as part of Robertson's colony. A few slaveholders in 1850s. County created from Milam County in 1850; named for Gov. P.H. Bell.

Race/Ethnicity: Anglo, 44.4%; Black, 21.2%; Hispanic, 26.2%; Asian, 3%; Other, 5%.

Vital Statistics, annual: Births, 6,496; deaths, 2,274; marriages, 3,865; divorces, 2,198.

Recreation: Fishing, hunting; lakes; historic sites; exposition center; Salado gathering of Scottish clans in November.

Minerals: Gravel.

Agriculture: Beef, corn, sorghum, wheat, cotton. Market value $77.0 million.

BELTON (22,695) county seat; University of Mary Hardin-Baylor; government/services; manufacturing; museum, nature center.

KILLEEN (151,463) Fort Hood; Texas A&M University–Central Texas and Central Texas College; regional airport; retail center, varied manufacturing; hospital; museums, planetarium; Four Winds Powwow in September.

TEMPLE (78,267) Major medical center with two hospitals and VA hospital; diversified industries; rail and wholesale distribution center; retail center; Temple College, Texas A&M College of Medicine; Azalee Marshall Cultural Activities Center; Czech museum; early-day tractor, engine show in October.

Other towns include: Harker Heights (32,665) Founder's Day in October;

Population	359,255
Change from 2010 (%)	15.8
Area (sq. mi.)	1,087.8
Land Area (sq. mi.)	1,051.0
Altitude (ft.)	390–1,227
Rainfall (in.)	36.1
Jan. mean min (°F)	35.6
July mean max (°F)	94.6
Civ. Labor	145,714
Unemployed (%)	6
Wages	$1,675,289,061
Per Capita Income	$43,919
Prop. Value	$30,136,088,721
Retail Sales	$5,299,888,552

Heidenheimer (224); **Holland** (1,170) corn festival in June; **Little River-Academy** (2,098).

Also, **Morgan's Point Resort** (4,736); **Nolanville** (5,533); **Pendleton** (369); **Rogers** (1,247); **Salado** (2,380) tourism, civic center, amphitheathre, art fair in August; **Troy** (1,982).

Also, part [714] of **Bartlett.**

Fort Hood has a population of 26,245.

Physical Features: On edge of Balcones Escarpment, Coastal Plain; heavy black to thin limestone soils; spring-fed streams; underground water; mesquite, other brush; Braunig Lake, Calaveras Lake.

Economy: Medical/biomedical research and services; government center with large federal payroll, military bases; tourism; education center.

History: Coahuiltecan Indian area; also Lipan Apache and Tonkawa tribes present. Mission San Antonio de Valero (Alamo) founded in 1718. Canary Islanders arrived in 1731. Anglo-American settlers began arriving in the late 1820s. County created and organized in 1836 from Spanish municipality named to honor the duke of Bexar; a colonial capital of Texas.

Race/Ethnicity: Anglo, 27%; Black, 7.3%; Hispanic, 60.4%; Asian, 2.8%; Other, 2.2%.

Vital Statistics, annual: Births, 28,172; deaths, 12,982; marriages, 13,456; divorces, 3,067.

Recreation: Historic sites include the Alamo, other missions, Casa Navarro, La Villita; River Walk, El Mercado (market), Tower of the Americas, Brackenridge Park, zoo, SeaWorld, HemisFair Park, Institute of Texan Cultures; museums, symphony orchestra; hunting, fishing; NBA Spurs; Fiesta in April, Folklife Festival in June.

Minerals: Gravel, sand, limestone.

Agriculture: Nursery crops, beef cattle, grain sorghum, hay, corn. Market value $67.9 million.

Education: Fourteen colleges including Our Lady of the Lake, St. Mary's University, Texas A&M University–San Antonio, Trinity University, the University of Texas at San Antonio.

SAN ANTONIO (1,548,248) county seat; Texas' second largest city; healthcare/biosciences, government/services, manufacturing, tourism, information technology, aerospace, education, energy; Alamodome. Leon Springs is now part of San Antonio.

Other towns include: **Alamo Heights** (8,614); **Balcones Heights** (3,362); **Castle Hills** (4,509); **China Grove** (1,321); **Converse** (29,210); **Elmendorf** (2,112); **Fair Oaks Ranch** (9,434); **Grey Forest** (566); **Helotes** (10,297) government/services, retail trade, Cornyval Festival in May, Highland games in April, John T. Floore Country Store, Gugger Homestead; **Hill Country Village** (1,102); **Hollywood Park** (3,367).

Also, **Kirby** (8,743); **Leon Valley** (11,799); **Live Oak** (16,451); **Macdona** (603); **Olmos Park** (2,508); **St. Hedwig** (2,488); **Selma** (11,795, parts in Guadalupe and Comal counties); **Shavano Park** (4,007); **Somerset** (1,996); **Terrell Hills** (5,344); **Universal City** (21,927); **Von Ormy** (1,320); **Windcrest** (5,933).

Part [1,157] of **Schertz** (38,084).

Lackland Air Force Base (9,124); **Randolph Air Force Base** (1,386).

Population	1,997,417
Change from 2010 (%)	16.5
Area (sq. mi.)	1,256.1
Land Area (sq. mi.)	1,239.8
Altitude (ft.)	400–1,896
Rainfall (in.)	32.3
Jan. mean min (°F)	40.7
July mean max (°F)	94.6
Civ. Labor	954,802
Unemployed (%)	5.8
Wages	$12,823,018,353
Per Capita Income	$47,830
Prop. Value	$212,733,203,664
Retail Sales	$31,711,528,500

Bexar County

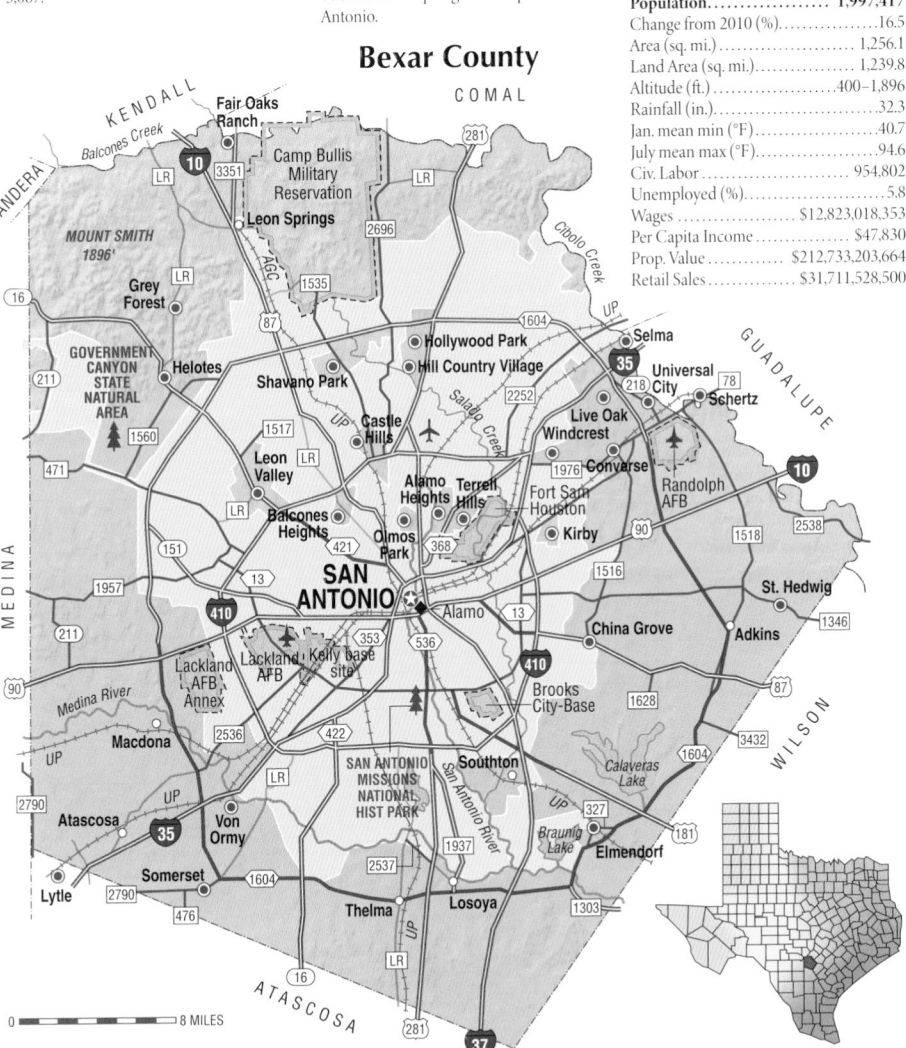

0 ▬▬▬▬ 8 MILES

Bowie County

Population	96,380
Change from 2010 (%)	4.1
Area (sq. mi.)	923.0
Land Area (sq. mi.)	885.0
Altitude (ft.)	200–480
Rainfall (in.)	52.0
Jan. mean min (°F)	33.1
July mean max (°F)	92.9
Civ. Labor	38,841
Unemployed (%)	6.2
Wages	$492,974,024
Per Capita Income	$41,172
Prop. Value	$8,802,773,070
Retail Sales	$1,807,983,759

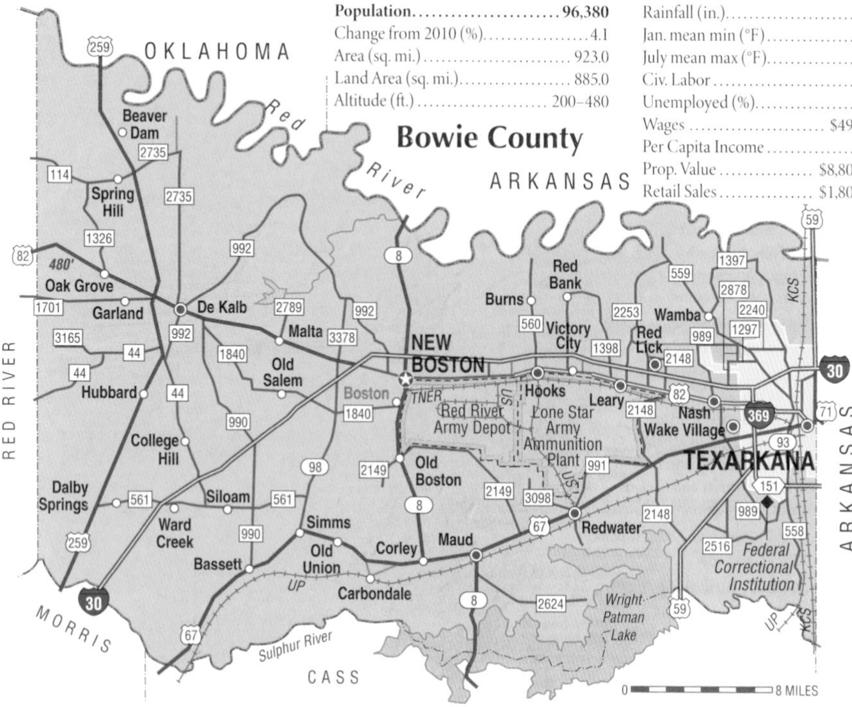

Physical Features: Forested hills at northeast corner of the state; clay, sandy, alluvial soils; drained by Red and Sulphur rivers; Wright Patman Lake.

Economy: Government/services, lumber, manufacturing, agribusiness.

History: Caddo tribal area, abandoned in the 1790s after trouble with the Osage tribe. Anglo-Americans began arriving 1815-20. County created and organized in 1840 from Red River County; named for the Alamo hero James Bowie.

Race/Ethnicity: Anglo, 63.4%; Black, 24.5%; Hispanic, 7.4%; Asian, 1%; Other, 3.5%.

Vital Statistics, annual: Births, 1,259; deaths, 1,076; marriages, 572; divorces, 377.

Recreation: Lake activities, Crystal Springs beach; hunting, fishing; historic sites; Four-States Fair in September, Octoberfest.

Minerals: Oil, gas, sand, gravel.

Agriculture: Beef cattle, pecans, hay, corn, poultry, soybeans, dairy, nurseries, wheat, rice, horses, milo. Market value $60.1 million. Pine timber, hardwoods, pulpwood harvested.

NEW BOSTON (4,556) site of county courthouse; army depot, lumber mill, steel manufacture, agribusiness, state prison; Pioneer Days in August. The area of Boston, officially designated as the county seat, has been annexed by New Boston.

TEXARKANA (39,059 in Texas, 29,901 in Arkansas) rubber company, paper manufacturing, distribution; hospitals; tourism; colleges; federal prison; Perot Theatre; Quadrangle Festival in September.

Other towns include: **De Kalb** (1,673) agriculture, government/services, commuting to Texarkana, Oktoberfest; **Hooks** (2,720); **Leary** (515); **Maud** (1,095); **Nash** (3,825); **Red Lick** (1,027); **Redwater** (1,109); **Simms** (300); **Wake Village** (5,669).

The public library in Brazoria is part of a county-wide library system. Photo by Djmaschek, CC 4/ Wikimedia Commons

Physical Features: Flat Coastal Plain, coastal soils, drained by Brazos and San Bernard rivers; Brazoria Reservoir, Eagle Nest Lake, Harris Reservoir, Mustang Lake East/West, San Bernard Reservoirs.

Economy: Petroleum and chemical industry, fishing, tourism, agribusiness. Part of Houston metropolitan area.

History: Karankawa area. Part of Austin's "Old Three Hundred" colony of families arriving in early 1820s. County created 1836 from Municipality of Brazoria, organized in 1837; name derived from Brazos River.

Race/Ethnicity: Anglo, 46.4%; Black, 13.6%; Hispanic, 30.7%; Asian, 6.8%; Other, 2.2%.

Vital Statistics, annual: Births, 4,939; deaths, 2,155; marriages, 2,205; divorces, 1,235.

Recreation: Beaches, water sports; fishing, hunting; wildlife refuges, historic sites, plantations; state and county parks; replica of the first capitol of the Republic of Texas at West Columbia.

Minerals: Oil, gas, sand, gravel.

Population	380,439
Change from 2010 (%)	21.5
Area (sq. mi.)	1,608.6
Land Area (sq. mi.)	1,357.7
Altitude (ft.)	sea level–146
Rainfall (in.)	56.5
Jan. mean min (°F)	45.6
July mean max (°F)	90.3
Civ. Labor	178,148
Unemployed (%)	7.6
Wages	$1,720,529,383
Per Capita Income	$48,374
Prop. Value	$62,464,812,811
Retail Sales	$4,889,945,756

Agriculture: Cattle, hay, rice, soybeans, sorghum, nurseries, corn, cotton, aquaculture, bees. Some 20,000 acres of rice irrigated. Market value $79.5 million.

ANGLETON (21,483) county seat; banking and distribution center for oil, chemical, agricultural area; fish-processing plant; hospital.

BRAZOSPORT (61,590) is a community of eight cities; chemical complex, deepwater seaport, commercial fishing, tourism; college; hospital. **Brazosport cities include: Clute** (11,919) mosquito festival in July, **Freeport** (12,990) museum, Riverfest in late April, **Jones Creek** (2,158), **Lake Jackson** (28,421) research & development, museum, sea center, Gulf Coast Bird Observatory; **Oyster Creek** (1,170); **Quintana** (20); Neotropical Bird Sanctuary, **Richwood** (4,341), **Surfside Beach** (571) tourism, St. Patrick's Day parade.

PEARLAND (122,331, parts in Harris, Fort Bend counties) trucking, metal fabrication, oilfield, chemical production; commuting to Houston, NASA; community college; Hindu temple; Winter Fest in January.

Other towns include: **Alvin** (29,391) petrochemical processing, agribusiness, rail, trucking; junior college; hospital; Crawfest and Shrimp Boil in April. **Bailey's Prairie** (789); **Bonney** (358); **Brazoria** (3,531) government/services, retail, manufacturing; library; No-Name Festival in June, Santa Anna Ball in July; **Brookside Village** (1,632).

Also, Damon (614); **Danbury** (1,883); **Danciger** (90); **Hillcrest Village** (758); **Holiday Lakes** (1,242); **Iowa Colony** (6,107); **Liverpool** (561); **Manvel** (12,671); **Old Ocean** (150); **Rosharon** (1,384); **Sandy Point** (237); **Sweeny** (4,047) petrochemicals, government/services, hospital, library, Pride Day in May; Levi Jordan Plantation; **West Columbia** (4,160) chemical industry, retail, cattle, rice farming, museum, historic sites, plantation, San Jacinto Festival in April, Stephen F. Austin funeral procession re-enactment in October.

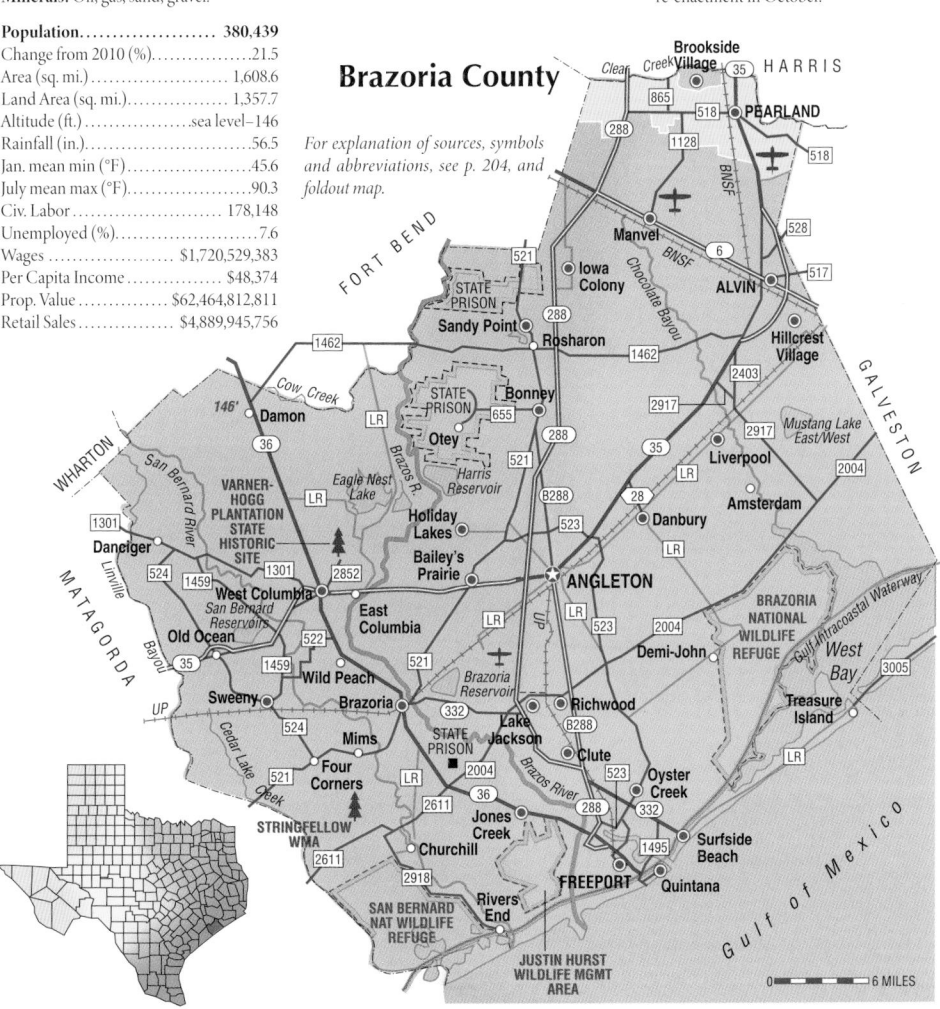

Brazoria County

For explanation of sources, symbols and abbreviations, see p. 204, and foldout map.

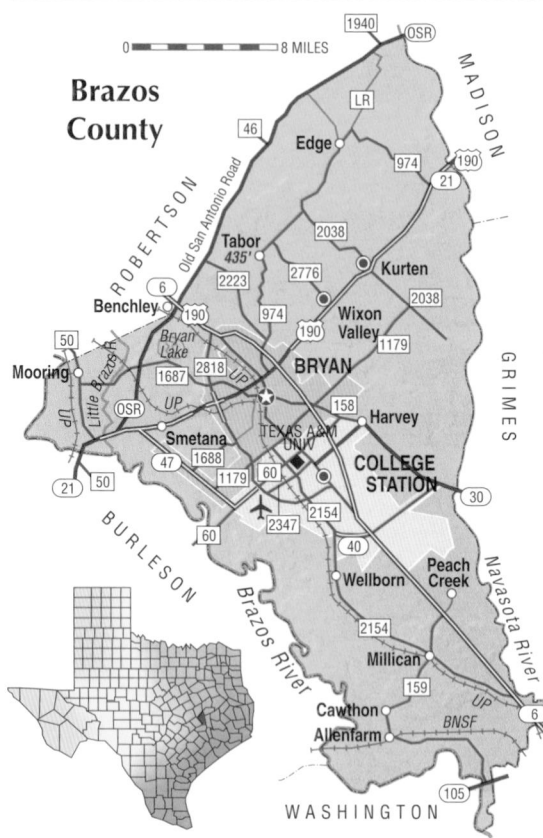

Brazos County

Physical Features: South central county between Brazos, Navasota rivers; Bryan Lake; rich bottom soils, sandy, clays on rolling uplands; oak trees.

Economy: Texas A&M University; market and medical center; agribusiness; computers, research and development; government/services; winery; industrial parks; tourism.

History: Bidais and Tonkawas; Comanches hunted in the area. Part of Stephen F. Austin's second colony of the late 1820s. County created in 1841 from Robertson, Washington counties and named Navasota; renamed for Brazos River in 1842, organized in 1843.

Race/Ethnicity: Anglo, 54.7%; Black, 11%; Hispanic, 26.1%; Asian, 5.8%; Other, 2.2%.

Vital Statistics, annual: Births, 2,903; deaths, 1,064; marriages, 1,498; divorces, 258.

Recreation: Fishing, hunting; raceway; many events related to Texas A&M activities; George Bush Presidential Library and Museum; winery harvest weekends in August.

Minerals: Sand and gravel, lignite, gas, oil.

Agriculture: Cattle, poultry, cotton, hay, horses and horticulture. Market value $91.6 million.

BRYAN (86,202) county seat; defense electronics, other varied manufacturing, agribusiness center; hospitals, psychiatric facilities; Blinn College extension; Brazos Valley African American Museum; steak & grape festival in June, Fiestas Patrias in September.

COLLEGE STATION (118,410) home of Texas A&M University, varied high-tech manufacturing, research; hospital.

Other towns include: **Kurten** (409); **Lake Bryan** (1,977); **Millican** (245); **Wellborn** (400); **Wixon Valley** (255).

Population.................... 230,789	Rainfall (in.)............................40.1	Wages $1,299,595,756
Change from 2010 (%)................18.4	Jan. mean min (°F)....................41.2	Per Capita Income $41,348
Area (sq. mi.).......................... 591.2	July mean max (°F)....................94.8	Prop. Value $27,070,353,454
Land Area (sq. mi.).................... 585.5	Civ. Labor 116,569	Retail Sales $3,156,412,407
Altitude (ft.)..................... 157–435	Unemployed (%)........................4.5	

The Brazos Valley African American Museum in Bryan was opened in July 2006. Photo by Larry D. Moore, CC 3/Wikimedia Commons

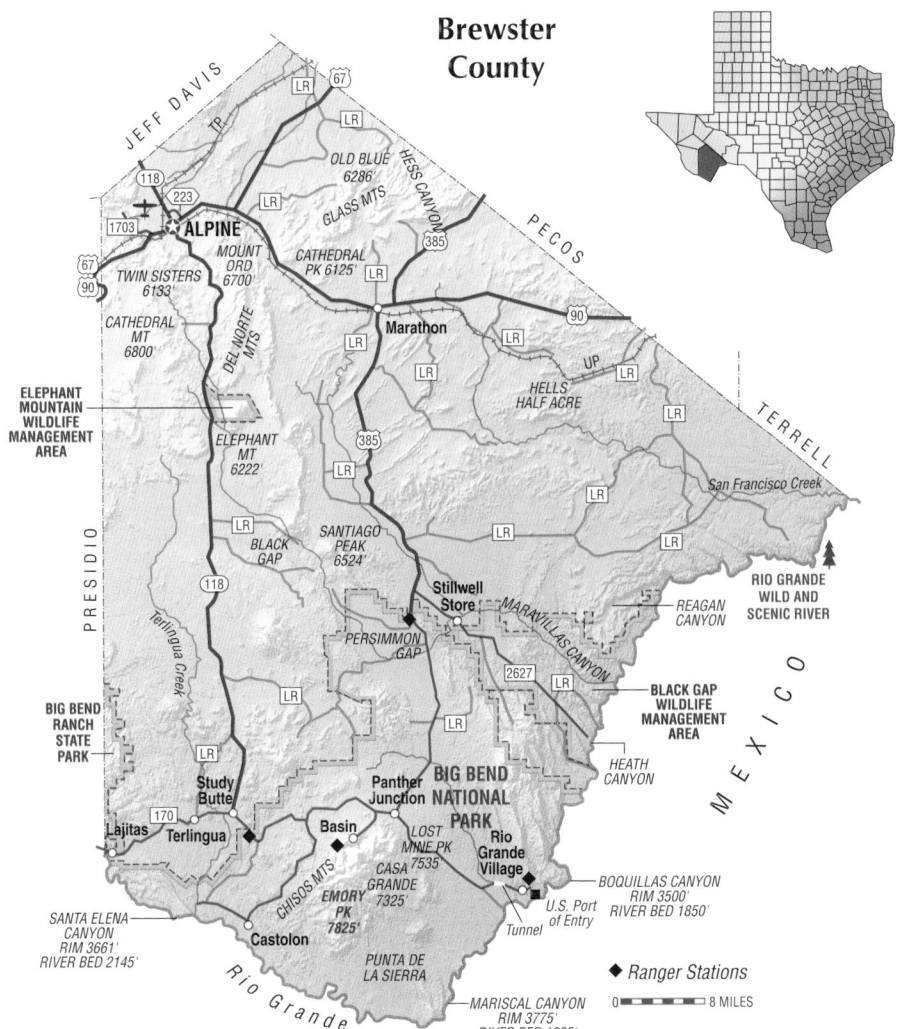

Brewster County

OLD BLUE 6286'

GLASS MTS

HESS CANYON

PECOS

JEFF DAVIS

ALPINE

MOUNT ORD 6700'

CATHEDRAL PK 6125'

TWIN SISTERS 6133'

CATHEDRAL MT 6800'

DEL NORTE MTS

Marathon

HELLS HALF ACRE

ELEPHANT MOUNTAIN WILDLIFE MANAGEMENT AREA

ELEPHANT MT 6222'

TERRELL

San Francisco Creek

PRESIDIO

BLACK GAP

SANTIAGO PEAK 6524'

Terlingua Creek

Stillwell Store

MARAVILLAS CANYON

REAGAN CANYON

RIO GRANDE WILD AND SCENIC RIVER

PERSIMMON GAP

2627

BLACK GAP WILDLIFE MANAGEMENT AREA

BIG BEND RANCH STATE PARK

HEATH CANYON

MEXICO

Study Butte

Panther Junction

BIG BEND NATIONAL PARK

Lajitas

Terlingua

Basin

LOST MINE PK 7535'

Rio Grande Village

CHISOS MTS

CASA GRANDE 7325'

BOQUILLAS CANYON RIM 3500' RIVER BED 1850'

SANTA ELENA CANYON RIM 3661' RIVER BED 2145'

EMORY PK 7825'

Castolon

U.S. Port of Entry Tunnel

PUNTA DE LA SIERRA

♦ Ranger Stations

0 ▬▬▬▬ 8 MILES

Rio Grande

MARISCAL CANYON RIM 3775' RIVER BED 1925'

For explanation of sources, symbols and abbreviations, see p. 204, and foldout map.

Physical Features: Largest county, with area slightly less than that of Connecticut plus Rhode Island; mountains, canyons, distinctive geology, plant life, animals.

Economy: Agriculture, tourism, government/services, Sul Ross State University, mining.

History: Pueblo culture had begun when Spanish explored in the 1500s. Mescalero Apaches in Chisos Mountains; Comanches raided in area. Ranching developed in northern part in the 1880s, with Mexican agricultural communities along river. County created, organized, 1887 from Presidio County; named for Henry P. Brewster, Republic secretary of war.

Race/Ethnicity: Anglo, 51.2%; Black, 0.9%; Hispanic, 43.8%; Asian, 0.9%; Other, 2.9%.

Vital Statistics, annual: Births, 96; deaths, 81; marriages, 83; divorces, 0.

Recreation: Big Bend National Park, Big Bend Ranch State Park, Rio Grande Wild and Scenic River; ghost towns, scenic drives; hunting; museum; rockhound areas; cavalry post.

Also, Barton Warnock Environmental Education Center at Lajitas; cowboy poetry and Western art show in Feburary; Terlingua chili cookoff in November.

Minerals: Bentonite.

Agriculture: Beef cattle, meat goats, horses. Market value $16.3 million. Hunting leases important.

ALPINE (5,928) county seat; ranch trade center, tourism, varied manufacturing; Sul Ross State University; hospital.

Marathon (399) tourism, ranching center, Gage Hotel, Marathon Basin quilt show in October.

Also, **Basin** (30); **Study Butte** (247), and **Terlingua** (50).

Population.	**9,092**
Change from 2010 (%).	-1.5
Area (sq. mi.)	6,192.3
Land Area (sq. mi.)	6,183.7
Altitude (ft.)	1,400–7,825
Rainfall (in.)	17.0
Jan. mean min (°F)	30.3
July mean max (°F)	88.5
Civ. Labor	3,967
Unemployed (%)	4.9
Wages	$48,141,900
Per Capita Income	$48,422
Prop. Value	$1,825,748,262
Retail Sales	$108,269,802

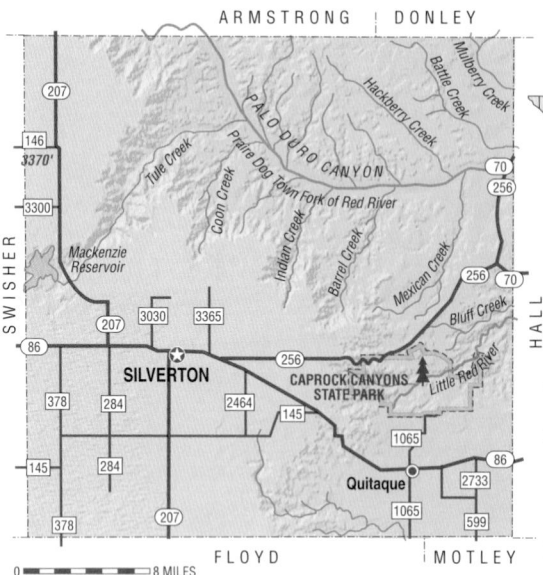

Briscoe County

Physical Features: Partly on High Plains, broken by Caprock Escarpment, fork of Red River; sandy, loam soils.

Economy: Agriculture, government/services.

History: Apaches in area, displaced by Comanches around 1700. Ranchers settled in the 1880s. County created from the Bexar District in 1876 and organized in 1892; named for Andrew Briscoe, Republic of Texas soldier.

Race/Ethnicity: Anglo, 66.5%; Black, 2.6%; Hispanic, 29.5%; Asian, 0%; Other, 1.3%.

Vital Statistics, annual: Births, 13; deaths, 20; marriages, 10; divorces, 7.

Recreation: Hunting, fishing; scenic drives; museum at Quitaque; Caprock Canyons State Park, trailway, bison herd, Clarity tunnel with bats, Mackenzie Reservoir; Briscoe County Celebration in August, Bison Music Festival in September.

Minerals: Insignificant.

Agriculture: Cotton, beef, grain sorghum, wheat, hay. Some 23,000 acres irrigated. Market value $36.6 million.

SILVERTON (687) county seat; agribusiness center, irrigation supplies manufactured; clinics.

Quitaque (392) agribusiness, nature tourism, government/services.

Population........................ 1,572	July mean max (°F).................... 90.9
Change from 2010 (%)................ -4.0	Civ. Labor 576
Area (sq. mi.)...................... 901.6	Unemployed (%)........................ 4.3
Land Area (sq. mi.).................. 900.0	Wages $3,850,918
Altitude (ft.)...................2,064–3,370	Per Capita Income $44,413
Rainfall (in.)......................... 22.4	Prop. Value $779,526,540
Jan. mean min (°F)..................... 23.2	Retail Sales $8,624,697

Brooks County

Physical Features: On Rio Grande plain; level to rolling; brushy; light to dark sandy loam soils.

Economy: Oil, gas, hunting leases, cattle, watermelons and hay.

History: Coahuiltecan Indians. Spanish land grants date to around 1800. County created from Hidalgo, Starr, Zapata counties, 1911; organized in 1912. Named for J.A. Brooks, Texas Ranger and legislator.

Race/Ethnicity: Anglo, 8.5%; Black, 0.2%; Hispanic, 90.6%; Asian, 0.2%; Other, 0.2%.

Vital Statistics, annual: Births, 117; deaths, 90; marriages, 65; divorces, 10.

Recreation: Hunting, fishing; Heritage Museum, Don Pedrito shrine; Fiesta del Campo in October.

Minerals: Oil, gas production; uranium.

Agriculture: Beef cow-calf operations, stocker; crops include hay, squash, watermelons, habanero peppers. Market value $26.2 million.

FALFURRIAS (4,916) county seat; oil and gas, agricultural, government/services.

Other towns include: **Encino** (145).

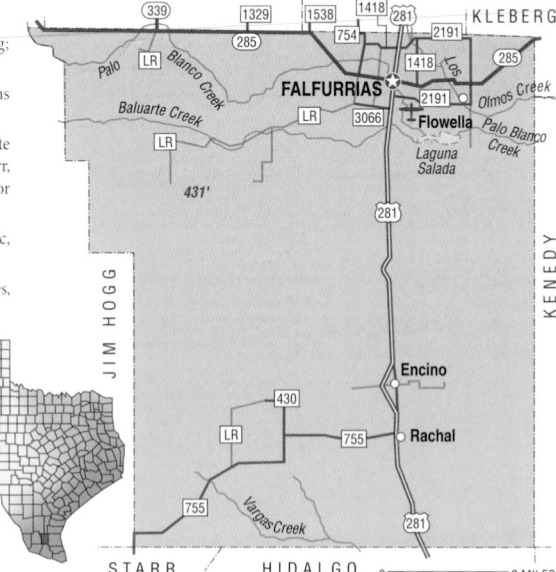

For explanation of sources, symbols and abbreviations, see p. 204, and foldout map.

Population........................ 7,115	Rainfall (in.)......................... 26.5	Wages $31,530,351
Change from 2010 (%)................ -1.5	Jan. mean min (°F).................... 42.5	Per Capita Income $36,558
Area (sq. mi.)...................... 943.7	July mean max (°F).................... 97.0	Prop. Value $1,305,570,827
Land Area (sq. mi.).................. 943.4	Civ. Labor 2,471	Retail Sales.................... $96,518,447
Altitude (ft.)...................... 46–431	Unemployed (%)....................... 10.2	

Brown County

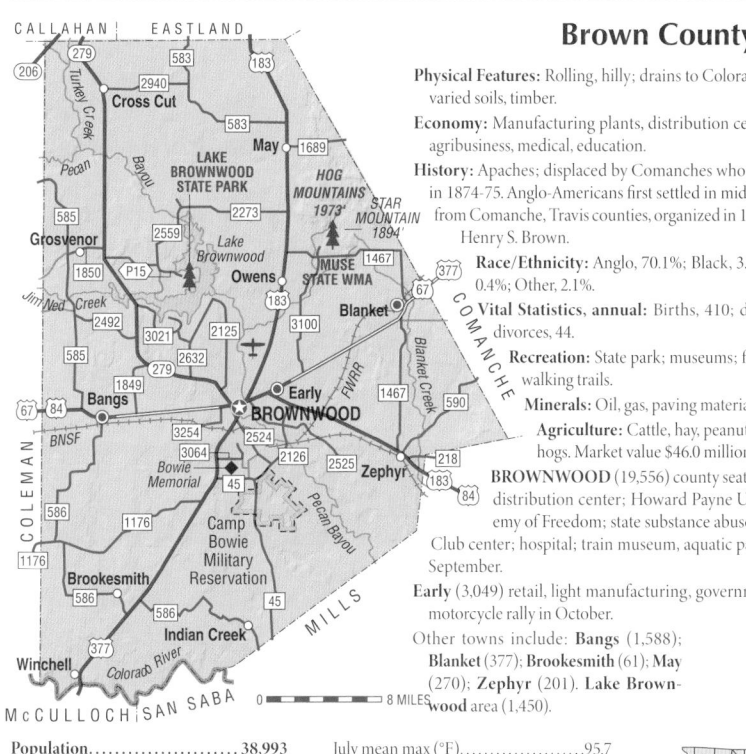

Physical Features: Rolling, hilly; drains to Colorado River; Lake Brownwood; varied soils, timber.

Economy: Manufacturing plants, distribution centers, government/services, agribusiness, medical, education.

History: Apaches; displaced by Comanches who were removed by U.S. Army in 1874-75. Anglo-Americans first settled in mid-1850s. County created 1856 from Comanche, Travis counties, organized in 1857. Named for frontiersman Henry S. Brown.

Race/Ethnicity: Anglo, 70.1%; Black, 3.8%; Hispanic, 23.3%; Asian, 0.4%; Other, 2.1%.

Vital Statistics, annual: Births, 410; deaths, 515; marriages, 303; divorces, 44.

Recreation: State park; museums; fishing, hunting; wildflowers, walking trails.

Minerals: Oil, gas, paving materials, gravel, clays.

Agriculture: Cattle, hay, peanuts, pecans, meat goats, wheat, hogs. Market value $46.0 million.

BROWNWOOD (19,556) county seat; manufacturing, retail trade, distribution center; Howard Payne University, MacArthur Academy of Freedom; state substance abuse treatment center; state 4-H Club center; hospital; train museum, aquatic park; Reunion Celebration in September.

Early (3,049) retail, light manufacturing, government/services, agribusiness; motorcycle rally in October.

Other towns include: **Bangs** (1,588); **Blanket** (377); **Brookesmith** (61); **May** (270); **Zephyr** (201). **Lake Brownwood** area (1,450).

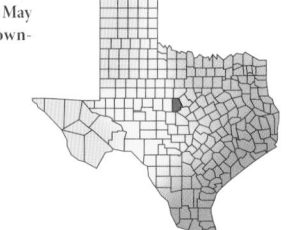

Population.......................38,993	July mean max (°F)....................95.7
Change from 2010 (%).................2.3	Civ. Labor............................14,786
Area (sq. mi.).........................957.0	Unemployed (%)........................5.5
Land Area (sq. mi.)..................944.4	Wages.......................$157,782,399
Altitude (ft.)...................1,230–1,973	Per Capita Income................$39,661
Rainfall (in.)...........................30.4	Prop. Value...............$5,055,612,244
Jan. mean min (°F)....................30.1	Retail Sales.................$528,378,906

The coliseum in Brownwood is home to the Howard Payne University Yellow Jackets basketball and volleyball teams. It was built in 1963 and has 4,000 seats. Photo by Larry D. Moore, CC by SA 4/ Wikimedia Commons

Burleson County

Physical Features: Rolling to hilly; drains to Brazos, Yegua Creek, Somerville Lake; loam and heavy bottom soils; oaks, other trees.

Economy: Oil and gas, tourism, commuters to Texas A&M University, agribusiness.

History: Tonkawa and Caddo tribes roamed the area. Mexicans and Anglo-Americans settled around Fort Tenoxtitlan in 1830. Black freedmen migration increased until 1910. Germans, Czechs, Italians migrated in the 1870s-80s. County created and organized in 1846 from Milam, Washington counties; named for Edward Burleson, a hero of the Texas Revolution.

Race/Ethnicity: Anglo, 62.5%; Black, 12.1%; Hispanic, 23.4%; Asian, 0.1%; Other, 1.6%..

Vital Statistics, annual: Births, 215; deaths, 214; marriages, 99; divorces, 2.

Recreation: Fishing, hunting; lake recreation; historic sites; Czech heritage museum.

Minerals: Oil, gas, sand, gravel.

Agriculture: Cattle, cotton, corn, hay, sorghum, broiler production, soybeans; some irrigation. Market value $58.6 million.

CALDWELL (4,515) county seat; agribusiness, oil and gas, manufacturing, distribution center, tourism; hospital; civic center, museum; Kolache Festival in September.

Somerville (1,502) tourism, railroad center, some manufacturing; museum; Country Cajun festival in March.

Other towns include: **Chriesman** (30); **Deanville** (130); **Lyons** (360); **Snook** (535) Snookfest in June.

Population		18,373
Change from 2010 (%)		6.9
Area (sq. mi.)		676.8
Land Area (sq. mi.)		659.0
Altitude (ft.)		177–566

Rainfall (in.)	38.7
Jan. mean min (°F)	36.8
July mean max (°F)	95.2
Civ. Labor	8,229
Unemployed (%)	5.5

Wages	$56,948,342
Per Capita Income	$45,970
Prop. Value	$4,796,149,557
Retail Sales	$188,056,525

Burnet County

Physical Features: Scenic Hill Country county with Lake Buchanan, Inks Lake, Lake Lyndon B. Johnson, Lake Travis, Lake Marble Falls; caves; sandy, red, black waxy soils; cedars, other trees.

Economy: Tourism, stone processing, hunting leases.

History: Tonkawas, Lipan Apaches. Comanches raided in area. Frontier settlers arrived in the late 1840s. County created from Bell, Travis, Williamson counties, 1852; organized 1854; named for David G. Burnet, provisional president of the Republic.

Race/Ethnicity: Anglo, 72.4%; Black, 1.5%; Hispanic, 23.8%; Asian, 0.4%; Other, 1.6%.

Vital Statistics, annual: Births, 526; deaths, 528; marriages, 310; divorces, 210.

Recreation: Water sports on lakes; sites of historic forts; hunting; state parks, wildlife refuge; wildflowers; birding, scenic train ride.

Minerals: Granite, limestone.

Agriculture: Cattle, goats, grapes, hay. Market value $14.1 million. Deer, wild hog, and turkey hunting leases.

BURNET (7,025) county seat; tourism, government/services, varied industries, ranching; hospital; museums; vineyards; bluebonnet festival in April.

MARBLE FALLS (7,098) tourism, retail, manufacturing; granite, limestone quarries; August drag boat race.

Other towns include: **Bertram** (1,576) Oatmeal festival on Labor Day; **Briggs** (172); **Cottonwood Shores** (1,359); **Granite Shoals** (5,337); **Highland Haven** (442); **Meadowlakes** (1,816); **Spicewood** (4,000). Also, part of **Horseshoe Bay** (3,192).

Population		48,716
Change from 2010 (%)		14.0
Area (sq. mi.)		1,021.3
Land Area (sq. mi.)		944.3
Altitude (ft.)		682–1,608
Rainfall (in.)		32.9
Jan. mean min (°F)		34.7

July mean max (°F)	93.0
Civ. Labor	23,785
Unemployed (%)	4
Wages	$196,378,144
Per Capita Income	$49,731
Prop. Value	$11,251,898,623
Retail Sales	$901,271,102

A lovely view of Marble Falls from a roadside park on U.S. Highway 281. Photo by Larry D. Moore, CC 3/Wikimedia Commons

Physical Features: Varied soils ranging from black clay to waxy; level, draining to San Marcos River.

Economy: Petroleum, varied manufacturing, government/services; part of Austin metro area, also near San Antonio.

History: Tonkawa area. Part of the DeWitt colony, Anglo-Americans settled in the 1830s. Mexican migration increased after 1890. County created from Bastrop and Gonzales counties and organized in 1848; named for frontiersman Mathew Caldwell.

Race/Ethnicity: Anglo, 38.9%; Black, 5.5%; Hispanic, 53.2%; Asian, 0.8%; Other, 1.4%.

Vital Statistics, annual: Births, 542; deaths, 320; marriages, 188; divorces, 125.

Recreation: Fishing, state park, nature trails, museums, barbecue havens; Luling Watermelon Thump and Lockhart Chisholm Trail roundup in June.

Minerals: Oil, gas, sand, gravel.

Agriculture: Eggs, beef cattle, hay, broilers. Market value $53.6 million.

LOCKHART (14,410) county seat; agribusiness center, government/services, tourism, light manufacturing, prison; renowned barbecue at Kreuz, Smitty's, Black's.

Luling (5,835) oil, tourism, agriculture; oil museum; hospital, barbecue cook-off in April.

Other towns include: **Dale** (300); **Fentress** (380); **Martindale** (1,262); **Maxwell** (500); part of **Mustang Ridge** (941, mostly in Travis County), and **Prairie Lea** (320).

Also, part of **Niederwald** (625), part of **Uhland** (1,331), and a small part of **San Marcos** (61,480), mostly in Hays County.

Caldwell County

Population...................	**43,199**
Change from 2010 (%)............	13.5
Area (sq. mi.).....................	547.2
Land Area (sq. mi.)...............	545.3
Altitude (ft.)....................	315–736
Rainfall (in.).....................	35.9
Jan. mean min (°F)................	37.8
July mean max (°F)................	94.8
Civ. Labor.......................	19,884
Unemployed (%)....................	5.3
Wages	$95,409,285
Per Capita Income	$34,617
Prop. Value	$5,007,638,506
Retail Sales	$390,566,181

For explanation of sources, symbols and abbreviations, see p. 204, and foldout map.

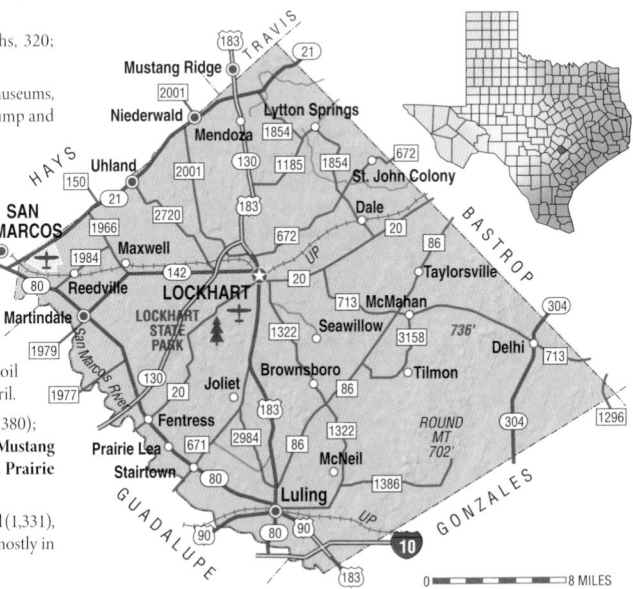

Calhoun County

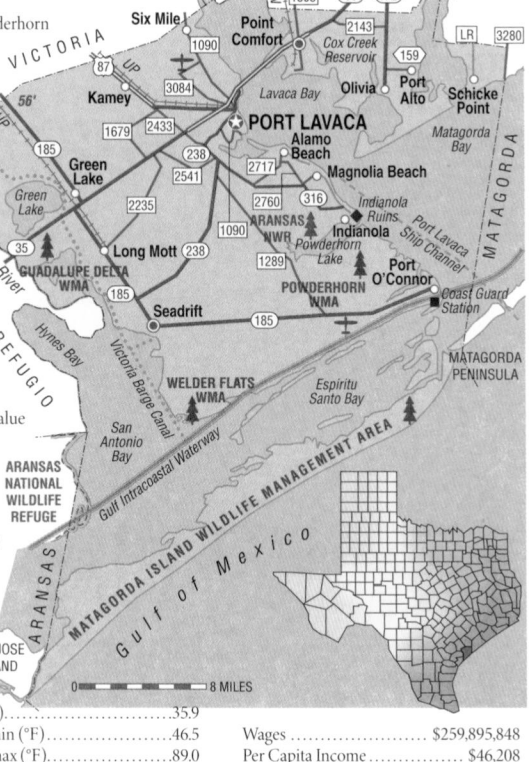

Physical Features: Sandy, broken by bays; Green Lake, Powderhorn Lake, Cox Creek Reservoir; partly on Matagorda Island.

Economy: Aluminum, plastics plants; marine construction; agribusinesses; petroleum; tourism; fish processing.

History: Karankawa tribal area. Empresario Martín De León brought 41 families in 1825. County created from Jackson, Matagorda, and Victoria counties in 1846; organized the same year. Named for John C. Calhoun, U.S. statesman.

Race/Ethnicity: Anglo, 41.8%; Black, 2.4%; Hispanic, 49.6%; Asian, 4.9%; Other, 1.1%.

Vital Statistics, annual: Births, 319; deaths, 198; marriages, 155; divorces, 20.

Recreation: Beaches, fishing, water sports, duck, goose hunting; historic sites, county park; La Salle Days in April.

Minerals: Oil, gas.

Agriculture: Cotton, cattle, corn, grain sorghum. Market value $32.1 million. Commercial fishing.

PORT LAVACA (12,641) county seat; commercial seafood operations, offshore drilling, tourist center; some manufacturing; convention center; hospital.

Other towns include: **Long Mott** (76); **Point Comfort** (694) aluminum, plastic plants, deepwater port; **Port O'Connor** (1,139) tourist center, seafood processing, manufacturing, lighted boat parade in December; **Seadrift** (1,496) commercial fishing, processing plants, Bayfront Park, Shrimpfest in June.

Population......................22,028	Rainfall (in.).........................35.9	
Change from 2010 (%).................3.0	Jan. mean min (°F).................46.5	Wages.......................$259,895,848
Area (sq. mi.).......................1,032.7	July mean max (°F)................89.0	Per Capita Income.................$46,208
Land Area (sq. mi.)...................506.8	Civ. Labor...........................12,338	Prop. Value................$6,183,538,209
Altitude (ft.)...................sea level–56	Unemployed (%)........................5.3	Retail Sales................$258,287,918

Callahan County

Population......................14,070	July mean max (°F)....................94.8
Change from 2010 (%).................3.9	Civ. Labor.............................6,070
Area (sq. mi.).........................901.3	Unemployed (%)........................4.8
Land Area (sq. mi.)...................899.4	Wages.......................$32,332,312
Altitude (ft.)...................1,350–2,204	Per Capita Income...............$41,962
Rainfall (in.)..........................27.4	Prop. Value............$2,042,572,399
Jan. mean min (°F)...............31.4	Retail Sales.................$176,551,968

Physical Features: On divide between Brazos, Colorado rivers; Lake Clyde, Lake Baird; level to rolling.

Economy: Ranching; feed and fertilizer business; many residents commute to Abilene; 200,000 acres in hunting leases.

History: Comanche territory until the 1870s. Anglo-American settlement began around 1860. County created in 1858 from Bexar, Bosque, and Travis counties; organized in 1877. Named for Texas Ranger J.H. Callahan.

Race/Ethnicity: Anglo, 85.5%; Black, 1%; Hispanic, 10.4%; Asian, 0.5%; Other, 2.3%.

Vital Statistics, annual: Births, 147; deaths, 179; marriages, 57; divorces, 34.

Recreation: Hunting, lakes; museums; Cross Plains Hunters' Feed at deer season.

Minerals: Oil and gas.

Agriculture: Cattle, wheat, sorghum, oats. Market value $31.2 million. Hunting leases important.

BAIRD (1,496) county seat; ranching/agricultural trade center, some manufacturing, shipping; historic sites; Railhead Day in May, depot museum.

Clyde (3,956) steel water systems manufacturing, government/services; library; Pecan Festival in October.

Other towns include: **Cross Plains** (1,014) oil and gas, agriculture, government/services, home of creator of Conan the Barbarian, museum, Barbarian Festival in June; **Putnam** (96).

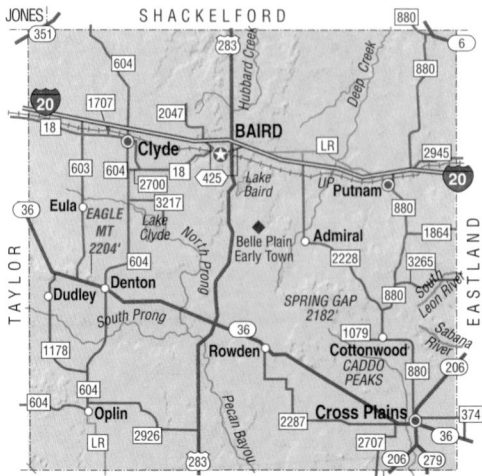

Physical Features: Southernmost county in rich Rio Grande Valley soils; flat landscape; semitropical climate; Loma Alta Lake.

Economy: Agribusiness, tourism, seafood processing, shipping, manufacturing, government/services.

History: Coahuiltecan tribal area. Spanish land grants date to 1781. County created from Nueces County, 1848; named for Capt. Ewen Cameron of Mier Expedition.

Race/Ethnicity: Anglo, 8.7%; Black, 0.3%; Hispanic, 89.8%; Asian, 0.6%; Other, 0.3%.

Vital Statistics, annual: Births, 7,238; deaths, 2,684; marriages, 2,305; divorces, 651.

Recreation: South Padre Island: year-round resort; fishing, hunting, water sports; historical sites, Palo Alto visitors center; gateway to Mexico, state parks; wildlife refuge; recreational vehicle center.

Minerals: Natural gas, oil.

Agriculture: Cotton, grain sorghums, vegetables, corn, citrus. Ranked second in sugar cane acreage. Wholesale nursery plants raised. Small feedlot and cow-calf operations. Some 112,000 acres irrigated, mostly cotton and grain sorghums. Market value $122.6 million. Ranked third in value of aquaculture.

BROWNSVILLE (184,500) county seat; international trade, varied industries, shipping, tourism; college, hospitals, crippled children health center; Gladys Porter

Cameron County

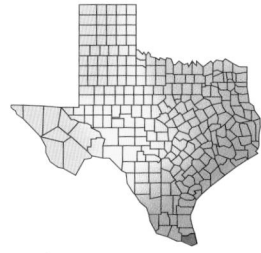

Zoo, historic Fort Brown; University of Texas–Rio Grande Valley, Texas Southmost College.

HARLINGEN (68,835) health care, government/services, tourism; hospitals; college extension campuses; nature center; birding festival in November.

SAN BENITO (24,581) retail center, tourism, agriculture; hospital; museums, arts center, historic buildings; recreation facilities, including walking/jogging trail; ResacaFest on July 4.

SOUTH PADRE ISLAND (2,766) beaches, tourism/convention center, real estate and construction; birding/nature center, Sandcastle Days in October, Spring Break in March.

Other towns include: **Bayview** (408); **Bluetown** (351); **Cameron Park** (7,417);

Combes (3,094); **Encantada-Ranchito El Calaboz** (2,201); **Indian Lake** (833); **La Feria** (7,703); **Laguna Heights** (4,219); **Laguna Vista** (3,348); **Laureles** (3,670); **Los Fresnos** (7,937) Little Graceland Museum, Butterfly Farm, library; **Los Indios** (1,075); **Olmito** (1,074); **Palm Valley** (1,241).

Also, **Port Isabel** (5,288) tourist center, fishing, museums, old lighthouse, Shrimp Cook-Off in November; **Primera** (4,905); **Rancho Viejo** (2,531); **Rangerville** (350); **Rio Hondo** (2,729); **Santa Maria** (651); **Santa Rosa** (2,766).

Population.................... 426,210	
Change from 2010 (%)................. 4.9	
Area (sq. mi.)...................... 1,276.5	
Land Area (sq. mi.)................... 890.9	
Altitude (ft.).................sea level–67	
Rainfall (in.)...........................27.4	
Jan. mean min (°F)....................51.6	
July mean max (°F)....................93.6	
Civ. Labor......................... 169,777	
Unemployed (%)........................9.1	
Wages..................... $1,379,306,529	
Per Capita Income................ $29,928	
Prop. Value.............. $25,473,967,448	
Retail Sales................ $5,066,926,858	

For explanation of sources, symbols and abbreviations, see p. 204, and foldout map.

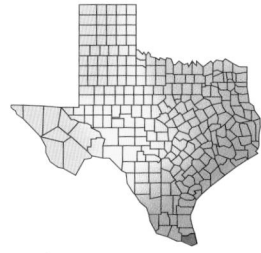

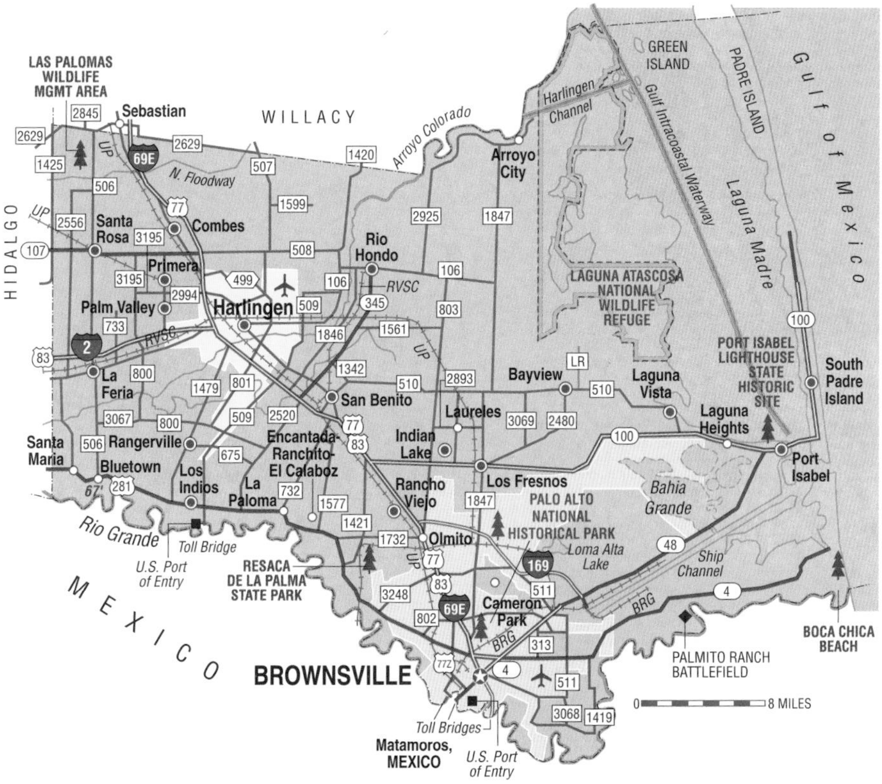

Physical Features: East Texas county with forested hills; drains to Big Cypress Creek on the north; Lake Bob Sandlin; third smallest county in Texas.

Economy: Agribusiness, chicken processing, timber industries, light manufacturing, retirement center.

History: Caddo area. Anglo-American settlers arrived in late 1830s. Antebellum slaveholding area. County created, organized from Upshur County 1874; named for jurist J.L. Camp.

Race/Ethnicity: Anglo, 55.5%; Black, 16.2%; Hispanic, 24.4%; Asian, 0.5%; Other, 3.1%.

Vital Statistics, annual: Births, 172; deaths, 132; marriages, 90; divorces, 22.

Recreation: Water sports, fishing on lakes; farmstead and airship museum; Pittsburg hot links; Chickfest in September.

Minerals: Oil, gas, clays, coal.

Agriculture: Poultry and products important; beef, dairy cattle, horses; peaches, hay, blueberries, vegetables. Market value $114.2 million. Forestry.

PITTSBURG (4,760) county seat; agribusiness, timber, tourism, food processing, light manufacturing, commuting to Longview, Tyler; hospital; community college; Prayer Tower.

Other towns include: **Leesburg** (128) and **Rocky Mound** (71).

Population	**12,914**
Change from 2010 (%)	4.1
Area (sq. mi.)	203.2
Land Area (sq. mi.)	195.8
Altitude (ft.)	236–538
Rainfall (in.)	45.1
Jan. mean min (°F)	33.1
July mean max (°F)	95.2
Civ. Labor	4,956
Unemployed (%)	6.5
Wages	$41,435,738
Per Capita Income	$37,111
Prop. Value	$1,506,904,810
Retail Sales	$121,104,756

Camp County

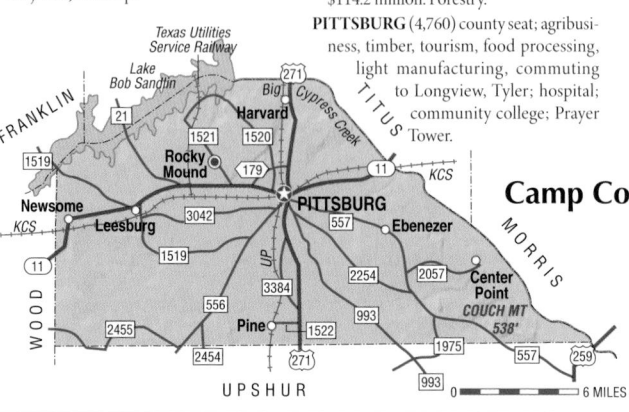

Carson County

Physical Features: In center of Panhandle on level, some broken land; loam soils.

Economy: Pantex nuclear weapons assembly/disassembly facility (U.S. Department of Energy), commuting to Amarillo, petrochemical plants, agribusiness.

History: Apaches, displaced by Comanches. Anglo-American ranchers settled in the 1880s. German, Polish farmers arrived around 1910. County created from Bexar District, 1876; organized 1888. Named for Republic secretary of state S.P. Carson.

Race/Ethnicity: Anglo, 85.9%; Black, 0.7%; Hispanic, 10.6%; Asian, 0.3%; Other, 2.3%.

Vital Statistics, annual: Births, 55; deaths, 58; marriages, 44; divorces, 6.

Recreation: Museum, The Cross at Groom; Square House Barbecue in fall.

Minerals: Oil, gas production.

Agriculture: Cattle, cotton, wheat, sorghum, corn, hay, soybeans. Market value $91.8 million.

PANHANDLE (2,315) county seat; government/services, agribusiness, petroleum center, commuters to Amarillo; Veterans Day celebration, car show in June.

Other towns include: **Groom** (542) farming center, government/services, Groom Day festival in August; **Skellytown** (436); **White Deer** (963) Polish sausage festival in November.

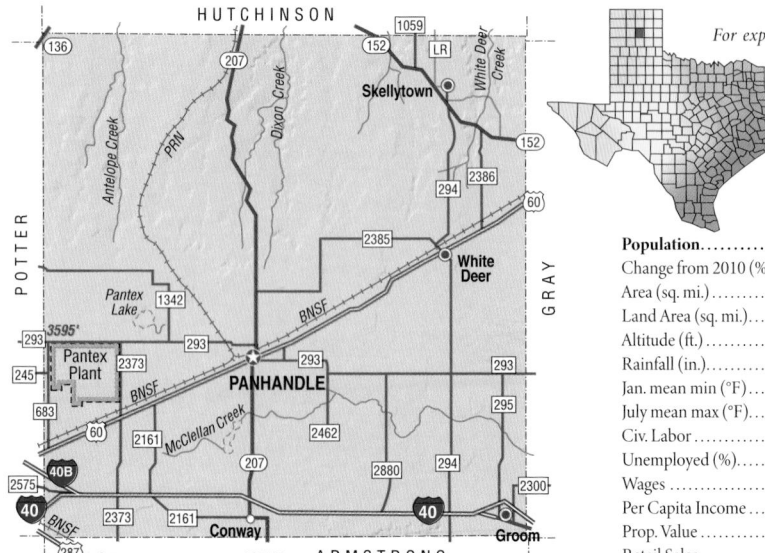

For explanation of sources, symbols and abbreviations, see p. 204, and foldout map.

Population	**5,951**
Change from 2010 (%)	-3.7
Area (sq. mi.)	924.1
Land Area (sq. mi.)	920.2
Altitude (ft.)	2,926–3,595
Rainfall (in.)	21.8
Jan. mean min (°F)	20.3
July mean max (°F)	92.2
Civ. Labor	3,020
Unemployed (%)	3.7
Wages	$118,461,840
Per Capita Income	$48,571
Prop. Value	$1,998,202,269
Retail Sales	$88,344,673

Cass County

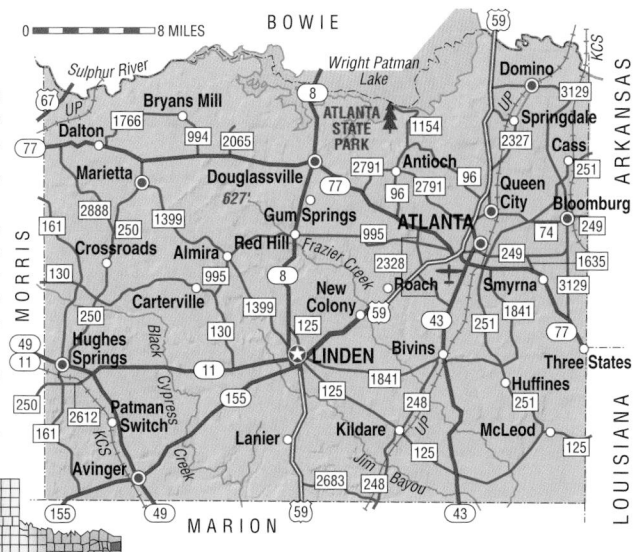

Physical Features: Forested Northeast county rolling to hilly; drained by Cypress Bayou, Sulphur River; Wright Patman Lake.

Economy: Timber and paper industries, government/services.

History: Caddoes, who were displaced by other tribes in the 1790s. Anglo-Americans arrived in the 1830s. Antebellum slaveholding area. County created and organized in 1846 from Bowie County; named for U.S. Sen. Lewis Cass.

Race/Ethnicity: Anglo, 76.2%; Black, 16.6%; Hispanic, 4.3%; Asian, 0.3%; Other, 2.3%.

Vital Statistics, annual: Births, 386; deaths, 414; marriages, 168; divorces, 152.

Recreation: Fishing, hunting, water sports; state park, county park; lake, wildflower trails.

Minerals: Oil, iron ore.

Agriculture: Cattle, poultry. Market value $53.4 million. Timber important.

LINDEN (2,034) county seat, timber, agribusiness, tourism; oldest courthouse still in use as courthouse, hospital; Rock and Roll Hall of Fame.

ATLANTA (5,610) Paper and timber industries, government/services, varied manufacturing, hospital, library; Forest Festival in August.

Other towns include: **Avinger** (431) timber, paper industry, steel plant, early cemetery, Glory Days celebration in October; **Bivins** (215); **Bloomburg** (406); **Domino** (100); **Douglassville** (225); **Hughes Springs** (1,733) varied manufacturing, warehousing, trucking school, Pumpkin Glow in October; **Kildare** (104); **Marietta** (129); **McLeod** (600); **Queen City** (1,477) paper industry, commuters to Texarkana, government/services, historic sites.

Population	30,451
Change from 2010 (%)	0.0
Area (sq. mi.)	960.3
Land Area (sq. mi.)	937.0
Altitude (ft.)	167–627
Rainfall (in.)	49.2
Jan. mean min (°F)	34.6
July mean max (°F)	92.1
Civ. Labor	12,169
Unemployed (%)	7.4
Wages	$80,481,168
Per Capita Income	$37,566
Prop. Value	$3,161,122,671
Retail Sales	$264,010,650

The public library in Atlanta, Texas. the largest town in Cass County. Photo by Michael Barera, CC by SA 4/Wikimedia Commons

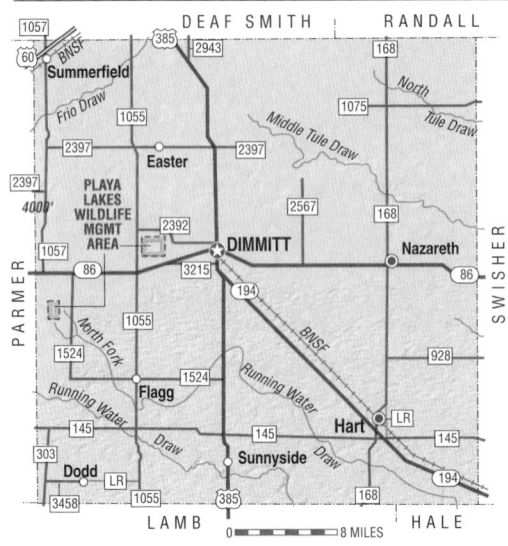

Castro County

Physical Features: Flat Panhandle county, drains to creeks, draws and playas; underground water.

Economy: Agribusiness.

History: Apaches, displaced by Comanches in the 1720s. Anglo-American ranchers began settling in the 1880s. Germans settled after 1900. Mexican migration increased after 1950. County created, 1876 from Bexar District, organized 1891. Named for Henri Castro, Texas colonizer.

Race/Ethnicity: Anglo, 32%; Black, 2.3%; Hispanic, 64.3%; Asian, 0.5%; Other, 0.8%.

Vital Statistics, annual: Births, 125; deaths, 65; marriages, 44; divorces, 16.

Recreation: Pheasant hunting; Italian POW camp site; Dimmitt Harvest Days celebrated in August.

Minerals: Insignificant.

Agriculture: Beef cattle, dairies (first in number of milk cows), corn, cotton, wheat, sheep. Market value $1.1 billion; third in state.

DIMMITT (4,063) county seat; agribusiness center; library, hospital; quilt festival in April.

Other towns include: Hart (1,014) and **Nazareth** (291) German festival/Suds & Sounds in July.

Population........................ 7,380	July mean max (°F)....................91.0
Change from 2010 (%)................ -8.5	Civ. Labor 3,458
Area (sq. mi.)........................899.3	Unemployed (%)........................3.5
Land Area (sq. mi.)..................894.4	Wages $26,693,020
Altitude (ft.) 3,565–4,000	Per Capita Income $64,427
Rainfall (in.)..........................21.2	Prop. Value $1,783,703,439
Jan. mean min (°F)....................21.3	Retail Sales $63,788,201

Chambers County

Physical Features: Gulf coastal plain, coastal soils; Lake Anahuac; some forests.

Economy: Water suppliers, banking, chemical distribution facilities, air services, carbon dioxide disposal.

History: Karankawa and other coastal tribes. Nuestra Señora de la Luz Mission established near present Wallisville in 1756. County created and organized in 1858 from Liberty, Jefferson counties. Named for Gen. T. J. Chambers, surveyor.

Race/Ethnicity: Anglo, 65.1%; Black, 8.2%; Hispanic, 23.9%; Asian, 0.9%; Other, 1.6%.

Vital Statistics, annual: Births, 512; deaths, 290; marriages, 216; divorces, 189.

Recreation: Fishing, hunting; water sports; camping; county parks; wildlife refuge; historic sites; Wallisville Heritage Museum; Texas Gatorfest at Anahuac in September.

Minerals: Oil, gas.

Agriculture: Beef cattle, rice, hay, aquaculture; significant irrigation. Market value $19.3 million. Hunting, fishing important.

ANAHUAC (2,491) county seat; canal connects with Houston Ship Channel; agribusiness; hospital; library.

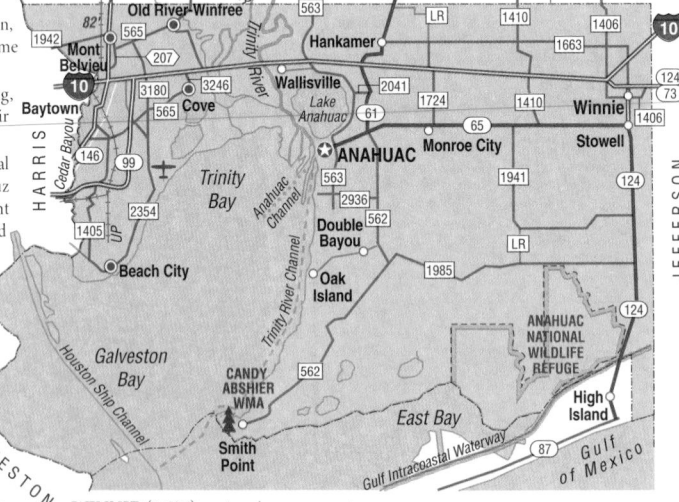

WINNIE (3,606) ecotourism; commuting to Beaumont, Houston; rice farming; antiques market; hospital; library, museum; Texas Rice Festival in early October.

Other towns include: **Beach City** (2,856), **Cove** (567), **Hankamer** (226), **Mont Belvieu** (6,666), **Old River-Winfree** (1,475), **Stowell** (2,096), and **Wallisville** (300). Part [4,180] of **Baytown.**

Population...................... 44,298	
Change from 2010 (%)................26.2	
Area (sq. mi.).......................871.2	
Land Area (sq. mi.)..................597.1	
Altitude (ft.) ....sea level–82	
Rainfall (in.)..........................57.1	
Jan. mean min (°F)....................42.2	
July mean max (°F)....................90.6	
Civ. Labor 20,031	
Unemployed (%)........................9.2	
Wages $272,257,418	
Per Capita Income $56,610	
Prop. Value $21,350,895,447	
Retail Sales $539,773,084	

Shops in downtown Jacksonville, in Cherokee County. Photo by Renelibrary, CC by SA 4.0/Wikimedia Commons

Cherokee County

Physical Features: East Texas county; hilly, partly forested; drains to Angelina, Neches rivers; many streams; Lake Palestine, Lake Striker, Lake Jacksonville; sandy, clay soils.

Economy: Government/services, varied manufacturing, agribusiness.

History: Caddo tribes attracted Spanish missionaries around 1720. Cherokees began settling area around 1820, and soon afterward Anglo-Americans began to arrive. Cherokees forced to Indian Territory 1839. Named for Indian tribe; created 1846 from Nacogdoches County.

Race/Ethnicity: Anglo, 60.3%; Black, 13.7%; Hispanic, 23.3%; Asian, 0.4%; Other, 2.1%..

Vital Statistics, annual: Births, 827; deaths, 557; marriages, 319; divorces, 152.

Recreation: Water sports; fishing, hunting; historic sites and parks, national wildlife refuge; Texas State Railroad; nature trails through forests; lakes.

Minerals: Gas, oil.

Agriculture: Nurseries (second in the state in value of sales), hay, beef cattle, dairies, poultry. Market value $115.7 million. Timber, hunting income significant.

RUSK (5,796) county seat; agribusiness, tourism, state mental hospital, prison unit; historic footbridge, heritage festival in October.

JACKSONVILLE (15,152) varied manufacturing, plastics, agribusiness, tourism, retail center; hospitals, junior colleges; Love's Lookout; Tomato Fest in June.

Other towns include: **Alto** (1,306) farming, timber, light manufacturing, pecan festival in November; **Cuney** (140); **Gallatin** (447); **Maydelle** (250); **New Summerfield** (1,227); **Reklaw** (395, partly in Rusk County); **Wells** (813). Part [68] of **Bullard** and part [66] of **Troup**.

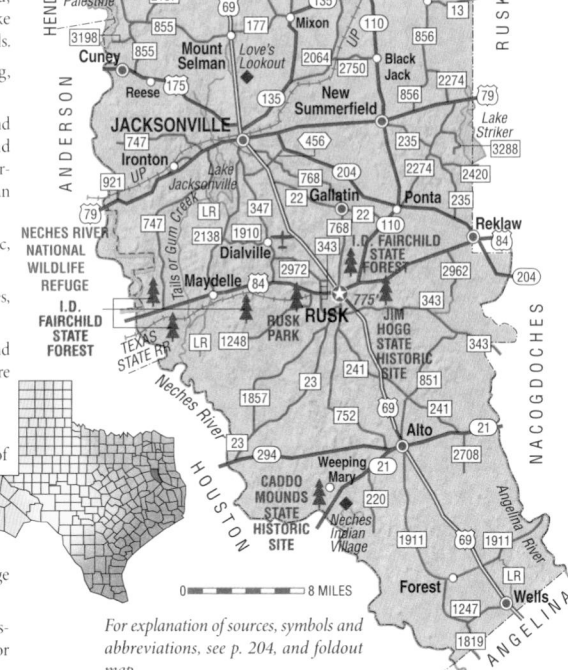

For explanation of sources, symbols and abbreviations, see p. 204, and foldout map.

Population	53,539
Change from 2010 (%)	5.3
Area (sq. mi.)	1,062.2
Land Area (sq. mi.)	1,052.9
Altitude (ft.)	187–775
Rainfall (in.)	49.5
Jan. mean min (°F)	36.3

July mean max (°F)	91.2
Civ. Labor	21,243
Unemployed (%)	6.8
Wages	$148,998,494
Per Capita Income	$35,245
Prop. Value	$4,907,715,917
Retail Sales	$478,740,093

Childress County

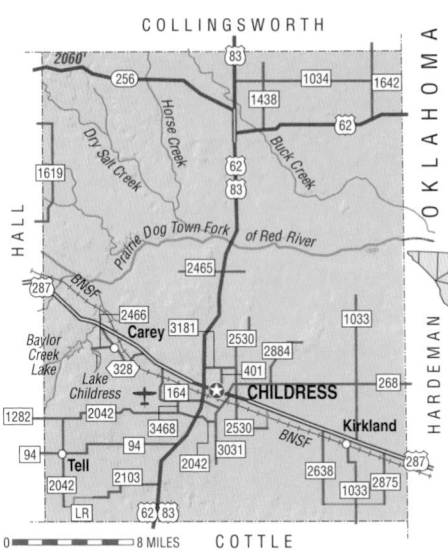

Physical Features: Rolling prairie, at corner of Panhandle, draining to fork of Red River; Baylor Creek Lake, Lake Childress; mixed soils.

Economy: Government/services, retail trade, tourism, agriculture.

History: Apache tribal area, displaced by Comanches. Ranchers arrived around 1880. County created in 1876 from Bexar, Young districts; organized in 1887; named for writer of Texas Declaration of Independence, George C. Childress.

Race/Ethnicity: Anglo, 57.3%; Black, 9.9%; Hispanic, 29.9%; Asian, 0.8%; Other, 1.8%.

Vital Statistics, annual: Births, 62; deaths, 75; marriages, 45; divorces, 16.

Recreation: Recreation on lakes and creeks, fishing; hunting of deer, turkey, wild hog, quail, dove; parks; county museum.

Minerals: Insignificant.

Agriculture: Cotton, beef cattle, wheat, hay, sorghum, peanuts; some 9,000 acres irrigated. Market value $27.2 million. Hunting leases.

CHILDRESS (6,289) county seat; agribusiness, hospital, prison unit; settlers reunion and rodeo in July.

Other towns include: **Tell** (20).

Population.......................... 7,038	Rainfall (in.)...........................26.4	
Change from 2010 (%)..................0.0	Jan. mean min (°F)...................26.8	Wages $29,353,367
Area (sq. mi.)....................... 713.7	July mean max (°F)...................95.7	Per Capita Income $30,731
Land Area (sq. mi.).................. 696.4	Civ. Labor 3,168	Prop. Value $1,146,283,645
Altitude (ft.) 1,560–2,060	Unemployed (%).........................3.6	Retail Sales $118,586,882

Clay County

Physical Features: Hilly, rolling; Northwest county drains to Red, Trinity rivers; Lake Arrowhead; sandy loam, chocolate soils; mesquites, post oaks.

Economy: Oil, agribusiness, commuting.

History: Wichitas arrived from north-central plains in mid-1700s, followed by Apaches and Comanches. Ranching attempts began in 1850s. County created from Cooke County, 1857; Indians forced disorganization, 1862; reorganized, 1873; named for Henry Clay, U.S. statesman.

Race/Ethnicity: Anglo, 90.6%; Black, 0.5%; Hispanic, 5.4%; Asian, 0.3%; Other, 2.9%.

Vital Statistics, annual: Births, 84; deaths, 131; marriages, 68; divorces, 20.

Recreation: Fishing, hunting, horses, water sports; state park; pioneer reunion in September.

Minerals: Oil and gas, stone.

Agriculture: Beef cattle, wheat, pecans, peaches, dairy cattle. Market value $55.7 million. Oaks, cedar, elms sold to nurseries, mesquite cut for firewood.

HENRIETTA (3,104) county seat; agribusiness, government/services, manufacturing; hospital; museum; Turkey Fest in April.

Other towns include: **Bellevue** (347), **Bluegrove** (135), **Byers** (474), **Dean** (463), **Jolly** (159), **Petrolia** (672).

For explanation of sources, symbols and abbreviations, see p. 204, and foldout map.

Population...................... 10,351	Rainfall (in.)...........................32.7	
Change from 2010 (%)................-3.7	Jan. mean min (°F)...................28.7	Wages $15,804,739
Area (sq. mi.)...................... 1,116.8	July mean max (°F)...................96.6	Per Capita Income $44,295
Land Area (sq. mi.)................ 1,088.7	Civ. Labor 4,852	Prop. Value $2,270,799,249
Altitude (ft.) 791–1,200	Unemployed (%).........................5.2	Retail Sales $67,009,797

Cochran County

Physical Features: South Plains bordering New Mexico with small lakes (playas); underground water; loam, sandy loam soils.

Economy: Farming, government/services, retail.

History: Hunting area for various Indian tribes. Ranches operated in the 1880s but population in 1900 was still only 25. Farming began in the 1920s. County created from Bexar and Young districts in 1876; organized in 1924; named for Robert Cochran, who died at the Alamo.

Race/Ethnicity: Anglo, 35.9%; Black, 3.4%; Hispanic, 58.9%; Asian, 0%; Other, 1.6%.

Vital Statistics, annual: Births, 39; deaths, 31; marriages, 9; divorces, 5.

Recreation: Museum; Last Frontier Trail Drive and Buffalo Soldier Day in June.

Minerals: Insignificant.

Agriculture: Cotton, peanuts, sorghum, peas, sunflowers, wheat. Crops 60 percent irrigated. Market value $87.6 million.

MORTON (1,846) county seat; oil, farm center, meat packing, light manufacture; hospital.

Other towns include: **Bledsoe** (126), **Whiteface** (432).

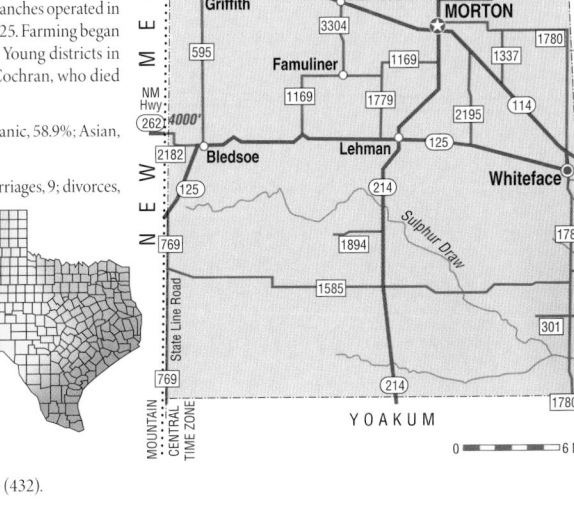

Population........................ 2,904	Rainfall (in.)............................18.9	
Change from 2010 (%)................-7.1	Jan. mean min (°F)....................24.4	Wages $8,110,083
Area (sq. mi.)........................ 775.2	July mean max (°F)....................91.5	Per Capita Income $39,333
Land Area (sq. mi.)................. 775.2	Civ. Labor 1,145	Prop. Value $766,027,380
Altitude (ft.) 3,565–4,000	Unemployed (%).......................5.6	Retail Sales $26,421,176

Coke County

Physical Features: West Texas prairie, hills, Colorado River valley; sandy loam, red soils; E.V. Spence Reservoir, Oak Creek Reservoir.

Economy: Oil and gas, government/services, agriculture.

History: From around 1700 to 1870s, Comanche bands roamed through the area. Ranches began operating after the Civil War. County was created and organized in 1889 from Tom Green County; named for Gov. Richard Coke.

Race/Ethnicity: Anglo, 78%; Black, 0.1%; Hispanic, 19.5%; Asian, 0.1%; Other, 2%.

Vital Statistics, annual: Births, 39; deaths, 53;marriages, 11; divorces, 12.

Recreation: Hunting, fishing, Caliche Loop birdwatching trail; lakes; Sumac hiking trail; historic sites, Fort Chadbourne, county museum, Fort Chadbourne Days in May; amphitheater.

Minerals: Oil, gas.

Agriculture: Beef cattle, small grains, sheep and goats, hay. Market value $7.8 million.

ROBERT LEE (1,092) county seat; oil and gas, wind farms, ranching, government/services; old jail museum.

BRONTE (1,025) ranching, oil.

Other towns include: **Silver** (34) and **Tennyson** (46). Also, a small part of **Blackwell** (295).

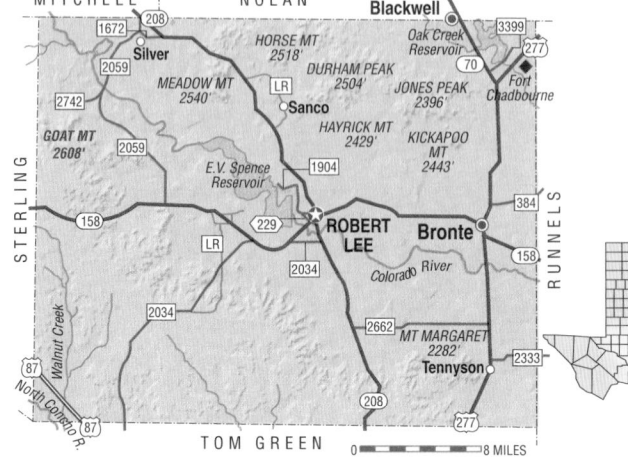

Population......................... 3,390	Rainfall (in.)............................22.8	
Change from 2010 (%).................2.1	Jan. mean min (°F).....................28.4	Wages $8,254,808
Area (sq. mi.).......................... 928.0	July mean max (°F).....................96.7	Per Capita Income $41,669
Land Area (sq. mi.)................... 911.5	Civ. Labor............................ 1,349	Prop. Value $1,023,620,554
Altitude (ft.)...................1,700–2,608	Unemployed (%)..........................5.3	Retail Sales.................. $22,155,760

Coleman County

Physical Features: Hilly, rolling; drains to Colorado River, Pecan Bayou; O.H. Ivie Reservoir, Hords Creek Lake, Lake Coleman; mesquite, oaks.

Economy: Agribusiness, petroleum, ecotourism, varied manufacturing.

History: Presence of Apaches and Comanches brought military outpost, Camp Colorado, before the Civil War. Settlers arrived after organization. County created in 1858 from Brown, Travis counties; organized in 1864; named for Houston's aide, R.M. Coleman.

Race/Ethnicity: Anglo, 74.8%; Black, 2.7%; Hispanic, 19.4%; Asian, 0.3%; Other, 2.5%.

Vital Statistics, annual: Births, 72; deaths, 131; marriages, 45; divorces, 30.

Recreation: Fishing, hunting; water sports; city park, historic sites; lakes; Santa Anna Peak; Santa Anna bison cook-off in May.

Minerals: Oil, gas, stone, clays.

Agriculture: Cattle, wheat, sheep, hay, grain sorghum, goats, oats, cotton. Market value $41.2 million. Mesquite for firewood and furniture.

COLEMAN (4,305) county seat; varied manufacturing; hospital, library, museums: Fiesta de la Paloma in October.

SANTA ANNA (1,010) agribusiness, oil, tourism; museum; Funtier days in May.

Other towns include: **Burkett** (90), **Goldsboro** (15), **Gouldbusk** (70), **Novice** (126), **Rockwood** (53), **Talpa** (127), and **Valera** (80).

Population......................... 8,191	Rainfall (in.)............................28.7	
Change from 2010 (%)................-7.9	Jan. mean min (°F).....................33.7	Wages $19,039,698
Area (sq. mi.)....................... 1,281.4	July mean max (°F).....................95.7	Per Capita Income $42,683
Land Area (sq. mi.)................. 1,262.0	Civ. Labor............................ 2,845	Prop. Value $1,806,985,326
Altitude (ft.)...................1,289–2,250	Unemployed (%)..........................6.4	Retail Sales.................. $67,723,793

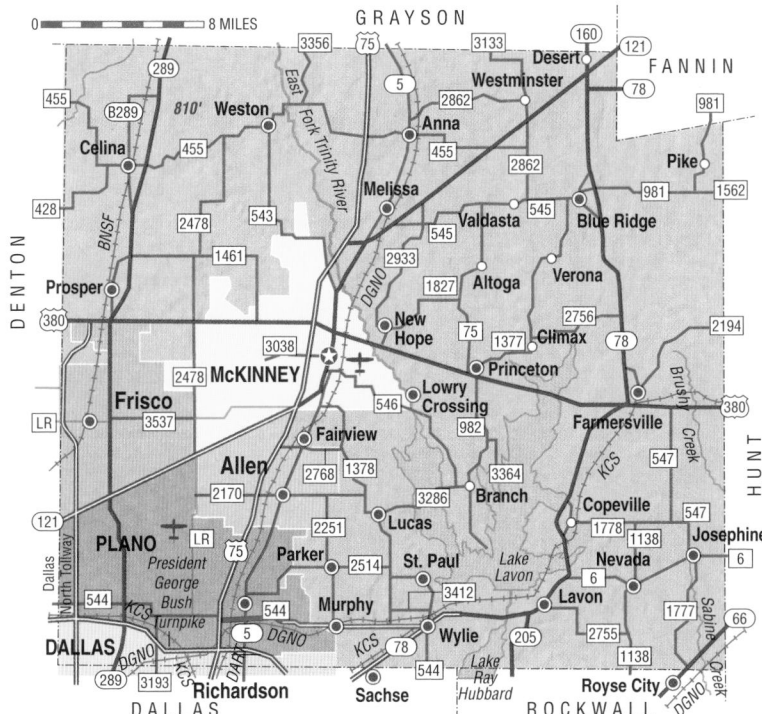

Collin County

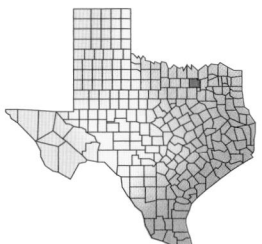

Physical Features: Heavy, black clay soil; level to rolling; drains to Trinity; Lake Lavon, Lake Ray Hubbard.

Economy: Government/services, manufacturing plants, retail and wholesale center, many residents work in Dallas.

History: Caddo tribal area until 1850s. Settlers of Peters colony arrived in the early 1840s. County created, organized, from Fannin County in 1846. Named for pioneer settler Collin McKinney.

Race/Ethnicity: Anglo, 56.5%; Black, 9.8%; Hispanic, 15.4%; Asian, 14.7%; Other, 3.3%.

Vital Statistics, annual: Births, 10,921; deaths, 4,005; marriages, 5,554; divorces, 2,374.

Recreation: Fishing, water sports; historic sites; old homes restoration, tours; natural science museum.

Minerals: Insignificant.

Agriculture: Landscape nurseries, corn, wheat, cattle, hay, grain sorghum. Market value $66.8 million.

McKINNEY (197,391) county seat; agribusiness, trade center, varied industry; hospital, community college; museums.

PLANO (290,855) professional services, banking, finance, insurance, health care/hospitals; community college, university extensions; museums, fine arts organizations, nature preserves, hiking trails;

balloon festival in September, AsiaFest in April.

FRISCO (190,974) technical, aerospace industry; hospital, community college.

Other towns include: **Allen** (105,524) retail, manufacturing, wholesale trade, hospital, community college, nature conservatory, natatorium, historic stone dam, Stampede rodeo in October; **Anna** (14,708); **Blue Ridge** (957); **Celina** (13,399) museum, historic town square, Fun Day in September.

Also, **Copeville** (243); **Fairview** (9,021) government/services, retail center, commuters, museum, old mill site, wildlife sanctuary, veterans celebration in November; **Farmersville** (4,534) agriculture, light industries, Audie Murphy Day in June.

Also, **Josephine** (1,750); **Lavon** (3,839); **Lowry Crossing** (1,753); **Lucas** (8,183);

Melissa (13,461) industrial plants, library, old town; **Murphy** (20,595); **Nevada** (1,098); **New Hope** (635); **Parker** (5,216); **Princeton** (15,222) manufacturing, commuters, Spring Onion festival in April.

Also, **Prosper** (24,579); **St. Paul** (1,105); **Westminster** (1,155); **Weston** (580); **Wylie** (53,514) manufacturing, retail, hospital, historic sites, big cat sanctuary, July Jubilee.

Also, part [52,147] of **Dallas**, part [34,920] of **Richardson** and part [8,172] of **Sachse**.

For explanation of sources, symbols and abbreviations, see p. 204, and foldout map.

Population..................	**1,033,046**
Change from 2010 (%).................	32.0
Area (sq. mi.)........................	886.1
Land Area (sq. mi.)...................	841.2
Altitude (ft.)......................	434–810
Rainfall (in.)...........................	42.3
Jan. mean min (°F)....................	30.1
July mean max (°F).....................	91.5
Civ. Labor..........................	576,083
Unemployed (%).......................	4.8
Wages	$8,485,909,167
Per Capita Income.................	$68,474
Prop. Value.............	$189,257,810,623
Retail Sales...............	$20,897,295,384

Collingsworth County

Physical Features: Panhandle county of rolling, broken terrain, draining to Red River forks; sandy and loam soils.

Economy: Agribusiness.

History: Apaches, displaced by Comanches. Ranchers from England arrived in the late 1870s. County created in 1876, from Bexar and Young districts, organized in 1890. Named for Republic of Texas' first chief justice, James Collinsworth (name misspelled in law).

Race/Ethnicity: Anglo, 58.4%; Black, 4.1%; Hispanic, 34.5%; Asian, 0.1%; Other, 2.7%.

Vital Statistics, annual: Births, 26; deaths, 39; marriages, 15; divorces, 2.

Recreation: Deer, quail hunting; children's camp, county museum, pioneer park; county fair/parade in September.

Minerals: Gas, oil production.

Agriculture: Cotton, peanuts, cow-calf operations, wheat, stocker cattle; 22,000 acres irrigated. Market value $39.7 million.

WELLINGTON (2,002) county seat; peanut-processing plants, varied manufacturing, agriculture; hospital, library; restored Ritz Theatre.

Other towns include: **Dodson** (104), **Quail** (18), **Samnorwood** (56).

Population		2,853
Change from 2010 (%)		-6.7
Area (sq. mi.)		919.3
Land Area (sq. mi.)		918.4
Altitude (ft.)		1,750–2,840
Rainfall (in.)		22.6
Jan. mean min (°F)		27.4
July mean max (°F)		97.6
Civ. Labor		1,082
Unemployed (%)		5.1
Wages		$9,825,687
Per Capita Income		$42,026
Prop. Value		$748,191,080
Retail Sales		$15,608,737

Colorado County

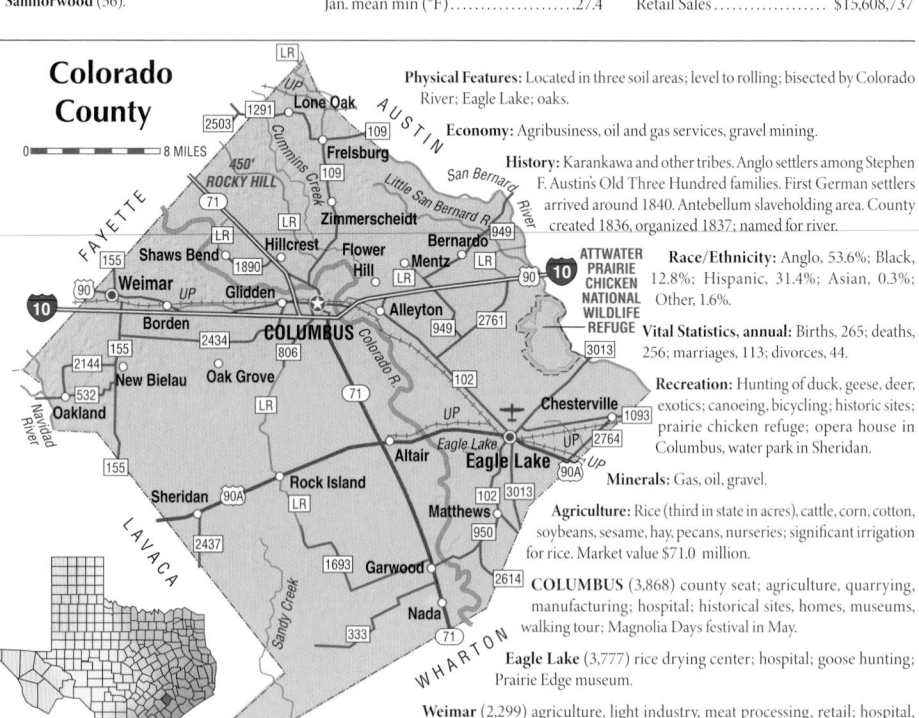

Physical Features: Located in three soil areas; level to rolling; bisected by Colorado River; Eagle Lake; oaks.

Economy: Agribusiness, oil and gas services, gravel mining.

History: Karankawa and other tribes. Anglo settlers among Stephen F. Austin's Old Three Hundred families. First German settlers arrived around 1840. Antebellum slaveholding area. County created 1836, organized 1837; named for river.

Race/Ethnicity: Anglo, 53.6%; Black, 12.8%; Hispanic, 31.4%; Asian, 0.3%; Other, 1.6%.

Vital Statistics, annual: Births, 265; deaths, 256; marriages, 113; divorces, 44.

Recreation: Hunting of duck, geese, deer, exotics; canoeing, bicycling; historic sites; prairie chicken refuge; opera house in Columbus, water park in Sheridan.

Minerals: Gas, oil, gravel.

Agriculture: Rice (third in state in acres), cattle, corn, cotton, soybeans, sesame, hay, pecans, nurseries; significant irrigation for rice. Market value $71.0 million.

COLUMBUS (3,868) county seat; agriculture, quarrying, manufacturing; hospital; historical sites, homes, museums, walking tour; Magnolia Days festival in May.

Eagle Lake (3,777) rice drying center; hospital; goose hunting; Prairie Edge museum.

Weimar (2,299) agriculture, light industry, meat processing, retail; hospital, library; "Gedenke" (remember) celebration on Mother's Day weekend.

Other towns include: **Altair** (30), **Garwood** (600), **Glidden** (762), **Nada** (165), **Oakland** (80), **Rock Island** (160), **Sheridan** (300).

Population		22,283
Change from 2010 (%)		6.8
Area (sq. mi.)		973.7
Land Area (sq. mi.)		960.3
Altitude (ft.)		125–450
Rainfall (in.)		43.9
Jan. mean min (°F)		40.8
July mean max (°F)		94.3
Civ. Labor		9,647
Unemployed (%)		5.1
Wages		$87,034,303
Per Capita Income		$46,909
Prop. Value		$5,910,988,837
Retail Sales		$386,611,198

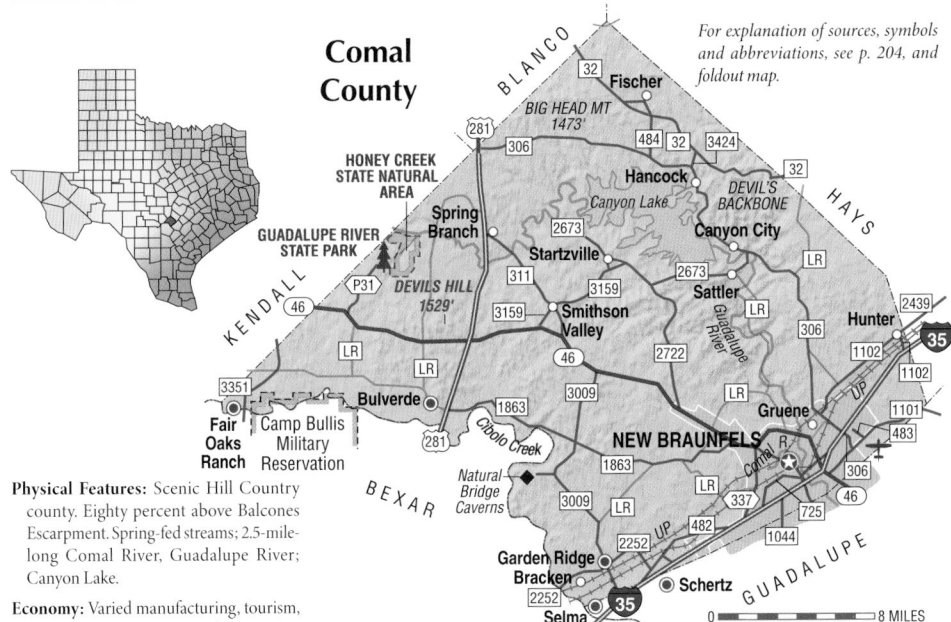

Comal County

For explanation of sources, symbols and abbreviations, see p. 204, and foldout map.

Physical Features: Scenic Hill Country county. Eighty percent above Balcones Escarpment. Spring-fed streams; 2.5-mile-long Comal River, Guadalupe River; Canyon Lake.

Economy: Varied manufacturing, tourism, government/services, agriculture; county in San Antonio metropolitan area.

History: Tonkawa, Waco Indians. A pioneer German settlement 1845. Mexican migration peaked during Mexican Revolution. County created from Bexar, Gonzales, Travis counties and organized in 1846; named for river, a name for Spanish earthenware or metal pan used for cooking tortillas.

Race/Ethnicity: Anglo, 66.6%; Black, 2.1%; Hispanic, 28.8%; Asian, 0.7%; Other, 1.5%.

Vital Statistics, annual: Births, 1,632; deaths, 1,108; marriages, 1,186; divorces, 197.

Recreation: Fishing, hunting; historic sites; scenic drives, Devil's Backbone; lake facilities; Prince Solms Park, other county parks; Landa Park with 76 species of trees; Gruene historic area; caverns; river resorts; river tubing; Schlitterbahn water park; Wurstfest in November, Wasselfest in December.

Minerals: Stone, lime, sand and gravel.

Agriculture: Cattle, goats, sheep, hogs, horses; nursery, hay, corn, sorghum, wheat. Market value $9.6 million.

NEW BRAUNFELS (87,388) county seat; manufacturing, retail, distribution center; picturesque city, making it a tourist center; Conservation Plaza; rose garden; hospital; library; mental health and retardation center. Gruene is now part of New Braunfels.

Canyon Lake (27,978), which includes Startzville, Sattler, Smithson Valley, Canyon City, Fischer, Hancock, and Spring Branch, retirement and recreation area, tourism, barbecue cook-off in April.

Other towns include: **Bulverde** (5,806) retail center; **Garden Ridge** (4,187);

Also in the county, parts of **Fair Oaks Ranch** [7,204], **Selma** [8,493], and **Schertz** [38,784].

Population	**156,317**
Change from 2010 (%)	44.1
Area (sq. mi.)	574.9
Land Area (sq. mi.)	559.5
Altitude (ft.)	560–1,529
Rainfall (in.)	34.0
Jan. mean min (°F)	38.1
July mean max (°F)	93.3
Civ. Labor	76,409
Unemployed (%)	4.8
Wages	$805,783,518
Per Capita Income	$60,056
Prop. Value	$30,269,959,001
Retail Sales	$2,410,863,876

A view of Canyon Lake and the dam from above. Photo by U.S. Army Corps of Engineers, PD/Wikimedia Commons

Comanche County

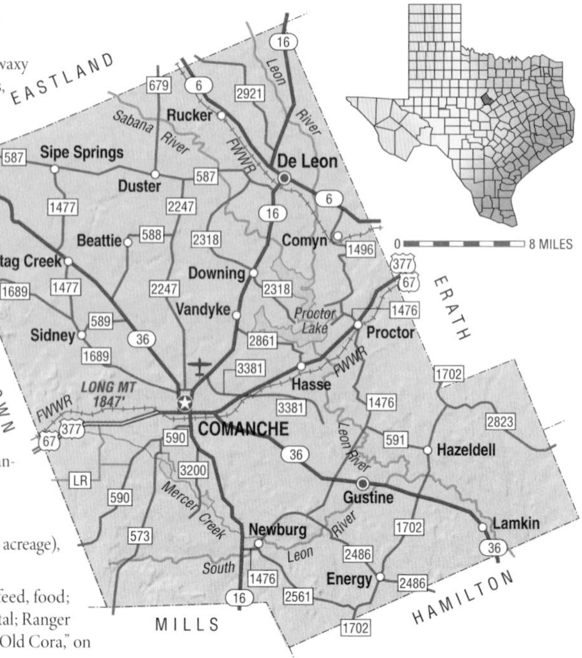

Physical Features: Rolling, hilly terrain; sandy, loam, waxy soils; drains to Leon River, Proctor Lake; pecans, oaks, mesquites, cedars.

Economy: Dairies, peanut-, pecan-shelling plants, manufacturing.

History: Comanche area. Anglo-American settlers arrived in 1854 on land granted earlier to Stephen F. Austin and Samuel May Williams. County created and organized in 1856 from Bosque and Coryell counties; named for the Indian tribe.

Race/Ethnicity: Anglo, 68.6%; Black, 0.2%; Hispanic, 29.2%; Asian, 0.2%; Other, 1.5%.

Vital Statistics, annual: Births, 174; deaths, 188; marriages, 93; divorces, 47.

Recreation: Hunting, fishing, water sports, nature tourism; parks, community center, museums; Comanche Pow-Wow in September, rodeo in July.

Minerals: Limited gas, oil, stone, clay.

Agriculture: Dairies, beef cattle, pecans (first in state in acreage), hay, wildlife, melons. Market value $173.3 million.

COMANCHE (4,336) county seat; plants process feed, food; varied manufacturing; agribusiness; winery; hospital; Ranger College branch; library; state's oldest courthouse, "Old Cora," on display on town square.

De Leon (2,233) pecans, light manufacturing; hospital; car museum, Peach and Melon Festival in August.

Other towns include: **Energy** (70), **Gustine** (484), **Proctor** (228), and **Sidney** (148).

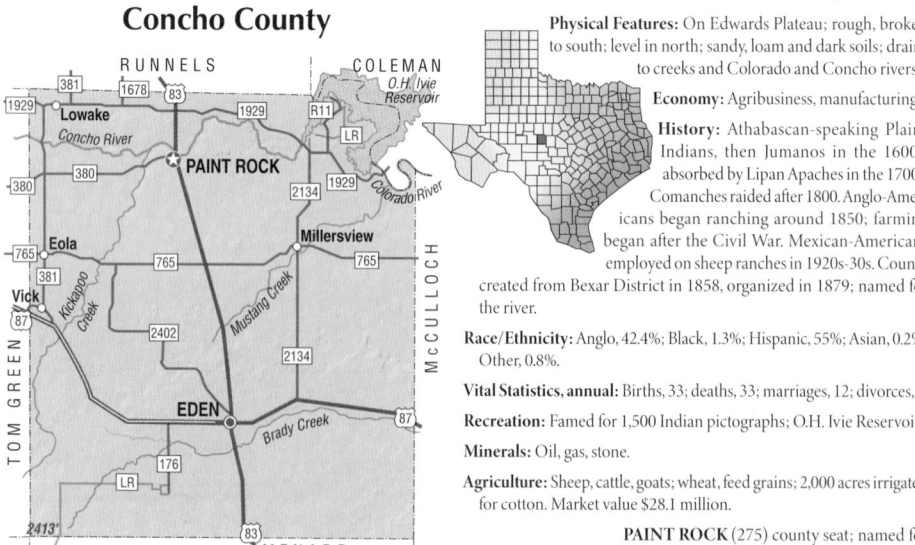

Population.......................... 13,878	July mean max (°F)....................95.7
Change from 2010 (%)................-0.7	Civ. Labor 5,729
Area (sq. mi.)......................... 947.7	Unemployed (%).......................5.1
Land Area (sq. mi.).................. 937.8	Wages $41,547,100
Altitude (ft.)..................1,020–1,847	Per Capita Income................ $43,242
Rainfall (in.)............................32.4	Prop. Value $2,984,617,487
Jan. mean min (°F)....................31.4	Retail Sales.................. $159,464,081

Concho County

Physical Features: On Edwards Plateau; rough, broken to south; level in north; sandy, loam and dark soils; drains to creeks and Colorado and Concho rivers.

Economy: Agribusiness, manufacturing.

History: Athabascan-speaking Plains Indians, then Jumanos in the 1600s, absorbed by Lipan Apaches in the 1700s. Comanches raided after 1800. Anglo-Americans began ranching around 1850; farming began after the Civil War. Mexican-Americans employed on sheep ranches in 1920s-30s. County created from Bexar District in 1858, organized in 1879; named for the river.

Race/Ethnicity: Anglo, 42.4%; Black, 1.3%; Hispanic, 55%; Asian, 0.2%; Other, 0.8%.

Vital Statistics, annual: Births, 33; deaths, 33; marriages, 12; divorces, 3.

Recreation: Famed for 1,500 Indian pictographs; O.H. Ivie Reservoir.

Minerals: Oil, gas, stone.

Agriculture: Sheep, cattle, goats; wheat, feed grains; 2,000 acres irrigated for cotton. Market value $28.1 million.

PAINT ROCK (275) county seat; named for Indian pictographs nearby; farming, ranching center.

EDEN (1,297) steel fabrication; hospital; fall fest.

Other towns include: **Eola** (215), **Lowake** (40), and **Millersview** (80).

Population.......................... 2,716	July mean max (°F)....................95.2
Change from 2010 (%)...............-33.5	Civ. Labor 1,364
Area (sq. mi.)......................... 993.7	Unemployed (%).......................4.5
Land Area (sq. mi.).................. 983.8	Wages $10,751,392
Altitude (ft.)..................1,421–2,413	Per Capita Income................ $35,758
Rainfall (in.)............................25.0	Prop. Value $1,242,955,512
Jan. mean min (°F)....................29.5	Retail Sales.................. $16,673,501

Cooke County

Physical Features: North Texas county; drains to Red, Trinity rivers; Ray Roberts Lake, Lake Texoma, Lake Kiowa, Hubert H. Moss Lake; sandy, red, loam soils.

Economy: Oil and gas, varied manufacturing, commuting to Dallas and Fort Worth.

History: Frontier between Caddoes and Comanches. Anglo-Americans arrived in the late 1840s. Germans settled western part around 1890. County created and organized in 1848 from Fannin County; named for Capt. W.G. Cooke of the Texas Revolution.

Race/Ethnicity: Anglo, 74.2%; Black, 2.9%; Hispanic, 19.3%; Asian, 0.7%; Other, 2.7%.

Vital Statistics, annual: Births, 545; deaths, 413; marriages, 442; divorces, 123.

Recreation: Water sports; hunting, fishing; zoo; museum; park, Gainesville Depot Day/car show in October.

Minerals: Oil, natural gas, sand, gravel.

Agriculture: Beef cattle, horses, forages, wheat. Market value $53.8 million. Hunting leases important.

GAINESVILLE (16,373) county seat; aerospace, plastics, energy; Victorian homes, walking tours; hospital; community college; juvenile correction unit; Camp Sweeney for diabetic children; World War II Camp Howze site.

Muenster (1,603) varied manufacturing, food processing, water utilities; hospital; museum; Germanfest late April, Oktoberfest.

Other towns include: Callisburg (365), **Era** (150), **Lindsay** (1,081) 1919 Romanesque-style church, **Myra** (150), **Oak Ridge** (190), **Rosston** (75), **Valley View** (785), and the residential community around **Lake Kiowa** (1,970).

For explanation of sources, symbols and abbreviations, see p. 204, and foldout map.

Population........................**40,477**	July mean max (°F)....................93.4
Change from 2010 (%).................5.3	Civ. Labor............................18,774
Area (sq. mi.).........................898.4	Unemployed (%).........................5.4
Land Area (sq. mi.)..................874.8	Wages $175,008,435
Altitude (ft.).....................617–1,217	Per Capita Income................$52,875
Rainfall (in.)............................42.7	Prop. Value $7,421,351,087
Jan. mean min (°F)....................31.3	Retail Sales..................$695,300,612

The headquarters of The Comanche Chief newspaper. The local paper is family-owned and published weekly. Photo by Leaflet, PD/Wikimedia Commons

Physical Features: Leon Valley in center, remainder rolling, hilly; Belton Lake.

Economy: Fort Hood, prisons, agribusiness, manufacturing.

History: Tonkawa area, later various other tribes. Anglo-Americans settled around Fort Gates in late 1840s. Permanent establishment of Fort Hood in 1950 changed cultural geography. County created from Bell County, organized 1854; named for local pioneer James Coryell.

Race/Ethnicity: (Anglo, 55.9%; Black, 15.7%; Hispanic, 19.4%; Asian, 1.7%; Other, 7.1%.

Vital Statistics, annual: Births, 1,045; deaths, 526; marriages, 466; divorces, 288.

Recreation: State park; deer hunting; fishing; lake, Leon River; bluebonnet area; historic homes; log jail; Shivaree in June.

Minerals: Oil and gas.

Agriculture: Beef, forages, oats, wildlife, row crops. Market value $36.3 million. Hunting leases, timber.

GATESVILLE (15,997) county seat; prisons, varied manufacturing; hospital; refurbished courthouse; museum; branch Central Texas College; Spurfest in September.

COPPERAS COVE (35,270) business center for Fort Hood; industrial filters, other manufacturing; hospital, library; Central Texas College; Rabbit Fest in May.

Other towns include: **Evant** (405, partly in Hamilton County), **Flat** (210), **Jonesboro** (125), **Mound** (125), **Oglesby** (466), **Purmela** (50), **South Mountain** (365). Part [14,415] of **Fort Hood**.

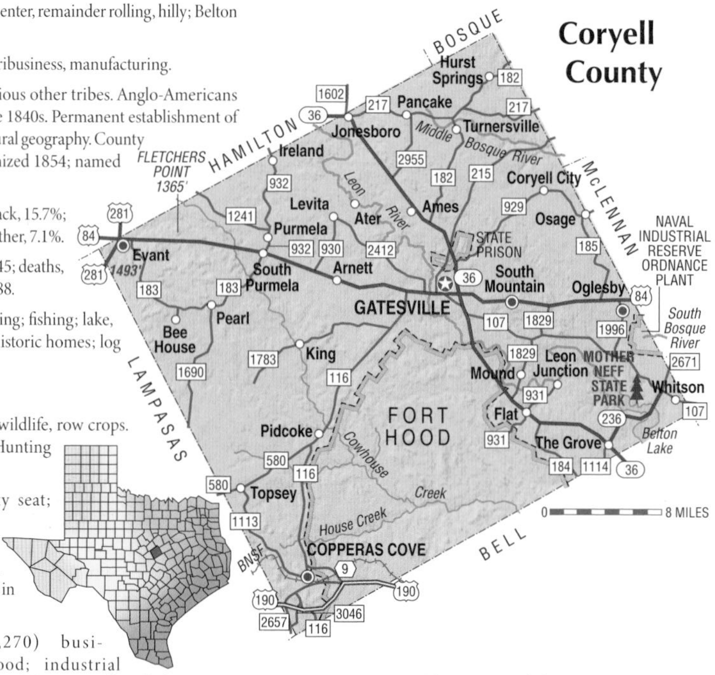

Coryell County

Population	75,137
Change from 2010 (%)	-0.3
Area (sq. mi.)	1,056.8
Land Area (sq. mi.)	1,052.1
Altitude (ft.)	600–1,493
Rainfall (in.)	33.7
Jan. mean min (°F)	31.9
July mean max (°F)	94.2
Civ. Labor	24,233
Unemployed (%)	5.8
Wages	$197,708,631
Per Capita Income	$35,570
Prop. Value	$5,080,751,637
Retail Sales	$563,571,745

The bell at Mother Neff State Park in Coryell County. It was used by the Civilian Conservation Corps, who built the park between 1934 and 1938. Photo by Larry D. Moore, CC 3/Wikimedia Commons

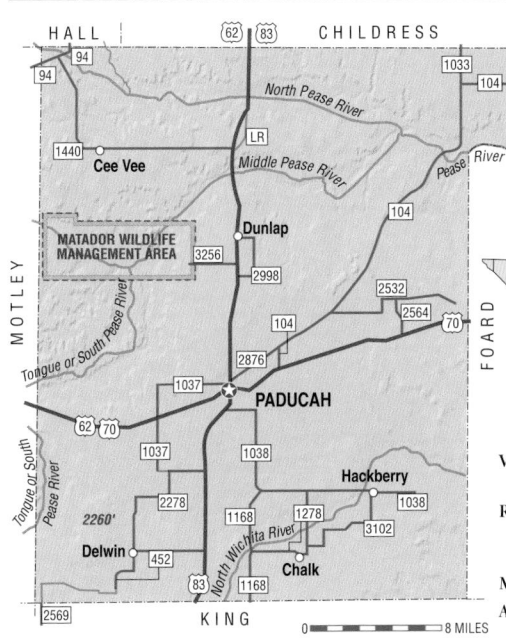

Cottle County

Physical Features: Northwest county below Caprock, rough in west, level in east; gray, black, sandy and loam soils; drains to Pease River.

Economy: Agribusiness, government/services.

History: Around 1700, Apaches were displaced by Comanches, who in turn were driven out by the U.S. Army in the 1870s. Anglo-American settlers arrived in the 1880s. County created in 1876 from Fannin County; organized in 1892; named for George W. Cottle, Alamo hero.

Race/Ethnicity: Anglo, 63.1%; Black, 10.1%; Hispanic, 25.2%; Asian, 0%; Other, 1.4%.

Vital Statistics, annual: Births, 0; deaths, 31; marriages, 0; divorces, 0.

Recreation: Hunting of quail, dove, wild hogs, deer; wildlife management area; museum, Fiestas Patrias in September, horse and colt show in April.

Minerals: Oil, natural gas.

Agriculture: Beef cattle, cotton, peanuts, wheat. 3,000 acres irrigated. Market value $27.7 million.

Population	1,354
Change from 2010 (%)	-10.0
Area (sq. mi.)	901.6
Land Area (sq. mi.)	900.6
Altitude (ft.)	1,470–2,260
Rainfall (in.)	24.9
Jan. mean min (°F)	27.9
July mean max (°F)	97.2
Civ. Labor	630
Unemployed (%)	4.6
Wages	$6,685,283
Per Capita Income	$60,260
Prop. Value	$686,745,401
Retail Sales	$6,653,507

PADUCAH (1,085) county seat; government/services, library.

Other towns include: Cee Vee (45).

For explanation of sources, symbols and abbreviations, see p. 204, and foldout map.

Physical Features: Rolling prairie, Pecos Valley, some hills; sandy, loam soils; Juan Cordona Lake (intermittent).

Economy: Oil and gas; agriculture; government/services.

History: Lipan Apache area. Ranching developed in the 1890s. Oil discovered in 1926. County created from Tom Green County in 1887, organized in 1927; named for Baylor University president W. C. Crane.

Race/Ethnicity: (Anglo, 29.8%; Black, 2.3%; Hispanic, 66.4%; Asian, 0.2%; Other, 1.1%.

Vital Statistics, annual: Births, 79; deaths, 36; marriages, 19; divorces, 4.

Recreation: Museum of the Desert Southwest; sites of pioneer trails and historic Horsehead Crossing on Pecos River; hunting of mule deer, quail; camping park; rodeo in May.

Minerals: Oil, gas production.

Agriculture: Beef cattle, goats. Market value $1.9 million.

CRANE (3,582) county seat; oil-well servicing and production, foundry, steel, surfboard manufacturing; hospital.

Population	4,678
Change from 2010 (%)	6.9
Area (sq. mi.)	785.7
Land Area (sq. mi.)	785.1
Altitude (ft.)	2,290–2,945
Rainfall (in.)	15.6
Jan. mean min (°F)	31.9
July mean max (°F)	93.3
Civ. Labor	1,525
Unemployed (%)	11.4
Wages	$17,294,941
Per Capita Income	$51,025
Prop. Value	$1,609,435,199
Retail Sales	$46,794,681

Crane County

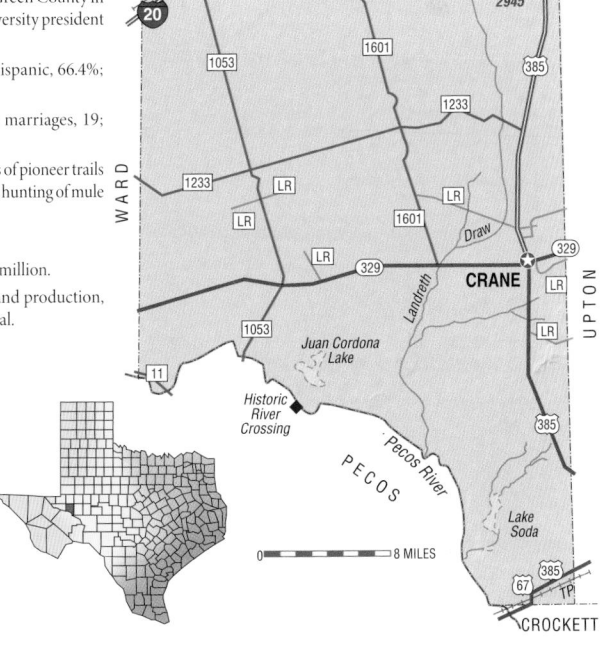

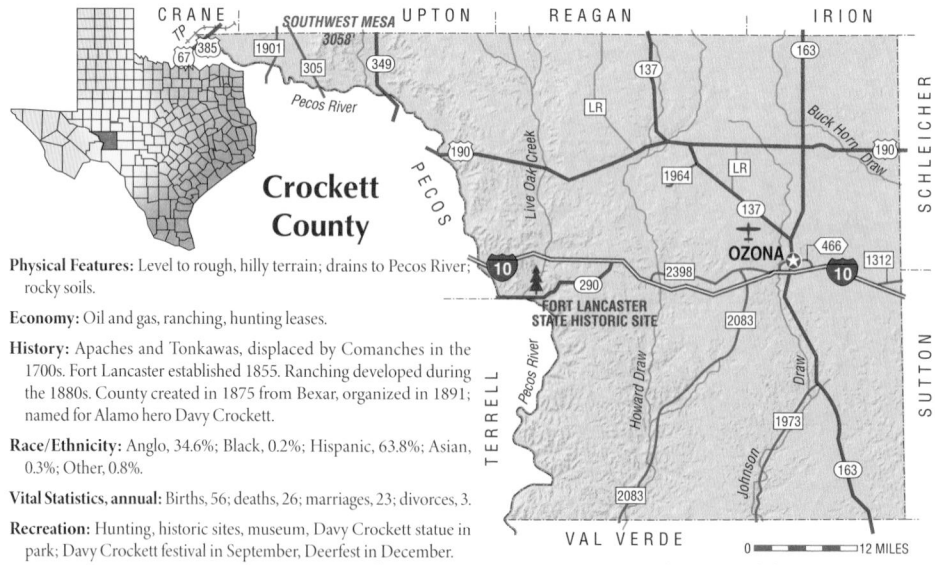

Crockett County

Physical Features: Level to rough, hilly terrain; drains to Pecos River; rocky soils.

Economy: Oil and gas, ranching, hunting leases.

History: Apaches and Tonkawas, displaced by Comanches in the 1700s. Fort Lancaster established 1855. Ranching developed during the 1880s. County created in 1875 from Bexar, organized in 1891; named for Alamo hero Davy Crockett.

Race/Ethnicity: Anglo, 34.6%; Black, 0.2%; Hispanic, 63.8%; Asian, 0.3%; Other, 0.8%.

Vital Statistics, annual: Births, 56; deaths, 26; marriages, 23; divorces, 3.

Recreation: Hunting, historic sites, museum, Davy Crockett statue in park; Davy Crockett festival in September, Deerfest in December.

Minerals: Oil, gas production.

Agriculture: Sheep (first in numbers), goats; beef cattle. Market value $15.4 million.

OZONA (2,912) county seat; ranching, oil & gas, hunting, tourism; health care clinics.

Population		3,461
Change from 2010 (%)		-6.9
Area (sq. mi.)		2,807.4
Land Area (sq. mi.)		2,807.3
Altitude (ft.)		1,720–3,058
Rainfall (in.)		18.9
Jan. mean min (°F)		30.2
July mean max (°F)		93.4
Civ. Labor		1,465
Unemployed (%)		7.5
Wages		$15,453,626
Per Capita Income		$44,458
Prop. Value		$2,531,974,282
Retail Sales		$37,370,638

Crosby County

Physical Features: Flat, rich soil above Caprock, broken below; drains into Brazos River forks and playas.

Economy: Agribusiness, tourism, commuters to Lubbock.

History: Comanches, driven out by U.S. Army in 1870s; ranching developed soon afterward. Quaker colony founded in 1879. County created from Bexar District 1876, organized 1886; named for Texas Land Commissioner Stephen Crosby.

Race/Ethnicity: Anglo, 36.5%; Black, 3.2%; Hispanic, 58.9%; Asian, 0%; Other, 1.1%.

Vital Statistics, annual: Births, 90; deaths, 77; marriages, 35; divorces, 16.

Recreation: White River Lake; Silver Falls Park; hunting.

Minerals: Sand, gravel, oil, gas.

Agriculture: Cotton, beef cattle, sorghum; about 112,000 acres irrigated. Market value $86.9 million.

CROSBYTON (1,602) county seat; agribusiness center; hospital, Pioneer Museum, Prairie Ladies Multi-Cultural Center, library; Cowboy Gathering in October.

Other towns include: **Lorenzo** (1,142); **Ralls** (1,824) government/services, agribusiness, museums, Cotton Boll Fest in September.

For explanation of sources, symbols and abbreviations, see p. 204, and foldout map.

Population		5,702
Change from 2010 (%)		-5.9
Area (sq. mi.)		901.7
Land Area (sq. mi.)		900.2
Altitude (ft.)		2,250–3,235
Rainfall (in.)		23.3
Jan. mean min (°F)		25.9
July mean max (°F)		92.3
Civ. Labor		2,520
Unemployed (%)		5.4
Wages		$13,629,379
Per Capita Income		$37,580
Prop. Value		$1,007,060,081
Retail Sales		$35,372,963

The east side of Blanco Canyon in Crosby County. The red area is the Ogallala formation and the white area is the Blanco formation. Photo by Leaflet, CC 3/Wikimedia Commons

Culberson County

Physical Features: Contains Texas' highest mountain; slopes toward Pecos Valley on east, Diablo Bolson on west; salt lakes; unique vegetation in canyons.

Economy: Tourism, government/services, talc mining and processing, agribusiness, sulfur mining.

History: Apaches arrived about 600 years ago. U.S. military frontier after Civil War. Ranching developed after 1880. Mexican migration increased after 1920. County created from El Paso County 1911, organized 1912; named for D.B. Culberson, Texas congressman.

Race/Ethnicity: Anglo, 23.6%; Black, 0.3%; Hispanic, 73.1%; Asian, 0.9%; Other, 1.9%..

Vital Statistics, annual: Births, 36; deaths, 14; marriages, 1; divorces, 1.

Recreation: National park; Guadalupe and El Capitan, twin peaks; scenic canyons and mountains; classic car museum, antique saloon bar; frontier days in June, big buck tournament.

Minerals: Sulfur, talc, marble, oil.

Agriculture: Beef cattle; crops include cotton, vegetables, melons, pecans; 6,000 acres in irrigation. Market value $15.9 million.

VAN HORN (1,913) county seat; agribusiness, tourism, rock crushing, government/services; hospital.

Other towns: **Kent** (30).

Population	2,211
Change from 2010 (%)	-7.8
Area (sq. mi.)	3,813.0
Land Area (sq. mi.)	3,812.8
Altitude (ft.)	2,900–8,749
Rainfall (in.)	11.6
Jan. mean min (°F)	28.3
July mean max (°F)	92.3
Civ. Labor	1,196
Unemployed (%)	4.5
Wages	$20,272,589
Per Capita Income	$59,506
Prop. Value	$3,417,603,577
Retail Sales	$100,308,865

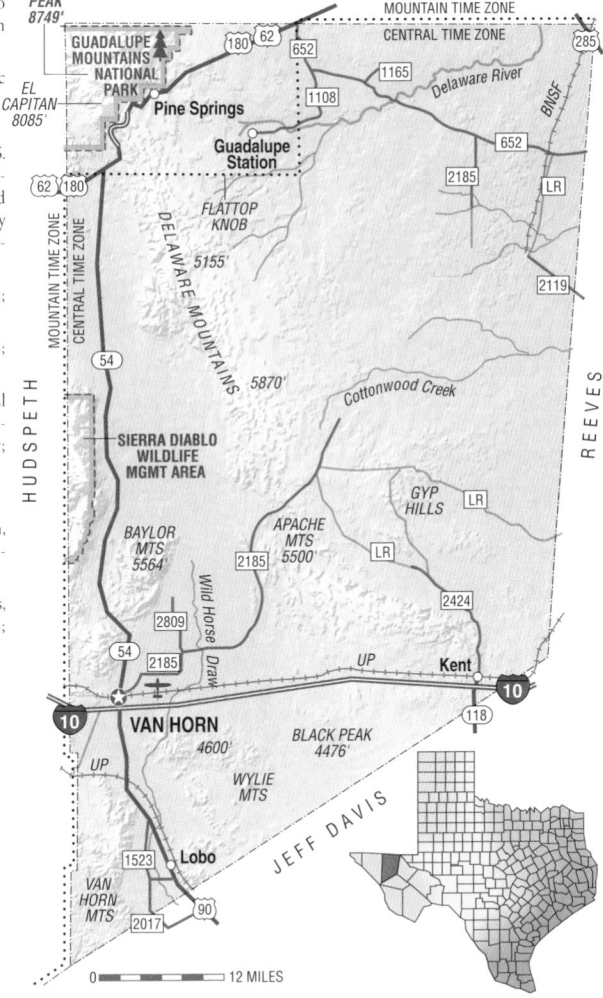

Dallam County

Physical Features: Prairie, broken by creeks; playas; sandy, loam soils; Rita Blanca National Grassland.

Economy: Agribusiness, dairies, cheese manufacturing, tourism.

History: Earliest Plains Apaches; displaced by Comanches and Kiowas. Ranching developed in late 19th century. Farming began after 1900. County created from Bexar District, 1876, organized 1891. Named for lawyer-editor James W. Dallam.

Race/Ethnicity: Anglo, 48%; Black, 1.2%; Hispanic, 46.2%; Asian, 0.4%; Other, 3.9%.

Vital Statistics, annual: Births, 157; deaths, 38; marriages, 304; divorces, 25.

Recreation: XIT museum, XIT rodeo in August, pheasant hunting, wildlife, grasslands.

Minerals: Petroleum.

Agriculture: A leader in production of grain (corn, wheat, sorghum). Cattle, hogs, dairies, potatoes, sunflowers, beans;

substantial irrigation. Market value $634.9 million.

DALHART (8,097, partly in Hartley County) county seat; government/services; agribusiness center for parts of Texas, New Mexico, Oklahoma; railroad; cheese plant; grain operations; junior college branch; hospital; prison.

Other towns include: **Kerrick** (35) and **Texline** (519).

Population	**7,053**
Change from 2010 (%)	5.2
Area (sq. mi.)	1,505.3
Land Area (sq. mi.)	1,503.3
Altitude (ft.)	3,655–4,780
Rainfall (in.)	17.6
Jan. mean min (°F)	18.3
July mean max (°F)	91.1
Civ. Labor	3,704
Unemployed (%)	2.6
Wages	$67,337,865
Per Capita Income	$64,756
Prop. Value	$1,851,197,600
Retail Sales	$130,804,819

Dallas County

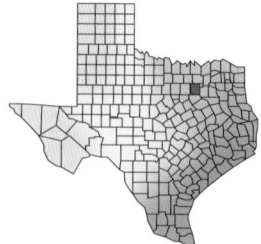

Physical Features: Mostly flat, heavy blackland soils, sandy clays in west; drains to Trinity River; Joe Pool Lake, White Rock Lake, Mountain Creek Lake, Lake Ray Hubbard, North Lake.

Economy: A national center for telecommunications, transportation, electronics manufacturing, data processing, conventions and trade shows; foreign-trade zone located at D/FW International Airport, U.S. Customs port of entry; government/services.

History: Caddoan area. Anglo-Americans began arriving in 1840. Antebellum slaveholding area. County created and organized in 1846 from Nacogdoches, Robertson counties; named for U.S. Vice President George Mifflin Dallas.

Race/Ethnicity: Anglo, 28.3%; Black, 22.6%; Hispanic, 40.2%; Asian, 6.6%; Other, 2%.

Vital Statistics, annual: Births, 40,112; deaths, 15,727; marriages, 17,207; divorces, 7,365.

Recreation: One of the state's top tourist destinations and one of the nation's most popular convention centers; State Fair, museums, zoo, West End shopping and

tourist district, historical sites, including Sixth Floor museum in the old Texas School Book Depository, site of the assassination of President Kennedy.

Also, the Morton H. Meyerson Symphony Center; performing arts; professional sports; Texas broadcast museum; lakes, state park, Audubon center; theme and amusement parks.

Minerals: Sand, gravel, oil and gas.

Agriculture: Horticultural crops, wheat, hay, corn, soybeans, horses. Market value $29.8 million.

Education: Southern Methodist University, University of Dallas, Dallas Baptist University, University of Texas at Dallas, University of North Texas at Dallas, University of Texas Southwestern Medical Center and many other education centers.

DALLAS (1,357,986) county seat; center of state's largest consolidated metropolitan area and third-largest city in Texas; D/FW International Airport is one of the world's busiest; headquarters for the U.S. Army and Air Force Exchange Service; Federal Reserve Bank; a leader in fashions and in computer operations; hospitals; many

Population	**2,647,576**
Change from 2010 (%)	11.8
Area (sq. mi.)	908.6
Land Area (sq. mi.)	871.3
Altitude (ft.)	350–870
Rainfall (in.)	37.6
Jan. mean min (°F)	37.3
July mean max (°F)	96.0
Civ. Labor	1,368,473
Unemployed (%)	6.2
Wages	$34,155,175,879
Per Capita Income	$62,782
Prop. Value	$374,526,283,216
Retail Sales	$46,609,884,668

hotels in downtown area offer adequate accommodations for most conventions.

GARLAND (242,493) varied manufacturing, community college branch, hospitals, performing arts center.

IRVING (245,941) finance, technology, tourism, distribution center; Boy Scout headquarters and museum; North Lake College; hospitals; parks; Dragon Boat Festival in May.

Other cities include: **Addison** (16,450) general aviation airport, theater center; **Balch Springs** (26,426); part [56,834] of **Carrollton** (139,248) residential community, distribution center, hospital; **Cedar Hill** (48,836) residential, light manufacturing, retail, distribution center, Northwood University, community college, state park, Penn Farm, Country Day on the Hill in October; **Cockrell Hill** (4,412); **Coppell** (41,250) distribution, varied manufacturing, office center, hike and bike trails; **DeSoto** (52,631) residential community,

light industry and distribution, hospitals; Toad Holler Creekfest in June.

Also: **Duncanville** (39,782) construction, health care, manufacturing; library, museums; Juneteenth celebration; **Farmers Branch** (41,093) distribution center, varied manufacturing, Brookhaven College, hospital; **Glenn Heights** (13,325, partly in Ellis County); most [133,445] of **Grand Prairie** (195,756) wholesale trade, aerospace, entertainment, hospital, library, Joe Pool Reservoir, Indian pow-wow in September, Lone Star horse-racing track; **Highland Park** (8,666); **Hutchins** (6,240) varied manufacturing; **Lancaster** (39,508) residential, industrial, distribution center, Cedar Valley College, Commemorative Air Force museum, Cold War air museum, Bear Creek nature preserve, depot, historic town square, Oktoberfest.

Also: **Mesquite** (142,030) shipping, rail port hub, retail, hospitals, arts center, championship rodeo July – September, rodeo parade in spring, Summer Sizzle

festival in June, community college, historical parks; most [86,403] of **Richardson** (124,695) telecommunications, software development, financial services, hospital, library, Wildflower Music Festival in May; **Rowlett** (67,818) residential, manufacturing, government/services, hospital, library, park, hike and bike trails; **Sachse** (26,126, partly in Collin County) commuting to Dallas, government/services, Fallfest in October; **Seagoville** (17,107) rural/suburban setting, federal prison, Seagofest in October; **Sunnyvale** (6,795) tile manufacturing, hospital, Samuell Farm, Sunnyfest on July 4; **University Park** (25,017); **Wilmer** (4,478).

Part of **Combine** (2,442) and part of **Ovilla** (4,167).

For explanation of sources, symbols and abbreviations, see p. 204, and foldout map.

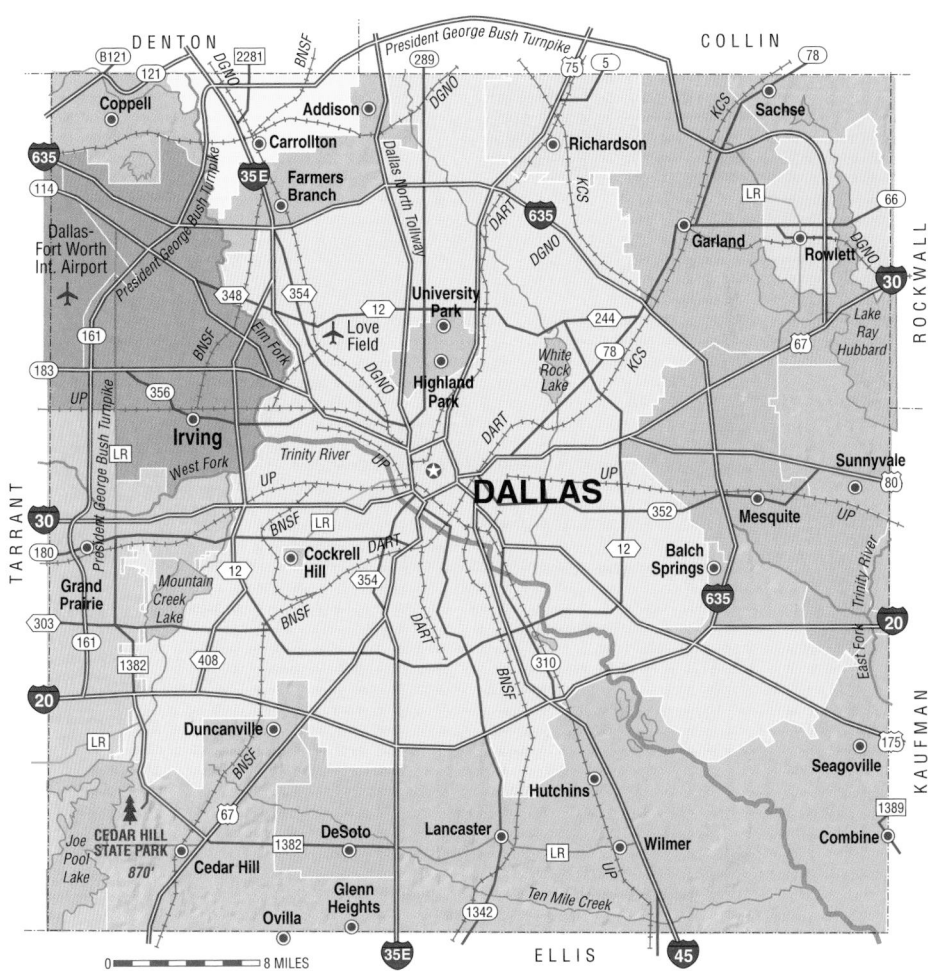

Dawson County

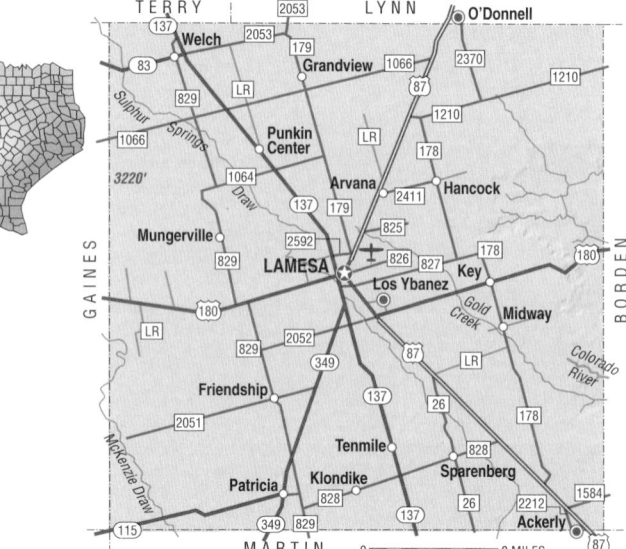

Physical Features: South Plains county, broken on the east; loam and sandy soils.

Economy: Agriculture, farm and gin equipment manufacturing, peanut plant, government/services.

History: Comanche, Kiowa area. Ranching developed in 1880s. Farming began after 1900. Hispanic population increased after 1940. County created from Bexar District, 1876, organized 1905; named for Nicholas M. Dawson, San Jacinto veteran.

Race/Ethnicity: Anglo, 34.7%; Black, 6.7%; Hispanic, 56.4%; Asian, 0.3%; Other, 1.6%.

Vital Statistics, annual: Births, 205; deaths, 129; marriages, 72; divorces, 37.

Recreation: Parks, museum, campground, part of Quanah Parker Trail; Lamesa poetry and music fest in May.

Minerals: Oil, natural gas.

Agriculture: Cotton, peanuts, sorghums, watermelons, alfalfa, grapes. 60,000 acres irrigated. Market value $121.3 million.

LAMESA (8,857) county seat; agribusiness, food processing, oil-field services, some manufacturing, computerized cotton-classing office; hospital, library; Howard College branch; prison unit; chicken-fried steak festival last weekend in April.

Other towns include: **Ackerly** (227, partly in Martin County), **Los Ybanez** (18) and **Welch** (230).

Also, **O'Donnell** (837, mostly in Lynn County) bust of Dan Blocker.

For explanation of sources, symbols and abbreviations, see p. 204, and foldout map.

Population..................... **12,720**	July mean max (°F).....................93.1
Change from 2010 (%)................-8.0	Civ. Labor............................4,522
Area (sq. mi.)........................ 902.1	Unemployment (%)........................7.7
Land Area (sq. mi.)................... 900.3	Wages $45,374,444
Altitude (ft.)...................2,580–3,220	Per Capita Income................$40,131
Rainfall (in.)............................19.1	Prop. Value $1,299,120,900
Jan. mean min (°F)....................26.0	Retail Sales.................. $211,886,234

Shops in the Erath County Courthouse Historic District. Photo by Renelibrary, CC by SA 4.0/Wikimedia Commons

Deaf Smith County

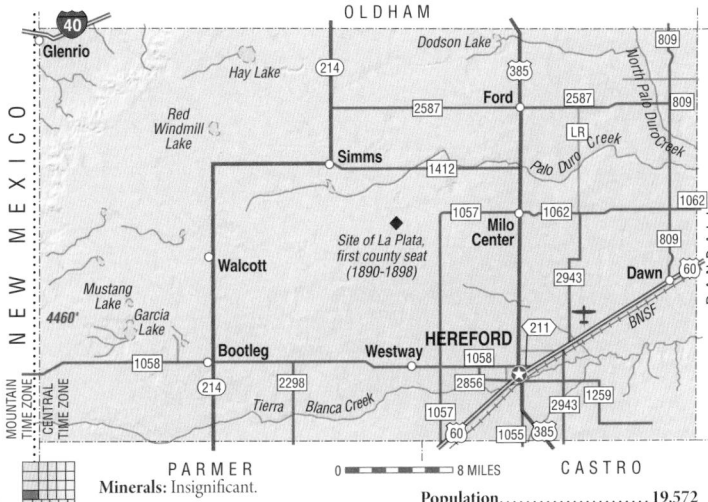

Physical Features: High Plains county, partly broken; chocolate and sandy loam soils; drains to Palo Duro and Tierra Blanca creeks.

Economy: Agriculture, varied industries, meat packing, offset printing.

History: Apache Indians, were displaced by Comanches and Kiowas. Ranching developed after the U.S. Army drove out the Indian tribes 1874-1875. Farming began after 1900. Hispanic settlement increased after 1950. County created in 1876 from the Bexar District; organized in 1890. Named for famed scout in Texas Revolution, Erastus "Deaf" Smith.

Race/Ethnicity: Anglo, 22.8%; Black, 0.9%; Hispanic, 74.7%; Asian, 0.3%; Other, 1%.

Vital Statistics, annual: Births, 348; deaths, 143; marriages, 139; divorces, 16.

Recreation: Museum, tours, POW camp chapel; Cinco de Mayo, Pioneer Days in May.

Minerals: Insignificant.

Agriculture: Leading agricultural county, dairies (second in number of milk cows), feedlot operations, cotton, wheat, sorghum, corn; 50 percent irrigated. Market value $1.6 billion, first in state.

HEREFORD (15,635) county seat; cattle feeding, agriculture, trucking; hospital; Amarillo College branch; aquatic center.

Other towns include: **Dawn** (52).

Population	19,572
Change from 2010 (%)	1.0
Area (sq. mi.)	1,498.4
Land Area (sq. mi.)	1,496.9
Altitude (ft.)	3,650–4,460
Rainfall (in.)	20.1
Jan. mean min (°F)	22.5
July mean max (°F)	91.4
Civ. Labor	8,892
Unemployed (%)	3.8
Wages	$98,459,221
Per Capita Income	$52,368
Prop. Value	$3,032,275,134
Retail Sales	$399,396,687

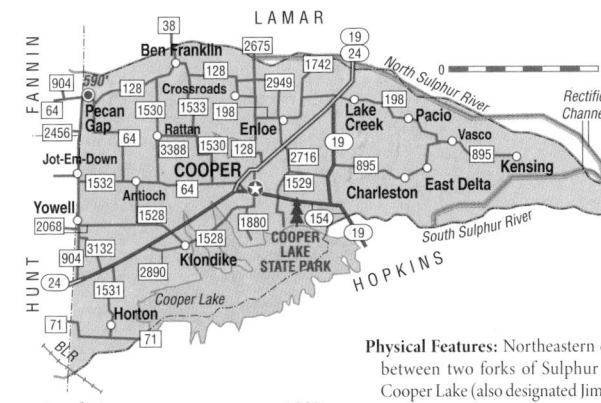

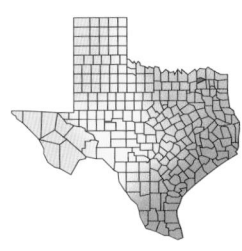

Delta County

Physical Features: Northeastern county between two forks of Sulphur River; Cooper Lake (also designated Jim Chapman Lake); black, sandy loam soils.

Economy: Agriculture, government/services, retirement location.

History: Caddo area, but disease, other tribes caused displacement around 1790. Anglo-Americans arrived in 1820s. County created from Lamar, Hopkins counties 1870. Greek letter delta origin of name, because of shape of the county.

Race/Ethnicity: Anglo, 79.5%; Black, 8%; Hispanic, 7.6%; Asian, 0.6%; Other, 4%.

Vital Statistics, annual: Births, 60; deaths, 73; marriages, 30; divorces, 23.

Recreation: Fishing, hunting; lake, state park; Cooper Chiggerfest in October.

Minerals: Insignificant.

Agriculture: Beef, hay, soybeans, wheat, corn, sorghum, cotton. Market value $36.3 million.

COOPER (1,933) county seat; commuters, industrial park, some manufacturing, agribusiness; museum, library; post office mural.

Other towns include: **Ben Franklin** (60), **Enloe** (90), **Klondike** (175), **Lake Creek** (55), and **Pecan Gap** (204).

Population	5,295
Change from 2010 (%)	1.2
Area (sq. mi.)	277.9
Land Area (sq. mi.)	256.8
Altitude (ft.)	322–590
Rainfall (in.)	44.80
Jan. mean min (°F)	30.0
July mean max (°F)	94.0
Civ. Labor	2,392
Unemployed (%)	4.8
Wages	$7,759,686
Per Capita Income	$40,622
Prop. Value	$740,154,595
Retail Sales	$57,583,027

For explanation of sources, symbols and abbreviations, see p. 204, and foldout map.

Denton County

Physical Features: North Texas county; partly hilly, draining to Elm Fork of Trinity River, Lewisville Lake, Ray Roberts Lake, Grapevine Lake; Blackland and Grand Prairie soils and terrain.

Economy: Varied industries, colleges, horse industry, tourism, government/services; part of Dallas-Fort Worth metropolitan area.

History: Land grant from Texas Congress 1841 for Peters colony. County created, organized, out of Fannin County in 1846; named for John B. Denton, pioneer Methodist minister.

Race/Ethnicity: Anglo, 58%; Black, 10.5%; Hispanic, 19.4%; Asian, 8.8%; Other, 3%.

Vital Statistics, annual: Births, 10,040; deaths, 3,374; marriages, 4,698; divorces, 2,763.

Recreation: Lake activities, parks; universities' cultural, athletic activities, including "Texas Women; A Celebration of History"; "First Ladies of Texas" collection of memorabilia; Little Chapel in the Woods; Texas Motor Speedway; Denton Jazz Festival in April.

Population....................	**886,563**
Change from 2010 (%)................	33.8
Area (sq. mi.)......................	953.0
Land Area (sq. mi.)..................	878.4
Altitude (ft.)......................	433–980
Rainfall (in.)......................	38.1
Jan. mean min (°F)..................	33.0

Minerals: Natural gas.

Education: University of North Texas, Texas Woman's University, and North Central Texas College.

Agriculture: Second in number of horses. Eggs, nurseries, turf, cattle; also, hay, sorghum, wheat, peanuts grown. Market value $123.2 million.

DENTON (142,944) county seat; universities, manufacturers of trucks (Peterbilt), medical, aviation; hospitals; historic courthouse square; storytelling festival in March.

LEWISVILLE (114,262) commuting to Dallas-Fort Worth, retail center, electronics and varied industries; hospital, library; Celtic Feis & Scottish Highland Games in March.

FLOWER MOUND (79,640) residential community, library, mound of native grasses, bike classic in spring.

Carrollton (139,248, also in Dallas County), hospital.

Other towns include: **Argyle** (4,555) horse farms/training, bluegrass festival in

July mean max (°F)..................	95.3
Civ. Labor........................	507,813
Unemployed (%)...................	4.9
Wages....................	$3,980,186,216
Per Capita Income...............	$59,414
Prop. Value.............	$134,731,479,596
Retail Sales.............	$12,121,926,016

March; **Aubrey** (4,855) horse farms/training, cabinet construction, museum, peanut festival early October; **Bartonville** (1,814); **Copper Canyon** (1,515); **Corinth** (23,304); **Cross Roads** (1,618); **Draper** (33); **Dish** (467); **Double Oak** (3,234); **Hackberry** (1,128); **Hebron** (449); **Hickory Creek** (4,425); **Highland Village** (17,300); **Justin** (4,320); **Krugerville** (2,013); **Krum** (5,589) commuters, old grain mill, heritage museum, North Pole Days in December; **Lake Dallas** (8,399) light manufacturing, marina, historic downtown, Mardi Gras.

Also: **Lakewood Village** (731); **Lantana** (8,473); **Little Elm** (53,126) real estate, retail, lake activities/beach area, summer concert series; **Northlake** (3,435); **Oak Point** (4,487); **Pilot Point** (4,590) light manufacturing, horse ranches, Fireman's Fest in April; **Ponder** (2,280); **Providence** (6,414); **Roanoke** (9,012); **Sanger** (9,388) distribution center, commuters, government/services, lakes, Sellabration in September; **Shady Shores** (3,200); **The Colony** (46,686) retail, business offices, industrial firms; parks, nature trails, salute to veterans on Veterans Day; and **Trophy Club** (13,947) commuters, retail.

Part [31,056] of **Dallas**, part [9,502] **Fort Worth**, part [77,073] **Frisco**, part [6,090] **Plano**, and small parts of **Coppell, Celina, Prosper, Southlake, Westlake.**

DeWitt County

Physical Features: Gulf Coastal Plain county drained by Guadalupe and tributaries; rolling to level; waxy, loam, sandy soils.

Economy: Oil, tourism.

History: Coahuiltecan area, then Karankawas and other tribes, finally the Comanches. Mexican and Anglo-American settlers arrived in the 1820s. County created, organized, in 1846 from Gonzales, Goliad, and Victoria counties; named for Green DeWitt, colonizer.

Race/Ethnicity: Anglo, 53.8%; Black, 8.1%; Hispanic, 35.8%; Asian, 0.2%; Other, 1.9%.

Vital Statistics, annual: Births, 270; deaths, 253; marriages, 136; divorces, 86.

Recreation: Hunting, fishing, historic homes, museums, wildflowers, German dance halls.

Minerals: Oil and natural gas, gravel.

Agriculture: Cattle, pecans, row crops. Market value $38.7 million.

CUERO (7,482) county seat; medical/hospital, government/services, retail, ranching, oil and gas; Turkeyfest in October.

YORKTOWN (2,112) oil and gas, agriculture; library, museum, park, hike/bike trail; Western Days in October.

Other towns include: **Hochheim** (70), **Meyersville** (110), **Nordheim** (304), **Thomaston** (45), **Westhoff** (410).

Part [2,118] of **Yoakum** (5,940 total) cattle, leather, meat processing, hospital, museum, Tom Tom festival in June.

For explanation of sources, symbols and abbreviations, see p. 204, and foldout map.

Population	20,611
Change from 2010 (%)	2.6
Area (sq. mi.)	910.5
Land Area (sq. mi.)	909.0
Altitude (ft.)	100–550
Rainfall (in.)	35.7
Jan. mean min (°F)	39.1
July mean max (°F)	96.5
Civ. Labor	8,933
Unemployed (%)	5.8
Wages	$83,731,638
Per Capita Income	$59,389
Prop. Value	$7,642,246,639
Retail Sales	$224,281,170

The Hurley Administration building on the campus of the University of North Texas in Denton. The school has historically been known for its jazz music department. Photo by Michael Barera, CC by SA 4.0/Wikimedia Commons

Dickens County

Physical Features: West Texas county; broken land, Caprock in northwest; sandy, chocolate, red soils; drains to Croton, Duck creeks.

Economy: Agriculture, government services/prison unit, hunting leases, wind farms.

History: Comanches driven out by U.S. Army 1874-75. Ranching and some farming began in late 1880s. County created 1876, from Bexar District; organized 1891; named for Alamo hero who is variously listed as James R. Demkins or Dimpkins and J. Dickens.

Race/Ethnicity: Anglo, 61.4%; Black, 4.4%; Hispanic, 31.7%; Asian, 0.7%; Other, 1.6%.

Vital Statistics, annual: Births, 25; deaths, 26; marriages, 10; divorces, 7.

Recreation: Hunting, fishing; Soldiers Mound site, Dickens Springs; downtown Spur.

Minerals: Oil, gas.

Agriculture: Cattle, horses, cotton, hay, small grains. Some irrigation. Market value $26.9 million. Hunting leases important.

DICKENS (253) county seat, market for ranching country.

SPUR (1,173) farming, ranching, hunting, government/services; museum; homecoming in October.

Other towns include: **Afton** (15) and **McAdoo** (75).

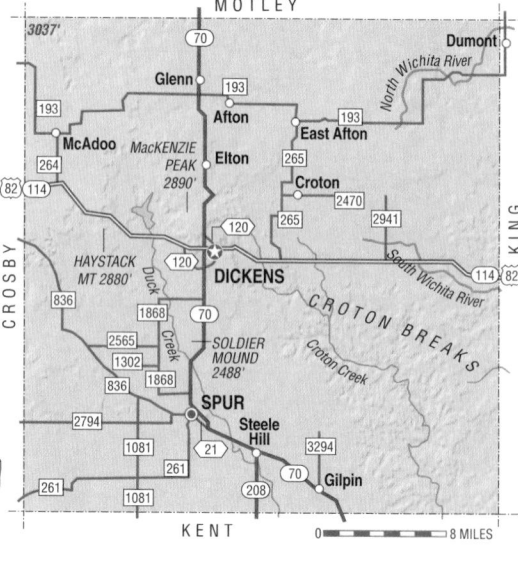

Population..........................	**2,119**	July mean max (°F).....................	94.7
Change from 2010 (%)...............	-13.3	Civ. Labor..............................	676
Area (sq. mi.)..........................	905.2	Unemployed (%)........................	6.1
Land Area (sq. mi.)...................	901.7	Wages.............................	$4,232,504
Altitude (ft.)....................	1,800–3,037	Per Capita Income................	$33,843
Rainfall (in.).............................	22.8	Prop. Value..................	$738,611,052
Jan. mean min (°F).....................	26.6	Retail Sales...................	$16,012,258

Physical Features: Southwest county; level to rolling; much brush; sandy, loam, red soils; drained by Nueces River.

Economy: Government/services, agribusiness, petroleum products, tourism.

History: Coahuiltecan area, later Comanches. John Townsend, a black man from Nacogdoches, led the first attempt at settlement before the Civil War. Texas Rangers forced out the Comanches in 1877. Mexican migration increased after 1910. County created 1858 from Bexar, Maverick, Uvalde, Webb counties; organized

Dimmit County

1880. Named for Philip Dimmitt of the Texas Revolution; law misspelled name.

Race/Ethnicity: Anglo, 12.4%; Black, 0.6%; Hispanic, 85.8%; Asian, 0.4%; Other, 0.5%.

Vital Statistics, annual: Births, 173; deaths, 109; marriages, 62; divorces, 3.

Recreation: Hunting, fishing, campsites,

wildlife area; winter haven for tourists; old jailhouse museum.

Minerals: Oil, natural gas.

Agriculture: Onions, pecans, cantaloupes, olives, tomatoes, tangerines, cattle, goats, horses, hay. Market value $28.5 million.

CARRIZO SPRINGS (5,567) county seat; agribusiness center, feedlot, food processing, oil, gas processing, hunting center; hospital; historic Baptist church; Mt. Hope cemetery with 17 Texas Rangers buried; bull riding event in April.

Other towns include: **Asherton** (1,018), **Big Wells** (694) Cinco de Mayo, and **Catarina** (100) Camino Real festival in April.

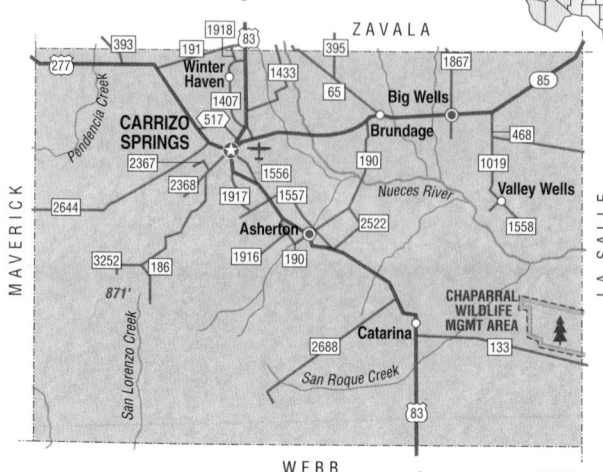

Population..........................	**9,709**
Change from 2010 (%)................	-2.9
Area (sq. mi.)......................	1,334.5
Land Area (sq. mi.).................	1,328.9
Altitude (ft.)......................	410–871
Rainfall (in.).........................	19.8
Jan. mean min (°F).....................	40.5
July mean max (°F).....................	97.8
Civ. Labor............................	6,017
Unemployed (%)........................	6.2
Wages........................	$76,251,324
Per Capita Income................	$38,800
Prop. Value...............	$8,032,398,170
Retail Sales.................	$125,796,131

For explanation of sources, symbols and abbreviations, see p. 204, and foldout map.

Donley County

Physical Features: Panhandle county bisected by Red River Salt Fork; Greenbelt Lake, Lelia Lake; rolling to level; clay, loam, sandy soils.

Economy: Agribusiness, government/services, tourism.

History: Apaches displaced by Kiowas and Comanches, who were driven out in 1874-75 by U.S. Army. Methodist colony from New York settled in 1878. County created in 1876, organized 1882, out of Bexar District; named for Texas Supreme Court Justice S.P. Donley.

Race/Ethnicity: Anglo, 81.1%; Black, 6.4%; Hispanic, 10.1%; Asian, 0.3%; Other, 1.8%.

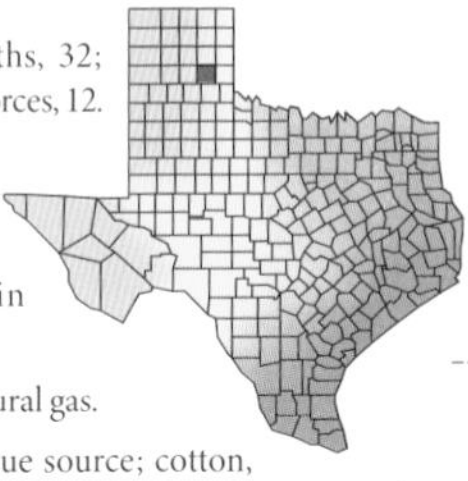

Vital Statistics, annual: Births, 32; deaths, 51; marriages, 24; divorces, 12.

Recreation: Lake, hunting, fishing, camping, water sports; Col. Goodnight Chuckwagon cook-off in September.

Minerals: Small amount of natural gas.

Agriculture: Cattle top revenue source; cotton, peanuts, alfalfa, wheat, hay, melons; 15,000 acres irrigated. Market value $94.2 million.

CLARENDON (1,772) county seat; higher education, agribusiness, tourism, medical center clinic; Saints Roost museum, library, junior college; restored historic buildings.

Other towns include: **Hedley** (287) cotton festival in October, **Howardwick** (368), and **Lelia Lake** (70).

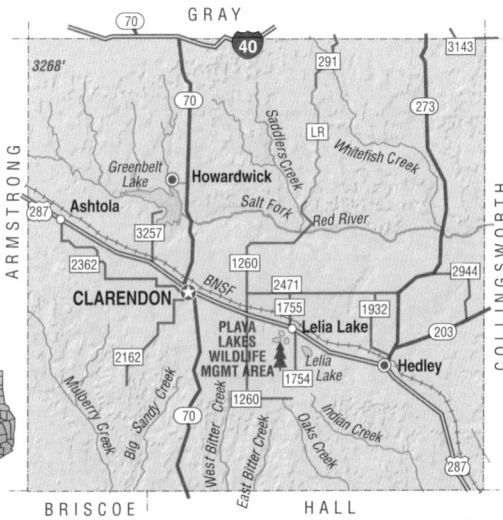

Population........................ **3,228**	July mean max (°F)....................94.7
Change from 2010 (%)................-12.2	Civ. Labor 1,426
Area (sq. mi.)........................ 933.1	Unemployed (%)........................4.3
Land Area (sq. mi.)................... 929.9	Wages $8,065,758
Altitude (ft.) 2,080–3,268	Per Capita Income $45,531
Rainfall (in.)...........................24.0	Prop. Value $899,367,510
Jan. mean min (°F).....................23.8	Retail Sales $44,330,694

The county courthouse for Donley, in downtown Clarendon. Photo by Avalliso, CC by SA 4.0/Wikimedia Commons

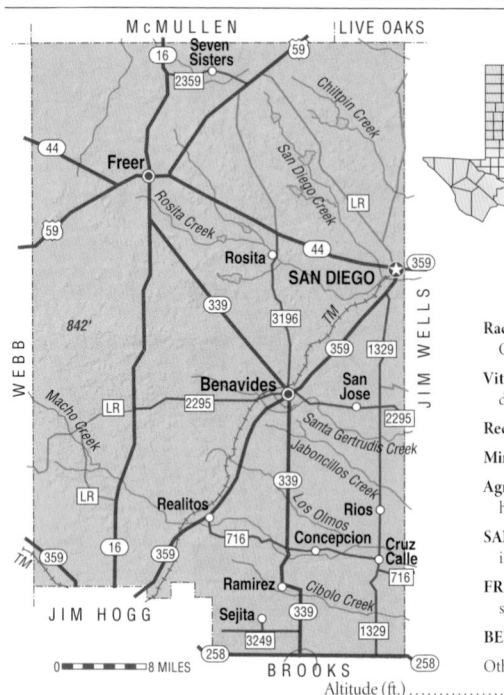

Duval County

Physical Features: South Texas county; level to hilly, brushy in most areas; varied soils.

Economy: Ranching, petroleum, tourism, government/services.

History: Coahuiltecans, displaced by Comanche bands. Mexican settlement began in 1812. County created from Live Oak, Nueces, and Starr counties in 1858, organized in 1876; named for Burr H. Duval, a victim of Goliad massacre.

Race/Ethnicity: Anglo, 10.4%; Black, 0.6%; Hispanic, 88.2%; Asian, 0.1%; Other, 0.4%.

Vital Statistics, annual: Births, 181; deaths, 149; marriages, 68; divorces, 4.

Recreation: Hunting, tourist crossroads.

Minerals: Oil, gas, salt, sand, gravel, uranium.

Agriculture: Most income from beef cattle; grains, cotton, vegetables, hay, dairy. Market value $11.0 million.

SAN DIEGO (4,217, part [879] in Jim Wells County) county seat; ranching, oil field, tourist center; hospital.

FREER (2,632) oil and gas, construction, ranching and hunting; rattlesnake roundup in May.

BENAVIDES (1,239) serves truck-farming area.

Other towns include: Concepcion (57) and Realitos (167).

Population	10,907	Altitude (ft.)	180–842	Unemployed (%)	11.4
Change from 2010 (%)	-7.4	Rainfall (in.)	26.0	Wages	$31,617,872
Area (sq. mi.)	1,795.6	Jan. mean min (°F)	43.1	Per Capita Income	$39,029
Land Area (sq. mi.)	1,793.5	July mean max (°F)	97.0	Prop. Value	$2,995,898,064
		Civ. Labor	4,622	Retail Sales	$46,351,098

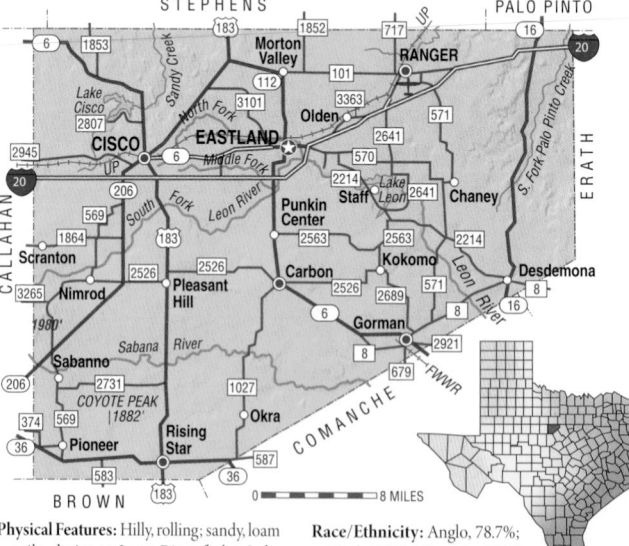

Eastland County

Population	18,307
Change from 2010 (%)	-1.5
Area (sq. mi.)	931.9
Land Area (sq. mi.)	926.5
Altitude (ft.)	960–1,980
Rainfall (in.)	29.0
Jan. mean min (°F)	28.8
July mean max (°F)	94.6
Civ. Labor	6,975
Unemployed (%)	6.6
Wages	$79,249,434
Per Capita Income	$78,826
Prop. Value	$3,102,327,320
Retail Sales	$325,525,149

EASTLAND (4,010) county seat; tourism, government/services, petroleum industries, varied manufacturing; hospital, library; Old Ripfest in September.

CISCO (3,834) manufacturing, distribution, oilfield services; Conrad Hilton's first hotel restored, museums; community college; folklife festival in April.

RANGER (2,444) oil center, varied manufacturing, junior college.

Other towns include: Carbon (270) livestock equipment manufacturing; Desdemona (180); Gorman (1,034) peanut processing, agribusiness, hospital; Olden (113), and Rising Star (820) cap manufacturing, plant nursery; Octoberfest.

Physical Features: Hilly, rolling; sandy, loam soils; drains to Leon River forks; Lake Cisco, Lake Leon.

Economy: Agribusiness, education, petroleum industries.

History: Plains Indian area. Frank Sánchez among first settlers in 1850s. County created from Bosque, Coryell, Travis counties, 1858, organized 1873; named for W.M. Eastland, Mier Expedition casualty.

Race/Ethnicity: Anglo, 78.7%; Black, 1.8%; Hispanic, 17.2%; Asian, 0.4%; Other, 1.7%.

Vital Statistics, annual: Births, 200; deaths, 265; marriages, 147; divorces, 53.

Recreation: Hunting, water sports; museums; historic sites and displays.

Minerals: Oil, natural gas.

Agriculture: Beef cattle, hay, cotton. Some 9,000 acres irrigated. Market value $23.5 million.

Ector County

Physical Features: West Texas county; level to rolling, some sand dunes; meteor crater; desert vegetation.

Economy: Center for Permian Basin oil field operations, plastics, electric generation plants.

History: First settlers in late 1880s. Oil boom in 1926. County created from Tom Green County, 1887; organized 1891; named for jurist M.D. Ector.

Race/Ethnicity: Anglo, 30.7%; Black, 4.4%; Hispanic, 62.2%; Asian, 1%; Other, 1.5%.

Vital Statistics, annual: Births, 2,991; deaths, 1,196; marriages, 1262; divorces, 327.

Recreation: Globe Theatre replica; presidential museum and Bush childhood home; ranching museum, art institute; second-largest U.S. meteor crater, museum; Stonehenge replica.

Minerals: More than 3 billion barrels of oil produced since 1926; gas, cement, stone.

Agriculture: Beef cattle, horses are chief producers; pecans, hay, poultry; minor irrigation. Market value $3.4 million.

Education: University of Texas of Permian Basin, Texas Tech University Health Sciences Center, Odessa (junior) College.

ODESSA (126,729, part [2,166] in Midland County) county seat; oil and gas, manufacturing, ranching; hospitals; cultural center; Permian Basin Fair and Expo in September.

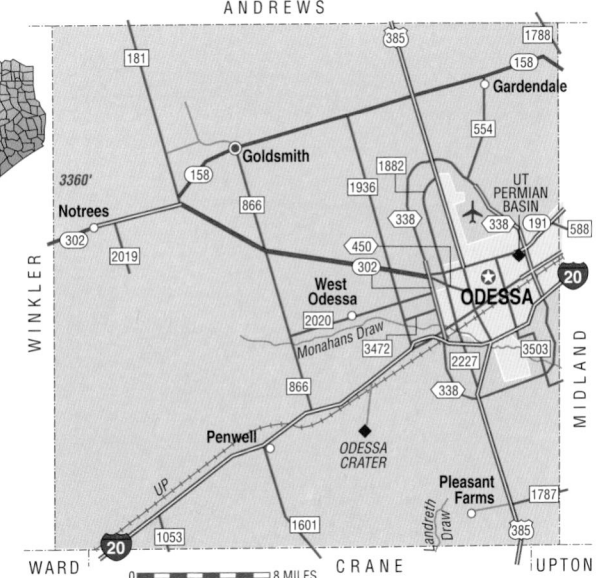

Other towns include: **Gardendale** (1,959), **Goldsmith** (286), **Notrees** (20), **Penwell** (41), and **West Odessa** (29,224).

For explanation of sources, symbols and abbreviations, see p. 204, and foldout map.

Population.................... 167,383		July mean max (°F)....................94.8
Change from 2010 (%)................22.1		Civ. Labor............................78,715
Area (sq. mi.)........................ 901.8		Unemployed (%).......................9.9
Land Area (sq. mi.).................. 897.7		Wages $1,010,325,242
Altitude (ft.) 2,780–3,360		Per Capita Income $50,161
Rainfall (in.)...........................13.5		Prop. Value $18,856,673,701
Jan. mean min (°F)....................31.8		Retail Sales $3,409,649,399

Edwards County

Physical Features: Rolling, hilly, with caves and spring-fed streams; rocky, thin soils; drained by Llano, Nueces rivers; varied timber.

Economy: Hunting leases, tourism, oil, gas production, ranching.

History: Apache area. First land sold in 1876. County created from Bexar District, 1858; organized 1883; named for Nacogdoches empresario Hayden Edwards.

Race/Ethnicity: Anglo, 43.3%; Black, 0.6%; Hispanic, 55.1%; Asian, 0.1%; Other, 0.7%.

Vital Statistics, annual: Births, 22; deaths, 33; mmarriages, 7; divorces, 1.

Recreation: Hunting, fishing; scenic drives; Devil's Sinkhole, Kickapoo Cavern state parks.

Minerals: Gas.

Agriculture: Second in number of goats. Mohair-wool production, Angora goats (first in numbers), sheep, cattle, some pecans. Market value $10.9 million. Cedar for oil.

ROCKSPRINGS (1,149) county seat; government/services, hunting, ranching, oil and gas, hunters' barbecue in November.

Other towns include: **Barksdale** (100).

Population........................ 1,959		July mean max (°F)....................90.4
Change from 2010 (%)................-2.1		Civ. Labor 1,357
Area (sq. mi.)....................... 2,119.9		Unemployed (%).......................4.2
Land Area (sq. mi.)................. 2,117.9		Wages $8,299,913
Altitude (ft.) 1,480–2,415		Per Capita Income $45,429
Rainfall (in.)...........................26.6		Prop. Value $2,318,827,959
Jan. mean min (°F)....................36.6		Retail Sales $24,104,267

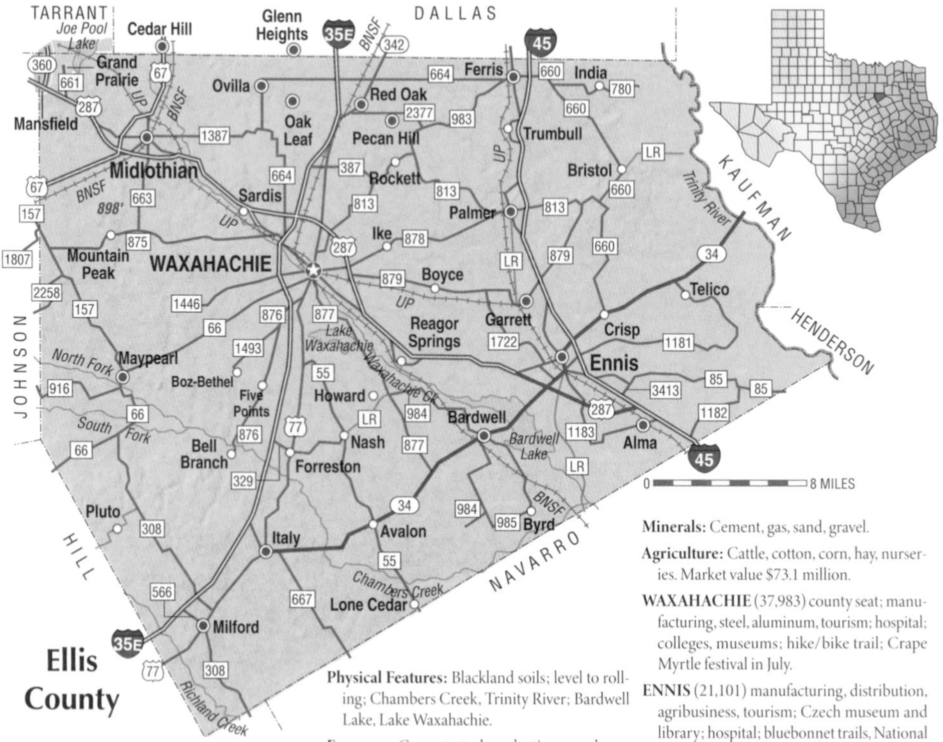

Ellis County

Map labels

TARRANT · Joe Pool Lake · Cedar Hill · Glenn Heights · DALLAS · 35E · BNSF · 342 · 45 · 360 · Grand Prairie · 661 · 67 · 664 · Ferris · 660 · India · 780 · Ovilla · Red Oak · 660 · Mansfield · 287 · 1387 · Oak Leaf · 2377 · 983 · Trumbull · LR · Midlothian · 664 · Pecan Hill · 387 · Rockett · Bristol · 660 · 67 · BNSF · 663 · Sardis · 813 · Palmer · 813 · 157 · 898' · 813 · Ike · 878 · 660 · 34 · 875 · 287 · Boyce · 879 · Telico · WAXAHACHIE · 879 · LR · Mountain Peak · 2258 · 1446 · 876 · 877 · Reagor Springs · Garrett · Crisp · 1181 · 157 · 66 · Lake Waxahachie · 1722 · 1493 · Ennis · 1231 · JOHNSON · North Fork · Maypearl · 55 · 3413 · 85 · 85 · 916 · Boz-Bethel · Five Points · Howard · 984 · Bardwell · 287 · 1182 · 66 · South Fork · 876 · 77 · Nash · 877 · Bardwell Lake · 1183 · Alma · 66 · Bell Branch · Forreston · LR · 45 · 329 · Pluto · 34 · 984 · BNSF · 0 ___ 8 MILES · 308 · Italy · Avalon · 985 · Byrd · 566 · 55 · NAVARRO · 667 · Lone Cedar · Chambers Creek · 35E · Milford · 77 · 308 · Richland Creek · HILL · KAUFMAN · Trinity River · HENDERSON

Population.................... 188,464

Change from 2010 (%)................26.0
Area (sq. mi.)........................951.8
Land Area (sq. mi.)...................935.5
Altitude (ft.).....................300–898
Rainfall (in.).........................39.1
Jan. mean min (°F)...................33.8
July mean max (°F)...................93.9
Civ. Labor........................364,592
Unemployed (%).........................6.9
Wages.................... $3,495,606,899
Per Capita Income............... $37,715
Prop. Value.............. $24,935,423,576
Retail Sales................ $2,354,874,161

Physical Features: Blackland soils; level to rolling; Chambers Creek, Trinity River; Bardwell Lake, Lake Waxahachie.

Economy: Cement, steel production, warehousing and distribution, government/services; many residents work in Dallas.

History: Tonkawa area. Part of Peters colony settled in 1843. County created 1849, organized 1850, from Navarro County. Named for Richard Ellis, president of convention that declared Texas' independence.

Race/Ethnicity: Anglo, 61%; Black, 9.8%; Hispanic, 26.6%; Asian, 0.4%; Other, 1.9%.

Vital Statistics, annual: Births, 2,126; deaths, 1,209; marriages, 1,140; divorces, 337.

Recreation: Lakes, fishing, hunting; bluebonnet trails, historic homes, courthouse; Medieval-theme Scarborough Faire in spring.

Minerals: Cement, gas, sand, gravel.

Agriculture: Cattle, cotton, corn, hay, nurseries. Market value $73.1 million.

WAXAHACHIE (37,983) county seat; manufacturing, steel, aluminum, tourism; hospital; colleges, museums; hike/bike trail; Crape Myrtle festival in July.

ENNIS (21,101) manufacturing, distribution, agribusiness, tourism; Czech museum and library; hospital; bluebonnet trails, National Polka Festival in May.

MIDLOTHIAN (34,164) cement plants, steel plant, distribution center, manufacturing; heritage park, cabin; spring fling in April.

Other towns include: **Alma** (402); **Avalon** (400); **Bardwell** (726); **Bristol** (736); **Ferris** (2,987); **Forreston** (400); **Garrett** (900); **Howard** (60); **Italy** (1,957); **Maypearl** (1,116); **Milford** (767); **Oak Leaf** (1,442); **Ovilla** (4,320); **Palmer** (2,203); **Pecan Hill** (706); and **Red Oak** (13,648) manufacturing, Founders Day in September.

Also, **Glenn Heights** (13,377, mostly in Dallas County). Part of **Grand Prairie** and **Mansfield**.

A tank at the Fort Bliss Main Post Historic District in El Paso. Photo by ForgottenColorado, CC by SA 4.0/Wikipedia Commons

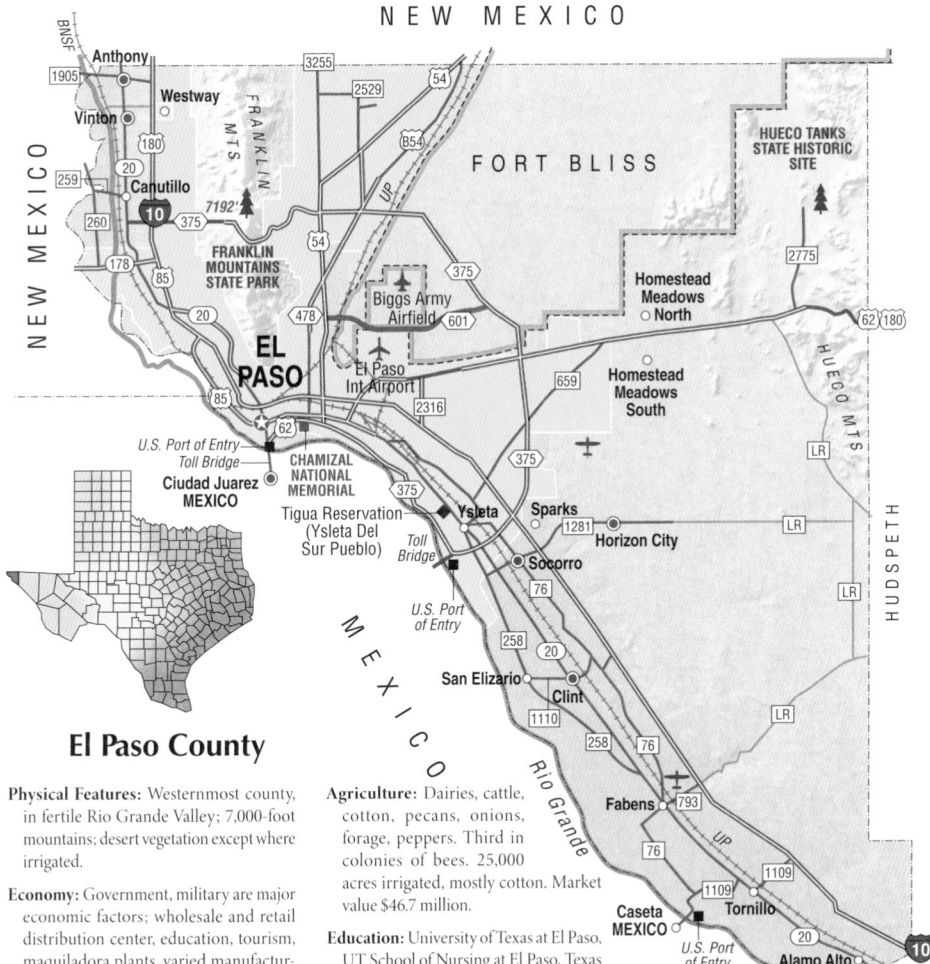

El Paso County

Physical Features: Westernmost county, in fertile Rio Grande Valley; 7,000-foot mountains; desert vegetation except where irrigated.

Economy: Government, military are major economic factors; wholesale and retail distribution center, education, tourism, maquiladora plants, varied manufacturing, oil refining, cotton, food processing.

History: Various Indian tribes inhabited the valley before Spanish civilization arrived in the late 1650s. Agriculture in area dates to at least 100 A.D. Spanish along with Tigua and Piro tribes fleeing Santa Fe uprising of 1680 sought refuge in the area. County created from the Bexar District in 1849; organized in 1850; named for historic pass (Paso del Norte), lowest all-weather pass through the southern Rocky Mountains.

Race/Ethnicity: Anglo, 13%; Black, 3.4%; Hispanic, 80.5%; Asian, 1.2%; Other, 1.7%.

Vital Statistics, annual: Births, 13,521; deaths, 5,296; marriages, 6,809; divorces, 98.

Recreation: Gateway to Mexico; Chamizal Museum; major tourist center; December Sun Carnival with football game; state parks, mountain tramway, missions and other historic sites.

Minerals: Production of cement, stone, sand and gravel.

Agriculture: Dairies, cattle, cotton, pecans, onions, forage, peppers. Third in colonies of bees. 25,000 acres irrigated, mostly cotton. Market value $46.7 million.

Education: University of Texas at El Paso, UT School of Nursing at El Paso, Texas Tech University Health Sciences Center, El Paso Community College.

EL PASO (686,265) county seat; Texas' sixth-largest city and metro area, largest U.S. city on Mexican border. A center for government operations. Federal installations include Fort Bliss, home of the U.S. Army 1st Armored Division, William Beaumont General Hospital, and La Tuna federal prison.

Manufactured products include clothing, electronics, auto equipment, plastics; trade and distribution; refining; processing oil, food, cotton, and other farm products. Hospitals; museums; convention center; theater, symphony orchestra.

Other towns include: **Anthony** (5,640 in Texas, 9,310 in New Mexico); **Canutillo** (7,073); **Clint** (1,163); **Fabens** (8,500); **Homestead Meadows North** (5,571); **Homestead Meadows South** (7,600); **Horizon City** (19,733); **Prado Verde** (266); **San Elizario** (14,313), red & green chile war festival in September; **Socorro** (34,740) settled in 1680; **Sparks** (5,501);

Tornillo (1,540); **Vinton** (2,042); **Westway** (4,297), and **Ysleta** (now within El Paso) settled in 1680, called the oldest town in Texas.

And, **Fort Bliss** (9,137).

For explanation of sources, symbols and abbreviations, see p. 204, and foldout map.

Population......................	**852,224**
Change from 2010 (%).................	6.4
Area (sq. mi.).......................	1,015.0
Land Area (sq. mi.).................	1,012.7
Altitude (ft.).....................	3,520–7,192
Rainfall (in.).............................	9.7
Jan. mean min (°F).....................	32.5
July mean max (°F).....................	94.7
Civ. Labor............................	94,893
Unemployed (%)........................	4.9
Wages	$714,885,134
Per Capita Income................	$45,968
Prop. Value	$57,122,910,826
Retail Sales...............	$11,436,167,636

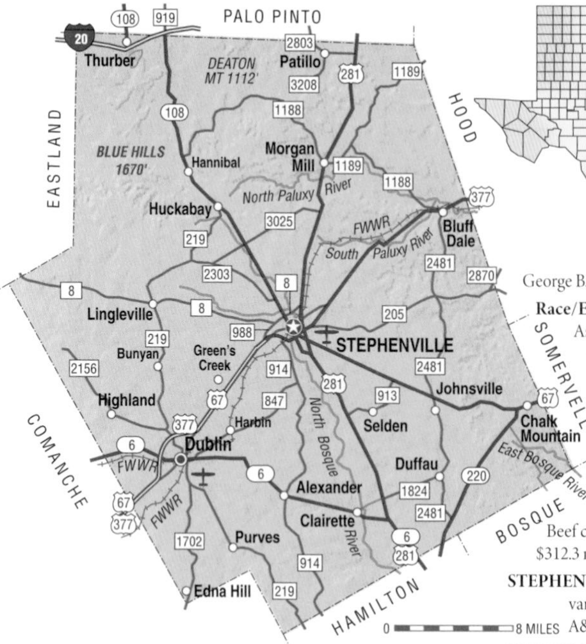

Erath County

Physical Features: On Rolling Plains; clay loam, sandy soils; drains to Bosque, Paluxy rivers.

Economy: Agricultural, industrial, and educational enterprises.

History: Caddo and Anadarko Indians were moved to Oklahoma in 1860. Anglo-American settlement began 1854-1855. County created from Bosque, Coryell counties in 1856, organized the same year; named for George B. Erath, Texas Revolution figure.

Race/Ethnicity: Anglo, 73.8%; Black, 1.2%; Hispanic, 22.5%; Asian, 0.6%; Other, 1.5%.

Vital Statistics, annual: Births, 448; deaths, 323; marriages, 285; divorces, 140.

Recreation: Old courthouse, log cabins, museums; nearby lakes, hunting, Bosque River Park; university fine arts center; Dairy Fest in June.

Minerals: Gas, oil.

Agriculture: Dairies (first in number of milk cows). Beef cattle, horticulture industry, horses raised. Market value $312.3 million.

STEPHENVILLE (21,245) county seat; Tarleton State University, varied manufacturing; hospital, mental health center; Texas A&M research and extension center.

DUBLIN (3,562) dairies, food processing, varied manufacturing, tourism; library; old Dr Pepper plant; grist mill; St. Patrick's Day celebration.

Other towns include: **Bluff Dale** (400); **Lingleville** (100); **Morgan Mill** (206); **Thurber** (48) former coal-mining town; Gordon Center for Industrial History of Texas.

Population		43,042
Change from 2010 (%)		13.6
Area (sq. mi.)		1,089.8
Land Area (sq. mi.)		1,083.1
Altitude (ft.)		820–1,670
Rainfall (in.)		31.5
Jan. mean min (°F)		31.0
July mean max (°F)		94.2
Civ. Labor		19,430
Unemployed (%)		4.9
Wages		$177,453,265
Per Capita Income		$40,462
Prop. Value		$6,910,048,560
Retail Sales		$630,238,007

Falls County

Physical Features: On rolling prairie; bisected by Brazos; blackland, red, sandy loam soils; mineral springs.

Economy: Government/services, agribusiness, varied manufacturing.

History: Wacos, Tawokanis, Anadarkos in conflict with Comanches. Cherokees alone in area 1830 until 1835 when Anglo-American settlement began. Antebellum slave-holding area. County created, organized, 1850 from Limestone, Milam counties; named for Brazos River falls.

Race/Ethnicity: Anglo, 50.6%; Black, 22.7%; Hispanic, 23.9%; Asian, 0.3%; Other, 2.3%.

Vital Statistics, annual: Births, 207; deaths, 178; marriages, 85; divorces, 16.

Recreation: Fishing, hunting, camping; Highland Mansion and Falls on the Brazos.

Minerals: Gravel, sand, oil.

Agriculture: Stocker cattle, cow-calf operations, corn, grain sorghum, soybeans, cotton, wheat, oats (first in acreage), goats, sheep, horses. Some cotton irrigated. Market value $157.9 million.

MARLIN (5,577) county seat; agriculture, prison; hospital; museum.

Other towns include: **Chilton** (958); **Golinda** (592); **Lott** (773); **Reagan** (300); **Rosebud** (1,345) feed, fertilizer processing, clothing manufactured; **Satin** (86). Part of **Bruceville-Eddy** (1,693).

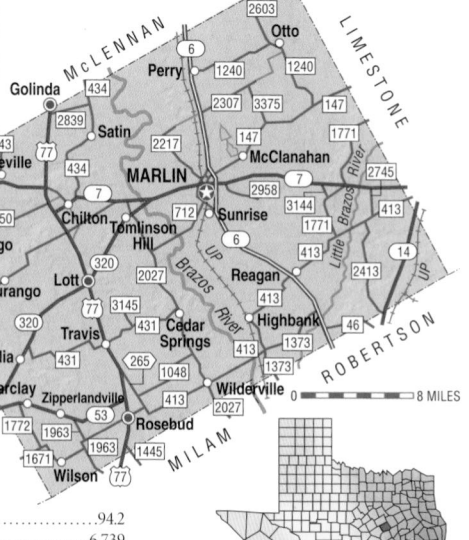

Population		17,401
Change from 2010 (%)		-2.6
Area (sq. mi.)		773.8
Land Area (sq. mi.)		765.5
Altitude (ft.)		282–731
Rainfall (in.)		38.5
Jan. mean min (°F)		35.4
July mean max (°F)		94.2
Civ. Labor		6,739
Unemployed (%)		5.4
Wages		$34,093,746
Per Capita Income		$35,258
Prop. Value		$2,242,390,726
Retail Sales		$128,318,538

Fannin County

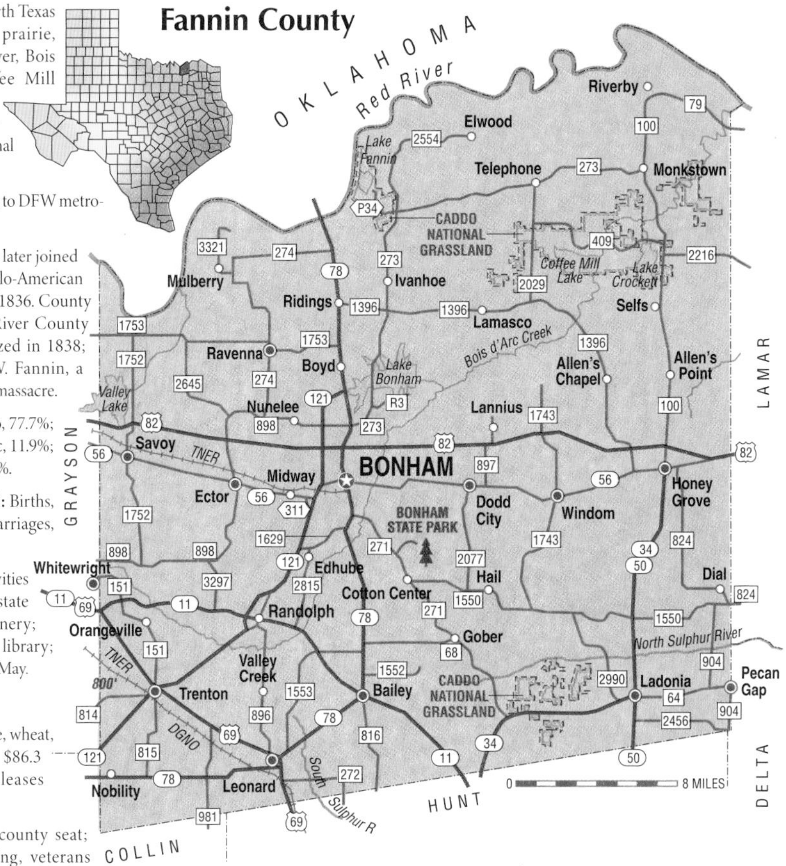

Physical Features: North Texas county of rolling prairie, drained by Red River, Bois d'Arc Creek; Coffee Mill Lake, Lake Bonham, Valley Lake; mostly blackland soils; national grasslands.

Economy: Commuting to DFW metroplex, agribusiness.

History: Caddoes who later joined with Cherokees. Anglo-American settlement began in 1836. County created from Red River County in 1837 and organized in 1838; named for James W. Fannin, a victim of the Goliad massacre.

Race/Ethnicity: Anglo, 77.7%; Black, 6.8%; Hispanic, 11.9%; Asian, 0.4%; Other, 3%.

Vital Statistics, annual: Births, 353; deaths, 458; marriages, 211; divorces, 127.

Recreation: Water activities on lakes; hunting; state park, fossil beds; winery; Sam Rayburn home, library; Bois D'Arc festival in May.

Minerals: Sand.

Agriculture: Beef cattle, wheat, corn. Market value $86.3 million. Hunting leases important.

BONHAM (10,786) county seat; varied manufacturing, veterans hospital/private hospital, state jail; Sam Rayburn birthday celebration in January.

Other towns include: **Bailey** (315); **Dodd City** (395); **Ector** (740); **Gober** (146); **Honey Grove** (1,732) agribusiness center, varied manufacturing, tourism, historic buildings, library, Davy Crockett Festival in October; **Ivanhoe** (110).

Also: **Ladonia** (632) restored historical downtown, tourism, varied manufacturing, commuters, rodeo; **Leonard** (2,092) government/services, power plant, retail, light industry, museums, community picnic in July; **Randolph** (600); **Ravenna** (221); **Savoy** (860); **Telephone** (210); **Trenton** (684); **Windom** (206).

Also, part of **Pecan Gap** (197) and part of **Whitewright** (1,713).

For explanation of sources, symbols and abbreviations, see p. 204, and foldout map.

Population	36,230
Change from 2010 (%)	6.8
Area (sq. mi.)	898.9
Land Area (sq. mi.)	890.8
Altitude (ft.)	450–800
Rainfall (in.)	46.1
Jan. mean min (°F)	30.9
July mean max (°F)	92.3
Civ. Labor	16,763
Unemployed (%)	4.3
Wages	$93,639,841
Per Capita Income	$39,830
Prop. Value	$5,014,592,019
Retail Sales	$355,967,365

Fayette County

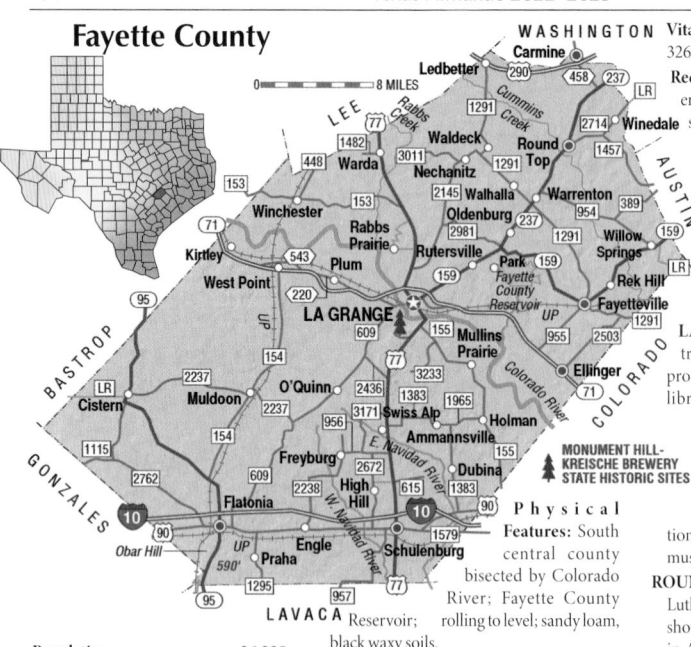

Population.................. 26,328
Change from 2010 (%)..............7.2
Area (sq. mi.).................959.8
Land Area (sq. mi.)..............950.0
Altitude (ft.)..................200–590
Rainfall (in.)........................40.5
Jan. mean min (°F).................39.2
July mean max (°F).................95.5
Civ. Labor......................11,368
Unemployed (%)....................4.8
Wages....................$108,002,539
Per Capita Income.............$54,552
Prop. Value.............$7,605,240,234
Retail Sales..............$467,737,178

Economy: Agribusiness, production of electricity, mineral production, government/services, small manufacturing, tourism.

History: Lipan Apaches and Tonkawas. Austin's colonists arrived in 1822. Germans and Czechs began arriving in 1840s. County created from Bastrop, Colorado counties in 1837; organized in 1838; named for hero of American Revolution, Marquis de Lafayette.

Race/Ethnicity: Anglo, 70.1%; Black, 6.8%; Hispanic, 21.1%; Asian, 0.2%; Other, 1.4%.

Vital Statistics, annual: Births, 282; deaths, 326; marriages, 125; divorces, 81.

Recreation: Monument Hill, Kreische brewery, Faison Home Museum, other historic sites including "Painted Churches"; hunting, fishing, lake; German and Czech ethnic foods; Prazska Pout in August, Octoberfests.

Minerals: Oil, gas, sand, gravel, bentonite clay.

Agriculture: Beef cattle, corn, hay, sorghum, pecans, dairies. Market value $47.4 million. Firewood sold.

LA GRANGE (4,759) county seat; electricity generation, manufacturing, food processing, retail trade, tourism; hospital, library, quilt museum, polka museum, archives; Czech heritage center; Best Little Cowboy Gathering in March.

SCHULENBURG (3,006) varied manufacturing, food processing; Blinn College extension; aircraft, International Festival Institute, July-August; polka music museums; sausagefest in April.

ROUND TOP (90) music center, tourism; old Lutheran church, heritage museum; antiques shows, April/October; Shakespeare festival in April, Schuetzenfest in September, and **Winedale** (67), historic restorations including Winedale Inn.

Other towns include: **Carmine** (262); **Ellinger** (386) Tomato Festival in May; **Fayetteville** (262) tourism, antiques, old precinct courthouse, Lickskillet festival in October; **Flatonia** (1,507) food production, manufacturing, government/services; rail history museum, parks, Czhilispiel in October; **Ledbetter** (83); **Muldoon** (95); **Plum** (145); **Warda** (121); **Warrenton** (186) antique Cadillac museum; **West Point** (213), and **Winchester** (232).

Fisher County

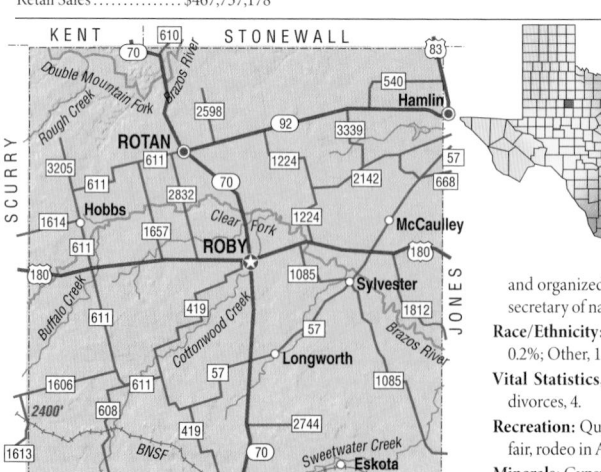

Population.................. 3,859
Change from 2010 (%).............-2.9
Area (sq. mi.)....................901.8
Land Area (sq. mi.)..............898.9
Altitude (ft.)...............1,720–2,405
Rainfall (in.)........................24.8
Jan. mean min (°F).................30.5
July mean max (°F)................94.6
Civ. Labor........................1,643
Unemployed (%)....................4.6
Wages....................$10,263,820
Per Capita Income............$44,630
Prop. Value...........$1,488,462,493
Retail Sales..............$15,847,143

Physical Features: On rolling prairie; mesquite; red, sandy loam soils; drains to forks of Brazos River.

Economy: Agribusiness, hunting, gypsum.

History: Lipan Apaches, disrupted by Comanches and other tribes around 1700. Ranching began in 1876. County created from the Bexar District in 1876 and organized in 1886; named for S.R. Fisher, Republic of Texas secretary of navy.

Race/Ethnicity: Anglo, 65.4%; Black, 3.3%; Hispanic, 29.8%; Asian, 0.2%; Other, 1.1%.

Vital Statistics, annual: Births, 50; deaths, 52; marriages, 13; divorces, 4.

Recreation: Quail, dove, turkey hunting; wildlife viewing; county fair, rodeo in August in Roby.

Minerals: Gypsum, oil.

Agriculture: Cattle, cotton, hay, wheat, sorghum, horses, sheep, goats. Irrigation for cotton and alfalfa. Market value $35.7 million.

ROBY (624) county seat; agribusiness, cotton gin; hospital between Roby and Rotan.

ROTAN (1,470) gypsum plant, oil mill, agribusiness.

Other towns include: **McCaulley** (96) and **Sylvester** (79). Part of **Hamlin** (2,021).

Floyd County

Physical Features: Flat High Plains, broken by Caprock on east, by White River on south; many playas; red, black loam soils.

Economy: Cotton, wind farm, varied manufacturing, government/services.

History: Plains Apaches in area, and later Comanches. First white settlers arrived in 1884. County created from the Bexar District in 1876 and organized in 1890. Named for Dolphin Ward Floyd, who died at the Alamo.

Race/Ethnicity: Anglo, 34.8%; Black, 3.7%; Hispanic, 60.1%; Asian, 0.1%; Other, 0.9%.

Vital Statistics, annual: Births, 75; deaths, 67; marriages, 21; divorces, 24.

Recreation: Hunting of pheasant, deer, quail; fishing; Blanco Canyon; Floydada Punkin Day in October; museum.

Minerals: Not significant.

Agriculture: Cotton, wheat, sorghum, corn; pumpkins. Some 260,000 acres irrigated. Market value $196.0 million.

FLOYDADA (2,562) county seat; trucking, agriculture, retail, medical clinic, museum.

LOCKNEY (1,637) agriculture center; manufacturing; hospital.

Other towns include: **Aiken** (52), **Dougherty** (91), and **South Plains** (67).

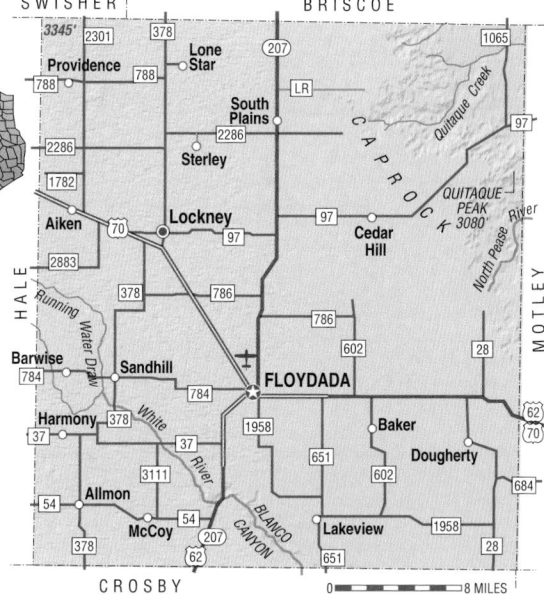

Population....................... **5,535**	
Change from 2010 (%)...............-14.1	
Area (sq. mi.)......................... 992.5	
Land Area (sq. mi.).................. 992.1	
Altitude (ft.) 2,440–3,345	
Rainfall (in.)...........................21.6	
Jan. mean min (°F)....................25.1	
July mean max (°F)....................92.4	
Civ. Labor 2,545	
Unemployed (%).........................5.9	
Wages $17,251,660	
Per Capita Income $44,646	
Prop. Value $1,408,049,053	
Retail Sales................... $42,100,168	

Foard County

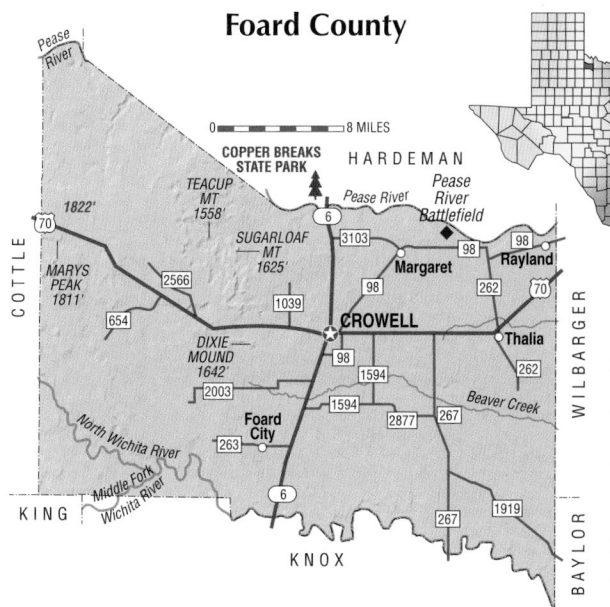

Physical Features: Northwest county drains to North Wichita, Pease rivers; sandy, loam soils, rolling surface.

Economy: Agribusiness, clothes manufacturing, government/service.

History: Comanches and Kiowas ranged the area until driven away in the 1870s. Ranching began in 1880. County created out of Cottle, Hardeman, King, and Knox counties in 1891, organized the same year; named for Maj. Robert L. Foard of the Confederate army.

Race/Ethnicity: Anglo, 76.2%; Black, 5%; Hispanic, 17.7%; Asian, 0.4%; Other, 0.4%.

Vital Statistics, annual: Births, 10; deaths, 16; marriages, 0; divorces, 1.

Recreation: Three museums; hunting; astronomy and ecotourism foundation; wild hog cook-off in November.

Minerals: Natural gas, some oil.

Agriculture: Wheat, cattle, alfalfa, cotton, sorghum, dairies. Market value $14.9 million. Hunting leases important.

CROWELL (813) county seat; retail center, clothing manufacturing; library, Fire Hall museum.

For explanation of sources, symbols and abbreviations, see p. 204, and foldout map.

Population....................... **1,139**	
Change from 2010 (%)...............-14.7	
Area (sq. mi.)......................... 707.7	
Land Area (sq. mi.).................. 704.4	
Altitude (ft.)...................1,210–1,822	
Rainfall (in.)...........................27.3	
Jan. mean min (°F)....................26.0	
July mean max (°F)....................98.0	
Civ. Labor 574	
Unemployed (%)..........................3	
Wages $3,125,283	
Per Capita Income $44,895	
Prop. Value $1,019,925,798	
Retail Sales................... $7,147,802	

Fort Bend County

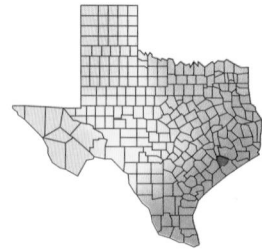

Physical Features: On Gulf Coastal Plain; drained by Brazos, San Bernard rivers; Smithers Lake; level to rolling; rich alluvial soils.

Economy: Agribusiness, petrochemicals, technology, government/services; many residents work in Houston.

History: Karankawa groups in area, who retreated to Mexico by the 1850s. Named for river bend where some of Austin's colonists settled in 1824 and built a blockhouse for protection against the Indians. Antebellum plantations made it one of six Texas counties with black majority in 1850. County created in 1837 from Austin County and organized in 1838.

Race/Ethnicity: Anglo, 33.2%; Black, 19.3%; Hispanic, 24.2%; Asian, 20.4%; Other, 2.7%.

Vital Statistics, annual: Births, 9,887; deaths, 2,984; marriages, 3,321; divorces, 1,871.

Recreation: Many historic sites, museums, memorials, parks; George Ranch historical park; Brazos Bend State Park with George Observatory; fishing, waterfowl hunting.

Minerals: Oil, gas, sulfur, salt, clays, sand and gravel.

Agriculture: Nursery crops, cotton, sorghum, corn, hay, cattle, horses; irrigation for rice. Market value $85.0 million.

RICHMOND (13,598) county seat; foundry; University of Houston branch, Wharton County Junior College branch; Richmond State supported-living center, hospital.

SUGAR LAND (131,448) government/services, prisons, commuting to Houston; hospitals; University of Houston branch; Museum of Southern History. New Territory and Greatwood are now part of Sugar Land.

MISSOURI CITY (80,681, part [6,276] in Harris County) hospital.

ROSENBERG (37,823) varied industry, railroad museum.

Other towns include: **Arcola** (2,360); **Beasley** (804); **Cinco Ranch** (24,176); **Fairchilds** (1,068); **Fresno** (28,243); **Fulshear** (13,914); **Guy** (239); **Katy** (21,729, mostly in Harris County) hospital; **Kendleton** (461); **Meadows Place** (4,591); **Mission Bend** (46,172).

Also: **Needville** (3,522) agriculture, commuting, historic Schendel house, historic cemetery, Czech soup supper in January; **Orchard** (434); **Pecan Grove** (20,569); **Pleak** (1,517); **Simonton** (965); **Stafford** (19,501, partly in Harris County); **Thompsons** (331); **Weston Lakes** (4,699).

Also, part [42,242] of **Houston**.

Population	805,788
Change from 2010 (%)	37.7
Area (sq. mi.)	885.3
Land Area (sq. mi.)	861.5
Altitude (ft.)	46–158
Rainfall (in.)	50.4
Jan. mean min (°F)	44.1
July mean max (°F)	94.9
Civ. Labor	395,859
Unemployed (%)	6.7
Wages	$2,743,891,540
Per Capita Income	$59,653
Prop. Value	$103,143,863,651
Retail Sales	$9,340,038,608

For explanation of sources, symbols and abbreviations, see p. 204, and foldout map.

Franklin County

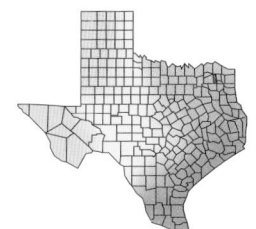

Physical Features: Small Northeast county with many wooded hills; drained by numerous streams; alluvial to sandy clay soils; Lake Bob Sandlin, Lake Cypress Springs.

Economy: Agribusiness, government/services, retirement area, distribution.

History: Caddoes abandoned the area in the 1790s because of disease and other tribes. First white settlers arrived around 1818. County created in 1875 from Titus County, organized the same year; named for jurist B.C. Franklin.

Race/Ethnicity: Anglo, 77.3%; Black, 4.5%; Hispanic, 15.2%; Asian, 0.5%; Other, 2.3%.

Population	10,791
Change from 2010 (%)	1.8
Area (sq. mi.)	294.8
Land Area (sq. mi.)	284.4
Altitude (ft.)	300–600
Rainfall (in.)	47.4
Jan. mean min (°F)	47.4
July mean max (°F)	92.0
Civ. Labor	5,004
Unemployed (%)	5.1
Wages	$42,085,288
Per Capita Income	$41,307
Prop. Value	$1,910,721,168
Retail Sales	$109,279,360

Vital Statistics, annual: Births, 123; deaths, 122; marriages, 62; divorces, 33.

Recreation: Fishing, water sports; historic homes; wild hog hunting, horse stables; stew cook-off in October.

Minerals: Lignite coal, oil and gas.

Agriculture: Beef cattle, milk production, poultry, hay. Market value $134.1 million. Timber marketed.

MOUNT VERNON (2,789) county seat; distribution center, manufacturing, tourism, antiques; hospital; nature preserves. museum with Don Meredith exhibit; wine festivals in May and October.

Other towns include: Scroggins (150), and **Winnsboro** (3,299, mostly in Wood County) commercial center, Autumn Trails.

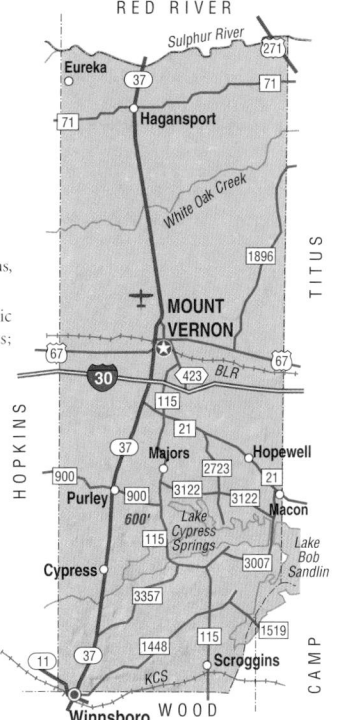

Freestone County

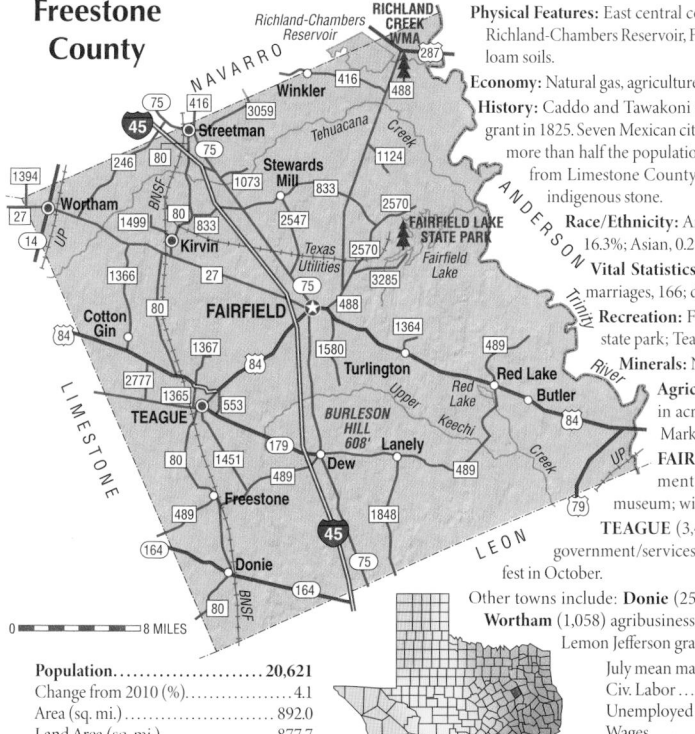

Physical Features: East central county bounded by the Trinity River; Richland-Chambers Reservoir, Fairfield Lake; rolling Blackland, sandy, loam soils.

Economy: Natural gas, agriculture.

History: Caddo and Tawakoni area. David G. Burnet received land grant in 1825. Seven Mexican citizens received grants in 1833. In 1860, more than half the population was black. County created in 1850 from Limestone County; organized in 1851. Named for the indigenous stone.

Race/Ethnicity: Anglo, 65.8%; Black, 15.9%; Hispanic, 16.3%; Asian, 0.2%; Other, 1.5%.

Vital Statistics, annual: Births, 215; deaths, 202; marriages, 166; divorces, 33.

Recreation: Fishing, hunting; lakes; historic sites; state park; Teague amateur rodeo in July.

Minerals: Natural gas, oil.

Agriculture: Beef cattle, peaches (second in acreage), hay, blueberries, horticulture. Market value $68.1 million. Hunting leases.

FAIRFIELD (2,984) county seat; government/services, trade center; hospital; museum; wild game supper in July.

TEAGUE (3,495) railroad terminal, oil and gas, government/services, agriculture; library, museum; Parkfest in October.

Other towns include: Donie (250), **Kirvin** (136), **Streetman** (259), **Wortham** (1,058) agribusiness, blues festivals in September, Blind Lemon Jefferson gravesite.

Population	20,621
Change from 2010 (%)	4.1
Area (sq. mi.)	892.0
Land Area (sq. mi.)	877.7
Altitude (ft.)	200–608
Rainfall (in.)	43.1
Jan. mean min (°F)	35.3
July mean max (°F)	93.5
Civ. Labor	6,244
Unemployed (%)	8
Wages	$49,296,705
Per Capita Income	$38,182
Prop. Value	$4,034,441,610
Retail Sales	$166,245,570

Frio County

Physical Features: South Texas county of rolling terrain with much brush; bisected by Frio River; sandy, red sandy loam soils.

Economy: Agribusiness, oil-field services, hunting leases.

History: Coahuiltecans; many taken into San Antonio missions. Comanches kept settlers out until after Civil War. Mexican citizens recruited for labor after 1900. County created in 1858 from Atascosa, Bexar, Uvalde counties, organized in 1871; named for the Frio (cold) River.

Race/Ethnicity: Anglo, 14.5%; Black, 2.7%; Hispanic, 80%; Asian, 1.9%; Other, 0.8%.

Vital Statistics, annual: Births, 242; deaths, 155; marriages, 96; divorces, 27.

Recreation: Hunting, Big Foot Wallace Museum, Winter Garden area, splash pad/skate parks.

Minerals: Oil, natural gas, stone.

Agriculture: Peanuts, potatoes, sorghum, cotton, corn, spinach, cucumbers, watermelons, bees (second in number of colonies). Second in vegetables harvested. Market value $124.4 million. Hunting leases.

PEARSALL (10,577) county seat; agriculture center, oil and gas, food processing, shipping, government/services; old jail museum; hospital, junior college extension; Cinco de Mayo celebration.

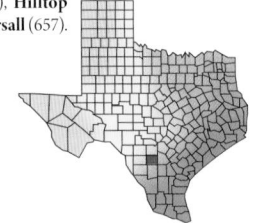

Dilley (4,269) shipping center for melons and peanuts; hospital.

Other towns include: **Bigfoot** (537), **Hilltop** (282); **Moore** (441), and **North Pearsall** (657).

Population...................... **19,103**	
Change from 2010 (%)................11.0	July mean max (°F).....................97.4
Area (sq. mi.)........................ 1,134.4	Civ. Labor............................. 9,238
Land Area (sq. mi.)................ 1,133.5	Unemployed (%)........................5.4
Altitude (ft.)...................... 400–763	Wages $90,709,167
Rainfall (in.)...........................24.7	Per Capita Income $30,223
Jan. mean min (°F)....................35.0	Prop. Value $3,808,188,908
	Retail Sales................. $167,656,307

Gaines County

Physical Features: On South Plains, drains to draws; playas; underground water.

Economy: Oil, gas, cotton, peanuts.

History: Comanche country until the U.S. Army campaigns of 1875. Ranchers arrived in the 1880s; farming began around 1900. County created from Bexar District in 1876; organized in 1905; named for James Gaines, signer of the Texas Declaration of Independence.

Race/Ethnicity: Anglo, 54.8%; Black, 1.4%; Hispanic, 42.5%; Asian, 0.3%; Other, 0.8%.

Vital Statistics, annual: Births, 460; deaths, 128; marriages, 231; divorces, 49.

Recreation: Cedar Lake one of largest alkali lakes on Texas plains.

Minerals: Oil, gas.

Agriculture: Cotton (first in bales produced), peanuts (first in acreage), small grains, pecans, paprika, rosemary; cattle, sheep, hogs; substantial irrigation. Market value $188.8 million.

SEMINOLE (7,660) county seat; manufacturing, oil and gas, agriculture; hospital, library, museum; Ag & Oil Day celebration in September.

SEAGRAVES (2,946) market for three-county area; cotton, peanut farming; library, museum; Celebrate Seagraves in July.

Other towns include: **Loop** (243). Also, part of **Denver City** (4,911).

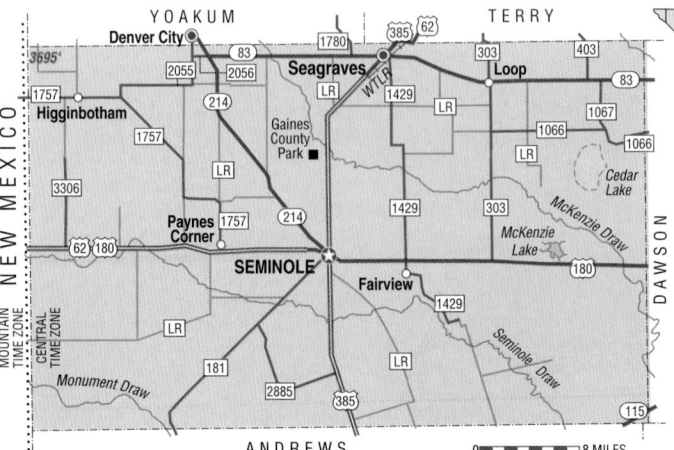

Population **21,170**	
Change from 2010 (%)............20.8	
Area (sq. mi.) 1,502.9	
Land Area (sq. mi.)........... 1,502.4	
Altitude (ft.) 2,935–3,695	
Rainfall (in.).......................18.4	
Jan. mean min (°F) 27.7	
July mean max (°F)................93.4	
Civ. Labor 9,731	
Unemployed (%)....................5.3	
Wages.................... $89,556,983	
Per Capita Income $44,405	
Prop. Value............ $4,661,042,737	
Retail Sales $300,682,571	

Physical Features: Partly island, partly coastal; flat, artificial drainage; sandy, loam, clay soils; broken by bays.

Economy: Port activities dominate economy; insurance and finance center, petrochemical plants, varied manufacturing, tourism, medical education, oceanographic research, ship building, commercial fishing.

History: Karankawa and other tribes roamed the area until 1850. French, Spanish, and American settlement began in 1815 and reached 1,000 by 1817.

County created from Brazoria County in 1838; organized in 1839; named for the Spanish governor of Louisiana Count Bernardo de Gálvez.

Race/Ethnicity: Anglo, 56.1%; Black, 12.7%; Hispanic, 25%; Asian, 3.6%; Other, 2.3%.

Vital Statistics, annual: Births, 4,219; deaths, 2,675; marriages, 1,770; divorces, 1,185.

Recreation: One of Texas' most historic cities; popular tourist and convention center; fishing, surfing, boating, sailing and other water sports; state park; historic homes tour in spring, Moody Gardens.

Also, Mardi Gras celebration; Rosenberg Library; museums; restored sailing ship, "Elissa," railroad museum; Dickens on the Strand in early December.

Minerals: Oil, gas, clays, sand and gravel.

Agriculture: Cattle, aquaculture, nursery crops, rice, hay, horses, soybeans, grain sorghum. Market value $9.2 million.

Galveston County

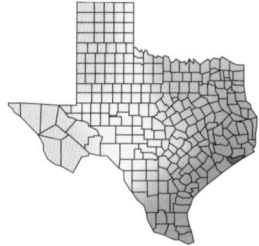

GALVESTON (50,372) county seat; tourist center, shipyard, other industries, insurance, port container facility; University of Texas Medical Branch; National Maritime Research Center; Texas A&M University at Galveston; Galveston College; hospitals.

LEAGUE CITY (108,604, part [1,987] in Harris County) residential community, commuters to Houston, hospital.

TEXAS CITY (51,178) refining, petrochemical plants, port, rail shipping; College of the Mainland; hospital, library; dike; Cinco de Mayo, Shrimp Boil in August.

Bolivar Peninsula (2,800) includes: **Port Bolivar** (700) lighthouse, free ferry; **Crystal Beach** (800) seafood industry, sport fishing, tourism, Fort Travis Seashore Park, shorebird sanctuary, Crab Festival in May; **Gilchrist** (400), and **High Island** (300).

Other towns include: **Bacliff** (10,073); **Bayou Vista** (1,645); **Clear Lake Shores** (1,190).

Also: **Dickinson** (21,576) manufacturing, commuters, strawberry festival in May; **Friendswood** (40,659, part [11,499] in Harris County); **Hitchcock** (7,895) residential community, tourism, fishing and shrimping, Good Ole Days in August, WWII blimp base, museum.

Also: **Jamaica Beach** (1,088); **Kemah** (2,006) tourism, boating, commuters, museum, Blessing of Fleet in August; **La Marque** (17,326) refining, greyhound racing, farming, hospital, library, Gulf Coast Grill-off in October; **San Leon** (5,439); **Santa Fe** (13,645); **Tiki Island** (1,083).

Population.	**339,931**
Change from 2010 (%).	16.7
Area (sq. mi.).	873.8
Land Area (sq. mi.).	378.4
Altitude (ft.).	sea level–40
Rainfall (in.).	50.8
Jan. mean min (°F).	48.6
July mean max (°F).	89.6
Civ. Labor.	164,318
Unemployed (%).	7.3
Wages.	$1,542,972,986
Per Capita Income.	$54,250
Prop. Value.	$46,645,264,094
Retail Sales.	$4,531,612,556

For explanation of sources, symbols and abbreviations, see p. 204, and foldout map.

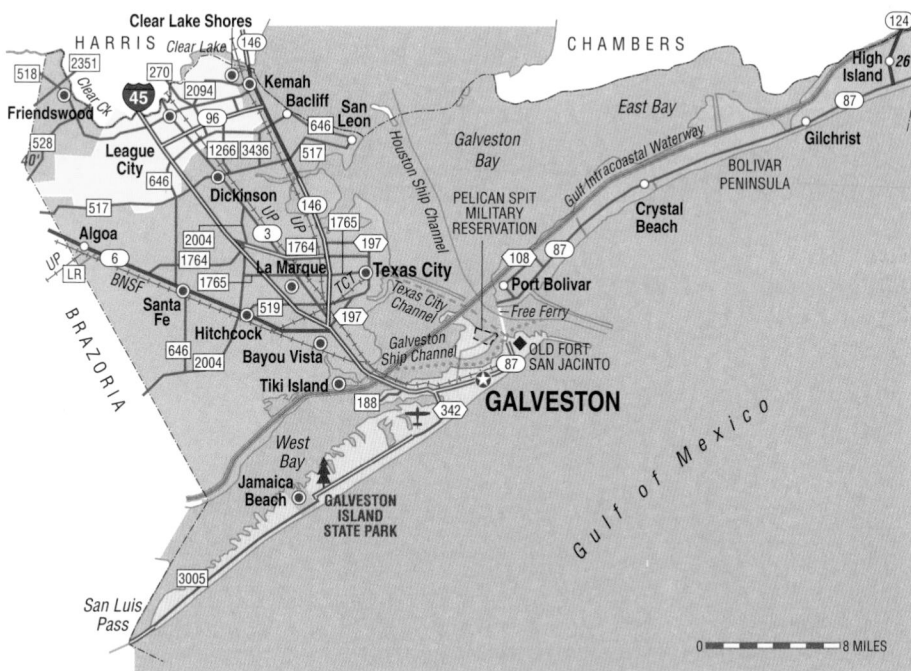

Garza County

Physical Features: On edge of Caprock; rough, broken land, with playas, gullies, canyons, Brazos River forks, Lake Alan Henry; sandy, loam, clay soils.

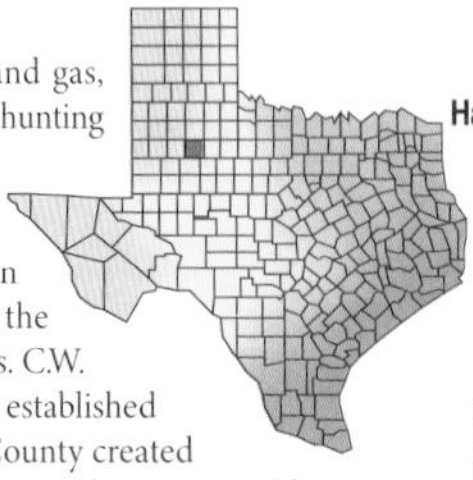

Economy: Agriculture, oil and gas, trade, government/services, hunting leases.

History: Kiowas and Comanches yielded to U.S. Army in 1875. Ranching began in the 1870s, farming in the 1890s. C.W. Post, the cereal millionaire, established enterprises here in 1906. County created from Bexar District 1876; organized 1907; named for a pioneer Bexar County family.

Race/Ethnicity: Anglo, 42.5%; Black, 6.2%; Hispanic, 50%; Asian, 0.1%; Other, 0.9%.

Vital Statistics, annual: Births, 71; deaths, 56; marriages, 29; divorces, 10.

Recreation: Scenic areas, lake activities, Post-Garza Museum, trade days monthly.

Minerals: Oil, gas, sand, gravel.

Agriculture: Cotton, beef cattle, hay. Some 8,000 acres irrigated. Market value $22.1 million. Hunting leases.

POST (5,138) county seat; founded by C.W. Post; agriculture, tourism, government/services, prisons; museums, theater.

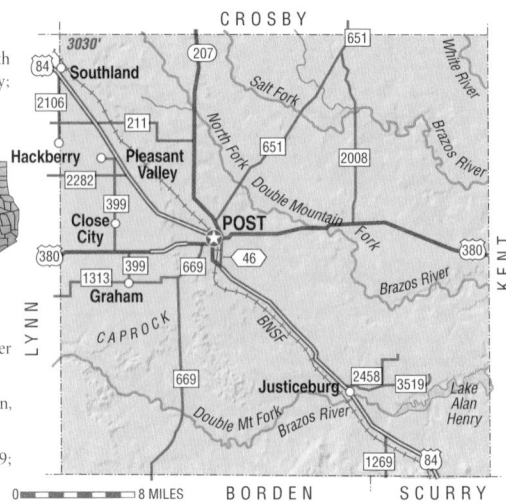

For explanation of sources, symbols and abbreviations, see p. 204, and foldout map.

Population........................ **6,115**	July mean max (°F)....................94.4
Change from 2010 (%)................-5.4	Civ. Labor............................ 1,939
Area (sq. mi.)........................ 896.2	Unemployed (%)........................5.5
Land Area (sq. mi.).................. 893.4	Wages $18,112,470
Altitude (ft.)....................2,140–3,030	Per Capita Income................ $32,601
Rainfall (in.)............................22.0	Prop. Value $1,139,614,447
Jan. mean min (°F).....................29.0	Retail Sales................... $30,557,378

A beautiful drive in Garza County, down FM 669. Photo by Leaflet, CC 3/Wikimedia Commons

Gillespie County

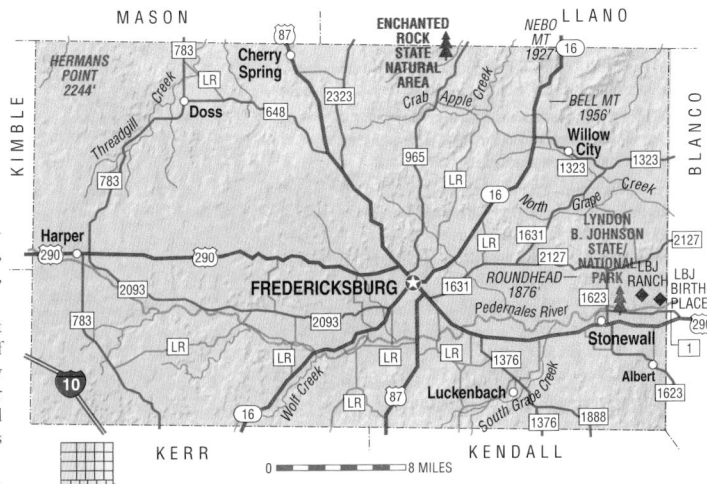

Physical Features: Picturesque Edwards Plateau area with hills, broken by spring-fed streams.

Economy: Tourism, government/services, agriculture, wine and specialty foods, hunting leases.

History: German settlement founded in 1846 in heart of Comanche country. County created in 1848 from Bexar and Travis counties, organized the same year; named for Texas Ranger Capt. R.A. Gillespie.

The birthplace of President Lyndon B. Johnson and Fleet Admiral Chester W. Nimitz.

Race/Ethnicity: Anglo, 72.9%; Black, 0.4%; Hispanic, 24.9%; Asian, 0.3%; Other, 1.2%.

Vital Statistics, annual: Births, 254; deaths, 318; marriages, 220; divorces, 84.

Recreation: Among leading deer-hunting areas; numerous historic sites and tourist attractions include LBJ Ranch, Nimitz Hotel and Pacific war museum; Pioneer Museum Complex, Enchanted Rock, wineries, produce stands.

Minerals: Sand, gravel.

Agriculture: Beef cattle, wine, hay, peaches (first in acreage). Market value $31.2 million. Hunting leases important.

FREDERICKSBURG (11,482) county seat; agribusiness, tourism, wineries, food processing; museum; tourist attractions; hospital; Easter Fires, Oktoberfest.

Other towns include: **Doss** (100); **Harper** (1,388) ranching, deer hunting, Dachshund Hounds Downs race and Trades Day in October; **Luckenbach** (25) saloon, general store and dance hall; **Stonewall** (543) agribusiness, wineries, tourism, hunting, Peach Jamboree in June, and **Willow City** (22) scenic drive.

Population	**27,375**
Change from 2010 (%)	10.2
Area (sq. mi.)	1,061.7
Land Area (sq. mi.)	1,058.2
Altitude (ft.)	1,040–2,244
Rainfall (in.)	31.5
Jan. mean min (°F)	34.3
July mean max (°F)	92.7
Civ. Labor	12,821
Unemployed (%)	3.7
Wages	$128,867,213
Per Capita Income	$63,291
Prop. Value	$10,071,369,340
Retail Sales	$577,736,080

Glasscock County

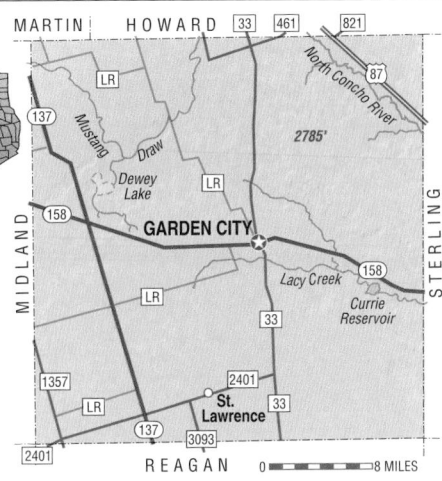

Physical Features: Western county on rolling plains, broken by small streams; sandy, loam soils.

Economy: Farming, ranching, hunting leases, oil and gas.

History: Hunting area for Kickapoos and Lipan Apaches. Anglo-American sheep ranchers and Mexican-American shepherds or pastores moved into the area in the 1880s. County created in 1887 from Tom Green County; organized in 1893; named for Texas pioneer George W. Glasscock.

Race/Ethnicity: Anglo, 65.3%; Black, 1%; Hispanic, 32.7%; Asian, 0.1%; Other, 0.7%.

Vital Statistics, annual: Births, 16; deaths, 3; marriages, 10; divorces, 0.

Recreation: Hunting of deer, quail, turkey, fox, bobcat, coyote; St. Lawrence Fall Festival in October.

Minerals: Oil, gas, stone/rock.

Agriculture: Cotton, watermelons, wheat, sorghum, hay; 25,000 acres irrigated. Cattle, goats, sheep, hogs raised. Market value $50.6 million.

GARDEN CITY (427) county seat; serves sparsely settled ranching, oil area.

Also, **St. Lawrence** (90) farming.

Population	**1,369**
Change from 2010 (%)	11.7
Area (sq. mi.)	901.1
Land Area (sq. mi.)	900.2
Altitude (ft.)	2,470–2,785
Rainfall (in.)	17.6
Jan. mean min (°F)	28.3
July mean max (°F)	92.6
Civ. Labor	824
Unemployed (%)	3
Wages	$9,646,690
Per Capita Income	$84,623
Prop. Value	$4,899,719,498
Retail Sales	$23,674,618

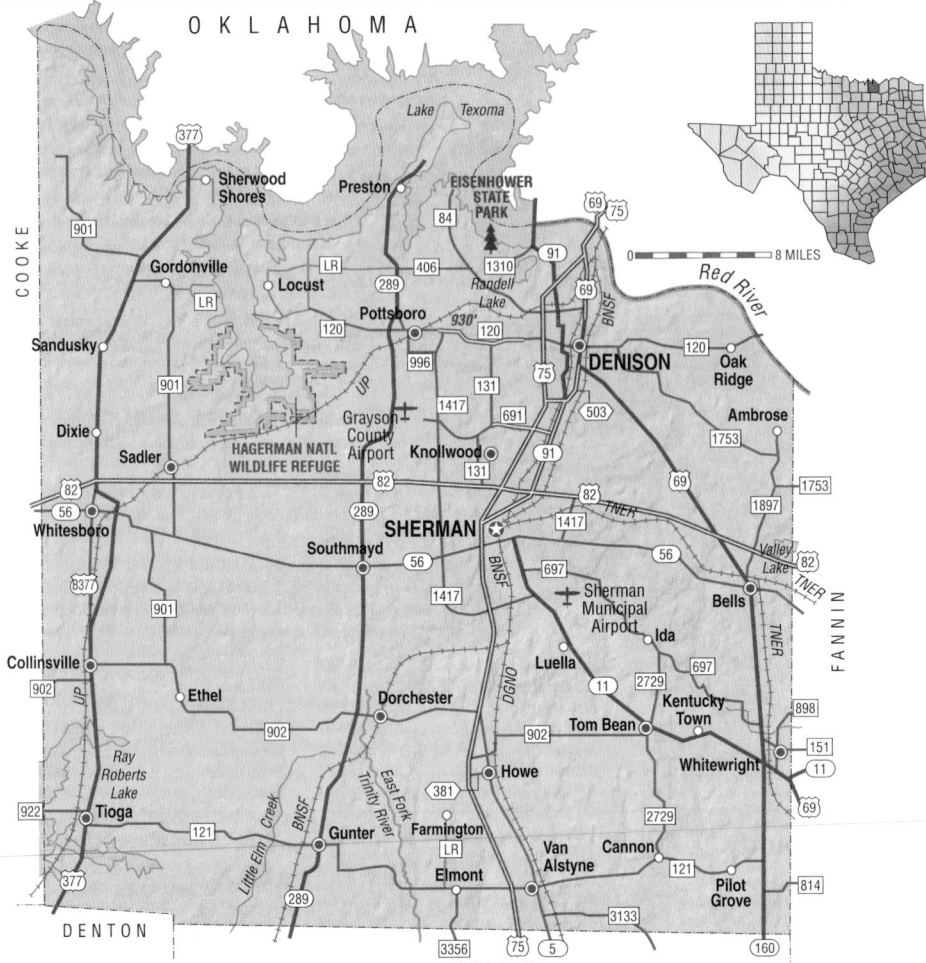

Physical Features: North Texas county; level, some low hills; sandy loam, blackland soils; drains to Red River and tributaries of Trinity River; Lake Texoma, Ray Roberts Lake, Valley Lake, Randell Lake.

Economy: A manufacturing, distribution and trade center for northern Texas and southern Oklahoma; nature tourism, mineral production.

History: Caddo and Tonkawa area. Preston Bend trading post established 1836-1837. Peters colony settlers arrived in the 1840s. County created in 1846 from Fannin County, organized the same year; named for Republic Attorney General Peter W. Grayson.

Race/Ethnicity: Anglo, 75%; Black, 5.7%; Hispanic, 13.8%; Asian, 1%; Other, 4.3%.

Vital Statistics, annual: Births, 1,579; deaths, 1,461; marriages, 919; divorces, 178.

Recreation: Lakes, fishing, hunting, water sports, state park, cultural activities, Hagerman National Wildlife Refuge, Pioneer Village, railroad museum.

Minerals: Oil, gas, gravel, sand.

Grayson County

Agriculture: Wheat, corn, hay, beef cattle, horses. Market value $66.2 million.

Education: Austin College in Sherman and Grayson County College located between Sherman and Denison.

SHERMAN (44,113) county seat; varied manufacturing, processors and distributors for major companies; Austin College; hospital.

DENISON (25,402) health care, manufacturing, retail center; hospital; Eisenhower birthplace, air force base museum; Main Street Fall festival in October.

Other towns include: **Bells** (1,542); **Collinsville** (1,934); **Dorchester** (167); **Gordonville** (165); **Gunter** (1,660); **Howe** (3,391) manufacturing, agriculture, trucking services, library, Founders' Day in May; **Knollwood** (591); **Pottsboro** (2,479) lake activities, marinas, education, Frontier Days in September; **Sadler** (341).

Also: **Southmayd** (1,122); **Tioga** (1,141) Gene Autry museum, festival in

September; **Tom Bean** (1,129); **Van Alstyne** (4,449) retail center, manufacturing, government/services, museum, Grayson County College-South Campus, Fall Der All in October; **Whitesboro** (4,075) agribusiness, tourism, manufacturing, library, Peanut Festival in October; **Whitewright** (1,721) government/services, retail, manufacturing, museum, truck & tractor pull in June.

Population	**135,612**
Change from 2010 (%)	12.2
Area (sq. mi.)	979.2
Land Area (sq. mi.)	932.8
Altitude (ft.)	500–930
Rainfall (in.)	43.6
Jan. mean min (°F)	33.1
July mean max (°F)	92.1
Civ. Labor	64,881
Unemployed (%)	4.8
Wages	$614,290,578
Per Capita Income	$43,987
Prop. Value	$18,607,634,688
Retail Sales	$2,194,234,733

Gregg County

Physical Features: A populous, leading petroleum county, heart of the famed East Texas oil field; bisected by the Sabine River; hilly, timbered; with sandy, clay, alluvial soils.

Economy: Oil but with significant other manufacturing; tourism, conventions, agribusiness, and lignite coal production.

History: Caddoes; later Cherokees, who were driven out in 1838 by President Lamar. First land grants issued in 1835 by Republic of Mexico. County created and organized in 1873 from Rusk, Upshur counties; named for Confederate Gen. John Gregg. In U.S. censuses 1880-1910, blacks were more numerous than whites. Oil discovered in 1931.

Race/Ethnicity: Anglo, 56.6%; Black, 20.1%; Hispanic, 19.4%; Asian, 1.1%; Other, 2.5%.

Vital Statistics, annual: Births, 1,858; deaths, 1,274; marriages, 1,240; divorces, 416.

Recreation: Water activities on Lake Cherokee, hunting, varied cultural events, East Texas Oil Museum in Kilgore.

Minerals: Leading oil-producing county with more than 3 billion barrels produced since 1931; also, sand, gravel and natural gas.

Agriculture: Cattle, horses, hay, nursery crops. Market value $4.1 million. Timber sales.

LONGVIEW (83,749, small part [1,958] in Harrison County) county seat; chemical manufacturing, oil industry, distribution and retail center; hospitals; LeTourneau University, University of Texas-Tyler Longview center; convention center; balloon race in July.

Kilgore (14,329, part [3,515] in Rusk County), oil, distribution center; Kilgore College, Rangerette museum; Shakespeare festival in summer.

Gladewater (6,788, part [2,496] in Upshur County) oil, manufacturing, tourism, antiques; library, airport, skydiving; Gusher Days in April; daffodils in February-March.

Other towns include: **Clarksville City** (932); **Easton** (639, partly in Rusk County); **Judson** (1,057); **Lakeport** (1,051); **Liberty City** (2,624) oil, tourism, government/services, Honor America Night in November.

Also: **Warren City** (277); **White Oak** (6,570) oil and gas, commuting to Longview, Tyler; park, Roughneck Days in spring every three years.

Population.	**126,116**
Change from 2010 (%)	3.6
Area (sq. mi.)	275.8
Land Area (sq. mi.)	273.3
Altitude (ft.)	240–530
Rainfall (in.)	48.1
Jan. mean min (°F)	34.2
July mean max (°F)	93.8
Civ. Labor	56,141
Unemployed (%)	7
Wages	$909,383,161
Per Capita Income	$47,109
Prop. Value	$11,982,080,454
Retail Sales	$3,205,849,271

For explanation of sources, symbols and abbreviations, see p. 204, and foldout map.

Grimes County

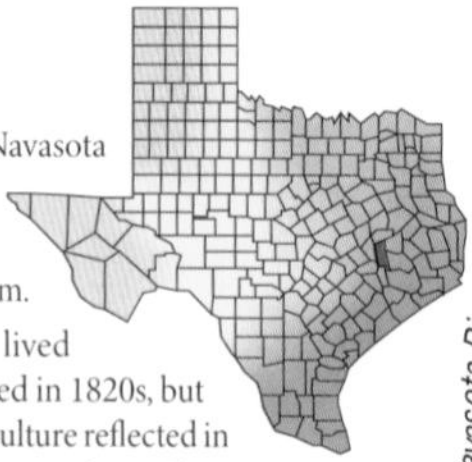

Physical Features: Rich bottom soils along Brazos, Navasota rivers; remainder hilly, partly forested; Gibbons Creek Reservoir.

Economy: Varied manufacturing, agribusiness, tourism.

History: Bidais (customs similar to the Caddoes) lived peacefully with Anglo-American settlers who arrived in 1820s, but tribe was removed to Indian Territory. Planter agriculture reflected in 1860 census, which listed 77 persons owning 20 or more slaves. County created from Montgomery County in 1846, organized the same year; named for Jesse Grimes, who signed Texas Declaration of Independence.

Race/Ethnicity: Anglo, 57.5%; Black, 15.2%; Hispanic, 24.5%; Asian, 0.2%; Other, 2.4%.

Vital Statistics, annual: Births, 328; deaths, 279; marriages, 139; divorces, 71.

Recreation: Hunting, fishing; Gibbons Creek Reservoir; historic sites; fall Renaissance Festival at Plantersville.

Minerals: Lignite coal, natural gas.

Agriculture: Cattle, forage, horses, poultry; berries, pecans, honey sales significant. Market value $47.5million. Some timber sold, Christmas tree farms.

ANDERSON (243) county seat; rural center; Fanthorp Inn historic site; Go-Texan weekend in February.

NAVASOTA (7,867) agribusiness center for parts of three counties; varied manufacturing; food, wood processing; hospital; prisons; La Salle statue; Blues Fest in August.

Other towns include: Bedias (474); **Iola** (435); **Plantersville** (869); **Richards** (300); **Roans Prairie** (64); **Shiro** (210); **Todd Mission** (117).

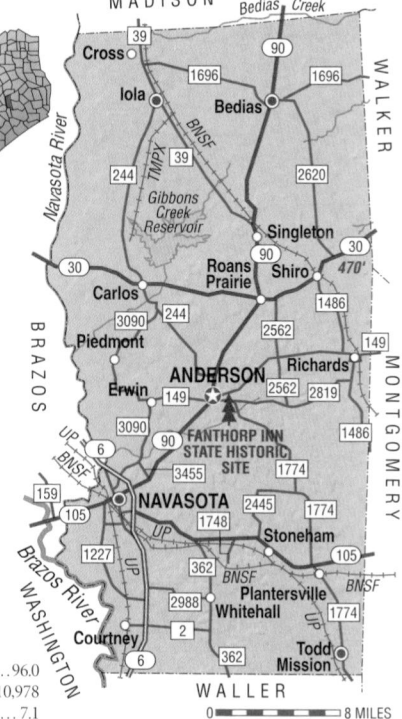

Population.................... **29,466**	July mean max (°F)...................96.0
Change from 2010 (%)..............10.8	Civ. Labor.........................10,978
Area (sq. mi.).......................801.6	Unemployed (%)......................7.1
Land Area (sq. mi.).................787.5	Wages $96,278,105
Altitude (ft.).....................150–470	Per Capita Income.............$36,909
Rainfall (in.)..........................43.5	Prop. Value..............$6,883,799,586
Jan. mean min (°F)...................40.0	Retail Sales................$216,825,003

For explanation of sources, symbols and abbreviations, see p. 204, and foldout map.

The City Hall building in Navasota in Grimes County. Photo by Larry D. Moore, CC by SA 4.0/Wikimedia Commons

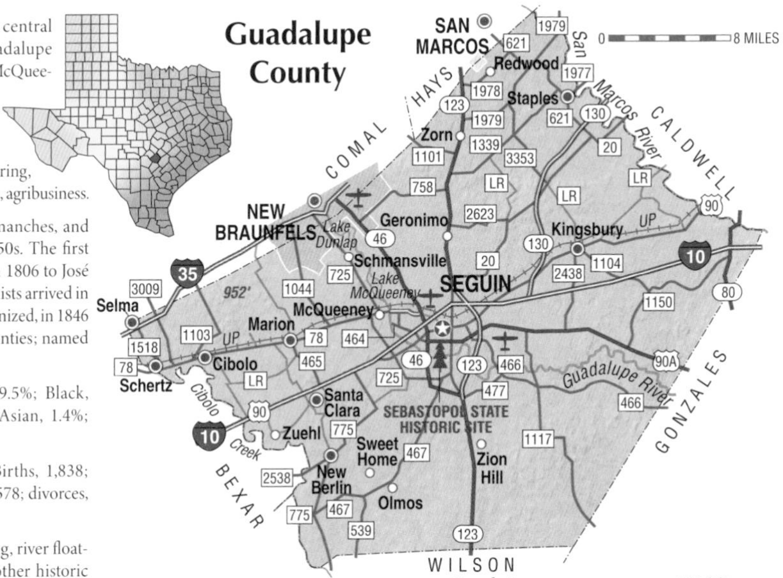

Physical Features: South central county bisected by Guadalupe River, Lake Dunlap, Lake McQueeney; level to rolling surface; sandy, loam, blackland soils.

Economy: Varied manufacturing, commuting to San Antonio, agribusiness.

History: Karankawas, Comanches, and other tribes until the 1850s. The first Spanish land grant was in 1806 to José de la Baume. DeWitt colonists arrived in 1827. County created, organized, in 1846 from Bexar, Gonzales counties; named for the river.

Race/Ethnicity: Anglo, 49.5%; Black, 7.8%; Hispanic, 38.8%; Asian, 1.4%; Other, 2.3%.

Vital Statistics, annual: Births, 1,838; deaths, 1,043; marriages, 578; divorces, 471.

Recreation: Fishing, hunting, river floating; Sebastopol House, other historic sites; river drive; Fiestas Juan Seguin in June, Diez y Seis in September in Seguin.

Minerals: Oil, gas, gravel, clays.

Agriculture: Cattle, corn, milo, wheat, cotton, hay, nursery crops, pecans. Market value $73.6 million.

SEGUIN (31,884) county seat; varied manufacturing/logistics, health care, government/services; hospital, museums, heritage village; Texas Lutheran University; Pecan Fest in late October.

Guadalupe County

Other towns include: **Cibolo** (31,951), **Geronimo** (1,374), **Kingsbury** (874), **Marion** (1,243), **McQueeney** (2,793), **New Berlin** (621), **Redwood** (4,219), **Santa Clara** (725), **Schertz** (42,709, parts in Bexar and Comal counties), **Staples** (272).

Also, part [15,408] of **New Braunfels**, part [2,612] of **Selma**, and a small part of **San Marcos**.

Population	**166,961**
Change from 2010 (%)	26.9
Area (sq. mi.)	714.8
Land Area (sq. mi.)	711.3
Altitude (ft.)	350–952
Rainfall (in.)	34.6
Jan. mean min (°F)	40.5
July mean max (°F)	95.2
Civ. Labor	82,056
Unemployed (%)	4.7
Wages	$543,634,031
Per Capita Income	$45,797
Prop. Value	$20,354,569,687
Retail Sales	$1,948,275,256

The Seguin Gazette building in Guadalupe County. The Gazette has been around since 1888 and publishes 5 days a week. Photo by Larry D. Moore, CC by SA 4.0/Wikimedia Commons

Hale County

Physical Features: High Plains; fertile sandy, loam soils; playas; large underground water supply.

Economy: Agribusiness, food processing/distribution, manufacturing, government/services.

History: Comanche hunters driven out by U.S. Army in 1875. Ranching began in 1880s. First motor-driven irrigation well drilled in 1911. County created from Bexar District in 1876; organized in 1888; named for Lt. J.C. Hale, who died at San Jacinto.

Race/Ethnicity: Anglo, 33%; Black, 5.4%; Hispanic, 59.3%; Asian, 0.4%; Other, 1.6%.

Vital Statistics, annual: Births, 483; deaths, 322; marriages, 223; divorces, 35.

Recreation: Llano Estacado Museum; art gallery, antiques stores; pheasant hunting; Cowboy Days in September at Plainview.

Minerals: Some oil.

Agriculture: Cotton, fed beef, sorghum, dairies, corn, vegetables, wheat. Market value $411.7 million. Irrigation of 200,000 acres.

PLAINVIEW (20,124) county seat; agriculture, distribution, corn milling; Wayland Baptist University, South Plains College branch; hospital, library, mental health center; prisons.

Hale Center (2,059) trade center; farm museum, library, parks, murals, cacti gardens.

Abernathy (2,699, part [752] in Lubbock County) government/services, farm supplies, textile plant, gins.

Other towns include: **Cotton Center** (300), **Edmonson** (101), **Petersburg** (1,108), **Seth Ward** (1,899).

Population	33,165	July mean max (°F)	91.0
Change from 2010 (%)	-8.6	Civ. Labor	11,818
Area (sq. mi.)	1,004.8	Unemployed (%)	6.4
Land Area (sq. mi.)	1,004.7	Wages	$125,039,648
Altitude (ft.)	3,180–3,620	Per Capita Income	$35,633
Rainfall (in.)	20.5	Prop. Value	$3,497,861,510
Jan. mean min (°F)	25.8	Retail Sales	$368,154,160

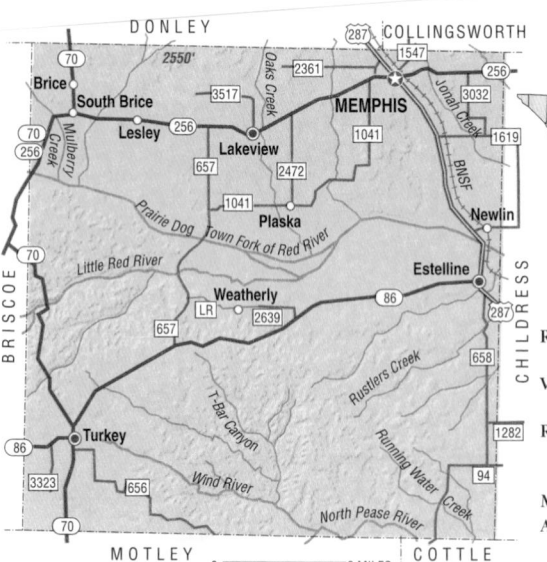

Hall County

Physical Features: Rolling to hilly, broken by Red River forks, tributaries; red and black sandy loam.

Economy: Agriculture, farm/ranch supplies.

History: Apaches displaced by Comanches, who were removed to Indian Territory in 1875. Ranching began in the 1880s. Farming expanded after 1910. County created in 1876 from Bexar, Young districts; organized in 1890; named for Republic of Texas secretary of war W.D.C. Hall.

Race/Ethnicity: Anglo, 53.3%; Black, 9%; Hispanic, 36.4%; Asian, 0%; Other, 1%.

Vital Statistics, annual: Births, 22; deaths, 57; marriages, 0; divorces, 8.

Recreation: Hunting of deer, wild hog, dove; Rails to Trails system; Bob Wills museum; Memphis Picnic festival in September.

Minerals: None.

Agriculture: Cotton (lint and seed), beef cattle, hay, alfalfa, peanuts. Market value $56.4 million. Hunting leases important.

MEMPHIS (2,063) county seat; agriculture, foundry, trucking; historic buildings including Presbyterian church (1911); amphitheater built by WPA.

Other towns include: **Estelline** (131), motorcycle rally/chili cookoff in August, **Lakeview** (92), **Turkey** (375) Bob Wills Day in April.

Population	3,017	July mean max (°F)	95.7
Change from 2010 (%)	-10.0	Civ. Labor	1,110
Area (sq. mi.)	904.1	Unemployed (%)	5.8
Land Area (sq. mi.)	883.5	Wages	$6,856,184
Altitude (ft.)	1,750–2,550	Per Capita Income	$33,095
Rainfall (in.)	22.6	Prop. Value	$726,721,041
Jan. mean min (°F)	26.0	Retail Sales	$39,172,687

Hamilton County

Physical Features: Hilly north central county broken by scenic valleys; loam soils.

Economy: Varied manufacturing, agri-business, hunting leases, tourism.

History: Waco and Tawakoni Indian area. Anglo-American settlers arrived in the mid-1850s. County created and organized in 1858, from Bosque, Comanche, Lampasas counties; named for South Carolina Gov. James Hamilton, who aided the Texas Revolution and Republic.

Race/Ethnicity: Anglo, 84.5%; Black, 0.4%; Hispanic, 13.3%; Asian, 0.3%; Other, 1.2%.

Vital Statistics, annual: Births, 92; deaths, 154; marriages, 50; divorces, 30.

Recreation: Deer, quail, dove hunting; Linear Pecan Creek park in Hamilton; old Bulman (bowstring) bridge over Leon River; Hamilton dove festival in October.

Minerals: Natural gas.

Agriculture: Beef, milk, hay. Market value $62.0 million. Hunting leases important.

HAMILTON (3,108) county seat; manufacturing, agribusiness; hospital and medical clinics; museum, historical homes.

Hico (1,428) tourism, agriculture, varied manufacturing; antiques shops, Billy the Kid museum; steak cookoff in May.

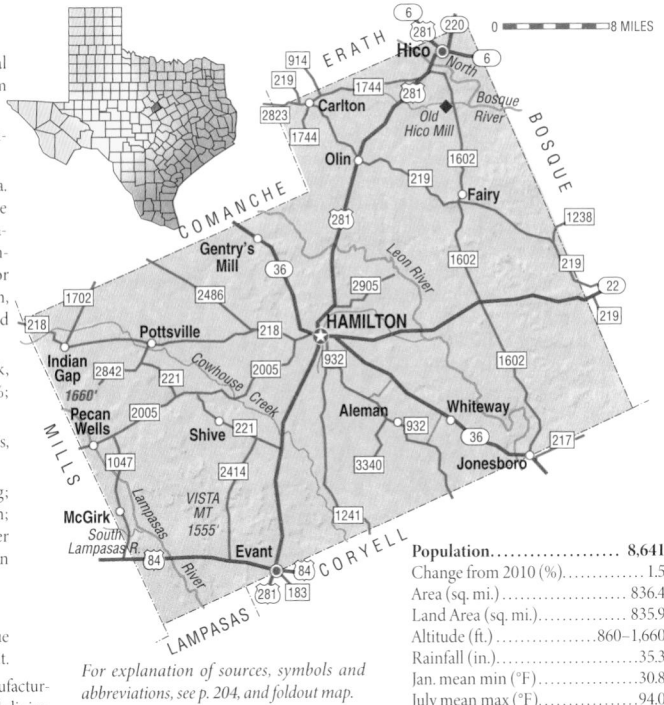

For explanation of sources, symbols and abbreviations, see p. 204, and foldout map.

Other towns include: **Carlton** (75), **Evant** (388, partly in Coryell County), **Jonesboro** (125, partly in Coryell County); **Pottsville** (105).

Population	**8,641**
Change from 2010 (%)	1.5
Area (sq. mi.)	836.4
Land Area (sq. mi.)	835.9
Altitude (ft.)	860–1,660
Rainfall (in.)	35.3
Jan. mean min (°F)	30.8
July mean max (°F)	94.0
Civ. Labor	3,743
Unemployed (%)	4.1
Wages	$29,356,682
Per Capita Income	$60,584
Prop. Value	$2,102,802,245
Retail Sales	$87,546,967

A scenic drive down State Highway 70 in Hall County. Photo by Leaflet, CC by SA 4.0/Wikimedia Commons

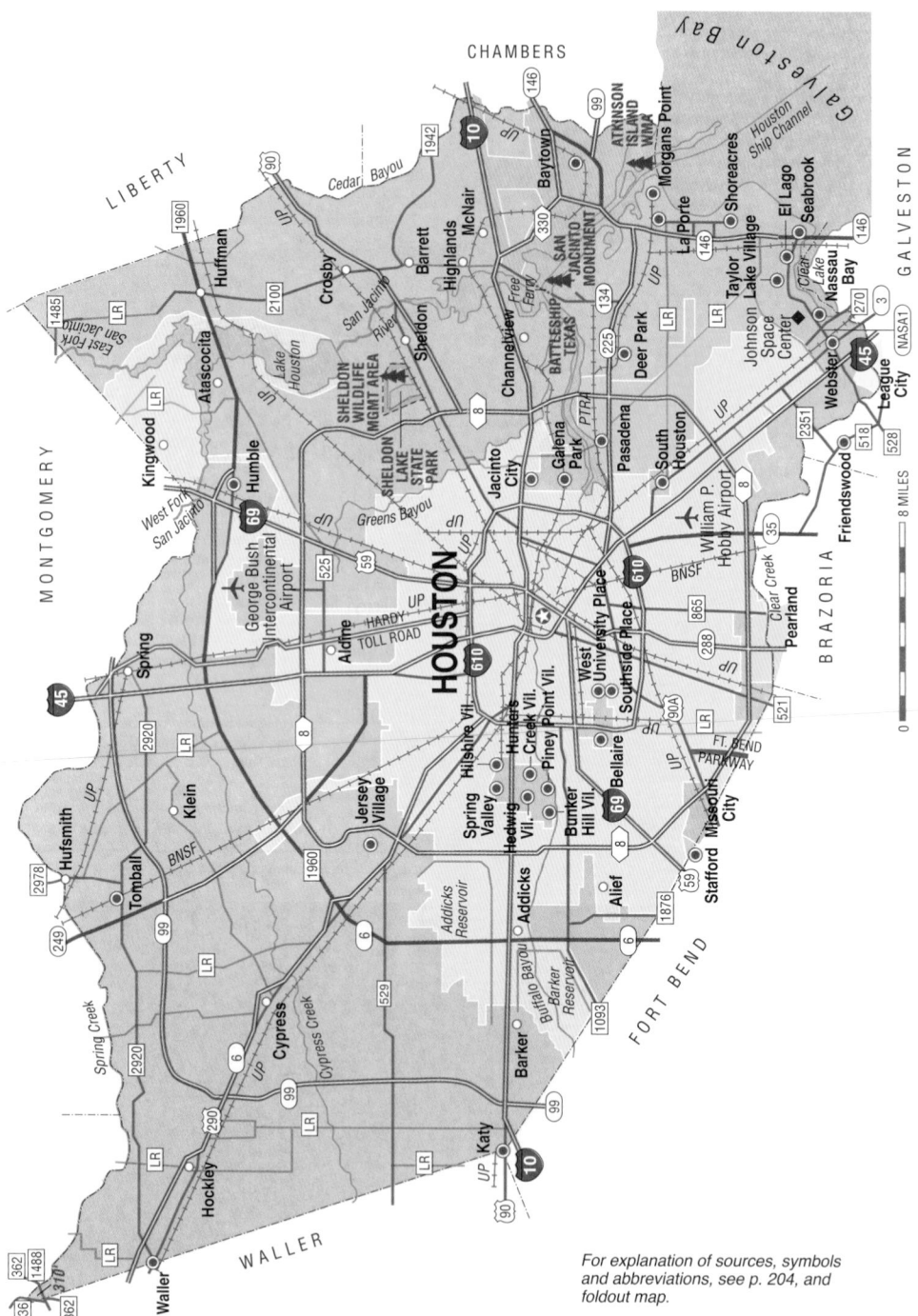

For explanation of sources, symbols and abbreviations, see p. 204, and foldout map.

Harris County

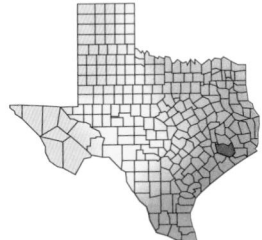

Physical Features: Largest county in eastern half of state; level; typically coastal surface and soils; many bayous, canals for artificial drainage; Lake Houston, Sheldon Reservoir; partly forested.

Economy: Highly industrialized county with largest population; more than 92 foreign governments maintain offices in Houston; corporate management center; nation's largest concentration of petrochemical plants; largest U.S. wheat-exporting port, among top U.S. ports in the value of foreign trade and total tonnage.

Petroleum refining, chemicals, food, fabricated metal products, non-electrical machinery, primary metals, scientific instruments; paper and allied products, printing and publishing; center for energy, space and medical research; center of international business.

History: Orcoquiza villages were visited by Spanish authorities in 1746. Pioneer settlers arrived by boat from Louisiana in 1822. Antebellum planters brought black slaves. Mexican migration increased after the Mexican Revolution. County created in 1836 and organized in 1837; named for John R. Harris, founder of Harrisburg (now part of Houston).

Race/Ethnicity: Anglo, 29.1%; Black, 18.5%; Hispanic, 42.6%; Asian, 7.4%; Other, 2.1%.

Vital Statistics, annual: Births, 73,427; deaths, 25,342; marriages, 29,882; divorces, 12,463.

Recreation: Professional baseball, basketball, football, soccer; rodeo and livestock show; Jones Hall for the Performing Arts; Nina Vance Alley Theatre; Convention Center; Toyota Center, a 19,000-seat sports and entertainment center; Reliant Stadium and downtown ballpark.

Sam Houston Park, with restored early Houston homes, church, stores; Museum of Fine Arts, Contemporary Arts Museum, Rice Museum; Wortham Theater; Hobby Center for Performing Arts; museum of natural science, planetarium, zoo in Hermann Park.

San Jacinto Battleground, Battleship Texas; Johnson Space Center.

Fishing, boating, other freshwater and saltwater activities.

Minerals: Among leading oil, gas, petrochemical areas; production of petroleum, cement, natural gas, salt, lime, sulfur, sand and gravel, clays, stone.

Agriculture: Nursery crops, grass (third in acreage of sod), cattle, hay, horses, vegetables, Christmas trees (first in acreage), goats, rice, corn. Market value $50.6 million. Substantial income from forest products.

Education: Houston is a major center of higher education, with more than 300,000 students enrolled in 28 colleges and universities in the county. Among these are Rice University, the University of Houston, Texas Southern University, University of St. Thomas, Houston Baptist University.

Medical schools include Houston Baptist University School of Nursing, University of Texas Health Science Center, Baylor College of Medicine, Institute of Religion and Human Development, Texas Chiropractic College, Texas Woman's University-Houston Center.

HOUSTON (2,325,298, small parts in Fort Bend and Montgomery counties) county seat; largest Texas city; fourth-largest in nation.

A leading center for manufacture of petroleum equipment, agricultural chemicals, fertilizers, pesticides, oil and gas pipeline transmission; a leading scientific center; manufacture of machinery, fabricated metals; a major distribution, shipping center; engineering and research center; food processing; 85 hospitals.

Plants make apparel, lumber and wood products; furniture, paper, chemical, petroleum and coal products; publishing center; one of the nation's largest public school systems; prominent corporate center; Go Texan Days (rodeo) in February/March, international festival in March/April.

PASADENA (156,841) residential city with large industrial area manufacturing petrochemicals and other petroleum-related products; civic center; San Jacinto College, Texas Chiropractic College; hospitals; historical museum; Strawberry Festival in May.

BAYTOWN (81,725, part [4,180] in Chambers County) refining, petrochemical center; commuters to Houston; Lee College; hospital, museum, library; historical homes; Chili When It's Chilly cookoff and the Great Bull Run in January.

The Clear Lake Area: which includes **El Lago** (2,680); **Nassau Bay** (4,095); **Seabrook** (14,059); **Taylor Lake Village** (3,594); **Webster** (11,989) — tourism, Johnson Space Center, University of Houston-Clear Lake, commuting to Houston; Bayport Industrial Complex includes Port of Bayport; 12 major marinas; hospitals; Christmas lighted boat parade.

Other towns include: **Aldine** (17,792); **Atascocita** (78,165); **Barrett** (3,483); **Bellaire** (18,283) residential city with several major office buildings; **Bunker Hill Village** (3,865); **Channelview** (46,373) hospital; **Crosby** (2,875) government/services, chemical plant, Czech Fest in October; **Cypress** (120,000); **Deer Park** (34,050) ship-channel industries, Totally Texas celebration in April; **Galena Park** (11,022); **Hedwig Village** (2,601); **Highlands** (7,793) commuters, heritage museum, Jamboree in October; **Hilshire Village** (793); **Hockley** (400); **Huffman** (15,000); **Humble** (15,704) oil-field equipment manufactured, retail center, hospital; **Hunters Creek Village** (4,738); **Jacinto City** (10,499); **Jersey Village** (7,907).

Also: **Katy** (21,912, partly in Fort Bend and Waller counties) corporate headquarters, distribution center, hospitals; museums, park; Rice Harvest festival in October; **Klein** (45,000); **La Porte** (34,757) petrochemical industry; depot museum; Sylvan Beach Festival in April; Galveston Bay; **Morgan's Point** (358); **Piney Point Village** (3,338); **Sheldon** (2,157); **Shoreacres** (1,580); **South Houston** (17,674).

Also: **Southside Place** (1,867); **Spring** (68,450); **Spring Valley** (4,248); **Tomball** (11,754) health care, oil and gas, retail, hospital, museum, junior college, parks and nature preserve, German festival in March; **West University Place** (15,699).

Parts of **Friendswood, League City, Missouri City, Pearland, Stafford,** and **Waller.**

Addicks, Alief, and Kingwood are now within the city limits of Houston.

Population	**4,698,655**
Change from 2010 (%)	14.8
Area (sq. mi.)	1,777.5
Land Area (sq. mi.)	1,703.5
Altitude (ft.)	sea level–310
Rainfall (in.)	56.8
Jan. mean min (°F)	43.4
July mean max (°F)	90.7
Civ. Labor	2,280,347
Unemployed (%)	7.1
Wages	$43,242,163,732
Per Capita Income	$60,002
Prop. Value	$720,163,806,322
Retail Sales	$90,436,159,789

Physical Features: Hilly in west, blackland in east; bisected by Blanco River; on edge of Balcones Escarpment.

Economy: Education, tourism, retirement area, some manufacturing; part of Austin metropolitan area.

History: Tonkawa area, also some Apache and Comanche presence. Spanish authorities attempted the first permanent settlement in 1807. Mexican land grants in early 1830s to Juan Martín Veramendi, Juan Vicente Campos and Thomas Jefferson Chambers. County created in 1843 from Travis County, organized the same year; named for Capt. Jack Hays, a famous Texas Ranger.

Race/Ethnicity: Anglo, 53.7%; Black, 2.5%; Hispanic, 39.6%; Asian, 1.5%; Other, 2.3%.

Vital Statistics, annual: Births, 2,467; deaths, 1,007; marriages, 1,056; divorces, 527.

Recreation: Fishing, hunting; college cultural, athletic events; African-American museum, LBJ museum; Cypress Creek and Blanco River resorts, guest ranches, Wonder World park.

Minerals: Sand, gravel, cement produced.

Agriculture: Beef cattle, goats, exotic wildlife; greenhouse nurseries; hay, corn, sorghum, wheat and cotton. Market value $21.8 million.

SAN MARCOS (69,731) county seat; Texas State University, outlet center, tourism, distribution center, commuting; hospital; San Marcos, Blanco rivers; jazz festival in February, Mermaid Fest in September.

KYLE (47,899) medical, education, retail center, Claiborne Kyle Log House, Katherine Anne Porter House, 5k Kyle-O-Meter in October.

Other towns include: **Bear Creek** (466); **Buda** (17,862) construction, manufacturing, retail, government/services, Stagecoach park, Weiner Dog races in April;

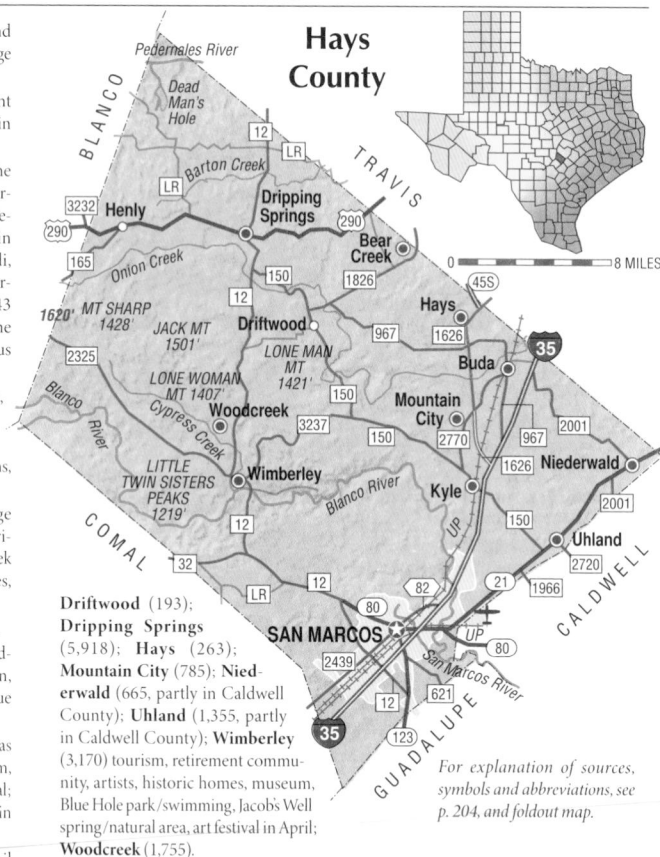

Hays County

Driftwood (193); **Dripping Springs** (5,918); **Hays** (263); **Mountain City** (785); **Niederwald** (665, partly in Caldwell County); **Uhland** (1,355, partly in Caldwell County); **Wimberley** (3,170) tourism, retirement community, artists, historic homes, museum, Blue Hole park/swimming, Jacob's Well spring/natural area, art festival in April; **Woodcreek** (1,755).

For explanation of sources, symbols and abbreviations, see p. 204, and foldout map.

Population....................	**228,364**	July mean max (°F)..................94.3	
Change from 2010 (%)...............45.4		Civ. Labor........................ 123,618	
Area (sq. mi.)........................ 679.9		Unemployed (%)........................4.5	
Land Area (sq. mi.)................. 678.0		Wages...................... $892,570,489	
Altitude (ft.)....................550–1,620		Per Capita Income............... $45,332	
Rainfall (in.)...........................35.7		Prop. Value.............. $33,283,505,777	
Jan. mean min (°F)....................38.7		Retail Sales............... $5,134,061,990	

An airplane at the Commemorative Air Force, Central Texas Wing hangar and museum, in San Marcos. Photo by Larry D. Moore, CC 3/ Wikimedia Commons

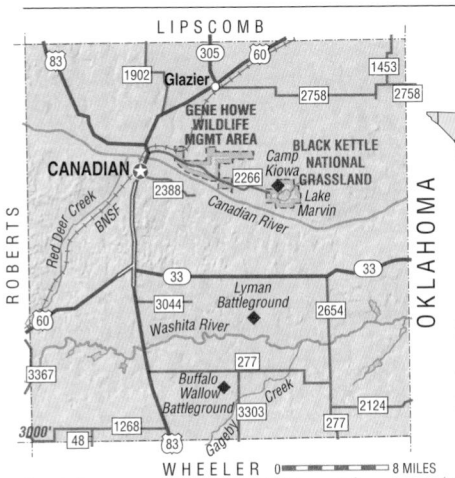

Hemphill County

Physical Features: Sloping surface, broken by Canadian, Washita rivers; sandy, red, dark soils.

Economy: Oil, gas, agriculture, tourism, hunting, government/services.

History: Apaches who were in the area were later pushed out by Comanches and Kiowas. The tribes were removed to the Indian Territory in 1875. Ranching began in the late 1870s. Farmers began to arrive after 1900. County created from the Bexar and Young districts in 1876 and organized in 1887; named for Republic of Texas Justice John Hemphill.

Race/Ethnicity: Anglo, 62%; Black, 0.1%; Hispanic, 36.4%; Asian, 0.3%; Other, 1%.

Vital Statistics, annual: Births, 76; deaths, 34; marriages, 47; divorces, 12.

Recreation: Lake Marvin; fall foliage tour; hunting, fishing; Indian Battleground, wildlife management area; museum; 4th of July rodeo; prairie chicken viewing in April.

Population	3,838
Change from 2010 (%)	0.8
Area (sq. mi.)	912.2
Land Area (sq. mi.)	906.3
Altitude (ft.)	2,170–3,000
Rainfall (in.)	21.8
Jan. mean min (°F)	21.2
July mean max (°F)	93.2
Civ. Labor	1,631
Unemployed (%)	4.5
Wages	$22,366,755
Per Capita Income	$57,053
Prop. Value	$1,466,667,565
Retail Sales	$29,647,534

Minerals: Oil, natural gas, caliche.

Agriculture: Cattle, wheat, horses, hay, alfalfa; some irrigation. Market value $138.9 million. Hunting, nature tourism.

CANADIAN (2,717) county seat; oil, gas production; hospital; art foundation.

Henderson County

Physical Features: East Texas county bounded by Neches and Trinity rivers; hilly, rolling; one-third forested; sandy, loam, clay soils; timber; Cedar Creek Reservoir, Lake Palestine, Lake Athens, Forest Grove Reservoir; Trinidad Lake.

Economy: Agribusiness, retail trade, varied manufacturing, minerals, recreation, tourism.

History: Caddo tribal area. Cherokees and other tribes migrated into the area in 1819-1820 ahead of white settlement. Cherokees were forced into Indian Territory in 1839. Anglo-American settlers arrived in the 1840s. County created in 1846 from Nacogdoches and Houston counties; organized the same year. County named for Gov. J. Pinckney Henderson.

Race/Ethnicity: Anglo, 77.5%; Black, 6.6%; Hispanic, 13%; Asian, 0.4%; Other, 2.3%.

Vital Statistics, annual: Births, 897; deaths, 1,084; marriages, 503; divorces, 38.

Recreation: Cedar Creek Reservoir, Lake Palestine, other lakes; Purtis Creek State Park; hunting, fishing, bird-watching; aerial ropeslide at New York; East Texas Arboretum.

Minerals: Oil, gas, clays, lignite, sulfur, sand and gravel.

Agriculture: Beef cattle, forages, nurseries/horticulture, rodeo stock. Market value $40.2 million. Hunting leases and fishing. Timber important.

ATHENS (13,649) county seat; agribusiness center, varied manufacturing, tourism, state fish hatchery and museum; hospital, mental health center; Trinity Valley Community College; Texas Fiddlers' Contest in May.

GUN BARREL CITY (6,222) recreation, retirement, retail center.

MALAKOFF (2,434) brick factory, varied industry, tourism, library, Cornbread Festival in April.

Other towns include: **Berryville** (1,075); **Brownsboro** (1,286); **Caney City** (230); **Chandler** (3,259) commuting to Tyler, retail trade, tourism, Pow Wow Festival in October; **Coffee City** (1,504); **Enchanted Oaks** (344); **Eustace** (1,007); **Larue** (250); **Log Cabin** (780); **Moore Station** (214); **Murchison** (618); **Payne Springs** (807); **Poynor** (315); **Seven Points** (1,558) agribusiness, retail trade, recreation, Monte Carlo celebration in November; **Star Harbor** (495); **Tool** (2,374), and **Trinidad** (882).

Also, **Mabank** (3,995, mostly in Kaufman County).

Population	82,989
Change from 2010 (%)	5.7
Area (sq. mi.)	949.3
Land Area (sq. mi.)	873.8
Altitude (ft.)	256–763
Rainfall (in.)	42.9
Jan. mean min (°F)	34.5
July mean max (°F)	92.6
Civ. Labor	37,256
Unemployed (%)	5.6
Wages	$196,421,634
Per Capita Income	$40,135
Prop. Value	$10,514,070,328
Retail Sales	$938,607,129

Hidalgo County

Physical Features: Rich alluvial soils along Rio Grande; sandy, loam soils in north; semitropical vegetation; Anzalduas Channel Dam, Delta Lake, Valley Acres Reservoir.

Economy: Food processing and shipping, other agribusinesses, tourism, mineral operations; Texas' fifth-largest metro area.

History: Coahuiltecan and Karankawa area. Comanches forced Apaches southward into valley in the 1700s; Comanches arrived in valley in the 1800s. Spanish settlement occurred 1750-1800. County created in 1852 from Cameron and Starr counties, organized the same year; named for leader of Mexico's independence movement of 1810, Father Miguel Hidalgo y Costillo.

Race/Ethnicity: Anglo, 6.2%; Black, 0.3%; Hispanic, 92%; Asian, 1%; Other, 0.2%.

Vital Statistics, annual: Births, 16,325; deaths, 4,179; marriages, 4,783; divorces, 0.

Recreation: Winter resort, retirement area; fishing, hunting; gateway to Mexico; historical sites; museum; Bentsen-Rio Grande Valley State Park; museums; All-Valley Winter Vegetable Show at Pharr.

Minerals: Oil, gas, stone, sand and gravel.

Agriculture: Ninety percent of farm cash receipts from crops (ranked first in state), principally from sugar cane (first in acreage), grain sorghum (first in acreage), vegetables (first in acreage), citrus, cotton; livestock includes cattle; 184,000 acres irrigated. Market value $311.0 million.

EDINBURG (99,454) county seat; vegetable processing and packing, petroleum operations, tourism, clothing; planetarium; the University of Texas-Rio Grande Valley; hospitals; behavioral health center; museum; Texas Cook'em High Steaks July 4 weekend, Fiesta Edinburg in February.

McALLEN (144,785) retail center, medical care/hospitals, government/services; community college; birding center,

For explanation of sources, symbols and abbreviations, see p. 204, and foldout map.

Population	886,294
Change from 2010 (%)	14.4
Area (sq. mi.)	1,582.9
Land Area (sq. mi.)	1,570.9
Altitude (ft.)	28–376
Rainfall (in.)	22.2
Jan. mean min (°F)	49.3
July mean max (°F)	96.2
Civ. Labor	364,476
Unemployed (%)	10.3
Wages	$2,608,704,301
Per Capita Income	$27,415
Prop. Value	$51,843,534,647
Retail Sales	$11,054,150,664

Mxlan arts/music celebration of Mexican culture in late July.

MISSION (86,214) citrus groves, agricultural processing/distribution; hospital; community college; international butterfly park; Citrus Fiesta in January.

PHARR (81,473) agriculture, trading center; trucking; tourism; old clock, juke box museums; folklife festival in February.

Other towns include: **Abram** (2,461); **Alamo** (20,208) live steam museum;

Alton (17,165); **Doffing** (5,722); **Donna** (17,235) citrus center, varied manufacturing; **Edcouch** (3,368); **Elsa** (7,174); **Granjeno** (320); **Hargill** (919); **Hidalgo** (13,984) trade zone, shipping, winter resort, agribusiness, historical sites, library, Borderfest in March; **La Blanca** (2,652); **La Homa** (12,102); **La Joya** (4,409); **La Villa** (2,544); **Los Ebanos** (313).

Also: Mercedes (17,096) "boot capital," citrus, and vegetable center, food processing, tourism, recreation vehicle show in January, Hispanic Fest July 4; **Mila Doce** (6,778); **Monte Alto** (1,976); **North Alamo** (3,926); **Murillo** (9,095); **Palmhurst** (2,737); **Palmview** (10,829); **Palmview South** (6,064); **Peñitas** (4,721); **Perezville** (6,022); **Progreso** (6,073); **Progreso Lakes** (268); **San Carlos** (3,486); **San Juan** (38,033) retirement area, trucking, Shrine of Our Lady of San Juan, Spring Fiesta in February; **San Manuel-Linn** (787); **South Alamo** (3,589); **Sullivan City** (4,273); **Weslaco** (42,047) agriculture, nature tourism, South Texas College, hospital, Dragonfly Days in May.

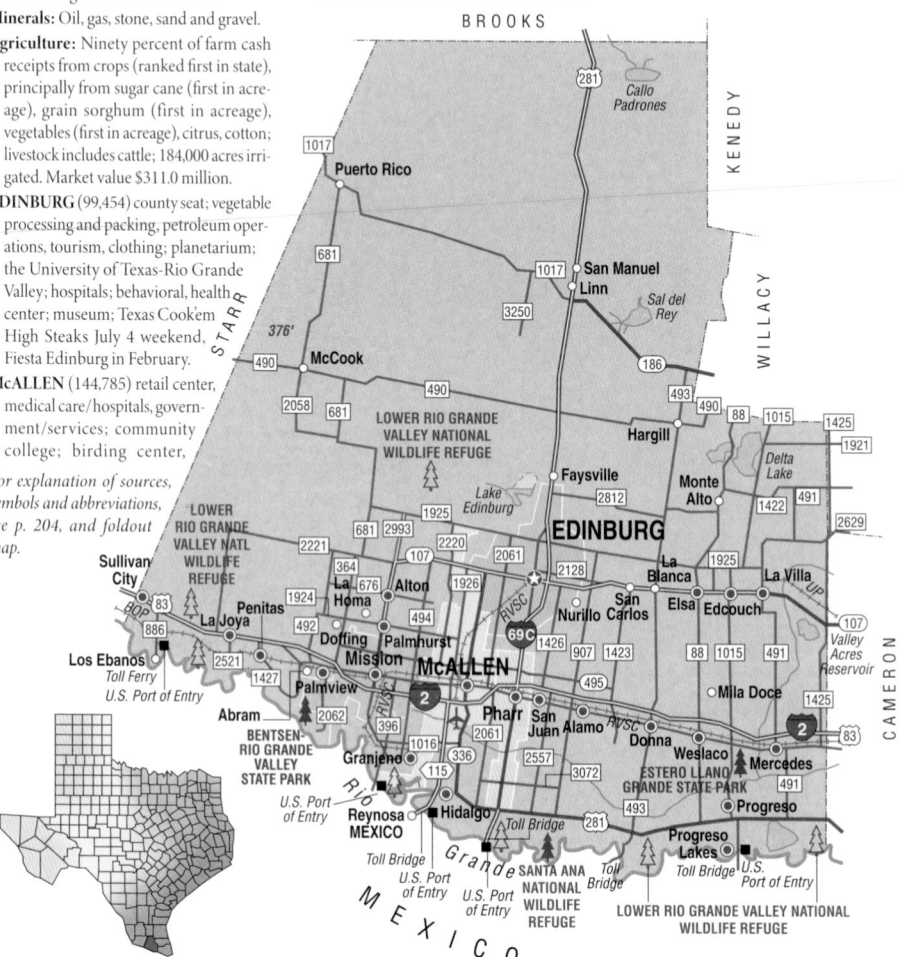

The old Hidalgo County jail in Edinburg. Photo by Larry D. Moore, CC by 4.0/Wikimedia Commons

Hill County

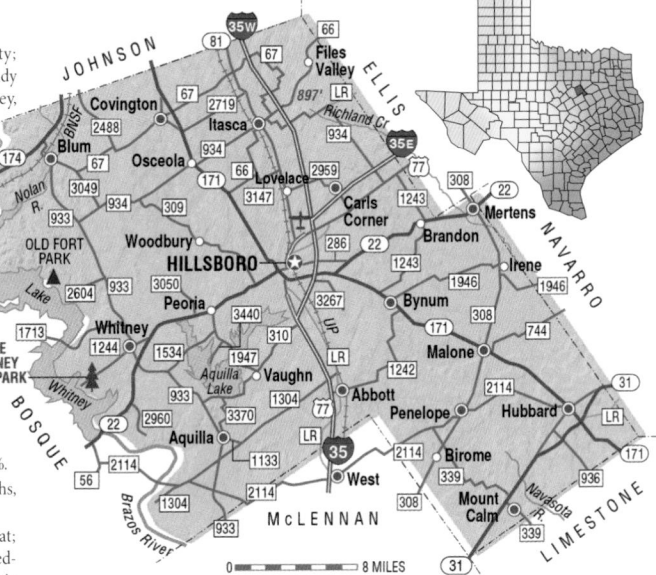

Physical Features: North central county; level to rolling; blackland soils, some sandy loams; drains to Brazos; Lake Whitney, Aquilla Lake.

Economy: Agribusiness, tourism, varied manufacturing.

History: Waco and Tawakoni area, later Comanches. Believed to be Indian "council spot," a place of safe passage without evidence of raids. Anglo-Americans of the Robertson colony arrived in the early 1830s. Fort Graham established in 1849. County created from Navarro County in 1853, organized the same year; named for G.W. Hill, Republic of Texas official.

Race/Ethnicity: Anglo, 69%; Black, 6.2%; Hispanic, 22%; Asian, 0.3%; Other, 2.3%.

Vital Statistics, annual: Births, 389; deaths, 455; marriages, 233; divorces, 135.

Recreation: Lake activities; excursion boat; Texas Heritage Museum including Confederate and Audie Murphy exhibits, historic structures, rebuilt frontier fort barracks; motorcycle track.

Minerals: Gas, limestone.

Agriculture: Corn, cattle, sorghum, wheat, cotton, dairies, turkeys. Market value $114.0 million. Some firewood marketed.

HILLSBORO (8,767) county seat; agribusiness, varied manufacturing, retail, outlet center, tourism, antiques malls; Hill College; hospital; Cell Block museum, restored courthouse; Cotton Pickin Fair in September.

WHITNEY (2,202) manufacturing, stone works, government/services; hospital; museum; Pioneer Days in October.

Other towns include: **Abbott** (375); **Aquilla** (114); **Blum** (471); **Brandon** (75); **Bynum** (210); **Carl's Corner** (187); **Covington** (276); **Hubbard** (1,405) agriculture, machine shop, antiques, museum, library, Magnolias & Mistletoe Victorian Christmas celebration; **Irene** (170); **Itasca** (1,761); **Malone** (279); **Mertens** (131); **Mount Calm** (336); **Penelope** (207).

Population	37,069
Change from 2010 (%)	5.6
Area (sq. mi.)	985.7
Land Area (sq. mi.)	958.9
Altitude (ft.)	417–897
Rainfall (in.)	37.9
Jan. mean min (°F)	34.8
July mean max (°F)	95.0
Civ. Labor	16,143
Unemployment (%)	5.6
Wages	$122,380,429
Per Capita Income	$41,240
Prop. Value	$5,017,877,080
Retail Sales	$404,487,424

Hockley County

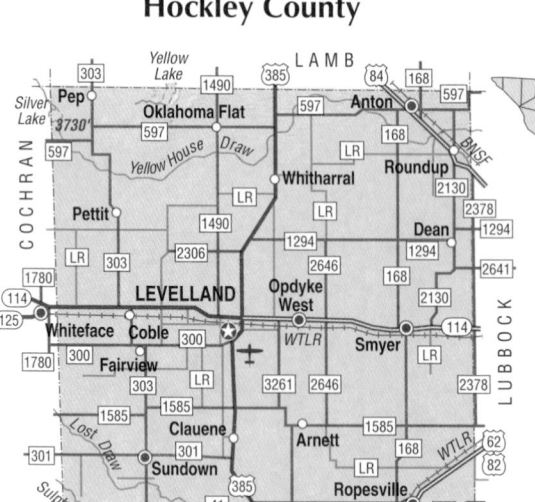

Physical Features: South Plains, numerous playas, drains to Yellow House Draw; loam, sandy loam soils.

Economy: Extensive oil, gas production and services; manufacturing; varied agribusiness.

History: Comanches displaced Apaches in the early 1700s. Large ranches of 1880s brought few residents. Homesteaders arrived after 1900. County created in 1876 from Bexar, Young districts; organized in 1921. Named for the Republic of Texas secretary of war Gen. G.W. Hockley.

Race/Ethnicity: Anglo, 44.4%; Black, 3.9%; Hispanic, 49.7%; Asian, 0.3%; Other, 1.5%.

Vital Statistics, annual: Births, 335; deaths, 224; marriages, 129; divorces, 79.

Recreation: Early Settlers' Day in July; Marigolds Arts, Crafts Festival in November.

Minerals: Oil, gas, stone; one of leading oil counties with more than 1 billion barrels produced.

Agriculture: Cotton, grain sorghum; cattle, hogs raised; substantial irrigation. Market value $92.0 million.

LEVELLAND (13,555) county seat; oil, cotton, cattle center; government/services; hospital; South Plains College; Hot Burrito & Bluegrass Music Festival in July.

Other towns include: **Anton** (1,100); **Opdyke West** (196); **Pep** (30); **Ropesville** (430); **Smyer** (477); **Sundown** (1,422); **Whitharral** (158).

Population......................22,862	July mean max (°F)....................91.6
Change from 2010 (%)................-0.3	Civ. Labor...........................10,275
Area (sq. mi.)..........................908.6	Unemployed (%).........................7.0
Land Area (sq. mi.)...................908.4	Wages $118,438,810
Altitude (ft.)....................3,300–3,730	Per Capita Income $42,162
Rainfall (in.)............................19.8	Prop. Value $3,298,901,811
Jan. mean min (°F)....................26.1	Retail Sales.................$249,333,994

Hood County

Physical Features: Hilly; broken by Paluxy, Brazos rivers; sandy loam soils; Lake Granbury, Squaw Creek Reservoir.

Economy: Tourism, commuting to Fort Worth and Dallas, nuclear power plant, agriculture.

History: Lipan Apache and Comanche area. Anglo-American settlers arrived in the late 1840s. County created in 1866 from Johnson and Erath counties, organized the same year; named for Confederate Gen. John B. Hood.

Race/Ethnicity: Anglo, 84.3%; Black, 0.4%; Hispanic, 13%; Asian, 0.5%; Other, 1.6%.

Vital Statistics, annual: Births, 676; deaths, 751; marriages, 389; divorces, 193.

Recreation: Lakes, fishing, scenic areas; summer theater; Gen. Granbury's Bean & Rib cookoff in March; Acton historic site; hike & bike trail.

Minerals: Oil, gas, stone.

Agriculture: Hay, turfgrass, beef cattle, nursery crops, pecans, peaches; some irrigation. Market value $18.9 million.

For explanation of sources, symbols and abbreviations, see p. 204, and foldout map.

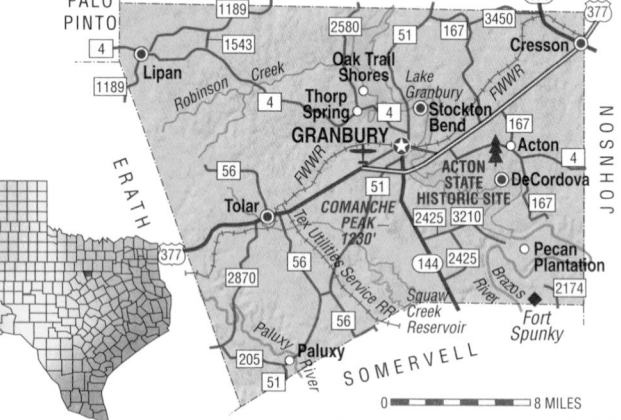

GRANBURY (10,454) county seat; retail, tourism, medical services; historic downtown area, opera house, museums; hospital, library, college extensions; Harvest Moon festival in October.

Other towns include: **Acton** (1,129) grave of Elizabeth Crockett, wife of Davy; **Cresson** (1,123); **DeCordova** (2,998); **Lipan** (500); **Oak Trail Shores** (3,411); **Pecan Plantation** (5,719); **Stockton Bend** (334); **Tolar** (983).

Population......................60,984	
Change from 2010 (%)................19.2	
Area (sq. mi.)..........................436.8	
Land Area (sq. mi.)...................420.6	
Altitude (ft.)....................600–1,230	
Rainfall (in.)............................35.1	
Jan. mean min (°F)....................30.1	
July mean max (°F)....................95.1	
Civ. Labor...........................27,911	
Unemployed (%).........................5.5	
Wages $185,348,660	
Per Capita Income $51,384	
Prop. Value $9,887,101,845	
Retail Sales...............$1,131,428,240	

Hopkins County

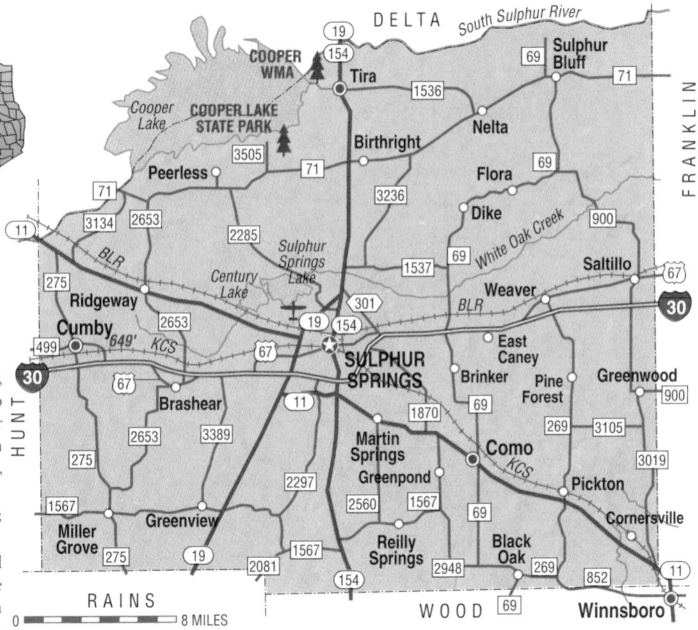

Physical Features: Varied timber, including pines; drains north to South Sulphur River; Cooper Lake (also known as Jim Chapman Lake), Sulphur Springs Lake; light, sandy to heavier black soils.

Economy: Agribusiness, feed mills; varied manufacturing.

History: Caddo area, displaced by Cherokees, who in turn were forced out by President Lamar in 1839. First Anglo-American settlement in 1837. County created in 1846 from Lamar and Nacogdoches counties, organized the same year; named for pioneer Hopkins family.

Race/Ethnicity: Anglo, 72.9%; Black, 7%; Hispanic, 16.9%; Asian, 0.5%; Other, 2.4%.

Vital Statistics, annual: Births, 444; deaths, 398; marriages, 276; divorces, 183.

Recreation: Fishing, hunting; state park, lake activities; dairy museum; dairy festival in June; stew contest in September.

Minerals: Lignite coal.

Agriculture: Dairies, beef cattle, hay (first in acreage). Market value $253.7 million. Firewood and hardwood lumber marketed.

SULPHUR SPRINGS (16,279) county seat; dairy farming, equine center, food processing and distribution, varied manufacturing, tourism; hospital; library, heritage park, music box gallery, civic center.

Other towns include: **Brashear** (280), **Como** (746), **Cumby** (826), **Dike** (170), **Pickton** (300), **Saltillo** (200), **Sulphur Bluff** (280), **Tira** (316).

Population	37,312
Change from 2010 (%)	6.1
Area (sq. mi.)	792.8
Land Area (sq. mi.)	767.2
Altitude (ft.)	340–649
Rainfall (in.)	47.2
Jan. mean min (°F)	32.9
July mean max (°F)	93.1
Civ. Labor	17,519
Unemployed (%)	4.7
Wages	$144,505,785
Per Capita Income	$41,562
Prop. Value	$3,592,266,686
Retail Sales	$632,933,308

The Granbury Square Plaza in Hood County. Photo by Michael Barera, CC by SA 4.0/Wikimedia Commons

Houston County

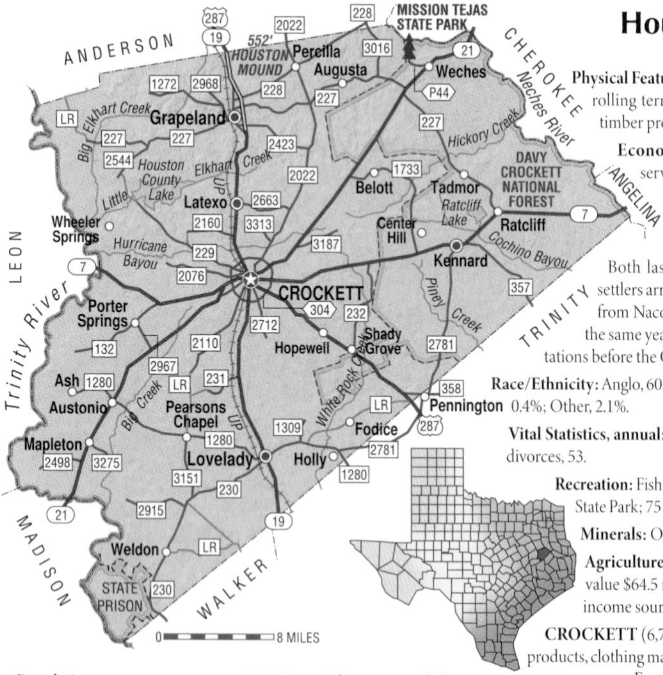

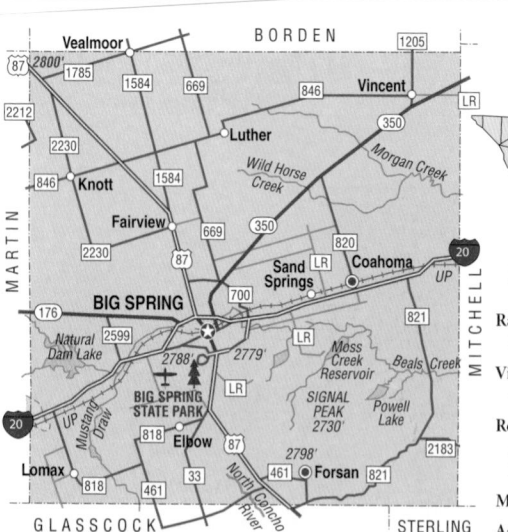

Physical Features: East Texas county over half forested; rolling terrain, draining to Neches, Trinity rivers; timber production.

Economy: Livestock, timber, government/services, manufacturing, tourism.

History: Caddo group attracted mission San Francisco de los Tejas in 1690. Spanish town of Bucareli established in 1774. Both lasted only a few years. Anglo-American settlers arrived in the 1820s. County created in 1837 from Nacogdoches County by Republic, organized the same year; named for Sam Houston. Cotton plantations before the Civil War had many slaves.

Race/Ethnicity: Anglo, 60.9%; Black, 24.2%; Hispanic, 12.1%; Asian, 0.4%; Other, 2.1%.

Vital Statistics, annual: Births, 231; deaths, 268; marriages, 124; divorces, 53.

Recreation: Fishing, hunting; national forest; Mission Tejas State Park; 75 historical markers; Houston County Lake.

Minerals: Oil, gas, gravel.

Agriculture: Cattle, hay, watermelons, cotton. Market value $64.5 million. Hunting leases. Timber principal income source.

CROCKETT (6,741) county seat; timber, steel and plastic products, clothing manufacturing, hospital; historic sites; Black Expo in February; fiddlers festival in June.

Other towns include: **Grapeland** (1,456) steel, agribusiness, oil and gas, Peanut Festival in October; **Kennard** (329); **Latexo** (338); **Lovelady** (639) Lovefest in February; **Ratcliff** (106).

Population	23,381
Change from 2010 (%)	-1.5
Area (sq. mi.)	1,236.6
Land Area (sq. mi.)	1,230.9
Altitude (ft.)	150–552
Rainfall (in.)	45.2
Jan. mean min (°F)	36.8
July mean max (°F)	93.4
Civ. Labor	9,771
Unemployed (%)	5.5
Wages	$110,956,318
Per Capita Income	$39,609
Prop. Value	$3,756,325,697
Retail Sales	$172,885,814

Howard County

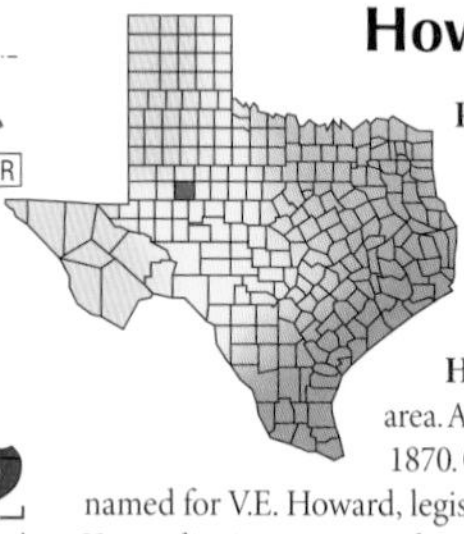

Physical Features: On edge of Llano Estacado; sandy loam soils; Natural Dam Lake.

Economy: Agriculture, petrochemicals, government/services.

History: Pawnee and Comanche area. Anglo-American settlement began in 1870. Oil boom in the mid-1920s. County named for V.E. Howard, legislator; created in 1876 from Bexar, Young districts; organized in 1882.

Race/Ethnicity: Anglo, 47.3%; Black, 6.2%; Hispanic, 43.9%; Asian, 0.6%; Other, 1.7%.

Vital Statistics, annual: Births, 484; deaths, 416; marriages, 247; divorces, 18.

Recreation: Lakes, state park; campground in Comanche Trail Park, Native Plant Trail, museum, historical sites, Pow Wow in April, Pops in the Park in July.

Minerals: Oil, gas, sand, gravel, and stone.

Agriculture: Cotton, beef, hay. Market value $26.9 million.

BIG SPRING (28,349) county seat; agriculture, petrochemicals, varied manufacturing; hospitals including a state institution and Veterans Administration hospital; federal prison; Howard College; railroad plaza.

Other towns include: **Coahoma** (948), **Forsan** (215), **Knott** (200), and **Sand Springs** (859).

Population	36,294
Change from 2010 (%)	3.7
Area (sq. mi.)	904.2
Land Area (sq. mi.)	900.8
Altitude (ft.)	2,180–2,800
Rainfall (in.)	19.5
Jan. mean min (°F)	31.3
July mean max (°F)	94.6
Civ. Labor	13,138
Unemployed (%)	7.0
Wages	$167,859,752
Per Capita Income	$43,348
Prop. Value	$6,861,060,684
Retail Sales	$569,307,386

Hudspeth County

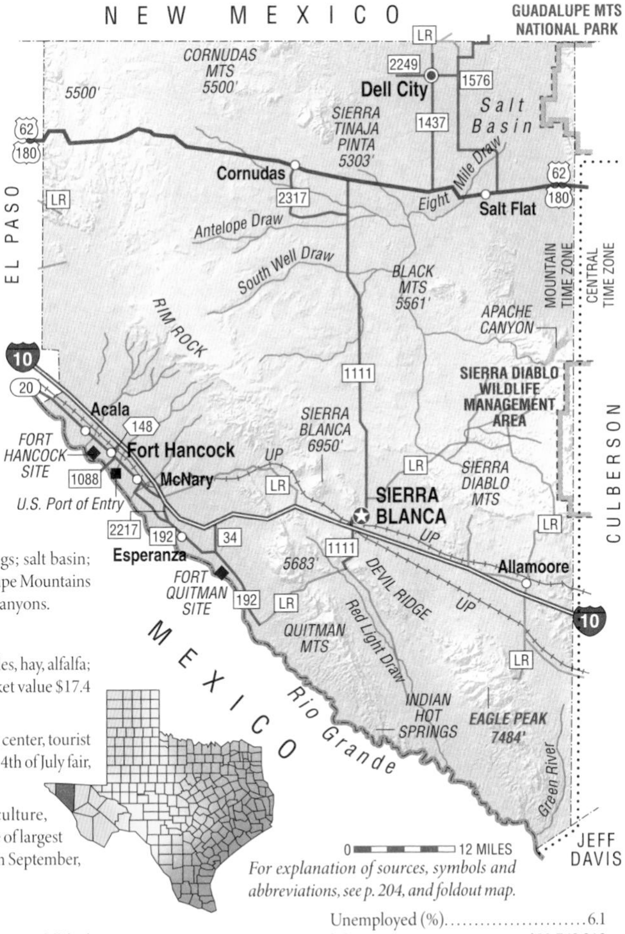

Physical Features: Plateau, basin terrain, draining to salt lakes; Rio Grande; mostly rocky, alkaline, clay soils and sandy loam soils, except alluvial along Rio Grande; desert, mountain vegetation. Fertile agricultural valley.

Economy: Agribusiness, mining, tourism, hunting leases.

History: Mescalero Apache area. Fort Quitman established in 1858 to protect routes to west. Railroad in 1881 brought Anglo-American settlers. Political turmoil in Mexico (1912–1929) brought more settlers from Mexico. County named for Texas political leader Claude B. Hudspeth; created in 1917 from El Paso County, organized the same year.

Race/Ethnicity: Anglo, 19.8%; Black, 0.9%; Hispanic, 77.7%; Asian, 0.3%; Other, 1%.

Vital Statistics, annual: Births, 45; deaths, 12; marriages, 1; divorces, 0.

Recreation: Scenic drives; fort sites; hot springs; salt basin; white sands; hunting; birding; part of Guadalupe Mountains National Park, containing unique plant life, canyons.

Minerals: Talc, stone, gypsum.

Agriculture: Most income from cotton, vegetables, hay, alfalfa; beef cattle raised; 18,000 acres irrigated. Market value $17.4 million.

SIERRA BLANCA (574) county seat; ranching center, tourist stop on interstate highway; adobe courthouse; 4th of July fair; livestock show in January.

Other towns include: **Dell City** (948) agriculture, government/services, telephone co-op; some of largest water wells in state, Dell Valley Hudspeth fair in September, and **Fort Hancock** (1,832).

For explanation of sources, symbols and abbreviations, see p. 204, and foldout map.

Population.......................	3,680
Change from 2010 (%).................	5.9
Area (sq. mi.).......................	4,571.8
Land Area (sq. mi.)................	4,571.0
Altitude (ft.)..................	3,117–7,484

Rainfall (in.)............................	11.2
Jan. mean min (°F)....................	25.7
July mean max (°F)....................	92.5
Civ. Labor.............................	1,894

Unemployed (%)........................	6.1
Wages	$23,762,212
Per Capita Income	$23,569
Prop. Value	$934,208,395
Retail Sales...................	$10,734,143

Forever view down Texas Ranch Road 1111 in Hudspeth County. Photo by Carol M. Highsmith, courtesy of the Library of Congress

Hunt County

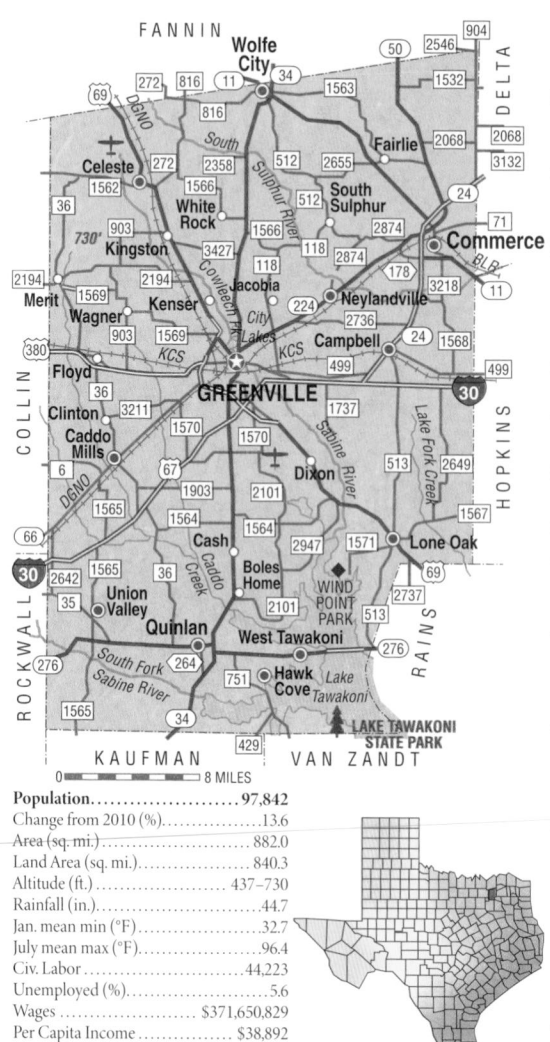

Population.......................97,842
Change from 2010 (%)..................13.6
Area (sq. mi.)........................882.0
Land Area (sq. mi.)...................840.3
Altitude (ft.).....................437–730
Rainfall (in.)........................44.7
Jan. mean min (°F)....................32.7
July mean max (°F)....................96.4
Civ. Labor..........................44,223
Unemployed (%).........................5.6
Wages.......................$371,650,829
Per Capita Income...............$38,892
Prop. Value..............$12,145,491,435
Retail Sales...............$1,550,355,394

Physical Features: Level to rolling surface; Sabine, Sulphur rivers; Lake Tawakoni, Greenville City Lakes; mostly heavy Blackland soil, some loam, sandy loams.

Economy: Education, varied manufacturing, agribusiness; several Fortune 500 companies in county; many residents employed in Dallas area.

History: Caddo Indians gone by 1790s. Kiowa bands in the area when Anglo-American settlers arrived in 1839. County named for Memucan Hunt, Republic secretary of navy; created in 1846 from Fannin, Nacogdoches counties, organized the same year.

Race/Ethnicity: Anglo, 70.4%; Black, 8.7%; Hispanic, 17%; Asian, 1.1%; Other, 2.5%.

Vital Statistics, annual: Births, 1,097; deaths, 958; marriages, 531; divorces, 216.

Recreation: Lake Tawakoni sports, catfish tournament in August; Texas A&M University–Commerce events.

Minerals: Sand and white rock, gas, oil.

Agriculture: Cattle, forage, greenhouse crops, top revenue sources; horses, wheat, oats, cotton, grain sorghum. Market value $55.3 million. Some firewood sold.

GREENVILLE (28,992) county seat; varied manufacturing, retail trade, health and government services, commuters to Dallas; hospital; branch of Paris Junior College; cotton museum, Audie Murphy exhibit; fiddle festival in October.

COMMERCE (9,696) Texas A&M University–Commerce, government/services, varied manufacturing; emergency medical center; planetarium, children's museum; Bois d'Arc Bash in September.

Other towns include: **Caddo Mills** (1,698); **Campbell** (675); **Celeste** (907); **Hawk Cove** (559); **Lone Oak** (696); **Merit** (225); **Neylandville** (105); **Quinlan** (1,541); **Union Valley** (425); **West Tawakoni** (1,844) tourist center, light industry, Lakefest in October; **Wolfe City** (1,543) manufacturing, antiques shops, commuters to Dallas; museum, library, car and truck show in October.

For explanation of sources, symbols and abbreviations, see p. 204, and foldout map.

This ditch was built in Irion County in the early 1900's as a source of water for plants, and it is still in use today. Photo by USDA NRCS Texas

Hutchinson County

Physical Features: High Plains, broken by Canadian River and tributaries, Lake Meredith; fertile valleys along streams.

Economy: Oil and gas, petrochemicals, carbon black plants. History: Antelope Creek Indian area. Later, Comanches were driven out in U.S. cavalry campaigns of 1874-75. Adobe Walls site of two Indian attacks, in 1864 and 1874. Ranching began in the late 1870s. Oil boom in the early 1920s. County created in 1876 from Bexar Territory; organized in 1901; named for pioneer jurist Anderson Hutchinson.

Race/Ethnicity: Anglo, 68.3%; Black, 2.6%; Hispanic, 24.5%; Asian, 0.5%; Other, 3.9%.

Vital Statistics, annual: Births, 287; deaths, 239; marriages, 133; divorces, 92.

Recreation: Lake Meredith activities, fishing, camping; Adobe Walls, historic Indian battle site; Alibates Flint Quarries.

Minerals: Oil and gas.

Agriculture: Beef cattle, corn, wheat; about 35,000 acres irrigated. Market value $44.9 million. Hunting important.

STINNETT (1,460) county seat; petroleum refining, farm center.

BORGER (12,331) petroleum refining, petrochemicals, nitrogen plant, carbon-black production, oil-field servicing, retail center; Frank Phillips College; museum; hospital; Downtown Merchants Beach Bash in June.

Other cities include: **Fritch** (1,961), **Sanford** (151).

Population	20,550
Change from 2010 (%)	-7.2
Area (sq. mi.)	895.0
Land Area (sq. mi.)	887.4
Altitude (ft.)	2,600–3,380
Rainfall (in.)	21.7
Jan. mean min (°F)	25.2
July mean max (°F)	93.8
Civ. Labor	8,181
Unemployed (%)	6.8
Wages	$126,611,146
Per Capita Income	$43,981
Prop. Value	$3,556,872,718
Retail Sales	$231,490,884

Irion County

Physical Features: West Texas county with hilly surface, broken by Middle Concho River, tributaries; clay, sandy soils.

Economy: Ranching, oil, gas production, wildlife recreation.

History: Tonkawa Indian area. Anglo-American settlement began in the late 1870s. County named for Republic leader R.A. Irion; created in 1889 from Tom Green County, organized the same year.

Race/Ethnicity: Anglo, 70.4%; Black, 0.6%; Hispanic, 27%; Asian, 0.2%; Other, 1.5%.

Vital Statistics, annual: Births 12; deaths, 20; marriages, 10; divorces, 2.

Recreation: Hunting; historic sites, including Dove Creek battlefield and stagecoach stops, old Sherwood courthouse built 1900; hunters appreciation dinner in November.

Minerals: Oil, gas.

Agriculture: Beef cattle, sheep, goats; hay, wheat. Market value $9.3 million.

MERTZON (797) county seat; farm center, wool warehousing.

Other towns include: **Barnhart** (110).

For explanation of sources, symbols and abbreviations, see p. 204, and foldout map.

Population	1,592
Change from 2010 (%)	-0.4
Area (sq. mi.)	1,051.6
Land Area (sq. mi.)	1,051.6
Altitude (ft.)	2,000–2,750
Rainfall (in.)	20.2
Jan. mean min (°F)	32.0
July mean max (°F)	95.0
Civ. Labor	774
Unemployed (%)	5.4
Wages	$12,597,469
Per Capita Income	$72,177
Prop. Value	$2,383,411,679
Retail Sales	$5,246,586

Jack County

Physical Features: Rolling Cross Timbers, broken by West Fork of the Trinity, other streams; sandy, dark brown, loam soils; Lake Bridgeport, Lake Jacksboro, Lost Creek Reservoir.

Economy: Petroleum production, oil-field services, livestock, manufacturing, tourism.

History: A Caddo and Comanche borderland. The first Anglo-American settlers arrived in 1855 as part of the Peters Colony. County named for brothers P.C. and W.H. Jack, who were leaders in Texas' independence effort; created in 1856 from Cooke County; organized in 1857 with Mesquiteville (original name of Jacksboro) as the county seat.

Race/Ethnicity: Anglo, 75.4%; Black, 3.9%; Hispanic, 18.8%; Asian, 0.3%; Other, 1.4%.

Vital Statistics, annual: Births, 104; deaths, 96; marriages, 54; divorces, 31.

Recreation: Hunting, wildlife leases; fishing; lake activities; Fort Richardson, Texas 4-H Museum (county is birthplace of 4-H clubs in Texas), other historic sites; Lost Creek Reservoir State Trailway.

Minerals: Oil, gas.

Agriculture: Cattle, hay, wheat, goats, sheep. Market value $23.2 million. Firewood sold.

JACKSBORO (4,648) county seat; agribusiness, petroleum production and services, tourism; hospital; library; Fort Richardson Living History Days in April.

Other towns include: **Bryson** (572), **Jermyn** (75), **Perrin** (443127).

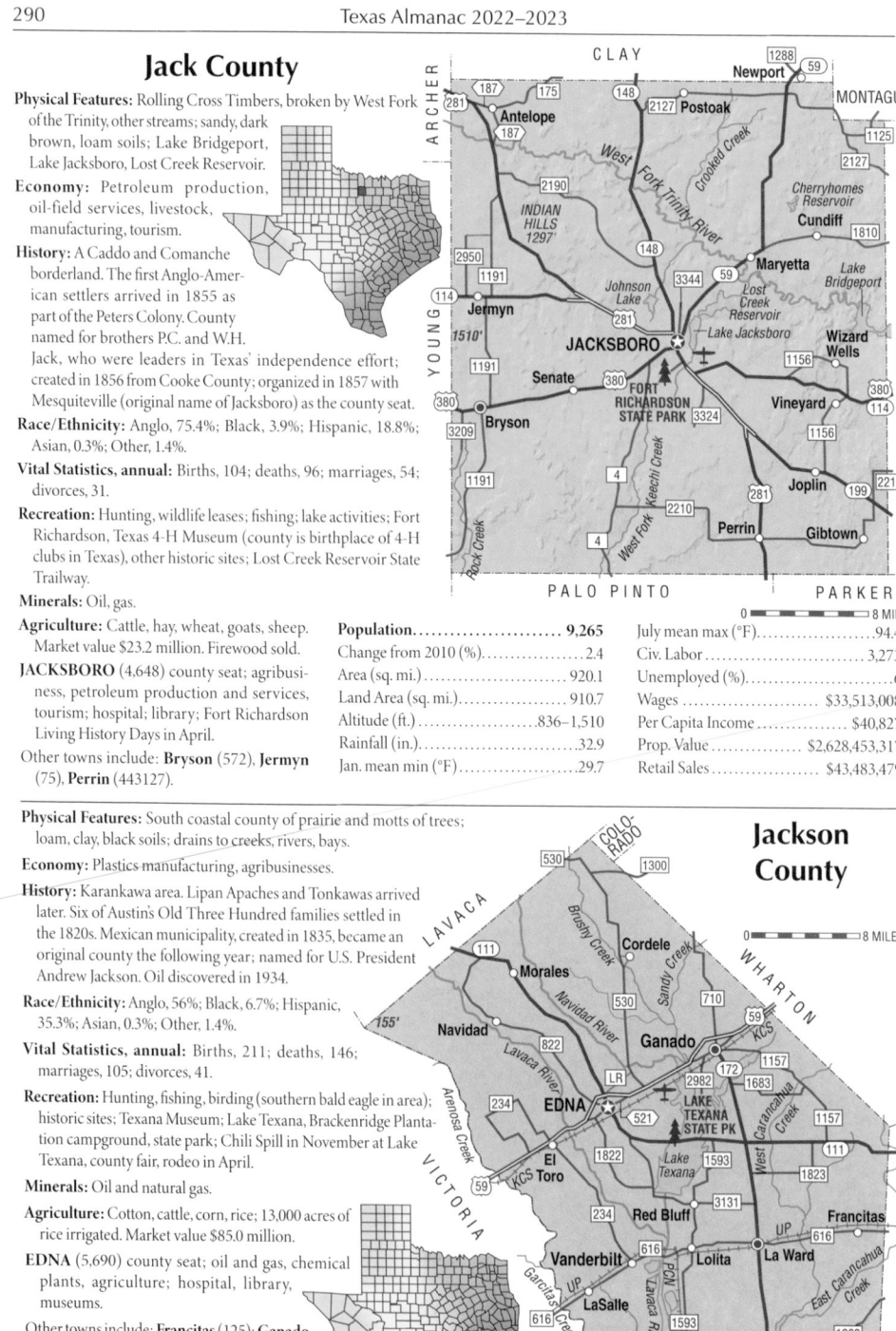

Population		**9,265**
Change from 2010 (%)		2.4
Area (sq. mi.)		920.1
Land Area (sq. mi.)		910.7
Altitude (ft.)		836–1,510
Rainfall (in.)		32.9
Jan. mean min (°F)		29.7
July mean max (°F)		94.4
Civ. Labor		3,273
Unemployed (%)		6
Wages		$33,513,008
Per Capita Income		$40,827
Prop. Value		$2,628,453,317
Retail Sales		$43,483,479

Jackson County

Physical Features: South coastal county of prairie and motts of trees; loam, clay, black soils; drains to creeks, rivers, bays.

Economy: Plastics manufacturing, agribusinesses.

History: Karankawa area. Lipan Apaches and Tonkawas arrived later. Six of Austin's Old Three Hundred families settled in the 1820s. Mexican municipality, created in 1835, became an original county the following year; named for U.S. President Andrew Jackson. Oil discovered in 1934.

Race/Ethnicity: Anglo, 56%; Black, 6.7%; Hispanic, 35.3%; Asian, 0.3%; Other, 1.4%.

Vital Statistics, annual: Births, 211; deaths, 146; marriages, 105; divorces, 41.

Recreation: Hunting, fishing, birding (southern bald eagle in area); historic sites; Texana Museum; Lake Texana, Brackenridge Plantation campground, state park; Chili Spill in November at Lake Texana, county fair, rodeo in April.

Minerals: Oil and natural gas.

Agriculture: Cotton, cattle, corn, rice; 13,000 acres of rice irrigated. Market value $85.0 million.

EDNA (5,690) county seat; oil and gas, chemical plants, agriculture; hospital, library, museums.

Other towns include: **Francitas** (125); **Ganado** (2,115) oil and gas, agriculture, historic movie theater, Crawfish Festival in May; **LaSalle** (110); **La Ward** (221); **Lolita** (606); **Vanderbilt** (418).

Population		**14,561**
Change from 2010 (%)		3.5
Area (sq. mi.)		856.9
Land Area (sq. mi.)		829.4
Altitude (ft.)		sea level–155
Rainfall (in.)		43.3
Jan. mean min (°F)		42.0
July mean max (°F)		94.0
Civ. Labor		7,163
Unemployed (%)		5.5
Wages		$69,559,738
Per Capita Income		$46,596
Prop. Value		$4,241,445,363
Retail Sales		$152,494,331

Jasper County

Physical Features: East Texas county; hilly to level; national forest; Sam Rayburn Reservoir, B.A. Steinhagen Lake; Neches River.

Economy: Timber industries; nature tourism, government/services.

History: Caddo and Atakapa Indian area. Land grants to John R. Bevil and Lorenzo de Zavala in 1829. County created in 1836, organized in 1837, from Mexican municipality; named for Sgt. William Jasper of American Revolution.

Race/Ethnicity: Anglo, 73.3%; Black, 16.1%; Hispanic, 7.3%; Asian, 0.6%; Other, 2.5%.

Vital Statistics, annual: Births, 472; deaths, 458; marriages, 249; divorces, 114.

Recreation: Lake activities; hunting, fishing; state park, Big Thicket; Butterfly Festival in October at Jasper.

Minerals: Oil, gas produced.

Agriculture: Cattle, plant nurseries, fruits, vegetables. Market value $9.1 million. Timber is major income producer. Hunting leases and fishing tournaments are major income producers.

JASPER (7,533) county seat; tourism, government/services, timber; hospital; Angelina College extension; museum; Azalea Festival in March.

Other towns include: **Browndell** (201); **Buna** (2,063) timber, oil, polka dot house, redbud festival in March; **Evadale** (1,545); **Kirbyville** (2,211) electric co-op, government/services, retail, commuters, Caboose museum, library, Magnolia Festival in April; **Sam Rayburn** (1,137).

Population.......................**35,726**	July mean max (°F)....................91.4
Change from 2010 (%)..................0.0	Civ. Labor............................12,689
Area (sq. mi.)........................969.7	Unemployed (%)......................10.4
Land Area (sq. mi.)..................938.9	Wages........................ $105,538,973
Altitude (ft.)........................10–580	Per Capita Income $40,834
Rainfall (in.)........................59.8	Prop. Value $4,175,046,833
Jan. mean min (°F)....................38.7	Retail Sales................. $473,013,286

For explanation of sources, symbols and abbreviations, see p. 204, and foldout map.

The building where Neri's Bistro operates in Jacksboro was built in 1939. Photo by Larry D. Moore, CC by SA 4.0/Wikimedia Commons

The Queen of Peace Shrine and Gardens in Port Arthur. Photo by Carol M. Highsmith, courtesy of The Library of Congress

Jeff Davis County

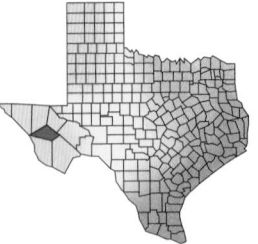

Physical Features: Highest average elevation in Texas; peaks (Mt. Livermore, 8,378 ft.), canyons, plateaus; intermountain wash, clay, loam soils; cedars, oaks in highlands.

Economy: Tourism, agriculture, McDonald Observatory.

History: Mescalero Apaches in area when Antonio de Espejo explored in 1583. U.S. Army established Fort Davis in 1854 to protect routes to west. Civilian settlers followed, including Manuel Músquiz, a political refugee from Mexico. County named for Jefferson Davis, U.S. Secretary of War, Confederate president; created 1887 from Presidio County, organized the same year.

Race/Ethnicity: Anglo, 56.2%; Black, 0.3%; Hispanic, 40.6%; Asian, 0.2%; Other, 2.3%.

Vital Statistics, annual: Births, 12; deaths, marriages, 12; divorces, 0.

Recreation: Scenic drives including loop along Limpia Creek, Mt. Livermore, Blue Mountain; hunting; Fort Davis National Historic Site; state park;

McDonald Observatory on Mt. Locke; Davis Mountain Preserve; Chihuahuan Desert Research Institute; hummingbird celebration in August.

Minerals: Not significant.

Agriculture: Greenhouse tomatoes, beef cattle, horses, meat goats. Market value $29.3. Hunting leases important.

FORT DAVIS (1,162), county seat; tourism, government/services, retail; library,

Overland and Old Spanish trail museums; "Coolest July 4th in Texas" celebration.

Other town: **Valentine** (123).

Population	**2,411**
Change from 2010 (%)	2.9
Area (sq. mi.)	2,264.6
Land Area (sq. mi.)	2,264.6
Altitude (ft.)	3,162–8,378
Rainfall (in.) Fort Davis	17.47
Rainfall (in.) Mt. Locke	20.37
Jan. mean min. (°F) Fort Davis	28.9
Jan. mean min. (°F) Mt. Locke	32.4
July mean max. (°F) Fort Davis	88.7
July mean max. (°F) Mt. Locke	84.5
Civ. Labor	996
Unemployed (%)	4.8
Wages	$8,283,460
Per Capita Income	$43,080
Prop. Value	$606,140,085
Retail Sales	$9,837,108

For explanation of sources, symbols and abbreviations, see p. 204, and foldout map.

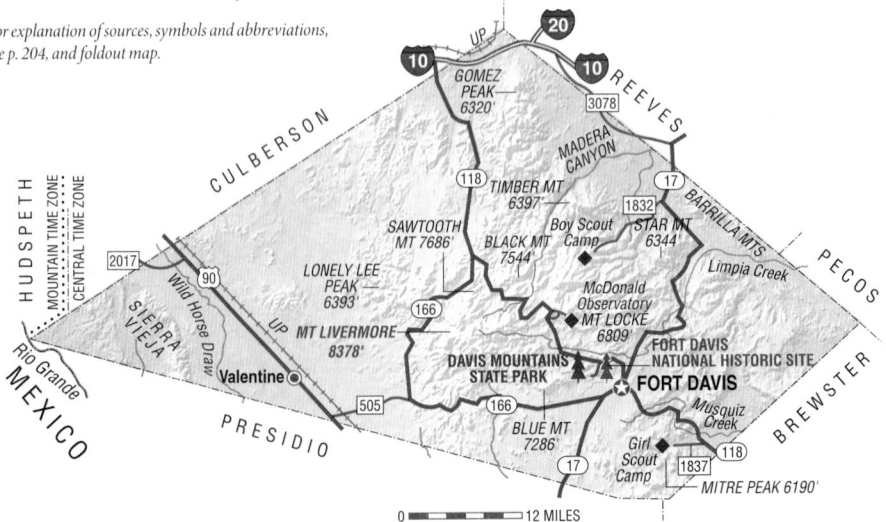

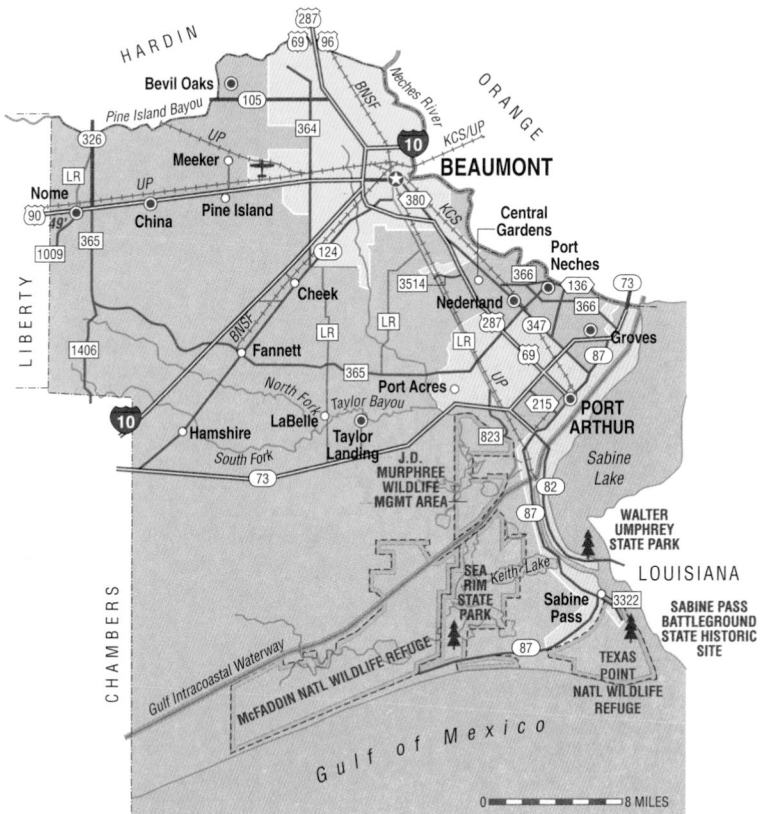

Jefferson County

Physical Features: Gulf Coast grassy plain, with timber in northwest; beach sands, sandy loams, black clay soils; drains to Neches River, Gulf of Mexico.

Economy: Government/services, petrochemical and other chemical plants, shipbuilding, steel mill, port activity, oil-field supplies.

History: Atakapas and Orcoquizas, whose numbers were reduced by epidemics or migration before Anglo-American settlers arrived in the 1820s. Cajuns arrived in the 1840s; Europeans in the 1850s. Antebellum slaveholding area. County created in 1836 from Mexican municipality; organized in 1837; named for U.S. President Thomas Jefferson.

Race/Ethnicity: Anglo, 39.7%; Black, 33%; Hispanic, 21%; Asian, 4.1%; Other, 1.9%.

Vital Statistics, annual: Births, 3,782; deaths, 2,514; marriages, 2,045; divorces, 537.

Recreation: Beaches, fresh and saltwater fishing; duck, goose hunting; water activities; Dick Dowling Monument and Park; Spindletop site, energy, fire museums; saltwater lake; J.D. Murphree WMA, McFaddin wildlife refuge, Texas Point wildlife refuge; Lamar University events; historic sites; South Texas Fair in March-April.

Minerals: Large producer of oil, gas, sulfur, salt, sand and gravel.

Agriculture: Rice, hay, beef cattle, crawfish; considerable rice irrigated. Market value $32.3 million. Timber sales significant.

BEAUMONT (118,078) county seat; oil and gas production, government/services, engineering and industrial services, port; Lamar University, Institute of Technology; hospitals; entertainment district; Neches River Festival in April.

PORT ARTHUR (54,563) oil, chemical activities, shrimping and crawfishing, shipping, offshore marine, tourism; hospitals; museum; prison; Asian New Year Tet, Janis Joplin Birthday Bash in January. Sabine Pass and Port Acres are now within the city limits of Port Arthur.

Other towns include: **Bevil Oaks** (1,226); **Central Gardens** (4,309); **China** (1,203); **Fannett** (2,333); **Groves** (15,953) retail center, some manufacturing, government/services, tourism; hospital; pecan festival in September; **Hamshire** (759).

Also, **Nederland** (17,439) petrochemical refining, retail center, education; Windmill and French/Acadian museums; extended-care hospital; Tex Ritter memorial and park; heritage festival in March (city founded by Dutch immigrants in 1898).

Also, **Nome** (607); **Port Neches** (12,638) chemical and synthetic rubber industry,

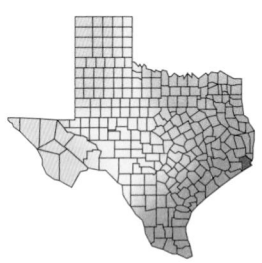

manufacturing, library, riverfront park with La Maison Beausoleil, RiverFest in May; **Taylor Landing** (238).

Population	**251,590**
Change from 2010 (%)	-0.3
Area (sq. mi.)	1,112.7
Land Area (sq. mi.)	876.3
Altitude (ft.)	sea level–49
Rainfall (in.)	60.4
Jan. mean min (°F)	41.7
July mean max (°F)	92.0
Civ. Labor	106,038
Unemployed (%)	10.6
Wages	$1,734,673,862
Per Capita Income	$44,613
Prop. Value	$34,593,396,848
Retail Sales	$4,254,144,615

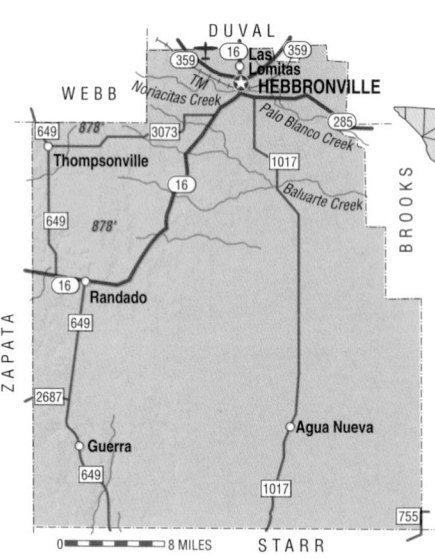

Jim Hogg County

Physical Features: South Texas county on rolling plain, with heavy brush cover; white blow sand and sandy loam; hilly, broken.

Economy: Oil, cattle operations.

History: Coahuiltecan area, then Lipan Apache. Spanish land grant in 1805 to Xavier Vela. County named for Gov. James Stephen Hogg; created and organized in 1913 from Brooks and Duval counties.

Race/Ethnicity: Anglo, 7.1%; Black, 0.3%; Hispanic, 91.2%; Asian, 0.4%; Other, 0.8%.

Vital Statistics, annual: Births, 90; deaths, 50; marriages, 32; divorces, 0.

Recreation: White-tailed deer and bobwhite hunting.

Minerals: Oil and gas.

Agriculture: Cattle, hay, milk goats; some irrigation. Market value $10.4 million.

HEBBRONVILLE (4,400) county seat; ranching, oil-field center.

Other towns include: **Guerra** (4), **Las Lomitas** (233), **South Fork Estates** (72), and **Thompsonville** (47).

Population........................ 5,092	Rainfall (in.).............................23.8	Wages $18,101,367
Change from 2010 (%)..................-3.9	Jan. mean min (°F).....................44.8	Per Capita Income................ $33,602
Area (sq. mi.)...................... 1,136.2	July mean max (°F)....................96.7	Prop. Value $1,001,110,910
Land Area (sq. mi.)................ 1,136.1	Civ. Labor............................ 1,856	Retail Sales.................. $36,856,203
Altitude (ft.) 230–878	Unemployed (%).........................9.5	

Jim Wells County

Physical Features: South Coastal Plains; level to rolling; sandy to dark soils; grassy with mesquite brush; Lake Corpus Christi.

Economy: Oil and gas production, agriculture, nature tourism.

History: Coahuiltecans, driven out by Lipan Apaches in 1775. Tomás Sánchez established settlement in 1754. Anglo-American settlement began in 1878. County created 1911 from Nueces County; organized 1912; named for developer J.B. Wells Jr.

Race/Ethnicity: Anglo, 17.1%; Black, 0.3%; Hispanic, 81.4%; Asian, 0.3%; Other, 0.6%.

Vital Statistics, annual: Births, 639; deaths, 424; marriages, 32; divorces, 0.

Recreation: Hunting; fiestas; Tejano Roots hall of fame; South Texas museum.

Minerals: Oil, gas, caliche.

Agriculture: Cattle, sorghum, corn, cotton, dairies, goats, wheat, watermelons, sunflowers, peas, hay. Market value $121.6 million.

ALICE (18,536) county seat; oil-field service center, agribusiness, government/services; hospital; Coastal Bend College campus; Fiesta Bandana (from original name of city) in May.

Other towns include: **Alfred** (80); **Ben Bolt** (1,600); **Orange Grove** (1,301); **Pernitas Point** (274, partly in Live Oak County); **Premont** (2,537) wildflower tour in spring; **Rancho Alegre** (1,636); **Sandia** (328).

Also, part [879] of **San Diego** (4,221).

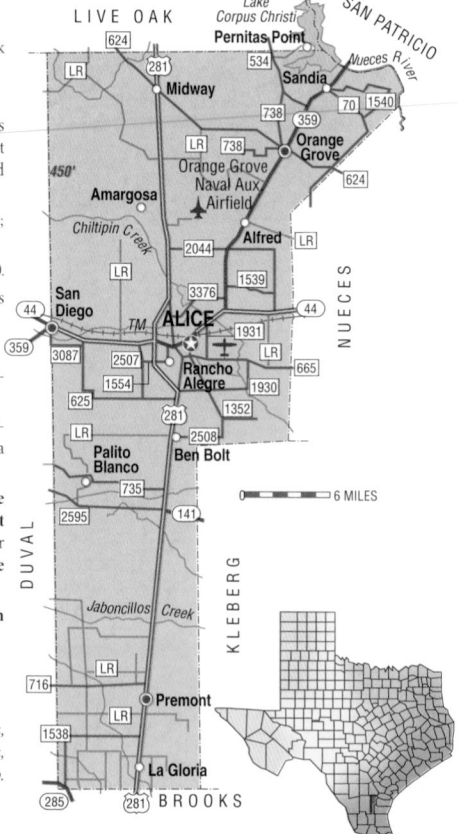

For explanation of sources, symbols and abbreviations, see p. 204, and foldout map.

Population........................ 40,204	
Change from 2010 (%)..................-1.6	
Area (sq. mi.)...................... 868.3	
Land Area (sq. mi.)................... 865.0	
Altitude (ft.) 50–450	
Rainfall (in.)........................28.4	
Jan. mean min (°F)....................44.9	
July mean max (°F)....................97.2	
Civ. Labor...........................15,212	
Unemployed (%).......................11.9	
Wages $145,314,454	
Per Capita Income $42,174	
Prop. Value $2,730,431,859	
Retail Sales................. $455,260,398	

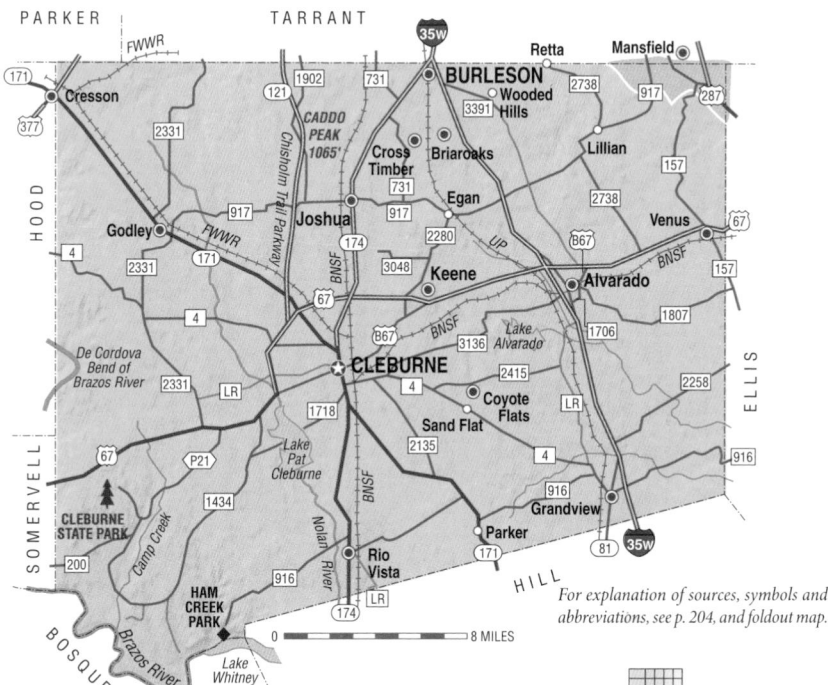

For explanation of sources, symbols and abbreviations, see p. 204, and foldout map.

Johnson County

Physical Features: North central county drained by tributaries of Trinity, Brazos rivers; lakes; hilly, rolling, many soil types.

Economy: Agribusiness, railroad shops; manufacturing, distribution, lake activities, many residents employed in Fort Worth and Dallas; part of Fort Worth-Arlington metropolitan area.

History: No permanent Indian villages existed in the area. Anglo-American settlers arrived in the 1840s. County named for Col. M.T. Johnson of the Mexican War and Confederacy; created and organized in 1854. Formed from McLennan, Hill, and Navarro counties.

Race/Ethnicity: Anglo, 71.1%; Black, 3.1%; Hispanic, 22.1%; Asian, 0.5%; Other, 2.8%.

Vital Statistics, annual: Births, 2,092; deaths, 1,340; marriages, 1,228; divorces, 510.

Recreation: Bird, deer hunting; water activities on Lake Pat Cleburne, Lake Whitney; state park; sports complex; museum; Chisholm Trail; Goatneck bike ride in July.

Minerals: Limestone, sand and gravel.

Agriculture: Cattle, hay, horses, dairies, cotton, sorghum, wheat, oats, hogs. Market value $57.9 million.

CLEBURNE (33,110) county seat; manufacturing, oil and gas; hospital, library, museum; Hill College campus; Whistle Stop Christmas.

BURLESON (47,403, part in Tarrant County) agriculture, retail center; hospital.

Other towns include: **Alvarado** (4,590) County Pioneer Days; **Briaroaks** (507); **Coyote Flats** (329); **Cross Timber** (319); **Godley** (1,377); **Grandview** (1,796); **Joshua** (7,805) many residents work in Fort Worth; **Keene** (6,755) Southwestern Adventist University; **Lillian** (1,160); **Rio Vista** (1,050), and **Venus** (4,806).

Also, part of **Cresson** (1,338), and part [2,153] of **Mansfield** (72,419, mostly in Tarrant County).

Population	174,777
Change from 2010 (%)	15.8
Area (sq. mi.)	734.5
Land Area (sq. mi.)	724.7
Altitude (ft.)	500–1,065
Rainfall (in.)	37.6
Jan. mean min (°F)	32.6
July mean max (°F)	95.7
Civ. Labor	83,641
Unemployed (%)	5.3
Wages	$656,892,513
Per Capita Income	$43,759
Prop. Value	$19,167,879,212
Retail Sales	$2,264,786,662

An old wall in Alice. Photo by Jay Phagan, CC 2/Wikimedia Commons

Jones County

Physical Features: West Texas Rolling Plains; drained by Brazos River fork, tributaries; Lake Fort Phantom Hill.

Economy: Agribusiness; government/services; varied manufacturing.

History: Comanches and other tribes hunted in the area. U.S. military presence began in 1851. Ranching established in the 1870s. County named for the last president of the Republic, Anson Jones; created in 1858 from Bexar and Bosque counties; re-created in 1876; organized in 1881.

Race/Ethnicity: Anglo, 57.1%; Black, 11.8%; Hispanic, 28.9%; Asian, 0.4%; Other, 1.6%.

Vital Statistics, annual: Births, 147; deaths, 214; marriages, 71; divorces, 22.

Recreation: Lake activities, hunting, Fort Phantom Hill, Cowboy Reunion July 4 in Stamford.

Minerals: Oil, gas, sand and gravel, stone.

Agriculture: Cotton, wheat, sesame and peanuts; cattle. Some 3,500 acres irrigated for peanuts and hay. Market value $41.5 million.

ANSON (2,357) county seat; farming center, government/services; hospital; old courthouse, opera house, museums; Cowboys Christmas Ball in December.

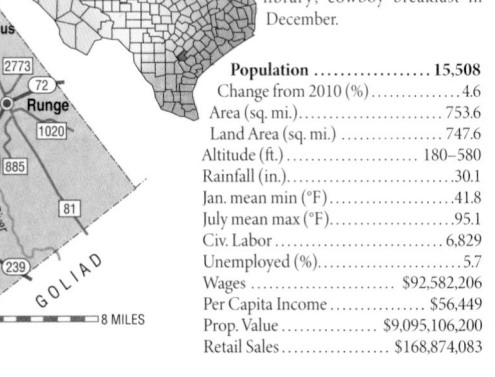

STAMFORD (2,934) trade center for three counties, hospital, historic homes, cowboy museum.

HAMLIN (2,040) farm and ranching, oil and gas, electricity/steam plant using mesquite trees, hunting; hospital; museums; Runnin' the Buff 5K in December.

Other towns include: **Hawley** (623), **Lueders** (331) limestone quarries.

Part [5,710] of **Abilene.**

Population	19,697
Change from 2010 (%)	-2.5
Area (sq. mi.)	937.1
Land Area (sq. mi.)	928.6
Altitude (ft.)	1,480–1,970
Rainfall (in.)	26.1
Jan. mean min (°F)	31.1
July mean max (°F)	96.2
Civ. Labor	5,859
Unemployed (%)	6.4
Wages	$35,380,970
Per Capita Income	$32,639
Prop. Value	$1,558,116,296
Retail Sales	$232,402,280

Karnes County

Physical Features: Sandy loam, dark clay, alluvial soils in rolling terrain; traversed by San Antonio River; mesquite, oak trees.

Economy: Oil and gas; agribusiness.

History: Coahuiltecan area. Spanish ranching began around 1750. Anglo-Americans arrived in 1840s; Polish in the 1850s. County created in 1854 from Bexar, Goliad, and San Patricio counties, organized the same year; named for Texas Revolutionary figure Henry W. Karnes.

Race/Ethnicity: Anglo, 36.4%; Black, 7.2%; Hispanic, 55%; Asian, 0.2%; Other, 0.9%.

Vital Statistics, annual: Births, 180; deaths, 131; marriages, 6; divorces, 28.

Recreation: Panna Maria, nation's oldest Polish settlement, founded 1854; Old Helena restored courthouse, museum; hunting, nature tourism, guest ranches.

Minerals: Oil, gas, uranium.

Agriculture: Beef cattle, grain, cotton, hay. Market value $29.4 million.

KARNES CITY (3,280) county seat; oil and gas, agribusiness, tourism, processing center, oil-field servicing, manufacturing; library; Lonesome Dove Fest in September.

KENEDY (3,577) farm and oil center, library, dove/quail hunting, prison, hospital; Bluebonnet Days in April.

Other towns include: **Falls City** (686) ranching, sausage making, library, city park on river; **Gillett** (120); **Hobson** (135); **Panna Maria** (45); **Runge** (1,144) oil and gas services, farming, museum, library; cowboy breakfast in December.

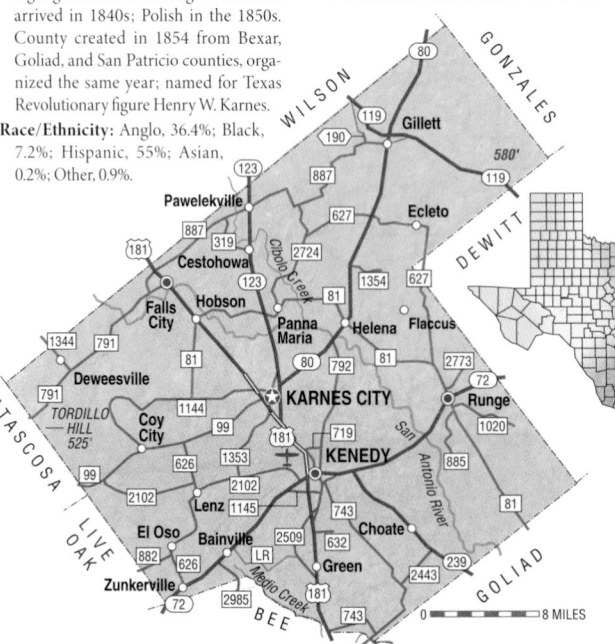

Population	15,508
Change from 2010 (%)	4.6
Area (sq. mi.)	753.6
Land Area (sq. mi.)	747.6
Altitude (ft.)	180–580
Rainfall (in.)	30.1
Jan. mean min (°F)	41.8
July mean max (°F)	95.1
Civ. Labor	6,829
Unemployed (%)	5.7
Wages	$92,582,206
Per Capita Income	$56,449
Prop. Value	$9,095,106,200
Retail Sales	$168,874,083

Physical Features: North Blackland prairie, draining to Trinity River; Cedar Creek Reservoir, Lake Ray Hubbard and Terrell City Lake.

Economy: Agriculture, commuting to Dallas, government/services.

History: Caddo and later Cherokee Indians in the area; removed by 1840 when Anglo-American settlement began. County created from Henderson County and organized in 1848; named for member of Texas and U.S. congresses D.S. Kaufman.

Race/Ethnicity: Anglo, 64.5%; Black, 10.6%; Hispanic, 21.6%; Asian, 0.8%; Other, 2.2%.

Vital Statistics, annual: Births, 1,539; deaths, 897; marriages, 686; divorces, 380.

Recreation: Lake activities; Porter Farm near Terrell is site of origin of U.S.-Texas Agricultural Extension program; antique centers near Forney; historic homes at Terrell.

Minerals: Gravel, sand, oil, gas.

Kaufman County

Agriculture: Beef cattle, horticulture, hay/forage, row crops, horses. Market value $57.1 million.

KAUFMAN (7,649) county seat; government/services, manufacturing and distribution, commuters to Dallas; hospital; Octoberfest.

TERRELL (19,183) agribusiness, varied manufacturing, large outlet center; private hospital, state hospital; community college, Southwestern Christian College; British flying school museum, Heritage Jubilee in April.

FORNEY (27,565) important antiques center, light industrial, commuters to Dallas, historic homes, barbecue cook-off in June.

Other towns include: **Combine** (2,270, partly in Dallas County); **Cottonwood** (212); **Crandall** (3,495) Cotton Festival in September; **Elmo** (1,049); **Grays Prairie** (379); **Kemp** (1,303); **Lawrence** (259);

Mabank (3,423, partly in Henderson County) varied manufacturing, tourism, retail trade, Western Week in June; **Oak Grove** (686); **Oak Ridge** (699); **Post Oak Bend** (701); **Rosser** (404); **Scurry** (769); **Talty** (2,879).

Population.................... **135,410**
Change from 2010 (%)................31.0
Area (sq. mi.)........................ 807.7
Land Area (sq. mi.).................. 780.7
Altitude (ft.)..................... 300–611
Rainfall (in.)...........................39.9
Jan. mean min (°F)....................33.1
July mean max (°F)....................94.3
Civ. Labor 68,197
Unemployed (%)........................5.5
Wages $444,184,053
Per Capita Income $43,972
Prop. Value $16,980,995,978
Retail Sales............... $1,728,310,428

For explanation of sources, symbols and abbreviations, see p. 204, and foldout map.

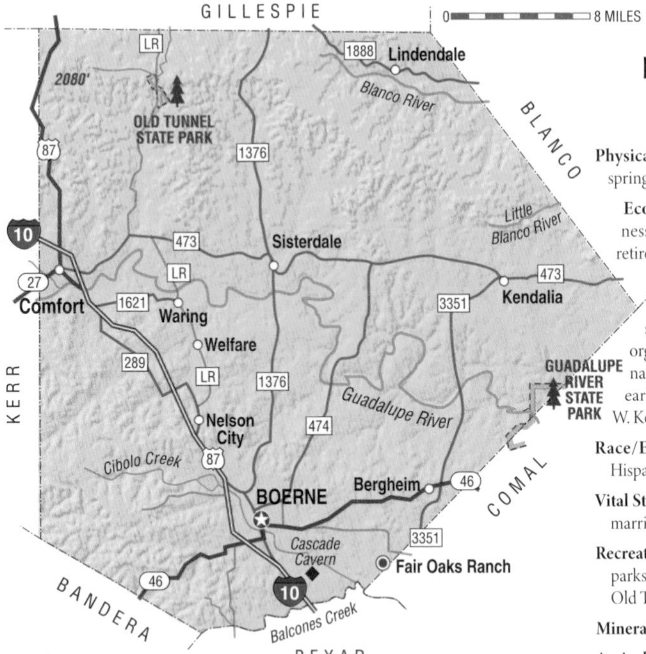

Kendall County

Physical Features: Hill Country, plateau, with spring-fed streams; caves; scenic drives.

Economy: Government/services, agribusiness, commuters to San Antonio, tourism, retirement area, some manufacturing.

History: Lipan Apaches, Kiowas and Comanches in area when German settlers arrived in 1840s. County created, organized, from Blanco, Kerr counties 1862; named for pioneer journalist-sheepman and early contributor to Texas Almanac, George W. Kendall.

Race/Ethnicity: Anglo, 72.5%; Black, 0.3%; Hispanic, 25.3%; Asian, 0.4%; Other, 1.2%.

Vital Statistics, annual: Births, 377; deaths, 377; marriages, 472; divorces, 21.

Recreation: Hunting, fishing, exotic wildlife, state parks; Cascade Cavern, Cave Without a Name, Old Tunnel; historic sites.

Minerals: Limestone rock, caliche.

Agriculture: Cattle, goats, sheep, hay. Market value $12.4 million. Cedar posts, firewood sold.

BOERNE (17,228) county seat; tourism, antiques, some manufacturing, ranching, commuting to San Antonio; library; Christmas in Comfort on Saturday after Thanksgiving.

Other towns include: **Comfort** (2,936) tourism, farming and ranching, manufacturing, Civil War monument honoring Unionists, library, museum, mountain bike trail; **Kendalia** (149); **Sisterdale** (110); **Waring** (73).

Part of **Fair Oaks Ranch** (10,042).

Population	47,284
Change from 2010 (%)	41.5
Area (sq. mi.)	663.0
Land Area (sq. mi.)	662.5
Altitude (ft.)	1,000–2,080
Rainfall (in.)	38.1
Jan. mean min (°F)	35.4
July mean max (°F)	92.5
Civ. Labor	22,722
Unemployed (%)	3.9
Wages	$246,675,316
Per Capita Income	$81,882
Prop. Value	$10,113,619,619
Retail Sales	$1,379,023,013

Grass returns to this ranch in Kent County, after years of brush removal and reclamation efforts. Photo by USDA NRCS Texas

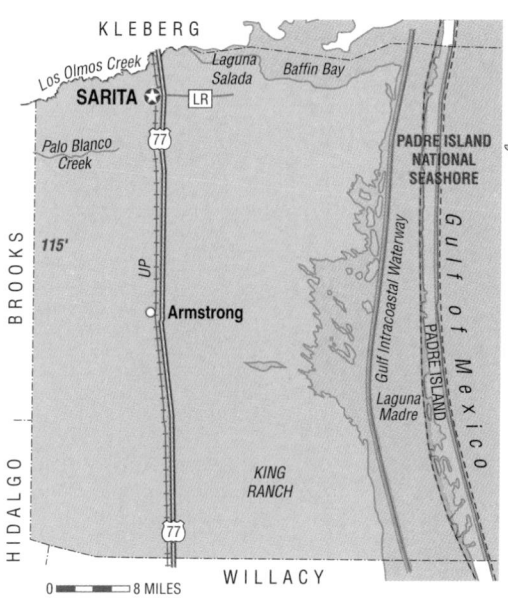

Kenedy County

Physical Features: Gulf coastal county; flat, sandy terrain, some loam soils; motts of live oaks.

Economy: Oil, ranching, nature tourism, hunting leases, wind farm.

History: Coahuiltecan Indians who assimilated or were driven out by the Lipan Apaches. Spanish ranching began in the 1790s. Anglo-Americans arrived after the Mexican War. Among last counties created, organized, 1921 from Cameron, Hidalgo, and Willacy counties; named for pioneer steamboat operator and cattleman, Capt. Mifflin Kenedy.

Race/Ethnicity: Anglo, 21.2%; Black, 0.2%; Hispanic, 75.8%; Asian, 0.2%; Other, 2.3%.

Vital Statistics, annual: Births, 0; deaths, 3; marriages, 5; divorces, 0.

Recreation: Hunting, fishing, nature tourism.

Minerals: Oil, gas.

Agriculture: Beef cattle, horses. Market value $19.7 million. Hunting leases, nature tourism important.

SARITA (244) county seat; cattle-shipping point, ranch headquarters, gas processing; one of state's least populous counties.

Also, **Armstrong** (4).

For explanation of sources, symbols and abbreviations, see p. 204, and foldout map.

Population............................ 390	July mean max (°F)...................94.6
Change from 2010 (%)................-6.3	Civ. Labor 175
Area (sq. mi.)..................... 1,945.8	Unemployed (%)........................7.4
Land Area (sq. mi.)................ 1,458.3	Wages $6,388,795
Altitude (ft.).................sea level–115	Per Capita Income $42,262
Rainfall (in.)..........................29.2	Prop. Value $2,127,810,195
Jan. mean min (°F)....................44.4	Retail Sales .... N/A

Kent County

Physical Features: Rolling, broken terrain; lake; drains to Salt and Double Mountain forks of Brazos River; sandy, loam soils.

Economy: Agribusiness, oil and gas operations, government/services, hunting leases.

History: Comanches driven out by the U.S. Army in the 1870s. Ranching developed in the 1880s. County created in 1876 from Bexar and Young territories; organized in 1892. Name honors Andrew Kent, one of 32 volunteers from Gonzales who died at the Alamo.

Race/Ethnicity: Anglo, 81.4%; Black, 0.9%; Hispanic, 15.9%; Asian, 0%; Other, 1.7%.

Vital Statistics, annual: Births, 0; deaths, 9; marriages, 4; divorces, 1.

Recreation: Hunting, fishing; scenic croton breaks and salt flat; Winterfest in December.

Minerals: Oil, gas.

Agriculture: Cattle, cotton, wheat, sorghum. Market value $9.9 million.

JAYTON (503) county seat; oil-field services, farming center; Summerfest in August.

Other towns include: **Girard** (44).

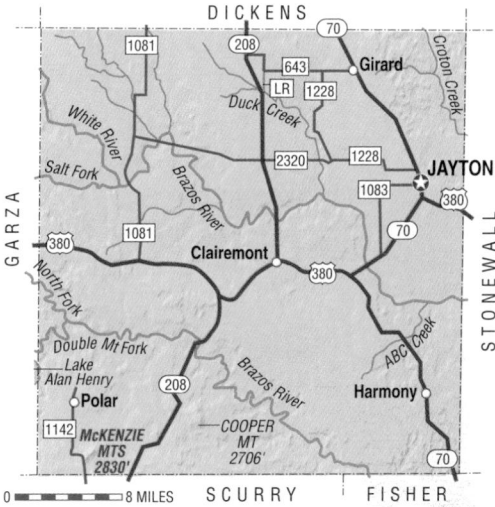

Population............................ 759	July mean max (°F)...................94.6
Change from 2010 (%)................-6.1	Civ. Labor 482
Area (sq. mi.)........................ 902.9	Unemployed (%)........................3.1
Land Area (sq. mi.)................... 902.5	Wages $3,054,100
Altitude (ft.)...................1,740–2,830	Per Capita Income $54,630
Rainfall (in.)..........................23.5	Prop. Value $861,646,559
Jan. mean min (°F)....................27.2	Retail Sales $4,857,067

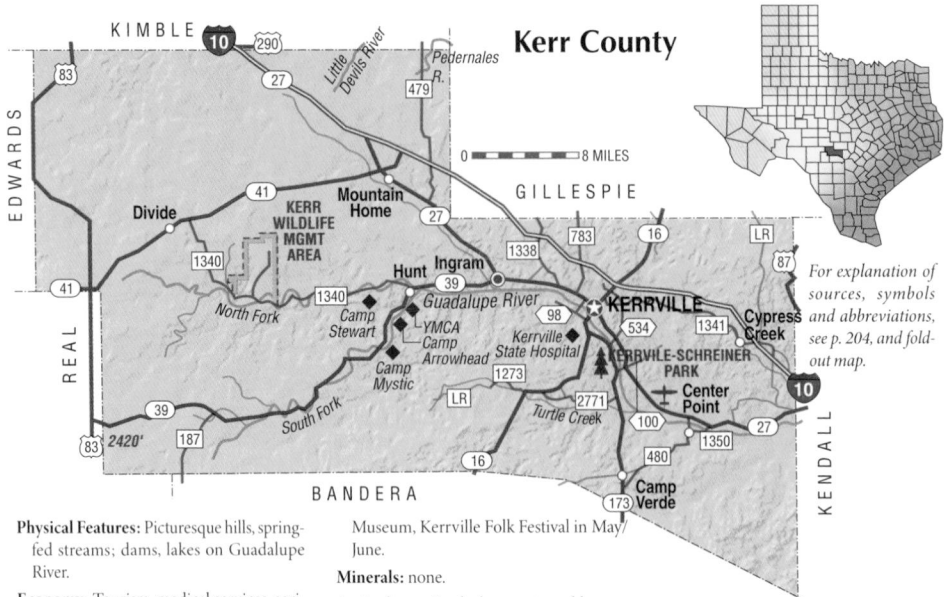

Kerr County

0 ——— 8 MILES

For explanation of sources, symbols and abbreviations, see p. 204, and foldout map.

Physical Features: Picturesque hills, spring-fed streams; dams, lakes on Guadalupe River.

Economy: Tourism, medical services, agribusiness, hunting leases.

History: Lipan Apaches, Kiowas and Comanches in area. Anglo-American settlers arrived in the late 1840s. County created in 1856 from Bexar County; organized the same year; named for a member of Austin's Colony, James Kerr.

Race/Ethnicity: Anglo, 66.8%; Black, 1.5%; Hispanic, 28.9%; Asian, 0.8%; Other, 1.8%.

Vital Statistics, annual: Births, 540; deaths, 774; marriages, 334; divorces, 184.

Recreation: Youth camps, dude ranches, park, Cailloux and Point theaters, wildlife management area, Cowboy Artists Museum, Kerrville Folk Festival in May/June.

Minerals: none.

Agriculture: Cattle, hay, goats and horses; deer (second in numbers as livestock). Market value $9.3 million. Hunting leases important.

KERRVILLE (24,005) county seat; tourist center, youth camps, agribusiness, aircraft and parts, varied manufacturing; Schreiner University; state hospital, veterans hospital, private hospital; retirement center; retail trade; state arts, crafts show in May.

Other towns include: **Camp Verde** (41); **Center Point** (800); **Hunt** (708) youth camps, hospital; **Ingram** (1,855) camps, cabins; **Mountain Home** (96).

Population	**52,829**
Change from 2010 (%)	6.5
Area (sq. mi.)	1,107.3
Land Area (sq. mi.)	1,103.3
Altitude (ft.)	1,404–2,420
Rainfall (in.)	32.1
Jan. mean min (°F)	33.8
July mean max (°F)	92.2
Civ. Labor	20,988
Unemployed (%)	4.8
Wages	$230,029,844
Per Capita Income	$51,768
Prop. Value	$8,787,901,328
Retail Sales	$1,044,363,659

The Kerrville-Schreiner Park Amphitheater. Photo by Larry D. Moore, CC by SA 4.0/Wikimedia Commons

Kimble County

Population........................ 4,604
Change from 2010 (%)................ -0.1
Area (sq. mi.)....................... 1,251.2
Land Area (sq. mi.)................. 1,251.0
Altitude (ft.)................... 1,476–2,460
Rainfall (in.)........................ 27.0
Jan. mean min (°F)................... 27.8
July mean max (°F)................... 94.3
Civ. Labor.......................... 1,818
Unemployed (%)....................... 4.5
Wages $12,810,435
Per Capita Income $44,371
Prop. Value $2,928,093,841
Retail Sales $94,121,010

Physical Features: Picturesque Edwards Plateau; rugged, broken by numerous streams; drains to Llano River; sandy, gray, chocolate loam soils.

Economy: Livestock production and market, tourism, cedar oil and wood products, metal building materials.

History: Apache, Kiowa and Comanche area until the 1870s. U.S. military outposts protected the first Anglo-American settlers in the 1850s. County created from Bexar County in 1858 and organized in 1876. Named for George C. Kimble, a Gonzales volunteer who died at the Alamo.

Race/Ethnicity: Anglo, 68.1%; Black, 0.3%; Hispanic, 30%; Asian, 0.4%; Other, 0.9%.

Vital Statistics, annual: Births, 39; deaths, 45; marriages, 24; divorces, 22.

Recreation: Hunting, fishing in spring-fed streams, nature tourism; among leading deer counties; state park; Kimble Kounty Kow Kick on Labor Day, Wild Game dinner on Thanksgiving Saturday.

Minerals: gravel.

Agriculture: Cattle, meat goats, sheep, Angora goats, pecans. Market value $10.9 million. Hunting leases important. Firewood, cedar sold.

JUNCTION (2,522) county seat; tourism, varied manufacturing, livestock production; two museums; Texas Tech University center; hospital; library; airport.

Other towns include: **London** (180); **Roosevelt** (14).

King County

Physical Features: Hilly, broken by Wichita, Brazos tributaries; extensive grassland; dark loam to red soils.

Economy: Oil and gas, ranching, government/services, horse sales, hunting leases.

History: Apache area until Comanches moved in about 1700. Comanches were removed by U.S. Army in 1874-75 after which ranching began. County created in 1876 from Bexar District; organized in 1891; named for William P. King, a volunteer from Gonzales who died at the Alamo.

Race/Ethnicity: Anglo, 85.4%; Black, 0%; Hispanic, 13.5%; Asian, 0%; Other, 1%.

Vital Statistics, annual: Births, 0; deaths, 0; marriages, 5; divorces, 0.

Recreation: 6666 Ranch visits, hunting, roping and ranch horse competitions.

Minerals: Oil, gas.

Agriculture: Cattle, horses, wheat, hay, cotton. Market value $13.8 million. Hunting leases important.

GUTHRIE (188) county seat; ranch-supply center, government/services; community center complex, library; Thanksgiving community supper.

Population........................ 274
Change from 2010 (%)................ -4.2
Area (sq. mi.)..................... 913.3
Land Area (sq. mi.)................ 910.9
Altitude (ft.) 1,450–2,250
Rainfall (in.)....................... 25.5
Jan. mean min (°F)................... 27.0
July mean max (°F)................... 95.9
Civ. Labor.......................... 285
Unemployed (%)....................... 1.4
Wages $2,218,449
Per Capita Income $78,849
Prop. Value $597,162,733
Retail Sales .... N/A

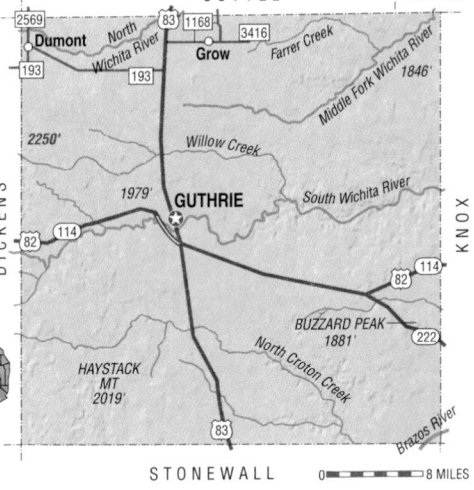

Lamar County

Physical Features: North Texas county on divide between Red, Sulphur rivers; soils chiefly blackland, except along Red; pines, hardwoods; Pat Mayse Lake and Lake Crook.

Economy: Varied manufacturing, agribusiness, medical, government/services.

History: Caddo Indian area. First Anglo-American settlers arrived about 1815. County created in 1840 from Red River County; organized in 1841; named for second president of Republic, Mirabeau B. Lamar.

Race/Ethnicity: Anglo, 73.7%; Black, 12.5%; Hispanic, 8.3%; Asian, 0.6%; Other, 4.7%.

Vital Statistics, annual: Births, 680; deaths, 641; marriages, 465; divorces, 254.

Recreation: Lake activities; Gambill goose refuge; hunting, fishing; state park; Trail de Paris rail-to-trail; Sam Bell Maxey Home; State Sen. A.M. Aikin Archives, other museums.

Minerals: Negligible.

Agriculture: Beef, hay, dairy, soybeans (first in acreage), wheat, corn, sorghum, cotton. Market value $73.4 million.

PARIS (25,297) county seat; varied manufacturing, food processing, government/services; hospitals; junior college; museums; Tour de Paris bicycle rally in July; archery pro-am tournament in March.

Other towns include: **Arthur City** (180), **Blossom** (1,558), **Brookston** (130), **Chicota** (150), **Cunningham** (110), **Deport** (556, partly in Red River County), **Pattonville** (180), **Petty** (130), **Powderly** (1,204), **Reno** (3,360), **Roxton** (647), **Sumner** (95), **Sun Valley** (77), **Toco** (80).

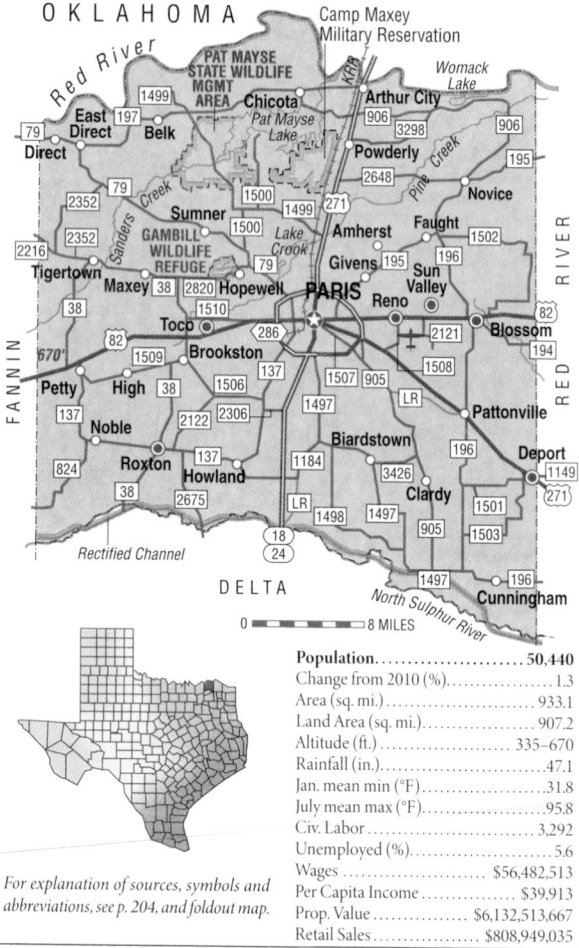

For explanation of sources, symbols and abbreviations, see p. 204, and foldout map.

Population	**50,440**
Change from 2010 (%)	1.3
Area (sq. mi.)	933.1
Land Area (sq. mi.)	907.2
Altitude (ft.)	335–670
Rainfall (in.)	47.1
Jan. mean min (°F)	31.8
July mean max (°F)	95.8
Civ. Labor	3,292
Unemployed (%)	5.6
Wages	$56,482,513
Per Capita Income	$39,913
Prop. Value	$6,132,513,667
Retail Sales	$808,949,035

Shops along Main Street in Paris. Photo by Adavyd, CC 3/Wikimedia Commons

Lamb County

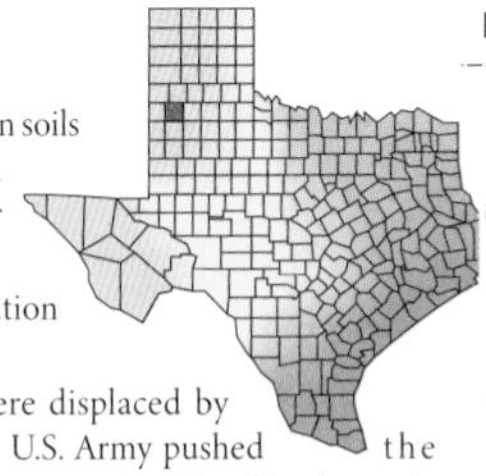

Physical Features: Rich, red, brown soils on the High Plains; some hills; drains to upper Brazos River tributaries; numerous playas.

Economy: Agribusiness; distribution center; denim textiles.

History: Apache tribes, who were displaced by Comanches around 1700. The U.S. Army pushed the Comanches into the Indian Territory in 1875. Ranching began in the 1880s; farming started after 1900. County created in 1876 from the Bexar District and organized in 1908; named for Lt. G.A. Lamb, who died in battle of San Jacinto.

Race/Ethnicity: Anglo, 37.9%; Black, 4.6%; Hispanic, 55%; Asian, 0.1%; Other, 2.1%.

Vital Statistics, annual: Births, 187; deaths, 147; marriages, 65; divorces, 3.

Recreation: Waylon Jennings Birthday Bash in June at Littlefield, museums, Earth Day in April.

Minerals: Oil, stone, gas.

Agriculture: Fed cattle; cotton, corn, wheat, grain sorghum, vegetables, soybeans, hay; sheep. 179,500 acres irrigated. Market value $575.3 million.

LITTLEFIELD (5,840) county seat; milk processing, agribusiness, manufacturing; hospital, prison, museum.

Olton (2,022) agribusiness, retail center; Sandcrawl museum; pheasant hunt in winter; Sandhills Celebration in August.

Other towns include: **Amherst** (630); **Earth** (957) farming center, dairies, feed lot; **Fieldton** (20); **Spade** (64); **Springlake** (96);

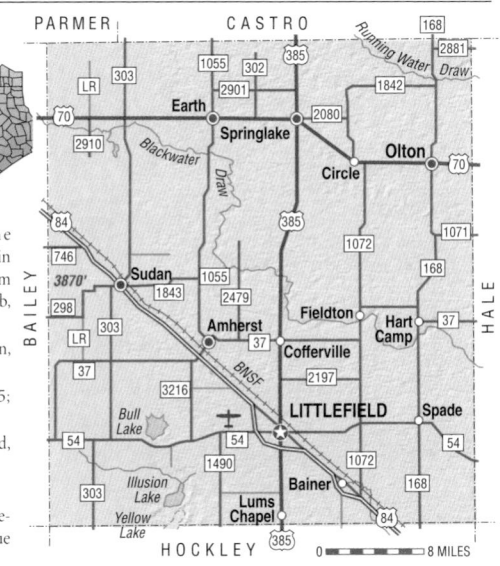

Sudan (892) farming center, government/services, Homecoming Day in fall.

Population	**12,565**
Change from 2010 (%)	-10.1
Area (sq. mi.)	1,017.7
Land Area (sq. mi.)	1,016.2
Altitude (ft.)	3,390–3,870
Rainfall (in.)	18.9
Jan. mean min (°F)	24.5
July mean max (°F)	92.0
Civ. Labor	23,650
Unemployed (%)	.6
Wages	$267,834,532
Per Capita Income	$43,063
Prop. Value	$1,564,372,299
Retail Sales	$128,952,656

Lampasas County

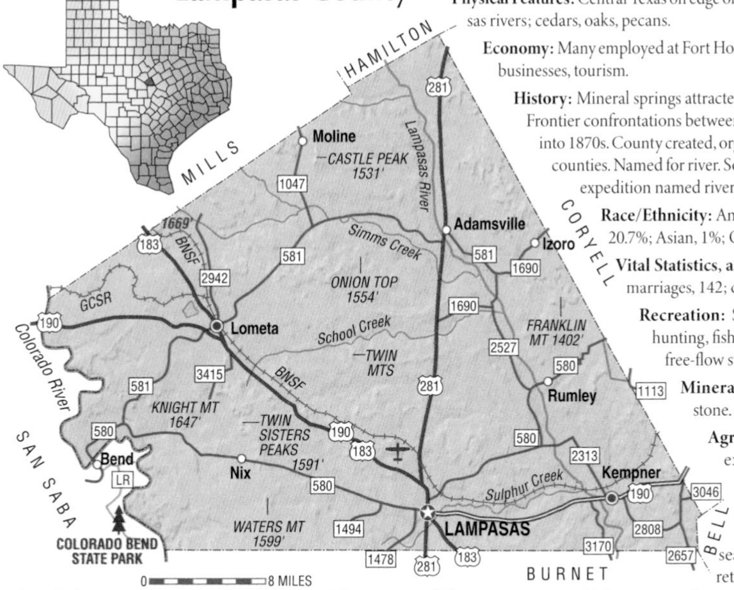

Physical Features: Central Texas on edge of Hill Country; Colorado, Lampasas rivers; cedars, oaks, pecans.

Economy: Many employed at Fort Hood, several industrial plants, agribusinesses, tourism.

History: Mineral springs attracted first Anglo-Americans in 1853. Frontier confrontations between settlers, Comanches continued into 1870s. County created, organized, in 1856 from Bell, Travis counties. Named for river. Some have speculated that an early expedition named river for city of Lampazos in Mexico.

Race/Ethnicity: Anglo, 70.9%; Black, 3%; Hispanic, 20.7%; Asian, 1%; Other, 4.1%.

Vital Statistics, annual: Births, 219; deaths, 197; marriages, 142; divorces, 79.

Recreation: Scenic drives; state park; deer hunting, fishing in streams; Hancock Springs free-flow swim area at Lampasas.

Minerals: Sand and gravel, building stone.

Agriculture: Beef cattle, hay, goats, exotic animals. Market value $18.4 million. Hunting leases, ecotourism.

LAMPASAS (7,787) county seat; manufacturing, health care, retail; historic downtown; hospital, college extensions; museum; Spring Ho in July.

Other towns include: **Bend** (115, partly in San Saba County); **Izoro** (17); **Kempner** (1,165); **Lometa** (887) market and shipping point; Diamondback Jubilee in March.

Population	**21,326**
Change from 2010 (%)	8.4
Area (sq. mi.)	713.9
Land Area (sq. mi.)	712.8
Altitude (ft.)	800–1,669
Rainfall (in.)	32.2
Jan. mean min (°F)	33.4
July mean max (°F)	95.6
Civ. Labor	5,427
Unemployed (%)	5.2
Wages	$49,421,250
Per Capita Income	$45,655
Prop. Value	$2,953,825,367
Retail Sales	$252,236,860

La Salle County

Physical Features: Brushy plain, broken by Nueces, Frio rivers and their tributaries; chocolate, dark gray, sandy loam soils.

Economy: Agribusiness, hunting leases, tourism, government services.

History: Coahuiltecans, squeezed out by migrating Apaches. U.S. military outpost in the 1850s, settlers of Mexican descent established nearby village. Anglo-American ranching developed in the 1870s. County created from Bexar District in 1858; organized in 1880; named for Robert Cavelier Sieur de La Salle, French explorer who died in Texas.

Race/Ethnicity: Anglo, 11.3%; Black, 0.2%; Hispanic, 87.5%; Asian, 0%; Other, 0.7%.

Vital Statistics, annual: Births, 104; deaths, 61; marriages, 34; divorces, 13.

Recreation: Nature trails; school where Lyndon B. Johnson taught; wildlife management area; deer, bird, javelina hunting, fishing; wild hog cookoff in March.

Minerals: Oil, gas.

Agriculture: Beef cattle, peanuts, watermelons, grain sorghum. Market value $6.3 million.

COTULLA (4,063) county seat; oil and lodging, state prison; hunting center; Brush Country museum.

Other towns include: **Encinal** (583), **Fowlerton** (48).

Population	7,426
Change from 2010 (%)	7.8
Area (sq. mi.)	1,494.2
Land Area (sq. mi.)	1,486.7
Altitude (ft.)	255–650
Rainfall (in.)	24.7
Jan. mean min (°F)	38.9
July mean max (°F)	9,609.0
Civ. Labor	9,222
Unemployed (%)	5.1
Wages	$48,508,877
Per Capita Income	$50,656
Prop. Value	$7,951,912,008
Retail Sales	$126,728,331

Lavaca County

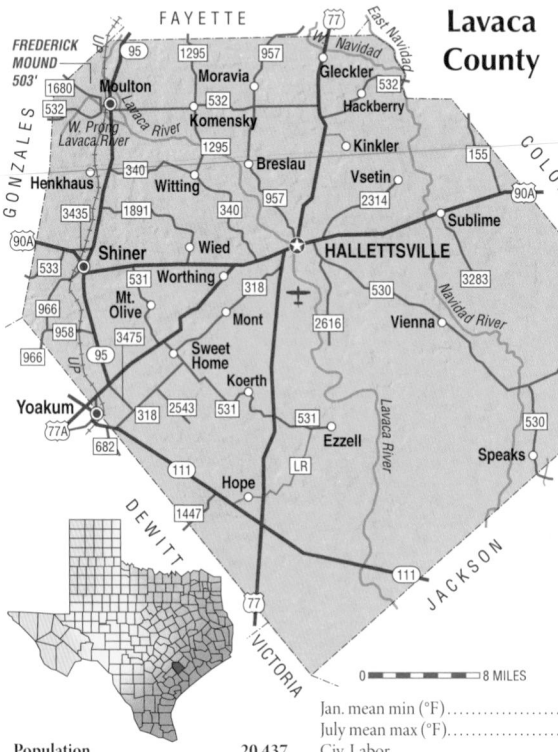

Physical Features: Coastal Plains county; north rolling; sandy loam, black waxy soils; drains to Lavaca, Navidad rivers.

Economy: Varied manufacturing, oil and gas production, agribusinesses, tourism.

History: Coahuiltecan area; later a Comanche area until 1850s. Anglo-Americans first settled in 1831. Germans and Czechs arrived 1880–1900. County created, organized, in 1846 from Colorado, Jackson, Gonzales, Victoria counties. Name is Spanish for cow, la vaca, from name of river.

Race/Ethnicity: Anglo, 71%; Black, 6.8%; Hispanic, 20.5%; Asian, 0.3%; Other, 1.3%.

Vital Statistics, annual: Births, 231; deaths, 269; marriages, 118; divorces, 31.

Recreation: Deer, other hunting, fishing; wildflower trails, historic sites, churches; Fiddlers Frolics in Hallettsville in April.

Minerals: Some oil, gas.

Agriculture: Cattle, forage, poultry, rice, corn, sorghum. Market value $50.5 million. Hunting leases.

HALLETTSVILLE (2,753) county seat; retail center; varied manufacturing; agribusiness; museum, library, hospital; domino, "42" tournaments; Kolache Fest in September.

Yoakum (6,173, partly in DeWitt County); cattle, leather, meat processing; hospital; museum; Tom Tom festival in June.

Shiner (2,230) Spoetzl brewery, varied manufacturing; museum; clinic; Half Moon Holidays in July.

Other towns include: **Moulton** (924) agribusiness, Town & Country Jamboree in July; **Sublime** (75); **Sweet Home** (360).

Population	20,437
Change from 2010 (%)	6.1
Area (sq. mi.)	970.4
Land Area (sq. mi.)	969.7
Altitude (ft.)	85–503
Rainfall (in.)	41.1
Jan. mean min (°F)	41.3
July mean max (°F)	93.4
Civ. Labor	8,293
Unemployed (%)	.5
Wages	$60,520,037
Per Capita Income	$53,483
Prop. Value	$5,867,239,715
Retail Sales	$221,744,786

Physical Features: Rolling terrain, broken by Yegua and its tributaries; red to black soils, sandy to heavy loams; Somerville Lake.

Economy: Varied manufacturing, agribusiness, lignite coal operations, government/services.

History: Tonkawas; removed in 1855 to the Brazos Reservation. Most Anglo-American settlement occurred after the Texas Revolution. Slaveholding area. Germans, Wends, and other Europeans began arriving in the 1850s. County created from Bastrop, Burleson, Fayette, Washington counties in 1874 and organized the same year; named for Gen. Robert E. Lee.

Race/Ethnicity: Anglo, 61.6%; Black, 10.5%; Hispanic, 25.4%; Asian, 0.3%; Other, 2%.

Vital Statistics, annual: Births, 208; deaths, 183; marriages, 111; divorces, 63.

Recreation: Fishing, hunting; lake activities, state park; pioneer village; historic sites.

Minerals: Lignite coal, iron ore, gravel.

Agriculture: Beef cattle, hay, nurseries, poultry, peanuts, goats, horses, aquaculture, corn; some irrigation. Market value $56.9 million. Firewood.

GIDDINGS (5,118) county seat; oil/gas, manufacturing, agriculture; museum, old Presbyterian church (1886); rodeo in May.

Other towns include: **Dime Box** (381); **Lexington** (1,216) utility plant, livestock-marketing center, small businesses, log cabins heritage center, homecoming rodeo and barbecue cookoff in May; **Lincoln** (336); **Serbin** (109) Wendish museum.

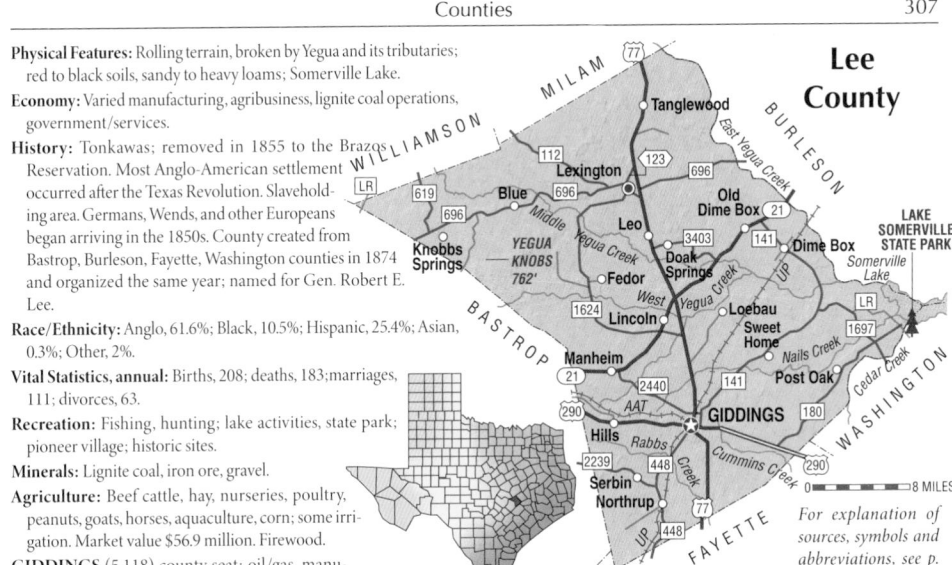

Lee County

For explanation of sources, symbols and abbreviations, see p. 204, and foldout map.

Population...................... 17,411	July mean max (°F)....................94.1
Change from 2010 (%)..................4.8	Civ. Labor............................9,080
Area (sq. mi.)......................631.1	Unemployed (%).......................4.4
Land Area (sq. mi.)..................629.0	Wages......................$89,261,484
Altitude (ft.).....................238–762	Per Capita Income................$50,665
Rainfall (in.)........................36.6	Prop. Value...............$4,070,242,167
Jan. mean min (°F)...................37.2	Retail Sales...............$1,040,885,721

Physical Features: Hilly, rolling, almost half covered by timber; drains to Navasota, Trinity rivers and tributaries; Lake Limestone; sandy, dark, alluvial soils.

Economy: Poultry farming, cattle ranching, hay.

History: Bidais, absorbed into the Kickapoos and other groups. Permanent settlement by Anglo-Americans occurred after the Texas Revolution; Germans arrived in the 1870s. County created and organized in 1846 from Robertson County; named for founder of Victoria, Martín de León.

Race/Ethnicity: Anglo, 75.8%; Black, 6.5%; Hispanic, 15.4%; Asian, 0.5%; Other, 1.5%.

Vital Statistics, annual: Births, 213; deaths, 223; marriages, 102; divorces, 45.

Recreation: Hilltop Lakes resort area; sites of Camino Real, Fort Boggy State Park; deer hunting.

Minerals: Oil, natural gas.

Agriculture: Poultry, cow-calf production, hay, small grains. Market value $169.4 million. Hardwoods, pine marketed.

CENTERVILLE (920) county seat; agriculture, government/services; Christmas on the Square in December.

BUFFALO (1,903) oil and gas; library; May Spring Fest with fiddlers' contest.

Other towns include: **Concord** (28); **Flynn** (81); **Hilltop Lakes** (1,020) resort and retirement center; **Jewett** (1,337) steel mill, civic center, museum, library, Classic Coon Hunt in January; **Leona** (186) candle factory; **Marquez** (297); **Normangee** (731, partly in Madison County) farming and tourism; library, museum, city park; **Oakwood** (517).

Leon County

Population...................... 17,588	July mean max (°F)....................93.2
Change from 2010 (%)..................4.7	Civ. Labor............................6,123
Area (sq. mi.)....................1,080.6	Unemployed (%).......................7.7
Land Area (sq. mi.)................1,073.2	Wages......................$67,424,128
Altitude (ft.).....................150–630	Per Capita Income................$40,056
Rainfall (in.)........................42.3	Prop. Value...............$4,697,314,390
Jan. mean min (°F)...................34.9	Retail Sales...............$181,378,332

Liberty County

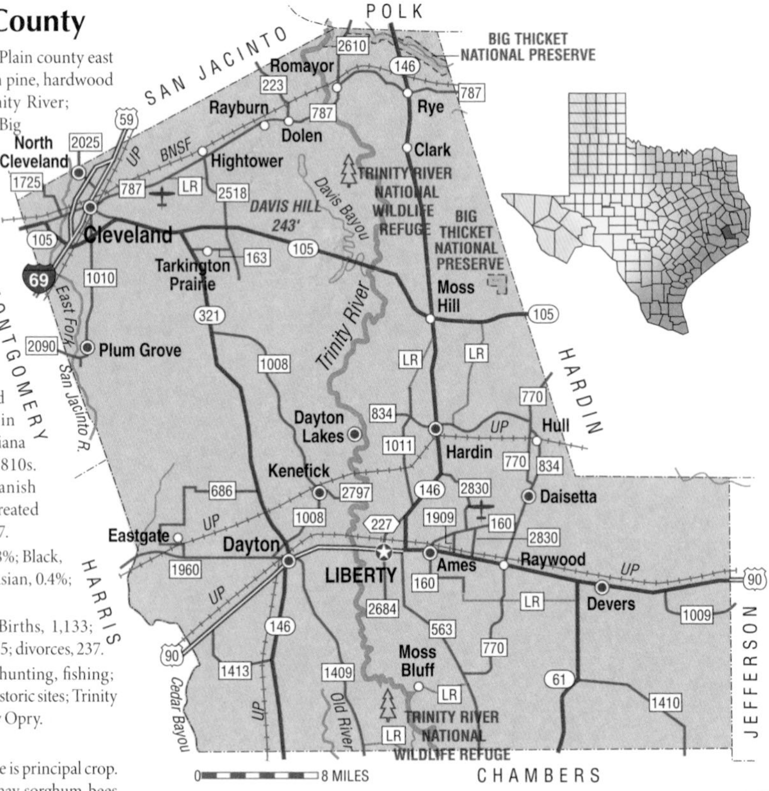

Physical Features: Coastal Plain county east of Houston; 60 percent in pine, hardwood timber; bisected by Trinity River; sandy, loam, black soils; Big Thicket.

Economy: Agribusiness; chemical plants; varied manufacturing; tourism; forest industries; prisons; many residents work in Houston; part of Houston metropolitan area.

History: Karankawa tribal area until the 1740s. Spanish established Atascosito settlement in 1756. Settlers from Louisiana began arriving in the 1810s. County named for Spanish municipality, Libertad; created in 1836, organized in 1837.

Race/Ethnicity: Anglo, 63.8%; Black, 9.3%; Hispanic, 24.3%; Asian, 0.4%; Other, 1.9%.

Vital Statistics, annual: Births, 1,133; deaths, 765; marriages, 555; divorces, 237.

Recreation: Big Thicket; hunting, fishing; national wildlife refuge; historic sites; Trinity Valley exposition; Liberty Opry.

Minerals: Oil, gas.

Agriculture: Beef cattle; rice is principal crop. Also nursery crops, corn, hay, sorghum, bees (first in number of colonies). Market value $29.9 million. Some lumbering.

LIBERTY (10,165) county seat; petroleum-related industry, agribusiness; library, museum; regional historical resource depository; Liberty Bell, Price Daniel House; hospital; Jubilee in March.

Cleveland (8,960) forest products processed, shipped; tourism; library; museum; hospital.

Dayton (9,186) rice, oil center.

Other towns include: **Ames** (1,218); **Daisetta** (1,151); **Dayton Lakes** (109); **Devers** (527); **Hardin** (979); **Hull** (803); **Kenefick** (686); **North Cleveland** (314); **Plum Grove** (717); **Raywood** (231); **Romayor** (135); **Rye** (150).

For explanation of sources, symbols and abbreviations, see p. 204, and foldout map.

Population......................**91,098**	July mean max (°F)....................92.1
Change from 2010 (%)................20.4	Civ. Labor............................34,054
Area (sq. mi.).......................1,176.3	Unemployed (%)......................10.4
Land Area (sq. mi.)................1,158.4	Wages $219,743,376
Altitude (ft.)........................3–243	Per Capita Income................ $37,874
Rainfall (in.)..........................61.3	Prop. Value $10,414,481,576
Jan. mean min (°F)....................41.2	Retail Sales.................. $936,024,230

A pair of white ibis wading at the Trinity River National Wildlife Refuge in Liberty County. Photo by William L. Pharr, CC by SA 4.0/ Wikimedia Commons

Limestone County

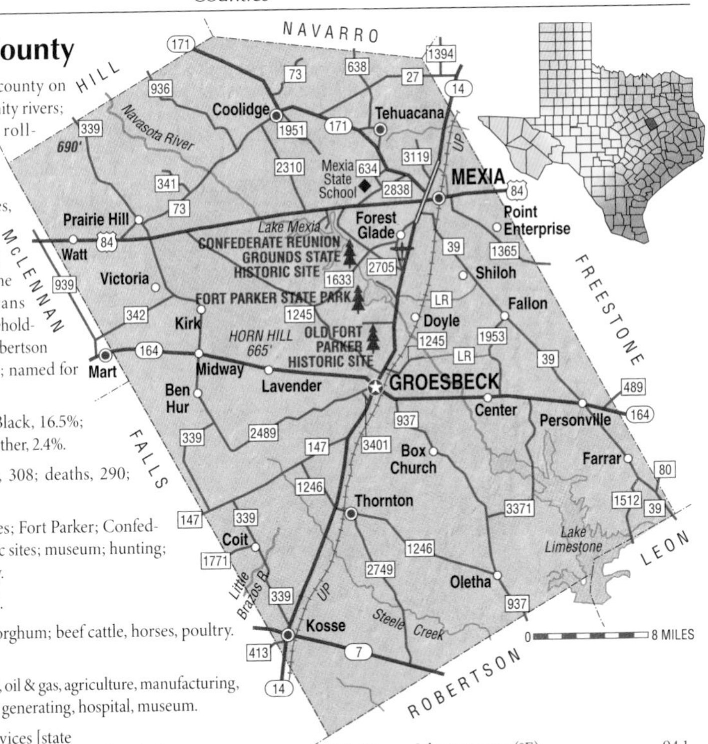

Physical Features: East central county on divide between Brazos and Trinity rivers; borders Blacklands, level to rolling; drained by Navasota and tributaries; Lake Limestone.

Economy: Government/services, electricity-generating plant.

History: Tawakoni (Tehuacana) and Waco area, later Comanche raiders. First Anglo-Americans arrived in 1833. Antebellum slaveholding area. County created from Robertson County and organized in 1846; named for indigenous rock.

Race/Ethnicity: Anglo, 57.3%; Black, 16.5%; Hispanic, 23.1%; Asian, 0.4%; Other, 2.4%.

Vital Statistics, annual: Births, 308; deaths, 290; marriages, 156; divorces, 12.

Recreation: Fishing, lake activities; Fort Parker; Confederate Reunion Grounds; historic sites; museum; hunting; Groesbeck fiddle festival in May.

Minerals: Natural gas, lignite coal.

Agriculture: Hay, corn, wheat, sorghum; beef cattle, horses, poultry. Market value $66.3 million.

GROESBECK (4,308) county seat, oil & gas, agriculture, manufacturing, hunting, mining, prison, power generating, hospital, museum.

MEXIA (7,605) government/services [state school], manufacturing; hospital, college extension campus; Boomtown History Day in April.

Other towns include: **Coolidge** (997), **Kosse** (473), **Prairie Hill** (150), **Tehuacana** (286), **Thornton** (541).

Population	23,709
Change from 2010 (%)	1.4
Area (sq. mi.)	933.2
Land Area (sq. mi.)	905.3
Altitude (ft.)	363–690
Rainfall (in.)	40.3
Jan. mean min (°F)	35.2
July mean max (°F)	94.1
Civ. Labor	8,211
Unemployed (%)	6.8
Wages	$85,421,058
Per Capita Income	$37,774
Prop. Value	$3,693,786,852
Retail Sales	$234,527,725

Lipscomb County

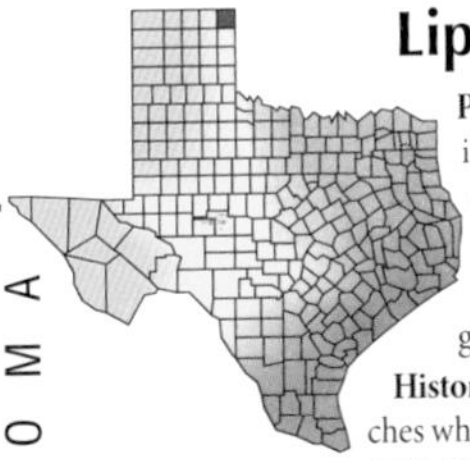

Physical Features: High Plains, broken in east; drains to tributaries of Canadian, Wolf Creek; sandy loam, black soils.

Economy: Oil and gas, agribusinesses, government/services.

History: Apaches, later Kiowas and Comanches who were driven into Indian Territory in 1875. Ranching began in late 1870s. County created in 1876 from Bexar District; organized in 1887; named for A.S. Lipscomb, Republic of Texas leader.

Race/Ethnicity: Anglo, 63.1%; Black, 0.2%; Hispanic, 34.1%; Asian, 0.4%; Other, 2%.

Vital Statistics, annual: Births, 48; deaths, 21 ;marriages, 12; divorces, 18.

Recreation: Hunting; Wolf Creek museum; prairie chicken booming grounds.

Minerals: Oil, natural gas.

Agriculture: Cattle, corn, wheat, grain sorghum, hay, sunflowers. Some 23,000 acres irrigated. Market value $79.3 million.

LIPSCOMB (28), county seat; livestock center.

BOOKER (1,487, partly in Ochiltree County) trade center, library.

Other towns include: **Darrouzett** (341) Deutsches Fest in July; **Follett** (440); **Higgins** (398) library, Will Rogers Day in August.

Population	3,208
Change from 2010 (%)	-2.8
Area (sq. mi.)	932.3
Land Area (sq. mi.)	932.2
Altitude (ft.)	2,220–2,892
Rainfall (in.)	22.3
Jan. mean min (°F)	18.1
July mean max (°F)	94.0
Civ. Labor	1,574
Unemployed (%)	3.8
Wages	$33,367,391
Per Capita Income	$77,810
Prop. Value	$606,600,750
Retail Sales	$19,146,598

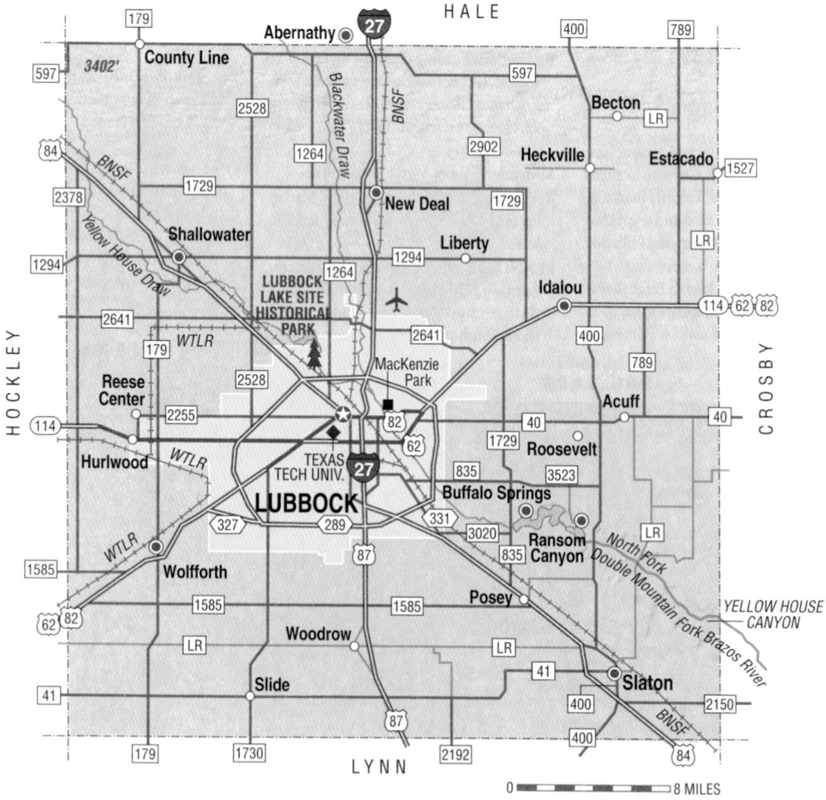

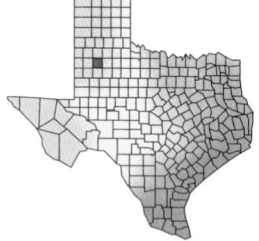

Physical Features: South Plains, broken by 1,500 playas, upper Brazos River tributaries; rich soils with underground water.

Economy: Among world's largest cottonseed processing centers, a leading agribusiness center, cattle feedlots, varied manufacturing, higher education center, medical center, government/services.

History: Evidence of human habitation for 12,000 years. In historic period, Apache Indians, followed by Comanche hunters. Sheep raisers from Midwest arrived in the late 1870s. Cotton farms brought in Mexican laborers in the 1940s-1960s. County named for Col. Tom S. Lubbock, an organizer of the Confederate Terry's Rangers; county created in 1876 from Bexar District; organized in 1891.

Race/Ethnicity: Anglo, 52.2%; Black, 7.2%; Hispanic, 36.3%; Asian, 2.2%; Other, 1.8%.

Vital Statistics, annual: Births, 4,112; deaths, 2,441; marriages, 2,163; divorces, 826.

Recreation: Lubbock Lake archaeological site; Texas Tech events; civic center; Buddy Holly statue, Walk of Fame, Lubbock Music Fest in fall; planetarium; Ranching Heritage Center; Panhandle-South

For explanation of sources, symbols and abbreviations, see p. 204, and foldout map.

Lubbock County

Plains Fair, National Cowboy symposium in September; wine festivals; Buffalo Springs Lake.

Minerals: Oil, gas, stone, sand and gravel.

Agriculture: Second in bales of cotton produced. Fed beef, cow-calf operations; poultry, eggs; hogs. Other crops, nursery, grain sorghum, wheat, sunflowers, soybeans, hay, vegetables; more than 155,000 acres irrigated, mostly cotton. Market value $219.5 million.

Education: Texas Tech University with law and medical schools; Lubbock Christian University; South Plains College branch; Wayland Baptist University off-campus center.

LUBBOCK (259,158) county seat; center for large agricultural area; manufacturing includes electronics, earth-moving equipment, food containers, fire-protection equipment, clothing, other products; distribution center for South Plains; feedlots; museum; government/services; hospitals, psychiatric hospital; wind power center.

Other towns include: **Buffalo Springs** (493); **Idalou** (2,301); **New Deal** (827); **Ransom Canyon** (1,113); **Shallowater** (2,528); **Slaton** (6,048) agriculture, government/services, Harvey House hotel, museums, sausagefest in October; **Wolfforth** (5,757) retail, government/services.

Also, part of **Abernathy** (2,706).

Population	**308,880**
Change from 2010 (%)	10.8
Area (sq. mi.)	900.7
Land Area (sq. mi.)	895.6
Altitude (ft.)	2,821–3,402
Rainfall (in.)	19.1
Jan. mean min (°F)	26.4
July mean max (°F)	92.8
Civ. Labor	158,123
Unemployment (%)	4.9
Wages	$1,800,105,667
Per Capita Income	$44,311
Prop. Value	$26,776,317,523
Retail Sales	$6,212,966,699

Lynn County

Physical Features: South Plains, broken by Caprock Escarpment, playas, draws; sandy loam, black, gray soils.

Economy: Agribusiness.

History: Apaches, ousted by Comanches who were removed to Indian Territory in 1875. Ranching began in 1880s. Farming developed after 1900. County created in 1876 from Bexar District; organized in 1903; named for Alamo victim W. Lynn.

Race/Ethnicity: Anglo, 46.3%; Black, 2%; Hispanic, 50.1%; Asian, 0.1%; Other, 1.2%.

Vital Statistics, annual: Births, 70; deaths, 51; marriages, 29; divorces, 13.

Recreation: Pioneer museum in Tahoka; Dan Blocker museum in O'Donnell; sandhill crane migration in winter.

Minerals: Oil, natural gas.

Agriculture: Cotton produces largest income (first in acreage); 72,000 acres irrigated. Also, ranching, grain sorghum. Market value $111.4 million.

TAHOKA (2,765) county seat; agricultural center, electric/telephone cooperatives; hospital; museum; Harvest Festival in the fall.

O'Donnell (840, partly in Dawson County) commercial center.

Other towns include: **New Home** (366); **Wilson** (496).

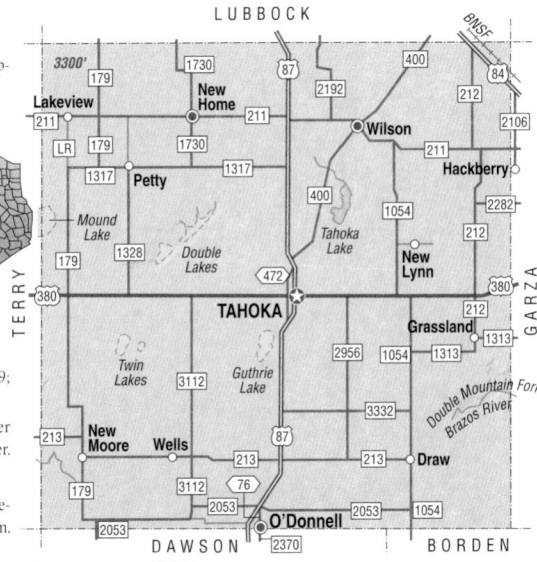

Population....................... **6,151**	July mean max (°F)...................91.9
Change from 2010 (%).................4.0	Civ. Labor............................2,746
Area (sq. mi.)........................893.5	Unemployed (%).........................7.5
Land Area (sq. mi.)...................891.9	Wages.....................$21,389,152
Altitude (ft.).................. 2,660-3,300	Per Capita Income................ $43,141
Rainfall (in.)...........................21.1	Prop. Value................$1,557,077,293
Jan. mean min (°F)....................28.0	Retail Sales....................$21,820,813

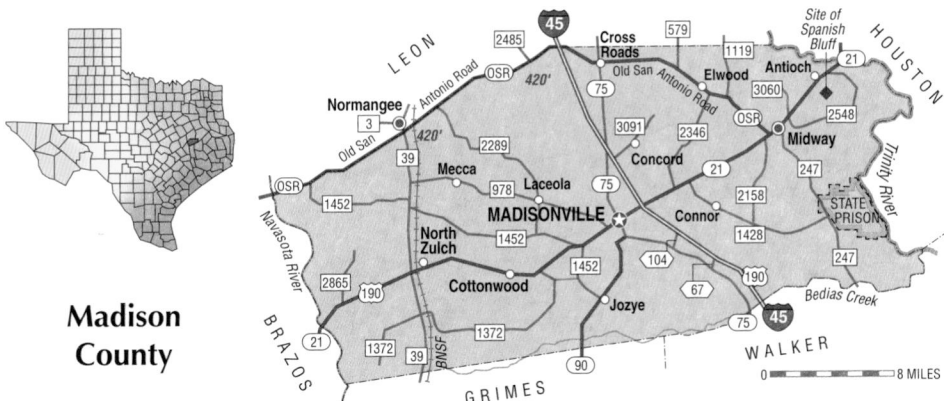

Madison County

Physical Features: Hilly, draining to Trinity, Navasota rivers, Bedias Creek; one-fifth of area timbered; alluvial, loam, sandy soils.

Economy: Prison, government/services, varied manufacturing, agribusiness, oil production.

History: Caddo, Bidai Indian area; Kickapoos migrated from the east. Spanish settlements established in 1774 and 1805. Anglo-Americans arrived in 1829. Census of 1860 showed 30 percent of population was black. County named for U.S. President James Madison; created from Grimes, Leon, and Walker counties 1853; organized 1854.

Race/Ethnicity: Anglo, 53%; Black, 19.1%; Hispanic, 24.5%; Asian, 0.5%; Other, 2.5%.

Vital Statistics, annual: Births, 145; deaths, 126; marriages, 111; divorces, 52.

Recreation: Fishing, hunting; Spanish Bluff where survivors of the Gutiérrez-Magee expedition were executed in 1813; other historic sites.

Minerals: sand, oil.

Agriculture: Nursery crops, cattle, horses, poultry raised; forage for livestock. Market value $124.1 million.

MADISONVILLE (4,734) county seat; farm-trade center, varied manufacturing; hospital, library; Spring Fling in April.

Other towns, **Midway** (229); **Normangee** (706, mostly in Leon County); **North Zulch** (600).

Population....................... **14,188**	
Change from 2010 (%).................0.5	
Area (sq. mi.)........................472.4	
Land Area (sq. mi.)...................466.1	
Altitude (ft.).....................131–420	
Rainfall (in.)...........................45.1	
Jan. mean min (°F)....................36.9	
July mean max (°F)....................94.4	
Civ. Labor............................4,439	
Unemployed (%)..........................7	
Wages.......................$47,011,455	
Per Capita Income................ $32,648	
Prop. Value................$2,677,160,200	
Retail Sales.................$277,792,588	

Marion County

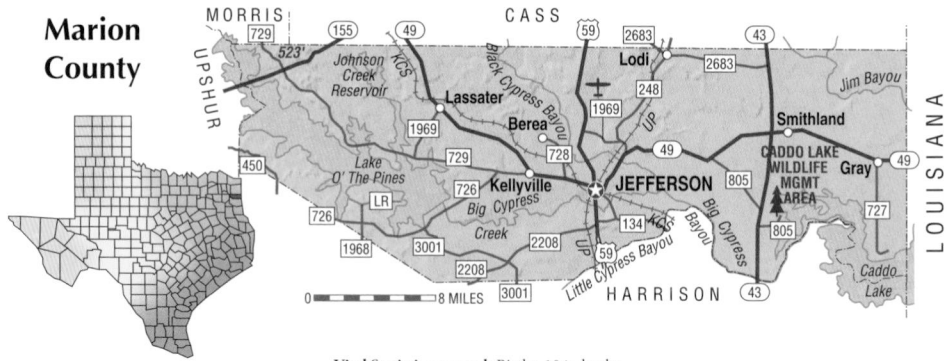

Physical Features: Northeastern county; hilly, three-quarters forested with pines, hardwoods; drains to Caddo Lake, Lake O' the Pines, Big Cypress Bayou; Johnson Creek Reservoir.

Economy: Agriculture, tourism, forestry, food processing.

History: Caddoes forced out in 1790s. Kickapoo in area when settlers arrived from Deep South around 1840. Antebellum slaveholding area. County created 1860 from Cass County, organized the same year; named for Gen. Francis Marion of American Revolution.

Race/Ethnicity: Anglo, 69.1%; Black, 22.7%; Hispanic, 3.8%; Asian, 0.6%; Other, 3.5%.

Vital Statistics, annual: Births, 104; deaths, 167; marriages, 79; divorces, 40.

Recreation: Lake activities, hunting, Excelsior Hotel, 84 medallions on historic sites including Jay Gould railroad car, museum, historical homes tour in May, Spring Festival.

Minerals: Iron ore, natural gas, oil.

Agriculture: Beef cattle, hay. Market value $5.9 million. Forestry is most important industry.

JEFFERSON (1,967) county seat; tourism, syrup works, forestry; museum, library; historical sites.

Other towns include: **Lodi** (175).

Population	**9,760**
Change from 2010 (%)	8.7
Area (sq. mi.)	420.3
Land Area (sq. mi.)	380.9
Altitude (ft.)	168–523
Rainfall (in.)	48.2
Jan. mean min (°F)	32.7
July mean max (°F)	92.6
Civ. Labor	4,202
Unemployed (%)	7.7
Wages	$20,212,989
Per Capita Income	$39,895
Prop. Value	$1,343,045,995
Retail Sales	$59,802,126

Martin County

Physical Features: South Plains; sandy, loam soils, broken by playas, creeks; Sulphur Springs Draw Reservoir.

Economy: Oil and gas production, agribusiness.

History: Apaches, ousted by Comanches who in turn were forced out by the U.S. Army in 1875. Farming began in 1881. County created from Bexar District in 1876; organized in 1884; named for Wylie Martin, senator of Republic of Texas.

Race/Ethnicity: Anglo, 47.7%; Black, 1.2%; Hispanic, 49.5%; Asian, 0.2%; Other, 1.2%.

Vital Statistics, annual: Births, 93; deaths, 52; marriages, 28; divorces, 17.

Recreation: Museum, settlers reunion in July at Stanton.

Minerals: Oil, gas.

Agriculture: Cotton, beef cattle, milo, wheat, horses, meat goats. Market value $54.3 million.

STANTON (3,002) county seat; oil and gas production, agribusiness; commuting to Midland, Big Spring; hospital; museum, historic monastery, other historic buildings; Old Sorehead trade days April, June, October.

Other towns include: **Ackerly** (237, partly in Dawson County); **Lenorah** (83); **Tarzan** (30). A small part of **Midland**.

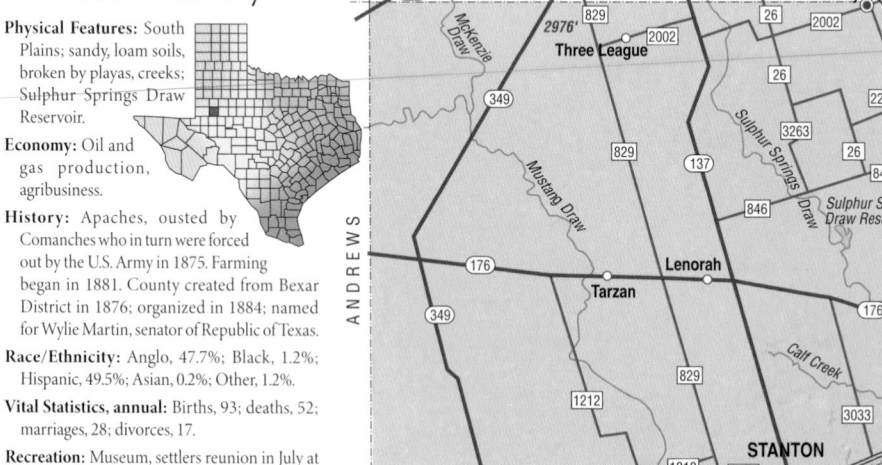

Population	**5,731**
Change from 2010 (%)	5.9
Area (sq. mi.)	915.7
Land Area (sq. mi.)	914.9
Altitude (ft.)	2,470–2,976
Rainfall (in.)	17.6
Jan. mean min (°F)	30.0
July mean max (°F)	94.0
Civ. Labor	2,548
Unemployed (%)	5.4
Wages	$29,924,455
Per Capita Income	$60,844
Prop. Value	$10,745,360,740
Retail Sales	$110,223,869

Mason County

Physical Features: Central county; hilly, draining to Llano and San Saba rivers and their tributaries; limestone, red soils; varied timber.

Economy: Sand plants, agriculture, tourism, hunting.

History: Lipan Apaches in area, driven south by Comanches around 1790. German settlers arrived in the mid-1840s, followed by Anglo-Americans. Mexican immigration increased after 1930. County created from Bexar and Gillespie counties in 1858, organized the same year; named for Mexican War victim U.S. Army Lt. G.T. Mason.

Race/Ethnicity: Anglo, 72.1%; Black, 0.4%; Hispanic, 26.3%; Asian, 0.1%; Other, 0.9%.

Vital Statistics, annual: Births, 51; deaths, 44; marriages, 23; divorces, 14.

Recreation: Hunting, fishing; kayaking, rock crawling, camping; historic homes of stone; prehistoric Indian artifacts exhibit; Fort Mason, where Robert E. Lee served; bat cave; wildflower drives in spring, Roundup rodeo in July.

Minerals: Sand, topaz, granite.

Agriculture: Beef cattle, hay, meat goats. Market value $21.7 million. Hunting leases important.

MASON (2,298) county seat; agriculture, hunting, nature tourism; museums, historical district, homes, rock fences built by German settlers; wild game dinner in November.

Other towns include: **Art** (14), **Fredonia** (55), **Pontotoc** (125).

For explanation of sources, symbols and abbreviations, see p. 204, and foldout map.

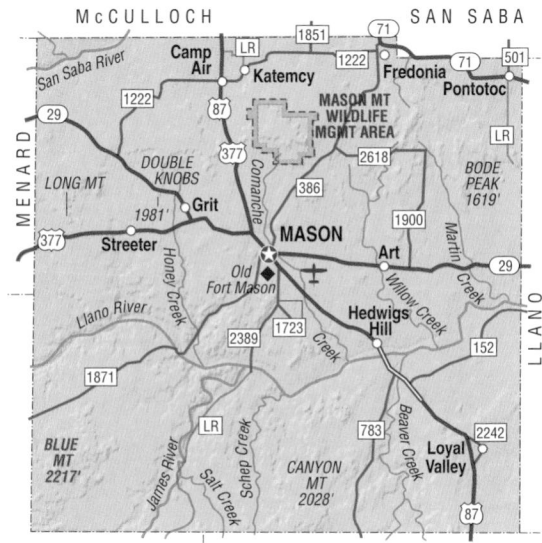

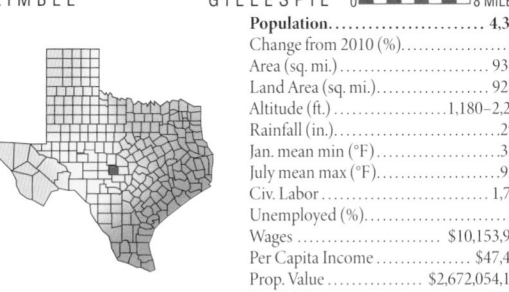

Population	**4,301**
Change from 2010 (%)	3.8
Area (sq. mi.)	932.2
Land Area (sq. mi.)	928.8
Altitude (ft.)	1,180–2,217
Rainfall (in.)	29.2
Jan. mean min (°F)	32.1
July mean max (°F)	92.3
Civ. Labor	1,755
Unemployed (%)	.5
Wages	$10,153,937
Per Capita Income	$47,439
Prop. Value	$2,672,054,104
Retail Sales	$23,218,007

A view of Lake O' the Pines in Marion County. Photo by the U.S. Army Corps of Engineers

This M114 155 mm howitzer is displayed in front of the McCulloch County courthouse in Brady. Photo by Larry D. Moore, CC by SA 4.0/ Wikimedia Commons

Physical Features: Gulf Coastal Plain; flat, broken by bays; many different soils; drains to Colorado River, creeks, coast; South Texas Project Reservoir.

Economy: Agribusiness, oil and gas fields, refinery.

History: Karankawa tribal area, Tonkawas in the area later.

Anglo-Americans arrived in 1822. Mexican immigration increased after 1920. An original county, created in 1836 from a Spanish municipality, named for canebrake; organized in 1837; settled by Austin colonists.

Race/Ethnicity: Anglo, 43.1%; Black, 10.6%; Hispanic, 42.8%; Asian, 1.9%; Other, 1.3%.

Vital Statistics, annual: Births, 533; deaths, 407; marriages, 304; divorces, 89.

Recreation: Wildlife hunting and viewing, fishing (fresh and salt water), beaches, sailing, historic sites, museums; Bay City rice festival in October.

Minerals: Oil and gas.

Agriculture: Cotton, rice, soybeans, corn, grain sorghum; some 33,000 acres of crops irrigated; cattle, turf, aquaculture (first in value). Market value $124.2 million.

BAY CITY (17,431) county seat; government/services, education, nuclear power plant; petrochemicals; agribusiness; hospital, junior college branch.

PALACIOS (4,589) tourism, seafood industry; hospital; Marine Education Center; public fishing piers; Bay Festival on Labor Day.

Other towns include: **Blessing** (989) historic sites; **Cedar Lane** (300); **Collegeport** (80); **Elmaton** (160); **Markham** (1,096); **Matagorda** (465); **Midfield** (305); **Pledger** (265); **Sargent** (900) retirement community, fishing, birding, commercial fishing, barbecue cookoff in April; **Van Vleck** (2,214); **Wadsworth** (160).

Matagorda County

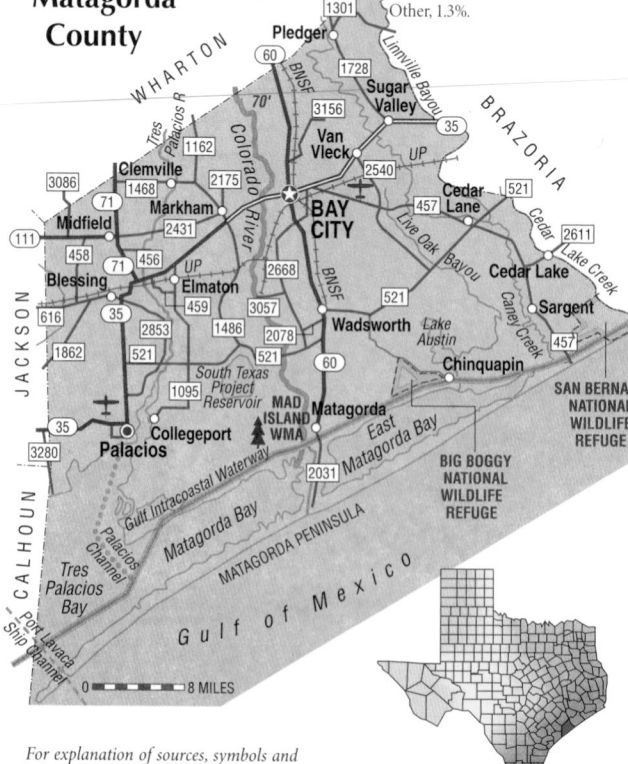

For explanation of sources, symbols and abbreviations, see p. 204, and foldout map.

Population......................	**36,292**
Change from 2010 (%).................	-7.5
Area (sq. mi.)......................	1,612.5
Land Area (sq. mi.)................	1,100.3
Altitude (ft.)...................	sea level–70
Rainfall (in.)............................	48.9
Jan. mean min (°F)...................	45.4
July mean max (°F)...................	91.5
Civ. Labor	16,106
Unemployed (%)........................	9.1
Wages	$147,337,009
Per Capita Income	$45,237
Prop. Value	$8,640,030,577
Retail Sales	$412,419,274

Maverick County

Physical Features: Southwestern county on the Rio Grande; broken, rolling surface, with dense brush; clay, sandy, alluvial soils.

Economy: Oil, government/services, agribusiness, tourism.

History: Coahuiltecan area; later Comanches arrived. Spanish ranching began in the 1760s. Anglo-Americans arrived in 1834. County named for Sam A. Maverick, whose name is now a synonym for unbranded cattle; created in 1856 from Kinney County; organized in 1871.

Race/Ethnicity: Anglo, 3.2%; Black, 0.1%; Hispanic, 95.1%; Asian, 0.2%; Other, 1.2%.

Vital Statistics, annual: Births, 1,150; deaths, 398; marriages, 594; divorces, 40.

Recreation: Tourist gateway to Mexico; white-tailed deer, bird hunting; fishing; historic sites, Fort Duncan museum.

Minerals: Oil, gas, sand, gravel.

Agriculture: Cattle feedlots; pecans, vegetables, sorghum, wheat; goats, sheep. Some irrigation from Rio Grande. Market value $43.0 million.

EAGLE PASS (28,992) county seat; government/services, retail center, tourism; hospital; junior college, Sul Ross college branch; entry point to Piedras Negras, Mex., Nacho Festival in Piedras Negras in October.

Other communities include: **Chula Vista** (3,980), **Eidson Road** (9,132), **El Indio** (169), **Las Quintas Fronterizas** (4,114), and **Rosita** (2,797), all immediately south of Eagle Pass. Also, **Elm Creek** (2,870) and **Quemado** (226).

Population.....................	**57,888**
Change from 2010 (%)................	19.4
Area (sq. mi.)......................	1,291.8
Land Area (sq. mi.)................	1,279.3
Altitude (ft.).....................	550–975
Rainfall (in.)...........................	20.4
Jan. mean min (°F)...................	41.5
July mean max (°F)....................	98.1
Civ. Labor..........................	23,914
Unemployed (%)......................	15.5
Wages	$171,400,673
Per Capita Income...............	$31,380
Prop. Value...............	$4,513,081,913
Retail Sales.................	$641,844,151

McCulloch County

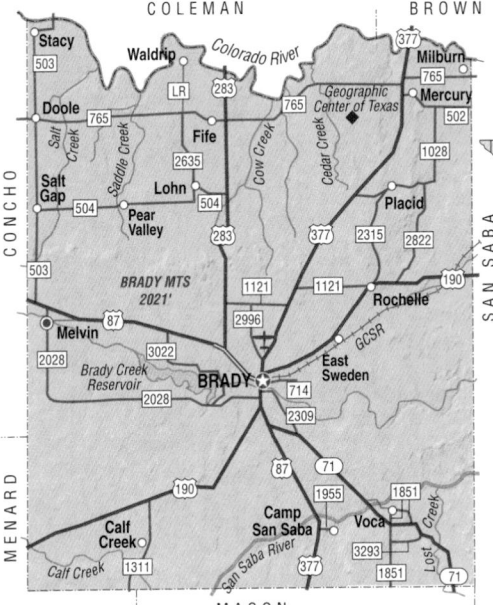

Physical Features: Hilly and rolling; drains to Colorado River, Brady Creek and Brady Creek Reservoir, San Saba River; black loams to sandy soils.

Economy: Agribusiness, industrial sand production, hunting leases.

History: Apache area. First Anglo-American settlers arrived in the late 1850s, but Comanche raids delayed further settlement until the 1870s. County created from Bexar District in 1856; organized in 1876; named for San Jacinto veteran Gen. Ben McCulloch.

Race/Ethnicity: Anglo, 63.4%; Black, 1.6%; Hispanic, 32.9%; Asian, 0.3%; Other, 1.5%.

Vital Statistics, annual: Births, 87; deaths, 117; marriages, 22; divorces, 50.

Recreation: Hunting, lake activities, museums, goat cookoff on Labor Day, Hogtoberfest in October, golf tournaments.

Minerals: Sand, oil, and gas.

Agriculture: Beef cattle and sheep; also small grains, goats, hay, cotton. Market value $22.5 million. Hunting leases.

BRADY (5,602) county seat; silica sand, oil-field equipment, ranching, tourism, other manufacturing; hospital; Heart of Texas car show in April, Cinco de Mayo.

Other towns: **Doole** (74), **Lohn** (149), **Melvin** (182), **Mercury** (166), **Rochelle** (163), and **Voca** (56).

Population.....................	**8,323**
Change from 2010 (%)................	7.2
Area (sq. mi.)......................	1,073.4
Land Area (sq. mi.)................	165.6
Altitude (ft.).....................	1,280–2,021
Rainfall (in.)...........................	27.6
Jan. mean min (°F)...................	32.2
July mean max (°F)...................	94.2
Civ. Labor..........................	3,169
Unemployed (%)......................	.7
Wages	$24,932,450
Per Capita Income...............	$38,895
Prop. Value...............	$1,817,827,259
Retail Sales.................	$99,521,939

McLennan County

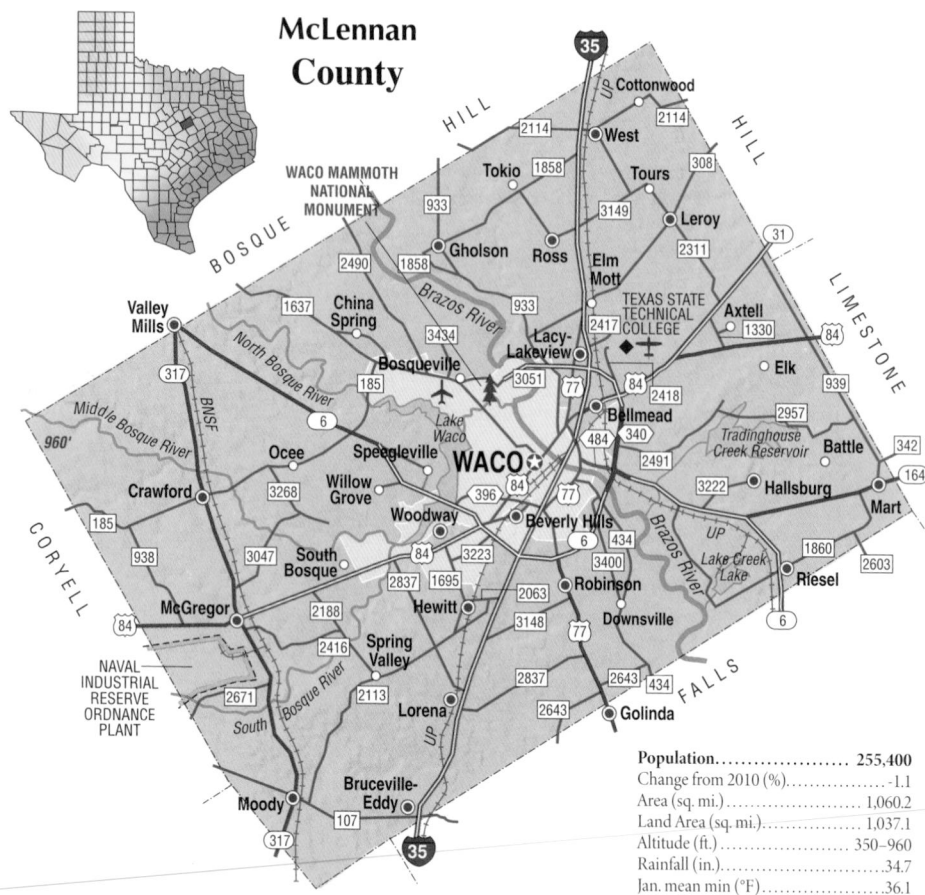

Population **255,400**
Change from 2010 (%) .... -1.1
Area (sq. mi.) 1,060.2
Land Area (sq. mi.) 1,037.1
Altitude (ft.) 350–960
Rainfall (in.) 34.7
Jan. mean min (°F) 36.1
July mean max (°F) 96.3
Civ. Labor 122,535
Unemployed (%) 5.1
Wages $1,549,288,666
Per Capita Income $28,490,833,687
Prop. Value $28,490,833,687
Retail Sales $3,841,047,862

Physical Features: Central Texas county of mostly Blackland prairie, but rolling hills in west; drains to Bosque, Brazos rivers and Lake Waco, Tradinghouse Creek Reservoir, Lake Creek Lake; heavy, loam, sandy soils.

Economy: Agribusiness, education, health services.

History: Tonkawas, Wichitas and Wacos in area. Anglo-American settlers arrived in the 1840s. Indians removed to Brazos reservations in 1854. County created from Milam County in 1850, organized the same year; named for settler, Neil McLennan Sr.

Race/Ethnicity: Anglo, 54.6%; Black, 14.4%; Hispanic, 26.9%; Asian, 1.6%; Other, 2.2%.

Vital Statistics, annual: Births, 3,528; deaths, 2,123; marriages, 1,666; divorces, 810.

Recreation: Texas Ranger Hall of Fame, museum; Texas Sports Hall of Fame; Dr Pepper Museum; Cameron Park; drag boat races April and May; zoo; historic sites, homes; museums; libraries; art center; symphony; civic theater; Baylor

University events; Heart o' Texas Fair in October.

Minerals: Sand, gravel, limestone.

Agriculture: Corn, silage, wheat, beef cattle, dairies. Market value $179.7 million.

Education: Baylor University; community college; Texas State Technical College; university extensions.

WACO (138,400) county seat; manufacturing, higher education, medical services/hospital, government/services, finance; riverside park, historic suspension bridge, zoo; Magnolia Silos market; Waco Mammoth National Monument; wine festivals in April and October.

HEWITT (14,820) medical services/hospital, construction, retail; car show and concert in April.

WEST (2,939) known for Czech foods; varied manufacturing; Westfest Labor Day weekend.

Other towns include: **Axtell** (300); **Bellmead** (10,731); **Beverly Hills** (1,993); **Bruceville-Eddy** (1,857, partly in Falls County);

China Spring (1,401); **Crawford** (765); **Elm Mott** (300); **Gholson** (1,114); **Hallsburg** (472); **Lacy-Lakeview** (6,914); **Leroy** (347); **Lorena** (1,785); **Mart** (1,971) agricultural center, some manufacturing, museum; juvenile correction facility.

Also: **McGregor** (5,264) agriculture, manufacturing, distribution; private telephone museum; Frontier Founders Day in September; **Moody** (1,415) agriculture, commuting to Waco, Temple; library; Cotton Harvest fest in September; **Riesel** (1,041); **Robinson** (11,883); **Ross** (294); **Woodway** (9,230).

Part of **Golinda** (589, mostly in Falls County) and part of **Valley Mills** (1,180, mostly in Bosque County).

For explanation of sources, symbols and abbreviations, see p. 204, and foldout map.

McMullen County

Physical Features: Southern county of brushy plain, sloping to Frio, Nueces rivers and tributaries, Choke Canyon Reservoir; saline clay soils.

Economy: Government/services, retail, agriculture, oil and gas services.

History: Coahuiltecans, squeezed out by Lipan Apaches and other tribes. Anglo-American settlers arrived in 1858. Sheep ranching of 1870s attracted Mexican laborers. County created from Atascosa, Bexar, Live Oak counties 1858; organized 1862, reorganized 1877; named for Nueces River pioneer-empresario John McMullen.

Race/Ethnicity: Anglo, 57.8%; Black, 0.4%; Hispanic, 40.8%; Asian, 0.4%; Other, 0.5%.

Vital Statistics, annual: Births, 0; deaths, 7; marriages, 11; divorces, 1.

Recreation: Hunting, wildlife viewing; lake activities, state park, wildlife management area; Labor Day rodeo.

Minerals: Gas, oil, lignite coal, caliche, kaolinite.

Agriculture: Beef cattle. Market value $8.3 million. Wildlife enterprises important.

Tilden (301), county seat; oil, gas, lignite mining, ranch center, government/services.

Other towns include: **Calliham** (100).

Population.......................... 749	Altitude (ft.) 150–642	Unemployed (%)..........................3
Change from 2010 (%)................6.7	Rainfall (in.)............................24.0	Wages $7,595,891
Area (sq. mi.)....................... 1,156.8	Jan. mean min (°F)....................42.6	Per Capita Income $65,250
Land Area (sq. mi.)................ 1,139.4	July mean max (°F)....................96.4	Prop. Value $4,164,609,958
	Civ. Labor 673	Retail Sales................... $19,354,234

Medina County

Physical Features: Southwestern county with scenic hills in north; south has fertile valleys, rolling surface; Medina River, Medina Lake.

Economy: Agribusiness, tourism, commuters to San Antonio.

History: Lipan Apaches and Comanches in area. Settled by Alsatians led by Henri Castro in 1844. Mexican immigration increased after 1900. County created and organized in 1848 from Bexar; named for river, probably for Spanish engineer Pedro Medina.

Race/Ethnicity: Anglo, 43%; Black, 1.8%; Hispanic, 53.1%; Asian, 0.5%; Other, 1.3%.

Vital Statistics, annual: Births, 585; deaths, 428; marriages, 255; divorces, 133.

Recreation: A leading deer area; scenic drives, camping, fishing, historic buildings, museum, market trail days most months.

Minerals: Oil and natural gas.

Agriculture: Cattle, corn, grains, cotton, hay, vegetables, aquaculture; 50,000 acres irrigated. Market value $93.9 million.

HONDO (9,618) county seat; flight training center, aerospace industry, agribusiness, varied manufacturing, hunting leases; hospital; prisons; wild game festival in January.

CASTROVILLE (3,114) farming; tourism; commuting to San Antonio; Landmark Inn, museum; St. Louis Day celebration in August.

DEVINE (5,001) commuters, shipping for truck crop-livestock; fall festival in October.

Other towns: **D'Hanis** (873), **La Coste** (1,293), **Natalia** (1,617), **Riomedina** (60), **Yancey** (209). Also, **Lytle** (3,066, mostly in Atascosa County).

Population...................... 53,794	July mean max (°F)....................94.9
Change from 2010 (%)................16.9	Civ. Labor 22,031
Area (sq. mi.)....................... 1,334.4	Unemployed (%)........................5.2
Land Area (sq. mi.)................ 1,325.4	Wages $112,659,440
Altitude (ft.) 570–1,995	Per Capita Income $41,095
Rainfall (in.)............................30.3	Prop. Value $7,064,827,834
Jan. mean min (°F)....................39.1	Retail Sales................... $763,427,302

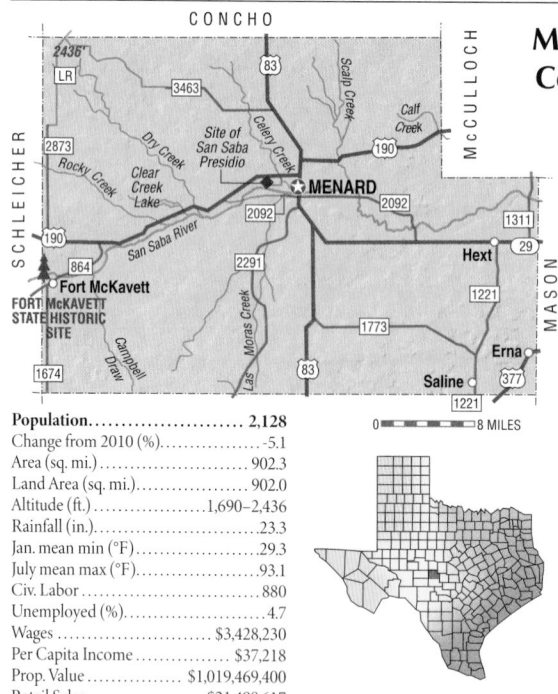

Menard County

Physical Features: West central county of rolling topography, draining to San Saba River and tributaries; limestone soils.

Economy: Agriculture, tourism, oil, gas production.

History: Apaches, followed by Comanches in 18th century. Mission Santa Cruz de San Sabá established in 1757. A few Anglo-American and German settlers arrived in 1840s. County created from Bexar County 1858, organized 1871; named for Galveston's founder, Michel B. Menard.

Race/Ethnicity: Anglo, 55.8%; Black, 0.5%; Hispanic, 42.9%; Asian, 0.1%; Other, 0.5%.

Vital Statistics, annual: Births, 15; deaths, 33; marriages, 4; divorces, 7.

Recreation: Hunting, fishing; historic sites, including Spanish presidio, mission, irrigation ditches; U.S. fort; railroad museum; Jim Bowie barbecue cook-off in May.

Minerals: Oil, gas.

Agriculture: Cattle, sheep, goats, pecans, hay. Market value $9.1 million. Hunting leases, ecotourism important.

MENARD (1,378) county seat; agribusiness, government/services; hunters blowout ball in early November.

Other towns include: **Fort McKavett** (50); **Hext** (75).

Population	2,128
Change from 2010 (%)	-5.1
Area (sq. mi.)	902.3
Land Area (sq. mi.)	902.0
Altitude (ft.)	1,690–2,436
Rainfall (in.)	23.3
Jan. mean min (°F)	29.3
July mean max (°F)	93.1
Civ. Labor	880
Unemployed (%)	4.7
Wages	$3,428,230
Per Capita Income	$37,218
Prop. Value	$1,019,469,400
Retail Sales	$21,499,617

Midland County

Physical Features: Flat western county, broken by draws; sandy, loam soils with native grasses.

Economy: Among leading petroleum-producing counties; distribution, administrative center for oil industry; varied manufacturing; government/services.

History: Comanches in area in 19th century. Sheep ranching developed in the 1880s. Permian Basin oil boom began in the 1920s. County created from Tom Green County in 1885 and organized the same year; name came from midway location on the railroad between El Paso and Fort Worth. The Chihuahua Trail and Emigrant Road were pioneer trails that crossed the county.

Race/Ethnicity: Anglo, 42.9%; Black, 6%; Hispanic, 47.3%; Asian, 1.8%; Other, 1.8%.

Vital Statistics, annual: Births, 3,032; deaths, 1,098; marriages, 1269; divorces, 714.

Recreation: Permian Basin Petroleum Museum, Library, Hall of Fame; Museum of Southwest; Commemorative Air Force and Museum; community theater; metropolitan events; homes of Presidents Bush.

Minerals: Oil, natural gas.

Agriculture: Beef cattle, horses, sheep and goats; cotton, hay, pecans; some 11,000 acres irrigated. Market value $16.3 million.

MIDLAND (146,701) county seat; petroleum, petrochemical center; varied manufacturing; livestock sale center; hospitals; cultural activities; community college; polo club, Texas League baseball; Celebration of the Arts in May.

Part [2,166] of **Odessa.**

Population	176,814
Change from 2010 (%)	29.2
Area (sq. mi.)	902.1
Land Area (sq. mi.)	900.3
Altitude (ft.)	2,550–2,980
Rainfall (in.)	14.8
Jan. mean min (°F)	31.5
July mean max (°F)	96.2
Civ. Labor	95,625
Unemployed (%)	6.8
Wages	$1,865,556,925
Per Capita Income	$130,983
Prop. Value	$42,741,588,887
Retail Sales	$3,876,792,295

Counties of Texas

A detailed county map accompanies each of 254 county articles on pages 191–369. Below is the legend to the symbols used on those maps:

Legend to counties

——	Principal road
——	Secondary road
—	Local road
≡≡≡	Divided highway
10	Interstate highway
(377)	U.S. highway
(81)	State highway
308	Farm-to-market road
LR	Local roads
28	Loop
+++++	Railway
BNSF	Railway name
〜	River or creek
◯	Lake
◌	Intermittent water source
▬▬▬	Intracoastal Waterway
✪	County seat
◉	Incorporated town
○	Unincorporated town
------	County boundary
P E C O S	Name of neighboring county
400'	Elevation
880'	Highest point in county
✈	Major airport with scheduled jet service
✛	Municipal airport
✦	Military airport
♠	National park or wildlife management area
⬚	Federal land
♠	State park or wildlife management area
⬚	State land
◆	Ranger station
········	Time zone line
⬚	Boundary of prison or military installation

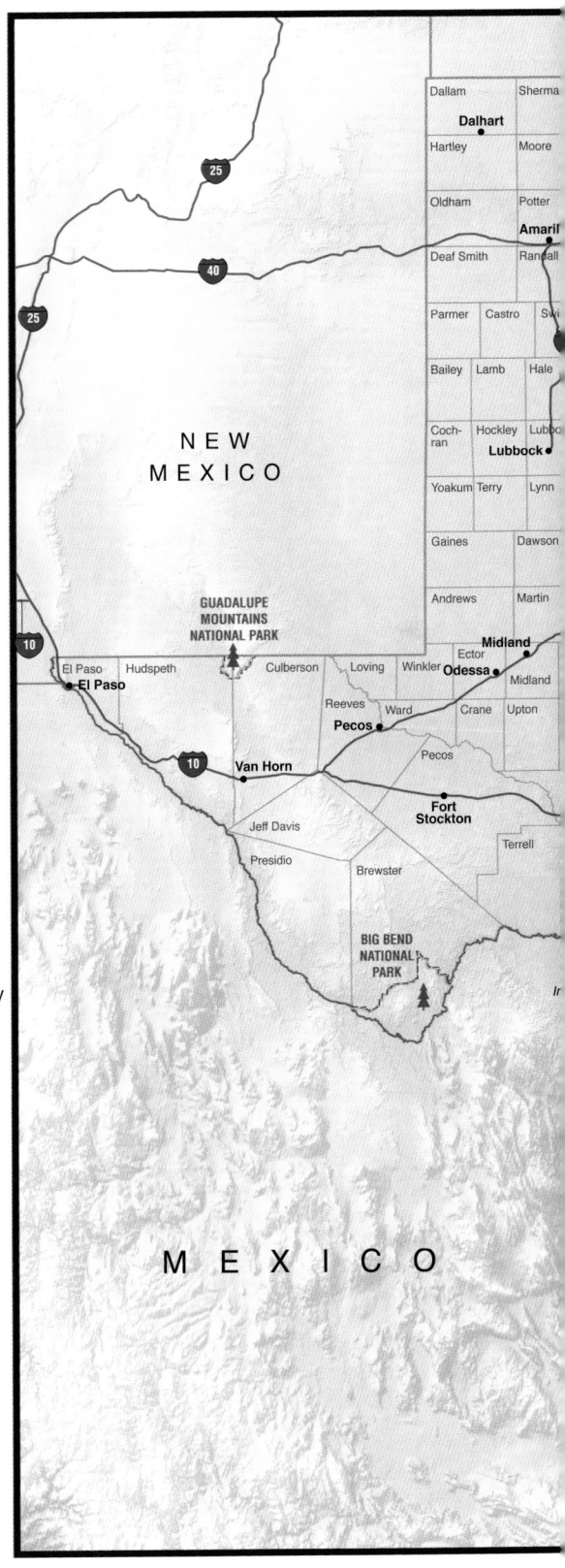

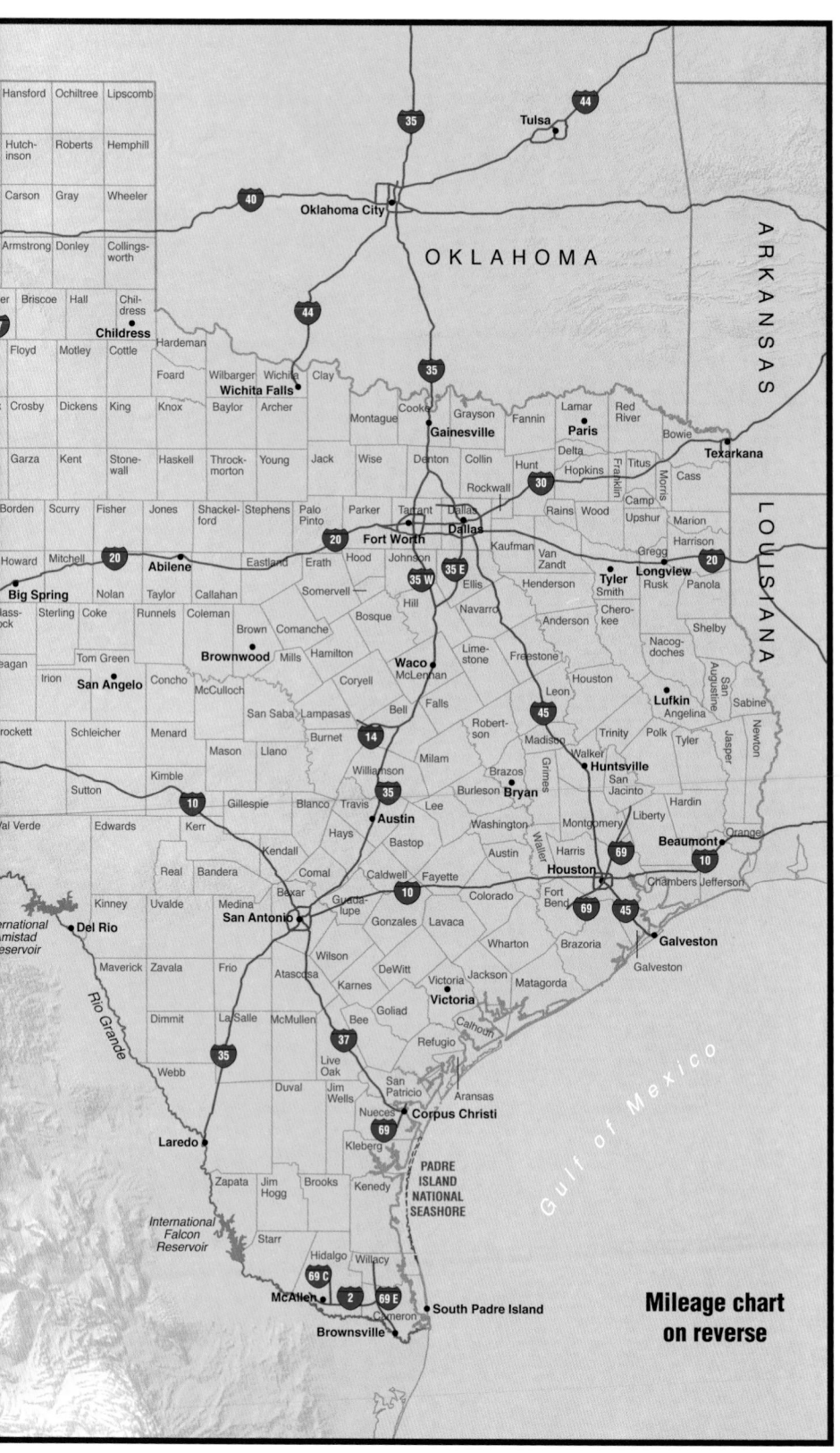

Mileage chart
on reverse

Milam County

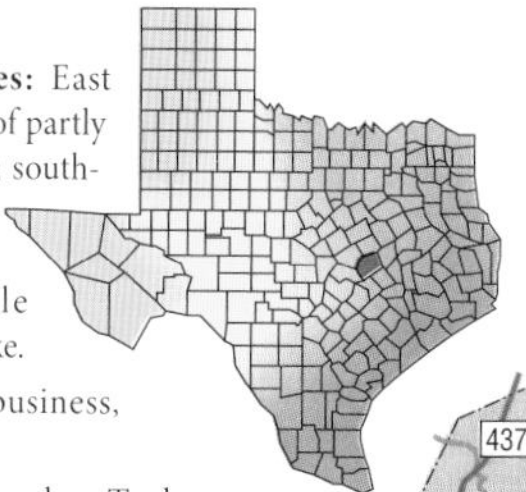

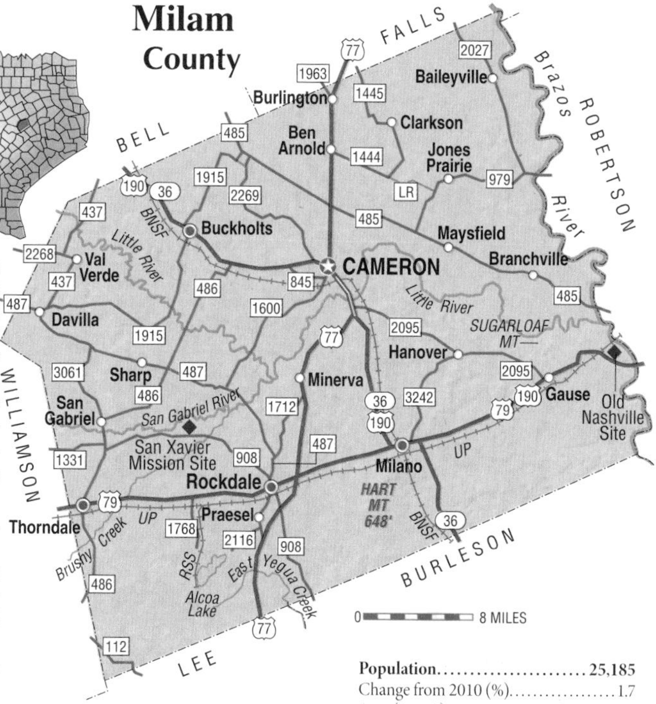

Physical Features: East central county of partly level Blackland; southeast rolling to Post Oak Belt; Brazos, Little rivers; Alcoa Lake.

Economy: Agribusiness, manufacturing.

History: Lipan Apaches, Tonkawas and Comanches in area. Mission San Francisco Xavier established 1745–1748. Anglo-American settlers arrived in 1834 and a private fort was established in 1840 at Bryant Station to help protect the settlers from Indian raids. County created in 1836 from municipality named for Ben Milam, a leader who died at the battle for San Antonio in December 1835; organized in 1837.

Race/Ethnicity: Anglo, 60%; Black, 8.8%; Hispanic, 29%; Asian, 0.4%; Other, 1.6%.

Vital Statistics, annual: Births, 320; deaths, 288; marriages, 147; divorces, 79.

Recreation: Fishing, hunting; historic sites include Fort Sullivan, Indian battlegrounds, mission sites; museum in old jail at Cameron, El Camino Real.

Minerals: Barite, limited oil and gas production.

Agriculture: Cattle, poultry (first in number of turkeys), corn. Market value $129.5 million.

CAMERON (5,619) county seat; government/services, manufacturing; hospital, library; dewberry festival in April.

ROCKDALE (5,656) government/services; hospital, juvenile detention center.

For explanation of sources, symbols and abbreviations, see p. 204, and foldout map.

Other towns include: **Buckholts** (546); **Burlington** (100); **Davilla** (191); **Gause** (425); **Milano** (445); **Thorndale** (1,394) agribusiness, farming, ranching, antiques, barbecue cook-off in June.

Population	25,185
Change from 2010 (%)	1.7
Area (sq. mi.)	1,021.8
Land Area (sq. mi.)	1,016.9
Altitude (ft.)	250–648
Rainfall (in.)	37.0
Jan. mean min (°F)	33.8
July mean max (°F)	88.7
Civ. Labor	9,852
Unemployed (%)	6.5
Wages	$58,430,624
Per Capita Income	$37,238
Prop. Value	$4,265,575,689
Retail Sales	$238,607,905

The historic Vaughn Building in Midland. Photo by Larry D. Moore, CC by SA 4.0

Mills County

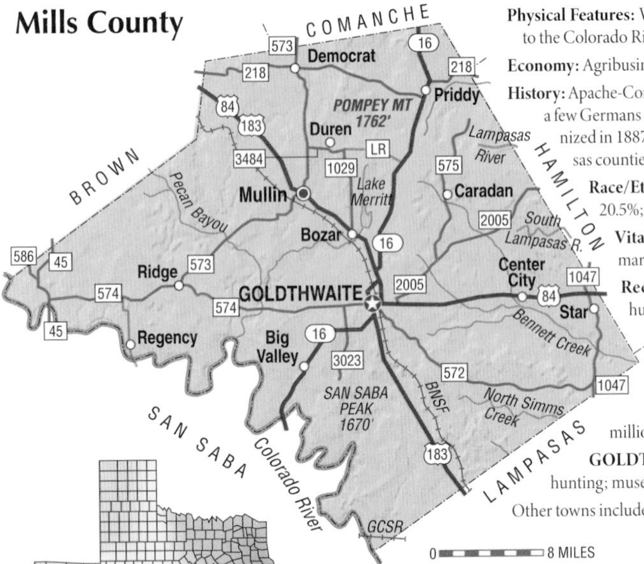

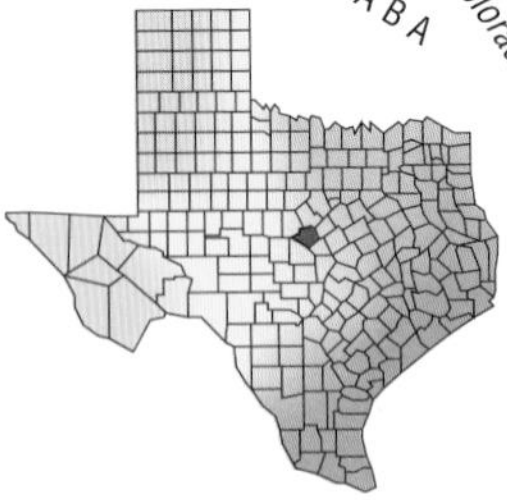

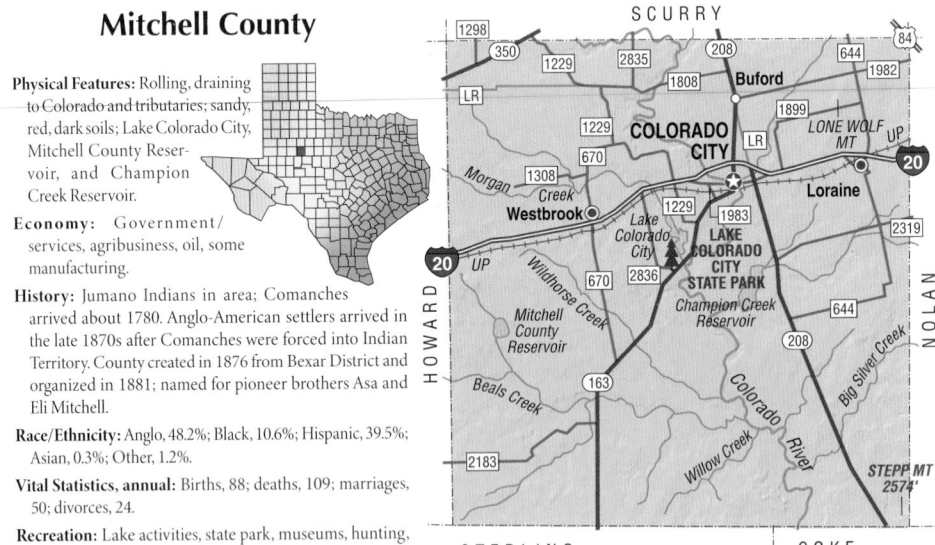

Physical Features: West central county of hills, plateau draining to the Colorado River; sandy, loam soils.

Economy: Agribusiness, hunting leases.

History: Apache-Comanche area of conflict. Anglo-Americans and a few Germans settled in the 1850s. County created and organized in 1887 from Brown, Comanche, Hamilton, Lampasas counties; named for pioneer jurist John T. Mills.

Race/Ethnicity: Anglo, 77.3%; Black, 0.5%; Hispanic, 20.5%; Asian, 0.1%; Other, 1.3%.

Vital Statistics, annual: Births, 30; deaths, 62; marriages, 27; divorces, 13.

Recreation: Fishing; deer, dove and turkey hunting; Regency suspension bridge; rangeland recreation.

Minerals: Not significant.

Agriculture: Cattle, dairies, sheep (first in numbers), goats, hay. Market value $30.9 million.

GOLDTHWAITE (1,888) county seat; agribusiness, hunting; museum; barbecue & goat cook-off in April.

Other towns include: **Mullin** (177); **Priddy** (215); **Star** (97).

Population	4,899
Change from 2010 (%)	-0.7
Area (sq. mi.)	749.8
Land Area (sq. mi.)	748.3
Altitude (ft.)	1,112–1,762
Rainfall (in.)	30.6
Jan. mean min (°F)	33.0
July mean max (°F)	91.5
Civ. Labor	1,937
Unemployed (%)	4.3
Wages	$13,001,014
Per Capita Income	$39,334
Prop. Value	$2,244,301,819
Retail Sales	$111,434,972

Mitchell County

Physical Features: Rolling, draining to Colorado and tributaries; sandy, red, dark soils; Lake Colorado City, Mitchell County Reservoir, and Champion Creek Reservoir.

Economy: Government/services, agribusiness, oil, some manufacturing.

History: Jumano Indians in area; Comanches arrived about 1780. Anglo-American settlers arrived in the late 1870s after Comanches were forced into Indian Territory. County created in 1876 from Bexar District and organized in 1881; named for pioneer brothers Asa and Eli Mitchell.

Race/Ethnicity: Anglo, 48.2%; Black, 10.6%; Hispanic, 39.5%; Asian, 0.3%; Other, 1.2%.

Vital Statistics, annual: Births, 88; deaths, 109; marriages, 50; divorces, 24.

Recreation: Lake activities, state park, museums, hunting, Colorado City playhouse.

Minerals: Oil.

Agriculture: Cotton principal crop, grains also produced. Cattle, sheep, goats, hogs raised. Market value $21.7 million.

COLORADO CITY (3,790) county seat; cotton, cattle, oil; hospital/medical services; opera house; poppy-mallow blooms at sports complex; goat cook-off in October.

Other towns include: **Loraine** (587) and **West-brook** (256), trade centers. The community around **Lake Colorado City** (570).

For explanation of sources, symbols and abbreviations, see p. 204, and foldout map.

Population	8,531
Change from 2010 (%)	-9.3
Area (sq. mi.)	915.9
Land Area (sq. mi.)	911.1
Altitude (ft.)	1,930–2,574
Rainfall (in.)	20.4
Jan. mean min (°F)	28.3
July mean max (°F)	95.0
Civ. Labor	2,362
Unemployed (%)	8.4
Wages	$22,255,322
Per Capita Income	$33,593
Prop. Value	$1,524,365,779
Retail Sales	$41,751,473

Montague County

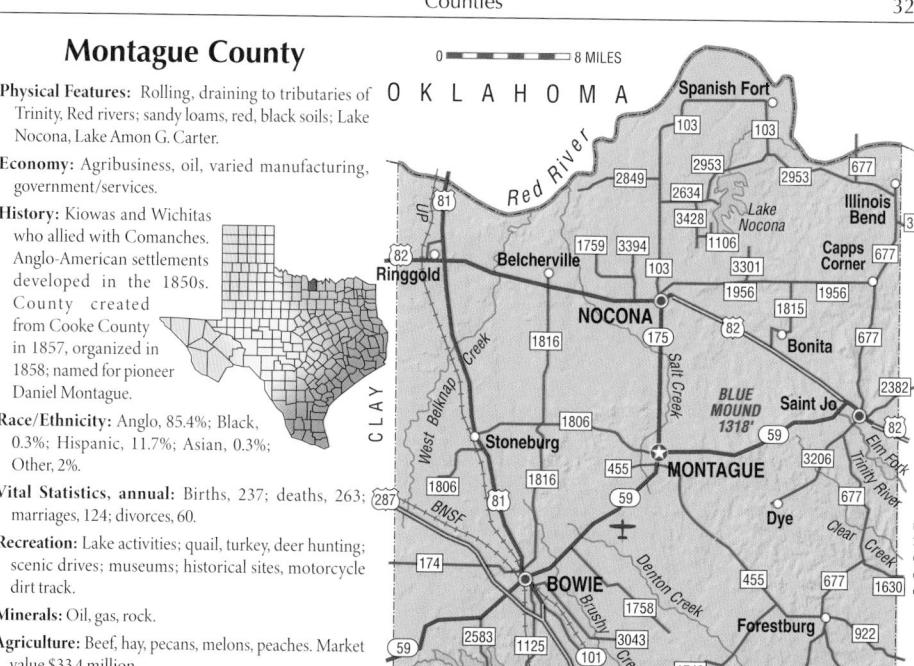

Physical Features: Rolling, draining to tributaries of Trinity, Red rivers; sandy loams, red, black soils; Lake Nocona, Lake Amon G. Carter.

Economy: Agribusiness, oil, varied manufacturing, government/services.

History: Kiowas and Wichitas who allied with Comanches. Anglo-American settlements developed in the 1850s. County created from Cooke County in 1857, organized in 1858; named for pioneer Daniel Montague.

Race/Ethnicity: Anglo, 85.4%; Black, 0.3%; Hispanic, 11.7%; Asian, 0.3%; Other, 2%.

Vital Statistics, annual: Births, 237; deaths, 263; marriages, 124; divorces, 60.

Recreation: Lake activities; quail, turkey, deer hunting; scenic drives; museums; historical sites, motorcycle dirt track.

Minerals: Oil, gas, rock.

Agriculture: Beef, hay, pecans, melons, peaches. Market value $33.4 million.

MONTAGUE (299) county seat.

BOWIE (5,133) varied manufacturing, oil and gas operations; hospital, library; Jim Bowie Days in June.

NOCONA (3,027) athletic goods, boot manufacturing; hospital; art galleries, museums; Wheels & Grills barbecue cook-off and car show in September.

Other towns include: **Forestburg** (50); **Ringgold** (100); **Saint Jo** (1,074) wineries, retail center, art galleries, museums, rodeo in August; **Sunset** (579).

Population...................... **19,695**	July mean max (°F)....................93.3
Change from 2010 (%)..................-0.1	Civ. Labor.............................8,832
Area (sq. mi.)..........................938.3	Unemployed (%).........................5.8
Land Area (sq. mi.)...................930.9	Wages.........................$48,689,055
Altitude (ft.).....................715–1,318	Per Capita Income................$42,230
Rainfall (in.)............................35.1	Prop. Value...............$3,880,218,587
Jan. mean min (°F)....................29.2	Retail Sales.................$222,622,731

The United Methodist Church in Montague. Photo by QuesterMark, CC 2/Wikimedia Commons

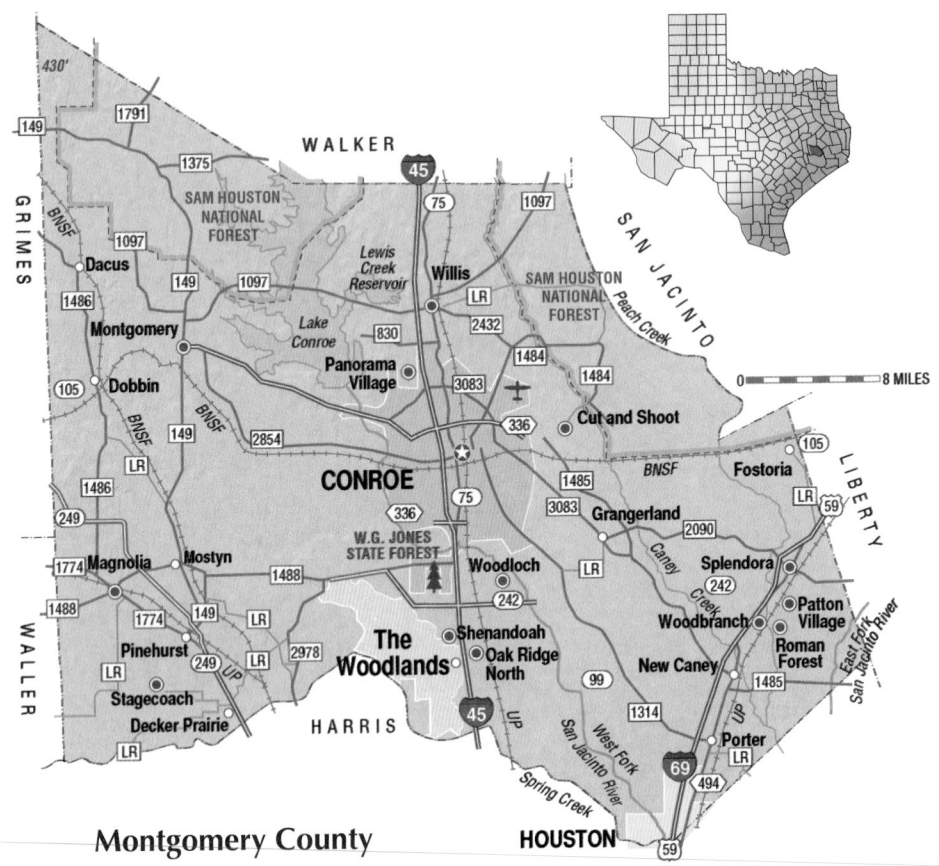

Montgomery County

Physical Features: Rolling, half timbered; Sam Houston National Forest; loam, sandy, alluvial soils; Lake Conroe and Lewis Creek Reservoir.

Economy: Varied manufacturing, oil production, medical research, government/services, many residents work in Houston.

History: Orcoquisac and Bidais tribes, removed from the area by the 1850s. Anglo-Americans arrived in the 1820s as part of Austin's colony. County created and organized in 1837 from Washington County; named for Richard Montgomery, American Revolution general.

Race/Ethnicity: Anglo, 64.8%; Black, 4.8%; Hispanic, 25.1%; Asian, 2.9%; Other, 2.2%.

Vital Statistics, annual: Births, 7,336; deaths, 3,623; marriages, 3,390; divorces, 1,809.

Recreation: Hunting, fishing; Lake Conroe activities; national and state forests; hiking, boating, horseback riding; historic sites.

Minerals: Natural gas.

Agriculture: Greenhouse crops, hay, beef cattle, horses. Market value $25.8 million. Timber important.

CONROE (90,276) county seat; government/services, hospital/medical services, commuters to Houston; new Sam Houston State University medical school; community college, museum; Cajun catfish festival in October.

The Woodlands (122,233) commuters to Houston, energy, tourism; college branches, hospitals, museums, parks, concerts, festivals at Mitchell Pavilion.

Other towns include: **Cut and Shoot** (1,409); **Dobbin** (310); **Grangerland** (300); **Magnolia** (2,118) government/services, drilling technology, construction, depot museum, Love Bug Fest in June; **Montgomery** (1,308) commuters to Houston and Conroe, antiques stores, pioneer museum, historic homes tour in April; **New Caney** (6,800); **Oak Ridge North** (3,382); **Panorama Village** (2,337); **Patton Village** (2,132).

Also: **Pinehurst** (5,448); **Porter** (4,200); **Porter Heights** (1,974); **Roman Forest** (2,061); **Shenandoah** (3,185); **Splendora** (2,240); **Stagecoach** (320); **Willis** (7,809) commuters to Conroe and Houston; **Woodbranch** (1,410); **Woodloch** (213).

Also, part [5,741] of **Houston** [Kingwood], hospital.

Population	**604,391**
Change from 2010 (%)	32.6
Area (sq. mi.)	1,076.9
Land Area (sq. mi.)	1,041.9
Altitude (ft.)	50–430
Rainfall (in.)	48.8
Jan. mean min (°F)	40.4
July mean max (°F)	93.5
Civ. Labor	285,994
Unemployed (%)	6.5
Wages	$3,017,993,587
Per Capita Income	$63,424
Prop. Value	$80,207,163,615
Retail Sales	$9,384,141,632

For explanation of sources, symbols and abbreviations, see p. 204, and foldout map.

Moore County

Physical Features: Flat to rolling, broken by creeks; sandy loams; Lake Meredith.

Economy: Varied agribusiness, petroleum, natural gas.

History: Comanches, removed to Indian Territory in 1874–1875; ranching began soon afterward. Farming developed after 1910. Oil boom in the 1920s. County created in 1876 from Bexar District; organized in 1892; named for Republic of Texas navy commander E.W. Moore.

Race/Ethnicity: Anglo, 31.3%; Black, 2.1%; Hispanic, 54.9%; Asian, 9.7%; Other, 1.8%.

Vital Statistics, annual: Births, 438; deaths, 164; marriages, 151; divorces, 97.

Recreation: Lake Meredith activities; pheasant, deer, quail hunting; historical museum; arts center; free overnight RV park; Dogie Days in June.

Minerals: Oil and gas.

Agriculture: Fed beef, corn, wheat, stocker cattle, sorghum, cotton, soybeans, sunflowers. Market value $478.1 million. Irrigation of 122,000 acres.

DUMAS (14,044) county seat; tourism, retail trade, varied agribusiness; hospital, hospice, retirement complex.

Other towns include: **Cactus** (3,241), **Sunray** (1,828). Small part of **Fritch**.

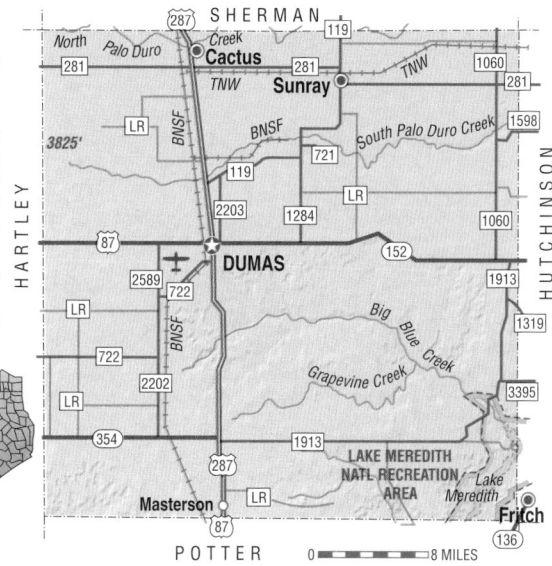

Population...................... **21,046**	July mean max (°F)...................91.6
Change from 2010 (%)................-3.9	Civ. Labor..........................10,629
Area (sq. mi.).......................909.6	Unemployed (%)........................3.6
Land Area (sq. mi.)..................899.7	Wages $148,846,177
Altitude (ft.)...................2,915–3,825	Per Capita Income $46,108
Rainfall (in.)............................18.4	Prop. Value $2,787,536,775
Jan. mean min (°F)....................22.1	Retail Sales $434,958,732

Morris County

Physical Features: East Texas county of forested hills; drains to streams, Lake O' the Pines, Ellison Creek Reservoir, Barnes Creek Reservoir.

Economy: Steel manufacturing, agriculture, timber, government/services.

History: Caddo Indians until the 1790s. Kickapoo and other tribes in area 1820s-30s. Anglo-American settlement began in mid-1830s. Antebellum slaveholding area. County named for legislator-jurist W.W. Morris; created from Titus County and organized in 1875.

Race/Ethnicity: Anglo, 64.4%; Black, 21.8%; Hispanic, 9.8%; Asian, 0.3%; Other, 3.4%.

Vital Statistics, annual: Births, 161; deaths, 179; marriages, 97; divorces, 18.

Recreation: Activities on Lake O' the Pines, small lakes; fishing, hunting; state park.

Minerals: Iron ore.

Agriculture: Beef cattle, broiler production, hay. Market value $44.2 million. Timber industry significant.

DAINGERFIELD (2,454) county seat; varied manufacturing, government/services; library, museum, city park, historic theater; Daingerfield Days in October.

Other towns include: **Cason** (173); **Lone Star** (1,508) oil-field equipment manufactured, catfish farming, Starfest in September; **Naples** (1,343) trailer manufacturing, livestock, watermelon festival in July; **Omaha** (980), retail center, government/services, commuters.

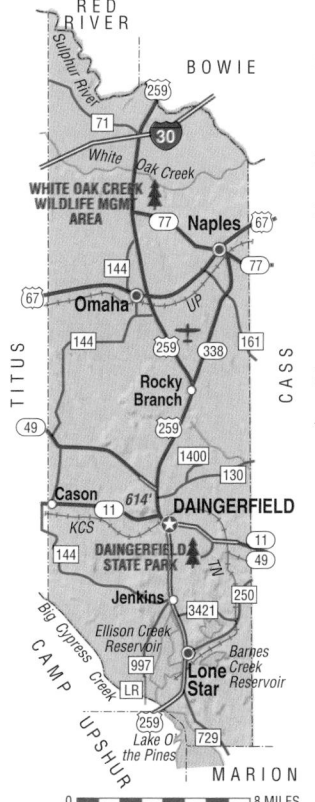

Population...................... **12,428**	
Change from 2010 (%)................-3.9	
Area (sq. mi.).......................258.7	
Land Area (sq. mi.)..................252.0	
Altitude (ft.)..................... 228–614	
Rainfall (in.)............................46.8	
Jan. mean min (°F)....................35.1	
July mean max (°F)....................94.1	
Civ. Labor 4,652	
Unemployed (%)......................11.3	
Wages $46,422,016	
Per Capita Income $41,068	
Prop. Value $1,235,264,463	
Retail Sales $98,628,526	

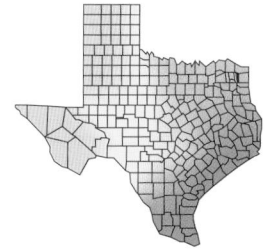

For explanation of sources, symbols and abbreviations, see p. 204, and foldout map.

Motley County

Physical Features: Western county just below Caprock; rough terrain, broken by Pease tributaries; sandy to red clay soils.

Economy: Agriculture, government/services, light manufacturing.

History: Comanche tribes in the area, removed to the Indian Territory by the U.S. Army in 1874–1875. Cattle ranching began in the late 1870s. County was created out of the Bexar District in 1876 and organized in 1891; named for Dr. J.W. Mottley, a signer of Texas Declaration of Independence (however, name was misspelled in legislative statute).

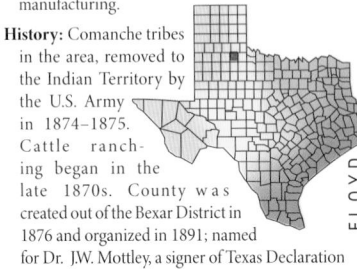

Race/Ethnicity: Anglo, 81.2%; Black, 2%; Hispanic, 15.8%; Asian, 0%; Other, 0.8%.

Vital Statistics, annual: Births, 0; deaths, 17; marriages, 21; divorces, 0.

Recreation: Quail, dove, turkey, deer, feral hog hunting; Matador Ranch headquarters; spring-fed pool at Roaring Springs; Motley-Dickens settlers reunion in August at Roaring Springs.

Minerals: Minimal.

Agriculture: Beef cattle, cotton, peanuts, hay, wheat. Some irrigation. Market value $15.2 million. Hunting leases important.

MATADOR (609) county seat; ranching, farming, government/services; museum, historic oil-derrick gas station; motorcycles race in April.

Other towns include: **Flomot** (181) bluegrass festival in May, and **Roaring Springs** (235).

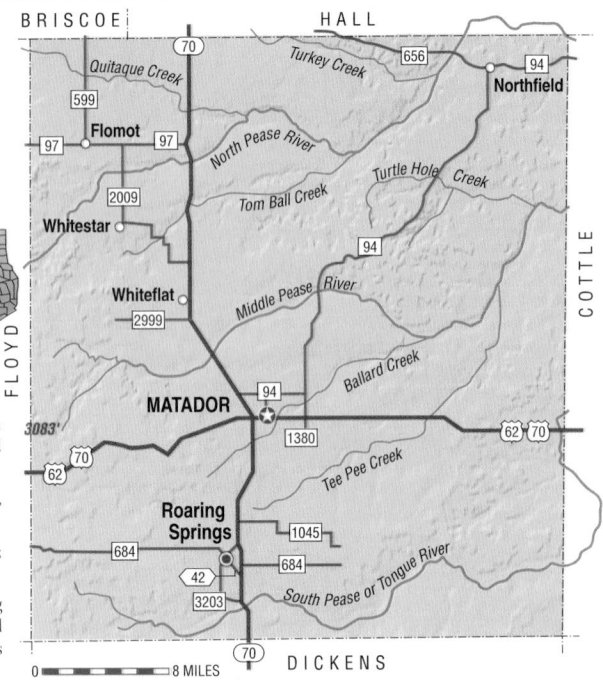

Population.	1,205
Change from 2010 (%).	-0.4
Area (sq. mi.)	989.8
Land Area (sq. mi.).	989.6
Altitude (ft.)	1,800–3,083
Rainfall (in.).	23.4
Jan. mean min (°F).	29.6
July mean max (°F).	94.2
Civ. Labor.	449
Unemployed (%).	5.1
Wages	$2,619,922
Per Capita Income	$32,988
Prop. Value	$360,305,810
Retail Sales	$6,798,587

The Pilgrim's Pride plant in Nacogdoches. Photo by Billy Hathorn, Public Domain/Wikimedia Commons

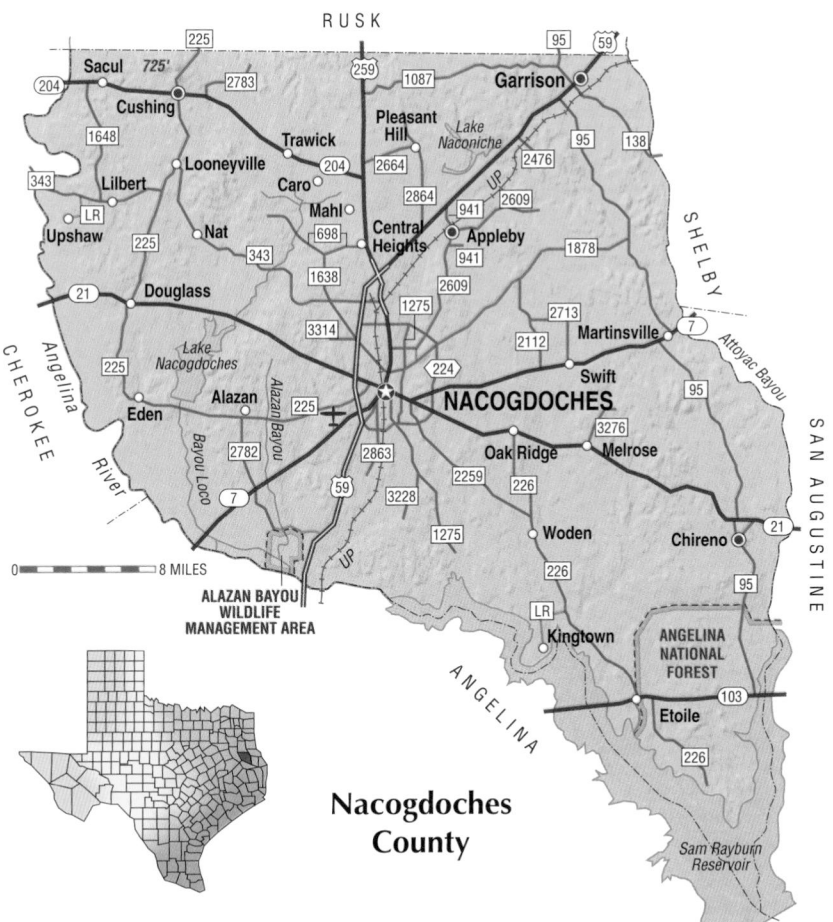

Nacogdoches County

Physical Features: East Texas county on divide between the Angelina River and Attoyac Bayou; hilly; two-thirds is forested; red, gray, sandy soils; Sam Rayburn Reservoir, Lake Nacogdoches, Lake Naconiche.

Economy: Agribusiness, timber, manufacturing, education, tourism.

History: Caddo tribes, joined by displaced Cherokees in the 1820s. Indian tribes moved west of the Brazos River by 1840. Spanish missions established in 1716. Spanish settlers arrived in the mid-1700s.

Anglo-Americans arrived in the 1820s. An original county of the Republic in 1836, organized in 1837. Name comes from Caddo tribe in the area.

Race/Ethnicity: Anglo, 59.1%; Black, 17.3%; Hispanic, 19.5%; Asian, 1.5%; Other, 2.4%.

Vital Statistics, annual: Births, 864; deaths, 605; marriages, 462; divorces, 160.

Recreation: Lake and river activities; Stephen F. Austin State University events; Angelina National Forest; historic site.

Tourist attractions include the Old Stone Fort, pioneer homes, museums, Millard's Crossing Historic Village, Piney Woods Native Plant Center; Azalea Trail in March, Blueberry Festival in June.

Minerals: First Texas oil discovered here, 1866; gas, oil, clay, and stone.

Agriculture: A leading poultry-producing county (third in number of broilers); beef cattle raised. Market value $370.7 million. Substantial timber sold.

NACOGDOCHES (33,677) county seat; varied manufacturing, lumber mills, wood products, trade center; hospitals; Stephen F. Austin State University; Nine Flags Festival in November/December.

Other towns include: **Appleby** (491), **Chireno** (386), **Cushing** (610), **Douglass** (380), **Etoile** (700), **Garrison** (881), **Martinsville** (350), **Sacul** (150), **Woden** (400).

For explanation of sources, symbols and abbreviations, see p. 204, and foldout map.

Population	**65,027**
Change from 2010 (%)	0.8
Area (sq. mi.)	981.2
Land Area (sq. mi.)	946.5
Altitude (ft.)	164–725
Rainfall (in.)	49.3
Jan. mean min (°F)	35.8
July mean max (°F)	93.2
Civ. Labor	27,901
Unemployed (%)	5.9
Wages	$244,202,306
Per Capita Income	$38,569
Prop. Value	$6,133,393,788
Retail Sales	$871,842,943

Navarro County

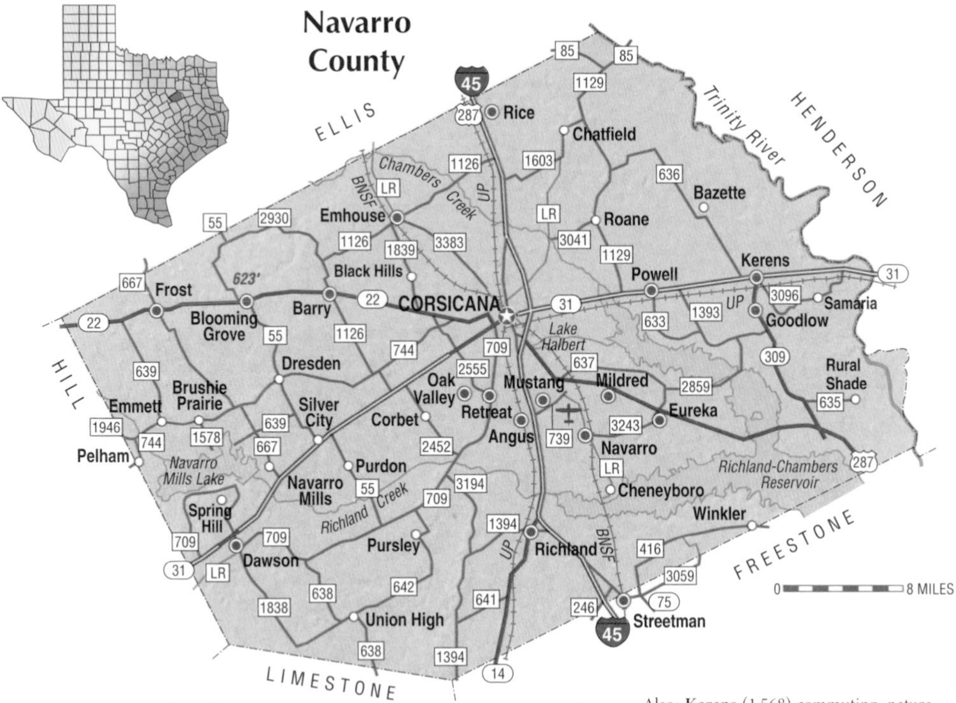

[Map of Navarro County showing towns including Rice, Chatfield, Bazette, Emhouse, Roane, Kerens, Black Hills, Powell, Samaria, Goodlow, CORSICANA, Frost, Barry, Blooming Grove, Dresden, Brushie Prairie, Emmett, Silver City, Oak Valley, Mustang, Mildred, Rural Shade, Eureka, Corbet, Retreat, Angus, Navarro, Pelham, Purdon, Cheneyboro, Winkler, Spring Hill, Navarro Mills, Dawson, Pursley, Richland, Streetman, Union High. Surrounding counties: ELLIS, HENDERSON, HILL, LIMESTONE, FREESTONE. Features: Trinity River, Chambers Creek, Lake Halbert, Navarro Mills Lake, Richland-Chambers Reservoir, Richland Creek.]

Physical Features: Level Blackland, some rolling; drains to creeks, Trinity River; Navarro Mills Lake, Richland-Chambers Reservoir, Lake Halbert.

Economy: Diversified manufacturing, agribusinesses, oil-field operations, distribution.

History: Kickapoo and Comanche area. Anglo-Americans settled in the late 1830s. Antebellum slaveholding area. County created in 1846 from Robertson County, organized the same year; named for Republic of Texas leader José Antonio Navarro.

Race/Ethnicity: Anglo, 56.6%; Black, 12.7%; Hispanic, 27%; Asian, 0.5%; Other, 3%.

Vital Statistics, annual: Births, 664; deaths, 568; marriages, 339; divorces, 165.

Recreation: Lake activities; Pioneer Village; historic buildings; youth exposition, Derrick Days in April.

Minerals: Longest continuous Texas oil flow; more than 200 million barrels produced since 1895; natural gas, sand and gravel also produced.

Agriculture: Beef cattle, cotton, sorghum, corn, wheat, sunflowers, herbs, horses, dairies. Market value $73.3 million.

CORSICANA (24,601) county seat; major distribution center, pecans, candy, fruitcakes; varied manufacturing; agribusiness; hospital; Navarro College; Texas Youth Commission facility.

Other towns include: **Angus** (455); **Barry** (265); **Blooming Grove** (863); **Chatfield** (40); **Dawson** (810); **Emhouse** (143); **Eureka** (318); **Frost** (653); **Goodlow** (194).

Also: **Kerens** (1,568) commuting, nature tourism, Cotton Harvest Festival in October; **Mildred** (405); **Mustang** (21); **Navarro** (221); **Oak Valley** (410); **Powell** (147); **Purdon** (133); **Retreat** (405); **Rice** (1,002); **Richland** (274).

Population.......................52,013
Change from 2010 (%)..................9.0
Area (sq. mi.).......................1,085.9
Land Area (sq. mi.)..................1,009.6
Altitude (ft.)..................... 250–623
Rainfall (in.)...........................39.8
Jan. mean min (°F).....................34.7
July mean max (°F).....................94.1
Civ. Labor.........................22,772
Unemployed (%)........................5.7
Wages $193,827,690
Per Capita Income $39,652
Prop. Value $6,509,663,456
Retail Sales $678,521,365

The Mustang Bowl in Sweetwater was built by the Works Progress Administration in 1939. Photo by Larry D. Moore, CC by SA 4.0/Wikimedia Commons

Newton County

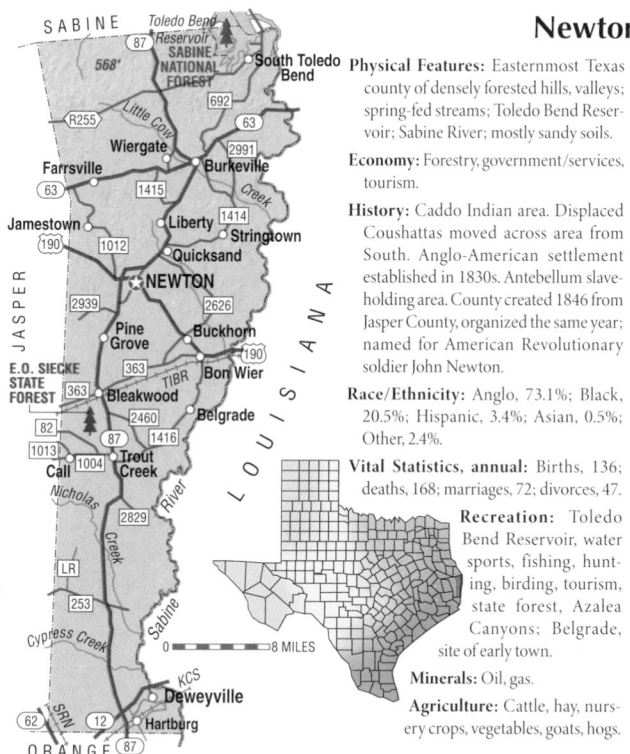

Physical Features: Easternmost Texas county of densely forested hills, valleys; spring-fed streams; Toledo Bend Reservoir; Sabine River; mostly sandy soils.

Economy: Forestry, government/services, tourism.

History: Caddo Indian area. Displaced Coushattas moved across area from South. Anglo-American settlement established in 1830s. Antebellum slave-holding area. County created 1846 from Jasper County, organized the same year; named for American Revolutionary soldier John Newton.

Race/Ethnicity: Anglo, 73.1%; Black, 20.5%; Hispanic, 3.4%; Asian, 0.5%; Other, 2.4%.

Vital Statistics, annual: Births, 136; deaths, 168; marriages, 72; divorces, 47.

Recreation: Toledo Bend Reservoir, water sports, fishing, hunting, birding, tourism, state forest, Azalea Canyons; Belgrade, site of early town.

Minerals: Oil, gas.

Agriculture: Cattle, hay, nursery crops, vegetables, goats, hogs.

Market value $1.6 million. Hunting leases. Major forestry area.

NEWTON (2,338) county seat; lumber manufacturing, plywood mill, private prison unit, tourist center; genealogical library, museum; Wild Azalea festival in March.

Deweyville (873) power plant, commercial center for forestry, farming area.

Other towns include: **Bon Wier** (375); **Burkeville** (603); **Call** (493); **South Toledo Bend** (454); **Wiergate** (350).

Population	**13,317**
Change from 2010 (%)	-7.8
Area (sq. mi.)	939.7
Land Area (sq. mi.)	933.7
Altitude (ft.)	10–568
Rainfall (in.)	54.9
Jan. mean min (°F)	36.5
July mean max (°F)	93.1
Civ. Labor	5,144
Unemployed (%)	10.7
Wages	$12,750,968
Per Capita Income	$34,265
Prop. Value	$2,582,808,227
Retail Sales	$38,910,205

For explanation of sources, symbols and abbreviations, see p. 204, and foldout map.

Nolan County

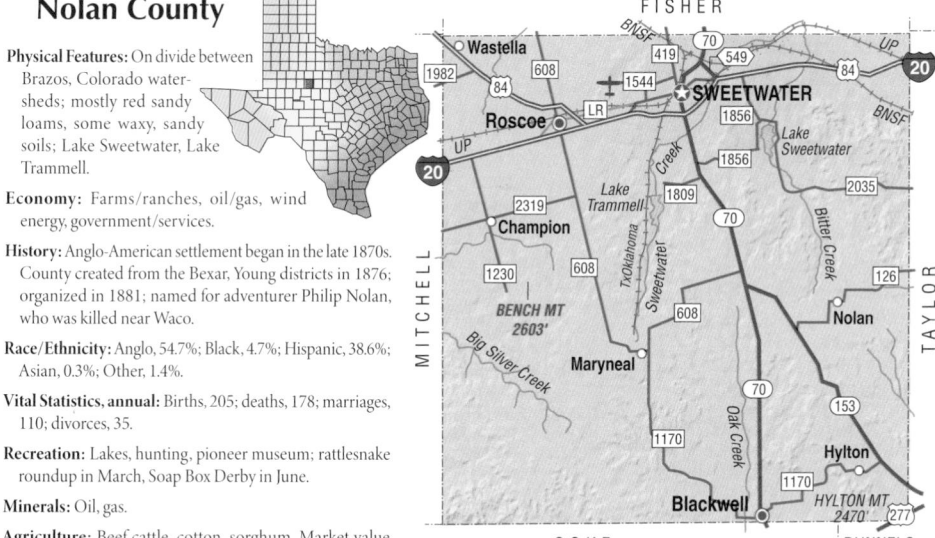

Physical Features: On divide between Brazos, Colorado watersheds; mostly red sandy loams, some waxy, sandy soils; Lake Sweetwater, Lake Trammell.

Economy: Farms/ranches, oil/gas, wind energy, government/services.

History: Anglo-American settlement began in the late 1870s. County created from the Bexar, Young districts in 1876; organized in 1881; named for adventurer Philip Nolan, who was killed near Waco.

Race/Ethnicity: Anglo, 54.7%; Black, 4.7%; Hispanic, 38.6%; Asian, 0.3%; Other, 1.4%.

Vital Statistics, annual: Births, 205; deaths, 178; marriages, 110; divorces, 35.

Recreation: Lakes, hunting, pioneer museum; rattlesnake roundup in March, Soap Box Derby in June.

Minerals: Oil, gas.

Agriculture: Beef cattle, cotton, sorghum. Market value $36.6 million. Some 3,300 acres irrigated.

SWEETWATER (10,285) county seat; wind energy, varied manufacturing, gypsum; hospital; Texas State Technical College; WWII museum.

Other towns include: **Blackwell** (286, partly in Coke County), Oak Creek Reservoir to south; **Maryneal** (50); **Nolan** (60); **Roscoe** (1,240).

Population	**14,256**
Change from 2010 (%)	-6.3
Area (sq. mi.)	914.0
Land Area (sq. mi.)	912.0
Altitude (ft.)	1,896–2,603
Rainfall (in.)	22.4
Jan. mean min (°F)	29.0
July mean max (°F)	93.9
Civ. Labor	7,263
Unemployed (%)	4.9
Wages	$75,291,142
Per Capita Income	$46,066
Prop. Value	$3,365,596,869
Retail Sales	$263,242,827

Nueces County

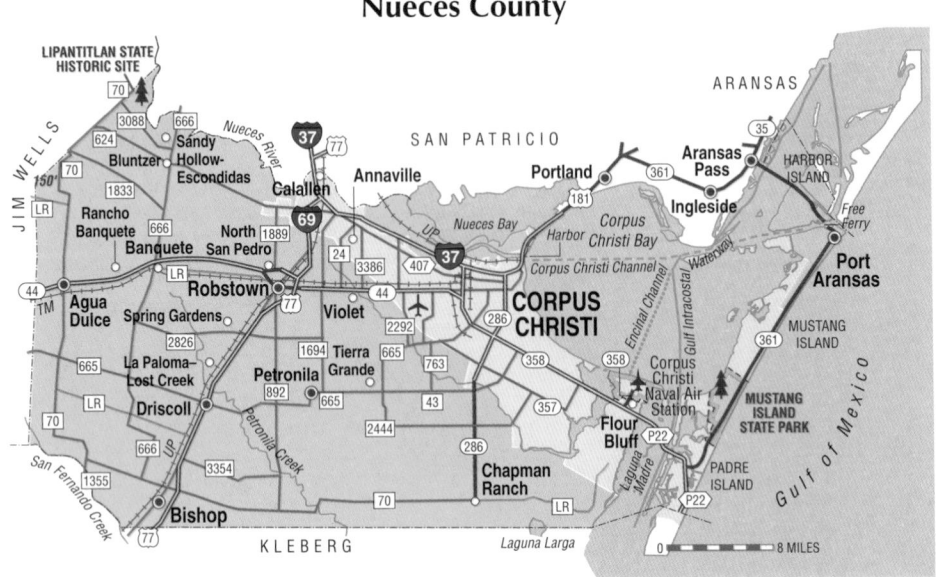

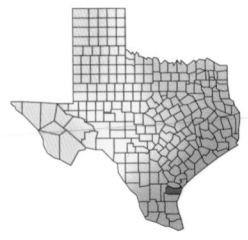

Physical Features: Southern Gulf Coast county; flat, rich soils, broken by bays, Nueces River, Petronila Creek; includes Mustang Island, north tip of Padre Island.

Economy: Petroleum processing, deepwater port facility, agriculture, tourism.

History: Coahuiltecan, Karankawa and other tribes who succumbed to disease or fled by 1840s. Spanish settlers arrived in the 1760s. Settlers from Ireland arrived around 1830. County name is Spanish for nuts; county named for river; created and organized in 1846 out of San Patricio County.

Race/Ethnicity: Anglo, 28.3%; Black, 3.6%; Hispanic, 64.4%; Asian, 2.1%; Other, 1.4%.

Vital Statistics, annual: Births, 5,054; deaths, 2,937; marriages, 2,436; divorces, 657.

Recreation: Major resort area; beaches, fishing, water sports, birding; Padre Island National Seashore, Mustang Island State Park, Lipantitlan State Historic Site; Art Museum of South Texas, Corpus Christi Museum of Science and History; Texas State Aquarium; Museum of Asian Cultures; professional baseball, hockey; greyhound race track.

Minerals: Oil, gas, sand, gravel.

Agriculture: Grain sorghum (second in acreage), cotton, cattle, wheat, hay, nurseries/turfgrass. Market value $161.0 million.

CORPUS CHRISTI (327,618) county seat; seaport, naval bases, varied manufacturing, petroleum processing, tourism; hospitals; museums; Army depot; Texas A&M University-Corpus Christi, Del Mar College; USS Lexington museum, Harbor Lights; Buccaneer Days in late April.

PORT ARANSAS (4,153) deepwater port, tourism, marine research, Coast Guard base, fishing industry; University of Texas Marine Science Institute; museum, beach; Celebration of Whooping Cranes in February; Texas Sand Fest in April.

ROBSTOWN (11,212) agriculture, transportation, tourism, petroleum processing; regional fairgrounds; Cottonfest in October, Fiesta Mexicana in March.

Other towns include: **Agua Dulce** (838); **Banquete** (795); **Bishop** (3,092) petrochemicals, agriculture, pharmaceuticals, plastics, nature trail, Old Tyme Faire in April; **Chapman Ranch** (200); **Driscoll** (744); **La Paloma-Lost Creek** (505); **North San Pedro** (868); **Petronila** (121); **Rancho Banquete** (415); **Sandy Hollow-Escondidas** (259); **Spring Gardens** (662); **Tierra Grande** (441); and **Tierra Verde** (320).

Annaville, Calallen, and Flour Bluff are now part of Corpus Christi.

Population	363,049
Change from 2010 (%)	6.7
Area (sq. mi.)	11,656.0
Land Area (sq. mi.)	835.5
Altitude (ft.)	sea level–150
Rainfall (in.)	32.5
Jan. mean min (°F)	46.6
July mean max (°F)	93.1
Civ. Labor	163,641
Unemployed (%)	7.6
Wages	$2,073,469,587
Per Capita Income	$44,889
Prop. Value	$46,061,562,283
Retail Sales	$5,658,049,252

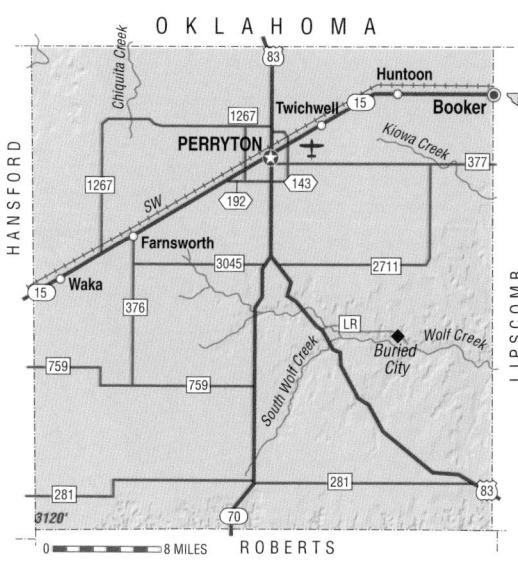

Ochiltree County

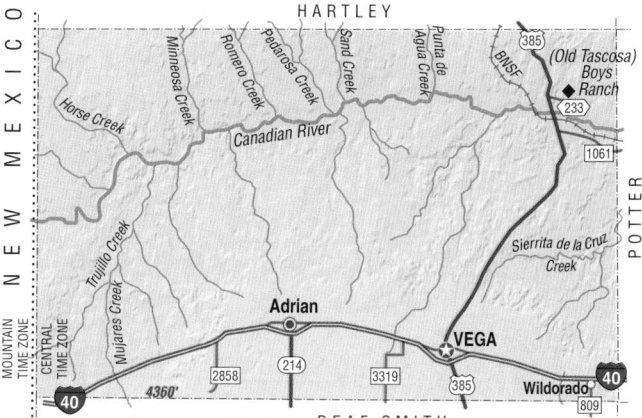

Physical Features: Panhandle county bordering Oklahoma; level, broken by creeks; deep loam, clay soils.

Economy: Agribusiness, oil/gas, government/services.

History: Apache groups, who were pushed out by Comanches in late 1700s. The Comanches were removed to the Indian Territory in 1874–1875 by U.S. Army. Ranching developed in 1880s; farming began after 1900. Created from the Bexar District in 1876, organized in 1889; named for Republic of Texas leader W.B. Ochiltree.

Race/Ethnicity: Anglo, 42.1%; Black, 0.2%; Hispanic, 56.1%; Asian, 0.2%; Other, 1.2%.

Vital Statistics, annual: Births, 184; deaths, 83; marriages, 95; divorces, 48.

Recreation: Wolf Creek park; Museum of the Plains; Prehistoric settlement site of "Buried City"; pheasant hunting, also deer and dove; Wheatheart of the Nation celebration in August.

Minerals: Oil, natural gas, caliche.

For explanation of sources, symbols and abbreviations, see p. 204, and foldout map.

Agriculture: Cattle, swine, corn, cotton, wheat (second in acreage), sorghum, hay and forages; some 50,000 acres irrigated. Market value $349.1 million.

PERRYTON (8,816) county seat; oil/gas, cattle feeding, grain center; hospital; college.

Other towns include: **Farnsworth** (130); **Waka** (65). Also, **Booker** (1,558, mostly in Lipscomb County).

Population.......................	**10,219**
Change from 2010 (%).................	0.0
Area (sq. mi.)........................	918.1
Land Area (sq. mi.)..................	917.6
Altitude (ft.)...............	2,550–3,120
Rainfall (in.)........................	22.1
Jan. mean min (°F)....................	19.0
July mean max (°F)...................	92.4
Civ. Labor...........................	3,818
Unemployed (%).......................	4.9
Wages.........................	$50,086,903
Per Capita Income................	$60,862
Prop. Value...............	$1,783,639,637
Retail Sales..................	$81,303,997

Oldham County

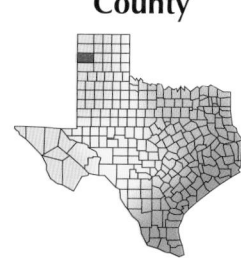

Physical Features: Northwestern Panhandle county; level, broken by Canadian River and tributaries.

Economy: Agriculture, wind energy, sand and gravel.

History: Apaches; followed later by Comanches, Kiowas. U.S. Army removed the Indians in 1875. Anglo ranchers and Spanish pastores (sheep men) from New Mexico were in the area in the 1870s. County created in 1876 from Bexar District; organized in 1880; named for editor-Confederate senator W.S. Oldham.

Race/Ethnicity: Anglo, 82.5%; Black, 2.5%; Hispanic, 12.5%; Asian, 0.7%; Other, 1.5%.

Vital Statistics, annual: Births, 23; deaths, 17; marriages, 9; divorces, 3.

Recreation: Old Tascosa, Cal Farley's Boys Ranch, Boot Hill Cemetery, museums;

midway point on old Route 66; County Roundup in August, Boys Ranch rodeo Labor Day weekend.

Minerals: Sand and gravel, oil, natural gas, stone.

Agriculture: Beef cattle; crops include wheat, grain sorghum. Market value $156.0 million.

VEGA (917) county seat; farm and ranch trade center; transportation; museums.

Other towns include: **Adrian** (167); **Wildorado** (210). Also, **Cal Farley's Boys Ranch** (297).

Population.......................	**2,126**
Change from 2010 (%).................	3.6
Area (sq. mi.)........................	1,501.4
Land Area (sq. mi.)..................	1,500.5
Altitude (ft.)..................	3,140–4,360
Rainfall (in.)........................	19.2
Jan. mean min (°F)...................	20.7
July mean max (°F)...................	92.3
Civ. Labor...........................	921
Unemployed (%).......................	3.5
Wages.........................	$12,364,279
Per Capita Income................	$55,479
Prop. Value...............	$1,390,655,307
Retail Sales..................	$54,080,952

Orange County

Physical Features: In southeastern corner of the state; bounded by Sabine, Neches rivers, Sabine Lake; coastal soils; two-thirds timbered.

Economy: Oil and gas production, electric power plants, commercial fishing.

History: Atakapan Indian area. French traders in area by 1720. Anglo-American settlement began in the 1820s. County created from Jefferson County in 1852, organized the same year; named for early orange grove.

Race/Ethnicity: Anglo, 80.9%; Black, 8.8%; Hispanic, 6.9%; Asian, 1%; Other, 2.1%.

Vital Statistics, annual: Births, 1,218; deaths, 947; marriages, 680; divorces, 211.

Recreation: Fishing, hunting, water sports, birding, county park, museums; historical homes, crawfish and crab festivals in spring.

Minerals: Oil and gas.

Agriculture: Beef cattle, forages, citrus, bees. Market value $5.0 million. Hunting leases. Timber important.

ORANGE (18,297) county seat; seaport, petrochemical plants, varied manufacturing, food and timber processing shipping; hospital, theater, museums; Lamar State College-Orange; Mardi Gras/gumbo festival in February.

BRIDGE CITY (7,868) varied manufacturing, ship repair yard, steel fabrication, fish farming, government/services; library; tall bridge and newer suspension bridge over Neches; stop for Monarch butterfly in fall during its migration to Mexico.

Vidor (10,570) steel processing, railroad-car refinishing; library; barbecue festival in April.

Other towns include: **Mauriceville** (3,804); **Orangefield** (725); **Pine Forest** (508); **Pinehurst** (2,077); **Rose City** (501); **West Orange** (3,181).

Population	82,461
Change from 2010 (%)	0.8
Area (sq. mi.)	379.5
Land Area (sq. mi.)	333.7
Altitude (ft.)	sea level–35
Rainfall (in.)	64.2
Jan. mean min (°F)	39.6
July mean max (°F)	91.2
Civ. Labor	36,235
Unemployed (%)	9.3
Wages	$315,343,215
Per Capita Income	$45,663
Prop. Value	$8,286,699,132
Retail Sales	$1,015,571,472

For explanation of sources, symbols and abbreviations, see p. 204, and foldout map.

The sign at Cal Farley's Boys Ranch in Oldham County. Photo by Nicholas Henderson, CC 2/Wikimedia Commons

Palo Pinto County

Physical Features: North central county; broken, hilly, wooded in parts; Possum Kingdom Lake, Lake Palo Pinto; sandy, gray, black soils.

Economy: Varied manufacturing, tourism, petroleum, agribusiness.

History: Anglo-American ranchers arrived in the 1850s. Conflicts between settlers and numerous Indian tribes who had sought refuge on the Brazos River resulted in Texas Rangers removing the Indians in 1856. County created in 1856 from Bosque and Navarro counties; organized in 1857; named for creek (in Spanish name means painted stick).

Race/Ethnicity: Anglo, 73.7%; Black, 2.4%; Hispanic, 21.4%; Asian, 0.5%; Other, 1.8%.

Vital Statistics, annual: Births, 353; deaths, 348; marriages, 190; divorces, 122.

Recreation: Lake activities, hunting, fishing, state parks, Rails to Trails hiking, biking, fossil park.

Minerals: Oil, gas, clays.

Agriculture: Cattle, dairy products, nursery crops, hay, wheat. Market value $43.2 million. Cedar posts marketed.

Palo Pinto (354) county seat; government center.

MINERAL WELLS (17,430, part [193] in Parker County) oil and gas, manufacturing, tourism; hospital, Weatherford College branch; art center; state park east of city in Parker County; Crazy Water Festival in October.

Other towns include: **Gordon** (488); **Graford** (620) retirement/recreation area, Possum Fest in October; **Mingus** (257); **Santo** (445), and **Strawn** (676).

Population.................... 29,008	July mean max (°F)................. 95.5
Change from 2010 (%).............. 3.2	Civ. Labor........................ 12,960
Area (sq. mi.)......................985.5	Unemployed (%).................... 6.3
Land Area (sq. mi.)................951.8	Wages..................... $92,741,547
Altitude (ft.)..................782–1,530	Per Capita Income............. $41,193
Rainfall (in.).......................32.1	Prop. Value.............. $5,632,372,747
Jan. mean min (°F)................32.2	Retail Sales.............. $369,698,342

Panola County

Physical Features: East Texas county; sixty percent forested, rolling plain; broken by Sabine, Murvaul Creek; Toledo Bend Reservoir, Lake Murvaul, Martin Creek Lake.

Economy: Gas, oil-field operations, food processing, agribusiness.

History: A Caddo tribal area. Anglo-American settlement established in 1833. Antebellum slaveholding area. County name is Indian word for cotton; created from Harrison, Shelby counties in 1846; organized the same year.

Race/Ethnicity: Anglo, 71.8%; Black, 16.2%; Hispanic, 9.6%; Asian, 0.3%; Other, 1.9%.

Vital Statistics, annual: Births, 287; deaths, 266; mmarriages, 157; divorces, 75.

Recreation: Fishing, water activities, hunting; Jim Reeves memorial, Tex Ritter museum and Texas Country Music Hall of Fame.

Minerals: Oil, gas, coal.

Agriculture: Broilers, cattle, forages. Market value $100.7 million. Timber sales significant.

CARTHAGE (6,941) county seat; petroleum processing, poultry, sawmills; hospital, junior college; Oil & Gas Blast in October.

Other towns include: **Beckville** (902), **Clayton** (125), **DeBerry** (200), **Gary** (311), **Long Branch** (150), **Panola** (305). Also, **Tatum** (1,416, mostly in Rusk County).

Population..................... 24,586	
Change from 2010 (%)...................3.3	
Area (sq. mi.).......................... 821.3	
Land Area (sq. mi.).................... 801.8	
Altitude (ft.)...................... 172–548	
Rainfall (in.)...........................51.4	
Jan. mean min (°F)......................35.2	
July mean max (°F).....................93.0	
Civ. Labor............................ 8,879	
Unemployed (%)........................7.8	
Wages..................... $96,297,706	
Per Capita Income................ $45,467	
Prop. Value............... $4,860,871,222	
Retail Sales.................. $262,434,385	

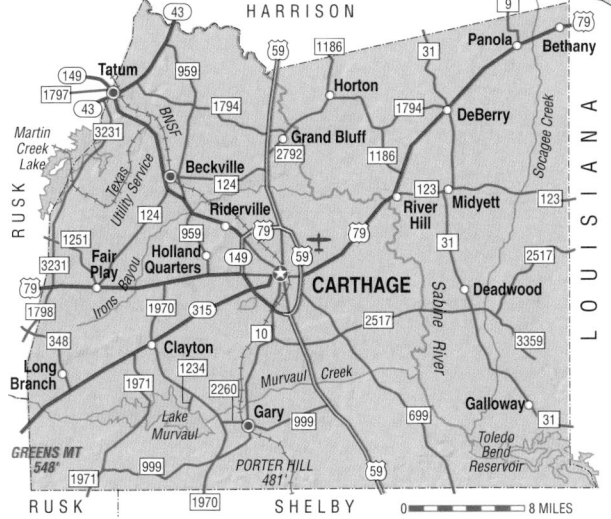

Parker County

Physical Features: Hilly, broken by Brazos, Trinity tributaries, Lake Mineral Wells, Lake Weatherford; varied soils.

Economy: Agriculture, varied manufacturing, retail sales, government/services, commuting to Fort Worth; part of Dallas-Fort Worth metropolitan area.

History: Comanche and Kiowa area in the late 1840s when Anglo-American settlers arrived. County named for pioneer legislator Isaac Parker; created in 1855 from Bosque, Navarro counties, organized the same year.

Race/Ethnicity: Anglo, 83.2%; Black, 1.4%; Hispanic, 12.5%; Asian, 0.4%; Other, 2.2%.

Vital Statistics, annual: Births, 1,484; deaths, 1,066; marriages, 777; divorces, 383.

Recreation: Water sports; state park and trailway; nature trails; hunting; Peach Festival in July and rodeo days in June; first Monday trade days monthly.

Minerals: Natural gas, oil, stone, sand and gravel, clays.

Agriculture: Beef cattle, greenhouses, hay, horses (first in number), peaches, sheep and goats, vegetables, pecans, aquaculture. Market value $65.0 million.

WEATHERFORD (32,587) county seat; retail center, manufacturing, warehousing, tourism, commuting to Fort Worth, government/services, equine industry; hospital, Weatherford College; museums, public gardens, historic buildings.

Other towns include: **Aledo** (4,423); **Annetta** (3,132), **Annetta North** (581) and

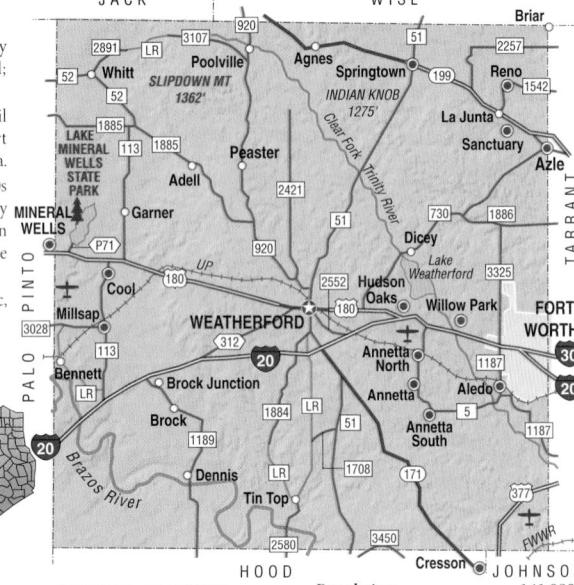

Annetta South (592); **Cool** (185); **Dennis** (953); **Hudson Oaks** (2,479); **Millsap** (474); **Peaster** (555); **Poolville** (520); **Reno** (3,146); **Sanctuary** (344); **Springtown** (3,142) commuters, government/services, Wild West Festival in September; **Whitt** (38); **Willow Park** (5,562).

Also, parts of **Azle** (13,351); **Briar** (6,116), and **Cresson** (1,338); part [193] of **Mineral Wells**. Also, a small part of **Fort Worth**.

Population	141,080
Change from 2010 (%)	20.7
Area (sq. mi.)	910.1
Land Area (sq. mi.)	903.5
Altitude (ft.)	700–1,362
Rainfall (in.)	35.8
Jan. mean min (°F)	30.1
July mean max (°F)	93.2
Civ. Labor	68,910
Unemployment (%)	4.8
Wages	$438,764,586
Per Capita Income	$55,811
Prop. Value	$21,511,240,430
Retail Sales	$2,800,469,549

Parmer County

Physical Features: High Plains, broken by draws, playas; sandy, clay, loam soils.

Economy: Cattle feeding, grain elevators, meatpacking plant, other agribusiness.

History: Apaches, pushed out in late 1700s by Comanches and Kiowas. U.S. Army removed Indians in 1874–1875. Anglo-Americans arrived in 1880s. Mexican migration increased after 1950. County named for Republic figure Martin Parmer of Bexar District in 1876, organized in 1907.

Race/Ethnicity: Anglo, 33.3%; Black, 1.5%; Hispanic, 64.1%; Asian, 0.2%; Other, 0.6%.

Vital Statistics, annual: Births, 159; deaths, 75; marriages, 20; divorces, 17.

Recreation: Hunting, playa lake, Border Town Days in July at Farwell.

Minerals: Not significant.

Agriculture: Cattle (second in numbers), dairies (third in number of cows); wheat, corn, cotton, sorghum, alfalfa, apples, potatoes. 163,000 acres irrigated. Market value $893.3 million.

FARWELL (1,255) county seat; agribusiness, grain storage, farm equipment plants.

FRIONA (3,815) farming, feed lots, feed mill; hospital; museum; Cheeseburger Festival in July.

Other towns include: **Bovina** (1,776) farm trade center; **Lazbuddie** (248).

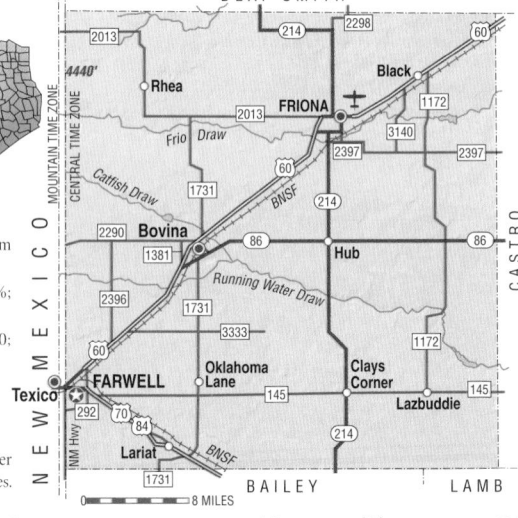

Population	9,501
Change from 2010 (%)	-7.5
Area (sq. mi.)	885.2
Land Area (sq. mi.)	880.8
Altitude (ft.)	3,785–4,440
Rainfall (in.)	20.1
Jan. mean min (°F)	22.5
July mean max (°F)	59.8
Civ. Labor	5,197
Unemployment (%)	2.6
Wages	$80,980,425
Per Capita Income	$49,541
Prop. Value	$1,727,491,539
Retail Sales	$77,556,903

Pecos County

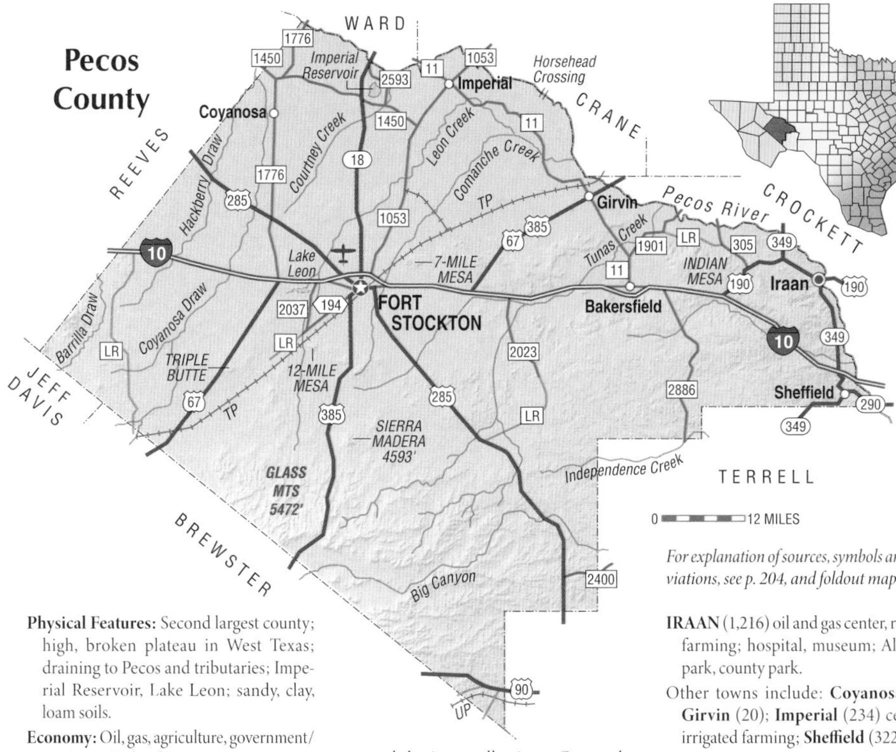

WARD

1776

1450

Imperial Reservoir

2593

11

1053

Imperial

Horsehead Crossing

CRANE

Coyanosa

1450

Leon Creek

11

REEVES

Hackberry Draw

Courtney Creek

1776

18

Comanche Creek

TP

285

1053

Girvin

Pecos River

CROCKETT

385

67

Tunas Creek

1901

LR

305

349

Lake Leon

7-MILE MESA

11

INDIAN MESA

190

Iraan

190

FORT STOCKTON

2037

194

LR

Bakersfield

12-MILE MESA

LR

2023

349

10

349

TRIPLE BUTTE

Coyanosa Draw

JEFF DAVIS

Barrilla Draw

LR

67

TP

385

285

LR

2886

Sheffield

290

SIERRA MADERA 4593'

GLASS MTS 5472'

BREWSTER

Independence Creek

TERRELL

Big Canyon

2400

0 ▭▬▬▭ 12 MILES

UP

90

For explanation of sources, symbols and abbreviations, see p. 204, and foldout map.

Physical Features: Second largest county; high, broken plateau in West Texas; draining to Pecos and tributaries; Imperial Reservoir, Lake Leon; sandy, clay, loam soils.

Economy: Oil, gas, agriculture, government/services, wind turbines.

History: Comanches in area when military outpost established in 1859. Settlement began after the Civil War. Created from Presidio County in 1871; organized in 1872; named for Pecos River, name origin uncertain.

Race/Ethnicity: Anglo, 25.2%; Black, 3.3%; Hispanic, 69.7%; Asian, 0.5%; Other, 1%.

Vital Statistics, annual: Births, 203; deaths, 114; marriages, 84; divorces, 14.

Recreation: Old Fort Stockton, Annie Riggs Museum, stagecoach stop, scenic drives, Dinosaur Track Roadside Park, cattle-trail sites, archaeological museum with oil and ranch-heritage collections; Comanche Springs Water Carnival in summer.

Minerals: Natural gas, oil, gravel, caliche.

Agriculture: Cattle, alfalfa, pecans, sheep, goats, onions, peppers, melons. Market value $46.2 million. Aquaculture firm producing shrimp. Hunting leases.

FORT STOCKTON (8,470) county seat, distribution center for petroleum industry, government/services, agriculture, tourism, varied manufacturing, winery, prison units, spaceport launching small satellites; hospital; historical tours.

IRAAN (1,216) oil and gas center, ranching, farming; hospital, museum; Alley Oop park, county park.

Other towns include: **Coyanosa** (172); **Girvin** (20); **Imperial** (234) center for irrigated farming; **Sheffield** (322) oil, gas center.

Population...........................**15,052**
Change from 2010 (%).................-2.9
Area (sq. mi.).......................4,764.8
Land Area (sq. mi.)..................4,763.9
Altitude (ft.)...................2,040–5,472
Rainfall (in.)..........................15.2
Jan. mean min (°F)......................33.2
July mean max (°F).......................94.3
Civ. Labor 6,645
Unemployed (%)...........................7.5
Wages $69,515,634
Per Capita Income $39,731
Prop. Value $5,327,610,221
Retail Sales.................. $493,753,119

A view of the lake at Lake Mineral Wells State Park in Parker County. Photo by Larry D. Moore, CC by SA 4.0/Wikimedia Commons

Polk County

Physical Features: Rolling; densely forested, with Big Thicket, unique plant, animal life; Neches, Trinity rivers, tributaries; lake.

Economy: Timber, lumber production, tourism, manufacturing.

History: Caddo area; Alabama and Coushatta Indians arrived from Louisiana in the late 1700s. Anglo-American and Hispanic families received land grants in the early 1830s. County named for U.S. President James K. Polk; created from Liberty County and organized 1846.

Race/Ethnicity: Anglo, 70.5%; Black, 10.7%; Hispanic, 15%; Asian, 0.4%; Other, 3.1%.

Vital Statistics, annual: Births, 562; deaths, 673; marriages, 324; divorces, 175.

Recreation: Lake and state park, water activities, fishing, hunting, Alabama-Coushatta Reservation, museum, Big Thicket, woodland trails, champion trees, historic homes.

Minerals: Oil, gas, sand, gravel.

Agriculture: Hay and greenhouse nurseries; vegetables raised; income also from beef cattle, horses. Market value $6.8 million. Timber and hardwood.

LIVINGSTON (5,247) county seat; lumber, tourism, oil; museum, hospital; Civil War re-enactment in February.

West Livingston (9,474) includes **Blanchard**, East Tempe, Moore Hill, and Polunsky prison unit.

Other towns include: **Ace** (40); **Camden** (1,200); **Corrigan** (1,683) plywood plant; **Dallardsville** (350); **Goodrich** (317); **Leggett** (500); **Moscow** (170) historic sites; **Onalaska** (2,464); **Seven Oaks** (118).

Population.................	**50,293**
Change from 2010 (%).........	10.7
Area (sq. mi.)................	1,109.7
Land Area (sq. mi.).........	1,057.1
Altitude (ft.).................	68–484
Rainfall (in.).................	51.5
Jan. mean min (°F)...........	39.6
July mean max (°F)...........	93.7

Civ. Labor	18,790
Unemployed (%)...............	8.6
Wages	$135,574,050
Per Capita Income	$39,818
Prop. Value	$5,998,481,422
Retail Sales	$554,657,489

Physical Features: Mostly level, part rolling; broken by Canadian River and tributaries; sandy, sandy loam, chocolate loam, clay soils; Lake Meredith.

Economy: Transportation and distribution hub for large area, manufacturing, agribusiness, tourism, government/services, petrochemicals, gas processing.

History: Apaches, pushed out by Comanches in the 1700s. Comanches removed to Indian Territory in 1874–1875. Ranching began in the late 1870s. Oil boom in the 1920s. County named for Robert Potter, Republic leader; created in 1876 from Bexar District; organized in 1887.

Race/Ethnicity: Anglo, 43.8%; Black, 9.3%; Hispanic, 38.7%; Asian, 5.4%; Other, 2.5%.

Population....................	**116,063**
Change from 2010 (%)...............	-4.1
Area (sq. mi.).........................	922.0
Land Area (sq. mi.)...................	908.4
Altitude (ft.)..................	2,915–3,910
Rainfall (in.)...........................	20.4
Jan. mean min (°F)...................	23.4
July mean max (°F)...................	91.4
Civ. Labor	54,717
Unemployed (%).......................	4.5
Wages	$1,043,142,033
Per Capita Income	$46,086
Prop. Value	$10,749,076,338
Retail Sales...............	$2,489,644,457

Vital Statistics, annual: Births, 1,944; deaths, 1,231; marriages, 1429; divorces, 415.

Recreation: Lake activities, Alibates Flint Quarries National Monument, hunting, fishing, Wildcat Bluff nature center, Cadillac Ranch car sculpture, professional sports events, Tri-State Fair in September.

Minerals: Natural gas, oil, helium.

Agriculture: Beef cattle production and processing; wheat, sorghum, cotton. Market value $24.8 million.

AMARILLO (202,314 total, part [97,022] in Randall County) county seat; hub for northern Panhandle oil and ranching, distribution and marketing center, tourism, manufacturing, food processing, prison; hospitals; Amarillo College, Texas Tech University medical, engineering, pharmacy schools; Quarter Horse Hall of Fame, museum.

Other towns include: **Bishop Hills** (173) and **Bushland** (1,485).

Potter County

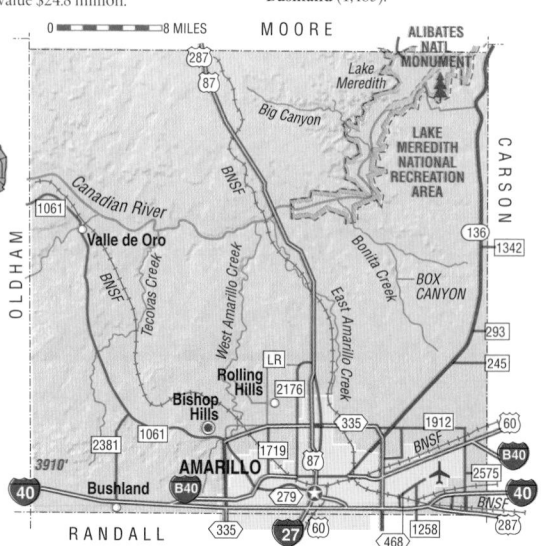

The Llano Cemetery in Amarillo. Photo by Ammodramus, CC/Wikimedia Commons

Presidio County

Physical Features: Rugged, some of Texas' tallest mountains; clays, loams, sandy loams on uplands; intermountain wash; timber sparse; Capote Falls, state's highest.

Economy: Government/services, ranching, hunting leases, tourism.

History: Presidio area has been cultivated farmland since at least 1200 A.D. Spanish explorers of the 1500s encountered permanent villages along Rio Grande. Jumanos, Apaches, and Comanches in the area when Spanish missions began in 1680s. Anglo-Americans arrived in the 1840s. County created in 1850 from Bexar District; organized in 1875; named for Spanish Presidio del Norte (fort of the north).

Race/Ethnicity: Anglo, 15.9%; Black, 0.5%; Hispanic, 81.1%; Asian, 1.2%; Other, 1%.

Vital Statistics, annual: Births, 108; deaths, 36; marriages, 42; divorces, 0.

Recreation: Hunting; scenic drives along Rio Grande, in mountains; ghost towns, mysterious Marfa Lights; Fort D.A. Russell; Big Bend Ranch State Park; hot springs; Cibolo Creek Ranch Resort; Chinati Foundation art festival in fall. (Chinati Mountains State Natural Area not yet open to public.)

Minerals: Sand, gravel, silver, zeolite.

Agriculture: Cattle, tomatoes, hay, onions, melons. Some irrigation near Rio Grande. Market value $48 million.

MARFA (1,650) county seat; ranching supply, Border Patrol headquarters, tourism, art center, gateway to mountainous area; Paisano Hotel, headquarters for movie Giant; Old Timers Roping on Memorial Day weekend.

PRESIDIO (3,774) international bridge to Ojinaga, Mex., gateway to Mexico's West Coast by rail; Fort Leaton historic site; asado cook-off in February.

Other towns include: **Redford** (67); **Shafter** (57) old mining town.

For explanation of sources, symbols and abbreviations, see p. 204, and foldout map.

Population.	**6,535**	
Change from 2010 (%)	-16.4	
Area (sq. mi.)	3,855.9	
Land Area (sq. mi.)	3,855.2	
Altitude (ft.)	2,400–7,728	
Rainfall (in.) Marfa	15.4	
Rainfall (in.) Presidio	10.8	Unemployed (%)	12.7
Jan. mean min. Marfa (°F)	23.2	Wages	$25,886,010
Jan. mean min. Presidio (°F)	34.5	Per Capita Income	$46,581
July mean max. Marfa (°F)	88.5	Prop. Value	$1,375,692,183
July mean max. Presidio (°F)	100.8	Retail Sales	$57,801,644
Civ. Labor	2,869		

Physical Features: Northeastern county; rolling; partly Blackland, sandy loams, sandy soils; Sabine River, Lake Tawakoni, Lake Fork Reservoir.

Economy: Agribusiness, some manufacturing.

History: Caddo area. In the 1700s, Tawakoni Indians entered the area. Anglo-Americans arrived in the 1840s. County, county seat named for Emory Rains, Republic leader; created in 1870 from Hopkins, Hunt, and Wood counties, organized the same year; birthplace of National Farmers Union, 1902.

Race/Ethnicity: Anglo, 86.2%; Black, 2.2%; Hispanic, 8.7%; Asian, 0.5%; Other, 2.2%.

Vital Statistics, annual: Births, 102; deaths, 150; marriages, 84; divorces, 52.

Recreation: Lake Tawakoni and Lake Fork Reservoir activities; birding, Eagle Fest in February.

Minerals: Gas, oil.

Agriculture: Beef, forages, dairies, vegetables (second in sweet potato acreage), fruits, nurseries. Market value $22.8 million.

EMORY (1,451) county seat; local trade, tourism, government/services, commuting to Greenville and Dallas; African-American museum.

Other towns include: **East Tawakoni** (976) and **Point** (922), manufacturing, tourism, tamale fest on July 4. Part of **Alba** (543), mostly in Wood County.

Rains County

Population	12,416	July mean max (°F)	91.4
Change from 2010 (%)	13.8	Civ. Labor	6,230
Area (sq. mi.)	258.8	Unemployed (%)	3.9
Land Area (sq. mi.)	229.5	Wages	$19,794,190
Altitude (ft.)	340–570	Per Capita Income	$34,819
Rainfall (in.)	44.5	Prop. Value	$1,441,315,968
Jan. mean min (°F)	31.4	Retail Sales	$110,520,875

Randall County

Physical Features: Panhandle county; level, but broken by scenic Palo Duro Canyon, Buffalo Lake; Bivins Lake; silty clay, loam soils.

Economy: Agribusiness, education, tourism, part of Amarillo metropolitan area.

History: Comanche Indians removed in the mid-1870s; ranching began soon afterward. County created in 1876 from the Bexar District; organized in 1889; named for Confederate Gen. Horace Randal (name misspelled in statute).

Race/Ethnicity: Anglo, 69.3%; Black, 3%; Hispanic, 23.8%; Asian, 1.4%; Other, 2.3%.

Vital Statistics, annual: Births, 1,667; deaths, 1,050; marriages, 481; divorces, 467.

Recreation: State park, with Texas outdoor musical drama each summer;

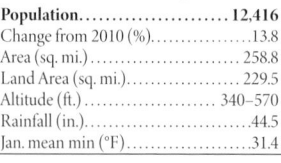

Panhandle-Plains Historical Museum; West Texas A&M University events; aoudad sheep, migratory waterfowl hunting in season; Buffalo Lake National Wildlife Refuge; cowboy breakfasts at ranches.

Minerals: Not significant.

Agriculture: Grain sorghum, beef cattle, wheat, silage, cotton, dairies, hay. Market value $479.5 million.

CANYON (16,179) county seat; West Texas A&M University, tourism, commuting to Amarillo, ranching, farm center, light manufacturing, gateway to state park.

AMARILLO (202,314 total, part [105,292] in Potter County) hub for northern Panhandle oil and ranching, distribution and marketing center, manufacturing; hospitals.

Other towns include: **Lake Tanglewood** (847); **Palisades** (364); **Timbercreek Canyon** (460); **Umbarger** (327) German sausage festival in November.

Part of **Happy** (651, mostly in Swisher County).

Population	139,034
Change from 2010 (%)	15.2
Area (sq. mi.)	922.4
Land Area (sq. mi.)	911.5
Altitude (ft.)	2,700–3,890
Rainfall (in.)	20.2
Jan. mean min (°F)	21.5
July mean max (°F)	91.7
Civ. Labor	73,278
Unemployed (%)	3.7
Wages	$417,147,039
Per Capita Income	$49,544
Prop. Value	$13,444,282,345
Retail Sales	$2,014,405,564

Reagan County

Physical Features: Western county; level to hilly, broken by draws, Big Lake (intermittent); sandy, loam, clay soils.

Economy: Oil and gas production, hunting, ranching.

History: Comanches in the area until the mid-1870s. Ranching began in the 1880s. Hispanic migration increased after 1950. County named for Texas' U.S. Sen. John H. Reagan, first chairman of the Texas Railroad Commission; county created and organized in 1903 from Tom Green County.

Race/Ethnicity: Anglo, 28.4%; Black, 1.7%; Hispanic, 69.1%; Asian, 0%; Other, 0.6%.

Vital Statistics, annual: Births, 70; deaths, 29; marriages, 25; divorces, 10.

Recreation: Site of 1923 discovery well Santa Rita No. 1 on University of Texas land.

Minerals: Gas, oil.

Agriculture: Cotton, cattle, sheep, goats. Market value $18.2 million. Hunting leases important.

BIG LAKE (3,661) county seat; center for oil activities, agriculture, government/services; hospital; Spring bluegrass festival, St. Rita festival in August.

For explanation of sources, symbols and abbreviations, see p. 204, and foldout map.

Population......................	**3,836**
Change from 2010 (%).................	13.9
Area (sq. mi.)......................	1,176.0
Land Area (sq. mi.).................	1,175.3
Altitude (ft.)....................2,370–2,960
Rainfall (in.)............................19.3
Jan. mean min (°F)....................30.8

July mean max (°F)....................93.5
Civ. Labor............................1,726
Unemployed (%)........................8.2
Wages........................ $31,895,262
Per Capita Income................ $51,945
Prop. Value................ $5,552,610,162
Retail Sales.................... $34,693,751

A marshy inlet of Lake Fork Reservoir in Rains County. Photo by Carol M. Highsmith, courtesy of the Library of Congress

Real County

Physical Features: Hill Country, spring-fed streams, scenic canyons; Frio, Nueces rivers; cedars, pecans, walnuts, many live oaks.

Economy: Ranching, tourism, government/services, cedar cutting.

History: Tonkawa area; Lipan Apaches arrived in early 1700s; later, Comanche hunters arrived in the area. Spanish mission established in 1762. Anglo-Americans arrived in 1850s. County created, organized in 1913 from Bandera, Edwards, and Kerr counties; named for legislator-ranchman Julius Real.

Race/Ethnicity: Anglo, 69.1%; Black, 0.5%; Hispanic, 28%; Asian, 0%; Other, 2.1%.

Vital Statistics, annual: Births, 41; deaths, 38; marriages, 20; divorces, 0.

Recreation: Tourist and hunting center, birding, fishing, camping, scenic drives, state natural area.

Minerals: Not significant.

Agriculture: Goats, sheep, beef cattle produce most income. Market value $1.3 million. Cedar posts processed.

LEAKEY (464) county seat; tourism, ranching; museums; July Jubilee.

CAMP WOOD (725) tourism, hunting, ranching; medical clinic; San Lorenzo de la Santa Cruz mission site; museum; Lindbergh Park, settlers reunion in August.

Other towns include: **Rio Frio** (50).

Population........................ 3,499	July mean max (°F).....................93.0
Change from 2010 (%)................5.7	Civ. Labor 1,129
Area (sq. mi.)...................... 700.1	Unemployed (%)........................6.7
Land Area (sq. mi.)................. 699.2	Wages $6,170,778
Altitude (ft.)...................1,400–2,400	Per Capita Income $36,070
Rainfall (in.)........................27.4	Prop. Value $1,313,608,351
Jan. mean min (°F)....................33.6	Retail Sales $32,489,826

Red River County

Physical Features: On Red-Sulphur rivers' divide; 39 different soil types; half timbered; River Crest Reservoir.

Economy: Manufacturing, government/services, agriculture.

History: Caddo Indians abandoned the area in the 1790s. One of the oldest counties; settlers were moving in from the United States in the 1810s. Kickapoo and other tribes arrived in the 1820s. Antebellum slaveholding area. County created in 1836 as original county of the Republic; organized in 1837; named for Red River, its northern boundary.

Race/Ethnicity: Anglo, 71%; Black, 17.6%; Hispanic, 7.5%; Asian, 0.2%; Other, 3.5%.

Vital Statistics, annual: Births, 115; deaths, 180; marriages, 58; divorces, 51.

Recreation: Historical sites include pioneer homes, birthplace of John Nance Garner; fall foliage; water activities; hunting of deer, turkey, duck, small game.

Minerals: Small oil flow.

Agriculture: Beef cattle, corn, soybeans, wheat, sorghum, hay. Market value $94.0 million. Timber sales substantial.

CLARKSVILLE (2,991) county seat; varied manufacturing; hospital, library; Historical Society bazaar in October.

Other towns include: **Annona** (285); **Avery** (433); **Bagwell** (150); **Bogata** (1,052); **Detroit** (675) commercial center in west. Part of **Deport** (558).

Population........................ 11,649	Rainfall (in.)...........................48.8	Wages $29,604,724
Change from 2010 (%)................-9.4	Jan. mean min (°F)....................30.8	Per Capita Income $43,039
Area (sq. mi.)...................... 1,056.7	July mean max (°F)....................91.9	Prop. Value $2,231,223,241
Land Area (sq. mi.)................ 1,036.6	Civ. Labor 5,238	Retail Sales $54,039,790
Altitude (ft.)...................... 260–560	Unemployed (%)........................6.4	

Reeves County

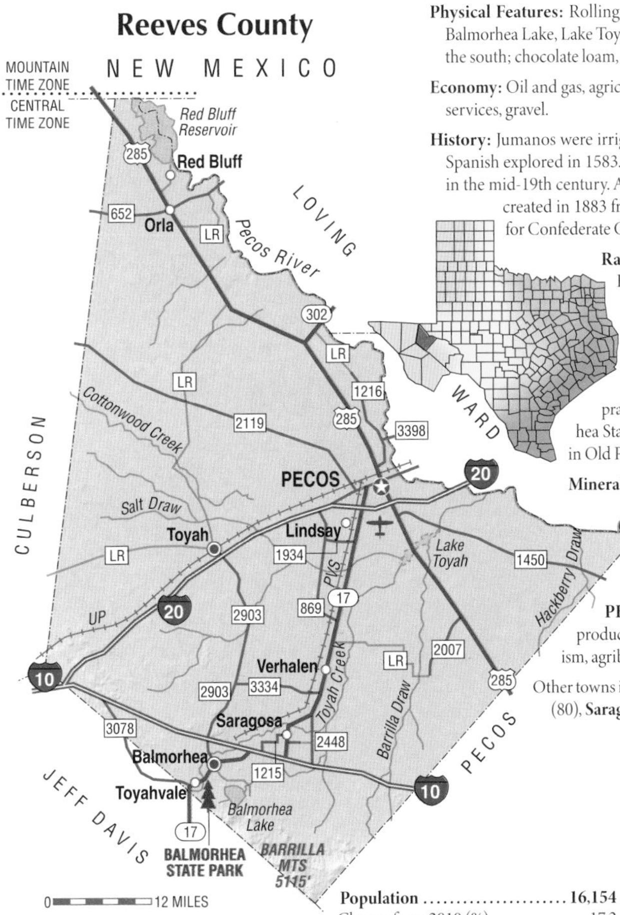

NEW MEXICO

Red Bluff
Reservoir

285 Red Bluff

652 Orla LR

LOVING

Pecos River

302

LR

1216

2119 285 3398

WARD

PECOS 20

CULBERSON

Cottonwood Creek

Salt Draw

Toyah LR

Lindsay
1934

Lake
Toyah 1450

PYS

UP 20 2903 869 17

Verhalen LR 2007

2903 3334

Saragosa

2448

3078

Balmorhea 1215

JEFF DAVIS

Toyahvale

17 Balmorhea
Lake

BALMORHEA BARRILLA
STATE PARK MTS
5115'

Hackberry Draw

Barrilla Draw

Toyah Creek

285

10

PECOS

10

0 ⊏■■■■⊐ 12 MILES

For explanation of sources, symbols and abbreviations, see p. 204, and foldout map.

Population **16,154**
Change from 2010 (%)................17.2
Area (sq. mi.) 2,642.1
Land Area (sq. mi.)................. 2,635.4
Altitude (ft.) 2,460–5,115

Physical Features: Rolling plains, broken by many draws, Pecos River, Balmorhea Lake, Lake Toyah, Red Bluff Reservoir; Barrilla Mountains on the south; chocolate loam, clay, sandy, mountain wash soils.

Economy: Oil and gas, agriculture, tourism, food processing, government/ services, gravel.

History: Jumanos were irrigating crops from springs (Balmorhea) when Spanish explored in 1583. Mexican farmers supplied nearby Fort Davis in the mid-19th century. Anglo-Americans arrived in the 1870s. County created in 1883 from Pecos County; organized in 1884; named for Confederate Col. George R. Reeves.

Race/Ethnicity: Anglo, 17.4%; Black, 4.5%; Hispanic, 76.6%; Asian, 0.8%; Other, 0.5%.

Vital Statistics, annual: Births, 206; deaths, 114; marriages, 85; divorces, 22.

Recreation: Replica of Judge Roy Bean store, West of Pecos museum; park with javelina, prairie dogs; scenic drives; water activities; Balmorhea State Park with San Solomon Springs pool; Night in Old Pecos, cantaloupe festival in July.

Minerals: Oil, gas, gravel.

Agriculture: Ranching, dairies, hay, cotton, cantaloupes, pecans, pistachios. Some 11,000 acres irrigated. Market value $10.9 million.

PECOS (10,574) county seat; food processing, produce shipping, government/services, prison, tourism, agribusiness; hospital; 16th of September fiesta.

Other towns include: **Balmorhea** (538), **Lindsay** (288), **Orla** (80), **Saragosa** (185), **Toyah** (96), **Toyahvale** (60).

Rainfall (in.) Pecos.................	11.61
Rainfall (in.) Balmorhea.............	13.54
Jan. mean min. Pecos (°F).............	28.1
Jan. mean min. Balmorhea (°F)........	30.3
July mean max. Pecos (°F)	98.5
July mean max. Balmorhea (°F)	94.4
Civ. Labor	7,910
Unemployed (%).......................	7.5
Wages	$98,975,585
Per Capita Income	$45,458
Prop. Value	$14,768,048,059
Retail Sales	$302,801,992

The public library in Leakey, county seat of Real County. Photo by Billy Hathorn, CC 3/Wikimedia Commons

Refugio County

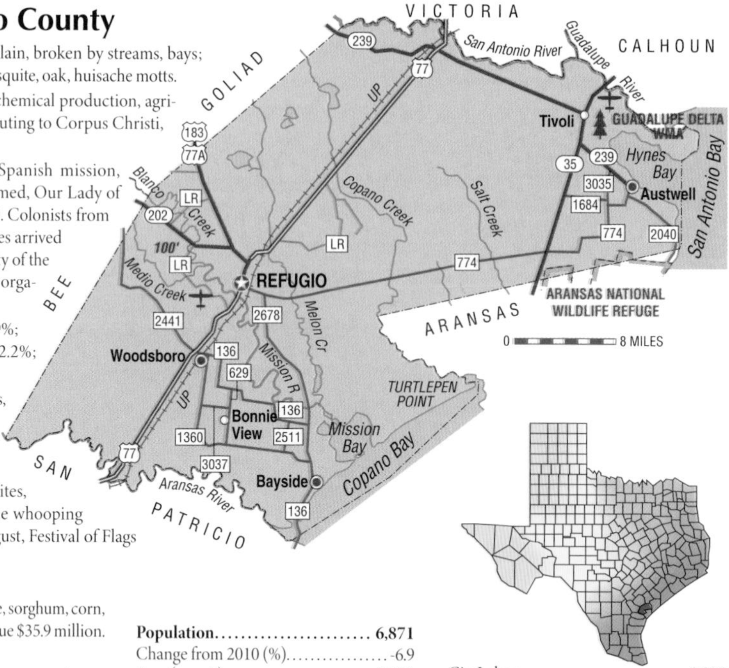

Physical Features: Coastal plain, broken by streams, bays; sandy, loam, black soils; mesquite, oak, huisache motts.

Economy: Petroleum, petrochemical production, agribusinesses, tourism, commuting to Corpus Christi, Victoria.

History: Karankawa area. Spanish mission, for which the county is named, Our Lady of Refuge, established in 1793. Colonists from Ireland and the United States arrived in the 1830s. Original county of the Republic created in 1836, organized in 1837.

Race/Ethnicity: Anglo, 39.9%; Black, 5.9%; Hispanic, 52.2%; Asian, 0.3%; Other, 1.3%.

Vital Statistics, annual: Births, 99; deaths, 108; marriages, 27; divorces, 20.

Recreation: Water activities, hunting, fishing, historic sites, wildlife refuge, home of the whooping crane; chili cook-off in August, Festival of Flags in October.

Minerals: Oil, natural gas.

Agriculture: Cotton, beef cattle, sorghum, corn, soybeans, horses. Market value $35.9 million. Hunting leases.

REFUGIO (2,695) county seat; petroleum, agribusiness center; hospital; museum; historic homes.

Other towns include: **Austwell** (144); **Bayside** (318) resorts; **Tivoli** (477); **Woodsboro** (1,447) commercial center.

Population	**6,871**
Change from 2010 (%)	-6.9
Area (sq. mi.)	818.2
Land Area (sq. mi.)	77.4
Altitude (ft.)	sea level–100
Rainfall (in.)	36.9
Jan. mean min (°F)	44.3
July mean max (°F)	92.0

Civ. Labor	3,037
Unemployed (%)	7.2
Wages	$23,044,134
Per Capita Income	$46,464
Prop. Value	$1,786,210,407
Retail Sales	$77,159,038

Roberts County

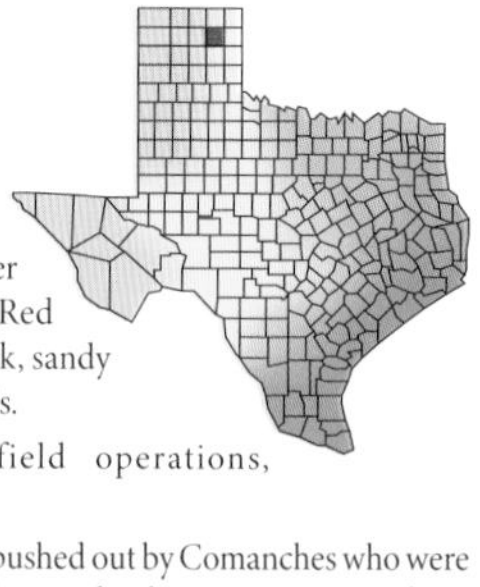

Physical Features: Rolling, broken by Canadian River and tributaries; Red Deer Creek; black, sandy loam, alluvial soils.

Economy: Oil-field operations, agribusiness.

History: Apaches; pushed out by Comanches who were removed in 1874–1875 by the U.S. Army. Ranching began in the late 1870s. County created in 1876 from Bexar District; organized in 1889; named for Texas leaders John S. Roberts and Gov. O.M. Roberts.

Race/Ethnicity: Anglo, 89.8%; Black, 0%; Hispanic, 8.5%; Asian, 0%; Other, 1.5%.

Vital Statistics, annual: Births, 0; deaths, 6; marriages, 6; divorces, 1.

Recreation: Scenic drives, hunting, museum; national cow-calling contest in June.

Minerals: Production of gas, oil.

Agriculture: Beef cattle; wheat, sorghum, corn, soybeans, hay; 6,300 acres irrigated. Market value $18.3 million.

MIAMI (553) county seat; ranching, oil center, some manufacturing.

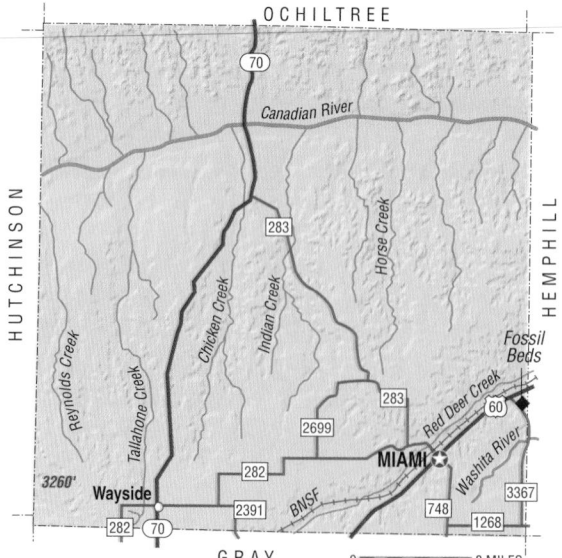

For explanation of sources, symbols and abbreviations, see p. 204, and foldout map.

Population	**851**
Change from 2010 (%)	-8.4
Area (sq. mi.)	924.2
Land Area (sq. mi.)	924.1
Altitude (ft.)	2,380–3,260
Rainfall (in.)	24.1
Jan. mean min (°F)	22.1

July mean max (°F)	92.1
Civ. Labor	411
Unemployed (%)	4.1
Wages	$3,096,028
Per Capita Income	$48,344
Prop. Value	$551,021,753
Retail Sales	$1,529,994

Physical Features: Rolling in north and east, draining to bottoms along Brazos, Navasota rivers; sandy soils, heavy in bottoms; Lake Limestone, Twin Oaks Reservoir, Camp Creek Reservoir.

Economy: Agribusiness, government/services, oil and gas.

History: Tawakoni, Waco, Comanche, and other tribes. Anglo-Americans arrived in the 1820s. Antebellum slave-holding area. County created in 1837, organized in 1838, subdivided into many others later; named for pioneer Sterling Clack Robertson.

Race/Ethnicity: Anglo, 56.1%; Black, 19.5%; Hispanic, 22.2%; Asian, 0.6%; Other, 1.3%.

Vital Statistics, annual: Births, 211; deaths, 173; marriages, 91; divorces, 34.

Recreation: Hunting, fishing; historic sites; dogwood trails, wildlife preserves.

Minerals: Gas, oil, lignite coal.

Agriculture: Poultry, beef cattle, cotton, hay, corn; 20,000 acres of cropland irrigated. Market value $158.1 million.

FRANKLIN (1,701) county seat; oil and gas, power plants, agriculture; Carnegie library.

HEARNE (4,637) railroad center; depot museum, historic homes, World War II POW camp; October Sticks & Stones golf and dominoes (Texas 42) tournament.

Other towns include: **Bremond** (978) mining, agriculture, power utilities, library, museum, Polish Days in late June; **Calvert** (1,124) agriculture, tourism, antiques, Maypole festival, tour of homes; **Mumford** (170); **New Baden** (150); **Wheelock** (225).

Robertson County

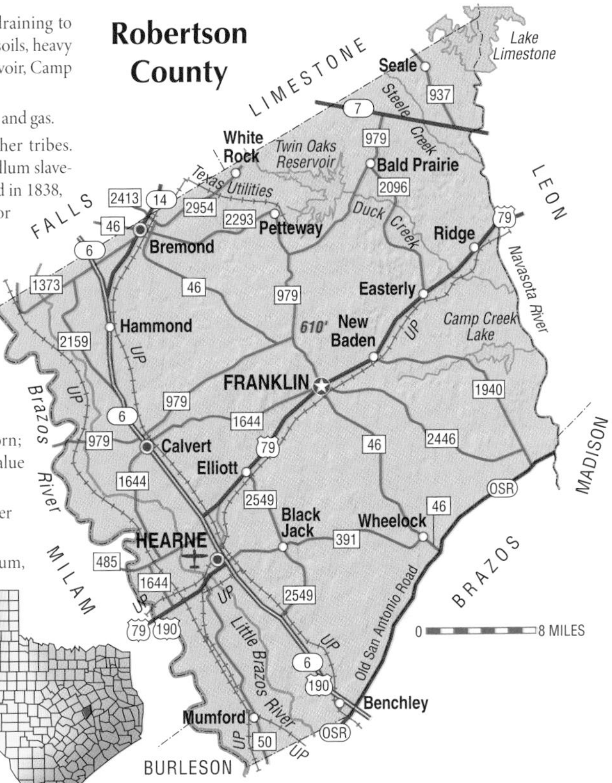

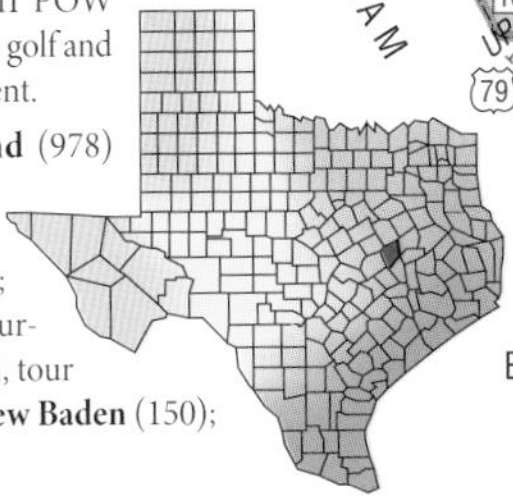

Population	17,708
Change from 2010 (%)	6.5
Area (sq. mi.)	865.4
Land Area (sq. mi.)	855.7
Altitude (ft.)	230–610
Rainfall (in.)	39.5
Jan. mean min (°F)	38.8
July mean max (°F)	94.9
Civ. Labor	7,422
Unemployed (%)	5.7
Wages	$61,268,508
Per Capita Income	$42,463
Prop. Value	$5,642,636,427
Retail Sales	$121,002,078

The Depot Museum in Hearne. Photo by Billy Hathorn, CC 3/Wikimedia Commons

Rockwall County

Physical Features: Rolling prairie, mostly Blackland soil; Lake Ray Hubbard. Texas' smallest county.

Economy: Industrial employment in local plants and in Dallas; in Dallas metropolitan area; residential development around Lake Ray Hubbard.

History: Caddo area. Cherokees arrived in the 1820s. Anglo-American settlers arrived in the 1840s. County created in 1873 from Kaufman, organized the same year; named for wall-like rock formation.

Race/Ethnicity: Anglo, 71%; Black, 6.1%; Hispanic, 17.9%; Asian, 2.8%; Other, 2%.

Vital Statistics, annual: Births, 1,034; deaths, 545; marriages, 1,463; divorces, 319.

Recreation: Lake activities; proximity to Dallas; unusual rock outcrop.

Minerals: Not significant.

Agriculture: Small grains, cattle, horticulture, horses. Market value $7.8 million.

ROCKWALL (45,641) county seat; commuters, varied manufacturing, government/services; hospital; harbor retail and entertainment district; Founders Day in April.

Other towns include: **Fate** (15,121); **Heath** (9,099); **McLendon-Chisholm** (3,541) chili cookoff in October; **Mobile City** (223); **Royse City** (13,191) government/services, varied manufacturing, agribusiness, museum, library, Funfest in October.

Part [8,267] of **Rowlett**, hospital, and a small part of **Wylie.**

Population.................... 103,363	Rainfall (in.)............................38.6	Wages $434,940,300
Change from 2010 (%)................31.9	Jan. mean min (°F)...................33.0	Per Capita Income................ $62,237
Area (sq. mi.).......................... 148.7	July mean max (°F)....................96.0	Prop. Value $15,720,293,005
Land Area (sq. mi.).................. 127.0	Civ. Labor 53,858	Retail Sales................ $2,112,468,140
Altitude (ft.)...................... 431–624	Unemployed (%).......................4.8	

Runnels County

Physical Features: Level to rolling; bisected by Colorado and tributaries; sandy loam, black waxy soils; O.H. Ivie Reservoir, Lake Ballinger.

Economy: Agribusiness, oil, government/services, manufacturing.

History: Spanish explorers found Jumanos in area in the 1650s; later, Apaches and Comanches driven out in the 1870s by U.S. military. First Anglo-Americans arrived in the 1850s; Germans, Czechs around 1900. County named for planter-legislator H.G. Runnels; created in 1858 from Bexar and Travis counties; organized in 1880.

Race/Ethnicity: Anglo, 60.5%; Black, 1.5%; Hispanic, 36.2%; Asian, 0.1%; Other, 1.5%.

Vital Statistics, annual: Births, 112; deaths, 140; marriages, 53; divorces, 18.

Recreation: Deer, dove and turkey hunting; lakes; fishing; antique car museum; historical markers in county.

Minerals: Oil, gas, sand.

Agriculture: Cattle, cotton, wheat, sorghum, dairies, sheep and goats. Market value $53.4 million.

BALLINGER (3,620) county seat; varied manufacturing, meat processing; Carnegie Library, hospital, Western Texas College extension; the Cross, 100-ft. tall atop hill; city park; Festival of Ethnic Cultures in April.

Other towns include: **Miles** (849); **Norton** (50); **Rowena** (349); **Wingate** (100); **Winters** (2,427) manufacturing, museum, hospital.

For explanation of sources, symbols and abbreviations, see p. 204, and foldout map.

Population....................... 10,121	July mean max (°F)....................94.4
Change from 2010 (%)................-3.6	Civ. Labor 4,531
Area (sq. mi.)...................... 1,057.1	Unemployed (%).......................3.9
Land Area (sq. mi.)................ 1,050.9	Wages $30,856,175
Altitude (ft.).................1,915–2,301	Per Capita Income................ $41,929
Rainfall (in.)...........................24.0	Prop. Value $1,716,913,212
Jan. mean min (°F)....................31.2	Retail Sales.................. $108,018,574

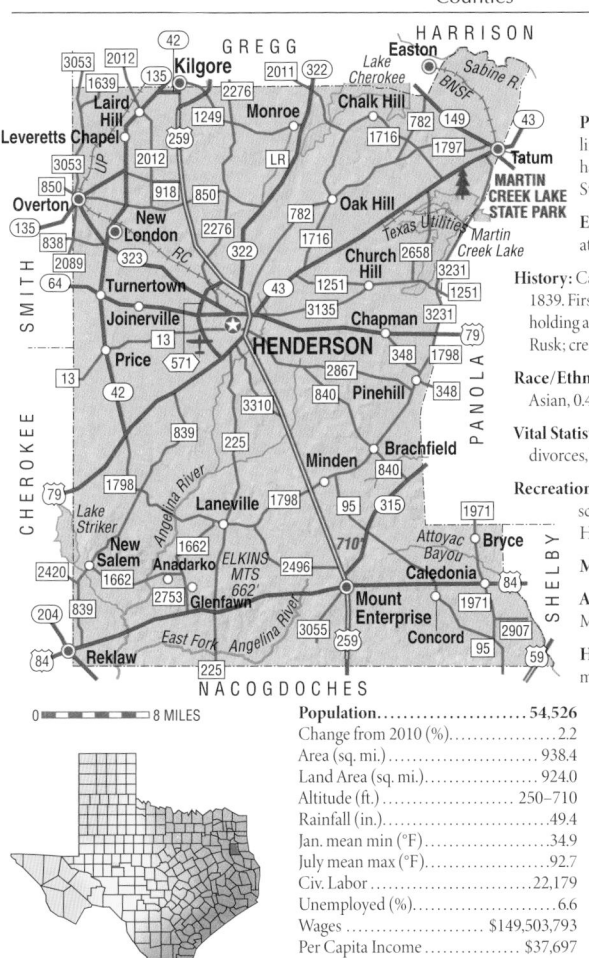

Rusk County

Physical Features: East Texas county on Sabine-Angelina divide; varied deep, sandy soils; over half in pines, hardwoods; Martin Creek Lake, Lake Cherokee, Lake Striker.

Economy: Oil and gas, lignite mining, electricity generation, agriculture.

History: Caddo area. Cherokees settled in the 1820s; removed in 1839. First Anglo-Americans arrived in 1829. Antebellum slaveholding area. County named for Republic, state leader Thomas J. Rusk; created and organized from Nacogdoches County in 1843.

Race/Ethnicity: Anglo, 63%; Black, 16.5%; Hispanic, 17.8%; Asian, 0.4%; Other, 2.1%.

Vital Statistics, annual: Births, 645; deaths, 544; marriages, 287; divorces, 225.

Recreation: Water sports, state park, historic homes and sites, scenic drives, site of East Texas Field discovery oil well; Henderson syrup festival in November.

Minerals: Oil, natural gas, lignite.

Agriculture: Beef cattle, forage, poultry, nursery plants. Market value $100.2 million. Timber income substantial.

HENDERSON (13,688) county seat; power plant, mining, lumber, state jails; hospital, museum.

Population	54,526
Change from 2010 (%)	2.2
Area (sq. mi.)	938.4
Land Area (sq. mi.)	924.0
Altitude (ft.)	250–710
Rainfall (in.)	49.4
Jan. mean min (°F)	34.9
July mean max (°F)	92.7
Civ. Labor	22,179
Unemployed (%)	6.6
Wages	$149,503,793
Per Capita Income	$37,697
Prop. Value	$5,738,694,952
Retail Sales	$391,561,242

Other towns include: **Joinerville** (140); **Laird Hill** (300); **Laneville** (169); **Minden** (150); **Mount Enterprise** (438); **New London** (1,011) site of 1937 school explosion that killed 293 students and faculty; **Overton** (2,558, partly in Smith County) oil, lumbering center, petroleum processing, prison, A&M research center, blue-grass music festival in July; **Price** (275); **Tatum** (1,419, partly in Panola County); **Turnertown-Selman City** (271).

Also: part of **Easton** (515, mostly in Gregg County), part of **Reklaw** (395, mostly in Cherokee County), and part [3,515] of **Kilgore** (14,852 total).

The post office in New London in Rusk County. Photo by Nsaum75, CC by SA 4.0/Wikimedia Commons

Sabine County

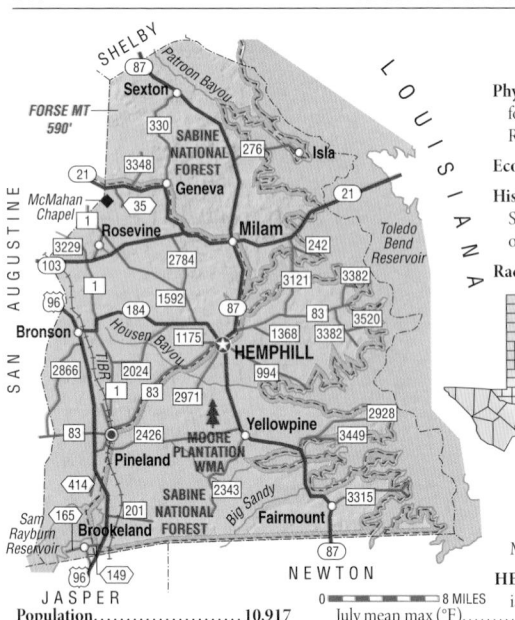

Physical Features: Eighty percent forested; 114,498 acres in national forest; Sabine River, Toledo Bend Reservoir on east; Sam Rayburn Reservoir on southwest.

Economy: Timber, government/services, tourism.

History: Caddo area. Spanish land grants in the 1790s brought first Spanish and Anglo settlers. An original county, created in 1836; organized in 1837. Name means cypress in Spanish.

Race/Ethnicity: Anglo, 83.3%; Black, 7.8%; Hispanic, 4.8%; Asian, 0.3%; Other, 3.5%.

Vital Statistics, annual: Births, 111; deaths, 168; marriages, 77; divorces, 6.

Recreation: Lake activities, hunting, campsites, hiking trails, marinas, historic homes; McMahan's Chapel, pioneer Protestant church; Sabine National Forest; Lobanillo Swales historic trail.

Minerals: Glauconite, oil.

Agriculture: Beef cattle; forage, fruit raised. Market value $17.7 million. Significant timber industry.

HEMPHILL (1,233) county seat; timber, lake activities, tourism; hospital; NASA Columbia museum, library; Boo Bash at Halloween.

Other towns include: **Bronson** (377); **Brookeland** (300); **Geneva** (200); **Milam** (1,512); **Pineland** (793) timber processing.

Population.....................**10,917**	July mean max (°F)...................92.7
Change from 2010 (%)................0.8	Civ. Labor............................3,972
Area (sq. mi.)........................592.3	Unemployed (%).......................9.9
Land Area (sq. mi.)..................530.7	Wages.......................$26,008,303
Altitude (ft.)......................164–590	Per Capita Income...............$36,627
Rainfall (in.)..........................51.9	Prop. Value.............$1,516,636,619
Jan. mean min (°F)...................35.6	Retail Sales..................$81,075,344

San Augustine County

Physical Features: Hilly East Texas county, 80 percent forested with 66,799 acres in Angelina National Forest, 4,317 in Sabine National Forest; Sam Rayburn Reservoir; varied soils, sandy to black alluvial.

Economy: Timber, poultry, tourism.

History: Presence of Ais Indians attracted Spanish mission in 1717. First Anglos and Indians from U.S. southern states arrived around 1800. Antebellum slaveholding area. County created and named for Mexican municipality in 1836; an original county; organized in 1837.

Race/Ethnicity: Anglo, 67%; Black, 23.3%; Hispanic, 7.8%; Asian, 0.2%; Other, 1.4%.

Vital Statistics, annual: Births, 79; deaths, 128; marriages, 54; divorces, 4.

Recreation: Lake activities, historic homes, tourist facilities in national forests; sassafras festival in October.

Minerals: Small amount of oil.

Agriculture: Poultry, cattle, horses; watermelons, peas, corn, truck crops. Market value $56.7 million. Timber sales significant.

SAN AUGUSTINE (1,918) county seat; logging, poultry farms, tourism; hospital; Mission Dolores museum.

Other towns include: **Broaddus** (203).

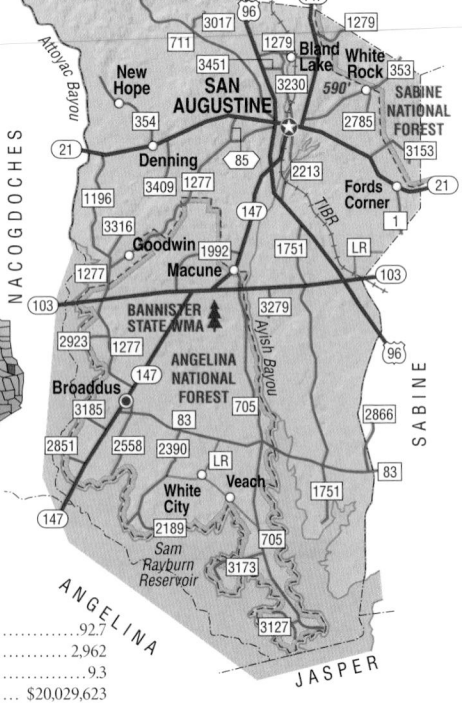

Population.....................**8,458**	July mean max (°F)...................92.7
Change from 2010 (%)...............-4.6	Civ. Labor............................2,962
Area (sq. mi.)........................592.3	Unemployed (%).......................9.3
Land Area (sq. mi.)..................530.7	Wages.......................$20,029,623
Altitude (ft.)......................164–590	Per Capita Income...............$42,299
Rainfall (in.)..........................51.9	Prop. Value.............$1,839,107,030
Jan. mean min (°F)...................35.6	Retail Sales..................$64,544,332

For explanation of sources, symbols and abbreviations, see p. 204, and foldout map.

San Jacinto County

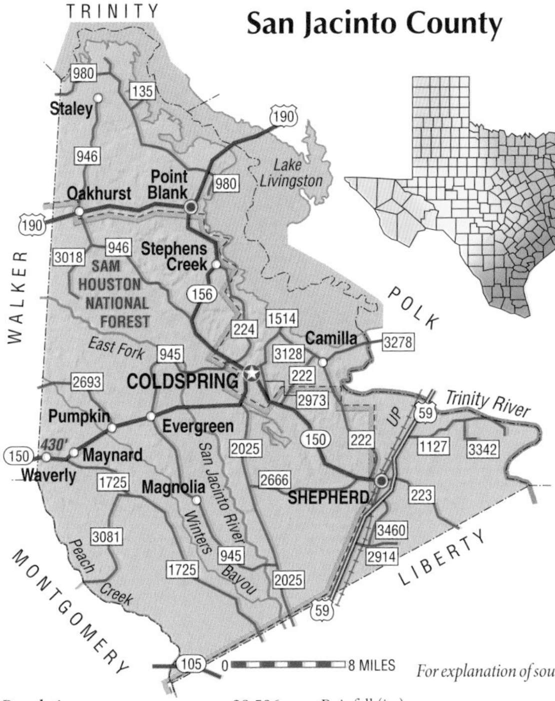

Physical Features: East Texas county north of Houston; rolling hills; eighty percent of area is forested; Sam Houston National Forest; Trinity and East Fork of San Jacinto rivers; Lake Livingston.

Economy: Timber and oil.

History: Atakapa Indian area. Anglo-Americans arrived in the 1820s. Land grants issued to Mexican families in the early 1830s. County created from Liberty, Montgomery, Polk, and Walker counties in 1869; organized in 1870; named for the battle.

Race/Ethnicity: Anglo, 72.9%; Black, 9.7%; Hispanic, 14.7%; Asian, 0.4%; Other, 2.1%.

Vital Statistics, annual: Births, 283; deaths, 313; marriages, 120; divorces, 118.

Recreation: Lake activities, hunting, old courthouse and jail; Wolf Creek car show in Coldspring in October. Approximately 60 percent of county in national forest.

Minerals: Oil, rock, gravel and iron ore.

Agriculture: Beef cattle and forages. Market value $7.2 million. Timber is a principal product.

COLDSPRING (976) county seat; lumbering, oil, farming center, tourism; historic sites.

SHEPHERD (2,649) lumbering, tourism, ranching.

Other towns include: **Oakhurst** (242); **Point Blank** (748) logging, agribusiness, construction.

For explanation of sources, symbols and abbreviations, see p. 204, and foldout map.

Population......................29,506	Rainfall (in.)............................50.7	Wages........................ $21,708,268
Change from 2010 (%)................11.8	Jan. mean min (°F).....................38.2	Per Capita Income................ $36,260
Area (sq. mi.).........................627.9	July mean max (°F)....................92.4	Prop. Value................ $3,606,160,151
Land Area (sq. mi.)...................569.2	Civ. Labor............................11,897	Retail Sales.................... $64,673,049
Altitude (ft.).........................62–430	Unemployed (%)..........................8	

The Sam Rayburn Reservoir can hold up to 2,857,077 acre-feet of water. Photo by Ricraider, CC 3/Wikimedia Commons

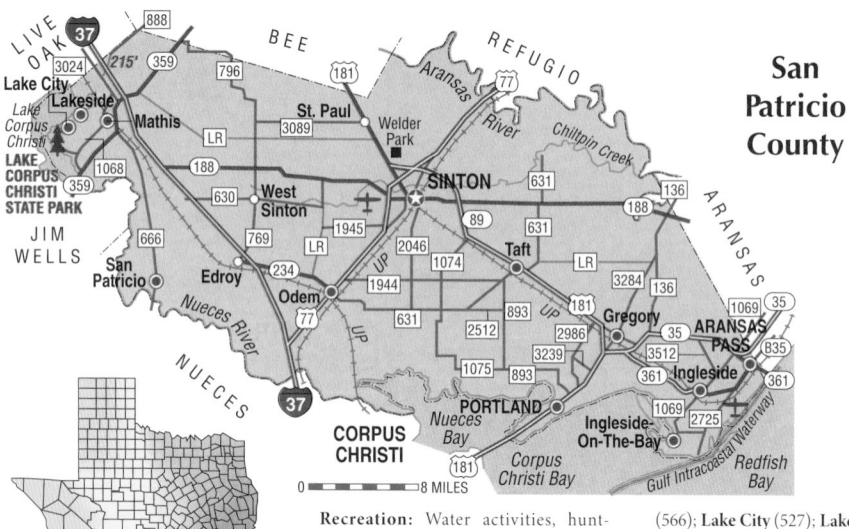

San Patricio County

Physical Features: Grassy, coastal prairie draining to Aransas, Nueces rivers and to bays; sandy loam, clay, black loam soils; Lake Corpus Christi.

Economy: Oil, petrochemicals, agribusiness, manufacturing, tourism, in Corpus Christi metropolitan area.

History: Karankawa area. Mexican sheep herders in the area before colonization. Settled by Irish families in 1830 (name is Spanish for St. Patrick). Created, named for municipality in 1836; organized in 1837, reorganized in 1847.

Race/Ethnicity: Anglo, 37.9%; Black, 1.3%; Hispanic, 58.4%; Asian, 0.7%; Other, 1.4%.

Vital Statistics, annual: Births, 1,021; deaths, 642; marriages, 290; divorces, 243.

Recreation: Water activities, hunting, Corpus Christi Bay, state park, Welder Wildlife Foundation and Park, birdwatching.

Minerals: Oil, gas, gravel, caliche.

Agriculture: Cotton, grain sorghum, beef cattle, corn. Market value $131.3 million. Fisheries income significant.

SINTON (5,240) county seat; oil, agribusiness, tourism; Go Texan Days in October.

ARANSAS PASS (8,388, part [808] in Aransas County) deepwater port, shrimping, tourism, offshore oil-well servicing, aluminum and chemical plants; hospital; Shrimporee in May.

PORTLAND (22,115) retail center, petrochemicals, commuters to Corpus Christi; Indian Point pier; Windfest in April.

Other towns include: **Edroy** (301); **Gregory** (1,854); **Ingleside** (9,895) offshore well servicing, chemical and manufacturing plants, commuters, birding, Round Up Days in April; **Ingleside-on-the-Bay**

(566); **Lake City** (527); **Lakeside** (300); **Mathis** (4,800); **Odem** (2,367); **St. Paul** (596); **San Patricio** (402); **Taft** (2,862) agriculture, drug rehabilitation center, commuters, wind farm, blackland museum, barbecue, tamale and hot sauce cook-off in December; **Taft Southwest** (1,342).

Population	**66,688**
Change from 2010 (%)	2.9
Area (sq. mi.)	707.8
Land Area (sq. mi.)	693.5
Altitude (ft.)	sea level–215
Rainfall (in.)	35.3
Jan. mean min (°F)	44.2
July mean max (°F)	93.4
Civ. Labor	29,426
Unemployed (%)	9.6
Wages	$270,186,138
Per Capita Income	$46,506
Prop. Value	$20,567,988,963
Retail Sales	$959,265,084

For explanation of sources, symbols and abbreviations, see p. 204, and foldout map.

West Texas Feed and Mercantile shop in Eldorado. Photo by Billy Hathorn, CC/Wikimedia Commons

San Saba County

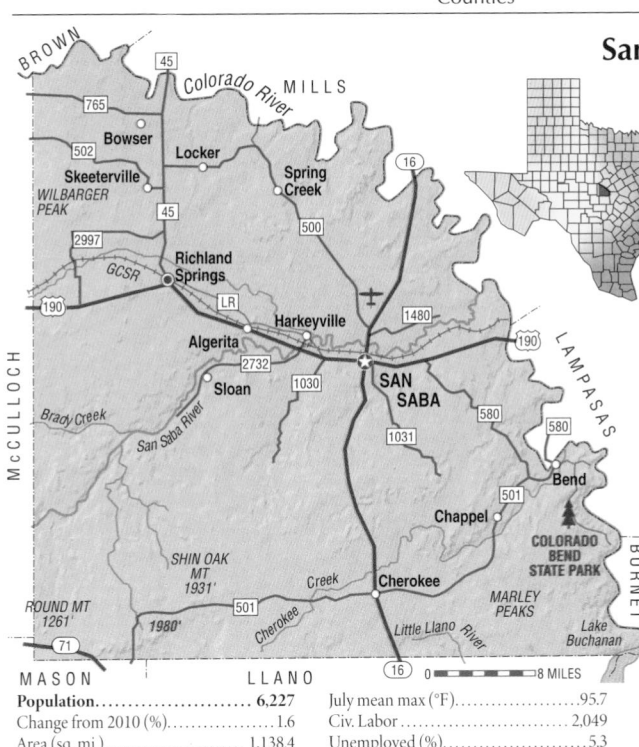

Physical Features: West central county; hilly, rolling; bisected by San Saba River; Colorado River on east; black, gray sandy loam, alluvial soils; northern tip of Lake Buchanan.

Economy: Pecan processing plants, tourism, hunting leases.

History: Apaches and Comanches in the area when Spanish explored. Anglo-American settlers arrived in 1850s. County created from Bexar District in 1856, organized the same year; named for river.

Race/Ethnicity: Anglo, 63.8%; Black, 3.2%; Hispanic, 31.3%; Asian, 0.1%; Other, 1.3%.

Vital Statistics, annual: Births, 73; deaths, 54; marriages, 13; divorces, 2.

Recreation: State park with Gorman Falls; deer hunting; historic sites; fishing; scenic drives; wildflower trail.

Minerals: Rock quarry, limestone and sand stone.

Agriculture: Cattle, pecans (second in acreage), wheat, hay, some sheep/goats. Market value $35.8 million. Hunting, wildlife leases.

SAN SABA (3,212) county seat; claims title "Pecan Capital of the World"; stone processing, varied manufacturing, prison; Cow Camp cookoff in May.

Other towns include: Bend (115, partly in Lampasas County); **Cherokee** (175); **Richland Springs** (330).

Population...................... **6,227**	July mean max (°F)....................95.7
Change from 2010 (%)................1.6	Civ. Labor............................ 2,049
Area (sq. mi.)...................... 1,138.4	Unemployed (%)........................5.3
Land Area (sq. mi.)................. 1,135.3	Wages $14,622,151
Altitude (ft.)...................1,020–1,980	Per Capita Income $40,521
Rainfall (in.)............................28.5	Prop. Value $2,540,849,995
Jan. mean min (°F)....................34.6	Retail Sales $35,289,743

Schleicher County

Physical Features: West central county on edge of Edwards Plateau, broken by Devils, Concho, San Saba tributaries; part hilly; black soils.

Economy: Oil, ranching, hunting.

History: Jumanos in the area in the 1630s. Later, Apaches and Comanches; removed in the 1870s. Ranching began in the 1870s. Census of 1890 showed third of population from Mexico. County named for Gustav Schleicher, founder of German colony; county created from Crockett County in 1887, organized in 1901.

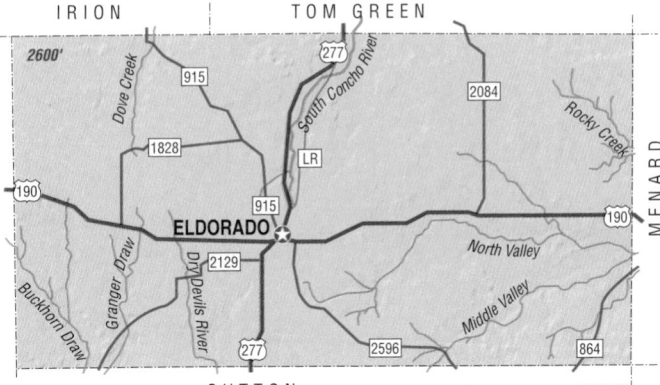

Race/Ethnicity: Anglo, 42.8%; Black, 1%; Hispanic, 55.3%; Asian, 0.1%; Other, 0.5%.

Vital Statistics, annual: Births, 23; deaths, 23; marriages, 11; divorces, 5.

For explanation of sources, symbols and abbreviations, see p. 204, and foldout map.

Recreation: Hunting, livestock show in January, youth and open rodeos, mountain bike events.

Minerals: Oil, natural gas.

Agriculture: Beef cattle, sheep, goats, and cotton, hay. Market value $17.8 million. Hunting leases important.

ELDORADO (1,584) county seat; oil activities, center for livestock, mohair marketing, woolen mill, government/services; hospital.

Population...................... **2,822**	
Change from 2010 (%)................-18.5	
Area (sq. mi.)...................... 1,310.7	
Land Area (sq. mi.)................. 1,310.6	
Altitude (ft.)...................2,070–2,600	
Rainfall (in.)............................23.2	
Jan. mean min (°F)....................31.1	
July mean max (°F)....................92.1	
Civ. Labor............................ 1,144	
Unemployed (%)........................5.9	
Wages $8,650,864	
Per Capita Income $42,255	
Prop. Value $1,362,126,357	
Retail Sales $10,018,720	

Scurry County

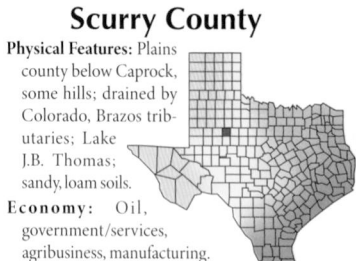

Physical Features: Plains county below Caprock, some hills; drained by Colorado, Brazos tributaries; Lake J.B. Thomas; sandy, loam soils.

Economy: Oil, government/services, agribusiness, manufacturing.

History: Apaches; displaced later by Comanches who were relocated to Indian Territory in 1875. Ranching began in the late 1870s. County created from Bexar District in 1876; organized in 1884; named for Confederate Gen. W.R. Scurry.

Race/Ethnicity: Anglo, 51%; Black, 4.2%; Hispanic, 43%; Asian, 0.3%; Other, 1.2%.

Vital Statistics, annual: Births, 230; deaths, 179; marriages, 134; divorces, 63.

Recreation: Lake J.B. Thomas water recreation; Towle Memorial Park; museums, community theater, White Buffalo Days and Bikefest in October.

Minerals: Oil, gas.

Agriculture: Cotton, wheat, cattle, hay. Market value $45.2 million.

SNYDER (11,073) county seat; oil, wind energy, agriculture; Western Texas College, hospital, museum; Western Swing days in June.

Other towns include: **Dunn** (75); **Fluvanna** (180); **Hermleigh** (308); **Ira** (250).

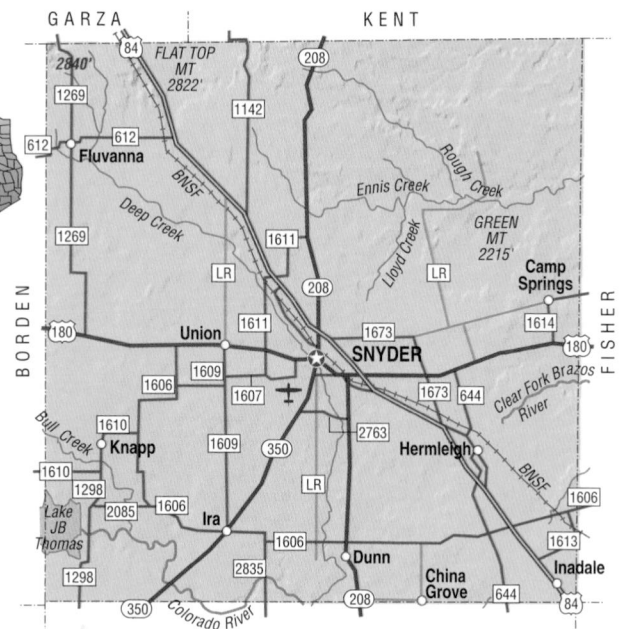

Population......................16,697	July mean max (°F)....................93.9
Change from 2010 (%).................-1.3	Civ. Labor............................5,962
Area (sq. mi.)......................907.5	Unemployed (%)........................7.5
Land Area (sq. mi.)..................905.4	Wages.........................$76,933,827
Altitude (ft.)..................1,800–2,840	Per Capita Income................$42,915
Rainfall (in.)......................22.7	Prop. Value...............$3,893,433,314
Jan. mean min (°F)....................28.2	Retail Sales..................$257,617,903

Shackelford County

Physical Features: Rolling, hilly, drained by tributaries of Brazos; sandy and chocolate loam soils; lake.

Economy: Oil and ranching, some manufacturing, hunting leases.

History: Apaches; driven out by Comanches. First Anglo-American settlers arrived soon after establishment of military outpost in the 1850s. County created from Bosque County in 1858; organized in 1874; named for Dr. Jack Shackelford (sometimes referred to as John), Texas Revolution hero.

Race/Ethnicity: Anglo, 86.5%; Black, 0.4%; Hispanic, 11.2%; Asian, 0.3%; Other, 1.4%.

Vital Statistics, annual: Births, 43; deaths, 27; marriages, 14; divorces, 15.

Recreation: Fort Griffin historic site, courthouse historical district, hunting, lake, outdoor activities, June Fandangle musical about area history.

Minerals: Oil, natural gas.

Agriculture: Beef cattle, wheat, hay, cotton. Market value $16.6 million. Hunting leases.

ALBANY (2,037) county seat; oil, ranching, hunting; medical clinics; historical district, Old Jail art center, car museum.

Other town: **Moran** (275).

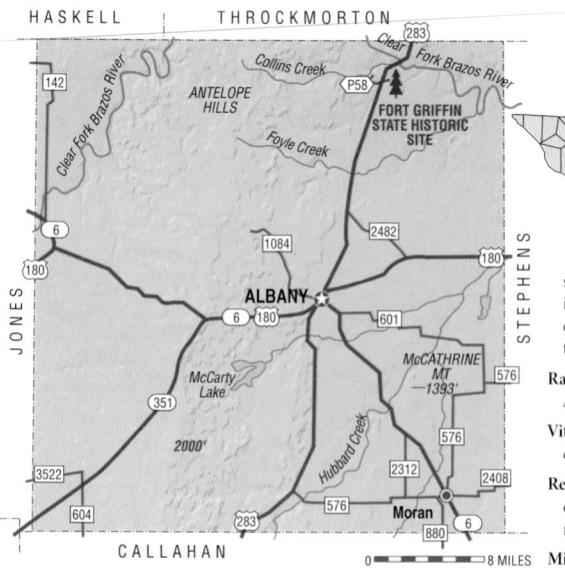

Population.......................3,382	July mean max (°F)....................94.4
Change from 2010 (%).................0.1	Civ. Labor............................1,759
Area (sq. mi.)......................915.6	Unemployed (%)........................4.2
Land Area (sq. mi.)..................914.3	Wages.........................$16,778,328
Altitude (ft.)..................1,150–2,000	Per Capita Income................$113,163
Rainfall (in.)......................28.4	Prop. Value...............$1,265,455,306
Jan. mean min (°F)....................30.2	Retail Sales..................$19,064,302

Shelby County

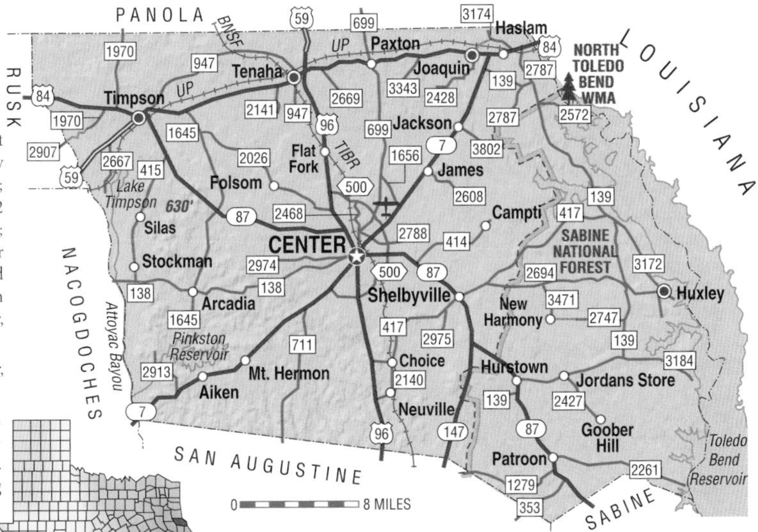

Physical Features: East Texas county; partly hills, much bottomland; well-timbered, 67,762 acres in national forest; Attoyac Bayou, other streams; Toledo Bend Reservoir, Pinkston Reservoir; sandy, clay, alluvial soils.

Economy: Poultry, timber, cattle, tourism.

History: Caddo Indian area. First Anglo-Americans settled in the 1810s. Antebellum slaveholding area. Original county of the Republic, created in 1836; organized in 1837; named for Isaac Shelby of the American Revolution.

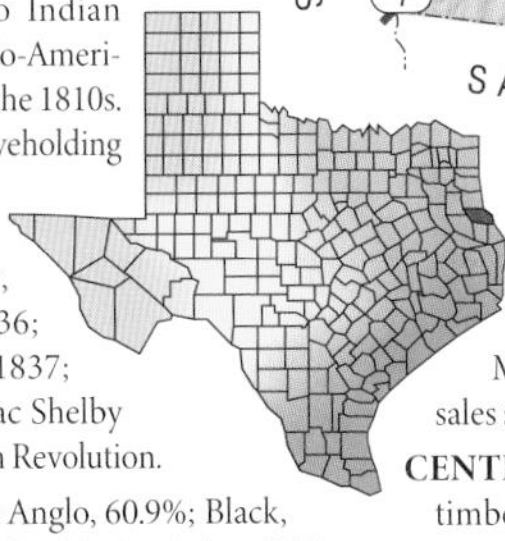

Race/Ethnicity: Anglo, 60.9%; Black, 16.9%; Hispanic, 20.1%; Asian, 0.5%; Other, 1.3%.

Vital Statistics, annual: Births, 390; deaths, 300; marriages, 189; divorces, 60.

Recreation: Toledo Bend Reservoir activities; Sabine National Forest; hunting, fishing, camping; historic sites, restored 1885 courthouse.

Minerals: Natural gas, oil.

Agriculture: First in poultry and egg production. Beef cattle and hay. Market value $467.6 million. Timber sales significant.

CENTER (5,335) county seat; poultry, timber, oil and gas, tourism; hospital, Panola College extension, museum; What-A-Melon festival in July, poultry festival in October.

Other towns include: **Huxley** (372); **Joaquin** (795); **Shelbyville** (600); **Tenaha** (1,144); **Timpson** (1,124) livestock, timber, farming, commuters, genealogy library, Frontier Days in July.

For explanation of sources, symbols and abbreviations, see p. 204, and foldout map.

Population.	**24,249**
Change from 2010 (%).	-4.7
Area (sq. mi.).	834.6
Land Area (sq. mi.).	795.6
Altitude (ft.).	174–630
Rainfall (in.).	54.2
Jan. mean min (°F).	35.1
July mean max (°F).	94.4
Civ. Labor.	11,346
Unemployed (%).	6.1
Wages.	$95,835,679
Per Capita Income.	$41,767
Prop. Value.	$2,830,567,285
Retail Sales.	$297,217,790

The police station and City Hall for Timpson in Shelby County. Photo by Hourick, public domain/Wikimedia Commons

Sherman County

Physical Features: A northern Panhandle county; level, broken by creeks, playas; sandy to dark loam soils; underground water.

Economy: Agribusiness, tourism.

History: Apaches; pushed out by Comanches in the 1700s. Comanches removed to Indian Territory in 1875. Ranching began around 1880; farming after 1900. County named for Republic of Texas Gen. Sidney Sherman; created from Bexar District in 1876; organized in 1889.

Race/Ethnicity: Anglo, 51.9%; Black, 0.4%; Hispanic, 46.3%; Asian, 0.1%; Other, 1.1%.

Vital Statistics, annual: Births, 39; deaths, 34; marriages, 16; divorces, 9.

Recreation: Depot museum; pheasant, pronghorn hunting, jamboree and rodeo in July, carriage driving event in September.

Minerals: Natural gas, oil.

Agriculture: Beef and stocker cattle, wheat, corn, milo, cotton; 127,000 acres irrigated. Market value $838.1 million.

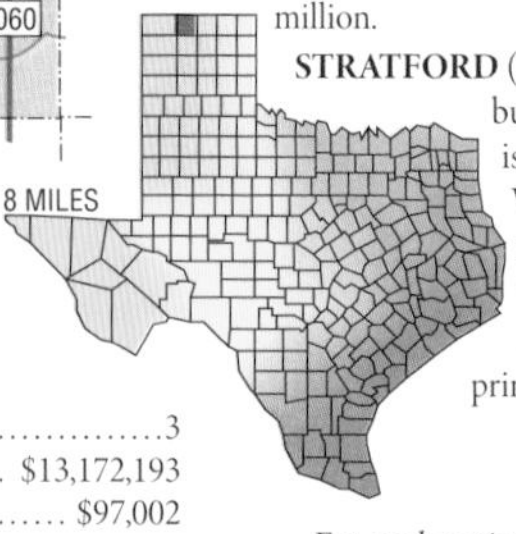

STRATFORD (2,049) county seat; agribusiness, petroleum, tourism, birdseed packaging; VA clinic; science and art museum.

Texhoma (1,142 [with 333 in Texas]) other principal town.

For explanation of sources, symbols and abbreviations, see p. 204, and foldout map.

Population	3,077
Change from 2010 (%)	1.4
Area (sq. mi.)	923.2
Land Area (sq. mi.)	923.0
Altitude (ft.)	3,200–3,805
Rainfall (in.)	17.8
Jan. mean min (°F)	19.5
July mean max (°F)	91.5
Civ. Labor	1,362
Unemployed (%)	3
Wages	$13,172,193
Per Capita Income	$97,002
Prop. Value	$1,067,975,244
Retail Sales	$47,992,202

Some nice old buildings across the street from Tyler City Square in Smith County. Photo by Rupak.bhattacharya, CC 3.0/Wikimedia Commons

Smith County

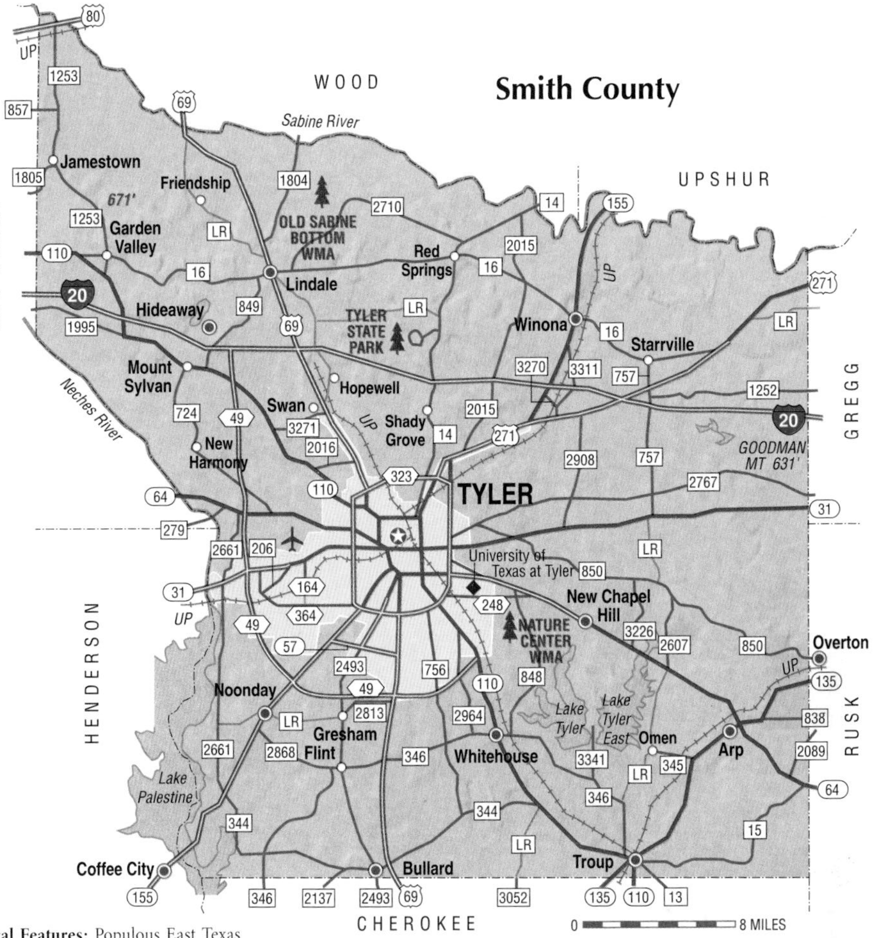

WOOD

UPSHUR

VAN ZANDT

GREGG

HENDERSON

RUSK

CHEROKEE

0 ■■■■■ 8 MILES

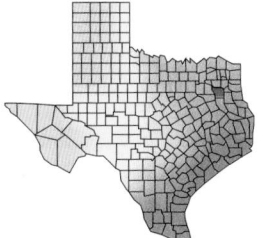

Physical Features: Populous East Texas county of rolling hills, many timbered; Sabine, Neches rivers, other streams; Lake Palestine, Lake Tyler, Lake Tyler East; alluvial, gray, sandy loam, clay soils.

Economy: Medical facilities, education, government/services, agribusiness, petroleum production, manufacturing, distribution center, tourism.

History: Caddoes of area reduced by disease and other tribes in the 1790s. Cherokees settled in the 1820s; removed in 1839. In the late 1820s, first Anglo-American settlers arrived. Antebellum slaveholding area. County named for Texas Revolution Gen. James Smith; county created and organized in 1846 from Nacogdoches County.

Race/Ethnicity: Anglo, 59%; Black, 16.9%; Hispanic, 20.1%; Asian, 1.6%; Other, 2.1%.

Vital Statistics, annual: Births, 3,109; deaths, 2,111; marriages, 1,717; divorces, 659.

Recreation: Activities on Palestine, Tyler lakes; Rose Garden; state park; Goodman Museum; Caldwell Zoo; collegiate events; Juneteenth celebration, Rose Festival in October, Azalea Trail, East Texas Fair in September/October.

Minerals: Oil, gas.

Agriculture: Horticultural crops and nurseries, beef cattle, forages, fruits and vegetables, horses, Christmas trees. Market value $53.6 million. Timber sales substantial.

TYLER (108,173) county seat; health services, education, retail center, varied manufacturing; University of Texas at Tyler, Tyler Junior College, Texas College, University of Texas Health Science Center; hospitals, nursing school; museums, Camp Ford historic park; styles itself, "City of Roses".

Other towns include: **Arp** (1,036) Strawberry Festival in April; **Bullard** (2,872, part in Cherokee County); **Flint** (2,500); **Hideaway** (3,191); **Lindale** (6,496) distribution center, foundry, varied manufacturing, Country Fest in October; **New Chapel Hill** (637); **Noonday** (811) Sweet Onion festival in June; **Troup** (1,980, part in Cherokee County) plastic manufacturing, motorcyle customization, Crawfish Boil in May; **Whitehouse** (8,899) commuters to Tyler, government/services, Yesteryear festival in June; and **Winona** (599).

Part of **Overton** (2,503, mostly in Rusk County).

Population	**231,516**
Change from 2010 (%)	10.4
Area (sq. mi.)	949.7
Land Area (sq. mi.)	921.5
Altitude (ft.)	275–671
Rainfall (in.)	46.6
Jan. mean min (°F)	36.4
July mean max (°F)	92.7
Civ. Labor	110,097
Unemployed (%)	5.6
Wages	$1,388,942,257
Per Capita Income	$56,292
Prop. Value	$25,760,133,062
Retail Sales	$4,238,328,465

Somervell County

Physical Features: Hilly terrain southwest of Fort Worth; Brazos, Paluxy rivers; Squaw Creek Reservoir; gray, dark, alluvial soils; second-smallest county.

Economy: Nuclear power plant, tourism.

History: Wichita, Tonkawa area; Comanches arrived later. Anglo-Americans arrived in the 1850s. County created in 1875 as Somerville County from Hood County, organized the same year. Spelling was changed in 1876; named for Republic of Texas Gen. Alexander Somervell.

Race/Ethnicity: Anglo, 74.8%; Black, 0.6%; Hispanic, 21.8%; Asian, 0.5%; Other, 2.1%.

Vital Statistics, annual: Births, 77; deaths, 98; mmarriages, 81; divorces, 22.

Recreation: Fishing, hunting; unique geological formations; dinosaur tracks in state park; Glen Rose Big Rocks Park; Fossil Rim Wildlife Center; nature trails, museums; exposition center; Paluxy Pedal bicycle ride in October.

Minerals: Sand, gravel, silica, natural gas.

Agriculture: Cattle, hay. Market value $4.1 million. Hunting leases important.

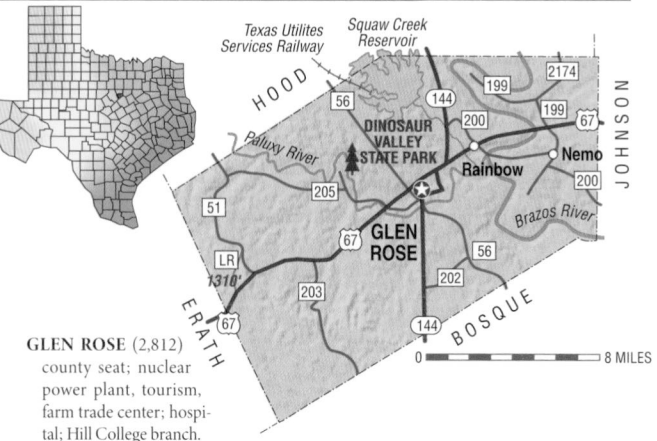

GLEN ROSE (2,812) county seat; nuclear power plant, tourism, farm trade center; hospital; Hill College branch.

Other towns include: **Nemo** (56); **Rainbow** (121).

Population	**9,569**
Change from 2010 (%)	12.7
Area (sq. mi.)	192.0
Land Area (sq. mi.)	186.5
Altitude (ft.)	550–1,310

Rainfall (in.)	36.9
Jan. mean min (°F)	27.4
July mean max (°F)	97.0
Civ. Labor	4,385
Unemployed (%)	5.7
Wages	$57,804,184
Per Capita Income	$45,812
Prop. Value	$3,743,194,579
Retail Sales	$54,402,437

Starr County

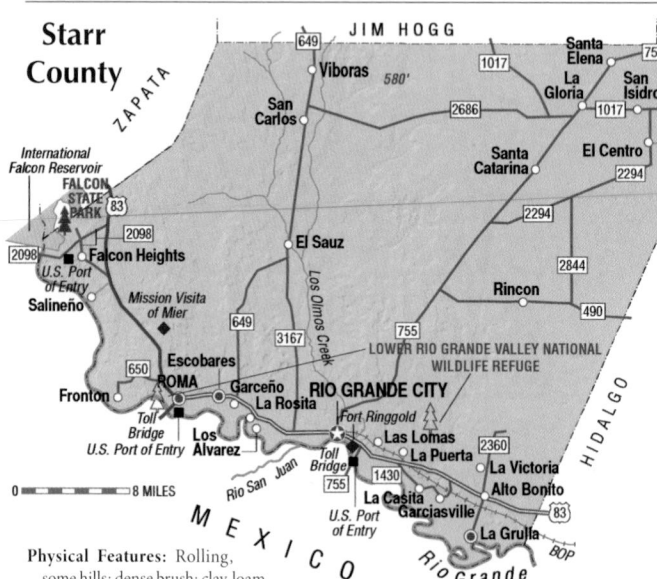

Population	**63,690**
Change from 2010 (%)	4.5
Area (sq. mi.)	1,229.1
Land Area (sq. mi.)	1,223.2
Altitude (ft.)	125–580
Rainfall (in.)	22.7
Jan. mean min (°F)	45.9
July mean max (°F)	98.4
Civ. Labor	26,452
Unemployed (%)	17.7
Wages	$136,437,394
Per Capita Income	$27,713
Prop. Value	$3,330,907,105
Retail Sales	$521,591,939

Physical Features: Rolling, some hills; dense brush; clay, loam, sandy soils, alluvial on Rio Grande; Falcon Reservoir.

Economy: Vegetable packing, other agribusiness, oil processing, tourism, government/services.

History: Coahuiltecan Indian area. Settlers from Spanish villages that were established in 1749 on south bank began to move across river soon afterward. Fort Ringgold established in 1848. County named for Dr. J.H. Starr, secretary of treasury of the Republic; county created from Nueces County and organized in 1848.

Race/Ethnicity: Anglo, 4.2%; Black, 0%; Hispanic, 95.4%; Asian, 0.1%; Other, 0.1%.

Vital Statistics, annual: Births, 1,283; deaths, 397; marriages, 409; divorces, 0.

Recreation: Falcon Reservoir activities; deer, white-wing dove hunting; access to Mexico; historic houses, Lee House at Fort Ringgold; grotto at Rio Grande City; Roma Fest in November.

Minerals: Oil, gas, sand, gravel.

Agriculture: Beef and fed cattle; vegetables, cotton, sorghum; 8,500 acres irrigated for vegetables. Market value $47.2 million.

RIO GRANDE CITY (15,074) county seat; government/services, tourism, agriculture; hospital, college branches; trolley tours; Vaquero Days in February.

ROMA-Los Saenz (11,221) agriculture center; La Purísima Concepción Visita.

Other towns include: **Delmita** (226); **Escobares** (2,837); **Falcon Heights** (56); **Fronton** (170); **Garceño** (391); **Garciasville** (59); **La Casita** (112); **La Grulla** (1,688); **La Puerta** (590); **La Rosita** (70); **Las Lomas** (3,295); **La Victoria** (156); **Los Alvarez** (286); **North Escobares** (108); **Salineño** (175); **San Isidro** (227); **Santa Elena** (35).

Stephens County

Physical Features: West central county; broken, hilly; Hubbard Creek Reservoir, Possum Kingdom Lake, Lake Daniel; Brazos River; loam, sandy soils.

Economy: Oil, agribusiness, manufacturing, recreation.

History: Comanches, Tonkawas in the area when Anglo-American settlement began in the 1850s. County created as Buchanan in 1858 from Bosque County; renamed in 1861 for Confederate Vice President Alexander H. Stephens; organized in 1876.

Race/Ethnicity: Anglo, 69.9%; Black, 2%; Hispanic, 25.8%; Asian, 0.4%; Other, 1.6%.

Vital Statistics, annual: Births, 119; deaths, 107; marriages, 61; divorces, 14.

Recreation: Lake activities, state park, hunting, campsites, historical points, Swenson Museum, Sandefer Oil Museum, aviation museum, festival and car show in fall.

Minerals: Oil, natural gas, stone.

Agriculture: Beef cattle, hogs, goats, sheep; wheat, oats, hay, peanuts, grain sorghum, cotton, pecans. Market value $10.6 million.

BRECKENRIDGE (5,684) county seat; oil, agriculture, oil-field equipment, aircraft parts; hospital, prison, Texas State Technical College branch, library.

Other towns include: **Caddo** (70) gateway to Possum Kingdom State Park.

For explanation of sources, symbols and abbreviations, see p. 204, and foldout map.

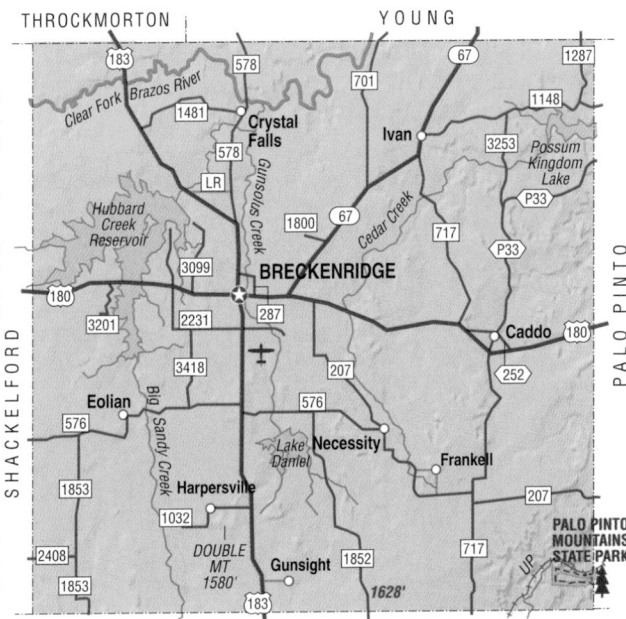

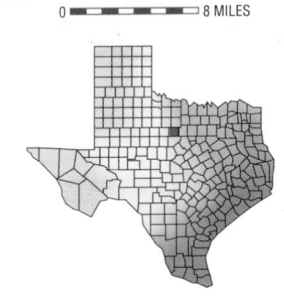

Population	9,556
Change from 2010 (%)	-0.8
Area (sq. mi.)	921.5
Land Area (sq. mi.)	896.7
Altitude (ft.)	995–1,628
Rainfall (in.)	30.0
Jan. mean min (°F)	30.3
July mean max (°F)	95.8
Civ. Labor	4,026
Unemployed (%)	5.4
Wages	$34,944,969
Per Capita Income	$43,971
Prop. Value	$1,571,009,951
Retail Sales	$89,794,858

An old stone building in Rio Grande City. Photo by Carol M. Highsmith, courtesy of the Library of Congress

Sterling County

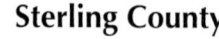

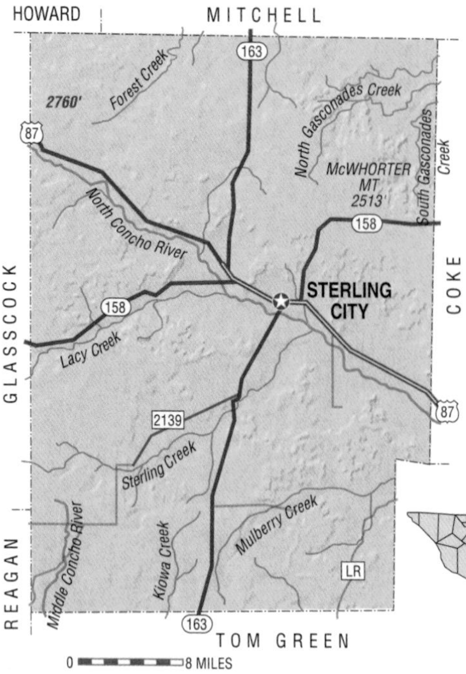

Physical Features: Central prairie, surrounded by hills, broken by Concho River and tributaries; sandy to black soils.

Economy: Ranching, oil and gas, government/services.

History: Ranching began in the late 1870s after the Comanches, Kickapoos, and other tribes were removed by the U.S. Army. County named for buffalo hunter W.S. Sterling; created in 1891 from Tom Green County, organized the same year.

Race/Ethnicity: Anglo, 63.5%; Black, 0.7%; Hispanic, 33%; Asian, 0%; Other, 2.5%.

Vital Statistics, annual: Births, 16; deaths, 9; marriages, 9; divorces, 1.

Recreation: Hunting of deer, quail, turkey, dove; hunters appreciation dinner in November; junior livestock show in December.

Minerals: Oil, natural gas.

Agriculture: Cattle, sheep/goats, horses, wheat, hay; about 600 acres irrigated. Market value $7.7 million. Hunting leases important.

STERLING CITY (964) county seat; farm, ranch trade center, oil-field services.

Population	1,254
Change from 2010 (%)	9.7
Area (sq. mi.)	923.5
Land Area (sq. mi.)	923.5
Altitude (ft.)	2,000–2,760
Rainfall (in.)	20.5
Jan. mean min (°F)	28.2
July mean max (°F)	93.6
Civ. Labor	579
Unemployed (%)	6.0
Wages	$6,729,972
Per Capita Income	$61,920
Prop. Value	$916,417,867
Retail Sales	$14,433,638

Stonewall County

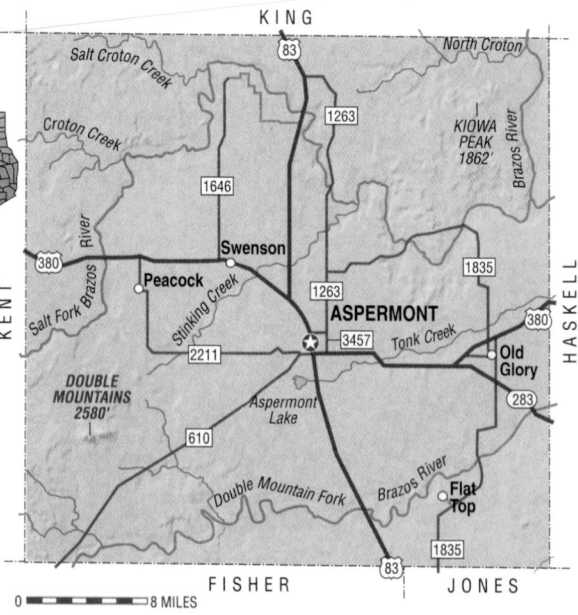

Physical Features: Western county on Rolling Plains below Caprock, bisected by Brazos forks; sandy loam, sandy, other soils; some hills.

Economy: Agribusiness, light fabrication, government/services.

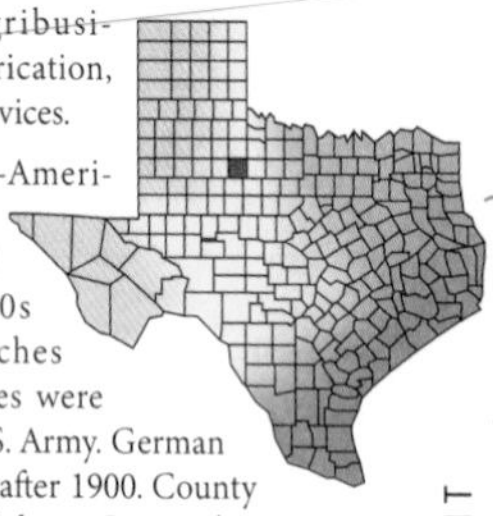

History: Anglo-American ranchers arrived in the 1870s after Comanches and other tribes were removed by U.S. Army. German farmers settled after 1900. County named for Confederate Gen. T.J. (Stonewall) Jackson; created from Bexar District 1876, organized in 1888.

Race/Ethnicity: Anglo, 78.5%; Black, 2%; Hispanic, 16.8%; Asian, 0.8%; Other, 1.5%.

Vital Statistics, annual: Births, 20; deaths, 29; marriages, 4; divorces, 3.

Recreation: Deer, quail, feral hog, turkey hunting; rodeos in June, September.

Minerals: Gypsum, gravel, oil.

Agriculture: Beef cattle, wheat, cotton, peanuts, hay. Also, grain sorghum, meat goats and swine. Market value $15.5 million.

ASPERMONT (861) county seat; oil field and ranching center, light fabrication; hospital; livestock show in February, Springfest.

Other towns include: **Old Glory** (100) farming center.

Population	1,382	July mean max (°F)	97.0
Change from 2010 (%)	-7.2	Civ. Labor	576
Area (sq. mi.)	920.2	Unemployed (%)	4.0
Land Area (sq. mi.)	916.3	Wages	$5,551,554
Altitude (ft.)	1,450–2,580	Per Capita Income	$58,541
Rainfall (in.)	23.8	Prop. Value	$758,272,926
Jan. mean min (°F)	28.5	Retail Sales	$23,653,596

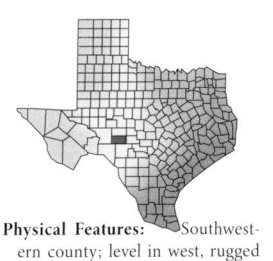

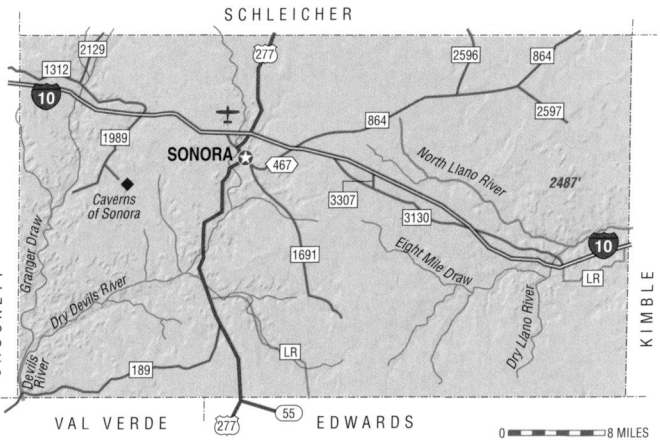

Physical Features: Southwestern county; level in west, rugged terrain in east, broken by tributaries of Devils, Llano rivers; black, red loam soils.

Economy: Natural gas, ranching, hunting.

History: Lipan Apaches drove out Tonkawas in 1600s. Comanches, military outpost, and disease forced Apaches south. Anglo-Americans settled in 1870s. Mexican immigration increased after 1890. County created from Crockett in 1887; organized in 1890; named for Confederate Col. John S. Sutton.

Race/Ethnicity: Anglo, 36.1%; Black, 0%; Hispanic, 63%; Asian, 0.2%; Other, 0.5%.

Vital Statistics, annual: Births, 50; deaths, 30; marriages, 25; divorces, 9.

Recreation: Hunting, Miers Museum, ranch museum, Caverns of Sonora, wildlife sanctuary, Cinco de Mayo.

Minerals: Oil, natural gas.

Sutton County

Agriculture: Meat goats (first in numbers), sheep, cattle, Angora goats (second in numbers). Exotic wildlife. Wheat and oats raised for grazing, hay; minor irrigation. Market value $10.4 million. Hunting leases important.

SONORA (2,967) county seat; natural gas production, ranching, tourism; Dry Devils River Music Flood in October.

Population	3,664
Change from 2010 (%)	-11.2
Area (sq. mi.)	1,454.4
Land Area (sq. mi.)	1,453.9
Altitude (ft.)	1,840–2,487
Rainfall (in.)	23.0
Jan. mean min (°F)	29.2
July mean max (°F)	94.4
Civ. Labor	1,158
Unemployed (%)	8.9
Wages	$19,513,451
Per Capita Income	$61,646
Prop. Value	$1,735,871,766
Retail Sales	$69,181,522

Swisher County

Physical Features: High Plains; level, broken by Tule Canyon and Creek; playas; large underground water supply; rich soils.

Economy: Cotton processing, manufacturing.

History: Apaches; displaced by Comanches around 1700. U.S. Army removed Comanches in 1874. Ranching began in the late 1870s. Farming developed after 1900. County named for J.G. Swisher of Texas Revolution; county created from Bexar, Young territories in 1876; organized in 1890.

Race/Ethnicity: Anglo, 45.9%; Black, 8%; Hispanic, 44%; Asian, 0%; Other, 1.8%.

Vital Statistics, annual: Births, 111; deaths, 81; marriages, 27; divorces, 4.

Recreation: Mackenzie battle site, Picnic celebration in July at Tulia.

Minerals: Not significant.

Agriculture: Cotton, cattle, wheat, corn, sorghum, cucumbers. Some 65,000 acres irrigated. Market value $623.9 million.

TULIA (4,698) county seat; agriculture, government/services, manufacturing; hospital, library, museum.

Other towns include: **Happy** (666, partly in Randall County); **Kress** (683); **Vigo Park** (36).

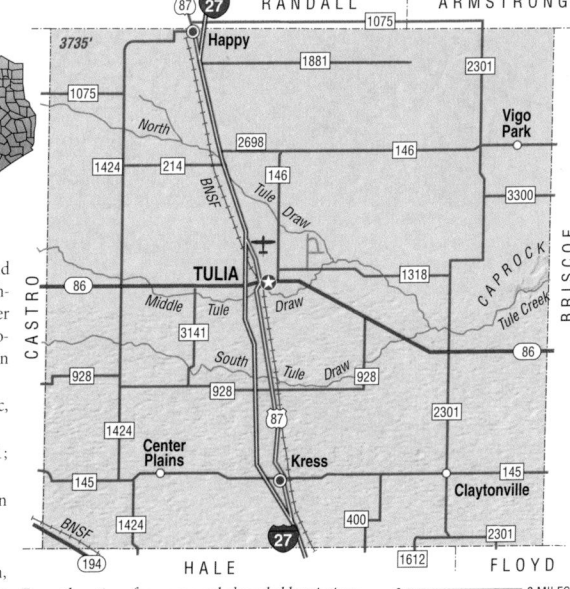

For explanation of sources, symbols and abbreviations, see p. 204, and foldout map.

Population	7,439
Change from 2010 (%)	-5.3
Area (sq. mi.)	900.7
Land Area (sq. mi.)	890.2
Altitude (ft.)	3,160–3,735
Rainfall (in.)	21.6
Jan. mean min (°F)	22.0
July mean max (°F)	91.9
Civ. Labor	2,596
Unemployed (%)	5.2
Wages	$18,972,203
Per Capita Income	$51,779
Prop. Value	$914,894,780
Retail Sales	$45,745,610

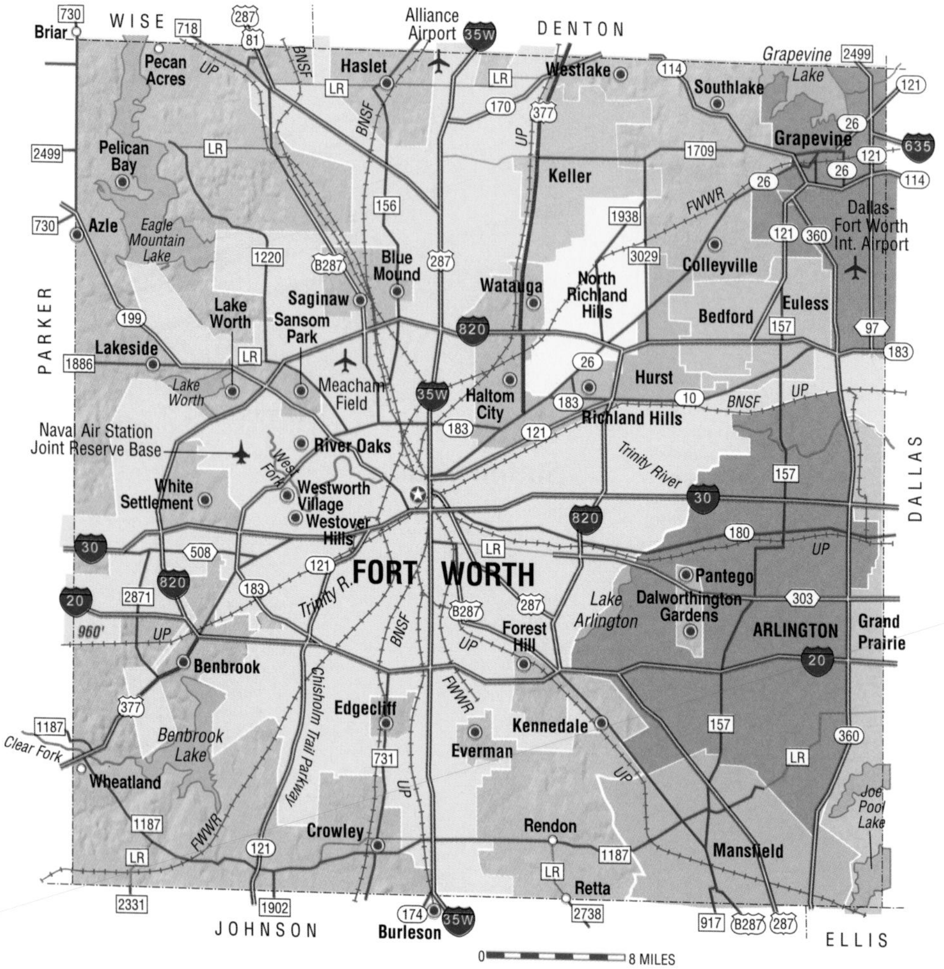

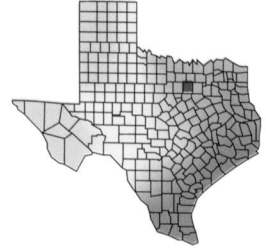

Tarrant County

Physical Features: Part Blackland, level to rolling; drains to Trinity; Lake Worth, Grapevine Lake, Eagle Mountain Lake, Benbrook Lake, Joe Pool Lake, Lake Arlington.

Economy: Tourism, planes, helicopters, foods, mobile homes, electronic equipment, chemicals, plastics among products of more than 1,000 factories, large federal expenditure, D/FW International Airport, economy closely associated with Dallas urban area.

History: Caddoes in area. Comanches, other tribes arrived about 1700. Anglo-Americans settled in the 1840s. Named for Republic of Texas Gen. Edward H. Tarrant, who helped drive Indian tribes from area. County created in 1849 from Navarro County; organized in 1850.

Race/Ethnicity: Anglo, 46%; Black, 16.3%; Hispanic, 29%; Asian, 5.6%; Other, 2.9%.

Vital Statistics, annual: Births, 28,364; deaths, 12,277; marriages, 14,067; divorces, 7,354.

Recreation: Scott Theatre; Amon G. Carter Museum; Kimbell Art Museum; Modern Art Museum; Museum of Science and History; Casa Mañana; Botanic Gardens; Fort Worth Zoo; Log Cabin Village, all in Fort Worth.

Also, Six Flags Over Texas at Arlington; Southwestern Exposition, Stock Show; Convention Center; Stockyards Historical District; Texas Rangers and Dallas Cowboys at Arlington, other athletic events.

Minerals: Production of cement, sand, gravel, stone, gas.

Agriculture: Hay, beef cattle, wheat, horses, horticulture. Market value $29.4 million. Firewood marketed.

Education: Texas Christian University, University of Texas at Arlington, Texas Wesleyan University, Texas A&M University School of Law, University of North Texas Health Science Center, Southwestern Baptist Theological Seminary, Tarleton State University branch, and several other academic centers including a junior college system with five campuses and various centers.

FORT WORTH (895,100, small parts in Denton, Parker and Wise counties) county seat; a major mercantile, commercial and financial center; airplane, helicopter and other manufacturing plants; hospitals/health care; distribution center; oil and gas; stock show and rodeo January/February.

A cultural center with renowned art museums, Bass Performance Hall; many conventions held in downtown center; agribusiness center for wide area with grain-storage and feed-mill operations; adjacent to D/FW International Airport.

ARLINGTON (391,791) University of Texas-Arlington, General Motors plant, tourism, the Texas Rangers baseball team, AT&T Stadium, retail, hospitals, bowling museum, art museum; Scottish festival in June.

Other towns include: **Hurst** (38,479); **Euless** (56,965); **Bedford** (49,530) helicopter plant, hospital, Celtic festival in fall (these three contiguous cities are sometimes referred to as H.E.B.).

Azle (13,285, partly in Parker County) government/services, retail, medical care/hospital, commuters to Fort Worth, museum, Sting Fling festival in September; **Benbrook** (23,912) varied manufacturing, hospitals; **Blue Mound** (2,435); **Briar** (6,301, parts in Wise and Parker counties).

Also, **Colleyville** (27,091) medical services, commuters, government/services, barbecue cookoff in April; **Crowley** (15,945) varied manufacturing, government/services, hospital; **Dalworthington Gardens** (2,333); **Edgecliff** (2,979); **Everman** (6,215); **Forest Hill** (12,894).

Also, **Grapevine** (54,277) tourist center, distribution, near the D/FW International Airport, hospitals, museums, art

Largest U.S. Media Markets

Rank	TV Homes
1. New York	7.10 million
2. Los Angeles	5.28 million
3. Chicago	3.25 million
4. Philadelphia	2.82 million
5. Dallas/Fort Worth	**2.62 million**
6. Washington, D.C.	2.48 million
7. Houston	**2.42 million**
8. San Francisco	2.41 million
9. Boston	2.36 million
10. Atlanta	2.34 million

Source: Nielsen Media Research, 2019.

galleries, Grapefest in September; **Haltom City** (43,003) light manufacturing, food processing, medical center; library; **Haslet** (1,928) commuters, government/services, chili fest and rodeo in May; **Keller** (46,651) Bear Creek Park, Wild West Fest.

Also, **Kennedale** (8,486) commuters, printing, manufacturing, library, drag strip, custom car show in May; **Lakeside** (1,635); **Lake Worth** (4,858) retail, tourism, museum, nature center; **Mansfield** (70,080, partly in Johnson, Ellis counties) varied manufacturing, retail, government/services, commuters, hospital, community college, library, museum, parks, Pecan festival in September; **North Richland**

Hills (71,210) hospital; **Pantego** (2,462); **Pelican Bay** (1,905); **Rendon** (14,490); **Richland Hills** (7,917).

Also, **River Oaks** (7,928); **Saginaw** (24,337) manufacturing, distribution/trucking, food processing/flour mill, Train & Grain festival in October; **Sansom Park** (5,625); **Southlake** (31,613) technology, financial, retail center, hospital, parks, Oktoberfest; **Watauga** (24,402); **Westlake** (1,725); **Westover Hills** (710); **Westworth Village** (2,772).

Also, **White Settlement** (17,719) aircraft manufacturing, drilling equipment, technological services, museums including Civil War museum, parks, historic sites; industrial park; settlers day festival in fall.

Also, part [9,983] of **Burleson**; part [61,070] of **Grand Prairie**, and part of **Pecan Acres** (4,745).

Population................... 2,060,239
Change from 2010 (%)................13.9
Area (sq. mi.)........................ 902.3
Land Area (sq. mi.)................. 863.6
Altitude (ft.)...................... 420–960
Rainfall (in.)..........................35.5
Jan. mean min (°F)................32.4
July mean max (°F).....................95.5
Civ. Labor.........................1,087,875
Unemployed (%)........................5.9
Wages $14,854,891,704
Per Capita Income $53,292
Prop. Value $269,626,851,344
Retail Sales $35,727,101,457

For explanation of sources, symbols and abbreviations, see p. 204, and foldout map.

A bird show featuring a hyacinth macaw at the Fort Worth Zoo. Photo by Jerry Tillery, CC 2/Wikimedia Commons

Physical Features: Prairies, with Callahan Divide, draining to Colorado River tributaries, Brazos River forks; Lake Abilene, Lake Kirby; mostly loam soils.

Economy: Agribusiness, oil and gas production, education, Dyess Air Force Base.

History: Comanches in the area about 1700. Anglo-American settlers arrived in the 1870s. Named for Alamo heroes Edward, James, and George Taylor, brothers; county created from Bexar, Travis counties in 1858 and organized in 1878.

Race/Ethnicity: Anglo, 62%; Black, 7.1%; Hispanic, 25.3%; Asian, 1.9%; Other, 3.4%.

Vital Statistics, annual: Births, 2,097; deaths, 1,378; marriages, 1285; divorces, 383.

Recreation: Abilene State Park, lake activities, Nelson Park Zoo, college events, Buffalo Gap historical tour and arts festival in April, Western Heritage ranch rodeo in May, as well as the West Texas Fair in September at Abilene.

Minerals: Oil, natural gas.

Taylor County

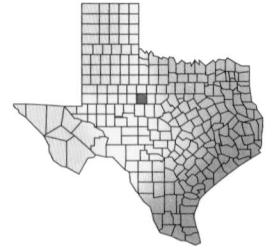

Agriculture: Beef cattle, small grains, cotton, milo. Market value $31.5 million.

Education: Abilene Christian University, Hardin-Simmons University, McMurry University, Texas Tech University pharmacy school, nursing school, and branch campus, and Cisco Junior College branch.

ABILENE (123,302, a small part in Jones County) county seat; retail center, oil and gas, military, colleges; hospitals, Abilene State School; Fort Phantom Hill (in Jones County). Wylie is now part of Abilene.

Other communities include: **Buffalo Gap** (512) historic sites; **Impact** (29); **Lawn** (315); **Merkel** (2,646) oil and wind energy, ranching, hunting, commuting, museum, health clinic, part of Bankhead Highway (early 1900s transcontinental route); classic car show in March; **Ovalo** (225); **Potosi** (3,574); **Trent** (347); **Tuscola** (753); **Tye** (1,318).

Population	139,044
Change from 2010 (%)	5.7
Area (sq. mi.)	919.3
Land Area (sq. mi.)	915.6
Altitude (ft.)	1,640–2,490
Rainfall (in.)	24.8
Jan. mean min (°F)	30.2
July mean max (°F)	94.2
Civ. Labor	66,701
Unemployed (%)	4.6
Wages	$790,472,878
Per Capita Income	$47,793
Prop. Value	$14,027,547,182
Retail Sales	$2,373,333,002

For explanation of sources, symbols and abbreviations, see p. 204, and foldout map.

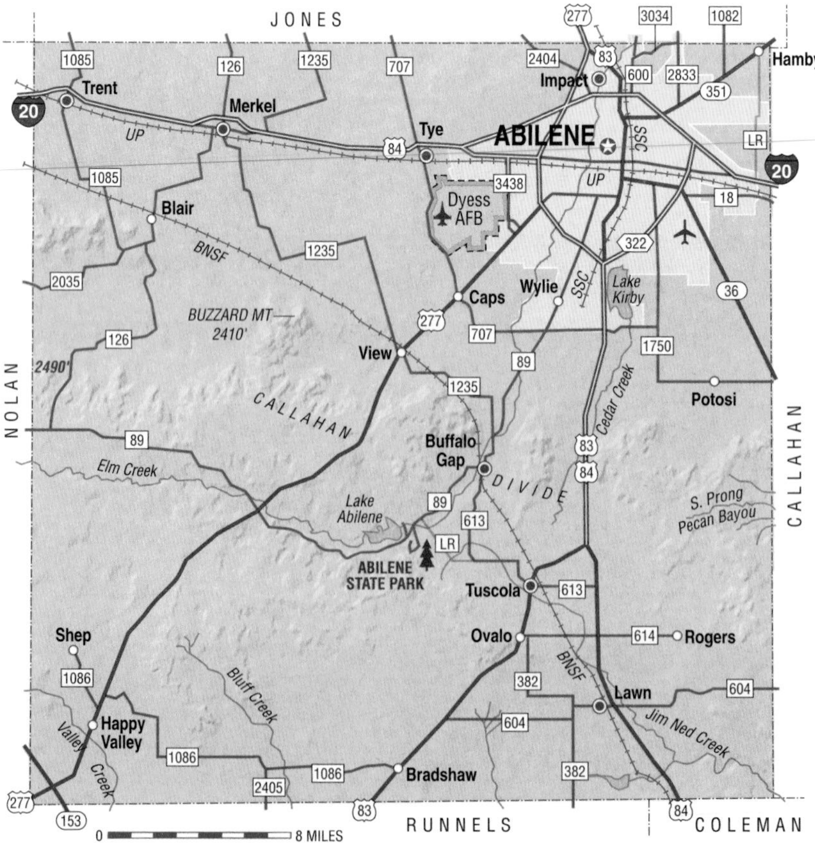

JONES

1085 | Trent | 126 | 1235 | 707 | 2404 | 83 | 277 | 3034 | 1082
600 | 2833 | Hamby
20 | Merkel | Tye | 84 | **ABILENE** | 351 | Impact
UP | SSC | LR
1085 | 3438 | UP | 20
Blair | Dyess AFB | 18
BNSF | 1235 | 322
2035 | Wylie | Lake Kirby | 36
126 | Caps | 277 | SSC
BUZZARD MT 2410' | 707 | 1750
2490' | View | 1235 | 89 | Potosi
CALLAHAN | Cedar Creek
89 | Buffalo Gap | 83 | 84
Elm Creek | 89 | DIVIDE | S. Prong Pecan Bayou
Lake Abilene | 613 | LR
ABILENE STATE PARK | Tuscola | 613
Shep | Ovalo | 614 | Rogers
1086 | 382 | BNSF | Lawn | 604
Happy Valley | 1086 | 604 | Jim Ned Creek
277 | 1086 | Bradshaw | 382 | 84
153 | 2405 | 83

NOLAN — CALLAHAN

0 ▬▬ 8 MILES

RUNNELS | COLEMAN

Terrell County

Physical Features: Trans-Pecos southwestern county; semi-mountainous, many canyons; rocky, limestone soils.

Economy: Ranching, hunting leases, oil/gas exploration, tourism.

History: Coahuiltecans, Jumanos, and other tribes left many pictographs in area caves. Sheep ranching began in the 1880s. Named for Confederate Gen. A.W. Terrell; county created in 1905 from Pecos County, organized the same year.

Race/Ethnicity: Anglo, 50%; Black, 0.6%; Hispanic, 47.8%; Asian, 0.1%; Other, 1.3%.

Vital Statistics, annual: Births, 0; deaths, 17; marriages, 6; divorces, 0.

Recreation: Nature tourism, hunting, especially white-tailed and mule deer, Rio Grande Wild and Scenic River, varied wildlife, hiking trail; Snake Days in June, Cactus Pachanga in October.

Minerals: Gas, oil, limestone.

Agriculture: Goats (meat, Angora); sheep (meat, wool); some beef cattle. Market value $4.2 million. Wildlife leases important.

Sanderson (681) county seat; ranching, hunting, tourism, government/services; museum.

Other town: **Dryden** (13).

Population.	794
Change from 2010 (%).	-19.3
Area (sq. mi.).	2,358.1
Land Area (sq. mi.).	2,358.0

Altitude (ft.)	1,180–3,765
Rainfall (in.).	14.7
Jan. mean min (°F).	31.5
July mean max (°F).	92.2
Civ. Labor	403

Unemployed (%).	4
Wages	$3,260,909
Per Capita Income	$49,591
Prop. Value	$599,540,811
Retail Sales	$3,030,796

Terry County

Physical Features: South Plains, broken by draws, playas; sandy, sandy loam, loam soils.

Economy: Oil-field services, agribusiness, peanut processing.

History: Comanches removed in the 1870s by U.S. Army. Ranching developed in the 1890s; farming after 1900. Oil discovered in 1940. County named for Confederate Col. B.F. Terry, head of the Eighth Texas Cavalry (Terry's Texas Rangers). Created from the Bexar District in 1876; organized in 1904.

Race/Ethnicity: Anglo, 38.9%; Black, 4.5%; Hispanic, 55.3%; Asian, 0.1%; Other, 0.9%.

Vital Statistics, annual: Births, 189; deaths, 139; marriages, 73; divorces, 43.

Recreation: Museum, aquatic center, vineyard festival in August, harvest festival in October.

Minerals: Oil, gas, salt mining.

Agriculture: Cotton is principal crop; peanuts (third in acreage), grain sorghum, guar, wheat, melons, cattle, grapes. 98,000 acres irrigated. Market value $136.9 million.

BROWNFIELD (9,707) county seat; oil-field services, government/services, vineyards, peanut processing; hospital; quilt trail displays in April.

Other towns include: **Meadow** (590); **Tokio** (6); **Wellman** (204).

Population.	12,544
Change from 2010 (%).	-0.8
Area (sq. mi.).	890.9
Land Area (sq. mi.).	888.8
Altitude (ft.).	3,080–3,600
Rainfall (in.).	19.6
Jan. mean min (°F).	26.9

July mean max (°F).	92.4
Civ. Labor	4,853
Unemployed (%).	6.7
Wages	$35,371,729
Per Capita Income	$37,741
Prop. Value	$1,322,663,540
Retail Sales	$215,154,561

Throckmorton County

Physical Features: Northwest county southwest of Wichita Falls; rolling, between Brazos forks; red to black soils.

Economy: Oil, agribusiness, hunting.

History: Site of Comanche Indian Reservation 1854-59. Ranching developed after Civil War. County named for Dr. W.E. Throckmorton, father of Gov. J.W. Throckmorton; county created from Fannin in 1858; organized in 1879.

Race/Ethnicity: Anglo, 84.5%; Black, 0.4%; Hispanic, 13.2%; Asian, 0.4%; Other, 1.2%.

Vital Statistics, annual: Births, 10; deaths, 30; marriages, 18; divorces, 2.

Recreation: Hunting, fishing; historic sites include Camp Cooper, site of former Comanche reservation, restored ranch home; Millers Creek Reservoir; wild game dinner in January.

Minerals: Natural gas, oil.

Agriculture: Beef cattle, horses, wheat, hay. Market value $27.3 million. Mesquite firewood sold. Hunting leases important.

THROCKMORTON (735) county seat; varied manufacturing, oil-field services; hospital; Old Jail museum.

Other towns include: **Elbert** (21), **Woodson** (234).

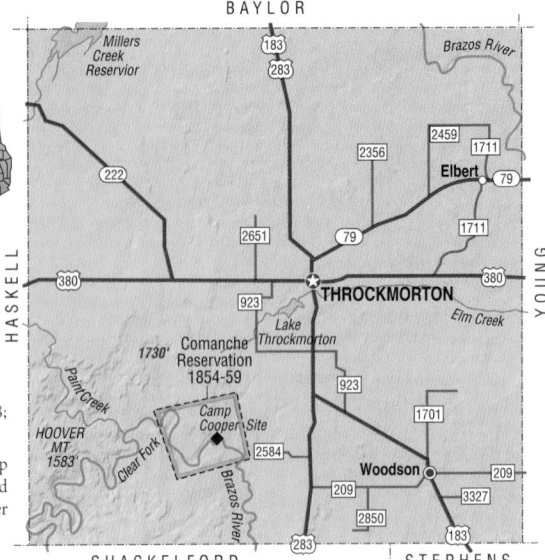

Population.................. 1,448	July mean max (°F).............. 95.8
Change from 2010 (%)...........-11.8	Civ. Labor..........................654
Area (sq. mi.)....................915.5	Unemployed (%)....................4.9
Land Area (sq. mi.)..............912.6	Wages $3,174,541
Altitude (ft.)...............1,100–1,730	Per Capita Income...........$41,454
Rainfall (in.)......................29.8	Prop. Value.............$960,145,352
Jan. mean min (°F)...............29.6	Retail Sales...............$8,006,418

Titus County

Physical Features: Northeast Texas county; hilly, timbered; drains to Big Cypress Creek, Sulphur River; Lake Bob Sandlin, Welsh Reservoir, Monticello Reservoir.

Economy: Agribusiness, varied manufacturing, electric power generation.

History: Caddo area. Cherokees and other tribes settled in the 1820s. Anglo-American settlers arrived in the 1840s. Named for pioneer settler A.J. Titus; county created from Bowie and Red River counties in 1846, organized the same year.

Race/Ethnicity: Anglo, 44%; Black, 9.7%; Hispanic, 43.6%; Asian, 0.7%; Other, 1.7%.

Vital Statistics, annual: Births, 500; deaths, 311; marriages, 237; divorces, 36.

Recreation: Fishing, hunting, lake activities, state park, rodeo, railroad museum, flower gardens.

Minerals: Lignite coal, oil, gas.

Agriculture: Poultry, beef cattle, hay, horticulture, horses. Market value $149.3 million. Timber sales significant.

MOUNT PLEASANT (17,064) county seat; tourism, varied manufacturing, food-processing plants; hospital; Northeast Texas Community College; jubilee and outhouse races in May.

Other towns include: **Cookville** (105), **Millers Cove** (161), **Talco** (499), **Winfield** (528).

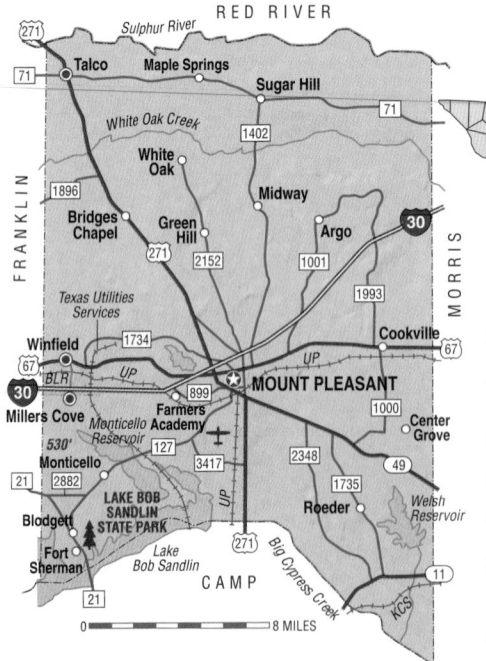

Population......................33,690	Rainfall (in.)............................47.7	Wages $218,658,464
Change from 2010 (%).................4.2	Jan. mean min (°F)....................31.1	Per Capita Income................$37,070
Area (sq. mi.)........................425.6	July mean max (°F)....................92.9	Prop. Value...............$3,590,285,664
Land Area (sq. mi.)..................406.1	Civ. Labor............................13,443	Retail Sales.................$861,305,538
Altitude (ft.)......................250–530	Unemployed (%)........................5.6	

Tom Green County

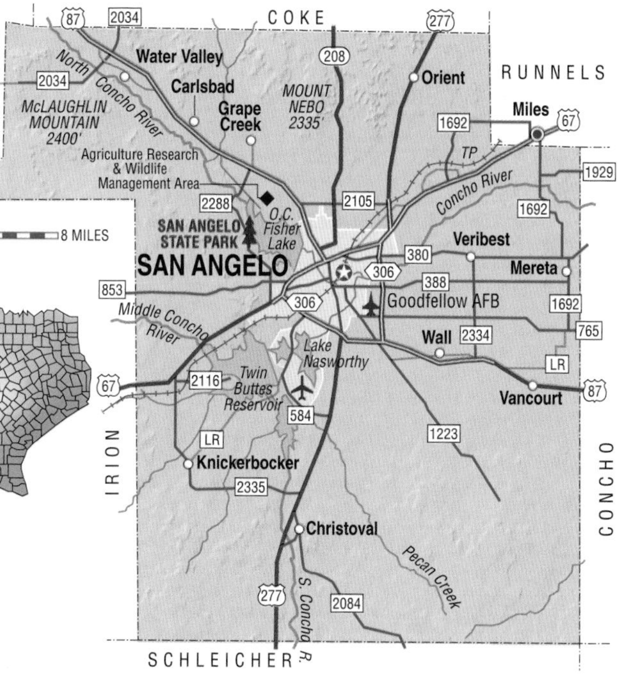

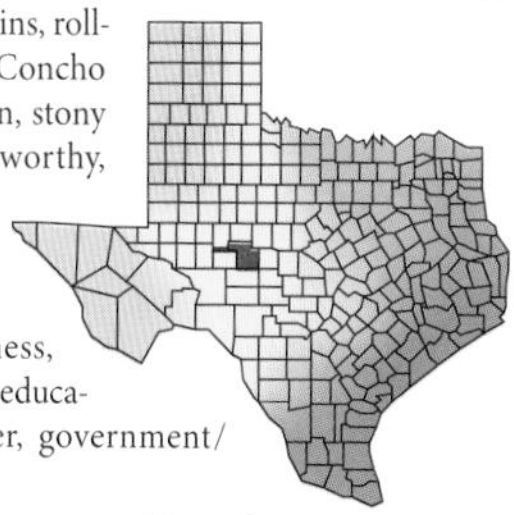

Physical Features: Plains, rolling hills, broken by Concho forks; loams in basin, stony hillsides; Lake Nasworthy, Twin Buttes Reservoir, O.C. Fisher Lake.

Economy: Agribusiness, trade center for area, education, medical center, government/services.

History: Jumano Indians attracted Spanish missionaries around 1630. Comanches controlled the area when the U.S. military established the first outpost in the 1850s. Anglo-American settlement occurred after the Civil War. County created from the Bexar District in 1874 and named for Gen. Tom Green of the Texas Revolution; organized in 1875; twelve other counties were created from the original area.

Race/Ethnicity: Anglo, 50.9%; Black, 3.7%; Hispanic, 42%; Asian, 1%; Other, 2.1%.

Vital Statistics, annual: Births, 1,721; deaths, 973; marriages, 926; divorces, 349.

Recreation: Water sports, hunting, Fort Concho museum, symphony, Christmas at Old Fort Concho, February rodeo.

Minerals: Oil, natural gas.

Agriculture: Cotton, beef cattle, goats, sheep (third in number), small grains, milo. About 30,000 acres irrigated. Market value $100.0 million.

SAN ANGELO (100,052) county seat; government/services, retail, transportation, education; hospitals, Angelo State University, Howard Junior College branch; riverwalk; Museum of Fine Arts, drag boat races in June.

Other towns include: **Carlsbad** (780); **Christoval** (576); **Grape Creek** (3,201); **Knickerbocker** (94); **Mereta** (131); **Vancourt** (131); **Veribest** (115); **Wall** (329); **Water Valley** (203).

Population	117,613
Change from 2010 (%)	6.7
Area (sq. mi.)	1,540.6
Land Area (sq. mi.)	1,522.0
Altitude (ft.)	1,675–2,600
Rainfall (in.)	23.0
Jan. mean min (°F)	29.6
July mean max (°F)	94.5
Civ. Labor	53,714
Unemployed (%)	5.2
Wages	$585,376,492
Per Capita Income	$48,876
Prop. Value	$10,112,719,265
Retail Sales	$2,150,771,436

For explanation of sources, symbols and abbreviations, see p. 204, and foldout map.

Farm animals spotted just outside Mount Pleasant in Titus County. Photo by Carol M. Highsmith, courtesy of the Library of Congress

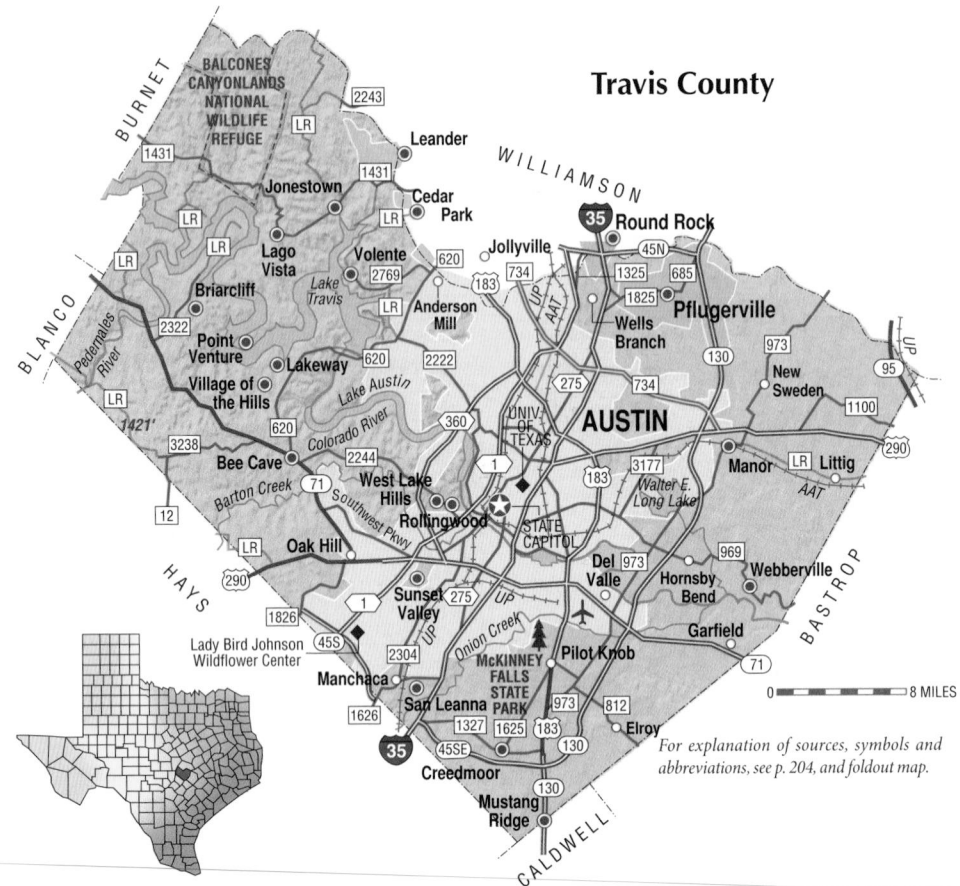

Travis County

For explanation of sources, symbols and abbreviations, see p. 204, and foldout map.

Physical Features: Central county of scenic hills, broken by Colorado River; Lake Travis, Lake Austin, Lady Bird Lake, Walter E. Long Lake; cedars, pecans, other trees; diverse soils, mineral deposits.

Economy: Government/services, education, technology, research, and industry.

History: Tonkawa and Lipan Apache area; Comanches, Kiowas arrived about 1700. Spanish missions from East Texas temporarily relocated near Barton Springs in 1730 before removing to San Antonio. Anglo-Americans arrived in the early 1830s. County created in 1840, when Austin became Republic's capital, from Bastrop County; organized in 1843; named for Alamo commander Col. William B. Travis; many other counties created from its original area.

Race/Ethnicity: Anglo, 47.8%; Black, 8.1%; Hispanic, 34.7%; Asian, 6.5%; Other, 2.7%.

Vital Statistics, annual: Births, 16,297; deaths, 5,380; marriages, 9,906; divorces, 2,469.

Recreation: Colorado River lakes, hunting, fishing; McKinney Falls State Park; LBJ Presidential Library, Lady Bird Johnson Wildflower Center; collegiate, metropolitan, governmental events; official buildings and historic sites; museums, including

Bullock state history museum; Sixth St. restoration area; scenic drives; many city parks; South by Southwest film, music festival in March.

Minerals: Production of lime, stone, sand, gravel, oil and gas.

Agriculture: Cattle, nursery crops, hogs; sorghum, corn, cotton, small grains, pecans. Market value $28.1 million.

Education: University of Texas, St. Edward's University, Concordia Lutheran University, Huston-Tillotson College, Austin Community College, Episcopal and Presbyterian seminaries.

AUSTIN (984,115, part [55,385] in Williamson County) county seat and state capital; state and federal payrolls, IRS center, high-tech industries, healthcare/hospitals, including state institutions for blind, deaf, mental illnesses; popular retirement area. Anderson Mill, Del Valle, and Oak Hill are now part of Austin.

Other towns include: **Bee Cave** (6,897) retail, tourism, SpringFest in April; **Briarcliff** (1,775); **Creedmoor** (222); **Garfield** (1,845); **Jonestown** (2,092) tourism, retail, commuters, Chili Pod chili cookoff in April; **Lago Vista** (7,335); **Lakeway** (15,981) residential real estate, retail, tourism, lake activities; **Manchaca** (1,233);

Population.................... 1,273,554
Change from 2010 (%).................24.3
Area (sq. mi.)...................... 1,023.0
Land Area (sq. mi.)...................990.2
Altitude (ft.).....................400–1,421
Rainfall (in.)...........................34.3
Jan. mean min (°F)....................36.3
July mean max (°F)....................95.2
Civ. Labor......................... 755,518
Unemployed (%).........................4.5
Wages $16,225,051,190
Per Capita Income................ $71,666
Prop. Value $282,103,045,807
Retail Sales.............. $20,675,125,912

Manor (13,817); **Mustang Ridge** (957, partly in Caldwell County).

Also, **Pflugerville** (67,738) high-tech industries, agriculture, government/services, Deutchenfest in May; **Point Venture** (1,043); **Rollingwood** (1,585); **San Leanna** (540); **Sunset Valley** (663); **The Hills** (2,480) residential community; **Volente** (597); **Webberville** (466); **Wells Branch** (13,772); **West Hills** (3,250).

Also, part [8,447] of **Cedar Park**, part [882] of **Jollyville**, and part [1,779] of **Round Rock**, all mostly in Williamson County.

Trinity County

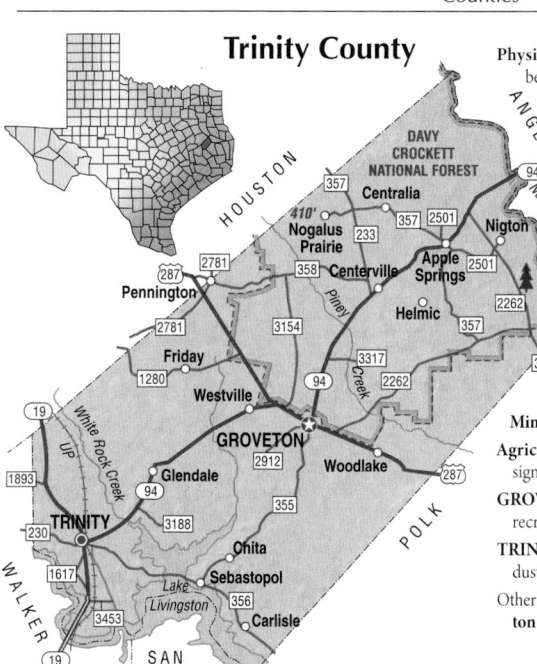

Physical Features: Heavily forested East Texas county of hills, between Neches and Trinity (Lake Livingston) rivers; rich alluvial soils, sandy upland; 67,910 acres in national forest.

Economy: Forestry, cattle, tourism, government/services.

History: Caddoes, reduced by disease in the late 1700s. Kickapoo, Alabama, and Coushatta in area when Anglo-Americans settled in the 1840s. Named for river; county created in 1850 out of Houston County, organized the same year.

Race/Ethnicity: Anglo, 78.5%; Black, 9.8%; Hispanic, 9%; Asian, 0.2%; Other, 2.1%.

Vital Statistics, annual: Births, 151; deaths, 225; marriages, 71; divorces, 40.

Recreation: Lake activities, fishing, hiking, hunting, national forest, historic site.

Minerals: Limited oil, gas, sand and gravel.

Agriculture: Beef cattle. Market value $8.2 million. Timber sales significant. Hunting leases, fishing.

GROVETON (1,055) county seat; logging, government/services, recreation; museum, library; Bear Chase marathon in April.

TRINITY (2,741) government/services, steel fabrication, forest-industries center, commuters; hospital.

Other towns include: **Apple Springs** (350); **Centralia** (190); **Pennington** (67); **Sebastopol** (300) historic town; **Woodlake** (180).

Population...................... **14,530**	Altitude (ft.).................... 131–410	Unemployed (%)........................7.7
Change from 2010 (%)................-0.4	Rainfall (in.)............................49.3	Wages $21,209,409
Area (sq. mi.)......................... 714.0	Jan. mean min (°F)....................35.1	Per Capita Income $36,062
Land Area (sq. mi.)................... 693.6	July mean max (°F)....................92.9	Prop. Value $2,405,853,452
	Civ. Labor 5,369	Retail Sales $82,961,027

Tyler County

Physical Features: Hilly East Texas county; densely timbered; drains to Neches River; B.A. Steinhagen Lake; Big Thicket is unique plant and animal area.

Economy: Lumbering, government/services, some manufacturing, tourism, hunting leases.

History: Caddoan area. Cherokees, Alabama, and Coushatta pushed into area from U.S. South in the 1820s. Anglo-Americans settled in the 1830s. Named for U.S. President John Tyler; county created in 1846 from Liberty County, organized the same year.

Race/Ethnicity: Anglo, 78.5%; Black, 11.5%; Hispanic, 7.4%; Asian, 0.2%; Other, 2.2%..

Vital Statistics, annual: Births, 213; deaths, 274; marriages, 138; divorces, 80.

Recreation: Big Thicket National Preserve; Heritage Village; lake activities; Allan Shivers Museum; state forest; historic sites; dogwood festival in spring; rodeo, frontier frolics in September; gospel music fest in June.

Minerals: Oil, natural gas.

Agriculture: Cattle, hay, nursery crops, blueberries, horses. Market value $14.9 million. Timber sales significant.

WOODVILLE (2,727) county seat; lumber, cattle market, varied manufacturing, tourism; hospital, prison.

Other towns include: **Chester** (324) **Colmesneil** (603), **Doucette** (160), **Fred** (300), **Hillister** (250), **Ivanhoe** (2,001), **Spurger** (590), **Warren** (882).

Population...................... **22,735**	Altitude (ft.)........................50–461	July mean max (°F)....................91.8
Change from 2010 (%)................4.5	Rainfall (in.)............................56.2	Civ. Labor 7,456
Area (sq. mi.)......................... 935.6	Jan. mean min (°F)....................37.5	Unemployed (%)........................9.1
Land Area (sq. mi.)................... 924.5		Wages $41,101,968
		Per Capita Income $32,978
		Prop. Value $2,797,139,982
		Retail Sales $147,313,630

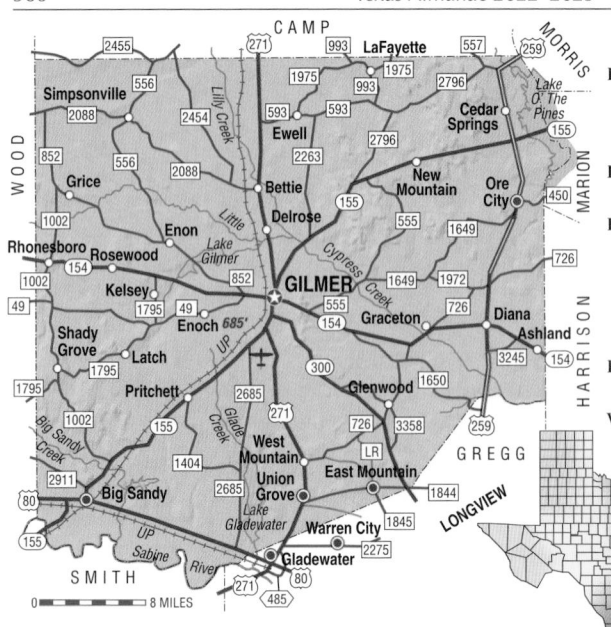

Upshur County

Physical Features: East Texas county; rolling to hilly, over half forested; drains to Sabine River, Little Cypress Creek, Lake O' the Pines, Lake Gilmer, Lake Gladewater.

Economy: Manufacturing, oil, gas, agribusiness, timber.

History: Caddoes; reduced by epidemics in the 1700s. Cherokees in area in the 1820s. Anglo-American settlement in the mid-1830s. County created from Harrison, Nacogdoches counties in 1846, organized the same year; named for U.S. Secretary of State A.P. Upshur.

Race/Ethnicity: Anglo, 78.9%; Black, 7.8%; Hispanic, 9.8%; Asian, 0.3%; Other, 2.8%.

Vital Statistics, annual: Births, 449; deaths, 471; marriages, 206; divorces, 174.

Recreation: Scenic trails, hunting, fishing, fall foliage, Yamboree in October at Gilmer.

Minerals: Oil, gas, sand, gravel.

Agriculture: Dairies, cattle, hay, vegetable crops, poultry. Market value $40.7 million. Timber a major product.

GILMER (5,085) county seat; agriculture, communications, electric power; museum; trails, parks; site of Cherokee village.

Other towns include: **Big Sandy** (1,402); **Diana** (585); **East Mountain** (851); **Ore City** (1,227); **Union Grove** (373). Part of **Gladewater** (6,341).

Population......................41,204	July mean max (°F)....................93.4	
Change from 2010 (%)................4.8	Civ. Labor............................17,433	
Area (sq. mi.).........................592.6	Unemployed (%).......................6.7	
Land Area (sq. mi.)..................583.0	Wages.........................$77,438,104	
Altitude (ft.)......................228–685	Per Capita Income...............$37,563	
Rainfall (in.)...........................47.1	Prop. Value...............$3,543,555,804	
Jan. mean min (°F)...................31.4	Retail Sales.................$294,717,018	

Upton County

Physical Features: Western county; north flat, south rolling, hilly; limestone, sandy loam soils, drains to creeks.

Economy: Oil, wind turbines, farming, ranching.

History: Apache and Comanche area until the tribes were removed by the U.S. Army in the 1870s. Sheep and cattle ranching developed in the 1880s. Oil discovered in 1925. County created in 1887 from Tom Green County; organized in 1910; the name honors brothers John and William Upton, Confederate colonels.

Race/Ethnicity: Anglo, 40.8%; Black, 1.2%; Hispanic, 56.4%; Asian, 0%; Other, 1.4%.

Vital Statistics, annual: Births, 61; deaths, 36; marriages, 32; divorces, 17.

Recreation: Historic sites, Mendoza Trail museum, scenic areas, dinosaur tracks west of McCamey.

Minerals: Oil, natural gas.

Agriculture: Cotton, sheep, goats, cattle, watermelons, pecans. Extensive irrigation. Market value $19.1 million.

RANKIN (846) county seat, oil, ranching, farming; hospital; Barbados cookoff in May, All Kid rodeo in June.

McCAMEY (2,065) government/services, wind and solar power, oil; hospital; Wind Energy cookoff and festival in September.

Other town: **Midkiff** (182).

Population......................3,619	Rainfall (in.)...........................15.1	Wages.........................$38,765,943
Change from 2010 (%)................7.9	Jan. mean min (°F)...................31.9	Per Capita Income...............$47,118
Area (sq. mi.).......................1,241.5	July mean max (°F)...................95.3	Prop. Value...............$8,038,930,930
Land Area (sq. mi.)...............1,241.3	Civ. Labor.............................1,931	Retail Sales.................$30,945,104
Altitude (ft.)..................2,310–3,141	Unemployed (%).......................5.3	

Uvalde County

Physical Features: Edwards Plateau, rolling hills below escarpment; spring-fed Sabinal, Frio, Leona, Nueces rivers; cypress, cedar, other trees, including maple groves.

Economy: Agribusinesses, hunting leases, light manufacturing, tourism.

History: Mission Nuestra Señora de la Candelaria founded in 1762 for Lipan Apaches near present-day Montell; Comanches harassed mission. U.S. military outpost established in 1849. County created from Bexar in 1850; re-created and organized in 1856; named for 1778 governor of Coahuila, Juan de Ugalde, with name Anglicized.

Race/Ethnicity: Anglo, 25.1%; Black, 0.4%; Hispanic, 73%; Asian, 0.4%; Other, 0.9%.

Vital Statistics, annual: Births, 429; deaths, 233; marriages, 159; divorces, 14.

Recreation: Deer, turkey hunting; Garner State Park; water activities on rivers; John Nance Garner museum; Uvalde Memorial Park; scenic trails, historic sites.

Minerals: Asphalt, stone, sand, gravel.

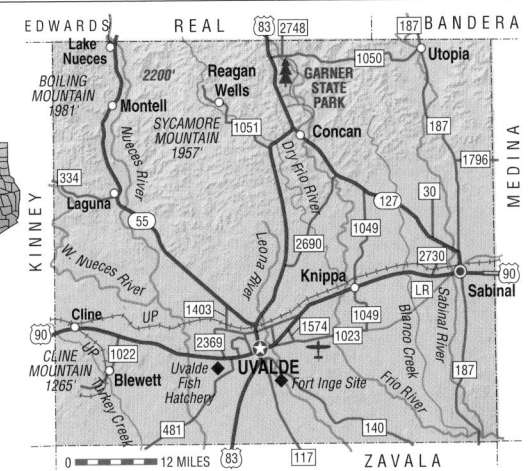

Agriculture: Cattle, vegetables, corn, cotton, sorghum, sheep, goats, hay, wheat. Substantial irrigation. Market value $87.1 million.

UVALDE (16,086) county seat; vegetable, wool, mohair processing, tourism; opera house; junior college, A&M research center; hospital; Fort Inge Day in April.

SABINAL (1,705) farm, ranch center, tourism, retirement area.

Other towns include: **Concan** (500); **Knippa** (639); **Utopia** (213) resort; **Uvalde Estates** (2,228).

Population	26,743
Change from 2010 (%)	1.3
Area (sq. mi.)	1,558.6
Land Area (sq. mi.)	1,552.0
Altitude (ft.)	650–2,200
Rainfall (in.)	24.6
Jan. mean min (°F)	38.6
July mean max (°F)	96.1
Civ. Labor	11,292
Unemployed (%)	6.1
Wages	$102,003,337
Per Capita Income	$41,116
Prop. Value	$4,394,155,349
Retail Sales	$399,754,064

Val Verde County

Physical Features: Southwestern county bordering Mexico, rolling, hilly, brushy; Devils, Pecos rivers, Rio Grande and Amistad Reservoir; limestone, alluvial soils.

Economy: Agribusiness, tourism, trade center, military, Border Patrol, hunting leases, fishing.

History: Apaches, Coahuiltecans, Jumanos present when Spanish came through in the late 1500s. Comanches arrived later. U.S. military outpost established in 1850s to protect settlers. Only county named for Civil War battle; Val Verde means green valley. Created in 1885 from Crockett, Kinney, Pecos counties, organized the same year.

Race/Ethnicity: Anglo, 15.2%; Black, 1.2%; Hispanic, 82%; Asian, 0.4%; Other, 1%.

Vital Statistics, annual: Births, 904; deaths, 353; marriages, 478; divorces, 172.

Recreation: Gateway to Mexico; deer hunting, fishing; Amistad lake activities; two state parks; Langtry restoration of Judge Roy Bean's saloon; ancient pictographs; San Felipe Springs; winery.

Minerals: Production sand and gravel, gas, oil.

Agriculture: Sheep, Angora goats, meat goats (second in numbers); cattle; minor irrigation. Market value $9.4 million.

DEL RIO (35,982) county seat; government/services including federal agencies/military, agribusiness, tourism; hospital, extension colleges; Fiesta de Amistad in October.

Laughlin Air Force Base (1,502).

Other towns and places include: **Cienegas Terrace** (3,804); **Comstock** (344); **Langtry** (30); **Val Verde Park** (2,648).

Population	50,853
Change from 2010 (%)	4.0
Area (sq. mi.)	323.7
Land Area (sq. mi.)	3,144.8
Altitude (ft.)	845–2,343
Rainfall (in.)	20.2
Jan. mean min (°F)	38.7
July mean max (°F)	96.4
Civ. Labor	21,726
Unemployed (%)	6.6
Wages	$194,649,485
Per Capita Income	$38,331
Prop. Value	$4,489,519,292
Retail Sales	$647,146,418

Van Zandt County

Physical Features: Eastern county in three soil belts; level to rolling; Sabine, Neches rivers; Lake Tawakoni; partly forested.

Economy: Agriculture, government/services, commuters to Dallas/Tyler.

History: Caddo tribes, reduced by epidemics before settlers arrived. Cherokees settled in the 1820s; removed in 1839 under policies of Republic President Lamar; Anglo-American settlement followed. County named for Republic leader Isaac Van Zandt; created from Henderson County in 1848, organized the same year.

Race/Ethnicity: Anglo, 83.3%; Black, 2.8%; Hispanic, 10.8%; Asian, 0.4%; Other, 2.5%.

Vital Statistics, annual: Births, 608; deaths, 621; marriages, 337; divorces, 201.

Recreation: Canton First Monday trade days, lake activities, state parks, historic sites.

Minerals: Oil, gas.

Agriculture: Nurseries, beef cattle, hay and foliage, dairies, vegetables. First in nursery stock acreage in the open and in sweet potato acreage. Market value $104.6 million.

CANTON (3,966) county seat; tourism, agribusiness, commuters; museums, bluegrass festival in June.

WILLS POINT (3,777) government/services, retail, tourism, commuters to Dallas and Tyler; depot museum, bluebird festival in April.

Other towns include: **Ben Wheeler** (504); **Edgewood** (1,554) commuters, heritage park, antiques; **Edom** (397) arts and crafts; **Fruitvale** (433); **Grand Saline** (3,311) salt plant, agriculture, medical services/hospital, Salt Palace museum, salt prairie marsh, birding, Salt Festival in June; **Van** (2,875) oil center, hay, cattle, oil festival in October.

Population.......................56,376	July mean max (°F)....................93.7
Change from 2010 (%)..................7.2	Civ. Labor............................26,225
Area (sq. mi.)..........................859.6	Unemployed (%).........................5.1
Land Area (sq. mi.)...................842.6	Wages.......................$114,324,765
Altitude (ft.)......................330–698	Per Capita Income................$39,609
Rainfall (in.)..........................44.2	Prop. Value.................$6,538,106,440
Jan. mean min (°F)....................33.7	Retail Sales...................$561,127,502

Victoria County

Physical Features: Rolling prairies, intersected by many streams; sandy loams, clays, alluvial soils.

Economy: Petrochemical plants, government/services, oil, manufacturing, agribusiness, tourism.

History: Karankawas and other tribes in the area when Spanish explored in 1528. Comanches, Tawakonis arrived later. La Salle's camp on Garcitas Creek 1685–1687. Spanish ranching developed in the 1750s. Anglo-Americans arrived after 1836. An original county, created in 1836 from Mexican municipality named for President Guadalupe Victoria of Mexico.

Race/Ethnicity: Anglo, 44.2%; Black, 6%; Hispanic, 46.9%; Asian, 1.1%; Other, 1.5%.

Vital Statistics, annual: Births, 1,363; deaths, 847; marriages, 621; divorces, 383.

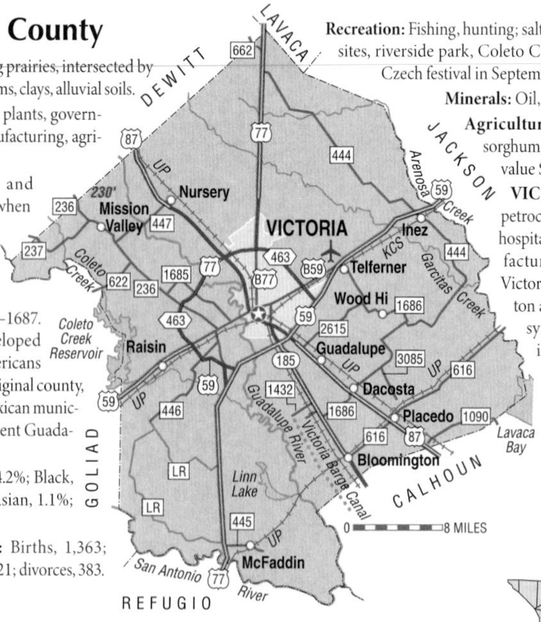

Recreation: Fishing, hunting; saltwater activities, historic homes, sites, riverside park, Coleto Creek Reservoir and park, zoo, Czech festival in September at Victoria.

Minerals: Oil, gas, sand, gravel.

Agriculture: Corn, beef cattle, grain sorghums, cotton, rice, soybeans. Market value $58.4 million.

VICTORIA (66,891) county seat; petrochemicals, government/services, hospitals/healthcare, retail, oil, manufacturing, agribusiness, tourism; Victoria College, University of Houston at Victoria; community theater, symphony, museums; Bootfeast in October.

Other towns include: **Bloomington** (2,488), **Inez** (2,357), **Nursery** (600), **Placedo** (753), **Telferner** (700).

Population.......................91,329	Jan. mean min (°F)....................40.7
Change from 2010 (%)..................5.2	July mean max (°F)....................94.1
Area (sq. mi.)..........................888.8	Civ. Labor............................40,682
Land Area (sq. mi.)...................882.1	Unemployed (%)...........................7
Altitude (ft.)..................sea level–230	Wages.......................$453,788,173
Rainfall (in.)..........................41.1	Per Capita Income................$48,938
	Prop. Value.................$9,964,443,013
	Retail Sales................$1,811,390,475

Walker County

For explanation of sources, symbols and abbreviations, see p. 204, and foldout map.

Physical Features: South central county north of Houston of rolling hills; more than 70 percent forested; national forest; San Jacinto, Trinity rivers; Lake Livingston, Lake Conroe.

Economy: State employment in prison system, education.

History: Coahuiltecans, Bidais in area when Spanish explored around 1690. Later, area became trading ground for many Indian tribes. Anglo-Americans settled in the 1830s. Antebellum slaveholding area. County created in 1846 from Montgomery County and organized the same year; first named for U.S. Secretary of the Treasury R.J. Walker; renamed 1863 for Texas Ranger Capt. S.H. Walker.

Race/Ethnicity: Anglo, 55.1%; Black, 22.6%; Hispanic, 19.2%; Asian, 1%; Other, 1.8%.

Vital Statistics, annual: Births, 667; deaths, 513; marriages, 435; divorces, 203.

Recreation: Fishing, hunting, lake activities; Sam Houston museum, homes, grave; prison museum; other historic sites, state park, Sam Houston National Forest; Sam Houston folk festival in spring.

Minerals: Clays, natural gas, oil, sand and gravel, stone.

Agriculture: Cattle, nursery plants, poultry, cotton, hay. Market value $33.8 million. Timber sales substantial.

HUNTSVILLE (43,899) county seat; state prison system, Sam Houston State University, forest products, varied manufacturing; hospital; museums, arts center.

Other towns include: **Dodge** (150), **New Waverly** (1,062), **Riverside** (585).

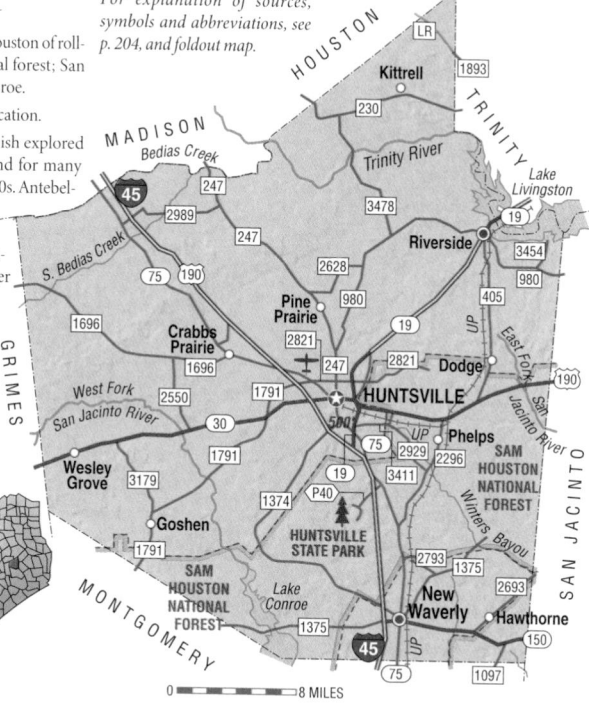

Population.	75,949
Change from 2010 (%).	11.9
Area (sq. mi.).	801.5
Land Area (sq. mi.).	784.2
Altitude (ft.).	131–500
Rainfall (in.).	49.1
Jan. mean min (°F).	39.7
July mean max (°F).	93.3
Civ. Labor.	24,013
Unemployed (%).	6.6
Wages.	$285,133,649
Per Capita Income.	$29,838
Prop. Value.	$7,225,783,075
Retail Sales.	$821,750,519

The Victoria County Monument in Memorial Square Park was designed for the Texas Centennial in 1936. It is on the National Register of Historic Places. Photo by Larry D. Moore, CC by SA 4.0/Wikimedia Commons

Waller County

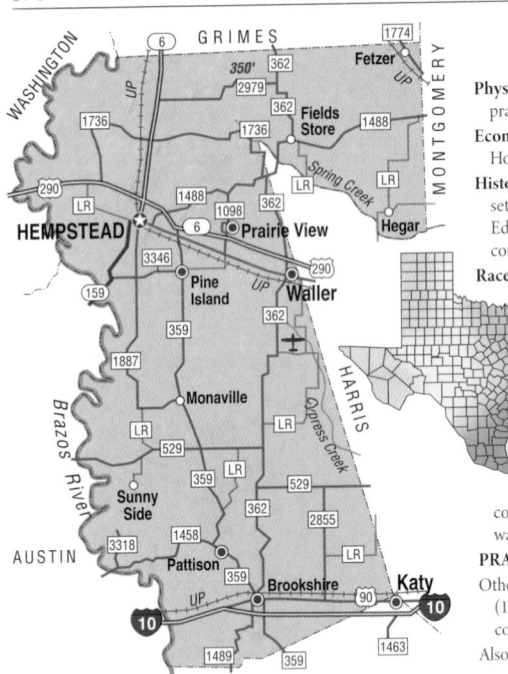

Physical Features: South central county west of Houston on rolling prairie; drains to Brazos; alluvial soils; about 20 percent forested.

Economy: Agribusiness, education, equine-related businesses, part of Houston metropolitan area.

History: Bidais Indians reduced to about 100 when Anglo-Americans settled in 1820s. Antebellum slaveholding area. County named for Edwin Waller, Republic leader; created in 1873 from Austin, Grimes counties, organized the same year.

Race/Ethnicity: Anglo, 43.7%; Black, 23.4%; Hispanic, 30.7%; Asian, 0.5%; Other, 1.5%.

Vital Statistics, annual: Births, 592; deaths, 305; marriages, 321; divorces, 103.

Recreation: Fishing, hunting; historic sites; museum.

Minerals: Oil, gas.

Agriculture: Cattle, hay, rice, greenhouse nurseries, turf grass. 10,000 acres irrigated. Market value $102.4 million. Some timber marketed.

HEMPSTEAD (7,507) county seat; varied manufacturing, commuting to Houston, agribusiness center, large vegetable market; watermelon fest in July.

PRAIRIE VIEW (6,625) home of Prairie View A&M University.

Other towns include: **Brookshire** (5,937), **Pattison** (628), **Pine Island** (1,200), **Waller** (3,119, partly in Harris County) agriculture, education, construction.

Also, part [2,081] of **Katy** (21,729, mostly in Harris County) hospitals.

Population.....................**54,822**	Rainfall (in.)...........................45.5	Wages $271,409,883
Change from 2010 (%)................26.9	Jan. mean min (°F)....................38.0	Per Capita Income $42,456
Area (sq. mi.).........................517.8	July mean max (°F)....................95.0	Prop. Value $11,554,542,051
Land Area (sq. mi.)..................513.4	Civ. Labor 24,052	Retail Sales.................. $566,535,524
Altitude (ft.) 100–350	Unemployed (%).........................7	

Ward County

Physical Features: Western county on Pecos River; plain covered by grass, brush; sandy, loam soils.

Economy: Oil, gas, government/services.

History: Jumano Indians in area when Spanish explored in the 1580s. Comanches arrived later. Railroad stations established in the 1880s. Oil discovered in the 1920s. County named for Republic leader Thomas W. Ward; county created from Tom Green County in 1887; organized in 1892.

Race/Ethnicity: Anglo, 37.1%; Black, 4.3%; Hispanic, 56.8%; Asian, 0.3%; Other, 1.2%.

Vital Statistics, annual: Births, 198; deaths, 134; marriages, 103; divorces, 26.

Recreation: Sandhills state park, camel treks, Million Barrel museum in Monahans, county park, Butterfield stagecoach festival in July.

Minerals: Oil, gas, caliche, sand, gravel.

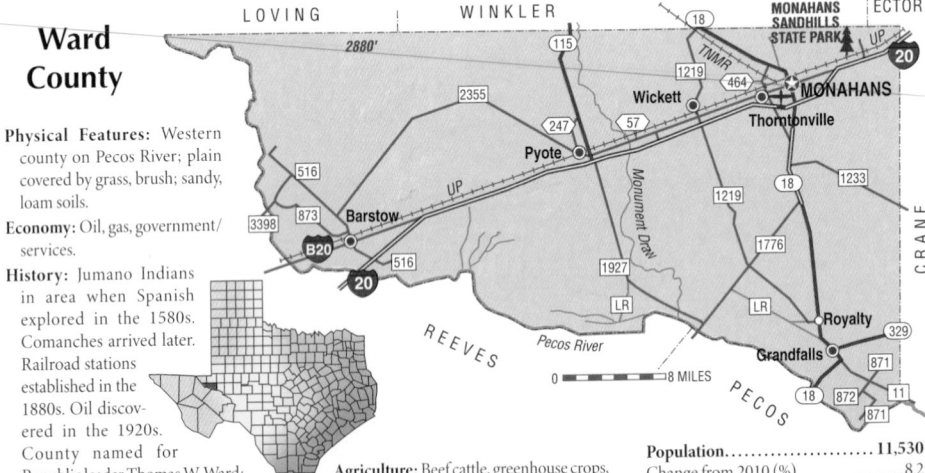

Agriculture: Beef cattle, greenhouse crops, alfalfa, horses. Market value $19.1 million. Hunting leases important.

MONAHANS (7,801) county seat; oil and gas, tourism, ranching; hospital, Odessa College extension.

Other towns include: **Barstow** (384); **Grandfalls** (398); **Pyote** (133) Rattlesnake bomber base museum; **Thorntonville** (543); **Wickett** (543).

Population.....................**11,530**	
Change from 2010 (%)................8.2	
Area (sq. mi.).........................835.8	
Land Area (sq. mi.)..................835.6	
Altitude (ft.)..................2,400–2,880	
Rainfall (in.).........................13.9	
Jan. mean min (°F)....................30.9	
July mean max (°F)....................94.9	
Civ. Labor 5,656	
Unemployed (%)........................8.8	
Wages $71,386,595	
Per Capita Income $53,870	
Prop. Value $5,449,344,564	
Retail Sales.................. $171,353,244	

Washington County

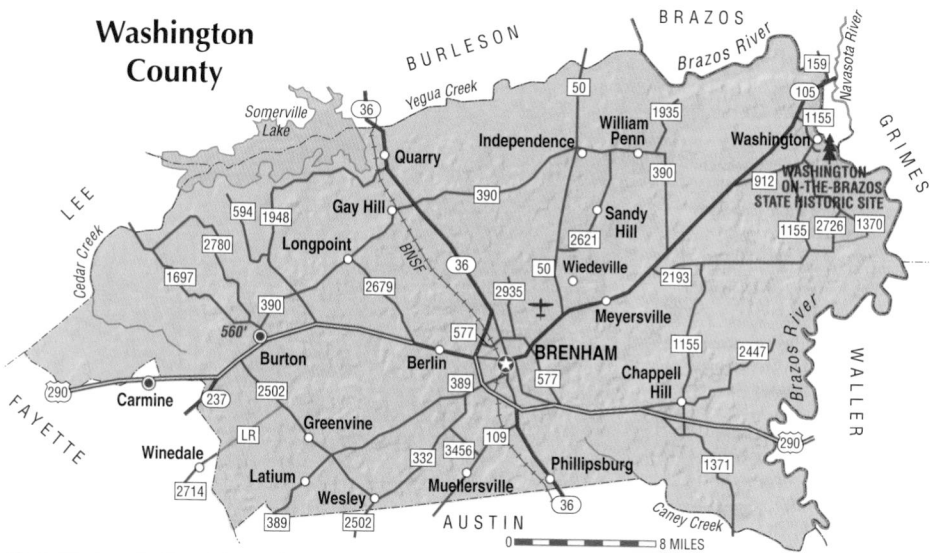

Physical Features: South central county in Brazos valley; rolling prairie of sandy loam, alluvial soils.

Economy: Agribusiness, oil, tourism, manufacturing, government/services.

History: Coahuiltecan tribes and Tonkawas in area when Anglo-American settlers arrived in 1821. Antebellum slaveholding area. Germans arrived around 1870. County named for George Washington; an original county, created in 1836, organized in 1837.

Race/Ethnicity: Anglo, 63.2%; Black, 17%; Hispanic, 17%; Asian, 1.3%; Other, 1.3%..

Vital Statistics, annual: Births, 402; deaths, 389; marriages, 221; divorces, 113.

Recreation: Many historic sites, including Washington-on-the-Brazos, Texas Baptist Historical Museum, Star of Republic Museum; wildflowers, Somerville Lake,

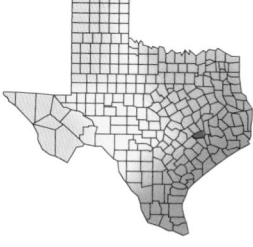

fishing, hunting, birding; antique rose nursery; Bluebonnet festival in April.

Minerals: Oil, gas and stone.

Agriculture: Cattle, poultry, dairy products, hogs, horses; hay, corn, sorghum, cotton, small grains, nursery crops. Market value $35.6 million.

BRENHAM (17,646) county seat; Blue Bell creamery, retail, tourism; hospital; Blinn College; Maifest.

Other towns include: **Burton** (302) agriculture, tourism, national landmark cotton gin, festival in April; **Chappell Hill** (750) agriculture, industrial, tourism, museum, historic homes, Scarecrow festival in October; **Washington** (100) site of signing of Texas Declaration of Independence.

Population.	**35,570**
Change from 2010 (%)	5.5
Area (sq. mi.)	621.8
Land Area (sq. mi.)	604.0
Altitude (ft.)	150–560
Rainfall (in.)	45.1
Jan. mean min (°F)	39.0
July mean max (°F)	94.2
Civ. Labor	15,180
Unemployed (%)	5.5
Wages	$180,791,155
Per Capita Income	$55,735
Prop. Value	$8,014,827,268
Retail Sales	$549,247,329

For explanation of sources, symbols and abbreviations, see p. 204, and foldout map.

Geese feeding in a fallow rice field in Waller County. Photo by Beverly Moseley, USDA NRCS Texas

Wichita County

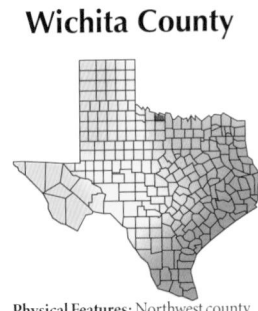

Physical Features: Northwest county in prairie bordering Oklahoma; drained by Red, Wichita rivers; North Fork Buffalo Creek Reservoir, Lake Wichita; sandy, loam soils.

Economy: Manufacturing, retail trade center, air base, government/services, agriculture.

History: Wichitas and other Caddoan tribes in the area in the 1700s; later, Comanches, Apaches also present until the 1850s. Anglo-American settlement increased after 1870. County named for tribe; created from Young Territory in 1858; organized in 1882.

Race/Ethnicity: Anglo, 64.3%; Black, 10%; Hispanic, 20.1%; Asian, 2.1%; Other, 3.2%.

Vital Statistics, annual: Births, 1,740; deaths, 1,304; marriages, 1,126; divorces, 404.

Recreation: Museums; historic sites; Texas-Oklahoma High School Oil Bowl football game; collegiate activities; water sports; Fiestas Patrias parade, Ranch Round-up in August.

Minerals: Oil.

Agriculture: Beef cattle, horticulture, wheat, hay. Seventy-five percent of hay irrigated; 10 percent of wheat/cotton. Market value $33.8 million.

WICHITA FALLS (105,754) county seat; distribution center for large area of Texas and Oklahoma, government/services, varied manufacturing, oil-field services; hospitals, including North Texas state hospital; Midwestern State University, vocational-technical training center; hiking trails; Hotter'n Hell bicycle race in August; Sheppard Air Force Base.

Other cities include: **Burkburnett** (11,194) some manufacturing, Trails and Tales of Boomtown USA display and tours; **Cashion** (355); **Electra** (2,719) oil, agriculture, manufacturing, commuters to Wichita Falls; hospital; goat barbecue in May; **Iowa Park** (6,379) manufacturing, prison, Parkfest in May; **Kamay** (640); **Pleasant Valley** (336).

Population	**132,920**
Change from 2010 (%)	1.1
Area (sq. mi.)	633.1
Land Area (sq. mi.)	627.8
Altitude (ft.)	912–1,240
Rainfall (in.)	28.9
Jan. mean min (°F)	29.8
July mean max (°F)	96.9
Civ. Labor	54,990
Unemployed (%)	5.7
Wages	$600,876,160
Per Capita Income	$44,479
Prop. Value	$10,150,475,799
Retail Sales	$1,852,390,217

An NRSC Conservationist talks to a farmer in his watermelon field in Raymondville. Photo by Ken Hammond, USDA NRCS

Wilbarger County

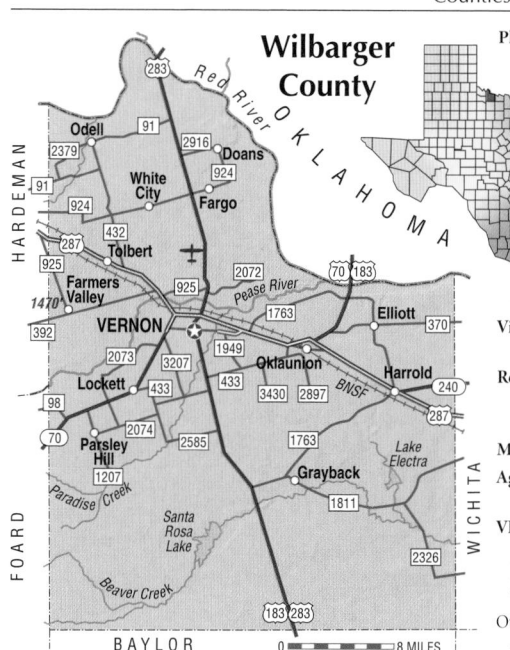

Physical Features: Gently rolling prairie draining to Red, Pease rivers, tributaries; sandy, loam, waxy soils; Santa Rosa Lake, Lake Electra.

Economy: Agribusiness, electricity generating plant, government/services.

History: Anglo-American settlement developed after removal of the Comanches into the Indian Territory in 1875. County named for pioneers Josiah and Mathias Wilbarger; created from the Bexar District in 1858 and organized in 1881.

Race/Ethnicity: Anglo, 55.9%; Black, 8.8%; Hispanic, 31.1%; Asian, 0.9%; Other, 3.1%.

Vital Statistics, annual: Births, 177; deaths, 163; marriages, 137; divorces, 25.

Recreation: Doan's Crossing, on route of cattle drives; Waggoner Ranch, other historic sites; hunting, fishing; Red River Valley Museum; Santa Rosa roundup in May.

Minerals: Oil.

Agriculture: Wheat, cattle, cotton, alfalfa, peanuts; 15,000 acres irrigated. Market value $51.9 million.

VERNON (10,307) county seat; government/services, agribusiness, manufacturing, electricity-generating plant; college; state hospital/mental health center, private hospital, prison; museums; vintage car show in August.

Other towns include: **Harrold** (200); **Lockett** (150) A&M extension center; **Odell** (100); **Oklaunion** (138).

Population......................12,465	Rainfall (in.)............................27.9	Wages.........................$66,261,865
Change from 2010 (%)................-7.9	Jan. mean min (°F)....................27.7	Per Capita Income................$46,314
Area (sq. mi.)........................977.9	July mean max (°F)....................96.6	Prop. Value................$2,321,946,178
Land Area (sq. mi.)..................970.8	Civ. Labor............................5,037	Retail Sales..................$328,610,842
Altitude (ft.)..................1,030–1,470	Unemployed (%).......................7.4	

Willacy County

Physical Features: Flat coastal prairie sloping toward Gulf; alluvial, sandy, marshy soils; Padre Island; La Sal Vieja, salt lake; wildlife refuge.

Economy: Agribusiness, oil, government/services.

History: Coahuiltecan area when Spanish explored in the 1500s. Spanish ranching began in the 1790s. County named for legislator John G. Willacy; created in 1911 from Cameron, Hidalgo counties, organized in 1912; reorganized in 1921 after most of its territory was given over to the newly created Kenedy County.

Race/Ethnicity: Anglo, 8.7%; Black, 1.7%; Hispanic, 88.3%; Asian, 0.5%; Other, 0.4%.

Vital Statistics, annual: Births, 291; deaths, 151; marriages, 108; divorces, 50.

Recreation: Fresh and saltwater fishing, hunting of deer, turkey, dove; mild climate attracts many winter tourists.

Minerals: Oil, natural gas.

Agriculture: Cotton, sorghum, corn, vegetables, sugar cane watermelon; 20 percent of cropland irrigated. Livestock includes cattle, horses, goats, hogs. Market value $88.1 million.

RAYMONDVILLE (10,998) county seat; agribusiness, oil, food processing, tourism, enterprise zone, prison; museum; Boot Fest in October.

Other towns include: **Lasara** (924); **Lyford** (2,539); **Port Mansfield** (168) charter fishing, bait and tackle, ecotourism/birding, nature trail, fishing tournament in July; **San Perlita** (554); **Sebastian** (1,805).

Population......................21,566	
Change from 2010 (%)................-2.6	
Area (sq. mi.)........................784.3	
Land Area (sq. mi.)..................590.6	
Altitude (ft.)..................sea level–94	
Rainfall (in.)............................26.1	
Jan. mean min (°F)....................47.6	
July mean max (°F)....................96.7	
Civ. Labor............................6,688	
Unemployed (%).......................12.2	
Wages.........................$40,118,044	
Per Capita Income................$27,584	
Prop. Value................$2,266,785,106	
Retail Sales..................$97,060,339	

For explanation of sources, symbols and abbreviations, see p. 204, and foldout map.

Williamson County

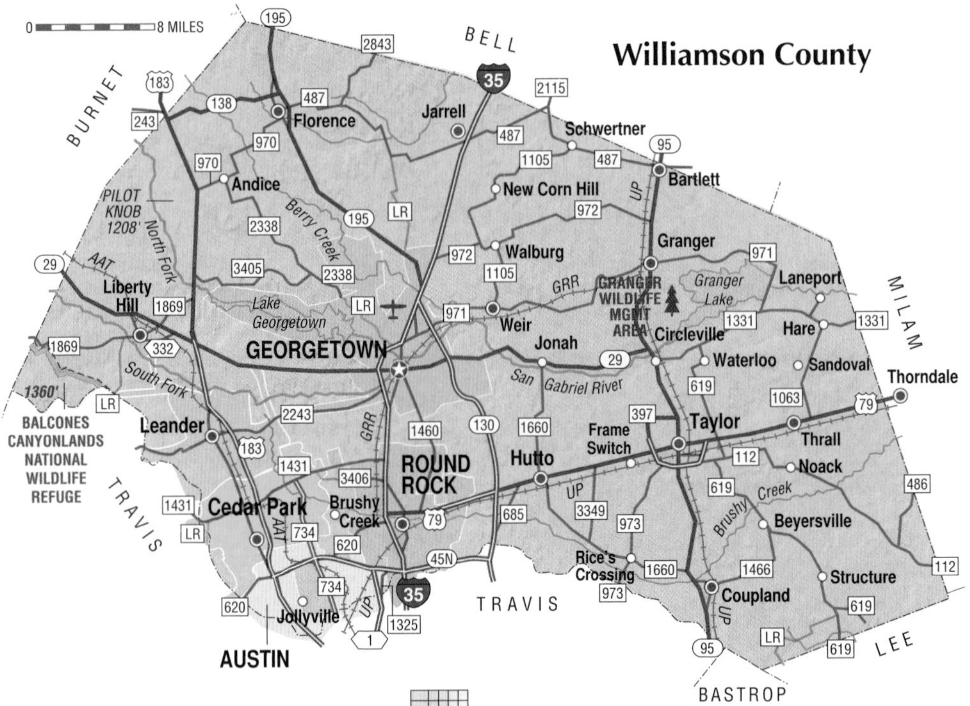

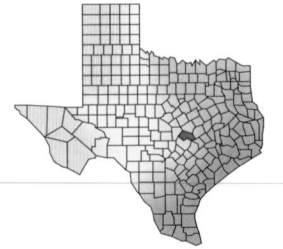

Physical Features: Central county near Austin. Level to rolling; mostly Blackland soil, some loam, sand; drained by San Gabriel River and tributaries; Granger Lake, Lake Georgetown.

Economy: Agribusinesses, varied manufacturing, education center, government/services; the county is part of Austin metropolitan area.

History: Tonkawa area; later, other tribes moved in. Comanches raided until the 1860s. Anglo-American settlement began in the late 1830s. County named for Robert M. Williamson, pioneer leader; created from Milam County and organized in 1848.

Race/Ethnicity: Anglo, 58.7%; Black, 6.3%; Hispanic, 24.8%; Asian, 6.9%; Other, 3%.

Vital Statistics, annual: Births, 6,428; deaths, 2,625; marriages, 2,646; divorces, 811.

Recreation: Lake recreation; Inner Space Cavern; historic sites; deer hunting, fishing; Gov. Dan Moody Museum at Taylor; San Gabriel Park; old settlers park; walking tours, rattlesnake sacking, barbecue cookoff, frontier days in summer; Round Rock minor league baseball; Cedar Park Center, home of Austin Spurs NBA developmental basketball team and the Texas Stars AHL hockey team.

Minerals: Building stone, sand and gravel.

Agriculture: Corn, cattle, sorghum, cotton, wheat, hay, nursery crops. Market value $114.9 million.

GEORGETOWN (75,756) county seat; education, health, government/services, manufacturing, retail; hospital; Southwestern University; Red Poppy festival in April.

ROUND ROCK (119,899, part [1,779] in Travis County) semiconductor, varied manufacturing, tourism and distribution center; hospital; Texas Baptist Children's Home.

CEDAR PARK (77,541, part [8,447] in Travis County) energy equipment manufacturing, millwork, concrete production, commuting to Austin; hospital, community college extension; steam-engine train; Cedar Fest in the spring.

TAYLOR (18,154) varied manufacturing, wholesale, transportation, government/services; hospital, college extension campuses, museum, parks; Blackland Prairie Day in May.

Other towns include: **Andice** (300); **Bartlett** (2,789, partly in Bell County) cotton, corn production, commuters, prison, first rural electrification in nation in 1933, clinic, library, Friendship Fest in September; **Brushy Creek** (27,199); **Coupland** (317); **Florence** (1,306).

Also, **Granger** (1,624); **Hutto** (26,801) agriculture, manufacturing, government/services, commuters to Austin, museum, Olde Tyme Days in October; **Jarrell** (1,870); **Jollyville** (18,409, partly in Travis County); **Leander** (59,110) varied manufacturing, government/services, community college campus, Old Town street festival in May, Leanderthal Lady prehistoric site; **Liberty Hill** (2,931) artisans center; **Schwertner** (175); **Thrall** (1,036); **Walburg** (277); **Weir** (544).

Also, part [55,385] of **Austin.**

For explanation of sources, symbols and abbreviations, see p. 204, and foldout map.

Population.	**589,216**
Change from 2010 (%).	39.4
Area (sq. mi.).	1,134.4
Land Area (sq. mi.).	1,118.3
Altitude (ft.).	400–1,360
Rainfall (in.).	35.7
Jan. mean min (°F).	36.5
July mean max (°F).	94.9
Civ. Labor.	325,591
Unemployed (%).	4.4
Wages.	$3,203,731,758
Per Capita Income.	$53,145
Prop. Value.	$89,578,669,179
Retail Sales.	$9,811,759,549

Physical Features: Upper Coastal Plains; mostly sandy soils, some heavier; San Antonio River, Cibolo Creek.

Economy: Agribusiness, oil and gas, commuters to San Antonio; part of San Antonio metropolitan area.

History: Coahuiltecan Indians in area when Spanish began ranching around 1750. Anglo-American settlers arrived in the 1840s. Germans, Polish settled in the 1850s. County created from Bexar, Karnes counties and organized in 1860; named for James C. Wilson, a member of the Mier Expedition.

Race/Ethnicity: Anglo, 56.8%; Black, 1.3%; Hispanic, 40.1%; Asian, 0.3%; Other, 1.3%.

Vital Statistics, annual: Births, 562; deaths, 410; marriages, 266; divorces, 157.

Recreation: Rancho de las Cabras mission ranch ruins, historic homes; the Stockdale watermelon jubilee in June; Floresville peanut festival in October.

Minerals: Oil, gas, clays.

Agriculture: Cattle, corn, sorghum, hay, cotton. Market value $68.6 million.

FLORESVILLE (8,104) county seat; government/services, distribution, retail trade; hospital; parks.

Other towns include: **La Vernia** (1,426); **Pandora** (110); **Poth** (2,344) agriculture, commuting to San Antonio; bicycle ride in September; **Stockdale** (1,702) agriculture, commuting to San Antonio, museum, nature center, watermelon jubilee in June; **Sutherland Springs** (420).

Part of **Nixon** (2,542, mostly in Gonzales County).

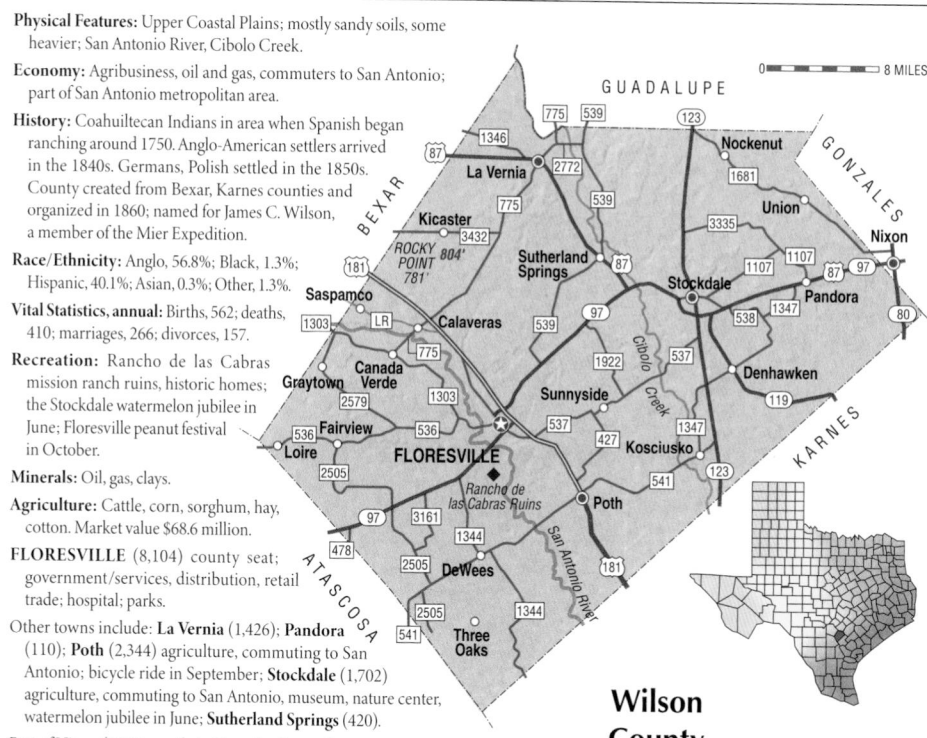

Wilson County

Population	52,127	Rainfall (in.)	29.1	Wages	$96,619,215
Change from 2010 (%)	21.5	Jan. mean min (°F)	32.2	Per Capita Income	$46,448
Area (sq. mi.)	808.4	July mean max (°F)	95.5	Prop. Value	$5,761,592,385
Land Area (sq. mi.)	803.7	Civ. Labor	25,055	Retail Sales	$533,777,666
Altitude (ft.)	300–804	Unemployed (%)	4.6		

Winkler County

Physical Features: Western county adjoining New Mexico on plains, partly sandy hills.

Economy: Oil and natural gas, ranching, prison, some farming.

History: Apache area until arrival of Comanches in the 1700s. Anglo-Americans began ranching in the 1880s. Oil discovered in 1926. Mexican migration increased after 1960. County named for Confederate Col. C.M. Winkler; created from Tom Green County in 1887; organized in 1910.

Race/Ethnicity: Anglo, 34.7%; Black, 1.8%; Hispanic, 61.2%; Asian, 0.2%; Other, 1.9%.

Vital Statistics, annual: Births, 136; deaths, 70; marriages, 32; divorces, 16.

Recreation: Part of Monahans Sandhills State Park; museum; Roy Orbison festival in June at Wink; Wink Sink, large sinkhole.

Minerals: Oil, gas.

Agriculture: Beef cattle. Market value $3.4 million.

KERMIT (6,494) county seat; oil, gas, ranching, some farming; hospital; Celebration Days in August.

WINK (1,066) oil, gas, ranching.

Population	7,990	July mean max (°F)	96.9
Change from 2010 (%)	12.4	Civ. Labor	3,927
Area (sq. mi.)	841.3	Unemployed (%)	8.1
Land Area (sq. mi.)	841.1	Wages	$56,534,519
Altitude (ft.)	2,665–3,400	Per Capita Income	$63,667
Rainfall (in.)	13.1	Prop. Value	$3,605,351,293
Jan. mean min (°F)	28.9	Retail Sales	$128,391,317

Wise County

Physical Features: Northwest county of rolling prairie, some oaks; clay, loam, sandy soils; Lake Bridgeport, Eagle Mountain Lake.

Economy: Petroleum, sand and gravel, agribusiness, many residents work in Fort Worth.

History: Caddo Indian groups. Delaware tribe present when Anglo-Americans arrived in the 1850s. County created in 1856 from Cooke County, organized the same year; named for Virginian, U.S. Sen. Henry A. Wise, who favored annexation of Texas.

Race/Ethnicity: Anglo, 76.5%; Black, 0.9%; Hispanic, 19.9%; Asian, 0.4%; Other, 2.1%.

Vital Statistics, annual: Births, 837; deaths, 554; mmarriages, 434; divorces, 278.

Recreation: Lake activities, hunting, exotic deer preserve, historical sites, Lyndon B. Johnson National Grassland, heritage museum; Decatur Chisholm trail days in June, Bridgeport Butterfield stage days in July.

Minerals: Gas, oil, sand, gravel.

Agriculture: Beef cattle, hay, dairies, horses, wheat, goats. Market value $46.3 million.

DECATUR (7,086) county seat; petroleum center, dairying, cattle marketing, some manufacturing; hospital.

BRIDGEPORT (7,077) trade center for lake resort, oil and gas production, manufacturing, prison release facility; time-share housing, art community.

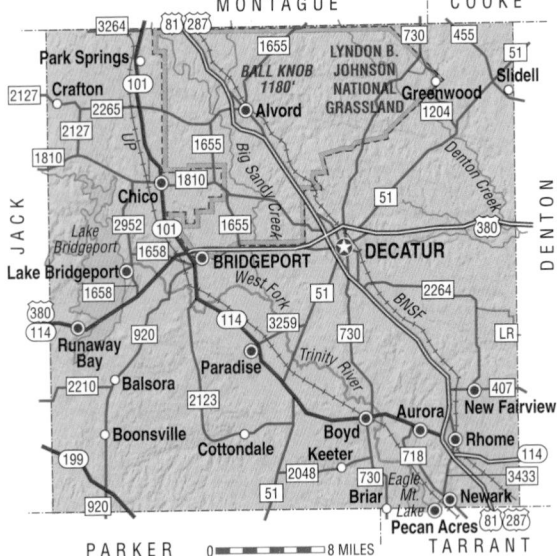

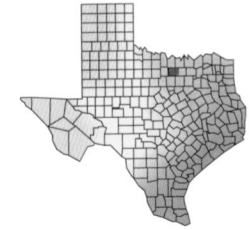

Other towns include: **Alvord** (1,576); **Aurora** (1,550) sand and gravel, manufacturing, equestrian center, "alien crash" site; **Boyd** (1,504) chili cookoff in May; **Briar** (6,116, mostly in Tarrant County); **Chico** (1,181); **Greenwood** (76); **Lake Bridgeport** (398); **Newark** (1,244); **New Fairview** (1,563); **Paradise** (560); **Pecan Acres** (4,480, partly in Tarrant County); **Rhome** (1,845); **Runaway Bay** (1,575) tourism, fishing, boating, golf club, Firecracker Scramble in July; **Slidell** (175).

For explanation of sources, symbols and abbreviations, see p. 204, and foldout map.

Population.......................**69,609**	Rainfall (in.)............................34.7	Wages $265,245,614
Change from 2010 (%)................17.7	Jan. mean min (°F)....................29.7	Per Capita Income $44,870
Area (sq. mi.)........................ 922.6	July mean max (°F)...................94.2	Prop. Value $12,978,854,947
Land Area (sq. mi.)................... 904.4	Civ. Labor 32,445	Retail Sales $840,335,495
Altitude (ft.)....................649–1,180	Unemployed (%)........................5.2	

The Select movie theater in Mineola. Photo by Renelibrary, CC by SA 4.0/ Wikimedia Commons

Wood County

Physical Features: Hilly northeastern county almost half forested; sandy to alluvial soils; drained by Sabine and tributaries; Lake Fork Reservoir, Lake Quitman, Lake Winnsboro, Lake Hawkins, Holbrook Lake.

Economy: Agribusiness, oil, gas, tourism.

History: Caddo Indians, reduced by disease. Anglo-American settlement developed in the 1840s. County created from Van Zandt County in 1850, organized the same year; named for Gov. George T. Wood.

Race/Ethnicity: Anglo, 81.7%; Black, 5.1%; Hispanic, 10.5%; Asian, 0.4%; Other, 2%.

Vital Statistics, annual: Births, 417; deaths, 613; marriages, 238; divorces, 176.

Recreation: Autumn trails; lake activities; hunting, fishing, birding; Gov. Hogg shrine and museum; historic sites; scenic drives; Mineola depot.

Minerals: Gas, oil, sand, gravel.

Agriculture: Cattle, dairies, poultry, forages, vegetables, nurseries. Market value $127.5 million. Timber production significant.

QUITMAN (1,850) county seat; tourism, food processing, some manufacturing; hospital; botanical gardens; Dogwood Fiesta.

MINEOLA (4,777) agriculture, railroad center (Amtrak), oil and gas, heritage and

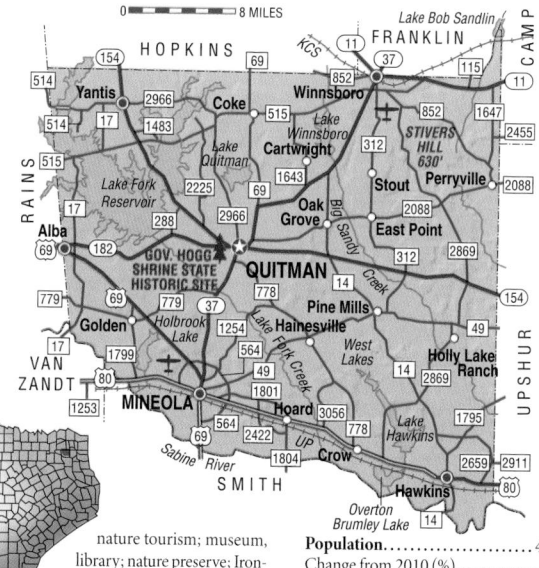

nature tourism; museum, library; nature preserve; Ironhorse Festival in November.

WINNSBORO (3,399, partly in Franklin County) poultry production, dairies, distribution, prison; hospital.

Other towns include: **Alba** (562, partly in Rains County); **Golden** (398) Sweet Potato festival in October; **Hawkins** (1,354) petroleum, water bottling, Jarvis Christian College; oil festival in October; **Holly Lake Ranch** (3,031); **Yantis** (419).

Population	45,084
Change from 2010 (%)	7.4
Area (sq. mi.)	695.7
Land Area (sq. mi.)	645.2
Altitude (ft.)	270–630
Rainfall (in.)	43.0
Jan. mean min (°F)	32.5
July mean max (°F)	94.4
Civ. Labor	18,144
Unemployed (%)	5.8
Wages	$112,713,190
Per Capita Income	$39,803
Prop. Value	$5,666,501,904
Retail Sales	$553,227,433

Yoakum County

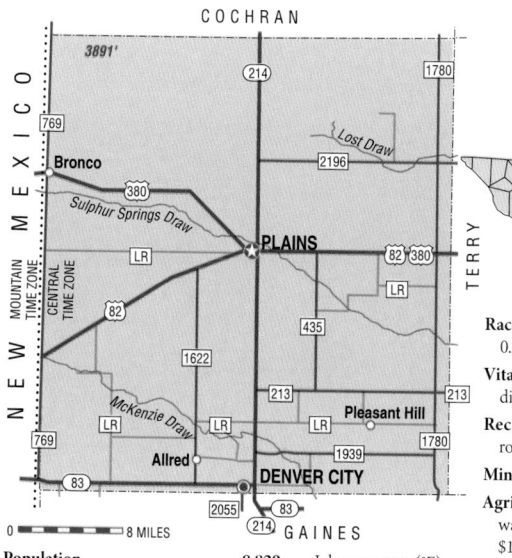

Physical Features: Western county is level to rolling; playas, draws; sandy, loam, chocolate soils.

Economy: Oil and gas, agriculture.

History: Comanche hunting area. Anglo-Americans began ranching in the 1890s. Oil discovered in 1936. Mexican migration increased in the 1950s. County named for Henderson Yoakum, pioneer historian; created from Bexar District in 1876; organized in 1907.

Race/Ethnicity: Anglo, 29.7%; Black, 0.7%; Hispanic, 68.1%; Asian, 0.2%; Other, 1.1%.

Vital Statistics, annual: Births, 162; deaths, 63; marriages, 55; divorces, 26.

Recreation: Tsa Mo Ga museum at Plains; Plains watermelon roundup on Labor Day weekend.

Minerals: Oil, natural gas.

Agriculture: Cotton, peanuts (third in acreage), sorghum, wheat, watermelons, cattle. Some 90,000 acres irrigated. Market value $100.2 million.

PLAINS (1,644) county seat; oil, agribusiness center.

DENVER CITY (5,044) center for oil, agriculture activities in two counties; hospital/medical services, library, museum; Annie Armstrong dugout shelter.

Population	8,829
Change from 2010 (%)	12.1
Area (sq. mi.)	799.7
Land Area (sq. mi.)	799.7
Altitude (ft.)	3,400–3,891
Rainfall (in.)	18.2
Jan. mean min (°F)	25.7
July mean max (°F)	91.7
Civ. Labor	3,264
Unemployed (%)	9.1
Wages	$43,242,110
Per Capita Income	$44,932
Prop. Value	$2,931,844,880
Retail Sales	$76,773,226

Young County

Physical Features: Hilly, broken; drained by Brazos and tributaries; Possum Kingdom Lake, Lake Graham.

Economy: Oil, agribusiness, tourism, hunting leases.

History: U.S. military outpost established in 1851. Site of Brazos Indian Reservation from 1854–1859 with Caddoes, Wacos, and other tribes. Anglo-American settlers arrived in the 1850s. County named for early Texan, Col. W.C. Young; created from Bosque and Fannin counties, and organized in 1856; reorganized in 1874.

Race/Ethnicity: Anglo, 76.1%; Black, 1.2%; Hispanic, 20.3%; Asian, 0.3%; Other, 1.9%.

Vital Statistics, annual: Births, 215; deaths, 239; marriages, 139; divorces, 82.

Recreation: Lake activities; hunting; Fort Belknap; marker at oak tree in Graham where ranchers formed forerunner of Texas and Southwestern Cattle Raisers Association.

Minerals: Oil, gas, sand, and gravel.

Agriculture: Beef cattle; wheat is the chief crop, also hay, cotton, pecans, nursery plants. Market value $21.7 million.

GRAHAM (9,158) county seat; oil and gas production, agriculture, tourism, government/services; hospital; old post office museum and art center; Western heritage days in September.

Other towns include: **Loving** (300); **Newcastle** (595) old coal-mining town; **Olney**

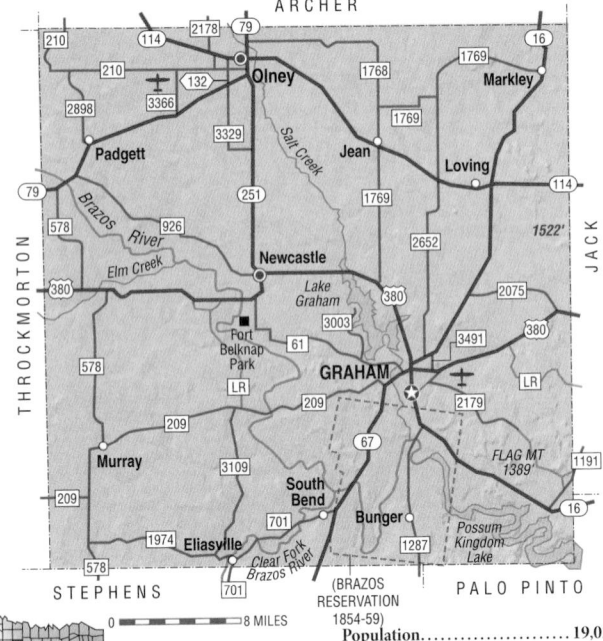

(3,235) aluminum, varied manufacturing, hospital; One-Arm Dove Hunt in September; **South Bend** (100).

Population	**19,029**
Change from 2010 (%)	2.6
Area (sq. mi.)	930.9
Land Area (sq. mi.)	914.5
Altitude (ft.)	995–1,522
Rainfall (in.)	31.5
Jan. mean min (°F)	28.3
July mean max (°F)	96.2
Civ. Labor	7,669
Unemployed (%)	5.4
Wages	$80,444,407
Per Capita Income	$50,732
Prop. Value	$2,533,051,623
Retail Sales	$288,056,231

For explanation of sources, symbols and abbreviations, see p. 204, and foldout map.

The welcome sign on U.S. 83 as you enter Crystal City in Zavala County. Photo by Barbara Brannon, CC 2/Wikimedia Commons

Zapata County

Physical Features: South Texas county of rolling, brushy topography; broken by tributaries of Rio Grande; Falcon Reservoir.

Economy: Natural gas and oil production and services, banking, tourism/Falcon Reservoir activities.

History: Coahuiltecan Indians in area when the ranch settlement of Nuestra Señora de los Dolores was established in 1750. Anglo-American migration increased after 1980. County named for Col. Antonio Zapata, pioneer rancher; created and organized in 1858 from Starr, Webb counties.

Race/Ethnicity: Anglo, 5.3%; Black, 0%; Hispanic, 94.1%; Asian, 0.2%; Other, 0.1%.

Vital Statistics, annual: Births, 270; deaths, 85; marriages, 25; divorces, 2.

Recreation: Lake, state park, hunting, fishing, bird watching, golfing, Dolores Hacienda site, rock hunting.

Minerals: Natural gas, caliche.

Agriculture: Beef cattle, sorghum, meat goats. Market value $6.3 million. Hunting/wildlife leases important.

Zapata (4,924) county seat; tourism, agribusiness, oil, retirement center; clinic; fajita cook-off in November.

Other towns include: **Falcon** (186); **Lopeño** (185); **Medina** (4,387), and **San Ygnacio** (558) historic buildings, museum.

Population...................... **14,196**	July mean max (°F).....................97.8
Change from 2010 (%)..................1.3	Civ. Labor.............................4,306
Area (sq. mi.)......................1,058.0	Unemployed (%).........................13
Land Area (sq. mi.)..................998.4	Wages................... $32,813,914
Altitude (ft.)......................301–860	Per Capita Income................ $28,936
Rainfall (in.)...........................19.8	Prop. Value............... $1,661,393,140
Jan. mean min (°F)....................46.3	Retail Sales................... $80,353,042

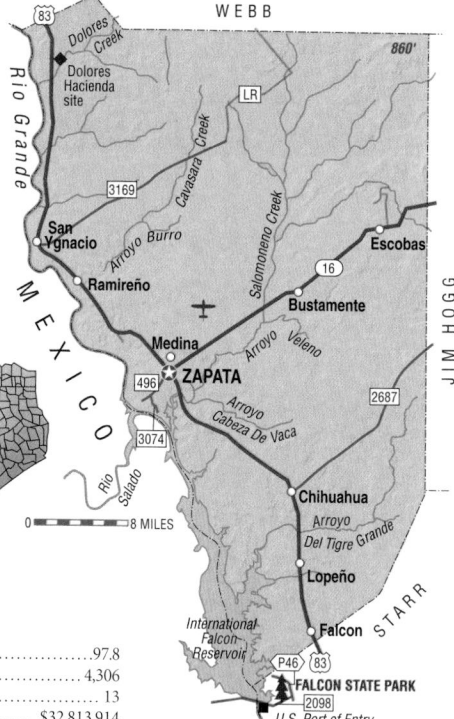

For explanation of sources, symbols and abbreviations, see p. 204, and foldout map.

Zavala County

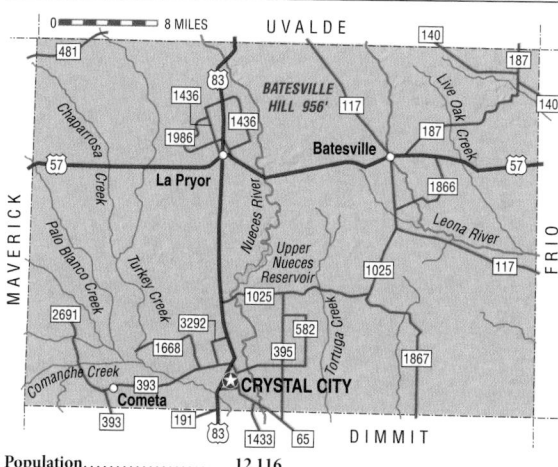

Physical Features: Southwestern county near Mexican border; rolling plains broken by much brush; Nueces, Leona, other streams; Upper Nueces Reservoir.

Economy: Agribusiness, food packaging, leading county in Winter Garden truck-farming area, government/services.

History: Coahuiltecan area; Apaches, Comanches arrived later. Ranching developed in the late 1860s. County created from Maverick and Uvalde counties in 1858; organized in 1884; named for Texas Revolutionary leader Lorenzo de Zavala.

Race/Ethnicity: Anglo, 5.3%; Black, 0.2%; Hispanic, 94%; Asian, 0%; Other, 0.2%.

Vital Statistics, annual: Births, 195; deaths, 111; marriages, 44; divorces, 0.

Recreation: Hunting, fishing; spinach festival in November.

Minerals: Oil, natural gas.

Agriculture: Cattle, grains, vegetables, cotton, pecans. About 30,000 acres irrigated. Market value $66.6 million. Hunting leases important.

CRYSTAL CITY (7,189) county seat; agribusiness, food processing, oil-field services; site of World War II detention center. Home of Popeye statue.

Other towns include: **Batesville** (1,039) and **La Pryor** (1,798).

Population...................... **12,116**
Change from 2010 (%)..................3.8
Area (sq. mi.)......................1,301.7
Land Area (sq. mi.)................1,297.4
Altitude (ft.)......................540–956
Rainfall (in.)...........................19.6
Jan. mean min (°F)....................43.6
July mean max (°F)....................97.2
Civ. Labor.............................3,417
Unemployed (%).......................13.6
Wages................... $24,988,737
Per Capita Income................ $30,779
Prop. Value............... $2,934,815,450
Retail Sales................... $59,020,478

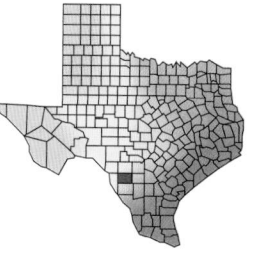

The Great Texas Land Rush

Stake your claim!

It seems unbelievable, but the **Great Texas Land Rush** has been active since 2011, and today it is stronger than ever! Funds raised through the Land Rush program are used to support the creation of each new edition of the Texas Almanac and improve our web presence at TexasAlmanac.com.

We'd like to extend a big *Thank You!* to our current adopters, listed below.

Ad Hall, adopted by Henry D. Hall Jr.
Alanreed, adopted by Margaret Gibson
Allen, adopted by Martinique Allen
Almeda, adopted by Margaret Gibson
Almedes, adopted by John
Alpine, adopted by Cindy Brandimarte
Amarillo, adopted by Joe & Mary Hughes
Anadarko, adopted by Ricardo Cruz
Annetta, adopted by Johnny D. Chapman
Appleby, adopted by David L Peavy
Aransas Pass, adopted by Marie Halff
Argyle, adopted by Kay Teer
Arlington, adopted by Floreen Henry & Family
Athens, adopted by Afred Smith, Marine Smith & Donald Lyles
Austin, adopted by Austin Faith LaPorte
Austin, adopted by Tommy & Sandy Hughes
Azle, adopted by Nancy Nation Jay
Bainville, adopted by Matt Mendiola
Baker, adopted by Judy G. Russell
Barnhart, adopted by Herbie R Taylor
Barton Creek, adopted by Weird Austin Productions, Inc.
Bastrop, adopted by Kevin & Debra DeWitt Jordan
Beaukiss, adopted by Karen & Connie Moss
Bee Cave, adopted by The Waldens
Bell Bottom, adopted by Tamarah Humphrey
Bells, adopted by Charming Grace Boutique
Bennett, adopted by Paula Wallace Cairns
Beth, adopted by Kimberly L
Bexar, adopted by Omega Delta Phi - Beta Theta Chapter
Blanco, adopted by Brenda Weeks Norris
Bland Lake, adopted by Kathleen Nelson
Boerne, adopted by Baby Girl
Bogata, adopted by Frank Vin Robinson
Borger, adopted by Robert & Laura Garrett
Bostick, adopted by Tina A. Griffith
Brad, adopted by Krista Fowles
Brady, adopted by Kailyn & HoneyGrove Smith
Brazosport, adopted by Carl Wolfe
Breckenridge, adopted by Herbie R Taylor
Brileytown, adopted by Jena L. Briley
Broaddus, adopted by Mayor Shirley J Parker
Brownsboro, adopted by Jacob Leon Cook
Brownsville, adopted by Felix Garza, Jr.
Brushy Creek, adopted by Round Rock Preservation
Bryans Mill, adopted by Brandy Luckey
Bryant Station, adopted by Denton Bryant KSJ
Buckner, adopted by Josh & Katie Asbill
Bunker Hill Village, adopted by Charlotte Lee
Bute, adopted by Joel Dixon
Caldwell, adopted by Kim & Doug Unerfusser
Cameron, adopted by Weird Austin Productions
Caney Head, adopted by Joe Moss
Canyon, adopted by Amanda Torrez

Carpenter, adopted by Jennifer, Eric, Andrew, Justin, & Katie
Cayote, adopted by Lloyd Tackitt
Center Point, adopted by Kate Crosby
Centerville, adopted by The Bain Family
Clear Creek, adopted by Ron & Beverly Little
Cleveland, adopted by Thomas Glenn Crawford
Clifton, adopted by = JE =
Colleyville, adopted by Andrew & Winnie Wayne
Cornelia, adopted by Chloe Cornelia Johnson
Crabapple, adopted by Peter Pehl II
Creedmoor, adopted by Peter Pehl II
Crockett, adopted by charles thompson
Cross Creek, adopted by Weird Austin Productions, Inc.
Cut & Shoot, adopted by Karen & Bob Yawn
D'Hanis, adopted by Mary Gilhooly
Dale, adopted by Emilie Jones Siarkiewicz
Dallas, adopted by Debra Polsky
Datura, adopted by Barbara Ribling
Diddy Wa Diddy, adopted by David M. Lanagan
Ding Dong, adopted by Barry Gidden
Doak Springs, adopted by Rachel Mae Cooper-Anderson
Dobbin, adopted by Ann & James Smith
Dodd City, adopted by Weird Austin Productions, Inc.
Dog Ridge, adopted by Phillip R Smith
Douglassville, adopted by Brandy Luckey
Douro, adopted by Ector County Utility District
Eagle'S Nest, adopted by Arrowhead Treazures, LLC
East Sweden, adopted by Mandie de Leon
Ecleto, adopted by Urrutia family
Edinburg, adopted by Ricardo Garza
Electra, adopted by Elaine Faucett
Elk, adopted by Charles Barton Family
Elroy, adopted by Todd Carlstrand
Ernest, adopted by Weird Austin Productions, Inc.
Erwin, adopted by Krista Fowles
Eureka Mills, adopted by The Notzon Family
Fairview, adopted by Crownover Family
Fairview, adopted by The Raymond Hall Family
Fedor, adopted by Fedor Mercantile & Gift Company
Flannagan'S Ranch, adopted by Rosemary Laverne Flanagan King
Florence, adopted by Roger & Cecelia Motzko
Fort Hood, adopted by Lane Abner Johnston
Fort Stockton, adopted by Kate Crosby
Fort Worth, adopted by Floreen Henry & Family
Fredericksburg, adopted by Liebeskind, A Children's Boutique
Frisco, adopted by Jim Whitten
Fruitvale, adopted by R&B Brand

Gainesville, adopted by Krista Fowles
Galveston, adopted by Dustin Henry
Gardendale, adopted by John N. Tyler
Garfield, adopted by Martin Legal Video
Gay Hill, adopted by Marissa Warner
George, adopted by Richard & Margaret George
Germantown, adopted by Claudia & Ford Frost
Giddings, adopted by Lone Star Back Roads, LLC
Gillespie, adopted by Friends of Gillespie County Country Schools, Inc
Gillett, adopted by Raul Degollado Serenil Sr
Glen Cove, adopted by Dennis & Bonnie Nelson
Glenrio, adopted by the Blu Turtle of Old Route 66 Association of Texas
Gonzales, adopted by Jose H Cantu
Good, adopted by personal
Grand Saline, adopted by Joel Robert Dixon
Grape Creek, adopted by Thomas J Mccarran
Grey Forest, adopted by Gus Van Steenberg & Family
Griffith, adopted by Tina A. Griffith
Guys Store, adopted by Angelica Proctor-Saddler
Hamilton Pool, adopted by Weird Austin Productions, Inc.
Harper, adopted by Mary Ann Walker
Harris, adopted by The Hughes Family
Harrold, adopted by Mindee Thweatt
Haskell, adopted by Kate Anger
Helotes, adopted by Edna Marnock Smith
Hishway, adopted by Jerald & Dee Lee
Hooleyan, adopted by Hoolyan Au Naturele Medical Cannabis Co
Houston, adopted by The Hughes Family
Houston Heights, adopted by Harley Grace LaPorte
Hughlett, adopted by Crownover Family
Hurst, adopted by Jay Ward
Independence, adopted by The Quinlan Family
Jacksboro, adopted by Jim Hawkins & Allen Hamilton
Jamaica Beach, adopted by Ron & Beverly Little
Jericho, adopted by Blair & Blanca Schaffer
Jerusalem, adopted by Amy Nelson
Johnsue, adopted by Taryn Peterson
Jot-Em-Down, adopted by Black Ranches
Jourdanton, adopted by Eye Care For Texans - Dr. Ron Mixon, OD
Judkins, adopted by Haskell Shelton Jr
Jumbo, adopted by JK Keeling Farms
Junction, adopted by Steve Palmer
Kamey, adopted by McKamey Bros
Katy, adopted by Scott & Jenny Wallace
Kelley, adopted by Kelley Miller
Keltys, adopted by Robert & John Hensley & Mary Hensley Johnson
Kennard, adopted by Paul Standley

Kerrville, adopted by Kate Crosby
Kleberg, adopted by Krista Fowles
Kolls, adopted by Adam Kolls
La Junta De Los Rios, adopted by juan
La Porte, adopted by Georgia Malone
Lake Jackson, adopted by Carl Wolfe
Laloma, adopted by ROBERT LEE MATTA
Langtry, adopted by Arrowhead Treazures, LLC
Las Islitas, adopted by Donna Dominguez-Lent Russell
Lauback, adopted by Megan Laubach
Lawrence Chapel, adopted by Jerry Moss
League City, adopted by John&Geri Paden
Leon, adopted by The Bain Family
Leon Springs, adopted by John Campbell
Lesley, adopted by Thelma L Hall Beasley
Lewisville, adopted by Kristie SS Steed
Lightner, adopted by Kelly Barker
Longview, adopted by Jim & Suzanne Bardwell
Lovelady, adopted by Mildred Brown & Donald Lyles
Loveless, adopted by Mark & Kara Bradbury
Luckenbach, adopted by Mary Hartwig
Lueders, adopted by LAURIE BEAL COOK
Lufkin, adopted by Jim Whitten
Magnet, adopted by William Loocke
Magnolia, adopted by Josey Reynolds/Helen Vandergriff
Mankins, adopted by David Pettijohn
Marfa, adopted by Cindy Brandimarte
Margaret, adopted by Margaret Gibson
Mathis, adopted by Dennis Parrish
Mcbride, adopted by Joshua McBride
Mcgregor, adopted by The Leslie Family
Medicine Mound, adopted by Bill Holcomb
Menard, adopted by Cynthia Womack
Midyett, adopted by Bob B. Midyett Jr
Miller Community, adopted by Gary S. King
Milligan, adopted by Lucy Anderson
Minden, adopted by Joe Earl Conway
Mineral Wells, adopted by Nanette & Dennis Sever
Mixon, adopted by Malachi Scott Dwaine Mixon
Mixon, adopted by Malachi Scott Dwaine Mixon
Mobeetie, adopted by Jan Hart
Mont, adopted by Irene Polansky Szwarc
Monterey, adopted by Rick Ferguson, Brooke Ferguson, Brittney Ferguson, Summer
Montgomery, adopted by Ken & Elisabeth Becker
Montgomery, adopted by Beth Blevins
Morgan'S Point, adopted by Claude Hunter
Morris, adopted by Krista Fowles
Mount Sharp, adopted by Dodie Juarez Scott
Mudville, adopted by All Things Texas@ John Mowey
Munn, adopted by Valerie Munn Hearn
Nacogdoches, adopted by Jim Whitten
New Braunfels, adopted by Gina Perryman
New Deal, adopted by Cindy Brandimarte
New York, adopted by Joel Dixon
North Waco, adopted by Michael Bauer
Nurillo, adopted by John Carlos Trevino
O'Donnell, adopted by TM
Oak Point, adopted by John Lusk
Oakalla, adopted by Wanda Williams Langford
Oakdale, adopted by HoganFarm
Odessa, adopted by Jane, Eileen & Joe Suggs, Jr.
Ogarita, adopted by Lee Webb
Orange Grove, adopted by Albert Sanchez Jr

Paradise, adopted by Camille Cobb
Pasche, adopted by Golda Marie Foster (grdaughter of John Q & Ora Ledbetter Triplett)
Pecos, adopted by Yolanda Lara Diaz
Peerless, adopted by Laura Lindley
Pelham, adopted by Michael Heiskell
Pernitas Point, adopted by Mr.&Mrs Albert (Yvette) Sanchez Jr.
Perry, adopted by Perry Barker
Perryman'S Crossing, adopted by Gina Perryman
Pflugerville, adopted by Tony Bain & Matt Burkhard
Pickett Valley, adopted by Fred Dillard
Pickton, adopted by Rose Bryant
Pilgrim, adopted by Michael & Kacie Pilgrim
Pinehill, adopted by Fred Buckner Vinson
Piney Point Village, adopted by Charlotte Lee
Pipe Creek, adopted by K. L. Backhaus
Pistol Hill, adopted by Joe Brown
Pittsburg, adopted by John R. Pitts, Jr.
Plains, adopted by Jean & Ed Callary
Pleasant Ridge, adopted by Robbie Pierce Ferguson
Pleasanton, adopted by Eye Care For Texans - Dr. Ron Mixon, OD
Pluto, adopted by PLUTO TV
Point Enterprise, adopted by Jennifer & Jack Dixon
Port Acres, adopted by the Bill & Delores Atkinson Family
Porvenir, adopted by Amanda Shields
Poteet, adopted by Eye Care for Texans - Dr. Ron Mixon, OD
Prairie View, adopted by Roy Elzie Donald Lyles Endowment College Fund
Presidio, adopted by Felix Salmeron
Presidio, adopted by CARAN DRIVER
Pringle, adopted by Mike Pringle
Quihi, adopted by John Germann
Rankin, adopted by Cynthia Rackley Cooper
Rath City, adopted by Bob Rogers, Robert Rogers & Clive Siegle
Raven Hill, adopted by Conchata Laferrel Clark
Rayner, adopted by Rick Ferguson, Brooke Ferguson, Brittney Ferguson, Summer
Redland, adopted by Airborne Excavation & Utility Jeff Tagert
Riceville, adopted by Ronny & Sheri Cortez
Richardson, adopted by FASTSIGNS of Richardson
Riesel, adopted by Sheryl Thompson
Roberts, adopted by David Fleming Bragg
Roberts, adopted by Cindy Roberts Bragg
Rockdale, adopted by JOY KORNEGAY
Rollingwood, adopted by Weird Austin Productions, Inc.
Roma (-Los Saenz), adopted by Now salinas
Rosenberg, adopted by Danny M. Diaz
Rosenfeld, adopted by Michael Rosenfeld
Round Rock, adopted by Caran Driver
Rowlett, adopted by Keep Rowlett Beautiful, Inc.
Ruidosa, adopted by Jumano Indian Nation
Salome, adopted by Eddie & Penelope Hernandez
San Antonio, adopted by His Eminence Archbishop Ray Gonia, ECLJ
San Benito, adopted by Hon. Daniel T. Robles & Linda D. Robles
San Felipe, adopted by Edith Elizabeth Pollitz
San Patricio, adopted by Mary Margaret Baldeschwiler

San Roman, adopted by Mario & Jeanette San Roman
San Ygnacio, adopted by GeorgiAnne Uribe Brochstein
Sand Branch, adopted by Thompson
Sanderson, adopted by Karen Elizabeth Balestrini (KERR)
Sandies Chapel, adopted by Melinda Clingman
Sandy Elm, adopted by Teddy & Gay Lynn Olsovsky
Sandy Hill, adopted by Mary & Joe Hughes
Sarahville De Viesca, adopted by Rancho Viesca
Savoy, adopted by Chucos Auto Repair llc
Seagoville, adopted by Krista Fowles
Shamrock, adopted by Nanette & Dennis Sever
Siloam, adopted by The Slone Family
Slaton, adopted by Jerry Kitten
Stephenville, adopted by Stephen Gilhooly
Stevenson, adopted by Caroline Brooks
Stinnett, adopted by Nanette & Dennis Sever
Study Butte, adopted by The DiBona Family
Sunset Valley, adopted by Weird Austin Productions, Inc.
Sweet Union, adopted by Glynis Riser
Swinney Switch, adopted by Paige Willett
Taylor, adopted by Lone Star Back Roads LLC
Taylors Creek, adopted by Fred Dillard Dillard Ranch
Telegraph, adopted by Chris & Beth Ann Kelm
Terlingua, adopted by The DiBona Family
Terlingua, adopted by The DiBona Family
Tevis Bluff, adopted by Sequila Tevis
Texarkana, adopted by John & Sakiko Willis
Travis, adopted by Liz, Tom & Austin Kaplan
Travis Ranch, adopted by Roy, Elzie & Donald Lyles Scholarship Fund (R)
Truby, adopted by Bill Truby
Tuff, adopted by Howard Purnell
Turkey Creek, adopted by Joel Dixon
Turlington, adopted by Lucas Garcia
Turnertown, adopted by THE CONTRACTORS BAND
Tusculum, adopted by Ben Adam
Tyler, adopted by Donald Lyles Doing Business As The Texas Telegram Telegraph (R) & The Texas Town Ta
Valentine, adopted by Dallas Love Ya
Verhalen, adopted by Michael Cate
Vreeland, adopted by Jack A. Muggli, Grandson of Jacob Martin Muggli Sr, the founder of Vreeland.
Waller, adopted by The McCaig Family
Webberville, adopted by Susan Hensley
Webster, adopted by Sue Craddock Hamm
Weisinger, adopted by the Warren Steffen family, descendants of the Dampier/Gibbs/Fultz family
Wheatland, adopted by Valerie Russell
Wheelock, adopted by Alice & Julia Hedrick
Whitewright, adopted by Molly Malinda M. Reed
Williamson Settlement, adopted by John C Poole
Wills Point, adopted by Letitia Wills-Smith
Wimberley, adopted by Margaux Vautherot
Woodward, adopted by Kaye Arnold
Zapata Ranch, adopted by Amanda Lynne Clements
Ziler, adopted by Howard County Judge Kathryn Wiseman
Zulu, adopted by TEXASZULU.COM

Population

NACOGDOCHES
CITY LIMIT
POP. 29914

U.S. CENSUS OF TOWNS

CENTER OF POPULATION BY DECADES

TEN LARGEST U.S. METRO AREAS

The population of Nacogdoches has grown by 13% since this photo was taken in 2002. Photo by Jeff Attaway, CC by 2.0/Flickr.

Population 2010 and 2019

Population: Numbers in parentheses are from the 2010 U.S. census. The Census Bureau counts only incorporated cities and a few unincorporated towns called Census Designated Places.

Population figures at the far right for incorporated cities and CDPs are the Texas Demographic Center estimates for July 1, 2019. (Note: The results of the 2020 U.S. Census were not yet available at press time.) Names of the incorporated cities are in capital letters, e.g., "ABBOTT".

The population figure given for other towns is an estimate received from local officials through a Texas Almanac survey.

When no 2010 census was conducted for a newly incorporated city, these places show "(nc)" for "not counted" in place of a 2010 population figure.

Location: The county in which the town is located follows the name of the town. If more than one county is listed, the town is principally in the first-named county, e.g., "ABERNATHY, Hale-Lubbock".

Businesses: For incorporated cities, the number following the county name indicates the number of businesses in the city as of January 2018 as reported by the state comptroller. For unincorporated towns, it is the number of businesses within the postal zip code as reported by the U.S. Bureau of the Census for 2016.

For example, "ABBOTT, Hill, 22" means Abbott in Hill County had 22 businesses.

Post Offices: Places with post offices, as of May 2021, are marked with an asterisk (*), e.g., "*Afton".

Town, County . . . . Pop. 2019	Town, County . . . . Pop. 2019	Town, County . . . . Pop. 2019
A	Aikin Grove, Red River. 15	Alleyton, Colorado, 14 165
	Airport Heights, Starr (161). 177	*Allison, Wheeler, 6 135
*ABBOTT, Hill, 22 (356). 375	Airport Road Addition, Brooks,	Allmon, Floyd 24
*ABERNATHY, Hale, Lubbock, 95	(93). 86	Allred, Yoakum 90
(2,805). 2,699	Airville, Bell 65	ALMA, Ellis, 14 (331). 402
*ABILENE, Taylor, Jones, 4,121	Alabama-Coushatta, Polk 572	Almira, Cass 30
(117,463). 123,302	*ALAMO, Hidalgo, 560	*ALPINE, Brewster, 336
Ables Springs, Kaufman 20	(18,353). 20,208	(5,905). 5,928
Abner, Kaufman. 75	Alamo Alto, El Paso 19	Alsa, Van Zandt 30
Abram, Hidalgo (2,067) 2,461	Alamo Beach, Calhoun 100	*Altair, Colorado, 6. 30
Acala, Hudspeth. 25	ALAMO HEIGHTS, Bexar, 333	*ALTO, Cherokee, 57 (1,225). 1,306
*Ace, Polk, 1. 40	(7,031). 8,614	Alto Bonito Heights, Starr (342). . . . 366
*ACKERLY, Dawson, Martin, 16	Alanreed, Gray, 1 48	Altoga, Collin 137
(220). 227	Alazan, Nacogdoches 100	ALTON, Hidalgo, 269
Acme, Hardeman. 7	*ALBA, Wood, Rains, 70 (504). 562	(12,298). 17,165
Acton, Hood 1,129	*ALBANY, Shackelford, 123	Alum Creek, Bastrop 70
Acuff, Lubbock 152	(2,034). 2,037	*ALVARADO, Johnson, 224
Acworth, Red River 50	Albert, Gillespie. 25	(3,785). 4,590
Adams Gardens, Cameron 350	Albion, Red River. 52	*ALVIN, Brazoria, 998
Adams Store, Panola. 12	Alderbranch, Anderson. 3	(24,236). 29,391
Adamsville, Lampasas 75	Aldine, Harris (15,869). 17,792	*ALVORD, Wise, 58 (1,334). 1,576
Addicks, Harris . . . . . . [part of Houston]	*ALEDO, Parker, 278 (2,716). 4,423	Amada Acres, Starr (92) 82
Addielou, Red River. 31	Aleman, Hamilton 50	Amargosa, Jim Wells (291) 311
*ADDISON, Dallas, 1,841	Alexander, Erath 40	*AMARILLO, Potter, Randall, 6,780
(13,056). 16,450	Aley, Henderson 45	(190,695). 202,314
Adell, Parker 100	Alfred, Jim Wells (91) 80	Amaya, Zavala (93). 87
*Adkins, Bexar, 36. 400	Algerita, San Saba. 10	Ambia, Lamar 16
Admiral, Callahan 18	Algoa, Galveston 135	Ambrose, Grayson 90
Adobes, Presidio 5	*ALICE, Jim Wells, 687	AMES, Liberty, 10 (1,003). 1,218
*ADRIAN, Oldham, 6 (166) 167	(19,104). 18,536	Ames, Coryell 10
Advance, Parker. 100	Alice Acres, Jim Wells (490). 466	*AMHERST, Lamb, 14 (721). 630
*Afton, Dickens, 4. 15	*Alief, Harris . . . . [part of Houston]	Amherst, Lamar. 125
Agnes, Parker 60	Allamoore, Hudspeth 10	Amistad, Val Verde (53). 45
*AGUA DULCE, Nueces, 20	*ALLEN, Collin, 2,916	Ammannsville, Fayette 137
(812). 838	(84,246). 105,524	Amphion, Atascosa. 26
Agua Dulce, El Paso (3,014). 3,428	Allenfarm, Brazos. 35	Amsterdam, Brazoria 193
Agua Nueva, Jim Hogg 5	Allenhurst, Matagorda 72	Anacua, Starr (12) 9
Aguilares, Webb (21) 23	Allen's Chapel, Fannin 30	Anadarko, Rusk 30
*Aiken, Floyd, 1 52	Allen's Point, Fannin. 40	*ANAHUAC, Chambers, 89
Aiken, Shelby. 150	Allentown, Angelina. 800	(2,243). 2,491

For a complete list of more than 17,000 Texas communities, past and present, go to www.texasalmanac.com

Town, County . . . . Pop. 2019	Town, County . . . . Pop. 2019	Town, County . . . . Pop. 2019
Anchor, Brazoria 150	Ashwood, Matagorda 132	**B**
*ANDERSON, Grimes, 48 (222) 243	Asia, Polk 83	
Anderson Mill, Williamson,	*ASPERMONT, Stonewall, 56	Back, Gray 6
Travis . . . . [part of Austin]	(919). 861	*Bacliff, Galveston, 90 (8,619) 10,073
Ander-Weser-Kilgore, Goliad 322	Atascocita, Harris (65,844) 78,165	*Bagwell, Red River, 1. 150
Andice, Williamson 300	*Atascosa, Bexar, 46 600	*BAILEY, Fannin, 10 (289) 315
*ANDREWS, Andrews, 518	Ater, Coryell 12	BAILEY'S PRAIRIE, Brazoria, 16
(11,088). 14,704	*ATHENS, Henderson, 595	(727). 789
*ANGLETON, Brazoria, 583	(12,710). 13,649	Baileyville, Milam 32
(18,862). 21,483	*ATLANTA, Cass, 273 (5,675). 5,610	Bainer, Lamb. 10
ANGUS, Navarro, 24 (414). 455	Atlas, Lamar 28	Bainville, Karnes 8
*ANNA, Collin, 276 (8,249). 14,708	Atoy, Cherokee 50	*BAIRD, Callahan, 78 (1,496) 1,496
Annaville, Nueces	*AUBREY, Denton, 208 (2,595) 4,855	Baker, Floyd 28
[part of Corpus Christi]	Augusta, Houston. 40	Bakersfield, Pecos 9
ANNETTA, Parker, 70 (1,288). 3,132	AURORA, Wise, 28 (1,220). 1,550	*BALCH SPRINGS, Dallas, 615
ANNETTA NORTH, Parker, 11	*AUSTIN, Travis, Williamson,	(23,728). 26,426
(518). 581	37,458 (790,491). 984,115	BALCONES HEIGHTS, Bexar,
ANNETTA SOUTH, Parker, 10	Austonio, Houston. 37	175 (2,941). 3,362
(526). 592	*AUSTWELL, Refugio, 9 (147) 144	Bald Hill, Angelina. 100
*ANNONA, Red River, 5 (315) 285	Authon, Parker 15	Bald Prairie, Robertson. 40
*ANSON, Jones, 102 (2,430) 2,357	*Avalon, Ellis, 3 400	*BALLINGER, Runnels, 202
Antelope, Jack 65	*AVERY, Red River, 21 (482) 433	(3,767). 3,620
ANTHONY, El Paso, 133	*AVINGER, Cass, 29 (444) 431	*BALMORHEA, Reeves, 18
(5,011). 5,640	Avoca, Jones, 2. 121	(479). 538
Antioch, Cass 45	*Axtell, McLennan, 21. 300	Balsora, Wise. 50
Antioch, Delta 10	*AZLE, Tarrant, Parker, 577	B and E, Starr (518) 571
Antioch, Madison 15	(10,947). 13,285	*BANDERA, Bandera, 286 (857). . . . 941
Antioch Colony, Hays. 25		
*ANTON, Hockley, 16 (1,126). 1,100		
APPLEBY, Nacogdoches (474). 491		
*Apple Springs, Trinity, 10 350		
*AQUILLA, Hill, 9 (109). 114		
*ARANSAS PASS, San Patricio,		
Aransas, 341 (8,204) 8,757		
Arbala, Hopkins. 41		
Arcadia, Shelby 35		
*ARCHER CITY, Archer, 66		
(1,834). 1,920		
ARCOLA, Fort Bend, 67		
(1,642). 2,360		
Arden, Irion 7		
Argo, Titus 90		
*ARGYLE, Denton, 271 (3,282) 4,555		
ARLINGTON, Tarrant, 10,904		
(365,438). 391,791		
Armstrong, Bell 25		
Armstrong, Kenedy, 3. 4		
Arneckeville, DeWitt 50		
Arnett, Coryell 15		
Arnett, Hockley. 5		
*ARP, Smith, 70 (970) 1,036		
Arroyo City, Cameron 600		
Arroyo Colorado Estates,		
Cameron, (997) 1,120		
Arroyo Gardens, Cameron (456) . . . 527		
*Art, Mason, 14 14		
Artesia Wells, La Salle, 2 35		
*Arthur City, Lamar, 6. 180		
Arvana, Dawson 8		
Asa, McLennan 46		
Ash, Houston. 19		
Ashby, Matagorda 60		
*ASHERTON, Dimmit, 15		
(1,084). 1,018		
Ashland, Upshur 45		
Ashtola, Donley. 20		

McCulloch County:
Geographic center of the state

Center of Texas Population

Shaded counties:
Centers of population for the state in the past.

The center means as many people live east, west, north and south of the point.

Locations of population centers for each decennial census.

Texas Business Review and other sources.

Town, County . . . . Pop. 2019	Town, County . . . . Pop. 2019	Town, County . . . . Pop. 2019
Bandera Falls, Bandera 90	*BELLMEAD, McLennan, 251	BEVIL OAKS, Jefferson, 29
*BANGS, Brown, 48 (1,603) 1,588	(9,901). 10,731	(1,274). 1,226
*Banquete, Nueces, 9 (726) 795	*BELLS, Grayson, 43 (1,392). 1,542	Bevilport, Jasper 12
Barbarosa, Guadalupe 46	*BELLVILLE, Austin, 290	Beyersville, Williamson 80
Barclay, Falls 58	(4,097). 4,602	Biardstown, Lamar. 75
*BARDWELL, Ellis, 4 (649) 726	Belmena, Milam 15	*Bigfoot, Frio, 10 (450) 537
*Barker, Harris, 11 2,500	Belmont, Gonzales, 6 55	Big Hill, Limestone. 9
*Barksdale, Edwards, 2 100	Belott, Houston 101	*BIG LAKE, Reagan, 146
Barnes, Polk 75	*BELTON, Bell, 838 (18,216). 22,695	(2,936). 3,661
*Barnhart, Irion, 11 110	Ben Arnold, Milam 100	*BIG SANDY, Upshur, 87
Barnum, Polk. 50	*BENAVIDES, Duval, 21 (1,362) . . . 1,239	(1,343). 1,402
Barrera, Starr (108) 112	*Ben Bolt, Jim Wells, 4 1,600	*BIG SPRING, Howard, 669
Barrett, Harris, 23 (3,199). 3,483	*BENBROOK, Tarrant, 682	(27,282). 28,349
*BARRY, Navarro (242) 265	(21,234). 23,912	Big Thicket Estates, Liberty, Polk,
*BARSTOW, Ward, 3 (349). 384	Benchley, Robertson, Brazos 110	(742). 882
*BARTLETT, Williamson, Bell, 61	*Bend, San Saba, Lampasas, 1 115	Big Valley, Mills 35
(2,684). 2,789	*Ben Franklin, Delta, 1 60	*BIG WELLS, Dimmit, 8 (697) 694
Barton Corners, Lipscomb 4	Ben Hur, Limestone 42	Biloxi, Newton 75
Barton Creek, Travis (3,077) 3,402	*BENJAMIN, Knox, 14 (258) 256	Birch, Burleson 200
BARTONVILLE, Denton, 116	Benjamin Perez, Starr (34) 30	Birome, Hill 30
(1,469). 1,814	Bennett, Parker 120	Birthright, Hopkins 100
Barwise, Floyd. 16	Benoit, Runnels. 10	Biry, Medina 24
*Basin, Brewster, 3 30	Bentonville, Jim Wells. 15	*BISHOP, Nueces, 62 (3,134). 3,092
Bassett, Bowie 100	*Ben Wheeler, Van Zandt, 70. 504	BISHOP HILLS, Potter (193) 173
*BASTROP, Bastrop, 764	*Berclair, Goliad, 3 253	*Bivins, Cass, 6 215
(7,218). 9,226	Berea, Houston 41	Bixby, Cameron (504). 598
Bateman, Bastrop. 12	Berea, Marion 200	Black, Parmer 100
*Batesville, Zavala, 10 (1,068) 1,050	Bergheim, Kendall, 17 1,213	Blackfoot, Anderson. 50
Batesville, Red River. 14	Berlin, Washington 40	Black Hill, Atascosa 60
*Batson, Hardin, 14 140	Bernardo, Colorado 155	Black Hills, Navarro 80
Battle, McLennan. 100	BERRYVILLE, Henderson, 8	Black Jack, Cherokee 47
Baxter, Henderson 150	(975). 1,075	Black Jack, Robertson. 45
*BAY CITY, Matagorda, 547	*BERTRAM, Burnet, Williamson,	Black Oak, Hopkins 150
(17,614). 17,431	86 (1,353) 1,576	*BLACKWELL, Nolan, Coke,
Baylor Lake, Childress 50	Bessmay, Jasper 400	16 (311). 286
BAYOU VISTA, Galveston, 34	Best, Reagan 2	Blair, Taylor. 25
(1,537). 1,645	Bethany, Panola. 50	Blanchard, Polk 500
*BAYSIDE, Refugio, 13 (325) 318	Bethel, Anderson 75	*BLANCO, Blanco, 248 (1,739). . . . 2,098
*BAYTOWN, Harris, Chambers, 1,940	Bethel, Henderson 125	Blanconia, Bee, Refugio 100
(71,802). 81,725	Bethel, Runnels. 20	Bland Lake, San Augustine 80
BAYVIEW, Cameron, 12 (383) 408	Bethlehem, Upshur 75	*BLANKET, Brown, 19 (390) 377
Bazette, Navarro 30	Bettie, Upshur 110	Blanton, Hill 5
BEACH CITY, Chambers (2,198) . . 2,856	Beulah, Limestone 12	Bleakwood, Newton. 450
BEAR CREEK, Hays (382) 466	BEVERLY HILLS, McLennan,	*Bledsoe, Cochran, 1 126
*BEASLEY, Fort Bend, 22 (641). . . . 804	99 (1,995) 1,993	*Bleiblerville, Austin, 4 125
Beattie, Comanche. 48		*Blessing, Matagorda, 22 (927) 989
*BEAUMONT, Jefferson, 3,768		
(117,267). 118,078		
Beaver Dam, Bowie 10		
Bebe, Gonzales 42		
Becker, Kaufman 300		
*BECKVILLE, Panola, 21 (847). . . . 902		
Becton, Lubbock 62		
*BEDFORD, Tarrant, 1,409		
(46,979). 49,530		
*BEDIAS, Grimes, 31 (443). 474		
BEE CAVE, Travis, 493 (3,925) 6,897		
Bee House, Coryell 15		
*BEEVILLE, Bee, 470 (12,863). . . . 13,554		
Belcherville, Montague. 25		
Belfalls, Bell. 30		
Belgrade, Newton 20		
Belk, Lamar. 58		
*BELLAIRE, Harris, 709		
(16,855). 18,283		
Bell Branch, Ellis 125		
*BELLEVUE, Clay, 18 (362) 347		

Ten Largest U.S. Metro Areas		
Rank	**Metro Area**	**2019 Estimates**
1.	New York	19,216,182
2.	Los Angeles	13,214,799
3.	Chicago	9,458,539
4.	**Dallas-Fort Worth**	**7,573,136**
5.	**Houston**	**7,066,141**
6.	Washington, D.C.	6,280,487
7.	Miami	6,166,488
8.	Philadephia	6,102,434
9.	Atlanta	6,020,364
10.	Phoenix	4,948,203

Source: U.S. Census.

CITIES & TOWNS

Town, County . . . . Pop. 2019	Town, County . . . . Pop. 2019	Town, County . . . . Pop. 2019
Blevins, Falls 36	Boyd, Fannin. 105	*BROWNSBORO, Henderson, 70
Blewett, Uvalde 7	*Boys Ranch, Oldham, 3 (282). 301	(1,039). 1,286
Blodgett, Titus. 60	Boz-Bethel, Ellis. 100	Brownsboro, Caldwell 50
*BLOOMBURG, Cass, 9 (404) 406	Bozar, Mills. 9	*BROWNSVILLE, Cameron, 4,930
*BLOOMING GROVE, Navarro,	Brachfield, Rusk. 40	(175,023). 184,500
19 (821). 863	Bracken, Comal 95	*BROWNWOOD, Brown, 639
*Bloomington, Victoria, 10	*BRACKETTVILLE, Kinney, 65	(19,288). 19,556
(2,459). 2,488	(1,688). 1,692	Broyles Chapel, Anderson. 60
*BLOSSOM, Lamar, 59 (1,494) 1,558	Brad, Palo Pinto. 16	*BRUCEVILLE-EDDY, McLennan, Falls,
Blue, Lee. 75	Bradford, Anderson 60	27 (1,475) 1,857
Blueberry Hill, Bee (866) 863	Bradshaw, Taylor 61	Brumley, Upshur 75
*Bluegrove, Clay 135	*BRADY, McCulloch, 243	Brundage, Dimmit (27) 23
BLUE MOUND, Tarrant, 49	(5,528). 5,602	*Bruni, Webb, 6 (379). 389
(2,394). 2,435	Branch, Collin. 530	Brushie Prairie, Navarro 35
*BLUE RIDGE, Collin, 50 (822) 957	Branchville, Milam. 127	Brushy Creek, Williamson,
Bluetown, Cameron (356). 351	*Brandon, Hill, 3 75	(21,764). 27,199
*Bluff Dale, Erath, 24 400	*Brashear, Hopkins, 15 280	Brushy Creek, Anderson. 125
*Bluffton, Llano, 5 75	*BRAZORIA, Brazoria, 214	*BRYAN, Brazos, 2,485
*BLUM, Hill, 16 (444) 471	(3,019). 3,531	(76,201). 86,202
Bluntzer, Nueces 150	Brazos, Palo Pinto 97	Bryans Mill, Cass. 150
Boca Chica Village, Cameron 34	BRAZOS COUNTRY, Austin, 16	Bryarly, Red River 3
*BOERNE, Kendall, 1,419	(469). 488	Bryce, Rusk. 15
(10,471). 17,228	Brazos Point, Bosque 20	*BRYSON, Jack, 12 (539) 572
*BOGATA, Red River, 52	Brazosport, Brazoria 60,138	*Buchanan Dam, Llano, 41
(1,153). 1,052	*BRECKENRIDGE, Stephens,	(1,519). 1,537
Bois d'Arc, Anderson 25	277 (5,780). 5,684	Buchanan Lake Village, Llano,
Bois d'Arc, Rains 6	*BREMOND, Robertson, 41 (929). . . 978	(692). 766
Bold Springs, Polk 100	*BRENHAM, Washington, 977	Buchel, DeWitt 45
Boles Home, Hunt 100	(15,716). 17,646	Buckeye, Matagorda. 16
*Boling, Wharton, 32 (1,122). 1,133	Breslau, Lavaca 65	*BUCKHOLTS, Milam, 14 (515). . . . 546
Bolivar, Denton 140	Briar, Tarrant, Wise, Parker,	Buckhorn, Austin. 50
Bolivar Peninsula, Galveston,	(5,665). 6,301	Buckhorn, Newton. 80
(2,417). 2,800	BRIARCLIFF, Travis, 53 (1,438) . . . 1,775	Buckner, Parker 10
Bomarton, Baylor. 15	BRIAROAKS, Johnson, 8 (492) 507	*BUDA, Hays, 719 (7,295) 17,862
Bonami, Jasper. 12	Brice, Hall, Briscoe. 20	Buena Vista, Starr (102) 117
Bonanza, Hopkins 26	*BRIDGE CITY, Orange, 227	Buena Vista, Shelby 20
Bonanza Hills, Webb (37) 41	(7,840). 7,868	*BUFFALO, Leon, 154 (1,856). 1,903
*BONHAM, Fannin, 353	*BRIDGEPORT, Wise, 302	*BUFFALO GAP, Taylor, 44
(10,127). 10,786	(5,976). 7,077	(464). 512
Bonita, Montague 25	Bridges Chapel, Titus 60	Buffalo Mop, Limestone 21
BONNEY, Brazoria (310) 357	*Briggs, Burnet, 9. 172	BUFFALO SPRINGS, Lubbock,
Bonnie View, Refugio 97	Bright Star, Rains 25	(453). 493
Bonus, Wharton 44	Brinker, Hopkins 100	Buffalo Springs, Clay 45
*Bon Wier, Newton, 6. 375	*Briscoe, Wheeler, 2 135	Buford, Mitchell. 30
*BOOKER, Lipscomb, Ochiltree,	Bristol, Ellis (668). 736	Bugscuffle, Rusk. 12
54 (1,516) 1,487	*BROADDUS, San Augustine, 26	Bula, Bailey. 35
Boonsville, Wise 52	(207). 203	Bulcher, Cooke 3
Booth, Fort Bend 50	Broadway, Lamar 25	*BULLARD, Smith, Cherokee,
Bootleg, Deaf Smith 10	BROCK, Parker, ... 967	200 (2,463). 4,183
Borden, Colorado 20	Brock Junction, Parker 100	Bull Run, Newton 90
*BORGER, Hutchinson, 414	Bronco, Yoakum 30	*BULVERDE, Comal, Bexar, 428
(13,251) 12,331	*Bronson, Sabine, 7 377	(4,630). 5,806
Bosqueville, McLennan 200	*BRONTE, Coke, 43 (999) 1,025	*Buna, Jasper, 87 (2,142) 2,063
Boston, Bowie . . . . . [part of New Boston]	*Brookeland, Sabine, 29 300	Buncombe, Panola. 95
Botines, Webb (117). 123	*Brookesmith, Brown, 1 61	Bunger, Young 24
*BOVINA, Parmer, 42 (1,868) 1,776	Brooks, Panola. 40	BUNKER HILL VILLAGE,
Bowers City, Gray 10	Brookshier, Runnels 15	Harris, 69 (3,633) 3,865
*BOWIE, Montague, 357	*BROOKSHIRE, Waller, 194	Bunyan, Erath 20
(5,218). 5,133	(4,702). 5,937	*BURKBURNETT, Wichita, 228
Bowman, Archer 300	BROOKSIDE VILLAGE, Brazoria,	(10,811). 11,194
Bowser, San Saba 20	39 (1,523) 1,632	BURKE, Angelina (737) 727
Box Canyon, Val Verde (34). 27	*Brookston, Lamar, 14 130	*Burkett, Coleman 90
Box Church, Limestone 45	Broom City, Anderson 20	*Burkeville, Newton, 25 603
Boxelder, Red River 100	BROWNDELL, Jasper (197). 201	Burleigh, Austin. 150
Boxwood, Upshur 20	*BROWNFIELD, Terry, 245	*BURLESON, Johnson, Tarrant,
Boyce, Ellis 125	(9,657). 9,707	1,452 (36,690) 47,403
*BOYD, Wise, 132 (1,207). 1,504	Browning, Smith 25	*Burlington, Milam, 3. 100

Town, County . . . . Pop. 2019	Town, County . . . . Pop. 2019	Town, County . . . . Pop. 2019

*BURNET, Burnet, 432 (5,987) 7,025
Burns, Bowie 400
Burns City, Cooke 45
Burrantown, Houston 70
*BURTON, Washington, 81 (300) . . . 302
*Bushland, Potter, 17 1,485
Bustamante, Zapata 10
Busterville, Hockley 6
Butler, Bastrop 40
Butler, Freestone 67
Butterfield, El Paso (114) 139
*BYERS, Clay, 14 (496) 474
*BYNUM, Hill, 9 (199) 210
Byrd, Ellis 30
Byrdtown, Lamar 22

C

*CACTUS, Moore, 35 (3,179) 3,241
*Caddo, Stephens, 4 70
*CADDO MILLS, Hunt, 133
   (1,338) 1,698
Cade Chapel, Navarro, Freestone 25
Cadiz, Bee 15
Calallen, Nueces . [part of Corpus Christi]
Calaveras, Wilson, Bexar 100
*CALDWELL, Burleson, 290
   (4,104) 4,515
Caledonia, Rusk 75
Calf Creek, McCulloch 23
Calina, Limestone 10
*Call, Newton, 5 493
Callender Lake, Van Zandt,
   (1,039) 1,290
*Calliham, McMullen, 4 100
CALLISBURG, Cooke (353) 379
Call Junction, Jasper 50
*CALVERT, Robertson, 50
   (1,192) 1,124
Camargito, Starr (388) 418
*CAMERON, Milam, 203
   (5,552) 5,619
Cameron Park, Cameron,
   (6,963) 7,417
Camilla, San Jacinto 200
Camp Air, Mason 12
*CAMPBELL, Hunt, 45 (638) 675
*Campbellton, Atascosa, 5 350
Camp Creek Lake, Robertson 350
Campo Verde, Starr (132) 148
Camp Ruby, Polk 35
Camp San Saba, McCulloch 36
Camp Seale, Polk 53
Camp Springs, Scurry 10
Camp Swift, Bastrop (6,383) 7,908
Camp Switch, Gregg 70
Campti, Shelby 25
Camp Verde, Kerr 41
*CAMP WOOD, Real, 37 (706) 725
Canada Verde, Wilson 40
*CANADIAN, Hemphill, 146
   (2,649) 2,717
Candelaria, Presidio 55
CANEY CITY, Henderson, 12
   (217) 230
Cannon, Grayson 50

*CANTON, Van Zandt, 812
   (3,581) 3,966
Cantu Addition, Brooks (188) 181
*Canutillo, El Paso, 197 (6,321) 7,073
*CANYON, Randall, 447
   (13,303) 16,179
Canyon City, Comal 800
Canyon Creek, Hood (916) 1,070
*Canyon Lake, Comal, 288
   (21,262) 27,978
Cape Royale, San Jacinto (670) 611
Caplen, Galveston 60
Capps Corner, Montague 30
Cap Rock, Crosby 6
Caps, Taylor 300
Caradan, Mills 20
Carancahua, Jackson 375
*CARBON, Eastland, 10 (272) 270
Carbondale, Bowie 10
Carey, Childress 25
Carlisle, Trinity 110
Carlos, Grimes 60
*Carlsbad, Tom Green, 10 (719) 780
CARL'S CORNER, Hill, 3 (173) 187
Carlson, Travis 20
*Carlton, Hamilton, 2 75
*CARMINE, Fayette, 51 (250) 262
Carmona, Polk 50
Caro, Nacogdoches 70
Carrizo Hill, Dimmit (582) 593
*CARRIZO SPRINGS, Dimmit,
   153 (5,368) 5,567
Carroll, Smith 60
Carroll Springs, Anderson,
   Henderson 20
*CARROLLTON, Dallas, Denton,
   5,038 (119,097) 143,325
Carson, Fannin 22
Carta Valley, Edwards 12
Carterville, Cass 39
*CARTHAGE, Panola, 365
   (6,779) 6,941
Cartwright, Wood 144
Casa Blanca, Starr (54) 63
Casa Piedra, Presidio 8
Casas, Starr (39) 49
Cash, Hunt 56
CASHION, Wichita (348) 355
*Cason, Morris, 1 173
Cass, Cass 100
Cassie, Burnet 496
Cassin, Bexar 200
*Castell, Llano, 2 72
CASTLE HILLS, Bexar, 302
   (4,116) 4,509
Castolon, Brewster 8
*CASTROVILLE, Medina, 194
   (2,785) 3,114
Catarina, Dimmit, 13 (118) 100
*Cat Spring, Austin, 24 200
Caviness, Lamar 90
Cawthon, Brazos 75
Cayote, Bosque 75
*Cayuga, Anderson, 2 137
Cedar Bayou, Harris 1,555
*Cedar Creek, Bastrop, 143 145
*CEDAR HILL, Dallas, Ellis,

   1,228 (45,028) 48,836
Cedar Hill, Floyd 24
Cedar Lake, Matagorda 160
*Cedar Lane, Matagorda, 3 300
*CEDAR PARK, Williamson,
   Travis, 2,495 (48,932) 77,541
Cedar Point, Polk (630) 624
Cedar Shores, Bosque 270
Cedar Springs, Falls 90
Cedar Springs, Upshur 100
Cedarvale, Kaufman 50
Cedar Valley, Bell 14
Cee Vee, Cottle 45
Cego, Falls 42
Cele, Travis 20
*CELESTE, Hunt, 34 (814) 907
*CELINA, Collin, Denton, 307
   (6,028) 13,399
*CENTER, Shelby, 349 (5,193) 5,335
Center, Limestone 76
Center City, Mills, Hamilton 27
Center Grove, Houston 39
Center Grove, Titus 35
Center Hill, Houston 105
Center Plains, Swisher 20
Center Point, Camp 41
*Center Point, Kerr, 39 800
Center Point, Upshur 50
Centerview, Leon 20
*CENTERVILLE, Leon, 83 (892) . . . 920
Centerville, Trinity 60
Central, Angelina 1,400
Central Gardens, Jefferson,
   (4,347) 4,309
Central Heights, Nacogdoches 300
Central High, Cherokee 30
*Centralia, Trinity 190
Cesar Chavez, Hidalgo (1,929) 2,210
Cestohowa, Karnes 110
Chalk, Cottle 17
Chalk Hill, Rusk 200
Chalk Mountain, Erath, Somervell 25
Chambliss, Collin 29
Champion, Nolan 10
Champions, Harris 21,250
Chances Store, Burleson 15
*CHANDLER, Henderson, 157
   (2,734) 3,259
Chaney, Eastland 35
*Channelview, Harris, 398
   (38,289) 46,373
*CHANNING, Hartley, 5 (363) 346
Chaparrito, Starr (114) 106
Chapeno, Starr (47) 51
Chapman, Rusk 20
*Chapman Ranch, Nueces 200
Chappel, San Saba 25
*Chappell Hill, Washington, 50 750
Charco, Goliad 96
Charleston, Delta, Hopkins 150
Charlie, Clay 70
*CHARLOTTE, Atascosa, 40
   (1,715) 1,865
*Chatfield, Navarro, 3 40
Cheapside, Gonzales, DeWitt 5
Cheek, Jefferson 1,096
Cheneyboro, Navarro 100

Town, County . . . . Pop. 2019	Town, County . . . . Pop. 2019	Town, County . . . . Pop. 2019
*Cherokee, San Saba, 10 175	Cinco Ranch, Fort Bend, Harris,	Clegg, Live Oak. 125
Cherry Spring, Gillespie 75	(18,274). 25,089	Clemville, Matagorda 25
*CHESTER, Tyler, 13 (312) 324	Cipres, Hidalgo 20	Cleo, Kimble 3
Chesterville, Colorado 30	Circle, Lamb 6	*CLEVELAND, Liberty, 492
*CHICO, Wise, 66 (1,002) 1,181	Circle Back, Bailey 8	(7,675). 8,960
*Chicota, Lamar 150	Circle D-KC Estates, Bastrop,	Cleveland, Austin. 125
Chihuahua, Zapata. 77	(2,393). 2,730	Cliffside, Potter 206
*CHILDRESS, Childress, 177	Circleville, Williamson 50	*CLIFTON, Bosque, 223 (3,442) . . . 3,594
(6,105). 6,289	*CISCO, Eastland, 159 (3,899). 3,834	Climax, Collin. 82
*CHILLICOTHE, Hardeman, 16	Cistern, Fayette 137	Cline, Uvalde. 15
(707). 665	Citrus City, Hidalgo (2,321). 2,883	*CLINT, El Paso, 63 (926). 1,163
*Chilton, Falls, 10 (911) 958	Citrus Grove, Matagorda 30	Clinton, Hunt 150
*CHINA, Jefferson, 30 (1,160). 1,203	Clairemont, Kent. 12	Close City, Garza. 65
CHINA GROVE, Bexar, 59	Clairette, Erath 55	Cloverleaf, Harris (22,942) 24,256
(1,179). 1,321	Clara, Wichita 100	*CLUTE, Brazoria, 355
China Grove, Scurry 15	Clardy, Lamar 160	(11,211). 11,919
*China Spring, McLennan, 63	*CLARENDON, Donley, 94	*CLYDE, Callahan, 174 (3,713) 3,956
(1,281). 1,401	(2,026). 1,772	*COAHOMA, Howard, 27
Chinati, Presidio 8	Clareville, Bee 25	(817). 948
Chinquapin, Matagorda 6	Clark, Liberty 75	Coble, Hockley 11
*CHIRENO, Nacogdoches, 17	Clarkson, Milam 10	Cochran, Austin. 200
(386). 386	*CLARKSVILLE, Red River, 123	COCKRELL HILL, Dallas, 92
Chita, Trinity. 81	(3,285). 2,991	(4,193). 4,412
Choate, Karnes 30	CLARKSVILLE CITY, Gregg,	COFFEE CITY, Henderson, 13
Chocolate Bayou, Brazoria 60	Upshur, 23 (865). 932	(278). 1,504
Choice, Shelby 35	*CLAUDE, Armstrong, 60	Coffeeville, Upshur 50
*Chriesman, Burleson, 1 30	(1,196). 1,210	Cofferville, Lamb. 4
*CHRISTINE, Atascosa (390) 439	Clauene, Hockley. 10	Coit, Limestone. 25
*Christoval, Tom Green, 26 (504) . . . 576	Clawson, Angelina 1,500	Coke, Wood 53
Chula Vista, Maverick (3,818) 3,980	Clay, Burleson 61	*COLDSPRING, San Jacinto, 92
Chula Vista, Zavala (450) 479	Clays Corner, Parmer 15	(853). 976
Chula Vista, Cameron (288) 263	*Clayton, Panola, 2. 125	*COLEMAN, Coleman, 207
Church Hill, Rusk 20	Claytonville, Swisher 85	(4,709). 4,305
Churchill, Brazoria. 90	Clear Creek, Burnet 78	Colfax, Van Zandt 94
*CIBOLO, Guadalupe, 474	CLEAR LAKE SHORES,	Colita, Polk, Trinity 50
(19,580). 31,951	Galveston, 85 (1,063). 1,190	College Hill, Bowie 40
Cienegas Terrace, Val Verde,	*CLEBURNE, Johnson, 1,126	College Mound, Kaufman. 500
(3,424). 3,804	(29,337). 33,110	*Collegeport, Matagorda 80

An old Santa Fe train station in Clifton. Photo by Larry D. Moore, CC by 4.0/Wikimedia Commons.

Town, County . . . . Pop. 2019	Town, County . . . . Pop. 2019	Town, County . . . . Pop. 2019
*COLLEGE STATION, Brazos, 2,576 (93,857) 118,410	Cornudas, Hudspeth 5	CROSS ROADS, Denton, 106 (1,563). 1,618
*COLLEYVILLE, Tarrant, 1,145 (22,807). 27,091	*CORPUS CHRISTI, Nueces, 9,140 (305,215). 327,618	Cross Roads, Henderson. 160
*COLLINSVILLE, Grayson, 51 (1,624). 1,934	*CORRIGAN, Polk, 66 (1,595) 1,683	Cross Roads, Madison 75
*COLMESNEIL, Tyler, 34 (596) 603	*CORSICANA, Navarro, 903 (23,770). 24,601	Cross Roads, Milam 35
Colony, Rains 35	Coryell City, Coryell 70	Crossroads, Cass 60
Colorado Acres, Webb (296) 338	*Cost, Gonzales, 7 84	Crossroads, Delta. 20
*COLORADO CITY, Mitchell, 175 (4,146). 3,790	Cotton Center, Fannin 33	Crossroads, Harrison 100
Coltharp, Houston. 40	*Cotton Center, Hale, 4. 300	Crossroads, Hopkins 50
Colton, Travis 50	Cottondale, Wise. 300	CROSS TIMBER, Johnson (268). . . . 319
*COLUMBUS, Colorado, 271 (3,655). 3,868	Cotton Gin, Freestone 28	Croton, Dickens 7
*COMANCHE, Comanche, 218 (4,335). 4,349	Cotton Patch, DeWitt 11	Crow, Wood 178
*COMBES, Cameron, 45 (2,895). . . 3,094	COTTONWOOD, Kaufman (185). 212	*CROWELL, Foard, 34 (948) 813
COMBINE, Kaufman, Dallas, 52 (1,942). 2,270	Cottonwood, Madison 40	*CROWLEY, Tarrant, 352 (12,838). 15,945
Cometa, Zavala 10	Cottonwood, McLennan 150	Crown, Atascosa 10
*Comfort, Kendall, 140 (2,363) . . . 2,936	Cottonwood, Somervell 24	Cruz Calle, Duval 12
*COMMERCE, Hunt, 237 (8,078). 9,696	COTTONWOOD SHORES, Burnet, 51 (1,123). 1,359	Cryer Creek, Navarro. 15
*COMO, Hopkins, 30 (702) 746	*COTULLA, La Salle, 144 (3,603). 4,063	Crystal Beach, Galveston 800
*Comstock, Val Verde. 344	Couch, Karnes. 10	*CRYSTAL CITY, Zavala, 101 (7,138). 7,189
Comyn, Comanche 30	Coughran, Atascosa 20	Crystal Falls, Stephens 10
*Concan, Uvalde, 36. 500	Country Acres, San Patricio (185) . . . 179	Crystal Lake, Anderson 12
*Concepcion, Duval (62) 57	County Line, Lubbock 59	Cuadrilla, El Paso. 67
Concord, Cherokee 50	County Line, Rains 40	*CUERO, DeWitt, 320 (6,841). . . . 7,482
*Concord, Leon, 1 28	*COUPLAND, Williamson, 19 317	Cuevitas, Hidalgo (40) 50
Concord, Madison. 50	Courtney, Grimes 60	*CUMBY, Hopkins, 42 (777). 826
Concord, Rusk. 23	COVE, Chambers, 22 (510) 567	Cumings, Fort Bend (981). 1,398
Concrete, DeWitt. 46	Cove Springs, Cherokee 49	Cundiff, Jack 45
Cone, Crosby 50	*COVINGTON, Hill, 19 (269) 276	*CUNEY, Cherokee, 2 (140) 140
Conlen, Dallam 14	Cox, Upshur 30	*Cunningham, Lamar, 2 110
Connor, Madison. 20	*Coyanosa, Pecos, 13 (163) 172	Currie, Navarro 25
*CONROE, Montgomery, 3,454 (56,207). 90,276	Coy City, Karnes. 30	Curtis, Jasper. 150
Content, Bell. 25	Coyote Acres, Jim Wells (508) 581	*CUSHING, Nacogdoches, 44 (612). 610
*CONVERSE, Bexar, 528 (18,198). 29,120	COYOTE FLATS, Johnson (312). . . . 329	Cusseta, Cass. 30
Conway, Carson 20	Crabbs Prairie, Walker 240	*CUT AND SHOOT, Montgomery, 62 (1,070) 1,409
Cooks Point, Burleson 60	Craft, Cherokee. 21	Cuthand, Red River 116
*Cookville, Titus, 10. 105	Crafton, Wise 100	Cyclone, Bell. 47
COOL, Parker, 6 (157). 185	*CRANDALL, Kaufman, 108 (2,858). 3,495	Cypress, Franklin. 20
*COOLIDGE, Limestone, 13 (955). 997	*CRANE, Crane, 101 (3,353) 3,582	Cypress Creek, Kerr. 200
*COOPER, Delta, 72 (1,969). 1,997	*CRANFILLS GAP, Bosque, 16 (281). 286	*Cypress, Harris, 2,552 120,000
Cooper, Houston 27	*CRAWFORD, McLennan, 40 (717). 765	Cypress Mill, Blanco 200
Copano Village, Aransas. 210	Creath, Houston 20	
*Copeville, Collin, 4. 243	Crecy, Trinity 15	**D**
*COPPELL, Dallas, Denton, 1,376 (38,659) 41,250	CREEDMOOR, Travis, 35 (202). . . . 222	Dacosta, Victoria 89
*COPPERAS COVE, Coryell, 658 (32,032). 35,270	Crescent Heights, Henderson 180	Dacus, Montgomery. 190
COPPER CANYON, Denton, 37 (1,334). 1,515	*CRESSON, Hood, Johnson, Parker, 87 (741) 1,123	Daffan, Travis 500
Corbet, Navarro 80	Crews, Runnels 30	*DAINGERFIELD, Morris, Titus, 90 (2,560) 2,454
Cordele, Jackson 51	Crisp, Ellis. 115	*DAISETTA, Liberty, 20 (966). 1,151
CORINTH, Denton, 490 (19,935). 23,304	*CROCKETT, Houston, 278 (6,950). 6,741	Dalby Springs, Bowie 75
Corinth, Jones. 10	*Crosby, Harris, 388 (2,299) 2,875	*Dale, Caldwell, 35. 300
Corinth, Leon 50	*CROSBYTON, Crosby, 51 (1,741). 1,602	*DALHART, Dallam, Hartley, 323 (7,930). 8,097
Corley, Bowie 35	Cross, Grimes 53	*Dallardsville, Polk, 1 350
Cornersville, Hopkins 200	Cross, McMullen 25	*DALLAS, Dallas, Collin, Denton, 41,922 (1,197,816). 1,357,986
Cornett, Cass 30	Cross Cut, Brown 22	Dalton, Cass 50
	Cross Mountain, Bexar (3,124) 3,708	DALWORTHINGTON GARDENS, Tarrant, 153 (2,259) 2,333
	*CROSS PLAINS, Callahan, 57 (982). 1,014	*Damon, Brazoria, 25 (552). 614
		*DANBURY, Brazoria, 48 (1,715). . . 1,883
		*Danciger, Brazoria, 1. 90
		*Danevang, Wharton, 5 61

CITIES & TOWNS

Town, County	Pop. 2019
Daniels, Panola	75
Danville, Gregg, Rusk.	200
Darby Hill, San Jacinto	25
Darco, Harrison.	10
Darden, Polk.	320
*DARROUZETT, Lipscomb, 16 (350).	341
Datura, Limestone	2
*Davilla, Milam	191
Davis, Atascosa	8
Davis Prairie, Limestone.	17
*Dawn, Deaf Smith	52
*DAWSON, Navarro, 23 (807).	810
*DAYTON, Liberty, 397 (7,242).	9,186
DAYTON LAKES, Liberty (93).	109
Deadwood, Panola.	106
DEAN, Clay, 9 (493).	463
Dean, Hockley.	20
*Deanville, Burleson, 4	130
*DeBerry, Panola, 23	200
*DECATUR, Wise, 495 (6,042).	7,086
Decker Prairie, Montgomery.	2,000
DeCORDOVA, Hood (2,683).	2,998
*DEER PARK, Harris, 959 (32,010).	34,050
*DE KALB, Bowie, 66 (1,699)	1,673
*DE LEON, Comanche, 115 (2,246).	2,217
Delhi, Caldwell.	150
Delia, Limestone	20
*DELL CITY, Hudspeth, 17 (365)	378
Del Mar Heights, Cameron (113).	97
*Delmita, Starr, 4 (216).	226
Delray, Panola	45
*DEL RIO, Val Verde, 882 (35,591).	35,982
Delrose, Upshur.	35
Del Sol, San Patricio (239)	231
*Del Valle, Travis, 118.	[part of Austin]
Delwin, Cottle.	12
Demi-John, Brazoria	300
Democrat, Mills, Comanche	8
Denhawken, Wilson.	52
*DENISON, Grayson, 843 (22,682).	25,402
Denning, San Augustine	100
*DENNIS, Parker, 2	953
Denson Springs, Anderson	60
*DENTON, Denton, 3,635 (113,383).	142,944
Denton, Callahan.	6
*DENVER CITY, Yoakum, Gaines, 159 (4,479).	5,044
*DEPORT, Lamar, Red River, 15 (578).	556
Derby, Frio	50
*Desdemona, Eastland	180
Desert, Collin	35
*DeSOTO, Dallas, 1,079 (49,047).	52,631
*DETROIT, Red River, 36 (732)	678
*DEVERS, Liberty, 20 (447)	527
*DEVINE, Medina, 233 (4,350).	5,001
Dew, Freestone	150
DeWees, Wilson	60
Deweesville, Karnes.	12
*Deweyville, Newton, 11 (1,023).	873

Town, County	Pop. 2019
Dewville, Gonzales	30
Dexter, Cooke	12
*D'Hanis, Medina, 21 (847).	873
Dial, Fannin	76
Dialville, Cherokee	200
*Diana, Upshur, 39.	585
*DIBOLL, Angelina, 113 (5,359)	5,279
Dicey, Parker.	40
*DICKENS, Dickens, 12 (286).	253
*DICKINSON, Galveston, 541 (18,680).	21,576
*Dike, Hopkins, 6.	170
*DILLEY, Frio, 86 (3,894).	4,269
Dilworth, Gonzales	18
Dilworth, Red River.	25
*Dime Box, Lee, 15	381
*DIMMITT, Castro, 117 (4,393).	4,063
Dimple, Red River.	60
Dinero, Live Oak, 1	344
Ding Dong, Bell.	301
Direct, Lamar	85
Dirgin, Rusk	50
DISH, Denton (201).	467
Divide, Kerr	50
Divot, Frio	30
Dixie, Grayson	17
Dixon, Hunt	31
Dixon-Hopewell, Houston	10
Doak Springs, Lee	50
Doans, Wilbarger.	20
*Dobbin, Montgomery, 1	310
Dobrowolski, Atascosa	10
Dodd, Castro.	12
*DODD CITY, Fannin, 17 (369)	395
*Dodge, Walker, 5	150
*DODSON, Collingsworth (109)	104
Dodson Prairie, Palo Pinto	18
Doffing, Hidalgo (5,091).	5,722
Dog Ridge, Bell.	215
Dogwood City, Smith.	800
Dolen, Liberty.	75
DOMINO, Cass, 8 (93)	100
*Donie, Freestone, 7.	250
*DONNA, Hidalgo, 536 (15,798).	17,235
*Doole, McCulloch	74
Doolittle, Hidalgo (2,769).	3,033
DORCHESTER, Grayson (148)	167
Dorras, Stonewall, Fisher	20
Doss, Cass.	15
*Doss, Gillespie, 7	100
Dot, Falls	17
Dotson, Panola	35
Double Bayou, Chambers	200
DOUBLE OAK, Denton, 100 (2,867).	3,234
DOUBLE HORN, Burnet.	238
*Doucette, Tyler, 3	160
*Dougherty, Floyd, 2	91
Dougherty, Rains.	40
*Douglass, Nacogdoches, 20	380
*DOUGLASSVILLE, Cass, 8 (229).	225
Downing, Comanche.	30
Downsville, McLennan	150
Downtown Texas, Milam	34
Doyle, San Patricio (254)	243

Town, County	Pop. 2019
Doyle, Limestone.	50
Dozier, Collingsworth	4
Drane, Navarro	16
DRAPER, Denton (27).	33
Drasco, Runnels.	15
Draw, Lynn	18
Dreka, Shelby	30
Dresden, Navarro	25
Dreyer, Gonzales	20
*Driftwood, Hays, 89 (144)	193
*DRIPPING SPRINGS, Hays, 622 (1,788).	5,918
*DRISCOLL, Nueces, 12 (739)	744
Drop, Denton	90
*Dryden, Terrell, 1	13
Dubina, Fayette	272
*DUBLIN, Erath, 156 (3,654)	3,562
Dudley, Callahan	25
Duffau, Erath.	76
*DUMAS, Moore, 378 (14,691).	14,044
Dumont, King, Dickens	19
Dunbar, Rains.	40
*DUNCANVILLE, Dallas, 1,139 (38,524).	39,782
Dundee, Archer.	12
Dunlap, Cottle.	10
Dunlap, Travis.	80
Dunlay, Medina.	145
Dunn, Scurry	75
Duplex, Fannin	25
Durango, Falls.	54
Duren, Mills	15
Duster, Comanche	25
Dye, Montague	30

E

Town, County	Pop. 2019
Eagle, Chambers	30
*EAGLE LAKE, Colorado, 106 (3,639).	3,777
*EAGLE PASS, Maverick, 902 (26,248).	28,992
*EARLY, Brown, 183 (2,762)	3,049
*EARTH, Lamb, 23 (1,065).	957
East Afton, Dickens	13
East Alto Bonito, Starr (824)	953
*EAST BERNARD, Wharton, 113 (2,272).	2,351
East Caney, Hopkins.	100
East Columbia, Brazoria	95
East Delta, Delta	60
East Direct, Lamar.	48
Easter, Castro	26
Easterly, Robertson	61
Eastgate, Liberty	200
East Hamilton, Shelby	25
*EASTLAND, Eastland, 211 (3,960).	4,010
East Lopez, Starr (166)	179
EAST MOUNTAIN, Upshur, 20 (797).	851
EASTON, Gregg, Rusk, 5 (510).	639
East Point, Wood	40
East Sweden, McCulloch	40
EAST TAWAKONI, Rains, 24 (883).	976
Ebenezer, Camp	55

Town, County . . . . Pop. 2019	Town, County . . . . Pop. 2019	Town, County . . . . Pop. 2019
Ebenezer, Jasper. 50	El Chaparral, Starr (464). 507	El Refugio, Starr (331) 392
Echo, Coleman 6	*ELDORADO, Schleicher, 67	Elroy, Travis 125
Ecleto, Karnes 22	(1,951). 1,584	*ELSA, Hidalgo, 158 (5,660) 7,174
*ECTOR, Fannin, 12 (695). 740	Eldorado Center, Navarro. 20	El Sauz, Starr. 50
*EDCOUCH, Hidalgo, 46	Eldridge, Colorado. 10	El Socio, Starr (130) 144
(3,161). 3,368	*ELECTRA, Wichita, 72 (2,791) . . . 2,719	Elton, Dickens. 4
*EDEN, Concho, 54 (2,766) 1,828	Elevation, Milam 12	El Toro, Jackson. 136
Eden, Nacogdoches 100	*ELGIN, Bastrop, 419 (8,135) 10,262	Elwood, Fannin 31
Edgar, DeWitt 8	Elias-Fela Solis, Starr (30) 36	Elwood, Madison. 50
Edge, Brazos 10	Eliasville, Young. 100	*Elysian Fields, Harrison, 7 500
EDGECLIFF, Tarrant (2,776) 2,979	*El Indio, Maverick, 1 (190). 169	Emberson, Lamar 80
Edgewater Estates, San Patricio (72). . . 73	Elk, McLennan 150	Emerald Bay, Smith (1,047). 1,080
*EDGEWOOD, Van Zandt, 97	*ELKHART, Anderson, 60	EMHOUSE, Navarro, 2 (133) 143
(1,441). 1,554	(1,371). 1,299	Emmett, Navarro. 100
Edgeworth, Bell. 15	EL LAGO, Harris, 67 (2,706). 2,680	*EMORY, Rains, 179 (1,239) 1,451
Edhube, Fannin. 40	*ELLINGER, Fayette, 9. 386	Encantada-Ranchito El Calaboz,
*EDINBURG, Hidalgo, 1,921	Elliott, Robertson 55	Cameron (2,255) 2,201
(74,569). 99,454	Elliott, Wilbarger. 50	ENCHANTED OAKS,
*EDMONSON, Hale, 5 (111) 101	*Elmaton, Matagorda, 3 160	Henderson, (326) 344
*EDNA, Jackson, 257 (5,499). 5,690	Elm Creek, Maverick (2,469). 2,870	*ENCINAL, La Salle, 28 (559). 583
Edna Hill, Erath. 32	*ELMENDORF, Bexar, 71	*Encino, Brooks, 6 (143). 145
EDOM, Van Zandt, 16 (375). 397	(1,488). 2,112	*Energy, Comanche, 2 70
*Edroy, San Patricio, 1 (331) 301	El Mesquite, Starr (38) 44	Engle, Fayette 141
Egan, Johnson 133	Elm Grove, Cherokee. 50	English, Red River 100
*Egypt, Wharton, 3 26	Elm Grove, San Saba 15	*Enloe, Delta, 1 90
Eidson Road, Maverick (8,960) 9,132	Elm Grove, Wharton 76	*ENNIS, Ellis, 685 (18,513). 21,101
Elam Springs, Upshur. 50	Elm Grove Camp, Guadalupe 88	Enoch, Upshur. 25
Elbert, Throckmorton (30). 21	*Elm Mott, McLennan, 70. 300	*Enochs, Bailey 80
Elbow, Howard 10	*Elmo, Kaufman, 1 (768). 1,049	Enon, Upshur 204
El Brazil, Starr (47). 50	Elmont, Grayson 15	*Eola, Concho, 4 215
El Camino Angosto, Cameron,	Elm Ridge, Milam 25	Eolian, Stephens 9
(253). 254	Elmwood, Anderson. 15	*Era, Cooke, 5 150
*EL CAMPO, Wharton, 609	Eloise, Falls 19	Ericksdahl, Jones 35
(11,602). 11,918	El Oso, Karnes. 35	Erin, Jasper 70
El Castillo, Starr (188) 219	*EL PASO, El Paso, 16,474	Erna, Menard, Mason. 27
El Cenizo, Starr (249). 283	(649,121). 686,265	Erwin, Grimes. 52
EL CENIZO, Webb, 25 (3,273) 3,127	El Quiote, Starr (208) 223	Escobares, Starr, 44 (1,188) 2,837
El Centro, Starr 50	El Rancho Vela, Starr (274) 291	Escobar I, Starr (324) 352

Humphries House in Edgewood. Photo by Renelibrary, CC by 4.0/Wikimedia Commons.

Town, County . . . . Pop. 2019	Town, County . . . . Pop. 2019	Town, County . . . . Pop. 2019
Escobas, Zapata 2	Farmers Academy, Titus 75	Folsom, Shelby 30
Eskota, Fisher 32	*FARMERS BRANCH, Dallas,	Ford, Deaf Smith 25
Esperanza, Hudspeth 75	1,975 (28,616) 41,093	Fords Corner, San Augustine 30
Espey, Atascosa 55	Farmers Valley, Wilbarger 30	Fordtran, Victoria 18
Estacado, Lubbock, Crosby 32	*FARMERSVILLE, Collin, 201	Forest, Cherokee 85
*ESTELLINE, Hall, 3 (145). 131	(3,301). 4,534	*Forestburg, Montague, 14 50
Estes, Aransas 300	Farmington, Grayson 40	Forest Chapel, Lamar 105
Ethel, Grayson. 40	*Farnsworth, Ochiltree, 6 130	Forest Glade, Limestone 340
*Etoile, Nacogdoches, 12. 700	Farrar, Limestone. 51	Forest Grove, Milam 60
Eugenio Saenz, Starr (159) 170	Farrsville, Newton 152	Forest Heights, Orange 250
Eula, Callahan 125	*FARWELL, Parmer, 47 (1,363). . . . 1,255	FOREST HILL, Tarrant, 328
*EULESS, Tarrant, 1,423	Fashing, Atascosa 35	(12,355). 12,894
(51,277). 56,965	*FATE, Rockwall, 261 (6,434) 15,121	Forest Hill, Lamar 50
Eulogy, Bosque 10	Faught, Lamar 25	Forest Hill, Wood. 30
EUREKA, Navarro, 9 (307). 318	Faulkner, Lamar. 10	*FORNEY, Kaufman, 761
Eureka, Franklin 18	Fawil, Newton. 183	(14,661). 27,565
*EUSTACE, Henderson, 57	*FAYETTEVILLE, Fayette, 69	*Forreston, Ellis, Navarro, 2. 400
(991). 1,007	(258). 262	*FORSAN, Howard, 9 (210) 215
*Evadale, Jasper, 16 (1,483) 1,545	Faysville, Hidalgo (439) 500	Fort Bliss, El Paso (8,591) 9,137
*EVANT, Coryell, Hamilton, 37	Fedor, Lee. 92	Fort Clark Springs, Kinney,
(426). 405	*Fentress, Caldwell, 8 380	(1,228). 1,231
Evergreen, Starr (73) 79	Fernando Salinas, Starr (15) 12	*Fort Davis, Jeff Davis, 59
Evergreen, San Jacinto 100	*FERRIS, Ellis, 101 (2,436) 2,987	(1,201). 1,162
EVERMAN, Tarrant, 117	Fetzer, Waller 150	*Fort Hancock, Hudspeth, 8
(6,108). 6,215	Fields Store, Waller. 500	(1,750). 1,832
Ewell, Upshur 20	*Fieldton, Lamb, 1 20	Fort Hood, Bell, Coryell,
Ezzell, Lavaca 55	Fife, McCulloch 32	(29,589). 26,245
	Fifth Street, Fort Bend (2,486) 3,338	*Fort McKavett, Menard. 50
	Files Valley, Hill 60	Fort Parker, Limestone 2
F	Fincastle, Henderson 75	Fort Parker State Park, Limestone 30
*Fabens, El Paso, 67 (8,257). 8,500	Finney, Hale 18	Fort Sherman, Titus 200
Fabrica, Maverick (923) 989	*Fischer, Comal, 17 400	Fort Spunky, Hood. 15
FAIRCHILDS, Fort Bend (763). . . . 1,068	Fisk, Coleman 40	*FORT STOCKTON, Pecos, 314
*FAIRFIELD, Freestone, 223	Five Points, Ellis 25	(8,283). 8,470
(2,951). 2,984	Flaccus, Karnes 15	*FORT WORTH, Tarrant, Denton,
Fairland, Burnet. 340	Flagg, Castro 26	Parker, Wise, 20,779
Fairlie, Hunt 80	*Flat, Coryell, 2 210	(741,206). 895,100
Fairmount, Sabine 1,500	Flat Fork, Shelby 10	Foster, Terry 6
Fair Oaks, Limestone 15	*FLATONIA, Fayette, 102	Fostoria, Montgomery 586
FAIR OAKS RANCH, Bexar, Comal,	(1,383). 1,507	Fouke, Wood. 30
Kendall, 154 (5,986) 9,434	Flat Prairie, Trinity. 33	Four Corners, Fort Bend,
Fair Play, Panola. 80	Flats, Rains 40	(12,382). 17,948
FAIRVIEW, Collin, 289 (7,248) 9,021	Flat Top, Stonewall. 5	Four Corners, Brazoria. 60
Fairview, Armstrong. 10	*Flint, Smith, 193 2,500	Four Corners, Chambers 18
Fairview, Cass 20	Flo, Leon 12	Four Corners, Montgomery 500
Fairview, Gaines 160	Flomot, Motley 181	Four Points, Webb (18). 15
Fairview, Hockley 20	Flora, Hopkins. 20	Fowlerton, La Salle, 4 (55). 48
Fairview, Hood 30	Flor del Rio, Starr (122) 134	Frame Switch, Williamson 25
Fairview, Howard 5	*FLORENCE, Williamson, 103	*Francitas, Jackson, 2 125
Fairview, Wilson 95	(1,136). 1,306	Frankel City, Andrews 2
Fairy, Hamilton 40	*FLORESVILLE, Wilson, 355	Frankell, Stephens 8
New Falcon, Zapata (191). 175	(6,448). 8,104	*FRANKLIN, Robertson, 83
Falconaire, Starr (132) 128	Florey, Andrews. 25	(1,564). 1,701
*Falcon Heights, Starr, 1 (53). 56	Flour Bluff, Nueces	*FRANKSTON, Anderson, 89
Falcon Lake Estates, Zapata,	. . . . [part of Corpus Christi]	(1,229). 1,216
(1,036). 1,155	Flowella, Brooks (118) 116	*Fred, Tyler, 6 300
Falcon Mesa, Zapata (405) 342	Flower Hill, Colorado. 20	*FREDERICKSBURG, Gillespie,
Falcon Village, Starr (47). 43	*FLOWER MOUND, Denton,	1,193 (10,530) 11,482
*FALFURRIAS, Brooks, 133	2,290 (64,669) 79,640	*Fredonia, Mason, San Saba, 2. 55
(4,981). 4,916	Floyd, Hunt. 90	Freedom, Rains 32
Fallon, Limestone. 100	*FLOYDADA, Floyd, 115	*FREEPORT, Brazoria, 309
*FALLS CITY, Karnes, 32 (611). . . . 686	(3,038). 2,562	(12,049). 12,990
Falman, San Patricio (76) 73	*Fluvanna, Scurry, 8 180	*FREER, Duval, 91 (2,818) 2,632
Famuliner, Cochran 5	*Flynn, Leon, 4 81	Freestone, Freestone. 100
Fannett, Jefferson (2,252) 2,333	Foard City, Foard. 10	Frelsburg, Colorado. 75
*Fannin, Goliad, 6 359	Fodice, Houston 49	Frenstat, Burleson 50
Fargo, Wilbarger 169	*FOLLETT, Lipscomb, 25 (459) 440	

CITIES & TOWNS

Town, County . . . . Pop. 2019	Town, County . . . . Pop. 2019	Town, County . . . . Pop. 2019
*Fresno, Fort Bend, 113 (19,069). 28,243	*GARY, Panola (311) 311	Goober Hill, Shelby 30
Fresno, Collingsworth 10	Garza-Salinas II, Starr (719) 785	Goodland, Bailey. 10
Freyburg, Fayette. 148	Gastonia, Kaufman 100	Goodlett, Hardeman 80
Friday, Trinity 70	*GATESVILLE, Coryell, 372 (15,751). 15,997	GOODLOW, Navarro, 4 (200) 194
Friendship, Dawson 40	*Gause, Milam, 6 425	Good Neighbor, Hopkins 40
Friendship, Smith. 200	Gay Hill, Washington 40	Goodnight, Armstrong. 20
Friendship, Upshur 25	Geneva, Sabine 200	*GOODRICH, Polk, 32 (271) 317
Friendship Village, Bowie 200	Geneview, Stonewall 3	Goodsprings, Rusk. 40
*FRIENDSWOOD, Galveston, Harris, 1,179 (35,805) 40,659	Gentry's Mill, Hamilton 20	Goodwill, Burleson 12
Frio Town, Frio 9	George's Creek, Somervell, Johnson, Hood 43	Goodwin, San Augustine 70
*FRIONA, Parmer, 86 (4,123) 3,815	*GEORGETOWN, Williamson, 2,136 (47,400). 75,756	*GORDON, Palo Pinto, 30 (478). . . . 488
*FRISCO, Collin, Denton, 5,120 (116,989). 190,974	*GEORGE WEST, Live Oak, 157 (2,445). 2,568	*Gordonville, Grayson, 21 165
*FRITCH, Hutchinson, Moore, 66 (2,117) 1,961	Georgia, Lamar 55	*GOREE, Knox, 8 (203) 203
Frog, Kaufman 90	Germany, Houston. 23	*GORMAN, Eastland, 43 (1,083). . . 1,034
Fronton, Starr (180) 170	Geronimo, Guadalupe, 5 (1,032) . . . 1,374	Goshen, Walker. 250
Fronton Ranchettes, Starr (113). 117	GHOLSON, McLennan, 21 (1,061). 1,114	Gould, Cherokee 20
*FROST, Navarro, 21 (643) 653	Gibtown, Jack 20	*Gouldbusk, Coleman, 3. 70
Fruitland, Montague 20	*GIDDINGS, Lee, 326 (4,881) 5,118	Graceton, Upshur 100
*FRUITVALE, Van Zandt, 11 (408). 433	Gilchrist, Galveston, 1 300	*GRAFORD, Palo Pinto, 30 (584). 620
Frydek, Austin 900	*Gillett, Karnes, 12. 120	*GRAHAM, Young, 515 (8,903) . . . 9,158
Fulbright, Red River. 150	Gilliland, Knox 20	Graham, Garza 60
*FULSHEAR, Fort Bend, 318 (1,134). 13,914	*GILMER, Upshur, 392 (4,905) 5,085	*GRANBURY, Hood, 1,249 (7,978). 10,454
*FULTON, Aransas, 98 (1,358) 1,437	Gilpin, Dickens 2	Grand Acres, Cameron (49) 43
Funston, Jones 26	Ginger, Rains. 70	Grand Bluff, Panola 115
Furrh, Panola. 40	*Girard, Kent (50) 44	*GRANDFALLS, Ward, 10 (360). . . . 398
	Girvin, Pecos. 20	*GRAND PRAIRIE, Dallas, Tarrant, Ellis, 4,737 (175,396). 195,756
G	Gist, Jasper 20	*GRAND SALINE, Van Zandt, 119 (3,136). 3,311
Gadston, Lamar. 35	Givens, Lamar 135	*GRANDVIEW, Johnson, 109 (1,561). 1,796
*Gail, Borden, 5 (231). 284	*GLADEWATER, Gregg, Upshur, 332 (6,441). 6,788	Grandview, Dawson. 8
*GAINESVILLE, Cooke, 773 (16,002). 16,709	Glaze City, Gonzales 10	Grandview, Gray 13
Galena, Smith 50	Glazier, Hemphill. 48	*GRANGER, Williamson, 54 (1,419). 1,624
*GALENA PARK, Harris, 160 (10,887). 11,022	Gleckler, Lavaca 78	Grangerland, Montgomery 300
Galilee, Smith 150	Glen Cove, Coleman 40	GRANITE SHOALS, Burnet, 90 (4,910). 5,337
*GALLATIN, Cherokee (419) 447	Glendale, Trinity 175	GRANJENO, Hidalgo, 2 (293) 320
Galloway, Panola 71	Glenfawn, Rusk. 100	Grape Creek, Tom Green, (3,154). 3,201
*GALVESTON, Galveston, 1,887 (47,745). 50,372	*Glen Flora, Wharton, 3 210	*GRAPELAND, Houston, 87 (1,489). 1,456
*GANADO, Jackson, 112 (2,003). . . 2,115	Glenn, Dickens 4	*GRAPEVINE, Tarrant, 2,825 (46,334). 54,277
Garceño, Starr (420). 391	GLENN HEIGHTS, Dallas, Ellis, 160 (11,278). 13,396	Grassland, Lynn. 40
*Garciasville, Starr, 2 (46) 59	Glenrio, Deaf Smith 10	Gray, Marion. 12
Garden City, Glasscock, 31 (334). . . . 427	*GLEN ROSE, Somervell, 235 (2,444). 2,812	Grayback, Wilbarger 10
*Gardendale, Ector, 45 (1,574). . . . 1,959	Glenwood, Upshur. 150	GRAYS PRAIRIE, Kaufman, 6 (337). 379
Gardendale, La Salle. 80	Glidden, Colorado, 1 (661). 762	Graytown, Wilson, Bexar 85
GARDEN RIDGE, Comal, 116 (3,259). 4,187	Globe, Lamar 60	Green, Karnes. 50
Garden Valley, Smith 150	Glory, Lamar. 30	Green Hill, Titus 80
Garfield, Travis (1,698). 1,845	*Gober, Fannin, 1. 146	Green Lake, Calhoun 51
Garfield, DeWitt 16	*GODLEY, Johnson, 65 (1,009) 1,377	Greenpond, Hopkins 150
*GARLAND, Dallas, 5,949 (226,876). 242,493	*Golden, Wood, 6 398	Green's Creek, Erath. 75
Garland, Bowie 45	Goldfinch, Frio 35	Green Valley, Denton 100
Garner, Parker. 196	*Goldsboro, Coleman, 1 15	Green Valley Farms, Cameron, (1,272). 1,526
Garner State Park, Uvalde. 50	*GOLDSMITH, Ector, 18 (257) 286	Greenview, Hopkins. 25
GARRETT, Ellis, 9 (806). 900	*GOLDTHWAITE, Mills, 82 (1,878). 1,888	*GREENVILLE, Hunt, 979 (25,557). 28,992
*GARRISON, Nacogdoches, 43 (895). 881	*GOLIAD, Goliad, 138 (1,908) 2,089	Greenvine, Washington 35
*Garwood, Colorado, 21. 600	GOLINDA, Falls, McLennan, 18 (559). 592	Greenwood, Hopkins. 100
	Golly, DeWitt 41	Greenwood, Midland 2,000
	Gomez, Terry 6	
	*GONZALES, Gonzales, 360 (7,237). 7,576	

Town, County . . . . Pop. 2019	Town, County . . . . Pop. 2019	Town, County . . . . Pop. 2019
Greenwood, Red River 20	*HAMLIN, Jones, Fisher, 70	HEDWIG VILLAGE, Harris, 253
*Greenwood, Wise, 3 76	(2,124). 2,040	(2,557). 2,601
*GREGORY, San Patricio, 38	Hammond, Robertson 44	Hefner, Knox. 3
(1,907). 1,854	Hamon, Gonzales 20	Hegar, Waller. 100
Gresham, Smith. 1,000	*Hamshire, Jefferson, 18 759	Heidelberg, Hidalgo (1,725) 1,877
GREY FOREST, Bexar, 16 (483) 566	Hancock, Comal 1,000	*Heidenheimer, Bell, 6 224
Grice, Upshur 20	Hancock, Dawson 20	Helena, Karnes 35
Griffith, Cochran. 12	*Hankamer, Chambers, 12 226	Helmic, Trinity 86
Grigsby, Shelby 15	Hannibal, Erath. 25	*HELOTES, Bexar, 515 (7,341) . . . 10,297
Grit, Mason 15	Hanover, Milam. 25	*HEMPHILL, Sabine, 136
*GROESBECK, Limestone, 131	*HAPPY, Swisher, Randall, 34	(1,198). 1,233
(4,328). 4,308	(678). 666	*HEMPSTEAD, Waller, 241
*GROOM, Carson, 32 (574). 542	Happy Union, Hale 25	(5,770). 7,507
Grosvenor, Brown 24	Happy Valley, Taylor. 12	*HENDERSON, Rusk, 606
*GROVES, Jefferson, 316	Harbin, Erath 21	(13,712). 13,688
(16,144). 15,953	*HARDIN, Liberty, 11 (819) 979	Henkhaus, Lavaca 88
*GROVETON, Trinity, 46	Hare, Williamson. 60	Henly, Hays. 140
(1,057). 1,055	*Hargill, Hidalgo, 3 (877) 919	*HENRIETTA, Clay, 123 (3,141). . . 3,104
Grow, King 9	*HARKER HEIGHTS, Bell, 662	Henry's Chapel, Cherokee. 75
Gruenau, DeWitt. 18	(26,700). 32,665	*HEREFORD, Deaf Smith, 395
Gruene, Comal . . . [part of New Braunfels]	Harkeyville, San Saba 12	(15,370). 15,635
*GRUVER, Hansford, 41 (1,194) . . . 1,133	*Harleton, Harrison, 22 390	Hermits Cove, Rains 40
Guadalupe, Victoria 70	*HARLINGEN, Cameron, 2,167	*Hermleigh, Scurry, 16 (345). 308
Guadalupe-Guerra, Starr (37) 57	(64,849). 68,835	Hester, Navarro 35
Guadalupe Station, Culberson. 10	Harmon, Lamar. 12	*HEWITT, McLennan, 398
*Guerra, Jim Hogg (6) 4	Harmony, Floyd. 42	(13,549). 14,820
Gum Springs, Cass. 59	Harmony, Grimes 12	*Hext, Menard, 1 75
GUN BARREL CITY, Henderson,	Harmony, Kent 10	HICKORY CREEK, Denton, 126
322 (5,672). 6,222	Harmony, Nacogdoches 50	(3,247). 4,924
Gunsight, Stephens 6	*Harper, Gillespie, 31 (1,192). 1,388	Hickory Creek, Houston. 31
*GUNTER, Grayson, 74 (1,498) . . . 1,660	Harpersville, Stephens 5	Hickory Creek, Hunt 40
Gus, Burleson 50	Harrison, McLennan 100	*HICO, Hamilton, 143 (1,379) 1,428
*GUSTINE, Comanche, 10 (476) . . . 490	Harrold, Wilbarger, 3 200	*HIDALGO, Hidalgo, 481
*Guthrie, King, 1 (160). 188	*HART, Castro, 23 (1,114). 1,014	(11,195). 13,984
Gutierrez, Starr (79). 84	Hartburg, Newton 893	HIDEAWAY, Smith (3,083). 3,191
*Guy, Fort Bend, 9 239	Hart Camp, Lamb 4	Higginbotham, Gaines 21
Guys Store, Leon 20	*Hartley, Hartley, 19 (540). 595	*HIGGINS, Lipscomb, 15 (397) 398
	Harvard, Camp 48	High, Lamar. 14
H	Harvey, Brazos. 1,000	Highbank, Falls 20
	Harwell Point, Burnet. 138	High Hill, Fayette. 176
Haciendito, Presidio. 10	*Harwood, Gonzales, 12. 118	*High Island, Galveston, 5. 300
HACKBERRY, Denton, 53 (968) . . . 1,128	*HASKELL, Haskell, 96 (3,322). . . . 3,169	Highland, Erath. 60
Hackberry, Cottle. 30	Haslam, Shelby 100	HIGHLAND HAVEN, Burnet,
Hackberry, Edwards. 3	*HASLET, Tarrant, 249 (1,517) . . . 1,928	(431). 442
Hackberry, Garza. 5	Hasse, Comanche 50	HIGHLAND PARK, Dallas, 457
Hackberry, Lavaca 40	Hatchel, Runnels 6	(8,564). 8,666
Hagansport, Franklin 40	Hatchettville, Hopkins 20	*Highlands, Harris, 120 (7,522) 7,793
Hagerville, Houston. 70	Havana, Hidalgo (407) 393	HIGHLAND VILLAGE, Denton,
Hail, Fannin 30	HAWK COVE, Hunt, 3 (483) 559	511 (15,056). 17,300
Hainesville, Wood 95	*HAWKINS, Wood, 86 (1,278) 1,354	Hightower, Liberty. 225
*HALE CENTER, Hale, 40	*HAWLEY, Jones, 55 (634) 623	HILL COUNTRY VILLAGE,
(2,252). 2,059	Hawthorne, Walker 100	Bexar, 98 (985). 1,102
Halfway, Hale 165	Haynesville, Wichita 65	Hillcrest, Colorado. 25
Hall, San Saba 25	HAYS, Hays, 2 (217). 263	HILLCREST VILLAGE, Brazoria,
*HALLETTSVILLE, Lavaca, 213	Hazeldell, Comanche 12	(730). 758
(2,550). 2,753	*HEARNE, Robertson, 160	*Hillister, Tyler, 11 250
Halls Bluff, Houston. 67	(4,459). 4,637	Hillje, Wharton 51
HALLSBURG, McLennan, 12	HEATH, Rockwall, Kaufman, 264	Hills, Lee. 20
(507). 472	(6,921). 9,099	*HILLSBORO, Hill, 385 (8,456) . . . 8,767
*HALLSVILLE, Harrison, 123	*Hebbronville, Jim Hogg, 84	Hillside Acres, Webb (30) 49
(3,577). 4,344	(4,558). 4,400	Hilltop, Frio (287) 282
*HALTOM CITY, Tarrant, 1,331	HEBRON, Denton, 43 (415) 449	Hilltop, Starr (77). 85
(42,409). 43,003	Heckville, Lubbock 91	*Hilltop Lakes, Leon (1,101) 1,020
Hamby, Taylor. 100	*HEDLEY, Donley, 7 (329) 287	HILSHIRE VILLAGE, Harris, 18
*HAMILTON, Hamilton, 181	Hedwigs Hill, Mason 12	(746). 793
(3,095). 3,108		Hinckley, Lamar. 40
		Hindes, Atascosa 14

Town, County . . . . Pop. 2019	Town, County . . . . Pop. 2019	Town, County . . . . Pop. 2019
Hinkles Ferry, Brazoria. 100	*HUBBARD, Hill, 64 (1,423). 1,405	*INGLESIDE, San Patricio, 215
Hiram, Kaufman 75	Hubbard, Bowie 350	(9,387). 9,895
*HITCHCOCK, Galveston, 175	Huber, Shelby 15	INGLESIDE-ON-THE-BAY,
(6,961). 7,895	Huckabay, Erath. 150	San Patricio, 13 (615) 566
Hitchland, Hansford. 15	HUDSON, Angelina, 81 (4,731) . . . 4,979	*INGRAM, Kerr, 174 (1,804) 1,855
Hix, Burleson 35	Hudson Bend, Travis (2,981). 3,617	*IOLA, Grimes, 11 (401) 435
Hoard, Wood 45	HUDSON OAKS, Parker, 153	IOWA COLONY, Brazoria, 26
Hobbs, Fisher 32	(1,662). 2,479	(1,170). 6,107
Hobson, Karnes, 11 135	Huffines, Cass 140	*IOWA PARK, Wichita, 173
Hochheim, DeWitt. 70	*Huffman, Harris, 155 15,000	(6,355). 6,379
*Hockley, Harris, 147 400	Hufsmith, Harris 500	*Ira, Scurry, 12. 250
Hodges, Jones 150	*HUGHES SPRINGS, Cass, 66	*IRAAN, Pecos, 58 (1,229) 1,216
Hogansville, Rains. 300	(1,760). 1,733	*IREDELL, Bosque, 19 (339). 343
Hogg, Burleson 20	*Hull, Liberty, 15 (669). 803	Ireland, Coryell 60
Holiday Beach, Aransas (514) 507	*HUMBLE, Harris, 1,834	*Irene, Hill 170
HOLIDAY LAKES, Brazoria, 5	(15,133). 15,704	Ironton, Cherokee 110
(1,107). 1,242	*Hungerford, Wharton, 16 (347) 305	*IRVING, Dallas, 6,682
*HOLLAND, Bell, 49 (1,121) 1,170	*Hunt, Kerr, 38 708	(216,290). 245,941
Holland Quarters, Panola 40	Hunter, Comal. 40	Isla, Sabine 350
*HOLLIDAY, Archer, 75 (1,758). . . 1,774	HUNTERS CREEK VILLAGE,	Israel, Polk. 25
Holly, Houston 95	Harris, 103 (4,367) 4,738	*ITALY, Ellis, 59 (1,863) 1,957
Holly Grove, Polk. 20	*HUNTINGTON, Angelina, 107	*ITASCA, Hill, 55 (1,644). 1,761
Holly Lake Ranch, Wood (2,774). . . 3,031	(2,118). 2,149	Ivan, Stephens 15
Holly Springs, Jasper, Newton 50	Huntoon, Ochiltree 22	IVANHOE, Tyler (1,425) 2,001
HOLLYWOOD PARK, Bexar, 121	*HUNTSVILLE, Walker, 1,135	*Ivanhoe, Fannin, 8 110
(3,062). 3,396	(38,548). 43,899	Izoro, Lampasas, Coryell. 17
Holman, Fayette. 101	Hurley, Wood 30	
Homer, Angelina 475	Hurlwood, Lubbock. 152	
Homestead Meadows North, El Paso	Hurnville, Clay 10	**J**
(5,124). 5,571	*HURST, Tarrant, 1,601	
Homestead Meadows South, El Paso	(37,337). 38,479	JACINTO CITY, Harris, 206
(7,247). 7,600	Hurstown, Shelby 20	(10,553). 10,499
*HONDO, Medina, 276 (8,803) . . . 9,618	Hurst Springs, Coryell 10	*JACKSBORO, Jack, 188 (4,511) . . . 4,648
*HONEY GROVE, Fannin, 63	*HUTCHINS, Dallas, 134	Jackson, Shelby 50
(1,668). 1,732	(5,338). 6,240	Jackson, Van Zandt. 25
Honey Island, Hardin. 200	*HUTTO, Williamson, 551	*JACKSONVILLE, Cherokee, 708
Hood, Cooke. 13	(14,698). 26,801	(14,544). 15,152
Hooker Ridge, Rains 250	HUXLEY, Shelby, 5 (385) 372	Jacobia, Hunt. 60
*HOOKS, Bowie, 50 (2,769) 2,720	*Hye, Blanco, 11 72	Jakes Colony, Guadalupe. 95
Hoover, Gray. 5	Hylton, Nolan 6	JAMAICA BEACH, Galveston, 43
Hoover, Lamar. 20		(983) 1,088
Hope, Lavaca. 45		James, Shelby. 75
Hopewell, Franklin 50	**I**	Jamestown, Newton 196
Hopewell, Houston 22		Jamestown, Smith 75
Hopewell, Lamar 90	Iago, Wharton (161). 151	Jardin de San Julian, Starr (22). 26
Hopewell, Red River 152	Ida, Grayson 30	*JARRELL, Williamson, 138
Hopewell, Smith 45	*IDALOU, Lubbock, 88 (2,250). . . . 2,301	(984). 1,870
HORIZON CITY, El Paso, 268	Iglesia Antigua, Cameron (413) 444	*JASPER, Jasper, 409 (7,590) 7,533
(16,735). 19,733	Ike, Ellis 50	*JAYTON, Kent, 21 (534) 503
Hornsby Bend, Travis (6,791) 8,332	Illinois Bend, Montague 40	Jean, Young 110
Horseshoe Bend, Cooke (789). 971	IMPACT, Taylor, 1 (35). 29	*JEFFERSON, Marion, 216
HORSESHOE BAY, Llano, Burnet,	*Imperial, Pecos, 6 (278) 234	(2,106). 1,967
168 (3,418). 4,016	Inadale, Scurry 12	Jenkins, Morris 350
Hortense, Polk. 20	Independence, Washington. 140	Jennings, Lamar. 85
Horton, Delta 40	India, Ellis 30	*Jermyn, Jack, 3 75
Horton, Panola 200	Indian Creek, Brown 28	JERSEY VILLAGE, Harris, 262
*HOUSTON, Harris, Fort Bend,	Indian Creek, Smith 300	(7,620). 7,907
Montgomery, 87,046	Indian Gap, Hamilton 35	*JEWETT, Leon, 67 (1,167). 1,337
(2,100,263). 2,325,298	Indian Hill, Newton. 7	JF Villarreal, Starr (104) 111
Howard, Ellis. 60	Indian Hills, Hidalgo (2,591) 3,079	Jiba, Kaufman 50
HOWARDWICK, Donley, 9	INDIAN LAKE, Cameron (640) 833	*JOAQUIN, Shelby, 40 (824). 795
(402). 368	Indianola, Calhoun 200	Joe Lee, Bell. 8
*HOWE, Grayson, 63 (2,600) 3,391	Indian Rock, Upshur 45	*JOHNSON CITY, Blanco, 146
Howland, Lamar 65	Indian Springs, Polk (785). 920	(1,656). 2,167
Hoxie, Williamson. 60	Indio, Starr (50). 66	Johnsville, Erath. 45
Hoyte, Milam 20	Indio, Presidio 5	Johntown, Red River 175
Hub, Parmer 25	*INDUSTRY, Austin, 44 (304). 331	*Joinerville, Rusk 140
	*Inez, Victoria, 51 (2,098) 2,357	Joliet, Caldwell 70

Town, County	Pop. 2019
JOLLY, Clay, 5 (172)	159
Jollyville, Williamson, Travis, (16,151)	18,409
Jonah, Williamson	60
*Jonesboro, Coryell, Hamilton, 8	125
JONES CREEK, Brazoria, 26 (2,020)	2,158
Jones Prairie, Milam	20
JONESTOWN, Travis, 89 (1,834)	2,092
*Jonesville, Harrison, 2	70
Joplin, Jack	15
Joppa, Burnet	84
Jordans Store, Shelby	20
*JOSEPHINE, Collin, 27 (812)	1,750
*JOSHUA, Johnson, 267 (5,910)	7,805
Josserand, Trinity	29
Jot-Em-Down, Delta, Hunt	8
*JOURDANTON, Atascosa, 152 (3,871)	4,522
Joy, Clay	110
Jozye, Madison	36
Juarez, Cameron (1,017)	1,169
Jud, Haskell	60
*Judson, Gregg, 9	1,057
Juliff, Fort Bend	100
Jumbo, Panola	60
*JUNCTION, Kimble, 182 (2,574)	2,522
Justiceburg, Garza, 3	45
*JUSTIN, Denton, 193 (3,246)	4,320

K

Town, County	Pop. 2019
Kalgary, Crosby	2
*Kamay, Wichita, 5	640
Kamey, Calhoun	25
Kanawha, Red River	90
*Karnack, Harrison, 22	350
*KARNES CITY, Karnes, 103 (3,042)	3,280
Karon, Live Oak	25
Katemcy, Mason	80
*KATY, Harris, Waller, Fort Bend, 2,528 (14,102)	21,912
*KAUFMAN, Kaufman, 366 (6,703)	7,649
K-Bar Ranch, Jim Wells (358)	337
Keechi, Leon	15
*KEENE, Johnson, 103 (6,106)	6,755
Keeter, Wise	250
Keith, Grimes	50
*KELLER, Tarrant, 1,437 (39,627)	46,651
Kellerville, Wheeler	15
Kellogg, Hunt	20
Kellyville, Marion	75
Kelsey, Upshur	50
Kelton, Wheeler	34
*KEMAH, Galveston, 339 (1,773)	2,006
*KEMP, Kaufman, 103 (1,154)	1,303
Kemper City, Victoria	16
*KEMPNER, Lampasas, 82 (1,089)	1,165
*Kendalia, Kendall, 12	149

Town, County	Pop. 2019
*KENDLETON, Fort Bend, 3 (380)	461
*KENEDY, Karnes, 142 (3,296)	3,577
KENEFICK, Liberty, 13 (563)	686
*KENNARD, Houston, 13 (337)	329
*KENNEDALE, Tarrant, 313 (6,763)	8,486
*Kenney, Austin, 3	957
Kenser, Hunt	100
Kensing, Delta	30
Kent, Culberson	30
Kentucky Town, Grayson	20
*KERENS, Navarro, 53 (1,573)	1,568
*KERMIT, Winkler, 200 (5,708)	6,494
Kerrick, Dallam, 2	35
*KERRVILLE, Kerr, 1,389 (22,347)	24,005
Kerrville South, Kerr	6,600
Key, Dawson	10
Kiam, Polk	24
Kicaster, Wilson	190
Kickapoo Indian Reservation, Maverick	366
*Kildare, Cass	104
*KILGORE, Gregg, Rusk, 863 (12,975)	14,329
*KILLEEN, Bell, 2,548 (127,921)	151,463
King, Coryell	30
King Ranch Headquarters, Kleberg	191
*KINGSBURY, Guadalupe, 19 (782)	874
*Kingsland, Llano, 161 (6,030)	7,348
Kingston, Hunt	140
*KINGSVILLE, Kleberg, 600 (26,213)	25,315
Kingtown, Nacogdoches	300
Kingwood, Harris, Montgomery	[part of Houston]
Kinkler, Lavaca	75
Kiomatia, Red River	50
KIRBY, Bexar, 118 (8,000)	8,743
*KIRBYVILLE, Jasper, 126 (2,142)	2,211
Kirk, Limestone	10
Kirkland, Childress, Hardeman	25
Kirtley, Fayette	93
*KIRVIN, Freestone (129)	136
Kittrell, Walker	126
Klein, Harris	45,000
Klondike, Dawson	50
*Klondike, Delta, 5	175
Klump, Washington	20
Knapp, Scurry	10
*Knickerbocker, Tom Green, 1	94
*Knippa, Uvalde, 13 (689)	639
Knobbs Springs, Lee	20
KNOLLWOOD, Grayson, 4 (432)	591
*Knott, Howard, 4	200
*KNOX CITY, Knox, 43 (1,130)	1,135
Koerth, Lavaca	45
Kokomo, Eastland	25
Komensky, Lavaca	75
*Kopperl, Bosque, 9	225
Kosciusko, Wilson	390
*KOSSE, Limestone, 22 (464)	473

Town, County	Pop. 2019
*KOUNTZE, Hardin, 115 (2,123)	2,217
*KRESS, Swisher, 22 (715)	683
KRUGERVILLE, Denton, 65 (1,662)	2,013
*KRUM, Denton, 179 (4,157)	5,589
*KURTEN, Brazos, 2 (398)	409
*KYLE, Hays, 923 (28,016)	47,899
Kyote, Atascosa	34

L

Town, County	Pop. 2019
LaBelle, Jefferson	40
*La Blanca, Hidalgo, 15 (2,488)	2,652
La Carla, Starr (70)	73
La Casita, Starr (128)	112
Laceola, Madison	10
La Chuparosa, Starr (49)	55
Lackland Air Force Base, Bexar, (9,918)	9,124
La Coma, Webb (48)	53
*LA COSTE, Medina, 27 (1,119)	1,293
Lacy, Trinity	44
LACY-LAKEVIEW, McLennan, 128 (6,489)	6,914
*LADONIA, Fannin, 22 (612)	632
La Escondida, Starr (153)	170
La Esperanza, Starr (229)	212
LaFayette, Upshur	80
*LA FERIA, Cameron, 194 (7,302)	7,703
La Feria North, Cameron (212)	231
Lagarto, Live Oak	735
La Gloria, Jim Wells	70
La Gloria, Starr	150
Lago, Cameron (204)	176
Lago Vista, Starr (115)	124
*LAGO VISTA, Travis, 292 (6,041)	7,335
*LA GRANGE, Fayette, 413 (4,641)	4,759
*LA GRULLA, Starr, 22 (1,622)	1,688
Laguna, Uvalde	8
Laguna Heights, Cameron, (3,488)	4,219
Laguna Park, Bosque, 4 (1,276)	1,261
Laguna Seca, Hidalgo (266)	274
LAGUNA VISTA, Cameron, 72 (3,117)	3,348
Laguna Vista, Burnet	94
La Homa, Hidalgo (11,985)	12,102
*Laird Hill, Rusk, 1	300
La Isla, El Paso	27
Lajitas, Brewster	75
*LA JOYA, Hidalgo, 75 (3,980)	4,409
La Junta, Parker	300
Lake Arrowhead, Clay	250
LAKE BRIDGEPORT, Wise, 6 (340)	398
Lake Brownwood, Brown, (1,532)	1,450
Lake Bryan, Brazos (1,728)	1,977
Lake Cherokee, Rusk (3,071)	3,198
Lake Cisco, Eastland	300
LAKE CITY, San Patricio (509)	527
Lake Colorado City, Mitchell, (588)	570

Town, County . . . . Pop. 2019	Town, County . . . . Pop. 2019	Town, County . . . . Pop. 2019

*Lake Creek, Delta, Lamar, 2 55
*LAKE DALLAS, Denton, 240
  (7,105). 8,399
Lake Dunlap, Guadalupe (1,934) . . . 2,303
Lakehills, Bandera (5,150). 5,912
*LAKE JACKSON, Brazoria, 754
  (26,849). 28,421
Lake Kiowa, Cooke (1,906) 1,809
Lake Leon, Eastland 75
Lake Medina Shores, Bandera,
  (1,235). 1,375
Lake Meredith Estates,
  Hutchinson, (437). 406
Lake Murvaul, Panola. 300
Lake Nueces, Uvalde 60
LAKEPORT, Gregg, 34 (974) 1,051
Lakeshore Gardens-Hidden Acres,
  San Patricio (504). 456
LAKESIDE, San Patricio (312) 300
LAKESIDE, Tarrant, 64 (1,307). . . . 1,635
LAKESIDE CITY, Archer, 24
  (997). 1,047
Lakeside Village, Bosque. 226
LAKE TANGLEWOOD, Randall,
  10 (796). 847
Lake Victor, Burnet 265
Lake View, Val Verde (199) 210
*LAKEVIEW, Hall, 5 (107) 92
Lakeview, Floyd. 39
Lakeview, Lynn 15
Lakeview, Orange 75
*LAKEWAY, Travis, 784
  (11,391). 15,981
Lakewood Harbor, Bosque 250

LAKEWOOD VILLAGE, Denton,
  (545). 731
*LAKE WORTH, Tarrant, 324
  (4,584). 4,858
La Loma de Falcon, Starr (95) 101
Lamar, Aransas, Refugio (636). 618
*LA MARQUE, Galveston, 389
  (14,509). 17,326
Lamasco, Fannin 32
*LAMESA, Dawson, 319
  (9,422). 8,857
La Minita, Starr (171). 176
Lamkin, Comanche 87
*LAMPASAS, Lampasas, 383
  (6,681). 7,787
Lanark, Cass 30
*LANCASTER, Dallas, 699
  (36,361). 39,508
*Lane City, Wharton, 4 111
Lanely, Freestone 27
Laneport, Williamson 40
*Laneville, Rusk, 5 169
*Langtry, Val Verde. 30
Lanier, Cass. 80
Lannius, Fannin. 79
Lantana, Denton (6,874). 8,473
La Paloma, Cameron (2,903). 3,526
La Paloma Addition, San Patricio,
  (330). 311
La Paloma-Lost Creek, Nueces,
  (408). 505
La Paloma Ranchettes, Starr,
  (239). 258
La Parita, Atascosa 48

*LA PORTE, Harris, 948
  (33,800). 34,757
La Presa, Webb (319) 291
*La Pryor, Zavala, 11 (1,643) 1,798
La Puerta, Starr (632) 590
*LAREDO, Webb, 6,909
  (236,091). 266,898
Laredo Ranchettes, Webb (22). 22
La Reforma, Starr. 20
Lariat, Parmer 100
La Rosita, Starr (85) 70
*Larue, Henderson, 23 250
*LaSalle, Jackson 110
Lasana, Cameron (84) 69
*Lasara, Willacy, 1 (1,039). 924
Las Escobas, Starr. 5
Las Haciendas, Webb (7) 4
Las Lomas, Starr (3,147) 3,295
Las Lomitas, Jim Hogg (244). 233
Las Palmas, Zapata (67) 75
Las Palmas II, Cameron (1,605). . . . 1,907
Las Pilas, Webb (28). 27
Las Quintas Fronterizas, Maverick,
  (3,290). 4,114
Lassater, Marion 60
Las Yescas, Cameron 221
Latch, Upshur 50
Latex, Harrison 75
*LATEXO, Houston, 9 (322) 338
La Tina Ranch, Cameron (618) 737
Latium, Washington. 30
Laughlin Air Force Base, Val Verde,
  (1,569). 1,502
Laurel, Newton 357
Laureles, Cameron (3,692) 3,670

The historic commercial district in Lancaster. Photo by Renelibrary, CC by 4.0/Wikimedia Commons.

Town, County	Pop. 2019
Lavender, Limestone	30
*LA VERNIA, Wilson, 217 (1,034).	1,426
La Victoria, Starr (171)	156
*LA VILLA, Hidalgo, 17 (1,957).	2,544
*LAVON, Collin, 120 (2,219).	3,839
*LA WARD, Jackson, 5 (213).	221
*LAWN, Taylor, 10 (314).	315
Lawrence, Kaufman	259
*Lazbuddie, Parmer, 5.	248
*LEAGUE CITY, Galveston, Harris, 2,813 (83,560).	108,604
Leagueville, Henderson	50
*LEAKEY, Real, 66 (425).	464
*LEANDER, Williamson, 1,135 (26,526).	59,110
LEARY, Bowie, 13 (495).	515
*Ledbetter, Fayette, Lee, 13	83
Leedale, Bell	24
*Leesburg, Camp, 11	128
*Leesville, Gonzales, 2	152
*LEFORS, Gray, 9 (497).	474
*Leggett, Polk, 5.	500
Lehman, Cochran	6
Leigh, Harrison	60
Lela, Wheeler	135
*Lelia Lake, Donley, 1.	70
*Leming, Atascosa, 6 (946).	1,028
*Lenorah, Martin, 6	83
Lenz, Karnes	50
Leo, Cooke	20
Leo, Lee	10
*LEONA, Leon, 8 (175).	186
*LEONARD, Fannin, 102 (1,990).	2,092
Leon Junction, Coryell	50
Leon Springs, Bexar.	[part of San Antonio]
*LEON VALLEY, Bexar, 475 (10,151).	11,799
*LEROY, McLennan, 10 (337).	347
Lesley, Hall	25
*LEVELLAND, Hockley, 424 (13,542).	13,555
Leverett's Chapel, Rusk.	400
Levi, McLennan	50
Levita, Coryell.	70
*LEWISVILLE, Denton, 3,655 (95,290).	114,262
*LEXINGTON, Lee, 74 (1,177).	1,216
*LIBERTY, Liberty, 448 (8,397).	10,165
Liberty, Lubbock	228
Liberty, Milam.	40
Liberty, Newton.	128
Liberty City, Gregg (2,351)	2,624
*LIBERTY HILL, Williamson, 363 (967).	2,931
Liberty Hill, Houston	73
Liberty Hill, Milam	25
Lilbert, Nacogdoches	100
*Lillian, Johnson, 9.	1,160
*Lincoln, Lee, 11	336
*LINDALE, Smith, 409 (4,818).	6,496
*LINDEN, Cass, 77 (1,988).	1,945
Lindenau, DeWitt	50
Lindendale, Kendall.	70
*LINDSAY, Cooke, 38 (1,018).	1,148

Town, County	Pop. 2019
Lindsay, Reeves (271).	288
*Lingleville, Erath	100
*Linn, Hidalgo, 4 (801).	749
Linn Flat, Nacogdoches	60
Linwood, Cherokee	40
*LIPAN, Hood, 44 (430).	500
*Lipscomb, Lipscomb (37)	28
*Lissie, Wharton, 5.	72
Littig, Travis	35
Little Cypress, Orange	900
*LITTLE ELM, Denton, 800 (25,898).	53,126
*LITTLEFIELD, Lamb, 147 (6,372).	5,840
Little Hope, Wood	25
Little Midland, Burnet	82
Little New York, Gonzales.	15
*LITTLE RIVER-ACADEMY, Bell, 36 (1,961).	2,098
Lively, Kaufman.	50
LIVE OAK, Bexar, 406 (13,131).	16,451
*LIVERPOOL, Brazoria, 21 (482).	561
*LIVINGSTON, Polk, 588 (5,335).	5,247
*LLANO, Llano, 240 (3,232).	3,529
Llano Grande, Hidalgo (3,008)	2,702
Locker, San Saba	16
Lockett, Wilbarger.	150
Lockettville, Hockley	20
*LOCKHART, Caldwell, 471 (12,698).	14,410
*LOCKNEY, Floyd, 46 (1,842).	1,637
Locust, Grayson.	118
*Lodi, Marion, 1	175
Loebau, Lee	35
Logan, Panola	40
LOG CABIN, Henderson, 6 (714).	780
*Lohn, McCulloch, 1	149
Loire, Wilson, Atascosa.	50
Lois, Cooke.	10
*Lolita, Jackson, 19 (555).	606
Loma Alta, McMullen.	25
Loma Alta, Val Verde	30
Loma Grande, Zavala (107).	101
Loma Linda, San Patricio (122)	123
Loma Linda East, Jim Wells (254)	267
Loma Linda East, Starr (44).	41
Loma Linda West, Starr (114)	134
Loma Vista, Starr (160).	170
Lomax, Howard.	25
*LOMETA, Lampasas, 38 (856).	887
*London, Kimble, 5	180
Lone Camp, Palo Pinto.	110
Lone Cedar, Ellis	18
Lone Grove, Llano	50
*LONE OAK, Hunt, 49 (598).	696
Lone Oak, Colorado	50
Lone Pine, Houston	81
*LONE STAR, Morris, 42 (1,581).	1,508
Lone Star, Cherokee	20
Lone Star, Floyd.	42
Lone Star, Lamar	35
*Long Branch, Panola, 4	150
Long Lake, Anderson	30
Long Mott, Calhoun	76
Longoria, Starr (92)	100

Town, County	Pop. 2019
Longpoint, Washington	30
*LONGVIEW, Gregg, Harrison, 3,509 (80,455).	83,749
Longworth, Fisher	47
Looneyville, Nacogdoches	50
*Loop, Gaines, 6 (225)	243
*Lopeño, Zapata (174)	185
Lopezville, Hidalgo (4,333).	4,197
*LORAINE, Mitchell, 15 (602)	587
*LORENA, McLennan, 150 (1,691).	1,785
*LORENZO, Crosby, 30 (1,147).	1,142
Los Altos, Webb (140).	147
Los Alvarez, Starr (303).	286
Los Angeles, La Salle.	15
Los Angeles Subdivision, Willacy, (121).	143
Los Arcos, Webb (127)	134
Los Arrieros, Starr (91)	93
Los Barreras, Starr (288)	302
Los Centenarios, Webb (87)	98
Los Corralitos, Webb (35).	44
Los Ebanos, Starr (280).	302
*Los Ebanos, Hidalgo, 1 (335)	313
Los Escondidos, Burnet	80
*LOS FRESNOS, Cameron, 219 (5,542).	7,937
Los Fresnos, Webb (67).	80
Los Huisaches, Webb (17).	14
*LOS INDIOS, Cameron, 21 (1,083).	1,075
Los Lobos, Zapata (9).	7
Los Minerales, Webb (20).	17
Los Nopalitos, Webb (62)	62
Losoya, Bexar	500
Lost Creek, Travis (4,509).	4,631
Lost Prairie, Limestone.	2
Los Veteranos I, Webb (24)	22
Los Veteranos II, Webb (24)	28
LOS YBANEZ, Dawson, 1 (19)	18
*LOTT, Falls, 49 (759)	773
*Louise, Wharton, 37 (995).	1,024
Lovelace, Hill	30
*LOVELADY, Houston, 33 (649).	639
*Loving, Young, 4.	300
*Lowake, Concho, 1	40
LOWRY CROSSING, Collin, 57 (1,711).	1,753
Loyal Valley, Mason	52
Loyola Beach, Kleberg	185
*Lozano, Cameron (404)	430
*LUBBOCK, Lubbock, 7,871 (229,573).	259,158
LUCAS, Collin, 209 (5,166)	8,183
Luckenbach, Gillespie	25
*LUEDERS, Jones, 10 (346).	331
Luella, Grayson	639
*LUFKIN, Angelina, 1,810 (35,067).	36,423
*LULING, Caldwell, 248 (5,411).	5,835
*LUMBERTON, Hardin, 449 (11,943).	12,816
Lums Chapel, Lamb	6
Luther, Howard.	3
Lutie, Collingsworth	10
Lydia, Red River	109
*LYFORD, Willacy, 44 (2,611).	2,539

Town, County . . . . Pop. 2019	Town, County . . . . Pop. 2019	Town, County . . . . Pop. 2019
Lynn Grove, Grimes. 25	Mars, Van Zandt, Henderson. 20	McNeil, Caldwell. 50
*Lyons, Burleson, 3. 360	*MARSHALL, Harrison, 853	*McQueeney, Guadalupe, 41
*LYTLE, Atascosa, Medina, Bexar,	(23,523). 23,950	(2,545). 2,793
190 (2,492). 3,069	Marston, Polk 25	*MEADOW, Terry, 16 (593) 590
Lytton Springs, Caldwell. 300	*MART, McLennan, 64 (1,897). . . . 1,971	Meadow Grove, Bell. 22
	*MARTINDALE, Caldwell, 49	MEADOWLAKES, Burnet, 41
M	(1,116). 1,262	(1,777). 1,816
	Martinez, Starr (69) 72	MEADOWS PLACE, Fort Bend,
*MABANK, Kaufman, Henderson,	Martins Mill, Van Zandt 158	111 (4,660). 4,591
222 (3,035). 4,178	Martin Springs, Hopkins. 200	Mecca, Madison, Grimes 48
Mabelle, Baylor 9	*Martinsville, Nacogdoches, 2 350	Medicine Mound, Hardeman 25
Mabry, Red River. 60	Marvin, Lamar 48	Medill, Lamar 50
*Macdona, Bexar, 4 (559) 603	Maryetta, Jack 7	Medina, Zapata (3,935). 4,387
Macon, Franklin 21	*Maryneal, Nolan, 5. 50	*Medina, Bandera, 31. 850
Macune, San Augustine 50	Marysville, Cooke 12	Meeker, Jefferson 2,280
*MADISONVILLE, Madison, 205	*MASON, Mason, 216 (2,114). 2,298	Meeks, Bell 6
(4,396). 4,734	Massey Lake, Anderson 30	*MEGARGEL, Archer, 11 (203). 196
Madras, Red River 61	Masterson, Moore, 2. 2	*MELISSA, Collin, 206 (4,695) . . 13,461
Magnet, Wharton 42	*MATADOR, Motley, 39 (607) 609	Melrose, Nacogdoches 400
*MAGNOLIA, Montgomery, 954	*Matagorda, Matagorda, 27 (503). . . . 465	*MELVIN, McCulloch, 4 (178) 182
(1,393). 2,118	*MATHIS, San Patricio, 141	*MEMPHIS, Hall, 74 (2,290). 2,063
Magnolia, San Jacinto. 150	(4,942). 4,800	*MENARD, Menard, 59 (1,471). . . . 1,378
Magnolia Beach, Calhoun. 250	Matthews, Colorado. 20	Mendoza, Caldwell 100
Magnolia Springs, Jasper. 20	*MAUD, Bowie, 37 (1,056) 1,095	Menlow, Hill. 12
Maha, Travis 200	*Mauriceville, Orange, 14	*Mentone, Loving, 5 (19) 29
Mahl, Nacogdoches 150	(3,252). 3,804	Mentz, Colorado 100
Mahomet, Burnet 97	Maverick, Runnels 35	*MERCEDES, Hidalgo, 502
Majors, Franklin 13	Maxdale, Bell. 25	(15,570). 17,096
*MALAKOFF, Henderson, 113	Maxey, Lamar 70	Mercury, McCulloch 166
(2,324). 2,434	*Maxwell, Caldwell, 26 500	*Mereta, Tom Green, 2 131
Mallard, Montague 12	*May, Brown, 13. 270	*MERIDIAN, Bosque, 78 (1,493). . . 1,515
*MALONE, Hill, 13 (269). 279	*Maydelle, Cherokee, 1. 250	*Merit, Hunt, 1 225
Malta, Bowie. 350	Mayfield, Hale. 26	*MERKEL, Taylor, 92 (2,590) 2,646
Malvern, Leon 12	Mayfield, Hill 25	Merle, Burleson 10
Mambrino, Hood. 74	Mayflower, Newton 50	Merriman, Eastland 14
*Manchaca, Travis, 106 (1,133) . . . 1,233	Maynard, San Jacinto 90	*MERTENS, Hill, 6 (125) 131
Manchester, Red River 185	*MAYPEARL, Ellis, 47 (934) 1,116	*MERTZON, Irion, 52 (781). 797
Mangum, Eastland. 15	Maysfield, Milam 140	*MESQUITE, Dallas, Kaufman,
Manheim, Lee 50	*McAdoo, Dickens, 2 75	3,193 (139,824). 142,030
Mankin, Henderson. 30	*McALLEN, Hidalgo, 5,480	Mesquite, Starr (505) 543
Mankins, Archer 10	(129,872). 144,785	Metcalf Gap, Palo Pinto 6
*MANOR, Travis, 276 (5,037). . . . 13,817	McBeth, Brazoria. 20	*MEXIA, Limestone, 260 (7,459). . . 7,605
*MANSFIELD, Tarrant, Johnson,	*McCAMEY, Upton, 69 (1,887). . . . 2,065	*Meyersville, DeWitt, 6. 110
Ellis, 2,003 (56,368). 70,080	*McCAULLEY, Fisher. 96	Meyersville, Washington. 15
Manuel Garcia, Starr (203) 180	McClanahan, Falls 30	*MIAMI, Roberts, 22 (597). 553
Manuel Garcia II, Starr (77) 72	McCook, Hidalgo 50	Mico, Medina 107
*MANVEL, Brazoria, 342	McCoy, Atascosa 30	Midcity, Lamar 50
(5,179). 12,671	McCoy, Floyd 20	Middleton, Leon 26
Maple, Bailey. 40	McCoy, Kaufman. 20	*Midfield, Matagorda, 4 305
Maple, Red River. 30	McCoy, Panola 30	*Midkiff, Upton, 14 182
Maple Springs, Titus. 25	McCoy, Red River 175	*MIDLAND, Midland, Martin,
Mapleton, Houston 32	*McDade, Bastrop, 17 (685) 746	5,000 (111,147). 146,701
*Marathon, Brewster, 18 (430) 399	*McFaddin, Victoria. 50	*MIDLOTHIAN, Ellis, 964
*MARBLE FALLS, Burnet, 706	McGirk, Hamilton, Mills 18	(18,037). 34,164
(6,077). 7,098	*McGREGOR, McLennan, 197	*MIDWAY, Madison, Montgomery,
*MARFA, Presidio, 148 (1,981) . . . 1,650	(4,987). 5,264	20 (228). 229
Margaret, Foard, Hardeman 50	*McKINNEY, Collin, 4,631	Midway, Dawson. 12
Marie, Runnels 10	(131,117). 197,391	Midway, Fannin. 51
*MARIETTA, Cass (134) 129	McKinney Acres, Andrews (815) . . . 1,079	Midway, Jim Wells 24
*MARION, Guadalupe, 106	*McLEAN, Gray, 24 (778) 747	Midway, Limestone 9
(1,066). 1,243	McLENDON-CHISHOLM,	Midway, Polk 525
*Markham, Matagorda, 13	Rockwall, 5 (1,373) 3,541	Midway, Red River 40
(1,082). 1,096	*McLeod, Cass, 3 600	Midway, Titus 110
Markley, Young 25	McMahan, Caldwell. 90	Midway, Upshur 20
*MARLIN, Falls, 154 (5,967) 5,577	McMillin, San Saba 15	Midway, Van Zandt 31
Marlow, Milam 45	McNair, Harris 2,039	Midway North, Hidalgo (4,752). . . . 5,011
*MARQUEZ, Leon, 31 (263) 297	McNary, Hudspeth. 100	Midway South, Hidalgo (2,239). . . . 2,562

Town, County . . . . Pop. 2019	Town, County . . . . Pop. 2019	Town, County . . . . Pop. 2019
Ottine, Gonzales 80	PARKER, Collin, 124 (3,811). 5,216	Pert, Anderson. 20
Otto, Falls 48	Parker, Johnson 93	Peters, Austin. 150
*Ovalo, Taylor, 3 225	Park Springs, Wise 90	*PETERSBURG, Hale, Floyd, 23
*OVERTON, Rusk, Smith, 87	Parsley Hill, Wilbarger 25	(1,202). 1,108
(2,554). 2,558	Parvin, Denton 44	Peter's Prairie, Red River 40
OVILLA, Ellis, Dallas, 132	*PASADENA, Harris, 3,246	Petersville, DeWitt 38
(3,492). 4,320	(149,043). 156,841	*PETROLIA, Clay, 12 (686) 672
Owens, Brown. 16	Patillo, Erath 10	PETRONILA, Nueces, 2 (113) 121
Owens, Crosby 4	Patman Switch, Cass. 40	Petteway, Robertson. 25
Owentown, Smith 100	Patonia, Polk 15	Pettibone, Milam 25
Owl Creek, Bell. 130	Patricia, Dawson 50	Pettit, Hockley. 30
Owl Ranch, Jim Wells (225) 193	Patroon, Shelby 25	*Pettus, Bee, 10 (558) 559
Oxford, Llano 18	*PATTISON, Waller, 32 (472) 628	*Petty, Lamar, 5 130
OYSTER CREEK, Brazoria, 34	PATTON VILLAGE, Montgomery,	Petty, Lynn 8
(1,111). 1,170	17 (1,557) 2,132	Peyton, Blanco. 30
*Ozona, Crockett, 125 (3,225) 2,912	Pattonfield, Upshur 20	*PFLUGERVILLE, Travis, 1,666
	*Pattonville, Lamar, 9 180	(46,936). 67,738
P	Pawelekville, Karnes. 110	Phalba, Van Zandt 73
	*Pawnee, Bee, 6 (166). 155	*PHARR, Hidalgo, 1,751
Pablo Pena, Starr (63). 67	Paxton, Shelby 50	(70,400). 81,473
Pacio, Delta. 35	Paynes Corner, Gaines 18	Phelps, Walker. 98
Padgett, Young. 18	PAYNE SPRINGS, Henderson, 26	Phillipsburg, Washington 75
*PADUCAH, Cottle, 48 (1,186). . . . 1,085	(767). 807	Pickens, Henderson 20
*Paige, Bastrop, 34 275	Peach Creek, Brazos. 150	Pickett, Navarro. 30
Paint Creek, Haskell. 150	Peacock, Stonewall. 100	*Pickton, Hopkins, 11. 300
*PAINT ROCK, Concho, 12	Peadenville, Palo Pinto 15	Pidcoke, Coryell 50
(273). 200	Pearl, Coryell. 50	Piedmont, Grimes 50
Paisano Park, San Patricio (130) 130	*PEARLAND, Brazoria, Harris,	Piedmont, Upshur 20
*PALACIOS, Matagorda, 113	Fort Bend, 3,428 (91,252). . . 122,331	*Pierce, Wharton, 2 51
(4,718). 4,589	Pearl City, DeWitt 4	Pike, Collin 47
*PALESTINE, Anderson, 776	*PEARSALL, Frio, 234 (9,146). . . . 10,577	Pilgrim, Gonzales 22
(18,712). 19,115	Pearson, Medina 24	Pilgrim Rest, Rains. 72
PALISADES, Randall (325). 364	Pearsons Chapel, Houston 95	Pilot Grove, Grayson 48
Palito Blanco, Jim Wells 750	Pear Valley, McCulloch 37	Pilot Knob, Travis 500
*PALMER, Ellis, 76 (2,000). 2,203	*PEASTER, Parker, ... 555	*PILOT POINT, Denton, 190
PALMHURST, Hidalgo, 109	Pecan Acres, Tarrant, Wise (4,099) . .4,745	(3,856). 4,590
(2,607). 2,737	*PECAN GAP, Delta, Fannin, 7	Pine, Camp. 78
PALM VALLEY, Cameron, 18	(203). 204	Pine Branch, Red River. 40
(1,304). 1,241	Pecan Grove, Fort Bend,	PINE FOREST, Orange, 15 (487). . . . 508
PALMVIEW, Hidalgo, 383	(15,963). 20,569	Pine Forest, Hopkins 100
(5,458). 10,829	PECAN HILL, Ellis, 12 (626) 706	Pine Grove, Cherokee 30
Palmview South, Hidalgo,	Pecan Plantation, Hood (5,294). . . . 5,719	Pine Grove, Newton. 180
(5,575). 6,064	Pecan Wells, Hamilton 6	Pine Harbor, Marion (810) 790
Palo Blanco, Starr (204) 234	*PECOS, Reeves, 345 (8,780) 10,574	Pinehill, Rusk 70
Paloduro, Armstrong 10	Peeltown, Kaufman 75	*Pinehurst, Montgomery, 108
Paloma Creek, Denton (2,501) 3,177	Peerless, Hopkins. 90	(4,624). 5,448
Paloma Creek South, Denton,	Peggy, Atascosa 22	PINEHURST, Orange, 210
(2,753). 3,569	Pelham, Navarro 75	(2,097). 2,077
*Palo Pinto, Palo Pinto, 8 (333) 354	PELICAN BAY, Tarrant, 12	PINE ISLAND, Waller (988). 1,200
Paluxy, Hood, Erath 36	(1,547). 1,905	Pine Island, Jefferson 350
*PAMPA, Gray, 553 (17,994) 17,277	Pena, Starr (118) 127	*PINELAND, Sabine, 29 (850) 793
Pancake, Coryell 11	*Pendleton, Bell, 1 369	Pine Mills, Wood 75
Pandale, Val Verde 25	*PENELOPE, Hill, 4 (198) 207	Pine Prairie, Walker 450
*Pandora, Wilson, 1 110	*PEÑITAS, Hidalgo, 98 (4,385) . . . 4,721	Pine Springs, Culberson 20
*PANHANDLE, Carson, 80	*Pennington, Trinity, Houston, 7 67	Pine Springs, Smith 150
(2,452). 2,315	*Penwell, Ector, 6 41	Pineview, Wood. 10
*Panna Maria, Karnes, 6 45	Peoria, Hill 105	Pinewood Estates, Hardin,
*Panola, Panola, 1 305	Percilla, Houston 95	(1,678). 1,698
PANORAMA VILLAGE,	Perezville, Hidalgo (5,376) 6,022	Piney, Austin 60
Montgomery, 31 (2,170) 2,337	Pernitas Point, Live Oak, Jim Wells. . . 274	PINEY POINT VILLAGE, Harris,
*PANTEGO, Tarrant, 393	*Perrin, Jack, 14 (398). 431	59 (3,125) 3,338
(2,394). 2,462	Perry, Falls. 76	Pin Hook, Lamar 48
Panther Junction, Brewster 130	*PERRYTON, Ochiltree, 404	Pioneer, Eastland 20
Papalote, Bee. 75	(8,802). 8,816	*Pipe Creek, Bandera, 116. 130
*PARADISE, Wise, 81 (441) 560	Perryville, Wood 35	Pitner Junction, Rusk 20
*PARIS, Lamar, 1,127 (25,171). . . . 25,297	Personville, Limestone 50	*PITTSBURG, Camp, 231
Park, Fayette 25		(4,497). 4,760

Town, County	Pop. 2019
*Placedo, Victoria, 4 (692)	753
Placid, McCulloch	32
Plain, Houston	30
*PLAINS, Yoakum, 52 (1,481)	1,644
*PLAINVIEW, Hale, 718 (22,194)	20,124
*PLANO, Collin, Denton, 10,742 (259,841)	290,855
*PLANTERSVILLE, Grimes, 56	869
Plaska, Hall	20
PLEAK, Fort Bend, 28 (1,044)	1,517
Pleasant Farms, Ector	800
Pleasant Grove, Falls	35
Pleasant Grove, Limestone	20
Pleasant Grove, Upshur	35
Pleasant Grove, Wood	30
Pleasant Hill, Polk (522)	597
Pleasant Hill, Eastland	15
Pleasant Hill, Nacogdoches	250
Pleasant Hill, Yoakum	30
*PLEASANTON, Atascosa, 461 (8,934)	10,912
PLEASANT VALLEY, Wichita, (336)	336
Pleasant Valley, Garza	5
*Pledger, Matagorda	265
Pluck, Polk	53
*Plum, Fayette, 2	145
PLUM GROVE, Liberty, 6 (600)	717
Pluto, Ellis	30
POETRY, Hunt, Kaufman	90
*POINT, Rains, 41 (820)	922
*POINT BLANK, San Jacinto, 17 (688)	748
*POINT COMFORT, Calhoun, 30 (737)	694
Point Enterprise, Limestone	200
POINT VENTURE, Travis, 19 (800)	1,043
Polar, Kent	15
*Pollok, Angelina, 34	400
*PONDER, Denton, 68 (1,395)	2,280
Ponta, Cherokee	50
*Pontotoc, Mason, 1	125
Poole, Rains	20
*Poolville, Parker, 28	520
Port Acres, Jefferson	[part of Port Arthur]
Port Alto, Calhoun	45
*PORT ARANSAS, Nueces, 418 (3,480)	4,153
*PORT ARTHUR, Jefferson, 1,082 (53,818)	54,563
*Port Bolivar, Galveston, 60	700
*Porter, Montgomery, 376	4,200
Porter Heights, Montgomery, (1,653)	1,974
Porter Springs, Houston	50
*PORT ISABEL, Cameron, 269 (5,006)	5,288
*PORTLAND, San Patricio, 487 (15,099)	22,115
*PORT LAVACA, Calhoun, 437 (12,248)	12,641
Port Mansfield, Willacy, 11 (226)	168
*PORT NECHES, Jefferson, 315 (13,040)	12,638

Town, County	Pop. 2019
*Port O'Connor , Calhoun, 46 (1,253)	1,139
Port Sullivan, Milam, Robertson	15
Porvenir, Presidio	3
Posey, Hopkins	12
Posey, Lubbock	225
*POST, Garza, 173 (5,376)	5,138
Post Oak, Blanco	10
Post Oak, Lee	100
Postoak, Jack, Clay	20
Postoak, Lamar	65
POST OAK BEND, Kaufman, 9 (595)	701
Post Oak Point, Austin	60
*POTEET, Atascosa, 124 (3,260)	3,554
*POTH, Wilson, 48 (1,908)	2,344
Potosi, Taylor (2,991)	3,574
*POTTSBORO, Grayson, 133 (2,160)	2,479
Pottsville, Hamilton	105
*Powderly, Lamar, 40 (1,178)	1,204
*POWELL, Navarro, 9 (136)	147
*POYNOR, Henderson, 11 (305)	315
Prado Verde, El Paso (246)	266
Praesel, Milam	115
Praha, Fayette	90
Prairie Chapel, McLennan	35
Prairie Dell, Bell	34
*Prairie Hill, Limestone, 4	150
Prairie Hill, Washington	20
*Prairie Lea, Caldwell, 6	320
Prairie Point, Cooke	22
*PRAIRIE VIEW, Waller, 44 (5,576)	6,625
Prairieville, Kaufman	75
*PREMONT, Jim Wells, 57 (2,653)	2,537
*PRESIDIO, Presidio, 93 (4,426)	3,774
Preston, Grayson (2,096)	2,016
*Price, Rusk, 4	275
*Priddy, Mills, 8	215
PRIMERA, Cameron, 33 (4,070)	4,905
Primrose, Van Zandt	26
*PRINCETON, Collin, 263 (6,807)	15,222
Pringle, Hutchinson	20
Pritchett, Upshur	125
*Proctor, Comanche, 5	228
*PROGRESO, Hidalgo, 55 (5,507)	6,073
PROGRESO LAKES, Hidalgo, 9 (240)	268
Progress, Bailey	49
Prospect, Rains	40
*PROSPER, Collin, Denton, 650 (9,423)	24,579
Providence, Floyd	78
Providence, Polk	350
PROVIDENCE VILLAGE, Denton, (4,786)	6,414
Pruitt, Cass	25
Pruitt, Van Zandt	45
Pueblo Nuevo, Webb (521)	555
Puerto Rico, Hidalgo	50
Pullman, Potter	31
Pumpkin, San Jacinto	100

Town, County	Pop. 2019
Pumpville, Val Verde	25
Punkin Center, Dawson	8
Punkin Center, Eastland	12
*Purdon, Navarro, 8	133
Purley, Franklin	100
*Purmela, Coryell, 1	50
Pursley, Navarro	40
Purves, Erath	50
*PUTNAM, Callahan, 2 (94)	96
*PYOTE, Ward, 7 (114)	133

Q

Town, County	Pop. 2019
*Quail, Collingsworth, 1 (19)	18
Quail Creek, Victoria (1,628)	1,739
*QUANAH, Hardeman, 100 (2,641)	2,480
Quarry, Washington	60
Quarterway, Hale	24
*QUEEN CITY, Cass, 74 (1,476)	1,477
*Quemado, Maverick, 9 (230)	226
Quesada, Starr (25)	34
Quicksand, Newton	50
Quihi, Medina	125
*QUINLAN, Hunt, 203 (1,394)	1,541
QUINTANA, Brazoria, 3 (56)	20
*QUITAQUE, Briscoe, Floyd, 14 (411)	392
*QUITMAN, Wood, 191 (1,809)	1,850

R

Town, County	Pop. 2019
Rabbs Prairie, Fayette	79
Raccoon Bend, Austin	775
Rachal, Brooks	36
Radar Base, Maverick (762)	917
Radium, Jones	10
Rafael Pena, Starr (17)	13
Ragtown, Lamar	30
*Rainbow, Somervell, 15	121
Raisin, Victoria	85
Raleigh, Navarro	40
*RALLS, Crosby, 50 (1,944)	1,824
Ramireno, Zapata (35)	27
Ramirez, Duval	42
Ramirez, Perez, Starr (78)	75
Ramos, Starr (116)	122
Ranchette Estates, Willacy (152)	143
Ranchitos Del Norte, Starr (112)	99
Ranchitos East, Webb (212)	231
Ranchitos Las Lomas, Webb, (266)	298
Rancho Alegre, Jim Wells (1,704)	1,636
Rancho Banquete, Nueces (424)	415
Rancho Chico, San Patricio (396)	494
Ranchos Penitas West, Webb, (573)	587
RANCHO VIEJO, Cameron, 43 (2,437)	2,531
Rancho Viejo, Starr (228)	265
Rand, Kaufman	70
Randado, Jim Hogg, Zapata	6
*Randolph, Fannin, 2	600
Randolph Air Force Base, Bexar (1,241)	1,386
*RANGER, Eastland, 83 (2,468)	2,444
RANGERVILLE, Cameron, (289)	350

CITIES & TOWNS

Town, County . . . . Pop. 2019	Town, County . . . . Pop. 2019	Town, County . . . . Pop. 2019
San Juan, Starr (129). 137	*SEAGRAVES, Gaines, 47	*Sheridan, Colorado, 14 300
SAN LEANNA, Travis (497). 540	(2,417). 2,946	*SHERMAN, Grayson, 1,517
San Leon, Galveston (4,970) 5,439	Seale, Robertson 60	(38,315). 44,113
*SAN MARCOS, Hays, Caldwell,	*SEALY, Austin, 366 (6,019). 6,805	Sherry, Red River. 15
Guadalupe, 1,953 (44,894) 69,731	Seaton, Bell 60	Sherwood, Irion, Tom Green. 170
SAN PATRICIO, San Patricio (395) . . . 402	Seawillow, Caldwell 75	Sherwood Shores, Grayson,
San Pedro, Cameron (530) 457	*Sebastian, Willacy, 10 (1,917). . . . 1,805	(1,190). 1,141
*SAN PERLITA, Willacy (573) 554	Sebastopol, Trinity. 300	Sherwood Shores, Bell 774
San Roman, Starr. 5	Seco Mines, Maverick (560) 597	Sherwood Shores, Burnet 920
*SAN SABA, San Saba, 157	Security, Montgomery 200	Shields, Coleman. 8
(3,099). 3,212	Sedalia, Collin 24	Shiloh, Leon 30
SANSOM PARK, Tarrant, 102	Segno, Polk 80	Shiloh, Limestone 250
(4,686). 5,625	Segovia, Kimble. 12	*SHINER, Lavaca, 146 (2,069) 2,230
Santa Anna, Starr (13). 13	*SEGUIN, Guadalupe, 1,223	Shirley, Hopkins. 20
*SANTA ANNA, Coleman, 57	(25,175). 31,884	*Shiro, Grimes, 3 210
(1,099). 1,010	Sejita, Duval 24	Shive, Hamilton. 60
Santa Catarina, Starr 15	Selden, Erath. 55	SHOREACRES, Harris, 21
SANTA CLARA, Guadalupe, 22	Selfs, Fannin 30	(1,493). 1,580
(725). 725	SELMA, Bexar, Guadalupe, Comal,	Short, Shelby. 15
Santa Cruz, Starr (54). 54	325 (5,540). 11,795	Shovel Mountain, Burnet 148
*Santa Elena, Starr, 2. 35	*SEMINOLE, Gaines, 376	*Sidney, Comanche, 3. 148
*SANTA FE, Galveston, 419	(6,430). 7,660	Sienna Plantation, Fort Bend,
(12,222). 13,654	Sempronius, Austin 25	(13,721). 19,403
*Santa Maria, Cameron, 2 (733). 651	Senate, Jack 20	*Sierra Blanca, Hudspeth, 12 (553). . . 574
Santa Monica, Willacy (83). 76	Serbin, Lee 109	Siesta Acres, Maverick (1,885) 2,011
*SANTA ROSA, Cameron, 39	Serenada, Williamson (1,641) 1,724	Siesta Shores, Zapata (1,382) 1,563
(2,873). 2,766	Seth Ward, Hale (2,025) 1,899	Silas, Shelby. 75
Santa Rosa, Starr (241) 242	SEVEN OAKS, Polk, 4 (111). 118	Siloam, Bowie 50
Santel, Starr (44) 42	Seven Pines, Gregg, Upshur 50	*SILSBEE, Hardin, 307 (6,611) 6,805
*Santo, Palo Pinto, 25 445	SEVEN POINTS, Henderson, 101	*Silver, Coke, 1. 34
*San Ygnacio, Zapata, 4 (667). 558	(1,455). 1,558	Silver City, Milam 25
*Saragosa, Reeves, 3 185	Seven Sisters, Duval 25	Silver City, Navarro 100
*Saratoga, Hardin, 11 1,000	Sexton, Sabine 29	Silver City, Red River 25
Sardis, Ellis 60	*SEYMOUR, Baylor, 120 (2,740). . . 2,740	Silver Creek Village, Burnet. 300
Sargent, Matagorda 900	Shadybrook, Cherokee (1,967) 2,115	Silver Lake, Van Zandt 42
*Sarita, Kenedy, 18 (238). 244	Shady Grove, Cherokee 30	*SILVERTON, Briscoe, 35 (731) 687
Saron, Trinity. 6	Shady Grove, Houston 83	Silver Valley, Coleman 15
Saspamco, Wilson 300	Shady Grove, Panola 45	Simmons, Live Oak 65
*Satin, Falls, 2 86	Shady Grove, Smith 250	*Simms, Bowie, 8. 300
Sattler, Comal 2,500	Shady Grove, Upshur 40	Simms, Deaf Smith. 6
Saturn, Gonzales 15	Shady Grove , Burnet 114	*SIMONTON, Fort Bend, 49 (814) . . 965
Savannah, Denton (3,318). 4,227	Shady Hollow, Travis (5,004). 5,196	Simpsonville, Matagorda 6
*SAVOY, Fannin, 29 (831). 860	Shady Oaks, Henderson 300	Simpsonville, Upshur 100
Scenic Oaks, Bexar (4,957) 5,678	SHADY SHORES, Denton, 71	Sinclair City, Smith. 50
Schattel, Frio 30	(2,612). 3,200	Singleton, Grimes 45
*SCHERTZ, Guadalupe, Comal,	Shafter, Presidio. 57	*SINTON, San Patricio, 183
Bexar, 1,107 (31,506). 42,709	*SHALLOWATER, Lubbock, 136	(5,665). 5,240
Schicke Point, Calhoun. 70	(2,484). 2,528	Sipe Springs, Comanche 70
Schroeder, Goliad 347	*SHAMROCK, Wheeler, 103	Sisterdale, Kendall 110
*SCHULENBURG, Fayette, 330	(1,910). 1,777	Sivells Bend, Cooke 36
(2,852). 3,006	Shangri La, Burnet 108	Six Mile, Calhoun 300
Schumansville, Guadalupe 678	Shankleville, Newton 35	Skeeterville, San Saba 10
Schwab City, Polk. 120	Shannon, Clay 20	*SKELLYTOWN, Carson, 12
*Schwertner, Williamson, 1 175	Sharp, Milam. 52	(473). 436
Scissors, Hidalgo (3,186). 3,460	SHAVANO PARK, Bexar, 100	*Skidmore, Bee, 17 (925). 932
*SCOTLAND, Archer, 19 (501). 512	(3,035). 4,007	Slate Shoals, Lamar. 10
*SCOTTSVILLE, Harrison, 20	Shawnee Prairie, Angelina. 20	*SLATON, Lubbock, 158 (6,121). . . . 6,048
(376). 391	Shaws Bend, Colorado 100	Slayden, Gonzales 10
Scranton, Eastland 40	*Sheffield, Pecos, 11 322	Slide, Lubbock. 245
Scrappin Valley, Newton. 25	Shelby, Austin 300	*Slidell, Wise, 2 175
*Scroggins, Franklin, 17 150	*Shelbyville, Shelby, 27 600	Sloan, San Saba 30
*SCURRY, Kaufman, 64 (681). 769	Sheldon, Harris (1,990). 2,157	Slocum, Anderson 150
*SEABROOK, Harris, 479	SHENANDOAH, Montgomery,	Smetana, Brazos. 80
(11,952). 14,059	330 (2,134). 3,185	*SMILEY, Gonzales, 8 (549). 571
*SEADRIFT, Calhoun, 52 (1,364). . . .1,496	Shep, Taylor 25	Smithland, Marion, Cass. 179
*SEAGOVILLE, Dallas, 486	*SHEPHERD, San Jacinto, 72	Smith Point, Chambers. 180
(14,835). 17,107	(2,319). 2,649	Smithson Valley, Comal 1,000

Town, County . . . . Pop. 2019	Town, County . . . . Pop. 2019	Town, County . . . . Pop. 2019

*SMITHVILLE, Bastrop, 254
  (3,817). 4,461
Smithwick, Burnet 102
*SMYER, Hockley, 7 (474) 477
Smyrna, Cass. 215
Smyrna, Rains. 25
*SNOOK, Burleson, 21 (511) 535
Snow Hill, Collin 23
Snow Hill, Upshur 75
*SNYDER, Scurry, 520 (11,202). . . . 11,073
*SOCORRO, El Paso, 590
  (32,013). 34,740
Soldier Mound, Dickens. 10
Solis, Cameron (512) 431
*SOMERSET, Bexar, 73 (1,631). . . . 1,996
*SOMERVILLE, Burleson, 77
  (1,376). 1,502
Sommer's Mill, Bell 27
*SONORA, Sutton, 133 (3,027). . . . 2,967
*SOUR LAKE, Hardin, 103
  (1,813). 1,944
South Alamo, Hidalgo (3,361). . . . 3,589
*South Bend, Young, 2 100
South Bosque, McLennan. 1,523
South Brice, Hall 19
South Fork Estates, Jim Hogg (70) 72
SOUTH FRYDEK, Austin 225
*SOUTH HOUSTON, Harris,
  629 (16,983). 17,674
*SOUTHLAKE, Tarrant, Denton, 1,743
  (26,575). 31,613
Southland, Garza. 157
South La Paloma, Jim Wells (345) . . . 324
*SOUTHMAYD, Grayson, 19
  (992). 1,122
SOUTH MOUNTAIN, Coryell,
  (384). 365
*SOUTH PADRE ISLAND,
  Cameron, 357 (2,816) 2,766
*South Plains, Floyd 67
South Point, Cameron (1,376). 1,388
South Purmela, Coryell 10
South Shore, Bell 60
SOUTHSIDE PLACE, Harris, 61
  (1,715). 1,867
South Sulphur, Hunt. 60
South Toledo Bend, Newton,
  (524). 454
Southton, Bexar. 113
*Spade, Lamb, 2 (73) 64
Spanish Fort, Montague 50
Sparenberg, Dawson 40
Sparks, El Paso (4,529) 5,501
Sparks, Bell 40
Speaks, Lavaca. 60
*SPEARMAN, Hansford, 111
  (3,368). 3,245
Speegleville, McLennan 1,655
*Spicewood, Burnet, 279. 4,000
Spider Mountain, Burnet 92
*SPLENDORA, Montgomery, 169
  (1,615). 2,240
SPOFFORD, Kinney (95). 96
Spraberry, Midland 46
*Spring, Harris, 2,188 (54,298). . . . 68,450
*SPRING BRANCH, Comal, 380 . . . 254
Spring Creek, Hutchinson. 20

Spring Creek, San Saba. 20
Springdale, Cass 55
Springfield, Anderson. 30
Spring Gardens, Nueces (563) 662
Spring Hill, Bowie 100
Spring Hill, Navarro 60
Spring Hill, San Jacinto 38
*SPRINGLAKE, Lamb, 9 (108) 96
*SPRINGTOWN, Parker, 306
  (2,658). 3,142
SPRING VALLEY, Harris, 142
  (3,715). 4,248
Spring Valley, McLennan 400
*SPUR, Dickens, 49 (1,318). 1,173
*Spurger, Tyler, 15 590
Stacy, McCulloch. 20
Staff, Eastland 65
*STAFFORD, Fort Bend, Harris,
  1,410 (17,693) 19,501
Stag Creek, Comanche 45
STAGECOACH, Montgomery, 11
  (538). 620
Stairtown, Caldwell 35
Staley, San Jacinto. 30
*STAMFORD, Jones, Haskell, 133
  (3,124). 2,934
Stampede, Bell. 6
Stamps, Upshur 45
*STANTON, Martin, 105 (2,492). . . 3,002
*Staples, Guadalupe, 5 (267) 272
*Star, Mills, 1 97
STAR HARBOR, Henderson, 13
  (444). 495
Star Route, Cochran. 15
Starrville, Smith. 75
Startzville, Comal 7,000
Steele Hill, Dickens 4
Stephens Creek, San Jacinto 385
*STEPHENVILLE, Erath, 908
  (17,123). 21,245
Sterley, Floyd. 31
*STERLING CITY, Sterling, 46
  (888). 964
Stewards Mill, Freestone 22
Stewart, Rusk. 15
Stiles, Reagan. 4
Stillwell Store, Brewster 2
*STINNETT, Hutchinson, 50
  (1,881). 1,760
Stith, Jones 50
*STOCKDALE, Wilson, 80
  (1,442). 1,702
Stockman, Shelby. 55
STOCKTON BEND, Hood (305) . . . 334
Stoneburg, Montague. 51
Stoneham, Grimes 15
*Stonewall, Gillespie, 25 (505). 543
Stony, Denton 25
Stout, Wood 302
*Stowell, Chambers, 9 (1,756). . . . 2,096
Stranger, Falls 12
*STRATFORD, Sherman, 65
  (2,017). 2,049
Stratton, DeWitt. 25
*STRAWN, Palo Pinto, 34 (653) 676
Streeter, Mason 85

*STREETMAN, Freestone, 26
  (247). 259
String Prairie, Bastrop. 40
Stringtown, Newton. 20
Structure, Williamson. 50
Stubblefield, Houston. 15
Stubbs, Kaufman 50
Study Butte, Brewster, 29 (233) 247
Sturgeon, Cooke 10
Styx, Kaufman. 50
Sublime, Lavaca. 75
*SUDAN, Lamb, 23 (958) 892
Sugar Hill, Titus. 90
*SUGAR LAND, Fort Bend, 4,317
  (78,817). 131,448
Sugar Valley, Matagorda 45
*SULLIVAN CITY, Hidalgo, 67
  (3,998). 4,273
*Sulphur Bluff, Hopkins, 4. 280
*SULPHUR SPRINGS, Hopkins,
  794 (15,449). 16,279
Summerfield, Castro, Parmer 48
Summerville, Gonzales. 45
*Sumner, Lamar, 31 95
*SUNDOWN, Hockley, 41
  (1,397). 1,422
Sunny Side, Waller 250
Sunnyside, Castro 64
Sunnyside, Wilson 100
SUNNYVALE, Dallas, 256
  (5,130). 6,795
*SUNRAY, Moore, 45 (1,926) 1,828
Sunrise, Falls 200
*SUNRISE BEACH, Llano, 36
  (713). 797
*Sunset, Montague, Wise, 15 (497). . . 579
Sunset, Starr (47). 50
Sunset Acres, Webb (23) 20
Sunset Oaks, Burnet. 198
SUNSET VALLEY, Travis, 142
  (648). 663
SUN VALLEY, Lamar, 32 (69) 77
SURFSIDE BEACH, Brazoria, 34
  (482). 571
*Sutherland Springs, Wilson, 6. 420
Swamp City, Gregg. 8
Swan, Smith 150
*SWEENY, Brazoria, 103 (3,684). . . 4,047
Sweet Home, Guadalupe. 294
*Sweet Home, Lavaca, 5 360
Sweet Home, Lee 30
Sweet Union, Cherokee 40
*SWEETWATER, Nolan, 373
  (10,906). 10,285
Swenson, Stonewall 80
Swift, Nacogdoches 210
Swiss Alp, Fayette. 17
Sylvan, Lamar 68
*Sylvester, Fisher, 1 79

T

Tabor, Brazos. 150
Tadmor, Houston. 67
*TAFT, San Patricio, 61 (3,048) . . . 2,862
Taft Southwest, San Patricio,
  (1,460). 1,342

CITIES & TOWNS

CITIES & TOWNS

Town, County . . . . Pop. 2019	Town, County . . . . Pop. 2019	Town, County . . . . Pop. 2019
*TAHOKA, Lynn, 70 (2,673). 2,765	*Thicket, Hardin, 2 306	Travis Ranch, Kaufman (2,556) 3,217
*TALCO, Titus, 16 (516). 499	*Thomaston, DeWitt 45	Trawick, Nacogdoches 375
*Talpa, Coleman, 8. 127	*THOMPSONS, Fort Bend, 6	Treasure Island, Brazoria. 152
TALTY, Kaufman, 30 (1,535). 2,879	(246). 331	Treasure Island, Guadalupe. 172
Tamina, Montgomery. 900	Thompsonville, Jim Hogg (46) 47	*TRENT, Taylor, 3 (337). 347
Tanglewood, Lee 60	Thompsonville, Gonzales 30	*TRENTON, Fannin, 58 (635) . . . 684
Tanquecitos South Acres, Webb,	Thornberry, Clay 75	Trickham, Coleman 29
(233). 240	*THORNDALE, Milam, 75	Trimmer, Bell 390
Tanquecitos South Acres II, Webb,	(1,336). 1,394	*TRINIDAD, Henderson, 28
(50). 51	*THORNTON, Limestone, 16	(886). 882
Tarkington Prairie, Liberty 300	(526). 541	*TRINITY, Trinity, 138 (2,697) 2,741
*Tarpley, Bandera, 6 30	THORNTONVILLE, Ward, 11	TROPHY CLUB, Denton, 290
*Tarzan, Martin, 7 30	(476). 543	(8,024). 13,947
Tascosa Hills, Potter 90	Thorp Spring, Hood. 222	*TROUP, Smith, Cherokee, 102
*TATUM, Rusk, Panola, 68	*THRALL, Williamson, 32 (839). . . 1,036	(1,869). 2,097
(1,385). 1,419	Three League, Martin. 20	Trout Creek, Newton 70
*TAYLOR, Williamson, 549	Three Oaks, Wilson 150	*TROY, Bell, 103 (1,645). 1,982
(15,191). 18,154	*THREE RIVERS, Live Oak, 101	Truby, Jones 26
TAYLOR LAKE VILLAGE, Harris,	(1,848). 2,018	Trumbull, Ellis. 100
66 (3,544) 3,594	Three States, Cass 45	Truscott, Knox. 50
TAYLOR LANDING, Jefferson,	*THROCKMORTON,	Tucker, Anderson 175
(228). 238	Throckmorton, 49 (828) 735	*Tuleta, Bee, 12 (288). 306
Taylorsville, Caldwell 35	Thunderbird Bay, Brown (663) 602	*TULIA, Swisher, 128 (4,967) 4,698
Taylor Town, Lamar. 40	Thurber, Erath. 48	Tulip, Fannin. 10
Tazewell, Hopkins 20	Tidwell, Hunt 50	Tulsita, Bee (14). 2
*TEAGUE, Freestone, 115	Tierra Bonita, Cameron (141). 119	Tundra, Van Zandt. 34
(3,560). 3,495	Tierra Dorada, Starr (28) 31	Tunis, Burleson 150
Teaselville, Smith 150	Tierra Grande, Nueces (403). 441	*TURKEY, Hall, 20 (421) 375
*TEHUACANA, Limestone, 3	Tierra Verde, Nueces (277). 320	Turlington, Freestone. 27
(283). 286	Tigertown, Lamar 400	Turnersville, Coryell 125
Telegraph, Kimble 3	TIKI ISLAND, Galveston, 31	Turnersville, Travis 90
*Telephone, Fannin, 7. 210	(968). 1,083	*Turnertown-Selman City, Rusk, 3. . . 271
*Telferner, Victoria, 5 700	*Tilden, McMullen, 42 (261). 301	Turtle Bayou, Chambers. 55
Telico, Ellis, Navarro. 115	Tilmon, Caldwell. 60	*TUSCOLA, Taylor, 73 (742) 753
*Tell, Childress, Cottle, Hall 20	TIMBERCREEK CANYON,	Tuxedo, Jones 42
*TEMPLE, Bell, 2,199 (66,102) . . . 78,267	Randall (418). 460	Twichell, Ochiltree. 22
*TENAHA, Shelby, 32 (1,160). . . . 1,144	Timberwood, Bexar (13,447). . . . 16,881	Twitty, Wheeler 12
Tenmile, Dawson. 30	*TIMPSON, Shelby, 68 (1,155) 1,124	*TYE, Taylor, 57 (1,242) 1,318
*Tennessee Colony, Anderson, 13 . . . 300	Tin Top, Parker 500	*TYLER, Smith, 4,648
*Tennyson, Coke, 1 46	*TIOGA, Grayson, 44 (803) 1,018	(96,901). 108,173
*Terlingua, Brewster, 2 (58). 50	TIRA, Hopkins (297) 316	*Tynan, Bee, 6 (278). 283
*TERRELL, Kaufman, 836	*Tivoli, Refugio, 5 (479). 477	Type, Williamson, Bastrop 40
(15,816). 19,183	TOCO, Lamar, 3 (75). 80	
TERRELL HILLS, Bexar, 113	Todd City, Anderson 10	**U**
(4,878). 5,344	TODD MISSION, Grimes, 93	
Terry Chapel, Falls 30	(107). 117	UHLAND, Hays, Caldwell, 22
Terryville, DeWitt 40	Tokio, McLennan. 250	(1,014). 1,355
*TEXARKANA, Bowie (Miller,	Tokio, Terry 6	*Umbarger, Randall, 2 327
Ark.), 3,467 (66,035). 69,491	*TOLAR, Hood, 48 (681). 983	UNCERTAIN, Harrison, 3 (94). 97
*TEXAS CITY, Galveston, 1,018	Tolbert, Wilbarger 15	Union, Scurry 20
(45,099). 51,178	Tolette, Lamar 40	Union, Terry 8
TEXHOMA, Sherman (Texas Co.,	Tolosa, Kaufman, Henderson 65	Union, Wilson 52
Okla.), 27 (1,295) 1,142	*TOMBALL, Harris, 1,459	UNION GROVE, Upshur, 2 (357). . . 373
*TEXLINE, Dallam, 26 (507) 519	(10,753). 11,754	Union Grove, Bell 12
Texroy, Hutchinson 50	*TOM BEAN, Grayson, 27	Union High, Navarro 30
Thalia, Foard. 50	(1,045). 1,129	Union Hill, Denton 25
*THE COLONY, Denton, 929	Tomlinson Hill, Falls 64	UNION VALLEY, Hunt (307). 425
(36,328) 46,686	TOOL, Henderson, 53 (2,240) . . . 2,374	Unity, Lamar 60
Thedford, Smith 65	Topsey, Coryell 35	*UNIVERSAL CITY, Bexar, 579
The Grove, Coryell 100	*Tornillo, El Paso, 12 (1,568). 1,540	(18,530). 21,927
THE HILLS, Travis (2,472). 2,480	Tours, McLennan. 130	UNIVERSITY PARK, Dallas, 861
Thelma, Bexar. 150	*Tow, Llano, 6 305	(23,068). 25,017
Thelma, Limestone 20	Town Bluff, Tyler 429	Upper Meyersville, DeWitt 33
Theon, Williamson 30	*TOYAH, Reeves, 3 (90). 96	Upshaw, Nacogdoches 400
Thermo, Hopkins 56	*Toyahvale, Reeves, 1 60	Upton, Bastrop 25
*The Woodlands, Montgomery,	Tradewinds, San Patricio (180) 186	Urbana, San Jacinto 15
766 (93,847). 122,233	Travis, Falls 48	Utley, Bastrop 30

Town, County . . . . Pop. 2019	Town, County . . . . Pop. 2019	Town, County . . . . Pop. 2019

*Utopia, Uvalde, 35 (227) 213
*UVALDE, Uvalde, 548
   (15,751). 16,086
Uvalde Estates, Uvalde (2,171). 2,228

V

Valdasta, Collin 82
*VALENTINE, Jeff Davis, 4 (134) . . . 123
*Valera, Coleman, 2 80
Valle de Oro, Potter 250
Valle Vista, Starr (469) 512
Valley Creek, Fannin 110
*VALLEY MILLS, Bosque,
   McLennan, 84 (1,203). 1,253
*Valley Spring, Llano 50
*VALLEY VIEW, Cooke, 87 (757) . . . 833
Valley View, Runnels 10
Valley View, Upshur 75
Valley View, Wichita. 210
Valley Wells, Dimmit 21
Val Verde, Milam 25
Val Verde Park, Val Verde (2,384) . . . 2,648
*VAN, Van Zandt, 137 (2,632) 2,875
*VAN ALSTYNE, Grayson, 184
   (3,046). 4,449
Vance, Real 20
*Vancourt, Tom Green, 1 131
Vandalia, Red River 35
*Vanderbilt, Jackson, 7 (395) 418
*Vanderpool, Bandera, 5. 20
Vandyke, Comanche. 20
*VAN HORN, Culberson, 94
   (2,063). 1,913
*Van Vleck, Matagorda, 27
   (1,844). 2,214
Vasco, Delta. 20
Vashti, Clay 70
Vattmann, Kleberg 25
Vaughan, Hill. 75
Veach, San Augustine 12
Vealmoor, Howard 5
*VEGA, Oldham, 39 (884) 917
*VENUS, Johnson, 84 (2,960) 4,806
Vera, Knox. 30
Verdi, Atascosa. 110
Verhalen, Reeves 12
*Veribest, Tom Green, 3 115
*VERNON, Wilbarger, 322
   (11,002). 10,307
Verona, Collin 34
Vessey, Red River 15
Viboras, Starr. 15
Vick, Concho 20
*VICTORIA, Victoria, 2,769
   (62,592). 66,891
Victoria, Limestone 25
Victoria Vera, Starr (110). 106
Victory City, Bowie 350
*VIDOR, Orange, 434 (10,579). . . 10,570
Vienna, Lavaca 40
View, Taylor 350
Vigo Park, Swisher 36
Villa del Sol, Cameron (175) 197
*Village Mills, Hardin, 17 200
Villa Pancho, Cameron (788) 936
Villarreal, Starr (131) 143

Villa Verde, Hidalgo (874). 875
Vincent, Howard 10
Vineyard, Jack 19
VINTON, El Paso, 78 (1,971) 2,042
Violet, Nueces 160
Vistula, Houston 21
*Voca, McCulloch, 7. 56
VOLENTE, Travis, 28 (520) 597
Volga, Houston 9
*VON ORMY, Bexar, 84 (1,085) . . . 1,320
Voss, Coleman, 2 20
*Votaw, Hardin, 1. 160
Vsetin, Lavaca 45

W

*WACO, McLennan, 4,335
   (124,805). 138,400
*Wadsworth, Matagorda, 10 160
*WAELDER, Gonzales, 32
   (1,065). 1,144
Wagner, Hunt 75
Waka, Ochiltree, 2 65
Wakefield, Polk 25
WAKE VILLAGE, Bowie, 108
   (5,492). 5,669
*Walburg, Williamson, 4. 277
Walcott, Deaf Smith 5
Waldeck, Fayette 34
Waldrip, McCulloch 15
Walhalla, Fayette 38
*Wall, Tom Green, 16. 329
Wallace, Van Zandt 70
*WALLER, Waller, Harris, 264
   (2,326). 3,119
*WALLIS, Austin, 54 (1,252). 1,344
*Wallisville, Chambers, 17 300
Walnut Bend, Cooke 45
Walnut Grove, Panola. 125
*WALNUT SPRINGS, Bosque, 23
   (827). 911
Walton, Van Zandt 60
Wamba, Bowie 430
Waneta, Houston. 19
Waples, Hood 155
*Warda, Fayette, 3 121
Ward Creek, Bowie 10
*Waring, Kendall, 7 73
*Warren, Tyler, 26 (757) 882
WARREN CITY, Gregg, Upshur, 8
   (298). 277
Warrenton, Fayette. 186
Warsaw, Kaufman 100
Washburn, Armstrong 120
*Washington, Washington, 24 100
*WASKOM, Harrison, 86
   (2,160). 2,263
Wastella, Nolan 12
*WATAUGA, Tarrant, 539
   (23,497). 24,402
Waterloo, Williamson. 70
Waterman, Shelby 40
*Water Valley, Tom Green, 7 203
Watson, Burnet 50
Watt, Limestone. 25
Waverly, San Jacinto, Walker 200

*WAXAHACHIE, Ellis, 1,272
   (29,621). 37,983
Wayne, Cass 15
Wayside, Armstrong, 2 25
Wayside, Roberts. 40
Wealthy, Leon 12
*WEATHERFORD, Parker,
   1,862 (25,250) 32,587
Weatherly, Hall 8
Weaver, Hopkins 35
WEBBERVILLE, Travis, 12 (392). . . . 466
Webbville, Coleman. 15
*WEBSTER, Harris, 826
   (10,684). 11,989
Weches, Houston. 46
Weedhaven, Jackson. 35
Weeping Mary, Cherokee 85
*Weesatche, Goliad, 3. 411
*WEIMAR, Colorado, 157
   (2,151). 2,299
*WEINERT, Haskell, 6 (172). 161
*WEIR, Williamson, 20 (450) 544
Wiess Bluff, Jasper 60
*Welch, Dawson, 4 (222). 230
Welcome, Austin 300
Weldon, Houston. 131
Welfare, Kendall 10
*Wellborn, Brazos, 7. 400
*WELLINGTON, Collingsworth,
   54 (2,189) 2,002
*WELLMAN, Terry, 3 (203) 204
*WELLS, Cherokee, 24 (790) 813
Wells, Lynn 10
Wells Branch, Travis (12,120) 13,772
*WESLACO, Hidalgo, 1,125
   (35,670). 42,047
Wesley, Washington, Austin. 65
Wesley Grove, Walker. 25
*WEST, McLennan, 177 (2,807). . . 2,939
West Alto Bonito, Starr (696). 743
*WESTBROOK, Mitchell, 15
   (253). 256
*WEST COLUMBIA, Brazoria, 168
   (3,905). 4,160
Westcott, San Jacinto 55
Westdale, Jim Wells (372) 404
Western Lake, Parker (1,525). 1,698
*Westhoff, DeWitt, 8. 410
WESTLAKE, Tarrant, Denton, 99
   (992). 1,725
*WEST LAKE HILLS, Travis, 374
   (3,063). 3,250
West Livingston, Polk (8,071) 9,474
West Mineola, Wood 20
*Westminster, Collin, 5 (861). 1,155
West Mountain, Upshur 325
West Odessa, Ector (22,707) 29,224
*WESTON, Collin, 14 (563) 580
WESTON LAKES, Fort Bend,
   (2,482). 4,699
WEST ORANGE, Orange, 107
   (3,443). 3,181
Westover, Baylor 18
WESTOVER HILLS, Tarrant,
   (682). 710
Westphalia, Falls 186
West Point, Fayette, 11 213

CITIES & TOWNS

Town, County . . . . Pop. 2019	Town, County . . . . Pop. 2019	Town, County . . . . Pop. 2019
West Sharyland, Hidalgo (2,309) . . . 2,207	Wilcox, Burleson 39	*Woodlawn, Harrison, 5 550
West Sinton, San Patricio 150	Wilderville, Falls 45	WOODLOCH, Montgomery,
WEST TAWAKONI, Hunt, 41	*Wildorado, Oldham, 10. 210	(207) 213
(1,576). 1,844	Wild Peach, Brazoria (2,452) 2,615	Woodrow, Fort Bend 190
WEST UNIVERSITY PLACE,	Wildwood, Hardin (1,235) 1,173	Woodrow, Lubbock 2,034
Harris, 280 (14,787) 15,699	Wilkins, Upshur. 75	Woods, Panola. 65
Westville, Trinity 46	William Penn, Washington 40	*WOODSBORO, Refugio, 58
Westway, El Paso (4,188). 4,297	*WILLIS, Montgomery, 459	(1,512). 1,447
Westway, Deaf Smith 15	(5,662). 7,809	*WOODSON, Throckmorton, 13
Westwood Shores, Trinity (1,162). . . . 1,053	Willow City, Gillespie, 3 22	(264). 234
WESTWORTH VILLAGE,	Willow Grove, McLennan. 100	Wood Springs, Smith 200
Tarrant, 67 (2,472). 2,772	WILLOW PARK, Parker, 173	*WOODVILLE, Tyler, 177
*WHARTON, Wharton, 335	(3,982). 5,562	(2,586). 2,727
(8,832). 8,653	Willow Springs, Fayette. 74	Woodville, Cherokee 20
Wheatland, Tarrant, Parker. 175	Willow Springs, Rains. 25	Woodward, La Salle 6
*WHEELER, Wheeler, 61 (1,592). . . . 1,550	*WILLS POINT, Van Zandt, 211	WOODWAY, McLennan, 352
Wheeler Springs, Houston 89	(3,524). 3,777	(8,452). 9,230
*Wheelock, Robertson, 4 225	*WILMER, Dallas, 66 (3,682) 4,478	Woosley, Rains 47
White City, San Augustine. 20	Wilmeth, Runnels 15	*WORTHAM, Freestone, 30
White City, Wilbarger 40	*WILSON, Lynn, 15 (489) 496	(1,073). 1,058
*WHITE DEER, Carson, 42	Wilson, Falls 42	Worthing, Lavaca. 55
(1,000). 963	*WIMBERLEY, Hays, 669	Wright City, Smith 172
*WHITEFACE, Cochran, 15 (449) . . . 432	(2,626). 3,170	Wrightsboro, Gonzales 10
Whiteflat, Motley. 4	Winchell, Brown 20	Wyldwood, Bastrop (2,505). 2,756
White Hall, Bell 262	Winchester, Fayette 232	*WYLIE, Collin, Rockwall, Dallas,
Whitehall, Grimes 30	WINDCREST, Bexar, 237	1,222 (41,427) 53,514
*WHITEHOUSE, Smith, 315	(5,364). 5,933	Wylie, Taylor . . . . [part of Abilene]
(7,660). 8,899	Windemere, Travis (1,037) 1,184	
*WHITE OAK, Gregg, 249	*WINDOM, Fannin, 14 (199). 206	
(6,469). 6,570	*WINDTHORST, Archer, 45 (409) . . . 395	**Y**
White Oak, Titus 60	Winedale, Fayette, Washington 67	*Yancey, Medina, 14 209
White River Lake, Crosby 83	*WINFIELD, Titus, 17 (524). 528	*YANTIS, Wood, 64 (388). 419
White Rock, Hunt 60	*Wingate, Runnels, 3 100	Yard, Anderson 50
White Rock, Red River 90	*WINK, Winkler, 33 (940) 1,066	Yarrellton, Milam 35
White Rock, Robertson 80	Winkler, Navarro, Freestone 26	Yellowpine, Sabine 97
White Rock, San Augustine 60	*Winnie, Chambers, 149 (3,254) . . . 3,606	*YOAKUM, Lavaca, DeWitt, 224
*WHITESBORO, Grayson, 202	*WINNSBORO, Wood, Franklin,	(5,815). 6,173
(3,793). 4,075	281 (3,252) 3,399	*YORKTOWN, DeWitt, 130
*WHITE SETTLEMENT, Tarrant,	*WINONA, Smith, 42 (576) 599	(2,092). 2,112
341 (16,116). 17,719	Winter Haven, Dimmit. 123	Youngsport, Bell. 49
White Star, Motley 6	*WINTERS, Runnels, 81 (2,562) . . . 2,427	Yowell, Delta, Hunt 30
Whiteway, Hamilton 8	Witting, Lavaca 90	Ysleta del Sur Pueblo, El Paso 350
*WHITEWRIGHT, Grayson,	WIXON VALLEY, Brazos, 18 (254) . . . 255	Yznaga, Cameron (91) 74
Fannin, 84 (1,604). 1,721	Wizard Wells, Jack 69	
*Whitharral, Hockley 158	*Woden, Nacogdoches, 3 400	
Whitman, Washington 25	*WOLFE CITY, Hunt, 53 (1,412). . . 1,543	**Z**
*WHITNEY, Hill, 184 (2,087) 2,202	*WOLFFORTH, Lubbock, 188	Zabcikville, Bell 76
Whitsett, Live Oak, 9 200	(3,670). 5,757	*Zapata, Zapata, 143 (5,089) 4,924
Whitson, Coryell 50	Womack, Bosque 25	Zapata Ranch, Willacy (108) 117
*Whitt, Parker 38	Woodbine, Cooke 250	Zarate, Starr (59) 63
Whon, Coleman 35	WOODBRANCH, Montgomery,	*ZAVALLA, Angelina, 40 (713) 730
*WICHITA FALLS, Wichita,	(1,282). 1,410	*Zephyr, Brown, 12 201
3,030 (104,553). 105,754	Woodbury, Hill 45	Zimmerscheidt, Colorado. 50
*WICKETT, Ward, 34 (498) 543	WOODCREEK, Hays, 37 (1,457) . . . 1,755	Zion Hill, Guadalupe 595
Wied, Lavaca. 65	Wooded Hills, Johnson. 580	Zipperlandville, Falls 22
Wiedeville, Washington 35	Wood Hi, Victoria 35	Zorn, Guadalupe 287
*Wiergate, Newton, 1 350	*Woodlake, Trinity, 1 180	Zuehl, Guadalupe (376) 393
Wigginsville, Montgomery 100	Woodland, Red River 128	Zunkerville, Karnes 15

Elections

Candidate placards for the 2020 General Election stand outside Collin College in McKinney, on November 1, 2020. Photo by Chris Zúniga/Flickr (CC).

2020 Presidential Election Results by County

Below are the official results by county. Listed are the leading candidates for U.S. president: Joseph Biden for the Democratic Party, Donald Trump for the Republican Party, Jo Jorgensen for the Libertarian Party, and Howie Hawkins for the Green Party.

The total number of votes counted in the presidential race, 11,315,056, was 66.73 percent of the registered voters. The voting-age population in November 2020 was estimated at 21,596,071. The statewide turnout in the previous presidential election in 2016 was 59.39 percent of the registered voters.

For historical election results, including presidential races since 1848, senator and primary races since 1906, governor races since 1845, and prohibition elections since 1854, see the "Elections" section at texasalmanac.com.

Source: Texas Secretary of State.

County	Registered Voters	Turnout %	Presidential Race							
			Trump	%	Biden	%	Jorgensen	%	Hawkins	%
Statewide	**16,955,519**	**66.73**	**5,890,347**	**52.06**	**5,259,126**	**46.48**	**126,243**	**1.12**	**33,396**	**0.30**
Anderson	29,274	65.68	15,110	78.59	3,955	20.57	134	0.70	22	0.11
Andrews	10,272	57.08	4,943	84.31	850	14.50	60	1.02	10	0.17
Angelina	53,166	65.03	25,076	72.53	9,143	26.44	274	0.79	75	0.22
Aransas	18,306	67.14	9,239	75.17	2,916	23.73	103	0.84	31	0.25
Archer	6,538	73.36	4,300	89.66	446	9.30	45	0.94	4	0.08
Armstrong	1,498	74.23	1,035	93.08	75	6.74	2	0.18	0	0.00
Atascosa	29,409	61.61	12,039	66.45	5,876	32.43	143	0.79	58	0.32
Austin	20,293	71.72	11,447	78.65	2,951	20.28	123	0.85	33	0.23
Bailey	3,539	52.56	1,434	77.10	409	21.99	14	0.75	2	0.11
Bandera	17,098	74.37	10,057	79.10	2,505	19.70	120	0.94	30	0.24
Bastrop	52,096	70.38	20,516	55.96	15,474	42.20	531	1.45	128	0.35
Baylor	2,408	70.68	1,494	87.78	183	10.75	22	1.29	1	0.06
Bee	16,033	58.75	6,006	63.76	3,288	34.90	93	0.99	27	0.29
Bell	215,974	58.98	67,893	53.30	57,014	44.76	1,980	1.55	440	0.35
Bexar	1,189,373	64.81	308,618	40.04	448,452	58.18	8,837	1.15	2,798	0.36
Blanco	9,344	79.63	5,443	73.15	1,911	25.68	72	0.97	15	0.20
Borden	499	83.37	397	95.43	16	3.85	2	0.48	1	0.24
Bosque	12,724	71.72	7,469	81.84	1,561	17.10	83	0.91	13	0.14
Bowie	61,407	62.31	27,116	70.87	10,747	28.09	300	0.78	91	0.24
Brazoria	224,256	69.11	90,433	58.35	62,228	40.15	1,860	1.20	417	0.27
Brazos	122,137	69.64	47,530	55.88	35,349	41.56	1,812	2.13	252	0.30
Brewster	7,524	64.09	2,461	51.04	2,258	46.83	89	1.85	14	0.29
Briscoe	1,025	70.73	639	88.14	78	10.76	7	0.97	1	0.14
Brooks	5,521	44.99	998	40.18	1,470	59.18	10	0.40	6	0.24
Brown	23,954	66.67	13,698	85.78	2,107	13.19	134	0.84	24	0.15
Burleson	12,440	69.20	6,743	78.33	1,788	20.77	63	0.73	15	0.17
Burnet	33,697	73.35	18,767	75.93	5,639	22.81	268	1.08	34	0.14
Caldwell	25,945	57.71	8,031	53.64	6,672	44.56	190	1.27	47	0.31
Calhoun	13,080	60.06	5,641	71.80	2,148	27.34	61	0.78	6	0.08
Callahan	9,773	69.91	6,012	88.00	734	10.74	71	1.04	15	0.22
Cameron	218,910	52.16	49,032	42.94	64,063	56.11	728	0.64	336	0.29
Camp	7,904	64.02	3,626	71.66	1,394	27.55	31	0.61	7	0.14
Carson	4,345	71.85	2,779	89.01	297	9.51	37	1.19	3	0.10
Cass	20,889	66.67	11,033	79.22	2,795	20.07	79	0.57	17	0.12
Castro	3,853	54.06	1,602	76.91	466	22.37	9	0.43	6	0.29
Chambers	30,709	70.51	17,353	80.15	3,997	18.46	250	1.15	50	0.23
Cherokee	29,166	66.89	15,101	77.41	4,210	21.58	161	0.83	36	0.18
Childress	3,658	62.30	1,943	85.26	310	13.60	18	0.79	8	0.35
Clay	7,959	72.17	5,069	88.25	614	10.69	46	0.80	12	0.21
Cochran	1,771	56.47	809	80.90	177	17.70	11	1.10	3	0.30
Coke	2,414	73.70	1,586	89.15	178	10.01	10	0.56	5	0.28
Coleman	5,960	69.19	3,641	88.29	451	10.94	23	0.56	9	0.22
Collin	648,670	75.67	252,318	51.40	230,945	47.05	6,075	1.24	1,246	0.25
Collingsworth	1,942	62.72	1,048	86.04	155	12.73	12	0.99	1	0.08
Colorado	14,378	69.38	7,472	74.91	2,420	24.26	50	0.50	19	0.19
Comal	115,876	76.71	62,740	70.58	24,826	27.93	1,106	1.24	191	0.21
Comanche	9,562	63.65	5,177	85.06	853	14.02	49	0.81	5	0.08
Concho	1,757	72.17	1,058	83.44	197	15.54	10	0.79	3	0.24
Cooke	27,268	69.66	15,596	82.10	3,210	16.90	156	0.82	26	0.14
Coryell	41,450	56.68	15,438	65.71	7,565	32.20	410	1.75	77	0.33

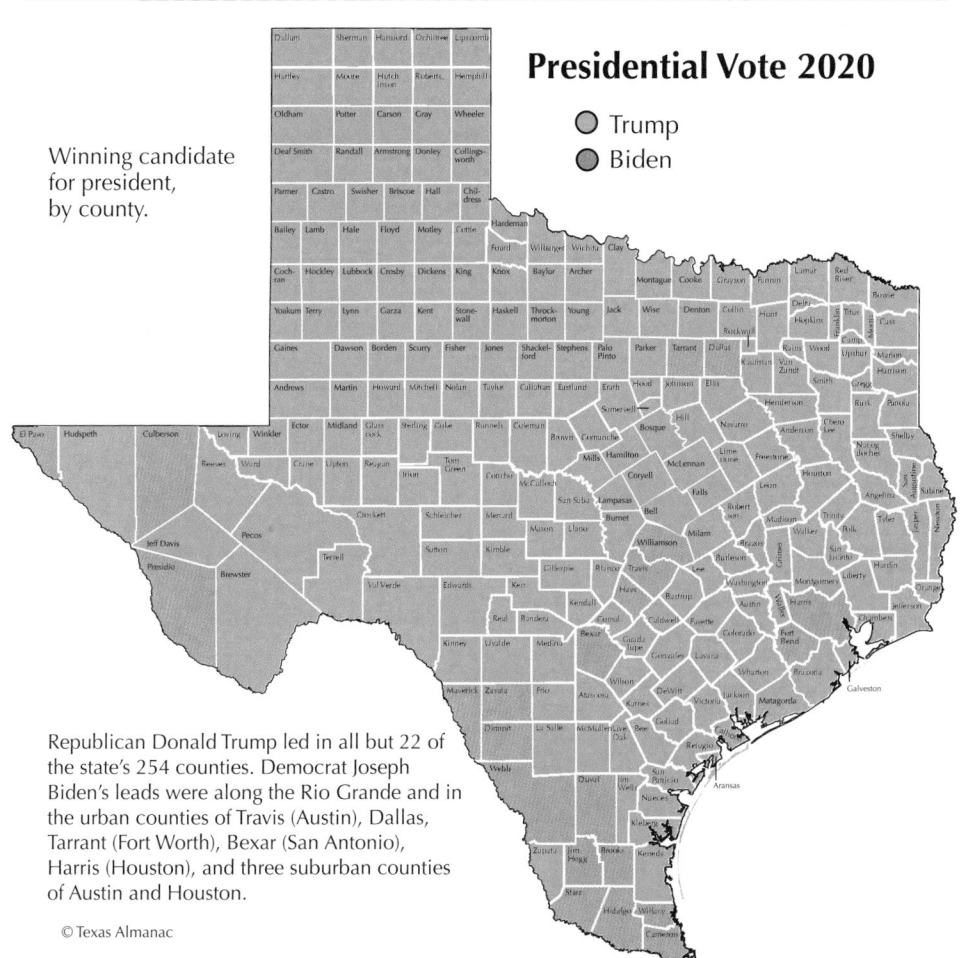

Presidential Vote 2020

Winning candidate for president, by county.

○ Trump
○ Biden

Republican Donald Trump led in all but 22 of the state's 254 counties. Democrat Joseph Biden's leads were along the Rio Grande and in the urban counties of Travis (Austin), Dallas, Tarrant (Fort Worth), Bexar (San Antonio), Harris (Houston), and three suburban counties of Austin and Houston.

© Texas Almanac

County	Registered Voters	Turnout %	Presidential Race							
			Trump	%	Biden	%	Jorgensen	%	Hawkins	%
Cottle	1,041	63.59	540	81.57	113	17.07	6	0.91	3	0.45
Crane	2,663	56.44	1,247	82.97	241	16.03	10	0.67	4	0.27
Crockett	2,473	63.65	1,220	77.51	344	21.86	9	0.57	1	0.06
Crosby	3,629	53.82	1,396	71.48	527	26.98	22	1.13	8	0.41
Culberson	1,709	50.56	415	48.03	438	50.69	9	1.04	2	0.23
Dallam	3,046	52.82	1,389	86.33	197	12.24	18	1.12	5	0.31
Dallas	1,398,469	65.75	307,076	33.40	598,576	65.10	9,635	1.05	3,667	0.40
Dawson	7,104	53.34	2,951	77.88	808	21.32	25	0.66	5	0.13
Deaf Smith	8,900	51.80	3,294	71.45	1,264	27.42	35	0.76	17	0.37
Delta	3,949	65.64	2,162	83.41	403	15.55	24	0.93	3	0.12
Denton	565,089	73.96	222,480	53.23	188,695	45.15	5,421	1.30	1,092	0.26
DeWitt	12,094	67.12	6,567	80.89	1,494	18.40	46	0.57	11	0.14
Dickens	1,328	74.40	853	86.34	130	13.16	3	0.30	2	0.20
Dimmit	7,341	49.94	1,384	37.75	2,264	61.76	10	0.27	8	0.22
Donley	2,322	70.97	1,438	87.26	198	12.01	11	0.67	1	0.06
Duval	8,346	60.54	2,443	48.35	2,575	50.96	22	0.44	13	0.26
Eastland	12,230	67.81	7,237	87.27	983	11.85	60	0.72	12	0.14
Ector	80,872	55.14	32,697	73.33	11,367	25.49	428	0.96	89	0.20
Edwards	1,499	71.11	893	83.77	168	15.76	5	0.47	0	0.00
Ellis	120,188	71.13	56,717	66.34	27,565	32.24	954	1.12	220	0.26
El Paso	488,470	54.60	84,331	31.62	178,126	66.78	2,746	1.03	1,445	0.54

County	Registered Voters	Turnout %	Presidential Race							
			Trump	%	Biden	%	Jorgensen	%	Hawkins	%
Erath	23,935	70.42	13,684	81.18	2,916	17.30	218	1.29	35	0.21
Falls	10,361	59.19	4,177	68.11	1,899	30.96	44	0.72	13	0.21
Fannin	22,199	67.60	12,171	81.10	2,655	17.69	155	1.03	23	0.15
Fayette	17,398	74.38	10,171	78.60	2,661	20.56	83	0.64	26	0.20
Fisher	2,646	69.01	1,448	79.30	352	19.28	21	1.15	5	0.27
Floyd	3,850	52.96	1,584	77.69	438	21.48	15	0.74	2	0.10
Foard	884	62.33	445	80.76	99	17.97	6	1.09	1	0.18
Fort Bend	482,368	74.12	157,718	44.12	195,552	54.70	3,028	0.85	1,091	0.31
Franklin	7,061	70.94	4,161	83.07	804	16.05	36	0.72	8	0.16
Freestone	12,481	69.79	6,991	80.25	1,635	18.77	67	0.77	18	0.21
Frio	8,984	58.76	2,823	53.48	2,422	45.88	23	0.44	11	0.21
Gaines	9,701	61.81	5,355	89.31	576	9.61	54	0.90	10	0.17
Galveston	228,482	67.87	93,911	60.56	58,842	37.95	1,913	1.23	393	0.25
Garza	2,681	61.66	1,413	85.48	231	13.97	5	0.30	4	0.24
Gillespie	20,404	77.68	12,514	78.95	3,176	20.04	140	0.88	16	0.10
Glasscock	800	81.63	611	93.57	39	5.97	3	0.46	0	0.00
Goliad	5,766	69.29	3,085	77.22	877	21.95	24	0.60	2	0.05
Gonzales	12,629	60.56	5,627	73.57	1,948	25.47	57	0.75	15	0.20
Gray	12,406	62.73	6,840	87.90	829	10.65	97	1.25	16	0.21
Grayson	86,740	68.57	44,163	74.26	14,506	24.39	634	1.07	136	0.23
Gregg	72,867	65.85	32,493	67.72	14,796	30.84	551	1.15	113	0.24
Grimes	17,877	69.44	9,432	75.98	2,833	22.82	118	0.95	30	0.24
Guadalupe	111,142	69.84	47,553	61.26	28,805	37.11	1,023	1.32	211	0.27
Hale	18,997	50.46	7,177	74.87	2,279	23.77	97	1.01	31	0.32
Hall	1,926	60.70	995	85.12	168	14.37	4	0.34	1	0.09
Hamilton	5,832	74.61	3,616	83.11	641	14.73	52	1.20	40	0.92
Hansford	3,009	68.03	1,849	90.33	166	8.11	27	1.32	3	0.15
Hardeman	2,486	63.56	1,330	84.18	241	15.25	9	0.57	0	0.00
Hardin	39,952	69.17	23,858	86.33	3,474	12.57	276	1.00	27	0.10
Harris	2,480,522	66.15	700,630	42.70	918,193	55.96	16,819	1.03	5,129	0.31
Harrison	45,933	64.70	21,466	72.23	7,908	26.61	294	0.99	42	0.14
Hartley	2,909	71.43	1,868	89.89	195	9.38	14	0.67	1	0.05
Haskell	3,377	65.56	1,840	83.11	353	15.94	15	0.68	6	0.27
Hays	152,840	71.57	47,680	43.59	59,524	54.41	1,735	1.59	418	0.38
Hemphill	2,355	73.04	1,486	86.40	206	11.98	25	1.45	3	0.17
Henderson	54,663	66.44	28,911	79.61	7,060	19.44	264	0.73	75	0.21
Hidalgo	391,309	56.45	90,527	40.98	128,199	58.04	1,261	0.57	865	0.39
Hill	23,625	63.20	11,926	79.87	2,860	19.15	119	0.80	26	0.17
Hockley	13,781	58.78	6,536	80.69	1,482	18.30	61	0.75	16	0.20
Hood	44,831	72.59	26,496	81.42	5,648	17.36	319	0.98	71	0.22
Hopkins	23,954	66.55	12,719	79.79	3,046	19.11	143	0.90	31	0.19
Houston	13,444	70.20	7,060	74.80	2,314	24.52	56	0.59	7	0.07
Howard	17,526	58.43	8,054	78.64	2,069	20.20	89	0.87	28	0.27
Hudspeth	2,085	55.88	779	66.87	371	31.85	10	0.86	5	0.43
Hunt	59,367	65.01	29,163	75.56	8,906	23.07	434	1.12	71	0.18
Hutchinson	13,533	64.83	7,681	87.55	965	11.00	115	1.31	10	0.11
Irion	1,298	68.49	759	85.38	120	13.50	8	0.90	2	0.22
Jack	5,254	71.98	3,418	90.38	331	8.75	24	0.63	9	0.24
Jackson	9,482	67.00	5,231	82.34	1,033	16.26	53	0.83	23	0.36
Jasper	23,374	66.79	12,542	80.34	2,954	18.92	105	0.67	7	0.04
Jeff Davis	1,670	78.14	784	60.08	501	38.39	17	1.30	3	0.23
Jefferson	149,372	63.44	47,570	50.20	46,073	48.62	897	0.95	199	0.21
Jim Hogg	3,800	53.58	833	40.91	1,197	58.79	4	0.20	2	0.10
Jim Wells	26,636	51.32	7,453	54.52	6,119	44.77	69	0.50	28	0.20
Johnson	105,574	68.22	54,628	75.85	16,464	22.86	771	1.07	142	0.20
Jones	9,635	69.96	5,660	83.96	999	14.82	63	0.93	19	0.28
Karnes	8,359	62.83	3,968	75.55	1,234	23.50	30	0.57	17	0.32
Kaufman	81,901	69.25	37,624	66.34	18,405	32.45	528	0.93	146	0.26
Kendall	33,836	78.18	20,083	75.92	6,020	22.76	289	1.09	46	0.17
Kenedy	296	65.54	127	65.46	65	33.51	1	0.52	1	0.52
Kent	592	78.04	411	88.96	47	10.17	1	0.22	3	0.65

County	Registered Voters	Turnout %	Presidential Race								
			Trump	%	Biden	%	Jorgensen	%	Hawkins	%
Kerr	37,726	73.54	20,879	75.25	6,524	23.51	283	1.02	51	0.18
Kimble	3,113	73.63	1,987	86.69	284	12.39	17	0.74	4	0.17
King	183	86.89	151	94.97	8	5.03	0	0.00	0	0.00
Kinney	2,270	70.62	1,144	71.37	446	27.82	11	0.69	2	0.12
Kleberg	18,749	58.37	5,504	50.29	5,314	48.56	97	0.89	29	0.26
Knox	2,391	60.90	1,180	81.04	265	18.20	7	0.48	4	0.27
Lamar	32,390	66.20	16,760	78.16	4,458	20.79	172	0.80	28	0.13
Lamb	8,085	54.55	3,521	79.84	840	19.05	40	0.91	7	0.16
Lampasas	15,424	67.42	8,086	77.76	2,144	20.62	145	1.39	24	0.23
La Salle	4,426	54.36	1,335	55.49	1,052	43.72	12	0.50	7	0.29
Lavaca	13,661	74.64	8,804	86.34	1,333	13.07	46	0.45	8	0.08
Lee	11,145	72.56	6,255	77.35	1,750	21.64	65	0.80	16	0.20
Leon	11,727	73.97	7,523	86.73	1,072	12.36	57	0.66	14	0.16
Liberty	46,155	63.56	23,302	79.44	5,785	19.72	218	0.74	29	0.10
Limestone	13,963	65.14	6,789	74.65	2,213	24.33	66	0.73	27	0.30
Lipscomb	1,977	68.44	1,205	89.06	131	9.68	17	1.26	0	0.00
Live Oak	7,572	66.75	4,199	83.08	819	16.20	30	0.59	6	0.12
Llano	16,688	75.86	10,079	79.61	2,465	19.47	99	0.78	16	0.13
Loving	111	59.46	60	90.91	4	6.06	2	3.03	0	0.00
Lubbock	183,320	65.90	78,861	65.27	40,017	33.12	1,617	1.34	276	0.23
Lynn	4,028	56.93	1,853	80.81	428	18.67	10	0.44	2	0.09
Madison	5,361	64.09	2,904	84.52	490	14.26	36	1.05	6	0.17
Marion	149,461	65.48	59,543	60.84	36,688	37.49	1,297	1.33	243	0.25
Martin	706	73.09	460	89.15	53	10.27	2	0.39	1	0.19
Mason	7,822	67.73	4,169	78.69	1,088	20.54	30	0.57	10	0.19
Matagorda	7,596	64.03	3,470	71.34	1,339	27.53	47	0.97	8	0.16
Maverick	3,467	62.30	1,857	85.97	288	13.33	13	0.60	2	0.09
McCulloch	3,168	78.09	1,991	80.48	457	18.47	19	0.77	2	0.08
McLennan	22,026	62.32	9,845	71.72	3,733	27.19	115	0.84	33	0.24
McMullen	33,050	46.43	6,881	44.84	8,332	54.29	73	0.48	60	0.39
Medina	33,763	67.11	15,642	69.04	6,773	29.89	184	0.81	45	0.20
Menard	1,469	69.98	823	80.06	197	19.16	6	0.58	2	0.19
Midland	90,392	65.12	45,624	77.51	12,329	20.95	777	1.32	126	0.21
Milam	15,838	66.79	7,984	75.48	2,496	23.60	72	0.68	24	0.23
Mills	3,429	73.05	2,217	88.50	271	10.82	15	0.60	2	0.08
Mitchell	4,524	57.01	2,170	84.14	397	15.39	11	0.43	1	0.04
Montague	14,001	70.13	8,615	87.74	1,097	11.17	78	0.79	24	0.24
Montgomery	370,060	73.38	193,382	71.22	74,377	27.39	3,166	1.17	526	0.19
Moore	9,995	55.11	4,359	79.14	1,062	19.28	66	1.20	21	0.38
Morris	8,583	65.09	3,872	69.30	1,669	29.87	36	0.64	10	0.18
Motley	859	75.90	604	92.64	46	7.06	2	0.31	0	0.00
Nacogdoches	38,786	69.06	17,378	64.88	9,000	33.60	302	1.13	83	0.31
Navarro	29,959	63.83	13,800	72.16	5,101	26.67	167	0.87	53	0.28
Newton	9,400	64.83	4,882	80.11	1,173	19.25	34	0.56	5	0.08
Nolan	8,871	60.39	4,131	77.11	1,162	21.69	53	0.99	10	0.19
Nueces	211,652	60.16	64,617	50.75	60,925	47.85	1,404	1.10	368	0.29
Ochiltree	5,192	60.79	2,812	89.10	302	9.57	37	1.17	3	0.10
Oldham	1,425	70.81	917	90.88	81	8.03	10	0.99	1	0.10
Orange	54,442	66.11	29,186	81.09	6,357	17.66	376	1.04	51	0.14
Palo Pinto	18,946	65.92	10,179	81.50	2,178	17.44	101	0.81	27	0.22
Panola	16,808	68.13	9,326	81.44	2,057	17.96	57	0.50	11	0.10
Parker	103,999	73.20	62,045	81.50	13,017	17.10	880	1.16	158	0.21
Parmer	4,537	58.41	2,135	80.57	488	18.42	23	0.87	4	0.15
Pecos	8,323	56.09	3,215	68.87	1,382	29.61	50	1.07	21	0.45
Polk	40,520	59.69	18,573	76.79	5,387	22.27	171	0.71	50	0.21
Potter	57,736	57.74	22,820	68.45	9,921	29.76	454	1.36	126	0.38
Presidio	4,789	46.29	721	32.52	1,463	65.99	21	0.95	12	0.54
Rains	8,320	72.75	5,155	85.16	842	13.91	43	0.71	13	0.21
Randall	93,313	69.31	50,796	78.54	12,802	19.79	910	1.41	129	0.20
Reagan	1,879	59.82	942	83.81	172	15.30	7	0.62	3	0.27
Real	2,702	73.35	1,643	82.90	320	16.15	14	0.71	5	0.25

County	Registered Voters	Turnout %	Presidential Race							
			Trump	%	Biden	%	Jorgensen	%	Hawkins	%
Red River	8,489	68.39	4,517	77.80	1,246	21.46	36	0.62	7	0.12
Reeves	7,558	48.81	2,254	61.10	1,395	37.82	30	0.81	8	0.22
Refugio	5,007	67.23	2,210	65.66	1,108	32.92	26	0.77	21	0.62
Roberts	680	80.88	529	96.18	17	3.09	4	0.73	0	0.00
Robertson	11,844	68.38	5,646	69.71	2,374	29.31	66	0.81	13	0.16
Rockwall	71,102	75.79	36,726	68.15	16,412	30.45	611	1.13	121	0.22
Runnels	7,025	62.76	3,807	86.35	552	12.52	39	0.88	11	0.25
Rusk	32,388	66.00	16,534	77.34	4,629	21.65	155	0.73	50	0.23
Sabine	8,050	68.21	4,784	87.12	669	12.18	27	0.49	7	0.13
San Augustine	6,108	65.52	3,007	75.14	980	24.49	13	0.32	2	0.05
San Jacinto	18,969	66.64	10,161	80.39	2,337	18.49	101	0.80	39	0.31
San Patricio	43,248	59.87	16,516	63.79	8,988	34.71	291	1.12	93	0.36
San Saba	3,776	68.91	2,308	88.70	287	11.03	7	0.27	0	0.00
Schleicher	1,709	67.82	940	81.10	211	18.21	6	0.52	2	0.17
Scurry	9,489	61.86	4,983	84.89	818	13.94	53	0.90	15	0.26
Shackelford	2,320	70.17	1,484	91.15	130	7.99	10	0.61	4	0.25
Shelby	15,570	64.78	7,975	79.06	2,068	20.50	37	0.37	4	0.04
Sherman	1,520	65.26	886	89.31	91	9.17	9	0.91	5	0.50
Smith	146,149	68.48	69,080	69.02	29,615	29.59	1,126	1.12	254	0.25
Somervell	6,712	73.70	4,105	82.98	768	15.52	56	1.13	10	0.20
Starr	34,050	51.47	8,247	47.06	9,123	52.06	92	0.52	63	0.36
Stephens	5,672	67.00	3,385	89.08	397	10.45	16	0.42	2	0.05
Sterling	939	68.05	584	91.39	51	7.98	1	0.16	3	0.47
Stonewall	953	77.23	615	83.56	116	15.76	4	0.54	1	0.14
Sutton	2,449	63.58	1,222	78.48	322	20.68	9	0.58	4	0.26
Swisher	3,941	59.76	1,845	78.34	478	20.30	22	0.93	10	0.42
Tarrant	1,212,524	68.84	409,741	49.09	411,567	49.31	10,368	1.24	2,617	0.31
Taylor	83,696	65.88	39,547	71.73	14,588	26.46	827	1.50	150	0.27
Terrell	673	68.05	334	72.93	119	25.98	3	0.66	2	0.44
Terry	6,589	54.82	2,812	77.85	757	20.96	33	0.91	10	0.28
Throckmorton	1,216	73.52	806	90.16	82	9.17	5	0.56	1	0.11
Titus	17,666	59.67	7,570	71.81	2,856	27.09	94	0.89	19	0.18
Tom Green	70,086	64.51	32,313	71.47	12,239	27.07	546	1.21	96	0.21
Travis	854,577	71.21	161,337	26.51	435,860	71.62	8,905	1.46	2,094	0.34
Trinity	11,541	60.12	5,579	80.41	1,323	19.07	25	0.36	11	0.16
Tyler	14,556	66.36	8,194	84.82	1,403	14.52	52	0.54	11	0.11
Upshur	28,619	66.01	15,809	83.68	2,877	15.23	179	0.95	22	0.12
Upton	2,207	61.98	1,178	86.11	170	12.43	13	0.95	7	0.51
Uvalde	17,420	59.38	6,174	59.69	4,073	39.38	66	0.64	29	0.28
Val Verde	28,927	52.82	8,284	54.21	6,771	44.31	170	1.11	47	0.31
Van Zandt	38,965	66.80	22,270	85.56	3,516	13.51	175	0.67	33	0.13
Victoria	56,612	60.39	23,358	68.32	10,380	30.36	339	0.99	103	0.30
Walker	35,038	67.39	15,375	65.12	7,884	33.39	287	1.22	63	0.27
Waller	35,116	64.74	14,260	62.73	8,191	36.03	201	0.88	82	0.36
Ward	6,880	59.01	3,241	79.83	764	18.82	29	0.71	26	0.64
Washington	23,947	72.77	12,959	74.36	4,261	24.45	178	1.02	20	0.11
Webb	137,840	49.62	25,898	37.86	41,820	61.14	446	0.65	233	0.34
Wharton	25,697	65.23	11,926	71.15	4,694	28.01	105	0.63	36	0.21
Wheeler	3,514	66.51	2,159	92.38	168	7.19	7	0.30	3	0.13
Wichita	83,575	55.09	32,069	69.65	13,161	28.59	675	1.47	125	0.27
Wilbarger	8,196	55.20	3,524	77.90	956	21.13	33	0.73	11	0.24
Willacy	12,804	43.34	2,441	43.99	3,108	56.01	0	0.00	0	0.00
Williamson	376,672	76.87	139,729	48.26	143,795	49.66	4,998	1.73	790	0.27
Wilson	35,036	71.39	18,463	73.81	6,350	25.39	151	0.60	39	0.16
Winkler	4,013	52.98	1,753	82.46	358	16.84	14	0.66	1	0.05
Wise	45,643	70.91	27,032	83.52	4,973	15.37	310	0.96	47	0.15
Wood	32,382	70.34	19,049	83.63	3,509	15.40	175	0.77	40	0.18
Yoakum	4,407	59.70	2,174	82.63	420	15.96	31	1.18	6	0.23
Young	11,769	70.01	7,110	86.30	1,034	12.55	76	0.92	18	0.22
Zapata	8,257	46.92	2,033	52.48	1,826	47.13	11	0.28	4	0.10
Zavala	8,066	54.29	1,490	34.03	2,864	65.40	13	0.30	12	0.27

General Election, 2020

Below are the official voting results for the general election held November 3, 2020, as canvassed by the State Canvassing Board. Federal races include presidential, Senate, and House of Representatives elections. Statewide races include railroad commissioner, courts of criminal appeals, and Texas Supreme Court. District races include the state senate and state board of education.

Omitted races include the state House of Representatives, judges for the court of appeals, and district judges, as well as races with single entrants; these can be found at our website, texasalmanac.com.

Abbreviations used are (Dem.) Democrat, (Rep.) Republican, (Lib.) Libertarian, (Ind.) Independent and (W-I) Write-in.

Federal Races

President

Donald J. Trump (Rep.)	5,890,347	52.06%
Joseph R. Biden (Dem.)	5,259,126	46.48%
Jo Jorgensen (Lib.)	126,243	1.12%
Howie Hawkins (Green)	33,396	0.30%
President R. Boddie (W-I)	2,012	0.02%
Brian Carroll (W-I)	2,785	0.02%
Todd Cella (W-I)	205	0.00%
Jesse Cuellar (W-I)	49	0.00%
Tom Hoefling (W-I)	337	0.00%
Gloria La Riva (W-I)	350	0.00%
Abram Loeb (W-I)	360	0.00%
Robert Morrow (W-I)	56	0.00%
Kasey Wells (W-I)	114	0.00%
Total vote	11,315,056	

U.S. Senate

John Cornyn (Rep.)	5,962,983	53.51%
Mary "MJ" Hegar (Dem.)	4,888,764	43.87%
Kerry Douglas Mckennon (Lib.)	209,722	1.88%
David B. Collins (Green)	81,893	0.73%
Ricardo Turullols-Bonilla (W-I)	678	0.01%
Total Vote	11,144,040	

U.S. House of Representatives

(See map of districts on p. 514.)

District 1

Louie Gohmert (Rep.)	219,726	72.58%
Hank Gilbert (Dem.)	83,016	27.42%
Total Vote	302,742	

District 2

Dan Crenshaw (Rep.)	192,828	55.61%
Sima Ladjevardian (Dem.)	148,374	42.79%
Elliott Robert Scheirman (Lib.)	5,524	1.59%
Total Vote	346,726	

District 3

Van Taylor (Rep.)	230,512	55.07%
Lulu Seikaly (Dem.)	179,458	42.87%
Christopher J. Claytor (Lib.)	8,621	2.06%
Total Vote	418,591	

District 4

Pat Fallon (Rep.)	253,837	75.14%
Russell Foster (Dem)	76,326	22.59%
Lou Antonelli (Lib.)	6,334	1.88%
Tracy Jones (W-I)	1,306	0.39%
Total Vote	337,803	

District 5

Lance Gooden (Rep.)	173,836	61.99%
Carolyn Salter (Dem.)	100,743	35.93%
Kevin A. Hale (Lib.)	5,834	2.08%
Total Vote	280,413	

District 6

Ron Wright (Rep.)	179,507	52.8%
Stephen Daniel (Dem.)	149,530	43.98%
Melanie A. Black (Lib.)	10,955	3.22%
Total Vote	339,992	

District 7

Lizzie Fletcher (Dem.)	159,529	50.79%
Wesley Hunt (Rep.)	149,054	47.45%
Shawn Kelly (Lib.)	5,542	1.76%
Total Vote	314,125	

District 8

Kevin Brady (Rep.)	277,327	72.51%
Elizabeth Hernandez (Dem.)	97,409	25.47%
Chris Duncan (Lib.)	7,735	2.02%
Total Vote	382,471	

District 9

Al Green (Dem.)	172,938	75.48%
Johnny Teague (Rep.)	49,575	21.64%
Jose R. Sosa (Lib.)	6,594	2.88
Total Vote	229,107	

District 10

Michael McCaul (Rep.)	217,216	52.48%
Mike Siegel (Dem.)	187,686	45.35%
Roy Eriksen (Lib.)	8,992	2.17%
Total Vote	413,894	

District 11

August Pfluger (Rep.)	232,568	79.71%
Jon Mark Hogg (Dem.)	53,394	18.3%
Wacey Alpha Cody (Lib.)	5,811	1.99%
Total Vote	291,773	

District 12

Kay Granger (Rep.)	233,853	63.72%
Lisa Welch (Dem.)	121,250	33.04%
Trey Holcomb (Lib.)	11,918	3.25%
Total Vote	367,021	

District 13

Ronny Jackson (Rep.)	217,124	79.38%
Gus Trujillo (Dem.)	50,477	18.46%
Jack B. Westbrook (Lib.)	5,907	2.16%
Total Vote	273,508	

District 14

Randy Weber (Rep.)	190,541	61.64%
Adrienne Bell (Dem.)	118,574	38.36%
Total Vote	309,115	

District 15

Vicente Gonzalez (Dem.)	115,605	50.5%
Monica de la Cruz-Hernandez (Rep.)	109,017	47.62%
Ross Lynn Leone (Lib.)	4,295	1.88%
Total Vote	228,917	

District 16

Veronica Escobar (Dem.)	154,108	64.72%
Irene Armendariz-Jackson (Lib..)	84,006	35.28%
Total Vote	238,114	

District 17

Pete Sessions (Rep.)	171,390	55.85%
Rick Kennedy (Dem.)	125,565	40.92%
Ted Brown (Lib.)	9,918	3.23%
Total Vote	306,873	

District 18

Sheila Jackson Lee (Dem.)	180,952	73.29%
Wendell Champion (Rep.)	58,033	23.51%
Luke Spencer (Lib.)	4,514	1.83%
Vince Duncan (Ind.)	3,396	1.38%
Total Vote	246,895	

District 19

Jodey C. Arrington (Rep.)	198,198	74.78%
Tom Watson (Dem.)	60,583	22.86%
Joe Burnes (Lib.)	6,271	2.37%
Total Vote	265,052	

District 20

Joaquin Castro (Dem.)	175,078	64.67%
Mauro Garza (Rep.)	89,628	33.11%
Jeffrey Blunt (Lib.)	6,017	2.22%
Total Vote	270,723	

2020 Presidential Primaries: Results by County

Below are the official canvass results by county in the party primaries for president held March 3, 2020.

This table lists the principal candidates in the Democratic primary: Joseph Biden, Bernie Sanders, and Michael Bloomberg.

Source: Texas Secretary of State.

In the Republican primary, the top candidate is listed; Donald Trump received 94.13% percent of votes cast in the Republican primary.

Alongside the number of votes received by each candidate is listed the percent of the total vote received.

Republican Primary		County	Democratic Primary					
Trump	%		Biden	%	Sanders	%	Bloomberg	%
1,898,664	94.13%	Statewide	725,562	34.64%	626,339	29.91%	300,608	14.35%
7,646	96.63%	Anderson	763	47.96%	336	21.12%	300	18.86%
2,281	93.41%	Andrews	81	35.06%	84	36.36%	33	14.29%
12,166	94.97%	Angelina	1,652	50.85%	648	19.94%	466	14.34%
3,820	92.14%	Aransas	504	42.75%	222	18.83%	176	14.93%
2,455	94.86%	Archer	74	44.31%	28	16.77%	31	18.56%
676	96.99%	Armstrong	11	39.29%	10	35.71%	4	14.29%
4,220	94.05%	Atascosa	806	29.48%	741	27.10%	585	21.40%
4,662	95.55%	Austin	460	44.79%	214	20.84%	205	19.96%
832	90.73%	Bailey	47	40.17%	34	29.06%	15	12.82%
3,997	95.76%	Bandera	443	38.59%	282	24.56%	171	14.90%
7,672	94.83%	Bastrop	2,371	32.14%	2,280	30.90%	1,000	13.55%
876	95.01%	Baylor	27	41.54%	5	7.69%	19	29.23%
1,596	95.17%	Bee	493	44.25%	242	21.72%	173	15.53%
21,480	94.10%	Bell	7,851	43.06%	4,798	26.32%	2,456	13.47%
75,555	93.40%	Bexar	49,552	28.79%	57,051	33.15%	26,231	15.24%
2,232	96.00%	Blanco	376	36.08%	240	23.03%	143	13.72%
235	97.92%	Borden	2	33.33%	1	16.67%	2	33.33%
3,647	95.87%	Bosque	293	40.98%	172	24.06%	114	15.94%
12,024	94.42%	Bowie	2,066	56.00%	700	18.98%	487	13.20%
33,464	93.40%	Brazoria	8,904	40.88%	5,860	26.90%	3,138	14.41%
17,063	90.63%	Brazos	4,099	31.58%	4,749	36.59%	1,002	7.72%
934	94.73%	Brewster	354	26.90%	408	31.00%	151	11.47%
470	91.98%	Briscoe	9	26.47%	4	11.76%	5	14.71%
69	95.83%	Brooks	289	18.63%	522	33.66%	424	27.34%
5,846	96.28%	Brown	369	48.17%	184	24.02%	69	9.01%
3,346	94.87%	Burleson	383	50.59%	122	16.12%	150	19.82%
6,480	95.65%	Burnet	1,028	39.51%	579	22.25%	432	16.60%
2,969	93.69%	Caldwell	987	32.89%	958	31.92%	432	14.40%
2,131	95.43%	Calhoun	427	46.01%	191	20.58%	159	17.13%
2,382	96.09%	Callahan	120	47.43%	74	29.25%	14	5.53%
7,645	92.69%	Cameron	7,554	23.95%	10,520	33.36%	6,402	20.30%
1,874	95.37%	Camp	350	52.63%	120	18.05%	114	17.14%
1,420	97.39%	Carson	66	49.62%	25	18.80%	18	13.53%
4,381	96.54%	Cass	626	55.99%	204	18.25%	151	13.51%
661	94.43%	Castro	51	30.18%	32	18.93%	60	35.50%
7,300	94.51%	Chambers	506	40.38%	342	27.29%	185	14.76%
7,547	95.90%	Cherokee	844	51.46%	299	18.23%	270	16.46%
1,196	94.92%	Childress	52	43.33%	32	26.67%	15	12.50%
2,771	95.19%	Clay	133	49.63%	43	16.04%	34	12.69%
397	92.76%	Cochran	17	53.13%	8	25.00%	4	12.50%
818	95.45%	Coke	26	36.62%	12	16.90%	14	19.72%
2,238	94.99%	Coleman	70	42.94%	36	22.09%	16	9.82%
64,574	93.61%	Collin	30,128	35.56%	25,628	30.25%	11,277	13.31%
687	95.02%	Collingsworth	22	34.92%	11	17.46%	15	23.81%
3,578	94.86%	Colorado	432	46.15%	167	17.84%	146	15.60%
20,429	94.80%	Comal	3,643	36.19%	2,417	24.01%	1,406	13.97%
2,601	94.41%	Comanche	146	38.52%	82	21.64%	85	22.43%
709	87.42%	Concho	27	41.54%	19	29.23%	10	15.38%
8,160	93.84%	Cooke	500	40.72%	310	25.24%	230	18.73%

2020

Leading candidates by county: Joseph R. Biden, Sen. Bernie Sanders, and Michael R. Bloomberg

(Sen. Elizabeth Warren received 5 delegates.)

© Texas Almanac

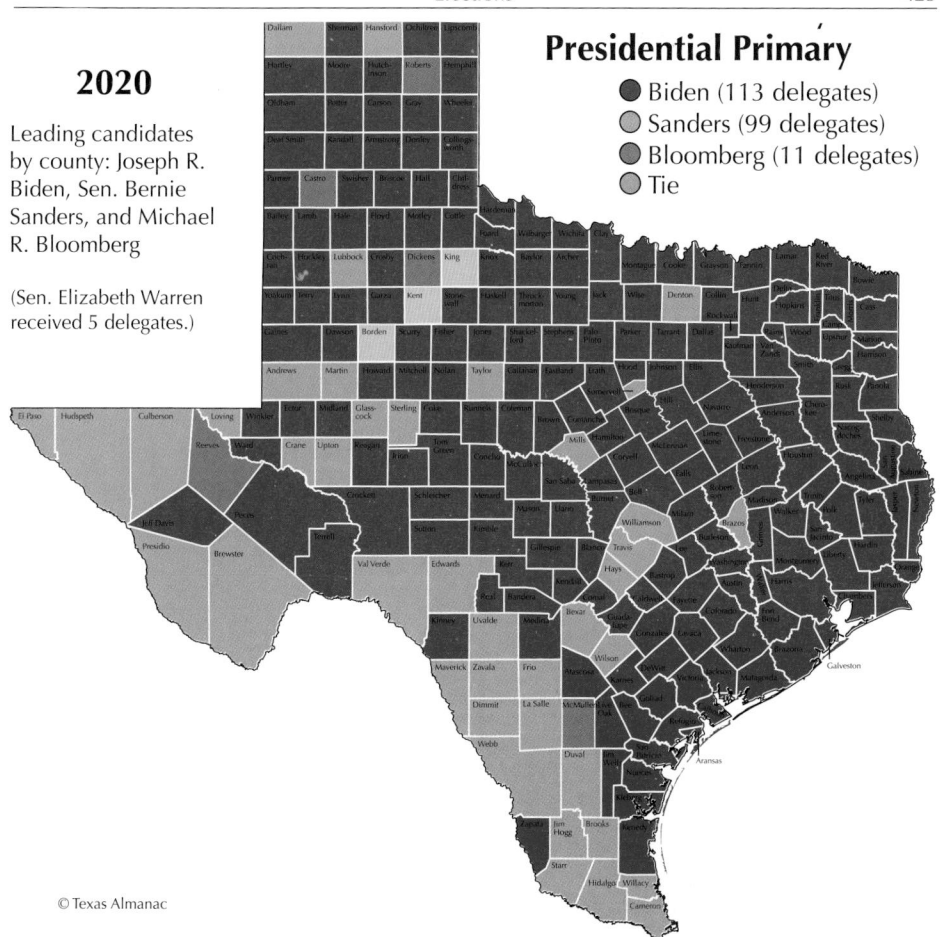

Presidential Primary

- ● Biden (113 delegates)
- ◐ Sanders (99 delegates)
- ● Bloomberg (11 delegates)
- ◐ Tie

Republican Primary		County	Democratic Primary					
Trump	%		Biden	%	Sanders	%	Bloomberg	%
6,586	93.18%	Coryell	982	40.08%	702	28.65%	337	13.76%
349	93.07%	Cottle	20	32.79%	18	29.51%	8	13.11%
571	94.38%	Crane	24	32.43%	25	33.78%	12	16.22%
517	89.45%	Crockett	84	26.84%	77	24.60%	42	13.42%
742	87.60%	Crosby	83	43.23%	55	28.65%	33	17.19%
28	100.00%	Culberson	128	21.81%	188	32.03%	137	23.34%
769	94.59%	Dallam	20	29.85%	26	38.81%	9	13.43%
79,464	92.71%	Dallas	98,192	40.66%	64,842	26.85%	32,702	13.54%
1,645	91.34%	Dawson	101	30.33%	71	21.32%	90	27.03%
1,408	94.62%	Deaf Smith	133	36.44%	85	23.29%	84	23.01%
1,303	90.93%	Delta	72	48.32%	33	22.15%	23	15.44%
62,385	93.33%	Denton	22,054	32.74%	22,301	33.10%	8,166	12.12%
2,689	95.46%	DeWitt	237	45.58%	109	20.96%	89	17.12%
458	94.05%	Dickens	16	27.59%	8	13.79%	18	31.03%
73	93.59%	Dimmit	433	18.55%	688	29.48%	536	22.96%
745	95.64%	Donley	33	45.83%	15	20.83%	11	15.28%
157	91.81%	Duval	515	22.33%	821	35.60%	505	21.90%
3,667	96.40%	Eastland	152	38.78%	124	31.63%	50	12.76%
10,681	95.92%	Ector	1,173	34.23%	1,018	29.71%	577	16.84%
569	89.61%	Edwards	3	8.57%	11	31.43%	4	11.43%
21,203	94.21%	Ellis	4,480	45.96%	2,388	24.50%	1,401	14.37%

Republican Primary		County	Democratic Primary					
Trump	%		Biden	%	Sanders	%	Bloomberg	%
16,913	91.90%	El Paso	19,363	28.25%	24,851	36.26%	14,090	20.56%
7,031	93.30%	Erath	376	33.84%	325	29.25%	154	13.86%
1,671	95.92%	Falls	349	48.14%	139	19.17%	156	21.52%
5,010	94.60%	Fannin	417	42.38%	191	19.41%	180	18.29%
4,774	95.58%	Fayette	529	42.97%	229	18.60%	235	19.09%
611	95.92%	Fisher	81	50.31%	29	18.01%	18	11.18%
854	89.61%	Floyd	53	46.09%	22	19.13%	17	14.78%
308	89.53%	Foard	15	50.00%	7	23.33%	2	6.67%
53,105	92.77%	Fort Bend	29,219	41.98%	18,297	26.29%	10,468	15.04%
1,662	97.42%	Franklin	188	50.54%	58	15.59%	69	18.55%
3,304	95.91%	Freestone	333	48.33%	167	24.24%	107	15.53%
397	94.75%	Frio	515	20.30%	697	27.47%	540	21.28%
1,595	97.61%	Gaines	71	39.23%	46	25.41%	31	17.13%
27,075	94.64%	Galveston	9,278	41.46%	5,504	24.60%	2,958	13.22%
565	96.91%	Garza	40	42.11%	21	22.11%	20	21.05%
5,608	94.13%	Gillespie	617	41.63%	240	16.19%	260	17.54%
354	98.88%	Glasscock	3	23.08%	6	46.15%	4	30.77%
1,357	95.23%	Goliad	187	49.47%	63	16.67%	66	17.46%
2,990	89.55%	Gonzales	239	38.00%	129	20.51%	135	21.46%
3,667	96.25%	Gray	117	42.55%	79	28.73%	38	13.82%
13,470	95.76%	Grayson	2,381	40.06%	1,548	26.04%	1,018	17.13%
10,705	96.90%	Gregg	2,876	52.14%	1,092	19.80%	796	14.43%
3,821	95.93%	Grimes	503	45.69%	246	22.34%	177	16.08%
16,023	92.81%	Guadalupe	3,812	37.90%	2,837	28.21%	1,402	13.94%
2,463	95.72%	Hale	243	37.50%	171	26.39%	111	17.13%
483	97.58%	Hall	42	49.41%	18	21.18%	20	23.53%
2,101	94.60%	Hamilton	162	44.51%	62	17.03%	68	18.68%
1,128	94.79%	Hansford	8	34.78%	12	52.17%	0	0.00%
654	95.47%	Hardeman	59	47.97%	20	16.26%	19	15.45%
8,808	97.70%	Hardin	692	48.87%	285	20.13%	222	15.68%
181,894	93.94%	Harris	121,866	37.69%	92,158	28.50%	47,459	14.68%
8,193	96.74%	Harrison	1,675	50.01%	617	18.42%	614	18.33%
1,089	95.69%	Hartley	36	64.29%	11	19.64%	0	0.00%
764	96.46%	Haskell	104	59.77%	20	11.49%	15	8.62%
14,248	92.43%	Hays	7,092	27.93%	9,817	38.66%	2,134	8.40%
768	95.40%	Hemphill	39	52.70%	8	10.81%	14	18.92%
11,381	96.27%	Henderson	1,389	45.98%	594	19.66%	529	17.51%
11,460	92.53%	Hidalgo	15,893	26.79%	16,721	28.18%	15,118	25.48%
5,255	95.63%	Hill	559	43.77%	284	22.24%	248	19.42%
3,089	93.46%	Hockley	160	40.92%	110	28.13%	72	18.41%
12,705	94.36%	Hood	943	39.44%	508	21.25%	453	18.95%
4,727	96.79%	Hopkins	563	46.03%	271	22.16%	204	16.68%
3,899	96.70%	Houston	496	55.30%	157	17.50%	132	14.72%
3,317	93.62%	Howard	299	38.28%	166	21.25%	173	22.15%
163	95.88%	Hudspeth	89	25.07%	103	29.01%	52	14.65%
12,280	93.83%	Hunt	1,287	39.32%	1,019	31.13%	468	14.30%
4,308	95.16%	Hutchinson	130	36.72%	89	25.14%	75	21.19%
458	94.43%	Irion	22	39.29%	16	28.57%	6	10.71%
1,813	96.85%	Jack	80	45.45%	33	18.75%	35	19.89%
2,408	94.69%	Jackson	192	52.03%	60	16.26%	55	14.91%
6,035	97.42%	Jasper	669	51.23%	220	16.85%	262	20.06%
448	93.92%	Jeff Davis	119	36.06%	81	24.55%	35	10.61%
13,921	96.95%	Jefferson	9,815	48.47%	3,981	19.66%	3,800	18.77%
12	92.31%	Jim Hogg	288	23.40%	343	27.86%	299	24.29%
1,165	93.57%	Jim Wells	1,619	34.40%	1,044	22.18%	1,021	21.70%
16,756	96.38%	Johnson	2,326	37.50%	1,790	28.86%	943	15.20%
2,556	92.37%	Jones	160	46.92%	83	24.34%	43	12.61%
1,613	94.05%	Karnes	210	33.87%	147	23.71%	129	20.81%
13,790	92.13%	Kaufman	2,351	42.39%	1,485	26.78%	819	14.77%

Presidential Primary

2020

Donald Trump
won every county.

○ Trump (117 delegates)
155 delegates were possible.

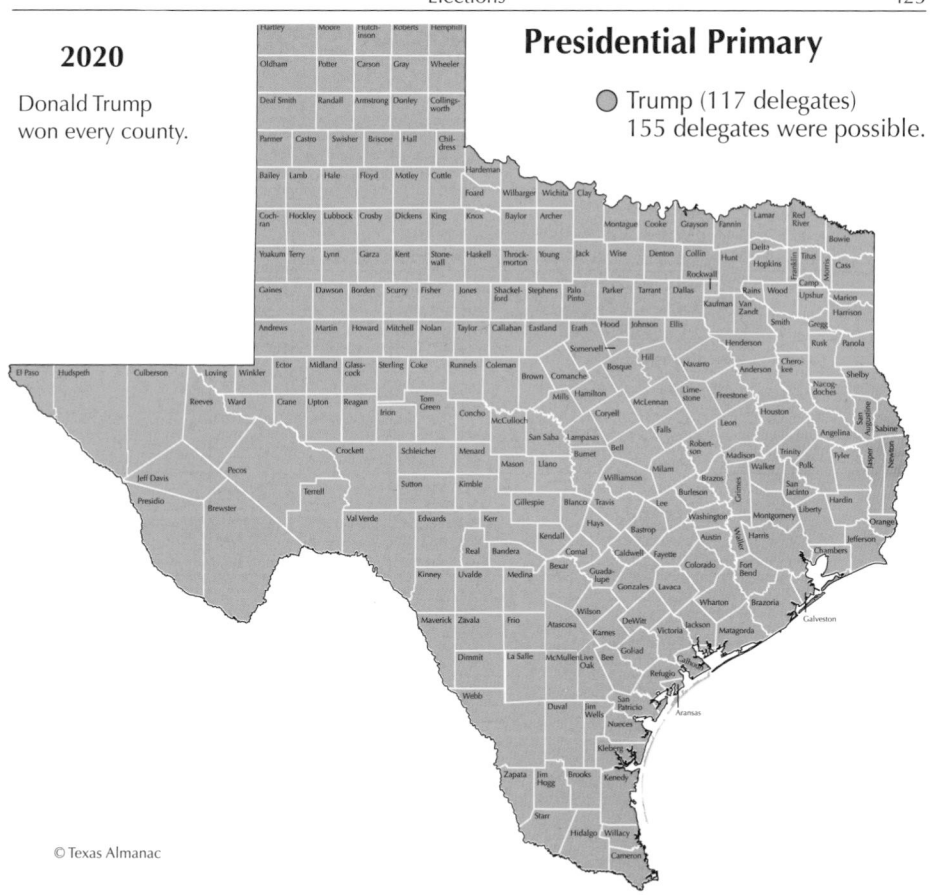

© Texas Almanac

Republican Primary		County	Democratic Primary					
Trump	%		Biden	%	Sanders	%	Bloomberg	%
6,793	95.29%	Kendall	924	35.79%	554	21.46%	432	16.73%
13	86.67%	Kenedy	30	24.79%	22	18.18%	23	19.01%
189	96.92%	Kent	14	33.33%	4	9.52%	14	33.33%
9,739	93.55%	Kerr	1,054	37.55%	628	22.37%	453	16.14%
1,296	93.04%	Kimble	41	40.20%	27	26.47%	14	13.73%
111	98.23%	King	0	0.00%	1	50.00%	1	50.00%
741	85.86%	Kinney	58	40.00%	23	15.86%	29	20.00%
1,602	94.12%	Kleberg	950	38.24%	629	25.32%	454	18.28%
721	91.27%	Knox	53	63.86%	14	16.87%	6	7.23%
6,836	97.41%	Lamar	864	46.80%	389	21.07%	303	16.41%
1,610	94.93%	Lamb	117	39.80%	75	25.51%	71	24.15%
2,860	96.01%	Lampasas	359	40.61%	182	20.59%	130	14.71%
81	91.01%	La Salle	262	21.34%	291	23.70%	248	20.20%
3,899	97.16%	Lavaca	234	41.86%	103	18.43%	97	17.35%
2,833	95.04%	Lee	338	47.74%	153	21.61%	114	16.10%
3,905	96.87%	Leon	247	55.88%	67	15.16%	69	15.61%
9,482	95.20%	Liberty	804	43.70%	471	25.60%	325	17.66%
4,009	92.18%	Limestone	354	45.74%	163	21.06%	153	19.77%
768	93.43%	Lipscomb	18	36.73%	9	18.37%	7	14.29%
1,731	95.85%	Live Oak	164	51.57%	48	15.09%	57	17.92%
4,810	95.46%	Llano	544	40.57%	245	18.27%	248	18.49%
24	82.76%	Loving	1	11.11%	3	33.33%	2	22.22%
28,165	93.71%	Lubbock	4,481	30.63%	4,577	31.29%	1,801	12.31%

Republican Primary		County	Democratic Primary					
Trump	%		Biden	%	Sanders	%	Bloomberg	%
864	87.18%	Lynn	36	49.32%	14	19.18%	17	23.29%
1,817	91.81%	Madison	69	44.23%	31	19.87%	27	17.31%
22,282	92.03%	Marion	5,384	41.68%	3,086	23.89%	1,687	13.06%
247	96.48%	Martin	8	42.11%	0	0.00%	10	52.63%
2,039	95.95%	Mason	160	51.45%	79	25.40%	32	10.29%
1,482	95.98%	Matagorda	373	59.97%	106	17.04%	83	13.34%
1,002	90.03%	Maverick	16	30.77%	20	38.46%	4	7.69%
1,409	89.18%	McCulloch	86	40.95%	35	16.67%	34	16.19%
4,613	93.02%	McLennan	680	48.33%	295	20.97%	217	15.42%
358	96.50%	McMullen	1,150	14.39%	2,726	34.10%	1,419	17.75%
5,665	96.59%	Medina	881	38.09%	561	24.25%	300	12.97%
478	91.22%	Menard	26	42.62%	18	29.51%	7	11.48%
18,832	92.74%	Midland	1,507	38.50%	994	25.40%	599	15.30%
3,892	93.24%	Milam	428	40.42%	270	25.50%	179	16.90%
1,306	95.47%	Mills	30	29.41%	32	31.37%	19	18.63%
1,186	94.13%	Mitchell	69	51.49%	25	18.66%	21	15.67%
3,837	96.38%	Montague	211	43.96%	112	23.33%	77	16.04%
61,272	95.31%	Montgomery	9,995	39.02%	6,483	25.31%	3,749	14.64%
2,222	93.87%	Moore	119	41.32%	77	26.74%	38	13.19%
1,196	98.03%	Morris	328	52.99%	120	19.39%	109	17.61%
384	97.71%	Motley	8	44.44%	3	16.67%	4	22.22%
7,393	93.69%	Nacogdoches	1,370	40.38%	988	29.12%	404	11.91%
6,753	93.74%	Navarro	891	46.87%	423	22.25%	343	18.04%
2,604	91.63%	Newton	196	55.21%	62	17.46%	67	18.87%
1,954	92.83%	Nolan	171	43.62%	107	27.30%	46	11.73%
16,137	96.38%	Nueces	8,588	37.92%	5,661	24.99%	4,268	18.84%
1,717	95.76%	Ochiltree	33	38.82%	21	24.71%	14	16.47%
600	97.24%	Oldham	16	40.00%	9	22.50%	8	20.00%
13,179	95.87%	Orange	1,163	44.02%	574	21.73%	495	18.74%
4,768	93.99%	Palo Pinto	347	39.08%	205	23.09%	170	19.14%
4,116	97.77%	Panola	493	58.69%	129	15.36%	117	13.93%
23,300	95.79%	Parker	2,064	38.74%	1,348	25.30%	809	15.18%
785	95.97%	Parmer	48	42.11%	31	27.19%	19	16.67%
1,236	93.99%	Pecos	222	25.61%	218	25.14%	219	25.26%
6,912	92.39%	Polk	580	35.41%	334	20.39%	315	19.23%
8,678	95.13%	Potter	1,215	34.64%	1,055	30.07%	520	14.82%
145	96.67%	Presidio	168	16.63%	415	41.09%	137	13.56%
2,379	96.28%	Rains	176	43.35%	71	17.49%	81	19.95%
19,662	95.14%	Randall	1,591	33.62%	1,414	29.88%	623	13.16%
541	89.42%	Reagan	9	33.33%	7	25.93%	8	29.63%
822	96.48%	Real	47	34.81%	39	28.89%	15	11.11%
1,862	98.15%	Red River	273	51.22%	114	21.39%	83	15.57%
90	100.00%	Reeves	328	22.45%	313	21.42%	345	23.61%
1,159	89.22%	Refugio	158	35.35%	67	14.99%	127	28.41%
425	99.07%	Roberts	1	9.09%	0	0.00%	6	54.55%
2,704	96.40%	Robertson	479	52.70%	159	17.49%	160	17.60%
11,910	94.10%	Rockwall	2,407	40.53%	1,507	25.37%	789	13.29%
1,861	95.34%	Runnels	77	46.11%	28	16.77%	18	10.78%
8,240	95.66%	Rusk	1,016	55.25%	282	15.33%	326	17.73%
2,248	97.61%	Sabine	167	50.45%	46	13.90%	64	19.34%
1,465	97.15%	San Augustine	274	57.44%	67	14.05%	91	19.08%
4,129	96.11%	San Jacinto	456	52.66%	169	19.52%	125	14.43%
5,053	94.17%	San Patricio	1,825	43.04%	1,077	25.40%	646	15.24%
1,358	96.52%	San Saba	22	21.15%	10	9.62%	19	18.27%
489	96.07%	Schleicher	45	36.89%	29	23.77%	21	17.21%
2,474	93.43%	Scurry	98	38.28%	77	30.08%	31	12.11%
737	97.10%	Shackelford	27	50.00%	13	24.07%	3	5.56%
4,960	92.92%	Shelby	261	57.24%	80	17.54%	72	15.79%
577	95.37%	Sherman	18	42.86%	10	23.81%	5	11.90%

Republican Primary		County	Democratic Primary					
Trump	%		Biden	%	Sanders	%	Bloomberg	%
26,907	95.59%	Smith	5,378	45.92%	2,636	22.51%	1,827	15.60%
2,193	93.68%	Somervell	94	29.56%	95	29.87%	56	17.61%
46	100.00%	Starr	1,048	13.77%	3,167	41.61%	1,258	16.53%
1,751	97.44%	Stephens	69	47.59%	24	16.55%	18	12.41%
298	96.13%	Sterling	5	27.78%	7	38.89%	1	5.56%
217	98.64%	Stonewall	35	47.30%	6	8.11%	14	18.92%
682	86.77%	Sutton	28	36.36%	20	25.97%	11	14.29%
944	94.78%	Swisher	94	45.63%	24	11.65%	52	25.24%
118,494	94.64%	Tarrant	59,267	38.21%	47,506	30.63%	19,273	12.43%
14,737	92.15%	Taylor	1,939	39.92%	1,388	28.58%	384	7.91%
87	97.75%	Terrell	36	20.93%	23	13.37%	28	16.28%
1,574	86.87%	Terry	75	31.65%	63	26.58%	60	25.32%
394	97.52%	Throckmorton	18	69.23%	4	15.38%	4	15.38%
3,692	95.18%	Titus	436	46.88%	205	22.04%	166	17.85%
14,676	94.42%	Tom Green	1,769	39.28%	1,309	29.06%	559	12.41%
37,832	89.80%	Travis	53,297	23.71%	84,224	37.47%	18,759	8.35%
3,197	94.36%	Trinity	260	45.45%	101	17.66%	117	20.45%
4,147	96.33%	Tyler	300	47.77%	104	16.56%	131	20.86%
5,978	97.14%	Upshur	705	53.01%	254	19.10%	180	13.53%
597	94.02%	Upton	19	20.21%	28	29.79%	23	24.47%
2,334	94.80%	Uvalde	631	24.81%	633	24.89%	593	23.32%
2,484	90.20%	Val Verde	832	26.21%	856	26.97%	674	21.24%
10,147	96.66%	Van Zandt	725	47.70%	340	22.37%	261	17.17%
10,605	93.03%	Victoria	1,763	44.75%	974	24.72%	461	11.70%
5,328	97.16%	Walker	1,164	43.16%	692	25.66%	347	12.87%
4,891	95.04%	Waller	1,014	38.70%	869	33.17%	346	13.21%
1,340	91.28%	Ward	112	28.21%	98	24.69%	111	27.96%
4,898	97.03%	Washington	676	41.86%	323	20.00%	280	17.34%
2,642	90.17%	Webb	5,372	19.93%	9,446	35.05%	5,903	21.90%
6,602	93.00%	Wharton	612	41.32%	364	24.58%	303	20.46%
1,535	96.48%	Wheeler	31	46.27%	14	20.90%	13	19.40%
12,006	93.50%	Wichita	1,707	37.54%	1,300	28.59%	606	13.33%
2,115	90.85%	Wilbarger	120	42.40%	59	20.85%	45	15.90%
162	97.01%	Willacy	682	22.71%	903	30.07%	684	22.78%
40,954	93.08%	Williamson	18,198	29.87%	19,322	31.71%	6,852	11.25%
6,720	95.00%	Wilson	848	36.54%	587	25.29%	429	18.48%
661	93.36%	Winkler	40	46.51%	17	19.77%	13	15.12%
9,773	96.75%	Wise	645	35.19%	491	26.79%	335	18.28%
9,114	95.63%	Wood	753	51.22%	256	17.41%	218	14.83%
957	94.57%	Yoakum	33	37.50%	30	34.09%	16	18.18%
3,540	95.37%	Young	185	43.33%	82	19.20%	61	14.29%
38	100.00%	Zapata	823	26.55%	814	26.26%	677	21.84%
109	99.09%	Zavala	721	26.13%	779	28.23%	706	25.59%

Political Party Organizations

Democratic State Executive Committee

txdemocrats.org

Chairman: Gilberto Hinojosa

P.O. Box 15707, Austin 78761

Republican State Executive Committee

texasgop.org

Chairman: Allen West

P.O. Box 2206, Austin 78768

Libertarian State Executive Committee

lptexas.org

Chair: Whitney Bilyeu

100 Congress Ave., Ste. 2000, Austin 78701

Green State Executive Committee

txgreens.org

Co-Chairs: Alfred Molison and Laura Palmer

P.O. Box 271080, Houston 77277

Texas Primary Elections, 2020

Following are the official results for the contested races in the Democratic and Republican primaries held March 3, 2020. Included are selected federal, statewide, and selected district races. Runoffs were held on July 14.

Some data was omitted for space, including the Texas House of Representatives, judges in the Court of Appeals, judges in the Criminal Court of Appeals, judges in the state Supreme Court, district-level races, races in which only a single candidate was running, select races in the US House of Representatives, and some party propositions.

For full and historical election results, see texasalmanac.com.

Source: Texas Secretary of State.

Democratic Primary

Federal Races

President

Joseph Biden	725,562	34.64%
Bernie Sanders	626,339	29.91%
Michael Bloomberg	300,608	14.35%
Elizabeth Warren	239,237	11.42%
Pete Buttigieg	82,671	3.95%
Amy Klobuchar	43,291	2.07%
Julián Castro	16,688	0.8%
Tom Steyer	13,929	0.67%
Michael Bennet	10,324	0.49%
Tulsi Gabbard	8,688	0.41%
Andrew Yang	6,674	0.32%
Roque "Rocky" De La Fuente	5,469	0.26%
Cory Booker	4,941	0.24%
Marianne Williamson	3,918	0.19%
John K. Delaney	3,280	0.16%
Robby Wells	1,505	0.07%
Deval Patrick	1,304	0.06%
Total vote		2,094,428

U.S. Senate

Mary "M.J." Hegar	417,160	22.31%
Royce West	274,074	14.66%
Cristina Tzintzun Ramirez	246,659	13.19%
Annie "Mamá" Garcia	191,900	10.27%
Amanda K. Edwards	189,624	10.14%
Chris Bell	159,751	8.55%
Sema Hernandez	137,892	7.38%
Michael Cooper	92,463	4.95%
Victor Hugo Harris	59,710	3.19%
Adrian Ocegueda	41,566	2.22%
Jack Daniel Foster Jr.	31,718	1.7%
D.R. Hunter	26,902	1.44%
Total Vote		1,869,419

U.S. House of Representatives

District 3

Lulu Seikaly	28,250	44.55%
Sean McCaffity	27,736	43.73%
Tanner Do	7,433	11.72%
Total Vote		63,419

District 10

Mike Siegel	35,651	43.99%
Pritesh Gandhi	26,818	33.09%
Shannon Hutcheson	18,578	22.92%
Total Vote		81,047

District 12

Lisa Welch	36,750	81.06%
Danny Anderson	8,588	18.94%
Total Vote		45,338

District 13

Gus Trujillo	6,998	42.09%
Greg Sagan	5,773	34.72%
Timothy W. Gassaway	3,854	23.18%
Total Vote		16,625

District 14

Adrienne Bell	26,152	61.83%
Eddie Fisher	4,967	11.74%
Sanjanetta Barnes	4,482	10.6%
Mikal Williams	4,055	9.59%

Robert "Puga" Thomas	2,640	6.24%
Total Vote		42,296

District 22

Sri Preston Kulkarni	34,664	53.07%
Derrick A. Reed	16,126	24.69%
Nyanza Davis Moore	9,449	14.47%
Carmine Petrillo III	5,074	7.77%
Total Vote		65,313

District 23

Gina Ortiz Jones	41,718	66.41%
Efrain V Valdez	6,964	11.09%
Rosalinda "Rosey" Ramos Abuabara	6,896	10.98%
Ricardo R. Madrid	4,518	7.19%
Jaime Escuder	2,725	4.34%
Total Vote		62,821

District 24

Kim Olson	24,442	41.04%
Candace Valenzuela	18,078	30.36%
Jan McDowell	5,965	10.02%
Crystal Fletcher	3,386	5.69%
Richard Fleming	3,010	5.05%
Sam Vega	2,677	4.5%
John Biggan	1,996	3.35%
Total Vote		59,554

District 26

Carol H. Iannuzzi	31,019	55.34%
Mat Pruneda	15,701	28.01%
Neil Durrance	9,329	16.64%
Total Vote		56,049

District 30

Eddie Bernice Johnson	58,804	70.63%
Shenita "Shae" Cleveland	11,358	13.64%
Barbara Mallory Caraway	10,452	12.55%
Hasani Burton	2,638	3.17%
Total Vote		83,252

District 31

Christine Eady Mann	24,145	34.7%
Donna Imam	21,352	30.69%
Tammy Young	9,956	14.31%
Michael Edward Grimes	7,542	10.84%
Eric Hanke	4,117	5.92%
Dan Janjigian	2,471	3.55%
Total Vote		69,583

Statewide Races

Railroad Commissioner

Chrysta Castañeda	598,638	33.85%
Roberto R. "Beto" Alonzo	506,748	28.65%
Kelly Stone	383,453	21.68%
Mark Watson	279,911	15.83%
Total Vote		1,768,750

Supreme Court

Chief Justice

Amy Clark Meachum	1,434,175	80.51%
Jerry Zimmerer	347,186	19.49%
Total Vote		1,781,361

State Senate

District 11

Susan Criss	26,155	53.01%
Margarita Ruiz Johnson	23,188	46.99%
Total Vote		49,343

District 12

Shadi Zitoon	32,831	57.48%
Randy Daniels	24,291	42.52%
Total Vote	57,122	

District 13

Borris L Miles	36,514	55.43%
Melissa Morris	22,840	34.67%
Richard R. Andrews	6,525	9.9%
Total Vote	65,879	

District 19

Xochil Peña Rodriguez	30,821	43.92%
Roland Gutierrez	26,550	37.83%
Freddy Ramirez	12,808	18.25%
Total Vote	70,179	

District 27

Eddie Lucio Jr	31,046	49.76%
Sara Stapleton Barrera	22,221	35.62%
Ruben Cortez	9,122	14.62%
Total Vote	62,389	

District Races
State Board of Education
District 5

Rebecca Bell-Metereau	143,351	68.51%
Letti Bresnahan	65,885	31.49%
Total Vote	209,236	

District 6

Michelle Palmer	52,028	46.8%
Kimberly Mcleod	38,439	34.57%
Debra Kerner	20,712	18.63%
Total Vote	111,179	

District 10

Marsha Burnett-Webster	133,862	84.5%
Stephen Wyman	24,549	15.5%
Total Vote	158,411	

Propositions
1 – Right to healthcare

In Favor	1,923,052	94.51%
Against	111,801	5.49%
Total Vote	2,034,853	

2 – Right to a 21st-century public education

In Favor	1,931,961	94.98%
Against	102,209	5.02%
Total Vote	2,034,170	

3 – Right to clean air, safe water, climate policy

In Favor	1,989,221	97.63%
Against	48,352	2.37%
Total Vote	2,037,573	

4 – Right to economic security

In Favor	1,919,677	94.95%
Against	102,152	5.05%
Total Vote	2,021,829	

Democratic Runoff
Federal Races
U.S. Senate
District 15

Mary "M.J." Hegar	502,516	52.24%
Royce West	459,457	47.76%
Total Vote	961,973	

U.S. House of Representatives
District 3

Lulu Seikaly	20,617	60.72%
Sean McCaffity	13,339	39.28%
Total Vote	33,956	

District 10

Mike Siegel	26,799	54.22%
Pritesh Gandhi	22,629	45.78%
Total Vote	49,428	

District 13

Gus Trujillo	4,988	66.36%
Greg Sagan	2,529	33.64%
Total Vote	7,517	

State Races
Railroad Commissioner

Chrysta Castañeda	579,698	62.02%
Roberto R. "Beto" Alonzo	355,053	37.98%
Total Vote	934,751	

State Senate
District 19

Roland Gutierrez	16,593	52.75%
Xochil Peña Rodriguez	14,864	47.25%
Total Vote	31,457	

District 27

Eddie Lucio Jr.	16,942	53.54%
Sara Stapleton Barrera	14,702	46.46%
Total Vote	31,644	

State Board of Education
District 6

Michelle Palmer	39,757	64.23%
Kimberly McLeod	22,139	35.77%
Total Vote	61,896	

Republican Primary
Federal Races
President

Donald J. Trump	1,898,664	94.13%
Uncommitted	71,803	3.56%
Bill Weld	15,824	0.78%
Joe Walsh	14,772	0.73%
Roque "Rocky" De La Fuente Guerra	7,563	0.37%
Bob Ely	3,582	0.18%
Matthew John Matern	3,512	0.17%
Zoltan G. Istvan	1,447	0.07%
Total vote	2,017,167	

U.S. Senate

John Cornyn	1,470,669	76.04%
Dwayne Stovall	231,104	11.95%
Mark Yancey	124,864	6.46%
John Anthony Castro	86,916	4.49%
Virgil Bierschwale	20,494	1.06%
Total Vote	1,934,047	

U.S. House of Representatives
District 7

Wesley Hunt	28,060	61%
Cindy Siegel	12,497	27.17%
Maria Espinoza	2,716	5.9%
Kyle Preston	1,363	2.96%
Jim Noteware	937	2.04%
Laique Rehman	424	0.92%
Total Vote	45,997	

District 11

August Pfluger	56,093	52.21%
Brandon Batch	16,224	15.1%
Wesley W. Virdell	7,672	7.14%
Jamie Berryhill	7,496	6.98%
J.Ross Lacy	4,785	4.45%
J.D. Faircloth	4,257	3.96%
Casey Gray	4,064	3.78%
Robert Tucker	3,137	2.92%
Ned Luscombe	2,066	1.92%
Gene Barber	1,641	1.53%
Total Vote	107,435	

District 13

Josh Winegarner	39,130	38.97%
Ronny Jackson	20,048	19.96%
Chris Ekstrom	15,387	15.32%
Elaine Hays	7,701	7.67%
Lee Harvey	3,841	3.82%
Vance Snider II	3,506	3.49%

Mark Neese .... 2,984 ....2.97%
Matt McArthur .... 1,816 ....1.81%
Diane Knowlton .... 1,464 ....1.46%
Richard Herman .... 915 ....0.91%
Asusena Reséndiz .... 818 ....0.81%
Jamie Culley .... 779 ....0.78%
Monique Worthy .... 748 ....0.74%
Catherine "I Swear" Carr .... 707 ....0.7%
Jason Foglesong .... 579 ....0.58%
   Total Vote 100,423

District 16
Sam Williams .... 5,097 ....31.26%
Irene Armendariz-Jackson .... 4,147 ....25.43%
Anthony Aguero .... 2,184 ....13.39%
Jaime Arriola Jr .... 2,115 ....12.97%
Blanca Ortiz Trout .... 1,662 ....10.19%
Patrick Hernandez-Cigarruista .... 1,100 ....6.75%
   Total Vote 16,305

District 17
Pete Sessions .... 21,706 ....31.61%
Renée Swann .... 13,072 ....19.04%
George W. Hindman .... 12,405 ....18.07%
Elianor Vessali .... 6,286 ....9.15%
Scott Bland .... 4,947 ....7.2%
Trent Sutton .... 3,662 ....5.33%
Todd Kent .... 2,367 ....3.45%
Kristen Alamo Rowin .... 1,183 ....1.72%
Laurie Godfrey McReynolds .... 1,105 ....1.61%
David Saucedo .... 975 ....1.42%
Jeff Oppenheim .... 483 ....0.7%
Ahmad Adnan .... 477 ....0.69%
   Total Vote.. 68,668

District 22
Troy Nehls .... 29,583 ....40.45%
Kathaleen Wall .... 14,201 ....19.42%
Pierce Bush .... 11,281 ....15.43%
Greg Hill .... 10,315 ....14.1%
Dan Mathews .... 2,165 ....2.96%
Bangar Reddy .... 1,144 ....1.56%
Joe Walz .... 1,039 ....1.42%
Shandon Phan .... 773 ....1.06%
Diana Miller .... 771 ....1.05%
Jon Camarillo .... 718 ....0.98%
Douglas Haggard .... 398 ....0.54%
Howard Steele .... 283 ....0.39%
Matt Hinton .... 274 ....0.37%
Brandon T. Penko .... 96 ....0.13%
Aaron Hermes .... 92 ....0.13%
   Total Vote 73,133

District 24
Beth Van Duyne .... 32,067 ....64.33%
David Fegan .... 10,295 ....20.65%
Desi Maes .... 2,867 ....5.75%
Sunny Chaparala .... 2,808 ....5.63%
Jeron Liverman .... 1,809 ....3.63%
   Total Vote 49,846

District 31
John Carter .... 53,070 ....82.28%
Mike Williams .... 5,560 ....8.62%
Christopher Wall .... 3,155 ....4.89%
Abhiram Garapati .... 2,717 ....4.21%
   Total Vote.. 64,502

District 32
Genevieve Collins .... 22,908 ....52.88%
Floyd Mclendon .... 14,699 ....33.93%
Jon Hollis .... 1,945 ....4.49%
Jeff Tokar .... 1,892 ....4.37%
Mark Sackett... 1,880 ....4.34%
   Total Vote.. 43,324

Statewide Race
Railroad Commissioner
James "Jim" Wright................................ 991,593 ....55.29%
Ryan Sitton .... 801,904 ....44.71%
   Total Vote... 1,793,497

District Races
State Senate
District 13
Milinda Morris....................................... 5,363 ....65.03%
William J. Booher .... 2,884 ....34.97%
   Total Vote 8,247

State Board of Education
District 5
Robert Morrow .... 54,460 ....40%
Lani Popp .... 46,276 ....33.99%
Inga Cotton... 35,425 ....26.02%
   Total Vote 136,161

District 14
Sue Melton-Malone .... 108,389 ....61.09%
Maria Y. Berry .... 69,048 ....38.91%
   Total Vote 177,437

Propositions
1 – No restriction on prayer in public schools
In Favor .... 1,768,450 ....88.62%
Against .... 227,105 ....11.38%
   Total Vote.. 1,995,555

2 – No restrictions on the right to bear arms
In Favor .... 1,700,394 ....85.38%
Against .... 291,190 ....14.62%
   Total Vote... 1,991,584

3 – Ban taxpayer-funded lobbying
In Favor .... 1,862,609 ....94.3%
Against .... 112,642 ....5.7%
   Total Vote 1,975,251

4 – Build wall along the southern border
In Favor .... 1,861,692 ....93.86%
Against .... 121,880 ....6.14%
   Total Vote 1,983,572

Republican Runoff
Federal Races
U.S. House of Representatives
District 13
Ronny Jackson .... 36,684 ....55.57%
Josh Winegarner .... 29,327 ....44.43%
   Total Vote... 66,011

District 15
Monica De La Cruz-Hernandez............... 7,423 ....75.95%
Ryan Krause .... 2,350 ....24.05%
   Total Vote... 9,773

District 16
Irene Armendariz-Jackson...................... 5,170 ....65.43%
Sam Williams .... 2,731 ....34.57%
   Total Vote... 7,901

District 17
Ipete Sessions .... 18,524 ....53.51%
Renée Swann... 16,096 ....46.49%
   Total Vote 34,620

District 18
Wendell Champion .... 4,000 ....71.81%
Irobert M. Cadena .... 1,570 ....28.19%
   Total Vote 5,570

District Races
State Board of Education
District 5
Lani Popp .... 55,990 ....77.96%
Robert Morrow .... 15,827 ....22.04%
   Total Vote 71,817

Government

87TH LEGISLATURE REPORT

HISTORICAL DOCUMENTS

CHIEF OFFICIALS, 1691–2021

STATE, LOCAL, & FEDERAL GOVERNMENT

The city hall in Strawn, in Palo Pinto County.
Photo by Nicholas Henderson, CC 2/Flickr

North Richland Hills Senator Kelly Hancock (far end of the table) chairs the Senate Business and Commerce Committee. Senate Media Photo.

Report on the 87th Legislature

By Carolyn Barta

In short, the 87th session of the Texas Legislature was unlike any other, with the regular session addressing unparalleled challenges, and the aftermath casting Texas into the national spotlight.

Lawmakers convened for the biennial five-month session on January 12, 2021, under a unique set of circumstances: in the midst of a global coronavirus pandemic that created health and economic issues, and less than a week after protesters stormed the nation's Capitol over a disputed presidential election, raising security and political concerns. Add to that, social and racial unrest across the nation.

Then a brutal winter snowstorm in February left more than 4.8 million Texans without electricity and water for days during a power blackout, resulting in an estimated at least 200 deaths, billions of dollars in damage to homes, farmers and businesses, and the exposure of a vulnerable electrical grid and regulatory system.

The political backdrop clearly favored Republicans, who maintained majorities in both the Texas House (83 to 67) and Senate (18 to 13) and whose major voice was Gov. Greg Abbott, gearing up to run for a third four-year term in 2022.

After quickly moving to repair regulatory problems affecting the power grid, the GOP-controlled Legislature pursued a social-issue agenda that would appeal to the most conservative voters who dominated the 2020 electorate. President Donald Trump easily carried the state by 5.6 percentage points, and the Democrats' highly touted effort to pick up nine seats to regain a Texas House majority failed miserably. Democrats' successes were confined largely to urban county elections.

Both state chambers had Republican leaders: Lt. Gov. Dan Patrick presided again over the Senate, and Dade Phelan, a four-term Beaumont Republican, was elected speaker by House members, succeeding one-term speaker Dennis Bonnen.

Emboldened by their 2020 electoral success, Republicans pushed through permitless carry of handguns, a near-total ban on abortion, penalties for cities that cut police budgets, a proposal targeting the teaching of critical race theory and a Patrick priority to require pro sports teams with state government contracts to play the national anthem at games. Gov. Abbott called it "the most conservative session in a generation."

The session solidified Texas' position as a "mega-red" state and a bedrock of the conservative movement in the Republican Party, with former President Trump continuing to cast a long shadow over Texas lawmakers and the state's electorate.

Still, it wasn't all easy sailing for the Republicans. One of Gov. Abbott's top priorities was a "voter integrity" bill. It would ban 24-hour and drive-through voting, bar unsolicited distribution of mail-in ballots, empower partisan poll watchers, impose uniform early-voting hours statewide and prohibit polling places from opening before 1 p.m. on Sundays, which critics said targeted Black voters who participated in "souls to the polls" voter drives on Sunday mornings.

Democrats individually walked out of the House just hours before adjournment on May 31 until a quorum of 100 (two-thirds of the 150-member body) was no longer present, thus thwarting the bill's passage — only the fourth time in history that the quorum-busting tactic was used.

Gov. Abbott retaliated by vetoing a portion of the budget that would leave some 2,100 Capitol staffers unpaid for two years but could be reversed in a special session if legislators finished their work to his satisfaction.

Despite the pandemic and partisan tensions, lawmakers passed the only required bill — the state budget taking effect September 1, 2021. Cobbling together the $248.6 billion no-tax-increase budget proved less onerous than expected. Consumers returned to the marketplace as people were vaccinated against COVID-19 and the state began to open up, and financial forecasts improved during the session.

Abbott, to the delight of his base but against some opposition, lifted mask mandates and declared the state to be reopened to 100% capacity as of March 10, 2021.

Lawmakers said the budget kept 2019 promises to better fund public schools and cut taxes, though it would spend about 5% less than the previous budget. Critics called it too lean to keep up with the state's fast-growing needs, as some 700,000 new residents were expected over the next two years.

After the winter storm, everything took a back seat to fixing the power grid. Reforms included required weatherization and emergency communication, and a restructuring of the Energy Reliability Council of Texas (ERCOT) board of directors and the Public Utility Commission (PUC). New laws would create power outage alerts so Texans could prepare for looming blackouts, impose more control by elected officials over the ERCOT board and expand the PUC from three to five members.

Gov. Abbott declared that "everything that needed to be done was done to fix the power grid." However, days after the session's close, facing temperatures in the high 90s, ERCOT called on consumers to cut back on energy use to avoid summer power outages.

Media attention focused on the session's so-called "red meat" conservative bills, including:

Abortion: The "heartbeat" bill banned abortions after a fetal heartbeat is detected, which could be as early as six weeks, before a woman might know she is pregnant.

Guns: Texans 21 and older who can legally possess a handgun would no longer need a state-issued license, a background check or pass a safety course to carry a handgun, openly or concealed. Permitless carry passed despite a 2019 mass shooting targeting Hispanics in an El Paso Walmart that killed 23 persons.

Border security: The budget included more than $1 billion for border security. After the session, Gov. Abbott declared that Texas would build the border wall that Trump began and diverted $250 million from state prisons to begin funding design and construction.

Defunding the police: A ban on defunding the police in the ten largest cities was approved, over the objection of local officials who said the state overstepped into areas of local control.

Critical race theory: Teaching "critical race theory" in public schools was restricted, which opponents feared would stifle teachers from adding context to teaching racial history, social justice and current events.

Among issues that failed:

- Expansion of health insurance coverage under the Affordable Care Act. Texas ranks No. 1 in the percent of children (12.7%) who lack health insurance. Expansion of Medicaid would have brought health insurance to around a million Texans without a tax.

- Air-conditioning in state-run jails and prisons. One in five of the state's 100 lockups have no air-conditioning and nearly half are only partially cooled.

- Virtual education funding. Texas schools are funded largely based on in-person attendance, and a bill to fund remote instruction failed, leaving online instruction uncertain in many districts.

Other bills passed:

- Booze-to-go. Texans can buy beer and wine starting at 10 a.m. on Sundays, and Texas businesses can continue to sell alcohol to go, which was allowed during the pandemic.

- Broadband. A State Broadband Development Office will award grants, low-interest loans and other incentives to build out broadband access. Nearly a million Texans, approximately 3.4% of the state's population, lack broadband access at home, including 90% in rural areas.

- Criminal justice/policing: Reforms in response to George Floyd's death by Minneapolis police included banning police chokeholds and requiring police to stop colleagues from misusing deadly force.

COVID-19 affected the session in many ways, from health protocols to reduced public interaction, such as the number of Texans willing to testify in committee hearings. A bill to rein in the governor's power to restrict business operations during a pandemic died, but the Legislature responded otherwise to COVID-19: assuring families access to nursing homes during health emergencies, providing a liability shield for businesses and protecting churches from closure by public officials.

COVID-19 also delayed U.S. Census results. Detailed population numbers needed to redraw legislative and congressional districts were unavailable in the regular session, requiring a special session in the fall.

Before that, Gov. Abbott called a 30-day special session beginning July 8, 2021, to address the failed voter bill and other issues, including an overhaul of bail-setting procedures, limiting access to school sports teams for transgender students, abortion-inducing drugs, social media censorship and border security.

Democrats again stymied passage of the voter bill when 50-plus legislators bolted the state on a chartered flight for Washington, D.C., where they lobbied for passage of federal voting legislation that would supersede state law. Several tested positive for COVID-19 while there. The exodus wasn't expected to permanently kill the Texas "elections integrity" bill, but it put Texas at the center of a national struggle on voting rights following the disputed presidential election. Abbott promised to keep calling special sessions until the Democrats capitulated.

The fall redistricting session would include the addition of two congressional seats, reflecting population growth, to Texas' 36-member delegation of 23 Rs, 13 Ds. New faces were assured as a result of several GOP retirements, but Republicans were poised to grow their strength, also controlling the redrawing of legislative districts required by new census numbers.

Carolyn Barta is a former political writer for The Dallas Morning News and retired journalism professor at Southern Methodist University. ☆

Declaration of Independence of the Republic of Texas

The Declaration of Independence of the Republic of Texas was adopted in general convention at Washington-on-the-Brazos, March 2, 1836.

Richard Ellis, president of the convention, appointed a committee of five to write the declaration for submission to the convention. However, there is much evidence that George C. Childress, one of the members, wrote the document with little or no help from the other members. Childress is therefore generally accepted as the author.

The text of the declaration is followed by the names of the signers of the document. The names are presented here as the signers actually signed the document.

Our thanks to the staff of the Texas State Archives for furnishing a photocopy of the signatures.

UNANIMOUS

Declaration of Independence,

BY THE
DELEGATES OF THE PEOPLE OF TEXAS,
IN GENERAL CONVENTION,
AT THE TOWN OF WASHINGTON,
ON THE SECOND DAY OF MARCH, 1836.

WHEN A GOVERNMENT has ceased to protect the lives, liberty and property of the people from whom its legitimate powers are derived, and for the advancement of whose happiness it was instituted; and so far from being a guarantee for the enjoyment of those inestimable and inalienable rights, becomes an instrument in the hands of evil rulers for their oppression; when the Federal Republican Constitution of their country, which they have sworn to support, no longer has a substantial existence, and the whole nature of their government has been forcibly changed without their consent, from a restricted federative republic, composed of sovereign states, to a consolidated central military despotism, in which every interest is disregarded but that of the army and the priesthood — both the eternal enemies of civil liberty, and the ever-ready minions of power, and the usual instruments of tyrants; When long after the spirit of the Constitution has departed, moderation is at length, so far lost, by those in power that even the semblance of freedom is removed, and the forms, themselves, of the constitution discontinued; and so far from their petitions and remonstrances being regarded, the agents who bear them are thrown into dungeons; and mercenary armies sent forth to force a new government upon them at the point of the bayonet. When in consequence of such acts of malfeasance and abdication, on the part of the government, anarchy prevails, and civil society is dissolved into its original elements: In such a crisis, the first law of nature, the right of self-preservation — the inherent and inalienable right of the people to appeal to first principles and take their political affairs into their own hands in extreme cases — enjoins it as a right towards themselves and a sacred obligation to their posterity, to abolish such government and create another in its stead, calculated to rescue them from impending dangers, and to secure their future welfare and happiness.

Nations, as well as individuals, are amenable for their acts to the public opinion of mankind. A statement of a part of our grievances is, therefore, submitted to an impartial world, in justification of the hazardous but unavoidable step now taken of severing our political connection with the Mexican people, and assuming an independent attitude among the nations of the earth.

The Mexican government, by its colonization laws, invited and induced the Anglo-American population of Texas to colonize its wilderness under the pledged faith of a written constitution, that they should continue to enjoy that constitutional liberty and republican government to which they had been habituated in the land of their birth, the United States of America. In this expectation they have been cruelly disappointed, inasmuch as the Mexican nation has acquiesced in the late changes made in the government by General Antonio Lopez de Santa Anna, who, having overturned the constitution of his country, now offers us the cruel alternative either to abandon our homes, acquired by so many privations, or submit to the most intolerable of all tyranny, the combined despotism of the sword and the priesthood.

It has sacrificed our welfare to the state of Coahuila, by which our interests have been continually depressed, through a jealous and partial course of legislation carried on at a far distant seat of government, by a hostile majority, in an unknown tongue; and this too, notwithstanding we have petitioned in the humblest terms, for the establishment of a separate state government, and have, in accordance with the provisions of the national constitution, presented the general Congress, a republican constitution which was without just cause contemptuously rejected.

It incarcerated in a dungeon, for a long time, one of our citizens, for no other cause but a zealous endeavor to procure the acceptance of our constitution and the establishment of a state government.

It has failed and refused to secure on a firm basis, the right of trial by jury; that palladium of civil liberty, and only safe guarantee for the life, liberty, and property of the citizen.

It has failed to establish any public system of education, although possessed of almost boundless resources (the public domain) and, although, it is an axiom, in political science, that unless a people are educated and enlightened it is idle to expect the continuance of civil liberty, or the capacity for self-government.

It has suffered the military commandants stationed among us to exercise arbitrary acts of oppression and tyranny; thus trampling upon the most sacred rights of the citizen and rendering the military superior to the civil power.

It has dissolved by force of arms, the state Congress of Coahuila and Texas, and obliged our representatives to fly for their lives from the seat of government; thus depriving us of the fundamental political right of representation.

It has demanded the surrender of a number of our citizens, and ordered military detachments to seize and carry them into the Interior for trial; in contempt of the civil authorities, and in defiance of the laws and constitution.

It has made piratical attacks upon our commerce; by commissioning foreign desperadoes, and authorizing them to seize our vessels, and convey the property of our citizens to far distant ports of confiscation.

It denies us the right of worshipping the Almighty according to the dictates of our own consciences, by the support of a national religion calculated to promote the temporal interests of its human functionaries rather than the glory of the true and living God.

It has demanded us to deliver up our arms; which are essential to our defense, the rightful property of freemen, and formidable only to tyrannical governments.

It has invaded our country, both by sea and by land, with intent to lay waste our territory and drive us from our homes; and has now a large mercenary army advancing to carry on against us a war of extermination.

It has, through its emissaries, incited the merciless savage, with the tomahawk and scalping knife, to massacre the inhabitants of our defenseless frontiers.

It hath been, during the whole time of our connection with it, the contemptible sport and victim of successive military revolutions and hath continually exhibited every characteristic of a weak, corrupt and tyrannical government.

These, and other grievances, were patiently borne by the people of Texas until they reached that point at which forbearance ceases to be a virtue. We then took up arms in defense of the national constitution. We appealed to our Mexican brethren for assistance. Our appeal has been made in vain. Though months have elapsed, no sympathetic response has yet been heard from the Interior. We are, therefore, forced to the melancholy conclusion that the Mexican people have acquiesced in the destruction of their liberty, and the substitution therefor of a military government — that they are unfit to be free and incapable of self-government.

The necessity of self-preservation, therefore, now decrees our eternal political separation.

We, therefore, the delegates, with plenary powers, of the people of Texas, in solemn convention assembled, appealing to a candid world for the necessities of our condition, do hereby resolve and DECLARE that our political connection with the Mexican nation has forever ended; and that the people of Texas do now constitute a FREE, SOVEREIGN and INDEPENDENT REPUBLIC, and are fully invested with all the rights and attributes which properly belong to the independent nations; and, conscious of the rectitude of our intentions, we fearlessly and confidently commit the issue to the decision of the Supreme Arbiter of the destinies of nations.

RICHARD ELLIS, president of the convention and Delegate from Red River.

Charles B Stewart

Tho⁵ Barnett
John S.D. Byrom

Fran^co Ruiz
J. Antonio Navarro
Jesse B. Badgett
Wm D. Lacey
William Menefee
Jn° Fisher
Mathew Caldwell
William Mottley
Lorenzo de Zavala
Stephen H. Everitt
Geo W Smyth

Elijah Stapp
Claiborne West

W^m B Scates

M.B. Menard
A.B. Hardin
J.W. Bunton
Tho⁵ J. Gasley
R. M. Coleman
Sterling C. Robertson
Benj Briggs Goodrich
G.W. Barnett
James G. Swisher
Jesse Grimes
S. Rhoads Fisher
John W. Moore
John W. Bower
Saml A Maverick from Bejar
Sam P. Carson
A. Briscoe
J.B. Woods
Jas Collinsworth
Edwin Waller
Asa Brigham
Geo. C. Childress
Bailey Hardeman
Rob. Potter

Thomas Jefferson Rusk
Chas. S. Taylor
John S. Roberts

Robert Hamilton
Collin McKinney
Albert H Latimer
James Power

Sam Houston
David Thomas

Edwd Conrad
Martin Parmer
Edwin O. LeGrand
Stephen W. Blount
Ja⁵ Gaines
Wm Clark, Jr
Sydney O. Penington
Wm Carrol Crawford
Jn° Turner

Test. H.S. Kimble, Secretary

Documents Concerning the Annexation of Texas to the United States

For an overview of the subject, please see these discussions: The New Handbook of Texas, Texas State Historical Association, Austin, 1996; Vol. 1, pages 192–193. On the web: **https://tshaonline.org/handbook/online/articles/mga02**. Also see, the Texas State Library and Archives website: **www.tsl.state.tx.us/ref/abouttx/annexation/index.html** and the Texas Almanac website: **https://texasalmanac.com/topics/history/timeline/annexation-and-statehood**.

Joint Resolution for Annexing Texas to the United States

Resolved

by the Senate and House of Representatives of the United States of America in Congress assembled,

That Congress doth consent that the territory properly included within and rightfully belonging to the Republic of Texas, may be erected into a new State to be called the State of Texas, with a republican form of government adopted by the people of said Republic, by deputies in convention assembled, with the consent of the existing Government in order that the same may by admitted as one of the States of this Union.

2. And be it further resolved, That the foregoing consent of Congress is given upon the following conditions, to wit:

First, said state to be formed, subject to the adjustment by this government of all questions of boundary that may arise with other government,

—and the Constitution thereof, with the proper evidence of its adoption by the people of said Republic of Texas, shall be transmitted to the President of the United States, to be laid before Congress for its final action on, or before the first day of January, one thousand eight hundred and forty-six.

Second, said state when admitted into the Union, after ceding to the United States all public edifices, fortifications, barracks, ports and harbors, navy and navy yards, docks, magazines and armaments, and all other means pertaining to the public defense, belonging to the said Republic of Texas, shall retain funds, debts, taxes and dues of every kind which may belong to, or be due and owing to the said Republic;

and shall also retain all the vacant and unappropriated lands lying within its limits, to be applied to the payment of the debts and liabilities of said Republic of Texas, and the residue of said lands, after discharging said debts and liabilities, to be disposed of as said State may direct; but in no event are said debts and liabilities to become a charge upon the Government of the United States.

Third — New States of convenient size not exceeding four in number, in addition to said State of Texas and having sufficient population, may, hereafter by the consent of said State, be formed out of the territory

thereof, which shall be entitled to admission under the provisions of the Federal Constitution;

and such states as may be formed out of the territory lying south of thirty-six degrees thirty minutes north latitude, commonly known as the Missouri Compromise Line, shall be admitted into the Union, with or without slavery, as the people of each State, asking admission shall desire;

and in such State or States as shall be formed out of said territory, north of said Missouri Compromise Line, slavery, or involuntary servitude (except for crime) shall be prohibited.

3. And be it further resolved, That if the President of the United States shall in his judgment and discretion deem it most advisable, instead of proceeding to submit the foregoing resolution of the Republic of Texas, as an overture on the part of the United States for admission, to negotiate with the Republic; then,

Be it resolved, That a State, to be formed out of the present Republic of Texas, with suitable extent and boundaries, and with two representatives in Congress, until the next appointment of representation, shall be admitted into the Union, by virtue of this act, on an equal footing with the existing States, as soon as the terms and conditions of such admission, and the cession of the remaining Texian territory to the United States shall be agreed upon by the governments of Texas and the United States:

And that the sum of one hundred thousand dollars be, and the same is hereby, appropriated to defray the expenses of missions and negotiations, to agree upon the terms of said admission and cession, either by treaty to be submitted to the Senate, or by articles to be submitted to the two houses of Congress, as the President may direct.

Approved, March 1, 1845.

Source: Peters, Richard, ed., The Public Statutes at Large of the United States of America, v.5, pp. 797–798, Boston, Chas. C. Little and Jas. Brown, 1850.

Twenty-Ninth Congress: Session 1 — Resolutions
[No. 1.] Joint Resolution for the Admission of the State of Texas into the Union

Whereas

the Congress of the United States, by a joint resolution approved March the first, eighteen hundred and forty-five, did consent that the territory properly included within, and rightfully belonging to, the Republic of Texas, might be erected into a new State, to be called _The State of Texas,_ with a republican form of government, to be adopted by the people of said republic, by deputies in convention assembled, with the consent of the existing government, in order that the same might be admitted as one of the States of the Union;

which consent of Congress was given upon certain conditions specified in the first and second sections of said joint resolution;

and whereas the people of the said Republic of Texas, by deputies in convention assembled, with the consent of the existing government, did adopt a constitution, and erect a new State with a republican form of government, and, in the name of the people of Texas, and by their authority, did ordain and declare that they assented to and accepted the proposals, conditions, and guaranties contained in said first and second sections of said resolution:

and whereas the said constitution, with the proper evidence of its adoption by the people of the Republic of Texas, has been transmitted to the President of the United States and laid before Congress, in conformity to the provisions of said joint resolution:

Therefore—

Resolved by the Senate and House of Representatives of the United States of America in Congress assembled, That the State of Texas shall be one, and is hereby declared to be one, of the United States of America, and admitted into the Union on an equal footing with the original States in all respects whatever.

Sec. 2. And be it further resolved, That until the representatives in Congress shall be apportioned according to an actual enumeration of the inhabitants of the United States, the State of Texas shall be entitled to choose two representatives.

Approved, December 29, 1845.

Source: Minot, Geo., ed., Statutes at Large and Treaties of the United States of America from Dec. 1, 1845, to March 3, 1851, V. IX, p. 108

Constitution of Texas

The complete official text of the Constitution of Texas, including the original document, which was adopted Feb. 15, 1876, plus all amendments approved since then, is available on the State of Texas website:

statutes.capitol.texas.gov

An index and search features at that website allow exploration of the 17 Articles and subsequent Sections of the Constitution, along with other Texas Statutes.

For election information, upcoming elections, amendment or other election votes, and voter registration information, go to:

sos.state.tx.us/elections/index.shtml

According to the **Legislative Reference Library of Texas**, "The Texas Constitution is one of the longest in the nation and is still growing. As of 2019 (the 86th Legislature), the Texas Legislature has proposed a total of 690 amendments. Of these, 507 have been adopted, and 180 have been defeated by Texas voters. Thus, the Texas Constitution has been amended 507 times since its adoption in 1876."

Amending the Texas Constitution requires a two-thirds favorable vote by both the Texas House of Representatives and the Texas Senate, followed by a majority vote of approval by voters in a statewide election.

Prior to 1973, amendments to the constitution could not be submitted by a special session of the Legislature. But the constitution was amended in 1972 to allow submission of amendments if the special session was opened to the subject by the governor.

Constitutional amendments are not subject to a gubernatorial veto. Once submitted, voters have the final decision on whether to change the constitution as proposed.

The table on the next page lists the total number of amendments submitted to voters by the Texas Legislature, how many were adopted, the year in which the Legislature approved them for submission to voters; e.g., the 70th Legislature in 1987 approved 28 bills proposing amendments to be submitted to voters, of which 20 were adopted.

For more information on bills and constitutional amendments, see the Legislative Reference Library of Texas website:

lrl.texas.gov

Amendments, 2019

The following 10 amendments were submitted to voters by the 86th Legislature in an election on **Nov. 5, 2019**.

HJR 4: The constitutional amendment providing for the creation of the flood infrastructure fund to assist in the financing of drainage, flood mitigation, and flood control projects. **Adopted.**

Votes for: 1,538,726; Votes against: 437,384

HJR 12: The constitutional amendment authorizing the legislature to increase by $3 billion the maximum bond amount authorized for the Cancer Prevention and Research Institute of Texas. **Adopted.**

Votes for: 1,259,398; Votes against: 77,939

HJR 34: The constitutional amendment authorizing the legislature to provide for a temporary exemption from ad valorem taxation of a portion of the appraised value of certain property damaged by a disaster. **Adopted.**

Votes for: 1,679,049; Votes against: 294,235

HJR 38: The constitutional amendment prohibiting the imposition of an individual income tax, including a tax on an individual's share of partnership and unincorporated association income. **Adopted.**

Votes for: 1,477,373; Votes against: 509,547

HJR 72: The constitutional amendment permitting a person to hold more than one office as a municipal judge at the same time. **Defeated.**

Votes for: 685,827; Votes against: 1,298,866

HJR 95: The constitutional amendment authorizing the legislature to exempt from ad valorem taxation precious metal held in a precious metal depository located in this state. **Adopted.**

Votes for: 982,881; Votes against: 932,885

HJR 151: The constitutional amendment allowing increase distributions to the available school fund. **Adopted.**

Votes for: 1,459,578; Votes against: 509,590

SJR 24: The constitutional amendment dedicating the revenue received from the existing state sales and use taxes that are imposed on sporting goods to the Texas Parks and Wildlife Department and the Texas Historical Commission to protect Texas' natural areas, water quality, and history by acquiring, managing,and improving state and local parks and historic sites while not increasing the rate of the state sales and use taxes. **Adopted.**

Votes for: 1,745,353; Votes against: 237,656

SJR 32: The constitutional amendment to allow the transfer of a law enforcement animal to a qualified caretaker in certain circumstances. **Adopted.**

Votes for: 1,858,876; Votes against: 123,648

SJR 79: The constitutional amendment providing for the issuance of additional general obligation bonds by the Texas Water Development Board in an amount not to exceed $200 million to provide financial assistance for the development of certain projects in economically distressed areas. **Adopted.**

Votes for: 1,294,936; Votes against: 677,619

Amendments, 2021

The following 8 amendments will be submitted to voters by the 87th Legislature in an election on Nov. 2, 2021.

HJR 99: Proposing a constitutional amendment authorizing a county to finance the development or redevelopment of transportation or infrastructure in unproductive, underdeveloped, or blighted areas in the county; authorizing the issuance of bonds and notes.

HJR 125: Proposing a constitutional amendment to allow the surviving spouse of a person who is disabled to receive a limitation on the school district ad valorem taxes on the spouse's residence homestead if the spouse is 55 years of age or older at the time of the person's death.

HJR 143: Proposing a constitutional amendment authorizing the professional sports team charitable foundations of organizations sanctioned by certain professional associations to conduct charitable raffles at rodeo venues.

HJR 165: Proposing a constitutional amendment providing additional powers to the State Commission on Judicial Conduct with respect to candidates for judicial office.

SJR 19: Proposing a constitutional amendment establishing a right for residents of certain facilities to designate an essential caregiver for in-person visitation.

SJR 27: Proposing a constitutional amendment to prohibit this state or a political subdivision of this state from prohibiting or limiting religious services of religious organizations.

SJR 35: Proposing a constitutional amendment authorizing the legislature to provide for an exemption from ad valorem taxation of all or part of the market value of the residence homestead of the surviving spouse of a member of the armed services of the United States who is killed or fatally injured in the line of duty.

SJR 47: Proposing a constitutional amendment changing the eligibility requirements for certain judicial offices.

Constitutional Amendments Submitted to Voters by the Texas Legislature
(Proposed/Adopted)

Year	No.	Year	No.	Year	No.
1879	1/1	1931	9/9	1979	12/9
1881	2/0	1933	12/4	1981	10/8
1883	5/5	1935	13/10	1982	3/3
1887	6/0	1937	7/6	1983	19/16
1889	2/2	1939	4/3	1985	17/17
1891	5/5	1941	5/1	1986	1/1
1893	2/2	1943	3/3	1987	28/20
1895	2/1	1945	8/7	1989	21/19
1897	5/1	1947	9/9	1990	1/1
1899	1/0	1949	10/2	1991	15/12
1901	1/1	1951	7/3	1993	19/14
1903	3/3	1953	11/11	1995	14/11
1905	3/2	1955	9/9	1997	15/13
1907	9/1	1957	12/10	1999	17/13
1909	4/4	1959	4/4	2001	20/20
1911	5/4	1961	14/10	2003	22/22
1913	8/0	1963	7/4	2005	9/7
1915	7/0	1965	27/20	2007	17/17
1917	3/3	1967	20/13	2009	11/11
1919	13/3	1969	16/9	2011	10/7
1921	5/1	1971	18/12	2013	10/10
1923	2/1	1973	9/6	2015	7/7
1925	4/4	1975	12/6	2017	7/7
1927	8/4	1977	15/11	2019	10/9
1929	7/7	1978	1/1	2021	8/NA

Source: Legislative Reference Library of Texas

Early Leaders of Texas

The presidents of the Republic of Texas and the state's first Governor, from top left: **David G. Burnet**, provisional president; **Sam Houston**, second and fourth presidents; **Mirabeau B. Lamar**, third president; **Anson Jones**, the Republic's last president; and **J. Pinckney Henderson**, the Lone Star State's first governor.

Texas' Chief Governmental Officials

On this and the following pages are lists of the principal administrative officials who have served the Republic and State of Texas with dates of their tenures of office. In a few instances, there are disputes as to the exact dates of tenures. Dates listed here are those that appear the most authentic.

★ ★ ★ ★ ★ ★ ★

Governors and Presidents

Spanish Royal Governors

(*Some authorities would include Texas under administrations of several earlier Spanish governors. The late Dr. C.E. Castañeda, Latin-American librarian of The University of Texas and authority on the history of Texas and the Southwest, would include the following four: Francisco de Garay, 1523–1526; Pánfilo de Narváez, 1526–28; Nuño de Guzmán, 1528–1530; and Hernando de Soto, 1538–1543.*)

Domingo Terán de los Rios..............................1691–1692
Gregorio de Salinas Varona..............................1692–1697
Francisco Cuerbo y Valdés 1698–1702
Mathías de Aguirre 1703–1705
Martín de Alarcón 1705–1708
Simón Padilla y Córdova 1708–1712
Pedro Fermin de Echevers y Subisa 1712–1714

Juan Valdéz..1714–1716
Martín de Alarcón 1716–1719
José de Azlor y Virto de Vera, Marqués de
   San Miguel de Aguayo.................................1719–1722
Fernando Pérez de Almazán..............................1722–1727
Melchor de Mediavilla y Azcona.........................1727–1731
Juan Antonio Bustillo y Ceballos........................1731–1734
Manuel de Sandoval 1734–1736
Carlos Benites Franquis de Lugo.........................1736–1737
Joseph Fernández de Jáuregui y Urrutia 1737–1737
Prudencio de Orobio y Basterra..........................1737–1741
Tomás Felipe Winthuisen (or Winthuysen) 1741–1743
Justo Boneo y Morales 1743–1744
Francisco García Larios 1744–1748
Pedro del Barrio Junco y Espriella.......................1748–1750
Jacinto de Barrios y Jáuregui............................1751–1759
Angel de Martos y Navarrete 1759–1767
Hugo Oconór 1767–1770
Juan María Vicencio, Barón de Ripperdá...............1770–1778
Domingo Cabello y Robles 1778–1786
Rafael Martínez Pacheco 1787–1790
Manuel Muñoz..1790–1799
Juan Bautista de Elguezábal 1799–1805
Antonio Cordero y Bustamante 1805–1808
Manuel María de Salcedo 1808–1813
   (*Mexico's War of Independence 1810–1812 created governmental instability.*)

J. W. Baines	Jan. 18, 1883–Jan. 21, 1887
John M. Moore	Jan. 21, 1887–Jan. 22, 1891
George W. Smith	Jan. 22, 1891–Jan. 17, 1895
Allison Mayfield	Jan. 17, 1895–Jan. 5, 1897
J. W. Madden	Jan. 5, 1897–Jan. 18, 1899
D. H. Hardy	Jan. 18, 1899–Jan. 19, 1901
John G. Tod	Jan. 19, 1901–Jan., 1903
J. R. Curl	Jan. 1903–April 1905
O. K. Shannon	April 1905–Jan. 1907
L. T. Dashiel	Jan. 1907–Feb. 1908
W. R. Davie	Feb. 1908–Jan. 1909
W. B. Townsend	Jan. 1909–Jan. 1911
C. C. McDonald	Jan. 1911–Dec. 1912
J. T. Bowman	Dec. 1912–Jan. 1913
John L. Wortham	Jan. 1913–June 1913
F. C. Weinert	June 1913–Nov. 1914
D. A. Gregg	Nov. 1914–Jan. 1915
John G. McKay	Jan. 1915–Dec. 1916
C. J. Bartlett	Dec. 1916–Nov. 1917
George F. Howard	Nov. 1917–Nov. 1920
C. D. Mims	Nov. 1920–Jan. 1921
S. L. Staples	Jan. 1921–Aug. 1924
J. D. Strickland	Sept. 1924–Jan. 1, 1925
Henry Hutchings	Jan. 1, 1925–Jan. 20, 1925
Mrs. Emma G. Meharg	Jan. 20, 1925–Jan. 1927
Mrs. Jane Y. McCallum	Jan. 1927–Jan. 1933
W. W. Heath	Jan. 1933–Jan. 1935
Gerald C. Mann	Jan. 1935–Aug. 31, 1935
R. B. Stanford	Aug. 31, 1935–Aug. 25, 1936
B. P. Matocha	Aug. 25, 1936–Jan. 18, 1937
Edward Clark	Jan. 18, 1937–Jan. 1939
Tom L. Beauchamp	Jan. 1939–Oct. 1939
M. O. Flowers	Oct. 26, 1939–Feb. 25, 1941
William J. Lawson	Feb. 25, 1941–Jan. 1943
Sidney Latham	Jan. 1943–Feb. 1945
Claude Isbell	Feb. 1945–Jan. 1947
Paul H. Brown	Jan. 1947–Jan. 19, 1949
Ben Ramsey	Jan. 19, 1949–Feb. 9, 1950
John Ben Shepperd	Feb. 9, 1950–April 30, 1952
Jack Ross	April 30, 1952–Jan. 9, 1953
Howard A. Carney	Jan. 9, 1953–Apr. 30, 1954
C. E. Fulgham	May 1, 1954–Feb. 15, 1955
Al Muldrow	Feb. 16, 1955–Nov. 1, 1955
Tom Reavley	Nov. 1, 1955–Jan. 16, 1957
Zollie Steakley	Jan. 16, 1957–Jan. 2, 1962
P. Frank Lake	Jan. 2, 1962–Jan. 15, 1963
Crawford C. Martin	Jan. 15, 1963–Mar. 12, 1966
John L. Hill	Mar. 12, 1966–Jan. 22, 1968
Roy Barrera	Mar. 7, 1968–Jan. 23, 1969
Martin Dies Jr.	Jan. 23, 1969–Sept. 1, 1971
Robert D. (Bob) Bullock	Sept. 1, 1971–Jan. 2, 1973
V. Larry Teaver Jr.	Jan. 2, 1973–Jan. 19, 1973
Mark W. White Jr.	Jan. 19, 1973–Oct. 27,1977
Steven C. Oaks	Oct. 27, 1977–Jan. 16, 1979
George W. Strake Jr.	Jan. 16, 1979–Oct. 6, 1981
David A. Dean	Oct. 22, 1981–Jan. 18, 1983
John Fainter	Jan. 18, 1983–July 31, 1984
Myra A. McDaniel	Sept. 6, 1984–Jan. 26, 1987
Jack Rains	Jan. 26, 1987–June 15, 1989
George Bayoud Jr.	June 19, 1989–Jan. 15, 1991
John Hannah Jr.	Jan. 17, 1991–Mar. 11, 1994
Ronald Kirk	April 4, 1994–Jan. 10, 1995
Antonio O. "Tony" Garza Jr.	Jan. 18, 1995–Dec. 2, 1997
Alberto R. Gonzales	Dec. 2, 1997–Jan. 10, 1999
Elton Bomer	Jan. 11, 1999–Dec. 31, 2000
Henry Cuellar	Jan. 2, 2001–Oct. 5, 2001
Gwyn Shea	Jan. 2, 2002–Aug. 4, 2003
Geoff Connor	Sept. 26, 2003–Jan. 1, 2005
J. Roger Williams	Jan. 1, 2005–July 1, 2007
Phil Wilson	July 1, 2007–July 6, 2008

The Capitals of Texas

The capitals of the six nations that have ruled Texas have been:

Spain: Valladolid (before 1551) and Madrid

France: Paris

Mexico: Mexico City, D.F.

Republic Of Texas: San Felipe de Austin, Washington-on-the-Brazos, Harrisburg, Galveston Island, Velasco, Columbia, Houston, and Austin

United States: Washington, D.C.

Confederate States Of America: Montgomery, Alabama and Richmond, Virginia

Learn more at TexasAlmanac.com

Esperanza (Hope) Andrade	July 23, 2008–Nov. 23,2012
John T. Steen Jr.	Nov. 27, 2012–Jan. 7, 2014
Nandita Berry	Jan. 7, 2014–Jan 21, 2015
Carlos H. Cascos	Jan 21, 2015–Jan 5, 2017
Rolando B. Pablos	Jan 5, 2017–Dec. 17, 2018
David Whitley	Dec. 17, 2018–May 27, 2019
(Senate refused to confirm)	
Ruth Ruggero Hughs	Aug. 19, 2019–May 31, 2021
(Resigned)	
Vacant	May 31, 2021

★ ★ ★ ★ ★ ★ ★

Attorneys General of the Republic

David Thomas and Peter W. Grayson	Mar. 2–Oct. 22, 1836
J. Pinckney Henderson, Peter W. Grayson, John Birdsall, and A.S. Thurston	1836–1838
J.C. Watrous	Dec. 1838–June 1, 1840
Joseph Webb and F.A. Morris	1840–1841
George W. Terrell, Ebenezer Allen	1841–1844
Ebenezer Allen	1844–1846

State Attorneys General

Volney E. Howard (D)	Feb. 21, 1846–May 7, 1846
John W. Harris (D)	May 7, 1846–Oct. 31, 1849
Henry P. Brewster	Oct. 31, 1849–Jan. 15, 1850
A. J. Hamilton	Jan. 15, 1850–Aug. 5, 1850

(The first few attorneys general held office by appointment of the governor. The office was made elective in 1850 by constitutional amendment. Ebenezer Allen was the first elected attorney general.)

Ebenezer Allen	Aug. 5, 1850–Aug. 2, 1852
Thomas J. Jennings	Aug. 2, 1852–Aug. 4, 1856
James Willie	Aug. 4, 1856–Aug. 2, 1858
Malcolm D. Graham (D)	Aug. 2, 1858–Aug. 6, 1860
George M. Flournoy (D)	Aug. 6, 1860–Jan. 15, 1862
N. G. Shelley (D)	Feb. 3, 1862–Aug. 1, 1864
B. E. Tarver (D)	Aug. 1, 1864–Dec. 11, 1865
Wm. Alexander (Unionist)	Dec. 11, 1865–June 25, 1866
W. M. Walton (D)	June 25, 1866–Aug. 27, 1867
Wm. Alexander (R)	Aug. 27, 1867–Nov. 5, 1867
Ezekiel B. Turner (I)	Nov. 5, 1867–July 11, 1870
Wm. Alexander (R)	July 11, 1870–Jan. 27, 1874
George Clark (D)	Jan. 27, 1874–Apr. 25, 1876
H. H. Boone (D)	Apr. 25, 1876–Nov. 5, 1878
George McCormick	Nov. 5, 1878–Nov. 2, 1880
J. H. McLeary (D)	Nov. 2, 1880–Nov. 7, 1882
John D. Templeton (D)	Nov. 7, 1882–Nov. 2, 1886
James S. Hogg (D)	Nov. 2, 1886–Nov. 4, 1890
C. A. Culberson (D)	Nov. 4, 1890–Nov. 6, 1894

M. M. Crane (D) ....Nov. 6, 1894–Nov. 8, 1898
Thomas S. Smith (D). ....Nov. 8, 1898–Mar. 15,1901
C. K. Bell (D) ....Mar. 20, 1901–Jan. 1904
R. V. Davidson (D) ....Jan. 1904–Dec. 31, 1909
Jewel P. Lightfoot (D) ....Jan. 1, 1910–Aug. 31, 1912
James D. Walthall (D).....................Sept. 1, 1912–Jan. 1, 1913
B. F. Looney (D)..............................Jan. 1, 1913–Jan., 1919
C. M. Cureton (D) ....Jan. 1919–Dec. 1921
W. A. Keeling (D)............................Dec. 1921–Jan. 1925
Dan Moody (D)...............................Jan. 1925–Jan. 1927
Claude Pollard (D)...........................Jan. 1927–Sept. 1929
R. L. Bobbitt (D) ....Sept. 1929–Jan. 1931
   (Appointed)
James V. Allred (D)..........................Jan. 1931–Jan. 1935
William McCraw (D)........................Jan. 1935–Jan. 1939
Gerald C. Mann (D) ....Jan. 1939–Jan. 1944
   (Resigned)
Grover Sellers (D)............................Jan. 1944–Jan. 1947
Price Daniel (D)...............................Jan. 1947–Jan. 1953
John Ben Shepperd (D).....................Jan. 1953–Jan. 1, 1957
Will Wilson (D)...........................Jan. 1, 1957–Jan. 15, 1963
Waggoner Carr (D) ....Jan. 15, 1963–Jan. 1, 1967
Crawford C. Martin (D)..............Jan. 1, 1967–Dec. 29, 1972
John Hill (D) ....Jan. 1, 1973–Jan. 16, 1979
Mark White (D)........................Jan. 16, 1979–Jan. 18, 1983
Jim Mattox (D)..........................Jan. 18, 1983–Jan. 15, 1991
Dan Morales (D)........................Jan. 15, 1991–Jan. 13, 1999
John Cornyn (R) ....Jan. 13, 1999–Dec. 2, 2002
Greg Abbott (R)..........................Dec. 2, 2002–Jan. 20, 2015
Ken Paxton (R) ....Jan. 20, 2015–present

★ ★ ★ ★ ★ ★ ★

Treasurers of the Republic

Asa Brigham... 1838–1840
James W. Simmons... 1840–1841
Asa Brigham...1841–1844
Moses Johnson...1844–1846

State Treasurers

James H. Raymond.......................Feb. 24, 1846–Aug. 2, 1858
C.H. Randolph ....Aug. 2, 1858–June 1865
   (Randolph fled to Mexico upon collapse of Confederacy. No
   exact date is available for his departure from office or for Harris'
   succession to the post. It is believed Harris took office Oct. 2, 1865.)
Samuel Harris............................Oct. 2, 1865–June 25, 1866
W.M. Royston.......................... June 25, 1866–Sept. 1, 1867
John T. Allan .... Sept. 1, 1867–Jan. 1869
George W. Honey ....Jan. 1869–Jan. 1874
   (Honey was removed from office for a short period in 1872 and B.
   Graham served in his place.)
B. Graham *(short term)* ....beginning May 27, 1872
A. J. Dorn ....Jan. 1874–Jan. 1879
F. R. Lubbock..................................Jan. 1879–Jan. 1891
W. B. Wortham................................Jan. 1891–Jan. 1899
John W. Robbins ....Jan. 1899–Jan. 1907
Sam Sparks ....Jan. 1907–Jan. 1912
J. M. Edwards..................................Jan. 1912–Jan. 1919
John W. Baker ....Jan. 1919–Jan. 1921
G. N. Holton...............................July 1921–Nov. 21, 1921
C. V. Terrell.............................Nov. 21, 1921–Aug. 15, 1924
S. L. Staples ....Aug. 16, 1924–Jan. 15, 1925
W. Gregory Hatcher.......................Jan. 16, 1925–Jan. 1, 1931
Charley Lockhart ....Jan. 1, 1931–Oct. 25, 1941
Jesse James...............................Oct. 25, 1941–Sept. 29, 1977
Warren G. Harding ....Oct. 7, 1977–Jan. 3, 1983
Ann Richards..............................Jan. 3, 1983–Jan. 2, 1991
Kay Bailey Hutchison.......................Jan. 2, 1991–June 1993
Martha Whitehead............................June 1993–Aug. 1996

The office of treasurer was eliminated by constitutional amendment in an election Nov. 7, 1995, effective the last day of August 1996.

Railroad Commissioners

After the first three names in the following list, each commissioner's name is followed by a surname in parentheses. The name in parentheses is the name of the commissioner whom that commissioner succeeded.

John H. Reagan..........................June 10, 1891–Jan. 20, 1903
L. L. Foster..............................June 10, 1891–April 30, 1895
W. P. McLean..........................June 10, 1891–Nov. 20, 1894
L. J. Storey (McLean)...................Nov. 21, 1894–Mar. 28,1909
N. A. Stedman (Foster)................... May 1, 1895–Jan. 4, 1897
Allison Mayfield (Stedman).............Jan. 5, 1897–Jan. 23, 1923
O. B. Colquitt (Reagan)..................Jan. 21, 1903–Jan. 17, 1911
William D. Williams (Storey) .... April 28, 1909–Oct. 1, 1916
John L. Wortham (Colquitt)..............Jan. 21, 1911–Jan. 1, 1913
Earle B. Mayfield (Wortham) ....Jan. 2, 1913–Mar. 1, 1923
Charles Hurdleston (Williams) ....Oct. 10, 1916–Dec. 31,1918
Clarence Gilmore (Hurdleston)........... Jan. 1, 1919–Jan. 1, 1929
N. A. Nabors (A. Mayfield) .... Mar. 1, 1923–Jan. 18, 1925
William Splawn (E. Mayfield)...........Mar. 1, 1923–Aug. 1, 1924
C. V. Terrell (Splawn) ....Aug. 15, 1924–Jan. 1, 1939
Lon A. Smith (Nabors).................Jan. 29, 1925–Jan. 1, 1941
Pat M. Neff (Gilmore).....................Jan. 1, 1929–Jan. 1, 1933
Ernest O. Thompson (Neff)...............Jan. 1, 1933–Jan. 8, 1965
G. A. (Jerry) Sadler (Terrell) ....Jan. 1, 1939–Jan. 1, 1943
Olin Culberson (Smith) ....Jan. 1, 1941–June 22, 1961
Beauford Jester (Sadler)................Jan. 1, 1943–Jan. 21, 1947
William J. Murray Jr. (Jester) ....Jan. 21, 1947–Apr. 10, 1963
Ben Ramsey (Culberson) ....Sept. 18, 1961–Dec. 31, 1976
Jim C. Langdon (Murray) ....May 28, 1963–Dec. 31, 1977
Byron Tunnell (Thompson)...........Jan. 11, 1965–Sept. 15, 1973
Mack Wallace (Tunnell)..............Sept. 18, 1973–Sept. 22, 1987
Jon Newton (Ramsey) ....Jan. 10, 1977–Jan. 4, 1979
John H. Poerner (Langdon) ....Jan. 2, 1978–Jan. 1, 1981
James E. Nugent (Newton) ....Jan. 4, 1979–Jan. 3,1995
Buddy Temple (Poerner)..................Jan. 2, 1981–Mar. 2, 1986
Clark Jobe (Temple).......................Mar. 3, 1986–Jan. 5, 1987
John Sharp (Jobe) ....Jan. 6, 1987–Jan. 2, 1991
Kent Hance (Wallace) .... Sept. 23, 1987–Jan. 2, 1991
Robert Krueger (Hance)..................Jan. 3, 1991–Jan. 22, 1993
   (Krueger resigned when Gov. Ann Richards appointed him interim
   U.S. senator on the resignation of Sen. Lloyd Bentsen.)
Lena Guerrero (Sharp).................Jan. 23, 1991–Sept. 25, 1992
James Wallace (Guerrero) ....Oct. 2, 1992–Jan. 4, 1993
Barry Williamson (Wallace)...............Jan. 5, 1993–Jan. 4, 1999
Mary Scott Nabers (Krueger) ....Feb. 9, 1993–Dec. 9, 1994
Carole K. Rylander (Nabers) ....Dec. 10, 1994–Jan. 4, 1999
Charles Matthews (Nugent)............Jan. 3, 1995–Jan. 31, 2005
Antonio Garza (Williamson)...........Jan. 4, 1999–Nov. 18, 2002
Michael Williams (Rylander) Jan.4, 1999–Mar. 31, 2011
Victor G. Carrillo (Garza) ....Feb. 19, 2003–Jan. 3, 2011
Elizabeth A. Jones (Matthews) .... Feb. 2, 2005–Feb. 28, 2012
David Porter (Carrillo) ....Jan. 5, 2011–Jan. 2, 2017
Barry T. Smitherman (Williams)..........July 8, 2011–Jan. 2, 2015
Buddy Garcia (Jones) .... April 16, 2012–Dec. 7, 2012
   (Appointed by Gov. Perry.)
Ryan Sitton (Smitherman)................ Jan 5, 2015–Jan. 4, 2021
Christi Craddick (Garcia) ....Dec. 17, 2012–present
Wayne Christian (Porter)..................... Jan 9, 2017–present
Jim Wright (Sitton)............................Jan. 4, 2021–present

★ ★ ★ ★ ★ ★ ★

Comptrollers of Public Accounts
For the Republic

John H. Money...........................Dec. 30, 1835–Jan. 17, 1836
H. C. Hudson............................Jan. 17, 1836–Oct. 22, 1836
Elisha M. Pease..............................June 1837–Dec. 1837
F. R. Lubbock.................................. Dec. 1837–Jan. 1839
Jas. W. Simmons.......................Jan. 15, 1839–Sept. 30, 1840
Jas. B. Shaw ....Sept. 30, 1840–Dec. 24, 1841
F. R. Lubbock............................Dec. 24, 1841–Jan. 1, 1842
Jas. B. Shaw ....Jan. 1, 1842–Jan. 1, 1846

State Comptrollers of Public Accounts

Jas. B. Shaw ....Feb. 24, 1846–Aug. 2, 1858
Clement R. Johns........................Aug. 2, 1858–Aug. 1, 1864
Willis L. Robards........................Aug. 1, 1864–Oct. 12, 1865
Albert H. Latimer ....Oct. 12, 1865–Mar. 27, 1866
Robert H. Taylor .... Mar. 27, 1866–June 25, 1866
Willis L. Robards.....................June 25, 1866–Aug. 27, 1867
Morgan C. Hamilton ....Aug. 27, 1867–Jan. 8, 1870
A. Bledsoe ....Jan. 8, 1870–Jan. 20, 1874
Stephen H. Darden.....................Jan. 20, 1874–Nov. 2, 1880
W. M. Brown ....Nov. 2, 1880–Jan. 16, 1883
W. J. Swain .... Jan. 16, 1883–Jan. 18, 1887
John D. McCall........................ Jan. 18, 1887–Jan. 15, 1895
R. W. Finley............................Jan. 15, 1895–Jan. 15, 1901
R. M. Love .... Jan. 15, 1901–Jan. 1, 1903
J. W. Stephen...........................Jan. 1903–Jan. 1911
W. P. Lane..............................Jan. 1911–Jan. 1915
H. B. Terrell............................Jan. 1915–Jan. 1920
M. L. Wiginton.........................Jan. 1920–Jan. 1921
Lon A. Smith ....Jan. 1921–Jan. 1925
S. H. Terrell............................Jan. 1925–Jan. 1931
Geo. H. Sheppard ....Jan., 1931–Jan. 17, 1949
Robert S. Calvert.......................Jan. 17, 1949–Jan., 1975
Robert D. (Bob) Bullock ....Jan. 1975–Jan. 3, 1991
John Sharp.................................Jan. 3, 1991–Jan. 2, 1999
Carole Keeton Strayhorn ....Jan. 2, 1999–Jan. 1, 2007
Susan Combs..............................Jan. 1, 2007–Jan. 1, 2015
Glenn Hegar................................. Jan. 2, 2015–present

★ ★ ★ ★ ★ ★ ★

U.S. Senators from Texas

U.S. Senators were selected by the legislatures of the states until the U.S. Constitution was amended in 1913 to require popular elections. In Texas, the first Senator chosen by the voters in a general election was Charles A. Culberson in 1916. Because of political pressures, however, the rules of the Democratic Party of Texas were changed in 1904 to require that all candidates for office stand before voters in the primary. Consequently, Texas' Senators faced voters in 1906, 1910 and 1912 before the U.S. Constitution was changed.

Following is the succession of Texas representatives in the United States Senate since the annexation of Texas to the Union in 1845:

Houston Succession

Sam Houston (I) ....Feb. 21, 1846–Mar. 4, 1859
John Hemphill (D)......................Mar. 4, 1859–July 11, 1861
Louis T. Wigfall and W. S. Oldham took their seats in the Confederate Senate, Nov. 16, 1861, and served until the Confederacy collapsed. After that event, the State Legislature on Aug. 21, 1866, elected David G. Burnet and Oran M. Roberts to the U.S. Senate,

anticipating immediate readmission to the Union, but they were not allowed to take their seats.
Morgan C. Hamilton (R) ....Feb. 22, 1870–Mar. 3, 1877
Richard Coke (D) ....Mar. 4, 1877–Mar. 3, 1895
Horace Chilton (D) ....Mar. 3, 1895–Mar. 3, 1901
Joseph W. Bailey (D) .... Mar. 3, 1901–Jan. 8, 1913
(Resigned.)
Rienzi Melville Johnston (D)..............Jan. 8, 1913–Feb. 3, 1913
(Appointed to fill vacancy.)
Morris Sheppard (D)......................Feb. 13, 1913–Apr. 9, 1941
(Died in office)
Andrew J. Houston (D) ....June 2–26, 1941
(Appointed to fill vacancy; died in office.)
W. Lee O'Daniel (D) ....Aug. 4, 1941–Jan. 3, 1949
Lyndon B. Johnson (D) ....Jan. 3, 1949–Jan. 20, 1961
(Resigned to become U.S. vice president.)
William A. Blakley (D)..................Jan. 20, 1961–June 15, 1961
(Appointed to fill vacancy.)
John G. Tower (R).......................June 15, 1961–Jan. 21, 1985
Phil Gramm (R)..........................Jan. 21, 1985–Dec. 2, 2002
John Cornyn (R) .... Dec. 2, 2002–present

Rusk Succession

Thomas J. Rusk (D) .... Feb 21, 1846–July 29, 1857
(Died in office.)
J. Pinckney Henderson (D).............. Nov. 9, 1857–June 4, 1858
(Died in office.)
Matthias Ward (D)......................Sept. 29, 1858–Dec. 5, 1859
(Appointed to fill vacancy.)
Louis T. Wigfall (D).....................Dec. 5, 1859–Mar. 23, 1861
(Succession was broken by secession. See note above under Houston Succession.)
James W. Flanagan (R)..................Feb. 22, 1870–Mar. 3, 1875
Samuel B. Maxey (D).....................Mar. 3, 1875–Mar. 3, 1887
John H. Reagan (D) ....Mar. 3, 1887–June 10, 1891
(Resigned to head Texas Railroad Commission.)
Horace Chilton (D) ....Dec. 7, 1891–Mar. 30,1892
(Appointed to fill vacancy.)
Roger Q. Mills (D) .... Mar. 30, 1892–Mar. 3, 1899
Charles A. Culberson (D)...............Mar. 3, 1899–Mar. 4, 1923
Earle B. Mayfield (D) ....Mar. 4, 1923–Mar. 4, 1929
Tom Connally (D) ....Mar. 4, 1929–Jan. 3, 1953
Price Daniel (D)..........................Jan. 3, 1953–Jan. 15, 1957
(Resigned to become governor.)
William A. Blakley (D)..................Jan. 15, 1957–Apr. 27, 1957
(Appointed to fill vacancy.)
Ralph W. Yarborough (D) ....Apr. 27, 1957–Jan. 12, 1971
Lloyd Bentsen (D) ....Jan. 12, 1971–Jan. 20, 1993
(Resigned to become U.S. Secretary of Treasury.)
Robert Krueger (D) ....Jan. 20, 1993–June 14, 1993
(Appointed to fill vacancy.)
Kay Bailey Hutchison (R).............. June 14, 1993–Jan. 20, 2013
Ted Cruz (R)..................................Jan. 20, 2013–present

★ ★ ★ ★ ★ ★ ★

General Land Office Commissioners
For the Republic

John P. Borden .... Aug. 23, 1837–Dec. 12, 1840
H. W. Raglin .... Dec. 12, 1840–Jan. 4, 1841
Thomas William Ward .... Jan. 4, 1841–Mar. 20, 1848
(Part of term after annexation.)

State Land Commissioners

George W. Smyth ....Mar. 20, 1848–Aug. 4, 1851
Stephen Crosby .... Aug. 4, 1851–Mar. 1, 1858
Francis M. White.......................Mar. 1, 1858–Mar. 1, 1862
Stephen Crosby ....Mar. 1, 1862–Sept. 1, 1865

The Texas Capitol cupola. Photo by Justtraveling.com.

Francis M. White	Sept. 1, 1865–Aug. 7, 1866
Stephen Crosby	Aug. 7, 1866–Aug. 27, 1867
Joseph Spence	Aug. 27, 1867–Jan. 19, 1870
Jacob Kuechler	Jan. 19, 1870–Jan. 20, 1874
J. J. Groos	Jan. 20, 1874–June 15, 1878
W. C. Walsh	July 30, 1878–Jan. 10, 1887
R. M. Hall	Jan. 10, 1887–Jan. 16, 1891
W. L. McGaughey	Jan. 16, 1891–Jan. 26, 1895
A. J. Baker	Jan. 26, 1895–Jan. 16, 1899
George W. Finger	Jan. 16, 1899–May 4, 1899
Charles Rogan	May 11, 1899–Jan. 10, 1903
John J. Terrell	Jan. 10, 1903–Jan. 11, 1909
J. T. Robison	Jan, 1909–Sept. 11, 1929
J. H. Walker	Sept. 11, 1929–Jan., 1937
William H. McDonald	Jan 1937–Jan. 1939
Bascom Giles	Jan. 1939–Jan. 5, 1955
J. Earl Rudder	Jan. 5, 1955–Feb. 1, 1958
Bill Allcorn	Feb. 1, 1958–Jan. 1, 1961
Jerry Sadler	Jan. 1, 1961–Jan. 1, 1971
Bob Armstrong	Jan. 1, 1971–Jan. 1, 1983
Garry Mauro	Jan. 1, 1983–Jan. 7, 1999
David Dewhurst	Jan. 7, 1999–Jan. 3, 2003
Jerry Patterson	Jan. 3, 2003–Jan. 2, 2015
George P. Bush	Jan. 2, 2015–present

★ ★ ★ ★ ★ ★ ★

Speakers of the House
For the Republic

Speaker	Term	Congress
Ira Ingram	1836–37	1st
Branch Tanner Archer	1837	2nd
Joseph Rowe	1838	2nd
John M. Hansford	1838–39	3rd
David Spangler Kaufman	1840–41	4th, 5th
Kenneth L. Anderson	1841–42	6th
Nicholas H. Darnell	1842–43	7th
Richardson A. Scurry	1843–44	8th
John M. Lewis	1844–45	9th

State Speakers of the House

Speaker, Residence	Term	Leg.
William E. Crump (D), Bellville	1846	1st
John Brown (D), Brownsboro	1846	1st
Edward T. Branch (D), Liberty	1846	1st
William H. Bourland (D), Paris	1846	1st
Stephen W. Perkins (D), Columbia	1846	1st
James W. Henderson (D), Houston	1847–48	2nd
Charles G. Keenan (D), Huntsville	1849–51	3rd
David C. Dickson (D), Anderson	1851–53	4th
Hardin R. Runnels (D), Boston	1853–55	5th
Hamilton P. Bee (D), Laredo	1855–57	6th
William S. Taylor (D), Larissa	1857–58	7th
Matt F. Locke (D), Lafayette	1858–59	7th
Marion DeKalb Taylor (D), Jefferson	1859–61	8th
Constantine W. Buckley (D), Richmond	1861	9th
Nicholas H. Darnell (D), Dallas	1861–62	9th
Constantine W. Buckley (D), Richmond	1863	9th
Marion DeKalb Taylor (D), Jefferson	1863–65	10th
Nathaniel M. Burford (Unionist), Dallas	1866	11th
(Vacant under Congressional Reconstruction and military administration, 1867-1870)		
Ira H. Evans (R), Corpus Christi	1870–71	12th
William H. Sinclair (R), Galveston	1871–73	12th
Marion DeKalb Taylor (D), Jefferson	1873–74	13th
Guy M. Bryan (D), Galveston	1874–76	14th
Thomas R. Bonner (D), Tyler	1876–79	15th
John H. Cochran (D), Dallas	1879–81	16th
George R. Reeves (D), Pottsboro	1881–83	17th
Charles R. Gibson (D), Waxahachie	1883–85	18th
Lafayette L. Foster (D), Groesbeck	1885–87	19th
George C. Pendleton (D), Belton	1887–89	20th
Frank P. Alexander (D), Greenville	1889–91	21st
Robert T. Milner (D), Henderson	1891–93	22nd
John H. Cochran (D), Dallas	1893–95	23rd
Thomas Slater Smith (D), Hillsboro	1895–97	24th

Speaker, Residence	Term	Leg.
L. Travis Dashiell (D), Jewett	1897–99	25th
J. S. Sherrill (D), Greenville	1899–1901	26th
Robert E. Prince (D), Corsicana	1901–03	27th
Pat M. Neff (D), Waco	1903–05	28th
Francis W. Seabury (D), Rio Grande City	1905–07	29th
Thomas B. Love (D), Lancaster	1907–09	30th
Austin M. Kennedy (D), Waco	1909	31st
(Resigned during 31st session)		
John W. Marshall (D), Whitesboro	1909–11	31st
Sam Rayburn (D), Bonham	1911–13	32nd
Chester H. Terrell (D), San Antonio	1913–15	33rd
John W. Woods (D), Rotan	1915–17	34th
Franklin O. Fuller (D), Coldspring	1917–19	35th
R. Ewing Thomason (D), El Paso	1919–21	36th
Charles G. Thomas (D), Lewisville	1921–23	37th
Richard E. Seagler (D), Palestine	1923–25	38th
R. Lee Satterwhite (D), Amarillo	1925–27	39th
Robert L. Bobbitt (D), Laredo	1927–29	40th
W. S. Barron (D), Bryan	1929–31	41st
Fred H. Minor (D), Denton	1931–33	42nd
Coke R. Stevenson (D), Junction	1933–37	43rd–44th
Robert W. Calvert (D), Hillsboro	1937–39	45th
R. Emmett Morse (D), Houston	1939–41	46th
Homer L. Leonard (D), McAllen	1941–43	47th
Price Daniel (D), Liberty	1943–45	48th
Claud H. Gilmer (D), Rocksprings	1945–47	49th
William O. Reed (D), Dallas	1947–49	50th
Durwood Manford (D), Smiley	1949–51	51st
Reuben Senterfitt (D), San Saba	1951–55	52nd–53rd
Jim T. Lindsey (D), Texarkana	1955–57	54th
Waggoner Carr (D), Lubbock	1957–61	55th–56th
James A. Turman (D), Gober	1961–63	57th
Byron M. Tunnell (D), Tyler	1963–65	58th
Ben Barnes (D), De Leon	1965–69	59th–60th
Gus F. Mutscher (D), Brenham	1969–72	61st–62nd
(Resigned during 62nd session)		
Rayford Price (D), Palestine	1972–73	62nd
Price Daniel Jr. (D), Liberty	1973–75	63rd
Bill Clayton (D), Springlake	1975–83	64th–67th
Gib Lewis (D), Fort Worth	1983–93	68th–72nd
Pete Laney (D), Hale Center	1993–2003	73rd–77th
Tom Craddick (R), Midland	2003–09	78th–80th
Joe Straus (R), San Antonio	2009–19	81st–85th
Dennis Bonnen (R), Angleton	2019–21	86th
Dade Phelan (R), Beaumont	2021– present	87th

★ ★ ★ ★ ★ ★ ★

Chief Justice of the Supreme Court Republic of Texas

James Collinsworth.....................Dec. 16, 1836–July 23, 1838
John Birdsall ....Nov. 19–Dec. 12, 1838
(Senate refused to confirm)
Thomas J. Rusk..........................Dec. 12, 1838–Dec. 5, 1840
John Hemphill ....Dec. 5, 1840–Dec. 29, 1845

Under Constitutions of 1845 and 1861

John Hemphill ....Mar. 2, 1846–Oct. 10, 1858
Royall T. Wheeler ....Oct. 11, 1858–April 1864
Oran M. Roberts......................Nov. 1, 1864–June 30, 1866

Under Constitution of 1866 (Presidential Reconstruction)

George F. Moore ....Aug. 16, 1866–Sept. 10, 1867
(Removed under Congressional Reconstruction by military authorities who appointed members of the next court.)

Under Constitution of 1866 (Congressional Reconstruction)

Amos Morrill............................Sept. 10, 1867–July 5, 1870

Under Constitution of 1869

Lemuel D. Evans ....July 5, 1870–Aug. 31, 1873
Wesley Ogden............................Aug. 31, 1873–Jan. 29, 1874
Oran M. Roberts.......................Jan. 29, 1874–Apr. 18, 1876

Under Constitution of 1876

Oran M. Roberts.........................Apr. 18, 1876–Oct. 1, 1878
George F. Moore ....Nov. 5, 1878–Nov. 1, 1881
Robert S. Gould ....Nov. 1, 1881–Dec. 23, 1882
Asa H. Willie ....Dec. 23, 1882–Mar. 3, 1888
John W. Stayton ....Mar. 3, 1888–July 5, 1894
Reuben R. Gaines ....July 10, 1894–Jan. 5, 1911
Thomas J. Brown.......................Jan. 7, 1911–May 26, 1915
Nelson Phillips ....June 1, 1915–Nov. 16, 1921
C. M. Cureton............................Dec. 2, 1921–Apr. 8, 1940
Hortense Sparks Ward.................Jan. 8, 1925–May 23, 1925
(Mrs. Ward headed a special Supreme Court to hear one case in 1925.)
W. F. Moore ....Apr. 17, 1940–Jan. 1, 1941
James P. Alexander.......................Jan. 1, 1941–Jan. 1, 1948
J. E. Hickman.............................Jan. 5, 1948–Jan. 3, 1961
Robert W. Calvert......................Jan. 3, 1961–Oct. 4, 1972
Joe R. Greenhill ....Oct. 4, 1972–Oct. 25, 1982
Jack Pope ....Nov. 29, 1982–Jan. 5, 1985
John L. Hill Jr.............................Jan. 5, 1985–Jan. 4, 1988
Thomas R. Phillips......................Jan. 4, 1988–Sept. 3 2004
Wallace B. Jefferson....................Sept. 14, 2004–Oct. 1, 2013
Nathan L. Hecht...............................Oct. 1, 2013–present

★ ★ ★ ★ ★ ★ ★

Presiding Judges, Court of Appeals (1876–1891) and Court of Criminal Appeals (1891–present)

Mat D. Ector..............................May 6, 1876–Oct. 29, 1879
John P. White............................Nov. 9, 1879–Apr. 26, 1892
James M. Hurt............................May 4, 1892–Dec. 31, 1898
W. L. Davidson ....Jan. 2, 1899–June 27, 1913
A. C. Prendergast.......................June 27, 1913–Dec. 31, 1916
W. L. Davidson ....Jan. 1, 1917–Jan. 25, 1921
Wright C. Morrow.......................Feb. 8, 1921–Oct. 16, 1939
Frank Lee Hawkins ....Oct. 16, 1939–Jan. 2, 1951
Harry N. Graves.........................Jan. 2, 1951–Dec. 31, 1954
W. A. Morrison............................Jan. 1, 1955–Jan. 2, 1961
Kenneth K. Woodley.....................Jan. 3, 1961–Jan. 4, 1965
W. T. McDonald..........................Jan. 4, 1965–June 25, 1966
W. A. Morrison...........................June 25, 1966–Jan. 1, 1967
Kenneth K. Woodley.....................Jan. 1, 1967–Jan. 1, 1971

John F. Onion Jr............................ Jan. 1, 1971–Jan. 1, 1989
Michael J. McCormick..................... Jan. 1, 1989–Jan. 1, 2001
Sharon Keller................................ Jan. 1, 2001–present

★ ★ ★ ★ ★ ★ ★

Administrators of Public Education, Superintendents of Public Instruction

Pryor Lea.............................. Nov. 10, 1866–Sept. 12, 1867
Edwin M. Wheelock.................... Sept. 12, 1867–May 6, 1871
Jacob C. DeGress......................... May 6, 1871–Jan. 20, 1874
O. H. Hollingsworth .... Jan. 20, 1874–May 6, 1884
B. M. Baker .... May 6, 1884–Jan. 18, 1887
O. H. Cooper .... Jan 18, 1887–Sept. 1, 1890
H. C. Pritchett.......................... Sept. 1, 1890–Sept. 15, 1891
J. M. Carlisle........................... Sept. 15, 1891–Jan. 10, 1899
J. S. Kendall............................. Jan. 10, 1899–July 2, 1901
Arthur Lefevre .... July 2, 1901–Jan. 12, 1905
R. B. Cousins........................... Jan. 12, 1905–Jan. 1, 1910
F. M. Bralley .... Jan. 1, 1910–Sept. 1, 1913
W. F. Doughty .... Sept. 1, 1913–Jan. 1, 1919
Annie Webb Blanton..................... Jan. 1, 1919–Jan. 16, 1923
S. M. N. Marrs......................... Jan. 16, 1923–April 28, 1932
C. N. Shaver .... April 28, 1932–Oct. 1, 1932
L. W. Rogers .... Oct. 1, 1932–Jan. 16, 1933
L. A. Woods.................................. Jan. 16, 1933–1951

The office of State Superintendent of Public Instruction was abolished by the **Gilmer-Aikin Laws of 1949** and the office of Commissioner of Education was created. The Commissioner is appointed by the State Board of Education, (also created by the Gilmer-Aikin Laws) the members of which are elected by the people.

State Commissioners of Education

J. W. Edgar............................ May 31, 1951–June 30, 1974
Marlin L. Brockette .... July 1, 1974–Sept. 1, 1979
Alton O. Bowen .... Sept. 1, 1979–June 1, 1981
Raymon Bynum.......................... June 1, 1981–Oct. 31, 1984
W. N. Kirby.............................. April 13, 1985–July 1, 1991
Lionel R. Meno........................... July 1, 1991–Mar. 1, 1995
Michael A. Moses .... Mar. 9, 1995–Aug. 18, 1999
Jim Nelson............................. Aug. 18, 1999–Mar. 25, 2002
Felipe Alanis........................... Mar. 25, 2002–July 31, 2003
Shirley J. Neeley......................... Jan. 12, 2004–July 1, 2007
Robert Scott.............................. July 1, 2007–July 2, 2012
Michael Williams .... Sept. 1, 2012–Dec. 31, 2015
Mike Morath .... Jan. 4, 2016–present

★ ★ ★ ★ ★ ★ ★

State Commissioners of Agriculture

Robert Teague Milner 1907–1908
Edward Reeves Kone..................................... 1908–1914
Fred Davis.. 1915–1920
George B. Terrell... 1921–1930
James E. McDonald....................................... 1931–1950
John C. White 1951–1977
Reagan V. Brown 1977–1982
Jim Hightower 1983–1990
Rick Perry 1991–1998
Susan Combs.. 1999–2006
Todd Staples... 2007–2015
Sid Miller 2015–present

Cecilia Abbott.
Photo courtesy of the Office of the First Lady.

First Ladies of Texas

Martha Evans Gindratt Wood........................ 1847–1849
Bell Administration.. 1849–1853
   (Gov. Peter Hansbrough Bell was not married while in office.)
Lucadia Christiana Niles Pease................ 1853–57; 1867–69
Runnels Administration................................. 1857–1859
   (Gov. Hardin R. Runnels never married.)
Margaret Moffette Lea Houston 1859–1861
Martha Evans Clark....................................... 1861
Adele Barron Lubbock................................... 1861–1863
Susie Ellen Taylor Murrah.............................. 1863–1865
Mary Jane Bowen Hamilton........................... 1865–1866
Annie Rattan Throckmorton.......................... 1866–1867
Ann Elizabeth Britton Davis.......................... 1870–1874
Mary Home Coke... 1874–1876
Janie Roberts Hubbard................................... 1876–1879
Frances Wickliff Edwards Roberts.................. 1879–1883
Anne Maria Penn Ireland................................ 1883–1887
Elizabeth Dorothy Tinsley Ross...................... 1887–1891
Sarah Stinson Hogg.. 1891–1895
Sally Harrison Culberson................................ 1895–1899
Orlene Walton Sayers..................................... 1899–1903
Sarah Beona Meng Lanham............................ 1903–1907
Fannie Brunner Campbell............................... 1907–1911
Alice Fuller Murrell Colquitt.......................... 1911–1915
Miriam A. Wallace Ferguson.......................... 1915–1917
   (Miriam A. Wallace Ferguson was Mistress of the Mansion while her husband, James E. Ferguson, was governor, 1915–1917. She served as both Governor and Mistress of the Mansion, 1925–1927 and 1933–1935.)
Willie Cooper Hobby...................................... 1917–1921
Myrtle Mainer Neff.. 1921–1925
Mildred Paxton Moody 1927–1931
Maud Gage Sterling.. 1931–1933
Jo Betsy Miller Allred..................................... 1935–1939
Merle Estella Butcher O'Daniel...................... 1939–1941
Fay Wright Stevenson..................................... 1941–1942
   (Died in the Governor's Mansion on Jan. 3, 1942.)
Edith Will Scott Stevenson............................ 1942–1946
   (Mother of Gov. Coke R. Stevenson and Mistress of the Mansion upon the death of the governor's wife.)
Mabel Buchanan Jester................................... 1946–1949
Marialice Shary Shivers.................................. 1949–1957
Jean Houston Baldwin Daniel......................... 1957–1963
Idanell Brill Connally..................................... 1963–1969
Ima Mae Smith.. 1969–1973
Betty Jane Slaughter Briscoe.......................... 1973–1979
Rita Crocker Bass Clements............................ 1979–1983
Linda Gale Thompson White.......................... 1983–1987
Rita Crocker Bass Clements............................ 1987–1991
Richards Administration................................. 1991–1995
   (Gov. Ann Richards was not married while in office.)
Laura Welch Bush... 1995–2000
Anita Thigpen Perry....................................... 2000–2015
   Cecilia Abbott...................................... 2015–present

State Government

Texas state government is divided into executive, legislative, and judicial branches under the Texas Constitution adopted in 1876.

The chief executive is the Governor, whose term is for four years. Other elected state officials with executive responsibilities include the Lieutenant Governor, Attorney General, Comptroller of Public Accounts, Commissioner of the General Land Office, and Commissioner of Agriculture. The terms of those officials are also four years.

The Secretary of State and the Commissioner of Education are appointed by the Governor.

Except for making numerous appointments and calling special sessions of the Legislature, the Governor's powers are limited in comparison with those in most states.

The Governor's office welcomes comments and concerns, which are relayed to government officials who may offer assistance. **Send a message through the webform at:**

https://gov.texas.gov/contact

Or call the **Citizen's Opinion Hotline:**

1 (800) 252-9600

State Government Income and Expenditures

Taxes are the state government's primary source of income. On this and the following pages are summaries of state income and expenditures, percent change from previous year, tax collections, tax revenue by type of tax, a summary of the state budgets for the 2018–2019 and 2020–2021 bienniums, Texas Lottery income and expenditures, and the amount of federal payments to state agencies. **Totals may not sum due to rounding.**

State Revenues by Source and Expenditures by Function
Amounts (in $ Millions) and Percent Change from Previous Year

Revenues by Source	2020	%	2019	%	2018	%	2017	%	2016	%
Tax Collections	57,380	–3.4	59,381	6.8	55,585	12	49,643	2.4	48,476	–6.2
Federal Income	58,117	38.7	41,904	5.8	39,618	3.3	38,366	–2.8	39,474	7.6
Licenses, Fees, Permits, Fines, and Penalties	6,241	–4.6	6,542	1.0	6,477	3.5	6,258	2.1	6,128	1.5
State Health Service Fees and Rebates	7,497	5.8	7,088	–6.7	7,599	13.4	6,702	201.9	8,071	32.8
Net Lottery Proceeds	2,392	–4.7	2,510	12.6	2,229	8.5	2,053	80.2	2,220	17.2
Land Income	1,809	–19.6	2,251	9.2	2,061	21.6	1,694	48.7	1,140	–26.4
Interest and Investment Income	2,529	1.0	2,504	35.4	1,849	9.3	1,691	24.1	1,362	–2.2
Settlements of Claims	624	–3.4	647	18.8	544	3.2	528	–19.1	652	20.5
Escheated Estates	715	3.2	693	9.0	636	–35	979	78.5	548	0.0
Sales of Goods and Services	255	–8.6	279	–2.2	285	–7.5	308	5.2	293	–36.1
Other Revenues	4,016	–3.0	4,142	26.2	3,282	10.4	2,973	1.9	2,918	13.2
Total Net Revenues	**141,576**	**10.7**	**127,941**	**6.5**	**120,166**	**8.1**	**111,195**	**–0.1**	**111,280**	**1.7**
Expenditures by Function	**2020**	**%**	**2019**	**%**	**2018**	**%**	**2017**	**%**	**2016**	**%**
Executive	3,165	4.2	3,038	5.4	2,883	3.6	2,783	7.1	2,599	5.5
Legislative	139	–8.0	151	8.4	139	–7.3	150	8.2	138	–2.5
Judicial	411	23	334	–7.9	362	4.8	346	3.6	333	5.0
General Government Total	3,714	5.4	3,522	4.1	3,384	3.2	3,279	6.8	3,071	5.1
Education	42,869	13.9	37,653	2.4	36,783	3.6	35,505	–1.3	35,964	3.4
Employee Benefits	4,972	0.2	4,961	4.2	4,760	0.1	4,755	5.6	4,502	11.2
Health and Human Services	57,197	10.3	51,873	2.9	50,421	2.7	49,075	–3.3	50,734	9.6
Public Safety and Corrections	4,877	–6.1	5,193	–3.4	5,375	9.1	4,928	2.0	4,829	5.8
Transportation	12,647	20.5	10,494	5.5	9,952	–3	10,261	6.8	9,608	12.9
Natural Resources/Recreational Services	3,116	10.8	2,812	2.4	2,746	34.2	2,046	–28.2	2,847	9.5
Regulatory Agencies	331	–1.5	336	7.5	312	–10.7	350	–42.8	611	26.4
Lottery Winnings Paid*	541	–20.9	684	9.0	628	12.7	557	–17.2	672	21.4
Debt Service – Interest	1,661	1.0	1,645	3.3	1,593	26.8	1,256	11.4	1,127	–4.2
Capital Outlay	1,192	40.2	851	42.1	599	–2.4	614	2.4	599	44.7
Total Net Expenditures	**133,118**	**10.9**	**120,025**	**3.0**	**116,554**	**3.5**	**112,625**	**–1.7**	**114,570**	**7.7**

* Does not include payments made by retailers.
All amounts rounded. Revenue and expenditures exclude trust funds. Fiscal years end August 31.

Source: 2020 State of Texas Annual Cash Report, Revenue and Expenditures of State Funds for the Year Ending August 31, 2021, Comptroller of Public Accounts' Office.

Governor Greg Abbott
P.O. Box 12428
Austin 78711
(512) 463-2000
gov.texas.gov/
Salary: $153,750

Lt. Governor Dan Patrick
P.O. Box 12068
Austin 78711
(512) 463-0001
www.ltgov.texas.gov/
Salary: Same as Senator when serving as President of the Senate, same as Governor when serving as Governor.

Attorney General
Ken Paxton
P.O. Box 12548
Austin 78711
(512) 463-2100
www.texasattorneygeneral.gov/
Salary: $153,750

Comptroller of Public Accounts Glenn Hegar
P.O. Box 13528
Austin 78711
(512) 463-4600
comptroller.texas.gov/
Salary: $153,750

Texas Land Commissioner
George P. Bush
P.O. Box 12873
Austin 78711
(512) 463-5256
www.glo.texas.gov
Salary: $140,938

Agriculture Commissioner
Sidney C. Miller
P.O. Box 12847
Austin 78711
(512) 463-7476
www.texasagriculture.gov
Salary: $140,938

Secretary of State
Vacant
P.O. Box 12697
Austin 78711
(512) 463-5770
www.sos.state.tx.us
Salary: $132,924

Education Commissioner
Michael H. Morath
1701 N. Congress Ave.
Austin 78701
(512) 463-8985
tea.texas.gov/
Salary: $220,375

State Government Budget Summary, 2022–2023 Biennium

Source: Legislative Budget Board; www.lbb.state.tx.us.

The Legislative Budget Board's (LBB) baseline appropriations for state government operations for the 2022–2023 biennium total $248.5 billion from All Funds functions of state government. The funding is a $13.5 billion, or 5.2 percent, decrease from the 2020–2021 biennial level of $262.1 billion.

General Revenue Funds, including funds dedicated within the General Revenue Fund, total $116.4 billion for the 2022–2023 biennium, an increase of $6.1 billion, or 5.5 percent, from the adjusted 2020–2021 biennial spending level of $110.3 billion. The table below details the difference in spending by article.

General Revenue Funds, by Article				
Article (Governmental Division)	Estimated/ Budgeted 2020–2021	2022–2023 Budget	Biennial Change	Percentage Change
Art. I: General Government	$3,977.4	$4,064.3	$86.9	2.2
Art. II: Health and Human Services	$33,629.6	$34,291.4	$661.8	2.0
Art. III: Agencies of Education	$60,402.8	$62,745.1	$2,342.3	3.9
Public Education	$44,561.5	$46,551.3	$1,989.8	4.5
Higher Education	$15,841.3	$16,193.8	$352.5	2.2
Art. IV: The Judiciary	$553.8	$551.6	–$2.3	–0.4
Art. V: Public Safety & Criminal Justice	$11,869.5	$12,055.0	$185.5	1.6
Art. VI: Natural Resources	$933.1	$1,002.1	$69.00	7.4
Art. VII: Business & Economic Dev.	$520.9	$490.1	–$30.8	–5.9
Art. VIII: Regulatory	$367.8	$301.7	–$66.1	–18.0
Art. IX: General Provisions		$456.8		
Art. X: The Legislature	$408.1	$410.2	$2.1	0.5
House Bill 2	–2,393.4			
Total, All Articles	**$110,269.6**	**$116,368.2**	**$6,098.60**	**5.5**

All figures in millions.

Source: Summary of Conference Committee Report For Senate Bill 1: Appropriations for the 2022–23 Biennium May 2021.

State Tax Collections 2002–2020				
FY	State Tax Collections (in millions)	Resident Population	Per Capita Tax Collections	Taxes as % of Personal Income
2020	$57,379.8	29,293,475	$1,959	3.6
2019	$59,380.7	28,950,175	$2,051	4.1
2018	$55,584.8	28,668,600	$1,939	4.0
2017	$49,643.4	28,255,300	$1,757	3.8
2016	$48,476.2	27,845,500	$1,741	3.8
2015	$51,683.1	27,389,200	$1,887	4.0
2014	$50,992.6	26,788,600	$1,896	4.3
2013	$47,781.0	26,399,510	$1,810	4.2
2012	$44,079.1	26,005,770	$1,695	4.0
2011	$38,856.2	25,592,790	$1,518	3.8
2010	$35,368.9	25,191,450	$1,404	3.7
2009	$37,822.5	24,737,000	$1,529	4.1
2008	$41,357.9	24,250,000	$1,705	4.3
2007	$36,955.6	23,778,000	$1,554	4.3
2006	$33,544.5	23,339,000	$1,437	4.1
2005	$29,838.3	22,808,000	$1,308	4.0
2004	$27,913.0	22,409,000	$1,246	4.1
2003	$26,126.7	22,052,000	$1,185	4.1
2002	$26,279.1	21,673,000	$1,213	4.2

Sources: 2020 State of Texas Annual Cash Report; historic data collected from older reports.

Tax Revenues, 2019–2020				
Type of Tax	FY 2019	% Change	FY 2020	% Change
Sales	$34,023.9	6.5	$34,099.1	0.2
Motor Vehicle Sales/Rentals*	$5,010.5	0.7	$4,815.2	–3.9
Motor Fuels	$3,743.0	1.9	$3,524.7	–5.8
Franchise	$4,217.8	14.4	$4,418.4	4.8
Oil Production	$3,886.8	14.6	$3,229.4	–16.9
Insurance	$2,599.0	3.6	$2,741.7	5.5
Cigarette & Tobacco	$1,410.3	6.8	$1,299.0	–7.9
Natural Gas Production	$1,685.7	17.8	$925.5	–45.1
Alcoholic Beverages	$1,369.4	6.0	$1,125.3	–17.8
Hotel	$636.1	5.8	$470.7	–26.0
Utility	$471.4	4.2	$478.2	1.4
Other Taxes	$326.5	3.4	$252.7	–22.6
Total	**$59,380.7**	**6.8**	**$57,379.8**	**–3.4**

All figures in millions.
*Includes tax on manufactured housing sales.
Source: 2020 State of Texas Annual Cash Report.

Federal Revenue by Agency

Texas received $58.1 billion in federal funds during fiscal 2020, an increase of $16.2 billion, or 38.7 percent from fiscal 2019. Federal funds accounted for 41.0 percent of total net revenue, the largest source of revenue in fiscal 2020.

	2017	2018	2019	2020
Health and Human Services	$24,418.8	$25,483.4	$27,279.5	$32,103.8
Governor – Fiscal	$179.7	$223.6	$310.5	$8,710.9
Texas Education Agency	$5,074.6	$5,168.8	$5,608.0	$5,226.7
Texas Dept. of Transportation	$4,250.5	$3,875.2	$4,026.4	$5,217.4
Texas Workforce Commission	$1,235.2	$1,296.9	$1,427.9	$2,384.8
General Land Office	$287.9	$341.0	$413.0	$925.8
Dept. of Agriculture	$580.6	$611.3	$638.6	$742.0
Texas Division of Emergency Management	–	–	–	$625.3
Dept. of Family and Protective Services	$447.5	$446.3	$491.7	$526.7
All other Agencies	$1,890.8	$2,171.9	$1,708.8	$1,653.4
Total	$38,365.6	$39,618.6	$41,904.5	$58,116.8

Totals may not sum due to rounding. All figures in millions.

Source: 2020 State of Texas Annual Cash Report

Texas Lottery

Source: Texas Lottery Commission; www.txlottery.org/

The State Lottery Act was passed by the Texas Legislature in July 1991. Texas voters approved a constitutional amendment authorizing a state lottery in an election on Nov. 5, 1991, by a vote of 1,326,154 to 728,994. Since the first ticket was sold on May 29, 1992, the Texas Lottery® has generated more than $115 billion in total sales and more than $33 billion in revenue for the state. More than $70 billion in prizes have been distributed to players through June 2021.

Since 1997, the Texas Lottery has contributed more than $23 billion to the Foundation School Fund, which supports public education. Before September 1997, revenues were only deposited in the General Revenue Fund.

As authorized by the state Legislature, certain Texas Lottery revenues have been earmarked to benefit state programs, including the Fund for Veterans Assistance, which is administered by the Texas Veterans Commission. Sales and unclaimed prizes from the veterans' designated scratch-off games have totaled $162.6 million since 2010.

Other Texas Lottery funds, such as unclaimed prizes, contribute to other causes and programs as authorized by the Texas Legislature.

Distribution of Texas Lottery proceeds for fiscal year 2020:

- 66.3 percent to prizes paid
- 37.4 percent to the Foundation School Fund
- 7.5 percent to retailer commissions
- 5.2 percent for lottery administration
- 0.5 percent to the Texas Veterans Commission. ☆

Texas Lottery Financial Data

Start-up to Aug. 31, 2020. All amounts in millions.

Period	Sales	Value of Prizes Won	Retailer Commissions	Revenue to State of Texas*
Start-up – FY 1992	$591.6	$268.9	$29.6	$250.0
FY 1993	$1,856.1	$981.7	$92.8	$656.8
FY 1994	$2,760.2	$1,528.7	$138.0	$927.7
FY 1995	$3,036.5	$1,689.3	$151.8	$1,015.0
FY 1996	$3,432.3	$1,951.1	$171.7	$1,098.3
FY 1997	$3,745.5	$2,151.7	$187.4	$1,182.8
FY 1998	$3,090.0	$1,648.1	$154.6	$1,097.8
FY 1999	$2,571.6	$1,329.0	$128.8	$953.4
FY 2000	$2,657.3	$1,508.8	$133.0	$862.8
FY 2001	$2,825.3	$1,643.2	$141.3	$864.0
FY 2002	$2,966.3	$1,715.4	$148.4	$928.9
FY 2003	$3,130.7	$1,845.2	$156.6	$949.1
FY 2004	$3,487.9	$2,068.6	$174.4	$1,051.0
FY 2005	$3,662.5	$2,228.0	$183.2	$1,070.3
FY 2006	$3,774.7	$2,310.6	$188.8	$1,090.3
FY 2007	$3,774.2	$2,315.3	$188.8	$1,093.0
FY 2008	$3,671.5	$2,281.1	$183.8	$1,034.9
FY 2009	$3,720.1	$2,299.8	$186.1	$1,062.2
FY 2010	$3,738.4	$2,300.2	$187.3	$1,063.1
FY 2011	$3,811.3	$2,387.2	$190.8	$1,023.8
FY 2012	$4,190.8	$2,632.6	$209.8	$1,155.5
FY 2013	$4,376.3	$2,767.4	$218.9	$1,214.1
FY 2014	$4,384.6	$2,741.2	$219.5	$1,220.7
FY 2015	$4,529.7	$2,858.3	$226.7	$1,242.7
FY 2016	$5,067.5	$3,186.4	$253.5	$1,392.3
FY 2017	$5,077.5	$3,257.4	$253.9	$1,334.0
FY 2018	$5,626.8	$3,666.1	$281.5	$1,450.5
FY 2019	$6,251.5	$4,056.5	$313.1	$1,636.6
FY 2020	$6,704.0	$4,442.4	$335.6	$1,683.7
Total	**$108,512.7**	**$66,060.2**	**$5,429.7**	**$31,605.3**

Revenue to the state presented on an accrual basis.

Muenster Senator Drew Springer with Secretary of the Senate Patsy Spaw. Senate Media Photo.

Texas Legislature

The Texas Legislature has **181 members: 31 in the Senate** and **150 in the House of Representatives**. Regular sessions convene on the second Tuesday of January in odd-numbered years, but the governor may call special sessions. Article III of the Texas Constitution deals with the legislative branch. On the web: **capitol.texas.gov**

The following lists are of members of the **87th Legislature**, which convened for its Regular Session on Jan. 12, 2021, and adjourned on May 31, 2021. The **88th Legislature** is scheduled to convene on Jan. 10, 2023, and adjourn May 29, 2023.

State Senate

Thirty-one members of the State Senate are elected to four-year, overlapping terms. Salary: The salary of all members of the Legislature, both Senators and Representatives, is $7,200 per year and $124 per diem during legislative sessions; mileage allowance at same rate provided by law for state employees. The per diem payment applies during each regular and special session of the Legislature.

Senatorial Districts include one or more whole counties; some counties have more than one Senator.

The **address of Senators** is Texas Senate, P.O. Box 12068, Austin 78711-2068; phone (512) 463-0200; Fax: (512) 463-0326. On the web: senate.texas.gov.

President of the Senate: Lt. Gov. Dan Patrick; **President Pro Tempore**: Brian Birdwell (R-Granbury); **Secretary of the Senate**: Patsy Spaw; **Sergeant-at-Arms**: Rick DeLeon.

Texas State Senators

District, Member, Party-Hometown, Occupation

1. Bryan Hughes, R-Mineola; attorney.
2. Bob Hall, R-Edgewood; retired military.
3. Robert Nichols, R-Jacksonville; engineer.
4. Brandon Creighton, R-Conroe; attorney.
5. Charles Schwertner, R-Georgetown; surgeon.
6. Carol Alvarado, D-Houston; small-business owner.
7. Paul Bettencourt, R-Houston; tax advisor.
8. Angela Paxton, R-McKinney; consultant, former educator.
9. Kelly G. Hancock, R-North Richland Hills; business owner.
10. Beverly Powell, D-Burleson; education advocate.
11. Larry Taylor, R-Friendswood; insurance agent.
12. Jane Nelson, R-Flower Mound; businesswoman.
13. Borris L. Miles, D-Houston; insurance and real estate developer.
14. Sarah Eckhardt, D-Austin; attorney.
15. John Whitmire, D-Houston; attorney.
16. Nathan Johnson, D-Dallas; attorney.
17. Joan Huffman, R-Houston; attorney.
18. Lois W. Kolkhorst, R-Brenham; business owner.
19. Roland Gutierrez, D-San Antonio; attorney.
20. Juan (Chuy) Hinojosa, D-McAllen; attorney.
21. Judith Zaffirini, D-Laredo; communications specialist, former educator.
22. Brian Birdwell, R-Granbury; retired military.
23. Royce West, D-Dallas; attorney.
24. Dawn Buckingham, R-Lakeway; physician.
25. Donna Campbell, R-New Braunfels; physician.
26. José Menéndez, D-San Antonio; businessman.
27. Eddie Lucio Jr., D-Brownsville; advertising executive.
28. Charles Perry, R-Lubbock; certified public accountant.
29. César Blanco, D-El Paso; consultant.
30. Drew Springer, R-Muenster; financial services.
31. Kel Seliger, R-Amarillo; business owner.

House of Representatives

This is a list of the current members of the House of Representatives. They were elected for two-year terms from the districts shown below. Representatives and senators receive the same salary.

The **address of all Representatives** is House of Representatives, P.O. Box 2910, Austin, 78768-2910; phone: (512) 463-1000; Fax: (512) 463-5896. On the web: house.texas.gov

Speaker, Dade Phelan (R-Beaumont). **Chief Clerk**, Robert Haney. **Sergeant-at-Arms**, Michael Black.

Texas State Representatives

District, Member, Party-Hometown, Occupation

1. Gary VanDeaver, R-New Boston; educator, retired.
2. Bryan Slaton, R-Royse City; business owner.
3. Cecil Bell, Jr., R-Magnolia; contractor.
4. Keith Bell, R-Forney; electrical contractor.
5. Cole Hefner, R-Mount Pleasant; insurance agent.
6. Matt Schaefer, R-Tyler; attorney.
7. Jay Dean, R-Longview; self-employed.
8. Cody Harris, R-Palestine; ranch broker.
9. Chris Paddie, R-Marshall; general manager.
10. Vacant.
11. Travis Clardy, R-Nacogdoches; attorney.
12. Kyle Kacal, R-College Station; rancher.
13. Ben Leman, R-Anderson; business, rancher.
14. John Raney, R-College Station; bookstore owner.
15. Steve Toth, R-The Woodlands; business owner.
16. Will Metcalf, R-Conroe; banker.
17. John Cyrier, R-Lockhart; general contractor.
18. Ernest Bailes IV, R-Shepherd; self-employed.
19. James White, R-Hillister; educator, rancher.
20. Terry M. Wilson, R-Marble Falls; military, retired.
21. Dade Phelan, R-Beaumont; real estate developer.
22. Joe Deshotel, D-Beaumont; attorney, contractor.
23. Mayes Middleton, R-Wallisville; oil & gas.
24. Greg Bonnen, R-Friendswood; neurosurgeon.
25. Cody Vasut, R-Angleton; attorney.
26. Jacey Jetton, R-Sugar Land; business owner.
27. Ron Reynolds, D-Missouri City; attorney.
28. Gary Gates, R-Richmond; real estate investor.
29. Ed Thompson, R-Pearland; insurance agent.
30. Geanie W. Morrison, R-Victoria; state representative.
31. Ryan Guillen, D-Rio Grande City; investor.
32. Todd Hunter, R-Corpus Christi; attorney.
33. Justin Holland, R-Heath; real estate broker.
34. Abel Herrero, D-Robstown; attorney.
35. Oscar Longoria, D-Peñitas; attorney.
36. Sergio Muñoz, Jr., D-Palmview; attorney.
37. Alex Dominguez, D-Brownsville; attorney.
38. Eddie Lucio III, D-Brownsville; attorney.
39. Armando Martinez, D-Weslaco; attorney.
40. Terry Canales, D-Edinburg; attorney.
41. R.D. "Bobby" Guerra, D-Mission; attorney.
42. Richard Peña Raymond, D-Laredo; mediator.
43. J. M. Lozano, R-Kingsville; business.
44. John Kuempel, R-Seguin; salesman.
45. Erin Zwiener, D-Driftwood; writer.
46. Sheryl Cole, D-Austin; lawyer, CPA.
47. Vikki Goodwin, D-Austin; real estate broker.
48. Donna Howard, D-Austin; community advocate.
49. Gina Hinojosa, D-Austin; attorney.
50. Celia Israel, D-Austin; realtor.
51. Eddie Rodriguez, D-Austin; business development consultant.
52. James Talarico, D-Round Rock; nonprofit director.
53. Andrew Murr, R-Junction; attorney, rancher.
54. Brad Buckley, R-Salado; veterinarian.
55. Hugh Shine, R-Temple; financial advisor.
56. Charles "Doc" Anderson, R-Waco; veterinarian.
57. Trent Ashby, R-Lufkin; title insurance executive.
58. DeWayne Burns, R-Cleburne; investor, farmer, rancher.
59. Shelby Slawson, R-Stephenville; attorney, entrepreneur, small-business owner.
60. Glenn Rogers, R-Graford; rancher.
61. Phil King, R-Weatherford; attorney.
62. Reggie Smith, R-Van Alstyne; attorney.
63. Tan Parker, R-Flower Mound; business consultant.
64. Lynn Stucky, R-Denton; veterinarian.
65. Michelle Beckley, D-Carrollton; business owner.
66. Matt Shaheen, R-Plano; technology executive.
67. Jeff Leach, R-Plano; attorney.
68. David Spiller, R-Jacksboro; attorney.
69. James B. Frank, R-Wichita Falls; business owner.
70. Scott Sanford, R-McKinney; minister.
71. Stan Lambert, R-Abilene; banker, retired.
72. Drew Darby, R-San Angelo; attorney, business.
73. Kyle Biedermann, R-Fredericksburg; business owner.
74. Eddie Morales, D-Eagle Pass; attorney.
75. Mary González, D-Clint; consultant.
76. Claudia Ordaz Perez, D-El Paso; consultant.
77. Lina Ortega, D-El Paso; attorney.
78. Joe Moody, D-El Paso; attorney.
79. Art Fierro, D-El Paso.
80. Tracy King, D-Batesville; business.
81. Brooks Landgraf, R-Odessa; attorney, rancher.
82. Tom Craddick, R-Midland; business development manager.
83. Dustin Burrows, R-Lubbock; attorney.
84. John Frullo, R-Lubbock; small-business owner.
85. Phil Stephenson, R-Wharton; CPA.

86. John Smithee, R-Amarillo; attorney.

87. Four Price, R-Amarillo; attorney.

88. Ken King, R-Canadian; oil & gas service executive.

89. Candy Noble, R-Lucas.

90. Ramón Romero, Jr., D-Fort Worth; CEO.

91. Stephanie Klick, R-Fort Worth; registered nurse.

92. Jeff Cason, R-Bedford.

93. Matt Krause, R-Fort Worth; attorney.

94. Tony Tinderholt, R-Arlington; retired.

95. Nicole Collier, D-Fort Worth; attorney.

96. David Cook, R-Mansfield; attorney.

97. Craig Goldman, R-Fort Worth; real estate, finance.

98. Giovanni Capriglione, R-Southlake; finance.

99. Charlie Geren, R-River Oaks; restaurant owner and rancher.

100. Jasmine Crockett, D-Dallas; attorney.

101. Chris Turner, D-Grand Prairie; communications.

102. Ana-Maria Ramos, D-Richardson; attorney, professor.

103. Rafael Anchía, D-Dallas; attorney.

104. Jessica González, D-Dallas; attorney.

105. Terry Meza, D-Irving; attorney.

106. Jared Patterson, R-Frisco; energy management.

107. Victoria Neave, D-Dallas; attorney.

108. Morgan Meyer, R-Dallas; attorney.

109. Carl Sherman, Sr., D-DeSoto; pastor, business.

110. Toni Rose, D-Dallas; mental health liaison.

111. Yvonne Davis, D-Dallas; small-business owner.

112. Angie Chen Button, R-Richardson; marketing.

113. Rhetta Bowers, D-Rowlett; educator.

114. John Turner, D-Dallas; attorney.

115. Julie Johnson, D-Farmers Branch; attorney.

116. Trey Martinez Fischer, D-San Antonio; contractor.

117. Philip Cortez, D-San Antonio; public relations.

118. Leo Pacheco, D-San Antonio; human resources.

119. Liz Campos, D-San Antonio; self-employed.

120. Barbara Gervin-Hawkins, D-San Antonio; education.

121. Steve Allison, R-San Antonio; attorney.

122. Lyle Larson, R-San Antonio; self-employed.

123. Diego Bernal, D-San Antonio; attorney.

124. Ina Minjarez, D-San Antonio; attorney.

125. Ray Lopez, D-San Antonio.

126. Sam Harless, R-Spring; automobile dealer.

127. Dan Huberty, R-Kingwood; finance.

128. Briscoe Cain, R-Deer Park; attorney.

129. Dennis Paul, R-Houston; engineer.

130. Tom Oliverson, R-Cypress; anesthesiologist.

131. Alma Allen, D-Houston; educational consultant.

132. Mike Schofield, R-Katy; attorney.

133. Jim Murphy, R-Houston; consultant.

134. Ann Johnson, D-Houston; attorney.

135. Jon Rosenthal, D-Houston; engineer.

136. John Bucy, III, D-Austin; education.

137. Gene Wu, D-Houston; attorney.

138. Lacy Hull, R-Houston.

139. Jarvis Johnson, D-Houston; business owner.

140. Armando Walle, D-Houston; legal assistant.

141. Senfronia Thompson, D-Houston; attorney.

142. Harold Dutton, Jr., D-Houston; attorney.

143. Ana Hernandez, D-Houston; attorney.

144. Mary Ann Perez, D-Houston; insurance agent.

145. Christina Morales, D-Houston; funeral director.

146. Shawn Thierry, D-Houston; attorney.

147. Garnet Coleman, D-Houston; business consulting.

148. Penny Morales Shaw, D-Houston; attorney.

149. Hubert Vo, D-Houston; business.

150. Valoree Swanson, R-Spring; business. ☆

Texas State House of Representatives 2021–2022

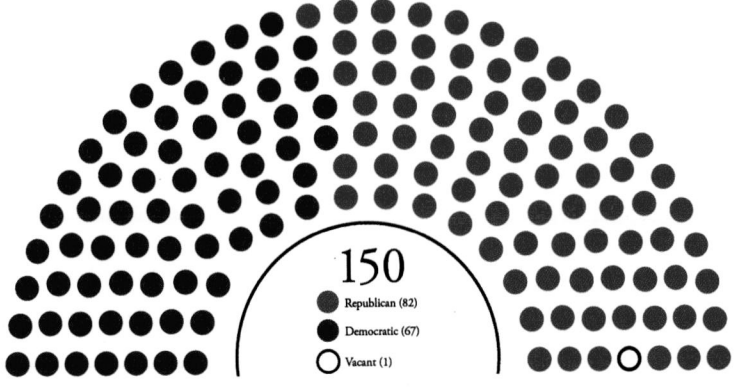

150

● Republican (82)

● Democratic (67)

○ Vacant (1)

The current Supreme Court with only eight members. In the top row, left to right: Justice Rebecca Huddle, Justice J. Brett Busby, Justice John Phillip Devine, Justice James Blacklock, Justice Jane Bland. Bottom row, left to right: Justice Debra Lehrmann, Chief Justice Nathan Hecht, and Justice Jeffrey Boyd. Photo by Ostler McCarthy.

Texas State Judiciary

The judiciary of the state consists of nine justices of the Supreme Court of Texas; nine judges of the Court of Criminal Appeals; 80 justices of the 14 Courts of Appeals; 459 judges of the State District Courts; 13 judges of the Criminal District Courts; 527 County Court judges; 805 Justice Court judges; and more than 1,200 Municipal Court judges in 944 cities.

Since 1876, judges at all levels are elected by voters in partisan elections. The Judicial Campaign Fairness Act was added to the Texas Election Code in 1995 by the 74th Legislature and limits individual campaign contributions to $5,000 for a statewide judicial office and $1,000–$5,000 for other judicial offices, depending on judicial district population. The exception is law firms, for which a $50 limit is set.

In addition to its system of formal courts, the State of Texas has established 18 **Alternative Dispute Resolution Centers**. The centers are headed by a director and help ease the caseload of Texas courts by using mediation, arbitration, negotiation, and moderated settlement conferences to handle disputes.

Centers are located in Amarillo, Austin, Beaumont, Bryan–College Station, Conroe, Corpus Christi, Dallas, Denton, El Paso, Fort Worth, Houston, Kerrville, Lubbock, Paris, Richmond, San Antonio, San Marcos, and Waco.

(The list of U.S. District Courts in Texas can be found in the Federal Government section, page 519.)

State Higher Courts

The state's higher courts include the Supreme Court, the Court of Criminal Appeals, the Courts of Appeals, and District Courts. Justices of the Supreme Court, Court of Criminal Appeals, and Courts of Appeals are elected to six-year, overlapping terms. District Court judges are elected to four-year terms.

Base judicial salaries as set by the 86th Legislature are: Supreme Court and Court of Criminal Appeals chief justices, $170,500, justices, $168,000; Court of Appeals chief justices, $156,500; justices, $154,000. Court of Appeals justices also may receive additional compensation paid by counties for extra judicial service, not to exceed $9,000 per year.

District Court judges receive $140,000 from the state. They may receive additional compensation paid by counties, not to exceed $18,000 per year.

The justices listed below are current as of August 2021. Notations in parentheses are term of office expiration dates. Elsewhere in this section are lists of District Court judges by district number, district court numbers in each county, and county court judges.

Supreme Court

Chief Justice, Nathan L. Hecht (12/31/26). **Justices**: J. Brett Busby (12/31/26); Jeffrey S. Boyd (12/31/26); Debra H. Lehrmann (12/31/22); John Phillip Devine (12/31/24); James D. "Jimmy" Blacklock (12/31/24); Jane Bland (12/31/24) and Rebecca Huddle (12/31/22). The ninth seat is vacant as of press time.

Clerk of Court, Blake A. Hawthorne. Location of court, Austin. Web: **txcourts.gov/supreme.**

Court of Criminal Appeals

Presiding Judge, Sharon Keller (12/31/24). **Judges**: Bert Richardson (12/31/26); Kevin Yeary (12/31/26); David Newell (12/31/26); Jesse F. McClure III (12/31/22); Mary Lou Keel (12/31/22), Scott Walker (12/31/22); Barbara Parker Hervey (12/31/24); and Michelle Slaughter (12/31/24). State Prosecuting Attorney, Stacey M. Soule.

Clerk of Court, Deanna Williamson. Location of court, Austin. Web: **http://www.txcourts.gov/cca.**

Courts of Appeals

These courts have jurisdiction within their respective supreme judicial districts. A constitutional amendment approved in 1978 raised the number of associate justices for Courts of Appeals where needed. Judges are elected from the district for six-year terms. An amendment adopted in 1980 changed the name of the old Courts of Civil Appeals to the Courts of Appeals and changed the jurisdiction of the courts. Terms end on 12/31 of the year in parentheses.

First District, Houston:* Chief Justice Sherry Radack (2022). Justices: Gordon Goodman (2024); Sarah Beth Landau (2024); Julie Countiss (2024); Richard Hightower (2024); Peter M. Kelley (2024); Veronica Rivas-Malloy (2026); and Amparo M. Guerra (2026). Clerk of Court, Christopher A. Prine. Counties in the First District: Austin, Brazoria, Chambers, Colorado, Fort Bend, Galveston, Grimes, Harris, Waller, Washington.

Second District, Fort Worth: Chief Justice: Bonnie Sudderth (2024). Justices: Dana Womack (2026); Elizabeth Kerr (2022); J. Wade Birdwell (2024); Dabney Bassel (2024); Mike Wallach (2024); and Brian Walker (2026). Clerk of Court, Debra Spisak. Counties in the Second District: Archer, Clay, Cooke, Denton, Hood, Jack, Montague, Parker, Tarrant, Wichita, Wise, Young.

Third District, Austin: Chief Justice Darlene Byrne (2026). Justices: Edward Smith (2024); Chari L. Kelly (2024); Melissa Goodwin (2022); Thomas Baker (2024); and Gisela Triana (2024). Clerk of Court, Jeffrey D. Kyle. Counties in the Third District: Bastrop, Bell, Blanco, Burnet, Caldwell, Coke, Comal, Concho, Fayette, Hays, Irion, Lampasas, Lee, Llano, McCulloch, Milam, Mills, Runnels, San Saba, Schleicher, Sterling, Tom Green, Travis, Williamson.

Fourth District, San Antonio: Chief Justice Rebeca C. Martinez (2026). Justices: Beth Watkins (2024); Patricia O'Connel Alvarez (2024); Luz Elena Chapa (2024); Liza Rodriguez (2024); Irene Alarcon Rios (2020); and Lori I. Valenzuela (2026). Clerk of Court, Keith E. Hottle. Counties in the Fourth District: Atascosa, Bandera, Bexar, Brooks, Dimmit, Duval, Edwards, Frio, Gillespie, Guadalupe, Jim Hogg, Jim Wells, Karnes, Kendall, Kerr, Kimble, Kinney, La Salle, Mason, Maverick, McMullen, Medina, Menard, Real, Starr, Sutton, Uvalde, Val Verde, Webb, Wilson, Zapata, Zavala.

Fifth District, Dallas: Chief Justice Robert D. Burns, III (2024). Justices: Robbie Partida-Kipness (2024); Lana Myers (2022); Erin Nowell (2024); David Schenck (2022); Bill Pedersen, III (2024); Amanda Reichek (2024); Cory Carlyle (2024); Ken Molberg (2024); Leslie L. Osborne (2024); Craig Smith (2026); Bonnie Lee Goldstein (2026); and Dennise Garcia (2026). Clerk of Court, Lisa Matz. Counties in the Fifth District: Collin, Dallas, Grayson, Hunt, Kaufman, Rockwall.

Sixth District, Texarkana: Chief Justice Josh R. Morris, III (2020). Justices: Scott Stevens (2024) and Ralph K. Burgess (2026). Clerk of Court, Debbie Autrey. Counties in the Sixth District: Bowie, Camp, Cass, Delta, Fannin, Franklin, Gregg, Harrison, Hopkins, Hunt, Lamar, Marion, Morris, Panola, Red River, Rusk, Titus, Upshur, Wood.

Seventh District, Amarillo: Chief Justice Brian P. Quinn (2026). Justices: Judy Parker (2024); Patrick A. Pirtle (2024); and Larry Doss (2022). Clerk of Court, Bobby Ramirez. Counties in the Seventh District: Armstrong, Bailey, Briscoe, Carson, Castro, Childress, Cochran, Collingsworth, Cottle, Crosby, Dallam, Deaf Smith, Dickens, Donley, Floyd, Foard, Garza, Gray, Hale, Hall, Hansford, Hardeman, Hartley, Hemphill, Hockley, Hutchinson, Kent, King, Lamb, Lipscomb, Lubbock, Lynn, Moore, Motley, Ochiltree, Oldham, Parmer, Potter, Randall, Roberts, Sherman, Swisher, Terry, Wheeler, Wilbarger, Yoakum.

Eighth District, El Paso: Chief Justice Yvonne Rodriguez (2022). Justices: Jeff Alley (2022) and Gina Palafox (2022). Clerk of Court, Elizabeth G. Flores. Counties in the Eighth District: Andrews, Brewster, Crane, Crockett, Culberson, El Paso, Hudspeth, Jeff Davis, Loving, Pecos, Presidio, Reagan, Reeves, Terrell, Upton, Ward, Winkler.

Ninth District, Beaumont: Chief Justice Scott Golemon (2026). Justices: Charles Kreger (2022); Leanne Johnson (2024); and Hollis Horton (2024). Clerk of Court, Carol Harley. Counties in the Ninth District: Hardin, Jasper, Jefferson, Liberty, Montgomery, Newton, Orange, Polk, San Jacinto, Tyler.

Tenth District, Waco: Chief Justice Thomas W. Gray (2024). Justices: Matt Johnson (2026) and John Neill. (2024). Clerk of Court, Nita Whitener. Counties in the Tenth District: Bosque, Brazos, Burleson, Coryell, Ellis, Falls, Freestone, Hamilton, Hill, Johnson, Leon, Limestone, Madison, McLennan, Navarro, Robertson, Somervell, Walker.

Eleventh District, Eastland: Chief Justice John Bailey (2024). Justices: W. Stacy Trotter (2022) and Bruce Williams (2026). Clerk of Court, Sherry Williamson. Counties in the Eleventh District: Baylor, Borden, Brown, Callahan, Coleman, Comanche, Dawson, Eastland, Ector, Erath, Fisher, Gaines, Glasscock, Haskell, Howard, Jones, Knox, Martin, Midland, Mitchell, Nolan, Palo Pinto, Scurry, Shackelford, Stephens, Stonewall, Taylor, Throckmorton.

Twelfth District, Tyler: Chief Justice James T. Worthen (2026). Justices: Brian Hoyle (2022) and Greg Neeley (2024). Clerk of Court, Katrina McClenny. Counties in the Twelfth District: Anderson, Angelina, Cherokee, Gregg, Henderson, Houston, Nacogdoches, Rains, Rusk, Sabine, San Augustine, Shelby, Smith, Trinity, Upshur, Van Zandt, Wood.

Thirteenth District, Corpus Christi: Chief Justice Dori Contreras (2024). Justices: Nora Longoria (2024); Leticia Hinojosa (2022); Jaime Tijerina (2024); Gina Benavides (2024); and Clarissa Silva (2026). Clerk of Court, Kathy S. Mills. Counties in the Thirteenth District: Aransas, Bee, Calhoun, Cameron, DeWitt, Goliad, Gonzales, Hidalgo, Jackson, Kenedy, Kleberg, Lavaca, Live Oak, Matagorda, Nueces, Refugio, San Patricio, Victoria, Wharton, Willacy.

Fourteenth District, Houston†: Chief Justice Tracy E. Christopher (2026). Justices: Kevin Jewell (2022); Jimmy Zimmerer (2024); Charles A. Spain (2024); Frances Bourliot (2024); Meagan Hassan (2024); Randy Wilson (2022); Margaret "Meg" Poissant (2024); and Kenneth Wise (2026). Clerk of Court, Christopher A. Prine. Counties in the Fourteenth District: Austin, Brazoria, Chambers, Colorado, Fort Bend, Galveston, Grimes, Harris, Waller, Washington.☆

*The location of the First Court of Appeals was changed from Galveston to Houston by the 55th Legislature, with the provision that all cases originated in Galveston County be tried in that city and with the further provision that any case may, at the discretion of the court, be tried in either city.

†Because of the heavy workload of the Houston-area Court of Appeals, the 60th Legislature in 1967 provided for the establishment of a Fourteenth Appeals Court in Houston.

District Judges in Texas

Sources: Texas Judicial Directory and Texas State Directory.

Below are the names of all district judges in Texas, as of July 2021, listed in district court order. To determine which judges have jurisdiction in specific counties, refer to the **Texas Courts by County** table, on pages 460–461.

Dist	Judge
1	Craig M. Mixson (R)
1-A	Delinda Gibbs-Walker (R)
2	Chris Day (R)
3	Mark A. Calhoon (R)
4	J. Clay Gossett (R)
5	Bill Miller (R)
6	Wes Tidwell (R)
7	Kerry L. Russell (R)
8	Eddie Northcutt (R)
9	Phil Grant (R)
10	Kerry Neves (R)
11	Kristen B. Hawkins (D)
12	David W. Moorman (R)
13	James Lagomarsino (R)
14	Eric V. Moyé (D)
15	Jim Fallon (R)
16	Sherry Shipman (R)
17	Melody Wilkinson (R)
18	Sydney B. Hewlett (R)
19	Thomas West (R)
20	John W. Youngblood (R)
21	Carson Campbell (R)
22	Bruce Boyer (R)
23	Ben Hardin (R)
24	Jack W. Marr (R)
25	William D. Old, III (R)
25-A	Jessica R. Crawford (R)
26	Donna King (R)
27	John Gauntt (R)
28	Nanette Hasette (D)
29	Michael Moore (R)
30	Jeff McKnight (R)
31	Steven R. Emmert (R)
32	Glen N. Harrison (R)
33	Allan Garrett (R)
34	William E. Moody (D)
35	Michael L. Smith (R)
36	Starr Bauer (R)
37	Nicole Garza (D)
38	Camile G. DuBose (R)
39	Shane Hadaway (R)
40	Bob Carroll (R)
41	Anna Perez (D)
42	James Eidson (R)
43	Craig Towson (R)
44	Ashley Wysocki (R)
45	Mary Lou Alvarez (D)
46	Dan Mike Bird (R)
47	Daniel L. Schaap (R)
48	David L. Evans (R)
49	Joe Lopez (D)
50	Jennifer A. Habert (R)
51	Carmen Symes Dusek (R)
52	Trent D. Farrell (R)
53	Maria Cantu Hexel (D)
54	Susan Kelly (R)
55	Latosha L. Payne (D)
56	Lonnie Cox (R)
57	Antonia Toni Arteaga (D)
58	Kent Walston (D)
59	Larry Phillips (R)
60	Justin Sanderson (D)
61	Fredericka Phillips (D)
62	Will Biard (R)
63	Roland Andrade (R)
64	Danah Zirpoli (R)

Dist	Judge
65	Yahara Lisa Gutierrez (D)
66	A. Lee Harris (R)
67	Donald J. Cosby (R)
68	Martin Hoffman (D)
69	Ron Enns (R)
70	Denn Whalen (R)
71	Brad Morin (R)
72	Ann-Marie Carruth (R)
73	David A. Canales (D)
74	Gary Coley (R)
75	Mark Morefield (R)
76	Angela Saucier (R)
77	Patrick Simmons (R)
78	Meredith Kennedy (R)
79	Richard Terrell (D)
80	Jeralynn Manor (D)
81	Lynn Ellison (R)
82	Bryan F. Rusty
83	Robert Cadena (R)
84	Curtis W. Brancheau (R)
85	Kyle Hawthorne (R)
86	Casey Blair (R)
87	Deborah Oakes Evans (R)
88	Earl Stover, III (R)
89	Charles M. Barnard (R)
90	Stephen Bristow (R)
91	Steven R. Herod (R)
92	Luis M. Singleterry (D)
93	Fernando Mancias (D)
94	Bobby Galvan (D)
95	Monica Purdy (D)
96	Joseph Patrick Pat Gallagher (R)
97	Jack McGaughey (R)
98	Rhonda Hurley (D)
99	Phillip Hays (R)
100	Stuart Messer (R)
101	Staci Williams (D)
102	Jeff M. Addison (R)
103	Janet Leal (D)
104	Jeff Propst (R)
105	Jack W. Pulcher (R)
106	Reed Filley (R)
107	Benjamin Euresti, Jr. (D)
108	Doug Woodburn (R)
109	John L. Pool (R)
110	William P. Smith (R)
111	Monica Zapata Notzon (D)
112	Pete Gomez, Jr. (D)
113	Rabeea Collier (D)
114	Austin Reeve Jackson (R)
115	Dean Fowler (R)
116	Tonya Parker (D)
117	Sandra Watts (D)
118	Timothy Yeats (R)
119	Ben Woodward (R)
120	Maria Salas-Mendoza (D)
121	John A. Trey Didway (R)
122	John Ellisor (R)
123	LeAnn Kay Rafferty (R)
124	F. Alfonso Charles (R)
125	Kyle Carter (D)
126	Aurora Martinez Jones (D)
127	R.K. Sandill (D)
128	Courtney Arkeen (R)
129	Michael Gomez (D)
130	Denise M. Fortenberry (R)

Dist	Judge
131	Norma Gonzales (D)
132	Ernie B. Armstrong (R)
133	Jaclanel McFarland (D)
134	Dale B. Tillery (D)
135	Stephen Williams (R)
136	Baylor Wortham (D)
137	John Trey McClendon (R)
138	Gabriela Gabby Garcia (D)
139	J. R. Bobby Flores (D)
140	Douglas H. Freitag (R)
141	John P. Chupp (R)
142	David G. Rogers (R)
143	Michael Swanson (R)
144	Michael Mery (D)
145	Jeff Davis (R)
146	Jack Jones (R)
147	Clifford A. Brown (D)
148	Carlos Valdez (D)
149	Terri Tipton Holder (R)
150	Monique Diaz (D)
151	Mike Engelhart (D)
152	Robert Schaffer (D)
153	Susan McCoy (R)
154	Felix Klein (R)
155	Jeff Steinhauser (R)
156	Patrick L. Flanigan (R)
157	Tanya Garrison (D)
158	Steve Burgess (R)
159	Paul E. White (R)
160	Aiesha Redmond (D)
161	Justin Low (R)
162	Maricela Moore (D)
163	Rex Wayne Peveto (R)
164	Cheryl E. Thornton (D)
165	Ursula A. Hall (D)
166	Laura Salinas (D)
167	Dayna Blazey (D)
168	Marcos Lizarraga (D)
169	Gordon G. Adams (R)
170	Jim Meyer (R)
171	Bonnie Rangel (D)
172	Mitch Templeton (R)
173	Dan Moore (R)
174	Hazel B. Jones (D)
175	Catherine Torres-Stahl (D)
176	Nikita Harmon (D)
177	Robert Johnson (D)
178	Kelli Johnson (D)
179	Ana Martinez (D)
180	DaSean Jones (D)
181	Titiana D. Frausto (R)
182	Danilo Danny Lacayo (D)
183	Chuck Silverman (D)
184	Abigail Anastasio (D)
185	Jason Luong (D)
186	Jefferson Moore (R)
187	Stephanie R. Boyd (D)
188	Scott Novy (R)
189	Scot Dollinger (D)
190	Beau Miller (D)
191	Gena Slaughter (D)
192	Kristina Williams (D)
193	Bridgett Whitmore (D)
194	Ernest B. White III (D)
195	Hector Garza (D)
196	Andrew Bench (R)

Dist	Judge	Dist	Judge	Dist	Judge
197	Adolfo Cordova (D)	267	Robert E. Bobby Bell (R)	337	Colleen Gaido (D)
198	Melvin Rex Emerson (R)	268	R. O'Neil Williams (D)	338	Ramona Franklin (D)
199	Angela Tucker (R)	269	Cory Sepolio (D)	339	Teiva Bell (D)
200	Jessica Mangrum (D)	270	Dedra Davis (D)	340	Jay Weatherby (R)
201	Amy Clark Meachum (D)	271	Brock Smith (R)	341	Beckie Palomo (D)
202	John Tidwell (R)	272	John Brick (R)	342	Kimberly Fitzpatrick (R)
203	Raquel Rocky Jones (D)	273	James A. Payne Jr. (R)	343	Janna Whatley (R)
204	Tammy Kemp (D)	274	Gary L. Steel (R)	344	Randy McDonald (R)
205	Francisco X. Dominguez (D)	275	Marla Cuellar (D)	345	Jan Soifer (D)
206	Rose Guerra Reyna (D)	276	Robert Rolston (R)	346	Paty Baca (D)
207	Jack H. Robison (R)	277	Stacey Mathews (R)	347	Missy Medary (R)
208	Greg Glass (D)	278	Hal R. Ridley (R)	348	Megan Fahey (R)
209	Brian Warren (D)	279	Randy Shelton (D)	349	Pam Foster Fletcher (R)
210	Alyssa G. Perez (D)	280	Barbara J. Stalder (D)	350	Thomas Wheeler (R)
211	Brody Shanklin (R)	281	Christine Weems Harris	351	Natalia Nata Cornelio (D)
212	Patricia V. Grady (R)	282	Amber Givens-Davis (D)	352	Josh Burgess (R)
213	Christopher R. Wolfe (R)	283	Lela D. Mays (D)	353	Madeleine Connor (R)
214	Inna Klein (R)	284	Kristin Bays (R)	354	Kelli Aiken (R)
215	Elaine H. Palmer (D)	285	Aaron Haas (D)	355	Bryan Bufkin (R)
216	Albert D. Patillo III (R)	286	Jay M. Pat Phelan (R)	356	Steven Thomas (R)
217	Robert K. Inselmann, Jr. (R)	287	Gordon H. Green (D)	357	Juan A. Magallanes (D)
218	Russell Wilson (R)	288	Cynthia Marie Chapa (D)	358	John F. Shrode (R)
219	Jennifer Edgeworth (R)	289	Carlos Quezada (D)	359	Kathleen A. Hamilton (R)
220	Shaun Carpenter (R)	290	Jennifer Peña (D)	360	Patricia Baca Bennett (R)
221	Lisa B. Michalk (R)	291	Stephanie Mitchell (D)	361	Steve Smith (R)
222	Roland Saul (R)	292	Brandon Birmingham (D)	362	Bruce McFarling (R)
223	Phil Vanderpool (R)	293	Maribel Flores (D)	363	Tracy Holmes (D)
224	Cathy Stryker (R)	294	Chris Martin (R)	364	William B. Billy
225	Peter Sakai (D)	295	Donna Roth (D)	365	Amado Abascal (D)
226	Velia J. Meza (D)	296	John Roach, Jr. (R)	366	Tom Nowak (R)
227	Kevin M. O'Connell (R)	297	David Hagerman (R)	367	Margaret Barnes (R)
228	Frank Aguilar (R)	298	Emily G. Tobolowsky (D)	368	Rick J. Kennon (R)
229	Baldemar Balde Garza (D)	299	Karen Sage (D)	369	C. Michael Davis (R)
230	Chris Morton (D)	300	Randall Hufstetler (R)	370	Noe Gonzalez (D)
231	Jesus Jesse Nevarez Jr. (R)	301	Mary Brown (D)	371	Mollee Westfall (R)
232	Josh Hill (D)	302	Sandra Jackson (D)	372	Scott Wisch (R)
233	Kenneth E. Newell (R)	303	Rhonda Hunter (D)	377	Eli Garza (R)
234	Lauren Reeder (D)	304	Andrea Martin (D)	378	William D. Doug Wallace (R)
235	Janelle M. Haverkamp (R)	305	Cheryl Lee Shannon (D)	379	Ron Rangel (D)
236	Tom Lowe (R)	306	Anne Darring (R)	380	Ben N. Smith (R)
237	Les Hatch (R)	307	Tim Womack (R)	381	Jose L. Garza (D)
238	Elizabeth Leonard (R)	308	Gloria Lopez (D)	382	Brett Hall (R)
239	Patrick Sebesta (R)	309	Linda Marie Dunson (D)	383	Lyda Ness Garcia (D)
240	Frank J. Fraley (D)	310	Sonya Heath (D)	384	Patrick M. Garcia (D)
241	Jack M. Skeen, Jr. (R)	311	Germaine Tanner (D)	385	Leah G. Robertson (R)
242	Lowell Kregg Hukill (R)	312	Clinton Chip Wells (D)	386	Jacqueline Jackie Valdez (D)
243	Selena N. Solis (D)	313	Natalia Oakes (D)	387	Janet Buening Heppard (D)
244	James Rush (R)	314	Michelle Moore (D)	388	Marlene Gonzalez (D)
245	Tristan H. Longino (D)	315	Leah Shapiro (D)	389	Leticia Letty Lopez (D)
246	Angela Graves-Harrington (D)	316	James Mosley (R)	390	Julie H. Kocurek (D)
247	Janice Berg (D)	317	Larry Thorne (D)	391	Brad Goodwin (R)
248	Hilary Unger (D)	318	David W. Lindemood (R)	392	Scott McKee (R)
249	Wayne Bridewell (R)	319	David Stith (R)	393	Doug Robison (R)
250	Karin Crump (D)	320	Pamela C. Sirmon (R)	394	Roy B. Ferguson (R)
251	Ana Estevez (R)	321	Robert Wilson (R)	395	Ryan D. Larson (R)
252	Raquel West (D)	322	James B. Munford (R)	396	George Gallagher (R)
253	Chap B. Cain III (R)	323	Alex Kim (R)	397	Brian Keith Gary (R)
254	Kim Brown (D)	324	Jerome S. Jerry Hennigan (R)	398	Keno Vasquez (D)
255	Kim Cooks (D)	325	Judith G. Wells (R)	399	Frank J. Castro (D)
256	David Lopez (D)	326	Paul Rotenberry (R)	400	Tameika Carter (D)
257	Sandra Peake (D)	327	Linda Chew (D)	401	George Flint (D)
258	Travis Kitchens (R)	328	Walter Armatys (R)	402	J. Brad McCampbell (R)
259	Brooks H. Hagler (D)	329	Randy M. Clapp (R)	403	Brenda Kennedy (D)
260	Steve Parkhurst (R)	330	Andrea Plumlee (D)	404	Ricardo M. Adobbati (D)
261	Lora Livingston (D)	331	Chantal Melissa Eldridge (D)	405	Jared Robinson (R)
262	Lori C. Gray (D)	332	Mario E. Ramirez, Jr. (D)	406	Oscar O.J. Hale, Jr. (D)
263	Amy Martin (D)	333	Brittanye Morris (D)	407	Tina Torres (D)
264	Paul LePak (R)	334	Dawn Deshea Rogers (D)	408	Angelica Jimenez (D)
265	Jennifer Bennett (D)	335	Reva Towslee-Corbett (R)	409	Sam Medrano, Jr. (D)
266	Jason Cashon (R)	336	Laurine J. Blake (R)	410	Jennifer Robin (R)

Dist	Judge
411	John Wells (R)
412	Justin R. Gilbert (R)
413	William C. Bosworth, Jr. (R)
414	Vicki Menard (R)
415	Graham Quisenberry (R)
416	Andrea Thompson (R)
417	Cynthia Wheless (R)
418	Tracy A. Gilbert (R)
419	Catherine A. Mauzy (D)
420	Edwin Allen Ed Klein (R)
421	Chris Schneider (R)
422	Shelton Gibbs IV (R)
423	Chris Duggan (D)
424	Evan Stubbs (R)
425	Betsy F. Lambeth (R)
426	Steve Duskie (R)
427	Tamara Needles (D)
428	William Bill Henry (R)
429	Jill R. Willis (R)
430	Israel Ramon (D)
431	Jim Johnson (R)
432	Ruben Gonzalez, Jr. (R)
433	Dibrell Dib Waldrip (R)
434	Christian Becerra (D)
435	Patty Maginnis (R)
436	Lisa K. Jarrett (R)

Dist	Judge
437	Melisa Skinner (R)
438	Rosie Alvarado (D)
439	David Rakow (R)
440	Grant Kinsey (R)
441	Jeff Robnett (R)
442	Tiffany Haertling (R)
443	Cindy Ermatinger (R)
444	David A. Sanchez (D)
445	Gloria M. Rincones (D)
446	Sara Kate Billingsley (R)
448	Sergio H. Enriquez (D)
449	Renee Rodriguez-Betancourt (D)
450	Brad Urrutia (D)
451	Kirsten Cohoon (R)
452	Robert Hofmann (R)
453	Sherri Tibbe (D)
454	Daniel J. Danny Kindred (R)
455	Dustin Howell (R)
456	Heather Hines Wright (R)
457	Vince Santini (R)
458	Robert L. Rolnick (D)
459	Maya Guerra Gamble (D)
460	Selena Alvarenga (D)
461	Patrick Bulanek (R)
462	Lee Ann Breading (R)
464	Joe Ramirez (D)

Dist	Judge
466	Stephanie Bascon (R)
467	Derbha Jones(R)
468	Lindsey Wynne (R)
469	Piper McCraw (R)
470	Emily Miskel (R)
471	Andrea Bouressa (R)
505	Kali Morgan (D)
506	Gary W. Chaney (R)
507	Julia Maldonado (D)

Criminal District Courts	
Dallas 1	Tina Yoo Clinton (D)
Dallas 2	Nancy Kennedy (D)
Dallas 3	Audra LaDawn Riley (D)
Dallas 4	Dominique Collins (D)
Dallas 5	Carter Thompson (D)
Dallas 6	Jeanine Howard (D)
Dallas 7	Chika Anyiam (D)
El Paso	Diane Navarette (D)
Jefferson	John B. "Johnny" Stevens (D)
Tarrant 1	Elizabeth Beach (R)
Tarrant 2	Wayne Francis Salvant (R)
Tarrant 3	Robb Catalano (R)
Tarrant 4	Mike Thomas (R)

Administrative Judicial Regions of Texas

There are 11 administrative judicial regions in the state for administrative purposes. Presiding Judges are appointed by the Governor to four-year terms. They must be active or retired region judges or active or retired appellate judges with judicial experience in a region court. They receive extra compensation of $5,000, paid by counties in the administrative region.

The Presiding Judge convenes an annual conference of judges in the administrative region to consult on business in the courts and to adopt rules for administering cases in the region.

The Presiding Judge may assign active or retired region judges residing within the administrative region to any of its region courts. The Presiding Judge of one administrative region may request the Presiding Judge of another administrative region to assign a judge from that region to sit in a region court in the requesting Judge's administrative region.

The Chief Justice of the Supreme Court of Texas convenes an annual conference of the 11 Presiding Judges to determine the need for assignment of judges and to promote the uniform administration of the assignments. The Chief Justice can assign judges of one administrative region for service in another region.

First Region: Ray Wheless, McKinney (3/2021): Collin, Dallas, Ellis, Fannin, Grayson, Kaufman, Rockwall.

Second Region: Olen Underwood, Conroe (5/2022): Angelina, Bastrop, Brazos, Burleson, Chambers, Grimes, Hardin, Jasper, Jefferson, Lee, Liberty, Madison, Montgomery, Newton, Orange, Polk, San Jacinto, Trinity, Tyler, Walker, Waller, Washington.

Third Region: Billy Ray Stubblefield, Georgetown (2/2022): Austin, Bell, Blanco, Bosque, Burnet, Caldwell, Colorado, Comal, Comanche, Coryell, Falls, Fayette, Gonzales, Guadalupe, Hamilton, Hays, Hill, Lampasas, Lavaca, Llano, McLennan, Milam, Navarro, Robertson, San Saba, Travis, Williamson.

Fourth Region: Sid L. Harle, San Antonio (12/2021): Aransas, Atascosa, Bee, Bexar, Calhoun, De Witt, Dimmit, Frio, Goliad, Jackson, Karnes, La Salle, Live Oak, Maverick, McMullen, Refugio, San Patricio, Victoria, Webb, Wilson, Zapata, Zavala.

Fifth Region: Missy Medary, Alice (11/2023): Brooks, Cameron, Duval, Hidalgo, Jim Hogg, Jim Wells, Kenedy, Kleberg, Nueces, Starr, Willacy.

Sixth Region: Stephen B. Ables, Kerrville (12/2024): Bandera, Brewster, Crockett, Culberson, Edwards, El Paso, Gillespie, Hudspeth, Jeff Davis, Kendall, Kerr, Kimble, Kinney, Mason, McCulloch, Medina, Menard, Pecos, Presidio, Reagan, Real, Sutton, Terrell, Upton, Uvalde, Val Verde.

Seventh Region: Dean Rucker, Midland (4/2023): Andrews, Borden, Brown, Callahan, Coke, Coleman, Concho, Crane, Dawson, Ector, Fisher, Gaines, Garza, Glasscock, Haskell, Howard, Irion, Jones, Kent, Loving, Lynn, Martin, Midland, Mills, Mitchell, Nolan, Reeves, Runnels, Schleicher, Scurry, Shackelford, Sterling, Stonewall, Taylor, Throckmorton, Tom Green, Ward, Winkler.

Eighth Region: David L. Evans, Fort Worth (12/2022): Archer, Clay, Cooke, Denton, Eastland, Erath, Hood, Jack, Johnson, Montague, Palo Pinto, Parker, Somervell, Stephens, Tarrant, Wichita, Wise, Young.

Ninth Region: Ana Estevez, Amarillo (2/2024): Armstrong, Bailey, Baylor, Briscoe, Carson, Castro, Childress, Cochran, Collingsworth, Cottle, Crosby, Dallam, Deaf Smith, Dickens, Donley, Floyd, Foard, Gray, Hale, Hall, Hansford, Hardeman, Hartley, Hemphill, Hockley, Hutchinson, King, Knox, Lamb, Lipscomb, Lubbock, Moore, Motley, Ochiltree, Oldham, Parmer, Potter, Randall, Roberts, Sherman, Swisher, Terry, Wheeler, Wilbarger, Yoakum.

Tenth Region: Alfonso Charles, Longview (2/2022): Anderson, Bowie, Camp, Cass. Cherokee, Delta, Franklin, Freestone, Gregg, Harrison, Henderson, Hopkins, Houston, Hunt, Lamar, Leon, Limestone, Marion, Morris, Nacogdoches, Panola, Rains, Red River, Rusk, Sabine, San Augustine, Shelby, Smith, Titus, Upshur, Van Zandt, Wood.

Eleventh Region: Susan Brown, Houston (3/2022): Brazoria, Fort Bend, Galveston, Harris, Matagorda, Wharton. ☆

Texas Courts by County

Below are listed the state district court or courts, court of appeals district, administrative judicial district, and U.S. judicial district for each county in Texas as of August 2021. For the names of the district court judges, see table by district number on page 457. Lists of other judges in the Texas court system begin on page 493.

County	State Dist. Court(s)	Ct. of Appeals Dist	Adm. Jud. Reg.	U.S. Jud. Dist.	County	State Dist. Court(s)	Ct. of Appeals Dist	Adm. Jud. Reg.	U.S. Jud. Dist.
Anderson	3, 87, 349, 369	12	10	E-Tyler	Dawson	106	11	7	N-Lubbock
Andrews	109	8	7	W-Midland	Deaf Smith	222	7	9	N-Amarillo
Angelina	159, 217	12	2	E-Lufkin	Delta	8, 62	6	10	E-Sherman
Aransas	36, 156, 343	13	4	S-C.Christi	Denton	16, 158, 211, 362, 367, 393, 431, 442, 462, 467	2	8	E-Sherman
Archer	97	2	8	N-W. Falls					
Armstrong	47	7	9	N-Amarillo	DeWitt	24, 135, 267	13	4	S-Victoria
Atascosa	81, 218	4	4	W-San Ant.	Dickens	110	7	9	N-Lubbock
Austin	155	1, 14	3	S-Houston	Dimmit	293, 365	4	4	W-San Ant.
Bailey	287	7	9	N-Lubbock	Donley	100	7	9	N-Amarillo
Bandera	198	4	6	W-San Ant.	Duval	229	4	5	S-C. Christi
Bastrop	21, 335, 423	3	2	W-Austin	Eastland	91	11	8	N-Abilene
Baylor	50	11	9	N-W. Falls	Ector	70, 161, 244, 358, 446	11	7	W-Midland
Bee	36, 156, 343	13	4	S-C. Christi	Edwards	452	4	6	W-Del Rio
Bell	27, 146, 169, 264, 426	3	3	W-Waco	Ellis	40, 378, 443	10	1	N-Dallas
Bexar	37, 45, 57, 73, 131, 144, 150, 166, 175, 186, 187, 224, 225, 226, 227, 285, 288, 289, 290, 379, 386, 399, 407, 408, 436, 437, 438	4	4	W-San Ant.	El Paso	34, 41, 65, 120, 168, 171, 205, 210, 243, 327, 346, 383, 384, 388, 409, 448, Cr. 1	8	6	W-El Paso
					Erath	266	11	8	N-Ft. Worth
					Falls	82	10	3	W-Waco
Blanco	33, 424	3	3	W-Austin	Fannin	336	6	1	E-Sherman
Borden	132	11	7	N-Lubbock	Fayette	155	3	3	S-Houston
Bosque	220	10	3	W-Waco	Fisher	32	11	7	N-Abilene
Bowie	5, 102, 202	6	10	E-Texark	Floyd	110	7	9	N-Lubbock
Brazoria	149, 239, 300, 412, 461	1, 14	11	S-Galves	Foard	46	7	9	N-W. Falls
Brazos	85, 272, 361	10	2	S-Houston	Fort Bend	240, 268, 328, 387, 400, 434, 458, 505	1, 14	11	S-Houston
Brewster	394	8	6	W-Pecos					
Briscoe	110	7	9	N-Amarillo	Franklin	8, 62	6	10	E-Texark
Brooks	79	4	5	S-C. Christi	Freestone	77, 87	10	10	W-Waco
Brown	35	11	7	N-S. Angelo	Frio	81, 218	4	4	W-San Ant.
Burleson	21, 335	10	2	W-Austin	Gaines	106	11	7	N-Lubbock
Burnet	33, 424	3	3	W-Austin	Galveston	10, 56, 122, 212, 306, 405	1, 14	11	S-Galves
Caldwell	22, 207, 421	3	3	W-Austin					
Calhoun	24, 135, 267	13	4	S-Victoria	Garza	106	7	7	N-Lubbock
Callahan	42	11	7	N-Abilene	Gillespie	216	4	6	W-Austin
Cameron	103, 107, 138, 197, 357, 404, 444, 445	13	5	S-Brownsville	Glasscock	118	11	7	N-S. Angelo
					Goliad	24, 135, 267	13	4	S-Victoria
Camp	76, 276	6	10	E-Marshall	Gonzales	25, 25-A	13	3	W-San Ant.
Carson	100	7	9	N-Amarillo	Gray	31, 223	7	9	N-Amarillo
Cass	5	6	10	E-Marshall	Grayson	15, 59, 397	5	1	E-Sherman
Castro	64, 242	7	9	N-Amarillo	Gregg	124, 188, 307	6, 12	10	E-Tyler
Chambers	253, 344	1, 14	2	S-Galves	Grimes	12, 506	1, 14	2	S-Houston
Cherokee	2, 369	12	10	E-Tyler	Guadalupe	25, 25-A, 274, 456	4	3	W-San Ant.
Childress	100	7	9	N-Amarillo	Hale	64, 242	7	9	N-Lubbock
Clay	97	2	8	N-W. Falls	Hall	100	7	9	N-Amarillo
Cochran	286	7	9	N-Lubbock	Hamilton	220	10	3	W-Waco
Coke	51	3	7	N-S. Angelo	Hansford	84	7	9	N-Amarillo
Coleman	42	11	7	N-S. Angelo	Hardeman	46	7	9	N-W. Falls
Collin	199, 219, 296, 366, 380, 401, 416, 417, 428, 429, 468, 469, 470, 471	5	1	E-Sherman	Hardin	88, 356	9	2	E-B'mont
					Harris	11, 55, 61, 80, 113, 125, 127, 129, 133, 151, 152, 157, 164, 165, 174, 176, 177, 178, 179, 180, 182, 183, 184, 185, 189, 190, 208, 209, 215, 228, 230, 234, 245, 246, 247, 248, 257, 262, 263, 269, 270, 280, 281, 295, 308, 309, 310, 311, 312, 313, 314, 315, 333, 334, 337, 338, 339, 351, 507	1, 14	11	S-Houston
Collingsworth	100	7	9	N-Amarillo					
Colorado	25, 25-A	1, 14	3	S-Houston					
Comal	22, 207, 274, 433, 463, 466	3	3	W-San Ant.					
Comanche	220	11	3	N-Ft. Worth					
Concho	119	3	7	N-S. Angelo					
Cooke	235	2	8	E-Sherman					
Coryell	52, 440	10	3	W-Waco					
Cottle	50	7	9	N-W. Falls	Harrison	71	6	10	E-Marshall
Crane	109	8	7	W-Midland	Hartley	69	7	9	N-Amarillo
Crockett	112	8	6	N-S. Angelo	Haskell	39	11	7	N-Abilene
Crosby	72	7	9	N-Lubbock	Hays	22, 207, 274, 428, 453	3	3	W-Austin
Culberson	205, 394	8	6	W-Pecos	Hemphill	31	7	9	N-Amarillo
Dallam	69	7	9	N-Amarillo	Henderson	3, 173, 392	12	10	E-Tyler
Dallas	14, 44, 68, 95, 101, 116, 134, 160, 162, 191, 192, 193, 194, 195, 203, 204, 254, 255, 256, 265, 282, 283, 291, 292, 298, 301, 302, 303, 304, 305, 330, 363, Cr. 1, Cr. 2, Cr. 3, Cr. 4, Cr. 5, Cr. 6, Cr. 7,	5	1	N-Dallas	Hidalgo	92, 93, 139, 206, 275, 332, 370, 389, 398, 430, 449, 464	13	5	S-McAllen
					Hill	66	10	3	W-Waco
					Hockley	286	7	9	N-Lubbock
					Hood	355	2	8	N-Ft. Worth

County	State Dist. Court(s)	Ct. of Appeals Dist	Adm. Jud. Reg.	U.S. Jud. Dist.
Hopkins	8, 62	6	10	E-Sherman
Houston	3, 349	12	10	E-Lufkin
Howard	118	11	7	N-Abilene
Hudspeth	205, 394	8	6	W-Pecos
Hunt	196, 354	5, 6	10	N-Dallas
Hutchinson	84, 316	7	9	N-Amarillo
Irion	51	3	7	N-S. Angelo
Jack	271	2	8	N-Ft. Worth
Jackson	24, 135, 267	13	4	S-Victoria
Jasper	1, 1-A	9	2	E-B'mont
Jeff Davis	394	8	6	W-Pecos
Jefferson	58, 60, 136, 172, 252, 279, 317, Cr. 1	9	2	E-B'mont
Jim Hogg	229	4	5	S-Laredo
Jim Wells	79	4	5	S-C. Christi
Johnson	18, 249, 413	10	8	N-Dallas
Jones	259	11	7	N-Abilene
Karnes	81, 218	4	4	W-San Ant.
Kaufman	86, 422	5	1	N-Dallas
Kendall	451	4	6	W-San Ant.
Kenedy	105	13	5	S-C. Christi
Kent	39	7	7	N-Lubbock
Kerr	198, 216	4	6	W-San Ant.
Kimble	452	4	6	W-Austin
King	50	7	9	N-W. Falls
Kinney	63	4	6	W-Del Rio
Kleberg	105	13	5	S-C. Christi
Knox	50	11	9	N-W. Falls
Lamar	6, 62	6	10	E-Sherman
Lamb	154	7	9	N-Lubbock
Lampasas	27	3	3	W-Austin
La Salle	81, 218	4	4	S-Laredo
Lavaca	25, 25-A	13	3	S-Victoria
Lee	21, 335	3	2	W-Austin
Leon	87, 278, 369	10	10	W-Waco
Liberty	75, 253	9	2	E-B'mont
Limestone	77, 87	10	10	W-Waco
Lipscomb	31	7	9	N-Amarillo
Live Oak	36, 156, 343	13	4	S-C. Christi
Llano	33, 424	3	3	W-Austin
Loving	143	8	7	W-Pecos
Lubbock	72, 99, 137, 140, 237, 364	7	9	N-Lubbock
Lynn	106	7	7	N-Lubbock
Madison	12, 278	10	2	S-Houston
Marion	115, 276	6	10	E-Marshall
Martin	118	11	7	W-Midland
Mason	452	4	6	W-Austin
Matagorda	23, 130	13	11	S-Galves.
Maverick	293, 365	4	4	W-Del Rio
McCulloch	452	3	6	W-Austin
McLennan	19, 54, 74, 170, 414	10	3	W-Waco
McMullen	36, 156, 343	4	4	S-Laredo
Medina	454	4	6	W-San Ant.
Menard	452	4	6	N-S. Angelo
Midland	142, 238, 318, 385, 441	11	7	W-Midland
Milam	20	3	3	W-Waco
Mills	35	3	7	N-S. Angelo
Mitchell	32	11	7	N-Abilene
Montague	97	2	8	N-W. Falls
Montgomery	9, 221, 284, 359, 410, 418, 435, 457	9	2	S-Houston
Moore	69	7	9	N-Amarillo
Morris	76, 276	6	10	E-Marshall
Motley	110	7	9	N-Lubbock
Nacogdoches	145, 420	12	10	E-Lufkin
Navarro	13	10	3	N-Dallas
Newton	1, 1-A	9	2	E-B'mont
Nolan	32	11	7	N-Abilene
Nueces	28, 94, 105, 117, 148, 214, 319, 347	13	5	S-C. Christi
Ochiltree	84	7	9	N-Amarillo
Oldham	222	7	9	N-Amarillo
Orange	128, 163, 260	9	2	E-B'mont
Palo Pinto	29	11	8	N-Ft. Worth
Panola	123	6	10	E-Tyler
Parker	43, 415	2	8	N-Ft. Worth
Parmer	287	7	9	N-Amarillo
Pecos	83, 112	8	6	W-Pecos
Polk	258, 411	9	2	E-Lufkin
Potter	47, 108, 181, 251, 320	7	9	N-Amarillo
Presidio	394	8	6	W-Pecos
Rains	8, 354	12	10	E-Tyler
Randall	47, 181, 251	7	9	N-Amarillo
Reagan	112	8	6	N-S. Angelo
Real	38	4	6	W-San Ant.
Red River	6, 102	6	10	E-Texark
Reeves	143	8	7	W-Pecos
Refugio	24, 135, 267	13	4	S-Victoria
Roberts	31	7	9	N-Amarillo
Robertson	82	10	3	W-Waco
Rockwall	382, 439	5	1	N-Dallas
Runnels	119	3	7	N-S. Angelo
Rusk	4	6, 12	10	E-Tyler
Sabine	1, 273	12	10	E-Lufkin
San Augustine	1, 273	12	10	E-Lufkin
San Jacinto	258, 411	9	2	S-Houston
San Patricio	36, 156, 343	13	4	S-C. Christi
San Saba	33, 424	3	3	W-Austin
Schleicher	51	3	7	N-S. Angelo
Scurry	132	11	7	N-Lubbock
Shackelford	259	11	7	N-Abilene
Shelby	123, 273	12	10	E-Lufkin
Sherman	69	7	9	N-Amarillo
Smith	7, 114, 241, 321	12	10	E-Tyler
Somervell	18, 249	10	8	W-Waco
Starr	229, 381	4	5	S-McAllen
Stephens	90	11	8	N-Abilene
Sterling	51	3	7	N-S. Angelo
Stonewall	39	11	7	N-Abilene
Sutton	112	4	6	N-S. Angelo
Swisher	64, 242	7	9	N-Amarillo
Tarrant	17, 48, 67, 96, 141, 153, 213, 231, 233, 236, 297, 322, 323, 324, 325, 342, 348, 352, 360, 371, 372, 396, 432, Cr. 1, Cr. 2, Cr. 3, Cr. 4	2	8	N-Ft. Worth
Taylor	42, 104, 326, 350	11	7	N-Abilene
Terrell	63, 83	8	6	W-Del Rio
Terry	121	7	9	N-Lubbock
Throckmorton	39	11	7	N-Abilene
Titus	76, 276	6	10	E-Texark
Tom Green	51, 119, 340, 391	3	7	N-S. Angelo
Travis	53, 98, 126, 147, 167, 200, 201, 250, 261, 299, 331, 345, 353, 390, 403, 419, 427, 450, 455, 459, 460	3	3	W-Austin
Trinity	258, 411	12	2	E-Lufkin
Tyler	1-A, 88	9	2	E-Lufkin
Upshur	115	6, 12	10	E-Marshall
Upton	112	8	6	W-Midland
Uvalde	38	4	6	W-Del Rio
Val Verde	63, 83	4	6	W-Del Rio
Van Zandt	294	12	10	E-Tyler
Victoria	24, 135, 267, 377	13	4	S-Victoria
Walker	12, 278	10	2	S-Houston
Waller	506	1, 14	2	S-Houston
Ward	143	8	7	W-Pecos
Washington	21, 335	1, 14	2	W-Austin
Webb	49, 111, 341, 406	4	4	S-Laredo
Wharton	23, 329	13	11	S-Houston
Wheeler	31	7	9	N-Amarillo
Wichita	30, 78, 89	2	8	N-W. Falls
Wilbarger	46	7	9	N-W. Falls
Willacy	197	13	5	S-Brownsville
Williamson	26, 277, 368, 395, 425	3	3	W-Austin
Wilson	81, 218	4	4	W-San Ant.
Winkler	109	8	7	W-Pecos
Wise	271	2	8	N-Ft. Worth
Wood	402	6, 12	10	E-Tyler
Yoakum	121	7	9	N-Lubbock
Young	90	2	8	N-W. Falls
Zapata	49	4	4	S-Laredo
Zavala	293, 365	4	4	W-Del Rio

Texas State Agencies

On the following pages is information about several of the many state agencies in Texas. Information was supplied to the Texas Almanac by the agencies, their websites, and from news reports. The web address for more information about state agencies, boards, and commissions is: https://www.tsl.texas.gov/apps/lrs/agencies/index.html.

Texas Commission on Environmental Quality

Source: Texas Commission on Environmental Quality; www.tceq.texas.gov

The Texas Commission on Environmental Quality (TCEQ) is the state's leading environmental agency. The TCEQ works to protect Texas' human and natural resources in a manner consistent with sustainable economic development. The agency has about 2,700 employees; of those, about 800 work in the 16 regional offices.

One of the TCEQ's major functions is issuing permits and other authorizations for the control of air pollution, the safe operation of water and wastewater utilities, and the management of hazardous and nonhazardous waste.

The agency promotes voluntary compliance with environmental laws through pollution prevention programs, regulatory workshops, and assistance to businesses and local governments. When environmental laws are violated, the TCEQ has the authority to levy penalties as much as $25,000 a day per violation for administrative cases. In a typical year, the agency conducts more than 105,000 investigations at regulated entities for compliance with state and federal laws and receives about 4,000 complaints.

TCEQ Budget for FYE 2022 and FYE 2023	
Assessment, Planning and Permitting	$245,820,762
Safe Drinking Water	$48,087,570
Enforcement and Compliance Support	$142,708,918
Pollution Cleanup	$87,475,953
River Compact Commissions	$5,982,211
Indirect Administration	$116,937,401
Total	**$647,012,815**

Source: SB1, General Appropriations Bill, 2021.

The TCEQ is also responsible for most state and federal regulatory programs that protect groundwater, administers permits for the discharge of wastewater and stormwater, and conducts Section 401 certifications of federal permits.

The agency enforces the federal Safe Drinking Water Act, oversees the protection of the state's approximately 7,000 public water systems providing drinking water to roughly 27 million customers, and has general supervision of water districts.

Office of Air

Texas is home to some of the largest U.S. cities, with several metropolitan populations of greater than 1 million people. With these concentrated populations, vehicular traffic and other emissions can create air quality issues among the most challenging in the country.

The state has a fast-growing population, a large industrial base concentrated along the Gulf Coast, and an oil and gas industry expanding throughout much of the state. The TCEQ conducts survey activities along with targeted and/or specialized monitoring activities to evaluate changing air quality conditions across the state.

The TCEQ measures air quality across the state for compliance with federal standards, as well as for localized compounds of concern. Texas' air toxic monitoring network is one of the most comprehensive in the country with more than 80 monitoring sites located across the state.

The TCEQ is responsible for developing a state implementation plan to bring metropolitan areas into compliance with federal air quality standards, such as the ozone standard. The leading areas of concern for ozone issues are the Houston-Galveston-Brazoria and Dallas–Fort Worth areas.

Office of Water

The TCEQ preserves and improves the quality of the state's surface waters by establishing surface water quality standards; monitoring, assessing, and reporting conditions; and implementing plans to reduce pollution and improve water quality. It protects surface water users through the water rights permitting process and the watermaster programs.

Office of Waste

Waste management projects at the TCEQ include Superfund projects, pesticide collections, and permits and authorizations for municipal and industrial waste management. Another major cleanup program focuses on leaking petroleum storage tanks. In 2019, there were 55 Superfund sites in the state, and work continues at another 1,344 sites.

The TCEQ issues permits and other authorizations for municipal and industrial waste management, including landfills and storage, processing, and recycling operations. In addition, the safe recycling of both municipal and industrial waste streams is encouraged.

The TCEQ also regulates the disposal of radioactive material, with the exception of naturally occurring radioactive material (NORM) generated as a result of oil and gas exploration. This includes the regulation of the receipt, processing, storage, and disposal of by-product and low-level radioactive waste, the licensing of uranium and thorium recovery facilities, decommissioning of inactive uranium-recovery facilities, permitting for underground injection control, and legacy radioactive material disposal sites.

Help With Understanding Environmental Rules

The TCEQ offers services to anyone interested in environmental stewardship and navigating TCEQ's programs and regulatory requirements. Staff members host workshops on recycling and disposal opportunities, and on regulatory and pollution prevention topics.

The TCEQ also offers free compliance assistance to thousands of small businesses and local governments each year. Contact the TCEQ at PO Box 13087, Austin, 78711; (512) 239-1000; www.tceq.texas.gov. ☆

Health and Human Services

Source: Texas Health and Human Services, hhs.texas.gov

Texas Health and Human Services (HHS) is the oversight agency for the state's health and human services system. HHS also administers state and federal programs that provide financial, health, and social services to Texans. Executive Commissioner Cecile Erwin Young was appointed on Aug. 14, 2020.

In 2003, the 78th Texas Legislature mandated an unprecedented transformation of the state's health and human services system, blending 12 agencies into five. The system transformed again in 2017, with the goal of removing bureaucratic silos, creating clear lines of accountability, and making it easier for people to find out about services or benefits they might qualify for.

Today's HHS consists of only two agencies: Texas Health and Human Services Commission (HHSC) and the Texas Department of State Health Services (DSHS). The executive commissioner is appointed by the governor and confirmed by the Senate. The Department of Family and Protective Services is an independent agency under the HHSC umbrella.

HHS is located at 4601 Guadalupe St., Austin, 78711-3247; Phone: 512-424-6500; TTY: 512-424-6597.

Health and Human Services Commission

The HHSC oversees the licensing and credentialing of facilities for long-term care, including nursing homes and assisted living; licenses child care providers; and manages daily operations at state-supported hospitals and living centers.

It also delivers benefits and services such as Medicaid, SNAP food benefits, and TANF cash assistance; services for women and people with special health needs; long-term care for the aging and those with disabilities; and behavioral health services.

Department of State Health Services

DSHS serves as the public health authority for Texas, providing vital statistics and health data to the public, leading the public-health response in times of disaster or outbreaks, and administering chronic and infectious disease prevention and testing. The department also licenses and regulates facilities on topics including youth camps and mobile food establishments. It is led by Commissioner of Public Health Dr. John Hellerstedt.

The client services DSHS previously provided were transferred to HHSC in 2016.

Department of Family and Protective Services

The Department of Family and Protective Services (DFPS) works to protect children and vulnerable adults through prevention programs, investigations, and services and referrals. DFPS has five major programs:

- Adult Protective Services
- Child Protective Services
- Investigations
- Prevention and Early Intervention
- Statewide Intake

HHS Budget for FYE 2022 and FYE 2023	
Dept. of Family and Protective Services	$4,602.1
Dept. of State Health Services	$1,865.6
Health and Human Services Commission	$78,600.1
Total	**$85,067.8**

All figures in millions. Total may not sum due to rounding.
Source: SB1, General Appropriations Bill, 2021.

To report abuse, neglect, or exploitation of children, the elderly or people with disabilities, call 1-800-252-5400 or report online at www.txabusehotline.org. For emergencies call 911.

DFPS headquarters address: 701 W. 51st St., Austin, 78751; Mailing address: PO Box 149030, Austin, 78714-9030; www.dfps.state.tx.us.

Other HHSC Programs

The Family Violence program offers emergency shelter and services to victims and their children.

The Disaster Assistance program processes grant applications for victims of presidentially declared disasters, such as tornados, floods, and hurricanes.

As of 2017, the HHS no longer provides refugee resettlement services. Nonprofit agencies, including U.S. Committee for Refugees and Immigrants (USCRI),l have stepped in to provide health services for these groups.☆

Major HHS Programs at a Glance

The **Medicaid** program provides healthcare coverage for one out of every three children in Texas, pays for half of all births, and accounts for 25 percent of the state's total budget. In 2018, an average of 4 million Texans received healthcare coverage through Medicaid.

The **Children's Health Insurance Program (CHIP)** is designed for families who earn too much money to qualify for Medicaid yet cannot afford private insurance.

The **Temporary Assistance for Needy Families (TANF)** program provides basic financial assistance for needy children and the parents or caretakers with whom they live. As a condition of eligibility, caretakers must sign and abide by a personal-responsibility agreement. Time limits for benefits have been set by both state and federal welfare-reform legislation.

SNAP food benefits, formerly known as food stamps, is a federally funded program that assists low-income families, the elderly, and single adults obtain a nutritionally adequate diet.

Both SNAP and TANF benefits are delivered via the electronic benefit transfer (EBT) system, through which clients access benefits at about 12,000 retail locations statewide with the Lone Star card. Information about Medicaid, CHIP, and other health and human services programs can be found at www.211texas.org, or by calling **2-1-1**, a toll-free local resource for information on HHS programs.

The General Land Office Building in Austin was completed in 1857. Photo by Larry D. Moore, CC by 3.0/Wikimedia Commons.

The General Land Office

Source: General Land Office of Texas, glo.texas.gov

History of the General Land Office

The Texas General Land Office (GLO) is one of the oldest governmental entities in the state, dating back to the Republic of Texas. The first General Land Office was established in 1836 by the Republic's constitution, and the first Texas Congress enacted the provision into law in 1837. The GLO was established to oversee distribution of public lands, register titles, issue patents on land, and maintain records of land granted.

In the early years of statehood, beginning in 1845, Texas established the precedent of using its vast public domain for public benefit. The first use was to sell or trade land to eliminate the huge debt remaining from Texas' War for Independence and the early years of the Republic.

Texas also gave away land to settlers as homesteads; to veterans as compensation for service; for internal improvements, including building railroads, shipbuilding, and improving rivers for navigation; and to build the state Capitol.

The public domain was closed in 1898 when the Texas Supreme Court declared there was no more vacant and unappropriated land in Texas. In 1900, all remaining unappropriated land was set aside by the Legislature to benefit public schools.

Today, 13 million acres of land and minerals, owned by the Permanent School Fund, the Permanent University Fund, various other state agencies, and the Veterans Land Board, are managed by the GLO and the Commissioner of the Texas General Land Office.

This includes over 4 million acres of submerged coastal lands, which consist of bays, inlets, and the area from the Texas shoreline to the three-marine-league line (10.36 miles) in the Gulf of Mexico. It is estimated that more than 1 million acres make up the public domain of the state's riverbeds and another 1.7 million acres are excess lands belonging to the Permanent School Fund.

The GLO is the steward of the Texas Gulf Coast, serving as the premier state agency for protecting and renourishing the coast and fighting coastal erosion. In 1999, the Legislature created the Coastal Erosion Planning and Response Act and put the GLO in charge of facilitating restoration and preservation of eroding beaches, dunes, wetlands, and other bay shorelines along the Texas coast.

The Permanent School Fund owns mineral rights alone in almost 7.4 million acres covered under the Relinquishment Act, the Free Royalty Act, and the various sales acts, and it has outright ownership to about 747,522 upland acres, mostly west of the Pecos River.

Historic Distribution of the Public Lands of Texas

PURPOSE	ACRES
Settlers	**68,027,108**
Spain and Mexico	24,583,923
Spanish and Mexican Grants south of the Nueces River, recognized by Act of Feb. 10, 1852	3,741,241
Headrights	30,360,002
Republic colonies	4,494,806
Preemption land	4,847,136
Military	**9,874,262**
Bounty	5,354,250
Battle donations	1,162,240
Veterans donations	1,377,920
Confederate	1,979,852
Improvements	**37,155,714**
Road	27,716
Navigation	4,261,760
Irrigation	584,000
Ships	17,000
Manufacturing	111,360
Railroads	32,153,878
Education	**52,329,168**
University, public school, and eleemosynary institutions	52,329,168
Total of distributed lands	**167,386,252**

Texas Veterans Land Board Programs

The Veterans Land Board (VLB) was formally established by the Legislature to administer benefits for Texas Veterans in 1946, with the first loan made in 1949.

Since then, the programs have evolved to include low-interest land, housing, and home improvement loans. VLB has funded more than 220,000 loans amounting to more than $11 billion for Texas veterans, military members, and their families since its inception.

VLB strives to offer the best benefits program in the nation and works to ensure that Texas veterans are aware of these benefits.

In a joint effort with the Texas Veterans Commission, the VLB operates the Texas Veterans Call Service Center to connect veterans, military members, and their families with the benefits and services they need. For more information, contact VLB at 1-800-252-VETS (8387) or https://vlb.texas.gov/

Texas State Veterans Homes

In 1997, the 75th Legislature approved legislation authorizing the Veterans Land Board to construct and operate Texas State Veterans Homes under a cost-sharing program with the U.S. Department of Veterans Affairs (USDVA). The homes provide affordable, quality, long-term care for Texas' veterans.

Texas State Veterans Cemeteries

The VLB owns and operates several cemeteries under USDVA guidelines. The USDVA funds the design and construction of the cemeteries, but the land must be donated.

The Alamo

In 2011, the 82nd Legislature granted authority over the Alamo to the GLO. The Alamo hosts millions of visitors from around the world each year. UNESCO designated the Alamo and four other Spanish missions in San Antonio as U.S. World Heritage sites in 2015.

Plans to create a museum and visitors center to house rock legend Phil Collins' donated collection of Alamo and Texana artifacts are underway. ☆

Texas Historical Commission

The Texas Historical Commission protects and preserves the state's historic and prehistoric resources. The Texas State Legislature established the Texas State Historical Survey Committee in 1953 to identify important historic sites across the state.

The Texas Legislature changed the agency's name to the Texas Historical Commission in 1973 and increased its mission and its protective powers. Today the agency's concerns include archaeology, architecture, community heritage development, historic sites, history programs, and education. The commission:

- Works with communities and individuals to help identify important historic resources and develop a plan to preserve them.

- Provides leadership and training to county historical commissions, heritage organizations, and museums in Texas' 254 counties.

- Helps protect Texas' diverse architectural heritage, including historic county courthouses.

- Partners with communities to stimulate tourism and economic development.

- Assists Texas cities in the revitalization of their historic downtowns through the Texas Main Street Program.

- Administers the state's historical marker program, which has around 15,000 markers across the state.

- Consults with citizens and groups to nominate properties as Recorded Texas Historic Landmarks, State Archeological Landmarks, and to the National Register of Historic Places.

- Operates 20 state historic sites including house museums, military forts, and archeological sites.

- Works with property owners to save archeological sites on private land and ensures archeological sites are protected as land is developed for highways and other public construction projects.

Mailing address: PO Box 12276, Austin 78711-2276; (512) 463-6100; www.thc.texas.gov.

Railroad Commission of Texas

The Railroad Commission of Texas has primary regulatory jurisdiction over the oil and natural gas industry, pipeline transporters, the natural gas and hazardous liquid pipeline industry, natural gas utilities, the liquefied petroleum gas (LP-gas) industry, rail industry, and coal and uranium surface mining operations. It also promotes the use of LP-gas as an alternative fuel in Texas through research and education.

The commission exercises its statutory responsibilities under provisions of the Texas Constitution, the Texas Natural Resources Code, the Texas Water Code, the Texas Utilities Code, the Coal and Uranium Surface Mining and Reclamation Acts, the Pipeline Safety Acts, and the Railroad Safety Act.

The commission has regulatory and enforcement responsibilities under federal law, including the Federal Railroad Safety Act, the Local Rail Freight Assistance Act, the Surface Coal Mining Control and Reclamation Act, the Pipeline Safety Acts, the Resource Conservation Recovery Act, and the Clean Water Act.

The Railroad Commission was established by the Texas Legislature in 1891 and given jurisdiction over rates and operations of railroads, terminals, wharves, and express companies. In 1917, the legislature declared pipelines to be common carriers and gave the commission regulatory authority over them. It was also given the responsibility to administer conservation laws relating to oil and natural gas production.

The Railroad Commission exists to protect the environment, public safety, and the rights of mineral interest owners; to prevent waste of natural resources; and to assure fair and equitable utility rates in those industries over which it has authority. Mailing address: PO Box 12967, Austin 78711-2967; (512) 463-7158; www.rrc.state.tx.us.

Texas Department of Juvenile Justice

The Texas Department of Juvenile Justice was created on Dec. 1, 2011, by Senate Bill 653, 82nd Legislature. Its creation abolished both the Texas Youth Commission and the Texas Juvenile Probation Commission.

The agency's executive director is Camille Cain, and it has a 13-member commission who are appointed to six-year terms. It is chaired by Wes Ritchey of Dalhart.

The **Texas Youth Commission (TYC)** had operated correctional facilities and halfway houses for serious youth offenders. In 2007, widespread sexual and physical abuse was uncovered at many of its facilities. After a number of supervisors were dismissed, the entire TYC board resigned on March 15, 2007, and their powers were transferred to a conservator. The 80th Texas Legislature approved a bill to overhaul the troubled agency.

The **Texas Department of Juvenile Justice** is a unified state juvenile justice agency that works in partnership with local county governments, courts, and communities to promote public safety by providing services to youth from initial contact through end of supervision. Its expressed goals are to:

- Support development of county-based programs and services for youth and families that reduce the need for out-of-home placement;
- Seek alternatives to placing youthful offenders in secure state facilities, while also addressing treatment of youth and protecting the public;
- Locate facilities as geographically close as possible to workforce and other services, and support youths' connection to their families;
- Encourage regional and county collaboration;
- Enhance the continuity of care throughout the juvenile justice system; and
- Use secure facilities of a size that supports effective youth rehabilitation and public safety.

The agency is located at Braker H Complex, 11209 Metric Blvd., Austin 78758. Mailing Address: PO Box 12757, Austin 78711-2757; (512) 490-7130; https://www.tjjd.texas.gov/.

Texas Workforce Commission

The Texas Workforce Commission (TWC) is the state government agency charged with overseeing and providing workforce development services to employers and job seekers of Texas. It is led by three appointed commissioners, representing the public (Bryan Daniel), labor (Julian Alvarez III), and employers (Aaron Demerson).

For employers, TWC offers recruiting, retention, training and retraining, outplacement services, and information on labor law and labor market statistics.

For job seekers, TWC offers career development information, job search resources, training programs, and, as appropriate, unemployment benefits. While targeted populations receive intensive assistance to overcome barriers to employment, all Texans can benefit from the services offered by TWC and its network of workforce partners.

The Texas Workforce Commission is part of a local and state network dedicated to developing the workforce of Texas. The network is composed of the statewide efforts of the commission coupled with planning and service provision on a regional level by 28 local workforce boards. This network gives customers access to local workforce solutions and statewide services in a single location — Texas Workforce Centers.

Primary services of the Texas Workforce Commission and its network partners are funded by federal tax revenue and are generally free to all Texans. Mailing address: 101 E. 15th Street, Austin 78778; (512) 463-2222; www.twc.state.tx.us. ☆

Texas State Boards and Commissions

Following is a list of appointees to state boards and commissions, as well as names of other state officials, revised to **August 18, 2021**. Information includes, where available, (1) date of creation; (2) whether the position is elective or appointive; (3) length of term; (4) compensation, if any; (5) number of members; (6) names of appointees, their hometowns, and expiration of terms. In some instances the date of term expiration has passed; in such cases, no new appointment had been made by press time, and the official is continuing to fill the position until a successor is named. Most positions marked "apptv." are appointed by the Governor. Where otherwise, appointing authority is given. Most advisory boards are not listed. Salaries for commissioners and administrators are those that were authorized by the appropriations bill passed by the 85th Legislature for the 2018–2019 biennium. They are "not-to-exceed" salaries: maximum authorized salaries for the positions. Actual salaries may be less than those stated here.

Accountancy, Texas State Board of Public: (1945 with 2-yr. terms; reorganized 1959 as 9-member board with 6-yr. overlapping terms; number of members increased to 12 in 1979; increased to 15 in 1989; per diem and expenses: Presiding Officer Manuel "Manny" Cavazos IV, Manor (1/31/23); Susan I. Adams, Colleyville (1/31/27); Kelly V. Aimone, Houston (1/31/25); Olivia Espinoza-Riley, Addison (1/31/27); Renee D. Foshee, San Marcos (1/31/25); Lisa A. Friel, San Antonio (1/31/25); Ray R. Garcia, Houston (1/31/27); Jamie D. Grant, Arlington (1/31/23); Jill A. Holup, Austin (1/31/25); James D. "Jim" Ingram IV, College Station (1/31/23); Kevin J. Koch, Temple (1/31/25); Debra D. Seefeld, Montgomery (1/31/25); Debra S. Sharp, Houston (1/31/23); Jeannette P. Smith, Mission (1/31/25); Sheila M. Vallés-Pankratz, Mission (1/31/27). Exec. Dir. William Treacy ($182,875), 505 E. Huntland Dr., Ste. 380, Austin 78752-3757; (512) 305-7800.

Acupuncture Examiners, Texas State Board of: (1993); apptv.; 6-yr.; per diem; 9 members: Presiding Officer Donna S. Guthery, Bellaire (1/31/23); Elisabeth Lee "Elle" Carlson, Garland (1/31/25); Sheri J. Davidson, Houston (1/31/25); Maria M. Garcia, Plano (1/31/27); Samantha A. Gonzalez, San Antonio (1/31/27); Raymond J. Graham, El Paso (1/31/27); Mary E. Hebert, Nacogdoches (1/31/25); Grant E. Weidler, Spring (1/31/23); Rey Ximenes, Spicewood (1/31/27). Exec. Dir. Stephen "Brint" Carlton, 333 Guadalupe, Tower 3, Ste. 610, PO Box 2018, Austin 78768-2018; (512) 305-7010.

Adjutant General's Dept. (See Military Dept., Texas.)

Administrative Hearings, State Office of: Created in 1991 by 72nd Leg.; apptv.; 2-yr.; 1 member: Chief Admin. Law Judge Kristofer Monson, Driftwood (5/15/22) ($180,000), 300 W. 15th St., Ste. 504, Austin 78701; (512) 475-4993.

Aging and Disability Services Council, Department of (DADS): Est. 2003 by the 78th Legislature; later abolished by 84th Legislature (Senate Bill 200) effective 9/1/2017 and services merged into Texas Health and Human Services Commission.

Alcoholic Beverage Commission, Texas: (1935 as Liquor Control Board; name changed in 1970); apptv.; 6-yr; per diem and expenses; administrator apptd. by commission; 5 members: Chair Kevin J. Lilly, Houston (11/15/21); M. Scott Adkins, El Paso (11/15/23); Jason E. Boatright, Dallas (11/15/23); Hasan K. Mack, Austin (11/15/25); Deborah Gray Marino, San Antonio (11/15/25). Exec. Dir. Bentley Nettles ($200,000), 5806 Mesa Dr., PO Box 13127, Austin 78711; (512) 206-3333.

Alzheimer's Disease and Related Disorders, Texas Council on: (1999); apptv.; 2-yr.; 15 members (3 ex officio; 12 appointed by Gov., Lt. Gov., and House Speaker: Chair Marc Diamond, Dallas; Byron Cordes, San Antonio; Laura DeFina, Dallas; Joe A. Evans Jr., Beaumont (8/31/21); Vaunette Fay, Houston; Ana Guerrero Gore, Galveston; Char Hu, Dallas; Eddie Patton, Jr., Sugar Land (3/31/21); Mary Quiceno, Dallas; Sudha Seshadri, San Antonio; Terrence Sommers, Amarillo; Angela Turner, Normangee. Ex officio members include 1 from Texas Dept. of State Health Services and 2 from Texas Health and Human Services Commission. 1100 W. 49th St., PO Box 149347, Austin 78714-9347; (800) 242-3399.

Angelina and Neches River Authority: (1935 as Sabine-Neches Conservation Dist.; reorganized in 1950 and name changed to Neches River Conservation Dist.; changed to present name in 1977); apptv.; expenses; 6-yr.; 9 members: Pres. Jody Anderson, Lufkin (9/5/25); Kimberly M. Childs, Nacogdoches (9/5/25); Eddie Hopkins, Jasper (9/5/23); Donnie R. Kee, Diboll (9/5/23); Virginia M. "Ginger" Lymbery, Lufkin (9/5/23); Dale Morton, Nacogdoches (9/5/21); Thomas R. "Tom" Murphy, Crockett (9/5/25); Skip Ogle, Tyler (9/5/21); Francis G. Spruiell, Center (9/5/21). Gen. Mgr. Kelley Holcomb, 2901 N. John Redditt Dr., Lufkin 75904; (936) 632-7795.

Animal Health Commission, Texas: (1893 as Texas Livestock Sanitary Commission; name changed in 1959; members increased to 9 in 1973; raised to current number in 1983); apptv.; per diem and expenses; 6-yr.; 13 members: Chair Coleman Locke, Hungerford (9/6/21); Jim Eggleston, Weatherford (9/6/21); Jimmie Ruth Evans, San Antonio (9/6/25); Melanie Johnson, Houston (9/6/25); Kenneth "Ken" Jordan, San Saba (9/6/21); Barret J. Klein, Boerne (9/6/25); Wendee C. Langdon, Lubbock (9/6/23); Joe Leathers, Guthrie (9/6/25); Thomas "Tommy" Oates, Huntsville (9/6/25); Joseph G. "Joe" Osterkamp, Muleshoe (9/6/23); Keith M. Staggs, Gonzales (9/6/23); Leo Vermedahl, Dalhart (9/6/23); Michael L. Vickers, Falfurrias (9/6/21). Exec. Dir. Andy Schwartz ($155,814), 2105 Kramer Ln., PO Box 12966, Austin 78711-2966; (512) 719-0700.

Appraiser Licensing & Certification Board, Texas: (1991); 6-yr.; apptv.; per diem on duty; 9 members; 1 ex officio: Texas General Land Office; 8 apptd: Chair Sara Oates, Austin (1/31/25); Clayton Black, Stanton (1/31/23); R. Chance Bolton, Bee Cave (1/31/27); Rolando Castro, Cypress (1/31/23); Paola Escalante-Castillo, Weslaco (1/31/27); Martha Gayle Reid Lynch, El Paso (1/31/27); Stephanie Robinson, McKinney (1/31/25); Lisa Sprinkle, El Paso (1/31/25). Comm. Chelsea Buchholtz, PO Box 12188, Austin 78711-2188; (512) 936-3001.

Architectural Examiners, Texas Board of: (1937 as 3-member board; raised to 6 members in 1951 and to 9 in 1977); apptv.; 6-yr.; per diem and expenses. Chair Debra Dockery, San Antonio (1/31/23); Tim A. Bargainer, Georgetown (1/31/25); Chase Bearden, Austin (1/31/21); Darren L. James, Lewisville (1/31/25); Rosa G. Salazar, Dallas (1/31/23); Joyce J. Smith, Burnet (1/31/23); Fernando Trevino Sr., San Antonio (1/31/25); Jennifer Nicole Walker, Lampasas (1/31/21); Robert Scott "Bob" Wetmore, Austin (1/31/21). Exec. Dir. Julie Hildebrand ($151,429), 505 E. Huntland Dr., Ste. 350, PO Box 12337, Austin 78711; (512) 305-9000.

Arts, Texas Commission on the: (1965 as Texas Fine Arts Commission; name changed to Texas Commission on the Arts and Humanities in 1971; to present form in 1979); apptv.; 6-yr.; expenses; members: Chair Dale W. Brock, Fort Worth (8/31/23); Theresa W. Chang, Houston (8/31/25); Mila Gibson, Sweetwater (8/31/21); Adrian Guerra, Roma (8/31/23); Mary Ann Apap Heller, Austin (8/31/25); Patty Nuss, Corpus Christi (8/31/23); Karen Partee, Marshall (8/31/25); Sean Payton, Killeen (8/31/21); Marci Roberts, Marathon (8/31/21). Exec. Dir. Gary Gibbs

($129,927), 920 Colorado St., Ste. 501, PO Box 13406, Austin 78711-3406; (512) 463-5535.

Assistive and Rehabilitative Services, Department of (DARS): (2004) apptv.; 6-yr.; 9 members: Department was dissolved in September 2016 and programs were transferred to Texas Workforce Commission.

Athletic Trainers, Advisory Board of: (1971 as Texas Board of Athletic Trainers; name changed in 1975); expenses; 6-yr.; 5 members: Chair Britney Webb, San Marcos (1/31/27); Michael Fitch, Dallas (1/31/23); Darrell Ganus, Kilgore (1/31/21); David Schmidt, San Antonio (1/31/23); David Weir, College Station (1/31/25). PO Box 12157, Austin 78711; (512) 463-5699.

Auditor's Office, State: (1929); 2-yr.; apptd. by Legislative Audit Committee, a joint Senate-House committee: State Auditor (vacant), Robert E. Johnson Bldg., 1501 Congress Ave., P.O. Box 12067, Austin 78711-2067; (512) 936-9500.

Autism and Pervasive Developmental Disorders, Texas Council on: (1987); abolished by the 84th Legislature in 2015. Duties transferred to Texas Health and Human Services Commission.

Banking, Texas Department of: (1923); 2-yr.; apptd. by State Finance Commission; Comm. Charles G. Cooper ($242,925); 2601 N. Lamar Blvd., Austin 78705; (512) 475-1300. (See also Finance Commission of Texas.)

Bar of Texas, State: (1939 as administrative arm of Supreme Court); 46 directors, 36 elected by membership, 6 apptd by Texas Supreme Court, 4 by bar president; 3-yr. terms; also 14 ex officio members, including immediate past chair and out-of-state members; expenses paid from dues collected from membership. Chair Santos Vargas, Texas Law Center, 1414 Colorado St., Austin 78711; (512) 427-1463.

Barbering, Advisory Board on: (1929 as 3-member Texas Board of Barber Examiners; members increased in 1975; name changed in 2005 and functions transferred to Texas Dept. of Licensing & Regulation); 6-yr.; apptd. by dept. commissioners; 5 members: Presiding Officer Ron Jemison, Houston (9/29/21); James Bowens, Round Rock (9/29/19); Jenny Hatch, Alpine (9/29/21); Michelle Wasser, Austin (9/29/25); Ronald Weathers, De Soto (9/29/23). PO Box 12157, Austin 78711; (512) 463-6599.

Behavioral Health Executive Council, Texas: (2019, created by Legislature to comprise 4 existing Boards of Examiners; 6-yr. for presiding member, 2-yr. for others; 9 members: Presiding Member Gloria Canseco, San Antonio (2/1/25); John K. Bielamowicz, Waxahachie (2/1/22); Brian C. Brumley, Sumner (2/1/23); Susan Fletcher, Frisco (2/1/23); George F. Francis IV, Georgetown (2/1/23); Steven Hallbauer, Rockwall (2/1/23); Ben Morris, Cleburne (2/1/22); Jeanene L. Smith, Austin (2/1/22); Christopher S. Taylor, Dallas (2/1/22). Exec. Dir. Darrel D. Spinks, 333 Guadalupe St., Ste. 3-900, Austin 78701; (512) 305-7700.

Blind, Texas Commission for the: as of September 2016 the commission was incorporated into the Texas Workforce Commission.

Blind and Visually Impaired, Texas School for the: (1979); apptv.; 6-yr.; expenses; 9 members: Pres. Lee Sonnenberg, Lubbock (1/31/19); Mary K. Alexander, Valley View (1/31/21); Dan Brown, Pflugerville (1/31/23); Michael Hanley, Leander (1/31/23); Beth Jones, Anna (1/31/25); Brenda Lee, Brownwood (1/31/21); Joseph Muniz, Harlingen (1/31/21); Julie Prause, Columbus (1/31/23); Elaine Robertson, Katy (1/31/25). Supt. Emily Coleman ($142,159), 1100 W. 45th St., Austin 78756; (512) 454-8631.

Bond Review Board, Texas: (1987); composed of Gov., Lt. Gov., House Speaker, and Comptroller; oversees debt financing for Texas' infrastructure and other public purposes, debt issuance, and debt management functions of state and local entities, and the state's private activity bond allocation; Exec. Dir. Rob Latsha ($117,500); 300 W. 15th St., Ste. 409, PO Box 13292, Austin 78711-3292; (512) 463-1741.

Brazos River Authority: (1929 as Brazos River Conservation and Reclamation District; name changed to present form in 1953); apptv.; 6-yr; expenses; 21 members: Presiding Officer Cynthia A. Flores, Round Rock (2/1/21); Thomas Abraham, Sugar Land (2/1/25); Gary Boren, Lubbock (2/1/25); Mike Fernandez, Abilene (2/1/25); Jennifer "Jen" Henderson, Round Rock (2/1/23); Rick Huber, Granbury (2/1/21); Judy Ann Krohn, Georgetown (2/1/23); Traci Garrett LaChance, Danbury (2/1/23); Jim Lattimore Jr., Graford (2/1/25); Royce Lesley, Comanche (2/1/23); Wesley D. Lloyd, Waco (2/1/25); John H. Luton, Granbury (2/1/23); W.J. "Bill" Rankin, Brenham (2/1/21); Austin Ruiz, Harker Heights (2/1/21); Alan K. Sandersen, Sugar Land (2/1/25); David Savage, Katy (2/1/25); Jarrod D. Smith, Danbury (2/1/23); Jeffery Scott Tallas, Sugar Land (2/1/21); W. Wintford "Ford" Taylor III, Waco (2/1/21); R. Wayne Wilson, Bryan (2/1/23); 1 vacancy. Gen. Mgr. David Collinsworth, 4600 Cobbs Dr., PO Box 7555, Waco 76714; (254) 761-3100.

Canadian River Compact Commission: (1951, negotiates with New Mexico and Oklahoma regarding waters of the Canadian); apptv.; 6-yr.; Comm. Roger S. Cox (12/31/21), PO Box 1750, Amarillo 79105-1750; (806) 242-9651.

Canadian River Municipal Water Authority: (1953); 2-yr.; 17 members apptd. by member cities: Pres. Richard Ellis, Levelland; Donnie Brumley, Plainview; Jerry Carlson, Pampa; James O. Collins, Lubbock; Tyke Dipprey, Plainview; Rickey Dunn, Brownfield; Charles Gillingham, Borger, Bill Hallerberg, Amarillo; Jay House, Lubbock; Jay Dee House, Tahoka; Glendon Jett, Borger; Buddy Moore, Levelland; Cris Norris, Lamesa; Mac Smith, Pampa; Roy Urrutia, Amarillo; Charlie Vaughn, O'Donnell; Chad Wilson, Slaton. Gen. Mgr. Kent Satterwhite, 9875 Water Authority Rd., PO Box 9, Sanford 79078; (806) 865-3325.

Cancer Prevention & Research Institute of Texas: (1985 as Texas Cancer Council; name changed in 2007); apptv.; 6-yr.; expenses; 9 members, 3 each apptd. by Gov., Lt. Gov., and House Speaker: Presiding Officer Donald "Dee" Margo, El Paso (1/31/27); David A. Cummings, San Angelo (1/31/23), Ambrosio Hernandez, Pharr (1/31/25); Will Montgomery, Dallas (1/31/23); Mahendra C. Patel, San Antonio (1/31/21); Cindy Barberio Payne, Spring Branch (1/31/25); William Rice, Austin (1/31/25); Craig Rosenfeld, Dallas (1/31/17); 1 vacancy. CEO Wayne Roberts ($281,875), 1701 Congress Ave., Ste. 6-127, PO Box 12097, Austin 78711; (512) 463-3190.

Cardiovascular Disease and Stroke, Texas Council on: (1999); apptv.; 6-yr.; 14 members: 3 ex officio: 1 each from Texas Workforce Commission, Health and Human Services Commission, Texas Dept. of State Health Services; 11 apptd.: Chair Suzanne Hildebrand, Live Oak (2/1/25); Elie R. Balesh, Houston (2/1/25); Stanley Duchman, Houston (2/1/27); Janet Hewlett, Florence (2/1/23); Samantha Kersey, Dickinson (2/1/25); Sherron D. Meeks, Odessa (2/1/27); J. Neal Rutledge, Austin (2/1/23); Shilpa Shamapant, Austin (2/1/27); Harry "Kyle" Sheets, Ovalo (2/1/23); E'Loria Simon-Campbell, Houston (2/1/25); Maricella "Marcie" Gonzalez Wilson, Lakeway (2/1/27). PO Box 149347, Austin 78714-9347; (512) 776-7111.

Cemetery, Texas State: (1997); apptv.; 6-yr.; 3 members: Chair Benjamin M. Hanson, Austin (2/1/21); James L. "Jim" Bayless Jr., Austin (2/1/23); Carolyn Hodges, Houston (2/1/25). Admin. Nathan Stephens, 909 Navasota St., Austin 78702; (512) 463-6600.

Central Colorado River Authority (See Colorado River Authority, Central.)

Chemist, Office of the Texas State: (1911); ex officio, indefinite term: State Chemist Tim Herrman, 445 Agronomy Rd., PO Box 3160, College Station 77841-3160; (979) 845-1121.

Chiropractic Examiners, Texas Board of: (1949); apptv.; 6-yr.; expenses; 9 members: Pres. Mark Bronson, Fort Worth (2/1/27); Sarah Abraham, Sugar Land (2/1/27); Brandon Allen, Austin

(2/1/25); Nicholas Baucum, Corpus Christi (2/1/27); Michael P. Henry, Austin (2/1/25); Mindy Neal, Bovina (2/1/23); Ebony Todd, Fort Hood (2/1/23); Debra White, Nacogdoches (2/1/23); Scott Wofford, Abilene (2/1/25). Exec. Dir. Patrick Fortner ($100,830), 333 Guadalupe St., Ste. 3-825, Austin 78701; (512) 305-6700.

Civil Commitment Office, Texas: (2011 as Office of Violent Sex Offender Management; took present name in 2015); apptv.; 6-yr.; 5 members: Chair Christy Jack, Fort Worth (2/1/23); Jose Aliseda, Beeville (2/1/25); Roberto Dominguez, Mission (2/1/23); Rona Stratton Gouyton, Fort Worth (2/1/27); Kathryn E. "Katie" McClure, Kingwood (2/1/27). Exec. Dir. Marsha McLane, 4616 W. Howard Ln., Bldg. 2, Ste. 350, Austin 72228; (512) 341-4421.

Coastal Water Authority: (1967 as Coastal Industrial Water Authority; name changed in 1985); 2-yr.; per diem and expenses; 7 members; 4 apptd. by Houston mayor; 3 by Gov.: Pres. D. Wayne Klotz, Houston (3/31/23); Tony L. Council, Houston (3/31/23); Thomas A. Reiser, Houston (4/1/19); Jon M. "Mark" Sjolander, Dayton (4/1/22); Joseph G. Soliz, Houston (3/31/18); Douglas E. Walker, Beach City (4/1/19); Giti Zarinkelk, Houston (3/31/18). Exec. Dir. Donald R. Ripley, 1801 Main St., Ste. 800, Houston 77002; (713) 658-9020.

Colorado River Authority, Central: (1935); Abolished December 1, 2017 by 85th Legislature. All assets were transferred to Coleman County.

Colorado River Authority, Lower: (1934 as 9-member board; members increased in 1951 and 1975); apptv.; 6-yr.; per diem on duty; 15 members: Chair Timothy Timmerman, Austin (2/1/25); Michael L. "Mike" Allen, Kerrville (2/1/25); Lori A. Berger, Flatonia (2/1/21); Melissa K. Blanding, Driftwood (2/1/27); Stephen F. Cooper, El Campo (2/1/23); Joseph M. "Joe" Crane, Bay City (2/1/27); Laura D. Figueroa, Brenham (2/1/23); Carol Freeman, Llano (2/1/27); Raymond A. "Ray" Gill Jr., Horseshoe Bay (2/1/23); Thomas L. "Tom" Kelley, Eagle Lake (2/1/23); Robert "Bobby" Lewis, Elgin, (2/1/25); Thomas Michael Martine, Cypress Mill (2/1/25); Margaret D. "Meg" Voelter, Austin (2/1/25); Martha Leigh M. Whitten, San Saba (2/1/27); Nancy Eckert Yeary, Lampasas (2/1/23). Gen. Mgr. Phil Wilson, 3700 Lake Austin Blvd., PO Box 220, Austin 78767; (512) 578-3200.

Colorado River Authority, Upper: (1935 as 9-member board; reorganized in 1965); apptv.; 6-yr.; per diem and expenses; 9 members: Chair Nancy Blackwell, Ballinger (2/1/27); Reese Braswell, Bronte (2/1/27); Erica Hall, Abilene (2/1/27); Fred Hernandez Jr., San Angelo (2/1/25); Leslie Lasater, San Angelo (2/1/27); Tanner Mahan, Menard (2/1/23); Kathryn Mews, Menard (2/1/23); Hugh "Che" Stone, San Angelo (2/1/23); Mason Vaughan, Eldorado (2/1/25). Director Scott McWilliams, 512 Orient, San Angelo 76903; (325) 655-0565.

Consumer Credit Commissioner, Texas Office of: Comm. Leslie L. Pettijohn ($196,000), 2601 N. Lamar Blvd., Austin 78705; (512) 936-7600. Consumer Help Line: (800) 538-1579.

Cosmetology, Advisory Board on: (1935 as 3-member State Board of Hairdressers and Cosmetologists; name changed and members increased in 1971; changed to current name in 2005 and functions transferred to Texas Dept. of Licensing and Regulation); apptv.; per diem and expenses; 6-yr.; 10 members: Presiding Officer Aleshia Rivera, Mount Pleasant (9/29/25); Anthony Anderson, Spring Branch (9/29/25); Aurora B. Farthing, Lubbock (9/29/25); Natalie Inderman, Shallowater (9/29/25); Betty Neff, Austin (9/29/23); Mary Paschal-Lindsay, Pearland (9/29/25); Vanessa Robbins, Houston (9/29/21); Ron Robinson, Waco (12/20/21); Sam Webb, Austin (9/29/21); 1 ex officio member representing Texas Education Agency. c/o Texas Dept. of Licensing & Regulation, 920 Colorado St., PO Box 12157, Austin 78711; (512) 463-6599.

Counselors, Texas State Board of Examiners of Professional: (1981); apptv.; 6-yr.; expenses; 9 members: Chair Steven Hallbauer, Rockwall (2/1/23); Carmelia "Lia" Amuna, Killeen

(2/1/27); Loretta J. Bradley, Lubbock (2/1/27); Brenda S. Compagnone, San Antonio (2/1/25); Vanessa Hall, Tomball (2/1/25); Garrett A. Narren, Dallas (2/1/25); Roy Smith, Midland (2/1/23); Carolyn Janie Stubblefield, Dallas (2/1/23); Christopher S. Taylor, Dallas (2/1/27). Admin. Cristina De Luna, 333 Guadalupe St., Ste. 2-450, Austin 78701; (512) 305-7700.

County and District Retirement System, Texas: (See Retirement System, Texas County and District.)

Court Administration, Office of: (1985); apptd. by State Supreme Court chief justice; 1 member who also serves as executive director of the Texas Judicial Council: Admin. Dir. David Slayton ($197,415), 205 W. 14th St., Ste. 600, PO Box 12066, Austin 78711-2066; (512) 463-1625.

Court Interpreter Advisory Board, Licensed: Apptv. by Texas Supreme Court; part of Judicial Branch Certification Commission; staggered terms; 6-yr., 5 members: Presiding Officer Laura Angelini, San Antonio (2/1/27); Luis Garcia, Keller (2/1/27); Robert Richter Jr., Houston (2/1/19); Melissa Wallace, San Antonio (2/1/19); Cynthia de Peña, McAllen (2/1/23). 205 W. 14th St., Ste. 600, PO Box 12066, Austin 78711-2066; (512) 463-1630.

Court Reporters Certification Advisory Board: Apptv. by Texas Supreme Court; part of Judicial Branch Certification Commission; staggered terms; 6-yr., 7 members: Presiding Officer Cathleen Stryker, San Antonio (2/1/27); Janice Eidd-Meadows, Tyler (12/31/27); Deborah K. Hamon, Rockwall (2/1/23); Shari J. Krieger, Mansfield (2/1/27); Molly Pela, Houston (2/1/19); Whitney Alden Riley, Boerne (2/1/19); Kim Tindall, San Antonio (2/1/23). 205 W. 14th St., Ste. 600, PO Box 12066, Austin 78711-2066; (512) 475-4368.

Credit Union Commission: (1949 as 3-member Credit Union Advisory Commission; name changed and members increased to 6 in 1969; increased again in 1981); apptv.; 6-yr.; expenses; 9 members: Chair Yusuf E. Farran, El Paso (2/15/21); Elizabeth L. "Liz" Bayless, Austin (2/15/25); Karyn C. Brownlee, Coppell (2/15/23); Steven "Steve" Gilman, Houston (2/15/21); Sherri Brannon Merket, Midland (2/15/23); James L. "Jim" Minge, Arlington (6/15/23); Kay Rankin-Swan, Monahans (2/15/25); David F. Shurtz, Hudson Oaks (2/15/23); Beckie Stockstill Cobb, Deer Park (2/15/21). Comm. John J. Kolhoff ($192,500), 914 E. Anderson Ln., Austin 78752; (512) 837-9236.

Crime Stoppers Council, Texas: (1981); apptv.; 4-yr.; per diem and expenses; 5 members: Chair Greg New, Waxahachie (9/1/24); Lauren Day, Austin (9/1/24); Perry Gilmore, Amarillo (9/1/21); Carlo Hernandez, Brownsville (9/1/21); Stephanie Vanskike, Beaumont (9/1/24). www.the texascrimestoppers.org.

Crime Victims' Institute: (1995 as function of attorney general's office; transferred to Sam Houston State University in 2003); apptv.; 2-yr.; 15 members: Justin Berry, Austin (1/31/23); Lee Ann Breading, Denton (1/31/23); Abigail Brookshire (1/31/23); Melissa Carter, Bryan (1/31/22); Matthew L. Ferrara, Austin (1/31/22); Libby Hamilton, Austin (1/31/23); Joan Huffman (1/31/23); Shawn Kennington, Pittsburg (1/31/22); Lindsay Kinzie, Fort Worth (1/31/22); Gene Pack, Houston (1/31/22); JD Robertson, Wimberley (1/31/22); Andrea Sparks, Austin (1/31/22); Hector Villarreal, Alice (1/31/22); James White, Hillister (1/31/23); Erleigh Wiley, Forney (1/31/23). Dir. Mary Breaux, 816 17th St., PO Box 2180, Huntsville 77341-2180; (936) 294-3100.

Criminal Justice, Texas Department of: (1989, assumed duties of former Department of Corrections, Adult Probation Commission and Board of Pardons and Paroles); apptv.; 6-yr.; expenses; 9 members: Chair Patrick O'Daniel, Austin (2/1/23); Rodney Burrow, Pittsburg (2/1/27); E.F. "Mano" DeAyala, Houston (2/1/23); Molly Francis, Dallas (2/1/2025); Faith Johnson, Dallas (2/1/25); Larry Miles, Amarillo (2/1/23); Eric Nichols, Austin (2/1/27); Derrelynn Perryman, Fort Worth (2/1/27); Sichan Siv, San Antonio (2/1/25). Exec. Dir. Bryan Collier ($275,501), 209

W. 14th St., Ste. 500, PO Box 13084, Austin 78711-3084; (512) 463-9988.

Deaf, Texas School for the: (1979); apptv.; 6-yr.; expenses; 9 members: Pres. Eric Hogue, Wylie (1/31/21); Shawn P. Saladin, Edinburg (1/31/23); Angie Wolf, Dripping Springs (1/31/21); Sha Cowan, Dripping Springs (1/31/23); Ryan D. Hutchison, Austin (1/31/21); Dina Lynne Moore, Round Rock (1/31/27); Christopher Moreland, New Braunfels (1/31/23); David Saunders, Waxahachie (1/31/25); Keith Sibley, Bedford (1/31/25); Heather Withrow, Austin (1/31/25). Supt. Claire Bugen ($148,908), 1102 S. Congress Ave., Austin 78704; (512) 462-5353.

Demographic Center, Texas: (2001); created by 77th Legislature; State Demographer Lloyd B. Potter, 1700 Congress Ave., PO Box 13455, Austin 78711; (512) 463-8390.

Dental Examiners, State Board of: (1919 as 6-member board; increased to 9 members in 1971; increased to 12 in 1981; increased to 15 in 1991; sunsetted in 1994; reconstituted with 18 members in 1995; reduced to present number in 2005); apptv.; 6-yr.; per diem and expenses; 11 members: Presiding Officer David H. Yu, Austin (2/1/25); Linda Treviño Burke, Harlingen (2/1/25); Bryan Henderson II, Dallas (2/1/23); Lorie Jones, Magnolia (2/1/23); Yvonne E. Maldonado, El Paso (2/1/27); Robert G. McNeill, Dallas (2/1/27); Margo Y. Melchor, Houston (2/1/27); Lois M. Palermo, League City (2/1/25); Marquita Pride, Little Elm (2/1/27); Jorge Quirch, Missouri City (2/1/23); Kathryn Sisk, Spring Branch (2/1/23). Exec. Dir. Casey Nichols ($105,000), 333 Guadalupe, Tower 3, Ste. 800, Austin 78701-3942; (512) 463-6400.

Diabetes Council, Texas: (1983; with 5 ex officio and 6 public members serving 2-yr. terms; changed in 1987 to 3 ex officio and 8 public members; changed to present in 1991; term length changed from 4 to 6 years in 1997); 6-yr.; 16 members: 11 apptv.: Chair Feyi Obamehinti, Keller (2/1/23); Gary Francis, San Antonio (2/1/27); Felicia Fruia-Edge, Rancho Viejo (2/1/23); Dirrell Jones, Farmers Branch (2/1/23); Aida "Letty" Moreno-Brown, El Paso (2/1/27); Ninfa Peña-Purcell, College Station (2/1/27); Stephen Ponder, Belton (2/1/25); Ardis Reed, Hideaway (2/1/23); ~~Jason Ryan, Houston~~ (2/1/25); Maryanne Strobel, Cypress (2/1/27); Christine Wicke, McKinney (2/1/25). The 5 ex officio members include 1 each from Texas Workforce Commission, Texas Health and Human Services Commission, Texas Dept. of State Health Services, Employees Retirement System, and Teacher Retirement System. Coord. Ashley Doyle, 1100 W. 49th St., PO Box 149347, Austin 78714-9347; (512) 776-2834.

Dietitians, State Board of Examiners of: All duties transferred to the Texas Department of Licensing and Regulation transferred to the Texas Department of Licensing and Regulation. Abolished in 2015 by the 84th Legislature, S.B. 202.

Disabilities, Governor's Committee on People with: (1949 as Gov.'s Committee on Employment of the Handicapped; re-created in 1983 as Gov.'s Committee for Disabled Persons; given current name and expanded duties in 1991); apptv.; 2-yr. and at pleasure of Gov.; 12 members: Chair Aaron W. Bangor, Austin (2/1/22); Kori A. Allen, Plano (2/1/22); Ellen M. Bauman, Joshua (2/1/23); Evelyn M. Cano, Pharr (2/1/22); Elyse L. Lieberman, Victoria (2/1/23); Eric N. Lindsay, San Antonio (2/1/23); Richard Martinez, San Antonio (2/1/22); Kristie L. Orr, College Station (2/1/23); Dylan Rafaty, Plano (2/1/23); Emma F. Rudkin, Boerne (2/1/22); Amy L. Scott, Austin (2/1/22); Kristopher A.W. "Kris" Workman, Sutherland Springs (2/1/23). Exec. Dir. Ron Lucey, 1100 San Jacinto Blvd., Austin 78701; (512) 463-5739; 7-1-1 TDD.

Disabilities, Texas Council for Developmental: (1971); apptv.; 6-yr.; 27 members; 19 apptv.: Chair Mary Durheim, Spring (2/1/23); Rebecca "Hunter" Adkins, Lakeway (2/1/21); Kimberly Blackmon, Fort Worth (2/1/21); Ronald "Ronnie" Browning, Spring (2/1/23); Gladys Cortez, McAllen (2/1/23); Kristen Cox, El Paso (2/1/21); Maverick Crawford III, San Antonio (2/1/25); Andrew "Andy" Crim, Fort Worth (2/1/25); Scott McAvoy, Cedar Park (2/1/21); Michael Peace, Poteet (2/1/25); Randell Resneder, Lubbock (2/1/21); Eric Shahid, Somerville (2/1/25); Molly Spratt, Austin (2/1/21); Emmett "Toby" Summers III, San Antonio (2/1/21); Robert Schier III, Elgin (2/1/23); Lora Taylor, Houston (2/1/25); John Thomas, Weatherford (2/1/23); Kimberly Torres, Houston (2/1/25), 1 vacancy. 8 ex officio members from various state agencies. Exec. Dir. Beth Stalvey ($138,433), 6201 E. Oltorf St., Ste. 600, Austin 78741-7509; (512) 437-5432.

Disabilities, Texas Council on Purchasing from People with: Duties transferred to Texas Workforce Commission in 2015. Abolished by the legislature in 2015.

Disabilities, Texas Office for Prevention of Developmental: Abolished in 2017.

Education, State Board of: (1866; re-created in 1928 and re-formed in 1949 by Gilmer-Aikin Act to consist of 21 elective members from districts co-extensive with 21 congressional districts at that time; increased to 24 with congressional redistricting in 1971; increased to 27 with congressional redistricting in 1981; reorganized by special legislative session as 15-member apptv. board in 1984; became elective board again in 1988); expenses; 4-yr.; 15 members: Dist. 1: Georgina C. Pérez (D), El Paso (1/1/23); Dist. 2: Ruben Cortez Jr. (D), Brownsville (1/1/23); Dist. 3: Marisa B. Perez-Diaz (D), Converse (1/1/23); Dist. 4: Lawrence A. Allen Jr. (D), Houston (1/1/23); Dist. 5: Rebecca Bell-Metereau (D), San Marcos (1/1/23); Dist. 6: Will Hickman (R), Houston (1/1/23); Dist. 7: Matt Robinson (R), Dickinson (1/1/23); Dist. 8: Audrey Young (R), Nacogdoches (1/1/23); Dist. 9: Chair Keven Ellis (R), Lufkin (1/1/23); Dist. 10: Tom Maynard (R), Florence (1/1/23); Dist. 11: Patricia Hardy (R), Fort Worth (1/1/23); Dist. 12: Pam Little (R), Fairview (1/1/23); Dist. 13: Aicha Davis (D), Dallas (1/1/23); Dist. 14: Sue Melton-Malone (R), Robinson (1/1/23); Dist. 15: Jay Johnson (R), Pampa (1/1/23). c/o Texas Education Agency, 1701 Congress Ave., Austin 78701-1494; (512) 463-9007.

Education Agency, Texas: (1949, established by Gilmer-Aikin Act, replacing office led since 1866 by State Superintendent of Public Instruction; presently led by Commissioner of Education, apptd. by Gov. since 1995; 4-yr.: Comm. Mike Morath ($220,375 plus supplement), 1701 Congress Ave., Austin 78701; (512) 463-9734.

Education Board, Southern Regional: (1969); apptv.; 4-yr.; 5 members: Gov. Greg Abbott (ex officio, 1/20/23); Harrison Keller, Austin (6/30/21); Pedro Martinez, San Antonio (6/30/23); Mike Morath, Austin (6/30/22); Larry Taylor, Friendswood (6/30/24). Pres. Stephen L. Pruitt, 592 10th St. N.W., Atlanta, GA 30318-5776; (404) 875-9211.

Educator Certification, State Board for: (1995); apptv.; 6-yr.; expenses; 15 members; 4 ex officio: rep. of Comm. of Education, rep. of Comm. of Higher Education, rep. of alternative certification program, dean of a college of education; 11 apptv.: Chair John P. Kelly, Pearland (2/1/23); Robert "Bob" Brescia, Odessa (2/1/23); Rohanna Brooks-Sykes, Spring (2/1/27); Tommy L. Coleman, Livingston (2/1/25); Julia Dvorak, Pflugerville (2/1/25); Rex Gore, Austin (2/1/27); Melissa Isaacs, Jewett (2/1/27); Andrew Kim, New Braunfels (2/1/27); Courtney Boswell MacDonald, Kerrville (2/1/23); Shareefah Mason, Dallas (2/1/25); Jean Streepey, Dallas (2/1/25). 1701 Congress Ave., 5th Fl., Austin 78701-1494; (512) 936-8400.

Edwards Aquifer Authority: (1993); 4-yr.; expenses; 17 members (2 apptv. and 15 elected from single-member districts). Apptv. members: Fohn Bendele, Medina & Uvalde Cos. (12/1/24); Gary Middleton, South Central Texas Water Advisory Committee (12/1/24). Elected members: Dist. 1: Carol Patterson, Bexar Co. (12/1/22); Dist. 2: Byron Miller, Bexar Co. (12/1/22); Dist. 3: Abelardo A. "Abe" Salinas III, Bexar Co. (12/1/22); Dist. 4: Benjamin Youngblood III, Bexar Co. (12/1/24); Dist. 5: Randall Perkins, Bexar Co. (12/1/22); Dist. 6: Deborah Carington, Bexar Co. (12/1/24); Dist. 7: Enrique Valdivia, Bexar Co. (12/1/22); Dist. 8: Kathleen Krueger, Comal Co. (12/1/24); Dist. 9: Ronald J. Walton, Comal & Guadalupe Cos. (12/1/22); Dist. 10: Austin

Bodin, Hays Co. (12/1/22); Dist. 11: Rachel Allyn Sanborn, Hays & Caldwell Cos. (12/1/22); Dist. 12: Scott Yanta, Medina Co. (12/1/24); Dist. 13: Chair Luana Buckner, Medina & Atascosa Cos. (12/1/22); Dist. 14: Donald W. Baker, Uvalde Co. (12/1/24); Dist. 15: Rader Gilleland, Uvalde Co. (12/1/22). Gen. Mgr. Roland Ruiz, 900 E. Quincy St., San Antonio 78215; (210) 222-2204.

Emergency Communications, Commission on State: (1985 as 17-member Advisory Commission on State Emergency Communications; name changed and members reduced to 12 in 2000); apptv.; 4-yr.; expenses; 12 members, 3 ex officio: reps. of Dept. of State Health Services, Public Utility Comm., and Dept. of Information Resources; 9 apptd.: Presiding Officer Debbie S. "Debi" Hays, Odessa (9/1/23); James Beauchamp, Midland (9/1/25); Sue A. Brannon, Midland (9/1/23); Lucille Maes, Angleton (9/1/25); Jack D. Miller, Denton (9/1/21); Clinton Sawyer, Amherst (9/1/25); Catherine A. "Cathy" Skurow, Portland (9/1/23); Larry L. "Chip" VanSteenberg, Conroe (9/1/21); Von C. Washington Sr., El Paso (9/1/21). Exec. Dir. Kelli Merriweather ($132,835), 333 Guadalupe St., Ste. 2-212, Austin 78701; (512) 305-6911.

Emergency Management, Texas Division of: (1951 as Division of Defense and Disaster Relief; incorporated into Dept. of Public Safety in 1963; took current name in 2009; became component of Texas A&M University System in 2019.) Chief W. Nim Kidd, 1033 La Posada Dr., Ste. 300, Austin 78752; (512) 424-2208.

Emergency Services Retirement System, Texas: (See Retirement System, Texas Emergency Services.)

Engineers and Land Surveyors, Texas Board of Professional: (1937 as 6-member Texas State Board of Registration for Professional Engineers; members increased to 9 in 1981; name changed to Texas Board of Professional Engineers in 1997, took current name in 2019 when merged with Texas Board of Professional Land Surveying); apptv.; per diem and expenses; 6-yr.; 10 members, inc. 1 rep from General Land Office with unlimited term (Mark J. Neugebauer, Round Rock); 9 termed members: Chair Sina K. Nejad, Beaumont (9/26/25); Ademola Adejokun, Arlington (9/26/23); Lamberto Ballí, Boerne (9/26/21); Albert Cheng, Houston (9/26/21); Coleen M. Johnson, Leander (9/26/25); Marguerite McClinton Stoglin, Grand Prairie (9/26/25); Cathy Norwood, Midland (9/26/21); Rolando Rubiano, Harlingen (9/26/23); Kiran Shah, Richmond (9/26/23). Exec. Dir. Lance Kinney ($176,040), 1917 S. Interstate 35, Austin 78741; (512) 440-7723.

Environmental Quality, Texas Commission on: (1913 as State Board of Water Engineers; name changed in 1962 to Texas Water Commission; reorganized and name changed in 1965 to Water Rights Commission; reorganized and name changed back to Texas Water Commission in 1977 to perform judicial function for the Texas Dept. of Water Resources; name changed to Texas Natural Resource Conservation Commission in 1993; changed to present form in 2002); apptv.; 6-yr.; 3 members full-time ($201,000): Chair Jon Niermann, Austin (8/31/21); Bobby Janecka, Austin (8/31/25); Emily Lindley, Austin (8/31/23). Exec. Dir. Toby Baker ($223,277), 12100 Park 35 Circle, PO Box 13087, Austin 78711-3087; (512) 239-1000.

Ethics Commission, Texas: (1991); apptv.; 4-yr.; 8 members: 4 apptd. by Gov., 2 by Lt. Gov., 2 by House Speaker: Chair Chad M. Craycraft, Dallas (11/19/23); Randall H. Erben, Austin (11/19/21); Chris Flood, Houston (11/19/19); Mary K. "Katie" Kennedy, Houston (11/19/23); Patrick W. Mizell, Houston (11/19/21); Richard S. Schmidt, Corpus Christi (11/19/21); Joseph O. Slovacek, Houston (11/19/21); Steven D. Wolens, Dallas (11/19/19). Exec. Dir. Anne Temple Peters ($139,097), 201 E. 14th St., 10th Fl., PO Box 12070, Austin 78711-2070; (512) 463-5800. Disclosure Filing Fax: (512) 463-8808.

Facilities Commission, Texas: (2007; formerly Texas Building and Procurement Commission); apptv.; 6-yr.; 7 members: Chair Steven Alvis, Houston (1/31/23); William Allensworth, Austin

(1/31/21); Brian Bailey, Austin (1/31/27); Eddy Betancourt, Mission (1/31/23); Patti C. Jones, Lubbock (1/31/21); C. Price Wagner, Dallas (1/31/25); 1 vacancy. Exec. Dir. Mike Novak ($177,982), 1711 San Jacinto Blvd., PO Box 13047, Austin 78711-3047; (512) 463-3446.

Family and Protective Services, Department of: (1991 as Dept. of Protective and Regulatory Services; reorganized to present form in 2004); apptv.; 6-yr.; 9 members: Chair Bonnie Hellums, Houston (2/1/23); Connie Almeida, Richmond (2/1/27); Omedi "Dee Dee" Cantu Arismendez, Alice (2/1/27); Liesa Hackett, Huntsville (2/1/23); Greg Hamilton, Hutto (2/1/27); Cortney Jones, Austin (2/1/25); Matt Kouri, Austin (2/1/23); Julie Krawczyk, Garland (2/1/25); Enrique Mata, El Paso (2/1/25). Comm. Jaime Masters ($215,000), 701 W. 51st St., PO Box 149030, Austin 78714-9030; (512) 438-4800. Abuse Hotline: (800) 252-5400. Ombudsman Hotline: (800) 720-7777.

Film Commission, Texas: (1971, became part of the Economic Development and Tourism Division in office of Gov. in 2015); Dir. Stephanie Whallon ($108,700), 1100 San Jacinto Blvd., Ste. 3.410, PO Box 12428, Austin 78711; (512) 463-9200.

Finance Commission of Texas: (1923 as Banking Commission; reorganized as Finance Commission in 1943 with 9 members; members increased to 12 in 1983; changed back to 9 members in 1989; increased to 11 in 2009); apptv.; 6-yr.; per diem and traveling expenses; Chair Phillip A. Holt, Bonham (2/1/22); Robin Armstrong, Friendswood (2/1/22); Robert "Bob" Borochoff, Houston (2/1/22); Hector J. Cerna, Eagle Pass (2/1/26); Larry Long, Dallas (2/1/26); William M. "Will" Lucas, Center (2/1/24); George "Cliff" McCauley, San Antonio (2/1/24); Sharon McCormick, Frisco (2/1/26); Vince E. Puente Sr., Fort Worth (2/1/24); Debbie Scanlon, Missouri City (2/1/22); Laura Nassri Warren, Palmhurst (2/1/26). Exec. Dir. Charles G. Cooper, 2601 N. Lamar Blvd., Austin 78705; (512) 936-6222. (See also Banking, Texas Department of.)

Fire Fighters' Pension Commissioner: (1937); Abolished by the 83rd Legislature, S.B. 220 in 2013. (See Retirement System, Texas Emergency Services.)

Fire Protection, Texas Commission on: (1991; formed by consolidation of Fire Dept. Emergency Board and Commission on Fire Protection Personnel Standards and Education); apptv.; 6-yr.; expenses; 13 members: Presiding Officer J.P. Steelman, Longview (2/1/23); Christopher G. Cantu, Round Rock (2/1/27); David Coatney, College Station (2/1/27); Sue De Villez, Georgetown (2/1/25); Michael Glynn, Roanoke (2/1/27); Paul Hamilton, Amarillo (2/1/25); Mike Jones, Burleson (2/1/23); Clyde Loll, Huntsville (2/1/27); Bob D. Morgan, Fort Worth (2/1/23); Mala Sharma, Houston (2/1/23); Tim Smith, Lubbock (2/1/27); Kelly Vandygriff, Abernathy (2/1/25); Rusty Wilson, Mesquite (2/1/25). Exec. Dir. Mike Wisko ($117,103), 1701 Congress, Ste. 1-105, PO Box 2286, Austin 78768-2286; (512) 936-3838.

Forensic Science Commission, Texas: (2005); apptv.; 2-yr.; 9 members: 4 apptd. by Gov., 3 by Lt. Gov., and 2 by Atty. Gen.: Presiding Officer Jeffrey J. Barnard, Dallas (9/1/21); Bruce Budowle, North Richland Hills (9/1/22); Patrick Buzzini, Spring (9/1/21); Michael Coble, Fort Worth (2/1/21); Mark Daniel, Fort Worth (9/1/21); Nancy Downing, Bryan (9/1/22); Jasmine Drake, Houston (9/1/22); Sarah Kerrigan, The Woodlands, (9/1/21); Jarvis Parsons, Bryan (9/1/2021). Coor. Kathryn Adams, 1700 Congress Ave., Ste. 445, Austin, TX 78701; (888) 296-4232.

Funeral Service Commission, Texas: (1903 as State Board of Embalming; 1935 as State Board of Funeral Directors and Embalmers; name changed to present form in 1987); apptv.; per diem and expenses; 6-yr.; 7 members: Presiding Officer Larry Allen, Mesquite (2/1/27); Timothy Brown, McAllen (2/1/27); Kevin Combest, Lubbock (2/1/25); Melanie Grammar, Whitewright (2/1/25); Dianne Hefley, Amarillo (2/1/23); Jonathan Scepanski, McAllen (2/1/25); Kristin Tips, San Antonio

(2/1/23). Exec. Dir. Glenn Bower ($99,721), 333 Guadalupe St., Ste. 2-110, Austin 78701; (512) 936-2474.

Geoscientists, Texas Board of Professional: (2001); apptv.; expenses; 3-yr.; 9 members (6 professional geoscientists, 3 public members): Chair Becky L. Johnson, Fort Worth (2/1/23); Bereket M. Derie, Georgetown (2/1/27); Margon Dillard, Richmond (2/1/25); Steven Fleming, Shavano Park (2/1/27); Edward F. Janak Jr., Fredericksburg (2/1/25); W. David Prescott II, Amarillo (2/1/25); Brandon Stowers, Austin (2/1/23); LaFawn Thompson, New Braunfels (2/1/27); Mark N. Varhaug, Dallas (2/1/23). Exec. Dir. Rene D. Truan ($109,157), 333 Guadalupe St., Ste. 1-530; PO Box 13225, Austin 78711; (512) 936-4408.

Guadalupe River Authority, Upper: (1939); apptv.; 6-yr.; 9 members: Pres. Blake W. Smith, Hunt (2/1/27); Lynda Ables, Kerrville (2/1/25); Gene Allen, Kerrville (2/1/25); Aaron C. Bulkley, Hunt (2/1/25); Austin Dickson, Kerrville (2/1/27); Mike Hughes, Ingram (2/1/23); Diane L. McMahon, Kerrville (2/1/27); William R. Rector, Kerrville (2/1/23); Maggie Snow, Kerrville (2/1/23). Gen. Mgr. Ray Buck, 125 Lehmann Dr., Ste. 100, Kerrville 78028; (830) 896-5445.

Guadalupe-Blanco River Authority: (1935); apptv.; per diem and expenses on duty; 6-yr.; 9 members: Chair Dennis L. Patillo, Victoria (2/1/27); William Carbonara, Cuero (2/1/25); Steve Ehrig, Gonzales (2/1/25); Oscar Fogle, Lockhart (2/1/23); Don B. Meador, San Marcos (2/1/25); Kenneth A. Motl, Port Lavaca (2/1/23); Sheila L. Old, Seguin (2/1/27); Andra Wisian, Boerne (2/1/27); 1 vacancy. Gen. Mgr. Kevin Patteson, 933 E. Court St., Seguin 78155; (830) 379-5822.

Guaranteed Student Loan Corporation, Texas: (1979 as nonprofit corp.); as of July 21, 2019, the organization is named Trellis Company.

Guardianship Certification Advisory Board: Apptv. by Texas Supreme Court; part of Judicial Branch Certification Commission; staggered terms; 6-yr., 5 members: Presiding Officer Jamie Maclean, Austin (2/1/27); Jason S. Armstrong, Lufkin (2/1/19); Gladys Burwell, Friendswood (2/1/19); Toni Rhodes Glover, Fort Worth (2/1/23); Chris Wilmoth, Dallas (2/1/27). 205 W. 14th St., Ste. 600, PO Box 12066, Austin 78711-2066; (512) 475-4368.

Gulf Coast Authority: (1969); apptv.; 2-yr.; per diem, expenses on duty; 9 members: 3 apptd. by Gov., 3 by County Commissioners Courts of counties in district, 3 by Mayors Councils of cities in district. Chair Franklin D. R. Jones, Jr., Harris Co. (8/31/21); Billy J. Enochs, Galveston Co. (8/31/21); Gloria Anays Millian Matt, Harris Co. (8/31/21); Lamont E. Meaux, Chambers Co. (8/31/22); W. Chris Peden, Galveston Co. (8/31/21); Mark Schultz, Chambers Co. (8/31/20); Kevin Scott, Galveston Co. (8/31/22); Rita E. Standridge, Chambers Co. (8/31/22); 1 vacancy. Gen. Mgr. Elizabeth Fazio Hale, 910 Bay Area Blvd., Houston 77058; (281) 488-4115.

Gulf States Marine Fisheries Commission: (1949 with members from Texas, Alabama, Florida, Louisiana and Mississippi); apptv.; 3-yr.; 3 Texas members: 2 ex officio: Texas Parks and Wildlife Dept. exec. dir. and 1 member of Legislature; 1 apptd. by Gov.: Douglass W. "Doug" Boyd, Boerne (3/17/23). Exec. Dir. David M. Donaldson, 2404 Government St., Ocean Springs, MS 39564; (228) 875-5912.

Health and Human Services Commission, Texas: (1939 as Dept. of Public Welfare; changed to Texas Dept. of Human Resources in 1977; changed to Texas Dept. of Human Services in 1985; changed to present name in 1992). Exec. Comm. Cecile Erwin Young ($290,258), 4601 W. Guadalupe St., PO Box 13247, Austin 78711-3247; (512) 424-6500.

Health Coordinating Council, Texas Statewide: (1977); apptv.; 6-yr.; 17 members (4 ex officio; 13 apptd. by Gov.): Chair Ayeez A. Lalji, Sugar Land (8/1/19); Dave Allen, San Antonio (8/31/23); Carol Boswell, Andrews (8/1/21); Salil V. Deshpande, Houston (8/1/19); Chelsea Elliott, Austin (8/31/23); Elva

Concha LeBlanc, Fort Worth (8/1/19); Elizabeth J. "Betty" Protas, League City (8/31/23); Melinda Rodriguez, San Antonio (8/1/21); Courtney Sherman, Fort Worth (8/1/21); D. Bailey Wynne, Dallas (8/31/23); Nancy Carolyn Williams Yuill, Sugar Land (8/1/19); Shaukat Ali Zakaria, Houston (8/1/21); Yasser Zeid, Longview (8/1/21). Ex-officio members include 1 each from Texas Dept. of State Health Services and Texas Higher Education Coordinating Board, and 2 from Texas Health and Human Services Commission. Coord. Matt Turner, PO Box 149347, Austin, TX 78714-9347; (512) 776-6541.

Health Professions Council: (1993); ex officio; 12 members: 1 from Gov.'s office and 1 each from the following 11 regulating agencies: Texas Board of Chiropractic Examiners, Texas State Board of Dental Examiners, Texas Medical Board, Texas Board of Nursing, Texas Optometry Board, Texas State Board of Pharmacy, Executive Council of Physical Therapy and Occupational Therapy Examiners, Texas Behavioral Health Executive Council, Texas Board of Veterinary Medical Examiners, Texas Funeral Service Commission, Texas Health and Human Services Licensing and Certification Unit. Admin. Officer John Monk ($100,000), 333 Guadalupe St., Ste. 2-220, Austin 78701; (512) 305-8550.

Health Services, Texas Department of State: (2003, merging Texas Dept. of Health, Texas Dept. of Mental Health and Mental Retardation, Texas Health Care Information Council, Texas Comm. on Alcohol and Drug Abuse); Comm. John William Hellerstedt ($271,083), 1100 W. 49th St., PO Box 149347, Austin 78714-9347; (512) 776-7111.

Health Services Authority, Texas: (2007); apptv.; 2-yr.; expenses; 2 ex officio plus 12 apptd. members: Chair Shannon Calhoun, Goliad (6/15/21); Paula Anthony-McMann, Tyler (6/15/21); Victoria Ai Linh Bryant, Houston (6/15/21); Lourdes Cuellar, Houston (6/15/21); Salil Deshpande, Houston (6/15/21); Emily Hartmann, El Paso (6/15/21); Kenneth James, Volente (6/15/21); Jerome Lisk, Tyler (6/15/21); Leticia Rodriguez, Monahans (6/15/21); Jonathan Sandstrom Hill, Lakeway (6/15/21); Siobhan Shahan, Amarillo (6/15/21); Carlos Vital, Friendswood (6/15/21). 901 S. MoPac Blvd., Bldg. 1, Ste. 300, Austin 78746; (512) 329-2730.

Health Services Council, Texas Department of State: (1975); Abolished August 31, 2016.

Hearing Instruments, State Committee of Examiners in the Fitting and Dispensing of: (1969); Abolished by the 84th Legislature, S.B 202. As of Oct. 1, 2016, all duties transferred to the Texas Department of Licensing and Regulation.

Higher Education Coordinating Board, Texas: (1953 as temporary board; became permanent 15-member Texas Commission on Higher Education in 1955; changed to Texas College and University Systems Coordinating Board in 1965; name and membership changed to present form in 1987); apptv.; 6-yr.; expenses; 9 members, plus 1 ex officio student rep. serving 1-yr.: Chair Fred Farias III, McAllen (8/31/25); S. Javaid Anwar, Midland (8/31/21); Ricky A. Raven, Sugar Land (8/31/21); Emma W. Schwartz, El Paso (8/31/25); Matthew B. Smith, Copperas Cove (5/31/22); R. Swan Torn, Houston (8/31/25); Donna N. Williams, Arlington (8/31/23); Welcome W. Wilson Jr., Houston (8/31/23); 2 vacancies. Comm. of Higher Education Harrison Keller ($299,813), 1200 E. Anderson Ln., PO Box 12788, Austin 78711-2788; (512) 427-6101.

Higher Education Tuition Board, Texas Prepaid: (1995); apptv.; expenses; 6 members, plus 1 ex officio chair: State Comptroller; 2 apptd. by Gov. and 4 by Lt. Gov. Members: Michele Purgason, Arlington (2/1/23); Ben Streusand, Spring (2/1/13); Judy Trevino, San Antonio (2/1/27); Javier Villalobos, McAllen (2/1/23); Jarrod Winkcompleck, Austin (2/1/23); Deborah Zuloaga, El Paso (2/1/19). c/o Educational Opportunities and Investment Division, Comptroller of Public Accounts, PO Box 13528, Austin 78711-3528; (800) 445-4723.

A group tours the Landmark Inn State Historic Site, which is maintained by the Texas Historical Commission. Photo courtesy of the Texas Historical Commission

Historian, Texas State: (2005); apptv.; 2-yr.; Monte L. Monroe, Lubbock (9/30/22).

Historical Commission, Texas: (1953); apptv.; expenses; 6-yr.; 15 members: Chair John L. Nau III, Houston (2/1/27); Donna Bahorich, Houston (2/1/25); Earl Broussard, Austin (2/1/23); Jim Bruseth, Austin (2/1/25); Monica Zárate Burdette, Rockport (2/1/27); John W. Crain, Dallas (2/1/25); Garrett Donnelly, Midland (2/11/23); Renee Dutia, Dallas (2/1/25); Lilia Garcia, Raymondville (2/1/27); David Gravelle, Dallas (2/1/27); Laurie Limbacher, Austin (2/1/23); Catherine McKnight, Dallas (2/1/23); Tom Perini, Buffalo Gap (2/1/27); Gilbert E. Peterson, Alpine (2/1/25); Daisy Sloan White, College Station (2/1/23). Exec. Dir. Mark Wolfe ($156,652), 1511 Colorado St., PO Box 12276, Austin 78711; (512) 463-6100.

Holocaust and Genocide Commission, Texas: (2009); created by 81st Legislature. apptv.; 4-yr.; 15 members: Chair Lynne Aronoff, Houston (2/1/23); Jeffrey L. Beck, Dallas (2/1/23); Fran Berg, Dallas (2/1/21); Anne U. Clutterbuck, Houston (2/1/19); Laura Ehrenberg-Chesler, San Antonio (4/13/21); Ilan Emanuel, Corpus Christi (2/1/23); Jonathan Gurwitz, San Antonio (2/1/21); Lucy Taus Katz, Austin (2/1/25); Matthew A. Kornhauser, Houston (2/1/19); Sandra B. Lessig, Houston (2/1/19); Elliott Naishtat, Austin (5/10/21); David A. Patterson, Dallas (4/13/21); Gilbert Tuhabonye, Austin (2/1/21); Providence Umugwaneza, San Antonio (2/1/25); Edward B. Westermann, San Antonio (2/1/21). Exec. Dir. Joy Nathan ($85,600), PO Box 12276, Austin 78711-2276; (512) 463-5108.

Housing and Community Affairs, Texas Department of: (1979 as Texas Housing Agency; merged with Department of Community Affairs and name changed in 1991); apptv.; expenses; 6-yr.; 7 members: Chair Leo Vasquez, Houston (1/31/23); Brandon Batch, Midland (1/31/21); Paul A. Braden, Dallas (1/31/23); Kenny Marchant, Coppell (1/31/25); Ajay Thomas, Austin (1/31/25); Sharon Thomason, Wolfforth (1/31/21); 1 vacancy. Exec. Dir. Bobby Wilkinson ($192,299), 221 E. 11th St., PO Box 13941, Austin 78711-3941; (512) 475-3800.

Housing Corporation, Texas State Affordable: (1994); 6 yrs.; 5 members: Chair Bill Dietz, Waco (2/1/25); Valerie V. Cardenas, San Juan (2/1/25); Courtney Johnson Rose, Missouri City (2/1/27); Andy Williams, Fort Worth (2/1/23); Lemuel Williams, Austin (2/1/27). Pres. David Long, 6701 Shirley Ave., Austin 78752; (512) 477-3555.

Human Rights, Texas Commission on: (2004 as part of the Texas Workforce Commission's Civil Rights Division); as of September 1, 2015, the duties and authority of the commission were transferred to the Texas Workforce Commissioners.

Indigent Defense Commission, Texas: (2001 as Texas Task Force on Indigent Defense, took present name and form in 2011); 13 members: 8 ex officio: Chief Justice of Supreme Court and 3 other judges, 2 reps. from Texas Senate, 2 from House of Reps.; 5 apptd., 2-yr.: Alex Bunin, Houston (2/1/23); Valerie Covey, Georgetown (2/1/22); Richard Evans, Bandera (2/1/22); Missy Medary, Corpus Christi (2/1/22); Gonzalo Rios, San Angelo (2/1/23). Exec. Dir. Geoff Burkhart ($146,000), 209 W. 14th St., Rm. 202, Austin 78701; (512) 936-6994. Toll-free: (866) 499-0656.

Industrialized Building Code Council, Texas: (1973); apptv.; 2-yr.; 12 members: Presiding Officer Roland L. Brown, Midlothian (2/1/21); Suzanne R. Arnold, Garland (2/1/22); Janet Hoffman, Galveston (2/1/22); Otis W. Jones, Houston (2/1/21); Binoy J. Kurien, Pearland (2/1/22); Edwin O. Lofton Jr., Horseshoe Bay (2/1/22); Edward Martin Jr., Austin (2/1/21); Scott A. McDonald III, Keller (2/1/21); Marcela A. Rhoads, Dallas (2/1/22); John D. Scholl, Claude (2/1/22); Stephen Shang, Austin (2/1/21); William F. "Dubb" Smith III, Dripping Springs (2/1/22); c/o Texas Dept. of Licensing and Regulation, PO Box 12157, Austin 78711; (512) 539-5735.

Information Resources, Texas Department of: (1981 as Automated Information and Telecommunications Council; name changed to current in 1990); 6-yr.; expenses; 10 members: 3 ex officio, reps of Dept. of Criminal Justice, Texas Education Agency, and Texas Parks and Wildlife Dept.; 7 apptv.: Chair Ben Gatzke, Fort Worth (2/1/23); Mike Bell, Spring (2/1/23); Stuart A. Bernstein, Austin (2/1/21); Stacey Napier, Austin (2/1/25); Jeffrey Tayon, Houston (2/1/21); Kara Thompson, Austin (2/1/25); 1 vacancy. Exec. Dir. Amanda Crawford ($194,182), 300 W.15thSt., Ste. 1300, PO Box 13564, Austin 78711-3564; (512) 475-4700.

Injured Employee Counsel, Office of: (2005; represents the interests of workers' compensation claimants); apptv.; 2-yr.; 1 member: Public Counsel Jessica Barta ($151,048), 7551 Metro Center Dr., Ste. 100, Austin 78744; (866) 393-6432.

Insurance, Texas Dept. of: (1876 as Dept. of Insurance; changed to Dept. of Agriculture, Insurance, Statistics and History in 1887; to Dept. of Insurance and Banking in 1907; to present name in 1923); Commissioner (apptv.; 2-yr.; position vacant), 333 Guadalupe St., PO Box 12030, Austin 78711; (512) 676-6000.

Insurance Counsel, Office of Public: (See Public Insurance Counsel, Office of.)

Interstate Commission for Adult Offender Supervision: (1937 as Interstate Compact for the Supervision of Parolees and Probationers; took present name in 2000); 50 member states; apptv.: Pam Alexander-Schneider, Lubbock (2/1/27). Compact Admin. for Texas Rene Hinojosa ($165,193). Chair Jeremiah

Stromberg, 3070 Lake Crest Circle, Ste. 400-264, Lexington KY 40513; (859) 721-1050.

Interstate Mining Compact Commission: (1970); 24 member states, plus 2 associate member states; ex officio or apptv., according to gov's. choice; Texas reps. are appointed from the Texas Railroad Commission: Jim Wright. Exec. Dir. Tom Clarke, 437 Carlisle Dr., Ste. A, Herndon, VA 20170; (703) 709-8654.

Interstate Oil & Gas Compact Commission: (1935); 30 member states, plus 8 associate member states; ex officio or apptv., according to gov's. choice; per diem and expenses. Official rep. for Texas: Wayne Christian. Exec. Dir. Lori Wrotenbery, 900 NE 23rd St., Oklahoma City, OK 73105; (405) 522-8380.

Jail Standards, Texas Commission on: (1975); apptv.; 6-yr.; expenses; 9 members: Chair Bill Stoudt, Longview (1/31/25); Patricia M. Anthony, Garland (1/31/25); Raul "Pinky" Gonzales, Refugio (1/31/27); Duane Lock, Southlake (1/31/23); Monica H. McBride, Alpine (1/31/25); Ben Perry, Waco (1/31/23); Esmaeil Porsa, Parker (1/31/23); Ross Garrick Reyes, Melissa (1/31/27); Kelly Rowe, Lubbock (2/1/27). Exec. Dir. Brandon Wood ($116,740), 300 W. 15th St., Ste. 503, PO Box 12985, Austin 78711-2985; (512) 463-5505.

Judicial Branch Certification Commission: (2015); apptv.; 6-yr.; 9 members, inc. 4 apptd by Supreme Court and 5 judges: Chair Sid L. Harle, San Antonio (2/1/23); Velma Arellano, Corpus Christi (2/1/21); Mark P. Blenden, Bedford (2/1/23); Don D. Ford III, Houston (2/1/19); Glen Harrison, Sweetwater (2/1/27); Ann Murray Moore, Edinburg (2/1/21); William C. Sowder, Lubbock (2/1/25); Polly Jackson Spencer, San Antonio (2/1/19); Victor Villarreal, Laredo (2/1/25). 205 W. 14th St., Se. 600, PO Box 12066, Austin 78711-2066; (512) 475-4368.

Judicial Compensation Commission: (2007); apptv.; 6-yr.; expenses; 9 members: Chair William Strawn, Austin (2/1/21); Carlos Amaral, Plano (2/1/25); Alejandro Cestero, Houston (2/1/21); Conrith Warren Davis, Sugar Land (2/1/23); Rebeca Aizpuru Huddle, Bellaire (2/1/25); Linda W. Kinney, Comfort (2/1/23); Curt Nelson, San Antonio (2/1/25); Scott J. Salmans, McGregor (2/1/21); 1 vacancy. 205 W. 14th St., PO Box 12066, Austin 78711-2066; (512) 463-1625.

Judicial Conduct, State Commission on: (1965 as 9-member Judicial Qualifications Commission; name changed to present in 1977); expenses; 6-yr.; 13 members: 6 apptd. by Supreme Court; 2 by State Bar; 5 by Gov.: Chair David C. Hall, Sweetwater (11/19/21); Ronald E. Bunch, Waxahachie (11/19/23); Sujeeth B. Draksharam, Sugar Land (11/19/21); Valerie Ertz, Dallas (11/19/23); Janis Holt, Silsbee (11/19/25); M. Patrick Maguire, Kerrville (11/19/21); Darrick L. McGill, Georgetown (11/19/21); David Patronella, Houston (11/19/21); Clifton Roberson, Tyler (11/19/25); David Schenck, Dallas (11/19/25); Frederick Tate, Colleyville (11/19/23); 2 vacancies. Exec. Dir. Jacqueline Habersham ($128,000), 300 W. 15th St., PO Box 12265, Austin 78711; (512) 463-5533.

Judicial Council, Texas: (1929 as Texas Civil Judicial Council; name changed in 1975); 6-yr.; expenses; 22 members: 16 ex officio and 6 apptd. from general public: Chair Nathan L. Hecht, Dallas (12/31/26); Sharon Keller, Dallas (12/31/24). Legislative Members: Brandon Creighton, Conroe; Jeff Leach, Plano; Reggie Smith, Van Alstyne; Judith Zaffirini, Laredo. Judicial Members: Bill Gravell Jr., Round Rock (2/1/23); Claudia Laird, Conroe (2/1/25); Missy Medary, Corpus Christi (2/1/25); Emily Miskel, McKinney (2/1/23); Valencia Nash, Dallas (2/1/25); Kathleen Person, Temple (2/1/23); Sherry Radack, Houston (2/1/23); Maggie Sawyer, Brady (2/1/23); Edward J. Spillane, College Station (2/1/25); Ken Wise, Houston (2/1/25). Citizen Members: Kevin Bryant, Dallas (6/30/23); Sonia Clayton, Houston (6/30/25); Jon Gimble, Waco (6/30/25); Rachel Racz, Fort Worth (6/30/23); Kenneth S. Saks, San Antonio (6/30/21); Evan Young, Austin (6/30/21). Exec. Dir. David Slayton ($197,415), 205 W. 14th St., Ste. 600, PO Box 12066, Austin 78711-2066; (512) 463-1625.

Judicial Districts Board: (1985); 13 ex officio members (term in other office); 1 apptv. (4 yrs.); ex officio: Chief Justice of Texas Supreme Court; Presiding Judge, Court of Criminal Appeals; Presiding Judge of each of 11 Administrative Judicial Districts; Gov. apptee.: Thomas Phillips, West Lake Hills (12/31/22). 205 W. 14th St., Austin 78701.

Juvenile Justice Department, Texas: (2011, combining the Texas Youth Commission and Texas Juvenile Probation Commission); apptv.; 6-yr.; expenses; 13 members: Chair Wes Ritchey, Dalhart (2/1/27); Edeska Barnes Jr., Jasper (2/1/27); James Castro, Bergheim (2/1/23); Mona Lisa Chambers, Houston (2/1/25); Pama Hencerling, Victoria (2/1/23); Pat Sabala Henry, Morton (2/1/23); Lisa K. Jarrett, San Antonio (2/1/27); Ann Lattimore, Cedar Park (2/1/27); Melissa Martin, Deer Park (2/1/25); David "Scott" Matthew, Georgetown (2/1/25); Vincent Morales Jr., Rosenberg (2/1/25); Allison Palmer, San Angelo (2/1/23); James Smith, Midland (2/1/23). Exec. Dir. Camille Cain ($216,725), 11209 Metric Blvd., PO Box 12757, Austin 78711-2757; (512) 490-7130. Abuse Hotline: (866) 477-8354.

Land Board, School: (1939); 2-yr.; per diem and expenses; 5 members: 1 ex officio: Comm. of General Land Office; 4 apptd.: 1 by Atty. Gen. and 3 by Gov.; ex officio chair: George P. Bush; members: Gilbert Burciaga, Austin (8/29/21); Michael A. Neill, Athens (8/29/21); Michael Scott Rohrman, Dallas (8/29/21); Todd A. Williams, Dallas (8/29/21). c/o General Land Office, 1700 Congress Ave., Austin 78701-1495; (512) 463-5001.

Land Board, Veterans: (1949 as 3-member ex officio board; reorganized 1956); 4-yr.; per diem and expenses; 3 members: 1 ex officio chair: Comm. of General Land Office; 2 apptd.: Grant Moody, San Antonio (12/29/24); Judson Scott, Bee Cave (12/29/22). Exec. Sec. Mark Havens ($233,171), 1700 Congress Ave. PO Box 12873, Austin 78711-2873; (512) 463-5001.

Land Surveying, Texas Board of Professional: (See Engineers and Land Surveyors, Texas Board of Professional.)

Lavaca-Navidad River Authority: (1954 as 7-member Jackson County Flood Control District; reorganized as 9-member board in 1959; name changed to present form in 1969); apptv.; 6-yr.; per diem and expenses; 9 members: Pres. Ronald Kubecka, Deutschburg (5/1/21); Jerry Adelman, Palacios (5/1/23); Callaway Aimone, Edna (5/1/25); Sandra "Sandy" Johs, La Ward (5/1/21); Lee Kucera, Edna (5/1/23); Terri Parker, Ganado (5/1/23); Leonard Steffek, Edna (5/1/25); Jennifer Storz, Edna (5/1/21); Charles Taylor, Cape Carancahua (5/1/25). Gen. Mgr. Patrick Brzozowski, 4631 FM 3131, Edna 77957; (361) 782-5229.

Law Enforcement, Texas Commission on: (1965 as Texas Commission on Law Enforcement Officer Standards & Education; changed name to present form in 2014); apptv.; 6-yr.; expenses; 9 members: Presiding Officer Kim Lemaux, Arlington (8/30/21); Janna Atkins, Abilene (8/30/23); Patricia Burruss, Dallas (8/30/25); Michael Griffis, Odessa (8/30/25); Jason Hester, Lago Vista (8/30/25); Ron E. Hood, Dripping Springs (8/30/25); Jack W. Taylor, Austin (8/30/23); Sharon Breckenridge Thomas, San Antonio (8/30/21); Tim Whitaker, Richmond (8/30/21). Exec. Dir. Kim Vickers ($136,649), 6330 E. Hwy. 290, Ste. 200, Austin 78723; (512) 936-7700.

Law Examiners, Texas Board of: (1919); 9 attorneys apptd. by Supreme Court biennially for 6-year terms expiring Sept. 30 of odd-numbered years. Chair Augustin Rivera Jr., Corpus Christi (9/30/23); Barbara Ellis, Austin (9/30/25); Teresa Ereon Giltner, Dallas (9/30/23); C. Alfred Mackenzie, Waco (9/30/21); Dwaine M. Massey, Houston (9/30/23); Anna M. McKim, Lubbock (9/30/21); Harold "Al" Odom, Houston (9/30/25); Cynthia Eva Hujar Orr, San Antonio (9/30/21); Carlos R. Soltero, Austin (9/30/25). Exec. Dir. Nahdiah Hoang, 205 W. 14th St., PO Box 13486, Austin 78711-3486; (512) 463-1621.

Law Library, Texas State: (1971); ex officio; expenses; 3 members: reps. of Atty. Gen., Chief Justice of Supreme Court, Presiding Judge of Court of Criminal Appeals. Dir. Dale Propp ($97,034),

205 W. 14th St., PO Box 12367, Austin 78711-2367; (512) 463-1722.

Legislative Budget Board: (1949); 10 members; 5 ex officio: Lt. Gov.; House Speaker; Chair, Senate Finance Comm.; Chair, House Appropriations Comm.; Chair, House Ways and Means Comm.; 5 other members of Legislature. Dir. Jerry McGinty ($220,000), 1501 Congress Ave., PO Box 12666, Austin 78711; (512) 463-1200.

Legislative Council, Texas: (1949); 14 ex officio members: Lt. Gov.; House Speaker; 6 senators apptd. by Lt. Gov.; 5 representatives by Speaker; Chair, House Administration Committee. Exec. Dir. Jeff Archer ($179,826), 1501 Congress Ave., PO Box 12128, Austin 78711-2128; (512) 463-1155.

Legislative Redistricting Board: (1951); 5 ex officio members: Lt. Gov., House Speaker, Atty. Gen., Comptroller of Public Accounts, Comm. of General Land Office; PO Box 12128, Austin 78711-2128; (512) 463-1151.

Legislative Reference Library: (1909); 3 ex officio members: Lt. Gov., House Speaker, Chair of House Appropriations Comm.; 3 Legislative members; indefinite term. Dir. Mary Camp ($165,000), 1100 Congress Ave., Rm. 2N.3, Austin 78701; (512) 463-1252.

Librarian, State: (1839; present office est. 1909); apptv., indefinite term: Mark Smith ($148,197), PO Box 12927, Austin 78711-2927; (512) 463-5455.

Library and Archives Commission, Texas State: (1909 as 5-member Library and State Historical Commission; name changed to present form in 1979); apptv.; per diem and expenses on duty; 6-yr.; 7 members: Chair Martha Wong, Houston (9/28/21); David C. Garza, Brownsville (9/28/25); F. Lynwood Givens, Plano (9/28/21); Arthur T. "Art" Mann, Hillsboro (9/28/23); Bradley S. "Brad" Tegeler, Austin (9/28/25); Darryl Tocker, Austin (9/28/23); 1 vacancy. Dir. and Librarian Mark Smith ($148,197), 1201 Brazos St., PO Box 12927, Austin 78711-2927; (512) 463-5474.

Licensing and Regulation, Texas Department of: (1989); apptv.; 6-yr.; expenses; 7 members: Chair Rick Figueroa, Brenham (2/1/21); Thomas F. Butler, Deer Park (2/1/25); Gerald R. Callas, Beaumont (2/1/23); Helen Callier, Kingwood (2/1/21); Nora Castañeda, Harlingen (2/1/25); Joel Garza, Pearland (2/1/21); Gary Wesson, Richmond (2/1/23). Exec. Dir. Brian E. Francis ($185,250), 920 Colorado St., PO Box 12157, Austin 78711; (512) 463-6599.

Lottery Commission, Texas: (1993); 6-yr.; apptv.; expenses; 5 members: Chair Robert G. Rivera, Dallas (2/1/21); Cindy Lyons Fields, El Paso (2/1/23); Mark A. Franz, Austin (2/1/25); Erik C. Saenz, Houston (2/1/23); Jamey Steen, Houston (2/1/25). Exec. Dir. Gary Grief ($213,344), 611 E. 6th St., PO Box 16630, Austin 78761-6630; (512) 344-5000.

Lower Colorado River Authority (See Colorado River Authority, Lower.)

Lower Concho River Water and Soil Conservation Authority (See Concho River Water and Soil Conservation Authority, Lower.)

Lower Neches Valley Authority (See Neches Valley Authority, Lower.)

Manufactured Housing Division: (1995, part of Texas Dept. of Housing and Community Affairs); apptv.; 6-yr.; 5 members: Chair Ronnie Richards, Clear Lake Shores; Jason R. Denny, Austin (1/31/25); Joe Gonzalez, Round Rock (1/31/27); Sylvia Guzman, Spring (1/31/25); Keith C. Thompson, Lubbock (1/31/23). Exec. Dir. Joe A. Garcia, 1106 Clayton Ln., Ste. 270W, PO Box 12489, Austin 78711-2489; (512) 475-2200.

Marriage and Family Therapists, Texas State Board of Examiners of: (1991); apptv.; 6-yr.; per diem and transportation expenses; 9 members: Presiding Member Lisa V. Merchant, Clyde (2/1/23); Russell F. "Russ" Bartee, Fort Worth (2/1/25); Jodie Elder, Dallas (2/1/27); George F. Francis IV, Georgetown (2/1/23); Evelyn

Husband-Thompson, Houston (2/1/27); Daniel W. Parrish, DeSoto (2/1/25); Anthony C. Scoma, Austin (2/1/27); Jeanene L. Smith, Austin (2/1/25); Richmond E. Stoglin, Arlington (2/1/23). Board Admin. Sarah Faszholz ($72,000), 333 Guadalupe St., Tower 3, Rm. 900, Austin 78701; (512) 305-7700.

Medical Board, Texas: (1907 as 11-member Texas State Board of Medical Examiners; members increased to 12 in 1931, 15 in 1981,18 in 1993 and 19 in 2003; changed to present name in 2005 by Senate Bill 419); apptv.; 6-yr.; per diem on duty; 19 members, inc. 12 doctors: Pres. Sherif Z. Zaafran, Houston (4/13/21); Devinder S. Bhatia, Houston (4/13/25); George L. De Loach, Livingston (4/13/23); James S. Distefano, College Station (4/13/25); Kandace B. Farmer, Highland Village (4/13/21); Jeffrey L. Luna, Livingston (4/13/21); Robert D. Martinez, Mission (4/13/25); Jayaram B. Naidu, Odessa (4/13/21); Satish Nayak, Andrews (4/13/25); Manuel "Manny" Quinones Jr., San Antonio (4/13/23); Jason K. Tibbels, Bridgeport (4/13/25); David G. Vanderweide, League City (4/13/23). 7 Public Members: Arun Agarwal, Dallas (4/13/25); Sharon J. Barnes, Rosharon (4/13/23); Michael E. Cokinos, Houston (4/13/21); Robert Gracia, Richmond (4/13/23); Tomeka M. Herod, Allen (4/13/25); LuAnn Morgan, Midland (4/13/21); 1 vacancy. Exec. Dir. Stephen Brint Carlton ($156,145), 333 Guadalupe St., Tower 3, Ste. 610, PO Box 2018, Austin 78768-2018; (512) 305-7010. Consumer Complaint Hotline: (800) 201-9353.

Medical Physicists, Texas Board of Licensure for Professional: (1991); abolished by the Legislature in 2015. All duties transferred to the Texas Medical Board.

Medical Radiologic Technology Board: (2015); apptv.; 6-yr.; 9 members: Presiding Officer Faraz Khan, Houston (2/1/25); Nicholas Beckmann, Houston (2/1/27); Linda Brown, Port Neches (2/1/23); Jennifer Flanagan, Fort Worth (2/1/23); Regan Landreth, Georgetown (2/1/25); Shannon Lutz, Cypress (2/1/23); Scott Morren, Anton (2/1/27); Shaila D. Parker, Dallas (2/1/27); Carol Waddell, West (2/1/25). Exec. Dir. Stephen "Brint" Carlton, 333 Guadalupe St., Tower 3, Ste. 610, Austin 78701; (512) 305-7010.

Midwestern State University Board of Regents: (1959); apptv.; 6-yr.; 9 members: Chair R. Caven Crosnoe, Wichita Falls (2/25/20); Warren T. Ayres, Wichita Falls (2/25/22); Tiffany Burks, Grand Prairie (2/25/22); Guy A. "Tony" Fidelie Jr., Wichita Falls (2/25/24); Shawn Hessing, Fort Worth (2/25/20); Nancy Marks, Wichita Falls (2/25/20); Oku Okeke, Wichita Falls (2/25/24); Karen Liu Pang, Irving (2/25/24); Shelley Sweatt, Wichita Falls (2/25/22). Pres. Suzanne Shipley, 3410 Taft Blvd., Wichita Falls 76308; (940) 397-4000.

Midwifery Board, Texas: (1999); abolished by the Legislature in 2015. All duties transferred to the Texas Department of Licensing and Regulation.

Military Dept., Texas: (1836 by Republic of Texas; Adjutant General's Dept. established 1905, renamed 2013); apptv.; commanded by Adjutant General, Maj. Gen. Tracy R. Norris, Austin (1/1/21); ($178,196); assisted by Army National Guard Maj. Gen. Gregory P. Chaney, Austin; Air National Guard Maj. Gen. Thomas M. Suelzer, Keller; State Air Guard Maj. Gen. Robert J. Bodisch, Austin. Officers serve at the pleasure of the Gov.; c/o Camp Mabry, PO Box 5218, Austin 78703; (512) 782-5001.

Military Preparedness Commission, Texas: (2003); apptv.; 6-yr.; 3 ex-officio members (1 Senator, 1 House Representative, 1 General); 13 apptv.: Chair Kevin Pottinger, Fort Worth (2/1/27); Patrick Akuna, Killeen (2/1/25); Carol Bonds, San Angelo (2/1/25); Garry Bradford, Corpus Christi (2/1/25); Darrell Coleman, Wichita Falls (2/1/25); Tom Duncavage, League City (2/1/23); Woody Gilliland, Abilene (2/1/23); Dennis Lewis, Texarkana (2/1/27); Benjamin Miranda, El Paso (2/1/23); Kenneth Sheets, Mesquite (2/1/27); Annette Sobel, Lubbock (2/1/23); Shannalea Taylor, Del Rio (2/1/27); James Whitmore,

New Braunfels (2/1/23). Dir. Keith Graf, PO Box 12428, Austin 78711; (512) 475-1475.

Motor Vehicles, Texas Department of: (2009); apptv.; 6-yr.; 9 members: Chair Charles Bacarisse, Houston (2/1/25); Christian Alvarado, Austin (2/1/27); Stacey Gillman, Houston (2/1/25); Brett Graham, Denison (2/1/23); Tammy McRae, Conroe (2/1/25); Sharla Omumu, Cypress (2/1/27); John M. Prewitt, Cypress (2/1/23); Manuel "Manny" Ramirez, Fort Worth (2/1/27); Paul R. Scott, Lubbock (2/1/23). Exec. Dir. Whitney Brewster ($202,739), 4000 Jackson Ave., Austin 78731; (888) 368-4689.

Municipal Retirement System, Texas (See Retirement System, Texas Municipal.)

Music Office, Texas: (1990, became part of the Office of Gov. in 1991); Dir. Brendon Anthony, 1100 San Jacinto Blvd., Ste. 3.418, PO Box 12428, Austin 78711; (512) 463-6666.

Neches River Municipal Water Authority, Upper: (1953 as 9-member board; members decreased to 3 in 1959); apptv.; 6-yr.; 3 members: Pres. Phil Jenkins, Palestine (2/1/23); Jay Herrington, Palestine (2/1/27); Paul Morris, Palestine (2/1/25). Gen. Mgr. Monty D. Shank, 210 FM 1892 (Frankston), PO Box 1965, Palestine 75802; (903) 876-2237.

Neches Valley Authority, Lower: (1933); apptv.; per diem and expenses on duty; 6-yr.; 9 members: Pres. Kal A. Kincaid, Beaumont (7/28/23); Lonnie B. Grissom, Woodville (7/28/21); Steve Lucas, Beaumont (7/28/25); Clint A. Mitchell, Nederland (4/28/23); Ivy Pate, Beaumont (7/28/21); James M. Scott, Beaumont (7/28/25); Charles "Caleb" Spurlock, Woodville (7/28/25); Jeanie Turk, Sour Lake (7/28/21); William D. "Bill" Voigtman, Silsbee (4/28/23). Gen. Mgr. Scott Hall, 7850 Eastex Fwy., PO Box 5117, Beaumont 77726-5117; (409) 892-4011.

Nueces River Authority: (1953 as Nueces River Conservation and Reclamation District; name changed to present form in 1971); apptv.; 6-yr.; per diem and expenses; 21 members: Pres. Dan Leyendecker, Corpus Christi (2/1/25); Alston Beinhorn, Catarina (2/1/23); Jane D. Bell, Corpus Christi (2/1/25); Allan P. Bloxsom III, Kendalia (2/1/21); Dane Bruun, Corpus Christi (2/1/25); ~~Eric Burnett, Portland (2/1/27)~~; ~~Amy M. Clark, Three Rivers (2/1/21)~~; Marshall Davidson, Ingleside (2/1/25); Chad Foster Jr., Uvalde (2/1/23); John W. Galloway, Beeville (2/1/21); Annelise Gonzalez, San Antonio (2/1/23); Lana P. Guthrie, Rocksprings (2/1/25); Debra Young Hatch, Corpus Christi (2/1/23); Karin E. Knolle, Sandia (2/1/27); Travis W. Pruski, Floresville (2/1/21); David Purser, Karnes City (2/1/25); Armandina "Dina" Ramirez, Karnes City (2/1/25); Tomas Ramirez III, Devine (2/1/21); Bill Schuchman, Jourdanton (2/1/23); Anita Shackelford, Leakey (2/1/25); Tony Wood, Corpus Christi (2/1/23). Exec. Dir. John Byrum, 539 Hwy. 83 S., Uvalde 78801; (830) 278-6810.

Nursing, Texas Board of: (1909 as 5-member Texas Board of Nurse Examiners; members increased to 6 in 1931 and to 9 in 1981; name changed to present and members increased to 13 in 2007); apptv.; per diem and expenses; 6-yr.; 13 members: Pres. Kathy Shipp, Lubbock (1/31/23); Daryl Chambers, Grand Prairie (1/31/27); Laura Disque, Edinburg (1/31/25); Carol Kay Hawkins, San Antonio (1/31/25); Mazie Mathews Jamison, Dallas (1/31/23); Kenneth D. "Ken" Johnson, San Angelo (1/31/27); Kathy Leader-Horn, Granbury (1/31/27); Allison Porter-Edwards, Bellaire (1/31/27); Tamara Rhodes, Amarillo (1/31/23); David Saucedo II, El Paso (1/31/27); Melissa Schat, Granbury (1/31/25); Rickey "Rick" Williams, Killeen (1/31/25); Kimberly "Kim" Wright, Big Spring (1/31/23). Exec. Dir. Katherine A. Thomas ($166,879), 333 Guadalupe St., Ste. 3-460, Austin 78701-3944; (512) 305-7400.

Occupational Therapy Examiners, Texas Board of: (1983 as 6-member board; increased to 9 in 1999); apptv.; 6-yr.; per diem and expenses; 9 members: Chair Stephanie Johnston, Magnolia (2/1/27); Jacob Boggus, Harlingen (2/1/27); Blanca Cardenas, Mission (2/1/23); Jennifer Clark, Iola (2/1/25); Karen Gardner, Brenham (2/1/23); DeLana Honaker, Amarillo (2/1/23); Eddie

Jessie, Houston (2/1/23); Sally Harris King, Houston (2/1/27); Todd Novosad, Bee Cave, (2/1/25). Exec. Dir. Ralph Harper ($100,893), 333 Guadalupe St., Ste. 2-510, Austin 78701-3942; (512) 305-6900.

Offenders with Medical or Mental Impairments, Texas Correctional Office on: apptv.; 6-yr.; 21 members: 11 ex officio from various state agencies; 10 apptd. by Gov.: Chair Robb Catalano, Fort Worth (2/1/25); Sanjay Adhia, Sugar Land (2/1/27); Allan Cain, Carthage (2/1/23); James B. Eby, Wichita Falls (2/1/25); Matthew Faubion, San Antonio (2/1/23); Scott MacNaughton, San Antonio (2/1/23); Trenton R. Marshall, Burleson (2/1/25); Casey O'Neal, Austin (2/1/25); Denise Oncken, Houston (2/1/27); Rogelio Rodriguez, El Paso (2/1/27). Dir. April Zamora ($135,599), 4616 W. Howard Ln., Ste. 200, Austin 78728; (512) 671-2134.

One-Call Board of Texas: (1997; created by the Underground Facility Damage Prevention and Safety Act and serves as the board for the Texas Underground Facility Notification Corp.); apptv.; 3-yr.; 12 members: Chair Robert DeLeon, Corpus Christi (8/31/22); Joe Canales, Austin (8/31/22); Joseph Costa, DeSoto (8/31/23); Sandy Galvan, San Antonio (8/31/22); William Geise, Austin (8/31/23); Sam Kannappan, Houston (8/31/22); Marcela Navarrete, El Paso (8/31/21); Christopher Nowak, Houston (8/31/23); Manish Seth, Missouri City (8/31/21); George Spencer, Austin (8/31/23); Les Stephens, San Marcos (8/31/21); Richard Tesson, Houston (8/31/21). Exec. Dir. Don Ward, 9415 Burnet Rd., Ste. 311, PO Box 9764, Austin 78766; (512) 467-2850.

Optometry Board, Texas: (1921 as 6-member State Board of Examiners in Optometry; name and number of members changed to present in 1981); apptv.; per diem; 6-yr.; 9 members: Chair Mario Gutierrez, San Antonio (1/31/23); Judith Chambers, Austin (1/31/25); John Todd Cornett, Amarillo (1/31/25); Ronald L. Hopping, Friendswood (1/31/27); Carey A. Patrick, Allen (1/31/27); Rene D. Peña, El Paso (1/31/27); Meghan Schutte, (1/31/25); Ty Sheehan, San Antonio (1/31/23); Bill Thompson, Richardson (1/31/23). Exec. Dir. Kelly Parker ($95,000), 333 Guadalupe St., Ste. 2-420, Austin 78701-3942; (512) 305-8500.

Orthotics and Prosthetics, Texas Board of: abolished by the Legislature in 2013. All duties transferred to the Texas Department of Licensing and Regulation.

Pardons and Paroles, Texas Board of: (1893 as Board of Pardon Advisers; changed in 1936 to Board of Pardons and Paroles with 3 members; members increased to 6 in 1983; made a division of the Texas Dept. of Criminal Justice in 1990); apptv.; 6-yr.; 7 members (chairman, $176,300; members, $112,750 each): Chair David Gutiérrez, Gatesville (2/1/27); D'Wayne Jernigan, Huntsville (2/1/25); Carmella Jones, Angleton (2/1/23); James LaFavers, Amarillo (2/1/23); Brian Long, Palestine (2/1/23); Linda Molina, San Antonio (2/1/27); Ed Robertson, Austin (2/1/27). Parole Commissioners: Elodia Brito, Amarillo; Lee Anne Eck-Massingill, Gatesville; Ira Evans, Angleton; Mary J. Farley, Huntsville; Troy Fox, Austin; Raymond Gonzalez, Amarillo; James Paul Kiel, Palestine; Tracy Long, Huntsville; Jeffrey Marton, Amarillo; Marsha Moberley, Austin; Anthony Ramirez, San Antonio; Wanda Saliagas, Palestine; Charles Speier, San Antonio; Roel Tejeda, Gatesville. Gen. Counsel Bettie L. Wells ($125,172), 8610 Shoal Creek Blvd., PO Box 13401, Austin 78711-3401; (512) 406-5452.

Parks and Wildlife Commission, Texas: (1963 as 3-member board; members increased to 6 in 1971 and to 9 in 1983); apptv.; expenses; 6-yr.; 9 members: Chair Arch H. "Beaver" Aplin III, Lake Jackson (2/1/23); James E. Abell, Kilgore (2/1/25); Oliver J. Bell, Houston (2/1/23); Paul L. Foster, El Paso (2/1/27); Anna B. Galo, Laredo (2/1/27); Jeffery D. Hildebran, Houston (2/1/25); Robert L. "Bobby" Patton Jr., Fort Worth (2/1/25); Travis B. "Blake" Rowling, Dallas (2/1/27); Dick Scott, Wimberley (2/1/23). Exec. Dir. Carter Smith ($200,643), 4200 Smith School Rd., Austin 78744; (512) 389-4800.

Pecos River Compact Commission: (1942, negotiates with New Mexico regarding waters of the Pecos); apptv.; 6-yr.; salary and expenses. Comm. Frederic "Rick" Tate (1/23/23), PO Box 340, Marfa 79843; (432) 729-3224.

Pension Review Board, Texas: (1979); apptv.; 6-yr.; 7 members: Chair Stephanie V. Leibe, Austin (1/31/27); Keith Brainard, Georgetown (1/31/25); Marcia Dush, Austin (1/31/25); Rossy Fariña-Strauss, Austin (1/31/23); Christopher Gonzales, Cypress (1/31/27); Robert D. "Rob" Ries, Austin (1/31/23); Christopher Zook, Houston (1/31/27). Exec. Dir. Anumeha Kumar ($126,730), 300 W. 15th St., PO Box 13498, Austin 78711-3498; (512) 463-1736.

Pharmacy, Texas State Board of: (1907 as 6-member board; members increased to current number in 1981); apptv.; 6-yr.; 11 members: Pres. Julie Spier, Katy (8/31/23); Rick Fernandez, Northlake (8/31/23); Daniel Guerrero, San Marcos (8/31/23); Lori Henke, Amarillo (8/31/23); Donnie Lewis, Athens (8/31/25); Bradley A. Miller, Austin (8/31/23); Donna Montemayor, San Antonio (8/31/25); Chip Thornsburg, San Antonio (8/31/21); Suzete Tijerina, Castle Hills (8/31/21); Rick Tisch, Spring (8/31/25); Jenny Downing Yoakum, Kilgore (8/31/21). Exec. Dir. Allison Vordenbaumen Benz ($132,490), 333 Guadalupe St., Ste. 3-500, Austin 78701; (512) 305-8000. Consumer complaints: (800) 821-3205.

Physical Therapy and Occupational Therapy Examiners, Executive Council of: (1971); apptv.; 2-yr.; expenses; 5 members: Presiding Officer Manoranjan "Mano" Mahadeva, Frisco (2/1/23); Donivan Hodge, Spicewood (2/1/23); Eddie Jessie, Houston (2/1/25); Stephanie Johnston, Magnolia (2/1/21); Barbara Sanders, Austin (2/1/23). Exec. Dir. Ralph Harper ($100,893), 333 Guadalupe St., Ste. 2-510, Austin 78701-3942; (512) 305-6900.

Physical Therapy Examiners, Texas Board of: (1971); apptv.; 6-yr.; expenses; 9 members: Chair Harvey Aikman, Mission (1/31/27); Glenda Clausell, Houston (1/31/27); Jacob Delgado, Hewitt (1/31/25); Manuel "Tony" Domenech, Austin (1/31/23); Donivan Hodge, Spicewood (1/31/23); Liesl Olson, Lubbock (1/31/27); Kathryn "Kate" Roby, Temple (1/31/25); Barbara Sanders, Austin (1/31/23); Melissa Skillern, Manvel (1/31/25). Exec. Dir. Ralph Harper ($100,893), 333 Guadalupe St., Ste. 2-510, Austin 78701-3942; (512) 305-6900.

Physician Assistant Board, Texas: (1993 as Physician Assistant Advisory Council; changed to present name in 1995); apptv.; 6-yr.; 13 members: Chair Karrie Lynn Crosby, Robinson (2/1/27); Steve S. Ahmed, Big Spring (2/1/25); Clay P. Bulls, Abilene (2/1/27); Jennifer L. Clarner, Austin (2/1/23); Victor S. Ho, Houston (2/1/27); Lawrence G. "Larry" Hughes, Frisco (2/1/25); Sandra Longoria, Harlingen (2/1/25); Cameron J. McElhaney, Austin (2/1/23); Janith K. Mills, Irving (2/1/23); Melinda Ann Moore Gottschalk, Round Rock (2/1/25); Gregory Rowin, Harlingen (2/1/23); Andrew Sauer, Amarillo (2/1/27); Lali Shipley, Austin (2/1/27). Exec. Dir. Stephen Brint Carlton ($156,145), 333 Guadalupe, Tower 3, Ste. 610, TX 78768; (512) 305-7010. Consumer Complaints: (800) 201-9353.

Plumbing Examiners, Texas State Board of: (1947 as 6-member board; members increased to 9 in 1981); apptv.; expenses; 6-yr.; Chair Frank S. Denton, Conroe (9/5/25); James "Ron" Ainsworth, Midland (9/5/23); Ben Friedman, Dallas (9/5/21); Milton Gutierrez, Fort Worth (9/5/21); Robert F. Jalnos, San Antonio (9/5/21); William "Bill" Klock, Houston (9/5/23); Thomas "Justin" MacDonald, Kerrville (9/5/25); Mark Savasta, Houston (9/5/23); David "Dave" Yelovich, Friendswood (9/5/25). Exec. Dir. Lisa G. Hill ($114,239), 929 E. 41st St., PO Box 4200, Austin 78765-4200; (512) 936-5200.

Podiatric Medical Examiners Advisory Board: (1923 as 6-member State Board of Chiropody Examiners; name changed to State Board of Podiatry Examiners in 1967; made 9-member board in 1981; name changed to present in 1996; in 2017 the licensing and regulation of the practice of Podiatry transferred to the Texas Department of Licensing and Regulation); apptv.; 6-yr.; expenses; 9 members: Presiding Officer Travis A. Motley, Fort Worth (2/1/23); Cory Brown, Abilene (2/1/23); Leslie Campbell, Allen (2/1/27); Maria "Yvette" Hernandez, Rio Grande City (2/1/23); James Michael Lunsford, Austin (2/1/25); Joe E. Martin, College Station (2/1/25); Amanda S. Nobles, Longview (2/1/27); Renee Pietzsch, Georgetown (2/1/27); Cirenia Hernandez Terrazas, Austin (2/1/25). PO Box 12157, Austin 78711; (512) 463-6599.

Port Freeport Commission: (1925); apptv.; 6-yr.; 6 elected members: Chair John Hoss, Freeport (5/31/23); Dan Croft, Jones Creek (5/31/25); Rob Giesecke, Damon (5/31/27); Shane Pirtle, Brazoria (5/31/23); Rudy Santos, Angleton (5/31/27); Ravi K. Singhania, Brazosport (5/31/25). Exec. Dir. Phyllis Saathoff, 1100 Cherry St., Freeport 77541; (979) 233-2667.

Prepaid Higher Education Tuition Board, Texas (See Higher Education Tuition Board, Texas Prepaid.)

Preservation Board, State: (1983); 2-yr.; 6 members (3 ex officio: Gov., Lt. Gov., House Speaker); 3 apptv.: 1 apptd. by Gov.: Alethea Swann Bugg, San Antonio (2/1/23); 1 senator apptd. by Lt. Gov.; 1 representative by Speaker. Exec. Dir. Rod Welsh ($175,990), 201 E. 14th St., PO Box 13286, Austin 78711; (512) 463-5495.

Prison Board (See Criminal Justice, Texas Dept. of.)

Private Security Advisory Committee, Texas: (1969 as Board of Private Investigators and Private Security Agencies; reorganized in 1998 as Texas Comm. on Private Security; re-established in 2004 as a bureau of the Texas Dept. of Public Safety named Texas Private Security Board and in 2020 took its current name); apptv.; expenses; 6-yr.; 8 members (1 ex officio: Dir., Dept. of Public Safety); 7 apptd. members: Chair Patricia James, Houston (1/31/21); D. Wade Hayden, San Antonio (1/31/23); Derrick A. Howard, Universal City (1/31/23); Alan S. Trevino, Austin (1/31/23); Debbra Ulmer, Houston (1/31/25); 2 vacancies. Service Dir. Chris Sims ($128,851), 6100 Guadalupe St., PO Box 4087, Austin 78773-0001; (512) 424-7293.

Process Server Certification Advisory Board: apptv. by Texas Supreme Court; part of Judicial Branch Certification Commission; staggered terms; 6-yr., 5 members: Presiding Officer Patrick J. Dyer, Missouri City, (2/1/27); Rhonda Hughey, Kaufman (2/1/19); Eric Johnson, Rosharon (2/1/27); Melissa K. Perez, Waxahachie (2/1/23); Justiss Rasberry, El Paso (2/1/19). 205 W. 14th St., PO Box 12066, Austin 78711-2066; (512) 475-4368.

Prosecuting Attorney, State: (1923) apptd. by Court of Criminal Appeals: Stacey M. Soule ($154,000), 209 W. 14th St., Austin 78701; (512) 463-1660.

Psychologists, Texas State Board of Examiners of: (1969 as 6-member board; members increased to 9 in 1981); apptv.; 6-yr.; per diem and expenses; 9 members: Presiding Member John K. Bielamowicz, Waxahachie (10/31/21); Herman Adler, Houston (10/31/23); Jamie Becker, Plano (10/31/25); Ryan T. Bridges, Houston (10/31/23); Jeanette Deas Calhoun, Tyler (10/31/25); Susan Fletcher, Frisco (10/31/21); Ronald S. "Ron" Palomares, Denton (10/31/21); Sangeeta Singg, San Angelo (10/31/25); Andoni Zagouris, McAllen (10/31/23). Board Admin. Diane Moore ($60,000), 333 Guadalupe St., Ste. 3-900, Austin 78701; (512) 305-7700.

Public Finance Authority, Texas: (1984, assumed duties of Texas Building Authority); apptv.; per diem and expenses; 6-yr.; 7 members: Chair Billy M. Atkinson Jr., Sugar Land (2/1/23); Larry G. Holt, College Station (2/1/27); Ramon Manning, Houston (2/1/21); Shanda Perkins, Burleson (2/1/25); Jay A. Riskind, Austin (2/1/23); Brendan Scher, Austin (2/1/25); Ben Streusand, Spring (2/1/25). Exec. Dir. Lee Deviney ($151,994), 300 W. 15th St., Ste. 411, PO Box 12906 Austin 78711-2906; (512) 463-5544.

Public Insurance Counsel, Office of: (1991). Public Counsel (apptv.; 2-yr.) Melissa R. Hamilton ($149,976), (2/1/21), 333 Guadalupe St., Ste. 3-120; Austin 78701; (512) 322-4143.

The Texas Racing Commission regulates horse and greyhound racing in the state. Photo by Travis Isaac, CC by 2.0/Flickr,

Public Safety Commission: (1935 with 3 members; members increased to 5 in 2007); apptv.; expenses; 6-yr.; 5 members: Chair Steven P. Mach, Houston (1/1/22); Nelda L. Blair, Conroe (1/1/26); Steve H. Stodghill, Dallas (1/1/24); Dale Wainwright, Austin (1/1/24); 1 vacancy. Dir. of Texas Dept. of Public Safety Steven C. McCraw ($247,981), 5805 N. Lamar Blvd., PO Box 4087, Austin 78773-0001; (512) 424-2000.

Public Utility Commission: (1975); apptv.; 6-yr.; 3 members ($201,000): Chair Peter Lake, Austin (9/1/23); Lori Cobos, Austin (9/1/21); Will McAdams, Austin (9/1/25). Exec. Dir. Thomas Gleeson ($200,000), 1701 Congress Ave., 7th Fl., PO Box 13326, Austin 78711-3326; (512) 936-7000.

Public Utility Counsel, Office of: (1983); apptv.; 2-yr.; Interim Public Counsel: Chris Ekoh ($110,538), 1701 Congress Ave., Ste. 9-180, PO Box 12397, Austin 78711-2397; (512) 936-7500.

Racing Commission, Texas: (1986); apptv.; 6-yr.; per diem and expenses; 9 members; 2 ex officio: Chair, Public Safety Comm. and Comm. of Agriculture; 7 apptv.: Chair Robert C. Pate, Corpus Christi (2/1/23); Margaret Martin, Boerne (2/1/21); Connie McNabb, Montgomery (2/1/21); Michael "Mike" Moore, Fort Worth (2/1/23); Arvel "A.J." Waight Jr., Willow City (2/1/21); 2 vacancies. Exec. Dir. Chuck Trout ($90,200), 8505 Cross Park Dr., Ste. 110, PO Box 12080, Austin 78711; (512) 833-6699.

Radiation Advisory Board, Texas: (1961); apptv.; 6-yr.; 18 members: Ronal Benke, Austin (4/16/27); Charles Cavnor, Little Elm (4/16/25); John Hageman, San Antonio (4/16/23); Mark C. Harvey, Houston (4/16/27); Frank "Neal" Leavell, Lampasas (4/16/21); Lisa Masters, San Antonio (4/16/27); Darlene Metter, San Antonio (4/16/25); Sanjay Narayan, Dallas (4/16/27); William Pate, League City (4/16/25); Kenneth "Ken" Peters, Granbury (4/16/25); Doug Posey, Corpus Christi (4/16/23); Gerald T. "Tim" Powell, Bay City (4/16/27); Kevin L. Raabe, Floresville (4/16/23); Robert "Bob" Redweik, Tomball (4/16/25); Darshan J. Sachde, Austin (4/16/25); Mark Silberman, Austin (4/16/23); Lynn Slaney Silguero, Frisco (4/16/23); Simon Trubek, Austin (4/16/27). 8407 Wall St., PO Box 149347, Austin 78714-9347; (888) 899-6688.

Radioactive Waste Disposal Compact Commission, Texas Low-Level: (1993); apptv.; 6-yr.; expenses; 6 Texas members, plus 2 members from Vermont; Texas apptees.: Chair Brandon T. Hurley, Grapevine (8/31/25); Richard H. Dolgener, Andrews (8/31/21); Lisa Edwards, Granbury (8/31/23); Linda Morris, Waco (8/31/21); Jeff Munday, Austin (8/31/25); John M. Salsman, Driftwood (8/31/23). Exec. Dir. Stephen Raines, 919 Congress Ave., Ste. 830, Austin 78701; (737) 300-2154.

Railroad Commission of Texas: (1891); elective; 6-yr.; 3 members, $140,937 each: Wayne Christian (12/31/22); Christi Craddick (12/31/24); Jim Wright (12/31/26). Exec. Dir. Wei Wang ($192,600), 1701 Congress Ave., PO Box 12967, Austin 78711-2967; (512) 463-7158.

Real Estate Commission, Texas: (1949 as 6-member board; members increased to current number in 1979); apptv.; per diem and expenses; 6-yr.; 9 members: Chair R. Scott Kesner, El Paso (1/31/25); Jason Hartgraves, Frisco (1/31/25); Leslie Lerner, Houston (1/31/27); Jan Fite Miller, Kemp (1/31/23); Benjamin "Ben" Peña, Bayview (1/31/27); Barbara Russell, Denton (1/31/25); DeLora Wilkinson, Cypress (1/31/23); Micheal Williams, Colleyville (1/31/23); Mark Woodroof, Houston (1/31/27). Exec. Dir. Chelsea Buchholtz ($180,250), 1700 Congress Ave., Ste. 400, PO Box 12188, Austin 78711-2188; (512) 936-3000.

Real Estate Research Center, Texas: (1971); apptv.; 6-yr.; 10 members; 1 ex officio: rep. of Texas Real Estate Commission; 9 apptv.: Chair Russell L. Cain, Port Lavaca (1/31/23); Troy C. Alley Jr., DeSoto (1/31/23); Doug Foster, San Antonio (1/31/27); Vicki Fullerton, The Woodlands (1/31/25); Patrick Geddes, Dallas (1/31/23); W. Douglas Jennings, Fort Worth (1/31/27); Besa Martin, Boerne (1/31/27); Walter F. "Ted" Nelson, Houston (1/31/25); Rebecca "Becky" Vajdak, Temple (1/31/25). Exec. Dir. Gary Maler ($247,367), 1700 Research Pkwy., Ste. 200, Texas A&M University, 2115 TAMU, College Station 77843-2115; (979) 845-2031.

Red River Authority of Texas: (1959); apptv.; 6-yr.; per diem and expenses; 9 members: Pres. Todd W. Boykin, Amarillo (8/11/21); Mary Lou Bradley, Memphis (8/11/25); Jerry Bob Daniel, Truscott (8/11/21); Jerry Dan Davis, Wellington (8/11/23); Michael R. Sandefur, Texarkana (8/11/23); George Wilson Scaling II, Henrietta (8/11/21); Zackary K. Smith, Canyon (8/11/25); Stephen A. Thornhill, Denison (8/11/25); Joe L. Ward, Telephone (8/11/23). Gen. Mgr. Randall W. Whiteman, 3000 Hammon Rd., PO Box 240, Wichita Falls 76307; (940) 723-8697.

Red River Compact Commission: (1949, negotiates with Oklahoma, Arkansas and Louisiana regarding waters of the Red); apptv.; 6-yr.; salary and expenses. Comm. Robin Phillips (2/1/23), 300 N. Travis St., Sherman 75090; (903) 814-7273.

Redistricting Board, Legislative (See Legislative Redistricting Board.)

Rehabilitation Council of Texas: (1973); apptv.; 3-yr.; at least 15 members: Chair Michael A. Ebbeler Jr., Austin (10/29/22);

Matt Berend, Scotland (10/29/21); Amanda Bowdoin, Forney (10/29/23); Jennifer Clouse, Temple (2/25/23); Lisa Cowart, Beaumont (10/29/21); JoAnn Fluke, Abilene (10/29/21); Cheryl A. Fuller, Austin; Lindsey Geeslin, Waco (10/29/23); Gennadiy Goldenshteyn, Dallas (2/25/23); Bobbie Hodges, Fort Worth (10/29/22); Paul Hunt, Austin (10/29/21); Elizabeth Kendell, San Antonio (10/29/22); Lisa Maciejewski-West, San Angelo (10/29/22); April Pollreisz, Amarillo (10/29/21); Joe Powell, Irving (10/29/21); Emily Robinson, Pflugerville (10/29/23); Rodrick Robinson, McKinney (10/29/23); Karen Stanfill, Houston (10/29/22); Crystal Stark, College Station (10/29/21); Abdi Warsame, Wylie (2/25/23). 101 E. 15th St., Rm. 144T, Austin 78788-0001; (512) 936-3445.

Respiratory Care Board: (2015); apptv.; 6-yr.; 9 members: Presiding Officer Latana T. Jackson, Cedar Hill (2/1/23); Samuel L. Brown Jr., Marshall (2/1/25); Tim R. Chappell, Plano (2/1/27); Sam Gregory "Gregg" Marshall, Round Rock (2/1/27); Debra E. Patrick, McKinney (2/1/25); Shad J. Pellizzari, Cedar Park (2/1/23); Kandace D. "Kandi" Pool, San Angelo (2/1/27); Hammad Nasir Qureshi, Tomball (2/1/25); Sonia K. Sanderson, Beaumont (2/1/23). Exec. Dir. Stephen "Brint" Carlton, 333 Guadalupe St., Tower 3, Ste. 610, Austin 78701; (512) 305-7010.

Retirement System, Texas County & District: (1967); apptv.; 6-yr.; 9 members: Chair Mary Louise Nicholson, Fort Worth (12/31/23); Tammy Biggar, Bonham (12/31/25); Chris Davis, Alto (12/31/21); Susan Fletcher, Frisco (12/31/23); Chris Hill, McKinney (12/31/21); Deborah Hunt, Georgetown (12/31/21); Kara Sands, Corpus Christi (12/31/23); Chris Taylor, Fort Worth (12/31/25); Holly Williamson, Houston (12/31/25). Exec. Dir. Amy Bishop, 901 S. MoPac Expwy., Bldg. IV, Ste. 500, Austin 78746; (512) 328-8889.

Retirement System, Texas Emergency Services: (1977; formerly the Fire Fighters' Relief and Retirement Fund); apptv.; expenses; 6-yr.; 9 members: Chair Jenny Moore, Lake Jackson (9/1/21); Courtney Gibson Bechtol, Rockport (9/1/21); Nathan Douglas, Seabrook (9/1/25); Matthew "Matt" Glaves, Alvin (9/1/25); Edward J. Keenan, Houston (9/1/23); Pilar Rodriguez, Edinburg (9/1/21); Jerry Romero, El Paso (2/1/25); Rodney Alan Ryalls, Burkburnett (9/1/23); Stephanie Lynn Wagner, Wimberley (9/1/23). Exec. Dir. Shirley Hays ($105,000), PO Box 12577, Austin 78711; (512) 936-3372.

Retirement System, Texas Municipal: (1947); apptv.; 6-yr.; expenses; 6 members: Chair David Landis, Perryton (2/1/21); Anali Alanis, Pharr (2/1/21); Jesús A. Garza, Victoria (2/1/23); Juan Diego Huizar, Pleasanton (2/1/23); Bill Philibert, Deer Park (2/1/25); Bob Scott, Carrollton (2/1/25). Exec. Dir. David Wescoe, 1200 N. I-35, PO Box 149153, Austin 78714-9153; (512) 476-5576.

Retirement System of Texas, Employees: (1949); apptv.; 6-yr.; 6 members: 1 apptd. by Gov., 1 by Chief Justice of State Supreme Court, 1 by House Speaker; 3 elected by ERS members: Chair I. Craig Hester, Austin (8/31/22); Brian R. Barth, Austin (8/31/25); Ilesa Daniels, Houston (8/31/21); James "Jim" Kee, San Antonio (8/31/26); Catherine Melvin, Austin (8/31/23); 1 vacancy. Exec. Dir. Porter Wilson ($316,117), 200 E. 18th St., PO Box 13207, Austin 78711-3207; (877) 275-4377.

Retirement System of Texas, Teacher: (1937 as 6-member board; members increased to 9 in 1973); 6-yr.; expenses; 9 members; 2 apptd. by State Board of Education, 3 by Gov., 4 by Gov. after being nominated by popular ballot of retirement system members: Chair Jarvis V. Hollingsworth, Missouri City (8/31/23); Michael Ball, Argyle (8/31/25); David Corpus, Humble (8/31/25); John Elliott, Austin (8/31/21); Christopher Moss, Lufkin (8/31/21); James Dick Nance, Hallettsville (8/31/23); Nanette Sissney, Whitesboro (8/31/23); Robert H. Walls, San Antonio (8/31/25); 1 vacancy. Exec. Dir. Brian Guthrie ($355,141), 1000 Red River St., Austin 78701-2698; (512) 542-6400.

Rio Grande Compact Commission: (1929, negotiates with Colorado and New Mexico regarding waters of the Rio Grande); apptv.; 6-yr.; salary and expenses; Comm. Robert "Bobby" Skov, Fabens (6/9/25), 401 E. Franklin Ave. Ste. 560, El Paso 79901; (915) 764-0014.

Risk Management, State Office of: apptv.; 2-yr.; 5 members: Chair Lloyd M. Garland, Lubbock (2/1/25); Ricardo "Rick" Galindo III, San Antonio (2/1/25); Rosemary Gammon, Plano (2/1/21); Tomas Gonzalez, El Paso (2/1/23); Gerald Ladner Sr., Austin (2/1/21). Exec. Dir. Stephen Vollbrecht ($150,563), 300 W. 15th St., 6th Fl., PO Box 13777, Austin 78711-3777; (512) 475-1440.

Sabine River Authority of Texas: (1949); apptv.; per diem and expenses; 6-yr.; 9 members: Cary "Mac" Abney, Marshall (7/6/21); Thomas "Tom" Beall, Milam (7/6/23); Jeffrey D. "Jeff" Jacobs, Rockwall (7/6/25); Joshua A. "Josh" McAdams, Center (7/6/25); Jeanette Sterner, Holly Lake Ranch (7/6/21); Cliff Todd, Long Branch (7/6/23); Janie Walenta, Quitman (7/6/23); Kevin M. Williams, Orange (7/6/25); Laurie Woloszyn, Longview (7/6/21). Exec. VP David Montagne, PO Box 579, Orange 77631-0579; (409) 746-2192.

Sabine River Compact Commission: (1953, negotiates with Louisiana regarding the waters of the Sabine); apptv.; 6-yr.; salary and expenses; 2 commissioners: Jerry F. Gipson, Longview (7/12/22); Michael H. Lewis, Newton (7/12/19); c/o PO Box 13087, Austin 78711; (512) 239-4730.

San Antonio River Authority: (1937); elective; 6-yr.; 12 members: Chair Darrell T. Brownlow, Wilson Co. (11/4/25); Jim Campbell, Bexar Co. (11/2/21); Alicia L. Cowley, Goliad Co. (11/2/21); John J. Flieller, Wilson Co. (11/2/21); James Fuller, Goliad Co. (11/4/25); Lourdes Galvan, Bexar Co. (11/4/25); Jerry G. Gonzales, Bexar Co. (11/4/25); Michael W. Lackey, Bexar Co. (11/2/21); Hector R. Morales, Bexar Co. (11/7/23); Gaylon J. Oehlke, Karnes Co. (11/4/25); Deb B. Prost, Bexar Co. (11/7/23); H.B. "Trip" Ruckman III, Karnes Co. (11/2/21). Gen. Mgr. Derek Boese, 100 E. Guenther St., San Antonio 78204; (210) 227-1373.

San Jacinto River Authority: (1937); apptv.; expenses while on duty; 6-yr.; 7 members: Pres. Ronnie Anderson, Mont Belvieu (10/16/21); Ed Boulware, Montgomery (10/16/23); Stacey Buick, Montgomery (10/16/21); William "Wil" Faubel, Montgomery (10/16/25); Mark Micheletti, Kingwood (10/16/23); Ricardo "Rick" Mora, The Woodlands (10/16/25); 1 vacancy. Gen. Mgr. Jace A. Houston, 1577 Dam Site Rd., PO Box 329, Conroe 77305; (936) 588-3111.

Savings and Mortgage Lending, Department of: (1961); commissioner apptd. by State Finance Commission. Comm. Caroline C. Jones ($194,750), 2601 N. Lamar Blvd., Ste. 201, Austin 78705; (512) 475-1350.

School Land Board (See Land Board, School.)

School Safety Center, Texas: (2001); apptv.; 2-yr.; 5 ex officio members from the Texas Higher Education Coord. Board, Texas Education Agency, Health and Human Services Comm., Attorney General's office, and the Texas Juvenile Justice Dept.; 12 apptd. members: Bill Avera, Jacksonville (2/1/22); Craig Bessent, Abilene (2/1/22); Kerri Brady, Georgetown (2/1/22); Lizeth Cuellar Olivarez, Laredo (2/1/23); Edwin S. Flores, Dallas (2/1/23); Bryan Hedrick, Hereford (2/1/22); James M. Mosley, Borger (2/1/23); Teresa K. Oldham, Jarrell (2/1/22); Michael L. Slaughter, Wylie (2/1/23); Jill M. Tate, Colleyville (2/1/23); Alan Trevino, Burnet (2/1/22); Robert W. Wilson, Silsbee (2/18/23). Director Kathy Martinez-Prather, 601 University Dr., San Marcos 78666; (512) 245-8082.

Securities Board, Texas State: (1957, the outgrowth of several amendments to the Texas Securities Act, originally passed in 1913); expenses; 6-yr.; 5 members: Chair E. Wally Kinney, Comfort (1/20/25); Robert Belt, Houston (1/20/23); Kenny Koncaba, Friendswood (1/20/23); Ejike E. Okpa, Dallas (1/20/27); Melissa Tyroch, Belton (1/20/25). Comm. Travis J. Iles ($162,491), 208 E. 10th St., Austin 78701; (512) 305-8301.

Sex Offender Treatment, Council on: (1983); apptv.; expenses; 6-yr.; 7 members: Presiding Officer Aaron Paul Pierce, Temple (2/1/23); Elizabeth Perez Aliseda, Beeville (2/1/23); Ezio Leite, North Richland Hills (2/1/27); Emily Orozco-Crousen, Abilene (2/1/27); Velma "Jean" Stanley, Lufkin (2/1/25); Tiffany Strother, Godley (2/1/25); James Taylor, San Antonio (2/1/21). Exec. Dir. Pamela Adams, c/o Texas Dept. of State Health Services, PO Box 149347, Austin 78714-9347; (512) 834-4530

Skill Standards Board, Texas: (1995); abolished and its powers and duties were transferred to the Texas Workforce Investment Council on September 1, 2015.

Social Worker Examiners, Texas State Board of: (1993); apptv.; 6-yr.; per diem and travel expenses; 9 members: Presiding Member Brian C. Brumley, Sumner (2/1/27); Katie Andrade, Mount Pleasant (2/1/27); Megan Marie Graham, Houston (2/1/23); Ben W. Morris, Cleburne (2/1/27); Martha Mosier, College Station (2/1/23); Audrey Ramsbacher, San Antonio (2/1/23); Asia Rodgers, Fort Worth (2/1/25); Dolores Saenz-Davila, McAllen (2/1/25); Jennifer Swords, Fort Worth (2/1/25). Admin. Sarah Faszholz ($72,000), 333 Guadalupe St., Tower 3, Rm. 900, Austin 78701; (512) 305-7700.

Soil & Water Conservation Board, Texas State: (1939); 2-yr.; 7 members: 2 apptd. by Gov.; 5 elected by district directors: Chair Marty H. Graham, Rocksprings (5/5/22); David Basinger, Deport (5/1/22); Scott Buckles, Stratford (5/7/23); José Dolan Jr., Zapata (5/7/23); Barry Mahler, Iowa Park (5/7/23); Gov. Apptees.: Tina Y. Buford, Harlingen (2/1/22); Carl Ray Polk Jr., Lufkin (2/1/23). Exec. Dir. Rex Isom ($150,283), 1497 Country View Ln., Temple 76504; (254) 773-2250.

Special Education, Continuing Advisory Committee for: (1997); apptv.; 4-yr.; 17 members: Shemica S. Allen, Allen (2/1/23); Teresa Bronsky, Plano (2/1/23); Jana S. Burns, Saginaw (2/1/21); Elizabeth A. "Beth" Donaldson, Stowell (2/1/21); Rachel A. Dreiling, Dallas (2/1/21); Alicia Giordano, Humble (2/1/21); Amy Litzinger, Austin (2/1/21); Stephanie Martinez, Laredo (2/1/23); Jana McKelvey, Austin (2/1/23); Kristine H. Mohajer, Leander (2/1/21); Susan Nichols, Carrollton (2/1/21); Laurie Goforth Rodriguez, Dickinson (2/1/21); Jen Stratton, Austin (2/1/23); Agata K. "Agatha" Thibodeaux, Katy (2/1/21); Ray Tijerina, San Antonio (2/1/21); Laura Villarreal, Universal City (2/1/23); Jo Ann Garza Wofford, New Braunfels (2/1/21). c/o Texas Education Agency, 1701 Congress Ave., Austin 78701; (512) 463-9734; Parent Information Line: (800) 252-9668.

Speech Language Pathologists and Audiologists Advisory Board: (2015); apptv.; 6-yr.; 9 members: Presiding Officer Sherry Sancibrian, Lubbock (3/3/22); Emanuel Bodner, Houston (9/1/21); Cheval Bryant, Sugar Land (9/1/25); Tammy Camp, Shallowater (9/1/23); Kristina Kelley, Dallas (9/1/23); Cristen Plummer-Culp, Round Rock (9/1/25); Kimberly Ringer, Pflugerville (9/1/25); Elizabeth Sterling, Austin (9/1/25); 1 vacancy. PO Box 12157, Austin 78711; (512) 463-6599.

Stephen F. Austin State University Board of Regents: (1969); apptv.; expenses; 6-yr.; 9 members: Chair Karen G. Gantt, McKinney (1/31/23); David Alders, Nacogdoches (1/31/25); Robert A. Flores, Nacogdoches (1/31/27); Brigettee Carnes Henderson, Lufkin (1/31/23); M. Thomas Mason, Dallas (1/31/23); Judy Larson Olson, The Woodlands (1/31/25); Laura Rectenwald, Longview (1/31/27); Nancy C. Windham, Nacogdoches (1/31/27); Jennifer Wade Winston, Lufkin (1/31/25). Pres. Scott Gordon, 1936 North St., Nacogdoches 75962; (936) 468-3401.

Sulphur River Basin Authority: (1985); apptv.; 6-yr.; 7 members: Chair Chris Spencer, Hughes Springs (2/1/23); Gary Cheatwood, Bogata (2/1/23); Emily Glass, Sulphur Springs (2/1/27); Reeves Hayter, Paris (6/15/25); Kirby Hollingsworth, Mount Vernon (2/1/27); Wallace E. "Wally" Kraft II, Paris (2/1/25); Kelly Mitchell, Texarkana (2/1/23). Exec. Dir. Chris Hartung, 911 N. Bishop St., Ste. C104, Wake Village 75501; (903) 223-7887.

Sunset Advisory Commission: (1977); 12 members: 5 members of House of Representatives, 5 members of Senate, 1 public member apptd. by Speaker, 1 public member by Lt. Gov.; 2-yr.; expenses. Public members: Ralph Duggins, Fort Worth (9/1/21); Julie Harris-Lawrence, Surfside Beach (9/1/21). Exec. Dir. Jennifer Jones ($190,000), 1501 Congress Ave., 6th Fl., PO Box 13066, Austin 78711; (512) 463-1300.

Teacher Retirement System (See Retirement System of Texas, Teacher.)

Texas A&M University System Board of Regents: (1875); apptv.; 6-yr.; expenses; 9 members: Chair Tim Leach, Midland (2/1/23); Robert L. Albritton, Fort Worth (2/1/27); James R. "Randy" Brooks, San Angelo (2/1/27); Jay Graham, Houston (2/1/25); Michael A. "Mike" Hernandez III, Fort Worth (2/1/25); Bill Mahomes, Dallas (2/1/27); Elaine Mendoza, San Antonio (2/1/23); Michael J. Plank, Houston (2/1/25); Cliff Thomas, Victoria (2/1/23). Chancellor John Sharp, 301 Tarrow St., College Station 77840; (979) 458-7700.

Texas Southern University Board of Regents: (1947); apptv.; expenses; 6-yr.; 9 members: Chair Albert H. Myres, Sr., Houston (2/1/25); Caroline Baker Hurley, Houston (2/1/27); James M. Benham, College Station (2/1/23); Marc C. Carter, Houston (2/1/23); Pamela A. Medina, Houston (2/1/25); Stephanie D. Nellons-Paige, Houston (2/1/25); Ron J. Price, Mesquite (2/1/23); Marilyn A. Rose, Houston (2/1/27); Mary Evans Sias, Richardson (2/1/27). Pres. Lesia L. Crumpton-Young, 3100 Cleburne St., Houston 77004; (713) 313-7011.

Texas State Technical College Board of Regents: (1960 as Board of the Texas State Technical Institute; changed to present name in 1991); apptv.; expenses; 6-yr.; 9 members: Chair Curtis Cleveland, Waco (8/31/21); Tony Abad, Waco (8/31/21); John K. Hatchel, Woodway (2/1/23); Keith Honey, Longview (8/31/25); Charles "Pat" McDonald, Richmond (8/31/23); Alejandro "Alex" Meade III, Mission (8/31/21); Kathy Powell, San Angelo (8/31/25); Tiffany Tremont, New Braunfels (8/31/23); Ron Widup, Arlington (8/31/25). Chancellor Mike Reeser, 3801 Campus Dr., Waco 76705; (254) 799-3611.

Texas State University System Board of Regents: (1911 as Board of Regents of State Teachers Colleges; name changed in 1965 to Board of Regents of State Senior Colleges; changed to present form in 1975); apptv.; per diem and expenses; 6-yr.; 9 members: Chair Charlie Amato, San Antonio (2/1/25); Duke Austin, Houston (2/1/23); Garry Crain, The Hills (2/1/23); Sheila Faske, Rose City (2/1/27); Dionicio "Don" Flores, El Paso (2/1/25); Nicki Harle, Baird (2/1/23); Stephen Lee, Beaumont (2/1/27); William F. Scott, Nederland (2/1/25); Alan L. Tinsley, Madisonville (2/1/27). Chancellor Brian McCall, 601 Colorado St., Austin 78701-2904; (512) 463-1808.

Texas Tech University System Board of Regents: (1923); apptv.; expenses; 6-yr.; 9 members: Chair J. Michael Lewis, Dallas (1/31/23); Arcilia Acosta, Dallas (1/31/27); Cody Campbell, Fort Worth (1/31/27); Pat Gordon, El Paso (1/31/27); Mark Griffin, Lubbock (1/31/25); Ginger Kerrick Davis, Webster (1/31/25); John Steinmetz, Dallas (1/31/23); John Walker, Houston (1/31/23); Dusty Womble, Lubbock (1/31/25). Chancellor Tedd L. Mitchell, 1508 Knoxville Ave., Ste. 302, PO Box 42011, Lubbock 79409-2011; (806) 742-2161.

Texas Woman's University Board of Regents: (1901); apptv.; expenses; 6-yr.; 9 members: Chair Kathleen Wu, Dallas (2/1/23); Bernadette C. Coleman, Denton (2/1/23); Teresa H. Doggett, Austin (2/1/21); Bob Hyde, Irving (2/1/25); Jill Jester, Denton (2/1/23); Stacie D. McDavid, Fort Worth (2/1/25); Janelle Shepard, Weatherford (2/1/27); Mary P. Wilson, Austin (2/1/25); Crystal Wright, Houston (2/1/27). Chancellor Dr. Carine M. Feyten, 304 Administration Dr., Denton 76204; (940) 898-2000.

Transportation Commission, Texas: (1917 as State Highway Commission; merged with Mass Transportation Commission and name changed to State Board of Highways and Public

Transportation in 1975; merged with Texas Dept. of Aviation and Texas Motor Vehicle Commission and name changed to present form in 1991); governs the Texas Department of Transportation; apptv.; 6-yr.; 5 members: Chair J. Bruce Bugg Jr., San Antonio (2/1/27); Alvin New, Christoval (2/1/27); Laura Ryan, Cypress (2/1/23); Robert C. Vaughn, Dallas (2/1/25); 1 vacancy. Exec. Dir. Marc D. Williams ($344,000), 125 E. 11th St., Austin 78701; (512) 463-8588.

Trinity River Authority: (1955); apptv.; per diem and expenses; 6-yr.; 25 members: Pres. Kevin Maxwell, Crockett (3/15/21); Cathy Altman, Midlothian (3/15/23); Whitney D. Beckworth, Fort Worth (3/15/21); Henry Borbolla III, Fort Worth (3/15/25); C. Cole Camp, Arlington (3/15/23); Megan W. Deen, Fort Worth (3/15/23); Tommy G. Fordyce, Huntsville (3/15/25); Lisa A. Hembry, Dallas (3/15/23); Jerry F. House, Leona (3/15/23); John W. Jenkins, Hankamer (3/15/21); David B. Leonard, Liberty (3/15/25); Victoria K. Lucas, Terrell (3/15/23); D. Joe McCleskey, Apple Springs (3/15/23); Robert F. McFarlane, Palestine (3/15/21); Lewis H. McMahan, Dallas (3/15/25); Manny Rachal, Livingston (3/15/21); Steven L. Roberts, Coldspring (3/15/23); William O. Rodgers, Fort Worth (3/15/25); Amir A. Rupani, Dallas (3/15/25); Kathryn L. Sanders, Athens (3/15/25); C. Dwayne Somerville, Mexia (3/15/25); Frank H. Steed Jr., Kerens (3/15/21); Brenda K. Walker, Palestine (3/15/25); David G. Ward, Madisonville (3/15/23); Edward C. Williams III, Dallas (3/15/21). Gen. Mgr. Kevin Ward, 5300 S. Collins St., PO Box 60, Arlington 76004; (817) 467-4343.

Tuition Board, Texas Prepaid Higher Education (See Higher Education Tuition Board, Texas Prepaid.)

University Lands, Board for Lease of: (1929 as 3-member board; members increased to 4 in 1985); 2-yr.; 4 members: Comm. of General Land Office, 2 members of Board of Regents of The University of Texas, 1 of Board of Regents of Texas A&M University. Ex officio Chair George P. Bush; Christina Melton Crain, Dallas (2/1/25); Mike Hernandez III, Fort Worth (2/1/25); Nolan Perez, Harlingen (2/1/27). Interim CEO: Joe Quoyeser, 825 Town and Country Ln., Ste. 1100, Houston 77024; (713) 352-3808.

University of Houston System Board of Regents: (1963); apptv.; expenses; 6-yr.; 9 members: Chair Tilman J. Fertitta, Houston (8/31/21); Durga D. Agrawal, Houston (8/31/25); Doug H. Brooks, Plano (8/31/23); Alonzo Cantu, McAllen (8/31/25); Steve I. Chazen, Bellaire (8/3123); Beth Madison, Houston (8/31/23); John A. McCall Jr., Crockett (8/31/25); Gerald W. McElvy, Southlake (8/31/21); Jack B. Moore, Houston (8/31/23). Chancellor Renu Khator, 4800 Calhoun Rd., Houston 77004; (832) 842-3444.

University of North Texas System Board of Regents: (1949); apptv.; 6-yr.; expenses; 9 members: Chair Laura Wright, Dallas (5/22/21); Melisa Denis, Southlake (5/22/25); Mary Denny, Aubrey (5/22/23); Daniel Feehan, Fort Worth (5/22/25); Milton B. Lee II, San Antonio (5/22/25); A.K. Mago, Dallas (5/22/21); Carlos Munguia, University Park (5/22/23); G. Brint Ryan, Dallas (5/22/25); John Scott Jr., Keller (5/22/25). Chancellor Lesa Roe, 1901 Main St., Dallas 75201; (214) 571-4800.

University of Texas System Board of Regents: (1881); apptv.; expenses; 6-yr.; 9 members: Chair Kevin P. Eltife, Tyler (2/1/27); Christina Melton Crain, Dallas (2/1/25); R. Steven Hicks, Austin (2/1/25); Jodie Lee Jiles, Houston (2/1/25); Janiece Longoria, Houston (2/1/23); Nolan Perez, Harlingen (2/1/27); Stuart W. Stedman, Houston (2/1/27); Kelcy L. Warren, Dallas (2/1/25); James C. "Rad" Weaver, San Antonio (2/1/23). Chancellor James B. Milliken, 210 W. Seventh St., Austin 78701-2982; (512) 499-4400.

Upper Colorado River Authority (See Colorado River Authority, Upper.)

Upper Guadalupe River Authority (See Guadalupe River Authority, Upper.)

Upper Neches River Municipal Water Authority (See Neches River Municipal Water Authority, Upper.)

Utility Commission, Public (See Public Utility Commission.)

Veterans Commission, Texas: (1927 as Veterans State Service Office; reorganized as Veterans Affairs Commission in 1947 with 5 members; name changed to present form in 1985); apptv.; 6-yr.; per diem while on duty and expenses; 5 members: Chair Laura Koerner, Fair Oaks Ranch (12/31/23); Kevin Barber, Houston (12/31/21); Mary Dale, Cedar Park (12/31/25); Mike Hernandez, Abilene (12/31/25); Kimberlee Shaneyfelt, Dallas (12/31/23). Exec. Dir. Thomas P. Palladino ($151,123), PO Box 12277, Austin 78711-2277; (512) 463-6564.

Veterans Land Board (See Land Board, Veterans.)

Veterinary Medical Examiners, Texas Board of: (1911; revised 1953; made 9-member board in 1981); apptv.; expenses on duty; 6-yr.; 9 members: Pres. Jessica Quillivan, Magnolia (8/26/21); Sue Allen, Waco (8/26/25); Sandra "Lynn" Criner, Needville (8/26/21); Samantha Mixon, Boerne (8/26/23); Raquel Olivier, Houston (8/26/23); Keith Pardue, Austin (8/26/21); Randall Skaggs, Perryton (8/26/23); Michael White, Conroe (8/26/25); Victoria Whitehead, Lubbock (8/26/25). Exec. Dir. John M. Helenberg ($113,413), 333 Guadalupe St., Ste. 3-810, Austin 78701; (512) 305-7555.

Water Development Board, Texas: (1957; legislative function for the Texas Dept. of Water Resources, 1977); apptv.; per diem and expenses; 6-yr.; 3 members: Chair Brooke T. Paup, Austin (2/1/25); Kathleen Jackson, Beaumont (12/31/23); 1 vacancy. Exec. Admin. Jeff Walker ($188,285), 1700 Congress Ave., Austin 78701; (512) 463-7847.

Women, Governor's Commission for: (1967); apptv.; 2-yr; up to 15 members: Chair Karen Harris, Lakehills (12/31/21); Tina Yturria Buford, Harlingen (12/31/21); Cynthia Conroy, El Paso (12/31/21); Starr Corbin, Georgetown (12/31/21); Sasha Crane, McAllen (12/31/21); Amy Henderson, Amarillo (12/31/21); Ashlee Kleinert, Dallas (12/31/21); Karen Manning, Houston (12/31/21); Nathali Parker, Round Rock (12/31/21); Rienke Radler, Fort Worth (12/31/21); Jinous Rouhani, Austin (12/31/21); Catherine Susser, Corpus Christi (12/31/21); Patsy Wesson, Fort Worth (12/31/21); Laura Koenig Young, Tyler (12/31/21). Exec. Dir. Christina McKinney ($63,600), 1100 San Jacinto Blvd., Rm. 2.256, PO Box 12428, Austin 78711; (512) 475-2615.

Workers' Compensation, Commissioner of: (1991; functions transferred to the Texas Dept. of Insurance Division of Workers' Compensation in 2005); apptv.; 2-yr.; Comm. Cassie Brown ($169,111), Austin (2/1/23), 7551 Metro Center Dr., Ste. 100, PO Box 12050, Austin 78711; (800) 252-7031.

Workforce Commission, Texas: (1936 as Texas Employment Commission; name changed 1995); apptv.; 6-yr.; 3 members ($201,000): Chair Bryan Daniel, Georgetown (2/1/25); Julian Alvarez III, Harlingen (2/1/23); Aaron Demerson, Austin (2/1/27). Exec. Dir. Ed Serna ($182,500), 101 E. 15th St., Austin 78778-0001; (512) 463-2222.

Workforce Investment Council, Texas: (1993); apptv.; 19 members: 5 ex officio members (representing Economic Development and Tourism Office, Higher Education Coord. Board, Texas Education Agency, Texas Health and Human Services Comm., Texas Workforce Comm.); 14 apptd.: Chair Mark Dunn, Lufkin (9/1/25); Gina Aguirre Adams, Jones Creek (9/1/21); Joe Arnold, Muldoon (9/1/21); Jesse Gatewood, Corpus Christi (9/1/23); Lindsey Geeslin, Waco (9/1/21); Lauren Gore, Houston (9/1/25); Thomas Halbouty, Southlake (9/1/25); Michael Hinojosa, Dallas (9/1/21); John Martin, San Antonio (9/1/23); Wayne Oswald, Houston (9/1/21); Paul Puente, Houston (9/1/21); Richard Rhodes, Austin (9/1/25); Rick Rhodes, Austin (9/1/23); Brandon Willis, Beaumont (9/1/25). Dir. Lee Rector ($125,000), 1100 San Jacinto Blvd., Ste. 1.100, Austin 78701; (512) 936-8100. ☆

Storefronts in Denton. Photo by Nicholas Henderson, CC by 2.0/Flickr

Local Government

Texas has **254 counties**, a number that has not changed since 1931 when Loving County was organized. Loving has a population of 169, according to the July. 1, 2019, Texas Demographic Center estimate, compared with 164 in 1970 and a peak of 285 in 1940. It is the **least-populous county** in Texas. In contrast, Harris County has **the most residents** in Texas, with a 2019 population estimate of **4,713,325**.

Counties range in area from Rockwall's 148.7 square miles to the 6,192.8 square miles in Brewster, which is equal to the combined area of the states of Connecticut and Rhode Island.

The Texas Constitution makes a county a legal subdivision of the state. Each county has a **commissioners court**. It consists of four commissioners, each elected from a commissioner's precinct, and a county judge elected from the entire county. In smaller counties, the county judge retains judicial

responsibilities in probate and insanity cases. **For names of county and district officials, see tables on pages 501–512.**

There are **1,223 incorporated municipalities** in Texas that range in size from 18 residents in Los Ybanez to Houston's 2,325,489, according to the July 1, 2019, Texas Demographic Center estimates. More than 80 percent of the state's population lives in cities and towns, meeting the U.S. Census Bureau definition of urban areas.

Texas had **348 incorporated towns with more than 5,000 population**, according to the 2019 Texas Demographic Center estimates. Under law, these cities may adopt their own charters (called home rule) by a majority vote. Cities of fewer than 5,000 may be chartered only under the general law.

Some home-rule cities may show fewer than 5,000 residents because population has declined since adopting home-rule charters.

Mayors and City Managers of Texas Cities

This list was compiled from online sources and phone calls. It includes the name of each city's mayor, as well as the name of the city manager, city administrator, city coordinator, or other managing executive for municipalities having

that form of government. **Home-rule cities are marked in this list by a single-dagger symbol (†) after the name.**

A

Abbott . . . . Anthony R. Pustejovsky
Abernathy . . . . Ron Johnson
 City Mgr., Joe Hines
Abilene (†) . . . . .Anthony Williams
 City Mgr., Robert Hanna
Ackerly . . . . Scott Ragle
Addison (†) . . . . .Joe Chow
 City Mgr., Wes Pierson
Adrian . . . . .Maggie Gruhlkey

Agua Dulce . . . . .John Howard
Alamo (†) . . . . .Diana Martinez
 City Mgr., Bobby Salinas
Alamo Heights (†) . . . . . . Bobby Rosenthal
 City Mgr., Buddy Kuhn
Alba . . . . Don Heinert
Albany . . . . Susan Montgomery
 City Mgr., Billy Holson
Aledo . . . . Kit Marshall
 City Admin., Bill Funderburk

Alice (†) . . . . .Cynthia Carrasco
 City Mgr., Michael Esparza
Allen (†) . . . . Ken Fulk
 City Mgr., Eric Ellwanger
Alma . . . . Ginger Gonzalez
 City Mgr., Jim Benton
Alpine (†) . . . . Andres (Andy) Ramos
 City Mgr., Megan Antrim, Interim
Alto . . . . Jimmy Allen

Alton (†) . . . . .Salvador Vela
City Mgr., Jeff Underwood
Alvarado . . . . Jacob Wheat
City Mgr., Paul DeBuss
Alvin (†) . . . . Paul Horn
City Mgr., Junru Roland
Alvord . . . . Jim Enochs
City Admin., Clint Mercer
Amarillo (†) . . . . .Ginger Nelson
City Mgr., Jared Miller
Ames . . . . .Cornelius Gilmore
Amherst . . . . Clinton Sawyer
Anahuac . . . . .Charlie Henry
City Admin., Kenneth Kathan
Anderson . . . . Karen McDuffie
Andrews (†) . . . . .Flora Braly
City Mgr., Steve Eggleston
Angleton (†) . . . . Jason Perez
City Mgr., Chris Whittaker
Angus . . . . .Julie Humphries
Anna (†) . . . . Nate Pike
City Mgr., Jim Proce
Annetta . . . . Sandy Roberts
Annetta North . . . . Robert Schmidt
Annetta South . . . . .Charles Marsh
Annona . . . . .George English, Sr.
Anson (†) . . . . Sara Alfaro
City Mgr., Sonny Campbell
Anthony . . . . Benjamin Romero
Anton . . . . .Blake Cate
City Mgr., Mike Sea
Appleby . . . . Gerald Hebert, Sr.
Aquilla . . . . .Justin Earl
Aransas Pass (†) . . . . Ram Gomez
City Mgr., Gary Edwards
Archer City . . . . .Kelvin Green
City Mgr., George Huffman
Arcola . . . . Fred A. Burton
City Admin., Annette Guajardo-Goldberg
Argyle . . . . .Bryan Livingston
Town Mgr., Richard Olson
Arlington (†) . . . . Jim Ross
City Mgr., Trey Yelverton
Arp . . . . Terry Lowry
Asherton . . . . Alex Bustamante, Jr.
Aspermont . . . . Steven Ellis
City Admin., Lorenzo Calamaco
Athens (†) . . . . Toni Clay
City Mgr., Elizabeth Borstad
Atlanta (†) . . . . .Travis Ransom
City Mgr., David Cockrell
Aubrey . . . . .Chris Rich
Town Admin., Mark Kaiser
Aurora . . . . .Terry Solomon
City Admin., Toni Wheeler
Austin (†) . . . . Steve Adler
City Mgr., Spencer Cronk
Austwell . . . . Molly Grace Garcia
Avery . . . . .Alex Ackley
Avinger . . . . .Marvin Parvino
Azle (†) . . . . Alan Brundrett
City Mgr., Tom Muir

B

Bailey . . . . .Kenneth Burks
Bailey's Prairie . . . . Tammy Mutina
Baird . . . . .Donny Smith
City Admin., Lori Higgins
Balch Springs (†) . . . . .Carrie Gordon
City Mgr., Susan Cluse
Balcones Heights . . . . . . Suzanne de Leon
City Admin., David J. Harris

Ballinger (†) . . . . .Dawni Seymore
City Mgr., Brian Frieda
Balmorhea . . . . .John L. Davis
Bandera . . . . Suzanne Schauman
City Admin., Terry Byrd
Bangs . . . . Eric Bishop
Bardwell . . . . .Jodie Odlozil
Barry . . . . Charles Worsham
Barstow . . . . .Olga Abila
Bartlett . . . . Chad Mees
City Admin., Joseph Resendez
Bartonville . . . . Bill Scherer
Town Admin., Sylvia Ordeman
Bastrop (†) . . . . Connie Schroeder
City Mgr., Paul A. Hofmann
Bay City (†) . . . . .Robert Nelson
City Mgr., Shawna Burkhart
Bayou Vista . . . . Lou Wortham
Bayside . . . . Donna Easton
Baytown (†) . . . . .Brandon Capetillo
City Mgr., Rick Davis
Bayview . . . . .Gary Paris
Beach City . . . . Ryan Dagley
Bear Creek . . . . .Mark Bohm
Beasley . . . . .Kenneth Reid
Beaumont (†) . . . . .Becky Ames
City Mgr., Kyle Hayes
Beckville . . . . Gene Mothershed
Bedford (†) . . . . Michael Boyter
City Mgr., Jimmy Stathatos
Bedias . . . . Gwen Boullion
Bee Cave (†) . . . . Kara King
City Mgr., Clint Garza
Beeville (†) . . . . . Francisco Dominguez, Jr.
City Mgr., John Benson
Bellaire (†) . . . . .Andrew S. Friedberg
City Mgr., Brant Gary, Interim
Bellevue . . . . .Robert Ratliff
Bellmead (†) . . . . .Gary Moore
City Mgr., Yousry (Yost) Zakhary
Bells . . . . Terry Crumby
City Admin., Beth Woodson
Bellville . . . . James Harrison
City Admin., Shawn Jackson
Belton (†) . . . . .Wayne Carpenter
City Mgr., Sam A. Listi
Benavides . . . . . Sijifredo (Chacho) Flores
Benbrook (†) . . . . .Jerry Dittrich
City Mgr., Andy Wayman
Benjamin . . . . .Sylinda Meinzer
Berryville . . . . Ron Hewlett
Bertram . . . . .Mike Dickinson
Beverly Hills . . . . .David Gonzales
Bevil Oaks . . . . .Rebecca (Becky) Ford
Big Lake . . . . Phil Pool
Big Sandy . . . . .Rex Rozell
City Admin., Laura Rex
Big Spring (†) . . . . . .Shannon D. Thomason
City Mgr., Todd Darden
Big Wells . . . . Robert D. Juarez, Jr.
Bishop . . . . Tem Miller
Bishop Hills . . . . Betty Benham
Blackwell . . . . .Laura Rozzlle
Blanco . . . . Rachel Lumpee
City Admin., Will Daves
Blanket . . . . B.J. McGinnis
Bloomburg . . . . .Delores Simmons
Blooming Grove . . . . .Gary Patterson
Blossom . . . . .Charlotte Burge
Blue Mound . . . . Darlene Copeland
Blue Ridge . . . . .Rhonda Williams
Blum . . . . Chryle Hackler
Boerne (†) . . . . Tim Handren
City Mgr., Ben Thatcher

Bogata . . . . Larry Hinsley
Bonham (†) . . . . .H.L. Compton
City Mgr., Sean Pate
Bonney . . . . Raymond Cantu
Booker . . . . B.J. Alvarado
Borger (†) . . . . Karen Felker
City Mgr., Garrett Spradling
Bovina . . . . .Frank Gonzalez, Jr.
City Mgr., Cesar Marquez
Bowie (†) . . . . Gaylynn Burris
City Mgr., Bert Cunningham
Boyd . . . . .Rodney Holmes
City Admin., Greg Arrington
Brackettville . . . . Eric J. Martinez
City Admin., Nora Y. Rivas
Brady (†) . . . . .Anthony Groves
City Mgr., Dennis Jobe
Brazoria . . . . Roger Shugart
City Mgr., Mike Collard
Brazos Country . . . . .Albert Sykes
Breckenridge (†) . . . . .Bob Sims
City Mgr., Erika McComis
Bremond . . . . .Rick Swick
Brenham (†) . . . . Milton Y. Tate, Jr.
City Mgr., James Fisher
Briarcliff . . . . .Al Hostetler
City Admin., Aaron Johnson
Briaroaks . . . . .Jerry D. Mabry
Bridge City (†) . . . . David Rutledge
City Mgr., Jerry D. Jones
Bridgeport (†) . . . . Randy Singleton
City Mgr., Chester Nolen
Broaddus . . . . Shirley Parker
Brock . . . . .Jay Hamilton
Bronte . . . . Paul Gohman
Brookshire . . . . .Darrell Branch
Brookside Village . . . . .Craig Bailey
Browndell . . . . .Tincy Brooks
Brownfield (†) . . . . Geronimo M. Gonzales
City Mgr., Jeff Davis
Brownsboro . . . . Dusty Wise
Brownsville (†) . . . Juan (Trey) Mendez, III
City Mgr., Noel Bernal
Brownwood (†) . . . . Stephen E. Haynes
City Mgr., Emily Crawford
Bruceville-Eddy . . . . Connally Bass
City Admin., Sonya Bishop
Bryan (†) . . . . Andrew Nelson
City Mgr., Kean Register
Bryson . . . . .Lutitia Ford
Buckholts . . . . Teresa Eaton
Buda (†) . . . . .Lee Urbanovsky
City Mgr., Kenneth Williams
Buffalo . . . . .Jerrod Jones
Buffalo Gap . . . . .David L. Perry
Buffalo Springs . . . . Meggan Wilkes
Bullard . . . . Pam Frederick
City Mgr., David Hortman
Bulverde (†) . . . . Bill Krawietz
City Mgr., Danny Batts
Bunker Hill Village . . . . . . Robert P. Lord
City Admin., Karen Glynn
Burkburnett (†) . . . . .Carl Law
City Mgr., Lawrence Cutrone
Burke . . . . John Thomas Jones
Burleson (†) . . . . Chris Fletcher
City Mgr., Bryan Langley
Burnet (†) . . . . .Crista Goble Bromley
City Mgr., David Vaughn
Burton . . . . David Zajicek
Byers . . . . .Norrieca Dalton
Bynum . . . . Casi D. Wood

C

Cactus . . . . .Socorro Marquez
    City Mgr., Aldo Gallegos
Caddo Mills . . . . .Ron Olson
    City Mgr., Matt McMahan
Caldwell . . . . Norris L. McManus
    City Admin., Camden White
Callisburg . . . . Nathan Caldwell
Calvert . . . . Marcus D. Greaves
    City Admin., Kevin O'Carroll
Cameron (†) . . . . .Bill Harris
    City Mgr., J. Rhett Parker
Campbell . . . . .Terry Trapp
Camp Wood . . . . Josh Cox
Canadian . . . . .Terrill Bartlett
    City Mgr., Joe Jarosek
Caney City . . . . Lamar Matthews
Canton . . . . .Lou Ann Everett
    City Mgr., Lonny Cluck
Canyon (†). . . . . Gary Hinders
    City Mgr., Joe Price
Carbon . . . . Corey Hull
Carl's Corner . . . . Susan Ezell
Carmine . . . . Wade Eilers
Carrizo Springs (†) . . . . .Wayne Seiple
    City Mgr., Ronnie J. Guest, Jr.
Carrollton (†) . . . . Kevin Falconer
    City Mgr., Erin Rinehart
Carthage (†) . . . . Olin Joffrion
    City Mgr., Stephen K. Williams
Cashion . . . . Debra Carr
Castle Hills . . . . .JR Trevino
    City Mgr., Ryan Rapelye
Castroville . . . . .Darrin Schroeder
    City Admin., Scott Dixon
Cedar Hill (†) . . . . Stephen Mason
    City Mgr., Greg Porter
Cedar Park (†) . . . . . Corbin Van Arsdale
    City Mgr., Brenda Eivens
Celeste . . . . Larry Godwin
Celina (†) . . . . .Sean Terry
    City Mgr., Jason Laumer
Center (†) . . . . David Chadwick
    City Mgr., Chad Nehring
Centerville . . . . Noal Ray Goolsby
Chandler . . . . Libby Fulgham
    City Admin., John Whitsell
Channing . . . . Troy Williams
Charlotte . . . . Buddy Lee Daughtry
Chester . . . . .Floyd Petri
Chico . . . . .Colleen Self
Childress (†) . . . . .Cary Preston
    City Mgr., Kevin Hodges
Chillicothe . . . . Cathy Young
China . . . . .William (Butch) Sanders
China Grove . . . . Mary Ann Hajek
    City Admin., Susan Conaway
Chireno . . . . Susan Higginbotham
    City Admin., Steven Spencer
Christine . . . . Jerry Flores
Cibolo (†) . . . . Stosh Boyle
    City Mgr., Robert T. Herrera
Cisco (†) . . . . Tammy Douglas
    City Mgr., Darwin Archer
Clarendon . . . . Sandy Skelton
    City Admin., David Dockery
Clarksville . . . . .Ann Rushing
    City Mgr., Damien Carrasco, Interim
Clarksville City . . . . Joe B. Spears
    City Mgr., Matt Maines
Claude . . . . Bill Wood
Clear Lake Shores . . . . Kurt Otten
    City Admin., Brent Spier

Cleburne (†) . . . . .Scott Cain
    City Mgr., Steve Polasek
Cleveland (†) . . . . .Richard Boyett
    City Mgr., Bobby Penington
Clifton . . . . Richard Spitzer
    City Admin., Pamela K. Harvey
Clint . . . . .Dora H. Aguirre
Clute (†) . . . . Calvin Shiflet
    City Mgr., CJ Snipes
Clyde . . . . Rodger Brown
    City Admin., Christopher McGuire
Coahoma . . . . .Warren Wallace
Cockrell Hill . . . . Luis D. Carrera
    City Admin., Bret Haney
Coffee City . . . . .Frank Serrato
Coldspring . . . . .Pat Eversole
Coleman (†) . . . . Tommy Sloan
    City Mgr., Diana Lopez
College Station (†) . . . . . . Karl Mooney
    City Mgr., Bryan Woods
Colleyville (†) . . . . Richard Newton
    City Mgr., Jerry Ducay
Collinsville . . . . Derek Kays
Colmesneil . . . . .Don Baird
Colorado City (†) . . . . .Robert Oliver
    City Mgr., David Hoover
Columbus . . . . Lori An Gobert
    City Mgr., Donald Warschak
Comanche . . . . .Mary A. Boyd
Combes . . . . Marco Sanchez
    Town Admin., Aida Gutierrez
Combine . . . . .Tim Ratcliff
Commerce (†) . . . . .Wyman Williams
    City Mgr., Howdy Lisenbee
Como . . . . Jerry Radney
Conroe (†) . . . . .Jody Czajkoski
    City Admin., Paul Virgadamo, Jr.
Converse (†) . . . . Alfred (Al) Suarez
    City Mgr., Le Ann Piatt
Cool . . . . .Dorothy Hall
Coolidge . . . . Jesse Ashmore
Cooper . . . . .Darren Braddy
Coppell (†) . . . . Wes Mays
    City Mgr., Mike Land
Copperas Cove (†) . . . . .Bradi Diaz
    City Mgr., Ryan Haverlah
Copper Canyon . . . . Ron Robertson
    Town Admin., Donna Welsh
Corinth (†) . . . . Bill Heidemann
    City Mgr., Bob Hart
Corpus Christi (†) . . . Paulette M. Guajardo
    City Mgr., Peter Zanoni
Corrigan . . . . .Johnna Gibson
    City Mgr., Darrian Hudman
Corsicana (†) . . . . .Don Denbow
    City Mgr., Connie Standridge
Cottonwood . . . . .Karen Deloney
Cottonwood Shores . . . . .Donald Orr
    City Admin., J.C. Hughes
Cotulla . . . . Javier Garcia
    City Admin., Larry Dovalina
Coupland . . . . Jack R. Piper
Cove . . . . .Leroy Stevens
Covington . . . . George Burnett
Coyote Flats . . . . .Doug Peterson
Crandall . . . . .Danny Kirbie
    City Mgr., Jana Shelton
Crane . . . . .Kelly Nichols
    City Admin., Dru Gravens
Cranfills Gap . . . . .David D. Witte
Crawford . . . . .Brian Porter
    City Mgr., Brian Bolfing
Creedmoor . . . . .Fran Klestinec
    City Admin., Robert Wilhite

Cresson . . . . .Teena Conway
Crockett (†) . . . . Ianthia Fisher
    City Admin., John Angerstein
Crosbyton . . . . .Dusty Cornelius
    City Admin., Amy Wallace
Cross Plains . . . . .Jerry Cassle
    City Admin., Debbie Gosnell
Cross Roads . . . . . . .T. Lynn Tompkins, Jr.
    Town Admin., Kristi Gilbert
Cross Timber . . . . Patti Meier
Crowell . . . . .Ronnie Allen
Crowley (†) . . . . Billy P. Davis
    City Mgr., Robert Loftin
Crystal City (†) . . . . . . .Frank Moreno, Jr.
    City Mgr., Santos Camarillo
Cuero (†) . . . . .Sara Post-Meyer
    City Mgr., Raymie Zella
Cumby . . . . Doug Simmerman
Cuney . . . . Jessie Johnson
Cushing . . . . Robert Sides
Cut and Shoot . . . . .Nyla Akin Dalhaus

D

Daingerfield (†). . . . . .Lou Irvin
    City Mgr., Keith Whitfield
Daisetta . . . . Kellie Taylor
Dalhart (†). . . . . Clinton Hale
    City Mgr., James Stroud
Dallas (†). . . . . Eric Johnson
    City Mgr., T.C. Broadnax
Dalworthington Gardens. . . Laurie Bianco
    City Admin., Lola Hazel,
Danbury . . . . Melinda Strong
Darrouzett . . . . .Jerry Reynolds
    City Mgr., Coleen Bradley
Dawson . . . . .Stephen Sanders
Dayton (†) . . . . Caroline Wadzeck
    City Mgr., Theo Melancon
Dayton Lakes . . . . Justin McCormick
Dean . . . . Steve L. Sicking
Decatur (†) . . . . .Mike McQuiston
    City Mgr., Brett Shannon
DeCordova . . . . .Dave Hanson
Deer Park (†) . . . . Jerry Mouton, Jr.
    City Mgr., James Stokes
De Kalb . . . . Lowell Walker
De Leon (†) . . . . Jan Grisham
    City Admin., David Denman
Dell City . . . . .Pamela Dean
Del Rio (†) . . . . . . Bruno (Ralphy) Lozano
    City Mgr., Matt Wojnowski
Denison (†) . . . . Janet Gott
    City Mgr., Greg Smith
Dennis . . . . .James Synowsky
Denton (†) . . . . .Gerard Hudspeth
    City Mgr., Sara Hensley, Interim
Denver City (†) . . . . Tommy Hicks
    City Mgr., Stan David
Deport . . . . Patrick Watson
DeSoto (†) . . . . .Rachel L. Proctor
    City Mgr., Brandon Wright
Detroit . . . . Kenneth Snodgrass
Devers . . . . Steven Horelica
Devine . . . . Cory Thompson
    City Admin., John Vidaurri
Diboll (†). . . . . Trey Wilkerson
    City Mgr., Gerry Boren
Dickens . . . . David Warren
    City Admin., Lillian Atkinson
Dickinson (†). . . . . Sean Skipworth
    City Mgr., Theo Melancon
Dilley . . . . Gilbert Villanueva Eguia
    City Admin., Juan F. Estrada

Dimmitt (†) . . . . Roger Malone
City Mgr., Daniel Jackson
Dish . . . . William Sciscoe
Dodd City . . . . Jackie Lackey
Dodson . . . . .Steve Kane
Domino . . . . Moria White
Donna (†) . . . . .Rick Morales
City Mgr., Carlos Yerena
Dorchester . . . . David Smith
Double Horn . . . . .Cathy Sereno
Double Oak . . . . Von Beougher
Douglassville . . . . DeWitt McCall
Draper . . . . Jamie Sue Harris
Dripping Springs . . . . Bill Foulds, Jr.
City Admin., Michelle Fischer
Driscoll . . . . Mark Gonzalez
Dublin . . . . .David Leatherwood
City Mgr., Bobby Mendez
Dumas (†) . . . . .Bob Brinkmann
City Mgr., Arbie Taylor
Duncanville (†) . . . . Barry L. Gordon
City Mgr., Aretha R. Ferrell-Benavides

E

Eagle Lake . . . . .Mary Parr
City Mgr., Melinda A. Landin
Eagle Pass (†) . . . . .Rolando Salinas, Jr.
City Mgr., George Antuna
Early . . . . .Robert G. Mangrum
City Admin., Tony Aaron
Earth . . . . Sawnya Bullock
East Bernard . . . . Marvin R. Holub
Eastland (†) . . . . .Larry Vernon
City Mgr., JJ Oznick
East Mountain . . . . Marc Covington
Easton . . . . Walter Ward
East Tawakoni . . . . Harold Chandler
Ector . . . . Jerry M. Newell
Edcouch . . . . Virginio Gonzalez, Jr.
City Mgr., Victor Hugo de la Cruz
Eden . . . . .Agapito Torres
City Admin., Laura Beeson

Edgecliff Village . .Dennis (Mickey) Rigney
City Admin., Veronica Gamboa
Edgewood . . . . Steve Steadham
Edinburg (†) . . . . Richard Molina
City Mgr., Ron Garza
Edmonson . . . . Sammy Shannon
Edna (†) . . . . Lance Smiga
City Mgr., Gary Broz
Edom . . . . Barbara Crow
El Campo (†) . . . . .Chris Barbee
City Mgr., Courtney Sladek
El Cenizo . . . . .Elsa Degollado
City Admin., Jaime Montes
Eldorado . . . . George Arispe
Electra (†) . . . . .Lynda Lynn
City Admin., Steve Bowlin
Elgin (†) . . . . .Ron Ramirez
City Mgr., Thomas Mattis
Elkhart . . . . .Jennifer McCoy
El Lago . . . . .Shawn Findley
Ellinger . . . . Matt Mikulenka
Elmendorf. . . . . Michael J. Gonzales
City Admin., Cody D. Dailey
El Paso (†) . . . . Oscar Leeser
City Mgr., Tommy Gonzalez
Elsa (†) . . . . .Alonzo Perez
City Mgr., JJ Ybarra
Emhouse . . . . .Jimmy Barkley
Emory . . . . .Earl Hill, III
City Admin., Mike Dunn
Enchanted Oaks . . . . Natalie Onate
Encinal . . . . Sylvano Sanchez
City Mgr., Velma Davila
Ennis (†) . . . . Angeline Juenemann
City Mgr., Marty Nelson
Escobares . . . . Lorena Cantu
Estelline . . . . .Jeff Jones
Euless (†) . . . . .Linda Martin
City Mgr., Loretta Getchell
Eureka . . . . .Tammy Cantrell
Eustace . . . . .Dustin Shelton
Evant . . . . Roger T. Kircus
Everman (†) . . . . Ray Richardson
City Mgr., Craig Spencer

F

Fairchilds . . . . .Lance Bertolino
Fairfield . . . . Kenneth Hughes
City Admin., Nate Smith
Fair Oaks Ranch (†) . . . . . . .Greg Maxton
City Mgr., Tobin Maples
Fairview (†) . . . . .Henry Lessner
Town Mgr., Julie Couch
Falfurrias . . . . Justo Ramirez
City Admin., Andy Garcia
Falls City . . . . .Brent Houdmann
Farmers Branch (†) . . . . Robert C. Dye
City Mgr., Charles S. Cox
Farmersville . . . . Bryon Wiebold
City Mgr., Benjamin L. White
Farwell . . . . Joe Stanton
Fate (†) . . . . David Billings
City Mgr., Michael Kovacs
Fayetteville . . . . Mike Stroup
Ferris . . . . Fred Pontley
City Admin., Gloria Perkins
Flatonia. . . . . Bryan Milson
City Mgr., Sarah Novo
Florence . . . . Mary Condon
Floresville (†)
. . . . .Cecelia (Cissy) Gonzalez-Dippel
City Mgr., Andy Joslin
Flower Mound (†) . . . . .Derek France
Town Mgr., Debra Wallace, Interim
Floydada . . . . .Bobby Gilliland
City Mgr., Darrell Gooch
Follett . . . . Lynn Blau
City Mgr., Robert Williamson
Forest Hill (†) . . . . .Gerald Joubert
City Mgr., Sheyi I. Ipaye
Forney (†) . . . . .Amanda Lewis
City Mgr., Charles Daniels, Interim
Forsan. . . . . Steve Park
Fort Stockton . . . . Joe Chris Alexander
City Mgr., Frank Rodriguez, III
Fort Worth (†) . . . . .Mattie Parker
City Mgr., David Cooke
Franklin . . . . .Molly Hedrick

Bottle Plant Cafe in Glen Rose. Photo by Nicholas Henderson, CC by 2.0/Flickr

Frankston . . . . .Tommy Carr
Fredericksburg (†). . . . . . . Charlie Kiehne
   City Mgr., Kent Myers
Freeport (†). . . . . .Brooks Bass
   City Mgr., Tim Kelty
Freer . . . . Arnold Cantu
   City Mgr., Ana A. Garcia
Friendswood (†) . . . . .Mike Foreman
   City Mgr., Morad Kabiri
Friona . . . . Ricky White
   City Mgr., Leander (Lee) Davila
Frisco (†). . . . . Jeff Cheney
   City Mgr., George Purefoy
Fritch . . . . .Richard Hein
   City Mgr., Drew Brassfield
Frost . . . . .Scott Dowdle
Fruitvale . . . . Vicki Ferguson
Fulshear (†). . . . . .Aaron Groff
   City Mgr., Jack Harper
Fulton . . . . Kelli Cole

G

Gainesville (†). . . . . .Tommy Moore
   City Mgr., Barry Sullivan
Galena Park (†) . . . . Esmeralda Moya
Gallatin . . . . .Juanita Cotton
Galveston (†) . . . . Craig Brown
   City Mgr., Brian Maxwell
Ganado . . . . Clinton Tegeler
Garden Ridge . . . . .Robb Erickson
   City Admin., Nancy Cain
Garland (†) . . . . Scott LeMay
   City Mgr., Bryan Bradford
Garrett . . . . Matt Newsom
Garrison . . . . .Russell Wright
Gary . . . . .Mark Thornton
Gatesville (†). . . . . .Gary Chumley
   City Mgr., William H. (Bill) Parry, III
Georgetown (†) . . . . .Josh Schroeder
   City Mgr., David Morgan
George West (†) . . . . .Andrew Garza
   City Mgr., Shirley Holm, Interim
Gholson . . . . Phillip Bagley
Giddings (†) . . . . John Dowell
   City Mgr., Ricky Jorgensen
Gilmer (†) . . . . Tim Marshall
   City Mgr., Greg Hutson
Gladewater (†). . . . . . . .John (JD) Shipp
   City Mgr., Ricky Tow
Glenn Heights (†) . . . . . . Harry A. Garrett
   City Mgr., David A. Hall
Glen Rose . . . . .Julia Douglas
   City Admin., Michael Leamons
Godley . . . . .Jan Whitegead
   City Mgr., David J. Wallis
Goldsmith . . . . .Richard Bradley
   City Mgr., Bennie Cope
Goldthwaite . . . . .Mike McMahan
   City Mgr., Robert E. Lindsey, III
Goliad . . . . Brenda Moses
Golinda . . . . Joyce Farar
Gonzales (†) . . . . .Connie L. Kacir
   City Mgr., Tim Patek
Goodlow . . . . .Nantambu Kambon
Goodrich . . . . Kelly Nelson
Gordon . . . . Jack Coleman
Goree . . . . .Randy Hibdon
Gorman (†) . . . . .David Perry
Graford . . . . Carl S. Walston
Graham (†) . . . . Neal Blanton
   City Mgr., Brandon Anderson
Granbury (†) . . . . .Nin Hulett
   City Mgr., Chris Coffman

Grandfalls . . . . Jeff Corean
   City Admin., Donna Edens
Grand Prairie (†). . . . . Ron Jensen
   City Mgr., Tom Hart
Grand Saline . . . . .Jeremy Gunnels
   City Admin., Tully Davidson
Grandview . . . . .Zachary Stewart
   City Mgr., David D. Henley
Granger . . . . .Trevor Cheatheam
   City Admin., Christy Cavness Bradshaw
Granite Shoals (†) . . . . Will Skinner
   City Mgr., Jeffery D. Looney
Granjeno . . . . .Yvette Cabrera
Grapeland . . . . .Mitchell Woody
Grapevine (†) . . . . .William D. Tate
   City Mgr., Bruno Rumbelow
Grays Prairie . . . . Lorenzo Garza, Jr.
Greenville (†) . . . . .Jerry Ransom
   City Mgr., Summer Spurlock
Gregory . . . . .Jeronimo B. Garcia
Grey Forest . . . . .Mitch Thornton
Groesbeck . . . . .Ray O'Docharty
   City Admin., Chris Henson
Groom . . . . .Tim Case
Groves (†) . . . . .Chris Borne
   City Mgr., D.E. Sosa
Groveton . . . . Tommy Walton
Gruver . . . . Buster Davis
   City Mgr., Johnnie Williams
Gun Barrel City (†) . . . . .David Skains
   City Mgr., Jeff Arnswald
Gunter . . . . Mark Millar
   City Mgr., Rick Chaffin
Gustine . . . . Ken Huey

H

Hackberry . . . . .Ronald Austin
   City Admin., Brenda Lewallen
Hale Center . . . . W.H. Johnson
   City Mgr., Mike Cypert
Hallettsville . . . . .Alice Jo Summers
   City Admin., Grace Ward
Hallsburg . . . . .Mike Glockzin
Hallsville . . . . Jesse Casey
Haltom City (†) . . . . .An Truong
   City Mgr., Rex L. Phelps
Hamilton . . . . Jim McInnis
   City Admin., Ryan Polster
Hamlin . . . . Curtis Collins
   City Admin., Bobby Evans
Happy . . . . Sara Tirey
Hardin . . . . .Harry Johnson
Harker Heights (†). . . . . . .Spencer H. Smith
   City Mgr., David R. Mitchell
Harlingen (†). . . . . Chris Boswell
   City Mgr., Dan Serna
Hart . . . . Eliazar Castillo
   City Admin., Adrian Rosas
Haskell . . . . .Alberto Alvarez, Jr.
   City Admin., June Ellis
Haslet . . . . Gary Hulsey
   City Admin., James Quin
Hawk Cove . . . . . . .Delores (Dotty) Spence
   City Admin., Rhonda McKeehan
Hawkins . . . . Stephen Lucas
Hawley . . . . Billy Richardson
Hays . . . . Larry Odom
Hearne (†). . . . . Ruben Gomez
   City Mgr., John Naron
Heath (†) . . . . Kelson Elam
   City Mgr., Aretha L. Adams
Hebron . . . . Kelly Clem
Hedley . . . . .Carrie Butler

Hedwig Village . . . . Tom Jinks
   City Admin., Kelly Johnson
Helotes . . . . .Rich Whitehead
   City Admin., Marian Mendoza
Hemphill . . . . .Robert Hamilton
   City Mgr., Thad Smith
Hempstead (†) . . . . Dave Shelburne
Henderson (†) . . . . .John (Buzz) Fullen
   City Mgr., Jay Abercrombie
Henrietta . . . . .Roy L. Boswell
   City Admin., Kelley Bloodworth
Hereford (†) . . . . Tom Simons
   City Mgr., Steve Bartels
Hewitt (†) . . . . .Steve Fortenberry
   City Mgr., Bo Thomas
Hickory Creek . . . . Lynn Clark
   Town Admin., John Smith
Hico . . . . .Eddie Needham
   City Admin., Adam Niolet
Hidalgo (†) . . . . Sergio Coronado
   City Mgr., Julian Gonzalez
Hideaway . . . . Ray Hutcheson
Higgins . . . . Brandon L. Range
   City Mgr., Kim Eggleston
Highland Haven . . . . .Olan Kelley
Highland Park (†) . . . . Margo Goodwin
   Town Admin., Bill Lindley
Highland Village (†) . . . .Charlotte Wilcox
   City Mgr., Paul Stevens
Hill Country Village Gabriel Durand-Hollis
   City Admin., Frank Morales
Hillcrest Village . . . . Tom Wilson
Hillsboro (†) . . . . Andrew L. Smith
   City Mgr., Megan Henderson
Hilshire Village . . . . .Russell Herron
   City Admin., Susan Blevins
Hitchcock (†). . . . . .Chris Armacost
   City Admin., Marie Gelles
Holiday Lakes . . . . Norman Schroeder
Holland . . . . .Johnny Kallus, Acting
Holliday . . . . Allen Moore
Hollywood Park . . . . . . Oscar Villareal, Jr.
Hondo (†) . . . . .James W. Danner
   City Mgr., Scott L. Albert
Honey Grove . . . . Claude Caffee
Hooks . . . . Alfred (Al) Turnage
Horizon City (†) . . . . Ruben Mendoza
Horseshoe Bay (†) . . . . Cynthia Clinesmith
   City Mgr., Stan R. Farmer
Houston (†) . . . . .Sylvester Turner
Howardwick . . . . Tony Clemishire
Howe . . . . .Bill French
   City Admin., Joe Shephard
Hubbard . . . . .Mary Alderman
   City Mgr., Jason Patrick
Hudson . . . . .Robert Smith
   City Admin., James Freeman
Hudson Oaks . . . . Marc Povero
   City Admin., Sterling Naron
Hughes Springs . . . . .James Samples
   City Mgr., Stephen Barnes
Humble (†) . . . . Norman Funderburk
   City Mgr., Jason Stuebe
Hunters Creek Village . . . . . . .Jim Pappas
   City Admin., Tom Fullen,
Huntington . . . . Frank Harris
   City Admin., Bill Stewart
Huntsville (†) . . . . .Andy Brauninger
   City Mgr., Aron Kulhavy
Hurst (†) . . . . Henry Wilson
   City Mgr., Clay Caruthers
Hutchins . . . . .Mario Vasquez
   City Admin., Trudy Lewis

Hutto (†) . . . . Mike Snyder
City Mgr., Warren Hutmacher
Huxley . . . . Larry Vaughn

I

Idalou . . . . Russ Perkins
City Admin., Suzette Williams
Impact . . . . Trevor Dickson
Indian Lake . . . . James Chambers
Industry . . . . Mable Meyers
Ingleside (†) . . . . Ronnie Parker
City Mgr., Linnette Barker
Ingleside on the Bay . . . . . Jo Ann Ehmann
Ingram . . . . Kathy Rider
Iola . . . . Christina Stover
Iowa Colony . . . . . Michael Byrum-Bratsen
City Mgr., Robert Hemminger
Iowa Park (†) . . . . Ray Schultz
City Mgr., Jerry Flemming
Iraan . . . . Darren Brown
Iredell . . . . Joel Wellborn
Irving (†) . . . . Rick Stopfer
City Mgr., Chris Hillman
Italy . . . . Bryant Cockran
City Admin., Shawn Holden
Itasca . . . . James Bouldin
City Admin., CinDee Garrett
Ivanhoe . . . . Cathy Bennett

J

Jacinto City (†) . . . . Ana Diaz
City Mgr., Lon Squyres
Jacksboro . . . . Joe Mitchell
City Mgr., Michael Smith
Jacksonville (†) . . . . Randy Gorham
City Mgr., Greg Smith
Jamaica Beach . . . . Clay Morris
City Admin., Brad Heiman, Interim
Jarrell . . . . Larry Bush
City Mgr., Vanessa Shrauner
Jasper (†) . . . . Randy Sayers
City Mgr., Denise Kelley
Jayton . . . . George Chisum
Jefferson . . . . Rob Baker
Jersey Village (†) . . . . Bobby Warren
City Mgr., Austin Bleess
Jewett . . . . John Sitton
Joaquin . . . . Frank Cooper
Johnson City . . . . Rhonda Stell
Jolly . . . . D. LeAnn Skinner
Jones Creek . . . . Terry Jeffers
Jonestown . . . . Paul Johnson
City Admin., Steve Jones
Josephine . . . . Joe Holt
Joshua (†) . . . . Joe Hollarn
City Mgr., Mike Peacock
Jourdanton . . . . Robert A. Williams
City Mgr., Lamar Schulz
Junction . . . . Russell Hammonds
Justin . . . . Liz Woodall
City Mgr., Chuck Ewings

K

Karnes City . . . . Leroy T. Skloss
City Mgr., Ken Roberts
Katy (†) . . . . Bill Hastings
City Admin., Byron J. Hebert
Kaufman (†) . . . . Jeff Jordan
City Mgr., Michael T. Slye
Keene (†) . . . . Gary Heinrich
City Mgr., Bernie Parker

Keller (†) . . . . Armin Mizani
City Mgr., Mark Hafner
Kemah . . . . Carl Joiner
City Admin., Walter Gant, III
Kemp . . . . Christi Neal
City Admin., Regina Kiser
Kempner . . . . John (JW) Wilkerson
Kendleton . . . . Darryl K. Humphrey, Sr.
Kenedy . . . . Joe Baker
City Mgr., William Linn
Kenefick . . . . Martin (Marty) Wells
Kennard . . . . Jesse Stephens
City Admin., Michael Deckard
Kennedale (†) . . . . Brian Johnson
City Mgr., George Campbell
Kerens . . . . Jeffrey Saunders
Kermit (†) . . . . Jerry L. Phillips
City Mgr., Frankie Davis
Kerrville (†) . . . . Bill Blackburn
City Mgr., E.A. Hoppe
Kilgore (†) . . . . Ronnie E. Spradlin, III
City Mgr., Josh Selleck
Killeen (†) . . . . Jose L. Segarra
City Mgr., Kent Cagle
Kingsbury . . . . Shirley Nolen
Kingsville (†) . . . . Sam R. Fugate
City Mgr., Mark McLaughlin
Kirby (†) . . . . . Kimberly McGehee Aldrich
City Mgr., Monique Vernon
Kirbyville . . . . Frank George
Kirvin . . . . J.W. Walthall
Knollwood . . . . Rosalie Dunn
Knox City . . . . Kent DeVille
City Admin., Sam Watson
Kosse . . . . Brooks Valls
Kountze . . . . Fred Williams
City Admin., Roderick Hutto
Kress . . . . Amparo Becerra
Krugerville . . . . Jeff Parrent
City Admin., Jeff Parrent
Krum . . . . Ronald G. Harris, Jr.
Kurten . . . . Chris Court
Kyle (†) . . . . Travis Mitchell
City Mgr., Scott Sellers

L

La Coste . . . . Andy Keller
City Admin., George Salzman
Lacy Lakeview (†) . . . . Sharon Clark
City Mgr., Keith Bond
Ladonia . . . . Jan Cooper
La Feria (†) . . . . Olga H. Maldonado
City Mgr., Jaime S. Sandoval
Lago Vista (†) . . . . Ed Tidwell
City Mgr., Tracie Hlavinka
La Grange (†) . . . . Jan Dockery
City Mgr., Shawn Raborn
La Grulla . . . . Pedro A. Flores
City Mgr., Marlen Garza
Laguna Vista (†) . . . . Nadine Smith
City Mgr., Ed Meza
La Joya (†) . . . . Isidro Casanova
City Admin., Jacqueline Bazan
Lake Bridgeport . . . . Sherry Pewitt
Lake City . . . . Dennis Veit
Lake Dallas (†) . . . . Andi Nolan
City Mgr., Mike Wilson, Interim
Lake Jackson (†) . . . . . Gerald Roznovsky
City Mgr., Modesto Mundo
Lakeport . . . . Johnny Sammons
Lakeside (San Patricio Co.) . . . . Jeff Mason
Lakeside (Tarrant Co.) . . . . Pat Jacob
Town Admin. Norman Craven,

Lakeside City . . . . Cory Glassburn
City Admin., Eric Stevens
Lake Tanglewood . . . . George Moore
Lakeview . . . . Kelly Clark
Lakeway (†) . . . . Thomas Kilgore
City Mgr., Julie Oakley
Lakewood Village . . . . . . Mark Vargus
Town Admin., Linda Asbell
Lake Worth (†) . . . . Walter Bowen
City Mgr., Stacey Almond
Lamesa (†) . . . . Josh Stevens
City Mgr., Wayne Chapman, Interim
Lampasas (†) . . . . TJ Monroe
City Mgr., Finley Degraffenried
Lancaster (†) . . . . Clyde C. Hairston
City Mgr., Opal Mauldin-Jones
La Porte (†) . . . . Louis R. Rigby
City Mgr., Corby Alexander
Laredo (†) . . . . Pete Saenz
City Mgr., Robert A. Eads
Latexo . . . . Robert Hernandez
La Vernia . . . . Robert W. Gregory
La Villa . . . . Alma Moron
Lavon . . . . Vicki Sanson
City Admin., Kim Dobbs
La Ward . . . . Richard Koch
Lawn . . . . Veronica Burleson
League City (†) . . . . Pat Hallisey
City Mgr., John Baumgartner
Leakey . . . . Hazel Pendley
Leander (†) . . . . Christine Sederquist
City Mgr., Rick Beverlin
Leary . . . . B.J. Martin
City Admin., Randy Mansfield
Lefors . . . . Michael Ray
Leona . . . . Ernest (Bubba) Oden
Leonard . . . . Michael Pye
City Admin., Terry McCalpin
Leon Valley (†) . . . . Chris Riley
City Mgr., Gilbert Perales
Leroy . . . . David Williams
Levelland (†) . . . . Barbra Pinner
City Mgr., Erik Rejino
Lewisville (†) . . . . Rudy Durham
City Mgr., Donna Barron
Lexington . . . . Allen Retzlaff
Liberty (†) . . . . Carl Pickett
City Mgr., Tom Warner
Liberty Hill . . . . Liz Branigan
City Admin., Lacie Hale
Lindale (†) . . . . Jeff Daugherty
City Mgr., Carolyn Caldwell
Linden . . . . Lynn Reynolds
City Admin., Lee Elliott
Lindsay . . . . Scott Neu
Lipan . . . . Mike Stowe
Little Elm (†) . . . . Curtis Cornelious
City Mgr., Matt Mueller
Littlefield (†) . . . . Eric Turpen
City Mgr., Mitch Grant
Little River-Academy . . . . . Drew Lanham
Live Oak (†) . . . . Mary M. Dennis
City Mgr., Scott Wayman
Liverpool . . . . Bill Strickland
Livingston (†) . . . . Judy B. Cochran
City Mgr., Bill Wiggins
Llano . . . . Gail Lang
City Mgr., Scott Edmonson
Lockhart (†) . . . . Lew White
City Mgr., Steve Lewis
Lockney . . . . Michael DeLeon
City Mgr., G.A. (Buster) Poling, Jr.
Log Cabin . . . . Jennifer Williams
Lometa . . . . Stephen Brister Hicks

Lone Oak . . . . Doug Williams
Lone Star . . . . Randy Hodges
Longview (†) . . . . Andy Mack
　City Mgr., Keith Bonds
Loraine . . . . Mark Overton
Lorena . . . . Tommy Ross
　City Mgr., Joseph R. Pace
Lorenzo . . . . Tim Tiner
　City Admin., Michael Chambers
Los Fresnos (†) . . . . Alejandro Flores
　City Mgr., Mark Milum
Los Indios . . . . Jaime Gonzalez
　City Admin., Jared Hockema
Los Ybanez . . . . Mary A. Ybanez
　City Mgr., John Castillo
Lott . . . . .Sue Tacker
Lovelady . . . . William B. Shoemaker
Lowry Crossing . . . . Derek Stephens
Lubbock (†) . . . . Dan Pope
　City Mgr., W. Jarrett Atkinson
Lucas (†) . . . . .Jim Olk
　City Mgr., Joni Clarke
Lueders . . . . Benny Jarvis
Lufkin (†) . . . . Mark Hicks
　City Mgr., Bruce Green
Luling (†) . . . . .Mike Hendricks
　City Mgr., Mark Mayo
Lumberton (†) . . . . .Don Surratt
　City Mgr., Steve Clark
Lyford . . . . .Rick Salinas
Lytle . . . . Ruben Gonzalez
　City Admin., Josie Campa

M

Mabank . . . . .Jeff Norman
　City Mgr., Bryant Morris
Madisonville . . . . .Bill Parten
　City Mgr., Camilla Viator
Magnolia . . . . Todd Kana
　City Admin., Don Doering
Malakoff . . . . Delois Pagitt
　City Admin., Ann Barker
Malone . . . . James Lucko
Manor (†) . . . . Larry Wallace, Jr.
　City Mgr., Thomas M. Bolt
Mansfield (†) . . . . .Michael Evans
　City Mgr., Joe Smolinski
Manvel (†) . . . . Debra Marz Davison
　City Mgr., Kyle J. Jung
Marble Falls (†) . . . . . . Richard Westerman
　City Mgr., Mike Hodge
Marfa . . . . .Manny Baeza
　City Admin., Amanda Roane
Marietta . . . .(vacant)
　City Mgr., Charles Elliott
Marion . . . . Victor Contreras
Marlin (†) . . . . Carolyn Lofton
　City Mgr., Cedric Davis, Sr.
Marquez . . . . Stynette Clary
　City Mgr., Lauren Powers
Marshall (†) . . . . .Amy Ware
　City Mgr., Mark Rohr
Mart . . . . .Len Williams
Martindale . . . . .Katherine Glaze
　City Admin., Jared Anable
Mason . . . . Whitney Leifeste
　City Admin., John Palacio
Matador . . . . Pat Smith
Mathis (†) . . . . Ciri Villarreal
　City Mgr., Michael Barrera
Maud . . . . Jimmy Clary
Maypearl . . . . .Joy Landry

McAllen (†) . . . . .Javier Villalobos
　City Mgr., Roel Roy Rodriguez
McCamey . . . . .Patty Jones
McGregor (†) . . . . James S. Hering
　City Mgr., Kevin Evans
McKinney (†) . . . . George Fuller
　City Mgr., Paul Grimes
McLean . . . . Tanner Hess
McLendon-Chisholm . . . . Keith Short
　City Admin., Lisa Palomba
Meadow . . . . .Natalie Howard
　City Admin., Terri McClanahan
Meadowlakes . . . . .Mark Bentley
　City Mgr., Johnnie Thompson
Meadows Place . . . . . Charles D. Jessup, IV
Megargel . . . . Melissa Latham
Melissa (†) . . . . Reed Greer
　City Mgr., Jason Little
Melvin . . . . Josephine Castillo
Memphis . . . . .Joe Davis
Menard . . . . .Barbara Hooten
　City Admin., Don Kerns
Mercedes (†) . . . . . . .Oscar D, Montoya, Sr.
　City Mgr., Alberto Perez
Meridian . . . . .Johnnie Hauerland
　City Admin., Marie Garland
Merkel . . . . .Mary Schrampfer
　City Mgr., Steve Campbell
Mertens . . . . .Don O. Dillard
Mertzon . . . . Bill Taylor
Mesquite (†) . . . . .Bruce Archer
　City Mgr., Cliff Keheley
Mexia (†) . . . . Geary Smith
　City Mgr., Eric Garretty
Miami . . . . .Chad Breeding
Midland (†) . . . . .Patrick Payton
　City Mgr., Robert Patrick
Midlothian (†) . . . . Richard Reno
　City Mgr., Chris Dick
Midway . . . . Brenda Ford
Milano . . . . Karl Westbrook
Mildred . . . . Bryan Roach
Miles . . . . Travis McMillan
Milford . . . . .Bruce Perryman
Miller's Cove . . . . Willie B. Garrett
Millsap . . . . .Jamie French
　City Mgr., Mark Barnes
Mineola . . . . Jayne Lankford
　City Mgr., Mercy L. Rushing
Mineral Wells (†) . . . . .Regan Johnson
　City Mgr., Randy Criswell
Mingus . . . . Milo Moffit
Mission (†) . . . . .Armando O'Caña
　City Mgr., Randy Perez
Missouri City (†) . . . . . . .Robin J. Elackatt
　City Mgr., Bill Atkinson, Interim
Mobeetie . . . . .Bobbie Walker
Mobile City . . . . .Kenny Phillips
Monahans (†) . . . . .Adam Steen
　City Mgr., Rex M. Thee
Mont Belvieu (†) . . . . Nick Dixon
　City Mgr., Nathan Watkins
Montgomery . . . . Sara Countryman
　City Admin., Richard Tramm
Moody . . . . Charleen Dowell
　City Admin., William A. Sterling
Moore Station . . . . Charles Anderson
Moran . . . . Steven W. Taggart
Morgan . . . . Jonathan W. Croom, II
Morgan's Point . . . . Michel J. Bechtel
　City Admin., Brian Schneider
Morgan's Point Resort . . . . . Dennis Green
　City Mgr., Dalton Rice,

Morton . . . . Kim Silhan
　City Mgr., Veronica Olguin
Moulton . . . . Mark Zimmerman
　City Admin., LuAnn D. Rogers
Mountain City . . . . . . .Ralph McClendon
　City Admin., Tiffany Cornutt
Mount Calm . . . . Jimmy Tucker
Mount Enterprise . . . . .Brandon Jones
Mount Pleasant (†) . . . . . . Tracy Craig, Sr.
　City Mgr., Ed Thatcher
Mount Vernon . . . . Brad Hyman
　City Admin., Tina Rose
Muenster . . . . .Tim Felderhoff
　City Admin., Adam Deweber
Muleshoe (†) . . . . .Colt Ellis
　City Mgr., Ramon Sanchez
Mullin . . . . Bo Mackey
Munday . . . . Robert Bowen
　City Admin., Ricky Ake
Murchison . . . . John Placyk
Murphy (†) . . . . .Scott Bradley
　City Mgr., Mike Castro
Mustang Ridge . . . . Alisandro Flores

N

Nacogdoches (†) . . . . .Jimmy Mize
　City Mgr., Mario Canizares
Naples . . . . David Betts
Nash . . . . Robert Bunch
　City Admin., Doug Bowers
Nassau Bay (†) . . . . Bob Warters
　City Mgr., Jason Reynolds
Natalia (†) . . . . .Tommy Ortiz
　City Admin., Rene Hinojosa
Navarro . . . . Vickie Lynn Farmer
Navasota (†). . . William A. (Bert) Miller, III
　City Mgr., Brad Stafford
Nazareth . . . . .Marlin Durbin
　City Mgr., Lacey Farris
Nederland (†) . . . . Don Albanese
　City Mgr., Christopher Duque
Needville . . . . Sandra Dorr
Nevada . . . . Ben Ponce
Newark . . . . Mark Wondolowski
New Berlin . . . . .Walter Williams
New Boston . . . . Ronald Humphrey
　City Admin., Elizabeth Lea
New Braunfels (†) . . . . . . Rusty Brockman
　City Mgr., Robert Camareno
Newcastle . . . .(vacant)
New Chapel Hill . . . . .Riley Harris
New Deal . . . . Regina Hobson
New Fairview . . . . . . Nolan Schoonmaker
New Home . . . . Steve Lisemby
New Hope . . . . Andy Reitinger
New London . . . . .Dale McNeel
New Summerfield . . . . .Jane Barrow
Newton . . . . Mark Bean
　City Admin., Donald H. Meek
New Waverly . . . . .Nathaniel James
Neylandville . . . . Kathy Wilson
Niederwald . . . . Reynell Smith
Nixon . . . . Dorothy Riojas
Nocona . . . . .Robert Fenoglio
　City Mgr., Lynn Henley
Nolanville (†) . . . . .Andy Williams
　City Mgr., Kara Escajeda
Nome . . . . Kerry Abney
Noonday . . . . Mike Turman
Nordheim . . . . Katherine Payne
Normangee . . . . .Troy Noey
North Cleveland . . . . .Bob Bartlett

The Luther Hotel in Palacios. Photo by Larry D. Moore, CC by 4.0/Wikimedia Commons

Northlake . . . . David Rettig
  Town Mgr., Drew Corn
North Richland Hills (†) . . . Oscar Trevino
  City Mgr., Mark Hindman
Novice . . . . Bobby Green

O

Oak Grove . . . . Jeffrey Davis
Oak Leaf . . . . .Tom Leverentz
Oak Point . . . . Dena Meek
  City Mgr., Stephen Ashley
Oak Ridge (Cooke Co.) . . . . Chad Ramsey
Oak Ridge (Kaufman Co.) . . . . . . Al Rudin
Oak Ridge North . . . . .Paul Bond
  City Mgr., Heather Neeley
Oak Valley . . . . .Jarrett Greer
Oakwood . . . . Jacquelyn Morrow
O'Brien . . . . Chris Casillas
Odem . . . . .Virginia Garza
Odessa (†) . . . . .Javier Joven
  City Mgr., Michael Marrero
O'Donnell . . . . Kim Parker
Oglesby . . . . .Bruce Pomerenke
Old River-Winfree . . . . .Joe Landry
Olmos Park . . . . Ronald Hornberger
  City Mgr., Celia DeLeon
Olney (†) . . . . Rue Rogers
  City Admin., Neal Welch
Olton . . . . Mark McFadden
  City Admin., Keeley Adams
Omaha . . . . Ernest Paul Pewitt
Onalaska . . . . .B. Milton (Chip) Choate
  City Admin., Angela Stutts
Opdyke West . . . . Wayne Riggins
Orange (†) . . . . Larry Spears, Jr.
  City Mgr., Mike Kunst
Orange Grove . . . . Carl Srp
  City Admin., Todd Wright
Orchard . . . . Rod Pavlock
Ore City . . . . Angie Edwards
Overton . . . . .C.R. Evans
  City Admin., Clyde Carter, Interim
Ovilla . . . . .Richard Dormier
  City Mgr., Pam Woodall
Oyster Creek . . . . .Justin Mills
  City Admin., Toby Guenter

P

Paducah . . . . .Rodger Brannen
Paint Rock . . . . .Ricky Donaldson
Palacios (†) . . . . .Linh Chau
  City Mgr., David Kocurek
Palestine (†) . . . . Dana Goolsby
  City Mgr., Teresa Herrera
Palisades . . . . .Jerry Lane
Palm Valley . . . . George Rivera
Palmer . . . . Kenneth Bateman
  City Admin., Alicia Baran
Palmhurst . . . . Ramiro J. Rodriguez, Jr.
  City Mgr., Lori A. Lopez
Palmview (†) . . . . Ricardo Villareal
  City Mgr., Michael Leo
Pampa (†) . . . . .Lance DeFever
  City Mgr., Shane Stokes
Panhandle . . . . .Doyle Robinson
  City Mgr., Terry Coffee
Panorama Village . . . . .Lynn Scott
Pantego . . . . .Doug Davis
  City Mgr., Joe Ashton
Paradise . . . . Roy Steel
Paris (†) . . . . Paula Portugal
  City Mgr., Grayson Path
Parker . . . . Lee Pettle
  City Admin., Luke Olson
Pasadena (†) . . . . Jeff A. Wagner
Pattison . . . . .Joe Garcia
Patton Village . . . . Scott Anderson
Payne Springs . . . .(vacant)
Pearland (†) . . . . Kevin Cole
  City Mgr., Clay Pearson
Pearsall (†) . . . . Mary Moore
  City Mgr., Federico Reyes
Peaster . . . . Don Smelley
Pecan Gap . . . . .Cole Hoskison
Pecan Hill . . . . .Don Schmerse
  City Admin., Shelley Martinez
Pecos (†) . . . . David Flores
  City Mgr., Heather Ramirez, Interim
Pelican Bay . . . . Glen Oberg
Penelope . . . . .Allen Neal
Peñitas (†) . . . . .Rodrigo (Rigo) Lopez
  City Mgr., Omar Romero
Perryton . . . . Kerry Symons
  City Mgr., David Landis

Petersburg . . . . .Misty Wilson
  City Mgr., Mario Martinez
Petrolia . . . . Buddy Alexander
Petronila . . . . Todd Wright
Pflugerville (†) . . . . .Victor Gonzales
  City Mgr., Sereniah Breland
Pharr (†) . . . . Ambrosio (Amos) Hernandez
  City Mgr., Edward M. Wylie, Interim
Pilot Point (†) . . . . . . Shea Dane-Patterson
  City Mgr., Britt M. Lusk
Pine Forest . . . . .Cathy Nagel
Pinehurst . . . . T.W. Permenter
  City Admin., Jerry Hood
Pine Island . . . . Steve Nagy
Pineland . . . . Joe Lane
Piney Point Village . . . . Mark Kobelan
  City Admin., Paul Davis, Interim
Pittsburg (†) . . . . .David Abernathy
  City Mgr., Clint Hardeman
Plains . . . . Shane McKinzie
  City Admin., Steve Vasquez
Plainview (†) . . . . Charles Starnes
  City Mgr., Jeffrey Snyder
Plano (†) . . . . .John B. Muns
  City Mgr., Mark D. Israelson
Plantersville . . . . Karen Hale
Pleak Village . . . . Larry Bittner
Pleasanton (†) . . . . Clinton J. Powell
  City Mgr., Johnny Huizar
Pleasant Valley . . . . Jerry Gholson
Plum Grove . . . . .Barbara Norris
Poetry . . . . Tara Senkevech
Point . . . . Johnny Northcutt
Point Blank . . . . .Mark T. Wood
  City Mgr., Kelly Hoot
Point Comfort . . . . John Warren
  City Admin., Robby Silva
Point Venture . . . . .Eric Love
Ponder . . . . Matthew Poole
Port Aransas (†) . . . . Charles R. Bujan
  City Mgr., David Parsons
Port Arthur (†) . . . . Thurman (Bill) Bartie
  City Mgr., Ron Burton
Port Isabel (†) . . . . . Juan Jose (JJ) Zamora
  City Mgr., Jared Hockema
Portland (†) . . . . Cathy Skurow
  City Mgr., Randy L. Wright
Port Lavaca (†) . . . . .Jack Whitlow
  City Mgr., Joanna P. (Jody) Weaver

Port Neches (†) . . . . .Glenn Johnson
City Mgr., André Wimer
Post . . . . .Marvin Self
City Mgr., J. Rhett Parker
Post Oak Bend . . . . Alison Novak
City Admin., Barbara A. Bedrick
Poteet . . . . Denise Sanchez
City Admin., Eric A. Jiminez
Poth . . . . .Chrystal Eckel
Pottsboro . . . . Frank Budra
City Mgr., Kevin Farley
Powell . . . . Clay Jackson
Poynor . . . . Dannie Smith
Prairie View (†) . . . . .Brian E. Rowland
Premont . . . . .Priscilla Vargas
Presidio . . . . .John Ferguson
City Admin., Brad Newton
Primera . . . . .Jorge Ledesma
City Admin., Celina Gonzales
Princeton . . . . .Brianna Chacón
City Mgr., Derek Borg
Progreso . . . . Gerardo Alanis
City Admin., Alfredo Espinosa
Progreso Lakes . . . . . . O.D. (Butch) Emery
Prosper (†) . . . . Ray Smith
Town Mgr., Harlan Jefferson
Providence Village (†) . . . . . . Linda Inman
Town Mgr., Brian Roberson
Putnam . . . . Hubert Donaway
Pyote . . . . Abigail Pritchard

Q

Quanah (†) . . . . Kathy Butler
City Admin., Paula Wilson
Queen City . . . . .Harold Martin
Quinlan . . . . .Jacky Goleman
City Admin., John Adel
Quintana . . . . Shari Wright
City Admin., Tammi Cimiotta
Quitaque . . . . Janice Henson
City Mgr., Maria Merrell
Quitman . . . . Randy Dunn
City Admin., Rodney D. Kieke

R

Ralls . . . . .Don Hamilton
City Admin., Kim Perez
Rancho Viejo . . . . . . .Maribel B. Guerrero
Town Admin., Fred Blanco
Ranger (†) . . . . John Casey
City Mgr., Gerald Gunstanson
Rangerville . . . . Wayne Halbert
Rankin . . . . .Brandon Brown
Ransom Canyon . . . . Jana Trew
City Admin., Maria Elena Quintanilla
Ravenna . . . . Claude L. Lewis
Raymondville (†) . . . . . . Gilbert Gonzales
City Mgr., Eleazar Garcia, Jr.
Red Lick . . . .(vacant)
Red Oak (†) . . . . .Mark Stanfill
City Mgr., Todd Fuller
Redwater . . . . Robert Lorance
Refugio . . . . Wanda Dukes
Reklaw . . . . Bob Parrott
Reno (Lamar Co.) . . . . .Bart Jetton
Reno (Parker Co.) . . . . Sam White
City Admin., Scott Passmore
Retreat . . . . Janice Barfknecht
Rhome . . . . .Jo Ann Wilson
City Admin., Cynthia Northrop
Rice . . . . .Vickie Young
City Admin., Tonya Roberts

Richardson (†) . . . . Paul Voelker
City Mgr., Dan Johnson
Richland . . . . Kenneth Guard
Richland Hills (†) . . . . Edward Lopez
City Mgr., Candice Edmondson
Richland Springs . . . . Johnie Reeves
Richmond (†) . . . . . Rebecca (Becky) Haas
City Mgr., Terri Vela
Richwood (†) . . . . Steve Boykin
City Mgr., Eric Foerster
Riesel . . . . .Kevin Hogg
Rio Bravo (†) . . . . Daisy Lee Valdez
City Admin., Jesus Olivares
Rio Grande City (†) . . . . . . .Joel Villarreal
City Mgr., Noe Castillo
Rio Hondo . . . . . .Gustavo (Gus) Olivares
City Admin., Ben Medina
Rio Vista . . . . .Jeff Faraizl
Rising Star . . . . .Jimmy Carpenter
City Admin., Jan Clark
River Oaks (†) . . . . .Joe Ashton
City Admin., Marvin Gregory
Riverside . . . . John LeMaire
Road Runner . . . . David Ortega, Jr.
Roanoke (†) . . . . Scooter Gierisch
City Mgr., Scott Campbell
Roaring Springs . . . . .Jeff Thacker
Robert Lee . . . . Jason Moran
City Supt., Luke Sheldon
Robinson (†) . . . . Bert Echterling
City Mgr., Craig Lemin
Robstown (†) . . . . .Gilbert Gomez
Roby . . . . Eli Sepeda
City Mgr., Jack W. Brown
Rochester . . . . .Lonnetta Farrar
City Admin., Gail Nunn
Rockdale (†) . . . . John King
City Mgr., Barbara Holly
Rockport (†) . . . . Patrick R. (Pat) Rios
City Mgr., Kevin Carruth
Rocksprings . . . . LaWanda Goller
Rockwall (†) . . . . .Kevin Fowler
City Mgr., Mary Smith
Rocky Mound . . . . .Noble T. Smith
Rogers . . . . .Billy Crow
City Admin., Chris Hill
Rollingwood . . . . Mike Dyson
City Admin., Amber Lewis
Roma (†) . . . . Jaime Escobar, Jr.
City Mgr., Crisanto Salinas
Roman Forest . . . . .Chris Parr
City Admin., Liz Mullane
Ropesville . . . . .Brenda Rabel
Roscoe . . . . Frank S. (Pete) Porter
City Mgr., Cody Thompson
Rosebud . . . . .Marlene Zipperlen
City Admin., Kenny Ray Murray
Rose City . . . . Bonnie Stephenson
Rose Hill Acres . . . . David Lang
Rosenberg (†) . . . . .Kevin Raines
City Mgr., John Maresh
Ross . . . . Jim Jaska
Rosser . . . . Shannon R. Corder
Rotan . . . . Pete Garcia
City Mgr., Carla Thornton
Round Mountain . . . . Alvin Gutierrez
Round Rock (†) . . . . Craig Morgan
City Mgr., Laurie Hadley
Round Top . . . . .Mark Massey
Rowlett (†) . . . . Tammy Dana-Bashian
City Mgr., Brian Funderburk
Roxton . . . . Paul Helms
City Mgr., Janet Wheeler

Royse City (†) . . . . .Clay Ellis
City Mgr., Carl Alsabrook
Rule . . . . Delle Watkins
Runaway Bay . . . . Herman White
City Admin., Pamela Woods
Runge . . . . .Homer Lott, Jr.
Rusk (†) . . . . .Ben Middlebrooks
City Mgr., Amanda Hill
Sabinal . . . . .Charles D. Story

S

Sachse (†) . . . . .Mike Felix
City Mgr., Gina Nash
Sadler . . . . .Jackie Moss
City Admin., Jaime Vannoy
Saginaw (†) . . . . .Todd Flippo
City Mgr., Gabe Reaume
Saint Hedwig . . . . .Dee Grimm
Saint Jo . . . . Tom Weger
Salado . . . . .Michael Coggin
Village Admin., Don Ferguson
San Angelo (†) . . . . .Brenda Gunter
City Mgr., Daniel Valenzuela
San Antonio (†) . . . . .Ron Nirenberg
City Mgr., Erik Walsh
San Augustine . . . . Leroy Hughes
City Mgr., John Camp
San Benito (†) . . . . . Ricardo (Rick) Guerra
City Mgr., Manuel De La Rosa
Sanctuary . . . . Megg Galloway
San Diego . . . . .Ruperto Canales, III
City Dir., Issabelle N. Garcia
Sandy Oaks . . . . Micki L. Ball
Sandy Point . . . . Charles J. Waller, Jr.
San Elizario . . . . Antonio Araujo
City Admin., Maya Sanchez
San Felipe . . . . Bobby Byars
Sanford . . . . Dallis Shelton
Sanger (†) . . . . Thomas Muir
City Mgr., John Noblitt
San Juan (†) . . . . Mario Garza
City Mgr., Benjamin Arjona
San Leanna . . . . Molly Quirk
City Admin., Rebecca Howe
San Marcos (†) . . . . Jane Hughson
City Mgr., Bert Lumbreras
San Patricio . . . . Jackie Hale
San Perlita . . . . George M. Guadiana
San Saba . . . . Ken Jordan
City Mgr., Stan Weik
Sansom Park . . . . .Art Minor
City Admin., Angela Winkle
Santa Anna . . . . .Harold Fahrlender
Santa Clara . . . . .Jeff Hunt
Santa Fe (†) . . . . .Jason Tabor
City Mgr., Glen Adams
Santa Rosa . . . . .Bobby de la Fuente
Savoy . . . . .Rick Berube
Schertz (†) . . . . .Ralph Gutierrez
City Mgr., Mark Browne
Schulenburg . . . . Elaine Kocian
City Admin., Tami Walker
Scotland . . . . .Ron Hoff
Scottsville . . . . Kerry L. Cade
Scurry . . . . Johnny Blazek
Seabrook (†) . . . . Thom Kolupski
City Mgr., Gayle Cook
Seadrift . . . . Elmer DeForest
Seagoville (†) . . . . Dennis K. Childress
City Mgr., Patrick Stallings
Seagraves . . . . .Rick Dollahan
Sealy (†) . . . . .Carolyn Bilski
City Mgr., Warren Escovy

Seguin (†) . . . . Donna Dodgen
  City Mgr., Steve Parker
Selma . . . . Tom Daly
  City Admin., Johnny Casias
Seminole (†) . . . . John Belcher
  City Admin., Tommy Phillips
Seven Oaks . . . . Centa Evans
Seven Points . . . . Skippy Waters
Seymour . . . . Jon Hrncirik
  City Admin., Jeff Brasher
Shady Shores . . . . .Cindy Aughinbaugh
  Town Admin., Wendy Admin.
Shallowater . . . . .Royking Potter
  City Mgr., Russel Moses
Shamrock . . . . .Lynn Ramsey
  City Mgr., Troy Potts
Shavano Park . . . . .Bob Werner
  City Mgr., Bill Hill
Shenandoah . . . . Ritch Wheeler
  City Admin., Kathie Reyer
Shepherd . . . . .Charles Minton
Sherman (†) . . . . .David Plyler
  City Mgr., Robby Hefton
Shiner . . . . .Fred Hilscher
Shoreacres . . . . David Jennings
  City Mgr., Troy Harrison
Silsbee (†) . . . . .Kevin Garner
  City Mgr., DeeAnn Zimmerman
Silverton . . . . Lane B. Garvin
  City Admin., Brian Barboza
Simonton . . . . Laurie Boudreaux
  City Admin., Jennifer Jones Ward
Sinton (†) . . . . Edward Adams
  City Mgr., John D. Hobson
Skellytown . . . . Amanda Dickerson
Slaton (†) . . . . Clifton Shaw
  City Admin., Mike Lamberson
Smiley . . . . Michael K. Mills
Smithville . . . . Joanna Morgan
  City Mgr., Robert Tamble
Smyer . . . . Joe Riddle
Snook . . . . John W. See, III
Snyder (†) . . . . Tony Wofford
  City Mgr., Merle Taylor
Socorro (†) . . . . Ivy Avalos
  City Mgr., Adriana Rodarte
Somerset . . . . Lydia P. Hernandez
  City Admin., Omar H. Pachecano
Somerville . . . . Tommy Thompson
  City Admin., Danny Segundo
Sonora . . . . .Juanita Gomez
  City Mgr., Arturo Fuentes
Sour Lake . . . . .Bruce Robinson
  City Mgr., Jack Provost
South Frydek . . . . Laura Meyer
South Houston . . . . .Joe Soto
Southlake (†) . . . . John Huffman
  City Mgr., Shana K. Yelverton
Southmayd . . . . .David Turner
South Mountain . . . . Donald Smart
South Padre Island (†) . . . Patrick McNulty
  City Mgr., Randy Smith
Southside Place . . . . Andy Chan
  City Mgr., David Moss
Spearman . . . . Tobe Shields
  City Mgr., Wade Willson
Splendora . . . . Dorothy Welch
Spofford . . . . .Alex Solis
  City Mgr., Sarah Terrazas
Spring Branch . . . . James Mayer
Springlake . . . . Gaylon Conner
Springtown . . . . Greg Hood
  City Admin., David Miller
Spring Valley Village . . . . . .Marcus Vajdos
  City Admin., Julie Robinson

Spur . . . . Louise Jones
St. Paul . . . . David Gensler
Stafford (†) . . . . .Cecil Willis, Jr.
Stagecoach . . . . Galen Mansee
Stamford (†) . . . . .James Decker
  City Mgr., Alan Plumlee
Stanton . . . . Sally Poteet
  City Admin., Jessie Montez
Staples . . . . .Ronnie Clark
Star Harbor . . . . .Warren Claxton
Stephenville (†) . . . . Doug Svien
  City Mgr., Allen Barnes
Sterling City . . . . Lane Horwood
  City Admin., Laura Arizola
Stinnett . . . . .Colin Locke
  City Admin., Durk Downs
Stockdale . . . . Ray Wolff
  City Mgr., Banks Akin
Stockton Bend . . . . Edward Reiter
Stratford . . . . Greg Wright
  City Admin., Tommy Bogart
Strawn . . . . Omer Mallory
  City Admin., Danny Miller
Streetman . . . . Johnny A. Robinson
Sudan . . . . Sam Miller
Sugar Land (†) . . . . .Joe R. Zimmerman
  City Mgr., Mike Goodrum
Sullivan City (†) . . . . . Leonel (Leo) Garcia
  City Mgr., Ana M. Mercado
Sulphur Springs (†) . . . . . . John A. Sellers
  City Mgr., Marc Maxwell
Sun Valley . . . . .Tom Wagnon
Sundown . . . . Jonathan Strickland
  City Admin., Billy Hernandez
Sunnyvale (†) . . . . Saji George
  Town Mgr., Susan Guthrie
Sunray . . . . Bruce Broxson
  City Mgr., K.J. Perry
Sunrise Beach Village. . . . . Tommy Martin
Sunset Valley . . . . Marc Bruner
  City Admin., Sylvia Carrillo
Surfside Beach . . . . Gregg Bisso
Sweeny (†) . . . . Jeff Farley
  City Mgr., Reese Cook
Sweetwater (†) . . . . Jim McKenzie
  City Mgr., David A. Vela

T

Taft . . . . Pedro Lopez
  City Mgr., Melissa Gonzalez
Tahoka . . . . .John B. Baker
  City Admin., Julie Arrington
Talco . . . . Mike Sloan
Talty . . . . Frank Garrison
  City Admin., James Stroman
Tatum . . . . .Clay Lassen
Taylor (†) . . . . .Brandt Rydell
  City Mgr., Brian Laborde
Taylor Lake Village . . . . Jon Keeney
Taylor Landing . . . . John Durkay
Teague . . . . .James Monks
  City Admin., Theresa Bell
Tehuacana . . . . Roy Cholopisa
Temple (†) . . . . Tim Davis
  City Mgr., Brynn Myers
Tenaha . . . . Mike William Ramsey
  City Mgr., Natalie Harris
Terrell (†) . . . . E. Rick Carmona
  City Mgr., Mike Sims
Terrell Hills (†) . . . . .John Low
  City Mgr., William Foley
Texarkana (†). . . . . .Bob Bruggeman
  City Mgr., David Orr, Interim

Texas City (†) . . . . . . .Dedrick Johnson, Sr.
Texhoma . . . . .Missy Cartwright
Texline . . . . Jeff Finnegan
  City Mgr., Marcia French
The Colony (†). . . . . Joe McCourry
  City Mgr., Troy Powell
The Hills (Village of-) . . . . .Greg Wharton
  City Mgr., Wendy L. Smith
Thompsons . . . . Freddie Newsome
Thorndale . . . . George Galbreath
  City Admin., William Kiesling
Thornton . . . . Kenneth Capps
  City Mgr., Victoria Winstead
Thorntonville . . . . .David Mitchell
Thrall . . . . .Troy Marx
Three Rivers . . . . .Felipe Q. Martinez
  City Mgr., Thomas Salazar
Throckmorton . . . . .Will Carroll
Tiki Island . . . . Vernon (Goldie) Teltschick
Timbercreek Canyon . . . . Bill Young
  City Mgr., Katie Paul
Timpson . . . . Debra Smith
Tioga . . . . Craig Jezek
Tira. . . . . Allen Joslin
Toco . . . . .John J. Waller
Todd Mission . . . . . . .George C. Coulam
  City Mgr., Neal Wendele
Tolar . . . . Terry Johnson
Tom Bean . . . . .Daniel Harrison
Tomball (†) . . . . .Gretchen Fagan
  City Mgr., David Esquivel
Tool . . . . .Tawnya Austin
  City Admin., Makenzie Lyons
Toyah . . . . Bobby Creamer
Trent . . . . Leanna West
Trenton. . . . . Rodney Alexander
Trinidad . . . . Larry Estes
  City Admin., Terri R. Newhouse
Trinity . . . . Wayne Huffman
  City Mgr., Steven Jones, Interim
Trophy Club (†) . . . . Alicia Fleury
  Town Mgr., Wade Carroll
Troup . . . . .Joe Carlyle
  City Mgr., Gene Cottle
Troy . . . . Michael Morgan
  City Admin., Jeff Straub
Tulia (†). . . . . Dusty George
  City Mgr., B.J. Potts
Turkey . . . . .Christy Yates
  City Mgr., Larry Plumlee
Tuscola . . . . Dale Martin
Tye . . . . .Bill Murphy
Tyler (†) . . . . Don Warren
  City Mgr., Edward Broussard

U

Uhland . . . . Naomi Schrock
  City Admin., Karen Gallaher
Uncertain . . . . Judye Patterson
Union Grove . . . . Mallory Dippold Shelton
Union Valley . . . . Craig Waskow
Universal City (†). . . . . John Williams
  City Mgr., Kim Turner
University Park (†)
  . . . . Thomas H. (Tommy) Stewart
  City Mgr., Robbie Corder
Uvalde (†) . . . . .Don McLaughlin
  City Mgr., Vince DiPiazza

V

Valentine. . . . . .Summer Webb
Valley Mills . . . . .Josh Thayer

Valley View . . . . Mike Chalke
Van . . . . .Don Smith
   City Mgr., Charles West
Van Alstyne . . . . Jim Atchison
   City Mgr., Lane Jones
Van Horn . . . . Becky Brewster
Vega . . . . Roudy Blasingame
Venus . . . . James Burgess
   City Admin., Tonya Roberts
Vernon (†) . . . . Pam Gosline
   City Mgr., Martin Mangum
Victoria (†) . . . . Jeff Bauknight
   City Mgr., Jesús A. Garza
Vidor (†) . . . . Kelly Carder
   City Mgr., Robbie Hood
Vinton . . . . Manuel (Manny) Leos
   Village Admin., Andrea Carrillo
Volente . . . . .Dan Thost
Von Ormy . . . . Sally Martinez

W

Waco (†) . . . . Dillon Meek
   City Mgr., Bradley Ford
Waelder . . . . Roy Tovar
   City Mgr., Steven McKay
Wake Village (†) . . . . .Sheryl Collum
   City Admin., Jim Roberts
Waller . . . . Danny L. Marburger
Wallis . . . . .Dennis L. Diggs
Walnut Springs . . . . .Sammy Ortega
Warren City . . . . Ricky Wallace
Waskom . . . . .Jesse Moore
Watauga (†) . . . . .Arthur L. Miner
   City Mgr., Andrea Gardner
Waxahachie (†) . . . . .David Hill
   City Mgr., Michael Scott
Weatherford (†) . . . . .Paul Paschall
   City Mgr., James Hotopp
Webberville . . . . Hector Gonzales
Webster (†) . . . . Donna Rogers
   City Mgr., Michael K. Ahrens
Weimar . . . . .Milton R. Koller
   City Mgr., Mike Barrow
Weinert . . . . David Caldwell
Weir . . . . Alber Walther

Wellington . . . . J.D. Hamby
   City Mgr., Jon Sessions
Wellman . . . . Eddie Garza
Wells . . . . .Tony McKnight
Weslaco (†) . . . . .David Suarez
   City Mgr., Mike R. Perez
West . . . . .Tommy Muska
   City Admin., Shelly Nors
Westbrook . . . . Lynn Gaston
West Columbia . . . . . Laurie B. Kincannon
   City Mgr., Debbie Sutherland
Westlake . . . . Laura Wheat
   Town Mgr., Amanda DeGan
West Lake Hills . . . . . . Linda Anthony
   City Admin., Travis Askey
Weston . . . . .Jim Marischen
Weston Lakes . . . . .Ramona Neal
West Orange (†) . . . . Randy Branch
Westover Hills . . . . Kelly Thompson
West Tawakoni . . . . Jim Turnipseed
   City Admin., Anette Lemons
West University Place (†) . . . .Susan Sample
   City Mgr., David J. Beach
Westworth Village . . . . .L. Kelly Jones
   City Admin., Mike Murray
Wharton (†) . . . . Tim Barker
   City Mgr., Andres Garza, Jr.
Wheeler . . . . Bob McCain
White Deer . . . . Robert Peets
Whiteface . . . . Judy Deavours
Whitehouse (†) . . . . .James Wansley
   City Mgr., Leslie Black
White Oak (†) . . . . .Kyle Kutch
   City Coord., Charles Smith
Whitesboro . . . . W.D. (Dee) Welch
   City Admin., Michael Marter
White Settlement (†) . . . . Ronald A. White
   City Mgr., Jeff James
Whitewright . . . . Tona Shiplet
Whitney . . . . Trey Jetton
   City Admin., Chris Bentley
Wichita Falls (†) . . . . . . .Stephen Santellana
   City Mgr., Darron Leiker
Wickett . . . . .Xavier Estrada
Willis (†) . . . . Leonard Reed
   City Mgr., Robert Evans

Willow Park . . . . .Doyle Moss
   City Admin., Bryan Grimes
Wills Point . . . . Mark Turner
   City Admin., Pam Pearson
Wilmer . . . . Sheila Petta
   City Admin., Rona Stringfellow
Wilson . . . . Randy Dunn
Wimberley . . . . Gina Fulkerson
   City Admin., Mike Boese
Windcrest (†) . . . . .Dan Reese
   City Mgr., Rafael Castillo
Windom . . . . Donny Cobb
Windthorst . . . . Greg P. Vieth
Winfield . . . . Debbie Cruitt
Wink . . . . .Eric Hawkins
Winnsboro . . . . Andrea Newsom
   City Admin., Craig Lindholm
Winona . . . . .Curtis Land
Winters . . . . .Lisa Yates
Wixon Valley . . . . James (Jim) Soefje
Wolfe City . . . . .Sharion Scott
Wolfforth . . . . Mike Wright
   City Mgr., Darrell Newsom
Woodbranch Village . . . . .Mike Tyson
Woodcreek . . . . Gloria Whitehead
   City Mgr., Brenton B. Lewis
Woodloch . . . . Ralph Leino, Jr.
Woodsboro . . . . .Kay Roach
Woodson . . . . Bobby Mathiews
Woodville . . . . .Paula M. Jones
   City Admin., Mandy K. Risinger
Woodway (†) . . . . .Jane Kittner
   City Mgr., Shawn Oubre
Wortham . . . . Pellie Goolsby
Wylie (†) . . . . Matthew Porter
   City Mgr., Chris Holsted

Y

Yantis . . . . John D. (Trey) Norris, III
Yoakum (†) . . . . .Carl O'Neill
   City Mgr., Kevin Coleman
Yorktown . . . . Bill Baker
   City Mgr., John Barth

Z

Zavalla . . . . .Carlos Guzman

The Innovation Pipeline in Tyler. Photo by Michael Barera, CC by SA 4.0/Wikimedia Commons

Polk County Courthouse in Livingston. Photo by Jim Evans, CC by 4.0/Wikimedia Commons.

County Courts

Each Texas county has one county court created by the Texas Constitution — a constitutional county court — which is presided over by the county judge (see table beginning on page 501 for a list of county judges). In more populated counties, the Legislature has created statutory county courts, including courts at law, probate courts, juvenile courts, domestic relations courts, and criminal courts at law. Following is a list of statutory county courts and judges, as reported in the Texas Judicial Directory as of July 2021. Other courts with jurisdiction in each county can be found on pages 456–461. Other county and district officials can be found on pages 501–512.

Anderson: Court at Law, Brendan Jeffrey Doran.

Angelina: Court at Law No. 1, Joe Lee Register; No. 2, Clyde M. Herrington.

Aransas: Court at Law, Richard Bianchi.

Atascosa: Court at Law, Bob Brendel.

Austin: Court at Law, Daniel W. Leedy.

Bastrop: Court at Law, M. Benton Eskew.

Bell: Court at Law No. 1, Jeanne Parker; No. 2, John Michael Mischtian; No. 3, Rebecca DePew.

Bexar: Court at Law No. 1, Helen Petry Stowe; No. 2, Grace M. Uzomba; No. 3, David J. Rodriguez; No. 4, Alfredo Ximenez; No. 5, John Amos Longoria; No. 6, Wayne A. Christian; No. 7, Michael DeLeon; No. 8, Mary D. Roman; No. 9, Gloria Saldana; No. 10, J. Frank Davis; No. 11, Carl T. Stolhandske; No. 12, Yolanda Huff; No. 13, Rosie Gonzalez; No. 14, Carlo R. Key; No. 15, Melissa Vara. **Probate Court**, No. 1, Oscar Kazen; No. 2, Veronica Vasquez.

Bosque: Court at Law, Luke A. Giesecke.

Bowie: Court at Law, Craig L. Henry.

Brazoria: Court at Law No. 1 & **Probate Court**, Courtney T. Gilbert; No. 2 & **Probate Court**, Marc W. Holder; No. 3 & **Probate Court**, Jeremy E. Warren; No. 4 & **Probate Court**, Lori L. Rickert.

Brazos: Court at Law No. 1, Amanda S. Matzke; No. 2, James White Locke.

Brown: Court at Law, Sam Clifton Moss.

Burnet: Court at Law, Linda M. Bayless.

Caldwell: Court at Law, Barbara L. Molina.

Calhoun: Court at Law, Alex R. Hernandez.

Cameron: Court at Law No. 1, Arturo A. McDonald Jr.; No. 2, Laura Betancourt; No. 3, David Gonzales III; No. 4, Sheila Garcia Bence; No. 5, Estela Chavez-Vasquez.

Cass: Court at Law, Donald W. Dowd.

Cherokee: Court at Law, Janice C. Stone.

Collin: Court at Law No. 1, Corinne Ann Mason; No. 2, Barnett Walker; No. 3, Lance S. Baxter; No. 4, David D. Rippel; No. 5, Dan K. Wilson; No. 6, Jay A. Bender; No. 7, David Waddill. **Probate Court**, Weldon S. Copeland Jr.

Comal: Court at Law No. 1, Randy C. Gray; No. 2 Charles A. Stephens II; No. 3, Deborah Wigington.

Cooke: Court at Law, John H. Morris.

Coryell: Court at Law, John R. Lee.

Dallas: Court at Law No. 1, D'Metria Benson; No. 2, Melissa Bellan; No. 3, Sally L. Montgomery; No. 4, Paula Rosales; No. 5, Mark Greenberg. County **Criminal Court** No. 1, Dan Patterson; No. 2, Julia Hayes; No. 3,

Audrey Moorhead; No. 4, Nancy Cutler Mulder; No. 5, Lisa Green; No. 6, Angela M. King; No. 7, Remeko Tranisha Edwards; No. 8, Carmen P. White; No. 9, Peggy Hoffman; No. 10, Etta J. Mullin; No. 11, Shequitta Kelly. **Probate Court** No. 1, Brenda Hull Thompson; No. 2, Ingrid Michelle Warren; No. 3, Margaret R. Jones-Johnson.

Denton: Court at Law No. 1 & **Juvenile Court**, Kimberly McCary; No. 2, Robert Ramirez. **Criminal Court at Law** No. 1, David W. Jahn; No. 2, Susan Piel; No. 3, Forrest Beadle; No. 4, Chance Oliver; No. 5, Charles (Coby) Waddill. **Probate Court**, Bonnie J. Robison.

Ector: Court at Law No. 1, Brooke Hendricks; No. 2, Christopher M. Clark.

Ellis: Court at Law No. 1, Jim Chapman; No. 2, A. Gene Calvert Jr.

El Paso: Court at Law No. 1, Ruth Reyes; No. 2, Julie Gonzalez; No. 3, Javier Alvarez; No. 4, Alejandro Gonzalez; No. 5, Jesus Rodriguez; No. 6, M. Sue Kurita; No. 7, Ruben Morales. **Criminal Court at Law** No. 1, Alma R. Trejo; No. 2, Robert S. Anchondo; No. 3, Carlos Carrasco; No. 4, Jessica Vazquez. **Probate Court** No. 1, Patricia B. Chew; No. 2, Eduardo Gamboa.

Erath: Court at Law, Blake B. Thompson.

Fannin: Court at Law, Charles Butler.

Fisher: Multicounty **Court at Law**, David C. Hall (also Mitchell and Nolan Counties)

Fort Bend: Court at Law No. 1, Christopher G. Morales; No. 2, Jeffery A. McMeans; No. 3, Juli Mathew; No. 4, Toni M. Wallace; No. 5, Teana V. Watson; No. 6, Sherman Hatton, Jr.

Galveston: Court at Law No. 1, John Grady; No. 2, Kerri M. Foley; No. 3, Jack Ewing. **Probate Court**, Kimberly A. Sullivan.

Gillespie: Court at Law, Christopher G. Nevins

Grayson: Court at Law No. 1, James C. Henderson; No. 2, Carol M. Siebman.

Gregg: Court at Law No. 1, R. Kent Phillips. No. 2, Vincent L. Dulweber.

Grimes: Court at Law, Tuck Moody McLain

Guadalupe: Court at Law No. 1, Bill Squires; No. 2, Kirsten Legore.

Harris: Civil **Court at Law** No. 1, Vacant; No. 2, Jim F. Kovach; No. 3, LaShawn A. Williams; No. 4, Lesley Briones. County **Criminal Court at Law** No. 1, Alex Salgado; No. 2, Ronnisha Bowman; No. 3, Erica Hughes; No. 4, Shannon Baldwin; No. 5, David M. Fleischer; No. 6, Kelley Andrews; No. 7, Andrew A. Wright; No. 8, Franklin Bynum; No. 9, Toria J. Finch; No. 10, Lee Harper Wilson; No. 11, Sedrick T. Walker II; No. 12, Genesis Draper; No. 13, Raul Rodriguez; No. 14, David L. Singer; No. 15, Tonya Jones; No. 16, Darrell William Jordan. **Probate Court** No. 1, Jerry W. Simoneaux; No. 2, Michael B. Newman; No. 3, Jason Cox; No. 4, James Horwitz.

Harrison: Court at Law, Joe M. Black IV.

Hays: Court at Law No. 1, Robert E. Updegrove; No. 2, Chris Johnson; No. 3, Dan O'Brien.

Henderson: Court at Law No 1, Scott S. Williams; No 2, Nancy Adams Perryman.

Hidalgo: Court at Law No. 1, Rodolfo Gonzalez; No. 2, Jaime Palacios; No. 4, Federico Garza Jr.; No. 5, Arnoldo Cantu; Jr. No. 6, Albert Garcia; No. 7, Sergio Valdez; No. 8, Omar Maldonado, No. 9, Patricia O'Caña-Oliveres; No. 10 Armando J. Marroquin. **Probate Court**, JoAnne Garcia.

Hill: Court at Law, Matthew S. Crain.

Hood: Court at Law, Vincent Messina.

Hopkins: Court at Law, Nicholas C. Harrison.

Houston: Court at Law, Sarah Tunnell Clark.

Hunt: Court at Law No. 1, Timothy S. Linden; No. 2, Joel D. Littlefield.

Jefferson: Court at Law No. 1, Gerald W. Eddins; No. 2, Terrence L. Holmes; No. 3, Clint M. Woods.

Jim Wells: Court at Law, Michael Ventura Garcia

Johnson: Court at Law No. 1, Robert B. Mayfield III; No. 2, F. Steven McClure.

Kaufman: Court at Law No. 1, Tracy Gray; No. 2, Bobby L. Rich, Jr.

Kerr: Court at Law, Susan F. Harris.

Kleberg: Court at Law, Jamie E. Carrillo.

Lamar: Court at Law, Bill H. Harris.

Liberty: Court at Law, Thomas A. Chambers; No. 2, Wesley N Hinch.

Lubbock: Court at Law No. 1, Mark J. Hocker; No. 2, Drue A. Farmer; No. 3, Benjamin Webb.

McLennan: Court at Law No. 1, Vikram Deivanayagam; No. 2, T. Bradley Cates.

Medina: Court at Law, Mark Cashion.

Midland: Court at Law No. 1, K. Kyle Peeler; No. 2, Marvin L. Moore.

Mitchell: Multicounty **Court at Law**, David C. Hall. (also Fisher and Nolan Counties)

Montgomery: Court at Law No. 1, Dennis D. Watson; No. 2, Claudia L. Laird; No. 3, Amy Tucker; No. 4, Mary Ann Turner; No. 5, Keith Mills Stewart.

Moore: Court at Law, Jerod Pingelton.

Nacogdoches: Court at Law, John A. (Jack) Sinz.

Navarro: Court at Law, Amanda D. Putman.

Nolan: Multicounty **Court at Law**, David C. Hall. (also Fisher and Mitchell Counties)

Nueces: Court at Law No. 1, Robert J. Vargas; No. 2, Lisa Elisabet Gonzales; No. 3, Deeanne Galvan; No. 4, Mark H. Woerner; No. 5, Timothy J. McCoy.

Orange: Court at Law No. 1, Mandy White-Rogers; No 2, Troy Johnson.

Panola: Court at Law, Terry D. Bailey.

Parker: Court at Law No. 1, Jerry D. Buckner; No. 2, Lynn Marie Johnson.

Polk: Court at Law, Tom Brown.

Potter: Court at Law No. 1, Walt Weaver; No. 2, Matt Hand.

Randall: Court at Law No. 1, James W. Anderson. No. 2, Matthew Martindale.

Reeves: Court at Law, Scott W. Johnson.

Rockwall: Court at Law No. 1, Brian Williams; No. 2 Stephani Woodward.

Rusk: Court at Law, Chad W. Dean.

San Patricio: Court at Law, M. Elizabeth Welborn.

Smith: Court at Law No. 1, Jason A. Ellis; No. 2, Taylor Heaton. No. 3, Floyd Thomas Getz.

Starr: Court at Law, Orlando Rodriguez.

Tarrant: Court at Law No. 1, Donald R. Pierson; No. 2, Jennifer Rymell; No. 3, Mike Hrabal. **Criminal Court at Law** No. 1, David Cook; No. 2, Carey F. Walker; No. 3, Bob McCoy; No. 4, Deborah L. Nekhom; No. 5, Jamie Cummings; No. 6, Molly S. Jones; No. 7, Cheril S. Hardy; No. 8, Charles L. Vanover; No. 9, Brent A. Carr; No. 10, Phil A. Sorrels. **Probate Court** No. 1, Christopher W. Ponder; No. 2, Brooke Ulrickson Allen.

Taylor: Court at Law No. 1, Robert Harper; No. 2, Harriett L. Haag.

Tom Green: Court at Law No. 1, Charles (Ben) Nolen; No. 2, Penny Anne Roberts.

Travis: Court at Law No. 1, J. Todd T. Wong; No. 2, Eric M. Shepperd; No. 3, John H. Lipscombe; No. 4, Dimple Malhotra; No. 5, Nancy Hohengarten; No. 6, Brandy Mueller; No. 7, Elisabeth A. Earle; No. 8, Carlos H. Barrera; No. 9, Kim Williams. **Probate Court**, Guy Herman.

Val Verde: Court at Law, Sergio J. Gonzalez.

Van Zandt: Court at Law, Joshua Wintters.

Victoria: Court at Law No. 1, Travis H. Ernst; No. 2, Daniel F. Gilliam.

Walker: Court at Law, Tracy M. Sorensen.

Waller: Court at Law, Carol A. Chaney.

Washington: Court at Law, Eric Thomas Berg.

Webb: Court at Law No. 1, Hugo D. Martinez; No. 2, Victor G. Villarreal.

Wichita: Court at Law No. 1, Gary Wayne Butler; No. 2, Greg King.

Williamson: Court at Law No. 1, Brandy Hallford; No. 2, Laura B. Barker; No. 3, Doug Arnold; No. 4, John B. McMaster.

Wise: Court at Law No. 1, Greg Lowery; No. 2, Stephen J. Wren. ☆

Regional Councils of Government

Source: Texas Association of Regional Councils; www.txregionalcouncil.org/

The concept of regional planning and cooperation, fostered by enabling legislation in 1965, has spread across Texas since organization of the **North Central Texas Council of Governments** in 1966.

Regional councils are voluntary associations of local governments that deal with problems and planning needs that cross the boundaries of individual local governments or that require regional attention.

These concerns include criminal justice, emergency communications, job-training programs, solid-waste management, transportation, and water-quality management. The councils make recommendations to member governments and may assist in implementing the plans. Financing is provided by local, state, and federal governments.

The **Texas Association of Regional Councils** is at 701 Brazos, Ste. 780, Austin 78701; (512) 478-4715. Following is a list of the 24 regional councils, member counties, executive director, and contact information:

1. **Panhandle Regional Planning Commission**: Armstrong, Briscoe, Carson, Castro, Childress, Collingsworth, Dallam, Deaf Smith, Donley, Gray, Hall, Hansford, Hartley, Hemphill, Hutchinson, Lipscomb, Moore, Ochiltree, Oldham, Parmer, Potter, Randall, Roberts, Sherman, Swisher, and Wheeler. Kyle Ingham, P.O. Box 9257, Amarillo 79105-9257; (806) 372-3381; www.theprpc.org.

2. **South Plains Association of Governments**: Bailey, Cochran, Crosby, Dickens, Floyd, Garza, Hale, Hockley, King, Lamb, Lubbock, Lynn, Motley, Terry, and Yoakum. Tim Pierce, P.O. Box 3730, Lubbock 79452-3730; (806) 762-8721; www.spag.org.

3. **Nortex Regional Planning Commission**: Archer, Baylor, Clay, Cottle, Foard, Hardeman, Jack, Montague, Wichita, Wilbarger, and Young. Dennis Wilde, P.O. Box 5144, Wichita Falls 76307-5144; (940) 322-5281; www.nortexrpc.org.

4. **North Central Texas Council of Governments**: Collin, Dallas, Denton, Ellis, Erath, Hood, Hunt, Johnson, Kaufman, Navarro, Palo Pinto, Parker, Rockwall, Somervell, Tarrant, and Wise. R. Michael Eastland, P.O. Box 5888, Arlington 76005-5888; (817) 695-9101; www.nctcog.org.

5. **Ark-Tex Council of Governments**: Bowie, Cass, Delta, Franklin, Hopkins, Lamar, Morris, Red River, and Titus. Chris Brown, 4808 Elizabeth St., Texarkana, Texas 75503; (903) 832-8636; www.atcog.org.

6. **East Texas Council of Governments**: Anderson, Camp, Cherokee, Gregg, Harrison, Henderson, Marion, Panola, Rains, Rusk, Smith, Upshur, Van Zandt, and Wood. David Cleveland, 3800 Stone Rd., Kilgore 75662-6297; (903) 984-8641; www.etcog.org.

7. **West Central Texas Council of Governments**: Brown, Callahan, Coleman, Comanche, Eastland, Fisher, Haskell, Jones, Kent, Knox, Mitchell, Nolan, Runnels, Scurry, Shackelford, Stephens, Stonewall, Taylor, and Throckmorton. Tom Smith, 3702 Loop 322, Abilene 79602-7300; (325) 672-8544; www.wctcog.org.

8. **Rio Grande Council of Governments**: Brewster, Culberson, El Paso, Hudspeth, Jeff Davis, Presidio, and Doña Ana County, N.M. Annette Gutierrez, 8037 Lockheed Dr., Ste. 100, El Paso 79925; (915) 533-0998; www.riocog.org.

9. **Permian Basin Regional Planning Commission**: Andrews, Borden, Crane, Dawson, Ector, Gaines, Glasscock, Howard, Loving, Martin, Midland, Pecos, Reeves, Terrell, Upton, Ward, and Winkler. Virginia Belew, PO Box 60660, Midland 79711-0660; (432) 563-1061; www.pbrpc.org.

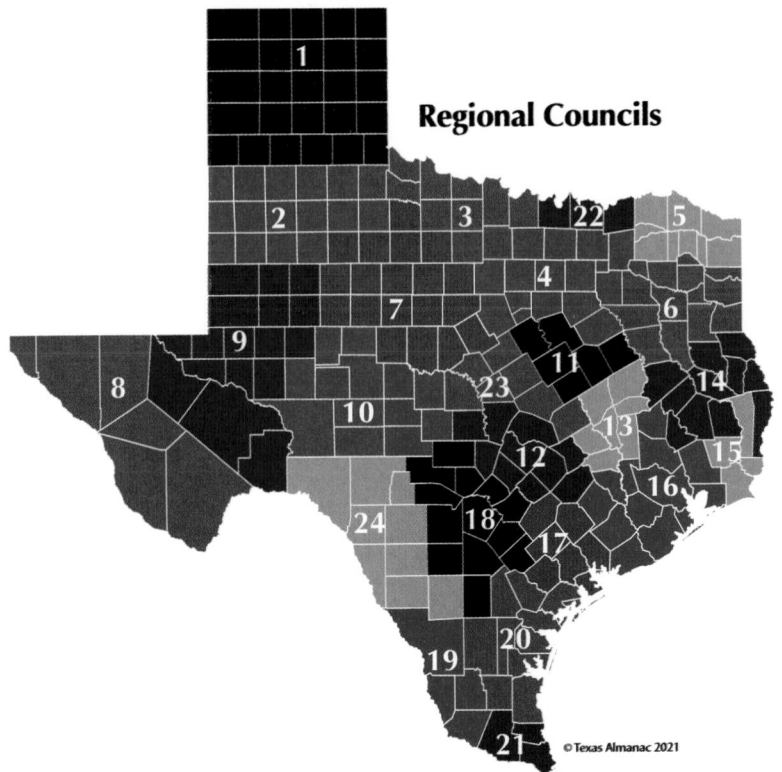

Regional Councils

© Texas Almanac 2021

10. **Concho Valley Council of Governments**: Coke, Concho, Crockett, Irion, Kimble, Mason, McCulloch, Menard, Reagan, Schleicher, Sterling, Sutton, and Tom Green. John Austin Stokes, 2801 W. Loop 206, Ste. A, San Angelo 76904; (325) 944-9666; www.cvcog.org.

11. **Heart of Texas Council of Governments**: Bosque, Falls, Freestone, Hill, Limestone, and McLennan. Russell Devorsky, 1514 S. New Road, Waco 76711; (254) 292-1800; www.hotcog.org.

12. **Capital Area Council of Governments**: Bastrop, Blanco, Burnet, Caldwell, Fayette, Hays, Lee, Llano, Travis, and Williamson. Betty Voights, 6800 Burleson Rd., Bldg. 310, Ste. 165, Austin 78744; (512) 916-6018; www.capcog.org.

13. **Brazos Valley Council of Governments**: Brazos, Burleson, Grimes, Leon, Madison, Robertson, and Washington. Tom Wilkinson Jr., P.O. Drawer 4128, Bryan 77805-4128; (979) 595-2800; www.bvcog.org.

14. **Deep East Texas Council of Governments**: Angelina, Houston, Nacogdoches, Newton, Polk, Sabine, San Augustine, San Jacinto, Shelby, Trinity, and Tyler. Lonnie Hunt, 1405 Kurth Dr., Lufkin, 75904; (963) 634-2247; www.detcog.gov.

15. **South East Texas Regional Planning Commission**: Hardin, Jasper, Jefferson, and Orange. Shanna Burke, 2210 Eastex Fwy., Beaumont 77703; (409) 899-8444; www.setrpc.org.

16. **Houston-Galveston Area Council**: Austin, Brazoria, Chambers, Colorado, Fort Bend, Galveston, Harris, Liberty, Matagorda, Montgomery, Walker, Waller, and Wharton. Chuck Wemple, 3555 Timmons Ln., Ste. 120, Houston 77227-2777; (713) 993-4514; www.h-gac.com.

17. **Golden Crescent Regional Planning Commission**: Calhoun, DeWitt, Goliad, Gonzales, Jackson, Lavaca, and Victoria. Michael Ada, 1908 N. Laurent, Ste. 600, Victoria 77901; (361) 578-1587; www.gcrpc.org.

18. **Alamo Area Council of Governments**: Atascosa, Bandera, Bexar, Comal, Frio, Gillespie, Guadalupe, Karnes, Kendall, Kerr, McMullen, Medina, and Wilson. Diane Rath, 82700 NE Loop 410, Ste. 101, San Antonio 78217; (210) 362-5200; www.aacog.com.

19. **South Texas Development Council**: Jim Hogg, Starr, Webb, and Zapata. Robert Mediola, 1002 Dicky Lane, Laredo 78044-2187; (956) 722-3995; www.stdc.cog.tx.us.

20. **Coastal Bend Council of Governments**: Aransas, Bee, Brooks, Duval, Jim Wells, Kenedy, Kleberg, Live Oak, Nueces, Refugio, and San Patricio. John P. Buckner, 2910 Leopard St, Corpus Christi 78408; (361) 883-5743; coastal-bendcog.org.

21. **Lower Rio Grande Valley Development Council**: Cameron, Hidalgo, and Willacy. Manny Cruz, 301 W. Railroad St., Weslaco 78596; (956) 682-3481; www.lrgvdc.org.

22. **Texoma Council of Governments**: Cooke, Fannin, and Grayson. Eric Bridges, 1117 Gallagher Dr., Ste. 470, Sherman 75090; (903) 813-3514; www.tcog.com.

23. **Central Texas Council of Governments**: Bell, Coryell, Hamilton, Lampasas, Milam, Mills, and San Saba. Jim Reed, P.O. Box 729, Belton 76513-0729; (254) 770-2210; www.ctcog.org.

24. **Middle Rio Grande Development Council**: Dimmit, Edwards, Kinney, La Salle, Maverick, Real, Uvalde, Val Verde, and Zavala. Nick Gallegos, 307 W. Nopal, Carrizo Springs 78834; (830) 876-3533; www.mrgdc.org. ☆

County Tax Appraisers

The following list of Chief Appraisers for Texas counties was furnished by the State Property Tax Division of the State Comptroller's office. It includes the mailing address for each appraiser and is current to August 2021.

Anderson: Adrienne Polk, P.O. Box 279, Palestine 75802

Andrews: Susan Brewer, 600 N. Main St. Andrews 79714

Angelina: Tim Chambers, P.O. Box 2357, Lufkin 75902

Aransas: Mike Soto, 11 Hwy 35 N, Rockport 78382

Archer: Kimbra York, P.O. Box 1141, Archer City 76351

Armstrong: Melissa Clement, P.O. Box 149, Claude 79019

Atascosa: Michelle L. Berdeaux, P.O. Box 600, Pleasanton 78065

Austin: Greg Cook, 906 E. Amelia St., Bellville 77418

Bailey: Jessica Rivera, 302 Main St., Muleshoe 79347

Bandera: Shawn Davis, P.O. Box 1119, Bandera 78003

Bastrop: Faun Cullens, P.O. Box 578, Bastrop 78602

Baylor: Mitzi Welch, 211 N. Washington, Seymour 76380

Bee: Patricia Davis, 401 N. Washington, Beeville 78102

Bell: Billy White, P.O. Box 390, Belton 76513

Bexar: Michael Amezquita, P.O. Box 830248, San Antonio 78283

Blanco: Candice Fry, P.O. Box 338, Johnson City 78636

Borden: Tracy Cooley, P.O. Box 298, Gail 79738

Bosque: Christopher Moser, P.O. Box 393, Meridian 76665

Bowie: Mike Brower, P.O. Box 6527, Texarkana 75505

Brazoria: Al Baird, 500 N. Chenango, Angleton 77515

Brazos: Mark Price, 4051 Pendleton Dr., Bryan 77802

Brewster: Denise Flores, 107 W. Avenue E, #2, Alpine 79830

Briscoe: Theresa Clinton, P.O. Box 728, Silverton 79257

Brooks: Daniel Garcia, P.O. Drawer A, Falfurrias 78355

Brown: Brett McKibben, 403 Fisk Ave., Brownwood 76801

Burleson: Tonya Barnes, P.O. Box 1000, Caldwell 77836

Burnet: Stan Hemphill, P.O. Box 908, Burnet 78611

Caldwell: Shanna Ramzinski, P.O. Box 900, Lockhart 78644

Calhoun: Jesse Hubbell, P.O. Box 49, Port Lavaca 77979

Callahan: Stephanie McPherson, 132 W. 4th St., Baird 79504

Cameron: Richard Molina, P.O. Box 1010, San Benito 78586

Camp: Jan Tinsley, 143 Quitman St., Pittsburg 75686

Carson: Shannon Hensley, P.O. Box 970, Panhandle 79068

Cass: Lacy Hicks, 502 N. Main St., Linden 75563

Castro: Steven Cole Pierce, 204 S.E. 3rd (Rear), Dimmitt 79027

Chambers: Mitchell McCullough, P.O. Box 1520, Anahuac 77514

Cherokee: J.L. Flowers, P.O. Box 494, Rusk 75785

Childress: Twila Butler, 1710 Ave. F NW, Childress 79201

Clay: Lisa Murphy, P.O. Box 108, Henrietta 76365

Cochran: David Greener, 109 S.E. First St., Morton 79346

Coke: Gayle Sisemore, P.O. Box 2, Robert Lee 76945

Coleman: Bill W. Jones, P.O. Box 914, Coleman 76834

Collin: Bo Daffin, 250 W. Eldorado, McKinney 75069

Collingsworth: Dwight Bowen, 800 West Ave., Box 9, Wellington, 79095

Colorado: Robert Maes., P.O. Box 10, Columbus 78934

Comal: Rufino Lozano, 900 S. Seguin Ave., New Braunfels 78130

Comanche: JoAnn Hohertz, 8 Huett Cir., Comanche 76442

Concho: D'Andra Warlick, P.O. Box 68, Paint Rock 76866

Cooke: Doug Smithson, 201 N. Dixon, Gainesville 76240

Coryell: Mitch Fast, 705 E. Main St., Gatesville 76528

Cottle: Nakia Hargrave, P.O. Box 459, Paducah 79248

Crane: Byron Bitner, 511 W. 8th St., Crane 79731

Crockett: Janet M. Thompson, P.O. Box 1569, Ozona 76943

Crosby: Gary Zeitler, P.O. Box 505, Crosbyton 79322

Culberson: Maricel Gonzalez, P.O. Box 550, Van Horn 79855

Dallam: Holly McCauley, P.O. Box 579, Dalhart 79022

Dallas: Ken Nolan, 2949 N. Stemmons Fwy., Dallas 75247

Dawson: Norma J. Brock, P.O. Box 797, Lamesa 79331

Deaf Smith: Danny Jones, P.O. Box 2298, Hereford 79045

Delta: Kim Gregory, P.O. Box 47, Cooper 75432

Denton: Hope McClure, P.O. Box 2816, Denton 76202

DeWitt: Denise Moore, 103 E. Bailey St., Cuero 77954

Dickens: Patti Abbott, P.O. Box 180, Dickens 79229

Dimmit: Norma Carrillo, 203 W. Houston St., Carrizo Springs 78834

Donley: Paula Lowrie, P.O. Box 1220, Clarendon 79226

Duval: Raul Garcia, P.O. Box 809, San Diego 78384

Eastland: Randy Clark, P.O. Box 914, Eastland 76448

Ector: Anita Campbell, 1301 E. 8th St., Odessa 79761

Edwards: Renn Rudasill Riley, P.O. Box 858, Rocksprings 78880

Ellis: Kathy Rodrigue, P.O. Box 878, Waxahachie 75168

El Paso: Dinah Kilgore, 5801 Trowbridge Dr., El Paso 79925

Erath: Jerry Lee, 1195 W. South Loop, Stephenville 76401

Falls: Andrew Hahn, 403 Craik St., Marlin 76661

Fannin: Michael Jones, 831 W. State Hwy. 56, Bonham 75418

Fayette: Richard Moring, P.O. Box 836, La Grange 78945

Fisher: Kellen Walker, P.O. Box 516, Roby 79543

Floyd: Jim Finley, P.O. Box 249, Floydada 79235

Foard: Debbie Stribling, P.O. Box 419, Crowell 79227

Fort Bend: Jordan Wise, 2801 B.F. Terry Blvd., Rosenberg 77471

Franklin: Genea Burnaman, P.O. Box 720, Mount Vernon 75457

Freestone: Bud Black, 218 N. Mount St., Fairfield 75840

Frio: Luciano R. Gonzales, P.O. Box 1129, Pearsall 78061

Gaines: Gayla Harridge, P.O. Box 490, Seminole 79360

Galveston: Tommy Watson, 9850 Emmet F Lowry Exp, Ste. A, Texas City 77591

Garza: Diane Josey, P.O. Drawer F, Post 79356

Gillespie: Scott Fair, 1159 S. Milam, Fredericksburg 78624

Glasscock: Priscilla A. Ginnetti, P.O. Box 155, Garden City 79739

Goliad: Robert Ckodre, P.O. Box 34, Goliad 77963

Gonzales: John Liford, P.O. Box 867, Gonzales 78629

Gray: Tyson Paronto, P.O. Box 836, Pampa 79066

Grayson: Shawn Coker, 515 N. Travis, Sherman 75090

Gregg: Libby Neely, 4367 W. Loop 281, Longview 75604

Grimes: Mark Boehnke, P.O. Box 489, Anderson 77830

Guadalupe: Peter Snaddon, 3000 N. Austin St., Seguin 78155

Hale: Nikki Branscum, P.O. Box 29, Plainview 79073

Hall: Gina Chavira, 512 W. Main St., Ste. 14, Memphis 79245

Hamilton: Heather Donahoo, 119 E. Henry St., Hamilton 76531

Hansford: Brandi Thompson, 709 W. 7th Ave., Spearman 79081

Hardeman: Richard Petree, P.O. Box 388, Quanah 79252

Hardin: Crystal Smith, P.O. Box 670, Kountze 77625

Harris: Roland Altinger, P.O. Box 920975, Houston 77292

Harrison: Robert Lisman, P.O. Box 818, Marshall 75671

Hartley: Juan Salazar, P.O. Box 405, Hartley 79044

Haskell: Wanda Hester, P.O. Box 467, Haskell 79521

Hays: Laura Raven, 21001 N. IH-35, Kyle 78640

Hemphill: Pam Scates, 223 Main St., Canadian 79014

Henderson: Linda Moncada, P.O. Box 430, Athens 75751

Hidalgo: Rolando Garza, P.O. Box 208, Edinburg 78540

Hill: Mike McKibben, P.O. Box 416, Hillsboro 76645

Hockley: Lorie Marquez, P.O. Box 1090, Levelland 79336

Hood: Greg Stewart, P.O. Box 819, Granbury 76048

Hopkins: Cathy Singleton, P.O. Box 753, Sulphur Springs 75483

Houston: Carey Minter, P.O. Box 112, Crockett 75835

Howard: Richard Petree, P.O. Box 1151, Big Spring 79721

Hudspeth: Adolfo Ramirez, P.O. Box 429, Sierra Blanca 79851

Hunt: Brent South, P.O. Box 1339, Greenville 75403

Hutchinson: Joe Raper, P.O. Box 5065, Borger 79008

Irion: Byron Bitner, P.O. Box 980, Mertzon 76941

Jack: Kathy Conner, P.O. Box 958, Jacksboro 76458

Jackson: Damon Moore, 404 N. Allen St., Edna 77957

Jasper: Lori Barnett, P.O. Box 1300, Jasper 75951

Jeff Davis: Lisa Reyna, P.O. Box 373, Fort Davis 79734

Jefferson: Angela Bellard, P.O. Box 21337, Beaumont 77720

Jim Hogg: Jorge Arellano, P.O. Box 459, Hebbronville 78361

Jim Wells: J. Sidney Vela, P.O. Box 607, Alice 78333

Johnson: Jim Hudspeth, 109 N. Main, Cleburne 76033

Jones: Kim McLemore, P.O. Box 348, Anson 79501

Karnes: Brian Stahl, 915 S. Panna Maria Ave., Karnes City 78118

Kaufman: Sarah Curtis, P.O. Box 819, Kaufman 75142

Kendall: Shelby Presley, 118 Market Ave., Boerne 78006

Kenedy: Thomas G. Denney, P.O. Box 39, Sarita 78385

Kent: Cindy Watson, P.O. Box 68, Jayton 79528

Kerr: Sharon Constantinides, P.O. Box 294387, Kerrville 78029

Kimble: Kenda McPherson, P.O. Box 307, Junction 76849

King: Kala Briggs, P.O. Box 117, Guthrie 79236

Kinney: Todd Tate, P.O. Box 1377, Brackettville 78832

Kleberg: Tina Flores, P.O. Box 1027, Kingsville 78364

Knox: Mitzi Welch, P.O. Box 47, Benjamin 79505

Lamar: Stephanie Lee, P.O. Box 400, Paris 75461

Lamb: Lesa Kloiber, P.O. Box 950, Littlefield 79339

Lampasas: Susan Jones, P.O. Box 175, Lampasas 76550

La Salle: Martin Villareal, P.O. Box 1530, Cotulla 78014

Lavaca: Pamela Lathrop, P.O. Box 386, Hallettsville 77964

Lee: James Orr, 898 E. Richmond, Ste. 100, Giddings 78942

Leon: Jeff Beshears, P.O. Box 536, Centerville 75833

Liberty: Lana McCarty, P.O. Box 10016, Liberty 77575

Limestone: Karen Wietzikoski, P.O. Drawer 831, Groesbeck 76642

Lipscomb: Angela Peil, P.O. Box 128, Darrouzett 79024

Live Oak: Debra Morin, P.O. Box 2370, George West 78022

Llano: Scott Dudley, 103 E. Sandstone, Llano 78643

Loving: Sherlene Burrows, P.O. Box 352, Mentone 79754

Lubbock: Tim Radloff, P.O. Box 10542, Lubbock 79408

Lynn: Rebecca Norris, P.O. Box 789, Tahoka 79373

Madison: Matt Newton, P.O. Box 1328, Madisonville 77864

Marion: Anna Lummus, 801 N. Tuttle St., Jefferson 75657

Martin: Marsha Graves, P.O. Box 1349, Stanton 79782

Mason: Liza Trevino, P.O. Box 1119, Mason 76856

Matagorda: Vince Maloney, 2225 Ave. G, Bay City 77414

The atrium at the Fayette County Courthouse. Photo by Jim Evans, CC by 4.0/Wikimedia Commons.

Maverick: Maggie Duran, P.O. Box 2628, Eagle Pass 78852

McCulloch: Zane Brandenberger, 306 W. Lockhart, Brady 76825

McLennan: Joe Don Bobbitt, 315 S. 26th St., Waco 76710

McMullen: Blaine Patterson, P.O. Box 338, Tilden 78072

Medina: Johnette Dixon, 1410 Ave. K, Hondo 78861

Menard: Kayla Wagner, P.O. Box 1008, Menard 76859

Midland: Jerry Bundick, P.O. Box 908002, Midland 79708

Milam: Leslie Sootoo, P.O. Box 769, Cameron 76520

Mills: Codi Ann McCarn, P.O. Box 565, Goldthwaite 76844

Mitchell: John Stewart, 2112 Hickory St., Colorado City 79512

Montague: Kim Haralson, P.O. Box 121, Montague 76251

Montgomery: Tony Belinoski, P.O. Box 2233, Conroe 77305

Moore: Samantha Trujillo, P.O. Box 717, Dumas 79029

Morris: Summer Golden, P.O. Box 563, Daingerfield 75638

Motley: Jim Finley, P.O. Box 249, Floydada 79235

Nacogdoches: Gary Woods, 216 W. Hospital St., Nacogdoches 75961

Navarro: Thomas Dally, P.O. Box 3118, Corsicana 75110

Newton: Margie L. Herrin, 109 Court St., Newton 75966

Nolan: Brenda Klepper, P.O. Box 1256, Sweetwater 79556

Nueces: Ronnie Canales, 201 N. Chaparral, Ste. 206, Corpus Christi 78401

Ochiltree: Donna Lee Stewart, 825 S. Main, Ste. 100, Perryton 79070

Oldham: Leann Voyles, P.O. Box 310, Vega 79092

Orange: Scott Overton, P.O. Box 457, Orange 77631

Palo Pinto: Donna E. Kozlovsky, P.O. Box 250, Palo Pinto 76484

Panola: Michael Douglas McPhail, 1736 Ballpark Dr., Carthage 75633

Parker: Rick Armstrong, 1108 Santa Fe Dr., Weatherford 76086

Parmer: Jill Timms, P.O. Box 56, Bovina 79009

Pecos: Sam Calderon III, P.O. Box 237, Fort Stockton 79735

P.O.lk: Chad Hill, 114 Matthews St., Livingston 77351

Potter: Jeff Dagley, P.O. Box 7190, Amarillo 79114

Presidio: Cynthia Ramirez, P.O. Box 879, Marfa 79843

Rains: Sherri McCall, P.O. Box 70, Emory 75440

Randall: Jeff Dagley, P.O. Box 7190, Amarillo 79114

Reagan: Jacquelyn Botello, P.O. Box 8, Big Lake 76932

Real: Juan Saucedo, P.O. Box 158, Leakey 78873

Red River: Christie Ussery, P.O. Box 461, Clarksville 75426

Reeves: John Huddleston, P.O. Box 1229, Pecos 79772

Refugio: Connie Raymond, P.O. Box 156, Refugio 78377

Roberts: Hether Williams, P.O. Box 458, Miami 79059

Robertson: Nancy Commander, P.O. Box 998, Franklin 77856

Rockwall: Kevin Passons, 841 Justin Rd., Rockwall 75087

Runnels: Paul Scott Randolph, P.O. Box 524, Ballinger 76821

Rusk: Weldon Cook, P.O. Box 7, Henderson 75653

Sabine: Cari Papania, P.O. Box 137, Hemphill 75948

San Augustine: Evelyn Watts, 122 N. Harrison St., San Augustine 75972

San Jacinto: Kelly Foxworth, P.O. Box 1170, Coldspring 77331

San Patricio: Robert Cenci, P.O. Box 938, Sinton 78387

San Saba: Jan Vanderburg, 423 E. Wallace St., San Saba 76877

Schleicher: Liza Trevino, P.O. Box 936, Eldorado 76936

Scurry: Jackie Martin, 2612 College Ave., Snyder 79549

Shackelford: Clayton Snyder, P.O. Box 2247, Albany 76430

Shelby: Robert N. Pigg, 724 Shelbyville St., Center 75935

Sherman: Teresa Edmond, P.O. Box 239, Stratford 79084

Smith: Carol Dixon, 245 South S.E. Loop 323, Tyler 75702

Somervell: Wes Rollen, 112 Allen Dr., Glen Rose 76043

Starr: Rosalva Guerra, 100 N. FM 3167, Ste. 300, Rio Grande City 78582

Stephens: Gary Zeitler, P.O. Box 351, Breckenridge 76424

Sterling: Ronnie Krejci, P.O. Box 28, Sterling City 76951

Stonewall: Debra Smith, P.O. Box 308, Aspermont 79502

Sutton: Mary Bustamante, 300 E. Oak St., Ste. 2, Sonora 76950

Swisher: Andrew Moritz, P.O. Box 8, Tulia 79088

Tarrant: Jeff Law, 2500 Handley-Ederville Rd., Fort Worth 76118

Taylor: Gary Earnest, P.O. Box 1800, Abilene 79604

Terrell: Blain Chriesman, P.O. Box 747, Sanderson 79848

Terry: Eddie Olivas, P.O. Box 426, Brownfield 79316

Throckmorton: DeDe Smith, P.O. Box 788, Throckmorton 76483

Titus: Shirley Dickerson, P.O. Box 528, Mount Pleasant 75456

Tom Green: Bill Benson, 2302 Pulliam St., San Angelo 76905

Travis: Marya Crigler, P.O. Box 149012, Austin 78714

Trinity: Greg Gallant, P.O. Box 950, Groveton 75845

Tyler: David Luther, P.O. Drawer 9, Woodville 75979

Upshur: Amanda Thibodeaux, 105 Diamond Loch, Gilmer 75644

Upton: Linda Zarate, P.O. Box 1110, McCamey 79752

Uvalde: Roberto Valdez, 209 N. High St., Uvalde 78801

Val Verde: Cherry Sheedy, 417 W. Cantu Rd., Del Rio 78842

Van Zandt: Scott Hyde, P.O. Box 926, Canton 75103

Victoria: John Haliburton, 2805 N. Navarro, Ste. 300, Victoria 77901

Walker: Raymond Kiser, P.O. Box 1798, Huntsville 77342

Waller: Becky Gurrola, P.O. Box 887, Hempstead 77445

Ward: Norma Valdez, P.O. Box 905, Monahans 79756

Washington: Dyann White, P.O. Box 681, Brenham 77834

Webb: Martin Villarreal, 3302 Clark Blvd., Laredo 78043

Wharton: Tylene Gamble, 308 E. Milam, Wharton 77488

Wheeler: Kimberly Morgan, P.O. Box 1200, Wheeler 79096

Wichita: Lisa Stephens-Musick, P.O. Box 5172, Wichita Falls 76307

Wilbarger: Sandy Burkett, P.O. Box 1519, Vernon 76385

Willacy: Agustin Lopez, 688 FM 3168, Raymondville 78580

Williamson: Alvin Lankford, 625 FM 1460, Georgetown 78626

Wilson: Jennifer Coldewey, 1611 Railroad St., Floresville 78114

Winkler: Gary Zietler, P.O. Box 1219, Kermit 79745

Wise: Michael Hand, 400 E. Business 380, Decatur 76234

Wood: Tracy Nichols, P.O. Box 1706, Quitman 75783

Yoakum: Brooks Barrett, P.O. Box 748, Plains 79355

Young: Luke Robbins, P.O. Box 337, Graham 76450

Zapata: Amada Gonzalez, 200 E. 7th Ave., Ste. 240, Zapata 78076

Zavala: Yolanda Lavenant, 323 W. Zavala, Crystal City 78839

☆

Wet-Dry Counties

Source: Texas Alcoholic Beverage Commission; www.tabc.state.tx.us

Although the laws regulating the alcoholic beverage industry are consistent statewide, the Alcoholic Beverage Code allows for local-option elections to determine the types of alcoholic beverages that may be sold and how they can be sold.

Elections can be held by counties, cities, or individual justice of the peace precincts. In the time since our last edition went to press, four counties have moved from Part Wet to Wet: Crane, Kerr, Mason, and Wilson.

As of August 2021, there were 59 completely wet counties in Texas and 5 completely dry counties.

Over time, Texas has been getting "wetter." In 2003, there were 35 completely wet counties and 51 completely dry. In 1995, there were 53 dry counties, and in 1986, there were 62 dry counties. The list below reflects the wet, part wet, and dry coding on the map.

Counties where all alcoholic beverage sales are legal everywhere (59): Aransas, Austin, Bexar, Brazos, Brewster, Brooks, Burnet, Cameron, Childress, Clay, Collingsworth, Colorado, Comal, Cottle, Crane, Crosby, Culberson, Dimmit, Donley, Duval, Ector, El Paso, Fayette, Fisher, Fort Bend, Goliad, Gonzales, Guadalupe, Hidalgo, Hudspeth, Jim Hogg, Kendall, Kenedy, Kerr, Kinney, Kleberg, La Salle, Mason, Midland, Mitchell, Nolan, Nueces, Ochiltree, Presidio, San Saba, Scurry, Sherman, Starr, Sutton, Val Verde, Victoria, Waller, Washington, Webb, Wharton, Wilbarger, Wilson, Zapata, Zavala.

Counties that are partially wet (190): Anderson, Andrews, Angelina, Archer, Armstrong, Atascosa, Bailey, Bandera, Bastrop, Baylor, Bee, Bell, Bosque, Bowie, Brazoria, Blanco, Briscoe, Brown, Burleson, Caldwell, Calhoun, Callahan, Camp, Carson, Cass, Castro, Chambers, Cherokee, Cochran, Coke, Coleman, Collin, Comanche, Concho, Cooke, Coryell, Crockett, Dallam, Dallas, Dawson, Deaf Smith, Delta, Denton, DeWitt, Dickens, Eastland, Edwards, Ellis, Erath, Falls, Fannin, Floyd, Foard, Franklin, Freestone, Frio, Gaines, Galveston, Garza, Gillespie, Glasscock, Gray, Grayson, Gregg, Grimes, Hale, Hall, Hamilton, Hansford, Hardeman, Hardin, Harris, Harrison, Hartley, Haskell, Hays, Henderson, Hill, Hockley, Hood, Hopkins, Houston, Howard, Hunt, Hutchinson, Irion, Jack, Jackson, Jasper, Jeff Davis, Jefferson, Jim Wells, Johnson, Jones, Karnes, Kaufman, Kimble, King, Knox, Lamar, Lamb, Lampasas, Lavaca, Lee, Leon, Liberty, Limestone, Lipscomb, Live Oak, Llano, Loving, Lubbock, Lynn, Madison, Marion, Martin, Matagorda, Maverick, McCulloch, McLennan, McMullen, Medina, Menard, Milam, Mills, Montague, Montgomery, Moore, Morris, Motley, Nacogdoches, Navarro, Newton, Oldham, Orange, Palo Pinto, Panola, Parker, Parmer, Pecos, Polk, Potter, Rains, Randall, Reagan, Real, Red River, Reeves, Refugio, Robertson, Rockwall, Runnels, Rusk, Sabine, San Augustine, San Jacinto, San Patricio, Schleicher, Shackelford, Shelby, Smith, Somervell, Stephens, Sterling, Stonewall, Swisher, Tarrant, Taylor, Terrell, Terry, Titus, Tom Green, Travis, Trinity, Tyler, Upshur, Upton, Uvalde, Van Zandt, Walker, Ward, Wheeler, Wichita, Willacy, Williamson, Winkler, Wise, Wood, Yoakum, Young.

Counties where no sales of alcoholic beverages are legal anywhere (5): Borden, Hemphill, Kent, Roberts, Throckmorton. ☆

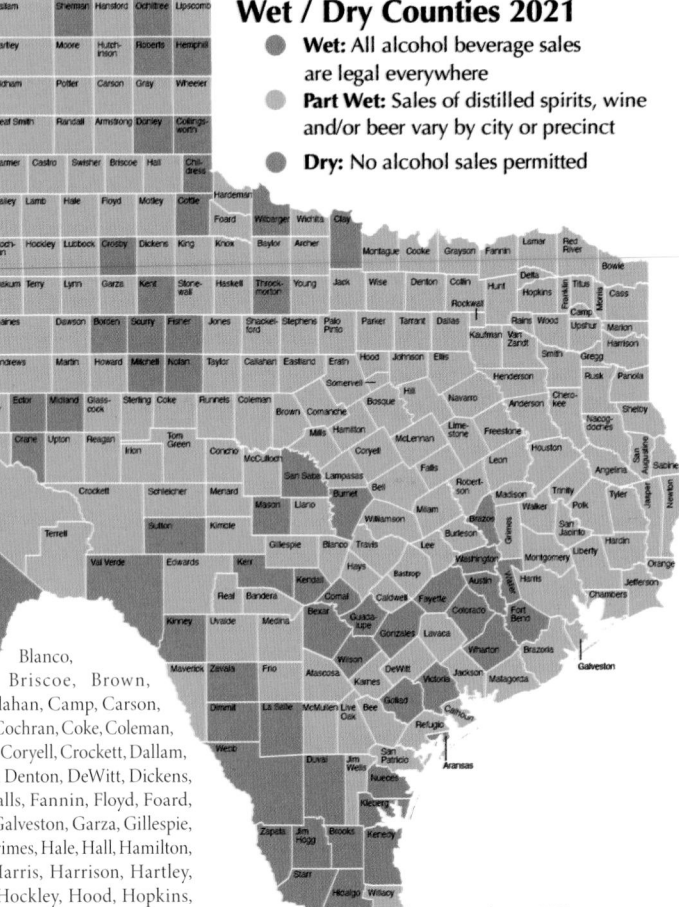

Wet / Dry Counties 2021

● **Wet:** All alcohol beverage sales are legal everywhere

● **Part Wet:** Sales of distilled spirits, wine and/or beer vary by city or precinct

● **Dry:** No alcohol sales permitted

© Texas Almanac 2021

Texas County and District Officials – Table No. 1

County Seats, County Judges, County Clerks, County Attorneys, County Commissioners, County Treasurers, Tax Assessors–Collectors, and Sheriffs

See Table No. 2 on **pages 507–512** for District Attorneys, District Clerks, District Attorneys, and County Commissioners. Judges in county courts at law, as well as probate courts, juvenile/domestic relations courts, county criminal courts, and county criminal courts of appeal, are on **pages 493–495**. The officials listed here are elected by popular vote. If no county attorney is listed, the district attorney, whose name is listed in Table No. 2, assumes the duties of that office.

County	County Seat	County Judge	County Clerk	County Attorney	County Treasurer	Assessor–Collector	Sheriff
Anderson	Palestine	Robert D. Johnston	Mark Staples	—	Tara Holliday	Margie Grissom	W.R. Flores
Andrews	Andrews	Charlie Falcon	Vicki Scott	Sean Galloway	Office abolished 1985.	Robin Harper	Rusty Stewart
Angelina	Lufkin	Don Lymbery	Amy Fincher	Cary Kirby	Jill Brewer	Billie Page	Greg Sanches
Aransas	Rockport	C.H. (Burt) Mills, Jr.	Carrie Arrington	Amanda Oster	Alma Cartwright	Anna Marshall	William (Bill) Mills
Archer	Archer City	Randall C. Jackson	Karren Winter	David Levy	Patricia A. Vieth	Dawn Vieth	Jack Curd
Armstrong	Claude	Hugh Reed	Tawnee Blodgett	—	Susan Overcast McGrath	Jamie Craig	Melissa Anderson
Atascosa	Jourdanton	Robert Hurley	Diane Gonzales	Lucinda A. Vickers	Laura Pawelek	Loretta Holley	David Soward
Austin	Bellville	Tim Lapham	Carrie Gregor	—	Bryan Haevischer	Kim Rinn	Jack Brandes
Bailey	Muleshoe	Sherri Harrison	Robin Dickerson	Jackie R. Claborn, II	Shonda L. Black	Maria Gonzalez	Richard Wills
Bandera	Bandera	Richard Evans	Tandie Mansfield	Janna Lindig	Beverly Schmidt	Rebekah (Reba) Dolphus	Dan Butts
Bastrop	Bastrop	Paul Pape	Rose Pietsch	—	Jo Dawn Bomar	Ellen Owens	Maurice Cook
Baylor	Seymour	Rusty A. Stafford	Chris Jakubicek	Cynthia Ayres-Walker	Kevin Hostas	Jeanette Holub	Sam Mooney
Bee	Beeville	George (Trace) Morill, III	Nickelle Gonzales	Michael Knight	Office abolished 1982.	Michelle Matus	Alden E. Southmayd, III
Bell	Belton	David Blackburn	Shelley Coston	James E. Nichols	Gaylon Evans	Shay Luedeke	Eddy Lange
Bexar	San Antonio	Nelson W. Wolff	Lucy Adame-Clark	Office abolished.	Office abolished 1985.	Albert Uresti	Javier Salazar
Blanco	Johnson City	Brett Bray	Laura Walla	Deborah Earley	Camille Swift	Kristen Spies	Don Jackson
Borden	Gail	Ross D. Sharp	Jana Underwood	Marlo Holbrooks	Shawna Gass	Benny Allison	Benny Allison
Bosque	Meridian	Cindy Vanlandingham	Tab Ferguson	Natalie Koehler	Carla Sigler	Arlene Swiney	Trace Hendricks
Bowie	New Boston	Bobby Howell	Tina Petty	—	Donna Burns	Josh Davis	Jeff Neal
Brazoria	Angleton	L.M. (Matt) Sebesta, Jr.	Joyce Hudman	—	Cathy Campbell	Kristin R. Bulanek	Bo Stallman
Brazos	Bryan	Duane Peters	Karen McQueen	Earl Gray	Laura Taylor Davis	Kristeen Roe	Wayne Dicky
Brewster	Alpine	Eleazar R. Cano	Sarah Vasquez	J. Steve Houston	Julie K. Morton	Sylvia Vega	Ronny Dodson
Briscoe	Silverton	Wayne Nance	Bena Hester	Emily Teegardin	Mary Jo Brannon	Jon Etta Ziegler	Garrett Davis
Brooks	Falfurrias	Eric Ramos	Elvaray B. Silvas	David T. Garcia	Alan Hernandez	Urbino (Benny) Martinez	Urbino (Benny) Martinez
Brown	Brownwood	Paul D. Lilly	Sharon Ferguson	Shane Britton	Ann Krpoun	Christine Pentecost	Vance Hill
Burleson	Caldwell	Keith Schroeder	Anna L. Schielack	Susan Deski	Stephanie Smith	Jessica Lucero	Gene Hermes
Burnet	Burnet	James Oakley	Janet Parker	Eddie Arredondo	Karrie Crownover	Sheri Frazier	Calvin Boyd
Caldwell	Lockhart	Hoppy Haden	Teresa Rodriguez	—	Angela Meuth Rawlinson	Darla Law	Mike Lane
Calhoun	Port Lavaca	Richard Meyer	Anna Goodman	—	Rhonda Kokena	Kerri Boyd	Bobbie Vickery
Callahan	Baird	G. Scott Kniffen	Nicole Crocker	Shane Deel	Ian Windham	Tammy Walker	Eric Pechacek
Cameron	Brownsville	Eddie Treviño, Jr.	Sylvia Garza-Perez	Luis V. Saenz	David A. Betancourt	Tony Yzaguirre, Jr.	Eric Garza
Camp	Pittsburg	A.J. Mason	Elaine Young	James W. Wallace, III	Kim Pittman	Missy Huffman	John Cortelyou
Carson	Panhandle	Dan Looten	Celeste Bichsel	Scott Sherwood	Denise Salzbrenner	Jackie Moore	Tam Terry
Cass	Linden	Becky Wilbanks	Amy L. Varnell	—	Melissa Shores	Angela Young	Larry Rowe
Castro	Dimmitt	Carroll Gerber	JoAnna Blanco	Shalyn Hamlin	Elaine D. Flynt	Pam Rickert	Salvador Rivera
Chambers	Anahuac	Jimmy Sylvia	Heather Hawthorne	Ashley Cain Land	Nicole M. Whittington	Denise Hutter	Brian C. Hawthorne
Cherokee	Rusk	Chris Davis	Laverne Lusk	Dana Young	Erin Curtis	Shonda McCutcheon Potter	Brent Dickson

County	County Seat	County Judge	County Clerk	County Attorney	County Treasurer	Assessor-Collector	Sheriff
Childress	Childress	Jay Mayden	Barbara Spitzer	Greg Buckley	Brenda Overstreet	Kathy Dobbs	Michael (Mike) Pigg
Clay	Henrietta	Mike Campbell	Sasha Kelton	Seth C. Slagle	Danja Bloodworth	Maribel Longoria	Jeffrey C. Lyde
Cochran	Morton	Pat Sabala Henry	Lisa Smith	Amanda Martin	Doris Sealy	Treva Jackson	Jorge De La Cruz
Coke	Robert Lee	Hal Spain	Monica Reyes	Nicholas E. Arrott, II	Therese Emert	Josie Dean	Wayne McCutchen
Coleman	Coleman	Billy D. Bledsoe	Stacey Mendoza	Hayden J. Wise	Jerri Ann Wilson	Jamie Dodgen	Les Cogdill
Collin	McKinney	Chris Hill	Stacey Kemp	—	—	Kenneth Maun	Jim Skinner
Collingsworth	Wellington	John A. James	Jackie Johnson	Gaylon Davis	Gina Harris	Sharon Chism	Kent Riley
Colorado	Columbus	Ty Prause	Kimberly Menke	Jay E. Johannes	Joyce Guthmann	Erica Kollaja	R.H. (Curly) Wied
Comal	New Braunfels	Sherman Krause	Bobbie Koepp	—	Renee Couch	Kristen H. Hoyt	Mark Reynolds
Comanche	Comanche	Stephanie L. Davis	Ruby Lesley	Craig Willingham	Patsy Phifer	Grace Everhart	Chris Pounds
Concho	Paint Rock	David Dillard	Phyllis F. Lovell	Bryan Clayton	Jenifer Gierisch	Chad Miller	Chad Miller
Cooke	Gainesville	Steve Starnes	Pam Harrison	Edmund J Zielinski	Patty Brennan	Brandy Ann Carr	Ray Sappington
Coryell	Gatesville	Roger A. Miller	Barbara Simpson	Brandon Belt	Randi McFarlin	Justin K. Carothers	Scott Williams
Cottle	Paducah	Karl Holloway	Vickey Wederski	Greg Buckley	Crystal Tucker	Nakia Hargrave	Mark Box
Crane	Crane	Roy Hodges	Janie Macias	Austin Rawls	Sheila Pahl	Judy Crumrine	Andrew Aguilar
Crockett	Ozona	Fred Deaton	Ninfa Preddy	Jody K. Upham	Laura Conner	Michelle M. Medley	Antonio Alejandro, III
Crosby	Crosbyton	Rusty Forbes	Tammy Marshall	Michael Sales	Debra Riley	Michele Cook	Ethan Villanueva
Culberson	Van Horn	Carlos G. Urias	Linda McDonald	Stephen Mitchell	Adrian Hinojos	Jose Morales	Oscar Carrillo
Dallam	Dalhart	Wes Ritchey	Terri Banks	Whitney Hill	Kenda McKay	Jami Parr	Shane Stevenson
Dallas	Dallas	Clay Jenkins	John F. Warren	—	Pauline Medrano	John R. Ames	Marian Brown
Dawson	Lamesa	Foy O'Brien	Clare Christy	Steven B. Payson	Terri Stahl	Sylvia Ortiz	Matt Hogg
Deaf Smith	Hereford	D.J. Wagner	Rachel Garman	—	Karen Smith	Teresa Garth	J. Dale Butler
Delta	Cooper	Jason Murray	Jane Jones	Jay Garrett	Debbie Huie	Dawn Stewart	Charla Singleton
Denton	Denton	Andy Eads	Juli Luke	—	Cindy Yeatts Brown	Michelle French	Tracy Murphree
DeWitt	Cuero	Daryl L. Fowler	Natalie Carson	A. Jay Condie	Carol Ann Martin	Ashley D. Mraz	Carl Bowen
Dickens	Dickens	Kevin Brendle	Becky Hill	Aaron Clements	Darla Thomason	Rebecca Haney	Terry Braly
Dimmit	Carrizo Springs	Francisco G. Ponce	Mario E. Garcia	Daniel Gonzalez	Estanislado Martinez	Mary E. Sandoval	Marion Boyd
Donley	Clarendon	John C. Howard	Vicky Tunnell	Landon Lambert	Wanda Smith	Kristy Christopher	Charles (Butch) Blackburn
Duval	San Diego	Gilbert N. Saenz	Elodia M. Garza	Baldemar Gutierrez	Sylvia Lazo	Roberto Elizondo	Romeo R. Ramirez
Eastland	Eastland	Rex Fields	Cathy Jentho	—	Christina Dodrill	Andrea May	Jason Weger
Ector	Odessa	Debi Hays	Jennifer Martin	Gregory Barber	Cleopatra Anderson-Callaway	Lindy Wright	Mike Griffis
Edwards	Rocksprings	Souli Asa Shanklin	Olga Lydia Reyes	Allen Ray Moody	Lupe S. Enriquez	Lorri Garcia Ruiz	James W. Guthrie
Ellis	Waxahachie	Todd Little	Krystal Valdez	Ann Montgomery	Cheryl Chambers	Richard Rozier	Brad Norman
El Paso	El Paso	Ricardo A. Samaniego	Delia Briones	Jo Anne Bernal	Office abolished 1989.	Ruben P. Gonzalez	Richard Wiles
Erath	Stephenville	Alfonso Campos	Gwinda Jones	Lisa Pence	Kimberly Barrier	Jennifer Carey	Matt Coates
Falls	Marlin	Jay Elliott	Elizabeth Perez	Kathryn (Jody) Gilliam	Sheryl Pringle	Kayci Nehring	Joe Lopez
Fannin	Bonham	Randy Moore	Tammy Biggar	Richard Glaser	David E. Woodson	Gail Young	Mark Johnson
Fayette	La Grange	Joe Weber	Brenda Fietsam	Peggy Supak	Office abolished 11-3-87.	Sylvia Mendoza	Keith Korenek
Fisher	Roby	Ken Holt	Pat Thomson	Michael Hall	Jeanna Parks	Jonnye Lu Gibson	Randy Ford
Floyd	Floydada	Marty Lucke	Ginger Morgan	Lex Herrington	Lori Morales	Delia Suarez	Paul Raissez
Foard	Crowell	Mark Christopher	Debra Hopkins	Marshall Capps	Darcy Moore	Mike Brown	Mike Brown
Fort Bend	Richmond	KP George	Laura Richard	Bridgette Smith-Lawson	Bill Rickert	Carmen P. Turner	Eric Fagan
Franklin	Mount Vernon	Scott Lee	Betty Crane	Landon Ramsay	Betty Sue Allen	Sue Ann Harper	Ricky Jones

County	County Seat	County Judge	County Clerk	County Attorney	County Treasurer	Assessor–Collector	Sheriff
Freestone	Fairfield	Linda Grant	Linda Jarvis	Brian Evans	Jeannie Keeney	Daniel M. Ralstin	Jeremy Shipley
Frio	Pearsall	Arnulfo C. Luna	Aaron Tomas Ibarra	Joseph Sindon	Pete Jasso Martinez	Anna Alaniz	Michael (Mike) Morse
Gaines	Seminole	Tom Keyes	Terri Berry	Joe H. Nagy, Jr.	Michael Lord, Jr.	Susan Shaw	Ronny Pipkin
Galveston	Galveston	Mark Henry	Dwight D. Sullivan	—	Kevin C. Walsh	Cheryl E. Johnson	Henry Trochesset
Garza	Post	Lee Norman	Jim Plummer	Ted Weems	LuAnne Terry	Nancy Wallace	Terry Morgan
Gillespie	Fredericksburg	Mark Stroeher	Mary Lynn Rusche	Steven A. Wadsworth	Kelly Eckhardt	Vicki I. Schmidt	Buddy Mills
Glasscock	Garden City	Billy Ray Reynolds	Rebecca Batla	Hardy Wilkerson	Alan Dierschke	Tina Flores	Keith Burnett
Goliad	Goliad	Mike Bennett	Mary Ellen Flores	Rob Baiamonte	Bryan Howard	Michelle Garcia	Roy Boyd
Gonzales	Gonzales	Patrick C. Davis	Lona Ackman	Paul Watkins	Sheryl Barborak	Crystal Cedillo	Robert Ynclan
Gray	Pampa	Chris Porter	Jeanne Horton	Josh Seabourn	Scott Hahn	Gaye Whitehead	Michael Ryan
Grayson	Sherman	Bill Magers	Deana Patterson	—	Gayla Hawkins	Bruce Stidham	Tom Watt
Gregg	Longview	Bill Stoudt	Michelle Gilley	—	Office abolished 1-1-1988.	Kirk Shields	Maxey Cerliano
Grimes	Anderson	Joe Fauth, III	Vanessa Burzynski	Jon C. Fultz	Tom Maynard	Mary Ann Waters	Donald G. Sowell
Guadalupe	Seguin	Kyle Kutscher	Teresa Kiel	Dave Willborn	Linda Douglass	Daryl John	Arnold S. Zwicke
Hale	Plainview	David Mull	Latrice Kemp	Jim Tirey	Ida A. Tyler	Roland Nash	David Cochran
Hall	Memphis	Ray Powell	Olivia M. Fisher	Harley Caudle	Janet Bridges	Teresa Altman	Tom Heck
Hamilton	Hamilton	W. Mark Tynes	Cynthia K. Puff	Mark Henkes	Shawna Dyer	Terry Payne Short	Justin Caraway
Hansford	Spearman	Benny D. Wilson	Janet Torres	Cheryl Nelson	Lynn French	Linda Cummings	Robert Mahaffee
Hardeman	Quanah	Ronald Ingram	Ellen London	Stanley Watson	Traysha Newsom	Ian Evans	Pat Laughery
Hardin	Kountze	Wayne McDaniel	Glenda Alston	Matthew Minick	Deborah McWilliams	Shirley Cook	Mark Davis
Harris	Houston	Lina Hidalgo	Teneshia Hudspeth	Christian D. Menefee	Dylan Osborne	Ann Harris Bennett	Ed Gonzalez
Harrison	Marshall	Chad Sims	Liz James	—	Sherry Rushing	Veronica King	Brandon (BJ) Fletcher
Hartley	Channing	Ronnie Gordon	Melissa Mead	Robert Elliott	Dinkie Parman	Chanze Fowler	Chanze Fowler
Haskell	Haskell	Kenny Thompson	Belia Abila	Kris Fouts	Stacia Leach	Connie Benton	David Halliburton
Hays	San Marcos	Ruben Becerra	Elaine Cárdenas	—	Britney Bolton Richey	Jenifer O'Kane	Gary Cutler
Hemphill	Canadian	George Briant	Lisa Johnson	Kyle Miller	Kay Smallwood	Chris Jackson	Brent Clapp
Henderson	Athens	Wade McKinney	Mary Margaret Wright	Clint Davis	Michael Bynum	Peggy Goodall	Botie Hillhouse
Hidalgo	Edinburg	Richard F. Cortez	Arturo Guajardo, Jr.	—	Lita Leo	Pablo (Paul) Villarreal, Jr.	J.E. (Eddie) Guerra
Hill	Hillsboro	Justin Lewis	Nicole Tanner	David Holmes	Rhonda Burkhart	Krissi Hightower	Rodney B. Watson
Hockley	Levelland	Sharla Baldridge	Jennifer Nicole Palermo	Anna Hord	Denise Bohannon	Debra C. Bramlett	Ray Scifres
Hood	Granbury	Ron Massingill	Katie Lang	Matthew A. Mills	Leigh Ann McCoy	Andrea Ferguson	Roger Deeds
Hopkins	Sulphur Springs	Robert Newsom	Tracy Smith	Dusty Rabe	Danny Davis	Debbie Pogue Mitchell	Lewis Tatum
Houston	Crockett	Jim L. Lovell	Terri Meadows	Daphne Lynette Session	Janis Omelina	Danette Millican	Randy Hargrove
Howard	Big Spring	Kathryn Wiseman	Brent Zitterkopf	Joshua Hamby	Sharon Adams	Tiffany Sayles	Stan Parker
Hudspeth	Sierra Blanca	Thomas D. Neely	Brenda Sanchez	Mary Anne Bramblett	Blanca Santana	Patricia Rose	Arvin West
Hunt	Greenville	Bobby W. Stovall	Jennifer Lindenzweig	G. Calvin Grogan	Brittni Turner	Randy L. Wineinger	Terry Jones
Hutchinson	Stinnett	Cindy Irwin	Jan Barnes	Craig Jones	Kathy Sargent	Carrie Kimmell	Blaik Kemp
Irion	Mertzon	Molly Criner	Shirley Graham	James Ridge	Carolyn Huelster	Joyce Gray	W.A. Estes
Jack	Jacksboro	Brian Keith Umphress	Vanessa James	Michael Brad Dixon	Brad Campsey	Sharon Robinson	Thomas Spurlock
Jackson	Edna	Jill S. Sklar	Katherine R. Brooks	—	Mary Horton	Monica Foltz	A.J. (Andy) Louderback
Jasper	Jasper	Mark Allen	Debbie Newman	—	Rene Kelley-Ellis	Bobby Biscamp	Mitchel Newman
Jeff Davis	Fort Davis	Curtis Evans	Jennifer Wright	Teresa L. Todd	Dawn Kitts	William (Bill) Kitts	William (Bill) Kitts
Jefferson	Beaumont	Jeff Branick	Theresa Goodness	—	Charlie Hallmark	Allison Nathan Getz	Zena Stephens
Jim Hogg	Hebbronville	Juan Carlos Guerra	Zonia G. Morales	Rodolfo Gutierrez	Gloria (Gigi) Benavides	Norma Liza S. Hinojosa	Erasmo Alarcon, Jr.

County	County Seat	County Judge	County Clerk	County Attorney	County Treasurer	Assessor–Collector	Sheriff
Jim Wells	Alice	Juan Rodriguez, Jr.	J.C. Perez, III	Michael Guerra	Mark Dominguez	Mary Lozano	Danny Bueno
Johnson	Cleburne	Roger Harmon	Becky Ivey	Bill Moore	Kathy Blackwell	Scott Porter	Adam King
Jones	Anson	Dale Spurgin	LeeAnn Jennings	Chad Cowan	Sandy Taber	Gloria Little	Danny Jimenez
Karnes	Karnes City	Wade J. Hedtke	Carol Swize	Jennifer M. Dillingham	Vi Swierc	Tammy Braudaway	Dwayne Villanueva
Kaufman	Kaufman	Hal Richards	Laura Hughes		Chuck Mohnkern	Brenda Samples	Bryan Beavers
Kendall	Boerne	Darrel L. Lux	Darlene Herrin		Sheryl D'Spain	James Hudson	Al Auxier
Kenedy	Sarita	Louis E. (Bud) Turcotte, III	Veronica Vela	Allison Strauss	Cynthia M. Salinas	Irma G. Longoria	Ramon Salinas, III
Kent	Jayton	Jim White	Craig Harrison	Katie Lackey	Christy Long	William Scogin	William Scogin
Kerr	Kerrville	Rob Kelly	Jackie (JD) Dowdy	Heather Stebbins	Tracy Soldan	Bob Reeves	Larry Leitha
Kimble	Junction	Delbert R. Roberts	Haydee Torres	Andrew James Heap	Jolene Williams	Allen Castleberry	Allen Castleberry
King	Guthrie	Duane Lee Daniel	Jammye D. Timmons	George (Trey) Poage	Maggie Oliver	Amy McCauley	Michael R. McWhirter
Kinney	Brackettville	Tully Shahan	Rick Alvarado	Brent Smith	Diana Gutierrez	Martha Peña-Padron	Brad Coe
Kleberg	Kingsville	Rudy Madrid	Stephanie G. Garza	Kira Talip Sanchez	Priscilla Alaniz Cantu	Maria Victoria Valadez	Richard Kirkpatrick
Knox	Benjamin	Stan Wojcik	Lisa Cypert	Lina Reyes Trevino	Julie Bradley	Penny Eaton	Hunter Embesi
Lamar	Paris	Brandon Bell	Ruth Sisson	Gary Young	Camey Boyer	Haskell Maroney	Scott Cass
Lamb	Littlefield	James M. DeLoach	Tonya Ritchie	Scott A. Say	Jerry Yarbrough	Brenda Goheen	Gary Maddox
Lampasas	Lampasas	Randall J. Hoyer	Connie Hartmann	John K. Greenwood	Melissa Karcher	Betty Salinas	Jesus (Jess) G. Ramos
La Salle	Cotulla	Joel Rodriguez, Jr.	Margarita Esqueda	Elizabeth Martinez	Maria Perez	Dora A. Gonzales	Anthony Zertuche
Lavaca	Hallettsville	Mark Myers	Elizabeth A. Kouba	Kyle A. Denney	Karen Bludau	Deborah A. Sevcik	Micah Harmon
Lee	Giddings	Paul E. Fischer	Sharon Blasig	Martin Placke	Melinda (Lyndy) Krause	David Matthietz	Casey Goetz
Leon	Centerville	Byron Ryder	Christie Wakefield	Keith Cook	Brandi S. Hill	Robin Shafer	Kevin Ellis
Liberty	Liberty	Jay H. Knight	Lee Haidusek Chambers	Matthew Poston	Kim Harris	Richard Brown	Robert (Bobby) Rader
Limestone	Groesbeck	Richard Duncan	Kerrie Cobb	William Roy DeFriend	Carol Pickett	Stacy L. Hall	Murray Agnew
Lipscomb	Lipscomb	Mickey Simpson	Kim Blau	Matthew D. Bartosiewicz	Kimberly L. Long	Gailan Winegarner	John Worthington
Live Oak	George West	Jim Huff	Ida Vasquez	Dwayne McWilliams	Kitley Moffatt-Wasicek	Deanna Atkinson	Larry Busby
Llano	Llano	Ron Cunningham	Marci Hadeler	Dwain K. Rogers	Teresa Kassell	Kris Fogelberg	Bill Blackburn
Loving	Mentone	Skeet Lee Jones	Mozelle Carr	Stephen Simonsen	Regina Wilkinson	Chris H. Busse	Chris H. Busse
Lubbock	Lubbock	Curtis Parrish	Kelly Pinion	Chris Winn		Ronnie Keister	Kelly S. Rowe
Lynn	Tahoka	Mike Braddock	Karen Strickland	Rebekah Filley	Amy Schuknecht	Donna Willis	Wanda Mason
Madison	Madisonville	A.J. (Tony) Leago	Susanne Morris		Judi Delesandri	Karen M. Lane	Bobby Adams
Marion	Jefferson	Leward J. LaFleur	Vickie Smith	Angela Smoak	Terrie S. Neuville	Karen Jones	David Capps
Martin	Stanton	Bryan Cox	Linda Gonzales	James Napper	Cynthia O'Donnell	Kathy Hull	Brad Ingram
Mason	Mason	Jerry Bearden	Pam Beam	Rebekah Whitworth	Polly McMillan	Joe Lancaster	Joe Lancaster
Matagorda	Bay City	Nate McDonald	Stephanie Wurtz	Jennifer Chau	Loretta K. Griffin	Becky Cook	Frank D. Osborne
Maverick	Eagle Pass	David Saucedo	Sara Montemayor	Jaime A. Iracheta	Rito Valdez	Isamari Villarreal	Tom Schmerber
McCulloch	Brady	Frank Trull	Christine A. Jones	Mark Marshall	Mikkie Williams	Silvia Campos	Matt Andrews
McLennan	Waco	Scott Felton	Andy Harwell		Bill Helton	Randy H. Riggs	Parnell McNamara
McMullen	Tilden	James E. Teal	Mattie S. Sadovsky	Kimberly Kreider-Dusek	Jill Atkinson	Bessilia (Bessie) Guerrero	Emmett Shelton
Medina	Hondo	Chris Schuchart	Gina Champion		Debbie Southwell	Melissa Lutz	Randy Brown
Menard	Menard	Brandon Corbin	Christy Eggleston	Luke Davis	Ron Wood	Tim Powell	Buck Miller
Midland	Midland	Terry Johnson	Alison Haley	Russell Malm	Mitzi Baker	Karen Hood	David Criner
Milam	Cameron	Steve Young	Jodi Morgan	Bill Torrey	Linda Acosta	Sherry Mueck	Mike Clore
Mills	Goldthwaite	Ed Smith	Sonya Scott	Gerald Hale	Summer Campbell	Lori King	Clint Hammonds

County	County Seat	County Judge	County Clerk	County Attorney	County Treasurer	Assessor–Collector	Sheriff
Mitchell	Colorado City	Mark Merrell	Carla Kern	Sterling T. Burleson, II	Jennifer Rivera	Sylvia Clanton	Patrick Toombs
Montague	Montague	Kevin Benton	Kim Jones	Clay V. Riddle	Jennifer Fenoglio	Kathryn Phillips	Marshall Thomas
Montgomery	Conroe	Mark J. Keough	Mark Turnbull	B.D. Griffin	Melanie K. Bush	Tammy J. McRae	Rand Henderson
Moore	Dumas	Rowdy Rhoades	Brenda McKanna	Scott Higginbotham	Kara Milligan	Chris A. Rivera	Morgan W. Hightower
Morris	Daingerfield	Doug Reeder	Scott Sartain	Ricky Shelton	Molly Cummings	Kim Thomasson	Jack Martin
Motley	Matador	James B. (Jim) Meador	Dianna Russell	Tom Edwards	Misty Jones	Ronda Miller	Robert Fisk
Nacogdoches	Nacogdoches	Greg Sowell	June Clifton	John Fleming	Denise Baublet	Kim Morton	Jason Bridges
Navarro	Corsicana	H.M. Davenport, Jr.	Sherry Dowd	—	Ryan Douglas	Mike Dowd	Elmer Tanner
Newton	Newton	Kenneth Weeks	Sandra K. Duckworth	—	Ginger Sims	Melissa J. Burks	Robert Burby
Nolan	Sweetwater	Whitley May	Sharla Keith	Samantha Morrow	Jeanne Wells	Kathy Bowen	David Warren
Nueces	Corpus Christi	Barbara Canales	Kara Sands	Jenny P. Dorsey	Office abolished 11-3-87.	Kevin Kieschnick	J.C. Hooper
Ochiltree	Perryton	Charles E. Kelly	Jeri Ann McGarraugh	Jose N. Meraz	Britney Meraz	Linda Womble	Terry Bouchard
Oldham	Vega	Don R. Allred	Darla Lookingbill	Kent Birdsong	Sherri Johnson	Linda Brown	Brent Warden
Orange	Orange	John Gothia	Brandy Robertson	John Kimbrough	Christy Khoury	Karen Fisher	Jimmy Lane Mooney
Palo Pinto	Palo Pinto	Shane Long	Janette K. Green	Maegan Kostiha	Tanya Fallin	Stacy L. Choate	Brett E. McGuire
Panola	Carthage	LeeAnn Jones	Bobbie Davis	—	Joni Reed	Holly Gibbs	Sarah Fields
Parker	Weatherford	Pat Deen	Lila Deakle	John Forrest	Jenny Barnwell	Jenny Gentry	Russ Authier
Parmer	Farwell	Trey Ellis	Susie Spring	Jeff W. Actkinson	Sharon May	Awyna Sanchez	Randy Geries
Pecos	Fort Stockton	Joe Shuster	Liz Chapman	Frank Lacy	Sonia Murphy	Santa Acosta	TJ Perkins
Polk	Livingston	Sydney Murphy	Schelana Hock	—	Terri Williams	Leslie Jones Burks	Byron A. Lyons
Potter	Amarillo	Nancy Tanner	Julie Smith	Scott Brumley	Leann Jennings	Sherri Aylor	Brian Thomas
Presidio	Marfa	Cinderela Guevara	Flor Zubia	Rod Ponton	Frances Garcia	Natalia Williams	Danny Dominguez
Rains	Emory	Wayne Wolfe	Linda Wallace	Robert Vititow	Teresa Northcutt	Sheila Floyd	David Traylor
Randall	Canyon	Christy Dyer	Susan Allen	—	Angie Parker	Christina McMurray	Christopher Forbis
Reagan	Big Lake	Jim O'Bryan	Terri Curry	Michele Dodd	Ginna Hruska	Cynthia Aguilar	Jeff N. Garner
Real	Leakey	Bella A. Rubio	D'Ann Green	Bobby Jack Rushing	Mairi Gray	Terrie Pendley	Nathan T. Johnson
Red River	Clarksville	L.D. Williamson	Shawn Weemes	Val Varley	Sandra Embrey	Tonya R. Martin	Jimmy Caldwell
Reeves	Pecos	Leo Hung	Dianne O. Florez	Alva Alvarez	Zulema Rodriguez	Rosemary Chabarria	Arturo (Art) Granado
Refugio	Refugio	Robert Blaschke	Ida Ramirez	Deborah A. Bauer	Rita Trojcak	Ida Turner	Raul (Pinky) Gonzales
Roberts	Miami	Rick L. Tennant	Toni Rankin	William P. Weiman	Amy Tennant	Hether Williams	Bruce Skidmore
Robertson	Franklin	Charles L. Ellison	Stephanie M. Sanders	W. Coty Siegert	Melinda Turner	Michael (Duba) Brewer	Gerald Yezak
Rockwall	Rockwall	David Sweet	Jennifer Fogg	—	David Peek	Kim Sweet	Terry Garrett
Runnels	Ballinger	Barry Hilliard	Julia Miller	Ben Clayton	Ann Strube	Robin Burgess	Carl L. Squyres
Rusk	Henderson	Joel Hale	Trudy McGill	Micheal E. Jimerson	Andy Vinson	Nesha Partin	Johnwayne Valdez
Sabine	Hemphill	Daryl Melton	Jamie Clark	Robert G. Neal, Jr.	Tricia Jacks	Martha M. Stone	Thomas N. Maddox
San Augustine	San Augustine	Jeff Boyd	Margo Noble	Wesley Hoyt	Pam Smith	Regina Barthol	Robert Cartwright
San Jacinto	Coldspring	Fritz Faulkner	Dawn Wright	—	Dianna (Dee Dee) Adams	Betty Davis	Greg Capers
San Patricio	Sinton	David Krebs	Gracie Alaniz-Gonzales	Tamara Cochran-May	Denise Janak	Marcela Thormaehlen	Oscar Rivera
San Saba	San Saba	Byron Theodosis	Kim Wells	Randall Robinson	Lois VanBeck	David Jenkins	David Jenkins
Schleicher	Eldorado	Charlie Bradley	Mary Ann Gonzalez	Clint T. Griffin	Jennifer L. Henderson	Vanessa Covarrubiaz	Jason Chatham
Scurry	Snyder	Dan Hicks	Melody Appleton	Michael Hartman	Kirsta Koennecke	Jana Young	Trey Wilson
Shackelford	Albany	Robert Skelton	Cheri Hawkins	Rollin Rauschl	Tammy Brown	Edward A. Miller	Edward A. Miller
Shelby	Center	Allison Harbison	Jennifer Fountain	Gary W. Rholes	Ann Blackwell	Debora Riley	Kevin Windham
Sherman	Stratford	Terri Beth Carter	Laura Rogers	Kim Allen	Alicia Law	Valerie McAlister	Ted Allen

County	County Seat	County Judge	County Clerk	County Attorney	County Treasurer	Assessor–Collector	Sheriff
Smith	Tyler	Nathaniel Moran	Karen Phillips	—	Kelli R. White	Gary Barber	Larry Smith
Somervell	Glen Rose	Danny L. Chambers	Michelle Reynolds	Andrew Lucas	Susanne Graves	April Campos	Alan West
Starr	Rio Grande City	Eloy Vera	Humberto Gonzalez	Victor Canales, Jr.	Romeo Gonzalez	Ameida Salinas	Rene (Orta) Fuentes
Stephens	Breckenridge	Michael Roach	Jackie Ensey	Gary Trammel	Sharon Trigg	Christie Latham	Kevin Roach
Sterling	Sterling City	Deborah Horwood	Terri McCutchen	Lilli Hensley	Rhea McGinnis	Julie McEntire	Tim A. Sanders
Stonewall	Aspermont	Ronnie Moorhead	Holly McLaury	Riley Branch	Anya Mullen	Jim B. Ward	William (Bill) Mullen
Sutton	Sonora	Rachel Chavez Duran	Pam Thorp	Dawn B. Cahill	Janell Schniers	Kathy Sanchez Marshall	Oscar Chavez
Swisher	Tulia	Harold Keeter	C.J. Chasco	J. Michael Criswell	Tricia Speer	Deborah Lemons	Jim McCaslin
Tarrant	Fort Worth	B. Glen Whitley	Mary Louise Nicholson		Office abolished 4-2-83	Wendy Burgess	Bill E. Waybourn
Taylor	Abilene	Downing A. Bolls, Jr.	Larry Bevill		Lesa Hart Crosswhite	Kay Middleton	Ricky Bishop
Terrell	Sanderson	Dale Lynn Carruthers	Raeline Thompson	Kenneth D. Bellah	Rebecca Luevano	Santiago Gonzalez, Jr.	Santiago Gonzalez, Jr.
Terry	Brownfield	J.D. Wagner	Kim Carter	JoShae Ferguson-Worley	Karen Grigsby	Rexann W. Furlow	Timothy Click
Throckmorton	Throckmorton	Trey Carrington	Dianna Moore	Kris Fouts	Brenda Rankin	Doc Wigington	Doc Wigington
Titus	Mount Pleasant	Brian P. Lee	Joan Newman	John Mark Cobern	Sheryl Preddy	Melissa Stevens	Tim C. Ingram
Tom Green	San Angelo	Stephen C. Floyd	Christina Ubando	Chris Taylor	Dianna Spieker	Becky Robles	J. Nick Hanna
Travis	Austin	Andy Brown	Dana DeBeauvoir	Delia Garza	Dolores Ortega Carter	Bruce Elfant	Sally Hernandez
Trinity	Groveton	Doug Page	Shasta Bergman	Colton Hay	B.L. Dockens	Nancy Shanafelt	Woody Wallace
Tyler	Woodville	Jacques L. Blanchette	Donece Gregory		Leann Monk	Lynnette Cruse	Bryan Weatherford
Upshur	Gilmer	Todd Tefteller	Terri Ross		Brandy Vick	Luana Howell	Larry Webb
Upton	Rankin	Dusty Kilgore	LaWanda McMurray	Paige Skehan	Vivian Venegas	Monica Zarate	Dan Brown
Uvalde	Uvalde	William R. Mitchell	Valerie Del Toro Romero	John Dodson	Joni Deorsam	Rita C. Verstuyft	Ruben Nolasco
Val Verde	Del Rio	Lewis Owens	Generosa Gracia-Ramon	David E. Martinez	Aaron D. Rodriguez	Elodia Garcia	Joe Frank Martinez
Van Zandt	Canton	Don Kirkpatrick	Susan Strickland		Kenny Edwards	Misty Stanberry	Steve Hendrix
Victoria	Victoria	Ben Zeller	Heidi Easley		Sean Kennedy	Ashley Hernandez	Justin Marr
Walker	Huntsville	Danny Pierce	Kari French	Elton Mathis	Amy Klawinsky	Diana L. McRae	Clint McRae
Waller	Hempstead	Carbett (Trey) J. Duhon, III	Debbie Hollan	Alan Nicholas	Joan Sargent	Ellen C. Shelburne	Troy Guidry
Ward	Monahans	Greg M. Holly	Denise Valles		Carleigh Ennis	Vicki Heflin	Franin Vale
Washington	Brenham	John Durrenberger	Beth A. Rothermel	Renee Ann Mueller	Peggy Kramer	Cheryl Gaskamp	Otto H. Hanak
Webb	Laredo	Tano E. Tijerina	Margie Ramirez Ibarra	Marco A. Montemayor	Raul Reyes	Patricia Barrera	Martin Cuellar
Wharton	Wharton	Phillip Spenrath	Barbara Svatek	G.A. (Trey) Maffett	Donna Thornton	Cindy Hernandez	Shannon Srubar
Wheeler	Wheeler	Terry Hefley	Margaret Dorman	Leslie Standerfer	Renee Warren	Cindy Brown	Johnny G. Carter
Wichita	Wichita Falls	Woodrow W. Gossom, Jr.	Lori Bohannon		Bob Hampton	Tommy Smyth	David Duke
Wilbarger	Vernon	Greg Tyra	Jana Kennon	Cornell Curtis	Joann Carter	Sherrie Campsey	Brian Fritze
Willacy	Raymondville	Aurelio (Keter) Guerra	Susana R. Garza	Annette C. Hinojosa	Ruben Cavazos	Elizabeth Barnhart	Joe Salazar
Williamson	Georgetown	Bill Gravell, Jr.	Nancy E. Rister	Doyle (Dee) Hobbs, Jr.	D. Scott Heselmeyer	Larry Gaddes	Mike Gleason
Wilson	Floresville	Richard L. Jackson	Eva S. Martinez	Tom Caldwell	Jan Hartl	Dawn Polasek Barnett	Jim Stewart
Winkler	Kermit	Charles M. Wolf	Pam Greene	Thomas Duckworth, Jr.	Susan Willhelm	Minerva Soltero	Darin Mitchell
Wise	Decatur	J.D. Clark	Sherry Lemon	James Stainton	Katherine Hudson	Monte Shaw	Lane Akin
Wood	Quitman	Lucy Hebron	Kelley Price		Becky S. Burford	Carol Taylor	Kelly Cole
Yoakum	Plains	Jim Barron	Summer Lovelace		Darla Welch	Ian Parrish	David Bryant
Young	Graham	John C. Bullock	Kay Hardin	Chris Baran	Ann Daily	Christy Centers	Travis Babcock
Zapata	Zapata	Joe Rathmell	Mary Jayne Villarreal-Bonoan	Said Alfonso Figueroa	Romeo Salinas	Delia Mendoza	Raymundo Del Bosque
Zavala	Crystal City	Joe Luna	Michelle Bonilla	Eduardo Serna	Elizabeth Tovar	Cindy Martinez-Rivera	Eusevio Salinas

Texas County and District Officials — Table No. 2

District Clerks, District Attorneys, and County Commissioners

See Table No. 1 on **pages 501–506** for County Seats, County Judges, County Clerks, County Attorneys, County Treasurers, Tax Assessors-Collectors, and Sheriffs. Judges in county courts at law, as well as probate courts, juvenile/domestic relations courts, county criminal courts, and county criminal courts of appeal, are on **pages 493–495**. If more than one district attorney is listed for a county, the district court number is noted in parentheses after each attorney's name. The officials listed here are elected by popular vote. If no district attorney is listed, the county attorney, whose name is listed in Table No. 1, assumes the duties of that office.

County	District Clerk	District Attorney	Comm. Precinct 1	Comm. Precinct 2	Comm. Precinct 3	Comm. Precinct 4
Anderson	Teresia Coker	Allyson Mitchell	Greg Chapin	Rashad Mims	Kenneth Dickson	Joey Hill
Andrews	Sherry Dushane	Sean Galloway	Kerry Pack	Mark Savell	Jeneane Anderegg	Jim Waldrop
Angelina	Reba Squyres	Janet Cassels	Rodney Paulette	Kermit Kennedy	Terry Pitts	Bobby Cheshire
Aransas	Pam Heard	—	Jack Chaney	Leslie (Bubba) Casterline	Pat Rousseau	Wendy Laubach
Archer	Lori Rutledge	Casey Polhemus	Wade Scarbrough	Darin Wolf	Pat Martin, III	Darryl Lightfoot
Armstrong	Tawnee Blodgett	Randall C. Sims	Adam Ensey	Dustin Sanders	Robert Harris	Mike Ollinger
Atascosa	Margaret E. Littleton	Audrey Gossett Louis	Mark Gillespie	Stuart Knowlton	Eliseo Perez	Kennard (Bubba) Riley
Austin	Sue Murphy	Travis J. Koehn	Mark Lamp	Robert (Bobby) Rinn	Leroy Cerny	Chip Reed
Bailey	Becky Espinoza	Kathryn Gurley	Gary Don Gartin	Mike Slayden	Cody Black	Jim Daniel
Bandera	Tammy Kneuper	Stephen Harpold	Bruce Eliker	Bobby Harris	Jack Moseley	Jordan (Jody) Rutherford
Bastrop	Sarah Loucks	Bryan Goertz	Mel Hamner	Clara Beckett	Mark Meuth	Donna Snowden
Baylor	Chris Jakubicek	Hunter Brooks	Rick Gillispie	Larry Elliott	Reed Slagle	Charlie Piatt
Bee	Zenaida Silva	Jose Aliseda	Kristofer Linney	Dennis DeWitt	Sammy G. Farias	Kenneth Haggard
Bell	Joanna Staton	Henry Garza	Russell Schneider	Bobby Whitson	Bill Schumann	John Driver
Bexar	Mary Angie Garcia	Joe Gonzales	Rebeca Clay-Flores	Justin Rodriguez	Trish DeBerry	Tommy Calvert
Blanco	Debby Elsbury	Wiley B. (Sonny) McAfee	Tommy Weir	Emil Ray Uecker	Chris Liesmann	Paul Granberg
Borden	Jana Underwood	Ben R. Smith	Norman (Jibber) Herridge	Randy Adcock	Ernest Reyes	Greg Stansell
Bosque	Juanita Miller	Adam Sibley	Billy Hall	Terry Townley	Larry (Shotgun) Philipp	Ronny Liardon
Bowie	Jill Harrington	Jerry Rochelle	Sammy Stone	Tom Whitten	James Strain	Mike Carter
Brazoria	Rhonda Barchak	Tom Selleck	Donald (Dude) Payne	Ryan Cade	Stacy Adams	David Linder
Brazos	Gabriel Garcia	Jarvis Parsons	Steve Aldrich	Russ Ford	Nancy Berry	Irma Cauley
Brewster	Jo Ann Salgado	Ori White	Jim Westermann	Sara Allen Colando	Ruben Ortega	Mike Pallanez
Briscoe	Bena Hester	Wade Jackson	Ken Wood	Jack Wellman	Danny Francis	John Burson
Brooks	Lesvia Gonzales	Carlos Omar Garcia	Eduardo (Eddie) Garza	Rolando Gutierrez	Horacio Villareal, III	Ernesto (Pepe) Williams
Brown	Cheryl Jones	Micheal Murray	Gary Worley	Joel Kelton	Wayne Shaw	Larry Traweek
Burleson	Dana Fritsche	Susan Deski	Dwayne Faust	Vincent Svec, Jr.	David Hildebrand	Carol Hill
Burnet	Casie Walker	Wiley B. (Sonny) McAfee	Jim Luther, Jr.	Damon Beierle	Billy Wall	Joe Don Dockery
Caldwell	Juanita Allen	Fred Weber	B.J. Westmoreland	Barbara Shelton	Edward (Ed) Theriot	Joe Roland
Calhoun	Anna Kabela	Dan Heard	David Hall	Vern Lyssy	Joel Behrens	Gary Reese
Callahan	Sharon Owens	Shane Deel	Rick McGowen	Bryan Farmer	Tom Windham	Erwin Clark
Cameron	Laura Perez-Reyes	Luis V. Saenz	Sofia C. Benavides	Joey Lopez	David A. Garza	Gus Ruiz
Camp	Teresa Bockmon	David Colley	George French	Steve Hudnall	Perry Weeks	Steve Lindley
Carson	Celeste Bichsel	Luke M. Inman	Mike Britten	James Martin	Mike Jennings	Kevin Howell
Cass	Jamie Albertson	Courtney Shelton	Brett Fitts	Danny Joe Shaddix	Paul Cothren	Darrell Godwin
Castro	JoAnna Blanco	Shalyn Hamlin	Paul Ramirez	Tim Elliott	Michael Goolsby	Ralph Brockman
Chambers	Patti L. Henry	Cheryl Swope Lieck	Jimmy Gore	Kenneth Mark Tice	Tommy Hammond	Billy Combs
Cherokee	Alison Dotson	Elmer Beckworth	Kelly Traylor	Steven Norton	Patrick Reagan	Billy McCutcheon
Childress	Barbara Spitzer	Luke M. Inman	Jeremy Hill	Mark Ross	Kevin Hackler	Rick Elliott

County	District Clerk	District Attorney	Comm. Precinct 1	Comm. Precinct 2	Comm. Precinct 3	Comm. Precinct 4
Clay	Marianne Bowles	Casey Polhemus	Richard Lowery	Johnny Gee	Retta Collins	Chase Broussard
Cochran	Lisa Smith	Angela L. Overman	Timothy Roberts	Matt Evans	Eric Silhan	Reynaldo Morin
Coke	Monica Reyes	Allison Palmer	Donald Robertson	Paul Williams	Marshall Millican	Joe Setcik
Coleman	Darlene Huddle-Boyd	Heath Hemphill	Matt Henderson	Jim Rice	Scotty Lawrence	Alan Davis
Collin	Lynne Finley	Greg Willis	Susan Fletcher	Cheryl Williams	Darrell Hale	Duncan Webb
Collingsworth	Jackie Johnson	Luke M. Inman	Farris Nation	James Ellis	Joel Sherwood	Kirby Campbell
Colorado	Linda Holman	Jay E. Johannes	Doug Wessels	Darrell Kubesch	Keith Neuendorff	Darrell Gertson
Comal	Heather Kellar	Jennifer Tharp	Donna Eccleston	Scott Haag	Kevin Webb	Jen Crownover
Comanche	Brenda Dickey	Adam Sibley	Gary (Corky) Underwood	Russell Gillette	Sherman Sides	Jimmy Dale Johnson
Concho	Phyllis F. Lowell	John Best	Trey Bradshaw	Ralph Willberg	Gary Gierisch	Aaron (Sonny) Browning
Cooke	Marci A. Gilbert	John Warren	Gary Hollowell	Jason Snuggs	Adam Arendt	Leon Klement
Coryell	Becky Moore	Dusty Boyd	Kyle Matthews	Daren Moore	Ryan Basham	Ray Ashby
Cottle	Vickey Wederski	Hunter Brooks	Jimmy Sweeney	Steven Beck, Jr.	Manuel Cruz	John B. Brothers
Crane	Janie Macias	Amanda Navarette	Manuella Kirkpatrick	Brian Brents	Domingo Escobedo	Cody Bob Harrelson
Crockett	Ninfa Preddy	Laurie English	Frank Tambunga	G.L. Bunger, V	Wesley Bean	Mike Medina
Crosby	Shari Smith	Michael Sales	Larry McCauley	Frank Mullins	Donald Kirksey	Kevin Langdon
Culberson	Linda McDonald	Yvonne Rosales	Javier Mendoza	Raul Rodriguez	Gilda Morales	Adrian Norman
Dallam	Terri Banks	Erin Lands	Carl McCarty	Corey Crabtree	Levi James	Floyd French
Dallas	Felicia Pitre	John Creuzot	Theresa Daniel	J.J. Koch	John Wiley Price	Elba Garcia
Dawson	Adreana Gonzalez	Philip Mack Furlow	Mark Shofner	Martha Hernandez	Nicky Goode	Russell Cox
Deaf Smith	Elaine Gerber	Chris Strowd	Chris Kahlich	Jerry O'Connor	Mike Brumley	Dale Artho
Delta	Jane Jones	Will W. Ramsay	Eric Lair	Jimmy Sweat	Bobby Asbill	Mark Brantley
Denton	David Trantham	Paul Johnson	Ryan Williams	Ron Marchant	Bobbie J. Mitchell	Dianne Edmondson
DeWitt	Esther Ruiz	Robert C. Lassmann	Curtis G. Afflerbach	James B. Pilchiek, Sr.	James Kaiser	Richard Randle
Dickens	Becky Hill	Wade Jackson	Dennis Wyatt	Mike Smith	Charles Morris	Jerry Alexander
Dimmit	Maricela G. Gonzalez	Roberto Serna	Mike Uriegas	Alonso G. Carmona	Juan Carmona	Valerie Rubalcaba
Donley	Fay Vargas	Luke M. Inman	Mark White	Daniel Ford	Neil Koetting	Dan Sawyer
Duval	Rachel S. Vela	Gocha Ramirez	Pete Guerra	Rene Perez	David Garza	Gilberto Uribe, Jr.
Eastland	Tessa K. Culverhouse	Russ Thomason	Andy Maxwell	James Crenshaw	Ronnie Wilson	Robert Rains
Ector	Clarissa Webster	Dusty Gallivan	Mike Gardner	Greg Simmons	Don Stringer	Armando S. Rodriguez
Edwards	Olga Lydia Reyes	Tonya Ahlschwede	Marty H. Graham	Lee D. Sweeten	Matt Fry	Kenneth Reed
Ellis	Melanie Reed	Ann Montgomery	Randy Stinson	Lane Grayson	Paul Perry	Kyle Butler
El Paso	Norma Favela Barceleau	Yvonne Rosales	Carlos Leon	David Stout	Iliana Holguin	Carl L. Robinson
Erath	Wanda Greer	Alan Nash	Dee Stephens	Albert Ray	Joe Brown	Jim Buck
Falls	Christy Wideman	Kathryn (Jody) Gilliam	Milton Albright	F.A. Green	Jason Willberg	Nita Wuebker
Fannin	Nancy Young	Richard Glaser	Edwina Lane	A.J. Self	Jerry Magness	Dean Lackey
Fayette	Linda Svrcek	Peggy Supak	Jason McBroom	Luke Sternadel	Harvey Berckenhoff	Drew Brossmann
Fisher	Gina Pasley	Richard Thompson	Gordon Pippin	Dexter Elrod	Preston Martin	Kevin Stuart
Floyd	Patty Davenport	Wade Jackson	Tanner R. Smith	Clint Bigham	Nathan Johnson	David Martinez
Foard	Debra Hopkins	John Staley Heatly	Rick Hammonds	Rockne Wisdom	Larry Wright	Anthony Hinsley
Fort Bend	Beverley McGrew Walker	Brian Middleton	Vincent Morales, Jr.	Grady Prestage	Andy Meyers	Ken DeMerchant
Franklin	Ellen Jaggers	Will W. Ramsay	Jerry Cooper	Larkin Jumper	Charlie Emerson	Sam Young
Freestone	Teresa Black	Brian Evans	Andy Bonner	Thomas Craig Oakes	Lloyd Lane	Clyde Ridge, Jr.

County	District Clerk	District Attorney	Comm. Precinct 1	Comm. Precinct 2	Comm. Precinct 3	Comm. Precinct 4
Frio	Otilia M. Trevino	Audrey Gossett Louis	Joe Vela	Richard Graf	Raul Carrizales	Jose Asuncion
Gaines	Susan Murphree	Philip Mack Furlow	Brian Rosson	Craig Belt	David Murphree	Biz Houston
Galveston	John D. Kinard	Jack Roady	Darrell Apffel	Joe Giusti	Stephen D. Holmes	Ken Clark
Garza	Jim Plummer	Philip Mack Furlow	Jeff Williams	Charles Morris	Ted Brannon	Jerry Benham
Gillespie	Ian Davis	Lucy Wilke	Charles Olfers	Keith Kramer	Dennis Neffendorf	Donnie Schuch
Glasscock	Rebecca Batla	Hardy Wilkerson	Charles Gully	Mark Halfmann	Gary Jones	John Seidenberger
Goliad	Mary Ellen Flores	Rob Lassmann	Kenneth Edwards	Alonzo Morales	Kirby Brumby	David Bruns
Gonzales	Janice Sutton		K.O. (Dell) Whiddon	Donnie R. Brzozowski	Kevin T. La Fleur	Collie Boatright
Gray	Jo Mays	Franklin McDonough	Logan Hudson	Lake Arrington	John Mark Baggerman	Jeff Haley
Grayson	Kelly Ashmore	Brett Smith	Jeff Whitmire	David Whitlock	Phyllis James	Bart Lawrence
Gregg	Trey Hattaway	Tom Watson	Ronnie L. McKinney	Darryl Primo	Floyd Wingo	Shannon E. Brown
Grimes	Diane Leflore	Andria Bender	Chad Mallett	David E. Dobyanski	Barbara Walker	Phillip Cox
Guadalupe	Linda Balk		Greg Seidenberger	Drew Engelke	Michael Carpenter	Judy Cope
Hale	Carla Cannon	Wally Hatch	Harold King	Chris Daniel	Kenny Kernell	Jimmy Kelly
Hall	Olivia M. Fisher	Luke M. Inman	Ronny Wilson	Terry Lindsey	Gary Proffitt	Troy Glover
Hamilton	Sandy Layhew	Adam Sibley	Johnny Wagner	Keith Allen Curry	Lloyd Huggins	Dickie Clary
Hansford	Janet Torres	Mark Snider	Ira G. (Butch) Reed	David L. Thomas	Tim Stedje	Danny Henson
Hardeman	Ellen London	Staley Heatly	Chris Call	Haden Braziel	Barry Haynes	Rodney Foster
Hardin	Dana Hogg	Rebecca Walton	L.W. Cooper, Jr.	Chris Kirkendall	Amanda Young	Alvin Roberts
Harris	Marilyn Burgess	Kim Ogg	Rodney Ellis	Adrian Garcia	Tom S. Ramsey	R. Jack Cagle
Harrison	Sherry Griffis	Reid McCain	William D. Hatfield	Zephaniah Timmins	Phillip Mauldin	Jay Ebarb
Hartley	Melissa Mead	Erin Lands	David Vincent	David Spinhirne	Chad Hicks	Robert (Butch) Owens
Haskell	Debbie Gressett	Mike Fouts	Jerry Don Garcia	Elmer Adams	Matt Sanders	Neal Kreger
Hays	Beverly Crumley	Wes Mau	Debbie Ingalsbe	Mark Jones	Lon Shell	Walt Smith
Hemphill	Lisa Johnson	Franklin McDonough	Dawn E. Webb	Tim Alexander	Curt McPherson	Nicholas Thomas
Henderson	Betty Herriage	Jenny Palmer	Wendy Spivey	Scott Tuley	Charles (Chuck) McHam	Mark Richardson
Hidalgo	Laura Hinojosa	Ricardo Rodriguez, Jr.	David L. Fuentes	Eduardo (Eddie) Cantu	Joe M. Flores	Ellie Torres
Hill	Marchel Eubank	Mark Pratt	Andrew Montgomery	Larry Crumpton	Scotty Hawkins	Martin Lake
Hockley	Dennis Price	Angela L. Overman	Alan Wisdom	Larry Carter	Seth Graf	Tommy Clevenger
Hood	Tonna Trumble Hitt	Ryan Sinclair	Kevin Andrews	Ron Cotton	Jack Wilson	Dave Eagle
Hopkins	Cheryl Fulcher	Will W. Ramsay	Mickey Barker	Greg Anglin	Wade Bartley	Joe Price
Houston	Carolyn Rains	Donna Gordon Kaspar	Gary Lovell	Willie Kitchen	Gene Stokes	Jimmy Henderson
Howard	Joanna Gonzales	Hardy Wilkerson	Eddilisa Ray	Craig Bailey	Jimmie Long	John Cline
Hudspeth	Brenda Sanchez	Yvonne Rosales	Andrew Virdell	Sergio Quijas	Johny Sheets	Delbert (Sonny) Berry
Hunt	Susan Spradling	Noble D. Walker	Mark Hutchins	Randy Strait	Phillip Martin	Steven Harrison
Hutchinson	Robin Stroud	Mark Snider	Gary Alexander	Dwight Kirksey	Ben Bentley	Chris Prock
Irion	Shirley Graham	Allison Palmer	Tia Paxton	Jeff Davidson	John Nanny	Bill (Beaver) McManus, III
Jack	Tracie Pippin	James Stainton	Gary Oliver	Darren Francis	Henry D. Birdwell, Jr.	Terry Ward
Jackson	Sharon Mathis	Pam Guenther	Wayne Hunt	Wayne Bubela	Glenn Martin	Dennis Karl
Jasper	Rosa Norsworthy	Anne Pickle	Seth Martindale	Roy Parker	Willie Stark	Vance Moss
Jeff Davis	Jennifer Wright	Ori White	Jody Adams	Todd Jagger	John Davis	Albert W. Miller
Jefferson	Jamie Smith	Bob Wortham	Vernon Pierce	Darrell Bush	Michael Sinegal	Everette (Bo) Alfred
Jim Hogg	Zonia G. Morales	Gocha Ramirez	Humberto Martinez	Abelardo Alaniz	Sandalio Ruiz	Cynthia Guerra Betancourt
Jim Wells	R. David Guerrero	Carlos Omar Garcia	Margie H. Gonzalez	Ventura Garcia	Renee Kirchoff Chapa	Wicho Gonzalez

County	District Clerk	District Attorney	Comm. Precinct 1	Comm. Precinct 2	Comm. Precinct 3	Comm. Precinct 4
Johnson	David Lloyd	Dale Hanna	Rick Bailey	Kenny Howell	Mike White	Larry Woolley
Jones	Lacey Hansen	Joe Edd Boaz	Roy Spalding	Lonnie Vivian	Todd McWilliams	Joel Spraberry
Karnes	Denise Rodriguez	Audrey Gossett Louis	Shelby Dupnik	Benny Lyssy	James Rosales	Sharon Chesser
Kaufman	Rhonda Hughey	Erleigh Norville Wiley	Mike Hunt	Skeet Phillips	Terry Barber	Ken Cates
Kendall	Susan Jackson	Nicole S. Bishop	Christina Bergmann	Richard W. Elkins	Richard Chapman	Don Durden
Kenedy	Veronica Vela	John T. Hubert	Joe Recio	Israel Vela, Jr.	Sarita Armstrong Hixon	Cindy Gonzales
Kent	Craig Harrison	Mike Fouts	Roy W. Chisum	Don Long	Daryl Ham	Robert Graham
Kerr	Dawn Lantz	Stephen Harpold (198th); Lucy Wilke (216th)	Harley David Belew	Tom Moser	Jonathan Letz	Don Harris
Kimble	Haydee Torres	Tonya Ahlschwede	Brady Schulze	Kelly Simon	Dennis Dunagan	Kenneth Hofmann
King	Tammye D. Timmons	Hunter Brooks	Reggie Hatfield	Larry Rush	Doris Tidmore	Jay Hurt
Kinney	Rick Alvarado	Suzanne West	Mark Frerich	Joe Montalvo	Dennis Dodson	Tim Ward
Kleberg	Jennifer Whittington	John T. Hubert	David Rosse	Chuck Schultz	Jerry Martinez	Marcus Salinas
Knox	Lisa Cypert	Hunter Brooks	Johnny McCown	Dan Godsey	Ray Herring	Nathan Urbanczyk
Lamar	Shawntel Golden	Gary Young	Alan Skidmore	Lonnie Layton	Ronnie Bass	Kevin Anderson
Lamb	Debbie Long	Scott A. Say	Cory DeBerry	Kent Lewis	Danny Short	Lee Logan
Lampasas	Edith Wagner Harrison	John K. Greenwood	Bobby Carroll	Jamie Smart	Lewis Bridges	Mark Rainwater
La Salle	Margarita Esqueda	Audrey Gossett Louis	Noel Niavez	Joaquin Alba	Erasmo Ramirez, Jr.	Raul Ayala
Lavaca	Lori A. Wenske	Kyle A. Denney	Edward Pustka	Ronald Berckenhoff	Kenny Siegel	Dennis W. Kocian
Lee	Lisa Teinert	Martin Placke	Mark Matthietz	Richard Wagner	Alan Turner	Steven Knobloch
Leon	Cassandra Noey	James (Caleb) Henson	Joey Sullivan	David Ferguson	Kyle Workman	David Grimes
Liberty	Delia Sellers	Jennifer L. Bergman	Bruce Karbowski	Greg Arthur	David S. Whitmire	Leon Wilson
Limestone	Carol Jenkins	William Roy DeFriend	Bill David Sadler	W.A. (Sonny) Baker	Stephen Friday	Bobby Forrest
Lipscomb	Kim Blau	Franklin McDonough	Juan Cantu	Merle Miller	Scotty Schilling	Dan Cockrell
Live Oak	Melanie Matkin	Jose Aliseda	Richard Lee	Donna Kopplin Mills	Mitchell Williams	Emilio Garza
Llano	Joyce Gillow	Wiley B. (Sonny) McAfee	Peter R. Jones	Linda Raschke	Mike Sandoval	Jerry Don Moss
Loving	Mozelle Carr	Randall (Randy) Reynolds	Harlan Hopper	Ysidro (Joe) Renteria	Raymond W. King	William (Bill) Wilkinson
Lubbock	Barbara Sucsy	K. Sunshine Stanek	Terence Kovar	Jason Corley	Gilbert A. Flores	Chad Seay
Lynn	Courtney Odom	Philip Mack Furlow	Mark Woodley	John Hawthorne	Don Blair	Larry Durham
Madison	Rhonda Savage	Brian Risinger	Ricky Driskell	Carl Wiseman	Carl L. Cannon	David Pohorelsky
Marion	Susan Anderson	Angela Smoak	J.R. Ashley	Jacob Pattison	Ralph Meisenheimer	Charles W. Treadwell
Martin	Linda Gonzales	Hardy Wilkerson	Kenny Stewart	Robin Barnes	Bobby Holland	Koy Blocker
Mason	Pam Beam	Tonya Spaeth Ahlschwede	Reggie Loeffler	Wil Frey	Buddy Schuessler	Stephen Mutschink
Matagorda	Janice L. Hawthorne	Steven Reis	Gerardo (Bubba) Cook	Kent Pollard	Troy Shimek	Charles (Bubba) Frick
Maverick	Leopoldo Vielma	Roberto Serna	Gerardo (Jerry) Morales	Rosy Cantu	Olga Ramos	Roberto Ruiz
McCulloch	Michelle Pitcox	Tonya Spaeth Ahlschwede	Carol Anderson	Randy Deans	Jason Behrens	Rick Kemp
McLennan	Jon Gimble	Barry Johnson	Jim Smith	Patricia Miller	Will Jones	Ben Perry
McMullen	Mattie S. Sadovsky	Jose Aliseda	Larry Garcia	Murray Swaim	Scotty McClaugherty	Max Quintanilla, Jr.
Medina	Cindy Fowler	Mark P. Haby	Tim Neuman	Larry Sittre	David Lynch	Jerry Beck
Menard	Christy Eggleston	Tonya Ahlschwede	Frank Davis	Jay Cunningham	Ed Keith	Larry Burch
Midland	Alex (Lex) Archuleta	Laura A. Noldolf	Scott Ramsey	Robin Donnelly	Luis D. Sánchez	Randy Prude
Milam	Karen Berry	Bill Torrey	Henry (Hub) Hubnik	Donald Shuffield	Art Neal	Jeff Muegge
Mills	Sonya Scott	Micheal Murray	Mike Wright	Jed Garren	Dale Partin	Jason Williams

County	District Clerk	District Attorney	Comm. Precinct 1	Comm. Precinct 2	Comm. Precinct 3	Comm. Precinct 4
Mitchell	Belinda Blassingame	Ricky Thompson	Dennis Jones	Jeremy Strain	Jesse Munoz	Ricky Bailey
Montague	Robin Woods	Casey Polhemus	Roy Darden	Mike Mayfield	Mark Murphey	Bob Langford
Montgomery	Melisa Miller	Brett Ligon	Robert C. Walker	Charlie Riley	James Noack	James Metts
Moore	Mayra Rivero	Erin Lands	Daniel Garcia	Miles Mixon	Dee Vaughan	Lynn Cartrite
Morris	Gwen Ashworth	Ricky Shelton	Greg Frazier	Kerry McCoy	Michael Clair	Todd Freeman
Motley	Danna Russell	Wade Jackson	Douglas Campbell	Roegan Cruse	Franklin Jameson	Timmy Brooks
Nacogdoches	Loretta Cammack	Andrew Jones	Jerry Don Williamson	Sandy McCorvey	Robin Dawley	Mark Harkness
Navarro	Joshua B. Tackett	William Thompson	Jason Grant	Eddie Perry	Eddie Moore	James Olsen
Newton	Bree Allen	Courtney Tracy Ponthier	Danny Bentsen	Phillip A. White	Gary Fomby	Wesley (Gene) Thompson
Nolan	Jamie Clem	Richard Thompson	Terry Willman	Seth Mahaffey	Tommy White	Henry Ortega, Jr.
Nueces	Anne Lorentzen	Mark A. Gonzalez	Robert Hernandez	Joe A. (JAG) Gonzalez	John Marez	Brent Chesney
Ochiltree	Shawn Bogard	Jose N. Meraz	Duane Phigoda	Joe Johnson	JW DeWitt	Kevin Walker
Oldham	Darla Lookingbill		Quincy Taylor	Larry Groneman	Roger Morris	Billy Don Brown
Orange	Vickie Edgerly	John Kimbrough	Johnny Trahan	Theresa Beauchamp	Kirk Roccaforte	Robert Viator
Palo Pinto	Jonna Banks	Kriste Burnett	Gary Glover	Mike Reed	Mike Pierce	Jeff Fryer
Panola	Lindsey Smith	Danny Buck Davidson	Billy Alexander	David A. Cole	Craig M. Lawless	Dale LaGrone
Parker	Sharena Gilliland	Jeff Swain	George Conley	Craig Peacock	Larry Walden	Steve Dugan
Parmer	Sandra Warren	Kathryn Gurley	Kirk Frye	Charles Wilkins	Kenny White	Casey Russell
Pecos	Gayle Henderson	Ori White (83rd); Laurie English (112th)	Tom Chapman	Robert Gonzales	Mickey Jack Perry	Santiago Cantu, Jr.
Polk	Bobbye Richards	Lee Hon	Guvlene Robertson	Ronnie Vincent	Milt Purvis	C.T. (Tommy) Overstreet
Potter	Stephnie Menke	Randall Sims	H.R. Kelly	Mercy Murguia	John Coffee	Alphonso Vaughn
Presidio	Flor Zubia	Ori White	Brenda Silva Bentley	Eloy Aranda	Jose Cabezuela	Frank (Buddy) Knight
Rains	Laura Pate	Robert Vititow	Jeremy Cook	Mike Willis	Korey Young	Joe Humphrey
Randall	Joel Forbis	Robert Love	Rusty Carnes	Mark Benton	Bob Robinson	Buddy Deford
Reagan	Terri Curry	Laurie English	Mike Vargas	Tim Sellman	Tommy Holt	Mary Loffin
Real	D'Ann Green	Christina Mitchell Busbee	Brad Hart	Shawn D. Gray	Ramon Ybarra	Charles E. Hunger
Red River	Janice Gentry	Val Varley	Donnie Gentry	David Hutson	Jeff Moore	Danny Halley
Reeves	Patricia Tarin	Randall W. Reynolds	Rojelio Alvarado	Israel Campos	Paul Hinojos	Tony Trujillo
Refugio	Sylvia M. Lopez	Robert C. Lassmann	Roy Payne	Stanley Tuttle	Gary Lee Wright	Blaine Wolfshohl
Roberts	Toni Rankin	Franklin McDonough	Cleve Wheeler	William Gill	Kelly Flowers	James F. Duvall
Robertson	Barbara W. Axtell	W. Cory Siegert	Ty Rampy	Donald Threadgill	Chuck Hairston	James Taylor
Rockwall	Lea Carlson	Kenda Culpepper	Cliff Sevier	Lee Gilbert	Dennis Bailey	Janet Nichol
Runnels	Tammy Burleson	John Best	Carl King	Ronald Presley	Brandon Poehls	Juan Ornelas
Rusk	Terri Pirtle Willard	Micheal E. Jimerson	Randy Gaut	Robert Kuykendall	Greg Gibson	Bennie Whitworth
Sabine	Lisa Pitre	J. Kevin Dutton	Brent Cox	Jimmy McDaniel	Stanley Jacks	James Lowe
San Augustine	Jeanette Bryan	J. Kevin Dutton	Tommy Pickard	Ed Wilson	Joey Holloway	Rodney Ainsworth
San Jacinto	Tammy Currie	Robert H. Trapp	Laddie McAnally	Donny Marrs	David Brandon	Mark Nettuno
San Patricio	Heather B. Marks	Samuel B. Smith	Sonia Lopez	Gary Moore	Lilly Wilkinson	Howard Gillespie
San Saba	Kim Wells	Wiley B. (Sonny) McAfee	James Lebow	Rickey Lusty	Kenley Kroll	Pat Pool
Schleicher	Mary Ann Gonzalez	Allison Palmer	Gary Gibson	Steve Nelson	Kirk Griffin	Chris Meador
Scurry	Candace Jones	Ben Smith	Terry D. Williams	Craig Merritt	Shawn McCowen	Jim Robinson
Shackelford	Cheri Hawkins	Joe Edd Boaz	Steve Riley	Ace Reames	Lanham Martin	Cody Jordan
Shelby	Lori Oliver	Karren Price	Roscoe McSwain	Jimmy Lout	Stevie Smith	Tom Bellmyer

County	District Clerk	District Attorney	Comm. Precinct 1	Comm. Precinct 2	Comm. Precinct 3	Comm. Precinct 4
Sherman	Laura Rogers	Erin Lands	Dana Buckles	Terry Mathews	Jeff Crippen	David Davis
Smith	Penny Clarkston	Jacob Putman	Neal J. Franklin	Cary Nix	Terry Lee Phillips	JoAnn Hampton
Somervell	Virginia Dixon	Dale Hanna	Jeff Harris	Dwayne Johnson	Tammy Ray	Wade Busch
Starr	Orlando Velasquez	Gocha Ramirez	Jaime Alvarez	Raul (Roy) Peña, III	Eloy Garza	Ruben D. Saenz
Stephens	Christie Coapland	Dee Hudson Peavy	David Fambro	Mark McCullough	William H. Warren	Eric O'Dell
Sterling	Jerri McCutchen	Allison Palmer	Ross Copeland	Edward Michulka, Jr.	Tommy Wright, Jr.	Reed Stewart
Stonewall	Holly McLaury	Mike Fouts	Donna McCoy	Jan Harris	Kirk Meador	Gary Myers
Sutton	Pam Thorp	Laurie K. English	Lee C. Bloodworth	Bob Brockman	Carl Teaff	Fred Perez
Swisher	C.J. Chasco	J. Michael Criswell	Lloyd Rahlfs	Danny Morgan	Joe Murrell	Larry Buske
Tarrant	Thomas A. Wilder	Sharen Wilson	Roy Charles Brooks	Devan Allen	Gary Fickes	J.D. Johnson
Taylor	Tammy Robinson	James Hicks	Randall D. Williams	Kyle Kendrick	Brad Birchum	Chuck Statler
Terrell	Raeline Thompson	Suzanne West	Adam Johnson	Mike Sanchez	Arnulfo Serna	Heather Gully
Terry	Paige Lindsey	JoShae Ferguson-Worley	Mike Swain	Kirby Keesee	Martin Lefevere	Ernesto Elizardo
Throckmorton	Dianna Moore	Mike Fouts	Casey Wells	Kasey Hibbitts	Lance Sullivan	Klay Mitchell
Titus	Marcus Carlock	David Colley	Jeff Parchman	John Fitch	Dana Applewhite	Jimmy Parker
Tom Green	Anthony Joseph Monico	Allison Palmer (51st); John H. Best (119th)	Ralph Hoelscher	Sammy Farmer	Rick Bacon	Bill Ford
Travis	Velva L. Price	José Garza	Jeff Travillion	Brigid Shea	Ann Howard	Margaret Gómez
Trinity	Kristen Raiford	Benny L. Schiro	Tommy Park	Mike Loftin	Neal Smith	Steven Truss
Tyler	Pamela Reneé Crews	Lucas Babin	Joe Blacksher	Stevan Sturrock	Mike Marshall	Charles (Buck) Hudson
Upshur	Karen Bunn	Billy Byrd	Gene Dolle	Dustin Nicholson	Michael Ashley	Jay Miller
Upton	LaWanda McMurray	Laurie English	Pete Jackson	Tommy Owens	Mike Smart	Gary Wolfe
Uvalde	Christina J Ovalle	Christina Mitchell Busbee	John Yeackle	Mariano Pargas, Jr.	Jerry W. Bates	Roland (Ronnie) Garza
Val Verde	Jo Ann Cervantes	Suzanne West	Martin Wardlaw	Juan Carlos Vazquez	Robert Beau Nettleton	Gustavo (Gus) Flores
Van Zandt	Karen L. Wilson	Tonda Curry	Chad LaPrade	Virgil Melton, Jr.	Keith Pearson	Tim West
Victoria	Kim Plummer	Constance Filley Johnson	Danny Garcia	Kevin M. Janak	Gary Burns	Clint Ives
Walker	Robyn Flowers	Will Durham	Danny Kuykendall	Ronnie White	Bill Daugette	Jimmy Henry
Waller	Liz Pirkle	Elton Mathis	John A. Amsler	Walter E. Smith	Kendric D. Jones	Justin Beckendorff
Ward	Patricia Overbides	Randall W. Reynolds	Tino Sanchez	Larry Hanna	Dexter Nichols	Eddie Nelms
Washington	Tammy Brauner	Julie Renken	Don Koester	Candice Bullock	Kirk Hanath	Joy Fuchs
Webb	Esther Degollado	Isidro (Chilo) Alaniz	Jesse Gonzalez	Rosaura (Wawi) Tijerina	John C. Galo	Cindy Liendo
Wharton	Kendra Charbula	Dawn Elizabeth Allison	Richard Zahn	Bud Graves	Steven Goetsch	Doug Mathews
Wheeler	Sherri Jones	Franklin McDonough	Jackie Don May, Jr.	Robert Hink	David Simpson	John Walker
Wichita	Patti Flores	John Gillespie	Mark Beauchamp	Mickey Fincannon	Barry Mahler	Jeff Watts
Wilbarger	Brenda Peterson	Staley Heatly	John Wright	Phillip Graf	Kelly Neel	Josh Patterson
Willacy	Isabel Adame	Annette C. Hinojosa	Eliberto (Beto) Guerra	(vacant)	Henry De La Paz	Eduardo (Eddy) Gonzales
Williamson	Lisa David	Shawn Dick	Terry Cook	Cynthia Long	Valerie Covey	Russ Boles
Wilson	Deborah Bryan	Audrey Gossett Louis	Gary Martin	Paul W. Pfeil	Jeffery Pierdolla	Larry A. Wiley
Winkler	Geneva Baker	Amanda Navarette	Billy J. Stevens	Robbie Wolf	Victor Berzoza	Billy Ray Thompson
Wise	Brenda Rowe	James Stainton	Biff Hayes	Kevin Burns	Danny Lambert	Gaylord Kennedy
Wood	Donna Huston	Angela Albers	Virgil Holland	Jerry Gaskill	Mike Simmons	Russell Acker
Yoakum	Sandra Roblez	Bill Helwig	Woodson W. Lindsey	Ray Marion	Tommy Box	Tim Addison
Young	Jamie Freeze Land	Dee Peavy	Stacy Creswell	Matt Pruitt	Stacey Rogers	Jimmy Wiley
Zapata	Dora Martinez Castañon	Isidro (Chilo) Alaniz	Paco Mendoza	Olga M. Elizondo	Jose A. Solis	Norberto Garza
Zavala	Rachel Ramirez	Robert Serna	Joe Cruz	Raul Gomez	Jesse Gonzales	Florencio (Flo) Melendrez

Texans in Congress

Besides the two members of the U.S. Senate allocated to each state, Texas was allocated 36 members in the U.S. House of Representatives for the 116th Congress. The term of office for members of the House is two years; the terms of all members will expire on Jan. 3, 2023. Senators serve six-year terms. Sen. John Cornyn's term will end in 2027. Sen. Ted Cruz's term will end in 2025.

Addresses and phone numbers of the lawmakers' Washington and district offices are below, as well as the committees on which they serve. Washington zip codes are 20515 for members of the House and 20510 for senators. The telephone area code for Washington is 202. On the Internet, House members can be reached through www.house.gov/writerep.

In 2018, members of Congress received a salary of $174,000. Members in leadership positions received $193,400.

U.S. SENATE

(Total members 100; Republicans 53, Democrats 45, Independents 2.)

CORNYN, John. Republican (Home: Austin); Washington Office: 517 HSOB; (202) 224-2934, Fax 228-2856. www.cornyn.senate.gov.

Texas Offices: 221 W. 6th, Ste. 1530, Austin 78701, (512) 469-6034; 5001 Spring Valley, Ste. 1125 E, Dallas 75244, (972) 239-1310; 222 E. Van Buren, Ste. 404, Harlingen 78550, (956) 423-0162; 5300 Memorial Dr., Ste. 980, Houston 77007, (713) 572-3337; 1500 Broadway, Ste. 1230, Lubbock 79401, (806) 472-7533; 600 Navarro, Ste. 210, San Antonio 78205, (210) 224-7485; 100 E. Ferguson, Ste. 1004, Tyler 75702, (903) 593-0902.

John Cornyn.

Committees: Finance, Judiciary, Select Committee on Intelligence.

CRUZ, Ted. Republican (Home: Houston); Washington Office: 404 RSOB; (202) 224-5922. www.cruz.senate.gov.

Texas Offices: 300 E. 8th, Ste. 961, Austin 78701, (512) 916-5834; 3626 N. Hall, Ste. 410, Dallas 75219, (214) 599-8749; 1919 Smith, Ste. 9047, Houston 77002, (713) 718-3057; 200 S. 10th, Ste. 1603, McAllen 78501, (956) 686-7339; 9901 IH-10W, Ste. 950, San Antonio 78230, (210) 340-2885 305; S. Broadway, Ste. 501, Tyler 75702, (903) 593-5130.

Ted Cruz.

Committees: Foreign Relations; Commerce, Science and Transportation; Judiciary; Rules and Administration; Joint Economic Committee.

U.S. HOUSE of REPRESENTATIVES

(Total districts 435; Republicans 212, Democrats 220, 3 vacant. Texas delegation of 36; 23 Republicans, 13 Democrats.)

District 1 — GOHMERT, Louie, R-Tyler; Washington Office: 2269 RHOB; (202) 225-3035, Fax 226-1230; District Offices: 1121 ESE Loop 323, Ste. 206, Tyler 75701, (903) 561-6349; 101 E. Methvin, Ste. 302, Longview 75601, (903) 236-8597; 300 E. Shepherd, Ste. 210, Lufkin 75901, (936) 632-3180; 102 W. Houston, Marshall 75670, (866) 535-6302; 101 W. Main, Ste. 160, Nacogdoches 75961, (936) 715-9514. Committees: Judiciary, Natural Resources.

District 2 — CRENSHAW, Dan, R-Kingwood; Washington Office: 413 CHOB; (202) 225-6565. District Office: 1801 Kingwood Dr., Ste. 240, Kingwood 77339. Committees: Energy and Commerce.

District 3 — TAYLOR, Van, R-Plano; Washington Office: 1404 LHOB; (202) 225-4201; District Office: 5600 Tennyson Parkway, Ste. 275, Plano 75204. Committees: Financial Services.

District 4 — FALLON, Pat, R-Sherman; Washington Office, 1118 LHOB; (202) 225-6673, Fax 225-3332: District Offices: 6531 Horizon, Ste. A, Rockwall 75032, (972) 771-0100; 100 W. Houston, Ste. 14, Sherman 75090, (903) 820-5170; 2500 N. Robison, Ste. 190, Texarkana 75599, (903) 716-7500. Committees: Armed Services, Oversight and Reform.

District 5 — GOODEN, Lance, R-Terrell; Washington Office: 1722 LHOB; (202) 225-3484. District Office: 18601 LBJ Freeway, Ste. 725, Mesquite 75150. Committee: Financial Services.

District 6 — ELLZEY, Jake, R-Midlothian; Washington Office: 428 CHOB; (202) 225-2002. Committees: Financial Services.

District 7 — FLETCHER, Lizzie Pannill, D-Houston; Washington Office: 119 CHOB; (202) 225-2571; District Office: 5599 San Felipe Rd., Ste. 950, Houston 77056. Committees: Energy and Commerce; Science, Space, and Technology.

District 8 — BRADY, Kevin, R-The Woodlands; Washington Office: 1011 LHOB; (202) 225-4901, Fax 225-5524. District Offices: 200 River Pointe, Ste. 304, Conroe 77304, (936) 441-5700; 1300 11th St., Ste 400, Huntsville 77340, (936) 439-9532. Committee: Joint Committee on Taxation, Ways and Means.

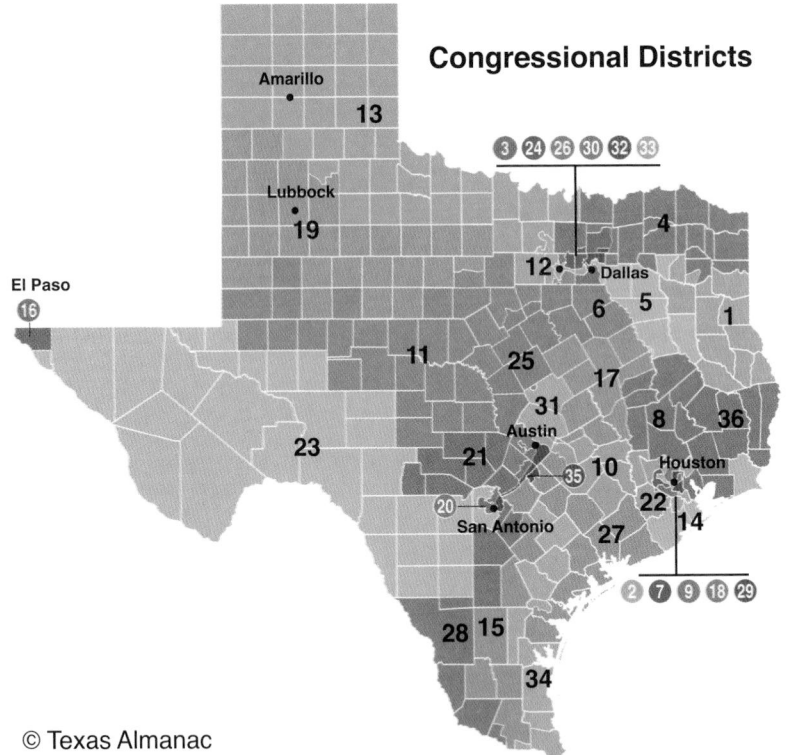

Congressional Districts

© Texas Almanac

District 9 — GREEN, Al, D-Houston; Washington Office: 2347 RHOB; (202) 225-7508; District Office: 3003 South Loop West, Ste. 460, Houston 77054, (713) 383-9234. Committees: Financial Services, Homeland Security.

District 10 — McCAUL, Michael, R-West Lake Hills; Washington Office: 2001 RHOB; (202) 225-2401, Fax 225-5955. District Offices: 3301 Northland Dr., Ste. 212, Austin 78731, (512) 473-2357; 2000 S. Market, Ste. 303, Brenham 77833, (979) 830-8497; 1773 Westborough Dr., Ste. 223, Katy 77449, (281) 398-1247; 990 Village Sq., Ste. B, Tomball 77375, (281) 255-8372. Committees: Foreign Affairs, Homeland Security.

District 11— PFLUGER, August, R-San Angelo; Washington Office: 1531 LHOB; (202) 225-3605. District Offices: 6 Desta Dr., Ste. 2000, Midland 79705, (432) 687-2390; 501 Center Ave., Brownwood 76801, (325) 646-1950; 132 Houston St., Granbury 76048, (682) 936-2577; 104 W. Sandstone, Llano 78643, (325) 247-2826; 119 W. 4th, Odessa 79761, (866) 882-3811; 33 E. Twohig, Ste. 307, San Angelo 76903, (325) 659-4010. Committees: Foreign Affairs, Homeland Security.

District 12 — GRANGER, Kay, R-Fort Worth; Washington Office: 1026 LHOB; (202) 225-5071, Fax 225-5683; District Office: 1701 River Run Rd., Ste. 407, Fort Worth 76107, (817) 338-0909. Committee: Appropriations.

District 13 — JACKSON, Ronny, R-Levelland; Washington Office: 118 CHOB; (202) 225-3706, Fax 225-3486; District Offices: 620 S. Taylor, Ste. 200, Amarillo 79101, (806) 371-8844; 2525 Kell Blvd., Ste. 406, Wichita Falls 76308, (940) 692-1700. Committee: Armed Services, Foreign Affairs.

District 14 — WEBER, Randy, R-Friendswood; Washington Office: 107 CHOB; (202) 225-2831. District Offices: 505 Orleans, Ste. 103, Beaumont 77701, (409) 835-0108; 122 West Way, Ste. 301, Lake Jackson 77566, (979) 285-0231; 174 Calder Rd., Ste. 150, League City 77573, (281) 316-0231. Committees: Science, Space and Technology; Transportation and Infrastructure.

District 15 — GONZALEZ, Vicente, D-McAllen; Washington Office: 113 CHOB; (202) 225-2531. District Offices: 131 W. Main St., Benavides 78341, (888) 217-0261; 217 E. Miller, Ste. 200, Falfurrias 78355, (361) 209-3027; 1305 W. Hackberry Ave., McAllen 78501, (956) 682-5545; 404 S. Mier St., San Diego 78384, (888) 217-0261; 1243 Cardinal Ln., Seguin 78155, (830) 358-0497. Committees: Financial Services, Foreign Affairs.

District 16 — ESCOBAR, Veronica, D-El Paso; Washington Office: 1330 LHOB; (202) 225-4831. District Office; 221 N. Kansas, Ste. 1500, El Paso 79901, (915) 541-1400. Committees: Armed Services, Judiciary, Ethics.

District 17 — SESSIONS, Pete, R-Waco; Washington Office: 2440 RHOB; (202) 225-6105; District Offices: 400 Austin Ave., Ste. 302, Waco 76701, (254) 732-0748; 2700 Earl Rudder Fwy, S. Hwy. 6, Ste. 4500, College Station 77845, (979) 431-6340. Committees: Financial Services, Oversight and Reform, Science, Space, and Technology.

District 18 — JACKSON LEE, Sheila, D-Houston; Washington Office: 2426 RHOB; (202) 225-3816, Fax 225-3317; District Offices: 1919 Smith, Ste. 1180, Houston 77002, (713) 655-0050; 420 W. 19th St., Houston 77008, (713) 861-4070; 6719 W. Montgomery, Ste. 204, Houston 77091, (713) 691-4882; 4300 Lyons Ave., Houston 77020, (713) 227-7740. Committees: Budget, Homeland Security, Judiciary.

District 19 — ARRINGTON, Jodey, R-Lubbock; Washington Office: 1107 LHOB; (202) 225-4005. District Offices: 500 Chestnut St., Abilene 79602, (325) 763-1611; 1312 Texas Ave., Ste. 219, Lubbock 79401, (806) 763-1611. Committee: Ways and Means.

District 20 — CASTRO, Joaquin, D-San Antonio; Washington Office: 2241 RHOB; (202) 225-3236. District Office: 727 E. Cesar E. Chavez Blvd., Ste. B-128, San Antonio 78206, (210) 348-8216. Committees: Education and Labor; Intelligence; Foreign Affairs.

District 21 — ROY, Chip S., R-Dripping Springs; Washington Office: 1005 LHOB; (202) 225-4236. District Office: 1100 NE Interstate 410 Loop, #640, San Antonio 78209, (210) 821-5024. Committees: Judiciary; Veterans' Affairs.

District 22 — NEHLS, Troy E., R-Richmond; Washington Office: 1104 LHOB; (202) 225-5951, Fax 225-5241. District Offices: 1117 FM 359, Ste. 210, Richmond, 77406, (346) 762-6600. Committees: Transportation and Infrastructure; Veterans' Affairs.

District 23 — GONZALES, Tony, R-San Antonio; Washington Office: 1104 LHOB; (202) 225-4511, Fax 225-2237. District Offices; 6333 De Zavala, Ste A216, San Antonio 78249, (210) 806-9920 (appt. only); 712 E. Gibbs, Ste. 101., Del Rio 78840, (830) 308-6200; 103 W. Callaghan, Fort Stockton 79735, (432) 299-6200; 124 S. Houston, Socorro 79927, (915) 990-1500 (appt only). Committees: Appropriations.

District 24 — VAN DUYNE, Beth, R-Irving; Washington Office: 1337 LHOB; (202) 225-6605, Fax 225-0074. District Office: 3100 Olympus Blvd, Ste. 440, Dallas, 75019, (972) 966-5500. Committees: Transportation and Infrastructure; Small Business.

District 25 — WILLIAMS, Roger, R-Austin; Washington Office: 1708 LHOB; (202) 225-9896. District Offices: 1005 Congress Ave., Ste. 925, Austin 78701, (512) 473-8910; 115 S. Main, Ste. 206, Cleburne 76033, (817) 774-2575. Committee: Financial Services; Small Business.

District 26 — BURGESS, Michael, R-Lewisville; Washington Office: 2161 RHOB; (202) 225-7772, Fax 225-2919. District Office: 2000 S. Stemmons Fwy., Ste. 200, Lake Dallas 75065, (972) 497-5031. Committees: Budget; Energy and Commerce; Rules.

District 27 — CLOUD, Michael, R-Victoria; Washington Office: 512 CHOB; (202) 225-7742. District Offices: 101 N. Shoreline Blvd., Ste. 300, Corpus Christi 78401, (361) 884-2222; 5606 N. Navarro, Ste. 203, Victoria 77904, (361) 894-6446. Committees: Agriculture; Oversight and Reform.

District 28 — CUELLAR, Henry, D-Laredo; Washington Office: 2372 RHOB; (202) 225-1640. District Offices: 602 E. Calton Rd., Laredo 78041, (956) 725-0639; 615 E. Houston, Ste. 451, San Antonio 78205, (210) 271-2851; 117 E. Tom Landry, Mission 78572, (956) 424-3942; 100 N. FM 3167, Rio Grande City 78582, (956) 487-5603. Committee: Appropriations.

District 29 — GARCIA, Sylvia, D-Houston; Washington Office: 1620 LHOB; (202) 225-1688; District Office: 11811 East Fwy., Ste. 430, Houston 77029. Committees: Financial Services, Judiciary.

District 30 — JOHNSON, Eddie Bernice, D-Dallas; Washington Office: 2306 RHOB; (202) 225-8885, Fax 225-1477; District Office: 1825 Market Center Blvd., Dallas 75207, (214) 922-8885. Committees: Science, Space, and Technology; Transportation and Infrastructure.

District 31 — CARTER, John, R-Round Rock; Washington Offices: 2208 RHOB; (202) 225-3864. District Offices: 1717 N. I-35, Ste. 303, Round Rock 78664, (512) 246-1600; 6544B S. General Bruce Dr., Temple 76502, (254) 933-1392. Committee: Appropriations.

District 32 — ALLRED, Colin, D-Dallas; Washington Office: 114 CHOB; (202) 225-2231; District Office: 12750 Merit Dr., Ste. 1434, Dallas 75251, (972) 392-0505. Committees: Foreign Affairs, Transportation and Infrastructure, Veterans' Affairs.

District 33 — VEASEY, Marc, D-Fort Worth; Washington Office: 2348 RHOB; (202) 225-9897. District Offices: 1881 Sylvan Ave., Ste 108, Dallas 75028, (214) 741-1387; 6707 Brentwood Stair Rd., Ste. 200, Fort Worth 76112, (817) 920-9086. Committees: Armed Services; Energy and Commerce.

District 34 — VELA, Filemon, D-Brownsville; Washington Office: 307 CHOB; (202) 225-9901. District Offices: 500 E. Main, Alice 78332, (361) 230-9776; 333 Ebony Ave., Brownsville 78520, (956) 544-8352; 1390 W. Expressway 83, San Benito 78586, (956) 276-4497; 301 W. Railroad, Weslaco 78596, (956) 520-8273. Committees: Agriculture, Armed Services.

District 35 — DOGGETT, Lloyd, D-Austin; Washington Office: 2307 RHOB; (202) 225-4865. District Offices: 300 E. 8th, 4th Floor, Austin 78701, (512) 916-5921; 217 W. Travis St., San Antonio 78205, (210) 704-1080. Committees: Agriculture; Armed Services.

District 36 — BABIN, Brian, R-Woodville; Washington Office: 2236 RHOB; (202) 225-1555, Fax 226-0396. District Offices: 203 Ivy Ave., Ste 600, Deer Park 77536, (832) 780-0966; 1201 Childers Rd., Orange 77630, (409) 883-8075; 100 W. Bluff Dr., Woodville 75979, (409) 331-8066. Committees: Transportation and Infrastructure; Science, Space and Technology. ☆

U.S. Tax Collections in Texas

Fiscal Year	Individual Income and Employment Taxes	Corporation Income Taxes	Estate Taxes	Gift Taxes	Excise Taxes	TOTAL U.S. Taxes Collected in Texas
	(in thousands) *Information for fiscal years furnished by the Internal Revenue Service.*					
2020	$ 239,159,253	$ 14,508,511	$ 1,023,884	$ 113,036	$ 17,291,862	$ 275,485,613
2019	245,361,121	18,470,193	1,620,965	148,057	22,661,021	292,330,171
2018	240,169,156	15,756,288	1,395,067	135,733	22,592,120	280,048,364
2017	225,236,761	22,939,596	1,314,828	123,822	21,340,788	270,955,237
2016	218,950,277	19,021,716	1,318,116	140,191	21,698,393	261,138,693
2015	226,945,577	32,083,819	1,167,572	115,516	19,591,942	279,904,425
2014	211,993,178	32,585,544	1,557,068	89,865	19,110,528	265,336,183
2013	195,542,035	33,933,242	890,069	596,861	18,950,003	249,912,209
2012	171,880,127	27,984,282	796,227	180,060	18,619,137	219,459,878
2011	160,086,749	21,880,905	117,936	359,987	15,850,240	198,295,817
2010	147,748,859	24,991,374	1,210,600	287,181	14,904,099	189,142,112
2009	158,798,111	24,235,172	1,780,030	242,918	15,465,279	200,521,512
2008	178,761,539	39,971,658	1,549,767	243,043	15,150,053	235,676,058
2007	160,306,445	41,823,425	1,473,490	218,194	21,569,350	225,390,904

Federal Funds Distribution in Texas

	2019		2020
Total all	$ 207.0 billion		$ 320.8 billion
Direct payments	$ 101.3 billion	Direct payments	$ 128.8 billion
Grants	50.7 billion	Grants	62.9 billion
Contracts	51.0 billion	Contracts	80.6 billion
Other financial assistance	5.0 billion	Other financial assistance	5.5 billion
Loans	–978.0 million	Loans	43.0 million
Top 5 by program			
Social Security retirement	$ 51.7 billion	Social Security retirement	$44.71 billion
Medical assistance	24.2 billion	Paycheck Protection Program	22.15 billion
Veterans compensation	9.2 billion	Medical assistance	3.92 billion
Social Security disability	9.1 billion	Coronavirus Relief Fund	7.47 billion
Social Security survivors	6.8 billion	Veterans compensation	6.34 billion
Top 5 by agency			
Social Security Administration	$ 72.0 billion	Social Security Administration	$ 76.2 billion
Department of Defense	44.1 billion	Department of Defense	72.0 billion
Department of Health and Human Svs	38.8 billion	Small Business Administration	46.1 billion
Department of Veterans Affairs	18.9 billion	Department of Health and Human Svs	46.1 billion
Department of Agriculture	9.7 billion	Department of Veterans Affairs	19.5 billion

Information for fiscal years from USAspending.gov.

Federal Funds Distribution to States, trailing 12 months

Rank	State	Total	Per Capita	Rank	State	Total	Per Capita
1	California	$ 474.8 billion	$12,008	12	Michigan	$ 117.5 billion	$11,806
2	Texas	305.2 billion	10,783	13	Arizona	115.5 billion	16,464
3	New York	268.2 billion	13,513	14	South Carolina	113.4 billion	22,593
4	Florida	258.1 billion	12,300	15	North Carolina	105.7 billion	10,285
5	Pennsylvania	234.8 billion	18,332	16	Georgia	105.6 billion	10,128
6	Indiana	160.9 billion	24,129	17	Massachusetts	101.9 billion	14,857
7	Minnesota	153.3 billion	27,484	18	Wisconsin	99.4 billion	17,147
8	Illinois	141.4 billion	11,045	19	Tennessee	99.0 billion	14,761
9	Virginia	138.5 billion	16,375	20	New Jersey	92.8 billion	10,309
10	Ohio	126.7 billion	10,868				
11	Kentucky	122.4 billion	27,489				

Source: USAspending.gov.

Major Military Installations

Below are listed the major military installations in Texas in 2018. Data are taken from the U.S. Department of Defense Base Structure Report 2017 and other sources. "Civilian" refers to Department of Defense and contractor personnel. *In October 2010, Fort Sam Houston, Lackland AFB, and Randolph AFB were merged into Joint Base San Antonio under the jurisdiction of the U.S. Air Force 502nd Air Base Wing.

U.S. Navy

Naval Air Station Corpus Christi

Location: Corpus Christi (est. 1941).

Address: NAS Corpus Christi, 11001 D St., Corpus Christi 78418

Main phone number: (361) 961-2811

Personnel: 1,369 active-duty; 395 reserve; 710 civilians.

Major units: Naval Air Training Command Headquarters; Training Air Wing 4; Marine Aviation Training Support Group; Coast Guard Air Group; Corpus Christi Army Depot (est. 1961).

Naval Air Station-Joint Reserve Base Fort Worth

Location: westside Fort Worth (est. 1994)

[Carswell, est. in 1942 as Fort Worth Army Air Field, closed in 1993].

Address: NAS-JRB, 1510 Chennault Ave., Fort Worth 76113

Main phone number: (817) 782-3058

Personnel: Active-duty — 2 Army, 232 Navy, 487 Marines, 159 Air Force; Reserve — 605 Army, 2,074 Navy, 1,366 Marines, 975 Air Force, 1,709 Air National Guard; 892 civilians.

Major units: Navy Fleet Logistics Support Squadrons 59; 8th Marine Corps District; Marine Air Group 41; 14th Marine Regiment; Marine Aviation Logistics Squadron 41; Marine Fighter Attach Squadron 112; 136th Airlift Wing, Texas Air National Guard; U.S. Army 90th Aviation Support Battalion; 10th Air Force, 301st Fighter Wing, Air Force Reserve.

Naval Air Station Kingsville

Location: Kingsville (est. 1942).

Address: NAS Kingsville, Texas 78363

Main phone number: (361) 516-6136

Personnel: 363 active-duty; 159 reserve; 243 civilians.

Major units: Training Air Wing Two; Training Squadrons 21 and 22; Naval Auxiliary Landing Field Orange Grove; McMullen Target Range, Escondido Ranch.

U.S. Army

Fort Bliss

Location: El Paso (est. 1849).

Address: Fort Bliss, Texas 79916

Main phone number: (915) 568-2121

Personnel: 25,546 active-duty; 260 reserve; 5,660 civilians.

Major units: 1st Armored Division; 32nd Air and Missile Defense Command; 15th Sustainment Brigade; 5th Armored Brigade; Air Defense Artillery School; 11th Air Defense Artillery Brigades; Joint Task Force North; 204th Military Intelligence Battalion; 212th Fires Brigade; 402nd Field Artillery Brigade; Biggs Army Airfield (est. 1916).

Fort Hood

Location: Killeen (est. 1942).

Address: Fort Hood, Texas 76544

Main phone number: (254) 286-5139

Personnel: 36,391 active-duty; 805 reserve; 6,915 civilians.

Major units: III Corps, Headquarters Command; First Army Division West; 1st Cavalry Division; 13th Sustainment Command; 89th Mili-tary Police Brigade; 3rd Cavalry Regiment; 41st Fires Brigade; 504th Battlefield Surveillance Brigade; Army Operational Test Command; Darnell Army Medical Center.

Fort Sam Houston*

Location: San Antonio (est. 1878).

Address: Fort Sam Houston, Texas 78234

Main phone number: (210) 221-1211

Personnel: 10,462 active-duty; 692 reserve; 10,506 civilians.

Major units: U.S. Army North; U.S. Army South; Brooke Army Medical Center; Institute of Surgical Research; Army Medical Command; Army Medical Dept. Center and School; 5th Recruiting Brigade; 12th Brigade, Western Region (ROTC); Camp Bullis (est. 1917), training area.

Red River Army Depot

Location: 18 miles west of Texarkana (est. 1941).

Address: Red River Army Depot, Texarkana 75507

Main phone number: (903) 334-2141

Personnel: 19 active-duty; 93 reserve; 3,059 civilians.

Major unit: Defense Distribution Center; U.S. Army Tank-Automotive and Armaments Command.

U.S. Air Force

Dyess Air Force Base

Location: Abilene (est. 1942 as Tye Army Airfield, closed at end of World War II, re-established in 1956).

Address: Dyess Air Force Base, Texas 79607

Main phone number: (325) 696-3113

Personnel: 4,221 active-duty; 425 reserve; 710 civilians.

Major units: 7th Bomb Wing (Air Combat Command); 317th Airlift Group.

Goodfellow Air Force Base

Location: San Angelo (est. 1940).

Address: Goodfellow AFB, San Angelo 76908

Main phone number: (325) 654-3876

Personnel: 3,195 active-duty; 29 reserve; 635 civilians.

Major units: 17th Training Wing; 517th Training Squadron; 17th Medical Group. 17th Mission Support Group.

Lackland Air Force Base*

Location: San Antonio (est. 1942 when separated from Kelly Field).

Address: Lackland Air Force Base, Texas 78236

Main phone number: (210) 671-1110

Personnel: 21,532 active-duty; 4,224 reserve; 9,296 civilians.

Major units: 37th Training Wing; 737th Training Group; 341th, 342nd, 343rd, 344th, and 345th Training Squadrons; Defense Language Institute; Inter-American Air Force Academy; Kelly Field Annex (was Kelly Air Force Base, est. 1916).

Laughlin Air Force Base

Location: Del Rio (est. 1942).

Address: Laughlin Air Force Base, Texas 78843

Main phone number: (830) 298-3511

Personnel: 1,288 active-duty; 82 reserve; 1,108 civilians.

Major unit: 47th Flying Training Wing.

Randolph Air Force Base*

Location: San Antonio (est. 1930).

Address: Randolph Air Force Base, Texas 78150

Main phone number: (210) 652-1110

Personnel: 2,649 active-duty; 538 reserve; 5,177 civilians.

Major units: 12th Flying Training Wing; 359th Medical Group; Air Education and Training Command; 902nd Mission Support Group; Air Force Recruiting Command; Air Force Manpower Agency.

Sheppard Air Force Base

Location: Wichita Falls (est. 1941).

Address: Sheppard Air Force Base, Texas 76311

Main phone number: (940) 676-2511

Personnel: 5,973 active-duty; 131 reserve; 1,603 civilians.

Presidential Medal of Freedom

President Donald Trump bestowed a Presidential Medal of Freedom to Babe Didricksen Zaharias posthumously in 2021.

Mildred Ella "Babe" Didricksen Zaharias was born in Port Arthur in 1911 and is widely regarded as one of the greatest athletes of all time. She competed in golf, baseball, basketball, and track and field, winning 2 gold medals in track and field in the 1932 Summer Olympics. Later she became a professional golfer and won 10 LPGA championships.

Major units: 82nd Training Wing; 80th Flying Training Wing; NCO Academy.

Texas Military Forces

Camp Mabry

Location: Austin. Just west of MoPac Blvd.

Address: Box 5218, Austin, Texas 78763

Main phone number: (512) 465-5101

Web site: https://tmd.texas.gov/

Adjutant General of Texas: Maj. General Tracy R. Norris

Major units: Joint Force Headquarters, the Standing Joint Interagency Task Force, the 36th Infantry Division, the 147th Reconnaissance Wing, 149th Fighter Wing, and the 136th Airlift Wing. Texas Air National Guard.

Texas Military Forces Museum: open Wednesday–Sunday, 10 a.m. - 4 p.m.

Tracing their history to early frontier days, the Texas Military Forces are organized into the Army and Air National Guard and the Texas State Guard.

The governor is commander-in-chief of the Texas Military Forces. This command function is exercised through the adjutant general appointed by the governor and approved by federal and state legislative authority.

When not in active federal service, Camp Mabry, in west Austin, serves as the administative and storage headquarters. Camp Mabry was established in the early 1890s as a summer encampment of the Texas Volunteer Guard, a forerunner of the Texas National Guard. The name honors Woodford Haywood Mabry, adjutant general from 1891–1898.

The State Guard, an all-volunteer backup force, was created by the Legislature in 1941. It became an active element of the state military forces in 1965 with a mission of reinforcing the National Guard in emergencies, and replacing National Guard units called into federal service. The State Guard had a membership of approximately 2,200 personnel in 2018.

The Army National Guard is available for state and national emergencies and has been used extensively during natural disasters. There were 17,000 Texans serving in the Texas Army National Guard in 2018.

When the military forces were reorganized following World War II, the Texas Air National Guard was added. Its units augment major Air Force commands. Approximately 3,000 men and women currently make up the Air Guard in the state.

Since 2003, some 31,000 National Guard troops from Texas have served in Iraq and Afghanistan.

In 2018, Adjutant General Norris commanded a total of some 22,000 soldiers, airmen, and civilians.

When called into active federal service, National Guard units come within the chain of command of the Army and Air Force units. ☆

Federal Courts in Texas

Source: The following list of U.S. appeals and district court judges and officials was compiled from court websites.

Texas is divided into four federal judicial districts, each of which is comprised of several divisions. Appeal from all Texas federal courts is to the U.S. Fifth Circuit Court of Appeals in New Orleans.

U.S. Court of Appeals, Fifth Circuit

The Fifth Circuit is composed of Louisiana, Mississippi, and Texas. Sessions are held in each of the states at least once a year and may be scheduled at any location having adequate facilities. U.S. circuit judges are appointed for life and received a salary of $231,800 in 2021.

Circuit Judges:
- Chief Judge, Priscilla R. Owen, Austin.
- Catharina Haynes, James C. Ho, and Don R. Willett, Dallas.
- Edith H. Jones, Gregg J. Costa, Jennifer Walker Elrod, and Jerry E. Smith, Houston.
- James E. Graves Jr., Leslie H. Southwick, and Cory Todd Wilson, Jackson, Miss.
- Stuart Kyle Duncan, Lafayette, La.
- James L. Dennis, Kurt Damian Engelhardt, and Stephen A. Higginson, New Orleans, La.
- Andrew Stephen Oldham, San Antonio.
- Carl E. Stewart, Shreveport, La.

Senior Judges: Fortunato P. Benavides and Patrick E. Higginbotham, Austin; Carolyn Dineen King and Thomas M. Reavley, Houston; Rhesa H. Barksdale and E. Grady Jolly, Jackson, Miss.; John M. Duhé Jr., Jacques L. Wiener Jr., W. Eugene Davis, and Edith Brown Clement, New Orleans, La.

Clerk of Court: Lyle W. Cayce, New Orleans, La.

U.S. District Courts

U.S. district judges are appointed for life and received a salary in 2021 of $218,600.

Northern Texas District

www.txnd.uscourts.gov

District Judges:
- Chief Judge, Barbara M.G. Lynn, Dallas.
- Matthew J. Kacsmaryk, Amarillo.
- Jane J. Boyle, Ada Brown, David C. Godbey, Ed Kinkeade, Sam A. Lindsay, Reed O'Connor, Karen Gren Scholer, and Brantley Starr, Dallas.
- Mark T. Pittman, Fort Worth.
- James Wesley Hendrix, Lubbock.

Senior Judges: A. Joe Fish and Sidney A. Fitzwater, Dallas; John H. McBryde and Terry R. Means, Fort Worth; Sam R. Cummings, Lubbock.

Clerk of District Court: Karen Sublett Mitchell, Dallas.

U.S. Attorney: Prerak Shah.

Federal Public Defender: Jason Hawkins.

U.S. Marshal: (vacant).

Bankruptcy Judges: Chief Judge, Harlin D. Hale, Dallas. Judges, Stacey G.C. Jernigan and Michelle V. Larson, Dallas; Edward L. Morris and Mark X. Mullin, Fort Worth; Robert L. Jones, Lubbock.

Following are the divisions of the Northern District and the counties in each division:

Abilene Division

Callahan, Eastland, Fisher, Haskell, Howard, Jones, Mitchell, Nolan, Shackelford, Stephens, Stonewall, Taylor, and Throckmorton. **Magistrate:** John R. Parker, Abilene. **Courtroom Deputy:** Jennifer Chittum.

Amarillo Division

Armstrong, Briscoe, Carson, Castro, Childress, Collingsworth, Dallam, Deaf Smith, Donley, Gray, Hall, Hansford, Hartley, Hemphill, Hutchinson, Lipscomb, Moore, Ochiltree, Oldham, Parmer, Potter, Randall, Roberts, Sherman, Swisher, and Wheeler. **Magistrate:** Lee Ann Reno, Amarillo. **Deputy-in-charge:** Christopher Kordes.

Dallas Division

Dallas, Ellis, Hunt, Johnson, Kaufman, Navarro, and Rockwall. **Magistrates:** David L. Horan, Irma Carrillo Ramirez, Rebecca Rutherford, and Renee H. Toliver, Dallas. **Courtroom Deputies:** Marie Gonzales, Lavenia Price, Shakira Todd, and Mervin Wright.

Fort Worth Division

Comanche, Erath, Hood, Jack, Palo Pinto, Parker, Tarrant, and Wise. **Magistrates:** Jeffrey L. Cureton and Hal R. Ray Jr., Fort Worth. **Courtroom Deputies:** Julie Harwell and Elsherie Moore.

Lubbock Division

Bailey, Borden, Cochran, Crosby, Dawson, Dickens, Floyd, Gaines, Garza, Hale, Hockley, Kent, Lamb, Lubbock, Lynn, Motley, Scurry, Terry, and Yoakum. **Magistrate:** D. Gordon Bryant Jr., Lubbock. **Courtroom Deputy:** Zelma Medrano.

San Angelo Division

Brown, Coke, Coleman, Concho, Crockett, Glasscock, Irion, Menard, Mills, Reagan, Runnels, Schleicher, Sterling, Sutton, and Tom Green. **Division Manager:** Erik Paltrow.

Wichita Falls Division

Archer, Baylor, Clay, Cottle, Foard, Hardeman, King, Knox, Montague, Wichita, Wilbarger, and Young. **Magistrate:** Hal R. Ray Jr., Wichita Falls.

Western Texas District

www.txwd.uscourts.gov

District Judges:
- Chief Judge, Orlando L. Garcia, San Antonio.
- Robert Pitman and Lee Yeakel, Austin.
- Alia Moses, Del Rio.
- Kathleen Cardone, David C. Guaderrama, and Frank Montalvo, El Paso.
- David Counts, Midland.
- Fred Biery, Jason Pulliam, and Xavier Rodriguez, San Antonio.
- Alan Albright, Waco.

Senior Judges: James R. Nowlin and Sam Sparks, Austin; David Briones, El Paso; Robert A. Junell, Midland and Pecos; David A. Ezra, San Antonio.

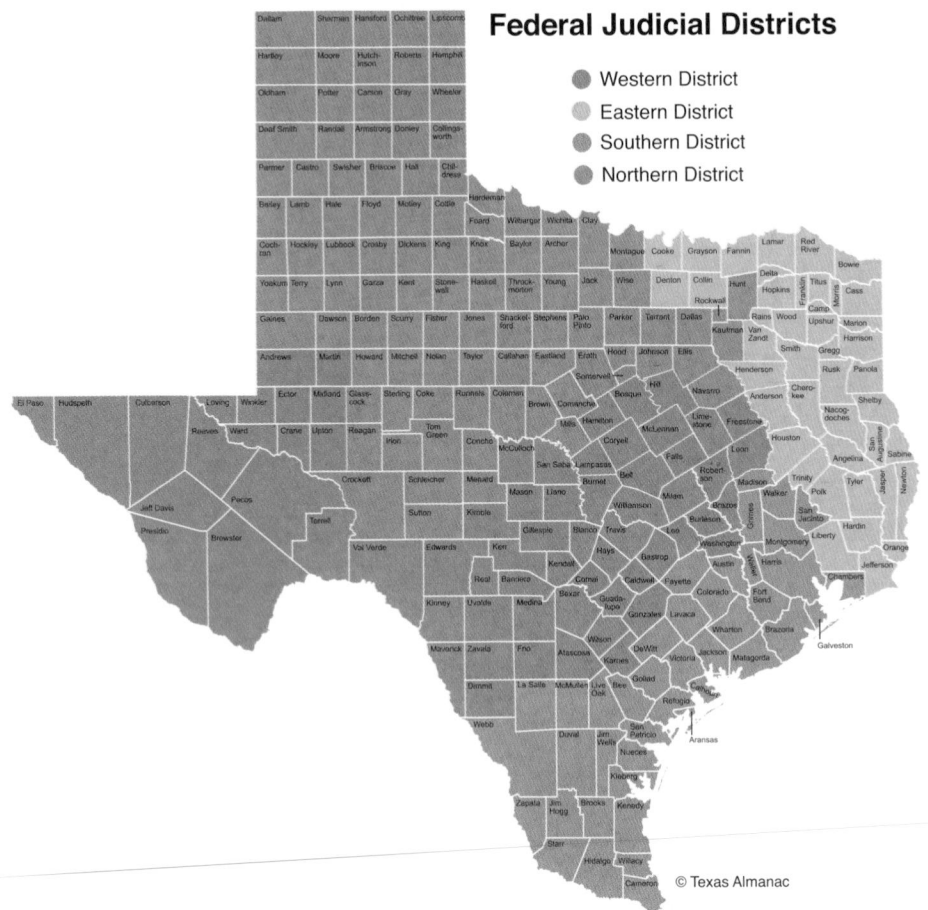

Federal Judicial Districts

- Western District
- Eastern District
- Southern District
- Northern District

© Texas Almanac

Clerk of District Court: Jeannette Clack, San Antonio.

U.S. Attorney: Ashley Hoff.

Federal Public Defender: Maureen Scott Franco.

U.S. Marshal: Susan L. Pamerleau.

Bankruptcy Judges: Chief Judge, Ronald B. King. Judges, H. Christopher Mott and Tony M. Davis, Austin; Craig A. Gargotta, San Antonio.

Following are the divisions of the Western District, and the counties in each division.

Austin Division

Bastrop, Blanco, Burleson, Burnet, Caldwell, Gillespie, Hays, Kimble, Lampasas, Lee, Llano, Mason, McCulloch, San Saba, Travis, Washington, and Williamson. **Magistrates:** Andrew W. Austin, Susan Hightower, and Mark Lane, Austin. **Courtroom Deputies:** Ka Kin "Zing" Cheng, Amanda Deichert, and James Ferrell.

Del Rio Division

Edwards, Kinney, Maverick, Terrell, Uvalde, Val Verde, and Zavala. **Magistrates:** Victor Roberto Garcia and Collis White, Del Rio. **Courtroom Deputies:** Mary Cienega and Carmen Levrie.

El Paso Division

El Paso, Hudspeth. **Magistrates**: Anne T. Berton, Robert F. Castañeda, Leon Schydlower, and Miguel A. Torres, El Paso. **Courtroom Deputies:** Veronica Medina, Veronica Montoya, Cecie Rodriguez, and Rita Velez.

Fort Hood Division

Fort Hood Military Reservation. **Courtroom Deputy:** Michelle Ortiz.

Midland-Odessa Division

Andrews, Crane, Ector, Martin, Midland, and Upton. Court for the Midland-Odessa Division is held at Midland, but may, at the discretion of the court, be held in Odessa. **Magistrate:** Ronald C. Griffin, Midland. **Courtroom Deputy:** Monica Ramirez.

Pecos Division

Brewster, Culberson, Jeff Davis, Loving, Pecos, Presidio, Reeves, Ward, and Winkler. **Magistrate:** David B. Fannin, Alpine. **Courtroom Deputy:** Yvette Lujan.

San Antonio Division

Atascosa, Bandera, Bexar, Comal, Dimmit, Frio, Gonzales, Guadalupe, Karnes, Kendall, Kerr, Medina, Real, and Wilson. **Magistrates:** Henry J. Bemporad, Elizabeth S.

"Betsy" Chestney, and Richard B. Farrer, San Antonio. **Courtroom Deputies:** Amy Jackson, Valeria Sandoval, and Crystal Sosa.

Waco Division

Bell, Bosque, Coryell, Falls, Freestone, Hamilton, Hill, Leon, Limestone, McLennan, Milam, Robertson, and Somervell. **Magistrate:** Jeffrey C. Manske, Waco. **Courtroom Deputy:** Jennifer Galindo-Beaver.

Eastern Texas District

www.txed.uscourts.gov

District Judges:

- Chief Judge, Rodney Gilstrap, Marshall.
- Ron Clark, Marcia A. Crone, Thad Heartfield, and Michael J. Truncale, Beaumont.
- Sean D. Jordan and Richard Schell, Plano.
- Amos L. Mazzant III, Sherman.
- Robert W. Schroeder III, Texarkana.
- J. Campbell Barker and Jeremy D. Kernodle, Tyler.

Clerk of District Court: David A. O'Toole.

U.S. Attorney: Nicholas J. Ganjei.

Federal Public Defender: John D. McElroy.

U.S. Marshal: John M. Garrison.

Bankruptcy Judges: Chief Judge, Brenda T. Rhoades, Plano; Joshua Searcy, Tyler.

Following are the divisions of the Eastern District and the counties in each division:

Beaumont Division

Hardin, Jasper, Jefferson, Liberty, Newton, and Orange. **Magistrates:** Keith F. Giblin and Zach Hawthorn, Beaumont. **Courtroom Deputies:** Tonya Piper and Sherre White.

Lufkin Division

Angelina, Houston, Nacogdoches, Polk, Sabine, San Augustine, Shelby, Trinity, and Tyler. **Deputy-in-charge:** Brandy Fairley.

Marshall Division

Camp, Cass, Harrison, Marion, Morris, and Upshur. **Magistrate:** Roy Payne, Marshall. **Courtroom Deputy:** Becky Andrews.

Sherman Division

Collin, Cooke, Delta, Denton, Fannin, Grayson, Hopkins, and Lamar. **Magistrates:** Christine A. Nowak, Sherman, and Kimberly C. Priest Johnson, Plano. **Courtroom Deputies:** Jane Amerson and Karen Lee.

Texarkana Division

Bowie, Franklin, Red River, and Titus. **Magistrate:** Caroline M. Craven, Texarkana. **Courtroom Deputy:** Hailey Amox.

Tyler Division

Anderson, Cherokee, Gregg, Henderson, Panola, Rains, Rusk, Smith, Van Zandt, and Wood. **Magistrates:** John D. Love and K. Nicole Mitchell, Tyler. **Courtroom Deputies:** Sharon Baum and Lisa Hardwick.

Southern Texas District

www.txs.uscourts.gov

District Judges:

- Chief Judge, Lee H. Rosenthal, Houston.
- Rolando Olvera and Fernando Rodriguez Jr., Brownsville.
- David S. Morales, Nelva Gonzales Ramos, and Drew B. Tipton, Corpus Christi.
- Jeffrey V. Brown, Galveston.
- Alfred H. Bennett, Keith P. Ellison, Charles Eskridge, Vanessa D. Gilmore, Andrew S. Hanen, George C. Hanks Jr., and Lynn N. Hughes, Houston.
- Marina Garcia Marmolejo and Diana Saldaña, Laredo.
- Micaela Alvarez, Randy Crane, and Ricardo H. Hinojosa, McAllen.

Senior Judges: Janis Graham Jack, Corpus Christi; David Hittner, Kenneth M. Hoyt, Sim Lake, Gray H. Miller, Hilda G. Tagle, and Ewing Werlein Jr., Houston; John D. Rainey, Victoria.

Clerk of Court: Nathan Ochsner, Houston.

U. S. Attorney: Jennifer Lowery, Houston.

Federal Public Defender: Marjorie A. Meyers.

U.S. Marshal: T. Michael O'Connor.

Bankruptcy Judges: Chief Judge, David Jones, Houston; Judges, Marvin Isgur, Christopher M. Lopez, and Jeffrey P. Norman, Houston; Eduardo V. Rodriguez, McAllen.

Following are the divisions of the Southern District and the counties in each division:

Brownsville Division

Cameron and Willacy. **Magistrates:** Ronald G. Morgan and Ignacio Torteya III, Brownsville. **Deputy-in-charge:** Rosy D'Venturi.

Corpus Christi Division

Aransas, Bee, Brooks, Duval, Jim Wells, Kenedy, Kleberg, Live Oak, Nueces, and San Patricio. **Magistrates:** Julie K. Hampton and Jason B. Libby, Corpus Christi. **Deputy-in-charge:** Jared Marks.

Galveston Division

Brazoria, Chambers, Galveston, and Matagorda. **Magistrate:** Andrew M. Edison, Galveston. **Deputy-in-charge:** Lucia Smith.

Houston Division

Austin, Brazos, Colorado, Fayette, Fort Bend, Grimes, Harris, Madison, Montgomery, San Jacinto, Walker, Waller, and Wharton. **Magistrates:** Peter Bray, Christina A. Bryan, Dena Hanovice Palermo, Sam S. Sheldon, and Frances H. Stacy, Houston. **Deputy-in-charge:** Darlene Hansen.

Laredo Division

Jim Hogg, La Salle, McMullen, Webb, and Zapata. **Magistrates:** Christopher A. dos Santos, John A. Kazen, and Diana Song Quiroga, Laredo. **Deputy-in-charge:** Aimee Veliz.

McAllen Division

Hidalgo and Starr. **Magistrates:** Juan F. Alanis, J. Scott Hacker, and Nadia S. Medrano, McAllen. **Deputy-in-charge:** Velma T. Barrera.

Victoria Division

Calhoun, DeWitt, Goliad, Jackson, Lavaca, Refugio, and Victoria. **Deputy-in-charge:** Lana Tesch. ☆

Law Enforcement

TEXAS CRIME HISTORY

CRIME PROFILE OF TEXAS COUNTIES

CORRECTIONAL INSTITUTIONS IN TEXAS

Texas Army National Guard soldiers were called in to support local law enforcement during a protest against police brutality in Austin, Texas on May 31, 2020. U.S. Army photo by Charles E. Spirtos/Flickr.

Crime in Texas

Source: Texas Department of Public Safety, Austin; www.dps.texas.gov

The crime statistics in this chapter are all thanks to the **Uniform Crime Reporting (UCR)** programs used by law enforcement agencies in Texas, and nationwide. The first of these programs in the United States was the Committee on Uniform Crime Records, developed by the International Association of Chiefs of Police (IACP) in the 1920s. The first IACP crime collection program, in 1930, was voluntary, and gathered information from 400 police agencies in 43 states. The FBI was authorized as the national clearinghouse for the information collected by that program.

UCR programs collect data on a summary basis, which provides reliable information about crime, but has many limitations. In 1985 a new system was outlined for **Incident Based Reporting (IBR)**, whereby crime data is collected electronically, and includes the circumstances of each incident. The national system, called NIBRS, has been slow to grow, but state programs and the FBI have worked in partnership to assist in the transition. In 2015, the Criminal Justice Information Services Division's Advisory Policy Board set a goal to **sunset summary reporting systems and adopt NIBRS by January 1, 2021.**

Texas first adopted the Uniform Crime Report in 1976, and the Department of Public Safety accepted the responsibility of collecting, validating, and tabulating reports from across the state. The Uniform Crime Reporting Section, created specifically for this purpose, is part of the Crime Records Service division of the department.

The state became certified to collect NIBRS data in 1998, and in 2015, House Bill 11 set a goal to transition all of Texas to NIBRS by September 1, 2019. About 550 agencies met that goal. Another 900 agencies pledged to transition by January 1, 2021. (We have not yet been able to confirm if this goal had been met.)

In Texas, the Department of Public Safety collects data for the national UCR program from police, sheriff's offices, and its own officers. Data are estimated for non-reporting agencies and those that did not have 12 months of data. Agencies that contributed data for the 2019 Crime in Texas report include: 76 college and university police departments, 58 independent school district and zero population police departments, 247 county sheriff's offices, and 673 city police departments.

Mass Attacks in Texas

According to the 2019 Crime in Texas report, the largest challenge facing the law enforcement community that year was mass attacks in public places. The FBI reported that Texas led the nation in active shooter events in 2019. The six that occurred in the state resulted in 36 deaths and 52 wounded. The U.S. Secret Service reported that Texas had 3 of the country's 34 mass attacks in public places that same year, resulting in the death of 33 people. Below is a summary of those three attacks.

- On May 29, 2019 a gunman shot three people in Liberty County, killing one, at a plumbing company. He fled the scene then shot and injured a sheriff's deputy during pursuit. The gunman shot and killed himself before he could be arrested.
- On August 3, 2019 a gunman killed 23 people and injured another 25 when he opened fire in a Wal-Mart in El Paso. Although the accused's trial began in 2020, it was delayed due to the COVID-19 pandemic.
- On August 31, 2019 a gunman fired at police officers before going on a shooting rampage through Midland-Odessa, killing 7 people and wounding 25. The attack ended when the gunman was shot and killed by police.

After these attacks, Governor Abbott created a task force of state legislators and subject matter experts to find ways to detect and prevent mass attacks before they happen.

Crime Summary, 2019

During 2019, there was a reported total of 805,879 index offenses in Texas. This represents a crime-volume increase of 1.1 percent when compared to 796,924 reported offenses in 2018.

In 2019, there were 2,779.3 crimes per 100,000 people, compared with 2,776.6 in 2018, according to data compiled by the Department of Public Safety's Uniform Crime Reporting (UCR) program. The 2019 crime rate is based on a population of 28,995,881.

Monthly crime variations show that, in general, crime occurrences peaked in the month of July. During 2019, Texas law enforcement officers made 698,834 arrests.

Index Crimes

Of the seven major crime categories, the UCR defines violent crime as murder, rape, robbery, and aggravated assault; property crime is defined as burglary, larceny-theft, and motor vehicle theft. The 2019 violent crime rate increased 1.6 percent from 2018, and the nonviolent, or property, crime rate increased 1.0 percent from 2018.

Texas Crime Rate* by Offense, 2019

Crime	2019	2018	% Change
Murder	4.8	4.6	4.9%
Rape	50.5	51.9	-2.6%
Robbery	99.5	98.5	1.0%
Aggravated Assault	260.7	258.4	0.9%
Violent Crime Total	**415.6**	**413.4**	**0.5%**
Burglary	387.7	409.4	-5.3%
Larceny-Theft	1,711.5	1,710.8	0.0%
Motor Vehicle Theft	264.5	242.9	8.9%
Property Crime Total	**2,363.7**	**2,363.2**	**0.0%**
Index Crime Total	**2,779.3**	**2,776.6**	**0.1%**

*Crime rate based on the 2019 Texas population of 28,995,881

Source: 2019 Crime in Texas, TDPS

The estimated value of property stolen during the commission of index crimes in 2019 was more than $2.2 billion, and about 26 percent of that property was recovered.

Arson

The reported number of arsons committed in Texas in 2019 was 2,366, a decrease of 3.0 percent from 2018. In 2019, arson victims suffered losses of $50.9 million, a 34.7-percent decrease when compared with 2018 arson losses of nearly $80 million.

Family Violence

Family violence decreased by 0.1 percent in 2019 from 2018. In 2019, there were 196,902 reported incidents of family violence involving 211,536 victims and 206,275 offenders. In 2016, there were 197,023 reported incidents of family violence involving 212,885 victims and 207,360 offenders.

DUI and Drug-Related Crimes

In 2019 there were 71,959 DUI arrests in Texas, a decrease of 2.7 percent from 2018. Of those arrests, 4,448 or 6.2 percent were of persons under the age of 21.

Texas reported 128,295 drug abuse arrests in 2019, a decrease of 13.6 percent from the previous year. Sales and manufacturing arrests accounted for 19,958 of the total (about 16 percent), and the remaining 108,337 arrests (84 percent) were for possession.

In a breakdown by drug type, the arrests for sales and manufacturing were 58.6 percent synthetic narcotics, 17.3 percent opium or cocaine, 9.4 percent marijuana, and 14.6 percent other. By contrast, possession arrests were 41.7 percent marijuana, 18.8 percent opium or cocaine, 9.6 percent synthetic narcotics, and 29.9 percent other.

Hate Crimes

There were 407 hate crimes incidents reported in Texas in 2019, an increase of 7.1 percent from 2018. Incidents involved a total of 521 victims and 499 offenders.

Reporting for Hate Crime bias improved dramatically in 2019. Broken down by bias motivation, 64.5 percent of incidents were motivated by race/ethnicity/ancestry, 15.5 percent by sexual orientation, 9.8 percent by religion, 4.5 percent by disability, 1.9 percent by gender, and 1 percent by gender identity. Crimes occurred most frequently in residences, and 55.7 percent of offenders were white, 21.2 percent were black, 3.3 percent were multi-racial, and the racial group of 18.7 percent of offenders was unknown.

Law Enforcement Assaults and Deaths

Assaults on law enforcement personnel increased 4.8 percent in 2019 to 4,838. Nine law officers were killed in the line of duty in 2019, and another five died in duty-related accidents. ☆

Texas Index Crimes by Volume 2000–2019

Year	Murder	Rape*	Robbery	Assault	Violent Crime Total	Change from Prior Year	Burglary	Larceny/ Theft	Motor Vehicle Theft	Property Crime Total	Change from Prior Year
2000	1,236	7,821	30,186	73,987	113,230	0.7%	188,205	634,575	92,878	915,658	2.1%
2001	1,331	8,191	35,330	77,221	122,073	7.8%	204,240	669,587	102,838	976,665	6.7%
2002	1,305	8,541	37,599	78,713	126,158	3.3%	212,702	690,028	102,943	1,005,673	3.0%
2003	1,417	7,986	37,000	75,706	122,109	–3.2%	219,733	697,790	98,174	1,015,697	1.0%
2004	1,360	8,401	35,811	75,983	121,555	–0.5%	220,079	696,220	93,844	1,010,143	–0.5%
2005	1,405	8,505	35,781	75,409	121,100	–0.4%	219,733	676,022	93,471	989,226	–2.1%
2006	1,385	8,407	37,271	74,624	121,687	0.5%	215,754	648,083	95,750	959,587	–3.0%
2007	1,415	8,430	38,777	73,570	122,192	0.4%	228,325	662,481	94,026	984,832	2.6%
2008	1,373	8.004	37,757	76,487	115,625	–5.4%	230,263	654,133	85,411	969,807	–1.5%
2009	1,327	8,286	38,041	74,135	121,789	5.3%	240,193	678,340	76,617	995,150	2.6%
2010	1,247	7,626	32,865	71,561	113,299	–7.0%	229,269	654,484	68,220	951,973	–4.3%
2011	1,089	7,445	28,399	68,028	104,961	–7.4%	215,512	613,528	63,379	892,419	–6.3%
2012	1,145	7,692	30,375	67,050	106,262	1.2%	204,976	605,362	64,982	875,320	–1.9%
2013	1,151	7,443	31,852	65,267	105,713	–0.5%	190,567	604,389	65,671	860,627	–1.7%
2014	1,187	11,466	30,857	65,338	108,848	3.0%	166,429	570,385	67,741	804,555	–6.5%
2015	1,314	12,208	31,883	67,358	112,763	3.6%	152,444	555,867	67,081	775,392	–3.6%
2016	1,473	13,320	33,250	72,609	120,652	7.0%	148,073	548,941	68,523	765,537	–1.3%
2017	1,412	14,332	32,120	75,347	123,211	2.1%	133,145	518,414	67,285	718,844	–6.1%
2018	1,324	14,891	28,273	74,165	118,653	–3.7%	117,513	491,028	69,730	678,271	–5.6%
2019	1,403	14,656	28,854	75,595	120,508	1.6%	112,405	496,279	76,687	685,371	1.0%

* In 2014, the FBI changed the definition of rape.

Source: Annual crime reports published by TDPS.

Crime Profile of Texas Counties, 2019

	No. Agencies Reporting	Murder	Rape	Robbery	Assault	Burglary	Larceny-Theft	Auto Theft	Total Index Crimes	Crime Rate per 100,000
Anderson	3	2	23	14	99	249	511	80	978	1,696.2
Andrews	2	0	13	3	68	69	188	23	364	1,970.4
Angelina	6	2	56	40	199	503	1,587	183	2,570	2,968.8
Aransas	4	0	25	12	110	282	728	64	1,221	3,924.5
Archer	1	0	3	0	3	2	0	0	8	451.9
Armstrong	1	0	0	0	1	10	5	3	19	1,011.2
Atascosa	6	1	9	11	66	219	653	122	1,081	2,106.0
Austin	5	0	5	3	38	80	147	30	303	1,009.7
Bailey	2	0	1	0	5	20	34	2	62	889.8
Bandera	1	0	2	1	9	95	143	27	277	1,205.4
Bastrop	5	6	57	30	178	271	793	136	1,471	1,649.3
Baylor	2	0	1	0	4	6	18	4	33	930.9
Bee	2	2	3	5	39	154	332	20	555	1,709.1
Bell	13	18	232	193	569	1,384	4,939	616	7,951	2,221.2
Bexar	27	122	1,818	2,122	8,128	9,707	58,687	8,623	89,207	4,436.8
Blanco	3	0	6	1	12	23	25	12	79	670.3
Borden	1	0	1	0	0	5	4	1	11	1,705.4
Bosque	3	0	3	0	25	44	42	11	125	729.5
Bowie	8	4	65	48	294	501	1,809	130	2,851	3,034.8
Brazoria	23	10	117	132	403	986	4,750	470	6,868	1,798.2
Brazos	4	3	157	101	366	817	3,421	337	5,202	2,266.4
Brewster	3	1	2	0	16	30	15	7	71	770.9
Briscoe	1	0	0	0	0	2	0	1	3	200.9
Brooks	2	0	0	1	15	48	62	1	127	1,799.6
Brown	4	0	28	7	85	192	643	58	1,013	2,689.4
Burleson	3	1	7	3	16	44	97	4	172	933.7
Burnet	6	0	26	7	87	164	390	57	731	1,466.2
Caldwell	4	0	13	3	61	67	259	23	426	986.4
Calhoun	3	0	16	3	58	81	174	14	346	1,796.5
Callahan	3	0	0	0	8	58	55	14	135	966.5
Cameron	21	4	233	236	1,115	1,674	8,677	353	12,292	2,903.8
Camp	2	0	6	1	22	38	82	11	160	1,227.7
Carson	2	1	2	3	23	21	23	6	79	1,328.2
Cass	5	1	19	6	70	110	281	27	514	1,742.6
Castro	2	0	4	0	25	24	38	10	101	1,335.6
Chambers	3	3	9	9	83	148	533	35	820	2,104.0
Cherokee	4	0	0	0	5	23	65	5	98	1,755.6
Childress	2	0	1	0	4	14	23	4	46	632.5
Clay	1	0	8	0	8	33	49	21	119	1,149.1
Cochran	1	0	0	0	3	12	15	0	30	1,078.4
Coke	1	0	0	0	2	10	0	4	16	476.8
Coleman	2	1	3	0	20	21	15	2	62	1,153.9
Collin	17	7	266	259	635	1,458	9,713	897	13,235	1,302.4

Source: Crime in Texas 2019 report, TDPS.

Crime Profile of Texas Counties, 2019

	No. Agencies Reporting	Murder	Rape	Robbery	Assault	Burglary	Larceny-Theft	Auto Theft	Total Index Crimes	Crime Rate per 100,000
Collingsworth	1	N/A	N/A	N/A	N/A	N/A	N/A	N/A	N/A	N/A
Colorado	4	1	12	3	22	54	154	19	265	1,254.3
Comal	4	2	61	34	263	405	1,267	166	2,198	1,316.9
Comanche	3	2	2	1	13	43	143	15	219	1,634.6
Concho	1	0	0	0	11	8	0	0	19	444.8
Cooke	3	3	20	8	91	97	350	23	592	1,489.4
Coryell	3	0	22	7	127	185	735	27	1,103	1,472.3
Cottle	1	0	0	0	0	0	0	0	0	0.0
Crane	2	0	3	0	4	7	7	6	27	560.2
Crockett	1	0	0	1	1	9	5	4	20	579.2
Crosby	3	0	1	1	3	29	13	4	51	1,120.1
Culberson	1	N/A	N/A	N/A	N/A	N/A	N/A	N/A	N/A	N/A
Dallam	2	0	5	0	27	54	101	19	206	2,085.4
Dallas	33	244	1,274	5,806	8,432	13,979	52,851	15,269	97,855	3,324.8
Dawson	2	2	7	12	55	136	296	30	538	4,379.7
Deaf Smith	2	0	2	5	82	85	249	36	459	2,473.5
Delta	1	0	0	0	1	10	16	1	28	525.4
Denton	25	7	358	177	457	1,009	6,250	672	8,930	1,322.5
DeWitt	2	1	11	0	70	75	214	15	386	2,426.6
Dickens	2	0	0	0	1	5	1	2	9	406.9
Dimmit	1	1	2	0	8	39	93	7	150	1,459.1
Donley	1	2	0	0	2	12	16	2	34	1,046.2
Duval	3	0	0	0	19	27	43	41	130	1,084.4
Eastland	6	3	15	1	18	65	89	14	205	1,181.9
Ector	4	17	155	149	1,153	715	3,689	866	6,744	4,044.7
Edwards	1	0	1	0	1	1	2	2	7	366.9
Ellis	9	3	37	39	132	379	1,672	174	2,436	1,404.1
El Paso	11	41	369	363	2,029	1,293	9,594	1,004	14,693	1,748.7
Erath	4	2	32	9	60	131	405	23	662	1,547.5
Falls	2	0	2	8	19	27	25	13	94	623.8
Fannin	4	2	18	2	42	84	262	41	451	1,388.3
Fayette	4	0	17	1	38	72	183	14	325	1,285.1
Fisher	1	0	0	0	0	9	5	0	14	368.5
Floyd	2	0	2	1	26	15	37	4	85	1,482.1
Foard	2	0	0	0	0	1	2	0	3	255.1
Fort Bend	11	15	216	235	1,016	1,251	7,190	568	10,491	1,358.3
Franklin	1	0	1	1	5	10	15	2	32	319.4
Freestone	4	1	8	3	38	92	138	18	298	1,513.9
Frio	3	0	0	1	24	93	123	25	266	1,327.7
Gaines	3	2	5	2	29	56	127	19	240	1,130.8
Galveston	17	16	255	200	447	1,022	5,284	752	7,976	2,242.6
Garza	1	0	5	0	10	17	11	2	45	686.9
Gillespie	2	1	3	1	20	17	163	6	211	784.9

Source: Crime in Texas 2019 report, TDPS.

Crime Profile of Texas Counties, 2019

	No. Agencies Reporting	Murder	Rape	Robbery	Assault	Burglary	Larceny-Theft	Auto Theft	Total Index Crimes	Crime Rate per 100,000
Glasscock	1	0	0	0	1	5	16	4	26	1,857.1
Goliad	1	1	3	2	16	19	49	11	101	1,331.9
Gonzales	4	1	18	1	92	57	217	22	408	1,958.2
Gray	2	0	18	8	115	165	517	32	855	3,941.9
Grayson	14	5	71	40	222	491	1,439	214	2,482	1,870.8
Gregg	7	9	96	77	344	639	2,453	293	3,911	2,981.7
Grimes	2	0	8	4	28	100	130	30	300	1,056.1
Guadalupe	4	3	75	31	160	320	1,535	120	2,244	1,471.6
Hale	4	0	5	4	56	158	421	32	676	2,111.1
Hall	2	1	0	1	2	9	9	0	22	774.4
Hamilton	2	0	5	0	9	16	30	4	64	908.7
Hansford	2	0	0	0	4	7	6	6	23	425.0
Hardeman	2	0	0	0	5	6	11	1	23	594.3
Hardin	5	3	5	7	75	132	347	79	648	1,133.7
Harris	45	392	2,469	11,920	19,935	26,031	112,958	20,770	194,475	4,071.5
Harrison	4	6	4	20	152	352	837	112	1,483	2,300.6
Hartley	1	0	0	0	0	3	3	4	10	348.8
Haskell	2	0	1	0	8	12	21	9	51	889.4
Hays	5	9	138	58	249	474	2,545	261	3,734	1,617.2
Hemphill	1	0	0	0	2	1	12	0	15	394.0
Henderson	10	2	73	14	123	414	524	128	1,278	1,602.4
Hidalgo	21	19	433	331	1,495	2,470	15,638	750	21,136	2,449.0
Hill	4	1	12	4	40	84	431	46	618	1,771.9
Hockley	3	2	25	10	117	143	318	30	645	2,822.5
Hood	2	1	15	8	57	133	595	72	881	1,458.0
Hopkins	3	1	15	7	37	37	144	49	290	788.4
Houston	3	1	2	0	35	72	157	12	279	1,215.1
Howard	2	3	15	21	166	226	903	193	1,527	4,192.8
Hudspeth	1	0	0	0	8	3	9	2	22	442.5
Hunt	5	7	38	37	394	302	947	166	1,891	2,065.8
Hutchinson	2	0	16	4	30	100	251	25	426	2,224.0
Irion	1	0	0	0	4	2	10	0	16	1,065.2
Jack	2	0	2	2	11	25	34	11	85	969.4
Jackson	3	1	4	2	9	28	92	13	149	3,001.3
Jasper	3	3	18	2	84	239	467	78	891	2,498.7
Jeff Davis	1	0	2	0	2	4	6	1	15	673.6
Jefferson	7	29	148	428	1,202	1,476	4,569	589	8,441	3,326.8
Jim Hogg	1	0	0	0	5	10	7	3	25	479.8
Jim Wells	3	0	11	11	188	362	778	51	1,401	3,654.1
Johnson	8	1	104	38	323	434	1,496	241	2,637	1,456.6
Jones	5	0	2	1	9	46	78	8	144	1,026.2
Karnes	3	1	2	2	50	99	158	29	341	2,178.9
Kaufman	7	4	54	32	149	417	1,297	226	2,179	1,662.9

Source: Crime in Texas 2019 report, TDPS.

Crime Profile of Texas Counties, 2019

	No. Agencies Reporting	Murder	Rape	Robbery	Assault	Burglary	Larceny-Theft	Auto Theft	Total Index Crimes	Crime Rate per 100,000
Kendall	2	0	7	4	31	45	350	49	486	1,086.7
Kenedy	1	0	0	0	0	2	3	3	8	1,810.0
Kent	1	0	0	0	4	2	3	0	9	1,265.8
Kerr	3	1	29	1	71	80	413	35	630	1,201.6
Kimble	2	0	1	1	5	7	3	1	18	418.0
King	1	0	0	0	0	0	0	0	0	0.0
Kinney	1	0	0	0	0	1	0	0	1	49.8
Kleberg	3	3	30	14	100	203	592	28	970	3,147.0
Knox	3	0	2	0	1	24	14	5	46	1,270.0
Lamar	4	1	40	21	228	222	609	70	1,191	2,410.7
Lamb	4	0	9	4	30	72	134	17	266	2,050.1
Lampasas	2	1	4	1	20	40	234	13	313	1,677.7
La Salle	2	0	0	1	5	7	37	0	50	660.9
Lavaca	5	2	7	3	33	91	107	9	252	1,135.6
Lee	2	0	9	3	39	28	146	15	240	1,508.9
Leon	1	0	0	0	11	36	70	10	127	824.9
Liberty	4	2	45	16	155	376	1,023	195	1,812	2,077.5
Limestone	3	0	3	2	28	83	102	10	228	975.5
Lipscomb	1	0	0	0	0	2	2	0	4	119.6
Live Oak	2	0	1	1	3	1	9	2	17	375.2
Llano	3	1	3	0	26	41	98	16	185	993.2
Loving	1	0	0	0	1	3	14	3	21	12,804.9
Lubbock	9	11	283	471	1,909	2,557	8,946	1,312	15,489	5,056.2
Lynn	3	0	0	0	1	8	8	5	22	369.7
Madison	2	0	1	4	23	40	32	21	121	844.0
Marion	2	0	0	5	17	40	37	10	109	1,112.5
Martin	2	0	0	0	0	2	6	0	8	136.8
Mason	1	0	1	0	7	4	5	1	18	419.8
Matagorda	5	0	36	12	113	247	818	53	1,279	3,523.1
Maverick	2	1	4	7	39	270	705	73	1,099	1,874.1
McCulloch	2	0	1	0	11	37	40	8	97	1,226.8
McLennan	16	12	159	159	769	1,153	4,968	557	7,777	3,068.2
McMullen	1	0	0	0	0	1	10	1	12	1,602.1
Medina	5	2	23	8	121	135	425	97	811	1,643.0
Menard	1	0	0	1	2	1	0	0	4	189.1
Midland	3	3	37	23	277	229	1,796	379	2,744	1,573.9
Milam	4	1	4	2	32	65	192	34	330	1,318.3
Mills	1	0	1	0	14	11	9	0	35	716.6
Mitchell	2	0	0	2	12	45	96	14	169	2,125.8
Montague	3	0	7	3	54	107	131	9	311	1,686.2
Montgomery	11	14	144	161	807	1,505	5,543	770	8,944	1,495.0
Moore	3	2	11	2	32	61	222	49	379	1,780.4

Source: Crime in Texas 2019 report, TDPS.

Crime Profile of Texas Counties, 2019

	No. Agencies Reporting	Murder	Rape	Robbery	Assault	Burglary	Larceny-Theft	Auto Theft	Total Index Crimes	Crime Rate per 100,000
Morris	5	0	4	4	18	35	98	12	171	1,403.4
Motley	1	0	1	0	0	1	2	0	4	325.2
Nacogdoches	4	4	26	28	120	247	827	95	1,347	2,058.8
Navarro	5	2	66	20	156	236	713	73	1,266	2,559.2
Newton	2	0	4	1	23	64	59	13	164	1,208.1
Nolan	3	0	2	4	29	121	166	18	340	2,552.4
Nueces	8	33	276	514	2,124	2,141	9,149	942	15,179	4,183.7
Ochiltree	2	0	2	0	9	31	86	9	137	1,389.5
Oldham	1	0	0	0	0	4	2	0	6	282.0
Orange	6	1	29	27	157	369	811	159	1,553	1,876.4
Palo Pinto	2	1	7	4	20	175	308	42	557	1,923.3
Panola	2	2	13	5	45	96	317	34	512	2,258.3
Parker	6	3	48	14	116	272	1,015	147	1,615	1,170.9
Parmer	4	0	1	1	7	17	27	10	63	646.0
Pecos	2	0	3	1	24	41	103	26	198	1,269.7
Polk	4	6	42	9	56	257	670	132	1,172	2,329.1
Potter	4	15	162	248	1,051	1,484	5,559	1,014	9,533	4,418.8
Presidio	3	0	2	0	4	2	6	0	14	205.9
Rains	2	0	0	0	10	22	30	7	69	563.4
Randall	3	0	30	6	41	132	264	40	513	1,273.1
Reagan	1	0	0	0	7	11	18	3	39	1,034.8
Real	1	0	0	0	3	15	39	5	62	1,783.1
Red River	3	0	2	2	24	42	45	10	125	1,040.5
Reeves	2	3	3	3	90	48	190	57	394	2,486.6
Refugio	3	0	2	0	7	36	34	7	86	1,237.9
Roberts	1	0	0	0	0	1	1	0	2	223.5
Robertson	2	1	1	3	25	93	168	33	324	1,876.2
Rockwall	5	2	31	10	60	125	877	116	1,221	1,275.3
Runnels	4	0	0	1	13	39	36	3	92	907.7
Rusk	4	5	16	5	86	231	695	86	1,124	2,198.8
Sabine	3	0	5	0	9	42	25	10	91	867.6
San Augustine	2	0	1	0	12	34	16	7	70	863.5
San Jacinto	1	0	26	1	17	115	173	42	374	1,297.2
San Patricio	8	2	29	15	113	218	703	92	1,172	1,990.1
San Saba	2	0	1	0	11	30	39	6	87	1,448.6
Schleicher	1	0	0	0	4	6	6	1	17	605.2
Scurry	2	0	9	3	155	89	163	19	438	2,614.5
Shackelford	1	0	0	0	5	1	2	0	8	248.7
Shelby	3	1	8	4	61	110	224	45	453	1,878.2
Sherman	2	0	0	0	0	3	5	0	8	260.8
Smith	10	7	132	82	550	918	3,655	427	5,771	2,495.0
Somervell	1	0	0	0	4	11	16	3	34	376.7
Starr	6	1	17	7	120	162	398	76	781	1,209.9

Source: Crime in Texas 2019 report, TDPS.

Crime Profile of Texas Counties, 2019

	No. Agencies Reporting	Murder	Rape	Robbery	Assault	Burglary	Larceny-Theft	Auto Theft	Total Index Crimes	Crime Rate per 100,000
Stephens	2	0	1	1	13	29	83	12	139	1,486.3
Sterling	1	0	0	1	1	3	8	2	15	1,130.4
Stonewall	1	0	0	0	1	0	0	0	1	74.7
Sutton	2	0	1	0	2	3	7	5	18	486.6
Swisher	3	0	4	7	25	40	114	8	198	2,926.4
Tarrant	39	101	998	1,690	4,666	7,035	37,547	5,950	57,987	2,828.4
Taylor	6	6	101	71	344	654	2,464	221	3,861	2,697.0
Terrell	1	N/A	N/A	N/A	N/A	N/A	N/A	N/A	N/A	N/A
Terry	2	0	6	0	20	41	89	21	177	1,455.4
Throckmorton	1	0	0	2	2	2	4	2	12	804.8
Titus	2	2	29	14	95	127	457	43	767	2,331.1
Tom Green	3	6	82	33	269	601	2,608	250	3,849	3,250.4
Travis	18	35	692	1,085	3,200	5,329	33,748	3,540	47,629	3,626.5
Trinity	2	0	1	1	4	28	35	10	79	664.9
Tyler	2	5	6	1	57	122	96	39	326	1,512.6
Upshur	4	0	10	8	61	108	206	29	422	1,113.0
Upton	1	0	0	0	2	3	25	3	33	893.6
Uvalde	3	2	10	4	53	106	588	23	786	2,940.7
Val Verde	2	2	13	10	42	153	497	47	764	1,561.5
Van Zandt	5	2	11	2	37	120	281	59	512	937.8
Victoria	2	6	85	58	292	510	1,698	165	2,814	3,054.7
Walker	2	0	31	24	187	167	589	91	1,089	1,500.6
Waller	6	3	26	19	80	98	389	51	666	1,260.1
Ward	2	1	8	4	50	56	279	18	416	3,526.6
Washington	2	0	26	8	109	110	355	36	644	1,836.5
Webb	5	6	110	167	605	768	3,862	325	5,843	2,142.5
Wharton	4	0	19	25	105	177	552	60	938	2,265.7
Wheeler	1	0	0	0	5	1	7	3	16	481.2
Wichita	6	4	115	92	227	676	2,688	278	4,080	3,108.1
Wilbarger	2	0	11	4	35	46	147	11	254	2,006.8
Willacy	5	0	18	4	134	158	221	12	547	2,598.1
Williamson	14	6	167	87	320	801	4,971	322	6,674	1,234.3
Wilson	4	0	7	0	13	94	111	23	248	633.9
Winkler	3	2	3	1	26	71	125	32	260	3,352.2
Wise	5	3	24	7	81	147	457	60	779	1,127.1
Wood	6	0	41	6	46	111	246	48	498	1,083.7
Yoakum	2	0	2	0	2	33	39	9	85	984.5
Young	3	1	11	3	21	50	87	15	188	1,051.9
Zapata	1	0	1	5	46	76	105	2	235	1,665.0
Zavala	2	0	4	0	17	41	27	5	94	787.3
TOTAL	**1,060**	**1,402**	**14,645**	**28,850**	**75,498**	**112,146**	**495,814**	**76,605**	**804,958**	**2,779.3**

Source: Crime in Texas 2019 report, TDPS.

Texas Department of Criminal Justice

Source: Texas Department of Criminal Justice, www.tdcj.texas.gov

The **Texas Board of Criminal Justice** is composed of nine non-salaried members who are appointed by the governor for staggered six-year terms. The board employs the Texas Department of Criminal Justice (TDCJ) executive director, sets rules and policies that guide the agency, and considers other agency actions at its meetings.

Board members serve in a separate capacity as the Board of Trustees for the **Windham School District** by hiring a superintendent and providing similar oversight. The Windham School District is a separate entity primarily funded through the Texas Education Agency (TEA).

In addition to hiring the TDCJ executive director, the board appoints an inspector general, a director of internal audits, a director of state counsel for offenders, and a prison rape elimination act ombudsman.

The TDCJ executive director is responsible for the administration and enforcement of statutes relative to the criminal justice system.

The Correctional Institutions Division, Private Facility Contract Monitoring and Oversight Division, Parole Division, and Community Justice Assistance Division are most involved in the everyday confinement and supervision of convicted felons.

The actual supervision of probationers is the responsibility of local community supervision and corrections departments. Victim Services coordinates a central mechanism for crime victims to participate in the criminal justice process.

Divisions of the TDCJ

The **Correctional Institutions Division** (CID) is responsible for the confinement of adult felony and state jail offenders who are sentenced to incarceration in a secure state-operated correctional facility. More about this division on the next page.

Private Facility Contract Monitoring and Oversight Division is responsible for oversight and monitoring contracts for privately operated secure facilities, as well as community-based facilities, which include substance abuse treatment services.

The **Parole Division** supervises all offenders released on parole or mandatory supervision; conducts release and transition planning; and verifies compliance with statutory provisions of release.

In addition, this division contracts for electronic monitoring and processing responses to violations, administers programs and services through District Resource Centers and Parole Offices, and coordinates the Interstate Compact for Adult Offender Supervision.

The **Community Justice Assistance Division** (CJAD) administers community supervision, also known as adult probation in Texas. CJAD is responsible for the distribution of formula and grant funds; the development of standards, including best-practice treatment standards; approval of Community Justice Plans and budgets; conducting program and fiscal audits; and providing training and certification

Operating Budget 2020		
Budget Item	**Total, All Funds ($ in millions)**	**Percent of Total**
A: Provide Prison Diversions	$248.0	7.0%
B: Special Needs Offenders	$27.6	0.8%
C: Incarcerate Felons	$2,909.0	81.8%
D: Board of Pardons and Paroles	$30.0	0.8%
E: Operate Parole System	$182.6	5.1%
F: Indirect Administration	$101.7	2.9%
G: Ensure Adequate Facilities	$58.0	1.6%
TOTAL	**$3,556.9**	**100%**

Source: TDCJ Fiscal Year 2020 Operating Budget

Inmate Profile	
As of Fiscal Year 2018	
Sex – Ethnicity – Age	
Male: 91.6%	Hispanic: 33.5%
Black: 32.7%	Other: 0.6%
White: 33.3%	Average age: 39.4
Average Sentences	
Prison: 19.5 years	State jail: 1.1 year
Average Part Of Sentence Served	
Prison: 61.0%	State jail: 99.5%
(Based on offenders released in Fiscal Year 2018.)	
Education	
Average IQ	90.7
Percent lacking high school diploma or GED:	81.3%

Source: TDCJ Annual Review 2018

of community supervision officers. The remaining divisions support the overall operation of the TDCJ. These include:

- **Office of the General Counsel**
- **Administrative Review and Risk Management**
- **Business and Finance**
- **Information Technology**
- **Manufacturing, Agribusiness and Logistics**
- **Facilities**
- **Rehabilitation Programs**
- **Re-entry and Integration Programs**
- **Health Services and Human Resources**

Correctional Institutions Division

In addition to the incarceration of offenders, the CID has the following support functions, including: classification and records; counsel substitute; laundry, food and supply; offender transportation; and correctional training and staff development.

The table below lists all of the correctional institutions in the state alphabetically by county. It includes both those operated by the CID as well as privately-operated facilities, which have been overseen by the **Private Facility Contract Monitoring and Oversight Division** since June 15, 2007.

The town listed is the nearest one to the facility, although the unit may actually be in another county. For instance, the Middleton Transfer Facility is in Jones County, but the nearest city is Abilene, which is in Taylor County. ☆

On-Hand Population	
As of Aug. 31, 2020	
Prisoners	
Prison	117,380
State Jails	1,748
SAFP (Substance Abuse)	1,412
TOTAL	**120,540**
Parole	
Mandatory Supervision Population	111,593
Probation	
Community Supervision Placements*	84,891

*Total adults on direct, indirect, and pretrial supervision, minus transfers

Source: TDCJ Statistical Report 2020

Correctional Institutions in Texas

County	Unit	Nearest Town	Max. Capacity, Gender	Employees	Type* (Operator**)
Anderson	Beto	Tennessee Colony	3,471 Male	633	Prison (CID)
Anderson	Coffield	Tennessee Colony	4,139 Male	879	Prison (CID)
Anderson	Gurney	Tennessee Colony	2,128 Male	437	Transfer (CID)
Anderson	Michael	Tennessee Colony	3,800 Male	816	Prison (CID)
Anderson	Powledge	Palestine	1,137 Male	290	Prison (CID)
Angelina	Diboll	Diboll	518 Male	136	Private Prison (MTC)
Angelina	Duncan	Diboll	606 Male	139	Geriatric (CID)
Bee	Garza East	Beeville	2,458 Male	442	Transfer (CID)
Bee	Garza West	Beeville	2,278 Male	401	Transfer (CID)
Bee	McConnell	Beeville	2,900 Male	542	Prison (CID)
Bexar	Dominguez	San Antonio	2,276 Male	382	State Jail (CID)
Bowie	Telford	New Boston	2,872 Male	706	Prison (CID)
Brazoria	Clemens	Brazoria	1,215 Male	348	Prison (CID)
Brazoria	Darrington	Rosharon	1,931 Male	546	Prison (CID)
Brazoria	Ramsey	Rosharon	1,891 Male	429	Prison (CID)
Brazoria	Scott	Angleton	1,130 Male	307	Prison (CID)
Brazoria	Stringfellow	Rosharon	1,212 Male	313	Prison (CID)
Brazoria	Terrell, C.T.	Rosharon	1,603 Male	466	Prison (CID)
Brazos	Hamilton	Bryan	1,166 Male	256	Pre-Release (CID)
Brown	Havins	Brownwood	596 Male	181	Pre-Release (CID)
Burnet	Halbert	Burnet	612 Female	135	SAFPF (CID)
Caldwell	Lockhart	Lockhart	500 Female, 500 Male	204	Private Prison/Work Program (MTC)
Cherokee	Hodge	Rusk	989 Male	333	DDP (CID)
Cherokee	Skyview	Rusk	562 Female/Male	295	Psychiatric (CID)

* **Prison types:** SAFPF (Substance Abuse Felony Punishment Facilities); DDP (Developmentally Disabled Program)
** **Operator abbreviations:** CID (TDCJ Correctional Institutions Division); MTC (Management and Training Corporation); LaSalle (LaSalle Corrections)
[1]. Employee and capacity data includes those working and held at the nearby Baten Intermediate Sanction Facility

Source: TDCJ Unit Directory

Correctional Institutions in Texas

County	Unit	Nearest Town	Max. Capacity, Gender	Employees	Type* (Operator**)
Childress	Roach	Childress	1,384 Male	289	Prison (CID)
Coryell	Crain	Gatesville	2,115 Female	711	Prison (CID)
Coryell	Hilltop	Gatesville	553 Female	268	Prison (CID)
Coryell	Hughes	Gatesville	2,984 Male	741	Prison (CID)
Coryell	Mountain View	Gatesville	645 Female	300	Prison (CID)
Coryell	Murray	Gatesville	1,341 Female	341	Prison (CID)
Coryell	Woodman	Gatesville	900 Female	270	State Jail (CID)
Dallas	Hutchins	Dallas	2,276 Male	399	State Jail (CID)
Dawson	Smith	Lamesa	2,234 Male	408	Prison (CID)
DeWitt	Stevenson	Cuero	1,384 Male	272	Prison (CID)
Duvall	Glossbrenner	San Diego	612 Male	123	SAFPF (CID)
El Paso	Sanchez	El Paso	1,100 Male	287	State Jail (CID)
Falls	Hobby	Marlin	1,384 Female	299	Prison (CID)
Falls	Marlin	Marlin	606 Female	126	Transfer (CID)
Fannin	Cole	Bonham	900 Male	226	State Jail (CID)
Fannin	Moore, C.	Bonham	1,224 Male	245	Transfer (CID)
Fort Bend	Jester I	Richmond	323 Male	119	SAFPF (CID)
Fort Bend	Jester III	Richmond	1,131 Male	288	Prison (CID)
Fort Bend	Jester IV	Richmond	550 Male	381	Psychiatric (CID)
Fort Bend	Vance	Richmond	378 Male	116	Prison (CID)
Freestone	Boyd	Teague	1,372 Male	298	Prison (CID)
Frio	Briscoe	Dilley	1,384 Male	233	Prison (CID)
Galveston	Hospital Galveston	Galveston	365 Female/Male	496	Medical (CID)
Galveston	Young	Galveston	455 Female	302	Medical (CID)
Gray	Jordan (Baten)	Pampa	1,008 Male[1]	289[1]	Prison (CID)
Grimes	Luther	Navasota	1,316 Male	323	Prison (CID)
Grimes	Pack	Navasota	1,478 Male	334	Prison (CID)
Hale	Formby	Plainview	1,100 Male	278	State Jail (CID)
Hale	Wheeler	Plainview	576 Male	127	State Jail (CID)
Harris	Kegans	Houston	667 Male	155	State Jail (CID)
Harris	Lychner	Humble	2,276 Male	413	State Jail (CID)
Hartley	Dalhart	Dalhart	1,398 Male	237	Prison (CID)
Hays	Kyle	Kyle	520 Male	117	Private Prison (MTC)
Hidalgo	Lopez	Edinburg	1,100 Male	257	State Jail (CID)
Hidalgo	Segovia	Edinburg	1,224 Male	233	Pre-Release (CID)
Houston	Eastham	Lovelady	2,474 Male	583	Prison (CID)
Jack	Lindsey	Jacksboro	1,031 Male	202	State Jail (MTC)
Jasper	Goodman	Jasper	612 Male	155	Transfer (CID)
Jefferson	Gist	Beaumont	2,276 Male	368	State Jail (CID)
Jefferson	Leblanc	Beaumont	1,224 Male	248	Pre-Release (CID)
Jefferson	Stiles	Beaumont	2,981 Male	756	Prison (CID)
Johnson	Estes	Venus	1040 Male	191	Private Prison (MTC)

* **Prison types:** SAFPF (Substance Abuse Felony Punishment Facilities); DDP (Developmentally Disabled Program)
** **Operator abbreviations:** CID (TDCJ Correctional Institutions Division); MTC (Management and Training Corporation); LaSalle (LaSalle Corrections)
[1]. Employee and capacity data includes those working and held at the nearby Baten Intermediate Sanction Facility

Source: TDCJ Unit Directory

Correctional Institutions in Texas

County	Unit	Nearest Town	Max. Capacity, Gender	Employees	Type* (Operator**)
Jones	Middleton	Abilene	2,128 Male	504	Transfer (CID)
Jones	Robertson	Abilene	2,984 Male	683	Prison (CID)
Karnes	Connally	Kenedy	2,148 Male	602	Prison (CID)
La Salle	Cotulla	Cotulla	606 Male	99	Transfer (CID)
Liberty	Cleveland	Cleveland	520 Male	134	Private Prison (MTC)
Liberty	Henley	Dayton	576 Female	124	State Jail (CID)
Liberty	Hightower	Dayton	1,384 Male	335	Prison (CID)
Liberty	Plane	Dayton	2,291 Female	418	State Jail (CID)
Lubbock	Montford	Lubbock	1,044 Male	705	Psychiatric (CID)
Madison	Ferguson	Midway	2,421 Male	578	Prison (CID)
Medina	Ney	Hondo	576 Male	134	State Jail (CID)
Medina	Torres	Hondo	1,384 Male	298	Prison (CID)
Mitchell	Wallace	Colorado City	1,448 Male	255	Prison (CID)
Pecos	Fort Stockton	Fort Stockson	606 Male	114	Transfer (CID)
Pecos	Lynaugh	Fort Stockton	1,416 Male	289	Prison (CID)
Polk	Polunsky	Livingston	2,984 Male	691	Prison (CID)
Potter	Clements	Amarillo	3,798 Male	1,050	Prison (CID)
Potter	Neal	Amarillo	1,732 Male	383	Prison (CID)
Rusk	Bradshaw	Henderson	1,980 Male	266	State Jail (MTC)
Rusk	East Texas	Henderson	224 Female, 2,012 Male	493	Multi-Use (MTC)
Rusk	Moore, B.	Overton	500 Male	109	Private Prison (MTC)
San Saba	San Saba	San Saba	606 Female	135	Transfer (CID)
Scurry	Daniel	Snyder	1,384 Male	224	Prison (CID)
Stephens	Sayle	Breckenridge	632 Male	146	SAFPF (CID)
Swisher	Tulia	Tulia	606 Male	117	Transfer (CID)
Terry	Rudd	Brownfield	612 Male	145	Transfer (CID)
Travis	Travis County	Austin	1,161 Male	264	State Jail (CID)
Tyler	Lewis	Woodville	2,231 Male	570	Prison (CID)
Walker	Byrd	Huntsville	1,365 Male	282	Prison (CID)
Walker	Ellis	Huntsville	2,482 Male	604	Prison (CID)
Walker	Estelle	Huntsville	3,480 Male	980	Prison (CID)
Walker	Goree	Huntsville	1,321 Male	315	Prison (CID)
Walker	Holliday	Huntsville	2,128 Male	435	Transfer (CID)
Walker	Huntsville	Huntsville	1,705 Male	446	Prison (CID)
Walker	Wynne	Huntsville	2,621 Male	697	Prison (CID)
Wichita	Allred	Iowa Park	3,722 Male	939	Prison (CID)
Willacy	Willacy County	Raymondville	1,069 Male	183	State Jail (La Salle)
Wise	Bridgeport	Bridgeport	520 Male	117	Private Prison (MTC)
Wood	Johnston	Winnsboro	612 Male	160	SAFPF (CID)

* **Prison types:** SAFPF (Substance Abuse Felony Punishment Facilities); DDP (Developmentally Disabled Program)
** **Operator abbreviations:** CID (TDCJ Correctional Institutions Division); MTC (Management and Training Corporation); LaSalle (LaSalle Corrections)
¹. Employee and capacity data includes those working and held at the nearby Baten Intermediate Sanction Facility

Source: TDCJ Unit Directory

Culture & the Arts

Visitors to the Dallas Museum of Art view a painting November 20, 2019.
Photo by risingthermals/Flickr (CC).

African American Texans
By Dr. Merline Pitre

African Americans have been part of the landscape of Texas as long as Europeans. Nearly spanning a period of five centuries, the African American presence began in 1528 with the arrival of an African slave, Esteban, who accompanied the first Spanish exploration of the land in the southwestern part of the United States that eventually became Texas. From this time forward, African American experience and journey included hardships and triumphs. Subjected to slavery, segregation and discrimination during this long history, African Americans have made significant contribution to the growth and development of Texas.

Spanish Texas

Esteban, one of four survivors of the Cabeza de Vaca expedition in 1528, established a pattern of Black involvement in Spanish Texas. Blacks accompanied most Spanish expeditions into Texas during the 16th and 17th centuries. By the late 18th century, the Black and mulatto inhabitants comprised more than 15% of the population. Although the Spanish introduced slavery into Texas, the majority of the Blacks living in the province were free. For example, in 1771 San Antonio listed a population of 1,779 Black males and of that number only four were slaves.

Free Blacks faced few, if any, restrictions on their freedom. They were socially accepted and followed whatever trade or profession they chose. These included teachers, shoemakers, teachers and landowners, to name a few. William Goyens is an example of a prominent Black businessman and landowner.

Slavery and Freedom

Unlike free Blacks who inhabited Spanish Texas, the majority of African Americans entered Texas as slaves. Slavery as an institution of significant impact came to Texas with Anglo Americans. The first Anglo Americans who settled in Texas came from the southern part of the United States, where slavery was a thriving institution, and, as such, brought their slaves along with them. During the time of the first Anglo settlement (1821) to the Texas Revolution (1836), slavery grew slowly. Upon gaining its independence from Mexico in 1836, the newly found Republic of Texas continued the "peculiar institution." During the Republic period, the slave population grew from 5,000 in 1836 to 30,000 in 1845, the year Texas was annexed to the United States. Slavery grew by leaps and bounds after annexation, reaching 58,161 in 1850. By the end of the Civil War, there were approximately 400,000 slaves in Texas. This increase was due in large part to the fact that many slave owners in

Above: The hat and saddle used by Fred Whitfield, a professional rodeo cowboy who specialized in tie-down roping. In his career he won eight world championships from the Professional Rodeo Cowboys Association and three National Finals Rodeo aggregate titles. The above display is from the National Multicultural Western Heritage Museum in Fort Worth. Photo by the Texas Historical Commission, www.thc. texas.gov.

other states had sent their slaves to East Texas since that area was far removed from the fighting. They came from as far away as Louisiana, Mississippi, Arkansas, and Virginia.

The overwhelming majority of the slaves were concentrated along the coast and river valleys of East Texas and labored in agricultural pursuits, primarily in cotton farming. Slaves were responsible for over 90% of the cotton grown in the state. Texans who engaged in rice farming and stock raising also depended on slave labor. So slavery was very profitable in East Texas.

The institution of slavery in Texas was similar to that of other southern states. The treatment of slaves varied from location to location, from plantation to plantation, from owner to owner. The typical slave faced a life replete with hardship. The majority of slaves were field hands who worked mostly on cotton plantations from sunup to sundown. The number of artisans, house servants and urban slaves was small, but still their work and behavior were regulated by a set of rules prescribed by the master. Living arrangements included crude cabins, inadequate clothing and only enough food for substance. Despite the restriction placed on them, the slaves showed a remarkable ability to cope with a hostile environment and to think and act in terms of survival and freedom.

The end of slavery came as a result of a bloody and costly civil war that lasted from 1861 to 1865. The collapse of the Confederacy and Robert E. Lee's surrender on April 9, 1865, meant freedom for the slaves. Although President Abraham Lincoln issued the Emancipation Proclamation on January 1, 1863, freeing slaves in the rebellion states, it was only in areas the Union troops had conquered that the slaves became freed people. For African Americans of Texas, freedom did not come until June 19, 1865 (commonly referred to as Juneteenth). On that date General Gordon Granger, the Union commander of the Department of Texas, arrived at the Port of Galveston and read General Order #3 and announced that the slaves of the state of Texas were free. Despite this reading of the official Emancipation Proclamation of Texas, not all slaves were freed. In isolated areas of the state where the army was unable to reach, the masters did not inform the slaves and, therefore, some slaves were not freed until 1868.

The immediate reaction of slaves on being set free varied. There was crying and weeping. Some slaves were confused and didn't know where to go. Others tested their freedom by walking off the plantations, only to return a short time afterward. Still others wanted the same things as their White counterparts — schooling, clothes and sufficient food. After their initial shock, African Americans had to rebuild their lives, locate family members and begin to live their lives as self-sufficient free men and women. The Freedmen's Bureau aided in the transition from slavery to freedom by providing legal assistance and helping to establish schools. But even before the Freedmen's Bureau could provide assistance, Blacks organized makeshift schools and began establishing their own religious institutions.

Yet the transition was not easy and was further complicated by the fact that the social order had changed and the racial animosity that separated Blacks and Whites still abided. The legal system was used to regulate Black behavior. A lack of land ownership and a reign of terror tied the masses of Blacks to a second form of slavery: sharecropping. Consequently, during the first year of freedom there was a mass migration of ex-slaves to urban centers such as Galveston, Houston, San Antonio, Marshall and Beaumont. Other migration occurred away from plantations in rural areas where Blacks established freedom colonies and on the outskirts of cities where they established freedmen's towns.

Reconstruction and Post Reconstruction

Reconstruction presented challenges and possibilities for White and Black Texans. In order to keep Blacks in a subservient position and to ensure that White supremacy prevailed, the 1866 Texas Constitution, drawn up and ratified by former Confederates, replaced slave codes with Black codes that denied freed people the right to vote, serve on juries or testify against Whites in court. But this denial of legal, civil and political rights did not endure. In March 1867 the United States Congress intervened through a series of Reconstruction Acts and demanded that all former Confederate states ratify the 14th amendment and grant legal and political rights to African Americans. These acts ordered southern states to summon constitutional conventions and write new constitutions denying constitutional rights to no one on account of race, color or previous condition of servitude. The result of which was that 11 African American delegates were elected to help write a new state constitution for Texas — a constitution that protected civil rights, established the state's first public education system and extended the franchise to all men.

After the ratification of the 1869 constitution and the passage of the 15th amendment, 42 men of color were elected to serve in the state legislature from 1870 to 1898 and helped to move the state toward democracy. These Black legislators' concern first and foremost was to further Black struggle for power and participation in the existing political, social and economic institutions. As members of the state legislature and constitutional conventions, Black lawmakers helped lay the foundation for public school systems of the state, make reforms in mental asylum and correctional institutions, and pass laws that granted universal suffrage and the protection of civil rights. Working along with these legislators was another Black, Norris Wright Cuney, who became the tutelary head of the state Republican Party from 1884 to 1896.

Reconstruction in Texas came to an end in 1873 when Democrats regained control of the state legislature. White Democrats then proceeded to reverse many of the democratic reforms instituted by Black and White Republicans. So from 1874 to 1900, even as Black Republicans tried to help move the state toward democracy, African Americans of Texas entered a period that some historians call the "nadir." That is, Whites suppressed Blacks politically, socially and economically. Additionally, lynching and other forms of violence were used to keep Blacks in their "place," most notably in East Texas.

The economic position of Blacks was not bright during the last half of the 19th century. The masses of Blacks were sharecroppers or tenant farmers. Of the Blacks who were not sharecroppers, 25% worked in towns and cities as restaurant workers, barbers, saloon keepers, launderers and as domestic help. Additionally, Black men worked in the lumber industry, on railroad construction and as longshoremen in towns like Galveston.

Given this economic reality, Blacks relied on education as a means of upward mobility. Still, education had its problems. The state established a segregated public-education system that underfunded African American schools and limited access to books, libraries and other educational resources. Black schools did not share equally in state money with Whites. As late as 1900, two-thirds of all Black schools met in churches or rented buildings. As for institutions of higher learning, church-affiliated institutions (Wiley, Bishop, Tillotson, Samuel Huston, Texas College and Mary Allen) along with Prairie View College carried the burden of educating Black students.

Despite the fact that Black public schools and Prairie View College were underfunded and double-taxed, between 1880 and 1900 the illiteracy rate among African Americans fell from 75.4% to 38%. This rate would continue to fall in the 20th century as the Julius Rosenwald Fund provided grants (which had to be matched by the Black community) for the construction of public schools in the rural areas of the South for African Americans. Between 1920 and 1932, Texas boasted of 527 Rosenwald schools, mostly in East and Central Texas. During the first half of the 20th century, the number of Black institutions of higher learning would increase from seven to nine.

Despite this glimmer of hope found in education, at the dawn of the 20th century the political gains that African Americans had made from 1870 to 1900 were virtually lost. The imposition of the poll tax and the purification of the ballot via the White Democratic primary that began in 1905 meant fewer African Americans would be voting. For example, there were 100,000 Black voters in 1890 compared to 5,000 in 1906. The majority of Blacks had been disenfranchised by the following methods: violence, economic coercion, literacy tests, poll taxes and the White Democratic primary. Coupled with these subterfuges, Blacks lived in a segregated world. Racial boundaries that were somewhat fluid during post-Reconstruction in Texas solidified throughout the 1880s and 1990s and culminated in the

Supreme Court decision in *Plessy v Ferguson* in 1896 that declared racial segregation legal.

Segregation (Jim Crow) and Black Response

In Texas, the nadir of the African American experience extended to the 20th century as segregation and violence deepened. Segregation was not just a system of physical separation of races. It was a social and legal system that denied Blacks equal access to everything from health care and jobs to education and justice. Coupled with segregation in keeping Blacks in their place was violence found most notably in the form of lynching and White-instigated race riots. Most notable among these were the following race riots and lynchings: Waco (1916), Houston (1917), Longview (1919), Kirvin Lynching (1922) and Beaumont (1943).

Black Texans responded to this violence and discrimination in several ways. Some fought back, some endured, some left the state for the North or the West, some moved from rural areas to towns and cities within the state. Still others formed self-help and protest organizations such as the fraternal orders, benevolent societies, literary clubs, the Urban League and the NAACP. Despite their second-class status, African Americans built viable and progressive communities throughout the state. As in the 19th century, they continued to organize churches, schools and social organizations that served their needs. As sharecroppers and tenant farmers, they organized a Black cooperative to raise prices for their produce. One also saw the rise of Black newspapers in large cities of the state, including the *Houston Informer, San Antonio Register* and *Dallas Express*.

One of the most significant achievements of African Americans of the 20th century was their participation in the Texas Centennial of 1936. There, under the leadership of A. Maceo Smith of the Dallas Chamber of Commerce and

Right: A sharecropper's wife preparing poke salad, 1939. Photo by Russell Lee/Wikimedia Commons.

Below: The lone remaining sharecropper's house at the Potter Farm, near Terrell. Photo by Carol M. Highsmith/Library of Congress.

Samuel W. Houston of Huntsville, the Hall of Negro Life was built in Fair Park in Dallas and October 19, 1936, was designated as Negro Day.

The establishment of the Hall of Negro Life was a way of preserving the history and culture of Black Texans. Among other things that were included in the hall were two exhibits: one highlighting Historically Black Colleges and Universities (HBCUs) and one dealing with aesthetics. The aesthetic exhibit featured Samuel A. Countee, Aaron Douglas and Frank Sheinall. Later, the world-renowned artist John T. Biggers' painting, along with that of James Thibodeaux, would also be on exhibit. Over the years other artists, musicians and writers were highlighted, such as Blind Lemon Jefferson, Huddie (Leadbelly) Ledbetter, Eddie Durham, Scott Joplin, Maud Cuney Hare and J. Mason Brewer.

In addition to highlighting outstanding personalities, events and organizations, Negro Day proved to be an opportunity for African American Texans to meet and plan strategies to end Jim Crow practices and discrimination. Out of this initial meeting came the idea of establishing the Texas Conference of State Branches of the NAACP, whereby all branches would coordinate their activities to eliminate Jim Crow through the Texas Conference. Two major cases sponsored by the Conference of State Branches were *Smith v Allwright* (1944) and *Sweatt v Painter* (1951). The first case involved the NAACP's effort to have the White Democratic primary statute (a law stating that only White men should vote in the Democratic primary) declared unconstitutional. Victory came in 1944 when the Supreme Court sided with the NAACP. The second case, *Sweatt v Painter*, centered around a frontal attack on segregated professional education. In its verdict the Supreme Court ordered a Black man, Heman Sweatt, admitted to the University of Texas Law School, notwithstanding a Black law school existed at Texas Southern University. *Sweatt v Painter* set precedence for *Brown v Board of Education* by implying that "separate but equal" was unconstitutional. *Brown v Board of Education* reversed *Plessy v Ferguson* and stated in writing that separate but equal was unconstitutional.

Civil Rights and Voting Rights

Viewing *Brown* as a pathway to equality and as a boost to the civil rights movement, Black activists became all the more determined to change the status quo. From 1955 to 1966, they launched a steady campaign to integrate public schools and to gain access to better jobs and public facilities. Within a decade many of the public schools in Texas had been integrated.

In the last half of the 20th century, each battle for civil rights required hard work, commitment and constant pressure on public officials. Sometimes it also required physically testing the law as many students at Texas Southern University, Wiley College, Bishop College and Prairie View University staged sit-in demonstrations in their respective cities. These sit-in demonstrations in large, as well as small, cities effectively desegregated many public facilities and helped bolster the Civil Rights Act of 1964, an act that legally assured integration in public accommodations in hotels, restaurants, swimming pools and golf courses.

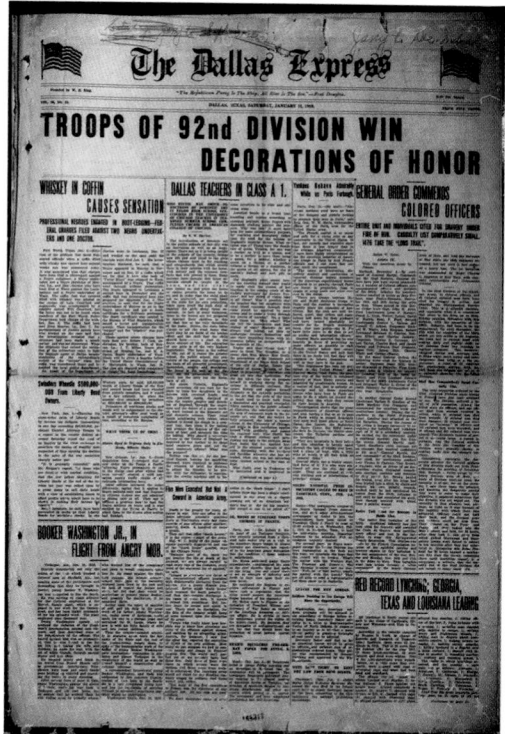

This edition of The Dallas Express was published on Jan. 11, 1919. The Dallas Express was the longest-running Black newspaper in Texas when it closed its doors in 1970. Photo found on Wikimedia Commons.

Much of the civil rights activities from the mid-20th century to the present have focused on consolidating the gains made during the last century. For Texas Blacks, most of the gains have come via voting rights. One cannot exaggerate the political significance of the overthrow of the White Democratic primary. Prior to *Smith v Allwright* (1944), only 30,000 Blacks were registered voters. In 1948 that number more than tripled to 100,000. In 1964 it reached 57% of the Black voting-age population. This percentage increased even more when the 24th amendment (1964) and the Voting Rights Act of 1965 struck down the poll tax and other subterfuges for voting. Moreover, the court-mandated reapportionment in 1966 made it possible for Blacks to send three members of their race to the Texas legislature, the first since Reconstruction — Curtis Graves and Joseph Lockridge to the House and Barbara Jordan to the Senate. Afterwards, Blacks led a campaign against at-large districts.

The Supreme Court concurrence in a lawsuit filed for single-member districts in Texas enabled African Americans to win legislative seats at the local, state and national levels. The result of which was that Barbara Jordan became the first Black female from the South to be elected to Congress. Today, five Black Texans have been elected to Congress. Twenty Blacks sit in the Texas legislature compared to three in 1968. Of that number, six are female. Most of the school boards, city councils and county commissioners in the state have at least one or more Black members. Coupled with this is the number of Black mayors who are or have been elected

Barbara Jordan sat on the House Judiciary Committee during the Watergate hearings. Photo by U.S. House of Representatives Photography Office

Conclusion

Without a doubt, African Americans' contribution and hard labor have made the state of Texas what it has become in the 21st century. In the latest census taken in 2020, African Americans are 12% of the state's population. Two-thirds of African Americans live in the Dallas-Fort Worth and Houston metropolitan areas. Making up a significant part of the population are cities such as Beaumont, Port Arthur, Austin and San Antonio. Yet the contribution of the African American history and culture of this state is not relegated to large or small cities, rural or urban centers, or to a geographic region. Their contribution attests to their abiding influence on Texas and American culture and institutions.

in small and large cities. For example, in 1995 Ronald Kirk became the first African American mayor in Dallas. In 1998 Lee P. Brown became the first African American to serve as mayor in Houston, and Sylvester Turner is currently serving as mayor in Houston. Also, in 1985 John Wiley Price and El Franco Lee became the first Black county commissioners in Dallas and Houston, respectively. The judiciary, an area that had been difficult for Blacks to get elected to office, now sees a large number of Blacks elected. In fact, 19 Black women were elected as judges in Harris County in 2018.

Despite the gains made by African Americans in the state of Texas, it would be premature to write the epitaph of the civil rights movement. Unfinished, the agendas abound. There are still pressing economic issues relating to employment, housing, and services. In point of fact, racial and gender income inequality is prevalent. The issue of affirmative action is still considered a divisive factor in many cities. Also, Texas has had a long history of Blacks dying at the hand of the police, and as such, one of its most current and pressing issues centers around police brutality and criminal justice reform. This issue was exacerbated when George Floyd, a Houston native, died in Minneapolis while in custody. In the aftermath of the state and nationwide protests against police brutality that erupted after Floyd's death, police reform efforts presented by state lawmakers still await a victory. There is no gainsaying that the problem of race remains in Texas. But by the same token, no one can deny that the civil rights movement in Texas changed the political landscape of the state.

Culture

As African Americans lived through the horrors of Jim Crow and the struggles of the civil rights movement, they continued to participate in the state's social and cultural life and to add their creative talents to the artistic development of both the state and the nation. For example, Juneteenth celebrations that started during Reconstruction have kept the memory of "first freedom" alive and are now celebrated in many other states and countries throughout the world, culminating in 2021 with its designation as an American national freedom holiday.

In keeping with the idea of preserving African American culture, there are a number of African American museums that have been established over the years. The most notable are the African American Museum of Dallas and the Buffalo Soldiers National Museum in Houston. Concomitant with preserving Black culture are the contributions of musicians, artists, writers and playwrights: Thomas Meloncon's *The Diary of Black Men* and Ntozake Shange's *For Colored Girls* made their way to Broadway. Shange's novel *Sassafrass, Cypress & Indigo* was a national best-seller. Musical icon Beyonce Knowles Carter of Houston and Erykah Badu have won Grammy and national awards for their music in the jazz, rhythm, blues and pop genres. Novelists J. California Cooper's *A Piece of Mine* and Anita Bunkley's *Emily: The Yellow Rose* also won national acclaim.

Celebrations, Festivals, and Events

Juneteenth (June 19, 1865). Celebrated since its inception as the day slaves were emancipated in Texas, Juneteenth became a state holiday in Texas in 1986 and ten years later a state holiday in Oklahoma. It is now recognized in 47 other states and several countries around the world. A bill in Congress making it a national holiday was passed in 2021 and signed into law by President Biden.

Kwanzaa is a celebration of life, prosperity and good harvest. It is observed from December 26 to January 1 each year. The seven principles commemorating Kwanzaa are self-determination, purpose, creativity, unity, community responsibility, economics and faith.

Black History Month started as Negro History Week by Carter G. Woodson in 1914. Its purpose was to expose and draw awareness to the contribution African Americans have made to this country and the world. Later, Negro History

The struggle never ended: Houston police chief Art Acevedo (center) and Black Lives Matter organizer DeRay Mckesson (right) discuss racial tension and police misconduct at The Summit on Race in America in 2019. Photo by Jay Godwin, courtesy of the LBJ Library

Week became Black History Week. In 1976 it became Black History Month in recognition of the need to expose African Americans' life history and contribution to the nation's society.

Martin Luther King Jr. Day celebrates the life of Martin L. King Jr. and his work in the civil rights movement. It became a national holiday in 1997 and is celebrated on the third Monday in January, which falls near King's birthday (January 15, 1929). In Texas the celebration takes on many forms — parades, public-speaking contests, church services and as a day of providing various forms of service to the community.

Harambee Festival, held in Dallas, is the oldest and largest African American cultural event in the state. This community-based festival celebrates African American culture with musical performances and free health screenings.

African American Book Festival is an interactive community gathering and cultural celebration of African American writers and their works and is held in Austin each year. Among other things, its program includes author presentations, book discussions, pop culture and conversations with children.

The Prairie View Trail Ride is the oldest African American trail ride in the United States. This 88-mile ride from Hempstead, Texas, to the Houston rodeo is held each year in the month of March.

Further Reading

Barr, Alwyn. *Black Texans: A History of African Americans in Texas 1528-1995.* Second Editions. Norman: University of Oklahoma Press, 1996.

Beil, Gail. "Four Marshallites' Role in the Passage of the Civil Rights Act of 1964," *Southwestern Historical Quarterly* 106 (July 2002) 1-24.

Campbell, Randolph B. *An Empire for Slavery: The Peculiar Institution in Texas, 1821-1865.* Baton Rouge: Louisiana State University Press, 1989.

Carrigan, William D. *The Making of a Lynching Culture: Violence and Vigilantism in Central Texas, 1836-1916.* Urbana: University of Illinois Press, 2004

Crouch, Barry A. *The Freedmen's Bureau and Black Texans.* Austin: University of Texas Press, 1992

Glasrud, Bruce and James M Smallwood. *The African American Experience in Texas,* Lubbock: Texas Tech University Press, 2007

Glasrud, Bruce and Merline Pitre. *Black Women in Texas History.* College Station: Texas A&M University Press, 2009

Hine, Darlene Clark. *Black Victory: The Rise and Fall of the White Primary in Texas.* Columbia: University of Missouri Press, 2003

Ladino, Robyn Duff. *Desegregating Texas Schools: Eisenhower, Shivers, and the Crisis At Mansfield High.* Austin: University of Texas Press, 1990.

Pitre, Merline. *Through Many Dangers, Toils and Snares: Black Leadership in Texas, 1868-1898.* College Station: Texas A&M University, 2017.

Pitre, Merline. *In Struggle against Jim Crow: Lulu B. White and the NAACP, 1900-1957.* College Station: Texas A & M University Press, 2010.

Pitre, Merline, *Born to Serve: A History of Texas Southern.* Norman: The University of Oklahoma Press, 2018.

Reid, Debra. "Racism and Sexism in Rural Texas: The Contested Nature of Progressive Reform 1870-1910" in *Seeking Inalienable Rights: Black Texans and their Quest for Justice.* College Station: Texas A & M University Press: 37-57.

Seals, Donald. "The Wiley-Bishop Student Movement: A Case Study of the 1960 Civil Rights Sit-ins." *Southwestern Quarterly* 106 (June 2003): 419-40.

Taylor, Quintard. *In Search of the Racial Frontier: African Americans in the American West, 1528-1990.* New York: W.W. Norton, 1998.

Texas Museums of Art, Science, History

Listed below are links to the websites of Texas museums. Where required, some have indication of the area of emphasis of the exhibits.

Abilene

Frontier Texas! (history)
frontiertexas.com

Grace Museum (art, history)
thegracemuseum.org

National Center for Children's Illustrated Literature (art)
nccil.org

Addison

Cavanaugh Flight Museum
cavflight.org

Albany

Old Jail Art Center (art)
theojac.org

Alpine

Museum of the Big Bend (history)
museumofthebigbend.com

Amarillo

Amarillo Museum of Art
amarilloart.org

American Quarter Horse Hall of Fame & Museum
aqha.com/museum

Don Harrington Discovery Center (science, children's)
discoverycenteramarillo.org

Texas Pharmacy Museum
ttuhsc.edu/pharmacy/museum

Angleton

Brazoria County Historical Museum
brazoriacountytx.gov/departments/museum

Austin

Blanton Museum of Art
blantonmuseum.org

Bob Bullock Texas State History Museum
thestoryoftexas.com

Capitol Visitors Center (history)
tspb.texas.gov/prop/tcvc/cvc/cvc.html

The Contemporary Austin (art)
thecontemporaryaustin.org

Elisabet Ney Museum (art, history)
austintexas.gov/elisabetney

French Legation Museum (history)
thc.texas.gov/historic-sites/french-legation-state-historic-site

Harry Ransom Humanities Research Center (history, literature)
hrc.utexas.edu

Lady Bird Johnson Wildflower Center
wildflower.org

Lyndon B. Johnson Presidential Library
lbjlibrary.org

Mexic-Arte Museum (art)
mexic-artemuseum.org

O. Henry Museum (history)
austintexas.gov/department/o-henry-museum

Pioneer Farms
pioneerfarms.org

Texas Memorial Museum (history, natural history)
tmm.utexas.edu

Texas Military Forces Museum
texasmilitaryforcesmuseum.org

Texas Music Museum
texasmusicmuseum.org

Thinkery (children's museum)
thinkeryaustin.org

Umlauf Sculpture Garden & Museum
umlaufsculpture.org

Wild Basin Wilderness Preserve
stedwards.edu/centers-institutes/wild-basin-creative-research-center

Women and Their Work
womenandtheirwork.org

Bay City

Matagorda County Museum and Children's Museum
visitbaycity.org/arts-culture/museum

Beaumont

Art Museum of Southeast Texas
amset.org

Edison Museum (science)
edisonmuseum.org

Fire Museum of Texas
firemuseumoftexas.org

Spindletop/Gladys City Boomtown Museum (history)
lamar.edu/spindletop-gladys-city

Texas Energy Museum (history)
texasenergymuseum.org

Beeville

Beeville Art Museum
facebook.com/pages/category/Art-Museum/Beeville-Art-Museum-103515313030905

Belton

Bell County Museum
bellcountymuseum.org

Big Spring

Heritage of Big Spring
heritagebigspring.com

Bonham

Fannin County Museum of History
fannincountymuseum.org

Fort Inglish Village
visitbonham.com/things-to-see/fort-inglish-village

Sam Rayburn Library/Museum
cah.utexas.edu/museums/rayburn.php

Borger

Hutchinson County Historical Museum
borgertx.gov/264/Hutchinson-County-Historical-Museum

Brownsville

Brownsville Heritage Museum (history)
brownsvillehistory.org

Brownsville Museum of Fine Art
bmfa.us

Children's Museum of Brownsville
cmofbrownsville.org

Costumes of the Americas Museum
cotam.net

RGV Commemorative Air Force Museum
rgvcaf.org/museum.html

Stillman House Museum (history)
www.brownsvillehistory.org/stillman-house-museum.html

Brownwood

Brown County Museum of History
browncountyhistory.org/bcmoh.html

Lehnis Railroad Museum
brownwoodtexas.gov/228/Lehnis-Railroad-Museum

Bryan-College Station

Brazos Valley African American Museum
bvaam.org

Brazos Valley Museum of Natural History
brazosvalleymuseum.org

Children's Museum of the Brazos Valley
cmbv.org

George H.W. Bush Presidential Library
bush41.org

University Art Galleries
uart.tamu.edu

Buffalo Gap

Buffalo Gap Historic Village
taylorcountyhistorycenter.com

Burton

Burton Cotton Gin and Museum
cottonginmuseum.org

Canadian

The Citadelle Art Museum
thecitadelle.org

River Valley Pioneer Museum
rivervalleymuseum.org

Canyon

Panhandle-Plains Historical Museum
panhandleplains.org

Carthage

Texas Country Music Hall of Fame & Tex Ritter Museum
tcmhof.com

Clarendon

Saints' Roost Museum (history)
saintsroostmuseum.com

Clifton

Bosque Museum (history)
bosquemuseum.org

Conroe

Heritage Museum of Montgomery County
heritagemuseum.us

Corpus Christi

Art Museum of South Texas
artmuseumofsouthtexas.org

Corpus Christi Museum of Science and History
ccmuseum.com

The facade of the Ellsworth Kelly "Austin" Chapel stands at the Blanton Museum of Art on the University of Texas campus in Austin, TX, on March 7, 2020. Photo by Keith Ewing/Flickr (CC).

Texas State Aquarium
texasstateaquarium.org

Texas State Museum of Asian Cultures
texasasianculturesmuseum.org

USS Lexington Museum
usslexington.com

Corsicana
Pearce Western Art/Civil War Museum
pearcemuseum.com

Cotulla
Brush Country Historical Museum
texastropicaltrail.com/plan-your-adventure/historic-sites-and-cities/sites/brush-country-museum

Dalhart
XIT Museum (history)
xitmuseum.com

Dallas
African American Museum
aamdallas.org

Crow Museum of Asian Art
crowcollection.org

Dallas Heritage Village
dallasheritagevillage.org

Dallas Historical Society (Fair Park)
dallashistory.org

Dallas Museum of Art
dma.org

Frontiers of Flight Museum
flightmuseum.com

George W. Bush Presidential Center
georgewbushlibrary.smu.edu

Perot Museum of Nature and Science
perotmuseum.org

Nasher Sculpture Center
nashersculpturecenter.org

Meadows Museum (art)
meadowsmuseumdallas.org

The Sixth Floor Museum (history)
jfk.org

Denison
Red River Railroad Museum
redriverrailmuseum.org

Denton
Courthouse-on-the-Square Museum
dentoncounty.gov/Facilities/Facility/Details/Courthouseonthe Square-Museum-11

Denton Firefighters Museum
discoverdenton.com/listing/denton-firefighters-museum/455

University of North Texas Art Galleries
galleries.cvad.unt.edu

Dublin
Dublin Bottling Works
dublinbottlingworks.com

Dublin Rodeo Heritage Museum
rodeoheritagemuseum.org

Dumas
Window on the Plains Museum
dumasmuseumandartcenter.org

Edgewood
Edgewood Heritage Park and Historical Village
edgewoodheritagepark.org

Edinburg
Museum of South Texas History
mosthistory.org

El Campo
El Campo Museum of Natural History
elcampomuseum.org

El Paso
Centennial Museum/Chihuahuan Desert Gardens
utep.edu/centennial-museum

El Paso Museum of Archaeology
archaeology.elpasotexas.gov

El Paso Museum of Art
epma.art

El Paso Museum of History
history.elpasotexas.gov

Fort Davis
Chihuahuan Desert Research Institute
cdri.org

Fort Stockton
Annie Riggs Museum (history)
historicfortstocktontx.com/attractions-2/annie-riggs-memorial-museum

Fort Worth
Amon Carter Museum (art)
cartermuseum.org

Cattle Raisers Museum
cattleraisersmuseum.org

Fort Worth Museum of Science and History
fwmuseum.org

Kimbell Art Museum
kimbellart.org

Log Cabin Village (history)
logcabinvillage.org

Modern Art Museum of Fort Worth
themodern.org

National Cowgirl Museum and Hall
of Fame
cowgirl.net

Sid Richardson Collection of Western Art
sidrichardsonmuseum.org

Texas Civil War Museum
texascivilwarmuseum.com

Fredericksburg

Gillespie County Historical Society
pioneermuseum.net

National Museum of the Pacific War
pacificwarmuseum.org

Frisco

Museum of the American Railroad
historictrains.org

National Videogame Museum
nvmusa.org

Galveston

The Bryan Museum (art, history)
thebryanmuseum.org

Galveston Children's Museum
galvestoncm.org

Moody Mansion
moodymansion.org

Offshore Energy Center/Ocean Star
(science, industry)
oceanstaroec.com

Texas Seaport Museum and Tallship
"Elissa"
galvestonhistory.org/sites/1877-
tall-ship-elissa-at-the-galveston-
historic-seaport

Gilmer

Flight of Phoenix Aviation Museum
flightofthephoenix.org

Greenville

Audie Murphy/American Cotton
Museum
cottonmuseum.com

Henderson

The Depot Museum (history)
depotmuseum.org

Houston

Blaffer Art Museum, University of
Houston
blafferartmuseum.org

Children's Museum of Houston
cmhouston.org

Contemporary Arts Museum
camh.org

Czech Center Museum
czechcenter.org

The Health Museum
thehealthmuseum.org

Houston Center for Contemporary
Craft
crafthouston.org

Houston Center for Photography
hcponline.org

Houston Fire Museum (history)
houstonfiremuseum.org

Houston Museum of Natural Science
hmns.org

Lawndale Art Center
lawndaleartcenter.org

Lone Star Flight Museum
lonestarflight.org

The Menil Collection (art)
menil.org

Museum of Fine Arts
mfah.org

Museum of Printing History
printingmuseum.org

San Jacinto Museum of History
sanjacinto-museum.org

Space Center Houston
spacecenter.org

Huntsville

Sam Houston Memorial Museum
samhoustonmemorialmuseum.com

Texas Prison Museum
txprisonmuseum.org

Kerrville

Museum of Western Art
museumofwesternart.com

Kilgore

East Texas Oil Museum
easttexasoilmuseum.kilgore.edu

Lake Jackson

Lake Jackson Historical Museum
ljhistory.org

Laredo

Republic of the Rio Grande Museum
webbheritage.org/museums

Texas A&M International University
Planetarium
tamiu.edu/planetarium

League City

Butler Longhorn Museum
butlerlonghornmuseum.com

West Bay Common School Children's Museum (history)
oneroomschoolhouse.org

Longview

Longview Museum of Fine Arts
lmfa.org

Lubbock

FiberMax Center for Discovery:
Agriculture
agriculturehistory.org

Buddy Holly Center (history, music)
buddyhollycenter.org

Museum of Texas Tech University
(art, humanities, science)
depts.ttu.edu/museumttu

National Ranching Heritage Center
depts.ttu.edu/nrhc

Science Spectrum
sciencespectrum.org

Lufkin

Naranjo Museum of Natural History
naranjomuseum.org

Texas Forestry Museum
treetexas.com

Marfa

The Chinati Foundation (art)
chinati.org

Marshall

Harrison County Historical Museum
harrisoncountymuseum.org

Michelson Museum of Art
michelsonmuseum.org

McAllen

International Museum of Art &
Science
theimasonline.org

McKinney

Heard Natural Science Museum &
Wildlife Sanctuary
heardmuseum.org

Midland

Museum of the Southwest (art,
science, children's)
museumsw.org

Petroleum Museum
petroleummuseum.org

Nacogdoches

Millard's Crossing Historic Village
mchvnac.com

New Braunfels

McKenna Children's Museum
mckennakids.org

Sophienburg Museum & Archives
www.sophienburg.com

Odessa

Ellen Noel Art Museum
noelartmuseum.org

Presidential Archives and Library
shepperdinstitute.com/
presidential-archives

Orange

Stark Museum of Art
starkculturalvenues.org

Panhandle

Carson County Square House
Museum
squarehousemuseum.weebly.com

Perryton

Museum of the Plains
museumoftheplains.com

Plano

Heritage Farmstead Museum
heritagefarmstead.org

Port Arthur

Museum of the Gulf Coast (history)
museumofthegulfcoast.org

Port Lavaca

Calhoun County Museum (history)
calhouncountymuseum.org

Richmond

George Ranch Historical Park
georgeranch.org

Rockport

Texas Maritime Museum
texasmaritimemuseum.com

Rosenberg

The Black Cowboy Museum
blackcowboymuseum.org

Rosenberg Railroad Museum
rosenbergrrmuseum.org

Round Top

Henkel Square (history)
henkelsquareroundtop.com

Winedale Historical Complex
cah.utexas.edu/museums/
winedale.php

San Angelo

Miss Hattie's Bordello Museum
misshatties.com

San Angelo Museum of Fine Arts and
Children's Art Museum
samfa.org

San Antonio

The Alamo
thealamo.org

Briscoe Western Art Museum
briscoemuseum.org

Holocaust Memorial Museum
hmmsa.org

Institute of Texan Cultures
texancultures.com

Magic Lantern Castle Museum
www.magiclanterns.org

The McNay (art)
mcnayart.org

San Antonio Art League & Museum
saalm.org

San Antonio Museum of Art
samuseum.org

Witte Museum (science, history)
wittemuseum.org

San Marcos

LBJ Museum San Marcos
lbjmuseum.org

Southwestern Writers Collection and
Wittliff Gallery of Southwestern &
Mexican Photography
thewittliffcollections.txstate.edu

Sarita

Kenedy Ranch Museum of South Texas
kenedy.org/museum

Schulenburg

Stanzel Model Aircraft Museum
stanzelmuseum.org

Serbin

Texas Wendish Heritage Museum
texaswendish.org/museum

Sherman

Sherman Jazz Museum
shermanjazzmuseum.com

The Sherman Museum (history)
theshermanmuseum.org

Snyder

Scurry County Museum
scurrycountymuseum.org

Sulphur Springs

SouthWest Dairy Museum and
Education Center
southwestdairyfarmers.com

Teague

The B-RI Railroad Museum
therailroadmuseum.com

Temple

Czech Heritage Museum
czechheritagemuseum.org

Railroad and Heritage Museum
templerrhm.org

Texarkana

Museum of Regional History
texarkanamuseum.org

The Woodlands

The Woodlands Children's Museum
woodlandschildrensmuseum.org

Thurber

W.K. Gordon Center for Industrial
History of Texas
tarleton.edu/gordoncenter

Tyler

Discovery Science Place
discoveryscienceplace.org

Historic Aviation Memorial Museum
tylerhamm.com

Smith County Historical Museum
tylertexasonline.com/tyler-
texas-museums.htm

Tyler Museum of Art
tylermuseum.org

Victoria

Children's Discovery Museum
cdmgoldencrescent.com

Museum of the Coastal Bend
(history)
museumofthecoastalbend.org

The Nave Museum (art)
navemuseum.com

Waco

Dr Pepper Museum (history)
drpeppermuseum.com

Martin Museum of Art
baylor.edu/martinmuseum/

Mayborn Museum Complex (history,
science)
baylor.edu/mayborn

Texas Ranger Hall of Fame/Museum
texasranger.org

Texas Sports Hall of Fame
tshof.org

Washington

Star of the Republic Museum
(history)
starmuseum.org

Weatherford

Museum of the Americas
museumoftheamericas.com

National Vietnam War Museum
nationalvnwarmuseum.org

Wharton

20th Century Technology Museum
20thcenturytech.com

White Settlement

White Settlement Historical Museum
wsmuseum.com

Wichita Falls

Kell House Museum (history)
wichita-heritage.org

Wichita Falls Museum of Art
wfma.msutexas.edu

Museum of North Texas History
museumofnorthtexashistory.org

Professional Wrestling
Hall of Fame & Museum
pro-wrestling-hall-of-fame-
museum.business.site

Yoakum

Yoakum Heritage Museum
yoakumareachamber.com/
visit-yoakum/experience-history ☆

Public Libraries in Texas

Texas public libraries continue to strive to meet the education and information needs of Texans by providing library services of high quality with often-times-limited resources.

Each year, services provided by public libraries increase, with more visits to public libraries and higher attendance in library programs.

The challenges facing public libraries in Texas are many and varied. The costs for providing electronic and online sources, in addition to traditional services, are growing faster than budgets.

Urban libraries are trying to serve growing populations, while libraries in rural areas are trying to serve remote populations and provide distance learning where possible.

National rankings of public libraries are published by the Institute of Museum and Library Services at imls.gov/research-evaluation/data-collection/public-libraries-survey.

When comparing Texas statistics to those nationally, Texas continues to rank below most of the other states in most categories, with the exception of public use of internet terminals.

Complete statistical information on public libraries is available on the Texas State Library's website: tsl.texas.gov/landing/statistics.html. There is also a listing of libraries at: tsl.texas.gov/texshare/libsearch. ☆

Source: Library Development Division of the Texas State Library and Archives in Austin.

Texas Institute of Letters Awards

Each year since 1939, the **Texas Institute of Letters** (texasinstituteofletters.org) has honored outstanding literature and journalism that is either by Texans or about Texas subjects.

Awards have been made for fiction, nonfiction, Southwest history, general information, magazine and newspaper journalism, children's books, translation, poetry, and book design. The awards of recent years are listed below; see previous recipients at tshaonline.org.

2021

Bryan Washington: *Memorial: A Novel*
Marisol Cortez: *Luz at Midnight*
Joe Holley: *Sutherland Springs*
Chera Hammons: *Maps of Injury*
David Meischen: *Anyone's Son*
Miguel Angel González-Quiroga: *War and Peace on the Rio Grande Frontier: 1830-1880*
Darcie Little Badger: *Elatsoe*
Francisco Stork: *Illegal*
Christina Soontornvat: *A Wish in the Dark*
Jerome Pumphrey and Jarrett Pumphrey: *The Old Truck*
Mary Ann Jacob: designer of *Daddy-O's Book of Big-Ass Art,* by Bob "Daddy-O" Wade
David Meischen: "Crossing the Light," *Storylandia*
ire'ne lara silva: "A Place Before Words," *Texas Highways*
Lon Tinkle Award (for career): Benjamin Alire Sáenz

2020

Oscar Cásares: *Where We Come From*
Bryan Washington: *Lot: Stories*
Holly George-Warren: *Janis: Her Life and Music*
Ron Tyler: *The Art of Texas: 250 Years*
Naomi Shihab Nye: *The Tiny Journalist*
Lupe Mendez: *Why I Am Like Tequila* (Aquarius Press)
Sergio Troncoso: "Rosary on the Border" in *A Peculiar Kind of Immigrant's Son*
Skip Hollandsworth: "Sabika's Story," in *Texas Monthly*
Rebecca Balcárcel: *The Other Half of Happy*
Rubén Degollado: *Throw: A Novel*
José M. Hernández: *The Boy Who Touched the Stars*
Cyrus Cassells: translator of *Still Life with Children: Selected Poems of Francesc Parcerisas*
Lon Tinkle Award (for career): John Rechy

2019

Ben Fountain: *Beautiful Country Burn Again: Democracy, Rebellion, and Revolution*
Natalia Sylvester: *Everyone Knows You Go Home*
Stephen Markley: *Ohio*
Tarfia Faizullah: *Registers of Illuminated Villages*
Megan Peak: *Girldom*
Brent Nongbri: *God's Library: The Archaeology of the Earliest Christian Manuscripts*
David Bowles: *The Feathered Serpent, Dark Heart of Sky: Myths of Mexico* and *They Call Me Güero*
Varian Johnson: *The Parker Inheritance*
Chris Barton: *What Can You Do with a Voice Like That?*
Clay Reynolds: "Railroad Man," *New Madrid,* and "Autumn Moon," *New Texas*
Lon Tinkle Award (for career): Naomi Shihab Nye

2018

Jan Reid: *Sins of the Younger Sons*
Chanelle Benz: *The Man Who Shot Out My Eye is Dead*
Roger D. Hodge: *Texas Blood: Seven Generations Among the Outlaws, Ranchers, Indians, Missionaries, Soldiers, and Smugglers of the Borderlands*
Jerry D. Thompson: *Tejano Tiger: José de los Santos Benavides and the Texas-Mexico Borderlands, 1823–1891*
Sasha Pimentel: *For Want of Water: and other poems*
Vanessa Villarreal: *Beast Meridian*
Brett Anthony Johnston: "Miss McElroy," *Ecotone*
Rose Cahalan: "Ride Like a Girl," *Texas Observer*
Michael Merschel: *Revenge of the Star Survivors*
Francisco X. Stork: *Disappeared*
Xelena González and Adriana M. Garcia: *All Around Us*
Philip Boehm: translator of *Chasing the King of Hearts,* by Hanna Krall
Mary Ann Jacob: designer, *The Nueces River, Rio Escondido,* by Margie Crisp and William B. Montgomery
Lon Tinkle Award (for career): Sandra Cisneros

2017

Paulette Jiles: *News of the World*
Amy Gentry: *Good as Gone*
Skip Hollandsworth: *The Midnight Assassin*
Max Krochmal: *Blue Texas: The Making of a Multiracial Democratic Coalition in the Civil Rights Era*
Bruce Bond: *Gold Bee*
Miriam Bird Greenberg: *In the Volcano's Mouth*
Stephen Harrigan: "Off Course," *Texas Monthly*
David Meischen: "Cicada Song," *Salamander*
Kathi Appelt and Alison McGhee: *Maybe a Fox*
Phillippe Diederich: *Playing for the Devil's Fire*
Dianna Hutts Aston: *A Beetle Is Shy*
Kristie Lee: *From Tea Cakes to Tamales*
Lon Tinkle Award (for career): Pat Mora

2016

Antonio Ruiz–Camacho: *Barefoot Dogs*
Mary Helen Specht: *Migratory Animals*
Jan Jarboe Russell: *The Train to Crystal City*
Andrew Torget III: *Seeds of Empire*
Laurie Ann Guerrero: *A Crown for Gumecindo*
J. Scott Brownlee: *Requiem for Used Ignition Cap*
W.K. Stratton: "My Brother's Secret," *Texas Monthly*
Brian Van Reet: "The Chaff," *Iowa Review*
Don Tate: *The Remarkable Story of George Moses Horton: Poet*
Brian Yansky: *Utopia, Iowa*
Pat Mora: *The Remembering Day/El dia de los muertos*
Andrea Caillouet: *The Luck Archive: Exploring Belief, Superstition, and Tradition*
Marian Schwartz: translator of *Anna Karenina,* by Leo Tolstoy
Lon Tinkle Award (for career): Sarah Bird

2015

Elizabeth Crook: *Monday, Monday*
Michael Morton: *Getting Life: An Innocent Man's 25-Year Journey from Prison to Peace*
Merritt Tierce: *Love Me Back*
Lawrence T. Jones: *Lens on the Texas Frontier*
Katherine Hoerth: *Goddess Wears Cowboy Boots*
Brian Van Reet: "Eat the Spoil," in *Missouri Review*

Chloe Honum: *The Tulip-Flame*

Pamela Colloff: "The Witness," *Texas Monthly*

Bill Wittliff and Ellen McKie: *The Devil's Backbone*, written by Bill Wittliff, illustrated by Jack Unruh

Nikki Lofton: *Nightingale's Nest*

Glaudia Guadalupe Martinez: *Pig Park*

Pat Mora and LiIbby Martinez: *I Pledge Allegiance*

Lon Tinkle Award (for career): Lawrence Wright

2014

Tom Zigal: *Many Rivers to Cross*

John Talifarro: *All The Great Prizes: The Life of John Hay from Lincoln to Roosevelt*

Lawrence Wright: *Going Clear: Scientology, Hollywood, and the Prison of Belief*

Nan Cuba: *Body and Bread*

Raúl Coronado: *A World Not to Come: A History of Latino Writing and Print Culture*

Pattiann Rogers: *Holy Heathen Rhapsody*

Bret Anthony Johnston: "To a Good Home," *Virginia Quarterly Review*

Sasha West: *Failure And I Bury The Body*

John MacCormack: "Life On The Shale," *San Antonio Express-News*, series

Lindsay Starr: *Two Prospectors: The Letters of Sam Shepard and Johnny Dark*

Xavier Garza: *Maximilian and the Mystery of the Bingo Rematch*

Kathi Appelt: *The True Blue Scouts of Sugar Man Swamp*

David Bowles: *Flower, Song, Dance: Aztec and Mayan Poetry*

Lon Tinkle Award (for career): Jan Reid

2013

Ben Fountain: *Billy Lynn's Long Halftime Walk*

Margie Crisp: *River of Contrasts*

Kevin Grauke: *Shadows of Men*

Kate Sayen Kirkland: *Captain James A. Baker of Houston: 1857–1941*

Ken Fontenot: *Kingdom of Birds*

James Sanderson: "Bankers," in *Descant*

Kathleen Winter: *Nostalgia for the Criminal Past*

Mellissa Del Bosque: "The Deadliest Place in Mexico," *The Texas Observer*, February, 12, 2012

Kristina Kachele: *In the Country of Empty Crosses*, written by Arturo Madrid

Donna Rubin: *Log Cabin Kitty*

Melodie Cuate: *Journey to Plum Creek*

Lon Tinkle Award (for career): Stephen Harrigan

2012

Stephen Harrigan: *Remember Ben Clayton*

Steven Fenberg: *Unprecedented Power: Jesse Jones, Capitalism, and the Common Good*

Siobhan Fallon: *You Know When the Men Are Gone*

Christopher Long: *The Looshaus*

Jennifer Grotz: *The Needle*

Bret Anthony Johnston: "Paradeability," *American Short Fiction*

Jose Antonio Rodriguez: *The Shallow End of Sleep*

Skip Hollandsworth: "The Lost Boys," *Texas Monthly*, April 2011

Jordan Smith: "The Science of Injustice," *Austin Chronicle*, August 19, 2011

Barbara Werden and Lindsay Starr: *Lone Star Law*, written by Michael Ariens

Dave Oliphant: *After-Dinner Declarations* by Nicanor Parra

Elaine Scott: *Space, Stars and the Beginning of Time*

J.L. Powers: *This Thing Called the Future*

Lon Tinkle Award (for career): Gary Cartwright

2011[1]

Jan Reid: *Comanche Sundown*

Gary Lavergne: *Before Brown: Heman Marion Sweatt, Thurgood Marshall and the Long Road to Justice*

Neil Foley: *Quest for Equality: The Failed Promise of Black-Brown Solidarity*

Bruce Machart: *The Wake of Forgiveness*

Barbara Ras: *The Last Skin*

Elyse Fenton: *Clamor*

Pamela Colloff: "Innocence Lost," *Texas Monthly*, October 2010

C.W. Smith: "Caustic," *Southwest Review*, Summer 2010

Tim Madigan: series on the surgery of a child, *Fort Worth Star-Telegram*

Julie Savasky and DJ Stout: *The Gernsheim Collection*

Diane Gonzales Bertrand: *The Party for Papa Luis/La Fiesta Para Papa Luis*

Dotti Enderle: *Crosswire*

Lon Tinkle Award (for career): C.W. Smith

2009

Scott Blackwood: *We Agreed to Meet Just Here*

Bryan Burrough: *The Big Rich: The Rise and Fall of the Greatest Texas Oil Fortunes*

John Pipkin: *Woodsburner*

Emilio Zamoro: *Claiming Rights and Righting Wrongs in Texas: Mexican Workers and Job Politics During World War II*

William Virgil Davis: *Landscape and Journey*

John Spong: "Holding Garmsir," *Texas Monthly*, January 2009.

Gwendolyn Zepeda: *Sunflowers/Girasoles*

Marjorie Kempner: "Discovered America," *Southwest Review*, Fall 2009

Lindsay Starr: *"I Do Not Apologize for the Length of This Letter": The Mari Sandoz Letters on Native American Rights, 1940–1965*

Lon Tinkle Award (for career): Larry L. King

2008

Brendan M. Greeley Jr.: *The Two Thousand Yard Stare: Tom Lea's World War II Paintings, Drawings, and Eyewitness Accounts*

Thomas Cobb: *Shavetail*

Ann Weisgarber: *The Personal History of Rachel DuPree*

Rick Bass: "Mary Katherine's First Deer" in *Gray's Sporting Journal*

Todd Benson and Guillermo Contreras: "Texas' Deadliest Export" in the *San Antonio Express-News*

Benjamin Alire Saenz: *The Perfect Season for Dreaming*

Claudia Guadalupe Martinez: *The Smell of Old Lady Perfume*

James Allen Hall: *Now You're the Enemy*

Kerry Neville Bakken: "Indignity" in *Gettysburg Review*

James M. Smallwood: *The Feud that Wasn't: The Taylor Ring, Bill Sutton, John Wesley Hardin, and Violence in Texas*

Barbara Whitehead: *Traces of Forgotten Places*

Reginald Gibbons: translator of *Sophocles, Selected Poems: Odes and Fragments*

Lon Tinkle Award (for career): Carolyn Osborn ☆

---

1   Beginning in 2011, the award date reflects the actual date of the presentation. For instance, Larry King's 2009 award was actually presented in 2010.

State Cultural Agencies Assist the Arts

Culture in Texas, as in any market, is a mixture of activity generated by both the commercial and the nonprofit sectors.

The commercial sector encompasses Texas-based profit-making businesses, including commercial recording artists, nightclubs, record companies, private galleries, assorted boutiques that carry fine art collectibles, and private dance and music halls.

Texas also has extensive cultural resources offered by nonprofit organizations that are engaged in charitable, educational, and humanitarian activities.

The Legislature has authorized five state agencies to administer cultural services and funds for the public good. The agencies are:

Texas Commission on the Arts; Texas Film Commission; Texas Historical Commission; Texas State Library and Archives Commission; and the State Preservation Board.

Although not a state agency, another organization that provides cultural services to the citizens of Texas is Humanities Texas.

The Commission on the Arts was established in 1965 to develop a receptive climate for the arts through the conservation and advancement of Texas' rich and diverse arts and cultural industries.

The Texas Commission on the Arts' goals are:

- Provide grants for the arts and cultural industries in Texas.
- Provide the financial, human, and technical resources necessary to ensure viable arts and cultural communities.
- Promote widespread attendance at arts and cultural performances and exhibitions in Texas.
- Ensure access to arts in Texas through marketing, fund raising, and cultural tourism.
- The commission is responsible for several initiatives including:
- Arts Education: programs that serve the curricular and training needs of the state's school districts, private schools, and home schools.
- Marketing and Public Relations: marketing and fund-raising expertise to generate funds for agency operations and increase visibility of the arts in Texas.
- Cultural Tourism: programs that develop and promote tourism destinations featuring the arts.

Information on programs is available on the Texas Commission on the Arts at arts.texas.gov. ☆

Source: Principally the Texas Commission on the Arts, along with other state cultural agencies.

Dancers perform in "The Good Fight Jam" in San Antonio, TX, on October 24, 2020. Photo by Cooper Chiu/Flickr (PD).

Performing Arts Organizations: Dance, music, theater

The Texas Commission on the Arts provides a listing of performing arts companies and artists in Texas at arts.texas.gov/artroster/roster/show/all. There are links arranged by category: dance, theater, music, etc.

There is also https://www.arts.texas.gov/resources/art-in-communities, which provides more information about community arts programs, as well as swpap.org, with performing arts organizations by city.

golf082/Flickr (CC) *Anthony V. Moulay/Flickr (CC)* *Dave Pinter/Flickr (CC)*

Wally Gobetz/Flickr (CC) *libby rosof/Flickr (CC)*

Clockwise: Jennifer Holliday sings in Northalsted, Chicago, IL, on August 7, 2010; Boz Scaggs performs at Bluesfest 2014 in LeBreton Flats, Ottawa, Canada, on April 18, 2014; Matthew McConaughey presents the Lincoln Navigator at the 2016 New York International Auto Show on March 22, 2016; a detail is shown of Trenton Doyle Hancock's "Flower Bed II: A Prelude to Damnation" from the Institute of Contemporary Art in Philadelphia, Pennsylvania, on April 24, 2008; The National September 11 Memorial & Museum, whose plaza was designed by Elaine Molinar and Craig Dykers, is shown in Battery Park City, New York, New York, on April 29, 2012.

Texas Medal of the Arts Awards

The Texas Medals of the Arts are presented to artists and arts patrons with Texas ties.

The awards are administered by the Texas Cultural Trust Council.

The council was established to raise money and awareness for the Texas Cultural Trust Fund, which was created

Source: Texas Commission on the Arts.

by the Legislature in 1993 to support cultural arts in Texas (txculturaltrust.org).

The medals, awarded every two years, were first presented in 2001. A concurrent proclamation by the state Senate and House of Representatives honors the recipients, and the governor presents the awards in Austin.

2019

Design: Brandon Maxwell, Longview, fashion designer, photographer.
Music: Boz Scaggs, Plano, singer/songwriter.
Visual arts: Trenton Doyle Hancock, Houston and Paris, TX, artist.
Music Ensemble: Conspirare, Austin, choral ensemble.
Literary: Stephen Harrigan, Austin, Abilene, and Corpus Christi, author, journalist.
Film: Matthew McConaughey, Austin, Uvalde, and Longview, actor.
Multimedia: Mark Seliger, Amarillo and Houston, photographer.
Theater: Jennifer Holliday, Houston, singer, actor.
Arts education: Vidal M. Treviño School of Communications and Fine Arts, Laredo.
Architecture: Elaine Molinar, El Paso, and Craig Dykers, San Antonio.

2017

Lifetime Achievement Award: Kenny Rogers of Houston.

Multimedia: Kris Kristofferson, Brownsville.
Music: Yolanda Adams, Houston.
Visual arts: Leo Villareal, El Paso, artist.
Dance: Lauren Anderson, Houston.
Literary: John Phillip Santos, San Antonio.
Film: Janine Turner, Euless, actor.
Journalism: Scott Pelley, San Antonio, news broadcaster.
Television: Jaclyn Smith, Houston, actor.
Theater: Renée Elise Goldsberry, Houston.
Arts education: Dallas Black Dance Theatre.
Architecture: Frank Welch, Dallas.
Individual arts patron: Lynn Wyatt, Houston.
Corporate arts patrons: John Paul and Eloise DeJoria, Austin.
Foundation arts patron: Tobin Endowment, San Antonio.

2015

Lifetime Achievement Award: The Gatlin Brothers of Seminole, Abilene, and Odessa.
Multimedia: Emilio Nicolas Sr. of San Antonio, for work as broadcaster.
Music: T Bone Burnett of Fort Worth.
Visual arts: Rick Lowe of Houston, artist.

Dance: Kilgore Rangerettes.

Literary: Lawrence Wright, Austin and Dallas.

Film: Jamie Foxx, Terrell, actor.

Television: Dan Rather, Wharton, news broadcaster.

Television: Chandra Wilson, Houston, actor.

Theater: Robert Schenkkan, Austin.

Arts education: Booker T. Washington High School for the Performing and Visual Arts, Dallas.

Architecture: Charles Renfro, Houston.

Individual arts patron: Margaret McDermott, Dallas.

Corporate arts patron: Dr Pepper Snapple Group, Plano.

Standing Ovation Award: Ruth Altshuler of Dallas.

2013

Multimedia: Eva Longoria of Corpus Christi, for work as actress, author, and philanthropist.

Music: Steve Miller of Dallas.

Visual arts: James Surls, Splendora, artist.

Dance: Houston Ballet.

Television/Film: Ricardo Chavira, San Antonio, actor.

Theater arts: Joe Sears and Jaston Williams, Austin (Greater Tuna fame).

Arts education: Big Thought / Gigi Antoni, Dallas.

Individual arts patron: Gene Jones and Charlotte Jones Anderson, Dallas.

Foundation arts patron: Kimbell Arts Foundation, Fort Worth.

Corporate arts patron: Texas Monthly.

2011

Lifetime Achievement Award: Barbara Smith Conrad from Center Point near Pittsburg, operatic mezzo-soprano and civil rights icon.

Music: ZZ Top of Houston, legendary band that sold over 50 million albums.

Literary: Robert M. Edsel, Dallas, author and founder/president of the Monuments Men Foundation for the Preservation of Art.

Visual arts: James Drake, Lubbock, artist.

Television: Bob Schieffer, Fort Worth, CBS news anchor.

Theater arts: Alley Theatre, Houston.

Multimedia: Ray Benson, Austin, front man for Asleep at the Wheel and co-writer of the play A Ride with Bob based on the life of Bob Wills.

Film: Marcia Gay Harden, UT-Austin graduate, Oscar-winning actress.

Film: Bill Paxton, Fort Worth, four-time Golden Globe nominee.

Arts education: Tom Staley, director of the Harry Ransom Center at UT-Austin.

Individual arts patron: Ernest and Sarah Butler of Austin, major donors to Austin arts groups.

Corporate arts patron: H-E-B, grocer with a long history of supporting the arts throughout Texas.

2009

A Standing Ovation Award was presented to former First Lady Laura Bush of Midland and Dallas.

Lifetime Achievement Award: posthumously to artist Robert Rauschenberg, born in Port Arthur.

Music: Clint Black of Katy, country music singer/songwriter.

Literary: T.R. Fehrenbach of San Antonio. Mr. Fehrenbach, born in San Benito, is the author of 18 nonfiction books, including Lone Star: A History of Texas and Texans.

Visual arts: Keith Carter of Beaumont, photographer.

Theater arts: Betty Buckley of Fort Worth, Tony Award winner and film actress.

Multimedia: Austin City Limits, the 30-year television series.

Film: Robert Rodriguez of Austin. Mr. Rodriguez, born in San Antonio, is a film director and writer.

Architecture: David Lake of Austin and Ted Flato of Corpus Christi, both now working in San Antonio.

Arts education: Pianist James Dick of Round Top, founder of the International Festival-Institute there.

Individual arts patron: Edith O'Donnell of Dallas.

Corporate arts patron: Anheuser-Busch of St. Louis and Houston.

2007

Lifetime Achievement Award: Broadcast newsman Walter Cronkite of Houston.

Music: Ornette Coleman of Fort Worth, jazz saxophonist.

Dance: Alvin Ailey American Dance Theater. The late Alvin Ailey, born in Rogers, was a creator of African American dance works.

Literary: writer Sandra Brown of Waco.

Visual arts: Jesús Moroles of Corpus Christi/Rockport, sculptor.

Theater arts: actress Judith Ivey of El Paso.

Multimedia: Bill Wittliff of Taft and Austin, publisher, writer, photographer, director, producer.

Arts education: Paul Baker of Hereford/Waelder. Headed drama departments at Baylor and Trinity universities.

Individual arts patron: Diana and Bill Hobby of Houston.

Corporate arts patron: Neiman Marcus, Dallas.

Foundation arts patron: Sid W. Richardson Foundation of Fort Worth.

2005

Lifetime Achievement Award: singer Vikki Carr of El Paso.

Television/theater: actress Phylicia Rashad of Houston.

Music: singer/songwriter Lyle Lovett of Klein.

Dance: Ben Stevenson of Houston and Fort Worth.

Literary arts: Naomi Shihab Nye of San Antonio.

Visual arts: Jose Cisneros of El Paso.

Theater: Robert Wilson of Waco.

Arts education: Ginger Head-Gearheart of Fort Worth, advocate of arts education in public schools.

Individual arts patrons: Joe R. and Teresa Lozano Long of Austin, philanthropists.

Foundation arts patron: Nasher Foundation/Dallas.

2003

Lifetime Achievement: John Graves of Glen Rose, author of Goodbye to A River.

Media-film/television acting: Fess Parker of Fort Worth.

Music: country singer Charley Pride of Dallas.

Dance: Tommy Tune of Wichita Falls and Houston.

Theater: Enid Holm of Odessa, actress and former executive director of Texas Nonprofit Theatres.

Literary arts: Sandra Cisneros of San Antonio.

Visual arts: sculptor Glenna Goodacre of Dallas.

Folk arts: Tejano singer Lydia Mendoza of San Antonio.

Architecture: State Capitol Preservation Project of Austin, headed by Dealey Herndon.

Arts education: theater teacher Marca Lee Bircher, Dallas.

Individual arts patron: philanthropist Nancy B. Hamon of Dallas.

Corporate arts patron: Exxon/Mobil based in Irving.

Foundation arts patron: Houston Endowment Inc.

2001

Lifetime Achievement: Van Cliburn of Fort Worth.

Film: actor Tommy Lee Jones of San Saba.

Music: singer-songwriter Willie Nelson of Austin.

Dance: Debbie Allen of Houston, choreographer, director, actress and composer.

Theater: Texas musical-drama producer Neil Hess of Amarillo.

Literary arts: playwright Horton Foote of Wharton.

Visual arts: muralist John Biggers of Houston.

Folk arts: musician brothers Santiago Jimenez Jr. and Flaco Jimenez of San Antonio.

Architecture: restoration architect Wayne Bell of Austin.

Arts education: theater arts director Gilberto Zepeda Jr. of Pharr.

Individual arts patron: philanthropist Jack Blanton of Houston.

Corporate arts patron: SBC Communications Inc. of San Antonio.

Foundation arts patron: Meadows Foundation of Dallas. ☆

Philosophical Society of Texas Awards of Merit

The Philosophical Society of Texas established the Award of Merit in 2000.

The categories were expanded in 2012 to separate categories, one for fiction and one for nonfiction.

In 2015, an award for poetry was introduced.

The book must be about Texas or the author must have been born in or have resided within the boundaries claimed by the Republic of Texas in 1836.

2000		Gregg Cantrell, *Stephen F. Austin, Empresario*, Yale University Press, 1999.
2001		Frank D. Welch, *Philip Johnson & Texas*, University of Texas Press, 2000.
2002		Hal K. Rothman, *LBJ's Texas White House: "Our Heart's Home,"* Texas A&M University Press, 2001.
2003		James L. Haley, *Sam Houston*, University of Oklahoma Press, 2002.
2004		Randolph B. Campbell, *Gone to Texas: A History of the Lone Star State*, Oxford University Press, 2003.
2005		David La Vere, *The Texas Indians*, Texas A&M University Press, 2004.
2006		Mavis P. Kelsey Sr. and Robin Brandt Hutchinon, *Engraved Prints of Texas, 1554–1900*, Texas A&M University Press, 2005
2007		Richard B. McCaslin, *At the Heart of Texas, 100 Years of the Texas State Historical Association, 1897–1997*, Texas State Historical Association Press, 2006.
2008		Stephen Fox, *The Country Houses of John F. Staub*, Texas A&M University Press, 2007.
2009		Pekka Hämäläinen, *The Comanche Empire*, Yale University Press, 2008.
2010		Emilio Zamora, *Claiming Rights and Righting Wrongs in Texas: Mexican Workers and Job Politics During World War II*, Texas A&M University Press, 2009.
2011		Dan K. Utley and Cynthia J. Beeman, *History Ahead: Stories beyond the Texas Roadside Markers*, Texas A&M University Press, 2011.
2012	Fiction	Gerald Duff, *Blue Sabine*, Moon City Press, 2011.
	Non-fiction	Michael Berryhill, *The Trails of Eroy Brown: The Murder Case that Shook the Texas Prison System*, University of Texas Press, 2011.
2013	Fiction	Ben Rehder, *The Chicken Hanger: A Novel*, Texas Christian University Press, 2012.
	Non-fiction	Jan Reid, *Let the People In: The Life and Times of Ann Richards*, UT Press, 2012.
2014	Fiction	Thomas Zigal, *Many Rivers to Cross*, Texas Christian University Press, 2013.
	Non-fiction	Raúl Coronado, *A World Not to Come: A History of Latino Writing and Print Culture*, Harvard University Press, 2013.
2015	Fiction	Sara Bird, *Above the East China Sea*, Knopf, 2014.
	Fiction	James Magnuson, *Famous Writers I have Known: A Novel*, W.W. Norton & Company, 2014.
	Non-fiction	Katie Robinson Edwards, *Midcentury Modern Art in Texas*, University of Texas Press, 2014.
	Poetry	Christian Wiman, *Once in the West*, Farrar, Straus and Giroux, 2014.
2016	Fiction	Sanderia Faye, *Mourner's Bench*, University of Arkansas Press, 2015.
	Non-fiction	Ron J. Jackson Jr. and Lee Spencer White, *Joe: The Slave Who Became an Alamo Legend*, University of Oklahoma Press, 2015.
	Poetry	James Hoggard, *New and Selected Poems*, TCU Press, 2015.
2017	Fiction	Dominic Smith, *The Last Painting of Sara de Vos*, 2016.
	Non-fiction	Kenneth Hafertepe, *The Material Culture of German Texans*, 2016.
	Poetry	Jonathan Fink, *Barbarossa*, 2016.
2018	Fiction	Chanelle Benz, *The Man Who Shot Out My Eye Is Dead*, 2017.
	Non-fiction	Andrew Sansom and William E. Reaves, *Of Texas Rivers and Texas Art*, 2017.
	Poetry	Dan Williams, *Past Purgatory, A Distant Paradise*, 2017.
2019	Fiction	Elizabeth Crook, *The Which Way Tree*, 2018.
	Non-fiction	Andrew Saansom, *Seasons at Selah: The Legacy of the Bamberger Ranch Prserve*, 2018.
	Poetry	Megan Peak, *Girldom*, 2018.
2020	Fiction	Leila Meachan, *Dragonfly*, 2019.
	Non-fiction	Stephen Harrigan, *Big Wonderful Thing: A History of Texas*, 2019.
	Poetry	Edward Vidaurre, *JazzHouse*, 2019.

Recent Movies Made in Texas

Following is a partial list of recent major productions filmed in Texas in descending order by date.

The date is for the year of release of the film, while actual location shots occurred earlier.

Location information is from the Texas Film Commission and other sources.

Sources: Texas Film Commission, and online.

The totals are not comprehensive.

When only a small portion of the movie is known to have been filmed in Texas, "(part)" is listed next to the movie title. Some of the major artists who worked on the project are listed in the column at far right.

Year	Movie	Locations	Artists
2019	Addict Named Hal	Austin, Pflugerville	Lane Michael Stanley (director)
2019	The Big Bend	Study Butte, Terlingua	Brett Wagner (director)
2019	Brother's Keeper	Abilene	Todd Randall (director)
2019	Caged Birds	Dallas	Fredrick Leach (director)
2019	The Dark and the Wicked	Granbury	Brett Wagner
2019	Flip Turn	Dallas, Irving	Alin Bijan (director)
2019	Fugitive Dreams	Austin, Bartlett, Bastrop, Elgin, Fredericksburg, Manor	Jason Neulander (director)
2019	The Get Together	Austin, Blanco, Hallettsville, Pflugerville, San Antonio	Laura Perez (director)
2019	Inbetween Girl	Austin, Galveston	Mei Makino (director)
2019	Marfa	Marfa, Lockney, Plainview	Andy Stapp (director)
2019	Miss Juneteenth	Fort Worth	Channing Godfrey Peoples (director)
2019	No Ordinary Love	Fort Worth	Chyna Robinson (director)
2019	Run Hide Fight	Dallas, Red Oak	Kyle Rankin (director)
2019	Twelve Mighty Orphans	Fort Worth, Weatherford	Ty Roberts (director)
2019	VFW	Dallas	Joe Begos (director)
2019	We Can Be Heroes	Austin	Robert Rodriguez (director)
2018	The Iron Orchard	Big Spring, Midland, Odessa, Austin	Ty Roberts (director), Austin Nichols
2018	1985	Dallas	Yen Tan (director), Michael Chiklis, Virginia Madsen
2016	Everybody Wants Some	Austin, Bastrop, Elgin, Manor, San Marcos, Taylor, Weimar, Wimberley	Richard Linklater (director), Blake Jenner
2015	My All American	Austin, Dallas, Fort Worth, San Antonio, Elgin, Manor, Smithville	Angelo Pizzo (director), Aaron Eckhart, Finn Wittrock
2013	Boyhood	Alpine, Austin, Houston, San Marcos, Big Bend, Webster, Pedernales State Park	Ethan Hawke, Patricia Arquette, Richard Linklater (director)
2013	Parkland	Dallas, Austin	Billy Bob Thornton, Zac Efron
2011	Bernie	Carthage, Smithville, Georgetown, Bastrop, Lockhart, Austin	Jack Black, Shirley MacLaine, Matthew McConaughey, Richard Linklater (director)
2011	The Tree of Life	Bastrop, Austin, Dallas, Houston, La Grange, Matagorda, San Marcos, Smithville, Waco	Brad Pitt, Sean Penn
2009	Friday the 13th	Austin, Bastrop, La Grange, Marshall, Wimberley	Marcus Nispel (director)
2006	No Country for Old Men (part)	Marfa	Ethan and Joel Coen (directors), Tommy Lee Jones

Number of Production Projects in Texas by Year

	2007	2008	2009	2010	2011	2014	2015	2016	2017	2018	2019
Feature Films	36	27	60	38	16	26	14	24	19	18	21
TV Series	14	12	20	17	15	14	20	15	23	26	39
Total	**50**	**39**	**80**	**55**	**31**	**40**	**34**	**39**	**42**	**44**	**60**

Sources: Texas Film Commission and the Motion Picture Association of America (2021).

Television series that were recently produced in Texas include *Fear the Walking Dead, The Son,* Emmy-nominated *The Long Road Home, Fixer Upper, The Leftovers, American Crime,* and some syndicated programs, in addition to the long-running *Austin City Limits.*

Film and Television Work in Texas

For almost a century, Texas has been one of the nation's top filmmaking states, after California and New York. More than 1,600 films have been made in Texas since 1910, including *Wings,* the first film to win an Academy Award for Best Picture, which was made in San Antonio in 1927.

Texas' attractions to filmmakers are its diverse locations, abundant sunshine and moderate winter weather, and a variety of support services. The economic benefits of hosting on-location filming over the past decade are estimated at more than $3 billion. Besides salaries paid to locally hired technicians and actors, as well as fees paid to location owners, the production companies do business with hotels, car rental agencies, lumberyards, restaurants, grocery stores, utilities, security services, and florists.

All types of projects come to Texas besides films, including television features and news organizations, commercials, corporate films, and game videos.

Many projects made in Texas originate in California studios, but Texas is also the home of many independent filmmakers who make films outside the studio system. Some films and television shows made in Texas have become icons. *Giant,* John Wayne's *The Alamo,* and the long-running TV series *Dallas* all made their mark on the world's perception of Texas.

The Texas Film Commission, a division of the Office of the Governor, markets to Hollywood Texas' locations, support services, and workforce availablity. The legislature funded the Texas Moving Image Incentive Program with $22 million in the 2018–2019 biennium.

The commission's free services include location research, employment referrals for production assistants, red-tape-cutting, and information on weather, travel, and other topics affecting production. ☆

Source: Texas Film Commission at gov.texas.gov/film/

Production still from Fugitive Dreams *(2019). Photo courtesy of Jason Neulander.*

Regional Commissions

Amarillo Film Office
1000 S. Polk, Amarillo 79101
(800) 646-3388
visitamarillo.com/media/film

Austin Film Office
111 Congress Ave., Ste. 700
Austin 78701,
(866) 462-8784
austinfilmcommission.com

Brownsville Border Film Commission
650 Ruben M. Torres Sr. Blvd.
Brownsville 78521,
(956) 546-3721
filmbtx.com

Corpus Christi Film Commission
101 N. Shoreline Dr., Ste. 430
Corpus Christi 78401
(800) 678-6232
visitcorpuschristitx.org/media

Dallas Film Commission
325 N. St. Paul St., Ste. 700
Dallas 75201,
(214) 571-1050
dallasfilmcommission.com

El Paso Film Commission
One Civic Center Plaza
El Paso 79901,
(915) 534-0600
filmelpaso.com

Fort Worth Film Commission
111 W. 4th St., Ste. 200
Fort Worth 76102, (817) 698-7842
filmfortworth.com

Houston Film Commission
701 Avenida de las Americas,
Ste. 200 Houston 77010,
(713) 853-8959
houstonfilmcommission.com

San Antonio Film Commission
203 S. St. Mary's St., Ste. 120
San Antonio 78205, (210) 207-6730
filmsanantonio.com

South Padre Island Film Commission
sopadre.com/about/
film-on-south-padre-island/

Holidays, Anniversaries, and Festivals, 2022–2023

Below are listed the principal federal and state government holidays; Christian, Jewish, and Islamic holidays and festivals; and special recognition days for 2021 and 2022.

Technically, the United States does not observe national holidays. Each state has jurisdiction over its holidays, which are usually designated by its legislature.

This list was compiled partially from the Texas Government Code, the U.S. Office of Personnel Management, and *Astronomical Phenomena 2021* and *Astronomical Phenomena 2022*, which are published jointly by the U.S. Naval Observatory and the United Kingdom Hydrographic Office.

See the footnotes for explanations of the symbols.

2022

New Year's Day	§	Sat., Jan. 1
Epiphany		Thurs., Jan. 6
Sam Rayburn Day	‡	Thurs., Jan. 6
Martin Luther King Jr. Day	§	Mon., Jan. 17
Confederate Heroes' Day	§	Wed., Jan. 19
Valentine's Day		Mon., Feb. 14
Presidents' Day	§	Mon., Feb. 21
Primary Election Day		Tues., March 1
Ash Wednesday		Wed., March 2
Texas Independence Day	§	Wed., March 2
Texas Flag Day	‡	Wed., March 2
César Chávez Day	§	Thurs., March 31
Ramadan, first day of		Sun., April 3
Former Prisoners of War Day	‡	Sat., April 9
Palm Sunday		Sun., April 10
Good Friday	§	Fri., April 15
Passover (Pesach), first day of		Sat., April 16
Easter Day		Sun., April 17
San Jacinto Day	§	Thurs., April 21
Mother's Day		Sun., May 8
Armed Forces Day		Sat., May 21
Ascension Day		Thurs., May 26
Memorial Day	§	Mon., May 30
Shavuot (Feast of Weeks)		Sun., June 5
Whit Sunday — Pentecost		Sun., June 5
Trinity Sunday		Sun., June 12
Flag Day (U.S.)		Tues., June 14
Emancipation Day in Texas (Juneteenth)	§	Sun., June 19
Father's Day		Sun., June 19
Independence Day	§	Mon., July 4
Islamic New Year		Fri., July 29
Lyndon Baines Johnson Day	§	Sat., Aug. 27
Labor Day	§	Mon., Sept. 5
Grandparents Day		Sun., Sept. 11
Rosh Hashanah (Jewish New Year)		Mon., Sept. 26
Yom Kippur (Day of Atonement)		Wed., Oct. 5
Sukkot (Tabernacles), first day of		Mon., Oct. 10
Columbus Day	‡	Mon., Oct. 10
Halloween		Mon., Oct. 31
Father of Texas Day	‡	Thurs., Nov. 3
General Election Day	§	Tues., Nov. 8
Veterans Day	§	Fri., Nov. 11
Thanksgiving Day	§	Thurs., Nov. 24
First Sunday in Advent		Sun., Nov. 27
Hanukkah, first day of		Mon., Dec. 19
Christmas Day	§	Sun., Dec. 25

2023

New Year's Day	§	Sun., Jan. 1
Epiphany		Fri., Jan. 6
Sam Rayburn Day	‡	Fri., Jan. 6
Martin Luther King Jr. Day	§	Mon., Jan. 16
Confederate Heroes' Day	§	Thurs., Jan. 19
Valentine's Day		Tues., Feb. 14
Presidents' Day	§	Mon., Feb. 20
Ash Wednesday		Wed., Feb. 22
Texas Independence Day	§	Thurs., March 2
Texas Flag Day	‡	Thurs., March 2
Ramadan, first day of		Thurs., Mar 23
César Chávez Day	§	Fri., March 31
Palm Sunday		Sun., April 2
Passover (Pesach), first day of		Thurs., April 6
Good Friday	§	Fri., April 7
Easter Day		Sun., April 9
Former Prisoners of War Day	‡	Sun., April 9
San Jacinto Day	§	Fri., April 21
Mother's Day		Sun., May 14
Ascension Day		Thurs., May 18
Armed Forces Day		Sat., May 20
Shavuot (Feast of Weeks)		Fri., May 26
Whit Sunday — Pentecost		Sun., May 28
Memorial Day	§	Mon., May 29
Trinity Sunday		Sun., June 4
Flag Day (U.S.)		Wed., June 14
Father's Day		Sun., June 18
Emancipation Day in Texas (Juneteenth)	§	Mon., June 19
Independence Day	§	Tues., July 4
Islamic New Year		Wed., July 19
Lyndon Baines Johnson Day	§	Sun., Aug. 27
Labor Day	§	Mon., Sept. 4
Grandparents Day		Sun., Sept. 10
Rosh Hashanah (Jewish New Year)		Sat., Sept. 16
Yom Kippur (Day of Atonement)		Mon., Sept. 25
Sukkot (Tabernacles), first day of		Sat., Sept. 30
Columbus Day	‡	Mon., Oct. 9
Halloween		Tues., Oct. 31
Father of Texas Day	‡	Fri., Nov. 3
General Election Day	§	Tues., Nov. 7
Veterans Day	§	Sat., Nov. 11
Thanksgiving Day	§	Thurs., Nov. 23
First Sunday in Advent		Sun., Dec. 3
Hanukkah, first day of		Fri., Dec. 8
Christmas Day	§	Mon., Dec. 25

Federal legal public holidays are shown in bold. If the holiday falls on a Sunday, the following Monday may be treated as a holiday. If the holiday falls on a Saturday, the preceding Friday may be treated as a holiday.

§ **State holiday in Texas.** For state employees, the Friday after Thanksgiving Day, Dec. 24, and Dec. 26 are also holidays. **Optional holidays** are César Chávez Day, Good Friday, Rosh Hashanah, and Yom Kippur. **Partial-staffing holidays** are Confederate Heroes Day, Texas Independence Day, San Jacinto Day, Emancipation Day in Texas, and Lyndon Baines Johnson Day. State offices will be open on optional holidays and partial-staffing holidays.

‡ **State Recognition Days**, as designated by the Texas Legislature.

Notes on holidays:

- Confederate Heroes Day combines the birthdays of Robert E. Lee (Jan. 19) and Jefferson Davis (June 3).
- Presidents' Day combines the birthdays of George Washington (Feb. 22) and Abraham Lincoln (Feb. 12).
- Jewish and Islamic holidays are tabular, meaning they begin at sunset on the previous evening.
- Between 1939 and 1957, Texas observed Thanksgiving Day on the last Thursday in November. As a result, in a November having five Thursdays, Texas celebrated national Thanksgiving on the fourth Thursday and Texas Thanksgiving on the fifth Thursday. In 1957, Texas changed the state observance to coincide with the national holiday.

Religious Affiliation Change: 2000 to 2010

Texas remains one of the nation's more "religious" states, even though a smaller portion of Texans is affiliated with a congregation than ten years ago.

At the same time, the estimated number of Muslims in the state increased to 421,972, making it the fifth-largest religious group in the state and making Texas first in the nation in number of Muslims.

Texas ranks in the upper half among the states in percentage of the population belonging to a denomination. According to the *2010 U.S. Religion Census*, at least **56.0 percent** of Texans are adherents to a religion. The national average is 48.8 percent.

The census, sponsored by the Association of Statisticians of American Religious Bodies, is the only U.S. survey to report religious membership down to the county level, as well as at the state level. The census relies on self-reports from congregations for membership numbers.

But in the past, the African-American churches did not participate in the study, and in 2010 less than half of those congregations participated.

Only 345,998 black Protestants were counted in Texas in 2010. According to the U.S. Census of 2010, there were 2,782,876 blacks in Texas, which would mean 87.6 percent of black Texans, who are predominately Protestant, were designated as unaffiliated to any church. This probably leaves out some one million Texas church members.

In 1990, it was estimated that there were 815,000 black Baptists in Texas. An estimate of the membership in black Pentecostal churches was about 300,000. And an estimate for black Methodists in Texas was approximately 200,000.

According to the *2010 U.S. Religion Census*, Texas ranks:

— **First** in number of evangelical Protestants, with 6,457,044.

— **First** in number that belong to nondenominational Christian churches, with 1,546,542.

— **First** in number of Muslims, with 421,972 estimated. New York is second with 392,953 estimated.

— **Second**, behind Pennsylvania, in number of Mainline Protestants at 1,641,527.

— **Second**, behind California, in number of Hindus.

— **Third** in number of Buddhists.

— **Third** in number of Catholics.

— **Fifth** in number of Mormons.

Carrying over those estimates into 2010 and adjusting for these additions, the percentage of Texans that are adherents* of a religion would be closer to **59.8 percent** in 2010.

[In addition, the religion census includes denominations that provide numbers of congregations but who have not enumerated the numbers of adherents in each congregation. Even with factoring in an average congregation size of 100 persons for Protestant congregations (a figure used by the census study), the total percentage would vary less than one percent, to **60.7 percent.**]

Although that is higher than the 56.0 percent figure compiled from the reporting churches, still it would be down from **67.1 percent** 20 years ago, indicating a move away from religious affiliation in Texas.

However, with the total state population booming, the churches still reported an **increase of 2.17 million** members, while the total population of Texas increased by 4.29 million from 2000 to 2010.

During the same period, the number of Texans not attached to a religion rose by **2.13 million.**

Thus, according to the Texas Almanac analysis from a variety of sources, there are **10.1 million** persons in the state who are not claimed by a religious group and about 15 million who are congregation members. (The U.S. census counted **25,145,561** persons in Texas in 2010.)

Largest Religious Bodies	Adherents*	Percent of Texas Population
1. Catholic Church	4,673,500	18.59 %
2. Southern Baptist Convention	3,722,194	14.80 %
3. Non-Denominational Christian	1,546,542	6.15 %
4. United Methodist Church	1,122,736	4.46 %
5. Muslim estimate	421,972	1.68 %
6. Church of Christ	351,129	1.40 %
7. Latter-Day Saints (Mormons)	296,141	1.18 %
8. Assembly of God	275,565	1.10 %
9. Presbyterian Church (U.S.A.)	155,046	0.62 %
10. Episcopal Church	148,439	0.59 %
11. Lutheran (Missouri Synod)	132,508	0.53 %
12. Lutheran (E.L.C.A.)	111,647	0.44 %
Unclaimed by any faith	10,103,455	40.20 %

__Adherents__ include all full members, their children, and others who regularly attend services. All figures used here by the Texas Almanac refer to these adherents.

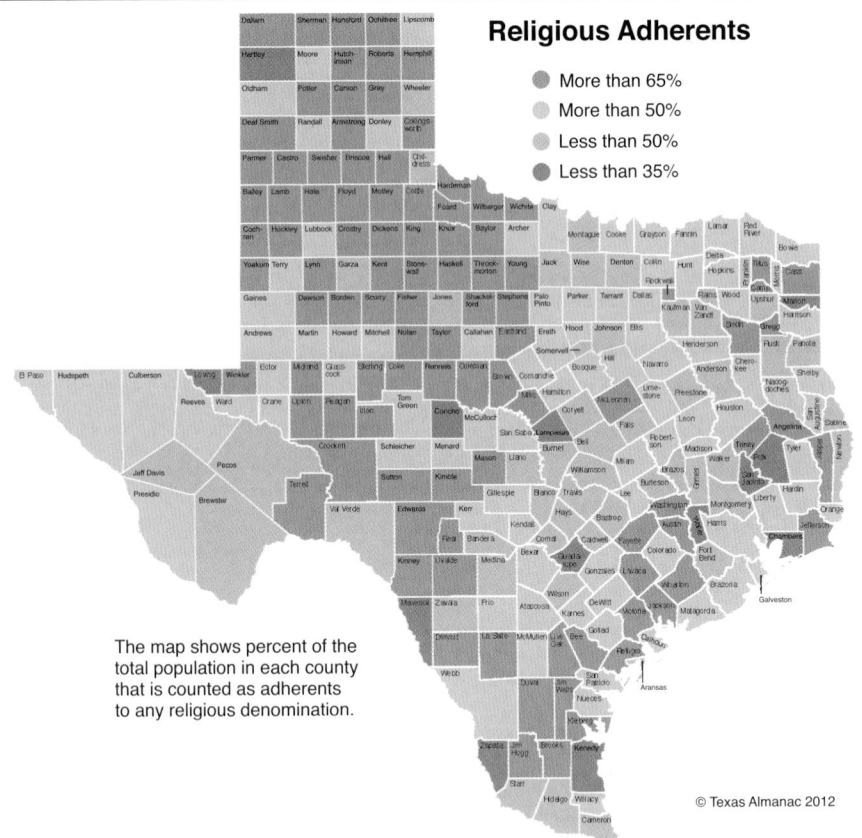

Religious Adherents

- More than 65%
- More than 50%
- Less than 50%
- Less than 35%

The map shows percent of the total population in each county that is counted as adherents to any religious denomination.

© Texas Almanac 2012

Numbers of Members Statewide by Denomination

Religious Groups in Texas	2000	Change	2010
Adventists	**46,323**	**+ 27,797**	**74,120**
Church of God (Seventh Day) (70 congregations)	—		—
Church of God General Conference	55		65
Seventh-Day Adventists	46,268		74,055
Baha'i	**10,777**	**+ 2,458**	**13,253**
Baptist	**4,537,918**	**+ 52,228**	**4,590,143**
Alliance of Baptists (9 congregations)			—
American Baptist Association	61,272		39,354
American Baptist Churches in the USA	7,057		7,172
Baptist General Conference	340		1,320
Baptist Missionary Association of America	123,198		—
Conservative Baptist Association of America (1 congregation)			—
Free Will Baptist, National Association of, Inc.	2,822		3,111
Independent Baptist Fellowship International (258 cong.)			—
Interstate & Foreign Landmark Missionary Baptists Association	93		—
Landmark Baptist, Indep. Assns. & Unaffil. Churches	964		—
National Primitive Baptist Convention, USA	4,463		—
North American Baptist Conference	1,569		1,157
Primitive Baptists Associations			—
Primitive Baptist Church — Old Line (118 congregations)			—
Progressive Primitive Baptists	197		—
Reformed Baptist Churches of America (27 congregations)			—
Regular Baptist Churches, General Assn. of (6 congregations)	684		—
Seventh Day Baptist General Conference			67

Religious Groups in Texas	2000	Change	2010
Southern Baptist Convention	3,519,459		3,722,194
Southwide Baptist Fellowship (13 congregations)			
Two-Seed-in-the-Spirit Predestinarian Baptists	29		—
Black Baptists (Estimate)*	(815,771)*		(815,771)*
National Baptist Convention of America, Inc.			89,050
National Baptist Convention, USA, Inc.			59,529
National Missionary Bapist Convention, Inc.			34,039
Progressive National Baptist Convention, Inc.			2,683
Full Gospel Baptist Church Fellowship (52 congregations)			—
Buddhist (95 congregations)	**—**		**66,116**
Mahayana			49,874
Theravada			13,461
Vajrayana			2,781
Catholic Church	**4,368,969**	**+ 304,531**	**4,673,500**
(Christian Scientists) Church of Christ, Scientist (64 cong.)	**—**		**—**
Churches of Christ	**424,907**	**– 30,843**	**394,064**
Church of Christ	377,264		351,129
Independent Christian Churches and Churches of Christ	43,602		40,078
International Churches of Christ	4,041		2,857
(Disciples of Christ) Christian Church	**111,288**	**– 36,471**	**74,817**
Episcopal	**177,910**	**– 29,471**	**148,439**
Episcopal Church, The	177,910		148,439
Reformed Episcopal Church			—
Anglican Church in North America (111 congregations)			—
Hindu (34 congregations in 2000)	**—**		**60,725**
Indian-American HIndu Temple Assn.			36,550
Post-Renaissance			968
Renaissance			98
Traditional Temples			23,109
Holiness	**86,942**	**– 1,738**	**85,204**
Christian & Missionary Alliance, The	3,858		5,465
Church of Christ (Holiness), U.S.A. (4 congregations)			—
Church of God (Anderson, Ind.)	4,669		3,990
Churches of Christ in Christian Union (2 congregations)			—
Free Methodist Church of North America	874		1,864
Missionary Church, The	403		3,119
Nazarene, Church of the	50,528		44,836
Salvation Army	25,070		23,761
Wesleyan Church, The	1,540		2,169
Jain (6 congregations)	**—**		**—**
Jehovah's Witnesses (426 congregations)	**—**		**—**
Judaism, (estimate) *	**(128,000)***	**– 67,355**	**60,645**
Conservative			**17,889**
Orthodox			**8,410**
Reconstructionist			**356**
Reform			**33,990**
Lutheran	**301,518**	**– 29,452**	**272,066**
Church of the Lutheran Brethren of America	—		72
Church of the Lutheran Confession (4 congregations)	—		
Evangelical Lutheran Church in America	155,019		111,647
Evangelical Lutheran Synod	—		—
Free Lutheran Congregations, The Assoc. of	368		75
Lutheran Church–Missouri Synod, The	140,106		132,508
Lutheran Congregations in Mission for Christ	—		20,936
North American Lutheran Church (26 congregations)	—		—
Wisconsin Evangelical Lutheran Synod	6,025		6,828

Religious Groups in Texas	2000	Change	2010
Mennonite/Amish	**4,930**	**– 1,330**	**3,600**
Amish, Old Order or Conservative Unaffiliated	24		309
Amish, undifferentiated	68		52
Apostolic Christian Church of America, Inc.	27		46
Beachy Amish Mennonite Churches	127		265
Brethren in Christ Church (1 congregation)			—
Church of God in Christ (Mennonite)	849		1,068
Church of the Brethren	284		118
Conservative Mennonite Conference	191		106
Evangelical Bible Churches, Fellowship of (was Ev. Menn. Bre.)			
Eastern Pennsylvania Mennonite Church	65		—
Grace Brethren Churches, Fellowship of (3 congregations)			—
Mennonite Brethren Churches, U.S. Conference of	425		403
Mennonite, other	1,655		—
Mennonite Church USA	1,215		1,233
Messianic Judaism	**—**		**—**
Association of Messianic Congregations (1 congregation)	—		—
Union of Messianic Jewish Congregations (5 congregations)	—		—
Methodist	**1,219,533**	**+ 94,912**	**1,314,445**
Black Methodists (estimate)*	(197,191)*		(150,000)*
African Methodist Episcopal Zion	(2,191)*		1,327
African Methodist Episcopal	(150,000)*		43,839
Christian Methodist Episcopal	(45,000)*		37,986
Congregational Methodist Church	—		2,396
Evangelical Methodist Church (11 congregations)			—
Southern Methodist Church (2 congregations)			
United Methodist Church, The	1,022,342		1,122,736
(Mormons)	**158,268**	**+ 142,323**	**300,591**
Church of Jesus Christ of Latter-day Saints, The	155,451		296,141
Community of Christ	2,817		4,450
Muslim, estimate	**114,999**	**+ 306,973**	**421,972**
Non-denominational (Evangelical Protestant)	**—**		**1,546,542**
Independent Non-Charismatic Churches	145,249		—
Independent Charismatic Churches	159,449		—
Orthodox (Eastern Christian)	**22,755**	**+ 9,695**	**32,450**
Antiochian Orthodox of North America	4,642		5,348
Armenian Apostolic Church/Cilicia	80		—
Armenian Apostolic Church/Etchmiadzin	1,275		515
Assyrian Apostolic Church			—
Coptic Orthodox Church (8 congregations)	—		3,866
Eritrean Orthodox	—		1,000
Ethiopian Orthodox (4 congregations)			—
Greek Orthodox Archdiocese of America	9,444		12,167
Greek Orthodox Archdiocese of Vasiloupulis	135		—
Malankara Archdiocese/Syrian Orthodox Church in North Amer.	825		1,260
Malankara Orthodox Syrian Church, American Diocese of the	2,675		2,433
Romanian Orthodox Archdiocese in Americas)	413		600
Orthodox Church in America (Territorial Dioceses)	2,096		2,657
Russian Orthodox Church Outside of Russia (4 congregations)			1,022
Serbian Orthodox Church in North America	1,110		1,372
Syrian Orthodox Church of Antioch	60		210
Pentecostal/Charismatic	**615,258**	**+ 61,825**	**677,083**
Apostolic Faith Mission of Portland, Ore.	—		135
Assemblies of God	228,098		275,565
Assemblies of God International Fellowship (3 congregations)	—		—
Black Pentecostals (estimate)*	(300,000)*		(300,000)*
Church of God in Christ (estimate)*	(300,000)*		77,545
Church of Our Lord Jesus Christ of Apostolic Faith (22 cong.)	—		—
Calvary Chapel Fellowship Churches (57 congregations)	—		—
Church of God (Cleveland, Tenn.)	38,259		47,709

Religious Groups in Texas	2000	Change	2010
Church of God of Prophecy	2,906		3,610
Church of God of the Apostolic Faith, Inc. (18 congregations)	—		—
Church of Our Lord Jesus Christ of Apostolic Faith (22 cong.)	—		—
Congregational Holiness Church	—		1,280
International Church of the Foursquare Gospel	12,501		11,047
Open Bible Standard Churches, Inc.			148
Pentecostal Church of God	11,592		13,486
Pentecostal Holiness Church, International	10,265		15,576
Pentecostal Church International, United (656 congregations)	—		—
Vineyard USA	11,637		8,527
Presbyterian	**204,804**	**– 21,514**	**183,290**
Associate Reformed Presbyterian Church	28		223
Cumberland Presbyterian Church	8,422		6,355
Cumberland Presbyterian Church in America (19 cong.)	—		—
Evangelical Presbyterian Church	1,449		2,883
Korean Presbyterian Church Abroad (2 congregations)	—		—
Korean Presbyterian Church in America (8 congregations)	—		—
Korean-American Presbyterian Church (4 congregations)	—		—
Orthodox Presbyterian Church, The	644		824
Presbyterian Church (USA)	180,315		155,046
Presbyterian Church in America	13,946		17,959
Reformed Presbyterian Church General Assembly (1 cong.)	—		—
Reformed Presbyterian Church Hanover Presbytery (1 cong)	—		—
Reformed Presbyterian Church in the United States (1 cong.)	—		—
(Quakers)	**1,074**	**+ 1,700**	**2,774**
Evangelical Friends Church International	—		1,845
Friends General Conference	—		929
Unaffiliated Friends Meetings (2 congregations)	—		—
Reformed/Congregational	**30,308**	**+ 2,599**	**32,907**
Communion of Reformed Evangelical Churches (5 cong.)	—		—
Christian Reformed Church in North America	1,936		1,416
Conservative Congregational Christian Conference	25		29
Evangelical Assn. of Reformed, and Congregational (5 cong.)	—		—
Evangelical Free Church of America, The	9,720		13,486
Hungarian Reformed Churches (2 congregations)	—		—
Reformed Church in America	2,040		512
United Church of Christ	16,587		17,464
Sikh (24 congregations)	**—**		**—**
Tao (1 congregation)	**—**		**—**
Unitarian Universalist Association	**6,872**	**+ 1,235**	**8,107**
Unity Churches, Association of (43 congregations)	**—**		**—**
Zoroastrian (3 congregations)	**NR**		**1,095**
OTHERS			
Christian Brethren (4 congregations)			—
Evangelical Covenant Church, The	1,022		1,393
Grace Gospel Fellowship (4 congregations)			—
Independent Fundamentalist Churches of America (1 cong.)			—
Metropolitan Community Churches, Universal Fellowship of	5,570		2,765
National Spiritualist Association of Churches (4 congregations)			—
New Apostolic Church of North America (13 congregations)			—
Polish National Catholic Church (3 congregations)	—		—
Statewide Totals**	**12,875,018**	**+ 2,167,088**	**15,042,106**
Unclaimed (not counted as adherent to religion)	7,976,802	+ 2,126,653	10,103,455

*Texas Almanac estimates. **2000 statewide totals include smaller denominations not reported in 2010 and not listed here.*

Compiled from the 2010 survey sponsored by the Association of Statisticians of American Religious Bodies, also other sources, including: Churches and Church Membership in the United States 2000, Glenmary Research Center, Nashville, Tenn., 2002. National Council of Churches of Christ in the USA, New York, Yearbook of American and Canadian Churches, annual. New Handbook of Texas, 1996, various: "Christian Methodist Episcopal Church," by Charles E. Tatum; "African-American Churches," "African Methodist Episcopal Church," and "African Methodist Episcopal Zion Church," by William E. Montgomery; "Religion," by John W. Storey.

Health & Science

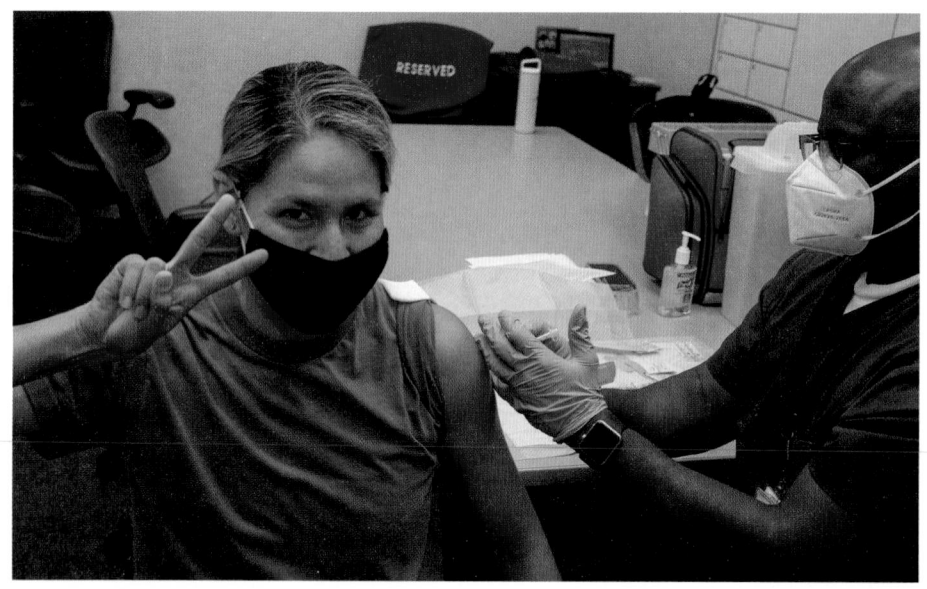

CORONAVIRUS PANDEMIC IN TEXAS

HONORED SCIENTISTS

VITAL STATISTICS

HOSPITALS

DRUG TREATMENT

MENTAL HEALTH CARE

Air Force Major Kimberly Bender recieves the first of two COVID-19 vaccine shots at Brooke Army Medical Center, Joint Base San Antonio, Fort Sam Houston. Photo by Joint Base San Antonio/Flickr.

COVID-19 art on 6th Street in Austin. Photo by Leah Rogers, CC by 4.0/Wikimedia Commons.

Coronavirus (COVID-19) Pandemic in Texas 2020–2021

by Dr. Ana Martinez-Catsam

On March 2, 2020, San Antonio city officials filed suit against the Centers for Disease Control and Prevention and other federal departments and officials, seeking to delay the release of individuals quarantined at Lackland Air Force Base. The previous month, Americans evacuated from Wuhan, China, where the novel coronavirus had been detected, arrived at Lackland AFB to undergo quarantine. In mid-February, 144 passengers from a cruise ship docked in Japan joined those already quarantined at Lackland.

By late February, San Antonio officials learned that a few released evacuees had tested positive for the novel coronavirus, referred to as COVID-19. The day the city filed suit, San Antonio Mayor Ron Nirenberg declared a public health emergency and prohibited those released from quarantine from traveling to or through San Antonio. Within days of San Antonio's actions, other Texas cities canceled events and restricted public gatherings.

On March 4, 2020, the Texas Department of State Health Services reported the state's first positive case not involving an evacuated quarantined person. On March 13, following an increase of positive cases, Governor Greg Abbott declared Texas a public health disaster, which allowed him to employ available resources, such as deploying Texas National Guard to assist health officials in addressing the crisis. Six days later, on March 19, the governor issued **Executive Order GA-08**, which prohibited gathering in groups of more than 10 and visiting nursing homes or other assisted living facilities, asked people to avoid specific businesses that required in-person congregation, and closed schools to in-person instruction.

Municipal governments experiencing an increase in positive cases issued declarations of local disaster and health emergency. The local proclamations outlined actions that either supplemented those already adopted or enhanced preventative measures.

On March 31, as the number of positive cases and deaths increased, Governor Abbott issued **Executive Order GA-14**, which would be in effect until April 30, 2020. While not referred to as a stay-at-home order, it required that services not deemed essential be conducted from home. Some counties issued "Stay Home, Work Safe" orders. Businesses, except for those exempt, were required to cease operation. Residents were encouraged to remain home except when seeking necessary services or engaging in allowable activities. Little did we know how long it would take before life would return to normal.

The Spread and Symptoms of COVID-19

It took time to discover exactly how the disease was being transmitted from person to person, but today we know. According to the Centers for Disease Control and Prevention (CDC), COVID-19 spreads through respiratory droplets or airborne transmission.

Respiratory Droplets

When individuals with COVID-19, whether symptomatic or asymptomatic, cough, talk, sneeze, and breathe, they create respiratory droplets that carry the virus. While medical experts are still learning about the virus, there is a consensus that direct contact, defined as within 6 feet, with an infected individual will increase the risk of infection and spread. When in close contact, respiratory droplets are inhaled through the nose or mouth and deposited on the mucous membranes.

Airborne Transmission

Airborne transmission occurs when droplets from people with COVID-19 remain in the air for minutes or hours. Poor ventilation in enclosed spaces allows for airborne transmission. Under such conditions, individuals who are more than 6 feet away or those who enter areas afterward can be exposed to the virus.

COVID-19

Symptoms	Recommendations to Protect Oneself and Prevent Spread	People at Greatest Risk
• Fever or chills • Cough • Shortness of breath or difficulty breathing • Fatigue • Muscle or body aches • Headache • New loss of taste or smell • Sore throat • Congestion or runny nose • Nausea or vomiting • Diarrhea	• Wear a mask over the nose and mouth • Maintain 6 feet apart • Avoid crowds • Wash hands with soap for 20 seconds or use alcohol-based hand sanitizer • Cover coughs and sneezes • Avoid touching eyes, nose, or mouth with unwashed hands • Clean and disinfect touched surfaces • Monitor health daily for symptoms • Avoid poorly ventilated spaces • Stay home when sick	• Older adults (risk increases with age 50 and older) • Adults of any age with underlying medical conditions

Counties with the Highest Confirmed Cases and Deaths (as of 6/1/2021)

County	Confirmed Cases	Fatalities
Harris County	400,436	6,442
Dallas County	260,526	4,079
Tarrant County	218,175	3,064
Bexar County	183,999	3,572
El Paso County	136,132	2,717

Peak Periods: Sample Daily Reporting Exceeding 10,000 New Cases

Date	Confirmed New Cases	New Fatalities
17-Jul-20	14,916	242
25-Nov-20	14,648	189
17-Dec-20	16,864	235
29-Dec-20	26,990	281
5-Jan-21	26,543	324
20-Jan-21	25,512	337

Daily Statewide Confirmed COVID-19 Cases

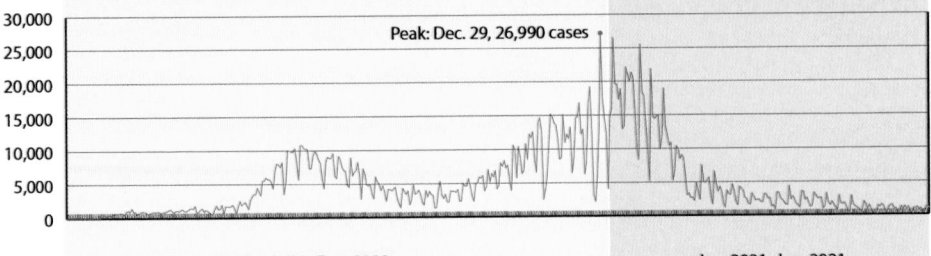

Peak: Dec. 29, 26,990 cases

Mar. 2020–Dec. 2020   Jan. 2021–Jun. 2021

Editor's note: Cases in Texas have risen once again since this feature was written, hitting a peak of 22,746 confirmed cases on Aug. 31, 2021.

State Response Timeline: March 2020–April 2021

The table below does not provide a comprehensive list of all state government responses. Furthermore, the summaries highlight only sections of the cited proclamations or orders. You can view all of the orders online at: **https://lrl.texas.gov/legeLeaders/governors/displayDocs.cfm?govdoctypeID=5&governorID=45**

Date	Selected Summary of Action
13-Mar-20	**Governor declares a State of Disaster**
19-Mar-20	**Executive Order GA-08**
	Avoiding gathering in groups of more than 10
	Avoiding in-person congregation in bars, eating establishments, gyms, massage parlors (drive-thru, delivery, and pickup encouraged)
	Shall not visit nursing, retirement, or other long-term care facilities
	Temporarily closes schools
24-Mar-20	**Executive Order GA-10**
	Requires daily reports of hospital bed capacity
	Requires daily reports of COVID-19 test results
26-Mar-20	**Executive Order GA-11**
	Mandatory self-quarantine for airline passengers making Texas their final destination and whose last point of departure or whose travel originated from certain areas
	A quarantine period of 14 days or until departure from Texas
31-Mar-20	**Executive Order GA-14**
	Requires all individuals to minimize in-person contact and social engagements except when engaging in or obtaining essential services
	Remote telework for services or activities not defined as essential services
	When engaging in essential daily activities, social distancing is recommended
17-Apr-20	**Executive Order GA-15**
	Requires hospitals to reserve at least 25% of their capacity for COVID-19 patients
17-Apr-20	**Executive Order GA-16 (reopening Texas)**
	Continual restriction on minimizing social engagement
	Reopened services starting April 24, 2020: retail services classified as non-essential provide service through pickup and mail or doorstep delivery
	Drive-thru, pickup, or delivery options for food establishments instead of dining in
	Visits to tattoo studios, gyms, massage parlors, and cosmetology salons discouraged
	Schools remain closed to in-person instruction
27-Apr-20	**Executive Order GA-18 (reopening Texas)**
	Continual restriction on minimizing social engagement
	25% occupancy for retail stores, restaurants, theaters, shopping malls, museums, and libraries
27-Apr-20	**Executive Order GA-19**
	Requires hospitals to reserve at least 15% of their capacity for COVID-19 patients
27-Apr-20	**Executive Order GA-20 (reopening Texas Travel)**
	Rescinds executive order GA-12, which required self-quarantine for 14 days for anyone who entered Texas through Louisiana
	Rescinds executive order GA-11 as it applies to travelers from Louisiana only
	GA-11 remains in effect for travelers from other points of origin
5-May-20	**Executive Order GA-21 (reopening Texas)**
	25% occupancy for listed establishments
	Excluded from the occupancy list: bars, massage establishments, tattoo and piercing studios, interactive amusement venues, and sexually-oriented establishments
	Schools remain closed to in-person instruction
3-Jun-20	**Executive Order GA-26 (reopening Texas)**
	50% occupancy for business establishments

Shortly after COVID-19 hit Texas, a wide range of products were out of stock at stores all over the state. Photos by 2C2K Photography CC by 2.0/ Wikimedia Commons.

Date	Selected Summary of Action
2-Jul-20	**Executive Order GA-29** Masks covering the nose and mouth required inside commercial and public spaces when social distancing is not possible Provides exemptions to mask requirement such as: under 10 years; those with medical conditions; while eating; while in a body of water; engaged in outdoor physical activity and maintaining social distance
17-Sep-20	**Executive Order GA-30 (reopening Texas)** Up to 75% occupancy for business establishments except in areas with high COVID-19 hospitalizations No occupancy limit, with at least 6 feet social distancing, for personal care and beauty service establishments 50% occupancy for amusement parks Bars and other establishments not defined as restaurants that hold a Texas Alcoholic Beverage Commission (TABC) permit remain closed to in-person occupancy Following health protocols recommended
17-Sep-20	**Executive Order GA-31** Hospitals are to suspend surgeries not deemed medically necessary as not to deplete their ability to cope with the COVID-19 crisis Requires hospitals to reserve at least 10% of their capacity for COVID-19 patients
7-Oct-20	**Executive Order GA-32 (reopening Texas)** No occupancy limit for outdoor events, establishments, areas unless restricted in other sections of the order 50% occupancy for professional, collegiate, or similar sporting events 50% on-premise occupancy for bars and similar TABC permit holding establishments if not in high hospitalization areas
2-Mar-21	**Executive Order GA-34 (reopening Texas)** Removal of occupancy limitations by the state if not in high hospitalization areas No state mandate requiring masks/face coverings, but those unable to maintain social distancing are encouraged to wear them This order does not prevent businesses or other establishments from requiring employees and customers to follow hygiene measures, including wearing face coverings
5-Apr-21	**Executive Order GA-35** No governmental entity can require individuals to receive the COVID-19 vaccine State agencies and political subdivisions can not require individuals to provide vaccination status as a condition to receive services or entering spaces Public or private entities receiving public funds can not require consumers to provide documentation regarding COVID-19 vaccination status This state order supersedes local orders
18-May-21	**Executive Order GA-36** Governmental entities or officials can not require individuals to wear face coverings

COVID-19 Impact: Economic

The coronavirus pandemic fueled a statewide economic crisis. Quarantines, capacity restrictions, and "Stay Home, Work Safe" orders adversely impacted all industries and businesses. Among the most affected by the pandemic were the leisure and hospitality industries. Restaurants, bars, retail stores, hotels/motels, amusement parks, gyms, and other such businesses saw a decline in sales revenue, experienced high unemployment rates, and closed their doors. Amid restrictions, some businesses launched or expanded online service and delivery and curbside pickup. Despite these pandemic adjustments and 2020 "reopening Texas" capacity limits ranging from 25%-75%, businesses continued to struggle. In September 2020, the Texas Restaurant Association projected that 15% of the state's restaurants would close permanently.

The lowest-paid workers, many of whom are in the service industries, suffered the most significant unemployment rate from the pandemic onset. In June 2020, the third month of a double-digit unemployment rate, the United Way of Texas conducted a statewide survey that found that workers in the hospitality and leisure industry reported the most significant impact from COVID-19. In 2019, the average wage for Texas hotel/motel housekeeping staff was $23,900, while desk clerks earned $23,300. In April 2021, The American Hotel & Lodging Association approximated that the hotel industry lost 296,387 jobs to the COVID-19 pandemic.

The United Way's survey further found that low-income households and those living below the Federal Poverty Level suffered the highest job losses. The survey revealed that 71% of the Dallas/Fort Worth metroplex, an area with high COVID-19 cases and fatalities, expressed economic concerns. Faced with economic uncertainty, Dallas/Fort Worth metroplex residents applied for unemployment (21%), applied for Supplemental Nutrition Assistance Program (SNAP) (12%), utilized food banks/pantries (17%), and relied on credit cards (22%). Thirty-four percent of those surveyed said their Coronavirus Aid, Relief, and Economic Security (CARES) Act stimulus check assisted with at most two weeks of expenses, including food and rent. As the health crisis continued, unemployment rates in Texas remained high compared to 2019.

The unemployment rate in Texas increased starting in March 2020 as the pandemic influenced state and local government response. COVID-19-related state and municipal closures and operation restrictions resulted in struggling industries and increased unemployment rates.

The highest unemployment rate occurred in April when Executive Order GA-14 and municipal "Stay Home, Work Safe" went into effect. The May rate remained in the double digits as the state enacted plans for limited reopening. Continual COVID-19 positive cases and deaths mandated continual business restrictions. While unemployment rates started declining during the fall of 2020, they were about double compared to the pre-COVID-19 rate of 3.4–3.7.

As unemployment increased, families and officials grew concerned about homelessness as many struggled to pay rents or mortgages. On September 1, 2020, a CDC order placed a moratorium on residential eviction to prevent the spread of COVID-19. The CARES Act further provided protective provisions for tenants. At the state level, the Texas Department of Housing and Community Affairs, the Supreme Court of Texas, and the Texas of Office Court Administration partnered to create the Texas Eviction Diversion Program (TEDP) to help tenants by providing property owners/landlords with alternatives to eviction. On September 25, 2020, Governor Abbott announced that over $171 million in funding from the federal CARES Act would support TEDP and other rental assistance programs. Some municipal governments, such as Dallas, Austin, San Antonio, and Houston, adopted ordinances to protect renters from eviction by providing or extending grace periods to resolve delinquencies.

Federal Poverty Level		
Household (persons in the family)	2020 Poverty Guideline (income)	2021 Poverty Guideline (income)
2	$17,240	$17,420
3	$21,720	$21,960
4	$26,200	$26,500
5	$30,682	$31,040

Office of the Assistant Secretary for Planning and Evaluation: 2020 Poverty Guidelines https://aspe.hhs.gov/2020-poverty-guidelines; 2021 Poverty Guidelines https://aspe.hhs.gov/2021-poverty-guidelines

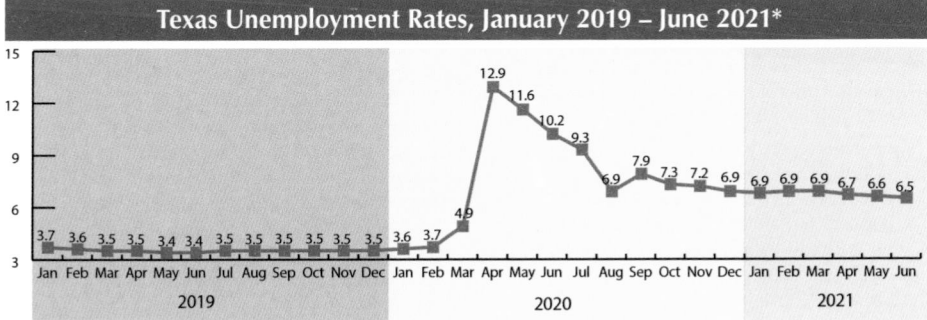

Texas Unemployment Rates, January 2019 – June 2021*

*As reported and revised by the U.S. Bureau of Labor Statistics on August 2, 2021. Data subject to revision by the U.S. Bureau of Labor Statistics: https://data.bls.gov/timeseries/LASST480000000000003

Staff from Harlandale Independent School District in San Antonio set out meal bags for families at a USDA-sponsored summer lunch program. Bagged meals of cold breakfasts and hot lunches are placed on a table for drivers to take at a safe distance. Photo by USDA/Wikimedia Commons.

Impact: Social

Homeless Population

The pandemic and associated restrictions proved challenging for the vulnerable homeless population. Capacity restrictions and social distancing measures forced homeless shelters to reduce the number of individuals they accommodated and slowed services to the unsheltered.

The limited access to shelters pushed more people to live on the streets. According to the CDC, unsheltered homeless populations were at greater risk for COVID-19 infection, especially in areas with high community spread. In response, municipalities, including San Antonio and El Paso, working with social organizations, opened auxiliary shelters and hotels to assist the homeless. Cities, among them Dallas, also allocated federal COVID-19 relief funds to address the homeless issue. Dallas designated funds toward supporting the renovation of hotels that serve as shelters.

When shelters and food pantries closed, charitable organizations and communities established resource hubs for the unsheltered that provided food, water, hygiene kits, masks, showers, and COVID-19 information. Volunteers also delivered food and water to the unsheltered. Cities relied on health department staff and volunteers to administer COVID-19 testing to the homeless.

Cities must conduct "point-in-time" counts of their homeless population every two years, with the latest slated for January 2021 to receive federal funds. The pandemic drove Texas cities to cancel or delay their counts. The South Alamo Regional Alliance for the Homeless, which usually attracts more than 400 volunteers to carry out the count in San Antonio, canceled its in-person survey. Many also requested exemptions for counting the unsheltered. While some cities decided against undertaking the count and relied on past data, others conducted the count using modified tactics to ensure the health safety of volunteers and the homeless. Houston's Coalition for the Homeless performed the survey in January 2021. Its data revealed that 15% of those surveyed had become homeless because of the pandemic. The count is far from accurate as the unsheltered can be missed in population counts. The extent of the pandemic's impact on the homeless population and how many Texans became homeless due to the health crisis are unknown.

Food Insecurity

The loss of jobs during the COVID-19 crisis further exacerbated food insecurities, especially among the working poor. In November 2020, a U.S. Census Bureau survey revealed that over 2.5 million Texas households, 66% being either Black or Hispanic, suffered from food insecurity. The same month Feeding Texas, a state network of food banks, reported that food banks assisted an average of 400,000 families weekly from March to August. Approximately half of those seeking assistance were doing so for the first time.

As more Texans experienced food insecurity, food banks lost 70% of their volunteers and 75% of their distribution partners (church pantries, Boys and Girls Clubs) due to the pandemic and associated restrictions. The Houston Food Bank, the largest in the state, usually relied on about 1,000 workers but was down to 150 in December 2020. The Texas Military Department deployed National Guard members to communities to assist food banks in distributing food to those in need. Faced with pandemic conditions, food banks employed drive-through distributions.

Food banks in highly impacted areas estimated they would be distributing millions of pounds worth of food but expected a shortfall that would outpace demand. The end of programs, such as the Farmers to Families Food Box, and the reduction of funding to the Texas Department of Agriculture, which provides fruits and vegetables to food banks, caused additional concern.

Food insecurity also led to an increase in Texans applying for Supplemental Nutrition Assistance Program (SNAP). Other federal programs available to Texans included The Child Nutrition Programs and Pandemic EBT (P-EBT). With school closures, low-income families who relied on school meals for their children were eligible for P-EBT, a one-time benefit. Despite attempts to address food insecurity amid the pandemic, the number of Texans suffering from hunger increased, with children being the most vulnerable.

Education

In June 2021, the Texas Education Agency (TEA) reported that approximately 11.3% (over 600,000) of students disengaged when schools closed at the onset of the pandemic. With school doors closed to in-person instruction, schools turned to virtual education. During the shift, schools reported losing contact with students. Moreover, the pandemic exposed inequity as many low-income families lacked access to computers or the internet to engage in online instruction. Approximately 15.5% of low-income students were not fully engaged compared to 5% of higher-income students. Hispanic and Black students had the highest percentage of disengagement. A survey of San Antonio conducted by the Urban Education Institute at the University of Texas at San Antonio further highlighted that children struggled with engagement because of hunger. The survey revealed that 22% of older students found it necessary to find employment or increase their hours to help their families, resulting in poor academic performance. For the 2020-2021 school year, teachers and school administrators were tasked with addressing the "COVID slide," an academic backslide, while developing methods of instruction that upheld social distancing requirements.

Mental Health

School closures and virtual instruction have created a sense of isolation and anxiety for many children. The stressors of the pandemic and limited access to mental health services have led to an increase in mental health-related issues among adolescents. According to the CDC, a nationwide rise in adolescent mental health-related emergency room visits began in April 2020 compared to 2019. The most significant increase at 31% was among adolescents aged 12-17 years. Hospitals also saw a 24% increase for children ages 5 to 11 years. In September 2020, Fort Worth's Cook Children's Medical Center admitted 37 adolescents after failed suicide attempts, the most significant number since they began tracking in 2015. In response, school districts, often partnering with local agencies or organizations, began offering on-campus and virtual counseling.

Adults also reported an increase in mental health issues since the onset of the pandemic. The CDC reported that during August 2020-February 2021, adults experiencing symptoms of depression or anxiety increased from 36.4% to 41.5%. The most significant increase was found among adults aged 18-29 years. According to a June 2020 CDC survey, 40% of adults in the United States struggled with mental health, with increased suicidal thoughts. According to the U.S. Office of National Drug Control Policy, substance and alcohol abuse has increased since March 2020.

Impact: Politics During a Pandemic

When the coronavirus pandemic struck the nation in the spring of 2020, the United States was experiencing a highly contentious election year. The partisan division influenced government response, further fueling the partisanship in the nation. Democrats generally supported stricter pandemic policies, including face-covering mandates and continued shutdowns, to ensure the virus slowdown. Republicans favored less stringent guidelines, opposing general mask mandates and supporting reopening by early summer 2020. A *U.S. News* report revealed that between May 1 and July 31, 2020, Democratic-led states not only implemented stricter pandemic policies but also rolled back their reopening in response to a new wave of confirmed cases. Republican-led states continued their scheduled reopening without making adjustments to the strictness of their pandemic response policies.

Tensions ran high between the Republican-dominated federal government and states, particularly those held by Democrats, over response to the health crisis. Among the criticisms levied at President Donald Trump's administration was the delayed response. By the time President Trump issued a state of emergency on March 13, 2020, several municipal and state governments had already introduced strategies to prevent the spread of COVID-19. States and municipal governments led the way in responding to the pandemic. The partisan conflict between Republican and Democratic was the most intense between Republican-led state governments and municipalities with strong Democratic-leaning leaders. In Texas, the cities (El Paso, San Antonio, Dallas-Fort Worth, Houston) with the largest populations are also Democratic pockets and reported the highest recorded COVID-19 cases and deaths. These cities criticized Governor Abbott's COVID-19 policies, which were in line with the Republican's less stringent response to the health crisis.

Face Covering

In June 2020, as COVID-19 cases increased, an ABC News/Ipsos poll found that more Americans wore a face covering when leaving home; however, mask usage has become a politically contentious issue. Democrats were more likely than Republicans to wear masks, support face-covering mandates, and comply with businesses requiring patrons to wear masks. Conservative Republicans were the least likely to wear masks or support action requiring face coverings. Republicans opposed to required mask mandates cited personal freedom or questioned the effectiveness of masks in slowing the spread of COVID-19 in spite of proven science. In response, Democrats accused those who refused to abide by health recommendations of endangering the public and possibly prolonging the pandemic and economic recovery. When Republican Governor Abbott issued Executive Order

GA-34, rescinding restrictions including mask-wearing, Democratic municipal leaders in the hardest-hit urban centers voiced their opposition. GA-34 prohibits municipal leaders from implementing local mask mandates.

The conflict over face coverings spilled over to malls, streets, and businesses. In July 2020, after Executive Order GA-29, which required masks under certain circumstances, anti-maskers rallied at the state capitol. Generally, anti-mask protests took place in larger urban centers with a higher count of confirmed COVID-19 cases. In December 2020, anti-maskers protested at North Star Mall in San Antonio. On March 2, 2021, when Abbott rescinded COVID-19 orders, including face coverings and local governments' or businesses' ability to require masks, Democratic leaders in highly impacted areas condemned the governor for acting prematurely. Having been denied the authority to implement face-covering mandates, municipal leaders encouraged Texans to continue wearing face-coverings to protect themselves and those around them.

Conflicts between Republican state and Democratic municipal leaders over face coverings, anti-mask protests, and confrontations in stores by those refusing to abide by mask requirements highlighted the pandemic's partisan divide in Texas.

Reopening Texas

Approximately one month after Governor Abbott declared a state of emergency, he issued the first executive order (GA-16) that commenced the reopening of Texas. Occupancy restrictions increased by 25% with each occupancy increase. When Texas experienced new waves of increased cases in the summer and fall, the governor's rollout plan remained in place without modification to occupancy percentages. When Governor Abbott announced on March 2, 2021, that he was rescinding COVID-19 restrictions and businesses would reopen at total capacity, Democratic leaders, such as San Antonio Mayor Ron Nirenberg, disapproved of the governor's decision. The governor reasoned that the COVID-19 vaccine and the decline in confirmed cases allowed for full reopening despite less than 50% of Texans being vaccinated in March 2021.

COVID-19 Vaccinations

Just as government response and face coverings revealed a partisan divide, so has the COVID-19 vaccine.

Since the federal government began the vaccine rollout, a national trend has emerged in which a growing number of Republicans have either refused vaccination or have expressed skepticism. Opposition or hesitancy stems from multiple factors, including distrust of science, distrust of government, and mixed partisan messages since the outset of the pandemic that downplayed the severity of the virus. In February 2021, a University of Texas/Texas Tribune Poll found that approximately 59% of Texas Republicans were hesitant or refused the COVID-19 vaccine. More than 60% of white Republicans in the state rejected vaccination. Twenty-five percent of Texas Democrats polled expressed opposition to vaccination.

Public health officials have expressed concerns that vaccination rates among Blacks and Hispanics continue to be lower than among Whites despite disproportionate COVID-19 hospitalization and death. As Blacks and Hispanics have a larger young population, the vaccine rollout excluded a sizable portion of these communities. Other barriers that limited vaccine access for low-income people, a large percentage being Black and Hispanic, include language, transportation, and occupational obstacles. A University of Pittsburgh and West Health Policy Center study revealed that Blacks in some Texas communities had to travel further to a vaccine hub than white residents. Socioeconomic and race/ethnicity divides continued as data showed that neighborhoods in the poorest sections received fewer doses or faced barriers in obtaining vaccines. After more than 50% of first-dose vaccines in Dallas went to wealthier white neighborhoods, city officials developed a plan to target zip codes in lower-socioeconomic communities of color. However, state officials threatened to slash their allocation if they moved forward with the project. In February, the Federal Emergency Management Agency (FEMA) set up vaccination sites in underserved communities in Dallas-Fort Worth and Houston, areas with high confirmed cases and fatalities. As vaccinations remained low among these vulnerable populations, health officials launched informational campaigns encouraging vaccination.

As of May 30, 2021, only 44.2% (12,804,890) of Texans have received the first dose of the COVID-19 vaccine, and only 35.4% (10,272,326) have been fully vaccinated. Texas has administered 75% of the doses provided.

1918 Spanish Influenza & Coronavirus: When the coronavirus appeared, comparisons to the Spanish Influenza pandemic of 1918 began to emerge. The table provides a general comparison.

Spanish Influenza*	COVID-19
Symptoms	
• fever/chills • cough • fatigue • breathing difficulty • headache • body aches • sore throat • congestion or runny nose • Death resulted from pneumonia, the deadly complication of Spanish influenza.	• fever/chills • cough • fatigue • difficulty breathing • headache • body aches • loss of taste or smell • sore throat • congestion or runny nose • nausea or vomiting • diarrhea
Recommendations to Slow Spread	
U.S. Public Health Service (PHS) Recommendations: • Avoid contact with others • Avoid indoor and outdoor crowds • Cover coughs and sneezes • Rest and avoid excessive fatigue • Do not spit on the floor or sidewalk • Do not share utensils, cups, or other items • Get fresh air by spending time outdoors away from crowds **PHS recommendations supplemented by local health department and other medical organization requirements or recommendations:** • Wearing gauze masks • Disinfection of public transit • Quarantine	**CDC Recommendations:** • Monitor daily health • Wear a mask that covers the nose and mouth • Social distancing indoors and outdoors: 6 feet distance between individuals who are not of the same household • Avoid crowds and poorly ventilated indoor spaces • Wash hands often with soap and water or use sanitizer with at least 60% alcohol if unable to use soap and water • Cover coughs and sneezes • Clean and disinfect high-touch surfaces • Get the COVID-19 vaccine
Most Affected Populations	
Age: healthy adults 20-40; those over 60; young children	**Age:** highest cases among 20-60-year-olds with higher confirmed case percentage in 30-39 age group
Reported Confirmed Cases in Texas*	
Second Wave: September 1918: 2,515 October 1918: 8,996	2,487,480 (as of May 10, 2021)
Reported Deaths in Texas*	
Second Wave: September 1918: 129 October 1918: 6,089	49,594 (as of May 10, 2021)
Similar Pandemic State/Municipal Response	
Municipal governments, advised by health officials (city health officers), took the lead in responding to the spread of influenza. Among the actions adopted by local governments: • prohibiting public gatherings (closing venues of entertainment, schools, churches) • requiring businesses to restrict customer capacity • forbidding jury trials • recommending people remain at home • some recommending masks (San Antonio encouraged those sneezing or coughing to wear masks; Cameron required barbers to wear masks)	Among the actions adopted by state & local governments: • prohibiting public gatherings (closing venues of entertainment, schools, churches) • restricting capacity • requiring businesses to disinfect • delaying jury trials • stay-at-home orders • required mask-wearing

*Spanish Influenza cases and deaths as reported by the State Registrar of Vital Statistics are considered underreported as influenza was not a reportable disease.

Works Sourced

Adeel, Abdul Basit, Michael Catalano, Olivia Catalano, Grant Gibson, etc. "COVID-19 Policy Response and the Rise of the Sub-National Governments." *Canadian Public Policy/Analyse de politiques* 46, Issue 4 (December 2020): 556-584.

AgriLife Today. "COVID-19 pandemic erases two decades of food security gains in Texas, U.S." Published October 14, 2020. https://agrilifetoday.tamu.edu/2020/10/14/covid-19-pandemic-erases-two-decades-of-food-security-gains-in-texas-u-s.

American Hotel & Lodging Association. "Texas: COVID-19 Impact on State's Hotel Industry."

Aratani, Lauren. "How did face masks become a political issue in America?" *The Guardian.* June 29, 2020.

Biediger, Shari. "To mask or not to mask: San Antonio reacts to new CDC guidance." San Antonio Report, May 15, 2021.

Bowen, Kacey. "Protesters gather at Texas Capitol for 'Shed the Mask' rally." FOX 7-Austin, July 4, 2020.

Cannon, Matt. "Police Break Up Face Mask Protest at Texas Mall, Arrest One Man." *Newsweek*, December 29, 2020.

Centers for Disease Control and Prevention (CDC). Accessed May 11, 2021. https://www.cdc.gov/coronavirus/2019-nCoV/index.html.

Centers for Disease Control and Prevention (CDC). "The Deadliest Flu: The Complete Story of the Discovery and Reconstruction of the 1918 Pandemic Virus."

Centers for Disease Control and Prevention (CDC). "History of 1918 Flu Pandemic."

Centers for Disease Control and Prevention. "Interim Guidance on People Experiencing Unsheltered Homelessness." Updated March 23, 2021.

Connelly, Christopher. "Report: Texas Does One of the Worst Jobs in the Nation at Caring for Kids during the Pandemic," KERA News, March 2, 2021.

Democrat and Chronicle.com. "Texas COVID-19 Vaccine Tracker." https://data.democratandchronicle.com/covid-19-vaccine-tracker/texas/48.

Diamond, Dan. "I'm still a zero: Vaccine-resistant Republicans warn that their skepticism is worsening." *The Washington Post*, April 20, 2021.

Dimmick, Iris. "San Antonio's Homeless Population Shows Surprising Trend as COVID-19 Rages in Bexar County." *San Antonio Report*, July 13, 2020.

Donald, Jessica and Spencer Grubbs. "Housing Affordability and Homelessness in Texas," FiscalNotes, March 2021.

Feeding Texas. "COVID-19 Impact: Texas Food Banking + Food Insecurity." November 2020.

Fernandez, Stacy. "230,000 Texas families filed for SNAP food assistance in March, twice as many as same month last year." *The Texas Tribune*, April 13, 2020.

Garnham, Juan Pablo. "Texas food banks may be less equipped to help hungry households in the new year." *The Texas Tribune*, December 7, 2020.

Garnham, Juan Pablo. "Texas' local officials blast Gov. Greg Abbott for 'irresponsible action' of lifting coronavirus restrictions." *The Texas Tribune*, March 2, 2021.

Gernhart, Gary, Office of PHS Historian. "A Forgotten Enemy: PHS's Fight Against the 1918 Influenza Pandemic." *Public Health Reports* 114, No. 6 (Nov.-Dec. 1999).

Harper, Karen Brooks. "Three FEMA-run vaccination sites aimed at underserved Texans to open later this month, Abbott says." *The Eagle*, February 10, 2021.

Henson, Jim and Joshua Blank. "Forget Fatigue — Political Leadership is Still Fueling COVID-19 in Texas." The Texas Politics Project, The University of Texas at Austin, December 7, 2020.

Huerta, Tiffany and Joe Herrera. "Researchers gather data to learn how COVID-19 pandemic affects teaching in San Antonio." KSAT.com, December 21, 2020.

Igielnik, Ruth. "Most Americans say they regularly wore a mask in stores in the past month; fewer see others doing it." Pew Research Center, June 20, 2020.

Influenza Encyclopedia. "The American Influenza Epidemic of 1918-1919." University of Michigan Center for the History of Medicine and Michigan Publishing.

Jaspers, Bret. "Dallas Leverages COVID-19 Pandemic to Address Long-Term Homelessness: Federal relief dollars are being used to buy and renovate hotels." *Texas Standard*, December 8, 2020.

Joy, William. "North Texas vaccines are going to mostly white, wealthy residents according to state, federal data." WFAA 8 ABC, March 14, 2021.

Leeb, Rebecca T., Rebecca H. Bitsko, Lakshmi Radhakrishnan, Pedro Martinez, Rashid Njai, and Kristin M. Holland. "Mental Health-Related Emergency Department Visits Among Children Aged <18 Years during the COVID-19 Pandemic — United States, January 1-October 17, 2020." Morbidity and Mortality Weekly Report-CDC, November 12, 2020.

Legislative Reference Library of Texas. "COVID-19 related Executive Orders by Governor Greg Abbott." https://lrl.texas.gov/legeLeaders/governors/displayDocs.cfm?govdoctypeID=5&governorID=45.

Lozano, Juan A. "Pandemic cited as cause of homelessness for some in Houston." AP News, March 24, 2021.

Luckingham, Bradford. *Epidemic in the Southwest*, 1918-1919. University of Texas-El Paso: Texas Western Press, 1984.

Luckingham, Bradford. "TO MASK OR NOT TO MASK: A Note on the 1918 Spanish Influenza Epidemic in Tucson." *The Journal of Arizona History* 25, No. 2 (Summer 1984).

Martinez, Marissa. "Texas no longer has a statewide mask mandate. But face coverings are still required in some businesses and public places." *The Texas Tribune*, March 10, 2021.

Martinez, Marissa, Juan Pablo Garnham and Mandi Cai. "COVID-19 vaccine demand drops in Texas, though less than a quarter of population is fully vaccinated." *The Texas Tribune*, April 23, 2021.

Martinez, Marissa and Sami Sparber. "As Texas expands COVID-19 vaccination eligibility, racial disparities persist among Black, Hispanic residents." *The Texas Tribune*, March 19, 2021.

Martinez-Catsam, Ana Luisa. "Desolate Streets: The Spanish Influenza in San Antonio." *The Southwestern Historical Quarterly* 116, No. 3 (January 2013).

Martinez-Catsam, Ana Luisa. "The Spanish Influenza of 1918: The Function of the *El Paso Morning Times* to a Community in Crisis." *Journal of the West* 52, No. 1 (Winter 2013).

Menchaca, Megan. "Texas cities face difficulties counting their unsheltered homeless population — at a time when their numbers matter most." *The Texas Tribune*, February 4, 2021.

Novak, Anna, Mitchell Ferman, and Mandi Cai. "10 months into pandemic, Texas' unemployment rate stays near Great Recession-level highs." *The Texas Tribune*, June 26, 2021.

Office of the Texas Governor. "Governor Abbott Announces Over $171 Million in CARES Act Funding for Rental Assistance, Texas Eviction Diversion Program." Published September 25, 2020. https://gov.texas.gov/news/post/governor-abbott-announces-over-171-million-in-cares-act-funding-for-rental-assistance-texas-eviction-diversion-program.

Office of the Texas Governor. "Governor Abbott's Proactive Response to the Coronavirus Threat."

Opdycke, Sandra. *The Flu Epidemic of 1918: America's Experience in the Global Health Crisis.* New York: Routledge Taylor & Francis Group, 2014.

Oxner, Reese. "White Republicans are refusing to get COVID-19 vaccine more than any other demographic group in Texas." *The Texas Tribune*, March 24, 2021.

Men lining up at a "spraying station" at Love Field for a preventative treatment for the influenza in November 1918. Source: U.S. National Archives and Records Administration, Public Domain

Platoff, Emma and Juan Pablo Garnham. "Dallas County axes plan to prioritize vaccinating communities of color after state threatens to slash allocation." *The Texas Tribune*, January 20, 2021.

Price, Sean. "Pandemic Pressures: COVID-19 Poses Serious Behavioral Health Challenges." Texas Medical Association, October 2020. https://www.texmed.org/TexasMedicineDetail.aspx?id=54816.

Russonello, Giovanni. "Nearly half of Republicans say they don't want a Covid vaccine, a big public health challenge." *The New York Times*, April 14, 2021.

Schneider, Andrew. "In Texas, All State Agencies Asked to Pare Budgets Due to COVID-19." NPR, August 3, 2020.

Sparber, Sami, Carrington Tatum, and Emma Platoff. "San Antonio mayor demands extension of coronavirus quarantine, bans evacuees from entering city." *The Texas Tribune*, March 2, 2020.

Stevenson, Stefan. "Texas health officials aim COVID-19 vaccine ad campaign at reluctant minority groups." *Fort Worth Star-Telegram*, April 20, 2021.

Swaby, Aliyya. "Warning of 'COVID slide,' Texas Education Agency reports 1 in 10 students have disengaged during the pandemic." *The Texas Tribune*, June 30, 2020.

Taboada, Melissa B. "As pandemic grinds on, Texas students increasingly feel alone and scared, and some are thinking about suicide." *The Texas Tribune*, December 22, 2021.

Texas Comptroller of Public Accounts Fiscal Notes. "Weathering the Pandemic: Texas Industries and COVID-19."

Texas Department of Housing and Community Affairs. "Texas Eviction Diversion Program (TEDP)." https://www.tdhca.state.tx.us/TEDP.htm.

Texas Department of State Health Services. https://txdshs.maps.arcgis.com/apps/dashboards/ed483ecd702b4298ab01e8b9cafc8b83.

United Way of Tarrant County. "COVID-19 Survey Results: Shedding Light on the Impact on Texas Communities." https://www.unitedwaytarrant.org/blog/general/covid-19-survey-results-shedding-light-on-the-impact-of-texas-communities.

University of Texas at Austin. "Protections for Texas Renters: COVID-19." https://sites.utexas.edu/covid19relief/tenant-protections.

U.S. Bureau of Labor Statistics. "Local Area Unemployment Statistics (Texas)."

U.S. Bureau of Labor Statistics. "State Employment and Unemployment Summary." Released January 26, 2021.

USA FACTS. "Texas Coronavirus Vaccination Progress." https://usafacts.org/visualizations/covid-vaccine-tracker-states/state/texas?utm_source=google&utm_medium=cpc&utm_campaign=ND-COVID-Vaccine&gclid=Cj0KCQjwna2FBhDPARIsACAEc_Wc6-uMTPXKX-Zvq0kbfF42lteVuIaWQCYsjtkP3vGQTVQnuqhywBoaAvLvEALw_wcB

Vahratian, Anjel, Stephen J. Blumberg, Emily P. Terlizzi, and Jeannine S. Schiller. "Symptoms of Anxiety or Depressive Disorder and Use of mental Health Care Among Adults during the COVID-19 Pandemic - United States, August 2020-February 2021." Morbidity and Mortality Weekly Report-CDC, April 2, 2021.

VanDusky-Allen, Julie and Olga Shvetsova. "How America's Partisan Divide over Pandemic Responses Played Out in the States," The Conversation, May 12, 2021.

Vela, Jorge A. "City of Laredo assists homeless people amid pandemic." Laredo Morning Times online, September 6, 2020.

Vela, Katie and Morjoriee White. "COVID-19 Response Prompts New Collaborations and Programs in San Antonio." Texas Homeless Network. https://www.thn.org/2020/09/11/sarah-covid-response.

Velasquez, JJ. "It's bullshit: County Judge Wolff says governor's repeal of COVID-19 measures leaves SA vulnerable." *San Antonio Report*, March 2, 2021.

Wellerman, Zak. "East Texas Food Bank receives help from Texas Army National." *Tyler Morning Telegraph*, April 15, 2020.

Zelinski, Andrea. "Why Eight Texas Republicans Broke From Their Party Over Mask Mandates." *Texas Monthly*, May 17, 2021. ☆

Death, Birth Rates Continue Trends in Texas Vital Statistics

Heart disease and cancer remained the major causes of death in 2015, the latest year for which statistical breakdowns were available from the Center for Health Statistics, Texas Department of State Health Services.

Of the 189,166 deaths, heart disease claimed 43,133 lives and cancer claimed 39,018 lives. These two diseases have been the leading causes of death in Texas and the nation since 1950. Chronic respiratory diseases (COPD) ranked third with 10,216 deaths.

These three diseases accounted for nearly half, 49 percent, of all Texas resident deaths in 2015.

The number of babies born to Texas mothers in 2015 was 403,439, an increase from 399,482 in 2014. The state's birth rate in 2015 was 14.7 per 1,000 population, down slightly from 14.8 in 2014. In 1960, the figure was 25.7.

In 2019, the number of induced abortions increased slightly to 57,929 from 2016's count of 54,507. The highest number of induced abortions was 81,591 in 2008.

Healthcare and Deaths in Texas Counties

County	2019 Physicians	2016 Hospital Beds	Total Deaths 2015	2015 Pregnancy rate*	2019 Abortions
Statewide Total	56,765	78,578	189,166	79.9	56,620
Anderson	67	156	655	82.3	47
Andrews	13	34	137	97.7	12
Angelina	195	446	871	75.5	77
Aransas	15	0	360	87.8	21
Archer	1	0	91	51.7	6
Armstrong	0	0	38	71.9	1
Atascosa	33	67	408	82.1	63
Austin	11	32	272	70.6	30
Bailey	2	25	50	110.5	4
Bandera	12	0	221	63.0	21
Bastrop	36	8	660	77.7	135
Baylor	8	49	61	79.1	1
Bee	22	69	271	94.3	43
Bell	899	1,005	2,274	97.5	932
Bexar	4,733	7,287	12,982	82.6	5,337
Blanco	4	0	122	64.8	14
Borden	0	0	10	103.4	1
Bosque	15	25	224	72.2	22
Bowie	278	840	1,076	75.5	8
Brazoria	396	272	2,155	81.7	634
Brazos	525	586	1,076	57.0	340
Brewster	16	25	81	68.9	12
Briscoe	0	0	20	59.6	0
Brooks	1	0	90	106.6	7
Brown	67	188	515	64.4	25
Burleson	5	25	214	78.2	18
Burnet	113	71	528	78.0	47
Caldwell	20	59	320	74.4	73
Calhoun	22	25	198	88.3	31
Callahan	3	0	179	59.4	3
Cameron	540	1,314	2,684	86.9	424
Camp	12	25	132	83.4	3
Carson	0	0	58	54.2	1
Cass	10	43	414	78.6	1
Castro	5	17	65	94.4	0
Chambers	16	39	290	76.3	43
Cherokee	66	97	557	96.5	123
Childress	12	39	75	68.2	1
Clay	5	25	131	49.7	4
Cochran	1	18	31	72.7	0
Coke	0	0	53	90.1	4
Coleman	4	25	131	58.1	2
Collin	2,673	2,384	4,005	62.4	1,631
Collings-wrth	1	13	39	54.4	0
Colorado	30	103	256	91.1	26
Comal	242	348	1,108	84.7	210
Comanche	14	25	188	88.6	10
Concho	2	16	33	87.9	3
Cooke	26	78	413	89.0	43

County	2019 Physicians	2016 Hospital Beds	Total Deaths 2015	2015 Pregnancy rate*	2019 Abortions
Coryell	39	25	526	62.3	77
Cottle	0	0	31	48.3	0
Crane	2	25	36	88.6	4
Crockett	1	0	26	94.9	2
Crosby	1	25	77	81.2	1
Culberson	23	14	14	94.8	2
Dallam	0	0	38	118.7	0
Dallas	7,103	7,807	15,727	85.5	7,595
Dawson	6	23	129	101.5	9
Deaf Smith	18	42	143	94.8	17
Delta	9	0	73	75.3	1
Denton	0	1,297	3,374	63.3	3
DeWitt	1,041	49	253	93.2	1,356
Dickens	0	0	26	98.5	2
Dimmit	8	48	109	102.6	19
Donley	1	0	51	52.3	0
Duval	0	0	149	105.3	23
Eastland	11	52	265	68.0	30
Ector	244	650	1,196	97.2	242
Edwards	1	0	33	83.3	0
Ellis	1,325	164	1,209	70.3	664
El Paso	181	2,419	5,296	82.7	693
Erath	34	98	323	54.4	68
Falls	2	36	178	66.3	23
Fannin	12	25	458	73.5	18
Fayette	27	65	326	78.9	19
Fisher	2	14	52	84.0	1
Floyd	4	25	67	74.4	2
Foard	0	0	16	61.5	2
Fort Bend	1,086	1,033	2,984	74.5	1,332
Franklin	3	0	122	73.9	7
Freestone	10	37	202	73.0	16
Frio	14	40	155	98.5	32
Gaines	9	25	128	119.8	7
Galveston	579	252	2,675	78.4	674
Garza	2	0	56	82.0	9
Gillespie	78	86	318	77.7	19
Glasscock	0	0	3	80.4	0
Goliad	1	0	87	69.6	2
Gonzales	16	33	187	106.5	28
Gray	19	115	267	92.0	2
Grayson	320	600	1,461	77.0	151
Gregg	390	738	1,274	78.2	31

Physicians – All M.D.s and D.O.s in direct patient care. (2020.)
Hospital Beds – Beds (2016) not including military and veteran's hospitals, nor beds in hospitals that were not in compliance with state regulations.
*Abortion total statewide includes abortions performed in Texas but county of residence unknown, plus abortions obtained outside the state by Texas residents.

County	2019 Physicians	2016 Hospital Beds	Total Deaths 2015	2015 Pregnancy rate*	2019 Abortions
Grimes	14	25	279	87.1	29
Guadalupe	121	125	1,043	65.0	200
Hale	31	68	322	76.2	22
Hall	0	0	57	42.6	1
Hamilton	14	42	154	79.0	7
Hansford	5	14	53	76.4	1
Hardeman	3	45	49	93.8	4
Hardin	12	0	536	69.1	42
Harris	12,117	14,807	25,342	88.0	14,475
Harrison	34	149	677	70.1	9
Hartley	9	21	51	63.8	0
Haskell	4	25	62	74.2	1
Hays	310	322	1,007	63.6	520
Hemphill	6	26	34	105.3	0
Henderson	78	127	1,084	70.8	58
Hidalgo	1,063	2,429	4,179	91.9	1,011
Hill	16	116	455	68.7	29
Hockley	12	48	224	76.7	9
Hood	87	73	751	87.3	39
Hopkins	32	96	398	73.0	26
Houston	9	25	268	78.3	42
Howard	40	150	416	85.5	32
Hudspeth	1	0	12	76.7	0
Hunt	109	181	958	68.5	110
Hutchinson	12	25	275	78.7	1
Irion	0	0	10	52.4	0
Jack	9	17	96	79.1	2
Jackson	9	25	146	91.5	17
Jasper	23	59	458	87.8	47
Jeff Davis	1	0	16	52.2	0
Jefferson	540	1,585	2,514	88.6	520
Jim Hogg	0	0	50	106.9	6
Jim Wells	33	135	424	94.3	60
Johnson	106	137	1,340	73.8	188
Jones	6	92	214	63.8	4
Karnes	6	25	131	97.3	17
Kaufman	74	91	897	71.8	196
Kendall	81	0	377	63.2	49
Kenedy	0	0	3	41.1	0
Kent	0	0	9	74.1	0
Kerr	134	124	774	79.0	53
Kimble	3	15	45	67.4	1
King	0	0	0	23.3	1
Kinney	0	0	42	102.7	1
Kleberg	22	96	243	75.2	40
Knox	2	28	61	76.2	2
Lamar	1	393	641	78.0	9
Lamb	126	75	147	84.7	52
Lampasas	5	25	197	68.8	2
La Salle	11	0	61	106.3	22
Lavaca	21	50	269	81.5	11
Lee	5	0	183	81.5	22
Leon	4	0	223	87.1	7
Liberty	46	29	765	77.0	133
Limestone	23	78	290	86.0	23
Lipscomb	0	0	21	76.6	0
Live Oak	1	0	143	81.0	11
Llano	15	30	311	86.3	10
Loving	0	0	0	–	0
Lubbock	758	1,556	2,441	67.3	283
Lynn	6	24	51	73.4	3
Madison	9	25	126	74.3	15
Marion	1	0	167	81.1	23
Martin	4	18	52	94.9	28
Mason	2	0	44	101.1	3
Matagorda	38	75	407	91.1	217
Maverick	48	101	398	106.4	26

County	2019 Physicians	2016 Hospital Beds	Total Deaths 2015	2015 Pregnancy rate*	2019 Abortions
McCulloch	6	25	117	70.9	13
McLennan	534	522	2,123	71.4	159
McMullen	0	0	7	96.5	2
Medina	25	25	428	76.2	59
Menard	1	0	33	57.6	2
Midland	261	563	1,098	98.1	191
Milam	9	35	288	87.2	18
Mills	2	0	62	45.1	3
Mitchell	5	25	109	80.2	2
Montague	12	87	263	79.3	13
Montgomery	1,393	1,237	3,623	75.3	753
Moore	20	25	164	104.6	4
Morris	4	0	179	73.6	6
Motley	0	0	17	42.6	0
Nacgdoches	140	392	605	62.4	52
Navarro	51	162	568	81.3	49
Newton	3	0	164	63.6	9
Nolan	14	86	178	86.4	8
Nueces	904	2,035	2,937	78.3	596
Ochiltree	7	25	83	89.8	2
Oldham	0	0	17	62.0	0
Orange	33	0	947	88.1	100
Palo Pinto	29	74	348	77.4	19
Panola	12	42	266	70.1	139
Parker	133	129	1,066	67.4	117
Parmer	2	25	75	89.3	1
Pecos	10	39	114	85.4	15
Polk	45	66	673	88.7	39
Potter	443	1,140	1,231	85.4	15
Presidio	3	0	36	82.3	9
Rains	1	0	150	62.7	5
Randall	86	4	1,050	66.5	15
Reagan	2	21	29	109.4	2
Real	0	0	38	100.0	3
Red River	3	0	180	65.5	5
Reeves	13	25	114	98.1	21
Refugio	3	20	108	88.6	4
Roberts	0	0	6	46.7	0
Robertson	0	0	173	76.6	15
Rockwall	203	170	545	62.9	103
Runnels	12	50	140	69.1	5
Rusk	44	96	544	72.9	27
Sabine	3	25	168	81.9	10
S. Augustine	2	18	128	66.8	57
San Jacinto	4	0	313	70.9	29
San Patricio	27	75	642	92.1	83
San Saba	1	0	54	102.2	3
Schleicher	1	14	23	37.7	1
Scurry	18	25	179	81.7	10
Shackelford	1	0	27	84.2	2
Shelby	7	0	300	89.6	7
Sherman	0	0	34	71.8	1
Smith	864	1,204	2,111	76.0	242
Somervell	13	16	96	53.1	7
Starr	22	48	397	100.9	54
Stephens	8	40	107	87.2	7
Sterling	0	0	9	82.5	0

Physicians – All M.D.s and D.O.s in direct patient care. (2020.)
Hospital Beds – Beds (2016) not including military and veteran's hospitals, nor beds in hospitals that were not in compliance with state regulations.
*Abortion total statewide includes abortions performed in Texas but county of residence unknown, plus abortions obtained outside the state by Texas residents.

County	2019 Physicians	2016 Hospital Beds	Total Deaths 2015	2015 Pregnancy rate*	2019 Abortions
Stonewall	2	12	29	96.6	0
Sutton	2	12	30	72.4	4
Swisher	4	20	81	95.0	0
Tarrant	4,530	6,284	12,277	76.6	4,672
Taylor	351	829	1,378	77.6	140
Terrell	0	0	17	91.7	1
Terry	4	45	139	97.5	6
Throck-mortn	2	0	30	51.9	1
Titus	61	174	311	79.5	26
Tom Green	298	574	973	78.7	135
Travis	3,627	2,881	5,380	70.5	3,452
Trinity	3	45	225	78.5	12
Tyler	4	49	274	76.5	19
Upshur	9	0	471	69.0	6
Upton	2	29	36	101.3	2
Uvalde	34	25	233	88.2	38
Val Verde	40	93	353	101.3	62
Van Zandt	14	52	621	71.7	26
Victoria	213	717	847	84.2	113
Walker	66	123	513	62.0	137
Waller	9	0	305	64.5	86
Ward	2	0	134	100.5	13
Washington	48	60	389	75.7	43

County	2019 Physicians	2016 Hospital Beds	Total Deaths 2015	2015 Pregnancy rate*	2019 Abortions
Webb	253	569	1,356	91.6	293
Wharton	35	208	417	89.6	61
Wheeler	6	41	72	84.2	1
Wichita	313	479	1,304	74.1	153
Wilbarger	13	47	163	85.8	8
Willacy	7	0	151	79.6	15
Williamson	1,100	833	2,625	66.6	991
Wilson	32	44	410	72.2	61
Winkler	2	19	70	99.1	7
Wise	79	148	554	76.9	63
Wood	26	50	613	72.2	16
Yoakum	6	24	63	99.2	7
Young	21	50	239	73.4	6
Zapata	1	0	85	97.8	17
Zavala	2	0	111	91.5	15

Physicians – All M.D.s and D.O.s in direct patient care. (2020.)

Hospital Beds – Beds (2016) not including military and veteran's hospitals, nor beds in hospitals that were not in compliance with state regulations.

*Abortion total statewide includes abortions performed in Texas but county of residence unknown, plus abortions obtained outside the state by Texas residents.

Marriage and Divorce

These charts are for certain years, including 1946, when there was a significant increase in marriages after World War II as well as a significant increase in divorces. Also included are the years 1979-81 when the marriage and divorce rates reached another peak. *Source: Statistical Abstracts of the United States, National Vital Statistics System.*

Texas

Year	Total marriages	Marriage rate*	Total divorces	Divorce rate**
1940	86,500	13.5	27,500	4.3
1946	143,092	20.5	57,112	8.4
1950	89,155	11.6	37,400	4.9
1955	91,210	10.4	34,921	4.0
1960	91,700	9.6	34,732	3.6
1965	111,500	10.5	41,300	3.9
1970	139,500	12.5	51,500	4.6
1975	153,200	12.5	76,700	6.3
1979	172,800	12.9	92,400	6.9
1980	181,800	12.8	96,800	6.8
1981	194,800	13.2	101,900	6.9
1985	213,800	13.1	101,200	6.2
1990	182,800	10.5	94,000	5.5
1995	188,500	10.1	98,400	5.3
2000	196,400	9.6	85,200	4.2
2005	169,300	7.4	74,000	3.2
2010	174,171	6.9	82,098	3.3
2015	187,415	6.8	71,123	2.6
2016	n/a	7.1	n/a	2.6
2017	n/a	7.1	n/a	2.2
2018	n/a	6.1	n/a	2.6
2019	n/a	4.9	n/a	2.1

*Rate per 1,000 population.

United States

Year	Total marriages	Marriage rate*	Total divorces	Divorce rate**
1940	1,595,879	12.1	264,000	2.0
1946	2,291,045	16.4	610,000	4.3
1950	1,667,231	11.1	385,144	2.6
1955	1,531,000	9.3	377,000	2.3
1960	1,523,381	8.5	393,000	2.2
1965	1,800,200	9.3	479,000	2.5
1970	2,159,000	10.6	708,000	3.5
1975	2,152,700	10.1	1,036,000	4.9
1979	2,331,300	10.6	1,181,000	5.4
1980	2,390,300	10.6	1,189,000	5.2
1981	2,422,100	10.6	1,213,000	5.3
1985	2,425,000	10.2	1,187,000	5.0
1990	2,443,000	9.8	1,182,000	4.7
1995	2,336,000	8.9	1,169,000	4.4
2000	2,329,000	8.2	**944,000	4.0
2005	2,230,000	7.5	847,000	3.6
2010	2,096,000	6.8	872,000	3.6
2015	2,221,579	6.9	800,909	3.1
2016	2,251,411	7.0	776,288	3.0
2017	2,236,496	6.9	787,251	2.9
2018	2,132,853	6.5	782,038	2.9
2019	2,015,603	6.1	746,971	2.7

**Since 2000, the total number of divorces does not include four to six states, including California.

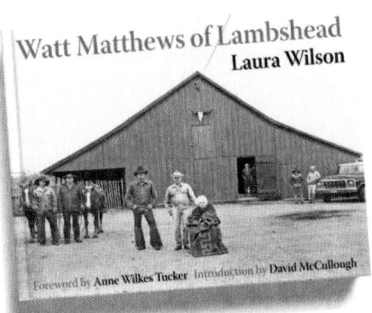

Texans in the National Academy of Sciences

The National Academy of Sciences is a private organization of researchers dedicated to the furtherance of science and its use for the general welfare. A total of 136 scientists who have had positions with Texas institutions have been named members or associates.

Established by congressional acts of incorporation, which were signed by President Lincoln in 1863, the academy acts as official adviser to the federal government in matters of science and technology. Election to the academy is one of the highest honors that can be accorded a scientist. As of May 2019, the number of active members was 2,537.

Elected from Texas in 2019 was Robert C. Kennicutt, Jr., of Texas A&M University.

Three foreign associates with ties to Texas institutions have been elected to the academy: in 1970, D.H.R. Barton from Texas A&M; in 1997, Johann Deisenhofer of UTSWMC in Dallas, and, in 2002, Jan-Ake Gustafsson of the University of Houston.

In 1931, Robert Moore (UT-Austin 1920–69) and Hermann Muller (Rice 1915-18, UT-Austin 1920–32) became the first scientists from Texas institutions elected to the academy. ☆

Source: National Academy of Sciences

Academy Member	Affiliation*	Elected
Perry L. Adkisson	A&M	1979
Richard W. Aldrich	UT-Austin	2008
James P. Allison	UT-MD Anderson	1997
Abram Amsel †	UT-Austin	1992
Neal R. Amundson †	U of H	1992
Dora E. Angelaki	Baylor Medical	2014
Charles J. Arntzen	A&M	1983
David H. Auston	Rice	1991
Paul F. Barbara †	UT-Austin	2006
Allen J. Bard	UT-Austin	1982
Bonnie Bartel	Rice	2016
Frederic C. Bartter †	UTHSC-San Antonio	1979
John D. Baxter †	HMRI	2003
Arthur L. Beaudet	Baylor Medical	2011
Brian J.L. Berry	UT-Dallas	1975
Bruce Beutler	UTSWMC	2008
Lewis R. Binford	SMU	2001
R.H. Bing †	UT-Austin	1965
Harold C. Bold †	UT-Austin	1973
Norman E. Borlaug	A&M	1968
Michael S. Brown	UTSWMC	1980
James J. Bull	UT-Austin	2016
Karl W. Butzer †	UT-Austin	1996
Horace R. Byers †	A&M	1952
Luis A. Caffarelli	UT-Austin	1991
C. Thomas Caskey	Baylor Medical	1993
Joseph W. Chamberlain †	Rice	1965
Zhijian (James) Chen	UTSWMC	2014
Wah Chiu	Baylor Medical	2012
C.W. Chu	U of H	1989
Melanie H. Cobb	UTSWMC	2006
Neal G. Copeland	HMRI	2009
F. Albert Cotton †	A&M	1967
Robert F. Curl Jr.	Rice	1997
Marcetta Darensbourg	A&M	2017
Ronald A. DePinho	UT-MD Anderson	2012
Gerard H. de Vaucouleurs †	UT-Austin	1986
Ronald DeVore	A&M	2017
Bryce DeWitt †	UT-Austin	1990
Robert E. Dickinson	UT-Austin	1988
Richard A. Dixon	UNT	2007
Stephen J. Elledge	Baylor Medical	2003
Ronald W. Estabrook †	UTSWMC	1979
Mary K. Estes	Baylor Medical	2007
Karl Folkers †	UT-Austin	1948
Marye Anne Fox	UT-Austin	1994
David L. Garbers †	UTSWMC	1993
Wilson S. Geisler	UT-Austin	2008
Quentin H. Gibson	Rice	1982
Alfred G. Gilman †	UTSWMC	1985
Joseph L. Goldstein	UTSWMC	1980
John B. Goodenough	UT-Austin	2012
William E. Gordon	Rice	1968
Verne E. Grant †	UT-Austin	1968
Norman Hackerman †	Welch	1971
Namoi J. Halas	Rice	2013
Carl G. Hartman †	UT-Austin	1937

Academy Member	Affiliation*	Elected
Dudley Herschbach	A&M	1967
David M. Hillis	UT-Austin	2008
Helen H. Hobbs	UTSWMC	2007
Lora Virginia Hooper	UTSWMC	2015
A. James Hudspeth	UTSWMC	1991
Thomas J.R. Hughes	UT-Austin	2009
Nancy A. Jenkins	MHRI	2008
Robert C. Kennicutt, Jr.	A&M	2019
James L. Kinsey †	Rice	1991
Steven A. Kliewver	UTSWMC	2015
Ernst Knobil †	UTHSC-Houston	1986
Jay K. Kochi †	U of H	1982
P. Kusch †	UT-Dallas	1956
Alan M. Lambowitz	UT-Austin	2004
David M. Lee	A&M	1991
Beth Levine	UTSWMC	2013
Herbert Levine	Rice	2011
Gardner Lindzey †	UT-Austin	1989
Guillermina Lozano	UT-MD Anderson	2017
Alan G. MacDiarmid †	UT-Dallas	2002
David J. Mangelsdorf	UT-Austin	2008
John L. Margrave †	Rice	1974
Martin M. Matzuk	Baylor Medical	2014
S.M. McCann †	UTSWMC	1983
Allan H. MacDonald	UT-Austin	2010
Steven L. McKnight	UTSWMC	1992
David J. Meltzer	SMU	2009
Robert Moore †	UT-Austin	1931
Nancy A. Moran	UT-Austin	2004
Hermann Muller †	Rice, UT-Austin	1931
Hans J. Muller-Eberhard †	UTHSC-Houston	1974
Ferid Murad	UTHSC-Houston	1997
Jack Myers †	UT-Austin	1975
Kyriacos C. Nicolaou	Rice	1996
Robert N. Noyce †	Sematech/Austin	1980
David R. Nygren	UT-Arlington	2000
Eric N. Olson	UTSWMC	2000
Bert W. O'Malley	Baylor Medical	1992
Jose N. Onuchic	Rice	2006
Theophilus Shickel Painter †	UT-Austin	1938
Luis F. Parada	UTSWMC	2011
John Patterson †	UT-Austin	1941
Kenneth L. Pike †	SIL	1985
William H. Press	UT-Austin	1994
Darwin J. Prockop	A&M	1991
Lester J. Reed †	UT-Austin	1973
Peter M. Rentzepis	A&M	1978
Rebecca Richards-Kortum	Rice	2015
Peter J. Rossky	UT-Austin	2011
David W. Russell	UTSWMC	2006
Marlan O. Scully	A&M	2001
Richard E. Smalley †	Rice	1990
Esmond E. Snell †	UT-Austin	1955
Richard C. Starr †	UT-Austin	1976
Patrick Stover	A&M	2016
Thomas Südhof	UTSWMC	2002
Max D. Summers	A&M	1989

Academy Member	Affiliation*	Elected
Harry L. Swinney	UT-Austin	1992
Joseph S. Takahashi	UTSWMC	2003
John T. Tate	UT-Austin	1969
Karen K. Uhlenbeck	UT-Austin	1986
Jonathan W. Uhr	UTSWMC	1984
Roger H. Unger	UTSWMC	1986
H.S. Vandiver †	UT-Austin	1934
Moshe Y. Vardi	Rice	2015
Ellen S. Vitetta	UTSWMC	1994
Salih J. Wakil	Baylor Medical	1990
Xiaodong Wang	UTSWMC	2004
Steven Weinberg †	UT-Austin	1972
D. Fred Wendorf	SMU	1987
John Archibald Wheeler †	UT-Austin	1952
Roger J. Williams †	UT-Austin	1946
Jean D. Wilson	UTSWMC	1983
Peter G. Wolynes	Rice	1991
James E. Womack	A&M	1999
Masahi Yanagisawa	UTSWMC	2003
Clarence Zener †	A&M	1959

Academy Member	Affiliation*	Elected
Huda Y. Zoghbi	Baylor Medical	2004

† Deceased
* **A&M** – Texas A&M University
Baylor Medical – Baylor College of Medicine, Houston
HMRI – Houston Methodist Research Institute
Rice – Rice University
SIL – Summer Institute of Linguistics
SMU – Southern Methodist University
U of H – University of Houston
UNT – University of North Texas
UT-Austin – The University of Texas at Austin
UT-Dallas – The University of Texas at Dallas
UTHSC – Houston—The University of Texas Health Science Center at Houston
UTHSC – The University of Texas Health Science Center at San Antonio
UT-MD – The University of Texas MD Anderson Cancer Center – Houston
UTSWMC – The University of Texas Southwestern Medical Center at Dallas
Welch – Robert A. Welch Foundation

Science Research Funding at Universities

The following chart shows funding for research and development by source at universities in Texas, in order of total R&D funding. The figures are from the National Science Foundation and are for fiscal year 2019.

(Thousands of dollars)	All R&D expenditures	Federal gov.	State/local gov.	Business	Nonprofit org.	Institutional funds
United States	$83,496,348*	$44,455,265	$4,495,452	$5,053,576	$5,683,937	$21,109,703
Texas (all colleges statewide)	**$5,967,210**	**$2,347,454**	**$854,553**	**$436,376**	**$446,322**	**$1,610,434**
1. U. Texas M.D. Anderson Ctr.	969,496	176,156	258,019	214,509	28,010	136,565
2. Texas A&M University	952,156	359,609	190,465	274,537	59,798	26,396
3. University of Texas-Austin	696,111	407,981	21,573	144,157	40,388	6,374
4. Baylor College of Medicine	651,920	309,354	32,232	193,449	85,736	0
5. U. Texas Southwestern Med. Dallas	496,697	203,544	79,363	68,457	59,096	54,920
6. U. Texas Health Sci., Houston	271,525	132,647	38,516	43,586	22,721	13,506
7. University of Houston	195,398	68,523	38,963	65,710	11,270	2,335
8. Texas Tech University	193,923	35,136	23,788	104,700	13,963	126
9. U. Texas Health Sci., San Antonio	188,483	96,502	20,807	42,551	19,715	409
10. Rice University	182,564	83,584	6,013	53,316	23,426	5,411
11. U. Texas Medical Branch	175,372	107,806	5,054	46,065	11,808	0
12. University of Texas-Dallas	126,661	48,466	12,133	38,469	22,831	0
13. University of Texas-Arlington	123,207	41,764	16,970	51,329	6,057	2,069
14. University of Texas-El Paso	106,809	41,261	17,507	33,594	4,587	8,988
15. University of Texas-San Antonio	84,326	34,588	12,247	27,509	2,408	2,181
16. University of North Texas, Denton	78,691	17,345	2,735	53,843	1,087	1,874
17. Texas State University	64,554	29,614	4,871	25,361	3,983	0
18. Uni. of Texas-Rio Grande Valley	52,016	13,629	6,309	27,496	3,996	368
19. U. North Texas, Health Science Ctr.	50,124	27,260	11,355	8,142	1,492	3
20. Texas Tech U., Health Sci. Ctr.	44,072	11,345	17,778	8,854	1,963	3,699
21. Southern Methodist University	42,562	17,869	1,092	18,220	2,034	4
22. Baylor University	33,304	6,955	1,157	19,443	2,955	1,642
23. Texas A&M U.-Corpus Christi	32,944	14,451	8,481	3,981	2,548	3,004
24. Texas A&M University-Kingsville	22,268	8,419	4,190	3,985	5,223	0
25. Prairie View A&M University	18,018	9,346	4,886	3,454	111	0
26. Uni. of Texas Health Science-Tyler	16,538	5,626	2,226	5,640	2,320	1
27. Tarleton State University	13,171	4,632	2,946	5,383	79	35
28. Texas Tech U. Health Sci., El Paso	11,883	2,279	2,544	6,306	335	56
29. St. Edward's University	9,650	6,500	1,500	700	500	300
30. Sam Houston University	9,445	3,723	183	5,310	115	61

Colleges and universities not listed received less.
*Total includes some $2.27 billion from other sources. Source: National Science Foundation.

National Health Expenditures

GDP and Expenditures ($ billion)	1970	1980	1990	2000	2010	2019
Total Health Expenditures	$74.9	$255.8	$724.3	$1,377.2	$2,593.6	$3,795.4
Percent of GDP	7.2	9.2	12.5	13.8	17.4	17.7
Per capita amount (in dollars)	$356	$1,110	$2,854	$4,878	$8,402	$11,582
Personal health care expenditure	$63.1	$217.0	$615.3	$1,161.5	$2,196.1	$9,787
Cost of private insurance	$1.4	$ 7.7	$ 29.1	$52.3	$108.5	$882
Hospital care expenditures	$27.2	$100.5	$250.4	$415.5	$822.3	$1192
Gross Domestic Product (GDP)	$1,038	$2,788	$5,801	$9,952	$14,527	$21,433.2

Source: U.S. Centers for Medicare and Medicaid Services.

Comparison of Vital Statistics

*Data from 2018 with states that either border Texas or have large populations. **Lowest and highest with number in bold.***

State/Country	Birthrate*	Death rate*	Life expectancy
Texas	13.0	7.0	78.4
Alaska	13.4	6.0	78.0
Arkansas	12.1	10.7	75.6
California	11.3	6.8	80.8
Florida	10.2	9.6	78.9
Georgia	11.9	8.1	77.2
Illinois	11.1	8.6	78.8
Louisiana	12.7	9.9	75.6
Michigan	10.8	9.9	77.7
New Mexico	10.9	9.1	77.2
New York	11.4	8.0	80.5
Ohio	11.5	10.6	76.8
Oklahoma	12.4	10.4	75.6
Utah	**14.6**	**5.8**	79.6
New Hampshire	**8.7**	9.4	79.1
West Virginia	10.1	**13.0**	74.4
United States	11.4	8.7	78.7
Japan	7.0	11.44	84.7
Brazil	13.4	6.8	75.0
Canada	10.2	8.1	83.6
Afghanistan	36.1	12.6	**53.3**
Germany	8.6	12.2	81.3
Italy	8.4	10.7	82.7
Monaco	**6.6**	10.5	**89.4**
Mexico	17.3	5.4	77.0
Angola	**42.2**	8.24	61.7
Russia	9.7	**13.4**	72.2
South Sudan	38.3	9.8	58.6
Qatar	9.4	**1.4**	79.6
United Kingdom	11.8	9.4	81.3
World	18.1	7.7	70.5

*Rates are number during 1 year per 1,000 persons.
Sources: National Vital Statistics System 2018; CIA World Factbook, 2018; Texas Vital Statistics Annual Report 2015.

Life Expectancy for Texans by Group

	All	Whites	Blacks	Hispanics
Total population	78.2	78.3	74.6	79.5
Males	75.8	75.8	71.5	76.9
Females	80.7	80.6	77.3	82.0

Source: Texas Department of State Health Services, for 2017.

Texas Births by Race/Ethnicity and Sex

	2019	2015	2000	1990
All Races	377,599	403,439	363,325	316,257
All Male	—	205,972	185,591	161,522
All Female	—	197,467	177,734	154,735
White Total	124,678	136,663	142,553	150,461
White Male	—	69,935	72,972	77,134
White Female	—	66,728	69,581	73,327
Black Total	47,326	47,515	41,180	43,342
Black Male	—	24,140	21,128	21,951
Black Female	—	23,375	20,052	21,391
Hispanic Total	179,689	191,080	166,440	115,576
Hispanic Male	—	97,469	84,750	58,846
Hispanic Female	—	93,611	81,690	56,730
Other* Total	28,181	28,181	13,152	6,687
Other Male	—	14,428	6,741	3,591
Other Female	—	13,753	6,411	3,287

*Other includes births of unknown race/ethnicity.
Source: Texas Department of State Health Services.*

Disposition of Bodies in Texas by Percent of Deaths

Year	Burial	Cremation	Donation of body	Removal from state/other
1989	83.7%	7.1%	0.7%	8.5%
1995	81.7%	11.6%	0.8%	5.8%
2001	75.5%	17.3%	0.8%	6.3%
2003	73.1%	19.7%	0.9%	6.2%
2014	52.0%	39.3%	-	-
2015	50.1%	41.2%	-	-
2016	48.2%	42.4%	1.4%	8.1%
2017	46.8%	43.9%	1.4%	7.9%

Sources: Texas DSHS (to 2003) and National Funeral Directors Association.

Nobel Prizes to Texans

John B. Goodenough received the Nobel Prize in Chemistry in 2019 for his work with others on the development of lithium-ion batteries, notably a cathode that provided a higher voltage than previously available.

Goodenough also received a doctorate in physics from the University of Chicago in 1952, and worked at the Massachusetts Institute of Technology and Oxford University in Great Britain.

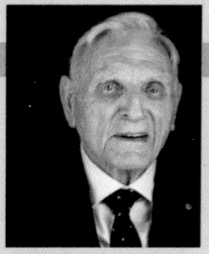

Community Hospitals in Texas

– Of the 652 reporting hospitals in Texas in 2020, 528 were considered community hospitals.

(A community hospital is defined as either a nonfederal, short-term general hospital or a special hospital whose facilities and services are available to the public. A hospital may include a nursing home-type unit and still be classified as short-term, provided that the majority of its patients are admitted to units where the average length of stay is less than 30 days.)

– The 528 hospitals employed 371,350 full-time equivalent people (FTEs) with a payroll, including benefits, of more than $31.7 billion.

– These hospitals contained some 66,844 beds.

– The average length of stay was 5.3 days in 2017, compared to 6.8 days in 1975. This was less than the U.S. average of 5.5 days.

– The average cost per adjusted admission in Texas was $12,357 or $2,552 per day. This was 5.8 percent less than the U.S. average of $13,126.

– There were 2.7 million admissions in Texas, which accounted for 14.5 million inpatient days.

– There were 45.1 million outpatient visits in 2017, of which 11.9 million were emergency room visits.

– Of the FTEs working in community hospitals within Texas, there were 122,050 registered nurses and 7,700 licensed vocational nurses. ☆

Source: The Texas Hospital Association.

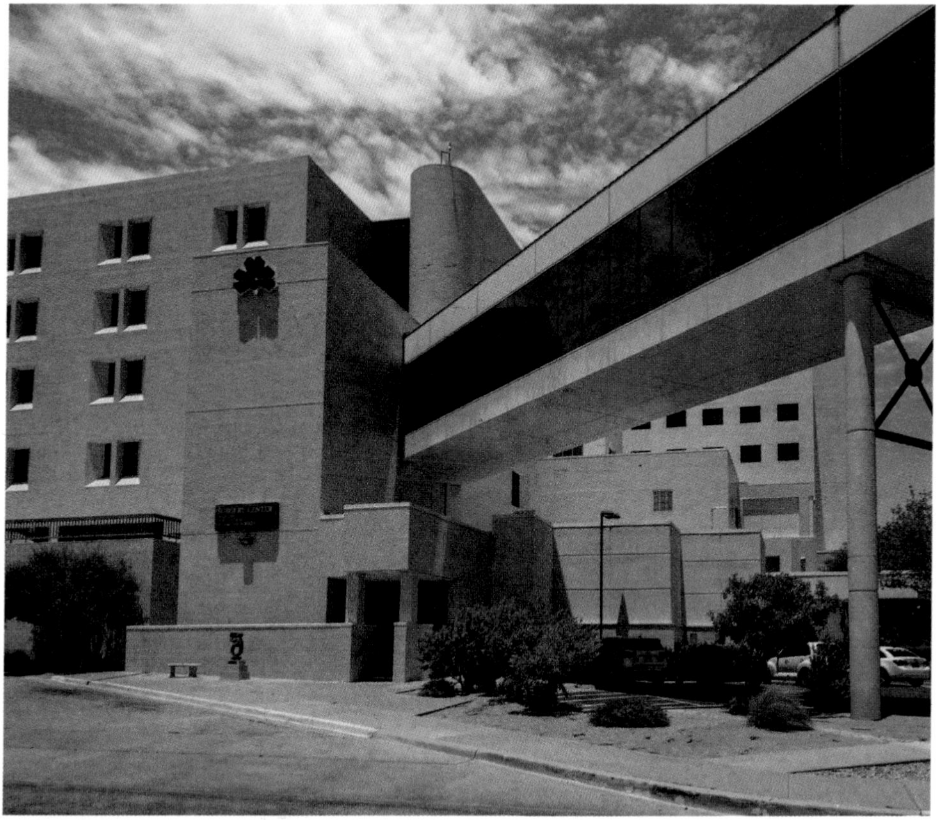

Shannon Medical Center Hospital is shown in San Angelo on July 13, 2020. Photo by Jonathan Cutrer/Flickr (CC).

Mental Health and Substance Abuse

Diagnosis of Adult Clients in Texas/United States: 2018–2019

Diagnosis	Texas clients	% of clients diagnosis		Employed as % of known employment
		Texas	United States	Texas
Schizophrenia	43,367	19.7	13.5	12.0
Bipolar disorder	137,410	62.4	42.0	27.0
Other psychoses	657	0.3	2.2	18.0
All other diagnoses	3,585	1.6	35.3	29.0
No diagnosis/deferred	35,017	15.9	6.9	25.9
Total	220,036	100.0	100.0	23.9

Source: U.S. Department of Health and Human Services, Center for Mental Health Services, Uniform Reporting System, 2019.

Readmission Within 180 Days of Mental Health Treatment: 2019

Age	Civil* Texas	Civil U.S.	States/Terr. reporting	Forensic* Texas	Forensic U.S.
		In percent of clients.			
0 to 12	17.6%	13.2%	11	50%	10.3%
13 to 17	12.6	15.1	19	1.4	9.6
18 to 20	13.3	15.6	34	3.3	9.3
21 to 64	18.3	18.6	51	7.9	10.9
65 to 74	9.4	13.6	34	8.1	10.5
75 and over	0	5.9	14	–	9.0
Age not available	–	66.7	1	–	–
Total	17.4	17.8	53	7.5	10.8

Forensic services are mental health services provided to persons directed into treatment by the criminal justice system; others are listed as "Civil." Source: U.S. Department of Health and Human Services, Center for Mental Health Services, Uniform Reporting System, 2019.

Substance Abuse Treatment in Texas: 2019

Facility operation	No.	%	Clients in treatment on March 29, 2019		
			No.	%	Clients under 18
Private nonprofit	196	38.3	11,137	30.9	783
Private for-profit	257	50.2	19,331	53.7	192
Local/county/community	27	5.3	894	2.5	132
State	9	1.8	1,278	3.6	19
Federal	22	4.3	3,343	9.3	–
Tribal	1	0.2	12	0.1	–
Total	512	100.0	35,995	100.0	1,126

Problem treated					. . . per 100,000 pop.
Alcohol and drug abuse	308	80.4	12,159	34.5	54
Drug abuse only	338	88.3	18,694	53.1	84
Alcohol abuse only	274	71.5	4,368	12.4	20

Source: National Survey of Substance Abuse Treatment Services, 2019.

Estimated Use of Drugs in Texas and Bordering States: 2018–2019

State	Any illicit drug	Marijuana	Other than marijuana[1]	Cigarettes	Binge alcohol[2]	Pain reliever misuse[4]
	*Current users[3] as **percent of population**, age 12+ years. Selected states.*					
U.S. total	12.34%	10.80%	3.31%	16.91%	11.24%	3.58%
Texas	8.75	7.19	2.93	16.67	9.43	3.62
Arkansas	9.45	8.46	2.91	22.55	10.22	3.66
Louisiana	9.41	7.74	3.26	22.07	10.86	3.85
Oklahoma	12.11	10.07	3.36	23.68	10.64	3.89
New Mexico	13.89	12.43	2.89	19.30	9.48	3.71

[1]Marijuana users who have also used another drug are included. [2]Binge use is defined as drinking five or more drinks on the same occasion on at least one day in the past 30 days. [3]Used drugs at least once within month. [4]Within the last year. *Source: U.S. Substance Abuse and Mental Health Services Administration, National Survey on Drug Use and Health, 2018-2019.*

State Institutions for Mental Health Services

Mental health services were provided to some 416,338 Texans in 2019 in various institutions, including community centers.

In 2004, the Texas Department of State Health Services was created (DSHS), bringing together:

— the Texas Department of Health,

— the Texas Department of Mental Health and Mental Retardation (MHMR),

— Commission on Alcohol and Drug Abuse,

— the Texas Health Care Information Council.

In 2016, Texas Health and Human Services was created by the Legislature with two agencies: the Texas Health and Human Services Commission (HHSC) and DSHS, with many direct client services transferred from DSHS to HHSC, including mental health services.

In 2019, state mental health agency expenditure was $1,095,727,077, with $541 million for community services, according to the federal Uniform Reporting System for the states.

Following is a list of the 10 state hospitals, the year each was founded, and number of beds in 2019, totalling 2,269.

Hospitals for Persons with Mental Illness

Austin State Hospital — Austin; 1857; 263 beds.
Big Spring State Hospital — Big Spring; 1937; 180 beds.
El Paso Psychiatric Center — El Paso; 1974; 71 beds.
Kerrville State Hospital — Kerrville; 1950; 220 beds.
North Texas State Hospital — Wichita Falls (1922), 268 beds and Vernon (1969); 294 beds.
Rio Grande State Center — Harlingen; 1962; 52 beds.
Rusk State Hospital — Rusk; 1919; 288 beds.
San Antonio State Hospital — San Antonio; 1892; 268 beds.
Terrell State Hospital — Terrell; 1885; 291 beds.
Waco Center for Youth — Waco; 1979; 74 beds.

Following is a list of community mental health centers, the year each was founded, and the counties each serves.

Community Mental Health Centers

Abilene — Betty Hardwick Center; 1971; Callahan, Jones, Shackelford, Stephens, and Taylor.
Amarillo — Texas Panhandle Centers; 1968; Armstrong, Carson, Collingsworth, Dallam, Deaf Smith, Donley, Gray, Hall, Hansford, Hartley, Hemphill, Hutchinson, Lipscomb, Moore, Ochiltree, Oldham, Potter, Randall, Roberts, Sherman, and Wheeler.
Austin — Integral Care; 1967; Travis.
Beaumont — Spindletop Center; 1967; Chambers, Hardin, Jefferson, and Orange.
Big Spring — West Texas Centers; 1997; Andrews, Borden, Crane, Dawson, Fisher, Gaines, Garza, Glasscock, Howard, Kent, Loving, Martin, Mitchell, Nolan, Reeves, Runnels, Scurry, Terrell, Terry, Upton, Ward, Winkler, and Yoakum.
Brownwood — Center for Life Resources; 1969; Brown, Coleman, Comanche, Eastland, McCulloch, Mills, and San Saba.
Bryan-College Station — MHMR Authority of Brazos Valley; 1972; Brazos, Burleson, Grimes, Leon, Madison, Robertson, and Washington.
Conroe — Tri-County Behavioral Healthcare; 1983; Liberty, Montgomery, and Walker.
Corpus Christi — Nueces Center for Mental Health & Intellectual Disabilities; 1970; Nueces.

Dallas — North Texas Behavioral Health Authority (NTBHA); 1967; Dallas, Ellis, Hunt, Kaufman, Navarro, and Rockwall.
Denton — Denton County MHMR Center; 1987; Denton.
Edinburg — Tropical Texas Behavioral Health; 1967; Cameron, Hidalgo, and Willacy.
El Paso — Emergence Health Network; 1968; El Paso.
Fort Worth — MHMR of Tarrant County; 1969; Tarrant.
Galveston — Gulf Coast Center; 1969; Brazoria and Galveston.
Granbury — Pecan Valley Centers for Behavioral & Developmental HealthCare; 1977; Erath, Hood, Johnson, Palo Pinto, Parker, and Somervell.
Houston — The Harris Center for Mental Health and IDD; 1965; Harris.
Jacksonville — Anderson-Cherokee Community Enrichment Services (ACCESS); 1995; Anderson and Cherokee.
Kerrville — Hill Country Mental Health & Developmental Disabilities Centers; 1997; Bandera, Blanco, Comal, Edwards, Gillespie, Hays, Kendall, Kerr, Kimble, Kinney, Llano, Mason, Medina, Menard, Real, Schleicher, Sutton, Uvalde, and Val Verde.
Laredo — Border Region Behavioral Health Center; 1969; Jim Hogg, Starr, Webb, and Zapata.
Longview — Community Healthcore; 1970; Bowie, Cass, Gregg, Harrison, Marion, Panola, Red River, Rusk, and Upshur.
Lubbock — StarCare Specialty Health System; 1969; Cochran, Crosby, Hockley, Lubbock, and Lynn.
Lufkin — Burke Center; 1975; Angelina, Houston, Jasper, Nacogdoches, Newton, Polk, Sabine, San Augustine, San Jacinto, Shelby, Trinity, and Tyler.
Lytle — Camino Real Community Services; 1996; Atascosa, Dimmit, Frio, La Salle, Karnes, Maverick, McMullen, Wilson, and Zavala.
McKinney — LifePath Systems; 1986; Collin.
Midland — PermiaCare; 1969; Brewster, Culberson, Ector, Hudspeth, Jeff Davis, Midland, Pecos, and Presidio.
Plainview — Central Plains Center; 1969; Bailey, Briscoe, Castro, Floyd, Hale, Lamb, Motley, Parmer, and Swisher.
Portland — Coastal Plains Community Center; 1996; Aransas, Bee, Brooks, Duval, Jim Wells, Kenedy, Kleberg, Live Oak, and San Patricio.
Rosenberg — Texana Center; 1996; Austin, Colorado, Fort Bend, Matagorda, Waller and Wharton.
Round Rock — Bluebonnet Trails Community Services; 1997; Bastrop, Burnet, Caldwell, Fayette, Gonzales, Guadalupe, Lee, and Williamson.
San Angelo — MHMR Services for the Concho Valley; 1969; Coke, Concho, Crockett, Irion, Reagan, Sterling, and Tom Green.
San Antonio — The Center for Health Care Services; 1966; Bexar.
Sherman — Texoma Community Center; 1974; Cooke, Fannin, and Grayson.
Temple — Central Counties Services; 1967; Bell, Coryell, Hamilton, Lampasas, and Milam.
Terrell — Lakes Regional MHMR Center; 1996; Camp, Delta, Franklin, Hopkins, Lamar, Morris, and Titus.
Tyler — Andrews Center Behavioral Healthcare System; 1970; Henderson, Rains, Smith, Van Zandt, and Wood.
Victoria — Gulf Bend Center; 1970; Calhoun, DeWitt, Goliad, Jackson, Lavaca, Refugio, and Victoria.
Waco — Heart of Texas Region MHMR Center; 1969; Bosque, Falls, Freestone, Hill, Limestone, and McLennan.
Wichita Falls — Helen Farabee Centers; 1969; Archer, Baylor, Childress, Clay, Cottle, Dickens, Foard, Hardeman, Haskell, Jack, King, Knox, Montague, Stonewall, Throckmorton, Wichita, Wilbarger, Wise, and Young. ☆

Source: U.S. Department of Health and Human Services and the Texas Health and Human Services.

Education

PUBLIC SCHOOLS

UIL WINNING SCHOOLS

TEXAS HISTORY DAY

UNIVERSITIES AND COLLEGES

Students of the San Antonio Academy of Texas engage in Upper School Field Day on April 12, 2019. Photo by San Antonio Academy of Texas (CC).

Texas Public Schools

Sources: Reports and online directory of the Texas Education Agency, tea.texas.gov; Summary of 2020—21 Conference Committee Report for HB1; additional reporting by A.J. Smuskiewicz.

Enrollment in Texas public schools continues to rise. In the 2019-2020 school year, 5,493,940 students were enrolled. That's an increase of 1.1 percent over enrollment in the 2018–2019 school year, and a jump of 13.9 percent above enrollment from 2009-2010, according to the Texas Education Agency.

In Texas, there are 1,202 independent and common school districts and 180 charter operators. Independent school districts are administered by an elected board of trustees and deal directly with the Texas Education Agency. Common districts are supervised by elected county school superintendents and county trustees. Charter schools are discussed later in this article.

There were 20 school districts with more than 50,000 students enrolled in their various schools, and 29.2 percent of all students in Texas attend school in those large districts. By contrast, only 1.8 percent of Texas students are enrolled at the 394 smallest districts in Texas, each of which has fewer than 500 students enrolled.

5 Largest School Districts, by Enrollment (May 2021)

School District	County	Enrollment
Houston ISD	Harris	196,943
Dallas ISD	Dallas	145,113
Cypress-Fairbanks ISD	Harris	114,881
Northside ISD	Bexar	103,151
Katy ISD	Harris, Fort Bend, Waller	84,176

5 Smallest School Districts, by Enrollment (May 2021)

School District	County	Enrollment
San Vicente ISD	Brewster	14
Doss Consolidated CSD	Gillespie	18
Divide ISD	Kerr	22
Valentine ISD	Jeff Davis	35
Comquest Academy CSD	Harris	38

Brief History of Public Education In Texas

Public education was one of the primary goals of the early settlers of Texas, who listed in the Texas Declaration of Independence the failure to provide education as one of their grievances against Mexico.

As early as 1838, President Mirabeau B. Lamar's message to the Republic of Texas Congress advocated setting aside public domain for public schools. His interest caused him to be called the "Father of Education in Texas." In 1839, Congress designated three leagues of land to support public schools for each Texas county and 50 leagues for a state university. In 1840, each county was allocated one more league of land.

The Republic, however, did not establish a public school system or a university. After Texas was admitted into the Union, the 1845 Texas State Constitution advocated public education, instructing the Legislature to designate at least 10 percent of the tax revenue for schools. Further delay occurred until Gov. Elisha M. Pease, on Jan. 31, 1854, signed the bill setting up the Texas public school system.

The public school system was made possible by setting aside $2 million out of $10 million Texas received for relinquishing its claim to land north and west of its present boundaries in the Compromise of 1850.

Early Funding and Administration Changes

During 1854, legislation provided for state apportionment of funds based upon an annual census. Also, railroads receiving grants were required to survey alternate sections to be set aside for public-school financing. The first school census that year showed 65,463 students; state fund apportionment was 62 cents per student.

When adopted in 1876, the present Texas Constitution provided: "All funds, lands, and other property heretofore set apart and appropriated for the support of public schools; all the alternate sections of land reserved by the state of grants heretofore made or that may hereafter be made to railroads, or other corporations, of any nature whatsoever; one half of the public domain of the state, and all sums of money that may come to the state from the sale of any portion of the same shall constitute a perpetual public school fund."

More than 52 million acres of the Texas public domain were allotted for school purposes. (See table "Distribution of the Public Lands of Texas" on page 465.)

In 1949, the Gilmer-Aikin Laws reorganized the state system of public schools by making sweeping changes in administration and financing. The Texas Education Agency, headed by the governor-appointed Commissioner of Education, administers the public-school system.

The policy-making body for public education is the 15-member State Board of Education, which is elected from separate districts for overlapping four-year terms. Current membership of the board is listed on page 501 in the State Government chapter.

Targeting Student Performance

The 68th Legislature passed one of the most historic education-reform bills of the past 50 years when lawmakers met in special session in the summer of 1984. House Bill 72 came in response to growing concern over deteriorating literacy among Texas' schoolchildren over two decades, reflected in students' scores on standardized tests.

Provisions of HB 72 raised teachers' salaries, but tied those raises to teacher performance. It also introduced more stringent teacher certification and initiated competency testing for teachers. Lawmakers also created the 22:1 class size ratio for kindergarten through fourth-grade classes and the no-pass, no-play rule.

Sweeping Reforms

In 1995, the 74th Legislature took on a monumental task and completely rewrote all the state's public education laws.

The Public Schools Reform Act of 1995 increased local control of public schools by limiting the Texas Education Agency to recommending and reporting on educational goals; overseeing charter schools; managing the permanent, foundation, and available school funds; administering an accountability system; creating and implementing the student testing program; recommending educator appraisal and counselor evaluation instruments; and developing plans for special, bilingual, compensatory, gifted and talented, vocational, and technology education.

It also reduced the authority of the State Board of Education. The goal was to return as much authority as possible to the local level. However, each subsequent legislature has reinstated some state-level control.

Charter Schools

Charter-school legislation in Texas provides for four types of charter schools: the home-rule school district charter, the campus or campus-program charter, the open-enrollment charter and a university-sponsored charter. A charter contract is typically granted for five years and can be revoked if the school violates its charter.

Since the inception of the charter school movement in Texas, the charter contracts have been granted by the State Board of Education (SBOE). However, SB2 passed during the 2013 legislative session shifted the authority to grant a charter to the commissioner of education. The State Board of Education, however, may veto any of his selections.

There are currently 175 active charter school districts in Texas. Since 1996, 338 charters have been approved and 157 have closed (including 38 closures due to the charter being revoked). So far, no district has created a home-rule charter, although citizens in Dallas ISD discussed it. There are 123 campus charter schools, which are created by school districts and overseen by each school district's board of trustees.

The most popular form of charter schools is the open-enrollment charter. These are public schools released from some Texas education laws and regulations. Many charter schools have focused efforts on educating young people who are at risk of dropping out of school or who have dropped out and then returned to school. There were 837 open-enrollment schools, representing 336,745 students during the 2019-2020 school year.

The state also approves university-sponsored charters; 29 of such schools are active and in operation, according to a search of TEA's online directory.

During the 2019-2020 school year, about 6.1 percent of the state's public school students attended open-enrollment charter schools.

State Appropriations

For FY22–23, general revenue financing for public education totals $46.6 billion, an increase of $2.0 billion over the FY20–21 funding level. Most of the funding for public education comes through the Foundation School Program system. The 86th Legislature increased FSP funding by $11.5 billion in General Revenue funding, with the intent to increase salaries for teachers and provide school district property tax relief.

Supplemental appropriation for public education include:

- $60 million for supplemental special education services.
- Increases the state's contribution rates at the Teacher Retirement System from 7.5 percent in 2020-21 to 7.75 percent in FY 2022 and 8.0 percent in FY 2023.
- Provides 897.6 million, an increase of $39.5 million, to maintain current helath insurance premiums and benefits for retired teachers.

Permanent School Fund

The Texas public school system was established and the Permanent School Fund (PSF) set up by the Fifth Legislature, Jan. 31, 1854.

The 158-year-old PSF is managed by the State Board of Education and is the second-largest educational endowment

Permanent School Fund		
Year	Fund Value* (in millions)	Funds Distributed to Schools (in millions)
2020	$46,675.6	$1,701.7
2019	$46,500.4	$1,535.8
2018	$44,067.5	$1,235.8
2017	$41,418	$1,056.4
2016	$37,263.9	$1,056.4
2015	$33,833.5	$8,38.7
2014	$34,951.2	$8,38.7
2013	$27,277	$1,020.9
2012	$25,503	$1,020.9
2011	$24,091.6	$1,092.8
2010	$22,107.8	$60.7
2009	$20,545.3	$716.5
2008	$23,142.4	$716.5
2007	$25,311.8	$843.1
2006	$22,802.7	$841.9
2005	$21,354.3	$880
2004	$19,261.8	$825.1
2003	$18,037.3	N/A
2002	$17,047.2	N/A
2001	$19,021.8	N/A
2000	$22,275.6	N/A
1999	$19,615.7	$698.5
1998	$16,296.2	$661.9
1997	$15,496.6	$690.8
1996	$12,995.8	$692.7
1995	$12,273.2	$740
1994	$11,330.6	$737
1993	$11,822.5	$737.7
1992	$10,944.9	$739.5
1991	$10,227.8	$739.2
1990	$7,328.2	$700.3
1980	$2,464.6	$3
1970	$842.2	$287.2
1960	$425.8	$164.2
1950	$161.2	$94
1940	$68.3	$34.6
1930	$38.7	$27.3
1920	$25.7	$18.4
1910	$16.8	$5.9

*Prior to 1991, the PSF reported cash, bonds at par, and stock at book value. From 1991 to the present, the PSF has reported cash, bonds and stocks at fair value.

Texas School Enrollment and Expenditures per Student

School Year	Enrollment	Spending per student
2019-2020	5,493,940	—
2018-2019	5,431,910	$12,861
2017–2018	5,399,682	$12,634
2016–2017	5,343,893	$12,264
2015–2016	5,284,306	$11,704
2014–2015	5,232,065	$10,971
2013–2014	5,151,925	$9,903
2012–2013	5,058,939	$9,969
2011–2012	4,978,120	$10,335
2010–2011	4,912,385	$11,142
2009–2010	4,824,778	$11,543
2008–2009	4,728,204	$11,567
2007–2008	4,651,516	$10,162
2006–2007	4,576,933	$9,629
2005–2006	4,505,572	$9,269

Graduates and Dropouts

School Year	Graduates	*Dropouts
2018-2019	355,615	34,477
2017-2018	347,893	33,697
2016–2017	334,424	33,050
2015–2016	324,311	33,466
2014–2015	313,397	33,437
2013–2014	303,109	35,358
2012–2013	301,418	34,696
2011–2012	292,636	36,276
2010–2011	290,581	34,363
2009–2010	280,520	33,235
2008–2009	264,275	40,923
2007–2008	252,121	45,796
2006–2007	241,193	55,306
2005–2006	240,485	51,841
2004–2005	239,716	18,290

* Grades 7–12.

in the United States. It is invested in global markets and broadly diversified.

Every year, a distribution is made from PSF to pay a portion of educational costs in each public school district. The amount distributed is subject to two constraints set in Article VII, Section 5 of the Texas Constitution:

- The SBOE may not approve a distribution rate or transfer to the Available School Fund (ASF) that exceeds 6 percent of the average market value of the fund, excluding real property.

- The total distributions over a 10-year period to the ASF may not exceed the total return on the PSF's investment assets over the same period.

The fund was first established in 1854 with $2.0 million. The funds distributed to schools that year was $40,587. By the year 1900 the fund had grown to $9.1 million. Funds distributed to schools in 1900 totalled $3.0 million. The PSF balance, as of Aug. 31, 2020, was $46.7 billion, an increase of $175.2 million from the prior year.

The PSF also provides a guarantee for bonds issued by local school districts, allowing districts to pay lower interest rates. As of Aug. 31, 2012, PSF assets guaranteed $77.7 billion in school district bonds to 844 public school districts and $1.4 billion in charter district bonds to 14 charter districts.

COVID-19 Pandemic

As the pandemic spread in early 2020, public schools throughout the United States ceased in-person learning. When a quick recovery became more unlikely, schools established online, or remote, learning for students. Many Texas public schools reopened to in-person education for the autumn term of 2020, ahead of schools in most other states. In July 2020, Governor Greg Abbott gave individual school districts the option of in-school classes. [1]

Public School Personnel and Salaries

Personnel Category	Personnel 2018—2019	Personnel 2019—2020	% Change from Previous	Average Base Salaries 2018—2019	Average Base Salaries 2019—2020	% Change from Previous
Teachers	358,445	363,098	1.30%	$54,121	$57,091	5.49%
Campus Administrators	21,812	21,960	0.68%	$78,947	$82,511	4.51%
Central Administrators	8,287	8,352	0.78%	$103,379	$108,366	4.82%
Professional Support*	73,190	74,966	2.43%	$64,063	$67,334	5.11%
Total Professionals	461,734	468,376	1.44%	—	—	—
Educational Aides	74,325	78,125	5.11%	$21,210	$22,067	4.04%
Auxiliary Staff	184,109	188,764	2.53%	$26,891	$28,279	5.16%
Total Staff	720,168	735,265	2.10%	—	—	—

*Personnel figures are full-time equivalent
** The Professional Support category includes supervisors, counselors, educational diagnosticians, librarians, nurses/physicians, therapists, and psychologists.

Source: TEA Staff Salary reports for 2018-2019 and 2019-2020

The closing and reopening of public schools generated much controversy. Some parents opposed remote learning, viewing it as substandard education, difficult for children psychologically, unhealthy for social development, and unnecessary because children and adolescents were at low risk for contracting, transmitting, or developing serious illness from COVID-19. [1] Others, including leaders of the Texas State Teachers Association, [1, 2] favored the school shutdowns for safety reasons, arguing that any in-person contact could increase the virus's spread among faculty, staff, and students.

As online learning continued and in-class learning remained nonmandatory, some students dropped out of the public school system entirely. [3] In some districts, teams of teachers visited the homes of missing students every few weeks. [3]

In May 2021, a study conducted by University of Kentucky researchers for the National Bureau of Economic Research reported that the reopening of Texas schools may have led to an acceleration in the number of COVID-19 cases in Texas. [1, 4] According to the researchers' computer model estimates, there may have been 43,000 additional cases and 800 additional deaths within two months of the autumn 2020 reopenings. However, a spokesperson for the Texas Education Agency (TEA) disputed those model estimates and maintained that allowing the option of in-class attendance was the correct decision. The spokesperson noted that only five percent of students, teachers, and staff had developed confirmed cases of COVID-19 during the 2020-21 school year. [1, 4]

Masks

In March 2021, Governor Abbott ended the state mandate ordering that face masks be worn in public settings, leaving mask policies up to individual school districts. [1, 5] However, he advised public schools to follow TEA's guidelines, which recommended wearing masks inside schools. [1, 6] Some parents and students opposed mask-wearing regulations, considering them to be unconstitutional intrusions on personal freedoms and individual decisions. [5] Others believed that masks should remain mandatory for everyone, arguing that they were needed for safety. [7]

Despite the loosening of the mask restrictions and the reopening of schools, Governor Abbott renewed the COVID-related public disaster declaration in May 2021. [8]

Vaccine

As of May 2021, about 40 percent of Texans were fully vaccinated against the coronavirus that causes COVID-19. [4] Even after vaccination became common in mid-2021, the mask-wearing recommendation continued because student and staff vaccination statuses could not be known with certainty. [1]

Enrollment

The TEA reported in January 2021 that enrollment in Texas public schools from early education through 12th grade decreased by about 157,000 students, or three percent, from October 2019 to October 2020. [9, 10] More than half of that decline occurred in the nonmandatory grade levels of early education, pre-kindergarten, and kindergarten. However, enrollment also declined for the mandatory grades (1 through 12) by about one percent. This was the first enrollment decline reported for Texas public schools since that data was first collected. The drop was likely related to students not returning to either in-class or online learning during the pandemic. [10]

Finances

During the summer of 2020, many school administrators and financial experts feared that a tight state budget, as well as the economic slowdown and school shutdowns, would have severe impacts on school-district budgets. [11]

However, according to a March 2021 report, sweeping COVID-related economic-relief legislation signed by President Joe Biden earlier that month was expected to provide local governments with financial windfalls. [11] In April 2021, state officials announced the release of $11.2 billion from the $18 billion in available federal COVID-relief funds to help public schools address pandemic-related problems, such as computer systems for remote learning and desk barriers for in-person learning. [12, 13]

Numerous school districts participated in a state-funded program in 2021 to incentivize teachers in poor communities to do extra intervention and tutoring for students during holiday and summer breaks and after-school hours. [14] The funds came from the TEA's Teacher Incentive Allotment. The districts hoped that the program, which raised some teacher salaries to more than $100,000, would help students catch up with lost learning stemming from school closures.

References

1. Martinez, Marissa. "Resuming in-person learning at Texas schools last fall accelerated spread of COVID-19, study says." *The Texas Tribune*. May 10, 2021. https://www.texastribune.org/2021/05/10/texas-schools-covid-19-increase-study/
2. "TSTA demands the governor shut down schools for the year, take other steps to protect Texans' health" [press release]. Texas State Teachers Association, Facebook. April 1, 2020. https://www.facebook.com/texasstateteachersassociation/photos/tsta-demands-the-governor-shut-down-schools-for-the-year-take-other-steps-to-pro/10158048809838433/
3. McNeel, Bekah. "In San Antonio, teachers hit the streets in search of students disappearing from online learning." *The Texas Tribune*. March 3, 2021. https://www.texastribune.org/2021/03/03/texas-schools-missing-students/
4. Lenthang, Marlene. "Rapid school reopenings may have led to thousands of COVID cases, hundreds of deaths in Texas." ABC News. May 20, 2021. https://abcnews.go.com/Health/rapid-school-reopenings-led-thousands-covid-cases-hundreds/story?id=77778717
5. Bohra, Neelam. "Parents sue Katy ISD for keeping mask mandate after Gov. Abbott lifted statewide requirement." *The Texas Tribune*. April 2, 2021. https://www.texastribune.org/2021/04/02/texas-katy-isd-mask-lawsuit/
6. SY 20-21 public health planning guidance. Texas Education Agency. March 25, 2021. https://tea.texas.gov/sites/default/files/covid/SY-20-21-Public-Health-Guidance.pdf
7. McNeel, Bekah. "'I've never done any of this': A Texas parent reluctantly dives into a school district's battle over masks." *The Texas Tribune*. April 12, 2021. https://www.texastribune.org/2021/04/12/texas-comal-isd-masks-coronavirus/
8. "COVID-19 support: Public health orders." Texas Education Agency. 2020-2021. https://tea.texas.gov/texas-schools/health-safety-discipline/covid/covid-19-support-public-health-orders
9. Summary of Texas public schools student enrollment trends: January 2021. Texas Education Agency. March 4, 2021. https://tea.texas.gov/sites/default/files/covid/SY21-Student-Enrollment-Summary-Table.pdf
10. Mitchell, Isaiah. "Enrollment drop hits Texas public schools." *The Texan*. January 14, 2021. https://thetexan.news/enrollment-drop-hits-texas-public-schools/
11. Ramsey, Ross. "Analysis: Government budgets looked terrible when COVID-19 started. A federal windfall has flipped the outlook." *The Texas Tribune*. March 12, 2021. https://www.texastribune.org/2021/03/12/texas-budget-coronavirus/
12. McGee, Kate. "Texas releases $11 billion of $18 billion in federal stimulus money for public schools." *The Texas Tribune*. April 28, 2021. https://www.texastribune.org/2021/04/28/texas-schools-stimulus-money/
13. Ramsey, Ross. "Analysis: A $5.5 billion shift in who pays for public education in Texas." *The Texas Tribune*. April 9, 2021. https://www.texastribune.org/2021/04/09/texas-education-property-taxes/
14. McNeel, Bekah. "Pay for some Texas teachers will top $100,000 in bid to aid poorer schools devastated by COVID-19." *The Texas Tribune*. May 17, 2021. https://www.texastribune.org/2021/05/17/texas-teacher-salaries-coronavirus/

University Interscholastic League Winning Schools for the 2018–2019 and 2020–2021 School Years

Source: University Interscholastic League, uiltexas.org

The **UIL Lone Star Cup** is awarded annually to six high schools, one in each of the six UIL classifications, based on their team performance in district and state championships. The winning schools receive the UIL Lone Star Cup trophy and a $1,000 scholarship. In the school year 2019-20, the Cup was not awarded due to the COVID-19 pandemic.

YEAR	1A	2A	3A	4A	5A	6A
Lone Star Cup Champions						
2020–21	Nazareth	Shiner	Brock	Argyle	Highland Park (Dallas)	The Woodlands (Conroe)
2018–19	Nazareth	Mason	Brock	Argyle	Highland Park (Dallas)	Southlake Carroll

The schools of individuals who won state championships in the academic, music, and the arts categories are listed first, then the winners in some sports categories. For other sports results, see page 180. A dash (—) in the box means there was no competition in that conference in that category for that year. In the year 2019-20, the spring state academic competitions were canceled due to the COVID-19 pandemic.

State Champions, Academics

YEAR	1A	2A	3A	4A	5A	6A
Overall State Meet Academic Champions						
2020–21	Slidell	Sabine Pass	Holliday	Lindale	PSJA Southwest	Clements (Sugar Land)
2018–19	Borden County	Sabine Pass	Holliday	Argyle	Lovejoy (Lucas)	Cypress Woods
Accounting						
2020–21	Happy	Vega	Holliday	Andrews	Tivy (Kerrville)	Keller
2018–19	Jayton	Union Grove (Gladewater)	Idalou	Argyle	Hallsville	Cypress Woods
Calculator Applications						
2020–21	Rankin	Sabine Pass	Brock	Spring Hill (Longview)	Canyon (New Braunfels)	North Shore (Houston)
2018–19	Santa Anna	Muenster	Ponder	Argyle	Canutillo (El Paso)	North Shore (Houston)
Computer Applications						
2020–21	Happy	Sanford Fritch	Elysian Fields	Andrews	Friendswood	Flower Mound
2018–19	Springlake-Earth	Vega	Chapel Hill (Mount Pleasant)	Melissa	Waller	Cypress Woods
Computer Science						
2020–21	Aspermont	San Augustine	Fairfield	School for Talented & Gifted (Dallas)	Lovejoy (Lucas)	Cypress Woods
2018–19	Borden County	Ozona	Ponder	Giddings	Austin LBJ	Cypress Woods
Number Sense						
2020–21	Jonesboro	Woodsboro	Sabine (Gladewater)	Salado	Highland Park (Dallas)	Clements (Sugar Land)
2018–19	Bellevue	Poolville	Sabine (Gladewater)	Wichita Falls Hirschi	Highland Park (Dallas)	Clements (Sugar Land)
Mathematics						
2020–21	Knippa	Woodsboro	Idalou	Calhoun (Port Lavaca)	Highland Park (Dallas)	Clements (Sugar Land)
2018–19	Fruitvale	Muenster	Sabine (Gladewater)	Salado	Highland Park (Dallas)	Dulles (Sugar Land)
Science						
2020–21	Guthrie	Eldorado	Skidmore-Tynan	Argyle	Sharyland Pioneer (Mission)	Martin (Arlington)
2018–19	Klondike (Lamesa)	Valley View	Whitney	La Feria	Lubbock	Dulles (Sugar Land)
Social Studies						
2020–21	Knippa	Lindsay	Llano	Wimberley	Montgomery Lake Creek	Lake Ridge (Mansfield)
2018–19	Hartley	Sabine Pass	Tolar	Hereford	Hallsville	Pearland Dawson
Current Issues						
2020–21	Fruitvale	Mason	New Caney Infinity ECHS	Wimberley	Montgomery Lake Creek	Health Careers (San Antonio)
2018–19	Borden County	Sabine Pass	Holliday	Argyle	College Station	Humble Atascosita

YEAR	1A	2A	3A	4A	5A	6A
Literary Criticism						
2020–21	Graford	Mason	S&S Consolidated (Sadler)	Argyle	Sulphur Springs	Seven Lakes (Katy)
2018–19	Graford	Sabine Pass	Holliday	Argyle	Sulphur Springs	McKinney
Poetry Interpretation						
2020–21	Irion County	West Hardin (Saratoga)	Chisum (Paris)	Tuloso-Midway (Corpus Christi)	PSJA Southwest	Judson (Converse)
2018–19	Irion County	Mason	Malakoff	Little Cypress-Mauriceville	Victoria West	Judson (Converse)
Prose Interpretation						
2020–21	Aspermont	Sundown	White Oak	Tuloso-Midway (Corpus Christi)	Corsicana	Judson (Converse)
2018–19	Petersburg	West Hardin (Saratoga)	Kemp	Little Cypress-Mauriceville	Tuloso-Midway (Corpus Christi)	Plano
Ready Writing						
2020–21	Prairie Lea	Falls City	East Chambers (Winnie)	Calallen (Corpus Christi)	Highland Park (Dallas)	Martin (Arlington)
2018–19	Woodson	Shelbyville	Franklin	Bullard	College Station	Pearland Dawson
Speech Team						
2020–21	Chireno	Mason	White Oak	Salado	Lovejoy (Lucas)	Plano
2018–19	Borden County	Shelbyville	London (Corpus Christi)	North Lamar (Paris)	Lovejoy (Lucas)	Pflugerville Hendrickson
Informative Speaking						
2020–21	Nazareth	Stamford	White Oak	Lampasas	Pflugerville	Plano West
2018–19	Lometa	Leon (Jewett)	Holliday	North Lamar (Paris)	Mount Pleasant	Plano West
Persuasive Speaking						
2020–21	Chireno	Schulenburg	Lexington	Salado	A&M Conslidated (College Station)	Plano West
2018–19	Borden County	Latexo	London (Corpus Christi)	North Lamar (Paris)	Dripping Springs	Plano West
Lincoln-Douglas Debate						
2020–21	Irion County	Shelbyville	Canadian	Hereford	Medina Valley (Castroville)	Cypress Lakes (Katy)
2018–19	Guthrie	Gary	London (Corpus Christi)	Bandera	Lovejoy (Lucas)	Plano West
Spelling & Vocabulary						
2020–21	San Isidro	Forsan	Henrietta	Hudson (Lufkin)	Sherman	Vandegrift (Austin)
2018–19	Irion County	Brackettville	Holliday	Snyder	Frisco Independence	Midway (Waco)
Spelling & Vocabulary Team						
2020–21	Moulton	Forsan	Henrietta	Giddings	Denton	Allen
2018–19	Kennard	Sabine Pass	Holliday	Burnet	Lubbock	El Paso Coronado
Journalism Team						
2020–21	Nazareth	Martin's Mill	Central (Pollok)	Lindale	Lovejoy (Lucas)	United South (Laredo)
2018–19	Savoy	San Isidro	Gateway (Georgetown)	Wimberley	Leander Rouse	Sterling (Baytown)
Editorial Writing						
2020–21	Nazareth	Albany	Paradise	Lindale	Joshua	Lamar (Houston)
2018–19	Grady (Lenorah)	San Isidro	Coleman	Devine	Lovejoy (Lucas)	Beaumont West Brook
Feature Writing						
2020–21	San Isidro	Shelbyville	Central (Pollok)	Chapel Hill (Tyler)	Ryan (Denton)	Hebron (Carrollton)
2018–19	Savoy	Mason	Gateway (Georgetown)	Argyle	Lindale	Mansfield
Headline Writing						
2020–21	Nazareth	Martin's Mill	Cole (San Antonio)	Kilgore	Aledo	Cinco Ranch (Katy)
2018–19	Nazareth	Martin's Mill	Van Alstyne	Bridgeport	PSJA Memorial (Alamo)	Stevens (San Antonio)
News Writing						
2020–21	Lasara	Archer City	Central (Pollok)	Center	Liberty Hill	Willis
2018–19	Savoy	Lindsay	Whitney	Henderson	Gregory-Portland	Sterling (Baytown)

State Champions, Publications

Year	Yearbooks (Gold Awards)	Print Newspapers (Gold Awards)
2020–21	Burges (El Paso); McKinney; Texas (Texarkana); Vista Ridge (Cedar Park); Westlake (Austin)	Albany; Bowie (Austin); McCallum (Austin); Pleasant Grove (Texarkana); St. Mark's (Dallas); Texas (Texarkana)
2019–20	Haltom; Highland Park; Kealing (Austin); Legacy (Mansfield); McKinney; Pleasant Grove (Texarkana); St. Thomas Episcopal (Houston); Texas (Texarkana); Vista Ridge (Cedar Park)	Albany; Pleasant Grove (Texarkana); St. Mark's (Dallas); Texas (Texarkana)

State Champions, Music and Theater

YEAR	1A	2A	3A	4A	5A	6A
One-Act Play						
2020–21	Rankin	Christoval	Shallowater	Corpus Christi Tuloso-Midway	Pharr-San Juan-Alamo Southwest	Northside Taft
2019–20	Spring state academic championships were canceled due to COVID-19 pandemic.					
State Marching Band Contest						
2020–21	—	Ganado	—	Lake Belton	—	Harlingen
2019–20	Irion	—	Mineola	—	Cedar Park	—

State Champions, Athletics

YEAR	1A	2A	3A	4A	5A	6A
Cross Country Team, Boys						
2020–21	Miller Grove (Cumby)	Port Aransas	Presidio	San Elizario	Grapevine	Carroll (Southlake)
2019–20	Miller Grove (Cumby)	Great Hearts Monte Vista (San Antonio)	Eustace	Decatur	Eastwood (El Paso)	Carroll (Southlake)
Cross Country Individual, Boys						
2020–21	Miller Grove	Poolville	Onalaska	Melissa	Grapevine	Wylie
2019–20	Miller Grove (Cumby)	Great Hearts Monte Vista (San Antonio)	Luling	Melissa	Aledo	La Porte
Cross Country Team, Girls						
2020–21	Nazareth	Sundown	Lago Vista	Canyon	Boerne Champion	Flower Mound (Lewisville)
2019–20	Miller Grove (Cumby)	Gruver	Holliday	Canyon	Boerne	Carroll (Southlake)
Cross Country Individual, Girls						
2020–21	Earth Springlake	Wellington	Cameron Yoe	Celina	Cedar Park	Denton Guyer
2019–20	Miller Grove (Cumby)	Lindsay	Whitesboro	Salado	McKinney North	Plano
Golf Team, Boys						
2020–21	Sterling City	Normangee	Brock	Argyle	Highland Park (Dallas)	Westlake (Austin)
2019–20	UIL state spring sports were canceled due to the COVID-19 pandemic.					
Golf Individual, Boys						
2020–21	Fort Elliott (Briscoe)	Tahoka	Columbus	Wimberley	Highland (Dallas)	Keller
2019–20	UIL state spring sports were canceled due to the COVID-19 pandemic.					
Golf Team, Girls						
2020–21	Robert Lee	Normangee	Wall	Andrews	Alamo Heights (San Antonio)	Hebron (Lewisville)
2019–20	UIL state spring sports were canceled due to the COVID-19 pandemic.					
Golf Individual, Girls						
2020–21	Eula (Clyde)	Martin's Mill	Chapel Hill (Mount Pleasant)	Carrollton (Ranchview)	Granbury	San Angelo Central
2019–20	UIL state spring sports were canceled due to the COVID-19 pandemic.					
Tennis, Team						
2020–21	—	—	—	Hereford	Highland Park (Dallas)	Westwood (Round Rock)
2019–20	—	—	—	Fredericksburg	Highland Park (Dallas)	Memorial (Houston)
Tennis, Boys Singles						
2020–21	Nueces Canyon (Barksdale)	Sabine Pass	Wall	Canyon	Lebanon Trail (Frisco)	Midland
2019–20	UIL state spring sports were canceled due to the COVID-19 pandemic.					

YEAR	1A	2A	3A	4A	5A	6A
Tennis, Boys Doubles						
2020–21	Crowell	Mason	Little River Academy	Wimberley	College Station A&M Consolidated	Westwood (Round Rock)
2019–20	UIL state spring sports were canceled due to the COVID-19 pandemic.					
Tennis, Girls Singles						
2020–21	Slidell	Mason	Franklin	Devine	Heritage (Frisco)	Bowie (Austin)
2019–20	UIL state spring sports were canceled due to the COVID-19 pandemic.					
Tennis, Girls Doubles						
2020–21	Nueces Canyon (Barksdale)	Mason	Reagan (Big Lake)	Stafford	Heritage (Frisco)	Houston Memorial
2019–20	UIL state spring sports were canceled due to the COVID-19 pandemic.					
Tennis, Mixed Doubles						
2020–21	Sterling City	Mason	Groesbeck	Hereford	Amarillo	Westwood (Round Rock)
2019–20	UIL state spring sports were canceled due to the COVID-19 pandemic.					
Track & Field, Boys Team						
2020–21	Paducah	Shiner	Brock	La Vega (Waco)	Liberty (Frisco)	Summer Creek (Humble)
2019–20	UIL state spring sports were canceled due to the COVID-19 pandemic.					
Track & Field, Girls Team						
2020–21	Ackerly Sands	Panhandle	Cameron Yoe	Kennedale	Lancaster	DeSoto
2019–20	UIL state spring sports were canceled due to the COVID-19 pandemic.					

Swimming & Diving, Team

	GIRLS		BOYS	
YEAR	5A	6A	5A	6A
2020–21	Lubbock	Conroe (The Woodlands)	Wakeland (Frisco)	Conroe (The Woodlands)
2019–20	Lubbock	Southlake Carroll	Kingwood Park (Humble)	Kingwood (Humble)

Wrestling, Boys

2020–21	**TEAM: 5A** Randall (Canyon) **6A** Allen **5A Weight Class 106**: Randall (Canyon) **113**: Creekview (Carrollton) **120**: Lubbock **126**: Randall (Canyon) **132**: Dumas **138**: Dumas **145**: Randall (Canyon) **152**: Heritage (Colleyville) **160**: Centennial (Burleson) **170**: Argyle **182**: Randall (Canyon) **195**: Lovejoy (Lucas) **220**: Creekview (Carrollton) **285**: Midlothian **6A** Weight Class **106**: Allen **113**: Martin (Arlington) **126**: Allen **132**: Martin (Arlington) **138**: West (Plano) **145**: Martin (Arlington) **152**: Martin (Arlington) **160**: Prosper **170**: Clemens (Schertz) **182**: Woodlands College Park (Conroe) **195**: Klein **220**: Martin (Arlington) **285**: Allen
2019–20	**TEAM: 5A** Randall (Canyon) **6A** Allen **5A Weight Class 106**: Carrollton (Creekview) **113**: East (Wylie) **120**: Lubbock **126**: Midlothian **132**:Lone Star (Frisco) **138**: Reedy (Frisco) **145**: Midlothian **152**: Dripping Springs **160**: Randall (Canyon) **170**: Randall (Canyon) **182**: New Waverly **195**: Creekview (Carrollton) **220**: Cedar Park **285**: Foster (Richmond) **6A Weight Class 106**: Ellison (Killeen) **113**: Allen **120**: Martin (Arlington) **126**: Martin (Arlington) **132**: Keller **138**: Vandegrift (Austin) **145**: Allen **152**: Vista Ridge (Cedar Park) **160**: Allen **170**: Katy **182**: Klein **195**: Allen **220**: Prosper **285**: New Braunfels

Wrestling, Girls

2020–21	**TEAM: 5A** Allen **6A** Randall (Canyon) **5A** Weight Class 95: Randall (Canyon) **102**: Randall (Canyon) **110**: Hanks (El Paso) **119**: Caprock (Amarillo) **128**: Centennial (Burleson) **138**: Kingwood Park (Humble) **148**: Friendswood **165**: The Colony (Lewisville) **185**: Hanks (El Paso) **215**: Kingwood Park (Humble) **6A** Weight Class 95: Woodlands College Park (Conroe) **102**: Allen **110**: Carroll (Southlake) **119:** Bowie (Austin) **128**: Cypress Ranch **138**: San Marcos **148**: Allen **165**: Tompkins (Katy) **185**: Woodlands College Park (Conroe) **215**: Steele (Cibolo)
2019–20	**TEAM: 5A** Eastwood (El Paso) **6A** Trinity (Euless) **5A Weight Class 95**: Eastlake (El Paso) **102**: Lovejoy (Lucas) **110**: Eastwood (El Paso) **119**: Independence (Frisco) **128**: Eastwood (El Paso) **138**: Kingwood Park (Humble) **148**: Burges (El Paso) **165**: Kimball (Dallas) **185**: Parkland (El Paso) **215**: Donna **6A Weight Class 95**: Woodlands College Park (Conroe) **102**: Cypress Creek **110**: Martin (Arlington) **119**: Weatherford **128**: West (Plano) **138**: Morton Ranch (Katy) **148**: West (Plano) **165**: Tompkins (Katy) **185**: Woodlands College Park (Conroe) **215**: Steele (Cibolo)

State and National History Day Contests, 2020–2021

Each year thousands of students, encouraged by teachers and parents statewide, participate in the National History Day program in Texas. Texas History Day, an affiliate of NHD, is a highly regarded academic program for 6th through 12th grade students. Students that place first or second at the state contest get the chance to compete in the national contest in Washington, D.C. Learn more at **texashistoryday.com.**

State History Day Winners 2020

Theme: Breaking Barriers

		Junior	Senior
Documentaries			
Individual		1st: *The International Space Station: A Symbol of Unity,* East Central Heritage MS (San Antonio)	1st: *"Kill the Indian, Save the Man"; How the Traumatic Shared Experience of Native American Boarding Schools Broke Intertribal Barriers and Led to the Formation of Pan-Indianism,* Livingston HS
		2nd: *Barbara Jordan: Breaking Racial and Gender Barriers. Equality for All; Privileges for None,* Santa Fe JH	2nd: *To Hell and Back,* IMPACT Early College HS (Baytown)
Group		1st: *Loving v. Virginia: Breaking Barriers in Anti-Miscegenation,* CM Rice MS (Plano)	1st: *Taking Giant Steps: Breaking Societal Barriers Through the Intellectual Growth of Jazz,* Goose Creek Memorial, Sterling HS
		2nd: *Flying the Hump,* Sartartia MS (Sugar Land)	2nd: *A Land Without Mercy: Robert Peary's Expedition to the North Pole,* Plano East SR HS
Exhibits			
Individual		1st: *Tearing Down the Barrier Between East West: The Fall of the Berlin Wall,* Gentry JH (Baytown)	1st: *The CCC: Breaking Barriers One Park At A Time,* New Caney HS
		2nd: *Mendez v. Westminster: Breaking Barriers for a Seat In the Classroom,* Shotwell MS (Houston)	2nd: *Joan Ganz Cooney: Breaking Barriers in Educational Broadcasting,* Belton New Tech HS at Waskow
Group		1st: *His Mission, His Legacy — Dr. Hector P. Garcia, A Man of the People,* St. Matthew Catholic School (San Antonio)	1st: *'B' is for Breaking Barriers: How Sesame Street Revolutionized Children's Television and Education,* Health Careers HS (San Antonio)
		2nd: *Swinging for Equality,* Hornedo MS (El Paso)	2nd: *The Equal Rights Amendment: Campaign Success to State ERAs,* Dickinson HS
Performances			
Individual		1st: *Madam CJ Walker,* Lewis MS (Houston)	1st: *The Catt in the Hat Breaks Barriers for the Rat,* Impact Early College HS (Baytown)
		2nd: *The BTT Shunt: Blalock's Diary,* Atlas Academy (Waco)	2nd: *little people, BIG DREAMS — A story of unwavering faith and resilience,* Liberty HS (Frisco)
Group		1st: *Mr. Rogers: Breaking Barriers,* Stillman MS (Brownsville)	1st: *King Henry VIII's Greatest Heir: Religious Freedom in America,* Highland Park HS (Dallas)
		2nd: *Penicillin: Breaking Barriers in the Health Care Field,* Sartartia MS (Sugar Land)	2nd: *Felix Tijerina: Breaking Barriers by opening doors for Latin Americans,* Veterans Memorial Early College HS (Brownsville)
Websites			
Individual		1st: *Breaking Barriers to Universal Vaccination,* Sartartia MS (Sugar Land)	1st: *Ethel Payne: Paving The Way To Equality Through Journalism,* Granbury HS
		2nd: *Turbulence Couldn't Shake Her: Bessie Coleman, Aviatrix,* Cedar Bayou JH (Baytown)	2nd: *"Deeds, Not Words!": The Suffragettes, Women Breaking Barriers,* Belton New Tech HS at Waskow
Group		1st: *Termination, Restoration, and Beyond: How the Alabama-Coushatta Tribe of Texas Continues to Face and Break Barriers in History,* Livingston JH	1st: *The Delano Grape Strike: How a Coalition of Immigrants Ended Labor Injustice,* Plano East SR HS
		2nd: *The Wright Brothers: Making the Impossible, Possible,* Sycamore Springs MS (Dripping Springs)	2nd: *Asking For the Moon: How the Space Race Created the Digital Age,* Plano East SR HS
Papers			
Individual		1st: *Breaking Barriers to Universal Vaccination,* Sartartia Middle School (Sugar Land)	1st: *Dr. Hector Garcia: The Driving Force Who Persuaded Lyndon Johnson to Break the Barrier of Racial Discrimination,* Sterling HS
		2nd: *The Fifth Circuit Four: The Unheralded Judges Who Helped to Break Legal Barriers in the Deep South,* Belmont Home School	2nd: *Breaking Economic Barriers: How the Woman's Commonwealth of Belton, Texas, Changed Their World,* Lorena HS

National History Day 2020

1st Place Senior Group Exhibit	1st Place Senior Individual Website	1st Place Junior Individual Paper	3rd Place Senior Group Performance
'B' is for Breaking Barriers: How Sesame Street Revolutionized Children's Television and Education, Health Careers HS (San Antonio)	*"Deeds, Not Words!": The Suffragettes, Women Breaking Barriers,* Belton New Tech HS at Waskow	*The Fifth Circuit Four: The Unheralded Judges Who Helped to Break Legal Barriers in the Deep South,* Belmont Home School	*Felix Tijerina: Breaking Barriers by opening doors for Latin Americans,* Veterans Memorial Early College HS (Brownsville)

State History Day Winners 2021

Theme: Communication in History: The Key to Understanding

	Junior	Senior
Documentaries		
Individual	1st: *Operation Rubicon: The Intelligence Coup of the Century*, Otto MS (Plano)	1st: *In the Words of Those Who Endured: How Slave Narratives are the Key to Understanding the Lives of Former Enslaved African Americans and Communicating an Accurate History of Slavery in America*, Livingston HS
	2nd: *Nikola Tesla: Lightning Fast Communication*, Lamar MS (Austin)	2nd: *Hidden on the "B" Side: Black Gospel Music of the Civil Rights Movement*, Waco HS
Group	1st: *Frances Ellen Watkins Harper: Protest Through Poetry*, Macario Garcia MS (Sugar Land)	1st: *Exposing the Lie: James Baldwin's Communication of the American Truth*, IMPACT Early College HS, Creek Memorial HS (Baytown)
	2nd: *Empowerment and Tragedy: American Propaganda During World War II*, Colleyville MS	2nd: *Music for Humanity: The Legacy of Live Aid*, Highland Park HS (Dallas)
Exhibits		
Individual	1st: *Margo Jones: A Pioneering Voice for Regional Theatre and Theatre-in-the-Round*, Livingston JH	1st: *The 1900 Storm*, New Caney HS
	2nd: *The Culper Spy Ring*, East Central Heritage MS (San Antonio)	2nd: *Glasnost: Transparency that Ended an Era*, Highland Park HS (Dallas)
Group	1st: *1st: Lewis Hine Child Labor Exposed*, Austin Peace Academy (Austin)	1st: *Jazz Diplomacy: The Cold War SWINGs in America's Favor*, Plano East Senior HS
	2nd: *Is It a Crime to Vote?*, Greenville Christian	2nd: *The Stories They Tell: Communicating the Daily Realities of Rural Americans during the Great Depression through FSA Photography*, Health Careers HS (San Antonio)
Performances		
Individual	1st: *Transformation of Songs to Hymns to Freedom*, Stovall MS (Houston)	1st: *Communication Amidst Chaos*, IMPACT Early College HS (Baytown)
	2nd: *The Importance of Communication in WWI and WWII*, Gentry JH (Baytown)	2nd: *The Unpublished Issue of the New-York Weekly Journal*, Carver HS (Houston)
Group	1st: *We Fight! We Sacrifice! We Triumph!*, Waco ATLAS Academy	1st: *Lady with the Lamp: Florence Nightingale's Mathematical Approach to Healthcare Reform*, Plano East Senior HS
	2nd: *Sacagawea: Translating Through the Heart of a New Nation*, Marathon ISD	2nd: *A Nation to Gain: Suffragettes Communicating Through Tactics*, Lorena HS
Websites		
Individual	1st: *Selling Space: The Significance of Propaganda During the Space Race*, Dripping Springs MS	1st: *There's Always Work at the Post Office: The United States Postal Service and Its Ongoing Fight for Financial Stability*, New Caney HS
	2nd: *Testing the Electoral College: The Letters that Influenced the Election of 1800*, Canyon Ridge MS (Austin)	2nd: *Cold War Propaganda: McCarthyism, the Space Race and Beyond*, Carnegie Vanguard HS (Houston)
Group	1st: *Marie Curie: Perception vs. Reality – How Bias and Miscommunication in Secondary Sources Distorts the Truth*, Sycamore Springs MS (Dripping Springs)	1st: *Won't You Be My Neighbor? The Story of Fred Rogers, a Television Program, and a Message to Millions*, Plano East Senior HS
	2nd: *Space Communication: Mission Control and the Apollo Program*, Gentry JH (Baytown)	2nd: *Bletchley Park: Cracking the 'Enigma' Codes*, El Paso HS
Papers		
Individual	1st: *Unlocking the Enemy's Secrets: How Bletchley Park Used the Communication of the Axis Powers to Aid the Allies*, Hornedo MS (El Paso)	1st: *The Stab-in-the-Back Legend: How Conspiracy-laden Communication Destroyed the Weimar Republic*, Plano East Senior HS
	2nd: *Dorothea Lange: Lens on the Great Depression*, Richards School for Young Women Leaders (Austin)	2nd: *Rosie the Housewife: Propaganda for Women to Leave the Workforce after World War II*, Lorena HS

National History Day 2021

1st Place Senior Exhibits	3rd Place Junior Individual Website
The 1900 Storm, New Caney HS	*Selling Space: The Significance of Propaganda During the Space Race*, Dripping Springs MS

Visiting graduate student from the University of Texas at Austin, Albina Khasanova, loads a plant seedling into an EcoFAB as part of a program with the DOE Joint Genome Institute and Environmental Genomics and Systems Biology Division at Berkeley Lab on February 6, 2020. Photo by Thor Swift via US Department of Energy Joint Genome Institute/Flickr (CC).

Colleges and Universities

Sources: Texas Higher Education Coordinating Board; highered.texas.gov; Legislative Budget Board, "Summary of 2020–21 Conference Committee Report for HB1"

Enrollment in Texas public, independent, career, and private colleges and universities in fall 2019 totaled 1,575,721 students, an increase of 4,000 students, 0.3 percent, above the fall 2018 enrollment of 1,571,721.

Enrollment in fall 2019 in the 37 public universities was 657,985, a 0.04 percent decrease from 2018's enrollment of 658,219. Health-related institutions had enrollment in 2019 of 26,169, a 1.5 percent increase from fall 2018 (25,786) but a decrease of 4.3 percent from fall 2016 (27,353).

The state's public community colleges, Lamar State Colleges, and Texas State Technical College System, which offer two-year degree programs, reported fall 2019 enrollments totaling 762,083 students, an increase of 0.5 percent over enrollment of 758,133 reported in fall 2017.

Enrollments for fall 2019 at independent and career colleges and universities was 129,484 students, down slightly from the 129,583 students enrolled in fall 2018.

Brief History of Higher Education in Texas

The first permanent institutions of higher education established in Texas were church-supported schools, although there were some earlier efforts:

Rutersville University was established in 1840 by Methodist minister Martin Ruter in Fayette County and was the predecessor of Southwestern University in Georgetown, which was established in 1843;

Baylor University, now at Waco, was established in 1845 at Independence, Washington County, by the Texas Union Baptist Association; and

Austin College, now at Sherman, was founded in 1849 at Huntsville by the Brazos Presbytery of the Old School Presbyterian Church.

Other historic Texas schools of collegiate rank included:

Larissa College, 1848, at Larissa, Cherokee County; McKenzie College, 1841, Clarksville, Red River County; Chappell Hill Male and Female Institute, 1850, Chappell Hill, Washington County; Soule University, 1855, Chappell Hill; Johnson Institute, 1852, Driftwood, Hays County; Nacogdoches University, 1845, Nacogdoches; Salado College, 1859, Salado, Bell County.

Cost of Public Higher Education in Texas 2020		
	2-Year Schools (82)	4-Year Schools (37)
Average Tuition and Fees	$2,760	$9,502
Average Debt	$15,422	$25,374
% of Students with Debt	28.9%	57.7%

Add-Ran College, established in 1873 at Thorp Spring, Hood County, was the predecessor of present-day Texas Christian University, Fort Worth.

Texas A&M University and The University of Texas

The Agricultural and Mechanical College of Texas (now Texas A&M University), authorized by the Legislature in 1871, opened its doors in 1876 to become the first publicly supported institution of higher education in Texas.

In 1881, Texans established The University of Texas in Austin, with a medical branch in Galveston. The Austin institution opened Sept. 15, 1883, and the Galveston school opened in 1891.

First College for Women

In 1901, the 27th Legislature established the Girls Industrial College, which began classes at its campus in Denton in 1903. A campaign to establish a state industrial college for women was led by the State Grange and Patrons of Husbandry.

A bill was signed into law on April 6, 1901, creating the college. It was charged with a dual mission, which continues to guide the university today, to provide a liberal arts education and to prepare young women with a specialized education "for the practical industries of the age."

In 1905, the name of the college was changed to the College of Industrial Arts; in 1934, it was changed to Texas State College for Women.

Since 1957, the institution, which is now the largest university principally for women in the United States, has been the Texas Woman's University.

Historic, Primarily Black Colleges

A number of Texas schools were established primarily for blacks, although collegiate racial integration has long been the status quo. Title III of the Higher Education Act of 1965 established the term Historically Black College/University (HBCU), defined as a school of higher learning that was established and accredited before the 1964 Civil Rights Act and was dedicated to educating African Americans.

Today there are ten HBCUs in Texas: state-supported Prairie View A&M University (originally established as Alta Vista Agricultural College in 1876) Prairie View; and Texas Southern University, Houston; privately supported Huston-Tillotson University, Austin; Jarvis Christian College, Hawkins; Wiley College, Marshall; Paul Quinn College, originally located in Waco, now in Dallas; and Texas College, Tyler.

Predominantly black colleges that are important in the history of higher education in Texas, but which have ceased operations, include Bishop College, established in Marshall in 1881, then moved to Dallas; Mary Allen College, established in Crockett in 1886; and Butler

---

Top 5 Undergrad Majors at Public Universities, 2019

1. Business, Management, Marketing, and Related Support Services (20,620 students)
2. Health Professions and Related Programs (11,559 students)
3. Multi/Interdisciplinary Studies (11,159 students)
4. Engineering (9,195 students)
5. Biological and Biomedical Sciences (7,073 students)

Source: Texas Public Higher Education Almanac 2020

College, originally named the Texas Baptist Academy, in 1905 in Tyler.

Hispanic-Serving Institutions

Title V of the Higher Education Act of 2008 established grant programs for public colleges that qualify as Hispanic-Serving Institutions (HSIs). An HSI is defined as a not-for-profit institution of higher learning with a full-time equivalent undergraduate student enrollment that is at least 25 percent Hispanic.

According to the Hispanic Association of Colleges & Universities, Texas has 100 HSIs, including many community colleges, operating today.

State Appropriations

The general revenue funds for higher education totaled $16.2 billion for FY22–23, an increase of 2.2 percent over the FY20–21 funding level. This amount represents about 14.0 percent of the total general revenue budget. Rates for all of the higher education formulas were increased over the FY22-23 rates.

The general revenue funds increase includes:

- $8.6 billion, a $486 million increase to the current biennium, to fund a number of higher education institutions, including $4.1 billion to General Academic Institutions, Lamar State Colleges and Texas State Technical Colleges; $2.6 billion to Health Related Institutions; and $1.8 billion to Community Colleges, with a continued focus on performance-based funding.

- $199 million for graduate medical education to maintain a 1.1 to 1.0 ratio for residency slots, and $118.5 million for the Texas Child Mental Health Care Consortium.

- $1.25 billion for financial aid programs, including $866 million for TEXAS Grants program; $178.6 million for Tuition Equalization Grants program; $88.5 million for Texas Educational Opportunity Grants (TEOG) Public Community Colleges; $7.5 million for TEOG State and Technical Colleges; and $110 million for Student Financial Aid to be allocated to TEXAS Grants, Tuition Equalization Grants, TEOG Public Community Colleges and TEOG Public State and Technical Colleges. ☆

Universities and Colleges

Sources: Texas Higher Education Coordinating Board (highered.texas.gov) and txhighereddata.org and individual institutions. Dates of establishment may differ from Brief History on page 595 because schools use the date when authorization was given rather than date of first classes.

Name of Institution, Location; (*type or ownership, if private sectarian institution); date of founding; president (unless otherwise noted)	Number of Faculty, 2019	Enrollment Fall Term, 2019	Enrollment Fall Term, 2020§	% Change
Abilene Christian University, Abilene; (3–Church of Christ); 1906 (as Childers Classical Institute; as Abilene Christian College, 1914; as university, 1976); Dr. Phil Schubert.	—	4,854	4,853	-0.02
ALAMO COLLEGES (9), Dr. Mike Flores, chancellor. 1978 (as San Antonio Community College District; 1982, as Alamo Community College District; current name, 2009). System consists of following colleges and presidents:	2,145	67,774	67,155	-0.91
Northeast Lakeview College, San Antonio; (7); 2007; Dr. Veronica Garcia.	197	6,540	6,551	0.17
Northwest Vista College, San Antonio; (7); 1995; Dr. Ric Baser.	544	18,010	18,186	0.98
Palo Alto College, San Antonio; (7); 1983; Dr. Robert Garza.	269	10,763	10,950	1.74
San Antonio College, San Antonio; (7); 1925; Dr. Robert Vela.	688	19,499	18,847	-3.34
St. Philip's College, San Antonio; (7); 1898; Dr. Adena Williams Loston.	447	12,962	12,621	-2.63
Alvin Community College, Alvin; (7); 1949; Dr. Christal Albrecht.	323	5,985	5,609	-6.28
Amarillo College, Amarillo; (7); 1929; Dr. Russell Lowery-Hart.	402	9,766	8,893	-8.94
Amberton University, Garland; (3); 1971 (as Amber University; current name, 2001); Dr. Melinda H. Reagan.	—	1,074	1,102	2.61
Angelina College, Lufkin; (7); 1968; Dr. Michael J. Simon.	265	4,564	4,067	-10.89
Angelo State University, San Angelo; Dr. Steven O'Day.	See **Texas Tech University**			
Arlington Baptist University, Arlington; (3–Baptist); 1939 (as Bible Baptist Seminary; 1965 as Arlington Baptist College; name changed to current in 2017); Dr. D. L. Moody.	—	—	—	—
Austin College, Sherman; (3–Presbyterian USA); 1849; Dr. Steven P. O'Day.	—	1,314	1,302	-0.91
Austin Community College, Austin; (7); 1972; Dr. Richard M. Rhodes.	1,886	38,730	36,898	-4.73
Baylor College of Medicine, Houston; (5); 1903 (in Dallas; moved to Houston, 1943; Baptist until 1969); Dr. Paul Klotman, M.D.	—	1,580	1,592	0.76
Baylor University, Waco; (3–Southern Baptist); 1845 (in Independence; merged with Waco University and moved to Waco, 1887); Dr. Linda A. Livingstone.	—	18,033	19,297	7.01
Blinn College, Brenham; (7); 1883 (as academy; jr. college, 1927); Dr. Mary Hensley Ed. D, chancellor.	665	19,183	17,906	-6.66
Brazosport College, Lake Jackson; (7); 1967; Dr. Millicent M. Valek.	180	4,212	3,911	-7.15
Brookhaven College, Farmers Branch	See **Dallas County Community College District**			
Cedar Valley College, Lancaster	See **Dallas County Community College District**			
Central Texas College, Killeen; (7); 1965; Dr. Jim Yeonopolus, chancellor.	582	9,492	8,091	-14.76
Cisco College, Cisco; (7); 1909 (as Cisco Junior College, a private institution; became state school in 1939; name changed to current in 2009); Dr. Thad J. Anglin, Chancellor.	179	3,539	3,226	-8.84
Clarendon College, Clarendon; (7); 1898 (as church school; became state school in 1927); Mr. Texas D. Buckhaults, Interim President.	74	1,579	1,433	-9.25
Coastal Bend College, Beeville; (7); (1966 as Bee County College, name changed in 1999); Dr. Justin Hoggard, President.	183	4,818	4,108	-14.74
College of the Mainland, Texas City; (7); 1967; Dr. Warren Nichols.	263	4,687	4,351	-7.17
Collin College, McKinney; (7); 1985 (as Collin County Community College); Dr. H. Neil Matkin, district president.	1,408	34,328	35,537	3.52
Concordia University Texas, Austin; (3–Lutheran Church–Missouri Synod); 1926 (as Concordia Lutheran College; current name, 1995); part of Concordia University System. Dr. Donald Christian.	—	2,511	2,253	-10.27
Criswell College, Dr. Barry Creamer, President.	—	—	—	—
Dallas Baptist University, Dallas; (3–Baptist); 1898 (as Decatur Baptist College; moved to Dallas, name changed to Dallas Baptist College, 1965; became university, 1985); Dr. Adam C. Wright, president.	—	4,487	4,247	-5.35
Dallas Christian College, Dallas; (3–Christian); 1950; Dr. Brian D. Smith.	—	—	—	—
DALLAS COUNTY COMMUNITY COLLEGE DISTRICT (9), Dr. Joe May, chancellor. System consists of following colleges and presidents:	2,618	82,246	69,210	-15.85
Brookhaven College, Farmers Branch; (7); 1978; Dr. Linda Braddy, president.	609	11,069	10,205	-7.81
Cedar Valley College, Lancaster; (7); 1977; Dr. Joseph Seabrooks.	285	7,646	5,943	-22.27
Eastfield College, Mesquite; (7); 1970; Dr. Eddie Tealer.	546	14,396	12,377	-14.02
El Centro College, Dallas; (7); 1966; Dr. Bradford Williams, president.	128	10,849	10,214	-5.85
Mountain View College, Dallas; (7); 1970; Dr. Beatriz Joseph, vice chancellor.	190	11,274	7,844	-30.42

*Type: (1) Public University System
(2) Public University
(3) Independent Senior College or University
(4) Public Medical School or Health Science Center
(5) Independent Medical, Dental or Chiropractic School

(6) Public Technical College System
(7) Public Community College
(8) Independent Junior College
(9) Public Community College System
(10) Public Lower-Level Institution

§ Preliminary numbers.

Name of Institution, Location; (*type or ownership, if private sectarian institution); date of founding; president (unless otherwise noted)	Number of Faculty, 2019	Enrollment		
		Fall Term, 2019	Fall Term, 2020§	% Change
North Lake College, Irving; (7); 1977; Dr. Christa Slejko, president.	325	9,598	8,587	-10.53
Richland College, Dallas; (7); 1972; Dr. Kathryn K. Eggleston, president.	597	17,414	14,040	-19.38
Del Mar College, Corpus Christi; (7); 1935; Dr. Mark Escamilla.	517	12,008	10,579	-11.90
Eastfield College, Mesquite	See **Dallas County Community College District**			
East Texas Baptist University, Marshall; (3–Baptist); 1913 (as College of Marshall; as East Texas Baptist College, 1944; as university, 1984); Dr. J. Blair Blackburn.	—	1,656	1,714	3.50
El Centro College, Dallas	See **Dallas County Community College District**			
El Paso Community College, El Paso; (7); 1969; five campuses: Mission del Paso, Northwest, Rio Grande, Transmountain, and Valle Verde; Dr. William Serrata.	1,234	28,124	25,357	-9.84
Frank Phillips College, Borger; (7); 1948; includes campus in Perryton; Dr. Jud Hicks.	89	1,492	1,558	4.42
Galveston College, Galveston; (7); 1967; Dr. W. Myles Shelton.	96	2,306	2,149	-6.81
Grayson College, Denison; (7); 1963; Dr. Jeremy McMillen.	202	4,473	4,012	-10.31
Hardin-Simmons University, Abilene; (3–Southern Baptist); 1891 (as Simmons College; as Simmons University, 1925; current name, 1934); Eric I. Bruntmyer.	—	2,324	2,128	-8.43
Hill College, Hillsboro; (7); 1923 (as Hillsboro Junior College; name changed to current, 1962); Dr. Pamela Boehm.	203	4,537	4,068	-10.34
Houston Baptist University, Houston; (3–Baptist); 1960; Dr. Robert B. Sloan Jr.	—	3,741	3,963	5.93
HOUSTON COMMUNITY COLLEGE (9), Cesar Maldonado, chancellor. Houston; 1971. System consists of following colleges and presidents:	2,296	47,697	37,676	-21.01
Central College, Houston; (7); Dr. Muddassir Siddiqi.	—	—	—	—
Coleman College for Health Sciences, Houston; (7); 2004; Dr. Phil Nicotera.	—	—	—	—
Northeast College, Houston; (7); Dr. Destry Dokes (interim).	—	—	—	—
Northwest College, Houston; (7); Dr. Zachary R. Hodges.	—	—	—	—
Southeast College, Houston; (7); Dr. Melissa Gonzalez.	—	—	—	—
Southwest College, Houston; (7); Dr. Madeline Burillo-Hopkins.	—	—	—	—
Online College, (7); Dr. Margaret Ford Fisher	—	—	—	—
Howard County Junior College District (9), Dr. Cheryl T. Sparks, president. Big Spring, 1945. System consists of the following:	157	47,697	37,676	-21.01
Howard College, Big Spring; (7); 1945; (also has campuses in Lamesa and San Angelo).	140	4,303	3,728	-13.36
Southwest Collegiate Institute for the Deaf, Big Spring; (7)	17	79	48	-39.24
Howard Payne University, Brownwood; (3–Baptist); 1889; Dr. Cory Hines.	—	1,031	468	-54.61
Huston-Tillotson University, Austin; (3–United Church of Christ and United Methodist); 1952 (as Huston-Tillotson College, the merger of Tillotson College, 1875, and Samuel Huston College, 1876; current name, 2005); Dr. Colette Pierce Burnette.	—	1,121	1,070	-4.55
Jacksonville College, Jacksonville; (8–Missionary Baptist); 1899; Dr. William Michael Smith.	—	511	524	2.54
Jarvis Christian College, Hawkins; (3); 1912; Dr. Lester Newman.	—	829	637	-23.16
Kilgore College, Kilgore; (7); 1935; Dr. Brenda Kays.	256	5,305	4,954	-6.62
Kingwood College, Kingwood	See **Lone Star College System**			
Lamar University and all branches	See **Texas State University System**			
Laredo Community College, Laredo; (7); 1946; Dr. Ricardo J. Solis.	264	10,165	5,243	-48.42
Lee College, Baytown; (7); 1934; Dr. Dennis Brown.	388	7,516	4,258	-43.35
LeTourneau University, Longview; (3); 1946 (as LeTourneau Technical Institute; became 4-yr. college, 1961); Dr. Dale A. Lunsford.	—	2,932	3,125	6.58
LONE STAR COLLEGE SYSTEM (9), Dr. Stephen C. Head., chancellor. 1973; formerly North Harris Montgomery Community College District. System consists of following colleges and presidents:	3,496	78,452	70,738	-9.83
Lone Star College–Cy-Fair, Houston; (7); 2003; Dr. Seelpa Keshvala.	897	20,946	20,568	-1.80
Lone Star College–Houston North, The Woodlands; (7); Dr. Stephen C. Head, chancellor	—	2,524	1,878	-25.59
Lone Star College–Kingwood, Humble; (7); 1984; Dr. Katherine Persson.	513	10,981	10,383	-5.45
Lone Star College–Montgomery, Conroe; (7); 1995; Dr. Rebecca L. Riley.	597	13,445	13,287	-1.18
Lone Star College–North Harris, Houston; (7); 1973; Dr. Gerald F. Napoles.	651	12,054	10,121	-16.04
Lone Star College–Tomball, Tomball; (7); 1986; Dr. Lee Ann Nutt.	343	7,146	5,768	-19.28
Lone Star College–University Park, Houston; (7); 2012; Shah Ardalan.	495	11,356	8,733	-23.10
Lubbock Christian University, Lubbock; (3–Church of Christ); 1957; Dr. L. Timothy Perrin.	—	1,755	1,664	-5.19
McLennan Community College, Waco; (7); 1965; Dr. Johnette McKown.	422	8,705	7,743	-11.05
McMurry University, Abilene; (3–Methodist); 1923; Dr. Sandra S. Harper.	—	1,175	1,094	-6.89
Midland College, Midland; (7); 1972; Dr. Steve Thomas.	255	5,115	5,006	-2.13
Midwestern State University, Wichita Falls; (2); 1922; Dr. Suzane Shipley.	340	5,500	5,860	6.55
Montgomery College, Conroe	See **Lone Star College System**			

*Type: (1) Public University System
(2) Public University
(3) Independent Senior College or University
(4) Public Medical School or Health Science Center
(5) Independent Medical, Dental or Chiropractic School
(6) Public Technical College System
(7) Public Community College
(8) Independent Junior College
(9) Public Community College System
(10) Public Lower-Level Institution

§ Preliminary numbers.

Name of Institution, Location; (*type or ownership, if private sectarian institution); date of founding; president (unless otherwise noted)	Number of Faculty, 2019	Enrollment		
		Fall Term, 2019	Fall Term, 2020§	% Change
Mountain View College, Dallas	See Dallas County Community College District			
Navarro College, Corsicana; (7); 1946; four campuses: Corsicana, Mexia, Midlothian and Waxahachie; Dr. Kevin G. Fegan.	417	8,036	7,154	-10.98
North Central Texas College, Gainesville; (7); 1924 (as Gainesville Jr. College; Cooke County College, 1960; present name, 1994); five campuses: Bowie, Corinth, Flower Mound, Gainesville, and Graham. Dr. Brent Wallace, chancellor.	445	9,382	8,197	-12.63
Northeast Lakeview College, San Antonio	See Alamo Colleges			
Northeast Texas Community College, Mount Pleasant; (7); 1984; Dr. Ron Clinton.	163	2,988	2,854	-4.48
North Harris College, Houston	See Lone Star College System			
North Lake College, Irving	See Dallas County Community College District			
Northwest Vista College, San Antonio	See Alamo Colleges			
Odessa College, Odessa; (7); 1946; Dr. Gregory Williams.	261	6,806	6,383	-6.22
Our Lady of the Lake University of San Antonio, San Antonio; (3–Roman Catholic); 1895 (as school for girls; as senior college, 1911; as university, 1975); two campuses: San Antonio and Houston; Dr. Diane E. Melby.	—	2,974	2,797	-5.95
Palo Alto College, San Antonio	See Alamo Colleges			
Panola College, Carthage; (7); 1947 (as Panola Junior College; name changed, 1988); Dr. Gregory S. Powell.	141	2,611	2,531	-3.06
Paris Junior College, Paris; (7); 1924; Dr. Pamela Anglin.	178	4,858	4,385	-9.74
Parker University, Dallas; (5); 1982 as Parker College of Chiropractic; name changed to present in 2011. Dr. William E. Morgan.	—	1,717	1,557	-9.32
Paul Quinn College, Dallas; (3–African Methodist Episcopal Church); 1872 (in Waco; moved to Dallas, 1990); Dr. Michael J. Sorrell.	—	554	468	-15.52
Prairie View A&M University, Prairie View	See Texas A&M University System			
Ranger College, Ranger; (7); 1926; Dr. William J. Campion.	135	2,342	2,302	-1.71
Rice University, Houston; (3); chartered, 1891; opened, 1912 (as Rice Institute; as William Marsh Rice University, 1960); Dr. David W. Leebron.	—	7,231	7,437	2.85
Richland College, Dallas	See Dallas County Community College District			
St. Edward's University, Austin; (3–Catholic); 1885; Dr. Montserrat Fuentes.	—	3,976	3,591	-9.68
St. Mary's University of San Antonio, San Antonio; (3–Roman Catholic); 1852; Dr. Thomas J. Mengler, J.D.	—	3,485	3,458	-0.77
St. Philip's College, San Antonio	See Alamo Colleges			
Sam Houston State University, Huntsville	See Texas State University System			
San Antonio College, San Antonio	See Alamo Colleges			
SAN JACINTO COLLEGE DISTRICT (9), Dr. Brenda Lang Hellyer, chancellor. San Jacinto consolidated its campuses in 2020. System consists of following colleges and provosts	1,296	32,452	30,840	-4.97
Central, Pasadena; (7); Dr. Van Wigginton.	523	15,302	15,015	-1.88
North, Houston; (7); Dr. William Raffetto.	351	10,043	10,963	9.16
South, Houston; (7); Dr. Brenda Jones.	422	12,550	13,519	7.72
Schreiner University, Kerrville; (3–Presbyterian); 1923; Dr. Charlie McCormick.	—	1,342	1,244	-7.30
Southern Methodist University, Dallas; (3–Methodist); 1911; Dr. R. Gerald Turner.	—	11,824	12,373	4.64
South Plains College, Levelland; (7); 1957; Dr. Robin Satterwhite.	369	9,179	8,799	-4.14
South Texas College, McAllen; (7); NA; Dr. Shirley A. Reed.	1,119	32,478	28,502	-12.24
South Texas College of Law, Houston; (3); 1923; Michael F. Barry.	—	977	1,003	2.66
Southwest Collegiate Institute for the Deaf, Big Spring	See Howard County Junior College District			
Southwest Texas Junior College, Uvalde; (7); 1946; Dr. Hector Gonzales.	219	6,911	6,514	-5.74
Southwest Texas State University, San Marcos	See Texas State University System			
Southwestern Adventist University, Keene; (3–Seventh-Day Adventist); 1893 (as Keene Industrial Academy; as Southwestern Junior College, 1916; as Southwestern Union College, 1963; as Southwestern Adventist College,1980; as university, 1996); Dr. Ken Shaw.	—	687	772	12.37
Southwestern Assemblies of God University, Waxahachie; (3–Assemblies of God); 1927 (in Enid, Okla., as Southwestern Bible School; moved to Fort Worth and merged with South Central Bible Institute, 1941; moved to Waxahachie as Southwestern Bible Institute, 1943; as Southwestern Assemblies of God College,1963; as university, 1996); Dr. Kermit S. Bridges.	—	2,061	1,985	-3.69
Southwestern Christian College, Terrell; (3–Church of Christ); 1948 (as Southern Bible Institute in Fort Worth; moved to Terrell and changed name, 1950); Dr. Ervin D. Seamster, Jr.	—	110	80	-27.27

*Type: (1) Public University System
(2) Public University
(3) Independent Senior College or University
(4) Public Medical School or Health Science Center
(5) Independent Medical, Dental or Chiropractic School

(6) Public Technical College System
(7) Public Community College
(8) Independent Junior College
(9) Public Community College System
(10) Public Lower-Level Institution

§ Preliminary numbers.

Name of Institution, Location; (*type or ownership, if private sectarian institution); date of founding; president (unless otherwise noted)	Number of Faculty, 2019	Enrollment		% Change
		Fall Term, 2019	Fall Term, 2020§	
Southwestern University, Georgetown; (3–United Methodist); 1840 (merger of Rutersville College, 1840; McKenzie College, 1841; Wesleyan College, 1846; and Soule University, 1855; first named Texas University; current name, 1875); Dr. Edward B. Burger.	—	1,502	1,506	0.27
Stephen F. Austin State University, Nacogdoches; (2); 1921; Dr. Scott Gordon.	709	12,862	12,620	-1.88
Sul Ross State University, Alpine (See **Texas State University System**)	134	1,644	1,559	-5.17
Sul Ross State University–Rio Grande College, Uvalde (See **Texas State University System**)	43	821	916	11.57
Tarleton State University, Stephenville	See **Texas A&M University System**			
TARRANT COUNTY COLLEGE DISTRICT (9), Eugene V. Giovannini, chancellor. Fort Worth; 1965 (as Tarrant County Junior College; name changed, 1999). System consists of following colleges and presidents:	2,440	54,378	57,856	6.40
Northeast Campus, Hurst; (7); Dr. Tahita Fulkerson (interim).	504	11,800	12,249	3.81
Northwest Campus, Fort Worth; (7); Dr. Zarina Blankenbaker.	355	7,838	9,066	15.67
South Campus, Fort Worth, (7); Dr. Peter Jordan.	387	7,555	8,081	6.96
Southeast Campus, Arlington, (7); Dr. William Coppola.	409	10,972	11,345	3.40
Trinity River Campus, Fort Worth, (7); Dr. S. Sean Madison.	380	6,236	6,780	8.72
Connect Campus, (7); Carlos Morales.	405	9,977	10,335	3.59
Temple College, Temple; (7); 1926; Dr. Christy Ponce.	230	4,887	4,929	0.86
Texarkana College, Texarkana; (7); 1927; Dr. Jason Smith.	213	4,087	3,838	-6.09
TEXAS A&M UNIVERSITY SYSTEM (1), Dr. John Sharp, chancellor. System consists of following colleges and presidents:	6,706	147,758	150,341	1.75
Texas A&M University, College Station; (2); 1876 (as Agricultural and Mechanical of Texas; current name,1963); includes College of Veterinary Medicine and College of Medicine at College Station; Dr. M. Katherine Banks.	2,518	63,859	65,370	2.37
Texas A&M University at Galveston, Galveston; (2); 1962 (as Texas Maritime Academy; as 4-yr. Moody College of Marine Sciences and Maritime Resources, 1971); Col. Michael E. Fossum USAFR (Ret.), COO.	138	1,644	1,660	0.97
Prairie View A&M University, Prairie View; (2); 1876 (as Alta Vista Agricultural College; as Prairie View State Normal Institute, 1879; as Prairie View Normal and Industrial College; as Prairie View A&M College, 1947, as branch of Texas A&M University System; current name, 1973); Dr. Ruth Simmons	454	8,940	9,449	5.69
Tarleton State University, Stephenville; (2); 1899 (as John Tarleton College; as state-run John Tarleton Agricultural College,1917; as Tarleton State College, 1949; current name, 1973); includes campus in Killeen; Dr. F. Dominic Dottavio.	750	13,177	14,033	6.50
Texas A&M International University, Laredo; (2); 1970 (as Laredo State University; current name, 1993); Dr. Pablo Arenaz.	343	8,305	8,464	1.91
Texas A&M University–Corpus Christi, Corpus Christi; (2); 1973 (as upper-level Corpus Christi State University; current name, 1993; 4-year in 1994); Kelly M. Quintanilla.	420	11,452	10,820	-5.52
Texas A&M University–Kingsville, Kingsville; (2); 1925 (as South Texas Teachers College; as Texas College of Arts and Industries, 1929; as Texas A&I University, 1967; joined University of South Texas System, 1977; joined Texas A&M University System, 1993); Dr. Mark Hussey.	478	7,479	6,917	-7.51
West Texas A&M University, Canyon; (2); 1910 (as West Texas State Normal College; as West Texas State Teachers College, 1923; as West Texas State College, 1949; as West Texas State Univ., 1963; current name, 1993); Dr.Walter Wendler.	430	9,970	10,103	1.33
Texas A&M University–Commerce, Commerce; (2); 1889 (as East Texas Normal College; as East Texas State Teachers College, 1923; as East Texas State College, 1957; university status conferred and named changed to East Texas State University, 1965; transferred to Texas A&M System, 1995); includes ETSU Metroplex Commuter Facility, Mesquite; Dr. Mark J. Rudin.	570	11,725	12,245	4.43
Texas A&M University–Texarkana, Texarkana; (2); 1971 (as East Texas State University at Texarkana; transferred to Texas A&M System and name changed, 1996); Dr. Emily Fourmy Cutrer.	141	2,053	2,153	4.87
Texas A&M University–Central Texas, Killeen; (2); Dr. Marc A. Nigliazzo.	163	2,440	2,341	-4.06
Texas A&M University–San Antonio, San Antonio; (2); Dr. Cynthia Teniente-Matson.	301	6,714	6,786	1.07
Texas A&M University Health Science Center, (4); Includes Baylor College of Dentistry, College of Medicine, Graduate School of Biomedical Sciences, Institute of Biosciences and Technology, School of Rural Public Health, and HSC satellite locations; Dr. Carrie L. Byington, M.D., Vice Chancellor for Health Services.	—	2,887	3,064	6.13
Texas Christian University, Fort Worth; (3–Disciples of Christ); 1873 (as AddRan Male and Female College at Thorp Spring; moved to Waco, 1895; as AddRan Christian University, 1889; current name,1902; moved to Fort Worth, 1910); Dr. Victor J. Boschini Jr., chancellor.	—	10,979	11,328	3.18
Texas Chiropractic College, Pasadena; (5); 1908; Dr. Stephen A Foster.	—	269	255	-5.20
Texas College, Tyler; (3–C.M.E.); 1894; Dr. Dwight J. Fennell.	—	940	765	-18.62
Texas College of Osteopathic Medicine, Fort Worth	See **University of North Texas Health Science Center at Fort Worth**			

*Type: (1) Public University System
(2) Public University
(3) Independent Senior College or University
(4) Public Medical School or Health Science Center
(5) Independent Medical, Dental or Chiropractic School

(6) Public Technical College System
(7) Public Community College
(8) Independent Junior College
(9) Public Community College System
(10) Public Lower-Level Institution

§ Preliminary numbers.

Name of Institution, Location; (*type or ownership, if private sectarian institution); date of founding; president (unless otherwise noted)	Number of Faculty, 2019	Enrollment		
		Fall Term, 2019	Fall Term, 2020§	% Change
Texas Lutheran University, Seguin; (3–Evangelical Lutheran); 1891 (as Evangelical Lutheran College in Brenham; as Lutheran College of Seguin, 1912; as Texas Lutheran College,1932; as university, 1996); Dr. Debbie Cottrell.	—	1,474	1,446	-1.90
Texas Southern University, Houston; (2); 1926 (as Houston Colored Junior College; as 4-yr. Houston College for Negroes, mid-1930s; as Texas State University for Negroes, 1947; present name, 1951); Dr. Lesia L. Crumpton-Young.	588	9,034	7,016	-22.34
Texas Southmost College, Brownsville; (7); 1926 (as The Junior College of the Lower Rio Grande Valley; 1931 as Brownsville Junior College; current name, 1949); Dr. Jesús Roberto Rodriguez.	248	8,628	8,780	1.76
TEXAS STATE TECHNICAL COLLEGE SYSTEM (6), Dr. Michael L. Reeser, chancellor. System consists of following colleges and provosts:	632	11,694	15,054	28.73
Texas State Technical College–Harlingen, Harlingen; (7) 1967; Cledia Hernandez.	187	4,297	5,356	24.65
Texas State Technical College–Marshall, Marshall; (7) 1991 (as extension center; as independent college, 1999); Barton Day.	41	628	1,057	68.31
Texas State Technical College–Waco, Waco; (7) 1965 (as James Connally Technical Institute; current name, 1969); Dr. Adam Hutchinson.	240	3,977	4,923	23.79
Texas State Technical College–West Texas, Abilene, Breckenridge, Brownwood and Sweetwater; (7) 1970; Rick Denbow.	111	1,963	2,454	25.01
Texas State Technical College–North Texas, Red Oak; (7) 2014; Marcus Balch	22	248	476	91.94
Texas State Technical College–Fort Bend, Rosenberg; (7) 2016; Randall Wooten	31	581	788	35.63
TEXAS STATE UNIVERSITY SYSTEM (1), Dr. Brian McCall, chancellor. System consists of following colleges and presidents:	3,886	85,942	87,468	1.78
Lamar University, Beaumont; (2); 1923 (as South Park Junior College; as Lamar College, 1932; as Lamar State College of Technology, 1951; present name, 1971; transferred from Lamar University System, 1995); Dr. Kenneth Evans.	543	14,811	15,845	6.98
Lamar State College–Orange, Orange; (10); 1969 (transferred from Lamar University System, 1995; current name, 2000); Dr. Thomas Johnson.	112	2,395	2,382	-0.54
Lamar State College–Port Arthur, Port Arthur; (10); 1909 (as Port Arthur College; joined Lamar University System, 1975; joined TSU System, 1995; current name, 2000); Dr. Betty J. Reynard.	123	2,710	2,687	-0.85
Lamar Institute of Technology, Beaumont; (10); (joined TSU System, 1995); Dr. Lonnie L. Howard.	183	4,011	4,576	14.09
Sam Houston State University, Huntsville; (2); 1879; Dr. Dana G. Hoyt.	979	21,363	21,654	1.36
Sul Ross State University, Alpine; (2); 1917 (as Sul Ross State Normal College; as Sul Ross State Teachers College, 1923; as Sul Ross State College, 1949; current name, 1969); Dr. William (Bill) Kibler.	119	1,644	1,559	-5.17
Sul Ross State University – Rio Grande College, Uvalde, Eagle Pass, Del Rio; (2); 1973 (current name, 1995); Dr. William (Bill) Kibler.	39	821	916	11.57
Texas State University, San Marcos; (2); 1903 (as Southwest Texas Normal School; as Southwest Texas State Normal College, 1918; as Southwest Texas State Teachers College, 1923; as Southwest Texas State College, 1959; as Southwest Texas State University, 1969; current name, 2003); Dr. Denise M. Trauth.	1,788	38,187	37,849	-0.89
TEXAS TECH UNIVERSITY SYSTEM (1), Tedd L. Mitchell M.D., chancellor. System consists of following colleges and presidents:	1,984	54,445	57,174	5.01
Angelo State University, San Angelo; (2); 1928 (was part of Texas State University System; joined Texas Tech system, 2007); Dr. Brian J. May.	420	10,289	10,722	4.21
Texas Tech University, Lubbock; (2); 1923 (as Texas Technological College; current name, 1969); Dr Lawrence Schovanec.	1,564	38,250	40,382	5.57
Texas Tech University Health Sciences Center, Lubbock; (4); 1972; Dr. Tedd L. Mitchell, M.D.	—	5,141	5,295	3.00
Texas Tech University Health Sciences Center, El Paso; (4); 2013; Dr. Richard Lange.	—	765	775	1.31
Texas Wesleyan University, Fort Worth; (3–United Methodist); 1891 (as college; current name, 1989); Dr. Frederick G. Slabach.	—	2,607	2,495	-4.30
Texas Woman's University, Denton; (2); 1901 (as College of Industrial Arts; as Texas State College for Women, 1934; current name, 1957); Carine M. Feyten, chancellor and president.	928	15,710	16,030	2.04
Tomball College, Tomball	See **Lone Star College System**			
Trinity University, San Antonio; (3–Presbyterian U.S.A.); 1869 (at Tehuacana; moved to Waxahachie, 1902; to San Antonio, 1942); Dr. Danny J. Anderson.	—	2,685	2,685	0.00
Trinity Valley Community College, Athens; (7); 1946 (as Henderson County Junior College); includes campus at Terrell; Dr. Jerry King.	266	6,432	5,662	-11.97
Tyler Junior College, Tyler; (7); 1926; Dr. L. Michael Metke, chancellor.	589	12,291	11,725	-4.60
University of Dallas, Irving; (3–Roman Catholic); 1956; Dr. John G. Plotts (interim).	—	2,481	2,489	0.32
UNIVERSITY OF HOUSTON SYSTEM (1), Dr. Renu Khator, chancellor. System consists of following colleges and presidents:	3,535	74,369	76,335	2.64
University of Houston, Houston; (2); 1927; Dr. Renu Khator.	2,092	46,148	47,066	1.99
University of Houston–Clear Lake, Houston; (2); 1974; Ira K. Blake.	514	9,082	9,060	-0.24
University of Houston–Downtown, Houston; (2); 1948 (as South Texas College; joined University of Houston System, 1974); Dr. Juan Sánchez Muñoz.	724	14,640	15,251	4.17

*Type: (1) Public University System
(2) Public University
(3) Independent Senior College or University
(4) Public Medical School or Health Science Center
(5) Independent Medical, Dental or Chiropractic School

(6) Public Technical College System
(7) Public Community College
(8) Independent Junior College
(9) Public Community College System
(10) Public Lower-Level Institution

§ Preliminary numbers.

Name of Institution, Location; (*type or ownership, if private sectarian institution); date of founding; president (unless otherwise noted)	Number of Faculty, 2019	Enrollment		
		Fall Term, 2019	Fall Term, 2020§	% Change
University of Houston–Victoria, Victoria; (2); 1973; Robert K. (Bob) Glenn.	205	4,499	4,958	10.20
University of the Incarnate Word, San Antonio; (3–Roman Catholic); 1881 (as Incarnate Word College; current name, 1996); Dr. Thomas M. Evans.	—	7,734	7,104	-8.15
University of Mary Hardin-Baylor, Belton; (3–Baptist); 1845; Dr. Randy O'Rear	—	3,846	3,876	0.78
UNIVERSITY OF NORTH TEXAS SYSTEM (1), Lesa B. Roe, chancellor. System consists of following colleges and presidents:	1,911	45,451	47,247	3.95
University of North Texas, Denton; (2); 1890 (as North Texas Normal College; as North Texas State Teachers College, 1923; as North Texas State College, 1949; as university, 1961; current name, 1988); Dr. Neal J. Smatresk.	1,682	39,192	40,727	3.92
University of North Texas at Dallas, Dallas; (2); (2000); Robert Mong.	229	4,040	4,190	3.71
University of North Texas Health Science Center at Fort Worth, Fort Worth; (4);1966 (as private college; part of North Texas State University, 1975; current name, 1993); Dr. Michael R. Williams.	—	2,219	2,330	5.00
University of St. Thomas, Houston; (3–Roman Catholic); 1947; Dr. Richard Ludwick.	—	3,438	3,693	7.42
THE UNIVERSITY OF TEXAS SYSTEM (1), James B. Milliken, chancellor. System consists of following colleges and presidents:	8,386	210,207	211,390	0.56
University of Texas at Austin, The, Austin; (2); 1883; Dr. Jay Hartzell.	2,798	50,894	50,287	-1.19
University of Texas at Arlington, The, Arlington; (2); 1895 (as Arlington College; as state-run Grubbs Vocational College, 1917; as North Texas Agricultural and Mechanical College, 1923; as Arlington State College, 1949; current name, 1967); Dr. Teile C. Lim (interim).	1,318	42,863	42,733	-0.30
University of Texas Rio Grande Valley, The, (2); 1973 (as branch of Pan American College; as University of Texas–Pan American at Brownsville, 1989; present name, 2015); Guy Bailey.	—	204	221	8.33
University of Texas at Dallas, The, Richardson; (2); 1961 (as Graduate Research of the Southwest; as Southwest Center for Advanced Studies, 1967; joined UT System with current name, 1969; full undergraduate program, 1975); Dr. Richard C. Benson.	1,229	29,543	28,669	-2.96
University of Texas at El Paso, The, El Paso; (2); 1913 (as Texas College of Mines and Metallurgy; as Texas Western College of UT, 1949; current name, 1967); Dr. Healther Wilson.	1,046	25,144	24,879	-1.05
University of Texas–Pan American, The, Edinburg. Merged with Brownsville campus in 2015 to form The University of Texas–Rio Grande Valley.				
University of Texas of the Permian Basin, The, Odessa; (2); 1969 (as 2-yr., upper-level institution; expanded to 4-yr., 1991); Dr. Sandra K. Woodley.	280	5,283	5,485	3.82
University of Texas at San Antonio, The, San Antonio; (2); 1969; Dr. Taylor Eighmy.	1,255	32,389	34,429	6.30
University of Texas at Tyler, The, Tyler; (2); 1971 (as Tyler State College; as Texas Eastern University, 1975; joined UT System, 1979); Dr. Michael V. Tidwell.	460	9,130	9,354	2.45
University of Texas Health Science Center at Houston, The, Houston; (4); 1972; includes Dental Branch (1905); Graduate School of Biomedical Sciences (1963); Medical School (1970); School of Allied Health Sciences (1973); School of Nursing (1972); School of Public Health (1967); Division of Continuing Education (1958); Dr. Giuseppe N. Colasurdo, M.D.	—	5,317	5,656	6.38
University of Texas Health Science Center at San Antonio, The, San Antonio; (4) 1968; includes Dental School (1970); Graduate School of Biomedical Sciences (1970); Health Science Center (1972); Medical School (1959 as South Texas Medical School of UT; present name, 1966); School of Allied Health Sciences (1976); School of Nursing (1969); Dr. William L. Henrich M.D.	—	3,383	3,464	2.39
University of Texas Health Science Center at Tyler, The, Tyler; (4); 1949 (as East Texas Tuberculosis Sanatorium; as East Texas Chest Hospital, 1971; joined UT system with current name, 1977); Dr. Kirk A. Calhoun M.D.	—	68	91	33.82
University of Texas M.D. Anderson Cancer Center, The, Houston; (4); 1941; Dr. Peter W.T. Pisters, M.D.	—	376	359	-4.52
University of Texas Medical Branch at Galveston, The, Galveston; (4) 1891; includes Graduate School of Biomedical Sciences (1952); Medical School (1891); School of Allied Health Sciences (1968); School of Nursing (1890); Vacant	—	3,314	3,464	4.53
University of Texas Southwestern Medical Center, The, Dallas; (4); 1943 (as private institution; as Southwestern Medical College of UT, 1948; as UT Southwestern Medical School at Dallas, 1967; joined UT Health Science Center at Dallas, 1972; includes Graduate School of Biomedical Sciences (1947); School of Allied Health Sciences (1968); Southwestern Medical School (1943); Dr. Daniel K. Podolsky M.D.	—	2,299	2,299	0.00
Vernon College, Vernon; (7); 1970; includes Wichita Falls campus; Dr. Dusty R. Johnston.	142	2,930	2,786	-4.91
Victoria College, Victoria; (7); 1925; Dr. David Hinds.	191	3,683	3,214	-12.73
Wayland Baptist University, Plainview; (3–Southern Baptist); 1910; Dr. Bobby Hall	—	2,948	2,539	-13.87
Weatherford College, Weatherford; (7); 1869 (as branch of Southwestern University; as denominational junior college, 1922; as municipal junior college, 1949); Dr. Tod Allen Farmer.	309	5,821	5,454	-6.30
Western Texas College, Snyder; (7); 1969; Dr. Barbara Beebe.	81	2,009	1,442	-28.22
Wharton County Junior College, Wharton; (7); 1946; Dr. Betty A. McCrohan.	289	6,904	6,097	-11.69
Wiley College, Marshall; (3–Methodist); 1873; Dr. Herman J. Felton, Jr.	—	715	615	-13.99

*Type: (1) Public University System
(2) Public University
(3) Independent Senior College or University
(4) Public Medical School or Health Science Center
(5) Independent Medical, Dental or Chiropractic School

(6) Public Technical College System
(7) Public Community College
(8) Independent Junior College
(9) Public Community College System
(10) Public Lower-Level Institution

§ Preliminary numbers.

Business

ECONOMY AND EMPLOYMENT

BANKING, INSURANCE, CONSTRUCTION

COMMERCIAL FISHING AND TOURISM

ELECTRIC GRIDS, OIL, GAS

MINERALS AND MEDIA

Many restaurants struggled to survive in 2020, but Campisi's "Egyptian" Restaurant is still serving pizza and spaghetti in Dallas. Photo by Lorie Shaull, CC 2/Flickr

COVID-19 Drains Texas Economy Through 2020

Source: Excerpted from the State of Texas Annual Cash Report 2020, Comptroller of Public Accounts.

Starting in August 2019, Texas nonfarm jobs stood at a total of 12,836,000. By August 2020, the Texas economy lost 616,600 nonfarm jobs, largely due to economic shocks from the COVID-19 pandemic and the recent fall in energy prices.

This decrease of 4.8 percent was the second-smallest percentage loss over this period among the ten most populous states (behind Georgia at 4.2 percent) and the sixteenth-smallest loss among all states.

Private-sector employment fell by 5.4 percent, while government employment (federal, state and local) fell by 1.4 percent.

Texas Industry Performance

Employment in the goods-producing industries decreased by 7.2 percent in fiscal 2020, while employment in the service-providing industries fell by 4.4 percent.

Employment decreased in all three of the goods-producing industries (mining and logging, manufacturing, and construction), led by a 24.6 percent fall in mining and logging. All but one of the service-providing industries also saw year-over-year declines in employment, with the largest percentage losses in the leisure and hospitality (17.7 percent) and information (6.3 percent) industries.

Financial activities was the only major industry in which employment increased over the year (by 0.4 percent, or 3,600 jobs).

Mining and Logging

Mining industry employment peaked in December 2014 at 321,900 and then declined steadily, reaching a low of 204,300 in September 2016. Industry employment then grew consistently for more than two years to reach 256,200 in January 2019. Since that time, mining employment has fallen by 27 percent.

From August 2019 to August 2020, mining employment decreased by 61,000, with most (49,600) of that loss occurring since March 2020. In addition to substantial exploration activities within the state and in the Gulf of Mexico, Texas is headquarters for many of the nation's largest oil and natural gas refining and distribution companies and has a large number of energy-related jobs in other industries.

As in the mining industry, employment in those industries and sectors has experienced significant declines over the year.

Consumer Spending

Consumer spending is a major component of the Texas economy. In fiscal 2016, for the first time since 2010, state sales tax collections fell (by 2.3 percent) from the previous year's total. The decline in state sales tax revenue was led by reduced collections from the oil- and natural gas-related exploration and production sectors, but collections from the manufacturing, retail trade, information, and real estate sectors also were down compared to 2015. Growth in sales tax collections resumed in 2017, with revenue up 2.3 percent over 2016. Sales tax revenue was up again in 2018, by 10.5 and by another 6.5 percent in 2019 to reach $34.0 billion.

Despite economic disruptions resulting from the COVID-19 virus, 2020 sales tax collections increased by a further 0.2 percent from 2019. State sales tax collections from all major sectors other than retail trade declined significantly from year ago levels, with the largest declines in the oil- and gas-related sectors.

However, collections from retail trade were up, as increased consumer spending on home improvements, home entertainment, distance learning and outdoor recreation in response to the COVID-19 pandemic spurred higher remittances from building materials, home furnishing, electronics and appliance, and sporting goods retailers.

Retail trade tax collections were also boosted by online out-of-state vendors and marketplace providers who did not have tax collection obligations a year ago. Tax remittances from the information sector were depressed, as federal law in July began prohibiting sales taxation of internet service.

The Consumer Confidence Index is a monthly measure of consumer optimism, an important factor affecting the sales of housing, automobiles and other major purchases. The index for the four-state West South Central (WSC) Region, which includes Texas, was down by 34 percent in fiscal 2020. The index for the nation as a whole was down 36 percent.

Gross Domestic Product in Current Dollars

	Millions of dollars			Percent of U.S. total			GDP* 2019	
	2018	2019	2020	2018	2019	2020	China	22,526,502
United States	20,611,861	21,433,226	20,936,558	100	100	100	United States	20,524,945
1. California	2,975,083	3,132,801	3,091,872	14.4	14.6	14.8	India	9,155,083
2. Texas	1,795,635	1,843,803	1,759,734	8.7	8.6	8.4	Japan	5,231,066
3. New York	1,705,010	1,772,261	1,699,045	8.3	8.3	8.1	Germany	4,482,448
4. Florida	1,050,298	1,106,500	1,095,888	5.1	5.2	5.2	Russia	3,968,180
5. Illinois	863,040	885,583	863,517	4.2	4.1	4.1	Indonesia	3,196,682
6. Pennsylvania	778,375	808,738	780,176	3.8	3.8	3.7	United Kingdom	3,118,396
7. Ohio	675,030	695,362	675,037	3.3	3.2	3.2	France	3,097,061
8. Georgia	602,024	625,714	619,240	2.9	2.9	3	Brazil	3,092,216
9. New Jersey	612,979	634,784	619,061	3	3	3	Italy	2,562,135
10. Washington	575,417	612,997	618,705	2.8	2.9	3	Mexico	2,525,481

Source: Bureau of Economic Analysis, U.S. Department of Commerce, 2020.

Estimated GDP in millions of U.S. dollars, from the World Factbook of the CIA.

Manufacturing

The Texas manufacturing industry lost 39,900 jobs over the past year, a decrease of 4.4 percent. Durable goods employment was down 32,800, with the largest losses in the fabricated metals (16,500) and machinery (10,200) manufacturing sectors. Both sectors are closely associated with oil and natural gas exploration and production, and employment in those sectors has been decreasing along with that in the mining industry.

Overall, durable goods employment decreased by 5.6 percent. Nondurable-goods manufacturing employment fell by 7,100 (2.2 percent). Total manufacturing employment in August 2020 was 869,100.

The value of Texas exports in 2014 was a record $289 billion, an increase of 3.3 percent from 2013. Those exports provided a substantial boost to manufacturing, notably for companies producing chemicals, computers and electronics, petroleum products, industrial machinery and transportation equipment. In 2015, the value of Texas exports fell sharply (to $251 billion, down 13.1 percent), hurt by falling oil prices and a stronger dollar. Texas exports continued to fall in 2016, down another 7.4 percent. However, Texas 2017 exports were up 13.5 percent from the 2016 level and increased by another 19.4 percent in 2018.

In November 2019, for the first time since October 2016, monthly Texas exports decreased on a year-over-year basis; total 2019 exports were still 4.8 percent higher than 2018 exports. However, exports have fallen sharply since March. For the period January 2020 to July 2020, the value of exports was 21.3 percent lower than that of the corresponding period of 2019.

Texas, however, remains the nation's leading exporting state, as it has been for more than a decade. Texas exports comprised 20 percent of total U.S. exports in 2019.

Construction

Construction employment decreased by 39,300 (5.0 percent) in fiscal 2020 to reach 739,800 in August 2020. Employment in the heavy and civil engineering construction sector decreased at the highest rate of any construction sector, falling by 7.9 percent (14,100).

Total housing construction activity in 2020 was up from 2019. Single-family building permits issued in the year ending in July 2020, at 130,862, were up 12.8 percent from the same period one year earlier. Building permits for multi-family units rose by 13.2 percent.

According to Multiple Listing Service data from the Texas A&M Real Estate Center, the median sales price for an existing Texas single-family home rose by 8.9 percent, from $246,000 in July 2019 to $268,000 in July 2020.

In July 2020, Texas had a 2.8-month inventory of existing homes for sale, the lowest level since at least 1990.

Professional and Business Services

Employment in the professional and business services industry fell by 23,000 jobs (1.3 percent) in fiscal 2020. Employment changes varied considerably among industry sectors, with the largest increases in accounting and bookkeeping services (6.3 percent) and architectural, engineering, and related services (4.8 percent).

The employment services sector, which includes temporary help agencies with many of its jobs in temporary and/or part-time positions, had both the largest absolute and percentage decreases in employment (28,600, 9.5 percent). Total professional and business services employment was 1,778,500 in August 2020.

Education and Health Services

The education and health services industry, composed of the educational services and health care and social assistance sectors, lost 70,200 jobs in fiscal 2020, a decrease of 4.0 percent. The relatively small educational services sector saw a decrease of 14,700 jobs (6.7 percent). Employment in the much larger health care and social assistance sector fell by 3.6 percent rate (55,500 jobs). In all, Texas education and health services employment fell to 1,675,100 in August 2020.

For more information

For a more detailed overview of population, income, jobs, wages and education trends of Texas' 12 economic regions, visit: https://comptroller.texas.gov/economy/economic-data/regions/

Financial Activities

In fiscal 2020, overall employment in the financial activities industry grew by 0.4 percent (3,600 jobs). The finance and insurance sector grew by 12,000 (2.1 percent) while the real estate and rental and leasing sector fell by 8,400 (3.7 percent). Credit intermediation (which includes financial institutions such as banks) is the industry's largest sector, employing 274,500 as of August 2020. Total Texas financial activities industry employment reached 809,700 in August 2020.

Trade, Transportation and Utilities

The trade, transportation and utilities industry, the state's largest employer with 20 percent of total nonfarm jobs in August 2020, lost 74,400 jobs (3.0 percent) over the year. Employment in all three industry sectors — retail trade, wholesale trade and transportation, warehousing and utilities — fell during fiscal 2020. Wholesale trade employment was down 6.8 percent (41,500), transportation, warehousing and utilities employment fell by 3,100 (0.5 percent), and employment in the retail trade sector decreased by 29,800 (2.3 percent). In all, the trade, transportation and utilities industry provided 2,438,400 Texas jobs in August 2020.

Information

The information industry is a collection of diverse sectors, representing established sectors of the economy (newspaper publishing, data processing, television broadcasting, and wired telephone services) as well as some newer sectors (cell phone service providers, Internet providers, and software). The publishing sector saw the largest percentage fall in employment over the year (7.0 percent, 2,700 jobs).

Total industry employment fell 6.3 percent (13,100) to reach 195,900 in August 2020.

Leisure and Hospitality

Employment in the leisure and hospitality industry decreased by 247,600 (17.7 percent) over the fiscal year. The majority of the industry's job losses occurred in the food services and drinking places sector, which lost 198,000 jobs (15.7 percent). The largest percentage loss was in the arts, entertainment, and recreation sector, which fell by 31.2 percent (49,400).

Total leisure and hospitality employment in August 2020 was 1,147,500, representing about 9 percent of total Texas employment.

Other Services

The other services industry is a varied mix of business activities including repair and maintenance services; laundry services; religious, political and civic organizations; funeral services; parking garages; beauty salons; and a wide range of personal services.

Personal and laundry services employment decreased by 15.3 percent, the highest rate among other service sectors. In all, other services industry employment fell by 23,100 to reach 423,600 in August 2020.

Government Employment

Government employment decreased by 1.4 percent (28,600) over the year. Federal government employment increased by 26,500, largely on the strength of temporary census hiring.

However, local government employment decreased by 31,100 and state government employment fell by 24,100. Total government employment in Texas was 1,954,000 in August 2020.

Texas Gross Domestic Product, 2011–2020, By Industry (in millions)

Industry	2011	2012	2013	2014	2015	2016	2017	2018	2019	2020
Agriculture, Forestry, Fishing/Hunting	$8,465	$8,218	$10,898	$10,403	$11,888	$8,709	$9,072	$10,898	$10,820	$12,460
% change*	(6.3)	(2.9)	32.6	(4.5)	14.3	(26.7)	4.2	20.1	20.5	15.2
Natural Resources and Mining	146,001	158,861	183,266	199,598	116,107	92,152	115,515	141,191	153,186	103,944
% change	19.6	8.8	15.4	8.9	(41.8)	(20.6)	25.4	22.2	-5.2	-32.1
Construction	56,842	63,588	68,103	75,385	81,424	85,386	87,540	95,486	100,869	100,421
% change	2.0	11.9	7.1	10.7	8.0	4.9	2.5	9.1	8.6	-0.4
Manufacturing	203,495	206,104	224,083	202,685	212,902	197,408	206,063	226,125	246,436	247,373
% change	15.3	1.3	8.7	(9.5)	5.0	(7.3)	4.4	9.7	3.7	0.4
Trade, Transportation, Utilities	244,618	266,982	275,782	289,279	306,115	307,889	322,390	345,636	353,621	347,552
% change	6.7	9.1	3.3	4.9	5.8	0.6	4.7	7.2	5.8	-1.7
Information	50,188	49,328	53,965	53,327	57,767	60,196	62,819	65,308	69,609	67,755
% change	0.2	(1.7)	9.4	(1.2)	8.3	4.2	4.4	4.0	5.5	-2.7
Financial Activities	178,923	192,555	202,323	221,251	234,397	249,593	254,810	265,853	293,873	292,945
% change	6.9	7.6	5.1	9.4	5.9	6.5	2.1	4.3	5.7	-0.3
Professional and Business Services	140,676	150,573	157,256	170,065	181,455	184,354	194,950	211,854	228,118	226,946
% change	6.8	7.0	4.4	8.1	6.7	1.6	5.7	8.7	7.4	-0.5
Educational and Health Services	89,109	92,472	95,613	99,694	107,190	112,839	117,308	121,979	129,974	127,535
% change	4.3	3.8	3.4	4.3	7.5	5.3	4.0	4.0	5.7	-1.9
Leisure and Hospitality Services	40,420	43,476	45,459	50,814	56,459	58,500	60,275	62,235	68,289	60,788
% change	3.8	7.6	4.6	11.8	11.1	3.6	3.0	3.3	5.3	-11
Other Private Services	25,735	27,658	28,889	31,213	32,584	32,924	33,911	35,700	38,083	37,539
% change	1.7	7.5	4.5	8.0	4.4	1.0	3.0	5.5	5.7	-1.4
Government and Schools	146,749	151,562	156,612	161,676	170,356	175,750	181,588	185,083	194,079	192,622
% change	0.6	3.3	3.3	3.2	5.4	3.2	3.3	5.5	3.9	-0.8
TOTAL	$1,331,221	$1,411,377	$1,502,249	$1,565,390	$1,568,644	$1,565,700	$1,646,211	$1,767,418	$1,886,957	1,817,880
% change	7.6	6.0	6.4	4.2	0.2	(0.2)	5.1	7.4	4.7	-3.7
TOTAL (in 2009 chained** dollars)	$1,343,791	$1,411,379	$1,472,104	$1,512,351	$1,590,409	$1,594,408	$1,615,822	$1,672,640	$1,788,527	1,729,047
% change	3.2	5.0	4.3	2.7	5.2	0.3	1.3	3.5	4.4	-3.3

*Percent change from the previous year. **In 1996, the U.S. Department of Commerce introduced the chained-dollar measure. The new measure is based on the average weights of goods and services in successive pairs of years. It is "chained" because the second year in each pair, with its weights, becomes the first year of the next pair. *Source: 2020 Comprehensive Annual Financial Report for the State of Texas.*

Per Capita Income by County, 2019

Below are listed data for 2019 for total personal income and per capita income by county. Total income is reported in millions of dollars. The middle column indicates the percent of change in total personal income from 2018 to 2019.

In the far right column is the county's rank in the state for per capita income. Midland County was first with $130,983. The lowest per capita income was in Hudspeth County at $23,569.

Source: Bureau of Economic Analysis, U.S. Department of Commerce, 2020.

Top Ten			Lowest Ten		
County	Major cities	PCI	County	Major cities	PCI
1. Midland	Midland	$130,983	245. Childress	Childress	$30,731
2. Shackelford	Albany	113,163	246. Frio	Pearsall	30,223
3. Sherman	Stratford	97,002	247. Cameron	Brownsville	29,928
4. Glasscock	Garden City	84,623	248. Walker	Huntsville	29,838
5. Kendall	Boerne	81,882	249. Bee	Beeville	29,792
6. Hartley	Dalhart, Channing	81,238	250. Zapata	Zapata	28,936
7. King	Guthrie	78,849	251. Starr	Rio Grande City	27,713
8. Eastland	Eastland, Cisco, Ranger	78,826	252. Willacy	Raymondville	27,584
9. Lipscomb	Lipscomb, Booker	77,810	253. Hidalgo	McAllen	27,415
10. Irion	Mertzon	72,177	254. Hudspeth	Fort Hancock	23,569

County	Total Income ($ mil)	% change 2018-19	Per capita income	Rank in State
United States	$18,542,262	3.9	$56,474	–
Metropolitan	16,588,018	4	58,650	–
Nonmetro	1,954,244	3.9	43,035	–
Texas	$1,531,346	4.6	$52,829	–
Metropolitan	1,399,196	4.7	54,064	–
Nonmetro	132,151	3.9	42,420	–
Anderson	2,080	4.4	36,027	223
Andrews	968	5.9	51,769	58
Angelina	3,438	1.8	39,644	189
Aransas	1,213	3.1	51,614	60
Archer	448	3.7	52,335	55
Armstrong	101	2.8	53,422	50
Atascosa	1,926	4.3	37,644	208
Austin	1,535	3.6	51,118	62
Bailey	313	2.2	44,665	117
Bandera	1,038	4.3	44,925	112
Bastrop	3,397	7	38,289	201
Baylor	164	3.6	46,615	86
Bee	970	4.1	29,792	249
Bell	15,939	5.1	43,919	134
Bexar	95,830	4	47,830	79
Blanco	654	5.6	54,814	43
Borden	40	-7.7	61,287	24
Bosque	792	3	42,366	147
Bowie	3,839	2.3	41,172	168
Brazoria	18,105	5	48,374	77
Brazos	9,478	4.6	41,348	164
Brewster	446	4.2	48,422	76
Briscoe	69	1.6	44,413	123
Brooks	259	4.2	36,558	219

County	Total Income ($ mil)	% change 2018-19	Per capita income	Rank in State
Brown	1,502	1.7	39,661	187
Burleson	848	4.2	45,970	97
Burnet	2,395	4.9	49,731	69
Caldwell	1,512	5.9	34,617	230
Calhoun	984	4.7	46,208	93
Callahan	585	4.5	41,962	157
Cameron	12,664	3.7	29,928	247
Camp	486	0.1	37,111	215
Carson	288	7.7	48,571	75
Cass	1,128	2.4	37,566	210
Castro	485	8	64,427	16
Chambers	2,482	7.4	56,610	37
Cherokee	1,855	1.9	35,245	228
Childress	225	2	30,731	245
Clay	464	4.7	44,295	128
Cochran	112	-0.8	39,333	194
Coke	141	3.4	41,669	160
Coleman	349	3	42,683	144
Collin	70,852	6.3	68,474	12
Collingsworth	123	6.5	42,026	155
Colorado	1,008	4.3	46,909	85
Comal	9,381	7.5	60,056	29
Comanche	590	6.7	43,242	137
Concho	97	8.1	35,758	224
Cooke	2,181	5.2	52,875	53
Coryell	2,702	4.8	35,570	226
Cottle	84	-1.6	60,260	28
Crane	245	5.9	51,025	63
Crockett	154	6	44,458	122
Crosby	216	2.6	37,580	209
Culberson	129	7.8	59,506	32
Dallam	472	7.9	64,756	15

County	Total Income ($ mil)	% change 2018-19	Per capita income	Rank in State
Dallas	165,463	3.5	62,782	20
Dawson	511	-2.8	40,131	178
Deaf Smith	971	5.2	52,368	34
Delta	217	4.8	40,622	54
Denton	52,713	6.8	59,414	174
De Witt	1,197	2.7	59,389	33
Dickens	75	2.8	33,843	232
Dimmit	393	3.2	38,800	198
Donley	149	-3.2	45,531	104
Duval	435	3	39,029	195
Eastland	1,447	1.7	78,826	8
Ector	8,338	6.3	50,161	67
Edwards	88	11.2	45,429	107
Ellis	8,496	7	45,968	206
El Paso	31,652	4	37,715	98
Erath	1,728	5.4	40,462	176
Falls	610	1.7	35,258	227
Fannin	1,415	5.3	39,830	183
Fayette	1,383	3.5	54,552	45
Fisher	171	-9	44,630	119
Floyd	255	6.9	44,646	118
Foard	52	-6.2	44,895	113
Fort Bend	48,420	6.2	59,653	31
Franklin	443	2.1	41,307	165
Freestone	753	2.9	38,182	202
Frio	614	4.1	30,223	246
Gaines	954	11.3	44,405	124
Galveston	18,561	4.6	54,250	46
Garza	203	3.8	32,601	240
Gillespie	1,708	3.6	63,291	19
Glasscock	119	-0.2	84,623	4
Goliad	349	5.1	45,589	103
Gonzales	933	-2.1	44,789	116
Gray	966	3.1	44,127	129
Grayson	5,991	5.4	43,987	130
Gregg	5,839	3.3	47,109	84
Grimes	1,066	6.1	36,909	217
Guadalupe	7,641	5.5	45,797	100
Hale	1,190	5.5	35,633	225
Hall	98	-3.6	33,095	235
Hamilton	513	4.2	60,584	27
Hansford	353	5.7	65,330	13
Hardeman	165	0.4	42,023	156
Hardin	2,720	3.3	47,221	82
Harris	282,809	3.8	60,002	30
Harrison	2,854	3.3	42,891	143
Hartley	453	12.2	81,238	6
Haskell	226	5.9	39,899	181
Hays	10,435	8	45,332	108
Hemphill	218	2.3	57,053	36
Henderson	3,321	4.4	40,135	177
Hidalgo	23,815	3.8	27,415	253
Hill	1,511	4.1	41,240	166
Hockley	971	2.5	42,162	153
Hood	3,167	5.7	51,384	61
Hopkins	1,541	4.5	41,562	161

County	Total Income ($ mil)	% change 2018-19	Per capita income	Rank in State
Houston	910	2.7	39,609	190
Howard	1,589	2.9	43,348	136
Hudspeth	115	6.9	23,569	254
Hunt	3,835	5.3	38,892	197
Hutchinson	921	3.5	43,981	131
Irion	111	2.5	72,177	10
Jack	365	-5.1	40,827	173
Jackson	688	9.2	46,596	87
Jasper	1,451	2	40,834	172
Jeff Davis	98	4.3	43,080	139
Jefferson	11,223	1.8	44,613	120
Jim Hogg	175	4.6	33,602	233
Jim Wells	1,707	3.3	42,174	152
Johnson	7,694	6.1	43,759	135
Jones	655	6.4	32,639	239
Karnes	881	5	56,449	38
Kaufman	5,987	9.1	43,972	132
Kendall	3,884	5.5	81,882	5
Kenedy	17	0	42,262	149
Kent	42	1.1	54,630	44
Kerr	2,723	3.4	51,768	59
Kimble	192	3.1	44,371	125
King	21	-10.6	78,849	7
Kinney	118	1.4	32,219	242
Kleberg	1,274	3.1	41,526	162
Knox	145	-0.9	39,587	192
Lamar	2,147	5	43,063	180
Lamb	589	6.6	45,655	140
Lampasas	1,085	3.1	50,656	102
La Salle	300	3.3	39,913	66
Lavaca	1,078	3.5	53,483	49
Lee	873	8.8	50,665	65
Leon	697	2.3	40,056	179
Liberty	3,341	5.5	37,874	203
Limestone	885	4.2	37,774	204
Lipscomb	252	3.3	77,810	9
Live Oak	457	4.1	37,415	212
Llano	1,088	4.6	49,905	68
Loving	9	18.6	53,734	48
Lubbock	13,762	4	44,311	126
Lynn	257	9.3	43,141	138
McCulloch	311	-0.6	38,895	196
McLennan	10,819	2.8	42,159	154
McMullen	48	3.2	65,250	14
Madison	466	3.5	32,648	238
Marion	393	3.3	39,895	182
Martin	351	-4.6	60,844	26
Mason	203	2.3	47,439	81
Matagorda	1,658	6.1	45,237	109
Maverick	1,843	3.7	31,380	243
Medina	2,120	4.8	41,095	170
Menard	80	4.1	37,218	214
Midland	23,162	3.8	130,983	1
Milam	924	3.9	37,238	213
Mills	192	2.8	39,334	193
Mitchell	287	0.4	33,593	234

County	Total Income ($ mil)	% change 2018-19	Per capita income	Rank in State
Montague	837	4.2	42,230	151
Montgomery	38,523	5.8	63,424	18
Moore	966	6.4	46,108	94
Morris	509	1.3	41,068	171
Motley	40	4.5	32,988	236
Nacogdoches	2,515	1.5	38,569	199
Navarro	1,987	4.4	39,652	188
Newton	466	1.7	34,265	231
Nolan	678	4.4	46,066	96
Nueces	16,263	3.5	44,889	114
Ochiltree	599	3.4	60,862	25
Oldham	117	-0.6	55,479	42
Orange	3,808	2.1	45,663	101
Palo Pinto	1,202	4.6	41,193	167
Panola	1,055	-0.2	45,467	105
Parker	7,974	6.6	55,811	40
Parmer	476	8	49,541	72
Pecos	629	4.9	39,731	186
Polk	2,045	4.2	39,818	184
Potter	5,411	2.8	46,086	95
Presidio	312	3.1	46,581	88
Rains	436	5.6	34,819	229
Randall	6,823	4.7	49,544	71
Reagan	200	0.1	51,945	56
Real	125	2.2	36,070	221
Red River	517	3.5	43,039	141
Reeves	726	12.2	45,458	106
Refugio	323	4.4	46,464	90
Roberts	41	-5	48,344	78
Robertson	725	2	42,463	145
Rockwall	6,530	7.4	62,237	21
Runnels	430	6.8	41,929	158
Rusk	2,051	2.6	37,697	207
Sabine	386	5	36,627	218
San Augustine	348	7.1	42,299	148
San Jacinto	1,046	4.6	36,260	220
San Patricio	3,103	3.2	46,506	89
San Saba	245	0.6	40,521	175
Schleicher	118	1	42,255	150
Scurry	717	-1	42,915	142
Shackelford	369	1	113,163	2
Shelby	1,056	-1.7	41,767	159
Sherman	293	13.1	97,002	3

County	Total Income ($ mil)	% change 2018-19	Per capita income	Rank in State
Smith	13,102	3.2	56,292	39
Somervell	418	4.3	45,812	99
Starr	1,791	3.7	27,713	251
Stephens	412	1.8	43,971	133
Sterling	80	0.9	61,920	22
Stonewall	79	-3.5	58,541	35
Sutton	233	-2	61,646	23
Swisher	383	1.4	51,779	57
Tarrant	112,047	4.4	53,292	51
Taylor	6,597	5	47,793	80
Terrell	38	1.8	49,591	70
Terry	466	9	37,741	205
Throckmorton	62	8.3	41,454	163
Titus	1,214	2.7	37,070	216
Tom Green	5,826	4.1	48,876	74
Travis	91,300	6	71,666	11
Trinity	528	3.2	36,062	222
Tyler	715	3.9	32,978	237
Upshur	1,568	3.6	37,563	211
Upton	172	6.3	47,118	83
Uvalde	1,099	3	41,116	169
Val Verde	1,879	5.6	38,331	200
Van Zandt	2,241	4.5	39,609	191
Victoria	4,506	4.4	48,938	73
Walker	2,177	3.7	29,838	248
Waller	2,346	6.6	42,456	146
Ward	646	11.5	53,870	47
Washington	2,000	4.2	55,735	41
Webb	8,982	3.7	32,466	241
Wharton	1,879	4.4	45,221	110
Wheeler	224	0.3	44,309	127
Wichita	5,881	4	44,479	121
Wilbarger	591	2.2	46,314	92
Willacy	589	0	27,584	252
Williamson	31,385	9.1	53,145	52
Wilson	2,372	4.9	46,448	91
Winkler	510	10.9	63,667	17
Wise	3,140	6	44,870	115
Wood	1,813	4.5	39,803	185
Yoakum	391	6.7	44,932	111
Young	914	1.5	50,732	64
Zapata	410	1.5	28,936	250
Zavala	364	5	30,779	244

8 Largest States' Unemployment Rates

Rank	State	June 2021	July 2021	Monthly Change
1.	Florida	11.5%	5.1%	−6.4%
2.	**Texas**	**6.5%**	**6.2%**	**−0.3%**
3.	Georgia	4.0%	3.7%	−0.3%
4.	Pennsylvania	6.9%	6.6%	−0.3%
5.	New York	14.7%	7.6%	−7.1%
6.	North Carolina	8.8%	4.4%	−4.4%
7.	Michigan	9.0%	4.8%	−4.2%
8.	California	13.2%	7.6%	−5.6%

Source: Bureau of Labor Statistics. August 2021.

Average Work Hours and Earnings

The following table compares the average weekly earnings, hours worked per week, and average hourly wage in Texas for production workers in selected industries in April 2020 and April 2021. Figures are provided by the Texas Workforce Commission.

Industry	Average Weekly Earnings		Average Weekly Hours		Average Hourly Earnings	
	April 2021	April 2020	April 2021	April 2020	April 2021	April 2020
Mining and Logging	$1,277.46	$1,188.14	45.3	44.6	$28.20	$26.64
Mining (including Oil & Gas)	1,283.68	1,185.91	45.2	44.6	28.40	26.59
Manufacturing						
Durable Goods	1,145.88	1,063.42	44.5	42.3	25.75	25.14
Fabricated Metal Product Mfg.	1,026.48	869.46	47.0	43.3	21.84	20.08
Nondurable Goods	788.16	852.52	41.2	43.1	19.13	19.78
Trade, Transportation, Utilities						
Wholesale Trade	1,023.00	944.15	42.2	40.4	24.83	23.37
Machinery, Equipment, Supplies	1,048.71	1,067.24	41.5	42.1	25.27	25.35
Retail Trade						
Auto Dealers/Parts	648.49	621.33	36.7	36.7	17.67	16.93
Building Material/Garden Equip.	462.35	499.46	32.4	34.0	14.27	14.69
Food/Beverage Stores	413.62	384.62	33.6	33.1	12.31	11.62
Gasoline Stations	377.48	376.88	32.5	34.2	11.63	11.02
Clothing/Accessories Stores	278.41	256.46	21.4	20.8	13.01	12.33

Employment in Texas by Industry

Employment in Texas reached 12,624,300 in June 2021, up 654,200 jobs since June 2020. The following table shows Texas Workforce Commission estimates of the nonagricultural labor force by industry for June 2021 and the percent change during the year in the number employed. *Source: Texas Workforce Commission. Additional information available at the website twc.texas.gov.*

Industry	June 2021	Monthly Change	Annual Change	Annual % Change
Total Nonagricultural	12,624,300	55,800	654,200	5.5%
Private	10,660,300	54,100	607,600	6
Goods-Producing	1,790,600	2,600	27,200	1.5
Mining & Logging (oil, gas)	189,200	2,900	12,200	6.9
Construction	726,600	-3,300	-100	0
Manufacturing	874,800	3,000	15,100	1.8
Service-Providing	10,833,700	53,200	627,000	6.1
Trade, Transportation, Utilities	2,564,700	6,600	129,100	5.3
Information	202,300	100	11,300	5.9
Financial Activities	827,200	800	30,600	3.8
Professional & Business Services	1,855,800	13,200	151,300	8.9
Education & Health Services	1,719,800	9,500	43,400	2.6
Leisure & Hospitality	1,291,500	19,000	184,600	16.7
Other Services	408,400	2,300	30,100	8
Government	1,964,000	1,700	46,600	2.4

Help Wanted: Top Online Postings of Job Vacancies

Occupation	July 2021	June 2021	Employer	July 2021	June 2021
Registered Nurses	31,826	30,879	Baylor Scott & White Health	8,029	7,102
Sales, Wholesale	21,386	21,656	Deloitte	4,548	4,337
Sales, Retail	19,571	19,430	HCA–Healthcare Company	4,131	4,197
Customer Service	19,517	19,581	Houston Methodist	3,475	3,084
Truck Drivers	17,222	16,475	Christus Health	2,642	3,181
Software Developers	17,173	16,135	UnitedHealth Group	2,552	2,123
Computer Tech	15,877	15,328	Anthem Blue Cross	2,505	2,337

Source: Texas Workforce Commission from Conference Board Help Wanted Online Data Series.

Largest Banks Operating in Texas by Asset Size

Source: Texas Department of Banking, December 31, 2018

Abbreviations: NA, not available; N.A. National Association.

	Name	City	Class	Assets (thousands of dollars)	Loans (thousands of dollars)
1	Charles Schwab Bank SSB	Westlake	State	351,075,000	25,537,000
2	JP Morgan Chase Bank	New York NY	National	246,711,590	NA
3	Bank of America	Charlotte NC	National	165,066,597	NA
4	USAA Federal Savings Bank	San Antonio	National	121,715,724	38,358,368
5	Comerica Bank	Dallas	State	86,257,000	50,582,000
6	Wells Fargo Bank	San Francisco CA	National	81,141,105	NA
7	BBVA USA	Birmingham AL	State	44,240,950	NA
8	Frost Bank	San Antonio	State	44,092,014	17,889,863
9	Texas Capital Bank N.A.	Dallas	National	40,035,375	24,393,255
10	Prosperity Bank	El Campo	State	35,563,929	19,617,895
11	Charles Schwab Premier Bank SSB	Westlake	State	33,115,000	0
12	Independent Bank	McKinney	State	18,110,591	12,770,197
13	Citibank	Sioux Falls SD	National	14,290,000	NA
14	Plains Capital Bank	University Park	State	14,229,718	7,290,482
15	Zions Bancoporation N.A.	Salt Lake City UT	National	12,993,040	NA
16	First Financial Bank N.A.	Abilene	National	12,065,711	5,322,562
17	International Bank of Commerce	Laredo	State	10,556,686	5,709,148
18	Capital One	New Orleans LA	National	10,391,469	NA
19	Woodforest National Bank	The Woodlands	National	9,792,477	4,868,649
20	Veritex Community Bank	Dallas	State	9,232,171	6,969,847
21	NexBank	Dallas	State	9,082,950	4,484,518
22	Truist Bank	Charlotte NC	State	7,572,143	NA
23	Amarillo National Bank	Amarillo	National	7,400,429	5,158,468
24	BOKF	Tulsa OK	National	7,005,971	NA
25	Southside Bank	Tyler	State	6,994,558	3,716,598
26	Allegiance Bank	Houston	State	6,423,375	4,659,169
27	Happy State Bank	Happy	State	6,326,783	3,429,087
28	TBK Bank SSB	Dallas	State	6,082,072	5,083,712
29	Cadence Bank N.A.	Birmingham AL	National	5,899,767	NA
30	Regions Bank	Birmingham AL	State	5,401,441	NA
31	Wells Fargo Bank South Central N.A.	Houston	National	5,262,057	340,038
32	Broadway National Bank	San Antonio	National	4,874,723	2,545,097
33	American National Bank of Texas	Terrell	National	4,448,694	2,406,771
34	Bancorp South Bank	Tupelo MS	State	4,433,845	NA
35	CommunityBank of Texas N.A.	Beaumont	National	4,029,141	2,891,632
36	First National Bank Texas	Killeen	National	3,889,580	1,351,218
37	First United Bank & Trust	Durant OK	State	3,860,938	NA
38	City Bank	Lubbock	State	3,730,641	2,242,676
39	Inwood National Bank	Dallas	National	3,667,073	1,967,049
40	TIB The Independent BankersBank	Farmers Branch	National	3,585,613	1,218,169
41	Texas Bank and Trust Company	Longview	State	3,580,389	2,484,802
42	VeraBank N.A.	Henderson	National	3,193,383	1,644,130
43	Spirit of Texas Bank SSB	College Station	State	3,166,882	2,430,939
44	First Bank & Trust	Lubbock	State	2,991,053	1,516,387
45	Guaranty Bank & Trust N.A.	Mount Pleasant	National	2,891,363	1,909,755
46	Lone Star National Bank	Pharr	National	2,737,786	1,302,827
47	Texas Exchange Bank SSB	Crowley	State	2,712,587	740,867
48	American Momentum Bank	College Station	State	2,700,117	1,822,788
49	Vantage Bank Texas	San Antonio	State	2,653,253	2,034,678
50	WestStar Bank	El Paso	State	2,520,224	1,587,625

Deposits/Assets of Commercial Banks by County

Source: Federal Reserve Bank of Dallas as of Dec. 31, 2018.

(in thousands of dollars)

County	Banks	Deposits	Assets	County	Banks	Deposits	Assets
Andrews	2	$786,813	$891,775	Fisher	1	72,316	79,543
Angelina	1	209,518	253,557	Floyd	1	98,753	110,149
Atascosa	2	156,141	179,741	Foard	1	35,591	39,756
Austin	5	2,247,370	2,640,246	Franklin	1	137,570	191,004
Bailey	1	82,066	95,914	Frio	2	651,437	747,255
Bandera	2	200,559	222,443	Galveston	4	2,443,359	2,818,052
Bastrop	2	732,743	832,163	Gillespie	1	856,602	1,027,574
Baylor	1	144,154	164,051	Gonzales	1	358,672	405,478
Bee	1	394,903	434,881	Gray	1	46,957	55,419
Bell	4	3,272,585	3,878,149	Grayson	3	531,304	603,838
Bexar	8	35,295,268	41,739,510	Gregg	3	2,738,363	3,154,115
Blanco	1	103,668	118,188	Grimes	2	286,326	329,785
Bosque	2	212,576	235,388	Guadalupe	3	740,993	840,515
Bowie	2	403,265	457,687	Hale	1	28,433	41,842
Brazoria	7	1,064,722	1,202,395	Hall	1	52,154	60,348
Brazos	2	1,376,265	1,702,781	Hansford	3	383,962	442,146
Briscoe	1	48,994	58,522	Hardeman	1	54,058	59,433
Brooks	1	70,721	78,668	Harris	17	19,229,546	22,831,273
Brown	2	597,258	692,419	Harrison	1	196,806	219,573
Burleson	1	518,430	585,429	Haskell	1	61,248	69,714
Burnet	1	216,982	246,255	Henderson	2	511,511	574,094
Caldwell	2	299,387	337,880	Hidalgo	5	2,837,932	3,245,212
Calhoun	1	288,038	317,838	Hill	1	147,021	174,653
Callahan	1	361,301	417,210	Hockley	2	169,732	189,546
Cameron	4	2,035,806	2,399,293	Hood	2	552,532	621,225
Camp	1	456,470	574,188	Hopkins	2	1,287,599	1,468,635
Carson	1	31,919	35,898	Houston	3	149,554	171,239
Cass	2	418,016	485,983	Howard	1	355,314	392,240
Castro	1	1,108,104	1,315,753	Hunt	1	45,217	49,406
Chambers	1	107,951	121,100	Irion	1	413,042	443,331
Cherokee	2	1,939,996	2,323,662	Jack	1	214,449	240,334
Childress	1	100,825	109,158	Jackson	1	52,037	55,733
Coke	1	35,596	41,227	Jasper	1	224,576	257,831
Coleman	2	146,726	164,425	Jeff Davis	1	77,685	85,847
Collin	4	15,351,268	19,740,097	Jefferson	2	2,811,864	3,280,197
Collingsworth	1	346,069	397,725	Jim Hogg	1	77,858	93,485
Colorado	4	429,944	509,599	Johnson	1	183,874	202,974
Comanche	1	84,215	92,919	Jones	1	57,552	62,995
Concho	2	180,945	205,992	Karnes	2	742,308	820,886
Cooke	2	1,105,043	1,257,696	Kaufman	2	2,934,672	3,243,517
Coryell	2	628,133	702,303	Kendall	1	131,506	147,556
Cottle	1	45,174	49,436	Kerr	1	144,894	159,550
Crockett	1	226,569	255,317	Kimble	2	104,219	114,513
Crosby	2	744,025	854,498	Kleberg	1	439,043	528,374
Dallas	24	98,710,887	124,594,733	Lamar	3	503,771	598,254
Dawson	1	317,970	350,327	Lamb	1	1,232,126	1,401,066
Deaf Smith	1	148,705	169,091	Lampasas	1	120,111	137,448
Delta	2	70,832	82,931	La Salle	1	87,693	98,237
Denton	4	1,014,778	1,154,602	Lavaca	2	901,613	1,014,153
DeWitt	2	373,066	426,164	Lee	1	188,031	209,953
Dickens	1	40,782	45,300	Leon	2	904,919	1,029,838
Dimmit	1	65,660	75,849	Liberty	1	265,398	307,164
Donley	1	35,155	42,941	Limestone	2	263,888	305,100
Duval	2	95,912	108,840	Live Oak	2	473,387	541,096
Ector	2	741,013	835,144	Llano	2	324,676	364,865
Edwards	1	69,285	79,024	Lubbock	9	7,202,629	8,437,114
Ellis	4	1,329,849	1,514,241	Lynn	1	48,239	53,804
El Paso	2	1,762,700	2,069,095	Martin	1	204,361	223,418
Erath	1	80,827	90,526	Mason	2	139,674	170,695
Fannin	1	86,664	99,674	McCulloch	2	246,566	275,947
Fayette	4	1,234,697	1,386,252	McLennan	12	3,601,061	4,121,667

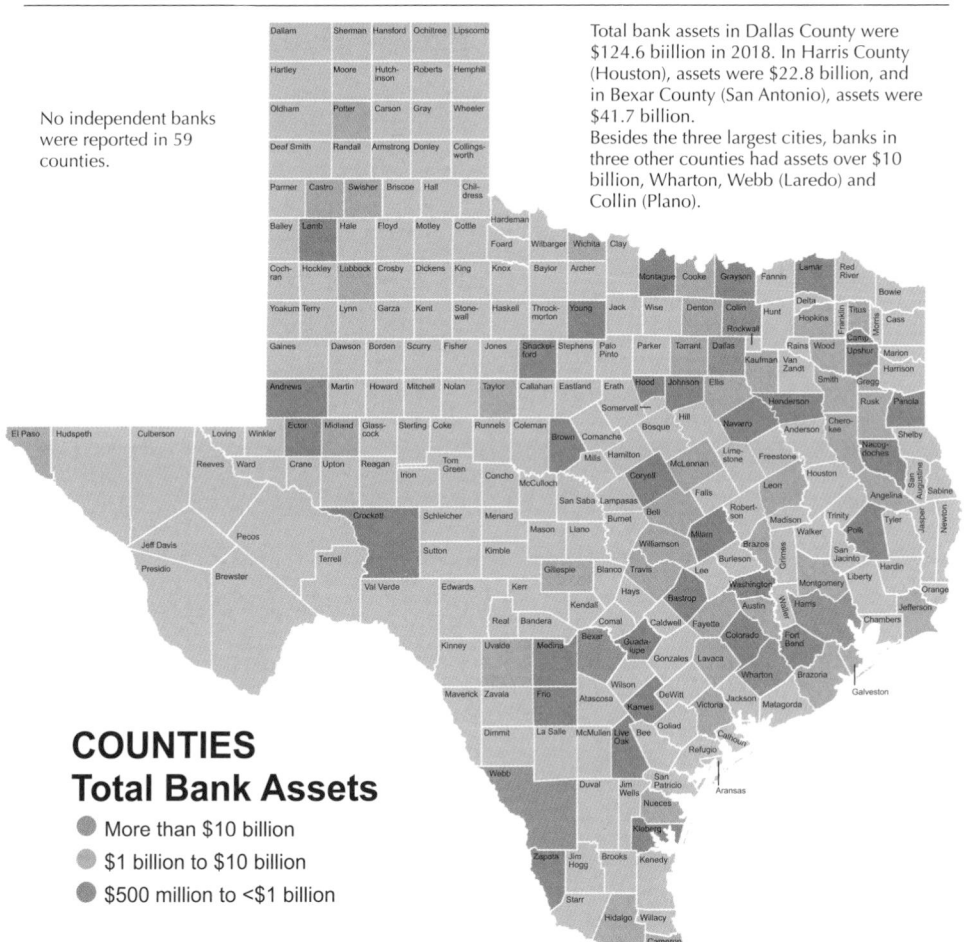

Total bank assets in Dallas County were $124.6 biillion in 2018. In Harris County (Houston), assets were $22.8 billion, and in Bexar County (San Antonio), assets were $41.7 billion.

Besides the three largest cities, banks in three other counties had assets over $10 billion, Wharton, Webb (Laredo) and Collin (Plano).

No independent banks were reported in 59 counties.

COUNTIES
Total Bank Assets

- ● More than $10 billion
- ● $1 billion to $10 billion
- ● $500 million to <$1 billion

County	Banks	Deposits	Assets
Medina	3	544,978	615,950
Menard	1	31,988	36,668
Midland	5	4,546,544	5,152,536
Milam	3	753,409	865,275
Mills	1	284,812	315,242
Mitchell	1	113,904	125,272
Montague	1	600,346	694,569
Montgomery	1	5,338,201	5,923,725
Morris	2	174,566	229,772
Nacogdoches	1	649,877	727,918
Navarro	4	865,304	999,160
Nolan	2	266,816	296,100
Nueces	5	2,322,016	2,636,085
Ochiltree	1	150,362	172,423
Orange	1	190,459	208,340
Palo Pinto	1	90,435	105,391
Panola	2	473,116	603,570
Parker	2	533,691	592,673
Parmer	1	140,134	158,719
Pecos	2	352,805	388,375
Polk	3	719,847	843,224
Potter	3	4,930,457	5,774,064
Presidio	1	111,062	129,531
Randall	1	140,739	159,818

County	Banks	Deposits	Assets
Rockwall	1	56,079	62,457
Runnels	3	354,889	393,200
Rusk	2	2,463,609	2,805,100
Sabine	1	53,507	61,500
San Jacinto	2	147,118	162,736
San Patricio	1	126,919	142,889
San Saba	1	52,416	60,969
Schleicher	1	50,905	60,537
Scurry	2	217,249	246,149
Shackelford	1	516,595	592,295
Shelby	2	395,923	455,099
Sherman	1	211,463	244,798
Smith	4	5,420,176	7,478,325
Starr	1	71,385	84,166
Sterling	1	173,449	183,532
Stonewall	1	57,348	67,891
Sutton	1	340,941	423,400
Swisher	2	2,902,560	3,488,531
Tarrant	9	3,270,178	3,860,943
Taylor	3	6,407,214	7,846,262
Titus	2	1,963,071	2,367,052
Tom Green	1	235,462	270,620
Travis	3	242,106	315,275
Trinity	1	52,297	57,825

County	Banks	Deposits	Assets		County	Banks	Deposits	Assets
Tyler	1	129,181	144,198		Wheeler	1	66,550	75,402
Upshur	2	510,368	587,879		Wichita	4	1,796,545	2,130,172
Uvalde	1	1,589,321	1,734,034		Wilbarger	1	248,340	294,284
Val Verde	1	23,455	28,288		Williamson	4	1,249,028	1,396,930
Van Zandt	1	125,454	145,753		Wilson	1	41,929	51,535
Walker	1	412,049	469,922		Wise	2	240,164	279,433
Ward	1	157,971	176,873		Wood	2	1,551,311	2,052,193
Washington	4	763,614	860,573		Young	3	650,882	767,275
Webb	4	8,811,325	11,650,632		Zapata	2	378,887	513,078
Wharton	3	18,334,982	23,884,829		Zavala	1	56,042	64,839

Texas Total Bank Resources and Deposits: 1905–2018

On Dec. 31, 2018, Texas had 409 national and state banks, the lowest number since our records began in 1905. In 1986, the number of independent banks in the state peaked at 1,972. In 2018, total assets were the highest ever at nearly $400 billion. Deposits peaked in 2018 at $328.9 billion. *Source: Federal Reserve Bank of Dallas.*

Date	National Banks			State Banks			Combined Total		
	No. Banks	Assets (in thousands)	Deposits (in thousands)	No. Banks	Assets (in thousands)	Deposits (in thousands)	No. Banks	Assets (in thousands)	Deposits (in thousands)
Sept. 30, 1905	440	$ 189,484	$ 101,285	29	$ 4,341	$ 2,213	469	$ 193,825	$ 103,498
Nov. 10, 1910	516	293,245	145,249	621	88,103	59,766	1,137	381,348	205,015
Dec. 29, 1920	556	780,246	564,135	1,031	391,127	280,429	1,587	1,171,373	844,564
Dec. 31, 1930	560	1,028,420	826,723	655	299,012	231,909	1,215	1,327,432	1,058,632
Dec. 31, 1940	446	1,695,662	1,534,702	393	227,866	179,027	839	1,923,528	1,713,729
Dec. 31, 1950	442	6,467,275	6,076,006	449	1,427,680	1,338,540	891	7,894,955	7,414,546
Dec. 31, 1960	468	10,520,690	9,560,668	532	2,997,609	2,735,726	1,000	13,518,299	12,296,394
Dec. 31, 1970	530	22,087,890	18,384,922	653	8,907,039	7,958,133	1,183	30,994,929	26,343,055
Dec. 31, 1980	641	75,540,334	58,378,669	825	35,186,113	31,055,648	1,466	110,726,447	89,434,317
Dec. 31, 1985	1,058	144,674,908	111,903,178	878	64,349,869	56,392,634	1,936	209,024,777	168,295,812
Dec. 31, 1986	1,077	141,397,037	106,973,189	895	65,989,944	57,739,091	1,972	207,386,981	164,712,280
Dec. 31, 1987	953	135,690,678	103,930,262	812	54,361,514	47,283,855	1,765	190,052,192	151,214,117
Dec. 31, 1988	802	130,310,243	106,740,461	690	40,791,310	36,655,253	1,492	171,101,553	143,395,714
Dec. 31, 1989	687	133,163,016	104,091,836	626	40,893,848	36,652,675	1,313	174,056,864	140,744,511
Dec. 31, 1990	605	125,808,263	103,573,445	578	45,021,304	40,116,662	1,183	170,829,567	143,690,107
Dec. 31, 1993	502	139,409,250	111,993,205	510	44,566,815	39,190,373	1,012	183,976,065	151,183,578
Dec. 31, 1994	481	140,374,540	111,881,041	502	47,769,694	41,522,943	983	188,144,234	153,403,984
Dec. 31, 1995	456	152,750,093	112,557,468	479	49,967,946	42,728,454	935	202,718,039	155,285,922
Dec. 31, 1996	432	152,299,695	122,242,990	445	52,868,263	45,970,674	877	205,167,958	168,213,664
Dec. 31, 1997	417	180,252,942	145,588,677	421	54,845,186	46,202,808	838	235,098,128	191,791,485
Dec. 31, 1998	402	128,609,813	106,704,893	395	50,966,996	42,277,367	797	179,576,809	148,982,260
Dec. 31, 1999	380	128,878,607	99,383,776	373	52,266,148	42,579,986	753	181,144,755	141,963,762
Dec. 31, 2000	358	112,793,856	88,591,657	351	53,561,550	43,835,525	709	166,355,406	132,427,182
Dec. 31, 2001	342	85,625,768	72,812,548	344	59,047,520	47,843,799	686	144,673,288	120,656,347
Dec. 31, 2002	332	95,308,420	79,183,418	337	62,093,220	49,715,186	669	157,401,640	128,898,604
Dec. 31, 2003	316	75,003,613	62,567,943	337	61,448,617	49,790,333	653	136,452,230	112,358,276
Dec. 31, 2004	311	82,333,800	67,977,669	328	69,127,411	54,950,601	639	151,461,211	122,928,270
Dec. 31, 2005	302	96,505,262	77,688,463	324	76,697,256	61,257,128	626	173,202,518	138,945,591
Dec. 31, 2006	286	97,936,270	79,389,737	322	83,910,356	66,132,394	608	181,846,626	145,522,131
Dec. 31, 2007	282	107,260,539	83,637,302	330	154,283,181	114,537,280	612	261,543,720	198,174,582
Dec. 31, 2008	267	108,816,852	84,802,191	327	164,658,101	115,186,285	594	273,474,953	199,988,476
Dec. 31, 2009	263	153,639,579	109,552,071	318	162,958,865	120,962,911	581	316,598,444	230,514,982
Dec. 31, 2010	253	149,498,073	120,827,780	314	162,772,458	127,925,865	567	312,270,531	248,753,645
Dec. 31, 2011	250	159,621,331	129,799,399	302	169,525,070	137,180,187	552	329,146,401	266,979,586
Dec. 31, 2012	227	156,392,247	139,945,006	293	205,788,318	169,156,089	520	362,180,565	302,101,095
Dec. 31, 2013	211	138,785,446	118,373,970	283	216,540,710	181,010,324	494	355,326,156	299,384,294
Dec. 31, 2014	203	128,134,221	108,506,074	267	235,388,932	197,078,456	470	363,523,153	305,584,530
Dec. 31, 2015	195	117,391,368	99,420,411	252	246,932,641	204,350,121	477	364,324,009	303,770,532
Dec. 31, 2016	186	122,431,838	104,027,309	244	254,560,238	208,323,981	430	376,992,076	312,351,290
Dec. 31, 2017	183	133,291,358	111,896,128	240	259,417,028	212,732,825	423	392,708,386	324,628,953
Dec. 31, 2018	176	$137,477,382	$114,245,832	233	$262,400,881	$214,562,067	409	$399,878,263	$328,907,699

Texas State Banks

Consolidated Statement, Foreign and Domestic Offices, as of Dec. 31, 2018

Source: Federal Reserve Bank of Dallas

Number of Banks	233

(thousands of dollars)

Assets

Cash and balances due from banks:
Non-interest-bearing balances
and currency and coin .... $ 4,962,045
Interest-bearing balances................................. 13,098,333
Held-to-maturity securities 13,547,370
Available-for-sale securities 47,367,624
Equity securities not held for trading..........................54,182
Federal funds sold in domestic offices...................1,365,496
Securities purchases under agreements to resell..........11,642
Loans and lease financing receivables:
Loans and leases held for sale 1,665,108
Loans and leases held for investment.............163,989,470
Less: allowance for loan and lease losses 1,811,630
Loans and leases, net 162,177,840
Trading Assets.. 141,420
Premises and fixed assets................................ 3,902,016
Other real estate owned 178,289
Investments in unconsolidated subsidiaries
and associated companies....................................... 49,909
Direct/indirect investments in real estate ventures...... 12,944
Intangible assets 6,070,415
Other assets...7,796,248
Total Assets .... **$ 262,400,881**

Liabilities

Deposits:
In domestic offices .... $ 214,164,380
Non-interest-bearing 79,784,426
Interest-bearing 134,379,960
In foreign offices, edge & agreement subsidiaries
and IBFs 497,687
Non-interest-bearing 264,633
Interest-bearing balances................................... 233,054
Federal funds purchased and securities sold under
agreements to repurchase:
funds in domestic offices....................................451,840
securities sold under agreement to repurchase 2,280,725
Trading liabilities 299,103
Other borrowed money (mortgages/leases)............ 9,615,243
Subordinated notes and debentures......................... 580,055
Other liabilities...2,000,675
Total Liabilities.. **$ 229,889,708**

Equity Capital

Perpetual preferred stock .... $ 4,906
Common stock 482,034
Surplus (exclude surplus related to
preferred stock) 16,457,220
Retained earnings... 16,645,362
Accumulated other comprehensive income.......... –1,077,974
Other equity capital components..................................–7,519
Total bank equity capital.......................................32,504,029
Minority interest in cons. subsidiaries................ 7,144
Total Equity Capital.................................... **$ 32,511,173**
Total liabilities, minority interest and
equity capital... **$ 262,400,881**

Texas National Banks

Consolidated Statement, Foreign and Domestic Offices, as of Dec. 31, 2018

Source: Federal Reserve Bank of Dallas

Number of Banks	176

(thousands of dollars)

Assets

Cash and balances due from banks:
Non-interest-bearing balances
and currency and coin .... $ 2,708,378
Interest-bearing balances................................. 9,238,424
Held-to-maturity securities 2,771,738
Available-for-sale securities 21,161,149
Equity securities not held for trading.......................... 37,944
Federal funds sold in domestic offices...................3,375,562
Securities purchases under agreements to resell........125,000
Loans and lease financing receivables:
Loans and leases held for sale 5,646,116
Loans and leases held for investment............... 87,674,263
Less: allowance for loan and lease losses 1,005,273
Loans and leases, net of allowance.................. 86,668,990
Trading Assets.. 27,594
Premises and fixed assets................................ 1,595,444
Other real estate owned 74,985
Investments in unconsolidated subsidiaries
and associated companies...29,807
Direct/indirect investments in real estate ventures......... 2,099
Intangible assets 847,772
Other assets...3,166,380
Total Assets .... **$ 137,477,382**

Liabilities

Deposits:
In domestic offices ....$ 114,245,638
Non-interest-bearing 30,220,646
Interest-bearing 84,024,992
In foreign offices, edge & agreement subsidiaries
and IBFs 0
Non-interest-bearing 0
Interest-bearing balances...................................0
Federal funds purchased and securities sold under
agreements to repurchase:
funds in domestic offices....................................792,297
securities sold under agreement to repurchase 883,402
Trading liabilities 21,011
Other borrowed money (mortgages/leases).............5,861,778
Subordinated notes and debentures..........................223,153
Other liabilities...975,172
Total Liabilities.. **$ 123,002,451**

Equity Capital

Perpetual preferred stock .... $ 160,750
Common stock 357,986
Surplus (exclude surplus related to
preferred stock) 4,607,653
Retained earnings... 9,621,463
Accumulated other comprehensive income........... – 278,689
Other equity capital components............................. – 7,973
Total bank equity capital....................................... 14,461,190
Minority interest in consolidated subsidiaries 13,741
Total Equity Capital.................................... **$ 14,474,937**
Total liabilities, minority interest and
equity capital... **$ 137,477,382**

Savings and Loan Associations in Texas

This table includes all thrifts that are not also classified as banks under federal law: that is, it includes federal savings and loan associations and federal savings banks. *Source: Texas Department of Savings and Mortgage Lending.*

Year ending	Number of Inst.	Total Assets	Mortgage Loans	Cash/ Securities	Deposits	FHLB/ Borrowed Money	†Net Worth
				in thousands of dollars			
Dec. 31, 2018	5	$83,782,803	$6,020,272	$43,883,996	$73,570,292	$153,368	$8,284,160
Dec. 31, 2017	5	82,642,161	7,155,350	41,128,877	73,813,038	62,068	7,559,159
Dec. 31, 2016	6	80,671,509	48,621,797	29,471,795	73,504,651	349,316	7,166,859
Dec. 31, 2015	6	73,722,445	47,512,693	24,727,034	65,397,606	213,039	6,703,177
Dec. 31, 2014	8	71,253,195	45,943,853	29,164,768	62,899,043	379,957	6,470,089
Dec. 31, 2013	8	66,605,862	41,812,008	34,083,458	59,101,594	196,784	5,941,114
Dec. 31, 2012	12	64,448,340	41,967,892	20,925,955	57,004,423	579,846	5,645,916
Dec. 31, 2011	12	57,857,491	40,757,220	15,671,590	50,819,345	657,598	5,079,133
Dec. 31, 2010	19	53,980,441	17,005,657	14,230,550	46,935,007	987,211	4,840,466
Dec. 31, 2009	19	46,524,327	17,810,587	9,702,023	40,272,742	973,610	4,254,794
Dec. 31, 2008	22	87,572,855	49,816,471	31,763,898	52,606,655	27,137,730	6,582,759
Dec. 31, 2005	19	55,755,096	42,027,293	9,140,789	30,565,411	11,299,136	4,228,103
Dec. 31, 2000	25	55,709,391	43,515,610	1,512,444	28,914,234	17,093,369	4,449,097
Dec. 31, 1995	45	52,292,519	27,509,933	5,971,364	28,635,799	15,837,632	3,827,249
Dec. 31, 1994	50	50,014,102	24,148,760	6,790,416	29,394,433	15,973,056	3,447,110
Dec. 31, 1990 §	131	72,041,456	27,475,664	20,569,770	56,994,387	17,738,041	−4,566,656
Conservatorship	51	14,952,402	6,397,466	2,188,820	16,581,525	4,304,033	−6,637,882
Privately Owned	80	57,089,054	21,078,198	18,380,950	40,412,862	13,434,008	2,071,226
Dec. 31, 1989 §	196	90,606,100	37,793,043	21,218,130	70,823,464	27,158,238	−9,356,209
Conservatorship	81	22,159,752	11,793,445	2,605,080	25,381,494	7,103,657	−10,866,213
Privately Owned	115	68,446,348	25,999,598	18,613,050	45,441,970	20,054,581	1,510,004
Dec. 31, 1988	204	110,499,276	50,920,006	26,181,917	83,950,314	28,381,573	−4,088,355
Dec. 31, 1985	273	91,798,890	60,866,666	10,426,464	72,806,067	13,194,147	3,903,611
Dec. 31, 1980	318	$34,954,129	$27,717,383	$3,066,791	$28,439,210	$3,187,638	$1,711,201

Texas Savings Banks

The savings bank charter was approved by the Legislature in 1993, and the first savings bank was chartered in 1994. Savings banks operate similarly to savings and loans associations in that they are housing-oriented lenders. Under federal law, a savings bank is categorized as a commercial bank and not a thrift. Therefore savings-bank information is also reported with state and national bank information. *Source: Texas Department of Savings and Mortgage Lending.*

Year ending	Number of Inst.	Total Assets	Mortgage Loans	Cash/ Securities	Deposits	FHLB/ Borrowed Money	†Net Worth
				in thousands of dollars			
Dec. 31, 2018	24	$24,434,061	$11,003,911	$9,104,353	$17,635,204	$3,653,055	$2,877,779
Dec. 31, 2017	24	22,355,393	10,721,196	7,199,404	16,479,408	3,194,283	2,462,036
Dec. 31, 2016	28	18,715,828	13,394,235	2,937,083	14,032,907	1,813,466	2,679,435
Dec. 31, 2015	28	13,790,890	10,291,788	2,597,416	10,218,604	1,199,403	2,202,693
Dec. 31, 2014	29	11,031,064	8,211,320	2,947,322	8,257,801	659,216	1,977,443
Dec. 31, 2013	30	10,194,983	7,148,798	3,389,771	7,739,381	499,261	1,812,736
Dec. 31, 2012	30	10,142,623	6,816,212	2,630,941	7,610,074	699,816	1,674,039
Dec. 31, 2011	30	9,530,011	6,132,972	2,650,324	7,247,147	568,547	1,543,269
Dec. 31, 2010	29	8,559,443	4,568,866	4,164,611	6,720,417	332,684	1,329,943
Dec. 31, 2009	29	8,372,892	4,283,372	1,237,215	6,330,896	307,494	1,201,409
Dec. 31, 2008	28	3,988,377	1,980,651	538,162	3,119,082	411,119	434,893
Dec. 31, 2007	26	9,967,678	6,471,833	1,027,709	6,162,709	2,328,467	1,372,231
Dec. 31, 2006	22	9,393,482	6,444,178	836,821	5,721,314	2,453,757	1,138,780
Dec. 31, 2005	19	8,720,497	5,605,678	985,535	5,308,639	1,967,673	1,352,882
Dec. 31, 2004	22	12,981,650	6,035,081	1,654,978	8,377,409	3,000,318	1,482,078
Dec. 31, 2003	23	17,780,413	8,396,606	3,380,565	11,901,441	3,315,544	2,422,317
Dec. 31, 2000	25	11,315,961	9,613,164	514,818	8,644,826	1,455,497	1,059,638
Dec. 31, 1995	13	7,348,647	5,644,591	1,106,557	4,603,026	2,225,793	519,827
Dec. 31, 1994	8	$6,347,505	$2,825,012	$3,139,573	$3,227,886	$2,628,847	$352,363

† Net worth includes permanent stock and paid-in surplus general reserves, surplus and undivided profits. § In 1989 and 1990, the Office of Thrift Supervision, U.S. Department of the Treasury, separated data on savings and loans (thrifts) into two categories: those under the supervision of the Office of Thrift Supervision (Conservatorship Thrifts) and those still under private management (Privately Owned).

Credit Unions: End of 2018

	# Credit Unions	Members	Surplus Funds	Savings	Loans	Assets
Texas	454	9.0 million	$21.6 billion	$88.8 billion	$78.1 billion	$104.4 billion
U.S.	5,572	117.5 million	$350.6 billion	$1,234.8 billion	$1,058.9 billion	$1,470.8 billion

Sources: Texas Credit Union Department and Credit Union National Association.

	U.S. Credit Union History				Texas Credit Union History			
Year	# Credit Unions	Members (million)	Savings ($ billion)	Loans ($ billion)	# Credit Unions	Members (million)	Savings ($ billion)	Loans ($ billion)
2017	5,800	113.6	1,181.0	978.4	NA	8.8	86.1	73.3
2016	6,022	109.2	1,114.4	889.5	NA	8.5	81.7	68.1
2015	6,259	105.0	1.029.1	804.9	478	8.3	77.6	63.2
2014	6,513	101.5	971.2	728.9	490	8.2	73.2	NA
2013	6,795	98.4	930.0	659.4	503	8.1	70.1	55.0
2010	7,605	92.6	804.3	580.3	550	7.5	58.9	43.3
2005	9,198	87.0	591.4	474.2	625	6.8	40.2	32.7
2000	10,860	79.8	380.9	309.3	714	6.5	28.4	22.6
1995	12,230	69.3	278.8	198.4	819	5.4	20.3	14.7
1990	14,549	61.6	201.1	141.3	954	4.4	13.9	8.9
1980	21,465	43.9	61.7	48.7	1,379	3.2	4.8	3.7
1970	23,687	22.8	15.4	14.1	1,435	1.5	1.0	1.0
1960	20,094	12.0	4.8	4.4	1,159	0.7	0.3	0.3
1950	10,586	4.6	0.9	0.7	484	0.2	0.04	0.04

Source: Credit Union National Association.

Credit Unions in Texas

Source: Texas Credit Union Department, National Credit Union Administration, and Credit Union National Association.

Credit unions are chartered at federal and state levels. The National Credit Union Administration (NCUA) is the regulatory agency for the federal-chartered credit unions in Texas.

The Texas Credit Union Department is the regulatory agency for the state-chartered credit unions. It was established in 1969 as a separate agency by the 61st Legislature. In 2018, it supervised 182 active credit unions. These state-chartered credit unions served 3.9 million Texans and had approximately $41.9 billion in assets in 2018.

The department is supervised by the nine-member Texas Credit Union Commission, which is appointed by the governor to staggered terms of six years, with the terms of one-third of the members expiring Feb. 15 of each odd-numbered year.

The Texas Credit Union League was the state association for federal and state credit unions beginning in 1934. It is now called Cornerstone Credit Union League and includes Oklahoma and Arkansas. The league's address is 6801 Parkwood Blvd., Ste. 300, Plano 75024.

The address for the Texas Credit Union Department is 914 East Anderson Lane, Austin 78752. Their website is cud.texas.gov. ☆

Comparison of Texas credit unions
as of Dec. 31, 2018

	State	Federal
No. of institutions	182	272
Total assets	$41.9 billion	$62.2 billion
Asset growth	3.4%	2.0%
Avg. asset size	$230.2 million	$229.8 million
No. with <$5 mil. asset	28	40
Net Income	$363.8 million	$508.6 million

Source: Texas Credit Union Department.

Credit Outstanding by Lenders 2018

	U.S. Outstanding ($ billion)	Market share
Banks/Savings Insti.	$1,682.0	42.0%
Finance Companies	534.0	13.3%
Credit Unions	469.2	11.7%
Federal Government*	1,236.6	30.8%
Educational Institutions*	30.4	0.8%
Nonfinancial business	38.6	1.0%
Pools of Securitized Assets	18.3	0.5%
Total	$ 4,009.2	

* Includes student loans. Source: Federal Reserve Board.

Insurance in Texas

Source: 2018 Annual Report, Texas Dept. of Insurance.

The Texas Department of Insurance reported that on Aug. 31, 2018, there were 2,819 entities licensed to handle insurance business in Texas and 641,371 agents and adjusters.

Under reforms in 1993-94, a three-member State Board of Insurance was replaced by the department, with a Commissioner of Insurance appointed by the governor for a two-year term in each odd-numbered year and confirmed by the Texas Senate.

On Sept. 1, 2005, legislation passed by the 79th Legislature took effect, transferring functions of the Texas Workers' Compensation Commission to the department and creating within it the Division of Worker's Compensation.

Also established was the office of Commissioner of Workers' Compensation, appointed by the governor, to enforce and implement the Texas Workers' Compensation Act.

Property/Casualty filings in Texas

A single-form filing submission may contain multiple policy forms and endorsements.

Type form	2017	2018	2019	2020
Personal liability	55	43	42	25
Bond/miscellaneous	363	304	197	208
Certificate of insurance	12	8	6	5
Commercial automobile	487	286	345	253
Commercial property	437	316	178	258
General liability	1,348	824	649	796
Homeowners	414	319	188	208
Inland marine	173	169	100	256
Identity theft	13	1	4	2
Commercial multi-peril	1,082	798	566	697
Personal automobile	431	256	271	512
Professional liability	512	375	288	327
Workers' compensation	103	98	109	71
Cyber risk	15	27	19	29
Total filing submissions	**5,588**	**3,930**	**3,041**	**3,763**
Actual forms received	**28,744**	**28,042**	**26,744**	**25,941**

Inspection Operations in Texas

The inspections office of the Texas Department of Insurance oversees amusement rides for building code standards as well as commercial and residential buildings for windstorm compliance.

Windstorm operations	2017	2018	2019	2020
Applications processed	33,983	50,341	30,959	42,698
Inspections completed	5,517	6,828	4,050	3,352
Certificates of compliance	32,020	41,784	29,044	28,054
Amusement ride safety	**2017**	**2018**	**2019**	**2020**
Inspection certif. approved	10,521	9,597	9,946	4,869
Injuries reported	89	77	75	19
Non-compliant operators	334	301	159	120

Agent/adjuster licensing

Licenses, certificates, and registrations.

Agents / Adjusters	2017	2018	2019	2020
Life, accident, health	236,521	240,844	251,850	271,049
Property, casualty	139,221	142,146	146,289	149,153
Adjusters	130,855	145,328	153,413	154,106
Life only	42,359	44,477	47,995	57,405
Total, including other types	**616,957**	**641,371**	**671,383**	**704,697**

Premium Rates Compared

Auto Insurance: Average for Coverage by State, 2021

The U.S. average is $1,758. Maine has the least expensive at $1,080. Most expensive states listed below:

1. Michigan	$3,141
2. Louisiana	$2,601
3. Nevada	$2,402
4. Kentucky	$2,368
5. DC	$2,188
6. Florida	$2,162
7. California	$2,125
8. New York	$2,062
9. Rhode Island	$2,040
10. Connecticut	$2,036
16. Texas	**$1,823**

In dollars, twelve-month rates. Information not available from some states. Source: carinsurance.com.

Homeowners Insurance: Average Premiums by State, 2021

The national average rate was $1,228. Most expensive states listed below:

1. Oklahoma	$3,572
2. Kansas	$3,174
3. Texas	**$2,940**
4. Florida	$2,876
5. Arkansas	$2,875
6. Louisiana	$2,656
7. Nebraska	$2,636
8. Mississippi	$2,625
9. Alabama	$2,599
10. South Dakota	$2,594

In dollars, twelve-month rates. $200,000 dwelling with $1,000 deductible and $100,000 liability. Source: insurance.com.

Texas Insurance Premiums, Payments

Year	Total Premiums	Claim Payments	Ratio
2019	$182.3 billion	$141.3 billion	77.5
2018	$175.8 billion	$134.2 billion	76.3
2017	$160.5 billion	$134.4 billion	83.7
2016	$152.3 billion	$119.3 billion	78.3

Texas Top 5 Auto Insurers/2020

Group	Premiums	% of market
State Farm	$3,255,666,985	14.01
Progressive	3,102,637,389	13.35
Berkshire Hathaway	3,082,237,706	13.26
Allstate	2,824,829,475	12.15
USAA	1,974,516,601	8.5

Texas Top 5 Homeowners Insurers/2020

State Farm	$1,861,662,578	18.52
Allstate	1,347,747,828	13.41
USAA	1,017,411,403	10.12
Farmers Ins.	1,005,685,319	10.01
Liberty Mutual	646,266,603	6.43

Texas Top 5 Health Insurers/2020

UnitedHealth	$18,032,763,135	22.67
Health Care Service Corp.	11,252,545,385	14.15
Centene	9,846,533,636	12.38
Humana	7,571,581,460	9.52
Anthem	5,667,059,885	7.13

Texas Top 5 Life Insurers/2020

New York Life	$770,242,872	5.96
Metropolitan	734,496,097	5.69
Northwestern Mutual	693,474,568	5.37
Prudential of America	584,510,373	4.53
Lincoln National	511,452,224	3.96

Personal Auto

Companies in state	177
Groups in state	60
Policies (liability)	19,834,608
Total Premiums	$23,241,970,616

Homeowners Insurance

Companies in state	154
Groups in state	70
Homeowners	4,882,463
Dwelling	775,441
Tenants	1,869,824
Total Premiums	$10,049,707,575

Health Insurance

Companies in state	476
Groups in state	189
Insured Texans	23,280,468
Texans without insurance	5,233,960
Texas estimated pop.	28,514,428
Total Premiums	$79,528,121,948

Life Insurance

Companies in state	432
Groups in state	159
Total Premiums	$12,914,861,552

Ten-year history, number of insurance companies operating in Texas

	2008	2009	2010	2011	2012	2013	2014	2015	2016	2017
Life/Health										
Texas	170	161	161	157	153	149	146	145	145	140
Non-Texas	520	514	504	499	485	483	479	477	475	474
Non-U.S.	0	0	0	0	7	6	6	6	6	6
subtotal	690	675	665	656	645	638	638	628	626	620
Property/Casualty										
Texas	250	250	243	238	236	225	224	235	245	221
Non-Texas	942	948	948	947	935	948	946	952	940	941
Non-U.S.	0	0	0	0	18	17	16	15	16	17
subtotal	1,192	1,198	1,191	1,185	1,189	1,190	1,186	1,202	1,201	1,179
Other*										
Texas	348	353	350	332	324	301	303	295	298	295
Non-Texas	486	504	515	512	487	464	467	462	480	494
Non-U.S.	0	0	0	0	7	6	6	6	6	7
subtotal	834	857	865	844	818	771	776	763	784	796
Grand Total	**2,716**	**2,730**	**2,721**	**2,685**	**2,652**	**2,599**	**2,600**	**2,593**	**2,611**	**2,595**

*Other** includes: Nonprofit legal services corporations, third-party administrators, continuing care retirement communities, and health maintenance organizations.

Source: 2017 Annual Report, Texas Department of Insurance.

Construction

Texas Non-Residential Contract Awards

The chart below shows the total value of non-residential construction contract awards in Texas by month in billions of dollars. The change over the period from January 2018 to January 2019 was an increase of 21.9 percent.

Month	Total Awards	Month	Total Awards	Month	Total Awards
September 2015	$ 2.572	November 2016	1.803	January 2018	2.212
October 2015	3.261	December 2016	2.312	February 2018	1.938
November 2015	2.140	January 2017	2.952	March 2018	2.194
December 2015	1.697	February 2017	2.007	April 2018	1.689
January 2016	2.410	March 2017	2.447	May 2018	2.907
February 2016	1.469	April 2017	2.938	June 2018	4.517
March 2016	2.540	May 2017	3.561	July 2018	4.595
April 2016	1.840	June 2017	2.904	August 2018	2.192
May 2016	2.147	July 2017	3.415	September 2018	1.774
June 2016	2.455	August 2017	2.469	October 2018	1.834
July 2016	2.009	September 2017	2.345	November 2018	1.998
August 2016	2.373	October 2017	4.794	December 2018	2.567
September 2016	3.090	November 2017	2.152	January 2019	$ 2.697
October 2016	2.517	December 2017	1.822	Source: State Comptroller, 2019.	

State Expenditures for Highways

The chart below shows net expenditures (excluding trusts) for state highway construction and maintenance by fiscal year and percent change from the previous year.

Year	Net Expenditures	Percent change
2007	$ 5,359,397,359	4.4
2008	$ 5,208,591,565	– 2.8
2009	$ 4,252,879,534	– 18.3
2010	$ 3,353,467,064	– 21.1
2011	$ 3,774,008,186	12.5
2012	$ 4,186,493,637	10.9
2013	$ 4,491,601,827	7.3
2014	$ 5,305,157,884	18.1
2015	$ 5,192,484,124	– 2.1
2016	$ 6,159,245,504	18.6
2017	$ 6,748,220,204	9.6
2018	$ 6,381,670,144	– 5.4
Source: Texas Annual Cash Reports.		

Federal Funds for Highways

The chart below shows fiscal 2019 dispersement of Federal Highway Administration funds for construction and maintenance in thousands of dollars. The column at right shows dollars per capita.

State	Highway Funds	
	Total	Lane-miles
U.S. Total	$ 42,355,403	8,804,092
1. California	3,963,775	394,383
2. Texas	3,790,154	679,917
3. Florida	2,046,153	274,149
4. New York	1,812,763	239,763
5. Pennsylvania	1,771,931	251,271
6. Illinois	1,535,424	306,614
7. Ohio	1,447,596	262,377
8. Georgia	1,394,444	272,017
9. Michigan	1,137,059	256,207
10. North Carolina	1,126,340	227,544
11. Virginia	1,098,983	163,648
Source: Federal Highway Administration, 2019.		

Texas Single-Family Building Permits

Year	No. of Dwelling Units		Avg. Value per Unit ($)	
	Units	% change	Value	% change
1980	67,870	–	$ 51.900	–
1981	66,161	– 2.5	55,700	7.3
1982	78,714	19.0	53,800	– 3.4
1983	103,252	31.2	63,400	17.8
1984	84,565	– 18.1	68,000	7.3
1985	67,964	– 19.6	71,000	4.4
1986	59,143	– 13.0	72,200	1.7
1987	43,975	– 25.6	77,700	7.6
1988	35,908	– 18.3	83,900	8.0
1989	36,658	2.1	90,400	7.7
1990	38,233	4.3	95,500	5.6
1991	46,209	20.9	92,800	– 2.8
1992	59,543	28.9	95,400	2.8
1993	69,964	17.5	96,400	1.0
1994	70,452	0.7	99,500	3.2
1995	70,421	0.0	100,300	0.8
1996	83,132	18.1	102,100	1.8
1997	82,228	– 1.1	108,900	6.7
1998	99,912	21.5	112,800	3.6
1999	101,928	2.0	118,800	5.3
2000	108,782	6.7	127,100	7.0
2001	111,915	2.9	124,700	– 1.9
2002	122,913	9.8	126,400	1.4
2003	137,493	11.9	128,800	1.9
2004	151,384	10.1	137,600	6.8
2005	166,203	9.8	144,300	4.9
2006	163,032	– 1.9	155,100	7.5
2007	120,366	– 26.2	169,000	9.0
2008	81,107	– 32.6	174,100	3.0
2009	68,230	– 15.9	167,900	– 3.6
2010	68,170	– 0.1	179,200	6.7
2011	67,254	– 1.3	191,100	6.6
2012	81,926	21.8	192,300	0.6
2013	93,478	14.1	197,500	2.7
2014	103,045	10.2	208,900	5.8
2015	105,448	2.3	217,100	3.9
2016	106,511	1.0	220,300	1.5
2017	116,766	9.6	$ 226,100	2.6
Real Estate Center at Texas A&M University, 2019.				

Commercial Fishing in Texas

Total Texas coastwide landings in 2017 were more than 93.3 million pounds, valued at more than $236.9 million. Shrimp accounted for most of the weight and value of all seafood landed (see chart at bottom).

The Coastal Fisheries Division of the Texas Parks and Wildlife Department manages the marine fishery resources of Texas' four million acres of saltwater, including the bays and estuaries and out to nine nautical miles in the Gulf of Mexico.

The division works toward sustaining fishery populations at levels that are necessary to ensure replenishable stocks of commercially and recreationally important species.

It also focuses on habitat conservation and restoration and leads the agency research on all water-related issues, including assuring adequate in-stream flows for rivers and sufficient freshwater inflows for bays and estuaries. ☆

Leading U.S. Ports in 2017		
Rank	Port	Value in Dollars (in millions)
1	New Bedford, MA	$ 389.5
2	Dutch Harbor, AK	173.0
3	Naknek-King Salmon, AK	154.0
4	Kodiak, AK	152.0
5	Alaska Peninsula, AK	111.5
14	**Brownsville–Port Isabel, TX**	**62.2**

Source: National Ocean Economics Program, 2019.

Top Fishing Ports for Texas in 2017		
Rank	Port	Pounds (000)	Dollars (000)
1	Brownsville–Port Isabel	23,000	$ 62,800
2	Palacios	20,200	54,500
3	Galveston	18,800	48,700
4	Port Arthur	17,100	37,100

Source: National Ocean Economics Program, 2019.

Landings by State 2017		
Rank	States	Pounds (000)	Dollars (000)
	Total, U.S.	9,923,678	$ 5,428,140
1	Alaska	6,004,882	1,764,462
2	Massachusetts	242,137	605,250
3	Maine	208,677	511,315
4	Louisiana	898,425	370,222
5	Washington	215,976	277,740
6	Florida	87,818	238,855
7	**Texas**	**93,361**	**236,993**
8	Virginia	343,964	183,203

Source: National Marine Fisheries Service, 2019.

Texas Commercial Fishery Landings by Species						
	2017		2015		2012	
Species	Pounds	Value	Pounds	Value	Pounds	Value
Shrimp, Brown	49,857,425	$ 115,006,107	52,552,655	$ 96,897,374	43,707,869	$ 92,254,541
Shrimp, White	28,914,208	74,195,669	16,644,175	45,591,742	24,100,143	62,970,321
Oyster, Eastern	3,503,518	20,403,679	1,582,685	8,232,088	5,817,191	21,302,111
Snapper, Red	2,212,786	9,881,455	2,151,587	9,387,187	1,122,665	4,447,884
Shrimp, marine, other	101,960	62,835	25,844	9,794	1,023,748	4,021,505
Crab, Blue	4,126,389	5,415,937	3,914,228	5,109,692	2,849,739	2,875,694
Drum, Black	1,926,052	2,457,801	1,812,617	2,003,383	1,612,023	1,485,663
Snapper, Vermilion	149.071	442.915	306,820	919,931	511,224	1,433,985
Croaker, Atlantic	87,768	766,557	90,084	745,8567	88,918	740,110
Total, including others	**93,361,097**	**$236,992,832**	**80,356,029**	**$173,418,614**	**90,557,774**	**$213,313,076**

Source: National Ocean Economics Program and National Marine Fisheries Service, 2019.

Tourism, Travel Impact Estimates by County, 2017

This analysis covers most travel in Texas including business, pleasure, shopping, to attend meetings and other destinations. **Spending** is all spending on goods and services by visitors at a destination. **Earnings** are wages and salaries of employees and income of proprietors of businesses that receive travel expenditures. Employment associated with these businesses are listed under **jobs**. **Local tax** receipts are from hotel taxes, local sales taxes, auto rental taxes, etc., as separate from state tax receipts, as well as spending by travel employees and property taxes attributable to travel businesses and employees. *Source: Office of the Governor, Economic Development and Tourism.*

County	Jobs	Spending	Earnings	Local tax
		(in thousands)		
Anderson	681	$54,813	$14,056	$1,575
Andrews	433	29,194	6,705	752
Angelina	1,530	130,608	31,166	3,140
Aransas	1,288	102,093	33,087	3,397
Archer	9	1,864	172	17
Armstrong	8	1,226	95	6
Atascosa*	740	64,047	21,762	2,178
Austin	420	42,686	10,011	847
Bailey	73	4,441	1,298	132
Bandera	734	29,633	21,615	2,178
Bastrop	1,973	155,312	69,207	6,997
Baylor	28	6,299	772	72
Bee*	393	40,094	9,350	1,009
Bell	5,352	445,138	137,258	14,207
Bexar	69,220	7,106,223	2,398,606	314,164
Blanco	194	15,969	4,366	522
Borden	1	108	12	0
Bosque	200	16,614	8,002	692
Bowie	1,874	189,350	36,794	4,247
Brazoria	4,843	372,276	111,490	11,817
Brazos	6,162	479,396	151,433	17,196
Brewster	1,583	74,300	39,438	3,489
Briscoe	8	1,271	166	10
Brooks	77	12,926	1,903	235
Brown	642	50,158	16,441	1,827
Burleson	161	14,514	4,256	342
Burnet	1,130	82,449	32,877	3,425
Caldwell	213	33,108	8,582	788
Calhoun	393	42,702	10,801	1,504
Callahan	54	3,839	1,065	74
Cameron	9,571	801,598	212,848	27,058
Camp	86	15,975	1,693	127
Carson	22	5,837	414	27
Cass	270	20,510	5,267	463
Castro	21	2,502	447	32
Chambers	248	39,120	8,064	1,630
Cherokee	449	34,960	8,793	784
Childress	188	14,453	3,241	619
Clay	44	20,575	778	56
Cochran	13	870	200	13
Coke	45	3,472	709	44
Coleman	80	6,742	1,518	154
Collin	15,658	1,500,619	645,351	66,202
Collingsworth	15	1,889	246	19

County	Jobs	Spending	Earnings	Local tax
		(in thousands)		
Colorado	507	55,988	13,652	1,195
Comal	4,690	405,262	148,845	15,611
Comanche	130	13,744	2,665	256
Concho	10	1,200	407	27
Cooke	577	60,728	16,502	1,792
Coryell	497	44,308	13,006	1,298
Cottle	10	1,677	181	12
Crane	36	3,322	626	85
Crockett	185	27,688	3,068	303
Crosby	25	1,609	442	30
Culberson	184	37,033	5,482	809
Dallam	283	14,121	6,144	618
Dallas	97,079	9,045,095	4,363,486	427,939
Dawson	210	17,710	3,443	373
Deaf Smith	178	16,175	3,605	461
Delta	14	1,515	311	21
Denton	6,806	713,091	245,921	27,936
DeWitt*	607	58,669	15,336	1,514
Dickens	7	483	137	11
Dimmit*	245	31,312	5,483	887
Donley	94	6,418	1,905	225
Duval	59	10,187	1,060	114
Eastland	245	16,171	4,416	555
Ector	2,522	425,258	86,756	14,726
Edwards	7	873	178	10
Ellis	1,256	167,432	47,721	5,452
El Paso	13,850	1,465,780	440,993	50,597
Erath	493	44,969	13,134	1,334
Falls	99	10,267	2,303	255
Fannin	119	14,966	2,640	310
Fayette	484	48,373	10,680	1,233
Fisher	7	992	167	13
Floyd	32	4,916	685	46
Foard	4	370	94	8
Fort Bend	4,998	518,759	173,847	18,545
Franklin	112	9,456	1,770	200
Freestone	380	46,148	5,662	666
Frio*	375	34,848	8,474	1,004
Gaines	166	16,778	3,689	439
Galveston	10,840	989,973	289,894	40,726
Garza	102	9,724	2,923	225
Gillespie	1,001	102,974	30,436	4,688

Oil and gas production in recent years may affect travel impact estimates.

Travel Impacts by Origin of Visitor, 2017

Origin	Spending ($Billions)	Earnings ($Billions)	Jobs (Thousand)	Tax Receipts ($Millions)		
				Local	State	**Federal
Other U.S.	$28.1	$10.3	283.8	$783	$1,459	$1,754
International	$6.8	$1.9	62.6	$150	$344	$280
Texas	$29.7	$9.0	284.6	$595	$1,536	$1,414
All visitors	**$64.6**	**$21.2**	**631.0**	**$1,528**	**$3,338**	**$3,448**
Other Travel*	$10.2	$4.5	46.6	0	0	$1,106
Total Travel	**$74.7**	**$25.7**	**677.6**	**$1,528**	**$3,338**	**$4,554**

*Other Travel includes resident air travel, travel arrangement, and convention / trade shows.
**Federal includes motor vehicle fuel and airline ticket taxes, as well as income taxes attributable to travel industry income.

Source: Survey for the Office of Governor.

County	Jobs	Spending	Earnings	Local tax
		(in thousands)		
Glasscock	3	258	44	2
Goliad	62	10,214	1,883	217
Gonzales*	217	28,781	5,255	680
Gray	537	42,017	13,062	1,246
Grayson	1,632	208,497	39,849	4,404
Gregg	2,586	219,822	60,375	6,303
Grimes	229	19,130	5,604	500
Guadalupe	2,002	165,633	70,231	6,524
Hale	703	48,242	12,610	1,382
Hall	13	2,283	311	34
Hamilton	56	6,171	1,365	160
Hansford	21	2,026	338	45
Hardeman	62	5,701	885	104
Hardin	493	43,916	10,275	1,138
Harris	109,463	12,165,938	5,247,543	594,078
Harrison	688	88,366	15,150	1,189
Hartley	12	1,053	205	15
Haskell	97	5,829	1,416	216
Hays	3,820	348,914	120,122	12,830
Hemphill	65	8,637	1,517	344
Henderson	496	110,527	21,561	1,980
Hidalgo	16,863	1,268,691	389,497	38,656
Hill	502	58,226	10,199	946
Hockley	347	24,281	6,627	548
Hood	532	63,134	17,087	1,951
Hopkins	532	66,320	13,099	1,230
Houston	237	32,484	5,913	433
Howard	862	114,305	19,329	3,079
Hudspeth	16	5,138	414	20
Hunt	826	108,037	30,989	2,747
Hutchinson	397	38,076	9,210	1,013
Irion	16	10,120	416	21
Jack	39	4,347	747	66
Jackson	102	11,836	2,443	252
Jasper	520	38,870	11,408	1,198

County	Jobs	Spending	Earnings	Local tax
		(in thousands)		
Jeff Davis	115	8,699	4,360	188
Jefferson	6,088	548,993	128,520	16,527
Jim Hogg	55	5,015	1,251	99
Jim Wells	736	66,125	16,358	1,251
Johnson	1,155	150,770	34,509	3,954
Jones	123	8,247	2,585	175
Karnes*	446	54,288	13,195	1,434
Kaufman	825	137,285	26,809	2,798
Kendall	1,276	87,004	32,197	2,814
Kenedy	13	829	320	13
Kent	7	714	142	7
Kerr	1,543	98,360	40,388	3,936
Kimble	138	16,466	2,580	388
King	0	43	7	0
Kinney	108	5,691	2,081	115
Kleberg	524	57,610	14,091	1,539
Knox	18	2,760	375	29
La Salle*	595	37,187	14,650	1,745
Lamar	867	70,867	21,008	2,099
Lamb	101	12,804	1,905	175
Lampasas	164	15,165	3,361	402
Lavaca	143	16,967	4,178	450
Lee	207	24,239	6,297	513
Leon	247	32,534	5,156	630
Liberty	438	53,195	18,276	1,633
Limestone	132	18,430	2,810	405
Lipscomb	8	2,232	200	12
Live Oak*	261	35,765	5,181	710
Llano	2,202	106,885	47,838	4,136
Loving	1	44	7	0
Lubbock	8,672	757,603	279,900	25,832
Lynn	15	1,096	252	17
Madison	104	10,890	2,260	308
Marion	129	8,540	2,062	213

*Oil and gas production in recent years may affect travel impact estimates.

County	Jobs	Spending	Earnings	Local tax	County	Jobs	Spending	Earnings	Local tax
		(in thousands)					(in thousands)		
Martin	93	17,482	1,737	101	Schleicher	7	457	130	9
Mason	52	3,045	738	85	Scurry	572	37,976	12,099	1,176
Matagorda	1,045	66,052	23,286	2,808	Shackelford	84	2,288	1,533	112
Maverick*	657	59,383	14,697	1,830	Shelby	527	34,918	8,878	893
McCulloch	156	18,494	2,546	471	Sherman	29	5,086	453	31
McLennan	5,772	556,876	149,083	16,348	Smith	3,924	354,399	104,858	10,487
McMullen*	13	1,960	468	19	Somervell	156	17,600	4,252	608
Medina	379	43,673	8,968	768	Starr	245	27,636	5,628	632
Menard	14	2,612	305	25	Stephens	82	7,147	1,766	192
Midland	3,687	544,447	104,044	16,187	Sterling	16	2,356	226	16
Milam	314	28,447	6,931	627	Stonewall	20	1,057	280	17
Mills	21	2,784	492	56	Sutton	138	7,937	2,059	326
Mitchell	62	9,703	1,863	242	Swisher	44	3,536	860	68
Montague	287	18,370	5,146	493	Tarrant	76,486	5,613,557	4,283,738	345,928
Montgomery	7,133	632,996	311,864	31,168	Taylor	3,789	422,356	100,711	12,755
Moore	389	42,936	7,343	1,287	Terrell	14	1,098	199	8
Morris	43	5,510	995	79	Terry	201	11,335	3,480	411
Motley	5	736	101	7	Throckmrton	11	3,336	202	13
Nacgdoches	1,120	78,953	21,569	2,620	Titus	518	55,034	11,298	1,326
Navarro	599	50,688	12,329	1,426	Tom Green	3,354	218,875	77,976	6,920
Newton	32	4,796	716	57	Travis	56,325	5,666,532	2,009,187	267,471
Nolan	399	25,312	9,195	1,235	Trinity	225	10,993	5,977	390
Nueces	14,895	1,140,074	385,275	49,230	Tyler	140	10,935	2,415	235
Ochiltree	196	18,856	3,658	527	Upshur	180	22,334	3,725	344
Oldham	53	8,595	934	87	Upton	54	3,252	801	94
Orange	1,099	120,943	27,933	2,940	Uvalde	834	82,685	20,689	2,964
Palo Pinto	555	71,755	13,719	1,178	Val Verde	662	55,972	16,178	1,854
Panola	194	17,446	3,559	567	Van Zandt	485	51,397	10,934	1,004
Parker	855	110,602	25,987	2,631	Victoria	1,524	215,854	41,638	5,326
Parmer	39	4,856	731	64	Walker	1,132	106,675	24,187	2,568
Pecos	586	62,303	9,803	2,496	Waller	229	50,695	8,400	1,223
Polk	795	56,603	18,565	1,490	Ward	856	53,952	15,760	2,459
Potter	8,312	755,558	207,026	26,748	Washington	672	91,919	17,082	1,904
Presidio	79	15,432	2,947	655	Webb*	6,103	568,444	154,510	16,024
Rains	92	8535	2,888	204	Wharton	484	41,084	9,963	1,292
Randall	1,260	113,680	23,831	2,411	Wheeler	155	19,477	3,033	409
Reagan	172	11,551	3,030	160	Wichita	3,371	219,588	56,433	6,643
Real	94	7,497	2,420	181	Wilbarger	255	22,532	5,211	705
Red River	33	4,298	1,002	70	Willacy	162	25,687	4,199	386
Reeves	1,342	120,899	25,076	5,471	Williamson	5,620	627,148	176,440	21,953
Refugio	108	21,609	2,531	257	Wilson*	395	34,179	10,101	850
Roberts	2	1,004	43	2	Winkler	93	11,658	1,667	294
Robertson	246	22,106	4,572	700	Wise	898	58,350	17,172	1,668
Rockwall	891	97,352	27,912	3,534	Wood	366	26,630	8,406	566
Runnels	82	6,898	1,441	126	Yoakum	73	6,360	1,435	199
Rusk	346	36,560	7,641	786	Young	313	23,258	7,276	666
Sabine	117	12,601	2,428	139	Zapata	181	15,747	2,947	218
S.Augustne	109	7,437	1,918	131	Zavala	45	7,351	902	80
SanJacinto	151	11,857	2,774	158					
SanPatricio	1,326	140,681	37,759	4,704					
San Saba	74	4,489	1,025	101					

*Oil and gas production in recent years may affect travel impact estimates.

Telecommunications Trends to High-Speed, Wireless

The chart below shows the move to wireless communications, and the decline in the number of telephone land lines in Texas and nationwide. The chart also shows the growth of high-speed Internet use in the state and in the United States. *Sources: Federal Communications Commission and Public Utility Commission of Texas.*

	2000	2005	2009	2011	2013	2016
Mobile Wireless Telephone Subscribers						
Texas	6,705,000	14,424,000	21,008,000	23,482,000	24,890,000	28,840,000
U.S.	90,643,000	192,053,000	261,284,000	290,304,000	310,691,000	395,900,000
Local Telephone Wirelines/Landlines						
Texas	13,657,444	12,310,000	10,500,000	9,590,000	8,840,000	8,110,000
U.S.	188,499,586	157,041,487	152,945,000	143,319,000	133,233,000	121,331,000
Internet Connections						
Texas	253,000	2,943,000	7,484,000	17,487,000	23,612,000	30,171,000
U.S.	4,107,000	42,518,000	102,043,000	206,124,000	275,608,000	369,416,000

U.S. Internet Lines by Technology (in thousands)

	aDSL	Cable Modem	Fiber	Satellite	Fixed Wireless	Mobile Wireless	Total
2013	30,657	52,760	7,250	1,623	810	190,706	284,692
2017	25,506	64,059	12,906	1,826	1,245	302,562	408,816

The chart below shows the percent of the population that in 2016 had access to advanced, high-quality voice, data, graphics, and video offerings. The chart shows that almost 28 percent of the rural population in Texas is without that access. *Source: Federal Communications Commission 2018 Broadband Progress Report.*

Percent with access to advanced telecommunications, 2016 (25 Mbps/3 Mbps)

	Population with access		Urban with access		Rural with access	
	Total	Percent	Population	Percent	Population	Percent
Texas	27,763,538	93.4 %	23,251,241	97.6 %	4,512,297	72.3 %
U.S.	313,389,000	81.2 %	226,701,000	89.7 %	27,694,000	45.7 %

A telecommunications repair employee works beside a strip mall on US I-10 and Fry Road in Katy on March 24, 2006. Photo by Bill Jacobus/Flickr (CC).

Texas Electric Grids: Demand and Capacity

- The Electric Reliability Council of Texas (**ERCOT**) operates the electric grid for 75 percent of the state.
- The Panhandle, South Plains, and a corner of Northeast Texas are under the Southwest Power Pool (**SPP**).
- El Paso and the far western corner of the Trans Pecos are under the Western Electric Coordinating Council (**WECC**).
- The southeast corner of Texas is under the **SERC** Reliability Corporation.

The councils were first formed in 1968 to ensure adequate bulk power supply.

	Actual (in megawatts)						**Estimate**		**Projected**
	2011	**2012**	**2013**	**2014**	**2015**	**2016**	**2017**	**2018**	**2019**
ERCOT demand	68,416	66,548	67,245	66,454	69,877	71,110	69,512	73,473	74,853
capacity	69,595	73,219	74,396	73,950	76,798	78,466	78,251	77,558	78,085
% margin*	1.7	9.1	9.6	10.1	9.0	9.4	11.1	9.3	7.4
SPP demand	54,991	53,177	47,647	46,076	48,894	51,883	51,577	51,687	52,422
capacity	62,044	72,802	71.897	65,302	63,426	63,350	67,780	68,714	67,618
% margin	11.4	27.0	33.8	29,4	22.9	18.1	31.4	32.9	29.0
WECC demand	117,755	130,465	132,875	127,092	131,072	139,431	136,903	136,679	136,244
capacity	147,147	147,527	167,171	162,119	164,417	165,881	160,337	164,960	163,492
% margin	20.0	11.6	20.5	21.6	20.3	15.9	14.6	17.1	16.1
SERC demand	161,995	158,041	121,810	123,866	127,742	128,985	127,575	128,851	129,811
capacity	201,103	198,140	165,171	159,822	159,279	160,896	160,253	161,117	162,434
% margin	19.4	20.2	26.3	22.5	19.8	19.8	20.4	20.3	20.1
U.S. demand	759,642	768,943	759,310	723,411	741,056	768,510	752,080	755,578	760,642
capacity	892,426	927,060	944,515	917,167	916,439	923,873	931,379	963,135	996,104
% margin	14.9	17.1	19.6	21.1	19.1	16.8	19.3	21.6	23.6

*Capacity Margin is the amount of unused available capability of an electric power system at **summer peak** load as a percentage of capacity resources. Source: Federal Energy Information Administration, March 2019. 2017–2019 data from ERCOT.

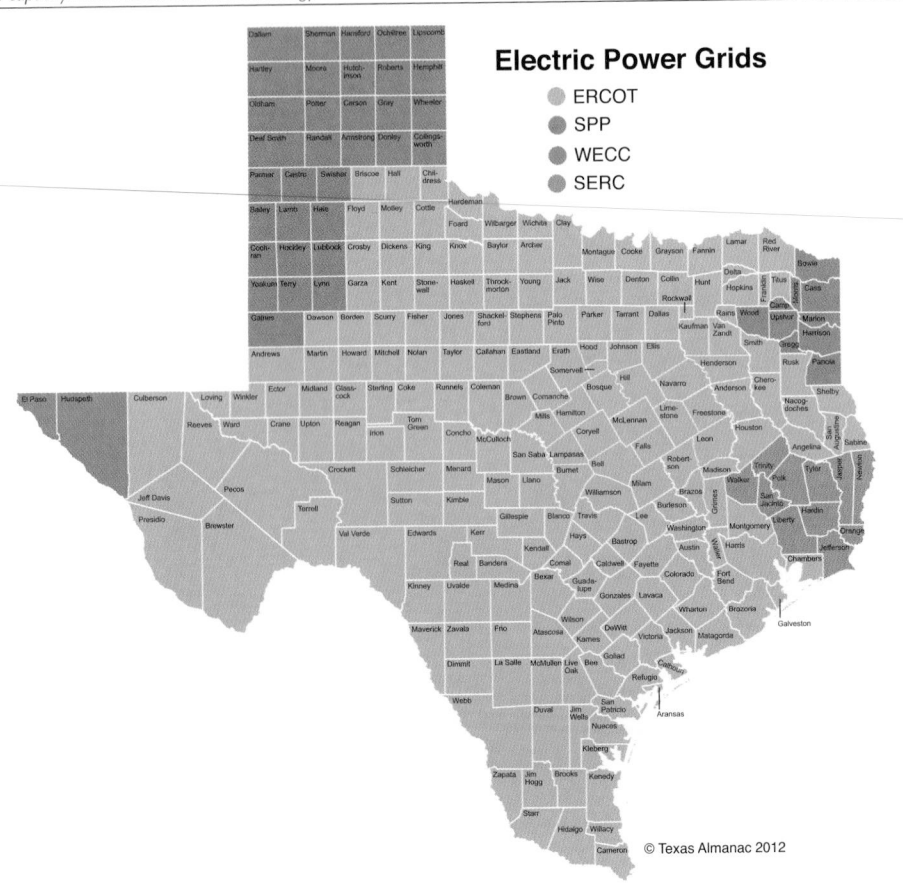

Electric Power Grids

- ERCOT
- SPP
- WECC
- SERC

© Texas Almanac 2012

Wind turbines stand in West Texas on February 13, 2019. Photo by Jonathan Cutrer/Flickr (CC).

Wind Energy Continues Expansion in State

Sources: U.S. Energy Information Administration and the American Wind Energy Association, 2019.

Texas continues to lead the nation in installed wind capacity and generation. In the first quarter of 2019, Texas had 25 percent of the nation's installed wind capacity, reaching almost 25,000 megawatts. Iowa was second in installed wind capacity, at 8,957 megawatts.

With Texas' significant growth in turbine development, wind generation was responsible for about 16 percent of total electricity generation in the state in 2018, more than double what it was in 2011 at 6.9 percent.

The Texas plains continue to see rapid growth in wind farms, while more recently expansion has begun offshore on the Gulf Coast.

In all, Texas has five of the ten largest wind generation projects in the country. Roscoe Wind Farm, which stretches across Nolan, Mitchell, Scurry, and Fisher counties, is the largest in the state, with a capacity of 782 MW.

It is third in the nation to Alta farm in California at 1,548 MW and Shepherds Flat in Oregon at 845 MW. ☆

Installed Wind Capacity in megawatts (MW)		
YEAR	Texas	U.S.
2019 (Q1)	24,895	97,227
2018	24,899	96,487
2017	22,637	89,078
2016	20,321	82,183
2015	14,208	66,008
2014	14,098	65,879
2013	12,354	61,110
2012	10,648	49,802
2011	10,394	46,919
2010	10,089	40,267
2009	9,403	34,863
2008	7,427	24,651
2007	4,296	16,596
2005	1,995	9,149
2000	181	2,566

2018 Renewable Energy as Portion of Net Generation of Electricity

(in thousand megawatt hours.)

State	Total Electric	Total Renewable	% Renewable	Hydroelectric	Wind
1. Washington	116,763	90,734	77.7 %	81,576	7,356
2. California	197,227	84,302	42.7 %	25,898	13,650
3. Texas	474,777	82,104	17.3 %	1,433	75,753
4. Oregon	84,836	45,679	53.8 %	36,729	7,137
5. New York	134,356	38,000	28.3 %	30,911	4,383
6. Iowa	64,187	22,922	35.7 %	999	21,685
United States	4,178,000	713,000	17.1 %	292,000	275,000

Source: Energy Information Administration, 2019.

Texas Oil Production History

The table shows the year of oil or gas discovery in each county, oil production in 2019 and 2020, and total oil production from date of discovery to Jan. 1, 2021. The counties omitted have not produced oil.

The table has been compiled by the *Texas Almanac* from information provided in past years by the Texas Mid-Continent Oil & Gas Assoc., which used data from the U.S. Bureau of Mines and the Texas state comptroller. Since 1970, production figures have been compiled from records of the Railroad Commission of Texas. The figures in the final column are cumulative of all previously published figures. The change in sources, due to different techniques, may create some discrepancies in year-to-year comparisons among counties.

County	Year of Discovery	Production in Barrels*		Total Production to Jan. 1, 2021
		2019	2020	
Anderson	1928	594,778	527,888	310,561,329
Andrews	1929	39,498,552	37,946,849	3,289,958,078
Angelina	1936	0	0	1,002,699
Aransas	1936	22,664	17,812	89,412,574
Archer	1911	893,043	765,033	510,779,083
Atascosa	1917	25,162,285	19,650,637	334,091,181
Austin	1915	356,351	284,575	122,191,361
Bandera	1995	1,532	512	46,409
Bastrop	1913	97,297	69,293	18,940,681
Baylor	1924	72,503	60,849	59,643,830
Bee	1929	236,212	191,588	115,266,222
Bell	1980	0	0	446
Bexar	1889	76,499	67,986	37,509,849
Borden	1949	7,878,426	6,628,106	469,855,575
Bosque	2006	0	0	309
Bowie	1944	22,958	22,679	7,242,524
Brazoria	1902	3,133,469	2,691,952	1,316,951,552
Brazos	1942	8,001,246	8,426,069	201,943,704
Brewster	1969	0	0	56
Briscoe	1982	0	0	4,065
Brooks	1935	136,260	72,949	183,252,609
Brown	1917	77,472	67,305	55,053,365
Burleson	1938	16,272,084	15,383,341	276,536,814
Caldwell	1922	1,077,222	942,118	299,445,335
Calhoun	1935	129,117	81,311	108,735,810
Callahan	1923	106,767	98,005	88,641,029
Cameron	1944	0	0	480,603
Camp	1940	80,903	55,998	31,447,023
Carson	1921	114,242	89,603	184,187,986
Cass	1936	463,886	485,392	119,458,572
Chambers	1916	2,426,819	1,987,292	943,279,000
Cherokee	1926	194,323	152,110	76,914,561
Childress	1961	4,914	1,928	1,814,292
Clay	1917	436,011	372,915	212,707,708
Cochran	1936	2,771,917	2,627,186	556,184,024
Coke	1942	317,812	234,446	231,848,743
Coleman	1902	196,538	152,607	98,874,429
Collin	1963	0	0	53,000
Collngswrth	1936	4,905	3,700	1,303,956
Colorado	1932	142,061	130,944	48,478,581
Comanche	1918	58,433	41,725	6,634,872
Concho	1940	274,724	219,546	31,210,035
Cooke	1924	1,038,153	875,117	420,601,518
Coryell	1964	0	0	1,100
Cottle	1955	95,657	81,695	6,688,838
Crane	1926	7,664,933	6,990,103	1,883,946,084

County	Year of Discovery	Production in Barrels*		Total Production to Jan. 1, 2021
		2019	2020	
Crockett	1925	6,254,570	5,260,862	471,729,509
Crosby	1955	919,997	663,291	38,613,028
Culberson	1953	897,535	482,202	101,433,832
Dallam	2015	0	0	116
Dallas	1986	0	0	232
Dawson	1934	3,327,123	3,124,305	440,937,183
Delta	1984	0	0	65,089
Denton	1937	21,372	11,132	11,951,483
DeWitt	1930	41,828,686	33,391,255	589,635,125
Dickens	1953	431,729	356,921	30,437,721
Dimmit	1943	41,036,494	31,896,966	541,740,208
Donley	1967	0	0	3,143
Duval	1905	882,327	772,410	603,867,578
Eastland	1917	146,574	124,332	160,530,151
Ector	1926	20,239,577	16,840,739	3,437,595,733
Edwards	1946	1,625	1,901	617,257
Ellis	1953	0	32	844,860
Erath	1917	1,267	476	2,298,570
Falls	1937	1,424	785	896,350
Fannin	1980	0	0	13,354
Fayette	1943	1,716,432	2,021,316	182,536,536
Fisher	1928	1,367,812	1,825,000	262,910,313
Floyd	1952	0	0	268,610
Foard	1929	74,338	64,062	25,524,946
Fort Bend	1919	745,937	696,511	715,398,653
Franklin	1936	398,058	284,625	184,009,930
Freestone	1916	24,202	16,925	47,299,677
Frio	1934	7,228,834	6,978,801	206,617,109
Gaines	1935	23,532,295	21,721,970	2,566,837,208
Galveston	1922	163,322	127,943	465,078,931
Garza	1926	2,196,451	1,909,215	382,013,465
Glasscock	1925	51,106,016	49,288,064	574,818,570
Goliad	1930	206,493	127,296	89,613,209
Gonzales	1902	41,688,233	36,270,882	383,273,749
Gray	1925	876,144	896,713	688,840,329
Grayson	1930	1,012,472	888,413	276,171,131
Gregg	1931	1,383,663	1,164,978	3,321,498,571
Grimes	1952	367,883	293,559	27,017,013
Guadalupe	1922	707,778	628,980	218,935,872
Hale	1946	1,131,070	979,498	206,585,490
Hamilton	1938	26	17	164,720
Hansford	1937	249,697	206,287	42,767,157
Hardeman	1944	795,020	568,807	97,232,986
Hardin	1893	913,367	760,190	464,372,711
Harris	1905	779,498	761,738	1,396,751,943

*Total includes condensate production.

County	Year of Discovery	Production in Barrels* 2019	2020	Total Production to Jan. 1, 2021
Harrison	1928	467,050	439,117	104,907,904
Hartley	1937	222,983	187,934	11,511,391
Haskell	1929	883,984	771,130	124,448,894
Hays	1956	0	0	296
Hemphill	1955	403,516	339,804	75,363,591
Henderson	1934	434,876	349,741	184,434,355
Hidalgo	1934	49,471	30,145	136,238,874
Hill	1929	0	0	80,670
Hockley	1937	11,965,204	10,814,434	1,876,844,456
Hood	1958	0	0	2,860,142
Hopkins	1936	153,160	139,621	93,161,245
Houston	1934	506,394	360,641	79,350,048
Howard	1925	87,623,802	96,471,676	1,208,960,682
Hudspeth	2008	0	0	59
Hunt	1942	459	467	2,027,944
Hutchnson	1923	474,216	376,819	541,468,656
Irion	1928	13,061,688	9,889,670	214,805,771
Jack	1923	845,674	820,078	220,308,421
Jackson	1934	2,326,311	1,758,113	700,716,814
Jasper	1928	302,886	260,298	46,404,824
Jeff Davis	1980	0	0	20,866
Jefferson	1901	519,563	398,709	578,631,223
Jim Hogg	1921	14,755	15,032	114,403,405
Jim Wells	1931	81,647	63,631	464,670,197
Johnson	1962	0	0	556,906
Jones	1926	420,371	483,981	230,656,349
Karnes	1930	107,666,119	93,733,010	993,166,760
Kaufman	1948	57,783	43,120	25,764,445
Kenedy	1947	115,691	81,073	43,323,490
Kent	1946	3,242,442	2,637,337	631,247,258
Kerr	1982	0	0	79,044
Kimble	1939	259	292	102,621
King	1943	1,808,002	1,475,697	204,357,798
Kinney	1960	0	0	402
Kleberg	1919	92,160	52,753	342,599,871
Knox	1946	176,789	174,992	65,121,138
Lamb	1945	226,387	203,522	428,431,680
Lampasas	1985	0	0	43,890,960
La Salle	1940	60,521,023	48,048,112	108569246
Lavaca	1941	7,026,029	6,219,215	87,317,545
Lee	1939	2,291,985	2,392,393	157,408,964
Leon	1936	605,774	429,998	79,863,595
Liberty	1904	791,523	600,442	562,936,406
Limestone	1920	63,382	59,905	121,426,749
Lipscomb	1956	991,813	739,650	99,614,806
Live Oak	1930	12,554,220	9,927,934	221,046,347
Llano	1978	0	0	647
Loving	1921	83,047,027	88,548,818	532,022,988
Lubbock	1941	955,535	824,244	89,020,852
Lynn	1950	275,045	179,177	24,593,435
Madison	1946	3,018,718	2,135,717	70,088,178
Marion	1910	493,628	354,591	59,982,745
Martin	1945	134,016,957	144,970,375	966,107,872
Matagorda	1901	187,670	189,534	292,046,458
Maverick	1929	1,162,465	968,981	69,882,459
McCulloch	1938	43,345	34,238	2,695,334
McLennan	1902	744	443	351,177
McMullen	1922	30,317,698	25,309,501	410,520,930
Medina	1901	95,691	77,546	12,513,738
Menard	1946	96,541	84,049	9,474,984
Midland	1945	189,503,922	189,294,777	1,537,052,962
Milam	1921	2,460,458	1,730,926	32,019,895
Mills	1982	0	0	28,122
Mitchell	1920	2,408,655	2,087,392	277,826,071
Montague	1919	946,145	794,511	356,696,403
Montgmry	1931	837,502	805,797	790,848,796
Moore	1926	244,833	191,405	34,438,439
Morris	2004	26,124	29,455	129,624
Motley	1957	38,937	33,134	11,487,581
Nacgdches	1866	9,393	7,855	7,365,112
Navarro	1894	131,865	114,488	222,821,568
Newton	1937	523,233	523,022	74,804,177
Nolan	1939	1,133,980	1,004,301	220,115,272
Nueces	1930	165,370	127,315	574,994,320
Ochiltree	1951	4,076,815	3,156,820	224,216,313
Oldham	1957	353,709	294,439	20,757,634
Orange	1913	424,871	338,203	172,365,391
Palo Pinto	1902	102,603	74,278	28,745,288
Panola	1917	239,893	205,001	122,174,798
Parker	1942	770	459	5,634,974
Parmer	1963	0	0	144,000
Pecos	1926	35,873,489	39,166,108	1,999,296,380
Polk	1930	445,335	380,073	145,187,923
Potter	1925	698,799	401,562	15,244,541
Presidio	1980	0	0	4,641
Rains	1955	0	0	148,911
Reagan	1923	52,531,529	46,612,896	847,090,468
Real	2003	1,015	781	31,231
Red River	1951	71,879	63,461	9,464,819
Reeves	1939	116,180,451	99,701,067	661,366,162
Refugio	1920	2,158,154	1,942,609	1,371,298,287
Roberts	1945	1,476,099	906,479	77,732,568
Robertson	1944	1,988,016	1,961,127	48,323,975
Runnels	1927	337,349	267,581	154,671,193
Rusk	1930	1,375,959	1,268,634	1,868,042,243
Sabine	1981	951	294	4,993,930
S.Augustine	1947	16,745	11,426	3,504,337
S. Jacinto	1940	47,299	53,113	30,125,349
S. Patricio	1930	377,708	248,037	498,453,039
San Saba	1982	0	0	499,480
Schleicher	1934	264,885	214,069	94,782,273
Scurry	1923	15,539,814	14,736,493	2,277,236,873
Shackelford	1910	352,865	313,047	191,308,614
Shelby	1917	25,672	18,141	6,118,387
Sherman	1938	62,066	69,958	10,445,628
Smith	1931	1,282,130	1,154,798	286,426,639
Somervell	1978	0	0	95,568
Starr	1929	341,690	245,817	318,023,085
Stephens	1916	1,790,012	1,572,887	373,137,393
Sterling	1947	670,508	548,698	104,506,171
Stonewall	1938	1,776,098	1,249,718	286,991,561

*Total includes condensate production.

County	Year of Discovery	Production in Barrels* 2019	2020	Total Production to Jan. 1, 2021
Sutton	1948	28,290	18,570	9,251,811
Swisher	1981	0	0	6
Tarrant	1969	0	0	368,843
Taylor	1929	351,957	347,958	150,999,769
Terrell	1952	29,592	21,966	10,843,539
Terry	1940	3,051,822	2,480,101	500,791,035
Thrckmrton	1925	689,937	572,084	233,210,423
Titus	1936	403,777	297,779	218,758,554
Tm Green	1940	477,033	336,014	100,079,472
Travis	1934	4,281	4,216	802,969
Trinity	1946	19,297	15,079	1,701,445
Tyler	1937	388,872	315,903	75,590,583
Upshur	1931	81,010	70,614	293,964,370
Upton	1925	74,270,073	77,466,624	1,365,581,514
Uvalde	1950	0	0	1,814
Val Verde	1935	1,306	539	161,366
Van Zandt	1929	448,849	423,875	560,231,986
Victoria	1931	1,717,604	1,004,628	266,906,405
Walker	1934	65,396	55,568	1,266,890
Waller	1934	152,145	108,605	35,716,695

County	Year of Discovery	Production in Barrels* 2019	2020	Total Production to Jan. 1, 2021
Ward	1928	49,180,683	47,101,254	1,070,771,906
Washngtn	1915	311,161	822,695	40,145,551
Webb	1921	325,223	1,144,254	285,301,712
Wharton	1925	677,916	629,313	366,697,137
Wheeler	1910	1,132,290	902,639	179,596,644
Wichita	1910	1,530,086	1,310,916	858,850,699
Wilbarger	1915	738,971	615,502	275,385,532
Willacy	1936	184,967	155,180	122,127,766
Williamson	1915	7,034	7,991	9,692,643
Wilson	1941	2,158,376	2,289,898	72,687,092
Winkler	1926	22,038,249	21,505,501	1,190,423,385
Wise	1942	172,739	149,865	116,577,630
Wood	1940	3,235,836	3,153,194	1,256,185,574
Yoakum	1936	27,419,490	26,111,179	2,440,437,070
Young	1917	888,987	783,830	327,697,866
Zapata	1919	55,556	25,771	50,941,907
Zavala	1937	7,161,114	6,841,813	110,003,489

Source: Railroad Commission, 2019–20 production reports.

*Total includes condensate production.

Rig Counts and Wells Drilled by Year

Year	Rotary rigs active* Texas	U.S.	Permits Texas	Texas wells completed Oil	Gas	Wells drilled** Texas
1990	348	1,009	14,033	5,593	2,894	11,231
1995	251	723	11,244	4,334	3,778	9,785
1996	283	779	12,669	4,061	4,060	9,747
1997	358	945	13,933	4,482	4,594	10,778
1998	303	827	9,385	4,509	4,907	11,057
1999	226	622	8,430	2,049	3,566	6,658
2000	343	918	12,021	3,111	4,580	8,854
2001	462	1,156	12,227	3,082	5,787	10,005
2002	338	830	9,716	3,268	5,474	9,877
2003	449	1,032	12,664	3,111	6,336	10,420
2004	506	1,192	14,700	3,446	7,118	11,587
2005	614	1,381	16,914	3,454	7,197	11,154
2006	746	1,649	18,952	4,761	8,534	12,764
2007	834	1,769	19,994	5,084	8,643	13,778
2008	898	1,880	24,073	6,208	10,361	16,615
2009	432	1,086	12,212	5,860	8,706	14,585
2010	659	1,541	18,029	5,392	4,071	9,477
2011	838	1,875	22,480	5,380	3,008	8,391
2012	899	1,919	22,479	10,936	3,580	14,535
2013	835	1,761	21,471	19,249	4,917	24,166
2014	882	1,862	25,792	24,999	3,585	29,554
2015	430	977	10,549	15,578	2,787	19,503
2016	236	510	8,113	7,813	2,129	10,468
2017	430	876	12,600	5,394	1,022	6,914
2018	513	1,032	13,307	8,588	1,813	10,986
2019	463	944	9,514	6,936	1,694	8,630
2020	206	436	5,322	8,867	2,032	10,899

Texas Railroad Commission. *Source for rig count: Baker Hughes Inc. This is an annual average from monthly reports.
Wells drilled in years before 2019 are oil and gas well **completions and dry holes drilled/plugged. Starting in 2019, only completions are counted.

Top Oil-Producing Counties since Discovery

There are 43 counties that have produced more than 500 million barrels of oil since discovery. The counties are ranked below. The column at right lists the number of regular producing oil wells in the county in February 2021.

Rank	County	Barrels	Oil Wells	Rank	County	Barrels	Oil Wells
1	Ector	3,437,595,733	6,248	23	Wichita	858,850,699	4479
2	Gregg	3,321,498,571	2,824	24	Reagan	847,090,468	4,296
3	Andrews	3,289,958,078	9,798	25	Montgomery	790,848,796	111
4	Gaines	2,566,837,208	3,555	26	Fort Bend	715,398,653	238
5	Yoakum	2,440,437,070	3,749	27	Jackson	700,716,814	266
6	Scurry	2,277,236,873	2,277	28	Gray	688,840,329	2,210
7	Pecos	1,999,296,380	3,272	29	Reeves	661,366,162	2576
8	Crane	1,883,946,084	3,706	30	Kent	631,247,258	590
9	Hockley	1,876,844,456	3,671	31	Duval	603,867,578	557
10	Rusk	1,868,042,243	1,749	32	De Witt	589,635,125	1188
11	Midland	1,537,052,962	6495	33	Jefferson	578,631,223	187
12	Harris	1,396,751,943	242	34	Nueces	574,994,320	124
13	Refugio	1,371,298,287	475	35	Glasscock	574,818,570	4,203
14	Upton	1,365,581,514	4983	36	Liberty	562,936,406	456
15	Brazoria	1,316,951,552	228	37	Van Zandt	560,231,986	218
16	Wood	1,256,185,574	609	38	Cochran	556,184,024	1,530
17	Howard	1,208,960,682	5,199	39	Dimmit	541,740,208	2113
18	Winkler	1,190,423,385	1,738	40	Hutchinson	541,468,656	1712
19	Ward	1,070,771,906	3,370	41	Loving	532,022,988	1554
20	Karnes	993,166,760	3097	42	Archer	510,779,083	2543
21	Martin	966,107,872	5,818	43	Terry	500,791,035	783
22	Chambers	943,279,000	138				

Source: Texas Railroad Commission.

Oil Production since Discovery

- More than 1 billion barrels
- 500 million to 1 billion
- 250 million to 500 million

Oil and Gas Production by County, 2020

In 2020 in Texas, the total natural gas production from gas wells was 6,567,517,206 thousand cubic feet (MCF) and total crude oil production from oil wells was 1,491,652,615 barrels (BBL). Total condensate was 267,073,743 barrels. Total casinghead production was 3,899,249,800 MCF. Counties not listed in the chart below had no production in 2020. Source: Texas Railroad Commission.

County	Oil (BBL)	Casinghead (MCF)	GW Gas (MCF)	Condensate (BBL)	County	Oil (BBL)	Casinghead (MCF)	GW Gas (MCF)	Condensate (BBL)
Anderson	527,486	725,709	1,608,489	23,355	Ector	16,540,414	39,016,330	2,291,933	4,726
Andrews	37,995,183	60,965,361	9,854,082	1,575,742	Edwards	1,901	0	1,855,697	193
Angelina	0	0	82,365,736	2,687	Ellis	32	12	2,453,483	0
Aransas	17,812	153,640	3,049,313	100,840	Erath	496	354	1,919,748	2,201
Archer	765,154	219,303	13,989	111	Falls	785	0	0	0
Atascosa	19,650,637	21,732,292	1,623,704	29,590	Fayette	2,009,558	5,605,396	23,829,546	1,107,930
Austin	284,542	297,977	8,448,693	25,174	Fisher	1,832,056	2,397,271	7,523	70
Bandera	512	0	0	0	Foard	64,083	7,663	40,029	0
Bastrop	69,293	47,478	26,727	4,609	Fort Bend	696,511	502,087	5,106,181	96,804
Baylor	60,584	4,367	0	0	Franklin	284,625	92,075	775,072	21,415
Bee	191,526	212,008	8,967,064	91,544	Freestone	16,925	56,448	79,020,942	44,712
Bexar	68,017	18	0	0	Frio	6,923,008	10,458,696	819,732	6,461
Borden	6,628,259	7,409,839	0	0	Gaines	21,710,218	20,422,598	234,767	2,862
Bowie	22,679	0	8,566	4,219	Galveston	127,803	34,213	850,606	78,574
Brazoria	2,706,047	625,107	8,177,472	317,758	Garza	1,909,215	206,599	0	0
Brazos	8,426,069	9,032,687	1,442,516	55,445	Glasscock	49,288,070	209,058,849	431,717	8,124
Brooks	72,819	131,354	11,621,428	254,681	Goliad	127,296	80,892	4,473,048	56,928
Brown	67,641	163,631	437,675	607	Gonzales	36,271,501	49,156,129	200,517	7,543
Burleson	15,416,834	12,280,093	1,644,681	63,732	Gray	896,545	1,314,455	5,364,217	9,327
Caldwell	942,101	34,252	0	0	Grayson	888,429	2,904,429	1,343,232	22,196
Calhoun	80,817	123,771	321,588	7,293	Gregg	1,165,644	1,694,069	23,126,217	112,778
Callahan	97,912	185,600	211,433	939	Grimes	293,559	1,756,573	7,315,244	41,383
Cameron	0	0	27,759	780	Guadalupe	628,736	40	0	0
Camp	55,998	0	34,373	0	Hale	972,809	1,121,877	0	0
Carson	89,968	380,755	7,012,129	29,447	Hamilton	17	0	47,357	0
Cass	485,545	311,528	165,093	1,243	Hansford	206,365	1,478,666	7,917,010	23,550
Chambers	1,980,215	717,539	3,061,069	36,088	Hardeman	568,855	119,835	0	0
Cherokee	152,102	366,619	18,834,266	167,913	Hardin	760,073	537,946	3,494,977	253,402
Childress	1,928	0	0	0	Harris	761,738	423,013	6,409,204	100,157
Clay	372,803	1,291,758	261,595	4,658	Harrison	439,062	1,038,625	272,386,920	364,227
Cochran	2,627,186	1,809,419	57,290	140	Hartley	187,888	67,514	853,689	0
Coke	234,436	1,237,914	242,724	2,679	Haskell	771,130	801,449	0	0
Coleman	152,471	258,981	226,233	1,432	Hemphill	361,897	3,521,572	77,204,876	1,429,170
Collngswrth	3,700	39,868	746,867	92	Henderson	349,642	2,755,689	6,372,836	15,248
Colorado	130,944	308,245	10,104,080	266,415	Hidalgo	30,145	1,553	41,439,799	508,237
Comanche	41,715	76,964	287,799	377	Hill	0	0	8,210,180	0
Concho	215,582	128,709	185,589	398	Hockley	10,814,410	5,805,143	17,014	1,416
Cooke	875,388	1,706,534	10,425,758	104,090	Hood	0	0	29,473,527	57,299
Cottle	81,695	8,885	1,811,884	19,818	Hopkins	139,688	73,180	30,354	3,480
Crane	6,988,445	33,784,540	7,756,882	66,474	Houston	360,641	417,061	2,029,755	102,064
Crockett	5,261,199	55,889,626	36,451,507	127,699	Howard	95,159,559	183,214,383	158,166	2,384
Crosby	663,291	6,149	0	0	Hunt	467	0	0	0
Culberson	482,202	2,140,720	403,044,647	37,756,293	Hutchinson	376,733	1,626,829	3,676,762	81,385
Dallas	0	0	6,328,446	0	Irion	9,884,321	138,849,017	1,067,130	12,394
Dawson	3,124,305	1,442,716	0	0	Jack	817,181	7,048,482	5,858,991	63,785
De Witt	33,224,351	95,487,693	165,265,355	20,948,511	Jackson	1,758,113	376,134	3,344,017	57,923
Denton	11,132	276,008	146,476,995	189,668	Jasper	260,298	400,951	8,622,986	472,130
Dickens	356,673	21,246	0	0	Jefferson	398,494	340,713	3,271,218	208,945
Dimmit	31,894,188	112,700,728	129,397,931	13,763,794	Jim Hogg	15,032	524	5,050,234	71,431
Donley	0	0	9,907	223	Jim Wells	63,644	197,226	2,310,400	11,394
Duval	772,136	114,729	5,369,459	23,831	Johnson	0	0	142,844,221	6,678
Eastland	124,217	315,400	1,203,461	17,173	Source: Texas Railroad Commission				

County	Oil (BBL)	Casinghead (MCF)	GW Gas (MCF)	Condensate (BBL)
Jones	484,170	168,713	14,938	452
Karnes	93,484,371	194,692,511	127,340,680	12,808,928
Kaufman	43,120	18,889	0	0
Kenedy	81,073	113,005	26,723,482	223,845
Kent	2,637,307	5,792,360	0	0
Kimble	292	0	0	0
King	1,475,697	203,762	75,217	40
Kleberg	52,753	124,046	5,342,501	107,905
Knox	174,988	189,769	0	0
La Salle	48,131,932	100,843,434	177,519,418	3,600,408
Lamb	210,397	189,056	0	0
Lavaca	6,216,928	9,935,400	26,518,618	1,240,019
Lee	2,392,492	4,426,313	564,292	20,512
Leon	430,132	1,063,419	32,631,642	31,546
Liberty	600,474	355,644	5,765,212	160,061
Limestone	59,905	12	27,498,791	16,514
Lipscomb	761,233	8,795,319	30,808,815	996,365
Live Oak	9,927,923	31,583,122	45,018,569	3,388,741
Loving	88,448,816	194,022,172	270,215,343	45,657,468
Lubbock	824,058	70,222	0	0
Lynn	179,177	55,944	0	0
Madison	2,135,224	5,702,848	1,667,108	88,149
Marion	354,436	295,078	1,099,176	20,578
Martin	144,405,379	292,095,499	6,762	110
Matagorda	185,730	201,105	10,855,908	310,103
Maverick	968,981	2,890,739	1,239,689	31,048
McCulloch	34,238	0	0	0
McLennan	443	0	0	0
McMullen	25,286,633	40,899,348	63,756,504	3,192,894
Medina	77,546	133	8,880	0
Menard	84,049	2,304	19,489	248
Midland	187,685,246	546,663,063	3,896,451	68,561
Milam	1,730,926	1,459,911	14,039	207
Mills	0	0	4,501	0
Mitchell	2,087,392	703,042	0	0
Montague	797,161	7,597,331	38,891,424	312,960
Montgomry	805,797	1,466,855	2,140,252	37,548
Moore	191,405	1,035,117	22,629,957	4,559
Morris	29,455	20,078	0	0
Motley	33,134	3,955	0	0
Nacogdchs	7,855	33,818	109,092,030	43,467
Navarro	114,488	120,222	299,663	10,693
Newton	523,024	686,218	1,771,067	100,950
Nolan	1,004,165	1,506,956	176,005	395
Nueces	127,355	195,984	7,033,611	156,233
Ochiltree	3,160,245	16,366,840	10,441,974	195,857
Oldham	284,628	473,941	37,004	0
Orange	338,203	691,806	1,699,477	138,531
Palo Pinto	74,271	1,489,544	4,418,819	31,147
Panola	205,128	1,274,745	508,695,130	1,364,474
Parker	459	124,832	51,240,410	64,321
Pecos	38,976,089	85,385,259	41,864,165	123,397
Polk	380,073	228,602	18,184,616	446,991
Potter	401,437	3,121,249	7,645,513	70,664
Reagan	46,673,113	309,463,793	847,350	11,295
Real	781	0	0	0
Red River	63,205	0	0	0

County	Oil (BBL)	Casinghead (MCF)	GW Gas (MCF)	Condensate (BBL)
Reeves	100,281,191	301,529,123	849,877,878	86,791,989
Refugio	1,931,069	5,963,814	1,415,282	21,543
Roberts	908,654	11,100,033	20,248,817	311,711
Robertson	1,961,127	940,544	51,782,645	3,448
Runnels	267,581	457,484	57,298	939
Rusk	1,268,753	1,715,657	96,554,264	537,400
Sabine	294	38	706,863	0
SanAugustn	11,426	197,326	214,958,585	16,289
San Jacinto	53,031	25,986	2,244,628	68,752
San Patricio	247,966	518,365	3,366,906	104,251
Schleicher	212,889	1,759,789	4,103,444	36,592
Scurry	14,647,692	40,946,476	0	0
Shackelford	313,103	413,902	746,107	9,405
Shelby	18,197	347,390	66,212,134	24,239
Sherman	73,274	76,412	13,129,374	4,682
Smith	1,154,808	1,269,363	19,618,205	260,120
Somervell	0	0	3,064,120	3,598
Starr	247,059	583,770	28,905,203	328,525
Stephens	1,572,741	1,951,212	5,698,423	36,263
Sterling	548,500	4,246,029	2,080,975	21,256
Stonewall	1,250,561	2,216,423	0	0
Sutton	18,570	33,529	19,169,476	31,089
Tarrant	0	0	356,151,886	10,901
Taylor	348,083	163,017	13,676	0
Terrell	21,908	330,693	11,532,068	57,316
Terry	2,480,003	390,628	0	0
Throckmrtn	572,076	1,934,970	105,965	3,686
Titus	297,779	1,233	0	84
Tom Green	334,825	2,263,359	307,159	6,945
Travis	4,216	0	0	0
Trinity	15,079	0	66,337	1,349
Tyler	315,903	282,509	8,298,581	921,824
Upshur	70,614	18,187	21,268,174	180,835
Upton	77,466,936	263,131,553	8,521,014	145,342
Val Verde	484	0	2,850,460	8
Van Zandt	423,875	203,311	1,641,179	2,009
Victoria	1,005,664	876,647	2,846,753	37,766
Walker	55,568	1,244,580	528,040	35,840
Waller	108,605	149	1,101,669	8,885
Ward	47,105,059	98,974,258	51,565,064	4,746,132
Washington	750,500	3,078,731	55,012,827	1,322,257
Webb	1,144,254	4,215,494	735,166,574	10,987,872
Wharton	629,125	795,732	7,635,295	129,350
Wheeler	899,289	7,571,749	72,837,978	1,645,850
Wichita	1,311,097	232,828	0	0
Wilbarger	615,492	93,466	0	0
Willacy	155,180	183,724	2,801,159	32,053
Williamson	7,991	0	0	0
Wilson	2,289,897	1,219,653	165	0
Winkler	21,588,063	42,378,962	12,560,911	867,420
Wise	149,207	3,052,471	163,145,260	313,729
Wood	3,153,194	49,177,534	4,719,366	167,309
Yoakum	26,111,179	38,646,237	40,642	0
Young	783,308	1,111,416	857,863	20,632
Zapata	25,771	51,207	65,485,719	52,891
Zavala	6,842,108	6,282,704	159,066	0

Source: Texas Railroad Commission

Top Gas-Producing Counties, 1993–2021

The top 37 natural gas-producing counties are listed in the chart below. The fourth column at the right lists the number of producing gas wells in the county in February 2021. Seventy-five counties have produced more than 500 billion cubic feet of natural gas since 1993 (see map). MCF is thousand cubic feet.

Rank	County	Gas (MCF)	Gas Wells	Rank	County	Gas (MCF)	Gas Wells
1	Webb	12,077,090,696	6,123	20	Nacogdoches	1,992,090,444	1,238
2	Panola	8,225,902,264	4,781	21	DeWitt	1,951,772,817	960
3	Tarrant	8,209,296,370	3,989	22	Dimmit	1,646,503,074	1,802
4	Zapata	6,505,149,450	2,661	23	Culberson	1,626,443,526	656
5	Hidalgo	5,247,132,874	1,204	24	Limestone	1,621,203,990	1,091
6	Johnson	5,106,839,554	2,843	25	Sutton	1,601,547,344	5,257
7	Freestone	4,562,558,413	2,918	26	Lavaca	1,571,944,409	429
8	Wise	4,486,680,589	4,085	27	La Salle	1,501,020,653	1,052
9	Pecos	4,194,566,316	1,200	28	Terrell	1,450,695,723	638
10	Denton	3,729,452,041	2,742	29	San Augustine	1,449,883,612	309
11	Reeves	3,324,471,873	1,596	30	Karnes	1,443,865,314	988
12	Hemphill	3,142,196,211	2,227	31	Parker	1,415,735,465	1,439
13	Starr	3,034,741,424	1,046	32	Leon	1,341,748,235	547
14	Harrison	2,993,972,409	2,119	33	Shelby	1,328,615,245	603
15	Wheeler	2,941,751,975	1,663	34	Brooks	1,327,773,404	357
16	Rusk	2,756,155,235	2,152	35	Gregg	1,317,820,663	782
17	Robertson	2,670,875,707	873	36	Duval	1,300,852,074	323
18	Crockett	2,654,199,501	5,492	37	Lipscomb	1,289,140,673	1,315
19	Loving	2,087,389,189	855				

Source: Texas Railroad Commission.

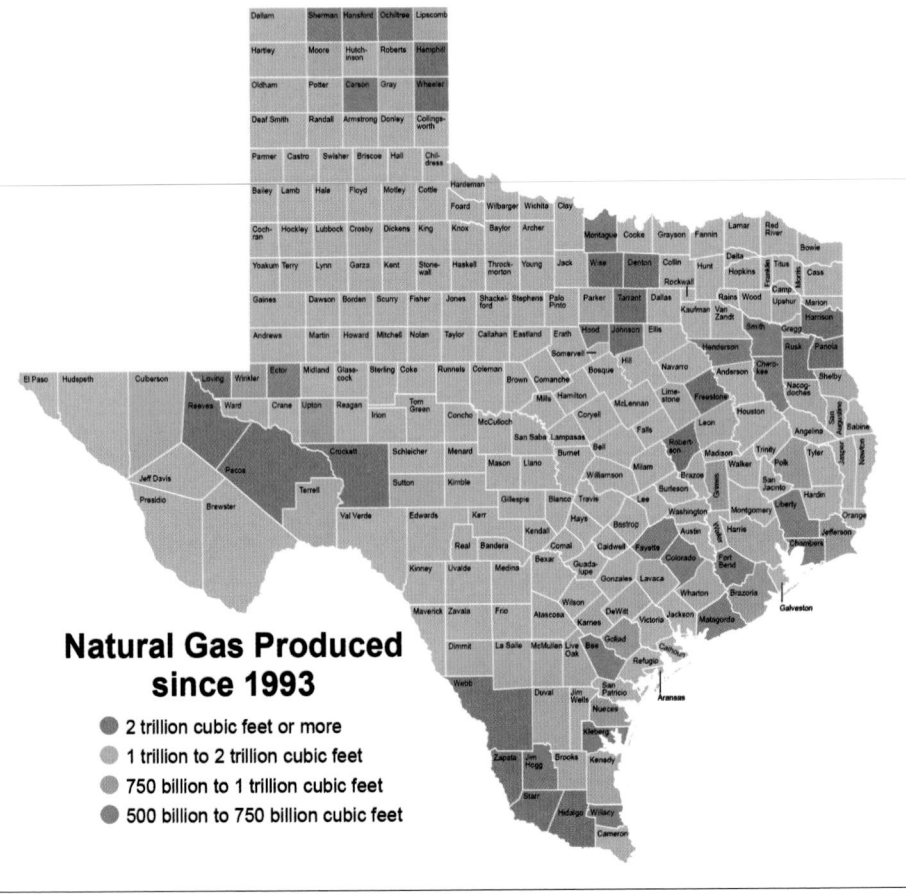

Natural Gas Produced since 1993

- 2 trillion cubic feet or more
- 1 trillion to 2 trillion cubic feet
- 750 billion to 1 trillion cubic feet
- 500 billion to 750 billion cubic feet

Petroleum Production and Income in Texas

Year	Crude Oil				Natural Gas		
	Production (thousand barrels)	Value (in thousands)	Average Price per barrel (nominal)	*Average price per barrel (2005 $)	Production (million cubic feet)	Value (in thousands)	Wellhead Price (cents per **Mcf)
1915	24,943	$ 13,027	$ 0 .52	NA	13,324	$ 2,594	19.5
1925	144,648	262,270	1.81	NA	134,872	7,040	5.2
1935	392,666	367,820	0.94	NA	642,366	13,233	2.1
1945	754,710	914,410	1.21	NA	1,711,401	44,839	2.6
1955	1,053,297	2,989,330	2.84	NA	4,730,798	378,464	8.0
1965	1,000,749	2,962,119	2.96	NA	6,636,555	858,396	12.9
1970	1,249,697	4,104,005	3.28	NA	8,357,716	1,203,511	14.4
1975	1,221,929	9,336,570	7.64	NA	7,485,764	3,885,112	51.9
1982	923,868	29,074,126	31.77	57.33	6,497,678	13,567,151	208.8
1983	876,205	22,947,814	29.35	50.95	5,643,183	14,672,275	225.0
1984	874,079	25,138,520	28.87	48.31	5,864,224	13,487,715	230.0
1985	860,300	23,159,286	26.80	43.52	5,805,098	12,665,114	218.0
1986	813,620	11,976,488	14.73	23.40	5,663,491	8,778,410	155.0
1987	754,213	13,221,345	17.55	27.10	5,516,224	7,612,389	138.0
1988	727,928	10,729,660	14.71	21.96	5,702,643	7,983,700	141.0
1989	679,575	12,123,624	17.81	25.62	5,595,190	8,113,026	145.0
1990	672,081	15,047,902	22.37	30.98	5,533,771	8,281,372	149.7
1991	672,810	12,836,080	19.04	25.47	5,509,990	7,713,986	143.0
1992	642,059	11,820,306	18.32	23.94	5,436,408	8,643,888	174.0
1993	572,600	9,288,800	16.19	20.70	5,606,498	7,365,800	204.0
1994	533,900	7,977,500	14.98	18.76	5,675,748	6,220,300	185.0
1995	503,200	8,177,700	16.38	20.09	5,672,105	5,305,200	155.0
1996	478,100	9,560,800	20.31	24.44	5,770,255	6,945,000	217.0
1997	464,900	8,516,800	18.66	22.07	5,814,745	8,134,200	232.0
1998	440,600	5,472,400	12.28	14.36	5,772,080	6,362,900	196.0
1999	337,100	5,855,800	17.29	19.93	5,538,929	6,789,700	219.0
2000	348,900	10,037,300	28.60	32.26	5,645,972	12,837,600	368.0
2001	325,500	7,770,500	23.41	25.82	5,668,602	13,708,700	400.0
2002	335,600	8,150,400	23.77	25.80	5,611,958	9,840,800	295.0
2003	333,300	9,708,600	29.13	30.96	5,671,689	14,797,800	488.0
2004	327,910	12,762,650	38.79	40.08	5,817,227	17,077,700	546.0
2005	327,600	12,744,600	52.61	52.61	5,700,613	16,399,400	733.0
2006	314,600	19,353,500	61.31	59.38	6,077,786	23,500,800	639.0
2007	311,830	21,341,100	68.30	64.30	6,421,375	22,968,420	625.0
2008	315,896	30,409,170	96.85	89.28	7,271,815	34,415,890	797.0
2009	349,391	18,455,530	57.40	52.31	7,573,033	12,167,800	367.0
2010	369,953	26,054,900	76.23	68.88	7,246,042	11,796,700	448.0
2011	448,903	39,420,500	91.99	81.15	7,051,594	13,646,300	395.0
2012	724,422	55,145,600	92.50	NA	7,128,775	12,959,100	266.0
2013	749,876	73,666,700	95.80	NA	7,725,119	15,358,900	373.0
2014	927,417	85,962,300	87.02	NA	8,171,230	18,034,000	428.0
2015	1,004,774	48,132,920	48.79	NA	7,871,200	8,827,180	263.0
2016	974,612	32,854,310	42.40	NA	6,996,000	20,566,930	255.0
2017	1,026,765	49,869,976	48.57	NA	6,300,292	20,664,957	328.0
2018	1,274,569	76,359,429	59.91	NA	5,742,978	19,468,695	339.0
2019	1,586,337	90,405,346	56.99	NA	6,775,942	14,907,072	220.0
2020	1,495,495	$ 58,563,584	$ 39.16	NA	6,593,494	$ 11,802,354	179.0

Revised May 2019. NA, not available.
*In chained (2005) dollars, from the U.S. Energy Information Administration (EIA).
**Mcf (thousand cubic feet)

Sources: Previously from the Texas Railroad Commission, Texas Mid-Continent Oil & Gas Association and, beginning in 1979, data are from Department of Energy. Data since 1993 are from the state comptroller and EIA and the railroad commission. Federal figures do not include gas that is vented or flared or used for pressure maintenance and repressuring, but do include non-hydrocarbon gases.

Offshore Production History – Oil and Gas

The cumulative offshore natural gas production as of Jan. 1, 2021, was 4,213,049,080 thousand cubic feet (Mcf). The cumulative offshore oil production was 42,776,352 barrels.

Production in Recent Years

Year	Crude Oil BBL	Casing-head Mcf	Gas Well Gas Mcf	Conden-sate BBL
2000	548,046	335,415	44,086,237	220,309
2005	450,378	389,301	38,589,312	451,692
2009	480,514	1,673,140	38,218,699	918,218
2010	477,303	1,160,607	28,143,515	866,959
2011	522,307	925,166	23,916,678	566,425
2012	605,389	902,900	17,011,234	435,049
2013	500,209	460,876	15,053,574	370,290
2014	424,191	574,464	12,280,841	354,585
2015	291,428	233,094	9,982,738	281,510
2016	154,005	48,816	8,337,712	231,975
2017	118,474	35,054	6,049,351	183,464
2018	129,485	59,654	4,117,566	203,940
2019	132,838	78,601	3,282,580	174,754
2020	105,514	56,486	2,477,909	126,695

2020 Production by Area

Offshore Area	Crude Oil BBL	Casing-head Mcf	Gas Well Gas Mcf	Conden-sate BBL
Brazos-LB	0	0	0	0
Brazos-SB	0	0	0	0
Galveston-LB	61,785	33,269	149,956	77,745
Galveston-SB	0	0	0	0
High Island-LB	0	0	537,149	0
High Island-SB	0	0	0	0
Matagrda Is.-LB	42,492	21,075	0	0
Matagrda Is.-SB	0	0	0	0
Mustang Is.-LB	0	0	620,239	9,647
Mustang Is.-SB	1,237	2,142	1,170,565	39,303
N. Padre Is.-LB	0	0	0	0
Sabine Pass	0	0	0	0
Total	**105,514**	**56,486**	**2,477,909**	**126,695**

Offshore Areas

Receipts by Texas from Tidelands

The Republic of Texas had proclaimed its Gulf boundaries as three marine leagues, recognized by international law as traditional national boundaries. These boundaries were never seriously questioned when Texas joined the Union in 1845.

In 1930 a congressional resolution authorized the U.S. Attorney General to file suit to establish offshore lands as properties of the federal government. Congress returned the disputed lands to Texas in 1953, and the U.S. Supreme Court confirmed Texas' ownership in 1960.

In 1978, the federal government also granted states a "fair and equitable" share of the revenues from offshore leases within three miles of the states' outermost boundary. States did not receive any such revenue until 1986.

The table shows annual receipts from tidelands in the Gulf of Mexico by the Texas General Land Office from 1963 to Aug. 31, 2018. It does not include revenue from bays and other submerged area owned by Texas. Totals include previous years not shown in this chart.

Source: General Land Office.

From	To	Total	Bonus	Rental	Royalty	Lease
9-01-1963	8-31-1964	$ 3,656,236.75	$ 2,435,244.36	$ 525,315.00	$ 695,677.39	...
9-01-1964	8-31-1965	54,654,576.96	53,114,943.63	755,050.12	784,583.21	...
9-01-1965	8-31-1966	22,148,825.44	18,223,357.84	3,163,475.00	761,992.60	...
9-01-1966	8-31-1967	8,469,680.86	3,641,414.96	3,711,092.65	1,117,173.25	...
9-01-1967	8-31-1968	6,305,851.00	1,251,852.50	2,683,732.50	2,370,266.00	...
9-01-1968	8-31-1969	6,372,268.28	1,838,118.33	1,491,592.50	3,042,557.45	...
9-01-1969	8-31-1970	10,311,030.48	5,994,666.32	618,362.50	3,698,001.66	...
9-01-1970	8-31-1971	9,969,629.17	4,326,120.11	726,294.15	4,917,214.91	...
9-01-1971	8-31-1972	7,558,327.21	1,360,212.64	963,367.60	5,234,746.97	...
9-01-1972	8-31-1973	9,267,975.68	3,701,737.30	920,121.60	4,646,116.78	...
9-01-1973	8-31-1974	41,717,670.04	32,981,619.28	1,065,516.60	7,670,534.16	...
9-01-1974	8-31-1975	27,321,536.62	5,319,762.85	2,935,295.60	19,066,478.17	...
9-01-1975	8-31-1976	38,747,074.09	6,197,853.00	3,222,535.84	29,326,685.25	...
9-01-1976	8-31-1977	84,196,228.27	41,343,114.81	2,404,988.80	40,448,124.66	...
9-01-1977	8-31-1978	118,266,812.05	49,807,750.45	4,775,509.92	63,683,551.68	...
9-01-1978	8-31-1979	100,410,268.68	34,578,340.94	7,318,748.40	58,513,179.34	...
9-01-1979	8-31-1980	200,263,803.03	34,733,270.02	10,293,153.80	155,237,379.21	...
9-01-1980	8-31-1981	219,126,876.54	37,467,196.97	13,100,484.25	168,559,195.32	...
9-01-1981	8-31-1982	250,824,581.69	27,529,516.33	14,214,478.97	209,080,586.39	...
9-01-1982	8-31-1983	165,197,734.83	10,180,696.40	12,007,476.70	143,009,561.73	...
9-01-1983	8-31-1984	152,755,934.29	32,864,122.19	8,573,996.87	111,317,815.23	...
9-01-1984	8-31-1985	140,561,690.79	32,650,127.75	6,837,603.70	101,073,959.34	...
9-01-1985	8-31-1986	516,503,771.08	6,365,426.23	4,241,892.75	78,289,592.27	$427,606,859.83
9-01-1986	8-31-1987	60,066,571.05	4,186,561.63	1,933,752.50	44,691,907.22	9,254,349.70
9-01-1987	8-31-1988	56,875,069.22	14,195,274.28	1,817,058.90	28,068,202.53	12,794,533.51
9-01-1988	8-31-1989	61,793,380.04	12,995,892.74	1,290,984.37	35,160,568.40	12,345,934.53
9-01-1989	8-31-1990	68,701,751.51	7,708,449.54	1,289,849.87	40,331,537.06	19,371,915.04
9-01-1990	8-31-1991	90,885,856.99	3,791,832.77	1,345,711.07	70,023,601.01	15,724,712.14
9-01-1991	8-31-1992	51,154,511.34	4,450,850.00	1,123,585.54	26,776,191.35	18,803,884.45
9-01-1992	8-31-1993	60,287,712.60	3,394,230.00	904,359.58	34,853,679.68	21,135,443.34
9-01-1993	8-31-1994	57,825,043.59	3,570,657.60	694,029.30	32,244,987.95	21,315,368.74
9-01-1994	8-31-1995	62,143,227.78	8,824,722.93	674,479.79	34,691,023.35	17,951,001.71
9-01-1995	8-31-1996	68,166,645.51	13,919,246.80	1,102,591.39	32,681,315.73	20,463,491.59
9-01-1996	8-31-1997	90,614,935.93	22,007,378.46	1,319,614.78	41,605,792.50	25,682,150.19
9-01-1997	8-31-1998	104,016,006.75	36,946,312.49	2,070,802.90	38,760,320.91	26,238,570.45
9-01-1998	8-31-1999	53,565,810.30	5,402,171.00	2,471,128.47	23,346,515.93	22,345,994.90
9-01-1999	8-31-2000	55,465,763.99	3,487,564.80	2,171,636.35	24,314,241.99	25,492,320.85
9-01-2000	8-31-2001	68,226,347.58	9,963,608.68	1,830,378.11	23,244,034.74	33,188,326.05
9-01-2001	8-31-2002	30,910,283.91	9,286,015.01	1,545,583.01	13,369,771.56	6,708,914.14
9-01-2002	8-31-2003	50,881,515.90	15,152,092.40	1,071,377.60	19,648,641.39	15,009,404.51
9-01-2003	8-31-2004	54,379,791.20	14,448,555.70	1,094,201.41	25,199,635.21	13,637,398.88
9-01-2004	8-31-2005	53,594,809.87	9,148,220.20	1,624,666.50	32,406,328.78	10,415,594.39
9-01-2005	8-31-2006	60,829,271.63	22,565,845.14	1,605,090.30	23,287,994.53	13,370,341.66
9-01-2006	8-31-2007	52,513,621.85	15,879,784.44	2,022,859.80	18,785,626.55	15,825,351.06
9-01-2007	8-31-2008	86,705,980.28	4,632,175.50	1,485,080.97	68,408,943.01	12,179,780.80
9-01-2008	8-31-2009	65,835,625.76	3,896,795.20	1,020,204.33	53,166,364.50	7,752,261.73
9-01-2009	8-31-2010	49,647,832.14	3,352,431.20	603,406.00	41,901,754.81	3,790,240.13
9-01-2010	8-31-2011	50,360,843.36	4,088,819.06	546,404.80	43,602,027.62	2,123,591.88
9-01-2011	8-31-2012	37,561,595.54	2,436,420.00	217,356.00	33,327,417.09	1,580,402.45
9-01-2012	8-31-2013	32,676,026.13	1,079,400.00	339,941.00	30,353,820.49	902,864.64
9-01-2013	8-31-2014	28,103,953.40	217,000.00	193,125.00	26,665,893.97	1,027,934.53
9-01-2014	8-31-2015	17,922,043.53	969,600.00	71,894.00	16,302,558.59	577,990.94
9-01-2015	8-31-2016	7,053,383.42	0.00	112,350.00	6,819,050.31	121,983.11
9-01-2016	8-31-2017	7,422,396.66	100,800.00	48,712.00	7,172,244.48	100,640.18
9-01-2017	8-31-2018	10,237,935.90	0.00	48,000.00	5,759,255.41	4,430,680.49
Totals		$ 3,974,612.907.55	$ 774,513,049,71	$ 147,166,154.10	$ 2,213,663,471.20	$ 839,270.232.54
Inside three-mile line		$ 533,256,002.78	$ 180,838,499.91	$ 39,193,553.27	$ 313,223,949.60	0.00
Between three-mile and three marine-league line		$ 2,599,261,306.65	$ 591,022,465.41	$ 107,734,519.64	$1,900,439,521.60	0.00
Outside three marine-league line		$ 842,095,598,12	$ 2,652,084.39	$ 173,281.19	0.00	$ 839,270,232,54

Nonpetroleum Minerals

Sources: U.S. Geological Survey's mineral industry surveys, www.usgs.gov/centers/nmic/mineral-industry-surveys; Bureau of Economic Geology, The University of Texas at Austin, www.beg.utexas.edu

There are many nonpetroleum, or nonfuel, minerals found in Texas. Although they are overshadowed by production of petroleum, natural gas, and natural gas liquids, many are important to the economy.

In 2020, Texas nonfuel mineral production was valued at **$6.0 billion**, a 5.9 percent decrease from the $6.5 billion in total value for 2019, and accounted for 7.4 percent of the total U.S. nonfuel mineral production value of $82.3 billion. Among all 50 states, **Texas ranked third in nonfuel mineral production** for the sixth year in a row (since 2015), behind Arizona ($7.0 billion in 2020) and Nevada ($8.2 billion).

The nonfuel mineral commodities produced in Texas in 2020 include: barite, cement (portland), gold, gypsum, helium, lime, ammonia, salt, sand and gravel (both construction and industrial), selenium, stone (both crushed and dimension), sulfur, talc, vanadium, and zeolites (clinoptilolite).

Texas was the leader in both crushed and dimension stone production, and second to California in sand and gravel (construction).

ALUMINUM: No aluminum ores are mined in Texas, but three Texas plants process aluminum materials in one or more ways. Plants in San Patricio and Calhoun counties produce aluminum oxide (alumina) from imported raw ore (bauxite), and a plant in Milam County reduces the oxide to aluminum.

ASBESTOS: Small occurrences of amphibole-type asbestos have been found in the state. In West Texas, richterite, a white, long-fibered amphibole, is associated with some of the talc deposits northwest of Allamoore in Hudspeth County. Another type, tremolite, has been found in the Llano Uplift of Central Texas where it is associated with serpentinite in eastern Gillespie and western Blanco counties. No asbestos is mined in Texas.

ASPHALT (NATIVE): Asphalt-bearing Cretaceous limestones crop out in Burnet, Kinney, Pecos, Reeves, Uvalde, and other counties. The most significant deposit is in southwestern Uvalde County, where asphalt occurs naturally in pore spaces of the Anacacho Limestone. The material is quarried and used extensively as road-paving material. Asphalt-bearing sandstones occur in Anderson, Angelina, Cooke, Jasper, Maverick, Montague, Nacogdoches, Uvalde, Zavala, and other counties.

BARITE: Deposits of a heavy, nonmetallic mineral, barite (barium sulphate), have been found in many localities, including Baylor, Brown, Brewster, Culberson, Gillespie, Howard, Hudspeth, Jeff Davis, Kinney, Live Oak, Llano, Taylor, Val Verde, and Webb counties. During the 1960s, there was small, intermittent production in the Seven Heart Gap area of the Apache Mountains in Culberson County, where barite was mined from open pits. Most of the deposits are known to be relatively small, but the Webb County deposit has not been evaluated. Grinding plants, which prepare barite mined outside of Texas for use chiefly as a weighting agent in well-drilling muds and as a filler, are located in Brownsville, Corpus Christi, El Paso, Galena Park, Galveston, and Houston.

BASALT (TRAP ROCK): Masses of basalt, a hard, dark-colored, fine-grained igneous rock, crop out in Kinney, Travis, Uvalde, and several other counties along the Balcones Fault Zone, and also in the Trans-Pecos area of West Texas. Basalt is quarried near Knippa in Uvalde County for use as road-building material, railroad ballast, and other aggregate.

BENTONITE (see CLAYS).

BERYLLIUM: Occurrences of beryllium minerals at several Trans-Pecos localities have been recognized for several years.

BRINE (see also SALT, SODIUM SULPHATE): Many wells in Texas produce brine by solution mining of subsurface salt deposits, mostly in West Texas counties such as Andrews, Crane, Ector, Loving, Midland, Pecos, Reeves, Ward, and others. These wells in the Permian Basin dissolve salt from the Salado Formation, an enormous salt deposit that extends in the subsurface from north of the Big Bend northward to Kansas, has an east-west width of 150 to 200 miles, and may have several hundred feet of net salt thickness. The majority of the brine is used in the petroleum industry, but it also is used in water softening, the chemical industry, and other uses. Three Gulf Coast counties, Fort Bend, Duval, and Jefferson, have brine stations that produce from salt domes.

BUILDING STONE (DIMENSION STONE): Granite and limestone currently are quarried for use as dimension stone. The granite quarries are located in Burnet, Gillespie, Llano, and Mason counties; the limestone quarries are in Shackelford and Williamson counties. Past production of limestone for use as dimension stone has been reported in Burnet, Gillespie, Jones, Tarrant, Travis, and several other counties. There also has been production of sandstone in various counties for use as dimension stone.

CEMENT MATERIALS: Cement is currently manufactured in Bexar, Comal, Dallas, Ector, Ellis, Hays, McLennan, Nolan, and Potter counties. Many of these plants utilize Cretaceous limestones and shales or clays as raw materials for the cement. On the Texas High Plains, a cement plant near Amarillo uses impure caliche as the chief raw material. Iron oxide, also a constituent of cement, is available from the iron ore deposits of East Texas and from smelter slag. Gypsum, added to the cement as a retarder, is found chiefly in the North-Central, Central, and Trans-Pecos areas.

A new greenfields white cement production plant has been proposed near Brady, but it has been delayed due to local opposition. It would be the third of its kind in the U.S.

Cement Production in Texas (metric tons)		
Type	**2020**	**2017**
Portland and Blended	11,858,581	11,465,785
Masonry	297,338	304,320
Clinker	10,864,668	10,128,636
Source: Industry surveys at USGS		

CHROMIUM: Chromite-bearing rock has been found in several small deposits around the margin of the Coal Creek serpentinite mass in northeastern Gillespie County and northwestern Blanco County. Exploration has not revealed significant deposits.

CLAYS: Texas has an abundance and variety of ceramic and nonceramic clays and is one of the country's leading producers of clay products.

Almost any kind of clay, ranging from common clay used to make brick and tile to clays suitable for manufacture of specialty whitewares, can be used for ceramic purposes. Fire clay suitable for use as refractories occurs chiefly in East and North-Central Texas; ball clay, a high-quality plastic ceramic clay, is found in East Texas.

Ceramic clay suitable for quality structural clay products, such as structural building brick, paving brick, and drain tile, is especially abundant in East and North-Central Texas. Common clay suitable for use in the manufacture of cement and ordinary brick is found in most counties of the state. Many of the Texas clays will expand or bloat upon rapid firing and are suitable for the manufacture of lightweight aggregate, which is used mainly in concrete blocks and highway surfacing.

Nonceramic clays are utilized without firing. They are used primarily as bleaching and absorbent clays, fillers, coaters, additives, bonding clays, drilling muds, catalysts, and potentially as sources of alumina. Most of the nonceramic clays in Texas are bentonites and fuller's earth. These occur extensively in the Coastal Plain and locally in the High Plains and Big Bend areas. Kaolin clays in parts of East Texas are potential sources of such nonceramic products as paper coaters and fillers, rubber fillers, and drilling agents. Relatively high in alumina, these clays also are a potential source of metallic aluminum.

COAL (see also LIGNITE): Bituminous coal, which occurs in North-Central, South, and West Texas, was a significant energy source in Texas prior to the large-scale development of oil and gas. During the period from 1895–1943, Texas mines produced more than 25 million tons of coal. The mines were inactive for many years, but the renewed interest in coal as a major energy source prompted a revaluation of Texas' coal deposits. In the late 1970s, bituminous coal production resumed in the state on a limited scale when mines were opened in Coleman, Erath, and Webb counties.

Much of the state's bituminous coal occurs in North-Central Texas. Deposits are found there in Pennsylvanian rocks within a large area that includes Coleman, Eastland, Erath, Jack, McCulloch, Montague, Palo Pinto, Parker, Throckmorton, Wise, Young, and other counties. Before the general availability of oil and gas, underground coal mines near Thurber, Bridgeport, Newcastle, Strawn, and other points annually produced significant coal tonnages. Preliminary evaluations indicate substantial amounts of coal may remain in the North-Central Texas area. The coal seams there are generally no more than 30 inches thick and are commonly covered by well-consolidated overburden. Ash and sulphur content are high. Beginning in 1979, two bituminous coal mine operations in North-Central Texas, one in southern Coleman County and one in northwestern Erath County, produced coal to be used as fuel by the cement industry. Neither mine is currently operating.

In South Texas, bituminous coal occurs in the **Eagle Pass district of Maverick County**, and bituminous cannel coal is present in the Santo Tomas district of Webb County. The Eagle Pass area was a leading coal-producing district in Texas during the late 1800s and early 1900s. The bituminous coal in that area, which occurs in the Upper Cretaceous Olmos Formation, has a high ash content and a moderate moisture and sulfur content. According to reports, Maverick County coal beds range from four to seven feet thick.

The cannel coals of western Webb County occur near the Rio Grande in middle Eocene strata. They were mined for more than 50 years and used primarily as a boiler fuel. Mining ceased from 1939 until 1978, when a surface mine was opened 30 miles northwest of Laredo to produce cannel coal for use as fuel in the cement industry and for export. An additional mine has since been opened in that county. Tests

Year	Total
2020	19,639,076
2019	23,306,720
2018	24,842,955
2017	35,415,535
2016	39,139,879
2015	36,277,112
2014	43,633,881
2013	42,449,594
2012	43,536,176
2011	45,587,404
2010	41,419,857
2009	37,099,067
2008	40,152,112
2007	38,403,681
2006	46,128,231
2005	47,168,916
2004	45,680,097
2003	48,179,875
2002	44,683,793
pre-2002	1,143,894,272

Texas Coal and Lignite Production (short tons)

Source: Railroad Commission of Texas

show that the coals of the Webb County Santo Tomas district have a high hydrogen content and yield significant amounts of gas and oil when distilled. They also have a high sulfur content. A potential use might be as a source of various petrochemical products.

Coal deposits in the Trans-Pecos country of West Texas include those in the Cretaceous rocks of the Terlingua area of Brewster County, the Eagle Spring area of Hudspeth County, and the San Carlos area of Presidio County. The coal deposits in these areas are believed to have relatively little potential for development as a fuel. They have been sold in the past as a soil amendment (see **LEONARDITE**).

COPPER: Copper minerals have been found in the Trans-Pecos area of West Texas, in the Llano Uplift area of Central Texas, and in redbed deposits of North Texas. No copper has been mined in Texas during recent years, and the total copper produced in the state has been relatively small. Past attempts to mine the North Texas and Llano Uplift copper deposits resulted in small shipments.

Practically all the copper production in the state has been from the Van Horn–Allamoore district of Culberson and Hudspeth counties in the Trans-Pecos area. Chief output was from the Hazel copper-silver mine of Culberson County that yielded over 1 million pounds of copper during 1891–1947. Copper ores and concentrates from outside of Texas are processed at smelters in El Paso and Amarillo.

CRUSHED STONE: Texas is among the leading states in the production of crushed stone. Most production consists of limestone; other kinds of crushed stone produced in the state include basalt (trap rock), dolomite, granite, marble, rhyolite, sandstone, and serpentinite. Large tonnages of crushed stone are used as aggregate in concrete, as road material, and in the manufacture of cement and lime. Some is used as riprap, terrazzo, roofing chips, filter material, and fillers, as well as other purposes. In 2018, Texas led the country in the production of crushed stone, followed by Pennsylvania, Florida, and North Carolina.

DIATOMITE (DIATOMACEOUS EARTH): Diatomite is a very lightweight siliceous material consisting of the remains of microscopic aquatic plants (diatoms). It is used chiefly as a filter and filler; other uses are for thermal insulation, as an abrasive, as an insecticide carrier, as a lightweight aggregate, and for other purposes. The diatomite was deposited in shallow, fresh-water lakes that were present in the High Plains during portions of the Pliocene and Pleistocene epochs. Deposits have been found in Armstrong, Crosby, Dickens, Ector, Hartley, and Lamb counties. No diatomite is mined in Texas.

DOLOMITE ROCK: Dolomite rock, which consists largely of the mineral dolomite (calcium-magnesium carbonate), commonly is associated with limestone in Texas. Areas in which dolomite rock occurs include Central Texas, the Callahan Divide, and parts of the Edwards Plateau, High Plains, and West Texas. Some of the principal deposits of dolomite rock are found in Bell, Brown, Burnet, Comanche, Edwards, El Paso, Gillespie, Lampasas, Mills, Nolan, Taylor, and Williamson counties. Dolomite rock can be used as crushed stone (although much of Texas dolomite is soft and not a good aggregate material), in the manufacture of lime, and as a source of magnesium.

FELDSPAR: Large crystals and crystal fragments of feldspar minerals occur in the Precambrian pegmatite rocks that crop out in the Llano Uplift area of Central Texas, including Blanco, Burnet, Gillespie, Llano, and Mason counties, and in the Van Horn area of Culberson and Hudspeth counties in West Texas. Feldspar has been mined in Llano County for use as roofing granules and as a ceramic material. Feldspar is currently mined in Burnet County for use as an aggregate.

FLUORSPAR: The mineral fluorite (calcium fluoride), which is known commercially as fluorspar, occurs in both Central and West Texas. In Central Texas, the deposits that have been found in Burnet, Gillespie, and Mason counties are not considered adequate to sustain mining operations. In West Texas, deposits have been

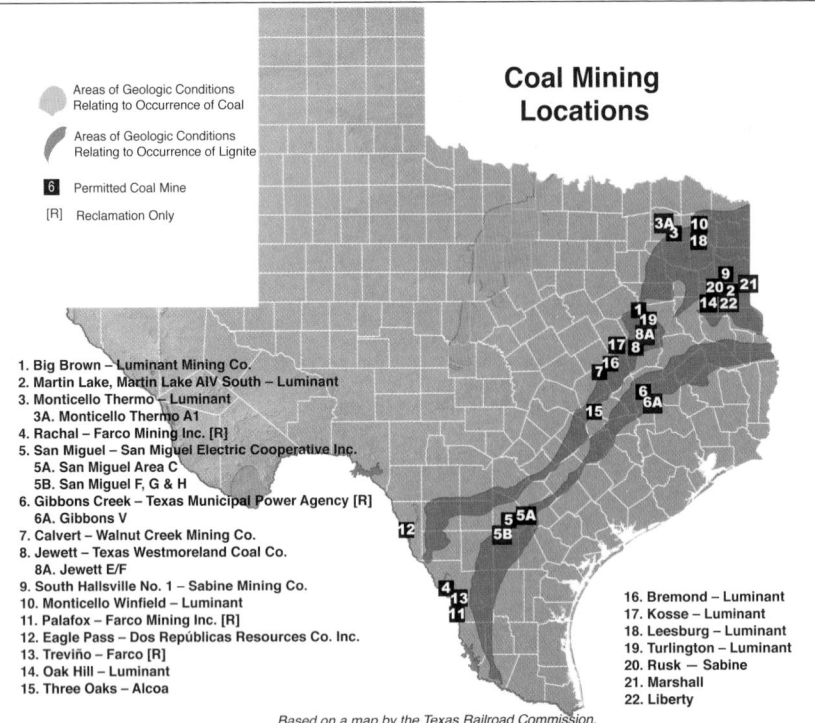

Areas of Geologic Conditions Relating to Occurrence of Coal

Areas of Geologic Conditions Relating to Occurrence of Lignite

6 Permitted Coal Mine

[R] Reclamation Only

Coal Mining Locations

1. Big Brown – Luminant Mining Co.
2. Martin Lake, Martin Lake AIV South – Luminant
3. Monticello Thermo – Luminant
   3A. Monticello Thermo A1
4. Rachal – Farco Mining Inc. [R]
5. San Miguel – San Miguel Electric Cooperative Inc.
   5A. San Miguel Area C
   5B. San Miguel F, G & H
6. Gibbons Creek – Texas Municipal Power Agency [R]
   6A. Gibbons V
7. Calvert – Walnut Creek Mining Co.
8. Jewett – Texas Westmoreland Coal Co.
   8A. Jewett E/F
9. South Hallsville No. 1 – Sabine Mining Co.
10. Monticello Winfield – Luminant
11. Palafox – Farco Mining Inc. [R]
12. Eagle Pass – Dos Repúblicas Resources Co. Inc.
13. Treviño – Farco [R]
14. Oak Hill – Luminant
15. Three Oaks – Alcoa

16. Bremond – Luminant
17. Kosse – Luminant
18. Leesburg – Luminant
19. Turlington – Luminant
20. Rusk — Sabine
21. Marshall
22. Liberty

Based on a map by the Texas Railroad Commission.

Coal and Lignite Mine Production
(in short tons)

Mine	Acres Bonded	2018	2019	2020	Cumulative Total
1. Big Brown	4,363.10	0	-	-	171,155,954
2. Martin Lake	17,167.70	2,471,147	924,947	-	315,950,912
Martin Lake AIV South	2,308.00	0	-	-	6,771,850
3. Monticello-Thermo	1,876.10	0	-	-	42,849,720
Monticello-Thermo A-1	278.9	0	-	-	792,213
4. Rachal	615.9	0	-	-	963,827
5. San Miguel	10,424.10	1,981,967	700,709	655,269	90,913,367
San Miguel Area C	3,668.20	195,081	-	-	22,747,139
San Miguel F, G, & H	1,996.00	787,644	2,303,071	1,992,447	5,083,162
6. Gibbons Creek	4,976.60	0	-	-	30,431,174
Gibbons Creek V	1,796.10	0	-	-	12,547,611
7. Calvert	6,072.00	2,030,297	2,156,794	1,972,073	57,569,286
8. Jewett	9,593.20	0	-	-	173,220,612
Jewett E/F	3,917.00	0	-	-	35,937,586
9. South Hallsville No. 1	16,299.90	1,221,253	1,065,829	693,180	114,303,250
10. Monticello-Winfield	13,269.00	0	-	-	277,049,944
11. Palafox	2,575.20	0	-	-	5,355,519
12. Eagle Pass	5,848.00	2,146,219	1,638,483	250,766	8,916,057
13. Treviño	531.9	0	-	-	890,453
14. Oak Hill	18,064.90	0	-	-	129,763,914
15. Three Oaks	11,654.90	93,632	-	-	75,274,333
16. Bremond	3,370.60	0	-	-	236
17. Kosse	11,440.60	8,683,043	9,594,365	10,104,902	99,379,810
18. Leesburg	4,293.00	0	-	-	0
19. Turlington	3,614.30	0	-	-	16,504,979
20. Rusk	8,825.00	2,313,432	2,073,093	933,156	14,746,033
21. Marshall	1,101.00	185,097	185,718	83,235	1,120,462
22. Liberty	3,424.80	2,734,143	2,663,711	2,954,048	16,168,176
Statewide Total	**173,446.80**	**24,842,955**	**23,306,720**	**19,639,076**	***1,886,638,233**

* Statewide cumulative total includes the cumulative amount mined from the following "no longer permitted" mines: Little Bull Creek (428,932), Powell Bend (1,569,875), Thurber (465,984), Darco (6,798,881), and Sandow (150,966,982).

Source: Coal Production through 2020 report, Railroad Commission of Texas

found in Brewster, El Paso, Hudspeth, Jeff Davis, and Presidio counties. Fluorspar has been mined in the Christmas Mountains of Brewster County and processed in Marathon. Former West Texas mining activity in the Eagle Mountains district of Hudspeth County resulted in the production of approximately 15,000 short tons of fluorspar during the peak years of 1942–1950. No production has been reported in Hudspeth County since that period. Imported fluorspar is processed in Brownsville, Eagle Pass, El Paso, and Houston. Fluorspar is used in the steel, chemical, aluminum, magnesium, ceramics, and glass industries, and for various other purposes.

FULLER'S EARTH (see CLAYS).

GOLD: No major deposits of gold are known in Texas. Small amounts have been found in the Llano Uplift region of Central Texas and in West Texas; minor occurrences have been reported on the Edwards Plateau and the Gulf Coastal Plain of Texas. Nearly all of the gold produced in the state came as a by-product of silver and lead mining at Presidio mine, near Shafter in Presidio County. Additional small quantities were produced as a by-product of copper mining in Culberson County and from residual soils developed from gold-bearing quartz stringers in metamorphic rocks in Llano County. No gold mining has been reported in Texas since 1952. Total gold production in the state from 1889–1952 amounted to more than 8,419 troy ounces, according to U.S. Bureau of Mines figures. Most of the production, at least 73 percent and probably more, came from the Presidio mine.

GRANITE: Granites in shades of red and gray and related intrusive igneous rocks occur in the Llano Uplift of Central Texas and in the Trans-Pecos country of West Texas. Deposits are found in Blanco, Brewster, Burnet, El Paso, Gillespie, Hudspeth, Llano, McCulloch, Mason, Presidio, and other counties. Quarries in Burnet, Gillespie, Llano, and Mason counties produce Precambrian granite for a variety of uses, such as dimension stone and crushed stone.

GRAPHITE: Graphite, a soft, dark-gray mineral, is a form of very high-grade carbon. It occurs in Precambrian schist rocks of the Llano Uplift of Central Texas, notably in Burnet and Llano counties. Crystalline-flake graphite ore formerly was mined from open pits in the Clear Creek area of western Burnet County and processed at a plant near the mine. The mill now occasionally grinds imported material. Uses of natural crystalline graphite are refractories, steel production, pencil leads, lubricants, foundry facings, and crucibles, as well as other purposes.

GRINDING PEBBLES (ABRASIVE STONES): Flint pebbles, suitable for use in tube-mill grinding, are found in the Gulf Coastal Plain, where they occur in gravel deposits along rivers and in upland areas. Grinding pebbles are produced from Frio River terrace deposits near the McMullen–Live Oak county line, but the area is now part of the Choke Canyon Reservoir area.

GYPSUM: Gypsum is widely distributed in Texas. Chief deposits are bedded gypsum in the area east of the High Plains, in the Trans-Pecos country, and in Central Texas. It also occurs in salt-dome caprocks of the Gulf Coast. The massive, granular variety, which is known as rock gypsum, is the kind most commonly used by industry. Other varieties include alabaster, satin spar, and selenite.

Gypsum is one of the important industrial minerals in Texas. Bedded gypsum is produced from surface mines in Culberson, Fisher, Gillespie, Hardeman, Hudspeth, Kimble, Nolan, and Stonewall counties. Gypsum was formerly mined at Gyp Hill salt dome in Brooks County and at Hockley salt dome in Harris County. Most of the gypsum is calcined and used in the manufacture of gypsum wallboard, plaster, joint compounds, and other construction products. Crude gypsum is used chiefly as a retarder in portland cement and as a soil conditioner.

HELIUM: Helium is a very light, nonflammable, chemically inert gas. The U.S. Interior Department has ended its helium operation near Masterson in the Panhandle. The storage facility at Cliffside

gas field near Amarillo and the 425-mile pipeline system will remain in operation until the government sells its remaining unrefined, crude helium. Helium is used in cryogenics, welding, pressurizing and purging, leak detection, synthetic breathing mixtures, and for other purposes. **In 2018, there were four helium extraction plants in Texas.**

IRON: Iron oxide (limonite, goethite, and hematite) and iron carbonate (siderite) deposits occur widely in East Texas, notably in Cass, Cherokee, Marion, and Morris counties, and also in Anderson, Camp, Harrison, Henderson, Nacogdoches, Smith, Upshur, and other counties. Magnetite (magnetic, black iron oxide) occurs in Central Texas, including a deposit at Iron Mountain in Llano County. Hematite occurs in the Trans-Pecos area and in the Llano Uplift of Central Texas. The extensive deposits of glauconite (a complex silicate containing iron) that occur in East Texas and the hematitic and goethitic Cambrian sandstone that crops out in the northwestern Llano Uplift region are potential sources of low-grade iron ore.

Limonite and other East Texas iron ores are mined from open pits in Cherokee and Henderson counties for use in the preparation of portland cement, as a weighting agent in well-drilling fluids, as an animal feed supplement, and for other purposes. East Texas iron ores also were mined in the past for use in the iron-steel industry.

KAOLIN (see CLAYS).

LEAD AND ZINC: The lead mineral galena (lead sulfide) commonly is associated with zinc and silver. It formerly was produced as a by-product of West Texas silver mining, chiefly from the Presidio mine at Shafter in Presidio County, although lesser amounts were obtained at several other mines and prospects. Deposits of galena also are known to occur in Blanco, Brewster, Burnet, Gillespie, and Hudspeth counties.

Zinc, primarily from the mineral sphalerite (zinc sulphide), was produced chiefly from the Bonanza and Alice Ray mines in the Quitman Mountains of Hudspeth County. In addition, small production was reported from several other areas, including the Chinati and Montezuma mines of Presidio County and the Buck Prospect in the Apache Mountains of Culberson County. Zinc mineralization also occurs in association with the lead deposits in Cambrian rocks of Central Texas.

LEONARDITE: Deposits of weathered (oxidized) low-Btu value bituminous coals, generally referred to as "leonardite," occur in Brewster County. The name leonardite is used for a mixture of chemical compounds that is high in humic acids. In the past, material from these deposits was sold as soil conditioner. Other uses of leonardite include modification of viscosity of drill fluids and as sorbants in water-treatment.

LIGHTWEIGHT AGGREGATE (see CLAYS, DIATOMITE, PERLITE, VERMICULITE).

LIGNITE: Almost all current coal production in Texas is located in the Tertiary-aged lignite belts that extend across the Texas Gulf Coastal Plain from the Rio Grande in South Texas to the Arkansas and Louisiana borders in East Texas. The Railroad Commission of Texas (RRC) reported that in 2018, Texas produced 24.8 million short tons of lignite from 12 mines. Cumulative production in 2018 was 1.8 billion short tons of lignite and coal. See the map and table opposite for more detail on coal and lignite mining.

The near-surface lignite resources, occurring at depths of less than 200 feet in seams of three feet or thicker, are estimated at 23 billion short tons. Recoverable reserves of strippable lignite, those that can be economically mined under current conditions of price and technology, are estimated by the EIA to be 722 million short tons.

Additional lignite resources of the Texas Gulf Coastal Plain occur as deep-basin deposits. Deep-basin resources, those that occur at depths of 200 to 2,000 feet in seams of five feet or thicker, are comparable in magnitude to near-surface resources. The deep-basin lignites are a potential energy resource that conceivably could be utilized by in situ (in place) recovery methods such as underground gasification.

As with bituminous coal, lignite production was significant prior to the general availability of oil and gas. Remnants of old underground mines are common throughout the area of lignite occurrence. Large reserves of strippable lignite have again attracted the attention of energy suppliers, and Texas is now the nation's sixth leading producer of coal, 99 percent of it lignite. Twelve large strip mines are now producing lignite that is burned for mine-mouth electric-power generation, and additional mines are planned. Mines are located in Atascosa, Franklin, Freestone, Harrison, Hopkins, Leon, Limestone, McMullen, Milam, Panola, Robertson, Rusk, and Titus counties.

LIME MATERIAL: Limestones, which are abundant in some areas of Texas, are heated to produce lime (calcium oxide) at a number of plants in the state. High-magnesium limestone and dolomite are used to prepare lime at a plant in Burnet County. Other lime plants are located in Bexar, Bosque, Comal, Hill, Johnson, and Travis counties. Lime production captive to the kiln's operator occurs in several Texas counties. Lime is used in soil stabilization, water purification, paper and pulp manufacture, metallurgy, sugar refining, agriculture, construction, removal of sulfur from stack gases, and for many other purposes.

LIMESTONE (see also BUILDING STONE): Texas is one of the nation's leading producers of limestone, which is quarried in more than 60 counties. Limestone occurs in nearly all areas of the state with the exception of most of the Gulf Coastal Plain and High Plains. Although some of the limestone is quarried for use as dimension stone, most of the output is crushed for uses such as bulk building materials (crushed stone, road base, concrete aggregate), chemical raw materials, fillers or extenders, lime and portland cement raw materials, agricultural limestone, and removal of sulfur from stack gases.

MAGNESITE: Small deposits of magnesite (natural magnesium carbonate) have been found in Precambrian rocks in Llano and Mason counties of Central Texas. At one time, there was small-scale mining of magnesite in the area; some of the material was used as agricultural stone and as terrazzo chips. Magnesite also can be calcined to form magnesia, which is used in metallurgical furnace refractories and other products.

MAGNESIUM: On the Texas Gulf Coast in Brazoria County, magnesium chloride is extracted from sea water at a plant in Freeport and used to produce magnesium compounds and magnesium metal. During World War II, high-magnesium Ellenburger dolomite rock from Burnet County was used as magnesium ore at a plant near Austin.

MANGANESE: Deposits of manganese minerals, such as braunite, hollandite, and pyrolusite, have been found in several areas, including Jeff Davis, Llano, Mason, Presidio, and Val Verde counties. Known deposits are not large. Small shipments have been made from Jeff Davis, Mason, and Val Verde counties, but no manganese mining has been reported in Texas since 1954.

MARBLE: Metamorphic and sedimentary marbles suitable for monument and building stone are found in the Llano Uplift and nearby areas of Central Texas and the Trans-Pecos area of West Texas. Gray, white, black, greenish black, light green, brown, and cream-colored marbles occur in Central Texas in Burnet, Gillespie, Llano, and Mason counties. West Texas metamorphic marbles include the bluish-white and the black marbles found southwest of Alpine in Brewster County and the white marble from Marble Canyon north of Van Horn in Culberson County. Marble can be used as dimension stone, terrazzo, and roofing aggregate, and for other purposes.

MERCURY (QUICKSILVER): Mercury minerals, chiefly cinnabar, occur in the Terlingua district and nearby districts of southern Brewster and southeastern Presidio counties. Mining began there about 1894, and from 1905–1935, Texas was one of the nation's leading producers of quicksilver. Following World War II, a sharp drop in demand and price, along with depletion of developed ore reserves, caused abandonment of all the Texas mercury mines.

With a rise in the price, sporadic mining took place from 1951–1960. In 1965, when the price of mercury moved to a record high, renewed interest in the Texas mercury districts resulted in the reopening of several mines and the discovery of new ore reserves. By April 1972, however, the price had declined, and the mines have reported no production since 1973.

MICA: Large crystals of flexible, transparent mica minerals in igneous pegmatite rocks and mica flakes in metamorphic schist rocks are found in the Llano Uplift area of Central Texas and the Van Horn area of West Texas. Most Central Texas deposits do not meet specifications for sheet mica, and although several attempts have been made to produce West Texas sheet mica in Culberson and Hudspeth counties, sustained production has not been achieved. A mica quarry operated for a short time in the early 1980s in the Van Horn Mountains of Culberson and Hudspeth counties to mine mica schist for use as an additive in rotary drilling fluids.

MOLYBDENUM: Small occurrences of molybdenite have been found in Burnet and Llano counties, and wulfenite, another molybdenum mineral, has been noted in rocks in the Quitman Mountains of Hudspeth County. Molybdenum minerals also occur at Cave Peak north of Van Horn in Culberson County, in the Altuda Mountain area of northwestern Brewster County, and in association with uranium ores of the Gulf Coastal Plain.

PEAT: This spongy organic substance forms in bogs from plant remains. It has been found in the Gulf Coastal Plain in several localities including Gonzales, Guadalupe, Lee, Milam, Polk, and San Jacinto counties. There has been intermittent, small-scale production of some of the peat for use as a soil conditioner.

PERLITE: Perlite, a glassy igneous rock, expands to a lightweight, porous mass when heated. It can be used as a lightweight aggregate, filter aid, horticultural aggregate, and for other purposes. Perlite occurs in Presidio County, where it has been mined in the Pinto Canyon area north of the Chinati Mountains. No perlite is currently mined in Texas, but perlite mined outside of Texas is expanded at plants in Bexar, Dallas, El Paso, Guadalupe, Harris, and Nolan counties.

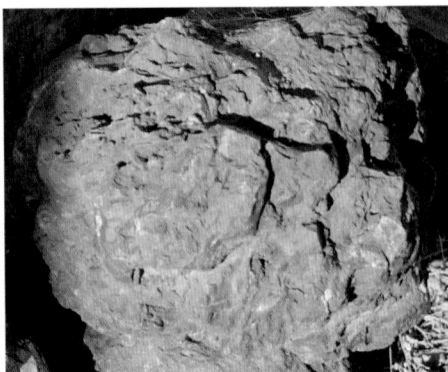

A sample of manganese ore at the Chihuahuan Desert Research Institute. Photo by Rosie Hatch

PHOSPHATE: Rock phosphate is present in Paleozoic rocks in several areas of Brewster and Presidio counties in West Texas and in Central Texas, but the known deposits are not large. In Northeast Texas, sedimentary rock phosphate occurs in thin conglomeratic lenses in Upper Cretaceous and Tertiary rock units; possibly some of these low-grade phosphorites could be processed on a small scale for local use as a fertilizer. Imported phosphate rock is processed at a plant in Brownsville.

POTASH: The potassium mineral polyhalite is widely distributed in the subsurface Permian Basin of West Texas and has been found in many wells in that area. During 1927–1931, the federal government drilled a series of potash-test wells in Crane, Crockett, Ector, Glasscock, Loving, Reagan, Upton, and Winkler counties. In addition to polyhalite, which was found in all of the counties, these wells revealed the presence of the potassium minerals carnallite and sylvite in Loving County and carnallite in Winkler County. The known Texas potash deposits are not as rich as those in the New Mexico portion of the Permian Basin and have not been developed.

PUMICITE (VOLCANIC ASH): Deposits of volcanic ash occur in Brazos, Fayette, Gonzales, Karnes, Polk, Starr, and other counties of the Texas Coastal Plain. Deposits also have been found in the Trans-Pecos area, High Plains, and in several counties east of the High Plains. Volcanic ash is used to prepare pozzolan cement, cleansing and scouring compounds, and soaps and sweeping compounds, as well as a carrier for insecticides and for other purposes. It has been mined in Dickens, Lynn, Scurry, Starr, and other counties.

QUICKSILVER (see MERCURY).

RARE-EARTH ELEMENTS AND METALS: The term "rare-earth elements" is commonly applied to elements of the lanthanide group (atomic numbers 57 through 71) plus yttrium. Yttrium, atomic number 39 and not a member of the lanthanide group, is included as a rare-earth element because it has similar properties to members of that group and usually occurs in nature with them. The metals thorium and scandium are sometimes termed "rare metals" because their occurence is often associated with the rare-earth elements.

The majority of rare-earth elements are consumed as catalysts in petroleum cracking and other chemical industries. Rare earths are widely used in the glass industry for tableware, specialty glasses, optics, and fiber optics. Cerium oxide has growing use as a polishing compound for glass, gem stones, cathode-ray tube faceplates, and other polishing. Rare earths are alloyed with various metals to produce materials used in the aeronautic, space, and electronics industries. The addition of rare-earth elements may improve resistance to metal fatigue at high temperatures, reduce potential for corrosion, and selectively increase conductivity and magnetism of the metal.

Various members of this group, including thorium, have anomalous concentrations in the rhyolitic and related igneous rocks of the Quitman Mountains and the Sierra Blanca area of Trans-Pecos, Texas.

SALT (SODIUM CHLORIDE) (see also BRINES): Salt resources of Texas are virtually inexhaustible. Enormous deposits occur in the subsurface Permian Basin of West Texas and in the salt domes of the Gulf Coastal Plain. Salt also is found in the alkali playa lakes of the High Plains, the alkali flats or salt lakes in the Salt Basin of Culberson and Hudspeth counties, and along some of the bays and lagoons of the South Texas Gulf Coast.

Texas is one of the leading salt-producing states. Rock salt is obtained from underground mines in salt domes at Grand Saline in Van Zandt County and Hockley Dome in Harris County. Salt is produced from rock salt and by solution mining as brines from wells drilled into the underground salt deposits.

SAND, INDUSTRIAL: Sands used for special purposes, due to high silica content or to unique physical properties, command higher prices than common sand. Industrial sands in Texas occur mainly in the Central Gulf Coastal Plain and in North-Central Texas. They include abrasive, blast, chemical, engine, filtration, foundry, glass, hydraulic-fracturing (proppant), molding, and pottery sands. Recent production of industrial sands has been from Atascosa, Colorado,

Hardin, Harris, Liberty, Limestone, McCulloch, Newton, Smith, Somervell, and Upshur counties.

SAND AND GRAVEL (CONSTRUCTION): Sand and gravel are among the most extensively utilized resources in Texas. Principal occurrence is along the major streams and in stream terraces. Sand and gravel are important bulk construction materials, used as railroad ballast, base materials, and for other purposes. In 2018, Texas was second only to California in production of sand and gravel (construction). Arizona and Washington were the next two largest producers.

SANDSTONE: Sandstones of a variety of colors and textures are widely distributed in a number of geologic formations in Texas. Some of the sandstones have been quarried for use as dimension stone in El Paso, Parker, Terrell, Ward, and other counties. Crushed sandstone is produced in Freestone, Gaines, Jasper, McMullen, Motley, and other counties for use as road-building material, terrazzo stone, and aggregate.

SERPENTINITE: Several masses of serpentinite, which formed from the alteration of basic igneous rocks, are associated with other Precambrian metamorphic rocks of the Llano Uplift. The largest deposit is the Coal Creek serpentinite mass in northern Blanco and Gillespie counties from which terrazzo chips have been produced. Other deposits are present in Gillespie and Llano counties. (The features that are associated with surface and subsurface Cretaceous rocks in several counties in or near the Balcones Fault Zone and that are commonly known as "serpentine plugs" are not serpentine at all, but are altered igneous volcanic necks and pipes, and mounds of altered volcanic ash, palagonite, that accumulated around the former submarine volcanic pipes.)

SHELL: Oyster shells and other shells in shallow coastal waters and in deposits along the Texas Gulf Coast have been produced in the past chiefly by dredging. They were used to a limited extent as raw material in the manufacture of cement, as concrete aggregate and road base, and for other purposes. No shell has been produced in Texas since 1981.

SILVER: During the period 1885–1952, the production of silver in Texas, as reported by the U.S. Bureau of Mines, totaled about 33 million troy ounces. For about 70 years, silver was the most consistently produced metal in Texas, although always in moderate quantities. All of the production came from the Trans-Pecos country of West Texas, where the silver was mined in Brewster County (Altuda Mountain), Culberson and Hudspeth counties (Van Horn Mountains and Van Horn–Allamoore district), Hudspeth County (Quitman Mountains and Eagle Mountains), and Presidio County (Chinati Mountains area, Loma Plata mine, and Shafter district).

Chief producer was the Presidio mine in the Shafter district, which began operations in the late 1800s, and, through September 1942, produced more than 30 million ounces of silver, more than 92 percent of Texas' total silver production. Water in the lower mine levels, lean ores, and low price of silver resulted in the closing of the mine in 1942. Another important silver producer was the Hazel copper-silver mine in the Van Horn–Allamoore district in Culberson County, which accounted for more than 2 million ounces.

An increase in the price of silver in the late 1970s stimulated prospecting for new reserves, and exploration began near the old Presidio mine, near the old Plata Verde mine in the Van Horn Mountains district, at the Bonanza mine in the Quitman Mountains district, and at the old Hazel mine. A decline in the price of silver in the early 1980s, however, resulted in reduction of exploration and mine development in the region. The recent rise in the value of silver has sparked new interest in the Shafter mining district of West Texas.

SOAPSTONE (see TALC AND SOAPSTONE).

SODIUM SULFATE (SALT CAKE): Sodium sulfate minerals occur in salt beds and brines of the alkali playa lakes of the High Plains in West Texas. In some lakes, the sodium sulfate minerals are present in deposits a few feet beneath the lakebeds. Sodium sulfate also is found in underground brines in the Permian Basin. Current production is from brines and dry salt beds at alkali lakes in Gaines and Terry counties. Past production was reported in Lynn and Ward counties. Sodium sulfate is used chiefly by the detergent and paper and pulp industries. Other uses are in the preparation of glass and other products.

STONE (see BUILDING STONE and CRUSHED STONE).

STRONTIUM: Deposits of the mineral celestite (strontium sulfate) have been found in a number of places, including localities in Brown, Coke, Comanche, Fisher, Lampasas, Mills, Nolan, Real, Taylor, Travis, and Williamson counties. Most of the occurrences are very minor, and no strontium is currently produced in the state.

SULFUR: Texas is one of the world's principal sulfur-producing areas. The sulfur is mined from deposits of native sulfur, and it is extracted from sour (sulfur-bearing) natural gas and petroleum. Recovered sulfur accounted for more than 90 percent of all 2018 sulfur production in the United States. Native sulfur is found in large deposits in the caprock of some of the salt domes along the Texas Gulf Coast and in some of the surface and subsurface Permian strata of West Texas, notably in Culberson and Pecos counties.

Native sulfur obtained from the underground deposits is known as Frasch sulfur, so called because of Herman Frasch, the chemist who devised the method of drilling wells into the deposits, melting the sulfur with superheated water, and forcing the molten sulfur to the surface. Most of the production now goes to the users in molten form.

Frasch sulfur is produced from only one Gulf Coast salt dome in Wharton County and from West Texas underground Permian strata in Culberson County. Operations at several Gulf Coast domes have been closed in recent years. During the 1940s, acidic sulfur earth was produced in the Rustler Springs district in Culberson County for use as a fertilizer and soil conditioner. Sulfur is recovered from sour natural gas and petroleum at plants in numerous Texas counties.

Sulfur in limestone mined in Texas. Photo by James St. John, CC by 2.0/Wikimedia Commons

Sulfur is used in the preparation of fertilizers and organic and inorganic chemicals, in petroleum refining, and for many other purposes.

TALC AND SOAPSTONE: Deposits of talc are found in the Precambrian metamorphic rocks of the Allamoore area of eastern Hudspeth and western Culberson counties. Soapstone, containing talc, occurs in the Precambrian metamorphic rocks of the Llano Uplift area, notably in Blanco, Gillespie, and Llano counties. Current production is from surface mines in the Allamoore area. Talc is used in ceramic, roofing, paint, paper, plastic, synthetic rubber, and other products.

TIN: Tin minerals have been found in El Paso and Mason counties. Small quantities were produced during the early 1900s in the Franklin Mountains north of El Paso. Cassiterite (tin dioxide) occurrences in Mason County are believed to be very minor. The only tin smelter in the United States, built at Texas City by the federal government during World War II and later sold to a private company, processes tin concentrates from ores mined outside of Texas, tin residues, and secondary tin-bearing materials.

TITANIUM: The titanium mineral rutile has been found in small amounts at the Mueller prospect in Jeff Davis County. Another titanium mineral, ilmenite, occurs in sandstones in Burleson, Fayette, Lee, Starr, and several other counties. Deposits that would be considered commercial under present conditions have not been found.

TRAP ROCK (see BASALT).

TUNGSTEN: The tungsten mineral scheelite has been found in small deposits in Gillespie and Llano counties and in the Quitman Mountains in Hudspeth County. Small deposits of other tungsten minerals have been prospected in the Cave Peak area north of Van Horn in Culberson County.

URANIUM: Uranium deposits were discovered in the Texas Coastal Plain in 1954 when abnormal radioactivity was detected in the Karnes County area. A number of uranium deposits have since been discovered within a belt of strata extending more than 250 miles from the middle Coastal Plain southwestward to the Rio Grande.

Various uranium minerals also have been found in other areas of Texas, including the Trans-Pecos, the Llano Uplift, and the High Plains. With the exception of small shipments from the High Plains during the 1950s, all the uranium production in Texas has been from the Coastal Plain. Uranium has been obtained from surface mines extending from northern Live Oak County, southeastern Atascosa County, across northern Karnes County, and into southern Gonzales County. Uranium is produced by in-situ leaching, brought to the surface through wells, and stripped from the solution at recovery operations.

In 1999, uranium mining shut down because of decreased value and demand. Production resumed in Texas in late 2004, when inventories were depleted and market prices rose to economic levels that allowed resumption of production. A total of 1.4 million pounds (606.5 tons) of eU$_3$O$_8$ was produced in South Texas in 2007.

There are no active uranium recovery operations in Texas, though as of 2017 there are 10 permits for uranium exploration in seven counties: Bee, Brooks, Duval, Goliad, Jim Hogg, Kleberg, and Live Oak.

VERMICULITE: Vermiculite, a mica-like mineral that expands when heated, occurs in Burnet, Gillespie, Llano, Mason, and other counties in the Llano Uplift region. It has been produced at a surface mine in Llano County. Vermiculite, mined outside of Texas, is exfoliated (expanded) at plants in Dallas, Houston, and San Antonio. Exfoliated vermiculite is used for lightweight concrete aggregate, horticulture, insulation, and other purposes.

VOLCANIC ASH (see PUMICITE).

ZEOLITES: The zeolite minerals clinoptilolite and analcime occur in Tertiary lavas and tuffs in Brewster, Jeff Davis, and Presidio counties in West Texas. Clinoptilolite also is found associated with Tertiary tuffs in the southern Texas Coastal Plain, including deposits in Karnes, McMullen, and Webb counties, and currently is produced in McMullen County. Zeolites, sometimes called "molecular sieves," can be used in ion-exchange processes to reduce pollution, as a catalyst in oil cracking, in obtaining high-purity oxygen and nitrogen from air, in water purification, and for many other purposes.

ZINC (see LEAD AND ZINC). ☆

Texas Newspapers, Radio, and Television Stations

Sources: 2021 Texas Newspaper Directory; FCC, https://www.fcc.gov/media/filing-systems-and-databases

Texas is rich with newspapers and broadcast media, many of which have long histories. In the following list, only printed, subscription newspapers appear, and their frequency of publication is indicated by the following codes: (D) daily or at least four days a week, (TW) triweekly, (S) semiweekly, (SM) semimonthly, (M) monthly; all others are weeklies. Radio and TV stations are those with valid operating licenses as of July 2021. Not included are those with construction permits or pending applications. ☆

—A—

Abernathy: Newspaper: *Abernathy Advocate.*

Abilene: Newspaper: *Abilene Reporter-News* (D). **Radio-AM:** KSLI, 1280 kHz; KWKC, 1340; KYYW, 1470; KZQQ, 1560. **Radio-FM:** KGNZ, 88.1 MHz; KACU, 89.5; KAGT, 90.5; KAQD, 91.3; KMWX, 92.5; KULL, 100.7; KEAN, 105.1; KKHR, 106.3; KEYJ, 107.9. TV Stations: KXVA-Ch. 15; KRBC-Ch. 29; KTAB-Ch. 30.

Agua Dulce: Radio-FM: KOUL, 107.7 MHz.

Alamo: Radio-FM: KJAV, 104.9 MHz.

Alamo Heights: Radio-AM: KDRY, 1100 kHz.

Albany: Newspaper: *Albany News.* **Radio-FM:** KQOS, 91.7 MHz.

Aledo: Newspaper: *The Community News.*

Alice: Newspaper: *Alice Echo-News Journal* (S). **Radio-AM:** KOPY, 1070 kHz. **Radio-FM:** KAWV, 88.3 MHz; KOPY, 92.1; KNDA, 102.9.

Allen: Newspaper: *Allen American.* **Radio-FM:** KESN, 103.3 MHz.

Alpine: Newspapers: *Alpine Avalanche; The Big Bend Gazette* (M). **Radio-AM:** KVLF, 1240 kHz. **Radio-FM:** KBAL, 90.3 MHz; KRTP, 91.7; KALP, 92.7.

Alvin: Newspaper: *Alvin Sun.* **Radio-AM:** KTEK, 1110 kHz. **Radio-FM:** KACC, 89.7 MHz. TV Station: KFTH-Ch. 36.

Amarillo: Newspaper: *Amarillo Globe-News* (D). **Radio-AM:** KGNC, 710 kHz; KIXZ, 940; KDJW, 1010; KZIP, 1310; KTNZ, 1360; KPUR, 1440. **Radio-FM:** KJRT, 88.3 MHz; KXLV, 89.1; KACV, 89.9; KAVW, 90.7; KXRI, 91.9; KQIZ, 93.1; KMXJ, 94.1; KXSS, 96.9; KGNC, 97.9; KPRF, 98.7; KBZD, 99.7; KXGL, 100.9; KATP, 101.9; KVWE, 102.9; KJJP, 105.7. TV Stations: KVII-Ch. 7; KACV-Ch. 9; KFDA-Ch. 10; KCIT-Ch. 15; KAMR-Ch. 19.

Anahuac: Newspaper: *The Progress.*

Andrews: Newspaper: *Andrews County News* (S). **Radio-AM:** KACT, 1360 kHz. **Radio-FM:** KACT, 105.5 MHz.

Anna: Newspaper: *Anna-Melissa Tribune.*

Anson: Newspaper: *Western Observer.* **Radio-FM:** KTLT, 98.1 MHz.

Aransas Pass: Newspaper: *Aransas Pass Progress.* **Radio-FM:** KKWV, 88.1 MHz.

Archer City: Newspaper: *Archer County News.* **Radio-FM:** KPMA, 91.9 MHz.

Arlington: Radio-FM: KLTY, 94.9 MHz. TV Station: KPXD-Ch. 25.

Arroyo: Radio-FM: KVJS, 88.1 MHz.

Athens: Newspaper: *Athens Daily Review* (D). **Radio-AM:** KLVQ, 1410 kHz.

Atlanta: Newspaper: *Cass County Citizen's Journal-Sun.* **Radio-AM:** KPYN, 900 kHz. **Radio-FM:** KNRB, 100.1 MHz.

Austin: Newspapers: *Austin American-Statesman* (D); *Austin Business Journal; West Austin News* (SM). **Radio-AM:** KLBJ, 590 kHz; KVET, 1300; KTSN, 1490. **Radio-FM:** KAZI, 88.7 MHz; KMFA, 89.5; KUT, 90.5; KVRX, 91.7; KLBJ, 93.7; KKMJ, 95.5; KVET, 98.1; KASE, 100.7; KPEZ, 102.3; KBPA, 103.5. TV Stations: KTBC-Ch. 7; KXAN-Ch. 21; KLRU-Ch. 22; KNVA-Ch. 23; KVUE-Ch. 33; KEYE-Ch. 34.

Austwell: Radio-FM: KIBQ, 105.9 MHz.

Azle: Newspaper: *The Azle News.* **Radio-FM:** KYDA,101.7 MHz.

—B—

Baird: Newspaper: *Baird Banner.* **Radio-FM:** KABW, 95.1 MHz.

Balch Springs: Radio-AM: KSKY, 660 kHz.

Ballinger: Newspaper: *Runnels County Register.* **Radio-AM:** KRUN, 1400 kHz. **Radio-FM:** KKCN, 103.1 MHz.

Bandera: Newspaper: *Bandera Bulletin.* **Radio-FM:** KEEP, 103.1 MHz.

Bangs: Radio-FM: KBNX, 97.9 MHz.

Bartlett: Newspaper: *Tribune-Progress.*

Bastrop: Newspaper: *Bastrop Advertiser* (S). **Radio-FM:** KHIB, 88.5 MHz; KLZT, 107.1.

Batesville: Radio-FM: KRZU, 90.7 MHz; KQSA, 97.9.

Bay City: Newspaper: *The Bay City Tribune* (S). **Radio-FM:** KQUE, 88.1 MHz; KZBJ, 89.5; KNTE, 101.7; KMKS, 102.5.

Baytown: Newspaper: *Baytown Sun* (D). **Radio-AM:** KWWJ, 1360. TV Station: KUBE-Ch. 31.

Beaumont: Newspaper: *The Beaumont Enterprise* (D). **Radio-AM:** KLVI, 560 kHz; KZZB, 990; KIKR, 1450. **Radio-FM:** KLBT, 88.1 MHz; KGHY, 88.5; KTXB, 89.7; KVLU, 91.3; KQXY, 94.1; KYKR, 95.1; KTCX, 102.5; KQQK, 107.9. TV Stations: KBMT-Ch. 12; KFDM-Ch. 15; KITU-Ch. 29.

Bee Cave: Radio-FM: KTXX, 104.9 MHz.

Beeville: Newspaper: *Beeville Bee-Picayune* (S). **Radio-AM:** KIBL, 1490 kHz. **Radio-FM:** KVFM, 91.3 MHz; KTKO, 105.7; KRXB, 107.1.

Bellaire: Radio-AM: KGOW, 1560 kHz.

Bellmead: Radio-FM: KBHT, 104.9 MHz.

Bells: Radio-FM: KMKT, 93.1 MHz.

Bellville: Newspaper: *The Bellville Times.* **Radio-AM:** KULF, 1090 kHz.

Belton: Newspaper: *The Belton Journal.* **Radio-FM:** KOOC, 106.3 MHz. TV Station: KNCT-Ch. 17.

Benavides: Radio-FM: KXTM, 94.3 MHz.

Benbrook: Radio-AM: KFLC, 1270 kHz. **Radio-FM:** KESS, 107.1 MHz.

Big Lake: Newspaper: *Big Lake Wildcat.*

Big Sandy: Newspaper: *Big Sandy–Hawkins Journal.* **Radio-FM:** KTAA, 90.7 MHz.

Big Spring: Newspaper: *Big Spring Herald* (D). **Radio-AM:** KBYG, 1400 kHz; KBST, 1490. **Radio-FM:** KBCX, 91.5 MHz; KBTS, 94.3; KBST, 95.7; KBUG, 100.9. TV Station: KCWO-Ch. 33.

Big Wells: Radio-FM: KHBE, 102.1 MHz.

Bishop: Radio-FM: KMZZ, 106.9 MHz.

Blanco: Newspaper: *Blanco County News.* TV Station: KNIC-Ch. 18.

Blanket: Radio-FM: KQMJ, 104.7 MHz

Bloomington: Radio-FM: KHVT, 91.5 MHz; KLUB, 106.9.

Blossom: Radio-FM: KISY, 92.7 MHz

Boerne: Newspaper: *The Boerne Star* (S). **Radio-AM:** KBRN,

1500 kHz.

Bogata: Newspaper: *Bogata News–Talco Times.*

Bonham: Newspaper: *The Fannin County Leader.* **Radio-AM:** KFYN, 1420 kHz.

Booker: Newspaper: *The Booker News.*

Borger: Newspaper: *Borger News-Herald* (D). **Radio-FM:** KWAS, 88.1 MHz; KQFX, 104.3; KQTY, 106.7. TV Station: KEYU-Ch. 31.

Bovina: Radio-FM: KKNM, 96.5 MHz.

Bowie: Newspaper: *The Bowie News* (S). **Radio-AM:** KNTX, 1410 kHz.

Brackettville: Newspaper: *Kinney County Post.* **Radio-FM:** KEDV, 90.3 MHz; KUDR, 94.7.

Brady: Newspaper: *Brady Standard-Herald.* **Radio-AM:** KNEL, 1490 kHz. **Radio-FM:** KNEL, 95.3 MHz.

Breckenridge: Newspaper: *Breckenridge American.* **Radio-AM:** KROO, 1430 kHz. **Radio-FM:** KQXB, 89.9 MHz; KLXK, 93.5.

Brenham: Newspaper: *The Banner-Press* (D). **Radio-AM:** KWHI, 1280 kHz. **Radio-FM:** KUBJ, 89.7 MHz; KLTR, 94.1; KTTX, 106.1.

Bridgeport: Radio-FM: KBOC, 98.3 MHz.

Brookshire: Radio-AM: KCHN, 1050 kHz.

Brownfield: Newspaper: *Brownfield News* (S). **Radio-AM:** KKUB, 1300 kHz. **Radio-FM:** KLTB, 89.7 MHz; KHLK, 104.3.

Brownsville: Newspapers: *The Brownsville Herald* (D); El Nuevo Heraldo (D). **Radio-AM:** KVNS, 1700 kHz. **Radio-FM:** KBNR, 88.3 MHz; KKPS, 99.5. TV: KVEO-Ch. 24.

Brownwood: Newspaper: *Brownwood Bulletin* (TW). **Radio-AM:** KXYL, 1240 kHz; KBWD, 1380. **Radio-FM:** KBUB, 90.3 MHz; KHBW, 91.7; KQBZ, 96.9; KPSM, 99.3; KOXE, 101.3.

Bryan: Newspaper: *The Eagle* (D). **Radio-AM:** KTAM, 1240 kHz; KAGC, 1510. **Radio-FM:** KORA, 98.3 MHz; KNFX, 99.5; KKYS, 104.7. TV Stations: KBTX-Ch. 16; KYLE-Ch. 29.

Buda: Radio-FM: KROX, 101.5 MHz.

Buffalo: Newspapers: *Buffalo Express.* **Radio-FM:** WTAW, 103.5 MHz.

Buffalo Gap: Radio-FM: KBGT, 93.3 MHz.

Bullard: Radio-FM: KZXM, 94.3 MHz.

Buna: Newspaper: *The Buna Beacon.*

Burkburnett: Newspaper: *Burkburnett Informer Star.* **Radio-FM:** KYYI, 104.7 MHz.

Burke: Radio-FM: KAGZ, 97.7 MHz.

Burleson: Radio-AM: KCLE, 1460 kHz.

Burnet: Newspapers: *Burnet Bulletin; Citizens Gazette.* **Radio-FM:** KMPN 95.9 MHz; KBEY, 103.9.

Bushland: Radio-FM: KTXP, 91.5 MHz.

—C—

Caldwell: Newspaper: *Burleson County Tribune.* **Radio-FM:** KALD, 91.9 MHz; KAPN, 107.3.

Callisburg: Radio-FM: KPFC, 91.9 MHz.

Cameron: Newspaper: *The Cameron Herald.* **Radio-AM:** KTON, 1330 kHz. **Radio-FM:** KMIL, 105.1 MHz.

Campbell: Radio-FM: KRVA, 107.1 MHz.

Canadian: Newspaper: *The Canadian Record.* **Radio-FM:** KHHC, 91.9 MHz.

Canton: Newspapers: *Canton Herald; Van Zandt News.* **Radio-AM:** KWJB, 1510 kHz.

Canyon: Newspaper: *The Canyon News* (S). **Radio-FM:** KWTS, 91.1 MHz; KARX, 107.1; KZRK, 107.9.

Carbon: Radio-FM: KJDE, 100.1 MHz.

Carrizo Springs: Newspaper: *The Carrizo Springs Javelin.* **Radio-AM:** KBEN, 1450 kHz. **Radio-FM:** KCZO, 92.1 MHz.

Carrollton: Newspaper: *Carrollton Leader.* **Radio-AM:** KJON, 850 kHz.

Carthage: Newspaper: *The Panola Watchman* (S). **Radio-AM:** KGAS, 1590 kHz. **Radio-FM:** KRTG, 88.3 MHz; KTUX, 98.9; KGAS, 104.3.

Cedar Lake: Radio-FM: KQVI, 89.9 MHz.

Cedar Park: Newspaper: *Hill Country News.* **Radio-FM:** KGSR, 93.3 MHz.

Celina: Newspaper: *Celina Record.*

Center: Newspaper: *The Light and Champion.* **Radio-AM:** KDET, 930 kHz. **Radio-FM:** KQBB, 100.5 MHz.

Centerville: Newspaper: *Centerville News.* **Radio-FM:** KKEE, 101.3 MHz; KUZN, 105.9.

Channing: Radio-FM: KAMT, 105.1 MHz.

Charlotte: Radio-FM: KSAQ, 102.3 MHz.

Childress: Newspaper: *The Red River Sun.* **Radio-AM:** KCTX, 1510 kHz. **Radio-FM:** KCTX, 96.1 MHz; KCHT 99.7.

Christine: Radio-FM: KWYU, 96.9 MHz.

Christoval: Radio-FM: KQTC, 99.5 MHz.

Clarendon: Newspaper: *The Clarendon Enterprise.* **Radio-FM:** KYCL, 88.9 MHz; KEFH, 99.3.

Clarksville: Newspaper: *Clarksville Times.* **Radio-AM:** KHDY, 1350 kHz. **Radio-FM:** KXQJ, 90.1 MHz; KHDY, 98.5.

Claude: Newspaper: *The Claude News.* **Radio-FM:** KPUR, 95.7 MHz.

Cleburne: Newspaper: *Cleburne Times-Review* (D). **Radio-AM:** KHFX, 1140 kHz.

Cleveland: Newspaper: *Cleveland Advocate.* **Radio-FM:** KTHT, 97.1 MHz.

Clifton: Newspaper: *The Clifton Record.* **Radio-FM:** KWOW, 104.1 MHz.

Clute: Newspaper: *The Facts* (D).

Clyde: Newspaper: *Clyde Journal.*

Coahoma: Radio-FM: KXCS, 105.5 MHz.

Cockrell Hill: Radio-AM: KRVA, 1600 kHz.

Coleman: Newspaper: *Chronicle & Democrat-Voice.* **Radio-AM:** KSTA, 1000 kHz. **Radio-FM:** KXYL, 102.3 MHz.

College Station: Radio-AM: KZNE, 1150 kHz; KWBC, 1550; WTAW, 1620. **Radio-FM:** KEOS, 89.1 MHz; KLGS, 89.9; KAMU, 90.9; KNDE, 95.1. TV Station: KAMU-Ch. 12.

Colorado City: Newspaper: *Colorado City Record.* **Radio-AM:** KVMC, 1320 kHz. **Radio-FM:** KEHM, 99.3 MHz; KAUM, 107.1

Columbus: Newspapers: *The Banner-Press Newspaper; The Colorado County Citizen.* **Radio-FM:** KULM, 98.3 MHz.

Comanche: Newspaper: *The Comanche Chief.* **Radio-AM:** KCOM, 1550 kHz. **Radio-FM:** KYOX, 94.3 MHz; KCXX 103.9.

Comfort: Newspaper: *The Comfort News.* **Radio-FM:** KMYO, 95.1 MHz.

Commerce: Radio-FM: KETR, 88.9 MHz; KYJC, 91.3.

Comstock: Radio-FM: KDER, 99.3 MHz.

Concan: Radio-FM: KHCU, 93.1 MHz.

Conroe: Newspaper: *The Courier* (D). **Radio-AM:** KJOZ, 880 kHz; KYOK, 1140. **Radio-FM:** KHPT, 106.9 MHz. TV Stations: KPXB-Ch. 32; KTBU-Ch. 33.

Converse: Radio-AM: KTMR, 1130 kHz.

Cooper: Newspaper: *Cooper Review.* **Radio-FM:** KPCO, 89.9 MHz; KIKT, 93.5.

Coppell: Newspapers: *Citizens' Advocate; Coppell Gazette.*

Copperas Cove: **Newspaper:** *Copperas Cove Leader-Press* (S). **Radio-FM:** KSSM, 103.1 MHz.

Corpus Christi: **Newspapers:** *Corpus Christi Caller-Times* (D); *Coastal Bend Daily Legal & Business News* (D). **Radio-AM:** KCTA, 1030 kHz; KCCT, 1150; KSIX, 1230; KKTX, 1360; KUNO, 1400; KEYS, 1440. **Radio-FM:** KPLV, 88.7 MHz; KEDT, 90.3; KBNJ, 91.7; KMXR, 93.9; KBSO, 94.7; KZFM, 95.5; KLTG, 96.5; KRYS, 99.1. TV Stations: KIII-Ch. 8; KZTV-Ch. 10; KRIS-Ch. 13; KSCC, Ch. 19; KEDT-Ch. 23; KORO-Ch. 27.

Corrigan: **Radio-FM:** KYTM, 99.3 MHz.

Corsicana: **Newspaper:** *Corsicana Daily Sun* (D). **Radio-AM:** KAND, 1340 kHz.

Cotulla: **Radio-FM:** KCOT, 96.3 MHz; KWMJ, 100.7.

Crane: **Newspaper:** *Crane News.* **Radio-AM:** KXOI, 810 kHz. **Radio-FM:** KMMZ, 101.3 MHz.

Creedmoor: **Radio-AM:** KZNX, 1530 kHz.

Crockett: **Newspaper:** *Houston County Courier.* **Radio-AM:** KIVY, 1290 kHz. **Radio-FM:** KCKT, 88.5 MHz; KIVY, 92.7; KBPC, 93.5.

Cross Plains: **Newspaper:** *Cross Plains Review.*

Crowell: **Newspaper:** *Foard County News.* **Radio-FM:** KTUT, 98.9 MHz.

Crystal City: **Newspaper:** *Zavala County Sentinel.* **Radio-FM:** KHER, 94.3 MHz.

Cuero: **Newspaper:** *Cuero Record.* **Radio-FM:** KTLZ, 89.9 MHz.

Cuney: **Radio-FM:** KVUT, 99.7 MHz.

—D—

Daingerfield: **Newspaper:** *The Steel Country Bee.*

Dalhart: **Newspaper:** *Dalhart Texan* (S). **Radio-AM:** KXIT, 1240 kHz. **Radio-FM:** KTDH, 89.3 MHz; KTDA, 91.7; KBEX 96.1.

Dallas: **Newspapers:** *The Dallas Morning News* (D); *Dallas Business Journal; Daily Commercial Record* (D); *Park Cities News; Texas Jewish Post.* **Radio-AM:** KLIF, 570 kHz; KGGR, 1040; KRLD, 1080; KFXR, 1190; KTCK, 1310; KNGO, 1480. **Radio-FM:** KNON, 89.3 MHz; KERA, 90.1; KCBI, 90.9; KKXT, 91.7; KZPS, 92.5; KBFB, 97.9; KLUV, 98.7; KJKK, 100.3; WRR, 101.1; KDMX, 102.9; KKDA, 104.5; KRLD, 105.3. TV Stations: WFAA-Ch. 8; KERA-Ch. 14; KDTX-Ch. 21; KDFI-Ch. 27; KDAF-Ch. 32; KDFW-Ch. 35; KXTX-Ch. 36.

Decatur: **Newspaper:** *Wise County Messenger* (S). **Radio-FM:** KDKR, 91.3 MHz; KRNB, 105.7. TV Station: KMPX-Ch. 30.

Deer Park: **Radio-FM:** KAMA, 104.9 MHz.

De Leon: **Newspaper:** *De Leon Free Press.*

Dell City: **Newspaper:** *Hudspeth County Herald.*

Del Mar Hills: **Radio-AM:** KVOZ, 890 kHz.

Del Rio: **Newspaper:** *The 830 Times.* **Radio-AM:** KDRN, 1230 kHz; KWMC, 1490. **Radio-FM:** KVFE, 88.5 MHz; KTPD, 89.3; KDLI, 89.9; KDLK, 94.1; KTDR, 96.3. TV Station: KYVV-Ch. 28.

Del Valle: **Radio-AM:** KIXL, 970 kHz.

Denison: **Radio-FM:** KYFB, 91.5 MHz.

Denton: **Newspaper:** *Denton Record-Chronicle* (D). **Radio-FM:** KFZO, 99.1 MHz; KHKS, 106.1. TV Station: KDTN-Ch. 29.

Denver City: **Newspaper:** *Denver City Press.*

Deport: **Newspaper:** *Deport-Blossom Times.*

DeSoto: **Newspaper:** *Focus Daily News* (D).

Detroit: **Newspaper:** *Detroit Weekly.* **Radio-FM:** KFYN, 104.3 MHz.

Devine: **Newspaper:** *The Devine News.* **Radio-FM:** KRPT, 92.5 MHz.

Diboll: **Radio-AM:** KSML, 1260 kHz. **Radio-FM:** KAFX,

95.5 MHz.

Dilley: **Radio-FM:** KKDL, 93.7 MHz; KVWG, 95.3; KLMO, 98.9.

Dimmitt: **Newspaper:** *The Castro County News.* **Radio-AM:** KDHN, 1470 kHz. **Radio-FM:** KNNK, 100.5 MHz.

Doss: **Radio-FM:** KGKV, 88.1 MHz.

Dripping Springs: **Newspapers:** *Dripping Springs Century News; News-Dispatch.* **Radio-FM:** KLLR, 91.9 MHz.

Dublin: **Newspaper:** *The Dublin Citizen.* **Radio-FM:** KSTV, 93.1 MHz.

Dumas: **Newspaper:** *Moore County News-Press* (S). **Radio-AM:** KDDD, 800 kHz. **Radio-FM:** KDDD, 95.3 MHz.

—E—

Eagle Lake: **Radio-FM:** KJJB, 95.3 MHz.

Eagle Pass: **Radio-AM:** KEPS, 1270 kHz. **Radio-FM:** KEPI, 88.7 MHz; KEPX, 89.5; KINL, 92.7. TV Station: KVAW-Ch. 18.

Early: **Radio-FM:** KJKB, 106.7 MHz.

East Bernard: **Newspaper:** *East Bernard Express.*

Eastland: **Newspaper:** *Eastland County Today.* **Radio-FM:** KQXE, 91.1 MHz; KATX, 97.7.

Eden: **Newspaper:** *Eden Echo.* **Radio-FM:** KPDE, 91.5 MHz.

Edinburg: **Radio-AM:** KURV, 710 kHz. **Radio-FM:** KOIR, 88.5 MHz; KBFM, 104.1; KVLY, 107.9.

Edna: **Newspaper:** *Jackson County Herald-Tribune.* **Radio-FM:** KIOX, 96.1 MHz.

El Campo: **Newspaper:** *El Campo Leader-News* (S). **Radio-AM:** KULP, 1390 kHz. **Radio-FM:** KXBJ, 96.9 MHz.

Eldorado: **Newspaper:** *Eldorado Success.* **Radio-FM:** KOPE, 88.9 MHz; KLDE, 104.9; KPEP, 106.5.

Electra: **Newspaper:** *Electra Star-News.* **Radio-FM:** KOLI, 94.9 MHz.

Elgin: **Newspaper:** *Elgin Courier.* **Radio-AM:** KTAE, 1260 kHz.

Elkhart: **Radio-FM:** KATG, 88.1 MHz.

Ellinger: **Radio-FM:** KTIM, 89.1 MHz.

El Paso: **Newspapers:** *El Paso Times* (D); *West Texas County Courier.* **Radio-AM:** KROD, 600 kHz; KTSM, 690; KAMA, 750; KQBU, 920; KXPL, 1060; KHRO, 1150; KVIV, 1340; KHEY, 1380; KELP, 1590; KSVE, 1650. **Radio-FM:** KTEP, 88.5 MHz; KKLY, 89.5; KVER, 91.1; KOFX, 92.3; KSII, 93.1; KINT, 93.9; KYSE, 94.7; KLAQ, 95.5; KHEY, 96.3; KBNA, 97.5; KTSM, 99.9; KPRR, 102.1. TV Stations: KCOS-Ch. 13; KFOX-Ch. 15; KTSM-Ch. 16; KVIA-Ch. 17; KDBC-Ch. 18; KTFN-Ch. 20; KSCE-Ch. 21; KINT-Ch. 25.

Emory: **Newspaper:** *Rains County Leader.*

Encinal: **Radio-FM:** KQBI, 91.7 MHz; KELT, 102.5; KZPL, 105.1.

Encino: **Radio-FM:** KZTX, 91.1 MHz.

Ennis: **Newspaper:** *The Ennis News.*

Escobares: **Radio-FM:** KERG, 104.7 MHz.

Estelline: **Radio-FM:** KZES, 91.3 MHz.

—F—

Fabens: **Radio-FM:** KPAS, 103.1 MHz.

Fairfield: **Newspapers:** *Freestone County Times; The Fairfield Recorder.* **Radio-FM:** KNES, 99.1 MHz.

Falfurrias: **Newspaper:** *Falfurrias Facts.* **Radio-AM:** KLDS, 1260 kHz. **Radio-FM:** KRVP, 91.5 MHz; KDFM, 103.3; KPSO, 106.3.

Fannett: **Radio-FM:** KZFT, 90.5 MHz.

Farmersville: **Newspaper:** *Farmersville Times.* **Radio-AM:** KFCD, 990 kHz. **Radio-FM:** KXEZ, 92.1 MHz.

Farwell: **Newspaper:** *The State Line Tribune.* **Radio-AM:**

KIJN, 1060 kHz. **Radio-FM:** KIJN, 92.3 MHz; KICA, 98.3. TV Station: KPTF-Ch. 18.

Ferris: Newspaper: *The Ellis County Press.* **Radio-AM:** KDFT, 540 kHz.

Flatonia: Newspaper: *The Flatonia Argus.*

Floresville: Newspaper: *Wilson County News.* **Radio-FM:** KJMA, 89.7 MHz; KTFM, 94.1.

Flower Mound: Radio-FM: KTCK, 96.7 MHz.

Floydada: Newspaper: *The Floyd County Hesperian-Beacon.* **Radio-AM:** KFLP, 900 kHz. **Radio-FM:** KFLP, 106.1 MHz.

Forney: Newspaper: *Forney Messenger.*

Fort Davis: Newspaper: *Jeff Davis County Mountain Dispatch.*

Fort Stockton: Newspaper: *Fort Stockton Pioneer.* **Radio-AM:** KFST, 860 kHz. **Radio-FM:** KRAF, 88.3 MHz; KFST, 94.3.

Fort Worth: Newspapers: *Fort Worth Star-Telegram* (D); *Commercial Recorder* (D); *Tarrant County Commercial Record* (S); *Fort Worth Business Press* (SM). **Radio-AM:** WBAP, 820 kHz; KFJZ, 870; KHVN, 970; KKGM, 1630. **Radio-FM:** KTCU, 88.7 MHz; KLNO, 94.1; KSCS, 96.3; KEGL, 97.1; KPLX, 99.5; KDGE, 102.1; KMVK, 107.5. TV Stations: KFWD-Ch. 9; KTXA-Ch. 18; KTVT-Ch. 19; KXAS-Ch. 24.

Franklin: Newspapers: *Franklin News Weekly; Franklin Advocate.* **Radio-FM:** KVLX, 103.9 MHz.

Frankston: Radio-FM: KOYE, 96.7 MHz.

Fredericksburg: Newspaper: *Fredericksburg Standard-Radio Post.* **Radio-AM:** KNAF, 910 kHz. **Radio-FM:** KIVM, 91.1 MHz; KBLC, 91.5; KNAF, 105.7. TV Station: KCWX-Ch. 5.

Freeport: Radio-FM: KJOJ, 103.3 MHz.

Freer: Radio-FM: KBTD, 89.1 MHz; KQCI, 91.5; KBRA, 95.9..

Friona: Newspaper: *Friona Star.* **Radio-FM:** KGRW, 94.7 MHz.

Frisco: Newspaper: *Frisco Enterprise.* **Radio-AM:** KATH, 910 kHz.

Fritch: Newspaper: *The Eagle Press.*

—G—

Gail: Newspaper: *Borden Star.*

Gainesville: Newspaper: *Gainesville Daily Register* (S). **Radio-AM:** KGAF, 1580 kHz. **Radio-FM:** KZMJ, 94.5 MHz.

Galveston: Newspaper: *The Galveston County Daily News* (D). **Radio-AM:** KGBC, 1540 kHz. **Radio-FM:** KOVE, 106.5 MHz. TV Stations: KTMD-Ch. 22; KLTJ-Ch. 23.

Gardendale: Radio-FM: KFZX, 102.1 MHz.

Garland: Radio-AM: KAAM, 770 kHz. TV Station: KUVN-Ch. 33.

Garwood: Radio-FM: KPUY, 97.3 MHz.

Gatesville: Newspaper: *Gatesville Messenger & Star-Forum* (S). **Radio-FM:** KVLW, 88.1 MHz.

Georgetown: Newspaper: *Williamson County Sun* (S). **Radio-FM:** KHFI, 96.7 MHz; KLJA, 107.7.

George West: Radio-FM: KGWT, 93.5 MHz; KXAF 97.9.

Giddings: Newspaper: *Giddings Times & News.* **Radio-FM:** KANJ, 91.1 MHz; KGID 96.3.

Gilmer: Newspaper: *Gilmer Mirror.* **Radio-FM:** KFRO, 95.3 MHz.

Ginger: Radio-FM: KYFA, 91.5 MHz.

Gladewater: Newspaper: *Gladewater Mirror.* **Radio-AM:** KEES, 1430 kHz.

Glen Rose: Newspaper: *Glen Rose Reporter.* **Radio-FM:** KTFW, 92.1 MHz.

Goldsmith: Radio-FM: KTXO, 94.7 MHz.

Goldthwaite: Newspaper: *The Goldthwaite Eagle.* **Radio-FM:** KRNR, 100.5 MHz.

Goliad: Newspaper: *Goliad Advance-Guard.* **Radio-FM:** KHMC, 95.9 MHz; KPQG 104.3.

Gonzales: Newspaper: *The Gonzales Inquirer.* **Radio-AM:** KCTI, 1450 kHz. **Radio-FM:** KCTI, 88.1 MHz; KMLR, 106.3.

Graham: Newspaper: *The Graham Leader* (S). **Radio-AM:** KSWA, 1330 kHz. **Radio-FM:** KWKQ, 94.7 MHz.

Granbury: Newspaper: *Hood County News* (S). **Radio-AM:** KPIR, 1420 kHz.

Grand Prairie: Radio-AM: KKDA, 730 kHz.

Grand Saline: Newspaper: *Grand Saline Sun.*

Granite Shoals: Radio-FM: KAJZ, 106.5 MHz.

Grape Creek: Radio-FM: KPTJ 104.5 MHz.

Grapeland: Newspaper: *The Messenger* (S).

Greenville: Newspaper: *Herald-Banner* (TW). **Radio-AM:** KGVL, 1400 kHz. **Radio-FM:** KTXG, 90.5 MHz. TV Station: KTXD-Ch. 23.

Greenwood: Radio-FM: KAGP 89.1 MHz.

Gregory: Radio-FM: KPUS, 104.5 MHz.

Groesbeck: Newspaper: *Groesbeck Journal.*

Groom: Newspaper: *The Groom News.*

Groves: Radio-FM: KCOL, 92.5 MHz.

Groveton: Radio-FM: KFON, 93.9 MHz.

Guthrie: Radio-FM: KJAG, 107.7 MHz

—H—

Hallettsville: Newspaper: *Hallettsville Tribune-Herald.* **Radio-FM:** KTXM, 99.9 MHz.

Hallsville: Radio-FM: KTLH, 107.9 MHz.

Haltom City: Radio-FM: KLIF, 93.3 MHz.

Hamilton: Newspaper: *Hamilton Herald-News.* **Radio-AM:** KCLW, 900 kHz.

Hamlin: Newspaper: *The Hamlin Herald.* **Radio-FM:** KCDD, 103.7 MHz.

Hardin: Radio-FM: KGBV, 90.7 MHz.

Harker Heights: Radio-FM: KUSJ, 105.5 MHz.

Harlingen: Newspaper: *The Valley Morning Star* (D). **Radio-AM:** KGBT, 1530 kHz. **Radio-FM:** KJJF, 88.9 MHz; KFRQ, 94.5; KBTQ, 96.1. TV Stations: KMBH-Ch. 16; KGBT-Ch. 18; KLUJ-Ch. 21.

Harper: Radio-FM: KZAH, 99.1 MHz.

Hartley: Radio-FM: KOGW, 90.5 MHz.

Haskell: Radio-FM: KVRP, 97.1 MHz.

Hawley: Radio-FM: KTJK, 101.7 MHz.

Hearne: Newspaper: *Robertson County News.* **Radio-FM:** KEDC, 88.5 MHz; KVJM, 103.1.

Hebbronville: Newspapers: *The Enterprise News; Hebbronville View* (SM). **Radio-FM:** KOTX 98.7 MHz; KEKO, 101.7; KUFA, 104.3.

Helotes: Radio-FM: KONO, 101.1 MHz.

Hemphill: Newspaper: *The Sabine County Reporter.* **Radio-FM:** KTHP, 103.9 MHz.

Hempstead: *The Waller County Express.* **Radio-FM:** KTWL, 105.3 MHz.

Henderson: Newspaper: *The Henderson News* (S). **Radio-AM:** KWRD, 1470 kHz.

Henrietta: Newspaper: *Clay County Leader.*

Hereford: Newspaper: *Hereford Brand* (S). **Radio-AM:** KPAN, 860 kHz. **Radio-FM:** KRLH, 90.9 MHz; KPAN, 106.3.

Hewitt: Radio-FM: KIXT, 106.7 MHz.

Hico: Newspaper: *The Hico News Review.* **Radio-FM:**

KCBN, 107.7.

Highland Park: Radio-AM: KBDT, 1160 kHz. **Radio-FM:** KVIL, 103.7 MHz.

Highlands: Newspaper: *Highlands Star-Crosby Courier.*

Highland Village: Radio-FM: KWRD, 100.7 MHz.

Hillsboro: Newspaper: *Hillsboro Reporter* (S). **Radio-AM:** KHBR, 1560 kHz. **Radio-FM:** KBRQ, 102.5 MHz.

Holliday: Radio-FM: KGVB, 90.9 MHz; KWFB, 100.9.

Hondo: Newspaper: *Hondo Anvil Herald.* **Radio-AM:** KCWM, 1460 kHz. **Radio-FM:** KZIC, 89.9 MHz; KAHL, 105.9.

Hooks: Radio-FM: KTRG, 94.1 MHz; KPWW, 95.9.

Hornsby: Radio-FM: KOOP, 91.7 MHz.

Houston: Newspapers: *Houston Chronicle* (D); *Daily Court Review* (D); *Houston Business Journal; Jewish Herald-Voice.* **Radio-AM:** KILT, 610 kHz; KTRH, 740; KBME, 790; KEYH, 850; KPRC, 950; KLAT, 1010; KNTH, 1070; KCOH, 1230; KXYZ, 1320; KSHJ, 1430; KMIC, 1590. **Radio-FM:** KUHF, 88.7 MHz; KPFT, 90.1; KTSU, 90.9; KXNG, 91.7; KQBT, 93.7; KTBZ, 94.5; KKHH, 95.7; KHMX, 96.5; KBXX, 97.9; KODA, 99.1; KILT, 100.3; KLOL, 101.1; KMJQ, 102.1; KLTN, 102.9; KRBE, 104.1; KHCB, 105.7. TV Stations: KUHT-Ch. 8; KHOU-Ch. 11; KTRK-Ch. 13; KTXH-Ch. 19; KZJL-Ch. 21; KETH-Ch. 24; KRIV-Ch. 26; KIAH-Ch. 34; KPRC-Ch. 35.

Howe: Radio-FM: KHYI, 95.3 MHz.

Hudson: Radio-FM: KZXL, 96.3 MHz.

Humble: Radio-AM: KGOL, 1180 kHz. **Radio-FM:** KSBJ, 89.3 MHz.

Hunt: Radio-FM: KYRT, 97.9 MHz; KLKV, 99.9.

Huntington: Radio-FM: KSML, 101.9 MHz.

Huntsville: Newspaper: *The Huntsville Item* (D). **Radio-AM:** KM2XVL, 1220 kHz; KHCH, 1410; KHVL, 1490. **Radio-FM:** KSHU, 90.5 MHz; KVST, 99.7; KSAM, 101.7.

Hurst: Radio-AM: KMNY, 1360 kHz.

Hutto: Radio-FM: KYLR, 92.1 MHz.

—I—

Idalou: Newspaper: *Idalou Beacon.* **Radio-FM:** KRBL, 105.7 MHz; KLZK, 107.7.

Ingleside: Newspaper: *The Ingleside Index.* **Radio-FM:** KAJE, 107.3 MHz.

Ingram: Newspaper: *West Kerr Current.* **Radio-FM:** KTXI, 90.1 MHz; KFXE, 96.5.

Iowa Park: Newspaper: *Iowa Park Leader.* **Radio-FM:** KXXN, 97.5 MHz.

Irving: Newspaper: *The Irving Rambler.* TV Station: KSTR-Ch. 34.

—J—

Jacksboro: Newspaper: *Jacksboro Herald-Gazette.* **Radio-FM:** KFWR, 95.9 MHz.

Jacksonville: Newspaper: *Jacksonville Progress* (S). **Radio-AM:** KEBE, 1400 kHz. **Radio-FM:** KBJS, 90.3 MHz; KEBE, 95.1; KLJT, 102.3; KOOI, 106.5. TV Station: KETK-Ch. 22.

Jasper: Newspaper: *The Jasper Newsboy.* **Radio-AM:** KCOX, 1350 kHz. **Radio-FM:** KTXJ, 102.7 MHz; KJAS, 107.3.

Jefferson: Newspaper: *Jefferson Jimplecute.* **Radio-FM:** KHCJ, 91.9 MHz; KJTX, 104.5.

Jewett: Newspaper: *Jewett Messenger.*

Johnson City: Newspaper: *Johnson City Record Courier.* **Radio-FM:** KFAN, 107.9 MHz.

Jourdanton: Radio-FM: KLEY, 95.7 MHz.

Junction: Newspaper: *Junction Eagle.* **Radio-AM:** KMBL, 1450 kHz. **Radio-FM:** KYKK, 93.5 MHz.

—K—

Karnes City: Newspaper: *The Karnes Countywide.* **Radio-FM:** KHHL, 103.1 MHz.

Katy: Newspaper: *Katy Times.* TV Station: KYAZ-Ch. 25.

Kaufman: Newspaper: *The Kaufman Herald.*

Keene: Radio-FM: KJRN, 88.3 MHz.

Kempner: Radio-FM: KOOV, 106.9 MHz.

Kenedy: Radio-AM: KAML, 990 kHz. **Radio-FM:** KCAF, 92.1 MHz.

Kerens: Radio-FM: KRVF, 106.9 MHz.

Kermit: Newspaper: *The Winkler County News.* **Radio-FM:** KDCJ, 91.5 MHz; KWXW, 93.7.

Kerrville: Newspapers: *The Kerrville Daily Times* (TW); *Hill Country Community Journal.* **Radio-AM:** KERV, 1230 kHz. **Radio-FM:** KKER, 88.7 MHz; KHKV, 91.1; KRNH, 92.3; KRVL, 94.3; KKVR, 106.1. TV Station: KMYS-Ch. 32.

Kilgore: Newspaper: *Kilgore News Herald* (S). **Radio-AM:** KDOK, 1240 kHz. **Radio-FM:** KZLO, 88.7 MHz; KKTX, 96.1.

Killeen: Newspaper: *Killeen Daily Herald* (D). **Radio-AM:** KRMY, 1050 kHz. **Radio-FM:** KNCT, 91.3 MHz; KIIZ, 92.3. TV Station: KAKW-Ch. 13.

Kingsland: Radio-FM: KHSB, 104.7 MHz.

Kingsville: Newspaper: *The Kingsville Record.* **Radio-AM:** KINE, 1330 kHz. **Radio-FM:** KTAI, 91.1 MHz; KKBA, 92.7; KFTX, 97.5.

Kirbyville: Newspaper: *Kirbyville Banner.*

Krum: Radio-FM: KNOR, 93.7 MHz.

Kurten: Radio-FM: KPWJ, 107.7 MHz.

Kyle: Newspaper: *Hays Free Press.*

—L—

La Feria: Newspaper: *La Feria News.*

La Grange: Newspaper: *The Fayette County Record* (S). **Radio-AM:** KVLG, 1570 kHz. **Radio-FM:** KBUK, 104.9 MHz.

Lake Dallas: TV Station: KAZD-Ch. 31.

Lake Jackson: Radio-FM: KYBJ, 91.1 MHz; KGLK, 107.5.

Lakeway: Newspaper: *Lake Travis View.*

Lamesa: Newspaper: *Lamesa Press Reporter* (S). **Radio-AM:** KPET, 690 kHz. **Radio-FM:** KBKN, 91.3 MHz; KTXC, 104.7.

Lampasas: Newspaper: *Lampasas Dispatch Record* (S). **Radio-AM:** KCYL, 1450 kHz.

La Porte: Newspaper: *Bay Area Observer.* **Radio-FM:** KHJK, 103.7 MHz.

Laredo: Newspaper: *Laredo Morning Times* (D). **Radio-AM:** KLAR, 1300 kHz; KLNT, 1490. **Radio-FM:** KHOY, 88.1 MHz; KBNL, 89.9; KJBZ, 92.7; KQUR, 94.9; KRRG, 98.1; KNEX, 106.1. TV Stations: KGNS-Ch. 8; KLDO-Ch. 19.

Laughlin AFB: Radio-FM: KDRX, 106.9 MHz.

La Vernia: Newspaper: *La Vernia News.*

League City: Radio-AM: KHCB, 1400 kHz.

Leander: Radio-FM: KUTX, 98.9 MHz.

Lefors: Radio-FM: KPWD, 91.7 MHz; KHNZ, 101.3.

Leonard: Newspaper: *The Leonard Graphic.*

Levelland: Newspaper: *Levelland & Hockley County News-Press* (S). **Radio-AM:** KLVT, 1230 kHz. **Radio-FM:** KJDL, 105.3 MHz.

Lewisville: Newspaper: *Lewisville Leader.* **Radio-FM:** KDXX, 107.9 MHz.

Lexington: Newspaper: *Lexington Leader.*

Liberty: Newspaper: *The Vindicator.* **Radio-FM:** KHIH, 99.9 MHz.

Liberty Hill: Newspaper: *The Liberty Hill Independent.*

Lindale: **Newspaper:** *Lindale News & Times.*

Lindsay: **Newspaper:** *Lindsay Letter.*

Little Elm: **Newspaper:** *Little Elm Journal.*

Littlefield: **Newspaper:** *The Lamb County Leader-News* (S). **Radio-AM:** KZZN, 1490 kHz.

Livingston: **Newspaper:** *Polk County Enterprise* (S). **Radio-AM:** KETX, 1440 kHz. **Radio-FM:** KEHH, 92.3 MHz.

Llano: **Newspaper:** *The Llano News.* **Radio-FM:** KVHL, 91.7 MHz; KTHE, 96.3; KITY, 102.9. TV Station: KBVO-Ch. 27.

Lockhart: **Newspaper:** *Lockhart Post-Register.* **Radio-AM:** KFIT, 1060 kHz.

Lometa: **Radio-FM:** KACQ, 101.9 MHz.

Longview: **Newspaper:** *Longview News-Journal* (D). **Radio-AM:** KFRO, 1370 kHz. **Radio-FM:** KYKX, 105.7 MHz. TV Stations: KFXK-Ch. 20; KCEB-Ch. 28.

Lorena: **Radio-FM:** KYAR, 98.3 MHz.

Lorenzo: **Radio-FM:** KKCL, 98.1 MHz.

Los Ybañez: **Radio-FM:** KJJT, 98.5 MHz.

Louise: **Radio-FM:** KABA, 90.3 MHz.

Lovelady: **Radio-FM:** KHMR, 104.3 MHz.

Lubbock: **Newspaper:** *Lubbock Avalanche-Journal* (D). **Radio-AM:** KRFE, 580 kHz; KFYO, 790; KJTV, 950; KKAM, 1340; KWBF, 1420; KBZO, 1460; KDAV, 1590. **Radio-FM:** KTXT, 88.1 MHz; KTTZ, 89.1; KAMY, 90.1; KKLU, 90.9; KLBB, 93.7; KFMX, 94.5; KLLL, 96.3; KQBR, 99.5; KONE, 101.1; KZII, 102.5; KXTQ, 106.5. TV Stations: KCBD-Ch. 11; KPTB-Ch. 16; KTTZ-Ch. 25; KAMC-Ch. 27; KLBK-Ch. 31; KJTV-Ch. 35.

Lufkin: **Newspaper:** *The Lufkin Daily News* (D). **Radio-AM:** KRBA, 1340 kHz. **Radio-FM:** KLDN, 88.9 MHz; KSWP, 90.9; KAVX, 91.9; KYBI, 100.1; KYKS, 105.1. TV Station: KTRE-Ch. 9.

Luling: **Newspaper:** *Luling Newsboy and Signal.* **Radio-FM:** KAMX, 94.7 MHz.

Lumberton: **Radio-AM:** KHTW, 1300 kHz. **Radio-FM:** KKHT, 100.7 MHz.

Lytle: **Radio-FM:** KZLV, 91.3 MHz.

—M—

Mabank: **Newspaper:** *The Monitor* (S). **Radio-AM:** KTXV, 890 kHz.

Madisonville: **Newspaper:** *Madisonville Meteor.* **Radio-AM:** KMVL, 1220 kHz. **Radio-FM:** KHML, 91.5 MHz; KAGG, 96.1; KMVL, 100.5.

Malakoff: **Radio-FM:** KCKL, 95.9 MHz.

Manor: **Radio-AM:** KTXW, 1120 kHz; KELG, 1440.

Marble Falls: **Newspaper:** *The Highlander* (S). **Radio-FM:** KBMD, 88.5 MHz.

Marathon: **Radio-FM:** KDKY, 91.5 MHz.

Marfa: **Newspaper:** *The Big Bend Sentinel.* **Radio-FM:** KRTS, 93.5 MHz.

Marion: **Radio-AM:** KBIB, 1000 kHz.

Markham: **Radio-FM:** KKHA, 92.5 MHz; KBYC, 104.5.

Marlin: **Newspaper:** *The Marlin Democrat.* **Radio-FM:** KRMX, 92.9 MHz.

Marshall: **Newspaper:** *Marshall News Messenger* (D). **Radio-AM:** KMHT, 1450 kHz. **Radio-FM:** KBWC, 91.1 MHz; KDPM, 92.3; KMHT, 103.9.

Mart: **Radio-FM:** KWAA, 88.9 MHz.

Mason: **Newspaper:** *Mason County News.* **Radio-FM:** KZZM, 101.7 MHz; KHLB, 102.5; KMSN, 104.1.

McAllen: **Newspaper:** *The Monitor* (D). **Radio-AM:** KRIO, 910 kHz. **Radio-FM:** KHID, 88.1 MHz; KVMV, 96.9; KGBT, 98.5. TV Station: KNVO-Ch. 17.

McCook: **Radio-FM:** KCAS, 91.5 MHz.

McCoy: **Radio-FM:** KMPI, 90.5 MHz.

McGregor: **Newspaper:** *The McGregor Mirror & Crawford Sun.*

McKinney: **Newspapers:** *Collin County Commercial Record* (S); *McKinney Courier-Gazette.* **Radio-FM:** KNTU, 88.1 MHz.

McQueeney: **Radio-FM:** KZAR, 97.7 MHz.

Memphis: **Radio-FM:** KHNZ, 101.5 MHz; KLSR, 105.3.

Menard: **Newspaper:** *Menard News and Messenger.* **Radio-FM:** KTCY, 105.3 MHz.

Mercedes: **Newspaper:** *The Mercedes Enterprise.* **Radio-FM:** KTEX, 100.3 MHz.

Meridian: **Newspaper:** *Meridian Tribune.* **Radio-FM:** KITT, 106.5 MHz.

Merkel: **Radio-AM:** KMXO, 1500 kHz. **Radio-FM:** KHXS, 102.7 MHz.

Mertzon: **Radio-FM:** KMEO, 91.9 MHz; KBTP, 101.1; KBJX, 103.5.

Mesquite: **Newspaper:** *Mesquite News.* **Radio-FM:** KEOM, 88.5 MHz.

Mexia: **Newspaper:** *The Mexia News* (S). **Radio-AM:** KEKR, 1590 kHz.

Meyersville: **Radio-FM:** KQBQ, 100.1 MHz.

Miami: **Newspaper:** *Miami Chief.*

Midland: **Newspaper:** *Midland Reporter-Telegram* (D). **Radio-AM:** KCRS, 550 kHz; KWEL, 1070; KLPF, 1180; KMND, 1510. **Radio-FM:** KVDG, 90.9 MHz; KNFM, 92.3; KZBT, 93.3; KQRX, 95.1; KCRS, 103.3; KCHX, 106.7. TV Stations: KUPB-Ch. 18; KMID-Ch. 26.

Midlothian: **Newspaper:** *Midlothian Mirror.*

Miles: **Newspaper:** *Miles Messenger.* **Radio-FM:** KMLS, 95.5 MHz.

Mineola: **Newspaper:** *Wood County Monitor.* **Radio-FM:** KMOO, 99.9 MHz.

Mineral Wells: **Radio-AM:** KVTT, 1110 kHz. **Radio-FM:** KYQX, 89.3 MHz.

Mirando City: **Radio-FM:** KBDR, 100.5 MHz.

Mission: **Newspaper:** *Progress Times.* **Radio-AM:** KIRT, 1580 kHz. **Radio-FM:** KQXX, 105.5 MHz.

Missouri City: **Radio-AM:** KBRZ, 1460 kHz.

Monahans: **Newspaper:** *The Monahans News.* **Radio-AM:** KCKM, 1330 kHz. **Radio-FM:** KMRA, 91.1 MHz; KBAT, 99.9.

Mont Belvieu: **Radio-FM:** KFNC, 97.5 MHz.

Moody: **Radio-FM:** KLTO, 99.1 MHz.

Moran: **Radio-FM:** KCKB, 104.1 MHz.

Morton: **Radio-FM:** KQOA, 91.1 MHz; KPGA, 91.9.

Moulton: **Newspaper:** *Moulton Eagle.*

Mountain Home: **Radio-FM:** KAXA, 103.7 MHz.

Mount Pleasant: **Newspaper:** *Mount Pleasant Tribune* (S). **Radio-AM:** KIMP, 960 kHz. **Radio-FM:** KYZQ, 88.3 MHz.

Mount Vernon: **Newspaper:** *Mount Vernon Optic-Herald.* **Radio-FM:** KDDM, 100.5 MHz.

Muenster: **Newspaper:** *Muenster Enterprise.* **Radio-FM:** KTMU, 88.7 MHz; KZZA, 106.7.

Muleshoe: **Newspaper:** *Muleshoe Journal.* **Radio-FM:** KVRQ, 93.3 MHz.

Munday: **Newspaper:** *The Knox County News-Courier.*

Murphy: **Newspaper:** *Murphy Monitor.*

—N—

Nacogdoches: **Newspaper:** *Nacogdoches Daily Sentinel* (S). **Radio-AM:** KSFA, 860 kHz. **Radio-FM:** KSAU, 90.1 MHz; KJCS, 103.3; KTBQ, 107.7. TV Station: KYTX-Ch. 15.

Naples: **Newspaper:** *The Monitor.*

Natalia: **Radio-FM:** KYRQ, 90.3 MHz.

Navasota: Newspaper: *The Navasota Examiner.* **Radio-FM:** KWUP, 92.5 MHz.

Nederland: Radio-AM: KBED, 1510 kHz.

Needville: Newspaper: *Hometown Journal.*

New Boston: Newspaper: *Bowie County Citizens Tribune.* **Radio-AM:** KLBW, 1530 kHz. **Radio-FM:** KEWL, 95.1 MHz; KZRB, 103.5; KTTY, 105.1.

New Braunfels: Newspaper: *New Braunfels Herald-Zeitung* (D). **Radio-AM:** KGNB, 1420 kHz. **Radio-FM:** KNBT, 92.1 MHz.

Newcastle: Radio-FM: KBLY, 100.5 MHz.

New Deal: Radio-FM: KTTU, 97.3 MHz.

Newton: Newspaper: *Newton County News.*

New Ulm: Newspaper: *New Ulm Enterprise.* **Radio-FM:** KNRG, 92.3 MHz.

New Waverly: Radio-FM: KNLY, 91.1 MHz.

Nocona: Newspaper: *Nocona News.*

Nolanville: Radio-FM: KLFX, 107.3 MHz.

Normangee: Newspaper: *The Normangee Star.*

—O—

Oakwood: Radio-FM: KDNT, 94.5 MHz.

O'Brien: Radio-FM: KZOB, 105.5 MHz.

Odem: Radio-FM: KXAI, 98.3 MHz.

Odessa: Newspaper: *Odessa American* (D). **Radio-AM:** KFLB, 920 kHz; KOZA, 1230. **Radio-FM:** KBMM, 89.5 MHz; KLVW, 90.5; KXWT, 91.3; KMRK, 96.1; KMCM, 96.9; KODM, 97.9; KHKX, 99.1; KQLM, 107.9. TV Stations: KOSA-Ch. 7; KWES-Ch. 9; KMLM-Ch. 15; KPEJ-Ch. 23; KPBT-Ch. 28; KWWT-Ch. 30.

O'Donnell: Newspaper: *O'Donnell Index-Press.*

Olney: Newspaper: *Olney Enterprise.*

Olton: Newspaper: *Olton Enterprise.*

Orange: Newspaper: *The Orange Leader* (S). **Radio-AM:** KOGT, 1600 kHz. **Radio-FM:** KKMY, 104.5 MHz; KIOC, 106.1.

Ore City: Radio-FM: KAZE, 106.9 MHz.

Overton: Radio-FM: KTYK, 100.7 MHz.

Ozona: Newspaper: *Ozona Stockman.* **Radio-FM:** KYXX, 94.3 MHz; KCMZ, 105.5.

—P—

Paducah: Newspaper: *Paducah Post.* **Radio-FM:** KPZX, 94.7 MHz.

Paint Rock: Newspaper: *The Concho Herald.*

Palacios: Newspaper: Palacios Beacon. **Radio-FM:** *KPAL, 91.3 MHz; KPLU, 100.7.*

Palestine: Newspaper: *Palestine Herald-Press* (TW). **Radio-AM:** KNET, 1450 kHz. **Radio-FM:** KYFP, 89.1 MHz; KYYK, 98.3.

Pampa: Newspaper: *The Pampa News* (TW). **Radio-AM:** KGRO, 1230 kHz. **Radio-FM:** KAVO, 90.9 MHz; KOMX, 100.3; KDRL, 103.3.

Panhandle: Newspaper: *Panhandle Herald & White Deer News.* **Radio-FM:** KPQP, 106.1 MHz.

Paris: Newspaper: *The Paris News* (TW). **Radio-AM:** KZHN, 1250 kHz; KPLT, 1490. **Radio-FM:** KHCP, 89.3 MHz; KQPA, 91.9; KOYN, 93.9; KBUS, 101.9; KPLT, 107.7.

Pasadena: Radio-AM: KIKK, 650 kHz; KLVL, 1480. **Radio-FM:** KFTG, 88.1 MHz; KKBQ, 92.9.

Pearland: Newspaper: *The Reporter News.*

Pearsall: Newspaper: *Frio-Nueces Current.* **Radio-AM:** KMFR, 1280 kHz. **Radio-FM:** KSAG, 103.3 MHz; KSAH, 104.1.

Pecan Grove: Radio-AM: KREH, 900 kHz.

Pecos: Newspaper: *Pecos Enterprise.* **Radio-AM:** KIUN, 1400 kHz. **Radio-FM:** KPKO, 91.3 MHz; KDNZ, 97.3;

KPTX, 98.3.

Perryton: Newspaper: *Perryton Herald* (S). **Radio-AM:** KEYE, 1400 kHz. **Radio-FM:** KEYE, 93.7 MHz.

Pflugerville: Radio-AM: KOKE, 1600 kHz.

Pharr: Newspaper: *Advance News Journal.* **Radio-AM:** KVJY, 840 kHz.

Pilot Point: Newspaper: *Pilot Point Post-Signal.* **Radio-FM:** KZMP, 104.9 MHz.

Pineland: Radio-FM: KFAH, 99.1 MHz.

Pittsburg: Newspaper: *The Pittsburg Gazette.* **Radio-FM:** KGWP, 91.1 MHz; KPIT, 91.7; KSCN, 96.9; KMPA, 103.1.

Plains: Radio-FM: KPHS, 90.3 MHz.

Plainview: Newspaper: *Plainview Herald* (TW). **Radio-AM:** KVOP, 1090 kHz; KREW, 1400. **Radio-FM:** KPMB, 88.5 MHz; KBAH, 90.5; KWLD, 91.5; KRIA, 103.9; KKYN, 106.9.

Plano: Newspaper: *Plano Star Courier.* **Radio-AM:** KTNO, 620 kHz.

Pleasanton: Newspaper: *Pleasanton Express.* **Radio-FM:** KWMF, 1380 kHz.

Pleasant Valley: Radio-FM: KZAM, 98.7 MHz.

Point Comfort: Radio-FM: KJAZ, 94.1 MHz.

Port Aransas: Newspaper: *Port Aransas South Jetty.*

Port Arthur: Newspaper: *The Port Arthur News* (TW). **Radio-AM:** KDEI, 1250 kHz; KOLE, 1340. **Radio-FM:** KQBU, 93.3 MHz; KTJM, 98.5. TV Station: KBTV-Ch. 27.

Port Isabel: Newspaper: *Port Isabel-South Padre Press.* **Radio-FM:** KNVO, 101.1 MHz; KLME, 105.5.

Portland: Radio-FM: KSGR, 91.1 MHz; KLHB, 105.5.

Port Lavaca: Newspaper: *Port Lavaca Wave.* **Radio-FM:** KNAL, 93.3 MHz.

Port Neches: Radio-AM: KBPO, 1150 kHz.

Port O'Connor: Radio-FM: KHPO, 91.9 MHz.

Post: Newspaper: *The Post Dispatch.* **Radio-FM:** KSSL, 107.3 MHz.

Prairie View: Radio-FM: KPVU, 91.3 MHz.

Premont: Radio-FM: KLBD, 88.1 MHz.

Presidio: Newspaper: *The Presidio International.*

Princeton: Newspaper: *Princeton Herald.*

Prosper: Newspaper: *Prosper Press.*

—Q—

Quanah: Newspaper: *Quanah Tribune-Chief.* **Radio-AM:** KOLJ, 1150 kHz. **Radio-FM:** KQTX, 98.1 MHz.

Quemado: Radio-FM: KQMD, 88.1 MHz.

Quitaque: Newspaper: *Valley Tribune.*

—R—

Ralls: Newspaper: *Crosby County News.*

Ranchitos Las Lomas: Radio-FM: KLIT, 93.3 MHz.

Ranger: Radio-FM: KWBY, 98.5 MHz.

Rankin: Radio-FM: KXFS, 93.7 MHz.

Raymondville: Newspaper: *Raymondville Chronicle/ Willacy County News.* **Radio-AM:** KSOX, 1240 kHz. **Radio-FM:** KVHI, 88.7 MHz; KBUC, 102.1; KBIC, 105.7.

Refugio: Newspaper: *Refugio County Press.* **Radio-FM:** KRIK, 100.5 MHz; KZAI, 103.7; KXHM, 106.1.

Reno: Radio-FM: KLOW, 98.9 MHz.

Richardson: Radio-AM: KKLF, 1700 kHz.

Riesel: Newspaper: *Riesel Rustler.*

Rio Grande City: Radio-FM: KXJT, 88.3 MHz; KRGX, 95.1; KQBO, 107.5. TV Station: KTLM-Ch. 14.

Robert Lee: Newspaper: *Observer/Enterprise.* **Radio-FM:** KJVI, 105.7 MHz.

Robinson: Radio-FM: KWPW, 107.9 MHz.

Robstown: Newspaper: *Nueces County Record-Star.* **Radio-AM:** KROB, 1510 kHz. **Radio-FM:** KLUX, 89.5 MHz; KSAB, 99.9; KMIQ, 104.9.

Rockdale: Newspaper: *Rockdale Reporter.* **Radio-FM:** KRXT, 98.5 MHz.

Rockport: Newspaper: *The Rockport Pilot* (S). **Radio-FM:** KKPN, 102.3 MHz.

Rocksprings: Newspaper: *Rocksprings Record and Texas Mohair Weekly.*

Rollingwood: Newspaper: *Westlake Picayune.* **Radio-AM:** KJCE, 1370 kHz.

Roma: Radio-FM: KRIO, 97.7 MHz.

Rosebud: Newspaper: *The Rosebud News.*

Rosenberg: Newspaper: *Fort Bend Herald and Texas Coaster* (TW). **Radio-AM:** KQUE, 980 kHz. TV Station: KXLN-Ch. 30.

Rotan: Newspaper: *Double Mountain Chronicle.*

Round Rock: Newspaper: *Round Rock Leader* (S). **Radio-FM:** KNLE, 88.1 MHz; KFMK, 105.9.

Rowena: Newspaper: *The Rowena Press.*

Roxton: Newspaper: *Roxton Progress* (SM).

Royse City: Newspaper: *Royse City Herald Banner.*

Rudolph: Radio-FM: KTER, 90.7 MHz.

Rusk: Newspaper: *Cherokeean Herald.* **Radio-AM:** KTLU, 1580 kHz.

—S—

Sabinal: Radio-FM: KHAV, 107.1 MHz.

Sachse: Newspaper: *Sachse News.*

Saint Jo: Newspaper: *Saint Jo Tribune.*

Salado: Newspaper: *Salado Village Voice.*

San Angelo: Newspaper: *San Angelo Standard-Times* (D). **Radio-AM:** KGKL, 960 kHz; KKSA, 1260; KCCE, 1340. **Radio-FM:** KLRW, 88.5 MHz; KNAR, 89.3; KNCH, 90.1; KLTP, 90.9; KDCD, 92.9; KSAO, 93.9; KIXY, 94.7; KGKL, 97.5; KELI, 98.7; KCLL, 100.1; KWFR, 101.9; KMDX, 106.1; KSJT, 107.5. TV Stations: KLST-Ch. 11; KSAN-Ch. 16; KIDY-Ch. 19.

San Antonio: Newspapers: *San Antonio Express-News* (D); *San Antonio Business Journal; The Hart Beat.* **Radio-AM:** KTSA, 550 kHz; KSLR, 630; KKYX, 680; KTKR, 760; KONO, 860; KRDY, 1160; WOAI, 1200; KZDC, 1250; KAHL, 1310; KXTN, 1350; KCHL, 1480; KEDA, 1540. **Radio-FM:** KPAC, 88.3 MHz; KSTX, 89.1; KSYM, 90.1; KYFS, 90.9; KRTU, 91.7; KROM, 92.9; KXXM, 96.1; KAJA, 97.3; KISS, 99.5; KCYY, 100.3; KQXT, 101.9; KJXK, 102.7; KZEP, 104.5; KVBH, 107.5. TV Stations: KLRN-Ch. 9; KSAT-Ch. 12; KVDA-Ch. 15; KHCE-Ch. 16; KWEX-Ch. 24; WOAI-Ch. 28; KENS-Ch. 29; KABB-Ch. 30.

San Augustine: Newspaper: *San Augustine Tribune.* **Radio-FM:** KXXE, 92.5 MHz.

San Benito: Newspaper: *San Benito News.* **Radio-FM:** KHKZ, 106.3 MHz.

Sanderson: Radio-FM: KEVK, 105.1 MHz.

San Diego: Radio-FM: KXAM, 102.5 MHz; KUKA, 105.9.

Sanger: Radio-FM: KAWA, 89.7 MHz.

San Juan: Radio-AM: KUBR, 1210 kHz.

San Marcos: Newspaper: *San Marcos Daily Record* (D). **Radio-FM:** KTSW, 89.9 MHz.

San Saba: Newspaper: *San Saba News & Star.* **Radio-AM:** KROY, 1410 kHz. **Radio-FM:** KNUZ, 106.1 MHz.

Santa Anna: Radio-FM: KXXU, 104.3 MHz; KSZX, 105.5.

Santa Fe: Radio-FM: KJIC, 90.5 MHz.

Savoy: Radio-FM: KQDR, 107.3 MHz.

Schertz: Radio-FM: KBBT, 98.5 MHz.

Schulenburg: Newspaper: *Schulenburg Sticker.*

Scotland: Radio-FM: KTWF, 95.5 MHz.

Seabrook: Radio-FM: KROI, 92.1 MHz.

Seadrift: Radio-FM: KMAT, 105.1 MHz.

Sealy: Newspaper: *The Sealy News.* **Radio-FM:** KQLC, 90.7 MHz.

Seguin: Newspaper: *The Seguin Gazette* (S). **Radio-AM:** KWED, 1580 kHz. **Radio-FM:** KSMG, 105.3 MHz.

Seminole: Newspaper: *Seminole Sentinel* (S). **Radio-AM:** KIKZ, 1250 kHz. **Radio-FM:** KSEM, 106.3 MHz.

Seymour: Newspaper: *The Baylor County Banner.* **Radio-AM:** KSEY, 1230 kHz. **Radio-FM:** KSEY, 94.3 MHz.

Shamrock: Newspaper: *County Star-News.* **Radio-FM:** KSNZ, 92.9 MHz.

Shepherd: Newspaper: *San Jacinto News-Times.*

Shenandoah: Radio-AM: KRCM, 1380 kHz.

Sherman: Newspaper: *Herald Democrat* (D). **Radio-AM:** KJIM, 1500 kHz. TV Station: KXII-Ch. 12.

Shiner: Newspaper: *The Shiner Gazette.*

Silsbee: Newspaper: *Silsbee Bee.* **Radio-FM:** KAYD, 101.7 MHz.

Silverton: Newspaper: *The Caprock Courier.*

Sinton: Newspaper: *The News of San Patricio.* **Radio-AM:** KDAE, 1590 kHz. **Radio-FM:** KNCN, 101.3 MHz.

Slaton: Newspaper: *The Slatonite.* **Radio-FM:** KVCE, 92.7 MHz.

Smiley: Radio-FM: KSXT, 90.3 MHz; KBQQ, 103.9.

Smithville: Newspaper: *Smithville Times.*

Snyder: Newspaper: *The Snyder News* (S). **Radio-AM:** KSNY, 1450 kHz. **Radio-FM:** KGWB, 91.1 MHz; KHMZ 94.9; KLYD, 98.9; KSNY, 101.5. TV Station: KPCB-Ch. 17.

Somerset: Radio-AM: KYTY, 810 kHz.

Somerville: Radio-FM: KXBT, 88.1 MHz.

Sonora: Newspaper: *The Devil's River News.* **Radio-FM:** KHOS, 92.1 MHz.

South Padre Island: Radio-FM: KESO, 92.7 MHz; KZSP, 95.3.

Spearman: Newspaper: *Reporter-Statesman.* **Radio-FM:** KTOT, 89.5 MHz; KXDJ, 98.3.

Springtown: Newspaper: *Springtown Epigraph.* **Radio-FM:** KSQX, 89.1 MHz.

Spur: Newspaper: *Texas Spur.*

Stamford: Newspapers: *The New Stamford American; The Stamford Star.* **Radio-AM:** KVRP, 1400 kHz. **Radio-FM:** KLGD, 106.9 MHz.

Stanton: Newspaper: *Martin County Messenger.* **Radio-FM:** KFLB, 88.1 MHz; KTPR, 89.9; KXQT, 105.9.

Stephenville: Newspaper: *Stephenville Empire Tribune* (S). **Radio-AM:** KSTV, 1510 kHz. **Radio-FM:** KQXS, 89.1 MHz; KEQX, 89.5; KTRL, 90.5.

Sterling City: Radio-FM: KNRX, 96.5 MHz.

Stockdale: Radio-AM: KQQB, 1520 kHz.

Stratford: Newspaper: *Sherman County Gazette.* **Radio-FM:** KUHC, 91.5 MHz.

Sulphur Bluff: Radio-FM: KETE, 99.7 MHz.

Sulphur Springs: Newspaper: *Sulphur Springs News-Telegram* (S). **Radio-AM:** KSST, 1230 kHz. **Radio-FM:** KGPF, 91.1 MHz; KZRF, 91.9; KSCH, 95.9.

Sunset Valley: Radio-FM: KVLR, 92.5 MHz.

Sweetwater: Newspaper: *Sweetwater Reporter* (TW). **Radio-AM:** KXOX, 1240 kHz. **Radio-FM:** KXOX, 96.7. TV Station: KTXS-Ch. 20.

—T—

Taft: Radio-FM: KYRK, 106.5 MHz.

Tahoka: Newspaper: *Lynn County News.* **Radio-FM:** KMMX, 100.3 MHz; KAMZ, 103.5.

Tatum: Radio-FM: KZQX, 100.3 MHz.

Taylor: Newspaper: *Taylor Press.* **Radio-FM:** KLQB, 104.3 MHz.

Teague: Newspaper: *Teague Chronicle.*

Temple: Newspaper: *Temple Daily Telegram* (D). **Radio-AM:** KTEM, 1400 kHz. **Radio-FM:** KVLT, 88.5 MHz; KBDE, 89.9; KLTD, 101.7. TV Station: KCEN-Ch. 9.

Terrell: Newspaper: *The Terrell Tribune.* **Radio-AM:** KPYK, 1570 kHz.

Terrell Hills: Radio-AM: KLUP, 930 kHz. **Radio-FM:** KTKX, 106.7 MHz.

Texarkana: Newspaper: *Texarkana Gazette* (D). **Radio-AM:** KCMC, 740 kHz; KTFS, 940; KKTK, 1400. **Radio-FM:** KTXK, 91.5 MHz; KTAL, 98.1; KKYR, 102.5. TV Station: KTAL-Ch. 26.

Texas City: Newspaper: *The Post Newspaper* (S). **Radio-AM:** KYST, 920 kHz.

The Colony: Newspaper: *The Colony Courier-Leader.*

Thorndale: Newspaper: *Thorndale Champion.* **Radio-FM:** KOKE, 99.3 MHz.

Three Rivers: Newspaper: *The Progress.* **Radio-FM:** KEMA, 94.5 MHz.

Throckmorton: Newspaper: *Throckmorton Tribune.*

Timpson: Newspaper: *East Texas Press.*

Todd Mission: Radio-FM: KTWL, 105.3 MHz.

Tolar: Radio-FM: KOME, 95.5 MHz.

Tomball: Radio-AM: KSEV, 700 kHz.

Tom Bean: Radio-FM: KLAK, 97.5 MHz.

Trenton: Newspaper: *Trenton Tribune.*

Trinity: Newspaper: *Trinity County News-Standard.* **Radio-FM:** KTYR, 89.7 MHz.

Troup: Radio-FM: KTBB, 97.5 MHz.

Tulia: Newspaper: *Swisher County News.* **Radio-FM:** KBTE, 104.9 MHz.

Turkey: Newpaper: *Caprock Courier.*

Tye: Radio-FM: KBCY, 99.7 MHz.

Tyler: Newspaper: *Tyler Morning Telegraph* (D). **Radio-AM:** KTBB, 600 kHz; KGLD, 1330; KYZS, 1490. **Radio-FM:** KVNE, 89.5 MHz; KGLY, 91.3; KRWR, 92.1; KTYL, 93.1; KNUE, 101.5; KKUS, 104.1. TV Station: KLTV-Ch. 7.

—U—

Umbarger: Radio-FM: KRBG, 88.7 MHz.

Universal City: Radio-AM: KSAH, 720 kHz.

University Park: Radio-AM: KEXB, 1440 kHz; KZMP, 1540.

Uvalde: Newspaper: *Uvalde Leader-News* (S). **Radio-AM:** KGWU, 1400 kHz. **Radio-FM:** KHPS, 88.9 MHz; KBNU, 93.9; KUVA, 102.3; KVOU, 104.9. TV Station: KPXL-Ch. 26.

Uvalde Estates: Radio-FM: KEWP, 103.5 MHz.

—V—

Valley Mills: Newspaper: *Valley Mills Progress* (SM).

Valley View: Radio-FM: KQFZ, 89.1 MHz.

Van Alstyne: Newspaper: *Van Alstyne Leader.*

Van Horn: Newspaper: *The Van Horn Advocate.* **Radio-FM:** KVHR, 91.5 MHz.

Vega: Newspaper: *Vega Enterprise.*

Vernon: Newspaper: *Vernon Record.* **Radio-AM:** KVWC, 1490 kHz. **Radio-FM:** KVED, 88.5 MHz; KVWC, 103.1.

Victoria: Newspaper: *Victoria Advocate* (D). **Radio-AM:** KVNN, 1340 kHz; KITE, 1410. **Radio-FM:** KAYK, 88.5 MHz; KBRZ, 89.3; KVRT, 90.7; KQVT, 92.3; KTXN, 98.7; KBAR, 100.9; KVIC, 104.7; KIXS, 107.9. TV Stations: KVCT-Ch. 11; KAVU-Ch. 20.

Vidor: Newspaper: *Vidor Vidorian.*

—W—

Waco: Newspaper: *Waco Tribune-Herald* (D). **Radio-AM:** KBBW, 1010 kHz; KWTX, 1230; KRZI, 1660. **Radio-FM:** KWBT, 94.5; KBGO, 95.7; KWTX, 97.5; WACO, 99.9; KWBU, 103.3. TV Stations: KWTX-Ch. 10; KXXV-Ch. 26; KWKT-Ch. 28.

Wake Village: Radio-FM: KHTA, 92.5 MHz.

Wallis: Newspaper: *Wallis News-Review.*

Waskom: Radio-FM: KQHN, 97.3 MHz.

Waxahachie: Newspapers: *Waxahachie Daily Light* (S); *The Waxahachie Sun.* **Radio-AM:** KBEC, 1390 kHz.

Weatherford: Newspaper: *Weatherford Democrat* (S). **Radio-AM:** KZEE, 1220 kHz. **Radio-FM:** KMQX, 88.5 MHz.

Webster: Newspaper: *Bay Area Citizen.*

Weimar: Newspaper: *Weimar Mercury.*

Wellington: Radio-FM: KSIF 91.7 MHz.

Wells: Radio-FM: KVLL, 94.7 MHz.

Weslaco: Radio-AM: KRGE, 1290 kHz. TV Station: KRGV-Ch. 13.

West: Newspaper: *The West News.*

West Lake Hills: Radio-AM: KTXZ, 1560 kHz.

West Odessa: Radio-FM: KFRI, 88.7 MHz.

Wharton: Newspaper: *Wharton Journal-Spectator* (S). **Radio-AM:** KANI, 1500 kHz.

Wheeler: Newspaper: *The Wheeler Times.* **Radio-FM:** KPDR, 90.3 MHz; KXNZ, 98.9.

Wheelock: Radio-FM: KVMK 100.9 MHz.

Whitehouse: Radio-FM: KISX, 107.3 MHz.

White Oak: Newspaper: *White Oak Independent.* **Radio-FM:** KAPW, 99.3 MHz.

Whitesboro: Newspaper: *Whitesboro News-Record.* **Radio-FM:** KMAD, 102.5 MHz.

Whitewright: Newspaper: *The Whitewright Sun.*

Wichita Falls: Newspaper: *Times Record News* (D). **Radio-AM:** KWFS, 1290. **Radio-FM:** KMCU, 88.7 MHz; KMOC, 89.5; KZKL, 90.5; KNIN, 92.9; KLUR, 99.9; KWFS, 102.3; KQXC, 103.9; KBZS, 106.3. TV Stations: KJTL-Ch. 15; KAUZ-Ch. 22; KFDX-Ch. 28.

Willis: Radio-FM: KAFR, 88.3 MHz.

Wills Point: Newspaper: *Wills Point Chronicle.*

Wimberley: Newspaper: *Wimberley View.*

Winfield: Radio-FM: KALK, 97.7 MHz.

Winnie: Newspapers: *The Hometown Press; The Seabreeze Beacon.* **Radio-FM:** KXXF 105.3 MHz.

Winnsboro: Newspaper: *Winnsboro News.* **Radio-FM:** KWNS, 104.7 MHz.

Winona: Radio-FM: KBLZ, 102.7 MHz.

Winters: Radio-FM: KORQ, 96.1 MHz.

Wixon Valley: Radio-FM: KBXT, 101.9 MHz.

Wolfforth: Radio-FM: KAIQ, 95.5 MHz. TV Station: KLCW-Ch. 23.

Woodville: Newspaper: *Tyler County Booster.*

Wylie: Newspaper: *The Wylie News.* **Radio-AM:** KHSE, 700 kHz.

—Y—

Yoakum: Newspaper: *Yoakum Herald-Times.* **Radio-FM:** KYKM, 94.3 MHz.

Yorktown: Newspaper: *Yorktown News-View.* **Radio-FM:** KGGB, 96.3 MHz.

—Z—

Zapata: Newspaper: *Zapata County News.* **Radio-FM:** KHEM, 89.3 MHz; KQHM 102.7; KJJS, 103.9. I

Transportation

RAILROADS

HIGHWAYS AND MOTOR VEHICLES

CONSULATES AND FOREIGN TRADE ZONES

PORTS AND AVIATION

The Texas Star discharges light crude oil from the Tranmere North Oil Jetty, River Mersey, in Liverpool, England, on April 20, 2019. She had loaded her cargo in Houston, TX. Photo by Darren Hillman/Flickr (CC).

Freight Railroads in Texas

In Texas in 2019, there were three Class I railroad companies operating. Short line railroads made up about 14.5 percent of the state's total track mileage. In 2019, railroads in the state carried some 118 million tons of freight. The leading commodities handled are listed below. A complete list of the 55 railroads in the state is in the Counties section on page 205.

Source: Association of American Railroads.

Railroads in State	Miles Operated
Class I (3, *see list at right*)	12,585
Regional	0
Short Line Railroads (51)	2,141
Total	**14,726**
Total excluding trackage rights*	**10,460**

Railroads in State	Miles Operated
Class I	12,585
Union Pacific Railroad Co.	6,356
BNSF Railway Co.	5,300
Kansas City Southern Railway Co.	929

*Trackage rights — track provided by another railroad.
Numbers in parentheses represent the number of railroad companies in each category.

Freight Traffic in Texas by Kind – 2019					
Carloads originated		**Tons**	**Carloads terminated**		**Tons**
Chemicals	471,000	45.0 million	Nonmetallic minerals	445,700	46.3 million
Nonmetallic minerals	279,400	29.0 million	Coal	383,400	44.9 million
Petroleum products	166,700	13.3 million	Chemicals	357,800	34.2 million
Intermodal	737,300	10.2 million	Farm products	159,200	16.5 million
Primary metal products	44,400	4.1 million	Intermodal	1,050,100	14.5 million
All Other	226,300	16.4 million	All Other	694,600	51.9 million
Total	**1,925,100**	**118.0 million**	**Total**	**3,090,800**	**208.3 million**

Texas Railroads
2020

- ● Union Pacific
- ● BNSF
- ● Kansas City Southern
- ● Texas Pacifico
- ● Other

Highway Miles, Construction, Maintenance, Vehicles: 2019

Texans drove more than 24 million motor vehicles in 2019 over 315,445 miles of roadways, including city- and county-maintained roads. That driving is calculated to have included more than 575.2 million miles driven daily on the 197,865 miles of state-maintained highways alone.

The Texas Department of Transportation (TxDOT) is responsible for state highway construction and maintenance, planning for future road expansion, administering Texas tollways and toll tags, and operating the state's 12 official Texas Travel Information Centers and 76 safety rest areas.

Mileage, maintenance, and construction figures (listed by county) refer only to roads that are maintained by the state: Interstates, U.S. highways, state highways, farm-to-market roads, and some loops around urban areas. Not included are city- or county-maintained streets and roads. A lane mile is one lane for one mile; i.e., one mile of four-lane highway equals four lane miles.

Sources: Texas Department of Transportation and Department of Motor Vehicles.

County	Vehicles Registered	Lane Miles of Highway	Vehicle Miles Driven Daily	State Construction Expenditures	Combined Construction Maintenance Expenditures	Total Vehicle Registration Fees	State Net Receipts	County Net Receipts
Anderson	48,835	1,013	1,299,188	$8,085,678	$24,258,395	$3,533,581	$2,568,624	$962,741
Andrews	21,045	556	1,034,777	5,819,889	22,119,691	1,946,443	1,470,451	474,563
Angelina	80,225	956	2,191,008	80,257,605	99,265,264	6,143,364	4,795,992	1,343,520
Aransas	25,750	203	531,860	6,958,282	12,075,825	1,556,014	1,038,655	513,472
Archer	11,638	572	404,090	3,181,966	10,045,987	780,839	330,550	449,398
Armstrong	2,624	379	408,889	2,093,175	10,894,164	162,851	8,861	153,947
Atascosa	49,302	1,011	2,143,042	9,308,954	42,365,399	3,425,822	2,550,527	872,939
Austin	41,408	649	1,553,989	126,241,336	132,938,009	2,777,160	1,989,174	785,325
Bailey	6,478	491	218,310	94,044	1,391,514	507,747	110,642	396,929
Bandera	28,016	414	444,877	1,494,155	6,494,464	1,650,249	1,033,387	613,257
Bastrop	98,313	806	2,647,823	54,418,416	94,753,738	7,001,110	5,474,698	1,517,305
Baylor	4,151	531	245,130	4,853,732	14,079,989	270,289	33,070	236,778
Bee	22,776	679	638,232	4,706,100	12,552,507	1,665,221	1,064,428	599,942
Bell	307,865	1,578	8,018,655	123,405,957	178,140,973	20,745,794	16,667,895	4,058,214
Bexar	1,574,939	3,389	33,536,530	399,841,080	585,220,525	137,676,180	100,903,637	36,666,568
Blanco	19,159	463	726,425	1,870,341	5,900,090	1,420,451	956,733	461,676
Borden	1,099	344	65,419	334,519	3,692,961	52,098	3,625	48,420
Bosque	23,289	695	553,104	3,619,072	12,597,224	1,343,836	759,663	582,246
Bowie	84,973	1,212	3,134,393	11,840,352	34,756,172	5,909,673	4,569,970	1,333,805
Brazoria	319,975	1,408	6,289,357	72,042,181	93,376,963	22,660,103	18,622,786	4,013,667
Brazos	154,822	978	4,130,973	19,598,686	61,143,631	11,647,478	9,244,305	2,371,749
Brewster	9,883	606	260,438	75,452	1,549,501	594,318	254,449	336,354
Briscoe	1,905	326	58,087	328,885	2,235,285	107,896	7,315	100,471
Brooks	5,961	346	669,101	10,296,250	12,917,592	368,037	112,559	255,407
Brown	40,466	773	851,643	1,104,784	6,567,859	2,988,526	2,132,759	853,576
Burleson	23,670	542	836,871	7,783,641	13,410,954	1,625,969	1,005,392	618,762
Burnet	59,348	794	1,691,869	7,259,653	14,617,360	4,112,570	3,024,197	1,081,330
Caldwell	42,869	716	1,396,600	11,845,264	17,227,520	2,923,124	2,068,854	852,276
Calhoun	22,929	406	613,239	2,875,795	12,853,623	1,826,850	1,248,946	576,290
Callahan	16,233	744	1,069,850	3,725,942	13,805,567	1,330,285	769,285	559,718
Cameron	330,796	1,913	6,826,523	40,273,685	60,859,433	27,802,389	19,724,469	8,065,270
Camp	17,597	265	269,553	322,925	2,347,833	1,542,613	1,056,485	485,488
Carson	7,354	778	789,337	11,795,600	38,307,707	514,405	116,202	398,025
Cass	32,251	975	873,597	7,240,826	16,644,265	1,979,543	1,296,143	682,514
Castro	8,012	533	258,256	1,373,465	6,941,902	836,755	384,916	451,611
Chambers	48,766	807	2,884,385	33,794,765	48,670,367	3,340,442	2,518,207	819,186
Cherokee	47,755	1,143	1,320,855	18,331,590	43,613,037	3,123,283	2,250,274	871,358
Childress	6,224	497	434,821	1,653,724	2,962,798	375,995	63,248	312,415
Clay	12,867	756	876,146	5,844,682	17,384,484	1,010,375	484,390	524,993
Cochran	2,898	467	102,556	240,412	1,710,061	202,018	10,044	191,864
Coke	4,609	369	191,373	6,019,594	8,503,228	259,688	39,377	220,179

County	Vehicles Registered	Lane Miles of Highway	Vehicle Miles Driven Daily	State Construction Expenditures	Combined Construction Maintenance Expenditures	Total Vehicle Registration Fees	State Net Receipts	County Net Receipts
Coleman	10,626	753	407,108	$548,438	$3,325,858	$624,438	$161,930	$462,232
Collin	824,623	1,555	9,180,969	85,811,082	122,100,697	62,459,107	50,938,033	11,431,064
Collingsworth	3,263	454	90,355	311,815	2,730,116	199,295	11,684	187,457
Colorado	29,424	767	1,963,436	16,128,214	35,286,823	2,152,512	1,465,463	684,826
Comal	179,303	736	5,166,329	46,383,728	96,163,543	14,893,568	12,210,769	2,656,038
Comanche	15,587	748	471,140	2,969,224	6,787,149	1,139,816	606,904	532,469
Concho	3,492	477	317,137	3,463,845	16,112,234	187,441	10,705	176,514
Cooke	54,943	850	1,959,676	27,761,433	40,332,650	4,235,173	3,220,002	1,011,167
Coryell	59,965	768	1,226,142	10,922,173	24,022,769	3,266,864	2,351,397	911,652
Cottle	1,532	390	67,443	178,258	1,923,597	84,292	5,430	78,695
Crane	4,962	319	406,326	14,813,585	22,010,146	329,597	123,595	205,936
Crockett	5,171	783	828,658	3,715,356	10,998,081	330,732	62,499	268,095
Crosby	5,568	569	190,923	608,068	3,667,573	336,332	32,322	303,702
Culberson	2,210	754	1,013,623	19,052,609	37,145,037	133,152	7,807	125,220
Dallam	8,068	699	431,707	8,616,330	13,433,979	712,900	266,987	445,664
Dallas	2,011,951	3,374	39,863,257	791,810,562	899,499,287	162,253,871	134,286,772	27,838,993
Dawson	11,522	741	606,777	2,693,910	10,127,069	870,362	371,673	497,095
Deaf Smith	20,529	603	417,751	1,733,855	9,227,889	1,936,365	1,320,969	614,489
Delta	6,460	373	179,949	775,582	4,944,927	353,922	88,223	265,499
Denton	701,437	1,666	11,373,574	195,870,655	226,765,241	50,249,014	41,163,017	9,016,943
DeWitt	25,073	673	751,660	7,672,184	24,799,667	1,723,961	1,104,479	618,347
Dickens	2,697	469	99,378	193,045	2,139,004	155,000	8,743	146,207
Dimmit	10,530	506	678,027	9,293,450	20,583,403	926,260	561,769	364,082
Donley	3,346	469	542,508	7,132,079	16,239,652	214,164	12,546	201,430
Duval	11,268	642	427,946	2,191,760	9,851,196	734,994	296,239	438,411
Eastland	23,048	1,027	1,478,965	35,589,454	45,936,309	1,993,607	1,373,093	619,600
Ector	171,036	971	3,428,545	19,573,332	43,002,398	15,803,702	13,432,196	2,365,621
Edwards	2,957	499	137,546	512,294	6,590,435	175,006	9,898	164,992
Ellis	183,201	1,542	5,720,296	74,976,522	115,462,052	56,488,127	42,075,025	14,392,377
El Paso	670,804	1,763	12,859,357	217,982,985	249,373,521	12,102,233	9,784,752	2,305,770
Erath	41,140	843	1,220,816	12,028,383	32,790,405	2,695,656	1,915,196	776,653
Falls	17,409	746	819,018	2,988,988	15,941,006	1,213,328	649,114	563,847
Fannin	37,673	988	803,884	35,907,610	68,466,741	2,510,746	1,751,297	757,458
Fayette	35,101	1,034	1,938,096	23,172,697	39,606,061	2,222,870	1,506,193	712,283
Fisher	4,579	558	182,446	3,008,168	14,100,638	254,241	14,365	239,644
Floyd	6,663	702	165,545	1,339,360	8,204,826	468,937	94,266	374,039
Foard	1,557	298	60,177	851,055	5,547,365	90,601	4,529	86,072
Fort Bend	621,823	1,306	8,363,712	153,620,601	183,673,190	45,872,683	37,462,849	8,352,166
Franklin	12,552	342	629,295	1,228,670	9,741,862	712,150	311,316	400,044
Freestone	22,725	823	1,594,356	2,721,563	10,053,571	1,488,787	897,859	589,782
Frio	13,884	759	1,441,514	12,743,076	63,760,887	921,823	457,823	463,566
Gaines	22,864	662	776,132	1,031,711	21,179,579	1,824,579	1,222,314	601,648
Galveston	288,583	1,070	5,355,748	185,126,685	206,386,014	19,980,172	16,352,509	3,596,100
Garza	4,702	457	503,500	445,863	10,134,292	299,468	61,672	237,572
Gillespie	37,215	685	844,856	2,569,367	10,669,523	2,348,338	1,565,517	777,071
Glasscock	2,677	357	391,835	3,208,687	27,095,135	148,157	9,491	138,535
Goliad	9,444	535	350,974	13,497,240	28,589,712	514,901	139,866	374,408
Gonzales	25,272	893	1,652,341	7,228,611	31,355,304	1,821,750	1,205,410	615,191
Gray	21,530	759	626,934	4,698,945	24,419,027	1,613,627	997,010	615,318
Grayson	134,892	1,270	3,807,660	39,856,023	84,363,891	9,789,723	7,821,279	1,956,967
Gregg	126,185	822	3,124,019	8,656,043	23,726,763	10,978,206	9,163,840	1,807,627
Grimes	34,412	615	1,166,493	79,904,609	87,949,468	2,216,285	1,509,836	704,488
Guadalupe	160,821	1,014	3,831,290	18,222,281	39,001,652	11,409,807	9,041,527	2,356,266
Hale	28,277	1,059	916,566	4,944,362	25,793,244	2,049,684	1,369,348	679,117
Hall	2,958	457	247,934	1,307,422	5,547,204	182,035	10,492	171,274
Hamilton	11,308	580	375,475	2,580,704	10,811,131	710,340	240,312	469,412

County	Vehicles Registered	Lane Miles of Highway	Vehicle Miles Driven Daily	State Construction Expenditures	Combined Construction Maintenance Expenditures	Total Vehicle Registration Fees	State Net Receipts	County Net Receipts
Hansford	6,405	526	129,151	$1,843,364	$12,617,412	$494,525	$112,528	$381,775
Hardeman	3,918	465	418,334	821,909	4,009,066	245,206	13,420	231,660
Hardin	57,875	581	1,381,487	5,509,366	14,078,624	4,268,910	3,209,743	1,055,495
Harris	3,231,688	5,373	66,955,261	649,899,667	828,948,615	263,555,904	219,268,026	44,033,288
Harrison	68,424	1,181	2,679,193	10,362,154	87,855,377	4,826,523	3,608,830	1,213,890
Hartley	6,826	551	455,947	7,300,214	17,281,887	736,809	387,047	349,426
Haskell	5,700	670	236,671	871,118	3,537,804	421,933	73,905	347,654
Hays	194,733	725	6,141,995	38,999,395	67,202,440	14,204,677	11,639,114	2,540,772
Hemphill	5,468	383	148,197	1,107,220	8,269,719	360,870	82,019	278,525
Henderson	91,183	1,063	1,905,071	26,578,053	37,238,726	5,757,286	4,428,363	1,323,624
Hidalgo	644,500	2,482	12,078,002	153,824,531	226,659,930	56,305,841	41,903,225	14,382,282
Hill	43,034	1,098	2,689,023	43,437,844	69,904,424	3,144,919	2,345,353	797,237
Hockley	24,873	751	629,566	1,004,952	17,469,079	1,817,715	1,197,385	617,837
Hood	71,497	405	1,078,670	23,528,147	26,161,472	5,249,743	4,064,500	1,178,179
Hopkins	42,549	1,006	1,888,031	4,691,736	21,161,560	3,023,307	2,157,101	863,626
Houston	22,059	868	653,426	3,595,959	18,216,976	1,281,962	714,037	566,740
Howard	29,250	885	1,527,118	18,544,068	40,361,718	2,042,603	1,364,081	676,870
Hudspeth	3,833	827	1,716,004	3,156,483	13,414,280	231,502	13,012	218,380
Hunt	95,174	1,379	3,140,975	6,902,330	16,217,884	6,658,571	5,138,532	1,513,874
Hutchinson	23,255	486	332,244	1,097,617	9,396,483	1,585,242	1,026,687	557,459
Irion	3,363	246	246,621	239,479	1,841,453	261,464	70,500	190,788
Jack	10,430	583	317,565	8,850,673	13,977,436	743,382	312,090	430,729
Jackson	17,800	637	974,977	5,184,872	27,934,628	1,156,240	616,427	538,957
Jasper	38,263	774	1,045,696	2,520,462	7,633,225	2,398,179	1,640,622	756,067
Jeff Davis	2,652	468	229,055	779,055	4,256,560	157,896	31,275	126,089
Jefferson	203,259	1,128	5,311,315	65,906,574	108,126,168	14,889,410	12,180,760	2,697,365
Jim Hogg	4,397	288	163,954	805,796	9,591,615	327,912	97,528	230,245
Jim Wells	38,289	715	1,254,386	21,873,219	30,790,908	2,916,565	2,109,655	805,050
Johnson	177,966	1,003	3,625,726	16,133,571	38,252,829	14,214,594	11,486,980	2,716,275
Jones	16,718	1,005	505,341	6,648,816	27,851,877	1,390,059	824,541	563,906
Karnes	19,938	708	922,937	17,850,877	48,683,446	1,303,705	766,852	536,348
Kaufman	131,709	1,208	4,330,054	42,128,058	90,964,088	8,704,384	6,794,910	1,903,361
Kendall	65,847	453	1,300,298	29,427,054	59,097,527	6,263,612	4,857,555	1,394,098
Kenedy	699	191	471,125	5,939,951	6,976,048	31,243	2,836	28,253
Kent	1,099	323	48,832	312,309	2,607,242	51,467	4,016	47,428
Kerr	58,941	712	1,350,651	17,529,439	31,943,164	3,985,815	2,981,460	992,242
Kimble	5,556	685	769,620	7,877,524	17,203,790	321,077	57,912	262,855
King	480	229	84,963	344,602	2,441,783	22,056	1,417	20,639
Kinney	3,621	407	230,773	4,846,497	7,667,763	230,389	61,876	168,337
Kleberg	24,432	379	805,348	5,560,547	8,622,571	1,800,188	1,258,175	540,592
Knox	4,134	467	136,294	4,005,268	10,763,269	286,182	30,779	255,249
Lamar	52,432	1,011	1,284,250	8,388,250	18,107,137	3,868,232	2,890,571	975,174
Lamb	12,632	799	437,393	509,913	6,636,250	874,109	375,700	497,545
Lampasas	26,795	527	730,589	780,713	5,017,277	1,935,160	1,245,517	687,475
La Salle	7,494	648	1,378,036	5,982,270	27,985,430	586,167	251,291	334,602
Lavaca	29,083	671	706,948	1,630,359	9,733,551	1,855,132	1,221,814	631,670
Lee	25,192	522	746,374	12,682,425	26,585,461	1,742,852	1,144,005	597,659
Leon	23,379	839	1,664,263	7,188,500	22,205,963	1,525,167	951,017	572,738
Liberty	78,692	871	2,254,984	40,327,249	53,385,133	5,426,423	4,248,523	1,175,009
Limestone	24,643	770	648,661	3,117,144	16,904,731	1,528,973	914,698	612,827
Lipscomb	4,080	413	97,208	907,053	3,498,392	340,826	54,108	286,540
Live Oak	12,649	1,012	1,688,673	4,195,819	22,702,145	773,350	297,520	475,073
Llano	28,378	509	549,502	4,580,037	12,396,465	1,733,212	1,052,806	676,580
Loving	225	68	230,636	3,599,902	21,912,005	14,090	717	13,374
Lubbock	244,501	1,737	4,137,571	78,467,047	118,665,561	19,881,782	16,475,774	3,368,477
Lynn	6,392	709	470,676	960,359	5,894,530	378,945	52,739	325,182

County	Vehicles Registered	Lane Miles of Highway	Vehicle Miles Driven Daily	State Construction Expenditures	Combined Construction Maintenance Expenditures	Total Vehicle Registration Fees	State Net Receipts	County Net Receipts
Madison	13,655	585	1,162,321	$8,175,767	$27,167,939	$1,295,643	$829,234	$465,669
Marion	10,065	330	270,303	200,566	2,581,737	611,909	200,512	411,002
Martin	7,187	642	1,122,147	3,637,365	30,266,949	618,648	183,365	434,864
Mason	6,547	422	205,441	837,624	4,141,513	354,940	77,559	277,042
Matagorda	34,493	709	944,585	7,671,603	29,177,611	2,182,211	1,471,869	708,514
Maverick	49,474	502	1,060,454	5,633,609	17,727,183	3,788,248	2,902,736	883,705
McCulloch	9,517	615	333,609	1,805,752	7,934,715	625,673	185,597	439,258
McLennan	221,458	1,700	7,048,218	102,126,987	215,238,901	17,095,106	13,787,125	3,292,442
McMullen	1,892	320	309,644	6,025,715	32,591,456	96,619	5,878	90,632
Medina	56,625	765	1,421,256	2,584,950	11,914,595	4,312,708	3,258,136	1,050,868
Menard	2,860	348	175,080	888,868	4,878,755	154,000	14,072	139,686
Midland	215,289	1,078	4,548,595	43,060,417	68,728,110	19,541,922	16,870,331	2,656,305
Milam	28,876	712	808,022	14,703,135	24,607,063	1,707,432	1,061,348	644,850
Mills	6,785	462	257,702	620,681	4,349,999	412,421	76,494	335,511
Mitchell	7,034	662	814,409	1,568,298	7,238,149	391,761	65,032	326,459
Montague	26,432	856	769,052	9,232,401	27,547,141	1,746,538	1,109,017	635,798
Montgomery	551,232	1,336	11,243,112	255,724,050	281,068,853	38,805,707	32,299,994	6,450,815
Moore	23,235	487	538,532	5,925,386	9,315,779	1,769,369	1,210,699	557,619
Morris	13,334	359	534,373	391,983	3,699,969	856,925	443,665	412,910
Motley	1,679	331	49,391	4,976,875	7,746,336	95,291	5,549	89,663
Nacogdoches	56,834	981	1,849,942	35,713,555	49,903,260	4,170,490	3,119,372	1,046,950
Navarro	45,639	1,253	2,185,137	48,413,665	78,939,201	3,255,136	2,392,338	860,417
Newton	13,146	554	370,184	1,591,593	9,502,882	795,145	302,560	491,849
Nolan	14,005	689	1,282,080	3,560,211	16,446,624	976,667	471,325	504,079
Nueces	269,227	1,584	7,006,047	355,035,650	414,115,039	20,544,854	17,015,908	3,509,399
Ochiltree	11,635	432	255,999	2,144,496	11,296,055	937,449	448,179	488,709
Oldham	3,020	467	818,952	618,825	4,103,841	213,344	37,578	175,665
Orange	78,388	640	2,961,057	18,673,016	34,227,145	5,003,022	3,826,864	1,171,352
Palo Pinto	31,306	828	1,132,108	3,574,392	15,921,066	2,052,319	1,388,640	661,740
Panola	25,953	774	997,554	11,787,874	34,098,785	1,544,849	1,098,140	445,457
Parker	159,291	889	3,910,675	15,294,764	45,782,034	12,662,581	10,072,312	2,573,751
Parmer	10,098	612	396,079	16,251,850	20,120,131	764,402	293,184	471,010
Pecos	16,203	1,684	1,345,186	4,420,767	13,144,160	1,262,499	723,433	538,274
Polk	55,549	865	1,798,239	9,134,952	20,948,304	4,406,626	3,364,035	1,039,129
Potter	101,723	921	2,490,550	21,395,617	64,259,775	8,349,519	6,862,959	1,477,501
Presidio	7,728	554	228,873	5,358,469	7,764,494	517,371	184,205	332,927
Rains	15,051	268	345,428	638,087	3,462,008	923,777	478,893	443,946
Randall	137,555	891	1,570,319	40,034,715	49,701,778	11,025,868	8,822,849	2,186,497
Reagan	5,025	319	399,895	1,858,128	8,321,482	402,321	117,911	284,366
Real	4,712	295	121,381	290,637	2,063,838	289,039	69,926	218,662
Red River	13,755	754	390,419	6,284,548	18,507,590	776,680	287,322	488,903
Reeves	14,500	1,182	1,884,671	33,701,940	113,540,486	1,284,886	750,321	534,331
Refugio	7,775	464	708,489	3,784,798	14,120,404	505,917	180,265	325,120
Roberts	1,245	244	88,652	728,964	8,015,873	59,394	3,963	55,383
Robertson	20,094	660	992,969	3,592,610	22,048,651	1,283,905	707,518	575,801
Rockwall	95,452	348	2,211,676	42,993,591	56,811,999	7,701,695	6,254,527	1,436,690
Runnels	12,804	734	416,469	5,799,468	24,796,418	847,197	359,192	487,349
Rusk	50,958	1,176	1,371,140	6,103,732	31,075,521	3,386,080	2,446,049	938,040
Sabine	12,709	482	296,061	802,200	5,604,654	771,183	321,232	449,182
San Augustine	9,352	539	297,023	2,178,165	11,056,118	677,958	271,587	405,843
San Jacinto	28,409	533	846,667	8,392,120	13,901,227	1,804,717	1,127,000	675,835
San Patricio	64,469	993	2,405,508	33,526,770	59,605,514	4,568,816	3,407,611	1,156,439
San Saba	7,955	437	186,881	911,425	7,187,156	470,104	95,104	374,615
Schleicher	4,196	361	131,040	374,945	1,328,345	255,210	46,787	208,237
Scurry	19,328	687	664,363	1,170,858	5,995,602	1,875,677	1,278,578	596,407
Shackelford	4,548	355	156,871	1,793,135	9,139,964	408,157	115,826	292,060

County	Vehicles Registered	Lane Miles of Highway	Vehicle Miles Driven Daily	State Construction Expenditures	Combined Construction Maintenance Expenditures	Total Vehicle Registration Fees	State Net Receipts	County Net Receipts
Shelby	26,976	877	805,921	$3,955,682	$11,346,678	$1,959,085	$1,277,533	$680,761
Sherman	2,832	445	257,217	9,733,082	17,095,014	257,630	16,367	241,216
Smith	219,949	1,610	5,820,322	37,541,409	76,218,573	17,077,994	13,664,182	3,395,763
Somervell	11,377	199	279,365	4,010,704	12,089,045	657,727	307,784	348,790
Starr	56,313	544	1,130,297	11,403,524	16,189,524	3,886,675	2,888,004	997,459
Stephens	9,905	559	220,889	4,814,746	17,393,730	650,179	244,506	405,331
Sterling	2,449	309	271,065	1,991,412	9,128,550	129,232	27,385	101,803
Stonewall	2,021	327	73,880	475,130	3,199,348	121,119	6,166	114,821
Sutton	5,386	590	782,446	675,586	2,636,706	358,452	101,605	256,452
Swisher	6,484	805	437,653	543,509	5,053,623	403,150	62,742	339,736
Tarrant	1,666,191	3,356	32,949,988	335,903,998	467,846,369	136,862,922	115,588,771	21,087,513
Taylor	126,220	1,210	2,657,940	22,211,040	36,078,149	10,182,805	8,313,134	1,859,986
Terrell	1,249	374	81,839	64,378	873,696	57,904	4,174	53,709
Terry	10,997	628	563,270	340,309	7,826,825	844,601	348,514	495,527
Throckmorton	1,959	343	74,000	1,028,480	4,616,761	130,291	5,798	124,407
Titus	30,614	581	1,367,036	12,366,865	22,896,316	2,476,519	1,735,869	738,997
Tom Green	114,296	1,041	1,909,474	18,262,560	34,417,612	8,830,610	6,916,232	1,904,426
Travis	931,348	2,162	22,069,950	172,539,381	290,513,590	70,987,738	58,458,593	12,383,616
Trinity	15,379	443	370,129	495,016	3,803,763	916,660	431,378	484,711
Tyler	21,184	517	517,929	8,080,594	21,951,643	1,274,830	691,288	582,730
Upshur	42,937	788	1,055,075	10,972,112	22,397,543	2,591,451	1,796,078	794,062
Upton	4,771	392	383,115	1,281,812	2,868,204	372,454	126,731	245,591
Uvalde	26,960	765	757,062	3,216,193	13,040,891	1,925,563	1,335,698	588,652
Val Verde	47,887	748	626,739	10,328,469	17,286,710	3,385,697	2,528,498	854,100
Van Zandt	60,520	1,173	2,467,786	8,690,648	26,530,992	3,832,231	2,783,007	1,046,936
Victoria	87,257	925	2,309,713	17,270,495	32,183,166	6,455,345	4,986,444	1,460,691
Walker	53,858	818	2,622,782	75,895,842	96,649,688	3,795,035	2,785,510	1,005,080
Waller	54,153	591	2,177,176	39,692,559	50,602,470	3,980,812	3,025,956	952,395
Ward	15,061	668	1,389,668	4,870,529	26,597,287	1,267,531	966,553	300,381
Washington	41,879	664	1,386,699	6,202,500	18,820,181	3,065,709	2,241,467	820,497
Webb	207,040	1,224	3,628,590	43,681,379	69,302,139	20,558,728	15,813,806	4,739,433
Wharton	47,250	916	1,691,227	35,384,259	85,459,966	3,554,593	2,673,509	878,928
Wheeler	6,654	674	557,804	2,425,343	13,833,555	432,327	85,309	346,713
Wichita	106,430	1,132	2,297,543	12,582,011	33,120,979	7,464,351	5,934,263	1,523,208
Wilbarger	12,180	718	688,806	2,954,538	15,530,415	973,423	452,423	519,958
Willacy	14,312	516	490,569	10,553,461	16,034,972	864,991	374,675	489,723
Williamson	478,792	1,674	9,659,026	44,073,718	105,560,783	36,462,000	29,693,549	6,701,265
Wilson	57,729	738	1,296,810	3,028,782	16,310,801	3,634,145	2,687,821	943,084
Winkler	9,739	292	823,465	5,419,275	18,413,321	743,307	433,609	309,449
Wise	88,508	917	2,424,272	4,438,857	11,167,119	6,487,178	5,139,777	1,342,819
Wood	52,185	911	967,216	5,139,950	19,549,134	3,448,892	2,507,519	936,838
Yoakum	10,549	430	317,635	2,794,173	20,396,438	868,903	397,303	471,022
Young	22,410	703	363,656	3,542,329	11,908,407	1,565,070	965,023	598,390
Zapata	11,789	288	313,888	2,711,008	4,206,029	779,613	395,841	383,559
Zavala	8,639	541	450,618	657,084	6,017,171	591,554	243,344	348,047
Total	**24,088,245**	**197,865**	**575,222,334**	**$7,013,552,109**	**$11,419,289,607**	**$1,871,685,316**	**$1,462,282,650**	**$407,448,167**

Texas Major Toll Roads

Facilities	Authority	2019	2016	2015	2010
Roads		(Tolls Collected in thousands of dollars)			
Camino Colombia Toll Road	TxDOT	$20,370	$6,997	$4,079	$3,352
Central Texas Toll Facilities[1]	Central Texas Turnpike System and Regional Authority	$306,830	$239,165	$202,582	$90,006
Fort Bend Toll Roads	Fort Bend Toll Road Authority	$40,167	$29,481	$26,860	$15,675
Harris County Toll Facilities[2]	Harris County Toll Road Authority	$854,849	$759,276	$745,373	$464,269
North Texas Toll Facilities	North Texas Tollway Authority	$911,046	$671,961	$698,454	$399,054
East Texas Toll Facilities	North East Texas Regional Authority	$12,222	$8,731	$8,340	–
Total, roads		**$2,145,484**	**$1,715,611**	**$1,685,688**	**$972,356**

[1]Including U.S. 183A and Manor Expressway. [2]Including Jesse Jones Memorial Toll Bridge.
Source: Highway Statistics annual, Federal Highway Administration; and local toll authorities.

Toll Bridges

Facilities	Authority	2019	2016	2015	2010
Bridge		(Tolls Collected in thousands of dollars)			
Cameron County International Toll Bridge	Cameron County	$20,664	$19,412	$21,273	$22,102
Del Rio International	City of Del Rio	$8,321	$10,268	$6,558	$4,144
Eagle Pass International	City of Eagle Pass	$13,857	$14,017	$10,737	$8,106
Laredo International	City of Laredo	$68,733	$68,887	$69,215	$41,449
McAllen International	City of McAllen	$19,013	$21,096	$19,799	$11,036
Pharr International	City of Pharr	$14,736	$18,156	$13,196	$10,639
Roma International	Starr County	$2,683	$2,561	$2,988	$2,081
San Luis Pass–Vacek	Galveston County	$579	$548	$3,128	$1,265
Zaragosa	City of El Paso	$25,275	$22,252	$21,499	$16,094
TOTAL, bridges		**$173,861**	**$177,197**	**$168,393**	**$116,916**

Source: Highway Statistics annual, Federal Highway Administration.

Driver Licenses

The following list shows the number of licensed drivers by year for Texas and for all the states. Sources are the Texas Department of Public Safety (for state figures) and the Federal Highway Administration.

Year	Texas licensed drivers	Total U.S. licensed drivers	Year	Texas licensed drivers	Total U.S. licensed drivers
2019	17,822,760	228,679,719	2007	16,330,825	205,741,845
2018	18,000,274	227,558,385	2006	16,096,985	202,810,438
2017	17,675,389	225,346,257	2005	15,831,852	200,548,972
2016	17,326,113	221,711,918	2004	15,562,484	198,888,912
2015	16,970,365	218,084,465	2003	15,091,776	196,165,666
2014	16,579,591	214,092,472	2002	14,639,132	194,295,633
2013	16,230,209	212,159,728	2001	14,303,799	191,275,719
2012	15,950,297	211,814,830	2000	14,024,305	190,625,023
2011	16,880,877	211,874,649	1995	12,369,243	176,628,482
2010	16,808,359	210,114,939	1990	11,136,694	167,015,250
2009	16,602,416	209,618,386	1985	10,809,078	156,868,277
2008	16,551,156	208,320,601	1980	9,287,286	145,295,036

Motor Vehicles Crashes, Losses in Texas

| Year | Number killed | †Number injured | Crashes by Kind | | | | Vehicle Miles Traveled | | Economic loss (in millions) |
			Fatal	†Injury	†Non-injury	†Total	Number (in millions)	Deaths per 100 mill miles	
1960	2,254	127,980	1,842	71,100	239,300	312,242	46,353	4.9	$350
1965	3,028	186,062	2,460	103,368	365,160	470,988	* 52,163	5.8	498
1966	3,406	208,310	2,784	115,728	406,460	524,972	55,261	6.2	557
1970	3,560	223,000	2,965	124,000	886,000	1,012,965	* 68,031	5.2	1,042
1975	3,429	138,962	2,945	92,510	373,141	468,596	84,575	4.1	1,440
1980	‡ 4,424	185,964	‡ 3,863	123,577	§ 305,500	432,940	103,255	4.3	3,010
1985	3,682	231,009	3,270	151,657	300,531	452,188	143,500	2.6	3,755
1990	3,243	262,576	2,882	162,424	216,140	381,446	163,103	2.0	4,994
1991	3,079	263,430	2,690	161,470	207,288	371,448	162,780	1.9	5,604
1992	3,057	282,025	2,690	170,513	209,152	382,355	162,769	1.9	6,725
1993	3,037	298,891	2,690	178,194	209,533	390,417	167,988	1.8	11,784
1994	3,142	326,837	2,710	192,014	219,890	414,614	172,976	1.8	12,505
1995	3,172	334,259	2,790	196,093	152,190	351,073	183,103	1.7	13,005
1996	3,738	350,397	3,247	204,635	§ 90,261	298,143	187,064	2.0	7,766
1997	3,508	347,881	3,079	205,595	97,315	305,989	194,665	1.8	7,662
1998	3,576	338,661	3,160	202,223	102,732	308,115	201,989	1.8	8,780
1999	3,519	339,448	3,106	203,220	105,375	311,701	213,847	1.6	8,729
2000	3,775	341,097	3,247	205,569	110,174	318,990	210,340	1.8	9,163
2001	3,739	340,554	3,319	207,043	113,596	323,958	216,276	1.73	9,348
2002	3,826	315,061	3,544	196,211	113,089	** 324,651	215,873	1.77	21,100
2003	3,823	308,543	3,372	190,926	§ 245,607	†† 460,025	218,209	1.75	20,700
2004	3,725	288,715	3,286	180,556	245,000	447,691	229,345	1.62	19,400
2005	3,559	293,583	3,157	184,093	257,532	464,541	234,232	1.52	19,200
2006	3,523	272,779	3,120	173,861	243,970	439,027	236,852	1.49	20,400
2007	3,463	267,305	3,098	173,052	264,098	459,689	241,746	1.43	20,600
2008	3,477	243,547	3,116	159,760	257,154	438,996	234,593	1.48	22,900
2009	3,108	234,704	2,807	154,685	251,850	428,273	232,055	1.34	20,300
2010	3,050	‡‡ 217,381	2,772	141,554	233,573	391,101	234,261	1.30	22,200
2011	3,015	211,006	2,751	138,624	226,949	381,463	235,602	1.28	21,900
2012	3,417	230,957	3,037	152,301	247,679	417,707	237,831	1.44	26,000
2013	3,407	232,599	3,065	154,458	272,601	445,829	244,536	1.39	27,800
2014	3,538	237,941	3,189	158,833	297,934	476,875	242,989	1.46	38,000
2015	3,582	247,652	3,186	165,199	332,891	521,389	258,122	1.39	36,600
2016	3,794	265,077	3,404	176,381	351,153	551,971	271,263	1.40	38,800
2017	3,721	253,852	3,432	160,926	343,680	537,970	274,580	1.36	38,401
2018	3,652	249,652	3,314	167,984	350,178	521,476	282,037	1.29	39,600
2019	3,610	256,338	3,288	172,768	363,111	539,167	286,268	1.26	39,200

(Note: The highest death rate was in 1966 at 6.2.)

*Method of calculating vehicle miles traveled revised. Last changed in 1982 by TxDOT.

†In August 1967, amended estimating formula received from National Safety Council (NCS). Starting 1972, actual reported injuries are listed rather than estimates.

‡Change in counting fatalities. In 1978, counted when injury results in death within 90 days of accident. In 1983, counted when injury results in death within 30 days.

§Change in counting Non-injury accidents. For 1996–2002, only crashes having at least **one vehicle towed** were tabulated.

¶Economic loss formula changed. Last changed in 2002, when figures are calculated using NCS Average Calculable Cost on a per death basis figure for the year identified. Figures are rounded to the nearest hundred million. For 1996–2001, only property damage in crashes having at least one vehicle towed was tabulated.

**Beginning with 2002 data, the "Total" crash figure includes "Unknown Severity Crashes" which are not included on this chart. Prior to 2002 these crashes were counted in the Non-injury or Injury category.

††Beginning with 2003 crashes, only those resulting in injury or death or damage to property to the apparent extent of $1,000 are tabulated.

‡‡Beginning in 2010, number injured includes incapacitating, non-incapacitating, and possible injuries.

Source: Texas Department of Transportation (TxDOT) since 2001. Earlier statistics are from the Texas Department of Public Safety (DPS).

Foreign Consulates in Texas

In the list below, these abbreviations appear after the name of the city: (CG) Consulate General; (C) Consulate; (VC) Vice Consulate. The letter "H" before the designation indicates honorary status. Compiled from "Foreign Consular Offices in the United States," U.S. Dept. of State, June 2021; also Texas Secretary of State and individual embassies..

Angola: Houston (CG); 3040 Post Oak Blvd., Ste. 780, 77056. (713) 212-3840. angolaconsulate-tx.org

Argentina: Houston (CG); 2200 West Loop S., 77027. (713) 871-8935. chous.cancilleria.gob.ar/en

Australia: Houston (CG); 3009 Post Oak Blvd., Ste. 1310, 77056. (832) 962-8420. usa.embassy.gov.au/houston

Austria: Houston (HC); 11000 Brittmoore Park Dr., 77041. (713) 723-9979. austrianconsulatehouston.org

Bahamas: Houston (HC); 7026 Old Katy Rd., Ste. 259, 77024. (713) 980-8791. bahamasembdc.org

Barbados: Houston (HC); 3027 Sleepy Hollow Dr., Sugar Land, 77479. (832) 725-5566.

Belgium: Austin (HC); 1404 Wilson St, Ste. B, Bastrop, 76092. (512) 571-3125.
Dallas (HC); 2525 E. Southlake Blvd, Ste. B, Southlake, 76092. (817) 748-4367.
Houston (HC); 2406 Cutter Court, Seabrook, 77586. (770) 402-4988.

Belize: Houston (HC); 1120 NASA Pkwy., Ste. 220R, 77058. (832) 390-4164.
San Antonio (HC); 3510 Pinto Pony Ln., 78247. (210) 859-8234.

Bolivia: Houston (CG); 2401 Fountain View Dr., Ste. 110, 77057. (832) 916-4200. boliviatx.org

Botswana: Houston (HC); 121 N. Post Oak Ln, Apt 2601, 77024. (713) 355-8614.

Brazil: Houston (CG); 5444 Westheimer Rd., Ste. 1900, 77056. (713) 961-3063. houston.itamaraty.gov.br/en-us

Canada: Dallas (CG); 500 N. Akard St., Ste. 2900, 75201. (214) 922-9806. international.gc.ca/country-pays/us-eu/dallas.aspx
Houston (C); 5847 San Felipe St., Ste. 1700, 77057. (713) 821-1440.
Austin (HC); P.O. Box 340069, 78734. (571) 217-4377.

Chile: Houston (CG); 1300 Post Oak Blvd., Ste. 1130, 77057. (713) 963-9066
Dallas (HC); 5200 Keller Springs Rd., Ste 633. 75248

Colombia: Houston (CG); 2400 Augusta Dr., Ste. 400, 77057. (713) 979-0844. houston.consulado.gov.co

Costa Rica: Houston (CG); 3100 Wilcrest, Ste. 260, 77042. (713) 266-0484.

Cote d'Ivoire: Houston (HC); 1302 Waugh Dr., Ste. 482, 77019. (713) 410-0472.

Croatia: Houston (HC); 3610 Rice Blvd., 77005. (713) 444-1442.

Cyprus: Houston (HC); 206 Voss Rd., 77024. (281) 704-6779.

Czech Republic: Houston (HC); Czech Center Museum, 4920 San Jacinto, 77004. (254) 931-4095.

Denmark: Houston (CG); Williams Tower, 2800 Post Oak Blvd., Ste. 1910, 77056. (713) 622-9018.
Dallas (HC); 2701 Hibernia St., 75204. (214) 680-7778.

Ecuador: Houston (CG); 2603 Augusta Dr., Ste. 810, 77057. (713) 572-8731. houston.consulado.gob.ec.
Dallas (HC); 6574 Gerrard St., Frisco, 75034. (972) 712-9107.

Egypt: Houston (CG); 5718 Westheimer, Ste. 1350, 77057. (713) 961-4915. consulateofegypthouston.com

El Salvador: Dallas (CG); 7610 Stemmons Fwy., Ste. 400, 75247. (214) 637-1500.
Houston (CG); 8300 Bissonet St., Ste. 400, 77074. (346) 571-5198.
McAllen (CG); 701 S. Broadway St., 78501. (956) 800-1363.
El Paso (C); 400 W. San Antonio St., Ste. B, 79901. (915) 600-5423.
Laredo (C); 6010 McPherson Rd., Ste. 140, 78041. (956) 701-3852.

Equatorial Guinea: Houston (CG); 6401 Southwest Fwy., 77074.

(713) 776-9900.

Estonia: Houston (HC); 3318 Spring Trail Dr., Sugar Land, 77479. (281) 770-3009.

Ethiopia: Houston (HC); 9301 Southwest Fwy., Ste. 250, 77074. (713) 271-7567.

Finland: Dallas (HC); 2021 McKinney Ave., Ste. 1600, 75201. (214) 999-3672.
Houston (HC); 2001 Kirby Dr., Ste. 1314, 77019. (281) 216-5132.

France: Houston (CG); 777 Post Oak Blvd., Ste. 600, 77056. (346) 272-5363. houston.consulfrance.org
Austin (HC); 3900 Petes Path, 78731.
Dallas (HC); 12720 Hillcrest, Ste. 730, 75230. (469) 438 3618.
El Paso (HC); 12270 Rojas Dr., 79936. (915) 892-1660.
San Antonio (HC); 311 Basin Dr., 78216. (210) 859-1308

Georgia: Houston (HC); 410 Pierce St., Ste. 220, 77002. (281) 766-7784.

Germany: Houston (CG); 1330 Post Oak Blvd., Ste. 1850, 77056. (713) 627-7770. houston.diplo.de
Austin (HC); 912 S. Capital of Texas Hwy., Ste. 450, 78746. (512) 852-4162.
Dallas (HC); 17130 Dallas Pkwy., Ste. 240, 75248. (972) 354-7000.

Greece: Houston (C); 2401 Fountain View Dr., Ste. 850, 77057. (713) 840-7522. mfa.gr/usa/en/consulate-in-houston

Guatemala: Houston (CG); 6300 Richmond Ave., Ste. 103, 77057. (713) 953-9531. conshouston.minex.gob.gt
Dallas (C); 4405 N. Beltwood Pkwy., Farmers Branch, 75244. (469) 886-9922.
Del Rio (C); 106 Foster Dr., 78840. (830) 422-2230. consdelrio.minex.gob.gt
McAllen (C); 705 S. Broadway St., 78501. (956) 429-3413. consmcallen.minex.gob.gt

Honduras: Dallas (CG); 3731 Briarpark Dr., Ste. 155, 77042.
Houston (CG); 3731 Briarpark Dr., Ste. 155, 77042. (346) 201-6711.
McAllen (CG); 1209 Galveston Ave., 78501. (956) 627-1210.
Irving (C); 2520 W. Irving Blvd., Ste. 400, 75061.(214) 347-4441.

Hungary: Houston (VC); 847 San Felipe St., Ste. 1700, 77057. (713) 914-1675. hungary.honoraryconsulate.network/houston

Iceland: Dallas (HC); 6827 Northwood Rd., 75225. (214) 415-2311.
Houston (HC); 777 S. Post Oak Ln., 17th floor, 77056. (713) 973-7880.

India: Houston (CG); 4300 Scotland St., 77007. (713) 626-2148. cgihouston.gov.in

Indonesia: Houston (CG); 10900 Richmond Ave., 77042. (713) 785-1691. kemlu.go.id

Ireland: Austin (CG); 515 Congress Ave., Ste. 1720, 78701. (512) 792-5500. dfa.ie/irish-consulate/austin
Houston (HC); 2630 Sutton Ct., 77027. (713) 961-3850.

Israel: Houston (CG); 24 Greenway Plz., Ste. 1500, 77046. (832) 301-3500. embassies.gov.il/houston

Italy: Houston (CG); 1330 Post Oak Blvd., Ste. 660, 77056. (713) 850-7520. conshouston.esteri.it
Dallas (HC); 8303 Elmbrook Dr., 75247. (214) 754-1832.
San Antonio (HC); 2255 W. Mistletoe Ave., 78201. (210) 735-7232.

Jamaica: Houston (HC); 6001 Savoy Dr.,Ste 509, 77036. (713) 782-8494.

Japan: Houston (CG); 2 Houston Center, 909 Fannin St., Ste. 3000, 77010. (713) 652-2977. houston.us.emb-japan.go.jp
Dallas (HC); 4524 Bentley Dr., Plano, 75093. (972) 596-5012.

Korea: Houston (CG); 1990 Post Oak Blvd., Ste. 1250, 77056.

(713) 961-0186. overseas.mofa.go.kr/us-houston-en
Dallas (C); 14001 N. Dallas Parkway, Ste. 450, 75240.
(972) 701-0180. overseas.mofa.go.kr/
us-dallas-en

Latvia: Houston (HC); 2120 Troon Rd., 77019. (713) 304-3831.

Lebanon: Houston (HC); 2400 Augusta Dr., Ste. 308, 77057.
(713) 268-1640.

Lithuania: Houston (HC); 4030 Case St., 77005. (713) 665-4218.

Luxembourg: Austin (HC); 2700 Via Fortuna Dr., Ste. 500.
(512) 413-3603.

Malawi: Wimberley (HC); (512) 569-7998.

Mali: Austin (HC); 2000 Lipanese Trail, 78733.

Malta: Dallas (HC); 7739 Southwestern Blvd., 75227. (972) 883 4785.

Mexico: Austin (CG); 5202 E. Ben White Blvd., Ste. 150, 78741.
(512) 478-2866. consulmex.sre.gob.mx/austin
Dallas (CG); 1210 River Bend Dr., 75247. (214) 932-8670.
consulmex.sre.gob.mx/dallas
El Paso (CG); 910 E. San Antonio Ave., 79901. (915) 747-3246.
consulmex.sre.gob.mx/elpaso
Houston (CG); 10555 Richmond Ave., 77042.
(713) 271-6800. consulmex.sre.gob.mx/houston
Laredo (CG); 1612 Farragut St., 78040. (956) 723-0990.
consulmex.sre.gob.mx/laredo
San Antonio (CG); 127 Navarro St., 78205. (210) 227-9145.
consulmex.sre.gob.mx/sanantonio
Brownsville (C); 301 Mexico Blvd., Ste. F2, 78520.
(956) 542-4431. consulmex.sre.gob.mx/brownsville
Del Rio (C); 2207 N. Bedell Ave., 78840. (830) 775-2352.
consulmex.sre.gob.mx/delrio
Eagle Pass (C); 2252 E. Garrison, 78852. (830) 773-9255.
consulmex.sre.gob.mx/eaglepass
McAllen (C); 600 S. Broadway, 78501. (956) 686-0243.
consulmex.sre.gob.mx/mcallen
Presidio (C); 319 W. De Marzo St., 79845. (432) 229-2788.
consulmex.sre.gob.mx/presidio

Monaco: Dallas (HC); 11020 Tibbs St., 75230. (214) 991-2916.

Mongolia: San Antonio (HCG); P.O. Box 399, Comfort, 78013.
(830) 995-5014.

Namibia: Houston (HC); 617 Caroline St., Ste. 3, 77002.
(832) 242-2426.
San Antonio (HC); 106 S. St. Mary's St., Ste. 200, 78205.
(210) 271-0630.

Netherlands: Dallas (HC); dallas@nlconsulate.com
Houston (HC); 10777 Westheimer Rd., Ste. 1055, 77042. (713) 783-7743.

New Zealand: Houston (HC); 3300 N. Sam Houston Pkwy. E,
77032. (713) 501-5418.

Nicaragua: Houston (CG); 6009 Richmond Ave., Ste. 100, 77057.
(713) 789-2762.

Norway: Houston (CG); 3410 W. Dallas St., Ste. 100,77019. (713)
620-4200.
Dallas (HC); P.O. Box 140918, 75214. (214) 707-2213.

Pakistan: Houston (CG); 11850 Jones Rd., 77070.(281) 890-2223.
pakistanconsulatehouston.org

Panama: Houston (CG); 24 Greenway Plaza, Ste. 1307, 77046.
(713) 622-4451. conpahouston.com
Austin (HC); 101 Knarr St., 78734. (512) 386-1461.

Paraguay: Houston (HC); 4707 Welford Dr., Bellaire, 77401.
(713) 444-9887.

Peru: Dallas (CG); 13601 Preston Rd., Ste. E650, 75240.
(972) 234-0005. consulado.pe/es/Dallas
Houston (CG); 5177 Richmond Ave. Ste. 695, 77056.
(713) 355-9438. consulado.pe.en/Houston

Philippines: Houston (CG); 9990 Richmond Ave., Ste. 100N,
77042. (832) 668-5139.

Poland: Houston (CG); 3040 Post Oak Blvd., Ste. 525, 77056.
(713) 993-9685. houston.msz.gov.pl/pl

Portugal: Houston (HC); 721 Buckingham Dr., 77024.
(713) 515-5272.

Qatar: Houston (CG); 1990 Post Oak Blvd., Ste. 900, 77056.
(713) 355-8221.

Romania: Dallas (HCG); 1412 Main St., Ste. 1800, 75202.
(214) 522-3799.
Houston (HC); 19927 Parsons Green Ct., Katy, 77450.
(713) 629-1551.

Russia: Houston (CG); 1333 W. Loop South, Ste. 1300, 77027.
(713) 337-3300. rusconhouston.mid.ru

Rwanda: Houston (HCG); 70 Terra Bella Dr., Manvel, 77578.

Saudi Arabia: Houston (CG); 5718 Westheimer Rd., Ste. 1500,
77057. (713) 785-5577.

Sierra Leone: Dallas (HC); 2301 Forest Ln., Ste. 400, Garland,
75042. (214) 552-5613.

Slovakia: Dallas (HC); 10830 N. Central Expwy., Ste. 400, 75231.
(214) 251-8020.

Slovenia: Houston (HC); 11300 Kingsworthy Lane, 77024.
(713) 278-1366.

South Africa: Dallas (HC); 1510 N. Hampton St., Ste. 340,
DeSoto 75115. (512) 463-5887.

Spain: Houston (CG); 1800 Bering Dr., Ste. 660, 77057.
(713) 783-6200. exteriores.gob.es/
Consulados/HOUSTON
Austin (HC); 327 Congress Ave., Ste. 450, 78701.
(512) 744-0044.
Corpus Christi (HC); P.O. Box 7589, 78467. (361) 994-7517.
Dallas (HC); 5454 La Sierra Dr., Ste. 200, 75231.
(214) 373-1200.
El Paso (HC); 5130 Gateway Blvd. E., Ste. 120, 79905.
(915) 274-9563.

Sri Lanka: Houston (HC); 6200 Savoy Dr., Ste. 270, 77036.
(832) 287-1677.

Sweden: Houston (CG); 3730 Kirby Dr., 77098. (713) 953-1417.
swedishconsulate.org
Dallas (HC); 3808 Miramar Ave., 75205. (214) 522-0148.

Switzerland: Dallas (HC); 2501 N. Harwood St., Ste. 1400,
75201. (214) 965-1025.
Houston (HC); 2000 Edwards St., 77007. (713) 467-9887.

Thailand: Houston (HCG); 3 Greenway Plaza, Ste. 800, 77046.
(713) 335-3995.
thaiconsulatehouston.com

Trinidad/Tobago: Houston (HC); 9 Parkside Rd., 78738. (713)
816-6477.

Tunisia: Dallas (HC); 4227 N. Capistrano Dr., 75287.(972)
267-4191.

Turkey: Houston (CG); 1990 Post Oak Blvd., Ste. 1300, 77056.
(713) 622-5849. houston.cg.mfa.gov.tr

Uganda: Dallas (HC); 12801 N. Central Expwy., Ste. 750, 75243.
(214) 675-7330.

Ukraine: Houston (HC); 123 N. Post Oak, Ste 410. (281)
242-6654.

United Arab Emirates: Houston (CG); 2200 Post Oak Blvd., Ste.
1500, 77056". (832) 956-6666.

United Kingdom: Houston (CG); 1301 Fannin St., Ste. 2400,
77002. (713) 210-4000.

Uruguay: Houston (HCG); 1220 Ripple Creek Dr., 77057. (713)
974-7855.
Dallas (HC); 2009 Chenault Dr., Ste. 100, Carrollton, 75006.
(214) 346-2919.

Vietnam: Houston (CG); 5251 Westheimer Rd., Ste. 1100, 77056.
(713) 850-1233.
vietnamconsulateinhouston.org/

Foreign-Trade Zones in Texas

Foreign-trade-zone status endows a domestic site with certain customs privileges, causing it to be considered outside customs territory and therefore available for activities that might otherwise be carried on overseas.

Operated as public utilities for qualified corporations, the zones are established under grants of authority from the Foreign-Trade Zones board, which is chaired by the

U.S. Secretary of Commerce. Zone facilities are available for operations involving storage, repacking, inspection, exhibition, assembly, manufacturing, and other processing.

A foreign-trade zone is especially suitable for export processing or manufacturing operations when foreign components or materials with a high U.S. duty are needed to make the end product competitive in markets abroad.

Source: U.S. Department of Commerce.

In 2021, there were 33 Foreign-Trade Zones in Texas.

Amarillo: FTZ 252
City of Amarillo
801 S. Fillmore St., Ste. 205,
Amarillo 79101

Athens: FTZ 269
Athens Economic Development Corp.
201 W. Corsicana St., Ste. 3,
Athens 75751

Austin: FTZ 183
FTZ of Central Texas Inc.
535 E. 5th St., Austin 78701

Beaumont: FTZ 115
Port Arthur: FTZ 116
Orange: FTZ 117
FTZ of Southeast Texas Inc.
P.O. Drawer 2297, Beaumont 77704

Bowie County: FTZ 258
TexAmericas Center
107 Chapel Ln., New Boston 75570

Brownsville: FTZ 062
Brownsville Navigation District
1000 Foust Rd., Brownsville 78521

Calhoun/Victoria Counties: FTZ 155
Calhoun-Victoria FTZ, Inc.
P.O. Drawer 397, Point Comfort 77978

Conroe: FTZ 265
City of Conroe
P.O. Box 3066, Conroe 77305

Corpus Christi: FTZ 122
Port of Corpus Christi Authority
222 Power St., Corpus Christi 78401

Dallas/Fort Worth: FTZ 039
D/FW International Airport Board
P.O. Box 619428, D/FW Airport 75261

Dallas/Fort Worth: FTZ 168
Metroplex International Trade
Development Corp.
P.O. Box 613307, Dallas 75261

Eagle Pass: FTZ 096
City of Eagle Pass
100 S. Monroe, Eagle Pass 78853

El Paso: FTZ 068
City of El Paso
501 George Perry, Ste. I,
El Paso 79925

El Paso: FTZ 150
Westport Economic Dev. Corp.
1865 Northwestern Dr.,
El Paso 79912

Ellis County: FTZ 113
Ellis County Trade Zone Corp.
P.O. Box 788
Midlothian 76065

Fort Worth: FTZ 196
Alliance Corridor Inc.
9800 Hillwood Pkwy., Ste. 300
Fort Worth 76177

The Port of Houston is shown./Photo by Carol M. Highsmith/rawpixel (CC).

Freeport: FTZ 149
Port Freeport
1100 Cherry St., Freeport 77541

Galveston: FTZ 036
Board of Trustees of the Galveston
Wharves
P.O. Box 328, Galveston 77553

Gregg County: FTZ 234
Gregg County
269 Terminal Cir., Longview 75603

Harris County: FTZ 084
Port of Houston Authority
111 East Loop North,
Houston 77029

Hidalgo County: FTZ 156
Hidalgo County Regional FTZ
100 E. Cano St., Ste. 201, Edinburg 78539

Laredo: FTZ 094
City of Laredo
5210 Bob Bullock Loop, Laredo 78041

Liberty County: FTZ 171
Liberty County Economic Development
Corporation
117 Cook St., Liberty 77535

Lubbock: FTZ 260
City of Lubbock

500 Broadway St., 6th Floor,
Lubbock 79401

Lufkin: FTZ 297
City of Lufkin
P.O. Box 190, Lufkin 75902

McAllen: FTZ 012
McAllen FTZ, Inc.
6401 S. 33rd St., McAllen 78503

Midland: FTZ 165
City of Midland
P.O. Box 60305, Midland 79711

San Antonio: FTZ 080
City of San Antonio Economic Development Department
100 W. Houston St., Ste. 1900,
San Antonio 78205

Starr County: FTZ 095
Starr County Industrial Foundation
P.O. Box 502, Rio Grande City 78582

Texas City: FTZ 199
Texas City FTZ Corp.
1801 9th Avenue N., Texas City 77590

Waco: FTZ 246
City of Waco
P.O. Box 1220, Waco 76703

Annual Tonnage Handled by Major/Minor Texas Ports

Table below gives consolidated tonnage (x1,000) handled by Texas ports. All figures are in short tons (2,000 lbs.). Note that "-" indicates no commerce was reported and "0" means tonnage reported was less than 500 tons. *Source: U.S. Corps of Engineers.*

Port	2019	2015	2010	2005	2000	1995	1990
Beaumont	101,090	87,170	76,959	78,887	76,894	20,937	26,729
Brownsville	6,633	7,779	4,616	5,105	3,268	2,656	1,372
Corpus Christi	111,224	85,647	73,663	77,637	81,164	70,218	60,165
Freeport	29,844	21,133	26,676	33,602	28,966	19,662	14,526
Galveston	10,958	10,381	13,949	8,008	10,402	10,465	9,620
Houston	284,944	240,933	227,133	211,666	186,567	135,231	126,178
Matagorda Channel (Port Lavaca)	5,221	11,821	8,879	11,607	10,552	9,237	6,097
Port Arthur	33,944	35,787	30,232	26,385	20,524	49,800	30,681
Sabine Pass	22,002	418	2,494	641	910	231	631
Texas City	40,889	42,924	56,591	57,839	58,109	50,403	48,052
Victoria Channel	2,673	6,733	2,792	3,224	5,104	4,624	3,740
Anahuac	-	-	-	-	-	-	0
Aransas Pass	45	917	173	128	6	181	169
Arroyo Colorado	666	260	411	791	837	994	765
Cedar Bayou	1,811	1,271	931	1,172	1,002	473	219
Chocolate Bayou	1,103	1,171	1,005	3,537	3,488	3,480	3,463
Clear Creek	-	-	-	-	-	-	0
Colorado River	760	848	671	501	445	576	476
Dickinson	450	491	93	688	904	657	556
Double Bayou	-	-	-	257	0	0	0
Greens Bayou	6,645	6,427	5,523	3,768	0	0	0
Harbor Island (Port Aransas)	121	28	1	10	151	209	-
Liberty Channel	3	16	5	-	-	-	0
Orange	1,574	838	684	627	681	693	710
Palacios	-	-	-	-	-	-	0
Port Isabel	-	0	0	-	5	130	269
Port Mansfield	-	-	-	-	-	20	102
Rockport	-	-	-	-	-	-	644
San Bernard River	194	317	371	773	633	653	534
Other Ports	0	0	0	0	0	0	0
TOTAL*	574,061	514,012	486,658	487,100	452,991	371,021	335,312

*Excludes duplication.

Foreign/Domestic Commerce: Breakdown for 2019

Data below represent inbound and outbound tonnage for major ports. Note that "-" means no tonnage was reported. All figures in short tons x1000.

Source: U.S. Corps of Engineers

Port	Foreign		Domestic		
	Imports	Exports	Receipts	Shipments	Local
Beaumont	16,500	47,677	9,595	24,218	3,100
Brownsville	3,269	671	2,425	265	4
Corpus Christi	18,564	66,757	6,063	15,533	4,187
Freeport	7,090	18,882	20	260	0
Galveston	2,348	3,722	2,755	1,979	154
Houston	48,587	115,128	1,936	7,006	14,966
Matagorda Chl. (Port Lavaca)	484	1,719	102	434	0
Port Arthur	6,929	15,746	4,004	2,609	51
Sabine Pass	0	21,137	0	34	-
Texas City	5,879	18,757	235	4,531	225
Victoria	-	-	761	1,912	-

Gulf Intracoastal Waterway by Commodity (Texas portion)

All figures in short tons x1000.

Source: U.S. Army Corps of Engineers

Commodity	2019	2015	2010	2005	2000
Coal	365	125	93	335	121
Petroleum products	53,738	57,224	49,219	39,538	34,816
Chemicals	16,060	17,475	17,553	20,668	21,382
Raw materials	4,056	3,910	3,123	4,898	5,822
Manufactured goods	2,130	1,631	1,646	2,449	2,301
Food, farm products	399	903	574	473	960
Total	76,748	81,268	72,917	69,549	66,440

U.S. ports ranked by tonnage, 2019 (millions)

1. Houston, 284.9
2. S. Louisiana, 238
3. New York, 136.6
4. Corpus Christi, 111.2
5. Beaumont, 101.1
6. New Orleans, 92.2
7. Long Beach, 80.7
8. Baton Rouge, 73.4
9. Los Angeles, 63.0
10. Virginia, 61.7

States ranked by tonnage, 2019 (x1,000)

1. Texas, 597,495
2. Louisiana, 530,269
3. California, 239,154
4. New Jersey, 142,731
5. Washington, 112,267
6. Florida, 98,803
7. Kentucky, 82,081
8. Ohio, 79,117
9. Illinois, 77,616
10. Alabama, 68,431

U.S. Freight Gateways, 2019

Top gateways ranked by value of shipments, with Texas gateways highlighted. In billions of dollars ($214.8 represents $214,800,000,000).

Source: U.S. Bureau of Transportation Statistics, National Transportation Statistics, annual.

Rank	Port	Mode	Exports	Imports	Total trade	Exports as a percent of total
1	Laredo, TX	Land	$94.5	$132.3	$226.8	41.7%
2	New York, NY	Water	42.4	162.3	204.8	20.7
3	Los Angeles, CA	Water	31.0	173.6	204.6	15.1
4	John F. Kennedy Internatl. Airport, NY	Air	84.1	100.2	184.3	45.6
5	Chicago, IL	Air	49.3	134.5	183.8	26.8
6	Long Beach, CA	Water	31.9	129.7	161.5	19.7
7	Houston, TX	Water	92.3	63.1	155.4	59.4
8	Detroit, MI	Land	75.5	57.2	132.7	56.9
9	Los Angeles International Airport, CA	Air	54.0	63.1	117.1	46.1
10	Savannah, GA	Water	28.6	77.5	106.1	27.0
11	Port Huron, MI	Land	39.7	46.7	86.4	45.9
12	New Orleans, LA	Air	38.6	46.0	84.6	45.6
13	Norfolk, VA	Water	28.9	49.9	78.8	36.7
14	El Paso, TX	Land	31.6	43.4	75.0	42.2
15	Charleston, SC	Water	27.3	47.5	74.8	36.5
16	Buffalo-Niagara Falls, NY	Land	35.1	33.9	69.0	50.8
17	Cleveland, OH	Air	39.8	24.4	64.2	62.0
18	San Francisco International Airport, CA	Air	29.6	31.9	61.5	48.2
19	Atlanta, GA	Air	21.2	37.4	58.6	36.2
20	Baltimore, MD	Water	15.0	43.4	58.4	25.6
21	Dallas-Fort Worth, TX	Air	23.3	34.1	57.5	40.6
22	Miami International Airport, FL	Air	34.7	22.5	57.2	60.7
23	Tacoma, WA	Water	20.1	31.5	51.6	39.0
24	Oakland, CA	Water	15.4	35.5	50.9	30.2
25	Atlanta, GA	Air	8.0	40.2	48.2	16.5
27	Hidalgo, TX	Land	13.0	22.2	35.1	36.9
29	Corpus Christi, TX	Water	29.2	5.8	35.0	83.4
32	Eagle Pass, TX	Land	7.5	21.9	29.4	25.4
36	Beaumont, TX	Water	19.7	5.9	25.6	76.9

Border Crossings at U.S. Ports of Entry, 2020

Below are statistics for selected states as to incoming border traffic at ports of entry into the United States. Data are from the U.S. Bureau of Transportation Statistics.

Total in thousands. Percent of U.S. total.

Entering at border (thousands 000)	U.S. total	%	Texas	California	New York	Arizona	Michigan
Vehicle passengers	4,795.9	38.2%	1,832.6	132.6	299.1	146.9	564.8
Personal vehicles	147,481.0	38.3%	56,413.3	57,649.7	5,177.8	15,260.7	4,504.6
Pedestrians	25,046.0	38.5%	9,644.4	11,362.8	22.0	3,870.6	0.4
Trucks	11,580.7	38.0%	4,396.4	1,386.2	1,370.1	423.2	2,120.8
Containers (truck)	11,628.4	37.6%	4,368.5	1,400.1	1,390.6	422.0	2,117.7

An American Airlines flight on a Boeing 737 arrives at Dallas/Fort Worth International Airport in Grapevine on October 23, 2019. Photo by Alan Wilson/Flickr (CC).

A plane rests at Matagorda Peninsula Airport on February 24, 2019. Photo by Adam Reeder/Flickr (CC).

Public Administration

In 1945, the Texas Aeronautics Commission (TAC) was created and directed by the legislature to encourage, foster, and assist in the development of aeronautics within the state, and to encourage the establishment of airports and air navigational facilities. The Commission's first annual report of Dec. 31, 1946, stated that Texas had 592 designated airports and 7,756 civilian aircraft.

The TAC's commitment to providing air transportation was strengthened in 1989 when the TAC became the Texas Department of Aviation (TDA). And on Sept. 1, 1991, when the Texas Department of Transportation (TxDOT) was created, the TDA became the Aviation Division within the department.

The primary responsibilities of the Aviation Division include providing engineering and technical services for planning, constructing, and maintaining aeronautical facilities in the state. It is also responsible for long-range aviation facility development planning (statewide system of airports) and applying for, receiving, and disbursing federal funds.

In the Texas Airport System Plan, TxDOT has identified 289 airports and three heliports. Of the airports, 26 are commercial airports, 24 are reliever airports, and 239 are general aviation airports.

Additionally, TxDOT's Aviation Division has requested Federal Aviation Administration Reliever status for five airports. These include the privately owned Austin Executive and Houston Executive airports, as well as the publicly owned New Braunfels Municipal, Mid-Way Regional (at Midlothian), and Cleburne municipal airports.

Commercial-service airports provide scheduled passenger service. Reliever airports are a special class of general aviation airports designated by the Federal Aviation Administration (FAA). They provide alternative landing facilities in the metropolitan areas separate from the commercial-service airports and, together with the business/corporate airports, provide access for business and executive turbine-powered aircraft.

The community-service and basic-service airports provide access for single- and multi-engine, piston-powered aircraft to smaller communities throughout the state. Some community-service airports are also capable of accommodating light jets.

TxDOT is charged by the legislature with planning, programming, and implementing improvement projects at the general aviation airports. In carrying out these responsibilities, TxDOT channels the Airport Improvement Program (AIP) funds provided by the FAA for all general aviation airports in Texas.

Since 1993, TxDOT has participated in the FAA's state block grant demonstration program. Under this program, TxDOT assumes most of the FAA's responsibility for the administration of the AIP funds for airports.

The Aviation Facilities Development Program (AFDP) oversees planning and research, assists with engineering and technical services, and provides financial assistance through state grants to public bodies operating airports for the purpose of establishing, constructing, reconstructing, enlarging, or repairing airports, airstrips, or navigational facilities.

The 85th Legislature appropriated funds to TxDOT, which subsequently allocated a portion of those funds to the Aviation Division. TxDOT allocated approximately $15 million annually for the 2018-2019 biennium to the Aviation Division to help implement and administer the AFDP. These funds are in addition to the block grant funds received through the FAA's AIP.

Source: Texas Transportation Institute

Drones

The past few years have seen the advent and proliferation of unmanned aircraft systems (UASs), commonly called drones.

They have woven their way into our everyday lives as hobbyists and various professionals use them for a variety of functions that include aerial photography, real estate, construction/industrial, agriculture, emergency management/law enforcement, and insurance.

Nationwide, more than 900,000 hobbyists registered UASs as of Dec. 31, 2018, and the FAA estimates there are some 1.25 million units that can be identified as distinctly hobbyist.

Commercial UAS operator registrations number more than 277,000 since online registration began in April 2016. The commercial UAS industry is still at a very early stage and growth is expected to accelerate in the years to come. The FAA says the fleet today exceeds 835,000.

Related to UASs are the remote pilots that fly them. The FAA issues Remote Pilot Certificates under the Small UAS Rule (14 CFR Part 107), which took effect on Aug. 29, 2016. This rule also provided the regulatory structure for the operation of small UASs for commercial purposes. As of December 2018, the FAA had issued more than 116,000 Remote Pilot Certificates.

A drone hovers just outside the borders of the Guadalupe Mountains National Park on August 22, 2020. Photo by Gary Seloff/Flickr (CC).

Passenger Enplanement by Airport

Airport	2009	2011	2013	2015	2017	Percent change	2019
Abilene	81,451	80,030	78,847	88,959	86,386	-5.29%	81,813
Amarillo	404,903	399,997	373,946	347,304	334,102	5.69%	353,124
Austin	4,019,088	4,409,094	4,809,854	5,643,251	6,580,031	29.29%	8,507,410
Beaumont	22,310	14,323	26,070	35,557	24,880	16.83%	29,068
Brownsville	77,438	84,465	88,292	147,831	119,912	7.92%	129,407
College Station	73,462	70,869	84,379	91,243	74,552	12.45%	83,832
Corpus Christi	353,868	327,534	309,480	339,105	318,810	2.92%	328,109
D/FW	26,548,401	27,464,158	28,946,438	31,356,173	31,433,095	13.82%	35,778,573
Dallas/Love	3,704,594	3,841,785	3,971,077	6,495,869	7,537,325	7.21%	8,080,506
Del Rio*	13,851	9,331	6,846	-	-	-	22,439
El Paso	1,489,619	1,469,168	1,377,876	1,370,243	1,442,605	21.02%	1,745,770
Harlingen	374,232	361,494	354,717	263,423	271,086	23.72%	335,381
Houston/Bush	19,168,962	19,491,854	18,821,429	20,346,164	19,556,778	12.01%	21,905,309
Houston/Hobby	4,032,037	4,646,710	5,213,512	5,765,544	6,392,225	10.60%	7,069,614
Killeen-Ft. Hood	202,226	189,330	175,992	153,698	131,836	33.98%	176,630
Laredo	100,308	105,631	106,524	113,176	94,970	-4.13%	91,043
Longview	24,201	21,360	20,207	19,871	20,682	31.32%	27,160
Lubbock	533,635	505,381	454,661	446,081	453,680	14.66%	520,181
McAllen	360,608	335,008	332,769	390,358	339,132	24.56%	422,434
Midland	435,979	472,177	502,303	533,049	498,248	34.95%	672,382
San Angelo	60,315	55,304	60,127	64,901	60,061	10.54%	66,390
San Antonio	3,809,114	3,967,764	3,998,343	4,057,345	4,300,499	16.80%	5,022,980
Texarkana	27,530	28,626	31,214	35,469	34,574	8.44%	37,492
Tyler	73,177	73,334	81,277	77,543	49,075	21.87%	59,807
Victoria	6,113	5,115	4,204	3,129	3,259	75.94%	5,734
Waco	66,116	60,479	59,809	63,256	61,340	2.55%	62,907
Wichita Falls	43,376	38,941	43,994	45,426	39,064	3.47%	40,418
Total	**70,702,726**	**66,106,914**	**68,529,262**	**70,334,187**	**78,293,968**	**14.20%**	**91,655,913**

Percent change 2017 to 2019. *Del Rio lost commercial service in 2013 and regained service in 2018. Calendar year data.

Sources: FAA Terminal Area Forecasts and Passenger Enplanement for US Airports 2019.

Texas Air History

Passengers enplaned in Texas by scheduled carriers. (Texarkana not included.) Fiscal year data.

Source: Federal Aviation Administration.

1950	1,169,051
1960	3,113,582
1965	5,757,689
1970	10,256,691
1975	13,182,957
1980	26,216,873
1985	40,659,223
1990	49,317,029
1995	57,166,515
2000	65,090,784
2005	65,718,669
2008	69,906,579
2009	66,155,323
2010	66,850,320
2011	68,505,347
2012	69,059,805
2013	70,305,633
2014	73,714,180
2015	78,261,315
2016	80,187,617
2017	80,223,633
2018	86,428,773
2019	91,618,421

Leading US Airlines, 2019

Rank	Airline	Passengers
1	**Southwest**	**162.681**
2	Delta	162.494
3	**American**	**155.785**
4	United	116.256
5	JetBlue	42.836
6	SkyWest	42.329
7	Alaska	35.452
8	Spirit	33.868

In millions. Texas-based airlines in bold. *Source: U.S. Department of Transportation.*

An airplane lands at Dallas/Fort Worth International AIrport on November 21, 2019. Photo by Roman K/Flickr (CC)..

Agriculture

PRINCIPAL CROPS

VEGETABLE CROPS

FRUITS AND NUTS

LIVESTOCK AND THEIR PRODUCTS

Hay is a primary feed crop for all of the farm animals in Texas. In 2020, we harvested 9.6 million tons of hay, valued at $1.3 billion. Photo by sbmeeper1/Public Domain

Agriculture in Texas

Information was collected from Texas A&M AgriLife Extension specialists, Texas Agricultural Statistics Service, U.S. Department of Agriculture, and U.S. Department of Commerce. Caroline Gleaton, Administrative Associate V; John Robinson, Professor and Extension Specialist-Cotton Marketing; and Mark Welch, Extension Economist-Grain Marketing, Texas A&M AgriLife Extension Service compiled the information. All references are to Texas unless otherwise specified. For information on the lumber industry, see page 71 in the Environment chapter.

Agribusiness, the combined phases of food and fiber production, processing, transporting and marketing, is a leading Texas industry. Most of the following discussion is devoted to the initial phase of production on farms and ranches.

Texas agriculture is an important industry. Cash receipts from agricultural producers in 2019 were estimated at $21.2 billion, compared with $21.7 billion in 2018. Agricultural production is associated with considerable upstream and downstream economic activity. Many businesses, financial institutions, and individuals are involved in providing supplies, credit, and services to farmers and ranchers, and in processing and marketing agricultural commodities.

The potential for further growth is favorable. With the increasing demand for food and fiber throughout the world, and because of the importance of agricultural exports to thw nation's trade balance, agriculture in Texas is destined to play an important role in the future.

Major efforts of research and educational programs by the Texas A&M University System are directed toward developing the state's agricultural industry to its fullest potential. The goal is to capitalize on natural advantages that agriculture has in Texas because of the relatively warm climate, productive soils, and availability of excellent export and transportation facilities.

Texas Farms

The number and nature of farms have changed over time. The number of farms in Texas has decreased from 420,000 in 1940 to 247,000 in 2020 with an average size of 510 acres. The number of small farms is increasing — but part-time farmers and ranchers operate them.

Mechanization of farming continues as new and larger machines replace manpower and smaller equipment. Even though machinery price tags are higher than in the past, machines are technologically advanced and efficient. Tractors, mechanical harvesters, and numerous cropping machines have virtually eliminated menial tasks that for many years were traditional to farming.

Revolutionary agricultural chemicals and genetically engineered traits have appeared along with improved plants and animals. Many of the natural hazards of farming and ranching have been reduced by better use of weather information, machinery and other improvements; but rising costs, labor availability, and high-energy costs have added to concerns of farmers and ranchers.

Changes in Texas agriculture in the last 50 years include:

1. More detailed record keeping that assists in management and marketing decisions

2. More restrictions on choice or inputs/practices

3. Precision agriculture is taking on new dimensions through the use of satellites, computers, Global Positioning Systems (GPS), and other high-tech tools to help producers manage inputs such as seed, fertilizers, pesticides, and water.

Farms have become fewer, larger, specialized, and much more expensive to own and operate, but are also far more productive. Meanwhile, the number of small farms operated by part-time farmers is increasing. Land ownership is becoming more of a lifestyle used mostly for recreational purposes. Off-farm landowners are increasing.

Irrigation continues to be an important factor in crop production. Crops and livestock have made major changes in production areas, as in the concentration of cotton on the High Plains and livestock industries in Central and East Texas. Pest and disease control methods have greatly improved. Herbicides are relied upon for weed control.

Feedlot finishing, commercial broiler production, artificial insemination, improved pastures and brush control, reduced feed requirements, and other changes have greatly increased livestock and poultry efficiency. Biotechnology and genetic engineering promise new breakthroughs in reaching even higher levels of productivity. Horticultural plant and nursery businesses have expanded. Improved wildlife management has increased deer, turkey and other wildlife populations. The use of land for recreation and ecotourism is growing.

Farmers and ranchers are better educated and informed, more science- and business-oriented. Today, agriculture operates in a global, high-tech, consumer-driven environment.

Cooperation among farmers in marketing, promotion and other fields has increased. Also, agricultural producers have become increasingly dependent on off-the-farm services to supply production inputs such as feeds, chemicals, credit, and other essentials.

Agribusiness

Texas farmers and ranchers have developed considerable dependence upon agribusiness. With many producers specializing in the production of certain crops and livestock, they look beyond the farm and ranch for supplies and services. On the input side, they rely on suppliers of production needs and services and, on the output side they need assemblers, processors, and distributors.

Since 1940, the proportion of Texans whose livelihood is linked to agriculture has changed greatly. In 1940, about 23 percent of Texans were producers on farms and ranches, and about 17 percent were suppliers or were engaged in assembly, processing, and distribution of agricultural products. The agribusiness alignment in 2008 reflected less than 2 percent on farms and ranches with about 15 percent of the labor force providing production or marketing supplies and services and retailing food and fiber products.

Cash Receipts

Farm and ranch cash receipts in 2019 totaled $21.3 billion, with estimates of $1.8 billion for direct government payments. Realized gross farm income totaled $26.1 billion, with farm production expenses of $20.6 billion and net farm income totaling $5.6 billion.

Percent of Income from Products

Livestock and livestock products accounted for 67.6 percent of the $21.3 billion cash receipts from farm marketings in 2019, with the remaining 32.4 percent from crops. Receipts from livestock have trended up largely because of increased feeding operations and reduced crop acreage associated with farm programs and low prices. However, these relationships change continuously because of variations in commodity prices and volume of marketings.

Cattle and calves accounted for 39.6 percent of total cash receipts (excluding government payments) received by Texas farmers and ranchers in 2019. Milk made up 12.4 percent of receipts, poultry and eggs 12.4 percent, hogs 1.1 percent, and miscellaneous livestock 2.0 percent.

Cotton accounted for 12.1 percent of total receipts, while feed crops was 8.7 percent, food grains 2.2 percent, vegetables and melons 1.3 percent, oil crops 0.7 percent, fruits and nuts 0.8 percent, and other crops 6.7 percent.

Texas' Rank Among states

Measured by cash receipts from crops and livestock, Texas ranked fourth in 2019; California ranked first; Iowa, second; and Nebraska, third.

Texas normally leads all other states in numbers of farms and ranches and farm and ranch land, cattle slaughtered, cattle on feed, calf births, sheep and lambs, goats, cash receipts from livestock marketings, cattle and calves, beef cows, sheep and lambs, wool production, mohair production, and exports of fats, oils, and greases. Texas also usually leads in production of cotton.

Texas Agricultural Exports

The value of Texas' share of agricultural exports in fiscal year 2019 was $6.3 billion. Cotton accounted for $2.1 billion of the exports; corn and processed grain products, $295.0 million; feed and other feedgrains, $255.4; wheat, $213.9 million; vegetable oils, $12.6 million; rice, $116.5 million; hides and skins, $102.9 million; beef and veal and pork, $1.1 billion; broiler meat and other poultry products, $322.0 million; fresh fruits, $38.3 million; processed fruits and tree nuts, $105.1 million; soybeans and soybean meal, $15.1 million; fresh and processed vegetables, $82.1 million; dairy products, $386.2 million; and miscellaneous and other products, $1.2 billion.

In 2018, Texas' exports of $6.9 billion of farm and ranch products compares with $6.9 billion in 2017 and $5.8 billion in 2016.

Cash Receipts by Commodities, 2015–2019

COMMODITIES	2015	2016	2017	2018	2019	Percent of 2019
	(All values in thousands of dollars)					
All Commodities	23,162,190	20,252,874	22,242,427	21,661,381	21,249,024	**100.00%**
Animals and products	**16,719,830**	**13,171,030**	**14,437,152**	**14,268,806**	**14,355,592**	**67.56%**
Meat animals	11,681,887	8,657,563	9,095,448	8,696,035	8,666,372	40.78%
Cattle and calves	11,459,962	8,467,800	8,899,836	8,473,061	8,424,033	39.64%
Hogs	221,925	189,763	195,612	222,974	242,339	1.14%
Dairy products, milk	1,818,675	1,848,140	2,213,152	2,168,608	2,640,193	12.43%
Poultry and eggs	2,845,330	2,289,041	2,702,579	2,984,390	2,626,194	12.36%
Broilers	2,030,358	1,835,520	2,231,814	2,374,520	2,165,130	10.19%
Misc. livestock †	373,938	376,286	425,973	419,773	422,833	1.99%
Crops	**6,442,360**	**7,081,843**	**7,805,274**	**7,392,575**	**6,893,431**	**32.44%**
Food grains	590,295	422,504	348,966	500,477	473,678	2.23%
Rice	127,907	122,768	147,896	155,112	171,896	0.81%
Wheat	460,006	297,599	198,545	342,506	298,337	1.40%
Feed crops	2,026,948	2,121,556	1,742,490	1,681,655	1,841,359	8.67%
Corn	1,067,346	1,170,850	1,010,355	1,029,645	1,104,563	5.20%
Sorghum	557,781	480,609	319,035	226,114	308,847	1.45%
Hay	395,753	460,479	410,626	410,581	419,469	1.97%
Cotton	1,710,731	2,366,886	3,443,599	2,991,571	2,566,232	12.08%
Oil crops	198,370	160,357	227,383	217,182	147,356	0.69%
Vegetables and melons	373,847	398,776	438,316	440,654	281,993	1.33%
Fruits and nuts	155,646	204,673	221,729	156,682	163,350	0.77%
All other crops ‡	1,386,522	1,407,090	1,382,791	1,404,354	1,419,462	6.68%

† Includes catfish, honey, mohair, wool, chicken eggs, farm chickens, turkeys, and other animals and products.
‡ Includes miscellaneous vegetables and other field crops.
Values are rounded to the nearest thousand. Sub-categories may not sum to total because not all sub-categories are reported.

Source: USDA/ERS Farm Income and Wealth Statistics.

Hunting

The management of wildlife as an economic enterprise through leasing for hunting makes a significant contribution to the economy of many counties. Leasing the right of ingress on a farm or ranch for the purpose of hunting is the service marketed. After the leasing, the consumer—the hunter—goes onto the land to seek the harvest of the wildlife commodity. Hunting lease income to farmers and ranchers in 2020 was estimated at $718 million.

The demand for hunting opportunities is growing while the land capable of producing huntable wildlife is decreasing. As a result, farmers and ranchers are placing more emphasis on wildlife management practices to help meet requests for hunting leases.

Irrigation

Agricultural irrigation in Texas peaked in 1974 at 8.6 million acres. Over the next 20 years, irrigation declined due to many factors including poor farm economics, falling water tables in certain regions, energy costs for irrigation pumping, and the movement of much of the vegetable production from South Texas to Mexico. For the past 15 years, total irrigated area has stabilized and fluctuates from year-to-year between 6 and 6.4 million acres. This puts Texas third in the nation, behind California and Nebraska in agricultural irrigation.

Although some irrigation is practiced in nearly every county of the state, about 60 percent of the total irrigated acreage is on the High Plains of Texas. Other concentrated areas of irrigation are the Upper Gulf Coast rice-producing area, the Lower Rio Grande Valley, the Winter Garden area of South Texas, and the Trans-Pecos area of West Texas.

Sprinkler irrigation is used on about 75 percent of the total irrigated acreage, with surface irrigation methods, primarily furrow and surge methods, on much of the remaining irrigated area. Texas growers are continuing the switch to center pivot irrigation machines. Texas farmers lead the nation in the adoption of efficient irrigation technologies, particularly LEPA (low energy precision application) and LESA (low elevation spray application) center pivot systems, both of which were developed by Texas A&M AgriLife Research and the Texas A&M AgriLife Extension Service.

The use of drip irrigation continues to increase and accounts for about 10 percent of the total irrigated acreage. Drip irrigation is routinely used for vegetables, vineyards and tree crops such as citrus, pecans and peaches. Some drip irrigation of cotton, forages and peanuts is being practiced in West Texas. Farmers continue to experiment with drip irrigation, but the relatively high costs and management requirements are limiting more widespread use. One exception is the Texas fast-growing wine industry, where drip irrigation is almost exclusively used for vineyards.

Agricultural irrigation uses about 58 percent of all freshwater in the state, and landscape irrigation accounts for about 40 percent of total municipal water use during the summer months. Texas is one of only a handful of states that require a state irrigator's license for the design and installation of landscape and residential irrigation systems. Cities of 20,000 persons or

Export Shares of Commodities					
Commodity*	2016	2017	2018	2019	2019 % of U.S. Total
	(All values in millions of dollars)				
Beef and veal	845.6	965.6	1,074.4	1,029.4	12.72%
Pork	59.2	60.3	69.8	76.5	1.10%
Hides and skins	200.9	195.2	146.5	102.9	9.82%
Other livestock products [1]	143.2	189.9	189.4	211.6	6.14%
Dairy products	251.3	313.6	338.1	386.2	6.52%
Broiler meat	201.8	232.2	235.8	246.8	7.65%
Other poultry products [2]	67.2	76.9	88.8	75.2	3.83%
Vegetables, fresh	42.1	45.3	43.5	30.6	1.14%
Vegetables, processed	81.7	84.9	73.0	51.4	1.14%
Fruits, fresh	39.5	42.7	41.2	38.3	0.88%
Fruits, processed	37.3	37.3	35.2	33.2	0.88%
Tree nuts	85.4	103.3	50.1	71.9	0.79%
Rice	92.9	105.1	105.5	116.5	6.25%
Wheat	180.0	138.2	163.3	213.9	3.43%
Corn	248.1	202.1	249.2	166.2	2.17%
Feeds and other feed grains [3]	346.6	278.7	258.4	255.4	3.05%
Grain products, processed	158.8	131.5	126.5	128.9	3.22%
Soybeans	20.6	28.0	18.8	12.2	0.07%
Soybean meal	3.7	5.1	5.6	2.9	0.07%
Vegetable oils	10.5	16.4	14.5	12.6	0.46%
Other oilseeds and products[4]	128.2	143.7	153.2	126.2	6.65%
Cotton	1,708.2	2,657.7	2,601.0	2,054.6	33.45%
Tobacco	0.0	0.0	0.0	0.0	0.00%
Other plant products [5]	832.0	835.3	801.6	855.2	4.70%
Total agricultural exports	**5,784.8**	**6,889.1**	**6,883.2**	**6,300.5**	**4.63%**
Total animal products	**1,769.2**	**2,033.7**	**2,142.8**	**2,128.6**	**6.94%**
Total plant products	**4,015.6**	**4,855.3**	**4,740.5**	**4,171.8**	**3.96%**

* Totals may not add due to rounding.
1 Includes other nonpoultry meats, animal fat, live farm animals, and other animal parts.
2 Includes turkey meat, eggs, and other fowl products.
3 Includes processed feeds, fodder, barley, oats, rye, and sorghum.
4 Includes peanuts (oilstock), other oil crops, corn meal, other oilcake and meal, protein substances, bran, and residues.
5 Includes sweeteners and products, other horticulture products, planting seeds, cocoa, coffee, and other processed foods.

Data sources: USDA, Economic Research Service; USDA, Foreign Agricultural Service, Global Agricultural Trade System.

This cotton harvest will be loaded into a module to be formed into a bale. Texas leads the U.S. in cotton production, and today our state's annual cotton harvest amounts to around 41.7 percent of the country's total production. Photo by USDA NRCS Texas/Flickr

larger are required to have irrigation inspectors to ensure that landscape irrigation systems meet state design and installation requirements. However, no license or certification is required for the design or installation of agricultural irrigation systems.

To meet future water demand for our rapidly growing cities and industries, several regions of the state are looking at water transfers from agriculture. The largest water transfer project is likely the San Antonio Water System Vista Ridge Pipeline, which is designed to transfer 16 billion gallons per year from the Carrizo and Simsboro aquifers in Burleson County to San Antonio. The long-term effects on water availability in Burleson County and surrounding areas are uncertain.

Texas water planning documents estimate that as much as 30 percent of future water demand could be met through agricultural irrigation conservation. However, state funding for such programs continues to decline. In about 20 percent of the irrigated area, water is delivered to farms through canals and pipelines by irrigation and other types of water districts and by river authorities. Many of these delivery networks are aging, in poor condition, and have high seepage losses. Estimates are that over 30 percent of all water diverted by irrigation districts is lost in the conveyance systems.

Approximately 80 percent of the state's irrigated acreage is supplied with water pumped from wells. Surface water sources supply the remaining area. Periods of droughts continue to plague Texas. The droughts over the last 20 years in particular have greatly impacted water availability from surface sources (rivers, reservoirs, etc.). As a result, the number of groundwater wells increased rapidly throughout South and West Texas, which could impact future water availability. Declining groundwater levels in several major aquifers is a serious problem, particularly in the Ogallala Aquifer in the Texas High Plains and the southern portion of the Carrizo-Wilcox formation.

Texas common law grants the landowner with broad rights to exploit the underlying groundwater. Laws and regulations governing groundwater use enacted in Texas over the last 50 years attempt to recognize the landowner's right to beneficially use the water, while giving water districts certain powers to manage and restrict water use. Legal battles are ongoing between these two interests. However, an increasing number of groundwater conservation districts are establishing water use limits for agricultural irrigation. The Edwards Aquifer Authority has a voluntary irrigation "opt-out" program, the first of its kind in Texas, where farmers receive payments in exchange for not irrigating during drought years.

Irrigation is an important factor in the productivity of Texas agriculture. The value of crop production from irrigated acreage is 50 to 60 percent of the total value of all crop production, although only about 30 percent of the state's total harvested cropland acreage is irrigated.

The Irrigation section was provided by Guy Fipps, Professor and Extension Agricultural Engineer, Texas A&M University.

Principal Crops

In most recent years, the value of crop production in Texas is less than 32 percent of the total value of the state's agricultural output. Cash receipts from farm sales of crops are reduced somewhat because some grain and roughage is fed to livestock on farms where produced. Drought has reduced receipts in recent years.

Receipts from all Texas crops totaled $6.9 billion in 2019, $7.4 billion in 2018, and $7.8 billion in 2017.

Cotton, corn, grain sorghum, and wheat account for a large part of the total crop receipts. In 2019, cotton contributed about 37.2 percent of the crop total; corn, 16.0 percent; and wheat, 4.3 percent. Hay, cottonseed, vegetables, peanuts, rice, soybeans, and grain sorghum are other important cash crops.

Cotton

Cotton has been a major crop in Texas for more than a century. Since 1880, Texas has led all states in cotton production in most years, and today the annual Texas cotton harvest amounts to around 41.7 percent of total production in the United States. The annual Texas cotton crop has averaged 5.7 million 480-lb. bales since 1996.

Value of upland cotton produced in Texas in 2020 was $1.4 billion. Cottonseed value in 2020 was $269.8 million — making the value of the Texas crop around $1.6 billion.

Upland cotton was harvested from 3.6 million acres in 2020 and American-Pima from 31,000 acres, for a total of 3.6 million acres. Yield for upland cotton in 2020 was 627 pounds per harvested acre, with American-Pima yielding 743 pounds per acre. Total cotton production for 2020 was 4.8 million 480 lb. bales. Upland cotton acreage harvested in 2019 totaled 5.25 million and American-Pima harvested 10,000 acres for total cotton acreage of 5.3 million acres. The yield for upland cotton was 578 pounds per acre and 816 pounds per acre for American-Pima. Total cotton production amounted to 6.3 million 480 lb. bales in 2019 and 6.9 million 480 lb. bales in 2018.

Cotton is the raw material for processing operations at gins, oil mills, compresses, and a small number of textile mills in Texas. Cotton in Texas is machine harvested. Field storage of harvested seed cotton has become common practice as gins decline in number. Most of the Texas cotton crop is exported. China, Turkey, Mexico and various Pacific Rim countries are major buyers. With the continuing development of fiber-spinning technology and the improved quality of Texas cotton, the export demand for Texas cotton has grown.

Grain Sorghum

Texas grain sorghum, in 2020, ranked number two in value of production in the U.S., with Kansas being number one. Much of the grain is exported, as well as being used in livestock and poultry feed throughout the state. Ethanol production is a more recent demand source for Texas sorghum.

Total production of grain sorghum in 2020 was 94.5 million bushels, with 63 bushels per acre yield from 1.5 million acres harvested. With an average price of $7.40 per cwt., the total value reached $391.6 million. In 2019, 1.4 million acres of grain sorghum were harvested, yielding an average of 61 bushels per acre for a total production of 85.4 million bushels. It was valued at $6.5 per cwt., for a total value of $310.4 million. In 2018, 1.4 million acres were harvested with an average of 46 bushels per acre, or

Value of Cotton & Cottonseed 1983–2020

Crop Year	Upland Cotton Production (Bales)	Upland Cotton Value	Cottonseed Production (Tons)	Cottonseed Value
	(All figures in thousands)			
1983	2,380	$680,870	1,002	$162,324
1984	3,680	962,688	1,563	157,863
1985	3,910	968,429	1,635	102,156
1986	2,535	560,945	1,053	82,118
1987	4,635	1,325,981	1,915	157,971
1988	5,215	1,291,651	2,131	238,672
1989	2,870	812,784	1,189	141,491
1990	4,965	1,506,182	1,943	225,388
1991	4,710	1,211,789	1,903	134,162
1992	3,265	769,495	1,346	145,368
1993	5,095	1,308,396	2,147	255,493
1994	4,915	1,642,003	2,111	215,322
1995	4,460	1,597,037	1,828	201,080
1996	4,345	1,368,154	1,784	230,136
1997	5,140	1,482,787	1,983	226,062
1998	3,600	969,408	1,558	204,098
1999	5,050	993,840	1,987	160,947
2000	3,940	868,061	1,589	162,078
2001	4,260	580,723	1,724	159,470
2002	5,040	967,680	1,855	191,065
2003	4,330	1,199,237	1,616	202,000
2004	7,740	1,493,510	2,895	301,080
2005	8,440	1,879,757	2,869	289,739
2006	5,800	1,288,992	2,066	243,776
2007	8,250	2,391,840	2,861	443,409
2008	4,450	935,568	1,547	351,192
2009	4,620	1,328,342	1,634	254,904
2010	7,840	3,006,797	2,685	413,490
2011	3,500	1,375,920	1,228	354,892
2012	5,000	1,675,200	1,669	442,285
2013	4,170	1,493,194	1,368	347,472
2014	6,175	1,739,868	1,946	354,579
2015	5,720	1,564,992	1,844	413,056
2016	8,100	2,593,296	2,528	490,432
2017	9,270	2,950,085	2,852	393,576
2018	6,850	2,232,552	2,088	331,992
2019	6,320	1,762,522	1,902	317,634
2020	4,700	1,373,904	1,443	269,841

Source: Texas Agricultural Facts@, USDA/NASS Crop Production Annual Summary, January; and Crop Values Annual Summary, February. USDA/NASS Quick Stats data system.

Year	**Realized Gross Farm Income	Farm Production Expenses	†Net Change In Farm Inventories	***Total Net Farm Income	***Total Net Income Per Farm
	(Values in millions of dollars)				(dollars)
1982	11,404.5	10,008.2	-127.8	1,396.3	7,197.60
1983	11,318.1	9,778.9	-590.7	1,539.2	7,933.80
1984	11,692.6	10,257.3	186.1	1,435.3	7,398.30
1985	11,375.3	9,842.8	-9.0	1,532.5	7,981.90
1986	10,450.1	9,272.8	-349.0	1,177.3	6,196.60
1987	12,296.6	10,038.7	563.2	2,257.9	12,010.10
1988	12,842.3	10,331.7	-128.4	2,510.6	13,076.20
1989	12,843.1	10,328.4	-798.6	2,514.7	12,962.10
1990	14,421.5	11,012.9	343.9	3,408.6	17,391.00
1991	14,376.4	11,270.3	150.0	3,106.1	15,767.00
1992	14,482.5	10,617.6	464.1	3,864.9	19,519.80
1993	15,817.0	11,294.6	197.0	4,522.5	20,745.40
1994	15,394.5	11,134.7	107.7	4,259.9	19,363.00
1995	15,678.9	12,537.3	243.7	3,141.6	14,151.30
1996	15,025.0	12,006.6	-290.1	3,018.4	13,475.10
1997	16,430.7	12,718.5	709.2	3,712.3	16,498.90
1998	15,506.0	12,047.4	-817.1	3,458.6	15,269.70
1999	17,469.5	12,441.9	196.0	5,027.6	22,099.30
2000	16,810.1	12,707.8	-50.2	4,102.3	17,968.90
2001	18,089.0	13,106.6	113.4	4,982.5	21,795.70
2002	16,567.9	11,372.8	436.8	5,195.1	22,686.00
2003	20,105.7	13,687.6	-137.7	6,418.1	28,026.60
2004	21,826.4	14,343.8	539.0	7,482.5	32,674.70
2005	21,928.5	15,371.6	306.7	6,556.8	28,507.90
2006	20,329.6	16,010.9	-753.8	4,318.7	18,777.00
2007	24,738.0	19,800.2	948.6	4,937.7	19,950.30
2008	22,523.4	19,674.0	-1,174.8	2,849.4	14,282.10
2009	20,648.8	18,562.9	-980.9	2,085.9	9,133.80
2010	23,474.2	18,807.4	46.6	4,666.6	22,404.40
2011	26,004.5	21,429.7	-2,494.0	4,574.7	21,811.90
2012	27,430.8	23,842.1	-1,075.4	3,588.8	NA
2013	29,303.2	24,202.8	-171.2	5,100.4	NA
2014	30,319.8	26,512.7	407.2	3,807.1	NA
2015	29,218.7	23,186.3	-416.4	6,032.4	NA
2016	24,629.3	22,105.5	-77.5	2,523.9	NA
2017	26,374.2	22,250.2	-789.1	4,124.0	NA
2018	25,707.6	21,545.2	-1,177.7	4,162.4	NA
2019	26,139.9	20,584.6	-998.9	5,555.3	NA

Realized Gross Income* and Net Income from Farming 1982–2019

* Details for items may not add to totals because of rounding.
**Cash receipts from farm marketings, government payments, value of home consumption and gross rental value of farm dwellings.
***Farm income of farm operators.
† A positive value of inventory change represents current-year production not sold by December 31. A negative value is an offset to production from prior years included in current-year sales.

Source: "Economic Indicators of the Farm Sector, State Financial Summary, 1985", 1987", 1989", 1993", USDA/ERS; "Farm Business Economics Report", August 1996, "Texas Agricultural Statistics Service, October, 2010". "Farm Income and Wealth Statistics", USDA/ERS. NA = Not available

230.9 million bushels. The season's average price was $6.6 per cwt. for a total value of $230.9 million.

Although grown to some extent in all counties where crops are important, the largest concentrations are in the High Plains, Coastal Bend, and the Lower Rio Grande Valley areas.

Research to develop high-yielding hybrids resistant to diseases and insect damage continues. A history of grain sorghum appeared in the 1972–73 edition of the *Texas Almanac.*

Rice

Rice, which is grown in about 20 counties on the Coastal Prairie of Texas, ranked third in value among Texas crops for a number of years. However, in 2018, cotton, corn, hay, wheat, and grain sorghum outranked rice.

Rice farms are highly mechanized, producing rice through irrigation and using airplanes for much of the planting, fertilizing, and application of insecticides and herbicides.

Texas farmers grow long- and medium-grain rice only. The Texas rice industry, which has grown from 110 acres in 1850 to a high of 642,000 planted acres in 1954, has been marked by significant yield increases and improved varieties. Record production was in 1981, with 27.2 million cwt. harvested. Highest yield was 8,370 pounds per acre in 2012.

Several different types of rice milling procedures are in use today. The simplest and oldest method produces a product known as regular milled white rice, the most prevalent on the market today.

During this process, rice grains are subjected to additional cleaning to remove chaff, dust, foreign seed, etc., and then husks are removed from the grains. This results in a product that is the whole unpolished grain of rice with only the outer hull and a small amount of bran removed. This product is called brown rice and is sometimes sold without further treatment other than grading. It has a delightful nutlike flavor and a slightly chewy texture.

When additional layers of the bran are removed, the rice becomes white in color and begins to appear as it is normally recognized at retail level. The removal of the bran layer from the grain is performed in a number of steps using two or three types of machines. After the bran is removed, the product is ready for classification as to size. Rice is more valuable if the grains are not broken. In many cases, additional vitamins are added to the grains to produce what is called "enriched rice."

Another process may be used in rice milling to produce a product called parboiled rice. In this process, the rice is subjected to a combination of steam and pressure prior to the time it is milled in the manner described above. This process gelatinizes the starch in the grain, the treatment aiding in the retention of much of the natural vitamin and mineral content. After cooking, parboiled rice tends to be fluffy, more separate, and plump.

Still another type of rice is precooked rice, which is actually milled rice that, after milling, has been cooked. Then the moisture is removed through a dehydration process. Precooked rice requires a minimum of preparation time since it needs merely to have the moisture restored to it.

The United States produces only a small part of the world's total rice, but it is one of the leading exporters. American rice is popular abroad and is exported to more than 100 foreign countries.

Texas rice production in 2020 totaled 14.6 million cwt. from 179,000 harvested acres, with a yield of 8,150 pounds per acre. The crop value totaled $195.6 million. Rice production was 11.0 million cwt. in 2019 on 150,000 harvested acres, yielding 8,150 pounds per acre. Total value in 2019 was $141.2 million. Rice production was 15.1 million cwt. in 2018 on 189,000 harvested acres. Production in 2018 was valued at $188.3 million with a yield of 7,970 pounds per acre.

Wheat

Wheat for grain is one of the state's most valuable cash crops. In 2020, wheat was exceeded in value by cotton, corn, hay, and sorghum. Wheat pastures also provide considerable winter forage for cattle that is reflected in value of livestock produced.

Texas wheat production totaled 61.5 million bushels in 2020 as yield averaged 30.0 bushels per acre. Planted acreage totaled 4.9 million acres and 2.1 million acres were harvested. With an average price of $5.10 per bushel, the 2020 wheat value totaled $313.7 million. In 2019, Texas wheat growers planted 4.6 million acres and harvested 2.1 million acres. The yield was 34.0 bushels per acre for 2019 with total production of 71.4 million bushels at $4.44 per bushel valued at $317.0 million.

Texas wheat growers planted 4.5 million acres in 2018 and harvested grain from 1.8 million acres. The yield was 32.0 bushels per acre for a total production of 56.0 million bushels valued at $289.5 million or $5.17 per bushel.

Wheat was first grown commercially in Texas near Sherman about 1833. The acreage expanded greatly in North Central Texas after 1850 because of rapid settlement of the state and introduction of the well-adapted Mediterranean strain of wheat. A major family flour industry was developed in the Fort Worth/Dallas/Sherman area between 1875 and 1900. Now, around half of the state's acreage is planted on the High Plains and about a third of this is irrigated. Most of the Texas wheat acreage is of the hard red winter class. Because of the development of varieties with improved disease resistance and the use of wheat for winter pasture, there has been a sizable expansion of acreage in Central and South Texas.

Most all wheat harvested for grain is used in some phase of the milling industry. The better-quality hard red winter wheat is used in the production of commercial bakery flour. Lower grades and varieties of soft red winter wheat are used in family flours. By-products of milled wheat are used for feed.

Corn

Interest in corn production throughout the state has increased since the 1970's as yields improved with new varieties. Once the principal grain crop, corn acreage declined as plantings of grain sorghum increased. Only 500 thousand acres were harvested annually until the mid-1970s, when development of new hybrids occurred.

Harvested acreage was 1.8 million in 2020; 2.2 million in 2019; and 1.8 million in 2018. Yields for the corresponding years (2020-2018) were 128, 133, and 108 bushels per acre, respectively.

Most of the acreage and yield increase has occurred in Central and South Texas. In 2020, corn ranked third in value of production among the state's crops. It was valued at $1.0 billion in 2020; $1.2 billion in 2019; and $780.6 million in 2018. The grain is largely used for livestock feed, but other important uses are in ethanol and food products.

Oats

Oats are grown extensively in Texas for winter pasture, hay, silage, and greenchop feeding, and some acreage is harvested for grain.

Of the 470 thousand acres planted to oats in 2020, 60 thousand acres were harvested. The average yield was 45.0 bushels per acre. Production totaled 2.7 million bushels with a value of $11.1 million, or $4.10 per bushel. In 2019, 400 thousand acres were planted. From the plantings, 40 thousand acres were harvested, with an average yield of 50.0 bushels per acre for a total production of 2.0 million bushels. Average price per bushel was $4.26 and total production value was $8.5 million.

Texas farmers planted 450 thousand acres of oats in 2018. They harvested 50 thousand acres that averaged 50.0 bushels per acre for a total production of 2.5 million bushels at an average price of $4.82 per bushel with an estimated value of $12.1 million. Most of the acreage was used for grazing.

Almost all oat grain produced in Texas is utilized as feed for livestock within the state. A small acreage is grown exclusively for planting seed.

Sugarcane

Sugarcane is grown from seed cane planted in late summer or fall. It is harvested 12 months later and milled to produce raw sugar and molasses. Raw sugar requires additional refining before it is in final form and can be offered to consumers.

The sugarcane grinding mill operated at Santa Rosa in Cameron County is considered one of the most modern mills in the United States. Texas sugarcane-producing counties include Cameron, Hidalgo, and Willacy.

At a yield of 31.7 tons per acre, sugarcane and seed production in 2020 totaled 1.1 million tons from 35.9 thousand harvested acres. In 2019, 33.5 thousand acres were harvested for total production of 1.1 million tons valued at $20.5 million. The yield was 33.8 tons per acre. In 2018, 38.9 thousand acres were harvested, from which 1.4 million tons of sugarcane were milled. The yield averaged 36.6 tons per acre for a total value of $27.2 million.

Hay, Silage, and Other Forage Crops

A large proportion of Texas' agricultural land is devoted to forage crop production. This acreage produces much of the feed requirements for the state's large domestic livestock population as well as game animals.

A field of sunflowers near the Mexico border. Photo by Craig O'Neal, CC 2/Flickr

Approximately 87.9 million acres of pasture and range-land, which are primarily in the western half of Texas, provide grazing for beef cattle, sheep, goats, horses, and game animals. An additional 8.3 million acres are devoted to cropland used only for pasture or grazing. The average annual acreage of forage land used for hay, silage, and other forms of machine-harvested forage is around 5 million acres.

All hay accounts for a large amount of this production with some corn and sorghum silage being produced. The most important hay crops are annual and perennial grasses and alfalfa. Production in 2020 totaled 9.6 million tons of hay from 5.0 million harvested acres at a yield of 1.9 tons per acre. Value of hay was $1.3 billion, or $147.00 per ton. In 2019, 9.2 million tons of hay were produced from 4.9 million harvested acres at a yield of 1.9 tons per acre. The value in 2019 was $1.1 billion or $130.00 per ton. In 2018, the production of hay was 8.7 million tons from 4.7 million harvested acres with a value of $1.1 billion or $143.00 per ton, at a yield of 1.8 tons per acre.

Alfalfa hay production in 2020 totaled 539,000 tons with 110,000 acres harvested and a yield of 4.9 tons per acre. At a value of $188 per ton, total value was $101.3 million. In 2019, 576,000 tons of alfalfa hay were harvested from 120,000 acres at a yield of 4.8 tons per acre. Value was $107.7 million, or $187 per ton. Alfalfa hay was harvested from 140,000 acres in 2018, producing an average of 5.6 tons per acre for total production of 784,000 tons valued at $159.9 million, or $204 per ton.

An additional sizable acreage of annual forage crops is grazed as well as much of the small grain acreage. Alfalfa, sweet corn, vetch, arrowleaf clover, grasses, and other forage plants also provide income as seed crops.

Peanuts

Well over three-fourths of the annual peanut production is from irrigated acreage. In 2020, Texas ranked fourth nationally in production of peanuts. Among Texas crops, peanuts ranked eighth in value.

Until 1973, essentially all of the Texas acreage was planted to the Spanish type, which was favored because of its earlier maturity and better drought tolerance than other types. The Spanish variety is also preferred for some uses due to its distinctive flavor. The Florunner variety, a runner market type, is now planted on a sizable proportion of the acreage where soil moisture is favorable. The variety is later maturing but better yielding than Spanish varieties under good growing conditions. Florunner peanuts have acceptable quality to compete with the Spanish variety in most products.

In 2020, peanut production totaled 490.0 million pounds from 190,000 acres planted and 175,000 harvested, yielding 2,800 pounds per acre. At 26.3 cents per pound, value of the crop was estimated at $128.9 million. In 2019, peanut production amounted to 488.0 million pounds from 165,000 acres planted and 160,000 harvested. With an average yield of 3,050 pounds per acre and average price of 28.1 cents per pound, the 2019 value of production was $137.1 million. Production in 2018 amounted to 464.0 million pounds of peanuts from 155,000 acres planted and 145,000 acres harvested, or an average of 3,200 pounds per harvested acre valued at 27.5 cents per pound for a $127.6 million value.

Soybeans

Soybean production is located in the areas of the Upper Coast, irrigated High Plains, and Red River Valley of Northeast Texas. Soybeans are adapted to the same general soil climate conditions as corn, cotton, or grain sorghum, provided moisture, disease, and insects are not limiting factors.

In low rainfall areas, yields have been too low or inconsistent for profitable production under dryland conditions. Soybeans' need for moisture in late summer minimizes economic crop possibilities in the Blacklands and Rolling Plains. In the Blacklands, cotton root rot seriously hinders soybean production. Limited moisture at critical growth stages may occasionally prevent economical yields, even in high-rainfall areas of Northeast Texas and the Coastal Prairie.

Because of day length sensitivity, soybeans should be planted in Texas during the long days of May and June to obtain sufficient vegetative growth for optimum yields.

Varieties planted during this period usually cease vegetative development and initiate reproductive processes during the hot, dry months of July and August. When moisture is insufficient during the blooming and fruiting period, yields are drastically reduced. In most areas of the state, July and August rainfall is insufficient to permit economical dryland production. The risk of dryland soybean production in the Coastal Prairie and Northeast Texas is considerably less when compared to other dryland areas because moisture is available more often during the critical fruiting period.

The 2020 soybean crop totaled 3.7 million bushels and was valued at $33.5 million, or $8.95 per bushel. Of the 120,000 acres planted, 110,000 were harvested with an average yield of 34.0 bushels per acre. In 2019, the Texas soybean crop averaged 28.0 bushels per acre from 73,000 acres harvested. Total production of 2.0 million bushels was valued at $15.7 million, or $7.70 per bushel. In 2018, the Texas soybean crop averaged 31.5 bushels per acre from 135,000 acres harvested. Total production of 4.3 million bushels was valued at $32.3 million, or $7.59 per bushel.

Sunflowers

Sunflowers constitute one of the most important annual oilseed crops in the world. The cultivated types, which are thought to be descendants of the common wild sunflower native to Texas, have been successfully grown in several countries including Russia, Argentina, Romania, Bulgaria, Uruguay, Western Canada, and portions of the northern United states. Extensive trial plantings conducted in the Cotton Belt states since 1968 showed sunflowers have considerable potential as an oilseed crop in much of this area including Texas. This crop exhibits good cold and drought tolerance, is adapted to a wide range of soil and climate conditions, and tolerates higher levels of hail, wind, and sand abrasion than other crops normally grown in the state.

In 2020, sunflower production totaled 80.0 million pounds and was harvested from 57,000 acres at a yield of 1,403 pounds per acre. With an average price of $22.90 per cwt., the crop was valued at $18.3 million. In 2019, 30,500 of the 33,000 acres planted to sunflowers were harvested with an average yield of 1,300 pounds per acre. Total production of 39.7 million pounds was valued at $7.3 million, or $18.30 per cwt.

In 2018, of 25,500 acres planted to sunflowers, 23,500 acres were harvested, yielding 1,174 pounds per acre for a total yield of 27.6 million pounds valued at $5.3 million, or $19.40 per cwt.

Reasons for growing sunflowers include the need for an additional cash crop with low water and plant nutrient requirements, the development of sunflower hybrids, and interest by food processors in Texas sunflower oil, which has high oleic acid content. Commercial users have found many advantages in this high oleic oil, including excellent cooking

Texas Crop Production, 2020

Crop	Harvested Acres (thousands)	Yield Per Acre	Unit	Total Production (thousands)	Cash Value (thousands)
Corn, grain	1,810.0	128	Bu.	231,680.0	$1,019,392.0
Corn, silage	270.0	18	Ton	4,860.0	—
Cotton, American-Pima	31.0	743	Lb : Bale	48.0	—
Cotton, Upland	3,600.0	627	Lb : Bale	4,700.0	1,373,904.0
Cottonseed	—	—	Ton	1,443.0	269,841.0
Grapefruit*	16.0	275	Box	—	68,731.0
Hay, Alfalfa	110.0	4.9	Ton	539.0	101,332.0
Hay, excluding alfalfa	4,900.0	1.85	Ton	9,065.0	1,232,840.0
Hay, All	**5,010.0**	**1.92**	**Ton**	**9,604.0**	**1,334,172.0**
Oats	60.0	45	Bu.	2,700.0	11,070.0
Onions, dry	11.0	338	Cwt.	3,718.0	73,467.0
Oranges*	7.8	172	Box	—	16,415.0
Pecans*	115.0	395	Lb.	45.4	63,365.0
Peanuts	175.0	2,800	Lb.	490,000.0	128,870.0
Potatoes	10.8	405	Cwt.	4,374.0	69,547.0
Rice	179.0	8,150	Lb : Cwt.	14,597.0	195,600.0
Sorghum, Grain	1,500.0	63	Lb : Cwt.	94,500.0	391,608.0
Sorghum, Silage	100.0	12.5	Ton	1,250.0	—
Soybeans	110.0	34	Bu.	3,740.0	33,473.0
Sugarcane for sugar & seed	35.9	31.7	Ton	1,138.0	—
Sunflowers	57.0	1,403	Lb.	79,980.0	18,329.0
Vegetables	47.9	—	Cwt.	12,841.7	215,990.0
Wheat, Winter	2,050.0	30	Bu.	61,500.0	313,650.0
Total of Listed Crops	**15,196.4**	**—**	**—**	**1,022,719.1**	**$5,597,424.0**

* Grapefruit, Texas 80-lb./box; Oranges, Texas 85-lb./box; Pecan production and value are utilized in-shell basis.

USDA/NASS, annual crop production, January; annual crop values, February.

stability, particularly for use as a deep-frying medium for potato chips, corn chips, and similar products.

Sunflower meal is a high-quality protein source free of nutritional toxins that can be included in rations for swine, poultry, and ruminants. The hulls constitute a source of roughage, which can also be included in livestock rations.

Nursery Crops

The trend to increase production of nursery crops continues to rise as transportation costs on long-distance hauling increases. This has resulted in a marked increase in the production of container-grown plants within the state. This increase is noted especially in the production of bedding plants, foliage plants, sod, and the woody landscape plants.

Plant rental services have become a multimillion-dollar business. This relatively new service provides the plants and maintains them in office buildings, shopping malls, public buildings, and even in some homes for a fee. The response has been good, as evidenced by the growth of companies providing these services.

The interest in plants for interior landscapes is confined to no specific age group as both retail nurseries and florist shops report that people of all ages are buying their plants— from the elderly in retirement homes to high school and college students in dormitory rooms and apartments.

Texas A&M AgriLife Extension specialists estimated cash receipts from nursery crops in Texas to be around $1.6 billion in 2020. Texans are creating colorful and green surroundings by improving their landscape plantings.

Vegetable Crops

Some market vegetables are produced in almost all Texas counties. In 2017, Hidalgo County was the leading Texas county in vegetable acres harvested, followed by Hartley and Frio counties. Other leading producing counties are: Terry, Guadalupe, Medina, Uvalde, Yoakum, and Waller.

Nationally, in 2020, Texas ranked eleventh in production, exceeded by California, Washington, Arizona, Florida, Oregon, Wisconsin, North Carolina, Georgia, Minnesota, and New York, respectively. Texas ranked eighth in value of fresh-market vegetables, exceeded by California, Florida, Arizona, Georgia, North Carolina, Washington, and New York, respectively.

In 2020, fresh market vegetable utilized production of 12.8 million cwt. in Texas was valued at $216.0 million. In 2019, Texas growers harvested total fresh market vegetable crops valued at $184.9 million from 47,800 acres with a utilized production of 12.6 million cwt. Texas growers harvested 15.8 million cwt. of fresh market vegetable crops from 62,000 acres, valued at $298.0 million, in 2018.

Onions

Onion production in 2020 totaled 3.7 million cwt. from 11,000 harvested acres and was valued at $73.5 million, at a yield of 338 cwt. per acre. In 2019, 3.0 million cwt. of onions were harvested from 9,000 acres and valued at $51.0 million, at a yield of 335 cwt. per acre. A total of 3.2 million cwt. of onions were produced from 11,000 harvested acres and valued at $61.3 million in 2018, yielding 300 cwt. per acre.

Carrots

Carrot production in 2018 totaled 400,000 cwt. from 1,600 harvested acres at a yield of 250 cwt. per acre. Production was valued at $3.8 million. In 2017, carrots were harvested from 1,900 acres with a value of $4.8 million. At a yield of 240 cwt. per acre, 2017 production was 456,000 cwt. Carrot production in 2016 totaled 590,000 cwt. from 2,000 harvested acres. At a yield of 295 cwt. per acre, production value was $6.6 million.

The winter carrot production from South Texas accounts for about three-fourths of total production during the winter season. *In 2019, data for carrots were discontinued.*

Vegetable Production, 2020

Crop	Harvested Acres	Yield Per Acre, Cwt.	Production, (000) Cwt.	Value (thousands of dollars)
Cabbage	6,400	290	1,856	40,832
Cucumbers	5,700	83	473	9,267
Dry Onions	11,000	338	3,718	73,467
Potatoes	10,800	405	4,374	69,547
Pumpkins	3,700	270	999	25,906
Spinach	2,100	136	286	5,485
Watermelons	19,000	290	5,510	61,033
Total	58,700	—	17,216	285,537

Numbers may not add due to rounding.

Source: USDA/NASS, Annual Vegetable Summary, February 2021; "2020 State Agriculture Overview, Texas"

All Potatoes

In 2020, all potatoes were harvested from 10,800 acres with production of 4.4 million cwt. valued at $69.5 million at a yield of 405 cwt. per acre. All potatoes were harvested from 14,800 acres with production of 7.1 million cwt. valued at $88.1 million in 2019, yielding 480 cwt. per acre. This compares with 17,500 acres harvested valued at $93.7 million in 2018 with a production of 7.4 million cwt. and a yield of 425 cwt. per acre.

Cantaloupes

Cantaloupe production in 2018 totaled 220,000 cwt. from 2,000 harvested acres and was valued at $5.1 million at a yield of 110 cwt. per acre. In 2017, cantaloupes were harvested from 2,000 acres for total production of 220,000 cwt. valued at $5.3 million, yielding 110 cwt. per acre. Of the 1,900 harvested acres in 2016, 237,500 cwt. cantaloupes were produced at a yield of 125 cwt. per acre and were valued at $5.2 million. *No data available after 2018.*

Watermelons

Watermelon production in 2020 was 5.5 million cwt. from 19,000 harvested acres with a value of $61.0 million, yielding 290 cwt. per acre. In 2019, at a yield of 290 cwt. per acre, 6.2 million cwt. watermelons were harvested from 21,500 acres and valued at $77.8 million. Watermelon production was 7.8 million cwt. from 23,000 harvested acres in 2018, with a value of $143.4 million at a yield of 340 cwt. per acre.

Cabbage

In 2020, 6,400 acres were harvested and yielded total production of 1.9 million cwt. that were valued at $40.8 million. Yield was 290 cwt. per acre. Numbers for 2019 were not reported. The 5,000 acres of cabbage harvested in Texas in 2018 brought a value of $27.4 million. At a yield of 270 cwt. per acre, total production was 1.4 million cwt.

Spinach

Spinach production is primarily concentrated in the Winter Garden area of South Texas.

The 2020 production value of spinach was estimated at $5.5 million. Production of 285,600 cwt. was harvested from 2,100 acres with a yield of 136 cwt. per acre. *In 2019, numbers were not reported for spinach.* The 2,800 acres, harvested in 2018, produced 322,000 cwt. at a yield of 115 cwt. per acre and valued at $6.1 million..

Pumpkin

Pumpkin production in 2020 was 999,000 cwt., harvested from 3,700 acres. The yield was 270 cwt. per acre and a value of $25.9 million. *Numbers for pumpkins in 2019 were not reported.* A production of 1.6 million cwt. was harvested from 4,900 acres with a yield of 330 cwt. per acre in 2018. The production value was $24.1 million.

Cucumbers

In 2020, 5,700 acres of cucumbers were harvested. Production totaled 473,100 cwt. and was valued at $9.3 million. The yield was 83 cwt. per acre. Numbers for cucumbers were not reported in 2019. At a yield of 97 cwt. per acre, the 475,300 cwt. cucumber crop in Texas during 2018 was harvested from 4,900 acres and valued at $8.7 million.

A couple picks out pumpkins at Barton Hill Farms in Bastrop. Photo courtesy of Barton Hill Farms, https://bartonhillfarms.com.

Fruits and Nuts

Texas is noted for producing a wide variety of fruits. The pecan is the only commercial nut crop in the state. The pecan is native to most of the state's river valleys and is the Texas state tree. Citrus is produced commercially in the three southernmost counties in the Lower Rio Grande Valley. Peaches represent the next most important Texas fruit crop, and there is considerable interest in growing apples.

Citrus

Texas ranks with Florida, and California as leading states in the production of citrus. Most of the Texas production is in Cameron, Hidalgo, and Willacy counties of the Lower Rio Grande Valley. In 2019/20, grapefruit utilized production was estimated at 4.4 million boxes at $11.01 per box or $68.7 million. Grapefruit production in 2018/19 was 6.1 million boxes for a total value of $65.2 million. Production in 2017/18 was 4.8 million boxes with a value of $54.1 million.

Production of oranges in 2019/20 was 1.3 million boxes for a total value of $16.4 million. In 2018/19, production was 2.5 million boxes for a total value of $24.6 million. Production was 1.9 million boxes in 2017/18 for a value of $35.5 million.

Peaches

Primary production areas are East Texas, the Hill Country, and the West Cross Timbers. Production varies substantially due to adverse weather conditions. Low-chilling varieties for early marketings are being grown in Atascosa, Frio, Webb, Karnes, and Duval counties.

The Texas peach crop's production totaled 2,420 tons in 2018. In 2017, utilized production was 2,500 tons. Value of production was $6.3 million. In 2016, utilized production was 4,200 tons that was valued at $9.2 million. *Numbers were not reported after 2018.*

Pecans

The pecan, the state tree, is one of the most widely distributed trees in Texas. It is native to over 150 counties and is grown commercially in some 30 additional counties. The pecan is also widely used as a dual-purpose yard tree. The commercial plantings of pecans have accelerated in Central and West Texas with many of the new orchards being irrigated. Many new pecan plantings are being established under trickle-irrigation systems.

In 2020, pecan orchards yielded 370 pounds per acre from 115,000 harvested acres. The utilized production was 45.4 million pounds with a value of $63.4 million or $1.52 per pound. In 2019, a yield of 335 pounds per acre was harvested from 112,000 acres. The utilized production was 37.5 million pounds with a value of $73.5 million, or $1.96 per pound. The 2018 crop totaled 33.6 million pounds from 112,000 harvested acres at a yield of 300 pounds per acre. The value was $56.1 million or $1.67 per pound.

Nationally, Texas ranked third with Georgia first and New Mexico second in utilized pecan production in 2020.

Livestock and Animal Products

Livestock and animal products accounted for about 67.6 percent of the agricultural cash receipts in Texas in 2019. The state ranks first nationally in all cattle, beef cattle, cattle on feed, sheep and lambs, wool, goats, and mohair.

Cattle and calves account for around 58.7 percent of cash receipts from marketings of livestock and animal products. Sales of livestock and animal products in 2019 totaled $14.4 billion, up from $14.3 billion in 2018.

Cattle and calves dominate livestock production in Texas, contributing around 58.7 percent of cash receipts from livestock and animal products. The January 1, 2021 inventory of all cattle and calves in Texas totaled 13.1 million head, valued at $12.7 billion, compared to 12.9 million as of January 1, 2020, valued at $12.5 billion, and 13.0 million as of January 1, 2019, valued at $12.9 billion.

On January 1, 2021, the sheep and lamb inventory stood at 730,000 head, valued at $132.9 million, compared with 735,000 head as of January 1, 2020, valued at $134.5 million. January 1, 2019 showed an inventory of 750,000 valued at $135.8 million. Sheep and lambs numbered 3.2 million on January 1, 1973, down from a high of 10.8 million in 1943. Wool production decreased from 26.4 million pounds valued at $23.2 million in 1973 to 1.4 million pounds valued at $2.4 million in 2020. Production was 1.7 million pounds in 2019 valued at $3.2 million, compared to 1.8 million pounds in 2018 and valued at $3.2 million. The price of wool per pound was 88 cents in 1973, compared to $1.80 in 2020, $1.90 in 2019, and $1.80 in 2018.

Mohair production in Texas has dropped from a 1965 high of 31.6 million pounds to 340,000 pounds in 2020. Production was valued at $2.4 million or $7.20 per pound. In 2019, production was 470,000 pounds valued at $3.8 million or $8.00 per pound. Mohair production in 2018 was 465,000 pounds valued at $3.3 million or $7.20 per pound.

Beef Cattle

Raising beef cattle is the most extensive agricultural operation in Texas. In 2019, cattle and calves were 39.6 percent of total cash receipts — $8.4 million of $21.2 million, compared with $8.5 million of $21.7 million in 2018 (39.1%) and $8.9 million of $22.2 million in 2017 (40.0%). The next leading commodity is dairy products such as milk.

Nearly all of the 254 counties in Texas derive more revenue from cattle than from any other agricultural commodity, and those that don't usually rank cattle second in importance.

Within the boundaries of Texas are 14.0 percent of all the cattle and calves in the U.S., as are 15.0 percent of the beef cows that have calved, and 13.1 percent of the calf crop as of January 1, 2021 inventory.

The number of all cattle and calves in Texas on January 1, 2021 totaled 13.1 million, compared with 12.9 million on January 1, 2020; and 13.0 million on January 1, 2019.

Calves born on Texas farms and ranches in January 1, 2021 totaled 4.6 million, compared with 4.5 million in 2020; and 4.7 million in 2019.

Dairying Product Manufacturing

The major dairy products manufactured in Texas include condensed, evaporated and dry milk, creamer, butter, and cheese. However, specifics of production and value are not available because of the small number of manufacturing plants producing these products.

Dairying

All cows' milk sold by Texas dairy farmers is marketed under the terms of Federal Marketing Orders. Most Texas dairymen are members of one of four marketing cooperatives. Associate Milk Producers, Inc. is the largest, representing the majority of the state's producers.

Texas dairy farmers received an average price for milk of $18.60 per hundred pounds in 2020, $19.10 in 2019, and $16.90 in 2018. A total of 14.8 billion pounds of milk was sold to plants and dealers in 2020, bringing in cash receipts from milk to dairy farmers of $2.8 billion. This compared with 13.8 billion pounds sold in 2019 that brought in $2.6 billion in cash receipts. In 2018, Texas dairymen sold 12.8 billion pounds of milk, which brought in cash receipts of $2.2 billion.

The annual average number of milk cows in Texas was 615,000 head as of January 1, 2021, inventory. This compared with 580,000 head as of January 1, 2020, and 545,000 as of January 1, 2019. Average milk production per cow in the state has increased steadily over the past several decades. The average milk production per cow in 2020 was 24,926 pounds. Milk per cow in 2019 was 24,513 pounds. In 2018, milk per cow was 23,948 pounds. Total milk production in Texas was 14.8 billion pounds in 2020, 13.9 billion pounds in 2019, and 12.9 billion pounds in 2018.

There were 467 farms reporting milk cows in Texas in 2017. In 2012, 985 farms reported milk cows, and in 2007, 1,293 farms reported milk cows in Texas.

Broiler hens in a chicken farm outside Luling. Photo by U.S. Department of Agriculture/Flickr

Hog Production 1974–2020

Year	Production (1,000 Lbs.)	Average Market Weight (Lbs.)	Average Price Per Cwt. ($)	Gross Income ($1,000)
1974	350,811	253	33.3	123,277
1975	271,027	244	43.7	127,323
1976	286,053	247	41.5	117,587
1977	292,290	247	38	109,634
1978	303,135	258	43.8	135,006
1979	320,790	261	39.7	125,183
1980	315,827	259	35.9	111,700
1981	264,693	256	41.7	121,054
1982	205,656	256	49.6	112,726
1983	209,621	256	45.2	95,343
1984	189,620	262	45.5	95,657
1985	168,950	266	43.4	72,512
1986	176,660	269	47.3	82,885
1987	216,834	NA	50.6	103,983
1988	236,658	NA	41.3	100,029
1989	230,004	NA	39.9	95,482
1990	196,225	NA	48.2	92,222
1991	207,023	NA	45.1	97,398
1992	217,554	NA	36.4	79,436
1993	221,071	NA	39.9	90,571
1994	224,397	NA	35.1	78,394
1995	221,323	NA	35.5	81,509
1996	204,476	NA	45.9	94,962
1997	224,131	NA	47.4	103,050
1998	271,444	NA	30.7	86,349
1999	274,572	NA	27.5	71,604
2000	328,732	NA	36.6	115,105
2001	260,875	NA	39.1	105,217
2002	223,441	NA	28.7	67,255
2003	197,876	NA	33.6	67,998
2004	202,199	NA	44.9	90,349
2005	223,375	NA	45.4	105,989
2006	257,644	NA	40.8	108,844
2007	273,213	NA	39.7	95,581
2008	328,356	NA	40.5	143,249
2009	286,069	NA	37.6	135,077
2010	149,934	NA	50.2	96,676
2011	168,718	NA	NA	153,517
2012	414,904	NA	NA	288,652
2013	285,822	NA	NA	240,322
2014	305,146	NA	NA	248,928
2015	376,691	NA	NA	224,328
2016	365,980	NA	NA	191,892
2017	366,121	NA	NA	197,572
2018	442,476	NA	NA	225,125
2019	494,912	NA	NA	244,954
2020	505,725	NA	NA	222,327

NA = not available

Source: "1985 Texas Livestock, Dairy and Poultry Statistics", USDA, Bulletin 235, June 1986, pp. 32, 46; 1991 "Texas Livestock Statistics", USDA,; "1993 Texas Livestock Statistics", Bulletin 252, Texas Agricultural Statistics Service, August 1994; "Texas Agricultural Facts, 2009", October, 2010; "Texas Ag Facts", various years. "Meat Animals - Prod., Disp., & Income", April 2020 and April 2021; (December 1 previous year); USDA/NASS Quick Stats. Numbers from previous years revised.

Poultry and Eggs

Poultry and eggs contribute about 12.4 percent of the total cash receipts of Texas farmers in 2019. On January 1, 2020, Texas ranked sixth among the states in broilers produced and sixth in eggs produced.

In 2019, cash receipts to Texas producers from the production of poultry and eggs totaled $2.6 billion. This compares with $3.0 billion in 2018 and $2.7 in 2017.

Broiler production in 2020 totaled 702.5 million birds, compared with 675.0 million in 2019 and 653.5 million in 2018.

Swine

Texas had 1.1 million head of swine on hand, December 1, 2020 — only 1.4 percent of the U.S. swine herd.

Although the number of farms producing hogs has steadily decreased, the size of production units has increased substantially. There is favorable potential for increased production.

In 2020, 3.2 million head of hogs were marketed in Texas, producing 505.7 million pounds of pork valued at $200.5 million. In 2019, 3.2 million head of hogs were marketed, producing 494.9 million pounds of pork valued at $230.3 million. Comparable figures for 2018 were 2.7 million head marketed, and 442.5 million pounds of pork produced with a value of $200.5 million.

Sheep and Wool

Sheep and lambs in Texas numbered 730,000 head on January 1, 2021, compared to 735,000 as of 2020, and 750,000 as of January 1, 2019. All sheep were valued at $132.9 million on January 1, 2021, compared with $134.5 million as of January 1, 2020, and $135.8 million as of January 1, 2019.

Breeding ewes one year old and over numbered 445,000 as of January 1, 2021; 445,000 as of January 1, 2020; and 455,000 as of January 1, 2019. Replacement lambs less than one year old totaled 90,000 head as of January 1, 2021; 100,000 as of January 1, 2020; and 100,000 as of January 1, 2019. Sheep and lamb farms in Texas were estimated to be 14,672 as of January 1, 2017; compared to 10,674 in 2012.

Texas wool production in 2020 was 1.4 million pounds from 180,000 sheep. Value totaled $2.4 million or $1.80 per pound. This compared with 1.7 million pounds of wool from 230,000 sheep valued at $3.2 million or $1.90 per pound in 2019; and 1.8 million pounds from 240,000 sheep valued at $3.2 million or $1.80 per pound in 2018.

Most sheep and lambs in Texas are concentrated in the Edwards Plateau area of West Central Texas and nearby counties.

San Angelo has long been the largest sheep and wool market in the nation and the center for wool and mohair warehouses, scouring plants and slaughterhouses.

Goats and Mohair

All goats in Texas numbered 827,000 on January 1, 2021. This compares with 869,000 on January 1, 2020, and 842,000 on January 1, 2019.

Sheep and Wool Production 1973–2021

Year	Sheep Number	Sheep Value	Wool Production (lbs)	Wool Value
1973	3,214,000	$64,280,000	26,352,000	$23,190,000
1974	3,090,000	80,340,000	23,900,000	15,535,000
1975	2,715,000	63,803,000	23,600,000	14,868,000
1976	2,600,000	81,900,000	22,000,000	17,380,000
1977	2,520,000	93,240,000	21,000,000	17,220,000
1978	2,460,000	111,930,000	18,500,000	15,355,000
1979	2,415,000	152,145,000	19,075,000	18,503,000
1980	2,400,000	138,000,000	18,300,000	17,751,000
1981	2,360,000	116,820,000	20,500,000	24,600,000
1982	2,400,000	100,800,000	19,300,000	16,212,000
1983	2,225,000	86,775,000	18,600,000	15,438,000
1984	1,970,000	76,830,000	17,500,000	16,100,000
1985	1,930,000	110,975,000	16,200,000	13,284,000
1986	1,850,000	107,300,000	16,400,000	13,284,000
1987	2,050,000	133,250,000	16,400,000	19,844,000
1988	2,040,000	155,040,000	18,200,000	35,854,000
1989	1,870,000	133,445,000	18,000,000	27,180,000
1990	2,090,000	133,760,000	17,400,000	19,662,000
1991	2,000,000	108,000,000	16,700,000	13,861,000
1992	2,140,000	111,280,000	17,600,000	16,896,000
1993	2,040,000	118,320,000	17,000,000	11,050,000
1994	1,895,000	106,120,000	14,840,000	15,582,000
1995	1,700,000	100,300,000	13,468,000	15,488,000
1996	1,650,000	108,900,000	9,900,000	8,316,000
1997	1,400,000	100,800,000	10,950,000	11,607,000
1998	1,530,000	122,400,000	9,230,000	5,815,000
1999	1,350,000	95,850,000	7,956,000	3,898,000
2000	1,200,000	94,800,000	7,506,000	3,678,000
2001	1,150,000	92,000,000	6,003,000	3,122,000
2002	1,130,000	88,140,000	5,950,000	4,046,000
2003	1,040,000	82,160,000	5,600,000	5,040,000
2004	1,100,000	105,600,000	5,600,000	5,712,000
2005	1,070,000	112,350,000	5,550,000	5,328,000
2006	1,070,000	124,260,000	4,900,000	4,459,000
2007	1,050,000	111,300,000	4,500,000	5,445,000
2008	960,000	97,920,000	4,200,000	4,872,000
2009	870,000	87,870,000	3,500,000	3,640,000
2010	830,000	83,000,000	3,450,000	5,451,000
2011	850,000	109,650,000	2,600,000	5,746,000
2012	670,000	102,510,000	2,100,000	3,507,000
2013	680,000	96,560,000	2,300,000	4,048,000
2014	730,000	118,990,000	2,100,000	3,297,000
2015	720,000	126,000,000	1,950,000	3,198,000
2016	725,000	131,950,000	1,800,000	3,150,000
2017	710,000	129,220,000	1,800,000	2,934,000
2018	750,000	138,750,000	1,760,000	3,168,000
2019	750,000	135,750,000	1,700,000	3,230,000
2020	735,000	134,505,000	1,350,000	2,430,000
2021	730,000	132,860,000	NA	NA

NA = not available

Source: "1985 Texas Livestock, Dairy and Poultry Statistics", USDA Bulletin 235, June 1986. "Texas Agricultural Facts" Annual Summary, Crop and Livestock Reporting Service, various years, "1993 Texas Livestock Statistics", Texas Agricultural Statistics Service, Bulletin 252, August 1994; "Texas Agricultural Statistics, 2009", October 2010, "Texas Ag Fact", February and March 2011; Texas Sheep and Wool report, January 29, 2021, Agricultural Prices, February 26, 2021, NASS/TASS Quick Stats.

Though data for the all-goat inventory is limited, the goatherd consists of Angora goats for mohair production. Angora goats totaled 61,000 as of January 1, 2021; 75,000 as of 2020; and 75,000 as of January 1, 2019.

Mohair production during 2020 totaled 340,000 pounds. This compares with 470,000 in 2019 and 465,000 pounds in 2018. Average price per pound in 2020 was $7.20 from 61,000 goats clipped for a total value of $2.4 million. In 2019, producers received $8.00 per pound from 75,000 goats clipped for a total value of $3.8 million. In 2018, producers received $7.20 per pound from 75,000 goats clipped for a total value of $3.3 million.

Over half of the world's mohair and 54 percent of the U.S. clipped are produced in Texas.

Mohair nanny with her newborn. Photo by Guy E. Connolly, courtesy of the National Wildlife Research Center/Wikimedia Commons

Horses

Nationally, Texas ranks as one of the leading states in horse numbers and is the headquarters for many national horse organizations. The largest single breed registry in America, the American Quarter Horse Association, has its headquarters in Amarillo. The National Cutting Horse Association and the American Paint Horse Association are both located in Fort Worth. In addition to these national associations, Texas also has active state associations that include Palominos, Arabians, Thoroughbreds, Appaloosas, and ponies.

Horses are still used to support the state's giant beef cattle and sheep industries. However, the largest horse numbers within the state are near urban and suburban areas where they are mostly used for recreational activities. Horses are most abundant in the heavily populated areas of the state. State participation activities consist of horse shows, trail rides, play days, rodeos, polo and horse racing. Residential subdivisions have been developed within the state to provide facilities for urban and suburban horse owners.

Goats and Mohair 1980–2021

Year	Goats		Angora Goats		Mohair	
	Number	Farm Value ($)	Number	Value ($)	Production (lbs)	Value ($)
1980	1,400,000	$64,400,000	NA	NA	8,800,000	$30,800,000
1981	1,380,000	53,130,000	NA	NA	10,100,000	35,350,000
1982	1,410,000	57,810,000	NA	NA	10,000,000	25,500,000
1983	1,420,000	53,250,000	NA	NA	10,600,000	42,930,000
1984	1,450,000	82,215,000	NA	NA	10,600,000	48,160,000
1985	1,590,000	76,797,000	NA	NA	13,300,000	45,885,000
1986	1,770,000	70,977,000	NA	NA	16,000,000	40,160,000
1987	1,780,000	82,592,000	NA	NA	16,200,000	42,606,000
1988	1,800,000	108,180,000	NA	NA	15,400,000	29,876,000
1989	1,850,000	100,270,000	NA	NA	15,400,000	24,794,000
1990	1,900,000	93,100,000	NA	NA	14,500,000	13,775,000
1991	1,830,000	73,200,000	NA	NA	14,800,000	19,388,000
1992	2,000,000	84,000,000	1,620,000	NA	14,200,000	12,354,000
1993	1,960,000	84,280,000	1,560,000	NA	13,490,000	11,197,000
1994	1,960,000	74,480,000	1,490,000	NA	11,680,000	30,602,000
1995	1,850,000	81,400,000	1,250,000	NA	11,319,000	20,940,000
1996	1,900,000	89,300,000	1,250,000	NA	7,490,000	14,606,000
1997	1,650,000	70,950,000	1,000,000	NA	6,384,000	14,556,000
1998	1,400,000	71,400,000	750,000	NA	4,650,000	12,044,000
1999	1,350,000	71,550,000	550,000	NA	2,550,000	9,384,000
2000	1,300,000	74,100,000	370,000	NA	2,346,000	10,088,000
2001	1,400,000	105,000,000	300,000	NA	1,716,000	3,775,000
2002	1,250,000	106,250,000	250,000	NA	1,944,000	3,110,400
2003	1,200,000	110,400,000	240,000	NA	1,680,000	2,856,000
2004	1,200,000	115,200,000	210,000	$13,860,000	1,620,000	3,402,000
2005	1,270,000	138,430,000	190,000	14,070,000	1,250,000	3,750,000
2006	1,310,000	137,388,000	178,000	15,200,000	1,100,000	4,400,000
2007	1,300,000	147,552,000	159,000	14,220,000	960,000	3,840,000
2008	1,185,000	120,870,000	134,000	11,250,000	820,000	3,116,000
2009	1,090,000	129,920,000	120,000	10,080,000	700,000	2,170,000
2010	1,020,000	$108,290,000	100,000	7,500,000	730,000	3,066,000
2011	980,000	NA	110,000	11,000,000	530,000	2,703,000
2012	905,000	NA	85,000	7,565,000	470,000	2,256,000
2013	872,000	NA	74,000	9,028,000	490,000	2,695,000
2014	906,000	NA	76,000	9,196,000	580,000	3,654,000
2015	908,000	NA	83,000	12,035,000	480,000	3,408,000
2016	865,000	NA	78,000	10,140,000	510,000	3,060,000
2017	892,000	NA	80,000	12,000,000	470,000	3,102,000
2018	869,000	NA	75,000	9,750,000	465,000	3,348,000
2019	842,000	NA	75,000	10,500,000	470,000	3,760,000
2020	869,000	NA	75,000	10,500,000	340,000	$2,448,000
2021	827,000	NA	61,000	$7,320,000	NA	NA

NA = Not Available

Source:"1985 Texas Livestock, Dairy and Poultry Statistics", USDA Bulletin 235, June 1986. "Texas Agricultural Facts", Crop and Livestock Reporting Service, various years; "1993 Texas Livestock Statistics", Texas Agricultural Statistics Service, Bulletin 252, August 1994; "Texas Agricultural Statistics, 2009", October 2010; "Texas Ag Facts", February and March 2011. USDA/TASS Texas Goat and Mohair, January 29, 2021; NASS Quick Stats.

Appendix

TEXAS OBITUARIES

PRONUNCIATION GUIDE

INDEX OF ENTRIES

Carol M. Highsmith and Rowdy, the mascot for the Dallas Cowboys, having fun in the endzone.
Photo by Carol M. Highsmith, courtesy of the Library of Congress/Wikimedia Commons

Obituaries: August 2019 – July 2021

Akers, Fred, 82; head coached the University of Texas at Austin football team from 1977–1986, including coaching Earl Campbell the year he won his Heisman Trophy; also coached at University of Wyoming (1975–1976) and Purdue (1987–1990) and ended his career with a record of 108–75–3; Arkansas native, moved to Horseshoe Bay in 2008; at his home in Horseshoe Bay, December 7, 2020.

Bass, Anne, 78; investor, documentary filmmaker, and philanthropist; directed *Dancing Across Borders* (2010) about a girl from Cambodia attending the School of American Ballet and becoming a professional dancer; native Hoosier rescued the Texas Ballet Theater from bankruptcy and supported the Modern Art Museum of Fort Worth and the Van Cliburn Foundation, among others; in New York City, April 1, 2020.

Benson, Cedric, 36; All-American running back for the Texas Longhorns and fourth overall pick in the NFL draft in 2005; Midland native's professional career highlights include rushing 1,000+ yards for three seasons back-to-back with the Cincinnati Bengals; ended his career after a Lisfranc injury in 2012; in Austin, August 17, 2019.

Brooks, David Owen, 65; one of a trio of men who committed what became known as the Houston Mass Murders from 1970–1973, when they abducted, tortured, raped, and murdered at least 28 young men and boys; although not the ringleader, he was found guilty and sentenced to 99 years in prison; in a hospital in Galveston, May 28, 2020.

Cochran, Cathy, 76; judge on the Texas Court of Criminal Appeals appointed by Governor Rick Perry in 2001 until retirement in 2014; earlier in her career, as Director of Criminal Justice for Governor George W. Bush, organized a committee that completely rewrote the Texas Code of Criminal Procedure; in Wimberley, February 7, 2021.

Cockrell, Lila, 97; two-time mayor of San Antonio and the second woman in the U.S. to be mayor of a major city; served four terms overall (1975-1981, 1989-1991), and inducted into the Texas Women's Hall of Fame in 1984; native of Fort Worth was denied a vote by the Texas voter ID laws in the 2019 San Antonio mayoral election when she went to the polls without the proscribed identification but was able to cast her vote two days later; in San Antonio, August 29, 2019.

Davis, Mac, 78; country music singer, songwriter, and native of Lubbock wrote several songs recorded by Elvis Presley including "A Little Less Conversation" and "In the Ghetto"; hosted the NBC television variety series *The Mac Davis Show* in the 1970s and played Will Rogers on Broadway; member of both the Nashville Songwriters Hall of Fame and the National Songwriters Hall of Fame; in Nashville, September 29, 2020.

Detmer, Hubert "Sonny," 76; legendary high school football coach amassed a record of 235-141-2 and many district titles over 35 seasons; coached his two sons, one a Heisman winner, and later his grandsons — all quarterbacks; in San Antonio, September 22, 2020.

Donley, Manuel "Cowboy," 92; pioneer of Tejano music; born in Mexico, his family moved to Austin when he was seven; played trumpet, alto saxophone, and Spanish, electric, and requinto guitars; formed Las Estrellas in 1955, which toured Texas and the Midwest for 20 years; inducted into Tejano Music Hall of Fame in 1986; in Austin, on June 28, 2020.

Edwards, David, 48; former point guard at Texas A&M, 1991-1994; native Virginian led the Aggies to first postseason tournament in the 90s in his senior year while totaling 256 assists (third best in the country); graduated as school record holder in assists (602) and steals (228); in New York, March 23, 2020.

Emmett, Andre, 37; Dallas-born professional basketball player, played four years at Texas Tech for Coach Bobby Knight; drafted in 2004 by Seattle then traded that night to the Memphis Grizzlies but played only 8 games that season; played for D-league and international teams, including the Austin Toros, Liège Basket (Belgium), and Shandong Lions (China); in Dallas, September 23, 2019.

English, Paul, 87; drummer for Willie Nelson inspired the song "Me and Paul"; described as "tough and flamboyant," the Vernon native joined the band in 1966 and also served as an unofficial bodyguard for Nelson; became a board member for Farm Aid in 1985 and held the office of treasurer for many years; on February 11, 2020.

Floyd, George Perry Jr., 46; his murder by a police officer in Minnesota sparked worldwide protests of police brutality against Blacks; his last words, "I can't breathe," became a rally for the protesters; grew up in Houston and laid to rest in Pearland; in Minneapolis, May 25, 2020.

Freeman, Dr. Thomas F., 100; lecturer and debate coach at TSU, and minister at Mount Horem Baptist Church in Houston; native Virginian coached his student debaters to multiple national and international titles; famous students included Representative Barbara Jordan and Dr. Martin Luther King, Jr.; received the Phoenix Award from the Congressional Black Caucus Foundation for "his profound influence on our nation as a legendary educator and prolific scholar"; in Houston, June 6, 2020.

George, Phyllis Ann, 70; crowned Miss Texas in 1970 and Miss America 1971 before her career as a sports reporter and news anchor for CBS; one of the first women to feature prominently in televised sports when she co-hosted live pregame shows for NFL games; later the Denton native founded the Kentucky Museum of Arts and Crafts and sold a Phyllis George Beauty line of cosmetics on HSN; in Kentucky, May 14, 2020.

Goodacre, Glenna, 80; sculptor from Lubbock, best known for designing the obverse of the Sacagawea dollar and the Vietnam

Left to right: Tejano musican Manuel "Cowboy" Donley, photo by Tom Pich, public domain; Country musician Mac Davis performing at the Alabama Music Hall of Fame 2010, photo by Carol M. Highsmith, public domain; Running back Cedric Benson playing for the Cincinnati Bengals, photo by Denverjeffrey, CC3.

Left to right: Specialist Vanessa Guillen, U.S. Army photo; Artist and musician Daniel Johnston, photo by Rich Jones, CC 2; Second baseman and broadcaster Joe Morgan , photo courtesy of the George Bush Presidential Library and Museum.

Women's Memorial; awarded the Texas Medal of Arts and inducted into the National Cowgirl Museum and Hall of Fame, both in 2003; in New Mexico, April 13, 2020.

Guillen, Vanessa, 20; U.S. Army soldier murdered in an armory at Fort Hood whose body was found buried in countryside more than two months later, focusing national attention on sexual harassment in the military; born and raised in Houston, trained as a 91F, small arms and artillery repairer; at Fort Hood, April 22, 2020.

Harris, Franklyn Allen "Tex," 81; discovered and exposed human rights abuses as a U.S. diplomat in Argentina; reported some 13,500 human rights violations at the risk of his life and career; grew up in Dallas, where he was an all-state basketball player; in Virginia, on February 23, 2020.

Holub, Emil Joseph "E.J.," 81; played center and linebacker for Texas Technical College (now Texas Tech) and professionally in the AFL and NFL; native of Schulenburg raised in Lubbock was drafted sixth overall in 1961 by the Dallas Texans (later the Kansas City Chiefs); with the AFL, was the first player to start on both offense and defense in more than one Super Bowl and the only player to start two Super Bowls at two different positions; inducted into the Kansas City Chiefs Hall of Fame (1976), the Texas Tech Hall of Fame (1977) and the National Football Foundation's College Hall of Fame (1986); in Midland, September 21, 2019.

Jalomo, Valentin, 81; Astros superfan known for his elaborately quaffed mustache and customary seat in left-center field; grew up in Taft and moved to Houston where he worked as a bilingual teacher at Houston ISD until retirement in 2002; in Houston, January 19, 2021.

Johnston, Daniel Dale, 58; cult-favorite singer-songwriter and visual artist; subject of the documentary *The Devil and Daniel Johnston* (2006) that explored his struggles with mental illness; created the famous "Hi, How Are You?" mural in Austin; at his home in Waller, September 11, 2019.

Knight, Shirley, 83; award-winning actress, including three Emmys and a Tony, never stopped working; native Kansan started in classic TV shows and nominated for Oscars for *The Dark at the Top of the Stairs* (1960) and *Sweet Bird of Youth* (1962); in later years helped build the Texas State University musical theater program to national prominence; at her daughter's San Marcos home, April 22, 2020.

Loyd, Nikki Araguz, 44; California-born author, speaker, and same-sex-marriage activist; after her husband, a sheriff's deputy and firefighter, was killed in a fire in 2010, her in-laws refused to allow her to see her stepchildren and filed two lawsuits to have the marriage annulled and to take away her firefighter's spousal benefits; a judge annulled the marriage in 2011 but she continued to fight, eventually having her marriage ruled legal in 2015; at home in Humble, November 6, 2019.

Lopez, Trinidad "Trini" III, 83; singer and guitarist, his debut album, *Trini Lopez at PJs*, sold more than a million copies and earned a gold disc; designed two guitars for Gibson in 1964 that are prized by collectors; also did some acting, including a role in *The Dirty Dozen* (1967); grew up in Dallas but started his career in Wichita Falls; in California, August 11, 2020.

Marion, Anne, 81; president of Burnett Ranches in West Texas since 1980, including the 6666 Ranch; Fort Worth native kept the Four Sixes ahead of the pack in land stewardship and breeding and has been recognized by the AQHA, the National Cowgirl Museum, and the Texas Cowboy Hall of Fame; started the Burnett Oil Company and served as chairman of the Fort Worth Chamber of Commerce; in California, February 11, 2020.

McAlester, Virginia Savage, 76; architectural historian and Dallas native, wrote *A Field Guide to American Houses*, which was named in the top ten outstanding reference books in 1984 by the American Library Association; helped found Preservation Dallas to conserve historic buildings and areas in the city; in Dallas, April 9, 2020.

McMurtry, Larry Jeff, 84; novelist and screenwriter born in Archer City, his works were mostly set in the Old West or contemporary Texas; won the Pulitzer Prize in 1985 for *Lonesome Dove*, which was adapted into a TV miniseries that won seven Emmy awards; wrote the adapted screenplay for *Brokeback Mountain* (2005) with cowriter Diana Ossana, for which they won the Academy Award for Best Adapted Screenplay; as president of the nonprofit PEN America in 1989, testified before the U.S. Congress against an immigration law that denied entry to foreign writers based on ideological differences; in Archer City, March 25, 2021.

McNally, Terrence, 81; decorated playwright with a six-decade long career; won his first Tony for *Kiss of the Spider Woman*; lived in Corpus Christi as a child, where his father owned a Schlitz distributorship; much later, wrote the controversial play *Corpus Christi*, in which Jesus and his disciples are homosexuals; in Florida, March 24, 2020.

Mobley, William Hodges, 78; former president of Texas A&M University and former chancellor of The Texas A&M University System; Ohio native promoted diversity and athletic integrity and expanded international opportunities for both

Left to right:Actress Shirley Knight, 1963 press photo; Musician Trini Lopez, photo courtesy the Dutch National Archives, CC ; Playwright Terrence McNally, Photo by ReadingRead43, CC4

students and faculty; later helped develop executive talent for corporations and academic institutions while living in Hong Kong and Shanghai; in Austin, March 25, 2020.

Moffett, Jim Bob, 82; Houston-raised oilman and philanthropist; played football at the University of Texas under coach Darrell Royal and became a major UT donor after finding success in oil; his New Orleans-based company's international operations drew intense criticism; a plan to develop land near the Barton Creek aquifer in Austin inspired activists to create the Save Our Spring Alliance and ultimately went to the U.S. Supreme Court, where the company lost; in Austin, January 8, 2021.

Morgan, Joe, 77; second baseman and member of the Big Red Machine at Cincinnati Reds; played with the Houston Colt .45s/Houston Astros, from 1963 to 1971 and again in 1980; born in Bonham before moving with his family to California; two-time National League MVP, 10-time All Star, won the Golden Glove 5 times; voted into the Baseball Hall of Fame in 1990; after retirement he gained acclaim as a broadcaster; at home in Danville, California, October 11, 2020.

Nash, Johnny, 80; best known for 1972 hit "I Can See Clearly Now," the Houston native also sang reggae and recorded an album in Kingston, Jamaica; got his start singing covers on local television show *Matinee*; his master tapes were among those destroyed in a fire at Universal Studios in 2008; in Houston, October 6, 2020.

Neal, Frederick "Curly," 77; featured ball handler for the Harlem Globetrotters; played in more than 6,000 games in 97 countries over his 22-year career; became the fifth Globetrotter to have his jersey (22) retired in 2008; averaged 23.1 points per game as a college player in his native North Carolina; at his home in Houston, March 26, 2020.

Ohlendorf, Norbert Kurt "Dutch," 87; "Junction Boy" who survived a brutal and dangerous football camp in Bear Bryant's first year as coach at Texas A&M; enrolled from Lockhart to study mechanics and earned a walk-on spot on the football team as a sophomore in 1951; served in the Army after graduation, then became a teacher, advancing to area superintendent; continued to teach in retirement, this time as a college lecturer; in Bryan, March 11, 2020.

Pickens, Thomas "T" Boone, Jr., 91; Oklahoma-born businessman and billionaire, well-known for his oil holdings and, later, support of alternative energy sources; announced the Pickens Plan in 2008, an energy proposal that aimed to move the U.S. away from OPEC sources of energy and toward domestic sources of natural gas, and wind and solar power; at his home in Dallas, September 11, 2019.

Pride, Charley, 86; country singer and professional baseball player; a native of Mississippi, along with his brother Mack pitched for several teams in the Negro American League in the 1950s until he was drafted into the army; returned to baseball but soon became more famous for his voice; won almost every major award possible for a country musician; part-owner of the Texas

Left to right: Country stars Charley Pride (photo by Greg Mathison, public domain) and Kenny Rogers (photo by John Mathew Smith & www.celebrity-photos.com CC 2)

Rangers and performed the national anthem at games; in Dallas, December 12, 2020.

Puga, Genoveva, 92; migrant farm worker who became a civil rights activist fighting citrus company Donna Fruit for worker's compensation for son's wife and child after her son, Juan Torrez, died while performing his job; after winning the case, worked to bring the same justice to other farm workers through the courts; a statute ending worker's compensation exclusion for contractors signed into law 1984; at her home in Alamo, November 22, 2020.

Reavley, Thomas, 99; served on the U.S. Court of Appeals for the Fifth Circuit from 1979 until his death in 2020; born in Quitman; drove President Franklin Roosevelt to a meeting with Winston Churchill and Joseph Stalin during Yalta Conference while serving as a lieutenant in the U.S. Navy; was Texas Secretary of State 1955-1957, state Supreme Court justice 1968-1977; in Houston, December 1, 2020.

Reid, Jan, 75; journalist and author of more than a dozen books; came to prominence writing for *Texas Monthly*, where his byline first appeared in 1973; grew up playing football and baseball in Wichita Falls; survived a shooting in 1998 and plagued by ill health; wrote both fiction and nonfiction, about history, politics, crime, sports, and occasionally music; in Austin, September 19, 2020.

Robinson, Charles P. "Charlie," 75; actor best known for playing "Mac" in the sitcom *Night Court*; native of Houston and member of the Actors Studio; performed theater in Houston before moving to Hollywood; returned to theater in 2010 and performed iconic roles including Willy Loman; in California, July 11, 2021.

Rogers, Kenneth Ray "Kenny," 81; beloved singer, songwriter, musician, and record producer born and raised in Houston; first began recording "teenage rock" in the 1950s, then became a country star; signature song "The Gambler" was a crossover hit in 1978 and won a Grammy in 1980; starred in the made-for-TV movie based on the song, as well as many other TV roles; at his home in Georgia, March 20, 2020.

Sessions, William S., 90; federal judge, appointed FBI director in 1987 by President Reagan; many associate him with the phrase "Winners Don't Use Drugs," which was included on all imported arcade games by law; the native Arkansan and Baylor graduate encouraged the FBI to develop a strong DNA program and automate the national fingerprinting process, reducing fingerprint search times from months to hours; attracted heavy criticism for the deadly

Left to right: Globetrotter Frederick "Curly" Neal, U.S Air Force photo by Airman First Class Brad Smith; Billionaire T. Boone Pickens, photo by David Shankbone, CC 3

Left to right: First baseman/outfielder Jimmy Wynn, photo by by Gary P Smith, CC 2; Artist Bob "Daddy-O" Wade, photo by Mbcoats, CC 4; Musician Billy Joe Shaver, photo by Giovanni Gallucci, www.LiveLoudTexas.com CC 2

confrontation with the Branch Davidians near Waco in 1993 and was dismissed by President Clinton later that year; in San Antonio, June 12, 2020.

Shaver, Billy Joe, 81; country music pioneer known for "Honky Tonk Heroes" and "Live Forever"; born in Corsicana where he lived with his mother and grandmother; worked as a songwriter in Nashville where he earned $50 a week; released debut album, *Old Five and Dimers Like Me*, in 1973; Willie Nelson called him the greatest living songwriter; in Waco, October 28, 2020.

Solinger, Johnny, 55; singer-songwriter and lead vocalist for Skid Row from 1999 to 2015; loved both rock and country music as a boy in the Dallas-Fort Worth area; released a solo country album in 2008; on June 26, 2021.

Solomon, Jimmie Lee, 64; attorney in Washington, D.C. hired by Major League Baseball; started in minor league relations, worked up the ladder to executive vice president of baseball development; grew up in Fort Bend County and played sports at Lamar Consolidated High School; attended Harvard Law after he was cut by the Oilers during training camp; at his home in Houston, October 8, 2020.

Stearns, Eldrewey, 89; civil rights activist, led demonstrations and sit-ins to desegregate Houston while attending law school at Texas Southern University; Galveston native won victories but no acclaim for imposing local media blackouts and once canceling a protest in exchange for integration of restaurants and theaters; in Texas City, December 23, 2020.

Villaronga, Raúl G., 82; Vietnam War veteran and first Puerto Rican mayor of Killeen for three terms (1992-1998); after serving 26 years, retired from the U.S. Army as a colonel in 1985 while stationed at Fort Hood; while mayor, negotiated an agreement with the Army to make Robert Gray Army Airfield in Fort Hood a Joint Use Airport, allowing more transportation to the area; in Killeen, March 20, 2021.

Wade, Bob "Daddy-O," 76; Austin-born artist raised in El Paso known for shaping the Texas Cosmic Cowboy counterculture in the 1970s; created outsized sculptures including the Lone Star Café Iguana, now displayed in the Fort Worth Zoo, and the World's Largest Cowboy Boots, which can be seen at the North

Star Mall in San Antonio; also created hand-tinted photographs he published in two books; at home in Austin, December 23, 2019.

Walker, Jerry Jeff, 78; country and folk singer-songwriter known for "Mr. Bojangles"; born Ronald Clyde Crosby in New York state, he roamed the country playing music under stage names "Jerry Ferris" and "Jeff Walker" before adopting the current one; settled in Austin in 1970s and joined the outlaw country scene; continued writing and performing until diagnosed with throat cancer in 2017; in Austin, October 23, 2020.

Watson, Robert José "Bob," 74; professional baseball player and executive; signed by the Houston Astros in 1965 as an amateur free agent; the Californian nearly quit the game when faced with discrimination in the South while playing in the minors; played outfield and first base for the Astros from 1966-1978, then traded to the Red Sox; ended his career batting .295 with 184 home runs and 989 RBI; credited with hitting the one-millionth home run in major league history; in Houston, May 14, 2020.

White, James, 81; owner of the iconic Broken Spoke dance hall in Austin, along with his wife Annetta White and his two daughters; brought joy to patrons through food, drinks, and Texas Two-Steppin' to live bands since 1964; Austin native; in Austin, January 24, 2021.

Williams, Clayton, 88; Midland businessman who ran for Texas governor against State Treasurer Ann Richards in 1990; initially led in polls by 20 points but made ill-advised comments on the campaign trail and ultimately lost the race; continued in business, taking Clayton Williams Energy, Inc. public in 1993 and diversifying into ranching and real estate; in Midland on February 14, 2020.

Williams, Frank S., 87; retired police officer, as a patrol officer in 1963 was sent to question Lee Harvey Oswald in connection with the shooting death of fellow officer J.D. Tippit, unaware that Oswald was also wanted for the death of President John F. Kennedy the same day; later became a detective, then a sergeant before retiring from the Dallas Police Department in 1978; in Dallas, November 25, 2020.

Wilson, Pamela Francis, 65; Houston photographer and graphic designer; known for using rich lighting and saturated color in her portraits, and earned the reputation as "the Annie Leibovitz of Texas"; her work has been featured in advertising campaigns, corporate reports, and magazines; photographed six U.S. presidents and many celebrities; at home in Houston, July 18, 2020.

Wynn, Jimmy, 78; outfielder and home run-hitter for the Colt .45s and Houston Astros over 11 seasons; nicknamed "The Toy Cannon" for his short stature and long home runs; three-time All-Star, native Ohioan became the first player to hit a homer into the upper deck of the Astrodome; after retirement, returned to the Astros as a community outreach executive; in Houston, March 26, 2020.

Left to right: Musician Johnny Solinger, photo by P. Schwichtenberg, CC 3; FBI Director William S. Sessions, FBI photo

TEXAS ALMANAC PRONUNCIATION GUIDE

Texas' rich cultural diversity is reflected nowhere better than in the names of places. Standard pronunciation is used in many cases, but purely colloquial pronunciation often is used, too.

In the late 1940s, George Mitchel Stokes, a graduate student at Baylor University, developed a list of pronunciations of 2,300 place names across the state. Stokes earned his doctorate and eventually was the director of the speech division in the communications studies department at Baylor University. He retired in 1983.

In the following list based on Stokes' longer list, pronunciation is by respelling and diacritical marking.

Respelling is employed as follows: "ah" as in the exclamation, ah, or the "o" in tot; "ee" as in meet; "oo" as in moot; "yoo" as in use; "ow" as in cow; "oi" as in oil; "uh" as in mud.

Note that ah, uh and the apostrophe(') are used for varying degrees of neutral vowel sounds, the apostrophe being used where the vowel is barely sounded. Diacritical markings are used as follows: bāle, băd, lĕt, rīse, rĭll, ōak, brōōd, fŏŏt.

The stressed syllable is capitalized. Secondary stress is indicated by an underline as in Atascosa — ăt uhs KŌ suh.

A

Abbott — Ă buht
Abernathy — Ă ber nă thĭ
Abilene — ĂB uh leen
Acala — uh KĀ luh
Ackerly — ĂK er lĭ
Acme — ĂK mĭ
Acton — ĂK t'n
Acuff — Ă kuhf
Adamsville — Ă d'mz vĭl
Addicks — Ă dĭks
Addielou — ă dĭ LŌŌ
Addison — A di s'n
Adkins — ĂT kĭnz
Adrian — Ā drĭ uhn
Afton — ĀF t'n
Agua Dulce — ah wuh DŌŌL sĭ
Agua Nueva — ah wuh nyŏŏ Ā vuh
Aiken — Ā kĭn
Alamo — ĂL uh mō
Alamo Heights — ăl uh mō HĪTS
Alanreed — ĂL uhn reed
Alba — ĂL buh
Albany — AWL buh nĭ
Albert — ĂL bert
Aledo — uh LEE dō
Alexander — ĕl ĭg ZĂN der
Alfred — ĂL frĕd
Algoa — ăl GŌ uh
Alice — Ă lĭs
Alief — Ā leef
Allen — Ā lĭn
Allenfarm — ălĭn FAHRM
Alleyton — Ă lĭ t'n
Allison — ĂL uh s'n
Alma — AHL muh
Alpine — ĂL pĭn
Altair — awl TĀR
Alto — ĂL tō
Altoga — ăl TŌ guh
Alvarado — ăl vuh RĀ dō
Alvin — ĂL vĭn
Alvord — ĂL vord
Amarillo — ăm uh RĬL ō
Amherst — AM herst
Ammannsville — ĂM 'nz vĭl

Anahuac — ĂN uh wăk
Anderson — ĂN der s'n
Andice — ĂN dĭs
Andrews — ĂN drōōz
Angelina — ăn juh LEE nuh
Angleton — ĂNG g'l t'n
Anna — ĂN uh
Annona — ă NŌ nuh
Anson — ĂN s'n
Antelope — ĂNT uh lōp
Anton — ĂNT n
Appleby — Ă p'l bĭ
Apple Springs — ă p'l SPRĬNGZ
Aquilla — uh KWĬL uh
Aransas — uh RĂN zuhs
Aransas Pass — uh răn zuhs PĂS
Arbala — ahr BĀ luh
Arcadia — ahr KĀ dĭ uh
Archer — AHR cher
Archer City — ahr cher SĬT ĭ
Arcola — ahr KŌ luh
Argo — AHR gō
Argyle — ahr GĪL
Arlington — AHR lĭng t'n
Arneckeville — AHR nĭ kĭ vĭl
Arnett — AHR nĭt
Arp — ahrp
Artesia Wells — ahr tee zh' WĔLZ
Arthur City — ahr ther SĬT ĭ
Asherton — ĂSH er t'n
Aspermont — ĂS per mahnt
Atascosa — ăt uhs KŌ suh
Athens — Ă thĕnz
Atlanta — ăt LĂN tuh
Atlas — ĀT l's
Attoyac — AT uh yăk
Aubrey — AW brĭ
Augusta — aw GUHS tuh
Austin — AWS t'n
Austonio — aws TŌ nĭ ō
Austwell — AWS wĕl
Avalon — ĂV uhl n
Avery — Ā vuh rĭ
Avinger — Ă vĭn jer
Avoca — uh VŌ kuh
Axtell — ĂKS t'l
Azle — Ā z'l

B

Bagwell — BĂG w'l
Bailey — BĀ lĭ
Baileyboro — BĀ lĭ ber ruh
Baileyville — BĀ lĭ vĭl
Baird — bărd
Bakersfield — BĀ kers feeld
Balch Springs — bawlch or bawlk SPRĬNGZ
Ballinger — BĂL ĭn jer
Balmorhea — băl muh RĀ
Bandera — băn DĔR uh
Bangs — băngz
Banquete — băn KĔ tĭ
Barclay — BAHRK lĭ
Bardwell — BAHRD w'l
Barker — BAHR ker
Barksdale — BAHRKS dāl
Barnhart — BAHRN hahrt
Barnum — BAHR n'm
Barry — BĂ rĭ
Barstow — BAHRS tō
Bartlett — BAHRT lĭt
Bassett — BĂ sĭt
Bastrop — BĂS trahp
Batesville — BĀTS v'l
Batson — BĂT s'n
Baxter — BĂKS ter
Bay City — ba SĬT ĭ
Baylor — BĀ ler
Bayside — BĀ sĭd
Baytown — BĀ town
Beasley — BEEZ lĭ
Beaukiss — bō KĬS
Beaumont — BŌ mahnt
Bebe — bee bee
Beckville — BĔK v'l
Becton — BĔK t'n
Bedias — BEE dĭs
Bee — bee
Beehouse — BEE hows
Beeville — BEE vĭl
Belcherville — BĔL cher vĭl
Bell — bĕl
Bellaire — bĕl ĂR
Bellevue — BĔL vyŏŏ

Diacritical markings are used as follows: bāle, băd, lĕt, rīse, rĭll, ōak, brōōd, fŏŏt. The stressed syllable is capitalized. Secondary stress is indicated by an underline as in Atascosa — ăt uhs KŌ suh. TEXAS ALMANAC ©.

A mural of local landmarks in Breckenridge. Photo by Kairos14, CC by SA 4.0/Wikimedia Commons

Bellmead — bĕl MEED
Bells — bĕlz
Bellville — BĔL vĭl
Belmont — BĔL mahnt
Belton — BĔL t'n
Ben Arnold — bĕn AHR n'ld
Benavides — <u>bĕn</u> uh VEE d's
Ben Bolt — bĕn BOLT
Benbrook — BĬN brŏŏk
Benchley — BĔNCH lĭ
Bend — bĕnd
Ben Franklin — bĕn FRĂNGk lĭn
Ben Hur — bĕn HER
Benjamin — BĔN juh m'n
Bennett — BĔN ĭt
Bentonville — BĔNT n vĭl
Ben Wheeler — bĭn HWEE ler
Berclair — ber KLĂR
Bertram — BERT r'm
Bessmay — bĕs MĀ
Best — bĕst
Bettie — BĔT ĭ
Bexar — BA är or băr
Beyersville — BĪRZ vĭl
Biardstown — BĂRDZ t'n
Bigfoot — BĬG fŏŏt
Big Lake — bĭg LĀK
Big Sandy — bĭg SĂN dĭ
Big Spring — bĭg SPRĬNG
Big Wells — bĭg WĔLZ
Birdville — BERD vĭl
Birome — bī RŌM
Birthright — BERTH rĭt
Bishop — BĬ sh'p
Bivins — BĪ vĭnz
Black — blăk
Blackfoot — BLĂK fŏŏt
Blackwell — BLĂK w'l
Blair — blăr

Blanchard — BLĂN cherd
Blanco — BLĂNG kō
Blanket — BLĂNG kĭt
Bleakwood — BLEEK wŏŏd
Bledsoe — BLĔD sō
Blessing — BLĔ sĭng
Blewett — BLŌŌ ĭt
Blooming Grove — <u>blōō</u> mĭng GRŌV
Bloomington — BLŌŌM ĭng t'n
Blossom — BLAH s'm
Blue Grove — blōō GRŌV
Blue Ridge — blōō RĬJ
Bluff Dale — BLUHF dāl
Bluffton — BLUHF t'n
Blum — bluhm
Boerne — BER nĭ
Bogata — buh GŌ duh
Boling — BŌL ĭng
Bolivar — BAH lĭ ver
Bomarton — BŌ mer t'n
Bonham — BAH n'm
Bonita — bō NEE tuh
Bonney — BAH nĭ
Bonus — BŌ n's
Bon Wier — bahn WEER
Booker — BŌŌ ker
Boonsville — BŌŌNZ vĭl
Booth — bŏŏth
Borden — BAWRD n
Borger — BŌR ger
Bosque — BAHS kĭ
Boston — BAWS t'n
Bovina — bō VEE nuh
Bowie — BŌŌ ĭ
Boxelder — bahks ĔL der
Boyce — bawĭs
Boyd — boĭd
Brachfield — BRĂCH feeld

Bracken — BRĂ kĭn
Brackettville — BRĂ kĭt vĭl
Bradford — BRĂD ferd
Bradshaw — BRĂD shaw
Brady — BRĀ dĭ
Brandon — BRĂN d'n
Brashear — bruh SHĬR
Brazoria — bruh ZŌ rĭ uh
Brazos — BRĂZ uhs
Breckenridge — BRĔK uhn rĭj
Bremond — <u>bree</u> MAHND
Brenham — BRĔ n'm
Brewster — BRŌŌ ster
Brice — brīs
Bridgeport — BRĬJ pōrt
Briggs — brĭgz
Briscoe — BRĬS kō
Britton — BRĬT n
Broaddus — BRAW d's
Brock — brahk
Bronson — BRAHN s'n
Bronte — brahnt
Brookeland — BRŌŌK l'nd
Brookesmith — BRŌŌK smith
Brooks — brŏŏks
Brookshire — BRŎŎK sher
Brookston — BRŎŎKS t'n
Brown — brown
Browndel — brown DĔL
Brownfield — BROWN feeld
Brownsboro — BROWNZ <u>buh</u> ruh
Brownsville — BROWNZ vĭl
Brownwood — BROWN wŏŏd
Bruceville — BRŌŌS v'l
Brundage — BRUHN dĭj
Bruni — BRŌŌ nĭ
Brushy Creek — bruh shĭ KREEK
Bryan — BRĪ uhn
Bryans Mill — brī 'nz MĬL

Diacritical markings are used as follows: bāle, bäd, lĕt, rīse, rĭll, ōak, brōōd, fŏŏt. The stressed syllable is capitalized. Secondary stress is indicated by an underline as in Atascosa — <u>ăt</u> uhs KŌ suh. © TEXAS ALMANAC.

Bryarly — BRĪ er lĭ
Bryson — BRĪ s'n
Buchanan Dam — buhk hăn uhn
  DĂM
Buckholts — BUHK hōlts
Buckhorn — BUHK hawrn
Buda — BYŌŌ duh
Buena Vista — bwā nuh VEES tuh
Buffalo — BUHF uh lō
Buffalo Gap — buhf uh lō GĂP
Buffalo Springs — buhf uh lō
  SPRĬNGZ
Bula — BYŌŌ luh
Bullard — BŌŌL erd
Bulverde — bōōl VER dĭ
Buna — BYŌŌ nuh
Burkburnett — berk ber NET
Burkett — BER kĭt
Burkeville — BERK vĭl
Burleson — BER luh s'n
Burlington — BER lĭng t'n
Burnet — BER nĕt
Burton — BERT n
Bushland — BŌŌSH l'nd
Bustamante — buhs tuh MAHN tĭ
Butler — BUHT ler
Byers — BĪ erz
Bynum — BĪ n'm
Byrd — berd

C

Cactus — KĂK t's
Caddo Mills — kă dō MĬLZ
Calallen — kăl ĂL ĭn
Calaveras — kăl uh VĔR's
Caldwell — KAHL wĕl
Calhoun — kăl HŌŌN
Call — kawl
Calliham — KĂL uh hăm
Callisburg — KĂ lĭs berg
Call Junction — kawl JUHNGK sh'n
Calvert — KĂL vert
Camden — KĂM dĭn
Cameron — KĂM uh r'n
Camilla — kuh MEEL yuh
Camp — kămp
Campbell — KĂM uhl
Campbellton — KĂM uhl t'n
Camp Wood — kămp WŌŌD
Canadian — kuh NĀ dĭ uhn
Candelaria — kăn duh LĔ rĭ uh
Canton — KĂNT n
Canyon — KĂN y'n
Caplen — KĂP lĭn
Caps — kăps
Caradan — KĂR uh dăn
Carbon — KAHR b'n
Carey — KĀ rĭ
Carlisle — KAHR lĭl
Carlsbad — KAHR uhlz băd
Carlton — KAHR uhl t'n
Carmine — kahr MEEN
Carmona — kahr MŌ nuh
Caro — KAH rō
Carrizo Springs — kuh ree zuh

  SPRĬNGZ
Carrollton — KĂR 'l t'n
Carson — KAHR s'n
Carthage — KAHR thĭj
Cash — kăsh
Cason — KĀ s'n
Cass — kăs
Castell — kăs TĔL
Castro — KĂS trō
Castroville — KĂS tro vĭl
Catarina — kăt uh REE nuh
Cat Spring — kăt SPRĬNG
Caviness — KĂ vĭ nĕs
Cayuga — kā YŌŌ guh
Cedar Bayou — see der BĪ ō
Cedar Creek — see der KREEK
Cedar Hill — see der HĬL
Cedar Lake — see der LĀK
Cedar Lane — see der LĀN
Cedar Park — see der PAHRK
Cedar Valley — see der VA lĭ
Cee Vee — see VEE
Celeste — suh LĔST
Celina — suh LĪ nuh
Center — SENT er
Center City — sĕn ter SĬT ĭ
Center Point — sĕn ter POINT
Centerville — sĕn ter vĭl
Centralia — sĕn TRĀL yuh
Chalk — chawlk
Chalk Mountain — chawlk MOWNT n
Chambers — CHĂM berz
Chandler — CHĂND ler
Channelview — chăn uhl VYŌŌ
Channing — CHĂN ĭng
Chapman Ranch — chăp m'n
  RĂNCH
Chappell Hill — chă p'l HĬL
Charco — CHAHR kō
Charleston — CHAHR uhls t'n
Charlie — CHAHR lĭ
Charlotte — SHAHR l't
Chatfield — CHĂT feeld
Cheapside — CHEEP sĭd
Cheek — cheek
Cherokee — CHĔR uh kee
Chester — CHĔS ter
Chico — CHEE kō
Chicota — chĭ KŌ tuh
Childress — CHĬL drĕs
Chillicothe — chĭl ĭ KAH thĭ
Chilton — CHĬL t'n
China — CHĪ nuh
China Spring — chī nuh SPRĬNG
Chireno — sh' REE nō
Chisholm — CHĬZ uhm
Chita — CHEE tuh
Chocolate Bayou — chah kuh lĭt
  BĪ ō
Choice — chois
Chriesman — KRĬS m'n
Christine — krĭs TEEN
Christoval — krĭs TŌ v'l
Cibolo — SEE bō lō
Circle Back — SER k'l băk

Circleville — SER k'l vĭl
Cisco — SĬS kō
Cistern — SĬS tern
Clairemont — KLĀR mahnt
Clairette — klăr ĭ ĔT
Clarendon — KLĂR ĭn d'n
Clareville — KLĂR vĭl
Clarksville — KLAHRKS vĭl
Clarkwood — KLAHRK wōōd
Claude — klawd
Clawson — KLAW s'n
Clay — klā
Clayton — KLĀT n
Clear Lake — KLĬR lăk
Clear Spring — klĭr SPRĬNG
Cleburne — KLEE bern
Clemville — KLĔM vĭl
Cleveland — KLEEV l'nd
Clifton — KLĬF t'n
Cline — klīn
Clint — klĭnt
Clodine — klaw DEEN
Clute — klōōt
Clyde — klīd
Coahoma — kuh HŌ muh
Cockrell Hill — kahk ruhl HĬL
Coke — kōk
Coldspring — KŌLD sprĭng
Coleman — KŌL m'n
Colfax — KAHL făks
Collegeport — kah lĭj PŌRT
College Station — kah lĭj STĀ sh'n
Collin — KAH lĭn
Collingsworth — KAH lĭnz werth
Collinsville — KAH lĭnz vĭl
Colmesneil — KŌL m's neel
Colorado — kahl uh RAH dō
Colorado City — kah luh rā duh or
  kah luh rah duh SĬT ĭ
Columbus — kuh LUHM b's
Comal — KŌ măl
Comanche — kuh MĂN chĭ
Combes — kōmz
Comfort — KUHM fert
Commerce — KAH mers
Como — KŌ mō
Comstock — KAHM stahk
Concan — KAHN kăn
Concepcion — kuhn sep sĭ ŌN
Concho — KAHN chō
Concord — KAHN kawrd
Concrete — kahn KREET
Cone — kōn
Conlen — KAHN lĭn
Conroe — KAHN rō
Converse — KAHN vers
Conway — KAHN wā
Cooke — kōōk
Cookville — KŌŌK vĭl
Coolidge — KŌŌ lĭj
Cooper — KŌŌ per
Copeville — KŌP v'l
Coppell — kahp pĕl or kuhp PĔL
Copperas Cove — kahp ruhs KŌV
Corbett — KAWR bĭt

Cordele — kawr DĚL
Corinth — KAH rĭnth
Corley — KAWR lĭ
Corpus Christi — <u>kawr</u> p's KRĬS tĭ
Corrigan — KAWR uh g'n
Corsicana — <u>kawr</u> sĭ KĂN uh
Coryell — kō rĭ ĔL
Cost — kawst
Cottle — KAH t'l
Cotton Center — <u>kaht</u> n SĔNT er
Cotton Gin — KAHT n jĭn
Cottonwood — KAHT n wo͞od
Cotulla — kuh TO͞O luh
Coupland — KŌP l'n
Courtney — KŌRT nĭ
Covington — KUHV ĭng t'n
Coy City — koi SĬT ĭ
Craft — krăft
Crafton — KRĂF t'n
Crandall — KRĂN d'l
Crane — krān
Cranfills Gap — krăn f'lz GĂP
Crawford — KRAW ferd
Creedmoor — KREED mōr
Cresson — KRĔ s'n
Crisp — krĭsp
Crockett — KRAH kĭt
Crosby — KRAWZ bĭ
Crosbyton — KRAWZ bĭ t'n
Cross — kraws
Cross Cut — KRAWS kuht
Cross Plains — kraws PLĀNZ
Cross Roads — KRAWS rōdz
Crow — krō
Crowell — KRŌ uhl
Crowley — KROW li
Crystal City — krĭs t'l SĬT ĭ
Crystal Falls — krĭs t'l FAWLZ
Cuero — KWĔR o
Culberson — KUHL ber s'n
Cumby — KUHM bĭ
Cuney — KYO͞O nĭ
Cunningham — KUHN ĭng hăm
Currie — KER rĭ
Cushing — KO͞O shĭng
Cuthand — KUHT hănd
Cyclone — SĪ klōn
Cypress — SĪ prĕs

D

Dabney — DĂB nĭ
Dacosta — duh KAHS tuh
Dacus — DĂ k's
Daingerfield — DĀN jer feeld
Daisetta — dā ZĔT uh
Dalby Springs — dĂl bĭ SPRĬNGZ
Dale — dāl
Dalhart — DĂL hahrt
Dallam — DĂL uhm
Dallas — DĂ luhs
Damon — DĀ m'n
Danbury — DĂN bĕrĭ
Danciger — DĂN sĭ ger
Danevang — DĂN uh văng
Darrouzett — dăr uh ZĔT

Davilla — duh VĬL uh
Dawn — dawn
Dawson — DAW s'n
Dayton — DĀT n
Deadwood — DĔD wo͞od
Deaf Smith — dĕf SMĬTH
Deanville — DEEN vĭl
DeBerry — duh BĔ rĭ
Decatur — <u>dee</u> KĀT er
Deer Park — dĭr PAHRK
De Kalb — dĭ KĂB
De Leon — da lee AHN
Del Rio — dĕl REE ō
Delta — DĔL tuh
Del Valle — dĕl VĂ lĭ
Delwin — DĔl wĭn
Denhawken — DĬN haw kĭn
Denison — DĔN uh s'n
Denning — DĔN ĭng
Dennis — DĔ nĭs
Denton — DĔNT n
Denver City — <u>dĕn</u> ver SĬT ĭ
Deport — DEE pōrt or dĭ PŌRT
Derby — DER bĭ
Desdemona — <u>dĕz</u> dĭ MŌ nuh
DeSoto — dĭ SŌ tuh
Detroit — dee TROIT
Devers — DĔ vers
Devine — duh VĬN
Dew — dyo͞o
Deweyville — DYO͞O ĭ vĭl
DeWitt — dĭ WĬT
Dewville — DYO͞O vĭl
Dexter — DĔKS ter
D'Hanis — duh HĂ nĭs
Dialville — DĬ uhl vil
Diboll — DĬ bawl
Dickens — DĬK ĭnz
Dickinson — DĬK ĭn s'n
Dike — dĭk
Dilley — DĬL i
Dilworth — DĬL <u>werth</u>
Dimebox — dīm BAHKS
Dimmit — DĬM ĭt
Dinero — dĭ NĔ rō
Direct — duh RĔKT
Dixon — DĬK s'n
Dobbin — DAH bĭn
Dobrowolski — <u>dah</u> bruh WAHL skĭ
Dodd City — dahd SĬT ĭ
Dodge — DAH j
Dodson — DAHD s'n
Donie — DŌ nĭ
Donley — DAHN lĭ
Donna — dah nuh
Doole — DOO lĭ
Dorchester — dawr CHĔS ter
Doss — daws
Doucette — DO͞O sĕt
Dougherty — DAHR tĭ
Douglass — DUHG l's
Douglassville — DUHG lĭs vĭl
Downing — DOWN ĭng
Downsville — DOWNZ vĭl
Dozier — DŌ zher
Draw — draw

Driftwood — DRĬFT wo͞od
Dripping Springs — drĭp ĭng
    SPRĬNGZ
Driscoll — DRĬS k'l
Dryden — DRĬD n
Dublin — DUHB lĭn
Duffau — DUHF ō
Dumas — DO͞O m's
Dumont — DYO͞O mahnt
Dundee — DUHN dĭ
Dunlap — DUHN lăp
Dunlay — DUHN lĭ
Dunn — duhn
Durango — duh RĂNG gō
Duval — DO͞O vawl

E

Eagle — EE g'l
Eagle Lake — <u>ee</u> g'l LĀK
Eagle Pass — <u>ee</u> g'l PĂS
Earth — erth
East Bernard — <u>eest</u> ber NAHRD
Easterly — EES ter lĭ
Eastland — EEST l'nd
Easton — EES t'n
Ector — ĔK ter
Edcouch — ĕd KOWCH
Eddy — E di
Eden — EED n
Edge — ĕj
Edgewood — ĔJ wo͞od
Edinburg — ĔD n <u>berg</u>
Edna — ED nuh
Edom — EE d'm
Edroy — ĔD roi
Edwards — ĔD werdz
Egan — EE g'n
Egypt — EE juhpt
Elbert — ĔL bert
El Campo — ĕl KĂM pō
Eldorado — <u>ĕl</u> duh RĂ duh
Electra — ĭ LĔK truh
Elgin — ĔL gĭn
Eliasville — <u>ee</u> LĪ uhs vĭl
El Indio — ĕl ĬN dĭ ō
Elkhart — ĔLK hahrt
Ellinger — ĔL ĭn jer
Elliott — ĔL ĭ 't
Ellis — ĔL uhs
Elmendorf — ĔLM 'n dawrf
Elm Mott — ĕl MAHT
Elmo — ĔL mō
Eloise — ĔL o <u>eez</u>
El Paso — ĕl PĂS ō
Elsa — ĔL suh
Elysian Fields — uh <u>lee</u> zh'n
    FEELDZ
Emhouse — ĔM hows
Emory — ĔM uh rĭ
Encinal — ĕn suh NAHL
Encino — ĕn SEE nō
Energy — ĔN er jĭ
Engle — ĔN g'l
English — ĬNG glĭsh

Enloe — ĔN lō
Ennis — ĔN ĭs
Enochs — EE nuhks
Eola — ee Ō luh
Era — EE ruh
Erath — EE răth
Esperanza — ĕs per RĂN zuh
Estelline — ĔS tuh leen
Etoile — ĭ TOIL
Etter — ĔT er
Eula — YŌO luh
Euless — YŌŌ lĭs
Eureka — yōō REE kuh
Eustace — YŌŌS t's
Evadale — EE vuh dāl
Evant — EE vănt
Evergreen — Ĕ ver green
Everman — Ĕ ver m'n

F

Fabens — FĀ b'nz
Fairbanks — FĀR bangks
Fairfield — FĀR feeld
Fairlie — FĀR lee
Fair Play — făr PLĀ
Fairview — FĀR vyōō
Fairy — FĀ rĭ
Falfurrias — făl FYŌŌ rĭ uhs
Falls — fawlz
Falls City — fawlz SĬT ĭ
Fannett — fă NĔT
Fannin — FĂN ĭn
Fargo — FAHR gō
Farmers Branch — fahr merz
  BRĂNCH
Farmersville — FAHRM erz vĭl
Farnsworth — FAHRNZ werth
Farrar — FĂR uh
Farrsville — FAHRZ vĭl
Farwell — FAHR w'l
Fashing — FĂ shĭng
Fate — făt
Fayette — fă ĔT
Fayetteville — FĀ uht vĭl
Fentress — FĔN trĭs
Ferris — FĔR ĭs
Field Creek — feeld KREEK
Fieldton — FEEL t'n
Fife — fif
Fischer — FĬ sher
Fisher — FĬSH er
Fisk — fĭsk
Flagg — flăg
Flat — flăt
Flatonia — flă TŌN yuh
Flint — flĭnt
Flomot — FLŌ maht
Florence — FLAH ruhns
Floresville — FLŌRZ vil
Florey — FLŌ ri
Floyd — floid
Floydada — floi DĀ duh
Fluvanna — flōō VĂN uh
Flynn — flĭn
Foard — fōrd

Foard City — fōrd SĬT ĭ
Fodice — FŌ dĭs
Follett — fah LĔT
Fordtran — fōrd TRĂN
Forest — FAW rĕst
Forestburg — FAW rĕst berg
Forney — FAWR nĭ
Forreston — FAW rĕs t'n
Forsan — FŌR săn
Fort Bend — fōrt BĔND
Fort Chadbourne — fōrt CHĂD bern
Fort Davis — fōrt DĀ vĭs
Fort Griffin — fōrt GRĬF ĭn
Fort Hancock — fōrt HĂN kahk
Fort McKavett — fōrt muh KĂ vĕt
Fort Stockton — fōrt STAHK t'n
Fort Worth — fōrt WERTH
Fowlerton — FOW ler t'n
Francitas — frăn SEE t's
Franklin — FRĂNGK lĭn
Frankston — FRĂNGS t'n
Fred — frĕd
Fredericksburg — FRĔD er rĭks
  berg
Fredonia — free DŌN yuh
Freeport — FREE pōrt
Freer — FREE er
Freestone — FREE stōn
Frelsburg — FRĔLZ berg
Fresno — FRĔZ nō
Friday — FRĪ dĭ
Friendswood — FRĔNZ wōōd
Frio — FREE ō
Friona — free Ō nuh
Frisco — FRĬS kō
Fritch — frĭch
Frost — frawst
Fruitland — FRŌŌT lănd
Fruitvale — FRŌŌT văl
Frydek — FRĪ dĕk
Fulbright — FŌŌL brĭt
Fulshear — FUHL sher
Fulton — FŌŌL t'n

G

Gail — gāl
Gaines — gānz
Gainesville — GĀNZ vuhl
Galena Park — guh lee nuh PAHRK
Gallatin — GĂL uh t'n
Galveston — GĂL vĕs t'n
Ganado — guh NĀ dō
Garceno — gahr SĀ nō
Garciasville — gahr SEE uhs vĭl
Garden City — GAHRD n sĭt ĭ
Gardendale — GAHRD n dāl
Garden Valley — gahrd n VĂ lĭ
Garland — GAHR l'nd
Garner — GAHR ner
Garrett — GĂR ĭt
Garrison — GĂ rĭ s'n
Garwood — GAHR wōōd
Gary — GĔ rĭ
Garza — GAHR zuh
Gatesville — GĀTS vil

Gause — gawz
Gay Hill — gā HĬL
Geneva — juh NEE vuh
Georgetown — JAWRJ town
George West — jawrj WĔST
Geronimo — juh RAH nĭ mō
Giddings — GĬD ĭngz
Gillespie — guh LĔS pĭ
Gillett — juh LĔT
Gilliland — GĬL ĭ l'nd
Gilmer — GĬL mer
Ginger — JĬN jer
Girard — juh RAHRD
Girvin — GER vĭn
Gladewater — GLĂD wah ter
Glasscock — GLĂS kahk
Glazier — GLĀ zher
Glen Cove — glĕn KŌV
Glendale — GLĔN dāl
Glenfawn — glĕn FAWN
Glen Flora — glĕn FLŌ ruh
Glenn — glĕn
Glen Rose — GLĔN rōz
Glidden — GLĬD n
Gober — GŌ ber
Godley — GAHD lĭ
Golden — GŌL d'n
Goldfinch — GŌLD fĭnch
Goldsboro — GŌLZ buh ruh
Goldsmith — GŌL smith
Goldthwaite — GŌLTH wāt
Goliad — GŌ lĭ ăd
Golinda — gō LĬN duh
Gonzales — guhn ZAH l's
Goodland — GŌŌD l'n
Goodlett — GŌŌD lĕt
Goodnight — GŌŌD nīt
Goodrich — GŌŌD rĭch
Gordon — GAWRD n
Gordonville — GAWRD n vĭl
Goree — GŌ ree
Gorman — GAWR m'n
Gouldbusk — GŌŌLD buhsk
Graford — GRĀ ferd
Graham — GRĀ 'm
Granbury — GRĂN bĕ rĭ
Grandfalls — grănd FAWLZ
Grand Saline — grăn suh LEEN
Grandview — GRĂN vyōō
Granger — GRĂN jer
Grapeland — GRĂP l'nd
Grapevine — GRĂP vīn
Grassland — GRĂS l'nd
Grassyville — GRĂ sĭ vĭl
Gray — grā
Grayburg — GRĀ berg
Grayson — GRA s'n
Green — green
Greenville — GREEN v'l
Greenwood — GREEN wōōd
Gregg — grĕg
Gregory — GRĔG uh rĭ
Grimes — grīmz
Groesbeck — GRŌZ bĕk
Groom — grōōm
Groveton — GRŌV t'n

Grow — grō
Gruene — green
Grulla — GROOL yuh
Gruver — GROO ver
Guadalupe — <u>gwah</u> duh LOO pĭ or
  <u>gwah</u> duh LOO pā
Guerra — GWĔ ruh
Gunter — GUHN ter
Gustine — GUHS <u>teen</u>
Guthrie — GUHTH rĭ
Guy — gī

H

Hackberry — HĂK bĕ rĭ
Hagansport — HĀ gĭnz pōrt
Hainesville — HĀNZ v'l
Hale — hāl
Hale Center — <u>hāl</u> SĔNT er
Hall — hawl
Hallettsville — HĂL ĕts vĭl
Hallsville — HAWLZ vĭl
Hamilton — HĂM uhl t'n
Hamlin — HĂM lĭn
Hammond — HĂM 'nd
Hamon — HĂ m'n
Hamshire — HĂM sher
Handley — HĂND lĭ
Hankamer — HĂN kăm er
Hansford — HĂNZ ferd
Happy — HĂ pĭ
Hardeman — HAHR duh m'n
Hardin — HAHRD n
Hare — hăr
Hargill — HAHR gĭl
Harleton — HAHR <u>uhl</u> t'n
Harlingen — HAHR lĭn juhn
Harper — HAHR per
Harris — HĂ rĭs
Harrison — HĂ rĭ s'n
Harrold — HĂR 'ld
Hart — hahrt
Hartburg — HAHRT berg
Hartley — HAHRT lĭ
Harwood — HAHR wŏŏd
Haskell — HĂS k'l
Haslam — HĂZ l'm
Haslet — HĂS lĕt
Hasse — HĂ sĭ
Hatchell — HĂ ch'l
Hawkins — HAW kĭnz
Hawley — HAW lĭ
Hays — hāz
Hearne — hern
Heath — heeth
Hebbronville — HĔB r'n vĭl
Hebron — HEE br'n
Hedley — HĔD lĭ
Heidenheimer — HĪD n hīmer
Helena — HĔL uh nuh
Helotes — hĕl Ō tĭs
Hemphill — HĔMP hĭl
Hempstead — HĔM stĕd
Henderson — HĔN der s'n
Henly — HĔN lĭ
Henrietta — hĕn rĭ Ĕ tuh

Hereford — HER ferd
Hermleigh — HER muh lee
Hewitt — HYOO ĭt
Hicks — hĭks
Hico — HĪ kō
Hidalgo — hĭ DĂL gō
Higgins — HĬ gĭnz
High — hī
Highbank — HĪ băngk
High Island — hī Ī l'nd
Highlands — HĪ l'ndz
Hightower — HĪ tow er
Hill — hĭl
Hillister — HĬL ĭs ter
Hillsboro — HĬLZ buh ruh
Hindes — hĭndz
Hiram — HĪ r'm
Hitchcock — HĬCH kahk
Hitchland — HĬCH l'nd
Hobson — HAHB s'n
Hochheim — HŌ hīm
Hockley — HAHK lĭ
Holland — HAHL 'nd
Holliday — HAH luh dā
Hondo — HAHN dō
Honey Grove — HUHN ĭ grōv
Honey Island — <u>huhn</u> ĭ Ī l'nd
Honey Springs — <u>huhn</u> ĭ SPRĬNGZ
Hood — hŏŏd
Hooks — hŏŏks
Hopkins — HAHP kĭnz
Houston — HYOOS t'n or YOOS t'n
Howard — HOW erd
Howe — how
Howland — HOW l'nd
Hubbard — HUH berd
Huckabay — HUHK uh bĭ
Hudspeth — HUHD sp'th
Huffman — HUHF m'n
Hufsmith — HUHF smĭth
Hughes Springs — hyōōz SPRĬNGZ
Hull — huhl
Humble — UHM b'l
Hungerford — HUHNG ger ferd
Hunt — huhnt
Hunter — HUHNT er
Huntington — HUHNT ĭng t'n
Huntsville — HUHNTS v'l
Hurlwood — HERL wŏŏd
Hutchins — HUH chĭnz
Hutchinson — HUH chĭn s'n
Hutto — HUH tō
Hye — hī
Hylton — HĬL t'n

I

Iago — ī Ā gō
Idalou — Ī duh lōō
Imperial — ĭm PĬR ĭ uhl
Inadale — Ī nuh dāl
Independence — ĭn duh PĔN d'ns
Indian Creek — ĭn dĭ uhn KREEK
Indian Gap — ĭn dĭ uhn GĂP
Industry — ĬN duhs trĭ
Inez — ī NĔZ

Ingleside — ĬNG g'l sīd
Ingram — ĬNG gr'm
Iola — ī Ō luh
Iowa Park — ī uh wuh PAHRK
Ira — Ī ruh
Iraan — ī ruh ĂN
Iredell — Ī ruh dĕl
Ireland — Ī rĭ l'nd
Irene — ī REEN
Irion — ĪR i uhn
Ironton — ĪRN t'n
Irving — ER vĭng
Italy — ĬT uh lĭ
Itasca — ī TĂS kuh
Ivan — Ī v'n
Ivanhoe — Ī v'n hō

J

Jack — jăk
Jacksboro — JĂKS buh ruh
Jackson — JĂK s'n
Jacksonville — JĂK s'n vĭl
Jamestown — JĀMZ town
Jardin — JAHRD n
Jarrell — JĂR uhl
Jasper — JĂS per
Jayton — JĀT n
Jean — jeen
Jeddo — JĔ dō
Jeff Davis — <u>jĕf</u> DA vĭs
Jefferson — JĔF er s'n
Jericho — JĔ rĭ kō
Jermyn — JER m'n
Jewett — JŌŌ ĭt
Jiba — HEE buh
Jim Hogg — jĭm HAWG
Jim Wells — jĭm WĔLZ
Joaquin — waw KEEN
Johnson — JAHN s'n
Johnson City — <u>jahn</u> s'n SĬT ĭ
Johntown — JAHN town
Johnsville — JAHNZ vĭl
Joinerville — JOI ner vĭl
Jolly — JAH lĭ
Jollyville — JAH lĭ vĭl
Jonah — JŌ nuh
Jones — jōnz
Jonesboro — JŌNZ <u>buh</u> ruh
Jonesville — JŌNZ vĭl
Josephine — JŌ suh <u>feen</u>
Joshua — JAH sh' wa
Jourdanton — JERD n t'n
Joy — joi
Joyce — jawĭs
Juliff — JŌŌ lĭf
Junction — JUHNGK sh'n
Juno — JŌŌ nō
Justiceburg — JUHS tĭs berg
Justin — JUHS tĭn

K

Kalgary — KĂL gĕ rĭ
Kamay — KĀ ĭm ā
Kanawha — KAHN uh wah

State Highway 97 passes through Jourdanton in Atascosa County. Photo by Billy Hathorn, CC 3/Wikimedia Commons

Karnack — KAHR năk
Karnes — kahrnz
Karnes City — kahrnz SĬT ĭ
Katemcy — kuh TĔM sĭ
Katy — KĀ tĭ
Kaufman — KAWF m'n
Keechi — KEE chĭ
Keene — keen
Kellerville — KĔL er vĭl
Kemah — KEE muh
Kemp — kĕmp or kĭmp
Kemp City — kĕmp SĬT ĭ
Kempner — KĔMP ner
Kendalia — kĔn DĀL yuh
Kenedy — KĔN uh dĭ
Kennard — kuh NAHRD
Kennedale — KĔN uh dāl
Kent — kĕnt
Kerens — KER 'nz
Kermit — KER mĭt
Kerr — ker
Kerrville — KER vĭl
Kildare — KĬL där
Kilgore — KĬL gŏr
Killeen — kuh LEEN
Kimble — KĬM b'l
King — kĭng
Kingsbury — KĬNGZ bĕ rĭ
Kingsland — KĬNGZ l'nd
Kingsmill — kĭngz MĬL
Kingston — KĬNGZ t'n
Kingsville — KĬNGZ vĭl
Kinney — KĬN ĭ
Kirby — KER bĭ
Kirbyville — KER bĭ vĭl
Kirkland — KERK l'nd
Kirvin — KER vĭn

Kleberg — KLĀ berg
Klondike — KLAHN dīk
Knickerbocker — NĬK uh <u>bah</u> ker
Knippa — kuh NĬP uh
Knott — naht
Knox — nahks
Knox City — nahks SĬT ĭ
Kosciusko — kuh SHOŌS kō
Kosse — KAH sĭ
Kountze — koōntz
Kress — kres
Krum — kruhm
Kurten — KER t'n
Kyle — kīl

L

La Blanca — lah BLAHN kuh
La Coste — luh KAWST
Ladonia — luh DŌN yuh
LaFayette — lah fĭ ĔT
Laferia — luh FĒ rĭ uh
Lagarto — luh GAHR tō
La Gloria — lah GLŌ rĭ uh
La Grange — luh GRĀNJ
Laguna — luh GOŌ nuh
Laird Hill — lärd HĬL
La Joya — luh HŌ yuh
Lake Creek — lāk KREEK
Lake Dallas — <u>lāk</u> DĂL uhs
Lake Jackson — lāk JĂK s'n
Laketon — LĀK t'n
Lake Victor — lāk VĬK ter
Lakeview — LĀK vyoō
Lamar — luh MAHR
La Marque — luh MAHRK
Lamasco — luh MĂS kō

Lamb — lăm
Lamesa — luh MEE suh
Lamkin — LĂM kĭn
Lampasas — lăm PĂ s's
Lancaster — LĂNG k's ter
Laneville — LĀN vĭl
Langtry — LĂNG trĭ
Lanier — luh NĬR
La Paloma — <u>lah</u> puh LŌ muh
La Porte — luh PŌRT
La Pryor — luh PRĪ er
Laredo — luh RĀ dō
Lariat — LĂ rĭ uht
Larue — luh ROŌ
La Salle — luh SĂL
Lasara — luh SĔ ruh
Lassater — LĂ sĭ ter
Latch — lăch
Latexo — luh TĔKS ō
Lavaca — luh VĂ kuh
La Vernia — luh VER nĭ uh
La Villa — lah VĬL uh
Lavon — luh VAHN
La Ward — luh WAWRD
Lawn — lawn
Lawrence — LAH r'ns
Lazbuddie — LĂZ buh dĭ
League City — <u>leeg</u> SĬT ĭ
Leakey — LĀ kĭ
Leander — lee ĂN der
Leary — LĬ er ĭ
Ledbetter — LĔD bĕt er
Lee — lee
Leesburg — LEEZ berg
Leesville — LEEZ vĭl
Lefors — lĭ FŌRZ
Leggett — LĔ gĭt

Leigh — lee
Lela — LEE luh
Lelia Lake — leel yuh LĀK
Leming — LĔ mĭng
Lenorah — lĕ NŌ ruh
Leo — LEE ō
Leon — lee AHN
Leona — lee Ō nuh
Leonard — LĔN erd
Leon Springs — lee ahn SPRĬNGZ
Leroy — LEE roi
Levelland — LĔ v'l lănd
Levita — luh VĪ tuh
Lewisville — LŌŌ ĭs vĭl
Lexington — LĔKS ĭng t'n
Liberty — LĬB er tĭ
Liberty Hill — <u>Ĭ</u> ber tĭ HĬL
Lillian — LĬL yuhn
Limestone — LĪM stōn
Lincoln — LĬNG k'n
Lindale — LĬN dāl
Linden — LĬN d'n
Lindenau — lĭn duh NOW
Lindsay — LĬN zĭ
Lingleville — LĬNG g'l vĭl
Linn — lĭn
Lipan — lĭ PĂN
Lipscomb — LĬPS k'm
Lissie — LĬ sĭ
Little Elm — <u>lĭt</u> l ĔLM
Littlefield — LĬT uhl feeld
Little River — <u>lĭt</u> uhl RĬV er
Live Oak — LĬV ōk
Liverpool — LĬ ver pōōl
Livingston — LĬV ĭngz t'n
Llano — LĂ nō
Locker — LAH ker
Lockett — LAH kĭt
Lockhart — LAHK hahrt
Lockney — LAHK nĭ
Lodi — LŌ dī
Lohn — lahn
Lolita — lō LEE tuh
Loma Alto — <u>lō</u> muh ĂL tō
Lometa — lō MEE tuh
London — LUHN d'n
Lone Grove — lōn GRŌV
Lone Oak — LŌN ōk
Long Branch — lawng BRĂNCH
Long Mott — lawng MAHT
Longview — LAWNG vyōō
Longworth — LAWNG werth
Loop — lōōp
Lopeno — lō PEE nō
Loraine — lō RĀN
Lorena — lō REE nuh
Los Angeles — laws AN juh l's
Los Ebanos — lōs ĔB uh nōs
Los Fresnos — lōs FRĔZ nōs
Los Indios — lōs ĬN dĭ ōs
Losoya — luh SAW yuh
Lott — laht
Louise — LŌŌ eez
Lovelady — LUHV lā dĭ
Loving — LUH vĭng
Lowake — lō WĀ kĭ

Lubbock — LUH buhk or LUH b'k
Lueders — LŌŌ derz
Luella — lōō ĔL uh
Lufkin — LUHF kĭn
Luling — LŌŌ lĭng
Lund — luhnd
Lutie — LŌŌ tĭ
Lyford — LĪ ferd
Lynn — lĭn
Lyons — LĪ 'nz
Lytton Springs — lĭt n SPRĬNGZ

M

Mabank — MĀ băngk
Macune — muh KŌŌN
Madison — MĂ dĭ s'n
Madisonville — MĂ duh s'n vĭl
Magnolia — măg NŌL yuh
Magnolia Springs — măg nol yuh SPRINGZ
Malakoff — MĂL uh kawf
Malone — muh LŌN
Malta — MAWL tuh
Manchaca — MĂN shăk
Manchester — MĂN chĕs ter
Manheim — MĂN hĭm
Mankins — MĂN kĭnz
Manor — MĂ ner
Mansfield — MĂNZ feeld
Manvel — MĂN v'l
Maple — MĀ puhl
Marathon — MĂR uh th'n
Marble Falls — mahr b'l FAWLZ
Marfa — MAHR fuh
Margaret — MAHR guh rĭt
Marietta — mĕ rĭ Ĕ tuh
Marion — MĔ rĭ uhn
Markham — MAHR k'm
Marlin — MAHR lĭn
Marquez — mahr KĀ
Marshall — MAHR sh'l
Mart — mahrt
Martin — MAHRT n
Martindale — MAHRT n dāl
Martinsville — MAHRT nz vĭl
Maryneal — mā rĭ NEEL
Marysville — MĂ rĭz vĭl
Mason — MĂ s'n
Matador — MĂT uh dōr
Matagorda — măt uh GAWR duh
Mathis — MĂ thĭs
Maud — mawd
Mauriceville — maw REES vĭl
Maverick — MĂV rĭk
Maxey — MĂKS ĭ
Maxwell — MĂKS w'l
May — mā
Maydell — MĀ dĕl
Maypearl — <u>mā</u> PERL
Maysfield — MĀZ feeld
McAdoo — MĂK uh dōō
McAllen — măk ĂL ĭn
McCamey — muh KĀ mĭ
McCaulley — muh KAW lĭ
McCoy — muh KOI

McCulloch — muh KUH luhk
McFaddin — măk FĂD n
McGregor — muh GRĔ ger
McKinney — muh KĬN ĭ
McLean — muh KLĀN
McLennan — muhk LĔN uhn
McLeod — măk LOWD
McMahan — măk MĂN
McMullen — măk MUHL ĭn
McNary — măk NĂ rĭ
McNeil — măk NEEL
McQueeney — muh KWEE nĭ
Meadow — MĔ dō
Medicine Mound — <u>mĕd</u> uhs n MOWND
Medill — mĕ DĬL
Medina — muh DEE nuh
Megargel — muh GAHR g'l
Melissa — muh LĬS uh
Melrose — MĔL rōz
Melvin — MĔL vĭn
Memphis — MĔM fĭs
Menard — muh NAHRD
Mendoza — mĕn DŌ zuh
Mentone — mĕn TŌN
Mercedes — <u>mer</u> SĂ deez
Mercury — MER kyuh ri
Mereta — muh RĔT uh
Meridian — muh RĬ dĭ uhn
Merit — MĔR ĭt
Merkel — MER k'l
Mertens — <u>mer</u> TĔNZ
Mertzon — MERTS n
Mesquite — muhs KEET
Mexia — muh HĂ uh
Meyersville — MĪRZ vĭl
Miami — mĭ ĂM uh or mĭ ĂM ĭ
Mico — MEE kō
Middleton — MĬD uhl t'n
Midfields — MĬD feeldz
Midland — MĬD l'nd
Midlothian — <u>mĭd</u> LŌ thĭ n
Midway — MĬD wā
Milam — MĪ l'm
Milano — mĭ LĂ nō
Mildred — MĬL drĕd
Miles — mīlz
Milford — MĬL ferd
Miller Grove — mĭl er GRŌV
Millersview — MĬL erz vyōō
Millett — MĬL ĭt
Millheim — MĬL hĭm
Millican — MĬL uh kuhn
Mills — mĭlz
Millsap — MĬL săp
Minden — MĬN d'n
Mineola — mĭn ĭ Ō luh
Mineral — MĬN er uhl
Mineral Wells — mĭn er uhl WĔLZ
Minerva — mĭ NER vuh
Mingus — MĬNG guhs
Minter — MĬNT er
Mirando City — mĭ răn duh SĬT ĭ
Mission — MĬSH uhn
Mission Valley — mĭsh uhn VĂ lĭ
Missouri City — muh zōōr uh SĬT ĭ

Mitchell — MĬ ch'l
Mobeetie — mō BEE tĭ
Moline — mō LEEN
Monahans — MAH nuh hănz
Monaville — MŌ nuh vĭl
Monkstown — MUHNGKS town
Monroe — MAHN rō
Monroe City — mahn rō SĬT ĭ
Montague — mahn TĀG
Montalba — mahnt ĂL buh
Mont Belvieu — mahnt BĔL vyōō
Montell — mahn TĔL
Montgomery — mahnt GUHM er ĭ
Monthalia — mahn THĀL yuh
Moody — MŌŌ dĭ
Moore — mōr
Morales — muh RAH lĕs
Moran — mō RĂN
Morgan — MAWR g'n
Morgan Mill — mawr g'n MĬL
Morse — mawrs
Morton — MAWRT n
Moscow — MAHS kow
Mosheim — MŌ shĭm
Moss Bluff — maws BLUHF
Motley — MAHT lĭ
Moulton — MŌL t'n
Mound — mownd
Mountain Home — mownt n HŌM
Mount Calm — mownt KAHM
Mount Enterprise — mownt ĔN
   ter prīz
Mount Pleasant — mownt PLĔ z'nt
Mount Selman — mownt SĔL m'n
Mount Sylvan — mownt SĬL v'n
Mount Vernon — mownt VER n'n
Muenster — MYŌŌNS ter
Muldoon — muhl DŌŌN
Muleshoe — MYŌŌL shōō
Mullin — MUHL ĭn
Mumford — MUHM ferd
Munday — MUHN dĭ
Murchison — MER kuh s'n
Murphy — MER fĭ
Mykawa—mĭ KAH wuh
Myra — MĪ ruh
Myrtle Springs — mert l SPRĬNGZ

Nacogdoches — năk uh DŌ chĭs
Nada — NĀ duh
Naples — NĀ p'lz
Nash — năsh
Natalia — nuh TĀL yuh
Navarro — nuh VĂ rō
Navasota — năv uh SŌ tuh
Nazareth — NĂZ uh r'th
Neches — NĀ chĭs
Nederland — NEE der l'nd
Needville — NEED vĭl
Nelsonville — NĔL s'n vĭl
Neuville — NYŌŌ v'l
Nevada — nuh VĀ duh
Newark — NŌŌ erk

New Baden — nyōō BĀD n
New Berlin — nyōō BER lin
New Boston — nyōō BAWS t'n
New Braunfels — nyōō BRAHN f'ls
   or BROWN fĕlz
Newby — NYŌŌ bĭ
New Caney — nyōō KĀ nĭ
Newcastle — NYŌŌ kăs uhl
New Gulf — nyōō GUHLF
New Home — NYŌŌ hōm
New Hope — nyōō HŌP
Newlin — NYŌŌ lĭn
New London — nyōō LUHN d'n
Newman — NYŌŌ m'n
Newport — NYŌŌ pōrt
New Salem — nyōō SĀ l'm
Newsome — NYŌŌ s'm
New Summerfield — nyōō SUHM
   er feeld
Newton — NYŌŌT n
New Ulm — nyōō UHLM
New Waverly — nyōō WĀ ver lĭ
New Willard — nyōō WĬL erd
Nimrod — NĬM rahd
Nineveh — NĬN uh vuh
Nixon — NĬKS uhn
Nocona — nō KŌ nuh
Nolan — NŌ l'n
Nolanville — NŌ l'n vĭl
Nome — nōm
Noonday — NŌŌN dā
Nopal — NŌ păl
Nordheim — NAWRD hīm
Normandy — NAWR m'n dĭ
Normangee — NAWR m'n jee
Normanna — nawr MĂN uh
Northrup — NAWR thr'p
North Zulch — nawrth ZŌŌLCH
Norton — NAWRT n
Novice — NAH vĭs
Nueces — nyōō Ā sĭs
Nugent — NYŌŌ j'nt
Nursery — NER suh rĭ

Oakalla — ō KĂL uh
Oak Grove — ōk GRŌV
Oak Hill — ōk HĬL
Oakhurst — ŌK herst
Oakland — ŌK l'nd
Oakville — ŌK vĭl
Oakwood — ŌK wōōd
O'Brien — ō BRĪ uhn
Ochiltree — AH k'l tree
Odell — Ō dĕl or ō DĔL
Odem — Ō d'm
Odessa — ō DĔS uh
O'Donnell — ō DAH n'l
Oenaville — ō EEN uh v'l
Oglesby — Ō g'lz bĭ
Oilton — OIL t'n
Oklaunion — ōk luh YŌŌN y'n
Olden — ŌL d'n
Oldenburg — ŌL dĭn berg
Oldham — ŌL d'm

Old Glory — ōld GLŌ rĭ
Olivia — ō LĬV ĭ uh
Olmito — awl MEE tuh
Olmos Park — ahl m's PAHRK
Olney — AHL nĭ
Olton — ŌL t'n
Omaha — Ō muh haw
Omen — Ō mĭn
Onalaska — uhn uh LĂS kuh
Oplin — AHP lĭn
Orange — AHR ĭnj
Orangefield — AHR ĭnj feeld
Orange Grove — AHR ĭnj GRŌV
Orchard — AWR cherd
Ore City — ōr SĬT ĭ
Osceola — ō sĭ Ō luh
Otey — Ō tĭ
Otis Chalk — ō tĭs CHAWLK
Ottine — ah TEEN
Otto — AH tō
Ovalo — ō VĂL uh
Overton — Ō ver t'n
Owens — Ō ĭnz
Ozona — ō ZŌ nuh

Paducah — puh DYŌŌ kuh
Paige — pāj
Paint Rock — pānt RAHK
Palacios — puh LĂ sh's
Palestine — PAL uhs teen
Palito Blanco — p' lee to BLAHNG
   kō
Palmer — PAH mer
Palo Pinto — pă lō PĬN tō
Paluxy — puh LUHK sĭ
Pampa — PĂM puh
Pandora — păn DŌR uh
Panhandle — PĂN hăn d'l
Panna Maria — păn uh muh REE
   uh
Papalote — pah puh LŌ tĭ
Paradise — PĂR uh dīs
Paris — PĂ rĭs
Parker — PAHR ker
Parmer — PAH mer
Parnell — pahr NĔL
Parsley Hill — pahrs lĭ HĬL
Pasadena — păs uh DEE nuh
Patricia — puh TRĬ shuh
Patroon — puh TRŌŌN
Pattison — PĂT uh s'n
Pattonville — PĂT n vĭl
Pawnee — paw NEE
Paxton — PĂKS t'n
Peacock — PEE kahk
Pearl — perl
Pearland — PĂR lănd
Pearsall — PEER sawl
Peaster — PEES ter
Pecan Gap — pĭ kahn GĂP
Pecos — PĀ k's
Penelope — puh NĔL uh pĭ
Penitas — puh NEE t's
Pennington — PĔN ĭng t'n

Penwell — PĬN wĕl
Peoria — pee Ō rĭ uh
Percilla — per SĬL uh
Perrin — PĔR ĭn
Perry — PĔ rĭ
Perryton — PĔ rĭ t'n
Peters — PEET erz
Petersburg — PEET erz berg
Petrolia — puh TRŌL yuh
Petteway — PĔT uh wā
Pettit — PĔT ĭt
Pettus — PĔT uhs
Petty — PĔT ĭ
Pflugerville — FLŌŌ ger vĭl
Pharr — fahr
Phelps — fĕlps
Phillips — FĬL uhps
Pickton — PĬK t'n
Pidcoke — PĬD kŏk
Piedmont — PEED mahnt
Pierce — PĬ ers
Pilot Point — pī l't POINT
Pine Forest — pĭn FAW rĕst
Pine Hill — pĭn HĬL
Pinehurst — PĬN herst
Pineland — PĬN land
Pine Mills — pĭn MĬLZ
Pine Springs — pĭn SPRĬNGZ
Pioneer — pī uh NĬR
Pipecreek — pīp KREEK
Pittsburg — PĬTS berg
Placedo — PLĂS ĭ dō
Placid — PLĂ sĭd
Plains — plānz
Plainview — PLĀN vyōō
Plano — PLĂ nō
Plantersville — PLĂN terz vĭl
Plaska — PLĂS kuh
Plateau — plă TŌ
Pleasant Grove—plĕ z'nt GRŌV
Pleasanton — PLĔZ uhn t'n
Pledger — PLĔ jer
Plum — pluhm
Point — point
Pointblank — pint BLĂNGK
Polk — pōlk
Pollock — PAHL uhk
Ponder — PAHN der
Ponta — pahn TĂ
Pontotoc — PAHNT uh tahk
Poolville — PŌŌL vĭl
Port Aransas — pōrt uh RĂN zuhs
Port Arthur — pōrt AHR ther
Port Bolivar — pōrt BAH lĭ ver
Porter Springs — pōr ter SPRĬNGZ
Port Isabel — pōrt ĬZ uh bĕl
Portland — PŌRT l'nd
Port Lavaca — pōrt luh VĂ kuh
Port Neches — pōrt NĂ chĭs
Port O'Connor — pōrt ō KAH ner
Posey — PŌ zĭ
Post — pōst
Postoak — PŌST ōk
Poteet — pō TEET
Poth — pōth

Potosi — puh TŌ sĭ
Potter — PAHT er
Pottsboro — PAHTS buh ruh
Pottsville — PAHTS vĭl
Powderly — POW der lĭ
Powell — POW w'l
Poynor — POI ner
Prairie Dell — prĕr ĭ DĔL
Prairie Hill — prĕr ĭ HĬL
Prairie Lea — prĕr ĭ LEE
Prairie View — prĕr ĭ VYŌŌ
Prairieville — PRĔR ĭ vĭl
Premont — PREE mahnt
Presidio — pruh SĬ dĭ ō
Priddy — PRĬ dĭ
Primera — pree MĔ ruh
Princeton — PRĬNS t'n
Pritchett — PRĬ chĭt
Proctor — PRAHK ter
Progreso — prō GRĔ sō
Prosper — PRAHS per
Purdon — PERD n
Purley — PER lĭ
Purmela — per MEE luh
Putnam — PUHT n'm
Pyote — PĬ ōt

Q

Quail — kwāl
Quanah — KWAH nuh
Queen City — kween SĬT ĭ
Quemado — kuh MAH dō
Quihi — KWEE hee
Quinlan — KWĬN l'n
Quintana — kwĭn TAH nuh
Quitaque — KĬT uh kwa
Quitman — KWĬT m'n

R

Rainbow — RĂN bō
Rains — rānz
Ralls — rahlz
Randall — RĂN d'l
Randolph — RĂN dahlf
Ranger — RĂN jer
Rangerville — RĂN jer vĭl
Rankin — RĂNG kĭn
Ratcliff — RĂT klĭf
Ravenna — rĭ VĔN uh
Rayburn — RĂ bern
Raymondville — RĂ m'nd vĭl
Raywood — RĂ wōōd
Reagan — RĂ g'n
Real — REE awl
Realitos — ree uh LEE t's
Redford — RĔD ferd
Red Oak — RĔD ōk
Red River — rĕd RĬ ver
Red Rock — rĕd RAHK
Red Springs — rĕd SPRĬNGZ
Red Water — RĔD wah ter
Reeves — reevz
Refugio — rĕ FYŌŌ rĭ ō

Reilly Springs — rī lĭ SPRĬNGZ
Reklaw — RĔK law
Reno — REE nō
Rhineland — RĬN l'nd
Rhome — rōm
Rhonesboro — RŌNZ buh ruh
Ricardo — rĭ KAHR dō
Rice — rīs
Richards — RĬCH erdz
Richardson — RĬCH erd s'n
Richland — RĬCH l'nd
Richland Springs — rĭch l'nd
    SPRĬNGZ
Richmond — RĬCH m'nd
Ridge — rĭj
Ridgeway — RĬJ wā
Riesel — REE s'l
Ringgold — RĬNG gōld
Rio Frio — ree ō FREE ō
Rio Grande City — ree ō grahn dĭ
    or ree ō grän SĬT ĭ
Rio Hondo — ree ō HAHN dō
Riomedina — ree ō muh DEE nuh
Rios — REE ōs
Rio Vista — ree ō VĬS tuh
Rising Star — rī zĭng STAHR
River Oaks — rĭ ver ŌKS
Riverside — RĬ ver sĭd
Riviera — ruh VĬR uh
Roane — rōn
Roanoke — RŌN ōk or RŌ uh
    nōk
Roans Prairie — rōnz PRĔR Ĭ
Roaring Springs — rōr ĭng
    SPRĬNGZ
Robert Lee — rah bert LEE
Roberts — RAH berts
Robertson — RAH bert s'n
Robinson — RAH bĭn s'n
Robstown — RAHBZ town
Roby — RŌ bĭ
Rochelle — rō SHĔL
Rochester — RAH chĕs ter
Rockdale — RAHK dāl
Rock Island — rahk Ĭ l'nd
Rockland — RAHK l'nd
Rockport — rahk PŌRT
Rocksprings — rahk SPRĬNGZ
Rockwall — rahk WAWL
Rockwood — RAHK wōōd
Roganville — RŌ g'n vĭl
Rogers — RAH jerz
Roma — RŌ muh
Romayor — rō MĂ er
Roosevelt — RŌ suh v'lt or RŌŌ
    suh v'lt
Ropesville — RŌPS vĭl
Rosanky — rō ZĂNG kĭ
Roscoe — RAHS kō
Rosebud — RŌZ b'd
Rose Hill — rōz HĬL
Rosenberg — RŌZ n berg
Rosenthal — RŌZ uhn thawl
Rosewood — RŌZ wōōd
Rosharon — rō SHĔ r'n

Diacritical markings are used as follows: bāle, băd, lĕt, rīse, rĭll, ōak, brōōd, fōōt. The stressed syllable is capitalized. Secondary stress is indicated by an underline as in Atascosa — ăt uhs KŌ suh. © TEXAS ALMANAC.

Rosita — rō SEE tuh
Ross — raws
Rosser — RAW ser
Rosston — RAWS t'n
Rossville — RAWS vĭl
Roswell — RAHZ w'l
Rotan — rō TĂN
Round Rock — ROWND rahk
Round Top — ROWN tahp
Rowena — rō EE nuh
Rowlett — ROW lĭt
Roxton — RAHKS t'n
Royalty — ROI uhl tĭ
Royse City — roi SĬT ĭ
Royston — ROIS t'n
Rugby — RUHG bĭ
Ruidosa — ree uh DŌ suh
Rule — rōol
Runge — RUHNG ĭ
Runnels — RUHN 'lz
Rural Shade — rŏŏr uhl SHĀD
Rusk — ruhsk
Rutersville — RŌŌ ter vĭl
Rye — rī

S

Sabinal — SĂB uh năl
Sabine — suh BEEN
Sabine Pass — suh been PĂS
Sabinetown — suh been TOWN
Sachse — SĂK sĭ
Sacul — SĂ k'l
Sadler — SĂD ler
Sagerton — SĂ ger t'n
Saginaw — SĂ guh naw
Saint Jo — sănt JŌ
Saint Paul — sănt PAWL
Salado — suh LĀ dō
Salesville — SĂLZ vĭl
Salineno — suh LEEN yō
Salmon — SĂL m'n
Salt Gap — sawlt GĂP
Saltillo — săl TĬL ō
Samfordyce — săm FOR dis
Sample — SĂM p'l
Samnorwood — săm NAWR wŏŏd
San Angelo — săn ĂN juh lō
San Antonio — săn ăn TŌ nĭ ō
San Augustine — săn AW g's teen
San Benito — săn buh NEE tuh
Sanderson — SĂN der s'n
Sandia — săn DEE uh
San Diego — săn dĭ Ā gō
Sandy Point — săn dĭ POINT
San Elizario — săn ĕl ĭ ZAH rĭ ō
San Felipe — săn fuh LEEP
Sanford — SĂN ferd
San Gabriel — săn GĀ brĭ uhl
Sanger — SĂNG er
San Jacinto — săn juh SĬN tuh or juh SĬN tō
San Juan — săn WAHN
San Marcos — săn MAHR k's
San Patricio — săn puh TRĬSH ĭ ō
San Perlita — săn per LEE tuh

San Saba — săn SĂ buh
Santa Anna — săn tuh ĂN uh
Santa Elena — săn tuh LEE nuh
Santa Maria — săn tuh muh REE uh
Santa Rosa — săn tuh RŌ suh
Santo — SĂN tō
San Ygnacio — săn ĭg NAH sĭ ō
Saragosa — sĕ ruh GŌ suh
Saratoga — sĕ ruh TŌ guh
Sargent — SAHR juhnt
Sarita — suh REE tuh
Saspamco — suh SPĂM kō
Satin — SĂT n
Savoy — suh VOI
Schattel — SHĂT uhl
Schertz — sherts
Schleicher — SHLĪ ker
Schroeder — SHRĀ der
Schulenburg — SHŌŌ lĭn berg
Schwertner — SWERT ner
Scotland — SKAHT l'nd
Scottsville — SKAHTS vĭl
Scranton — SKRĂNT n
Scurry — SKUH rĭ
Scyene — sī EEN
Seabrook — SEE brŏŏk
Seadrift — SEE drĭft
Seagoville — SEE gō vĭl
Seagraves — SEE grăvz
Seale — seel
Sealy — SEE lĭ
Sebastopol — suh BĂS tuh pōol
Sebastian — suh BĂS tĭ 'n
Security — sĭ KYŌŌR ĭ tĭ
Segno — SĔG nō
Segovia — sĭ GŌ vĭ uh
Seguin — sĭ GEEN
Selfs — sĕlfs
Selma — SĔL muh
Seminole — SĔM uh nōl
Seymour — SEE mōr
Shackelford — SHĂK uhl ferd
Shady Grove — shā dĭ GRŌV
Shafter — SHĂF ter
Shallowater — SHĂL uh wah ter
Shamrock — SHĂM rahk
Shannon — SHĂN uhn
Sharp — shahrp
Sheffield — SHĔ feeld
Shelby — SHĔL bĭ
Shelbyville — SHĔL bĭ vĭl
Sheldon — SHĔL d'n
Shepherd — SHĔ perd
Sheridan — SHĔ rĭ dn
Sherman — SHER m'n
Sherwood — SHER wood
Shiner — SHĪ ner
Shiro — SHĪ rō
Shive — shĭv
Sidney — SĬD nĭ
Sierra Blanca — sĭer ruh BLĂNG kuh
Siloam — suh LŌM
Silsbee — SĬLZ bĭ
Silver Lake — sĭl ver LĀK

Silverton — SĬL ver t'n
Silver Valley — sĭl ver VĂ lĭ
Simms — sĭmz
Simonton — SĪ m'n t'n
Singleton — SĬNG g'l t'n
Sinton — SĬNT n
Sipe Springs — SEEP sprĭngz
Sisterdale — SĬS ter dāl
Sivells Bend — sĭ v'lz BĔND
Skellytown — SKĔ lĭ town
Skidmore — SKĬD mōr
Slaton — SLĀT n
Slayden — SLĀD n
Slidell — sli DĔL
Slocum — SLŌ k'm
Smiley — SMĪ lĭ
Smith — smĭth
Smithfield — SMĬTH feeld
Smithland — SMĬTH l'nd
Smithson Valley — smĭth s'n VĂ lĭ
Smithville — SMĬTH vĭl
Smyer — SMĪ er
Snook — snŏŏk
Snyder — SNĪ der
Somerset — SUH mer sĕt
Somervell — SUH mer vĕl
Somerville — SUH mer vĭl
Sonora — suh NŌ ruh
Sour Lake — sowr LĀK
South Bend — sowth BĔND
South Bosque — sowth BAHS kĭ
South Houston — sowth HYŌŌS t'n
Southland — SOWTH l'nd
Southmayd — sowth MĀD
South Plains — sowth PLĀNZ
Spade — spād
Spanish Fort — spă nĭsh FŌRT
Sparenberg — SPĂR ĭn berg
Speaks — speeks
Spearman — SPĬR m'n
Spicewood — SPĪS wŏŏd
Splendora — splĕn DŌ ruh
Spofford — SPAH ferd
Spring — sprĭng
Springdale — SPRĬNG dāl
Springlake — sprĭng LĀK
Springtown — SPRĬNG town
Spur — sper
Spurger — SPER ger
Stacy — STĀ sĭ
Stafford — STĂ ferd
Stamford — STĂM ferd
Stanton — STĂNT n
Staples — STĀ p'lz
Starr — stahr
Stephens — STEE vĕnz
Stephenville — STEEV n vĭl
Sterley — STER lĭ
Sterling — STER lĭng
Sterling City — ster lĭng SĬT ĭ
Stiles — stīlz
Stinnett — stĭ NĔT
Stockdale — STAHK dāl
Stoneburg — STŌN berg
Stoneham — STŌN uhm
Stone Point — stōn POINT

Diacritical markings are used as follows: bāle, băd, lĕt, rise, rĭll, ōak, brōōd, fŏŏt. The stressed syllable is capitalized. Secondary stress is indicated by an underline as in Atascosa — ăt uhs KŌ suh. TEXAS ALMANAC ©.

The watertower in Tenaha in Shelby County. Photo by Hourick, Public Domain/ Wikimedia Commons

Tehuacana — tuh WAW kuh nuh
Telephone — TĔL uh fōn
Telferner — TĔLF ner
Tell — tĕl
Temple — TĔM p'l
Tenaha — TĔN uh haw
Tennyson — TĔN uh s'n
Terlingua — TER lĭng guh
Terrell — TĔR uhl
Terrell Hills — ter uhl HILZ
Terry — TĔR ĭ
Texarkana — tĕks ahr KĂN uh
Texas City — tĕks ĕz SĬT ĭ
Texhoma — tĕks Ō muh
Texline — TĔKS līn
Texon — tĕks AHN
Thalia — THĂL yuh
The Grove — th' GRŌV
Thicket — THĬ kĭt
Thomaston — TAHM uhs t'n
Thompsons — TAHMP s'nz
Thorndale — THAWRN dāl
Thornton — THAWRN t'n
Thorp Spring — thawrp SPRING
Thrall — thrawl
Three Rivers — three RĬ verz
Throckmorton — THRAHK mawrt n
Thurber — THER ber
Tilden — TĬL d'n
Timpson — TĬM s'n
Tioga — tī Ō guh
Titus — TĪT uhs
Tivoli — tī VŌ luh
Tokio — TŌ kĭ ō
Tolar — TŌ ler
Tolbert — TAHL bert
Tolosa — tuh LŌ suh
Tomball — TAHM bawl
Tom Bean — tahm BEEN
Tom Green — tahm GREEN
Tool — tōol
Topsey — TAHP sī
Tornillo — tawr NEE yō
Tow — tow
Toyah — TOI yuh
Toyahvale — TOI yuh văl
Trawick — TRĀ wĭk
Travis — TRĀ vĭs
Trent — trĕnt
Trenton — TRĔNT n
Trickham — TRĬK uhm
Trinidad — TRĬN uh dăd
Trinity — TRĬN ĭ tĭ
Troup — trōop
Troy — TRAW ĭ
Truby — TRŌO bĭ
Trumbull — TRUHM b'l
Truscott — TRUHS k't
Tucker — TUHK er
Tuleta — tōo LEE tuh
Tulia — TŌOL yuh
Tulsita — tuhl SEE tuh
Tundra — TUHN druh
Tunis — TŌO nĭs
Turkey — TER kĭ
Turlington — TER lĭng t'n

Stonewall — STŌN wawl
Stout — stowt
Stowell — STO w'l
Stranger — STRĂN jer
Stratford — STRĂT ferd
Strawn — strawn
Streeter — STREET er
Streetman — STREET m'n
Study Butte — styōo dĭ BYŌOT
Sublime — s'b LĪM
Sudan — SŌO dän
Sugar Land — SHŌO ger länd
Sullivan City — suh luh v'n SĬT ĭ
Sulphur Bluff — suhl fer BLUHF
Sulphur Springs — suhl fer
    SPRĬNGZ
Summerfield — SUHM er feeld
Sumner — SUHM ner
Sundown — SUHN down
Suniland — SUH nĭ länd
Sunny Side — SUH nĭ sīd
Sunray — SUHN rā
Sunset — SUHN sĕt
Sutherland Springs — suh ther l'nd
    SPRĬNGZ

Sutton — SUHT n
Swan — swahn
Sweeny — SWEE nĭ
Sweet Home — sweet HŌM
Sweetwater — SWEET wah ter
Swenson — SWĔN s'n
Swift — swĭft
Swisher — SWĬ sher
Sylvester — sil VES ter

Taft — tăft
Tahoka — tuh HŌ kuh
Talco — TĂL kō
Talpa — TĂL puh
Tanglewood — TĂNG g'l wōod
Tankersley — TĂNG kers lĭ
Tarrant — TAR uhnt
Tarzan — TAHR z'n
Tascosa — täs KŌ suh
Tatum — TĀ t'm
Tavener — TĂV uh ner
Taylor — TĀ ler
Teague — teeg

Turnersville — TER nerz vĭl
Turnertown — TER ner town
Turney — TER nĭ
Tuscola — tuhs KŌ luh
Tuxedo — TUHKS ĭ dō
Twin Sisters — twĭn SĬS terz
Twitty — TWĬ tĭ
Tye — tĭ
Tyler — TĪ ler
Tynan — TĪ nuhn

U

Uhland — YŌŌ l'nd
Umbarger — UHM bahr ger
Union — YŌŌN y'n
Upshur — UHP sher
Upton — UHP t'n
Urbana — er BĀ nuh
Utley — YŌŌT lĭ
Utopia — yōō TŌ pĭ uh
Uvalde — yōō VĂL dĭ

V

Valdasta — văl DĂS tuh
Valentine — VĂL uhn tīn
Valera — vuh LĬ ruh
Valley Mills — vă lĭ MĬLZ
Valley Spring — vă lĭ SPRĬNG
Valley View — vă lĭ VYŌŌ
Van — văn
Van Alstyne — văn AWLZ teen
Vancourt — VĂN kört
Vanderbilt — VĂN der bĭlt
Vanderpool — VĂN der pōōl
Van Horn — văn hawrn
Van Vleck — văn VLĔK
Van Zandt — văn ZĂNT
Vashti — VĂSH tĭ
Vaughan — vawn
Vega — VĀ guh
Velasco — vuh LĂS kō
Venus — VEE n's
Vera — VĬ ruh
Veribest — VĔR ĭ bĕst
Verhalen — ver HĂ lĭn
Vernon — VER n'n
Vickery — VĬK er ĭ
Victoria — vĭk TŌ rĭ uh
Vidor — VĪ der
Vienna — vee ĔN uh
View — vyōō
Village Mills — vĭl ĭj MĬLZ
Vincent — VĬN s'nt
Vinegarone — vĭn er guh RŌN
Vineyard — VĬN yerd
Violet — VĪ ō lĕt
Voca — VŌ kuh
Von Ormy — vahn AHR mĭ
Voss — vaws
Votaw — VŌ taw

W

Waco — WĀ kō

Wadsworth — WAHDZ werth
Waelder — WĔL der
Waka — WAH kuh
Walberg — WAWL berg
Waldeck — WAWL dĕk
Walker — WAWL ker
Wall — wawl
Waller — WAW ler
Wallis — WAH lĭs
Wallisville — WAH lĭs vĭl
Walnut Springs — wawl n't SPRĬNGZ
Walton — WAWL t'n
Warda — WAWR duh
Ward — wawrd
Waring — WĂR ĭng
Warren — WAW rĭn
Warrenton — WAW rĭn t'n
Washburn — WAHSH bern
Washington — WAHSH ĭng t'n
Waskom — WAHS k'm
Wastella — wahs TĔL uh
Watauga — wuh TAW guh
Water Valley — wah ter VĂ lĭ
Waxahachie — wawks uh HĂ chĭ
Wayland — WĀ l'nd
Weatherford — WĔ ther ferd
Weaver — WEE ver
Webb — wĕb
Webberville — WĔ ber vĭl
Webster — WĔBS ter
Weches — WEE chĭz
Weesatche — WEE săch
Weimar — WĪ mer
Weinert — WĪ nert
Weir — weer
Welch — wĕlch
Welcome — WĔL k'm
Weldon — WĔL d'n
Wellborn — WĔL bern
Wellington — WĔL ĭng t'n
Wellman — WĔL m'n
Wells — wĕlz
Weser — WEE zer
Weslaco — WĔS luh kō
West — wĕst
Westbrook — WĔST brōōk
Westfield — WĔST feeld
Westhoff — WĔS tawf
Westminster — wĕst MĬN ster
Weston — WĔS t'n
Westover — WĔS tō ver
Westphalia — wĕst FĀL yuh
West Point — wĕst POINT
Wharton — HWAWRT n
Wheeler — HWEE ler
Wheelock — HWEE lahk
White Deer — HWĪT Deer
Whiteface — HWĪT făs
Whiteflat — hwĭt FLĂT
Whitehouse — HWĪT hows
Whitesboro — HWĪTS buh ruh
Whitewright — HWĪT rīt
Whitharral — HWĪT hăr uhl
Whitney — HWĪT nĭ
Whitsett — HWĪT sĭt

Whitson — HWĪT s'n
Whitt — hwĭt
Whon — hwahn
Wichita — WĪCH ĭ taw
Wichita Falls — wĭch ĭ taw FAWLZ
Wickett — WĪ kĭt
Wiergate — WEER găt
Wilbarger — WĬL bahr ger
Wildorado — wĭl duh RĀ dō
Willacy — WĬL uh sĭ
Williamson — WĬL yuhm s'n
Willis — WĪ lĭs
Wills Point — wĭlz POINT
Wilmer — WĬL mer
Wilson — WĬL s'n
Wimberley — WĬM ber lĭ
Winchester — WĬN ches ter
Windom — WĬN d'm
Windthorst — WĬN thr'st
Winfield — WĬN feeld
Wingate — WĬN găt
Winkler — WĬNGK ler
Winnie — WĬ nĭ
Winnsboro — WĬNZ buh ruh
Winona — wĭ NŌ nuh
Winterhaven — WĬN ter hă v'n
Winters — WĬN terz
Wise — wīz
Wizard Wells — wĭ zerd WĔLZ
Woden — WŌD n
Wolfe City — wōōlf SĬT ĭ
Wolfforth — WŌŌL forth
Wood — wōōd
Woodbine — WŌŌD bīn
Woodlake — wōōd LĀK
Woodland — WŌŌD l'nd
Woodlawn — wōōd LAWN
Woodrow — WŌŌD rō
Woodsboro — WŌŌDZ buh ruh
Woodson — WŌŌD s'n
Woodville — WŌŌD v'l
Wortham — WERTH uhm
Wright City — rīt SĬT ĭ
Wrightsboro — RĪTS buh ruh
Wylie — WĪ lĭ

Y

Yancey — YĂN sĭ
Yantis — YĂN tĭs
Yoakum — YŌ k'm
Yorktown — YAWRK town
Young — yuhng
Youngsport — YUHNGZ pört
Ysleta — ĭs LĔT uh

Z

Zapata — zuh PAH tuh
Zavalla — zuh VĂL uh
Zephyr — ZĔF er
Zuehl — ZEE uhl

Diacritical markings are used as follows: bāle, băd, lĕt, rīse, rĭll, ōak, brōōd, fŏŏt. The stressed syllable is capitalized. Secondary stress is indicated by an underline as in Atascosa — ăt uhs KŌ suh. TEXAS ALMANAC ©.

ADVERTISER INDEX

GENERAL INDEX

- For cities and towns not listed in the index, see lists of towns on pages 385-412. For full information about cities, see "Cities and towns" entry in this index.
- For full information about counties, also look under the cities and towns in the county, as well as the "Counties" index entry.
- Page numbers in *italics* refer to photographs and artwork and their captions.

The Point Bolivar Lighthouse at Port Bolivar near Galveston. Photo by Jim Evans, CC by SA 4.0/ Wikimedia Commons

C

Dallas El Centro is the downtown campus of Dallas Community College. It opened its doors in 1966. Photo by Michael Barera, CC by SA 4.0/Wikimedia Commons

Feral hogs can be dangerous and problematic. Photo by USDA NRCS Texas

For CITIES and TOWNS not listed in the Index, see complete list on pages 385-412.

The rolling landscape of the Texas Hill Country. Photo by Zereshk, CC 3/Wikimedia Commons

For CITIES and TOWNS not listed in the Index, see complete list on pages 385–412.

LNG tanker passing Ingleside on the Bay through a channel into the Gulf of Mexico and beyond. Photo by Rosie Hatch

M

The lightning whelk is our state seashell. Photo by James St. John, CC 2/Flickr

An old oil pumpjack in West Texas. Photo by Jonathan Cutrer/jcutrer.com

For CITIES and TOWNS not listed in the Index, see complete list on pages 385-412.

The Western diamondback rattlesnake can reach lengths of up to seven feet. Photo by Peter Paplanus, CC 2/Flickr

For CITIES and TOWNS not listed in the Index, see complete list on pages 385-412.

For CITIES and TOWNS not listed in the Index, see complete list on pages 385–412.

A blooming agave in a West Texas sunrise. Photo by Jonathan Cutrer, jcutrer.com

For CITIES and TOWNS not listed in the Index, see complete list on pages 385-412.

A waterlily in the pond at the International Waterlily Collection in San Angelo. Photo by Jason Trbovich, CC2/Flickr

Fodor's 07

IRELAND

Where to Stay and Eat
for All Budgets

Must-See Sights
and Local Secrets

Ratings You Can Trust

Fodor's Travel Publications   New York, Toronto, London, Sydney, Auckland
www.fodors.com

FODOR'S IRELAND 2007

Editors: Robert I. C. Fisher, Constance Jones, Matthew Lombardi

Editorial Production: Eric B. Wechter

Editorial Contributors: John Daly, Alannah Hopkin, Anto Howard, Allison Morris

Maps: David Lindroth, *cartographer*; Rebecca Baer and Bob Blake, *map editors*

Design: Fabrizio La Rocca, *creative director*; Guido Caroti, *art director*; Ann McBride, *designer*; Moon Sun Kim, *cover designer*; Melanie Marin, *senior picture editor*

Production/Manufacturing: Angela L. McLean

Cover Photo (Early Celtic footpath on Skellig Island): Michael St. Maur Shell/Corbis

COPYRIGHT

Copyright © 2007 by Fodor's Travel, a division of Random House, Inc.

Fodor's is a registered trademark of Random House, Inc.

All rights reserved under International and Pan-American Copyright Conventions. Published in the United States by Fodor's Travel Publications, a division of Random House, Inc., and simultaneously in Canada by Random House of Canada Limited, Toronto. Distributed by Random House, Inc., New York.

No maps, illustrations, or other portions of this book may be reproduced in any form without written permission from the publisher.

ISBN-10: 1–4000–1717–3

ISBN-13: 978–1–4000–1717–1

ISSN: 0071–6464

SPECIAL SALES

This book is available at special discounts for bulk purchases for sales promotions or premiums. Special editions, including personalized covers, excerpts of existing books, and corporate imprints, can be created in large quantities for special needs. For more information, write to Special Markets/Premium Sales, 1745 Broadway, MD 6-2, New York, New York 10019, or e-mail specialmarkets@randomhouse.com.

AN IMPORTANT TIP & AN INVITATION

Although all prices, opening times, and other details in this book are based on information supplied to us at press time, changes occur all the time in the travel world, and Fodor's cannot accept responsibility for facts that become outdated or for inadvertent errors or omissions. So **always confirm information when it matters,** especially if you're making a detour to visit a specific place. Your experiences—positive and negative—matter to us. If we have missed or misstated something, **please write to us.** We follow up on all suggestions. Contact the Ireland editor at editors@fodors.com or c/o Fodor's at 1745 Broadway, New York, NY 10019.

PRINTED IN THE UNITED STATES OF AMERICA

10 9 8 7 6 5 4 3 2 1

Be a Fodor's Correspondent

Your opinion matters. It matters to us. It matters to your fellow Fodor's travelers, too. And we'd like to hear it. In fact, we *need* to hear it.

When you share your experiences and opinions, you become an active member of the Fodor's community. That means we'll not only use your feedback to make our books better, but we'll publish your names and comments whenever possible. Throughout our guides, look for "Word of Mouth," excerpts of your unvarnished feedback.

Here's how you can help improve Fodor's for all of us.

Tell us when we're right. We rely on local writers to give you an insider's perspective. But our writers and staff editors—who are the best in the business—depend on you. Your positive feedback is a vote to renew our recommendations for the next edition.

Tell us when we're wrong. We're proud that we update most of our guides every year. But we're not perfect. Things change. Hotels cut services. Museums change hours. Charming cafés lose charm. If our writer didn't quite capture the essence of a place, tell us how you'd do it differently. If any of our descriptions are inaccurate or inadequate, we'll incorporate your changes in the next edition and will correct factual errors at fodors.com *immediately.*

Tell us what to include. You probably have had fantastic travel experiences that aren't yet in Fodor's. Why not share them with a community of like-minded travelers? Maybe you chanced upon a pub or country house museum that you don't want to keep to yourself. Tell us why we should include it. And share your discoveries and experiences with everyone directly at fodors.com. Your input may lead us to add a new listing or highlight a place we cover with a "Highly Recommended" star or with our highest rating, "Fodor's Choice."

Give us your opinion instantly at our feedback center at www.fodors.com/feedback. You may also e-mail editors@fodors.com with the subject line "Ireland Editor." Or send your nominations, comments, and complaints by mail to Ireland Editor, Fodor's, 1745 Broadway, New York, NY 10019.

You and travelers like you are the heart of the Fodor's community. Make our community richer by sharing your experiences. Be a Fodor's correspondent.

Happy Landings!

Tim Jarrell, Publisher

CONTENTS

CLOSEUPS

IRELAND IN FOCUS

DUBLIN

6 <

CONTENTS

ABOUT THIS BOOK

Our Ratings

Sometimes you find terrific travel experiences and sometimes they just find you. But usually the burden is on you to select the right combination of experiences. That's where our ratings come in.

As travelers we've all discovered a place so wonderful that its worthiness is obvious. And sometimes that place is so experiential that superlatives don't do it justice: you just have to be there to know. These sights, properties, and experiences get our highest rating, **Fodor's Choice,** indicated by orange stars throughout this book.

Black stars highlight sights and properties we deem **Highly Recommended,** places that our writers, editors, and readers praise again and again for consistency and excellence.

By default, there's another category: any place we include in this book is by definition worth your time, unless we say otherwise. And we will.

Disagree with any of our choices? Care to nominate a place or suggest that we rate one more highly? Visit our feedback center at www.fodors.com/feedback.

Budget Well

Hotel and restaurant price categories from ¢ to $$$$ are defined in the opening pages of each chapter. For attractions, we always give standard adult admission fees; reductions are usually available for children, students, and senior citizens. Want to pay with plastic? **AE, D, DC, MC, V** following restaurant and hotel listings indicate if American Express, Discover, Diners Club, MasterCard, and Visa are accepted.

Restaurants

Unless we state otherwise, restaurants are open for lunch and dinner daily. We mention dress only when there's a specific requirement and reservations only when they're essential or not accepted—it's always best to book ahead.

Hotels

Hotels have private bath, phone, TV, and air-conditioning and operate on the European Plan (aka EP, meaning without meals), unless we specify that they use the Continental Plan (CP, with a Continental breakfast), Breakfast Plan (BP, with a full breakfast), or Modified American Plan (MAP, with breakfast and dinner) or are all-inclusive (including all meals and most activities). We always

list facilities but not whether you'll be charged an extra fee to use them, so when pricing accommodations, find out what's included.

Many Listings
- ★ Fodor's Choice
- ★ Highly recommended
- ⊠ Physical address
- ✛ Directions
- ⌖ Mailing address
- ☎ Telephone
- 🖷 Fax
- ⊕ On the Web
- ✉ E-mail
- 🎟 Admission fee
- ☉ Open/closed times
- ► Start of walk/itinerary
- Ⓜ Metro stations
- ▭ Credit cards

Hotels & Restaurants
- 🏨 Hotel
- 🛏 Number of rooms
- ☖ Facilities
- ⅋⊘⅃ Meal plans
- ✕ Restaurant
- ⌕ Reservations
- 🎩 Dress code
- ⌥ Smoking
- ⅋⅋ BYOB
- ✕🏨 Hotel with restaurant that warrants a visit

Outdoors
- 🏌 Golf
- ⛺ Camping

Other
- ☺ Family-friendly
- 🛈 Contact information
- ⇨ See also
- ⊠ Branch address
- ☞ Take note

WHAT'S WHERE

"My darlin' Dublin's dead and gone" goes the old ballad, and in many ways it is. Once the sleepy port city of a peripheral nation, it has been transformed into the thriving, trendsetting, triumphalist capital of Europe's fastest-growing economy during the past decade. But the visitor to Dublin, with a little work, can still uncover, behind the hustle and bustle of the "Celtic Tiger" economy, an intimate capital that's an utterly beguiling mix of elegant Georgian buildings, wrought-iron canals and bridges, an army of booksellers, and more than 1,000 pubs.

The heart of a city is its river, and Dublin's Liffey runs east to west to split the city neatly in two. This divide is not simply physical; the more affluent and slightly snobbish Southside can seem a world apart from the more working-class, sometimes blighted (but increasingly gentrified), fiercely proud Northside. North or south, Dublin is a great walking city, compact and easily navigated. The majority of areas of interest to the visitor can be found in the center of the **Southside**. **Christ Church Cathedral** sits atop the hill where Dublin is said to have been founded over a thousand years ago. It looks down with solemn authority on the river as it meanders up toward the merely 400-year-old splendor of **Trinity College**—whose Old Library is home to the *Book of Kells*—and its enclosed, cobblestoned campus.

Between these two sights—Christ Church to the west, Trinity College to the east—are the most famous sights of the city center. Here, you'll find the historic patina of Dublin buffed to its highest gloss around **Merrion Square**, the heart of the city's fabled 18th-century Georgian district. Here, **No. 29 Lower Fitzwilliam Street** can introduce you to the elegant period interiors of the 18th century.

Just to the west is "Museum Central"—a bevy of blocks home to the city's most august institutions, including the **National Gallery of Art**, the **National Museum of Archaeology and History**, **Leinster House**, the **National Library**, and the **National Museum of Natural History**. Continuing west, follow the throngs of upscale shoppers to **Grafton Street**, Dublin's most famous pedestrian street, running south to famed **St. Stephen's Green** and its gloriously Georgian **Newman House**. Head north instead and you'll hit **Temple Bar**, the area that has been transformed into Dublin's hottest scene-arena.

Crossing the famed Ha'Penny Bridge, you arrive in the **Northside**. This part of town once harbored the likes of James Joyce

and Brendan Behan, so you'll want to make a beeline for the **James Joyce Centre** and the **Dublin Writers Museum**. Other must-dos include the **Hugh Lane Municipal Gallery of Modern Art**, aglow with Picassos in a grand Palladian town house, and the grand **Custom House**. Today, Dublin is in the throes of its most dramatic transformation since the Georgian era. Both the old Dublin and the new are colossally entertaining.

DUBLIN ENVIRONS 	**Counties Meath, Louth, Kildare & Wicklow** Ireland's tumultuous history of conflict, myth, romance, and war are deeply present in the beautiful landscape of the Pale, the area immediately surrounding Dublin. County Meath is at the center of Irish Celtic mythology, and the ancient passage graves at **Newgrange** in the Boyne Valley and the Druidic stronghold of the **Hill of Tara** stand as solemn reminders of a vibrant pre-Christian Ireland. Stunning ancestral homes of the dwindling members of the Anglo-Irish ascendancy dot the landscape. The Palladian masterpiece of **Castletown House** in Celbridge, County Kildare, the Old Masters that virtually wallpaper the walls of **Russborough House**, and the studied grandeur of **Powerscourt House and Gardens** stand out as examples of the golden age of the Big House. From many of Dublin's wider streets you can still turn south and enjoy the verdant, rolling hills of the Wicklow Mountains, tantalizingly close to the capital's southern edge. The county of Wicklow contains arguably the most peaceful place in Ireland, the evocative monastic settlement at **Glendalough**. Wicklow's scenic wooded valley is also home to abbeys, castles, great houses, and gardens. Other delights await, including the 18th-century town of **Drogheda; Mellifont Abbey,** the first Cistercian monastery in Ireland; the high cross found at **Monasterboice**; and **Mount Usher Gardens.**
THE MIDLANDS 	**Counties Laois, Kildare, Offaly, Westmeath, Cavan, Monaghan, Leitrim, Longford, Roscommon, Galway & Tipperary** For the visitor and, indeed, for many Irish natives, the Midlands is the hidden Ireland. Most tourists stay in Dublin and then head straight for the West, neglecting to explore the largely untapped treasures of central Ireland. Perfect for the relaxed visitor who values the subtle over the spectacular, the flat, fertile plain at the center of Ireland is full of relatively undiscovered and uncrowded treasures such as historic towns, abbey ruins,

WHAT'S WHERE

grand houses, and a gamut of outdoor activities, including some of Europe's finest fishing. And don't miss a chance to cruise up the mighty Shannon at your leisure, docking at charming riverside hostelries.

The unique, chocolate-brown landscape of Irish boglands is prevalent around the town of **Shannonbridge,** in County Offaly. The glories of the fading Anglo-Irish tradition are still visible in old stately homes like **Strokestown House, Birr Castle Gardens,** and **Belvedere House Gardens;** in the romantic, neo-Gothic toy castles of **Charleville Forest** and **Tullynally;** and at those landmarks of Irish Palladian elegance, **Emo Court** and **Bellamont Forest.** Early-Christian Ireland found a spiritual home in parts of the Midlands, as witnessed by the beautifully melancholic monastic ruins of **Clonmacnoise.**

THE SOUTHEAST

Counties Carlow, Wexford, Kilkenny, Tipperary & Waterford

Ireland's "Sunny Southeast" is reputed to have the most average daily sunshine in Ireland. But beware, this is Ireland we're talking about: bring your raincoat anyway. Historically, the Southeast has been an invitation to invasion. First the Vikings and later the Normans heeded the call and changed the history of Ireland forever. County Wexford was named by the Vikings after the consort of their one-eyed god Odin; it still bears the stamp of those fearless, seagoing settlers in the steep pathways (and fine seafood) of **Wexford Town.**

Kilkenny is one of Ireland's finest medieval cities, known for its artisans and dominated by mighty **Kilkenny Castle,** home of the once-great Butler family for more than 500 years. **Waterford City** is home to the eponymous crystal, made at the confluence of three great rivers—the Nore, the Barrow, and the Suir. There's beautiful, rolling, 40-shades-of-green landscape in Tipperary's Golden Vale, but everything else is put in the shade by the stunning **Rock of Cashel.** Seat of the kings of Munster for 700 years, the extensive complex of medieval buildings is where St. Patrick said his first mass in Ireland.

THE SOUTHWEST

Counties Cork, Kerry, Limerick & Clare

If you've ever seen a stereotypical postcard of Ireland—you know the type: thatched, whitewashed cottage, stone walls, a donkey meandering down Main Street—chances are the picture was taken somewhere in the Southwest. **Killarney, Kinsale, Bantry**

Bay; even the names are evocative of everything Irish, and anyone who visits the counties of Cork, Kerry, and Limerick is guaranteed a visual and emotional taste of the Emerald Isle.

"The People's Republic of **Cork**" is what locals like to call this Rebel county, emphasizing their determination, Texas-style, to be different from the rest of the country. The county lends its name to Ireland's second-largest city, a port town that's full of canals and bridges and has a bustling shopping district, as well as the country's best food market. Many are seduced by Cork's quiet charm, but others find it a gray, unexciting place best considered a gateway to the Southwest.

Foodies head on to the historic seaside village of **Kinsale,** famous for its quality restaurants. But be warned: prices can be steep and service less stellar than you would expect for top dollar. An excursion to **Blarney Castle,** a few miles west of Cork city, is a must for first-time visitors, but bear in mind that the castle, although intact and impressively large, is not furnished. The coastal road from Kinsale to wooded **Glengarriff** takes you through the rugged splendor of West Cork. The wild, tempestuous sea is the undoubted star of the trip. Plan to meander along the many coastal roads, stopping to dawdle in small towns and villages, including **Timoleague,** with its romantically ruined waterside abbey and the brightly painted market town of **Clonakilty.**

Kerry, too, has a nickname: "The Kingdom." Its natives will argue with all comers that it remains the most beautiful and inspirational county in Ireland. Two great peninsulas dominate the county's wild, rocky coast. The Iveragh Peninsula, known to everyone as **the Ring of Kerry,** is arguably Ireland's most popular tourist drive. Once you've escaped Killarney, the Ring passes through tiny villages like **Sneem** to the magisterial, world's-end, rock islands of the **Skelligs** (once seen, never forgotten), before ending at **Kenmare,** a market town on the Kenmare River estuary jam-packed with craft shops and restaurants. The celebrity-popular (Julia Roberts has been spotted hiding out here) town of **Dingle** is the only town on the **Dingle Peninsula.** In deciding whether or not to visit the peninsula, weather is all important; if the mist comes down, give it a miss.

Frank McCourt's best-selling *Angela's Ashes* paints a grim picture of **Limerick City.** But Ireland's fourth-largest city, sitting proudly on the banks of the Shannon, although still beset

WHAT'S WHERE

with social problems, is home to the pocket-size Hunt Museum, whose compact interior has a magnificent collection of Celtic and medieval treasures. The surrounding countryside is not as wild and romantic as Cork or Kerry, but it does possess a couple of Ireland's most impressive stately homes, both open to lodgers: the Irish Gothic dottiness of **Glin Castle**, where you can dine with the owner and his wife, and the high Victorian Gothic **Adare Manor**, now an American-owned hotel.

THE WEST

Counties Clare, Galway & Mayo

"Haunting" might be the best word to describe the mysterious West, the least populated part of Ireland, where you can sometimes go a half day across the beautiful, barren landscape without sight or sound of another human being. A journey through the counties of Clare, Galway, and Mayo will take you from the limestone moonscape of the **Burren** to the majestic **Cliffs of Moher** to the looming **Twelve Bens**.

Galway is Ireland's fastest-growing city, a buzzing university town with a new high-style profile (wait until you see the "g" Hotel) and a different arts festival every second month. Galway is also the departure point for the sublime and spooky **Aran Islands**, celebrated by playwright J. M. Synge in *Riders to the Sea*. Here you'll hear lilting Irish spoken as a first language, just as it was a thousand years ago. Don't expect to be alone on the islands; tourism is now the chief industry here, with planes and ferries bringing day-trippers all summer long. (For a memorable stay, be sure to stay over one night.)

To the west are the wild shores and dark, brooding mountains of **Connemara**, loved by painters, writers, and seekers of silence. Towns like **Clifden** and **Leenane** (on Ireland's only fjord) ring out with the sound of pipe, whistle, and fiddle, as nearly every pub hosts wild and impromptu traditional-music sessions. It is another Gaeltacht (Irish-speaking area). **Westport** is an attractive market town on an inlet of Clew Bay, a wide expanse of sea dotted with islands and framed by mountains. Other must-dos include Lady Gregory's **Coole Park**; the picture-perfect village of **Kinvara**; the spectacular Gothic Revival house of **Kylemore Abbey**; and, for those with a generous budget, some of the grandest hotels in the land, including **Dromoland Castle** and **Ashford Castle**, the latter set near **Cong**, the village where *The Quiet Man* was filmed.

| THE NORTHWEST  | **Counties Sligo, Leitrim & Donegal** |

In a region of self-sufficiency and confidence, where the greeting you receive is all the warmer because of the dearth of visitors, you can observe the rural Northwest at work and play amid some of the most stunning natural backdrops anywhere.

If Galway belongs to Synge, then Sligo will forever be Yeats Country. Ireland's greatest poet drew much of his inspiration from the fickle skies that change color with a whisper of wind, the incredible spectrum of reds and purples thrown up by the gorse- and heather-filled fields surrounded by dry stone walls, and the unforgiving Atlantic Ocean, which beats a relentless rhythm against ancient rocks at Rosses Point.

The county is overwhelmingly rural, but lively **Sligo Town** is a charming oasis of culture and good food. County Donegal, in the far northwest, is ruggedly beautiful, with a rocky coast, turbulent surf, forlorn mountains, and windswept plateaus, full of legends about giants and witches, not to mention fairies known as *pishogues*. Heading north you'll find the waters of the astonishingly beautiful **Gartan Lough** and the 19th-century folly castle that lords over haunted **Glenveagh National Park**.

| NORTHERN IRELAND  | **Counties Down, Antrim, Derry, Tyrone & Fermanagh** |

The return of peace to Northern Ireland in the mid-1990s, after three decades of the Troubles, has at last opened up this relatively undiscovered country to the adventurous traveler. From the countless new bars and restaurants of reborn **Belfast** north to the geological freak of the **Giant's Causeway,** through the wild Sperrin Mountains, inside the medieval walls of historic **Derry,** and down to serene Lough Erene, the whole province seems to have come back to life. The region is also known for the beauty of the Antrim Coast, a truly spectacular one-day drive from Carncastle to Bushmills. Inland lie the Celtic homelands of the **Glens of Antrim,** one of the fabled redoubts of the "wee folk"; the rich farmlands and lake-lands of Fermanagh, where you'll experience the Irish farmer in all his stubborn splendor; the austere Mourne Mountains looking out over the Irish Sea; and many of the most beautiful 18th-century Anglo-Irish treasure houses, including **Florence Court**—its forest is reputedly haunted by the fairy world—and **Castle Coole, Castle Ward,** and **Mount Stewart.**

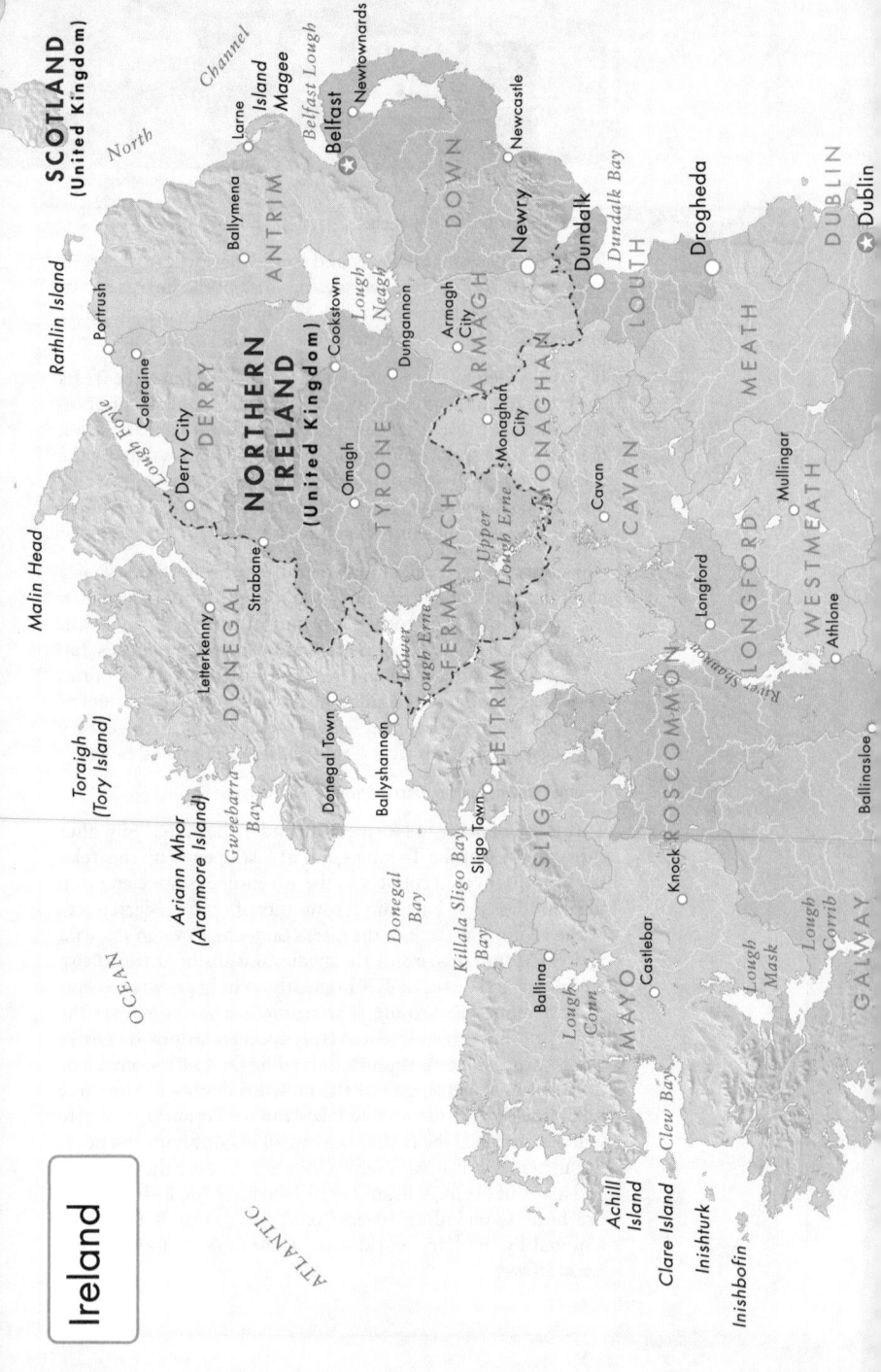

Ireland

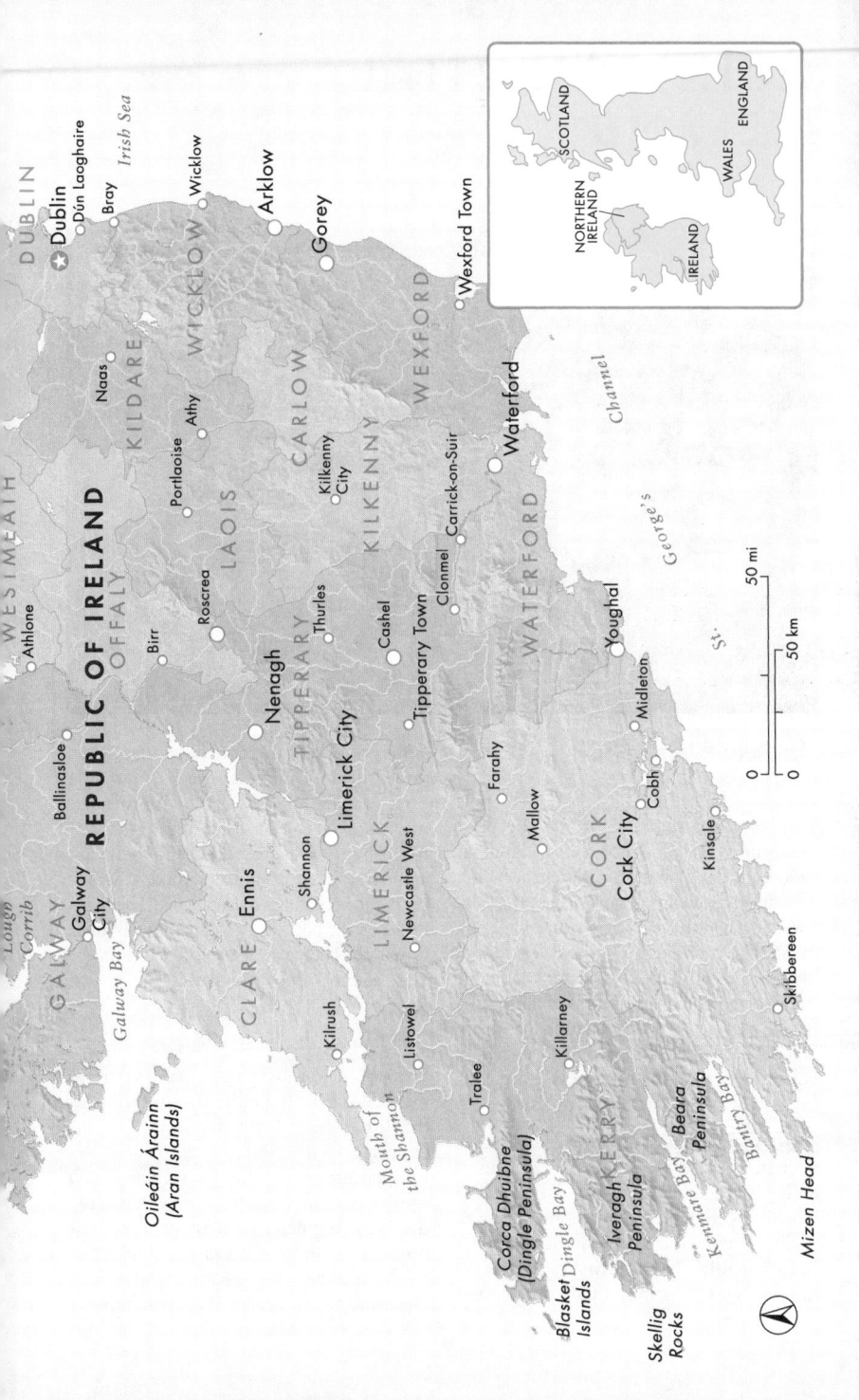

QUINTESSENTIAL IRELAND

The Pub: Pillar of Irish Social Life

It's been said that the pub is the poor man's university. If this is true, Ireland has more than 10,000 opportunities for higher education. Even if you only order an Evian, a visit to a pub (if not two or three) is a must. The Irish public house is a national institution—down to the spectacle, at some pubs, of patrons standing at closing time for the playing of Ireland's national anthem. Samuel Beckett would often repair to a pub, believing a glass of Guinness stout was the best way to ward off depression.

Pubs remain pillars of Irish social life—places to chat, listen, learn, gossip, and, of course, enjoy a throaty sing-along. Impromptu concerts often break out, and if you're really enjoying the *craic*—quintessentially Irish friendly chat and lively conversation—it's good form to buy a pint for the performers.

Wherever you go, remember that when you order a Guinness, the barman first pours it three-quarters of the way, then lets it settle, then tops it off and brings it over to the bar. The customer should then wait again until the top-up has settled, at which point the brew turns a deep black. The mark of a perfect pint? As you drink the liquid down, the brew will leave thin rings on the glass to mark each mouthful.

"Fleadhs" & Festivals

From bouncing-baby competitions to traditional-music festivals, the tradition of the *fleadh* (festival, pronounced "flah") is alive and well in Ireland year-round. Before you leave home, check on regional Irish tourist Web sites or, upon arrival, discuss the local happenings with local tourist boards or your hotel concierge. Music festivals rule the roost—Kinvara's Cuckoo Fleadh, Galway's Festival of Irish Popular

If you want to get a sense of contemporary Irish culture and indulge in some of its pleasures, start by familiarizing yourself with the rituals of daily life. These are a few highlights—things you can take part in with relative ease.

Music, the giant Fleadh Cheoil na hÉireann, and the World Irish Dancing Championships (held every April in Ennis) are some major events.

But there are also village festivals dedicated to hill-walking, fishing, poetry, art, and food; the Mullaghmore Lobster Festival in August always proves mighty tasty.

Keep A'Clappin & A'Tappin

Ceol agus craic, loosely translated as "music and merriment," are not simply recreations in Ireland. They are part of the very fabric of the national identity. Ask most Irish men or women in exile what they miss most about home and, more than likely, those words "the craic" will be uttered. And the beat and rhythm that accompany Irish fun are the "4/4" of the reel and the jig.

Wherever you go you'll find that every town buzzes with its own blend of styles

and sounds. In its most exciting form, "trad" music is an impromptu affair, with a single guitar or fiddle player belting out a few tunes until other musicians—flute, whistle, uilleann pipes, concertina, and bodhrán drum—seem to arrive out of the pub's dark corners and are quickly drawn into the unstoppable force of the session.

A check of local event guides will turn up a wealth of live entertainment—if you're lucky you'll find a world-class artist in performance whose talents are unsung outside a small circle of friends and fans.

On some nights, Dublin itself—with more than 120 different clubs and music pubs to choose from—almost becomes one giant traditional-music jam session. Where to head first? Just take a walk down Grafton Street and keep your ears open.

IF YOU LIKE . . .

The Most Beautiful Villages

Nearly everyone has a mind's-eye view of the perfect Irish village. Cozy huddles filled with charming calendar cottages, mossy churchyards, and oozing with thatched-roof-pewter-and-china-dog-atmosphere, these spots have a sense of once-upon-a-time-fied tranquility that not even tour buses can ruin. Should you be after medicine for over-tired nerves—a gentle peace in beautiful sur-roundings with a people so warm you'll be on first-name terms in five minutes—these will be your Arcadias. Many are so nestled away they remain the despair of motorists, but then no penciled itinerary is half as fun as stumbling upon these four-leaf clovers. Here are four of the most famous—but why not summon up courage, venture out on the lesser roads, and throw away the map?

Kinvara, Co. Galway. This village is picture-perfect, thanks to its gorgeous bay-side locale, great walks, and numerous pubs. North of the town is spectacularly sited Dun-guaire Castle, noted for its medieval-ban-quet evenings.

Cong, Co. Mayo. John Ford's *The Quiet Man* introduced this charmer to the world and the singular beauty of its whitewashed sin-gle-story cottages with tied-on thatched roofs.

Adare, Co. Limerick. Right out of a story-book, this celebrated village of low-slung Tudor cottages is adorned with ivied churches and a moated castle from the days when knighthood was in flower.

Lismore, Co. Tipperary. Set within some of Ireland's lushest pasturelands and lorded over by the Duke of Devonshire's castle, dreamy Lismore is popular with both ro-mantic folk and anglers (the sparkling Blackwater here teems with salmon).

New Irish Cuisine

To the astonishment—and delight—of many visitors, Ireland is in the throes of a food rev-olution. Not far out of Dublin you begin to see some of the reasons all about you: live-stock grazing in impossibly green fields, clear waters to spawn the freshest fish, and acres of produce thriving in the temperate climate. But it is Ireland's chefs who are the stars of the rapidly changing food scene. Hav-ing traveled the world, they're now produc-ing a Pan-European, postmodern cuisine. This New Irish cuisine—sometimes referred to as *cuisine Irelandaise*—marries simple treat-ments of traditional dishes, such as Clon-akilty black pudding, Clare nettle soup, Galway oysters, and Cong wild salmon, with exotic influences from Europe, North America, and the Pacific Rim. That noted, the Irish are a feisty lot not about to let new-fangled food get the better of them. Food in Ireland has become more international in flavor, but there has also been a renais-sance of authentically Irish cuisine based on regional cooking, thanks to the teachings and cookbooks of Myrtle Allen.

Thornton's, Dublin. Newer-than-now-nou-velle and grand-ol'-Irish ingredients col-lide in the kitchen of culinary wizard Kevin Thornton. Don't miss his moonshine sauce.

Ballymaloe House, Shanagarry. Presided over by Myrtle Allen, this famed outpost of Irish country-house cuisine uses marvelously fresh local produce, including seafood from the picturesque port of Ballycotton.

The Tannery, Dungarvan. Sir Andrew Lloyd Webber is just one foodie who raves over culinary wizard Paul Flynn's creations, in-cluding such gastro-pub fare as breast of wood pigeon on toasted brioche with truf-fle oil.

Celtic Sites

From rush hour on busy O'Connell Street in Dublin it's a long way to Tipperary's Cashel of the Kings, a group of ancient church relics—the largest in all Ireland—perched high above the plain on its famous rock. The journey is worth it, since it takes you back in time to the legendary days when Celtic Christianity conquered the isle of Eire. Beginning in the 5th century AD, hallowed shrines and monasteries sprung up across the land, often dotted with treasures sacred—the famous High Crosses, inscribed with biblical symbols and stories—and profane, such as the lofty Round Towers, lookouts for Viking raids. Just north of Dublin, around the Boyne Valley, you'll find three great sites: Tara, where "The Harp That Once Through Tara's Halls" played; Newgrange, once seat of the High Kings of Ireland; and Monasterboice, home to Muirdeach's High Cross, the finest in the land.

Clonmacnoise, Co. Offaly. This isolated monastery at the confluence of two rivers was famous throughout Europe as a center of learning. It's also a royal burial ground.

Glendalough, Co. Wicklow. A monastery founded by a hermit in the 6th century, attacked by Vikings in the 9th and 10th centuries, and plundered by English soldiers in the 12th century—your typical Irish ruins.

Rock of Cashel, Co. Tipperary. A cluster of ruins—cathedral, chapel, round tower—crowning a circular, mist-shrouded rock that rises from a plain.

Tara, Co. Meath. Fabled home of one of Ireland's titular High Kings, the ageless Hill of Tara has fired up people's imaginations from early Christians to Scarlett O'Hara.

The Stateliest Houses

Ireland's stately homes are either proud reminders of a shared history with Britain or symbols of an oppressive colonial past. If you're interested in luxurious pomp and reliving the decadence of yesteryear, there's no denying the magnificence of these country estates and lavish mansions, erected by the Anglo-Irish Protestant Ascendancy in the 17th, 18th, and 19th centuries. The wealthy settlers constructed ornate houses in various architectural styles, with Palladian designs popular in the first half of the 18th century, before the Neoclassical and neo-Gothic influences took over. In the last century, several majestic piles—notably Ashford Castle in Cong, Castle Leslie in Monaghan, and Dromoland Castle in Newmarket-on-Fergus—became hotels, so anyone can now enjoy a queen-for-a-stay fantasy.

Castle Leslie, Glaslough, Co. Monaghan. The most glorious hotel in Ireland, period. Hard to say which is more beautiful: the 1870 Gothic and Italianate structure or the reflection of it in the nearby lake.

Castle Ward, Co. Down. An architectural curiosity, in that it was built inside and out in two distinct styles, Classical and Gothic—perhaps because Viscount Bangor and his wife never could agree on anything.

Castletown House, Co. Kildare. Renaissance architect Andrea Palladio would surely have approved of this exceedingly large and grand Palladian country house.

Florence Court, Co. Down. With magnificent Georgian-period stuccoed salons, this shimmering white mansion is strikingly set against the Cuilcagh Mountains where, legend has it, you can hear the "song of the little people."

Natural Wonders

It's not always easy to conjure up leprechauns and druids in today's Ireland, but head to any of its famously brooding landscapes and those legendary times will seem like yesterday. With its romantic coastlines, wild bogs, and rugged seascapes, the Emerald Isle is especially rich in rugged, wildly gorgeous spectacle. Around its natural splendors, the countryside is dotted with villages where sheep outnumber residents by 100 to 1. Unfortunately, sheep don't also outnumber tourists.

The Aran Islands, Galway Bay. The islands battle dramatically with sea and storm and now welcome droves of visitors who fall under the spell of their brooding beauty.

The Skelligs, Ring of Kerry. Be warned: these spectacular pinnacles of rock soaring out of the sea will haunt you for days.

The Burren, Co. Clare. A 300-square-km (116-square-mi) expanse that is one of Ireland's strangest landscapes, the Burren stretches off as far as the eye can see in a gray, rocky, lunar landscape that becomes a wild rock garden in spring.

Cliffs of Moher, Co. Clare. One of Ireland's most breathtaking natural sights, these majestic cliffs stretch for 5 mi. At some points, the only thing separating you from the sea, 700 feet below, is a patch of slippery heather.

Giant's Causeway, Co. Antrim, Northern Ireland. There are equal measures of legend and science surrounding this rock formation—a cluster of 37,000-odd volcanic basalt pillars.

Glens of Antrim, Northern Ireland. This enchanted area is made up of nine wooded river valleys—don't miss Glenariff Forest Park, called "Little Switzerland" by Thackeray.

Retail Therapy

Once you get past all the traditional Irish leprechauns with a MADE IN CHINA sticker on their bottoms, you'll find that Ireland has some of Europe's finest-quality goods. Objects like a Donegal tweed hat or a hand-knit Aran sweater, a Belfast linen tablecloth or a piece of Waterford or Cavan crystal can be pricey but will last a lifetime. In Dublin look for antiques, vintage books, or au courant European and Irish fashions, many showcased at hot-cool shops like Costume and Platform. Galway has its share of galleries and offbeat boutiques and is a great spot for book shopping, especially the Irish antiquarian section at famed Kenny's Bookshop. Keep an eye open for signs indicating craft workshops, where independent craftspeople sell directly from their studios. The best of the North's traditional products, many made according to time-honored methods, include exquisite linen, laces, and superior handmade woolen garments. Traditional music CDs and the unadorned blackthorn walking stick are two good choices at the other end of the price scale.

John Molloy, Ardara. One of many shops in town where you can stake your claim to an heirloom Aran sweater or dream-woven Donegal tweed scarf.

O'Sullivan Antiques, Dublin. Mia Farrow and Liam Neeson are just two fans of this purveyor of 19th-century delights.

Waterford Crystal Factory and Shop, Waterford. Sunglasses might come in handy on a tour of this razzle-dazzle place.

Belleek Pottery, Co. Fermanagh. Any bride would be honored to receive a "Blessing Plate" of Parian china from this famed maker.

The Perfect Links

What makes Irish golf so great—and increasingly popular—is the natural architecture. The wild, wonderful coastline seems to be made for links golf; unlike many international courses, these courses have few forests, ponds, or short roughs. Most famous of these links courses is the celebrated Ballybunion. Fortunately, the courses can be played year-round—an asset in rainy Ireland. Pack plenty of sweaters and rain gear, and make sure you're in good shape: electric carts are available only at the most expensive courses. Golf clubs and bags can be rented almost anywhere. With the exception of the ancient Royal Belfast, all golf clubs in Ireland are happy to have visitors (and charge well for the privilege), and several tour operators have made golf excursions an art, so it's easy to have the golf trip of a lifetime. For information on the best courses in Ireland, see the Irish Greens chapter of this book.

Ballybunion Golf Club, Co. Kerry. On the Old Course, one of the country's classics, each and every hole is a pleasure.

The K Club, Co. Kildare. You'd have to be a nongolfer *and* a hermit not to have heard of this course, one of the country's most prestigious and demanding.

Portmarnock Golf Club, Co. Dublin. One of the nation's "Big Four" golf clubs (along with Ballybunion, Royal County Down, and Royal Portrush), Portmarnock is a links course near Dublin.

Royal County Down, Northern Ireland. A lunar landscape makes this course as beautiful as it is difficult.

Literary Haunts

Irish literature developed its distinctive traits largely because of Ireland's physical and political isolation. Yet the nation has produced a disproportionately large number of internationally famous authors for a country of its size. Ireland has produced no fewer than four Nobel prize winners—George Bernard Shaw, W. B. Yeats, Samuel Beckett, and Seamus Heaney. But the list of literary notables is a whole lot longer and includes James Joyce, Oscar Wilde, Sean O'Casey, Sean O'Faolain, Brian Friel, and Edna O'Brien. Indeed, the country's literary heritage is evident everywhere you go. In Dublin you'll find Joyce's Liffey; Dean Swift's cathedral; and the Abbey Theatre, a potent symbol of Ireland's great playwrights. An anthology of Irish verse is a travel guide in itself: Yeats opens up the county of Sligo; the Aran Islands were the inspiration of J. M. Synge; Cork inspired the works of Frank O'Connor; and Oliver Goldsmith was nurtured by Lissoy. Wherever you are in Ireland, its literary heritage is never far away.

Trinity College, Dublin. Founded by Queen Elizabeth I, this university provided the greats—Beckett, Wilde, Stoker—with 30 acres of stomping grounds.

Limerick City, Co. Limerick. Frank McCourt's *Angela's Ashes* has thousands heading here to tour Angela's city and partake of the tearfulness of it all.

Sligo Town, Co. Sligo. Take in the town where William Butler Yeats grew up, then visit his grave in Drumcliff to view his beloved mountain, Ben Bulben.

GREAT ITINERARIES

THE EAST & THE SOUTH

5 to 10 days

Dublin's literary charm and Georgian riches, and rugged County Wicklow and the historic Meath plains are all just a few hours' drive from each other. Here you'll find the Boyne Valley, the cradle of native Irish civilization—no one will want to miss sacred Tara, Kells, Newgrange, and Glendalough, all time-burnished sites that guard the roots of Irishness. More idyllic pleasures can be found at Powerscourt, the grandest gardens in the land. In the south you'll find fishing towns and bustling markets, coastal panoramas, and—just outside of crazy Killarney (oh, and it is crazy, an emerald-green Orlando)—stunning mountain-and-lake scenery.

Dublin

1 to 3 days. Dublin's pleasures are uncontainable. James Joyce's Dublin holds treasures for all sorts. Literary types: explore Trinity College, Beckett's stomping grounds, and its legendary *Book of Kells*. Visit key Joyce sites and the Dublin Writers Museum, and indulge in the Dublin Literary Pub Crawl. Joyce fanatics: arrive a week before Bloomsday (June 16) for Bloomstime celebrations. Literary or not, stroll around the city center and take in the elegant Georgian architecture around St. Stephen's Green, austere Dublin Castle, and the national treasures in the museums around Merrion Square and pedestrianized Grafton Street. Check out Temple Bar, Dublin's hip zone, and join locals in this city-of-1,000-pubs for a foamy pint in the late afternoon. Pubs are the center of Dublin activity, and the locals never lose their natural curiosity about "strangers."

You will frequently be asked, "Are you enjoying your holiday?" "Yes" is not good enough: What they're really after is your life story, and if you haven't got a good one you might want to make one up. Pay your respects by taking a tour of the ever-popular Guinness Brewery and Storehouse. Night options: catch a show at W. B. Yeats's old haunt, the Abbey Theatre; see some Victorian music hall shows at the Olympia Theatre; or listen to traditional or alternative music at a pub or other venue. Last call arrives early at pubs, even here, so if you're still revved, go to Lesson Street and hit the nightclubs. For a dose of unmitigated Irish enthusiasm, join the roaring crowds at Croke Park and see some traditional Gaelic football and hurling.

Boyne Valley & County Wicklow

2 days. Walt Disney couldn't have planned it better. The small counties immediately to the north, south, and west of Dublin—historically known as the Pale—seem expressly designed for the sightseer. The entire region is like an open-air museum, layered with legendary Celtic sites, spectacular gardens, and elegant Palladian country estates. First head to the Boyne Valley, a short trip north of the capital. Spend the morning walking among the Iron Age ruins of the rolling Hill of Tara. After a picnic lunch on top of the hill, drive through ancient Kells—one of the centers of early Christianity in Ireland—and then to Newgrange, famous for its ancient passage graves. One thousand years older than Stonehenge, the great white-quartz structure merits two or three hours. Spend the

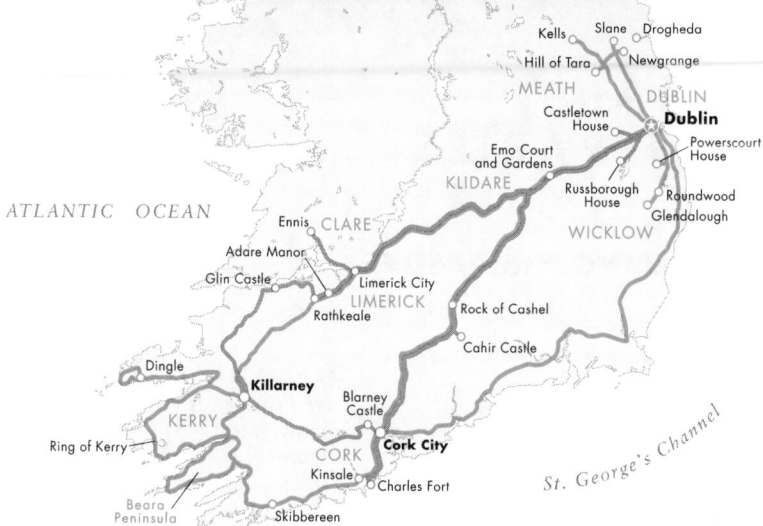

rest of your day driving through the low hills and valleys of County Meath and to Georgian-era Slane, a manorial town planned by the Conynghams. Dominating the town are elegant Slane Castle and 500-foot Slane Hill. Backtrack to Kells or continue to Drogheda and spend the night. The following day, head south of Dublin through the County Wicklow mountains. You might want to stop in one of the small, quiet towns along the Wicklow Way hiking trail and go for a short hike. Drive on to stately Powerscourt House, whose gardens epitomize the glory and grandeur of the Anglo-Irish aristocracy. From the profane to the sacred, head next to the "monastic city" of Glendalough and the medieval monastery of the hermit St. Kevin. Repair to Ireland's highest village, Roundwood, for lunch at the town's 17th-century inn.

West Cork & Kerry

4 days. Head about 250 km (155 mi) southwest to Cork City, filled with tall Georgian houses and old quays and perfect for a half day of walking. The place has few don't-miss attractions, but that's not the point: unlike many other towns, Cork is very much alive. As Europe's 2005 City of Culture, it has a progressive university, art galleries, offbeat cafés, a formidable pub

scene, and some of the country's best traditional music. Drive south to Kinsale, once heralded as the gourmet capital of Ireland, an old fishing town turned resort, with many good restaurants. A slow three- or four-hour drive along the coast and up through the small towns of West Cork takes you through the kind of landscape that inspired Ireland's nickname, the Emerald Isle. Spend the night in the market town of Skibbereen. Next morning, cross into County Kerry and head straight for Killarney, at the center of a scattering of azure lakes and heather-clad mountains. Although it has been almost transformed into a Celtic theme park by a flood of tourists, it's a good base for exploring your pick of three great Atlantic-pounded peninsulas: the strikingly desolate Beara Peninsula, the Ring of Kerry, and the Dingle Peninsula. All offer stunning ocean views, hilly landscapes (like the Macgillycuddy's Reeks mountains), and welcoming towns with good B&Bs. To do justice to the fabulous views of the Ring, you need a minimum of two days, especially if traveling by bus. The five-hour drive back to Dublin takes you through Limerick City and the lakes of the Midlands.

GREAT ITINERARIES

IRISH MANORS & CASTLES

5 to 7 days

Here's your chance to play lord of the manor. A tour of Ireland's magnficent manors and castles is just the thing if you have an interest in architecture, interior design, and history (including the sinister and macabre kind). You might even decide to splurge and stay at one of the grand country-house hotels along the way. It's best to go between June and September, when most houses are open.

Dublin & Environs

2 to 3 days. Right in the center of Dublin are historic Dublin Castle and the elegant, 18th-century Royal Hospital Kilmainham. Walk along the inner-city stretch of the River Liffey for excellent views of two of architect James Gandon's Georgian masterpieces, the Custom House and the Four Courts. South of the river, Georgian domestic town architecture is at its best on Merrion Square and Fitzwilliam Street. On Day 2 go west of Dublin to Castletown House, one of Ireland's most magnificent Georgian structures, in Celbridge, County Kildare; it has some striking interiors, including halls with Rococo stucco work by the Lafranchini brothers. From here head south into County Wicklow to visit Russborough House near Blessington, which flaunts the longest facade of any house in Ireland. Modesty did not suddenly strike when it came to decorating the interior, where Baroque exuberance was given free rein. The salons are still hung with Sir Alfred Beit's Old Master paintings, although his great Vermeer is now at Dublin's National Gallery.

The Road to Cork

1 day. Leave early from Dublin, heading southwest to Cork. On the way, stop in Portarlington to visit the Emo Court and Gardens, another James Gandon design and one of the finest large country houses near Dublin that is open to the public. You'll pass the venerated holy site of the Rock of Cashel on your way to Cahir Castle; take in its spectacular vista. Continue to Cork City. If you have time, stop at the coastal bulwark Charles Fort, about a half hour south of the city. Spend the night in Cork.

Around Killarney

2 to 3 days. From Cork City, a short detour off the main road to Killarney leads to ruined 15th-century Blarney Castle. Here you can pucker up for its famous stone and, ostensibly, be reciprocated with the gift of the gab. Nearby Blarney House was built in 1784, in Scottish baronial style. In Killarney National Park, Muckross House, a mid-Victorian manor, is worth seeing for its grounds full of flowers and for its outstanding rock garden. After a night in Killarney, head north to the Shannon estuary, on whose shore looms Glin Castle, the fairytale neo-Gothic ancestral home of the FitzGerald clan. This is not only one of Ireland's most enchanting houses, it is also one of its most remarkable hotels. Then head 40 km (25 mi) to the east to see one of Ireland's most beauteous villages, Adare, with requisite castle, friary, thatched cottages, and a great country-house hotel, Adare Manor, a mock-castle that can also welcome you just for tea or dinner. Stay here overnight or in nearby Limerick City or Ennis.

THE WEST & THE NORTH

6 to 7 days

"To hell or to Connaught" was the choice given the native population by Cromwell, and indeed the harsh, barren landscape of parts of the west and north might appear cursed to the eye of an uprooted farmer. But there's an appeal in the very wildness of Counties Clare, Galway, Mayo, Sligo, and Donegal, with their stunning, steep coastlines hammered and shaped for aeons by the Atlantic. Here, in isolated communities, you'll hear locals speaking Irish as they go about their business. The arrival of peace has opened the lush pastures of long-suffering Northern Ireland to travelers.

Galway & Clare

2 days. A three-hour drive west from Dublin leads straight to the 710-foot-high Cliffs of Moher, perhaps the single most impressive sight in Ireland. Using the waterside village of Ballyvaughan as your base, spend a day exploring the lunar landscape of the harsh, limestone Burren. In spring it becomes a mighty rock garden of exotic colors. The next morning, head north out of Ballyvaughan toward Galway City. On the way you'll pass 2-million-year-old Ailwee Cave and the picture-perfect village of Kinvara. Galway City, spectacularly overlooking Galway Bay, is rapidly growing, vibrant, and packed with culture and history. If time allows, drive west to Ros an Mhil (Rossaveal) and take a boat to the fabled Aran Islands. Spend the night in Galway City.

North & West to Donegal

2 days. Northwest of Galway City is tiny Clifden, with some of the country's best Atlantic views. From here, head east through one of the most beautiful stretches of road in Connemara—through Kylemore Valley, home of Kylemore Abbey, a huge Gothic Revival castle. After seeing the castle and its grounds, head north through tiny Leenane (the setting of the hit Broadway play, *The Beauty Queen of Leenane*) and on to the most attractive town in County Mayo, Westport. It's the perfect spot to spend the night: the 18th-century planned town is on an inlet of Clew Bay, and some of the west coast's finest beaches are nearby. Your drive north leads through the heart of Yeats Country in Sligo. Just north of cozy Sligo Town is the stark outline of a great hill, Ben Bulben, in whose shadow poet Yeats wanted to be buried. South of town, follow the signposted Yeats Trail around woody, gorgeously scenic Lough Gill. Continuing north, you pass Yeats's simple grave in unassuming Drumcliff, a 3000 BC tomb in Creevykeel, and small Donegal Town. Head north through Letterkenny on the tight, meandering roads, into the windswept mountains and along the jagged coastline of northern Donegal. A trip on a fishing boat to one of the many islands off the coast is a must, as is a slow drive along the coast from the Gweedore Headland, covered with heather and gorse, to the former plantation village of Dunfanaghy (Dun Fionnachaid), heart of Donegal's Irish-speaking Gaeltacht region and a friendly place to spend the night.

Northern Ireland

2 days. Begin exploring the province in historic, divided Derry City (called Londonderry by Unionists), Northern Ireland's second city. A few hours are sufficient to take in the views from the old city walls and the fascinating murals of the Catholic Bogside district. Continue on to two of the region's main attractions, the 13th-century Norman fortress of Dunluce Castle and the Giant's Causeway, shaped from volcanic rock some 60 million years ago. Heading south, sticking to coastal roads for the best scenery, you'll soon pass through the Glens of Antrim, whose green hills roll down into the sea. Tucked in the glens are a number of small, unpretentious towns with great hotels. Early in the morning, head straight to Northern Ireland's capital, Belfast. The old port city, gray and often wet, is a fascinating place, recovering from years of strife. A morning of driving through its streets will have to suffice before you head west through the rustic, pretty countryside to Lough Neagh, the largest lake in the British Isles. It's time to head back to Dublin, but if you're ahead of schedule, take the longer route that passes through the glorious Mountains of Mourne and around icy-blue Carlingford Lough.

BY CAR: SOME TIPS

1. Road signs are generally in both Irish and English, although in Gaeltacht (Irish speaking) areas new laws now mandate signs in Irish *only* (most such regions are located in the counties along the Western coast of the country, Donegal and Connemara in particular). Thus, if traveling in these areas, invest in a good, detailed map with both Irish and English names.

2. Another new law has mandated that all speed limit signs now need to be posted in kilometers—not miles—per hour (a bit of a nuisance, as most cars have speedometers in miles). Signage is currently being changed throughout Ireland.

3. Remember to slow down on smaller, countryside lanes and roads: traffic jams can sometimes be caused by flocks of sheep and cattle, not cars.

4. Brand-new divided highways are the fastest way to get from one point to another, but use caution: highways sometimes end as abruptly as they begin.

WHEN TO GO

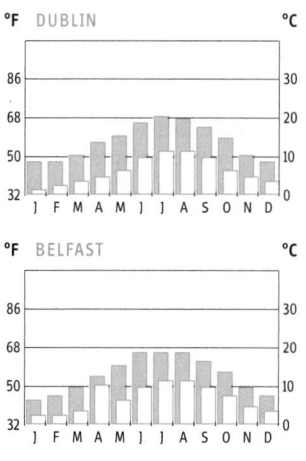

°F DUBLIN °C

°F BELFAST °C

In summer the weather is pleasant, the days are long (daylight lasts until after 10 in late June and July), and the countryside is green. But there are crowds in popular holiday spots, and prices for accommodations are at their peak. As British and Irish school vacations overlap from late June to mid-September, vacationers descend on popular coastal resorts in the south, west, and east. Unless you're determined to enjoy the short (July and August) swimming season, it's best to visit Ireland outside peak travel months. Fall and spring are good times to travel (late September can be dry and warm, although the weather can be unpredictable). Seasonal hotels and restaurants close from early or mid-November until mid-March or Easter. During this off-season, prices are lower than in summer, but your selection is limited, and many minor attractions close. St. Patrick's Week gives a focal point to a spring visit, but some Americans may find the saint's-day celebrations a little less enthusiastic than the ones back home. Dublin, however, has a weekend-long series of activities, including a parade and the Lord Mayor's Ball. If you're planning an Easter visit, don't forget that most theaters close from Thursday to Sunday of Holy Week (the week preceding Easter), and all bars and restaurants, except those serving hotel residents, close on Good Friday. Many hotels arrange Christmas packages. Mid-November to mid-February is either too cold or too wet for all but the keenest golfers, although some of the coastal links courses are playable.

Climate

🚩 Forecasts **Irish Meteorological Service** (☎ 01/806–4200 ⊕ www.meteireann.ie). **Marine Call** (☎ 0891/505–365 for marine forecasts). **Weathercall** (☎ 0891/500–427 for Northern Ireland forecasts). **Weather Channel Connection** (☎ 900/932–8437 95¢ a minute from a Touch-Tone phone ⊕ www.weather.com).

ON THE
CALENDAR

		Hundreds of festivals and events are held annually in Ireland. Here are some of the better known and better attended. If you plan to visit during one of them, book well in advance.
WINTER	Dec.	On December 26, St. Stephen's Day, the traditional Wren Boys in blackface and fancy dress wander through towns asking for money and singing (much of the money goes to charity); the most extravagant celebration takes place on Sandymount Green in Dublin.
SPRING	Mar.	The Adare Jazz Festival fills the town's pubs with great music. Castle Ward Opera (⊕ www.castlewardopera.com) performs at Belfast's Grand Opera House. For three weeks on either side of St. Patrick's Day, the Celtic Spring Festival brings theater, rock music, and an Irish-language festival to Derry. Ireland's major St. Patrick's event is the Dublin Festival and Parade (⊕ www.stpatricksday.ie), which includes fireworks and bands from the United States.
		For 10 days, the Dublin Film Festival (⊕ www.dublinfilmfestival.com) presents films from Ireland and around the world. Dublin's Feis Ceoil is a festival of traditional Irish music. Bands of every stripe march in step in the Limerick International Band Festival, which follows the city's St. Patrick's Day celebrations.
	Apr.	The World Irish Dancing Championships (⊕ www.clrg.ie/oireachtas.htm) are held in early April, with five days of furious dancing and more than 3,000 contenders. One of the biggest Celtic events, the Féilte Pan Cheilteach (⊕ homepage.eircom.net/~panceltic2002), or Pan Celtic Festival, kicks off for a week in late April, in Letterkenny, County Donegal. The Antiques and Collectibles Fair brings dealers from all parts of Ireland to Dublin. With Easter comes one of the biggest events of the horse-racing calendar, the two-day Fairyhouse Easter Racing Festival, about 19 km (12 mi) north of Dublin.
	May	Twenty-one days of concerts, competitions (including a marathon), and exhibitions take place during the Belfast Civic Festival. Heritage properties and private gardens open to the public during the County Wicklow Garden Festival. The Fleadh Nua, the annual festival of traditional Irish music, song, and dance, takes place in Ennis, County Clare. During the first week of May, Dingle hosts a grand festival celebrating storytelling, song, music, and dance: the Féile na Bealtaine (⊕ www.feilenabealtaine.ie).
		The Galway Early Music Festival (⊕ www.galwayearlymusic.com) fills Galway City with pre-Baroque Irish and European music. Sixty-plus traditional music sessions take place over the first weekend in

		May at **Kinvara's Cuckoo Fleadh**. The **Murphy's International Mussel Fair** in Bantry, County Cork, celebrates the peak of the harvest for this delicacy. Theater, literary readings, and plenty of music fill the calendar of the **Sligo Arts Festival** (⊕ www.sligofestival.com).
SUMMER	June	Devoted Joyceans celebrate *Ulysses* on June 16 (the day the novel was set, in 1904) in Dublin with **Bloomsday**. The **Budweiser Irish Derby** at the Curragh Racecourse, County Kildare, is the biggest horse race of the year. Carlow celebrates the arts in its annual **Éigse Carlow Arts Festival**.
		Ballycastle puts on a lively three-day music and dance festival, the **Fleadh Amhrán agus Rince**. **Listowel Writers' Week,** one of Ireland's leading literary festivals, brings writers, poets, and lovers of literature together in this County Kerry town. The **Weavers' Fair and Vintage Weekend** comes to Ardara in County Donegal; the fair has as much to do with music and dance as it does with homespun.
	July	On July 12 towns throughout the north commemorate the 1690 **Battle of the Boyne**. The **Coalisland International Music Festival** (⊕ www.geocities.com/coalisland) attracts folk bands from all over Europe to County Tyrone. On the last Sunday in July, thousands of pilgrims climb the rocky slopes of **Croagh Patrick** in County Mayo to honor Saint Patrick. The **Eagle Wing Festival** at Groomsport in County Down celebrates 300 years of links with America.
		Galway is jam-packed for the two-week **Galway Arts Festival** (⊕ www.galwayartsfestival.ie), which includes theater, film, music, and a parade. Bachelors from throughout the country strut their stuff in Mullingar for the **Guinness International Bachelor Festival**. The streets and pubs of Dublin's Temple Bar district resound day and night to jazz and blues during the **Temple Bar Blues Festival**.
	Late July–early Aug.	Across the whole of County Derry, the country's best musicians take part in the **Festival of Popular Irish Music**. The **Galway Races** start the day after Galway's Arts Festival ends, for a week of revelry. Would-be beauty queens come to County Donegal from as far away as Australia to compete in the **Mary of Dungloe International Festival**.
	Aug.	The **Ballyshannon Folk and Traditional Music Festival** (⊕ www.ballyshannonfolkfestival.com) in County Donegal is one of the best trad fests of the season. Kinvara, County Galway, hosts the **Cruinniú na mBád** (Festival of the Gathering of the Boats), in which brown-sailed hookers (a type of craft indigenous to the regions around Galway) are laden with turf and race across Galway Bay.

ON THE
CALENDAR

		The highlight of the traditional-music calendar is the Fleadh Cheoil na hÉireann (⊕ www.clonmelfleadh.com), held during the last weekend in August or the first weekend in September. The extravaganza is held in varying towns across the country and showcases some 4,000 traditional musicians in a dazzling array of céilithe, concerts, sessions, and street entertainments. The Kerrygold Dublin Horse Show attracts a fashionable set to watch the best in Irish bloodstock. The Kilkenny Arts Week is a marvelous assemblage of classical music, art exhibits, and theater. If you're in the neighborhood of Ballycastle, County Antrim, don't miss Ireland's oldest fair, Oul' Lammas Fair, held every year since 1606 on the last Monday and Tuesday in August.
		The three-day Puck Fair (⊕ www.puckfair.ie), in Killorglin, County Kerry, retains vestiges of old pre-Christian fertility rites, like the garlanding with flowers of a large billy goat to signify his being crowned king. The world-famous Rose of Tralee International Festival (⊕ www.roseoftralee.ie) selects a "Rose of Tralee" from an international lineup of young women of Irish descent. The competition coincides with the Tralee Races. Everyone's got the beat at the Waterford Spraoi (⊕ www.spraoi.com), an international street-theater festival.
FALL Sept.		The Appalachian and Bluegrass Music Festival traces Appalachian music back to Ireland at the Ulster American Folk Park in Omagh, County Tyrone. Indulge in the food of the gods at the Galway International Oyster Festival (⊕ www.galwayoysterfest.com).
		Troupes from all over Europe compete at Waterford's International Festival of Light Opera. Single people of all ages flock to County Clare for the Lisdoonvarna Matchmaking Festival in the hopes of finding a spouse—or at least a date.
Oct.		At the Cork Film Festival (⊕ www.corkfilmfest.org), feature-length films share the bill with shorts. The festival usually takes place during the second week of October. The Cork Jazz Festival (⊕ www.corkjazzfestival.com) draws jazz lovers late in the month. Runners fill the streets of Dublin in the Dublin City Marathon. The Dublin Theatre Festival (⊕ www.dublintheatrefestival.com) puts on 10 international productions, 10 Irish plays, a children's festival, and a fringe of 60-plus plays. The Wexford Opera Festival (⊕ www.wexfordopera.com) brings in international stars to perform three rarely heard operas in a tiny Georgian theater.
Nov.		The Belfast Festival at Queen's University (⊕ www.belfastfestival.com) is the city's preeminent arts festival, with hundreds of music, film, theater, and ballet performances.

ANCESTOR HUNTING

Over 46 million Americans, and millions more around the world, claim Irish ancestry, and the desire to trace those long-lost roots back in the "auld sod" can run deep. Here are some pointers for how you can make your trip to Ireland a journey into your past.

Before You Go

The more you can learn about your ancestors before you arrive in Ireland, the more fruitful your search is going to be once you're on Irish soil. Crucial facts include:

- The name of your ancestor who emigrated from Ireland
- Names of that ancestor's parents and spouse
- His or her date of birth, marriage, and death (even approximate dates help)
- County and parish of origin in Ireland
- Religious denomination

The first place to seek information is directly from members of your family (usually the older generation). Even if the details are hazy, a grandparent or a great aunt with a story to tell can be the source of important clues. And relatives who don't know any family history may have documents stored away that can help with your sleuthing—old letters, wills, diaries, birth certificates, photos.

If family resources aren't leading you anywhere, try turning to the Mormon Church. They've made it their mission to collect mountains of genealogical information, much of which it makes available free of charge at the Web site ⊕familyresearch.org; plug in the name a relative, and you may find records that include parents' names and places of origin. You can also visit one of hundreds of research centers throughout the U.S. (addresses for which are available on the Web site).

On the Ground in Ireland

Ancestor hunters have long traveled throughout Ireland to comb parish church records, but most of these records are now available on microfilm in Dublin at the **National Library** (✉ Kildare St. ☎ 01/603–0200 ⊕ www.nil.ie). The library is a great place to begin your hunting; you can consult a research adviser there free of charge.

Civil records dating back to 1865 are available at the **General Register Office** (✉ 8-11 Lombard St. East, Dublin ☎ 01/635–4423 ⊕ www.groireland.ie). Records for Anglican marriages date from 1845. The **National Archives** (✉ Bishop Street, Dublin ⊕ www.nationalarchives.ie) has census records, and like the National Library, provides free genealogy consultations.

For Northern Ireland, you can find information at the **Centre for Migration Studies** at the Ulster American Folk Park (✉ Mellon Rd, Castletown, Omagh ☎028/8225–6315 ⊕ www.qub.ac.uk/cms/) and the **Public Records Office** (✉ Balmoral Avenue, Belfast ☎ 028/9025–5905 ⊕ www.proni.gov.uk).

None of these places has their actual records available on line, but their Web sites provide information about genealogical research; reading up in advance will shorten your learning curve once you're there. The National Library site is particularly helpful.

If you'd rather not spend your vacation in a record hall, you can hire a professional to do your spadework. The Association of Professional Genealogists in Ireland (⊕www.irishgenealogy.ie) will present you with a "package of discovery" upon your arrival. The *Irish Times* newspaper also has ancestor-hunting resources (⊕ www.ireland.com/ancestor). And the National Library provides references for professionals.

IRISH FAMILY NAMES

Antrim
Lynch
McDonnell
McNeill
O'Hara
O'Neill
Quinn

Armagh
Hanlon
McCann

Carlow
Kinsella
Nolan
O'Neill

Cavan
Boylan
Lynch
McCabe
McGovern
McGowan
McNally
O'Reilly
Sheridan

Clare
Aherne
Boland
Clancy
Daly
Lynch
McGrath
McInerney
McMahon
McNamara
Molon(e)y
O'Brien
O'Dea
O'Grady
O'Halloran
O'Loughlin

Cork
Barry
Callaghan
Cullinane
Donovan
Driscoll
Flynn
Hennessey
Hogan
Lynch
McCarthy
McSweeney
Murphy
Nugent
O'Casey
O'Cullane
(Collins)

O'Keefe
O'Leary
O'Mahony
O'Riordan
Roche
Scanlon
Sheridan

Derry
Cahan
Hegarty
Kelly
McLaughlin

Donegal
Boyle
Clery
Doherty
Friel
Gallagher
Gormley
McGrath
McLoughlin
McSweeney
Mooney
O'Donnell

Down
Lynch
McGuinness
O'Neil
White

Dublin
Hennessey
O'Casey
Plunkett

Fermanagh
Cassidy
Connolly
Corrigan
Flanagan
Maguire
McManus

Galway
Blake
Burke
Clery
Fah(e)y
French
Jennings
Joyce
Kelly
Kenny
Kirwan
Lynch
Madden
Moran
O'Flaherty
O'Halloran

Kerry
Connor
Fitzgerald
Galvin
McCarthy
Moriarty
O'Connell
O'Donoghue
O'Shea
O'Sullivan

Kildare
Cullen
Fitzgerald
O'Byrne
White

Kilkenny
Butler
Fitzpatrick
O'Carroll
Tobin

Laois
Dempsey
Doran
Dunn(e)
Kelly
Moore

Leitrim
Clancy
O'Rourke

Limerick
Fitzgerald
Fitzgibbon
McKeough
O'Brien
O'Cullane
(Collins)
O'Grady
Woulfe

Longford
O'Farrell
Quinn

Louth
O'Carroll
Plunkett

Mayo
Burke
Costello
Dugan
Gormley
Horan
Jennings
Jordan
Kelly
Madden
O'Malley

Meath
Coffey
Connolly
Cusack
Dillon
Hayes
Hennessey
Plunkett
Quinlan

Monaghan
Boylan
Connolly
Hanratty
McKenna
McMahon
McNally

Offaly
Coghlan
Dempsey
Fallon
Malone
Meagher
(Maher)
Molloy
O'Carroll
Sheridan

Roscommon
Fallon
Flanagan
Flynn
Hanley
McDermot
McKeough
McManus
Molloy
Murphy

Sligo
Boland
Higgins
McDonagh
O'Dowd
O'Hara
Rafferty

Tipperary
Butler
Fogarty
Kennedy
Lynch
Meagher
(Maher)
O'Carroll
O'Dwyer
O'Meara
Purcell
Ryan

Tyrone
Cahan
Donnelly
Gormley
Hagan
Murphy
O'Neill
Quinn

Waterford
Keane
McGrath
O'Brien
Phelan
Power

Westmeath
Coffey
Dalton
Daly
Dillon
Sheridan

Wexford
Doran
Doyle
Hartley
Kavanagh
Keating
Kinsella
McKeogh
Redmond
Walsh

Wicklow
Cullen
Kelly
McKeogh
O'Byrne
O'Toole

Dublin

School kids in Dublin's Merrion Square

WORD OF MOUTH

"'Tis a great day for any tourist if they kick off their Ireland trip with a visit to darlin' Dublin. Let Heaven send what weather it may—I think the last time Dubliners enjoyed three days of sunshine in a row was back in Viking times—the city can't be beat as a curtain raiser to Erin's Isle. Whether it be lovely Georgian houses or quaint pubs or fetching folks ye'd be after, Dublin's the place to savor the 'pluck' of the Irish. For conversation, sit at the bar and ask for great oysters. Put a little horseradish on them and count your blessings." –WiseOwl

WELCOME TO DUBLIN

Ha'penny Bridge over the Liffey

TOP REASONS TO GO

★ **Georgian elegance:** Dublin's signature architectural style makes its most triumphant showing in Merrion, Fitzwilliam, Montjoy, and Parnell squares.

★ **The Guiness Brewery and Storehouse:** A high-tech museum tells the story of Guinness, Dublin's black blood. At the top, the Gravity Bar has the city's best views.

★ **The Chester Beatty Library:** This stunning collection of Islamic and Far Eastern art—one of the finest in the Western world—has an elegant home in the clock tower of Dublin Castle.

★ **Temple Bar:** This hyper-trendy neighborhood has two identities: quirky shopping district by day, raucous pub quarter by night.

★ **Trinity College:** An oasis of books, granite, and grass sits at the heart of the city. Highlights are the exquisitely illustrated *Book of Kells* and the ornate Long Room.

1 **The Southside.** Between **Christ Church Cathedral** and **Trinity College** lies a concentration of famous sights. **Merrion Square** is the heart of the Georgian district; to its west, four major museums sit side by side. Southwest from there is quaint **St. Stephen's Green**, which connects to Trinity via stylish, pedestrian-only **Grafton Street**.

2 **Temple Bar.** The cobblestone streets and small lanes bounded by Wellington Quay and Dame Street have been transformed into Dublin's trendiest neighborhood. The nightlife doesn't stop at "last call," and on weekends the streets are packed with young people from all over Europe.

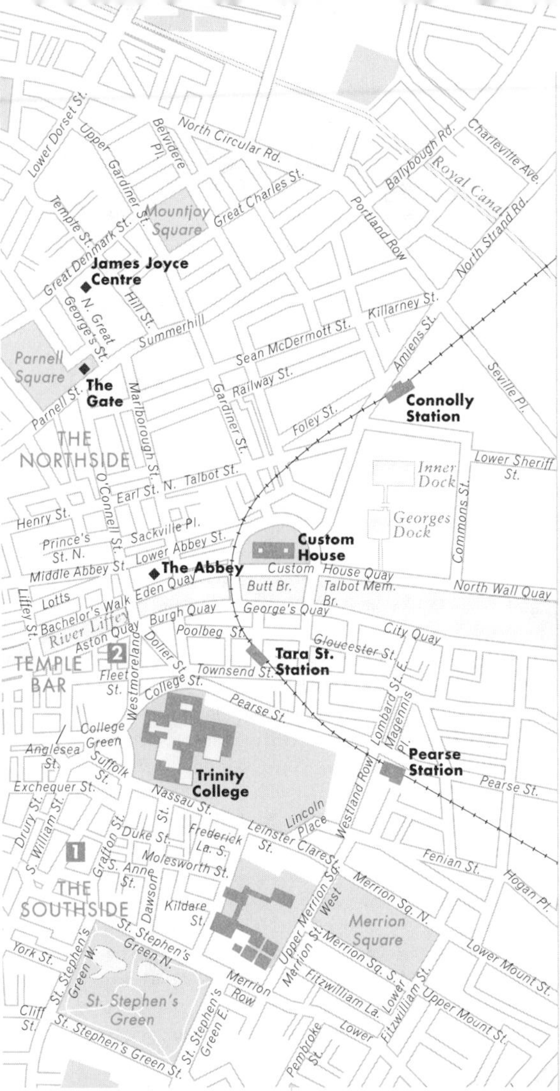

GETTING ORIENTED

Despite the hustle and bustle generated by Ireland's flourishing economy, Dublin remains an intimate capital that mixes elegant Georgian buildings, wrought-iron bridges, an army of book-sellers, and more than 1,000 pubs. The heart of the city is the river Liffey, which runs east to west, splitting Dublin neatly in two. The more affluent Southside has a greater concentration of sights, and it can seem a world apart from the more working-class (though increasingly gentrified) Northside. North or south, Dublin is compact and easily navigated, making it a great walking city.

3 The Northside. Less affluent but more eloquent than the Southside, this neighborhood was once home to James Joyce; today it's the site of the **Dublin Writers Museum** and the **James Joyce Centre**. Other highlights are the grand **Custom House**, historic **O'Connell Street**, and Dublin's two great theaters, the **Abbey** and the **Gate**.

4 Dublin West. This former industrial district stretches from **Christ Church Cathedral** west to another Dublin shrine, the **Guinness Brewery**. Imposing **Dublin Castle** houses the **Chester Beatty Library**—arguably the most impressive museum in Ireland. **Phoenix Park**, Europe's largest public city park, hugs the north bank of the Liffey.

DUBLIN PLANNER

Getting Around

Central Dublin is compact, so walking is the first choice for getting pretty much everywhere. Main thoroughfares can become crowded with pedestrians, especially at rush hour, so if you prefer less bustle, plan routes along quieter side streets.

When your feet need a break, turn to public transit. There's an extensive network of buses (mainly green double-deckers), and the pleasant LUAS tram system has two lines running through the city center. You can hail a taxi, wait at a stand, or phone a taxi company in order to get one. Because they're allowed to use bus lanes, taxis get through traffic faster than private vehicles do. Navigating the city on your own in a rental car is an expensive headache. For the details about getting around, see "Transportation" in the Essentials section at the end of this chapter.

DAY-TRIPPING ON THE DART

The DART (Dublin Area Rapid Transit) train line is great for jaunts out of the city. It runs from the fishing village of Howth, at the northern tip of Dublin Bay, south to the seaside resort of Bray in Wicklow. The route hugs the coastline, providing one spectacular view after another. And with tickets running a little over €3, the price is right.

Making the Most of Your Time

The city-center area south of the Liffey is a logical place to begin your exploration of Dublin: many of the top sights are there, set among graceful squares and terraces dating from the city's elegant Georgian heyday. You haven't really seen Dublin until you've toured this area.

Begin at **O'Connell Bridge**—the closest thing Dublin has to a central landmark—and head south down Westmoreland Street to view the **Bank of Ireland,** one of Dublin's most spectacular buildings. Across the street is the genteel campus of **Trinity College,** where your priority should be the Old Library, with its staggering Long Room and Ireland's greatest art treasure, the *Book of Kells*.

From there, a stroll along **Grafton Street,** Dublin's busiest shopping avenue, brings you to lovely **St. Stephen's Green.** At the Green's northeast corner you'll find the epicenter of Dublin cultural institutions: standing side by side are the **National Museum of Archaeology and History,** the **National Gallery of Ireland, the National Library,** and the **National Museum of Natural History.**

Other must-sees on the Southside are nearby **Merrion Square,** the happening **Temple Bar** district along the Liffey's banks, and, further west, **St. Patrick's Cathedral,** the **Guinness Brewery and Storehouse,** and the **Chester Beatty Library**—a gem of a museum. Cross the river to experience the grittier (though gentrifying) side of central Dublin. It's here that Dublin's literary heart beats strongest—the **Dublin Writers Museum** is a highlight, and the area is filled with landmarks from events in Irish literary history, both real and imagined. (⇨ Check out "Literary Dublin" later in this chapter.)

Meeting the Dubs

The most appealing thing about Dublin isn't the sights, or even the great pubs and restaurants. It's the people—the citizens, the Dubs. They're fun, funny, and irreverent, and most of them love nothing better than talking to strangers. So, to get the most out of your visit, make a point of rubbing elbows with the locals. The pub is a natural spot to do this (see "A Trip to the Pub" later in this chapter), but almost any place will suffice. Ask for directions on a street corner (even if you don't need them), and you might be on your way to a brilliant conversation.

MIND THE SLAG

"Slagging" is the Dubliner's favorite type of humor. It consists of mildly—or not so mildly—insulting a friend or a soon-to-be-friend in sharp but jovial fashion. It's best employed to deflate vainity or hubris, but clearly marks out the victim as well-liked and worthy. Packed buses and late-night chip shops are classic slagging venues.

Dublin with a Guiding Hand

Dublin is a walkers' city, and it's a city full of storytellers. Put two and two together, and it's little surprise that Dublin is a particularly good place for guided walking tours. There are scores of informative, jovial guides eager to reveal the mysteries of "dirty, darling Dublin"—specific recommendations are found under "Contacts & Resources" in the Essentials section at the end of this chapter. Tours usually have a theme that falls into one of three categories: history, culture, or music. While you're learning about the city and getting to know a garulous local, you can also swap stories and recommendations with other visitors along for the walk.

How's the Weather?

When is it best—and worst—to pay a call on the Irish capital? The summer offers a real lift, as the natives spill out of the pubs into the slew of sidewalk cafés and open-air restaurants. The week around St. Patrick's Day (March 17th) is, naturally, a nonstop festival of parades, cultural happenings, and "hooleys" (long nights of partying) throughout the city.

Christmas in Dublin seems to last a month, and the city's old-style illuminations match the genteel, warm mood of the locals. The downside quickly follows, however, for January and February are damp hangover months.

A warm sweater is a must all year round, as even summer nights can occasionally get chilly. Dublin gets its share of rain (though a lot less than other parts of Ireland), so an umbrella is a good investment—and best to make it a strong one, as the winds show no mercy to cheaper models.

Book of Kells

Updated by
Anto Howard

IN HIS INIMITABLE, IRRESISTIBLE WAY, James Joyce immortalized the city of Dublin in *Ulysses, Dubliners,* and *A Portrait of the Artist as a Young Man,* filling these works with the people he knew, speaking in their own words, and adding many more of his own. Disappointed with the city's provincial outlook and small-town manners, he left it in 1902, at the age of 20 (his famed peers Sean O'Casey and Samuel Beckett soon followed). Later he said he chose Dublin as the setting for his work because it was a "center of paralysis" where nothing much ever changed. Which only proves that even the greats get it wrong sometimes. Indeed, if Joyce were to return to his once genteel hometown today and take a quasi-Homeric odyssey through the city (as he so famously does in *Ulysses*), would he even recognize Dublin as his "Dear Dirty Dumpling, foostherfather of fingalls and dotthergills"?

For instance, what would he make of Temple Bar—the city's erstwhile down-at-the-heels neighborhood, now crammed with restaurants and stylish hotels in its made-over state as Dublin's "Left Bank"? Or the old market area of Smithfield, whose Cinderella transformation has changed it into an impressive plaza and winter ice-skating venue? Or of the new Irishness, where every aspect of Celtic culture results in sold-out theaters, from Martin McDonagh's Broadway hit *The Beauty Queen of Leenane,* to *Riverdance,* the old Irish mass-jig recast as a Las Vegas extravaganza? Plus, the resurrected Joyce might be stirred by the songs of U2, fired up by the films of Neil Jordan, and moved by the poems of Nobel laureate Seamus Heaney. In short, Irish has become cool. As for Ireland's capital, elegant shops and hotels, galleries, art-house cinemas, coffeehouses, and a stunning variety of restaurants are springing up on almost every street in Dublin, transforming the genteel city that suffocated Joyce into a place almost as cosmopolitan as the Paris to which he fled.

Dublin's popularity has provoked a few of its citizens to protest that the rapid transformation of their heretofore tranquil city has changed its spirit and character. Mundane topics like "house prices" and "the bloody traffic" have found their way into pub conversation. These skeptics (skepticism long being a favorite pastime in the capital city) await the outcome of "Dublin: The Sequel"—can the "new Dublin" get beyond the rage stage without losing its very essence? Their greatest fear is the possibility that the tattered old lady on the Liffey is becoming like everywhere else. Oh ye of little faith: the rare aul' gem that is Dublin is far from buried. The fundamentals—the Georgian elegance of Merrion Square, the Norman drama of Christ Church Cathedral, the foamy pint at an atmospheric pub—are still on hand to gratify. Most of all, there are the locals themselves: the nod and grin when you catch their eye on the street, the eagerness to hear half your life story before they tell you all of theirs, and their paradoxically dark but warm sense of humor.

EXPLORING DUBLIN

Coverage in this chapter is organized into six sections exploring the main neighborhoods of Dublin city (plus two excursions into County Dublin—one to the southern suburbs, and one to the northern). The first two sections—City Center and Georgian Dublin—focus on many of the South-side's major sights: Trinity College, St. Stephen's Green, Merrion Square, and Grafton Street. The third section—Temple Bar—takes you through this revived neighborhood, still the hottest, hippest zone in the capital.

The Northside section covers major cultural sights north of the Liffey and east of Capel Street, including the James Joyce Centre, Gate Theatre, Dublin Writers Museum, and the Hugh Lane Municipal Gallery of Modern Art. The next section—Dublin West—picks up across Dame Street from Temple Bar and continues west though the historic, working-class Liberties neighborhood to

> ### DUBLIN REBORN
>
> "My darlin' Dublin, dead and gone" goes a traditional ballad, but the recent rebirth, although at times difficult and a little messy, has been a spectacular success.

the Guinness Brewery and Storehouse, the city's most popular attraction. It also includes the two main cathedrals and the rapidly developing Smith-field district, which locals are hailing as the future "Temple Bar of the North-side." Finally, the Phoenix Park and Environs section covers the most western fringe of the Northside and the great public park itself. If you're planning to take in all the sights, you may wish to invest in the city's special tourist ticket, the **Dublin Pass**—for more information, see the entry in the Essentials section at the end of this chapter.

If you're visiting Dublin for more than two or three days, you'll have time to explore farther afield. There's plenty to see and do a short distance from the city center—in the suburbs of both north and south County Dublin. Worthwhile destinations in these parts of the county are covered in the Side Trips section.

Dublin's City Center: Trinity College to St. Stephen's Green

Dublin's center of gravity had traditionally been O'Connell Bridge, a diplomatic landmark in that it avoided locating the center either north or south of the river—as strong local loyalties still prevailed among "Northsiders" and "Southsiders," and neither group would ever accept that the city's center lay elsewhere than on their own side. The 20th century, however, saw diplomacy fall by the wayside—Dublin's heart now beats loudest southward across the Liffey, due in part to a large-scale refurbishment and pedestrianization of Grafton Street, which made this already upscale shopping address the main street on which to shop, stop, and be seen. At the foot of Grafton Street is the city's most famous and recognizable landmark, Trinity College; at the top of it is Dublin's most popular strolling retreat, St. Stephen's Green, a 27-acre landscaped park with flowers, lakes, bridges, and Dubliners enjoying their time-outs.

Numbers in the margin correspond to numbers on the Dublin South-side map.

TIMING To merely walk the streets of Dublin's compact city center would take only an hour, but it is so crammed with pleasures and treasures, you'll want to set aside at least a half a day to explore it. After all, Trinity College can easily take an hour or two. And who would ever want to rush

DUBLIN PAST & PRESENT

Until 500 AD, Dublin was little more than a crossroads—albeit a critical one—for four of the main thoroughfares that traversed the country. It had two names: Baile Atha Cliath, meaning City of the Hurdles, bestowed by Celtic traders in the 2nd century AD; and Dubhlinn, or "dark pool," after a body of water believed to have been where Dublin Castle now stands.

In 837, Norsemen carried out the first invasion of Dublin, to be followed by new waves of warriors staking their claim to the city—from the 12th-century Anglo-Normans to Oliver Cromwell in 1651. Not until the 18th century did Dublin reach a golden age, when the patronage of wealthy nobles turned the city into one of Europe's most prepossessing capitals. But the aura of "the glorious eighteenth" was short-lived; in 1800, the Act of Union brought Ireland and Britain together in a United Kingdom, and power moved to London.

The 19th century proved to be a time of political turmoil, although Daniel O'Connell, the first Catholic lord mayor of Dublin, won early success with the introduction of Catholic Emancipation in 1829. During the late 1840s, Dublin escaped the worst effects of the famine that ravaged much of southern and western Ireland.

The city entered another period of upheaval in the first decades of the 20th century, marked by the Easter Uprising of 1916. A war for independence from Britain began in 1919, followed by establishment of the Irish Free State in December 1921 and subsequent civil war. In its aftermath Dublin entered an era of political and cultural conservatism, which continued until the late 1970s. A major turning point occurred in 1972, when Ireland joined the European Economic Community. In the 1980s, while the economy remained in recession, Irish musicians stormed the American and British barricades of rock-and-roll music, with U2 climbing to the topmost heights.

The 1990s and first years of the 21st century have truly been Ireland's boom time, set in motion to a great extent by the country's participation in the European Union. When Ireland approved the new EU treaty in 1992, it was one of the poorest member nations, qualifying it for grants of all kinds. Since then, Ireland has transformed itself into the economic envy of the world, propelled by massive investment from multinational corporations, particularly in the telecommunications, software, and service industries. In 2000 the government announced that Ireland was the world's largest exporter of software. Recent years have seen such rapid growth that local wags suggest the economy needs to be tested for steroids.

Today, roughly a third of the Irish Republic's 3.9 million people live in Dublin and its suburbs. It's a city of young people—astonishingly so. Students from all over Ireland attend Trinity College and the city's dozen other universities. After graduating, more and more stick around, filling the new jobs and contributing to the hubbub.

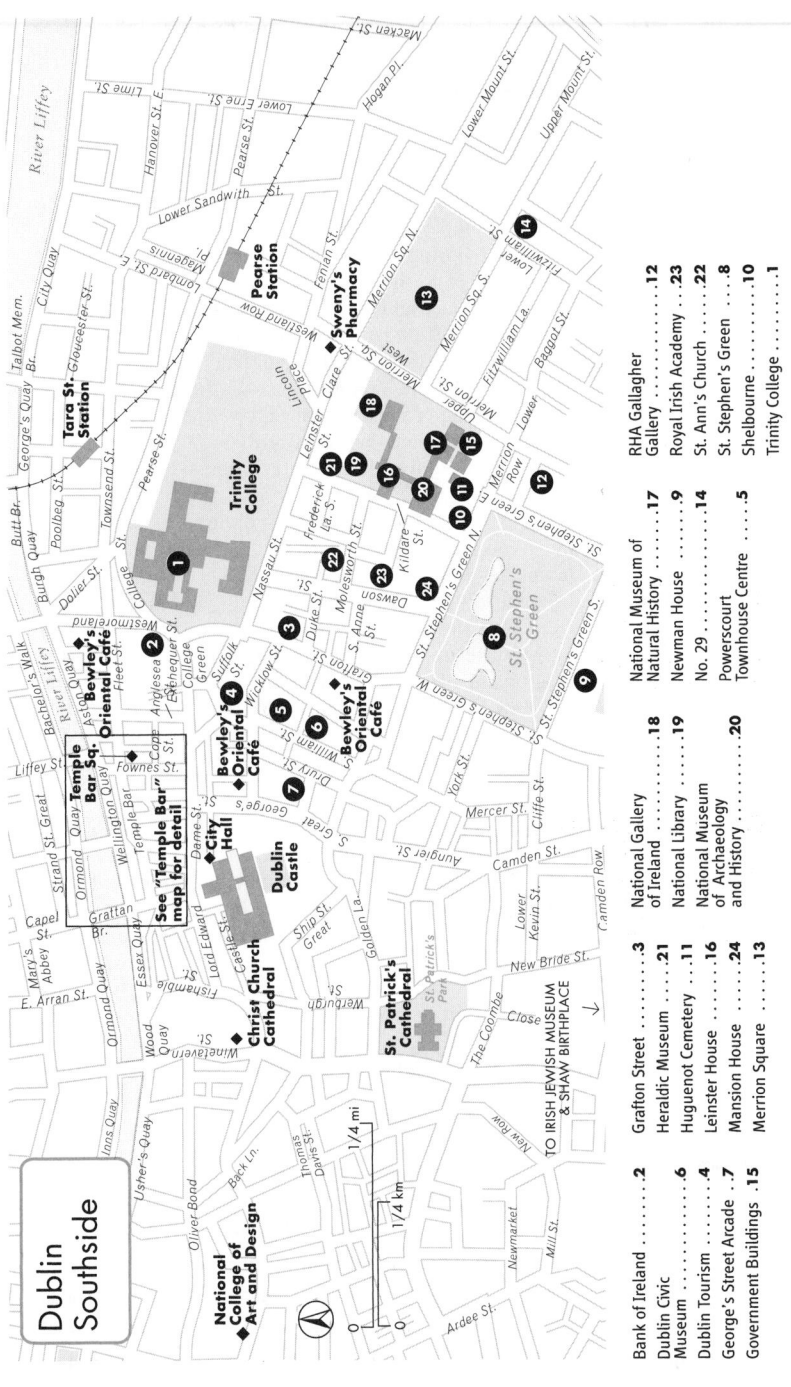

Dublin Southside

National College of Art and Design **2**
Dublin Civic Museum **6**
Dublin Tourism **4**
George's Street Arcade ..**7**
Government Buildings .**15**

Grafton Street **3**
Heraldic Museum **21**
Huguenot Cemetery ...**11**
Leinster House **16**
Mansion House **24**
Merrion Square **13**

National Gallery of Ireland **18**
National Library **19**
National Museum of Archaeology and History **20**

National Museum of Natural History ...**17**
Newman House **9**
No. 29 ....**14**
Powerscourt Townhouse Centre **5**

RHA Gallagher Gallery **12**
Royal Irish Academy ...**23**
St. Ann's Church **22**
St. Stephen's Green **8**
Shelbourne **10**
Trinity College **1**

See "Temple Bar" map for detail

♦ Bewley's Oriental Café

♦ Sweny's Pharmacy

Pearse Station

Tara St. Station

Trinity College

St. Stephen's Green

Dublin Castle

Christ Church Cathedral

City Hall

St. Patrick's Cathedral

National College of Art and Design

TO IRISH JEWISH MUSEUM & SHAW BIRTHPLACE

up Grafton Street? Take a leisurely amble and then stroll through St. Stephen's Green for a fitting finale.

The Main Attractions

2 Bank of Ireland. Across the street from the west facade of Trinity College stands one of Dublin's most striking buildings, formerly the original home of Irish Parliament. Sir Edward Lovett Pearce designed the central section in 1729; three other architects would ultimately be involved in the remainder of the building's construction. A pedimented portico fronted by six massive Corinthian columns dominates the grand facade, which follows the curve of Westmoreland Street as it meets College Green, once a Viking meeting place and burial ground. Two years after Parliament was abolished in 1801 under the Act of Union, which brought Ireland under the direct rule of Britain, the building was bought for the equivalent of €50,790 by the Bank of Ireland. Inside, stucco rosettes adorn the coffered ceiling in the pastel-hued, colonnaded, clerestoried main banking hall, at one time the Court of Requests, where citizens' petitions were heard. Just down the hall is the original House of Lords, with an oak-panel nave, a 1,233-drop Waterford glass chandelier, and tapestries depicting the Battle of the Boyne and the Siege of Derry; ask a guard to show you in. Visitors are welcome during normal banking hours; the Dublin historian and author Éamonn Mac Thomáis conducts brief guided tours every Tuesday at 10:30, 11:30, and 1:45. Accessed via Foster Place South, the small alley on the bank's east flank, the Bank of Ireland Arts Centre frequently mounts displays of contemporary Irish art and has a permanent exhibition, "Journey Through 200 Years." ✉ *2 College Green, Southside* ☎ *01/677–6801 bank, 01/671–1488 Arts Centre* ⊕ *www.visitdublin.com* ✉ *Bank free, Arts Centre €1.50* ☉ *Bank Mon.–Wed. and Fri. 10–4, Thurs. 10–5; Arts Centre Tues.–Fri. 10–4, Sat. 2–5, Sun. 10–1.*

3 Grafton Street. It's no more than 200 yards long and about 20 feet wide, but brick-lined Grafton Street, open only to pedestrians, can claim to be the most humming street in the city, if not in all of Ireland. It's one of Dublin's vital spines: the most direct route between the front door of Trinity College and St. Stephen's Green, and the city's premier shopping street, with Dublin's most distinguished department store, Brown Thomas, as well as tried and trusted Marks & Spencer. Grafton Street and the smaller alleyways that radiate off it offer dozens of independent stores, a dozen or so colorful flower sellers, and some of the Southside's most popular watering holes. In summer, buskers from all over the world line both sides of the street, pouring out the sounds of drum, whistle, pipe, and string.

NEED A BREAK?

The granddaddy of the capital's cafés, **Bewley's Oriental Café** (✉ 78 Grafton St., Southside ☎ 01/677–6761) recently came within a heartbeat of extinction, after having served coffee and sticky buns to Dubliners since its founding by the Quakers in 1842. Fortunately the old dame has been saved and turned into a combination café, pizza, and pasta joint, with a quality fish restaurant on the first floor. Best of all the new owners have brought back some of the old grandeur associated with Bewley's, including the exotic picture wallpaper and trademark stained-glass windows, designed by the distinguished early-20th-century artist Harry Clarke. The place is worth a visit if only to sit in the super-comfortable velvet seats over a cup of quality coffee, and people-watch just like Dubliners have for well over 150 years. There's even a cute little theater upstairs with lunchtime shows. The ticket price (€14) incudes homemade soup and a sandwich.

❾ Newman House. One of the greatest glories of Georgian Dublin, Newman House is actually two imposing town houses joined together. The earlier of the two, No. 85 St. Stephen's Green (1738), was originally known as Clanwilliam House. Designed by Richard Castle, favored architect of Dublin's rich and famous, it features a winged Palladian window on the Wicklow granite facade. It has two landmarks of Irish Georgian style: the Apollo Room, decorated with stuccowork depicting the sun god and his muses; and the magnificent Saloon, "the supreme example of Dublin Baroque," according to scholars Jacqueline O'Brien and Desmond Guinness. The Saloon is crowned with an exuberant ceiling aswirl with cupids and gods, created by the Brothers Lafranchini, the finest *stuccadores* (plaster-workers) of 18th-century Dublin. Next door at No. 86 (1765), the staircase, on pastel walls, is one of the city's most beautiful Rococo examples—with floral swags and musical instruments picked out in cake-frosting white. Catholic University (described by James Joyce in *A Portrait of the Artist as a Young Man*) was established in this building in 1850, with Cardinal John Henry Newman as its first rector. To explore the houses you must join a guided tour. At the back of Newman House lies Iveagh Gardens, a delightful hideaway with statues and sunken gardens that remains one of Dublin's best-kept secrets (you can enter via Earlsfort Terrace and Harcourt Street). ✉ *85–86 St. Stephen's Green, Southside* ☎ *01/716–7422* ⊕ *www.visitdublin.com* ✆ *House and garden €5* ☉ *Tours June–Aug., Tues.–Fri. at noon, 2, 3, and 4.*

❺ Powerscourt Townhouse Centre. Lucky man, the Viscount Powerscourt. In the mid-18th century, not only did he build Ireland's most spectacular country house, in Enniskerry, County Wicklow (which bears the family name), but he also decided to rival that structure's grandeur with one of Dublin's largest stone mansions. Staffed with 22 servants and built of granite from the viscount's quarry in the Wicklow Hills, Powerscourt House was a major statement in the Palladian style. Designed by Robert Mack in 1771, it's a massive edifice that towers over the little street it sits on (note the top story, framed by large volutes, which was intended as an observatory). Inside, there are Rococo salons designed by James McCullagh, splendid examples of plasterwork in the Adamesque style and—surprise!—a shopping atrium, installed in and around the covered courtyard. The stores here include high-quality Irish crafts shops and numerous food stalls. The mall exit leads to the Carmelite Church of St. Teresa's and Johnson's Court. Beside the church, a pedestrian lane leads onto Grafton Street. ✉ *59 S. William St., Southside* ☎ *01/679–4144* ☉ *Mon.–Wed. and Fri. 10–6, Thurs. 10–8, Sat. 9–6, Sun. noon–6; limited shops open Sun.*

8 St. Stephen's Green. Dubliners call it simply Stephen's Green, and green

FodorśChoice ★

it is (year-round)—a verdant, 27-acre Southside square that was used for the public punishment of criminals until 1664. After a long period of decline, it became a private park in 1814—the first time in its history that it was closed to the public. Its fortunes changed again in 1880, when Sir Arthur Guinness, later Lord Ardiluan (a member of the Guinness brewery family), paid for it to be laid out anew. Flower gardens, formal lawns, a Victorian bandstand, and an ornamental lake with lots of waterfowl are all within

> **WORD OF MOUTH**
>
> "We meandered around St. Stephen's Green for a bit. Reminded me of Central Park but with more of a garden feel to it. Very very nice." –Ocnmeg

the park's borders, connected by paths guaranteeing that strolling here or just passing through will offer up unexpected delights (such as palm trees). Among the park's many statues are a memorial to Yeats and another to Joyce by Henry Moore, and the *Three Fates*, a dramatic group of bronze female figures watching over human destiny. In the 18th century the walk on the north side of the green was referred to as the Beaux Walk because most of Dublin's gentlemen's clubs were in town houses here. Today it's dominated by the legendary Shelbourne Hotel. On the south side is the alluring Georgian-gorgeous Newman House. ⊠ *Free* ⊙ *Daily sunrise–sunset.*

10 Shelbourne. The redbrick, white-wood-trim Shelbourne hotel has commanded "the best address in Dublin" from the north side of St. Stephen's Green since 1865. After a major renovation and expansion, it reopened in the fall of 2006; a new restaurant, new lounge bar, and 75 additional guest rooms constitute a major facelift for Dublin's most iconic hotel. In 1921 the Irish Free State's constitution was drafted here, in a first-floor suite. Elizabeth Bowen wrote her novel *The Hotel* about this very place. ⊠ *27 St. Stephen's Green, Southside* ☎ *01/676–6471* ⊕ *www. marriott.com.*

1 Trinity College. Founded in 1592 by Queen Elizabeth I to "civilize" (Her

FodorśChoice ★

Majesty's word) Dublin, Trinity is Ireland's oldest and most famous college. The memorably atmospheric campus is a must; here you can track the shadows of some of the noted alumni, such as Jonathan Swift (1667–1745), Oscar Wilde (1854–1900), Bram Stoker (1847–1912), and Samuel Beckett (1906–89). Trinity College, Dublin (familiarly known as TCD), was founded on the site of the confiscated Priory of All Hallows. For centuries Trinity was the preserve of the Protestant Church; a free education was offered to Catholics—provided that they accepted the Protestant faith. As a legacy of this condition, until 1966 Catholics who wished to study at Trinity had to obtain a dispensation from their bishop or face excommunication.

Trinity's grounds cover 40 acres. Most of its buildings were constructed in the 18th and early 19th centuries. The extensive **West Front,** with a classical pedimented portico in the Corinthian style, faces College Green and is directly across from the Bank of Ireland; it was built between 1755 and 1759, and is possibly the work of Theodore Jacobsen, architect of London's Foundling Hospital. The design is repeated on the interior, so the view is the same from outside the gates and from the quadrangle inside. On the lawn in front of the inner facade stand statues of two alumni, orator Edmund Burke (1729–97) and dramatist Oliver Goldsmith (1730–74). Like the West Front, **Parliament Square** (commonly known as Front Square), the cobblestone quadrangle that lies just beyond this first patch of lawn, dates from the 18th century. On the right side of the square is Sir William Chambers's theater, or Examination Hall, dating from the mid-1780s, which contains the college's most splendid Adamesque interior, designed by Michael Stapleton. The hall houses an impressive organ retrieved from an 18th-century Spanish ship and a gilded oak chandelier from the old House of Commons; concerts are sometimes held here. The chapel, left of the quadrangle, has stucco ceilings and fine woodwork. The theater and the chapel were designed by Scotsman William Chambers in the late 18th century. The looming campanile, or bell tower, is the symbolic heart of the college; erected in 1853, it dominates the center of the square. To the left of the campanile is the Graduates Memorial Building, or GMB. Built in 1892, the slightly Gothic building now contains the offices of Philosophical and Historical societies, Trinity's ancient and fiercely competitive debating groups. At the back of the square stands old redbrick Rubrics, looking rather ordinary and out of place among the gray granite and cobblestones. Rubrics, now used as housing for students and faculty, dates from 1690, making it the oldest campus building still standing.

The **Old Library** houses Ireland's largest collection of books and manuscripts; its principal treasure is the *Book of Kells,* generally considered to be the most striking manuscript ever produced in the Anglo-Saxon world and one of the great masterpieces of early Christian art. The book, which dates to the 9th century, is a splendidly illuminated version of the Gospels. It was once thought to be lost—the Vikings looted the book in 1007 for its jeweled cover but ultimately left the manuscript behind. In the 12th century, Guardius Cambensis declared that the book was made by an angel's hand in answer to a prayer of St. Bridget; in the 20th century, scholars decided instead that the book originated on the island of Iona off Scotland's coast, where followers of St. Colomba lived until the island came under siege in the early to mid-9th century. They fled to Kells, County Meath, taking the book with them. The 680-page work was rebound in four volumes in 1953, two of which are usually displayed at a time, so you typically see no more than four original pages. (Some wags have taken to calling it the "Page of Kells.") However, such is the incredible workmanship of the *Book of Kells* that one folio alone is worth the entirety of many other painted manuscripts. On some pages, it has been determined that within a quarter inch, no fewer than 158 interlacements of a ribbon pattern of white lines on a black background can be discerned—little wonder some historians feel this book contains all the designs to be found in Celtic art. Note, too, the extraordinary colors, some of which were derived from shellfish, beetles' wings, and crushed pearls. The most famous page shows the "XPI" monogram (symbol of Christ), but if this page is not on display, you can still see a replica of it, and many of the other lavishly illustrated pages, in the adjacent exhibition—dedicated to the history, artistry, and conservation of the book—through which you must pass to see the originals.

Because of the fame and beauty of the *Book of Kells*—now the centerpiece of an exhibition called "Turning Darkness into Light"—it's all too easy to overlook the other treasures in the library. They include the *Book of Armagh*, a 9th-century copy of the New Testament that also contains St. Patrick's Confession, and the legendary *Book of Durrow*, a 7th-century Gospel book from County Offaly. You may have to wait in line to enter the library if you don't get there early in the day.

The main library room, also known as the **Long Room,** is one of Dublin's most staggering sights. At 213 feet long and 42 feet wide, it contains in its 21 alcoves approximately 200,000 of the 3 million volumes in Trinity's collection. Originally the room had a flat plaster ceiling, but in 1859–60 the need for more shelving resulted in a decision to raise the level of the roof and add the barrel-vault ceiling and the gallery bookcases. Since the 1801 Copyright Act, the college has received a copy of every book published in Britain and Ireland, and a great number of these publications must be stored in other parts of the campus and beyond. Of

note are the carved Royal Arms of Queen Elizabeth I above the library entrance—the only surviving relic of the original college buildings—and, lining the Long Room, a grand series of marble busts, of which the most famous is Roubiliac's depiction of Jonathan Swift. The Trinity College Library Shop sells books, clothing, jewelry, and postcards. ⊠ *Front Sq., Southside* ☎ *01/608–2308* ⊕ *www.tcd.ie* 🎫 *€8* ⊗ *May–Sept., Mon.–Sat. 9:30–5, Sun. 9:30–4:30; Oct.–Apr., Mon.–Sat. 9:30–5, Sun. noon–4:30.*

Trinity College's starkly modern Arts and Social Sciences Building, with an entrance on Nassau Street, houses the **Douglas Hyde Gallery of Modern Art,** which concentrates on contemporary art exhibitions and has its own bookstore. Also in the building, down some steps from the gallery, is a snack bar serving coffee, tea, and sandwiches, where students willing to chat about life in the old college frequently gather. ⊠ *Nassau St., Southside* ☎ *01/608–1116* 🎫 *Free* ⊗ *Mon.–Wed. and Fri. 11–6, Thurs. 11–7, Sat. 11–4:45.*

The **Berkeley Library,** the main student library at Trinity, was built in 1967 and named after the philosopher and alumnus George Berkeley (pronounced "Barkley," like the basketball player). The small open space in front of the library contains a spherical brass sculpture designed by Arnaldo Pomodoro. A very modern, sleek extension dominates the Nassau Street side of the campus. The library is not open to the public. ⊠ *Nassau St., Southside* ☎ *01/677–2941* ⊕ *www.tcd.ie* ⊗ *Grounds daily 8 AM–10 PM.*

In the Thomas Davis Theatre in the arts building, the **"Dublin Experience,"** a 45-minute audiovisual presentation, explains the history of the city over the last 1,000 years. ⊠ *Nassau St., Southside* ☎ *01/608–1688* ☐ *€5* ☉ *Late May–early Oct., daily 10–5; shows every hr on the hr.*

Also Worth Seeing

6 **Dublin Civic Museum.** Built between 1765 and 1771 as an exhibition hall for the Society of Artists, this building later was used as the City Assembly House, precursor of City Hall. The museum's esoteric collection includes Stone Age flints, Viking coins, old maps and prints of the city, and the sculpted head of British admiral Horatio Nelson, which used to top Nelson's Pillar, beside the General Post Office on O'Connell Street; the column was toppled by an IRA explosion in 1966 on the 50th anniversary of the Easter Uprising. The museum also holds temporary exhibitions relating to the city. ⊠ *58 S. William St., Southside* ☎ *01/679–4260* ⊕ *www.dublincity.ie* ☐ *Free* ☉ *Tues.–Sat. 10–6, Sun. 11–2.*

4 **Dublin Tourism.** Medieval St. Andrew's Church, deconsecrated and fallen into ruin, has been resurrected as the home of Dublin Tourism, a private organization that provides the most complete information on Dublin's sights, restaurants, and hotels; you can even rent a car here. The office has reservations facilities for all Dublin hotels, as well as guided tours, a plethora of brochures, and a gift shop. A pleasant café upstairs serves sandwiches and drinks. ⊠ *St. Andrew's Church, Suffolk St., Southside* ☎ *01/605–7700, 1850/230330 in Ireland* ⊕ *www.visitdublin.com* ☉ *July–Sept., Mon.–Sat. 8:30–6, Sun. 11–5:30; Oct.–June, daily 9–6.*

7 **George's Street Arcade.** This Victorian covered market fills the block between Drury Street and South Great George's Street. Two dozen or so stalls sell books, prints, clothing (new and secondhand), exotic foodstuffs, and trinkets. ⊠ *S. Great George's St., Southside* ☉ *Mon.–Sat. 9–6.*

NEED A BREAK? With its mahogany bar, mirrors, and plasterwork ceilings, the **Long Hall Pub** (⊠ 51 S. Great George's St., Southside ☎ 01/475–1590) is one of Dublin's most ornate traditional taverns. It's a good place to take a break with a sandwich and a pint of Guinness.

11 **Huguenot Cemetery.** One of the last such burial grounds in Dublin, this cemetery was used in the late 17th century by French Protestants who had fled persecution in their native land. The cemetery gates are rarely open, but you can view the grounds from the street—it's on the northeast corner across from the square. ⊠ *27 St. Stephen's Green N, Southside.*

12 **RHA Gallagher Gallery.** The Royal Hibernian Academy, an old Dublin institution, is housed in a well-lighted building, one of the largest exhibition spaces in the city. Besides its permenant collection, the gallery holds adventurous exhibitions of the best in contemporary art, both from Ireland and abroad. ⊠ *15 Ely Pl., off St. Stephen's Green, Southside* ☎ *01/661–2558* ⊕ *www.royalhibernianacademy.com* ☐ *Free* ☉ *Mon.–Wed., Fri., and Sat. 11–5, Thurs. 11–8, Sun. 2–5.*

Georgian Dublin: Museums & Marvels

If there's one travel poster that signifies "Dublin" more than any other, it's the one that depicts 50 or so Georgian doorways—door after colorful door, all graced with lovely fanlights upheld by columns. A building boom began in Dublin in the early 18th century as the Protestant Ascendancy constructed terraced town houses for themselves, and civic structures for their city, in the style that came to be known as Georgian, after the four successive British Georges who ruled from 1714 through 1830. The Georgian architectural rage owed much to architects such as James Gandon and Richard Castle. They and others were influenced by the great Italian Andrea Palladio (1508–80), whose *Four Books of Architecture* were published in the 1720s in London and helped to precipitate the revival of his style, which swept through England and its colonies. Never again would Dublin be so "smart," its visitors' book so full of aristocratic names, its Southside streets so filled with decorum and style. "Serene red and pink houses showed beautifully designed doorways, the one spot of variation in the uniformity of facade," as architectural historian James Reynolds puts it. Today, Dublin's Southside remains a veritable shop window of the Georgian style, though there are many period sights on the Northside as well (for instance, the august interiors of the Dublin Writers Museum and Belvedere College, or James Gandon's great civic structures, the Custom House and the Four Courts, found quayside).

But Georgian splendor is just the icing on the cake of this neighborhood. For there are also four of the most fascinating and glamorous museums in Ireland, conveniently sitting cheek to jowl: the National Gallery of Ireland, the National Library, the National Museum of Natural History, and the National Museum of Archaeology and History. Priceless old master paintings, legendary Celtic treasures, mythic prehistoric "Irish elks," and George Bernard Shaw manuscripts—there is enough here to keep you occupied for days.

Numbers in the margin correspond to numbers on the Dublin Southside map.

TIMING   This area is so compact you could stroll by all of the sights in a couple of hours, if you didn't linger or set foot in the museums. But that is unthinkable—after all, the treasures at the National Gallery and the National Museum of Archaeology and History, and the green tranquility of Merrion Square are some of Dublin's most fabled attractions. In addition, many of Dublin's finest Georgian mansions line these streets (as do dozens of the city's most historic pubs). Take a full day to savor the sights here, then plan on returning to visit your favorites at greater leisure.

The Main Attractions

⓰ **Leinster House.** Commissioned by the Duke of Leinster and built in 1745, this residence—Dublin's Versailles—almost single-handedly ignited the Georgian style that dominated Dublin for 100 years. It was not only the largest private home in the city but Richard Castle's first structure in Ireland (Castle–or Casells, to use his original German spelling—was

Dublin's Gorgeous Georgians

1

"EXTRAORDINARY DUBLIN!" sigh art lovers and connoisseurs of the 18th century. It was during the "gorgeous eighteenth" that this duckling of a city was transformed into a preening swan, largely by the Georgian style of art and architecture that flowered between 1714 and 1820 during the reigns of the three English Georges.

Today Dublin remains in good part a sublimely Georgian city, thanks to enduring grace notes: the commodious and uniformly laid out streets, the genteel town squares, the redbrick mansions accented with demilune fan windows. The great 18th-century showpieces are **Merrion, Fitzwilliam, Mountjoy,** and **Parnell squares. Merrion Square East,** the longest Georgian street in town, reveals scenes of decorum, elegance, polish, and charm, all woven into a "tapestry of rosy brick and white enamel," to quote the 18th-century connoisseur Horace Walpole.

Setting off the facades are fanlighted doors (often lacquered in black, green, yellow, or red) and the celebrated "patent reveal" window trims—thin plaster linings painted white to catch the light. These half-moon fanlights—as iconic of the city as clock towers are of Zurich—are often in the Neoclassical style known as the Adamesque (which was inspired by the designs of the great English architect, Robert Adam).

Many facades appear severely plain, but don't be fooled: just behind their stately front doors are entry rooms and stairways aswirl with tinted Rococo plasterwork, often the work of *stuccadores* (plasterworkers) from Italy (including the talented Lafranchini brothers). Magnificent **Newman**

House, one of the finest of Georgian houses, is open to the public. **Belvedere College** (✉ 6 Great Denmark St., Northside ☎ 01/874–3974) is open by appointment only.

The Palladian style—as the Georgian style was then called—began to reign supreme in domestic architecture in 1745, when the Croesus-rich earl of Kildare returned from an Italian grand tour and built a gigantic Palladian palace called **Leinster House** in the seedy section of town.

"Where I go, fashion will follow," he declared, and indeed it did. By then, the Anglo-Irish elite had given the city London airs by building the **Parliament House** (now the Bank of Ireland), the **Royal Exchange** (now City Hall), the **Custom House,** and the **Four Courts** in the new style.

But this phase of high fashion came to an end with the Act of Union: according to historian Maurice Craig, "On the last stroke of midnight, December 31, 1800, the gaily caparisoned horses turned into mice, the coaches into pumpkins, the silks and brocades into rags, and Ireland was once again the Cinderella among the nations."

It was nearly 150 years before the spotlight shone once again on 18th-century Dublin. In recent decades, the conservation efforts of the **Irish Georgian Society** (✉ 74 Merrion Sq., Southside ☎ 01/676-7053 ⊕ www. irishgeorgiansociety.org) have done much to restore Dublin to its Georgian splendor. Thanks to its founders, the Hon. Desmond Guinness and his late wife, Mariga, many historic houses including that of George Bernard Shaw on Synge Street, have been saved and preserved.

a follower of the 16th-century Italian architect Palladio and designed some of the country's most important 18th-century country houses). Inside, the grand salons were ornamented with coffered ceilings, Rembrandts, and Van Dycks—fitting settings for the parties often given by the duke's wife (and celebrated beauty), Lady Emily Lennox. The building has two facades: the one facing Merrion Square is designed in the style of a country house; the other, on Kildare Street, resembles that of a town house. The latter facade—ignoring the ground floor—was a major inspiration for Irishman James Hoban's designs for the White House in Washington, D.C. Built in hard Ardbracan limestone, the exterior of the house makes a cold impression, and, in fact, the duke's heirs pronounced the house "melancholy" and fled. Today, the house is the seat of Dáil Éireann (the House of Representatives, pronounced dawl e-rin) and Seanad Éireann (the Senate, pronounced shanad e-rin), which together constitute the Irish Parliament. When the Dáil is not in session, tours can be arranged weekdays; when the Dáil is in session, tours are available only on Monday and Friday. The Dáil visitor gallery is included in the tour, although it can be accessed on days when the Dáil is in session and tours are not available. To arrange a visit, contact the public relations office. ⊠ *Kildare St., Southside* ☎ *01/618–3000 public relations office* ⊕ *www.irlgov.ie* ⊒ *Free.*

⑬ Merrion Square. Created between 1762 and 1764, this tranquil square
Fodor'sChoice a few blocks east of St. Stephen's Green is lined on three sides by some
★ of Dublin's best-preserved Georgian town houses, many of which have brightly painted front doors crowned by intricate fanlights. Leinster House, the National Museum of Natural History, and the National Gallery line the west side of the square. It's on the other sides, however, that the Georgian terrace streetscape comes into its own—the finest houses are on the north border. Even when the flower gardens here are not in bloom, the vibrant, mostly evergreen grounds, dotted with sculpture and threaded with meandering paths, are worth strolling through. Several distinguished Dubliners have lived on the square, including Oscar Wilde's parents, Sir William and "Speranza" Wilde (No. 1); Irish national leader Daniel O'Connell (No. 58); and authors W. B. Yeats (Nos. 52 and 82) and Sheridan LeFanu (No. 70). As you walk past the houses, read the plaques on the house facades, which identify former inhabitants. Until 50 years ago the square was a fashionable residential area, but today most of the houses serve as offices. At the south end of Merrion Square, on Upper Mount Street, stands the Church of Ireland St. Stephen's Church. Known locally as the "pepper canister" church because of its cupola, the structure was inspired in part by Wren's churches in London. ⊠ *Southside* ☉ *Daily sunrise–sunset.*

⑱ National Gallery of Ireland. Caravaggio's *The Taking of Christ* (1602),
Fodor'sChoice Reynolds's *First Earl of Bellamont* (1773), Vermeer's *Lady Writing a*
★ *Letter with Her Maid* (circa 1670) . . . you get the picture. The National Gallery of Ireland—the first in a series of major civic buildings on the west side of Merrion Square—is one of Europe's finest smaller art museums—with "smaller" being a relative term: the collection holds more than 2,500 paintings and some 10,000 other works. But unlike Europe's

largest art museums, the National Gallery can be thoroughly covered in a morning or afternoon without inducing exhaustion. An 1854 Act of Parliament provided for the establishment of the museum, which was helped along by William Dargan (1799–1867), who was responsible for building much of Ireland's rail network (he is honored by a statue on the front lawn). The 1864 building was designed by Francis Fowke, who was also responsible for London's Victoria & Albert Museum.

A highlight of the museum is the major collection of paintings by Irish artists from the 17th through 20th centuries, including works by Roderic O'Conor (1860–1940), Sir William Orpen (1878–1931), and William Leech (1881–1968). The Yeats Museum section contains works by members of the Yeats family. Jack B. Yeats (1871–1957), the brother of writer W. B. Yeats, is by far the best-known Irish painter of the 20th century. Yeats painted portraits and landscapes in an abstract expressionist style not unlike that of the Bay Area Figurative painters of the 1950s and '60s. His *The Liffey Swim* (1923) is particularly worth seeing for its Dublin subject matter (the annual swim is still held, usually on the first weekend in September).

The collection also claims exceptional paintings from the 17th-century French, Dutch, Italian, and Spanish schools. Among the highlights are those mentioned above

> ### HIDDEN TREASURE
>
> The National Gallery's spectacular Caravaggio was discovered in the late 1980s, hanging unidentified in a Jesuit house not far from the museum.

and Rembrandt's *Rest on the Flight into Egypt* (1647), Poussin's *The Holy Family* (1649), and *Lamentation over the Dead Christ* (circa 1655–60), and Goya's *Portrait of Doña Antonia Zárate* (circa 1810). Don't miss the portrait of the *First Earl of Bellamont* (1773) by Reynolds; the earl was among the first to introduce the Georgian fashion to Ireland, and this portrait flaunts the extraordinary style of the man himself. The French Impressionists are represented with paintings by Monet, Sisley, and Pissarro. The British collection and the Irish National Portrait collection are displayed in the north wing of the gallery, while the Millennium Wing, a standout of postmodern architecture in Dublin, houses part of the permanent collection and also stages major international traveling exhibits. The amply stocked gift shop is a good place to pick up books on Irish artists. Free guided tours are available on Saturday at 3 and on Sunday at 2, 3, and 4. ✉ *Merrion Sq. W, Southside* ☎ *01/661–5133* ⊕ *www.nationalgallery.ie* 🎟 *Free; special exhibits €10* ⊗ *Mon.–Wed., Fri., and Sat. 9:30–5:30, Thurs. 9:30–8:30, Sun. noon–5:30.*

NEED A BREAK?

Fitzer's (✉ Merrion Sq. W, Southside ☎ 01/661–4496), the National Gallery's self-service restaurant, is a find—one of the city's best spots for an inexpensive, top-rate lunch. The 16 to 20 daily menu items are prepared with an up-to-date take on European cuisine. It's open Monday–Saturday 10–5:30 (lunch is served noon–2:30) and Sunday 2–5.

⑲ National Library. Happily, Ireland is one of the few countries in the world where you can admit to being a writer. And few countries as geographically diminutive as Ireland have garnered as many recipients of the Nobel Prize for Literature. Along with works by W. B. Yeats (1923), George Bernard Shaw (1925), Samuel Beckett (1969), and Seamus Heaney (1995), the National Library contains first editions of every major Irish writer, including books by Jonathan Swift, Oliver Goldsmith, and James Joyce (who used the library as the scene of the great literary debate in *Ulysses*). In addition, almost every book ever published in Ireland is kept here, along with an unequaled selection of old maps and an extensive collection of Irish newspapers and magazines—more than 5 million items in all.

The library is housed is a rather stiff Neoclassical building with collonaded porticoes and an excess of ornamentation—its not one of Dublin's architectural showpieces. But inside, the main Reading Room, opened in 1890 to house the collections of the Royal Dublin Society, has a dramatic domed ceiling, beneath which countless authors have researched and written. The library also has a free genealogical consultancy service that can advise you on how to trace your Irish ancestors. ⊠ *Kildare St., Southside* ☎ *01/661-8811* ⊕ *www.nli.ie* ✇ *Free* ☉ *Mon.–Wed. 10–9, Thurs. and Fri. 10–5, Sat. 10–1.*

★ ⑳ National Museum of Archaeology and History. Set just to the south of Leinster House, Ireland's National Museum of Archaeology and History houses a fabled collection of Irish artifacts dating from 7000 BC to the present. Organized around a grand rotunda, the museum is elaborately decorated, with mosaic floors, marble columns, balustrades, and fancy ironwork. It has the largest collection of Celtic antiquities in the world, including gold jewelry, carved stones, bronze tools, and weapons.

The Treasury collection, including some of the museum's most renowned pieces, is open on a permanent basis. Among the priceless relics on display are the late Bronze Age gold collar known as the Gleninsheen Gorget; the 8th-century Ardagh Chalice, a two-handled silver cup with gold filigree ornamentation; the bronze-coated iron St. Patrick's Bell, the oldest surviving example (5th–8th centuries) of Irish metalwork; the 8th-century Tara Brooch, an intricately decorated piece made of white bronze, amber, and glass; and the 12th-century bejeweled oak Cross of Cong, covered with silver and bronze panels.

The Road to Independence Room is devoted to the 1916 Easter Uprising and the War of Independence (1919–21); displays here include uniforms, weapons, banners, and a piece of the flag that flew over the General Post Office during Easter Week, 1916. Upstairs, Viking Age Ireland is a permanent exhibit on the Norsemen, featuring a full-size Viking skeleton, swords, leather works recovered in Dublin and surrounding areas, and a replica of a small Viking boat. The newest attraction is Medieval Ireland, bringing to life the age of cathedrals, monasteries, and castles.

In contrast to the ebullient late-Victorian architecture of the main museum building, the design of the National Museum Annex is purely functional; it hosts temporary shows of Irish antiquities. The 18th-century

Collins Barracks, near Phoenix Park (*see below*), houses the National Museum of Decorative Arts and History, a collection of glass, silver, furniture, and other decorative arts. ⊠ *Kildare St.; Annex, 7–9 Merrion Row, Southside* ☎ *01/677-7444* ⊕ *www.museum.ie* ⊠ *Free* ⊙ *Tues.–Sat. 10–5, Sun. 2–5.*

Also Worth Seeing

⓯ Government Buildings. The swan song of British architecture in the capital, this enormous complex, a landmark of Edwardian Baroque, was the last Neoclassical edifice to be erected by the British government. It was designed by Sir Aston Webb, who did many of the similarly grand buildings in London's Piccadilly Circus, to serve as the College of Science in the early 1900s. Following a major restoration, these buildings became the offices of the Department of the *taoiseach* (the prime minister, pronounced *tea*-shuck) and the *tánaiste* (the deputy prime minister, pronounced tawn-*ish*-ta). Fine examples of contemporary Irish furniture and carpets populate the offices. A stained-glass window, known as "My Four Green Fields," was made by Evie Hone for the 1939 New York World's Fair. It depicts the four ancient provinces of Ireland: Munster, Ulster, Leinster, and Connacht. The government offices are accessible only via 45-minute guided tours on Saturday, though they are dramatically illuminated every night. ⊠ *Upper Merrion St., Southside* ☎ *01/662–4888* ⊠ *Free; pick up tickets from National Gallery on day of tour* ⊙ *Tours Sat. 10:30–3:30.*

㉑ Heraldic Museum. Looking for something original for your wall? If you're a Fitzgibbon from Limerick, a Cullen from Waterford, or a McSweeney from Cork, chances are that your family designed, begged, borrowed, or stole a coat of arms somewhere in its history. The Heraldic Museum has hundreds of family-crest flags, coins, stamps, and silver, all highlighting the uses and evolution of heraldry in Ireland. ⊠ *2 Kildare St., Southside* ☎ *01/661–4877* ⊕ *www.nli.ie* ⊠ *Free* ⊙ *Mon.–Wed. 10–8:30, Thurs. and Fri. 10–4:30, Sat. 10–12:30; guided tours by appointment.*

㉔ Mansion House. The mayor of Dublin resides at the Mansion House, which dates from 1710. It was built for Joshua Dawson, who later sold the property to the government on the condition that "one loaf of double refined sugar of six pounds weight" be delivered to him every Christmas. In 1919 the Declaration of Irish Independence was adopted here. The house is not open to the public. ⊠ *Dawson St., Southside.*

㉖ ⓱ National Museum of Natural History. The famed explorer of the African interior, Dr. Stanley Livingstone (of "Dr. Livingstone, I presume?" fame), inaugurated this museum when it opened in 1857. It's little changed from Victorian times and remains a fascinating repository of mounted mammals, birds, and other flora and fauna. The Irish Room houses the most famous exhibits: skeletons of the extinct, prehistoric, giant "Irish elk." The World Animals Collection includes a 65-foot whale skeleton suspended from the roof. Don't miss the very beautiful Blaschka Collection, finely detailed glass models of marine creatures, the zoological accuracy of which has never been achieved again in glass. The museum is next door to the Government Buildings. ⊠ *Merrion Sq. W,*

Southside ☎ *01/677–7444* ⊕ *www.museum.ie* 🎫 *Free* ⊙ *Tues.–Sat. 10–5, Sun. 2–5.*

⑭ No. 29. Everything in this carefully refurbished 1794 home, known simply as Number Twenty-Nine, is in keeping with the elegant lifestyle of the Dublin middle class between 1790 and 1820, the height of the Georgian period, when the house was owned by a wine merchant's widow. From the basement to the attic—in the kitchen, nursery, servant's quarters, and the formal living areas—the National Museum has re-created the period's style with authentic furniture, paintings, carpets, curtains, paint, wallpapers, and even bell pulls. ⊠ *29 Lower Fitzwilliam St., Southside* ☎ *01/702–6165* ⊕ *www.esb.ie/numbertwentynine* 🎫 *€4.50* ⊙ *Tues.–Sat. 10–5, Sun. 1–5.*

㉓ Royal Irish Academy. The country's leading learned society houses important documents in its 18th-century library, including a large collection of ancient Irish manuscripts, such as the 11th- to 12th-century *Book of the Dun Cow,* and the library of the 18th-century poet Thomas Moore. ⊠ *19 Dawson St., Southside* ☎ *01/676–2570* ⊕ *www.ria.ie* 🎫 *Free* ⊙ *Weekdays 9:30–5.*

㉒ St. Ann's Church. St. Ann's plain, neo-Romanesque granite exterior, built in 1868, belies the rich Georgian interior of the church, which Isaac Wills designed in 1720. Highlights of the interior include polished-wood balconies, ornate plasterwork, and shelving in the chancel dating from 1723—and still in use for organizing the distribution of bread to the parish's poor. ⊠ *Dawson St., Southside* ☎ *01/676–7727* 🎫 *Free* ⊙ *Weekdays 10–4, Sun. for services.*

Off the Beaten Path

Irish Jewish Museum. Roughly 5,000 European Jews fleeing the pogroms of Eastern Europe arrived in Ireland in the late 19th and early 20th centuries. Today the Jewish population hovers around 1,800. The museum, opened in 1985 by Israeli president Chaim Herzog (himself Dublin educated), includes a restored synagogue and a display of photographs, letters, and personal memorabilia culled from Dublin's most prominent Jewish families. Exhibits trace the Jewish presence in Ireland back to 1067. In homage to Leopold Bloom, the Jewish protagonist of Joyce's *Ulysses,* every Jewish reference in the novel has been identified. The museum is a 20-minute-or-so walk southwest from St. Stephen's Green. ⊠ *3–4 Walworth Rd., Grand Canal* ☎ *01/453–1797* 🎫 *Free* ⊙ *May–Sept., Tues., Thurs., and Sun. 11–3:30; Oct.–Apr., Sun. 10:30–2:30.*

Sandymount Strand. South of the city center, a few blocks west of the Sydney Parade DART station, the Sandymount Strand stretches for 5 km (3 mi) from Ringsend to Booterstown. It was cherished by James Joyce and his beloved, Nora Barnacle from Galway, and it figures as one of the settings in *Ulysses.* (The beach is "at the lacefringe of the tide," as Joyce put it.) When the tide recedes, the beach extends for 1½ km (1 mi) from the foreshore, but the tide sweeps in again very quickly. A sliver of a park lies between Strand Road and the beach, whose water is not suitable for swimming.

Shaw Birthplace. "Author of many plays" is the simple accolade to George Bernard Shaw (1856–1950) on the plaque outside his birthplace. The Nobel laureate was born here to a once prosperous family fallen on hard times. Shaw lived in this modest, Victorian terrace house until he was 10 and remembered it as having a "loveless" feel. The painstaking restoration of the little rooms highlights the cramped, claustrophobic atmosphere. All the details of a family home—wallpaper, paint, fittings, curtains, furniture, utensils, pictures, rugs—remain, and it appears as if the family has just gone out for the afternoon. You can almost hear one of Mrs. Shaw's musical recitals in the tiny front parlor. The children's bedrooms are filled with photographs and original documents and letters that throw light on Shaw's career. ✉ *33 Synge St., Southside* ☎ *01/475–0854* ⊕ *www.visitdublin.com* 🎫 *€6.70* ☉ *May–Sept., Mon., Tues., Thurs. and Fri. 10–1 and 2–5, weekends 2–5.*

Temple Bar: The Changing Face

Locals complain about the late-night noise, visitors sometimes say the place has the feel of a "Dublin Theme Park," but a visit to modern Dublin wouldn't be complete without spending some time in the city's most vibrant area. More than any other neighborhood in the city, Temple Bar represents the dramatic changes (good and bad) and ascending fortunes of Dublin that came about in the last decade of the 20th century. The area, which takes its name from one of the streets of its central spine, was targeted for redevelopment in 1991–92 after a long period of neglect, having survived widely rumored plans to turn it into a massive bus depot and/or a giant parking lot. Temple Bar took off as Dublin's version of New York's SoHo, Paris's Bastille, London's Notting Hill—a thriving mix of high and alternative culture distinct from what you'll find in any other part of the city. Dotting the area's narrow cobblestone streets and pedestrian alleyways are new apartment buildings (inside they tend to be small and uninspired, though bearing sky-high rents), vintage-clothing stores, postage-stamp-size boutiques selling €250 sunglasses and other expensive gewgaws, art galleries, a hotel resuscitated by U2, hip restaurants, pubs, clubs, European-style cafés, and a smattering of cultural venues.

Temple Bar's regeneration was no doubt abetted by that one surefire real estate asset: location. The area is bordered by Dame Street to the south, the Liffey to the north, Fishamble Street to the west, and Westmoreland Street to the east. In fact, Temple Bar is situated so perfectly between everywhere else in Dublin that it's difficult to believe this neighborhood was once largely forsaken. It's now sometimes called the "playing ground of young Dublin," and for good reason: on weekend evenings and daily in summer it teems with young people—not only from Dublin but from all over Europe—drawn by its pubs, clubs, and lively *craic* (good conversation and fun).

Some who have witnessed Temple Bar's rapid gentrification and commercialization complain that it's losing its artistic soul—*Harper's Bazaar* said it was in danger of becoming "a sort of pseudoplace," like Lon-

Temple Bar

don's Covent Garden Piazza or Paris's Les Halles. Over the next few years the more cautiously developed Smithfield area may replace Temple Bar at the cutting edge of Dublin culture, but for the moment there's no denying that this is one of the best places to get a handle on the city.

Numbers in the margin correspond to numbers on the Temple Bar map.

TIMING   You can easily breeze through Temple Bar in an hour or so, but if you've got the time, plan to spend a morning or afternoon here, drifting in and out of the dozens of stores and galleries, relaxing at a café over a cup of coffee or at a pub over a pint. If you're looking for a change from sightseeing, you can even try catching a film.

The Main Attractions

30   **Gallery of Photography.** Dublin's premier photography gallery has a permanent collection of early-20th-century Irish photography and also puts on monthly exhibits of work by contemporary Irish and international photographers. The gallery is an invaluable social record of Ireland. The bookstore is the best place in town to browse for photography books and to pick up arty postcards. ⊠ *Meeting House Sq. S, Temple Bar* ☏ *01/671–4654* ⊕ *www.irish-photography.com* ⊠ *Free* ◷ *Tues.–Sat. 11–6, Sun. 1–6.*

25 **Ha'penny Bridge.** Every Dubliner has a story about meeting someone on this cast-iron Victorian bridge, a heavily trafficked footbridge that crosses the Liffey at a prime spot—Temple Bar is on the south side, and the bridge provides the fastest route to the thriving Mary and Henry Street shopping areas to the north. Until early in the 20th century, a halfpenny toll was charged to cross it. Congestion on the Ha'penny has been relieved with the opening of the Millennium Footbridge a few hundred yards up the river. A refurbishment, including new railings, a return to the original white color, and tasteful lighting at night has given the bridge a new lease on life.

> **TOO GREAT A TOLL**
>
> William Butler Yeats was one of many Dubliners who found halfpenny toll of Ha'penny Bridge too steep. He detoured to O'Connell Bridge instead.

27 **Irish Film Institute (IFI).** The opening of the IFI in a former Quaker meetinghouse helped to launch the revitalization of Temple Bar. It has two comfortable art-house cinemas showing revivals and new independent films, the Irish Film Archive, a bookstore for cineastes, and a popular bar and restaurant-café, all of which make this one of the neighborhood's most vital cultural institutions and *the* place to be seen. On Saturday nights in summer, the center screens films outdoors on Meeting House Square. ✉ *6 Eustace St., Temple Bar* ☎ *01/679–5744* ⊕ *www.fii.ie* ☞ *Free* ☉ *Weekdays 9:30 AM–midnight, weekends 11 AM–midnight.*

NEED A BREAK? The trendy **Irish Film Institute Café** (✉ 6 Eustace St., Temple Bar ☎ 01/679–5744) is a pleasant place for a lunchtime break. Sandwiches are large and healthful, with plenty of vegetarian choices, and the people-watching is unmatched.

28 **Meeting House Square.** The square, which is behind the Ark and accessed via Curved Street, takes its name from a nearby Quaker meetinghouse. Today it's something of a gathering place for Dublin's youth and artists. Numerous summer events—classic movies (Saturday nights), theater, games, and family programs—take place here. (Thankfully, seats are installed.) The square is also a favorite site for the continuously changing street sculpture that pops up all over Temple Bar (artists commissioned by the city sometimes create oddball pieces, such as half of a Volkswagen protruding from a wall). Year-round, the square is a great spot to sit, people-watch, and take in the sounds of the performing buskers who swarm to the place. There's also an organic food market here every Saturday morning.

★ **33** **Olympia Theatre.** One of the best places in Europe to see musical acts, the Olympia is Dublin's second oldest and one of its busiest theaters. This classic Victorian music hall, built in 1879, has a gorgeous red wrought-iron facade. The Olympia's long-standing Friday and Saturday series, "Midnight at the Olympia," has brought numerous musical performers to Dublin, and the theater has also seen many notable actors strut across its stage, including Alec Guinness, Peggy Ashcroft, Noël Coward, and even the old-time Hollywood team of Laurel and

Hardy. Big-name performers like Van Morrison often choose the intimacy of the Olympia over larger venues. It's really a hot place to see some fine performances, so if you have a chance, by all means go. Conveniently, there are two pubs here—through doors directly off the back of the theater's orchestra section. ⊠ *72 Dame St., Temple Bar* ☎ *01/ 677–7744.*

★ ❸❷ **Wall of Fame.** If you're strolling through Temple Bar and suddenly come upon a group of slack-jawed young people staring wide-eyed at a large wall, then you've probably stumbled upon the Wall of Fame. The whole front wall of the Temple Bar Music Centre has become a giant tribute to the giants of Irish rock music. Twelve huge photos adorn the wall, including a very young and innocent U2, a very beautiful Sinead O'Connor, and a very drunk Shane McGowan. ⊠ *Curved St., Temple Bar* ☎ *01/ 607–9202.*

> **NEED A BREAK?** The creamiest, frothiest coffees in all of Temple Bar can be had at the **Joy of Coffee/Image Gallery Café** (⊠ 25 E. Essex St., Temple Bar ☎ 01/679–3393); the wall of windows floods light onto the small gallery where original photographs adorn the walls.

Also Worth Seeing

☾ ❸❶ **The Ark.** If you're traveling with children and looking for something fun to do, stop by the Ark, Ireland's cultural center for children, housed in a former Presbyterian church. Its theater opens onto Meeting House Square for outdoor performances in summer. A gallery and workshop space host ongoing activities. ⊠ *Eustace St., Temple Bar* ☎ *01/670– 7788* ⊕ *www.ark.ie* 🖃 *Free* ☉ *Weekdays 9:30–5:30, weekends only if there's a show.*

❷❻ **Central Bank.** Everyone in Dublin seems to have an opinion on the Central Bank. Designed by Sam Stephenson in 1978, the controversial, ultramodern glass-and-concrete building suspends huge concrete slabs around a central axis. It was originally one story higher, but the top floor had to be lopped off as it was hazardous to low-flying planes. Watch out for—or just watch—the skateboarders and in-line skaters who have taken over on the little plaza in front of the building. ⊠ *Dame St., Temple Bar* ☎ *01/671–6666* ⊕ *www.centralbank.ie* ☉ *Weekdays 10–6.*

❷❾ **National Photographic Archive.** Formerly housed in the National Library's main building, the National Photographic Archive now has a stylish home in Temple Bar. The collection comprises approximately 600,000 photographs, most of which are Irish, making up a priceless visual history of the nation. Although most of the photographs are historical, dating as far back as the mid-19th century, there's also a large number of contemporary pictures. Subject matter ranges from topographical views to studio portraits, from political events to early tourist photographs. You can also buy a print of your favorite photo. ⊠ *Meeting House Sq., Temple Bar* ☎ *01/603–0374* ⊕ *www.nli.ie* 🖃 *Free* ☉ *Weekdays 10–5, Sat. 10–2.*

A GOOD WALK: THE GRAND CANAL

If the excitement of the new Dublin gets to be too much for you, try a saunter along the grassy banks of the tranquil Grand Canal, the southern border of the city center. At its completion in 1795, the 547-km (340-mi) canal was celebrated as the longest in Britain and Ireland. It connected Dublin to the River Shannon, and horse-drawn barges carried cargo (mainly turf) and passengers to the capital from all over the country. After the arrival of the railroad in the mid-19th century, the great waterway slowly fell into decline, until the last commercial traffic ceased in 1960. But the 6-km (4-mi) loop around the capital is ideal for a leisurely stroll.

Begin by walking east along the Pearse Street side of Trinity College until you arrive at the Ringsend Road Bridge. Raised on stilts above the canal is the **Waterways Visitors Centre,** an airy wood-and-glass building where you can learn about the history of Irish rivers and canals. Head south and then southwest along the bank until you reach the **Mount Street Bridge,** which has a wooden lock on either side. It's the perfect spot from which to watch these original gateways to the canal in operation. A small stone monument at the southwest corner of the bridge commemorates the battle of Mount Street Bridge in 1916 and the Irish Volunteers who died on the spot. On the southeast side of the canal is Percy Place, a street with elegant, three-story terrace houses. On the northwest side, a small lane leads up to the classy, wood-and-brass **Scruffy Murphy's** pub, where many

a backroom deal has been made by the country's political power brokers.

Walk southwest along Herbert Place. You can get really close to the dark green water here as it spills over one of the many wood-and-iron locks (all still in working order) that service the canal. James Joyce lost his virginity to a prostitute on the next stretch of the canal, around Lower Baggot Street Bridge, but these banks belong to the lonesome ghost of another writer, Patrick Kavanagh (1905–67), Ireland's great rural poet. He spent the later years of his life sitting on a bench here writing about the canal, which flowed from his birthplace in the Midlands to the city where he would die. A life-size statue of Kavanagh now occupies his spot on the bench.

Less than 2 km (1 mi) past the statue, the canal narrows as it approaches Richmond Bridge. To finish your walk in style, take a right onto Richmond Street and stroll past a few antiques stores until you arrive at **Bambrick's,** a pub in the best Irish tradition: half empty, frequented mostly by men over 50, and with a long, dark-wood bar and a staff whose sharp, grinning humor verges on rudeness.

You could walk from Waterways Visitors Centre to Bambrick's pub in as little as a half hour. If you give yourself a couple of hours, you can add a visit the Irish Jewish Museum, which is just beyond Richmond Bridge, and explore the old streets off the canal.

Across the Liffey: The Northside

"What do you call a Northsider in a suit? The accused." So went the old joke. But old stereotypes about the Northside being Dublin's poorer and more deprived half have been washed away beneath the wave of Celtic Tiger development. Locals and visitors alike are discovering the no-nonsense, laid-back charm of the Northside's revamped Georgian wonders, understated cultural gems, high-quality restaurants, and buzzing ethnic diversity.

If you stand on O'Connell Bridge or the pedestrian-only Ha'penny span, you'll get excellent views up and down the River Liffey, known in Gaelic as the *abha na life*, transcribed phonetically as Anna Livia by James Joyce in *Finnegan's Wake*. Here, framed with embankments like those along Paris's Seine, the river nears the end of its 128-km (80-mi) journey from the Wicklow Mountains to the Irish Sea. And near the bridges, you begin a pilgrimage into James Joyce country—north of the Liffey, in the center of town—and the captivating sights of Dublin's Northside, a mix of densely thronged shopping streets and genteelly refurbished homes.

For much of the 18th century, the upper echelons of Dublin society lived in the Georgian houses in the Northside—around Mountjoy Square— and shopped along Capel Street, which was lined with stores selling fine furniture and silver. But development of the Southside—Merrion Square in 1764, the Georgian Leinster House in 1745, and Fitzwilliam Square in 1825—changed the Northside's fortunes. The city's fashionable social center crossed the Liffey, and although some of the Northside's illustrious inhabitants stuck it out, the area gradually became run-down. The Northside's fortunes have now changed back, however. Once-derelict swaths of houses, especially on and near the Liffey, have been rehabilitated, and large shopping centers have opened on Mary and Jervis streets. The high-rise Docklands area, east of the Custom House, is the new hot place to live; a ferry taxi on the Liffey will soon connect it with Temple Bar, while a swing bridge has already been added between City Quay and the Northside. A huge shopping mall and entertainment complex is planned for O'Connell Street, right where the defunct Carlton Cinema stands, and there's even talk of moving the Abbey Theatre here. O'Connell street itself has been partially pedestrianized, and most impressive of all is the Spire, the street's new 395-foot-high stainless-steel monument. Precisely because the exciting redevelopment that transformed Temple Bar is still in its early stages here—because it's a place on the cusp of transition—the Northside is an intriguing part of town.

Numbers in the margin correspond to numbers on the Dublin Northside map.

TIMING   The two greatest cultural institutions of the Northside—the Dublin Writers Museum and the Dublin City Gallery, The Hugh Lane—deserve several hours each. Also, a number of additional sights connected with James Joyce and *Ulysses* are in the vicinity, so devoted Joyce fans will want to devote more time to the area.

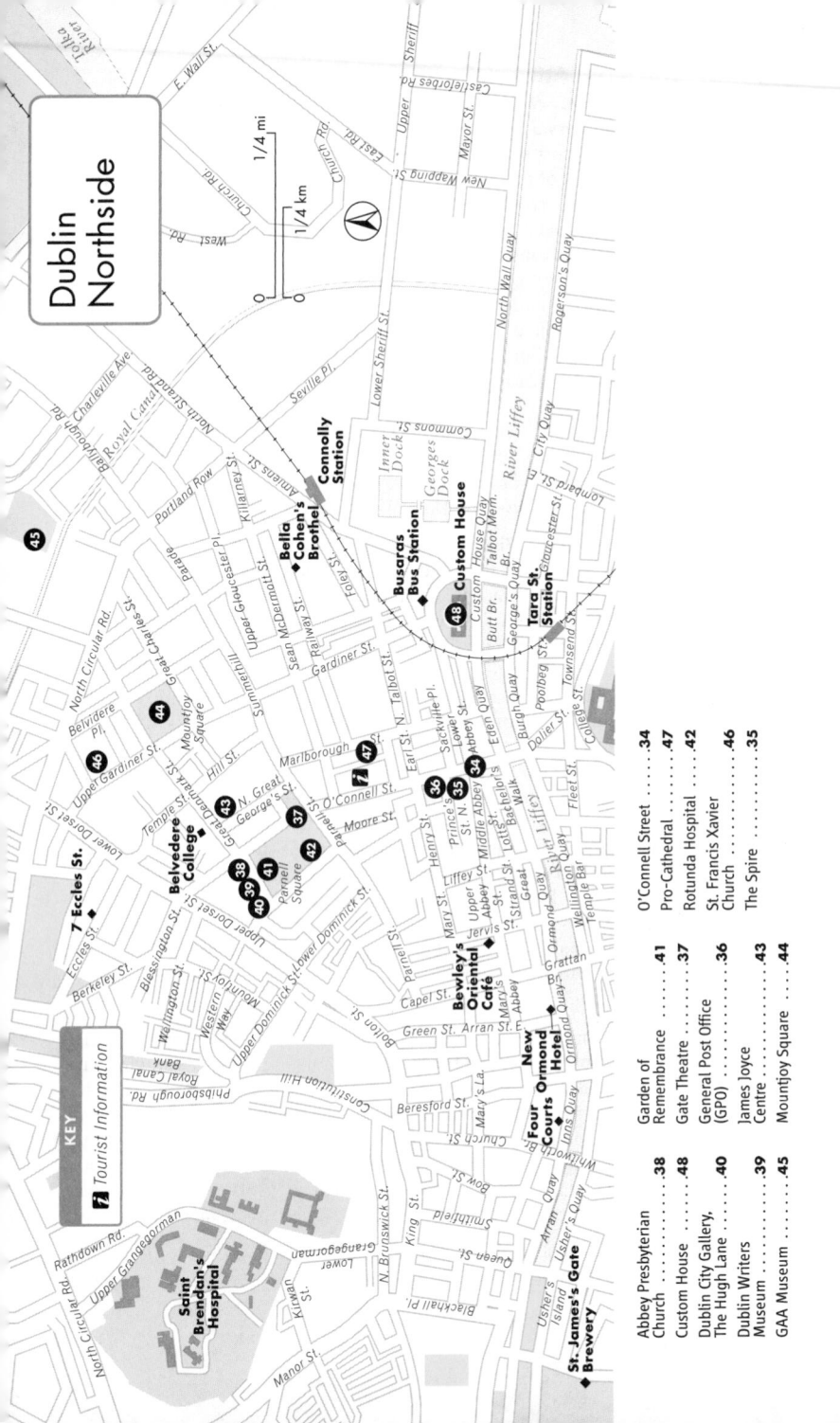

Dublin Northside

KEY

ℹ Tourist Information

1/4 mi

1/4 km

Abbey Presbyterian
Church **38**
Custom House **48**
Dublin City Gallery,
The Hugh Lane **40**
Dublin Writers
Museum **39**
GAA Museum **45**

Garden of
Remembrance **41**
Gate Theatre **37**
General Post Office
(GPO) **36**
James Joyce
Centre **43**
Mountjoy Square **44**

O'Connell Street **34**
Pro-Cathedral **47**
Rotunda Hospital **42**
St. Francis Xavier
Church **46**
The Spire **35**

The Main Attractions

48 Custom House. Seen at its best reflected in the waters of the Liffey during the short interval when the high tide is on the turn, the Custom House is the city's most spectacular Georgian building. Extending 375 feet on the north side of the river, this is the work of James Gandon, an English architect who arrived in Ireland in 1781, when the building's construction commenced (it continued for 10 years). Crafted from gleaming Portland stone, the central portico is linked by arcades to pavilions at either end. A statue of Commerce tops the copper dome, whose puny circumference, unfortunately, is out of proportion to the rest of the building. Statues on the main facade are based on allegorical themes. Note the exquisitely carved lions and unicorns supporting the arms of Ireland at the far ends of the facade. After Republicans set fire to the building in 1921, it was completely restored and reconstructed to house government offices. A visitor center traces the building's history and significance, and the life of Gandon. ✉ *Custom House Quay, Northside* ☎ *01/888–2538* ⊕ *www.visitdublin.com* 🎟 *€1* ☽ *Mid-Mar.–Oct., weekdays 10–12:30, weekends 2–5; Nov.–mid-Mar., Wed.–Fri. 10–12:30, Sun. 2–5.*

★ **40 Dublin City Gallery, The Hugh Lane.** Built as a town house for the Earl of Charlemont in 1762, this residence was so grand its Parnell Square street was nicknamed "Palace Row" in its honor. Sir William Chambers, who also built the Marino Casino for Charlemont, designed the structure in the best Palladian manner. Its delicate and rigidly correct facade, extended by two demilune (half-moon) arcades, was fashioned from the "new" white Ardmulcan stone (now seasoned to gray). Charlemont was one of the cultural locomotives of 18th-century Dublin—his walls were hung with Titians and Hogarths, and he frequently dined with Oliver Goldsmith and Sir Joshua Reynolds—so he would undoubtedly be delighted that his home is now a gallery, named after Sir Hugh Lane, a nephew of Lady Gregory (Yeats's aristocratic patron). Lane collected both Impressionist paintings and 19th-century Irish and Anglo-Irish works. A complicated agreement with the National Gallery in London (reached after heated diplomatic dispute) stipulates that a portion of the 39 French paintings amassed by Lane shuttle between London and here. Time it right and you'll be able to see Pissarro's *Printemps,* Manet's *Eva Gonzales,* Morisot's *Jour d'Été,* and, the jewel of the collection, Renoir's *Les Parapluies.*

In something of a snub to the British art establishment, the late Francis Bacon's partner donated the entire contents of the artist's studio to the gallery. The studio of arguably Britain's premier 20th-century artist has been reconstructed here in all its gaudy glory as a permanent display. It gives you a unique opportunity to observe the bravura technique of the artist responsible for such masterpieces as *Study After Velázquez* and the tragic splash-and-crash *Triptych.* Also on display are Bacon's diary, books, and apparently everything else picked up off his floor.

Between the collection of Irish paintings in the National Gallery of Ireland and the superlative works on display here, you can quickly become familiar with Irish 20th-century art. Irish artists represented include

Roderic O'Conor, well known for his views of the west of Ireland; William Leech, including his *Girl with a Tinsel Scarf* and *The Cigarette*; and the most famous of the group, Jack B. Yeats (W. B.'s brother). The museum has a dozen of his paintings, including *Ball Alley* and *There Is No Night*. There's also strikingly displayed stained-glass work by early-20th-century Irish master-artisans Harry Clarke and Evie Hone. ⊠ *Parnell Sq. N, Northside* ☎ *01/222–5550* ⊕ *www.hughlane.ie* 🖼 *Gallery free; Bacon Studio €7, €3.50 Tues. 9:30–noon* ☉ *Tues.–Thurs. 9:30–6, Fri. and Sat. 9:30–5, Sun. 11–5.*

★ ㉝ **Dublin Writers Museum.** "If you would know Ireland—body and soul—you must read its poems and stories," wrote Yeats in 1891. Further investigation into the Irish way with words can be found at this unique museum, in a magnificently restored 18th-century town house on the north side of Parnell Square. The mansion, once the home of John Jameson, of the Irish whiskey family, centers on the Gallery of Writers, an enormous drawing room gorgeously decorated with paintings, Adamesque plasterwork, and a deep Edwardian lincrusta frieze. Rare manuscripts, diaries, posters, letters, limited and first editions, photographs, and other mementos commemorate the lives and works of the nation's greatest writers—and there are many of them, so leave plenty of time—including Joyce, Shaw, J. M. Synge, Lady Gregory, Yeats, Beckett, and others. On display are an 1804 edition of Swift's *Gulliver's Travels,* an 1899 first edition of Bram Stoker's *Dracula,* and an 1899 edition of Wilde's *Ballad of Reading Gaol.* There's a "Teller of Tales" exhibit showcasing Behan, O'Flaherty, and O'Faoláin. Readings are periodically held. The bookshop and café make this an ideal place to spend a rainy afternoon. If you lose track of time and stay until the closing hour, you might want to dine at Chapter One, a highly regarded restaurant in the basement, which would have had Joyce ecstatic over its currant-sprinkled scones. ⊠ *18 Parnell Sq. N, Northside* ☎ *01/872–2077* ⊕ *www. visitdublin.com* 🖼 *€6.25* ☉ *July and Aug., weekdays 10–6, Sat. 10–5, Sun. 11–5; Sept.–June, Mon.–Sat. 10–5, Sun. 11–5.*

㉞ **Gate Theatre.** The show begins here as soon as you walk into the auditorium, a gorgeously Georgian masterwork designed by Richard Johnston in 1784 as an assembly room for the Rotunda Hospital complex. The Gate has been one of Dublin's most important theaters since its founding in 1929 by Micháel MacLiammóir and Hilton Edwards, who also founded Galway City's An Taibhdhearc as the national Irish-language theater. The Gate stages many innovative productions by Irish as well as foreign playwrights—and plenty of foreign actors have performed here, including Orson Welles (his first paid performance) and James Mason (early in his career). ⊠ *Cavendish Row, Northside* ☎ *01/874–4045* ☉ *Shows Mon.–Sat.*

㉟ **General Post Office.** One of the great civic buildings of Dublin's Georgian era, the GPO's fame is based on the role it played in the Easter Uprising. The building, with its impressive

THE SCARS OF HISTORY

Look for the bullet marks on the pillars of the General Post Office—they're remnants of the 1916 Easter Uprising.

Neoclassical facade, was designed by Francis Johnston and built by the British between 1814 and 1818 as a center of communications. This gave it great strategic importance—and was one of the reasons it was chosen by the insurgent forces in 1916 as a headquarters. Here, on Easter Monday, 1916, the Republican forces, about 2,000 in number and under the guidance of Pádrig Pearse and James Connolly, stormed the building and issued the Proclamation of the Irish Republic. After a week of shelling, the GPO lay in ruins; 13 rebels were ultimately executed, including Connolly, who was dying of gangrene from a wound in a leg shattered in the fighting and had to be propped up in a chair in front of the firing squad. Most of the original building was destroyed, though the facade survived, albeit with the scars of bullets on its pillars. Rebuilt and reopened in 1929, it became a working main post office with an attractive two-story main concourse. A bronze sculpture depicting the dying Cuchulainn, a leader of the Red Branch Knights in Celtic mythology, sits in the front window. The 1916 Proclamation and the names of its signatories are inscribed on the green marble plinth. ⊠ *O'Connell St., Northside* ☎ *01/872–8888* ⊕ *www. anpost.ie* 🖾 *Free* ⊙ *Mon.–Sat. 8–8, Sun. 10:30–6.*

NEED A BREAK?

For a classic Dublin pub with a bustling all-day atmosphere, stop in at **Kiely's** (⊠ 37/38 Middle Abbey St., Northside ☎ 01/872–2100). It's popular with media folk and does a great pub lunch and a smooth pint of the black stuff.

㊹ James Joyce Centre. Few may have read him, but everyone in Ireland has at least heard of James Joyce (1882–1941)—especially since a copy of his censored and suppressed *Ulysses* was one of the top status symbols of the early 20th century. Joyce is of course now acknowledged as one of the greatest modern authors, and his *Dubliners, Finnegan's Wake,* and *A Portrait of the Artist as a Young Man* can even be read as quirky "travel guides" to Dublin. Open to the public, this restored 18th-century Georgian town house, once the dancing academy of Professor Denis J. Maginni (which many will recognize from a reading of *Ulysses*), is a center for Joycean studies and events related to the author. It has an extensive library and archives, exhibition rooms, a bookstore, and a café. The collection includes letters from Beckett, Joyce's guitar and cane, and a celebrated edition of *Ulysses* illustrated by Matisse. The center is the main organizer of "Bloomstime," which marks the week leading up to the Bloomsday celebrations. (Bloomsday, June 16, is the single day *Ulysses* chronicles, as Leopold Bloom winds his way around Dublin in 1904.) ⊠ *35 N. Great George's St., Northside* ☎ *01/878–8547* ⊕ *www.jamesjoyce.ie* 🖾 *€5, guided tour €10* ⊙ *Tues.–Sat. 10–5.*

㉞ O'Connell Street. Dublin's most famous thoroughfare, which is 150 feet wide, was previously known as Sackville Street, but its name was changed in 1924, two years after the founding of the Irish Free State. After the devastation of the 1916 Easter Uprising, the Northside street had to be almost entirely reconstructed, a task that took until the end of the 1920s. At one time the main attraction of the street, Nelson's Pillar, a Doric column towering over the city center and a marvelous vantage point, was blown up in 1966, on the 50th anniversary of the Easter

Uprising. The 395-foot-high Spire was built in its place in 2003, and today this gigantic, stainless-steel monument dominates the street. A major clean up and repaving have returned to the street some of its old glory. The large monument at the south end of the street is dedicated to Daniel O'Connell (1775–1847), "The Liberator," and was erected in 1854 as a tribute to the orator's achievement in securing Catholic Emancipation in 1829. Seated winged figures represent the four Victories—Courage, Eloquence, Fidelity, and Patriotism—all exemplified by O'Connell. Ireland's four ancient provinces—Munster, Leinster, Ulster, and Connacht—are identified by their respective coats of arms. Look closely and you'll notice that O'Connell is wearing a glove on one hand, as he did for much of his adult life, a self-imposed penance for shooting a man in a duel. But even the great man himself is dwarfed by the newest addition to O'Connell Street, the silver Spire.

NEED A BREAK?

Conway's (✉ Parnell St. near Upper O'Connell St., Northside ☎ 01/873–2687), founded in 1745, is reputed to be Dublin's second-oldest pub. Guinness-drinking men who like "a flutter on the gee gees" (to gamble on horse racing) mix with office workers on their lunch breaks availing themselves of the unpretentious pub grub. One of Dublin's oldest hotels, dating to 1817, the **Gresham** (✉ Upper O'Connell St., Northside ☎ 01/874–6881) was once the bastion of Dublin high society. Its high-ceiling Georgian dining area is still a pleasant, old-fashioned spot for morning coffee or afternoon tea.

47 **Pro-Cathedral.** Dublin's principal Catholic cathedral (also known as St. Mary's) is a great place to hear the best Irish male voices—a Palestrina choir, in which the great Irish tenor John McCormack began his career, sings in Latin here every Sunday morning at 11. The cathedral, built between 1816 and 1825, has a classical church design—on a suitably epic scale. The church's facade, with a six-Doric-pillared portico, is based on the Temple of Theseus in Athens; the interior is modeled after the Grecian-Doric style of St. Philippe du Roule in Paris. But the building was never granted full cathedral status, nor has the identity of its architect ever been discovered; the only clue to its creation is in the church ledger, which lists a "Mr. P." as the builder. ✉ *Marlborough St., Northside* ☎ *01/874–5441* ⊕ *www.procathedral.ie* ⌨ *Free* ☉ *Daily 8–6.*

35 **The Spire.** Christened the "Stiletto in the Ghetto" by local smart alecks, this needlelike monument is the most exciting thing to happen to Dublin's skyline in decades. The Spire, also known as the Monument of Light, was originally planned as part of the city's millennium celebrations. But Ian Ritchie's spectacular 395-foot-high monument wasn't erected until the beginning of 2003. Seven times taller than the nearby General Post Office, the stainless-steel structure rises from the spot where Nelson's Pillar once stood. Approximately 10 feet in diameter at its base, the softly lighted monument narrows to only 1 foot at its apex—the upper part of the Spire sways gently when the wind blows. The monument's creators envisioned it serving as a beacon for the whole of the city, and it will certainly be the first thing you see as you drive into Dublin from the airport. ✉ *O'Connell St., Northside.*

Continued on page 76

LITERARY DUBLIN

A PLAYWRIGHT ON EVERY CORNER

A ramble through literary Dublin is a crash course in Irish soul.

As any visit to the Dublin Writers Museum will prove, this city packs more literary punch per square foot than practically any other spot on the planet. While the Irish capital may be relatively small in geographic terms, it looms huge as a country of the imagination. Dubliners wrote some of the greatest works of Western literature, including these immortal titles: *Ulysses, Gulliver's Travels, Dracula, The Importance of Being Earnest,* and *Waiting for Godot.* Today Dublin is a veritable literary theme park: within a few minutes' walk you can visit the birthplace of George Bernard Shaw, see where Sean O'Casey wrote *Juno and the Paycock,* and pop into the pub where Brendan Behan loved to get marinated.

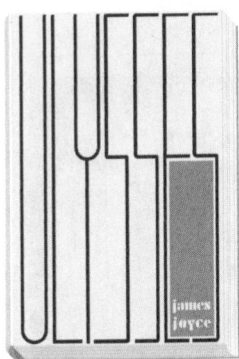

Ulysses, First American Edition

Shaw's proof copy of *Pygmalion*, his Nobel prize, and his Oscar

A Way with Words

As tellers of the tallest tales, speakers of Gaelic (reputedly the world's most perfect medium for prayers, curses, and seduction), and the finest practitioners of the art of blarney, it's little surprise that the Hibernian race produced no fewer than four Nobel prize winners: Shaw, W. B. Yeats, Samuel Beckett, and Seamus Heaney. But what is surprising is that this tiny, long-colonized island on the outskirts of Europe somehow managed to maneuver itself to the very heart of literature in the language of the invader itself, English. And at that heart's core lies Dublin.

> "All the world's a stage and most of us are desperately unrehearsed."
> —Sean O'Casey

For Better or Verse

By the 18th century, the Gaelic tradition was trumped by the boom of literature written in English, often by second- or third-generation descendants of English settlers, such as William Congreve, Richard Brinsley Sheridan, and Oliver Goldsmith. With the Easter Uprising of 1916, so many Irish writers found themselves censored that "being banned" became a matter of prestige (it also did wonders for book sales abroad, with a smuggled copy of *Ulysses* becoming the ultimate status symbol). Sadly, many writers became exiles; most famously, Joyce was joined in Paris by Beckett in 1932.

Dublin B(u)y the Book

Book lovers know that a guidebook to this city is an anthology of Irish literature in itself. Dublin's Northside is studded with landmarks immortalized in James Joyce's novels. A stone's throw from the Liffey is the Abbey Theater, a potent symbol of Ireland's great playwrights. To the south lies Trinity College, alma mater of Jonathan Swift, Bram Stoker, Oscar Wilde, and Samuel Beckett. And scattered around the city are thousands of pubs where storytelling evolved as the incurable Irish "disease." They are the perfect places to take a time-out while touring Dublin's leading literary shrines and sites.

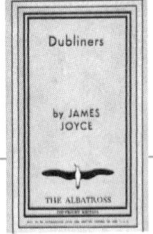

Arrow Books

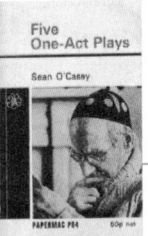

Macmillan

THE TRAIL OF TALES

Allowing you to turn the pages of the city, as it were, with your feet, a literary ramble through Dublin is a magical mystery tour through more than 400 years of Irish history.

Dublin Writers Museum, Gallery of Writers

DUBLIN WRITERS MUSEUM. The best place to start any literary tour of the city, this gloriously restored 18th-century mansion was once the home of the Jameson Whiskey family (booze and writers are never too far apart in Dublin). Its Edwardian rooms are filled with inky treasures like the 1804 edition of Swift's *Gulliver's Travels* and the 1899 first edition of Stoker's *Dracula*. ⇨ p. 64 ⊠ 18 Parnell Sq. N ☎ 01/872-2077 ⊕ www.visitdublin.com.

GATE THEATER. Landmarked by its noble Palladian portico, this magnificent Georgian theater (built 1784) today sees the premieres of some of Ireland's most talked-about plays. Orson Welles and James Mason got their starts here. ⊠ Cavendish Row ⊠ ☎ 01/874-4045 ⊕ www.gate-theater.ie.

JAMES JOYCE CENTRE. Now an extensive library dedicated to arguably the greatest novelist of the 20th century, this sumptuously decorated

18th-century town house was featured in *Ulysses* as a dancing academy. Letters from Beckett, Joyce's guitar and cane, and a Joyce edition illustrated by Matisse are collection highlights. ⇨ p. 66. ⊠ 35 N. Great George's St. ☎ 01/878-8547 ⊕ www.jamesjoyce.ie.

SEAN O'CASEY HOUSE. A one-time construction laborer, O'Casey became Ireland's greatest modern playwright and this is the house where he wrote all his famous Abbey plays, including *Juno and the Paycock* and *The Plough and the Stars.* ⊠ 422 N. Circular Rd.

ABBEY THEATRE. Hard to believe this 1950s modernist eyesore is the fabled home of Ireland's national theater company, established on a wave of nationalist passion by Yeats and his patron, Lady Gregory, in 1904. Here premiered J.M. Synge's scandalous *Playboy of the Western World* and the working-class plays of Sean O'Casey. The foyer and bar display mementos of the

theater's fabled "Abbeyists." ⊠ Lower Abbey St. ☎ 01/878-7222 ⊕ www.abbeytheater.ie.

TRINITY COLLEGE DUBLIN. This 400-year-old college has an incredible record for turning out literary giants like Swift, Goldsmith, Wilde, Synge, Stoker, and Beckett. Majestically presiding over its famous library is the 9th-century Book of Kells, mother of all Irish tomes. ⇨ pp. 46–49. ⊠ Front Sq. ☎ 01/608-2308 ⊕ www.tcd.ie.

NATIONAL LIBRARY. Joyce used the 1890 Main Reading Room, with its dramatic domed ceiling, as the scene of the great literary debate in *Ulysses.* At No. 30 Kildare Street a plaque marks a former residence of *Dracula*'s creator, Bram Stoker. ⇨ p. 54. ⊠ Kildare St. ☎ 01/661-8811 ⊕ www.nli.ie.

MERRION SQUARE. An elegant mansion, which can be toured, No. 1 Merrion Square is the former Oscar Wilde family residence. A statue of Oscar reclines in

Neary's Pub

the park opposite. Around the square, note the plaques that indicate former residents, including W.B. Yeats and Sheridan le Fanu, Dublin's most famous ghost-story teller ⇨ p. 52.

ST. STEPHEN'S GREEN. This pretty, flower-filled little park is home to a wonderful statue of Joyce ⇨ p. 46.

GEORGE BERNARD SHAW BIRTHPLACE. Shaw lived in this modest, Victorian terrace house until he was 10 and the painstaking restoration of the little rooms highlights a cramped, claustrophobic atmosphere Eliza Doolittle would have felt at home in. ⇨ p. 57. ✉ 33 Synge St. ☎ 01/475-0854 ⊕ www.visitdublin.com.

NEARY'S PUB. The exotic, Victorian-style interiors here were once haunted by Dublin's literary set, most notably the master bar raconteur Brendan Behan. ✉ 1 Chatham St. ☎ 01/677-7371.

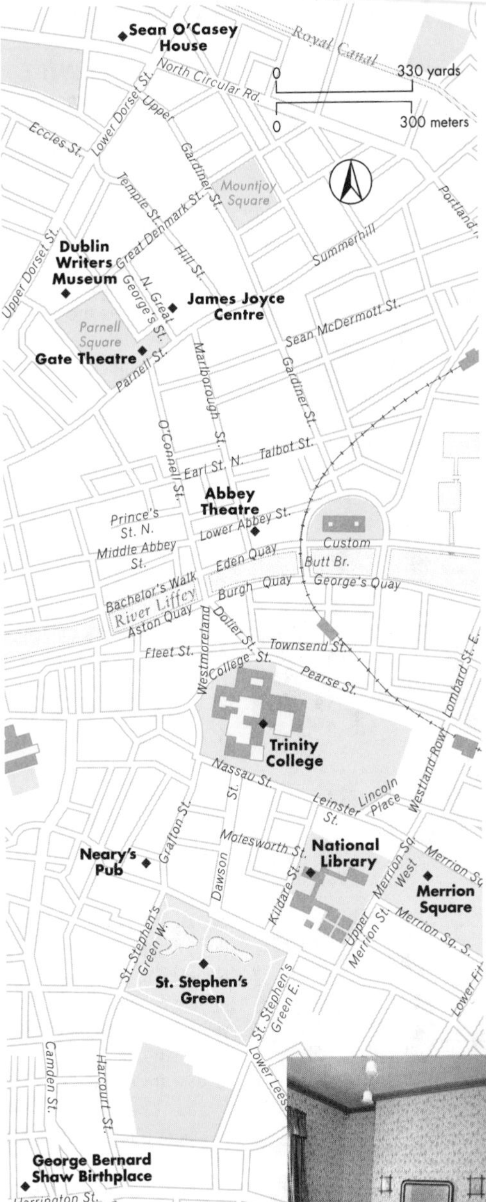

Sean O'Casey House

Royal Canal

North Circular Rd.

0 ─── 330 yards
0 ─── 300 meters

Eccles St. · Lower Dorset St. · Upper Dorset St. · Temple St. · Denmark St. · Gardiner St. Upper · Hill St. · Mountjoy Square · Summerhill · Portland

Dublin Writers Museum · Great Denmark St. · N. Great George's St.

James Joyce Centre

Sean McDermott St.

Parnell Square

Gate Theatre · Parnell St. · Marlborough St. · Gardiner St.

O'Connell St. · Earl St. N. · Talbot St.

Prince's St. N. · **Abbey Theatre** · Lower Abbey St.

Middle Abbey St. · Eden Quay · Custom

Bachelor's Walk · Burgh Quay · Butt Br. · George's Quay

River Liffey · Aston Quay

Fleet St. · Westmoreland St. · D'Olier St. · College St. · Townsend St. · Pearse St. · Lombard St. E.

Trinity College · Nassau St. · Leinster St. · Lincoln Place · Westland Row

Grafton St. · Molesworth St. · **National Library** · Upper Merrion St. · Merrion Sq.

Neary's Pub · Dawson St. · Kildare St. · **Merrion Square** · Merrion Sq. S.

St. Stephen's Green W. · St. Stephen's Green N. · **St. Stephen's Green** · St. Stephen's Green E. · Lower Fitzwilliam

Camden St. · Harcourt St. · Lower Leeson St.

George Bernard Shaw Birthplace · Harrington St. · S. Richmond St. · Charlemont St.

Shaw Birthplace

A DUBLIN PANTHEON

JONATHAN SWIFT

"Where fierce indignation can no longer tear his heart": Swift, one of the great satirists in the English language, willed these words be carved on his tomb at Dublin's St. Patrick's Cathedral. Swift was born on November 30th, 1667, in the Liberties area of Dublin. Life would deal him many misfortunes, but he gave as good as he got, venting his great anger with a pen sharper than any sword. His rage at the British government's mistreatment of the Irish was turned into the brilliant satire *A Modest Proposal* where he politely recommends a solution to the dual problems of hunger and overpopulation: breed babies for meat. Best remembered for the brilliant moral fable *Gulliver's Travels*, he died on October 19, 1745, and is buried in Dublin's St. Patrick's Cathedral, where he was dean.

OSCAR WILDE

The greatest wit of his age and arguably any other, Wilde was born on October 16th, 1834, at 21 Westland Row in Dublin, the son of an eminent eye doctor. He was educated at Trinity College, where he was a promising boxer and was quoted as saying his greatest challenge was learning to live up to the blue china he had installed in his rooms. Wilde moved to London in 1879, where he married, had children, and became celebrated for the plays *The Importance of Being Earnest* and *Salome* and his titillating novel *The Picture of Dorian Gray*. But his life was always more famous than his work and a scandalous affair with the aristocratic Alfred Douglas finally led to his ruin and imprisonment.

W. B. YEATS

Poet, dramatist, and prose writer, Yeats—winner of the Nobel Prize for Literature in 1923—stands as one of the greatest English-language poets of the 20th century. And yet in Ireland itself he is best remembered for his key role in the struggle for Irish freedom and the revival of Irish culture, including his part in forming the Abbey Theatre (National Theatre). Born in the seaside suburb of Sandymount in Dublin in 1865, his fascination with Celtic folklore and the stories of Cuchulainn can be seen throughout his early poems and plays. But many of his greatest poems are haunted by the dashing figure of Maud Gonne, actress, revolutionary, and unrequited love. He died in 1939 in Paris but his body was buried in Drucliffe, at the foot of Ben Bulben mountain in his beloved County Sligo.

GEORGE BERNARD SHAW

G. Bernard Shaw—he hated George, and never used it either personally or professionally—was born in Dublin in 1856. His father was a boozing corn merchant and his mother a professional singer. When Shaw was a boy his mother ran away with her voice coach, and it may be no coincidence that his plays are dotted with problem child/parent relationships. In 1886 he went to London where plays such as *Pygmalion* and *Saint Joan* helped propel him to international stardom. Pacifist, socialist, and feminist, Shaw was a true original, a radical in the real sense of the word, his work always challenging the norms of his day. He lived to the ripe old age of 94 and died in 1950 after falling off a ladder while trimming trees outside his house.

SEAN O'CASEY

The first working-class Irish literary great, dramatist O'Casey was born at 85 Upper Dorset Street in the inner-city Dublin slums in 1880. Problems with his eyes as a child kept him indoors where he gleaned a love of reading. An early advocate of Yeats's Celtic Revival, he later found his true faith in the socialism of union leader Jim Larkin. His trilogy of great tragicomedies—*Shadow of a Gunman*, *Juno and the Paycock*, and *The Plough and the Stars*—all deal with ordinary families caught up in the maelstrom of Irish politics and were performed at Yeats's Abbey in the 1920s. Their playful language and riotous action have made them classics ever since. He spent his later life in England and died in Devon in 1964.

BRENDAN BEHAN

Writer, fighter, drinker, and wit, Brendan Francis Behan was born in Dublin's Holles Street Hospital in 1923 into an educated, political working-class family. Urged on by his fiercely patriotic grandmother, he joined Fiánna Eireann, the youth wing of the IRA and, in 1939, was jailed for three years for possessing explosives. In prison he began to write but it wasn't until the 1950s that he hit it big with *The Quare Fellow*, a play based on his prison experiences, and later works *The Hostage* and *Borstal Boy*. But it was in the bars of Dublin that the "demon drinker" Behan delivered many of his greatest lines—alas, lost now forever. A self-proclaimed "drinker with a writing problem," he died in 1964 at the age of only 41.

REJOICE!: The Darlin' Dublin of James Joyce

If Joyce fans make one pilgrimage in their lives, let it be to Dublin on June 16th for Bloomsday. June 16th, of course, is the day Leopold Bloom toured Dublin in *Ulysses*, and commemorative events take place all week long leading up to the big day (and night).

Grown men and women stroll the streets attired in black suits and carrying fresh bars of lemon soap in their pockets, imitating the unassuming hero of what is arguably the 20th century's greatest novel. Denounced as obscene, blasphemous, and unreadable when it was first published in 1922 (and then banned in the U.S. until 1933), this 1,000-page riff on Homer's *Odyssey* portrays three characters—Leopold Bloom, a Jewish ad salesman, his wife, Molly, and friend Stephen Daedelus—as they wander through Dublin during the span of one day, June 16th, 1904. Dedicated Joyceans flock to the weeklong event, now called "Bloomstime," for Bloomsday breakfasts (where they can enjoy, like Bloom himself, "grilled mutton kidneys... which gave to his palate a fine tang of faintly scented urine"), readings, performances, and general merriment.

But don't despair if you miss Bloomsday, because you can experience the Dublin that inspired the author's novels year-round. James Joyce (1882-1941) set all his major works—*Dubliners, A Portrait of the Artist as a Young Man, Ulysses,* and *Finnegan's Wake*—in the city where he was born and spent the first 22 years of his life. Joyce knew and remembered Dublin in such detail that he bragged (and that's the word) that if the city were destroyed, it could be rebuilt in its entirety from his written works.

Above Left: Joyce Statue, Earl Street
Above Right: Bloomsday celebrations
Left: A portrait of the author by photographer Berenice Abbott

BEGIN IN THE HEART OF THE NORTHSIDE, on Prince's Street, next to the GPO (General Post Office), where the office of the old and popular *Freeman's Journal* newspaper (published 1763–1924) was once located and where Bloom once worked. Head north up O'Connell Street down Parnell Square before turning right onto Dorset Street and then left onto Eccles Street. Leopold and Molly Bloom's fictional home stood at 7 Eccles Street, north of Parnell Square.

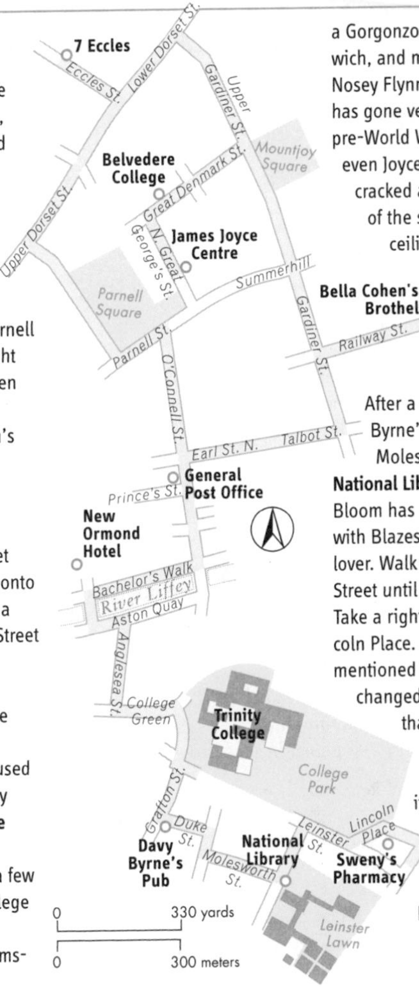

Head back to Dorset Street and go east. Take a right onto Gardiner Street and then a left onto Great Denmark Street and Belvedere College. Between 1893 and 1898, Joyce studied at Belvedere College (☎ 01/874–3974) under the Jesuits; it's housed in a splendid 18th-century mansion. The **James Joyce Centre** (☎ 01/878–8547 🌐 www.jamesjoyce.ie), a few steps from Belvedere College on North Great George's Street, is the hub of Bloomsday celebrations.

Go back to Gardiner Street and then south until you come to Railway Street on your left. The site of **Bella Cohen's Brothel** (✉ 82 Railway St.) is in an area that in Joyce's day contained many houses of ill repute. A long walk back down O'Connell Street to the bridge and then a right will take you to Ormond Quay. On the western

Map labels: 7 Eccles · Eccles St. · Lower Dorset St. · Upper Gardiner St. · Mountjoy Square · Belvedere College · Great Denmark St. · N. Great George's St. · Upper Dorset St. · James Joyce Centre · Summerhill · Parnell Square · Parnell St. · O'Connell St. · Gardiner St. · Bella Cohen's Brothel · Railway St. · Earl St. N. · Talbot St. · Prince's St. · General Post Office · New Ormond Hotel · Bachelor's Walk · River Liffey · Aston Quay · Anglesea St. · College Green · Trinity College · College Park · Grafton St. · Duke St. · Davy Byrne's Pub · Molesworth St. · National Library · Leinster St. · Lincoln Place · Sweny's Pharmacy · Leinster Lawn

0 — 330 yards
0 — 300 meters

edge of the Northside, the **New Ormond Hotel** (✉ Upper Ormond Quay ☎ 01/872–1811) was an afternoon rendezvous spot for Bloom.

Across the Liffey, walk up Grafton Street to **Davy Byrne's Pub** (✉ 21 Duke St., ☎ 01/671–1298). Here, Bloom comes to settle down for a glass of Burgundy and a Gorgonzola cheese sandwich, and meets his friend Nosey Flynn. Today, the pub has gone very upscale from its pre-World War II days, but even Joyce would have cracked a smile at the sight of the shamrock-painted ceiling and the murals of Joycean Dublin by Liam Proud.

After a stop at Davy Byrne's, proceed via Molesworth Street to the **National Library**—where Bloom has a near meeting with Blazes Boylan, his wife's lover. Walk up Molesworth Street until you hit Trinity. Take a right and walk to Lincoln Place. No establishment mentioned by Joyce has changed less since his time than **Sweny's Pharmacy** (✉ Lincoln Pl.), which still has its black-and-white exterior and an interior crammed with potions and vials.

Davy Byrne's Pub

Also Worth Seeing

38 Abbey Presbyterian Church. Built on the profits of sin—well, by a generous wine merchant actually—and topped with a soaring Gothic spire, this church anchors the northeast corner of Parnell Square, an area that was the city's most fashionable address during the gilded days of the 18th-century Ascendancy. Popularly known as Findlater's Church—after the merchant Alex Findlater—the church was completed in 1864 with an interior that has a stark Presbyterian mood despite stained-glass windows and ornate pews. For a bird's-eye view of the area, climb the small staircase that leads to the balcony. ⊠ *Parnell Sq., Northside* 🕾 *01/837–8600* 🎟 *Free* ⊙ *Hrs vary.*

45 GAA Museum. The Irish are sports crazy, and reserve their fiercest pride for their native games. In the bowels of Croke Park, the main stadium and headquarters of the GAA (Gaelic Athletic Association), this museum gives you a great introduction to native Irish sport. The four Gaelic games (football, hurling, camogie, and handball) are explained in detail, and if you're brave enough you can have a go yourself. High-tech displays take you through the history and highlights of the games. *National Awakening* is a really smart, interesting short film reflecting the key impact of the GAA on the emergence of the Irish nation and the forging of a new Irish identity. The exhilarating *A Day in September* captures the thrill and passion of All Ireland finals day—the annual denouement of the intercounty hurling and Gaelic football seasons—which is every bit as important to the locals as the Super Bowl is to sports fans in the U.S. Tours of the stadium, the fourth largest in Europe, are available. ⊠ *New Stand, Croke Park, North County Dublin* 🕾 *01/855–8176* ⊕ *www.gaa.ie* 🎟 *Museum €5.50, museum and stadium tour €9.50* ⊙ *July and Aug., Mon.–Sat. 9:30–6, Sun. noon–5; Sept.–June, Mon.–Sat. 9:30–5, Sun. noon–5.*

41 Garden of Remembrance. Opened 50 years after the Easter Uprising of 1916, the garden in Parnell Square commemorates those who died fighting for Ireland's freedom. At the garden's entrance is a large plaza; steps lead down to the fountain area, graced with a sculpture by contemporary Irish artist Oisín Kelly, based on the mythological Children of Lír, who were turned into swans. The garden serves as an oasis of tranquility in the middle of the busy city. ⊠ *Parnell Sq., Northside* 🎟 *Free* ⊙ *Daily 9–5.*

44 Mountjoy Square. Built over the course of the two decades leading up to 1818, this Northside square was once surrounded by elegant terraced houses. Today only the northern side remains intact. The houses on the once derelict southern side have been converted into apartments. Irishman Brian Boru, who led his soldiers to victory against the Vikings in the Battle of Clontarf in 1014, was said to have pitched camp before the confrontation on the site of Mountjoy Square. Playwright Sean O'Casey lived here, at No. 35, and used the square as a setting for *The Shadow of a Gunman.*

42 Rotunda Hospital. The Rotunda, founded in 1745 as the first maternity hospital in Ireland and Britain, was designed on a grand scale by architect Richard Castle (1690–1751), with a three-story tower and a copper cupola. It's now most worth a visit for its chapel, with elaborate plasterwork, appropriately honoring motherhood, executed by

Bartholomew Cramillion between 1757 and 1758. The Gate Theatre, in a lavish Georgian assembly room, is on the O'Connell Street side of this large complex. ⊠ *Parnell St., Northside* ☎ *01/873–0700.*

46 **St. Francis Xavier Church.** One of the city's finest churches in the classical style, the Jesuit St. Francis Xavier's was begun in 1829, the year of Catholic Emancipation, and was completed three years later. The building is designed in the shape of a Latin cross, with a distinctive Ionic portico and an unusual coffered ceiling. The striking, faux-marble high altarpiece, decorated with lapis lazuli, came from Italy. The church appears in James Joyce's story "Grace." ⊠ *Upper Gardiner St., Northside* ☎ *01/836–3411* ☞ *Free* ☉ *Daily 7 AM–8:30 PM.*

Dublin West: Cathedrals & Guinness

A cornucopia of things quintessentially Dublin, this area is studded with treasures and pleasures ranging from the opulent 18th-century salons of Dublin Castle to time-burnished St. Patrick's Cathedral, from the Liberties neighborhood—redoubt of the city's best antiques stores—to the Irish Museum of Modern Art (housed at the strikingly renovated Royal Hospital Kilmainham). You can time-travel from the 10th-century crypt at Christ Church Cathedral—the city's oldest surviving structure—to the modern plant of the Guinness Brewery and its storehouse museum. You can also cross the Liffey for a visit to Smithfield. Bordered on the east by Church Street, on the west by Blackhall Place, to the north by King Street, and to the south by the Liffey, Smithfield is Dublin's old market area where flowers, fruit, vegetables, and even horses have been sold for generations. Chosen as a flagship for north inner-city renovation, the area has seen a major face-lift in the last few years. The beautiful cobblestones of its streets have been taken up, refinished, and replaced, and giant masts topped with gaslights send 6-foot-high flames over Smithfield Square— now the venue for the occasional major rock concert (the square was where U2 were awarded the keys to Dublin city in 1999). Early morning is a special time in Smithfield, as the wholesale fruit and veg sellers still ply their trade in the wonderful 19th-century covered market. Traditional music bars like the Cobblestone, a favorite of the market traders, now sit side by side with modern hotels like Chief O'Neills and the award-winning Old Jameson Distillery museum.

Keep in mind that Dublin is compact. The following sights aren't far from those in the other city-center neighborhoods. In fact, City Hall is just across the street from the Temple Bar, and Christ Church Cathedral is a short walk farther west. The westernmost sights covered here— notably the Royal Hospital and Kilmainham Gaol—are, however, at some distance, so if you're not an enthusiastic walker, you may want to drive or catch a cab or a bus to them.

Numbers in the margin correspond to numbers on the Dublin West & Phoenix Park map.

TIMING   Allow a few hours for this area, especially if you want to include the Guinness Brewery and Storehouse and the Irish Museum of Modern Art at the Royal Hospital. Keep in mind that if you want to cover the easternmost sights—Dublin Castle, City Hall, Christ Church Cathedral, and environs—you can easily append them to a tour of Temple Bar.

The Main Attractions

⑤ Chester Beatty Library. A connoisseur's delight, this "library" is considered by many to be the most impressive museum in Ireland. After Sir Alfred Chester Beatty (1875–1968), a Canadian mining millionaire and a collector with a flawless eye, assembled one of the most significant collections of Islamic and Far Eastern art in the Western world, he donated it to Ireland. Housed in the gorgeous clock-tower building of Dublin Castle, and voted European Museum of the Year in 2002, the library is one of Dublin's real gems. Among the exhibits are clay tablets from Babylon dating from 2700 BC, Japanese wood-block prints, Chinese jade books, and Turkish and Persian paintings. The second floor, dedicated to the major religions, houses 250 manuscripts of the Koran from across the Muslim world, as well as one of the earliest Gospels. Life-size Buddhas from Burma and rhino cups from China are among the other curios on show. Guided tours of the library are available on Tuesday and Saturday at 2:30 PM. On sunny days the garden is one of the most tranquil places in central Dublin. The shop is full of unique and exotic souvenirs relating to the collection. ⊠ *Castle St., Dublin West* ☎ *01/407–0750* ⊕ *www.cbl.ie* ✆ *Free* ⊗ *May–Sept., weekdays 10–5, Sat. 11–5, Sun. 1–5; Oct.–Apr., Tues.–Fri. 10–5, Sat. 11–5, Sun. 1–5.*

Fodor'sChoice ★

★ **⑤ Christ Church Cathedral.** You'd never know from the outside that the first Christianized Danish king built a wooden church at this site in 1038; because of the extensive 19th-century renovation of its stonework and trim, the cathedral looks more Victorian than Anglo-Norman. Construction on the present Christ Church—the flagship of the Church of Ireland and one of two Protestant cathedrals in Dublin (the other is St. Patrick's just to the south)—was begun in 1172 by Strongbow, a Norman baron and conqueror of Dublin for the English crown, and continued for 50 years. By 1875 the cathedral had deteriorated badly; a major renovation gave it much of the look it has today, including the addition of one of Dublin's most charming structures: a Bridge of Sighs–like affair that connects the cathedral to the old Synod Hall, which now holds the Viking multimedia exhibition, Dublinia. Remains from the 12th-century building include the north wall of the nave, the west bay of the choir, and the fine stonework of the transepts, with their pointed arches and supporting columns. Strongbow himself is buried in the cathedral, beneath an impressive effigy. The vast, sturdy **crypt**, with its 12th- and 13th-century vaults, is Dublin's oldest surviving structure and the building's most notable feature. The Treasures of Christ Church exhibition includes manuscripts, various historic artifacts, and the tabernacle used when James II worshiped here. At 6 PM on Wednesday and Thursday you can enjoy the glories of a choral evensong. ⊠ *Christ Church Pl. and Winetavern St., Dublin West* ☎ *01/677–8099* ⊕ *www.cccdub.ie* ✆ *€5* ⊗ *June–Aug., daily 9–6; Sept.–May, daily 9:45–5.*

㊾ City Hall. Facing the Liffey from Cork Hill at the top of Parliament Street, this grand Georgian municipal building (1769–79), once the Royal Exchange, marks the southwest corner of Temple Bar. Today it's the seat

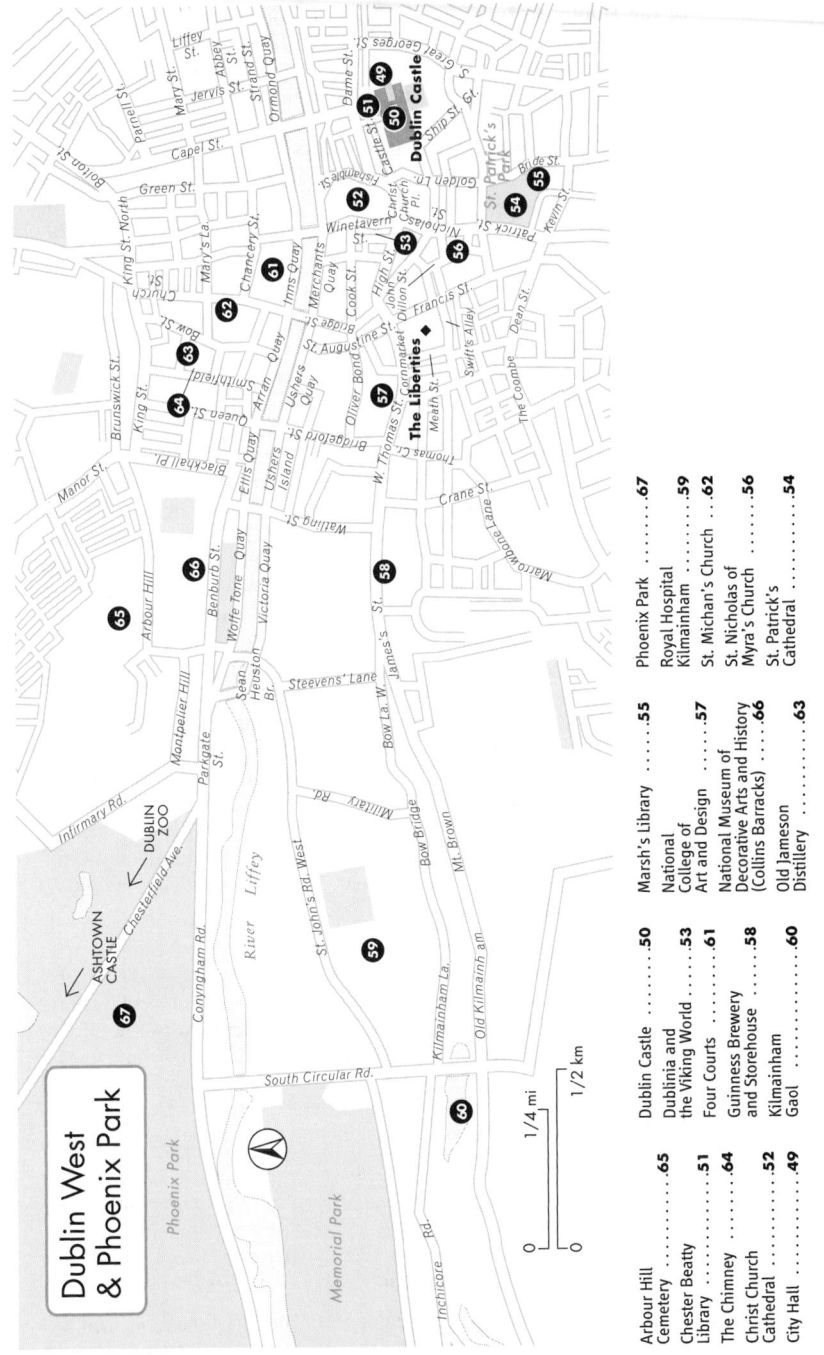

Dublin West & Phoenix Park

Arbour Hill Cemetery **65**
Chester Beatty Library **51**
The Chimney **64**
Christ Church Cathedral **52**
City Hall **49**

Dublin Castle **50**
Dublinia and the Viking World **53**
Four Courts **61**
Guinness Brewery and Storehouse **58**
Kilmainham Gaol **60**

Marsh's Library **55**
National College of Art and Design **57**
National Museum of Decorative Arts and History (Collins Barracks) **66**
Old Jameson Distillery **63**

Phoenix Park **67**
Royal Hospital Kilmainham **59**
St. Michan's Church **62**
St. Nicholas of Myra's Church **56**
St. Patrick's Cathedral **54**

1/2 km
1/4 mi

of the Dublin Corporation, the elected body that governs the city. Thomas Cooley designed the building with 12 columns that encircle the domed central rotunda, which has a fine mosaic floor and 12 frescoes depicting Dublin legends and ancient Irish historical scenes. The 20-foot-high sculpture to the right is of Daniel O'Connell, "The Liberator." He looks like he's about to begin the famous speech he gave here in 1800. The building houses a multimedia exhibition—with artifacts, kiosks, graphics, and audiovisual presentations—tracing the evolution of Ireland's 1,000-year-old capital. ⊠ *Dame St., Dublin West* ☎ *01/672–2204* ⊕ *www.dublincity.ie/your_council/city_hall* 🎫 *€4* ☼ *Mon.–Sat. 10–5:15, Sun. 2–5.*

⑤⓪ Dublin Castle. Neil Jordan's film *Michael Collins* captured Dublin Castle's near indomitable status well: seat and symbol of the British rule of Ireland for more than seven centuries, the castle figured largely in Ireland's turbulent history early in the 20th century. It's now mainly used for Irish and EU governmental purposes. The sprawling Great Courtyard is the reputed site of the Black Pool (Dubh Linn, pronounced *dove-lin*) from which Dublin got its name. In the Lower Castle Yard, the Record Tower, the earliest of several towers on the site, is the largest remaining relic of the original Norman buildings, built by King John between 1208 and 1220. The clock tower building now houses the Chester Beatty Library. Guided tours are available of the principal State Apartments (on the southern side of the Upper Castle Yard), formerly the residence of the English viceroys and now used by the president of Ireland to host visiting heads of state and EU ministers. The State Apartments are lavishly furnished with rich Donegal carpets and illuminated by Waterford glass chandeliers. The largest and most impressive of these chambers, St. Patrick's Hall, with its gilt pillars and painted ceiling, is used for the inauguration of Irish presidents. The Round Drawing Room, in Bermingham Tower, dates from 1411 and was rebuilt in 1777; numerous Irish leaders were imprisoned in the tower from the 16th century to the early 20th century. The blue oval Wedgwood Room contains Chippendale chairs and a marble fireplace. The Castle Vaults now hold an elegant little patisserie and bistro.

Carved oak panels and stained glass depicting viceroys' coats of arms grace the interior of the Church of the Holy Trinity (formerly called Chapel Royal), on the castle grounds. The church was designed in 1814 by Francis Johnston, who also designed the original General Post Office building on O'Connell Street. Once you're inside, look up—you'll see an elaborate array of fan vaults on the ceiling. More than 100 carved heads adorn the walls outside: among them, St. Peter and Jonathan Swift preside over the north door, St. Patrick and Brian Boru over the east.

One-hour guided tours of the castle are available every half hour, but the rooms are closed when in official use, so call ahead. The easiest way into the castle is through the Cork Hill Gate, just west of City Hall. ⊠ *Castle St., Dublin West* ☎ *01/677–7129* ⊕ *www.dublincastle.ie* 🎫 *State Apartments €4.50, including tour* ☼ *Weekdays 10–5, weekends 2–5.*

⑥① Four Courts. The stately Corinthian portico and the circular central hall warrant a visit here, to the seat of the High Court of Justice of Ireland.

The distinctive copper-cover dome topping a colonnaded rotunda makes this one of Dublin's most instantly recognizable buildings. The view from the rotunda is terrific. Built between 1786 and 1802, the Four Courts are James Gandon's second Dublin masterpiece—close on the heels of his Custom House, located downstream on the same side of the River Liffey. In 1922, during the Irish Civil War, the Four Courts was almost totally destroyed by shelling—the adjoining Public Records Office was gutted, and many priceless legal documents, including innumerable family records, were destroyed. Restoration took 10 years. Tours of the building are not given, but you're welcome to sit in while the courts are in session. ⊠ *Inns Quay, Dublin West* ☎ *01/872–5555* ⊕ *www.courts. ie* ⊙ *Daily 10–1 and 2:15–4.*

⑤⑧ Guinness Brewery and Storehouse. Ireland's all-dominating brewer— founded by Arthur Guinness in 1759 and at one time the largest stout-producing brewery in the world—spans a 60-acre spread west of Christ Church Cathedral. Not surprisingly, it's the most popular tourist destination in town—after all, the Irish national drink is Guinness stout, a dark brew made with

FodorsChoice
★

> **WORD OF MOUTH**
>
> "Given that Guinness is synonymous with Dublin, not making the trip to the Storehouse might be akin to visiting Boston and passing on a visit to Fenway Park."
> –DavidD

roasted malt. The brewery itself is closed to the public, but the Guinness Storehouse is a spectacular attraction, designed to woo you with the wonders of the "dark stuff." In a 1904 cast-iron-and-brick warehouse, the museum display covers six floors built around a huge, central glass atrium. Beneath the glass floor of the lobby you can see Arthur Guinness's original lease on the site, for a whopping 9,000 years. The exhibition elucidates the brewing process and its history, with antique presses and vats, a look at bottle and can design through the ages, a history of the Guinness family, and a fascinating archive of Guinness advertisements. You might think it's all a bit much (it's only a drink, after all), and parts of the exhibit do feel a little over the top. The star attraction is undoubtedly the top-floor **Gravity Bar,** with 360-degree floor-to-ceiling glass walls that offer a nonpareil view out over the city at sunset while you sip your free pint. One of the bar's first clients was one William Jefferson Clinton. The Guinness Shop on the ground floor is full of funky lifestyle merchandise associated with the "dark stuff." ⊠ *St. James' Gate, Dublin West* ☎ *01/408–4800* ⊕ *www.guinness.com* ⊡ *€14* ⊙ *July and Aug., daily 9:30–8; Sept.–June, daily 9:30–5.*

⑥⓪ Kilmainham Gaol. Leaders of many failed Irish rebellions spent their last days in this grim, forbidding structure, and it holds a special place in the myth and memory of the country. The 1916 commanders Pádrig Pearse and James Connolly were held here before being executed in the prison yard. Other famous inmates included the revolutionary Robert Emmet and Charles Stewart Parnell, a leading politician. You can visit the prison only as part of a guided tour, which leaves every hour on the hour. The cells are a chilling sight, and the guided tour and a 30-minute audiovisual presentation relate a graphic account of Ireland's political history over the past 200 years—from an Irish Nationalist viewpoint. A new exhibition displays items that haven't been seen together since Robert Emmet's failed rebellion of 1803. A small tearoom is on the premises. ☒ *Inchicore Rd., Dublin West* ☎ *01/453–5984* ⊕ *www. heritageireland.ie* ☒ *€5* ⊗ *Apr.–Sept., daily 9:30–5; Oct.–Mar., Mon.–Sat. 9:30–4, Sun. 10–5.*

★ ❺❾ **Royal Hospital Kilmainham.** This replica of Les Invalides in Paris is regarded as the most important 17th-century building in Ireland. Commissioned as a hospice for disabled and veteran soldiers by James Butler—the duke of Ormonde and viceroy to King Charles II—the building was completed in 1684, making it the first building erected in Dublin's golden age. It survived into the 1920s as a hospital, but after the founding of the Irish Free State in 1922, the building fell into disrepair. The entire edifice has since been restored to what it once was.

The structure's four galleries are arranged around a courtyard; there's also a grand dining hall—100 feet long by 50 feet wide. The architectural highlight is the hospital's Baroque chapel, distinguished by its extraordinary plasterwork ceiling and fine wood carvings. "There is nothing in Ireland from the 17th century that can come near this masterpiece," raved cultural historian John FitzMaurice Mills. The Royal Hospital also houses the **Irish Museum of Modern Art,** which concentrates on the work of contemporary Irish artists such as Richard Deacon, Richard Gorman, Dorothy Cross, Sean Scully, Matt Mullican, Louis Le Brocquy, and James Colman. The museum also displays works by some non-Irish 20th-century greats, including Picasso and Miró, and regularly hosts touring shows from major European museums. The Café Musée serves light fare such as soups and sandwiches. The hospital is a short ride by taxi or bus from the city center. ☒ *Kilmainham La., Dublin West* ☎ *01/612–9900* ⊕ *www.modernart.ie* ☒ *Free* ⊗ *Royal Hospital Tues.–Sat. 10–5:30, Sun. noon–5:30; tours every ½ hr. Museum Tues.–Sat. 10–5:30, Sun. noon–5:30; tours Wed. and Fri. at 2:30, Sat. at 11:30.*

❺❹ **St. Patrick's Cathedral.** The largest cathedral in Dublin and also the national cathedral of the Church of Ireland, St. Patrick's is the second of the capital's two Protestant cathedrals. (The other is Christ Church, and the reason Dublin has two cathedrals is because St. Patrick's originally stood outside the walls of Dublin, while its close neighbor was within the walls and belonged to the see of Dublin.) Legend has it that in the 5th century, St. Patrick baptized many converts at a well on the site of the cathedral. The original building, dedicated in 1192 and early English Gothic in style, was an unsuccessful attempt to assert supremacy over Christ Church Cathedral. At 305 feet, this is the longest church in the country, a fact Oliver Cromwell's troops—no friends to the Irish— found useful as they made the church's nave into their stable in the 17th century. They left the building in a terrible state; its current condition is largely due to the benevolence of Sir Benjamin Guinness—of the brewing family—who started financing major restoration work in 1860.

FodorśChoice
★

Make sure you see the gloriously heraldic Choir of St. Patrick's, hung with colorful medieval banners, and find the tomb of the most famous of St. Patrick's many illustrious deans, Jonathan Swift, immortal author of *Gulliver's Travels*, who held office from 1713 to 1745. Swift's tomb is in the south aisle, not far from that of his beloved "Stella," Mrs. Esther Johnson. Swift's epitaph is inscribed over the robing-room door. Yeats—who translated it thus: "Swift has sailed into his rest; Savage indignation there cannot lacerate his breast"—declared it the greatest epitaph of all time. Other memorials include the 17th-century Boyle Monument, with its numerous painted figures of family members, and the monument to Turlough O'Carolan, the last of the Irish bards and one of the country's finest harp players. Immediately north of the cathedral is a small park, with statues of many of Dublin's literary figures and St. Patrick's Well. "Living Stones" is the cathedral's permanent exhibition celebrating St. Patrick's place in the life of the city. If you're a music lover, you're in for a treat; matins (9:40 AM) and evensong (5:45 PM) are still sung on most days. ⊠ *Patrick St., Dublin West* ☎ *01/453–9472* ⊕ *www.stpatrickscathedral. ie* 🖾 *€5* ⊙ *May, Sept., and Oct., weekdays 9–6, Sat. 9–5, Sun. 10–11 and 12:45–3; June–Aug., weekdays 9–6, Sat. 9–4, Sun. 9:30–3 and 4:15–5:15; Nov.–Apr., weekdays 9–6, Sat. 9–4, Sun. 10–11 and 12:45–3.*

> ### FROM PEW TO VIEW
>
> While in the shadow of St. Patrick's Cathedral, head from Patrick Close to Patrick Street; look down the street toward the Liffey for a glorious view of Christ Church.

Also Worth Seeing

The Chimney. Just in front of the Chief O'Neill Hotel stands one of the original brick chimneys, built in 1895, of the Old Jameson Distillery, which has been turned into a 185-foot-tall observation tower with the first 360-degree view of Dublin. The redbrick chimney now has a two-tier, glass-enclosed platform at the top. The trip aloft in the glass elevator is just as thrilling as the view from the platform. ⊠ *Smithfield Village, Dublin West* ☎ *01/817–3820* ⊕ *www.chiefoneills.com* 🖾 *€5* ⊙ *Daily 10–5:30.*

Dublinia and the Viking World. Ever wanted a chance to put your head in the stocks? Dublin's Medieval Trust has set up an entertaining and informative reconstruction of everyday life in medieval Dublin. The main exhibits use high-tech audiovisual and computer displays; you can also see a scale model of what Dublin was like around 1500, a medieval maze, a life-size reconstruction based on the 13th-century dockside at Wood Quay, and a fine view from the tower. For a more modern take on the city, check out the James Malton series of prints of 18th-century Dublin, hanging on the walls of the coffee shop. Dublinia is in the old Synod Hall (formerly a meeting place for bishops of the Church of Ireland), joined via a covered stonework Victorian bridge to Christ Church Cathedral. An exhibition on "The Viking World" consists of a similar reconstruction of life in even earlier Viking Dublin. ⊠ *St. Michael's Hill, Dublin West* ☎ *01/679–4611* ⊕ *www.dublinia.ie* 🖾 *Exhibit €6* ⊙ *Apr.–Sept., daily 10–5; Oct.–Mar., Mon.–Sat. 11–4, Sun. 10–4:30.*

55 Marsh's Library. When Ireland's first public library was founded and endowed in 1701 by Narcissus Marsh, the Archbishop of Dublin, it was made open to "All Graduates and Gentlemen." The two-story brick Georgian building has remained virtually the same since then. It houses a priceless collection of 250 manuscripts and 25,000 15th- to 18th-century books. Many of these rare volumes were locked inside cages, as were the readers who wish to peruse them. The cages were to discourage students who, often impecunious, may have been tempted to make the books their own. The library has been restored with great attention to its original architectural details, especially in the book stacks. The library is a short walk west from St. Stephen's Green and accessed through a charming little cottage garden. ⌧ *St. Patrick's Close off Patrick St., Dublin West* ☎ *01/454–3511* ⊕ *www.marshlibrary.ie* ⌧ *€2.50* ☽ *Mon. and Wed.–Fri. 10–1 and 2–5, Sat. 10:30–1.*

57 National College of Art and Design. The delicate welding of glass and iron onto the redbrick Victorian facade of this onetime factory makes this school worth a visit. A walk around the cobblestone central courtyard often gives the added bonus of viewing students working away in glass, clay, metal, and stone. ⌧ *Thomas St., Dublin West* ☎ *01/671–1377* ⊕ *www.ncad.ie* ⌧ *Free* ☽ *Weekdays 9–7.*

63 Old Jameson Distillery. Founded in 1791, this distillery produced one of Ireland's most famous whiskeys for nearly 200 years, until 1966, when local distilleries merged to form Irish Distillers and moved to a purpose-built, ultramodern distillery in Middleton, County Cork. Part of the complex was converted into the group's head office, and the distillery itself became a museum. There's a short audiovisual history of the industry, which had its origins 1,500 years ago in Middle Eastern perfume making. You can also tour the old distillery, and learn about the distilling of whiskey from grain to bottle, or view a reconstruction of a former warehouse, where the colorful nicknames of former barrel makers are recorded. The 40-minute tour includes a complimentary tasting (remember: Irish whiskey is best drunk without a mixer—try it straight or with water); four attendees are invited to taste different brands of Irish whiskey and compare them against bourbon and Scotch. If you have a large group and everyone wants to do this, phone in advance to arrange it. ⌧ *Bow St., Dublin West* ☎ *01/807–2355* ⊕ *www.jamesondistillery.ie* ⌧ *€8.75* ☽ *Daily 9:30–6; tours every ½ hr.*

62 St. Michan's Church. However macabre, St. Michan's main claim to fame is down in the vaults, where the totally dry atmosphere has preserved several corpses in a remarkable state of mummification. They lie in open caskets. Most of the resident deceased are thought to have been Dublin tradespeople (one was, they say, a religious crusader). Except for its 120-foot-high bell tower, this Anglican church is architecturally undistinguished. The church was built in 1685 on the site of an 11th-century Danish church (Michan was a Danish saint). Another reason to come is to see the 18th-century organ, which Handel supposedly played for the first performance of *Messiah*. Don't forget to check out the Stool of Repentance—the only one still in existence in the city. Parishioners judged to be "open and notoriously naughty livers" used it to do public penance. ⊠ *Lower Church St., Dublin West* ☎ *01/872–4154* ☎ *€3.50* ⊗ *Mid-Mar.–Oct., weekdays 10–12:45 and 2–4:45, Sat. 10–12:45, Sun. service at 10 AM; Nov.–mid-Mar., weekdays 12:30–3:30, Sat. 10–12:45, Sun. service at 10 AM.*

⑤⑥ St. Nicholas of Myra's Church. A grand Neoclassical style characterizes this church, completed in 1834. The highly ornate chapel inside includes ceiling panels of the 12 apostles, and a pietà raised 20 feet above the marble altar, guarded on each side by angels sculpted by John Hogan while he was in Florence. The tiny nuptial chapel to the right has a small Harry Clarke stained-glass window. ⊠ *St. Nicholas St., Dublin West* ☎ *Free* ⊗ *Hrs vary.*

"Take it aisy": Phoenix Park & Environs

Far and away Dublin's largest park, Phoenix Park (the name is an anglicization of the Irish *Fionn Uisce,* meaning clear water) is a vast, green, arrowhead-shape oasis north of the Liffey, about a 20-minute walk from the city center. It's the city's main escape valve and sports center (cricket, soccer, Gaelic games, and polo), and the home of the noble creatures of the Dublin Zoo. A handful of other cultural sights near the park also merit a visit.

Numbers in the margin correspond to numbers on the Dublin West & Phoenix Park map.

TIMING   Phoenix Park is *big;* exploring it on foot could easily take the better part of a day. If you're looking for a little exercise, head here: jogging, horseback riding, and bicycling are the ideal ways to explore the park. To make a full day of it, you could couple a trip to the park with visits to several of the sights in the Dublin West area; the Smithfield neighborhoods and the Old Jameson Distillery closest, and the Guinness Brewery and Storehouse, across the river, is also fairly close.

The Main Attactions

★ **⑥⑥ National Museum of Decorative Arts and History.** Connoisseurs of the decorative arts have always had a special fondness for Irish style, whose glories range from Bronze Age Celtic jewels to the moderne 20th-century furniture of Eileen Gray. Here, in one gigantic treasure chest, is the full panoply of the National Museum's collection of glass, silver, furniture, and other decorative arts. The setting is spectacular: the huge Collins Barracks, named for the assassinated Irish Republican leader Michael Collins (1890–1922). Built in the early 18th century, designed by Captain Thomas Burgh, these erstwhile "Royal Barracks" were stylishly renovated to become a showcase for the museum, which opened in September 1997. The displays are far ranging, covering everything from one of the greatest collections of Irish silver in the world to Irish period furniture—you'll see that the country's take on Chippendale was far earthier than the English mode—to "The Way We Wore: 250 Years of Irish Clothing and Jewelry." Headlining the collections are some extraordinary objects, including the Fonthill Vase, the William Smith O'Brien Gold Cup, and the Lord Chancellor's Mace. ⊠ *Benburb St., Dublin West* ☎ *01/677-7444* ⊕ *www.museum.ie* ☎ *Free* ⊗ *Tues.–Sat. 10–5, Sun. 2–5.*

Phoenix Park. Europe's largest public park, which extends about 5 km (3 mi) along the Liffey's north bank, encompasses 1,752 acres of verdant green lawns, woods, lakes, and playing fields. Sunday is the best time to visit: games of cricket, football (soccer), polo, baseball, hurling (a combination of lacrosse, baseball, and field hockey), and Irish football are likely to be in progress. Old-fashioned gas lamps line both sides of Chesterfield Avenue, the main road that bisects the park for 4 km (2½ mi), which was named for Lord Chesterfield, a lord lieutenant of Ireland, who laid out the road in the 1740s. To the right as you enter the park is the People's Garden, a colorful flower garden designed in 1864.

Among the park's major monuments are the Phoenix Column, erected by Lord Chesterfield in 1747, and the 198-foot obelisk, built in 1817 to commemorate the Duke of Wellington, the Irish general who defeated Napoléon for the British. (Wellington was born in Dublin but, true to the anti-Irish prejudice so prevalent in 19th-century England, balked at the suggestion that he was Irish: "If a man is born in a stable, it doesn't mean he is a horse," he is reputed to have said.) A tall white cross marks the spot where Pope John Paul II addressed more than a million people during his 1979 visit to Ireland. Wild deer can be seen grazing in the many open spaces of the park, especially near here.

> ### THE DUBS' CUBS
>
> There's something about Dublin Zoo that lions must find agreeable—it's one of the few places in the world where they will breed in captivity.

You're guaranteed to see wildlife at the **Dublin Zoo** (⊠ Dublin West ☎ 01/677–1425 ⊕ www.dublinzoo.ie), the third-oldest public zoo in the world, founded in 1830, and just a short walk beyond the People's Garden. The place looks a little dilapidated, but a five-year renovation is scheduled for completion in 2006. Animals from tropical climes are kept in unbarred enclosures, and Arctic species swim in the lakes close to the reptile house. Some 700 lions have been bred here since the 1850s, one of whom became familiar to movie fans the world over when MGM used him for its trademark. (As they will tell you at the zoo, he is in fact yawning in that familiar shot: an American lion had to be hired to roar and the "voice" was dubbed.) The African Plains section houses the zoo's larger species; the Nakuru Safari is a new 25-minute tour of this area. Pets Corner and City Farm has goats, guinea pigs, and lambs. In summer the Lakeside Café serves ice cream and drinks. Admission to the Dublin Zoo is €12.50. Hours are March through September, Monday through Saturday, 9:30 to 6, and Sunday, 10:30 to 6; from October through February, Monday through Saturday, 9:30 to 5, and Sunday, 10:30 to 5.

Both the president of Ireland and the U.S. ambassador have official residences in the park (the president's is known as Aras an Uachtarain), but neither building is open to the public. Also within the park is a **visitor center** (⊠ Dublin West ☎ 01/677–0095 ⊕ www.heritageireland. ie), in the 17th-century fortified Ashtown Castle; it has information about the park's history, flora, and fauna. Admission to the center is €2.75. Hours are mid-March through end of March, daily 10–5:30, April to September, daily 10 to 6; October, daily 10 to 5:30; November to mid-March, Wednesday–Sunday, from 10 to 5.

NEED A BREAK? **Ryan's Pub (⊠ 28 Parkgate St., Dublin West ☎ 01/677–6097), one of Dublin's last remaining genuine late-Victorian-era pubs, has changed little since its last remodeling—in 1896. It's right near the entrance to Phoenix Park.**

Also Worth Seeing

65 Arbour Hill Cemetery. All 14 Irishmen executed by the British following the 1916 Easter Uprising are buried here, including Pádrig Pearse, who led the rebellion; his younger brother Willie, who played a minor role in the uprising; and James Connolly, a socialist and labor leader wounded in the battle. Too weak from his wounds to stand, Connolly was tied to a chair and then shot. The burial ground is a simple but formal area, with the names of the dead leaders carved in stone beside an inscription of the proclamation they issued during the uprising. ⊠ *Arbour Hill, Dublin West* 🖃 *Free* ⊙ *Mon.–Sat. 9–4:30, Sun. 9:30–noon.*

WHERE TO EAT

By Anto Howard

"Come in! Come in! Your dinner's poured out!" goes the old North Dublin joke. In truth, its description of Irish food as being best when hidden in soup wasn't so far off the mark. For years, "Irish cuisine" used to be nothing more than a convenient way of grouping potatoes and stout under the same heading. However, the days when critics bemoaned the *pot* luck of the Irish are thankfully gone. Today, be prepared to have your preconceptions overturned, and, on occasion, to be enthralled and very happily sated in the process.

The Irish dine later than Americans. They stay up later, too, and reservations are usually not booked before 6:30 or 7 PM and up to around 11 PM. Lunch is generally served from 12:30 to 2:30. Pubs often serve food through the day—until 8:30 or 9 PM. Most pubs are family-friendly and welcome children until 7 PM. The Irish are an informal bunch, so smart casual dress is typical. The more formal restaurants, however, do expect you to wear a jacket and tie (noted below). And remember: shorts and sneakers are out here.

Prices

A word of warning: forget about singing, you will pay for your supper in Dublin. High overhead and staffing costs have pushed up prices, especially in upscale places. Alas, Dublin recently got its first Starbucks, but there are scores of inexpensive cafés serving excellent coffee, and often good sandwiches. Other eateries, borrowing trends from all around the world, serve inexpensive pizzas, focaccia, pitas, tacos, and wraps (which are fast gaining popularity over the sandwich). It's worthwhile to see if the restaurant of your choice offers an early-bird and/or pre- or posttheater menu, with significantly lower set prices at specific times, usually up to 7:30 PM and after the show. Value Added Tax (V.A.T.)—

EATING WELL IN DUBLIN

It's only a decade since "ethnic" food in Dublin meant sitting at home in front of the TV with a very uninspired Chinese dish of sweet-and-sour chicken. A flood of foreign restaurants has resuscitated the once staid and boring Dublin dining scene and forced native chefs to rethink their menus and reinvent old favorites.

The abundant high-quality produce the country is famous for is finally receiving the care and attention of world-class chefs in the capital city's restaurants. Salmon is mixed with smoked haddock for fish cakes served with anchovy and parsley butter; black pudding is butter-fried and covered in an apple compote; and Irish beef is spiced and topped with a tangy avocado salsa.

Even the humble potato is being shaped and transformed into potato cakes and boxty (potato-and-flour pancake), and colcannon—a traditional Irish dish with bacon and cabbage—is getting a nouvelle spin.

Being an agricultural country with a maritime industry, Ireland benefits from a copious supply of freshly grown and readily available produce and seafood. Excellent Irish beef, pork, ham, and lamb appear on almost every menu.

Keep an eye out, too, for seasonal specials, such as wild or farmed quail and pheasant. Rich seafood harvests mean you can find fresh and smoked salmon, oysters, mussels, and shellfish in many guises—all vying with tender cuts of meat and an appetizing selection of quality vegetables.

Excellent dairy products are also essential to Irish cuisine. Dollops of fresh cream with home-baked desserts promise some exciting conclusions to these feasts—though you could also opt to finish a meal with a selection of native cheeses.

Leave room for the mature cheddars and luscious blue cheeses, the slightly sweet Dubliner, St. Tola goat's cheese from Clare, and Carrigburne Brie from Wexford—only a few of the many fine artisan cheeses produced around the country.

While you're in Dublin, do indulge at least once in the traditional Irish breakfast, which is often served all day. It includes rashers (bacon), sausages, black-and-white pudding (types of sausage), mushrooms, tomatoes, and a fried egg—with lots of traditional homemade brown and soda breads and the famous Irish creamery butter. You'll need a pot or two of tea to wash this down. Known as an "Ulster Fry" in Northern Ireland, this breakfast is often the biggest—and best—meal of the day.

a 13.5% tax on food and a government excise tax on drinks—will automatically be added to your bill. Before paying, check to see whether a service charge has been included on your bill, which is often the case. If so, you can pay the entire bill with a credit card; if not, it's usual to leave a tip in cash (10% to 15%) if paying the main bill by credit card.

WHAT IT COSTS in euros				
	$$$$	$$$	$$	$	¢
AT DINNER	over €30	€25–€30	€18–€24	€10–€17	under €10

Prices are per person for a main course.

City Center: The Southside

American

$$$$ ✕ **Shanahans on the Green.** The management describes this as an "American-style steak house" and if they mean big steaks—Texas-big—they deliver. Happily, quantity doesn't necessarily diminish quality and Shanahans arguably serves the best beef in the country, all certified Irish Angus, of course. In fact, the only things "American" here are those humongous portions and the basement bar, the Oval Office, full of Americana and presidential paperwork. The building itself is an Irish Georgian glory, designed by Richard Cassels, Dublin's leading 18th-century architect. Glowing with gilded chandeliers and graced with a few marble fireplaces, this restored town house offers a sleekly elegant setting in which to chow down on some of the tenderest beef this side of Kobe (they cook it in a special high-temperature oven, searing the outside to keep the inside good and juicy). If steak doesn't float your boat, they also do a mean pan-roasted Alaskan halibut with lump-crap stuffed artichoke, cherry-vine tomatoes, and gremolata. Oreo-cookie-crust cheesecake is the perfect way to finish off the feast but many will consider the decor—think sash windows, gilt mirrors, and plush carpets—rich enough. ⊠ *119 St. Stephen's Green, City Center* ☎ *01/407–0939* ⊕ *www.shanahans.ie* ⌕ *Reservations essential* ⊟ *AE, DC, MC, V* ☉ *No lunch Sat.–Thurs.*

FodorsChoice
★

Café

¢ ✕ **Busyfeet & Coco Café.** This bustling, quirky café emphasizes good, wholesome food. Organic ingredients play a prominent role on a menu that's laden with delicious salads and sandwiches. Try the grilled goat-cheese salad served with walnut-and-raisin toast and sun-dried-tomato tapenade on a bed of arugula. The delicious homemade hummus sandwich—served on poppy-seed bread, and topped with roasted red and yellow peppers, red onions, and zucchini—is a must. ⊠ *41–42 S. William St., City Center* ☎ *01/671–9514* ⊟ *No credit cards.*

FodorsChoice
★

Continental

★ $$$$ ✕ **Locks.** Near poet Patrick Kavanagh's favorite spot on the Grand Canal where "here by a lock Niagariously roars," a genuinely warm welcome awaits you at this adorably soigné country house–style restaurant. The dining room is all "Irish mother," meaning cozy and old-fashioned, with banquette seating, open fires, and starched table linens. Hearty portions are served on antique ironstone plates. The mouthwatering menu combines the best of peasant French fare with a modern Irish touch. Classic starters include Locks's special potato skins—dished up with prawns, tomato, and spinach and served with a fabulous hollandaise sauce—and excellent smoked salmon. The roast rack of lamb with ratatouille, pomme puree, and a rosemary jus is nonpareil in the city. ⊠ *1 Wind-*

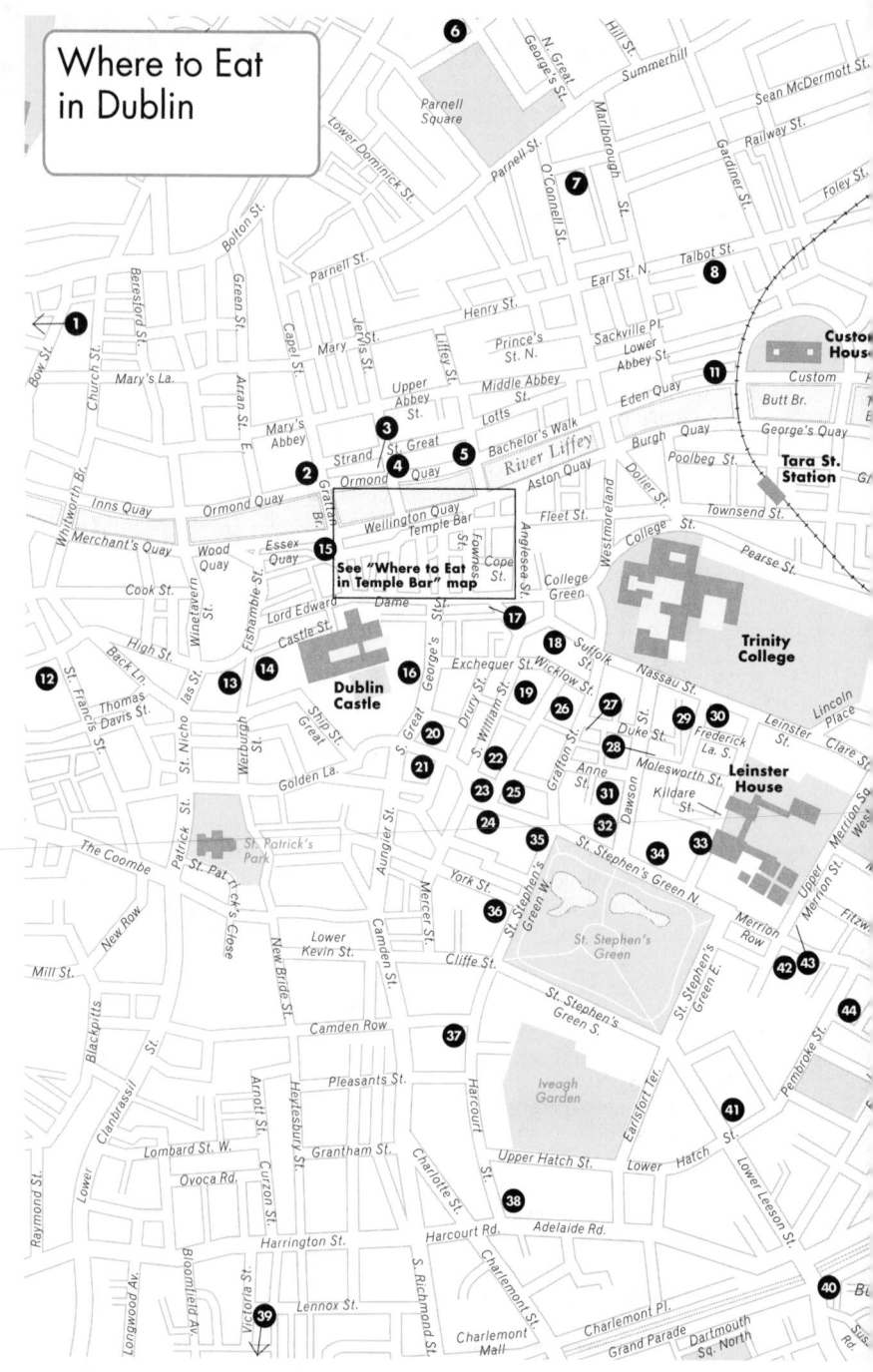

Where to Eat in Dublin

Parnell Square

River Liffey

See "Where to Eat in Temple Bar" map

Dublin Castle

Trinity College

Leinster House

St. Stephen's Green

Iveagh Garden

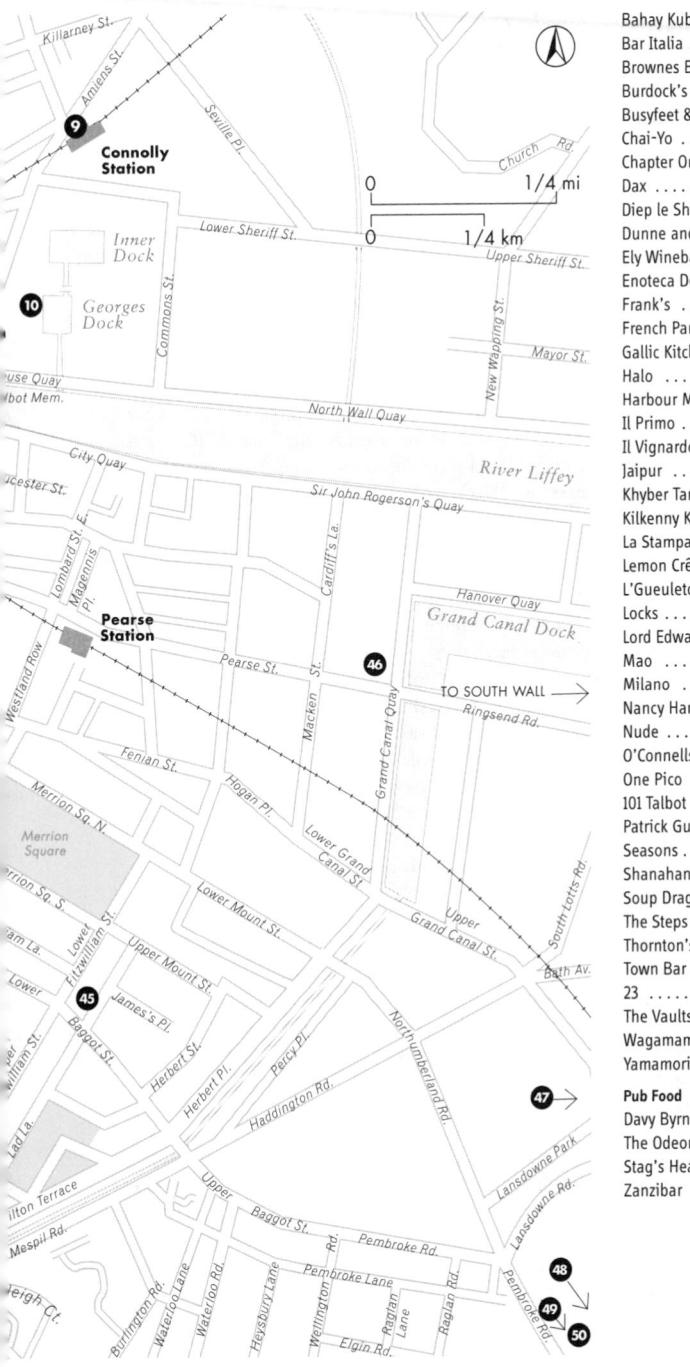

sor Terr., Portobello, City Center ☎ 01/454–3391 ⚇ *Reservations essential* ⊟ *AE, DC, MC, V* ⊘ *Closed Sun. No lunch Sat.*

French

★ **$$$$** ✕ **Thornton's.** If there has been something of a revolution in Irish cooking in the last decade then Kevin Thornton has been the movement's Lenin, and his permanently full restaurant is the Kremlin. Forget the stretched metaphors; if you're passionate about food, this place is a must. Thornton's cooking style is light, and his dishes are small masterpieces of structural engineering, piled almost dangerously high in towers of food. A highlight is the braised suckling pig served with trotter and loin in a *poitín* (Irish moonshine made from potatoes) sauce. Desserts range from banana ice cream to warm chocolate tartlet with raspberries. Sheridans of Dublin supplies the enormous selection of cheeses. The dining room is simple and elegant—there's little to distract you from the exquisite food. ⊠ *Fitzwilliam Hotel, St. Stephen's Green, City Center* ☎ 01/478–7008 ⊕ *www.thorntonsrestaurant.com* ⚇ *Reservations essential* ⊟ *AE, DC, MC, V* ⊘ *Closed Sun. and Mon.*

★ **$$–$$$$** ✕ **Brownes Brasserie.** "Dress to Impress" would seem to be the motto of this established brasserie; as soon as you walk up the granite steps into the small drawing room, the eclectic, luxurious decor almost assaults you. Italian-style friezes, jewel-color walls covered in gilded mirrors, velvet-draped tall windows, and crystal chandeliers all vie for your attention. In a sort of culinary fantasy, the food matches the decor in richness and variety. Favorites include char-grilled brochette of swordfish served on a bed of garlic potato with garlic puree and salsa verde, and escalopes of veal marinated in Parma ham and garlic, served with globe artichokes, linguine, and saffron cream. The lavender-scent crème brûlée is a lovely finish to a meal. ⊠ *22 St. Stephen's Green, Southside* ☎ 01/638–3939 ⊕ *www.brownesdublin.com* ⚇ *Reservations essential* ⊟ *AE, DC, MC, V* ⊘ *No lunch Sat.*

$$–$$$
Fodor'sChoice
★ ✕ **L'Gueuleton.** Dubliners don't do waiting, but you'll see hungry crowds hanging around waiting for a table outside this exceptional new eatery just off George's Street. Definitely the best new restaurant in Dublin, L'Gueuleton's tiny size doesn't put off the crowds who head here for authentic French food at a people's price. Start with the braised ray wings with capers or the warm poached egg and watercress salad. For a main course, the Toulouse sausages with choucroute and Lyonnaise potatoes somehow manages to be hearty and adventurous at the same time. Desserts have a devilishly childish touch to them, with the jelly and ice cream with raspberry cookie a typical example. All in all, this is most definitely worth the wait. Speaking of which: although you can't phone in a reservation, you can go there early in the evening and put your name down for a table along with your cell-phone number. They will give you a call 20 minutes before your table is ready. People also gather outside hoping to be fitted in during the evening. ⊠ *1 Fade St., City Center* ☎ *01/675–3708* ⊟ *MC, V* ⊘ *Closed Sun.*

¢ ✕ **Lemon Crêpe and Coffee Co.** Avoid this place on Fat Tuesday (known as Pancake Tuesday in Ireland) because there will be a line halfway down the street. On any other day this tiny place has the best crepes in town, and hungry Dubliners know it. The space is compact, white, and minimalist. A few sidewalk tables—complete with an outdoor heater—make this a great spot for a tasty snack while you watch Dublin saunter by. Ham, cheese, bacon, and spinach are a few of the savory filling choices. Favorite sweet fillings include banana, Nutella, cream, and the old classic, lemon juice and sugar. Take-out service is swift. ✉ *66 S. William St., City Center* ☎ *01/672–9044* ▭ *No credit cards.*

Indian

$–$$ ✕ **Jaipur.** Call to mind all the stereotypes of bad, production-line Indian restaurants. Then consign them to the flames, for Jaipur is something different altogether. A spacious room with a sweeping staircase and contemporary furnishings reflects Jaipur's modern, cutting-edge approach to Indian cuisine. Mixed with traditional dishes, such as chicken tikka masala, are more unusual preparations, such as *rara gosdh* (lamb slowly cooked with black-eyed peas). The delightful *karwari* is a sweet and sour butterfish in a tamarind-flavor broth redolent of coastal-south-Indian spices. Try the Jaipur Jugalbandi, a selection of five appetizers. Dishes can be toned down or spiced up to suit your palate, and service is courteous and prompt. Another plus: the wine list is well thought out. ✉ *41 S. Great George's St., City Center* ☎ *01/677–0999* ⊕ *www.jaipur.ie* ⌂ *Reservations essential* ▭ *AE, MC, V.*

$–$$ ✕ **Khyber Tandoori.** The Khyber Tandoori doorman, dressed in traditional colorful costume complete with a dashing white turban, has become something of a living landmark in modern Dublin. A short walk from St. Stephen's Green, this gem of a restaurant specializes in Pakistani cuisine but also serves a broad selection of Indian dishes. Try the *shami* (Syrian) kebabs—dainty, spiced patties of minced lamb and lentils—or *kabuli chicken tikka shashlik* (marinated, diced chicken with onions and red and green peppers), which comes bright red and sizzling on an iron platter. Settle in and admire the richly embroidered wall hangings and the great gusts of steam coming from the tandoori oven in the glassed-in area. ✉ *44–45 S. William St., City Center* ☎ *01/670–4855* ▭ *AE, DC, MC, V* ☺ *No lunch Sun.*

Irish

¢–$ ✕ **Kilkenny Kitchen.** Take a break from shopping and sightseeing at this big self-service restaurant on the upper floor of the Kilkenny Shop. Homemade soup, casseroles, cold meats, and salads are arranged on a long buffet, along with lots of tasty breads and cakes. Try to get a table by the window overlooking the playing fields of Trinity College. Lunchtime is busy, but Kilkenny is very pleasant for morning coffee or afternoon tea. ✉ *5–6 Nassau St., Southside* ☎ *01/677–7066* ⊕ *www.kilkennyshop.com* ▭ *AE, DC, MC, V.*

Italian

$$–$$$ ✕ **Il Primo.** Eccentric, gregarious Dieter Bergman likes to run his little two-story Italian restaurant like an intimate dinner party. So don't be surprised if he joins you at your table for a chat. Old wooden tables and chairs give the two small dining rooms a casual feel, and the friendly, if cramped, surroundings attract a devoted clientele. The *gnocchi di patate*, potato dumplings with tomato, spinach, and ricotta, is typical of the hearty fare. For the more adventurous the *Ravioli il Primo*—open ravioli stuffed with chicken, Parma ham, and wild mushrooms and smothered in a cream sauce—is a must. The wine list is, to quote a local phrase, as long as your arm. ⊠ *Montague St. off Harcourt St., City Center* ☎ *01/478–3373* ⊟ *AE, DC, MC, V* ☽ *No lunch weekends.*

$ ✕ **The Steps of Rome.** Discerning natives flock to this place for a cheap lunch, or a good takeout. Just a few steps from Grafton Street, this Italian eatery is also popular for a late-night bite. Slices of delicious, thin-crust pizza, with all the traditional toppings, are the main attraction. The *funghi* (mushroom) pizza is particularly good. The few tables are usually full, but it's worth waiting around for the classic Italian pasta dishes. Some diners just opt for the fresh salads with focaccia. Follow it all with cheesecake or tiramisu, and good strong espresso. ⊠ *1 Chatham Ct., City Center* ☎ *01/670–5630* ⊟ *No credit cards.*

¢–$ ✕ **Dunne and Crescenzi.** Nothing
FodorsChoice   succeeds like success. So popular is
★   this classy little Italian joint just off Nassau Street that they've expanded into the premises two doors down. Pity the poor little coffee shop in between trying to compete with the unpretentious brilliance of this brother-and-sister restaurant and deli. The menu couldn't be simpler: *paninis* (sandwiches), antipasti, a single pasta special, and desserts.

> **A TASTY TIP**
>
> A welcome addition is the arrival of little, family-run Italian joints with great food, no fuss, and real coffee, all at a good price. Bar Italia and bustling Dunne and Crescenzi are two of the best.

But the all-Italian kitchen staff work wonders with high-quality imported ingredients. The antipasto *misto,* an assortment of thinly sliced Parma ham, three types of salami, sun-dried tomatoes, cheeses, peppers in olive oil, and artichoke hearts makes a great light lunch. A couple of long tables make it perfect for a group, and the hundreds of bottles of wine on shelves cover every inch of the walls. ⊠ *14 S. Fredrick St., City Center* ☎ *01/677–3815* ⊕ *www.dunneandcrescenzi.com* ⊟ *AE, MC, V.*

Japanese

$–$$ ✕ **Yamamori.** Dublin's young and mobile folk went noodle-mad a few years ago and Yamamori jumped to the top of the list for these ramen addicts. The open plan and family-style tables have kept it popular with the buzz crowd. The meals-in-a-bowl are a splendid slurping experience, and although you'll be supplied with a small Chinese-style soup spoon, the best approach is with chopsticks. The *yasai yaki soba,* Chinese-style noodles with Asian vegetables and egg, garnished with menma and spring onions is a favorite example. You can also get sushi and sashimi, plus delicious chicken teriyaki. ⊠ *71–72 S. Great George's St., City Center* ☎ *01/475–5001* ⊟ *AE, MC, V.*

$ ✕ **Wagamama.** Canteen food wasn't like this at your school. Modeled on a Japanese canteen, Wagamama, with its long wooden tables and benches and high ceilings with exposed metal piping, ensures a unique communal dining experience. It attracts a young, loud crowd and is constantly busy. Formal courses aren't acknowledged—food is served as soon as it's ready, and appetizers and main courses arrive together. *Edamame—*

steamed and salted green soybeans in the pod—are a delicious starter and great fun to pop open and eat. Choose from filling bowls of *cha han* (fried rice with chicken, prawns, and vegetables) or chili beef ramen, and wash it down with fresh fruit or vegetable juice. There's also a fine selection of beers and sakes for the less abstentious. ⊠ *S. King St., City Center* ☎ *01/478–2152* ▭ *AE, DC, MC, V.*

Pan-Asian

$–$$ ✕ **Mao.** Everything is Asian-fusion at this bustling café, from the little Andy Warhol pastiche of Chairman Mao on the washroom door to the eclectic mix of dishes on the menu, which combine Thai, Vietnamese, and other Southeast Asian elements. Top choices include the Malaysian chicken, chili squid, and the *nasi goreng* (Indonesian fried rice with chicken and shrimp). Go early to be sure of a seat. ⊠ *2 Chatham Row, City Center* ☎ *01/670–4899* ⌲ *Reservations not accepted* ▭ *MC, V.*

Vegetarian

¢–$ ✕ **Nude.** One-word titles for restaurants and cafés were all the rage in Dublin about five years ago. Many of them have fallen by the wayside, but Nude, a sleek, ecofriendly fast-food café, has been such a success that owner Norman Hewson—brother of U2's Bono—has opened another branch for takeout only on Upper Leeson Street. The canteen-style tables set the extremely casual atmosphere—don't be surprised if your neighbor strikes up a conversation. You order at the counter and someone delivers to your table in double-quick time. The menu is mostly vegetarian, and everything on it is made with organic and free-range ingredients. Choose from homemade soups and vegetable wraps (hummus and peppers is a classic), smoothies, and fresh-squeezed juices. ⊠ *21 Suffolk St., City Center* ☎ *01/677–4804* ⊕ *www.nude.ie* ▭ *DC, MC, V.*

Georgian Dublin: Around Merrion Square

Contemporary

★ $$–$$$$ ✕ **La Stampa.** "Like eating on stage at the Met in the middle of Act Two" is how one wag described the sheer opulence of the jaw-dropping dining room at this classic French brasserie. Roman urns, little bronze cupids, busts of emperors, huge Regency mirrors, elaborate candelabras, and a large stained-glass skylight create a gloriously over-the-top Neoclassical ambience under the intricately plastered high ceilings. Such an operatic setting gives every meal a sense of fun and occasion. The food is in danger of being upstaged, but try the beautiful crispy confit duck leg with butter bean and merguez (sausage) stew; roasted scallops with artichoke mash and tomato vinaigrette; or giant prawns served with garlic or mango mayonnaise. Expect brisk but friendly service. ⊠ *35 Dawson St., Georgian Dublin* ☎ *01/677–4444* ⊕ *www.lastampa.ie* ▭ *AE, DC, MC, V.*

$$–$$$$ ✕ **One Pico.** Grown women have been known to swoon when chef–owner Eamonn O'Reilly walks into the dining room of his little restaurant tucked away in a quiet lane only a few minutes from Stephen's Green. Eamonn cuts quite a dash, but it's his sophisticated, daring, contemporary cuisine that tends to seduce visitors to One Pico. Try the incredible parsley and garlic soup with poached quail egg to start. Dishes such as roast rump of veal with fricassee of girolles, pearl onion and truffle, and *pomme sarladaise* demonstrate a savvy use of native ingredients. Follow this with the baked chèvre cheesecake garnished with praline chocolate and orange confit. As is usual with Dublin's luxe eateries, the fixed-price lunch menu offers great value. ⊠ *5–6 Molesworth Pl., off Schoolhouse La., Georgian Dublin* ☎ *01/676–0300* ⊕ *www.onepico.com* ⌔ *Reservations essential* ▤ *AE, DC, MC, V* ☉ *Closed Sun.*

★ $$–$$$ ✕ **Dax.** When is a wine bar not a wine bar? When it's the city's best new restaurant. Opened as a basement wine bar by Olivier Meisonnave, the former sommelier at stellar Thornton's, Dax is quickly becoming the dining spot of choice for Dubliners who care about food. You can choose to drink or dine (tapas style) at the bar, in the lush armchairs of the open-plan lounge, or in the more formal, restrained-modern dining room. The sautéed foie gras is a stand-out starter, while the chestnut risotto has quickly become one of the favorite main courses. The cold meat platter is a finger-lickin' little bar dish. With Olivier in charge the wine list is the envy of many a more expensive eatery, and with a couple of dozen wines poured by the glass you can dare to try something really special. ⊠ *23 Pembroke St. Upper Georgian Dublin* ☎ *01/676–1494* ⊕ *www.dax.ie* ⌔ *Reservations essential* ▤ *AE, DC, MC, V* ☉ *Closed Sun and Mon. No lunch Sat.*

French

$$$$ ✕ **Patrick Guilbaud.** The words
Fodor'sChoice "Dublin's finest restaurant" often
★ share the same breath as the name of this do-be-impressed place on the ground floor of the Merrion Hotel. The menu is described as French, but Guilbaud's genius lies in his occasional daring use of traditional Irish ingredients—so often abused and taken for granted—to create the unexpected. With the eponymous chef in charge, you can

> **A TASTY TIP**
>
> Patrick Guilbaud, Chapter One, One Pico, and other high-end places prove the simple adage: great chefs make great restaurants. Many have fixed-price lunch menus that are great bargains for the cash-conscious epicurean.

always expect superb cooking. His best dishes are simple—and flawless: Châlons duck à l'orange, Connemara lobster in season, and braised pig's trotters. Follow that, if you can, with the *assiette au chocolat* (a tray of five hot-and-cold chocolate desserts). The ambience is just as delicious—if you're into modern art, that is. There are no Georgian Gainsboroughs to be found here. Instead, you'll think you've wandered into skyscraper Manhattan, thanks to the marvelously lofty dining room and minimalist art hanging on the walls (the Roderick O'Connor and Louis LeBrocquys are all from the owner's private collection). Nearly as impressive is the 70-page wine list, the view of the Merrion's manicured gardens, and the lunch special for under €30. Soaring white vaults and empty white walls won't make you feel warm and cozy but you can always go somewhere else for that. What you won't find anywhere else is Guilbaud. ⊠ *21 Upper Merrion St., Georgian Dublin* ☎ *01/676–4192* ⊕ *www.merrionhotel.com* ⌔ *Reservations essential* ▤ *AE, DC, MC, V* ☉ *Closed Sun. and Mon.*

Irish

$–$$$ ✕ **Ely Winebar.** Almost equidistant from the twin dames of Dublin hotel elegance, the Shelbourne and the Merrion, Ely started out as a mere wine bar—and oh, what a selection of wines they have, many of them by the glass. But it has quickly grown into a wonderful little eatery with genuinely organic meat and veg from the owner's family farm in County Clare, guaranteeing a tasty mouthful every bite. Dishes tend to be simple—bangers and mash, a scrumptious lamb stew, Killaha oysters with brown bread—but incredibly fresh and succulent. The plate of mature Irish and Continental cheeses is the perfect finish—with a glass of wine of course. ✉ *22 Ely Pl., Georgian Dublin* ☎ *01/676–8986* ⊕ *www. elywinebar.ie* ▤ *AE, DC, MC, V* ⊗ *Closed Sun.*

Italian

$$–$$$$ ✕ **Town Bar and Grill.** Even basements can surprise, and an old wine merchant's cellar on Kildare Street has been transformed into this cozy, modern-Italian trattoria. The elegant, New York–vibe dining room has a definite buzz, and numerous Irish celebrities have already made this a regular haunt. Chef Temple Garner likes to take traditional Italian classics and give them a little—just a little—twist. The cured salmon carpaccio with shaved fennel, olives, and minted yogurt dressing is one of the most exciting starters. For mains try the monkfish *zuppa di pesce* with chorizo, red pepper, and saffron aioli crostini. Gingered sticky toffee pudding with *caramelita* (caramel ice cream with soft toffee pieces) is a nice guilty way to finish. ✉ *21 Kildare St., Georgian Dublin* ☎ *01/662–4724* ⊕ *www.townbarandgrill.com* ▤ *AE, DC, MC, V* ⊗ *No lunch Sun.*

¢–$ ✕ **Milano.** The big, open kitchen at this bright, cheerful place turns out tasty, flashy pizzas, with such combinations as tomato and mozzarella, ham and eggs, Cajun with prawns and Tabasco, spinach and egg, and ham and anchovies. There are also simple salads such as tomato and mozzarella with dough balls, and some baked pasta dishes. This is a good place to dine late, with last orders at midnight. Three other branches have opened: one in Temple Bar, another on Bachelor's Walk, and the third in the Irish Financial Services Centre. ✉ *38 Dawson St., Georgian Dublin* ☎ *01/670–7744* ▤ *AE, DC, MC, V.*

Pan-Asian

$–$$$ ✕ **Diep le Shaker.** Don't be surprised to see people ordering champagne with their meals—there's a permanent party vibe at this flamboyant Thai restaurant, which attracts Ireland's wealthy in droves. Comfortable high-back chairs, pristine table linen, and elegant stemware make this a stylish place to dine. But half the reason for going is to see and be seen. Try the steamed scallops and ginger, or lobster in garlic pepper and Thai herbs. It's slightly off the beaten track, on a narrow lane off Pembroke Street. ✉ *55 Pembroke La., Georgian Dublin* ☎ *01/661–1829* ⊕ *www. diep.net* ⌑ *Reservations essential* ▤ *AE, DC, MC, V* ⊗ *No lunch Sun.*

$–$$ ✕ **Chai-Yo.** Be educated while you eat. There's always something thrilling about getting close up and watching a master at work. The Japanese teppanyaki area at this classy pan-Asian restaurant on bustling Baggot Street, where the chef cooks your food right on your tabletop, is a feast for the eye as well as the palate. Choose from a selection of scallops, sea bass, steak, teriyaki chicken, and prawns, and watch as a beautiful grilled dish is whipped up before your eyes. The white walls and dark lacquered furnishings give Chai-Yo a serene ambience, enhanced by the delicate glassware and fine, green-washed-porcelain plates. The menu picks the best from Chinese, Thai, and Japanese dishes. The deep-fried crispy quail eggs are a tasty starter, and the king scallops in Thai chili oil with scallion and onion is the place's most popular main course. ⊠ *100 Lower Baggot St., Georgian Dublin* ☎ *01/662–2767* ▤ *AE, DC, MC, V* ⊘ *No lunch Sun.*

Temple Bar

American–Casual

$–$$ ✕ **Elephant & Castle.** The Elephant was long established in Temple Bar before the Tiger (Celtic, that is) changed the neighborhood forever. Large windows are great for people-watching in the city's trendiest area, but "nothing fancy" would be a good motto for the traditional American food. Charcoal-grilled burgers, salads, omelets, sandwiches, and pasta comprise the much-thumbed menu. Sunday brunch is always packed. The portions are some of the most generous in Dublin. When the service is good, the turnover tends to be quick, although you may be inclined to linger. New Yorkers take note: yes, this is a cousin of the restaurant of the same name in Greenwich Village. ⊠ *18 Temple Bar, Temple Bar* ☎ *01/679–3121* ⌂ *Reservations not accepted* ▤ *AE, DC, MC, V.*

¢–$$ ✕ **Bad Ass Café.** If you want to make a Dublin native wince, mention with excitement that Sinéad O'Connor used to wait tables at this lively café in a converted warehouse between the Central Bank and Ha'penny Bridge. (A "Rock 'n Stroll" tour plaque notes O'Connor's past here.) Old-fashioned cash shuttles whiz around the ceiling of the barnlike space, with bare floors and primary colors inside and out. You can indulge in some great people-watching behind the wall of glass here. The food—mainly pizzas and burgers—is unexceptional, but the Bad Ass can be a lot of fun and appetites of all ages love it. ⊠ *9–11 Crown Alley, Temple Bar* ☎ *01/671–2596* ⊕ *www.badasscafe.com* ▤ *AE, MC, V.*

Cajun–Creole

$–$$$ ✕ **Tante Zoe's.** The Deep South comes to Dublin with this dark, bustling restaurant, a firm favorite with vacationers and large parties. Images from the heyday of the antebellum South, bamboo, and dark-wood set a broody, atmospheric scene for colorful creole cooking. Seafood fans shouldn't miss the Cajun popcorn—a mountain of spicy baby shrimp coated in bread crumbs and served with a creamy tomato mayonnaise. Spicy blackened chicken with savory rice is another favorite. Desserts are reliably good, particularly the Mississippi mud pie. ⊠ *1 Crow St., Temple Bar* ☎ *01/679–4407* ⊕ *www.tantezoes.com* ⌂ *Reservations essential* ▤ *AE, DC, MC, V.*

Contemporary

$$$$ ✕ **The Tea Room.** In the Clarence Hotel, you can sit around all day and
Fodor's Choice   hope that Bono and the boys of U2—they own the joint after all—might
★   turn up for a quick snack. Other stars of stage and screen often stay at

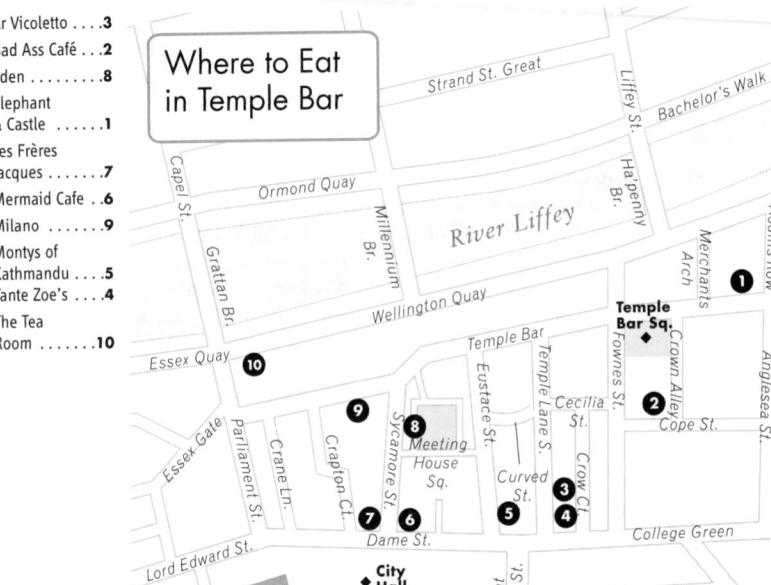

Where to Eat in Temple Bar

the hotel and stop in at the Tea Room. Minimalistically hued in golden oak, eggshell white, and light yellows, the high-ceiling room is a perfect stage for off-duty celebs. The contrast between this high-vaulted cocoon and busy Essex Street—whose madding crowds can be glimpsed through the double-height windows—is nowhere else as dramatic. Drama is also found on the newer-than-now nouvelle menu. You can opt for either adventurous specials—Spatchcock Quail with pea puree, truffled wild mushroom, and pistachio vinaigrette, anyone?—or such consistently good, typically mouthwatering delights as the panfried foie gras with caramelized onion tatin, "wicked apple" cider, and muscat raisins, or the risotto of Carlingford mussels and courgettes. Obviously, the menu is as chic as the customers. ⊠ *Clarence Hotel, 6–8 Wellington Quay, Temple Bar* ☎ *01/407–0813* ⊕ *www.theclarence.ie* ⌂ *Reservations essential* ⊟ *AE, DC, MC, V* ⊙ *No lunch Sat.*

$$–$$$$ ✕ **Mermaid Café.** Hope you don't mind sharing your dinner conversation with the people next to you. The Mermaid has the simple, crowded feel of a very upmarket canteen, with large tables set close together and casual, but classy, service. One of the chef–owners dabbles in fine art, and his tastes in this area are reflected in his artistic and decorative style of bistro cooking. It's not cheap, but the food is reliable. Lunch is an exceptional value—piquant crab cakes, huge hearty seafood casseroles, rib-eye steak, or butternut squash risotto with grilled squash, spinach, and Parmesan. Attention to detail and a thoughtful wine list make this modest restaurant with tall windows looking onto busy Dame Street one of the most popular eateries in Temple Bar. ⊠ *69 Dame St., Temple Bar* ☎ *01/670–8236* ⊕ *www.mermaid.ie* ▤ *MC, V.*

★ **$$–$$$** ✕ **Eden.** One of Dublin's hippest places, Eden is where arty and media types are likely to gather to talk about, well, themselves. It has an open kitchen and a high wall of glass through which you can observe one of Temple Bar's main squares. Patio-style doors lead to an outdoor eating area—a major plus in a city with relatively few alfresco dining spots. On weekend nights in summer you can enjoy an outdoor movie in Meeting House Square while you eat. Seasonal menus are in vogue here, but standout dishes include panfried fillet of vension, and fried brill with mangetout, chervil, and a prawn beurre blanc. Desserts include rhubarb crème brûlée and homemade ice creams and sorbets. ⊠ *Meeting House Sq., Temple Bar* ☎ *01/670–5372* ⊕ *www.edenrestaurant.ie* ⌂ *Reservations essential* ▤ *AE, DC, MC, V.*

French

★ **$$$–$$$$** ✕ **Les Frères Jacques.** Many restaurants call themselves French, but this elegant eatery next to the Olympia Theatre positively reeks of Gallic panache. Old prints of Paris and Deauville hang on the green-paper walls, and the French waiters, dressed in white Irish linen and black bow ties, exude a European charm without being excessively formal. Expect traditional French cooking that nods to the seasons. Seafood is a major attraction, and lobster (fished right from the tank—a "plus" that people with delicate sensibilities will find a definite minus) is typically roasted and flambéed with Irish whiskey. Others prefer the curry-dusted rack of seasonal lamb with game chips (fried potatoes marinated in game jus) and fennel mousse dip. Also recommended are the seasonal game specialties. A piano player performs Friday and Saturday evenings and on the occasional weeknight. ⊠ *74 Dame St., Temple Bar* ☎ *01/679–4555* ⊕ *www.lesfreresjacques.com* ⌂ *Reservations essential* ▤ *AE, MC, V* ☉ *Closed Sun. No lunch Sat.*

Italian

$–$$$ ✕ **Ar Vicoletto.** Learn Italian for free! Simply book a table and eavesdrop on the people next to you at this cheerful eatery where members of Dublin's Italian community congregate in the evenings to enjoy authentic Roman cuisine and lament the Irish weather. Specialties include sea bass on the bone stuffed with garlic and lemon, a delicious *melanzane parmigiani* (baked eggplant, cheese, and tomato sauce), and the excellent cream-based pastas, such as spaghetti Alfredo and carbonara. Beware of finishing the meal with too many flaming *sambucas* (anise-flavor, semisweet Italian liqueurs). The best table, by the window, overlooks the street. ⊠ *5 Crow St., Temple Bar* ☎ *01/670–8662* ▤ *AE, DC, MC, V.*

¢–$ ✕ **Milano.** Like the original Milano eatery on the Southside, in Dublin's Georgian Heart, this branch turns out flashy pizzas, salads, and pasta dishes. ⊠ *19 Essex St. E, Temple Bar* ☎ *01/670–3384* ▤ *AE, DC, MC, V.*

Nepalese

$–$$ ✕ **Montys of Kathmandu.** Montys proudly declares itself the "only Nepalese restaurant in Dublin." Was there ever any doubt? The bland decor is nothing to write home about, but the food at this little eatery in the middle of hypermodern Temple Bar is as authentic as it is unique. *Poleko* squid—lightly spiced and barbecued in a tandoori oven and served in a sizzler; or lamb *Choila*—lamb with fresh chilies, ginger, garlic, herbs, and a dash of red wine—are the more adventurous starters. For a main course try *Mo Mo,* dumplings served with Mo Mo chutney, a favorite street dish in Kathmandu. The wine cellar is surprisingly varied. ⊠ *28 Eustace St., Temple Bar* ☎ *01/670–4911* ⊕ *www.montys.ie* ▭ *AE, DC, MC, V* ⊗ *No lunch Sun.*

The Northside

Contemporary

$$$$ ✕ **Chapter One.** If you spot the maitre d' strolling between tables and handing out tickets, you know you're at the hugely popular pretheater special at Chapter One. Yes, they actually go pick up your tickets from the nearby Abbey or Gate theaters, and you can return after your show for dessert. The place gets its name from its location, downstairs in the vaulted, stone-wall basement of the Dublin Writers Museum; the natural stone and wood setting gives it a cozy cavelike feel. This contemporary French eatery is currently the culinary king of the Northside, thanks to chef-proprietor Ross Lewis's way with roasted venison with mustard and herb lentils, pancetta, chestnut dumplings, and roasted beetroot. Yeats himself would have loved the Challans (an heirloom variety) duck breast pie, parsnip puree, and green peppercorn jus, while Synge probably would have fancied the Dublin version of Proust's madeleine: rich bread-and-butter pudding, a favorite of working-class Irish mothers for generations, here turned into an outrageously filling work of art. ⊠ *18–19 Parnell Sq., Northside* ☎ *01/873–2266* ⊕ *www.chapteronerestaurant.com* ✍ *Reservations essential* ▭ *AE, DC, MC, V* ⊗ *Closed Sun. and Mon. No lunch Sat.*

Fodor'sChoice
★

$$–$$$$ ✕ **23.** Where now the glories of Babylon? It's a long time since O'Connell Street was the social center of Dublin and the Gresham Hotel was *the* place to be seen dining. But recent years have seen something of a comeback for the famous old hotel, and the ultramodern 23 is a big part of that revival. The decor leaves some cold, but the blend of droplights, tubular tables, and contemporary art against the backdrop of a dramatic glass wall would certainly delight the readers of *Wallpaper.* The brasserie-style cooking makes use of local ingredients in seafood, duck, chicken, steak, and vegetarian dishes. The pavlova trio, crammed with raspberries, blueberries, and strawberries, is a firm favorite, and a short but varied wine list has been well thought out. The breakfast—buffet-style or from a menu that includes eggs and a full Irish breakfast—attracts early-rising tourists and locals. ⊠ *Gresham Hotel, 23 Upper O'Connell St., Northside* ☎ *01/817–6116* ⊕ *www.gresham-hotels.com* ✍ *Reservations essential* ▭ *AE, DC, MC, V* ⊗ *Closed Sun. No lunch.*

$$–$$$ ✕ **Halo.** Judges from the nearby Four Courts rest their wigs on empty seats while the fashion crowd sits over multicolor drinks at this chic restaurant in the even more chic Morrison Hotel. With a soaring ceiling and minimalist decor, the dramatic two-story dining room, devised by fashion designer John Rocha, looks moody and mysterious by night, and a little forbidding by day. French and fusion are the two Fs favored by chef Jean-Michel Poulot, with seafood comprising his star dishes. Monkfish Wellington for two with market veg and spuds is one of the ever-changing specialties. The baked oysters starter is imaginatively combined with good old green cabbage and lemon and chive sabayon. Desserts are miniature works of art on enormous china platters. ⊠ *Morrison Hotel, Ormond Quay, Northside* ☎ *01/887–2421* ⊕ *www.morrisonhotel.ie* ▭ *AE, DC, MC, V.*

\$–\$\$ ✕ **Harbour Master.** You just have to look out the window to understand why this big, airy restaurant and bar in the Irish Financial Services Center north of the Liffey is so popular: it overlooks the serene and calming canal basin. At lunch the place is packed with stockbrokers and lawyers; dinner is more subdued. You can dine bistro-style at the cavernous bar, but it's better to head for the more spacious—and relaxing—dining area. Try the blackened salmon on a basil polenta mash, served with sautéed chorizo and poppy-seed yogurt dressing. ⊠ *Custom House Docks, Northside* ☎ *01/670–1688* ⊕ *www.harbourmaster.ie* ▭ *AE, DC, MC, V.*

\$–\$\$ ✕ **The Vaults.** Come eat under the train station. Not exactly the best sales pitch you've ever heard—yet this wonderful, long-neglected space beneath Connolly Station was imaginatively revamped in 2002 to create one of the city's most fashionable dining spots. Cavernous arches, smooth Portland stone floors, striking furniture, and dramatic lighting create the background for a mostly young business set. Each of the vaults is decorated in its own style, ranging from hypermodern to turn-of-the-20th-century elegant. Cocktails are a specialty, although it's worth a visit for the food alone. The Italian chef makes everything from scratch, including the pizza dough. A wide-ranging menu covers light snack options alongside more substantial dishes like the house pizza, a blend of tomato, mozzarella, prawns, red onion, and herbs. Be sure to leave room for the excellent lemon and raspberry tart. Note that dinner is served only until 8. ⊠ *Harbourmaster Pl., Northside* ☎ *01/605–4700* ⊕ *www. thevaults.ie* ⌲ *Reservations essential* ▭ *AE, DC, MC, V.*

Irish

¢ ✕ **Soup Dragon.** This tiny café and take-out soup shop serves an astonishing array of fresh soups daily. Soups come in three sizes, and you can get vegetarian soup or soups with meat- or fish-based broth. Best bets include red pepper, tomato, and goat cheese soup; fragrant Thai chicken soup; and hearty mussel, potato, and leek soup. The friendly staff makes fine coffee and delicious smoothies. The cost of soup includes bread and a piece of fruit for dessert—an excellent value. ⊠ *168 Capel St., Northside* ☎ *01/872–3277* ▭ *No credit cards* ⊘ *Closed Sun. No dinner.*

Italian

\$–\$\$ ✕ **Il Vignardo.** Sometimes when it comes to dining, the where is more important than the what. Il Vignardo serves some of Dublin's tastiest cheap and cheerful pizzas and pasta, but it's the unique decor that elevates this place a little above the rest. The dramatically vaulted ceilings, painted with creeping vines and branches, burst into bloom as they rise from Tuscan columns and evoke thoughts of Italian vineyards and sunshine. Outside, the sheltered courtyard garden, a real oasis in a city center setting, is perfect for summer dining or just a little aperitif. The extra-hot Mexican special is a great pizza, while the penne entrecote is the best of the pastas. If you want to spend a little extra, try the veal il Vignardo, sliced and cooked in a white-wine cream sauce. But who can resist the lasagna, served up with minced Irish beef? ⊠ *Hotel Isaccs, Store St., Northside* ☎ *01/855–3099* ⊕ *www.isaacs.ie* ⊟ *AE, DC, MC, V.*

¢–$ ✕ **Enoteca Delle Langhe.** Officially called Quartier Bloom in tribute to Joyce's most famous character, a charming little (very little) Italian quarter has sprung up just off Ormond Quay. It consists of a communal plaza area, a fabulous mural that's a modern take on Leonardo da Vinci's *The Last Supper,* and a couple of places to eat, including Enoteca delle Langhe. Italian-owned and -operated, Delle Langhe serves up the full enoteca experience: quality, affordable Italian wines (more than 75% are sourced from the Langhe district), a limited but enticing selection of appetizers, and warm, friendly, family-style service. In summer they even have tango dancers outside. ⊠ *Blooms La., Northside* ☎ *01/888–0834* ⊟ *AE, DC, MC, V.*

Mediterranean

$–$$ ✕ **101 Talbot.** Sardi's it's not, but the 101 has that certain buzz that only comes from restaurants popular with the artistic and literary set. Close to the Abbey and Gate theaters, so there's no danger of missing a curtain call, this comfortable upstairs restaurant showcases an ever-changing exhibition of local artists' work. The creative contemporary food—with Mediterranean and Middle Eastern influences—uses fresh local ingredients. Try the roast pork fillet marinated in orange, ginger, and soy, served with fried noodles. The cashew and red-pepper *rissole* (turnover) with chili and ginger jam, served with wild and basmati rice, also impresses. Healthful options and several vegetarian choices make this a highly versatile restaurant. ⊠ *101 Talbot St., Northside* ☎ *01/ 874–5011* ⌂ *Reservations essential* ⊟ *AE, DC, MC, V* ⊘ *Closed Sun. and Mon.*

South Dublin: The Grand Canal & Ballsbridge

Contemporary

$$$–$$$$ ✕ **Seasons.** The Four Seasons group prides itself on luxury service and attention to detail, and you should expect no less at the Dublin branch of the hotel's restaurant, with its large, slightly overwhelming, silver-service dining room. But this place is relatively new and has taken a little while to find its feet in and out of the kitchen. Highly dramatic dishes creatively incorporate Irish, often organic, ingredients. A starter of crisp basil-wrapped prawns with burnt citrus and melon chutney might be followed by roasted loin and braised shank of lamb with sauce *paloise* (hollandaise flavored with mint). Sommelier Simon Keegan is one of the best in the country. Sunday brunch has become a ritual for many well-to-do Dublin families. ⊠ *Four Seasons Hotel, Simmonscourt Rd., Balls-*

bridge ☎ 01/665–4642 ⊕ *www.fourseasons.com* ⚱ *Reservations essential* ▤ *AE, DC, MC, V.*

$$–$$$$ ✕ **Franks.** Snugly tucked into the arches under the Old Malting Tower Bridge at Grand Canal Quay, this relaxed new bar and restaurant is one of the most unusual Dublin locations in which to eat. They have plenty of snack and salad dishes available if you don't fancy splurging for a full meal. The main, bistro-style menu is strong on comfort meat dishes, including a signature steak tartare and wonderful homemade beef burgers. During Sunday brunch, which is a big hit here, the cozy atmosphere takes on a delightful busy hum. A great choice of wine in full and half bottles helps keep that buzz going. ✉ *The Malting Tower, Grand Canal Quay, Grand Canal* ☎ 01/662–5870 ▤ *AE, DC, MC, V.*

$–$$ ✕ **O'Connells.** When it comes to cooking, pedigree counts. Owner Tom
Fodor**'s**Choice   O'Connell is a brother to Ireland's favorite celebrity chef, Darina Allen,
★   famed for her "slow food" Ballymaloe Cookery School in Cork. Tom follows the family blueprint by showcasing locally produced meats and game that can be traced back to its source (in many cases, an individual farm). Add to this a focus on fresh Irish produce and baked goods cooked in a unique wood-fire oven and you have the makings of a feast that is deliriously, quintessentially Irish. Spiced beef is prepared according to an old Cork recipe, salmon fillet is "hot smoked" by the restaurant itself, while Ashe's Annascaul Black Pudding is handmade on the Dingle peninsula. You can also try the spit-roasted duck or the monkfish with a lemon and garlic sauce, and an omelet made from organic eggs from free-range chickens, peppers, zucchini, and a sweet chili sauce. A tremendous selection of fresh breads is on display in the open kitchen, which turns into a buffet for breakfast and lunch. The cheese board is a who's who of Irish farmhouse cheeses, including the Ferguson family's tangy Gubbeen. Serving as a cool backdrop, O'Connell's vast modern space is beautifully fitted out with sleek timber paneling and floor-to-ceiling windows. ✉ *Merrion Rd., Ballsbridge* ☎ 01/647–3304 ⊕ *www.oconnellsballsbridge.com* ▤ *AE, DC, MC, V.*

French

$ ✕ **French Paradox.** Like the people of the south of France that inspired the place, relaxed but stylish would best describe decor and dining at this little restaurant set over a wine shop. French Paradox has found a real niche in the Dublin scene. Wine buffs, Francophiles, and gourmets flock here for the hearty traditional fare and Mediterranean environment. Share the *assiette le fond de barrique,* a selection of charcuterie, pâté, and cheese, or perhaps indulge in a smoked-duck salad or a selection from the foie gras menu. Select a nice bottle from the ground-floor wineshop (mostly French labels) and sip it in situ for a mere €8 corkage fee. Seating is limited. ✉ *53 Shelbourne Rd., Ballsbridge* ☎ 01/660–4068 ⚱ *Reservations essential* ▤ *AE, MC, V* ⊙ *Closed Sun.*

Philippine

$$ ✕ **Bahay Kubo.** Don't always believe what you read. The very basic English translations on the menu fail miserably to capture the excitement and diversity of the dishes at Ireland's only Philippine restaurant. Persevere and you'll find a fine selection of authentic Philippine cooking with touches of Chinese and Malaysian cuisines. Chicken, beef, and prawns all feature heavily, with red-curry chicken in coconut milk the most popular choice with regulars. Desserts have been brought in frozen, so it's best to stick to starters and entrées and finish up with a coffee. The starched white linen and pale-wood flooring give the place an open and light feel. ✉ *14 Bath Ave., Ballsbridge* ☎ *01/660–5572* ⌖ *Reservations essential* ▱ *AE, MC, V* ⊘ *Closed Mon. No lunch Sat.–Wed.*

Dublin West

Café

¢–$ ✕ **Gallic Kitchen.** Canny Dubliners make regular pilgrimages to Sarah Webb's bakery, where some of the best pastries in town are available daily. There's no seating in this powerhouse patisserie, but long counters allow space for perching your coffee and tucking into the finest sweet and savory treats. Pop in for morning coffee and pear tart; for lunch try quiche or salmon roulade with homemade salsa; and take afternoon tea with a scrumptious scone. Expect queues at lunchtime, and be sure to buy in bulk for the tastiest take-out picnic in town. ✉ *49 Francis St., Liberties* ☎ *01/454–4912* ⊕ *www.gallickitchen.com* ▱ *No credit cards* ⊘ *Closed Sun. No dinner.*

Irish

¢ ✕ **Burdock's.** Old man Burdock has moved on and the place hasn't been the same since. But the hordes still join the inevitable queue at Dublin's famous take-out fish-and-chips shop, right next door to the Lord Edward pub. You can eat in the gardens of St. Patrick's Cathedral, a five-minute walk away. ✉ *2 Werburgh St., Dublin West* ☎ *01/454–0306* ▱ *No credit cards.*

Italian

¢–$ ✕ **Bar Italia.** We hope you're not shy about being seen eating, because the front of tiny Bar Italia is a sheer wall of glass that looks out onto the Liffey and the Civic Offices at Wood Quay. If the weather is good, snag one of the tables on the patio and grin at the office workers trudging back to work after lunch. The menu is short and simple, but everything on it is guaranteed to be fresh and cooked like your mother back in Naples would have done. The minestrone soup is, without question, the best in Ireland, and the melt-on-your-tongue gnocchi is served in a few different sauces. People travel miles to have their coffee here and the house wines never let you down. They now have a second, slightly more formal restaurant in the new "Italian Quarter," almost directly across the river on Ormond Quay. ✉ *Essex Quay, Dublin West* ☎ *01/679–5128* ▱ *MC, V.*

Seafood

$$ ✕ **Lord Edward.** Culinary trends and fashions may come and go but Dublin's oldest seafood restaurant remains resolutely traditional. On the cozy top floor above a lovely old bar of the same name, the Lord Edward looks out on the front entrance of Christchurch Cathedral. They do a mean Irish stew but the stars here are definitely the seafood dishes, usually smothered in a totally unhip but delicious, calorie-packed creamy

sauce. The salmon and the cod are two favorites. ⊠ *23 Christchurch Pl., Dublin West* ☏ *01/454–2420* ▤ *AE, DC, MC, V* ⊗ *Closed Sun.*

Phoenix Park & Environs

Eclectic

$–$$ ✕ **Nancy Hands.** It's a fine line to walk; re-create tradition without coming across like a theme bar. Nancy Hands just about pulls it off. A galleylike room juxtaposes old wood, raw brick, and antiques with contemporary art to create a convivial, cozy dining area. The bar food is good, but the upstairs restaurant operates on a more serious level. Specialties include Flanagan's Twist—a mousseline of scallop and crab encased in fresh salmon—and a Mediterranean skewer laden with succulent chicken and beef. The menu includes Thai- and Japanese-style dishes, too. Numerous wines are served by the glass, and the selection of spirits is one of the most impressive in the country. ⊠ *30–32 Parkgate St., Dublin West* ☏ *01/677–0149* ⌲ *Reservations essential* ▤ *AE, DC, MC, V.*

WHERE TO STAY

If you're lucky enough to stay at one of the classy hotels and elegant B&Bs in former Georgian town houses on both sides of the Liffey, you'll quickly realize that entering one of these little domestic palaces really is a trip back in time. But this does not mean the 21st century has not arrived. "An absolute avalanche of new hotels" is how the *Irish Times* characterized Dublin's recent hotel boom. New lodgings have sprung up all over the city, including the much-talked-about Westin at College Green, the Four Seasons, and a few others in Ballsbridge, an inner "suburb" that's a 20-minute walk from the city center.

Dublin has a decent selection of inexpensive accommodations, including many moderately priced hotels with basic but agreeable rooms. Many B&Bs, long the mainstay of the economy end of the market, have upgraded their facilities and now provide rooms with private bathrooms or showers, as well as cable color televisions and direct-dial telephones. The bigger hotels are all equipped with in-room data ports. If you've rented a car and you're not staying at a hotel with secure parking facilities, it's worth considering a location out of the city center, such as Dalkey or Killiney, where the surroundings are more pleasant and you won't have to worry about parking on city streets.

Prices

Demand for rooms means that rates are high at the best hotels by the standards of any major European or North American city (and factoring in the exchange rate means a hotel room can take a substantial bite out of your budget). Service charges range from 15% in expensive hotels to zero in moderate and inexpensive ones. Be sure to inquire when you make reservations.

As a general rule of thumb, lodgings on the north side of the Liffey River tend to be more affordable than those on the south. B&Bs charge as little as €46 a night per person, but they tend to be in suburban areas—

More Bang for Your Buck

1

YOU GET WHAT YOU PAY FOR. For decades Dublin was synonymous with cheap but unexciting accommodation. The Celtic Tiger has transformed expectations for visitors to Dublin. When it comes to their hotels, it is indeed the best of times and the worst of times. Choice and quality have expanded exponentially, but so have prices. So it's more important than ever to get the best deal for your dollar. If location is a priority but you don't want to spend a fortune, try the moderately priced, redbrick **Central Hotel,** which lives up to its name: it's 100 yards from the front gate of Trinity College. The rooms are small but stylish, and you have easy access to the wonderful Library Bar, the most serene drinking spot in Dublin. To stay just off the ever-trendy Grafton Street for less than €150 is a real treat, and the **Grafton House** also throws in beautifully furnished rooms in a Victorian town house. Or, in Victorian-era Ballsbridge, head to the charming **Hibernian,** decorated in best smoking-room Edwardian style. A pleasant outdoor courtyard, en suite showers, a peat fire, and a delicious all-you-can-eat breakfast—does that sound like a hostel to you? Well, it is— **Globetrotters Tourist Hostel** is the pick of its kind in the city, and it even has a cute B&B next door. Perhaps because the **Clifden Guesthouse** is on the Northside, its prices do not reflect its spacious comfort. Add in the free parking and oversize rooms and you know you've found a real bargain.

generally a 15-minute bus ride from the center of the city. This is not in itself a great drawback, and savings can be significant. Many hotels have a weekend, or "B&B," rate that's often 30% to 40% cheaper than the ordinary rate; some hotels also have a midweek special that provides discounts of up to 35%. These rates are available throughout the year but are harder to get in high season. Ask about them when booking a room (they are available only on a prebooked basis), especially if you plan a brief or weekend stay.

WHAT IT COSTS in euros				
	$$$$	$$$	$$	$	¢
FOR 2 PEOPLE	over €230	€180–€230	€130–€180	€80–€130	under €80

Prices are for a standard double room in high season, including V.A.T. and a service charge (often applied in larger hotels). Most hotels operate on the European Plan (EP), with no meals included in the basic room rate, or, if indicated, with Breakfast Plan (BP).

City Center: The Southside

$$$$ ☒ **Shelbourne.** This grande dame of Stephen's Green, is set to reopen in early 2007 after a head-to-toe, years-long renovation, graces the north side of the square, resplendent in its broad, ornamented, pink-and-white, mid-Victorian facade. The hotel has been long famed as the Dublin home of the nation's literati, Anglo-Irish marquesses, and touring Boston Brahmins. The renovation has brought a new restaurant, a new lounge bar, and 21st-century amenities to the guest rooms. Rooms in front overlook the Green; those in the back, without a view, are quieter. ⊠ *27 St. Stephen's Green, City Center, 2* ☎ *01/663–4500, 800/ 543–4300 in U.S.* 🖷 *01/661–6006* ⊕ *www.marriott.com* ↩ *265 rooms, 9 suites* ♨ *Restaurant, bar.*

$$$$ 🏨 **Westbury.** A favorite with the platinum credit-card set, this luxurious, chandelier-filled, modern hotel is just off Grafton Street, the shopping mecca of Dublin. You can join elegantly dressed Dubliners for afternoon tea in the spacious mezzanine-level main lobby, furnished with a grand piano and a great view out onto the busy streets. Alas, the utilitarian rooms—painted in pastels—don't share the lobby's elegance. More inviting are the suites, which combine European stylings with tasteful Japanese screens and prints. The flowery Russell Room serves formal lunches and dinners; the downstairs Sandbank, a seafood restaurant and bar, looks like a turn-of-the-20th-century establishment. ⊠ *Grafton St., City Center, 2* ☎ *01/679–1122* 🖷 *01/679–7078* ⊕ *www.jurysdoyle. com* ↩ *188 rooms, 17 suites* ♨ *2 restaurants, room service, minibars, cable TV, in-room VCRs, in-room data ports, bar, dry cleaning, laundry service, free parking, no-smoking rooms* ▤ *AE, DC, MC, V.*

$$$$ 🏨 **Westin Dublin.** If you've ever dreamed of spending the night in a bank, here's your chance. Reconstructed from three 19th-century landmark buildings (including a former bank) across the road from Trinity College, the Westin is all about location. The public spaces re-create a little of the splendor of yesteryear: marble pillars, tall mahogany doorways, blazing fireplaces, and period detailing on the walls and ceilings. The bedrooms, on the other hand, are functional and small, with the crisp, white Indian linen and custom-made beds the only luxurious touches. The rooms that overlook Trinity College are a little more expensive, but the chance to watch the students in a leisurely game of cricket on a summer weekend makes all the difference. The restaurant and Mint Bar are in the original vaults of the bank. ⊠ *College Green, City Center, 2* ☎ *01/645–1000* 🖷 *01/645–1401* ⊕ *www.westin.com* ↩ *142 rooms, 22 suites* ♨ *Restaurant, room service, minibars, cable TV, in-room data ports, 2 bars, dry cleaning, laundry service, concierge, business services, meeting rooms, free parking, no-smoking rooms* ▤ *AE, DC, MC, V.*

$$$–$$$$ 🏨 **Brooks.** This hotel likes to describe itself as a boutique property even though it has nearly 100 rooms, and it does manage to convey the classy, personal touch of a much smaller establishment. A two-minute walk from Grafton Street, Brooks is the perfect place to sit and recover if the Irish rain plays havoc with your plans: public spaces and the bar are warm and full of leather chairs, high-veneer oak panelling, and decorative bookcases. The rooms exude an old-school elegance—deep burgundy curtains, heavy bedspreads, and beds so big you could get lost in them. Each also has a high-tech, wireless audiovisual setup. Situated so near to the Gaety Theatre, the hotel's Jasmin Bar is an ideal spot for a pre- or posttheater drink. ⊠ *Drury St, City Center, 2* ☎ *01/670–4000* 🖷 *01/670–4455* ⊕ *www.sinnotthotels.com/brooks* ↩ *98 rooms* ♨ *Restaurant, room service, cable TV, in-room data ports, gym, bar,* *dry cleaning, laundry service, concierge, business services, meeting rooms, free parking, no-smoking rooms* ⊟ *AE, DC, MC, V.*

★ **$$–$$$$** ▦ **Central Hotel.** Every modern city needs its little oases of sanctuary and the Central's book-and-armchair-filled Library bar—warmed by its Victorian fireplace—nicely fits the bill. Established in 1887, this grand, old-style redbrick spot is in the heart of the city center, steps from Grafton Street, Temple Bar, and Dublin Castle. Recently renovated rooms are snug but you'll hardly notice the dimensions thanks to the high ceilings and the cosseting and stylish furnishings—flocked bedspreads, racing paintings, and 19th-century bric-a-brac make some of these rooms *World of Interiors*–worthy. The stately hotel dining room delights with its pastel-green walls, bookcases, and gilt-frame pictures. Much less soigné and a good deal more lively is Molly Malone's Tavern, adjacent to the hotel, with plenty of regulars who come for the atmosphere and the live, traditional Irish music on Friday and Saturday nights. ⊠ *1–5 Exchequer St., City Center, 2* ☎ *01/679–7302* ▦ *01/679–7303* ⊕ *www.centralhotel.ie* ⟿ *67 rooms, 3 suites* ♨ *Restaurant, room service, in-room data ports, 2 bars, dry cleaning, laundry service, concierge, business services, meeting rooms* ⊟ *AE, DC, MC, V.*

$$–$$$ ▦ **Drury Court Hotel.** With a hint of the Munich beer hall, the cozy, parquet-floor rathskeller dining room is the most charming thing about this small, good-value hotel. Public areas are purely functional but subtle greens, golds, and burgundies add a certain warmth to the rooms. The location is ideal, a two-minute walk from Grafton Street and just around corner from some of the city's best restaurants. Lunch is served in the casual Digges Lane Bar, frequented by many new-money, young Dubliners. ⊠ *28–30 Lower Stephens St., City Center, 2* ☎ *01/475–1988* ▦ *01/478–5730* ⊕ *www.drurycourthotel.com* ⟿ *42 rooms* ♨ *Restaurant, room service, bar, dry cleaning, laundry service, meeting room* ⊟ *AE, DC, MC, V.*

$–$$ ▦ **Grafton House.** A stone's throw from the famous shopping street that gave it its name, this Victorian Gothic–style building has been tastefully transformed into one of central Dublin's best bargains. The rooms are a little cramped, but they're brightly decorated with cheerful pine furnishings, and the small size of the place ensures warm, friendly service. ⊠ *26–27 S. Great George's St., City Center, 2* ☎ *01/679–2041* ▦ *01/677–9715* ⊕ *www.graftonguesthouse.com* ⟿ *17 rooms* ♨ *No-smoking rooms; no a/c* ⊟ *AE, MC, V* ⥀ *BP.*

Georgian Dublin: Around Merrion Square

$$$$ ▦ **Conrad Dublin International.** Ask for, no, insist on a room on the top three floors. The best thing about the seven-story, redbrick and smoked-glass Conrad are the spectacular views out over the city. Just off St. Stephen's Green, the Conrad firmly aims for international business travelers. Gleaming light-color marble graces the large formal lobby. Rooms are rather cramped but are nicely outfitted with natural-wood furnishings, painted in sand colors and pastel greens, and have Spanish marble in the bathrooms. A note to light sleepers: the air-conditioning–heating system can be noisy. The hotel has two restaurants: the informal Plurabelle and the plusher Alexandra Room. ⊠ *Earlsfort Terr., Georgian*

Dublin, 2 ☎ *01/676–5555* 🖷 *01/676–5424* ⊕ *www.conradhotels.com* 🛏 *182 rooms, 10 suites △ 2 restaurants, room service, in-room safes, minibars, cable TV, in-room VCRs, in-room data ports, gym, bar, concierge, business services, meeting rooms, free parking, no-smoking floor* 🖃 *AE, DC, MC, V.*

★ **$$$$** 🎫 **Merrion.** Arthur Wellesley, the Duke of Wellington and hero of Waterloo, once famously commented when queried about his Irish birth: "Just because a man is born in a stable doesn't make him a horse." His "stable," directly across from Government Buildings between Stephen's Green and Merrion Square, is one of the four exactingly restored Georgian town houses that make up this luxurious hotel. Some of the stately guest rooms are appointed in classic Georgian style—from the crisp linen sheets to the Carrara-marble bathrooms. Some are vaulted with delicate Adamesque plasterwork ceilings, and others are graced with magnificent, original marble fireplaces. Still, the decor is almost too spiffy—if this is the 18th century it has been buffed to a shiny 21st-century gloss. The staff is obviously accustomed to dealing with heads of state and royalty, so ladies shouldn't be surprised if they are addressed as "Madame." Clearly, this place must be very special, since leading Dublin restaurateur Patrick Guilbaud has moved his eponymous and fabulous restaurant here. ⊠ *Upper Merrion St., Georgian Dublin, 2* ☎ *01/603–0600* 🖷 *01/603–0700* ⊕ *www.merrionhotel.com* 🛏 *122 rooms, 20 suites △ 2 restaurants, room service, in-room safes, minibars, cable TV, in-room VCRs, in-room data ports, indoor pool, health club, hair salon, massage, 2 bars, dry cleaning, laundry service, concierge, business services, meeting rooms, free parking, no-smoking floor* 🖃 *AE, DC, MC, V.*

★ **$$–$$$$** 🎫 **Number 31.** Sam Stephenson, Dublin's most famous and highly controversial modernist architect, strikingly renovated two Georgian mews in the early 1960s as a private home. They are now connected via a small garden to the grand house they once served. Together they form a marvelous guesthouse a short walk from St. Stephen's Green, which give you a choice of bedroom styles: Georgian elegance or cool modern. Owners Deirdre and Noel Comer serve made-to-order breakfasts at refectory tables in the balcony dining room. The white-tile sunken living room, with its black leather sectional sofa and modern artwork that includes a David Hockney print, may make you think you're in California. If that essay in *Wallpaper*–modern doesn't send you, you'll be happy enough ensconced in one of the period-style guest rooms, one of which—No. 21—has a ceiling so lofty and corniced even a royal would feel at home. ⊠ *31 Leeson Close, Georgian Dublin, 2* ☎ *01/676–5011* 🖷 *01/676–2929* ⊕ *www.number31.ie* 🛏 *18 rooms △ Dry cleaning, laundry service, free parking, no-smoking rooms; no a/c* 🖃 *AE, MC, V.*

$$$ 🎫 **La Stampa.** Definitely a good thing in a very pretty, small package, this intimate town-house hotel, above the ever-popular and spectacular La Stampa restaurant and 50 yards from Trinity College, is the classiest new arrival on the Dublin scene. Each suite is individually decorated with an Asian theme—lots of wood, simple color schemes, and velvet bedspreads imported from Paris add to the luxury. For the price, there are few bet-

Fodor'sChoice
★

ter spots in town. ⊠ *35 Dawson St., Georgian Dublin, 2* ☏ *01/677–4444* 🖷 *01/677–4411* ⊕ *www.lastampa.ie* ⏎ *22 suites* ☖ *Restaurant, room service, minibars, cable TV, in-room VCRs, dry cleaning, laundry service, free parking, no-smoking rooms* ⊟ *AE, DC, MC, V.*

$$–$$$ 🏨 **Stephen's Hall Hotel & Suites.** Get a top-floor suite and lord it over the whole Southside in this all-suites hotel situated in a tastefully modernized Georgian town house just off St. Stephen's Green. The suites, considerably larger than the average hotel room, include one or two bedrooms, a separate sitting room, a fully equipped kitchen, and bath. The modern, motel-functional furniture is nondescript, but top-floor suites have spectacular city views, and ground-floor suites have private entrances. The Romanza restaurant serves breakfast, lunch, and dinner with an Italian flavor. ⊠ *14–17 Lower Leeson St., Georgian Dublin, 2* ☏ *01/ 661–0585* 🖷 *01/661–0606* ⊕ *www.stephens-hall.com* ⏎ *34 suites* ☖ *Restaurant, room service, kitchens, cable TV, 2 bars, meeting rooms, free parking, no-smoking rooms* ⊟ *AE, DC, MC, V.*

$–$$ 🏨 **Georgian House Hotel.** The name says it all. The owners of this hotel took three classic Georgian houses near St. Stephen's Green, added a modern extension, and opened one of Dublin's best value hotels. So you get an 18th-century-Dublin experience—high ceilings, original fireplaces, antique gilded mirrors—at guesthouse prices. Within the hotel, Maguires is a cozy, unpretentious little pub. ⊠ *18 Lower Bagott St., Georgian Dublin, 2* ☏ *01/661–8832* ⊕ *www.georgianhotel.ie* 🖷 *01/ 661–8834* ⏎ *20 rooms* ☖ *Restaurant, bar, free parking; no a/c* ⊟ *AE, MC, V* ⏏ *BP.*

$–$$ 🏨 **Kilronan House.** A good guesthouse should cheer you up when you come home at the end of a long day's touring. This large, late-19th-century terraced house with an elegant white facade will bring a smile to your face every time. A five-minute walk from St. Stephen's Green, Kilronan flaunts richly patterned wallpaper and carpets in its guest rooms, while orthopedic beds (rather rare in Dublin hotels, let alone in guesthouses) help to guarantee a restful night's sleep. ⊠ *70 Adelaide Rd., Georgian Dublin, 2* ☏ *01/475–5266* 🖷 *01/478–2841* ⊕ *www.dublinn. com* ⏎ *12 rooms* ☖ *Free parking, no-smoking room; no a/c* ⊟ *MC, V.*

Temple Bar

$$$–$$$$ 🏨 **The Clarence.** If coolness is contagious you definitely want a room at Temple Bar's most prestigious hotel. You might well bump into celebrity friends of co-owners Bono and the Edge of U2. Dating to 1852, the grand old hotel was given a total, no-expense-spared overhaul by its new owners in the early 1990s. The unique shapes and Arts and Crafts style of the old hotel were maintained in the Octagon Bar and the sleekly fabulous Tea Room Restaurant. Guest rooms are decorated in a mishmash of earth tones accented with deep purple, gold, cardinal red, and royal blue. With the exception of those in the penthouse suite, rooms are small. The laissez-faire service seems to take its cue from the minimalist style, so if you like to be pampered, stay elsewhere. ⊠ *6–8 Wellington Quay, Temple Bar, 2* ☏ *01/407–0800* 🖷 *01/407–0820* ⊕ *www.theclarence. ie* ⏎ *43 rooms, 5 suites* ☖ *Restaurant, minibars, cable TV, in-room data* ports, bar, dry cleaning, laundry service, meeting rooms, free parking, no-smoking rooms ☐ AE, DC, MC, V.

$$–$$$$ 🏨 **The Morgan.** In the sparkling heart of Temple Bar, the brand-new Morgan boasts about its chic design and decor, and the individually designed bedrooms and luxurious, colorful bathrooms are indeed pleasing to the eye. It is the hotel's extended-stay suites, however, that really sets it apart from the crowd. With a fully equipped kitchen and a spacious, gadget-filled living room, you can hunker down and make yourself comfortable for a week or two. The generously heated outside courtyard is perfect for cocktails. ✉ *10 Fleet St., Temple Bar, 2* ☎ *01/643–7000* 📠 *01/643–7060* ⊕ *www.themorgan.com* 🛏 *106 rooms* 🍴 *Restaurant, minibars, cable TV, in-room data ports, bar, dry cleaning, laundry service, no-smoking rooms* ☐ *AE, DC, MC, V.*

$$–$$$$ 🏨 **Paramount.** This medium-size hotel in the heart of trendy Temple Bar has opted to maintain its classy Victorian facade. The foyer continues this theme of solid elegance, with incredibly comfortable leather couches, bleached-blond-oak floors, and burgundy curtains. Dark woods and subtle colors decorate the bedrooms—very 1930s (if not Bogie and Bacall). If you're fond of a tipple, try the hotel's Art Deco Turks Head Bar and Chop House. ✉ *Parliament St. and Essex Gate, Temple Bar, 2* ☎ *01/417–9900* 📠 *01/417–9904* ⊕ *www.paramounthotel.ie* 🛏 *70 rooms* 🍴 *Restaurant, cable TV, in-room data ports, bar, laundry service, no-smoking rooms* ☐ *AE, DC, MC, V.*

$–$$$ 🏨 **Parliament.** As with many Dublin hotels, the interiors of the Parliament do not quite live up to the fabulous facade of one of Dublin's finest Edwardian buildings. Inside, the atmosphere is very much functional, if tidy, and appeals to mainly a business clientele—drawn by the location near the Central Bank and Trinity College. But rooms are a good size, with a simple, slightly monotonous beige and off-white color scheme. The Forum bar keeps up the democratic theme with reliable selection of bar food. ✉ *Lord Edward St., Temple Bar, 2* ☎ *01/670–8777* 📠 *01/670–8787* ⊕ *www.regencyhotels.com* 🛏 *63 rooms* 🍴 *Cable TV, bar, no-smoking rooms* ☐ *AE, DC, MC, V.*

$–$$$ 🏨 **Temple Bar.** Dublin doesn't usually do Art Deco, so the 1920s-style lobby of the Temple Bar—with its old-fashioned cast-iron fireplace, natural-wood furniture, and legions of exotic plants—is a refreshing change. Off the lobby are a small cocktail bar and the bright, airy, glass-roof Terrace restaurant, great spots to hang out and enjoy a pretheater martini. Mahogany wood and autumn green and rust colors characterize the guest rooms, nearly all of which have big double beds (which can leave them a little cramped). The Boomerang nightclub on the premises is open to both guests and the public. The hotel is in a former bank building, around the corner from Trinity College. ✉ *Fleet St., Temple Bar, 2* ☎ *01/677–3333* 📠 *01/677–3088* ⊕ *www.templebarhotel.com* 🛏 *129 rooms* 🍴 *Restaurant, cable TV, 2 bars, nightclub, parking (fee)* ☐ *AE, DC, MC, V.*

The Northside

$$$$ 🏨 **Clarion Hotel IFSC.** Built with business guests in mind, this high-rise hotel has been a surprise hit with tourists. Smack in the middle of the

International Financial Services Centre, the Clarion—with an office-block-like exterior—is indistinguishable from many of the financial institutions that surround it. The public spaces are bright and cheery, if a little uninspired, but the bedrooms—big by Dublin standards—are all straight lines and contemporary light-oak furnishings. Shades of blue and taupe do create a calm environment (the hotel claims its environment is guided by Eastern philosophy, no less), but for true serenity try to get a room at the front with great views out over the Liffey. Because the hotel mainly caters to business travelers, weekend bargains are a definite possibility—make sure you ask. ✉ *IFSC, Northside, 1* ☎ *01/433–8800* 🖷 *01/433–8811* ⊕ *www.clarionhotelifsc.com* ⤴ *145 rooms, 17 suites* ⌂ *Restaurant, room service, minibars, cable TV, in-room data ports, indoor pool, health club, massage, bar, dry cleaning, laundry service, free parking, no-smoking rooms* ▭ *AE, DC, MC, V.*

$$$$ ▥ **The Morrison.** How do you make a Dublin hotel instantly trendy? Simple: get the country's top fashion guru to design the interiors. John Rocha had the last word on everything at this übermodern trendsetting hotel, down to the toiletries and staff uniforms. Past the 18th-century Georgian facade, the superstriking, *Wallpaper*-ready public areas contrast with the very unfussy, almost Scandinavian bedrooms. Some visitors complain that the place leaves them a little cold, others that the Morrison is as good as a London boutique hotel, though many times the size. A new wing with a 49 rooms and private art gallery opened in 2005. Halo, the hotel's nouvelle Irish restaurant, is super-stylish and has one of the most ambitiously delicious menus in town. Halfway between the Ha'penny and Capel Street bridges, the Morrison is no more than a 10-minute walk from Trinity College. ✉ *Ormond Quay, Northside, 1* ☎ *01/887–2400* 🖷 *01/874–4039* ⊕ *www.morrisonhotel.ie* ⤴ *124 rooms, 14 suites* ⌂ *2 restaurants, room service, minibars, cable TV, in-room VCRs, in-room data ports, 2 bars, dry cleaning, laundry service, concierge, business services, meeting rooms, free parking, no-smoking rooms* ▭ *AE, DC, MC, V.*

$$ ▥ **Royal Dublin Hotel.** No, the Queen never stayed here and O'Connell Street is not what it once was, but new life has been brought to this old lady. One of the big pluses of this beige-plush and chandelier-lighted hotel is its perfect location at the top of the thoroughfare, near the Northside's major attractions (a 10-minute walk south deposits you at Trinity College). The public spaces are subtly lighted and decorated in slightly loud glass and brass. Rooms are spacious, and the hotel has built a solid reputation for extra-friendly service. The Georgian Room and Raffles bar try to put on posh English airs (think crisp linens), but the casual warmth of the staff undoes the stuffiness. ✉ *O'Connell St., Northside, 1* ☎ *01/873–3666* 🖷 *01/873–3120* ⊕ *www.royaldublin. com* ⤴ *117 rooms, 3 suites* ⌂ *Restaurant, room service, minibars, cable TV, in-room VCRs, in-room data ports, bar, dry cleaning, laundry service, no-smoking rooms* ▭ *AE, MC, V.*

★ **$–$$** ▥ **Charleville Lodge.** If Dublin's city center is a Georgian wonder, a short commute out to the historic Phibsborough area of Dublin's Northside will transport you to the elegantly Victorian 19th century. Here, in a row of beautifully restored terraced houses you can enjoy quality time

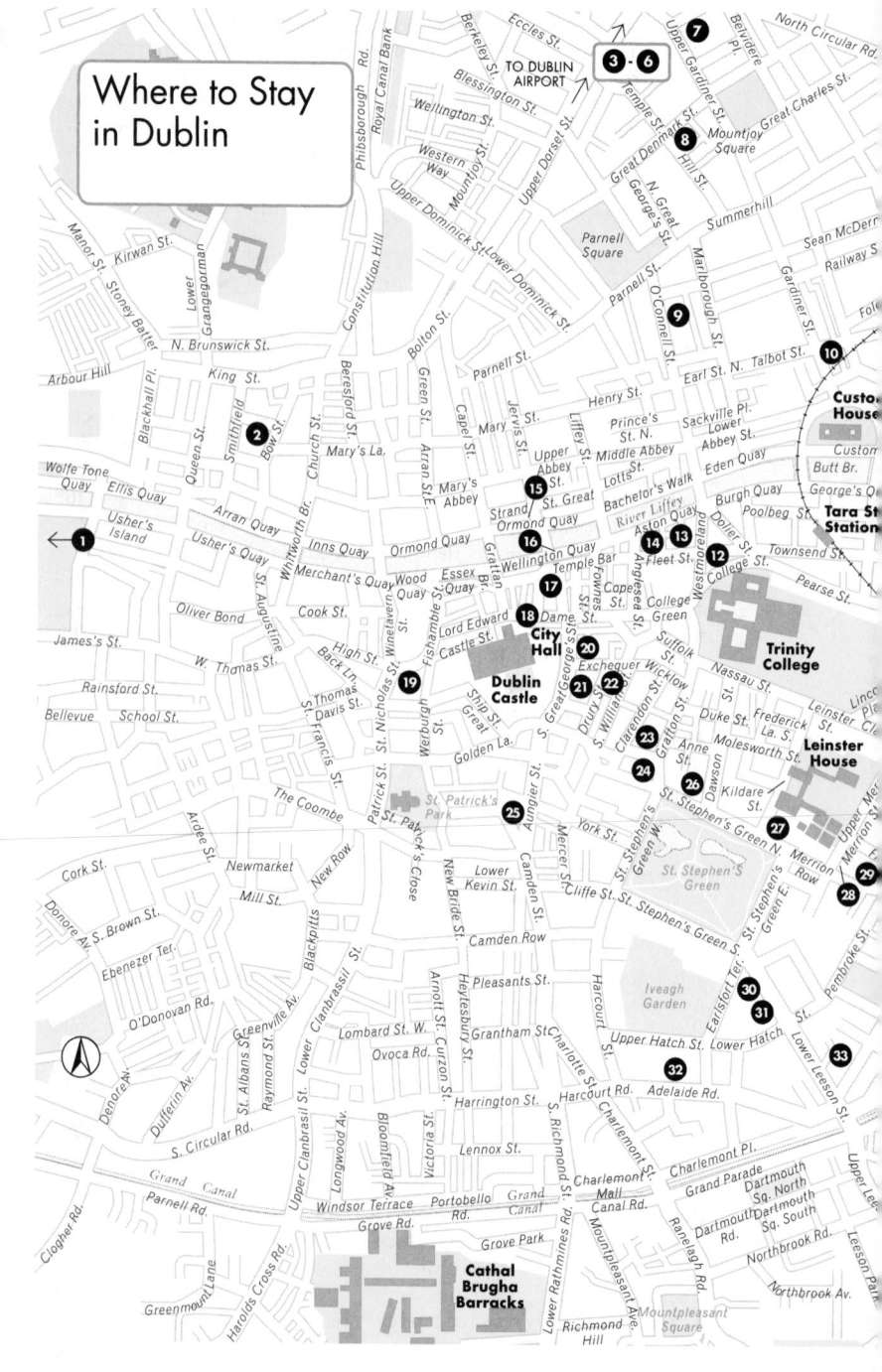

Where to Stay
in Dublin

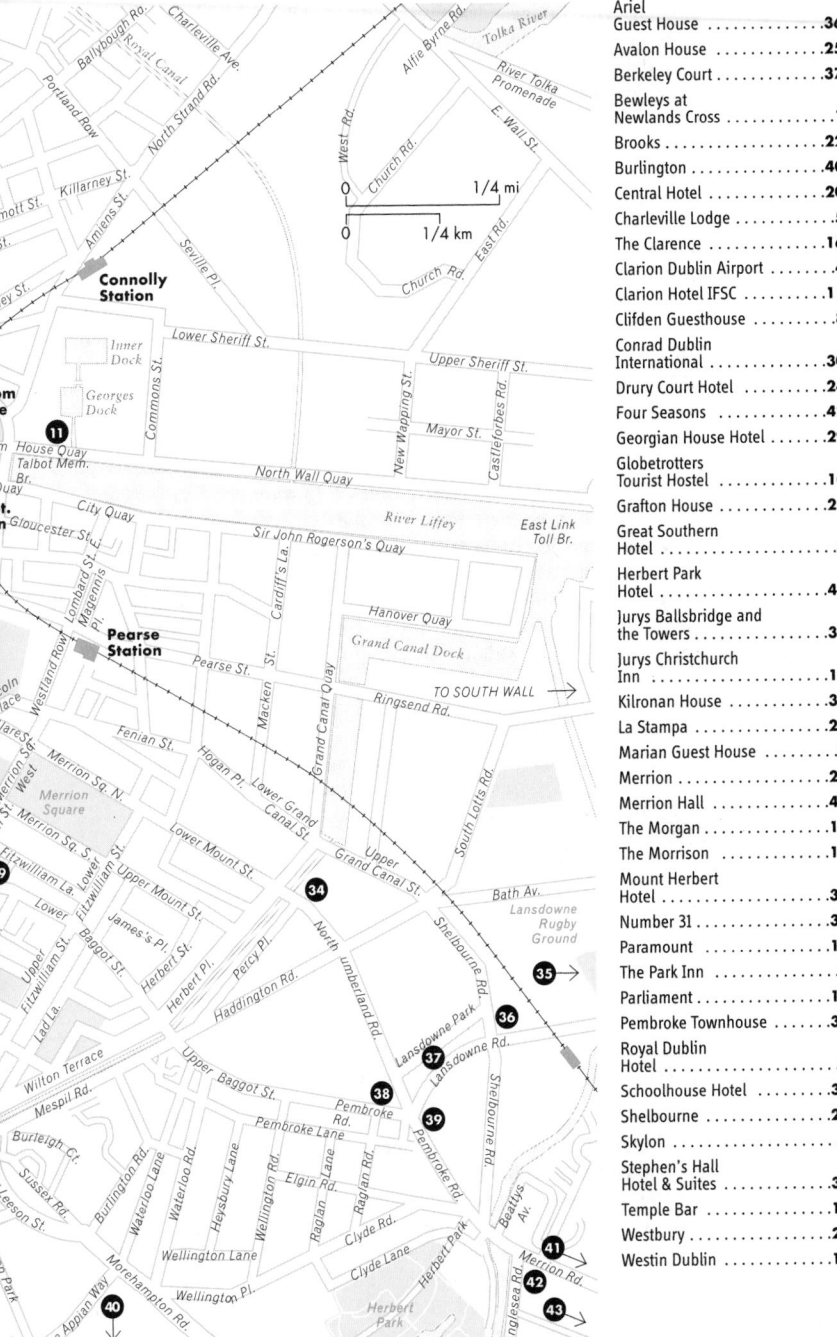

in Charleville Lodge's dramatically lighted residents' lounge, all twinkling chandeliers, plush wing chairs, and working fireplace. An antiquarian's delight, this grand salon is a great spot to chat with other travelers who have dared to stray off the beaten path. Upstairs, guest rooms are brightly colored, wide, and have refreshingly high ceilings. As for the commute, the No. 10 bus takes but five minutes and it's even a great walk in good weather. All in all, this hostelry offers a touch of luxury at great value. ⊠ *268–272 N. Circular Rd., Northside, 7* ☎ *01/838–6633* 🖷 *01/838–5854* ⊕ *www.charlevillelodge.ie* ⇨ *30 rooms* ⚘ *Free parking, no-smoking rooms; no a/c* ▭ *MC, V* �𝍌❙ *BP.*

$ 🖻 **Clifden Guesthouse.** The Gardiner Street area deservedly gets some bad press, as it's home to a host of cheap, poor-quality guesthouses. But there are a few diamonds in the rough, and the Clifden, although still certainly a bargain, is a cut above the rest. The Georgian building has been stylishly refurbished, and the rooms are huge, with simple furnishings and wonderfully tall, period windows. O'Connell Street is a five-minute walk away. As an added bonus, you can park here free even after you have checked out. ⊠ *32 Gardiner Pl., Northside, 1* ☎*01/874–6364* 🖷*01/874–6122* ⊕ *www.clifdenhouse.com* ⇨ *15 rooms* ⚘ *Free parking, no-smoking rooms; no a/c* ▭ *MC, V* �𝍌❙ *BP.*

¢–$ 🖻 **Globetrotters Tourist Hostel.** Globetrotters is a giant step up from many Dublin hostels, with a pleasant outdoor courtyard; clean, locking dorm rooms with en suite showers; a turf fire; comfortable bunk beds (with lamps for late-night reading); and a delicious all-you-can-eat breakfast. Plus, you're within walking distance of the city center, one block from the bus station, and two blocks from the train station. The owners also run Town House, a cute B&B in the same building. ⊠ *47–48 Lower Gardiner St., Northside, 1* ☎ *01/873–5893* 🖷 *01/878–8787* ⊕ *www. globetrottersdublin.com* ⇨ *94 dorm beds with shared bath, 38 double rooms* ⚘ *Restaurant, no-smoking rooms; no a/c, no room TVs* ▭ *MC, V* �𝍌❙ *BP.*

¢ 🖻 **Marian Guest House.** A veritable Everest of fine Irish meats, the Marian's mighty full Irish breakfast, with black pudding and smoked bacon, is reason enough to stay at this family-run guesthouse (the whole family can speak Irish, by the way). The place only has six rooms, so you get lots of attention and pampering. Rooms are fairly basic, but clean and pleasant. ⊠ *21 Upper Gardiner St., Northside, 1* ☎ *01/874–4129* ⊕ *www.marianguesthouse.ie* ⇨ *6 rooms* ⚘ *Free parking; no a/c* ▭ *MC, V* ⌾❙ *BP.*

South Dublin: The Grand Canal & Ballsbridge

$$$$ 🖻 **Berkeley Court.** A beauty-and-the-beast combination, the Berkeley Court is a somewhat ugly, glass-and-concrete building designed in a modern, blocklike style surrounded by serene and verdant grounds. The interior may be the most quietly elegant in any of Dublin's large modern hotels. The vast white and plushly carpeted lobby, with its huge central chandelier, has roomy sofas and antique planters. Golds, yellows, and greens decorate the large guest rooms, filled with antiques or period reproductions; bathrooms are tiled in marble. The Berkeley Room has table d'hôte and à la carte menus; the more informal Conservatory Grill, with large windows, serves grilled food and snacks. ⊠ *Lansdowne Rd., Ballsbridge, 4* ☏ *01/660–1711, 800/550–0000 in U.S.* 🖷 *01/661–7238* ⊕ *www.jurysdoyle.com* ↪ *156 rooms, 30 suites* ⚸ *2 restaurants, room service, cable TV, in-room data ports, gym, hair salon, some hot tubs, bar, shops, dry cleaning, laundry service, business services, meeting rooms, free parking, no-smoking rooms* ▭ *AE, DC, MC, V.*

$$$$ 🎞 **Four Seasons.** Much controversy surrounds the brash postmodern—critics would say faux-Victorian-Georgian hybrid—architecture of this hotel, in its own 4-acre gardens. The six-floor building mixes pre-20th-century design with modern glass and concrete. The impressive landscaping aims to makes the hotel seem like an oasis; a big effort has been made to ensure that a bit of greenery can be seen from most rooms. Guest rooms are spacious, with large windows that allow light to flood in. A selection of landscapes on the hotel walls lends the place a warm touch. The lower-level spa is one of the finest in the country, with a naturally lighted lap pool. ⊠ *Simmonscourt Rd., Ballsbridge, 4* ☏ *01/665–4000* 🖷 *01/665–4099* ⊕ *www.fourseasons.com* ↪ *192 rooms, 67 suites* ⚸ *Restaurant, coffee shop, room service, cable TV, in-room data ports, indoor pool, hot tub, bar, shop, dry cleaning, laundry service, business services, meeting rooms, free parking, no-smoking rooms* ▭ *AE, DC, MC, V.*

$$$$ 🎞 **Herbert Park Hotel.** For maximum pleasure secure a room overlooking the park of the same name adjacent to this hotel, which is also beside the Dodder River. Two of the suites even have large balconies with views of the park or the leafy suburbs. Relaxing shades of blue and cream predominate in the spacious rooms; all have individually controlled air-conditioning, a large desk, and two telephone lines. The hotel's large, light-filled lobby has floor-to-ceiling windows and a slanted glass roof. The spacious bar, terrace lounge, and restaurant are Japanese-inspired-minimalist in style. You can dine on the restaurant terrace in warm weather. ⊠ *Merrion Rd., Ballsbridge, 4* ☏ *01/667–2200* 🖷 *01/667–2595* ⊕ *www.herbertparkhotel.ie* ↪ *150 rooms, 3 suites* ⚸ *Restaurant, cable TV, gym, bar, business services, free parking, no-smoking rooms* ▭ *AE, DC, MC, V.*

$$$–$$$$ 🎞 **Burlington.** A genuine institution, Ireland's largest hotel is one of those landmarks where nearly every Irish person seems to have spent at least one night (or so they claim). In high contrast to the hotel's impersonal, 1972 glass-and-concrete facade, the staff here is famously friendly and attentive. Public rooms, especially the large bar, have mahogany counters and hanging plants that enhance the conservatory-style setting and take the edge off the uninspired building. The generous-size rooms, furnished in modern minimalist style, with neutral tones, have large picture windows. At night, Annabel's nightclub and the seasonal Irish cabaret are both lively (sometimes too lively!) spots. The Burlington has no sports and health facilities, but the Doyle hotel group, which runs it, has an arrangement that allows you to use the RiverView Sports Club in nearby Clonskeagh for €6.35 a visit. ⊠ *Upper Leeson St., Ballsbridge, 4* ☏ *01/660–5222* 🖷 *01/660–8496* ⊕ *www.jurysdoyle.com* ↪ *504 rooms* ⚸ *2 restaurants, room service, some minibars, cable TV with movies, in-room data ports, Wi-Fi, gym, bar, lobby lounge,*

lounge, cabaret, nightclub, dry cleaning, laundry service, shop, business services, meeting rooms, no-smoking rooms.

$$$–$$$$ 🏨 **Jurys Ballsbridge and the Towers.** Farmers and their families up in "the big smoke" for a shopping weekend have always favored the laid-back atmosphere of Jurys. These adjoining seven-story hotels, also popular with businesspeople, have more atmosphere than most comparable modern hotels. The Towers has an edge over its older, larger, less-expensive companion, Jurys Ballsbridge. Rooms in the Towers are decorated in blue and gold with built-in, natural-wood furniture; the large beds and armchairs are great for lounging. Jurys Ballsbridge, on the other hand, has large, plainly decorated rooms with light walls and brown drapes; furnishings are functional and uninspired. Early May through early October, Jury's Irish Cabaret has live entertainment Wednesday through Sunday. ⊠ *Pembroke Rd. (Jurys Ballsbridge) and Lansdowne Rd. (the Towers), Ballsbridge, 4* ☎ *01/660–5000* 🖷 *01/679–7078* ⊕ *www. jurysdoyle.com* 🖙 *Jurys Ballsbridge: 300 rooms, 3 suites. The Towers: 100 rooms, 5 suites* ⚐ *2 restaurants, coffee shop, some kitchenettes, indoor-outdoor pool, hot tub, bar, cabaret, shop, dry cleaning, laundry service, business services, meeting rooms, free parking* ⊟ *AE, DC, MC, V.*

$$$–$$$$ 🏨 **Pembroke Townhouse.** Dublin is at its most beautiful when it wears its Georgian face, and the Pembroke, a superb example of classic 18th-century grandeur, captures the city on a very good hair day. Town house does not do justice to the splendor of the place, but does hint at the cozy, relaxed atmosphere. The fan-windowed front door leads into a stately reception area, complete with Grecian pillars. The bright, airy, high-ceiling rooms are all individually designed in a gentle clash of contempory chic and Georgian symmetry. Nearly every wall bears a striking piece of contemporary Irish art. The hearty breakfast—including sautéed lamb's liver if desired—is served in the serene dining room. ⊠ *90 Pembroke Rd., Ballsbridge, 4* ☎ *01/660–0277* 🖷 *01/660–0291* ⊕ *www. pembroketownhouse.ie* 🖙 *48 rooms* ⚐ *In-room data ports, dry cleaning, laundry service, free parking* ⊟ *AE, DC, MC, V.*

$$$ 🏨 **Schoolhouse Hotel.** "Ahead of its class" exclaims the terrible slogan, but this converted Victorian parochial school just off the Grand Canal really is A-plus. The rooms—each named for a famous Irish writer and hung with a corresponding portrait—are very old-school (excuse the pun) luxury, with thick rugs matching the quilted bedspreads, plus beautiful oak chairs and desk. Though its name is hardly promising, the Canteen Restaurant is actually a classy, modern-Irish eatery in a beautiful, light-filled former classroom with a barrel ceiling. ⊠ *2-8 Northumberland Rd., Ballsbridge, 4* ☎ *01/667–5014* 🖷 *01/667–5015* ⊕ *www. schoolhousehotel.com* 🖙 *31 rooms* ⚐ *Restaurant, in-room data ports, dry cleaning, laundry service, meeting rooms, free parking* ⊟ *AE, DC, MC, V.*

$$–$$$ 🏨 **Merrion Hall.** When your hotel is surrounded by embassies you know you're in a classy part of town. Four-poster beds and whirlpool spas are some of the luxuries showered upon you at this quaintly elegant Edwardian town-house hotel in Ballsbridge. Ivy covers the secluded redbrick building, and a *Room with a View* atmosphere is created with a wonderfully stuffy afternoon tea (and also fine wines) served in the bay-win-

dowed drawing room—a great chance to meet the other happy guests. ⊠ *7 Herbert Rd., Ballsbridge, 4* ☎ *01/668–1426* 🖷 *01/668–4280* ⊕ *www.halpinsprivatehotels.com* ➴ *34 rooms* ⚭ *Cable TV, free parking, no-smoking rooms* ⊟ *AE, DC, MC, V.*

★ **$–$$$** 🏨 **Ariel Guest House.** The homemade preserves and oven-warm scones are reason enough to stay at this redbrick 1850 Victorian guesthouse in one of Dublin's poshest tree-lined suburbs. It's a few steps from a DART stop and a 15-minute walk from St. Stephen's Green. Restored rooms in the main house are lovingly decorated with Georgian antiques, Victoriana, and period wallpaper and drapes. The 13 rooms at the back of the house are more spartan, but all are immaculate. A Waterford-crystal chandelier hangs over the comfortable leather and mahogany furniture in the gracious, fireplace-warmed drawing room. Owner Michael O'Brien is an extraordinarily helpful and gracious host. ⊠ *52 Lansdowne Rd., Ballsbridge, 4* ☎ *01/668–5512* 🖷 *01/668–5845* ⊕ *www.arielhouse.net* ➴ *37 rooms* ⚭ *Free parking; no a/c* ⊟ *MC, V* ❏ *BP.*

$–$$$ 🏨 **Mount Herbert Hotel.** The Loughran family's sprawling accommodation includes a number of large, Victorian-era houses. The hotel overlooks some of Ballsbridge's fine rear gardens and is near the main rugby stadium; the nearby DART will have you in the city center in seven minutes. The simple rooms are painted in light shades and contain little besides beds. The lounge is a good place to relax. The restaurant, which overlooks the English-style back garden (floodlighted at night) and children's play area, serves three meals a day; at dinner you can dine on steaks and stews. ⊠ *7 Herbert Rd., Ballsbridge, 4* ☎ *01/668–4321* 🖷 *01/660–7077* ⊕ *www.mountherberthotel.ie* ➴ *177 rooms* ⚭ *Restaurant, cable TV, sauna, bar, shop, business services, meeting rooms, free parking, no-smoking rooms; no a/c* ⊟ *AE, DC, MC, V.*

Dublin West

$$–$$$ 🏨 **The Park Inn.** Formerly Chief O'Neills, this strikingly modern hotel anchors the rejuvenation of the old fruit market area, known as Smithfield Village, north of the Liffey. The top floors have delightful rooftop gardens with views of the city on both sides of the Liffey. Smallish, high-tech rooms all have in-room data ports and look thoroughly up-to-date, thanks to their glass-tile walls, hot-and-cool Miami Beach colors, 1960s-mod and minimalist furnishings (chrome, anyone?), and feng shui–inspired bathrooms. The café-bar has live traditional music and contemporary Irish food, and Asian cuisine is available in Kelly & Ping, a bright, airy restaurant off Duck Lane, a shopping arcade that's part of the hotel complex. ⊠ *Smithfield Village, Dublin West, 7* ☎ *01/817–3838* 🖷 *01/817–3839* ⊕ *www.chiefoneills.com* ➴ *70 rooms, 3 suites* ⚭ *Restaurant, room service, minibars, cable TV, in-room VCRs, in-room data ports, gym, bar, shops, dry cleaning, laundry service, free parking, no-smoking rooms* ⊟ *AE, DC, MC, V.*

$–$$ 🏨 **Jurys Christchurch Inn.** Expect few frills at this functional budget hotel, part of a Jurys minichain that offers a low, fixed room rate for up to three adults or two adults and two children. (The branch at Custom House Quay operates according to the same plan.) The biggest plus is the pleasant location, facing Christ Church Cathedral and within walking distance of most city-center attractions. The rather spartan rooms are decorated in pastel colors and have utilitarian furniture. ⊠ *Christ Church Pl., Dublin West, 8* ☎ *01/454–0000* 🖷 *01/454–0012* ⊕ *www.jurysdoyle.com* ➘ *182 rooms* ⚬ *Restaurant, bar, parking (fee), no-smoking rooms* ☰ *AE, DC, MC, V.*

¢ 🏨 **Avalon House.** Many young, independent travelers rate this cleverly restored redbrick Victorian building, a five-minute walk southwest from Grafton Street and 5 to 10 minutes from some of the city's best music venues, the most appealing of Dublin's hostels. Avalon House has a mix of dormitories, rooms without bath, and rooms with bath. The dorm rooms and en suite quads all have loft areas that offer more privacy than you'd typically find in a multibed room. The Avalon Café serves food until 10 PM but is open as a common room after hours. ⊠ *55 Aungier St., Dublin West, 2* ☎ *01/475–0001* 🖷 *01/475–0303* ⊕ *www.avalon-house.ie* ➘ *40 4-bed rooms, 35 with bath; 26 twin rooms, 4 with bath; 4 single rooms with shared bath; 5 12-bed dorms, 1 10-bed dorm, and 1 26-bed dorm, all with shared bath* ⚬ *Café, bar; no a/c, no room TVs* ☰ *AE, MC, V.*

¢ 🏨 **Bewleys at Newlands Cross.** Cheap and cheerful would best sum up this four-story hotel on the southwest outskirts of the city. It's ideal if you're planning to head out of the city early (especially to points in the southwest and west) and don't want to deal with morning traffic. The hotel is emulating the formula popularized by Jurys Inns, in which rooms—here each has a double bed, a single bed, and a sofa bed—are a flat rate for up to three adults or two adults and two children. ⊠ *Newlands Cross at Naas Rd., Dublin West, 22* ☎ *01/464–0140* 🖷 *01/464–0900* ⊕ *www.bewleyshotels.com* ➘ *258 rooms* ⚬ *Café, free parking, no-smoking rooms; no a/c* ☰ *AE, MC, V.*

Around Dublin Airport

$$–$$$$ 🏨 **Great Southern Hotel.** You could sleepwalk to your plane from the Great Southern. Near the main terminal, and next to the main road into the city center is this modern five-story hotel that's part of one of Ireland's most respected chains. Rooms are spacious and comfortable, if unexciting, but the service is exceptional. Double glazing ensures the roar of a 747 doesn't interrupt any beauty sleep. Twelve of the rooms are designated "Lady Executive." ⊠ *Dublin Airport, County Dublin, North County Dublin* ☎ *01/844–6000* 🖷 *01/844–6001* ⊕ *www.gsh.ie* ➘ *223 rooms, 6 suites* ⚬ *Restaurant, room service, in-room data ports, bar, free parking* ☰ *AE, DC, MC, V.*

$–$$ 🏨 **Clarion Dublin Airport.** Seen one, seen 'em all. The saying is fairly accurate when talking about airport hotels, and this Clarion is no exception. But the low-rise redbrick structure with a plain exterior has one big plus; rooms big enough to make you forget about the cookie-cutter decor. The Bistro Restaurant serves fish, meat, and vegetarian dishes; Sampans serves Chinese cuisine and is open for dinner only. There's live music in the bar on weekends. Guests have access to a nearby health club. ⊠ *Dublin Airport, County Dublin, North County Dublin* ☎ *01/808–0500* 🖷 *01/844–6002* ⊕ *www.clariondublinairport.com* ➘ *247* rooms ⚘ 2 *restaurants, room service, in-room data ports, bar, free parking, no-smoking rooms* ▭ *AE, DC, MC, V.*

$ ▣ **Skylon.** Location, location . . . and spacious rooms; the three reasons for choosing the Skylon. On the main road into Dublin city center from the airport stands this modern five-story hotel with a concrete-and-glass facade and generous-size rooms, plainly decorated in cool, sea-bright colors. Double beds and a pair of easy chairs are almost the only furniture in the rooms. A glass-fronted lobby with a large bar and the Rendezvous Room restaurant dominate the public areas. The cooking is adequate but uninspired, with dishes such as grilled steak, poached cod, and omelets. ✉ *Upper Drumcondra Rd., 9 North County Dublin* ☎ *01/837–9121* 🖷 *01/837–2778* ⊕ *www.skylon.org* ⇥ *90 rooms* ⚘ *Restaurant, bar, free parking* ▭ *AE, DC, MC, V.*

NIGHTLIFE & THE ARTS

Long before Stephen Dedalus's excursions into "nighttown" in James Joyce's *Ulysses,* Dublin was proud of its lively after-hours scene, particularly its thriving pubs. But the Celtic Tiger economy, the envy of all Europe, turned Dublin into one of the most happening destinations on the whole continent. Some of the old watering holes were replaced with huge, London-style "superbars," which, with the ubiquitous DJ in the corner, walk the fine line between pub and club. Most nights, the city's nightspots overflow with young cell phone–toting Dubliners and Europeans who descend on the capital for weekend getaways. The city's 900-plus pubs are its main source of entertainment; many public houses in the city center have live music—from rock to jazz to traditional Irish.

Theater is an essential element of life in the city that was home to O'Casey, Synge, Yeats, and Beckett. Today Dublin has eight major theaters that reproduce the Irish "classics," and also present newer fare from the likes of Martin Macdonagh and Conon Macpherson. Opera, long overlooked, now has a home in the restored old Gaiety Theatre.

Check the following newspapers for informative listings: the *Irish Times* publishes a daily guide to what's happening in Dublin and the rest of the country, and has complete film and theater schedules. The *Evening Herald* lists theaters, cinemas, and pubs with live entertainment. The *Big Issue* is a weekly guide to film, theater, and musical events around the city. The *Event Guide,* a weekly free paper that lists music, cinema, theater, art shows, and dance clubs, is available in pubs and cafés around the city. In peak season, consult the free Bord Fáilte (Irish Tourist Board) leaflet "Events of the Week." The **Temple Bar Web site** (⊕ www.temple-bar.ie) provides information about events in the Temple Bar area.

Nightlife

Dubliners have always enjoyed a night out, but in the last decade or so they have turned the pleasure into a work of art: the streets of the city center are the scene of what appears to be a never-ending party. In loud, brash dance clubs, where style and swagger rule, you're as likely to find crowds at 2 AM on a Wednesday as you are at the same time on a Saturday. In Dublin's clubs the dominant sound is hip-hop and electronic dance music, and the crowd that flocks to them every night of the week is of the trendy, under-thirty generation. Leeson Street—just off St. Stephen's Green, south of the Liffey, and known as "the strip"—is a main nightclub area that revs up at pub closing time and lasts until 4 AM. It has lost its gloss since a number of lap-dancing establishments have opened. The dress code at Leeson Street's dance clubs is informal, but jeans and sneakers are not welcome. Most of these clubs are licensed only to sell wine, and the prices can be exorbitant (up to €26 for a mediocre bottle); the upside is that most don't charge to get in.

There are plenty of alternatives to the electronic dance scene, including nightclubs where the dominant sounds range from soul to salsa—such as the weekend nightclub "Play" at the Gaiety Theatre and the totally Latin Sugar Club. Although jazz isn't a big part of the nightlife here, a few regular venues do draw the best of local and international talent. And if you're looking for something more mellow, the city doesn't disappoint: there are wine bars, bistros, cafés, and all manner of other late-night eateries where you can sit, sip, and chat until 2 AM or later.

Some of Dublin's classic pubs—arguably some of the finest watering holes in the world—have been reinvented with modern interiors and designer drinks, to attract a younger, upwardly mobile crowd. Beware Dublin Tourism's "Official Dublin Pub Guide," which has a tendency to recommend many of these bland spots. Despite the changes, however, the traditional pub has steadfastly clung to its role as the primary center of Dublin's social life. The city has nearly 1,000 pubs ("licensed tabernacles," writer Flann O'Brien calls them). And although the vision of elderly men enjoying a chin wag over a creamy pint of stout has become something of a rarity, there are still plenty of places where you can enjoy a quiet drink and a chat. Last drinks are called at 11:30 PM Monday to Wednesday, 12:30 AM Thursday to Saturday, and 11 PM on Sunday. Some city-center pubs have extended opening hours and don't serve last drinks until 1:45 AM.

A word of warning: although most pubs and clubs are perfectly safe, the lads can get lively—public drunkenness is very much a part of Dublin's nightlife. Whereas this is for the most part seen as the Irish form of unwinding after a long week (or, well, day), it can sometimes lead to regrettable incidents (fighting, for instance). In an effort to keep potential trouble at bay, bouncers and security guards maintain a visible presence in all clubs and many pubs around the city. At the end of the night, the city center is full of young people trying to get home, which makes for extremely long lines at taxi stands and late-night bus stops, especially on weekends. The combination of drunkenness and impatience can sometimes lead to trouble, so act cautiously. If you will need late-night transportation, try to arrange it with your hotel before you go out.

Irish Cabaret, Music & Dancing

CITY CENTER **Bewley's Cafe Theatre** (⊠ Grafton St., City Center ☎ 086/878-4001), with its "Live at The Oriental Room" nights, has become the atmospheric cabaret hot spot in Dublin.

BALLSBRIDGE **Burlington Hotel** (✉ Upper Leeson St., Ballsbridge ☎ 01/660–5222) has a high-class lounge featuring a well-performed Irish cabaret—with dancing, music, and song.

Jurys Hotel (✉ Pembroke Rd., Ballsbridge ☎ 01/660–5000) stages a traditional Irish cabaret.

DUBLIN WEST **Castle Inn** (✉ Christ Church Pl., Dublin West ☎ 01/475–1122) is really just a huge pub that has traditional Irish music and dancing with dinner in a medieval-style banquet hall.

Jazz

Globe (✉ 11 S. Great George's St., City Center ☎ 01/671–1220), has live "easy listening" jazz every Sunday afternoon.

JJ Smyth's (✉ 12 Aungier St., City Center ☎ 01/475–2565) is an old-time jazz venue where Louis Stewart, the granddaddy of Irish jazz, is a regular visitor.

Jurys Ballsbridge (✉ Pembroke Rd., Ballsbridge ☎ 01/660–5000) attracts the country's top jazz musicians and voices to its lively Sunday-evening sessions.

Nightclubs

NORTHSIDE **Spirit** (✉ 57 Middle Abbey St., Northside ☎ 01/677–9999) attracts a party-time, young crowd, which is serious about two things: dancing and more dancing. Spirit likes to call itself a "holistic venue" and its three floors are loosely designed around the themes of Mind, Body, and Soul. Mind is the basement level full of scented candles, chill-out couches, and ambient sounds; Body is the main dance floor with full-on dance tracks; and Soul is more funky.

CITY CENTER **Lillie's Bordello** (✉ Grafton St., City Center ☎ 01/679–9204) is a popular spot for a trendy professional crowd, as well as for rock and film stars.

The Pod (✉ Harcourt St., City Center ☎ 01/478–0166), also known as the "Place of Dance," qualifies as Dublin's most renowned dance club, especially among the younger set. Whether you get in depends as much on what you're wearing as on your age.

Red Box (✉ Old Harcourt St. Station, Harcourt St., City Center ☎ 01/478–0166), adjacent to the Pod and the Crawdaddy music venue, can pack in more than 1,000 people and surround them with state-of-the-art sound and light. It regularly hosts Irish and international rock acts, and celebrity DJs from Europe and the United States. It has full bar facilities.

Renards (✉ St. Fredrick St., Georgian Dublin ☎ 01/677–5876) is where you'll find upmarket thirtysomethings who like to let their hair down. The music can be a bit predictable, but you might just bump into Bono.

Rí Ra (✉ Dame Ct., City Center ☎ 01/677–4835) is part of the hugely popular Globe bar. The name means "uproar" in Irish, and on most nights the place does go a little wild. It's one of the best spots in Dublin for fun, no-frills dancing. Upstairs is more low-key.

Spy (⌧ 59 South William St., City Centre ☎ 01/679–0014) is a split-level space broken up into four distinct rooms, each with its own bar and vibe. Downstairs is an all-out dance club know as Wax.

Temple Bar Music Centre (⌧ Curved St., Temple Bar ☎ 01/670–9202) claims to provide a different sound every night, including house, tribute bands, guitar-driven rock, and Latin music.

Viper Room (⌧ 5 Aston Quay, Temple Bar ☎ 01/672–5566), decorated in rich reds and purples, is a delightfully decadent late-night club that plays funk, chart, and rhythm and blues. Downstairs there's live jazz and salsa.

Pubs

"When I die I want to decompose in a barrel of porter and have it served in all the pubs in Dublin." Author J. P. Donleavy realized that it's impossible to think of Dublin without also thinking of its 1,000 or so "public houses." These are what gives Dublin so much of its character, and they're largely to blame for the fierce loyalty Dublin inspires among locals and visitors. Some wag once asked if it was possible to cross Dublin without passing a single pub along the way. The answer was "Yes, but only if you go into every one." As a general rule, the area between Grafton and Great George's streets is a gold mine for classy pubs. Another good bet is the Temple Bar district (though some of the newer ones are all plastic and mirrors). And if it be real spit-on-the-floor hideaways you're after, head across the Liffey to the area around Parnell Square.

Conways (⌧ 70 Parnell St., Northside ☎ 01/873–2687) is an old-school, "spit-and-sawdust" public house with the beat of modern live music upstairs.

The Flowing Tide (⌧ Lower Abbey St., Northside ☎ 01/874–0842), directly across from the Abbey Theatre, draws a lively pre- and posttheater crowd. No TVs, quality pub talk, and a great pint of Guinness make it a worthwhile visit.

GUBU (⌧ Capel St., Northside ☎ 01/874–0710), run by the hugely successful owners of the Globe, is a mixed gay and straight bar. The music is loud and dance-driven, and the downstairs pool table is an added bonus.

Morrison Bar (⌧ Morrison Hotel, Upper Ormond Quay, Northside ☎ 01/878–2999) is a stylish late-night bar where cocktails are the drink of choice for the well-to-do Dublin set, which gathers on the long, lounging sofas. Downstairs, Lobo is a late-night bar open to 3 AM on weekends.

Cassidy's (⌧ 42 Lower Camden St., City Center ☎ 01/475–1429), is a quality neighborhood pub with a pint of stout so good that former president Bill Clinton dropped in for one during a visit to Dublin.

Cellar Bar (⌧ 24 Upper Merrion St., Georgian Dublin ☎ 01/603–0600), at the Merrion Hotel, is in a stylish 18th-century wine vault with bare brick walls and vaulted ceilings. It tends to draw a well-heeled crowd.

Davy Byrne's (⌧ 21 Duke St., City Center ☎ 01/671–1298) is a pilgrimage stop for Joyceans. In *Ulysses,* Leopold Bloom stops in here for a glass

CLOSE UP

Pub Grub

MOST PUBS SERVE FOOD at lunchtime, many throughout the day and into the early evening. This is an inexpensive way to eat out, and the quality of the food is often quite good.

Davy Byrne's. James Joyce immortalized this pub in *Ulysses*. Nowadays it's more akin to a cocktail bar than a Dublin pub, but it's good for fresh and smoked salmon, salads, fresh oysters, and a hot daily special. ⊠ *21 Duke St., Southside* ☎ *01/671-1298* ▭ *AE, MC, V.*

The Odeon. The converted main building of Harcourt Street's old railway station houses this large, modern bar. Both the lunch and dinner menus include fresh-grilled panini, beef-and-Guinness stew, chicken wings, and homemade sausages. Sunday brunch is served between noon and 5. ⊠ *57 Harcourt St., Southside* ☎ *01/478-2088* ▭ *AE, MC, V.*

The Old Stand. This pub, one of the oldest in Dublin, is close to Grafton Street, and serves grilled food, including steaks. ⊠ *37 Exchequer St., Southside* ☎ *01/677-7220* ▭ *AE, MC, V.*

Stag's Head. The most beautiful pub in Dublin, period. Built in 1895, it's a Victorian-era mahogany masterpiece. Serving one of Dublin's best pub lunches, this place is a favorite among Trinity students. ⊠ *1 Dame Ct., Southside* ☎ *01/679-3701* ▭ *No credit cards.*

Zanzibar. This spectacular, immense bar on the Northside looks as though it might be more at home in downtown Marrakech. Laze an afternoon away in one of the wicker chairs and enjoy hearty pastas, burgers, salads, and cocktails. ⊠ *34-35 Lower Ormond Quay, Northside* ☎ *01/878-7212* ▭ *AE, MC, V.*

---

of Burgundy and a Gorgonzola-cheese sandwich. He then leaves the pub and walks to Dawson Street, where he helps a blind man cross the road. Unfortunately, the pub is greatly changed from Joyce's day, but it still serves some fine pub grub.

Doheny & Nesbitt (⊠ 5 Lower Baggot St., Georgian Dublin ☎ 01/676–2945), a traditional spot with snugs, dark wooden furnishings, and smoke-darkened ceilings, has hardly changed over the decades.

Doyle's (⊠ 9 College St., City Center ☎ 01/671–0616), a small, cozy pub, is a favorite with journalists from the *Irish Times* office, just across the street.

George (⊠ 89 S. Great George's St., City Center ☎ 01/478–2983), Dublin's two-floor main gay pub, draws an almost entirely male crowd; its nightclub stays open until 2:30 AM except Tuesday. The "alternative bingo night," with star drag act Miss Shirley Temple Bar, is a riot of risqué fun.

Globe (⊠ 11 S. Great George's St., City Center ☎ 01/671–1220), one of the hippest café-bars in town, draws arty, trendy Dubliners who sip espresso drinks by day and pack the place at night. There's live jazz on Sunday.

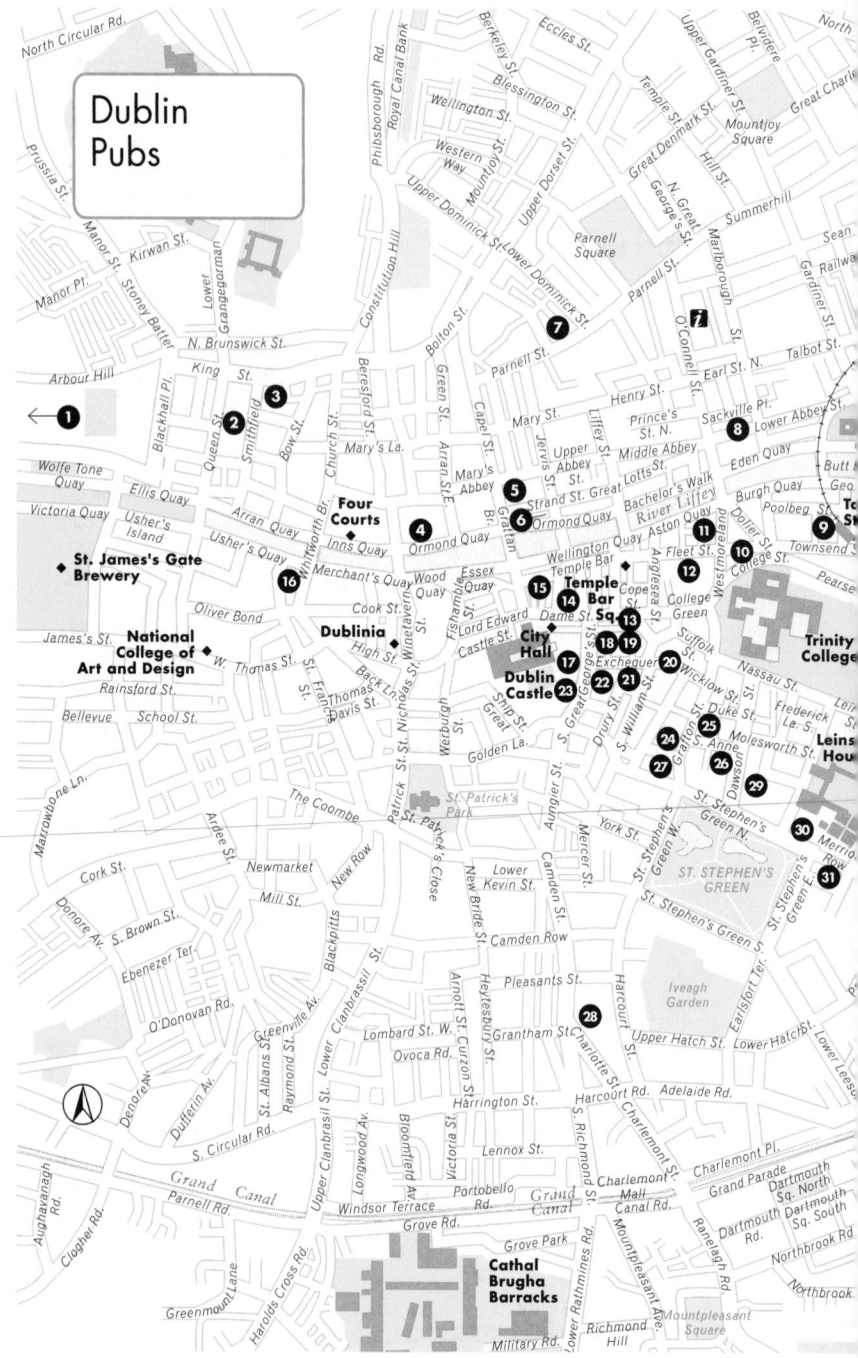

Dublin Pubs

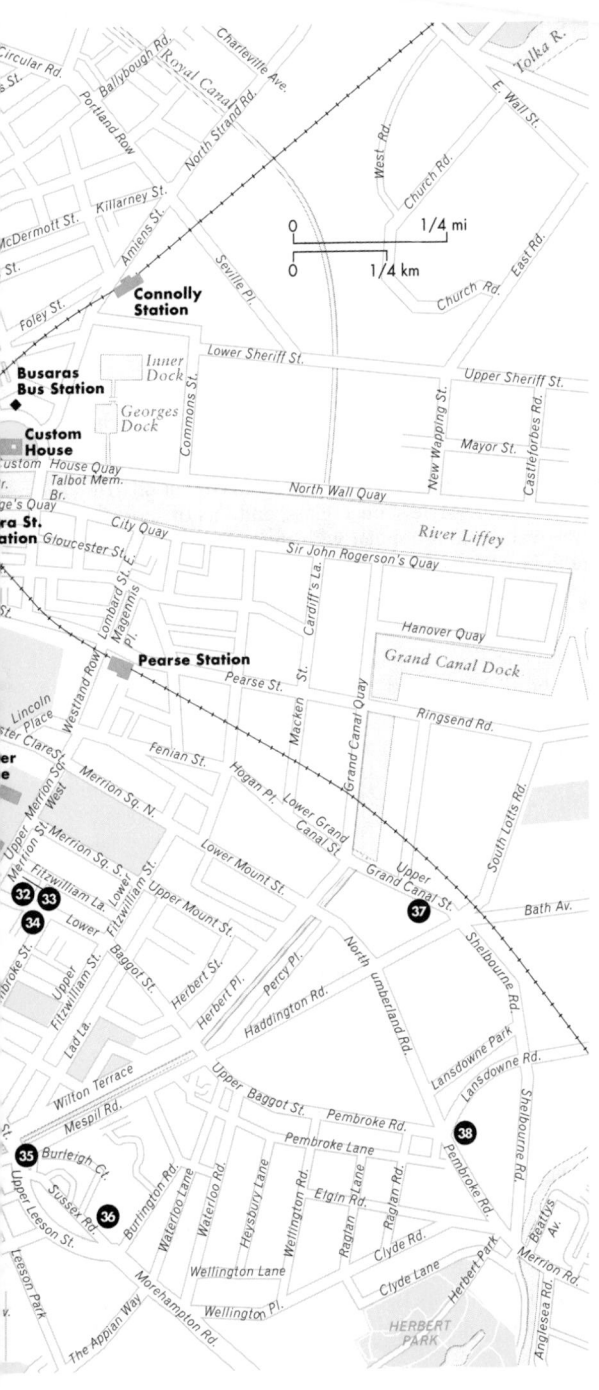

Fodor'sChoice **Grogans** (✉ 15 S. William St., City Center ☎ 01/677–9320), also known
★ as the Castle Lounge, is a small place packed with creative folk. Owner
Tommy Grogan is known as a patron of local artists, and his walls are
covered with their work.

Hogan's (✉ 35 Great St. George's St., City Center ☎ 01/677–5904), a
huge space on two levels, gets jammed most nights, but the old place
maintains its style through it all.

Horseshoe Bar (✉ Shelbourne, 27 St. Stephen's Green, City Center ☎ 01/
676–6471) is a popular meeting place for Dublin's businesspeople and
politicians, though around the semicircular bar there's comparatively
little space for drinkers. The bar is currently closed for a major renovation and hopes to reopen by late 2006.

Kehoe's (✉ 9 S. Anne St., City Center ☎ 01/677–8312) is popular with
Trinity students and academics. The tiny back room is cozy, and the upstairs is basically the owner's living room, open to the public.

Kitty O'Shea's (✉ Upper Grand Canal St., Georgian Dublin ☎ 01/660–
9965) has Pre-Raphaelite–style stained glass, and lots of sports paraphernalia on the walls, and is popular with sports fans of all types. Its
sister pubs are in Brussels and Paris; this is the original.

Lesson Lounge (✉ 148 Upper Lesson St., Georgian Dublin ☎ 01/660–
3816) has the look of a classic old Dublin "boozer," with one notable
exception: it has a television. The Lesson is known as a place to watch
televised sports of all kinds, and
it's always pleasant and inclusive.

Library Bar (✉ Central Hotel, 1–5
Exchequer St., City Center ☎ 01/
679–7302) is the place to go when
you're ready to get away from all
the madness. The book-lined
shelves, big armchairs and sofas,
and blazing fire make this first-
floor hideaway one of the most
serene nighttime spots in Dublin.

> **BONO RECOMMENDS**
>
> Irish rock & roll hero Bono has one
> prevailing test for judging a pub:
> "My favorite pubs are any that let
> you drink in after hours. As for tra-
> ditional music, it's all over Temple
> Bar in Dublin. If in Howth Head,
> check out Sharon Shannon—still a
> genius."

Long Hall Pub (✉ 51 S. Great
George's St., City Center ☎ 01/
475–1590), one of Dublin's most ornate traditional taverns, has Victorian lamps, a mahogany bar, mirrors, chandeliers, and plasterwork ceilings, all more than 100 years old. The pub serves sandwiches and an
excellent pint of Guinness.

McDaid's (✉ 3 Harry St., City Center ☎ 01/679–4395) attracted boisterous Brendan Behan and other leading writers in the 1950s; its wild
literary reputation still lingers, although the bar has been discreetly
modernized and is altogether quieter.

Mulligan's (✉ 8 Poolbeg St., City Center ☎ 01/677–5582) is synonymous
in Dublin with a truly inspirational pint of Guinness. Until a few years

ago no women were admitted. Today journalists, locals, and students of both genders flock here for the perfect pint.

Neary's (⊠ 1 Chatham St., City Center ☎ 01/677–7371), with an exotic, Victorian-style interior, was once the haunt of music-hall artists and a certain literary set, including Brendan Behan. Join the actors from the adjacent Gaiety Theatre for a good pub lunch.

O'Donoghue's (⊠ 15 Merrion Row, City Center ☎ 01/676–2807), a cheerful smoky hangout, has impromptu musical performances that often spill out onto the street.

The Old Stand (⊠ 37 Exchequer St., City Center ☎ 01/677–7220), one of the oldest pubs in the city, is named after the Old Stand stadium at Lansdowne Road, home to Irish rugby and football. The pub is renowned for great pints and fine steaks.

Ron Black's (⊠ 37 Dawson St., City Center ☎ 01/677–7220) is one of three "superbars" along Dawson Street. Celtic Tiger cubs jam the place, trying to meet each other over kicking house music and six or seven drinks.

Fodor'sChoice ★ **Stag's Head** (⊠ 1 Dame Ct., City Center ☎ 01/679–3701) dates from 1770 and was rebuilt in 1895. Theater people from the nearby Olympia, journalists, and Trinity students gather around the unusual Connemara red marble bar. The interior is a Victorian beaut.

Toner's (⊠ 139 Lower Baggot St., City Center ☎ 01/676–3090), though billed as a Victorian bar, actually goes back 200 years, with an original flagstone floor to prove its antiquity, as well as wooden drawers running up to the ceiling—a relic of the days when bars doubled as grocery shops. Oliver St. John Gogarty, who was the model for Buck Mulligan in James Joyce's *Ulysses,* accompanied W. B. Yeats here, in what was purportedly the latter's only visit to a pub.

TEMPLE BAR **Front Lounge** (⊠ 33 Parliament St., Temple Bar ☎ 01/679–3988), a modern pub, caters to a mixed crowd of young professionals, both gay and straight.

Oliver St. John Gogarty (⊠ 57 Fleet St., Temple Bar ☎ 01/671–1822) is a lively bar that attracts all ages and nationalities; it overflows with patrons in summer. On most nights there's traditional Irish music upstairs.

Palace Bar (⊠ 21 Fleet St., Temple Bar ☎ 01/677–9290), scarcely changed since the 1940s, is tiled and rather barren looking, but is popular with journalists and writers (the *Irish Times* is nearby). The walls are lined with cartoons drawn by the illustrators who used to spend time here.

The Porterhouse (⊠ 16–18 Parliament St., Temple Bar ☎ 01/679–8847) is one of the few bars in Ireland to brew its own beer. The Plain Porter has won the best stout at the "Brewing Oscars," beating out the mighty Guinness. The tasteful interior is all dark woods and soft lighting.

BALLSBRIDGE **Dubliner Pub** (⊠ Jurys Hotel, Pembroke Rd., Ballsbridge ☎ 01/660–5000), an old-fashioned Irish pub, is a busy meeting place during lunch and after work.

O'Brien's (✉ Sussex Terr., Ballsbridge ☎ 01/668–2594), beside the Doyle Burlington Hotel, is a little antique gem of a pub, scarcely changed since the 1950s, with traditional snugs.

DUBLIN WEST **Brazen Head** (✉ Bridge St., Dublin West ☎ 01/677–9549), Dublin's oldest pub (the site has been licensed since 1198), has stone walls and open fires—it has hardly changed over the years. The pub is renowned for traditional-music performances and lively sing-along sessions on Sunday evenings. On the south side of the Liffey quays, it's a little difficult to find—turn down Lower Bridge Street and make a right into the old lane.

Cobblestone (✉ N. King St., Dublin West ☎ 01/872–1799) is a glorious house of ale in the best Dublin tradition, popular with Smithfield Market workers. Its chatty imbibers and live traditional music are attracting a wider, younger crowd from all over town.

Company Cafe Bar (✉ 27 Ormond Quay, Dublin West ☎ 01/872–2480) is the renamed, polished-up incarnation of one of Dublin's old reliable gay hangouts.

Dice Bar (✉ 79 Queen St., Dublin West ☎ 01/674–6710), partly owned by one of the Fun Lovin' Criminals band, may look like the dive that it is, but the DJ-driven music always rocks and the hipster folks are friendly and laid-back.

Ryan's Pub (✉ 28 Parkgate St., Dublin West ☎ 01/677–6097) is one of Dublin's last genuine, late-Victorian-era pubs, and has changed little since its last (1896) remodeling.

The Arts

Classical Music & Opera

CITY CENTER **The Bank of Ireland Arts Center** (✉ Foster Pl. S, City Center ☎ 01/671–1488) is great at lunchtime, when classical music and opera recitals take place.

National Concert Hall (✉ Earlsfort Terr., Georgian Dublin ☎ 01/475–1666 ⊕ www.nch.ie), just off St. Stephen's Green, is Dublin's main theater for classical music of all kinds, from symphonies to chamber groups. The slightly austere Neoclassical building was transformed in 1981 into one of Europe's finest medium-size concert halls. It houses the cream of Irish classical musicians, the National Symphony Orchestra of Ireland. A host of guest international conductors and performers—Maxim Vengerov, Radu Lupu, and Pinchas Zukerman are just a few of the soloists who have appeared—keep the standard very high, and performances continue throughout the year. The concert year picks up speed in mid-September and sails through to June but July and August also get many dazzling troupes.

Opera Ireland (✉ John Player House, 276–288 S. Circular Rd., City Center ☎ 01/453–5519 ⊕ www.operaireland.com) performs at the Gaiety Theatre; call to find out what's on and when.

St. Stephen's Church (✉ Merrion Sq., Georgian Dublin ☎ 01/288–0663) stages a regular program of choral and orchestral events under its glorious "pepper canister" cupola.

Continued on page 136

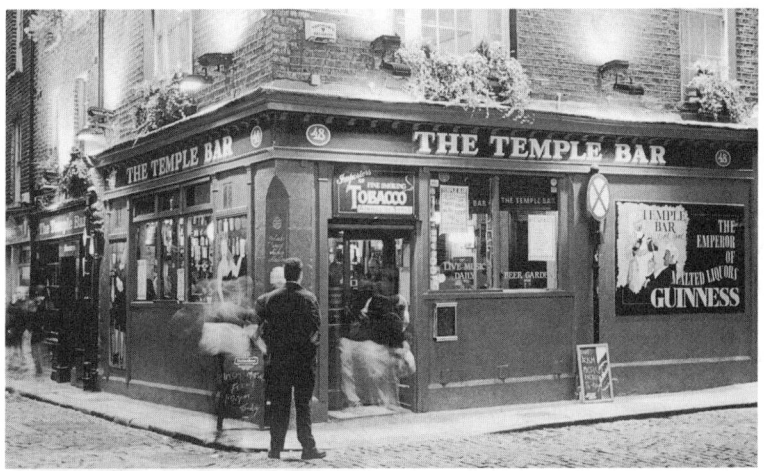

A TRIP TO THE PUB

For any visitor to Ireland who wants to see the natives in their bare element—to witness them at full pace, no-holds-barred—a trip to a busy pub is a must. Luckily for you, the pub is above all a welcoming place, where a visitor is seen as a source of new, exotic stories and, more importantly, as an unsullied audience for the locals and their tall tales.

WELCOME TO IRELAND'S LIVING ROOM...

The term "pub" is shorthand for "public house," which is an apt name for one of Ireland's great institutions. Stepping into a pub (and there seems to be one on every corner) is the easiest way to transport yourself into the thick of Irish life.

A pub, of course, is a drinking establishment, and for better or worse the Irish have a deep, abiding relationship with drink—particularly their beloved black stout. The point, however, isn't what you drink, but where: in the warmth of the public house, in company. It's the place to tell stories, most of them true, and to hear music. It's where locals go to mark the key stages of their lives: to wet a new baby's head; to celebrate a graduation; to announce an engagement; and finally to wake a corpse.

HOW TO CHOOSE A PUB

Not all pubs are created equal. Throughout this book we recommend some of the finest, but here are a few ways to distinguish the real gold from the sparkling pyrite:

- Qualified, experienced bar staff—not grubby students dreaming of the round-the-world trip they are working to save up for. A uniform of white shirt and black trousers is often a good sign.

- At least one man over sixty (preferably with a cap of some description) drinking at the bar (not at a table). He should know the good bars by now, right?

- No TV. Or, if there is a TV it should be hidden away in a corner, only to be used for horse racing and other major sporting events.

- No recorded music. A pub is a place to talk and listen. Occasional live music is okay, especially a traditional session.

- Bathrooms are clean but not *too* clean. They are purely functional, not polished chambers for hanging out and chatting with friends about your new Blackberry.

THE QUEST FOR THE CRAIC

Pub-going at its best has a touch of magic to it: conversation flows, spirits rise, and inhibitions evaporate. There's a word in Gaelic for this happy condition: the *craic*, which roughly translates as "lively talk and good times." The craic is the sort of thing that's difficult to find only when you're looking too hard for it. Large crowds, loud music, and one pint too many can also make the craic elusive. When your companions all seem clever and handsome, and you can't imagine better company in the world, that's when you know you've found it.

PUB ETIQUETTE

Some things to keep in mind if you want to get the most out of your trip to the pub:

- First, if you want to meet people and get into the craic, belly up to the bar counter and pass up a seat at a table.

- Always place your drink order at the bar and don't heckle the barkeepers to get their attention. They're professionals—they'll see you soon enough.

- If you do take a table, bring your dirty glasses back to the bar before you leave, or when you order another round.

- In present-day Ireland, male and female pubgoers usually get equal treatment. At the most traditional places, though, it's still customary in mixed company for the man to order drinks at the bar while the woman takes a table seat.

- Don't tip the barkeepers, except at Christmas, when you can offer to buy them a drink.

- Never sip from your Guinness until it has fully settled. You'll know this from the deep black color and perfectly defined white head.

- Don't smoke in the bar; it's against the law. But feel free to gather outside in the rain and chat with the other unfortunates. It's a great spot to start a romance.

- You have to be at least 18 years old to *drink* in a pub, but kids are welcome during the day, and nondrinking minors as young as 14 are often tolerated at night.

MAKING THE ROUNDS

You may get caught up in the "rounds" system, in which each pub mate takes turns to "shout" an order. Your new friends may forget to tell you when it's your round, but any failure to "put your hand in your pocket" may lead to a reputation that will follow you to the grave. To miss your "shout" is to become known for "short arms and long pockets" and to be shunned by decent people.

LAST CALL

Technically, pubs have to stop serving at 11:30 on weekdays, 12:30 on weekends, though they can remain open later. At the end of the night, ignore the first five calls of "Time please, ladies and gentlemen!" from the barman. You'll know he's getting serious by the roar of his voice.

THE "BLACK STUFF"

Stout, a dark beer made using roasted malts or barley, originated in Ireland, and it's the country's national drink, consumed in pubs with unflagging allegiance.

— Rich, creamy head.

— Nearly black in color, with a very slight coffee-like aftertaste.

— As you drink, the head will leave "rings of pleasure" down the side of the glass.

There are three main brands:

GUINNESS For most Irish, the name Guinness is synonymous with stout. With massive breweries in Africa and the Americas, it really is a world brand, but the "true" pint still flows from the original brewery at St. James Gate in Dublin. While some old-timers still drink the more malty bottled version, draught Guinness is now the standard. A deep, creamy texture and slightly bitter first taste is followed by a milder, more "toasty" aftertaste.

MURPHY'S The Murphy Brewery was founded by James Murphy in 1856 in Cork City. Murphy's is very much a Cork drink, and often suffers from "second city" complex in relation to its giant rival Guinness. Corkonians say Murphy's is a less bitter, more nutty flavor than the "Dublin stout."

BEAMISH Another Cork drink, a little sweeter and less dry than either Guinness or Murphy's, and so a little easier on the novice palate. Beamish and Crawford Brewery began making beer in 1792, after purchasing an existing brewery in the heart of Cork's medieval center that dates back to at least 1650 (and possibly 1500).

THE POUR

The storage and pouring of a pint of stout is almost as important as the brewing. The best quality is usually found in older bars that sell a lot of pints—meaning the beer you get hasn't been sitting in the keg too long and the pipes are well coated.

Pouring a pint consists of two stages: The glass is filled three-quarters full, then allowed to sit. After the head settles, the glass is filled to the top (stage two).

Why the painstaking ritual? Because the barkeeper knows you don't want your first sip to be a mouthful of foam. And because the flavor's that much sweeter for the waiting.

FOOD, SONG, AND ADDITIONAL DRINK

Although the majority of your companions will be drinking stout, you do have other options.

■ A lager is always available–Harp is the most popular brand.

■ If you're thirsting for something stronger, take a nip of Irish whiskey, which tends to be less smoky and intensely flavored than its Scotch cousin. Jameson and Bushmills, both smooth blends, are the standard varieties, and you can usually find a single-malt as well.

■ On the other hand, if the booze isn't your thing, you can always choose tea, soda, or a bottle of water. (Ballygowan is the Irish Evian.) It's fine to order nonalcoholic drinks–many people who drive do so.

■ Pub food is a lunchtime thing; the prices are reasonable, and the quality can be quite good. Ask for a menu at the bar. If you're near a coast, look for seafood specialties, from oysters and mussels to smoked salmon. With beef-and-Guinness stew, you can drink your stout and eat it too.

"TRAD" MUSIC IN ITS NATURAL DOMAIN

The pub is an ideal place to hear traditional Irish music. Performances can have a spontaneous air to them, but they don't start up just anywhere. Pubs that accommodate live sessions have signs saying so; and they're more common outside Dublin than in the city. To learn more about Irish music, see "Gael Force" in chapter 6.

Top photo: Traditional Irish stew
Above: Jameson whiskey

TEMPLE BAR **Opera Theatre Company** (✉ Temple Bar Music Centre, Curved St., Temple Bar ☎ 01/679–4962) is Ireland's only touring opera company. It performs at venues in Dublin and throughout the country.

DUBLIN WEST **Royal Hospital Kilmainham** (✉ Military Rd., Dublin West ☎ 01/671–8666 ⊕ www.rhk.ie) presents frequent classical concerts in its magnificent 17th-century interior.

Film

NORTHSIDE **Cineworld** (✉ Parnell Center, Parnell St., Northside ☎ 01/872–8400), a 17-screen theater just off O'Connell Street, is the city center's only multiplex movie house; it shows the latest commercial features.

Savoy Cinema (✉ O'Connell St., Northside ☎ 01/874–6000), just across from the General Post Office, is a four-screen theater with the largest screen in the country.

TEMPLE BAR **Irish Film Institute** (✉ 6 Eustace St., Temple Bar ☎ 01/677–8788) shows classic and new independent films.

CITY CENTER **Screen Cinema** (✉ 2 Townsend St., City Center ☎ 01/671–4988), between Trinity College and O'Connell Street Bridge, is a popular three-screen art-house cinema.

Rock & Contemporary Music

NORTHSIDE **The Ambassador** (✉ 1 Parnell Sq., Northside ☎ 01/889–9403) was once a cinema attached to the Gate Theatre. The plush interior and seats have been removed, and the stripped-down venue now houses visiting bands and "school-disco" nights with music from the '70s and '80s.

The Point (✉ Eastlink Br., Northside ☎ 01/836–3633 ⊕ www.thepoint. ie), a 6,000-capacity arena about 1 km (½ mi) east of the Custom House on the Liffey, is Dublin's premier venue for internationally renowned acts. Call or send a self-addressed envelope to receive a list of upcoming shows; tickets can be difficult to obtain, so book early.

CITY CENTER **Crawdaddy** (✉ Old Harcourt Station., Harcourt St. City Center ☎ 01/478–0166) is an intimate venue at the center of the hot POD nightclub complex. Predecessor to *Rolling Stone, Crawdaddy* was the very first rock magazine in the United States. It's an homage to that bygone era of sweat, three chords, and the truth.

International Bar (✉ Wicklow St., City Center ☎ 01/677–9250) has a long-established, tiny, get-close-to-the-band venue upstairs. It hosts theater in the afternoons.

The Village (✉ 26 Wexford St., City Center ☎ 01/475–8555), set in a striking, glass-fronted building, isn't too fussy about the kind of bands it hosts, so long as their amps are turned up full and the lead singer knows how to scream.

Whelan's (✉ 25 Wexford St., City Center ☎ 01/478–0766), just off the southeastern corner of St. Stephen's Green, is one of the city's best— and most popular—music venues. Well-known performers play everything from rock to folk to traditional music. The same owners run the Village bar and venue next door.

TEMPLE BAR **Olympia Theatre** (✉ 72 Dame St., Temple Bar ☎ 01/677–7744) puts on "Midnight from the Olympia" shows every Friday and Saturday from midnight to 2 AM, with everything from rock to country.

Temple Bar Music Centre (✉ Curved St., Temple Bar ☎ 01/670–0533) is a music venue, rehearsal space, television studio, and pub rolled into one. It buzzes with activity every day of the week. Live acts range from rock bands to world music to singer-songwriters.

DUBLIN WEST **Vicar Street** (✉ 58–59 Thomas St., Dublin West ☎ 01/454–5533), just across from Christ Church Cathedral, is a venue for intimate concerts. It often plays host to folk music, jazz, and comedy, as well as rock performances.

Theater

NORTHSIDE **Abbey Theatre** (✉ Lower Abbey St., Northside ☎ 01/878–7222 ⊕ www. abbeytheatre.ie) is the fabled home of Ireland's national theater company. In 1904 W. B. Yeats and his patron, Lady Gregory, opened the theater, which became a major center for the Irish literary renaissance—the place that first staged works by J. M. Synge and Sean O'Casey, among many others. The year 2004 celebrated the 100th anniversary of this landmark theater. Plays by recent Irish drama heavyweights like Brian Friel, Tom Murphy, Hugh Leonard, and John B. Keane have all premiered here, and memorable productions of international greats like Mamet, Ibsen, and Shakespeare have also been performed. You should not, however, arrive expecting 19th-century grandeur: the original structure burned down in 1951. Unfortunately, an ugly concrete boxlike auditorium was built in its place—but what it may lack in visuals it makes up for in space and acoustics. Some say the repertoire is overly reverential and mainstream, but such chestnuts as Dion Boucicault's *The Shaughran* wound up being applauded by many. Happily, the Abbey's sister theater at the same address, the Peacock, offers more experimental drama. But the Abbey will always be relevant since much of the theatergoing public still looks to it as a barometer of Irish culture.

Gate Theatre (✉ Cavendish Row, Parnell Sq., Northside ☎ 01/874–4045 ⊕ www.gate-theatre.ie), an intimate 371-seat theater in a jewellike Georgian assembly hall, produces the classics and contemporary plays by leading Irish writers, including Beckett, Wilde (their production of *Salome* was worldwide hit), Shaw, and the younger generation of dramatists such as Conor McPherson.

CITY CENTER **Andrew's Lane Theatre** (✉ 9–11 Andrew's La., City Center ☎ 01/679–5720) presents experimental productions.

Gaiety Theatre (✉ S. King St., City Center ☎ 01/677–1717) is the home of Opera Ireland when it's not showing musical comedy, drama, and revues. On weekends this elegant theater is taken over by a nightclub with live music and cabaret.

Samuel Beckett Centre (✉ Trinity College, City Center ☎ 01/608–2266) is home to Trinity's drama department, as well as visiting European groups. Dance is often performed here by visiting troupes.

New Project Arts Centre (✉ 39 E. Essex St., Temple Bar ☎ 01/671–2321) is a theater and performance space in an ugly modern building at the center of Temple Bar. Fringe and mainstream theater, contemporary music, and experimental art have all found a home here.

Olympia Theatre (✉ 72 Dame St., Temple Bar ☎ 01/677–7744) is Dublin's oldest and premier multipurpose theatrical venue. In addition to its high-profile musical performances, it has seasons of comedy, vaudeville, and ballet.

SPORTS

Football

Soccer—called football in Europe—is very popular in Ireland, largely due to the euphoria resulting from the national team's successes since the late 1980s. However, the places where you can watch it aren't ideal—they tend to be small and out-of-date. **Lansdowne Road Stadium** (✉ 62 Lansdowne Rd., Ballsbridge ☎ 01/668–4601), a vast rugby stadium, is the main center for international matches. A huge redevelopment of the stadium has recently been approved by the government and is due to start in 2008.

League of Ireland matches take place throughout the city on Friday evenings or Sunday afternoons from March to November. For details, contact the **Football Association of Ireland** (✉ 80 Merrion Sq. S, Georgian Dublin ☎ 01/676–6864).

Gaelic Games

The traditional games of Ireland, Gaelic football and hurling, attract a huge following, with roaring crowds cheering on their county teams. Games are held at Croke Park, the stunning, high-tech national stadium for Gaelic games, just north of the city center. For details of matches, contact the **Gaelic Athletic Association** (GAA; ✉ Croke Park, North County Dublin ☎ 01/836–3222 ⊕ www.gaa.ie).

Horse Racing

Horse racing—from flat to hurdle to steeplechase—is one of the great sporting loves of the Irish. The sport is closely followed and betting is popular, but the social side of attending races is equally important to Dubliners. The main course in Dublin is **Leopardstown** (✉ Leopardstown Rd., South County Dublin ☎ 01/289–3607 ⊕ www.leopardstown.com), an ultramodern course that in February hosts the Hennessey Gold Cup, Ireland's most prestigious steeplechase. Summertime is devoted to flat racing, and the rest of the year to racing over fences. You can also nip in for a quick meal at the restaurant.

The **Curragh** (☎ 045/441–205 ⊕ www.curragh.ie), southwest of Dublin off M7, hosts the five Classics, the most important flat races of the season, from May to September. There are numerous bars here and two restaurants. **Fairyhouse** (✉ Co. Meath ☎ 01/825–6167) hosts the Grand National, the most popular steeplechase of the season, every Easter Monday. **Punchestown** (☎ 045/897–704), outside Naas, County Kildare, is the home of the ever-popular Punchestown National Hunt Festival in April.

SHOPPING

The only known specimens of leprechauns or shillelaghs in Ireland are those in souvenir-shop windows, and shamrocks mainly bloom around the borders of Irish linen handkerchiefs and tablecloths. But in Dublin's shops you can find much more than kitschy designs. There's a tremendous variety of stores here, many of which are quite sophisticated—as a walk through Dublin's central shopping area, from O'Connell to Grafton Street, will prove. Department stores stock internationally known fashion-designer goods and housewares, and small (and often pricey) boutiques sell Irish crafts and other merchandise. Don't expect too many bargains here. And be prepared, if you're shopping in central Dublin, to push through crowds—especially in the afternoons and on weekends. Most large shops and department stores are open Monday to Saturday 9 to 6. Although nearly all department stores are closed on Sunday, some smaller specialty shops stay open. Those with later closing hours are noted below. You're particularly likely to find sales in January, February, July, and August.

Shopping Streets

Each of Dublin's dozen or so main shopping streets has a different character. Visit them all to appreciate the wide selection of items for sale here. The main commercial streets north of the river have both chain and department stores that tend to be less expensive (and less design-conscious) than their counterparts in the city center on the other side of the Liffey.

Northside

Henry Street, where cash-conscious Dubliners shop, runs westward from O'Connell Street. Arnotts department store is the anchor here; smaller, specialty stores sell CDs, footwear, and clothing. Henry Street's continuation, Mary Street, has a branch of Marks & Spencer and the Jervis Shopping Centre.

O'Connell Street, the city's main thoroughfare, more downscale than Southside city streets (such as Grafton Street), is still worth a walk. One of Dublin's largest department stores, Clery's, is here, across from the GPO. On the same side of the street as the post office is Eason's, a large book, magazine, and stationery store.

City Center

Dawson Street, just east of Grafton Street between Nassau Street to the north and St. Stephen's Green to the south, is the city's primary bookstore avenue. Waterstone's and Hodges Figgis face each other from opposite sides of the street.

Francis Street and surrounding areas, such as the Coombe, have plenty of shops where you can browse. It's all part of the Liberties, the oldest part of the city and the hub of Dublin's antiques trade. If you're looking for something in particular, dealers will gladly recommend the appropriate store to you.

Dublin à la Mode

THE SUCCESS OF SHOPS LIKE Costume and Platform has given young Irish designers the confidence to produce more original and impressive work. One of Costume's most popular designers, **Helen James**, graduated from NCAD textile design in 1992. She went straight to New York, where she worked for Donna Karan, Club Monaco, and Victoria's Secret, among others. She returned to Ireland in 2002 and developed her line of unique, hand-printed textile accessories. Many people say there is a delicate Japanese feel to her work.

Footwear has long been an area overlooked by Irish designers, but Irishwoman **Eileen Shields** has been living and working in New York since 1988; for almost 10 years she designed footwear for Donna Karan. Her own premiere collection is all about clean, bold lines. Materials include antique kid, fine suede, python, and soft patent leather. Textures are often strongly contrasting, while colors are sensual and sophisticated. You can get the shoes online at www. eileenshields.com, or in her store on Scarlett Row in Temple Bar.

The Tucker family has been a key player in Irish fashion since the 1960s, and daughter **Leigh Tucker** has quickly established herself as one of Dublin's classiest young designers. Fine tailoring is her trademark—the finish on her evening wear is nonpareil—and beaded French lace and draped jersey are her favorite materials. Her line can be found in boutiques across Ireland and at Costume in Dublin.

Grafton Street, Dublin's bustling pedestrian-only main shopping street, has two upscale department stores: Marks & Spencer and Brown Thomas. The rest of the street is taken up by shops, many of them branches of international chains, such as the Body Shop and Bally, and many British chains. This is also the spot to buy fresh flowers, available at reasonable prices from outdoor stands. On the smaller streets off Grafton Street—especially Duke Street, South Anne Street, and Chatham Street—are worthwhile crafts, clothing, and designer housewares shops.

Nassau Street, Dublin's main tourist-oriented thoroughfare, has some of the best-known stores selling Irish goods, but you won't find many locals shopping here. Still, if you're looking for classic Irish gifts to take home, you should be sure at least to browse along here.

Temple Bar, Dublin's hippest neighborhood, is dotted with small, precious boutiques—mainly intimate, quirky shops that traffic in a small selection of *très* trendy goods, from vintage clothes to some of the most avant-garde Irish garb anywhere in the city.

Shopping Centers

Northside

Ilac Center (⊠ Henry St., Northside) was Dublin's first large, modern shopping center, with two department stores, hundreds of specialty shops, and several restaurants. The stores are not as exclusive as those at some of the other centers, but there's plenty of free parking.

Jervis Shopping Centre (⊠ Jervis and Mary Sts., Northside ☎ 01/878–1323) is a slightly high-end center housing some of the major British chain stores. It has a compact design and plenty of parking.

City Center

Powerscourt Townhouse Centre (⊠ 59 S. William St., City Center), the former town home of Lord Powerscourt, built in 1771, has an interior courtyard that has been refurbished and roofed over; a pianist often plays on the dais at ground-floor level. Coffee shops and restaurants share space with a mix of stores selling antiques and crafts. You can also buy original Irish fashions here by young designers, such as Gráinne Walsh.

Royal Hibernian Way (⊠ Off Dawson St. between S. Anne and Duke Sts., City Center ☎ 01/679–5919) is on the former site of the two-centuries-old Royal Hibernian Hotel, a coaching inn that was demolished in 1983. The pricey, stylish shops—about 20 or 30, many selling fashionable clothes—are small in scale and include a branch of Leonidas, the Belgian chocolate firm.

St. Stephen's Green Centre (⊠ Northwest corner of St. Stephen's Green, City Center ☎ 01/478–0888), Dublin's largest and most ambitious shopping complex, resembles a giant greenhouse, with Victorian-style ironwork. On three floors overlooked by a vast clock, the 100 mostly small shops sell crafts, fashions, and household goods.

Tower Design Centre (⊠ Pearse St., City Center ☎ 01/677–5655), east of the heart of the city center (near the Waterways Visitors Centre), has more than 35 separate crafts shops in a converted 1862 sugar-refinery tower. On the ground floor are workshops devoted to heraldry and Irish pewter; the other six floors have stores that sell hand-painted silks, ceramics, hand-knit items, jewelry, and fine-art cards and prints.

Westbury Mall (⊠ Westbury Hotel, off Grafton St., City Center) is an upmarket shopping mall where you can buy designer jewelry, antique rugs, and decorative goods.

Department Stores

Arnotts (⊠ Henry St., Northside ☎ 01/872–1111 ⊠ Grafton St., Southside ☎ 01/872–1111), on three floors, stocks a wide selection of clothing, household, and sporting goods. The smaller Grafton Street branch sells new fashion and footwear.

Brown Thomas (⊠ Grafton St., City Center ☎ 01/679–5666), Dublin's most exclusive department store, stocks the leading designer names (including many Irish designers) in clothing and cosmetics, plus lots of stylish accessories. There's also a good selection of crystal.

Clery's (⊠ O'Connell St., Northside ☎ 01/878–6000), once the city's most fashionable department store, is still worth a visit. You'll find all kinds of merchandise—from fashion to home appliances—on its four floors. Note that goods sold here reflect a distinctly modest, traditional sense of style.

Dunnes Stores (⊠ St. Stephen's Green Centre, City Center ☎ 01/478–0188 ✉ Henry St., Northside ☎ 01/872–6833 ⊠ Ilac Center, Mary St., Northside ☎ 01/873–0211) is Ireland's largest chain of department stores. All of the branches stock fashion (including the exciting Savida range), household, and grocery items, and have a reputation for value and variety.

Eason's (⊠ O'Connell St., Northside ☎ 01/873–3811 ✉ Ilac Center, Mary St., Northside ☎ 01/872–1322) is known primarily for its large selection of books, magazines, and stationery; the larger O'Connell Street branch sells tapes, CDs, records, videos, and other audiovisual goodies.

Marks & Spencer (⊠ Grafton St., City Center ☎ 01/679–7855 ✉ Henry St., Northside ☎ 01/872–8833), perennial competitor to Brown Thomas, stocks everything from fashion (including lingerie) to tasty unusual groceries. The Grafton Street branch even has its own bureau de change, which doesn't charge commission.

Roches Stores (⊠ Henry St., Northside ☎ 01/873–0044), once Dublin's home of "sensible" clothes, has undergone a radical face-lift, with top European brands like Zara drawing crowds of fashion- and price-conscious shoppers.

Outdoor Markets

Cows Lane Market, held on weekends in summer at the west edge of Temple Bar, is home to some of the most innovative young fashion and accessory designers in the country.

Meeting House Square Market, held Saturday mornings at the heart of Temple Bar, is a good place to buy homemade foodstuffs: breads, chocolate, and organic veggies. On Sunday it transforms into a craft and furniture bazaar spotlighting Irish and international artists and designers.

Moore Street, on the Northside behind the Ilac Center, is open Monday through Saturday from 9 to 6. Stalls, which line both sides of the street, sell fruits and vegetables; this is also a good place to buy shoes and boots. Moore Street vendors are known for their sharp wit, so expect the traditional Dublin repartee when you're shopping.

Wolfe Tone Market fills Wolfe Tone Square (beside Jervis Shopping Center) every Saturday from 10 to 6. Artists and artisans operate their own stalls, offering everything from paintings and drawings to candles, glass, and textiles. There's a gourmet food market on the same spot every Friday from 10 to 4.

Specialty Shops

Antiques

Dublin is one of Europe's best cities in which to buy antiques, largely due to a long and proud tradition of restoration and high-quality craftsmanship. The Liberties, Dublin's oldest district, is, fittingly, the hub of the antiques trade, and is chockablock with shops and traders. Bachelor's Walk, along the quays, also has some decent shops. It's quite a seller's market, but bargains are still possible.

Antiques Fairs Ireland (⊠ Hilton Hotel, Charlemont Pl., City Center ☎ 01/453–7323) takes place monthly, alternating between the Hilton Hotel in Dublin city center and Clontarf Castle, in south county Dublin.

Ha'penny Bridge Galleries (⊠ 15 Bachelor's Walk, Northside ☎ 01/872–3950) has four floors of curios, with a particularly large selection of bronzes, silver, and china.

O'Sullivan Antiques (⊠ 43–44 Francis St., Dublin West ☎ 01/454–1143 or 01/453–9659) specializes in 18th- and 19th-century furniture and has a high-profile clientele, including Mia Farrow and Liam Neeson. They even have a sister shop in New York.

Books

You won't have any difficulty weighing down your suitcase with books. Ireland, after all, produced four Nobel literature laureates in just under 75 years. If you're at all interested in modern and contemporary literature, be sure to leave yourself time to browse through the bookstores, as you're likely to find books available here you can't find back home. Best of all, thanks to an enlightened national social policy, there's no tax on books, so if you only buy books, you don't have to worry about getting V.A.T. slips.

Books Upstairs (⊠ 36 College Green, City Center ☎ 01/679–6687) carries an excellent selection of special-interest books, including gay and feminist literature, psychology, and self-help books.

Cathach Books (⊠ 10 Duke St., City Center ☎ 01/671–8676) sells first editions of Irish literature and many other books of Irish interest, plus old maps of Dublin and Ireland.

Dublin Bookshop (⊠ 24 Grafton St., City Center ☎ 01/677–5568) is an esteemed, family-owned store that sells mass-market books.

Eason's/Hanna's (⊠ 29 Nassau St., City Center ☎ 01/677–1255) sells secondhand and mass-market paperbacks and hardcovers, and has a good selection of works on travel and Ireland.

Greene's (⊠ Clare St., City Center ☎ 01/676–2554) carries an extensive range of secondhand volumes and new educational and mass market books.

Hodges Figgis (⊠ 56–58 Dawson St., Georgian Dublin ☎ 01/677–4754), Dublin's leading independent bookstore, stocks 1½ million books on three floors. There's a pleasant café on the first floor.

Hughes & Hughes (⊠ St. Stephen's Green Centre, City Center ☎ 01/478–3060) has strong travel and Irish-interest sections. There's also a store at Dublin Airport.

Stokes (⊠ George's Street Arcade, City Center ☎ 01/671–3584) is a gem of an antique book store with a great used-book section.

Waterstone's (⊠ 7 Dawson St., Georgian Dublin ☎ 01/679–1415), a large two-story branch of the British chain, features a fine selection of Irish and international books.

China, Crystal, Ceramics & Jewelry

Ireland is *the* place to buy Waterford crystal, which is available in a wide selection of products, including relatively inexpensive items. Other lines are now gaining recognition, such as Cavan, Galway, and Tipperary crystal.

Appleby's (⊠ Johnson's Court, City Center ☎ 01/679–9572) is the best known of the several classy, old-style jewelry shops that line tiny Johnson's Court, a delightful little lane off busy Grafton Street.

Barry Doyle Design (⊠ Georges Street Arcade, City Center ☎ 01/671–2838) is a true original with his Celtic modern jewelry. You can even watch him at work in his adjoining studio.

Blarney Woollen Mills (⊠ 21–23 Nassau St., City Center ☎ 01/671–0068) is one of the best places for Belleek china, Waterford and Galway crystal, and Irish linen.

Designyard (⊠ Cows La., Temple Bar ☎ 01/474–1011) carries beautifully designed Irish and international tableware, lighting, small furniture, and jewelry.

House of Ireland (⊠ 37–38 Nassau St., City Center ☎ 01/671–1111) has an extensive selection of crystal, jewelry, tweeds, sweaters, and other upscale goods.

Kilkenny Shop (⊠ 5–6 Nassau St., City Center ☎ 01/677–7066) specializes in contemporary Irish-made ceramics, pottery, and silver jewelry, and regularly holds exhibits of exciting new work by Irish craftspeople.

McDowell (⊠ 3 Upper O'Connell St., Northside ☎ 01/874–4961), a jewelry shop popular with Dubliners, has been in business for more than 100 years.

Weir & Sons (⊠ 96 Grafton St., City Center ☎ 01/677–9678), Dublin's most prestigious jeweler, sells not only jewelry and watches, but also china, glass, lamps, silver, and leather.

Clothing Stores

A-Wear (⊠ Grafton St., City Center ☎ 01/872–4644) has become something of a fashion institution for both men and women. Leading Irish designers including John Rocha supply A-Wear with a steady stream of exciting new looks.

BT2 (⊠ Grafton St., City Center ☎ 01/605–6666) is swanky Brown Thomas's impressive attempt to woo a younger crowd. Most of the major labels are present, including DKNY and Paul Smith.

Costume (⊠ 10 Castel Market, City Center ☎ 01/679–4188) is a classy boutique where Dubliners with fashion sense and money like to shop for colorful, stylish clothes. Local designers include Leigh, Helen James, and Antonia Campbell-Hughes; Temperley and Preen are among the international designers featured.

Dolls (✉ 32 Clarendon Stl, City Center ☎ 01/672–9004), an independent boutique, likes to boast of its unusual designer pieces. Featured international designers include Karen Walker and Future Classics.

Scarlet Row (✉ 5 Scarlet Row, Temple Bar ☎ 01/672–9534), opened by an ex-Donna Karan shoe designer and a Dublin art curator, is a high-concept shoe store, fashion outlet, and gallery—great for browsing and buying alike.

Smock (✉ West Essex St., Temple Bar ☎ 01/613–9000) is a tiny designer shop with great, left-field taste. International labels include Pearson, Veronique, and A. F. Vandevoft. They also carry a beautiful line in fine jewelry.

Urban Outfitters (✉ 4 Cecilia St., Temple Bar ☎ 01/670–6202) is a U.S. chain shop that has become hugely popular with the locals. The music is almost as loud as the clothes, but this is a great place to shop with teenagers and young adults. Besides all the major street labels, they have a wide range of accessories.

Museum Stores

National Gallery of Ireland Shop (✉ Merrion Sq. W, Georgian Dublin ☎ 01/678–5450) has a terrific selection of books on Irish art, plus posters, postcards, note cards, and lots of lovely bibelots.

National Museum of Archaeology and History Shop (✉ Kildare St., Georgian Dublin ☎ 01/677–7444 Ext. 327) carries jewelry based on ancient Celtic artifacts in the museum collection, contemporary Irish pottery, a large selection of books, and other gift items.

Trinity College Library Shop (✉ Old Library, Trinity College, City Center ☎ 01/608–2308) sells Irish-theme books, *Book of Kells* souvenirs, clothing, jewelry, and lovely Irish-made items.

Music

Celtic Note (✉ 12 Nassau St., City Center ☎ 01/670–4157) is aimed at the tourist market, with lots of compilations and greatest-hits formats.

Claddagh Records (✉ 2 Cecilia St., Temple Bar ☎ 01/679–3664) has a good selection of traditional and folk music.

Gael Linn (✉ 26 Merrion Sq., City Center ☎ 01/676–7283) specializes in traditional Irish music and Irish-language recordings; it's where the aficionados go.

HMV (✉ 65 Grafton St., City Center ☎ 01/679–5334 ✉ 18 Henry St., Northside ☎ 01/872–2095) is one of the larger record shops in town.

McCullogh Piggott (✉ 25 Suffolk St., City Center ☎ 01/671–2410) is the best place in town to buy instruments, sheet music, scores, and books about music.

Tower Records (✉ 6–8 Wicklow St., City Center ☎ 01/671–3250) is the best-stocked international chain.

Sweaters & Tweeds

Don't think Irish woolens are limited to Aran sweaters and tweed jackets. You can choose souvenirs from a wide selection of hats, gloves, scarves, blankets, and other goods here. If you're traveling outside of Dublin, you may want to wait to make purchases elsewhere, but if Dublin is it, you still have plenty of good shops from which to choose. The tweed sold in Dublin comes from two main sources: Donegal and Connemara. Labels inside the garments guarantee their authenticity. Kilkenny Shop and House of Ireland listed under China, Crystal, Ceramics and Jewelery above are also great places for all things woolen. The following are the other largest retailers of traditional Irish woolen goods in the city.

Avoca Handweavers (⊠ 11–13 Suffolk St., City Center ☎ 01/677–4215) is a beautiful store with an eclectic collection of knitwear from contemporary Irish designers. The children's wear section on the second floor is a real joy. They also stock original ceramics.

Blarney Woollen Mills (⊠ 21–23 Nassau St., City Center ☎ 01/671–0068) stocks a good selection of tweed, linen, and wool sweaters from their mills in County Cork, in all price ranges.

Cleo Ltd (⊠ 18 Kildare St., Georgian Dublin ☎ 01/676–1421) sells hand-knit sweaters and accessories made only from natural fibers; it also carries its own designs.

Kevin and Howlin (⊠ 31 Nassau St., City Center ☎ 01/677–0257) specializes in handwoven tweed men's jackets, suits, and hats, and also sells tweed fabric.

Monaghan's (⊠ Grafton Arcade, 15–17 Grafton St., City Center ☎ 01/677–0823) specializes in cashmere.

Vintage

Flip (⊠ 4 Upper Fownes St., Temple Bar ☎ 01/671–4299), one of the original stores in Temple Bar, sells vintage and retro clothing from the '50s, '60s, and '70s.

Harlequin (⊠ Castle Market, City Center ☎ 01/671-0202) isn't cheap, but the owner–buyer has great taste in classic men's and women's wear.

Jenny Vander (⊠ Drury St., City Center ☎ 01/677–0406) is the most famous name in Irish vintage and retro clothing. Just browsing through her collection is a pleasure.

SIDE TRIPS FROM DUBLIN

Dubliners are undeniably lucky. Few populaces enjoy such glorious—and easily accessible—options for day trips. Just outside the city lie some of the region's most unique sights, including the James Joyce Martello Tower, Marino Casino, and Malahide Castle. Beyond the southern neighborhood of Ballsbridge, sights are too spread out to cover on foot, and it's necessary to use either a car or public transportation (the bus or DART). If you have a car, then head to Rathfarnham, directly south of the city. Alternatively, head east and follow the coast road south to

Dun Laoghaire and points even farther south. Traveling to and from each of the suburbs will take up most of a day, so you need to pick and choose the excursions you prefer.

South County Dublin

Dublin's southern suburbs are home to its more affluent and well-heeled citizens. As is usually the case, the wealthy folk have chosen some of the most scenic parts of the city, with the beautiful coastline to the east and Wicklow and its mountains to the south.

Numbers in the text correspond to numbers in the margin and on the South County Dublin map.

Rathfarnham

❶ *Bus 47A from Hawkins St. in city center goes to both parks in Rathfarnham. Or drive, leaving city center via Nicholas St. just west of Christ Church Cathedral and following it south through Terenure.*

Two parks lie in the suburb of Rathfarnham, due south of the city at the edge of the Dublin Mountains. The 18th-century house in **St. Enda's National Historic Park** has been turned into the **Pearse Museum**, commemorating Pádrig Pearse, leader of Dublin's 1916 Easter Uprising. In the early 20th century, the house was an Irish-language boys' school, which Pearse and his brother Willie founded. The museum preserves Pearse-family memorabilia, documents, and photographs. A lake and nature trails are also on the park's 50-acre grounds, and guides are available for tours of the park or simply for information. ⊠ *Grange Rd., South County Dublin* ☎ *01/493–4208* ⊕ *www.heritageireland.ie* ⊠ *Free* ☉ *Park daily 8:30–dusk. Museum May–Aug., daily 10–1 and 2–5:30; Sept., Oct., and Feb.–Apr., daily 10–1 and 2–5; Nov.–Jan., daily 10–1 and 2–4.*

☼ **Marlay Park** marks the start of the Wicklow Way, a popular walking route that crosses the Wicklow Mountains for 137 km (85 mi), through some of the most rugged landscapes in Ireland. In addition to its woodlands and nature walks, the 214-acre park has a cobbled courtyard, home to brightly plumaged peacocks. Surrounding the courtyard are crafts workshops, where you're welcome to observe bookbinding, jewelry making, and furniture making in process. Every Saturday from 3 to 5, kids can take a free ride on the model steam railway. To get here, leave St. Enda's Park via Grange Road and walk up the hill for about 1 km (½ mi), turning left at the T junction and continuing another ½ km (¼ mi). ⊠ *Grange Rd., South County Dublin* ☎ *01/493–4059* ⊠ *Free* ☉ *Feb. and Mar., daily 10–6; Apr. and Sept., daily 10–8; May–Aug., daily 10–9; Oct., daily 10–7; Nov.–Jan., daily 10–5.*

NIGHTLIFE **Johnnie Fox's** (⊠ Glencullen, South County Dublin ☎ 01/295–5647), 12 km (7½ mi) from the city center and 1½ km (1 mi) from Rathfarnam, sits 1,000 feet up in the Dublin Mountains, making it the highest licensed pub in Ireland. You approach it by a winding and steeply climbing route that turns off the main Dublin–Enniskerry road at Stepaside. Refusing to bow to the whims of modernization, the owners have steadfastly maintained its traditional character—oak tables, rough-stone

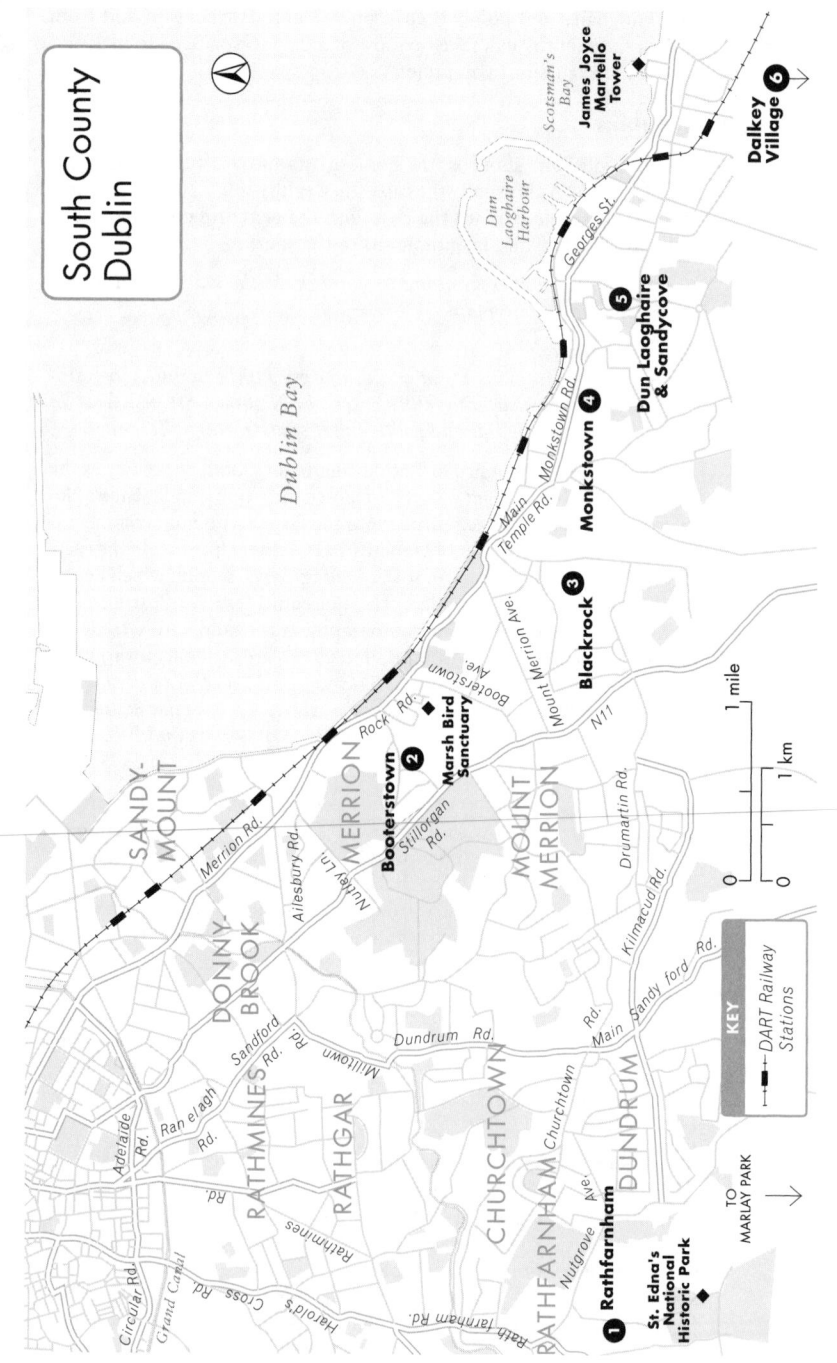

South County Dublin

1 Rathfarnham
St. Edna's National Historic Park

2 Booterstown
Marsh Bird Sanctuary

3 Blackrock

4 Monkstown

5 Dun Laoghaire & Sandycove

6 Dalkey Village

James Joyce Martello Tower

Dublin Bay

Scotsman's Bay

Dun Laoghaire Harbour

KEY

DART Railway Stations

TO MARLAY PARK

0   1 mile
0   1 km

floor flags strewn with sawdust, and ancient bric-a-brac, including copper kettles, crockery, old prints, and guns—and it appears very much as it did in the early 19th century, when Daniel O'Connell used it as a safe house for his seditious meetings. You can get lunch and dinner here; the specialty is seafood, and it alone is worth the journey. In the evenings expect to hear traditional Irish music.

Booterstown

❷ *Take DART local train from Tara St. or Pearce St. Or take R118 from corner of Lower Merrion St. and Merrion Sq.*

Booterstown stretches along Dublin Bay south of Sandymount. The **Booterstown Marsh Bird Sanctuary** is the largest wildlife preserve in the Dublin area. Curlews, herons, kingfishers, and other fairly rare migratory species come to nest here; information boards along the road describe the birds. Also on this main road is Glena, the house where Athlone-born John McCormack, one of the best and most popular tenors in the first quarter of the 20th century, died on September 16, 1945. ⊠ *Between DART line and Rock Rd.* ☎ *01/454–1786.*

Blackrock

❸ *3 km (2 mi) south of Booterstown on Rock Rd. Take DART line from city center to Blackrock.*

Fine sea views, swimming, a weekend market, and a major shopping center draw Dubliners down to Blackrock, a bedroom community where James Joyce's parents lived with their large brood for most of 1892. Above the Blackrock DART station, at **Idrone Terrace**—lined with restored, old-fashioned lamps—you can take in a lovely view across the bay to Howth Peninsula.

SHOPPING The **Blackrock Shopping Centre** (☎ 01/283–1660) is one of the most customer-friendly shopping centers around. It's built on two levels, looking onto an inner courtyard, with the giant Superquinn Foodstore, cafés, and restaurants, as well as shops selling clothes, electronics, and crafts. Blackrock can be reached conveniently on the DART train line; it has its own stop.

Monkstown

❹ *3 km (2 mi) south of Blackrock on R119. Take DART train from city center to Monkstown/Seapoint station.*

One of Dublin's most exclusive suburbs, Monkstown is known for its two architectural curiosities. John Semple, the architect of Monkstown's **Anglican parish church,** built in 1833, was inspired by two entirely different styles, the Gothic and the Moorish, which he joined into an unlikely hybrid of towers and turrets. The church, which is in the town's main square, is only open during Sunday services. The well-preserved ruins of **Monkstown Castle** lie about 1 km (½ mi) south of the suburb; it's a 15th-century edifice with a keep, a gatehouse, and a long wall section, all surrounded by greenery. The **Lambert Puppet Theatre** (⊠ Clifton La., South County Dublin ☎ 01/280–0974), which stages regular puppet shows every weekend, houses a puppetry museum, which can only be viewed after a show.

Comhaltas Ceoltóiri Éireann (✉ 35 Belgrave Sq., South County Dublin ☎ 01/
280–0295) is the place to go for a boisterous summer evening of Irish
music and dancing.

Dun Laoghaire & Sandycove

❺ *2½ km (1½ mi) southeast of Monkstown along R119, the Monkstown
Crescent.*

After the British monarch King George IV disembarked for a brief visit
in 1821, Dun Laoghaire (pronounced dun *lear*-ee) was renamed
Kingstown, but it reverted to its original Irish name 99 years later. Its
Irish name refers to Laoghaire, the High King of Tara who in the 5th
century permitted St. Patrick to begin converting Ireland to Christianity. The town was once a Protestant stronghold of the old ruling elite;
in some of the neo-Georgian squares and terraces behind George's
Street, the main thoroughfare, a little of the community's former elegance can still be seen.

Dun Laoghaire has long been known for its great harbor, enclosed by
two piers, each 2½ km (1½ mi) long. The harbor was constructed between 1817 and 1859 using granite quarried from nearby Dalkey Hill;
the west pier has a rougher surface and is less favored for walking than
the east pier, which has a bandstand where musicians play in summer.
The workaday business here includes passenger-ship and freight-serv-
ices sailings to Holyhead in north Wales, 3½ hours away. Dun Laoghaire
is also a yachting center, with the members-only Royal Irish, National,
and Royal St. George yacht clubs, all founded in the 19th century, lining the harbor area. A 15-minute walk south of Dun Laoghaire along
the coast road brings you to the village of Sandycove, with a lovely little beach and the famous Martello Tower.

The **National Maritime Museum,** west of the harbor and across from the
Gresham Royal Marine Hotel and the People's Park, is in the former
Mariners' church. Its nave makes a strangely ideal setting for exhibits
like the longboat captured during an aborted French invasion at Bantry,
County Cork, in 1796. A particularly memorable exhibit is the old
optic from the Baily Lighthouse on Howth Head, across Dublin Bay;
the herringbone patterns of glass reflected light across the bay until several decades ago. ✉ *Haigh Terr., South County Dublin* ☎ *01/280–
0969* ⊕ *www.dun-laoghaire.com/dir/maritime* ✇ *€1.90* ☾ *May–Sept.,
Tues.–Sun. 1–5.*

From the harbor area, Marine Parade leads alongside Scotsmans Bay
for 1¼ km (¾ mi), as far as Sandycove and the **Forty Foot Bathing Pool,**
a traditional bathing area that attracts mostly nude older men. Women
were once banned from here, but now hardy swimmers of both genders
are free to brave its cold waters.

★ Built in 1804, when Napoléon's invasion seemed imminent, the **James
Joyce Martello Tower** was demilitarized in the 1860s along with most of
the rest of the 34 Martello towers that ring Ireland's coast (the name
"Martello" derives from the small tower fort on Mortello Point in Cor-
sica, which inspired the English to create their own version). They're

known for their squat and solid construction, rotating cannon at the top, and—most importantly—their proximity to one another, so that each one is within visible range of the one next to it. In 1904, this tower was rented to Oliver St. John Gogarty, a medical student who was known for his poetry and ready wit, for £8 a year. He wanted to create a nurturing environment for writers and would-be literati. Joyce spent a week here in September 1904 and described it in the first chapter of *Ulysses*, using his friend as a model for the character Buck Mulligan. The tower now houses the **Joyce Museum**, founded in 1962 thanks to Sylvia Beach, the Paris-based first publisher of *Ulysses*. The tower stands a few steps away from the Forty Foot Bathing Pool. ⊠ *Sandycove* ☎ *01/280–9265* ⊕ *www.visitdublin.com* ⊠ *€6.70* ☉ *Mar.–Oct., Mon.–Sat. 10–1 and 2–5, Sun. 2–6; Nov.–Jan. by appointment.*

WHERE TO EAT ✗ **Brasserie Na Mara.** Chef Derek Breen serves Irish dishes with a mod-
$$–$$$ ern twist in this brasserie. *Na mara* means "of the sea" in Gaelic, and although he kept the name when he took over, he jettisoned the exclusive emphasis on seafood. Fish is nonetheless one specialty, and sesame crusted mackerel tops the list. For serious carnivores the rack of lamb with sautéed spinach, herb potatoes, and garlic jus is a cleverly jazzed-up Irish standard. The building has an unusual history: the first railway in Ireland, opened in 1834, was built from Westland Row (now Pearse Station) in Dublin to Dun Laoghaire. Much of the original station's entrance and ticketing area has been converted into this restaurant—now tall Georgian windows overlook the busy Dun Laoghaire ferry port. Reservations are essential on weekends. ⊠ *Dun Laoghaire Harbour, Dun Laoghaire, South County Dublin* ☎ *01/280–6767* ⊟ *AE, DC, MC, V* ☉ *Closed Sun. No lunch Sat.*

$–$$$ ✗ **Caviston's.** Stephen Caviston and his family have been dispensing fine food for years from their fish counter and delicatessen in Sandycove, and their name is synonymous with quality produce served in a stylish formula. The fish restaurant next door to the deli is an intimate place, with a few cozy tables and the friendliest service you could ask for. Typical entrées include panfried scallops served in the shell with a thermidor sauce, and char-grilled marinated swordfish with mango and melon chili chutney. You can also get a halved lobster with a simple butter sauce for an exceptionally good price. Other than seafood, organic vegetables, regional cheeses, and local meats fill out the mouthwatering menu. ⊠ *58–59 Glasthule Rd., Sandycove, South County Dublin* ☎ *01/280– 9120* ⊕ *www.cavistons.com* ⊟ *MC, V* ☉ *Closed Sun., Mon., and late Dec.–early Jan. No dinner.*

$ ✗ **The Forty Foot.** From the wall of windows that dominates this ultra-modern, two-story bar and restaurant you can look out onto the sea and the famous 40-foot-wide rocky cove (and bathing spot) that gave the place its name. The brightness and large open spaces give the Forty Foot a very casual feel, and it's popular with a young, business crowd. The long, New York–style bar is the perfect spot to have a drink while waiting to be seated. The menu changes regularly, but usually offers the very popular starter tian of salmon and crab in a cream sauce with tomato-and-oil dressing. European influences can be found in most of the main courses, including chicken stuffed with chorizo, and fillet of pork wrapped in pancetta. ☒ *Pavilion Centre, Dun Laoghaire, South County Dublin* ☎ *01/284–2982* ⊕ *www.40foot.ie* ⊟ *MC, V.*

Dalkey Village

⑥ *From James Joyce Martello Tower in Sandycove, it's an easy walk or quick drive 1 km (½ mi) south to Dalkey. Or take DART line from city center to Dalkey.*

Along Castle Street, the town's main thoroughfare, are the substantial stone remains—resembling small, turreted castles—of two 15th- and 16th-century fortified houses. From the mainland's Vico Road, beyond Coliemore Harbour, are astounding bay views as far as Bray in County Wicklow. On Dalkey Hill stands **Torca Cottage**, home of the Nobel prize–winning writer George Bernard Shaw from 1866 to 1874. You can return to Dalkey Village by Sorrento Road. The cottage is closed to the public. The **Heritage Centre** attached to Dalkey Castle has exhibits on local history, including a script written by playwright and local resident Hugh Leonard. While there you can head up into the 15th-century Towerhouse. ☒ *Castle St., South County Dublin* ☎ *01/285–8366* ⊕ *www.dalkeycastle.com* ☲ *Free* ☉ *Weekdays 9:30–5, weekends 11–5.*

In summer small boats make the 15-minute crossing from Coliemore Harbour to **Dalkey Island,** covered with long grass, uninhabited except for a herd of goats, and graced with its own Martello tower—and an excellent bird sanctuary. The 8th-century ruins of St. Begnet's church sit right beside the bird sanctuary.

WHERE TO STAY   ▦ **Fitzpatrick Castle Dublin.** Like a storybook vision out of an Irish Dis-

★ **$$$–$$$$** neyland, this 18th-century stone "castle" comes complete with gorgeous lime-green dressed-stone walls, white machicolations, and fairy-tale turrets. Add in its sweeping views over Dun Laoghaire and Dublin Bay and you can see why the Fitzpatrick is well worth the 15-km (9-mi) drive from the Dublin city center. Not a castle per se, but a stately home built to look like one, this popular landmark now has an interior renovated to within its eyeteeth, but happily its modern hallways and public spaces sport some antiques. Some will opt for a room and the four-poster beds in the 18th-century wing; others will like the cool calm of the rooms in the substantial modern addition. In all cases, bathrooms are large. The hotel is convenient to golfing, horseback riding, and fishing, and the fitness facilities include a heated pool. The views from Killiney Hill, behind the hotel, are spectacular, and the seaside resort village of Dalkey and Killiney Beach are both within walking distance. ☒ *Killiney, South County Dublin* ☎ *01/230–5400* 🖷 *01/230–5466* ⊕ *www. fitzpatrickcastle.com* ⇨ *113 rooms* ♨ *Restaurant, cable TV, in-room data ports, indoor pool, health club, bar, meeting rooms, free parking* ⊟ *AE, DC, MC, V* ⍻ *BP, EP.*

North County Dublin

Dublin's northern suburbs remain largely residential, but there are a few places worth the trip, such as the architectural gem Marino Casino. As with most suburban areas, walking may not be the best way to get around. It's good, but not essential, to have a car. Buses and trains serve most

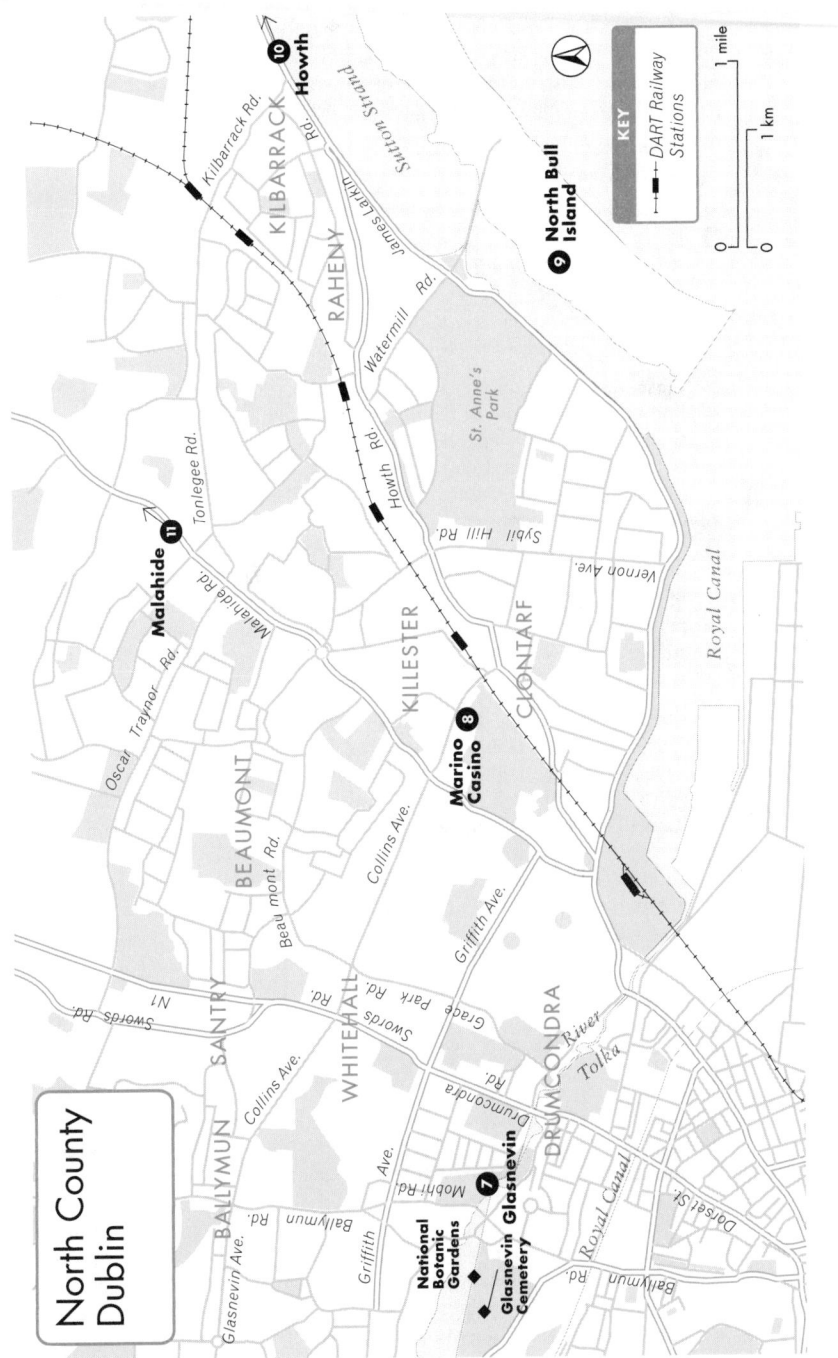

North County Dublin

Howth ⑩

KILBARRACK

Kilbarrack Rd.

RAHENY

James Larkin

Sutton Strand

Watermill Rd.

St. Anne's Park

North Bull Island ⑨

Tonlegee Rd.

Malahide ⑪

Malahide Rd.

Howth Rd.

Sybil Hill Rd.

Vernon Ave.

KILLESTER

CLONTARF

Royal Canal

Oscar Traynor Rd.

BEAUMONT

Beaumont Rd.

Collins Ave.

Marino Casino ⑧

N1

Swords Rd.

SANTRY

Collins Ave.

BALLYMUN

Glasnevin Ave.

Griffith Ave.

WHITEHALL

Griffith Ave.

Grace Park Rd.

Drumcondra Rd.

DRUMCONDRA

River Tolka

Ballymun Rd.

Mobhi Rd.

National Botanic Gardens ◆

Glasnevin Cemetery ◆ Glasnevin ⑦

Royal Canal

Ballymun Rd.

Dorset St.

KEY

▪▪▪ DART Railway Stations

0 ——— 1 km

0 ——— 1 mile

of these areas—the only drawback is that to get from one suburb to another by public transportation, you have to backtrack through the city center. Even if you're traveling by car, visiting all these sights will take a full day, so plan your trip carefully before setting off.

Numbers in the text correspond to numbers in the margin and on the North County Dublin map.

Glasnevin

❼ *Drive from north city center by Lower Dorset St., as far as bridge over Royal Canal. Turn left, go up Whitworth Rd., by side of canal, for 1 km (½ mi); at its end, turn right onto Prospect Rd. and then left onto Finglas road, N2. You can also take Bus 40 or Bus 40A from Parnell St., next to Parnell Sq., in northern city center.*

Glasnevin Cemetery, on the right-hand side of the Finglas road, is the best-known burial ground in Dublin. It's the site of the graves of many distinguished Irish leaders, including Eamon De Valera, a founding father of modern Ireland and a former Irish *taoiseach* (prime minister) and president, and Michael Collins, the celebrated hero of the Irish War of Independence. Other notables interred here include the late-19th-century poet Gerard Manley Hopkins and Sir Roger Casement, an Irish rebel hanged for treason by the British in 1916. The large column to the right of the main entrance is the tomb of "The Liberator" Daniel O'Connell, perhaps Ireland's greatest historical figure, renowned for his nonviolent struggle for Catholic rights and emancipation, achieved in 1829. The cemetery is freely accessible 24 hours.

The **National Botanic Gardens,** on the northeastern flank of Glasnevin Cemetery and the south banks of the Tolka River, date from 1795 and have more than 20,000 varieties of plants, a rose garden, and a vegetable garden. The main attraction is the beautifully restored Curvilinear Range—400-foot-long greenhouses designed and built by a Dublin iron-master, Richard Turner, between 1843 and 1869. The Great Palm House, with its striking double dome, was built in 1884 and houses orchids, palms, and tropical ferns. ⊠ *Glasnevin Rd., North County Dublin* ☎ *01/837–4388* ⊕ *www.botanicgardens.ie* ⊠ *Free* ⊙ *Apr.–Sept., Mon.–Sat. 9–6, Sun. 11–6; Oct.–Mar., Mon.–Sun. 10–4:30.*

Marino Casino

❽ *Take Malahide road from Dublin's north city center for 4 km (2½ mi). Or take Bus 20A or Bus 24 to Casino from Cathal Brugha St. in north city center.*

FodorśChoice
★

One of Dublin's most exquisite, yet also most underrated, architectural landmarks, the Marino Casino (the name means "little house by the sea," and the building overlooks Dublin Harbour) is a small-scale, Palladian-style Greek temple, built between 1762 and 1771 from a plan by Sir William Chambers. Often compared to the Petit Trianon at Versailles, it was commissioned by the great Irish grandee Lord Charlemont as a summerhouse. Inside, highlights are the china-closet boudoir, the huge golden sunset in the ceiling of the main drawing room, and the signs of the zodiac in the ceiling of the bijou library. When you realize that the structure has, in fact, 16 rooms—there are bedrooms upstairs—Sir

William's sleight-of-hand is readily apparent: from its exterior, the structure seems to contain only one room. It makes a good stop on the way to Malahide, Howth, or North Bull Island. ☒ *Malahide Rd., Marino, North County Dublin* ☎ *01/833–1618* ⊕ *www.heritageireland.ie* ☒ *€2.75* ☉ *Feb., Mar., and Nov., Sun. and Thurs. noon–4; Apr., Sun. and Thurs. noon–5; May and Oct., daily 10–5; June–Sept., daily 10–6.*

North Bull Island

❾ *From Dublin's north city center, take Clontarf road for 4 km (2½ mi) to causeway.*

A 5-km-long (3-mi-long) island created in the 19th century by the action of the tides, North Bull Island is one of Dublin's wilder places— it's a nature conservancy with vast beach and dunes. The island is linked to the mainland via a wooden causeway that leads to Bull Wall, a 1½-km (1-mi) walkway that stretches as far as the North Bull Lighthouse. The island is also accessible via a second, northerly causeway, which takes you to Dollymount Strand. (The two routes of entry don't meet at any point on the island.) You can reach this causeway from the mainland via James Larkin Road. The small **visitor center** here largely explains the island's bird life. ☒ *Off northerly causeway, North County Dublin* ☎ *01/833–8341* ☒ *Free* ☉ *Mar.–Oct., Mon.–Wed. 10:15–1 and 1:30–4, Thurs. 10:15–1 and 1:30–3:45, Fri. 10:15–1 and 1:30–2:30, weekends 10–1 and 1:30–5:30; Nov.–Feb., Mon.–Wed. 10:15–1 and 1:30–4, Thurs. 10:15–1 and 1:30–3:45, Fri. 10:15–1 and 1:30–2:30, weekends 10–1 and 1:30–4:30.*

On the mainland directly across from North Bull Island is **St. Anne's Park,** a public green with extensive rose gardens (including many prize hybrids) and woodland walks. ☒ *James Larkin Rd. and Mt. Prospect Ave., North County Dublin.*

Howth

❿ *From Dublin, take DART train, or Bus 31B from Lower Abbey St. in city center. Or, by car, take Howth road from north city center for 16 km (10 mi).*

A fishing village at the foot of a long peninsula, Howth (derived from the Norse *hoved*, meaning head; it rhymes with "both") was an island inhabited as long ago as 3250 BC. Between 1813 and 1833, Howth was the Irish terminus for the sea crossing to Holyhead in north Wales, but it was then superseded by the newly built harbor at Kingstown (now Dun Laoghaire). Today, its harbor, which supports a large fishing fleet, includes a marina. Both arms of the harbor pier form extensive walks. Separated from Howth Harbour by a channel nearly 1½ km (1 mi) wide is **Ireland's Eye,** with an old stone church on the site of a 6th-century monastery, and an early-19th-century Martello tower. In calm summer weather, local boatmen make the crossing to the island from the East pier in Howth Harbour. Contact head boatman **Frank Doyle** (☎ 087/ 267–8211) for times and details.

At the King Sitric restaurant on the East Pier, a 2½-km (1½-mi) cliff walk begins, leading to the white **Baily Lighthouse,** built in 1814. In some places, the cliff path narrows and drops close to the water, but the views out over the Irish Sea are terrific. Some of the best views in the whole Dublin area await from the parking lot above the lighthouse, looking out over the entire bay as far south as Dun Laoghaire, Bray, and the north Wicklow coast. You can also see quite a bit of Dublin.

Until 1959 a tram service ran from the railway station in Howth over Howth Summit and back down to the station. One of the open-top Hill of Howth trams that plied this route is now the star at the **National Transport Museum**, a short, 800-yard walk from Howth's DART station. Volunteers spent several years restoring the tram, which stands alongside other unusual vehicles, including horse-drawn bakery vans. ☎ *01/848–0831 or 01/847–5623* ⊕ *www.nationaltransportmuseum.org* ✉ *€3* ⊙ *June–Aug., Mon.–Sat. 10–5; Sept.–May, weekends 2–5.*

The **Howth Castle Gardens,** next door to the Transport Museum and accessible from the Deer Park Hotel, were laid out in the early 18th century. The many rare varieties in its fine rhododendron garden are in full flower April through June; there are also high beech hedges. The rambling castle, built in 1654 and considerably altered in the following centuries, is not open to the public, but you can access the ruins of a tall, square, 16th-century castle and a Neolithic dolmen. ⊠ *Deer Park Hotel, North County Dublin* ☎ *01/832–2624* ⊕ *www.deerpark-hotel.ie* ✉ *Free* ⊙ *Daily 8–dusk.*

WHERE TO EAT
★ **$$$$**

✕ **King Sitric.** Sitric was an 11th-century Norse king of Dublin who seemed to be very fond of Howth. Joan and Aidan MacManus's well-known seafood restaurant down by the harbor attracts many contemporary visitors to the old town. It's in a Georgian house, with the yacht marina and port on one side and sea views from which you can watch the boats land the very fish that might be tomorrow's special. The upstairs seafood bar is great for informal lunches in summer. A house specialty is black sole meunière, grilled and finished with a nut-brown butter sauce, but lobster, caught just yards away in Balscadden Bay, is the big treat—it's best at its simplest, in butter sauce. Crab is equally fresh, dressed with mayonnaise or Mornay sauce. Game and other meat dishes are also on offer, and Aidan is something of a collector when it comes to fine wines. ⊠ *East Pier, North County Dublin* ☎ *01/832–5235* ⊕ *www.kingsitric. ie* ⊟ *AE, DC, MC, V* ⊙ *Closed Sun. No lunch Sat.*

$–$$$

✕ **Wrights Findlater.** On Harbour Road right as you enter the village, this all-in-one bar, cocktail lounge and Asian-fusion restaurant is causing quite a stir on the north coast. It's really about about the harbor views, taken in from the many windows of the crisp modern dining rooms and from heated outdoor patios. The ground-floor bar serves a café-style menu and the top-floor cocktail lounge has to be one of Dublin's cooler spots to wait for a table. Sandwiched in between, the Lemongrass Restaurant presents Thai, Chinese, Vietnamese, and Indonesian dishes from an open kitchen—the *nasi goreng,* Indonesian rice served with prawn, chicken sate, and a fried egg is a standout. ⊠ *Wrights Findlater, Harbour Rd.* ☎ *01/832–4488* ⊕ *www.wrightsfindlaterhowth.com* ⌂ *Reservations essential* ⊟ *AE, DC, MC, V.*

Malahide

⑪ *By car, drive from north city center on R107 for 14½ km (9 mi). Or catch hourly train from Connolly Station. Or board Bus 42 to Malahide, which leaves every 15 minutes from Beresford Pl. behind Custom House.*

★ ♨ Malahide is chiefly known for its glorious **Malahide Castle,** a picture-book castle occupied by the Talbot family from 1185 until 1976, when it was sold to the Dublin County Council. The great expanse of park-land around the castle has more than 5,000 different species of trees and shrubs, all clearly labeled. The castle itself combines styles and crosses centuries; the earliest section, the three-story tower house, dates from the 12th century. Hung with many family portraits, the medieval great hall is the only one in Ireland that is preserved in its original form. Au-thentic 18th-century pieces furnish the other rooms. Within the castle, the **Fry Model Railway Museum** houses rare, handmade models of the Irish railway and one of the world's largest miniature railway displays, which covers an area of 2,500 square feet. ⊠ *10 km (6 mi) north of Howth on Coast Rd., North County Dublin* ☎ *01/846–2184* ⊕ *www. malahidecastle.com* ✉ *€6.50* ☼ *Apr.–Sept., Mon.–Sat. 10–5, Sun. 11–6; Oct.–May, Mon.–Sat. 10–5, Sun. 11–5.*

★ ♨ One of the greatest stately homes of Ireland, **Newbridge House,** in nearby Donabate, was built between 1740 and 1760 for Charles Cobbe, Arch-bishop of Dublin. The sober exterior and even more sober entrance hall—all Portland stone and Welsh slate—don't prepare you for the splendor of Newbridge's Red Drawing Room, with its crimson walls, fluted Corinthian columns, dozens of Old Masters, and a glamorous Rococo-style plaster ceiling. Elsewhere in the house are fascinating family heir-looms: the kitchens still have their original utensils; crafts workshops and some examples of old-style transportation, such as coaches, are in the courtyard; and there's even a Museum of Curiosities, complete with the mummified ear of an Egyptian bull. Beyond the house's walled gar-den are 366 acres of parkland and a restored 18th-century animal farm. Tara's Palace dollhouse is also here; it has 25 rooms, all fully furnished in miniature. You can travel from Malahide to Donabate by train, which takes about 10 minutes. From the Donabate train station, it's a 15-minute walk to the Newbridge House grounds. ⊠ *Donabate, 8 km (5 mi) north of Malahide, signposted from N1, North County Dublin* ☎ *01/843–6534* ⊕ *www.fingalcoco.ie* ✉ *€6.50* ☼ *Apr.–Sept., Tues.–Sat. 10–1 and 2–5, Sun. 2–6; Oct.–Mar., weekends 2–5.*

WHERE TO EAT ✕ **Bon Appetit.** The striking floral decor creates a cozy traditional air at
$$–$$$$ this stylish basement restaurant, an impression heightened by the staff of black-jacketed waiters and the collection of paintings daubed by local artists. Owner–chef Patsy McGuirk's Continental menu includes such entrées as roast fillet of John Dory on creamed leeks with spring onion and garlic cream, or the delicious sole McGuirk—filleted, stuffed with prawns and turbot, and baked with white wine and cream. ⊠ *9 James's Terr., North County Dublin* ☎ *01/845–0314* ⊕ *www.bonappetit. ie* ⊟ *AE, DC, MC, V* ☼ *Closed Sun. No lunch Sat.*

DUBLIN ESSENTIALS

Transportation

BY AIR

Dublin Airport, 10 km (6 mi) north of the city center, serves international and domestic flights. Three airlines have regularly scheduled flights from the United States to Dublin. Aer Lingus flies direct from New York, Boston, Los Angeles, Baltimore, Washington, and Chicago to Dublin. Continental flies from New York (Newark Liberty International Airport) to Dublin. Delta flies from Atlanta to Dublin via New York.

There are daily services to Dublin from all major London airports. Flights to Dublin also leave from Birmingham, Bristol, East Midlands, Liverpool, Luton, Manchester, Leeds/Bradford, Newcastle, Edinburgh, and Glasgow.

Within Ireland, Aer Lingus operates flights from Dublin to Belfast, Cork, Derry, Kerry, Shannon, Galway, Knock in County Mayo, Donegal, and Sligo. Ryanair flies to Belfast, and Aer Arann fly to Cork, Kerry, Sligo, Knock, Galway, and Donegal.

🛈 Carriers **Aer Arann** ☎ 01/814-5240. **Aer Lingus** ☎ 01/844-4747. **Air Wales** ☎ 800/465-193. **British Airways** ☎ 800/626-747. **BMI** ☎ 01/283-8833. **City Jet** ☎ 01/870-0300. **Continental** ☎ 1890/925-252. **Delta** ☎ 01/844-4166 or 01/676-8080. **Logan Air** ☎ 800/626-747. **Ryanair** ☎ 01/844-4411. **Thompsonfly** ☎ 01/247-7723.

🛈 Airport Information **Dublin Airport** ☎ 01/844-4900 ⊕ www.dublin-airport.com.

TRANSFERS Dublin Bus operates the Airlink shuttle service between Dublin Airport and the city center, with departures outside the arrivals gateway. Service runs from 5:45 AM to 11:30 PM, at intervals of about 10 minutes (after 8 PM buses run every 20 minutes), to as far as O'Connell Street and then Dublin's main bus station (Busaras), behind the Custom House on the Northside. Journey time from the airport to the city center is normally 30 minutes, but it may be longer in heavy traffic. The single fare is €5; pay the driver inside the bus. If you have time, you can save money by taking a regular bus for €2. Aircoach's comfortable coaches run from the airport to the city center 24 hours a day for €7 one way and €12 return. The service stops at the major hotels. A taxi is a quicker alternative than the bus to get from the airport to Dublin center. A line of taxis waits by the arrivals gateway; the fare for the 30-minute journey to any of the main city-center hotels is about €18 to €20 plus tip (tips don't have to be large but they are increasingly expected). Ask about the fare before leaving the airport.

🛈 **Aircoach** ☎ 01/844-7118 ⊕ www.aircoach.ie. **Busaras** ☎ 01/830-2222. **Dublin Bus** ☎ 01/873-4222 ⊕ www.dublinbus.ie.

BY BOAT & FERRY

Irish Ferries runs a regular high-speed car and passenger service directly into Dublin port from Holyhead in Wales. The crossing takes 1 hour and 40 minutes. Stena Line has services to both Dublin and nearby Dun Laoghaire port to Holyhead (3½ hours) and a high-speed service, known

1

as "HSS," which takes about 1 hour and 40 minutes. P & O sails from Dublin to Liverpool in a very slow 7 hours. Prices and departure times vary according to season, so call to confirm. In summer, reservations are strongly recommended; book online or through a travel agent. Dozens of taxis wait to take you into town from both ports, or you can take DART or a bus to the city center.

🚢 Boat & Ferry Lines **Irish Ferries** ✉ Merrion Row, Southside ☎ 01/661-0511 ⊕ www.irishferries.com. **P & O** ✉ Terminal 3, Dublin Port, City Center ☎ 01/407-3434 ⊕ www.poferries.com. **Stena Line** ✉ Ferryport, Dun Laoghaire, South County Dublin ☎ 01/204-7777 ⊕ www.stenaline.co.uk.

BY BUS

Busaras, just behind the Custom House on the Northside, is Dublin's main station for buses to and from the city. Bus Éireann is the main intercity bus company, with service throughout the country. Aircoach has direct bus connections to Cork and Belfast, and is usually a bit cheaper than Bus Éireann. In town, there's an extensive network of buses, most of which are green double-deckers. Some bus services run on cross-city routes, including the smaller "Imp" buses, but most buses start in the city center. Buses to the north of the city begin in the Lower Abbey Street–Parnell Street area, while those to the west begin in Middle Abbey Street and in the Aston Quay area. Routes to the southern suburbs begin at Eden Quay and in the College Street area. Several buses link the DART stations, and another regular bus route connects the two main provincial railway stations, Connolly and Heuston. If the destination board indicates AN LÁR, that means that the bus is going to the city center. Museumlink is a shuttle service that links up the National Museum of Natural History, National Museum of Archaeology and History, and the National Museum of Decorative Arts and History. You can catch it outside any of the three museums.

FARES & SCHEDULES   Intercity fares vary with the distance traveled. The Irish Rover Tourist pass, valid for all Bus Éireann services in the republic and for Ulsterbus services in Northern Ireland, costs €70 for three days' travel over eight consecutive days, and €158 for eight days' travel over 15 consecutive days. Timetables (€3.20) are available from Dublin Bus, staffed weekdays 9–5:30, Saturday 9–1. In the city, fares begin at 90 cents and are paid to the driver, who will accept inexact fares, but you'll have to go to the central office in Dublin to pick up your change as marked on your ticket. Change transactions and the city's heavy traffic can slow service considerably. Most bus lines run to 11:30 at night, but some late-night buses run Monday to Saturday until 3 AM on all major routes; the fare is €4–€6.

🚌 **Aircoach** ☎ 01/844-7118 ⊕ www.aircoach.ie. **Busaras** ☎ 01/830-2222. **Bus Éireann** ☎ 01/873-4222 ⊕ www.buseireann.ie. **Dublin Bus** ✉ 59 Upper O'Connell St., Northside ☎ 01/873-4222 ⊕ www.dublinbus.ie.

BY CAR

Renting a car in Dublin is very expensive, with high rates and a 12½% local tax. Gasoline is also expensive by U.S. standards, at around €1 a liter. Peak-period car-rental rates begin at around €260 a week for the smallest stick models, like a Ford Fiesta. Dublin has many car-rental companies, and it pays to shop around and to avoid "cowboy" outfits without proper licenses. A dozen car-rental companies have desks at Dublin Airport; all the main national and international firms also have branches in the city center. Traffic in Ireland has increased exponentially in the last few years, and nowhere has the impact been felt more than in Dublin, where the city's complicated one-way streets are congested not only during the morning and evening rush hours but often during much of the day. If possible, avoid driving a car except to get in and out of the city (and be sure to ask your hotel or guesthouse for clear directions to get you out of town).

🚗 Agencies **Avis** ✉ 1 Hanover St. E, Southside ☎ 01/677-5204 ⊕ www.avis.ie ✉ Dublin Airport, North County Dublin ☎ 01/844-5204. **Budget** ✉ 151 Lower Drumcondra Rd., North County Dublin ☎ 01/837-9802 ⊕ www.budget.ie ✉ Dublin Airport, North County Dublin ☎ 01/844-5919. **Dan Dooley** ✉ 42–43 Westland Row, Southside ☎ 01/677-2723 ⊕ www.dan-dooley.ie ✉ Dublin Airport, North County Dublin ☎ 01/844-5156. **Hertz** ✉ Leeson St. Bridge, Southside ☎ 01/660-2255 ⊕ www.hertz.ie ✉ Dublin Airport, North County Dublin ☎ 01/844-5466. **Europcar Murray's Rent-a-Car** ✉ Baggot St. Bridge, Southside ☎ 01/668-1777 ⊕ www.europcar.ie ✉ Dublin Airport, North County Dublin ☎ 01/844-4179.

BY TAXI

There are taxi stands beside the central bus station, and at train stations, O'Connell Bridge, St. Stephen's Green, College Green, and near major hotels; the Dublin telephone directory has a complete list. The initial charge is €3.40, with an additional charge of about €2 per kilometer thereafter. The fare is displayed on a meter (make sure it's on). You may, instead, want to phone a taxi company and ask for a cab to meet you at your hotel, but this may cost up to €2.55 extra. Many taxis run all night, but the demand, especially on weekends (and particularly near clubs on the Leeson Street strip and elsewhere, which stay open until 4 AM or later), can make for long lines at taxi stands. Hackney cabs, which also operate in the city, have neither roof signs nor meters and will sometimes respond to hotels' requests for a cab. Negotiate the fare before your journey begins. Although the taxi fleet in Dublin is large, the cabs are nonstandard and some cars are neither spacious nor in pristine condition. Cab Charge has a reliable track record. Metro is one of the city's biggest but also the busiest. VIP Taxis usually has a car available for a longer trip.

🚕 Taxi Companies **Cab Charge** ☎ 01/677-2222. **Metro** ☎ 01/668-3333. **VIP Taxis** ☎ 01/478-3333.

BY TRAIN & TRAM

Connolly Station provides train service to and from the east coast, Belfast, the north (with stops in Malahide, Skerries, and Drogheda), the northwest, and some destinations to the south, such as Wicklow and Arklow. Heuston Station is the place for trains to and from the south and west; trains run from here to Kildare Town, west of Dublin, via Celbridge, Sallins, and Newbridge. Pearse Station is for Bray and connections via Dun Laoghaire to the Liverpool-Holyhead ferries. Contact the Irish Rail Travel Centre for information.

An electric railway system, the Dublin Area Rapid Transit (DART), connects Dublin with Howth to the north and Bray to the south on a fast, efficient line. There are 25 stations on the route, which is the best means of getting to seaside destinations, such as Howth, Blackrock, Dun Laoghaire, Dalkey, Killiney, and Bray.

The LUAS tram service runs two lines right into the heart of the city. One line carries the super-sleek silver trams from Tallaght in the southwest to the Abbey Street station, located north of the Liffey, and on down to the city center's Connolly Station. This line also takes you from Royal Hospital Killmainham and carries you across the Liffey, through Smithfield, and down to the Abbey Street hub. The other line runs from the Sandyford residential suburb in the south sector of the city north to St. Stephen's Green—this line is useful for ferrying the tourist between the city district of Ballsbridge to St. Stephen's Green in the city center. Together, these lines cross the city center north and south, and so the LUAS is ideal for short hops across those areas.

FARES & SCHEDULES DART service starts at 6:30 AM and runs until 11:30 PM; at peak periods, 8–9:30 AM and 5–7 PM, trains arrive every five minutes. At other times of the day, the intervals between trains are 15 to 25 minutes. Call ahead to check precise departure times (they do vary, especially on bank holidays). Tickets can be bought at stations, but it's also possible to buy weekly rail tickets, as well as weekly or monthly "rail-and-bus" tickets, from the Irish Rail Travel Centre. Individual fares begin at €1.15 and range up to €3.60. You'll pay a heavy penalty for traveling the DART without a ticket. LUAS trams run from 5:30 AM until 12:30 AM Monday to Saturday and 7 AM until 11:30 PM on Sunday. They come every 7 to 10 minutes at peak times and every 15 to 20 minutes after that. Fares begin at €1.25 and increase according to the number of zones traveled.

🚆 Train Information **Irish Rail–Iarnod Éireann** ⊕ www.irishrail.ie/home. **Connolly Station** ✉ Amiens St., Northside. **DART** ☎ 01/836-6222 ⊕ www.irishrail.ie/dart. **Heuston Station** ✉ End of Victoria Quay, Dublin West. **Irish Rail Travel Centre** ✉ 35 Lower Abbey St., Northside ☎ 01/836-6222 ⊕ www.irishrail.ie/home. **LUAS** ☎ 800/300-604 ⊕ www.luas.ie. **Pearse Station** ✉ Westland Row, Southside.

Contacts & Resources

DUBLIN PASS

Like many tourist capitals around the world, Dublin now features a special pass to help travelers save on admission prices. In conjunction with Dublin Tourism, the Dublin Pass is issued for one, two, three, or six days, and allows free (or, rather, reduced, since the cards do cost something) admission to 30 sights, including the Guinness Brewery, the Dublin Zoo, the Dublin Writers Museum, and Christ Church Cathedral. Prices are €29 for one day; €49 for two days; €59 for three days; and €89 for six days; children's prices are much lower. You can buy your card online and have it waiting for you at one of Dublin's tourist information offices when you arrive. Another plus: you can jump to the head of any line at participating museums and sights.

🎫 **Dublin Tourism** ⊠ Suffolk St., off Grafton St., Southside ☎ 01/605-7700 in Dublin, 1850/230-330 in rest of Ireland ⊕ www.visitdublin.com/dublinpass.

EMERGENCIES

Call the Eastern Regional Health Authority for the names of doctors in the area. The Dublin Dental Hospital has emergency facilities and lists of dentists who provide emergency care. Hamilton Long, a Dublin pharmacy, is open Monday–Wednesday and Saturday 8:30–6, Thursday 8:30–8, and Friday 8:30–7. Temple Bar Pharmacy is open Monday–Wednesday, Friday, and Saturday 9–7, Thursday 9–8.

🎫 **Doctors & Dentists Dublin Dental Hospital** ⊠ 20 Lincoln Pl., Southside ☎ 01/662-0766 ⊕ web1.dental.tcd.ie. **Eastern Regional Health Authority** ☎ 01/679-0700 ⊕ www.erha.ie.

🎫 **Emergency Services Ambulance, fire, police (gardaí)** ☎ 999.

🎫 **Hospitals Beaumont** ⊠ Beaumont Rd., North County Dublin ☎ 01/837-7755 ⊕ www.beaumont.ie. **Mater** ⊠ Eccles St., Northside ☎ 01/830-1122 ⊕ www.mater. ie. **St. James's** ⊠ 1 James St., Dublin West ☎ 01/453-7941 ⊕ www.stjames.ie. **St. Vincent's** ⊠ Elm Park, South County Dublin ☎ 01/269-4533 ⊕ www.stvincents.ie.

🎫 **Late-Night Pharmacies Hamilton Long** ⊠ 5 Upper O'Connell St., Northside ☎ 01/874-8456. **Temple Bar Pharmacy** ⊠ 20 E. Essex St., Temple Bar ☎ 01/670-9751.

INTERNET CAFÉS

In the city center are a number of Internet cafés, which charge between €3 and €6 an hour. Some of the cheapest places are on Thomas Street, as it's not smack in the center of town. Central Cybercafe is one of the city's best, with top-notch computers and a good coffee bar.

🎫 **Central Cybercafe** ⊠ 6 Grafton St., Southside ☎ 01/677-8298 ⊕ www.globalcafe. ie. **Surf Centre One** ⊠ 79a Talbot Street St., Northside ☎ 01/855-2560 ⊕ www. worldlink.ie.

SIGHTSEEING TOURS

BUS TOURS Dublin Bus has three- and four-hour "City Tours" of the city center that include Trinity College, the Royal Hospital Kilmainham, and Phoenix Park. The one-hour City Tour, with hourly departures, allows you to hop on and off at any of the main sights. Tickets are available from the driver or Dublin Bus. There's also a continuous guided open-top bus tour (€12.50), run by Dublin Bus, which allows you to hop on and off the bus as often as you wish and visit some 15 sights along its route. The company also conducts a north-city coastal tour, going to Howth, and a south-city tour, traveling as far as Enniskerry.

Gray Line Tours runs city-center tours that cover the same sights as the Dublin Bus itineraries. Bus Éireann organizes day tours out of Busaras, the main bus station, to country destinations such as Glendalough.

🎫 **Bus Éireann** ☎ 01/836-6111 ⊕ www.buseireann.ie/site/home. **Dublin Bus** ☎ 01/873-4222 ⊕ www.dublinbus.ie/home. **Gray Line Tours** ☎ 01/670-8822 ⊕ www.grayline.com.

CARRIAGE TOURS Horse-drawn-carriage tours are available around Dublin and in Phoenix Park. For tours of the park, contact the Department of the Arts, Culture and the Gaeltacht. Carriages can be hired at the Grafton Street corner of St. Stephen's Green, without prior reservations.

🎫 **Department of the Arts, Culture and the Gaeltacht** ☎ 01/661-3111.

PUB & MUSICAL TOURS Dublin Tourism has a booklet to its self-guided "Rock 'n Stroll" Trail, which covers 16 sights with associations to such performers as Bob Geldof, Christy Moore, Sinéad O'Connor, and U2. Most of the sights are in the city center and Temple Bar. The Traditional Musical Pub Crawl begins at Oliver St. John Gogarty and moves on to other famous Temple Bar pubs. Led by two professional musicians who perform songs and tell the story of Irish music, the tour is given May–October, daily at 7:30 PM; the cost is €9. Discover Dublin runs the Musical Bus every Friday and Saturday night, with musicians on board leading you on a pub crawl of Dublin's best rock-and-roll pubs. It costs €22. The award-winning Viking Splash Tour is a big hit with kids. The amphibious ex–U.S. military vehicle takes your on a tour of the city center before launching onto the water down by the IFSC. Kids get a Viking helmet to wear and love terrifying native pedestrians with the "Viking Roar." An adult ticket is €16–€18.

Colm Quilligan arranges highly enjoyable evening tours of the literary pubs of Dublin, where "brain cells are replaced as quickly as they are drowned." The *Dublin Literary Pub Crawl* is a 122-page guide to those Dublin pubs with the greatest literary associations; it's widely available in the city's bookstores.

🎵 **Colm Quilligan** ☎ 01/454-0228 ⊕ www.dublinpubcrawl.com. **Music Bus** ☎ 01/475-3313. **Oliver St. John Gogarty** ✉ 57 Fleet St., Temple Bar ☎ 01/671-1822. **Traditional Musical Pub Crawl** ✉ Discover Dublin, 20 Lower Stephens St., Southside ☎ 01/478-0191 ⊕ www.discoverdublin.ie. **Viking Splash** ☎ 01/707-6000 ⊕ www.vikingsplashtours.com.

WALKING TOURS Historical Walking Tours of Dublin, run by Trinity College history graduate students, are excellent two-hour introductions to the city. The Bord Fáilte–approved tours take place from May to September, starting at the front gate of Trinity College, daily at 11 AM and 3 PM, with an extra tour on weekends at noon; tours are also available October–April, Friday–Sunday at noon. The cost is €10.

Dublin Footsteps conducts a Georgian/Literary Walking Tour that leaves from the Grafton Street branch of Bewley's Oriental Café June–September, daily at 11; each tour lasts approximately two hours and costs €9. Trinity Tours organizes walks of the Trinity College campus on weekends from March 17 (St. Patrick's Day) through mid-May and from mid-May to September daily. The half-hour tour costs €7.60 and includes the *Book of Kells* exhibit; tours start at the college's main gate every 40 minutes from 10:15 AM. There are generally nine tours a day. The Zozimus Experience is an enjoyable walking tour of Dublin's medieval past, with a particular focus on the seedy, including great escapes, murders, and mythical happenings. Tours, which are led by a guide in costume, are by arrangement only and start at the main gate of Dublin Castle at 6:45 PM; the cost is €10 per person. (Prepare yourself for a surprise.)

🎵 **Dublin Footsteps** ☎ 01/496-0641 ⊕ www.dublintourist.com. **Historical Walking Tours of Dublin** ☎ 01/878-0227 ⊕ www.historicalinsights.ie. **Trinity Tours** ☎ 01/608-2320. **Zozimus Experience** ☎ 01/661-8646 ⊕ www.zozimus.com.

VISITOR INFORMATION

Fáilte Ireland, the Irish Tourist Board, has its own visitor information offices in the entrance hall of its headquarters at Baggot Street Bridge; it's open weekdays 9:15–5:15. A suburban tourist office in Tallaght is open March–December, daily 9:30–5.

The main Dublin Tourism center is in the former (and still spectacular) St. Andrew's Church on Suffolk Street and is open July–September, Monday–Saturday 8:30–6, Sunday 11–5:30, and October–June, daily 9–6. On-site are many service counters, souvenir stands, and even a sandwich bar. The Dublin Airport branch is open daily 8 AM–10 PM; the branch at the Ferryport, Dun Laoghaire, is open daily 10–9.

The Temple Bar Information Centre produces the easy-to-use, annually updated *Temple Bar Guide,* which provides complete listings of the area's stores, pubs, restaurants, clubs, galleries, and other cultural venues.
🚩 Tourist Information **Fáilte Ireland** ✉ Baggot St. Bridge, Southside ☎ 01/602–4000 in Dublin, 1850/230–330 in rest of Ireland ✉ The Square, Tallaght ☎ 1850/230–330 ⊕ www.failteireland.ie. **Dublin Tourism** ✉ Suffolk St., off Grafton St., Southside ☎ 01/605–7700 in Dublin, 1850/230–330 in rest of Ireland ⊕ www.visitdublin.com. **Temple Bar Information Centre** ✉ 18 Eustace St., Temple Bar ☎ 01/671–5717.

Dublin Environs

INCLUDING COUNTIES CAVAN, DUBLIN, KILDARE,
LOUTH, MEATH, AND WICKLOW

Hiking in County Wicklow

WORD OF MOUTH

"As I am fascinated by Celtic history, the Hill of Tara was a must. I arrived early, around 9:30 AM. There was no one around, so I walked up to the hill and earthworks. I could see what looked like the whole of Ireland spread out before me. Warning: here is where I go hippie and mystical! I could feel the power of the land coursing through me, like I was a conduit for the lightning of the island traveling into the sky. It was incredible! I went back later with the official tour group, around 11 AM, and it just wasn't the same."   —GreenDragon

www.fodors.com/forums

WELCOME TO DUBLIN ENVIRONS

TOP REASONS TO GO

★ **Newgrange at Sunset:** Just standing amid these 5,000-year-old tombs (which pre-date the Pyramids), you'll wonder: how did they build them?

★ **A Day at the Races:** The Irish may like a drink, but they really love to gamble, as you'll discover in Kildare, center of the Irish bloodstock world.

★ **Georgian Country Houses:** Modesty never struck the rich Anglo-Irishman, whose propensity to flaunt his riches led to such over-the-top stately homes as Castletown, Russborough, and Powerscourt.

★ **Wicklow is for Walkers:** There's no better way to meet the locals and see the land than trekking out on the 132-km-long Wicklow Way, Ireland's most popular trail.

★ **Early Morning at Glendalough:** Before the tour buses arrive, channel the spirit of the 6th-century, isolation-seeking St. Kevin.

St Kevin's Church, Glendalough

1 The Boyne Valley. Set 48 km (30 mi) north of Dublin, this entire area is redolent with prehistoric and pagan sites. You don't have to be an Indiana Jones to be awed by the Hill of **Tara** or **Newgrange**, a Neolithic burial ground and solar observatory still evocative of the mysteries of pre-Celtic civilization.

Powerscourt Waterfall

2 County Wicklow. Set with dense woods and idyllic lakes, "the garden of Ireland" is a favorite day-out for Dubliners, thanks to sylvan estates like **Powerscourt** and **Glendalough**, a 6th-century monastic site so serene you may be tempted to renounce the profane world.

Old Lighthouses, Wicklow Head, County Wicklow

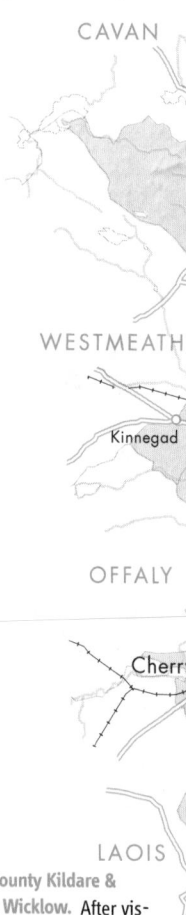

3 County Kildare & West Wicklow. After visiting stately **Castletown** and **Russborough**—two monuments to Ireland's Georgian age of elegance—check out Derby Day at the **Curragh** racecourse. The grinning bookmakers are just waiting to take your money.

NORTHERN IRELAND

ARMAGH

DOWN

MONAGHAN

Omeath

Carlingford Lough

N53

Dundalk

Inniskeen

N52

Dundalk Bay

N2

Ardee

N52

N2

LOUTH

Kells

1

Boyne Valley

Slane

Drogheda

N51

N3

Newgrange

N51

Navan

N1

N2

Irish Sea

Hill of Tara

N3

DUBLIN

Trim

MEATH

Swords

Lambay Island

M1

Drumleck Point

M4

Dublin

KILDARE

N7

Castletown

N81

3

Russborough House

N7

Bray

M11

Naas

Powerscourt

2

The Curragh

WICKLOW

Kilmacanoge

Kildare

N78

Kilcullen

Ballinalea

Wicklow Mountains

Wicklow Way

Glendalough

Wicklow

Wicklow Head

N9

CARLOW

0   10 mi

0   10 km

Arklow

N11

WEXFORD

GETTING ORIENTED

Dublin Environs includes three main regions: County Wicklow's coast and mountains, the Boyne Valley, and County Kildare. The Boyne Valley includes much of counties Meath and Louth to the north and east of Dublin. Kildare and Wicklow are to the southeast and south of the capital. Tour this small region, or opt for day-trips from Dublin, especially to the Wickow mountains, which rise up suddenly at the fringes of the city.

Malahide Castle, County Dublin

DUBLIN ENVIRONS PLANNER

Finding a Place to Stay

A lot of people opt to stay in Dublin and take day trips to the environs. If that's the case a hotel on the south side of the city or in South County Dublin might be a good idea if you're planning to spend time in Wicklow or East Kildare. For Meath and Louth a hotel on the north side or to the west of the city might work better. If don't want to "commute" from the city then the noted country-house hotels around Kildare and Wicklow are a great option. They are surprisingly good value for the unique, luxurious experience they offer. But they do tend to get booked up well in advance, especially at weekends when they fill up with Dubliners chilling out for a couple of days. B&B's are another good option and though the ones in this region tend to be a little more expensive than other parts of Ireland, they also are a little classier and more stylish. Reservations are recommended year-round.

Muiredach Cross, Monasterboice.

Getting Around

Driving distances to the nether reaches of this chapter from Dublin are less than two hours (in decent traffic) so the best option might be to base yourself in the city and make a couple of day trips into this region. For example, a trip to Newgrange, Tara, and the National Stud might take up one day. Then you can head into the Wicklow Mountains to Powerscourt House and then to Glendalough on another day. Country-house buffs can easily knock off Castletown and Russborough—two of the grandest in the land—in one afternoon. A car is handy, of course, and gives you flexibility to get off the beaten track and explore the numerous small towns and villages of Wicklow and west Kildare. But if you don't fancy driving on small country roads then there are numerous one-day and half-day bus tours from the city that take in the major sights.

The Big Two

Glendalough and Newgrange really are unique places, historically and indeed spiritually. They are not sights to be rushed through with a check-list of things to see. It's all about the atmosphere, the serenity, and the silence. So, in both places give yourself plenty of time.

They are also best enjoyed in relative tranquility, so try go as early in the morning as you can and beat the crowds. Strangely enough both places may in fact be at their best outside the summer months.

Newgrange was designed around the winter solstice, and seems to take on a special, etherial feel at that time of year.

Glendalough can be breathtaking on a clear spring day when the flora and fauna assault the senses.

Pack for the possibility of bad weather in both places, and bring along some food as you don't want to be forced to track back to the visitor center to get a snack.

Kerb stones with carvings around the great mound at Knowth

Guided Tours

Bus Éireann (☎ 01/836–6111, ⊕ www.buseireann.ie/site/home) runs guided bus tours to many of the historic and scenic locations throughout the Dublin environs daily in summer. Visits include trips to Glendalough in Wicklow; Boyne Valley and Newgrange in County Louth; and the Hill of Tara, Trim, and Navan in County Meath. All tours depart from Busaras Station, Dublin; information is available by phone Monday–Saturday 8:30–7, Sunday 10–7. Gray Line Tours (☎ 01/670–8822, ⊕ www.grayline.com), a privately owned touring company, also runs many guided bus tours throughout the Dublin environs between May and September. Their Grand Wicklow Tour lasts seven hours, as does their day trip to Newgrange and Mellifont Abbey. Prices start at €32. Wild Wicklow Tours (☎ 01/280–1899, ⊕ www.wildwicklow.ie) uses small minibuses that can handle smaller groups and take you off the beaten track. Their full-day trips to Glendalough also take in Avoca Handweavers and a Dublin coastal drive. Prices start at €28. Railtours Ireland (☎ 01/856–0045, ⊕ www.railtoursireland.com) has a half-day rail tour into the Wicklow Mountains. The train stops at Arklow and then a bus takes you through Avoca and on to Glendalough. The cost is €39.

Dining & Lodging Price Categories (in Euros)				
$$$$	**$$$**	**$$**	**$**	**¢**
Restaurants over €29	€22–29	€15–22	€8–15	under €8
Hotels over €230	€180–230	€130–180	€80–130	under €80

Restaurant prices are for a main course at dinner. Hotel prices are for a standard double room in high season.

The Great Outdoors

Although the counties surrounding Dublin comprise a small region, they have mountains, seashore, lakes, rivers, and flat plains. This varied topography makes it perfect for a host of outdoor activities.

Wicklow is Ireland's premier walking county, with the mighty Wicklow Way trail the central attraction. Many of Ireland's best golf courses are also in the region, with the majestic K club in Kildare topping the list as home of the 2006 Ryder Cup.

Sailing and water sports are popular all along the coast north and south of the city, with Brittas Bay north of Arklow a favorite beach and Carlingford Loch east of Dundalk a center for water sports. Lessons and equipment are usually available at each location, for a price of course. The Boyne, Liffey, and many smaller rivers and lakes make the area perfect for course and salmon fishing. Tackle and boats are usually rentable nearby.

HOW'S THE WEATHER?

While certainly not the wettest part of Ireland (the West gets that dubious distinction), the counties around Dublin do get their fair share of rain. So always plan for the worst and bring a warm sweater and a light raincoat. June, July, August, and September tend to be the driest months and the good news is that the rain in the region in summer is usually light and short-lived. Wicklow, with all its hills and valleys, seems to have an obscure microclimate of its own, so don't rely too much on the weatherman to get it right.

Updated by
Anto Howard

LIKE AN OPEN-AIR MUSEUM layered with legendary Celtic sites, grand gardens, and elegant Palladian country estates, the small counties immediately north, south, and west of Dublin—historically known as the Pale—seem expressly designed for the sightseer. Due to its location on the Irish Sea, facing Europe, the region has always been the first to attract conquerors, and the first over which they exercised the greatest influence. Traces of each new wave remain: the Celts chose Tara as the center of their kingdom; the Danes sailed the Rivers Boyne and Liffey to establish many of today's towns; and the region's great Protestant-built houses of the 18th century remind us that the Pale was the starting point and administrative center for the long, violent English colonization of the whole island.

The Dublin environs include three basic geographical regions: County Wicklow's coast and mountains, the Boyne Valley, and County Kildare. Lying tantalizingly close to the south of Dublin is the mountainous county of Wicklow, which contains some of the most *et-in-Arcadia-ego* scenery in the Emerald Isle. Here, the gently rounded Wicklow Mountains—to some, they are Ireland's finest—contain the evocative monastic settlement at Glendalough, many later abbeys and churches, and scores of the most beguiling attractions for the art lover: these are the great 18th-century estates of the Anglo-Irish aristocracy, whose reigning lords and ladies, prone to a certain sense of inferiority, were determined not to be outdone by the extravagant efforts of their English compatriots. The result was a string of spectacular stately home extravaganzas, such as Castletown, Powerscourt, and Russborough. Once you see their astonishingly elegant decoration, you may give thanks for the existence of vanity. A quick change of pace is nearby—an impressive eastern coastline that stretches from counties Wicklow to Louth, punctuated by delightful harbor towns and fishing villages. The coast is virtually unspoiled for its entire length.

North of Dublin lies the Boyne Valley, with its abundant ruins of Celtic Ireland extending from counties Meath to Louth. Some of the country's most evocative Neolithic ruins—including the famous passage graves at Newgrange—are nestled into this landscape, where layer upon layer of history reach back into earlier, unknowable ages. It was west of Drogheda—a fascinating town settled by the Vikings in the early 10th century—that the Tuatha De Danann, onetime residents of Ireland, went underground when defeated by invading Milesians and became, it's said, "the good people" (or fairies) of Irish legend. In pagan times this area was the home of Ireland's high kings, and the center of religious life. All roads led to Tara, the fabled Hill of Kings, the royal seat, and the place where the national assembly was held. Today, time seems to stand still—and you should, too, for it's almost sacrilegious to introduce a note of urgency here.

Southwest of Dublin are the flat pastoral plains of County Kildare; the plains stretch between the western Midlands and the foothills of the Dublin and Wicklow mountains—both names actually refer to the same mountain range, but each marks its county's claim to the land. Kildare is the flattest part of Ireland, a natural playing field for breeding, training, and racing some of the world's premier Thoroughbreds.

Rapid, carnivorous expansion of the capital city in the last decade has seen its suburban limits spread deep into the once bucolic areas of Meath and Kildare and the natives of these areas fear that their more rural way of life is under threat. Don't be surprised to hear Dublin accents starting to dominate in towns like Navan and Nass. But the new prosperity has meant the local young men and women no longer have to head off up to "the big smoke" of Dublin or even further afield to find work and the counties of the Pale are seeing their populations rise for the first time in decades.

Exploring Dublin Environs

This chapter is organized into three sections, each of which makes a reasonable day trip. Keep in mind that it's easy to lose an hour or so making detours, chatting with locals, and otherwise enjoying the unexpected. The itineraries above cover the area's highlights; if you have fewer than three days, use parts of each day's suggested itinerary to plan your excursion. A car is essential for visiting most sights, and don't plan on visiting both the north and south of Dublin during the same day. There are some points of interest accessible by public transport: bus tours from Dublin cover County Wicklow as far as Glendalough in the southwest and the Boyne Valley to the north; suburban bus services reach into the foothills of the Dublin Mountains; and Bus Éireann services take in the outlying towns. Some popular sights have direct connections to Dublin, including Enniskerry and Powerscourt Estate, which can be reached by taking the No. 44 bus from the Dublin quays area.

THE BOYNE VALLEY

For every wistful schoolboy in Ireland the River Boyne is a name that resonates with history and adventure. It was on the banks of that river in 1014 that the Celtic chieftain Brian Boru defeated the Danish in a decisive battle that returned the east of Ireland to native rule. It was also by this river that Protestant William of Orange defeated the Catholic armies of exiled James II of England, in 1690. In fact this whole area, only 48 km (30 mi) north of cosmopolitan Dublin, is soaked in stories and legends that predate the pyramids. You can't throw a stick anywhere in the valley without hitting some trace of Irish history. The great prehistoric, pagan, and Celtic monuments of the wide arc of fertile land known as the Boyne Valley invariably evoke a sense of wonder. You don't have to be an archaeologist to be awed by Newgrange and Knowth—set beside the River Boyne—or the Hill of Tara, Mellifont Abbey, or the High Cross of Monasterboice. One way to approach exploring this area is to start at the town of Trim, the locale closest to Dublin, and work your way north. Keep in mind that Omeath and the scenic Cooley Peninsula at the end of this section are on the border of Northern Ireland. (If you make it this far north, consult Chapter 8, particularly the

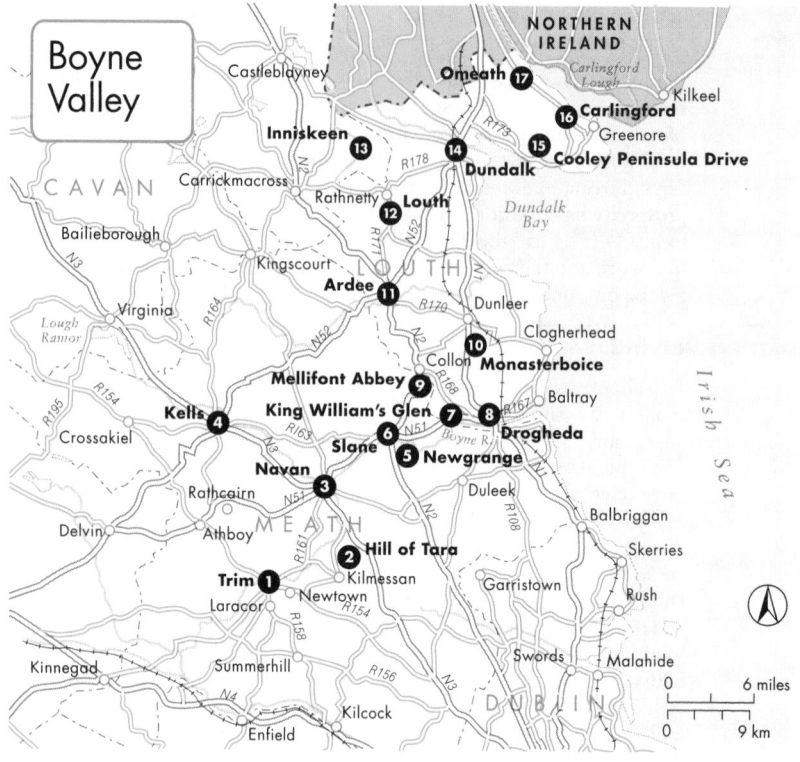

Boyne
Valley

coverage of the Mountains of Mourne, which are just across Carlingford Lough.)

Trim

1 *51 km (32 mi) northwest of Dublin via N3 to R154.*

The heritage town of Trim, on the River Boyne, contains some of the
finest medieval ruins in Ireland. In 1359, on the instructions of King Edward III, the town was walled and its fortifications strengthened. In the
15th century several parliaments were held here. Oliver Cromwell massacred most of its inhabitants when he captured the town in 1649.

Trim Castle, the largest Anglo-Norman fortress in Ireland, dominates present-day Trim from its 2½-acre site, which slopes down to the river's placid
waters. Built by Hugh de Lacy in 1173, the castle was soon destroyed, and
then rebuilt from 1190 to 1220. The ruins include an enormous keep
with 70-foot-high turrets flanked by rectangular towers. The outer castle wall is almost 500 yards long, and five D-shape towers survive. So
impressive is the castle it was used as a medieval backdrop in Mel Gibson's movie *Braveheart*. The admission price includes a house tour.
✉ *Trim* ☎ *046/943–8619* ⊕ *www.heritageireland.ie* ⚑ *Keep and*

DUBLIN ENVIRONS THROUGH THE AGES

You might think the counties that surround Dublin—Meath, Louth, Kildare, and Wicklow—suffer something of an inferiority complex in the shadow of the historic capital city on the Liffey. But the area historically known as the Pale can boast the oldest traces of civilization on the island of Ireland. Newgrange, the Neolithic burial chamber and solar observatory, dates from around 3200 BC and stands as a mysterious, enigmatic trace of a pre-Celtic civilization. The Celts, too, when they came, found a special resonance in this region and the Hill of Tara became the center of their spiritual and, to a lesser extent, political life. Next came the Normans, who quickly conquered the Pale and built great castles and walled towns to hold back the hordes of natives beyond. A long, gradual conquest of the rest of the island followed, but the aristocracy liked to remain near the political cauldron of Dublin. Thus, in the 18th-century Golden Age of the Irish nobility, they chose to build many of their great houses and ornate gardens in the counties surrounding the capital: the lavish Xanadus of Castletown, Russborough, and Powerscourt stand as monuments to their pride and prodigality. With the decline of the Irish gentry and the rise of the native farmer the land around Dublin became prized as some of the most fertile in the country. But now the bittersweet arrival of the Celtic Tiger's booming economy has seen rapid expansion of Dublin and a rude suburban intrusion into the once pastoral areas on its borders. But Kildare, Meath, Louth, and Wicklow have seen enough invasions come and go to know that history is a long tale whose outcome always surprises.

grounds €3.50, grounds only €1.50 ⊗ *Easter–Oct., daily 10–6; Nov.–Easter, weekends 10–5.*

Facing the river is the **Royal Mint,** a ruin that illustrates Trim's political importance in the Middle Ages. It produced coins with colorful names like "Irelands" and "Patricks" right up into the 15th century. The **Yellow Steeple** overlooks Trim from a ridge situated opposite the castle. The structure was built in 1368 and is a remnant of the Augustinian abbey of St. Mary's, founded in the 13th century, which itself was the site of a great medieval pilgrimage to a statue of the Blessed Virgin. Much of the tower was deliberately destroyed in 1649 to prevent its falling into Cromwell's hands, and today only the striking, 125-foot-high east wall remains. The Church of Ireland **St. Patrick's Cathedral** (⊠ Loman St.) dates from early in the 19th century, but the square tower is from an earlier structure built in 1449.

In the old town hall, the "The Power and the Glory" audiovisual display of the **Visitor Center** tells the story of the arrival of the Normans and of medieval Trim. ⊠ *Castle St.* ☎ *046/943-7227* ⊕ *www. meathtourism.ie* ✉ *€3.20 for audiovisual show* ⊗ *Mon., Tues., Fri., and Sat. 10:30–5, Sun. noon–5:30.*

If your ancestors are from County Meath, take advantage of the family-history tracing service at the **Meath Heritage and Genealogy Center.** ✉ *Castle St.* ☎ *046/943–6633* ✉ *Free* 🕐 *Mon.–Thurs. 9–1 and 1:30–5, Fri. 9–2.*

At **Newtown,** 1¼ km (¾ mi) east of Trim on the banks of the River Boyne, are the ruins of what was once the largest cathedral in Ireland, built beginning in 1210 by Simon de Rochfort, the first Anglo-Norman bishop of Meath. At **Laracor,** 3 km (2 mi) south of Trim on R158, a wall to the left of the rectory is where Jonathan Swift (1667–1745), the satirical writer, poet, and author of *Gulliver's Travels,* was rector from 1699 until 1714, when he was made dean of St. Patrick's Cathedral in Dublin. Nearby are the walls of the cottage where Esther Johnson, the "Stella" who inspired much of Swift's writings, once lived. One of the most pleasant villages of south County Meath, **Summerhill,** 8 km (5 mi) southeast of Laracor along R158, has a large square and a village green with a 15th-century cross. **Cnoc an Linsigh,** an attractive area south of Summerhill with forest walks and picnic sites, is ideal for a half day of meandering. Many of the lanes that crisscross this part of County Meath provide delightful driving between high hedgerows, and afford occasional views of the lush, pastoral countryside.

Where to Stay & Eat

$–$$ ✕🏨 **Castle Arch Hotel.** This newly refurbished hotel unashamedly hypes up the "castle" theme with its almost fairy-tale, lush decor in the guest rooms, not to mention the solid stone wall (complete with shooting window) that now adorns the bar–restaurant area. But behind all the hype there's a solid, reliable, small hotel with a great location right near the center of town and on the bank of the river. The bar has a good carvery and lively weekend entertainment, and the cozy restaurant plays it safe but sure with quality produce and typical Irish dishes like rack of lamb. ✉ *Trim, Co. Meath* ☎ *046/943–1516* 🖷 *046/943–6002* 🛏 *22 rooms* ♨ *Restaurant, bar* ▭ *AE, MC, V* ¶◎¶ *BP.*

¢ 🏨 **Tigh Catháin.** The "House of O'Catháin" is a Tudor-style country cottage about 1 km (½ mi) outside of town on the Longwood road. Owner Marie Keane has artfully decorated the three large bedrooms in different color schemes echoing the natural colors of the region. But the real wonders here are the lovely gardens out back and in front, perfect for lounging around in the sun. Family rooms include a double and two single beds. ✉ *High St., Co. Meath* ☎ *046/943–1996* ⊕ *www.tighcathaintrim.com* 🛏 *3 rooms* ¶◎¶ *BP.*

Hill of Tara

❷ In the legends and the popular imagination of the Irish this ancient site has taken on mythic proportions. As with much of the idealization of the Celtic past, it was the 19th-century revival led by Yeats and Lady Gregory that was responsible for the near-religious veneration of this Celtic site, set at the junction of the five ancient roads of Ireland, and known in popular folklore as the seat of the High Kings of Ireland. The 19th-century ballad by Thomas Moore, "The Harp That Once Through Tara's Halls," was also a major factor in the long over-romanticized view

Calling All Hike-a-holics

WHETHER YOU'RE A NOVICE or veteran hiker, Wicklow's gentle, rolling hills are a terrific place to begin an Irish walking vacation. Devoted hikers come from all over the world to traverse the 137-km (85-mi) Wicklow Way (☎ 01/493-4059), the first long-distance trail to open in Ireland and one of the best. Wicklow is Ireland's little Alps, with bracing fresh air guaranteed among the blue skies and mountain heather and gorse. Much of the route lies above 1,600 feet and follows rough sheep tracks, forest firebreaks, and old bog roads (rain gear, windproof clothing, and sturdy footwear are essential). The trail is picked up in the outskirts of Dublin suburbs, in Marlay Park, just south of Dublin city center, then ascends into the Wicklow mountain foothillls, before passing glens, farms,

and historic sights like Rathgall, home to the Kings of Leinster, and the Mill of Purgatory—a venerated "wardrobe" in Aghowle Church—before finishing up in Clonegal. Consider participating in one of the walking festivals held at Easter, in May, and in autumn. If your feet are less than bionic, you might opt for biking, another excellent way to see the area.

County Wicklow sponsors three annual walking festivals. The two-day Rathdrum Easter Walking Festival (☎ 0404/46262) includes hill walks of varying lengths over Easter weekend. The first weekend of May, the Wicklow Mountains May Walking Festival (☎ 0404/66058) is centered on Blessington. The Wicklow Mountains Autumn Walking Festival (☎ 0404/66058) is based in the Glenmalure area.

---

of Tara. Today, its ancestral banqueting hall and great buildings (one was the former palace of the Ard Rí, or High King) have all vanished but for a few columns. Still, the site is awe-inspiring. From the top of the Hill—it rises more than 300 feet above sea level—you can see across the flat central plain of Ireland, with the mountains of east Galway visible from nearly 160 km (100 mi) away. In the mid-19th century, the nationalist leader Daniel O'Connell staged a mass rally here that supposedly drew more than a million people—which would be nearly a third of Ireland's current population. On-site, first pay a call on the Interpretative Center housed in an old Church of Ireland church on the hillside. Here, you can learn the story of Tara and its legends. Without this background it will be difficult to identify many of the earthworks at Tara. Or just call upon your imagination to evoke the millennia-old spirit of the place and picture it in its prime, with the tribes congregating for some great pagan ceremony.

Systematic excavation by 20th-century archaeologists has led to the conclusion that the largest remains are those of an Iron Age fort that had multiple ring forts, some of which were ruined in the 19th century by religious zealots from England searching for the Ark of the Covenant here. The "Mound of the Hostages," a Neolithic passage grave, most likely gave the place its sacred air. During the hill's reign as a royal seat, which lasted to the 11th century, a great *feis* (national assembly) was held here every third year, during which laws were passed and tribal disputes settled. Tara's influence waned with the arrival of Christianity; the last king to live here was Malachy II, who died in 1022. But like with so many other prominent sites of the Irish pre-Christian era, Christianity remade Tara in its own image. Today a modern statue of St. Patrick stands here, as does a pillar stone that may have been the coronation stone (it was reputed to call out in approval when a king was crowned). In the graveyard of the adjacent Anglican church is a pillar with the worn image of a pagan god and a Bronze Age stone standing on end. ⊠ *Hill of Tara* ☎ *046/902–5903* ⊕ *www.heritageireland.ie* ✉ *€2* ⊙ *May–Oct., daily 10–6.*

> ### FIRES OF FAITH
>
> The Hill of Tara's decline was predicted one Easter Eve in the 5th century when, in accordance with the Druid religion, the lighting of fires was forbidden. Suddenly, on a hillside some miles away, flames were spotted. "If that fire is not quenched now," said a Druid leader, "it will burn forever and will consume Tara." The fire had been lit by St. Patrick at Slane, to celebrate the Christian rites of the Paschal.

Navan

❸ *10 km (6 mi) northwest of Hill of Tara on N3, 48 km (30 mi) north of Dublin on N3.*

Navan, at the crucial juncture of the Rivers Blackwater and Boyne, is a busy market and mining town with evidence of prehistoric settlements. It took off in the 12th century, when Hugh de Lacy, lord of Trim, had the place walled and fortified, making it a defensive stronghold of the English Pale in eastern Ireland. It's now the administrative center of Meath. At **St. Mary's Church,** built in 1839, you can find a late-18th-century wood carving of the Crucifixion, the work of a local artist, Edward Smyth—who at the time was the greatest sculptor Ireland had produced since the Middle Ages. On Friday, the **Fair Green,** beside the church, hosts a bustling outdoor market. ⊠ *Trimgate St.* ✉ *Free* ⊙ *Daily 8–8.*

The best views of town and the surrounding area are from the top of the **Motte of Navan,** a grassy mound said to be the tomb of Odhbha, the deserted wife of a Celtic king who, the story goes, died of a broken heart. It's more likely that the 50-foot-high mound is a natural formation. In the 12th century, D'Angulo, the Norman baron, adapted it into a motte and bailey (a type of medieval Norman castle), but there are no structural remains here from this period.

Kells

❹ *16 km (10 mi) northwest of Navan on N3.*

In the 9th century, a group of monks from Iona in Scotland took refuge at Kells (Ceanannus Mór) after being expelled by the Danes. St. Columba had founded a monastery here 300 years earlier, and although some historians think it was indigenous monks who wrote and illustrated the

Book of Kells—the Latin version of the four Gospels, and one of Ireland's greatest medieval treasures—most scholars now believe that the Scottish monks brought it with them. Reputed to have been fished out of a watery bog at Kells, the legendary manuscript was removed for safekeeping during the Cromwellian wars to Trinity College, Dublin, where it remains. A large exhibit is now devoted to it in the college's Old Library, where a few of the original pages at a time are on view. A copy of the *Book of Kells* is on display in the Church of Ireland **St. Columba's** in Kells; it's open until 5 on weekdays and until 1 on Saturday. Four elaborately carved High Crosses stand in the church graveyard; you'll find the stump of a fifth in the marketplace—during the 1798 uprising against British rule it was used as a gallows.

Similar in appearance to St. Kevin's Church at Glendalough and Cormac's Chapel at Cashel, **St. Colmcille's House** is a small, two-story, 7th-century church measuring about 24 feet square and nearly 40 feet high, with a steeply pitched stone roof. The nearly 100-foot-high **round tower,** adjacent to St. Colmcille's House, dates prior to 1076 and is in almost perfect condition. Its top story has five windows, each facing an ancient entrance into the medieval town.

Newgrange

5 Expect to see no less than one of the most spectacular prehistoric tombs in Europe when you come to Newgrange. Built in the 4th millennium BC—which makes it roughly 1,000 years older than Stonehenge—Newgrange was constructed with some 250,000 tons of stone, much of which came from the Wicklow Mountains, 80 km (50 mi) to the south. How the people who built this tumulus transported the stones to the spot remains a mystery. The mound above the tomb measures more than 330 feet across and reaches a height of 36 feet at the front. White quartz stone was used for the retaining wall, and egg-shape gray stones were studded at intervals. The passage grave may have been the world's earliest solar observatory. It was so carefully constructed that, for five days on and around the winter solstice, the rays of the rising sun still hit a roof box above the lintel at the entrance to the grave. The rays then shine for about 20 minutes down the main interior passageway to illuminate the burial chamber. The site was restored in 1962 after years of neglect and quarrying. The geometric designs on some stones at the center of the burial chamber continue to baffle experts.

FodorśChoice ★

The prehistoric sites of nearby Dowth and Knowth have been under excavation since 1962, and although Dowth is still closed to the public, **Knowth** is open at last. The great tumulus at Knowth is compa-

LET THERE BE A LIGHT SHOW

A visit to Newgrange's passage grave during the winter solstice is considered to be a memorable experience. You'll have to get on the nine-year waiting list to reserve one of the 24 places available on each of the five mornings (December 19–23). And then pray that no clouds obscure the sun and ruin the light show the Bronze Age builders intended.

rable in size and shape to New-grange, standing at 40 feet and having a diameter of approximately 214 feet. Some 150 giant stones, many of them beautifully decorated, surrounded the mound. More than 1,600 boulders, each weighing from one to several tons, were used in the construction. The earliest tombs and carved stones date from the Stone Age (3000 BC), although the site was in use until the early 14th century. In the early

Christian era (4th–8th centuries AD) it was the seat of the High Kings of Ireland. Much of the site is still under excavation, and you can often watch archaeologists at work here. Access to Newgrange and Knowth is solely via **Brú na Bóinne** (Palace of the Boyne), the Boyne Valley visitor center. Arrive early if possible, because Newgrange often sells out. The last tour leaves the visitor center one hour and 45 minutes before closing. ⊠ *Off N2, signposted from Slane, Donore* ☎ *041/988–0300* ⊕ *www.heritageireland.ie* ✉ *Newgrange and interpretive center €5.50; Knowth and interpretive center €4.25* ☼ *Newgrange and Knowth daily, Nov.–Feb., 9:30–5; Mar., Apr., and Oct., 9:30–5:30; May, 9–6:30; June–mid-Sept., 9–7; mid- to late-Sept., 9–6:30.*

Slane

❻ *2½ km (1½ mi) north of Newgrange, 46 km (29 mi) northwest of Dublin on N2.*

Slane Castle is the draw at this small, Georgian village, built in the 18th century around a crossroads on the north side of the River Boyne. The 16th-century building known as the **Hermitage** was constructed on the site where St. Erc, a local man converted to Christianity by St. Patrick himself, led a hermit's existence. All that remains of his original monastery is the faint trace of the circular ditch, but the ruins of the later church includes a nave and a chancel with a tower in between.

The stately 18th-century **Slane Castle** is beautifully situated overlooking a natural amphitheater. In 1981 the castle's owner, Anglo-Irish Lord Henry Mountcharles, staged the first of what have been some of Ireland's largest outdoor rock concerts; REM's show holds the record for attendance, with 70,000. In 2001, after a decade of renovation following a devastating fire, the castle reopened to the public. The tour includes the main hall, with its delicate plasterwork and beautiful stained glass, the dazzling red, neo-Gothic ballroom completed in 1821 for the visit of King George IV, and other rooms. The stunning parklands were laid out by Capability Brown, the famous 18th-century landscape gardener. ☎ *041/988–4400* ⊕ *www.slanecastle.ie* ✉ *€7* ☼ *May–early Aug., Sun.–Thurs. noon–5.*

North of Slane town is the 500-foot-high **Slane Hill,** where St. Patrick proclaimed the arrival of Christianity in 433 by lighting the Paschal Fire.

From the top, you have sweeping views of the Boyne Valley. On a clear day, the panorama stretches from Trim to Drogheda, a vista extending 40 km (25 mi).

A two-hour tour of farmer Willie Redhouse's fully functioning arable and livestock **Newgrange Farm** includes feeding the ducks, bottle-feeding the lambs, a tour of the aviaries with their exotic birds, and a donkey ride for the kids. Demonstrations of sheepdog work, threshing, and horseshoeing are given. Every Sunday at 3 PM the "Sheep Derby" takes place, with teddy bears tied astride the animals in the place of jockeys. Visiting children are made "owners" of individual sheep for the duration of the race. The farm lies 3 km (2 mi) east of Slane on N51. ☎ *041/982–4119* 🖂 *€7* ☼ *Easter–mid-Sept., Sun.–Fri. 10–5.*

Where to Stay & Eat

$–$$ ✕🏨 **Conyngham Arms Hotel.** Although built in the mid-19th century, the Conyngham Arms, at the crossroads in Slane, maintains a village-inn look. Four-poster beds in the guest rooms let you imagine sleeping like the aristocracy. The Gamekeeper's Lodge Bistro ($$) serves simple but delightful fresh meat and fish dishes. Try the salmon in season. Quality bar and snack food is also available. ⊠ *Co. Meath* ☎ *041/988–4444* 🖨 *041/982–4205* ⊕ *www.conynghamarms.com* 🛏 *16 rooms* ♿ *Restaurant, bar; no a/c* ⊟ *AE, MC, V* ⦷ *BP, FAP, MAP.*

King William's Glen

❼ On the northern bank of the River Boyne, King William's Glen is where a portion of King William of Orange's Protestant army hid before the Battle of the Boyne in 1690. They won by surprising the Catholic troops of James II, who were on the southern side, but many of the Protestant-Catholic conflicts in present-day Northern Ireland can be traced to the immediate aftermath of this battle. The site is marked with an orange-and-green sign; part of the site is also incorporated in the nearby, early-19th-century **Townley Hall Estate,** which has forest walks and a nature trail (the house is not open to the public).

Drogheda

❽ *6½ km (4 mi) east of King William's Glen on N51, 45 km (28 mi) north of Dublin on N1.*

Drogheda (pronounced draw-*hee*-da) is one of the most enjoyable and historic towns on the east coast of Ireland—and a setting for one of the most tragic events in Irish history (*see* the Bloody Cromwell CloseUp box). It was colonized in 911 by the Danish Vikings; two centuries later, the town was taken over by Hugh de Lacy, the Anglo-Norman lord of Trim, who was responsible for fortifying the towns along the River Boyne. At first, two separate towns existed, one on the northern bank, the other on the southern bank. In 1412, already heavily walled and fortified, Drogheda was unified, making it the largest English town in Ireland. Today, large 18th-century warehouses line the northern bank of the Boyne. The center of town, around West Street, is the historic heart of Drogheda. Towering over the river is the long **railway viaduct.** Built around 1850

Bloody Cromwell!

IN MUCH OF THE English-speaking world Oliver Cromwell is regarded as something of a hero, a deeply religious self-made man, master general, and leader of the victorious parliamentary side in the English Civil Wars.

But in Ireland, Cromwell's name is usually followed by a spit and a curse. In 1649 Old Ironsides arrived in Ireland to subdue a Royalist and Catholic rebellion once and for all. His methods were simple: burn every building, and kill every person that stood in his way.

"To Hell or to Connaught" (the latter being the most westerly of Ireland's four provinces) was the dire choice he offered the native population as he drove them ever westward and off the more fertile lands of the east and south. When he approached the walled town of Drogheda, the gates were closed to him.

Led by the Anglo-Irish Sir Arthur Aston, the native Catholic population bravely defended their town against Cromwell's relentless siege, twice driving back the advancing army. On the third attempt the town fell, and the order went out that no mercy was to be shown.

It's estimated that up to 3,500 men, women, and children were slaughtered. One group hid in the steeple of St. Peter's Church, so Cromwell burned it down with them all inside. Sir Arthur was beaten to death with his own wooden leg.

While the massacre at Drogheda frightened many Irish towns into submission (and thereby prevented other battles) the bloody stain on Cromwell's reputation was permanent.

as part of the railway line from Dublin to Belfast, it's still used and is a splendid example of Victorian engineering. Its height above the river makes the viaduct Drogheda's most prominent landmark.

The bank building on the corner of West and Shop streets, called the **Tholsel,** is an 18th-century square granite edifice with a cupola. The 13th-century **St. Laurence's Gate,** one of the two surviving entrances from Drogheda's original 11 gates in its town walls, has two four-story drum towers and is one of the most perfect examples in Ireland of a medieval town gate. **Butler's Gate,** near the Millmount Museum, predates St. Laurence's Gate by 50 years or more.

The Gothic-Revival Roman Catholic **St. Peter's Church** (⊠ West St.) houses the preserved head of St. Oliver Plunkett. Primate of all Ireland, he was martyred in 1681 at Tyburn in London; his head was pulled from the execution flames. A severe, 18th-century church within an enclosed courtyard, the Anglican **St. Peter's** (⊠ Fair St.) is rarely open except for Sunday services. It's worth a peek for its setting and the fine views over the town from the churchyard.

Perhaps the main attraction in Drogheda lies across the river from the town center. The **Millmount Museum and Martello Tower,** off the Dublin road (N1) south of Drogheda, shares space in a renovated British Army barracks with crafts workshops, including a pottery- and picture-gallery and studio. It was on the hill at Millmount that the townsfolk made their last stand against the bloodthirsty Roundheads of Cromwell. Perhaps in defiance of Cromwell's attempt to obliterate the town from the map, the museum contains relics of eight centuries of Drogheda's commercial and industrial past, including painted banners of the old trade guilds, a circular willow and leather coracle (the traditional fishing boat on the River Boyne), and many instruments and utensils from domestic and factory use. Most moving are the mementos of the infamous 1649 massacre of 3,000 people by Cromwell. There are also geological and archeaological displays. The exhibit inside the Martello Tower adjacent to the museum focuses on the military history of Drogheda. ⊠ *Millmount* ☎ *041/983–3097* ⊕ *www.millmount.net* ⚲ *Museum €4.50, tower €3* ⊘ *Mon.–Sat. 10–5:30, Sun. 2:30–5.*

Across the Meath border in County Dublin, 18 km (11 mi) south of Drogheda, is **Ardgillan Demesne,** one of the prettiest parks along the coast. Its 194 acres consist of rolling pastures, mixed woodland, and gardens overlooking the Bay of Drogheda, with splendid views of the coastline. The castle here, built in 1738 for a landowning family, rises two stories. Ground-floor rooms are decorated in Georgian and Victorian styles; first-floor rooms house a permanent display of 17th-century maps, and host an annual program of exhibitions. Guided tours are the only way to see the rest of the castle. ⊠ *Balbriggan* ☎ *01/849–2212* ⊕ *www.fingalcoco.ie* ⚲ *€6 for tour* ⊘ *Apr.–June and Sept., Tues.–Sun. 11–6; Oct.–Mar., Tues.–Sun. 11–4:30; July and Aug., daily 11–dusk.*

Where to Stay & Eat

¢–$ ✕ **Monk's.** This little café on the river is always full of locals looking for healthful food at a decent price. Monk's specializes in delicious, somewhat off-center sandwiches, including a wonderful goat-cheese bruschetta and a spicy Mexican chicken sandwich. The hot breakfasts are a treat, chunky French toast and fruit being the most popular dish. ⊠ *North Quay* ☎ *041/984–5630* ⊟ *MC, V.*

$$ ✕⚎ **Boyne Valley Hotel and Country Club.** A 1-km (½-mi) drive leads to this 19th-century mansion on 16 acres that was once owned by a Drogheda brewing family. The newer wing of this owner-run hotel has double rooms, all with contemporary furnishings and bright color schemes full of pinks and pastels. The public spaces have been restored in period fashion, with Neoclassical pillars, intricate plasterwork, and crystal chandeliers. A large conservatory houses a bar and overlooks the grounds, while a spacious hall is decorated with antiques and comfy chairs. The Cellar Restaurant specializes in fresh fish. ⊠ *Dublin Rd., Co. Louth* ☎ *041/983–7737* ⚐ *041/983–9188* ⊕ *www.boyne-valley-hotel. ie* ⚲ *71 rooms, 1 suite* ⚐ *Restaurant, 18-hole golf course, 2 tennis courts, indoor pool, health club, bar* ⊟ *AE, DC, MC, V* ⦿ *BP.*

Mellifont Abbey

❾ On the eastern bank of the River Mattock, which creates a natural border between Counties Meath and Louth, lie the remains of Mellifont Abbey, the first Cistercian monastery in Ireland. Founded in 1142 by St. Malachy, archbishop of Armagh, it was inspired by the formal structure surrounding a courtyard of St. Bernard of Clairvaux's monastery, which St. Malachy had visited. Among the substantial ruins are the two-story chapter house, built in 12th-century English-Norman style and once a daily meeting place for the monks; it now houses a collection of medieval glazed tiles. Four walls of the 13th-century octagonal lavabo, or washing place, still stand, as do some arches from the Romanesque cloister. At its peak Mellifont presided over almost 40 other Cistercian monasteries throughout Ireland, but all were suppressed by Henry VIII in 1539 after his break with the Catholic Church. Adjacent to the car park is a small **architectural museum** depicting the history of the abbey and the craftsmanship that went into its construction. ⊠ *Near Collon* ☎ *041/ 982–6459* ⊕ *www.heritageireland.ie* ⊠ *€2* ☉ *May–Sept., daily 10–5.*

Where to Eat

$$$–$$$$ ✕ **Forge Gallery Restaurant.** For generations the local forge was the burning heart of any rural Irish community and this well-established restaurant is still something of a beacon to locals and visitors for miles around. Warm rose and plum tones and antique furnishings decorate this two-story eatery in a converted forge, and an old fireplace fills the place with a comforting warmth and light. The cuisine mixes French Provençal with a strong hint of traditional Irish cooking. Two popular specialties are roast duckling served on a bed of pak choi, with spring onion, soy, and ginger sauce, and braised brace of quail with apricot, raisin, and apple stuffing. Make sure you try one of the seasonal homemade soups. Paintings by local artists hang in the reception area and are for sale. Reservations are essential on weekends. ⊠ *North of Slane on N2, Collon* ☎ *041/982–6272* ▤ *AE, DC, MC, V* ☉ *Closed Sun., Mon., and 2nd wk of Jan. No lunch Sat.*

Monasterboice

⑩ *8 km (5 mi) northeast of Mellifont Abbey on N1, 8 km (5 mi) north of Drogheda.*

Ireland has more carved-stone High Crosses than any other European country, and an outstanding collection is in the small, secluded village of Monasterboice, a former monastic settlement. Dating to AD 923, the **Muireadach Cross** stands nearly 20 feet high and is considered to be the best-preserved example of a High Cross in Ireland. Its elaborate panels depict biblical scenes, including Cain slaying Abel, David and Goliath, and a centerpiece of the Last Judgment. (Figurative scenes are not a characteristic of earlier High Crosses, such as those found in Ahenny, County Clare.) The **West Cross** stands a couple of feet taller than Muiredach's, making it one of the tallest in Ireland. Its engravings are less impressive—many of them having been worn away by centuries of Irish wind and rain. From the adjacent, 110-foot-high **round tower,** the extent of the former monastic settlement at Monasterboice is apparent. The key to the tower door is kept at the nearby gate lodge.

EATING WELL IN DUBLIN ENVIRONS

The counties around Dublin are not an obvious place to go to find good food. They are often perceived as being caught between the exotic charms of city dining and the true, rustic fare of the wilder west and south coasts. And yes, there's a lot of mediocre, overcooked, overpriced food in the region. The increase in population and influx of Dubliners and immigrants has brought some finer, more daring establishments in its wake, including the French Provençal delights of the Forge Gallery (just north of Slane) and the Scandinavian treats of Rolf's Bistro (in Ardee). But the real dining treasure here lies in the fact that the area is blessed with an abundance of old estates and country houses, which combine the most romantic and elegant of accommodations with some of the most exciting and mouthwatering dining rooms in Ireland. A deep respect for fresh, locally grown and raised produce and meats is a common theme, usually melded with a European outlook to the menu. It's a tour of the best of Irish home cooking: from the seafood gems of Ballymascanlon House on the Cooley Peninsula, west to the hearty game dishes of Moyglare Manor, and south to the haute-Irish menu at Rathsallagh House. And somehow each house manages to mix the dazzlingly elegant surroundings and menu with an informal, family atmosphere that makes the Irish country house the great-value wonder that it is.

Ardee

🕚 *14½ km (9 mi) northwest of Monasterboice on N2.*

In this market town, formerly at the northern edge of the Pale (originally the Pale referred to the area of eastern Ireland ruled directly by the Normans), stand two 13th-century castles: Ardee Castle and Hatch's Castle. The town of Ardee (Baile Átha Fhirdia or Ferdia's Ford), interestingly, was named after the ford where the mythical folk hero Cuchulainn fought his foster brother Ferdia. There's a statue depicting this battle at the start of the riverside walk. **Ardee Castle** (the one with square corners) was founded by Roger de Peppard in 1207, but much of the present building dates to the 15th century and later. The castle faces north—its objective to protect the Anglo-Irish Pale from the untamed Celtic tribes of Ulster. It was converted into a courthouse in the 19th century. **Hatch's Castle** (with rounded corners) is a private residence and not open to the public. Built in the 13th century, it was given by Cromwell as a gift to the loyal Hatch family. If you look closely you can see it still flaunts two 18th-century cannons at its entrance. **St. Mary's Church of Ireland** on Main Street incorporates part of a 13th-century Carmelite church burned by Edward the Bruce in 1316, including the holy water font. The current building was constructed in the 19th century.

Where to Eat

★ **$$–$$$** ✕ **Rolf's Bistro.** When the husband-and-wife team of Paul and Bernadette Svender (Rolf is Paul's father's name) opened their new restaurant in Ardee they knew what they wanted: an informal atmosphere with high-quality food. They renovated an old house in the middle of town, retaining much of its cozy charm with the help of discreet lighting, old pine floors, and a luxurious antique sofa in the waiting area. The menu reflects chef Paul's Scandinavian background, with Swedish caviar and beef Lindstrom (minced meat with capers and beetroot), a popular starter and main course. The steamed mussels served with chili sauce and aioli bread are refreshingly spicy. ⊠ *52 Market St.* ☎ *041/685–7949* ▤ *MC, V* ☉ *No lunch.*

$–$$$ ✕ **Carlito's.** Drinking a lazy aperitif before sitting down to eat is standard civilized behavior at this cozy Italian eatery in the small town of Dunleer, a few miles east of Ardee on the R170. The decor is nothing fancy, but the staff is sizeable and the commodious menu includes delicious homemade bread to go along with the real minestrone soup. The pizzas and pastas are streets ahead of your average joint, and the herb-crusted cod is a favorite main course. Save room for the killer tiramisu. ⊠ *Main St., Dunleer* ☎ *041/686–1366* ▤ *MC, V* ☉ *Closed Mon. No lunch.*

Louth

⑫ *11½ km (7 mi) north of Ardee on R171.*

Louth warrants a visit, if only for the splendidly preserved oratory here. St. Patrick, Ireland's patron saint, was reputed to have built his first church (which is no longer here) in this hilltop village in the 5th century. He also made St. Mochta (d. 534) the first bishop of Louth. Standing at the center of the village is the excellently preserved **St. Mochta's House,** an oratory dating from the 11th century, whose steeply pitched stone roof can be reached by a stairway. The house is freely accessible—but watch out for cattle (and their droppings) in the surrounding field.

Inniskeen

⑬ *6½ km (4 mi) north of Louth.*

On the road to Dundalk and just over the Louth county boundary in Monaghan lies Inniskeen, a small farming town that doubles as a social hearth for the area's far-flung community. Patrick Kavanagh (1906–69), the area's most famous poet, is commemorated at the **Inniskeen Folk Museum,** housed in a converted church next to a round tower. Born and raised here, Kavanagh immortalized the town in his early poem "Inniskeen Road"—where as a child he spied on young lovers and their "wink and elbow language of delight"—before becoming one of Ireland's leading poets. His remains were brought back to the village for burial. ☎ *042/937–8109* ▤ *Donations accepted* ☉ *May–Sept., Sun. 3–6, or by appointment.*

Dundalk

 14½ km (9 mi) east of Inniskeen, 80 km (50 mi) north of Dublin on N1.

Dundalk is a thriving, if uninspiring, frontier town—only 9½ km (6 mi) from the Northern Ireland border—with some fine historic buildings. It's the main town of County Louth (Ireland's smallest county), and it dates from the early Christian period, around the 7th century.

On Mill Street, the **bell tower** of a Franciscan monastery with Gothic windows dates from the 13th century. The **St. Patrick's Cathedral** was built between 1835 and 1847, when the Gothic Revival was at its height. With its buttresses and mosaics lining the chancel and the side chapel walls, the cathedral was modeled on the 15th-century King's College Chapel at Cambridge, England. The fine exterior was built in Newry granite, and the high altar and pulpit are of carved Caen stone. ⊠ *Town center* ⊙ *Daily 8–6.*

The Market House, the Town Hall, and the Courthouse are examples of the town's 19th-century heritage; the **Courthouse** is the most impressive of the three, built in the 1820s in a severe Greek Revival style, with Doric columns supporting the portico. It stands north of St. Patrick's Cathedral.

The **Dundalk County Museum** is dedicated to preserving the history of the dying local industries, such as beer brewing, cigarette manufacturing, shoe and boot making, and railway engineering. Other exhibits deal with the history of Louth from 7500 BC to the present. ⊠ *Joycelyn St.* ☎ *042/ 932–7056* ⊕ *www.louthcoco.ie* ⊠ *€3.80* ⊙ *June–Sept., Mon.–Sat. 10:30–5:30, Sun. 2–6; Oct.–May, Tues.–Sat. 10:30–5:30, Sun. 2–6.*

Where to Stay & Eat

$$–$$$$ ✕⌂ **Ballymascanlon House Hotel.** On 130 acres on the scenic Cooley Peninsula just north of Dundalk, you can find this converted Victorian mansion with a reputation for comfort and good cuisine. Reproduction period pieces fill the large guest rooms, which overlook either the spacious gardens or old stable yard. The restaurant ($$$) serves a set menu of Irish and French cuisine; it specializes in fresh seafood, such as lobster in season. Vegetarian plates are also available. ⊠ *Dundalk, Co. Louth* ☎ *042/935–8200* 🖷 *042/ 937–1598* ⊕ *www.ballymascanlon. com* 🖙 *90 rooms* ⚭ *Restaurant, 18-hole golf course, 2 tennis courts, indoor pool, health club, 2 bars* 🖃 *AE, DC, MC, V* ⚭❘ *BP.*

¢–$ ⌂ **Balrobin House.** This Georgian house was the home of Sir Lionel Harty and his wife Lady Lucy, who in the late 19th century would wine and dine Ireland's elite in its lush

> **UNWELCOME WAGON**
>
> The area around Dundalk is closely connected with Cuchulainn (pronounced coo-chu-lain)—"a greater hero than Hercules or Achilles," as Frank McCourt, in *Angela's Ashes*, quotes his father. Cuchulainn, the warrior of the Irish epic *Táin Bó Cuailnge* (Cattle Raid of Cooley), heroically defended this area of ancient Ulster against invaders.

surroundings. A marble fireplace, a walled garden, and antique gates are among the many original features of the house. The rooms maintain a period look with high, plasterwork ceilings and ornate furnishings. ⊠ *Kilkerley, Co. Louth* ☎ *042/937–7701* ⟿ *4 rooms* ☰ *MC, V* ⍰ *BP.*

Cooley Peninsula Drive

⓯ *Beginning in Dundalk, 80 km (50 mi) north of Dublin.*

A soft, misty rain falling on the ancient, mysterious Cooley Peninsula is a quintessential Irish scene. If you have a car and three or four free hours, go for a scenic drive around the peninsula and take in some of the finest views of the east coast of Ireland. A 64-km (40-mi) round-trip beginning and ending in Dundalk will take you by the Carlingford Lough on the north side of the peninsula, with the Mountains of Mourne rising in the distance. The area is steeped in Celtic mythology, especially with the daring feats of the doomed hero Cuchulainn. You could do worse for a travel guide than a modern translation of the *Táin Bó Cuailnge* epic itself. From Gyles Quay, a small coastal village with a clean, safe beach, you can take in excellent views southward along the County Louth coast to Clogher Head. A coast road winds east around the Cooley Peninsula to Greenore, a town built in Victorian times as a ferry terminal. If you feel like getting out of your car, the Táin Trail is a 25-mi meandering hike up through the Windy Gap and Clermont Cairn, and then down through Ravensdale Forest and back to the R174 road. This trail begins in Carlingford and passes through such towns as Omeath before ending in Ravensdale—so you can find plenty of places to stay along the way. Shorter walks are also marked.

Carlingford

⓰ *21 km (13 mi) east of Dundalk, 6½ km (4 mi) south of Omeath on R173.*

The appeal of the small, medieval fishing town of Carlingford is its natural scenery, as well as its striking whitewashed, thatched cottages. The mountains of the Cooley Peninsula back right up to the town, the Carlingford Lough lies at its feet, and the Mountains of Mourne rise only 5 km (3 mi) away across the lough. Some remnants from the area's medieval days include a tower from the town wall and one of its gates, which later became the town hall. The 15th-century **Mint Tower House,** in an alley off Market Square, is notable for its mullioned, limestone windows. **Taaffe's Castle,** a 16th-century fortified town house on the quay, has classic Norman defensive features. A massive, 13th-century fortress that rises up over the entrance to Carlingford Lough, **King John's Castle** has an unusual trait: its west gateway is only wide enough to admit one horseman. It was built in the 1190s and named for the English king who paid a brief visit in 1210. The highlight of the **Holy Trinity Heritage Centre,** in a beautifully restored medieval church, is a mural depicting the village at the height of the Middle Ages. An audiovisual display focuses on village history and the efforts to preserve Carlingford's medieval heritage. ⊠ *Churchyard Rd.* ☎ *042/937–3888* ✉ *€2* ⊗ *Weekdays 9:30–1 and 2–4:30.*

Where to Stay & Eat

$ ✕⬚ **The Oystercatcher Lodge and Bistro.** Right in the middle of town, this cute little lodge on Market Square will surprise you with the spaciousness of its "minisuite" rooms. Each one is beautifully finished with warm wood floors, off-white linens and drapes, and huge beds. The bistro is, of course, renowned for its oysters, and they use warm-water fish in the kitchen, unlike most Irish restaurants. ⊠ *Carlingford, Co. Louth* ☎ *042/ 937–3922* ⊕ *www.theoystercatcher.com* ⇗ *7 rooms* ⊟ *MC, V* ⏐◯⏐ *BP.*

$ ⬚ **Beaufort House.** Michael and Glynnis Caine's award-winning bed-and-breakfast is a little gem set right on the waters of the lough and only a few minutes from the village. Guest rooms are simply but warmly decorated. They also run a yacht charter and sea school, so there's a real nautical feel to the place. In a past life the Caines were restaurateurs, and dinner is available by arrangement for parties of eight or more. ⊠ *Carlingford, Co. Louth* ☎ *042/937–3879* ⊕ *www.beauforthouse.net* ⇗ *5 rooms* ⊟ *MC, V* ⏐◯⏐ *BP.*

Omeath

⓱ *6½ km (4 mi) northwest of Carlingford on R173.*

This northernmost town on Cooley Peninsula is blessed with a stunning landscape and the distinction of having outdoor Stations of the Cross that Catholics pray before in a solemn procession every Good Friday. Omeath was the last main Gaeltacht (Irish-speaking) village in this part of Ireland (most extant Gaeltacht villages are in the southwest and the west). There's a narrow road that climbs the mountains behind Omeath. As you ascend, the views become ever more spectacular, stretching over the Mountains of Mourne in the north and as far south as Skerries, 32 km (20 mi) north of Dublin. This narrow road leads back to Dundalk.

On the eastern side of the Omeath, on the outside of a shrine, are the open-air **Stations of the Cross**—14 pictures of the key moments during Christ's last days—at the monastery of the Rosminian Fathers. Jaunting cars (horse-drawn carts) take visitors to the site from the quayside. Daily from June to September, stalls at the **quay** sell all kinds of shellfish, including oysters and mussels, from the nearby lough. In July and August, a ferry service runs until 6 PM from here to Warrenpoint, across the lough in Northern Ireland; the trip takes five minutes.

COUNTY WICKLOW

Make your way to the fourth or fifth story of almost any building in Dublin that faces south and you can see off in the distance—amazingly, not *that* far off in the distance—the green, smooth hills of the Dublin and Wicklow mountains. On a clear day the mountains are even visible from some streets in and around the city center. If your idea of solace is green hills, and your visit to Ireland is otherwise limited to Dublin, County Wicklow—or Cill Mhantain (pronounced kill *wan*-tan), as it's known in Irish—should be on your itinerary. Not that the secret isn't out; rugged and mountainous with dark, wooded forests, central Wicklow, known as the "garden of Ireland," is a popular picnic area among

Dubliners. It has some of Ireland's grandest 18th-century mansions, and cradles one of the country's earliest Christian retreats: Glendalough. Nestled in a valley of dense woods and placid lakes, Glendalough and environs can seem (at least during the off-season) practically untouched since their heyday 1,000 years ago. The granite mountains that have protected Glendalough all these years run into the sea along the east coast, which has several popular sandy beaches. Journey from Dublin down to Arklow, sticking to the east side of the Wicklow Mountains. A quick note about getting here: it takes stamina to extract yourself from the unmarked maze of the Dublin exurbs (your best bet is to take N11, which becomes M11, and then again N11). Once you've accomplished that feat, this gorgeous, mysterious terrain awaits.

Bray

⑱ *22 km (14 mi) south of Dublin on N11, 8 km (5 mi) east of Enniskerry on R755.*

One of Ireland's oldest seaside resorts, Bray is a trim village known for its dilapidated summer cottages and sand-and-shingle beach, which stretches for 2 km (1 mi). When the trains first arrived from Dublin in 1854, Bray became the number-one spot for urban vacationers and subsequently took on the appearance of an English oceanfront town. Some Dubliners still flock to the faded glory of Bray's boardwalk to push baby carriages and soak up the sun. It's the terminus of the DART train from Dublin, so it's easy to get here without a car. Uncrowded trails for hiking and mountain-biking crisscross the mountains bordering Bray to the south. One of the best is a well-marked path leading from the beach to the 10-foot-tall cross that crowns the spiny peak of Bray Head, a rocky outcrop that rises 791 feet from the sea. The semi-difficult, one-hour climb affords stunning views of Wicklow Town and Dublin Bay.

The **Heritage Centre,** opposite the Royal Hotel, in the old courthouse, houses on its lower level a re-created castle dungeon with a 1,000-years-of-Bray exhibition. Upstairs is a huge model railway and a display about modern Bray. ⊠ *Lower Main St.* ☎ *01/286–6796* 📷 €3 ⊗ *June–Aug., weekdays 9–1 and 2–5, Sat. 10–3; Sept.–May, weekdays 9:30–1 and 2–4:30, Sat. 10–3.*

One Martello Terrace (☎ 01/286–8407), at the harbor, is Bray's most famous address. James Joyce (1882–1941) lived here between 1887 and 1891 and used the house as the setting for the Christmas dinner in *A Portrait of the Artist as a Young Man.* Today the house is owned by an Irish Teachta Dála (member of Parliament, informally known as a "TD"). The phone number listed above rings at her constituency office; someone there should be able to help scholars and devotees arrange a visit. (Call on Thursday between 10 AM and 1 PM.) Although the residence has been renovated, the dining room portrayed in Joyce's novel maintains the spirit of his time.

National Sealife is an aquarium and museum dedicated to the creatures of the sea, with an emphasis on those that occupy the waters around Ireland. Besides massive sea tanks that contain all manner of swimming

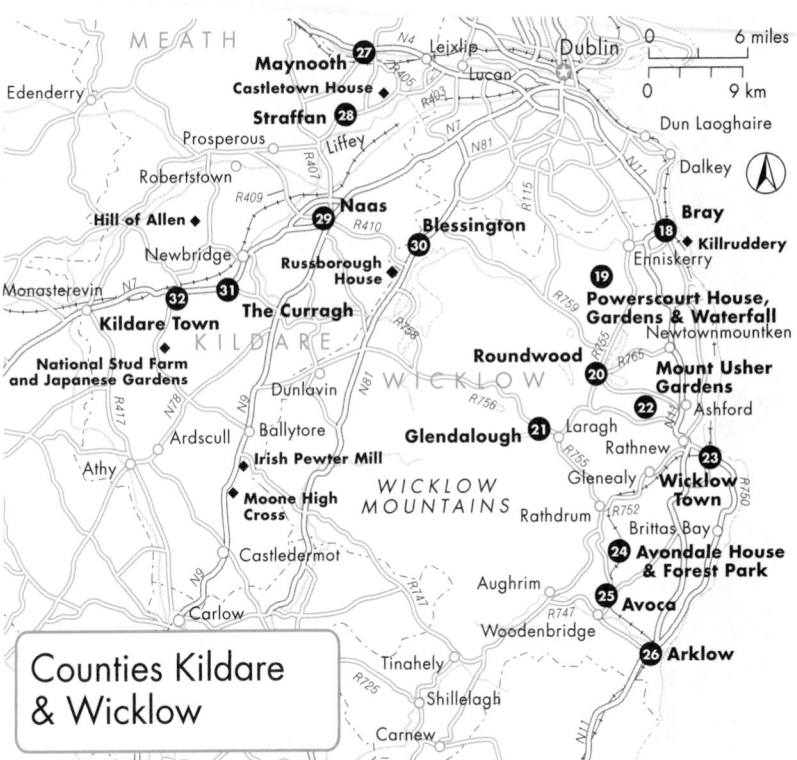

Counties Kildare & Wicklow

things, there's a major conservation project with captive breeding of sea horses. **FinZone** is an undersea adventure trail perfect for kids, including puzzles to solve. Touch-screen computers and video games give the whole thing a high-tech feel. In winter, call to confirm opening times before visiting. ⊠ *Strand Rd.* ☎ *01/286–6939* ⊕ *www.sealife.ie* ⊡ *€9.75* ☉ *May–Sept., daily 10–6; Oct.–Apr. weekdays 11–5, weekends 11–6.*

The 17th-century formal gardens at **Killruddery House** are precisely arranged, with fine beech hedges, Victorian statuary, and a parterre of lavender and roses. The Brabazon family, the earls of Meath, have lived here since 1618. In 1820 they hired William Morris to remodel the house as a revival Elizabethan mansion. The estate also has a Crystal Palace conservatory modeled on those at the botanic gardens in Dublin. ⊠ *Off Bray–Greystones Rd., 3 km (2 mi) south of Bray, Killruddery* ☎ *01/ 286–3405* ⊕ *www.killruddery.com* ⊡ *House and gardens €8, gardens only €5* ☉ *Gardens: Apr., weekends 1–5; May–Sept., daily 1–5; house May–June and Sept., daily 1–5.*

Where to Eat

$$–$$$$
FodorsChoice
★

✕ **Hungry Monk.** The cloisters and refectory-style decor is definitely tongue in cheek at this upbeat, fun bistro in sleepy Greystones, an old-fashioned seaside resort a couple miles south of Bray. Owner Pat Keown is a great host and his laughter and love of good food and fine wine are catching. Dinner is served by candlelight and the menu specializes in un-cluttered seafood dishes in summer and wild game on those cold winter nights. The "Seafood Symphony" is a particular favorite as is the roast Gressingham duck. Sunday lunches are famous for the length of time they go on (often into the early evening) and for the lively atmosphere. ✉ *1 Church Rd., Greystones* ☎ *01/287–5759* 🖃 *AE, DC, MC, V* ⊘ *Closed Mon. and Tues. No lunch Wed.–Sat.*

¢–$ ✕ **Summerville Country Cooking.** This restaurant's ceilings are high, the space is airy and bright, and the food—ranging from shepherd's pie to vegetarian quiche—tastes absolutely delicious. In summer take advantage of the sun-drenched garden terrace. ✉ *1 Trafalgar Rd., Greystones* ☎ *01/287–4228* 🖃 *V.*

Powerscourt House, Gardens & Waterfall

☾ ⓳ *25 km (16 mi) south of Dublin on R117, 22 km (14 mi) north of Glendalough on R755.*

Within the shadow of famous Sugar Loaf mountain, Enniskerry is one of the prettiest villages in Ireland. It's built around a sloping central triangular square with a backdrop of the wooded Wicklow Mountains. From Dublin you can get to Enniskerry directly by taking the No. 44 bus from the Dublin quays area. The main reason to visit the area around Enniskerry is the Powerscourt Estate.

They really had the life, those old aristocrats. At more than 14,000 acres, including stunning formal gardens and a 400-foot waterfall, **Powerscourt** must have been some place to call home. The grounds were originally granted to Sir Richard Wingfield, the first viscount of Powerscourt, by King James I of England in 1609. Richard Castle (1690–1751), the architect of Russborough House, was hired to design the great house. His was an age not known for modesty, and he chose the grand Palladian style. The house took nine years to complete and was ready to move in 1740, truly one of the great houses of Ireland and, indeed, all of Britain. Unfortunately, you won't be able to see much of it. A terrible fire almost completely destroyed the house in 1974, cruelly on the eve of a huge party to celebrate the completion after a long period of restoration by the Slazenger family. A second period of renovation is currently under way and the original ballroom on the first floor—once "the grandest room in any Irish house," according to historian Desmond Guinness—is the only room that gives a sense of the place's former glory. It was based on Palladio's version of the "Egyptian Hall" designed by Vitruvius, architect to Augustus, emperor of Rome.

Powerscourt Gardens, considered among the finest in Europe, were laid out from 1745 to 1767 following the completion of the house—and were radically redesigned in the Victorian style, from 1843 to 1875, by Daniel Robertson. The Villa Butera in Sicily inspired him to set these gardens with sweeping terraces, antique sculptures, and a circular pond and fountain flanked by winged horses. There's a celebrated view of the Italianate patterned ramps, lawns, and pond across the beautiful, heavily wooded Dargle Valley, which stair-steps to the horizon and the noble profile of Sugar Loaf mountain. The grounds include many specimen trees (plants grown for exhibition), an avenue of monkey puzzle trees, a parterre of brightly colored summer flowers, and a Japanese garden. The kitchen gardens, with their modest rows of flowers, are a striking antidote to the classical formality of the main sections. A self-serve restaurant, crafts center, garden center, and a children's play

> ### GENIUS IN A BOTTLE
>
> Powerscourt's grand Victorian gardens were designed by an eccentric boozer, Daniel Robertson, who liked to be tooled around the gardens-in-progress in a wheelbarrow while taking nips from a bottle of sherry.

area are also on the grounds. ⊠ *Enniskerry* ☎ *01/204–6000* ⊕ *www. powerscourt.ie* ⊠ *House €7, house and gardens €9* ⊙ *Mar.–Oct., daily 9:30–5:30; Nov.–Feb., daily 9:30–dusk.*

One of the most inspiring sights to the writers and artists of the Romantic generation, the 400-foot **Powerscourt Waterfall,** 5 km (3 mi) south of the gardens, is the highest in the British Isles. ⊠ *Enniskerry* ⊠ *€4.50* ⊙ *Mar.–Oct., daily 9:30–7; Nov.–Feb., daily 10:30–dusk.*

Where to Eat

$ ✕ **Poppies Country Cooking.** This cozy café—with a pine-panel ceiling,
Fodor'sChoice   farmhouse furniture, and paintings of poppies on the walls—is a great
★   place for breakfast, lunch, or late-afternoon tea. Expect potato cakes, shepherd's pie, lasagna, vegetarian quiche, house salads, and soup. But the most popular dishes are Poppies chicken (a casserolelike concoction) and homity pie (pot pie with potatoes, onion, garlic, and cream cheese). For dessert try the apple pie or the rhubarb crumble, which is so good that the Irish rugby team stops by for it after practice. They now open Friday night for dinner. ⊠ *The Square, Enniskerry* ☎ *01/282–8869* ▤ *MC, V* ⊙ *No dinner Sat.–Thurs.*

Roundwood

★ ⑳   *18 km (11 mi) south of Enniskerry on R755.*

At 800 feet above sea level, Roundwood is the highest village in Ireland. It's also surrounded by spectacular mountain scenery. The Sunday-afternoon market in the village hall, where cakes, jams, and other homemade goods are sold, livens up what is otherwise a sleepy place. From the broad main street, by the Roundwood Inn, a minor road leads west for 8 km (5 mi) to two lakes, Lough Dan and Lough Tay, lying deep between forested mountains like Norwegian fjords.

Where to Eat

★ ¢–$$$ ✕ **Roundwood Inn.** Travel back to the 17th century at this inn evocatively furnished in a traditional style, with wooden floors, dark furniture, and diamond-shape windows. It's best known for its good, reasonably priced bar food—eaten at sturdy tables beside an open fire. The restaurant offers a combination of Continental and Irish cuisines, reflecting the traditions of the German proprietor, Jurgen Schwalm, and his Irish wife, Aine. The separate bar and lounge also serve an excellent menu that includes a succulent seafood platter of salmon, oysters, lobster, and shrimp. ✉ *Main St., Roundwood village center* ☎ *01/281–8107* ♨ *Reservations essential* ▤ *AE, MC, V* ☺ *Closed Mon. and Tues. No dinner Sun.*

Glendalough

㉑

Fodor'sChoice

★

Nestled in a lush, quiet valley deep in the rugged Wicklow Mountains, among two lakes, evergreen and deciduous trees, and acres of windswept heather, Gleann dá Loch ("Glen of Two Lakes") is one of Ireland's premier monastic sites. The hermit monks of early Christian Ireland were drawn to the Eden-like quality of some of the valleys in this area, and this evocative settlement remains to this day a sight to calm a troubled soul. Stand here in the early morning (before the crowds and the hordes of schooltrippers arrive), and you can appreciate what drew the solitude-seeking St. Kevin to this spot. St. Kevin—or Coemghein, "fair begotten" in Irish (d. 618)—was a descendant of the royal house of Leinster who renounced the world and came here to live as a hermit before opening the monastery in 550. Glendalough then flourished as a monastic center until 1398, when English soldiers plundered the site, leaving the ruins that you see today. (The monastery survived earlier 9th- and 10th-century Viking attacks.) The visitor center is a good place to orient yourself and pick up a useful pamphlet. Many of the ruins are clumped together beyond the visitor center, but some of the oldest surround the Upper Lake, where signed paths direct you through spectacular scenery absent of crowds. Most ruins are open all day and are freely accessible.

Probably the oldest building on the site, presumed to date from St. Kevin's time, is the **Teampaill na Skellig** (Church of the Oratory), on the south shore of the Upper Lake. A little to the east is **St. Kevin's Bed,** a tiny cave in the rock face, about 30 feet above the level of the lake, where St. Kevin lived his hermit's existence. It's not easily accessible; you approach the cave by boat, but climbing the cliff to the cave can be dangerous. At the southeast corner of the Upper Lake is the 11th-century **Reefert Church,** with the ruins of a nave and a chancel. The saint also lived in the adjoining, ruined beehive hut with five crosses, which marked the original boundary of the monastery. You get a superb view of the valley from here.

The ruins by the edge of the Lower Lake are the most important of those at Glendalough. The **gateway,** beside the Glendalough Hotel, is the only surviving entrance to an ancient monastic site anywhere in Ireland. An extensive **graveyard** lies within, with hundreds of elaborately decorated crosses, as well as a perfectly preserved six-story **round tower.** Built in the 11th or 12th century, it stands 100 feet high, with an entrance 25 feet above ground level.

The largest building at Glendalough is the substantially intact 7th- to 9th-century **cathedral,** where you can find the nave (small for a large church, only 30 feet wide by 50 feet long), chancel, and ornamental oolite limestone window, which may have been imported from England. South of the cathedral is the 11-foot-high Celtic **St. Kevin's Cross.** Made of granite, it's the best-preserved such cross on the site. **St. Kevin's Church** is an early barrel-vaulted oratory with a high-pitched stone roof. ☎ *0404/45325*

⊕www.heritageireland.ie ⛁*€2.90* ⊗ *Mid-Mar.–mid-Oct., daily 9:30–6; mid-Oct.–mid-Mar., daily 9:30–5; last admission 45 min before closing.*

Where to Stay & Eat

$$–$$$ ✕⊡ **Glendalough Hotel.** Purists object to the proximity of this old-fashioned, early-19th-century hotel to the ruins at Glendalough, but to others it's a convenience. Some of the bedrooms, decorated in pastel colors, overlook the monastery and the wooded mountain scenery; others face the grounds. The burble of running water from the Glendassan River audibly enhances the experience. The restaurant ($$–$$$) also has views of the lawn. The Irish menu is simple, but portions are hearty and the pub is the only one for miles around. ✉ *Co. Wicklow* ☎ *0404/45135* 📠 *0404/45142* ⊕ *www.glendaloughhotel.com* 🛏*44 rooms* ⚙ *Restaurant, fishing, bar; no a/c* ▤ *AE, DC, MC, V* ⊗ *Closed Dec. and Jan.* ⊙❙ *BP.*

> **CURVES AHEAD**
>
> Getting to hallowed Glendalough from Dublin is easy, thanks to the St. Kevin's bus service. If you're driving, consider taking the scenic route along R155, but be prepared for awesome, austere mountaintop passes. Don't take this route if you're in a hurry, and don't expect a lot of signage—just concentrate on the glorious views.

Mount Usher Gardens

★ ㉒ Settled into more than 20 acres on the banks of the River Vartry, the gardens here were first laid out in 1868 by textile magnate Edward Walpole. Succeeding generations of the Walpole family further planted and maintained the grounds, which today have more than 5,000 species. The "Robinsonian" (that is, informal) gardener has made the most of the riverside locale by planting eucalypti, azaleas, camellias, and rhododendrons. The river is visible from nearly everyplace in the gardens; miniature suspension bridges bounce and sway underfoot as you cross the river. Near the entrance, you'll find a cluster of crafts shops (including a pottery workshop) as well as a bookstore and self-service restaurant. The twin villages of Ashford and Rathnew are to the south and east, and Newtownmountkennedy is to the north. ✉ *Ashford* ☎ *0404/40205* ⊕ *www.dublingardens.com* ⛁*€6.50* ⊗ *Mid-Mar.–Oct., daily 10:30–6.*

Where to Stay & Eat

★ **$$–$$$$** ✕⊡ **Tinakilly House.** All aboard who's going aboard! William and Bee Power have restored beautifully this Victorian-Italianate mansion, built in the 1870s by Captain Robert Halpin. The lobby has mementos of Captain Halpin and his nautical exploits, including paintings and ship models; Victorian antiques fill the house. Some bedrooms have four-poster beds, sitting areas, and views of the Wicklow landscape, the Irish Sea, or the lovely gardens on the 7-acre grounds. In the dining room ($$$–$$$$), expect to be served French-influenced Irish cuisine, with fresh vegetables from the garden. Brown and fruit breads are baked daily. ✉ *Rathnew, Co. Wicklow* ☎ *0404/69274* 📠 *0404/67806* ⊕ *www.tinakilly.ie* 🛏 *52 rooms, 5 suites* ⚙ *Restaurant, tennis court, bar; no a/c* ▤ *AE, DC, MC, V* ⊙❙ *BP.*

Wicklow Town

㉓ *26 km (16 mi) east of Glendalough on R763, 51 km (32 mi) south of Dublin on N11.*

At the entrance to the attractive, tree-lined Main Street of Wicklow Town—its name, from the Danish *wyking alo*, means "Viking meadow"—sprawl the extensive ruins of a 13th-century Franciscan friary. The **friary** was closed down during the 16th-century dissolution of the monasteries, but its ruins are a reminder of Wicklow's stormy past, which began with the unwelcome reception given to St. Patrick on his arrival in AD 432. Inquire at the nearby **priest's house** (⌧ Main St. ☎ 0404/67196) to see the ruins. The streets of Wicklow ran with blood during the 1798 rebellion when Billy Byrne, member of a wealthy local Catholic family, led rebels from south and central Wicklow against the forces of the Crown. Byrne was eventually captured and executed at Gallow's Hill just outside town. There is a memorial to him in the middle of Market Square.

The old **Wicklow Historic Gaol,** just above Market Square, has been converted into a museum and heritage center, where it's possible to trace your genealogical roots in the area. Computer displays and life-size models tell the gruesome history of the jail, from the 1798 rebellion to the late 19th century. ⌧ *Market Sq.* ☎ *0404/61599* ⊕ *www.wicklowshistoricgaol.com* ⌧ *€6.80* ⊙ *Mid–Mar.–Oct., daily 10–5.*

The **harbor** is Wicklow Town's most appealing area. Take Harbour Road down to the pier; a bridge across the River Vartry leads to a second, smaller pier, at the northern end of the harbor. From this end, follow the shingle beach, which stretches for 5 km (3 mi); behind the beach is the broad lough, a lagoon noted for its wildfowl. Immediately south of the harbor, perched on a promontory that has good views of the Wicklow coastline, is the ruin of the **Black Castle.** This structure was built in 1169 by Maurice Fitzgerald, an Anglo-Norman lord who arrived with the English invasion of Ireland. The ruins (freely accessible) extend over a large area; with some difficulty, you can climb down to the water's edge.

Between one bank of the River Vartry and the road to Dublin stands the Protestant **St. Lavinius Church,** which incorporates various unusual details: a Romanesque door, 12th-century stonework, fine pews, and an atmospheric graveyard. The church is topped off by a copper, onion-shape cupola, added as an afterthought in 1771. ⌧ *Free* ⊙ *Daily 10–6.*

Where to Stay & Eat

$–$$ ✕ **Rugantinos.** The heated deck overlooking the river is best spot to enjoy the hearty comfort food at this cozy little eatery on the South Quay. The spicy chicken wings in a Louisiana hot sauce are a specialty and the steaks are big and char-grilled to perfection. The early-bird menu (before 7:30 PM) is a big draw. ⌧ *Schooner House, South Quay* ☎ *0404/61900* ▤ *AE, MC, V* ⊙ *No lunch.*

$$$ ▥ **Wicklow Head Lighthouse.** This 95-foot-high stone tower—first built in 1781—once supported an eight-sided lantern, and has been renovated by the Irish Landmark Trust as a lodging. It sleeps four to six people in two delightfully quirky octagonal bedrooms and one double sofa bed in the sitting room. The kitchen–dining room at the top has stunning views out over the coast. Don't forget anything in the car; it's a long way down. You rent the entire lighthouse, and you must book for at least two nights. The old lighthouse is just south of town on Wicklow Head, right next to the new, automated one. ⊠ *Wicklow Head, Co. Wicklow* ☎ *01/670–4733* 📠 *01/670–4887* ⊕ *www.irishlandmark.com* ➷ *2 rooms sleep up to 6 people* ⚇ *Kitchenette; no a/c, no room TVs* ⊟ *MC, V.*

$$ 🏨 **Grand Hotel.** A traditional Irish town hotel, the Grand doesn't really deserve that adjective but has a great location in the center of Wicklow and is known for its small-town quality service and atmosphere. Guest rooms are big, if a little over-decorated, and most have large windows, which flood the rooms with light. Wynne's bar is well known for its lively traditional-music sessions and also serves up excellent pub grub. ⊠ *Wicklow Town, Co. Wicklow* ☎ *0404/67337* 📠 *0404/69607* ➷ *33 rooms* ⚇ *Restaurant, bar* ⊟ *AE, MC, V* ⦿ *BP.*

Avondale House & Forest Park

㉔ *17 km (10½ mi) southwest of Wicklow Town on R752.*

Outside the quaint village of Rathdrum, on the west bank of the Avondale River, is the 523-acre **Avondale Forest Park.** Part of a then-burgeoning movement to preserve and expand the Irish forest, it was, in 1904, the first forest in Ireland to be taken over by the state. There's a fine 5½-km (3½-mi) walk along the river, as well as pine and exotic-tree trails. **Avondale House,** on the grounds of the park, resonates with Irish history. The house was the birthplace and lifelong home of Charles Stewart Parnell (1846–91), the "Uncrowned King of Ireland," the country's leading politician of the 19th century and a wildly popular campaigner for democracy and land reform. Parnell's house, built in 1779, has been flawlessly restored—except for the reception and dining rooms on the ground floor, which are filled with Parnell memorabilia, including some of his love letters to Kitty O'Shea and political cartoons portraying Parnell's efforts to secure home rule for Ireland. ☎ *0404/46111* ⊕ *www.heritageireland.com* 🎫 *€5.50* ⊗ *May–Aug., daily 11–6; mid-Mar.–Apr., Sept., and Oct., Tues.–Sun. 11–6.*

> ### HERE, KITTY KITTY
>
> Parnell's mighty career came to a halt after he fell in love with a married woman, Kitty O'Shea—her husband started divorce proceedings and news of the scandal ruined Parnell, who died a year later. James Joyce dramatized the affair in a keenly contested argument during a Daedalus family dinner in *Portrait of the Artist as a Young Man.*

Avoca

㉕ *6½ km (4 mi) south of Avondale Forest Park on R754.*

Heavily forested hills surround the small, lovely hamlet of Avoca, at the confluence of the Rivers Avonbeg and Avonmore. Beneath a riverside tree here, the Irish Romantic poet Thomas Moore (1779–1852) composed his 1807 poem, "The Meeting of the Waters." There are some pleasant forest walks nearby, with scenic views of the valley. The oldest hand-weaving mill in Ireland, dating to 1723, **Avoca Handweavers** offers a short tour of the still-operating mill. The store sells a wide selection of its superb fabrics and woven and knit apparel, some of which is difficult to find elsewhere. There's even a cute café for a snack. ☎ *0402/35105* ✉ *Free* ⊗ *Mill: weekdays 8:30–4:30, weekends 10–5. Shop: May–Oct., daily 9–6; Nov.–Apr., daily 9:30–5:30.*

Arklow

㉖ *11 km (7 mi) southeast of Avoca on R754.*

An ideal point to access the rolling hills and forest walks of the intensely pastoral Vale of Avoca, the small beach town of Arklow is wrapped around an old port. The **Maritime Museum,** in the public library building near the railway station, traces Arklow's distinguished seafaring tradition. Exhibits include old photographs, historic boats, and the shipping diaries of long-dead captains. To get here, take a left at St. Peter's Church as you're heading out of town in the direction of Gorey and Wexford. ✉ *St. Mary's Rd.* ☎ *0402/32868* ✉ *€7* ⊗ *May–Sept., Mon.–Sat. 10–1 and 2–5; Oct.–Apr., weekdays 10–1 and 2–5.*

Immediately north of Arklow is **Brittas Bay,** an expanse of white sand, quiet coves, and rolling dunes—perfect for adventurous kids. In summer it's popular with vacationing Dubliners.

Shopping

If you love bread or have a sweet tooth, stop in at **Stone Oven Bakery** (✉ 65 Lower Main St. ☎ 0402/39418) at the bottom of the hill. The German-born baker, Egon Friedrich, prepares sourdough breads and delicious sweet treats, including hazelnut-chocolate triangles. You can also get simple cheese-and-bread sandwiches to go—or you can eat in the tiny, slightly haphazard café.

COUNTY KILDARE TO WEST WICKLOW

Of all the artistic delights that beckon both north and south of Dublin, few impress as much as the imposing country estates of County Wicklow. Here, during the "glorious eighteenth," great Anglo-Irish estates were built by English "princes of Elegance and Prodigality." Only an hour or two from Dublin, these estates—Russborough, Powerscourt, and Castletown are but three of the most famous—were profoundly influenced by the country villas of the great Italian architect Andrea Palladio, who erected the estates of the Venetian aristocracy along the Brenta Canal, only a short distance from the city on the lagoon. As in other parts of Ireland, the ancestral homes of the dwindling members of the Anglo-Irish ascendancy dot the landscape in the Pale.

Horse racing is a passion in Ireland—just about every little town has at least one betting shop—and County Kildare is the country's horse capital. Nestled between the basins of the River Liffey to the north and the River Barrow to the east, its gently sloping hills and grass-filled plains

2

are perfect for breeding and racing Thoroughbreds. For some visitors, the fabled National Stud Farm just outside Kildare Town provides a fascinating glimpse into the world of horse breeding. And don't forget the fabled Japanese Gardens, adjacent to the National Stud, which are among Europe's finest. You may want to pick up this leg from Glendalough—the spectacular drive across the Wicklow Gap, from Glendalough to Hollywood, makes for a glorious entrance into Kildare. One last note: consult Chapter 4, the Southeast, if you make it as far south as Castledermot, because Carlow and environs are only 10 km (6 mi) farther south.

Maynooth

27 *21 km (13 mi) southwest of Dublin.*

A few minutes south of the tiny Georgian town of Maynooth is the hamlet of Celbridge, official address to Ireland's largest country house, **Castletown** (see "Treasure Hunt: The Anglo-Irish Georgian House," in this chapter). After touring this grand mansion, head slightly to the west to find Maynooth's **St. Patrick's College.** What was once a center for the training of Catholic priests is now one of Ireland's most important lay universities. The visitor center chronicles the college's history and that of the Catholic Church in Ireland. Stroll through the university gardens—the Path of Saints or the Path of Sinners. At the entrance to St. Patrick's College are the ruins of Maynooth Castle, the ancient seat of the Fitzgerald family. The Fitzgeralds' fortunes changed for the worse when they led the rebellion of 1536 (it failed). The castle keep, which dates from the 13th century, and the great hall are still in decent condition. Mrs. Saults at 9 Parson Street has the key. ☎ *01/628–5222* ⊕ *www.may.ie* 🖾 *Free* ☉ *St. Patrick's May–Sept., Mon.–Sat. 11–5, Sun. 2–6; guided tours every hr.*

Where to Stay & Eat

$$$$ ✕🏨 **Moyglare Manor.** Owner Nora Devlin has exuberantly decorated this majestic Georgian manor house with her renowned antiques collection. Velvet chairs, oil paintings, and thickly draped windows furnish the drawing room, and the grand bedrooms have four-poster canopy beds, roomy wardrobes, marble fireplaces, and comfortable, chintz-covered armchairs. Lamp-shaded wall sconces add a romantic touch to the formal dining room, where a wonderful game-dominated, five-course set menu is served. The manor, which occupies 16 pastoral acres dotted with sheep and cows, is 29 km (18 mi) west of Dublin. ⊠ *Maynooth, Co. Kildare* ☎ *01/628–6351* 🖷 *01/628–5405* ⊕ *www.moyglaremanor.ie* ⇦ *17 rooms* ⚒ *Restaurant, 2 bars* 🚭 *AE, DC, MC, V* 🍽 *BP, MAP.*

Straffan

28 *5 km (3 mi) southwest of Castletown House on R403, 25½ km (16 mi) southwest of Dublin.*

Its attractive location on the banks of the River Liffey, its unique butterfly farm, and the Kildare Hotel and Country Club—where Arnold Palmer designed the K Club, one of Ireland's most renowned 18-hole golf courses—are what make Straffan so appealing. The only one of its kind in Ireland, the **Straffan Butterfly Farm** has a tropical house with exotic plants, butterflies, and moths. Mounted and framed butterflies are for sale. ☎ *01/627–1109* ⊕ *www.straffanbutterflyfarm.com* ✉ €7 ⊗ *June–Aug., daily noon–5:30.*

The **Steam Museum** covers the history of Irish steam engines, handsome machines used both in industry and agriculture—churning butter, threshing corn. There's also a fun collection of model locomotives. Engineers are present on "live steam days" every Sunday and bank holiday. The adjoining Lodge Park Walled Garden is included in the price and is perfect for a leisurely summer stroll. ✉ *Lodge Park* ☎ *01/627–3155* ⊕ *www.steam-museum.com* ✉ *€7.50* ⊗ *June–Aug., Wed.–Sun. 2–6; May and Sept., by appointment only.*

Where to Stay & Eat

$$$$
Fodor'sChoice
★

✕ ⌂ **Kildare Hotel and Country Club.** Manicured gardens and the renowned Arnold Palmer–designed K Club golf course surround this mansard-roof country mansion. The spacious, comfortable guest rooms are each uniquely decorated with antiques, and all have large windows that overlook either the Liffey or the golf course. (The rooms in the old house are best.) The hotel also has a leasing agreement with several privately owned cottages on the property. Chef Michel Flamme serves an unashamedly French menu—albeit with the hint of an Irish flavor—at the Byerly Turk Restaurant (named after a famous racehorse). The K-Club had the honor of hosting the biennial Ryder Cup golf tournament in 2006. ✉ *Co. Kildare* ☎ *01/601–7200* 🖷 *01/601–7299* ⊕ *www.kclub.ie* ⊷ *69 rooms, 26 apartments* ⌂ *3 restaurants, 2 18-hole golf courses, indoor pool, hair salon, spa, fishing, horseback riding, 3 bars* ▭ *AE, DC, MC, V* ⎮◎⎮ *BP, MAP.*

$$$–$$$$
Fodor'sChoice
★

✕ ⌂ **Barberstown Castle.** With a 13th-century castle keep at one end, an Elizabethan central section, a large Georgian country house at the other, and a whole new modern wing, Barberstown represents 750 years of Irish history. Ask for a room in one of the old sections where turf fires blaze in ornate fireplaces in the three sumptuously decorated lounges. Reproduction pieces fill the bedrooms, some of which have four-poster beds. The Georgian-style restaurant serves creatively prepared French food, also on tap for special parties in the banqueting room of the castle keep. ✉ *Co. Kildare* ☎ *01/628–8157* 🖷 *01/627–7027* ⊕ *www.barberstowncastle.ie* ⊷ *59 rooms* ⌂ *Restaurant, bar* ▭ *AE, DC, MC, V* ⎮◎⎮ *BP, MAP.*

Naas

➋➒ *13 km (8 mi) south of Straffan on R407, 30 km (19 mi) southwest of Dublin on N7.*

The seat of County Kildare and a thriving market town in the heartland of Irish Thoroughbred country, Naas (pronounced nace) is full of pubs with high stools where short men (trainee jockeys) discuss the merits of their various stables. Naas has its own small racecourse, but **Punchestown Racecourse** (✉ 3 km [2 mi] south of Naas on R411 ☎ 045/897–704) has a wonderful setting amid rolling plains, with the Wicklow Mountains a

TREASURE HUNT
THE ANGLO-IRISH GEORGIAN HOUSE

For an upclose look at the Lifestyles of the Rich and Famous, 18th-century style, nothing beats a visit to the great treasure houses of Castletown and Russborough. Set just a half-hour south of Dublin and located only 20 miles apart, they offer a unique peek through the keyhole into the extravagant world of Ireland's "Princes of Elegance and Prodigality."

When the Palladian architectural craze swept across England, the Anglo-Irish---determined not to be outdone---set about building palaces in their own domain that would be the equal of anything in the mother country. Both Castletown House and Russborough House set new benchmarks in symmetry, elegance, and harmony for the Georgian style, which reigned supreme from 1714 to 1830, and was named after the four Georges who successively sat on the English throne. This style was greatly influenced by the Italian architect, Andrea Palladio, who promulgated his Neoclassical villa designs in his *Four Books of Architecture*.

Published in 1570, this treatise created Palladian wannabees overnight from England to Virginia (including Thomas Jefferson, whose Monticello is Palladian in spirit).

Although Castletown remains the largest private house in Ireland, and Russborough has the longest façade of any domicile in the country, Georgian groupies know that the real treasures lie inside: ceilings lavishly worked in Italianate stuccowork, priceless Old Master paintings, and an intimate look at the glory and grandeur of the Anglo-Irish lords.

Above: Castletown House and its impressive grounds.

CASTLETOWN: A GEORGIAN VERSAILLES

Reputedly the inspiration for a certain building at 1600 Pennsylvania Avenue, Castletown remains the finest example of an Irish Palladian–style house.

In 1722, William Conolly (1662–1729) decided to build himself a house befitting his new status as the speaker of the Irish House of Commons and Ireland's wealthiest man. On an estate 20 km (12 mi) southwest of Dublin, he began work on Castletown, designed in the latest Neoclassical fashion by the Florentine architect Alessandro Galilei. As it turns out, a young Irish designer and Palladian aficionado by the name of Sir Edward Lovett Pearce (1699–1733) was traveling in Italy, met Galilei, and soon signed on to oversee the completion of the house. Inspired by the use of outlying wings to frame a main building—the "winged device" used in Palladio's Venetian villas— Lovett Pearce added Castletown's striking colonnades and side pavillons in 1724. It is said that between them a staggering total of 365 windows were built into the overall design of the house—legend has it that a team of four servants were kept busy year-round keeping them all clean.

Conolly died before the interior of the house was completed, and work resumed in 1758 when his great nephew Thomas, and more importantly, his 15-year-old wife, Lady Louisa Lennox, took up residence there. Luckily, Louisa's passion for interior decoration led to the creation of some of Ireland's most stunning salons, including the Print Room and the Long Gallery. Little of the original furnishings remain today, but there is plenty of evidence of the ingenuity of Louisa and her artisans, chief among whom were the Lafranchini brothers, master craftsmen who created the famous wall plasterwork, considered masterpieces of their kind. Rescued in 1967 by Desmond Guinness of the brewing family, Castletown was deeded to the Irish state and remains the headquarters for the Irish Georgian Society.

Above: Castletown House inside and out.
Center: The family crest of William Conolly.

Castletown House:

- ⊠ Celbridge
- ☎ 01/628-8252
- 🌐 www.heritageireland.ie
- 🎫 € 3.70
- 🕐 Open Easter.–Sept., week-days 10-6, weekends 1-6; Oct., weekdays 10-5, Sun. 1-5.

The Entrance Hall

Studded with 17th-century hunting scenes painted by Paul de Vos, this soaring white-on-white entryway showcases one of Ireland's greatest staircases. Also extraordinary are the walls festooned with plasterwork sculpted by the Brothers Lafranchini, famous for their stuccoed swags, flora, and portraits.

The Long Gallery

Upstairs at the rear of the house, this massive room—almost 80 feet by 23 feet—is the most notable of the public rooms. Hued in a vibrant cobalt blue and topped by a coved ceiling covered with Italianate stuccowork and graced by three Venetian Murano glass chandeliers, it is a striking exercise in the antique Pompeian style.

The Print Room

Smaller but even more memorable is the Print Room, the only example in Ireland of this elegant fad. Fashionable young women loved to glue black-and-white prints—here, looking like oversize postage stamps in a giant album—onto salon walls. This was the 18th-century forerunner of today's teens covering their walls with posters of rock-star icons.

Above left: The Grand Staircase. Upper right: 18th-century Italian engravings decorate the Print Room. Bottom right: A marble statue within the Long Gallery. Far right: Mahogony bureau made for Lady Louisa, circa 1760.

WHAT A WAY TO GO

"I do not get any idea of the beauty of my house if I live in it... only if I can gaze upon the house from far off," proclaimed Lady Louisa in 1821 of her beloved Castletown. In her late seventies, she had a tent built on the front lawn so she could study the house at her leisure. After one evening on the lawn she promptly caught a chill and died.

5 Other Great Georgian Houses:

Newbridge, County Dublin
Emo Court, County Laois
Westport House, County Mayo
Florence Court, County Fermanagh
Castle Coole, County Fermanagh

RUSSBOROUGH: A TEMPLE TO ART

An Irish Xanadu, Russborough House pulls out all the stops to achieve Palladian perfection.

Another conspicuously grand house rising seemingly in the middle of nowhere—actually the western part of County Wicklow—Russborough was an extravagance paid for by the wages of beer. In 1741, a year after inheriting a vast fortune from his brewer father, Joseph Leeson commissioned architect Richard Castle to build him a home of palatial stature, and was rewarded with this slightly over-the-top house, whose monumental 700-foot-long façade one-upped every other great house in Ireland. Following Castle's death, the project was taken over and completed by his associate, Francis Bindon. Today, the house serves as a showcase for the celebrated collection of Old Master paintings of Sir Alfred Beit, a descendant of the De Beers diamond family, who had bought and majestically restored the property in 1952.

Princely Magnificence

The first sight of Russborough draws gasps from visitors: a mile-long, beech-lined avenue leads to a distant embankment on which sits the longest house frontage in Ireland. Constructed of silver-gray Wicklow granite, the façade encompasses a seven-bay central block, from either end of which radiate semicircular loggias connecting the flanking wings—the finest example in Ireland of Palladio's "winged device."

The interiors are full of grand period rooms that were elegantly refurbished in the 1950s by their new, moneyed owner under the eye of the legendary 20th-century decorator, Lady Colefax. The Hall is centered around a massive black Kilkenny marble chimneypiece and has a ceiling modeled after one in the Irish Parliament. Four 18th-century Joseph Vernet marine landscapes—once missing but

A look at the 700-foot façade of Russborough House. Bottom left: The grand Saloon. Above right: The Hall. Opposite, top: Drawing Room. Opposite: Vermeer's *Lady Writing a Letter*.

found by Sir Alfred—once again grace the glorious stucco moldings created to frame them in the Drawing Room. The grandest room, the Saloon, is famed for its 18th-century stucco ceiling by the Lafranchini brothers; fine Old Masters hang on walls covered in 19th-century Genoese velvet. The views out the windows take in the foothills of the Wicklow Mountains and the famous Poulaphouca reservoir in front of the house.

VERMEER, DIAMONDS, AND GANGSTERS

If it can be said that beer paid for the house, then diamonds paid for the paintings. Russborough House is today as famed for its art collection—and the numerous attempts, some successful, to steal it—as for its architecture. Credit for this must go to Sir Alfred Beit (1903–1994), nephew of the cofounder of De Beers Diamonds. One evening in 1974 while Alfred was enjoying a quiet dinner with his wife, the door burst open and in marched Rose Dugdale, an English millionaire's daughter turned IRA stalwart. Her gang "liberated" 19 of the Beit masterpieces, including Vermeer's fabled *Lady Writing a Letter*, hopefully to bargain for the release of two IRA members jailed in London. Once the

paintings were recovered a week later, Sir Alfred decided to donate 17 works to the National Gallery of Ireland. Alas, a week before the handing-over ceremony in 1986, Sir Alfred and his wife were again settling down to dine when in marched Martin Cahill, a.k.a. "The General," Dublin's most notorious underworld boss (and subject of three major movies). He made off with the Vermeer and 16 other paintings. They didn't bring him much luck though, as he was subsequently shot to death in Dublin by the IRA for his Ulster affiliations. Seven years of secret negotiations resulted in the return of the paintings, which now sit safely (we hope) in the National Gallery.

Russborough House:

✉ Off N81, Blessington

☎ 045/865–239

💶 € 6

🕙 Open May–Sept., daily 10:30–5; April and Oct., Sun. 10:30–5.

STUCCADORES

Sounds better than plasterworkers, no? Baroque exuberance reigns in the house's lavishly ornamented plasterwork ceilings executed by the celebrated *stuccadores*, the Brothers Lafranchini, who originally hailed from Switzerland and worked in other great houses in Ireland, including Castletown. Their decorative flair adorns the Music Room and Library, but even these pale compared to the plasterwork done by an unknown artisan in the Staircase Hall—an extravaganza of whipped-cream moldings, cornucopias, and Rococo scrolls: "the ravings of a maniac," according to one 19th-century critic, who guessed that only an Irishman would have had the blarney to pull it off.

TREASURE HUNT: THE ANGLO-IRISH GEORGIAN HOUSE

2

spectacular backdrop. Horse races are held regularly here, but the most popular event is the Punchestown National Hunt Festival in April.

Blessington

 10 km (6 mi) southeast of Naas on R410, 23 km (14 mi) southwest of Dublin on N181.

Just outside the small village of Blessington are two of the marvels of Ireland: fabulous, art-filled, 18th-century **Russborough House** (see "Treasure Hunt: The Anglo-Irish Georgian House" in this chapter) and its adjacent **Poulaphouca Reservoir.** Known locally as the Blessington Lakes, Poulaphouca (pronounced pool-a-*fook*-a) is a large, meandering, artificial lake minutes from Russborough House that provides Dublin's water supply. You can drive around the entire perimeter of the reservoir on minor roads; on its southern end lies Hollywood Glen, a particularly beautiful natural spot. On the western shore of the lakes, the small market town of **Blessington,** with its wide main street lined on both sides by tall trees and Georgian buildings, is one of the most charming villages in the area. It was founded in the late 17th century, and was a stop on the Dublin–Waterford mail-coach service in the mid-19th century. Until 1932, a steam train ran from here to Dublin. Beyond the southern tip of the Poulaphouca Reservoir, 13 km (8 mi) south of Blessington on N81, look for a small sign for the **Piper's Stones,** a Bronze Age stone circle that was probably used in a ritual connected with worship of the sun. It's just a short walk from the road. You can take in splendid views of the Blessington Lakes from the top of **Church Mountain,** which you reach via a vigorous walk through Woodenboley Wood, at the southern tip of Hollywood Glen. Follow the main forest track for about 20 minutes and then take the narrow path that heads up the side of the forest to the mountaintop for about another half hour.

Where to Stay & Eat

$$$$ ✕⊞ **Rathsallagh House.** At the end of a long drive that winds through
Fodor'sChoice   a golf course and set in 530 acres of parkland is Rathsallagh House, which
★   came into being when low-slung, ivy-covered Queen Anne stables were converted into a farmhouse in 1798. Enveloping couches and chairs, fresh flower arrangements, large windows, fireplaces, and lots of lamps furnish the two drawing rooms. Large rooms have enchanting, pastoral names like Buttercup and Over Arch and the Yellow Room, with its claw-foot bath set in an alcove. Try to get a room overlooking the walled garden, where the scent of wildflowers wafts in through the beautiful French doors. The cozy Eagle Lodge bungalow has three bedrooms and sleeps up to six people. The outstanding haute-Irish dinner menu changes daily. Specialties include paupiette of herb-filled salmon with onion and chive beurre blanc. ⊠ *Dunlavin, Co. Wicklow* ☎ *045/403–112* 🖷 *045/403–343* ⊕ *www.rathsallagh.com* ⊷ *29 rooms, 1 bungalow* ⚒ *Restaurant, 18-hole golf course, tennis court, hot tub, massage, sauna, croquet, bar, meeting rooms* ▤ *AE, DC, MC, V* ⦿ *BP, MAP.*

The Curragh

 8 km (5 mi) southwest of Naas on M7, 25½ km (16 mi) west of Poulaphouca Reservoir.

The broad plain of the Curragh, bisected by the main N7 road, is the biggest area of common land in Ireland, encompassing about 31 square km (12 square mi) and devoted mainly to grazing. This is Ireland's major racing center, home of the **Curragh Racecourse** (⊠ N7 ☎ 045/441–205 ⊕ www.curragh.ie); the Irish Derby and other international horse races are run here.

Kildare Town

② *5 km (3 mi) west of the Curragh on M7, 51 km (32 mi) southwest of Dublin via N7 and M7.*

Horse breeding is the cornerstone of County Kildare's thriving economy, and Kildare Town is the place to come if you're crazy about horses. Right off Kildare's main market square, the **Silken Thomas** (☎ 045/522–232) pub re-creates an old-world atmosphere with open fires, dark wood, and leaded lights; it's a good place to stop for lunch before exploring the sights here.

The Church of Ireland **St. Brigid's Cathedral** is where the eponymous saint founded a religious settlement in the 5th century. The present cathedral, with its stocky tower, is a restored 13th-century structure. It was partially rebuilt around 1686, but restoration work wasn't completed for another 200 years. The stained-glass west window of the cathedral depicts three of Ireland's greatest saints: Brigid, Patrick, and Columba. In pre-Christian times druids gathered around a sacred oak that stood on the grounds and from which Kildare (*Cill Dara*), or the "Church of the Oak," gets its name. Also on the grounds is a restored fire pit reclaimed from the time of Brigid, when a fire was kept burning—by a chaste woman—in a female-only fire temple. Interestingly, Brigid started the place for women, but it was she who asked monks to move here as well. ⊠ *Off Market Sq.* ☎ *No phone* ☎ *€1.50* ⊗ *Daily 10–6.*

The 108-foot-high **round tower,** in the graveyard of St. Brigid's Cathedral, is the second highest in Ireland (the highest is in Kilmacduagh in County Galway). It dates from the 12th century. Extraordinary views across much of the Midlands await you if you're energetic enough to climb the stairs to the top. ☎ *045/521–229* ☎ *€3* ⊗ *May–Sept., daily 10–1 and 2–5.*

If you're a horse aficionado, or even just curious, check out the **National Stud Farm,** a main center of Ireland's racing industry. The Stud was founded in 1900 by brewing heir Colonel William Hall-Walker, and transferred to the Irish state in 1945. It's here that breeding stallions are groomed, exercised, tested, and bred. Spring and early summer, when mares have foals, are the best

HORSEFEATHERS!

Besides being nutty about horses, Colonel Walker may just have been more than a little eccentric— a believer in astrology, he had charts drawn up for his foals. Those with unfavorable predictions were sold right away. He even built the stallion stalls with lantern roofs to allow the moon and stars to work their magic on the equine occupants.

times to visit. The **National Stud Horse Museum,** also on the grounds, recounts the history of horses in Ireland. Its most outstanding exhibit is the skeleton of Arkle, the Irish racehorse that won major victories in Ireland and England during the late 1960s. The museum also contains medieval evidence of horses, such as bones from 13th-century Dublin, and some early examples of equestrian equipment. ⊠ *½ km (⅓ mi) south of Kildare Town* ☏ *045/521–617* ⊕ *www.irish-national-stud.ie* 🎫 *€9, includes entry to Japanese Gardens* ☉ *Mid-Feb.–mid-Nov., daily 9:30–5.*

★ Adjacent to the National Stud Farm, the **Japanese Gardens** were created between 1906 and 1910 by the Stud's founder, Colonel Hall-Walker, and laid out by a Japanese gardener, Tassa Eida, and his son Minoru. The gardens are recognized as among the finest Asian gardens in the world, although they're more of an East–West hybrid than authentically Japanese. The Scots pine trees, for instance, are an appropriate stand-in for traditional Japanese pines, which signify long life and happiness. The gardens symbolically chart the human progression from birth to death, although the focus is on the male journey. A series of landmarks runs along a meandering path: the Tunnel of Ignorance (No. 3) represents a child's lack of understanding; the Engagement and Marriage bridges (Nos. 8 and 9) span a small stream; and from the Hill of Ambition (No. 13), you can look back over your joys and sorrows. It ends with the Gateway to Eternity (No. 20), beyond which lies a Zen Buddhist meditation sand garden. This is a worthwhile destination any time of the year, though it's particularly glorious in spring and fall. ⊠ *About 2½ km (1½ mi) south of Kildare Town, clearly signposted off Market Sq.* ☏ *045/521–617* ⊕ *www.irish-national-stud.ie* 🎫 *€9, includes entry to National Stud* ☉ *Mid-Feb.–mid-Nov., daily 9:30–5.*

Where to Stay & Eat

$$–$$$ ✕🏨 **Keadeen Hotel.** The luxurious spa and health center are the big attraction at this family-owned hotel on 10 acres of award-winning, flower-filled gardens. Light is a constant theme in the spacious bedrooms with pastel color finishings and big windows overlooking the lawns below. Giant wall murals in the Derby Room restaurant are dedicated to the true heroes of Kildare, those famous race horses. Don't miss the chance to take a dip in the ancient Roman-style pool; it's a real miniature sea of tranquillity. ⊠ *Newbridge, Co. Kildare* ☏ *045/431–666* 🖷 *045/434–402* ⊕ *www.keadeenhotel.ie* 🛏 *75 rooms* ☖ *Restaurant, indoor pool, health club, meeting rooms* ▤ *AE, DC, MC, V* ⏹ *BP, MAP.*

DUBLIN ENVIRONS ESSENTIALS

To research prices, get advice from other travelers, and book travel arrangements, visit www.fodors.com.

Transportation

BY BUS

Bus services link Dublin with the main and smaller towns in the area. All buses for the region depart from Dublin's Busaras, the central bus station, at Store Street. For bus inquiries, contact Bus Éireann. You can reach Enniskerry and the Powerscourt Estate by taking Dublin Bus No. 44 from the Dublin quays area. The No. 45 and No. 45a head to Bray and the No. 84 goes to Greystones from near Merrion Square.

St. Kevin's, a private bus service, runs daily from Dublin (outside the Royal College of Surgeons on St. Stephen's Green) to Glendalough, stopping off at Bray, Kilmacanogue, Roundwood, and Laragh en route. Buses leave Dublin daily at 11:30 AM and 6 PM (7 PM on Sunday); buses leave Glendalough weekdays at 7:15 AM and 4:30 PM (9:45 AM and 4:30 PM on Saturday, 9:45 AM and 5:30 PM on Sunday). One-way fare is €11; a round-trip ticket costs €18.

Bus Information Bus Éireann ☎ 01/836-6111 ⊕ www.buseireann.ie. **Dublin Bus** ☎ 01/873-4222 ⊕ www.dublinbus.ie. **St. Kevin's** ☎ 01/281-8119 ⊕ www.glendaloughbus.com.

BY CAR

The easiest and best way to tour Dublin's environs is by car, because many sights are not served by public transportation, and what service there is, especially to outlying areas, is infrequent. (⇨ If you need to rent a car, *see* Car Rental *in* Dublin Essentials *in* Chapter 1.) To visit destinations in the Boyne Valley, follow N3, along the east side of Phoenix Park, out of the city and make Trim and Tara your first stops. Alternatively, leave Dublin via N1/M1 toward Belfast. Try to avoid the road during weekday rush hours (8 AM–10 AM and 5 PM–7 PM); stay on it as far as Drogheda and start touring from there.

To reach destinations in County Kildare, follow the quays along the south side of the River Liffey (they are one-way westbound) to St. John's Road West (N7); in a matter of minutes, you're heading for open countryside. Avoid traveling this route during the evening peak rush hours, especially on Friday, when Dubliners are themselves making their weekend getaways.

To reach destinations in County Wicklow, N11/M11 is the fastest and most clearly marked route. The two more scenic routes to Glendalough are R115 to R759 to R755, or R177 to R755.

BY TRAIN

Irish Rail (Iarnród Éireann) trains run the length of the east coast, from Dundalk to the north in County Louth to Arklow along the coast in County Wicklow. Trains make many stops along the way; there are stations in Drogheda, Dublin (the main stations are Connolly Station and Pearse Station), Bray, Greystones, Wicklow, and Rathdrum. From Heuston Station, the Arrow, a commuter train service, runs westward to Celbridge, Naas, Newbridge, and Kildare Town. Contact Irish Rail for schedule and fare information.

Train Information Irish Rail–Iarnod Éireann ⊕ www.irishrail.ie/home. **Connolly Station** ✉ Amiens St., Northside, Dublin. **Heuston Station** ✉ Victoria Quay and St. John's Road W, Dublin West, Dublin. **Irish Rail** ☎ 01/836-6222. **Pearse Station** ✉ Westland Row, Southside, Dublin.

Contacts & Resources

EMERGENCIES

Ambulance, fire, police ☎ 999.

TOUR OPTIONS

Bus Éireann runs guided bus tours to many of the historic and scenic locations throughout the Dublin environs daily in summer. Visits include trips to Glendalough in Wicklow; Boyne Valley and Newgrange in County Louth; and the Hill of Tara, Trim, and Navan in County Meath. All tours depart from Busaras Station, Dublin; information is available by phone Monday–Saturday 8:30–7, Sunday 10–7. Gray Line, a privately owned touring company, also runs many guided bus tours throughout the Dublin environs between May and September. Their Grand Wicklow Tour lasts seven hours, as does their day trip to Newgrange and Mellifont Abbey. Prices start at €32. Wild Wicklow Tours uses small minibuses that can handle smaller groups and take you off the beaten track. Their full-day trips to Glendalough also take in Avoca Handweavers and a Dublin coastal drive. Prices start at €28. Railtours Ireland have a half-day rail tour into the Wicklow Mountains. The train stops at Arklow and then a bus takes you through Avoca and on to Glendalough. The cost is €39.

🚌 Bus Tours **Bus Éireann** ☎ 01/836-6111 ⊕ www.buseireann.ie/site/home. **Gray Line Tours** ☎ 01/670-8822 ⊕ www.grayline.com. **Railtours Ireland** ☎ 01/856-0045 ⊕ www.railtoursireland.com. **Wild Wicklow Tour** ☎ 01/280-1899 ⊕ www.wildwicklow.ie.

VISITOR INFORMATION

For information on travel in the Dublin environs and for help in making lodging reservations, contact one of the following Tourist Information Offices (TIOs) year-round: Dublin Tourism and Bord Fáilte, Dundalk, Mullingar, Trim, or Wicklow Town. Mullingar is the head office of tourism for Counties Louth, Meath, and Kildare; it can give you contact information for temporary TIOs in these areas. In summer, temporary TIOs are open throughout the environs, in towns such as Arklow in County Wicklow, Drogheda and Dundalk in County Louth, and Kildare Town in County Kildare. **East Coast Midlands Tourism** is the department of Bord Fáilte directly involved for the Dublin Environs area and their Web site—www.eastcoastmidlands.ie—is very useful.

🏛 Tourist Information **Arklow** ✉ The Coach House East Coast & Midlands Tourism, County Westmeath, Ireland ☎ 0402/32484. **Drogheda** ✉ Bus Éireann Depot ☎ 041/983-7070. **Dublin Tourism** ✉ Suffolk St. ☎ 01/605-7700 or 01/602-4129. **Dundalk** ✉ Jocelyn St. ☎ 042/933-5484. **East Coast Midlands Tourism** ✉ Dublin Rd., Mullingar ☎ 044/934-8761 📠 044/934-0413 ⊕ www.eastcoastmidlands.ie. **Kildare** ✉ Market House ☎ 045/521-240. **Mullingar** ✉ Market House, Market Sq. ☎ 044/934-8650. **Trim** ✉ Old Town Hall, Castle St. ☎ 046/943-7227. **Wicklow Town** ✉ Rialto House, Fitzwilliam Sq. ☎ 0404/69117.

The Midlands

INCLUDING COUNTIES CAVAN, KILDARE, LAOIS,
LEITRIM, LONGFORD, MONAGHAN, OFFALY,
ROSCOMMON, TIPPERARY, AND WESTMEATH

Athlon Town, County Westmeath

WORD OF MOUTH

"In Cavan, we remember a group of men who were clearly on a meal break, who started playing the spoons and toe-tap dancing along to the traditional music tape. It was a moment of Ireland we treasure. Cavan doesn't make all the tour books, but it stays in our memory as a grand place."

–Danna

WELCOME TO THE MIDLANDS

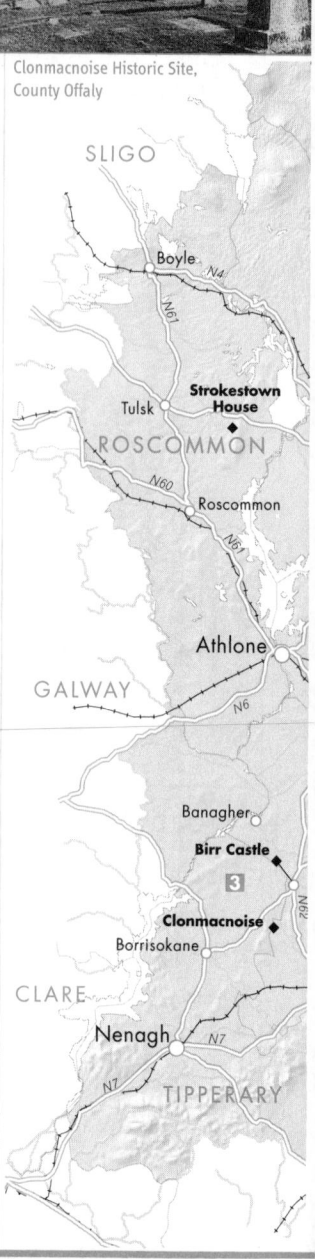

Clonmacnoise Historic Site, County Offaly

TOP REASONS TO GO

★ **Stately Clonmacnoise:** Atmospheric and still spirit-warm, this great early Christian monastery survived Viking, Norman, and English invaders over the centuries.

★ **Green Mansions:** "The biggest farm in the world," the Midlands is also home to stately homes and gardens, including fairy-tale Tullynally Castle and Birr Castle.

★ **Hiking the Slieve Bloom Mountains:** Dip in and out of the 20-mi Slieve Bloom Trail, ideal hiking country for those with a yen to rise above their surroundings.

★ **Bord na Mona Bog Rail Tour:** In a region where bogland reigns supreme, this rail tour on a narrow-gauge railway stops at turf banks and archaeological finds.

★ **Castle Leslie's Suite Temptation:** Owned by the extraordinary Leslie family, this neo-baronial hotel has been delighting guests from Winston Churchill to Paul McCartney.

1 The Eastern Midlands. Just an hour from Dublin, this region is essentially rich farmland but is studded with even richer sights: grand homes like **Emo Court, Belvedere House,** and **Tullynally Castle;** once-a-time-fied villages such as **Abbeyleix;** and the historic treats of **Fore Abbey** and **Locke's Distillery.**

2 The Northern Midlands. Leaving the ancient kingdom of Leinster, you come to two counties of Ulster: Cavan and Monaghan. Beyond **Cavan Town** you enter the heart of the Northern Lakelands, dotted with hundred of lakes and some of Ireland's poshest country-house hotels, including **Cabra Castle** and **Castle Leslie.**

3 The Western Midlands. One of the corners of "hidden Ireland," this region is unblighted by crowds. While some of the country's most distinctive boglands are here, cultural treasures also beckon: stately **Birr Castle** and **Strokestown House,** postcard-perfect **Terryglass,** and the great early Christian monastery of **Clonmacnoise.**

Birr Castle, County Offaly

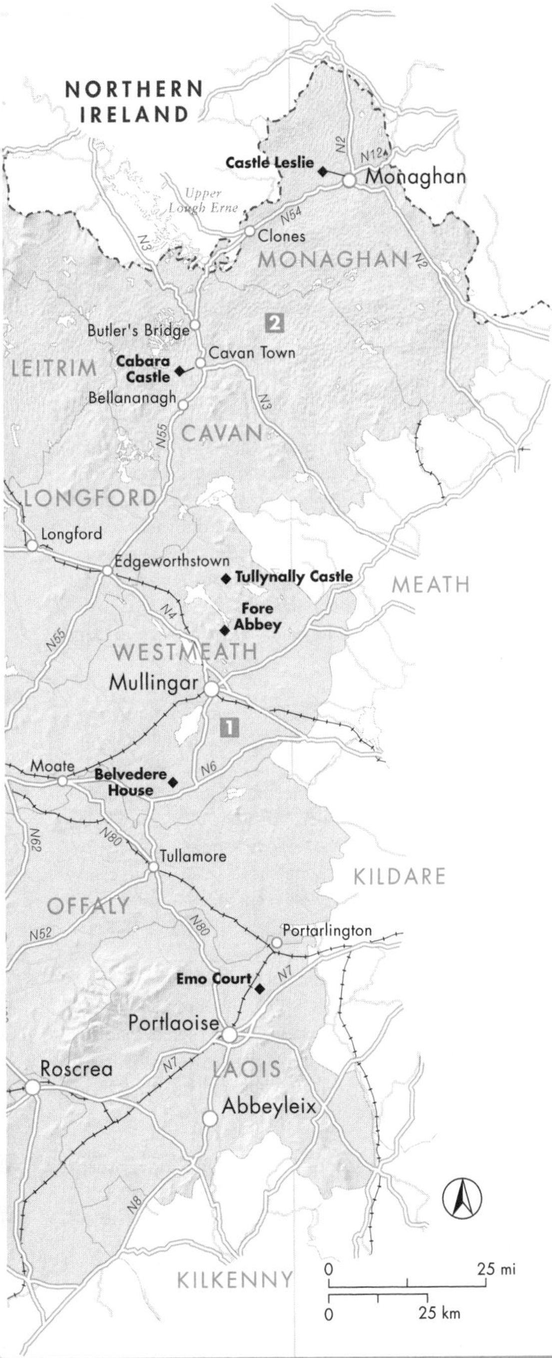

NORTHERN
IRELAND

Castle Leslie ◆ ○ Monaghan
N2 N12↗
Upper
Lough Erne
N54
Clones
MONAGHAN
N2
Butler's Bridge
LEITRIM   Cabara   Cavan Town
            Castle ◆
Bellananagh
N3
N55   CAVAN
LONGFORD
Longford
Edgeworthstown
N4   ◆ Tullynally Castle   MEATH
N55   Fore
            WESTMEATH   ◆ Abbey
            Mullingar
                              1
Moate   Belvedere ◆
N62 N80 House
N62   Tullamore
                    KILDARE
OFFALY
N52   N80   Portarlington
            Emo Court ◆   N7
       Portlaoise
Roscrea   N7
            LAOIS
            Abbeyleix

◆ (compass)   0   25 mi
KILKENNY   0   25 km
N8

GETTING ORIENTED

Perfect for the relaxed visitor who values the subtle over the spectacular, the flat, fertile plain at the center of Ireland is full of relatively undiscovered historic towns, abbey ruins, and grand houses. While just two hours from the chaotic rush of Dublin, Cork or Galway, the region is carpeted with countryside perfect for bicycling: no wonder stressed-out Dubliners love to head here to chill out.

Whispering Door, Clonmacnoise, County Offaly

MIDLANDS PLANNER

Getting Around

For the first-time visitor, the roads of the Midlands offer an easier intro to Irish driving than the hairpin bends of West Cork and Connemara. With a decent network of main arteries and off-the-beaten-track byroads, a car may deliver the best option for covering the widest itinerary of curiosity.

Happily, bus and train routes into and through the region have improved greatly over the past two decades. Public transport services are regular through the main towns—Athlone, Portarlington, Abbeyleix, Nenagh, and Longford. Of course, you may be forced to stop and change to reach a particular place—give time and attention to the appropriate timetables when planning your jaunts.

No one will deny, however, that the freedom of your own wheels will bring ample rewards in transporting you to the area's many hidden lakes and villages. This is Ireland at its most rural, so don't be surprised to round a bend only to confront a herd of sheep idly grazing with little hurry about them—do what the locals do, slow to a stop and wait for an opening in the woolly mass to occur.

The same goes for cows—especially when farmers move them from fields to barn at evening time. Refrain from honking your horn on these occasions—it will only confirm your status as an impatient tourist and, besides, the sheep won't take a bit of notice.

Finding a Place to Stay

The Irish B & B still reigns supreme in the Midlands—farmhouses and homes geared to paying guests offering a direct contact with local families and the lore of their area. Time was when these kinds of accommodations veered to the spartan—not anymore. Good beds, decent heating, en-suite bathrooms, and the legendary Irish breakfast are now the norm—add broadband, 32-inch TVs, and computer games courtesy of the landlady's kids often as part of the bargain.

Although B & Bs may not offer the same kind of privacy as hotels, they still work delightfully well as the ultimate way to meet genuine Irish folk, a bird's-eye view into working families and the organized chaos of a country household. As commercial progress has blossomed in the Midlands, so, too, have the options in hotels, country houses, and cottage rentals increased. Pretty much every town now has more than one decent hotel—most with health centers and spa facilities.

From June to early September, tourism gets into a serious stride bolstered by the many Irish families using their holiday homes and getaway cottages in the region. Finding accommodation is never a major problem—except for those weekends when towns are having their annual music festival or whatever.

Tourist offices generally cope bravely with these seasonal influxes and if you arrive without local knowledge or reservations, there's rarely a problem that can't be solved with a few phone calls. At a rock concert in Abbeyleix a few years ago, we heard that four travelers found temporary lodgings in a convent, but that's another story altogether . . .

Heading Out on the Water

Whether it's water sports, fishing, or nature-watching you seek, Ireland's heartland is full of waterborne opportunities for the visitor. The entire Midlands region is littered with thousands of loughs (the Irish terms for lakes) and rivers as well as an extensive canal system. Historically, these waterways were the lifeblood of Ireland's commercial life. In the 18th century, the construction of the Royal and Grand canals allowed the transport of food, livestock, and, of course, Guinness brew, from Dublin to the west. The Shannon, flowing majestically through the center of the region, is the longest river in Ireland and Britain and one of Europe's great waterways. Along the course of the river lie two major lakes, Lough Ree (north of Athlone) and Lough Derg (north of Limerick city). The best way to see the Shannon is by river cruiser. These boats are for hire at riverside towns like Carrick-on-Shannon in County Leitrim and Ballina in County Offaly. These "self-drive" boats accommodate up to 12 people and allow amateur mariners to take a relaxing meander along the river, with opportunities for fishing, swimming, and "refueling stops" at pretty shoreside villages like Terryglass, County Tipperary, where cozy pubs and excellent restaurants are the order of the day. Other activities, like waterskiing and canoeing, are also popular along the Shannon. You can also navigate the Shannon-Erne Waterway, a canal linking the majestic expanse of Upper and Lower Lough Erne in Northern Ireland to the Shannon. The link, created in 1994, is Europe's longest (750 km, 466 mi) navigable leisure waterway. Or if you just want to take in the riverscape at leisure, opt for a cruise on the Viking, which sets sail from Athlone. The northern Midlands are known as Ireland's Lakelands, thanks to thousands of pristine lakes and rivers dotting the landscape. The area is a paradise for anglers (note that fishing gear and tackle are usually rentable) and many boast of having an entire lake to themselves. The loughs of Cavan and Monaghan are also famed for their huge and rather fearsome pike fish.

How's the Weather?

C'mon, this is Ireland, after all—a rain mac or windbreaker should never be far from your side. Though, in fairness, it must be said that the legendary "soft" weather has become noticeably more clement; since 2000, Ireland has been recording more hours of sunshine. The incremental increase in the number of sunny days each year has prompted many philosophical discussions in Irish pubs on whether that itty-bitty hole in the ozone is really such a bad thing . . .

ACTIVITIES

Dotted with historical monuments like Clonmacnoise, Fore Abbey, and the Rock of Dunamase, as well as many fine ancient architectural gems like Emo Court and Carriglas Manor, you'll never be more than 10 mi from ancient history. Like all of Ireland's regions during the summer months, the Midlands rocks with festivals, literary gatherings, and small-town fairs—check out the tourist boards for listings. If you just want to wander where your nose takes you for a few days, the relatively quiet roads, unpopulated countryside, and tucked-away vistas around the Slieve Blooms will deliver many quiet rewards.

Dining & Lodging Price Categories (in Euros)					
	$$$$	**$$$**	**$$**	**$**	**¢**
Restaurants	over €29	€22–29	€15–22	€8–15	under €8
Hotels	over €230	€180–230	€130–180	€80–130	under €80

Restaurant prices are for a main course at dinner. Hotel prices are for a standard double room in high season.

Updated by
John Daly

IRISH SCHOOL CHILDREN WERE ONCE TAUGHT TO THINK of their country as a saucer, with mountains edging the rim and a dip in the middle. The dip is the Midlands—or the Lakelands, as it's sometimes referred to—and this often-overlooked region comprises nine counties: Cavan, Laois (pronounced leash), Westmeath, Longford, Offaly, Roscommon, Monaghan, Leitrim, and Tipperary. Ask people from other parts of Ireland what the purpose of the Midlands is and they will jest that the region exists simply to hold the rest of the country together.

Indeed, the Midlands is sometimes looked upon with disdain by the Irish people, a few of whom consider it dull and mundane (the worst of offenses in Ireland). The perception is a bit true, the flat plains of the Midlands being the kind of terrain you rush through on the way to someplace else; with no major city in the region (Dublin lies to the east, Galway and Limerick to the west, and Cork to the south), it remains a quiet and geographically unspectacular place. Night owls should probably keep going—the wildest thing in these parts is the wind.

But that is precisely why many travelers consider the Midlands a gem in the making. For when it comes to studying how Ireland gets on with its daily life, there are few better places. Here, a town's main hotel is usually one of the prime social centers and can be a good place from which to partake of local life. If you miss out witnessing a wedding reception, First Communion supper, or meeting of the Lion's Club, you can still get to know the locals just with a walk along a village's main street. Happily so, since there are plenty of folks who have nothing to do but be pleasant. Hereabouts, the pace of life is slower, every neighbor's face is familiar, and there are plenty of minor roads linking the more scenic areas—and if you're in no particular hurry, these are the ones to take. Spend enough time in the region and you might even get to recognize the difference between a Cavan twang and a Tipperary brogue.

The people and the slow pace of life hereabouts are a throwback to the Ireland of 20 years ago—the hurry and bustle of modernity found elsewhere in the Celtic Tiger is still blessedly absent. Long the butt of comedians' jokes for their supposed carefulness with cash (like the Cavan farmer who eats his dinner out of a drawer so he can hide it quickly should neighbors arrive unexpectedly), Midlanders have long met big-city ridicule with breezy nonchalance. Visitors, and the prosperity they bring to the local economy, are still prized in these flatland counties. The welcome is genuine, and the regional pride is abundantly evident once you get beyond those initial shy, self-deprecating shrugs.

The tourist sun also shines brightly on the region because of its notable cultural highlights. Among them are Clonmacnoise, Ireland's most important monastic ruins; historic towns with age-old industries, such as lace making and crystal making; the gorgeous gardens of Birr Castle; and some of Ireland's finest Anglo-Irish houses, including Strokestown Park House and Emo Court, and probably Ireland's most historically delightful hotel, Castle Leslie. As for scenic pleasures, this region of the country has a fair share of Ireland's 800 bodies of water. Speckling this lush countryside, many of these lakes were formed by glacial action some

10,000 years ago. Because of all the water, much of the landscape lies under blanket bog, a unique ecosystem that's worth exploring. The River Shannon, one of the longest rivers in Europe and the longest in the British Isles, bisects the Midlands from north to south, piercing a series of loughs (lakes): Lough Allen, Lough Ree, and Lough Derg. The Royal Canal and the Grand Canal cross the Midlands from east to west, ending in the Shannon north and south of Lough Ree.

These days, the Midlands is being "recolonized" by many young couples unable to afford the high property prices in Dublin: Small towns in the region have expanded with new housing for city commuters who make daily two-hour round-trip journeys to work. In a region historically depopulated by emigration, the influx of new residents has reenergized many of the small towns. Eateries, farmers' markets, and renovated pubs are the order of the day as touches of big city cosmopolitanism take root. On weekends, Midland towns and villages are hives of activity as young families make their homes in this pastoral, and infinitely more affordable, region beyond the Pale. They reckon if Charlotte Brontë spent her honeymoon here and Anthony Trollope settled in one of the region's villages to write two of his novels, it's good enough for them.

Exploring the Midlands

This chapter is organized into three Midlands sections: the eastern, northern, and western. The first two areas can be easily covered in an extended visit to the Midlands region, as they chart a course almost due north from the initial starting point in Abbeyleix, County Laois. The third section includes sights west of those in the first two, which means they can easily be visited if you're flying into Shannon and beginning your explorations of Ireland in the western half of the country. In fact, because parts of the Midlands border on virtually every major county of Ireland, there are three places in this chapter where you should be alert to nearby locales covered in other chapters: the easternmost sights in the Midlands (Emo Court and Coolbanagher) are within a few miles of the westernmost sites in the Dublin environs; the westernmost sights in the Midlands (Boyle and Lough Key Forest Park) are just across the border from County Sligo; and the northernmost sights and towns of the Midlands are just across the border from Northern Ireland.

THE EASTERN MIDLANDS

The eastern fringe of the Midlands is about an hour's drive from Dublin, and a visit to the area could easily be grafted onto a trip to the Dublin environs. In spite of its proximity to the capital, or perhaps because of it, this area is a bit removed from the regular tourist trail, and is a source of constant surprises. Unspoiled Georgian villages, ruined castles, and quaint "towns-that-time-forgot" dot the landscape. There are also plenty of opportunities for hill walking, horse riding, and other outdoor pursuits. Stately home-buffs are in for a treat, as Emo Court and Gardens, Charleveille Forest Castle, Belvedere House Gardens, and Tullynally Castle await them. The Eastern Midlands fan out from the central

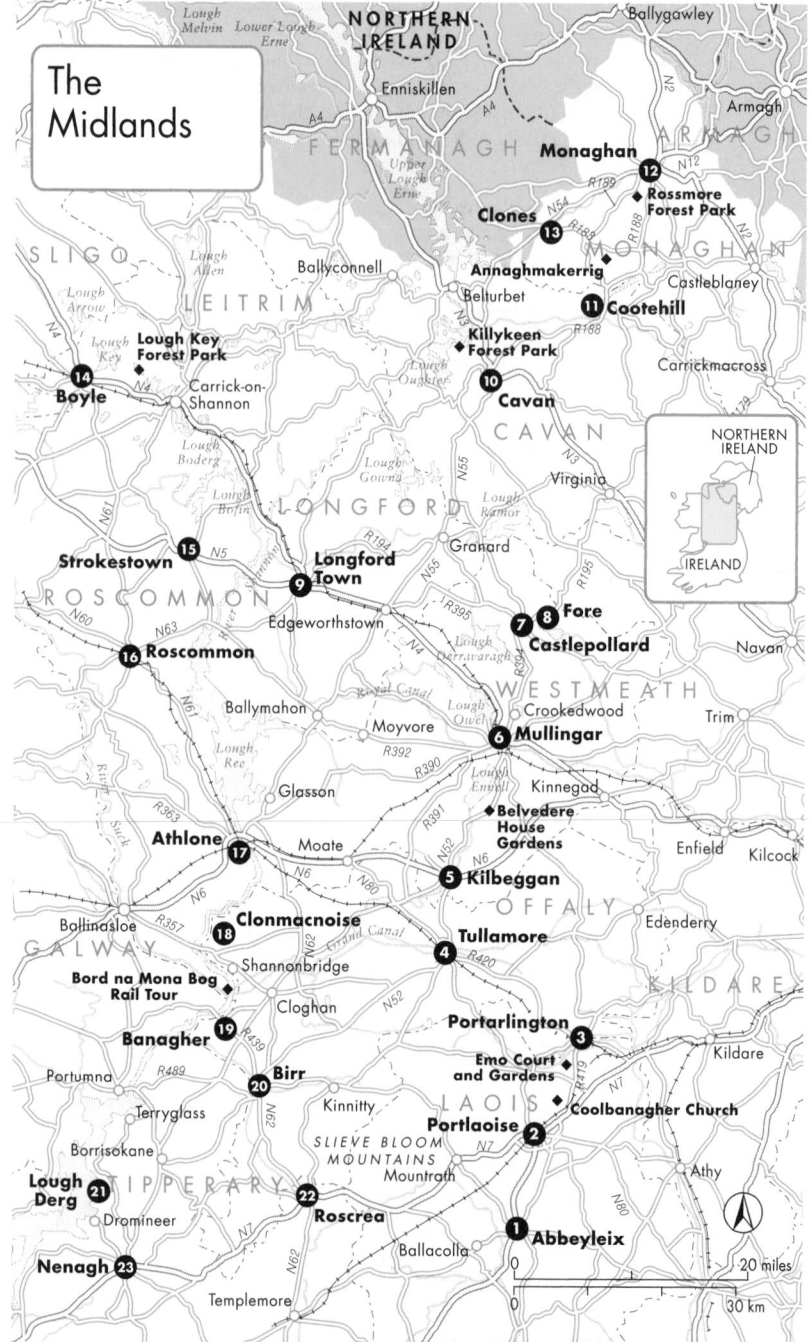

The
Midlands

point of Mullingar. With richer farmland than is found in the northern area of the Midlands, the eastern region tends toward agriculture. But the Dublin commuter culture means that you're as likely to be delayed on a back road by a badly parked BMW as by a slow-moving tractor on its way home from the dairy. A good tour begins at Abbeyleix and moves northwest to Castlepollard and environs, stopping just short of Longford, the jumping-off point for the northern Midlands.

Abbeyleix

❶ *99 km (61 mi) southwest of Dublin.*

"One of the most pleasing villages in Leinster, with each cottage having a useful garden!" Thus spoke J. M Brewer, a noted 19th-century writer, of Abbeyleix in 1826. Today it happily remains one of the most elegant small towns in Ireland, having retained its charming Georgian ambience and its broad main street, which is lined with well-appointed, stone-cut buildings and original shop fronts in the traditionally ornate Irish style. The entire tree-lined village was built in the 18th century, on the orders of the Viscount de Vesci, to house servants and tradesmen working on his nearby estate. Many town houses and vernacular buildings date from the 1850s but more recent buildings, including the Market House, erected in 1906, and the Hibernian Bank, from 1900, contribute greatly to the town's tranquil and refined character.

★ Don't miss **Morrissey's Pub and Grocery Store** (✉ Main St. ☎ 0502/ 31281), which has been a working public house since 1775. One of Ireland's best-loved drinking emporiums, it has a dark, wood-panel interior furnished with antique bar fittings. Customers can warm themselves by an ancient potbelly stove. Until 2005 this award-winning establishment still functioned as a shop and while it retains its stocks of groceries, they are no longer for sale. An evocative time capsule, it serves as a reminder of times when you could purchase a pound of butter, the newspaper, and cattle feed while enjoying the obligatory pint of Guinness.

The **Heritage House,** the former North Boys School, has fascinating informative displays on the de Vesci family and the history of Abbeyleix. The school was originally constructed for the education of Catholics while at the other end of the town you'll find the South School, built for Protestants. Also accessible through the Heritage House, ask to see the original Sexton's House (no extra charge), which boasts a stylish interior from the turn of the 19th century. ✉ *Top of town* ☎ *0502/31653* ⊕ *www.abbeyleixheritagetown.com* 🎟 *€3* ⊙ *Apr.–Sept., weekdays 9–5, weekends, 1–5; Oct.–Mar. weekdays 9–5.*

Ballinakill, a pretty Georgian village about 5 km (3 mi) south of Abbeyleix, contains the **Heywood Gardens,** designed by the English architect Sir Edward Lutyens in the early 20th century within an existing 18th-century park. The Lutyenses' house burned down, but the

---

WRECKED RUGS

The carpets for the ill-fated *Titanic* were woven at a now defunct carpet factory in Abbeyleix.

gardens, with landscaping most likely attributable to the famed Gertrude Jeckyll, are worth a detour. Guided tours are available through this gardener's paradise where a formal lawn flanked by traditional herbaceous borders leads to a sunken Italian garden. ⊠ *Ballinakill* ☎ *0502/ 33563* ⊕ *www.heritageireland.ie* ✉ *Free* ☉ *Daily 9–dusk.*

Where to Stay & Eat

$$ ✕🏠 **Preston House.** This ivy-clad Georgian building on the main Cork–Dublin road was a schoolhouse until the 1960s. Now it's a popular lunch and coffee stop by day, renowned for good traditional home cooking. By night the restaurant ($$, closed Sunday and Monday) takes on a more formal aspect. Owner Allison Dowling offers a menu featuring hearty, heartwarming dishes such as honey roast duck with plum and port sauce and sautéed venison with cream potatoes and red currants. The spacious guest rooms, furnished with solid Victorian antiques, have views of the long back gardens and fields beyond. ⊠ *Main St., Co. Laois* ☎ *0502/31432* ➺ *4 rooms* ⬧ *Restaurant, some pets allowed; no a/c, no smoking* ⊟ *MC, V* ⦿ *BP.*

¢ 🏠 **Foxrock Inn.** A friendly red setter by the name of Grouse greets new arrivals at this modest but friendly guesthouse in the picturesque heart of the County Laois countryside. The main attraction of this inn, set in the tiny village of Clough, are its owners, Sean and Marian Hyland, who extend a genuinely warm welcome. This enthusiastic young couple can bring you up-to-date on the 200-year history of the inn and adjacent pub, advise you on hiking in the Slieve Bloom Mountains, and organize golf and angling packages. Traditional music on Tuesday nights in summer is a big local draw. Rooms are plain but clean and comfortable. Simple, home-cooked dinners and packed lunches are available. Clough is located 8 km (5 mi) west of Abbeyleix (signposted off the R434 road to Borris-in-Ossary). ⊠ *Clough, Ballacolla, Co. Laois* ☎ *0502/ 38637* ⊕ *www.foxrockinn.com* ➺ *5 rooms* ⬧ *Dining room; no a/c, no room phones, no room TVs* ⊟ *AE, V* ⦿ *BP.*

Shopping

The Rathdowney Designer Outlet (⊠ Rathdowney ☎ 0505/48900 ⊕ www. rathdowneyoutlet.ie) would not look out of place in Midwestern America and offers the usual mix of top labels at easy-on-the-pocket prices. The extraordinary thing about this huge indoor mall is its location. The investors behind the venture adopted a "build it and they will come" approach. It is (as the Irish would say) in the "back of beyond," on the outskirts of a sleepy country town in County Laois. It's perfect for the addicted label hunter and also has attractions—craft and produce sales, occasional circus shows, a kids' active-play center—for nonshoppers curious to experience a surreal slice of pure Americana in rural Ireland. To get here from Abbeyleix, follow R433 west for 19 km (12 mi).

Portlaoise

❷ *14 km (9 mi) north of Abbeyleix.*

Near the heart of County Laois, the rich farmland south and west of Portlaoise, an hour by train or car from Dublin, is one of Ireland's undiscovered gems. Golf, fishing, hiking, and horseback riding are traditional

EATING WELL IN THE MIDLANDS

An old Irish joke concerns the tourist seeking sustenance in a country pub. "Toasted ham and cheese special" offers the barkeep as the total menu available to the famished visitor. "Wouldn't you have anything just a bit more exotic?" inquires the timid tourist. After a thoughtful pause, the barkeep replies: "Well, I suppose I could get the wife to take out the cheese."

Things have changed greatly in Ireland's food scene in tandem with EU membership and the more demanding customer. Those previously unheard words—tapas, latte, coriander, pesto, plus a whole lexicon of culinary adventure—have now become the norm across the country as a new breed of innkeeper responds to a changed cultural landscape.

The Midland town of Birr is known as the "belly button of Ireland" because of its central location, not because this region is known as a culinary hot spot. Nevertheless, the good news is that, as throughout Ireland, the economic boom that started in the 1990s has improved the standards and variety of the area's restaurants. Indeed, the Irish Food Board (An Bord Bia) has been making efforts to promote the use of locally produced and in-season produce through its Féile Bia program, so keep an eye out for eateries that have been awarded a Féile Bia certificate.

Happily, there are still restaurants that will pull you off the street, especially those offering beef—Mullingar, in the center of the Midlands, is the beef capital of Ireland—and the more upmarket restaurants usually serve fish freshly caught in one of the innumerable lakes that dot the landscape. By and large, however, the mainstay of the Midlands culinary scene remains the traditional carvery—a buffet-style "meat and two veg" dinner. Those not worried about their waistline will also enjoy the traditional breakfast of the region. The "Full Irish" or "Ulster Fry," as it's known in the northern part of the region, is about as hearty as breakfasts come—the standard version consists of eggs, bacon, sausages, white and black puddings, and grilled tomato with a side order of Irish soda bread, and all washed down with a nice cup of tea. Not surprisingly, after all that, many travelers even skip lunch.

---

sports hereabouts, and the development of the Grand Canal for recreational purposes is adding to the area's attractions. Explore the pretty villages and romantic, ivy-covered ruins by car, or follow one of the many hiking trails.

Portlaoise's name is derived from the Irish for "Fort of Laois" and refers to the town's strife-filled history. In terms of its architecture, it's rather eclectic—it feels as if bits of other towns were picked up and dropped randomly onto the site. Once best known for having Ireland's highest-security prison, which still looms over the town—it housed the IRA's most notorious members during the 1970s and '80s—the town is undergoing a renaissance. The main street, which once formed part of the main Dublin-Cork road, is now largely given over to pedestrians; pubs and restaurants are beginning to flourish; and the thriving Dunamaise Arts Centre adds that extra dash of culture to the proceedings. At the Tourist Information Office in Portlaoise you can pick up a map of the **Laois Heritage Trail**

(⊕ www.laoistourism.ie/HeritageTrail.asp), a signposted, daylong drive on quiet back roads that takes in 13 heritage sites, ranging from Abbeyleix to Emo Court; the circular trail starts in Borris-in-Ossary on N7.

A dramatic 150-foot-high limestone outcrop, the famous **Rock of Dunamase** dominates the landscape east of Portlaoise. For this reason, it was used as a military stronghold. As far back as AD 140 its occupants kept watch against marauders and it was fought over in turn by the Vikings, Normans, Irish, and English. Today it's crowned by the ruins of a 12th-century castle, once home to Diarmuid Mac Murrough, king of Leinster, who precipitated the Norman invasion when he invited the famed and feared Norman leader Strongbow to Ireland to marry his daughter, whose dowry included the Rock. Some of the castle's thick walls still stand. The main reason for visiting the Rock today is to take the short walk to its summit to enjoy the view of the Slieve Bloom Mountains to the north and the Wicklow Mountains to the south. ⊠ *5 km (3 mi) east of Portlaoise on N80 Stradbally Rd.*

Where to Stay & Eat

$$–$$$ ✕ **The Lemon Tree.** Although on Portlaoise's main street, this spot is its best-kept culinary secret. It combines an informal atmosphere with modern-but-cozy surroundings. Owner Kevin Hennessy used to be front-of-house supremo at swanky Dublin eatery Shanahans on the Green, and has here managed to import the style without the snobbishness. Starters might include duck confit with hoisin sauce while many enjoy the prime Irish Angus sirloin for the main course. Luncheon is only served for group parties who reserve in advance. ⊠ *Main St.* ☎ *0502/62200* ▤ *AE, MC, V.*

★ **$–$$** ✕ **Kingfisher.** In the town center, this is a particularly lively and stylish spot. The high-ceiling room was once a banking hall, but now its softly lighted walls glow with warm terra-cotta tones, the perfect complement to the spicy-but-not-too Punjabi cuisine. *Pappadams* (crunchy lentil-flour bread) and condiments appear on the table before you order, and the friendly staff in traditional dress will guide you expertly through the long menu. Dishes vary from mild and creamy *kormas* (curried meat dishes) to fresh cod with a mild blend of spices and lemon juice, to chicken "cooked with angry green chilies." Last orders for dinner are taken as late as 11:30 PM, so this is definitely the place to go when your tummy rumbles late on a summer's eve. Check out their very snazzy Web site. ⊠ *Old AIB Bank, Main St.* ☎ *0502/62500* ⊕ *www.kingfisherrestaurant. com* ▤ *AE, MC, V* ⊗ *No lunch Sat.–Tues.*

★ $ ⊡ **Ivyleigh House.** Owners Dinah and Jerry Campion say they like to give their guests "the best of everything" and that maxim is certainly in evidence the minute you step inside this elegant Georgian town house next to the Portlaoise railway station. Open fires, antiques, and sumptuously cozy sofas await you in the beige-on-brown, wood-accented sitting room. Upstairs, luxurious drapes grace the sash windows of the spacious bedrooms, most done in dramatic hues like pink and emerald. A virtual avalanche of plump cushions scattered on your antique bed reinforces the tone of rest and relaxation. Guests find it hard to decide from all the goodies in the scrumptious breakfast menu. Suffice to say the bread is home-baked, the food is locally produced, and no one can resist the Cashel blue-cheese cakes with mushrooms and tomatoes. Room TVs are available by request. ⊠ *Bank Pl., Co. Laois* ☎ *0502/22081* 🖷 *0502/63343* ⊕ *www.ivyleigh.com* 📨 *6 rooms* ⚿ *No a/c, no room TVs, no smoking* ⊟ *MC, V* ⊙❙ *BP.*

Nightlife & the Arts

Also known as Turley's bar, the canal-side **Anchor Inn** (⊠ Grand Canal, near Stradbally, Vicarstown ☎ 0502/25454), 10 km (6 mi) east of Portlaoise on N80, is popular for its lively Monday-night traditional-music sessions, which start around 9. Sessions take place more frequently in summer. Fishing, boating, and canal-bank walks are all accessible from
★ this location. The lively **Dunamaise Arts Centre** (⊠ Main St. ☎ 0502/63355 ⊕ www.dunamaise.ie), formerly the town jail, built into the back of the 18th-century stone courthouse, has a 240-seat theater, an art gallery, and a friendly coffee shop (open 8:30–5:30). You may catch a professional production on tour or a local amateur show. The exhibition space displays the work, usually of a surprisingly high standard, of contemporary Irish artists. It's behind the courthouse on Church Street.

Sports & the Outdoors

The **Heritage Golf & Heritage Club** (⊠ Killenard ☎ 0502/45500), just off the main Dublin-Cork road, is an 18-hole, par-72 course. This parkland championship course was codesigned by Seve Ballesteros and features challenging doglegs, as well as five lakes and a number of streams, to keep those fond of dodging water traps happy.

Portarlington

❸ *13 km (8 mi) northeast of Portlaoise.*

Built on the River Barrow in the late 17th century, Portarlington was originally an English settlement. Later, a Huguenot colony developed here, and French surnames are still common in the area. Some good examples of Georgian architecture can be seen in the town. A quintessential landmark of Irish Palladian elegance lies just 7 km (4½ mi) south
★ of Portarlington: **Emo Court and Gardens,** one of the finest large-scale country houses near Dublin open to the public. If you elect to skip over much of the Midlands, at least try to tack on a visit to Emo, especially if you're in County Kildare or Wicklow. To come upon the house from the main drive, an avenue lined with magisterial Wellingtonia trees, is to experience one of Ireland's great treasure-house views. Begun in

1790 by James Gandon, architect of the Custom House and the Four Courts in Dublin, Emo (the name derives from the Italian version of the original Irish name Imoe) is thought to be Gandon's only domestic work matching the grand scale of his Dublin civic buildings. Construction continued on and off for 70 years, as family money troubles followed the untimely death of Emo's original patron and owner, the first earl of Portarlington.

In 1996 Emo's English-born owner, Mr. Cholmeley-Harrison, donated the house to the Irish nation. The ground-floor rooms have been beautifully restored and decorated and are a prime example of life on the grand scale. Among the highlights are the entrance hall, with trompe l'oeil paintings in the apses on each side, and the library, which has a carved Italian-marble mantel with putti frolicking among grapevines. But the showstopper, and one of the finest rooms in Ireland, is the domed rotunda—the work of one of Gandon's successors, the Irish architect William Caldbeck—inspired by the Roman Pantheon. Marble pilasters with gilded Corinthian capitals support the rotunda's blue-and-white coffered dome. Emo's 55 acres of grounds include a 20-acre lake, lawns planted with yew trees, a small garden (the Clocker) with Japanese maples, and a larger one (the Grapery) with rare trees and shrubs. ⊠ *Emo* ☎ *0502/26573* ⊕ *www.heritageireland.ie* ⊡ *Gardens free, house €2.75* ☉ *Gardens daily 9–dusk; house mid-June–mid-Sept., Tues.–Sun. 10–5; last tour at 4:30.*

★ **Coolbanagher Church,** the familiar name for the exquisite Church of St. John the Evangelist, was, like Emo Court and Gardens, designed by James Gandon. On view inside are Gandon's original 1795 plans; there's also an elaborately sculpted 15th-century font from an earlier church that stood nearby. Adjacent to the church is Gandon's mausoleum for Lord Portarlington, his patron at Emo. The church is open daily from spring through autumn; at other times, ask around in the tiny village for a key, or at the rectory, a 10-minute drive away. ⊠ *8½ km (5 mi) south of Portarlington on R419* ☎ *0502/24143 rectory* ⊡ *Free* ☉ *May–Oct., daily 9–6.*

Where to Stay

$$ 🏨 **Roundwood House.** There's a dreamlike beauty to this place. As you
Fodor'sChoice arrive, a dark tree-lined avenue suddenly opens up to reveal a dramat-
★ ically gorgeous Palladian villa. A flock of white geese and a collection of friendly dogs form the welcoming party to this "chateauesque" mansion nestling on the slopes of the Slieve Bloom Mountains amid 18 acres of mature woodland and pasture. Antique family portraits of the builders, the Sharps—a prominent Quaker family whose wealth derived from the mid-1600s woolen industry—adorn the walls of the curio-filled drawing room. The bedrooms in the main house are elegant, airy, and painted in dramatic greens, yellows, and blues. If you prefer a cozier option, there are several rooms in the adjacent 17th-century Old House, or on the grounds in the picturesque Coach House and Forge. Tiniest of all is the Cottage, a stone charmer whose original tenants may have been Hansel and Gretel, at least according to hosts Frank and Rosemarie Kennan, who often share your table at dinner. The house is 3 mi from Moun-

trath on the scenic road to Kinnitty. ⊠ *Mountrath, Co. Laois* ☎ *0502/ 32120* 📠 *0502/32711* ⊕ *www.hidden-ireland.com/roundwood.html* ➡ *10 rooms* 🍴 *Dining room; no a/c, no room phones, no room TVs* ▤ *AE, DC, MC, V* 🍴 *BP.*

₵ 🏠 **Eskermore House.** In summertime, a delightful display of rambling roses adorns the doorway of this charming farmhouse. The old-world quirks of these lovely lodgings also include a chiming grandfather clock and an organ in the sitting room for musically gifted guests (those without a talent for ivory tinkling are gently urged to refrain). Located 8 km (5 mi) north of Portarlington on R402, this is a good base for hiking in the Slieve Bloom Mountains. The guest rooms are simply but comfortably furnished and face south over a beech tree-lined avenue and semi-wild gardens; room TVs are available on request. The sitting room has an open turf fire, a piano, and cable TV. Host Ann Mooney will prepare a wholesome dinner with advance notice. ⊠ *Mount Lucas, Edenderry, Co. Offaly* ☎ *0506/53079* ⊕ *www.eskermore.com* ➡ *3 rooms* 🍴 *Some pets allowed; no a/c, no room phones* ▤ *MC, V* 🍴 *BP.*

Tullamore

❹ *27 km (17 mi) northwest of Portarlington.*

The county seat of Offaly, Tullamore is a bustling market town that has really begun to thrive since Ireland's "Celtic Tiger" boom took off in the mid-1990s. Its most famous native is Ireland's finance minister Brian Cowen and the people here share his down-to-earth approach to life. The town's historical success was based on its location on the Grand Canal, one of Ireland's most important trading links during the 18th and 19th centuries. One relic of its former splendor is found on the southwestern edge of town, where, if you take the road heading to Birr from the center of Tullamore, you'll find a storybook vision in splendid Tin Soldier Fortress style: **Charleville Forest Castle.** Perhaps the finest neo-Gothic, British-style 19th-century castle in Ireland, its Flag Tower and turrets rise above its domain of 30 acres of woodland walks and gardens. The Georgian–Gothic Revival castellated house was built as a symbol (in fact, the floor plan is even modeled on the Union Jack) of English might triumphant over French force—the French revolutionary forces, to be exact, who had become a little too cozy with the Irish locals. Commissioned by Baron Tullamore and dating from 1812, the castle is a rural example of the work of architect Francis Johnston, responsible for many of Dublin's stately Georgian buildings. The interiors are somewhat the worse for wear—most are gigantic chambers with a few sticks of furniture—but the William Morris–designed dining room still has its original stenciled wallpaper. Guided tours of the interior are available. Descended through the Bury family, fortunes depleted and without heirs, the castle became an orphan in the 1960s but has been slowly restored. The surrounding forest is said to be the haunting grounds of the ancient Druids. ⊠ *1½ km (1 mi) outside Tullamore on N52 to Birr* ☎ *0506/21279* ⊕ *www.charlevillecastle.com* 🎫 *€16 for one adult or couple. Additional members of same party €6* ⊙ *May, weekends 2–5; June–Sept., Wed.–Sun. 2–5; Oct.–Apr.*

Sports & the Outdoors

BOATING   Exploring the inland waterways steering your own boat is a leisurely way to discover the unspoiled scenery, hidden villages, and abundant wildlife of Ireland's interior. You can rent a river cruiser for a floating holiday from **Celtic Canal Cruisers Ltd** (✉ 24th Lock ☎ 0506/21861).

GOLF   **Esker Hills Golf & Country Club** (✉ 5 km [3 mi] north of Tullamore on N80 ☎0506/55999) is a challenging 18-hole, par-71 championship course with natural lakes and woodlands.

Kilbeggan

❺ *11 km (7 mi) north of Tullamore.*

It's the whiskey (the Irish spell their traditional tipple with an "e") that brings most people to the unassuming little town of Kilbeggan. The town is the home of **Locke's Distillery,** which is the oldest pot-still distillery in the world and the last of its type in Ireland. This whiskey-lover's mecca was established in 1757 but was closed down as a functioning distillery in 1954. It has found new life as a museum of industrial archaeology illustrating the process of Irish pot-whiskey distillation and the social history of the workers. ☎ *0506/32134* ⊕ *www.lockesdistillerymuseum.com* ✉*€5.50* ☽ *Apr.–Oct., daily 9–6; Nov.–Mar., daily 10–4.*

Mullingar

❻ *24 km (15 mi) northeast of Kilbeggan.*

The Irish are great ones for wrapping an insult up in a lyrical turn of phrase. Rather than describe a woman as overweight they'll say with a wink she's "beef to the ankle, like a Mullingar heifer." Of course, the phrase also illustrates Mullingar's role as Ireland's beef capital—a town surrounded by rich countryside where cattle trading has historically been one of the chief occupations. It's also County Westmeath's major town—a busy commercial and cattle-trading center on the Royal Canal, midway between two large, attractive lakes, Lough Owel and Lough Ennel. Buildings here date mostly from the 19th century. Although best used as a base to tour the surrounding countryside, Mullingar has some interesting sights. The town's largest structure is the Renaissance-style Catholic **Cathedral of Christ the King,** completed in 1939. Note the facade's finely carved stonework and the mosaics of St. Patrick and St. Anne by the Russian artist Boris Anrep in the spacious interior. ✉ *Mary St.* ☎ *044/48338* ☽ *Daily 9–5:30.*

Mullingar Bronze and Pewter Centre offers free tours of its workshop, where the 800-year-old craft of pewter making is still practiced. Sculptured bronze figures are also made here (by Genesis Fine Art).

> ### BRIGHT ELIXIR
>
> "Irish" is a straight pot-still whiskey, and has a characteristic flavor that distinguishes it from Scotch, bourbon, or rye. Irish is not drunk until it has matured for at least seven years in wooden casks. It's best quaffed without a mixer, so try it straight or with water.

One of the joys of an Irish vacation can be a splurge at a castle-hotel, especially if it is enjoyed at Dromoland, a jewel set in County Clare.

(above) Listen for ancient echoes on the windswept Aran Islands. (opposite page, top) Enjoy close encounters with wild ponies in County Limerick. (opposite page, bottom) The River Lee Foot Bridge in Cork City is a handsome landmark.

(top) Even if you order only an Evian, a visit to a Dublin pub—or two or three—is a must. (bottom) A cruise along the Connemara coast can take you to Inis Mór, one of the Aran Islands. (opposite page) Imagine yourself the squire of Castletown House, Celbridge.

(top) Muckross House in Killarney National Park now houses the Kerry Folklife Centre. (bottom left) Relentlessly picturesque Adare has some storybook cottages. (bottom right) Dublin is noted for its 18th-century Georgian doorways.

(top) The sunny colors of these houses in Cork brighten even the rainiest days. (bottom) Span the centuries within a few blocks of Dublin Castle.

Begorra! It's the Strawberry Festival in Enniscorthy, Wexford.

You can purchase everything from whiskey measures to baby gifts made from both pewter and bronze in the showroom. There's also a coffee shop on the premises. ⊠ *Great Down, the Downs* ☎ *044/48791* ⊕ *www.mullingarpewter.com* ⊠ *Free* ☉ *Weekdays 9:30–5:30, Sat. 10–5:30.*

★ ☺ **Belvedere House Gardens** occupies a beautiful spot: the northeast shore of Lough Ennel. Access to this stately mid-18th-century hunting lodge with extensive gardens is through the servants' entrance—so you can see what life behind the scenes was like back then. Cries and whispers haunt this estate. Built in 1740 by architect Richard Cassels for Robert Rochfort, first earl of Belvedere, it became a byword for debauchery and dissipation, thanks to the hijinks of Rochfort's wife, the "very handsome" Mary Molesworth. After falling passionately in love with Rochfort's younger brother (and bearing him a child), she was locked up in another family house for decades. Robert regaled guests with the "scandal" while offering sumptuous dinners at this house under its great 18th-century plasterwork ceilings. He spent much of his family fortune dotting the gardens of the estate with "follies," including the Jealous Wall, a gigantic mock-castle ruin that served to cover up a view of the adjoining estate, owned by another brother, also hated. Today, the interiors are a quirky mix of Georgian stateliness and Victorian charm. The noted bow and Palladian windows have great parkland views sloping down to the lake and its islands. You can tour the 160 acres of the estate and woodland trails on the Belvedere tram. Also on the estate are a coffee shop, an animal sanctuary, and a children's play area. ⊠ *4 km (2½ mi) south of Mullingar on N52* ☎ *044/49060* ⊕ *www.belvedere-house.ie* ⊠ *House and parkland €8, tram €1.30* ☉ *Mar., Apr., and Sept., daily 10:30–6; May–Aug., daily 9:30–6; Oct.–Feb., daily 10:30–4:30.*

Where to Stay & Eat

★ $$ ✕⌷ **Crookedwood House.** This former rectory has stunning views of Lough Derravaragh—the magical lake where legend tells us the poor Children of Lir were forced to spend some 300 years after being turned into swans by their nasty stepmom. Legends aside, this is one of the premier restaurants in the Midlands. Chef–owner Noel Kenny has conjured up an exciting, German-inspired take on modern Irish cuisine ($$–$$$$). Venison goulash, anyone? In winter try the Hunter's Plate—a selection of pheasant, wild duck, and pigeon. Also irresistible is the trio of salmon, sole, and scallops with lobster sauce. The unusual combination of honey-roasted pork steak and salmon is wrapped in phyllo pastry and baked with grapes. The restaurant's decor—rough white walls and oak beams—won't do too much for the digestive juices, but the guest rooms upstairs are tranquil and some are even accented with 19th-century style pieces. The house is 13 km (8 mi) north of Mullingar on the R394 Castlepollard road. ⊠ *Co. Westmeath* ☎ *044/72165* ⊟ *044/72166* ⊕ *www.crookedwoodhouse. com* ⤳ *18 rooms* ⚮ *Restaurant, cable TV* ⊟ *AE, MC, V* ☉ *No dinner Sun. and Mon.* ⊚⎪ *BP*

★ $ ✕⌷ **An Tintáin.** In the quiet backwater village of Multyfarnham, this B&B (with restaurant) is set in one of the quaint cut-stone cottages along the main street, cheek by jowl with an old forge with a traditional horseshoe-shape entrance. An Tintáin translates in English as "The Hearth" and true to its name, there's a blazing fire and a cozy glow of homeliness inside. The rooms are simply but comfortably furnished and to complete the family-friendly mood, under-fives are even welcomed. In the restaurant ($$–$$$, no dinner Monday or Tuesday, lunch only on Sunday), locals mingle with visitors and hearty fare is the order of the day with the famous local beef being the star of the menu. ⊠ *Main St., Multyfarnham, 17 km (10 mi) north of Mullingar, Co. Westmeath* ☎ *044/71411* 🖷 *044/71434* ⊕ *www.antintain.info* ⬎ *6 rooms* ⚭ *Restaurant* ⊟ *AE, MC, V* ¶◎¶ *BP.*

Sports

GOLF **Delvin Castle Golf Club** (⊠ Delvin ☎ 044/64315) is an 18-hole course in a mature parkland setting. It has beautiful views across north Westmeath.

Castlepollard

❼ *21 km (13 mi) north of Mullingar.*

Fodor's Choice ★

A pretty village of multihue 18th- and 19th-century houses laid out around a large, triangular green, Castlepollard is also home to **Tullynally Castle and Gardens,** the largest castle in Ireland that still functions as a family home. This is not just any family, but the Pakenhams, that famous Irish tribe that has given us Elizabeth Longford (whose biography of Queen Victoria is in most libraries) and Antonia Fraser, wife of Harold Pinter and best-selling biographer of Mary, Queen of Scots, among others. In fact, Tullynally—the name, literally translated, means "Hill of the Swans"—has been the home of 10 generations of this family, which also married into the earldom of Longford. Lady Fraser's brother Thomas, a historian, is the current earl but does not use the title. As a result of the 18th-century "Gothicization," the former Georgian house was transformed into a faux-castle (by architect Francis Johnston); the resulting 600 feet of battlements were not just for bluff as the earls were foes of Catholic emancipation. Inside, the family has struggled to make the vast salons warm and cozy—a bit of a losing battle. Where the house really comes into its own is as a stage set for the surrounding park since the gray-stone structure is so long and has so many towers it looks like a miniature town from a distance. The total circumference of the building's masonry adds up to nearly ½ km (¼ mi) and includes a motley agglomeration of towers, turrets, and crenellations that date from the first early fortified building, circa 1655, up through the mid-19th century, when additions in the Gothic Revival style went up one after another.

Today, more attention is given to the beautiful parkland, in part because Thomas Pakenham is a tree-hugger extraordinaire. Author of several books, his most famous is *Meetings*

> ### BE IT EVER SO HUMBLE (NOT)
>
> Two wings designed by Sir Richard Morrison in 1840 joined the main block of Tullynally Castle to the stable court. They served dramatically different purposes: one was given over entirely to luxurious quarters for the dowager countess; the other housed 40 *indoor* servants.

with Remarkable Trees (1996), an exceptional art book that includes many of his magnificent photographs. The estate's rolling parkland was laid out in 1760, much along the lines you see today, with fine rhododendrons, numerous trees, and two ornamental lakes. A garden walk through the grounds in front of the castle leads to a spacious flower garden, a pond, a grotto, and walled gardens. The kitchen garden here is one of the largest in Ireland, with a row of old Irish yew trees. Don't miss the forest path, which takes you around the perimeter of the parkland and affords excellent views back to the romantic castle. ☒ *1½ km (1 mi) west of Castlepollard on the R395 road to Granard* ☎ *044/61159* ⊕ *www.tullynallycastle.com* ☒ *€5* ⊙ *June–Aug., daily 2–6.*

Fore

❽ *5 km (3 mi) east of Castlepollard.*

You've heard of the "seven wonders of the ancient world," but here in the heart of the Irish Midlands is a tiny village with seven wonders all to itself! According to Irish myth this is the place where water runs uphill, there's a tree that will not burn, and water that will not boil, among other fantastical occurrences. The village is known not only for its legend, but also for its medieval church and the remains (supposedly the largest in Ireland) of a Benedictine abbey. The spectacular remains of **Fore Abbey** dominate the simple village—its structure is massive and its imposing square towers and loophole windows make it resemble a castle rather than an abbey. Elsewhere in town, St. Fechin's Church, dating from the 10th century, has a massive, cross-inscribed lintel stone.

THE NORTHERN MIDLANDS

Our Northern Midlands coverage starts in Longford and works its way north, leaving the ancient kingdom of Leinster for Ulster's two most southerly counties, Cavan and Monaghan. The land in the north of County Cavan is known as "drumlin country," after the thousands of small, round hills consisting of boulder clay left behind by the glacial retreat of 10,000 years ago. The boulder clay also filled in many of the pre-glacial river alleys, causing the rivers to change course and resulting in the creation of many shallow lakes, which provide superb fishing and angling. Little wonder this region is also rightly heralded as the Northern Lakelands.

Longford Town

❾ *37 km (23 mi) west of Castlepollard, 124 km (77 mi) northwest of Dublin.*

Longford, the seat of County Longford and a typical small market-town community, is rich in literary associations, though after Oliver Goldsmith, the names in the county's writers' pantheon may draw a blank from all but the most dedicated Irish literature enthusiasts. Longford Town provides a good base for exploring the largely untouristed countryside surrounding it. A day trip to the pretty heritage village of Ardagh (10 km [7 mi] southeast of Longford Town), with its quaint houses and

Go for the Green

FEW REGIONS IN IRELAND equal the Midlands for pure greenness. It not only seems the entire area is planted with clover, but green-thumbers will rejoice in the abundance of elegant gardens, many of them designed and planted 250 years ago.

Most of these green oases are found on the grounds of the famed stately homes that dot the region. Many of the Anglo-Irish gentry were enthusiastic botanists and went to great lengths to find rare plant specimens from far-flung parts of the world. The earls of Rosse have been planting exotic plants from as far away as South America since the 17th century in the demesne of their castle in Birr.

The adventurer-botanist archetype is very much alive in the person of Thomas Pakenham, the current earl of Longford, and author of *Meetings with Remarkable Trees*. He has traveled the globe searching for exotic plants. The gardens in his home at Pakenham Hall in County Westmeath continue to evolve from their 18th-century origins. An "Oriental" garden added in the early 1990s features rare magnolias and lilies he collected as seed in China and other Asian countries.

Elsewhere, the gardeners at Strokestown House in County Roscommon have restored a 6-acre walled garden and now tend it with methods used in the 1700s. But you can visit modern gardens, too. The best example is Heywood Gardens in County Laois, which was completed in 1912. These formal gardens, featuring wonderful water terraces, were designed by the famous architect Sir Edwin Lutyens.

What typifies all the gardens in this part of Ireland is a lush serenity and the profusion of growth that is synonymous with the Irish landscape.

---

village green, is a popular option. Another lovely spot is Newtowncashel on the banks of Lough Ree where you can visit **Bogwood Crafts,** a fascinating workshop run by sculptors Michael and Kevin Casey. The center displays sculptures and keepsakes made from bogwood, which is hewn from the 5,000-year-old trees submerged and ultimately preserved by the area's ancient peatlands. To get there from Longford drive 9 mi on the N63 to Lanesborough, then take the R392 for 1 mi and follow signs for Turreen–Newtowncashel. ⊠ *Barley Harbour, Newtowncashel* ☎ *043/ 25297* ⊕ *www.bogwood.net* ☜ *Free* ☉ *Mon.–Sat. 10–6.*

Where to Stay & Eat

$–$$ ✕ **The Purple Onion.** A perfect resting place for tired and hungry travel-
Fodor's Choice   ers on the road to the west of Longford Town, this pub–restaurant is
★   on the main street of a tiny Shannon-side village. This place was originally a standard public house with the obligatory low ceilings, nooks,
crannies, and snugs, but under the patronage of Pauline Roe and Paul

Dempsey it has been transformed into a gourmet's delight—a special "gastro pub," now abustle with locals, cruise-boat tourists, and food lovers from all over. Specialties include a divine whiskey-flamed sirloin in a cream sauce, while potatoes and vegetables are abundant and even served (untypically, for an Irish pub) al dente. The huge servings of panfried mussels and crab claws in spicy garlic butter leave you blissfully sated, and all at an affordable price. An upstairs gallery has work by some of the finest and best-known Irish artists including Jack B. Yeats and Paul Henry, among 100 others. To get there from Longford Town drive 10 km (6 mi) west on the N5. ⊠ *Tarmonbarry* ☎ *0902/74376* ▤ *AE, MC, V.*

> ## THE HOUSE THAT DARCY BUILT
>
> Jane Austen—that most British of writers—is linked to Carrigglas Manor, a romantic Tudor-Gothic house near Longford. It was built in 1837 by Thomas Lefroy, who was at one point romantically involved with the novelist. Why they never married is a mystery, but it's believed that Austen based the character of Mr. Darcy in *Pride and Prejudice* on Mr. Lefroy. His descendants recently sold the house to golf-resort developers.

¢–$ ✕ **Keenans.** Assuming you are in the market for some liquid refreshment, try this lovingly restored pub of yore, set right next door to the Purple Onion. Inside, the fifth generation of Keenans still ply their trade and traditional music is on the menu on Monday nights. Keenans also serves excellent pub food. ⊠ *Tarmonbarry* ☎ *043/26052* ⊕ *www.keenans.ie* ▤ *AE, MC, V.*

★ $ ✕▦ **Viewmount House.** This sweet and exquisite Georgian home was once owned by the earl of Longford and has been restored to its former charm by James and Beryl Kearney. The bedrooms are full of character and have impressive period wallpapers and antique mahogany wardrobes and beds. Breakfast is served in a vaulted room, cheerily painted in robin's-egg blue. The 4 acres of grounds that surround the house are a gardener's paradise with an old orchard, a formal garden, and a Japanese garden replete with full-size pagoda. A courtyard restaurant ($$–$$$$) serves contemporary Irish and European delicacies. The house is 2 km (1 mi) outside Longford Town, just off the old Dublin road (R393). ⊠ *Dublin Rd., Co. Longford* ☎ *043/41919* ▤ *043/42906* ⊕ *www.viewmounthouse.com* ✑ *5 rooms, 1 suite* ♿ *No a/c* ▤ *AE, MC, V* ▯*BP.*

Nightlife & the Arts

The center of a thriving local arts scene is the **Backstage Theatre** (⊠ Farneyhoogan ☎043/47888 ⊕www.backstage.ie). In a country where many patriotic souls see the indigenous sports of Gaelic football and hurling as "art forms," it's perhaps appropriate that the venue is on the grounds of the local Gaelic Athletic Association club, with the intimidating title of the "Longford Slashers." An ideal opportunity to catch a local match and then head into the theater for a dose of drama, dance, classical music, or opera, the theater and club are located a mile outside Longford on the road to Athlone.

Cavan

10 *53 km (33 mi) northeast of Longford, 114 km (71 mi) northwest of Dublin.*

Like all the larger towns of the region, this is a growing and increasingly prosperous town, perhaps best known for its crystal factory. There are two central streets. With its pubs and shops, Main Street is like many other streets in similar Irish towns. Farnham Street has Georgian houses, churches, and a courthouse. **Cavan Crystal** is an up-and-coming rival to Waterford in the cut-lead-crystal line; the company offers guided factory tours and access to its factory shop. This is a good opportunity to watch skilled craftspeople at work if you can't make it to Waterford. A major building attached to the factory houses a visitor center, glass museum, restaurant, and coffee shop. ⊠ *Dublin Rd.* ☎ *049/433–1800* ⊕ *www.cavancrystaldesign.com* ⊠ *Free* ⊙ *Guided tours weekdays at 9:30, 10:30, and 11:30.*

OFF THE BEATEN PATH

KILLYKEEN FOREST PARK – This park is part of the beautiful, mazelike network of lakes called Lough Oughter. Within the park's 600 acres are a number of signposted walks and nature trails, stables offering horseback riding, and boats and bicycles for rent. Twenty-eight fully outfitted two- and three-bedroom cottages are available for weeklong, weekend, or midweek stays. Rates vary according to the season; call for details. ⊠ *11 km (7 mi) north of Cavan* ☎ *049/433–2541* ⊕ *www.coillte. ie* ⊠ *Free, parking €1.90* ⊙ *Daily 9–5.*

Where to Stay & Eat

$$–$$$ ✕ **Pol O'D Restaurant.** Consisting of two rooms spread over two floors, this characterful restaurant of stripped pine and exposed stonework is a busy lunch and dinner place much favored by locals. Chef–owner Paul O'Dowd opts for contemporary Irish fare with a little adventure in dishes such as smoked duck salad, quail's egg salad, and seafood medley of prawn and lemon sauce. Standard dishes reflecting traditional rural tastes include steak, lamb, and duck. Pristine starched tablecloths, simple candlelight and local staff make Pol O'D an unexpected pleasure in an area not generally blessed with multiple options come dinnertime. Children are welcome, as is traditional music, which seems to happen on a spontaneous basis. ⊠ *Main St., Ballyconnell* ☎ *049/95–6391* ⊟ *AE, MC, V* ⊙ *Closed Sun.*

★ **$$–$$$** ✕⬚ **Cabra Castle.** A collection of mock-Gothic towers, turrets, and crenellations, this hotel-castle stands sentinel amid a charming parkland of mature trees and pristine lawns. Cabro boasts rooms of all shapes and sizes from cozy attic rooms to elaborate "super-size" suites. Rooms in the castle are recommended but many of the bedrooms are in the adjoining courtyard area, a carefully restored stone outbuilding development overlooking a walled garden. The Victorian-Gothic theme of the main castle is carried through in the bar and the restaurant ($$–$$$, fixed-price Continental menu) with varying degrees of success. But don't miss the castle gallery, which has hand-painted ceilings and leaded-glass windows. ⊠ *65 km (40 mi) south of Cavan, Kingscourt, Co. Cavan* ☎ *042/966–7030* ⬚ *042/966–7039* ⊕ *www.cabracastle.com*

🛏 *80 rooms ⚹ Restaurant, cable TV, 9-hole golf course, fishing, horseback riding, bar, meeting rooms, some pets allowed; no a/c ☰ AE, MC, V ⦿ BP.*

★ $ ✕▦ **The Olde Post Inn.** In the village of Cloverhill, this lovingly restored former post office (if you hadn't guessed from the name) has won a clutch of awards and, as a result, is often booked solid. That magic formula of a genuine Irish welcome and fine food is what draws people here. Big open turf fires and cut stone walls provide the key to the warm feeling you get when you step inside. As for the guest bedrooms, in 2003–04 they were refurbished in a cheerful country-house style. In the restaurant ($$–$$$$), chef Gearoid Lynch gives a modern twist to some Irish classics including fillet of beef served with colcannon (a traditional mash with cabbage and onion) and bacon and cabbage terrine. To get here, take the N53 to Cloverhill from Cavan Town. ✉ *Cloverhill, Co. Cavan* ☎ *047/55555* 🖷 *047/55111* ⊕ *www.theoldepostinn.com* 🛏 *8 rooms ⚹ Restaurant; no a/c ☰ MC, V ⦿ BP.*

¢–$ ✕▦ **MacNean House & Bistro.** Nestled in the quietest of backwaters on
Fodor'sChoice the border with Northern Ireland, you would not expect the village of
★ Blacklion to have even the faintest whiff of glamour. You'd be wrong, for this is home to Ireland's best known TV chef, Neven Maguire. They come from all over just to find out if the food ($$–$$$) tastes as good as it looks on the television and his guests are not disappointed. Maguire creates dishes to drool for—scallops wrapped in Parma ham or crab ravioli in a lobster cream sauce are two winners—while he also offers several inspired takes on traditional Irish dishes, such as a delicious lamb in an herb crust. Desserts are Neven's specialty—try the hazelnut nougat glacé. The guest bedrooms are simply furnished in a modern Irish style and, given the remoteness of Blacklion, you might want to book a room when reserving a table, to avoid a post-dinner, late-night drive. The 65-km (40-mi) detour makes sense if you are heading from Dublin northwest to Sligo or Donegal. ✉ *Blacklion, Co. Cavan* ☎ *071/985–3022* 🖷 *071/9853404* 🛏 *4 rooms ⚹ Restaurant; no a/c ☰ MC, V ⦿ BP.*

Cootehill

⓫ *26 km (16 mi) northeast of Cavan.*

One of the most underestimated small towns in Ireland, Cootehill commands a lovely outpost on a wooded hillside in the heart of County Cavan. Its wide streets, with intriguing old shops, are always busy without being congested. Most who come here are anglers from Europe, the United Kingdom, and the rest of Ireland. Only pedestrians are allowed through the gates of the Bellamont Forest park. After about a mile of woodland, a gorgeous trail leads to **Bellamont Forest,** designed in 1728 by Edward Lovett

CRAZY LIKE A FOX

Famously, Charles Coote, the earl of Bellamont, gave his 1789 inaugural speech as quartermaster-general of Ireland in *French* and continually referred to his County Cavan neighbors as "Hottentots." He wound up marrying the daughter of the super-rich duke of Leinster, thereby providing for his three illegitimate daughters—as well as his three legitimate daughters—in his will.

Pearce, architect of Dublin's Bank of Ireland. Considered by some to be Ireland's loveliest 18th-century house, it was built for the Coote family in 1729 by Sir Edward Lovett Pearce, who was greatly inspired by the Palladian villas he saw on his Italian Grand Tour. He was also related by marriage to the house's most infamous owner, the earl of Bellamont, Charles Coote. A notorious seducer of women (leading to his nickname, the "Hibernian Seducer"), he was shot in the groin by Lord Townshend—giving rise to much speculation about his future extracurricular activities—then gloriously painted by Sir Joshua Reynolds in pink silks and ostrich plumes (the life-size canvas is now in the National Gallery of Ireland). Small but perfectly proportioned, his house has remained virtually unaltered since it was built. It's now a private home, but is occasionally opened to the public. If you're interested, inquire locally or at the Tourist Information Office (TIO) in Cavan. Walk up the main street of Cootehill to "the top of the town" (past the White Horse hotel), and you'll see the entrance to Bellamont Forest opposite St. Michael's Church. The parkland is quintessentially Irish and allows some views of the private Bellamont Forest mansion.

Where to Stay

¢ 🖬 **Riverside House.** Peace, quiet and the "Céad Míle Fáilte" (Irish for "a hundred thousand welcomes") is what keeps them coming back, according to Una Smith, owner of this quaint farmhouse overlooking the River Analee. In the main, serious anglers and those seeking a little bit of peace and pastoral solitude favor this off-the-beaten-track retreat. All rooms have peaceful views and are individually decorated with modest antiques and family hand-me-downs. Dinner can be served by arrangement. Bring your boots if you want to explore around this working dairy farm. The lodging is signposted 1 km (½ mi) outside town off R188. ⊠ Co. Cavan ☎ 049/555–2150 🖨 049/555–2150 ⊕ www. irishfarmholidays.com ⋑ 6 rooms, 5 with bath ⚏ Dining room, boating, fishing; no a/c, no room phones ⊟ MC ❑❘ BP.

Monaghan

★ ⓬ *24 km (15 mi) north of Cootehill.*

This handsome town with its elegant limestone civic buildings is built around a "Diamond"—a kite-shape, central plaza so typical of the "Plantation Towns" created by English and Scots settlers in the northern part of Ireland during the 1600s. Just above the Diamond, set in the middle of Market Square, is the town's old Market House, a neoclassically refined Georgian gem decorated with exquisite carvings and now home to the town's arts center. Across the road on neighboring Hill Street the **County Museum** houses an eclectic collection of more than 70,000 objects, which help to tell the story of the county. Exhibits include everything from the remains of a Giant Irish Red Deer (an extinct species that roamed the area 9,000 years ago) to one of the first televisions to arrive in the county. The most important artifact in the museum is the Cross of Clogher, a religious relic thought to date from the 14th century. ⊠ Hill St. ☎ 047/82928 ⊕ www.monaghan.ie ⋑ Free ⊙ Weekdays 11–5, Sat. noon–5.

The Great Hunger

IN HIS EPIC POEM "*The Great Hunger*," generally regarded as one of the masterpieces of Irish literature, poet Patrick Kavanagh (1904–67) summed up his native Monaghan as a place whose peasant populace remained "locked in a stable with pigs and cows forever."

The intellectual and sexual paralysis reflected in the work is undoubtedly a thing of the past, but the unremitting barrenness of Kavanagh's vision is still evident in the county's unvarying landscape. Given the acerbic nature of the poem, it's rather ironic that Kavanagh-centered tourism is big business in the region.

Kavanagh worked on the family farm in his youth: though closed to the public, the farmhouse, a plain building dating from 1791, is signposted off the R179 Carrickmacross road.

Kavanagh's bittersweet relationship with Monaghan led to self-imposed exile in Dublin. A lover of controversy in his lifetime, Kavanagh in death remains a source of conflict and debate: in 1998, 31 years after he died, a monument at his grave in memory of his widow, Katherine, was extensively damaged and anonymously replaced by an old wooden cross and stepping stones removed from the garden of his family home at Mucker, a short distance from the village in which he was reared.

Today, the **Patrick Kavanagh Center** (☎ 042/937-8560 ⊕ www.patrickkavanaghcountry.com) in Inniskeen hosts poetry competitions and writer's weekends.

Where to Stay & Eat

★ **$–$$** ✕ **Andy's Bar & Restaurant.** A real Monaghan institution, this eatery has won the Ulster region "pub of the year" award no less than eight times. The downstairs is pure Victorian with ornate high ceilings and mahogany booths; bar food is served all day. Upstairs, the formal restaurant was refurbished in 2004, but it retains an old style, cozy ambience. The menu is uncomplicated French-influenced fare with local produce high on the agenda. Expect to choose from starters like garlic Monaghan mushrooms and main courses like locally produced steak and crispy duck in a brandy and orange sauce. ⊠ *12 Market St.* ☎ *047/82277* ⊕ *www.andysmonaghan.com* ▭ *MC, V.*

¢ ✕ **Tommy's.** The Irish may not be the world's most gastronomically minded people but they know a good chip (french fry) when they taste it. This local spot is not pretty but the chips are wonderful—beautifully crispy chunks of home-cut comfort food. Sometimes it's good to go downmarket. ⊠ *Glasslough St.*

$$$$ ✕⌂ **Castle Leslie.** From Sir Winston Churchill to W. B. Yeats, from Queen **Fodor'sChoice** Margaret of Sweden to Sir Paul McCartney, they came, they saw, and ★ they were completely conquered—and you will be, too. Half baronial palace, half charming home, this ne plus ultra of Irish hotels has been pleasing guests—whether they were on an Edwardian weekend party or are today's sophisticated travelers—since 1870, when Sir John Leslie built this family seat on the shores of shimmering Glaslough lake. Mixing in "Free Range Gothic" with "Late Rothschild" and "Jacobean Bloody," he and his son came up with a grand granite castle eminence. Step inside and you'll see that although there are many magnificent historic houses doing double duty as hotels, none are as sensationally atmospheric as this. Grand reception rooms are full of lush delights—heavily carved and deeply cushioned furniture, velvet curtains, Wordsworth's harp, lovely 19th-century paintings (Sir John was a noted Pre-Raphaelite painter), Persian rugs, a Della Robbia fireplace, and the feeling of wraparound comfort that only this kind of companionable Victorian splendor can give. Better yet, at almost every turn you will find mementos of this noted family, which is said to have descended from Attila the Hun, funded the education of the Duke of Wellington (his death mask is displayed here), married into the Jennie Jerome family, and sprouted a bumper crop of writers and biographers (when Jonathan Swift stayed here, he wrote in the guest book: "Glaslough with rows of books upon its shelves/written by the Leslies about themselves").

You can almost hear the spirits of Uncle Shane or Aunt Alice rattling the doorknobs of the exquisitely appointed bedrooms: the Mauve Room welcomed the Duke and Duchess of Connaught and many other titled honeymooners ("Hence the loo beyond the bathroom is called 'The Throne Room' in honor of all the royalty who have rained," according to the hotel's delightful Web site); the Chinese Room is a symphony in regal Regency reds;

> ### WORD OF MOUTH
>
> "Castle Leslie has tons of character and was a wonderful place to stay. Some of the Irish castle-hotels are very elegant (requiring coat and tie to dinner) but Castle Leslie was more casual and a place that I would love to go back to."
>
> –Judy

the Red Room is filled with Renaissance-style treasures brought back from Perugia; Norman's Room, with brooding Jacobean bed and framed photos, honors Uncle Norman ("top cadet of his class at Sandhurst Military College"); while others will fancy Sir John's magisterial green-velvet bedroom. For dinner, head downstairs to the sumptuous dining room ($$$$, evening meals only), lined with 19th-century paintings, to dine on fine Irish fare served by candlelight by waitresses in Victorian dress; try the smashing noisettes of Irish lamb with sweet potato and rosemary gratin. Outside, a 1,000-acre park beckons, with fishing and golfing to fill the hours, but many will simply repair to the castle's beguilingly venerable Drawing Room with a glass of sherry to dream the afternoon away as Lord or Lady of the Manor. ⊠ *11 km (7 mi) northeast of Monaghan, Glaslough, Co. Monaghan* ☎ *047/88100* 🖷 *047/88256* ⊕ *www.castleleslie.com* ⇗ *14 rooms* ⌂ *Dining room, boating, fishing; no a/c, no room phones, no room TVs, no kids, no smoking* ⊟ *MC, V* ⍾ *BP.*

Clones

⑬ *28 km (18 mi) southwest of Monaghan.*

Although in terms of its population Clones is a relatively unimportant Midlands town, culturally it has had an impact far beyond its size. Among the more famous citizens of the town are Barry McGuigan, former world featherweight boxing champion and one of the most popular sports figures ever to emerge in Ireland; Thomas Bracken, the man who penned New Zealand's national anthem; and, currently the area's most celebrated citizen, novelist Patrick McCabe, whose novels perfectly capture the vaguely time-locked quality of life in the town. McCabe's novel *The Butcher Boy* put Clones on the map internationally, particularly when Neil Jordan, Ireland's preeminent movie director, made a film based on the book in and around the town.

Nowadays Clones (pronounced clo-*nez*), a small, agricultural market town 1 km (½ mi) from the Northern Ireland border, is one of two lace-making centers in County Monaghan (the other is Carrickmacross). It also has some ruins worth seeing. In early Christian times, Clones was the site of a monastery founded by St. Tighearnach, who died here in AD 458. An **Augustinian abbey** replaced the monastery in the 12th century, and its remains can still be seen near the 75-foottall round tower on Abbey Street. A 10th-century Celtic **High Cross,** with carved panels depicting scriptural scenes, stands in Clones's central diamond. In an attempt to earn some income in the 19th century, the wives of local rectors took up lace making. Crochet work and small raised dots are two hallmarks of Clones lace. A varied selection of Clones lace is on display around town and can be purchased at the **Clones Lace Centre.** ⊠ *Cara St.* ☎ *047/52125* ⊗ *Mon. and Wed.–Sat. 10–6.*

Where to Stay & Eat

★ **$$$–$$$$** ✕☒ **Hilton Park.** A wonderfully romantic ancestral home, Hilton Park makes you feel like you are houseguests of the estate owners, Johnny and Lucy Madden, the eighth generation of the family to live here. An imposing house, with colonnaded facade framed by 500 acres of parkland, lakes, and woods, it's positively dripping with delightful family heirlooms (including an Erard concert grand piano, which Chopin reputedly played). Bedrooms—some with four-poster beds— have beautiful views of the lakes and parkland. But in spite of all this history and opulence there's a serenely informal air to the place. The only "rule," according to Johnny, is that guests should refrain from wearing short trousers to the dinner table (thankfully, he says he has never had to enforce the regulation). Speaking of dinners ($$$$, for guests only), they are prepared from organic vegetables from the garden, fish from the lakes, and local produce. Lucy does the cooking and is also the author of *The Potato Year,* a quirky mix of recipe book and a history of the humble spud. Guests can play for free on Clones Golf Club, which forms part of the estate. To find Hilton Park, look for large black gates adorned with silver falcons. ⊠ *R183 Ballyhaise Rd., 5 km (3 mi) outside Clones, Co. Monaghan* ☎ *047/56007* 🖷 *047/56033* ⊕ *www.hiltonpark.ie* ⤳ *6 rooms* ♨ *Dining room, 18-hole golf course, lake, boating, fishing, croquet; no a/c, no room phones, no room TVs, no kids under 8, no smoking* ▤ *MC, V* ⊗ *Closed Oct.–Mar.* ⍾ *BP.*

THE WESTERN MIDLANDS

This section covers the area's western fringe, picking up in the town of Boyle in County Roscommon. It skirts Lough Key, Lough Ree, Lough Derg, and the River Shannon. Depending on how you travel south, you may journey through the hilly landscape of County Leitrim, dappled with lakes and beloved of anglers for its fish-filled waters. The region is the country's most sparsely populated (though it has a light sprinkling of villages and is the home of one of Ireland's leading writers, John McGahern). Moving south through Roscommon, western Offaly, and the northern part of Tipperary, the scenery is generally low on spectacle but high on unspoilt, lush, and undulating countryside. The towns are small and undistinguished, except Birr and Strokestown, both designed to complement the "big houses" that share their names. However, this is one of the parts of the country where you're most likely to encounter the "hidden Ireland"—a place unblighted by the plastic leprechaun syndrome of the more touristy areas to the south and west. The historic highlight in this region is the ancient site of Clonmacnoise, an important monastery of early Christian Ireland. The route then takes you southward, to northern County Tipperary.

Boyle

14 *190 km (118 mi) northwest of Dublin.*

An old-fashioned town on the Boyle River midway between Lough Gara and Lough Key, Boyle makes a good starting point for visits to the nearby Curlew Mountains. **King House,** a massive edifice in the center of town, was built about 1730 by the King family, which moved 50 years later to larger quarters at Rockingham in what is now Lough Key Forest Park; that house burned down in 1957. The King family came from Staffordshire, England, and aggressively worked to establish themselves as local nobility. Edward King, an ancestor of the Kings who settled here, drowned in the Irish Sea in 1636; he was the subject of Milton's poem "Lycidas." After extensive renovations, the house is now open to the public, with exhibits

> ### EXTREME HOUSE-GUESTS
>
> From 1788 to 1922 King House was used as a barracks for the Connaught Rangers. Known as the fiercest regiment of the British Army—Wellington called them the "Devil's Own"—they were notorious for their savagery in putting down the Irish.

on the Connaught Rangers and the Kings of Connaught, many done with waxwork figures in full period costume. A coffee shop serves traditional Irish breakfasts and hearty lunches, both with plenty of homemade baked goods on the menu. ☎ *071/966–3242* ⊕ *www.roscommoncoco.ie/kinghouse.htm* ✉ *€7* ⊙ *Apr.–mid-Oct., daily 10–6; last tour at 5.*

The ruins of the **Cistercian abbey** reflect its long history. The church was founded in the late 12th century, when the Romanesque style still prevailed, but as construction went on, the Gothic style arrived in Ireland, evident in the arches on the north side. A 17th-century gatehouse, through which you enter the abbey, has a small exhibition. ⊠ *On N4* ☎ *071/966–2604* ⌸ *Free* ⊙ *Apr.–Oct., daily 9:30–6:30.*

Where to Stay

$ 🖼 **Royal Hotel.** This traditional small-town hotel has a touch of the Far East to it. The restaurant serves traditional Irish fare but also does a tasty chow mein due to the fact that co-owner Nelson Chung hails from Hong Kong. Other than that, this is a comfortable if standard establishment. The chief reason to stay here, apart from good angling nearby, is to experience the slower pace of life of an old-fashioned Irish small town. Rooms vary in shape and size and are plainly but adequately furnished and well equipped. The restaurant overlooks a pretty stretch of river and serves both Chinese and Continental food. ⊠ *Bridge St., Co. Roscommon* ☎ *071/966–2016* 🖶 *071/966–2016* � *16 rooms* ⌂ *Restaurant, coffee shop, cable TV, in-room data ports, bar; no a/c* ▤ *AE, DC, MC, V* ⍟ *BP.*

The Outdoors

Boyle is a good starting point for bicycling over the lake-dotted landscape that extends north into neighboring County Leitrim and west into County Sligo. The 40-km (25-mi) scenic Arigna Drive from Boyle to Cootehall winds through unspoiled countryside on the shores of Lough Key and Lough Arrow on narrow, quiet roads that are ideal for cycling. **Brendan Sheerin** (⊠ Main St. ☎ 079/62010) rents bicycles.

Strokestown

⑮ *28 km (17 mi) south of Boyle.*

Strokestown is a town of strange dimensions. It boasts the widest main street in Ireland—laid out to rival the Ringstrasse in Vienna—and yet is home to only a couple of hundred people. At one end of this usually deserted boulevard the streetscape melts away into the undulating Roscommon countryside while at the other three large Gothic archways

★ announce the entrances to the vast **Strokestown Park House,** occupied by the Pakenham Mahon family from 1660 to 1979. The house once sat on 27,000 acres and was the second-largest estate in County Roscommon, after the King family's Rockingham. To some degree, the complicated architectural history mirrors the histories of other Anglo-Irish houses. The oldest parts of the house date from 1696; Palladian wings were added in the 1730s to the original block; and the house was extended again in the early 19th century. Its contents are a rich trove specific to the site, as they were never liquidated in the auctions that plagued so many other stately houses. The interior is full of curiosities, such as the gallery above the kitchen, which allowed the lady of the house to supervise domestic affairs from a safe distance. Menus were dropped from the balcony on Monday mornings with instructions to the cook for the week's meals. The 4-acre walled pleasure garden has the longest herbaceous border in Britain and Ireland. The **Irish Famine Museum,** in the stable yards, documents in detail the disastrous famine (1845–49) and the subsequent mass emigration. ☎ *071/963–3013* ⊕ *www.strokestownpark.ie* ⌸ *House €5; house, museum, and garden €13* ⊙ *Apr.–Oct., daily 9:30–5:30; Nov.–Mar. by appointment.*

Strokestown also has a charming selection of old-world shops and pubs. The pick of the bunch has to be **Beirne's Pub** (✉ Bridge St. ☎ 071/963–3049). Unlike so many ersatz "trad pubs" you may encounter, this is the real deal. Owned and occupied for four generations by the Beirne family, they still sell everything from cornflakes to chimney brushes in their little grocery–hardware store. After you've done the shopping you can get refreshments in the atmospheric little bar tucked away at the back of the shop. Then (if you're not over the limit) you might like to fill up with gas at the sidewalk pumps out front. They really don't make them like this anymore.

FodorsChoice
★

Roscommon

🔟 *19 km (12 mi) south of Strokestown.*

Sheep- and cattle-raising are the main occupations here in the capital of County Roscommon, a pleasant little town with many solid stone buildings, including the Bank of Ireland (in the former courthouse). On the southern slopes of a hill in the lower part of town sit the remains of **Roscommon Abbey,** founded in the 12th century. In the abbey's principal ruin, a church, are eight sculpted figures that represent gallowglasses (medieval Irish professional soldiers) and stand at the base of the choir. The ruins are freely accessible. As you head north out of Roscommon town you will pass the romantic sight of Roscommon Castle, a large Norman stronghold with impressive tumbledown curtain walls.

Where to Eat & Stay

$$–$$$$ ✕ **The Old Fort.** In a great location by the Shannon, this restored fort-turned-restaurant oozes character. Owner Fergal Moran, who grew up in the area and acquired the fort in the mid-1990s, took almost a decade to restore it; his labor of love greets visitors with low lighting, blazing fires, and plentiful sofas. The ambience is exposed beams, wooden floors, and vast bowls of fresh flowers in every nook. You have three dining options, the early-bird dinner, a set dinner, and an à la carte menu. The well-balanced assortment of fish and meat dishes appeals to traditional tastes—doing the simple things well seems to be the ethos here. Reservations are advised, especially in peak summer months. ✉ *Shannonbridge, Co. Roscommon* ☎ *090/9674973* ⊕ *www.theoldfortrestaurant.com* ▤ *MC, V* ☉ *Closed Mon. and Tue., and Nov.–mid.-Jan. No lunch.*

★ $$$ 🏨 **Clonalis House.** In a modern Ireland where many grand old family houses have been snapped up by tech millionaires as trophy country homes, Pyers O'Conor-Nash still lives in this legacy of his ancestry, which he can trace back 1,500 years to the original O'Conors of Connaught. The last High King of Ireland, Rory O'-Conor, was a direct descendant. This impressive 45-room mansion dates to 1878 and is widely regarded as being amongst the most historic of Ireland's Great Houses. Combining characteristics of Queen Anne

> ### RETAIL REFORMATORY
>
> The former county jail, a large stone building in Roscommon town center, has been transformed into a shopping mall—an unlikely venture that has to be seen to be believed.

and Italianate architectural styles, with large southwest-facing windows, bright and airy Clonalis defies the perception of Victorian architecture as rather dark and gloomy. Everything in the house—reception areas, bedrooms, and dining space—runs large scale. Bedrooms have four-poster beds and bathrooms of a similar scale, and a pair of cottages in the courtyard are also available to rent. In these grand surroundings, the food (guests only, no dinner Sunday and Monday, no lunch) runs to simple, unpretentious fare. With a minimum of fuss from Pyers and his wife Marguerite, this intriguing place manages to mix tradition with the daily routine of contemporary family life. As might be expected of the man who inhabits this glorious link to ancient Ireland, Pyers is a mine of information on the locality and its history. The library contains correspondence, heirlooms, and portraits of the O'Conors from the past 600 years; among its 7,000 volumes is the last judgment made under Brehon Law (the ancient Irish legal system that the English outlawed), handed down in 1580. ⊠ *Castlerea, Co. Roscommon, on the N60 west of Castlerea* ☎ *094/9620014* 🖶 ⊕ *www.clonalis.com* ⇋ *4 rooms, 3 cottages* ⚑ *Dining room, tea shop, some kitchens, tennis court, boating, fishing, library; no TV in some rooms* ⊟ *MC, V* ⊖⊖ *BP.*

★ $$–$$$ 🏠 **Castlecoote House.** A grand house that stands in the crook of a bend in the River Suck, Castlecoote was the birthplace of the Gunning sisters, two of the 18th century's most famous "It girls." From relatively modest beginnings this pair of beauties ended up as Duchess of Hamilton and Countess of Coventry; their portraits by celebrated portrait artist Sir Joshua Reynolds still hang in the main hall here. This is just one of the colorful stories that attend this house, which was built in the 17th century on the remains of a medieval castle, then won in a poker game by the Gunning family, and partially gutted in a fire during the 1980s. Owner Kevin Finnerty has meticulously restored the house to its authentic Georgian splendor and installed under-floor heating (a luxury previous owners never dreamt of as they huddled round the hearth for warmth). The bedrooms are luxurious, with four-poster beds, while the main salon—all crystal chandeliers, pale emerald walls, and white-trim doorways—is pure elegance in the 18th-century Irish fashion. Dinner must be booked by noon. To get here, drive 5 km (3 mi) on the R366 from Roscommon to Castlecoote. The limestone entrance gate, which is unmarked, is next to Castlecoote Stores. ⊠ *Castlecoote, Co. Roscommon* ☎ *090/666–3794* 🖶 *01/833–0666* ⊕ *www.castlecootehouse.com* ⇋ *5 rooms* ⚑ *Tennis court, fishing, croquet; no a/c, no room phones, no room TVs, no kids under 12, no smoking* ⊟ *MC, V* ⊖⊖ *BP.*

Athlone

ⓘ *29 km (18 mi) southeast of Roscommon, 127 km (79 mi) west of Dublin, 121 km (75 mi) east of Limerick.*

The mighty Shannon flows majestically through the heart of Athlone, yet for years it seemed as if the town was happy to turn its back on one of Europe's great waterways. That trend has now been well and truly reversed and with it has come a real buzz of regeneration. The area around Athlone Castle has transformed into a veritable "Left Bank" and on both sides of the Shannon, new restaurants and stylishly modern architec-

Goldsmith Country

ALL THAT GLITTERS may not be Goldsmith but that hasn't prevented the Irish tourist board from promoting the Northern Lakelands to the burgeoning literary tourism market as "Goldsmith Country." Yes, this is the region that gave birth to the writer Oliver Goldsmith (1730–74), celebrated for his farcical drama *She Stoops to Conquer* and his classic novel *The Vicar of Wakefield*. Goldsmith, however, left his homeland as a teenager and returned rarely. He is thought to have drawn on memories of his native Longford for his most renowned poem, "The Deserted Village." At Goldsmith's childhood home in Lissoy in County Longford, only the bare walls of the family house remain standing. At Pallas, near Ballymahon in County Longford, his birthplace, there's a statue in his memory but little else. The plot of *She Stoops to Conquer* involves a

misunderstanding in which a traveler mistakes a private house for an inn. This actually happened to Goldsmith at Ardagh House, now a college, in the center of the village of Ardagh (just off N55) in County Longford. In the same play the character Tony Lumpkin sings a song about a pub called the Three Jolly Pigeons; today the pub of the same name, on the Ballymahon road (N55) north of Athlone, is the headquarters of the Oliver Goldsmith Summer School. Every year on the first weekend in June, leading academics from around the world speak on Goldsmith at this pub and other venues, and there are readings by the best of Ireland's contemporary poets and evening traditional-music sessions in this tiny, atmospheric, traditional country pub. Call 0902/85162 for more information.

ture are beginning to spring up along streets lined with 200-year-old buildings. Once upon a time, tourists were few and far between in what was cuttingly termed the "dead center" of Ireland—but the renaissance has made Athlone an increasingly attractive destination. Beside the River Shannon, at the southern end of Lough Ree, stands **Athlone Castle**, built in the 13th century. After their defeat at the Battle of the Boyne in 1691, the Irish retreated to Athlone and made the river their first line of defense. The castle, a fine example of a Norman stronghold, houses a small museum of artifacts relating to Athlone's eventful past. The castle gatehouse also houses the town's tourist office. Admission includes access to an interpretive center depicting the siege of Athlone in 1691, the flora and fauna of the Shannon, and the life of the tenor John McCormack (1884–1945), an Athlone native and perhaps the finest lyric tenor Ireland has produced. ⊠ *Town Bridge* ☎ *090/647–2107* 🖃 *€5.50* 🕓 *May–Sept., daily 10–5; Oct.–Apr. by appointment.*

Where to Stay & Eat

★ **$$–$$$** ✕ **Le Château.** Owners Martina and Stephen Linehan have created a wonderfully atmospheric restaurant in Athlone's old quarter. As in cooking, the raw ingredients are the key. They've transformed a former Presbyterian church into a lovely riverside bistro where, on summer evenings, light streams in through the original stained-glass windows and candles illuminate the nautically themed dining room at nightfall. Stephen Linehan's menu does not attempt to reinvent the wheel but emphasizes wonderfully fresh local produce. The dishes are mainly traditional favorites with an emphasis on locally reared beef and lamb. Seafood dishes like roast monkfish wrapped in bacon are also popular while there is also usually some vegetarian delight like a trio of golden Brie, garlic mushrooms, and Caesar salad. ⊠ *St. Peter's Port, the Docks* ☎ *090/649–4517* ▤ *AE, DC, MC, V.*

★ **$$$–$$$$** ✕▣ **Wineport Lodge.** Once a wooden boathouse and current headquarters of Lough Ree Yacht Club, this lakeside restaurant-with-rooms is now billed as Ireland's first "wine hotel." Stylishly modern—all orange cedarwood and plate-glass windows—and set against parkland groves of trees, the striking light-filled wood-and-glass building seems like it was airlifted from Sweden. Inside, guests make a beeline to the restaurant ($$$–$$$$), where chef Feargal O'Donnell draws praise for his imaginative cooking and the way he matches food to the extensive wine menu. Mouthwatering offerings like sauté of tiger prawns and mango with coriander, lime, and pickled ginger or Clare Island organic salmon orzo with leek stew are standard fare. However, bar food ($) is also available from 4 PM to 6 PM. The guest rooms are minimalist but filled with stylish touches like leopard-skin prints. Once you've wined and dined, treat yourself to one of the alluring spa treatments Bliss Dublin provides to guests. Glasson lies 5 km (3 mi) north of Athlone on the shores of Lough Ree. ⊠ *Glasson, Co. Westmeath* ☎ *090/643–9010* 🖶 *090/648–5471* ⊕ *www.wineport.ie* ↪ *10 rooms* 🜂 *Restaurant, minibars, in-room data ports, fishing, bar* ▤ *AE, DC, MC, V* ⦿ *BP.*

Sports & the Outdoors

BICYCLING A combination of unfrequented back roads and lakeside scenery makes this attractive biking country. Rent bikes from **M. R. Hardiman** (⊠ Irishtown ☎ 090/647–8669).

BOATING A boat trip reveals the importance of Athlone's strategic location on the River Shannon as well as the beauty of the region. *The Viking* (⊠ The Strand ☎ 090/647–9277) is a replica of a Viking longboat that travels up the Shannon to nearby Lough Ree. The cost is €7.50; sailings take place daily from July through September at 11, 2:30, and 4. A river cruiser for a floating holiday can be rented by the week from **Athlone Cruisers Ltd** (⊠ Jolly Mariner Marina ☎ 090/647–2892).

GOLF **Athlone Golf Club** (⊠ Hodson Bay ☎ 0902/92073) is a lakeside 18-hole parkland course. **Glasson Golf & Country Club** (⊠ Glasson ☎ 090/648–5120), an 18-hole parkland course, is bordered on three sides by Lough Ree and the River Shannon. **Mount Temple Golf Club** (⊠ Campfield Lodge, Moate ☎ 090/648–1841) is an 18-hole parkland course 8 km (5 mi) east of Athlone.

Clonmacnoise

★ ⑱ *20 km (12 mi) south of Athlone, 93 km (58 mi) east of Galway.*

Many ancient sites dot the River Shannon, but Clonmacnoise is early-Christian Ireland's foremost monastic settlement and, like Chartres, a royal site. The monastery was founded by St. Ciaran between 543 and

549 at a location that was not as remote as it now appears to be: near the intersection of what were then two of Ireland's most vital routes—the Shannon River, running north–south, and the Eiscir Riada, running east–west. Like Glendalough, Celtic Ireland's other great monastic site, Clonmacnoise benefited from its isolation; surrounded by bog, it's accessible only via one road or via the Shannon. Thanks to this location, it almost survived everything thrown at it, including raids by feuding Irish tribes, Vikings, and Normans. But when the English garrison arrived from Athlone in 1552, they ruthlessly reduced the site to ruin. Still, with a little imagination, you can picture life here in medieval times, when the nobles of Europe sent their sons to be educated by the local monks.

The monastery was founded on an esker (natural gravel ridge) overlooking the Shannon and a marshy area known as the Callows, which today is protected habitat for the corncrake, a wading bird. Numerous buildings and ruins remain. The small **cathedral** dates as far back as the 10th century but has additions from the 15th century. It was the burial place of kings of Connaught and of Tara, and of Rory O'Conor, the last high king of Ireland, buried here in 1198. The two round towers include **O'Rourke's Tower,** which was struck by lightning and subsequently rebuilt in the 12th century. There are eight **smaller churches,** the littlest of which is thought to be the burial place of St. Ciaran. The only church of this group not built within the monastery walls is Nun's Church, about 1 km (½ mi) to the east. The High Crosses have been moved into the visitor center to protect them from the elements (copies stand in their original places); the best preserved of these is the Cross of the Scriptures, also known as Flann's Cross. Some of the treasures and manuscripts originating from Clonmacnoise are now housed in Dublin; most are at the National Museum, although the 12th-century *Book of the Dun Cow* is at the Royal Irish Academy Library.

Clonmacnoise has always been a prestigious burial place. Among the ancient stones are many other graves dating from the 17th to the mid-20th century, when a new graveyard was consecrated on adjoining land. The whole place is time-burnished, though in midsummer it can be difficult to avoid the throngs of tourists. ✉ *Near Shannonbridge* ☎ *090/ 574195* ⊕ *www.heritageireland.ie* 💷 *€5* ⊙ *Nov.–mid-Mar., daily 10–5:30; mid-Mar.–mid-May and mid-Sept.–Oct., daily 10–6; mid-May–early Sept., daily 9–7. Last admission 45 min before closing.*

Banagher

 31 km (19 mi) south of Clonmacnoise.

"Well, that beats Banagher!" This small Shannon-side town is best known in Ireland because of this common phrase, which dates from the 19th century when the town was the very worst example of a "rotten borough"—a corrupt electoral area controlled by the local landed gentry. In short, if something "beats Banagher" it's either pretty bad or rather extraordinary. Nowadays, Banagher is a lively marina town that is a popular base for water-sports enthusiasts. Anthony Trollope (1815–82), who came to Ireland as a post office surveyor in 1841, lived here while he wrote his first book, *The Macdermots of Ballycloran*. Charlotte Brontë

Getting Bogged Down

LIKE THE ESKIMOES with their 100 different words for snow, the natives of the Midlands retain a historic attachment to their vast boglands and will extol its virtues in great detail if prompted by a stranger.

In rural parts, turf, or peat, still accounts for much of the winter fuel supply and locals can always be counted upon to discuss in great detail the quality and consistency of this uniquely native resource.

"Grand year for the turf" will generally indicate a sunny August—key drying time when the "sods" are cut and allowed to dry along the banks. Conversely, "wicked bad turf" denotes a typically soft Irish summer with poor drying.

Along country lanes, the sight of reeks of cut turf is still commonplace. If you're tired of using the weather as a conversational ice-breaker, try turf as an alternative and virtually guaranteed discourse igniter.

No matter that from a distance an Irish peat bog looks like a flat, treeless piece of waterlogged land. A close-up view shows a much more exciting landscape.

Bogs support an extraordinary amount of wildlife, including larks and snipe, pale-blue dragonflies, and Greenland white-fronted geese. Amid the pools and lakes of the peat bog, amazing jewel-like wildflowers thrive, from purple bell heather to yellow bog asphodel, all alongside grasses, lichens, and mosses.

As you pass through the small town of Shannonbridge, 10 km (6 mi) south of Clonmacnoise, on either side of the road are vast stretches of chocolate-brown boglands and isolated industrial plants for processing the area's natural resource.

Bord na Móna, the same government agency that makes commercial use of other boglands, has jurisdiction over the area.

To take a closer look at the bog, join the **Bord na Móna Bog Rail Tour** (✉ Near Shannonbridge, Uisce Dubh ☎ 0905/74114 ⊕ www.bnm.ie 💶 €5.50 ☉ Tour Apr.–Oct., daily 10–5 on the hr), which leaves from Uisce Dubh.

A small, green-and-yellow diesel locomotive pulls one coach across the bog while the driver provides commentary on a landscape unchanged for millennia.

There are more than 1,200 km (745 mi) of narrow-gauge bog railway, and the section on the tour, known as the Clonmacnoise and South Offaly Railway, is the only part accessible to the public.

(1816–55) also famously spent her honeymoon here. **Flynn's** (✉ Main St. ☎ 0509/51312), in the center of town, is worth visiting to appreciate its light and spacious Victorian-style design. The lunch menu includes generously filled sandwiches, salad platters, a roast meat of the day, and chicken, fish, or burgers with chips.

If you happen to be in Banagher on a Thursday or a Sunday in summer, consider taking a two-hour **Shannon cruise** on *The River Queen*, an enclosed launch that seats 54 passengers and has a full bar on board. *Sil-*

ver Line Cruisers Ltd. ⊠ *The Marina* ☎ *0509/51112* 🖭 *€10* ☉ *Cruises June–mid-Sept., Thurs. at 3, Sun. at 2:30 and 4:30, weather permitting.*

Paddling a canoe is a nice alternative to a river cruise. **Shannon Adventure Canoeing and Camping Holidays** rents Canadian-class canoes, which allow you to explore the Shannon and other waterways on your own terms. ⊠ *The Marina* ☎ *0509/51411* ⊕ *www.iol.ie/~advcanoe/index. html* ☉ *May–Oct.*

Birr

⑳ *12 km (7 mi) southeast of Banagher, 130 km (81 mi) west of Dublin.*

Beautifully reminiscent of an English county town with its tree-lined malls and well-preserved houses, the heritage town of Birr has roots that go back to the 6th century. Still, it's that mid-18th-century Georgian building boom that sets the tone.

Fodor'sChoice
★

All roads in Birr lead to the gates of **Birr Castle Demesne,** a gorgeous Gothic Revival castle (built around an earlier 17th-century castle that was damaged by fire in 1823) that is still the home of the earls of Rosse. It's not open to the common man, but you can visit the surrounding 150 acres of gardens. The present earl and countess of Rosse continue the family tradition of making botanical expeditions all over the world for specimens of rare trees, plants, and shrubs. The formal gardens contain the tallest (32 feet) box hedges in the world and vine-sheltered hornbeam allées. In spring check out the wonderful display of flowering magnolias, cherries, crab apples, and naturalized narcissi; in autumn, the maples, chestnuts, and weeping beeches blaze red and gold. The grounds are laid out around a lake and along the banks of two adjacent rivers; above one of these stands the castle. The grounds also contain **Ireland's Historic Science Centre,** an exhibition on astronomy, photography, botany, and engineering housed in the stable block. The giant (72-inch-long) reflecting telescope, built in 1845, remained the largest in the world for 75 years. Allow at least two hours to see everything. ⊠ *Rosse Row* ☎ *0509/20336* ⊕ *www.birrcastleireland.com* 🖭 *Castle and grounds €9* ☉ *Nov.–Mar., daily 10–4; Apr.–Oct., daily 9–6.*

Where to Stay & Eat

$–$$ ✕ **The Thatch Bar.** It's worth venturing 2 km (1 mi) south of Birr, just off the N62 Roscrea road, into this thatched country pub and restaurant, which offers a warm welcome and imaginative food. Inexpensive meals are available at the bar at lunchtime and early evening (until 7:30), although in the evening the restaurant offers a choice of a five-course dinner menu or an à la carte menu. Pigeon and rabbit terrines, sirloin steak with mushrooms in garlic vie for diners' attention with more exotic dishes like kangaroo and (locally farmed) ostrich. ⊠ *Crinkle* ☎ *0509/20682* 🖃 *DC, MC, V* ☉ *Closed Mon. Oct.–Apr. and Sun.–Tues. May–Sept.*

$$–$$$$
Fodor'sChoice
★

✕🖼 **Kinnitty Castle.** Venture over to the foot of the Slieve Bloom Mountains, 16 km (10 mi) east of Birr, to this exuberant, turreted, Gothic Revival edifice, rebuilt in 1927 of ashlar granite. Everything is on a grand scale and some of the guest bedrooms here will time-warp you back to the 17th century. Some are fitted out with grand four-poster beds, such

3

as O'Carroll Baronial, blushing with red tartan throws. Or opt for the dazzler that is peaked with a wood-and-timber cathedral ceiling (even some bathrooms have wood beams here). Accommodations in the "new" wing (built 1994) are smaller, while the Moneyguyneen Country House on the castle grounds has cheaper B&B rooms. The dining room has enormously tall windows and a dark-wood floor. The Sli Dala is the hotel's main restaurant ($$–$$$$) with a table d'hôte menu offering dishes like fillet of salmon in a champagne cream sauce, while the Monk's Kitchen restaurant offers more down-home fare. And for purest relaxation, there's a full-scale spa offering massages, wraps, and beauty treatments. ⊠ *Kinnitty, Co. Offaly* ☎ *0509/37318* ☐ *0509/ 37284* ⊕ *www.kinnittycastle.com* ⊅ *48 rooms* ⌂ *2 restaurants, tennis court, spa, fishing, horseback riding, bar, meeting rooms; no a/c, no room TVs* ⊟ *AE, DC, MC, V* ¶◯ *BP.*

> **PARTY CRASHER**
>
> Kinnitty Castle is said to play host to a collection of ghostly guests. The most famous of these is "the friendly monk," who always appears dressed in black. The staff says the smiling specter particularly likes to show up at weddings and other festive events held in the castle's Great Hall of the O'Carrolls.

$$ ✕▦ **Dooly's.** This unpretentious country hotel began life as a coach house some 250 years ago and it has retained a charming old-style atmosphere. Floral patterns, open fires, and a relaxed welcome all form part of the decor. It's in Birr's central square, and a five-minute walk from the castle. The bustling bar and coffee shop are popular with locals. For a more formal dining experience you could try the Emmet Restaurant ($–$$), where fish dishes like baked sea bass in phyllo pastry and honey-glaze cod steak are specialties. ⊠ *Emmet Sq., Co. Offaly* ☎ *0509/20032* ☐ *0509/21332* ⊕ *www.doolyshotel.com* ⊅ *18 rooms* ⌂ *Restaurant, coffee shop, cable TV, fishing, horseback riding, bar, meeting rooms; no a/c* ⊟ *AE, DC, MC, V* ¶◯ *BP.*

¢ ✕▦ **The Maltings.** Sheltering beneath the eaves of Birr Castle on a riverbank, this converted stone-cut storehouse is a good option for families and offers special rates for children. The spacious rooms have small windows, country pine furniture, and simple matching floral drapes and spreads. All have en suite facilities with bath and shower, and are equipped with direct-dial telephones. The cheerful, low-ceiling restaurant ($–$$) overlooks the river and serves good value in plain Irish cooking. ⊠ *Castle St., Co. Offaly* ☎☐ *0509/21345* ⊅ *13 rooms* ⌂ *Restaurant, cable TV; no a/c* ⊟ *MC, V* ¶◯ *BP.*

Lough Derg

㉑ *16 km (10 mi) west of Birr on R489.*

Between Portland and Portumna, the River Shannon widens into 32,000 acres of unpolluted water, known as Lough Derg, a popular center for water sports, including waterskiing, yachting, and motor-cruising. Anglers flock here as well for pike and coarse fishing. Excellent woodland walks wind around the shore of the lake. (Be sure not to confuse this Lough Derg with the lake of the same name in County Donegal.) The well-signposted, scenic **Lough Derg Drive**, approximately 90 km (56 mi) long, encircles the lake, passing through a number of pretty waterside villages, from Portumna in the north to Killaloe in the south. **Terryglass**, on the eastern shore of Lough Derg and well signposted on R439 from Birr, is particularly popular with water-sports enthusiasts and anglers, as well as regular vacationers seeking an away-from-it-all destination; replete with grand church, tree-tunnel street, and cute cottages, it's considered one of the prettiest villages in Ireland.

Where to Stay

$ ⊡ **Kylenoe.** Virginia Moeran is famed for breeding racehorses, including top stallion Vinnie Roe (the only horse ever to win the Irish St. Leger three times in a row), owned by Irish movie director Jim Sheridan. But she and her family also find time to welcome guests to their 200-year-old stone house, which stands on 150 acres of farm and woodland close to Lough Derg. Relax in front of the log fire, explore the countryside on foot or horseback, or enjoy water sports. Rooms are spacious, with modest antique furnishings and family heirlooms. Children are welcome. Virginia Moeran's breakfasts have won awards, and she also cooks dinner (for guests only), which must be booked by 2:30 PM, from fresh local produce. To get here follow the lakeside road from Terryglass in the Ballinderry direction. ⊠ *Nenagh, Terryglass, Co. Tipperary* ☎ *067/ 22015* 🖶 *067/22275* ⬅ *4 rooms, 2 with bath* ♿ *Dining room, some pets allowed; no a/c, no room phones, no smoking* ▭ *MC, V* ⎮Ⓞ⎮ *BP.*

Sports & the Outdoors

BOATING **Shannon Sailing** (⊠ New Marina Complex, Dromineer ☎ 067/24499) organizes cruises of scenic Lough Derg by water bus and also hires out cruisers and sailboards. **Lough Derg Powerboat School** (⊠ Sallybay House, Ballina ☎ 061/375–474 ⊕ www.powerboat-training.co.uk/schools/ schools-loughderg.htm) runs powerboat and motor-cruiser training courses. Courses vary in length from half a day to four days.

GOLF Discerning golfers love the 18-hole parkland course at **Birr Golf Club** (⊠ The Glens ☎ 0509/20082). It's one of the best parkland courses in the country. Even though it's miles from the sea, the undulating fairways and dry sod make it reminiscent of a links course.

HIKING Birr is in the heart of an excellent hiking area. The Offaly Way and the Grand Canal Way are marked trails to the north of town; to the east is the 50-km (31-mi) Slieve Bloom Trail, a circular route that winds through some infrequently visited areas with spectacular views and rich plant and wildlife. Pick up brochures and maps locally, or consult the expert, **Christine Byrne** (⊠ Ardmore House, Kinnitty ☎ 0509/37009 ⊕ www.kinnitty.net), who organizes guided walks for all levels.

Roscrea

㉒ *19 km (12 mi) south of Birr.*

Every corner you turn in this charming town will offer reminders of its rich and sometimes turbulent past. Ancient castles, towers, and churches dot the town's skyline, proof of a heritage that goes back to the 7th century. Roscrea is on the main N7 road between Dublin and Cork, making it ideal as a stopover en route to the south. The road cuts right through the remains of a monastery founded by St. Cronan. It also passes the west facade of a 12th-century Romanesque church that now forms an entrance gate to a modern Catholic church. Above the structure's round-headed doorway is a hood-molding enclosing the figure of a bishop, probably St. Cronan. In the very center of town is **Roscrea Castle,** a Norman fortress dating from 1314, given by King Richard II to the duke of Ormond. Inside are vaulted rooms graced with tapestries and 16th-century furniture. A ticket to it also gains entry to the adjacent **Damer House,** a superb example of an early-18th-century town house on the grand scale. It was built in 1725 within the curtain walls of the castle, at a time when homes were often constructed beside or attached to the strongholds they replaced. The house has a plain, symmetrical facade and a magnificent carved-pine staircase inside; on display are exhibits about local history. To get here, start with your back to St. Cronan's monastery, turn left, and then right onto Castle Street. ⊠ *Castle St.* ☎ *0505/21850* ⊕ *www.heritageireland. ie* ☑ *€3.10* ⊙ *May–Sept., daily 9:30–6; Oct.–Apr., weekends 10–5.*

Where to Eat

★ **$$$$** ✕ **Fiacrí Country House Restaurant.** In just a few years, this cozy farmhouse restaurant has built up a legion of fans in spite of its remote location in the midst of the rolling Tipperary countryside. Chef Ailish Hennessy prepares modern country-house fare with an emphasis on locally produced meats. Meals are only served prix fixe but five courses are a fine value at €45. Specialties include panfried medallions of pork with caramelized apple, cider, and whole-grain mustard-cream sauce. Husband Enda does a charming turn overseeing the dining rooms, which also double as a cooking school. To get there take the Knock road off the Roscrea bypass; after 3 km (2 mi) turn right for Erril—the restaurant is signposted after 3 km (2 mi). ⊠ *Boulrea, Knock* ☎ *0505/ 43018* ⊕ *www.fiacrihouse.com* ▭ *AE, MC, V* ⊙ *Closed Sun.–Tues.*

Sports & the Outdoors

Three marked trails—measuring 9 km (5½ mi), 3 km (2 mi), and 1½ km (1 mi)—run through the 450-acre, organic **Fairymount Farm** (⊠ Ballingarry ☎ 067/21139 ⊕ www.fairymountfarm.com), with woodlands, horses, and sheep. Points of interest are explained in a booklet you can pick up here. The trails can also be followed on horseback (the farm's rangers can help you arrange this), and you can fish for pike or perch in the farm's 25-acre lake. Access to the farm costs €5.

Nenagh

㉓ *35 km (22 mi) west of Roscrea, 35 km (22 mi) east of Limerick.*

Originally a Norman settlement, Nenagh grew into a market town in the 19th century. Standing right in the center of Nenagh, the **Castle Keep** is all that remains of the original town. Once one of five round towers linked by a curtain wall, and measuring 53 feet across the base, it rises to 100 feet, with 19th-century crenellations at the top. The gatehouse and governor's house of Nenagh's old county jail now form the **Nenagh**

Heritage Centre, which has permanent displays of rural life before mechanization, as well as temporary painting and photography exhibits. ✉ *Kickham St.* ☎ *067/44587* 🎫 *€5* 🕐 *Easter–Oct., weekdays 9:30–5, Sun. 2:30–5; Nov.–Easter, weekdays 9:30–5.*

Where to Stay & Eat

¢–$ ✕ **Country Choice.** A foodies' favorite, this lovely shop has won countless awards for its well-stocked pantry of delicacies. Owner Peter Ward is an expert on Irish cheeses, and local varieties like Baylough farmhouse cheddar are particularly popular with customers. You can also find home-cooked fare in the simple coffee shop at the back of the store. Specialties include a soup of broccoli and Cashel Blue (an Irish blue cheese), as well as slow-cooked meat dishes like lamb ragout or beef in Guinness casserole. Home-baked bread and pastries are made with local flour. ✉ *25 Kenyon St.* ☎ *067/32596* 💳 *No credit cards* 🕐 *Closed Sun. No dinner.*

$ 🏨 **Ashley Park House.** The plantation-style verandas that adorn the front of this distinctly Irish Georgian home lend an intriguing and eccentric feel to this enchanting lakefront mansion. This tone is echoed by the charmingly offbeat welcome extended to guests by manager Sean Mounsey. This genial tweed-clad gent will want to show you every antique-crammed nook of the building and to recount its history—if you have time. The house has a walled garden where guests are encouraged to pick fruit from the orchard. In fact, there are extensive woodland walks here and you can borrow the property's row boat and explore Lough Ourna, the small lake in front of the house that bristles with ducks, herons, and other wildlife. Dinners created from fresh local produce may include the trout you'll hopefully catch in the lake. Book early for one of the large rooms with lake views. ✉ *Ardcroney, Co. Tipperary* ☎ *067/38223* 🛏 *5 rooms* ⚙ *Boating, fishing, some pets allowed; no a/c, no room phones, no TV in some rooms* 💳 *No credit cards* ⏏ *BP.*

MIDLANDS ESSENTIALS

To research prices, get advice from other travelers, and book travel arrangements, visit www.fodors.com.

Transportation

If traveling extensively by public transportation, be sure to load up on information (the best taxi-for-call companies, rail and bus schedules, etc.) upon arriving at the ticket counter or help desk of the bigger train and bus stations in the area, such as Belfast, Derry, and Armagh.

BY AIR

Dublin Airport is the principal international airport that serves the Midlands; car-rental facilities are available here. Sligo Airport has daily flights from Dublin on Aer Lingus.

🛂 Airport Information **Aer Lingus** ☎ 0818/365-000 ⊕ www.dublin-airport.com. **Dublin Airport** ☎ 01/814-1111. **Sligo Airport** ☎ 071/68280 ⊕ www.Sligoairport.com.

BY BUS

Bus Éireann runs an express bus from Dublin to Mullingar in 1½ hours, with a round-trip fare of €17.10. Buses depart three times daily. A regular-speed bus, leaving twice daily, makes the trip in two hours. Express buses also make stops at Longford (2¼ hours), Carrick-on-Shannon (3 hours), Boyle (3¼ hours), and Sligo (4¼ hours). There's also a daily bus from Mullingar to Athlone and an express service connecting Galway, Athlone, Longford, Cavan, Clones, Monaghan, and Sligo. Details of all bus services are available from the Bus Éireann depots listed below.

🚌 Bus Information **Athlone Railway Station** ☎ 090/648–4406. **Bus Éireann** ☎ 01/836–6111 in Dublin ⊕ www.buseireann.ie. **Cavan Bus Office** ☎ 049/433–1353. **Longford Railway Station** ☎ 043/45208. **Monaghan Bus Office** ☎ 047/82377. **Sligo Railway Station** ☎ 071/916–0066.

BY CAR

A car is necessary to really explore the region. Mullingar, Longford, and Boyle are on the main N4 route between Dublin and Sligo. It takes one hour to drive the 55 km (34 mi) from Dublin to Mullingar and two hours from Mullingar to Sligo (150 km [93 mi]). To get from Mullingar to southwestern Ireland, you can take N52 to Nenagh, where it meets N7, and follow that into Limerick. R390 from Mullingar leads you west to Athlone, where it connects with N6 to Galway. The 120-km (75-mi) drive takes about 2½ hours.

ROAD CONDITIONS: Most of the winding roads in the Midlands are uncongested, although you may encounter an occasional animal or agricultural machine crossing the road. In Mullingar, the cattle-trading town, roads can become badly crowded.

BY TRAIN

A direct-rail service links Longford (via Mullingar) to Dublin (Connolly Station), with on average eight trains every day making the 1½-hour journey. It costs €31.50 one way and €34.50 round-trip. Contact Irish Rail for information. Trains from Mullingar, departing three times daily weekdays and Sunday, stop at Longford (35 minutes), Carrick-on-Shannon (1 hour), Boyle (1¼ hours), and Sligo (2 hours). Portlaoise is served by a good commuter service and many of the intercity Dublin-Cork trains stop there. The intercity service to Galway City from Dublin Heuston serves Portarlington, Tullamore, and Athlone. Roscrea and Nenagh are served by a twice-daily train to Limerick City.

🚆 Train Information **Irish Rail** ☎ 01/836–6222 ⊕ www.irishrail.ie/home.

Contacts & Resources

CAR RENTAL

🚗 Agencies **Gerry Mullin** ✉ North Rd., Monaghan ☎ 047/81396. **Griffiths Mullingar Ltd.** ✉ Harbour St., Mullingar ☎ 044/48403. **Longford Car & Van Rentals** ✉ Longford Town, Longford ☎ 043/44099.

EMERGENCIES

The general emergency number in the area is 999. For medical service, contact the General Hospital in Mullingar

🚑 Emergency services **Ambulance, fire, police** ☎ 999. **General Hospital** ✉ Mullingar ☎ 044/40221. **Portlaoise Midland Regional Hospital** ✉ Portlaoise ☎ 0502/21364. 💊 Pharmacy **Weir's Chemist** ✉ Market Sq., Mullingar ☎ 044/48462.

INTERNET CAFÉS

Even though much of Ireland has gone Wi-Fi over the past two years, in some of the more rural regions you'll need to rely on the local Internet café to catch up on messages from home. As well as good places to find a decent cup of java, they are generally quite cheap; expect to pay around €2 an hour.

🛈 Internet Cafés **Ego Internet Cafe** ✉ Convent Building, Main St., Cavan ☎ 049/437-3488. **Bishop Business Ventures** ✉ 7a Mardyke St., Athlone ☎ 090/647-7633.

TOUR OPTIONS

To plan a trip within any particular county or area, you're best off starting with the local tourist office. They will have a thorough list of the must-see attractions in their areas. Several of the region's larger travel agencies organize tours.

🛈 Tour Companies **Trikon Travel** ✉ Castle St., Roscommon ☎ 090/662-6243. **Grenham Travel** ✉ 1 Connaught St., Athlone ☎ 090/649-2028. **O'Hanrahan Travel** ✉ 59 Dublin St., Monaghan ☎ 047/81133. **Airboran Travel** ✉ 4 Lismard Ct., Portlaoise ☎ 0502/21226.

VISITOR INFORMATION

Five Midlands Tourist Information Offices (TIOs) are open all year: Carrick-on-Shannon, Cavan, Monaghan, Mullingar, and Portlaoise. The Mullingar TIO has information on Counties Westmeath, Offaly, Monaghan, Cavan, and Laois. Another six Midlands TIOs are open seasonally: Athlone (April–October), Birr (May–September), Clonmacnoise (April–October), Longford (June–September), Tipperary (May–October), and Tullamore (mid-June–mid-September). For inquiries about Boyle and Roscommon, consult the Sligo TIO. For off-season inquiries about Tipperary, contact the Waterford City TIO.

🛈 Tourist Information **Athlone** ✉ Church St., Co. Westmeath ☎ 090/649-4630. **Birr** ✉ Rosse Row, Co. Offaly ☎ 0509/20110. **Carrick-on-Shannon** ✉ The Marina, Co. Leitrim ☎ 078/20170. **Cavan** ✉ Farnham St., Co. Cavan ☎ 049/433-1942 ⊕ www.cavantourism.com. **Clonmacnoise** ✉ Near Clonmacnoise ruins, Co. Offaly ☎ 0905/74134. **Longford** ✉ Main St., Co. Longford ☎ 043/46566. **Monaghan** ✉ Market House, Co. Monaghan ☎ 047/84786 ⊕ www.monaghantourism.com. **Mullingar** ✉ Dublin Rd., Co. Westmeath ☎ 044/48650 📠 044/40413 ⊕ www.ecoast-midlands.travel.ie. **Portlaoise** ✉ James Fintan Lawlor Ave., Co. Laois ☎ 0502/21178 ⊕ www.laoistourism.ie. **Sligo Town TIO** ✉ Temple and Charles Sts., Co. Sligo ☎ 071/916-1201 ⊕ www.irelandnorthwest.ie. **Tipperary** ✉ Excel Centre, Co. Tipperary ☎ 062/51457. **Tullamore** ✉ Bury Quay, Co. Offaly ☎ 0506/52617. **Waterford City TIO** ✉ 41 the Quay, Co. Waterford ☎ 051/875-823 ⊕ www.southeastireland.com.

The Southeast

INCLUDING COUNTIES CARLOW, KILKENNY, TIPPERARY, WATERFORD, AND WEXFORD

Farm in Tipperary

WORD OF MOUTH

"Cahir Castle is one of Ireland's best. There are many winding spiral staircases to explore and lots of nooks and crannies to see—but beware of the 'stumble steps' deliberately built into the castle."
—irisheyes

"The Rock of Cashel is a spectacular ruin and is one of the most important religious sites in Ireland. Its position overlooking the plains is quite amazing."
—wojazz3

WELCOME TO THE SOUTHEAST

TOP REASONS TO GO

★ **Glittering Waterford.** Long before Kleenex and Xerox turned their brand names into the thing itself, the Waterford Crystal Factory set a standard for cut crystal that all the world knows by name.

★ **Kilkenny, Ireland's Medieval Capital.** With its famous 14th-century "witch" Petronilla, Camelot-worthy Black Abbey, and storybook Kilkenny Castle, Kilkenny still conjures up the days of knights and damsels.

★ **Pretty-as-a-postcard Lismore.** Presided over by the castle of the Dukes of Devonshire, this enchanting, thatched-roof village has attracted visitors ranging from Sir Walter Raleigh to Fred Astaire.

★ **Cashel of the Kings.** Ireland's "Rock of Ages," this 200-foot-tall rock bluff was the seat of the kings of Munster and is still crowned with spectacular medieval ruins.

★ **Ireland in a Park.** From pre-Christian burial sites to a Norman castle, the Irish National Heritage Park is a top Wexford sight.

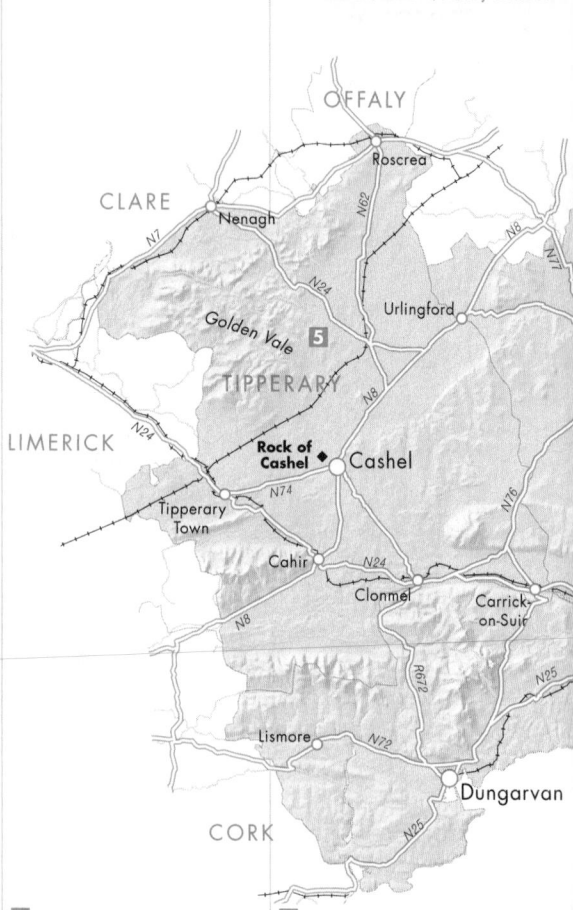

1 **Kilkenny City.** Creativity is evident in every aspect of this town, from its medieval stonework to its array of modern and traditional craft and design found in galleries and studios as well as the many festivals and events held here year-round.

2 **Southeast Inlands.** Redolent of the Middle Ages, this once-upon-a-timefied region is home to some thrilling medieval sights, including **Carlow Castle, Leighlinbridge's Black Castle,** the tiny village of **Old Leighlin,** and **Jerpoint Abbey,** the most famous Cistercian ruins in Ireland.

3 Wexford. The warm welcome, the ancient Viking streets and the tiny, atmospheric Theatre Royal add to the cultural pleasures as this proud town puts on its Sunday best for the Wexford Opera Festival, a week-long binge of arias and charm held every October.

4 Waterford & the Southeast Coast. Combining the best of Ireland's climate with some wonderful sand-and-sea settings, this coastal headland is noted for quaint villages like **Kilmore Quay** and **Ballyhack,** the bustling and historic city of **Waterford,** and beachfront locations that attract Dubliners by the droves.

GETTING ORIENTED

Set around Tipperary—Ireland's largest inland county—the Southeast is a vast region that stretches from the town of Carlow near the border of County Wicklow in the north to Ardmore near the border of County Cork in the south. While main towns can be packed with camera-wielding tourists, you can easily escape the tour buses thanks to endless expanses of tranquil countryside.

Parliament Street, Kilkenny City, County Kilkenny

Inside Saint Patrick's Rock of Cashel in County Tipperary

5 In & Around County Tipperary. The greatest group of monastic ruins in Ireland—the **Rock of Cashel**—lords it over miles of the idyllic region known as the Golden Vale along with some relentlessly romantic sights, like the 19th-century village of **Lismore** and **Cahir's** charming Swiss Cottage.

SOUTHEAST PLANNER

Getting Around

One of Ireland's main commercial hubs outside of Dublin, the Southeast is well served with transportation infrastructure. Waterford Airport allows easy access to the United Kingdom, while Rosslare allows the option of ferry crossings to France and beyond. Train and bus services are plentiful all across the region with Waterford, Kilkenny, and Wexford the main hubs for connections to Dublin and Cork. A car allows for the best option to cover ground quickly and easily, as the independence of your own wheels can top any form of scheduled transport. Unlike the Midlands where the volume of traffic is generally mellow, roads in this Southeast corner can be busy during the summer months—be sure to allow sufficient time going from A to B when it involves passing through a main town.

Finding a Place to Stay

Festivals, the good weather, plus the ongoing commerce from Dublin and Cork make the Southeast one of Ireland's hottest corners, so plan way ahead for a stay in any of the main towns (and many country manors have less than 6 bedrooms and fill up fast). As always, the local tourist offices are a mine of assistance if you arrive without reservations. Assume that all hotel rooms reviewed in this chapter have air-conditioning, in-room phones, TVs, and private bathrooms, unless otherwise indicated.

Talk Radio

As you'll no doubt spend a goodly portion of your time behind the wheel during your travels, tune into Irish radio for another angle on the country. If you want to feel the true pulse of the nation, check out any of the RTE Radio 1's morning programs with well-known jocks like Pat Kenny, Joe Duffy, and Marian Finucane allowing the nation to give full vent to their spleens across the airwaves. In a country still reeling from clerical scandals and government corruption of the 1990s, the radio has become Ireland's modern confessional and a serious insight into what makes the Irish tick.

Eating Well in the Southeast

Other than its fabled strawberries, the Southeast is probably best known for its rich seafood—especially Wexford mussels, crab, and locally caught salmon. Kilmore Quay, noted for lobster and deep-sea fishing, hosts an annual Seafood Festival the second week of July. Many restaurants serve local lamb, beef, and game in season.

Food is usually prepared in a simple, country-house style, but be ready for some pleasant surprises, as there are a number of ambitious Irish chefs at work in the Southeast's restaurants and hotels. The best of the region's cuisine rests on modern interpretations of classic dishes.

One leading light in the area, Chef Kevin Dundon at Dunbrody House, expounds a philosophy of understated but delicious food both in his cooking school and in his cookbook, *Full On Irish*. Informed by his culinary experience, dishes such as tea-smoked chicken and tarragon-glazed lamb exemplify Dundon's modern, international take on his Irish roots.

Another of the Southeast's prominent chefs, Jim Aherne of Kelly's hotel still prepares the traditional dishes—Rosslare mackerel, Slaney salmon—that have shone for 30 years. But, sign of the times: he has introduced more exotic fare, such as ostrich.

Cahir Town, County Tipperary

Passion on the High "C"s

Held in late October–early November, the two-week-long annual Wexford Opera Festival is the biggest social and artistic event in the entire southeast of the country. From mid-September until the final curtain comes down, Wexford becomes home to a colorful cast of international singers, designers, and musicians, as the town prepares for the annual staging of three grand opera productions at the tiny Theatre Royal. The festival has a huge international cachet, and the actual productions are expensive, full-dress affairs. The selection of operas runs toward the recherché and the choice is usually the envy of opera maestros around the world. In 2006 the operas presented two extraordinary rarities: Gaetano Donizetti's *Don Grigorio* and Conrad Susa's 1973 version of the Brothers Grimm, *Transformations*. Prices are €75–€95 a ticket, but the extensive fringe events and concerts are usually around €15, and sometimes far more fun. Best thing about the festival for nonopera buffs, though, is the excitement in the air: art exhibitions, street music, parades, and window-dressing contests are held every year, and local bars compete in a Singing Pubs competition. The bad news: nearly every single bed within a large radius of Wexford is booked during the festival weeks, and usually for months before the actual event kicks off.

Feeling Festive?

With practically every hamlet and village across the country glorying in its own festival or excuse for later pub opening, the Southeast delivers some of Ireland's most popular gatherings. Carlow's Eigse Arts festival is a 10-day celebration of visual arts in June; In August the Spraoi festival is a display of talented exuberance in Waterford City using the city's extensive pedestrian areas; and Kilkenny's Arts Festival attracts many global premieres to its weeklong calendar in August. Check with the tourist boards for listings and dates of all events, big and small.

How's the Weather?

As well as having some of the richest land in the country, the Southeast is the envy of all Ireland for that most elusive element—sunshine. The region is also the driest in Ireland, which is saying something in a country where seldom do more than three days pass without some rain. Compared to an average of 80 inches on parts of the west coast, the Southeast gets as little as 40 inches of rainfall per year, varying from the finest light drizzle (a soft day, thank goodness!) to full-blown downpours.

Hurling

Dining & Lodging Price Categories (in Euros)				
$$$$	**$$$**	**$$**	**$**	**¢**
Restaurants over €29	€22–29	€15–22	€8–15	under €8
Hotels over €230	€180–230	€130–180	€80–130	under €80

Restaurant prices are for a main course at dinner. Hotel prices are for a standard double room in high season.

4

Updated by
John Daly

THE IRISH LIKE TO LABEL THEIR REGIONS, and "Ireland's Sunny Southeast" is the tag they've applied to Counties Wexford, Carlow, Kilkenny, Tipperary, and Waterford. The moniker is by no means merely fanciful: the weather station on the coast at Rosslare reports that this region receives more hours of sunshine than any other part of the country. Little wonder the outdoors-loving Irish have made the Southeast's coast a popular warm-weather vacation destination. Receiving almost double the rays found anywhere else, the shore resorts buzz with activity from May to October. Thousands of families take their annual summer holidays here, where picnics and barbecues—often a rain-washed fantasy elsewhere in Ireland—are a golden reality.

The entire Southeast is rich with natural beauty: not the rugged and wild wonders found to the north and west, but a coast that alternates between long, sandy beaches and rocky bays backed by low cliffs, and an inland landscape of fertile river valleys and lush, undulating pastureland. The landscape of the region is diverse, the appeal universal: seaside fishing villages with thatched cottages, Tipperary's verdant, picturesque Golden Vale. Anglers appreciate the variety of fishing and scenery along the Barrow, Nore, and Suir rivers, and especially in the Blackwater Valley area.

The region doesn't lack for culture, either. History-rich Carlow Town, the cities of Kilkenny and Waterford, and Wexford Town have retained traces of their successive waves of invaders—Celt, Viking, and Norman. The most beautiful of these destinations is Kilkenny City, an important ecclesiastic and political center until the 17th century and now a lively market town. Its streets still hold remnants from medieval times—most notably St. Canice's Cathedral—and a magnificent 12th-century castle that received a sumptuous Victorian makeover. Wexford's narrow streets are built on one side of a wide estuary, giving it a delightful maritime air. Fans flock here for its Opera Festival, which draws top talent from around the world. Waterford, although less immediately attractive than Wexford, is also built at the confluence of two of the region's rivers, the Suir and the Barrow. It offers a rich selection of Viking and Norman remains, some attractive Georgian buildings, and the famed Waterford Glass Factory, which is open to visitors.

Deeper into the countryside, rustic charms beckon. The road between Rosslare and Ballyhack passes through quiet, atypical, flat countryside dotted with thatched cottages. Beyond Tramore, level, sandy beaches give way to rocky Helvick Head and the foothills of the Knockmealdown Mountains at Dungarvan. In the far southwest of County Waterford, near the Cork border, Ardmore presents early Christian ruins on an exposed headland, while in the wooded splendor of the Blackwater Valley, the tiny cathedral town of Lismore has a hauntingly beautiful fairy-tale castle.

Exploring the Southeast

The Southeast is a large region, stretching from the town of Carlow near the border of County Wicklow in the north to Ardmore near the border of County Cork in the south. A car is not essential for getting around but it does help: you may find the frequency of public transport somewhat patchy once you leave the major towns and cities. The flow of summer visitor traffic has long been an economic lifeline for the Southeast, so main road networks have improved a great deal in recent years and travel between popular areas is fairly speedy. Apart from June, July, and August, when the Irish stream here for vacations, the region is relatively free of traffic, making it ideal for leisurely exploration. Wexford, Waterford, and Kilkenny have compact town centers easily explored on foot, and they make good touring bases.

KILKENNY CITY

4

Dubbed "Ireland's Medieval Capital" by its tourist board, and also called "the Oasis of Ireland" for its many pubs and watering holes, Kilkenny is one of the country's most alluring destinations. It demands to be explored by foot or bicycle, thanks to its easily circumnavigated town center, a 900-year-old Norman citadel that is now a lovely place of Georgian streets and Tudor stone houses. The city (population 20,000) is impressively preserved and attractively situated on the River Nore, which forms the moat of the magnificently restored Kilkenny Castle. In the 6th century, St. Canice (aka "the builder of churches") established a large monastic school here. The town's name reflects Canice's central role: Kil Cainneach means "Church of Canice." Kilkenny did not take on its medieval look for another 400 years, when the Anglo-Normans fortified the city with a castle, gates, and a brawny wall.

Exploring Kilkenny City

The city center is small, and despite the large number of historic sights and picturesque streets—in particular, Butter Slip and High Street—you can easily cover it in less than three hours. One of the most pleasant cities south of Dublin (and one of its most sports-minded—during June and July, practically the only topic of conversation is the fate of the city's team at the All-Ireland Hurling Championship), Kilkenny City has become in recent years something of a haven for artists and craft workers seeking an escape from Dublin. At such venues as the Kilkenny Design Centre, you can find an array of crafts, especially ceramics and sweaters, for sale. The city has more than 60 pubs, many of them on Parliament and High streets, which also support a lively music scene. Many of the town's pubs and shops have old-fashioned, highly individualized, brightly painted facades, created as part of the town's 1980s revival of this Victorian tradition. So after taking in Kilkenny Castle and the Riverfront Canal Walk—an overgrown pathway that meanders along the castle grounds—mosey down High and Kieran streets. These parallel avenues, considered the historic center of Kilkenny, are connected by a series of horse cart–wide lanes and are fronted with some of the city's best-preserved pubs and Victorian flats. Be sure to look up over the existing modern storefronts to catch a glimpse of how the city looked in years past, as many of the buildings still have second-floor facades reflecting historic decorative styles. High and Kieran streets eventually merge into Parliament Street—the main commercial street—which stretches down to Irishtown.

Kilkenny holds a special place in the history of Anglo-Irish relations. The infamous 1366 Statutes of Kilkenny, intended to strengthen English authority in Ireland by keeping the heirs of the Anglo-Norman invaders from assimilating into the Irish way of life, was an attempt at apartheid. Intermarriage became a crime punishable by death. Anglo-Norman settlers could lose their estates for speaking Irish, for giving their children Irish names, or for dressing in Irish clothing. The native Irish were forced to live outside the town walls in shantytowns. Ironically, Irish and Anglo-Norman assimilation was already well under way by the time the statutes went into effect; perhaps if this intermingling had been allowed to evolve naturally, Anglo-Irish relations in the 20th century might have been more harmonious.

By the early 17th century, Irish Catholics began to chafe under such repression; they tried to bring about reforms with the Confederation of Kilkenny, which governed Ireland from 1642 to 1648, with Kilkenny as the capital. Pope Innocent X sent money and arms. Cromwell responded in 1650 by overrunning the town and sacking the cathedral, which he then used as a stable for his horses. This marked the end of Kilkenny's "Golden Age"; however, the succeeding centuries were not uneventful. In 1798 the city was placed under martial law due to a revolt by the United Irishmen; in 1904 King Edward VII paid a visit; and in 1923, at the height of Ireland's civil war, forces opposed to a government peace deal with the British briefly occupied Kilkenny Castle.

❶ In spite of Cromwell's defacements, **St. Canice's Cathedral** is still one of the finest cathedrals in Ireland; it's the country's second-largest medieval church, after St. Patrick's Cathedral in Dublin. The bulk of the 13th-century structure (restored in 1866) was built in the early-English style. Inside the massive walls is an exuberant Gothic interior, given a somber grandeur by the extensive use of a locally quarried black marble. Many of the memorials and tombstone effigies represent distinguished descendants of the Normans, some depicted in full suits of armor. Look for a female effigy in the south aisle wearing the old Irish, or Kinsale, cloak; a 12th-century black-marble font at the southwest end of the nave; and St. Ciaran's Chair in the north transept, also made of black marble, with 13th-century sculptures on the arms. The biggest attraction on the grounds is the 102-foot-high round tower, which was built in 847 by King O'Carroll of Ossory and is all that remains of the monastic development reputedly begun in the 6th century, around which the town developed. If you have the energy, climb the tower's 167 steps for the tremendous 360-degree view

---

WORD OF MOUTH

"My most treasured Ireland travel memory is stumbling into a bar in Kilkenny to find it packed with people singing along to a few musicians. I figured it was one of those things tourists 'think' happen, but really don't. Surprise!"

–MerryTravel

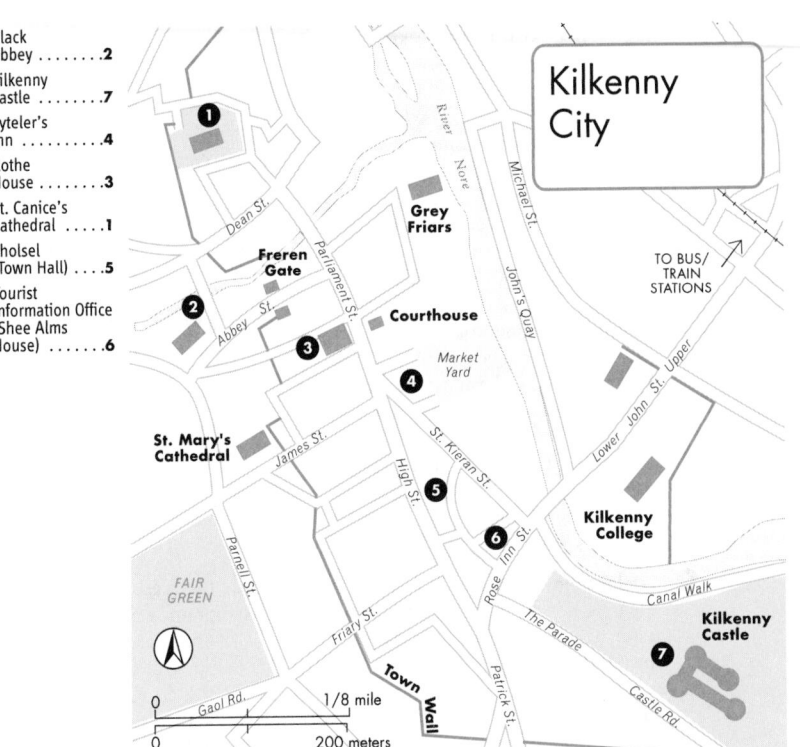

from the top, as well as for the thrill of mounting 102 steps on makeshift wooden stairs. Next door is St. Canice's Library, containing some 3,000 16th- and 17th-century volumes. ⊠*Dean St.* ☏*056/776–4971* 🖃*Cathedral €3, tower €2* ⊘ *Cathedral Easter–Sept., Mon.–Sat. 9–1 and 2–6, Sun. 2–6; Oct.–Easter, Mon.–Sat. 10–1 and 2–4, Sun. 2–4; tower access depends on weather.*

★ ❷ With a stained-glass, carved-stone interior that seems right out of the musical *Camelot*, the 13th-century **Black Abbey** is one of the most evocative and beautiful of Irish medieval structures. Note the famous 1340 five-gabled Rosary Window, an entire wall agleam with ruby and sapphire glass, depicting the life of Christ. Home to a Dominican order of monks since 1225, the abbey was restored as a church by this order (whose black capes gave the abbey its name). Interestingly, it's also one of the few medieval churches still owned by the Roman Catholic church, as most of the oldest churches in Ireland were built by the Normans and reverted to the Church of Ireland (Anglican) when the English turned to Protestantism. Nearby is the Black Freren Gate (14th century), the last remaining gateway to the medieval city of yore. ⊠*South of St. Canice's Cathedral* ☏ *056/772–1279* 🖃 *Free* ⊘ *Daily 9–1 and 2–6.*

❸ Set with splendidly sturdy stonework, **Rothe House** is one of the finest examples in Ireland of a Tudor-era merchant's house. There's a feeling of time travel as you step off the busy main street and into this medieval complex with its stone-wall courtyards, one of which houses a medieval well. Built by John Rothe between 1594 and 1610, it's owned by the Kilkenny Archaeological Society and houses a collection of Bronze Age artifacts, ogham stones, and period costumes. There's also a genealogical research facility that can help you trace your ancestors. ✉ Parliament St. ☎ 056/772–2893 ✉ €3 ⊙ Mar.–Oct., Mon.–Sat. 10:30–5, Sun. 3–5; Nov.–Feb., Mon.–Sat. 1–5.

> **THROW AWAY THE KEY**
>
> Across the road from Rothe House stands the stern limestone facade of Kilkenny Courthouse, below which lies an extremely spooky dungeon. Up to the early 19th century, convicts were locked up, four or five to a darkened cell, and literally left to rot. Those who managed to live through the experience emerged in a deranged state. You can visit the prison as part of a walking tour of the city, arranged through the city's tourist information office.

❹ **Kyteler's Inn,** the oldest in town, is notorious as the place where Dame Alice Le Kyteler, a member of a wealthy banking family and an alleged witch and "brothel keeper," was accused in 1324 of poisoning her four husbands. So, at least, said the enemies of this apparently very merry widow. The restaurant retains its medieval aura, thanks to its 14th-century stonework and exposed beams down in the cellar, built up around Kieran's Well, which predates the house itself. Food and drink in this popular pub are as simple and plentiful as they would have been in Dame Alice's day—but minus her extra ingredients (⇨ the CloseUp box "From Stake to Steak" for more information). ✉ Kieran St. ☎ 056/772–1064.

❺ The **Tholsel,** or town hall, which was built in 1761 on Parliament Street, stands near the site of the medieval Market Cross. With its distinctive clock tower and grand entrance portico, this limestone-marble building stands on the site of the execution of poor Petronilla, the "witch" burned at the stake in the 14th century in lieu of her mistress, Dame Alice Kyteler. The building itself burned down in 1985, but has since been completely rebuilt and now houses the city's municipal archives. Adjacent to the Thosel is **Alice's Castle**, a town jail rather grandly fitted out in 18th-century architectural ornamentation.

❻ The **Tourist Information Office** (TIO) is housed in the Shee Alms House (off the east side of High Street). The building was erected in 1582 by Sir Richard Shee as a hospital for the poor and functioned as such until 1895. ✉ Rose Inn St. ☎ 056/775–1500 ⊕ www.southeastireland.com ⊙ Apr.–Oct., Mon.–Sat. 9–6; Nov.–Mar., Mon.–Sat. 9–5.

★ ❼ A bewitching marriage of Gothic and Victorian styles, **Kilkenny Castle** dominates the south end of town. Amid rolling lawns beside the River Nore, the gray-stone castle stands on 50 acres of landscaped parkland (look for the garden shaped in the form of a gigantic Celtic cross). Its

From Stake to Steak

KYTELER'S INN IS FAMOUS for having been owned by the notorious Dame Alice Kyteler—a beautiful enchantress from the Middle Ages who went through four wealthy husbands quicker than you can say "poison." Her behavior aroused suspicion in the superstitious Kilkenny farm folk, and she was charged with witchcraft and finally convicted of sacrificing animals to an evil demon she referred to as "Art."

The story picks up speed when the bishop of Ossory, Richard de Ledrede, paid a Lenten visit to the priory. Following an inquisition into a Kilkenny sect of heretics, Dame Le Kyteler and her former brother-in-law, one Roger Outlawe, were ordered to appear before the bishop to answer charges of witchcraft. Outlawe was supported by Arnold de Paor, lord of Kells, who arrested the bishop and had him imprisoned in Kilkenny Castle

for 17 days. This, in turn, caused great scandal among the townsfolk and on his release the bishop managed to successfully prosecute the "heretics."

Dame Alice wound up being tossed into the dungeons of Kilkenny Castle, but thanks to her quick tongue—and the fact that her guards were beaten senseless (on order of Ireland's chancellor)—she managed to flee to England. The only problem is that she forgot to take her maid, Petronilla de Meath, who promptly became Ireland's first heretic to be burned at the stake in 1324.

Kyteler's Inn (✉ Kieran St. ☎ 056/ 772–1064) is now a popular pub-restaurant serving excellent bar food as well as traditional meals and good-quality steaks. Head down to the cellar for some pub grub and a chance to vent your hurrahs—or curses—at an effigy of Dame Alice.

4

battlements, spired towers, and numerous chimneys conjure up fairy-tale images of knights and damsels. Built in 1172, Kilkenny Castle served for more than 500 years, beginning in 1391, as the seat of one of the more powerful clans in Irish history, the Butler family, members of which were later designated earls and dukes of Ormonde. Around 1820, William Robert, son of the first marquess of Ormond, over-hauled the castle to make it a wonderland in the Victorian Feudal Revival style. In 1859 John Pollen was called in to redo the most impressive part of the interior, the 150-foot-long, aptly named Long Gallery, a refined, airy hall. Its dazzling green walls are hung with a vast collection of family portraits and frayed tapestries, while above hangs a sky-lighted, marvelously decorated ceiling, replete with oak beams carved with Celtic lacework and adorned with brilliantly painted animal heads. The main staircase was also redone in the mid-1800s to become a show-piece of Ruskinian Gothic. In 1967 the sixth marquess of Ormonde handed over the building to the state for the rather pathetic sum of £75. A guided tour visits many of the salons, and the castle's Butler Gallery houses a superb collection of Irish modern art, including examples by Nathaniel Hone, Jack B. Yeats, Sir John Lavery, Louis Le Brocquy, and James Turrell. ✉ *The Parade* ☎ *056/772–1450* ⊕ *www.heritageireland.ie* ✎ *Cas-*

tle tour €5, grounds and Butler Gallery free ⊙ *Apr. and May, daily 10:30–5; June–Sept., daily 10–7; Oct.–Mar., daily 10:30–12:45 and 2–5.*

Where to Stay & Eat

$–$$$ ✕ **Ristorante Rinuccini.** A warm glow emanates from this excellent Italian restaurant as you descend the steps into its dining room in the basement of a Georgian town house. Owner-chef Antonio Cavaliere is intensely involved in preparing the luscious pasta dishes—such as tortellini stuffed with ricotta cheese and spinach, served in a Gorgonzola sauce. Other specialties, such as organic Irish veal, go particularly well with Antonio's garlic roasted potatoes—highly recommended as a side dish. A splendid all-Italian wine list complements the menu, and there's a host of delicious homemade desserts. Across from Kilkenny Castle, this is one of the best Italian options in town. The restaurant accommodates overnight guests in the town house above. ⊠ *1 the Parade* ☎ *056/776–1575* ⊕ *www.rinuccini.com* ⌂ *Reservations essential* ▭ *AE, DC, MC, V.*

$–$$ ✕ **Café Sol.** There's always a lively buzz about this small eatery, with its tropics-tinted decor and chirpy staff. Chef Liam O'Hanlon gives Continental flair to the best of local produce, famous Kilkenny beef, and fish bought daily off the quays at Dunmore East. The emphasis is on contemporary Mediterranean-influenced cuisine. During the day, light meals and sandwiches are on offer; by night, the restaurant takes on a more formal aspect. ⊠ *William St.* ☎ *056/776–4987* ▭ *MC, V* ⊙ *Closed Sun.*

$ ✕ **Chez Pierre.** A friendly spot, Pierre's serves nicely prepared meals for all times of the day. From breakfast time to lunch it offers homemade cakes, sandwiches, and soups. But come evening, it plays true to its Gaelic name when chef Pierre Yves Schneider serves up bistro-style fare. The dishes are simple and fresh and are accompanied by a charming cast-iron skillet of roasted vegetables, ceremoniously placed on your candlelit table. ⊠ *Parliament St.* ☎ *056/776–4655* ▭ *No credit cards* ⊙ *Closed Sun and Mon.*

$$$ ✕⊡ **Langton's.** When it comes to restaurants and pubs, this is Kilkenny Central. A landmark since the 1940s, Langton's is a labyrinth of interconnected bars and eateries. Most of the seating areas, with open fires, have different personalities—from the leather-upholstered gentlemen's club in the Horseshoe Bar to an attempt at Art Deco in the spacious dining room ($$–$$$). Up front is one of Ireland's most famous "eating pubs," often crammed with punters to the rafters of its low ceiling. For more tranquil environs, head out back, where you can chow down in a neo-Gothic garden framed by a stretch of the old city walls. The main restaurant has a great reputation and offers well-prepared traditional dishes, including (of course) Irish stew. Upstairs, creams and browns decorate the Art Deco–style guest rooms, which have king-size beds and bathrooms with chic massaging showers. ⊠ *69 John St., Co. Kilkenny* ☎ *056/776–5133* ⊟ *056/776–3693* ⇨ *28 rooms, 2 suites* ⌂ *No a/c* ▭ *AE, DC, MC, V* ⊙⌷ *BP.*

$$ ✕⊡ **Zuni Townhouse and Restaurant.** This popular hotel boasts the chi-chi gloss of a big-city boutique lodging but without the icy cool reception you get in some fashionable joints. The clientele is mainly Dublin weekenders in search of Kilkenny's legendary nightlife. Relaxed and welcoming, room decor is minimalist with walls painted in strong modern colors. Zuni also has one of the city's leading nouvelle restaurants ($$–$$$), where the food, like the decor, is contemporary and light. The pervading signature here is the Asian influence, as seen in such dishes as spice-crusted cod with a mango and mint dressing. ⊠ *26 Patrick St., Co. Kilkenny* ☎ *056/772–3999* 🖶 *056/775–6400* ⊕ *www.zuni.ie* 🛏 *12 rooms, 1 suite* ⚙ *Restaurant, bar; no a/c* ⊟ *AE, DC, MC, V* 🍴 *BP.*

★ **$$–$$$** 🏨 **Butler House.** The closest you'll get to living in Kilkenny Castle during your stay in the city, the dowager duchess of Ormonde's 18th-century former town house is still an integral part of the castle complex. It's a charming piece of Georgian grandeur with an ivy-covered, three-bay facade and walled garden. Inside, the reception salon has a magnificent plastered ceiling and marble fireplaces. Upstairs, any grande dame might look askance—a gradual renovation of the guest rooms is ongoing, so the decor ranges from muted 1970s minimalist to bright modern. The rooms vary in size, with some big as a house and others on the snug side. If you can, treat yourself to one of the huge, high-ceiling bedrooms overlooking the garden and castle. The only slight disadvantage (if you look at things that way) is that breakfast is not served on the premises; for your morning meal you must saunter through the walled rose garden to the adjoining Kilkenny Design Centre. ⊠ *16 Patrick St., Co. Kilkenny* ☎ *056/776–5707* 🖶 *056/776–5626* ⊕ *www.butler.ie* 🛏 *12 rooms, 1 suite* ⚙ *Meeting rooms; no a/c* ⊟ *AE, DC, MC, V* 🍴 *BP.*

Nightlife & the Arts

Every August, Kilkenny becomes the focus for Ireland's culture vultures when the **Kilkenny Arts Festival** (☎ 056/776–3663 ⊕ www.kilkennyarts. ie) takes over the city for about two weeks. The emphasis in the past was on classical music, but the program has grown increasingly populist. Street theater, elaborate parades, and even a rock concert (staged in the conveniently named Woodstock Desmesne) have lent the festival a more contemporary air and there's even speculation that it might soon eclipse Ireland's premier arts festival in Galway.

If you're craving a pint, you have a choice of pubs along Parliament and High streets. **John Cleere's** (⊠ 22 Parliament St. ☎ 056/776–2573) is the best pub in town for a mix of live traditional music, poetry readings, and theatrical plays. The **Pumphouse** (⊠ 26 Parliament St. ☎ 056/776–3924) has traditional music during the week and live rock and pop on weekends. **Tynan's Bridge House** (⊠ 2 Horseleap Slip ☎ 056/21291) is set on one of Kilkenny's famous "slips," and was first used as an exercise run for dray horses. Inside, you can guess that the pub is more than 200 years old from all the gas lamps, silver tankards, and historic teapots on display. The **Widow McGraths** (⊠ 29 Parliament St. ☎ 056/775–2520) celebrates July 4 with a barbecue in its beer garden. It's also a good spot for live music.

The **Watergate Theatre** (⊠ Parliament St. ☎ 056/61674) hosts opera, plays, concerts, comedy, and other entertainment at reasonable prices.

Hurling: Fast & Furious

GET CHATTING WITH THE LOCALS in almost any pub across the Southeast, mention the sport of hurling, and an enthusiastic and often passionate conversation is bound to ensue. The region is the heartland of this ancient sport whose followers have an almost religious obsession with the game. It's a kind of aerial field hockey with players wielding curved sticks. Its history comes from Ireland's Celtic ancestors, but it bears about the same relation to field hockey as ice hockey does to roller-skating. It's no accident that prowess on the hurling field is regarded as a supreme qualification for election to public office. A man who succeeds at hurling is eminently capable of dealing with anything that fate and the spite of other politicians can throw at him. Hurling is also an extremely skillful sport. A player must have excellent hand-eye coordination combined with an ability to run at high speeds while balancing a small golf-ball-size ball on his camán (hurling stick). Fans will also proudly tell you it's also the world's fastest team sport. Ireland's other chief sporting pastimes, including soccer and hurling's cousin, Gaelic football, take a back seat in this part of the country. Stars like Kilkenny's D. J. Carey, rather than professional soccer players, are sporting icons for local kids. Counties Tipperary, Wexford, and Waterford are among the top teams in the region, but Kilkenny (nicknamed "The Cats") is currently the undisputed top team in the country. It has won three out of the last five All-Ireland hurling championships and is considered the best in the game.

There's an intense rivalry between the counties, especially between old foes Tipperary and Kilkenny. When it gets down to club level, passions run even higher. Almost every parish in the region has a hurling club, and a quick inquiry with locals will usually be enough to find out when the next game is on. Even for the uninitiated, hurling is a great spectator sport. Sporty types wishing to give it a go, be warned; it's fast, furious, and entails more than a hint of danger, as players flail the air to capture the bullet-fast *sliotar* (hurling ball).

Sports & the Outdoors

BICYCLING Bikes for exploring the quiet countryside around Kilkenny can be rented through **J. J. Wall** (⊠ 88 Maudlin St. ☎ 056/772–1236).

GAELIC FOOTBALL & HURLING The 1366 Statutes of Kilkenny expressly forbade the ancient Irish game of hurling. No matter: today, Kilkenny is considered one of the great hurling counties. Like its neighbor and arch-enemy, Wexford, Kilkenny has a long history of success in hurling, and as the annual All-Ireland Hurling Championships draws to its final stages during June and July, interest in the county's team runs to fever pitch. Catch the home team at matches held at **Kilkenny GAA Grounds** (⊠ Nowlan Park ☎ 056/777–0008 ⊕ www.gaa.ie).

Shopping

Kilkenny is a byword for attractive, original crafts that combine traditional arts with modern design elements. You can see glass being blown at the **Jerpoint Glass Studio** (⊠ Stoneyford ☎ 056/772–4350), where the glass is heavy, modern, uncut, and hand finished. The studio's factory shop is a good place to pick up a bargain. The town's leading outlet, the **Kilkenny Design Centre** (⊠ Kilkenny Castle ☎ 056/772–2118), in the old stable yard opposite the castle, sells ceramics, jewelry, sweaters, and handwoven textiles. **Murphy's Jewellers** (⊠ 85 High St. ☎ 056/772–1127) specializes in heraldic jewelry.

★ **Nicholas Mosse Pottery** (⊠ Bennettsbridge ☎ 056/772–7505) is the best-known name in Irish ceramics. Nicholas first set up his potter's wheel in an old flour mill in this quiet village (10 mi south of Kilkenny) in 1975. Since then, the business has boomed and the rustic floral-pattern pottery created here is instantly recognizable for its "spongeware" designs. A visit here allows you to see the pottery being made, and the adjoining factory shop often has good bargains. **Rudolf Heltzel** (⊠ 10 Patrick St. ☎ 056/772–1497) is known for its striking, modern designs of gold and silver jewelry. **Stoneware Jackson Pottery** (⊠ Bennettsbridge ☎ 056/772–7175) makes distinctive, hand-thrown tableware and lamps. The **Sweater Shop** (⊠ 81 High St. ☎ 056/776–3405) carries great sweaters.

SOUTHEAST INLANDS

North of Kilkenny City is a region notably rich in historical sights. Travel through the farmlands of the Barrow Valley to the small county seat of Carlow Town, with scenic detours to Leighlinbridge's picturesque castle and Old Leighlin's time-stained cathedral.

Carlow Town

▶ ❽ *36 km (22 mi) northeast of Kilkenny City on N10.*

Carlow Town was established on the banks of the River Barrow by the Anglo-Normans in the 12th century. Its position on the border of the English Pale—the area around Dublin that was dominated by the English from Elizabethan times onward—made it an important strategic center and hence the scene of many bloody battles and sieges. Today Carlow is a lively market town about an hour and a half by car from central Dublin. The presence of the large Institute of Technology here gives the town a lively buzz. It also has a thriving indigenous arts-and-crafts community. The ruins of the 13th-century **Carlow Castle,** once a strategically important fortification on the southeastern corner of the Pale, afford imposing views of the River Barrow. After withstanding a siege by Cromwell's troops in 1650, the castle was accidentally destroyed in 1814 when a Dr. Philip Middleton attempted to renovate the castle for use as a mental asylum; while setting off explosives to reduce the thickness of the walls, he managed to demolish all but the west-side curtain wall and its two flanking towers.

The Gothic-style, Roman Catholic **Cathedral of the Assumption,** completed in 1883, is notable for its stained-glass windows and a magnificently sculpted marble monument of its builder, Bishop James Doyle (1786–1834), a champion of Catholic emancipation. The monument was

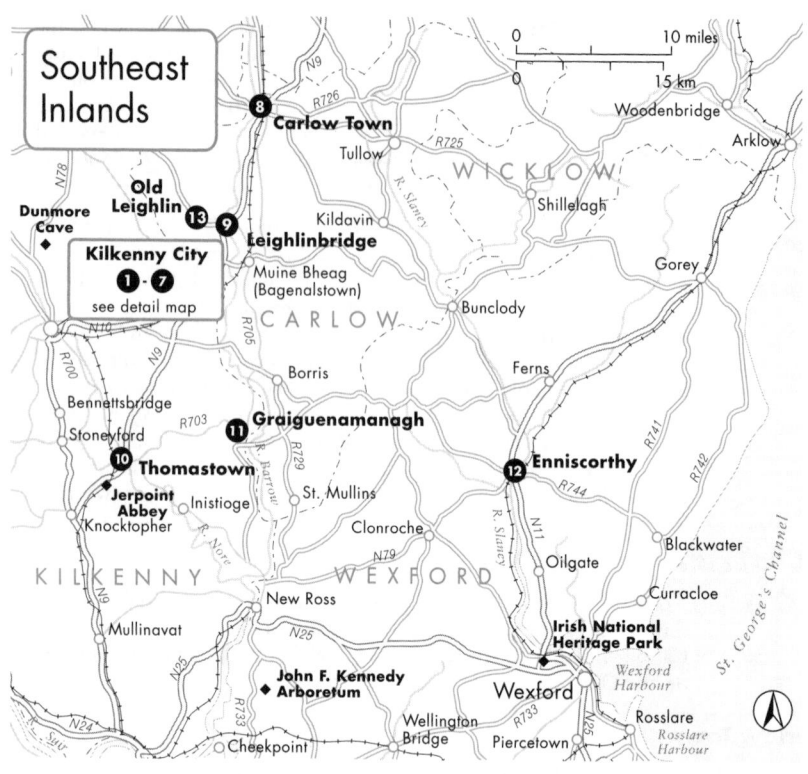

Southeast Inlands

carved by the Irish sculptor John Hogan (1800–58). ⊠ *College St.*
☎ *059/913–1227* ☑ *Free* ⊘ *Daily 7:30–7:30.*

One of the most poignant sites in Carlow Town is the **Croppies Grave**
(⊠ 98 St. off Maryborough St.), a small memorial garden where the bodies of 640 United Irishmen—called "Croppies" because they cropped
their hair to mark their allegiance to a free, independent Ireland—were
buried in a mass grave, following the Battle of Carlow during the 1798
rebellion against English rule. Two of the trees planted by a widowed
mother of three young men slain in the battle still stand; the third fell
in a storm, and its two halves are inscribed with a testimonial to the
courage of the Croppies.

The famous **Browne's Hill Dolmen,** a stone monument dating from 2500
BC with a capstone weighing in at 100 tons, is one of the largest dolmens in Europe. The Stone Age megalithic tomb is thought to mark the
burial place of a local king. The dolmen is reached via a pathway from
the parking lot. ⊠ *Hacketstown Rd., 3 km (2 mi) east of Carlow Town
on R726* ☑ *Free.*

Where to Stay & Eat

$$–$$$ ✕ **The Beams Restaurant.** Originally a coaching inn, this building re-
stored by the O'Gorman family evokes the past in massive wooden beams

dating back to 1760. Classic Continental cuisine is the speciality of French chef Romain Chall, who has overseen the kitchen for many years. Dishes include game in season and simply prepared fish. House specialties include breads baked on the premises, seafood pancakes, and delicious housemade ice creams. Vegetarian dishes regularly feature on the menu. This establishment has a loyal local following in an area not blessed with choice; it has become even busier with the addition of a wineshop. ⊠ *Dublin St.* ☎ *059/913–1824* ⊟ *AE, MC, V* ⊘ *Closed Sun. and Mon.*

$ 🏨 **Barrowville Town House.** Comfort, good food, and a refined atmosphere typify this elegant Regency-style house minutes from the center of Carlow Town. The house is handsomely decorated throughout, with a grand piano and a welcoming fireplace adorning the drawing room. Guest rooms vary in size, so it's advisable to book early for more spacious accommodation. This place is renowned for its breakfasts—not just for the food (you have the option of the traditional Irish fare or a buffet including cheese board and smoked salmon) but also for the location, as the first meal of the day is served in a light-filled conservatory under a twisting grapevine, with views of a delightful semiformal garden. Ex-hoteliers Marie and Randal Dempsey have run the place since 1989. ⊠ *Kilkenny Rd., Co. Carlow* ☎ *059/914–3324* 🖷 *059/914– 1953* ⊕ *www.barrowvillehouse.com* 🛏 *7 rooms* ♨ *Croquet; no a/c* ⊟ *AE, MC, V* 🍽 *BP.*

Nightlife & the Arts

Started in 1979 as a weekend event to bring together the visual and performing arts, literature, and the Irish language, **Éigse,** Carlow's annual festival, takes over the town in June for 10 days. Drama, classical and pop music, and street entertainments vie with impressive visual-arts exhibitions—including works by international artists—all around town. Irish music and dance play a prominent part in the celebrations. For information, contact the **Éigse Festival Office** (☎ 059/914–0491).

Sports & the Outdoors

GAELIC FOOTBALL & HURLING — Gaelic football and hurling are played at **Dr. Cullen Park GAA** (☎ 01/836– 3222 Gaelic Athletic Association in Dublin ⊕ www.gaa.ie).

GOLF — **Carlow Golf Club** (⊠ Deerpark ☎ 059/913–1695), 3 km (2 mi) north of town on the Dublin road, is in a wild deer park; the 18-hole course remains open all year.

Leighlinbridge

❾ *10 km (6 mi) south of Carlow Town on N9.*

Shure, Ireland 'tis a land of sweet vistas, and one of the most romantic is found here on the east bank of Leighlinbridge: romantic, Norman-era **Black Castle,** poetically mirrored in the waters of the River Barrow and framed by the bulk of a grandly medieval bridge. With five stone arches spanning the river since 1320, this is reputed to be one of the oldest functioning bridges in Europe and makes a magnificent repoussoir for the castle. Built in 1181 as one of the earliest Norman fortresses in Ireland, it has been the scene of countless battles and sieges. Its hulking, 400-year-old main tower still stands, all but daring you to set up your easel and canvas on the adjoining ageless towpath.

Where to Eat

$$$ ✕ **Lord Bagenal Inn.** This famous old pub nestles on the banks of the River Barrow in the heart of Leighlinbridge and is a perfect stopover point for weary southbound travelers. Built in the early 1800s, its maze of nooks and fireplaces gives away its age in spite of renovations in 2003. A quaint walled garden replete with water accents adds to the charm and there's even a small glassed-in playroom for children (open until 8 PM). Owner James Kehoe is a connoisseur of all the finer things in life. His establishment has an award-winning wine cellar and he stocks a pungent array of fine cigars, although with Ireland's smoking ban now in full effect, you will be asked to enjoy your Cohiba outside. Kehoe is also an art buff, as you can see from the modern Irish artworks that line the walls. As for the kitchen, signature dishes include pig's *crubeen* (pickled pigs' feet) braised in port and stuffed with truffles and sweetbreads, baked monkfish fillet wrapped in Serrano ham with a mango, mint, and tomato salsa, or fresh turbot with asparagus in beurre blanc. The inn has 12 rooms ($), should you want to stay overnight in Leighlinbridge. ⊠ *Main St.* ☎ *059/912–1668* ⊕ *www.lordbagenal.com* ▭ *DC, V.*

Thomastown

➓ *14½ km (9 mi) south of Kilkenny on R700 and N9.*

Thomastown, originally the seat of the kings of Ossory (an ancient Irish kingdom), is a pretty, stone-built village on the River Nore. It takes its name from Thomas FitzAnthony of Leinster, who encircled the town with a wall in the 13th century. Fragments of this medieval wall remain, as do the partly ruined 13th-century church of St. Mary and Mullins Castle, adjacent to the town bridge. Landmarked by its rearing and massive 15th-century tower, **Jerpoint Abbey**, near Thomastown, is one of the most notable Cistercian ruins in Ireland, dating from about 1160. The church, tombs, and the restored cloisters are a must for lovers of the Irish Romanesque. The vast cloister is decorated with affecting carvings of human figures and fantastical mythical creatures, including knights and knaves (one with a stomachache) and the assorted dragon or two. Dissolved in 1540, Jerpoint was taken over, as was so much around these parts, by the earls of Ormonde. The one part of the abbey that remains alive, so to speak, is its hallowed cemetery—the natives are still buried here. Guided tours of the impressive complex are available from mid-June to mid-September (last admission is 45 minutes before closing). ⊠ *2 km (1 mi) south of Thomastown on N9* ☎ *056/24623* ⊕ *www.heritageireland.ie* ☑ *€2.75* ☉ *Mar.–May and Oct.–mid-Nov., daily 10–5; June–Sept., daily 9:30–6:30.*

FodorsChoice ★ (Jerpoint Abbey)

Where to Stay & Eat

$$$$ ✕▥ **Mount Juliet.** Once part of the nearby medieval Jerpoint Abbey estate, later owned by the earls of Carrick, and then famous as the seat of a horse-racing stud, Mount Juliet has long been an address of note in County Kilkenny. Today, this 1,500-acre kingdom is still lorded over by its three-story Georgian mansion, which the second earl of Carrick

FodorsChoice ★ (Mount Juliet)

built along the banks of the River Nore and named in honor of his wife, Lady Juliana. Now a Conrad hotel, this estate still gives you the full princely treatment, thanks to a spa, famous golf course, and an array of restaurants that tempt one never to leave the grounds. Be sure to take a tour of the complex in the capable hands of estate manager Eamonn Houlihan, a mine of good cheer and information. The imposing mansion, whose elegant sash windows and mansard roof are creeper-covered in the best stately house manner, was subjected to full-blast renovation treatment in 1968. Begone, creaky floors and time-stained walls (and yesteryear's charm?); hello, large accommodations decorated with vibrant hues and fine fabrics, and suites with super-king-size beds and original fireplaces. Rooms are also available in a separate building, the Hunters Yard, plus there are 11 modern two-room lodges, including the Rose Garden suites, each of which comes with two bedrooms, a kitchen, and very luxe decor. For many, the Jack Nicklaus–designed golf course—which has hosted the Irish Open on three occasions—is *the* reason to head here. More sedate types will enjoy a sherry in the Tetrarch Bar (named for the greatest horse to come out of this estate's stud), a light lunch in Kendalls—a wood-trim casual bistro in the Yard complex—or fine Irish haute cuisine in the Lady Helen McAlmont Restaurant ($$$$), its tables adorned with crystal, silverware, and fine linen, and its windows with a grand vista over the Nore Valley. ✉ *Co. Kilkenny* ☎ *056/777–3000* 📠 *056/777–3009* 🌐 *www.mountjuliet.com* 🛏 *48 rooms, 11 lodges* 🖒 *2 restaurants, 18-hole golf course, tennis court, indoor pool, sauna, spa, fishing, archery, croquet, horseback riding, 3 bars; no a/c* 💳 *AE, DC, MC, V.*

★ $ **Ballyduff House.** This wonderfully picturesque house was used as a location in the nostalgic movie of Maeve Binchy's *Circle of Friends*. As this clematis-clad mansion comes into view at the top of a gently curving driveway you can understand why. Relaxation, long walks, and a warm welcome are the order of the day here. Three large, period bedrooms (one is a heavenly, superstylish vision in multiple hues of green) are decorated with Georgian furniture and ornate wallpaper and afford wonderful views of the river. You are welcome to walk around the gardens and participate in trout and salmon fishing. Mount Juliet Golf Course is less than a five-minute drive away. ✉ *Co. Kilkenny* ☎📠 *056/775–8488* 🌐 *www.ballyduffhouse.com* 🛏 *3 rooms* 🖒 *Fishing; no a/c* 💳 *No credit cards* ⏲ *Closed Nov.–Feb.* 🍽 *BP.*

Sports & the Outdoors

GOLF Visitors are welcome at the 18-hole **Mount Juliet Golf Course** (✉ Mount Juliet Estate ☎ 056/772–4455), a championship parkland course. The course was designed by Jack Nicklaus and includes practice greens and a driving range.

Graiguenamanagh

⓫ *15 km (9 mi) northeast of Thomastown on R703.*

The village of Graiguenamanagh (pronounced *graig-na-manna*) sits on the banks of the River Barrow at the foot of Brandon Hill. This is good walking country; ask for directions to the summit of **Brandon Hill** (1,694 feet), a 7-km (4½-mi) hike. In the 13th century the early-English-style church of **Duiske Abbey** was the largest Cistercian church in Ireland. The choir, the transept, and a section of the nave of the original abbey church are now part of a Catholic church. Purists will be disappointed by the modernization, carried out between 1974 and 1980, although medieval building techniques were used. ☎ *059/972–4238* ⊘ *Daily 9:30–7.*

Where to Stay & Eat

★ **$** ✕▣ **Waterside.** A growing mecca for boating enthusiasts, anglers, and those escaping the "big smoke," this wonderfully restored cut-stone corn mill certainly enjoys the perfect location, as it's perched on the banks of the River Barrow. This is an unpretentious and friendly accommodation. The mill's original pitch-pine beams have been retained in the guest rooms, which are simply and brightly decorated in reds and yellows. The restaurant ($$), which occupies the ground floor, also has exposed beams and decorated windows; it serves Continental cuisine and has a good wine list. Hill-walking trips, including transport and packed lunches, can be arranged for small groups. ⊠ *The Quay, Co. Kilkenny* ☎ *059/972–4246* 🖷 *059/972–4733* ⊕ *www.watersideguesthouse.com* ⇌ *10 rooms* ⚫ *Restaurant, fishing; no a/c* ▤ *AE, MC, V* ❍ *BP.*

Enniscorthy

⑫ *32 km (20 mi) east of Graiguenamanagh on R744.*

Enniscorthy, on the sloping banks of the River Slaney and on the main road between Dublin and Wexford, to the south of the popular resort of Gorey, is a thriving market town that is rich in history. The town is dominated by **Enniscorthy Castle**, built in the first quarter of the 13th century by the Prendergast family. The imposing Norman castle was the site of fierce battles against Oliver Cromwell in the 17th century and during the Uprising of 1798. Its square-towered keep now houses the County Wexford Museum, which contains thousands of historic items, including military memorabilia from the 1798 and 1916 uprisings. ⊠ *Castle Hill* ☎ *054/35926* 🖷 *€4.50* ⊘ *May–Sept., Mon.–Sat. 10–6, Sun. 2–5:30.*

The **National 1798 Center** tells the tale of the United Irishmen and the ill-fated 1798 rebellion. ⊠ *Arnold's Cross* ☎ *054/37596* 🖷 *€6* ⊘ *Mid-Mar.–Nov., Mon.–Sat. 9:30–5, Sun. 11–5; Dec.–mid-Mar., weekdays 9:30–4, weekends 11–4.*

St. Aidan's Cathedral stands on a commanding site overlooking the Slaney. This Gothic Revival structure was built in the mid-19th century under the direction of Augustus Welby Pugin, architect of the Houses of Parliament in London. ⊠ *Cathedral St.* ☎ *054/35777* 🖷 *Free* ⊘ *Daily 10–6.*

Where to Stay

$$$ ▣ **Ballinkeele House.** Built in 1840, the ancestral home of the Maher family is beautifully maintained by the present generation. The house is on 350 acres of game-filled parkland with fine stands of mature trees, lakes, and ponds, and an atmosphere of complete tranquillity. Throughout is a mix of antique ornaments, paintings, and furniture original to the house, while the spacious bedrooms have pleasant views across the countryside. Bicycles are available for you to explore the surrounding countryside, or you can simply enjoy a game of croquet on the lawn. One of Margaret's large breakfasts will set you up for a day of exploration; she is a keen cook and a member of Euro-Toques. At dinner ($$$$, guests only, Tue.–Sun.), she gives a touch of European flair to traditional dishes. Ballinkeele is 10 mi from Wexford town center. ⊠ *Ballymurn* ☎ *053/38105* 🖨 *053/38468* ⊕ *www.ballinkeele.com* 🛏 *5 rooms* 🍴 *Dining room, bicycles, croquet; no room phones, no room TVs, no smoking* ▭ *MC, V* ⊗ *Closed Dec.–Feb.* ⑩ *BP.*

$ 🏨 **Salville House.** Local legend has it that this fine Victorian farmhouse was once the home of a couple of "disreputable" ladies who danced at the Folies Bergères in Paris. Things are much more respectable nowadays: Gordon and Jane Parker have created a hilltop haven where food and relaxation are the order of the day. Gordon's inspired contemporary cuisine has a growing group of fans. Guests dine around a large mahogany table and are invited to bring their own wine. The bedrooms are spacious, with plenty of books on the shelves and a great view of the River Slaney. In summer a grass tennis court in front of the house adds to its charm. To get there, look for the signpost, 2 km (1 mi) out of Enniscorthy on the Wexford road. ⊠ *Wexford Rd.* ☎ *054/35252* 🖨 *054/35252* ⊕ *www.salvillehouse.com* 🛏 *5 rooms* 🍴 *Tennis court; no a/c, no room phones, no room TVs* ▭ *No credit cards* ⑩ *BP.*

Shopping

Carley's Bridge Pottery (⊠ Carley's Bridge ☎ 054/33512), established in 1654, specializes in large terra-cotta pots. **Kiltrea Bridge Pottery** (⊠ Kiltrea, Caime ☎ 054/35107) stocks garden pots, plant pots, and country kitchen crocks.

Old Leighlin

⑬ *5¼ km (3 mi) west of Leighlinbridge, signposted to right off N9.*

Home to one of Ireland's undiscovered gems of late medieval architecture, the tiny village of Old Leighlin first found fame as the site of a monastery, founded in the 7th century by St. Laserian, that once accommodated 1,500 monks. It hosted the church synod in 630 at which the Celtic Church first accepted the Roman date for the celebration of Easter (the date was officially accepted at the Synod of Whitby in 664); this decision marked the beginning of a move away from old Brehon Law and the deliberalization of the Church. This old monastery was rebuilt in the 12th century as **St. Laserian's Cathedral.** Sitting among green fields, with a castellated tower and Irish-Gothic windows, it evokes a stirring sense of Wordsworthian forlornness. Enlarged in the 16th century, its interior is noted for its 11th-century

TO THE TAVERN BORN

Carey's pub, which for centuries has served up glasses of ale to Old Leighlin residents, has been in the same family since 1542.

font, a 200-year-old grand wind organ, and a fine wood vaulted ceiling. Guided tours are available. ☎ 059/972–1411 ⊕ *www.cashel. anglican.org/laserians.shtm* ✉ *Free* ☉ *July and Aug., weekdays 10–5.*

WEXFORD TOWN

Wexford's history goes back to prehistoric times, though you'll find scant traces of it now. Much more obvious are the Viking and Norman associations, evident in alleys as well as in the town walls, some of which are still standing. Today, this coastal town is most famed for its Wexford Opera Festival, usually held in October, which has been seducing the world with wonderful productions of rare opera for over fifty years. The warm and vivacious welcome, the narrow and ancient Viking streets, and the tiny, atmospheric Theatre Royal add to pleasures of this event and any visit to Wexford Town.

Exploring Wexford Town

From its appearance today, you would barely realize that Wexford is an ancient place, but in fact it was defined on maps by the Greek cartographer Ptolemy as long ago as the 2nd century AD. Its Irish name is Loch Garman, but the Vikings called it Waesfjord—the harbor of the mud flats—which became Wexford in English. Wexford became an English garrison town after it was taken by Oliver Cromwell in 1649.

The River Slaney empties into the sea at Wexford Town. The harbor has silted up since the days when Viking longboats docked here; nowadays only a few small trawlers fish from here. Wexford Town's compact center is on the south bank of the Slaney. Running parallel to the quays on the riverfront is the main street (the name changes several times)—the major shopping street of the town, with a pleasant mix of old-fashioned bakeries, butcher shops, stylish boutiques, and a share of Wexford's many pubs. It can be explored on foot in an hour or two. Allow at least half a day in the area if you also intend to visit the Heritage Park at nearby Ferrycarrig, and a full day if you want to take in Johnstown Castle Gardens and its agricultural museum, or walk in the nature reserve at nearby Curracloe Beach. The town is at its best in late October and early November, when the presence of the Wexford Opera Festival creates a carnival atmosphere.

Rising above the town's rooftops are the graceful spires of two elegant examples of 19th-century Gothic architecture. These **twin churches** have identical exteriors, their foundation stones were laid on the same day, and their spires each reach a height of 230 feet. The **Church of the Assumption** is on Bride Street. The **Church of the Immaculate Conception** is on Rowe Street.

> **FOREIGN ACCENT**
>
> The Anglo-Norman conquest of Ireland began in County Wexford in 1169, so the British presence has deep roots and Wexford has been an English-speaking county for centuries.

⑭ The **Tourist Information Office** (TIO; ✉ Crescent Quay ☎ 053/23111) is a good place from which to start exploring Wexford Town on foot and to find out about guided walking tours organized by local historians.

⑮ Standing in the center of Crescent Quay, a large bronze **statue of Commodore John Barry** (1745–1803) commemorates the man who came to be known as the father of the American Navy. Born in 1745 in nearby Ballysampson, Barry settled in Philadelphia at age 15, became a brilliant naval fighter during the War of Independence (thus avenging his Irish ancestors), and trained many young naval officers who went on to achieve fame.

⑯ The **Franciscan Church** has a ceiling worth noting for its fine, locally crafted stuccowork. ✉ *School St.* ☎ *053/22758* 🎟 *Free* 🕙 *Daily 8:30–6:30.*

⑰ The **Wexford Bull Ring** (✉ Quay St., back toward quays) was once the scene of bull baiting, a cruel medieval sport that was popular among the Norman nobility. Also in this arena, in 1649, Cromwell's soldiers massacred 300 panic-stricken townspeople who had gathered here to pray as the army stormed their town. The legacy of this heartless leader has remained a dark folk memory for centuries and is only now beginning to fade. A housing development at the old Cromwell's Fort is one of the ritzier addresses in town.

⑱ The red sandstone **Westgate Tower** (✉ Westgate) was the largest of five fortified gateways in the Norman and Viking town walls, and it's the only one remaining. The early-13th-century tower has been sensitively restored. Keep an eye out as you wander this part of town for other preserved segments of the old town walls.

⑲ The ruins of the 12th-century **Selskar Abbey** (✉ Selskar St., south of Westgate Tower) still stand. Here the first treaty between the Irish and the Normans was signed in 1169.

⑳ The **Wexford Wildfowl Reserve** is a nature-lover's paradise. Just a short walk across the bridge from the main part of town, it shelters one-third of the world's Greenland white-fronted geese. As many as 10,000 of them spend their winters on the mud flats, known locally as slobs, which also draw ducks, swans, and other waterfowl. Observation hides are provided for bird-watchers, and an audiovisual show and exhibitions are available at the visitor center. Lectures on the teeming birdlife of the reserve can be arranged on request. ✉ *North Slob, Wexford Harbor* ☎ *053/23129* 🎟 *Free* 🕙 *Mid-Apr.–Sept., daily 9–6; Oct.–mid-Apr., daily 10–5.*

★ ☺ **㉑** The **Irish National Heritage Park,** a 35-acre, open-air living history museum beside the River Slaney, is one of Ireland's most successful and enjoyable family attractions. In about 1½ hours, a guide takes you through 9,000 years of Irish history—from the first evidence of humans on this island, at around 7000 BC, to the Norman settlements of the mid-12th century. Full-scale replicas of typical dwelling places illustrate the changes in beliefs and lifestyles. Highlights of the tour include a prehistoric homestead, a *crannóg* (lake dwelling), an early Christian *rath* (fortified farmstead), a Christian monastery, a horizontal water mill, a Viking long-

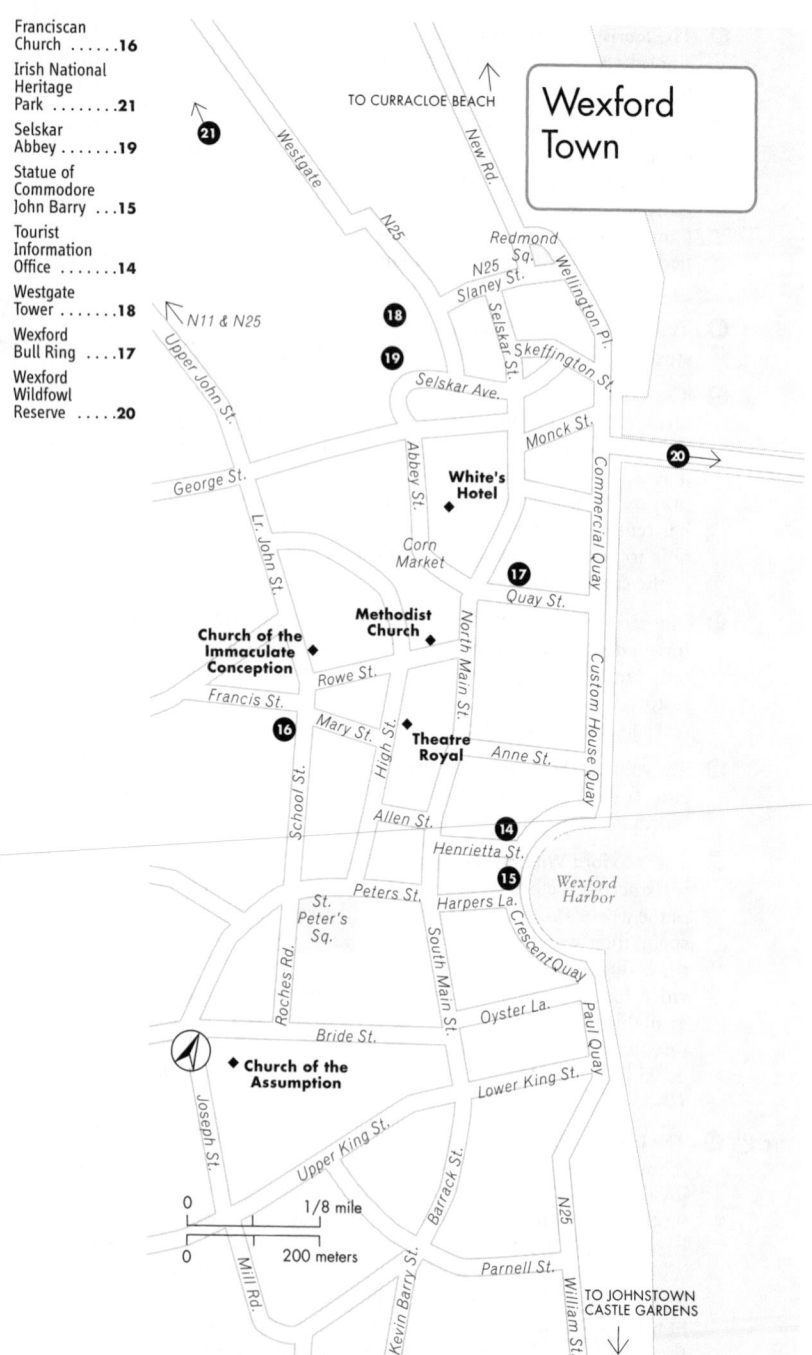

Wexford
Town

TO CURRACLOE BEACH

house, and a Norman castle. There are also examples of pre-Christian burial sites and a stone circle. Most of the exhibits are "inhabited" by students in appropriate historic dress who will answer questions. The riverside site includes several nature trails. ✉ *5 km (3 mi) north of Wexford Town on N11, Ferrycarrig* ☎ *053/20733* ⊕ *www.inhp.com* ✐ *€7.50* ⊙ *Mar.–Oct., daily 9:30–6:30; Nov.–Feb., daily 9:30–5:30.*

Only Walt Disney might have bettered the storybook look of the massive, Victorian-Gothic, gray-stone castle at **Johnstown Castle Gardens,** 5 mi (3 mi) southwest of Wexford following the N25 (direction Rosslare). A magical Gothic Revival extravaganza, this turreted, battlemented, and machicolated edifice, which bristles in silver-gray ashlar, was built for the Grogan-Morgan family between 1810 and 1855. Magnificent parklands—with splendid towering trees, lakes, and ornamental gardens—now frame the grand castle. Unfortunately, you can't tour the house (it houses a national agricultural college) other than its entrance hall, but the well-maintained grounds are open to the public. The centerpiece is the 5-acre lake, one side of which has a terrace, replete with statues, from which to take in the panorama of the mirrored castle. Because there's such a variety of trees framing the view—Japanese cedars, Atlantic blue cedars, golden Lawson cypresses—there's color through much of the calendar. Nearby are the Devil's Gate walled garden—a woodland garden set around the ruins of the medieval castle of Rathlannon—and the **National Museum of Agriculture and Rural Life.** The latter, housed in the quadrangular stable yards, shows what life was once like in rural Ireland. It also contains a 5,000-square-foot exhibition on the potato and the Great Famine (1845–49). ✉ *Signposted just off N25, 6 km (4 mi) southwest of Wexford Town* ☎ *053/42888* ⊕ ✐ *Gardens May–Sept. €2, Oct.–Apr. free. Museum €5* ⊙ *Gardens daily 9:30–5:30; museum Apr., May, and Sept.–Nov., weekdays 9–12:30 and 1:30–5, weekends 2–5; June–Aug., weekdays 9–5, weekends 11–5; Dec.–Mar., weekdays 9–12:30 and 1:30–5.*

OFF THE BEATEN PATH

CURRACLOE BEACH – Steven Spielberg filmed the terrifyingly gory D-Day landing scenes from his blockbuster *Saving Private Ryan* along this beautiful strand. In real life it's a popular swimming place in summer and is home to many migratory birds in winter. It's 9 km (5½ mi) long, with a 1 km (½ mi) nature trail in the seashore sand dunes. ✉ *11 km (7 mi) northeast of Wexford Town on R742.*

Where to Stay & Eat

$$–$$$ ✕ **Heavens Above.** This cozy wood-panel loft restaurant has legion of fans—not least because of the unusual (for Ireland) wine policy. Owners John and Nuala Barron also run the off-license next door and allow you to choose a bottle from their extensive range of more than 250 wines and beers, with no corkage charge to sully the taste of this sweet deal. The food has also been acclaimed, as you'll understand with your first bite of their Slaney salmon fillet en paupiette with black pepper and lime butter. ✉ *112 S. Main St.* ☎ *053/21273* ▭ *MC, V.*

$$–$$$ ✕ **La Riva.** In summertime the evening sun floods this quayside eatery with light, and the warm glow is reflected in the cooking—a colorful modern take on Mediterranean and Irish cuisine. Chef Warren Gillen

THE SOUTHEAST THROUGH THE AGES

The Southeast's coastal and inland areas have long, interesting histories. The kings of Munster had their ceremonial center on the Rock of Cashel, a vast, cathedral-topped rock rising above the plain. Legend has it that St. Patrick converted the High King of Ireland to Christianity here. In the 7th century Cashel became an important monastic settlement and bishopric, and there were also thriving early Christian monasteries at Kilkenny, Ardmore, and Lismore.

But the quiet life of Christian Ireland was disrupted from the 9th century onward by a series of Viking invasions. Liking what they found here—a pleasant climate, rich, easily cultivated land, and a series of sheltered harbors—the Vikings stayed on, founding the towns of Wexford and Waterford. (Waterford's name comes from the Norse Vadrefjord, Wexford's from Waesfjord.)

But less than two centuries later, the Southeast was the location of the most significant turning point in Ireland's recorded history. In 1169 the Normans (who had conquered England a hundred years before) landed at Bannow Bay in County Wexford. It was the beginning of what Irish patriots commonly describe as "800 years of English oppression."

The English were invited into Ireland by the former king of Leinster, Dermot MacMurrough, who hoped to regain his crown with the help of the Norman earl, Richard FitzGilbert de Clare, famously known as "Strongbow." To seal their pact, Dermot's daughter Aoife married Strongbow. It was symbolic of the way that the Normans, once they had conquered the country, integrated into Irish life. It wasn't long before the Normans were described as being "more Irish than the Irish themselves."

To this day, reminders of the Norman influence on Ireland remain strongest in the Southeast. Norman surnames are the most obvious indicator of the region's history, as names like Butler, Fitzgerald, Roche, and Fitzmaurice are all commonplace hereabouts. The architectural legacy of the Normans is also easy to spot in this part of Ireland.

The streetscapes of Kilkenny, Wexford, and Waterford cities owe their origins to the Normans. Travel the rural side roads of the region and it won't be long before you come across the ruins of a Norman castle, or "keep." Some are used to house animals or hay, while the best preserved are those that were integrated into later medieval or Georgian structures.

The Anglo-Normans and the Irish chieftains soon started to intermarry, but the process of integration came to a halt in 1366 with the Statutes of Kilkenny, based on English fears that if such intermingling continued they would lose whatever control over Ireland they had. The last great crisis was Oliver Cromwell's Irish campaign of 1650, which, in attempting to crush Catholic opposition to the English parliament, brought widespread woe.

sources organic and locally grown produce for his menu, which shows through in the delicately presented dishes. Expect to choose from entrées including spring lamb with shiitake mushrooms and spinach served with a warm red wine and strawberry vinaigrette. The service is good, too—friendly without being over-attentive, giving you a chance to take in the pretty views of the harbor. ⊠ *Crescent Quay* ☎ *053/24330* ⊟ *MC, V.*

$–$$ ✕ **Oak Tavern.** Ferrycarrig Castle and an 18th-century round tower stand sentinel over this lovely old-fashioned, family-run spot. The outdoor terrace overlooking the River Slaney is a lovely place for a relaxing repast. In cold weather you can warm yourself beside the log fires that blaze in the lounge. Specialties on the menu include locally produced steaks and salmon. The daytime bar menu offers better value. The tavern is about 2 km (1 mi) from town, and is not far from the gates of the Irish National Heritage Park on the N11 Dublin road. Unfortunately, as we went to press, the tavern suffered a major fire and will be shuttered for restoration for the foreseeable future. ⊠ *Enniscorthy Rd., Ferrycarrig* ☎ *053/20922* ⊕ *www.oaktavern.com* ⊟ *AE, MC, V.*

$$ ✕🖭 **Ferrycarrig.** A real favorite with families, this spot offers plenty of peace and tranquillity for parents thanks to its pleasant riverside location. All the bedrooms have wonderful views of the river, and some also have balconies. Tides restaurant ($$$–$$$$) overlooks its pleasant waterside location with a menu concentrating on seafood—scallops, salmon, and prawns prepared in simple lemon and butter sauces. For the kids there's a day-care facility and swimming pool. There's also a well-equipped health center. The hotel is to be found 3 km (2 mi) from Wexford Town on the N11. ⊠ *Ferrycarrig Bridge, Co. Wexford* ☎ *053/20999* 🖷 *053/20982* ⊕ *www.griffingroup.ie* ⇦ *102 rooms* 🖧 *Restaurant, indoor pool, health club, fishing, bar; no a/c* ⊟ *AE, DC, MC, V* ⦿ *BP.*

$ 🖭 **McMenamin's Town House.** From opera divas to Hollywood stars, they've all stayed here in this cozy Victorian villa. It's become one of the lodgings of choice for the annual opera festival held in the town each autumn and is also popular as a last stop-off for travelers heading for the Rosslare ferry to France. The bedrooms are spacious, warm, and immaculate, with large pieces of highly polished Victorian furniture and antique beds, including a mahogany half-tester. There are about eight choices at breakfast, including fresh fish of the day and hot porridge. Make sure you taste Kay and Seamus McMenamin's homemade whiskey marmalade. ⊠ *3 Auburn Terr., Redmond Rd., Co. Wexford* ☎ *053/46442* ⊕ *www.wexford-bedandbreakfast.com* ⇦ *5 rooms* 🖧 *No a/c, no room phones* ⊟ *MC, V* ⊙ *Closed last 2 wks of Dec.* ⦿ *BP.*

¢ 🖭 **Darral House.** A handsome Georgian town house, Darral House offers a good base for exploring Wexford Town and is within a five-minute walk of the town center. Constructed at the turn of the 19th century, it was renovated in 2005: guest rooms are tastefully decorated in harmony with the history of the house. Run by Sean and Kathleen Nolan, it's well known for an excellent "Full Irish"—the classic Irish breakfast. ⊠ *Spawell Rd., Co. Wexford* ☎ *053/24264* 🖷 *053/24284* ⇦ *4 rooms* 🖧 *Free parking; no a/c, no room phones* ⊟ *MC, V* ⦿ *BP.*

VOICES OF IRELAND

Ursula Sinnott
Director, Wexford Opera Festival

Wexford Opera is one of those festivals that everybody has always heard about. Held in October, it usually includes over forty daytime events as well as the eighteen evening performances of three major productions. Opera is the beating heart of the festival, and the Wexford company of artists are drawn from all over the world. It's a event that makes even the opera lovers of New York and Paris pea-green with envy.

"The success of the festival over the years is largely due to the overall Wexford experience, the relative uniqueness of coming here to find opera that is rarely performed anywhere else," notes Ms. Sinnott. "There is a constant sense of surprise among audiences here—an anticipation of 'what will this be like?' Moving along the narrow streets of the town from one event to the next, going in and out of shops where everybody is so well informed—little wonder the festival is so unique."

"It was originally founded through the efforts of a surgeon and a postman—and that all-

encompassing ethos continues to drive the event. We have a volunteer corps of 350 people that covers every strata of life: retired bank managers, police officers, doctors, unemployed people, farmers, shopkeepers. The running joke in the town is that volunteers can only 'retire' after 20 years service."

"Of course, we never rest on laurels—one week after this year's festival ends, the preparations for next year begin. Looking outward around the world and seeing what's happening is another factor in our success here—we've been so fortunate to have top class artistic directors over the years, some of which have been quite controversial, and all to the good of pushing the artistic envelope."

"Looking to the future, we are now in the second year of our Young Artists Development program. The other bright light in our future is the opening of our new theatre in 2008, still a venue where audiences will pass through the local neighborhoods to get to. This festival will never be above or away from the local people—it will always run through the town like a thread that binds us all together."

Nightlife & the Arts

Touring companies and local productions can be seen in Wexford at the **Theatre Royal** (⊠ 27 High St. ☎ 053/22400). The **Wexford Opera Festival** (☎ 053/22144 box office ⊕ www.wexfordopera.com), held during the last two weeks of October and the beginning of November, is the town's leading cultural event. The festival, which has been going strong since 1951, features seldom-performed operas sung by top talent from all over the world. Along with an ever-expanding of-fering of more populist fare performed in small venues and pubs, the festival supplies a feast of concerts and recitals that start at 11 AM and continue until midnight. For the full aria, see "Passion on the High C's" (page 255).

As the saying goes, if you can find a street without at least one bar on it, you're not still in Wexford. **Centenary Stores** (⊠ Charlotte St. ☎ 053/24424) is a Victorian-style pub. The adjoining night club makes it a popular place for the young crowd. Lunch is Monday through Saturday, and there's traditional music every Sunday morning. The **Sky and the Ground** (⊠ 112 S. Main St. ☎ 053/21273) is one of the best pubs in town and is a mecca for Irish music sessions, which pack in the crowds from Monday through Thursday. Dating to the 13th century, the **Thomas Moore Tavern** (⊠ Cornmarket ☎ 053/24348) is Wexford's oldest pub, named after the renowned Irish poet whose parents lived here. The pub has its original medieval walls and fine old beams along the ceiling. It's the perfect place for a quiet drink by the fire. Light lunches and snacks are served on weekdays between noon and 3.

Sports

GAELIC FOOTBALL & HURLING

You can watch Gaelic football and hurling at the **Wexford Park GAA** (⊠ Clonard Rd. ☎ 01/836–3222 GAA of Ireland in Dublin ⊕ www.gaa.ie).

Shopping

Barker's (⊠ 36 S. Main St. ☎ 053/23159) stocks Waterford crystal, local pottery, and crafts. **Martins Jewelers** (⊠ Lower Rowe St. ☎ 053/22635) specializes in handmade Celtic jewelry. **Simone Walsh** (⊠ 85 S. Main St. ☎ 053/23567) features Irish art and design and original paintings. **Westgate Design** (⊠ 22 N. Main St. ☎ 053/23787) carries a good selection of Irish crafts, clothing, pottery, candles, and jewelry; there's also a restaurant here. **The Wool Shop** (⊠ 39–41 S. Main St. ☎ 053/22247) is a good place to buy souvenirs, knitting yarn, and hand-loomed Aran sweaters.

WATERFORD & THE SOUTHEAST COAST

This journey takes you along mainly minor roads through the prettiest parts of the coast in Counties Wexford and Waterford, pausing midway to explore Waterford city—home of the dazzling cut glass—on foot. Along the way expect to see long golden beaches, quaint fishing villages like Kilmore Quay and Ballyhack, some of the country's best nature reserves, and Tramore, Ireland's most unredeemable family waterside resort. If you're coming from the Continent or England, chances are you'll end up on a ferry bound for Rosslare Harbour, one of Ireland's busiest ferry ports.

Rosslare

㉒ *16 km (10 mi) southeast of Wexford Town on R470.*

Sometimes called Ireland's sunniest spot, the village of Rosslare is a seaside getaway with an attractive beach. Vacationers generally head here to hike, golf, sun, and swim. **Rosslare Harbor,** 8 km (5 mi) south of the village, is the terminus for car ferries from Fishguard and Pembroke in Wales (a four-hour trip) and from Cherbourg and Roscoff in France (a 22-hour trip). Indeed, taking the ferry is the only reason you should find yourself in this otherwise dull little town. The two ferry companies, Irish Ferries and Stena Sealink (contact information in Southeast Essentials, *below*), serving Rosslare Harbour have small information kiosks in the ultramodern terminal, which also has lockers, a sprawling waiting room, and a café. You can purchase ferry tickets at the terminal. Reservations are also a must if you're traveling by car because onboard parking space is at a premium. The **Rosslare Harbour rail depot** (☎ 053/57937), adjacent to the ferry terminal, is served by frequent trains to Dublin's Connolly Station and Cork (change at Limerick Junction). Bus Éireann's Rosslare Harbour depot also adjoins the rail station.

> **TRAVEL TIP**
>
> Ferries to and from Rosslare frequently sell out, particularly in summer and any time the Irish soccer team is playing in a major tournament abroad. To be sure of getting a ticket on the boat of your choice, try to reserve your space in advance through the ferry companies' Cork or Dublin offices.

Where to Stay & Eat

★ **$$** ✕▥ **Kelly's.** This hotel has become somewhat of a legend with Irish vacationers. The reasons are numerous—a stunning beachfront location, second-to-none entertainment and leisure facilities, a child-friendly approach, and a reputation for excellent food being just a few. The guest rooms are comfort-laden havens decked out with rustic furnishings. Waterford-glass chandeliers hang in the Beaches restaurant ($$), where the menu includes dishes like Wicklow venison with wild mushrooms and Madeira jus or roast crispy Barbary duck with sauce curaçao. You can also dine in La Marine ($$), a casual, bistro-style restaurant that does a fine job of cooking up Irish produce in Mediterranean style. In July and August there's a one-week minimum stay. ⊠ Co. Wexford ☎ 053/32114 🖶 053/32222 ⊕ *www.kellys.ie* ⤴ 106 rooms ⚹ 2 restaurants, 18-hole golf course, 2 tennis courts, indoor pool, wading pool, gym, hair salon, hot tub, outdoor hot tub, sauna, spa, steam room, bicycles, croquet, playground ▭ AE, MC, V ⊗ Closed Dec.–Feb. ⋈ BP.

Nightlife & the Arts

The Strand Bar (⊠ Rosslare Harbor ☎ 053/33110), at the Hotel Rosslare, is a trendy spot with designer decor featuring stonework and fish tanks. It's popular for live music on weekends.

Sports

Rosslare Golf Club (⊠ Rosslare Strand ☎ 053/32203) is a 27-hole, par-72 championship links. A mixture of links and parkland can be found at the 27-hole **St. Helen's Bay** (⊠ Kilrane ☎ 053/33234).

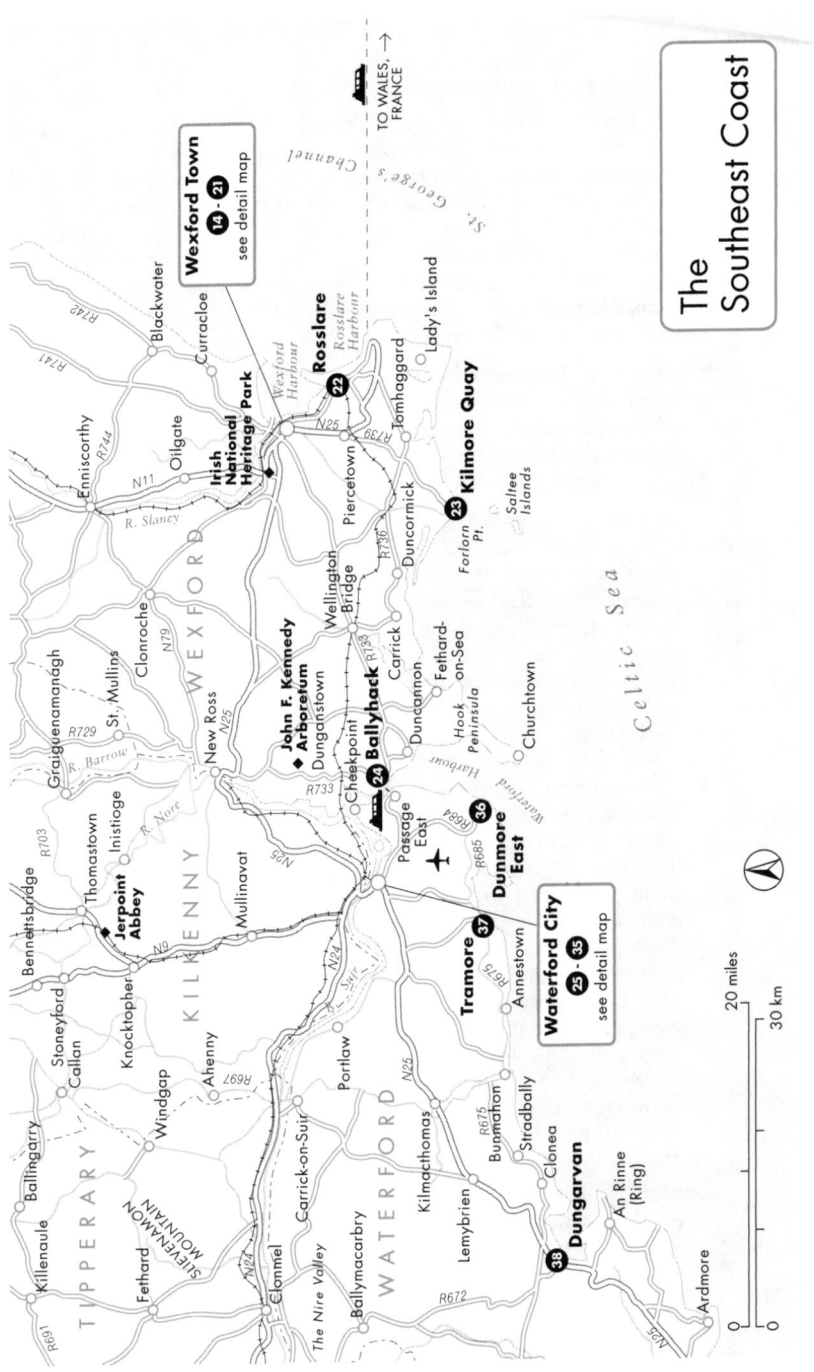

The Southeast Coast

TO WALES, FRANCE →

St. George's Channel

Wexford Town 14 · 21
see detail map

Rosslare 22

Blackwater

Curracloe

Rosslare Harbour

Lady's Island

Wexford Harbour

R742

R741

Enniscorthy

Oilgate

R744

N11

Tomhaggard

Irish National Heritage Park

N25

Piercetown

Piercetown

R739

Kilmore Quay 23

Saltee Islands

R. Slaney

Forlorn Pt.

R736

WEXFORD

Clonroche

N79

Wellington Bridge

Duncormick

Celtic Sea

R729

St. Mullins

R730

John F. Kennedy Arboretum

Dunganstown

Carrick

Fethard-on-Sea

Graiguenamanagh

R. Barrow

New Ross

N25

Checkpoint

Ballyhack 24

R733

Duncannon

Hook Peninsula

Churchtown

R. Nore

Inistioge

Jerpoint Abbey

Thomastown

R703

Bennettsbridge

Mullinavat

N25

Passage East

R684

R685

Dunmore East 36

Waterford Harbour

KILKENNY

Knocktopher

N10

N24

Ahenny

R697

Portlaw

Tramore 37

Annestown

R675

Waterford City 25 · 35
see detail map

Stoneyford

Callan

Windgap

Carrick-on-Suir

N24

WATERFORD

Ballingarry

Killenaule

Fethard

SLIEVENAMON MOUNTAIN

Clonmel

The Nire Valley

R672

Ballymacarbry

Kilmacthomas

Lemybrien

R675

Bunmahon

Stradbally

Clonea

Dungarvan 38

An Rinne (Ring)

R691

TIPPERARY

N72

Ardmore

N25

20 miles

30 km

0

0

Kilmore Quay

㉓

Fodor's Choice
★

22 km (14 mi) south of Rosslare on R739.

Noted for its fishing industry, this quiet, old-fashioned seaside village of thatched and whitewashed cottages is also popular with recreational anglers and bird-watchers. From the harbor there's a pleasant view to the east over the flat coast that stretches for miles. **Kehoe's Pub** (✉ Kilmore Quay ☎ 053/29830) is the hub of village activity; its collection of maritime artifacts is as interesting as that of many museums. During two weeks in July (generally mid-month), the village hosts a lively **seafood festival** (☎ 053/29922 or 086/3893278) with a parade, seafood barbecues, and other events.

★ The **Kilmore Quay Maritime Museum** is onboard the lightship *Guillemot*. Built in 1923, this is the last Irish lightship to be preserved complete with cabins and engine room, and it contains models and artifacts relating to the maritime history of the area. ✉ *Kilmore Quay* ☎ *053/21572* 🏷 *€5* ⊙ *June–Aug., daily noon–6; Sept. and Apr., weekends noon–6.*

Where to Stay & Eat

$$–$$$$ ✕ **Silver Fox.** A busy family-run seafood restaurant, this is considered one of the best in the area. Naturally, given its quayside location, seafood is the specialty here. Lemon sole gratin is a real favorite here—a scrumptious fillet with a creamy sauce of fresh prawns, scallops, mushrooms, and onions, plus a sprinkling of cheese. Nonseafood options include chicken angelica—stuffed with potatoes and leeks and wrapped in bacon with mushroom sauce. Simplicity and freshness define the food here. ✉ *Kilmore Quay* ☎ *053/29888* 🪑 *Reservations essential* ▭ *AE, MC, V* ⊙ *Closed mid-Jan.–mid-Feb. No lunch Mon.–Sat.*

$ 🏠 **Quay House.** A perfect base for those interested in boating or fishing, this guesthouse is a three-minute walk from the pier. The homey interior has Douglas fir pine floors throughout and country pine bedroom furniture. If you're the outdoor type you'll feel right at home: nearby are great waterside walks and boating options (a room for drying and storing diving and fishing equipment is available). ✉ *Kilmore Quay, Co. Wexford* ☎ *053/29988* 📠 *053/29808* 🌐 *www.kilmorequay.net* 🛏 *10 rooms* 🍴 *Restaurant, fishing; no a/c* ▭ *MC, V* ⊙ *BP.*

Shopping

Country Crafts (✉ Kilmore Quay ☎ 053/29885), which overlooks the harbor of Kilmore Quay, sells Irish-made crafts, country-style furniture, and paintings by local artists.

ROOKERY ON THE ROCKS

The Saltee Islands, Ireland's largest bird sanctuary, make a fine day trip from Kilmore Quay. You can see kittiwakes, puffins, guillemots, cormorants, gulls, and petrels, especially in late spring and early summer, when several million seabirds nest among the dunes and rocky scarp on the southern of the two islands. From mid-May to mid-September, look for boats at the village waterfront or on the marina to take you to the islands, weather permitting.

**EN
ROUTE**

On leaving Kilmore Quay, make your way north to R736, and then head west through Duncormick and on to Wellington Bridge. Past the bridge, head toward Fethard-on-Sea on the **Ring of Hook** drive. This is a strange and atypical part of Ireland, where the land is exceptionally flat and the narrow roads run straight.

Ballyhack

24   *34 km (21 mi) west of Kilmore Quay.*

Fodor'sChoice
★

On the upper reaches of Waterford Harbor, this pretty village with a square castle keep, wooden buildings, thatched cottages, and green, hilly background is admired by painters and photographers. A small car ferry makes the five-minute crossing to Passage East and Waterford. The gray-stone keep of **Ballyhack Castle** dates from the 16th century. It was once owned by the Knights Templars of St. John of Jerusalem, who held the ferry rights by royal charter. The first two floors have been renovated and house local-history exhibits. Guided tours are available by appointment, and the last admission is 45 minutes before closing. ☎ 051/389–468 ⊕ *www.heritageireland.ie* 🖃 €2.50 ⊙ *Mid-June–mid-Sept., weekdays 10–1 and 2–6, weekends 10–6.*

Twelve kilometers (8 mi) to the north of Ballyhack lies the **John F. Kennedy Arboretum**, with more than 600 acres of forest, nature trails, and gardens, plus an ornamental lake. The grounds contain some 4,500 species of trees and shrubs, and serve as a resource center for botanists and foresters. Go to the top of the park to get fine panoramic views. The arboretum is clearly signposted from New Ross on R733, which follows the banks of the Barrow southward for about 5 km (3 mi). The cottage where the president's great-grandfather was born is in Dunganstown; Kennedy relatives still live in the house. About 2 km (1 mi) down the road at Slieve Coillte you can see the entrance to the arboretum. ⊠ *Dunganstown* ☎ 051/388–171 ⊕ *www.heritageireland.ie* 🖃 €2.75 ⊙ *May–Aug., daily 10–8; Apr. and Sept., daily 10–6:30; Oct.–Mar., daily 10–5.*

Where to Stay & Eat

$$$$
Fodor'sChoice
★

✕🏨 **Dunbrody Country House.** A rural jewel, this sprawling two-story 1830s Georgian manor house used to be the digs of the seventh marquess of Donegal, Dermot Chichester (who now lives nearby). Under the magic touch of current chatelains, Kevin and Catherine Dundon, the gardens are soul-restoring, the manse's public salons are a soigné symphony of mix-and-match tangerine-hue fabrics and stuffed arm chairs, the views over the Barrow estuary remain grand, and the guest rooms charm with a judiciously luxe combination of period antiques and fine reproductions. Gourmands come here to stuff themselves cross-eyed in the ruby-red Harvest Room ($$$$), irresistibly drawn by master chef Kevin's Barbary duck in

> **SLOW BOAT TO WATERFORD**
>
> The Knights Templars of St. John of Jerusalem were required to keep a boat at Ballyhack to transport injured knights to the King's Leper Hospital at Waterford.

burnt-orange sauce, medallions of beef in Rhône wine jus, and chocolate "selection of indulgences." (In fact, you may learn how to cook these delights yourself; Kevin runs a cooking school on the premises, with classes conveniently scheduled for weekends). After a dinner that is likely to be memorable sip-to-sup, sit back with a goblet of Irish mist in hand and catch a dramatic sunset fading over the Hook Peninsula. No need to rush the next morn: the famous breakfasts are served until 11:30. ✉ *Arthurstown, New Ross, Co. Wexford* ☎ *051/389–600* 🖷 *051/ 389–601* ⊕ *www.dunbrodyhouse.com* ↪ *15 rooms, 7 suites* ⚷ *Restaurant, bar; no a/c* ▤ *AE, DC, MC, V* ⦿*BP.*

Waterford City

10 km (6 mi) west of Ballyhack by ferry and road (R683), 62 km (39 mi) southwest of Wexford Town, 158 km (98 mi) southwest of Dublin.

The largest town in the Southeast and Ireland's oldest city, Waterford was founded by the Vikings in the 9th century and was taken over by Strongbow, the Norman invader, with much bloodshed in 1170. The city resisted Cromwell's 1649 attacks, but fell the following year. It did not prosper again until 1783, when George and William Penrose set out to create "plain and cut flint glass, useful and ornamental," and thereby set in motion a glass-manufacturing industry without equal.

Waterford has better-preserved city walls than anywhere else in Ireland but Derry. Initially, the slightly run-down commercial center doesn't look promising. You need to park your car and proceed on foot to discover the heritage that the city has made admirable efforts since the mid-1990s to preserve, in particular the grand 18th-century Georgian buildings that Waterford architect John Roberts (1714–96) built, including the town's Protestant and Catholic cathedrals. The compact town center can be visited in a couple of hours. Allow at least another hour if you intend to take the Waterford crystal factory tour.

The **city quays**—at the corner of Custom House Parade and Peter Street— are a good place to begin a tour of Waterford City. (The TIO is also down here, at the Granary on Merchant's Quay.) The city quays stretch for nearly 2 km (1 mi) along the River Suir and were described in the 18th century as the best in Europe.

㉕ **Reginald's Tower,** a waterside circular tower on the east end of Waterford's quays, marks the apex of a triangle containing the old walled city of Waterford. Built by the Vikings for the city's defense in 1003, it has 80-foot-high, 10-foot-thick walls; an interior stairway leads to the top. The tower served in turn as the residence for a succession of Anglo-Norman kings (including Henry II, John, and Richard II), a mint for silver coins, a prison, and an arsenal. It's said that Strongbow's marriage to Eva, the daughter of Dermot MacMurrough, took place here in the late 12th century, thus uniting the Norman invaders with the native Irish. It has been restored to its original medieval appearance and furnished with appropriate 11th- to 15th-century artifacts. ✉ *The Quay* ☎ *051/ 304–220* 🖼 *€2* ⊙ *Mid-Mar.–Sept., daily 10–6; Oct., daily 10–5; Nov.–mid-Mar., Wed. and Thurs. 10–5.*

26 One of Waterford's finer Georgian buildings, **City Hall**, on the Mall, dates from 1783 and was designed by John Roberts, a native of the city. Nearby are some good examples of domestic Georgian architecture—tall, well-proportioned houses with typically Irish semicircular fanlights above the doors. The arms of Waterford hang over City Hall's own entrance, which leads into a spacious foyer that originally was a town meeting place and merchants' exchange. The building contains two lovely theaters, an old Waterford dinner service, and an enormous 1802 Waterford glass chandelier, which hangs in the Council Chamber (a copy of the chandelier hangs in Independence Hall in Philadelphia). The Victorian horseshoe-shape Theatre Royal is the venue for the annual Festival of Light Opera in September. ⊠ *The Mall* 🕾 *051/309–900* 🖃 *Free* ☉ *Weekdays 9–5.*

> **ONE WAY OR ANOTHER**
>
> Although there are several theories about the origin of the phrase, some experts credit Cromwell with coining the expression "by hook or by crook." Planning two siege routes to Waterford—one via Hook Head, the other via Crooke Village on the estuary of the River Suir—Cromwell declared that he would take the city "by Hooke or by Crooke."

27 The **Bishop's Palace** is among the most imposing of the remaining Georgian town houses. Only the foyer is open to the public. ⊠ *Alongside City Hall on Mall* 🖃 *Free* ☉ *Weekdays 9–5.*

★ **28** Lovers of Georgian decorative arts will want to visit the late-18th-century Church of Ireland **Christ Church Cathedral**, designed by local architect John Roberts and the only Neoclassical Georgian Cathedral in Ireland. Inside, all is cup-of-tea elegance—yellow walls, white-stucco trim in designs of florets and laurels, grand Corinthian columns—and you can see why architectural historian Mark Girouard called this "the finest 18th-century ecclesiastical building in Ireland." It stands on the site of a great Norman Gothic cathedral. The then Bishop Cheneix, it's oft told, wouldn't consider knocking that great edifice down—never, that is, until it was arranged for a little stone vaulting to fall in his path. Medievalists will be sad, but those who prize Age-of-Enlightenment high style will rejoice. ⊠ *Henrietta St.* 🕾 *051/858–958* ⊕ *www. christchurchwaterford.com* 🖃 *€3* ☉ *Easter–Sept., Mon.–Sat. 10–1 and 2–5; Sun. 11–1 and 2–5.*

29 Roofless ruins are all that remain of **French Church** (⊠ Greyfriar's St.), a 13th-century Franciscan abbey. The church, also known as Greyfriars, was given to a group of Huguenot refugees (hence the "French") in 1695. A splendid east window remains amid the ruins. The key is available at Reginald's Tower.

30 **St. Olaf's Church** (⊠ St. Olaf's St.) was built, as the name implies, by the Vikings in the mid-11th century. All that remains of the old church is its original door, which has been incorporated into the wall of the existing building (a meeting hall).

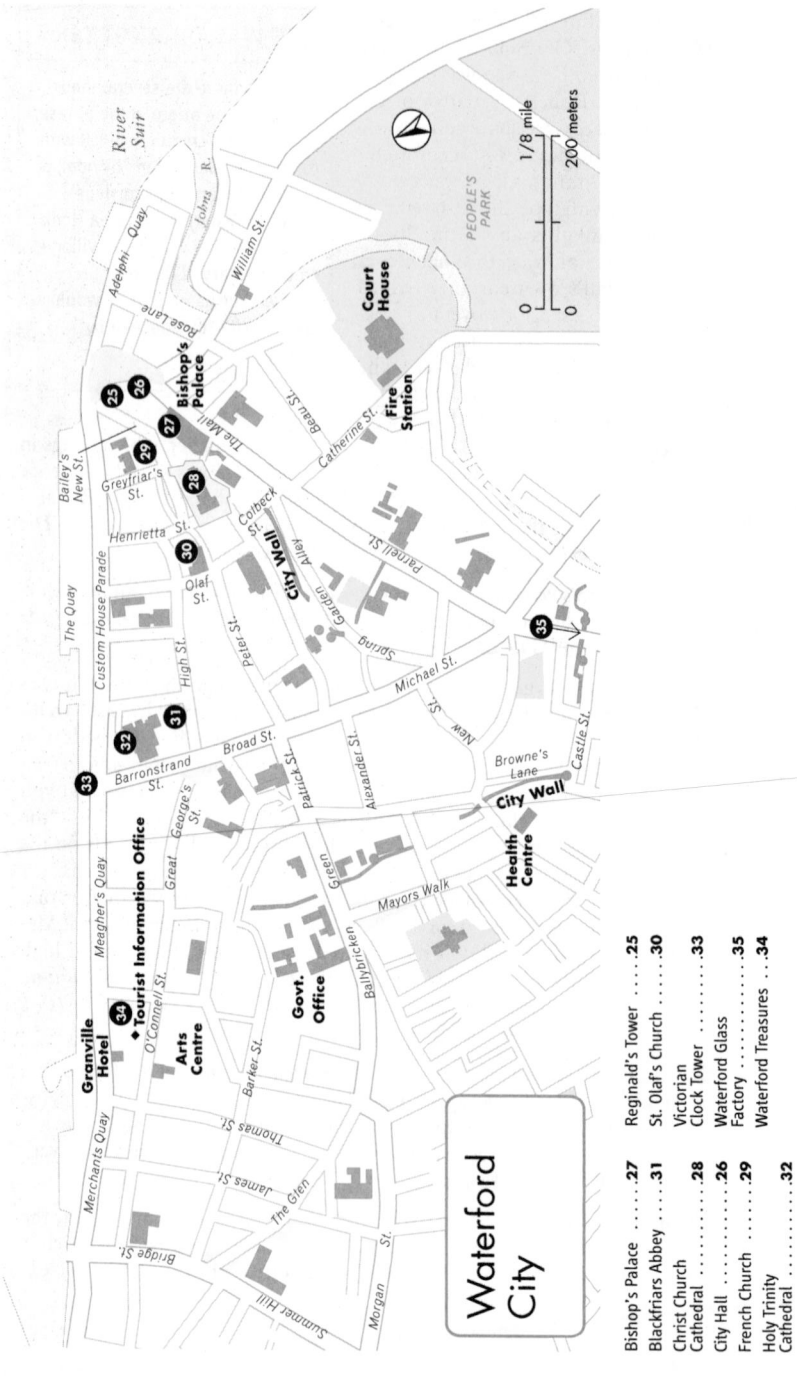

Waterford City

③ The ruined tower of **Blackfriars Abbey** (⊠ High St.) belonged to a Dominican abbey founded in 1226 and returned to the crown in 1541 after the dissolution of the monasteries. It was used as a courthouse until Cromwellian forces destroyed it in the 17th century.

③ The Roman Catholic **Holy Trinity Cathedral** has a simple facade and a richly (some would say garishly) decorated interior with high, vaulted ceilings and ornate Corinthian pillars. It was designed in Neoclassical style by John Roberts, who also designed Christ Church Cathedral and City Hall. Surprisingly, it was built in the late 18th century—when Catholicism was barely tolerated—on land granted by the Protestant city fathers. ⊠ *Barronstrand St. between High St. and clock tower on quays* ☎ *051/ 875–166* ✆ *Free* ☉ *Daily 8:30–5:30.*

③ The **Victorian Clock Tower** (⊠ Merchant's Quay) was built in 1864 with public donations. Although it has no great architectural merit, it serves as a reminder of the days when Waterford was a thriving, bustling port.

③ **Waterford Treasures**, above the Southeast's main TIO, uses interactive audiovisual technology to guide you through 1,000 years in the history of Waterford. Entertaining and educational, the exhibition displays Waterford's rich inheritance of rare and beautiful artifacts—from the Charter Roll of 1372, a list of all charters granted to Waterford up to that time, written in Latin on vellum, to the sword of King Edward IV to 18th-century crystal. A restaurant and a shop are also on the premises. ⊠ *The Granary, Merchant's Quay* ☎ *051/304–500* ✆ *€6* ☉ *Apr.–Sept., weekdays 9–5, Sat. 10–5, Sun. 11–5; Oct.–Mar., weekdays 10–5, Sun. 11–5.*

Fodor'sChoice
★

③ The city's most popular attraction is the **Waterford Glass Factory**, about 2 km (1 mi) from the TIO, where the world-famous crystal is created. The factory opened in 1783, crafting elegant and ornate stemware, chandeliers, and other pieces. Over the years, its clientele and product line diversified, and today the United States is the biggest market. The tour of the factory takes you through the specialized crafts of blowing, cutting, and polishing glass—all carried out against a noisy background of glowing furnaces and ceaseless bustle. An extensive selection of crystal is on view (and for sale) in the showroom. Tours are offered on weekends (often booked solid weeks in advance during summer), but on weekdays you're allowed to go at a more relaxed pace, which is infinitely preferable. To reserve a place in a 60-minute tour, which includes an optional 18-minute audiovisual show, call the factory or the tourist office. To get here, take the N25 Waterford–Cork road south from the quay, or ask at the tourist office about the regular bus service. ⊠ *Cork Rd., Kilbarry* ☎ *051/358–398* ⊕ *www.waterfordvisitorcentre.com* ✆ *€9* ☉ *Tours daily 9–4; factory daily 8:15–6.*

> ### WATERFORD CITY LIMITS
>
> Off Colbeck Street along Spring Garden Alley, you can see one of the remaining portions of the old city wall; there are sections all around the town center.

Rolls-Royce of Crystal

SILICA SAND + potash + litharge = Waterford crystal: it reads like cold science, but something magical happens when the craftsmen of Waterford produce arguably the top crystal in the world (although France's Baccarat might have something to say about that).

When the Waterford Glass Factory opened in 1783, it provided English royalty and nobility with a regular supply of ornate handcrafted stemware, chandeliers, and decorative knickknacks. Since then Waterford crystal has graced the tables of heads of state the world over, and Waterford's earlier pieces have become priceless heirlooms.

The best Waterford glass was produced from the late 18th century to the early 19th century. This early work, examples of which can be found in museums and public buildings all over the country, is characterized by a unique, slightly opaque cast that is absent from the modern product.

Crystal glass is not cheap: each piece is individually fashioned by almost two-dozen pairs of hands before it passes final inspection and receives the discreet Waterford trademark.

If you're in Waterford, put a tour of the factory at the top of your itinerary. There you can see master craftspeople at work, fashioning the molten glass, blowing it into bulbous shapes, and then cutting and carving to give each piece those wonderful light-catching facets that cast multicolor reflections. You probably won't need any protective eye gear, but considering all the razzle-dazzle, sunglasses might come in handy.

If the weather is favorable, consider taking a **cruise** along Waterford's harbor and the wide, picturesque estuary of the River Suir. You can enjoy lunch, afternoon tea, or dinner aboard a luxury river cruiser or simply take in the sights. The boat departs from the quay opposite the TIO, where you can purchase tickets. ☎ *051/421–723 Galley Cruises* ⊕ *www.rivercruises.ie* ☉ *Cruises Apr.–Oct., daily at 12:30, 3, and 7, weather permitting.*

Where to Stay & Eat

$$–$$$ ✕ **Chez Ks Steak & Seafood Restaurant.** There's always a lively buzz about this fine American-style eatery—especially on weekends when the resident piano man plays a baby grand in the center of the restaurant. The mood is modern, with pieces of contemporary art adorning the walls, and grilled food is the specialty. After choosing from such house favorites as steak fillet with pepper sauce, and tempura of monkfish served with a pineapple and pear chutney, customize your meal with a choice of trimmings, sauces, and side dishes. You can watch your meal being prepared in the open kitchen. Another plus is the excellent service. ⊠ *20–22 William St.* ☎ *051/844–180* ⌖ *Reservations essential* ⊟ *AE, DC, MC, V.*

$$–$$$ ✕ **Fitzpatricks Restaurant.** When he acquired the place in 2004, the new
FodorsChoice owner of the much-loved former O'Grady's Restaurant and Guesthouse
★ had a tough act to follow, but somehow Billy Fitzpatrick has managed to pull it off. Housed in a beautifully restored lodge house on the outskirts of the city, the interior has had a pleasing makeover but the am-

bience remains subtly traditional so as not to shock the regulars. The cuisine is firmly in the fine-dining camp with a Gallic flavor to the seafood-rich dishes on offer. ⊠ *Cork Rd.* ☎ *051/378–851* ▤ *DC, MC, V.*

$$–$$$ ✕ **Goose's Barbecue & Wine House.** The rustic dining room complements the ranch-style cooking that's served at this unusual restaurant in the historic quarter of the city. Exposed brick, robust furniture, and bright walls make convivial surroundings for a meat-heavy menu. Specialties include "Boozy beef steaks"—a prime Irish cut marinated in soy sauce and stout, and the "sticky finger spare ribs" barbecued with hickory. Efficient table service, good desserts, and hearty food guarantee a satisfying night out. ⊠ *19 Henrietta St.* ☎ *051/858–426* ⚓ *Reservations essential* ▤ *MC, V* ⊘ *Closed Sun. and Mon.*

$–$$ ✕ **The Wine Vault.** You'd never know it but underneath this modern build-
Fodor'sChoice ing lies the cellar of an Elizabethan town house, thought to have been
★ built by Peter Rice, the mayor of Waterford back in 1426. Famed for forging links between Waterford and the Spanish shrine of Santiago de Compostela, Rice was also a wealthy wine merchant and for centuries his fortified town house held stocks of Bordeaux, port, Madeira, claret, and hock. Today, fittingly, you can sit down at the polished wooden tables of a restored bonded warehouse to enjoy the creations of chef Fergal Phelan, who likes to buy wines to match food. Expect to choose from dishes like roast skewered monkfish with vegetables and rice plus an apricot, mango and red currant salsa or braised duo of Waterford venison and beef sausages with thyme mash. On your way out, be sure to peruse the vintages, hailing from Australia to Alsace, on sale in the basement wineshop. ⊠ *High St.* ☎ *051/853–444* ⊕ *www.waterfordwinevault. com* ▤ *AE, MC, V* ⊘ *Closed Sun.*

$$$$ ✕▣ **Waterford Castle.** Not only does this fairy-tale castle come with an
Fodor'sChoice 800-year history, it sits in the middle of a 310-acre island, and allows
★ lucky guests to be bed-and-boarded in the grandest Irish style. Back in Norman times, the Kfyeralds built a keep here and over the centuries—as their name became Fitzgeralds, "Kings of Ireland in all but name"—they expanded, adding two Elizabethan-style wings in the 17th century, fitting them out with rooftop gargoyles brought from Castle Irwell in Manchester. Today, the air of exclusivity lingers as the private ferry picks you up on the shores of the River Suir, and heightens with one step inside the Great Hall, a magnificent faux-baronial room in Portland stone and hung with medieval tapestries. Nearby is the Munster Dining Room ($$$$), whose luxe—oak paneling, darkened with age, and ancestral portraits spotlit in gilt frames—compliments one of the most stylish menus around. Most guest rooms are exquisitely done in real "country-house" style, some with canopied beds, chintz armchairs, and dark mahogany furniture. To top it all off, a prize-winning 18-hole golf course adjoins the castle. Obviously, the last great Fitzgerald to occupy the house, Mary Frances (whose son, Edward Fitzgerald, translated the *Rubaiyat of Omar Khayyam* into English) would be happy to see her former domain so lovingly cared for. ⊠ *The Island, Ballinakill, Co. Waterford* ☎ *051/878–203* 🖷 *051/879–316* ⊕ *www.waterfordcastle.com* ⤳ *14 rooms, 5 suites* ⟨ *Restaurant, 18-hole golf course, 2 tennis courts, fishing, croquet; no a/c* ▤ *AE, DC, MC, V.*

$–$$$ ✕▢ **Faithlegg House Hotel.** A gorgeous 18th-century mansion in mature
Fodor'sChoice woodlands has been converted into one of the Southeast's most popu-
★ lar getaway destinations for those who are out for both indulgence and
relaxation. There's an acclaimed 18-hole golf course and a gym for healthy
types. For those less inclined to such vigorous pursuits there's also the
full gamut of pampering treatments available at the Estuary Club spa.
Chef Eric Theze lends a French influence to the cuisine served in the hotel's
restaurant, the Roseville Rooms ($$–$$$), which includes two of the
house's original drawing rooms, replete with ornate stucco plasterwork
ceilings. Self-catering accommodation is also available and good mid-
week deals are usually available. To get there, take the Dunmore road
out of Waterford for 3 mi (2 km), then follow the sign for Passage East
and veer right under the railway bridge at Jack Meades' pub. ⊠ *Faith-
legg, Co. Waterford* ☎ *051/382–000* ⊟ *051/382–010* ⊕ *www.faithlegg.
com* ⇌ *68 rooms, 14 suites* ⌂ *Restaurant, 18-hole golf course, tennis
courts, pool, spa, fishing, billiards; no a/c* ⊟ *AE, DC, MC, V* ⍥ *BP.*

$–$$$ ▢ **Dooley's Hotel.** A friendly air pervades this unpretentious family-run
hotel on the banks of the river Suir. Dooley's is also just minutes' walk
from all the main attractions and is perfect for families. The rooms are
simple, bright, and decorated in vibrant colors. The service is excellent
and the traditional-style bar is popular with locals. The New Ship
restaurant serves Continental dishes and has an early-bird menu. ⊠ *30
The Quay, Co. Waterford* ☎ *051/873–531* ⊟ *051/870–262* ⊕ *www.
dooleys-hotel.ie* ⇌ *115 rooms* ⌂ *Restaurant, bar; no a/c* ⊟ *AE, DC,
MC, V* ⍥ *BP.*

$ ▢ **Foxmount Farm & Country House.** For a pleasant change of pace, you
can stay on a working dairy farm in the peaceful countryside. This elegant 17th-century creeper-clad country house on extensive grounds has
an informal style, with welcoming log fires and intriguing antiques. It's
about 5 km (3 mi) outside town on the road to the Passage East ferry.
Your host, Margaret Kent, has been welcoming guests for 40 years and
is renowned for her cooking. Sadly, she no longer provides dinners, but
the breakfast remains legendary. Enjoy seasonal fruit and fresh farm produce accompanied by Margaret's home-baked bread. ⊠ *Passage East
Rd., Co. Waterford* ☎ *051/874–308* ⊟ *051/854–906* ⊕ *www.
foxmountcountryhouse.com* ⇌ *5 rooms* ⌂ *Dining room, tennis court;
no a/c, no room TVs* ⊟ *No credit cards* ⊙ *Closed Nov.–mid-Mar.*
⍥ *BP.*

Nightlife & the Arts

The **Spraoi Festival** (☎ 051/841–808 ⊕ www.spraoi.com) is billed as the
"biggest street carnival in Ireland"—with street theater, live music, and
fireworks. This free outdoor festival, which appeals to children and adults
alike, takes place annually during the August bank holiday, the first weekend of the month. The **Waterford International Festival of Light Opera**
(☎ 051/874–402 ⊕ www.waterfordfestival.com), the only competitive
event of its kind, is a great draw for amateur musical societies from Ireland and Great Britain. The festival runs for 17 nights every September
at the **Theatre Royal** (⊠ City Hall, The Mall ☎ 051/874–402). The **Waterford Show** tells the story of Waterford's culture and heritage through
music, song, and dance. The show begins at 9 PM on Tuesday, Thurs-

day, and Saturday at City Hall from May through September. The admission cost of €11 includes a preshow drink and a glass of wine during the show. Book at Waterford Glass Factory or the **Waterford Tourist Information Office** (☎ 051/875–788).

You can see a wide selection of work by contemporary artists at the **Dyehouse Gallery and Waterford Pottery** (✉ Dyehouse La. ☎ 051/844–770 ⊕ www.dyehouse-gallery.com), one of Ireland's only modern purpose-built galleries. The building is an attraction in itself and has won numerous awards for its architectural design. The **Forum** (✉ The Glen ☎ 051/871–111 ⊕ www.forumwaterford.com) is a large entertainment venue that houses a 300-seat theater. Here you can watch local productions or those of traveling theater companies. Two music venues host big names as well as local acts performing all kinds of music. Culture buffs shouldn't miss the **Garter Lane Arts Centre** (✉ 22A O'Connell St. ☎ 051/855–038), which hosts concerts, exhibits, and theater productions. The five-screen **Waterford Cineplex** (✉ Patrick St. ☎ 051/874–595) shows current releases.

Geoffs (✉ 9 John St. ☎ 051/874–787) is a dimly lighted pub frequented by a mixed crowd including students and locals. Big flagstones cover the floors, and seating is on old wooden benches. An outdoor area is available for those keen to avoid Ireland's smoking ban. A wide selection of food is served until 9, every day. Housed in an 800-year-old building, the **Old Ground** (✉ 10 The Glen ☎ 051/852–283) is a popular pub with locals. Lunch is served daily, and traditional-music sessions are held every Friday night. The circa-1700 **T & H Doolan's Bar** (✉ 32 George's St. ☎ 051/872–764), reputed to be one of the oldest pubs in Ireland, hosts traditional Irish music most summer nights and Monday through Wednesday year-round. Known to the natives as Meade's Under the Bridge, **Jack Meades** (✉ Cheekpoint Rd., Halfway House, Ballycanavan ☎ 051/873–187) is snug under a time-stained stone bridge. In centuries past it was a stop on the coach road from Waterford to Passage East. There's a pub menu from May through September, and sing-along sessions are held throughout the year on the weekends. In winter the fireplaces roar, illuminating the wood beams and bric-a-brac. As in many pubs, the proprietors have created a patio area for the smoking fraternity, but this is an outdoor area with a difference—it also has a children's playground and a "minizoo" with a collection of cute farmyard animals.

Sports

GAELIC FOOTBALL & HURLING
Watch Gaelic football and hurling at the **Waterford GAA Grounds** (✉ Walsh Park ☎ 01/836–3222 GAA in Dublin ⊕ www.gaa.ie).

GOLF
Faithlegg Golf Club (✉ Faithlegg House, Checkpoint ☎ 051/382–241) is an 18-hole, par-72 course set in mature landscape on the banks of the River Suir. **Waterford Castle Golf Club** (✉ The Island, Ballinakill ☎ 051/871–633) is an 18-hole, par-72 course that claims to be Ireland's only true island course.

Shopping

City Square Shopping Centre (⌧ City Sq. ☎ 051/853–528) has more than 40 shops, ranging from small Irish fashion boutiques to large international department stores. Fashion shows and other forms of entertainment take place on the stage area in the center of the mall. **Joseph Knox** (⌧ 3 Barronstrand St. ☎ 051/875–307 ⊕ www.josephknox.com) displays the best selection of crystal in Waterford City. **Kellys** (⌧ 75–76 The Quay ☎ 051/873–557) has excellent Irish souvenirs, including traditional musical instruments, dolls, Irish linen, jewelry, Waterford crystal, and CDs. Even if you don't take the plant tour, pay a visit to the famed **Waterford Glass Factory** (⌧ Cork Rd., Kilbarry ☎ 051/332–500 ⊕ www.waterfordvisitorcentre.com). The showroom displays an extensive selection of Waterford crystal and Wedgwood china.

Dunmore East

36 *16 km (10 mi) southeast of Waterford City via R683 and R684.*

Dunmore East is a quaint, one-street fishing village of thatched cottages and an attractive lighthouse at the head of Waterford Harbor. Note the colorful but noisy kittiwakes that nest in the steep cliffs overlooking the harbor. Many small beaches and cliff walks are nearby, and you get a wonderful view of the estuary from the hill behind the village.

Where to Eat

$$–$$$ ✕ **The Ship Restaurant & Bar.** Chefs Paul Power and Emma Beckett emphasize fresh, local seafood at this simply furnished restaurant set in a 19th-century house overlooking the bay. Typical dishes include panfried John Dory and char-grilled swordfish. For those in the mood for a nonfishy alternative there are pan-roasted veal chops with roast pearl onions, crispy potatoes, and mustard tarragon cream sauce. ☎ 051/383–141 ⊕ www.theshiprestaurant.com ▤ AE, DC, MC, V.

Tramore

37 *11 km (7 mi) south of Waterford City on R675, 4 km (2½ mi) west of Dunmore East.*

☺ Tramore's 5-km-long (3-mi-long) **beach** is a popular escape for families from Waterford and other parts of the Southeast, as the many vacation homes and camper parks indicate. This is Ireland's biggest seaside resort and a dream-come-true for young children, but it's not to everybody's taste. A 50-acre amusement park, a miniature railway, and vacation-home developments overshadow part of the seafront. (The upper half of town is more quiet and reserved.)

Where to Stay

$ ⌂ **Annestown House.** The wonderful setting, the warm welcome, and the
Fodor's Choice feeling that you've stumbled upon a little piece of yesteryear make this
★ place a must if you're seeking a romantic hideaway. This Victorian rectory, perched on its own promontory in the quainter-than-quaint village of Annestown, is something out of an Enid Blighton adventure and seems more reminiscent of 1950s Cornwall than modern Ireland. The house overlooks a craggy cove with a white sandy beach and (of course)

there's a secret private pathway down to the beach. Inside, the rambling interior is full of old books and antiques and a snooker room. The house has been in the family of John Galloway since 1820. John and his wife, Pippa, are relaxed yet attentive hosts and delight in recounting the history of the house and the village, which was once owned in its entirety by the family. Bedrooms are generally large and full of character, most with wonderful sea views. ✉ *Annestown, Co. Waterford* ☎ *051/396–160* 🖷 *051/ 396–474* ⊕ *www.annestown.com* ⌂ *5 rooms* ⚬ *Dining room, tennis court, billiards, croquet; no a/c, no room TVs* 🖭 *AE, MC, V* ⊘ *Closed Nov.–mid-Mar.* ⍾ *BP.*

> ## THREE'S A CHARM
>
> At the western end of Tramore's beach, the sand gives way to rocky cliffs guarded by the Metal Man, a giant cast-iron figure that stands atop a great pillar. It's said that if a young woman hops on one foot around the base of the pillar three times, she will be married within a year. This custom, which is still observed in a lighthearted way, can be traced back to a stone that stood on the spot centuries ago and was used in ancient Celtic fertility rites.

Dungarvan

㊳ *42 km (26 mi) southwest of Tramore on R675.*

With their covering of soft grasses, the lowlands of Wexford and eastern Waterford gradually give way to heath and moorland; the wetter climate of the hillier western Waterford countryside creates and maintains the bog. The mountains responsible for the change in climate rise up behind Dungarvan, the largest coastal town in County Waterford. This bustling fishing and resort spot sits at the mouth of River Colligan, which empties into Dungarvan Bay here. It's a popular base for climbers and hikers. In **Ring (An Rinne)**, a Gaeltacht area on Dungarvan Bay, the Irish language is still in daily use—this is unusual in the south and east of the country. At Colaiste na Rinne, a language college, courses in Irish have been taught since 1909. ✉ *7 km (4¼ mi) southeast of Dungarvan, off N674F.*

Where to Stay & Eat

$$ ✕ **The Tannery.** Clearly, out there in Knockmealdown, the mountain air

FodorsChoice must do something to clear the brain and allow chefs to focus and pu-

★ rify. Perhaps that's why this place is besieged on weekends, when Dubliners head here to taste the creations of culinary wizard Paul Flynn. He worked for almost a decade with London culinary legend Nico Ladenis and now wins raves from the likes of Sir Andrew Lloyd Webber. The dishes on offer may look slightly odd on the menu but they taste sensational on the palate. Check out crab crème brûlée with pickled cucumber and onion marmalade served with melba toast. Or if that doesn't tickle your taste buds opt for homemade black pudding with risotto of parsley, pine nuts, and raisins or the roast rump of lamb with mild garlic crème and cocoa beans. Fanatical foodies who want to stay as close to the culinary action as possible can now overnight in the adjoining guesthouse, opened by the Flynns in 2005. Your waistline may never be the same again. ☒ *10 Quay St.* ⊕ *www.tannery.ie* ☎ *058/45420* ☐ *AE, DC, MC, V* ☺ *Closed Mon. and 2 wks in Jan. No dinner Sun.*

$–$$ 🏨 **The Gold Coast Golf Hotel.** Overlooking Dungarvan Bay, this hotel is part of a family-run and family-friendly property, including 21 self-catering holiday cottages (built around the 37-bedroom hotel) and 10 golf villas on the edge of a woodland course on a links setting. Rooms are bright, comfortable, and spacious. Guests can use the facilities of the Gold Coast's sister hotel, the Clonea Strand, just 2½ km (1½ mi) away, which include a games room, a leisure complex, and Clonea's 3-km-long (2-mi-long) sandy beach. ☒ *Co. Waterford* ☎ *058/42249 or 058/42416* 🖶 *058/43378* ⊕ *www.clonea.com* 🛏 *37 rooms, 16 cottages, 10 villas* △ *Restaurant, 18-hole golf course, tennis court, indoor pool, gym, fishing, bar, playground* ☐ *AE, DC, MC, V* ⊠ *BP.*

Nightlife & the Arts

Several miles away from Dungarvan, a *ceilí* (Irish dance) is held nightly in summer at **Colaiste na Rinne** (☒ Ring ☎ 058/46104).

IN & AROUND COUNTY TIPPERARY

"It's a long way to Tipperary . . .": so run the words of that famed song sung all over the world since World War I. Actually, Tipperary is *not* so far to go, considering that, as Ireland's biggest inland county, it's within easy striking distance of Waterford and Cork. Moving in from the coastline, you can travel through some of Ireland's most lush pasturelands and to some of its most romantic sights, such as Lismore Castle. The Blackwater Valley is renowned for its beauty, peacefulness, and excellent fishing. Some of the finest racehorses in the world are raised in the fields of Tipperary, which is also the county where you can find the Rock of Cashel—the greatest group of monastic ruins in all Ireland.

Lismore

39 *40 km (25 mi) northwest of Ardmore on N72 and R671.*

Fodor'sChoice
★

Popular with both anglers and romantics, the enchanting little town of Lismore is built on the banks of the Blackwater, a river famous for its trout and salmon. From the 7th to the 12th century it was an important monastic center, founded by St. Carthac (or Carthage), and it had one of the most renowned universities of its time. The village has two cathedrals; a Roman Catholic one from the late 19th century and the Church of Ireland St. Carthage's, which dates from 1633 and incorporates fragments of an earlier church. Glamour arrived in the form of the dukes of Devonshire, who built their Irish seat here (their main house is Chatsworth in England); in the 1940s, Fred Astaire, whose sister, Adele, had married Lord Charles Cavendish, younger son of the ninth duke, would bend the elbow at the town's Madden's Pub. There were darker interludes to the town's history: Lismore was hard hit by the Great Famine of 1845 and its Famine Graveyard bears poignant witness.

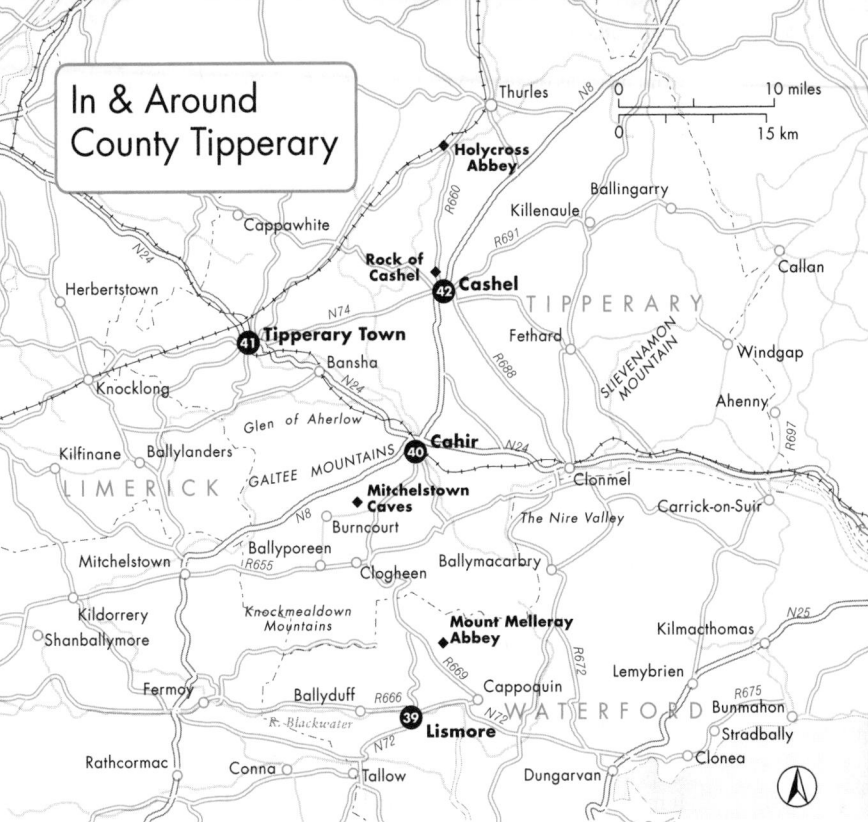

As you cross the bridge entering Lismore, take in the dramatic view of the magnificent **Lismore Castle**, a vast, turreted gray-stone building atop a rock that overhangs River Blackwater. There has been a castle here since the 12th century, but the present structure, built by the sixth duke of Devonshire, dates from the mid-19th century. Today, the house remains the Irish estate of the current duke and duchess and is not open to the public (although you can call it your own for a very posh rental fee). But the upper and lower gardens, which consist of woodland walks, including an unusual yew walk said to be more than 800 years old (Edmund Spencer is said to have written parts of *The Faerie Queen* there), are open during certain months of the year. Comprising 7 acres set with 17th-century defensive walls, the gardens have an impressive display of magnolias, camellias, and shrubs, and are adorned with examples of contemporary sculpture. ☎ *058/54424* ⊕ *www.lismorecastle. com* ✉ €6 ☉ *Apr., May, Sept., and Oct., daily 1:45–4:45; June–Aug., daily 11–4:45.*

Almost the definitive example in these Islands of an Estate town, Lismore has in recent years taken the firm decision to project a pride of place linked with a deep sense of history. The **Lismore Heritage Center**, housed in the former town courthouse, lies at the core of the town and exhibits focus on the town's Celtic origins and its links to many famous people from Sir Walter Raleigh to Prince Charles to Fred Astaire. An award-winning video presentation on the history of the town from its monastic 7th century origins up to the present day is shown. ⊠ *The Old Courthouse* ☎ *058/54975* ⊕ *www.discoverlismore.com* ✉ *€4* ☉ *Apr.–Sept., weekdays 9:30–5:30, Sat. 10–5:30, Sun. noon–5:30.*

Mount Melleray Abbey was the first post-Reformation monastery, founded in 1832 by the Cistercian Order in what was then a barren mountainside wilderness. Over the years the order has transformed the site into more than 600 acres of fertile farmland. The monks maintain strict vows of silence, but you're welcome to join in services throughout the day and are permitted into most areas of the abbey. It's also possible to stay in the guest lodge by prior arrangement. If you're heading into the Knockmealdown Mountains from Lismore, you can easily stop on the way at the abbey for a visit. ⊠ *South of Vee Gap, signposted off R669, 13 km (8 mi) from Lismore, Cappoquin* ☎ *058/54404* ⊕ *www. cappoquin.org/abbey.shtml* ✉ *Free* ☉ *Daily 8:30–5:45.*

Leaving Lismore, heading east on N72 for 6½ km (4 mi) toward Cappoquin, a well-known coarse-angling center, you can pick up R669 north into the **Knockmealdown Mountains.** Your route is signposted as the Vee Gap road, the Vee Gap being its summit, from where you'll have superb views of the Tipperary plain, the Galtee Mountains in the northwest, and a peak called Slievenamon in the northeast. If the day is clear, you should be able to see the Rock of Cashel, ancient seat of the kings of Munster, some 32 km (20 mi) away. Just before you enter the Vee Gap, look for a 6-foot-high mound of stones on the left side of the road. It marks the grave of Colonel Grubb, a local landowner who liked the view so much that he arranged to be buried here standing up so that he could look out over the scene for all eternity.

Where to Stay & Eat

$$–$$$$ ✕ **Buggy's Glencairn Inn.** Ken and Cathleen Buggy's country pub oozes character and welcomes patrons from all over the world. Here, God is in the details, from the cozy fires to the good food, and especially the genuine sense of hospitality. Ken's mantra—"when we say fresh, we mean it"—comes through in preparations of organic fowl and meat, and fish direct from Helvic head. Paté de campagne, smoked eel with horseradish sauce and salad, simple fish dishes cooked in butter and lemon, and pot-roasted guinea fowl issue from the kitchen, along with house-baked brown soda bread. Deserts run to fresh lime cake, homemade ice cream, and a farmhouse cheese selection that includes Durrus, Milleens, Carrigaline, Cashel Blue, and Dubliner. ⊠ *Glencairn, Co. Waterford* ☎ *058/ 56232* ⊕ *www.lismore.com* ⊟ *MC, V* ☉ *Closed Mon.*

★ $$–$$$ ✕⊡ **Richmond House.** It's been 300 years since the Earl of Cork and Burlington built this handsome country house and it still retains its imposing aura of courtly elegance. Today, happily, owners Claire and Paul Deevy give it a relaxed and welcoming touch. The public rooms, with log fires and traditional rust-and-cream decor, are reminiscent of a classic country hotel, although one graced with silver plate, a tapestry, and a stuffed owl. The pièce de résistance here, however, is the restaurant

($$$$), where Paul and his small staff wow critics and diners alike. Famous for his warm asparagus wrapped in smoked salmon, he prides himself on using local game in season and fish from Helvic, Dunmore, and Ardmore, adding his personal flair. Triumphs include wild Blackwater salmon with Thai spices, a spring roll with smoked duck breast, and rabbit with black pudding. Reservations are essential for the restaurant. ⊠ *Cappoquin, Co. Waterford* ☎ *058/54278* 🖷 *058/54988* ⊕ *www. richmondhouse.net* 🛏 *9 rooms* ⟐ *Restaurant, fishing, horseback riding, bar; no a/c* ▭ *AE, DC, MC, V* ⊗ *Closed late Dec.–mid-Jan.* ⊚| *BP.*

Cahir

⓾ *37 km (23 mi) north of Lismore, at crossroads of R668, N24, and N8.*

A pleasant Georgian square lies at the heart of this easygoing town, but **Cahir Castle** remains the unavoidable focal point. Perched on a rocky island on the River Suir, it's one of Ireland's largest and best-preserved castles, retaining its dramatic keep, tower, and much of its original defensive structure. An audiovisual show and guided tour are available upon request. ☎ *052/41011* ⊕ *www.heritageireland.ie* 🖷 *€2.90* ⊗ *Mid-Mar.–mid-June and mid-Sept.–mid-Oct., daily 9:30–5:30; mid-June–mid-Sept., daily 9–7; mid-Oct.–mid-Mar., daily 9:30–4:30; last admission 45 min before closing.*

If there's little storybook allure to the brute mass of Cahir Castle, fairytale looks grace the first earl of Glengall's 1812 **Swiss Cottage,** a dreamy relic from the days when Romanticism conquered 19th-century Ireland. A mile south of town on a particularly picturesque stretch of the River Suir, this "cottage orné" was probably designed by John Nash, one of the Regency period's most fashionable architects. Half thatched-roof cottage, half mansion, bordered by verandas constructed of branched trees, it was a veritable theater set that allowed the lordly couple to fantasize about being "simple folk" (down to the fact that secret doorways were constructed to allow servants to bring drinks and food without being noticed). Inside, some of the earliest Dufour wallpapers printed in Paris charm the eye. The Cottage is signposted from the R670 along the Cahir to Ardfinnan road, or you can hike from Cahir Castle on a footpath along the enchanting river. In peak season, crowds can be fierce. ☎ *052/41144* ⊕ *www.heritageireland.ie* 🖷 *€2.75* ⊗ *Mid-Mar.–mid-Apr., Tues.–Sun. 10–1 and 2–6; Mid-Apr.–mid-Oct., daily 10–6; mid-Oct.–mid-Nov., Tues.–Sun. 10–1 and 2–4:30.*

FodorśChoice ★

Where to Stay

$ ▦ **Bansha Castle.** Venture into the heart of quiet, wooded country backed by the Glen of Aherlow, about 8 km (5 mi) from Cahir on the N24 Tipperary road, to this 18th-century stone house with a Norman-style round tower. Large rooms, all with great views, are simply furnished with plain carpets and mahogany reproduction pieces, but walls are decorated in strong, vibrant colors. The drawing room has marble fireplaces, polished wooden floors, and floral patterned furniture. Locally grown organic produce is used in the good home cooking. Dinner ($$, guests only) should be booked in advance. Outdoor activities, such as walking, golfing, salmon and trout fishing, and horseback riding, are nearby. ✉ *Bansha, Co. Tipperary* ☎ *062/54187* 🖷 *062/54294* ⬎ *7 rooms* ⚱ *Dining room; no a/c, no room TVs* ▭ *No credit cards* ⦿ *BP.*

Tipperary Town

④ *22 km (14 mi) northwest of Cahir on N24.*

Tipperary Town, a dairy-farming center at the head of a fertile plain known as the Golden Vale, is a good starting point for climbing and walking in the hills around the Glen of Aherlow; but the small country town, on the River Ara, is worth visiting in its own right. In New Tipperary, a neighborhood built by local tenants during Ireland's Land War (1890–91), buildings such as Dalton's Heritage House have been restored; you can visit the Heritage House by calling the offices of Clann na hEireann. You can also visit the old Butter Market on Dillon Street; the Churchwell at the junction of Church, Emmet, and Dillon streets; and the grave of the grandfather of Robert Emmett—one of the most famous Irish patriots—in the graveyard at St. Mary's Church. A statue of Charles Kickham, whose 19th-century novel *The Homes of Tipperary* chronicled the devastation of this county through forced emigration, has a place of honor in the center of town. Adjacent to Bridewell Jail on St. Michael's Street is St. Michael's Church, with its stained-glass window depicting a soldier killed during World War I. The **headquarters of Clann na hEireann** (✉ 45 Main St. ☎ 062/33188) researches the origins and history of surnames throughout Ireland, and promotes clan gatherings.

Cashel

④ *17 km (11 mi) northeast of Tipperary Town on N74.*

Cashel is a market town on the busy Cork–Dublin road, with a lengthy history as a center of royal and religious power. From roughly AD 370 until 1101, it was the seat of the kings of Munster, and it was probably at one time a center of Druidic worship. Here, according to legend, St. Patrick arrived in about AD 432 and baptized King Aengus, who became Ireland's first Christian ruler. One of the many legends associated with this event is that St. Patrick plucked a shamrock to explain the mystery of the Trinity, thus giving a new emblem to Christian Ireland. The awe-inspiring, oft-mist-shrouded **Rock of Cashel** is one of Ireland's most visited sites. For complete information, see "Towering Glory: The Rock of Cashel" in this chapter.

Fodor'sChoice ★

In the same building as the town TIO, the **Cashel of the Kings Heritage Center** explains the historic relationship between the town and the Rock and includes a scale model of Cashel as it looked during the 1600s. ✉ *City Hall, Main St.* ☎ *062/62511* ⊕ *www.heritagetowns.com/cashel.html* ⊡ *Free* ☉ *Daily 9:30–5:50.*

The **G. P. A. Bolton Library**, on the grounds of the St. John the Baptist Church of Ireland Cathedral, has a particularly fine collection of rare books, manuscripts, and maps, some of which date from the beginning of the age of printing in Europe. ⊠ *John St.* ☎ *062/61944* ✉ €2 ⊙ *Daily 10–4.*

Where to Stay & Eat

★ **$$–$$$$**   ╳ **Chez Hans.** It's rather fitting that this restaurant is housed in a converted church as it's become something of a foodies' shrine. Gourmands travel from Dublin and Cork to get their fix of chef Jason Matthia's cuisine, which is contemporary with a hint of nouvelle. He works wonders with fresh Irish ingredients, especially seafood—go for the salmon, hake, or mussels served in a light chive velouté. Another specialty is diced lamb with ratatouille and couscous. The atmosphere is wonderful, too, with dark-wood decor and tapestries providing an elegant background for the white-linen tables. ⊠ *Rockside* ☎ *062/61177* ⚓ *Reservations essential* ▤ *AE, DC, MC, V* ⊙ *Closed Sun. and Mon. and late Jan.–early Feb. No lunch.*

★ **$$$–$$$$**   ╳▥ **Cashel Palace.** Built in 1730 for archbishop Theophilus Bolton, this grand house truly is a palace in every sense. It was designed by Sir Edward Lovett Pearce, who also created the Old Parliament House in Dublin—and is gorgeously offset by a parkland replete with fountains and centuries-old trees. Inside, red-pine paneling, barley-sugar staircases, Corinthian columns, and a surfeit of cosseting antiques all create an air of Georgian volupté. Guest rooms on the second floor are cozier, though not small. The Bishop's Buttery restaurant ($$–$$$$) relies on game in season, local lamb and beef, and fresh fish creatively prepared, and also serves simple, light meals all day. Don't miss the lovely gardens at the rear of the house, where you can see the descendants of the original hop plants used by Richard Guinis to brew the first "Wine of Ireland." Guinis went on, with his son, Arthur, to found the Guinness Brewery in Dublin. ⊠ *Main St., Co. Tipperary* ☎ *062/62707* 🖷 *062/61521* ⊕ *www. cashel-palace.ie* ⇥ *23 rooms* ⚲ *2 restaurants, fishing, bar; no a/c* ▤ *AE, DC, MC, V* ⦿ *BP.*

$$ ▥ **Dundrum House Hotel.** Nestled beside the River Multeen, 12 km (7½ mi) outside busy Cashel, is this imposing, four-story Georgian house. Sixteen high-ceiling bedrooms take up the main house; the rest are in a three-story wing built during the house's previous incarnation as a convent. Although highly renovated, many of the older rooms have accent pieces of early-Victorian furniture. A big plus: lovely views of the surrounding parkland. The old convent chapel, stained-glass windows intact, is now a cocktail bar. Elaborate plaster ceilings, attractive period furniture, and open fires make the spacious dining room and lounge inviting. ⊠ *Dundrum, Co. Tipperary* ☎ *062/71116* 🖷 *062/71366* ⊕ *www. dundrumhousehotel.com* ⇥ *85 rooms* ⚲ *2 restaurants, 18-hole golf course, pool, gym, sauna, steam room, fishing, 3 bars; no a/c* ▤ *AE, DC, MC, V* ⦿ *BP.*

Nightlife & the Arts

You can enjoy folksinging, storytelling, and dancing from mid-June through September, Tuesday through Saturday, at the **Bru Boru Center** (☎ 062/61122) at the foot of the Rock of Cashel. Entertainment usually begins at 9 PM and costs €15, €40 with dinner.

TOWERING GLORY: THE ROCK OF CASHEL

Haunt of St. Patrick, Ireland's "rock of ages" is a place where history, culture, and legend collide

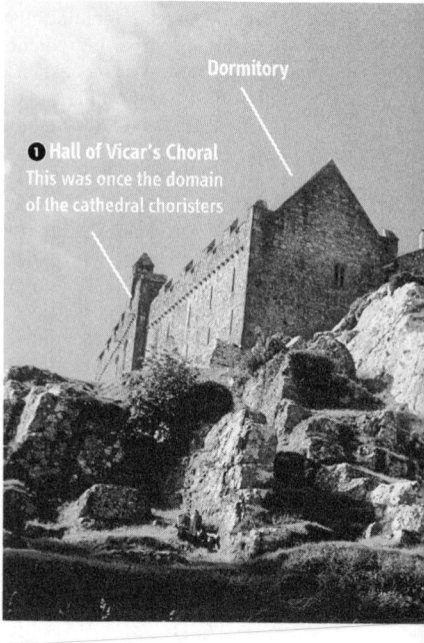

Dormitory

❶ Hall of Vicar's Choral This was once the domain of the cathedral choristers

Seat of the Kings of Munster and the hallowed spot where St. Patrick first plucked a shamrock to explain the mystery of the Trinity, the Rock of Cashel is Ireland's greatest group of ecclesiastical ruins. Standing like an ominous beacon in the middle of a sloped, treeless valley, the Rock's titanic grandeur and majesty creates what one ancient scribe called "a fingerpost to Heaven."

Historians theorize the stupendous mass was born during the Ice Age. This being Ireland, however, fulsome myths abound: There are those who believe it was created when the Devil himself took a huge bite of the Slieve Bloom Mountains only to spit it out right in the middle of the Golden Vale. Today, the great limestone mass still rises 300 feet to command a panorama over all it surveys—fittingly, the name derives from the Irish *caiseal*, meaning stone fort, and this gives a good idea of the strategic importance of Cashel in days of yore.

For centuries, Cashel was known as the "city of the kings"—from the 5th century, the lords of Munster ruled over much of southern Ireland from here. In 1101, however, they handed Cashel over to the Christian fathers, and the rock soon became the center of the reform movement that reshaped the Irish Church. Along the way, the church fathers embarked on a centuries-long building campaign that resulted in the magnificent group of chapels, round towers, and walls you see at Cashel today. View them from afar on the N8 highway and the complex looks so complete you're surprised upon arriving to discover guides in modern dress and not knights in medieval uniform.

■ TIP➔ The best approach to the rock is along the Bishop's Walk, a 10-minute hike that begins outside the drawing room of the Cashel Palace hotel on Main Street in the town of Cashel, just to the south of the rock.

Southeastern View of the Rock

❷ **Cormac's Chapel**
The finest example of Hiberno-
Romanesque architecture

❸ **The Choir**
Look for the noted Tomb
of Myler McGrath

4

TOWERING GLORY: THE ROCK OF CASHEL

Bishop's
Castle

Nave

St. Patrick's
Cathedral

South
Transept

Tickets

Dormitory

❼
❹
❺
❸
❷
❻
❶

❶ HALL OF THE VICAR'S CHORAL

Built in the 15th century—though topped with a
modern reconstruction of a beautifully corbeled
medieval ceiling—this was once the domain of
the cathedral choristers.

The Museum Located in the hall's undercroft,
this collection includes the original St. Patrick's
Cross and fast-forwards you to the present
thanks to a striking audiovisual display on the
Rock entitled the "Stronghold of the Faith."

❷ CORMAC'S CHAPEL

The real showpiece of Cashel is this chapel,
built in 1127 by Cormac McCarthy, King of
Desmond and Bishop of Cashel. A rare jewel
in gleaming red sandstone, it is the finest
example of Hiberno-Romanesque
architecture. The entry archway carries a

tympanum featuring a centaur in a helmet
with a bow and arrow aimed at a lion,
perhaps a symbol of good over evil. Such
work was rare in Irish architecture and points
to possible European influence. Preserved
within the chapel is a splendid but broken
sarcophagus, once believed to be Cormac's
final resting place. At the opposite end of the
chapel is the nave, where you can look for
wonderful medieval paintings now showing
through old plasterwork.

ST. PATRICK'S CATHEDRAL

With thick walls that attest to its origin as a fortress, this now roofless cathedral is the largest building on the site. Built in 1169, it was dedicated on March 17th–St. Patrick's Day. On the theory that ancient churches were oriented to the sunrise on the feast day of their dedicated saint, the cathedral points east, a direction agreeing closely with March 17th. The original cathedral, constructed in a flamboyant variation on Irish Romanesque style, was destroyed by fire in 1495. In ❸ **The Choir**, look for the noted Tomb of Myler McGrath. Note the tombs in the ❹ **North Transept** whose carvings–of the apostles, other saints, and the Beasts of the Apocalypse–are remarkably detailed. The octagonal staircase turret that ascends the cathedral's central tower leads to a series of defensive passages built into the thick walls–

St. Patrick's Cathedral

from the top of the tower, you'll have wonderful views. At the center of the cathedral is the area known as ❺ **The Crossing**, a magnificently detailed arch where the four sections of the building come together.

COMING OF AGE

450 AD–St. Patrick comes to Cashel, bringing the advent of Christianity when King Aengus accepts baptism from Ireland's patron saint.

King Brian Boru

990–Cashel is fortified by King Brian Boru, the legendary figure who broke the stranglehold of the Danes at the Battle of Clontarf in 1014.

1101–King Murtagh O'Brien, grandson of Brian Boru, proclaims the royal fortress "for God, St. Patrick, and St. Ailbe," making Cashel center of the Irish Church.

1317–The arrival of the Scots: Edward Bruce, brother of Robert I, is inaugurated king of Ireland, and attends Mass on the Rock where he later holds a parliament.

1749–Protestant archbishop Price earns undying infamy by pulling down the roof of the cathedral to rebuild his own church.

❼ Round Tower
As the oldest building on the Rock, the Round Tower rises 92 feet.

❹ North Transept

❻ST. PATRICK'S CROSS

Directly beyond the Rock's main entrance is this 7-foot-tall High Cross carved from one large block and resting upon what is said to have been the original coronation stone of the Munster kings. The cross was erected in the saint's honor to commemorate his famous visit to Cashel in 450. Upon both sides carved in high relief are two figures—the face of Christ crucified and a robed St. Patrick with his feet resting upon an ox head. Unique among High Crosses, this one has vertical supports on either side, perhaps allusions to the crosses of the good and bad thieves. A sort of early Irish bible class, these large stone crosses (which were sculpted from the 9th to the 12th centuries) were perfect teaching tools for a population that was largely illiterate. This cross is a faithfully rendered replica—the original now rests in the site museum.

❼THE ROUND TOWER

As the oldest building on the Rock, the Round Tower rises 92 feet to command a panoramic view of the entire Vale of Tipperary. Dating back to 995, its construction followed the grim reality of the Viking invasions. A constant lookout was posted here to warn of any advancing armies and food was always provisioned in the tower so as to outlast any prolonged siege. Note the door 10 feet from the ground, allowing ladders to be pulled up to thwart attackers, some of whom attempted to chip the rock at the base, with little effect.

4

TOWERING GLORY: THE ROCK OF CASHEL

Central Tower   Bishop's Castle

❺ The Crossing   Nave

Northern View of the Rock

THE ST. PATRICK CONNECTION

Baptism, St. Paddy Style

Set in front of the Archbishop's Castle, the Rock of Cashel's famed 12th-century St. Patrick's Cross reputedly marks the spot where St. Patrick made a breakthrough in his conversion of Ireland by baptising King Aengus and his son in 450. During the baptism, Patrick accidentally stuck his crozier through Aengus's foot. Asked why he did not cry out, the king said he thought the pain was part of the initiation ceremony.

Enduring a crozier point in his foot without protest gives some notion of the bravery of King Aengus, a royal patron who played a crucial part in St. Patrick's mission. While no records exist, a close bond clearly grew between king and saint—the pair spoke for hours walking around Cashel's grounds. The young king provided the financial assistance for many of the churches St. Patrick founded over the 11 years he remained in Munster. Such acceptance by a king opened many doors that might otherwise have remained firmly shut for Patrick.

Properly known as St. Patrick's Rock, Cashel has many fabled associations with Ireland's patron saint.

Shamrocks & Snakes

Before converting King Aengus, St. Patrick picked a shamrock on the Rock of Cashel, and used it to explain the mystery of the Holy Trinity, three Gods in One, a central tenet of Christianity, to him. The other famous myth associated with St. Patrick is the banishment of the snakes from Ireland, who fled when St. Patrick rang his bell at the end of his 40-day fast on Croaghpatrick in County Mayo. Of course, the island of Ireland, being cut off from the European mainland, never had any snakes in the first place . . . but why ruin a good story?

But Who Was St. Patrick?

While many legends surround this saint, he was an actual historical figure—his writings, a Latin text dating from the 5th century AD, yield the few undoubted facts about him. Born into a wealthy family in Roman-occupied Britain, he was kidnapped as a young man by Irish marauders and enslaved for six years as a sheepherder on the slopes of Slemish in County Antrim. He escaped, and returned to Britain, but a vision called him back to Ireland to convert the people to Christianity. Arriving in 433, he defied the pagan priests of Tara by kindling the Easter fire on Slane but went on in a peaceful conversion of Ireland to Christianity—not a drop of blood was shed—until his death in AD 460.

St. Patrick's conversion of Ireland was characterized by clever diplomacy: his missionaries were careful to combine elements of then-current druidic ritual with new Christian practice. For example, the Irish Christian church popularized the Feast of all Saints, and arranged for it to be celebrated on November 1, the same day as the great Celtic harvest festival, Samhain. Today's Halloween evolved from this linking of Celtic and Christian holidays.

Clearly a skilled negotiator as well as missionary, St. Patrick wisely preserved the social structure of Ireland, converting the people tribe by tribe. He first attempted to establish the Roman system of dioceses and bishops, but—since Ireland had never been conquered by the Romans—this arrangement did not suit a society without large cities. Instead, the Celts preferred a religious institution introduced by the desert fathers: the monastery, an idea of a "family" of monks being easy to grasp in a tribal society where kinship ties were

strong. Over 70 monasteries were founded in the 5th and 6th centuries, and by AD 700 abbots had replaced bishops as the leaders of the Catholic church.

In 457 St. Patrick retired to Saul, where he died. The only relic that can be tied to him is the famous 5th century iron bell in Dublin's National Museum. Even if it was not, as is traditionally believed, used by the saint, he carried one very like it, and used it to announce his approach.

4

TOWERING GLORY: THE ROCK OF CASHEL

St. Patrick stepping on a snake.

Sports

GAELIC FOOTBALL & HURLING About 20 km (12 mi) north of Cashel, **Semple GAA Stadium** (⊠ Thurles ☎ 0504/22702 ⊕ www.gaa.ie) is where major hurling and Gaelic football championships in the Southeast take place, as well as many exciting minor contests.

GOLF The natural features of the mature Georgian estate at Dundrum House Hotel have been incorporated into an 18-hole, par-72 course for the **County Tipperary Golf and Country Club** (⊠ Dundrum House Hotel, Dundrum ☎ 062/71717).

SOUTHEAST ESSENTIALS

To research prices, get advice from other travelers, and book travel arrangements, visit www.fodors.com.

Transportation

If traveling extensively by public transportation, be sure to load up on information (schedules, the best taxi-for-call companies, etc.) upon arriving at the ticket counter or help desk of the bigger train and bus stations in the area, such as Kilkenny City, Wexford Town, and Waterford City.

BY AIR

Aer Arann flies once daily in both directions between Waterford City and London's Luton Airport. There are also flights three times per week to Manchester.

🛪 Carrier **Aer Arann** ☎ 1890/462-726 ⊕ www.aerarann.ie.

AIRPORT

Waterford Regional Airport is on the Waterford–Ballymacaw road in Killowen. Waterford City is less than 10 km (6 mi) from the airport. A hackney cab from the airport into Waterford City costs approximately €15.

🛪 Airport Information **Waterford Regional Airport** ☎ 051/875-589 ⊕ www. flywaterford.com.

BY BOAT & FERRY

The region's primary ferry terminal is just south of Wexford Town at Rosslare. Irish Ferries connects Rosslare to Pembroke, Wales, and France's Cherbourg and Roscoff. Stenaline sails directly between Rosslare Ferryport and Fishguard, Wales.

🛥 Boat & Ferry Information **Irish Ferries** ☎ 053/33158 or 0818/300-400 ⊕ www. irishferries.com. **Stenaline** ☎ 053/61590 ⊕ www.stenaline.ie.

BY BUS

Bus Éireann makes the Waterford–Dublin journey 10 times a day for about €11 one way and return €16. There are six buses daily between Waterford City and Limerick, and four between Waterford City and Rosslare. The Cork–Waterford bus runs 13 times a day. In Waterford City, the terminal is Waterford Bus Station.

🚌 Bus Information **Bus Éireann** ☎ 01/836-6111 in Dublin, 051/879-000 in Waterford ⊕ www.buseireann.ie.

BY CAR

Waterford City, the regional capital, is easily accessible from all parts of Ireland. From Dublin, take N7 southwest, change to N9 in Naas, and continue along this highway through Carlow Town and Thomastown until it terminates in Waterford. N25 travels east–west through Waterford City, connecting it with Cork in the west and Wexford Town in the east. From Limerick and Tipperary Town, N24 stretches southeast until it, too, ends in Waterford City.

ROAD CONDITIONS For the most part, the main roads in the Southeast are of good quality and are free of congestion. Side roads are generally narrow and twisting, and you should keep an eye out for farm machinery and animals on country roads.

BY TRAIN

Waterford City is linked by Irish Rail service to Dublin. Trains run from Plunkett Station in Waterford City to Dublin four times daily, making stops at Thomastown, Kilkenny, Bagenalstown, and Carlow Town. The daily train between Waterford City and Limerick makes stops at Carrick-on-Suir, Clonmel, Cahir, and Tipperary Town. The train between Rosslare and Waterford City runs twice daily.

🚆 Train Information **Irish Rail** ☎ 01/836-6222 in Dublin, 051/873-401 in Waterford ⊕ www.irishrail.ie/home.

Contacts & Resources

CAR RENTAL

The major car-rental companies have offices at Rosslare Ferryport, and in most large towns rental information is available through the local tourism office. Typical car-rental prices start at about €55 per day (€32 per day for seven days) with unlimited mileage, and they usually include insurance and all taxes. Budget has offices in Rosslare Harbor and at Waterford Airport. Hertz has offices in Rosslare Harbor.

🚗 Agencies **Budget** ✉ The Ferryport, Rosslare Harbor ☎ 053/33318 ✉ Waterford Airport ☎ 051/421-670. **Hertz** ✉ The Ferryport, Rosslare Harbor ☎ 053/33238.

EMERGENCIES

🚑 Emergency Services **Ambulance, fire, police** ☎ 112 or 999.
🏥 Hospital **Waterford Regional Hospital** ✉ Ardkeen ☎ 051/848-000.

INTERNET CAFÉS

Even though much of Ireland has gone Wi-Fi over the past two years, in some of the more rural regions you'll need to rely on the local Internet café to catch up on messages from home. As well as good places to find a decent cup of java, they are generally quite cheap; expect to pay around €2 an hour.

🔢 Internet Access **I.O. Internet** ✉ 5 Cornmarket, Wexford Town ☎ 053/23729. **Voyager Internet Café** ✉ 85 The Quay, Waterford City ☎ 051/843-843.

TOUR OPTIONS

Irish City Tours in Kilkenny operates open-top coach tours from the castle gate Easter through September, daily 10:30–5.

Burtchaell Tours in Waterford City leads a Waterford walk at noon and 2 PM daily from March through September. Tours depart from the Granville Hotel. Walking tours of Kilkenny are arranged by Tynan Tours from the Kilkenny TIO; tours take place daily April through October, and Tuesday through Saturday, November to March. Walking tours of historic Wexford Town can be prebooked for groups by contacting Seamus P. Molloy of Wexford Town Walking Tours.

🔢 Bus Tour **Irish City Tours** ☎ 01/458-0054.

🔢 Walking Tours **Burtchaell Tours** ☎ 051/873-711. **Tynan Tours** ☎ 087/265-1745. **Wexford Town Walking Tours** ☎ 053/22663.

VISITOR INFORMATION

Eight Tourist Information Offices (TIOs) in the Southeast are open all year. They are Carlow Town, Dungarvan, Enniscorthy, Gorey, Kilkenny, Lismore, Waterford City, and Wexford Town. Another seven TIOs are open seasonally: Ardmore (June–mid-September); Cahir (May–September); Cashel (April–September); New Ross (May–September); Rosslare (April–September); Tipperary Town (May–October); Tramore (June–August).

🔢 Tourist Information **Ardmore** ✉ Co. Waterford ☎ 024/94444. **Cahir** ✉ Castle Car Park, Co. Tipperary ☎ 052/41453. **Carlow Town** ✉ College St., Co. Carlow ☎ 059/913-1554. **Cashel** ✉ Cashel Heritage Centre, Co. Tipperary ☎ 062/62511. **Dungarvan** ✉ The Courthouse, Co. Waterford ☎ 058/41741. **Enniscorthy** ✉ Wexford Museum, The Castle, Castle Hill, Co. Wexford ☎ 054/34699. **Gorey** ✉ Markethouse, Main St., Co. Wexford ☎ 055/21248. **Kilkenny** ✉ Shee Alms House, Rose Inn St., Co. Kilkenny ☎ 056/775-1500. **Lismore** ✉ Heritage Centre, Co. Waterford ☎ 058/54975. **New Ross** ✉ Harbour Centre, The Quay, Co. Wexford ☎ 051/421-857. **Rosslare** ✉ Rosslare Ferry Terminal, Kilrane, Rosslare Harbor, Co. Wexford ☎ 053/33232. **Tipperary Town** ✉ 3 Mitchel St., Co. Tipperary ☎ 062/51457. **Tramore** ✉ Town Centre, Co. Waterford ☎ 051/381-572. **Waterford City** ✉ 41 The Quay, Co. Waterford ☎ 051/875-823 ⊕ www.southeastireland.com. **Wexford Town** ✉ Crescent Quay, Co. Wexford ☎ 053/23111.

The Southwest

INCLUDING COUNTIES CORK, KERRY,
LIMERICK AND CLARE

Gallarus Oratory on the Dingle Peninsula, County Kerry

WORD OF MOUTH

"I adore Cork—both the county and the city. The people are extremely friendly, the countryside is gorgeous, there are great places to eat, some decent clubs, excellent chippers for late-night snacking, and the Cork accent is absolutely delightful. Blarney, Kinsale, Clonakilty—what more can you ask for?"

—SAM

WELCOME TO THE SOUTHWEST

TOP REASONS TO GO

★ **Blarney Castle:** Visitors line up to kiss the Blarney Stone and acquire the gift of gab. Kissing aside, this is an impressive 15th-century tower-house castle with unusual gardens, at their best in daffodil season—early to mid-March.

Blarney Castle

★ **Kinsale:** This picturesque port, long a favored haven of sailors, is famed for its fine dining in tiny front-parlor eateries. It's also a chic place to see and be seen—the Irish San Tropez.

★ **The Cork Coastline:** On the drive from Kinsale to Skibbereen you'll encounter friendly locals, charming little villages, unspoiled scenery, and excellent restaurants and pubs.

★ **The Gap of Dunloe:** A half-day tour lets you walk or ride horseback through Killarney's purple mountains and cross the glittering blue lake by row boat.

★ **Skellig Michael:** The rocky, twin-peaked island looms offshore as you follow the Ring of Kerry, beckoning you to visit.

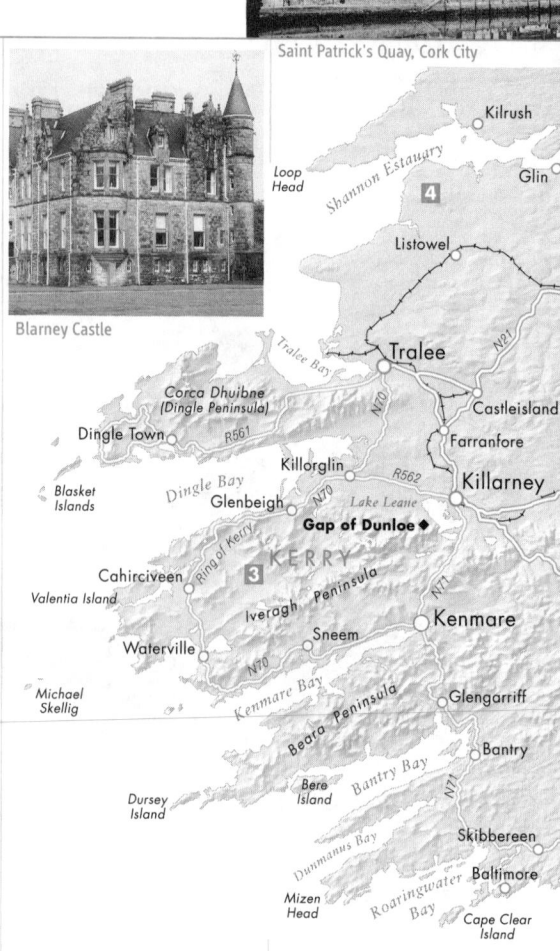

1 **Cork City.** Identifying Cork as Ireland's second-largest city is misleading—it has just a 10th the population of Dublin, and its character is more along the lines of a college town (which it is) than a metropolis. That means lively pubs, quirky cafés, and lots of good music, trad and otherwise.

2 **County Cork.** South of Cork City, the resort town of **Kinsale** is the gateway to a rocky, attractive coastline containing **Roaring Water Bay** and the wide, magnificent **Bantry Bay.** To the north of the city, some of the best salmon fishing in the world is to be had on the peaceful **Blackwater River.**

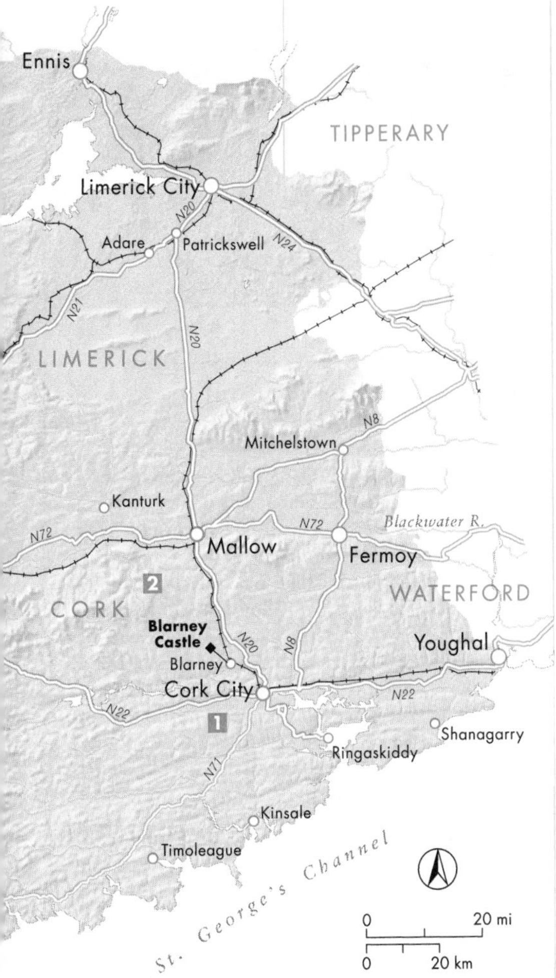

GETTING ORIENTED

In the Southwest, five-star scenery is everywhere. This is Ireland's picture-postcard country, from Kinsale on the south coast of County Cork, across Bantry Bay, inland to the mountains and lakes of Killarney, and out to Kerry's craggy western peninsulas. Brightly painted villages and small harbors encourage you to stop and linger—and when you do, you're rewarded with exceptional food, particularly in Kinsale and Kenmare, towns that vie for the title of Ireland's culinary capital. Off the western coast, the Skelligs rank as the region's most awesome sight, though it takes an often choppy boat ride to reach them.

5

3 County Kerry. The county's coast is formed by the **Iveragh Peninsula** (home to the **Ring of Kerry**), and **Corca Dhuibne** (a.k.a. **Dingle Peninsula**); both are among the most beautiful places in Ireland. **Killarney's** blue lakes and sandstone mountains, inland from the peninsulas, have a unique and romantic splendor.

4 Shannon Estuary. Along the mouth of Ireland's greatest river is "castle country," an area dotted with ruined castles and abbeys, the result of Elizabeth I's 16th-century attempt to subdue the province of Munster. **Limerick City**, too, bears the scars of history, from a different confrontation with the English—the 1691 Siege of Limerick.

Dingle Peninsula

THE SOUTHWEST PLANNER

Getting Around

Scenery is the main attraction in the Southwest, and unless you're a biker or hiker, the best option for taking it in is to rent a car. Once behind the wheel, plan to adopt the local pace—which is slow. Covering about 60 miles a day is ideal, with many stops along the way. Speed is dictated to some degree by the roads: most are small, with one lane in each direction and plenty of bends and hills.

Without a car, your best bet is to base yourself in Cork or Killarney, both accessible by train from Dublin, and take organized day trips or use the local buses (where available) from there.

For the details about getting around, *see* "Transportation" *in* the Essentials section at the end of this chapter.

Stone Circle, County Cork

Making the Most of Your Time

If you're here for a short stay—three days or fewer—you'd do well to base yourself in **Killarney** and devote your time to exploring the surrounding area, then heading out to the **Ring of Kerry** or the **Dingle Peninsula**. With more time at your disposal, spend a day driving through **Kenmare** to **Glengarriff** on the famous tunnel road, and take a boat out to **Illnacullin** (Garnish Island). Other highlights are the drive from **Kinsale** to the **Mizen Head** along the coast of West Cork; elegant **Glin Castle** on the Shannon Estuary; **Adare**, one of Ireland's prettiest villages; and the magnificently restored **Bunratty Castle**. Though the scenery is the top draw in the Southwest, **Cork City** is good for a day or two of urban fun, topped off with a visit to nearby **Blarney Castle.**

PICKING A PENINSULA

Two of Ireland's most scenic destinations sit side by side on the map: the Iveragh Peninsula (also known as the Ring of Kerry, for its scenic drive), and the Dingle Peninsula (also known by its Irish name, Corca Dhuibne). If you like wild, rugged scenery, archaeological remains, and Irish music, Dingle is for you. The most scenic part of the peninsula is at its tip, to the west of An Daingean/Dingle Town. The town itself is a lively spot, with craft shops, restaurants, and music bars. In contrast, the Ring of Kerry is a longer drive with more varied scenery, ranging from lush subtropical vegetation between Kenmare and Sneem, to rocky coves at Caherdaniel, and long sandy beaches near Glenbeigh. The scenery is punctuated by a series of small villages, all much quieter than Dingle.

Husseys Folly located near Dingle Bay

What to Bring Home

Locally made ceramics, knitwear, and jewelry can be found in the region's crafts shops, but it's also worth stopping to investigate signposts on the road directing you to the studios of the craftspeople themselves. Between Youghal and Midleton you can follow a "crafts trail" known as **East Cork Creates** (☎ 021/463–4758) that runs past 15 studios.

Where to Eat & Where to Stay

The Southwest is a great place for good food. County Cork in particular has become Ireland's top foodie destination. Adventurous, well-traveled chefs make the most of the first-rate local specialties: succulent meats, fresh seafood, and farmhouse cheeses.

For another kind of dining experience, check out the medieval banquets at Bunratty and Knappogue castles, near Shannon—they're an undeniably touristy good time.

For accommodations, the Southwest has some of the great country houses, including Longueville House on the Blackwater River in County Cork, Adare Manor in County Limerick, the Park Hotel Kenmare, and the Sheen Falls Lodge, also in Kenmare.

At the other spectrum is the uniquely Irish experience of a farmhouse B & B, such as Ballymakeigh House, near Youghal, where you can watch the cows coming home as you breakfast. In between is a range of excellent family-owned and -run traditional hotels, such as the Seaview in Ballylickey on Bantry Bay, The Butler Arms in Waterville, and the secluded Caragh Lodge near Killorglin.

How's the Weather?

The best times to visit the Southwest are mid-March to June, and September and October. In July and August it's the peak holiday period, meaning roads are more crowded, prices are higher, and the best places are booked up far in advance. March can be chilly, with daily temperatures averaging 40 and 50 degrees Fahrenheit. The average high in June is 65 degrees, which is about as hot as it gets. May and June are the sunniest months, May and September the driest. The further west you go, the more likely you'll get rain, but passing showers are much more common than daylong downpours. From November to March daylight hours are short, the weather damp, and many places close—attractions as well as restaurants and hotels.

Best Fests

■ Cork is known as Ireland's festival city, the longest-running being the **Cork Film Festival** in the second week in October, and the biggest the **Guinness Jazz Festival** on the last weekend in October.

■ The **West Cork Chamber Music Festival** brings internationally renowned musicians to perform in the intimate surroundings of the library of Bantry House for ten days in late June.

■ People come back year after year to the **Kinsale Festival of Fine Food,** which creates a party atmosphere all over town for the first weekend in October.

Dining & Lodging Price Categories (in Euros)					
	$$$$	**$$$**	**$$**	**$**	**¢**
Restaurants	over €32	€24–32	€18–24	€12–18	under €12
Hotels	over €280	€200–280	€140–200	€100–140	under €100

Restaurant prices are for a main course at dinner. Hotel prices are for a standard double room in high season.

Updated by
Alannah
Hopkin

CORK, KERRY, LIMERICK, AND CLARE—these southwest Ireland county names promise a rural idyll, miles and miles of pretty country lanes meandering though rich but sparsely populated farmland. The coast is a long, drawn-out highlight, from Kinsale west to Mizen Head in the far southwest corner of Cork, to the magical Ring of Kerry and the fabled Dingle Peninsula. Inland the glorious mountains and lakes of Killarney are famed for their wild beauty. Thanks to its accomplished chefs and the bounty of farms, lakes, and coast, County Cork has become a little paradise of fresh, rustic Irish cuisine. You'll also find a mild climate, Irish-speaking areas, and Ireland's second- and third-largest cities—Cork and Limerick. But it's the countryside that will make you want to linger. To be in a hurry here is to be ill-mannered. It was probably a Kerryman who first remarked that when God made time, he made plenty of it.

The Irish economic boom has been a mixed blessing. The southwest's main routes are no longer traffic-free, but the roads themselves are better. There's a greater choice of accommodations, with improved facilities, but many of the newer hotels and bed-and-breakfasts are short on character. Even the traditional warm Irish welcome is less ubiquitous, given the increased pace of everyday life.

Although the southwest has several sumptuous country-house hotels, it's basically an easygoing, unpretentious region, where informality and simplicity prevail. As in the rest of Ireland, social life revolves around the pub, and a visit to any neighborhood favorite is the best way to find out what's going on.

Exploring the Southwest

This chapter starts in Cork City and makes a clockwise sweep. It ends on the northern fringe of the region, crossing over the border from County Kerry into County Limerick and then briefly dipping into the southeastern reaches of County Clare in the area immediately around Shannon Airport. (If you're flying into Shannon, you may want to start with that section of the chapter and work your way backward.)

CORK CITY

254 km (158 mi) south of Dublin, 105 km (65 mi) south of Limerick City.

The major metropolis of the south, Cork is Ireland's second-largest city—but it runs a distant second, with a population of 175,000, roughly a tenth the size of Dublin. Cork is a spirited place, with a formidable pub culture, a lively traditional music scene, a respected and progressive university, attractive art galleries, and offbeat cafés. The city received a major boost in 2005 when it was named a Capital of Culture by the EU—the smallest city ever to receive the designation. The result was a burst in development; one of the lasting legacies is a striking but controversial redesign of the city center (Patrick Street and Grand Parade) by Barcelona-based architect Beth Gali.

In late summer and early autumn, the city hosts some of Ireland's premier festivals, including October's huge Cork Jazz Festival, which draws about 50,000 visitors from around the world, and the Cork Film Festival, also in October.

Exploring Cork City

"Cork is the loveliest city in the world. Anyone who does not agree with me either was not born there or is prejudiced." Whether Cork merits this accolade of native poet and writer Robert Gibbings, the city does have plenty to recommend it, including several noteworthy historic sites. They're spread out a bit, but still the best way to see the city is on foot. Patrick Street is the city center's main thoroughfare.

You can tour the center of the city, in a morning or an afternoon, depending on how much you plan to shop along the way. To really see everything, however, allow a full day, with a break for lunch at the Farmgate Café in the English Market. Also note that the Crawford Gallery and the English Market are closed on Sunday.

5

What to See

❶ Bishop Lucey Park. This tiny green park in the heart of the city opened in 1985 in celebration of the 800th anniversary of Cork's Norman charter. During its excavation, workers unearthed portions of the city's original fortified walls, now preserved just inside the arched entrance. Sculptures by contemporary Cork artists are found throughout the park. ⊠ *Grand Parade, Washington Village* ☞ *Free.*

❿ Cork City Gaol. This castlelike building contains an austere, 19th-century prison. Life-size figures occupy the cells, and sound effects illustrate the appalling conditions that prevailed here from the early 19th century through the founding of the Free State, after the 1916 Uprising. **The Radio Museum Experience** in the Governor's House tells the history of broadcasting in Cork, and features genuine artifacts from Cork's 1923 studio. ⊠ *Sunday's Well Rd., Sunday's Well* ☏ *021/430–5022* ⊕ *www.corkcitygaol.com* ☞ €6 ☾ *Nov.–Feb., daily 10–4; Mar.–Oct., daily 9:30–5.*

❻ Cork Opera House. It's an unattractive concrete hulk that went up in 1965 to replace an ornate and much-loved opera house that was ruined in a fire. Later attempts to integrate the opera house with its neighbor, the Crawford Municipal Art Gallery, have softened the grim facade. The piazza outside has sidewalk cafés and street performers. ⊠ *Lavitt's Quay, City Center South* ☏ *021/427–0022* ⊕ *www.corkoperahouse.ie.*

❹ Cork Vision Centre. This historical society, which is in an area that was once the bustling heart of medieval Cork, provides an excellent introduction to the city's geography and history. The highlight is a detailed 1:500 scale model of Cork, showing how it has grown and changed over the ages. ⊠ *N. Main St., Washington Village* ☏ *021/427–9925* ⊕ *www.corkvisioncentre.com* ☞ *Suggested donation. Guided tours of city model on request, €1.50* ☾ *Tues.–Sat. 10–5.*

❸ Court House. A landmark in the very center of Cork, this magnificent classical building has an imposing Corinthian portico and is still used

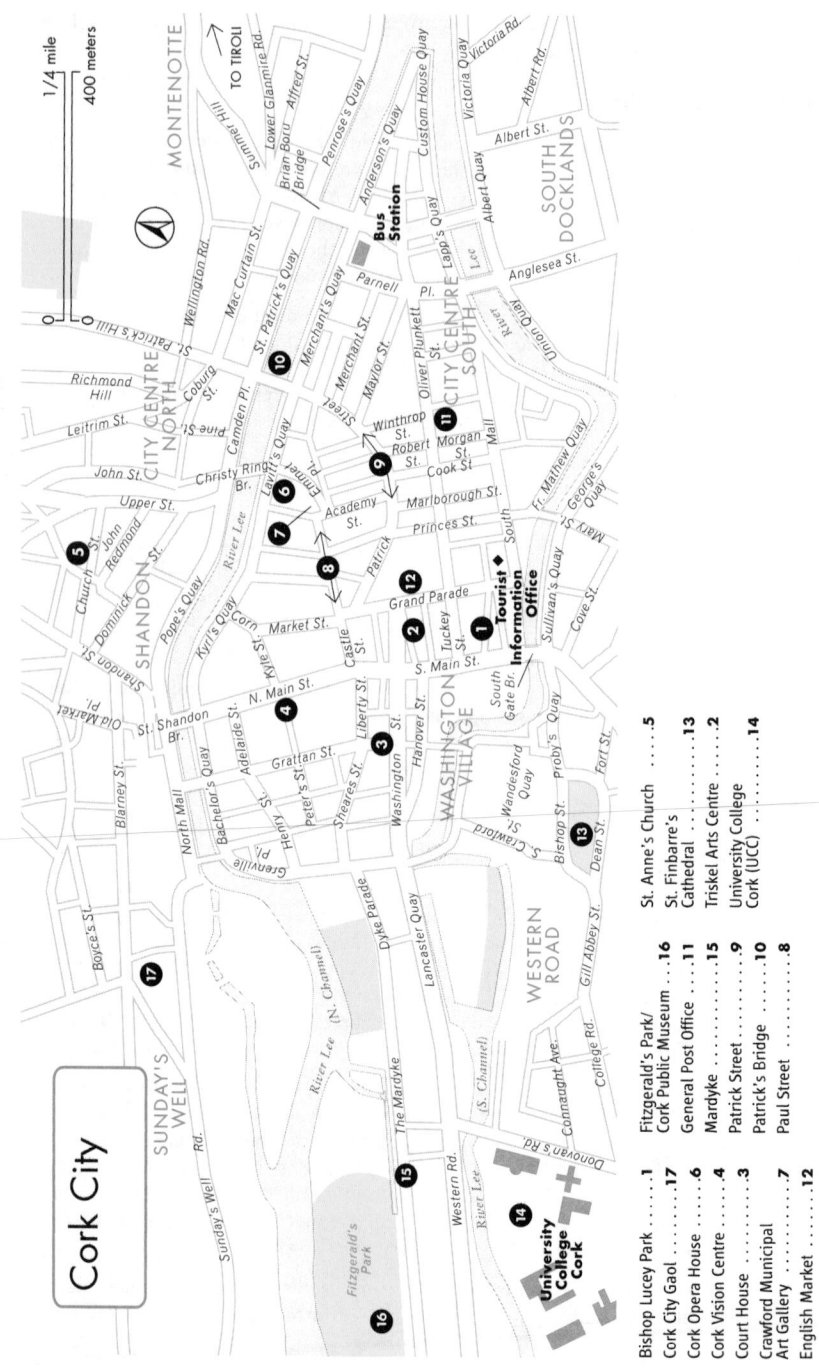

Cork City

University College Cork

Bishop Lucey Park **1**
Cork City Gaol **17**
Cork Opera House **6**
Cork Vision Centre **4**
Court House **3**
Crawford Municipal
Art Gallery **7**
English Market **12**

Fitzgerald's Park/
Cork Public Museum ...**16**
General Post Office **11**
Mardyke **15**
Patrick Street **9**
Patrick's Bridge **10**
Paul Street **8**

St. Anne's Church **5**
St. Finbarre's
Cathedral **13**
Triskel Arts Centre **2**
University College
Cork (UCC) **14**

TO TIROLI

Tourist ♦
Information
Office

as the district's main courthouse. The exterior has been cleaned and fully restored and looks every bit as good as it did when it was built in 1835. ☒ *Washington St., Washington Village* ☎ *021/427–2706* ☺ *Weekdays 9–5.*

★ ❼ **Crawford Municipal Art Gallery.** The large redbrick building was built in 1724 as the customs house and is now home to Ireland's leading provincial art gallery. An imaginative expansion has added an extra 10,000 square feet of gallery space for visiting exhibitions and adventurous shows of modern Irish artists. The permanent collection includes landscape paintings depicting Cork in the 18th and 19th centuries. Take special note of works by Irish painters William Leech (1881–1968), Daniel Maclise (1806–70), James Barry (1741–1806), and Nathaniel Grogan (1740–1807). The café, run by the Allen family of Ballymaloe, is a good place for a light lunch or a homemade sweet. ☒ *Emmet Pl., City Center South* ☎ *021/427–3377* ⊕ *www.crawfordartgallery.com* ☐ *Free* ☺ *Weekdays 9–5, Sat. 9–1.*

5

★ ⓬ **English Market.** Food lovers: head for one of the misleadingly small entrances to this large market in an elaborate, brick-and-cast-iron Victorian building. (Its official name is the Princes Street Market, and it's also known locally as the Covered Market.) Among the 140 stalls, keep an eye out for the Alternative Bread Co., which produces more

> ### WORD OF MOUTH
>
> "Cork's English Market is the best food market in Ireland and great fun to visit. Buy some cheeses, have a look at the fish stalls, and enjoy the banter."   —ter2000

than 40 varieties of handmade bread every day. Iago, Sean Calder-Potts's deli, has fresh pasta, lots of cheeses, and charcuterie. The Olive Stall sells olive oil, olive-oil soap, and olives from Greece, Spain, France, and Italy. Kay O'Connell's Fish Stall, in the legendary fresh-fish alley, purveys local smoked salmon. O'Reilly's Tripe and Drisheen is the last existing retailer of a Cork specialty, tripe (cow's stomach) and *drisheen* (blood sausage). Upstairs is the Farmgate, an excellent café. ☒ *Entrances on Grand Parade and Princes St., City Center South* ⊕ *www.corkcity.ie* ☺ *Mon.–Sat. 9–5:30.*

☝ ⓰ **Fitzgerald's Park.** This small, well-tended park is beside the River Lee's north channel in the west of the city. The park contains the **Cork Public Museum,** a Georgian mansion that houses a well-planned exhibit about Cork's history since ancient times, with a strong emphasis on the city's Republican history. ☒ *Western Rd., Western Road* ☎ *021/427–0679* ⊕ *www.corkcity.ie* ☐ *Free* ☺ *Museum weekdays 11–1 and 2:15–5, Sun. 3–5.*

⓫ **General Post Office.** This Neoclassical building with an elegant colonnaded facade was once Cork's opera house. It dominates a street otherwise occupied by boutiques, jewelry stores, and antiques shops. ☒ *Oliver Plunkett St., City Center South* ☎ *021/427–2000* ☺ *Weekdays 9–5:30, Sat. 9–5.*

NEED A
BREAK?

The friendly, old **Long Valley** (✉ Winthrop St., City Center South ☎ 021/427–2144), popular with artists, writers, students, and eccentrics, serves tea, coffee, pints, and sandwiches. The dark, mismatched interior is like a time warp taking you back to early-20th-century Cork. Some of the booths are built from wood salvaged from wrecked ocean liners—ask to be told the story. The generously filled sandwiches, made to order from home-cooked meat and thickly cut bread, also seem to belong to another age.

⑮ Mardyke. This popular riverside walk links the city center with Fitzgerald's Park. Beside it is a field where cricket, very much a minority sport in Ireland, is played on summer weekends. ✉ *Western Rd., Western Road.*

❾ Patrick Street. Extending from Grand Parade in the south to Patrick's Bridge in the north, Panna (as it's known locally) is Cork's main shopping thoroughfare. It has been designed as a pedestrian-priority area with wide walks and special street lights. A mainstream mix of department stores, boutiques, pharmacies, and bookshops line the way. If you look above some of the plate-glass storefronts, you can see examples of the bowfront Georgian windows that are emblematic of old Cork. The street saw some of the city's worst fighting during the War of Independence. ✉ *City Center South.*

❿ Patrick's Bridge. From here you can look along the curve of Patrick Street and north across the River Lee to St. Patrick's Hill, with its tall Georgian houses. The hill is so steep that steps are cut into the pavement. Tall ships that served the butter trade used to load up beside the bridge at Merchant's Quay before heading downstream to the sea. The design of the large, redbrick shopping center on the site evokes the warehouses of old. ✉ *Patrick St., City Center South* ⊕ *www.corkcity.ie.*

❽ Paul Street. A narrow street between the River Lee and Patrick Street and parallel to both, Paul Street is the backbone of the trendy shopping area that now occupies Cork's old French Quarter. The area was first settled by Huguenots fleeing religious persecution in France. Musicians and other street performers often entertain passersby in the Rory Gallagher Piazza, named for the rock guitarist (of the band Taste), whose family was from Cork. The shops here offer the best in modern Irish design—from local fashions to handblown glass—and antiques, particularly in the alley north of the piazza. ✉ *City Center South.*

❺ St. Anne's Church. The church's pepper-pot Shandon steeple, which has a four-sided clock and is topped with a golden, salmon-shape weather vane, is visible from throughout the city and is the chief reason why St. Anne's is so frequently visited. The Bells of Shandon were immortalized in an atrocious but popular 19th-century ballad of that name. Your reward for climbing the 120-foot-tall tower is the chance to ring the bells, with the assistance of sheet tune cards, out over Cork. Beside the church, Firkin Crane, Cork's 18th-century butter market, houses two small performing spaces. Adjacent is the Shandon Craft Market. ✉ *Church St., Shandon* ⊕ *www.corkcity.ie* ✉ *€1.50 church, €2 church and bell tower* ☉ *May–Oct., Mon.–Sat. 9:30–4:30; Nov.–Apr., Mon.–Sat. 10–3:30.*

Rebel Cork

CORK CITY RECEIVED ITS FIRST charter in 1185 from Prince John of Norman England, and it takes its name from the Irish word *corcaigh*, meaning "marshy place." The original 6th-century settlement was spread over 13 small islands in the River Lee. Major development occurred during the 17th and 18th centuries with the expansion of the butter trade, and many attractive Georgian-design buildings with wide bowfront windows were constructed during this time. As late as 1770, Cork's present-day main streets—Grand Parade, Patrick Street, and the South Mall—were submerged under the Lee. Around 1800, when the Lee was partially dammed, the river divided into two streams that now flow through the city, leaving the main business and commercial center on an island, not unlike Paris's Île de la Cité. As a result, the city features a number of bridges and quays, which, although initially confusing, add greatly to the port's unique character.

"Rebel Cork" emerged as a center of the Nationalist Fenian movement in the 19th century. The city suffered great damage during the War of Independence in 1919–21, when much of its center was burned down. Cork is now regaining some of its former glory as a result of sensitive commercial development and an ongoing program of inner-city renewal.

⑬ St. Finbarre's Cathedral. This was once the entrance to medieval Cork. According to tradition, St. Finbarre established a monastery on this site around AD 650 and is credited as being the founder of Cork. The present, compact, three-spire Gothic cathedral, which was completed in 1879, belongs to the Church of Ireland and houses a 3,000-pipe organ. ⌧ *Bishop St., Washington Village* ☎ *021/496–3387* ⊕ *www.cathedral.cork.anglican.org* ⌧ *Free* ☉ *Oct.–Mar., Mon.–Sat. 10–12:45 and 2–5; Apr.–Sept., Mon.–Sat. 10–5:30.*

❷ Triskel Arts Centre. An excellent place to get the pulse of artsy goings-on in town, Triskel Arts Centre occupies a converted pair of town houses, also home to a coffee shop and a small auditorium that hosts films and plays. Often on display are exhibitions devoted to contemporary art and crafts. ⌧ *Tobin St., Washington Village* ☎ *021/427–2022* ⊕ *www.triskelartscentre.com* ⌧ *Free* ☉ *Weekdays 11–6, Sat. 11–5.*

★ ⑭ University College Cork. The Doric, porticoed gates of UCC stand about 2 km (1 mi) from the center of the city. The college, which has a student body of roughly 10,000, is a constituent of the National University of Ireland. The main quadrangle is a fine example of 19th-century university architecture in the Tudor-Gothic style, reminiscent of many Oxford and Cambridge colleges. Several ancient ogham stones are on display, as are occasional exhibitions of archival material from the old library. The Honan Collegiate Chapel, east of the quadrangle, was built in 1916 and modeled on the 12th-century, Hiberno-Romanesque style, best exemplified by the remains of Cormac's Chapel at Cashel. The UCC chapel's stained-glass windows, as well as its collection of art and crafts, altar furnishings, and textiles in the Celtic Revival style, are noteworthy. Three large, modern buildings have been successfully integrated with the old, including the Boole Library, named for mathematician George Boole (1815–64), who was a professor at the college. Both indoors and out the campus is enhanced by works from the campus's outstanding collection of contemporary Irish art. The Lewis Glucksman Gallery opened in late 2004, in a striking new building in a wooded gully beside the college's entrance gates. Besides displaying works from the college's collection, it will host cutting-edge contemporary art exhibits. ⊠ *Western Road* ☎ *021/490–3000* ⊕ *www.ucc.ie* ✇ *Free* ⊙ *Weekdays 9–5, but call to confirm hrs Easter wk, July and Aug., and mid-Dec.–mid-Jan.*

> ### GRANDDAD OF THE COMPUTER
>
> George Boole (1815–64), a University College professor, is one of the heroes of the computer age. Despite growing up in a working-class family with limited access to education, he developed into a mathematical genius, inventing Boolean algebra—the foundation upon which computer science was built.

ST. MARY'S PRO-CATHEDRAL – It's worth hiking up to St. Mary's, which dates from 1808, only if you're interested in tracing your Cork ancestors. Its presbytery has records of births and marriages dating from 1784. ⊠ *Cathedral Walk, Shandon* ✇ *Free* ⊙ *Daily 9–6.*

OFF THE
BEATEN
PATH

Where to Stay & Eat

$$$$ ✕ **Ivory Tower.** Seamus O'Connell, the adventurous owner-chef here, is famous in Ireland through his television series, *Soul Food.* He describes his approach as "trans-ethnic fusion." He has cooked in Mexico and Japan, so his accomplished menu has such brilliantly eclectic dishes as wild duck with vanilla, sherry, and jalapeños; pheasant tamale; and wild sea trout smoked to order over oak, with whiskey and scallion sauce. Imaginative presentation, including a surprise taster to set the mood, compensates for the bare wooden floors and somewhat stark decor of the first-floor corner dining room. ⊠ *35 Princes St., Washington Village* ☎ *021/427–4665* ▭ *AE, DC, MC, V* ⊙ *Closed Mon. and Tues. No lunch.*

$$$–$$$$ ✕ **Les Gourmandises.** With a Breton sommelier, Soizic, working the front of the house, and her U.K.-and-Dublin-trained Irish husband, Pat, in the kitchen, you can expect a genuinely interesting eating experience. The restaurant is in a small but high-ceiling room. Natural light pours in from an overhead skylight, brightening the quarry-tile floor and red-velvet chairs that are arrayed around the tables. Crisp white linen and fresh flowers are typical of Soizic's attention to detail. Pat's training with Marco Pierre White, John Burton Race, and Patrick Guilbaud shows in his mastery of robust modern French repertoire. Roasted fillet of cod is served with braised lentils, thyme-and balsamic dressing, while roast guinea fowl comes with buttered cabbage and Madeira sauce. Desserts include coffee crème brûlée with a Swiss meringue and chocolate madeleine. Good-value set menus are also available. ✉ *17 Cook St., City Center South* ☎ *021/425–1959* 🖃 *MC, V* ⊗ *Closed Easter wk, last wk Aug., 1st wk Sept.*

$$–$$$$ ✕ **Jacobs on the Mall.** Mercy Fenton's imaginative cooking is one attraction; the other is the location—an erstwhile Victorian-style Turkish bath. The dining room has a high ceiling, an enormous skylight, cast-iron pillars, modern art, and a tall banquette room divider. Starters include duck liver parfait with plum chutney and oysters with ginger and lime relish. For a main course, try seared John Dory with coconut rice or roast haunch of venison with celeriac and parsnip puree and beetroot confit. Look for such desserts as date and butterscotch pudding with bourbon cream. ✉ *30A South Mall, City Center South* ☎ *021/425–1530* 🖃 *AE, DC, MC, V* ⊗ *Closed Sun.*

$$–$$$$ ✕ **Lovett's.** Since 1977 the Lovett family has been setting high culinary standards in the formal, portrait-lined dining room of a Georgian house 5 km (3 mi) south of Cork City. The extensive wine list emphasizes vineyards whose owners have Irish roots, but who left for Bordeaux and other wine-making regions in the 18th century. Try the hot black-and-white pudding terrine with onion and raisin confit, followed perhaps by black sole on the bone with citrus butter, and finish up with the Irish farmhouse cheese platter. There's also a vegetarian menu featuring local produce. The brasserie is less formal. ✉ *Churchyard La., off Well Rd., Douglas* ☎ *021/429–4909* 🖃 *AE, DC, MC, V* ⊗ *Closed Sun., Mon., 1st wk of Aug., and Christmas wk. No lunch.*

$$–$$$ ✕ **Café Paradiso.** The Mediterranean-style food is so tasty that even dedicated meat eaters forget that it's vegetarian. Australian owner-chef Denis Cotter, who has published two acclaimed cookbooks, garners raves for his risottos with seasonal vegetables, his *gougère-choux* (cheese-flavored pastries) with savory fillings, and his homemade desserts. The simple café-style dining room is busy and colorful, with enthusiastic young waiters who love to recite the daily specials. The food is creatively arranged on massive platters or bowls, which add a sense of occasion. The restaurant is midway between the courthouse and the university. You can also stay the night here: there are three small but attractive rooms available for around €180 a night. ✉ *16 Lancaster Quay, Western Road* ☎ *021/427–7939* 🖃 *AE, MC, V* ⊗ *Closed Sun., Mon., and last 2 wks of Aug.*

$$–$$$ ✕ **Fenn's Quay.** This tiny city-center restaurant, on the ground floor of a 250-year-old Georgian house, is always buzzing with a faithful local clientele—legal eagles from the nearby courthouse at lunch, theater- and moviegoers at dinner. The owners are also in the meat business; their baked ham is outstanding, and the char-grilled fillet steak with chunky chips has achieved legendary status: some regulars can't bring themselves to order anything else. But there are other good options: fish from the nearby market is given robust, unfussy treatment, and vegeterian options include twice-baked goat's cheese soufflé with apple and walnut salad. The ginger and toffee sticky pudding is a dessert specialty. Simple decor, with bright red cafe-style chairs and tan banquettes, gets a dose of character from striking modern paintings. ✉ *Fenn's Quay, Sheares St., Washington Village* ☎ *021/427–9527* 🖃 *AE, MC, V* ⊗ *Closed Sun.*

$$–$$$ ✕ **Jacques.** Hidden away in a tiny side street is one of Cork's favorite restaurants. Its windowless interior with its warm terra-cotta walls and

EATING WELL IN THE SOUTHWEST

The Southwest, especially County Cork, rivals Dublin as Ireland's food-culture epicenter. Cork has astonishing resources: waters full of a wide array of fish, acre after acre of potato fields, cows galore, wild mushrooms and berries—not to mention inventive chefs who transform this bounty into feasts. In tiny Shanagarry, Darina Allen trains hundreds of chefs every year at the Ballymaloe Cookery School. Whether trained at home or abroad, area chefs put a premium on fresh, local (often organically grown) produce.

Mussels and scallops are farmed in the waters off the coast of Cork and Kerry, while the rivers teem with wild salmon. Small smokeries process salmon, trout, mussels, and mackerel over either oak or beech wood chips, with mouthwatering results. Most restaurants in the region bake their own bread daily, often producing both yeast breads and Irish soda bread, which uses buttermilk or bicarbonate of soda in place of yeast. Kerry is famous for its delicately flavored mountain lamb, while local beef ensures a wide selection of tender steak cuts. Organic pork from heirloom breeds of pigs might remind you how tasty pork can be. And while in the southwest, make a point of trying some local farmhouse cheeses; look out for Milleens, Coolea, Durrus, Coomkeen, Gubbeen, or the superb hard cheeses, Desmond and Gabriel, made by West Cork Natural Cheeses.

The smaller country restaurants ooze ambience, but service can be a little slow, especially in the peak season of July and August. The food is freshly prepared and usually worth waiting for, so meanwhile sample some of that home-baked bread, and maybe a glass of local stout or your usual aperitif, or maybe chat with the people at the next table to pass the time. It's all part of the Irish experience.

curved Art Deco–style bar is carefully lighted to provide a calming ambience that makes you forget the world outside. Sisters Jacque and Eithne Barry have run the place for 25 years, and know their business. Food is always sourced locally, so it's as fresh as it comes. Eithne's cooking lets the flavor shine through, whether in a starter of fresh crab and baby spinach salad, or a main course of traditional roast duck with potato and apricot stuffing and red cabbage. For dessert try the fruited bread and butter pudding, or indulge in a chocolate and hazelnut torte. There's a special-value early dinner menu from 6 PM, and on Sunday a light menu is served from 4:30 PM. ⊠ *Phoenix St., off Oliver Plunkett St. near GPO, City Center South* ☎ *021/427–7387* ▤ *MC, V* ☉ *No lunch Sun.*

$$–$$$ ✕ **Proby's Bistro.** Proby's striking modern building, in a riverside location near St. Finbarre's Cathedral, sets the tone for stylish modern cooking that gives a Mediterranean treatment to fresh local produce. Patio tables and sun umbrellas optimistically placed on the terrace reinforce the Continental feel, and the interior dining room has an open fire and bold modern furnishings that complement the light, flavorful food. West Cork black pudding with grainy mustard and mashed potatoes is a favorite starter, while honey-glazed roast duck is a popular daily special. A pianist plays in the evening. ⊠*Proby's Quay, Crosses Green, Washington Village* ☎*021/431–6531* ▭ *AE, MC, V* ☻ *Closed Sun. and Mon.*

$–$$$ ✕ **Isaac's.** Cross Patrick's Bridge to the River Lee's north side and turn right to reach this large, atmospheric brasserie in a converted 18th-century warehouse. Modern art, jazz, high ceilings, and well-spaced tables covered in oilcloth set an eclectic tone. The East-meets-Mediterranean menu includes many tempting dishes, such as warm salads with Clonakilty black pudding, and king prawns in spicy tomato sauce. Reservations are advisable Friday and Saturday evenings. ⊠ *MacCurtain St., City Center North* ☎ *021/450–3805* ▭ *AE, DC, MC, V* ☻ *No lunch Sun.*

¢–$$ ✕ **Boqueria.** A gloomy old tavern on the street to the north of Patrick's Bridge has been transformed into an atmospheric tapas bar. The bar itself remains long and narrow, but skylights wipe out the gloom, and the walls are lined with attractive racks of Spanish wine. It's a popular breakfast spot, offering freshly squeezed orange and grapefruit juice, great coffee, and croissants, as well as a fine rendition of the traditional Irish fry. The tapas offerings cut loose from their Spanish roots to become showcases for artisanal Irish food: *queso raciones* is a plate of five Irish farmhouse cheeses and one Manchego, while four of the six elements in *charcuteria raciones* are made in west Cork. The results are enormously popular, so there's always a great buzz in the place. ⊠ *6 Bridge St.* ☎ *021/455–9049* ▭ *No credit cards.*

¢–$$ ✕ **Farmgate Café.** One of the best—and busiest—informal lunch spots in town is on a terraced gallery above the fountain at the Princes Street entrance to the covered English Market. One side of the gallery opens onto the market and is self-service; the other side is glassed in and has table service (reservations advised). Tripe and drisheen is one dish that is always on the menu; daily specials include less challenging but no less traditional dishes, such as corned beef with colcannon (potatoes and cabbage mashed with butter and seasonings) and loin of smoked bacon with *champ* (potatoes mashed with scallions or leeks). ⊠ *English Market, City Center South* ☎ *021/427–8134* ▭ *DC, MC, V* ☻ *Closed Sun. No dinner.*

★ $$$$ ✕▥ **Hayfield Manor.** The Manor, a surprisingly soigné modern homage to the country-house style, is beside the UCC campus, five-minutes' drive from the city center. Ruddy with red brick and classy white-sash windows, its exterior hints at the comfy luxe within. Beyond a splendid, carved-wood double staircase, you can find the Drawing Room—a symphony of gilded silk, with white-marble fireplace, 19th-century chandelier, and chic armchairs—and the wood-panel library, which overlooks a walled patio and garden. Rooms are spacious and ever-so-elegantly furnished in a version of the Louis XV style. The Victorian-style bar serves lunch, and then bar food until 7 PM, when the Manor Room restaurant opens for dinner. There's wireless Internet throughout. ⊠ *College Rd., Western Road, Co. Cork* ☎ *021/431–5900* ▭ *021/431–6839* ⊕ *www.hayfieldmanor.ie* ➥ *53 rooms* ♨ *Restaurant, cable TV, in-room data ports, Wi-Fi, indoor pool, health club, bar, meeting rooms* ▭ *AE, DC, MC, V* ⊠ *BP.*

$$$ ✕▥ **Hotel Isaac's.** A stylish renovation transformed an old, city-center warehouse into a busy restaurant and hotel complex. Rooms are bright and cheerful, with polished wood floors and rustic pine furniture. The restaurant and some of the rooms overlook a tiny courtyard garden with a waterfall cascading down one side. The dining room also operates as Greene's restaurant, where they serve seafood—king prawns with chili sauce, oysters poached in Guinness, brill, swordfish, and hake—as well as other intriguing concoctions, such as veal with apricot stuffing, Asian vegetables, and ginger soufflé. ⊠ *48 MacCurtain St., City Center North, Co. Cork* ☎ *021/450–0011* ⊟ *021/450–6355* ⊕ *www.isaacs.ie* ⤳ *47 rooms* ♢ *Restaurant, cafeteria, cable TV, in-room data ports, Wi-Fi, Ping-Pong* ⊟ *AE, MC, V* ⦿ *BP.*

$$$ ✕⊞ **Kingsley Hotel.** The riverside location is a boon, being close to open countryside yet a 10-minute walk from the city center. The Kingsley overlooks a rowing club on a pretty section of the River Lee, beside the Lee Fields, a big meadow whose paths are popular with joggers. The lobby and lounge of this spanking-new establishment are paneled with dark wood and furnished with upright velvet armchairs, like an old-style gentlemen's club. Guest rooms have large bathrooms, super-king-size beds, mahogany furniture, workstations, and CD players. Otters, the more formal restaurant, serves imaginative local seafood and seasonal game dishes; a lighter menu is served in the bar and library. The health center has a 20-meter pool and an outdoor hot tub. ⊠ *Victoria Cross, Western Road, Co. Cork* ☎ *021/480–0500* ⊟ *021/480–0527* ⊕ *www.kingsleyhotel.com* ⤳ *69 rooms* ♢ *Restaurant, in-room fax, some minibars, cable TV, in-room data ports, Wi-Fi, indoor pool, health club, bar* ⊟ *AE, DC, MC, V* ⦿ *BP.*

★ **$$** ✕⊞ **The Ambassador.** It's not the fanciest hotel in Cork, nor the hippest, but it has the most character and the best view—which you pay for by a steep 10-minute walk up from the town center. It's worth visiting the bar here just to enjoy the panoramic view of Cork City's docks, river, railway line, church steeples, and distant surrounding hills. An imposing redbrick and cut-limestone Victorian-era nursing home now converted into a comfortable hotel (affiliated with the Best Western group), the Ambassador is near the army barracks in a hilly area made famous by Frank O'Connor's short stories, an area now favored by style-conscious academics and bohos. Architecture buffs may question some features, such as the modern, double-glaze windows, but overall the interior retains its Victorian charm and spaciousness. The corridors are so wide you could drive a car down them, but patterned carpet runners help dispel any remaining institutional atmosphere. The Embassy Bar has dark-wood paneling and a large bay window overlooking the city, while the cocktail lounge, with book-filled shelves and chesterfields by an open fire, is a quieter venue. Guest rooms are massive, with large bathrooms, patterned wallpapers, small sitting areas, and matching floral curtains and drapes. There are three floors of bedrooms and the higher you go, the better the view—some rooms even have splendid walk-out balconies at no extra charge. ⊠ *Military Hill, St. Luke's, City Center North* ☎ *021/455–1996* ⊟ *021/455–1997* ⊕ *www.ambassadorhotel. ie* ⤳ *58 rooms* ♢ *Restaurant, cable TV, in-room data ports, Wi-Fi, health club, 2 bars, meeting rooms; no a/c* ⊟ *AE, DC, MC, V* ⦿ *BP.*

$$ ✕⊞ **Clarion.** Black-clad receptionists standing behind simple wooden desks at the far end of the vast, marble-floor lobby are the first indication that this place aspires to boutique-hotel chic. Occupying a corner block beside the River Lee, the Clarion is the first arrival of a huge docklands development. It's kitty-corner across the river from City Hall, and a short walk from shopping and dining. Rooms are built around a central, top-lighted atrium, and have views either of the river or the hotel's swanky main staircase. Decor is stark and hard-edged, with stylish pale-wood trim complemented by curtains and flooring in a khaki-olive theme. Kudos bar ($) spills out onto a riverside walkway and serves food from an open wok station until 8 nightly. The more formal restaurant Sinergie ($$) serves a light Mediterranean menu amid minimalist Japanese-inspired decor. ⊠ *Lapp's Quay, City Center South* ☎ *021/422–4900* 🖷 *021/422–4901* ⊕ *www.clarionhotelcorkcity.com* ⇥ *191 rooms* ⏦ *Restaurant, cable TV, in-room data ports, Wi-Fi, indoor pool, gym, sauna, steam room, bar* ⊟ *AE, DC, MC, V* ⵙ *BP.*

$ ✕⛱ **Flemings.** On a hillside overlooking the river, this stately Georgian house is set in extensive grounds, which include a kitchen garden that supplies the restaurant. The grounds could be tidier, but owner-chef Michael Fleming is more interested in cooking. Classical French food is his forte, and is served, appropriately, in a dining room decorated in the French Empire style with plush Louis XV–style chairs, gilt-framed portraits, and crystal chandeliers. Local ingredients are important; a starter of panfried foie gras is accompanied by black pudding from West Cork and glazed apple. Grilled monkfish from Michael's home town, Courtmacsherry, is served with a basil oil dressing and red wine sauce. The quiet, large guest rooms have high ceilings and elegant brocade fabrics. Ask about the special-value "dine and stay" package. ⊠ *Silver Grange House, Tivoli, Co. Cork* ☎ *021/482–1621* 🖷 *021/482–1178* ⇥ *4 rooms* ⏦ *Restaurant, cable TV, bar; no a/c* ⊟ *AE, DC, MC, V* ⵙ *BP.*

$$$ ⛱ **Rochestown Park.** On seven lovely acres of mature gardens in the fashionable suburb of Douglas, 5 km (3 mi) south of the city, this stylish hotel was built around a Victorian manor house once used as a convent. The grounds help it to retain a peaceful, otherwordly air. Rooms are modern, with cotton spreads, wool carpets, and light-oak fixtures. There's good access to the city's four-lane ring road—and a distant view of same from some rooms, which is compensated for by a view of the river estuary beyond. The large health center specializes in thalassotherapy—seaweed wraps and baths. ⊠ *Rochestown Rd., Douglas, Co. Cork* ☎ *021/489–0800* 🖷 *021/489–2178* ⊕ *www.rochestownpark.com* ⇥ *160 rooms* ⏦ *Restaurant, cable TV, indoor pool, health club, bar, meeting rooms* ⊟ *AE, DC, MC, V* ⵙ *BP.*

$$ ⛱ **Brookfield Hotel.** Next door to the campus of University College Cork, this budget hotel sits in 10 acres of private parkland with mature trees and is surrounded by blocks of redbrick, Georgian-style student accommodations, which double as a self-catering holiday village outside term time. This pleasant, quiet location, complete with secure car parking, is less than a mile from the city center. The hotel shares its main door with the pool and gym (a bonus in this price range), with a staircase leading up to reception, and three floors of guest rooms. Rooms are a bit boxy, with blond-wood desks, plain walls and carpets, patterned spreads, and dark-hue drapes, but are redeemed by the pretty views of

green lawns and pine trees from the windows. ⊠ *Brookfield Holiday Village, College Rd., Western Road* ☎ *021/480–4700* 🖷 *021/480–4793* ⊕ *www.brookfieldcork.ie* ⤴ *24 rooms* ♨ *Restaurant, cable TV, Wi-Fi, tennis court, indoor pool, health club, bar; no a/c* ⊟ *AE, DC, MC, V* ☉ *Closed Dec. 23–Jan. 2.*

$$ 🏨 **Lancaster Lodge.** Free city-center parking, a great location next to the lively Jurys Hotel, and value are the main reasons to stay at this modern, four-story inn. Rooms look out over the car park or across a narrow, fast-flowing branch of the River Lee, to the main road, but in compensation they're spacious and stylish, with pale-wood furniture and large bathrooms. A hearty breakfast from an extensive menu—served in your room or in the bright, contemporary dining room—is another plus. ⊠ *Lancaster Quay, Western Road, Co. Cork* ☎ *021/425–1125* 🖷 *021/425–1126* ⊕ *www.lancasterlodge.com* ⤴ *37 rooms, 2 suites* ♨ *Dining room, cable TV, in-room data ports, Wi-Fi, free parking; no a/c* ⊟ *AE, DC, MC, V* ⑩ *BP.*

Nightlife & the Arts

See the *Examiner* or the *Evening Echo* for details about movies, theater, and live music performances.

Galleries

The **Fenton Gallery** (⊠ Wandesford Quay, Washington Village ☎ 021/431–5294 ⊕ www.artireland.net) shows work by important Irish artists. The **Lewis Glucksman Gallery** (⊠ UCC Campus, Western Road, corner of Donovan's Rd., Western Road ☎ 021/490-1844 ⊕ www.glucksman.org), part of Cork's university, has won several awards for its striking modern architecture. The **Lavit Gallery** (⊠ 5 Father Mathew St., off South Mall, City Center South ☎ 021/427–7749) sells work by members of the Cork Arts Society and other Irish artists. Offbeat exhibits can be found at the **Triskel Arts Centre** (⊠ Tobin St. off S. Main St., Washington Village ☎ 021/427–2022 ⊕ www.triskelart.com). The **Vangard Gallery** (⊠ Carey's La., Paul St., City Center South ☎ 021/427–8718 ⊕ www.vangardgallery.com) exhibits leading contemporary Irish artists.

Performing Arts & Film

Cork Opera House (⊠ Lavitt's Quay, City Center South ☎ 021/427–0022) is the city's major hall for touring productions and variety acts. Smaller theatrical productions are staged at the **Everyman Palace** (⊠ MacCurtain St., City Center North ☎ 021/450–1673), which has an ornate Victorian interior. **The Kino** (⊠ Washington St., Washington Village ☎ 021/427–1571) is Cork's only art-house cinema. Three films are usually showing, from 2 PM onward.

Pubs & Nightclubs

La Bodega (⊠ Cornmarket St., City Center South ☎ 021/427–2878), a converted wine warehouse, is the hip meeting spot for Cork's thirtysomethings. Traditional music sessions can happen anytime at **An Bodhrán** (⊠ 42 Oliver Plunkett St., City Center South ☎ 021/437–1392). You can hear Cajun, folk, or Irish music from Sunday to Wednesday at the **Corner House** (⊠ 7 Coburg St., City Center North ☎ 021/450–0655). Night owls flock to **Half Moon** (⊠ Half Moon St., City Center South ☎ 021/427–0022), the Cork Opera House's late-night music club. It showcases local, up-and-coming jazz and blues bands most weekends starting at 11 PM.

Loafers (✉26 Douglas St., South Docklands ☎021/431–1612) is a friendly gay bar with a beer garden. **The Lobby** (✉ Union Quay, South Docklands ☎ 021/431–1113) has nightly music sessions: traditional and acoustic in the bar, folk and rock upstairs. **Long Valley** (✉ Winthrop St., South City Center ☎021/427–2144) is a Cork institution, famous for its doorstep sandwiches (made with very thick slices of bread and lots of fillings) that are impossible to eat tidily, and its conversation, which is always lively. The bar at the **Metropole Hotel** (✉ MacCurtain St., City Center North ☎021/450–8122) is one of Cork's best jazz spots. **Redz Bar and Club** (✉ Liberty St., Washington Village ☎ 021/425–1855 ⊕ www.rebelbargroup.com) has late-night live entertainment and DJs every night but Monday.

Shopping

Department Stores
Brown Thomas (✉ 18 Patrick St., City Center South ☎ 021/427–6771), Ireland's high-end department store, carries items by Irish and international designers. The ground floor has an excellent cosmetics hall and a good selection of menswear and Irish crystal. Refuel at the coffee shop, which sells healthful open sandwiches and homemade soups. **Dunnes Stores** (✉Merchant's Quay, City Center South ☎021/427–4200) began in Cork as a family-owned drapery store and became the place where all of Ireland buys its socks, underwear, and much more. The British retail giant **Marks & Spencer** (✉ 6–8 Patrick St., Merchant's Quay, City Center South ☎021/427–5555) is as popular for its foods (great for picnics) and housewares as for its clothing basics. For inexpensive rain gear, T-shirts, underwear, and any other garments you forgot to pack, head for **Penney's** (✉ 27 Patrick St., City Center South ☎ 021/427–1935). **Roches Stores** (✉ Patrick St., City Center South ☎ 021/427–7727), Cork's largest department store, is a family-owned business that occupies a beautiful landmark building with a central glass dome.

Malls
Mahon Point Shopping Centre (✉ Mahon Point, South Link Rd. ☎ 021/ 497–2800) is a massive out-of-town shopping center just south of the Lee Tunnel, with an emphasis on fashion. The **Merchant's Quay Shopping Centre** (✉ Merchant's Quay, City Center South ☎ 021/427–5466) is a large downtown mall.

Specialty Shops
ANTIQUES **Gallery 44** (✉44A MacCurtain St., City Center North ☎ 021/450–1319) stocks antique glass, porcelain, paintings, and prints. **Irene's** (✉ 22 Marlboro St., City Center South ☎021/427–0642) sells antique jewelry. **Mills Antiques** (✉ 3 Paul's La., City Center South ☎021/427–3528) carries Irish, English, and European paintings, prints, silver, porcelain, and small furniture. **Victoria's** (✉2 Oliver Plunkett St., City Center South ☎021/ 427–2752) carries interesting jewelry and Victoriana.

BOOKS **Connolly's Bookshop** (⊠ Paul St. Piazza, City Center South ☎ 021/427–5366) has an extensive stock of new and secondhand books, with a good selection of Irish-interest titles. **Mainly Murder Bookstore** (⊠ 2A Paul St., City Center South ☎ 021/427–2413) is a must for lovers of crime fiction. **Vibes & Scribes** (⊠ 3 Bridge St., City Center North ☎ 021/450–5370) attracts a loyal following of avid readers, with three floors of new, secondhand, and discount books as well as CDs and videos. **Waterstones** (⊠ Patrick St., City Center South ☎ 021/427–6522) is the biggest bookshop in town, with a great choice of new fiction and nonfiction as well as a wide selection of locally published books.

CLOTHING **Cocoon** (⊠ 6 Emmet Pl., City Center South ☎ 021/427–3393), a little shop in a hexagonal tower, has a ravishing selection of sexy Italian boots and shoes alongside unusual jewelry and accessories. Fashion lovers adore the evening and business attire at the **Dressing Room** (⊠ 8 Emmet Pl., City Center South ☎ 021/427–0117), a tiny but tony boutique opposite the entrance to the Cork Opera House. **Monica John** (⊠ French Church St., City Center South ☎ 021/427–1399) sells locally designed high-fashion ladies' wear as well as some imported lines. **Quills** (⊠ 107 Patrick St., City Center South ☎ 021/427–1717) has a good selection of Irish-made apparel for women and men. **Samui** (⊠ 17 Drawbridge St., City Center South ☎ 021/427–8080) stocks dramatic—often quirky, but always flattering—clothes from Ireland, France, Germany, and the United Kingdom. For casual weatherproof clothing, try the **Tack Room** (⊠ Unit 3, Academy St., City Center South ☎ 021/427–2704).

JEWELRY **Marlboro Gold Arts Ltd** (⊠ 33 Marlboro St., City Center South ☎ 021/427–7052) has imaginative, modern jewelry. **IMB Design** (⊠ 10a Paul St. shopping center, City Center South ☎ 021/425–1800) designs and sells contemporary jewelry in silver and gold.

MUSIC This **HMV** (⊠ Patrick St. ☎ 021/427–4433) has a good selection of Irish traditional music in its classical and jazz sections. The best place for recordings of Irish music is **Living Tradition** (⊠ 40 MacCurtain St., City Center North ☎ 021/450–2040). **Vibes & Scribes** (⊠ 3 Bridge St., City Center North ☎ 021/450–5370) has a good selection of bargain and secondhand CDs, DVDs, and videotapes. Chart hits are the main business of the **Virgin Megastore** (⊠ Queen's Old Castle, City Center South ☎ 021/427–9299), but you can find some traditional Irish music for sale in the small classical and jazz sections.

SPORTING GOODS The **Golf Addict** (⊠ 6 Emmet Pl., City Center South ☎ 021/427–3393) stocks everything the serious golfer could need, as well as a range of nonessential golf paraphernalia and gifts. The **Great Outdoors** (⊠ 23 Paul St., City Center South ☎ 021/427–6382) caters to most outdoor sports needs. **Matthews** (⊠ Academy St., City Center South ☎ 021/427–7633) has a wide selection of sporting gear.

Side Trips from Cork City

Blarney, northwest of Cork City on R617, and Cork Harbour, east of the city on N25 (follow signposts to Waterford), make perfect day trips. Blarney's attractions are Blarney Castle and the famous Blarney Stone.

Cork Harbour's draws include Fota Island, with an arboretum, a wildlife park, and Fota House—a renovated hunting lodge and estate—and the fishing port of Cobh.

Blarney

18 *10 km (6 mi) northwest of Cork City.*

"On Galway sands they kiss your hands, they kiss your lips at Carney, but by the Lee they drink strong tea, and kiss the stone at Blarney." This famous rhyme celebrates one of Ireland's most noted icons—the Blarney Stone, which is the main reason most people journey to this small community built around a village green.

> **WORD OF MOUTH**
>
> "Although I was a teeny bit scared of the height, it was completely amazing to kiss the Blarney Stone. Truly, now I have the gift of gab. Aside from the castle, there's the Blarney woolen mills, and various tiny shops for souvenirs and such." –Rachael

In the center of Blarney is **Blarney Castle,** or what remains of it: the ruined central keep is all that's left of this mid-15th-century stronghold. The castle contains the famed Blarney Stone; kissing the stone, it's said, endows the kisser with the fabled "gift of gab." It's 127 steep steps to the battlements. To kiss the stone, you must lie down on the battlements, hold on to a guardrail, and lean your head way back. It's good fun and not at all dangerous. Expect a line from mid-June to early September; while you wait, you can admire the views of the wooded River Lee valley and chuckle over how the word "blarney" came to mean what it does. As the story goes, Queen Elizabeth I wanted Cormac MacCarthy, Lord of Blarney, to will his castle to the crown, but he refused her requests with eloquent excuses and soothing compliments. Exhausted by his comments, the queen reportedly exclaimed, "This is all Blarney. What he says he rarely means."

You can take pleasant walks around the castle grounds; Rock Close contains oddly shaped limestone rocks landscaped in the 18th century and a grove of ancient yew trees that is said to have been the site of Druid worship. In early March there's a wonderful display of naturalized daffodils. ☎ *021/438–5252* 🌐 *www.blarneycastle.ie* 🎫 *Blarney Castle: €8* ⏲ *Blarney Castle: May and Sept., Mon.–Sat. 9–6:30, Sun. 9–5:30; June–Aug., Mon.–Sat. 9–7, Sun. 9–5:30; Oct.–Apr., Mon.–Sat. 9–sundown, Sun. 9–5:30.*

WHERE TO STAY & EAT

$–$$$

✕ **Blair's Inn.** Surrounded by woods five minutes from Blarney, Blair's Inn—noted for its exuberant window-box displays—is the perfect retreat from Blarney's tour-bus crowds. This is a real "local," complete with genial owner-hosts, John and Anne, as well as a busy restaurant. In summer enjoy the beer garden; in winter, warm wood fires flicker in the cozy interior. Freshly prepared local produce is served in generous portions: best bets include Irish stew with lamb, carrots, and potatoes, as well as corned beef and a memorable gratin of prawns, crab and salmon, served piping hot. There's live entertainment every Sunday at 9 PM as well as on Monday from May to October. ✉ *Cloghroe* ☎ *021/438–1470* 💳 *MC, V.*

¢–$ 🏠 **Maranatha Country House.** This gray-stone Victorian manor surrounded by pretty gardens and 27 woodland acres makes an excellent base for exploring Blarney, Cork City, and even Killarney, 1½ hours away. The guest rooms in Olwen and Douglas Venn's impeccably run family home are individually decorated with antiques (Olwen has a passion for French inlaid furniture) and striking textiles. The Regal Suite has a four-poster bed swathed in pink, green, and white-sprigged fabric that matches the ruched drapes, as well as a sunken bath with a hot tub. Breakfast is served in the conservatory, which overlooks rolling lawns and majestic trees. To get here drive through Blarney village on the R617 for 3 km (2 mi) to the village of Tower. ⊠ *Tower, Co. Cork* ☎ *021/438–5102* ⊕ *www.maranathacountryhouse.com* ⬅ *6 rooms* ⌂ *No a/c, no room TVs, no smoking* ☰ *MC, V* ☉ *Closed Dec.–mid-Jan.* ⦿ *BP.*

SHOPPING Blarney has lots of crafts shops south and west of the village green, a two-minute walk from the castle. **Blarney Woolen Mills** (☎ 021/438–5280 ⊕ www.blarney.ie) has the largest stock and the highest turnover of Blarney's crafts shops. It sells everything from Irish-made high fashion to Aran hand-knit items to leprechaun key rings.

Cork Harbour

⑲ *16 km (10 mi) east of Cork City.*

☾ The 70-acre **Fota Island Wildlife Park** is 12 km (7 mi) east of Cork via N25, R624, and the main Cobh road. It's an important breeding center for cheetahs and wallabies, and also is home to monkeys, zebras, giraffes, ostriches, flamingos, emus, and kangaroos. ☎ *021/481–2678* ⊕ *www.fotawildlife.ie* ⊡ *€11* ☉ *Mon.–Sat. 10–4:30, Sun. 11–4:30; last admission an hr before closing.*

Next to the Fota Island Wildlife Park is **Fota House,** the Smith-Barry ancestral estate: its name is derived from the Irish Fód te, which means "warm soil," a tribute to the unique tidal estuary microclimate here and the reason why one of Ireland's most exotic botanical gardens was established here. The original lodge house was built in the mid-18th century for the Smith-Barry family, which owned vast tracts of land in South Cork, including the whole of Fota Island. The next generation of the powerful family employed the renowned architects Richard and William Vitruvius Morrison to convert the structure into an impressive Regency–style house that has now been painstakingly restored. The symmetrical facade is relatively unadorned and stands in contrast to the resplendent Adamesque plasterwork of the formal reception rooms (somewhat denuded of furniture). The servants' quarters are almost as big as the house proper. Fota's glories continue in the gardens, which include an arboretum, a Victorian fernery, an Italian garden, an orangerie, and a special display of magnolias. You can relax over cake and scones in the tearoom after visiting the gift shop. ☎ *021/481–5543* ⊕ *www.fotahouse.com* ⊡ *€5.50* ☉ *Apr.–Sept., Mon.–Sat. 10–5:30, Sun. 11–5:30; Oct.–Mar., daily 11–4.*

Many of the people who left Ireland on immigrant ships for the New World departed from **Cobh,** a pretty fishing port and seaside resort 24 km (15 mi) southeast of Cork City on R624. The **Queenstown Story at**

Cobh Heritage Center, in the old Cobh railway station, re-creates the experience of the million emigrants who left from here between 1750 and the mid-20th century. It also tells the stories of great transatlantic liners, including the *Titanic,* whose last port of call was Cobh, and the *Lusitania,* which was sunk by a German submarine off this coast on May 7, 1915. Many of the *Lusitania's* 1,198 victims are buried in Cobh, which has a memorial to them on the local quay. ☎ *021/481–3591* ⊕ *www. cobhheritage.com* ✉ *€6* ⊙ *Oct.–Apr., daily 9:30–5; May–Sept., daily 9:30–6.*

The best view of Cobh is from **St. Colman's Cathedral,** an exuberant neo-Gothic granite church designed by the eminent British architect E. W. Pugin in 1869, and completed in 1919. Inside, granite niches portray scenes of the Roman Catholic Church's history in Ireland, beginning with the arrival of St. Patrick. ☎ *021/481–3222* ⊕ *www.cloyne. irl.com* ✉ *Free.*

ART GALLERIES Philip Gray served as a diver in the Irish navy, and left to paint, which he does extremely well. The sea in all its guises is his subject. **The Philip Gray Gallery of Fine Art** (✉ Slipway Two, Cork Dockyard, Rushbrooke, Cobh ☎ 021/481–4170 ⊕ www.philipgray.com) is on a slipway of a dockyard in Cork Harbour.

SPORTS & THE OUTDOORS Explore the sheltered, island-studded waters of Cork Harbour by renting a sailing dinghy from **International Sailing Center** (✉ Fort Lisle, Cobh ☎ 021/481–1237).

EAST CORK & THE BLACKWATER VALLEY

Although most visitors to Cork head west out of the city for the coastal areas between Cork and Glengarriff, the east and the north of the county are also worth exploring. East Cork, Youghal in particular, is popular with Irish tourists, who love the long sandy beaches here. North Cork's main attraction is the Blackwater River, which crosses the county from east to west. It's famous for its trout and salmon fishing and its scenery.

Youghal

㉀ *48 km (30 mi) east of Cork City on N25, 74 km (46 mi) south of Waterford.*

Youghal (pronounced yawl), an ancient walled seaport with a fine natural harbor, has a long sandy beach, making it popular with summer day-trippers. The opening of a new section of the main N25 enabling through traffic to bypass the town has restored its quiet charm, though renovation of the center is still ongoing. The town is at the mouth of the Blackwater River, on the border between Counties Cork and Waterford. It was included in a 40,000-acre land grant given to Sir Walter Raleigh by Elizabeth I in the late 16th century. According to local legend, Sir Walter Raleigh planted the first potatoes in Ireland here, a claim disputed by residents of several other locations (and by all accounts he spent little time here). The town is in the throes of some major in-

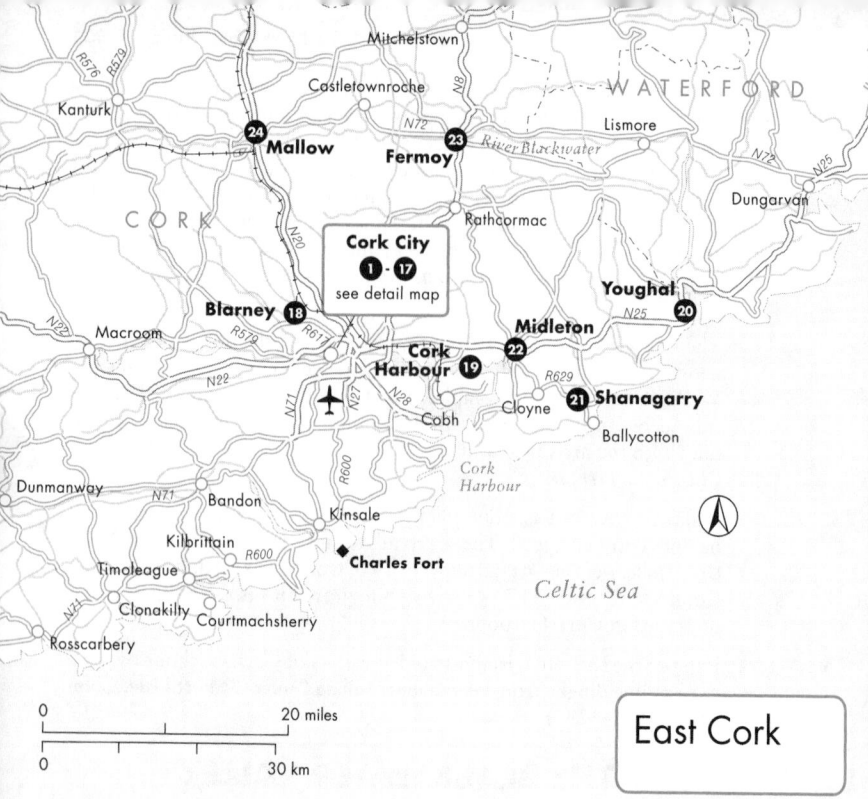

East Cork

vestment, aimed at updating its appeal. Rising above it all is Main Street's clock tower, which dates from 1776 and was built as a jail. Steps beside the tower lead to a well-preserved stretch of the old town walls. From here there's a magnificent panorama of the town and the estuary.

The **Youghal Heritage Centre** relates the town's history through an audiovisual presentation. If this whets your appetite, trained guides are available to show you the town; a walking tour takes about 90 minutes. ⊠ *Market Sq.* ☎ *024/20170* ⊕ *www.youghal.ie* ✉ *€2, tour €5* ☽ *June–mid-Sept., daily 9:30–7; mid-Sept.–May, weekdays 9:30–5:30.*

The **Moby Dick Lounge Bar** (⊠ Market Sq. ☎ 024/92756) contains memorabilia of the filming here of John Huston's version of Melville's *Moby-Dick,* in which Youghal masqueraded as New Bedford, Massachusetts.

St. Mary's Collegiate Church dates from the 13th century and contains many interesting monuments, including the tomb of Richard Boyle (1566–1643), who succeeded Sir Walter Raleigh as Mayor of Youghal and became the first earl of Cork. The brightly painted monument commemorates his three wives and 16 children and is similar to the monument in St. Patrick's Cathedral in Dublin, which Sir Richard ordered because he was not sure whether he would die in Dublin or Youghal. ⊠ *Emmet Pl.* ☎ *024/92350* ✉ *Free* ☽ *Key available from adjacent lodge.*

Where to Stay & Eat

$$–$$$ ✕⊡ **Aherne's.** In the Fitzgibbon family since 1923, Aherne's has a highly regarded seafood restaurant-bar ($$–$$$) with a magnetic appeal—it even draws food lovers from Cork City (less than an hour drive away). Popular main courses include hot buttered lobster, grilled salmon with fresh fennel, and plaice (flounder) stuffed with oysters in a red-wine sauce. The inexpensive bar food includes seafood pie topped with mashed potatoes. The 12 bedrooms, which occupy their own modern wing, are furnished with Victorian and Georgian antiques. ⊠ *163 N. Main St., Co. Cork* ☎ *024/92424* ⊟ *024/93633* ⊕ *www.ahernes.com* ➷ *13 rooms* ⟁ *Restaurant, cable TV, fishing, bar* ⊟ *AE, DC, MC, V* ⓍⓄⓁ *BP.*

$ ✕⊡ **Ballymakeigh House.** Consider this the Irish farmhouse of your
Fodor'sChoice dreams, the kind of place where you can easily end up staying a day or
★ two longer than planned. From the conservatory behind the creeper-clad house—with its cozy, impeccably kept guest rooms—you can breakfast on one of Margaret Browne's fresh strawberry muffins while watching the cows amble out to pasture after milking time. Reserve by 5 PM for her legendary six-course dinners, often made with herbs and edible flowers straight from the garden. The house is signposted off N25, 9½ km (6 mi) west of Youghal. ⊠*Killeagh, Co. Cork* ☎*024/95184* ⊟*024/95370* ⊕ *www.ballymakeighhouse.com* ➷ *6 rooms* ⟁ *Cable TV, tennis court, bicycles, Ping-Pong; no a/c* ⊟ *MC, V* Ⓧ *Closed Nov.–Mar.* ⓍⓄⓁ *BP.*

Shanagarry

㉑ *27 km (17 mi) southwest of Youghal via N25 and R632.*

There are two reasons to come to Shanagarry, a farming village known chiefly for its Quaker connections: Ballymaloe House, one of Ireland's first country-house hotels, and Ballymaloe Cookery School and Gardens, a top destination for chefs-in-training.

The most famous Shanagarry Quaker was William Penn (1644–1718), the founder of the Pennsylvania colony, who grew up in **Shanagarry House,** still a private residence in the center of the village. The entry gates are across from Shanagarry Castle, now owned and being restored by the potter and entrepreneur Stephen Pearce. The house's most famous tenant since William Penn was Marlon Brando, who stayed here in the summer of 1995 while filming *Divine Rapture* in nearby Ballycotton.

Where to Stay & Eat

$$$–$$$$ ✕⊡ **Ballymaloe House.** Ballymaloe is world famous as the fountainhead
Fodor'sChoice of the New Irish Cuisine (for more information, see "A Taste of Ireland"
★ in this chapter). Originally a farmhouse and family home, albeit on a gracious scale, Ballymaloe still functions partly as a working farm, one reason why the grounds—pleasant lawns, "which way home?" paths, and vegetable gardens—don't aspire to grandeur. Inside, past the doorway's demilune window, guests like to gather in the drawing room, a symphony of whites and beiges, with fine modern Irish paintings on the walls and not an antique in sight. A bigger dose of country charm can be found in some guest rooms (notably the ones cocooned in floral wallpapers). Nearly every corner of the former Norman manor is used,

down to the charming "stable" bedrooms on the first floor and the tiny, ivy-covered gatekeeper's cottage—perhaps the cutest accommodation in all Ireland. Newer, more spacious rooms downstairs have direct access to the pool and tennis court, and to views of the river and the garden's abundant bird life. This arcadia has been overseen by three generations of the Allen family, and their loyal staff have the knack of making a guest feel like a cosseted member of the family. ⊠ *Co. Cork* ☎ *021/465–2531* 🖷 *021/465–2021* ⊕ *www.ballymaloe.ie* 🛏 *33 rooms* 🍴 *Restaurant, 9-hole golf course, tennis court, pool, bar, some pets allowed; no a/c, no TV in some rooms* 🖃 *AE, DC, MC, V* ⦿ *BP.*

$–$$ ✕🏠 **Barnabrow House.** Owners John and Geraldine O'Brien stylishly combined the old and the new when they renovated the interior of this rambling 17th-century house. Specially made modern wood furniture from Africa sits beside Victorian antiques and against intensely colored walls. The results are romantic and relaxed and are helped by the stunning views across the countryside to Ballycotton Bay. The garden is lovely, and wildflowers are encouraged. The O'Briens pride themselves on the informal, relaxed atmosphere, which includes a cockerel that announces the break of day (you have been warned). Main house rooms have high ceilings and canopy beds; courtyard rooms are cozier and have low, beamed ceilings. The Trinity Rooms restaurant ($$–$$$), closed to nonresidents Monday through Wednesday, resembles a medieval banqueting hall, with a high-beam ceiling and church windows, and is painted wine-red. It serves imaginative dishes made with local produce, including fish from nearby Ballycotton. ⊠ *Cloyne, Co. Cork* ☎🖷 *021/465–2534* ⊕ *www. barnabrowhouse.ie* 🛏 *21 rooms* 🍴 *Restaurant, bar, some pets allowed; no a/c, no room TVs, no smoking* 🖃 *DC, MC, V* ⦿ *BP.*

Shopping

The ceramicist Stephen Pearce makes tablewares and bowls in four signature styles that are available in many Irish crafts shops. He sells a wide selection at his own **Stephen Pearce Emporium** (⊠ Near Cloyne ☎ 021/ 464–6262), where he also stocks an interesting range of Irish-made crafts.

Midleton

㉒ *15 km (9 mi) northwest of Shanagarry on R629, 12 km (8 mi) east of Cork City on N25.*

Midleton is famous for its school, Midleton College, founded in 1696, and its distillery, founded in 1825 and modernized in 1975, which manufactures spirits—including Irish whiskey—for distribution worldwide. A pleasant market town set at the head of the Owenacurra estuary, near the northeast corner of Cork Harbour, it has many gray-stone buildings dating mainly from the early 19th century.

The **Jameson Heritage Centre** has tours of the Old Midleton Distillery, to show you how Irish whiskey—*uisce beatha* (pronounced ishka bahhah), "the water of life"—was made in the old days. The old stone buildings are excellent examples of 19th-century industrial architecture, the impressively large old waterwheel still operates, and the pot still—a copper dome that can hold 32,000 imperial gallons of whiskey—is the

Continued on page 342

A TASTE OF IRELAND

Queen scallops with aubergine caviar

Great ingredients and innovative chefs are shaping West Cork into one of the most foodie-friendly places around.

The next time you wander into a time-burnished 19th-century Irish pub bent on downing a platter of steak, bland potatoes, and mushy peas, don't be surprised if you end up with a meal of skewered John Dory in clonmel cider Sauce and a finale of Cooleeney Camembert ganache with lavender jelly. Begorrah—you've encountered the much-vaunted Irish food revolution! Since the mid-1990s, the New Irish Cuisine has changed the beige, boiled, and boring food of yore into a bounty of gourmet delights. Today, haute-hungry gourmands packing chubby wallets (and the cookbooks of Margaret Johnson and Noel Cullen) are all abuzz discovering emerging culinary wizards; artisanal producers of farmhouse cheeses; organic beef and smoked fish; and some of the best farmers' markets and provisioners around. Leading the charge of Ireland's food revolution are superstar chefs, and few have done more to transform the Irish kitchen than Myrtle Allen and her daughter-in-law, Darina Allen. The trip to bountiful Ireland begins with them.

Gubbeen Farmhouse

BALLYMALOE: A TRIP TO BOUNTIFUL

Bacon chop with Irish Whiskey sauce, Ballymaloe Cookery School

When Myrtle Allen opened a restaurant at her Georgian farm-estate, Ballymaloe (east of Cork City and pronounced Bah-lee-mal-oo), in 1964, she hadn't set out to change the way Ireland eats.

Moving to the historic Quaker stronghold of Shangarry in 1948, she and her husband, Ivan, began the restoration of an old Georgian farm estate. Before too long, their 400-acre cropland became the breeding ground for a new gastronomy as the couple reaped harvests of sea kale, parsnips, carrageen moss, rutabagas, gooseberries, globe artichokes, and other heritage veggies. Long before organic became a buzzword, Myrtle made freshness her mantra: eggs from her own hens, produce from her own garden, freshly landed fish from nearby Ballycotton. So, when she opened The Yeats Room at Ballymaloe in 1964, her refashioning of her great-grandparents food was embraced by a generation reared on frozen pizza. In no time, food critics were raving about Myrtle's everything-old-is-new-again-but-better take.

The Herb Garden at Ballymaloe

Now retired, Myrtle has passed the torch on to her son-in-law, Rory O'Connell, whose balanced touch in the kitchen is almost Quaker-like in its subtlety. Dinners here are the real thing: fresh-picked coriander from the greenhouse for the leg of lamb, the eggs in the Carageen Pudding—a custard mixed with Cork seaweed and bittersweet Irish-coffee sauce—the gift of hens with squatters' rights, and if the plaice weren't biting that day, it won't be on the menu. Under the hosts' celebrated collection of modern Irish paintings, diners can enjoy a kaleidoscope of specialties (selections change seasonally, weekly, and daily) be it a radish-leaf soup, a Ballymaloe cheddar cheese fondue, or a roast Ballycotton cod with Ulster champ. A final testimony to Myrtle's practice of supporting small-scale, local food purveyors is the adieu offering: the amazing cheese board, which conveys local artisanship at its best. Ballymaloe House has lovely overnight accomodations (⊕ www.ballymaloe.ie ⇨ review under Shanagarry), just one reason why many diners enjoy a leisurely repast at night.

NOW WE'RE COOKING

If Myrtle Allen is the Alice Waters of Ireland, Darina Allen is its Martha Stewart. Thanks to her eight television series, her bestselling cookbooks, and the happy status of being the daughter-in-law of Myrtle, Darina's celebrity in Ireland is about on a par with U2's. She arrived in 1963 to apprentice at Ballymaloe and promptly fell in love with Myrtle's son, Tim, and her culinary dream. So, in 1983, she and Tim opened the Ballymaloe Cookery School, setting up shop two miles east on the other side of Shanagarry village at Kinoith House. The ultimate spot for a don't-just-visit, stay-and-become-an-Irish-chef experience, the school offers everything from two-hour starter lessons to the famed 12-week Certificate Course (run three times a year for 58 students), which many Irish chefs regard as a rite of passage. Half-day courses can be combined with an indulgent stay at

Darina Allen

Ballymaloe House—choose from "Sushi Made Simple," "The Magic of Phyllo," or "Discovering Tapas." A new departure is the "forgotten skills" series, day-long courses on chicken keeping, beekeeping, and organic gardening. Evidence that history repeats itself: Darina's daughter-in-law, Rachel Allen, is now making her second TV series, and publishing her second cook book.

MENU BEST BETS

Goujons of Ballycotton Haddock with Tartare Sauce

John's Rosemary, Red Wine & Garden Leek Risotto

Gubbeen Ham Braised in Chablis & Cream Served with Peperonata & Chives

Roast East Cork Beef with Roast Garlic Mayonnaise, with Fondant Potato & Vegetable Pakorash

Ballymaloe Cheddar Cheese Fondue

Grilled Ballycotton Hake with Scallops & Lobster, Herb Relish & French Beans

THE BALLYMALOE COOKERY SCHOOL is in Kineath, just outside Shanagarry (☎ 021/464-6785 ⊕ www.cookingisfun.ie). Classes range from afternoon demonstrations (€75) to half-day classes (€95) to 1, 2½, and 5 day courses to the full 12-week Certificate (€8,775). Students can stay in charming cottages on the grounds.

CORK CORNUCOPIA: THE FOOD ARTISANS

Compare a traditionally made butcher's sausage with the plastic-wrapped supermarket version, and you'll understand what all the fuss is about: flavor, texture, and general deliciousness.

You'll see why Ireland's new artisanal foodstuff makers, fed up with the formulaic, tasteless foods of big industry, have stepped in to pioneer the production of farmhouse cheeses, organic beef, and organic herb cultivation and fish smoking. They got a big boost with the 1998 founding of Slow Food Ireland (⊕ www.slowfoodireland.com), a loose collective of specialty producers and restaurateurs whose aim was to encourage careful food sourcing. West Cork has played an important role in the revival of Irish traditional foods, since incomers moving to the area seeking a change in lifestyle found that their small-business interests dovetailed with those of the traditional butchers, bakers, and farmers who had stayed put. These new artisans are now often listed on restaurant menus: Gubbeen Cheese, Ummera Smoked Salmon, Krawczyk's West Cork Salamis, Glenilen Dairy Products, and many others. Here are three of the best:

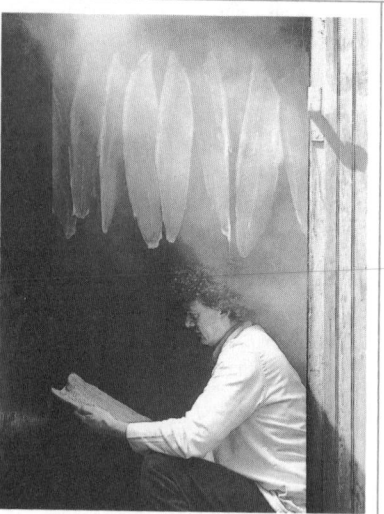

GUBBEEN FARMHOUSE PRODUCTS

Farmer Tom Ferguson tends a herd of prize cows, whose rich milk is made into creamy cheese by his wife Giana. The fresh-straw piggery allows its lucky pigs to have a view of Roaring Water Bay, one of the most scenic corners of Ireland. Tom and Giana's son, Fingal, runs the smokehouse (great smoked bacon, chorizo, and salamis), while daughter Clovisse grows organic vegetables and herbs. Products are sold at Neal's Yard in London and West Cork's Farmer's Markets. ⊠ *Gubbeen, Schull, near Skibbbereen, Co. Cork* ☎ *028/28231* ⊕ *www.gubbeen.com*

BELVELLY SMOKEHOUSE
Frank Hederman smokes his eels, mackerel, salmon, trout, and mussels over beech rather than oak, giving them an unusually mild flavor. His smoked salmon is sold in London's Fortnum & Mason. The smokehouse is open for tastings, and his products can be bought at Cork City's English Market and Midleton Farmer's Market. ⊠ *Cobh* ☎ *021/481-1089*

MACROOM OATMEAL
Since the early 1800s, Donal Creedon's porridge oats have been hand-roasted on the traditional cast-iron plate at Walton's Mills before being shelled and ground, giving them a distinctive smoky, nutty flavor. Great for breadmaking, the meal is sold at many food shops. ⊠ *Kanturk, Co. Cork* ☎ *026/41800* ⊕*macroomoatmealmills£eircom.net*

BLESSED ARE THE CHEESEMAKERS

Thirty years ago Irish cheese came in bright-orange blocks and tasted like salted plastic. Today, a thriving cheesemaking culture—a mix of native ingenuity and French, Swiss, German, and Dutch expertise—produces a wide range of artisanal farmhouse cheeses from the milk of goats and sheep, as well as from purebred cows. **Here are the best:**

Ardsallagh Goat's Cheese. A popular salad ingredient, this cheese can be bought from its maker, Jane Murphy, at the Midleton Farmer's Market.

Cashel Blue. The most famous Irish blue, this mild, creamy delight is made in Fethard, Co. Tipperary—it is as much used in cooking as on the cheese board.

Crozier Blue. Made from sheep's milk, this has a cult following.

Gabriel and Desmond. Using only summer-season raw milk from local herds grazed near the sea, these hard cheeses created by Americans Bill Hogan and Sean Ferry have a long maturation period, resulting in a piquant, aromatic bouquet.

Knockalara Sheep's Milk Cheese. Made by Wolfgang and Agnes Schiebitz, this is popular with chefs thanks to its soft, crumbly texture.

Milleens. This pungent, washed-rind winner is made from the milk of cows raised by Norman and Veronica Steele on their Beara Peninsula family farm.

FINDING THE FEAST

Long known as the "belly of Ireland," the West Cork region is celebrated for its rich fishing and even richer farming. These days, gourmets are busy rooting out the best Irish chorizo, sampling a new Durrus cheese and nutmeg pizza, or wolfing down Galway Bay oysters (heaven when served with Guinness!). Like a world-class picnic, this cook's tour is the tastiest recipe for a day trip through the region.

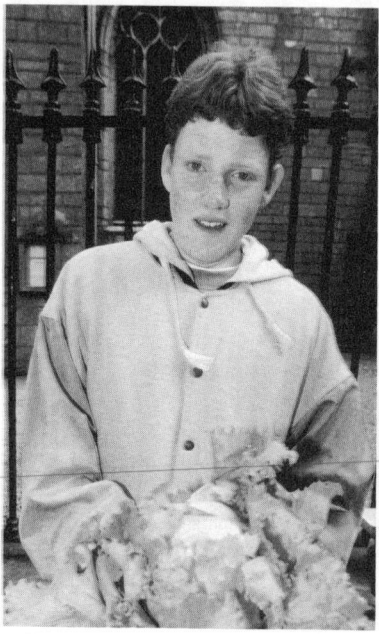

The best places to track down top temptations from Cork's gastronomic cornucopia are the area's food markets, often set in small villages and averaging only about a dozen stalls. Low overheads mean bargains for the buyers, who enjoy an amazing array of artisanal foodstuffs, from organic vegetables to sauces and relishes, Breton pancakes, handmade bread, home-cured ham, preserves, smoked salmon, and a great range of cheeses. And the markets' festive atmosphere (often livened up with a jazz trio or street performers) is complemented by the camaraderie of the stall-holders—this is often their main contact with the buying public. Darina Allen, with typical energy, can be found most Saturday mornings selling produce from her Ballymaloe Cookery School at a stall in Midleton. Check out the ever-changing market scene on its Web site (⊕ www.irelandmarkets.com) for up-to-date information. Here is a tip sheet:

COUNTY CORK

Bantry, Main Square, Friday 9 am to 1 pm. A traditional street market, with a strong presence of growers of organic plants and veggies.

Clonakilty, Thursday and Saturday, 10 am to 2 pm. Indoor market in MacCurtain Hall, with artisan food sold by its makers on Thursday and food and crafts sold by their makers on Saturday.

Kinsale, Market Square, Tuesday 10–1. Snack on a Breton crepe while stocking up on chutneys, smoked salmon, famhouse cheeses, fresh fish, and organic veg and fruit at this cute piazza market.

Midleton, Saturday 10 am–2 pm. One of the liveliest farmers' markets, it's held in a small car park, with buskers creating a festive vibe.

Schull, Sunday 11–3. At its best in summer and at Christmas, this foodie's market showcases superb products from local bakers, fish smokers and cheesemakers, and Gubbeen smoked pork products, all sold by their makers.

COUNTY KERRY

Kenmare, Wednesday 10 am–5 pm, closed Jan. and Feb. About 15 outdoor stalls offer local organic produce and a few exotic imports to an appreciative local clientele. Look out for Knockatee cheese from Tuosist down the road, Olivier's smoked trout from Killorglin, organic vegs, homemade pâtés, fresh fish, and French soaps and sweets.

Killarney, Parochial Hall, Country Market, Friday 11:30 am–1:30 pm. Famed for cakes, bread, savory tarts, jams, and farm-fresh eggs, the produce is all genuinely homemade, much of it from local farms, and sold at bargain prices.

Milltown, Old Church Market, Saturday 10 am–2pm. Organic producers converge on this church, on the main road (N70) between Killorglin and Castlemaine—specialist bakers, organic growers, a wheatgrass stall, and an herbalist are highlights.

OTHER FOODIE FAVES

THE ENGLISH MARKET Today, this famous city-center covered market is a thriving hub of artisanal butchers, fishmongers, and greengrocers. Organic fruits and vegs, top-quality meat and fresh fish, imported coffees and teas, locally made charcuterie, farmhouse cheeses—even a champagne from a local wine merchant, Bubble Brothers. ⊠ *Grand Parade, Cork City* ⊕ *www.corkcity.ie*

THE LETTERCOLLUM SHOP Founders of the Lettercollum Kitchen Project, Con McLaughlin and Karen Austin are masters of the vegetarian and ethnic repertory (and also offer cooking classes). Their shop/bakery sells specialist breads, cooks' ingredients, sandwiches, and savory herb tarts. Pick up a picnic. ⊠ *22 Connolly St., Clonakilty* ☎ *023/46251* ⊕ *www.lettercollum.ie*

URRU Once Ruth Healy took the Ballymaloe Certificate Cookery Course she left the corporate treadmill behind to open the ultimate cook's shop, which aims to bring urban chic to rural Ireland. Sip a latte while browsing among local artisanal foods, including homemade pâtés and patisserie, and a tempting range of cookbooks, cookwares, and chocolates. ⊠ *The Mill, MacSwiney Quay, Bandon, Co. Cork* ☎ *023/54731* ⊕ *www.urru.ie*

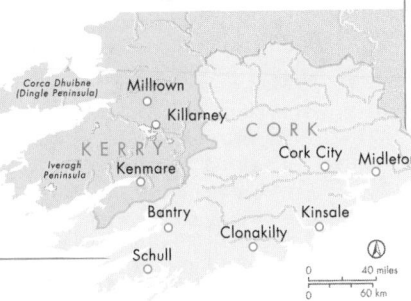

world's largest. Early in the tour, requests are made for a volunteer "whiskey taster"—so be alert if this option appeals. Tours end with a complimentary glass of Jameson's Irish whiskey (or a soft drink). A crafts center and café are also on the premises. ☎ 021/461–3594 ⊕ *www. whiskeytours.ie* ⛁ *€8.50* ⊘ *Mar.–Oct., daily 9–4:30; Nov.–Feb., tours only, weekdays at 12:30 and 3, weekends at 2 and 4.*

Fermoy

㉓ *35 km (22 mi) north of Cork City on N8, 43 km (27 mi) west of Youghal on R634, Tallow Rd., which adjoins N72.*

An army town dating mainly from the mid-19th century, Fermoy is a major crossroads on the Dublin–Cork road (N8); the east–west road that passes through town (N72) is an attractive 98-km (61-mi) alternative route to Killarney. The bridge that spans the Blackwater is flanked by two weirs dating from 1689. From mid-April to early July you can watch salmon working their way back to their spawning grounds. A few miles upstream on the same river is Castlehyde, a fine Georgian house which is now the home of the lord of Irish dance, Michael Flatley. It's easy to see why he was so charmed by the quiet, lush country that surrounds this famous salmon river.

Where to Stay & Eat

$$
Fodor'sChoice
★

×⊞ **Ballyvolane House.** With Georgian splendor in the terra-cotta, gilded, and black Italianate pillared hall and Regency coziness nonpareil in the daffodil yellow sitting room, Ballyvolane offers a setting as elegant as it is charming. Although this 1728 stone house looks imposing, life here unfolds with country-house informality. Expect to find old fishing gear and walking sticks lying about and the family dog greeting your return. The spacious bedrooms are decorated with a rich assortment of antiques and heirlooms, but also display an unpredictable sense of humor—the tub in Roland's Room, on a wooden pedestal perched to give a garden view, always raises a smile. The guest rooms look out onto wonderful gardens, with a 100-acre dairy farm beyond. Dinner is served at a large table in the formal dining room ($$$$), with family silver set on white linens (both dinner and rooms must be booked at least 24 hours in advance). The village of Castlelyons is signposted off N8 in Rathcormac, just south of Fermoy. ⊠ *Castlelyons, Co. Cork* ☎ *025/36349* ⊜ *025/ 36781* ⊕ *www.ballyvolanehouse.ie* ⇆ *6 rooms* ⚬ *Dining room, fishing; no a/c, no room phones, no smoking* ⊟ *AE, MC, V* �ⓞ *BP.*

Mallow

㉔ *30 km (18 mi) west of Fermoy on N72.*

Mallow, an angling center and market town, was, in the 18th century, a popular spa. Mallow lies at the intersection of the Cork–Limerick and Waterford–Killarney roads, within an hour's drive of all four towns. Today it's a small, sleepy town, with little trace of its 18th-century heyday, when it was the headquarters of the Rakes of Mallow Club, a notorious crowd of gamblers and drinkers immortalized in the song "The Rakes of Mallow." The ruins of the late-16th-century **Mallow Castle** are at the bottom of the main street, freely accessible behind ornamental gates. The castle was burned by the Jacobites in 1689, and its stables were later converted into a house, which is still in use as a private home. From here you can view the white fallow deer that are unique to Mallow and were presented by Elizabeth I.

Where to Stay & Eat

$$$ ✕⌷ **Longueville House.** Perched over the Blackwater Valley—the Irish
Fodor'sChoice Rhine—this imposing Georgian white-stone mansion graces one of the
★ most beautiful of all Irish river valleys. Built about 1720 by the Longfields—who changed their names to Longueville to favor the French side of the family and distance themselves from any Cromwellian associations—this family seat is framed by limestone quoins around a classically symmetrical facade. Inside, Georgian grace notes continue, with a few 18th-century plaster ceilings, Adamesque fireplaces, and a glowing dining salon lined with ancestral portraits. The Presidents' Restaurant ($$$$) serves an outstanding Irish-French–style menu prepared in large measure with produce from the house's farm, garden, and river. This is not a place for jeans and sneakers: the surroundings will make you want to dress up for dinner. The bedrooms are roomy and elegant, with a peaceful air and color-coordinated in restful pastel shades. ⊠ *Co. Cork* ☎ *022/47156* 🖷 *022/47459* ⊕ *www.longuevillehouse.ie* 🛏 *20 rooms* ⚑ *Restaurant, cable TV, fishing, bar, meeting rooms; no a/c* 🖃 *AE, DC, MC, V* ☺ *Closed mid-Feb.–mid-Mar.* ⍾ *BP.*

Sports

Mallow Golf Club (⊠ Ballyellis, Co. Cork ☎ 022/21145) is an 18-hole, par-72 parkland course with excellent views of the Blackwater Valley.

KINSALE TO GLENGARRIFF

The historic old port—and now booming seaside town—of Kinsale is the perfect place to begin the 136-km (85-mi) trip, via Bantry Bay and through a variety of seascapes, to the lush vegetation of Glengarriff. If you tackle this scenic West Cork coastal route nonstop, the drive takes less than two hours, but the whole point of this journey is to linger in places that tickle your fancy. Must-dos include the famed 18th-century manse of Bantry House and the romantic island gardens of Ilnacullin.

Kinsale

㉕ *29 km (18 mi) southwest of Cork City on R600.*

Foodies flock to Kinsale, a picturesque port that pioneered the Irish small-town tradition of fine dining in unbelievably small restaurants. Back in the early '80s, Kinsale had a village-size population of 2,000 souls and at least a dozen top-grade restaurants, mostly run by enthusiastic owner-chefs. Things have leveled out since then—the town has grown, while the number of restaurants has remained nearly the same, and most of the original chefs have moved on—but there is still a great buzz during the annual Autumn Flavours Festival. In the town center, at the tip of the wide, fjordlike harbor that opens out from the River Bandon, upscale shops and eateries with brightly painted facades line small streets. Kinsale has two yacht marinas, and skippers with deep-sea angling boats offer day charters. The Kinsale Yacht Club hosts racing and cruising events during the sailing season, which runs from March to October for hardy souls and from June to August for everyone else. This town is also where you can find Ireland's largest bareboat charter company.

The **Desmond Castle and the International Museum of Wine** are in a 15th-century fortified town house—originally a custom house—that has a dark history. It was used as a prison for French and American seamen in the 1700s, and was subsequently a jail and then a workhouse. Now it contains displays that tell the story of the wine trade and its importance to the Irish diaspora to France, America, Australia, and New Zealand. ⊠ *Cork St.* ☎ *021/477–4855* ⊕ *www.heritageireland.ie* ⛀ *€2.75* ☉ *Mid–Apr.–mid-June, Tues.–Sun. 10–6; mid-June–mid-Oct., daily 10–6.*

Memorabilia from the wreck of the *Lusitania* are among the best artifacts in the **Kinsale Museum,** which is in a 17th-century, Dutch-style courthouse. The 1915 inquest into that ship's sinking took place in the courtroom, briefly making it the focus of the world's attention; it has been preserved as a memorial. Because the staff consists of volunteers, it's best to call to confirm opening times. ⊠ *Old Courthouse, Market Pl.* ☎ *021/477–2044* ⛀ *€2.50* ☉ *Mon.–Sat. 11–5, Sun. 3–5.*

★ The British built **Charles Fort** on the east side of the Bandon River estuary in the late 17th century, after their defeat of the Spanish and Irish forces. One of Europe's best-preserved "star forts" encloses some 12 clifftop acres and is similar to Fort Ticonderoga in New York State. If the sun is shining, take the footpath signposted Scilly Walk; it winds along the harbor's edge under tall trees and then through the village of Summer Cove. ⊠ *3 km (2 mi) east of town* ☎ *021/477–2263* ⊕ *www.heritageireland.ie* ⛀ *€3.50* ☉ *Mid-Mar.–Oct., daily 10–6; Nov.–mid-Mar., weekends 10–5.*

The **Spaniard Inn** (⊠ Scilly ☎ 021/477–2436) looks over the town and harbor from a hairpin bend on the road to Charles Fort. Inside, sawdust-covered floors and a big open fire make this onetime fishermen's bar a cozy spot in winter. In summer you can take a pint to the veranda and watch the world go by on land and sea.

Where to Stay & Eat

★ **$$–$$$$** ✕ **Crackpots.** A grocery was transformed into Carole Norman's "ceramic café," a simple but elegant eatery with warm yellow walls, an open fire, and cozy dining areas. The most popular tables are in the front "shop window" area. Behind the restaurant is Carole's pottery workshop; if

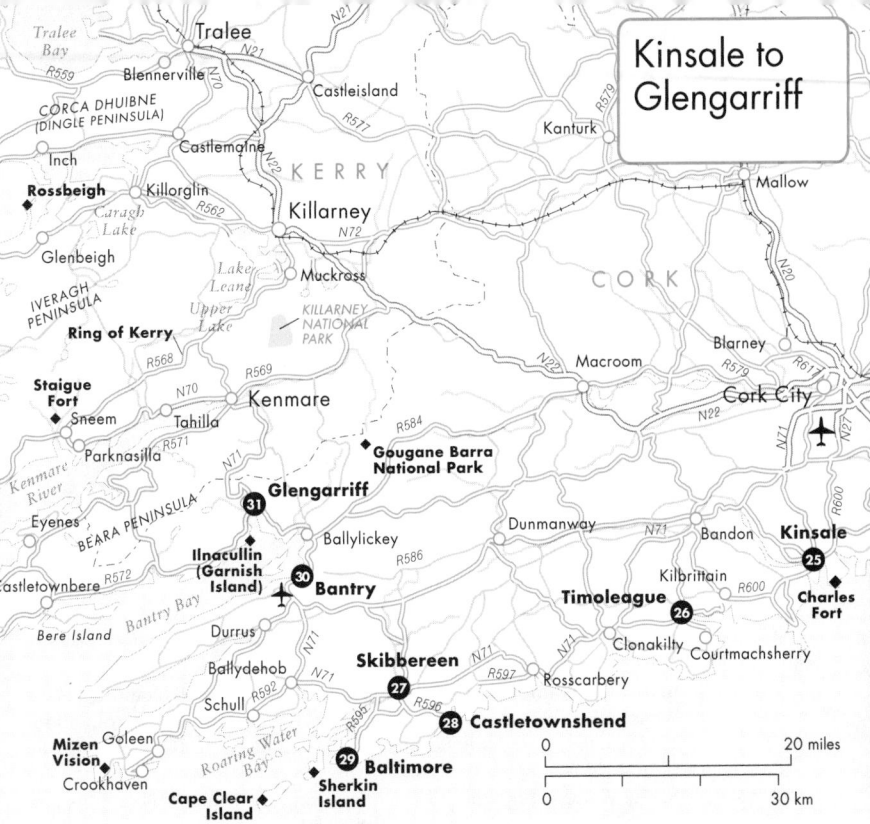

you like your dinner plate, you can buy it. The eclectic menu has plenty of light dishes in the lower price range, with vegetarian dishes a strong point. Choices range from spinach and ricotta cheese filo baked with red pepper sauce to Moroccan meatballs with couscous to Thai-style prawns with fragrant rice. There's always a steak option, too. ⊠ 3 Cork St. ☎ 021/477–2847 ▤ MC, V ⊙ Closed Mon.–Wed. in Nov.–Mar.

★ $$–$$$$ ✕ **Man Friday.** Yes, the name refers to Kinsale's alleged connection with the original Robinson Crusoe, Alexander Selkirk, for the town was reputedly his last port of call before shipwreck. Set about 1 km (½ mi) outside town, next to the Spaniard Inn, on a hilltop overlooking the harbor, the restaurant focuses on steaks and seafood, prepared in an unpretentious Continental style. A rustic downhill walkway leads to a series of interconnected rooms and a terrace where diners enjoy drinks in fine weather. The generous portions and the warm atmosphere make it the sort of place you'll want to revisit. ⊠ Scilly ☎ 021/477–2260 ▤ AE, DC, MC, V ⊙ Closed Sun. No lunch.

$$–$$$ ✕ **Max's Wine Bar.** Low-beam ceilings and polished antique tables of different shapes and sizes lend this town house considerable charm. Lunches are light; it's a good place if you're keen on salads. At dinner, owner-chef Olivier Queva's classical French background is evident in his treatment of the daily catch and in his clever ways with such unusual cuts

A Battle Lost

BEFORE KINSALE BECAME the foodie capital of Ireland, it was chiefly famous for the Battle of Kinsale in 1601, when the Irish and the Spanish joined forces against the English—and lost. As generations of Irish schoolchildren could tell you, the Battle of Kinsale was a turning point in Irish history. It precipitated an event known as "the Flight of the Earls" (the subject of Brian Friels' play *Making History*), in which the Irish aristocracy left for Europe, to seek help in furthering their cause from the Catholic king of Spain. The Irish earls never returned, leaving their lands to be colonized by the English settlers,

who also filled the power vacuum created by their absence. The Spanish influence that can be traced back to this battle can be seen in Kinsale's older houses, which have slate roofs and unusual slate fronts. Because of its geographical position (approximately 800 km [500 mi] of open sea due north of La Coruna) Kinsale continued to trade with Spain, and even today, Spanish trawlers regularly fish in the waters off the coast of County Cork. Kinsale went on to become an important fishing port as well as a British army and naval base.

of meat as oxtail and trotters. The wine list is long and includes a good selection of French and New World wines, ranging in price from about €15 to €85. ⊠ *Main St.* ☎ *021/477–2443* ▤ *MC, V* ⊗ *Closed Nov.–mid-Mar.*

★ **$$–$$$** ✕ **The Vintage.** Frank and Diana Ferguson, owners of this famous cottage restaurant, have adopted a bistro-style menu that is perfectly in tune with the simple, rustic interior. The ancient stone walls are exposed, under a low-beamed ceiling, and tables are simply set with oilcloth covers. The bar is tiny enough to be a novelty—it's likely to be the smallest you've ever seen. Daily specials are up on the blackboard: whole baked sea bass with sea asparagus and herb butter, perhaps. Or opt for a rib-eye steak with fondant potatoes and baby onions from the main menu. Starters are strong on local sea food (oysters, prawns, mussels), and desserts are homemade. ⊠ *50 Main St.* ☎ *021/477–2502* ▤ *AE, DC, MC, V* ⊗ *Tues.–Sun., 6 PM–10 PM. Closed Jan.–mid-Feb.*

♻ **$–$$$** ✕ **The Bulman.** Kinsale has other pub-restaurants, but none with such an idyllic waterside location. In summer drinks are taken outside, either at tables or on the big stone quay, which looks back to the town and out to the unspoiled outer harbor. At lunch, simple pub grub—mussels steamed in white wine or a meaty burger and chips—is served at the bar, and a more extensive menu in the restaurant. In the evening, the first-floor restaurant has tables with splendid views of the sun setting over the harbor. The menu includes steaks, tempura prawns, and local salmon. ⊠ *Summercove* ☎ *021/477–2131* ▤ *MC, V* ⊗ *No lunch Sun.*

$$$ ✕▥ **Blue Haven.** A restaurant and small hotel occupy this attractive, yellow-stucco, blue-trim town house. Rooms in the main house, though small, are cheerful and have paintings by local artists; newer rooms in an adjacent building have dark-oak furniture, antique canopy beds, and more spacious baths. Inexpensive bar food is served until 9:30 PM in the lounge, the patio, and the conservatory, all of which have swagged curtains and nautical brass. Some nights a pianist entertains, and there's always a pleasant buzz, as the bar is a popular local haunt. The quiet, pastel-color restaurant overlooks a garden and fountain, and is renowned for its seafood. ⊠ *3 Pearse St., Co. Cork* ☎ *021/477–2209* 📠 *021/477–4268* ⊕ *www.bluehavenkinsale.com* ⌦ *17 rooms* ♨ *Restaurant, coffee shop, cable TV, fishing, bar; no a/c* ⊟ *AE, DC, MC, V* ⦿⊙ *BP.*

$$ ✕⊡ **The White House.** One of Kinsale's oldest inns has maintained the tradition of a warm Irish welcome. Bedrooms vary in size, but all have fully tiled bathrooms and pastel color schemes. A bar menu is served both in the bar and in the quieter side room called Chelsea's Bistro; the boiled bacon and cabbage—served with enormous potatoes—and the fish of the day are good bets. Ask about the two- and three-day dinner-and-lodging specials. ⊠ *Pearse St. and Glen, Co. Cork* ☎ *021/477–2125* 📠 *021/477–2045* ⊕ *www.whitehouse-kinsale.ie* ⌦ *10 rooms* ♨ *Restaurant, cable TV, bar; no a/c* ⊟ *AE, DC, MC, V* ⦿⊙ *BP.*

★ $$$ ⊞ **Perryville House.** Pretty in pink-and-white stone trim, offset by a black wrought-iron veranda, and boasting a perch overlooking the inner harbor, Perryville House is in an adorable nook of town where homes often flower with hanging baskets and window boxes. The main salon hits all the right notes—emerald green walls, gilt-frame portrait, white fireplace—and one gets the impression of being in a private home. Front bedrooms have sea views, but rooms at the rear are quieter—key in July and August, when the town gets busy. All guest rooms are imaginatively furnished with Victorian antiques and have large beds and such extras as robes and fresh flowers. The lodging has a wine license, so you can buy by the glass or the bottle. ⊠ *Long Quay, Co. Cork* ☎ *021/477–2731* 📠 *021/477–2298* ⊕ *www.perryvillehouse.com* ⌦ *27 rooms* ♨ *Cable TV; no a/c, no kids under 13, no smoking* ⊟ *AE, DC, MC, V* ⊙ *Closed Nov.–Mar.* ⦿⊙ *BP.*

$$ ⊞ **Innishannon House.** A pretty country house built in 1720 in the Petit Château style on the banks of the Bandon, Innishannon retains plenty of casual character. Bar and dining room are hung with contemporary Irish art, and have a busy local trade. Guest rooms vary greatly in shape and size, as do the windows, but have a variety of interesting antiques and strong color schemes. The hotel is surrounded by gardens and woods, with an attractive stretch of the Bandon River running through it, bordering the grounds. It's in a quiet rural location just off N7, about 6 km (4 mi) from Kinsale; it's quite perfect both as a retreat and as a base for touring the area. ⊠ *Innishannon, Co. Cork* ☎ *021/477–5121* 📠 *021/477–5609* ⊕ *www.innishannon-hotel.ie* ⌦ *12 rooms* ♨ *Restaurant, cable TV, boating, fishing, bar, meeting rooms; no a/c* ⊟ *AE, DC, MC, V* ⦿⊙ *BP.*

★ $$ ⊞ **Old Bank House.** Owners Michael and Marie Riese manage this Georgian town house with flair and loving attention to detail. The large, high-ceiling rooms have fresh-flower arrangements, original Irish art, and tall double-glazed windows. The whole look is not, however, period Georgian but vacation casual, with throw pillows and plants setting a most

5

informal note. The higher the room, the better the view, and there's an elevator for your convenience. Michael was previously an award-winning full-time chef—no wonder his breakfasts are so memorable. ⊠ *Pearse St., Co. Cork* ☎ *021/477–4075* 🖷 *021/477–4296* ⊕ *www. oldbankhousekinsale.com* ⇨ *17 rooms* ⌂ *Cable TV; no a/c* ⊟ *AE, MC, V* ☺ *Closed Dec. 1–28* ❢❍❢ *BP.*

¢ ⌺ **Kilcaw House.** Low room rates and off-street parking make this attractive, modern country guesthouse a good choice. On busy weekends, when the town buzz continues into the small hours, Kilcaw's location— 2 km (1 mi) outside town on the Cork side of the R600—guarantees peace and quiet. An open fire in the lobby, polished pine floors, and striking colors add character to the farmhouse-style building. Rooms are well-equipped, spacious, and uncluttered, with country pine furniture and throw rugs on wooden floors. ⊠ *Pewter Hole Cross, on R600, Co. Cork* ☎ *021/477–4155* 🖷 *021/477–4755* ⊕ *www.kilcawhouse.com* ⇨ *7 rooms* ⌂ *Cable TV; no a/c* ⊟ *AE, MC, V* ❢❍❢ *BP.*

Nightlife

The **Shanakee** (⊠ Market St. ☎ 021/477–4472) is renowned for live music—both rock and Irish traditional. Check out the **Spaniard Inn** (⊠ Scilly ☎ 021/477–2436) for rock and folk groups. There's a traditional Irish session on Wednesday from 10 PM year-round.

Sports & the Outdoors

BICYCLING Rent a bike from **D&C Cycles** (⊠ 18 Main St. ☎ 021/477–4884) to explore the picturesque hinterland of Kinsale.

FISHING For deep-sea angling off the Old Head of Kinsale contact **William Van Dyk** (☎ 021/477–8944) or **Arthur Long** (☎ 021/477–8969), both of whom operate out of **Castlepark Marina** (⊠ Castlepark, Co. Cork). For bareboat charters or skippered cruises—of a day or longer—contact **Sail Ireland Charters** (⊠ Trident Hotel, Kinsale, Co. Cork ☎ 021/477–2927 ⊕ www.sailireland.com).

WATER SPORTS & TENNIS The **Oysterhaven Holiday and Activity Center** (⊠ Signposted off R600, Oysterhaven ☎ 021/477–0738) is in a sheltered inlet 10 km (6 mi) east of Kinsale. Rental of sailboarding equipment and wet suits starts at €20 per hour. Topaz dinghies rent for €30 per hour. If Irish weather permits, you can also book a tennis court here for €10 an hour.

Shopping

Boland's Craft Shop (⊠ Pearse St. ☎ 021/477–2161) sells some unusual items, including sweaters, designer rain gear, and linen shirts exclusive to this shop. **Giles Norman Photography Gallery** (⊠ 44 Main St. ☎ 021/477–4373) sells black-and-white photographs of Irish scenes. **Granny's Bottom Drawer** (⊠ 53 Main St. ☎ 021/477–4839) has fine linen and lace in classic and contemporary styles. The **Keane on Ceramics** (⊠ Pier Rd. ☎ 021/477–2085) gallery represents the best of Ireland's ceramics artists.

You can spend quite a bit of time browsing through the excellent selection of Irish poetry and books on local history at the **Kinsale Bookshop** (⊠ 8 Main St. ☎ 021/477–4244). **Kinsale Crystal** (⊠ Market St. ☎ 021/

Monks & Wine

CLOSE UP

A MID-13TH-CENTURY Franciscan abbey at the water's edge is Timoleague's most striking monument. (Walk around the back to find the entrance gate.) The view of the sea framed by its ruined Gothic windows is an unmissable photo-op.

The abbey was built before the estuary silted up, and its main business was the importing of wine from Spain. A tower and walls with Gothic-arch windows still stand, and you can trace the ground plan of the old friary–chapel, refectory, cloisters, and the extensive wine cellar. It was sacked by the English in 1642 but, like many other ruins of its kind, was used as a burial place until the late 20th century, hence the modern gravestones.

5

477–4463) is a studio that sells 100% Irish, handblown, hand-cut crystal. **Hilary Hale** (✉ Rincurran Hall, Summercove ☎ 021/477–2010 ⊕ www.hilaryhale.com) is a wood turner who uses storm-felled locally grown timber to make lamps, bowls, and platters. **The Trading House** (✉ 54 Main St. ☎ 021/477–7497) has exclusive housewares from France, Spain, and Scandinavia alongside Irish and French antiques. **Victoria Murphy** (✉ Market Quay ☎ 021/477–4317) sells small antiques and antique jewelry.

EN ROUTE

Leave Kinsale through its center and follow the quays, driving west along the Bandon River toward the bridge on R600. This takes you through **Garretstown Woods** (signposts for Clonakilty on R600), carpeted with wild bluebells in April. You'll then travel past the edge of Courtmacsherry Bay, along a wide, saltwater inlet that teems with curlew, plover, and other waders. The road leads to Clonakilty, where you pick up the main N71 to Skibbereen.

Timoleague

 19 km (12 mi) west of Kinsale on R600.

The romantic silhouette of its ruined abbey dominates the view when you're approaching Timoleague, a village of multicolor houses on the Argideen River estuary. The town marks the eastern end of the Seven Heads Peninsula, which stretches around to Clonakilty.

You can glimpse **Courtmacsherry,** the postcard village of multicolor cottages, just across the water. It has a sandy beach that makes it a favorite for vacationers. To reach it follow the signposts from Timoleague. Farther on you can find that many storefronts in **Clonakilty,** a small market town 9½ km (6 mi) west of Timoleague on R600/N71, have charmingly traditional, hand-painted signs and wooden facades. **Inchydoney,** 3 km (2 mi) outside Clonakilty, is one of the area's finest sandy beaches backed by sheltered sand dunes.

**OFF THE
BEATEN
PATH**

BIRTHPLACE OF MICHAEL COLLINS – The birthplace of Michael Collins (1890–1922) is signposted 9 km (6 mi) west of Timoleague off N71 (past the village of Lissavaird). You can see the ground plan of the simple homestead where the controversial founder of the modern Irish Army was born. There's also a bronze memorial (freely accessible), and another memorial in the nearest village, Woodfield, opposite the pub where Collins is said to have had his last drink on the day he was shot in an ambush.

Where to Stay & Eat

$$–$$$
Fodor's Choice
★

✕ **Casino House.** Stop midway between Kinsale and Timoleague, on coastal route R600, for a meal at this farmhouse, which has been renovated in a cool, minimalist style and converted to a restaurant. The two small but airy and well-lighted dining rooms—one blue and one green—have private sitting rooms for predinner drinks next to an open fire, a treat that sets the tone of gentle pampering that typifies the highly professional co-owner Kerrin Relja's hospitality. Menu highlights from talented Croatian owner-chef Michael Relja include garlic prawn salad, lobster risotto, a fine roast loin of lamb served with Roman gnocchi, and, as one of the top seasonal desserts, summer fruits with sabayon. ⊠ *Coolmaine, Kilbrittain* ☎ *023/49944* ▤ *MC, V* ⊘ *Closed Wed. and mid-Jan.–mid-Mar. No dinner Sun., no lunch Mon.–Sat.*

¢ 🏠 **Kilbrogan House.** Bandon is a market town on the Bandon River, midway between Kinsale and Clonakilty, a good, peaceful base for touring that's off the beaten tourist trail. Kilbrogan House stands at the highest point of town and has been the community's architectural star since it was built in 1818. Owner Catherine FitzMaurice spent 12 years restoring it to its Georgian splendor. The ornate plasterwork could easily grace a much larger country mansion, as could the elaborate flying staircase. Large windows afford garden views and bring streams of sunlight into the spacious rooms, which are furnished with well-selected antiques, original art, and handmade rugs over polished wood floors. An open fire warms the breakfast rooms in colder weather, and the geranium-filled conservatory glows with sun on clear days. An evening meal can be provided on request. ⊠ *Kilbrogan Hill, Bandon* ☎ *023/44935* 🖷 *023/44935* ⊕ *www.kilbrogan.com* ⇨ *5 rooms* ⟨ *Croquet; no a/c* ▤ *AE, MC, V* ⊘ *Closed Jan.* ⦿I *BP.*

Shopping

The handcrafted gifts and housewares at **Clonakilty Craft Centre** (⊠ Strand Rd., Clonakilty ☎ 023/35802) showcase contemporary Irish design. **Delaney's** (⊠ Clonakilty ☎ 023/48361) is full of small antiques as well as antiquarian and secondhand books. **Edward Twomey** (⊠ 16 Pearse St., Clonakilty ☎ 023/33365) is a traditional butcher's shop famed for its Clonakilty Black Pudding, a breakfast product that's prominently featured on the shop's nifty T-shirts—the ultimate West Cork souvenirs. Assemble a superior picnic at the **Lettercollum Kitchen Shop** (⊠ 22 Connolly St., Clonakilty ☎ 023/36938), a bakery and deli selling tasty breads and local organic produce. **Spiller's Lane Gallery** (⊠ Spiller's La., Clonakilty ☎ 023/38416), in a converted grain store at a pretty mews, sells Irish-made jewelry, cutlery, pottery, and paintings.

Skibbereen

 35 km (22 mi) west of Timoleague.

Skibbereen is the main market town in this neck of southwest Cork, and a good base for nearby sights. The Friday country market and the plethora of pubs punctuated by bustling shops and coffeehouses keep the place jumping year-round. A thoughtful renovation of a stone gasworks building has created an attractive, architecturally appropriate home for the **Skibbereen Heritage**

Center. An elaborate audiovisual exhibit on the Great Famine presents dramatized firsthand accounts of what it was like to live in this community when it was hit hard by hunger. Other attractions include displays on area marine life, walking tours, access to local census information, and a varying schedule of special programs. ⊠ *Upper Bridge St.* ☎ *028/ 40900* ⊕ *www.skibbheritage.com* 🖼 *€5* ۞ *Mid-Mar.–late May and mid-Sept.–mid-Oct., Tues.–Sat. 10–6; mid-May–mid-Sept., daily 10–6; mid-Oct.–mid-Mar. by appointment.*

The **Mizen Vision Visitor Centre,** which occupies a lighthouse at the tip of the Mizen Head (follow the R591 through Goleen to the end of the road), is the Irish mainland's most southerly point. The lighthouse itself is on a rock at the tip of the headland; to reach it, you must cross a dramatic 99-step suspension footbridge. The lighthouse was completed in 1910; the Engine Room and Keepers' House have been restored by the local community. The exhilaration of massive Atlantic seas swirling 164 feet below the footbridge and the great coastal views guarantee a memorable outing. ⊠ *Harbour Rd., Goleen* ☎ *028/35115* ⊕ *www. mizenhead.ie* 🖼 *€5* ۞ *Mid-Mar.–May and Oct., daily 10:30–5; June–Sept., daily 10–6; Nov.–mid-Mar., weekends 11–4.*

Where to Stay & Eat

$$$$ ✕ **Annie's.** A meal at this mildly eccentric cottage, in an offbeat village 16 km (10 mi) west of Skibbereen, is a true West Cork experience. Annie Barrie and her chef husband, Dano, have been running the place since the early '80s. When you arrive, chances are that Annie will send you across the road to Levi's Pub, where you can wait for your table, peruse the menu, and eventually give Annie your order. Dano's simple, well-judged cooking lends the restaurant considerable magic. Dishes are made from outstanding farmhouse cheeses, locally reared cattle, and the freshest seafood. ⊠ *Main St., Ballydehob* ☎ *028/37292* ⊟ *MC, V* ۞ *Closed Sun., Mon., and Nov.*

★ **$$$$** ✕ **Island Cottage.** On Heir Island, this unlikely venture is a pilgrimage spot for food lovers, who praise the high standard of cooking and the location. The five-course meals focus on local produce, some of it picked in the wild on the island. Expect good, honest, unfussily prepared food—

the best of new Irish Traditional. The restaurant is country-casual and tables seat 10, so be prepared to share. Cape Clear turbot with sea spinach is typical; for dessert, try the terrine of vanilla ice cream with meringue in blackberry sauce. The proprietors, John Desmond and Ellmary Fenton, also operate "the world's smallest cooking school" here. Advance booking for the restaurant and courses is necessary; call for details about the four-minute ferry ride to the island from Cunnamore, which is about 15 km (9 mi) west of Skibbereen (follow signs on the road to Ballydehob). ⊠ *Heir Island* ☎ *028/38102* ⊕ *www.islandcottage.com* ▱ *No credit cards* ⊙ *Closed mid-Sept.–mid-May and Mon. and Tues. June–mid-Sept. No lunch.*

¢ ✕▣ **Heron's Cove.** Although this hotel is only minutes by foot from the main road and Goleen's village center, this harborside retreat is a peaceable kingdom—expect to see herons outside your window. Sue Hill's modern house, on the edge of a secluded inlet, is well-run and extremely civilized. The well-equipped guest rooms, furnished in part with antiques, have excellent views from every window. In summer, fresh local seafood stars on the menu ($$–$$$), including John Dory in caper butter sauce, and you can pick out a great wine to accompany it from the racks along the wall. Off-season (November–March), evening meals are prepared for guests only. ⊠ *The Harbour, Goleen, Co. Cork* ☎ *028/35225* 🖷 *028/35422* ⊕ *www.heronscove.com* ↴ *5 rooms* ⚬ *Restaurant, cable TV, fishing; no a/c, no smoking* ▱ *AE, DC, MC, V* ⏐◯⏐ *BP.*

The Arts

The **West Cork Arts Center** (⊠ North St., Skibbereen ☎ 028/22090) has regular exhibits of work by local artists and an on-site crafts shop.

Castletownshend

28 *8 km (5 mi) southeast of Skibbereen.*

This town has an unusual number of large, gracious stone houses, most of them dating from the mid-18th century, when it was an important trading center. The main street runs steeply downhill to the 17th-century castle (built by the noted regional family of the Townshends) and the sea. The sleepy town awakens in July and August, when its sheltered harbor bustles. Sparkling views await from cliff-top St. Barrahane's Church, which has a medieval oak altarpiece and three stained-glass windows by early-20th-century Irish artist Harry Clarke.

Where to Eat

★ $–$$$$ ✕ **Mary Ann's.** Writer Edna O'Brien calls this her favorite pub in the world. Low-beamed, and one of Ireland's oldest, Mary Ann's attracts wealthy visitors from the United Kingdom and from other parts of Ireland, who mingle happily with the few locals left in the village in the front barroom, the quieter back room, or the large garden beyond. Energetic ownermanager Fergus O'Mahony is a brilliant host, and is always on the spot, supervising operations and contributing to the *craic* (lively conversation). Upstairs, the 32-seat restaurant nearly always buzzes, so reservations are a good idea. Try the trademark baked avocado stuffed with crab meat, the massively generous platter of Castlehaven Bay shellfish and seafood, or the succulent T-bone steak. ✉ *Main St.* ☎ *028/36146* ⊕ *www.maryannsbarrestaurant.com* ▤ *MC, V* ⊘ *Restaurant closed Nov.–Mar.; bar food available daily Apr.–Oct., Tues.–Sun. in Nov.–Mar.*

Baltimore

㉙ *13 km (8 mi) southwest of Skibbereen on R595.*

The beautiful, crescent-shape fishing village of Baltimore is a popular sailing center and attracts its share of vacationing families from Ireland and abroad, especially in summer. The village was sacked in 1631 by a band of Algerian sailors; as a result, watchtowers were installed at the harbor mouth. **Sherkin Island** (☎ 028/20125 ferry information) is 1 km (½ mi) off the coast, a 10-minute ferry ride away. On the island, you can find the ruins of Dún Na Long Castle and Sherkin Abbey, both built around 1470 by the O'Driscolls, a seafaring clan known as the "scourge of the Irish seas." The island's population today is 90, and there are several safe, sandy beaches and abundant wildlife. Simply walking on Sherkin's almost-traffic-free roads and taking in the scenery is memorable.

The rugged, dramatic **Cape Clear Island** (☎ 028/39119 ferry information ⊕ www.oilean-chleire.ie) is part of the West Cork Gaeltacht, or Irish-speaking area. The ferry to the 2- by 5-km (1- by 3-mi) island, which is 6 km (4 mi) offshore, takes about an hour from Baltimore. It's exciting to watch the skipper thread his way through the rocks and islets of Roaring Water Bay. You'll get excellent views of the Fastnet Rock Lighthouse, which is the focus of a biennial yachting race. Sparsely populated (about 150 residents), the island has little road traffic, a few bars, a youth hostel, and a few simple B&Bs. Bird-watchers should relish their time here—Cape Clear is the southernmost point of Irish territory, and its observatory, the country's oldest, has racked up all kinds of sightings of rare songbird migrants. Whales, dolphins, and large flocks of ocean-going birds can be seen offshore in summer. In late August the island hosts the International Story-telling Festival, a long weekend of simple entertainment for adults and kids; beware, it gets packed.

Where to Stay & Eat

✗⊡ **Rolf's Holiday Hostel.** Oozing a memorable, offbeat charm, with its chunky stone buildings, stone-built garden terrace, semi-wild garden, and stunning coastal views, this family-run establishment is just outside Baltimore, surrounded by wild gorse and above Roaring Water Bay. More like a Continental pension than a true hostel, its stone outbuildings (originally farmyard structures) house the communal kitchen and some of the unpretentious, cheery guest rooms. Café Art, the contemporary yet rustic restaurant ($–$$), offers local produce, steaks, and seafood. The menu prepared by chef Johannes Haffner includes Continental treats—beef Stroganoff cooked with vodka, for example, and Flemish apple tart—along with innovative contemporary dishes like mussels steamed with lemongrass and ginger. ✉ *Baltimore Hill, Co. Cork* ☎ *028/20289* ⊕ *www.rolfsholidays.com* ⇨ *12 rooms, 12-bed dorm room* ⌂ *Restaurant, kitchen, laundry facilities; no a/c, no room phones, no room TVs* ▤ *MC, V.*

The Outdoors

Baltimore Sailing School (⊠ The Pier ☎ 028/20141 ⊕ www. baltimoresailingschool.com) offers five-day sailing courses for adults and teenagers, in National 18 dinghies, costing €295.

Bantry

30 *25 km (16 mi) northwest of Skibbereen on N71.*

As you enter Bantry—an unprepossessing town at the head of Bantry Bay (topped out with a large market square and long plaza, which attracts artisans, craftspeople, and musicians in summer)—on the right-hand side of the road you'll see the porticoed entrance to **Bantry House.** One of Ireland's most enchanting manors, it's famed for its picture-perfect perch: on a hillock above the south shore of Bantry Bay, it's surrounded by a series of stepped gardens and parterres that comprise "the stairway to the sky." Spreading out below the Georgian mansion lies the bay and, in the far distance, the spectacular range of the Caha Mountains—one of the great vistas of Ireland. Built in the early 1700s and altered and expanded later that century, the house was the ancestral seat of the White family. The house as it looks today is largely the vision of Richard White, the second earl of Bantry, who traveled extensively through Europe and brought a lot of it back with him: fabulous Aubusson tapestries—said to have been commissioned by Louis XV—adorn the Rose Drawing Room, while state portraits of King George III and Queen Charlotte glitter in floridly Rococo gilt frames in the hyperthreatrical, Wedgwood-blue-and-gold dining room.

FodorśChoice
★

Outside, the drama continues in the stepped garden terraces, set with marble statues, framed by stone balustrades, and showcasing such delights as an embroidered parterre of dwarf box. Next to Bantry House is the **Bantry 1796 French Armada Center,** a small but worthwhile museum illustrating the abortive attempt by Irish Nationalist Wolfe Tone and his French ally General Hoche to land 14,000 troops in Bantry Bay to effect an uprising. In summer the house hosts concerts in the grand library room, notably the West Cork Chamber Music Festival (held during the first week of July). ⊠ *Bantry House is on right-hand side of N71 as you enter town from easterly Cork City direction* ☎ *027/50047* ⊕ *www.bantryhouse.ie* ⊠ *House, museum, and gardens €10; museum and gardens €5* ⊙ *Mar.–Oct., daily 10–6.*

Where to Stay & Eat

$$$ ✕🏠 **Blair's Cove House.** In the converted stables of a Georgian mansion, gleaming silverware, pink tablecloths, and a large crystal chandelier are set off against stone walls and exposed beams. A covered, heated terrace overlooks a fountain and a rose-filled courtyard. The owners are French, and the cuisine ($$$$) is a mixture of French and Irish. Starters are displayed on a self-service buffet; a popular main course is steak or local lamb cooked on the open wood-fired grill. Stone outbuildings have been converted into well-equipped guest rooms furnished with country antiques and morning views of the still-blue waters of Dunmanus Bay (which are breathtaking). ⊠ *Blair's Cove, Durrus, Co. Cork* ☎ *027/*

61041 ⊡ *3 rooms* ⚒ *Cable TV, some pets allowed; no a/c* ☰ *DC, MC, V* ☺ *Restaurant closed Sun. and Mon. and Nov.–mid-Mar. Guest rooms closed Nov.–mid-Mar.* ⦿| *BP.*

★ **$$** ▦ **Sea View House.** Among private, wooded grounds overlooking Bantry Bay, you'll find this large, three-story, 19th-century country house. Owner-manager Kathleen O'Sullivan keeps an eagle eye on what was, until 1980, her private home and today remains an oasis of calm, nestled in its own gardens well away from the main road. Antique furniture, plump sofas, polished brass, and ornate curtains provide comfort and elegance. Some bedrooms have sea views and small sofas in bay windows; others have views of the wooded gardens. In the dining room, polished tables are set with crocheted mats and linen napkins; service is friendly and informal. ⊠ *Ballylickey, Co. Cork* ☎ *027/50073* 🖷 *027/51555* ⊕ *www.seaviewhousehotel.com* ⊡ *25 rooms* ⚒ *Restaurant, cable TV, fishing, bar; no a/c* ☰ *AE, DC, MC, V* ☺ *Closed mid-Nov.–mid-Mar.* ⦿| *BP.*

Sports

Bantry Park Golf Club (⊠ Donemark, Co. Cork ☎ 027/50579) is an 18-hole, par-71 course that overlooks Bantry Bay.

Shopping

Manning's Emporium (⊠ Ballylickey ☎ 027/51049) is a showcase for locally made farmhouse cheeses, pâtés, and salamis—an excellent place to put together a picnic or just to browse.

Glengarriff

❸ *14 km (8 mi) northwest of Bantry on N71, 21 km (13 mi) south of Kenmare.*

One of the jewels of Bantry Bay is Glengarriff, the "rugged glen" much loved by Thackeray and Sir Walter Scott. The descent into wooded, sheltered Glengarriff reveals yet another landscape: thanks to the Gulf Stream, it's mild enough down here for subtropical plants to thrive. Trails along the shore are covered with rhododendrons and offer beautiful views of the nearby inlets, loughs, and lounging seals. You're very much on the beaten path, however, with crafts shops, tour buses, and boatmen soliciting your business by the roadside. Many are heading this way because

★ of that Irish Eden, Ilnacullin. Set on Garnish Island, **Ilnacullin,** about 10 minutes offshore from Glengariff and beyond islets populated by comical-looking basking seals, you can find one of the country's horticultural wonders. In 1910 a Belfast businessman, John Annan Bryce, purchased this rocky isle, and, with the help of famed English architect Howard Peto and Scottish plantsman Murdo Mackenzie, transformed it into a botanical Disneyland. The main showpiece is a wisteria-covered "Casita"—a rather strange-looking half-shed, half-mansion Peto cooked up—which is over a sunken Italian garden. A touch of Japan is supplied by the bonsai specimens lining the terrace. In fact, Ilnacullin has a little bit of everything, from a Grecian temple to a Martello tower (from which the British watched for attempted landings by Napoleonic forces) to a Happy Valley, all bedded with extraordinary shrubs, trees, and many unusual subtropical flowers. You get to Ilnacullin by taking a Blue Pool ferry, which departs for the island from Glengarriff. George Bernard Shaw found Il-nacullin peaceful enough to allow him to begin his *St. Joan* here; maybe you'll find Garnish inspiring, too. ☎ *027/63040* ⊕ *www.heritageireland. ie* ✍ *Gardens: €3.50. Boat ride: €10 round-trip* ☉ *July and Aug., Mon.–Sat. 9:30–6:30, Sun. 11–7; Apr.–June and Sept., Mon.–Sat. 10–6:30, Sun. 1–7; Mar. and Oct., Mon.–Sat. 10–4:30, Sun. 1–5.*

Glengarriff is the gateway to the **Ring of Beara,** a 137-km (85-mi) scenic drive that circles the Beara Peninsula on R572. The least famous of the southwest's three peninsulas is also the least frequented—and, some would say, the most ruggedly beautiful. One of the main attractions is the Beara Way, a 196-km (120-mi) marked walking route that takes one to many prehistoric archaeological sites. Dursey Island, at the peninsula's tip, is a bird-watcher's paradise that you reach by cable car. From Dursey Island, head for tiny Allihies, the former site of a huge copper mine, now the home of several leading Irish artists, some of whom invite studio visits—watch for signs. This is also great hiking country—known for some of the most scenic stretches of the Beara Way. Continue along a breathtaking coastal road to Eyeries—a village overlooking Coulagh Bay—and then up the south side of the Kenmare River to Kenmare. If you have time left over after exploring the Ring of Beara, you might want to backtrack to R584 and visit **Gougane Barra Forest Park** (⊕ www.coillte.ie), where the hermit St. Finbarr had his mountain retreat. It's the source of the River Lee, and it has nature trails.

THE RING OF KERRY

Along the perimeter of the Iveragh Peninsula, the dramatic Ring of Kerry is probably Ireland's single most popular tourist route. Stunning mountain and coastal views are around almost every turn. The only drawback: on a sunny day, it seems like half the nation's visitors are traveling along this two-lane road, packed into buses, riding bikes, or backpacking. The route is narrow and curvy, and the local sheep think nothing of using it for a nap; take it slowly. Tour buses tend to start in Killarney and ply the Ring counterclockwise, so consider jumping ahead and starting in Killorglin or following the route clockwise, starting in Kenmare (although this means you risk meeting tour buses head-on on narrow roads). Either way, bear in mind that most of the buses leave Killarney between 9 and 10 AM. The trip covers 176 km (110 mi) on N70 (and briefly R562) if you start and finish in Killarney; the journey will be 40 km (25 mi) shorter if you only venture between Kenmare and Killorglin. Because rain blocks views across the water to the Beara Peninsula in the east and the Dingle Peninsula in the west, hope for sunshine. It makes all the difference.

Kenmare

 21 km (13 mi) north of Glengarriff on N71, 34 km (21 mi) south of Killarney.

A lively touring base, this market town is set at the head of the sheltered Kenmare River estuary. It's currently a matter of lively debate as to whether Kenmare has displaced Kinsale as the culinary capital of Ireland. Kenmare offers an amazing number of stylish little restaurants for a town its size, and also boasts two of Ireland's most highly reputed hotels, the Park and the Sheen Falls. The shopping is pretty good, too, with Irish high fashion, crafts, and original art vying for your attention. The town was founded in 1670 by Sir William Petty (Oliver Cromwell's surveyor general, a multitasking entrepreneur), and most of its buildings date from the 19th century, when it was part of the enormous Lansdowne Estate—itself assembled by Petty. The **Kenmare Heritage Centre** explains the town's history and can outline a walking route to Kenmare's places of interest. ⊠ *The Sq.* ☎ *064/41233* ◻ *Free* ☉ *Easter–Sept., Mon.–Sat. 9:30–5:30.*

Where to Stay & Eat

$$–$$$ ✕ **An Leath Phingin.** The name means "The Half Penny." It's a stylish little place with stone walls and modern pine tables, and it specializes, oddly enough, in northern Italian cuisine. The explanation lies in owner-chef Con Guerin's links with Bologna, where he learned the art of making fresh pasta. The combination of Irish and Italian dishes is reflected in a starter of baked aubergine with olive oil, tomato, local goat's cheese, and basil, or a 12-inch *quattro formaggi* pizza with four Irish cheeses—Milleens, Cashel Blue, local goat's, and Gubeen. ⊠ *35 Main St.* ☎ *064/41559* ◻ *AE, MC, V* ☉ *Closed Tues. and Wed., Dec. and Jan. No lunch.*

$$–$$$ ✕ **Lime Tree.** An open fire, stone walls, and a minstrel's gallery on a large balcony above the main room lend considerable character to this restaurant in a former schoolhouse. Try one of the imaginative vegetarian options—deep-fried eggplant with slow-roasted tomatoes—or go for Kerry lamb oven-roasted with honey-mint jus. Leave room for a warm dessert, such as blackberry and pear fruit crumble. ⊠ *Shelburne St.* ☎ *064/41225* ◻ *MC, V* ☉ *Closed Nov.–Mar.*

$$–$$$ ✕ **Packies.** Owner Maura O'Connell Foley established Kenmare's original first-class restaurant, the Lime Tree, but has since opted for a quieter life at this smaller, cozier venue. She's passed her chef's toque to Martin Hallissey, who continues her practice of using local organic produce whenever possible. Stone walls, fireplace, and floors are warmed up by colorful local paintings, and the buzz of expectation among the closely packed diners. The contemporary Irish menu may feature crab cakes with tartar sauce, or rack of lamb with rosemary and garlic gravy. Leave room for desserts, which include homemade praline ice cream and a memorable sticky toffee pudding. ⊠ *Henry St.* ☎ *064/41508* ◻ *AE, MC, V* ☉ *Closed Sun. and mid-Jan.–Feb. No lunch.*

$$$$ ✕▦ **Park Hotel.** One of Ireland's premier country-house hotels, this
Fodor's Choice 1897 stolid and vast stone château has spectacular views of the Caha
★ Mountains. No one can fault its setting: an 11-acre parkland, where every tree seems manicured and where magnificent terraced lawns sweep down to the bay. A welcoming fire is always burning in the lobby—a cute and traditional setting, replete with tall grandfather clock. Beyond lies a drawing room aglow with ivory flocked wallpapers and any number of comfy chairs. Each of the spacious bedrooms is unique, though

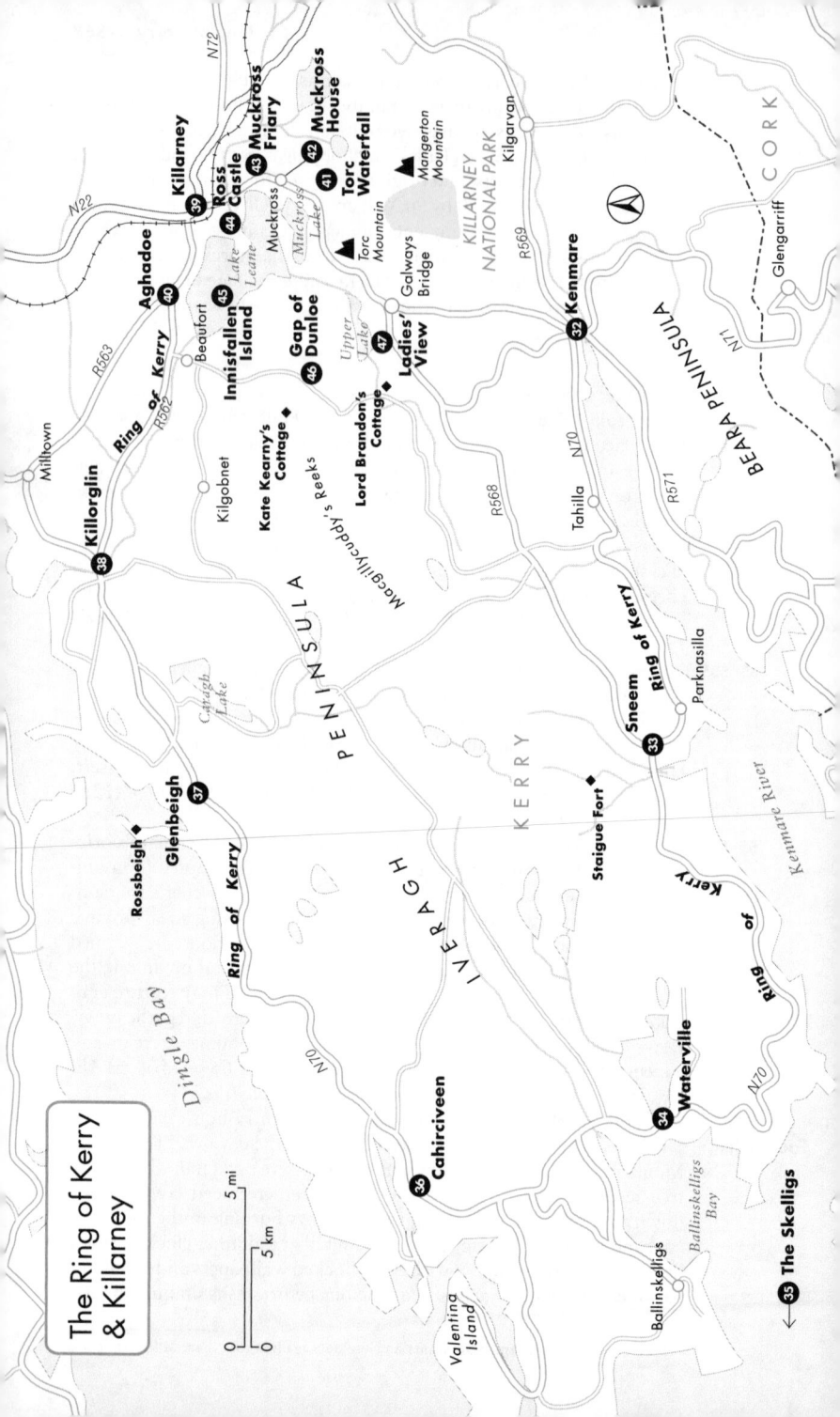

most have late-Victorian pieces; suites have walnut or mahogany beds, wardrobes, and chests of drawers. The restaurant ($$$$) serves justly famed modern Irish cuisine in an elegant dining room with lovely views of rolling lawns. The deluxe spa, on a wooded knoll neighboring the hotel, has individualized "Lifestyle" programs, which incorporate outdoor activities, including tai chi, meditation walks, mountain biking, golf, horseback riding, and walks on the Kerry Way. ⊠ *Shelburne Rd., Co. Kerry* ☎ *064/41200* 🖷 *064/41402* ⊕ *www.parkkenmare.com* 🛏 *35 rooms, 9 suites* ⚶ *Restaurant, cable TV, in-room data ports, 18-hole golf course, tennis court, pool, spa, fishing, bicycles, croquet, Ping-Pong, bar, library, some pets allowed; no a/c* ▭ *AE, DC, MC, V* ⊘ *Closed Jan. 4–mid-Feb.* ⊺⊘⊩ *BP.*

$$$$ ✕▥ **Sheen Falls Lodge.** The magnificence of this bright yellow, slate-roof
Fodor'sChoice stone manor is matched only by its setting: 300 secluded acres of lawns,
★ gardens, and forest between Kenmare Bay and the falls of the River Sheen. La Cascade restaurant ($$$$), which overlooks the falls, headlines modern Irish cuisine, while Oscar's Bistro ($–$$$) serves Mediterranean fare. The public salons are painted in warm, terra-cotta tones, and the mahogany-panel library has more than 1,000 books, mainly on Ireland. Guest rooms—all modern-traditional, in bright yellows and tranquil beiges—have bay or river views. You can hire one of the hotel's vintage cars, which include a Bentley and a Rolls, for picnics, trips into town, and other excursions. ⊠ *Sheen Falls, Co. Kerry* ☎ *064/41600* 🖷 *064/ 41386* ⊕ *www.sheenfallslodge.ie* 🛏 *55 rooms, 11 suites* ⚶ *2 restaurants, cable TV, tennis court, indoor pool, health club, spa, fishing, bicycles, billiards, croquet, horseback riding, 2 bars, library* ▭ *AE, DC, MC, V* ⊘ *Closed Jan.* ⊺⊘⊩ *BP.*

$$ ▥ **Sallyport House.** Across the bridge on the way into Kenmare, this 1932 family home has been enlarged to serve as a comfortable B&B. The spotless rooms, all with harbor or mountain views, are furnished with a variety of Victorian and Edwardian antiques. Owner Janey Arthur has placed family heirlooms everywhere; if you're interested in old Irish furniture, ask for a tour. A varied breakfast menu—which might include apples from Sallyport's own orchard—is served in a sunny room overlooking the garden. ⊠ *Glengarriff Rd., Co. Kerry* ☎ *064/42066* 🖷 *064/42067* ⊕ *www.sallyporthouse.com* 🛏 *5 rooms* ⚶ *Cable TV; no a/c* ▭ *No credit cards* ⊘ *Closed Nov.–Mar.* ⊺⊘⊩ *BP.*

$ ▥ **Sea Shore Farm.** Mary Patricia O'Sullivan offers a warm but professional welcome to her spacious farmhouse on Kenmare Bay. In fair weather there are views across the sea to the hills on the Beara Peninsula, and although the place is very close to Kenmare, you can walk across her farmland to the deserted seashore and view its plentiful wildlife. You can also walk—or run—the mile into town along a scenic back road. Rooms are furnished with ornate heirlooms and have good-size bathrooms and placid views. Breakfast includes a choice of pancakes, kippers, or smoked salmon as well as the usual fry. ⊠ *Tubrid, Co. Kerry* ☎☎ *064/41270* 🛏 *6 rooms* ⚶ *No a/c, no smoking* ▭ *MC, V* ⊘ *Closed Nov.–Feb.* ⊺⊘⊩ *BP.*

Nightlife

Try **O Donnabhain** (⊠ Henry St. ☎ 064/41361) for traditional Irish tunes.

Shopping

Avoca Handweavers (⊠ Moll's Gap, on N71 road to Killarney ☎ 064/34720) sells wool clothing and mohair rugs and throws in remarkable palettes and a variety of weaves. **Black Abbey Crafts** (⊠ 28 Main St. ☎ 064/42115) specializes in fine Irish-made crafts. **Brenmar Jon** (⊠ 25 Henry St. ☎ 064/41138) sells sophisticated knitwear. **Cleo's** (⊠ 2 Shelbourne St. ☎ 064/41410) stocks Irish-made woolens and linens that have striking designs, often drawn from Ireland's past.

Kenmare Art Gallery (⊠ Bridge St. ☎ 064/42999 ⊕ www.kenmareartgallery.com) has a good selection of works by contemporary artists, all of whom live locally but show internationally. **Noel & Holland** (⊠ 3 Bridge St. ☎ 064/42464) stocks secondhand books, including Irish-interest and children's titles. At **PFK** (⊠ 18 Henry St. ☎ 064/42590), Paul Kelly makes striking, modern jewelry in gold and silver.

Sneem

③③ *27 km (17 mi) southwest of Kenmare on N70.*

The pretty village of Sneem (from the Irish for "knot") is settled around an English-style green on the Ardsheelaun River estuary, and its streets are filled with houses washed in different colors. Beside the parish church are the "pyramids," as they're known locally. These 12-foot-tall, traditional stone structures with stained-glass insets look as though they've been here forever. In fact, the sculpture park was completed in 1990 to the design of the Kerry-born artist James Scanlon, who has won international awards for his work in stained glass.

The approximately 2,500-year-old, stone **Staigue Fort,** signposted 4 km (2 mi) inland at Castlecove, is almost circular and about 75 feet in diameter with a single south-side entrance. From the Iron Age (from 500 BC to the 5th century AD) and early Christian times (6th century AD), such "forts" were, in fact, the fortified homesteads for several families of one clan and their cattle. The walls at Staigue Fort are almost 13 feet wide at the base and 7 feet wide at the top; they still stand 18 feet high on the north and west sides. Within them, stairs lead to narrow platforms on which the lookouts stood. (Private land must be crossed to reach the fort, and a "compensation for trespass" of €1 is often requested by the landowner.)

Where to Stay

$$$$
Fodor's Choice
★

🏨 Parknasilla Great Southern. "Parknasilla": for many travelers in decades past, this word alone conjured up an Irish Xanadu—a towering, awe-inspiring, faux-baronial pile, stunningly set by the waters of the Kerry coast, with the sort of grand, slightly stuffy, early-20th-century sensibility that welcomed visitors with a porter in a frock coat and striped gray pants. So it's little wonder everyone from Charles de Gaulle to Princess Grace headed here; George Bernard Shaw found it so accommodating he wrote much of *Saint Joan* here. Although some rooms are a bit plain, most are tastefully decorated in soft pinks and blues. Continental cuisine is served in the Pygmalion restaurant, and you can down your sherry in the Doolittle Bar. There are some great ways to relax here, ranging from a hot tub perched over the lake and a golf course set around

Continued on page 368

GETTING OUTSIDE ALONG THE RING OF KERRY

When you travel Ireland's most popular scenic route, leaving your car behind makes all the difference.

The Ring of Kerry is one of Europe's great drives. The common wisdom, though, is that it suffers from its own popularity: tour buses dominate the road from sunup to sundown. There's more than a grain of truth to this reputation, but that doesn't mean you should scratch the Ring from your itinerary. Instead, plan to turn off the main road and get out of your car. You'll make a blissful discovery: the Iveragh Peninsula—one of the most beautiful locations in all of Ireland—remains largely unspoiled. It's full of fabulous places to hike, bike, and boat—and best of all, there are views the tour-bus passengers can only dream of.

Top: Looking from the island of Skellig Michael to Little Skellig Below left: Biking the Ring of Kerry Below right: On horseback at Rossbeigh Strand

AROUND THE RING
BY FOOT & BY BIKE

HIKING THE RING

Option number one for getting outdoors around the Ring of Kerry is to go by foot. There are appealing walking options for every degree of fitness and experience, from gentle, paved paths to an ascent up Ireland's tallest mountain.

The Kerry Way

The main hiking route across the peninsula is the Kerry Way, a spectacular 133-mile footpath that's easily broken down into day-trip-size segments. The path winds from **Killarney** through the foothills of the **MacGillicuddy's Reeks** and the **Black Valley** to **Glencar** and **Glenbeigh**, from where it parallels the Ring through **Cahirciveen, Waterville, Caherdaniel,** and **Sneem,** before ending in **Kenmare.** The route, indicated by way markers, follows grassy old paths and unpaved drovers' roads situated at higher elevations than the Ring—meaning better, and more tranquil, views.

Hiking the entire Kerry Way can take from 10 to 12 days. Numerous outfitters organize both guided and unguided tours. For a great day trip, hike the 10 km (6 mi) section from **Waterville** to **Caherdaniel,** which has great views of small islands and rocky coves. In the **Glencar** area near **Blackstones Bridge,** a series of shorter signposted walks, from 3 km (2 mi) upward, put you in the shadow of **Carrauntuohill,** Ireland's highest mountain.

> ### HIKING RESOURCES
> A copy of the **Kerry Way Map Guide,** available from Cork Kerry Tourism, is invaluable. For organized tours of the Way, try **Activity Ireland,** based in Caherdaniel (☎ 66/9475277 ⊕ www.activity-ireland.com). Climbers should check out the website of the **Mountaineering Council of Ireland,** ⊕ www.mountaineering.ie.

Taking It Easy: Three Gentle Strolls

🚶 Muckross Park in Killarney is a car-free zone with four signposted nature trails. Try the 4 km (2½ mi) Arthur Young's Walk through old yew and oak woods frequented by sika deer. You can also take an open boat from Ross Castle to the head of the **Upper Lake,** then walk back along the lakeside to Muckross House—about 10 km (6 mi).

🚶 The trails in Derrynane National Park, a 320-acre estate, run through mature woodland, bordering on rocky outcrops that lead to wide sandy beaches and dunes. At low tide, you can walk to **Abbey Island** offshore.

🚶 Even in high summer, Valentia Island is a peaceful spot for walking, with little traffic. Walk the road from **Knightstown** through the subtropical vegetation of the Knight of Kerry's estate, to the historic **Slate Quarry** (3 km/2 mi), 900 ft above the sea, with views of the Skelligs offshore.

Canglass Point *Dingle Bay* Kells

Ring of Kerry

Doulus Head   Cahirciveen

Slate Quarry ◆
            Knightstown
Valentia
Island   ○ Chapeltown

            Portmagee   R565   Mastergeehy

St Finan's Bay

Puffin
Island St Finan's Bay   Ballinskelligs   Waterville   Lough
                                                          Currane

Little Skellig

Skellig
Michael   Bolus Head   Ballinskelligs Bay
                        Hog's Head   Caherdaniel

                        Deenish   Abbey Island
                        Island
                Scariff   Derrynane
                Island   National Park

Kerry Way Trail

N70
R566   R567

CYCLING THE RING

The Ring of Kerry Cycle Route follows the main road for about a third of its 134 miles, but the rest is on deserted roads, including a long, scenic loop through Ballinskelligs, Portmagee, and Valentia Island. There are significant climbs and strong winds along the way, so good fitness is a prerequisite.

Easy Rides

From **Killarney,** the N71 road past **Muckross Park** and the **Upper Lake** takes you through ancient woodlands to **Ladies' View** (about 12 km/7.5 mi). From here you have one of the area's best panoramas, with the sparkling blue lakes backed by purple mountains. The scene will be in front of you as you make the ride back.

From **Glenbeigh,** escape the traffic by riding inland to peaceful **Caragh Lake** through a bog and mountain landscape that's rich in wildlife. You might spot a herd of long-bearded wild goats, or a peregrine falcon hovering above its prey. The full circuit of the lake, returning to Glenbeigh, is about 35 km (22 mi).

BIKING RESOURCES

You can rent bikes and get route information at **O'Sullivan's Cycles** (☎ 064/31282) in Killarney. Along the Ring at Glenbeigh, bikes are for rent at **Glenross Caravan & Camping Park** (☎ 066/976-8451 ⊕ www.killarneycamping.com/glenross.html).

For an organized tour, contact **Irish Cycling Safaris** (⊕ www.cyclingsafaris. com), which has trips along quiet back roads with local guides and support vans to carry luggage.

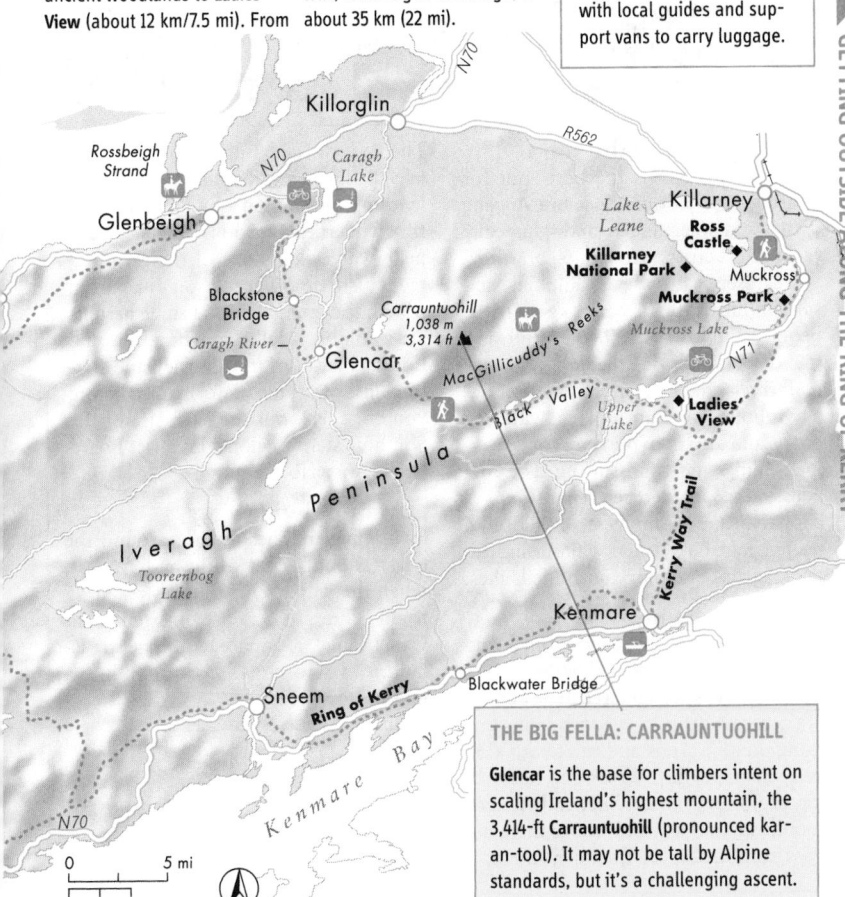

THE BIG FELLA: CARRAUNTUOHILL

Glencar is the base for climbers intent on scaling Ireland's highest mountain, the **3,414-ft Carrauntuohill** (pronounced karan-tool). It may not be tall by Alpine standards, but it's a challenging ascent.

TESTING THE WATERS

Boating around the Ring . . .

Kenmare Bay is the best spot for boating expeditions. **Kenmare Angling** (⊕ www.kenmareanglingandisghtseeing. com) offers customized tours, on which you can see castles, seals, dolphins, and salmon farms. Boats can take up to 10 people, and cost €300 for a full day, €200 for a half day. **Seafari** (⊕ www. seafariireland.com) at Kenmare Pier has a two-hour econature and seal watching cruise and also is an outfitter for kayaking, sailing, and wind-surfing. The **Cappanalea Outdoor Education Centre** (⊕ www. cappanalea.ie), 7 mi west of Killorglin, near Caragh Lake, offers windsurfing, canoeing, rock climbing and guided hikes.

. . . and Fishing

There's good fishing here, both inland and at sea. **Portmagee** and **Waterville** are the main deepsea angling centers; outings are generally from small open boats carrying up to 10 rods and run about €30 per person per day. Wreck and reef fishing promises pollock, ling, cod, conger, monkfish, and shark. Inshore there are bass, turbot, dogfish, flounder, and tope.

The **Caragh Lake** and the rivers **Laune, Inny, Roughty,** and **Caragh** are all excellent for wild salmon—and all are beautiful wilderness locations. **Lough Currane** near Waterville is one of the great sea trout fisheries. The season runs from March to September, and fishing permits are available locally from hotels. You'll find tackle shops in Killarney and Waterville. For detailed information before you go, check out the Web site of the South Western Regional Fisheries Board (⊕ www.swrfb.com).

. . . and Swimming

Swimming off the beaches around the coast is confined to July and August, when the water temperatures reach 55 to 60 degrees. There are dive centers at Caherdaniel, Kenmare, and Valentia Island; ⊕ www.scuba.ie is a good information resource.

Top Left: St Finian's Bay Right: Derrynane Bay
Bottom: Arriving by boat at Skellig Michael

THE TWIN PEAKS OF YOUR TRIP

The distinctive conical **Skellig Rocks** hover offshore at the western end of the Iveragh Peninsula, surrounded by swirling blue sea. They're a haunting presence that seems to follow along as you travel the mainland from Valentia to Waterville and Caherdaniel.

A venture out to the twin peaks of **Skellig Michael** (shown above, also known as Great Skellig) is a truly awesome experience. Boats leave from Waterville, Ballinskelligs, and Portmagee for a white-knuckle ride lasting about 45 minutes. Along the way you pass Michael's companion, **Little Skellig,** where people aren't allowed but gannets flourish.

Skellig Michael rises steeply for 700 feet; you reach the summit by climbing 600 steps cut into the rockface. Once there, you find, amazingly, the remains of a monastery, occupied by hermit monks from the 7th to 12th century. Looking back to the mainland and out at the wild expanse of open sea, you get an inkling of the monks' isolation from all things worldly. A visit to Skellig Michael may not be the most comfortable outing of you trip, but it will probably be the most memorable.

Birds of the Skelligs

The Ring of Kerry is one of the best places in Europe for observing seabirds, and the Skelligs are a particular treasure for birders. The **gannet** (below) with a wing span of 2 yards, is Ireland's largest seabird, and up to 22,000 nesting pairs reside on Little Skellig, where they dive for food from heights of up to 120 feet.

If you are lucky enough to get out to Skellig Michael in May, you'll be warned to watch out for comical-looking **puffins** (left) nesting in burrows underfoot.

THE RING ON HORSEBACK

Horses hold a special place in the hearts of the Irish. Horsemanship and breeding are sources of national pride—it's an oft-quoted fact that the Duke of Wellington rode an Irish horse at the Battle of Waterloo, while Napoleon's horse came from County Wexford. All over the country you'll find horses grazing in the fields, being ridden down country lanes, and galloping along beaches. If you share the Irish passion for all things equine, there's no better way to see the Ring than from the back of a horse.

🐴 You can gallop along the 3 mile stretch of **Rossbeigh Strand**, or take a trek around quiet country roads, on a horse from **Burke's Horse Trekking Center** in Glenbeigh (☎ 087/237–9110). They've been in the business for years and use mainly quiet-colored cobs (black and white all-rounders). Hats and boots are included in the price, which ranges from €20 to €30.

🐴 The six-day **Reeks Trail** riding led by **Killarney Riding Stables** (☎ 064/31–686 ⊕ www.killarney-reeks-trail.com) takes you through the mountains and woodland of MacGillicuddy's Reeks. The stables also book half- and full-day rides.

🐴 Near **Cahirciveen**, the **Final Furlong Farmhouse B & B** has a riding stable and a gorgeous location overlooking the sea. Ride as little or as much as you like during your stay, in small groups supervised by members of the proprietors, the O'Sullivan family. Contact Kathleen O'Sullivan (☎ 066/947 –3300 ✉ finalfurlong@eircom.net).

Top: Horse Racing in Rossbeigh Strand
Above Left: Gap of Dunloe. Right: Lakes of Killarney

THE WET AND MILD RING...

Rossdohan Pier, Sneem

... Courtesy of the Gulf Stream

The warm waters flowing from the Gulf of Mexico across the Atlantic, known as the Gulf Stream, give Ireland a mild climate, and the effects are particularly felt along the Ring of Kerry. The area is frost-free year round, with temperatures averaging 45 degrees Fahrenheit in winter and 60 in summer. But rain is a constant threat, brought in from the Atlantic by the prevailing southwesterly winds. Console yourself with this though: it may be wet, but it is never freezing.

Don't bother touring the Ring in heavy sea mist: you won't see a thing. But don't let other forms of rain deter you. Part of the attraction of the Ring is the interplay of light with sea, mountain, and distant horizons. Rain often enhances the view, and can give delightful effects. The sun is often shining before the rain has finished, so rainbows abound. Any weather, good or bad, seldom lasts more than half a day: if it's wet in the morning, it will probably be sunny in the afternoon, and vice versa.

Sock It to Me

Bring a rain jacket and a warm fleece or sweater: sea winds can be chilly. Above all, wear sensible footwear. If you're venturing off-road, even in summer, you will be glad of strong, waterproof shoes. And bring plenty of socks. There's nothing more miserable than wet feet!

Land of Exotic Palms

With no frost, Killarney and the Iveragh Peninsula are havens for subtropical vegetation. The New Zealand fern tree and the banana tree thrive. The "palm trees" you see here are usually yuccas that have been allowed to grow tall. Flax also grows to enormous size, and is often used as a shelter belt. The leaves of the gunnera can grow to the size of a compact car—look for them in Muckross Park. The lakes of Killarney are surrounded by luxuriant woods of oak, arbutus, birch, holly and mountain ash, with undergrowth of ferns, saxifrages, and mosses. Rhododendron and azaleas thrive on pockets of acid soil, and are at their best from mid-April to May.

5

GETTING OUTSIDE ALONG THE RING OF KERRY

THE ICE AGE COMETH, AND GOETH

Some 60 million years ago, the great rias, or drowned rivers, that became the bays of Bantry, Kenmare, and Dingle were formed. The sea penetrated far inland, forming the peninsulas of Beara, Iveragh, and Dingle. A million years ago, these lands were gripped by the Ice Age. When the ice receded, some 10,000 years ago, it left corries (or glacial hollows) gouged out of the mountains, great rocks scattered on the landscape (giving rise to legends of giants throwing stones), and outcrops of ice-smoothed sandstone.

Valentia Island

the ruins of Derryquin Castle. The sheltered coastal location—3 km (2 mi) south of Sneem—and excellent sporting facilities make this hotel an ideal retreat and an incomparable little world in County Kerry. ⊠ *Parknasilla, Co. Kerry* ☎ *064/45122* 🖨 *064/45323* ⊕ *www.gshotels.com* 🛏 *84 rooms* ⚐ *Restaurant, some minibars, cable TV, 12-hole golf course, tennis court, indoor pool, sauna, boating, fishing, horseback riding, bar, some pets allowed; no a/c* 🖃 *AE, DC, MC, V* ☯ *BP.*

★ $ 🏨 **Tahilla Cove Country House.** An idyllic location—with its own stone jetty in a sheltered private cove—gives this place its particular charm. The house itself is modern and much added to over the years, and has the appeal of a modest but comfortable private home. No doubt it won't be difficult to enjoy the plump chintz armchairs and open log fire in the large sitting room, or to laze on the terrace overlooking 14 acres of subtropical gardens and the cove. Rooms vary in size and are comfortably furnished, and all but two have sea views. ⊠ *Tahilla Cove, Co. Kerry* ☎ *064/45204* 🖨 *064/45104* ⊕ *www.tahillacove.com* 🛏 *9 rooms* ⚐ *Restaurant, cable TV, fishing, bar, some pets allowed; no a/c* 🖃 *AE, DC, MC, V* ☯ *Closed mid-Oct.–Apr.* ☯ *BP.*

EN ROUTE — **Derrynane House** was the home of Daniel O'Connell (1775–1847), "The Liberator," who campaigned for Catholic Emancipation (the granting of full rights of citizenship to Catholics), which became a reality in 1828. The house, with its lovely garden and 320-acre estate, now forms Derrynane National Park. The south and east wings of the house (which O'Connell himself remodeled) are open to visitors and contain much of the furniture and other items associated with O'Connell. ⊠ *Near Caherdaniel, 30 km (18 mi) west of Sneem off N70* ☎ *066/947–5113* 🎟 *€2.50* ☯ *Nov.–Mar., weekends 1–5; Apr. and Oct., Tues.–Sun. 1–5; May–Sept., Mon.–Sat. 9–6, Sun. 11–7.*

Waterville

34 *35 km (22 mi) west of Sneem.*

Waterville is famous for its game-fishing, its 18-hole championship golf course (adopted as a warm-up spot for the British Open by Tiger Woods, who was a big hit with the locals), and for the fact that Charlie Chaplin and Charles de Gaulle spent summers here. Besides all that, the village, like many others on the Ring of Kerry, has a few restaurants and pubs, but little else. There's excellent salmon and trout fishing at nearby Lough Currane. Outside Waterville and 1 km (½ mi) before Ballinskelligs, an Irish-speaking fishing village, is the **Cill Rialaig,** an artistic retreat. Here, a cluster of derelict stone cottages in a deserted village were given new life as artists' studios. Cill Rialaig attracts both Irish and international artists for residencies, and their work, and ceramics, metalwork, jewelry, and other handmade crafts, are exhibited and sold at the

> **TIGER AT THE TEE**
>
> The demanding Waterville Golf Links was adopted by Tiger Woods as his warm-up spot for the British Open. He was a big hit with the locals.

attractively designed, beehive-shape store. There's also a coffee shop. ⊠ *R566* ☎ *066/947–9277* 🖅 *Free* 🕙 *Daily 11–5.*

Where to Stay

🐾 **$$$** 🏨 **Butler Arms.** Charlie Chaplin loved it here. The rambling building—with white, castellated corner towers—is a familiar landmark on the Ring. It has been in the same family for four generations, and the clientele returns year after year for the excellent fishing and golf facilities nearby and the proximity of long, sandy, windswept beaches. Many regulars like the smallish rooms in the old part of the hotel, which are neither smart nor chic. More spacious rooms, with streamlined decor and sensational sea views, can be had in a newer wing, and there are 12 junior suites. The rambling old lounges with open turf fires are comfortable places to relax and read or converse. ⊠ *Waterville, Co. Kerry* ☎ *066/947–4144* 🖷 *066/947–4520* ⊕ *www.butlerarms.com* 🛏 *40 rooms* ♨ *Restaurant, cable TV, in-room data ports, tennis court, fishing, horseback riding; no a/c* ⊟ *AE, DC, MC, V* 🕙 *Closed Nov.–Mar.* 🍽 *BP.*

Nightlife

Head to the **Inny Tavern** (⊠ Inny Bridge, Waterville ☎ 066/947–4512) for live Irish music.

Sports

Waterville Golf Links (⊠ Co. Kerry ☎ 066/947–4102), an 18-hole, par-72 course, is one of the toughest and most scenic in Ireland or Britain.

The Skelligs

㉟ *21 km (13 mi) northwest of Waterville.*

In the far northwestern corner of the Ring of Kerry, across Portmagee Channel, lies Valentia Island, which is reachable by a bridge erected in 1971. Visible from Valentia, and on a clear day from other points along the coast are the **Skelligs,** one of the most spectacular sights in Ireland. Sculpted as if by the hand of God, the islands of Little Skellig, Great Skellig, and the Washerwoman's Rock are distinctively cone-shape, surrounded by blue swirling seas. The largest island, the Great Skellig, or Skellig Michael, distinguished by its twin peaks, rises 700 feet from the Atlantic. It has the remains of a settlement of early Christian monks, reached by climbing 600 increasingly precipitous steps. In spite of a thousand years of battering by Atlantic storms, the church, oratory, and beehive-shape living cells are surprisingly well preserved.

Fodor'sChoice ★

To visit the Skelligs, you can take a half-day trip in an open boat—perfect for adventurers who pack plenty of Dramamine. The entire visit takes three to four hours, with 1½ hours on the Skellig Michael, where visitors are supervised by resident guides, and the remaining time in transit (the duration varies depending on the weather and tides). During the journey you'll pass Little Skellig, the breeding ground of more than 22,000 pairs of gannets. Puffin Island, to the north, has a large population of shearwaters and storm petrel. Puffins nest in sand burrows on the Great Skellig in the month of May. But the masterpiece is the phenomenal Skellig Michael, home to that amazing 7th–12th-century village of monastic beehive dwellings, and offering vertigo-inducing views. Note that the waters are choppy at the best of times, and trips are made when the weather permits. Even in fine weather, it can be a rough, white-knuckle ride as you cross the swell of the open sea, lasting at least 45 minutes, and is not suitable for small children. One worthy outfitter is **Pat Joe Murphy** (✉ Portmagee ☎ 066/947–7156 💶 €30 ☉ Cruises daily at 10 AM, weather permitting, May–Aug.).

Where the bridge joins Valentia Island, **Skellig Experience** (✉ Valentia Island ☎ 066/947–6306 ⊕ www.skelligexperience.com 💶 €4.40 ☉ Apr.–June and Sept., daily 9:30–5; July and Aug., daily 9:30–7) offers an alternative to the less adventurous traveler. This center contains exhibits on local bird life, the history of the lighthouse and keepers, and the life and work of the early Christian monks. There's also a 15-minute audiovisual show that allows you to "tour" the Skelligs without leaving dry land. But if you're up for it, don't miss the boat ride out to the rocks; Skellig Michael is something you won't soon forget.

Where to Stay

★ ¢ 🏠 **Shealane Country House.** Cows graze in the adjoining field, and the breakfast room at this easily reached island retreat overlooks the ocean and the mainland hills. The large, modern detached house is on Valentia Island, beside the bridge to the mainland. The Skellig Experience Visitor Centre is across the road, and a brisk five-minute walk across the bridge leads you to Port Magee and should sharpen your appetite for hearty bar food. Alternately, you can drive 10 minutes north on the island to Knightstown, which offers additional modest dining options. Host Mary Lane is native to the area, and can organize boat trips to the Skelligs, fishing, horseback riding, and golf, and can recommend the local bars for live music. Her home is a delight, with bright airy rooms, polished pine floors, and large traditional wooden windows framing the peaceful views guests often dream about long after leaving. ✉ Corha-Mor, Valentia Island ☎ 066/947–6354 ✉ marylane@eircom.net ⬅ 5 rooms ♿ No a/c, no room phones, no room TVs ☉ Closed Nov.–Feb. ⍟ BP.

Cahirciveen

🌀 *18 km (11 mi) north of Waterville on N70.*

Cahirciveen (pronounced cah-her-sigh-*veen*), at the foot of Bentee Mountain, is the gateway to the western side of the Ring of Kerry and the main market town for southern Kerry. Following the tradition in this part of the world, the modest, terraced houses are each painted in different colors (sometimes two or three)—the brighter the better. The **O'Connell Memorial Church,** a large, elaborate, neo-Gothic structure that dominates the main street, was built in 1888 of Newry granite and black limestone to honor the local hero Daniel O'Connell. It's the only church in Ireland named after a layman. The **Cahirciveen Heritage Centre** is in the converted former barracks of the Royal Irish Constabulary, an imposing, castle-like structure built after the Fenian Rising of 1867 to suppress further revolts. The center has well-designed displays depicting scenes from times of famine in the locality, the life of Daniel O'Connell, and the restoration of this fine building from a blackened ruin. ⊠ *Barracks* ☎ *066/947-2777* ⊒ *€3.50* ☉ *June–Sept., Mon.–Sat. 10–6, Sun. 2–6; Mar.–May and Oct., weekdays 9:30–5:30.*

Glenbeigh

㊲ *27 km (17 mi) northeast of Cahirciveen on N70.*

The road from Cahirciveen to Glenbeigh is one of the Ring's highlights. To the north is Dingle Bay and the jagged peaks of the Dingle Peninsula, which will, in all probability, be shrouded in mist. If they aren't, the gods have indeed blessed your journey. The road runs close to the water here, and beyond the small village of Kells it climbs high above the bay, hugging the steep side of Drung Hill before descending to Glenbeigh. Note how different the stark character of this stretch of the Ring is from the gentle, woody Kenmare Bay side.

On a boggy plateau by the sea, the block-long town of Glenbeigh is a popular holiday base, with excellent hiking in the Glenbeigh Horseshoe, as the surrounding mountains are known, and exceptionally good trout fishing in Lough Coomasaharn. The area south of Glenbeigh and west of Carrantouhill Mountain, around the shores of the Caragh River and the village of Glencar, is known as the Kerry Highlands. The scenery is wild and rough but strangely appealing. A series of circular walks have been signposted, and parts of the Kerry Way pass through here. The area attracts serious climbers who intend to scale Carrantouhill, Ireland's highest peak (3,408 feet).

Worth a quick look, the **Kerry Bog Village Museum** is a cluster of reconstructed, fully furnished cottages that vividly portray the daily life of the region's working class in the early 1800s. ⊠ *Beside Red Fox Bar* ☎ *066/976-9184* ⊒ *€4* ☉ *Mar.–Nov., daily 8:30–7; Jan. and Feb. by request.*

A signpost to the right outside Glenbeigh points to **Caragh Lake**, a tempting excursion south to a beautiful expanse of water set among gorse- and heather-covered hills and majestic mountains. The road hugs the shoreline much of the way. North of Glenbeigh, the beach at **Rossbeigh** consists of about 3 km (2 mi) of soft, sandy coast backed by high dunes. It faces Inch Strand, a similar formation across the water on the Dingle Peninsula.

Where to Stay & Eat

$$ ✕▦ **Caragh Lodge.** Seven acres of gardens filled with azaleas, camellias, and magnolias surround this mid-19th-century fishing lodge by Caragh Lake. Two large rooms in the main house are furnished with Victorian and Georgian antiques. Rooms in the courtyard and the garden annexes are smaller, and another block has six larger rooms and one suite. Comfortable sitting rooms overlook the lake, as does the dining room. Owner Mary Gaunt supervises the quiet, relaxing dining room ($$–$$$; reservations essential for nonguests). The food is Irish, with produce from the gardens, homemade bread, and local meats and seafood. ⊠ *Caragh*

Lake, Killorglin, Co. Kerry ☎ 066/976–9115 📠 066/976–9316 ⊕ *www.caraghlodge.com* 🖃 15 rooms ⚒ *Restaurant, tennis court, sauna, boating, fishing; no a/c, no room TVs* ⊟ *AE, DC, MC, V* ⊗ *Closed mid-Oct.–mid-Apr. No lunch* ⍰ *BP.*

$$$$
Fodor's Choice
★
⌂ **Ard na Sidhe.** "Sidhe" (pronounced *sheen*) means "Hill of the Fairies," and this secluded, gabled Edwardian mansion certainly looks like it belongs in a fairy tale. Its courtly, ivy-covered stone walls are punctuated by casement windows set in gorgeous stone mullions, while the neatly manicured lakeside gardens contrast with the surrounding wilderness. The storybook mansion, built by Lady Gordon in 1913, has attractive, large rooms furnished with coordinated carpets and spreads, and floral drapes on bay windows; rooms in the main building are the nicest. Antiques and fireplaces dot the traditionally furnished lobby and lounges, but most of the furnishings are reproduction quality. Still, the setting and the house itself are incomparable. ⊠ *Caragh Lake, Co. Kerry* ☎ 066/976–9105 📠 066/976–9282 ⊕ *www.killarneyhotels.ie* 🖃 18 rooms ⚒ *Restaurant, boating, fishing, bar; no a/c, no room TVs* ⊟ *AE, DC, MC, V* ⊗ *Closed Oct.–Apr.* ⍰ *BP.*

$
⌂ **Glencar House.** A hunting lodge—built in 1670 by the earl of Lansdowne—on the Caragh River is now an unpretentious guesthouse with huge elk antlers over its fireplace and taxidermy hung at every turn. The large rooms have country pine furniture and breathtaking views of Killarney's famous mountains, MacGillicuddy's Reeks. The house is a 20-minute drive from Killarney, Waterville, and Kenmare, and is a popular base for golfers. (From Killarney, turn off the N72 Killorglin road for Beaufort, and follow signs for Glencar.) When asked if the hotel had installed air-conditioning, the concierge replied "No, we have real air!" ⊠ *Glencar, Co. Kerry* ☎ 066/976–0102 📠 066/976–0167 ⊕ *www.glencarhouse.com* 🖃 20 rooms ⚒ *Restaurant, cable TV, tennis court, fishing, Ping-Pong, bar; no a/c* ⊟ *AE, MC, V* ⊗ *Closed mid-Oct.–mid-Mar.* ⍰ *BP.*

🐾 ¢
⌂ **Blackstones House.** Padraig and Breda Breen's farmhouse is a rambling old building on Caragh River in Lickeen Wood, where a gentle stretch of rapids leads to a salmon pool. With four golf courses within 20 minutes' drive, and fishing and hiking on the doorstep, the conversion to guesthouse was a good move. All rooms have a river view and are simply furnished with country pine bedsteads and pink, blue, and yellow floral drapes and spreads against plain walls and carpets. Breda provides a simple evening meal on request. ⊠ *Glencar Co. Kerry* ☎ 066/976–0164 📠 066/976–0269 ⊕ *www.glencar-blackstones.com* 🖃 9 rooms ⚒ *Dining room, fishing, bicycles; no a/c, no room phones, no TV in some rooms* ⊟ *MC, V* ⊗ *Closed Nov.–Mar.* ⍰ *BP.*

Killorglin

❸ *14 km (9 mi) east of Glenbeigh, 22 km (14 mi) west of Killarney.*

The hilltop town of Killorglin is the scene of the Puck Fair, three days of merrymaking during the second weekend in August. A large billy goat with beribboned horns, installed on a high pedestal, presides over the fair. The origins of the tradition of King Puck are lost in time. Though some horse, sheep, and cattle dealing still occurs at the fair, the main attractions these days are free outdoor concerts and extended drinking hours. The crowd is predominantly young and invariably noisy, so avoid Killorglin at fair time if you've come for peace and quiet. On the other hand, if you intend to join in the festivities, be sure to book accommodations well in advance.

Where to Eat

$$$–$$$$ ✕ **Nick's Seafood and Steak.** Owner Nick Foley comes from the family that established Killarney's famous eatery, Foley's, and has made a name for himself as a chef. The old stone town house has a bar-cum-dining room at street level and a quieter dining room on the floor above. Foley is known for his generous portions, his wide choice of local seafood, and his steaks. Nick's is famous for its generous seafood plate, served with an individual sauce for each item. In winter sample the haunch of Kerry venison in red-wine and juniper sauce. ✉ *Lower Bridge St.* ☎ *066/976–1219* ▤ *MC, V* ☉ *Closed Nov. and Mon. and Tues. Dec.–Easter.*

IN & AROUND KILLARNEY

One of southwest Ireland's most attractive locales, Killarney is also the most heavily visited town in the region (its proximity to the Ring of Kerry and to Shannon Airport helps to ensure this). Light rain is typical of the area, but because of the topography, it seldom lasts long. And the clouds' approach over the lakes and the subsequent showers can actually add to the spectacle of the scenery. The rain is often followed within minutes by brilliant sunshine and, yes, even a rainbow.

Exploring Killarney & Environs

39–**47** *Killarney: 87 km (54 mi) west of Cork City on N22, 19 km (12 mi) southeast of Killorglin, 24 km (15 mi) north of Glengarriff.*

With its glacial landscape enhanced by subtropical vegetation, Killarney's views are legendary. Yes, the lakes really are sapphire-blue (at least when the sun is out), and seen from a distance the MacGillicuddy Reeks really are purple. Add a scattering of large gray rocks (large, as in big as a car), and acres of lush green flowering shrubs and trees, and you're starting to get the picture.

Much of the area is part of Killarney National Park, which has more than 24,000 acres and is famous for such native habitats and species as oak holly woods, yew woods, and red deer. Signposted self-guiding trails within the park introduce these habitats. At the park's heart is Muckross Demesne; the entrance is 4 km (2½ mi) from Killarney on N71. The National Park Visitor Centre is at Muckross House. Cars aren't allowed in Muckross Demesne; you can either walk, rent a bicycle, or take a traditional jaunting car—that is, a pony and a trap.

The air here smells of damp woods and heather moors. The red fruits of the Mediterranean strawberry tree (*Arbutus unedo*) are at their height

A Romantic Past

SUCH GREAT WRITERS AS Sir Walter Scott and William Thackeray struggled to find the superlatives to describe Killarney's heather-clad peaks, subtropical vegetation, and deep-blue waters dotted with wooded isles. Indeed the lakes and the mountains have left a lasting impression on a long stream of people, beginning in the 18th century with the English travelers Arthur Young and Bishop Berkeley. Visitors in search of the natural beauty so beloved by the Romantic movement began to flock to the southwest. By the mid-19th century, Killarney's scenery was considered as exhilarating and awe-inspiring as anything in Switzerland. The influx of affluent visitors that followed the 1854 arrival of the railway transformed the lives of Kerry's impoverished natives and set in motion the commercialization that continues today.

in October and November, which is also about the time when the bracken turns rust, contrasting with the evergreens. In late April and early May, the purple flowers of the rhododendron *ponticum* put on a spectacular display.

39 You may want to limit time spent in **Killarney** itself if discos, Irish cabarets, and singing pubs—the last a local specialty with a strong Irish-American flavor—aren't your thing. The nightlife is at its liveliest from May to September; the Irish and Europeans pack the town in July and August. Peak season for Americans follows in September and October. At other times, particularly from November to mid-March, when many of the hotels are closed, the town is quiet to the point of being eerie. Given the choice, go to Killarney in April, May, or early October.

40 **Aghadoe** (⊠ 5 km [3 mi] west of Killarney on R562 Beaufort–Killorglin Rd.) is an outstanding place to get a feel for what Killarney is all about: lake and mountain scenery. Stand beside Aghadoe's 12th-century ruined church and round tower, and watch the shadows creep gloriously across Lower Lake, with Innisfallen Island in the distance and the Gap of Dunloe to the west.

41 You reach **Torc Waterfall** (⊠ Killarney National Park, N71 [Muckross Rd.], 8 km [5 mi] south of Killarney) by a footpath that begins in the parking lot outside the gates of the Muckross Demesne. After your first view of the roaring cascade, which will appear after about 10 minutes' walk, it's worth the climb up a long flight of stone steps to the second, less-frequented clearing.

★ **42** **Muckross House**, a 19th-century, Elizabethan-style manor, now houses the Kerry Folklife Centre, where bookbinders, potters, and weavers demonstrate their crafts. Upstairs, elegantly furnished rooms portray the lifestyle of the landed gentry in the 1800s; downstairs in the basement you can experience the conditions of servants employed in the house. Inside you'll also find the Killarney National Park Visitor Centre. The informal grounds are noted for their rhododendrons and azaleas, the water garden, and the outstanding limestone rock garden. In the park beside the house, the Muckross Traditional Farms comprise reconstructed farm buildings and outbuildings, a blacksmith's forge, a carpenter's workshop, and a selection of farm animals. It's a reminder of the way things were done on the farm before electricity and the mechanization of farming. Meet and chat with the farmers and their wives as they go about their work. The visitor center has a shop and a restaurant. ⊠ *Killarney National Park, Muckross Demesne, Muckross Rd. (N71), 6½ km (4 mi) south of Killarney* ☎ *064/31440* ⊕ *www. heritageireland.ie* 🖾 *Visitor center free, farms or house €5.50, farms and house €8.25* ⊙ *House Sept.–June, daily 9–5:30. Visitor center Nov.–mid-Mar., daily 9–5.30; mid-Mar.–June, Sept., and Oct., daily 9–6; July and Aug., daily 9–7. Farms mid-Mar.–Apr., weekends 2–6; May, daily 1–6; June–Sept., daily 10–7; Oct., daily 2–6.*

43 The 15th-century Franciscan **Muckross Friary** is amazingly complete, although roofless. The monks were driven out by Oliver Cromwell's army in 1652. An ancient yew tree rises above the cloisters and breaks out over the abbey walls. Three flights of stone steps allow access to the upper floors and living quarters, where you can visit the cloisters and what was once the dormitory, kitchen, and refectory. ⊠ *Killarney National Park, Muckross Demesne, Muckross Rd. (N71), 4 km (2½ mi) south of Killarney* 🖾 *Free* ⊙ *Mid-June–early Sept., daily 10–5.*

44 **Ross Castle,** a fully restored 14th-century stronghold, was the last place in the province of Munster to fall to Oliver Cromwell's forces in 1652. A later dwelling has 16th- and 17th-century furniture. ⊠ *Knockreer Estate, off Muckross Rd. (N71), 2 km (1 mi) south of Killarney* ☎ *064/ 35851* 🖾 *€5* ⊙ *Apr. and Oct., daily 10–5; May and Sept., daily 9–6; June–Aug., daily 9–6:30.*

45 The romantic ruins on **Innisfallen Island** date from the 6th or 7th century. Between 950 and 1350 the *Annals of Innisfallen* were compiled here by monks. (The book survives in the Bodleian Library in Oxford.) To get to the island, which is on Lough Leane, you can rent a rowboat at Ross Castle (€4 per hour), or you can join a cruise (€8) in a covered, heated launch.

> ## WORD OF MOUTH
>
> "At Ross Castle, you can continue on to a boat ride on the lakes of Killarney, where you connect by pony-drawn jaunting cart to pass over the gap. It is a bit touristy, or even more than a bit. But in the end, it's a ride through gorgeous scenery up the lakes from the bottom to the top, and it's very memorable."   —Clifton

★ ☻ **46** Massive, glacial rocks form the side of the **Gap of Dunloe,** a narrow mountain pass that stretches for 6½ km (4 mi) between MacGillicuddy's Reeks and the Purple Mountains. The rocks create strange echoes: give a shout to test it out. Five small lakes are strung out beside the road. Cars are banned from the gap, but in summer the first 3 km (2 mi) are busy with horse and foot traffic, much of which turns back at the halfway point.

At the entrance to the Gap of Dunloe, **Kate Kearney's Cottage** (⊠ 19 km [12 mi] west of Killarney ☎ 064/44116) is a good place to rent a jaunting car or pony. Kate was a famous beauty who sold illegal *poteen* (moonshine) from her home, contributing greatly, one suspects, to travelers' enthusiasm for the scenery. Appropriately enough, Kearney's is now a pub and a good place to pause for an Irish coffee.

The gap's southern end is marked by **Lord Brandon's Cottage,** a tea shop serving soup and sandwiches. From here, a path leads to the edge of Upper Lake, where you can journey onward by rowboat. It's an old tradition for the boatman to carry a bugle and illustrate the echoes. The boat passes under Brickeen Bridge and into Middle Lake, where 30 islands are steeped in legends, many of which your boatman is likely to recount. Look out for caves on the left-hand side on this narrow stretch of water. ⊠ *7 km (4½ mi) west of Killarney* ⊙ *Easter–Sept., 10 AM–dusk.*

★ ㊼ If the weather is fine, head southwest 19 km (12 mi) out of Killarney on N71 to **Ladies' View,** a famed panorama of the three lakes and the surrounding mountains. The name goes back to 1905, when Queen Victoria was a guest at Muckross House. Upon seeing the view, her ladies-in-waiting were said to have been dumbfounded by its beauty.

Where to Stay & Eat

$$$–$$$$ ✕ **Gaby's Seafood.** Expect the best seafood in Killarney from Belgian owner-chef Gert Maes. Inside the rustic exterior is a little bar beside an open fire; steps lead up to the main dining area. Try the seafood platter (seven or eight kinds of fish in a cream-and-wine sauce) or lobster Gaby (shelled, simmered in a cream-and-cognac sauce, and served back in the shell). ⊠ *27 High St.* ☎ *064/32519* ▤ *AE, DC, MC, V* ⊙ *Closed Sun. and mid-Feb.–mid-Mar. No lunch.*

★ $$–$$$ ✕ **Old Presbytery.** This beautiful Georgian house is across the road from Killarney's cathedral and was once a residence for the clergy. Its interior has been transformed into a spacious, two-floor restaurant. Proceed past the bar area, with its open fire and leather sofas, into a room with wooden floors, brocade-upholstered chairs, and candlelighted tables. Chef Mark Ascott's imaginative menu is served by a friendly, efficient staff. Try the panfried John Dory with braised fennel and Japanese dressing, or Barbary duck breast with potato galette, carrot puree, and port jus. ⊠ *Cathedral Pl.* ☎ *064/30555* ▤ *AE, DC, MC, V* ⊙ *Closed Tues. and Jan. 7–Feb. 7. No lunch, except Sun. in Nov., Dec., and Feb.*

¢–$ ✕ **Panis Angelicus.** Daylight streams in through the large plate-glass shop windows of this stylish, contemporary café, and mellow jazz plays softly in the background. Add black-tile floors, original art on dark-red walls, and the smell of freshly ground coffee, and you have the ideal place to take a break. There are home-baked breads and cakes as well as a good selection of sandwiches, and the hot Irish potato cake with garlic butter and green salad is delicious. Dinner menus feature pasta specials, seafood salad, and other light bites. ⊠ *15 New St.* ☎ *064/39648* ▤ *MC, V* ⊙ *No dinner Oct.–Apr.*

$$$$ ✕▦ **Aghadoe Heights.** The lake views from here are unforgettable, and the 8 acres of grounds ensure absolute peace. The interior is an agreeable combination of antique and modern styles but the building itself

is modern—not the most atmospheric of styles. Most bedrooms have mountain vistas, and all are large, with good-size bathrooms, floral fabrics, lace-covered cushions, and natural wood furniture. Fredericks, the rooftop restaurant ($$$$; jacket and tie required), is romantic with silver candelabras, white linen, and upholstered chairs. Chef Robin Suter prepares a seasonal French menu. Main courses include both classics—black sole grilled or meunière—and more unusual dishes, such as medallions of veal with crab soufflé. ⊠ *Aghadoe Heights, 4 km (2½ mi) outside Killarney, on Tralee side, signposted off N22, Co. Kerry* ☎ *064/ 31766* 🖷 *064/31345* ⊕ *www.aghadoeheights.com* ⬑ *66 rooms, 3 suites* ⌂ *Restaurant, minibars, cable TV, in-room data ports, Wi-Fi, tennis court, indoor pool, health club, fishing, bar, meeting rooms* ⊟ *AE, DC, MC, V* ⊗ *Closed Jan.–Mar.* ⧖ *BP.*

$$$$ ✕⊡ **The Brehon.** If you ever get tired of 19th-century porcelain china dogs, thatched roofs, and country charm, head here for a blast of urbane sophistication. Past the rather institutional exterior, you'll enter a lobby that is pure New York City Tribeca: soaring ceilings, distressed brick walls, expensive wood and marble accents, and plush French Moderne–style seating. For more swank, repair to the hyper-handsome dark-wood bar, the striking white-on-black restaurant (a 21st-century spin on Charles Rennie Mackintosh), or the Angsana Spa, a spectacular symphony of blue pools and while columns where you can indulge in the latest holistic Asian healing treatments. Guest rooms are beige-on-beige islands of tranquillity; the priciest have spectacular wood four-posters and headboards. ⊠ *Co. Kerry* ☎ *064/30700* 🖷 *064/30701* ⊕ *www.thebrehon.com* ⬑ *115 rooms, 10 suites* ⌂ *Restaurant, minibars, cable TV, Wi-Fi, spa, bar, library, meeting rooms* ⊟ *AE, DC, MC, V.*

$ ✕⊡ **Foley's Townhouse and Restaurant.** Rooms in this 19th-century row of interconnected town houses have Victorian antiques and rustic, pine furniture. Windows are double-glazed, so the rooms are quieter than you would expect for a hotel right in the center of Killarney. In the restaurant ($$–$$$$) chef-owner Carol Hartnett makes use of local ingredients, including superior Irish cream and butter. Roulade of trout stuffed with prawn mousse and grilled T-bone steak with garlic butter are typical dishes. The wine list has more than 300 selections, and a pianist entertains in summer. ⊠ *23 High St., Co. Kerry* ☎ *064/31217* 🖷 *064/34683* ⊕ *www. foleystownhouse.com* ⬑ *28 rooms* ⌂ *Restaurant, cable TV, in-room data ports; no a/c* ⊟ *AE, DC, MC, V* ⊗ *Closed mid-Nov.–Feb.* ⧖ *BP.*

¢ ✕⊡ **Mills Inn.** If you wince at tour-bus crowds, consider this coaching inn in Ballyvourney, a village 15-minutes outside Killarney and on the main Cork–Killarney road. The inn is beside the rapid-flowing River Sullane, and its grounds have old castle ruins as well as a stable yard and gardens. Its bar, established in 1755, is popular with Irish-speaking locals and has music on Wednesday and Sunday nights. Rooms are well insulated from bar and traffic noise and have mahogany four-poster beds and a cream-and-gold color scheme. The restaurant ($$–$$$) serves generous portions of local beef and seafood; at the bar you'll get simple fare, such as Irish stew. ⊠ *Ballyvourney, Macroom, Co. Cork* ☎ *026/45237* 🖷 *026/45454* ⊕ *www.millsinn.ie* ⬑ *14 rooms* ⌂ *Restaurant, cable TV, 2 bars; no a/c* ⊟ *MC, V* ⧖ *BP.*

$$ ⊡ **Earls Court House.** In a quiet suburb within walking distance of Killarney's center, this comfortable guesthouse is furnished with interesting antiques collected by Emer Moynihan, who likes to greet her guests with tea or coffee and scones. Bedrooms are spacious, with large bathrooms and a mix of antique and reproduction Victorian furniture. Breakfast is served at mahogany tables in a large, sunny, wooden-floored room; menu choices include pancakes and kippers. The house has a wine license. ⊠ *Woodlawn Junction, Muckross Rd., N71, Co. Kerry* ☎ *064/34009* 🖷 *064/34366* ⊕ *www.killarney-earlscourt.ie* ⤼ *24 rooms* ♤ *Dining room, in-room data ports; no a/c* ⊟ *MC, V* ⊙ *Closed Dec. and Jan.* ❙❍❙ *BP.*

$$ ⊡ **Fuchsia House.** Tom and Mary Treacy come from a long line of Killarney hoteliers, which explains their professional approach. The house is in a strip of newly built, depressingly standardized B&Bs that have sprung up between the town and Muckross Park, but this one is different. It was built in 1992 in a gracious Edwardian style, with square bay windows beneath high gables and a redbrick ground floor, promising a spacious, comfortable interior. Tea and homemade cake are served to guests on arrival in the drawing room; guests can also enjoy a large conservatory that overlooks the garden (Tom is a keen gardener). Bedrooms are luxuriously furnished with coordinating fabrics, and better equipped than many hotels. The home-baked goodies on offer have made Mary's breakfasts legendary. ⊠ *Woodlawn Junction, Muckross Rd., Co. Kerry* ☎ *064/33743* 🖷 *064/36588* ⊕ *www.fuchsiahouse.com* ⤼ *10 rooms* ♤ *No a/c, no smoking* ⊟ *MC, V* ❙❍❙ *BP.*

¢ ⊡ **Lime Court.** On the Muckross Road between Killarney and the national park—yet only a five-minute walk from the town center and the railway station—this modern guesthouse has two large bay windows in front. Rooms are in an extension at the back and away from the road. Antiques and large potted plants decorate the reception area; a baby grand piano anchors the spacious lounge. Although guest rooms are plain, they're comfortable and light; all have small sitting areas. There are four pubs nearby, all offering Irish music and good food. ⊠ *Muckross Rd., N71, Co. Kerry* ☎ *064/34547* 🖷 *064/34121* ⊕ *www.hoztel.com* ⤼ *16 rooms* ♤ *No a/c* ⊟ *MC, V* ❙❍❙ *BP.*

Nightlife & the Arts

Bars where a professional leads the songs and encourages audience participation and solos are popular in Killarney. Try the **Laurels** (⊠ Main St. ☎ 064/31149). **Buckley's Bar** (⊠ College St. ☎ 064/31037) in the Arbutus Hotel has traditional Irish entertainment nightly from June to September. **Gleneagles** (⊠ Muckross Rd. ☎ 064/31870) is the place for big-name cabaret—from Sharon Shannon to the Wolfe Tones. It also has a late-night disco. **McSorleys Nite Club** (⊠ College St. ☎ 064/39770) is a lively late-night venue for the over-25s.

Sports & the Outdoors

BICYCLING A bicycle is the perfect way to enjoy Killarney's mild air, whether within the confines of Muckross Park or farther afield in the Kerry Highlands. Rent by the day or week from **O'Sullivan's Cycles** (⊠ Bishop's La., off New St. ☎ 064/31282).

FISHING Salmon and brown trout populate Killarney's lakes and rivers. **O'Neill's** (✉ Plunkett St. ☎ 064/31970) provides fishing tackle, bait, and licenses.

GOLF **Beaufort Golf Course** (✉ Churchtown, Beaufort ☎ 064/44440) has an 18-hole, par-71 course surrounded by magnificent scenery, and unlike most other Irish golf clubs, it has buggy-, trolley-, and club-rental facilities. For many, the three courses at the legendary **Killarney Golf and Fishing Club** (✉ Mahony's Point ☎ 064/31034) are the chief reason for coming to Killarney.

HIKING The **Kerry Way,** a long-distance walking route, passes through the Killarney National Park on its way to Glenbeigh. You can get a detailed leaflet about the route from the tourist information office. For the less adventurous, four safe and well-signposted nature trails of varying lengths are in the national park. Try the 4-km (2½-mi) Arthur Young's Walk, which passes through old yew and oak woods frequented by Sika deer. You can reach the **Mangerton walking trail,** a small tarred road leading to a scenic trail that circles Mangerton Lake, by turning left off N71 midway between Muckross Friary and Muckross House (follow the signposts). The summit of **Mangerton Mountain** (2,756 feet) can be reached on foot in about two hours—less if you rent a pony. It's perfect if you want a fine, long hike with good views of woodland scenery. **Torc Mountain** (1,764 feet) can be reached off Route N71; it's a satisfying 1½-hour climb, with lake views. Don't attempt mountain climbing in the area in misty weather; visibility can quickly drop to zero.

Shopping

Bricín Craft Shop (✉ 26 High St. ☎ 064/34902) has interesting handicrafts, including candles, ceramics, and woolens. **Christy's Design Store** (✉ 3 New St. ☎ 064/35406) stocks contemporary Irish pottery, ironwork, woodwork, crystal, and jewelry. Visit the **Frank Lewis Gallery** (✉ 6 Bridewell La., beside General Post Office ☎ 064/34843) for original paintings and sculptures. If you have Irish roots, you can learn all about your name and buy an item with its heraldic crest—from key rings to crystal to sweaters—at **House of Names** (✉ Kenmare Pl. ☎ 064/36320).

The **Killarney Bookshop** (✉ 32 Main St. ☎ 064/34108) has local-interest books as well as fiction, biography, and travel titles. Bargain hunters should head for **Killarney Outlet Centre** (✉ Fair Hill ☎ 064/36744 ⊕ www.killarneyoutletcentre.com) adjacent to the Great Southern Hotel and the Railway Station. The Nike Factory Store and Blarney Woolen Mills are the anchor tenants of this discount shopping center. **MacBee's** (✉ New St. ☎ 064/33622) is a modern boutique stocking the best of Irish high fashion. **Quills Woolen Market** (✉ Market Cross ☎ 064/32277) has the town's biggest selection of Irish knitwear. It also carries tweeds, linens, and Celtic jewelry.

CORCA DHUIBNE: THE DINGLE PENINSULA

The brazenly scenic Dingle Peninsula stretches for some 48 km (30 mi) between Tralee (pronounced tra-*lee*) in the east and Ceann Sleibne (Slea Head) in the west. Often referred to by its Irish name, Corca Dhuibne (pronounced *corca-guiney*), the peninsula is made up of rugged mountains, seaside cliffs, and softly molded glacial valleys and lakes. Long sandy beaches and Atlantic-pounded cliffs unravel along the coast. Dry-stone walls enclose small, irregular fields, and exceptional prehistoric and early Christian remains dot the countryside. As you drive over its mountain passes, looking out past prehistoric remains to the wild Atlantic sea, Dingle can be a magical destination that makes you feel like you're living in an ancient legend. Unfortunately, Dingle is notorious for its heavy rainfall and impenetrable sea mists, which can strike at any time of year. If they do, sit them out in An Daingean (Dingle Town) and enjoy the friendly bars, cafés, and crafts shops. West of Annascaul, the peninsula is Irish-speaking: English is considered a second language. A good Irish–English map can prove handy.

You can cover the peninsula in a long day trip of about 160 km (99 mi). If mist or continuous rain is forecast, postpone your trip until visibility improves. From Killarney, Killorglin, or Tralee, head for Castlemaine, and take the coast road (R561 and R559) to Dingle Town. You'll pass through the sheltered seaside resort of Inch, 19 km (12 mi) west of Castlemaine and 45 km (28 mi) northwest of Killarney, where the head of Dingle Bay is cut off by two sand spits that enclose Castlemaine Harbour. Inch has a 6½-km (4-mi) beach backed by dunes that are home to a large colony of natterjack toads.

Annascaul

 7 km (4½ mi) west of Inch.

An important livestock center until the 1930s, this village—near the junction of the Castlemaine and Tralee roads—has a wide road as cattle trading was once carried out in the streets. The town also has many pubs. Photographers will be tempted to snap **Dan Foley's** (☎ 066/915–7252) flamboyantly painted pub. Wander in for a pint; the legendary Dan Foley, who was a magician, a farmer, and an expert on local history, is no longer with us, but tales about him are still told in Annascaul.

The South Pole Inn (☎ 066/915–7388) was built by local hero Tom Crean (1877–1938). Crean enlisted in the English navy at the age of 15, and served on three expeditions to Antarctica—the Discovery, 1901–04, the Terra Nova 1910–13 (both under Captain Robert Falcon Scott) and the Endurance (1914–16) where he was second officer to Ernest Shackleton. Crean himself failed to reach the South Pole on any of these expeditions, and named his pub so that in his retirement he could go to work at the South Pole every day. Memorabilia at the pub will fill in the details of Crean's Antarctic adventures. Crean was famed for his amazing strength and resilience. He walked 35 mi through an Antarctic blizzard to bring help to his colleagues, with only two bars of chocolate and three biscuits for sustenance. For this he received the Albert Medal for Bravery. On another occasion he survived a 15-day journey across 800 mi of ocean in an open boat. The pub is the headquarters of the Tom Crean Society, which hosts occasional lectures and festivals, has been addressed by Sir Edmund Hillary and the grandsons of both Scott and Shackleton.

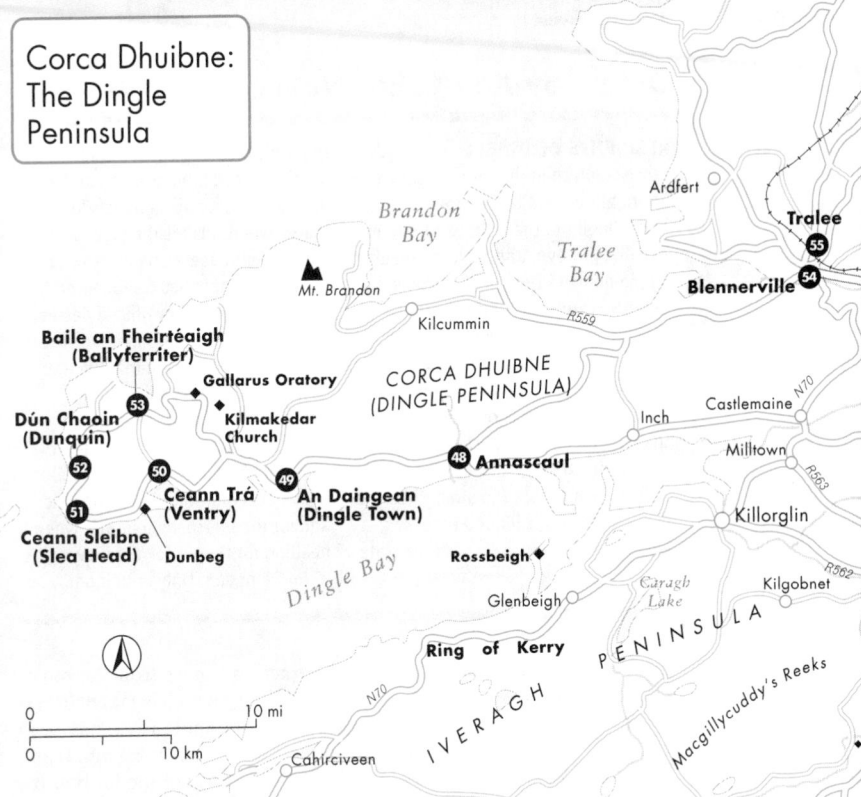

**Corca Dhuibne:
The Dingle
Peninsula**

An Daingean (Dingle Town)

49 *18 km (11 mi) west of Annascaul, 67 km (42 mi) west of Killarney, 45 km (28 mi) west of Killorglin on R561.*

Backed by mountains and facing a sheltered harbor, An Daingean, the chief town of its eponymous peninsula, has a year-round population of 1,400 that more than doubles in summer. Although many expect Dingle (to use its English name) to be a quaint and undeveloped Gaeltacht village, it has many crafts shops, seafood restaurants, and pubs. Still, you can explore its main thoroughfares—the Mall, Main and Strand streets, and the Wood—in less than an hour. Celebrity hawks, take note: off-season Dingle is favored as a hideaway by the likes of Julia Roberts, Paul Simon, and Dolly Parton. These and others have their visits commemorated on Green Street's "path of stars."

An Daingean's pubs are well known for their music, but among them **O'Flaherty's** (✉ Bridge St., at entrance to town ☎ 066/915–1983), a simple, stone-floor bar, is something special and a hot spot for traditional musicians. Spontaneous sessions occur most nights in July and August, less frequently at other times. Even without music, this pub is a good place to compare notes with fellow travelers.

Dingle by Any Other Name

RESIDENTS OF DINGLE, especially those involved in the tourist business, are fighting a battle with the government for the right to continue to call their town and their peninsula by the name of Dingle. The problem arises because the western part of Dingle Peninsula—known in Irish as Corca Dhuibme (pronounced *corca-guiney*) and its main town, Dingle—An Daingean in Irish—is officially an Irish-speaking area, part of the Kerry Gaeltacht. The Official Languages Act 2003 was introduced to strengthen the rights of Ireland's 90,000 Irish speakers to do business with the state in their native tongue—officially Ireland's first language. A side effect of this act was the necessity, under the new law, for all signposts for places where Irish is the official spoken language, to be in Irish. So the name Dingle has disappeared from all signposts, by official decree, to be replaced by An Daingean. The traders of Dingle claim that the name of their town is equivalent to an internationally recognized brand name, and are demanding that an exception be made in their case. But the wheels of government grind slow, and for the foreseeable future, when heading for Dingle Town, follow signs to An Daingean. Only in Ireland.

Since 1985, An Daingean's central attraction, apart from its music scene, has been a winsome bottle-nosed dolphin who has taken up residence in the harbor. The Dingle dolphin, or **Fungi**, as he has been named, will play for hours with swimmers (a wet suit is essential) and scuba divers, and he follows local boats in and out of the harbor. It's impossible to predict whether he will stay, but boatmen have become so confident of a sighting that they offer trippers their money back if Fungi does not appear. Boat trips (€8) leave the pier hourly in July and August between 11 and 6, weather permitting. At other times, call **Jimmy Flannery Sr.** (☎ 066/915–1967), who also rents wet suits and can arrange a swim with the dolphin.

Where to Stay & Eat

★ **$$–$$$** ✕ **Chart House.** Host Jim McCarthy is often found in the early evening leaning over the red half-door of the low, cabinlike stone building. The exterior gives little hint of the spacious, cleverly lighted dining room within, nor of the beautiful pair of windows at the back that frame lovely views of Dingle Harbor's trawler fleet. Nautical artifacts, including an antique compass, complement the rusty-red walls and matching tablecloths. Have a drink at the smart little bar while studying the night's menu. The atmosphere is pleasantly informal, but both food and service are polished and professional. The signature starter is a phyllo parcel of Annascaul black pudding with chutney. Move on to roast cod fillet with a basil mash, or roast guinea fowl, served with a simple but perfectly judged port-wine jus. Finish the meal with a selection of Irish cheeses, served with a glass of port, or a homemade apple and clove tartlet with ginger nut crumble and a glass of calvados. ⊠ *The Mall* ☎ *066/915–2255* ▤ *MC, V* ☻ *Closed Jan.–mid-Feb. Phone to confirm Oct.–May. No lunch.*

$$–$$$ ✕ **Out of the Blue.** Every fishing port should have a simple waterfront bistro like this one, serving the best seafood (owner Tim Mason won't open his tiny restaurant if there's no fresh-caught seafood available, which is almost never). Lobster, scallops, and crayfish are specialties, but also expect turbot, black sole, plaice, brill, monkfish, and even the humble pollack on the daily blackboard menu. Breton chef Eric Maillard puts modern twist on seafood classics, perhaps sole on the bone with almond cream, or John Dory with a pepper sauce and garlic eggplant. There's a short but well-chosen wine list, and a basic dessert selection. ⊠ *Waterside, beside pier* ☎ *066/915–0811* ♨ *Reservations essential* ▭ *MC, V* ⊙ *Closed Wed.*

$$ ✕ **Fenton's.** Step beyond the yellow door of this town house to find a cozy, cottage-style restaurant with quarry-tile floors, a stone fireplace, and local art (for sale) on the soft-blue walls. Rush-seat ladder-back chairs are drawn up to wood-top candlelighted tables. The bistro-style menu is unfussy, allowing for quick turnovers during Dingle's hectic high season. Some dishes, such as the *moules mariniers* (steamed mussels), are available in starter or main-course portions. Lamb and beef come from the Fenton family farm. Sirloin steak may be served with caramelized onions and a red-wine sauce, or try local black sole on the bone with fresh herb butter. ⊠ *Green St.* ☎ *066/915–1209* ▭ *AE, DC, MC, V* ⊙ *Closed mid-Nov.–Easter.*

> **WORD OF MOUTH**
>
> "We hiked to the mouth of Dingle Bay and the lighthouse. What a day! Fungi and his buddies were playing in the bay, locals brought their horses to the bay for a bath, and we ate lunch on the rocks at the mouth of the bay."   —dlcarter

$$$ ✕▥ **Dingle Skellig.** Rambling and modern as this building may be, its center is occupied by a beehivelike shape that's intended to echo local *clocháns* (prehistoric beehive huts). The octagonal reception area has wood cladding, contemporary stained-glass doors, and original paintings. Modern, pale-wood furniture and bold fabrics adorn the spacious rooms, which are in separate wings, most of which have sea views. The Peninsula Spa features an outdoor hot tub with stunning day views. The bar is a busy local meeting place where anything can—and does—happen. Floor-to-ceiling windows in the Coastguard restaurant look out over Dingle Bay. As you'd expect, the specialty is seafood. ⊠ *Co. Kerry* ☎ *066/915–0200* ⎙ *066/915–1501* ⊕ *www.dingleskellig.com* ↴ *110 rooms* ♿ *Restaurant, cable TV, indoor pool, gym, health club, spa, bar, meeting rooms* ▭ *AE, DC, MC, V* ⯒ *BP.*

$$$ ▥ **Emlagh House.** You'll be right on the waters' edge in this spacious, yellow, mansard-roof family home. Although most accommodations in An Daingean are cottagelike, the Kavanagh family chose the grander Georgian style: Emlagh looks like a historic mansion but actually dates from the late 20th century. The marble-floor lobby, with its exquisite mahogany side table and large vase of fresh flowers, sets a tone of quiet, unostentatious luxury. Relax on the goose-down–filled velvet sofas in front of the drawing room's open fire while sipping a drink from the honor bar. Bedrooms are large, with sitting areas in the bay windows. Each one is color-themed to a local wildflower, with plush carpets, Regency-stripe drapes, and Victorian antiques. There are more than 185 pieces of original Irish art in the house from the family's private collection. For rainy days, there's a piano in the drawing room, history books and Internet access in the library, and CD players in the bedrooms. It's a short, water's edge walk into town to sample Dingle's famous seafood. ⊠ *An Daingean Harbour, Co. Kerry* ☎ *066/915–2345* 🖷 *066/915–2369* ⊕ *www.emlaghhouse.com* ⤳ *10 rooms* ⟟ *Cable TV, in-room data ports* ▤ *AE, DC, MC, V* ⊙ *Closed Nov.–mid-Mar.* ⓪| *BP.*

$$ ▦ **Greenmount House.** Wonderful views of the town and harbor await at this modern B&B, a short walk uphill from the town center (turn right at the traffic circle at the entrance to An Daingean and right again when you come to the first T-junction). It looks just like many modern bungalows, but the interior has been cleverly redesigned by a local architect, with bright color schemes enlivening the traditional chintzy look. There are six suites in a connecting wing, each with a sitting room and balcony. Rooms in the original house, though smaller, are impeccable and comfortable, with pine beds and floral fabrics. Mary Curran is known for her baking, so an outstanding breakfast is served in the conservatory, which connects the two buildings. ⊠ *Upper John St., Co. Kerry* ☎ *066/915–1414* 🖷 *066/915–1974* ⊕ *www.greenmounthouse. com* ⤳ *9 rooms* ⟟ *Cable TV, lobby lounge; no a/c* ▤ *MC, V* ⊙ *Closed Dec. 10–27* ⓪| *BP.*

$$ ▦ **Pax House.** You can stand on the outdoor terrace of this modern bungalow and watch the boats return with their catch while the sun sets slowly in the west. Rooms are simple but well equipped. Breakfast is a generous affair, with fresh seafood on the menu and a selection of Irish cheeses on the buffet. Pax House is 1 km (½ mi) from the town center. ⊠ *Upper John St., Co. Kerry* ☎ *066/915–1518* 🖷 *066/915–2461* ⊕ *www.pax-house.com* ⤳ *12 rooms* ⟟ *Cable TV, lobby lounge; no a/c* ▤ *MC, V* ⊙ *Closed Nov.–Mar.* ⓪| *BP.*

$ ▦ **Alpine House.** The landmark Alpine is neither spanking-new nor old-world. One of An Daingean's original guesthouses—dating from 1963—is a plain, family-run, three-story establishment located in spacious grounds on the edge of town that has many admirers; book well in advance. Pine pieces furnish bright, cheerful, well-equipped rooms. The location, at the entrance to town with views over Dingle Bay, is superb: it's quiet, yet the harbor, pubs, and restaurants are only a two-minute walk away. ⊠ *Mail Rd., Co. Kerry* ☎ *066/915–1250* 🖷 *066/915–1966* ⊕ *www.alpineguesthouse.com* ⤳ *10 rooms* ⟟ *Cable TV, free parking; no a/c, no smoking* ▤ *AE, MC, V* ⓪| *BP.*

Nightlife

Nearly every bar on the Corca Dhuibne (Dingle Peninsula), particularly in the town of An Daingean, offers live music nightly in July and August. **O'Flaherty's** (⊠ Bridge St., at entrance to town ☎ 066/915–1983) is a gathering place for traditional musicians—you can hear impromptu music sessions most nights in July and August. For sing-along and dancing, try **Máire de Barra** (⊠ The Pier Head ☎ 066/912–1215).

The Outdoors

You're likely to remember a bike ride around Slea Head for a long time. You can rent bicycles at **Dingle Bicycle Hire** (⊠ The Tracks ☎ 066/915–2166).

Shopping

Don't miss An Daingean's café-bookshop, **An Cafe Liteartha** (⊠ Bothar An Dadhgaide ☎ 066/915–2204), which locals insist is one of the world's first (it has been here since the 1970s). Regardless, you can find friendly conversation as well as new and secondhand books. You can watch **Brian de Staic** (⊠ Green St. ☎ 066/915–1298) and his team make modern, Celtic-inspired jewelry in his studio, which is also a shop. **Greenlane Gallery** (⊠ Holy Ground ☎ 066/915–2018) has shows of contemporary Irish art with an emphasis on local landscapes. **Leác a Ré** (⊠ Strand St. ☎ 066/915–1138) sells handmade Irish crafts. One of Ireland's more unusual culinary success stories is **Murphys Ice Cream** (⊠ Strand St. ☎ 066/915–2644), which has won international awards: find out why at this flagship parlor. Lisbeth Mulcahy at the **Weaver's Shop** (⊠ Green St. ☎ 066/915–1688) sells outstanding handwoven, vegetable-dyed woolen wraps, mufflers, and fabric for making skirts.

Ceann Trá (Ventry)

50 *8 km (5 mi) west of An Daingean (Dingle Town) on R561.*

The next town after An Daingean along the coast, Ceann Trá has a small outcrop of pubs and small grocery stores (useful, since west of Dingle Town you'll find few shops of any kind), and a long sandy beach with safe swimming and ponies for rent. Between Ventry and Dún Chaoin (Dunquin) are several interesting archaeological sites on the spectacular cliff-top road along Ceann Sleibne (Slea Head).

Continuing west along the coast road beyond **Dunbeg,** you can see signs for PREHISTORIC BEEHIVE HUTS, called clocháns (pronounced cluck-*awns*) in Irish. Built of drystone on the southern slopes of Mt. Eagle, these cells were used by hermit monks in the early Christian period; some 414 exist between Ceann Sliebne and Dún Chaoin. Some local farmers, on whose land these monuments stand, charge a "trespass fee" of €1 to €2.

Ceann Sleibne (Slea Head)

51 *16 km (10 mi) west of An Daingean (Dingle Town) on R561, 8 km (5 mi) west of Ceann Trá.*

From the top of the towering cliffs of Ceann Sleibne at the southwest extremity of the Dingle Peninsula, the view of the Blasket Islands and the Atlantic Ocean is guaranteed to stop you in your tracks. Alas, Slea Head—to use its English name—has become so popular that tour buses, barely able to negotiate the narrow road, are causing traffic jams, particularly in July and August. Coumenole, the long sandy strand below, looks beautiful and sheltered, but swimming here is dangerous. This treacherous stretch of coast has claimed many lives in shipwrecks—most recently in 1982, when a large cargo boat, the *Ranga,* foundered on the rocks and sank. In

1588 four ships of the Spanish Armada were driven through the Blasket Sound; two made it to shelter, and two sank. One of these, the *Santa Maria de la Rosa,* is being excavated by divers in summer.

The largest of the **An Bhlaskaoid Mhóir (Blasket Islands)** visible from Ceann Sleibne, the Great Blasket was inhabited until 1953. The Blasket islanders were great storytellers and were encouraged by Irish linguists to write their memoirs. *The Islandman,* by Tomás O Crohán, gives a vivid picture of a hard way of life. "Their likes will not be seen again," O Crohán poignantly observed. The Blasket Centre explains the heritage of these islanders and celebrates their use of the Irish language with videos and exhibitions. ☒ *Dún Chaoin (Dunquin)* ☎ *066/915–6444* ⊕ *www.heritageireland.ie* ☒ *€3.50* ☉ *Easter–June and Sept., daily 10–6; July and Aug., daily 10–7.*

Fodor'sChoice ★

Dún Chaoin (Dunquin)

52 *13 km (8 mi) west of Ceann Trá on R559, 5 km (3 mi) north of Ceann Sleibne (Slea Head).*

Once the mainland harbor for the Blasket islanders, Dún Chaoin is at the center of the Gaeltacht, and attracts many students of Irish language and folklore. David Lean shot *Ryan's Daughter* hereabouts in 1969. The movie gave the area its first major boost in tourism, though it was lambasted by critics—"Gush made respectable by millions of dollars tastefully wasted," lamented Pauline Kael—sending Lean into a dry spell he didn't come out of until 1984's *A Passage to India.* **Kruger's Pub** (☎ 066/915–6127), Dunquin's social center, has long been frequented by artists and writers, including Brendan Behan; it's also the only eatery for miles.

Dún Chaoin's **pier** (signposted from main road) is surrounded by cliffs of colored Silurian rock, more than 400 million years old and rich in fossils. Down at the pier you can see *curraghs* (open fishing boats traditionally made of animal hide stretched over wooden laths and tarred) stored upside down, usually covered in canvas. Three or four men walk the curraghs out to the sea, holding them over their heads. Similar boats are used in the Aran Islands, and when properly handled they're extraordinarily seaworthy. In good weather **Blasket Island Boatmen** (☒ Dún Chaoin Pier ☎ 066/915–6455 ⊕ www.greatblasketisland.com) vessels ferry you from Dún Chaoin Pier to the Great Blasket Island, a 20-minute trip. Landing is by transfer to rubber dinghy, and the island is steep and rocky, so you need to be fit and agile. (At the time of this writing, the Irish government is in the process of buying the island for the nation. By 2007 a new pier might be in place on the island. Then again, it might not. Check with Dingle TIO near your travel date.) Still, the unique experience offered by the deserted village and old cliff paths of the island makes it well worth the effort. The cost of the boat ride is €20 round-trip. Boats run from 10 to 4, weather permitting, between Easter and September.

EN ROUTE   **Clogher Strand,** a dramatic, windswept stretch of rocks and sand, is not a safe spot to swim, but it's a good place to watch the ocean dramatically pound the rocks when a storm is approaching or a gale is blow-

CLOSE UP

The Silence Strikes You at Once

THE GREAT BLASKET, which measures roughly 2 mi by a half mile, has no traffic, no pub, no hotel, and no electricity. Yet this island–centerpiece of the An Bhlaskaoid Mhóir (Blasket Islands)–is probably one of the most memorable places in Ireland to visit.

These days it takes only 20 minutes from Dún Chaoin (Dunquin) Pier to make the 2-mi crossing of the Blasket Sound, but even on a calm day the swell can be considerable. In summer the island is inaccessible on about one day in five; in winter, the island can be cut off for weeks. Until 1954 a small community of hardy fisherfolk and subsistence farmers eked out a poor living here.

Today, visitors are usually attracted by the literary heritage of the island–the Irish-language writings of Tomás O Criomhthain, Muiris Ó Suilleabhain, and Peig Sayers–but what makes people return is something else: a rare quality of light and an intense peace and quiet in beautiful, unspoiled surroundings.

The inadequacy of the existing piers limits visitors to the island to a maximum of about 400 per day, a figure that is reached only rarely, with the average under 200. Most visitors stay for three or four hours, walking, sketching, or taking photographs.

The pier leads straight to a bank of springy maritime grass, typical of the island paths, which makes you want to tear off your walking boots and run about barefoot, like the island children of old.

The silence strikes you at once. The sea birds, stone chats, and swallows sound louder than on the mainland; sheep graze silently on the steep hillside.

The simple domestic ruins are very touching; you do not need to know the history to work out what happened to their owners (most departed for other locales, with many settling in Springfield, Massachusetts).

When the last boat of day-trippers leaves, the foreshore teems with rabbits, and seals bask on the white strand. At the time of this writing, camping is permitted, but it may well be banned in the near future. You can book a bed in the small hostel and self-cater, or eat an evening meal in the island café before sitting outside to watch the stars.

Many visitors, including John Milington Synge, have warned that there's something addictive about the Great Blasket. "I have a jealousy for that Island," he wrote after his 1907 sojourn, " . . . like the jealousy of men in love."

The **Blasket Island Boatman** (☎ 066/915-6455 or 066/915-1344) makes the 20-minute crossing from Dún Chaoin Pier to the island daily from May to September, weather permitting, costing €20 round-trip. Peig Sayers ferry sails from An Daingean (Dingle Town) to the island and takes about 30 minutes, costing €30 for a round-trip ticket.

Visitors may want to call in advance if the weather looks bad to see if these ferries are running. As for accommodations on the island, the only option is a sporadically open **Hostel** (☎ 086/852-2321 or 086/848-6687). If it's open, a bed will cost you around €20. Before you go, get a copy of Maurice O'Sullivan's *Twenty Years a-Growing*, which gives a fascinating account of a simple way of life that has only recently disappeared on the Blaskets.

5

ing. Overlooking the beach is **Louis Mulcahy's pottery studio.** One of Ireland's leading ceramic artists, Mulcahy produces large pots and urns that are both decorative and functional. You can watch the work in progress and buy items at workshop prices. ⊠ *Clogher Strand* ☎ *066/ 915–6229* ⊘ *Daily 9:30–6.*

Baile an Fheirtéaigh (Ballyferriter)

㊾ *5 km (3 mi) northeast of Dún Chaoin (Dunquin), 14 km (9 mi) west of An Daingean (Dingle Town) on R559.*

Like the other towns at this end of the Dingle Peninsula, Baile an Fheirtéaigh is a Gaeltacht village and mainly a spot for vacationers with RVs, many of them German or Dutch. The area around here is great for walking. A top sight in Ballyferriter itself is one of Ireland's best-preserved, early Christian churches, **Gallarus Oratory.** It dates from the 7th or 8th century and ingeniously makes use of corbeling—successive levels of stone projecting inward from both side walls until they meet at the top to form an unmortared roof. The structure is still watertight after more than 1,000 years. ⊠ *8 km (5 mi) northeast of Baile an Fheirtéaigh on R559* 🖮 *€2.50.*

Kilmalkedar Church is one of the finest surviving examples of Romanesque architecture. Although the Christian settlement dates from the 7th century, the present structure was built in the 12th century. Native builders integrated foreign influences with their own traditions, keeping the blank arcades and round-headed windows but using stone roofs, sloping doorway jambs, and weirdly sculpted heads. Ogham stones and other interestingly carved, possibly pre-Christian stones are on display in the churchyard. ⊠ *8 km (5 mi) northeast of Baile an Fheirtéaigh on R559* 🖮 *Free.*

OFF THE BEATEN PATH

CONNOR PASS – This mountain route, which passes from south to north over the center of the peninsula, offers magnificent views of Brandon Bay, Tralee Bay, and the beaches of North Kerry. The road is narrow, and the drops on the hairpin bends are precipitous. Be sure to nominate a confident driver who isn't scared of heights—such a soul is especially important in misty weather. It was from Brandon Bay that Brendan the Navigator (AD 487–577) is believed to have set off on his voyages in a specially constructed curragh. On his third trip he may have reached Newfoundland or Labrador, then Florida. Brendan was an inspiration to many voyagers, including Christopher Columbus.

The summit of Mt. Brandon (3,127 feet) is on the left as you cross the Connor Pass (from south to north). It's accessible only to hikers. Don't attempt the climb in misty weather. The easiest way to make the trek is to follow the old pilgrims' path, Saint's Road; it starts at Kilmalkedar Church and rises to the summit from Ballybrack, which is the end of the road for cars. At the summit you reach the ruins of an early Christian settlement. You can also approach the top from a path that starts just beyond Cloghane (signposted left on descending the Connor Pass); the latter climb is longer and more strenuous.

Blennerville

54 *60 km (37 mi) east of Baile an Fheirtéaigh (Ballyferriter), 5 km (3 mi) west of Tralee on R560.*

The five-story **windmill** with black-and-white sails is the main attraction in Blennerville, a village on the western edge of Tralee. The surrounding buildings have been turned into a visitor center, with crafts workshops and an exhibition recalling the town's past as County Kerry's main point of emigration during the Great Famine (1845–49). ☎ *066/712–1064* ✉ *€5* ⊘ *Apr.–Oct., daily 9–6.*

A popular **steam railway** shuttles along the 3 km (1½ mi) of tracks between Blennerville and Tralee, with departures from each terminus every half hour from May through September. ☎ *066/712–7444* ✉ *€5.*

Tralee

55 *5 km (3 mi) northeast of Blennerville, 50 km (31 mi) northeast of An Daingean (Dingle Town) on R559.*

County Kerry's capital and its largest town, Tralee (population 21,000) has long been associated with the popular Irish song "The Rose of Tralee," the inspiration for the annual Rose of Tralee International Festival. The last week of August, Irish communities worldwide send young women to join native Irish competitors; one of them is chosen as the Rose of Tralee. Visitors, musicians, and entertainers pack the town then. A two-day horse-race meeting—with seven races a day—runs at the same time, which contributes to the crowds. Tralee is also the home of Siamsa Tíre—the National Folk Theatre of Ireland—which stages dances and plays based on Irish folklore.

Kerry County Museum, Tralee's major cultural attraction, traces the history of Kerry's people since 5000 BC, using dioramas and an entertaining audiovisual show. You can also walk through a life-size reconstruction of a Tralee street in the Middle Ages. ✉ *Ashe Memorial Hall, Denny St.* ☎ *066/712-7777* ⊕ *www.kerrymuseum.ie* ✉ *€8* ⊘ *Jan.–Mar., Tues.–Fri. 10–4:30; Apr. and May, Tues.–Sat. 9:30–5:30; June–Aug., daily 9:30–5:30; Sept.–Dec., Tues.–Sat. 9:30–5.*

Where to Stay & Eat

$$–$$$ ✗ **Restaurant David Norris.** A modest terrace of modern buildings on the edge of the town park is home to this pleasant first-floor restaurant. You're greeted in a small reception area with sofa and stool, and offered a drink at the small bar while you peruse the owner-chef's menu of the day. Pale wood furniture in a crisp Art Deco style is complemented by a dusky pink-and-cream decor, with linen cloths and fresh flowers on the well-spaced tables. The menu is built around seasonal local produce, and everything is made on the premises, including bread, pasta, and ice cream. Roast fillet of Kerry beef may be served with black pepper mash, fried mushrooms, and caramelized onions and garlic. Seafood is always well-represented, and there's always a vegetarian option. For extra value for money, try the "early-bird menu" served until 7:30. ✉ *Ivy House, Ivy*

Terr. ☎ *066/718–5654* ▤ *AE, MC, V* ⊘ *Closed Sun., Mon., and 1 wk in Nov. and 2 wks in late Jan.–early Feb. No lunch.*

$$ ✕▦ **Meadowlands.** In a quiet suburb on the road to Listowel, 10 minutes' walk from Tralee's city center, this lively luxury hotel is turreted in the French château style and done up in exuberant, sumptuously stylish decors. Touches of nouvelle country-house style are everywhere, from the grand barrel-vaulted reception area to the two-story bar, which has a balcony library. A light bar menu is offered here, but for the full treatment, repair to the restaurant, a cozy bedazzlement of stonework, timber beams, and stone pillars. The hotel's owner runs a fleet of fishing boats in Dingle, so seafood is a major draw, with seared west coast scallops with lime and butter sauce and panfried Annascaul black pudding, or a kilo of steamed Atlantic mussels being two top choices. Large and exceptionally comfortable in an unfussy way, with dark-wood, Victorian-style furniture and plaster cornices on the ceiling, the guest rooms are decorated in sumptuous hues or tranquil beiges. The hotel is popular with golfers, who generally find the small extra fee for upgrading to an even larger room with two double beds well worth it. A festive, friendly, and stylish place, Meadowlands turns up the charm on weekends, when the bar hosts live music. ⊠ *Oakpark, Co. Kerry* ☎ *066/718–0444* 🖷 *066/718–0694* ⊕ *www.meadowlands-hotel.com* ⤳ *58 rooms* ⚐ *Restaurant, cable TV, bar, parking (fee)* ▤ *AE, DC, MC, V* ⵑ◯ⵑ *BP.*

$$ ▦ **Abbeygate.** Built on the site of Tralee's old marketplace, in a quiet spot behind the main shopping street, Abbeygate is an attractive modern hotel. Rooms have country-style wood furniture and large, tiled bathrooms. The Old Market Place Pub, a rambling, imaginatively designed bar, seats 500 people and is built in the traditional style, with wooden floors and open fireplaces. There's bar food at lunch and music and dancing nightly from June to September and at least three nights a week at other times. ⊠ *Maine St., Co. Kerry* ☎ *066/712–9888* 🖷 *066/712–9821* ⊕ *www.abbeygate-hotel.com* ⤳ *100 rooms* ⚐ *Restaurant, cable TV, 2 bars, meeting rooms; no a/c* ▤ *AE, DC, MC, V* ⵑ◯ⵑ *BP.*

Nightlife & the Arts

Ballad sessions are more popular here than traditional Irish music. **Horan's Hotel** (⊠ Clash St. ☎ 066/712–1933) has dance music and cabaret acts nightly during July and August and on weekends only during the off-season. Try to catch the **National Folk Theater of Ireland** (Siamsa Tíre). Language is no barrier to this colorful entertainment, which re-creates traditional rural life through music, mime, and dance. ⊠ *Godfrey Pl.* ☎ *066/712–3055* ⊘ *Shows July and Aug., Mon.–Sat. at 8:30 PM; May, June, and Sept., Tues. and Thurs. at 8:30 PM.*

Sports & the Outdoors

BICYCLING You can rent bicycles from **Tralee Bicycle Supplies** (⊠ Strand St. ☎ 066/712–2018).

GOLF Tralee is the heart of great golfing country. The **Ballybunion Golf Club** (Old Course; ⊠ Ballybunion ☎ 068/27146) is universally regarded as one of golf's holiest grounds. The **Tralee Golf Club** (⊠ West Barrow, Ardfert ☎ 066/713–6379) is a seaside links, designed by Arnold Palmer, with cliffs, craters, and dunes.

NORTH KERRY & SHANNONSIDE

Until several decades ago, Shannon meant little more to most people—if it meant anything at all—than the name of the longest river in Ireland and Great Britain, running for 273 km (170 mi) from County Cavan to Limerick City in County Clare. But mention Shannon nowadays and people think immediately of the airport, which has become western Ireland's principal gateway. In turn, what also comes to mind are many of the glorious sights of North Kerry and Shannonside: a slew of castles, including Bunratty, Glin, and Knappogue; Adare, sometimes called "Ireland's Prettiest Village," and the neighboring Adare Manor, a grand country-house hotel; and Limerick City, which attracts visitors tracing the memories so movingly captured in Frank McCourt's international bestseller *Angela's Ashes*. You could begin a tour of the area in Listowel, in northwest County Kerry, and then jump across the Kerry–Limerick border to Glin, on the south side of the Shannon River estuary. Limerick City and those parts of County Clare on the north side of the Shannon round out the tour.

5

Listowel

56 *27 km (16 mi) northeast of Tralee on N69.*

The small, sleepy market town of Listowel comes alive for its annual horse-racing festival during the third week of September. Writers' Week in June attracts international names for a more restrained but still festive event. You reach the town from the west by driving along a plain at the base of Stack's Mountain.

Where to Stay & Eat

$ ✕🏠 **Allo's Bar and Bistro.** Just off Listowel's main square, this cheerful, welcoming bar, which dates from 1859, serves the best local foods. Chef Armel Whyte and his partner, Helen Mullane, are known for their lively combinations of traditional and contemporary Irish cooking ($–$$$). The spacious bedrooms are furnished with Baroque-style mirrors, designer lamp shades, cherubs, and oil paintings, and have four-poster beds and large, Connemara marble bathrooms. If you like Irish whiskey, Armel will be pleased to introduce you to his collection; be warned, one vintage malt costs €60 a shot. ✉ *41 Church St.* 📠 *068/22880* 🛏 *3 rooms* ⚷ *Restaurant, bar; no a/c* ☐ *AE, MC, V* ☻ *Bar and bistro closed Sun. and Mon.* ⑩ *BP.*

Glin

57 *6½ km (4 mi) east of Tarbert on N69, 51 km (32 mi) north of Tralee on N69.*

Fodor\$Choice ★
If you're into Irish decorative arts of the 17th and 18th centuries, you'll want to make a beeline for **Glin Castle**, a fantastical neo-Gothic crenellated structure, set on the banks of the Shannon, which has been home to the FitzGerald family for centuries. The rich, red dining room is set with baronial Jacobean-style furniture, the Morning Room is lined with

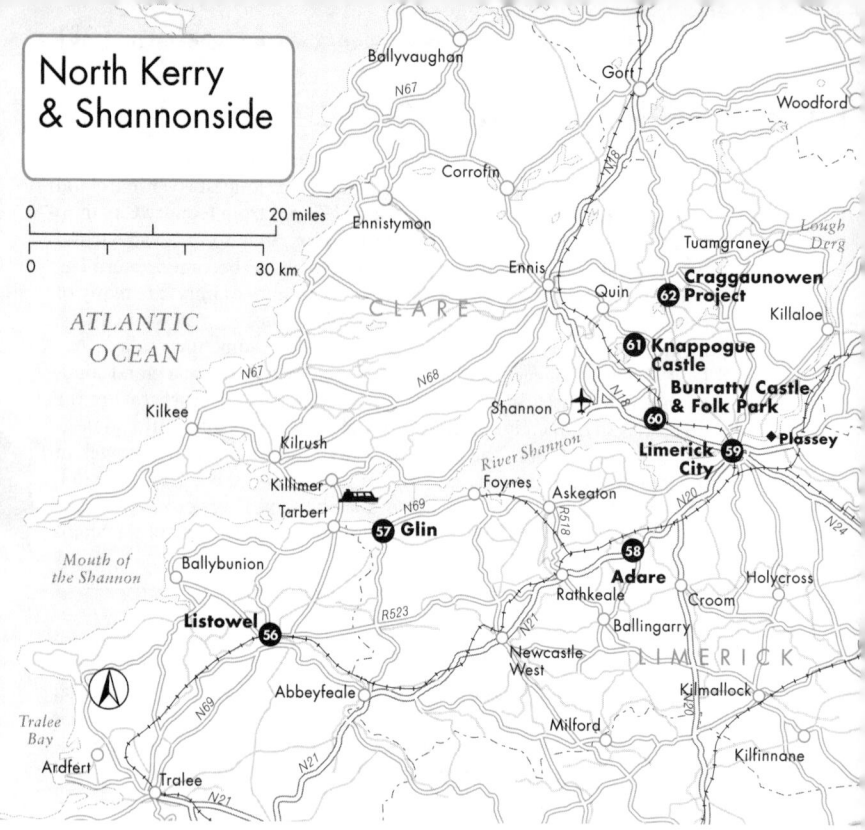

North Kerry & Shannonside

family curios, and the main Hall is set with Corinthian columns and a dazzling Dublin-style Georgian plaster ceiling. Everywhere you look are exceptional antiques, most with the vibrant, virile Irish touch. It wasn't always so. The family has seen more than its fair share of decapitations, bankruptcies, and other hair-raising tales (one knight was tied to a cannon by Cromwell's forces and threatened with being blown apart; another was drawn and quartered during the Middle Ages). The family was, in fact, of English origin but became "more Irish than Irish" by marrying into the Gaelic chieftainry families. Their latest house was built in 1785, then largely expanded between 1820 and 1836 into a full-fledged Irish Gothic mansion by the 25th knight, who added castellations and pepper-pot towers, which look like gigantic chess pieces. Inside, many marvel at the splendid "flying" staircase, the full-length family portraits, the equine paintings of Lady Rachel FitzGerald, and the famous mahogany furniture. Outside, clipped yews, walled gardens, an "antique" temple, and a neo-Gothic henhouse cast their own spell. ☎ 068/34173 ⊕ www.glincastle.com ☑ €8 ⊗ May and June, daily 10–noon and 2–4; other times by appointment.

Where to Stay & Eat

$$$$ ✕🏠 **Glin Castle.** Experience top-of-the-scale Irish castle living at the knight of Glin's imposing ancestral home, which has been in the FitzGerald family for 700 years. The palatial rooms showcase Glin's famous collection of 18th-century Irish furniture, and are superbly comfortable. The guest rooms are magnificent exercises in country-house style, with four-poster beds, export china–adorned walls, and furnishings that are the height of historic Irish chic. Traditional cuisine is served in the red dining room ($$$$), beneath portraits of FitzGerald ancestors. On the menu you'll find locally produced meat and poultry, freshly caught fish, and produce from the walled garden. Nonresidents are welcome for dinner but must reserve in advance. ⊠ *Co. Limerick* ☎ *068/34112* 🖷 *068/ 34364* ⊕ *www.glincastle.com* ➫ *15 rooms* ⚹ *Dining room, cable TV, tennis court, boating, fishing, croquet, horseback riding, meeting rooms, some pets allowed; no a/c, no kids under 10* ▤ *AE, DC, MC, V* ⊗ *Closed Nov.–Mar.* ⫶⊙⫶ *BP.*

Adare

⑤⑧ *19 km (12 mi) southwest of Limerick City on N21, 82 km (51 mi) north-*
Fodor's Choice *east of Tralee on N21, 40 km (25 mi) east of Glin.*
★

A once-upon-a-time village with several thatched cottages amid wooded surroundings on the banks of the River Maigue, Adare is famed as one of Ireland's prettiest villages. Perhaps it's more correct to say it's actually one of England's: the place was given a beauty makeover by a rich Anglo lord, the third earl of Dunraven, in the 1820s and 1830s, in an effort to create the "perfect rustic village." Few local feathers were ruffled since he won goodwill by restoring many villagers' houses. Playing into the mid-19th century vogue for romantic rusticity, the earl "picturesquely" restored many of the town's historic sights, including the remains of two 13th-century abbeys, a 15th-century friary, and the keep of the 13th-century **Desmond Castle** (now the centerpiece of a private golf course). Adjacent to the Adare Heritage Centre you'll find the **Trinitarian Priory,** founded in 1230 and now a convent. From the main bridge (where you can best view the castle), head to the **Augustinian Priory** and its gracious cloister. The most fetching time-burnished allure is provided by Adare's stone-built, thatched-roof cottages, often adorned with colorful, flower-filled window boxes and built for the earl's estate tenants. Some now house boutiques selling Irish crafts and antiques, along with a fine restaurant called the Wild Geese. Adare Manor, an imposing Tudor–Gothic Revival mansion, which was once the grand house of the Dunraven peerage, is now a celebrated hotel; on its grounds you can view two 12th-century ruins, the **St. Nicholas Chapel** and the **Chantry Chapel. Adare Heritage Centre** has an exhibition on the town's history since 1223, with a 15-minute audiovisual display. There's also a restaurant and three retail outlets: one sells sweaters, another crafts, and the third heraldry items. Guided walking tours of the village (€5) are offered from July to September. ⊠ *Main St.* ☎ *061/396–666* ⊕ *www. adarevillage.com* 🖻 *Free to heritage center; €5 to exhibition center* ⊙ *Daily 9–6. Historical exhibition: Mar.–June, daily 9–5; July–Sept., daily 9–5:30; Oct.–Dec., weekdays 9–5, weekends 9:30–5:30; Jan. and Feb., weekdays 10–4, weekends 10–5.*

Where to Stay & Eat

★ **$$$$** ✕ **The Wild Geese.** There's a charming, old-world atmosphere in the series of small dining rooms in this low-ceiling thatched cottage, one of the prettiest in a village famed for its fairy-tale looks. Co-owner and chef David Foley uses the best local produce to create imaginative and seriously good dishes. Try roast rack of lamb with tempura vegetables or roast breast of duck with an onion tartlet and mushroom-flavor rice. Lobster—grilled with snow peas and shallots and topped with a chive mayonnaise—is a popular summer option. The house dessert platter for two lets you sample all desserts, including the fantastic homemade ice cream. The restaurant is opposite the Dunraven Arms. ⊠ *Rose Cottage* ☎ *061/396–451* 🖃 *AE, DC, MC, V* ⊙ *Closed Mon. May–Sept.; Sun. and Mon. Oct.–Apr., and 3 wks in Jan.*

$$$$ ✕🏠 **Dunraven Arms.** Adare's landmark coach-stop inn, established in 1792, makes a popular first port of call if you're arriving at Shannon Airport, 40 km (25 mi) northwest—Charles Lindbergh, in fact, stayed in Room 6 while he advised on the airport's design. He might still cotton to the tranquil, antiques-adorned, but somewhat over-restored and generic look of this place. Paintings and prints of horseback riders decorate the pale-yellow walls of the cozy bar and lounges; the county hunt still meets here regularly, continuing a centuries-old tradition. The comfortable bedrooms (and there are lots of them) are tastefully furnished with antiques, and have large, luxurious bathrooms. Junior suites in the newer wing have antique four-poster beds. The elegant Maigue restaurant ($$–$$$$) specializes in modern Irish cuisine; in winter local game, including pheasant, is a popular option. You can dine informally in the bright, airy bar overlooking the rose garden. Service is impeccable, yet the staff also manages to find time to have a friendly chat, knowing the difference this can make. ⊠ *Main St., Co. Limerick* ☎ *061/396–633* 🖃 *061/396–541* ⊕ *www.dunravenhotel.com* 🛏 *76 rooms, 20 suites* ⟶ *Restaurant, cable TV, in-room data ports, Wi-Fi, indoor pool, health club, fishing, horseback riding, bar, meeting rooms; no a/c* 🖃*AE, DC, MC, V* ⦿*BP.*

$$ ✕🏠 **Fitzgeralds Woodlands House Hotel and Spa.** In the energetic, capable hands of the Fitzgerald family, what was once a small B&B has evolved into a thriving modern hotel. It's on 44 acres of landscaped grounds at the Limerick side of the village. Rooms are spacious, individually decorated in various modern styles, and well maintained. Expect to see locals in Timmy Mac's bar. The Brennan Rooms ($$) serves a traditional Irish table d'hôte menu: lamb, pork, and beef. More adventurous cooking takes place in the bistro-style restaurant in Timmy Mac's ($), which serves locally grown organic food. ⊠ *Knockanes, Co. Limerick* ☎ *061/605–100* 🖃 *061/396–073* ⊕ *www.woodlands-hotel.ie* 🛏 *84 rooms, 8 suites* ⟶ *2 restaurants, cable TV, in-room data ports, Wi-Fi, indoor pool, health club, spa, fishing, horseback riding, bar, meeting rooms; no a/c* 🖃 *AE, DC, MC, V* ⦿ *BP.*

★ **$$** ✕🏠 **Mustard Seed at Echo Lodge.** Dan Mullane's spacious Victorian country-house hotel and restaurant ($$$$) has flamboyantly decorated themed guest rooms—black-and-white, carnival, Chinese, and so on—and commands a view over the countryside. Chef Tony Schwartz uses only the best local produce, plus herbs and vegetables from his organic garden. Shark is an unusual seafood option in summer; more typical is the honey-glazed lamb shank with a cassoulet of beans and homegrown baby vegetables. His basil-flavored potato cakes are renowned. Fruits from the garden are used in such desserts as hot crunchy apple-and-black-currant crumble with calvados, cream, and caramel sauce. The hotel is 13 km (8 mi) southwest of Adare in Ballingarry. ⊠ *Ballingarry, Co. Limerick* ☎ *069/68508* 🖷 *069/68511* ⊕ *www.mustardseed.ie* 🛏 *14 rooms, 3 suites* 🍴 *Restaurant, bar, library; no a/c* 🖃 *AE, MC, V* ⊗ *Closed 2 wks in Feb.* ⦿| *BP.*

★ **$$$$** 🖽 **Adare Manor.** Play king or queen for a day at this spectacular (and, interestingly, American-owned) Victorian Gothic mansion, once the abode of the earls of Dunraven. The castellated mansion is enormous and set amid French-style gardens. Inside is a wonderland of vast stone arches and heavy wood carvings. Center stage is taken by the decorated ceiling in the baronial central hall and the 36-foot-high, 100-foot-long Minstrels' Gallery, wainscoted in oak. As for decor, a period air is retained but several of the color schemes are as bright as today and, thus, much of the time-burnished ambience is lost. The eight "staterooms" in the original house are the most sumptuous, with huge marble bathrooms and stone-mullioned windows. Most rooms have super-king-size beds; all have heavy drapes and carpets and overlook the 840 acres of grounds. Adare's golf course, designed by Robert Trent Jones Sr., is one of Ireland's best. (Note that breakfast is a hefty €23 extra here; plan accordingly.) ⊠ *Co. Limerick* ☎ *061/396–566* 🖷 *061/396–124* ⊕ *www.adaremanor.ie* 🛏 *63 rooms* 🍴 *Restaurant, cable TV, Wi-Fi, 18-hole golf course, indoor pool, sauna, fishing, horseback riding, 2 bars, meeting rooms; no a/c* 🖃 *AE, DC, MC, V.*

Sports

GOLF **Adare Manor Golf Course** (☎ 061/396–204) is an 18-hole, par-69 parkland course.

Shopping

Adare Gallery (⊠ Main St. ☎ 061/396–898) sells Irish-made jewelry, porcelain, and woodwork, as well as original paintings. **Carol's Antiques** (⊠ Main St. ☎ 061/396–977) has antique furniture, silver, china, and art objects from one of Adare's tiny cottages. At **George Stacpoole** (⊠ Main St. ☎ 061/396–409) you can find antiques and books.

Limerick City

59 *19 km (12 mi) northeast of Adare, 198 km (123 mi) southwest of Dublin.*

Before you ask, there's *no* direct connection between Limerick City and the facetious five-line verse form known as a limerick, which was first popularized by the English writer Edward Lear in his 1846 *Book of Nonsense*. The city, at the head of the Shannon estuary and at the intersection of a number of major crossroads, is an industrial port and the republic's third-largest city (population 75,000). If you fly into or out of Shannon Airport, and have a few hours to spare, do take a look around. The area around the cathedral and the castle is dominated by mid-18th-century buildings with fine Georgian proportions. What's more, the city has undergone considerable revitalization since the days recounted in Frank McCourt's childhood memoir, *Angela's Ashes*. Limerick is trying hard to counter a reputation for gang warfare, confined primarily to its less privileged outer suburbs. You need have no fear of violence in the city center: it still has the aura of a ghost town once the workers have gone home at the end of the day, in spite of the large sums of money spent recently on revitalising Limerick's quays. It doesn't help that the things for which Limerick is famous—rugby football, lace, and (Catholic) religious devotion—are all so uncool.

In the Old Customs House on the banks of the Shannon in the city center, the **Hunt Museum** has the finest collection of Celtic and medieval treasures outside the National Museum in Dublin. Ancient Irish metalwork, European objets d'art, and a selection of 20th-century European and Irish paintings—including works by Jack B. Yeats—are on view. A café overlooks the river. ⊠ *Rutland St.* ☎ *061/312–833* ⊕ *www.huntmuseum. com* ⌨ *€6* ⊙ *Mon.–Sat. 10–5, Sun. 2–5.*

Limerick is a predominantly Catholic city, but the Protestant **St. Mary's Cathedral** is the city's oldest religious building. Once a 12th-century palace—pilasters and a rounded Romanesque entrance were part of the original structure—it dates mostly from the 15th century (the black-oak carvings on misericords in the choir stalls are from this period). ⊠ *Bridge St.* ☎ *061/416–238* ⊙ *Daily 9–5.*

☺ First built by the Normans in the early 1200s, **King John's Castle** still bears traces on its north side of a 1691 bombardment. If you climb the drum towers (the oldest section), you'll have a good view of the town and the Shannon. Inside, a 22-minute audiovisual show illustrates the history of Limerick and Ireland; an archaeology center has three excavated, pre-Norman houses; and two exhibition centers display scale models of Limerick from its founding in AD 922. ⊠ *Castle St.* ☎ *061/411–201* ⌨ *€7* ⊙ *Daily 9:30–5.*

☺ The **Georgian House and Garden** will show you how people lived in Limerick's 18th-century heyday. A tall, narrow row house has been meticulously restored and filled with furnishings from the period, and the garden has been planted in a manner true to the time. The coach house at the rear of the house gives on to a Limerick lane and contains displays relating to the filming of *Angela's Ashes,* including a life-size reconstruction of the McCourt family home. ⊠ *Tontine Buildings, 2 Pery Sq.* ☎ *061/ 314–130* ⊕ *www.shannon-dev.ie* ⌨ *€5* ⊙ *Weekdays 10–4, weekends by appointment.*

On **O'Connell Street** you can find the main shopping area, which mainly consists of modest chain stores. However, the street lies one block inland from (east of) the Arthur's Quay Shopping Centre, a mall, which, along with the futuristic tourist information center, is one of the first fruits of a civic campaign to develop the Shannonside quays. **Cruises Street,** an inviting pedestrian thoroughfare, has chic shops and occasional street entertainers. It's on the opposite side of O'Connell Street from the Arthur's Quay Shopping Centre.

Guardian of the Shannon

LIMERICK WAS FOUNDED by Vikings who sailed up the Shannon in the year 922 and established a colony on an island in the estuary between the Rivers Shannon and Abbey, now known as King's Island. In 1194, after the death of Dónal Mór O'Brien, King of Munster, the Normans appropriated Limerick, and Richard I granted its charter in 1197. The great castle of King John and the cathedral of St. Mary's, both on King's Island, date from this period. Later a wall was built around this city, known as Englishtown, to divide it from Irishtown across the Abbey River. In the 18th-century the walls came down, the slums of Irishtown were cleared, and in its place stand the elegant Georgian buildings of Limerick's old town center.

Because of its strategic position at the crossing of the Shannon, the river that divides the old Irish province of Munster from the province of Connaught in the west, the taking of Limerick was a key feature in the wars of the 16th and 17th centuries. In 1691, after the Battle of the Boyne, the Irish retreated to the walled city, where they were besieged by William of Orange, who made three unsuccessful attempts to storm the city but then raised the siege and marched away. A year later, another of William's armies overtook Limerick for two months, and the Irish opened negotiations. The resulting Treaty of Limerick—which guaranteed religious tolerance—was never ratified, and 11,000 men of the Limerick garrison joined the French Army rather than fight in a Protestant "Irish" army. The stone on which the Treaty was signed can still be seen on Thomond Bridge.

Plassey, 5–10 minutes from Limerick on the ring road (signposted Dublin N7), is the setting for the University of Limerick, which has a small, but very attractive, campus notable for its rolling lawns and several striking architectural features.

Where to Stay & Eat

$$$ ✕ **Brulées Restaurant.** The dining rooms in this redbrick Georgian town house, on a corner a block from the River Shannon, are elegantly furnished in a simple, classical style. Chef and co-owner Teresa Murphy uses only the finest local ingredients, and gives a contemporary touch to Irish fare. Try the beef fillet with black-pudding mash or the grilled liver and bacon with grain mustard and mushroom cream. And, yes, the menu does include a classic crème brûlée among the tempting desserts—served with a crunchy bandy snap. ⊠ *8 Lower Mallow St.* ☎ *061/319–931* ▭ *AE, DC, MC, V* ⊘ *Closed Sun. No lunch Mon. and Sat.*

$$–$$$ ✕ **Freddy's Bistro.** On a quiet lane between busy O'Connell and Henry streets, this informal two-story restaurant fills a charming 18th-century coach house. Old brick walls are complemented by a warm color scheme that glows in candlelight. Steak with brandy, bacon, and mushroom sauce and monkfish with basil and lemon pesto are popular main courses. For dessert try the hot, sticky, toffee pudding. ⊠ *Theatre La., off Lower Glentworth St.* ☎ *061/418–749* ▭ *MC, V* ⊘ *Closed Sun. and Mon. No lunch.*

$–$$ ✕ **Green Onion Café.** The Irish-French chef team of Marie Munnelly and Geoff Gloux produces a witty, stylish menu at this hip eatery across from the Hunt Museum. The large room, which used to comprise the town hall, is split into two levels, which are, in turn, divided into intimate spaces through a judicious use of booths. Typical dishes include smoked Irish cheese (Gubbeen) and spinach tartlet, pork fillet coated in pistachio nuts with herb butter, jerk chicken with jalapeño salsa, and salmon with basil beurre blanc. For dessert, try the prune-and-toffee pudding with roasted nutty butterscotch. ⊠ *Old Town Hall Bldg., Rutland St.* ☎ *061/400–710* ⊟ *AE, DC, MC, V* ☾ *Closed Sun.*

¢–$ ✕ **Mortell's.** For fish-and-chips, this is *the* place. It's a simple café, but it serves only the freshest local seafood. You can also get full Irish breakfasts and baked goods. Mortell's has been in the family for more than 40 years, and everything, from the doughnuts to the brown bread to the mayo, is made on the premises. It's in the main shopping area. ⊠ *49 Roches St.* ☎ *061/415–457* ⊟ *AE, DC, MC, V* ☾ *Closed Sun. No dinner.*

$$$ ✕⊡ **Castletroy Park.** This large, redbrick-and-stone hotel, which grandly crowns a hill on the outskirts of town, is close to the university campus, and has splendid views of the Clate hills. The lobby, with its polished woods and Asian rugs, leads to a conservatory–cum–coffee shop overlooking an Italian-style courtyard. Guest rooms, scented with potpourri, have solid wood furniture, muted floral drapes and spreads, and rag-rolled walls. The fitness center is one of the best in the region. You can mix with the locals in the Merry Pedlar Pub and Bistro ($) or enjoy a formal meal in MacLaughlin's restaurant ($$). ⊠ *Dublin Rd., Co. Limerick* ☎ *061/335–566* ⊟ *061/331–117* ⊕ *www.castletroy-park.ie* ⌷ *101 rooms, 6 suites* ⌕ *2 restaurants, cable TV, in-room data ports, Wi-Fi, indoor pool, health club, bar, meeting rooms* ⊟ *AE, DC, MC, V* ⍾⌷ *BP.*

$–$$$ ✕⊡ **Clarion Hotel.** Limerick's tallest building, this dramatic, 17-story, boat-shape structure towers over the rest of the city, and is the focal point of Limerick's dock redevelopment. The interior is a bold statement in modern design—from the cutlery to the carpets—with simple geometric lines and earthy color schemes. Rooms are spacious and restful with bold color schemes and white Egyptian-cotton comforters, large windows, and views of the twinkling cityscape upriver or the wide estuary downriver. The Kudos bar ($) offers Thai food, and the boldly minimalist, waterside Sinergie ($$) restaurant serves imaginative Continental cuisine. There's high-speed wireless Internet. ⊠ *Steamboat Quay, Co. Limerick* ☎ *061/444–100* ⊟ *061/444–101* ⊕ *www.clarionhotellimerick. com* ⌷ *93 rooms* ⌕ *Restaurant, cable TV, in-room data ports, Wi-Fi, indoor pool, health club, bar, meeting rooms* ⊟ *AE, DC, MC, V* ⍾⌷ *BP.*

$ ⊡ **Sarsfield Bridge Hotel.** This modern budget accommodation has a great location beside the Sarsfield Bridge, midway between old Limerick and the shopping area. The popular, ground-floor Pier One bar-restaurant has leather sofas overlooking the river. Rooms above are built in a square around an enclosed courtyard; those on the inside have no views but are truly quiet. Red-velvet armchairs are the only touches of luxury in otherwise plain, small rooms, but overall, the hotel offers good value.

⊠ *Sarsfield Bridge, Co. Limerick* ☎ *061/317–179* 🖷 *061/317–182* ⊕ *www.tsbh.ie* ⤳ *55 rooms* ⚭ *Restaurant, cable TV; no a/c* ☰ *AE, MC, V* ⭕ *BP.*

¢ ⌂ **Jurys Inn.** Clean, airy, and in good shape, unlike some of Limerick's other inner-city lodgings, this big, well-run hotel is part of the Jurys budget chain. Rooms are a good size and have light-wood furnishings. The hotel overlooks an urban stretch of the Shannon being converted from industrial to leisure use and is a short step from the main shopping and business district. ⊠ *Lower Mallow St., Mount Kennett Pl., Co. Limerick* ☎ *061/207–000* 🖷 *061/400–966* ⊕ *www.jurysdoyle.com* ⤳ *151 rooms* ⚭ *Restaurant, cable TV, in-room data ports, Wi-Fi, bar; no a/c* ☰ *AE, DC, MC, V* ⭕ *BP.*

Nightlife & the Arts

ART GALLERIES The **Belltable Arts Center** (⊠ 69 O'Connell St. ☎ 061/319–866) has exhibition space and a small auditorium for touring productions. The **Limerick City Gallery** (⊠ Pery Sq. ☎ 061/310–633) owns a small permanent collection of Irish art and mounts exhibits of contemporary art.

PUBS, CABARET **Dolan's Pub** (⊠ 3–4 Dock Rd. ☎ 061/314–483) is a lively waterfront & DISCOS spot with traditional Irish music every night, and dancing classes from September to May. Dolan's Warehouse, under the same management and in the same location, is a live-music venue with top national and international acts. **Hogan's** (⊠ 20–24 Old Clare St. ☎ 061/411–279) has a traditional music session every Monday, Wednesday, and Saturday. The riverside **Locke's Bar** (⊠ 3 George's Quay ☎ 061/413–733) is one of Limerick's oldest bars, dating from 1724, and has Irish music Sunday, Monday, and Tuesday nights. It's also a great place for outdoor drinking in summer. There's traditional music at **Nancy Blake's Pub** (⊠ 19 Denmark St. ☎ 061/416–443) year-round Sunday–Wednesday from 9 PM. **William G. South's Pub** (⊠ The Crescent ☎ 061/318–850) is an old-fashioned pub that's typical of the age of Frank McCourt's *Angela's Ashes*. There's no music, but do drop by for lunchtime bar food (Mon.–Sat. 12:30–3) or a drink.

Shopping

DEPARTMENT Limerick has a branch of **Brown Thomas** (⊠ O'Connell St. ☎ 061/472– STORES 222), Ireland's upscale department store. **Dunnes Stores** (⊠ 130 Sarsfield St. ☎ 061/412–666) is, perhaps, Ireland's favorite department store chain. **Penneys** (⊠ 137 O'Connell St. ☎ 061/227–244) sells inexpensive clothing; it's a great place for low-price rain gear. **Roches Stores** (⊠ O'Connell St. ☎ 061/415–622) is a large, mid-range department store.

MALLS The shops in **Arthur's Quay Shopping Centre** (⊠ Arthur's Quay ☎ 061/ 419888) mainly sell clothing and accessories. The **Crescent Shopping Center** (⊠ Dooradoyle ☎ 061/228560), Limerick's biggest, swankiest mall, with branches of most High Street fashion chains, is a five-minute bus or car ride from the city center.

SPECIALTY SHOPS The **Celtic Bookshop** (⊠ 2 Rutland St. ☎ 061/401–155) specializes in books of Irish interest. **Davern & Bell** (⊠ 22 Thomas St. ☎ 061/481—967) is a gallery of contemporary Irish crafts, mainly ceramics. **Deoidín** (⊠ 6 Sarsfield St. ☎ 061/318–011) has an interesting selection of crafts, jewelry, and gifts. **Lane Antiques** (⌗ 45 Catherine St. ☎ 061/339–307) sells collectibles, antiquarian books, prints, and paintings.

Bunratty Castle & Folk Park

★ ☾ **60**   *18 km (10 mi) west of Limerick City on N18 road to Shannon Airport.*

Bunratty Castle and Folk Park are two of those rare attractions that appeal to all ages and manage to be both educational and fun. Built in 1460, the castle—a stolid, massive affair with four square keep towers—has been fully restored and decorated with 15th- to 17th-century furniture and furnishings. It gives wonderful insight into the life of those times. As you pass under the walls of Bunratty, look for the three "murder holes" that allowed defenders to pour boiling oil on attackers below.

The castle is the site of medieval banquets, which are held nightly at 5:45 and 8:45; the cost is €51.95. You're welcomed by Irish colleens in 15th-century dress, who bear the traditional bread of friendship. Then you're led off to a reception, where you'll quaff mead made from fermented honey, apple juice, clover, and heather. Before sitting down at long tables in the candlelighted great hall, you can don a bib. You'll need it, because you eat the four-course meal medieval-style—with your fingers. Serving "wenches" take time out to sing a few ballads or pluck harp strings. The banquets may not be authentic, but they're fun; they're also popular, so book as far in advance as possible.

On the castle grounds the quaint **Bunratty Folk Park** re-creates a 19th-century village street and has examples of traditional rural housing. Exhibits include a working blacksmith's forge; demonstrations of flour milling, bread making, candle making, thatching, and other skills; and a variety of farm animals. An adjacent museum of agricultural machinery can't compete with the furry and feathered live exhibits. If you can't get a reservation for the medieval banquet at the castle, a *ceilí* (known as the Traditional Irish Night; held nightly May to September at 5:45 and 9 for €43.25) at the folk park is the next best thing. The program features traditional Irish dance and song and a meal of Irish stew, soda bread, and apple pie. No visit to Bunratty is complete without a drink in **Durty Nelly's** (☎ 061/364072), an old-world (but touristy) pub beside the folk park entrance. Its fanciful decor has inspired imitations around the world. ☎ *061/361–511* ⊕ *www.shannonheritage.com* ✉ €11 ☾ *Sept.–May, daily 9:30–5:30, last entry 4:15; June–Aug., daily 9:30–7, last entry 6.*

Knappogue Castle

★ ☾ **61**   *21 km (13 mi) north of Bunratty.*

With a name that means "hill of the kiss," Knappogue is one of Ireland's most beautiful medieval tower-house castles. A 15th-century MacNamara stronghold, Knappogue Castle was renovated in the Victorian era and fitted with storybook details. Restored by a wealthy American family, the castle has now been retro-ed in 15th-century style. By day you can enjoy a castle tour, including the walled garden, which looks like something out of a medieval Book of Hours. In the evenings it hosts fun and fabulous "medieval-style" banquets (€49.95). You're first greeted at the main door by the Ladies of the castle who escort you to the Dalcassian Hall, where you enjoy a goblet of mead (honey wine), listen to Harp and Fiddle, then proceed to the banqueting hall for a four-course meal, great Irish choral music, and a theatrical set-piece in which the Butler and the Earl argue the virtues of Gallantry. As an added allure, the castle looks spectacular when floodlit. Who can resist? ⊠ *5 km (3 mi) southeast of Quin on R649* ☎ *061/368–103* ⊕ *www.shannonheritage. com* ⊠ *€5.95* ⊗ *May–Sept., daily 9:30–4:30.*

Craggaunowen Project

62 *6 km (4 mi) northeast of Knappogue Castle.*

★ ☾ It's a strange experience to walk across the little wooden bridge above reeds rippling in the lake into Ireland's Celtic past as a jumbo jet passes overhead on its way into Shannon Airport—1,500 years of history compressed into an instant. But if you love all things Celtic, you'll have to visit the **Craggaunowen Project.** The romantic centerpiece is Craggaunowen Castle, a 16th-century tower house restored with furnishings from the period. Huddling beneath its battlements are two replicas of early-Celtic-style dwellings. On an island in the lake, reached by a narrow footbridge, is a clay-and-wattle *crannóg*, a fortified lake dwelling; it resembles what might have been built in the 6th or 7th century, when Celtic influence still predominated in Ireland. The reconstruction of a small ring fort shows how an ordinary soldier would have lived in the 5th or 6th century, at the time Christianity was being established here. Characters from the past explain their Iron Age (500 BC–AD 450) lifestyle; show you around their small holding, stocked with animals; and demonstrate crafts skills from bygone ages. ⊠ *Signposted off road to Sixmilebridge about 10 km (6 mi) east of Quin, Kilmurry, Sixmilebridge* ☎ *061/360–788* ⊕ *www. shannonheritage.com* ⊠ *€8* ⊗ *May–Oct., daily 10–6.*

THE SOUTHWEST ESSENTIALS

To research prices, get advice from other travelers, and book travel arrangements, visit www.fodors.com.

Transportation

BY AIR

The southwest has two international airports: Cork (ORK) on the southwest coast, and Shannon (SNN) in the west. Cork Airport, 5 km (3 mi) south of Cork City on the Kinsale road, has direct flights daily to Dublin, London (Heathrow, Gatwick, and Stanstead), Manchester, East Midlands, Paris, and Brussels, and direct flights to many other European cities.

Shannon Airport, 26 km (16 mi) west of Limerick City, is the point of arrival for many transatlantic flights, including direct flights from Atlanta, Chicago, Philadelphia, Toronto (summer only), and New York

City (from both JFK and Newark); it also has regular flights from the United Kingdom and many European cities. Kerry County Airport (KIR) at Farranfore, 16 km (10 mi) from Killarney, has daily flights from London (Stansted), Liverpool, and Frankfurt (Hahn) operated by Ryanair, and a regular service to Dublin and Manchester operated by Aer Arran.

🛈 Airport Information **Cork Airport** ☎ 021/431-3131 ⊕ www.cork-airport.com. **Kerry County Airport** ☎ 066/976-4644 ⊕ www.kerryairport.ie. **Shannon Airport** ☎ 061/471-444 ⊕ www.shannon-airport.com.

TRANSFERS Bus service runs between Cork Airport and the Cork City Bus Terminal every 30 minutes, on the hour and the half hour. The ride takes about 10 minutes and costs about €3. Bus Éireann runs a regular bus service from Shannon Airport to Limerick City between 8 AM and midnight. The ride takes about 40 minutes and costs €5.

All buses running from Cork to Galway are now routed via Shannon Airport, giving direct connections to those cities. For buses to Dublin, Waterford, Tralee, and Killarney, change at Limerick.

You can find taxis outside the main terminal building at Shannon and Cork airports. The ride from Shannon Airport to Limerick City costs about €30; from Cork Airport to Cork City costs about €10.

🛈 Shuttles **Bus Éireann** ☎ 061/474-311 ⊕ www.buseireann.ie. **Cork City Bus Terminal** ✉ Parnell Pl. ☎ 021/450-6066.

BY BUS

Bus Éireann operates express services from Dublin to Limerick City, Cork City, and Tralee. Most towns in the region are served by the provincial Bus Éireann network. The main bus terminals in the region are at Cork, Limerick, and Tralee. The U.K. bus company National Express jointly with Bus Eireann run services from most U.K. cities to most Irish cities. The journey from London to Cork via Rosslare is by bus and ferry, and, at about 14 hours, arduous.

FARES & The provincial bus service, cheaper and more flexible than the train, SCHEDULES covers all the region's main centers. Express services are available between Cork City and Limerick City (seven times a day); Cork, Killarney, and Tralee (seven times a day); and Killarney, Tralee, Limerick, and Shannon.

If you plan to travel extensively by bus, a copy of the Bus Éireann timetable (€1.50 from bus terminals) is essential. It's possible to tour the region by bus, but you need careful timing. Buses tend to stop running in the early evening, which is fine if you want to stay overnight and leave the next morning, but rules out many day trips—unless you want to spend most of the day on the bus. As a general rule, the smaller the town, and the more remote, the less frequent its bus service. For example, Kinsale, a well-developed resort 29 km (18 mi) from Cork, is served by at least seven buses a day, both arriving and departing, while some of the smaller villages on the remote Corca Dhuibne (Dingle Peninsula) have bus service only one day a week in winter. Bus Éireann runs a regular bus service around the Ring of Kerry between mid-June and mid-September, but there are only two buses a day, leaving Killarney at 8:45 AM or 1:45 PM. The trip takes more than four hours. Consult with hotel concierges, tourist board staffers, or the bus line Web site for the full scoop on bus schedules.

🚌 **Bus Information Bus Éireann** ☎ 01/836-6111 in Dublin, 061/313-333 in Limerick, 021/450-8188 in Cork, 066/712-3566 in Tralee ⊕ www.buseireann.ie. **Cork Bus Station** ✉ Parnell Pl. ☎ 021/450-8188. **Limerick Bus Station** ✉ Colbert Station ☎ 061/313-333. **National Express** ✉ London U.K. ☎ 087/058-08080, drop the initial zero and add prefix 00-44 if dialing from Ireland. **Tralee Bus Station** ✉ Casement Station ☎ 066/712-3566.

BY CAR

The main driving route from Dublin is N7, which goes 192 km (120 mi) directly to Limerick City; from Dublin, pick up N8 in Portlaoise and drive 257 km (160 mi) to Cork City. The journey time between Dublin and Limerick runs just under three hours; between Dublin and Cork it takes about three hours. From Rosslare Harbour by car, take N25 208 km (129 mi) to Cork; allow 3½ hours for the journey. You can pick up N24 in Waterford for the 211-km (131-mi) drive to Limerick City, which also takes about 3½ hours.

A car is the ideal way to explore this region, packed as it is with scenic routes, attractive but remote towns, and a host of out-of-the-way restaurants and hotels that deserve a detour. That said, the Celtic Tiger is not all gain; increased prosperity has led to an enormous growth in car ownership. Road upgrading has not kept up with the increased usage, and the result is our old friend, the peak-hour traffic jam. This is especially bad in the mornings between 8 AM and 9 AM on all major roads around Cork City, Limerick, and even Killarney. The evening rush hour has a wider spread, and can build up anytime between 4 PM and 6 PM.

Cork, Kinsale, Killarney, Tralee, and Limerick all have strict parking by-laws. Kinsale, Killarney, and Tralee are all amply provided with ground-level car parks: follow the blue "P" signs. In Cork and Limerick it's advisable to use a multistory car park, as on-street parking can be hard to find. If you do get lucky, you'll have to become familiar with "disk" parking regulations, which involve buying a ticket (or disk) for around €2 an hour from a machine or a shop and displaying it. In Cork and Limerick car clampers are active, especially during peak traffic times.

🚌 **Rental Agencies Alamo** ✉ Cork Airport ☎ 021/431-8623 ⊕ www.carhire.ie. **Avis** ✉ Cork Airport ☎ 021/428-1111 ⊕ www.avis.com ✉ Killarney ☎ 064/36655 ✉ Shannon Airport ☎ 061/471-094. **Budget** ✉ Cork Airport ☎ 021/431-4000 ⊕ www.budget.ie ✉ Killarney ☎ 064/34341 ✉ Shannon Airport ☎ 061/471-361. **Dan Dooley** ✉ Shannon Airport ☎ 061/471-098 ⊕ www.dan-dooley.ie. **Enterprise** ✉ Cork Airport ☎ 021/497-5133 ⊕ www.enterprise.com. **Hertz** ✉ Cork Airport ☎ 021/496-5849 ✉ Kerry Airport ☎ 066/976-3270 ✉ Shannon Airport ☎ 061/471-369 ⊕ www.hertz.ie. **Europcar** ✉ Cork Airport ☎ 021/491-7300 ✉ Shannon Airport ☎ 061/701-200 ⊕ www.europcar.ie. **Irish Car Rentals** ✉ Shannon Airport ☎ 061/328-328, 021/431-8644 Cork ⊕ www.irishcarrentals.ie ✉ Ennis Rd., Limerick ☎ 061/206-088.

BY TAXI

There are taxi stands at Cork Airport, Cork Railway Station, and on Patrick Street. It costs €3.10 to hire a taxi on the street (€4.20 by night,

€5 on Sunday and bank holidays); add €1.50 to book one by phone, and €1.80 per kilometer or part of a mile. For journeys outside the 6-km city limit, the average price is €2 per kilometer, and the price should be agreed before setting off.

Taxis will also be found at railway stations in Tralee, Killarney, Limerick, and at Shannon and Kerry airports.

🚹 Taxi Companies **Cork Taxi Co Op** (☎ 021/477-2222 ⊕ corktaxicoop.ie). **Killarney Cabs** (☎ 064/34888). **Tralee Radio Cabs** (☎ 066/721-5451). **Speedi Taxis Limerick** (☎ 061/314-444).

BY TRAIN

From Dublin Heuston Station the region is served by three direct rail links, to Limerick City, Tralee (via Killarney), and Cork City. Journey time from Dublin to Limerick is 2½ hours; to Cork, 2¾ hours; to Tralee, 3¾ hours.

The rail network, which covers only the inner ring of the region, is mainly useful for moving from one touring base to another. A major upgrade of the Dublin-Cork line is due in 2007, with promises of hourly service in each direction. There are currently four trains a day from Cork to Tralee, but this too is scheduled to improve in 2007. The journey from Cork to Tralee takes about 2 hours; from Cork to Limerick, about 1¼ hours; from Limerick to Tralee, about 3 hours.

A suburban rail service runs up to four times hourly from Kent Station and has stops at Fota Island and Cobh and offers better Cork Harbour views than the road.

🚹 Train Information **Irish Rail-Iarnod Éireann** ⊕ www.irishrail.ie/home. **Dublin Heuston Station** ☎ 01/836-6222. **Inquiries** ☎ 061/315-555 in Limerick, 021/450-6766 in Cork, 066/712-3522 in Tralee. **Kent Station** ☎ 021/450-6766 for timetable.

Contacts & Resources

EMERGENCIES

🚹 **Ambulance, fire, police** ☎ 999. **Mid-Western Health Board** ✉ 31-33 Catherine St., Limerick ☎ 061/316-655. **Southern Health Board** ✉ Dennehy's Cross, Cork City ☎ 021/454-5011.

🚹 Pharmacies **Phelan's** ✉ 9 Patrick St., Cork City ☎ 021/427-2511. **P. O'Donoghue** ✉ Main St., Killarney ☎ 064/31813. **Roberts** ✉ 105 O'Connell St., Limerick City ☎ 061/414-414.

TOURS

BUS TOURS Bus Éireann, part of the state-run public-transport network, offers a range of day and half-day guided tours from June to September. You can book them at the bus stations in Cork or Limerick or at any tourist office. A full-day tour costs about €30, half-day €15. Bus Éireann also offers open-top bus tours of Cork City on Tuesday and Saturday in July and August for €5.10.

Dero's Tours and Corcoran's Tours organize full-day and half-day trips by coach or taxi around Killarney and the Ring of Kerry.

Keating Coaches offer day trips and half-day tours of the Shannon region from Limerick City. Themes include "castles and gardens;" "waterways, highways, and byways;" and "flying boats, monks, and dolphins."

🚌 **Fees & Schedules Bus Éireann** ☎ 01/836-6111 in Dublin, 061/313-333 in Limerick, 021/450-8188 in Cork, 066/712-3566 in Tralee ⊕ www.buseireann.ie. **Corcoran's Tours** ✉ 10 College St., Killarney ☎ 064/36666. **Dero's Tours** ✉ 22 Main St., Killarney ☎ 064/31251 ⊕ www.derostours.com. **Keating Coaches** ✉ Ballingarry, Co. Limerick ☎ 069/68201 ⊕ www.limericktours.com.

SPECIAL-INTEREST TOURS Gerry Coughlan of Arrangements Unlimited can prearrange special-interest group tours of the region. Half-day and full-day tours are individually planned for groups of 10 or more to satisfy each visitor's needs. Country House Tours organizes self-driven or chauffeur-driven group tours with accommodations in private country houses and castles. It also conducts special-interest tours, including gardens, architecture, ghosts, and golf, while Killorglin-based Go Ireland offers comprehensive packages for walking, cycling, fishing golfing and equestrian holidays on the ring of Kerry and the Dingle Peninsula with experienced local guides.

Destination Killarney is the foremost Killarney tour operator. Besides offering full-day and half-day tours of Killarney and Kerry by coach or taxi, the group will prearrange your visit, lining up accommodations, entertainment, special-interest tours, and sporting activities in one package. A full-day (10:30–5) tour costs from €16 to €20 per person, excluding lunch and refreshments. The Killarney Local Circuit tour is an excellent half-day (10:30–12:30) orientation. The memorable Gap of Dunloe tour at €20 includes a coach and boat trip. Add €15 for a horseback ride through the gap. More conventional day trips can also be made to the Ring of Kerry, the Loo Valley, and Glengarriff; the city of Cork and Blarney Castle; An Daingean (Dingle) and Ceann Sleibne (Slea Head); and Caragh Lake and Rossbeigh.

Jaunting cars (pony and trap) that carry up to four people can be rented at a stand outside the Killarney tourist office. They can also be found at the entrance to Muckross Estate and at the Gap of Dunloe. A ride costs between €16 and €32, negotiable with the driver, depending on duration (one to two hours) and route. Tangney Tours is the leading jaunting-car company and will also organize tours by coach or water bus, as well as entertainment.

🚌 **Fees & Schedules Arrangements Unlimited** ✉ 1 Woolhara Park, Douglas, Cork City, Co. Cork ☎ 021/429-3873 🖷 021/429-2488 ⊕ www.arrangements.ie. **Country House Tours** ✉ 71 Waterloo Rd., Dublin 4 ☎ 01/668-6463 🖷 01/668-6578 ⊕ www.tourismresources.ie. **Destination Killarney** ✉ Scott's Gardens, Killarney, Co. Kerry ☎🖷 064/32638 ⊕ www.gleneaglehotel.com. **Shannon Castle Tours** ✉ Bunratty Folk Park, Bunratty, Co. Clare ☎ 061/360-788 ⊕ www.shannonheritage.com. **Tangney Tours** ✉ Kinvara House, Muckross Rd., Killarney, Co. Kerry ☎ 064/33358.

WALKING TOURS SouthWest Walks Ireland has a variety of packages for all levels of walkers along the coast of West Cork, around the Sheep's Head and Beara Peninsula in Bantry Bay as well as in Kerry. Trips include accommodation, baggage transfer, and evening meals for self-guided or escorted groups. Activity Ireland organizes customized walking and climbing tours on the Ring of Kerry. Go Ireland specializes in active vacations, included walking and cycling excursions along the Kerry Way or the Dingle Peninsula. Michael Martin's Titanic Trail, a 90-minute guided walking tour of Cobh takes its name from the *Titanic,* but in fact covers the whole of Cobh's fascinating history, from coffin ships to ocean liners via naval fire power and tall ships. Trips are daily at 11 AM starting from outside the Commodore Hotel; the cost is €7.50. Martin can also customize a walk or tour by minibus.

Richard Clancy, an expert on the legends and history of Killarney, offers a two-hour guided walk in Killarney National Park daily at 11 AM (other times by arrangement). Trips leave from the Shell gas station on Lower New Street. The cost is €8. Limerick City Tours provides inexpensive walking tours of Limerick from June to September (and by arrangement other months). St. Mary's Action Centre has walking tours of Limerick's historic centers and of locations highlighted in Frank McCourt's *Angela's Ashes.* They're conducted daily at 11 and 2:30.

🏃 **Activity Ireland** ⊠ Caherdaniel, Co. Kerry ☎ 066/947-5277 ⊕ www.activity-ireland. com. **Go Ireland** ⊠ Killorglin ☎ 066/976-2094 ⊕ www.goactivities.com. **Limerick City Tours** ⊠ Noel Curtin, Rhebogue ☎ 061/311935. **Richard Clancy** ☎ 064/33471 ⊕ www. killarneyguidedwalks.com. **St. Mary's Action Centre** ⊠ 44 Nicholas St., Limerick ☎ 061/318-106 ⊕ www.iol.ie/~smidp. **SouthWest Walks Ireland** ⊠ 6 Church St., Tralee ☎ 066/712-8733 ⊕ www.southwestwalksireland.com. **Titanic Trail** ⊠ Cobh ☎ 021/481-5211 ⊕ www.titanic-trail.com.

VISITOR INFORMATION

Bord Fáilte provides a free information service; its tourist information offices (TIOs) also sell a selection of tourist literature. For a small fee it will book accommodations anywhere in Ireland.

Seasonal TIOs in Bantry, Cahirciveen, and Clonakilty are open from May to October; offices in An Daingean (Dingle Town) and Kinsale are open from March to November; the TIO in Kenmare is open April to October, and the one in Youghal is open May to mid-September. All of the seasonal TIOs are generally open Monday–Saturday 9–6; in July and August they are also open Sunday 9–6. Year-round TIOs can be found in An Daingean, Blarney, Clonakilty, Cork City, Killarney, Limerick, Shannon, Skibbereen, and Tralee and are open Monday–Saturday 9–6; in July and August TIOs are also open Sunday 9–6.

🏃 **Tourist Information Adare** ⊠ Heritage Centre ☎ 061-396-255 ⊕ www.shannon-dev.ie. **Bantry** ⊠ Co. Cork ☎ 027/50229 ⊕ www.corkkerry.ie. **Blarney** ⊠ Co. Cork ☎ 021/438-1624 ⊕ www.corkkerry.ie. **Cahirciveen** ⊠ The Old Barracks, Co. Kerry ☎ 066/947-2589 ⊕ www.corkkerry.ie. **Clonakilty** ⊠ Co. Cork ☎ 023/33226 ⊕ www.corkkerry.ie. **Cork City** ⊠ Grand Parade, Co. Cork ☎ 021/425-5100 🖷 021/425-5199 ⊕ www. corkkerry.ie. **An Daingean (Dingle Town)** ⊠ The Quay, Co. Kerry ☎ 066/915-1188. **Kenmare** ⊠ Co. Kerry ☎ 064/41233. **Killarney** ⊠ Aras Fáilte, Beech Rd., Co. Kerry ☎ 064/31633 🖷 064/34506 ⊕ www.corkkerry.ie. **Kinsale** ⊠ Pier Rd., Co. Cork ☎ 021/477-2234, 021/477-4417 off-season 🖷 021/477-4438. **Limerick** ⊠ Arthur's Quay, Co. Limerick ☎ 061/317-522 ⊕ www.shannon-dev.ie. **Shannon Airport** ⊠ Co. Clare ☎ 061/471-664 ⊕ www.shannon-dev.ie. **Skibbereen** ⊠ North St., Co. Cork ☎ 028/21766. **Tralee** ⊠ Ashe Memorial Hall, Denny St., Co. Kerry ☎ 066/712-1288 ⊕ www.shannon-dev. ie. **Youghal** ⊠ Co. Cork ☎ 024/92390.

The West

INCLUDING COUNTIES CLARE, GALWAY, MAYO, AND THE ARAN ISLANDS

Thatched Roof Repair, County Clare

WORD OF MOUTH

"The Aran Islands are everything you imagine Ireland to be: green, rolling land, quaint village life, and much hospitality."

—abuster

"The Cliffs of Moher were every bit as dramatic as we imagined. We arrived late in the afternoon and there weren't huge crowds. Beautiful."

—Tennischick

www.fodors.com/forums

WELCOME TO
THE WEST

Ashleram Bay, Achill Island, County Mayo

TOP REASONS
TO GO

★ **Ancient Aran:** Spend at least one night on one of the Oileáin Arainn (Aran Islands), three outposts of Gaelic civilization, which still have a strong whiff of the "old ways"—and not just the whiff of turf smoke.

★ **Foot-tapping in Doolin and Ennis:** Tap your foot in time to "trad" Irish music and sip your pint as you while away an afternoon—and maybe an evening as well—in one of Doolin's or Ennis's noted music bars.

★ **High-style Galway:** A university town and booming, buzzing hive of activity, with great theaters, bars, nightlife, shopping and restaurants, Galway is the city that loves to celebrate and, as one of Europe's fastest growing townships, has much to offer.

★ **The Mighty Cliffs of Moher:** Rising straight out of the sea to a height of 700 feet, these cliffs— standing in silence as they look out over the wild Atlantic—give you a new understanding of the word "awesome."

1 Connemara & County Mayo. Gorgeous **Clifden** would be considered just a village elsewhere, but out here in rugged, sparsely populated Connemara, set between Galway City and the coast, it's a booming metropolis. Opt for **Cong**—famed setting of *The Quiet Man*—or Georgian-flavored **Westport** as other bases for exploring the glacial lakes and silent mountains of this beautiful wilderness area.

Cottage, Inis Mor, Aran Islands
County Galway

2 County Clare & the Aran Islands. Set with postcard-perfect villages like **Doolin, Kinvara,** and **Lisdoonvarna,** the lunar landscape of the **Burren,** and the towering **Cliffs of Moher,** County Clare is pure tourist gold. An hour or less on a ferry away are the ageless **Aran Islands**—once famed for their isolation, they are now disturbed a bit by 200,000-plus curious annual visitors.

ROSCOMMON

WESTMEATH

GALWAY

N6

Loughrea

N65

Gort

Lough Derg

TIPPERARY

LIMERICK

Cliffs of Moher, County Clare

3 Galway City. Easily the liveliest city in Ireland after Dublin, you've got to get your fill of its buzz when visiting, best done by checking out its eyepopping "g" hotel, stylish new boutiques and craft shops, and dazzling weekend festivals.

GETTING ORIENTED

With the most westerly seaboard in Europe, this region remains a place apart—the most Irish part of Ireland. The "west" here refers to the counties west of the River Shannon. Rich in Nature's magnificence— the Burren and the Cliffs of Moher—they are also home to sophisticated outposts like Galway City and Westport. Last outpost before America: the Aran Islands, which do constant battle with the Atlantic.

6

Galway City, County Galway

WEST PLANNER

Getting Around

Public transport is not a strong point in the West. Trains arrive from Dublin on separate lines to Ennis, Galway, and Ballina via Westport, but do not run between these towns.

The bus network is more flexible, but there are not many services a day, and you will need to do some serious planning to get around.

Both the Burren and Connemara can be explored on guided day trips from Galway City. But to do full justice to the region, you really need a car—and a good map.

How's the Weather?

It will most likely rain, but the locals just call it "soft" weather. Average rainfall in the rest of Ireland is between 800mm (31 in) and 1200mm (47 in), but here on the west coast, it can exceed 2000mm (79 in). It is said to rain in the west on at least 300 of the 365 days in the year.

Take comfort from the thought that it may be damp, but it is never really cold, with mean daily temperatures around 6 degrees celsius (42 F) in January and February, the coldest months.

In the warmest months, July and August, average temperatures are around 15 C (60 F).

Church ruins in the Burren

Traveling to the Aran Islands

The spell of the Aran Islands is such that many travelers can't resist their siren call and make for the first ferry leaving from Doolin. While this chapter is organized to accommodate such anticipation, locals will tell you that it may be best to wait until you are in Galway City before you make arrangements to travel to the famed Oileáin Arainn (Aran Islands). That way you can postpone your trip if the weather looks bad, and shop around for the best deals.

You can do a day trip, leaving the city at 9:30 or 12 noon and returning by 6:30, but staying overnight is more rewarding. Everyone wants to go to the islands, and it is made as easy as possible to organize by the various transport companies. They are all genuine and licensed: no one is going to rip you off. Book at the Tourist Information Office in Forster Place, where the ferry companies and Aer Arran have concessions.

The standard ferry deal is €25 round-trip and €6 for bus transfer to the ferry port at Rossaveal. Look out for money-saving offers that may include B & B accommodation, free transfers to Rossaveel, or Connemara airport (both 40 minutes away), bicycle hire on the islands, or a ferry-out, flight-back plan.

There are three different ferry operators, and tickets are not transferable, so check the return sailing times of your operator when you get on board.

If you opt for the five-minute flight, for safety reasons, you (yes, you, not your bags!) will be weighed at check-in, and allocated an appopriate seat.

For more information, *see* By Boat & Ferry *in* The West Es-

When Ireland Celebrates

For both visitors and locals, festivals provide both free entertainment and a chance to meet people from all backgrounds who share a common interest.

Some festivals are traditional events, now tarted up with entertaining side shows: Kinvara's Criuinniú na mBád on the third Thursday in August centers around turf-laden "hookers" (heavy wooden sailing boats) racing across Galway Bay, while on the third weekend in August the Connemara Pony Show in Clifden attracts a nationwide equine entry, and creates a terrific buzz.

The Fleadh Nua in Ennis in late May is one of the country's biggest traditional music festivals, and a great place to make friends. There is plenty of free entertainment there, and also at the Lisdoonvarna Matchmaking Festival held in late September, an outing which may well change your life—stranger things have happened!

In contrast, the Galway Arts Festival, in the middle two weeks of July, hosts an international array of the best of contemporary theater, film, rock, jazz, traditional music, poetry readings, comedy acts, visual arts exhibitions, and an open-air parade by the street theater company Macnas, one of several local troupes to gain international recognition.

This is followed immediately by the Galway Races, the "only place" for Irish socialites to be seen in late July. These Thoroughbred horse races now feature a new sport: the game of Spot the Celebrity (usually arriving by helicopter).

Both Galway and neighboring Clarinbridge have Oyster Festivals in September, celebrating the local product with oyster-opening competitions and lots of free entertainment.

Finding a Place to Stay

Some of Ireland's finest country-house and castle hotels are in the West. Ashford and Dromoland castles provide a standard of luxury and baronial charm that you should experience at least once, if you can stretch your budget.

Star country house destinations include antique-filled Cashel House and the more simply elegant fishing hideaway, Delphi Lodge. Try to sample some of the smaller B & Bs as well: the home-cooking at Kilmurvey House on the Aran Islands is renowned, as is the fare at Berry Lodge near Lahinch. Other memorable destinations include the cliff-top Moy House, picture-perfect Gregan's Castle in the Burren, the gracious creeper-clad Newport House in Mayo, and Renvyle House, in a stunning location between ocean and mountain in scenic Connemara.

One of the great attractions of the West's hotels and guesthouses, however much you pay for the night, is their restful environment: many lodgings sit in the middle of a large private estate beside a lake or river, overlooking the sea or a hilly valley. The accommodation may be inexpensive, but the view would please the most demanding millionaire. Most of the moderately priced hotels are relatively new, and thus more modern than charming, but these newer hotels often have facilities—tennis courts and indoor pools—that are scarce at B & Bs and older hotels. Assume that all hotel rooms in this chapter have air-conditioning, in-room phones, TVs and private bathrooms, unless otherwise indicated.

6

Dining & Lodging Price Categories (in Euros)				
$$$$	**$$$**	**$$**	**$**	**¢**
Restaurants over €29	€22–29	€15–22	€8–15	under €8
Hotels	over €230	€180–230	€130–180	€80–130	under €80

Restaurant prices are for a main course at dinner. Hotel prices are for a standard double room in high season.

Updated by
Alannah
Hopkin

THE MOST WESTERLY SEABOARD IN EUROPE, Ireland's West is richly endowed by nature: the majestic Cliffs of Moher; the rocky expanse of the Burren (whose gray rocks hide a profusion of wild plants); Connemara's combination of rugged coastline, mountains, moorland, and lakes; and the famous Oileáin Árainn (Aran Islands), which do constant battle with the fury of the Atlantic. But the West also abounds in characterful small country towns and villages, such as Kinvara, Ballyvaughan, Clifden, and Westport, rife with good restaurants and pubs, and Galway, the city that loves to celebrate.

The West refers to the region that lies west of the River Shannon; most of this area falls within the old Irish province of Connaught. This region faces its nearest North American neighbors across 3,200 km (2,000 mi) of the Atlantic Ocean: next parish, New York, as they say in the West.

Towns as communities were unknown in pre-Christian Irish society, and even today, more than 150 years after the famine, many residents still live on isolated small farms rather than in towns and villages. Especially during the wet, wintry months, you can still walk out of your country house, hotel, or bed-and-breakfast in the morning and smell turf fires burning nearby.

Today, the West is, for many, the most typically Irish part of the country. Particularly in western County Galway, the region has the highest concentration of Gaeltacht (Irish-speaking) communities in all Ireland, with roughly 40,000 native Irish speakers making their homes here. The country's first Irish-language TV station broadcasts from the tiny village of An Spidéal (Spiddle), on the north shore of Galway Bay in the heart of the Gaeltacht. Throughout this area, you'll see plenty of signs printed in Irish only. Who would suspect that Gaillimh is Irish for Galway? But wherever you go in the West, you'll not only see, but more importantly *hear,* the most vital way in which traditional Irish culture survives here: musicians play in pubs all over the West, and they are acknowledged to be the best in the Republic.

A major factor in the region's economic development has been the lure of its spectacular scenery to visitors. So far, the development that typically comes with the cultivation of tourism has been mercifully low-key in the West. The Irish people are well aware of what a jewel they have in the largely unspoiled wilderness, grazed by sheep and herds of wild ponies, that is Connemara. The 5,000-acre Connemara National Park is the result of a successful lobby for landscape preservation. Peatlands, or bogs as they are called around here, are at last being valued for their unique botanical character. Ireland's last remaining peat-burning electricity-generating station—at Bellacorick in County Mayo—has closed. Galway City's suburbs have spread in all directions, and throughout the region the landscape is marked by newly built bungalows and houses. With increasing prosperity, the West of Ireland is undoubtedly losing some of its old-style visual charm. But while this is regrettable in terms of unspoiled views, for the people who live in the area, it is a boon.

It's nothing new that the West's greatest virtue for visitors—apart from its glorious scenery and the vibrant capital city of Galway—is its peo-

THE WEST THROUGH THE AGES

Although Ireland's East, Southwest, and the North were influenced by either Norman, Scots, or English settlers, the West largely escaped systematic resettlement and, with the exception of the walled town of Galway, remained purely Irish in language, social organization, and general outlook far longer than the rest of the country. The land in the West, predominantly mountains and bogs, did not immediately tempt the conquering barons. Oliver Cromwell was among those who found the place thoroughly unattractive, and he gave the Irish chieftains who would not conform to English rule the choice of going "to Hell or Connaught."

It wasn't until the late 18th century, when better transport improved communications, that the West began to experience the so-called foreign influences that had already Europeanized the rest of the country.

The West was, in effect, propelled from the 16th century into the 19th. Virtually every significant building in the region dates either from before the 17th century or from the late 18th century onward. As in the southwest, the population of the West was decimated by the Great Famine (1845–49) and by the waves of emigration that persisted until the 1950s.

6

ple. No matter how many times you get out of the car for a photo-op (and you should expect to *fly* through megabytes of memory here), the stories that you'll most likely tell when you show your friends and family those pictures are going to be about the *seisún,* or sessions (informal performances of traditional music) you stumbled upon in a small pub; the tiny, far-from-the-madding-crowd lake in Connemara that you made your own; and the great *craic* ("crack," or good conversation and fun) you're likely to discover wherever you go.

Exploring the West

This chapter is organized into four parts, covering the territory from south to north. The first section, the Burren and Beyond—West Clare to South Galway—picks up minutes from Shannon Airport and is not far from Ennis, the gateway to coastal County Clare. The second section takes you through the best of buzzing, bustling Galway City, and the third takes you out to the three Oileáin Árainn (Aran Islands), standing guard at the mouth of Galway Bay. The fourth section, covering Connemara and County Mayo, brings you north of Galway Bay and west of Galway City into fabled Connemara, and its spectacularly situated "capital," Clifden. Beyond lie the highlights of County Mayo: monumental Croagh Patrick, the pretty town of Westport, the Museum of Country Life in Turlough, and Ballina. Allow at least four days for exploring the region, six days if you include a visit to the Oileáin Árainn islands. Although distances between sights are not great, you may want to take scenic—meaning slower—national secondary routes. Covering 80 km to 112 km (50 mi to 70 mi) per day on these roads is a comfortable target.

COUNTY CLARE: THE BURREN & BEYOND

County Clare claims two of Ireland's unique natural sights: the awesome Cliffs of Moher and the stark, mournful landscape of the Burren, which hugs the coast from Black Head in the north to Doolin and the Cliffs of Moher in the south. Yet western County Clare (West Clare for short) is widely beloved among native Irish for a natural phenomenon significantly less unique than these: its sandy beaches. Though just another Irish beach town to some, Kilkee, to name just one, is a favorite summer getaway. So whether you're looking for inimitable scenery or just a lovely beach to plunk down on to relax in the sun (if you're lucky!) for a few hours, you can find it in West Clare.

This journey begins at Newmarket-on-Fergus, within minutes of Shannon Airport, a good jumping-off point for a trip through the West if you've just arrived in Ireland and are planning to head for Galway. This route also follows directly from the end of Chapter 5, which concludes 10 km (6 mi) down the road, at Bunratty Castle and Folk Park (and the Knappogue Castle and Craggaunowen Project, also nearby), so be sure to take a moment to glance at those sights to decide whether to include them as you get under way. The Shannon region is also the connecting link between County Limerick (and other points in the southwest) and Galway City. If you're approaching it from the southwest and you're not going into Limerick City, it makes sense to begin exploring the region from Killimer, reached via the ferry from Tarbert.

Newmarket-on-Fergus

❶ *13 km (8 mi) north of Shannon Airport on N18.*

A small town in County Clare, Newmarket-on-Fergus is chiefly remarkable as the village nearest the famed hotel of Dromoland Castle, formerly the home of Lord Inchiquin, chief of the O'Brien clan.

Where to Stay & Eat

$$$$ ✕🏨 **Dromoland Castle.** This massive, turreted, neo-Gothic castle—the
Fodor'sChoice ancestral home of the O'Briens, descendants of Brian Boru, High King
★ of Ireland—certainly looks the part. Dating from the 19th century (it replaced the 16th-century original) and now one of Ireland's grandest and best loved hotels, it bristles with towers and crenellations that rise up over the forest and a picture-perfect lake, looking like a storybook illustration from King Arthur and his knights. Inside, Dromoland really sets out to give you the full country-house treatment: oak paneling, ancestral portraits, plushly carpeted rooms, crystal chandeliers, Irish-Georgian antiques—all the creature comforts any high-born duke would want. But the cordiality of the long-serving staff, and the pervading aroma of wood smoke help to create an easygoing, relaxing ambience. Bedrooms (suites, in fact) in the main wing are the largest and most elaborate, with massive four-poster beds, tall, draped windows, custom fabrics, and genuine Hepplewhite armoires. Rooms in the discreetly added newer wings are more hotel-like, with Regency-style furniture, but all have luxurious bathrooms. The neo-Gothic, oak-wainscoted Earl of

Thomond Restaurant is magnificent, with beautifully presented tables decked with crystal and Irish linen, a harpist providing gentle background music, period wallpapers, Japanese vases, and spectacular chandeliers. Classic French cuisine is served with appropriate ceremony—perhaps poached lobster with steamed greens for the main course, or roast Clare lamb with salsa vert. The Green Room Bar and the Fig Tree restaurant offer more casual dining. For activities, the estate offers a full golf course, golf academy, tennis, fishing, a spa, and those idyllic woodlands and gardens—perfect for jogging, cycling, or a blissful stroll. ⊠ *5 km (3 mi) west of Newmarket-on-Fergus, signposted from N18, Co. Clare* ☎ *061/368–144* 🖷 *061/363–355* ⊕ *www.dromoland.ie* ➴ *100 rooms* ♨ *2 restaurants, in-room data ports, Wi-Fi, 18-hole golf course, 2 tennis courts, indoor pool, spa, fishing, bicycles, bar; no a/c* ☰ *AE, DC, MC, V* ⏐⊙⏐ *EP.*

$ ✕🖾 **Hunter's Lodge.** A good first or last stop for those arriving at Shannon, this unpretentious village pub with rooms is only 12 km (7 mi) from the airport. The village itself is still basking in the pleasure of no longer being on the main road, since it was bypassed by a new highway in 2003. The resulting cheerful little community will suit those who like to get to know "the real people" when arriving in a new country. Downstairs is a plush, upmarket version of an Irish pub, with dark mahogany furniture and brass trim in the bar, where locals congregate around a roaring open fire. Select pieces of old oak furniture dot the attractive, well-equipped guest rooms, and scatter rugs decorate the timber floors. The restaurant ($–$$), known for its cheerful service, has an uncomplicated menu of old familiars like sirloin steak in pepper sauce, burgers béarnaise, pasta Alfredo, and, the most popular of all, salmon *en croute* (wrapped in pastry with a seafood sauce). ⊠ *The Square, Co. Clare* ☎ *061/368–577* 🖷 *061/368–057* ➴ *6 rooms* ♨ *Restaurant, bar, free parking; no a/c* ☰ *AE, DC, MC, V* ⏐⊙⏐ *BP.*

Sports & the Outdoors

Dromoland Golf Course (☎ 061/368–144) is one of the most scenic in the country, set in a 700-acre estate of rich woodland on the grounds of Dromoland Castle. The 18-hole, par-71 course has a natural lake that leaves little room for error on a number of holes. Improvers take note: a state-of-the-art golf academy is scheduled to open in time for the 2007 season.

Ennis

❷ *9½ km (6 mi) north of Newmarket-on-Fergus on N18, 37 km (23 mi) northwest of Limerick, 142 km (88 mi) north of Tralee.*

A major crossroads and a convenient stop between the West and the Southwest, Ennis is the main town of County Clare. The pleasant market town has an attractively renovated, pedestrian-friendly center, bisected by the fast-flowing River Fergus. Ennis has always fostered the traditional arts, especially fiddle-playing and step-dancing (a kind of square dance). The **Fleadh Nua** (pronounced fla-*nooa*) festival at the end of May attracts both performers and students of Irish music and serves as the venue for the National Dancing Championships.

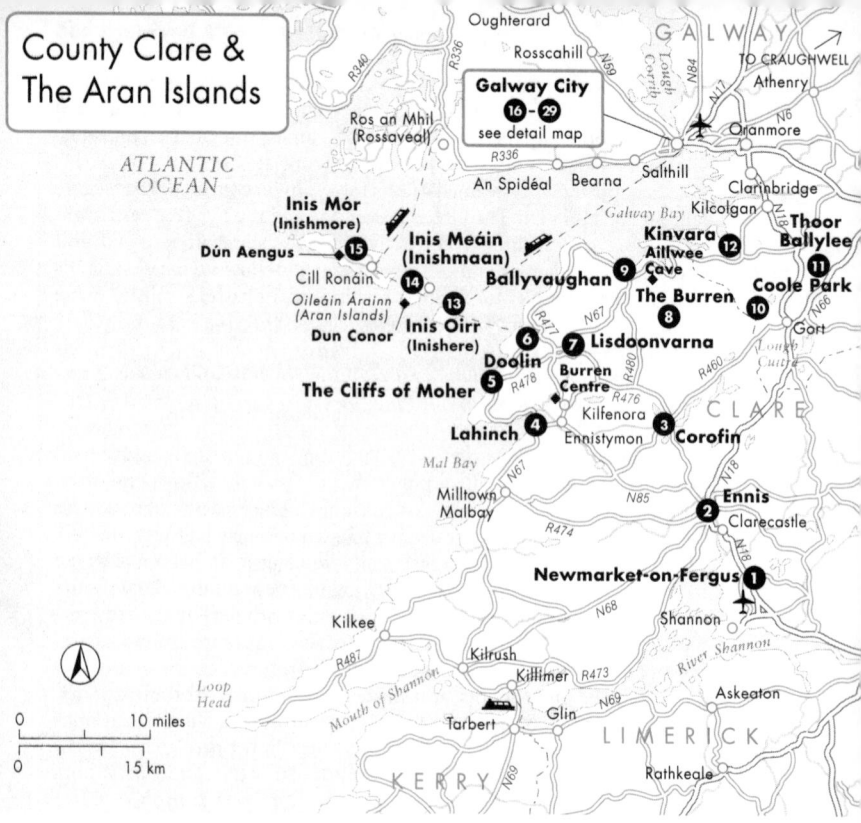

County Clare & The Aran Islands

Where to Stay & Eat

$ ✕🏨 **Lynch West County.** You will meet both leisure and business travelers from all walks of life at this popular stopping point on the Limerick–Galway road (N18), a lively modern hostelry affiliated with Best Western. It's a five-minute walk from Ennis's town center. Rooms are ample; most overlook the car park but at least are quiet. Service is helpful and friendly, despite the hotel's relatively large size. In July and August there's nightly Irish cabaret-style entertainment in the large bar, Boru's Porterhouse, which also serves bar food. The County Grill is a more intimate venue ($$) serving an à la carte menu of traditional Irish fare, while the Pine Room ($) offers a value-for-money four-course set menu. ⊠ *Clare Rd., Co. Clare* ☎ *065/682–3000* 🖷 *065/682–3759* ⊕ *www.lynchotels.com* 🛏 *152 rooms* 🍴 *3 restaurants, coffee shop, Wi-Fi, indoor pool, health club, bar; no a/c* 🖃 *AE, DC, MC, V* 🍽 *BP.*

$$ 🏨 **Temple Gate.** Before its conversion, this lodging was a Gothic-

> ### SPICY IRISH STEW
>
> These days the Ennis town center has a pleasantly multicultural ambience, as many emigrants arriving at Shannon Airport from faraway locations—including Brazil and West Africa—have settled here.

Local Heroes

THE MEMBER OF PARLIAMENT (or Dáil Éireann as it became known after independence) for Ennis has twice been a national leader at a time of great significance for Irish democracy, and each is commemorated by a town statue.

On a tall limestone column above a massive pediment in Ennis's town center stands a **statue of Daniel O'Connell** (1775–1847), "The Liberator," a member of Parliament for County Clare between 1828 and 1831 who was instrumental in bringing about Catholic Emancipation.

Outside the courthouse (in the town park, beside the River Fergus, on the west side of Ennis) stands a larger-than-life bronze **statue of Eamon De Valera** (1882–1975), who successfully contested the election here in 1917, thus launching a long political career.

He was the dominant figure in Irish politics during the 20th century, serving as prime minister for most of the years from 1937 until 1959, when he resigned as leader of Fianna Fáil, the party he founded, and went on to serve as president of Ireland until 1973.

Although De Valera was born in the United States, his maternal forebears were from County Clare.

6

---

style convent, and remnants of its previous existence (including the chapel, which is now a banquet hall) give character to this bright, modern hotel in the town center. Coordinated drapes and bedspreads in warm, earthy colors decorate the compact, well-equipped rooms, which have unusual views of pretty corners of Ennis's historic center. Preacher's Bar is popular with locals, while the guest lounge is a country house–style library. The entrance is via a cobblestoned courtyard adorned with Victorian street lamps. ⊠ *The Square, Co. Clare* ☎ *065/682–3300* 📠 *065/692–3322* ⊕ *www.templegatehotel.com* ➥ *70 rooms* ⌂ *Restaurant, in-room data ports, Wi-Fi, bar, library; no a/c* ▤ *AE, DC, MC, V* ⧄ *BP.*

Nightlife & the Arts

Glór - Irish Music Centre (⊠ Friar's Walk ☎ 065/684–3103 ⊕ www.glor.ie) is Ennis's venue for large concerts, hosting competitions of Irish music, song, and dance, and big name touring acts on the Irish music scene including Mary Black, Paul Brady, and Aslan. There's also a craft gallery and coffee shop, and free parking.

Although Ennis is not as fashionable as, say, Galway, it's one of the West's traditional-music hot spots. You're likely to hear sessions at the following pubs, but keep in mind that sessions don't necessarily take place every night and that the scene is constantly changing. Phone ahead to check whether a session is happening.

Cruise's (⊠ Abbey St. ☎ 065/684–1800). **Fawl's** (⊠ The Railway Bar, 69 O'Connell St. ☎ 065/682–4463). **Kerins'** (⊠ Lifford ☎ 065/682–0582). **Knox's** (⊠ Abbey St. ☎ 065/682–9264). **Poet's Corner Bar** (⊠ Old Ground Hotel, Main St. ☎ 065/682–8155). **Preachers** (⊠ Temple Gate Hotel, the Sq. ☎ 065/682–3300).

EATING WELL IN THE WEST

Because the West has a brief high season—from mid-June to early September—and a quiet off-season, it doesn't have as broad a choice of small, owner-operated restaurants as do other parts of Ireland. Often the best place to eat is a hotel—Sheedy's Restaurant and Country Inn in Lisdoonvarna, for example, which has one of the best chefs in County Clare, or Rosleague Manor in Letterfrack. The dominant style of cuisine in the West is an unfussy, traditional approach that allows the natural flavors of fresh local delights—locally reared lamb and beef, and freshly landed seafood—to shine through. Look out for wild salmon or sea trout, fresh from one of the region's fast-flowing rivers, and Connemara mountain lamb, which has a particular flavor from grazing on mountain herbs and grass: these three regional delicacies that are well worth the premium. Most of the chefs working in the region have traveled widely, and on many menus you will find a whiff of Asia—Thailand especially—along with the expected classic French repertoire. A handful of restaurants, including Kirwan's Lane Creative Cuisine and K. C.

Blake's in Galway, showcase adventurous contemporary Irish cooking with a bold fusion element. But many of the best things to eat in these parts are extremely simple, which makes a bar-food lunch a tempting option. It's hard to beat a platter of freshly sliced smoked salmon with half a lemon squeezed over it, home-baked brown bread with butter, and a glass of dry white wine. Oysters, too, (the local one is the European oyster, *ostrea edulis*) are often ordered in their shells and slipped directly into the mouth, followed by a bite of soda bread and butter and a sip of black stout; a combination made in heaven, many say. Galway oysters are in season from September to April. Fans say they taste of the sea, but not everyone likes the rubbery texture—the good news is each oyster contains only seven calories. Home-baked brown bread, whether soda (made with buttermilk) or yeast, is one of the great pleasures of the region, and another is the home-baking—porter cake, fruit scones, breakfast muffins—which is on offer at many of the region's B&Bs and inns.

Sports & the Outdoors

BICYCLING You can follow the scenic Burren Cycleway (69 km [43 mi]) to the famous Cliffs of Moher on a bike rented from **Tierney Cycles & Fishing** (✉ 17 Abbey St. ☎ 065/682–9433 ⊕ www.ennisrentabike.com).

Shopping

Stop in at the **Antique Loft** (✉ Clarecastle ☎ 065/684–1969) for collectibles and pine and mahogany antiques. The **Belleek Shop** (✉ 36 Abbey St. ☎ 065/682–9607) carries Belleek china, Waterford crystal, and Donegal Parian china, as well as Lladró, Hummel, and other collectible china. **Carraig Donn** (✉ 29 O'Connell St. ☎ 065/682–8188) sells its own line of knitwear. **Clare Craft and Design** (✉ 20 Parnell St. ☎ 065/684–4723) exhibits and sells art, pottery, and crafts produced by local artists.

The Rock Shop (✉ 2 O'Connell St. ☎ 065/682–2636) displays polished gemstones, fossils, and other rocks alongside jewelry and small sculptures in stone and marble.

Corofin

❸ *14 km (10 mi) northwest of Ennis via N18.*

Corofin? It's not a town but a tiny village of perhaps 200 people, just a line of houses and some lovely, unspoiled country pubs—but perhaps that is all you're looking for today. Corofin's **Clare Heritage and Genealogical Center** has a genealogical service and advice for do-it-yourselfers researching their Irish roots. Displays on west-Ireland 19th-century history cover culture, traditions, emigration, and famine. ✉ *Church St. ☎ 065/683–7955 ⊕ www. clareroots.com 🖾€4 ◷ Apr.–Oct., weekdays 9:30–5:30; Nov.–Mar. by appointment.*

> **POPULATION IMPLOSION**
>
> In 1841 the population of County Clare was 286,394. Fifty years later, famine and emigration had reduced this number to 112,334, and the population continued to decline, reaching an all-time low of 73,597 in 1956. It's now heading back to the 90,000 mark.

A 15th-century castle on the edge of Corofin houses the **Clare Archaeology Centre,** which has an exhibition on the antiquities of the Burren. Twenty-five monuments stand within a 1½-km (1-mi) radius of the castle; these date from the Bronze Age to the 19th century, and all are described at the center. ✉ *Dysert O'Dea Castle ☎ 065/683–7794 🖾€4 ◷ May–Sept., daily 10–6.*

Lahinch

❹ *30 km (18 mi) west of Ennis on N85.*

Lahinch, a busy resort village beside a long, sandy beach backed by dunes, is best known for its links golf courses and—believe it or not—its surfing. In 1972 the European Surfing Finals were held here, putting Lahinch on the world surfing map, where it has stayed ever since. But the center ring here is occupied by golf—with three world-class courses and a dazzling bay-view backdrop, Lahinch is often called the "St. Andrews of Ireland."

Where to Stay & Eat

¢ ✕🏠 **Berry Lodge.** Just south of Milltown Malbay, 8 km (5 mi) south of Lahinch (near the turn-off for Spanish Point) and way out in the country but within view of the sea, this is a good choice for people who relish peace and quiet, birdsong, and simple home comforts. The traditional two-story, white-paint, slate-roof house dates from 1775,

> **GNARLY, DUDE**
>
> Tom and Rosemary Buckley's Lahinch Surf Shop (☎ 065/708–1543) in The Promenade is the main center for County Clare surfers. Contact their Web site, www.lahinchsurfshop.com, for today's surf report.

and has been in Rita Meade's family for three generations. At an age when most of us would be putting our feet up, Rita not only runs the guesthouse and restaurant but hosts a popular local radio show on cooking. The country-pine pieces in her crisply clean rooms are genuine antiques, beds are covered in patchwork quilts, and the sprigged curtains have pretty tiebacks. Floors are genuine old pine, fireplaces are original, and the rooms are dotted with local craft work. You eat in a large room with a sofa and armchairs at one end, and a tall dresser laden with family treasures (reservations essential; telephone to confirm restaurant is open from September to June, when opening is subject to demand—otherwise open daily July and August). Cooking is simple and unfussy, the fresh local ingredients first-rate. A typical main course might be slow-roasted spiced duckling with red onion marmalade and a Guinness, honey, and orange sauce. ⊠ *Annagh, Milltown Malbay, Co. Clare* ☎ *065/708-7022* 🖷 *065/708-7011* ⊕ *www.berrylodge.com* 📩 *5 rooms* △ *No a/c, no room phones* ⊟ *MC, V* ⊘ *Closed Jan.–mid-Feb.* ⊺◯⊺ *BP.*

$$$$ 🏨 **Moy House.** Built for Sir Augustine Fitzgerald, this enchanting, 18th-

Fodor's Choice century Italianate-style lodge sits amid 15 private acres on an exhila-

★ rating, "Wuthering Heights"–like windswept cliff-top that's a three-minute drive from Lahinch. It's a world away from the bustling seaside resort—a peaceful haven, where you are made to feel like you're a guest in a privately owned country house. The decor is most alluring, with period velvet sofas, marble fireplaces, and gilt-framed paintings. Upstairs, brocade curtains and Oriental rugs complement the guest rooms' Georgian and Victorian polished-mahogany antiques. Some rooms have open fires, some have free-standing cast-iron bathtubs, six have stunning sea views, and two overlook the pretty, sheltered garden. Once you settle in, enjoy a drink at the "honesty bar" in the elegant drawing room (help yourself, and write it down), one of many touches that make the place so relaxing. In bad weather, curl up with a book in the peaceful library on the lower floor. Guests are given the run of the kitchen should they need to rustle up a snack in the night. The cozy dining room (guests only) serves an imaginative four-course dinner (€50) of contemporary cuisine. The real dessert is the vista from the veranda over Lahinch Bay. ⊠ *Milltown Malbay Rd., Co. Clare* ☎ *065/708-2800* 🖷 *065/708-2500* ⊕ *www.moyhouse.com* 📩 *9 rooms* △ *Dining room, in-room data ports; no a/c* ⊟ *AE, MC, V* ⊺◯⊺ *BP.*

$$ 🏨 **The Greenbrier Inn.** A well-designed modern building, this inn was designed as a guesthouse and both the guest rooms and the large lounge–dining room overlook Lahinch's famous golf links, Liscannor Bay, and the Atlantic Ocean. Set 250 yards from the beach, with ample parking, this is a practical, good-value choice for golfers and for those who like things traditional-modern and uncomplicated. The location and the views are the strong points here. Rooms are a good size, and have double-glazed windows with great views; some have small balconies. ⊠ *Ennistymon Rd., Co. Clare* ☎ *065/708-1242* 🖷 *065/708-1247* ⊕ *www.greenbrierinn.com* 📩 *14 rooms* ⊟ *MC, V* ⊘ *Closed Dec. 20–early Mar.* ⊺◯⊺ *BP.*

Nightlife & the Arts

For traditional music try the **19th Bar** (⊠ Main St. ☎ 065/708–1440). **O'Looney's** (⊠ The Promenade ☎ 065/708–1414) is known as Lahinch's

The Great Outdoors

WHILE THE WEST'S RUGGED SCENERY has always been popular with outdoor types, the biggest growth area in recent years has been in provision of facilities for walkers and hikers. The last decade has seen the completion of various "way-marked" (signposted) walking routes. Better, there are also several new tour operators specializing in customized walking holidays, providing accommodation and a guide, or annotated walking maps (see Tour Options in Essentials at end of this chapter). If you like challenging hills and relatively rough terrain, the West is excellent hiking country. The unusual, almost lunar landscape of the Burren in County Clare is less demanding than the terrain in Connemara. Here, and in the area north of Connemara in South County Mayo, the countryside is sparsely populated and subject to sudden changes in weather, usually a shower of rain. There are four signposted trails in the area, but it's always advisable to buy a good map locally before setting out. The **Burren Way** runs from Lahinch to Ballyvaughan on the shores of Galway Bay, a distance of 35 km (22 mi). The most spectacular part of the trail runs along the top of the Cliffs of Moher from Doolin to the coast near Lisdoonvarna, a distance of about 5 km (3 mi). The trails continue through the heart of the Burren's gray, rocky limestone landscape, with ever-changing views offshore of the Aran Islands and Galway Bay. The **Western Way's County Galway section** extends from Ougheterard on Lough Corrib through the mountains of Connemara to Leenane on Killary Harbour, a distance of 50 km (30 mi). Its 177-km (110-mi) County Mayo section, known as the Western Way (Mayo), continues past Killary Harbor to Westport on Clew Bay to the Ox Mountains east of Ballina; this trail includes some of the finest mountain and coastal scenery in Ireland. A new, 224-km (140-mi) hiking route, *slí Chonamara* through Irish-speaking Connemara, stretches along the shores of Galway Bay from An Spidéal to Carraroe, Carna, Lettterfrack, and Recess.

surfers' pub; there's music every night in summer and on Saturday nights in winter.

Sports & the Outdoors

Doonbeg Golf Club (⊠ On main N67 between Lahinch and Kilkee, Doonbeg ☎ 065/905–5246 ⊕ www.doonbeggolfclub.com), an 18-hole links course designed by Greg Norman, winds along 2½ km (1½ mi) of crescent-shape beach; the ocean is visible from almost every hole. The 6,613-yard, 18-hole, par-72 championship course at **Lahinch Golf Club** (⊠ The Seafront ☎ 065/708–1003), which opened in 1892, has challenging links that follow the natural contours of the dunes. The 18-hole, par-72 **Castle Course** (⊠ The Seafront ☎ 065/708–1003) is ideal for a carefree round of seaside golf, with shorter holes than the championship course at Lahinch Golf Club.

Shopping

The small **Design Lodge** (⊠ Main St. ☎ 065/708–1744) specializes in ladies' fashions and carries several Irish labels.

The Cliffs of Moher

★ ❺ *10 km (6 mi) northwest of Lahinch on R478.*

One of Ireland's most breathtaking natural sights, the majestic Cliffs of Moher rise vertically out of the sea in a wall that stretches over a long, 8-km (5-mi) swath and in places reaches a height of 710 feet. Stratified deposits of five different rock layers are visible in the cliff face. This was considered a venerated place in the Celtic era and a favorite hunting retreat by Brian Boru, the High King of Ireland. Numerous seabirds, including a large colony of puffins, make their homes in the shelves of rock on the cliffs. On a clear day you can see the Aran Islands and the mountains of Connemara to the north, as well as the

> ### CONCERTS IN THE CAR PARK
>
> The visitor center parking area at O'Brien's Tower is a favorite spot of performers. In high season, you're likely to be treated to some free entertainment—step dancers, fiddle players, or even a one-man band.

lighthouse on Loop Head and the mountains of Kerry to the south. Built in 1835 by Cornelius O'Brien—of Bunratty Castle fame and a descendant of the Kings of Thomond—**O'Brien's Tower** is a defiant, broody sentinel located on the cliffs' highest point, having been built to encourage tourism (yes, there were even tourists back then). Cornelius also erected here a wall of Moher flagstones (noted for their imprints of prehistoric eels). His tower is near the village of Liscannor. The **Visitor Centre**, a good refuge from passing rain squalls, has a gift shop and tearoom. ☎ 065/708–1565 ⊕ *www.shannonheritage.com* ✉ *Free, parking* €*2.50* ☉ *Cliffs daily 24 hrs; visitor center daily 9:30–5:30; O'Brien's Tower May–Sept., daily 9:30–5:30, weather permitting.*

Doolin

❻ *6 km (4 mi) north of the Cliffs of Moher on R479.*

A tiny village consisting almost entirely of B&Bs, hostels, pubs, and restaurants, Doolin is widely reputed to have three of the best pubs for traditional music in Ireland. But with the worldwide surge of interest in Irish music during the last decade, the village is more of a magnet for European musicians than it is for young, or even established, Irish artists. On **Doolin Pier**, about 1½ km (1 mi) outside the village, fisherfolk sell their fresh catches right off the boat—lobster, crayfish, salmon, and mackerel.

Doolin Ferries (☎ 065/707–4455 ⊕ www.doolinferries.com) makes the 30-minute trip from Doolin Pier to Inis Oirr (Inisheer), the smallest of the Aran Islands, from spring until early fall (weather permitting). There are at least three round-trip sailings a day, and up to eight in July and

August, but inquire on the day you plan to embark, as schedules vary according to weather and demand. Sometimes more than one ferry company operates out of Doolin; your return ticket will only be valid with the company that took you out, so when boarding the outbound ferry, be sure to check the return schedule. A sea voyage under the command of Captain P. J. Garrihy of **Cliffs of Moher Cruises** (⊠ Doolin Pier ☎ 065/708–6060 ⊕ www.mohercruises.com ⊠ €20 for 1½ hrs) will allow you to view the awesome Cliffs of Moher from beneath, and get an even better view of more than 20 species of seabirds that nest on its ledges. You could even meet some friendly dolphins. April through October there are six sailings per day, starting at 10 AM. By advance request, you can take a sunrise or sunset cruise.

Where to Stay & Eat

Because Doolin is known as a center of traditional music, it gets quite crowded with foreign visitors. If you're having trouble finding a room or you want to stay somewhere other than a B&B, you may want to follow the lead of the many Irish vacationers who tend to stay in nearby Lisdoonvarna, which is 5 km (3 mi) away and has a wider selection of lodgings.

★ $$$ ✕⊞ **Ballinalacken Castle.** One hundred acres of wildflower meadows surround this restored, low-slung Victorian lodge, which was built alongside the 16th-century ruins of an O'Brien castle (hence its somewhat bogus name). It's one of the most memorably sited of Ireland's coastal inns, with panoramic views of the Atlantic, the Aran Islands, and distant Connemara. The sense of spaciousness is exhilarating, and manager Marian Sheedy reports that many guests regularly oversleep due to the quietness. The public rooms display a mix of comfy old armchairs and antique, baronial-style Irish oak, amid floral wallpaper and rampant pots of aspidistra. Guest rooms in the older house have massive four-poster beds, marble fireplaces, and high ceilings. Some large, sunny rooms have bay windows to frame that stunning view; nice but plainer rooms in the new wing, with antique-style decor, are equally sought after. Chef Frank Sheedy, who has cooked in some of Ireland's best restaurants, serves an imaginative and sophisticated Continental menu ($$$$)—you'll want to finish off your feast of roast loin of Burren lamb with a platter of Cashel blue, Cooney, and smoked Gubeen cheeses. Book in advance or you may not get a table. Ballinalacken is about 1 km (½ mi) outside Doolin on the Lisdoonvarna road. ⊠ *Coast Rd., Co. Clare* ☎ *065/707–4025* 🖷 *065/707–4025* ⊕ *www.ballinalackencastle.com* ⬎ *19 rooms, 2 suites* ⚲ *Restaurant, bar; no a/c* ▤ *AE, DC, MC, V* ☽ *Closed Nov.–mid-Apr.* ⑩ *BP.*

$$ ✕⊞ **Aran View House.** This extensively modernized 1736 house on 100 acres of farmland offers magnificent views in nearly every direction: the Aran Islands to the west, the Cliffs of Moher to the south, and the gray limestone rocks of the Burren to the north. The interior is decorated with antique touches, such as four-poster beds and Georgian reproduction furniture. You can savor the view from the restaurant's bay windows while enjoying Continental cuisine ($$–$$$$), featuring top seafood, with an atmosphere nicely enhanced by Regency chairs and dusky pink

napery. It's on the coast road in the Fanore direction, about a 10-minute walk north from Doolin village. ⊠ *Coast Rd., Co. Clare* ☎ *065/707–4061* 🖷 *065/707–4540* ⊕ *www.aranview.com* ➥ *19 rooms* ♿ *Restaurant, bar; no a/c* ▭ *AE, DC, MC, V* ⊗ *Closed Nov.–mid-Apr.* ⦿❘ *BP.*

¢–$ ✕🖽 **Cullinan's Seafood Restaurant and Guesthouse.** The small restaurant ($$–$$$) here, in the back of a modest traditional farmhouse, is famed for its fresh, simply prepared seafood, but vegetarian and meat dishes are also served. Local ingredients—Inagh goat cheese, Burren smoked salmon, Doolin crabmeat, and Aran scallops—form the basis of a light, imaginative menu. A €25 early-bird set menu is served from 6 to 7. The floor-to-ceiling windows on two sides of the restaurant overlook the Aille River. The cottage-style rooms have simple pine furniture, fresh cotton-cover comforters, pleasant country views, and room TVs on request. ⊠ *Coast Rd., Co. Clare* ☎ *065/707–4183* 🖷 *065/707–4239* ⊕ *www. cullinansdoolin.com* ➥ *8 rooms* ♿ *Restaurant; no a/c, no room TVs* ▭ *MC, V* ⊗ *Guesthouse closed Christmas wk, restaurant closed Oct.–Easter* ⦿❘ *BP.*

Nightlife & the Arts

Famous for their traditional-music sessions, Doolin's three pubs are designed to hold big crowds, which means you should expect minimal comfort: hard benches or bar stools if you're lucky, and spit-and-sawdust flooring. The theory is that the music will be so good, you won't notice anything else. However, interesting music-related memorabilia hang on the walls, and O'Connors and McGann's serve simple bar food from midday until 9 (Irish stew is a good bet). **Gus O'Connor's** (⊠ Fisher St. ☎ 065/707–4168) sits midway between the village center and the pier and has tables outside near a stream. **McDermott's** (⊠ Lisdoonvarna Rd. ☎ 065/707–4700) is popular with locals. Autumn through spring it's sometimes closed during the daytime. **McGann's** (⊠ Lisdoonvarna Rd. ☎ 065/707–4133), across the road from McDermott's, is the smallest of Doolin's three famous pubs and has been run by the same family for 70 years.

Sports & the Outdoors

Cycle along the coast on a bike rented from **Patrick Moloney, Doolin Hostel** (⊠ Coast Rd. ☎ 065/707–4006).

Shopping

★ **Doolin Crafts Gallery** (⊠ Coast Rd. ☎ 065/707–4309), beside the cemetery and the church, carries a diverse range of unusual Irish-made goods, including jewelry, sweaters, scarves, pottery, and leatherwork, from local craftspeople, reflecting the cosmopolitan background of the Irish-Dutch owners. Don't miss the 1-acre garden, which has more than 600 plants from all over the world. The garden and the Flagship Restaurant, which serves only home-cooked food and mounts art exhibits, are open daily from Easter through September.

Lisdoonvarna

❼ *5 km (3 mi) east of Doolin on R478.*

One of only three spa towns in Ireland (the others are Enniscrone, in western County Sligo, and Ballybunion, in County Kerry), Lisdoonvarna has several sulfurous and iron-bearing springs with radioactive properties, all containing iodine. In the late 19th century the town grew to accommodate visitors who wanted to "take the waters"; today, a major refurbishment of the spa facilities is underway. The modest buildings reflect a mishmash of mock architectural styles: Scottish baronial, Swiss chalet, Spanish hacienda, and American motel. Depending on your taste, it's either lovably kitschy or just plain tacky. It's a popular weekend spot for Dubliners and other Irish vacationers, who stay at the big hotels (not those below) and many of these roustabouts like to party well into the night. If you're curious about health cures, the **Lisdoonvarna Spa Wells** is worth a visit. Iron and magnesia elements make the drinking water taste terrible (as does most spa water), but the bathing water is pleasant, if enervating. Electric sulfur baths, massage, wax baths, a sauna, and a solarium are available at the spa complex, which is on the edge of town in an attractive parkland setting. ⊠ *Town Park* ☎ *065/707–4023* ⊡ *Complex free, sulfur baths €6.50, book in advance* ☉ *Early June–early Oct., daily 10–6, subject to refurbishment: check in advance by phone.*

> **MAKE ME A MATCH**
>
> Lisdoonvarna is the traditional vacation spot for the West's bachelor farmers, who used to congregate here at harvest time in late September with the vague intention of finding wives. (Irish farmers are notoriously shy with women; many don't marry until their mid- or late fifties, if ever.) This tradition is now formalized in the Matchmaking Festival, held during late September. Middle-age singles (and some in their sixties, seventies, and eighties) dance to the strains of country-and-western bands, and a talent contest is held to name the most eligible bachelor.

Where to Stay & Eat

★ **$$$** ✕⊡ **Sheedy's Restaurant and Country Inn.** A 17th-century farmhouse just a short walk from the town center and the spa wells has been converted into this small, friendly hotel. It's been in the hands of the Sheedy family since 1855. Proprietor John Sheedy, who was chef de cuisine at Ashford Castle until moving back home, makes creative use of local produce in contemporary French-Irish fare ($$–$$$), and has turned Sheedy's into a much-lauded gastronomic destination. The green-gray dining room with plain, candlelighted tables provides a suitably sophisticated background for John's unusual and confident cooking. Try his fresh prawn soup, or a starter of warm salad of roasted monkfish with smoked bacon, mushrooms, and champagne dressing. His menu also features classic dishes like slow-roasted crispy duck with potato stuffing and apple sauce. The guest rooms are spacious and well-designed, with hip touches like power showers and CD players. All have relaxing views of the surrounding hilly countryside. ⊠ *Spa Rd., Co. Clare* ☎ *065/707–4026* 🖷 *065/707–4555* ⊕ *www.sheedys.com* ⊅ *11 rooms* ⌂ *Restaurant, bar; no a/c* ➘ *MC, V* ☉ *Closed Oct.–mid-Mar.* ⏐⍥ *BP.*

★ **$$** ✕⊡ **Carrigann.** Hikers love this small, friendly hotel, ensconced in trim, pretty gardens, and a two-minute walk from the village center. You get exceptional comfort here for the price. Hosts Mary and Gerard Howard keep a library of books on the Burren beside the turf fire in the sitting room, and are themselves generous sources of information. Choose between setting off with one of Mary's specially prepared walk sheets, join a guided group (most weekends—see hotel Web site), or hire your own guide. On return, if your gear is wet it will be taken off to a drying room by one of the friendly staff. Guest rooms are large, quiet, and comfortable, with dark, polished, Victorian-style furniture, quilted cream spreads, and plain *eau de nil*—green carpets. Gerard also runs his own butcher shop, guaranteeing top-quality beef and lamb on the dinner menu ($$–$$$). The dining room is pleasantly unfussy, with cream linen cloths and napkins, fresh flowers on the tables, and comfortable cream upholstered chairs. Try a starter of pan-seared sea scallops with black pudding on potato blini with whole-grain mustard sauce, or a more conventional platter of local smoked salmon, trout, mackerel, and eel with a dill dressing. Menus usually showcase char-grilled sirloin steak, while a simpler bar-food menu is also available. ⊠ *Carrigann Rd., Co. Clare* ☎ *065/707–4036* 🖷 *065/707–4567* ⊕ *www.gateway-to-the-burren.com* ↪ *20 rooms* ⚲ *Restaurant, fishing; no a/c* ☰ *MC, V* ☻ *Closed Nov.–Feb.* ⊠◍ *BP.*

Nightlife & the Arts

Country music and ballad singing are popular in the bars of Lisdoonvarna. For traditional music try the **Roadside Tavern** (⊠ Doolin Rd. ☎ 065/707–4084).

Shopping

To see an audiovisual presentation on the technique of smoking Atlantic salmon, plus live demonstrations of the oak-smoking process, visit the **Burren Smokehouse Ltd** (⊠ Ballyvaughan Rd. ☎ 065/707–4432). Neatly packaged whole sides of salmon, organic treats, and unusual crafts are for sale.

The Burren

★ *Extending throughout western County Clare from Cliffs of Moher in south to Black Head in north, and as far southeast as Corofin.*

As you travel north toward Ballyvaughan, the landscape becomes rockier and stranger. Instead of the seemingly ubiquitous Irish green, gray becomes the prevailing color. You're now in the heart of the Burren, a 300-square-km (116-square-mi) expanse that is one of Ireland's strangest landscapes. The Burren is aptly named: it's an Anglicization of the Irish word *bhoireann* (a rocky place). Stretching off in all directions, as far as the eye can see, are vast, irregular slabs of fissured limestone, known as karst, with deep cracks between them. From a distance, it looks like a lunar landscape, so dry that nothing could possibly grow on it. But in spring (especially from mid-May to mid-June), the Burren becomes a wild rock garden, as an astonishing variety of wildflowers blooms in the cracks between the rocks, among them at least 23 native species of orchid. The Burren also supports an incredible diversity of wildlife, including frogs, newts, lizards, badgers, stoats, sparrow hawks, kestrels, and dozens of other birds and animals. The wildflowers and other plants are given life from the spectacular caves, streams, and potholes that lie beneath the rough, scarred pavements. With the advent of spring, *turloughs* (seasonal lakes that disappear in dry weather) appear on the plateau's surface. Botanists are particularly intrigued by the cohabitation of Arctic and Mediterranean plants, many so tiny (and so rare, so please do not pick any) you can't see them from your car window; make a point of exploring some of this rocky terrain on foot. Numerous signposted walks run through both coastal and inland areas. For a private guided tour, contact **Mary Angela Keane** (☎ 065/707–4003 ✉ €35 per hour), or Shane Connolly of **Burren Hill Walks** (☎ 065/707–7168 ✉ €15 per person). May and June are peak months for flora, but a tour is worthwhile at any time of year.

The tiny **Burren Centre** has a modest audiovisual display and other exhibits that explain the Burren's geology, flora, and archaeology. Also here are a café and a crafts shop with good maps and locally published guides. ⊠ *8 km (5 mi) southeast of Lisdoonvarna on R476, Kilfenora* ☎ *065/708–8030* ⊕ *www.theburrencentre.ie* ✉ *€5* ⊙ *Mid-Mar.–May, Sept., and Oct., daily 10–5; June–Aug., daily 9:30–6.*

Beside the Burren Centre in Kilfenora, the ruins of a small 12th-century church, once the **Cathedral of St. Fachtna,** have been partially restored as a parish church. There are some interesting carvings in the roofless choir, including an unusual, life-size human skeleton. In a field about 165 feet west of the ruins is an elaborately sculpted high cross that is worth examining, though parts of it are badly weathered.

Nightlife & the Arts

Vaughan's Pub (⊠ Main St., Kilfenora ☎ 065/708–8004) is known for its traditional-music sessions.

Ballyvaughan

❾ *16 km (10 mi) north of Lisdoonvarna on N67.*

A pretty little waterside village and a good base for exploring the Burren, Ballyvaughan attracts walkers and artists who enjoy the views of Galway Bay and access to the Burren. **Aillwee Cave** is the only such chamber in the region accessible to those who aren't spelunkers. This vast 2-million-year-old cave is illuminated for about 3,300 feet and contains an underground river and waterfall. Above ground, there are a big craft shop, and cheese- and honey-making demonstrations. ⊠ *5 km (3 mi) south of Ballyvaughan on R480* ☎ *065/707–7036* ⊕ *www.aillweecave. ie* ✉ *€10* ⊙ *Sept.–June, daily 10–6, last tour at 5:30; July and Aug., daily 10–7, last tour at 6:30.*

Where to Stay & Eat

★ **$$$** ✕☐ **Gregan's Castle Hotel.** Sharon Stone, Gabriel Byrne, and Edna O'Brien have all been guests at this quiet, meticulous, creeper-covered and highly romantic Victorian country house, set at the base of the aptly named Corkscrew Hill (on N67, midway between Ballyvaughan and Lisdoonvarna). The Haden family obviously knows a thing or two about hospitality. They certainly know how to decorate in the loveliest fashion—the Corkscrew Bar is a cozy corner hung with copper pots, the guest bedrooms are lined with wallpaper patterns based on William Morris designs and stocked with Georgian and Victorian antiques, while the dining room allures in brilliant red. The house is surrounded by gardens and overlooks Galway Bay and the gray mountains of the Burren. The spacious ground-floor rooms have private patio gardens but lack the splendid views of the rooms upstairs. Ask about special deals for three-day stays. The restaurant ($$$–$$$$; jacket and tie required) serves updated French cuisine. ⊠ *Base of Corkscrew Hill, Co. Clare* ☎ *065/707–7005* 🖷 *065/707–7111* ⊕ *www.gregans.ie* ⇗ *18 rooms, 4 suites* ⚬ *Restaurant, Wi-Fi, fishing, bicycles, croquet, bar; no a/c, no room TVs* ▤ *AE, MC, V* ⊙ *Closed Nov.–Mar.* ⑩ *BP.*

$$ ✕⌂ **Hyland's Burren Hotel.** A turf fire greets you in the lobby of the hotel, a cheerful, welcoming spot with a reputation for friendliness and good entertainment. This unpretentious yellow-and-red coaching inn, in the heart of the Burren, dates from the early 18th century, and has been much extended and added-to. Rooms vary in size and shape, but all have pine furniture and color-coordinated drapes and spreads. Ask for a room overlooking the Burren. The restaurant ($$), cheerfully furnished with country pine and red tablecloths, specializes in simply prepared local produce. The bar hosts live music most nights from June to mid-September, and Irish storytelling once a week. Ask about special weekend rates. ⊠ *Main St., Co. Clare* ☎ *065/707–7037* 🖷 *065/707–7131* ⊕ *www.hylandsburren. com* ⇗ *30 rooms* ⚬ *Restaurant, bar; no a/c* ▤ *AE, DC, MC, V* ⑩ *BP.*

$ ⌂ **Drumcreehy House.** The pretty gabled facade with dormer windows is traditional in style, but, in fact, Bernadette Moloney and her German husband, Armin Grefkes, designed and built this house specifically as a B&B. It's just across the road from the sea, about 1 mi north of the village, just beyond the Whitethorn Craft Shop. The interior has character and style, thanks to a mix of imposing 19th-century German antiques, stripped-pine floors, and comfortable sofas and armchairs. Rooms are spacious and well-aired, with small sitting areas overlooking the peaceful countryside. Each room is individually styled on a wildflower theme, with plain walls, color-coordinated quilts and curtains, brass bedsteads, and attractive small antiques. A light, bar-food–style menu is served in the lounge, where you can also take a glass of wine; from April to October you can reserve for a more formal evening meal. The breakfast menu offers an unusually wide choice, including French toast, kippers, or creamed mushrooms on toast. Your hosts are knowledgeable and enthusiastic about the area, and have a good supply of books and maps. ☎ *065/707–7377* 🖷 *065/707–7379* ⊕ *www.drumcreehyhouse. com* ⇗ *12 rooms* ⚬ *No a/c, no smoking* ▤ *MC, V* ⑩ *BP.*

Nightlife & the Arts

Fodor'sChoice ★ The friendly **Monk's Pub** (⊠ Main St. ☎ 065/707–7059), near the waterfront, hosts great sessions of traditional and folk music. The bar food is excellent.

Coole Park

❿ *24 km (15 mi) northeast of Corofin on N18.*

Coole Park, north of the little town of Gort, was once the home of Lady Augusta Gregory (1859–1932), patron of W. B. Yeats and cofounder with the poet of Dublin's Abbey Theatre. Yeats visited here often, as did almost all the other writers who contributed to the Irish literary revival in the first half of the 20th century, including George Bernard Shaw (1856–1950) and Sean O'Casey (1880–1964). Douglas Hyde (1860–1949), the first president of Ireland, was also a visitor. The house fell derelict after Lady Gregory's death and was demolished in 1941; the grounds are now a national forest and wildlife park. Picnic tables make this a lovely alfresco lunch spot. The only reminder of its literary past is the Autograph Tree, a copper beech on which many of Lady Gregory's famous guests carved their initials. There's also a visitor center with displays on Lady Gregory and Yeats. ⊠ *Galway Rd.* ☎ *091/631–804* ⊠ *Park free, visitor center €3* ⊙ *Park daily 10–dusk; visitor center Apr.–mid-June, Tues.–Sun. 10–5; mid-June–Aug., daily 9:30–6:30; Sept., daily 10–5.*

Thoor Ballylee

⓫ *5 km (3 mi) north of Coole Park, signposted from N66.*

Thoor Ballylee is a sight Yeats fans won't want to miss. (It's one of the few major Yeats-related sights in the West that's not in County Sligo.) In his fifties and newly married, Yeats bought this 14th-century Norman "thoor," or tower, as a ruin in 1916 for £35 (about €44). The tower stands beside a whitewashed, thatched-roof cottage with a tranquil stream running alongside it. Its proximity to Lady Gregory's house at Coole Park made this a desirable location, though it required significant work on Yeats's part to make the ruin livable. He stayed here intermittently until 1929 and penned some of his more mystical works here, including *The Tower* and *The Winding Stair*. It's now fully restored and some rooms showcase the poet's original furnishings. The audiovisual display is a useful introduction to Yeats and his times. High up the tower's parapet you can get some great views of Coole's Seven Woods. ⊠ *N66, 2 km (3 mi) north of Gort* ☎ *091/631–436* ⊕ *www. irelandwest.ie* ⊠ *€5* ⊙ *June–Sept., Mon.–Sat. 9:30–5.*

Kinvara

★ ⓬ *13½ km (8 mi) east of Ballyvaughan, 15 km (9 mi) northwest of Gort on N67, 25 km (15½ mi) south of Galway City.*

The picture-perfect village of Kinvara is a growing holiday base, thanks to its gorgeous bay-side locale, great walking and sea angling, and numerous pubs. It's well worth a visit, whether you're coming from Ballyvaughan or Gort. Kinvara is best known for its long-standing early August sailing event, Cruinniú na mBád (Festival of the Gathering of the Boats), in which traditional brown-sailed Galway hookers laden with turf race across the bay. Hookers were used until the early part of this century to carry turf, provisions, and cattle across Galway Bay and out to the Aran Islands. A sculpture in Galway's Eyre Square honors their local significance.

★ On a rock north of Kinvara Bay, the 16th-century **Dunguaire Castle** spectacularly commands all the approaches to Galway Bay. It's said to stand on the site of a 7th-century castle built by the King of Connaught. Built in 1520 by the O'Hynes clan, the tiny, storybook castle takes its name from the fabled King of Connaught, Guaire. In 1929 it was purchased by Oliver St. John Gogarty, the noted surgeon, man of letters, and model for Buck Mulligan, a character in James Joyce's *Ulysses*. To his outpost came many of the leading figures of the 19th-century Celtic revival in Irish literature. Today Dunguaire is used for a "Middle-Ages" style banquet that honors local writers and others with ties to the West, including Lady Gregory, W. B. Yeats, Sean O'Casey, and Pádraic O'-Conaire. ⊠ *West Village* ☎ *091/637–108* ⊕ *www.shannonheritage. com* ⊠ *Castle €5.95, banquet €46.95* ⊘ *Mid-Apr.–Oct., daily 9:30–5; banquet at 5:30 and 8:30.*

Where to Stay & Eat

★ **$-$$$** ✕ **Moran's Oyster Cottage.** Signposted off the main road on the south side of Clarinbridge, this waterside thatched cottage, the home of the Moran family since 1760, houses at its rear a simply furnished restaurant that serves only seafood: Gigas oysters, chowder, smoked salmon, seafood cocktail, lobster with boiled potatoes and garlic butter, and fresh crab salad. It's *the* place to sample the local oysters, grown on a nearby bed owned by the Moran family, who have had the pub for six generations. Hope for good weather, so that you can eat outside overlooking the weir and watch the swans float by. The front bar has been preserved in the "old style," which means it's small and cramped, but very interesting if you want to get an idea of what most pubs around here were like 50 years ago. ⊠ *The Weir, Kilcolgan* ☎ *091/796–113* ⊟ *AE, MC, V.*

$$ ✕ **Merriman Inn.** Don't let its traditional looks deceive you: this white-washed, thatched inn on the shores of Galway Bay is, in fact, a midsize hotel, decorated with locally made, well-designed furniture, and original crafts, paintings, and sculpture. Guest rooms are medium-size with smallish, cottage-style windows at head height, and modern pine furniture; small paintings of local scenes provide the principal color. If you're lucky you could get a room with a breathtaking view of Galway Bay; less than half have one, so if it matters, ask when booking. The Quilty Room is a large, airy restaurant ($-$$$) hung with interesting landscape and still-life paintings by an artist named Quilty. Its menu is French-influenced—try the outstanding tournedos of salmon pan-seared with a confit of fennel and a sharp, spicy jus. ⊠ *Main St., Co. Galway* ☎ *091/ 638–222* ⊟ *091/637–686* ⊕ *www.merrimanhotel.com* ⬎ *32 rooms* ♢ *Restaurant, bar; no a/c* ⊟ *AE, DC, MC, V* ⊘ *Closed Jan.–mid-Mar.* ⑩ *BP.*

$ **Burren View Farm.** A million-dollar view awaits you at this modest, yellow, two-story B&B on the edge of Galway Bay, 5 km (3 mi) west of Kinvara. Set on a working sheep and cattle farm, it's relatively isolated amid stone-walled fields dotted with sheep. The breakfast room, sun lounge, and front bedrooms look out across a wide sea inlet to the gray expanse of the Burren. Rooms are plain and homey but clean and well maintained. Wholesome evening meals, Irish or continental style, are cooked on request, and food is also available in the local pub, a five-minute walk away. ⊠ *Doorus, Co. Galway* ☎ *091/637–142* ⊕ *www. kinvara.com* ⇩ *5 rooms, 2 with bath* ♿ *Dining room, fishing; no a/c, no room phones, no room TVs* ⊘ *Closed Nov.–Apr.* †○† *BP.*

Nightlife & the Arts

The first weekend in May, Kinvara hosts the annual **Cuckoo Fleadh** (⊠ Main St. ☎ 091/637–145), a traditional-music festival. Traditional music is played most nights at the **Winkles Hotel bar** (⊠ The Sq. ☎ 91/ 637–137), where Sharon Shannon got her start in the music business.

THE OILEÁIN ÁRAINN (ARAN ISLANDS)

No one knows for certain when the Aran Islands—Inis Mór (Inishmore), Inis Meáin (Inishmaan), and Inis Oirr (Inisheer)—were first inhabited, but judging from the number of Bronze Age and Iron Age forts found here (especially on Inis Mór), 3000 BC is a safe guess. Why wandering nomads in deerskin jerkins would be attracted to these barren islets remains a greater mystery, not the least because fresh water and farmable land were (and still are) scarce commodities. Remote western outposts of the ancient province of Connaught (though they are not the country's westernmost points; that honor belongs to the Blasket Islands), these three islands were once as barren as the limestone pavements of the Burren, of which they are a continuation. Today, the land is parceled into small, human-made fields surrounded by stone walls: centuries of erosion, generations of backbreaking labor, sheep, horses, and their attendant tons of manure have finally transformed this rocky wasteland into reasonably productive cropland.

While traditional Irish culture fights a rear-guard battle on the mainland, the islanders continue to preserve as best as they can a culture going back generations. Still, the Irish-speaking inhabitants enjoy a daily air service to Galway (subsidized by the government), motorized curraghs, satellite TV, and all the usual modern home conveniences. Yet they have retained a distinctness from mainlanders, preferring simple home decor, very plain food, and tightly knit communities, like the hardy fishing and farming folk from whom they are descended. Crime is virtually unknown in these parts; at your B&B, you'll likely find no locks on the guest-room doors, and the front-door latch will be left open. Many islanders have sampled life in Dublin or cities abroad but have returned to raise families, keeping the population stable at around 1,500. Tourists now flock here, to see the ancient

6

ISLAND NIGHTS

To appreciate the fierce loneliness of the Aran islands you must spend the night on one. Because all the islands, especially Inishmore, crawl with day-trippers, it's difficult to let their rugged beauty sink into your soul until 10 PM, when the sky is dark and the pubs fill with the acrid smell of peat smoke and Guinness. Once the day-trippers clear out, the islands' stunningly fierce and brooding beauty is disturbed only by the "baa" of the sheep and the incessant rush of the wind.

Aran Rediscovered

DURING THE 1800S, the islands, wracked by famine and mass emigration, were virtually forgotten by mainland Ireland. At the turn of the 20th century, however, the books of J. M. Synge (1871–1909)—who learned Irish on Inishmaan and wrote about its people in his famous play *Riders to the Sea*—prompted Gaelic revivalists to study and document this isolated bastion of Irish culture. To this day, Synge's travel book *The Aran Islands*, first published in 1907, and reissued by Penguin with a brilliant introduction by artist and map-maker, Tim Robinson in 1992, remains the best book ever written about the islands. Liam O'Flaherty became one of the most famous sons of Inishmore through his novels, such as *Famine*. And in 1934, American director Robert Flaherty filmed his classic documentary *Man of Aran* on Inishmore, recording the islanders' dramatic battles with sea and storm, and bringing the islands into the world spotlight. The film is shown in the *Ionad Árainn* (Aran Heritage Center) in Cill Rónáin (Kilronan) on Inishmore daily during July, August, and early September. Flaherty, incidentally, continues to be a common surname on the islands; it is hard to visit the islands *without* meeting a Flaherty.

sights and savor the spectacular views: the uninterrupted expanse of the Atlantic on the western horizon; the Connemara coast and its Twelve Bens to the northeast; and County Clare's Burren and the Cliffs of Moher to the southeast.

There's a small hotel on Inisheer, and two others on Inishmore, but there's no shortage of guesthouses and B&Bs, mostly in simple family homes. The best way to book is through the Galway City TIO. Each island has at least one wine-licensed restaurant serving plain home cooking. Most B&Bs will provide a packed lunch and an evening meal (called high tea) on request.

Inis Oirr (Inisheer)

 4 km (2½ mi) east of Inis Meáin (Inishmaan), 8 km (5 mi) northwest of Doolin docks.

The smallest and flattest of the islands, Inis Oirr can be explored on foot in an afternoon, though if the weather is fine you may be tempted to linger on the long, sandy beach between the quay and the airfield. Only one stretch of road, about 500 yards long, links the airfield and the sole village. "The back of the island," as Inis Oirr's uninhabited side facing the Atlantic is called, has no beaches, but people swim off the rocks.

It's worth making a circuit of the island to get a sense of its utter tranquillity. A maze of footpaths runs between the high stone walls that divide the fields, which are so small that they can support only one cow each, or two to three sheep. Those that are not cultivated or grazed turn into natural wildflower meadows between June and August, overrun with harebells, scabious, red clover, oxeye daisies, saxifrage, and tall grasses. It seems almost a crime to walk here—but how can you resist taking a rest in the corner of a sweet-smelling meadow on a sunny afternoon, sheltered by high stone walls with no sound but the larks above and the wind as it sifts through the stones?

The **Church of Kevin**, signposted to the southeast of the quay, is a small, early-Christian church that gets buried in sand by storms every winter. Each year the islanders dig it out of the sand for the celebration of St. Kevin's Day on June 14. A pleasant walk through the village takes you up to **O'Brien's Castle**, a ruined 15th-century tower on top of a rocky hill—the only hill on the island.

Where to Stay & Eat

$ ✕🖳 **Hotel Inisheer.** A pleasant, modern low-rise in the middle of the island's only village, a few minutes' walk from the quay and the airstrip, this simple, whitewashed building with a slate roof and half-slated walls has bright, plainly furnished rooms. The restaurant (open to nonguests) is the best bet on the island, although some of the food is imported frozen. The social life of the island centers on "the hotel," as it is called, and there are nightly sessions of traditional music. ⊠ *Lurgan Village, Co. Galway* ☎ *099/75020* 🖷 *099/75099* 📨 *27 rooms* ⚙ *Restaurant, bicycles, bar; no a/c, no room phones, no room TVs* 🖃 *AE, DC, MC, V* ⊘ *Closed Oct.–Mar.* ⦵ *BP.*

Inis Meáin (Inishmaan)

⓮ *3 km (2 mi) east of Inis Mór (Inishmore).*

The middle island in both size and location, Inis Meáin has a population of about 300 and can be comfortably explored on foot. In fact, you have no alternative if you want to reach the island's major antiquities: **Dun Conor (Conor Fort)**, a smaller version of Dún Aengus; the ruins of two **early-Christian churches;** and a chamber tomb known as the **Bed of Diar-**

muid and Grainne, dating from about 2000 BC. You can also take wonderful cliff walks above secluded coves. It's on Inishmaan that the traditional Aran lifestyle is most evident. Most islanders still don hand-knitted Aran sweaters, though nowadays they wear them with jeans and sneakers.

Shopping

Inis Meáin Knitting (⊠ Carrown Lisheen ☎ 099/73009) is a young company producing quality knitwear in luxury fibers for the international market—including Liberty of London, Barneys New York, and Bergdorf Goodman—while providing much-needed local employment. The factory showroom has an extensive selection of garments at discount prices. To get here from the pier, walk five minutes due west.

Inis Mór (Inishmore)

★ ⓯ *31 km (18 mi) southwest of Salthill docks, 5 km (3 mi) northwest of Doolin docks, 48 km (30 mi) west of Galway docks.*

With a population of 900, Inis Mór is the largest of the islands and the closest to the Connemara coast. It's also the most commercialized, its appeal slightly diminished by road traffic. In summer, ferries arriving at Cill Ronáin (Kilronan), Inis Mór's main village and port, are met by minibuses and pony-and-cart drivers, all eager to show visitors "the sights." More than 8 km (5 mi) long and about 3 km (2 mi) wide at most points, with an area of 7,640 acres, the island is just a little too large to explore comfortably on foot in a day. The best way to see it is really by bicycle; bring your own or rent one from one of the vendors operating near the quay. The **Ionad Árainn (Aran Heritage Centre)** explains the history and culture of the islanders, who for many years lived in virtual isolation from the mainland. ⊠ *Cill Ronáin (Kilronan)* ☎ *099/61355* ⊕ *www.visitaranislands.com* ✉ *€3* ⊙ *Apr., May, Sept. and Oct., daily 11–5, June- Aug. daily 10–7; Nov.–Mar., by appointment.*

Even if you only have a few hours to explore Inis Mór, rent a bike (next to the pier) and head straight for **Dún Aengus,** one of the finest prehistoric monuments in Europe, dating from about 2000 BC. Spectacularly set on the edge of a 300-foot-tall cliff overlooking a sheer drop, the fort has defenses consisting of three rows of concentric circles. Whom the builders were defending themselves against is a matter of conjecture. From the innermost rampart there's a great

> ### WORD OF MOUTH
>
> "In my opinion, the visit to Dún Aengus made the trip to Ireland worthwhile. It is a stunningly beautiful fort situated on cliffs that drop off dramatically into the Atlantic Ocean. The views are exhilarating. I can't begin to imagine how beautiful it would be on a sunny day" –Desidero

view of the island and the Connemara coast. In order to protect this fragile monument from erosion, you should approach it only through the visitor center, which gives access to a 1-km (½-mi) uphill walk over uneven terrain—wear sturdy footwear. ⊠ *7 km (4 mi) west of Cill Ronáin (Kilronan), Kilmurvey* ☎ *099/61010* ⊕ *www.heritageireland.ie* ✉ *€1.20* ⊙ *Mar.–Oct., daily 10–6; Nov.–Feb., daily 10–4.*

Where to Stay & Eat

★ $ ✕🏨 **Kilmurvey House.** This rambling 200-year-old stone farmhouse is the first choice of many visitors to the island. It's at the foot of Dún Aengus fort, a three-minute walk from the beach, and about 6½ km (4 mi) from the quay and the airport (accessible by minibus). The old stone house has been cleverly extended to provide extra guest rooms. The neatly kept front garden leads to a large, high-ceiling hall and wide stairs, giving a pleasant sense of space. The walls are hung with portraits of the house's previous owners, the warrior clan of O'Flahertys—one of whom was Oscar Wilde's godfather—and whose descendants include the famed writers Liam and Robert. Rooms are spacious and comfortable, with wonderful sea views. Dinners ($) are cooked about five nights a week by the warm, chatty owner, Treasa Joyce, and are not to be missed. Vegetables and herbs come from the back garden, the floury potatoes are island-grown, and wild Atlantic salmon is a popular main course. ⊠ *Cill Ronáin, Kilronan, Co. Galway* ☎ *099/61218* 🖷 *099/61397* ⊕ *www. kilmurveyhouse.com* 🗗 *12 rooms* ⚠ *Dining room; no a/c, no room TVs, no smoking* ⊟ *MC, V* ⊗ *Closed Nov.–Mar.* ⦿ *BP.*

$ 🖭 **Ard Einne Guesthouse.** Almost every window at this B&B on Inishmore looks out to the sea, making it the perfect place to de-stress. The rambling 80-year-old house, with its distinctive dormer windows, is close to both the beach and the town; many guests base themselves here for two or three nights, to make a thorough exploration of the island. The public rooms and guest rooms are relaxed, with modern decor including light-color linens and walls paneled with blond wood. Simple evening meals ($) are prepared by your host, Clodagh Ní Ghoill, who will discuss the four-course set menu in advance. ⊠ *Cill Ronáin, Kilronan, Co. Galway* ☎ *099/61126* 🖷 *099/61388* ⊕ *www.ardeinne.com* 🗗 *14 rooms* ⚠ *Dining room, fishing; no a/c, no room phones, no room TVs* ⊟ *MC, V* ⊗ *Closed mid-Dec.–Jan.* ⦿ *BP.*

Nightlife

The place to go for traditional music is the **American Bar** (⊠ Cill Ronáin, Kilronan ☎ 099/61130). **Joe Mac's** (⊠ Cill Ronáin ☎ 099/61248), right off the pier, is a good place for a pint while waiting for the ferry home. **Joe Watty's** (⊠ Main Rd., Cill Ronáin ☎ 099/61155) is a good bet for traditional music virtually every night in summer.

GALWAY CITY

Galway is often said to be a state of mind as much as it is a specific place. The largest city in the West today (population 65,000 and growing) and the ancient capital of the province of Connaught, Galway is also one of the fastest-growing cities in Europe, with an annual growth rate of 29.5%, compared to Ireland's national average of 11%. It's an astonishing fact, and you have to wonder where this city can possibly grow. For despite Galway's size, its commercially busy ring road, and its ever-spreading suburbs, its heart is *tiny*—a warren of streets so compact that if you spend more than a few hours here, you'll soon be strolling along with the sort of easy familiarity you'd feel in your hometown.

For many Irish people, Galway is a favorite weekend getaway: known as the city of festivals, it's the liveliest place in the Republic. It's also a university town: University College Galway (or UCG as it's locally known) is a center for Gaelic culture (Galway marks the eastern gateway to the West's large Gaeltacht). A fair share of UCG's 9,000 students pursue their studies in the Irish language. Galway is, in fact, permeated by youth culture. On festival weekends, you'll see as many

6

pierced and tattooed teenagers and twentysomethings here as you'd find at a rock concert. (If you're looking for the quiet, quaint side of Ireland depicted on travel posters, have a quick look at Galway and push on to Clifden or Westport, where you can still savor the atmosphere of a small old-world town.) But its students aren't its only avant-garde, as Galway has long attracted writers, artists, and musicians. The latter whip up brand-new jigs while also keeping the traditional-music pubs lively year-round. And the city's two small but internationally acclaimed theater companies draw a steady stream of theater people.

Although you're not conscious of it when you're in the center of town, Galway is spectacularly situated, on the north shore of Galway Bay, where the River Corrib flows from Lough Corrib to the sea. The seaside suburb of Salthill, on the south-facing shore of Galway Bay, has spectacular vistas across the vividly blue bay to Black Head on the opposite shore.

Galway's growth and popularity mean that at its busiest moments, its narrow, one-way streets are jam-packed with pedestrians, while cars are gridlocked. If there's a city in Ireland that never sleeps, this must be it. In fact, if you want to be guaranteed a quiet night's sleep, ask either for a room in the back of your center-city hotel or simply stay outside of town.

Exploring Galway City

Most of the city's sights, aside from the cathedral and the university campus, can be found in a narrow sector of the medieval town center that runs in a southwesterly direction from Eyre Square to the River Corrib. Eyre Square is easily recognizable, as it's the only open space in central Galway. It only takes five minutes to walk straight down Galway's main shopping street, the continuation of the north side of Eyre Square, to the River Corrib,

> **TRAVEL TIP**
>
> If you have postcards to mail, you may want to stop at the General Post Office at the start of your walking tour. It's on the left side of Eglinton Street, the first right off Williamsgate Street as you head toward the river from Eyre Square.

where it ends (note that the name of this street changes several times). Not only is the city center compact, it's also largely pedestrian-friendly, so the best way to explore it is on foot. Even the farthest point, the university campus, is less than a 15-minute walk from Eyre Square. A walk (or drive, for that matter) to Galway's seaside suburb, Salthill, 3 km (2 mi) west of Galway, with its long seaside promenade, is a favorite local occupation, traditionally undertaken on a Sunday afternoon.

What to See

🟤 **Cathedral of Our Lady Assumed into Heaven and St. Nicholas.** On Nun's Island, which forms the west bank of the River Corrib beside the Salmon Weir Bridge, stands Galway's largest Catholic church, dedicated by Cardinal Cushing of Boston in 1965. The cathedral was built on the site of the old Galway jail; a white cross embedded in the pavement of the adjacent parking lot marks the site of the cemetery that stood beside the prison. 🖅 *Free* ⏱ *Freely accessible.*

City of the Tribes

GALWAY'S FOUNDERS were Anglo-Normans who arrived in the mid-13th century and fortified their settlement against "the native Irish," as local chieftains were called.

Galway became known as "the City of the Tribes" because of the dominant role in public and commercial life of the 14 families that founded it.

Their names are still common in Galway and elsewhere in Ireland:

Athy, Blake, Bodkin, Browne, D'Arcy, Dean, Font, French, Kirwan, Joyce, Lynch, Morris, Martin, and Skerret.

The city's medieval heritage, a fusion of Gaelic and Norman influences, is apparent in the intimate two- and three-story stone buildings, the winding streets, the narrow passageways, and the cobblestones underfoot.

28 Claddagh. On the west bank of the Corrib estuary, this district was once an Irish-speaking fishing village outside the walls of the old town. The name is an Anglicization of the Irish *cladach,* which means "marshy ground." It retained a strong, separate identity until the 1930s, when its traditional thatched cottages were replaced by a conventional housing plan and its unique character and traditions were largely lost. One thing has survived: the Claddagh ring, composed of two hands clasped around a heart with a crown above it (symbolizing love, friendship, and loyalty), is still used by many Irish people as a wedding ring. Reproductions in gold or silver are favorite Galway souvenirs.

20 Collegiate Church of St. Nicholas. Built by the Anglo-Normans in 1320 and enlarged in 1486 and again in the 16th century, the church contains many fine carvings and gargoyles dating from the late Middle Ages, and it's one of the best-preserved medieval churches in Ireland. Legend has it that Columbus prayed here on his last stop before setting off on his voyage to the New World. On Saturday mornings, a street market, held in the pedestrian way beside the church, attracts two dozen or so vendors and hundreds of shoppers. ⊠ *Lombard St., Center* 🎫 *Free* ☉ *Daily 8–dusk.*

16 Eyre Square. The largest open space in central Galway and the heart of the city, on the east side of the River Corrib, Eyre Square incorporates a sculpture garden and children's play area on its east side, while its west side is bound by a heavily traveled road. A controversial renovation saw the removal of several well-loved landmarks, including most of the trees in the square (they were diseased). They were replaced by 95 new trees that will take time to mature. In the center is **Kennedy Park,** a patch of lawn named in honor of John F. Kennedy, who spoke here when he visited the city in June 1963. At the north end of the park, a 20-foot-high steel sculpture standing in the pool of a fountain represents the brown sails seen on Galway hookers, the area's traditional sailing boats. Now the entrance to Kennedy Park, the **Browne Doorway** was taken in 1905 from the Browne family's town house on Upper Abbeygate Street; it has

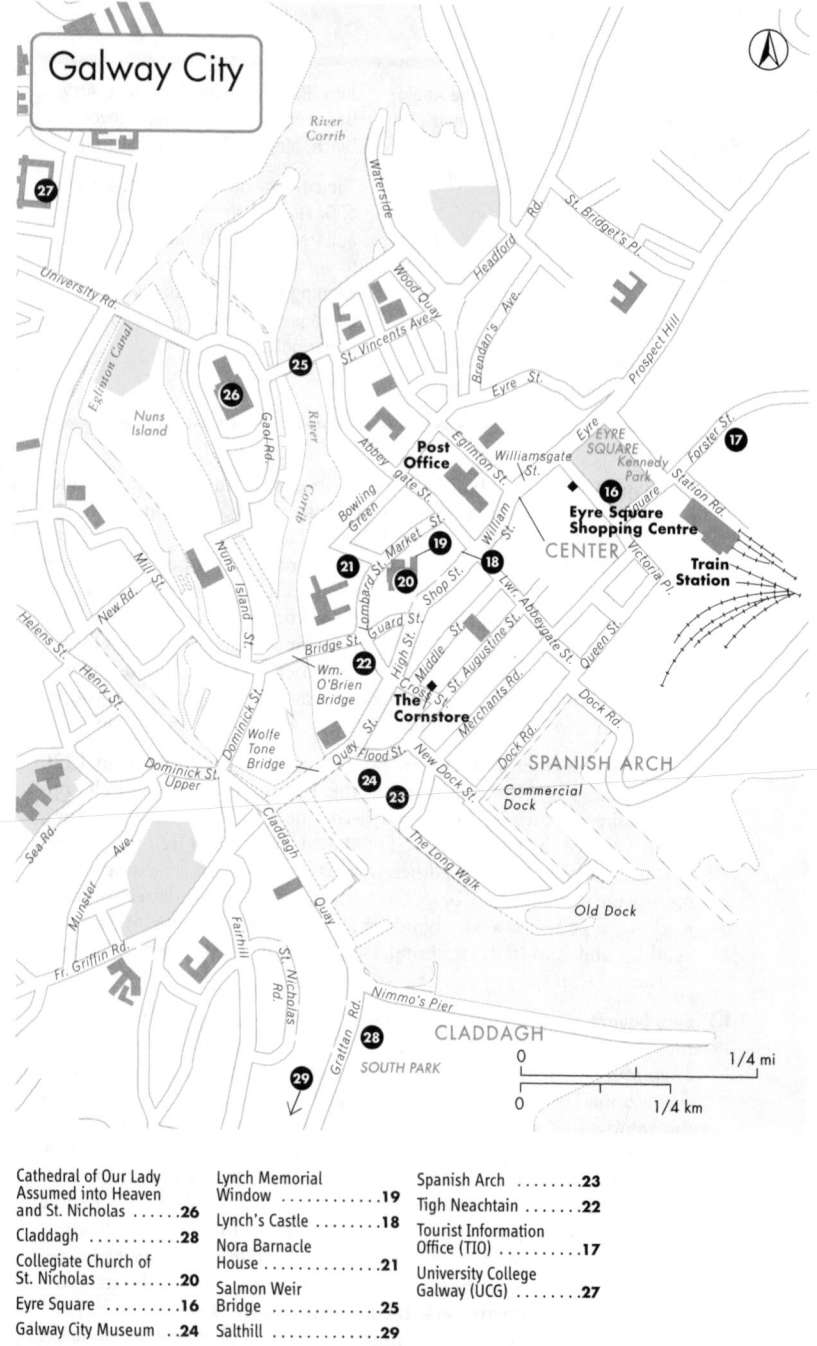

Galway City

Designer Galway (How to Get the Look): A Walk

There's no question about it: they have a different look in Galway. People have always dressed differently, because they dress for the Galway weather, which can be wet and windy at any time of year. But ever since Galway was transformed by Ireland's "Celtic Tiger" economic boom, they have also dressed—and decorated—with a real sense of style. Want proof? Just join all the locals on the following walk.

Pick up a free map of Galway from the swanky new **Tourist Information Office** on Forster Place. Turn left out the front door to reach the **Great Southern Hotel,** a monumental 19th-century grande dame in cut stone (its lobby is just the place for "scene-iors" to take their coffee or tea). Turn left beyond the hotel and right into Merchants Road to find the lively **Bold Art Gallery.** Then turn left into **Flood Street,** the heart of medieval Galway, a tiny area where all the cutest shops are jam-packed together, including **Cobwebs,** abrim with offbeat antique jewelry, old binoculars, and bronze model airplanes. For a feel of the essential Galway, cross the road to the banks of the **River Corrib** and walk to your left to the **Spanish Arch.** When natives feel homesick, this is the view they think of: white water breaking on the dark surface of the swift-flowing Corrib, the fishing boats of the Claddagh, and as many as a hundred swans floating by.

Staying on this side of the Corrib, cross over the bridge and take the riverside footpath past the contempo Jury's Inn and some old warehouses. Turn left over O'Brien's Bridge for the historic **Bridge Mills,** now outfitted with a

designer swap shop, a fun haberdashery, and **Tús Craft Design.** Continue along Bridge Street, turning right into Cross Street and right into Kirwan's Lane. Here, **Design Concourse Ireland/Judy Greene Pottery** has locally made turned-wood objects, basketware, and perfumery. Medieval Kirwan's Lane leads you on to Quay Street and **Twice as Nice,** a vintage and antique clothing boutique with old Irish linen. Continue up High Street to **Faller's Sweaters and Tweeds,** just the place to buy an Aran sweater and **The Kilkenny Shop,** Galway's largest emporium of Irish-designed products, with a dazzling selection of chic John Rocha crystal, Newbridge Silver, and Nicholas Mosse pottery. Across High Street, **Kenny's Gallery,** run by Tom Kenny, shows mainly artists working in the area. Farther up on the right, **Maille** has some great mohair wraps and *the* essential Galway fashion item, a Jack Murphy raincoat. Choose between a short version or a caped version (for those really wet days)—top one off with a rainproof Stetson with a feather in it and you'll pass for a local. High Street leads into William Street, where you'll find **The Treasure Chest,** a three-story shop selling upmarket Irish goods. Its exterior, painted in Wedgwood blue with white swags, just like the famous china, is a favorite with photographers. **Brown Thomas,** on William at the corner of Eglinton, has long been Galway's most upscale department store. A few steps up Williamsgate Street brings us back to Eyre Square and your starting point at the TIO.

6

the 17th-century coats of arms of both the Browne and Lynch families (two of Galway's 14 founding families), called a "marriage stone" because when the families were joined in marriage their coats of arms were, too. Keep an eye out for similar if less elaborate Browne doorways as you walk around the old part of town.

㉔ Galway City Museum. The city's civic museum, housed in a modern building behind the Spanish Arch, contains materials relating to local history: old photographs, antiquities (the oldest is a stone ax head carbon-dated to 3500 BC), and other historical gewgaws. At the time of writing it was undergoing restoration, but it should reopen by Easter 2007. ⊠ *Fishmarket, Spanish Arch* ☎ *091/567–641* ⊠ *€2* ☉ *Daily 10–1 and 2:15–5:15.*

㉚ Lynch Memorial Window. Embedded in a stone wall above a built-up Gothic doorway off Market Street, the window marks the spot where, according to legend, James Lynch FitzStephen, mayor of Galway in the early 16th century, condemned his son to death after the young man confessed to murdering a Spanish sailor who had romanced his girlfriend. When no one could be found to carry out the execution, Judge Lynch hanged his son himself, ensuring that justice prevailed, before retiring into seclusion. ⊠ *Market St., Center.*

㉘ Lynch's Castle. Now a branch of the Allied Irish Banks, this is the finest remaining example in Galway of a 16th-century fortified house—fortified because neighboring Irish tribes persistently raided the village, whose commercial life excluded them. The decorative details on its stone lintels are of a type usually found only in southern Spain. Like the Spanish Arch, it serves as a reminder of the close trading links that once existed between Galway and Spain. ⊠ *Shop St., Center.*

㉑ Nora Barnacle House. On June 16, 1904, James Joyce (1882–1941) had his first date with Nora Barnacle, who would later become his wife. He subsequently chose to set *Ulysses* on this day, now known universally as Bloomsday—"a recognition of the determining effect upon his life of his attachment to her," as Joyce's biographer Richard Ellman has said. Nora, the daughter of a poor baker, was born here. Today it has a modest collection of photographs, letters, and memorabilia, and a small gift shop. ⊠ *4 Bowling Green, Center* ☎ *091/564–743* ⊠ *€2.50* ☉ *Mid-May–Aug., Mon.–Sat. 10–5; mid-Sept.–mid-May by appointment.*

★ ㉕ Salmon Weir Bridge. The bridge itself is nothing special, but in season—from mid-April to early July—shoals of salmon are visible from its deck as they lie in the clear river water before making their way upstream to the spawning grounds of Lough Corrib. ⊠ *West end of St. Vincent's Ave., Center.*

㉙ Salthill. A lively, hugely popular seaside resort, Salthill is beloved for its seaside promenade—the traditional place "to sit and watch the moon rise over Claddagh, and see the sun go down on Galway Bay," as Bing Crosby used to croon in the most famous song about the city. The main attraction of the village, set 3 km (2 mi) west of Galway, is the long sandy

The Galway Saturday Market

LOCALS GET UP very early on Saturday in Galway in order to get the pick of the goods on offer at the Saturday food market. About 90 colorful stall-holders, many of whom follow an alternative lifestyle, set out their wares in the area behind the Collegiate Church of St. Nicholas in the city center. Take your pick of the Mediterranean goods on offer at the Real Olive Company, or sample some Aran Smoked Salmon, or treat yourself to an outdoor lunch at the Madras Curry Stall, or sushi from the Japanese-run Da Kappa-ya Sushi, followed by dessert from Yummy Crêpes. Organic vegetable sellers, plant sellers, herbalists, cheesemongers, and bakers are joined by hat sellers, wood carvers, and knitwear stalls, while a selection of Galway's famously wacky buskers entertain with music, juggling, and dance. Who could resist?

beach along the edge of Galway Bay and the promenade above it. The building of big new hotels along the seafront has nevertheless left plenty of room for the traditional amusement arcades (full of slot machines), seasonal cafés, and a fairground.

23 Spanish Arch. Built in 1584 to protect the quays where Spanish ships unloaded cargoes of wines and brandies, the arch now stands in the parking lot opposite Jurys Galway Inn. It's easily (and often) mistaken for a pile of weathered stones, yet it's another reminder of Galway's—and Ireland's—past links with Spain. ⊠ *The Long Walk, Spanish Arch.*

22 Tigh Neachtain (Naughton's Pub). You can hear traditional music every
Fodor'sChoice night at this popular pub, which stands at a busy little crossroads in the
★ heart of the old town. Grab a spot at one of its old-fashioned partitioned snugs at lunchtime for an inexpensive selection of imaginative bar food. It's a good place to mingle with local actors, writers, artists, musicians, and students, although it can become sardine-can crowded. ⊠ *17 Cross St., Spanish Arch* ☎ *091/566–172.*

17 Tourist Information Office (TIO). Just off Eyre Square, east of the bus and train station and the Great Southern Hotel, this is the place to make reservations for events around town and find out about the latest happenings. You can also book tickets to the Aran Islands here. ⊠ *Forster Pl., Center* ☎ *091/537–700* ⊕ *www.irelandwest.ie* ☉ *Weekdays 9–6, Sat. 9–1.*

27 University College Galway (UCG). Opened in 1846 to promote the development of local industry and agriculture, the UCG today is a center for Irish-language and Celtic studies. The Tudor Gothic–style quadrangle, completed in 1848, is worth a visit, though much of the rest of the campus is architecturally undistinguished. The library here has an important archive of Celtic-language materials, and in July and August the university hosts courses in Irish studies for overseas students. The cam-

6

VOICES OF IRELAND

Tom Kenny
Owner, The Kenny Gallery

Tom Kenny grew up in old Galway, a run-down city where nothing much happened. As a member of the legendary family behind the city's old landmark, Kenny's Bookshop, he has experienced the boom years first-hand. Founded by his mother in the 1940s, Kenny's had become world-famous by the 1980s. Continuing their trend of moving with the times, in 2006 Kenny's Bookshop closed its retail premises, but continues to trade online (⊕ www.kennys.ie), employing three generations of the family. Today, Tom Kenny runs an art gallery in the former shop: The Kenny Gallery (✉ High St. ☎ 091/534760 ⊕ www.thekennygallery.ie. "It was a great help that in 1984 Galway celebrated a Quincentennial," he recalls. "We were 500 years a city. It was like a year-long birthday bash, but more importantly, a whole new sense of civic pride was generated, a new sense of *duchas* (heritage) and our history. At the same time, curiously, it was forward-looking and since then, the city center has

been transformed. Up until then, it had been like a mouthful of bad teeth, with streets that were run-down, derelict, decaying—a terrible relic from the years of poverty in the mid-20th century and the effects of emigration. That's changed utterly. Galway is now known as a city of young people, because the prosperity allows them to stay here.

"When we opened our gallery in the 1960s, there wasn't one full-time professional artist working in County Galway. Artists, yes, but they needed day jobs. Today, there's an army of artists. And an army of art troupes and festivals: the Druid Theater Company, the Mánas street theater, the Galway Arts Festival, the Cúirt literary festival, the festivals devoted to film, children's arts, traditional music, and comedy. Galway has become an attractive place to live for people with young children, and when the children grow up, they don't want to leave. And for those of us who are not so young anymore, all the artistic activity keeps us young."

pus is across the River Corrib, in the northwestern corner of the city. ✉ *Newcastle Rd., University.*

Where to Stay & Eat

$$$ ✕ **Nimmo's.** Good food and a great ambience, due partly to the friendly, enthusiastic staff, makes this bustling bistro one of Galway's most popular restaurants. The central location in an old stone building overlooking the Corrib River adds to the pleasure. The long, spacious, second-floor room has original paintings on the walls and well-spaced tables set with white linen. The menu is short but well balanced, and while presentation is flamboyant, the food also tastes good. Try the salmon and chive terrine wrapped in smoked almonds, or rack of lamb with roasted red peppers and spring-onion mashed potatoes. There's a separate wine bar downstairs. ⊠ *The Long Walk, Spanish Arch* ☎ *091/561–114* ☱ *AE, DC, MC, V* ⊘ *Closed Mon. No lunch weekdays.*

$$–$$$ ✕**Kirwan's Lane Creative Cuisine.** Look for Mike O'Grady's stylish modern restaurant in a revamped alley at the river end of Quay Street. Blue-stained wooden tables, narrow floor-to-ceiling windows, and a quarry-tile floor set the stage for an informal, bistro-style menu. Fresh prawn cocktail is served with sauce Marie-Rose and a passion-fruit mayonnaise; confit of duck leg comes with braised red cabbage, star anise, and balsamic oil. Main courses have similarly unpredictable twists—rack of lamb is accompanied by sweet potato mash, basil oil, and apricots, and monkfish tails are dressed with a simple lemon and coriander dressing. ⊠ *Kirwan's La., Spanish Arch* ☎ *091/568–266* ☱ *AE, DC, MC, V* ⊘ *Closed Sun.*

$$–$$$ ✕**Malt House.** Hidden away in a flower-filled courtyard off High Street in the center of old Galway, Barry and Therese Cunningham's cozy pub-restaurant has long been popular with locals and visitors. In a city where the dining scene is trend-driven and youth-oriented, this is an oasis of calm and tradition, where nothing ever changes much, and you wouldn't want it to—just like your favorite armchair. You can either eat in the bar itself or just off the bar in the restaurant, a square room with beamed ceilings, rough-cast walls and appointments in the Galway team colors–white and maroon. Try the five-course seafood sampler menu, or choose à la carte. Fresh prawns panfried in garlic butter are popular; the sirloin steak with green-peppercorn sauce and the rack of lamb with a parsley crust should please landlubbers. ⊠ *Old Malte Arcade, High St., Center* ☎ *091/563–993* ☱ *AE, DC, MC, V* ⊘ *Closed Sun.*

★ ¢–$$$ ✕**McDonagh's Seafood House.** This longtime Galway landmark is partly a fish-and-chips bar and partly a "real" fish restaurant. If you haven't yet tried fish-and-chips, this is the place to start: cod, whiting, mackerel, haddock, or hake is deep-fried in a light batter while you watch. The fish is served with a heap of freshly cooked chips (french fries). Or go for the more sophisticated (and expensive) Seafood Bar menu: Galway oysters au naturel, perhaps, or a bowl of mussels steamed in wine and garlic, followed by flame-grilled black sole. The McDonaghs are one of Galway's most entrepreneurial families, in charge of several hotels in addition to this spot. ⊠ *22 Quay St., Spanish Arch* ☎ *091/565–001* ☱ *DC, MC, V* ⊘ *No lunch Sun. Oct.–Apr.*

¢–$$ ✕**K. C. Blake's.** K. C. stands for Casey, as in owner-chef John Casey, a larger-than-life character, who turned a medieval stone town house once associated with the Blake family—one of the families that founded Galway—into an ultramodern eatery. The hard-edge, minimalist decor, which features sleek black walls, provides a strong contrast with the old stone building. Dishes range from traditional beef-and-Guinness stew to funky starter combinations like black pudding croquettes with pear and cranberry sauce. ⊠ *10 Quay St., Spanish Arch* ☎ *091/561–826* ☱ *AE, MC, V.*

$$$$ ✕▣**Glenlo Abbey.** With distant views of Lough Corrib and a golf course on its 138-acre estate, Glenlo Abbey is a rural hideaway just 5 km (2 ½ mi) from Galway. Built as a private home in 1740, it takes its name from the vast church built next door for the owner's ailing wife, who died before it

was consecrated. Today, the church is used as a conference center and banquet room. The Abbey's lobby resembles a gentlemen's club, with parquet floors, chesterfields, and leather-bound books. Upstairs, official and correct Georgian-style furniture, brass lamps, and king-size beds fill the spacious bedrooms. Warming everything up, happily, is the genuinely friendly service. The delightfully unstuffy atmosphere is best seen in the Pullman Restaurant ($$$–$$$$), Glenlo's most popular feature. This is set in two *Orient Express* carriages installed on the grounds (and used in the famous Agatha Christie film of that name), offering a fun dining experience, complete with background click-clacks and train whistles. For more formal surroundings, repair to the classical River Room restaurant. Chandeliers hang from high, stucco ceilings and tall windows framed by peach-color curtains overlook the river. The food, beautifully served, includes delights like marinated venison on a bed of braised red cabbage. ⊠ *Bushy Park, Co. Galway* ☎ *091/526–666* 🖷 *091/527–800* ⊕ *www.glenlo.com* ➫ *38 rooms, 6 suites* ♙ *2 restaurants, cable TV, in-room data ports, Wi-Fi, 18-hole golf course, sauna, fishing, bar* ☰ *AE, DC, MC, V* ⦿ *EP.*

$$$$
Fodor'sChoice
★

✕⊡ **Radisson SAS.** The striking contemporary design of the Radisson has revived a run-down area a stone's throw from Eyre Square and overlooking a land-locked in-flow of Galway Bay, Lough Atalia. Against several newcomers, the hotel has successfully defended its reuptation as Galway's hippest hotel. Potted 20-foot bamboo sways at the entrance, while four palm trees grow in the spacious reception area. Two glass-wall elevators divide the lobby from the bar and waft you upstairs while delivering breathtaking views of Galway Bay. Rooms are spacious, with fully tiled bathrooms, restful, unfussy color schemes, Scandinavian-design contemporary furniture, and comfortable sitting areas. Double-glazing and altitude (starting on the third story) insulate the rooms from noise even on the loudest Galway night. The Atrium lounge and bar, its triple-height windows framing views of the water, is a popular lunch spot and buzzes with life from early to late. A pianist entertains on weekends, and in summer the large terrace with its views of the sea and the distant hills is a lively spot. Also overlooking the Lough, the spacious blue-and-white Marinas Restaurant ($$–$$$$) offers a wide selection of local seafood, as well as a good choice of international dishes. ⊠ *Lough Atalia Rd., Center, Co. Galway* ☎ *091/538–300* 🖷 *091/538–380* ⊕ *www.radissonhotelgalway.com* ➫ *217 rooms* ♙ *Restaurant, 2 bars, in-room data ports, Wi-Fi, minibars, indoor pool, hot tub, sauna, spa, parking (fee)* ☰ *AE, DC, MC, V* ⦿ *BP.*

★ **$$$$**
✕⊡ **St. Cleran's.** Once home to famed director John Huston, this gray-stone, veddy, veddy proper Georgian mansion has been dramatically restored by its present owner, entertainer Merv Griffin, into a super-luxe inn. Subtle it is not, and some people are overwhelmed by the deep-pile carpets and ubiquitous crystal chandeliers; others find the furnishings delightful and revel in all the top-quality antiques. You can also expect superb views of the rolling countryside, and excellent opportunities for country sports. The elegant, formal restaurant ($$$$, reservations essential) has a highly renowned Japanese chef, who cooks mainly in the classic French style with just the odd Japanese touch—tempura of tiger prawns with wasabi mayonnaise may be featured alongside a French classic like honey-roasted duck breast with orange-Cointreau sauce. It's

35 km (22 mi) east of Galway on the N6 Dublin road. ✉ *Craughwell, Loughrea, Co. Galway* ☎ *091/846–555* 🖶 *091/846–752* ⊕ *www. stclerans.com* ⇥ *12 rooms* ⏃ *Restaurant, miniature golf, fishing, horse-back riding, bar, library, Internet room; no a/c* ⊟ *AE, MC, V* ⏌◉ *BP.*

$$$$ 🖼 **the g.** G is for glamor—or good grief, depending on your taste—at this flamboyant addition to the top end of Galway's hotel scene. The g is in a new retail and leisure complex beside a busy roundabout, about 15 minutes' walk from Eyre Square; it's an oddly unhip location for a style icon. The architects worked with superstar hat designer Philip Treacy, a native of Galway, to create an interior that is every bit as extreme as Treacy's hats. The reception area is in black glass and black marble, lit by a tank of sedately bobbing, Connemara-bred seahorses. Yes, seahorses. Black and white op-art whorls feature on the aptly named Vertigo carpet in the vivid Pink Room, where afternoon tea (€45 for two) is popular with the ladies. There are also a self-consciously stylish bar and a more serene, silvery salon. Dimly lighted corridors with pink carpet lead to rooms where the decor is thankfully more restrained. Massive, extremely comfortable beds are dressed in white linen and graceful custom-made furniture with an art deco air is upholstered in soothing gray and *eau de nil* upholstery. Mirrors are everywhere, and outside the windows pebbled areas with greenery distract from the mundane views. Seashell–theme bathrooms are luxurious havens of marble and fine porcelain. Perched on scallop-shape purple velvet banquettes or jelly-tot–bright chairs in the ordinary but expensive Restaurant at the g ($$–$$$$), you can order from an Italian menu with an imaginative range of pasta (taglioni with fresh crab), classic fish dishes (grilled turbot with salsa verde), veal, and grilled meat. The ESPA spa takes pampering to serious extremes. ✉ *Wellpark, Co. Galway* ☎ *091/865–200* 🖶 *091/865–203* ⊕ *www. monogramhotels.ie* ⇥ *98 rooms* ⏃ *Restaurant, 2 bars, cable TV, in-room data ports, Wi-Fi, minibars, indoor pool, health club, sauna, steam room, bar, helipad* ⊟ *AE, DC, MC, V* ⏌◉ *BP.*

¢–$$$$ 🖼 **Jurys Galway Inn.** Expect good-quality budget accommodation at this four-story hotel beside the historic Spanish Arch and the river. Each room is big enough for three adults, or two adults and two children, and the fixed-price policy applies to all options. The light, airy rooms have modern pine fittings, plain carpets and walls, double-glaze windows, and fully equipped bathrooms. Those overlooking the river are quieter than those in front. The atmosphere runs toward anonymous-international, but the inn is central—at the foot of Galway's busy Quay Street, right on the bank of the Corrib—and the level of comfort is high for the price range (note that rates shoot up at peak times, such as during the Galway Races). ✉ *Quay St., Spanish Arch, Co. Galway* ☎ *091/566–444* 🖶 *091/568–415* ⊕ *www.jurysinn.com* ⇥ *130 rooms* ⏃ *Restaurant, in-room data ports, bar, parking (fee); no a/c* ⊟ *AE, DC, MC, V.*

$$$ 🖼 **Galway Great Southern.** Built in 1845 right on Eyre Square, to coincide with the arrival of the railway, this is still the classiest address in town, and a popular gathering spot. Tastefully muted, color-coordinated schemes and Georgian-style tables and chairs decorate all the guest rooms. The deluxe rooms in the original building have tall ceilings and windows and are particularly elegant, though those at the front directly above the bar can be noisy late into the night. Rooms in the back, on

GAEL FORCE
THE BOOM IN IRISH MUSIC & DANCE

Traditional Irish music and dance has taken the world by storm—but you need to journey to the West of Ireland to really get in step.

Folkloric music and dance may have faded in countries around the globe but don't tell that to the thousands of young Irish who are learning to play hornpipes and concertinas, sing the old shanties, and dance the old jigs. Once languishing, these "old-fashioned" arts have taken on a modern chic here at home and the reason why can be summed up in one word: Riverdance.

When this eye-popping spectacular first "tapped" its way into the Irish psyche in 1995 by jazzing up traditional step dancing and moving it from the local parish hall to the stages of Dublin's Point Theatre, it immediately sent its audiences reeling—in more ways than one. The first troupe to introduce the Irish jig to world theaters, it has since performed before 18 million people and, having taken in more than $1 billion at the box office, has danced all the way to the bank. Hand in hand with the fiddle-fueled rise of traditional Irish music—the wistful drone of an Irish tin whistle helped make 1997's *Titanic* the best-selling film soundtrack

Riverdance Irish Dance Troupe

HARPING ON

Ireland is the only country to have a musical instrument as its national emblem. The harp appears on *garda* (police) caps, Irish Euro coins, and government stationery. The original Irish harp was a small, triangular instrument designed to be held on the knee (not the large version of today's concert halls). The harp was first used as a logo for Guinness stout in 1850. The Guinness harp faces right, while the national emblem faces left.

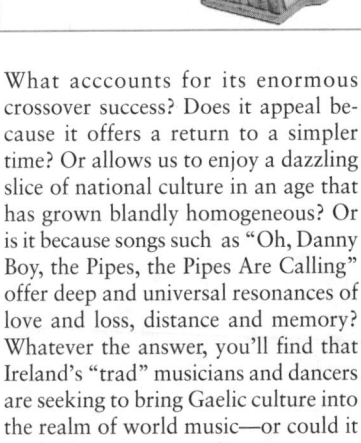

6

GAEL FORCE

of all time—Riverdance has resulted in the spectacular rebirth of old Gaelic culture over the past decade. And today, the world has fallen in step—literally. Riverdance's most fervent audiences are now found in far-off lands like Japan and Estonia; there's practically an Irish Step Dancing *Feis* (Irish for festival) every week somewhere in the U.S., and the sensational success of Celtic Woman—their Eire-savvy fusion of new-age pop, Celtic music, and classical crossover has catapulted their CDs to the top of the charts—are all signs that the tree of Irish music has deep roots around the globe.

What acccounts for its enormous crossover success? Does it appeal because it offers a return to a simpler time? Or allows us to enjoy a dazzling slice of national culture in an age that has grown blandly homogeneous? Or is it because songs such as "Oh, Danny Boy, the Pipes, the Pipes Are Calling" offer deep and universal resonances of love and loss, distance and memory? Whatever the answer, you'll find that Ireland's "trad" musicians and dancers are seeking to bring Gaelic culture into the realm of world music—or could it be the other way round?

COME AND MEET THOSE DANCING FEET

Ireland was swept off its feet, and its collective feet onto the boards, by the spectacular success of Riverdance. Thanks to that phenonemon, the thunderous dancing, stomping, clacking feet of today's Irish youth have once again taken up the trigger-quick step dances of old and the traditional music of the past.

Before Riverdance, Irish dancing was something schoolchildren performed chiefly for competitions, and sometimes on civic occasions, with their arms rigidly held by their sides (only the legs would move—a holdover from religious teachings that felt that dancing was sinful), and an expression of grave concentration on their faces. Today, it's a big thing for young people and also, due to those glitzy costumes and contests, a very expensive hobby.

Riverdance was a conscious attempt to project a more modern image of Ireland, and central to its roaring success were two American step dancers, Michael Flatley and Jean Butler. Their dazzling innovations reflected their origin in the more flexible American step dance competition world. Before Riverdance, the only options for prize-winning Irish step-dancers

were to teach or to retire—now hundreds of dancers are employed worldwide in touring shows inspired by Riverdance, such as Flatley's Celtic Tiger and Butler's Dancing on Dangerous Ground.

Set Dancing

Set dancing is also the name given to social dancing in which four couples face one another in a square in dances based on the French cotillion and the quadrilles. Set dancing has enjoyed a huge revival in recent years and nearly every town in Ireland once again has dancing at least one evening a week. Set dancing's successful revival is often attributed to the Willie Clancy Summer School in Co. Clare. Set dancing is fast and exhilarating and great social fun, so no wonder it caught on a second time.

Riverdance

STEPS & SETS

Ireland has a long tradition of solo dancing, first introduced by the jigs, reels, and hornpipes that traveling dancing masters taught in the 18th century. Some are performed in hard shoes, with the dancer beating out rhythms on the floor to complement the music, while others are danced with soft shoes to emphasize their graceful, airborne nature. In both cases, the main interest of the dance is in the foot and lower leg. Some solo dances have specific patterns of steps and are only danced to one tune and are known as "set dances"—in some places, set dances are known as table dances because the dancer often jumped up on the table to display his or her skills.

> The main interest of the dance is in the foot and lower leg

FANCY FOOTWORK

Because there were no accompanying drums, the sound of the feet on wooden floors has always been an important element in Irish dancing. When dancing really took off in the 18th century, many cabins only had earth floors, so the custom was to remove the top half of the half-door, and dance on that. Dancing masters used to display their prowess on fair days by dancing on soapy barrel lids, so they developed the ability to vary their steps in a confined space. From this came the tradition of dancing solos on one spot.

JUST FOLLOW THE SOUND OF THE MUSIC...

If you're interested in "Trad" music, the beat of a bodhrán or the tap of a shoe will likely lead you to Galway and County Clare's great folk *fleadhs* (festivals) and pub *seisiuns* (sessions).

THE BIGGEST FLEADH

The biggest festival of all is a three-day event called the All-Ireland finals at Fleadh Cheoil na hÉireann (pronounced flah-kwoil–"festival of music"). The 2006 event was held in Letterkenny, County Donegal, August 25–27, and was attended by nearly 11,000 musicians and 250,000 visitors, many of them second-generation Irish from overseas. This noncommercial festival of traditional music takes over a whole town, whose pubs become centers for casual music making. The All-Ireland rotates to different towns every year, much to the delight of the pub owners in the chosen town (⊕ www.comhaltas.com/fleadh/eireann.htm).

THE ENNIS BLOW-OUT

During the last week in May, the pleasant county town of Ennis hosts the **Fleadh Nua** (⊕ http://fleadhnua.com/), a massive eight-day-long celebration of dancing and song, with concerts, workshops, competitions, and *céilis*. Many of the events are open-air and free, and there is a great festive buzz. Ennis is home to a growing cadre of musicians: the Custys, Siobhán and Tommy Peoples, flute player Kevin Crawford, and accordion whiz kid Murty Ryan. Check out **Knox's Pub** (⊠ Abbey St. ☎ 065/682–9264) and **Cruise's Bar** (⊠ Abbey St. ☎ 065/684–1800) for lively evening sessions.

TOE-TAPPING IN MILTOWN

Held during the first week in July, the **Willie Clancy Summer School** (⊕ http://www.setdancingnews.net/wcss) is Ireland's biggest traditional music summer school. Classes, lectures, and recitals attract around 1,500 students from 42 countries to this tiny village on the west coast of Clare near Spanish Point. Set dancing is a big draw here, and a surefire way to make friends.

CEOL AGUS RINCE

Ceol (pronounced coil) is the Irish for music. And what always goes with the Irish for music? *Rince* (pronounced rincha), the Irish for dance: Music and Dance: you often see *Ceol agus Rince* on a poster advertising a traditional session or a céili.

Traditional Folk Music, Sligo, Co. Sligo, Ireland

Members of Kila mid-performance

DARLIN' DOOLIN

Doolin, County Clare, is little more than a dot on the map on the west coast of Clare (and to confuse things some maps have it down as "Roadford"). To traditional musicians its three main pubs—O'Connor's (✉ Fisher St. ☎ 065/707-4168 ⊕ www.oconnorspubdoolin.com), McDermott's (✉ Lisdoonvarna Rd. ☎ 065/707-4700 ⊕ www.mcdermottspubdoolin.com), and McGann's (✉ Lidoonvarna Rd. ☎ 065/707-4133 ⊕ www.esatclear.ie/mcgannsdoolin) are an irresistible magnet, as is the village's legendary charm. Some young musicians camp here all summer to learn from old masters.

CUCKOOS AND WINKLES

Kinvara, County Galway, is a pretty waterside village with an especially strong traditional music tradition. During the first weekend in May Kinvara hosts the annual **Cuckoo Fleadh** (✉ Main St. ☎ 091/637-145), a traditional music festival. Resident musicians like De Danann alumni Jackie Daly and Charlie Piggott play regularly at the town's **Winkles Hotel** (✉ The Square ☎ 091/637-137). Back in 1989, a young accordion player got together with her friends for a casual recording session. The resulting album, *Sharon Shannon*, became the most successful Trad-music recording ever released.

GIGGING IN GALWAY

Galway is the heart of Trad—the city and its environs have nurtured some of the most durable names in Irish music: Dé Danann, Arcady, singers Dolores and Seán Keane, and the mercurial accordion genius, Mairtìn O'Connor. Seán Ryan, master of the tin whistle,

has been playing every Sunday at Crane's (✉ 2 Sea Rd. ☎ 091/587-419) since the 1980s. **Tigh Coili** (✉ Mainguard St. ☎ 091/561-294) has traditional Irish music sessions every day at 5:30 and 10 PM. **Monroe's Tavern** (✉ Dominick St. ☎ 091/583-397) has traditional music every night from 9:30 PM, and invites you to join the locals in set dancing. There is also plenty of music to be found at old favorites in the city center like **Tigh Neachtain** (✉ 17 Cross St. ☎ 091/568-820), **Taaffe's** (✉ 19 Shop St. ☎ 091/564-066), and **Aras na Gael** (✉ 45 Lower Dominick St. ☎ 091/526-509). **The Bard's Den** (✉ Main St. ☎ 091/41042) in Letterfrack, Co. Galway, is noted for its Trad sessions. **Molloy's Bar** (✉ Bridge St. ☎ 098/26655) in Westport, Co. Mayo, is owned by Matt Molloy, flute player of the Chieftains, and is renowned for its great sessions.

■ **TIP→** For details, log on to www.comhaltas.com or get a copy of the "trad" bible, *Walton's Guide to Irish Music* (www.waltonmusic.com). All together now: "Too-ra-loo-ra-loo-ra, Too-ra-loo-ra-li!"

GOOD BEHAVIOR

If you happen on a pub session there are a few ground rules. Don't talk during the solo, and don't stare at the singer; most people look at the floor. Buy the musicians a drink if it's a small session, and if at all possible, have a party piece to contribute yourself. If you can't sing or play, recite a poem or tell a joke, even a short one. It's the gesture that counts.

FIDDLING AROUND

Irish Traditional music is very much the music of the people, played on relatively simple, portable instruments: fiddle, flute, tin whistle, accordion, handheld drum, and, recent additions, guitar or banjo.

UILLEANN PIPES

The uilleann (pronounced "illun") pipes, literally "elbow" pipes, are a quieter indoor version of bagpipes. The player sits while playing with a bag under one arm, the bellows under the other, and the "chanter," which plays the melody, on the thigh. A temperamental instrument, it can be heartrenderingly beautiful in the hands of a master like Liam O'Flynn or Paddy Keenan of the Bothy Band.

FIDDLE

The classical violin all but in name, this is the most popular instrument in Trad music for its singing, swooping versatility, its portability, and its relative affordability. Local fiddle styles still persist, especially in Donegal, Sligo, and the Sliabh Luachra region of Cork and Kerry and virtuosos such as Frankie Gavin of Dé Dannan, Martin Hayes, Tommy Peoples, and Liz Doherty are famed for their rhythm, color, and ornamentation.

SQUEEZE-BOXES & ACCORDIONS

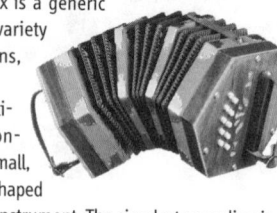

Squeeze-box is a generic term for a variety of melodeons, accordions, and concertinas. The concertina is a small, hexagonal-shaped button-key instrument. The simplest accordion is the one-row button accordion, usually called a melodeon. Styles of playing can vary enormously. Sharon Shannon is rooted in the highly rhythmic East Clare style but can veer into swing and Cajun styles as she plays her wildly energetic dance music.

FLUTES & WHISTLE

The tin whistle is the ideal beginner's instrument, but be sure to buy one in the key of D. It is still called the penny whistle because it costs so little to buy. But the flute used in Irish music is usually a simple wooden flute–hear it at its best in the hands of Matt Molloy and Paddy Moloney of the Chieftains, Mary Bergin, and Gavin Whelan.

BODHRÁN

The Bodhrán (pronounced "bow-rawn") is a simple goat's skin drum played with the back of the hand or a small wooden stick. When played well, by Mel Mercier, John Joe Kelly, or Tommy Hayes, it makes an exciting addition to the running rhythms of Trad music. They make it look easy, but in the hands of an untrained amateur, a badly played bodhrán can wreck a session.

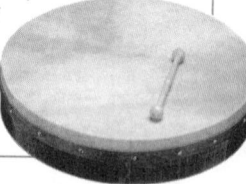

HAPPY LISTENING!

Traditional Irish pub music

SEÁN Ó RIADA The father of "modern" Trad music, this composer and visionary Irish language enthusiast (1931–71)–noted for his film score *Míse Éire* and his Irish language *Mass Cúil Aodha*–established the prototype traditional Irish group, Ceoltóiríc Chualann, in 1963, who evolved into the Chieftains.

THE CHIEFTAINS If you've seen a poster of Irish musicians wearing unhip cardigans, baggy trousers, and bad haircuts, it was probably the Chieftains, who went professional in 1975. Outstanding musicians, they include uilleann-piper Paddy Moloney, flute player Matt Molloy, harper Derek Bell (recently deceased), and Seán Keane and Martin Fay (fiddlers). Any of their famous 35 albums are worth owning.

PLANXTY The word *planxty* means a lively tune (without words) written to honor a patron, but it is now forever associated with a "super-group" formed in 1972 by singer Christy Moore, with Dónal Lunny, Andy Irvine, and Liam O'Flynn. Their haunting debut album, *Planxty* (1972), is a must. Reincarnated in the later '70s as The Bothy Band, their 1975 debut album remains a classic.

DÉ DANNAN This famed group grew from regular sessions in Hughe's bar in Spiddal, Co. Galway, in 1974. Brilliant fiddle and flute player Frankie Gavin, bouzouki whiz Alec Finn, banjo master Carlie Piggot, and Johnny "Ringo" McDonagh on bodhrán were joined by singers Dolores Keane, Mary Black, and Maura O'Connell (all now solo artists). *Dé Dannan* (1975) and *Mist-Covered Mountain* (1980) are their timeless evocations of the West of Ireland.

ALTAN Donegal-born husband-and-wife duo, Frankie Kennedy on flute and Máiréead Mhaonaight (fiddle and vocals), showcase the special Donegal way with fiddle and flute.

ANÚNA This vocal and instrumental ensemble, founded in the 1990s, represents the mystical, spiritual aspect of Celtic music, and is widely known through performances with the original Riverdance production. *Anúna* (1993), their first album, is still their best.

KILA Touted by the under-30s to be the future of Irish music, you can discern African percussion, Andean flute, and Eastern European folk music among the influences on their debut album, *Tóg É Go Bog É*–roughly translated as "The Living is Easy."

6

GAEL FORCE

Altan

the fifth floor, have views of the docks and Galway Bay. The rooftop spa includes an open-air hot tub. French-Irish cuisine is served at the formal, pleasantly old-fashioned Oyster Room. ⊠ *Eyre Sq., Center, Co. Galway* ☎ *091/564–041* 🖷 *091/566–704* ⊕ *www.gsh.ie* ↯ *112 rooms, 3 suites* ♧ *Restaurant, in-room data ports, Wi-Fi, hot tub, sauna, spa, 2 bars; no a/c* ▤ *AE, DC, MC, V* ⭐ *BP.*

☾ **$$** 🖾 **Cregg Castle.** Half country manor, half fortified keep, this 17th-century castle, on a 165-acre wildlife preserve, remains pleasantly informal thanks to its warm and laid-back hosts, the Brodericks. The house dog Magoo gives all guests a warm welcome, and the menagerie includes four other dogs, Scuttles the cat, a donkey, and a tame sheep called Ziggy. In addition, the farm has a flock of hens and turkeys, sheep, and a few cattle. The Brodericks all play musical instruments; traditional-music sessions often take place around the huge log-and-turf fire in the Great Hall. Bedrooms, which vary in shape and size, are decorated mainly with sturdy Victorian bygones. Breakfast is served until noon around an antique dining table that seats 18 people. It's about 15 km (9 mi) north of Galway on N17 (turn left for Corrandulla just beyond Claregalway). ⊠ *Tuam Rd., Corrandulla, Co. Galway* ☎🖷 *091/791–434* ↯ *8 rooms, 7 with bath* ♧ *Bicycles, some pets allowed; no smoking* ▤ *AE, MC, V* ☾ *Closed Nov.–Feb.* ⭐ *BP.*

$$ 🖾 **Killeen House.** Proper tea—served to you on the finest china—will welcome you here as you ease into a high-back armchair in Catherine Doyle's impeccable drawing room. Her peaceful country home is only 7 km (4 mi) from the city, but it could be in another world. In fact, you can walk through the immaculately kept garden and on for 10 minutes to the shore of Lough Corrib, which can be seen from some of the rooms. These are spacious and furnished with highly polished antiques, each on a different theme—Victorian, Edwardian, or Regency. The large beds are made up with crisp white bed linen, the furniture is in dark woods, and curtains and handwoven rugs are in calming neutral shades. The location, on the N59 Clifden road, makes this a fine location for both exploring the Connemara countryside by day and enjoying the considerable buzz of Galway City by night. ⊠ *Killeen, Bushypark, Co. Galway* ☎ *091/524–179* 🖷 *091/528–065* ⊕ *www.killeenhousegalway.com* ↯ *5 rooms* ♧ *Dining room, free parking; no a/c* ▤ *MC, V* ☾ *Closed Christmas wk* ⭐ *BP.*

$ 🖾 **Adare Guest House.** A five-minute walk from the city center, this family-run guesthouse, managed by the son of the original owners, makes a handy base for exploring Galway. There's ample space to park your car, and there's none of the nighttime noise of the city center. Rooms are relatively spacious for the price, extremely well equipped, and plainly decorated in browns and creams. The multichoice breakfast is served in a sunny room, with country-pine furniture and floors, that overlooks a flower-filled patio. ⊠ *9 Father Griffin Pl., Spanish Arch, Co. Galway* ☎ *091/582–638* 🖷 *091/583–693* ⊕ *www.adarebedandbreakfast.com* ↯ *11 rooms* ♧ *Dining room, free parking; no a/c* ▤ *AE, MC, V* ⭐ *BP.*

Nightlife & the Arts

Because of its small size and concentration of pubs and restaurants, Galway can seem even livelier at 11 PM than it does at 11 AM. On weekends, when there are lots of students and other revelers in town, Eyre Square and environs can be rowdy after pub-closing time. On the plus side, if you've been staying out in the country and you're ready for a little nightlife, you're certain to find plenty of it here.

Clubs & Pubs

The best spot for traditional music is the area between Eyre Square and the Spanish Arch. There's a big post-nightclub (open until 1 or 2) scene here—there are some clubs in town, but most everyone heads to Salthill, the small suburban community 3 km (2 mi) west of Galway. The main road, Upper Salthill, is lined with clubs.

CLUBS **Cuba** (⊠ Eyre Saure, Center ☎ 091/565–991), in the heart of Galway City, with three floors, draws diners and salsa lovers for Cuban cocktails and cigars to the beat of Latin music from DJs and live bands. Busy with students from the university, **GPO** (⊠ Eglinton St., Center ☎ 091/563–073) is perhaps the most popular dance club in the city center. Try **Club**

> ### LET'S RENDEVOUS
>
> Because noise levels in Galway's busy bars can make conversation difficult, the city's hotel lobbies are popular meeting places for people who want a quiet spot.

Q (⊠ Radisson SAS Hotel, Lough Atalia Rd., Center ☎ 091/583–300), which has resident DJs, hip-hop, chart, two dance floors, and big-name gigs. **McSwiggan's** (⊠ 3 Eyre St., Wood Quay, Center ☎ 091/568–917) is a huge Galway City place, with everything from church pews to ancient carriage lamps contributing to its eclectic character. **Roisin Dubh** (⊠ Dominick St., Spanish Arch ☎ 091/586–540) is a serious venue for emerging rock and traditional bands; it often showcases big, if still-struggling, talents. For late-night sounds heard from the comfort of your own table, try **Sally Longs** (⊠ Upper Abbeygate St., Center ☎ 091/565–756), Galway's hard rock pub, much loved by bikers. **Warwick** (⊠ O'Connor's Warwick Hotel, Lower Salthill, Salthill ☎ 091/521–244) has a DJ on Friday nights and a band on Saturday, both playing rock and pop oldies. Admission is €4 to €10.

PUBS **Tigh Neachtain** (⊠ 17 Cross St., Spanish Arch ☎ 091/568–820) is *the* place for traditional music in Galway City, and each visit will be an experience.

Aras na Gael (⊠ 45 Lower Dominick St., Spanish Arch ☎ 091/526–509) is one of the few pubs in the city center where Irish is spoken. Master of the tin whistle Seán Ryan plays every Sunday at **Crane's** (⊠ 2 Sea Rd. ☎ 091/587–419). You can usually find a session after about 9 PM at **King's Head** (⊠ 15 High St., Center ☎ 091/566–630). **Paddy's** (⊠ Prospect Hill, Center ☎ 091/567–843) is a good place for a pint near the bus and train station. **Taaffe's** (⊠ 19 Shop St., Center ☎ 091/564–066), in the midst of the shopping district, is very busy on afternoons. Up-and-coming young musicians play at the cozy **Tigh Coili Bar** (⊠ Mainguard St., Center ☎ 091/561–294) in traditional sessions daily at 5:30 and 10 PM.

Theater

An Taibhdhearc (⊠ Middle St., Center ☎ 091/562–024 ⊕ www.antaibhdearc.com), pronounced "on *tie*-vark," was founded in 1928 by

Hilton Edwards and Mícheál Macliammóir as the national Irish-language theater. It continues to produce first-class shows, mainly of Irish works in both the English and the Irish languages.

The **Druid Theatre Company** (⊠ Chapel La., Center ☎ 091/568–617 ⊕ www.druidtheatre.com) is esteemed for its adventurous and accomplished productions, mainly of 20th-century Irish and European plays. The players perform at the Royal Court's small stage in London. When they're home, they usually appear at the Town Hall, and they host many productions during the Galway Arts Festival in late July.

Macnas (⊠ Fisheries Field, Salmon Weir Bridge, Center ☎ 091/561–462 ⊕ www.macnas.com) is an internationally renowned, Galway-based troupe of performance artists who have raised street theater to new levels. Their participation in the Galway Arts Festival's annual parade is always much anticipated.

Visual Arts & Galleries

Bold (⊠ Merchants Rd. and Augustien St., Center ☎ 091/539–900 ⊕ www.boldartgallery.com) shows work by big name and up-and-coming Irish artists.

Kenny's Gallery (⊠ High St., Center ☎ 091/534–760 ⊕ www.kennys. ie) specializes in artists who paint scenes of Galway and Connemara. Reflecting a passion for modern Irish art, **Norman Villa Gallery** (⊠ 86 Lower Salthill, Salthill ☎ 091/521–131 ⊕ www.normanvillagallery. com) shows work in the gallery owner's home. The art gallery at **University College Galway** (⊠ Newcastle Rd., University ☎ 091/524–411) has a number of exhibits each year.

Sports & the Outdoors

Bicycling

Set off to explore the Galway area, especially its coast, by renting a bike from **Mountain Trail Bike Shop** (⊠ The Cornstore, Middle St., Center ☎ 091/569–888).

Fishing

Galway City is the gateway to Connemara, and Connemara is the place to fish. You can get fishing licenses, tackle, and bait, and arrange to hire a traditional fly-fishing guide or book a sea-angling trip at **Freeny's Sports** (⊠ 19–23 High St., Center ☎ 091/562–609). **Murt's** (⊠ 7 Daly's Pl., Woodquay ☎ 091/561–018) can handle your fishing needs.

Golf

Galway Bay Golf and Country Club (⊠ Renville, Oranmore ☎ 091/790–500) is an 18-hole, par-72 parkland course, designed by Christy O'Connor Jr., on the shores of Galway Bay. The **Galway Golf Club** (⊠ Blackrock, Salthill ☎ 091/522–033) is an 18-hole, par-71 course with excellent views of Galway Bay, the Burren, and the Aran Islands. Some of the fairways run close to the ocean.

River Cruising

A **Corrib Cruise** (☎ 091/592–447 ⊕ www.corribprincess.ie) from Wood Quay, behind the Town Hall Theatre at the Rowing Club, is a lovely way to spend a fine afternoon; it lasts 1½ hours and travels 8 km (5 mi) up the River Corrib and about 6 km (4 mi) around Lough Corrib. There's a bar on board, tea and coffee, and a commentary. The trip costs €12, and boats depart daily at 2:30 and 4:30 from May through September, with an additional departure at 12:30 July through August. You can also rent the boat for an evening.

Shopping

Antiques
Connaught Antiques (⊠ 9 Eyre Square St., Center ☎ 091/567–840 ⊕ www.connaughtantiques.com) stocks a wonderful selection of Irish, English, and French antiques, clocks, and *objets d'art,* mainly from the 18th and 19th centuries.

Books
Charlie Byrne's Bookshop (⊠ Middle St., Center ☎ 091/561–766) sells a large, varied selection of used books and remainders. **Hughes and Hughes** (⊠ Galway Shopping Centre, Headford Rd., ☎ 091/563–903) is the biggest bookshop in Galway.

Clothing
Faller's Sweater Shop (⊠ 25 High St., Center ☎ 091/564–833 ⊠ 35 Eyre Sq., Center ☎ 091/561–255) has the choicest selection of Irish-made sweaters, competitively priced. **O'Máille's** (⊠ 16 High St., Center ☎ 091/562–696) carries Aran sweaters, handwoven tweeds, and classically tailored clothing.

Crafts & Gifts
★ Don't miss **Design Concourse Ireland** (⊠ Kirwan's La., Center ☎ 091/566–927), a spectacular one-stop shop for the best in Irish handcrafted design. Ceramics, small pieces of furniture, contemporary basketware, handmade jewelry, wood turnings, handblown glass—in fact just about anything for the home that can be handmade—will be found in this two-story treasure trove. **Galway Irish Crystal** (⊠ Dublin Rd., Merlin Park ☎ 091/757–311 ⊕ www.galwaycrystal.ie), a factory outlet on the city's ring road, has hand-cut Irish glass, an informative heritage center on Galway lore, a crystal workshop you can visit, and a restaurant with a view of Galway Bay. The **Kilkenny Shop** (⊠ 6 High St., Center ☎ 091/566–110) is synonymous with good modern design in Ireland. This shop stocks the best ceramics, crystal, leatherware, clothing, and other craft items from around the country. **Meadows & Byrne** (⊠ Castle St., Center ☎ 091/567–776) sells the best in modern household items. Browse in **Tempo** (⊠ 9 Cross St., Center ☎ 091/562–282), which has a good selection of dec-

> **CLOTHES MAKE THE MAN**
>
> The grease in the wool of a hand-knit, heirloom-quality Aran sweater will make it feel very stiff for the first few months—or even years. Locals of all ages wear the traditional sweaters in Galway and on the Aran islands, but in other parts of Ireland the assumption is usually that anyone wearing an Aran is a visitor.

orative pieces, gifts, and antique furniture. Browse in **Treasure Chest** (⊠ William St., Center ☎ 091/563–862) for china, crystal, gifts, and classic clothing.

Food
Sheridan's Cheesemongers (⊠ 16 Churchyard St. ☎ 091/564–829 ⊕ www.sheridanscheesemongers.com) is run by Seamus and Kevin Sheridan. Together, they know all of Ireland's artisan cheese makers personally and stock the widest possible range of delectable cheeses, complemented by charcuterie (mainly Italian). The wineshop upstairs will complete your picnic.

Jewelry
Phyllis MacNamara's cute two-story boutique, **Cobwebs** (⊠ 7 Quay St., Spanish Arch ☎ 091/564–388 ⊕ www.cobwebs.ie) is filled with an irresistible selection of antique jewelry (real and costume) and collectibles for men and women, all with a witty twist. Dating from 1750, **Thomas Dillon's** (⊠ 1 Quay St., Spanish Arch ☎ 091/566–365 ⊕ www.claddaghring.ie) claims to be the original maker of Galway's famous Claddagh ring. In the back of the shop there's a small but interesting display of antique Claddagh rings and old Galway memorabilia.

Malls
The spacious indoor **Galway Shopping Centre** (⊠ Headford Rd.) is a mall with more than 60 outlets, 10 minutes' walk from Eyre Square with ample car parking. On the southwest side of Eyre Square and imaginatively designed to incorporate parts of the old town walls, the **Eyre Square Shopping Centre** is a good spot to pick up moderately priced clothing and household goods.

Music
Back2Music (⊠ 30 Upper Abbeygate St., Center ☎ 091/565–272) specializes in traditional Irish musical instruments, including the handheld drum, the *bodhrán* (pronounced bau-*rawn*). **Mulligan** (⊠ 5 Middle St. Ct., Center ☎ 091/564–961) carries thousands of CDs, records, and cassettes, with a large collection of traditional Irish music. **P. Powell and Sons** (⊠ The Four Corners, William St., Center ☎ 091/562–295) sells traditional Irish musical instruments and CDs, and has a knowledgable staff.

Vintage Goods
Twice as Nice (⊠ 5 Quay St., Spanish Arch ☎ 091/566–332) sells a mix of new and vintage men's and women's clothing, linens, lace, and jewelry at reasonable prices.

CONNEMARA & COUNTY MAYO

Bordered by the long expanse of Lough Corrib on the east and the jagged coast of the Atlantic on the west is the rugged, desolate region of western County Galway known as Connemara. Like the American West, it's an area of spectacular, almost myth-making geography—of glacial lakes; gorgeous, silent mountains; lonely roads; and hushed, uninhabited boglands. The Twelve Bens, "the central glory of Connemara," as author Brendan Lehane has called them, together with the Maamturk Mountains to their north, lord proudly over the area's sepia boglands. In the midst of this wilderness there are few people, since Connemara's population is sparse even by Irish standards. Especially in the off-season, you're far more likely to come across sheep strolling its roads than another car.

> ### THE WEARING OF THE GREEN
>
> Stands of Scotch pine, Norwegian spruce, Douglas fir, and Japanese Sitka grow in Connemara's valleys and up hillsides—the result of a concerted national project that has thus far reforested 9% of Ireland.

Two main routes—one inland, the other coastal—lead through Connemara. To take the inland route described below, leave Galway City on the well-signposted outer-ring road and follow signs for N59—Moycullen, Oughterard, and Clifden. If you choose to go the coastal route, you can travel due west from Galway City to Ros an Mhil (Rossaveal) on R336 through Salthill, Bearna, and An Spidéal—all in the heart of the West's strong Gaeltacht, home to roughly 40,000 Irish speakers (note that most place signage hereabouts will be in Irish, so a map with both English and Irish names will prove handy). You can continue north on R336 from Ros an Mhil (Rossaveal) to Maam Cross and then head for coastal points west, or pick up R340 and putter along the coast.

Oughterard

30 *27 km (17 mi) northwest of Galway City on N59.*

Bustling Oughterard (pronounced *ook*-ter-ard) is the main village on the western shores of Lough Corrib and one of Ireland's leading angling resorts. The prettiest part of the village is on the far (Clifden) side, beyond the busy commercial center, beside a wooded section of the River Corrib. The lough is signposted to the right in the village center, less than 1½ km (1 mi) up the road. From mid-June to early September, local boatmen offer trips on the lough, which has several islands. It's also possible to take a boat trip to the village of Cong, at the north shore of the lough. Midway between Oughterard and Cong, Inchagoill Island (the Island of the Stranger), a popular destination for a half-day trip, has several early-Christian church remains. The cost of boat rides is negotiable; expect to pay about €10 per person.

Where to Stay & Eat

★ **$$$** ✕🏠 **Ross Lake House.** Well off the beaten path, this surprisingly stylish country hideaway sits near a stream and is surrounded by 5 acres of colorful gardens. Built by James Edward Jackson, land agent for Lord Iveagh at Ashford Castle, the white-trim Georgian house, managed by the enthusiastic Henry and Elaine Reid, has a suavely furnished interior, with 19th-century antiques and welcoming open fires. Guest rooms in the converted stables are simpler and a little smaller than those in the house, but all have peaceful garden views. A table d'hôte dinner menu, set in a salon with Regency-stripe wallpapers, offers good-quality, plain country-house cooking featuring local delicacies, including the much-sought after Connemara mountain lamb. The house is 5 km (3 mi) from

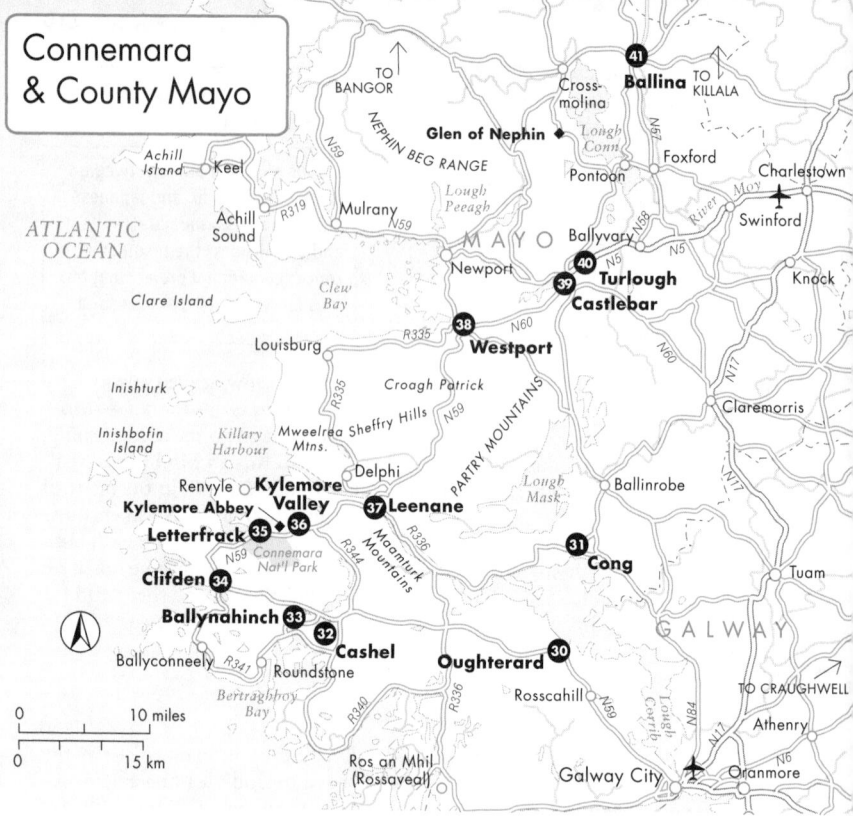

Connemara & County Mayo

Oughterard. ✉ *Rosscahill, Co. Galway* 📠 *091/550–109* ⊕ *www.rosslakehotel.com* 🛏 *13 rooms* ⚐ *Restaurant, tennis court, horseback riding, bar; no a/c* ➜ *AE, DC, MC, V* ⊙ *Closed Nov.–mid-Mar.* ⊙I *BP.*

Nightlife

For good traditional music try **Flaherty's** (✉ Main St. 📞 091/552–194).

EN ROUTE As you continue northwest from Oughterard on N59, you'll soon pass a string of small lakes on your left; their shining blue waters reflecting the blue sky are a typical Connemara sight on a sunny day. About 16 km (10 mi) northwest of Oughterard, the continuation of the coast road (R336) meets N59 at Maam Cross in the shadow of Leckavrea Mountain. Once an important meeting place for the people of north and south Connemara, it's still the location of a large monthly cattle fair. Walkers will find wonderful views of Connemara by heading for any of the local peaks visible from the road. Beyond Maam Cross, some of the best scenery in Connemara awaits on the road to Recess, 16 km (10 mi) west of Maam Cross on N59. At many points on this drive, a short walk away from either side of the main road will lead you to the shores of one of the area's many small loughs. Stop and linger if the sun is out—even intermittently—for the light filtering through the clouds gives splendor to the distant, dark-gray mountains and creates patterns on the brown-green moorland below. In June and July, it stays light until 11 PM or so, and it's worth taking a late-evening stroll to see the sun's reluctance to set. In Recess, **Joyce's** (☎ 095/34604) is a crafts shop owned by a family that is famed for its traditional Connemara tweeds. The emporium has a good selection of tweed, and also carries an enticing selection of contemporary ceramics, handwoven shawls, books of Irish interest, original paintings, and small sculptures.

Cong

❸❶ *23 km (14 mi) northeast of Maam Cross on N59.*

Fodor'sChoice
★
On a narrow isthmus between Lough Corrib and Lough Mask on the County Mayo border, the pretty, old-fashioned village of Cong, near Maam Cross, is dotted with ivy-covered thatched cottages, dilapidated farmhouses, and one immensely posh hotel, Ashford Castle. Cong is surrounded by many stone circles and burial mounds, but its most notable ruins are those of the **Augustine Abbey** (✉ Abbey St.), dating from the early 13th century and still exhibiting some finely carved details. It can be seen overlooking a river near fabulous Ashford Castle, now a hotel.

Cong's 15 minutes of fame came in 1952, when John Ford filmed *The Quiet Man,* one of his most popular films, here; John Wayne plays a prizefighter who goes home to Ireland to court the fiery Maureen O'Hara. (Film critic Pauline Kael called the movie "fearfully Irish and green and hearty.") The **Quiet Man Heritage Cottage,** in the village center, is an exact replica of the cottage used in the film, with reproductions of the furniture and costumes, a few original artifacts, and pictures of actors Barry Fitzgerald and Maureen O'Hara on location. For much of the year, Margaret and Gerry Collins host "Quiet Man" tours, originating at the cottage and exploring such Cong village sites as the river fight scene, the "hats in the air" scene, and Pat Cohan's Bar. ✉ *Cong Village Center* ☎ *094/954–6089* ⊕ *www.quietman-cong.com* 🔖 *€4* ☉ *Mar.–Nov., daily 10–6.*

Where to Stay

★ **$$$$** 🏨 **Ashford Castle.** Nearly bigger than the neighboring village of Cong, this famed mock-Gothic baronial showpiece was built in 1870 for the Guinness family and has been wowing visitors ever since—that is, if your guest list runs to Prince Rainier, John Travolta, and Jack Nicholson. Massive, flamboyantly turreted, built of stone with towers and bridges, crenellations and mullioned windows, Ashford is the very picture of a romantic Irish castle. As a world apart from the normal hubbub of Irish life, it remains strong on luxury, charm, and good service, but—some pundits would say—light on authenticity as time-stained charm has given way to too many creature comforts. Still, this is the reason why Pierce Brosnan took over the whole castle for two days for his wedding to Keely Shaye Smith, and it remains a popular destination with honeymooners from all over the world. The 82 bedrooms include presidential and executive suites—and for once the name isn't just hopeful, as presidents of both the United States (Reagan, on his trip back to his ancestral homeland) and France have stayed here. Inside, large paintings in gilt frames hang from the castle's carved stone walls above polished wood paneling, illuminated by crystal chandeliers. Deluxe rooms have generous sitting areas, heavily carved antique furniture, open fireplaces and extra-large bathrooms. Standard bedrooms in the discreetly added new wing are smaller, with marble bathroom fittings and Victorian-style antiques, have ample amenities but lack the scale and baronial flamboyance of the rest of the castle. The suites in the original castle building are vast, with double-height windows, furnished with Georgian antiques, and blissfully comfortable. The Prince of Wales Cocktail Bar (named for the one who visited in the 1890s) is the venue for elegant predinner drinks. The cuisine, by distinguished Swiss chef, Stefan Matz, is stylish and unfussy, showcasing fresh local ingredients. The hotel makes the most of its superb location at the head of Lough Corrib and the surrounding formal lawns and gardens are possibly the most neatly manicured outdoor space in Ireland. Accordingly, fly-fishing is a popular outdoor sport, and the river bank has recently been landscaped to facilitate anglers—typical of the no-expense-spared Ashford approach—while there has also been massive investment in the hotel's spa facilities. ⊠ *Co. Mayo* ☎ *094/954–6003* 🖷 *094/954–6260* ⊕ *www.ashford.ie* ⇥ *72 rooms, 11 suites* △ *2 restaurants, cable TV, in-room data ports, Wi-Fi, 9-hole golf course, 2 tennis courts, health club, boating, fishing, bicycles, horseback riding, 2 bars; no a/c* ☰ *AE, DC, MC, V* ⅋⊙⅋ *EP.*

Cashel

㉜ *8 km (5 mi) south of Recess on R340, 49½ km (31 mi) west of Cong.*

Cashel is a quiet, extremely sheltered angling center at the head of Bertraghboy Bay. General de Gaulle is among the many people who have sought seclusion here. A word of caution: stray sheep, bolting Connemara ponies, cyclists, and reckless local drivers are all regular hazards on the narrow mountain roads hereabouts.

Where to Stay & Eat

★ **$$$** 🏨 **Zetland Country House.** On a hill overlooking secluded Cashel Bay, John and Mona Prendergast's mid-Victorian country retreat offers an idyllic experience of quiet, elegant country living. Once a 19th-century sporting lodge favored by the earl and countess of Zetland, the rambling white house is surrounded by large old trees, wooded grounds, and flowering shrubs. A dining room with massive antique sideboards adorned with family silver overlooks the bay, as does the large and blissfully serene sitting room. The main drawing room is a picture of Georgian grace, replete with chandelier, marble fireplace, and glowing-yellow walls. Upstairs, guest bedrooms are large, and many have sea views, but those with garden views are also attractive. Fine Georgian and Victorian antiques of polished mahogany decorate the comfortable quarters. ⊠ *Cashel Bay, Co. Galway* ☎ *095/31111* 🖷 *095/31117* ⊕ *www.zetland.com* ⇥ *20 rooms* △ *Restaurant, tennis court, fishing, bar; no a/c* ☰ *AE, DC, MC, V* ⅋⊙⅋ *BP.*

Sports & the Outdoors

Cashel Equestrian Center (✉ Cashel House, Cashel Bay ☎ 095/31001) offers scenic treks and the chance to ride a Connemara pony on its home ground.

Ballynahinch

33 *10 km (6 mi) west of Cashel on R341.*

Forested country runs along the shores of Ballynahinch Lake, which nowadays is accessible to the general public. Woodland in this part of Ireland indicates the proximity of a "big house" whose owner can afford to plant trees for pleasure and prevent their being cut down for fuel. Surely enough, soon after the woodland hereabouts begins, you will come to the gate lodge of the noted country-house hotel, Ballynahinch Castle. This being Connemara, with its Irish settlement pattern, there's no village as such, just an area named Ballynahinch.

Where to Stay & Eat

$$$$ Fodor's Choice ★ **Ballynahinch Castle.** Built in the late 18th century on the Owenmore River amid 40 walkable wooded acres, this huge, rambling, castellated, and gorgeous country house was the home of Richard Martin (1754–1834), known as "Humanity Dick," the founder of the Royal Society for the Prevention of Cruelty to Animals. Set in the midst of 300 of the most beautiful acres of Connemara, this has long been a favored forgetaway for the famous, from the O'Flaherty Chieftains to Grace O'Malley—the Pirate Queen of Connemara—to H.R.H. the Maharajah Ranjitsinji, "Prince of Cricketeers." Comfort without ostentation is the hallmark here, and because many guests are here for the fishing, the bar and restaurant are pleasantly informal. The tiled lobby with Persian rugs has two inviting leather chesterfields in front of an open fire. The biggest bedrooms, all most stylishly decorated, in the ground-floor wing, have four-poster beds and floor-to-ceiling windows opening onto lawns that run down the river. Rooms in the old house are equally comfortable and quiet. The Owenmore restaurant enjoys a panoramic riverside perch and high style cuisine. The castle is signposted off N59 between Recess and Clifden. ✉ *Ballynahinch, Recess, Co. Galway* ☎ *095/31006* 📠 *095/31085* 🌐 *www.ballynahinch-castle.com* *30 rooms, 10 suites* *Restaurant, in-room data ports, tennis court, fishing, bar; no a/c* 💳 *AE, DC, MC, V* ⏲ *Closed last wk of Dec. and Feb.* 🍽 *BP.*

OFF THE BEATEN PATH

ROUNDSTONE MUSICAL INSTRUMENTS – From Ballynahinch, take N59 to the small seaside town of Roundstone, where you can find this delightful music shop and museum. Artisans here have been handcrafting bodhráns (Irish drums) here for dozens of years. The workshop is in an old Franciscan monastery with a beautiful bell tower. Besides the bodhráns, you can buy traditional CDs, books, and coffee—and you can also expect a good chat. If you wish, you can have your drum hand-painted with your family crest, a Celtic design, or your initials while you wait. ✉ *I.D.A. Craftcenter, Roundstone* ☎ *095/35808* 🌐 *www.bodhran.com* ⏲ *May, June, Sept., and Oct., daily 9:30–6; July and Aug., daily 9–7; Nov.–Apr., Mon.–Sat. 9:30–6.*

6

Clifden

★ *23 km (14 mi) west of Recess, 79 km (49 mi) northwest of Galway City on N59.*

With roughly 1,100 residents, Clifden would be called a village by most, but in these parts it's looked on as something of a metropolis. It's far and away the prettiest town in Connemara, as well as its unrivaled "capital." Clifden's first attraction is its location—perched high above Clifden Bay on a forested plateau, its back to the spectacular Twelve Ben Mountains. The tapering spires of the town's two churches add to its alpine feel. A selection of small restaurants, lively bars with music most summer nights, pleasant accommodations, and excellent walks make the town a popular base. It's quiet out of season, but in July and August crowds flock here, especially for August's world-famous Connemara Pony Show.

> **TRAVEL TIP**
>
> Clifden's popularity necessitates a chaotic one-way traffic system, and loud techno music blasts out of certain bars. If you're over 25 and value your peace and quiet, you'd best choose a base outside town.

A 2-km (1-mi) walk along the beach road through the grounds of the ruined **Clifden Castle** is the best way to explore the seashore. The castle was built in 1815 by John D'Arcy, the town's founder, who laid out the town's wide main street on a long ridge with a parallel street below it. D'Arcy was High Sheriff of Galway, and his greatest wish was to establish a center of law and order in what he saw as the lawless wilderness of Connemara. Before the founding of Clifden, the interior of Connemara was largely uninhabited, with most of its population clinging to the seashore. Take the aptly named **Sky Road** to really appreciate Clifden's breathtaking scenery. Signposted at the west end of town, this high, narrow circuit of about 5 km (3 mi) heads west to Kingstown, skirting Clifden Bay's precipitous shores.

Where to Stay & Eat

$–$$ ✕ **Mitchell's Seafood.** A town-center shop has been cleverly converted into a stylish, two-story eatery. On the first floor, beyond the plate-glass windows, there's a welcoming open fire, and you can eat at the bar or at one of the polished wood tables. Exposed stone walls and wooden floors are alluring accents on the quieter second level. Braised whole sea bass with fennel butter typifies the simple treatment given to seafood. The all-day menu also features lighter options like homemade spicy fish cakes and fresh crab salad. There are several meat options, including traditional Irish stew of Connemara lamb and fresh vegetables. ✉ Market St. ☎ 095/21867 ▭ MC, V ⊘ Closed Nov.–Feb.

★ $$$ ✕▯ **Rock Glen Manor House.** You will probably be "greeted" by a pair of braying donkeys who graze beside the driveway. Enter this realm and you can see riding boots and tennis rackets in the hall—clearly, Peadar Nevin's beautifully converted 1815 shooting lodge feels more like a private home than a top-class hotel. A turf fire warms the large, sumptuous drawing room—an eye-knocking symphony in red, chicly fitted out with houndstooth-check armchairs and gilt-frame mirrors (plus a lovely array of magazines, books, and board games). Fluffy mohair or chintz spreads cover the beds in the sweetly furnished guest rooms. In the Victorian-style restaurant ($$–$$$), you can expect such winners as roasted rack of lamb with an herb crust and duxelles. To get here from Clifden, cross the bridge at the west end of town and walk less than 1 km (½ mi) down the R341 Roundstone road. ⊠ *Co. Galway* ☎ *095/21035* 🖶 *095/21737* ⊕ *www.rockglenhotel.com* 🛏 *27 rooms* ⚏ *Restaurant, tennis court, fishing, horseback riding, bar; no a/c* 🖃 *AE, MC, V* ☾ *Closed Jan. and Feb. No lunch* ⊺⊙⊺ *BP.*

$$$ 🏨 **Abbeyglen Castle Hotel.** Creeper-covered, as if under a Sleeping Beauty spell, gorgeous Abbeyglen sits framed by towering trees at the foot of the glorious Twelve Bens Mountains. If time hasn't completely stopped here, it has certainly slowed down—but that's just the way the relaxed guests want it. Surrounded by gardens with waterfalls and streams, the Victorian castle-manor was built in 1832 by John D'Arcy, the founder of Clifden and builder of Clifden Castle. Inside, each guest room is uniquely decorated with heavy, ornate, dark-wood furniture and rich colors befitting a castle. Although it's in a very quiet and seemingly secluded location, the hotel becomes busy during complimentary afternoon tea, and has a busy nightlife scene, with live traditional music in its bar and big-name touring acts in its function room. This makes it a particularly popular weekend destination with Irish city-dwellers. ⊠ *Sky Rd., Co. Galway* ☎ *095/22832* 🖶 *095/21797* ⊕ *www.abbeyglen.ie* 🛏 *38 rooms* ⚏ *Restaurant, tennis court, pool, sauna, fishing, bar; no a/c* 🖃 *AE, DC, MC, V* ☾ *Closed Jan.* ⊺⊙⊺ *BP.*

$$ 🏨 **Quay House.** A roaring turf fire in the sitting room greets you at this three-story Georgian house, Clifden's oldest building (1820). It's a short walk from the busy town center, and an oasis of calm beside the harbor quay. Rooms are unusually spacious, and those in the main house are imaginatively decorated with deep-color walls and witty bygones; all but one have sea views. There's also a new wing with seven studio rooms with balconies overlooking the harbor. Proprietors Julia and Patrick Foyle have tucked in homey touches, such as books and model boats. ⊠ *The Quay, Connemara, Co. Galway* ☎ *095/21369* 🖶 *095/21608* ⊕ *www.thequayhouse.com* 🛏 *20 rooms* ⚏ *Some kitchenettes, fishing; no a/c* 🖃 *MC, V* ☾ *Closed Nov.–mid-Mar., except by arrangement.*

¢ 🏨 **Dun Rí.** An old town house in the lower, quieter part of Clifden has been extended and converted into a comfortable guesthouse with private parking. The town's bars and restaurants are only two minutes' walk away, yet there can be sheep grazing on a vacant lot across the road. Rooms are a good size, with hotel-like features including adjustable radiators, swagged floral curtains and efficient showers. Help yourself to tea and coffee in the residents' lounge, a good place to compare notes with fellow travelers. The breakfast room has pine floor and white damask cloths, and the toast is accompanied by butter-balls (shaped by butter-pats, once ubiquitous in country hotels, now seldom seen) and homemade jam. ⊠ *Hulk St.* ☎ *095/21625* 🖶 *095/21635* ⊕ *www.connemara. net/dun-ri* 🛏 *13 rooms* ⚏ *Lounge; no a/c* 🖃 *MC, V* ⊺⊙⊺ *BP.*

Nightlife

Abbeyglen Castle Hotel (⊠ Sky Rd. ☎ 095/21201) hosts musical sessions in the bar most nights from June to September and occasional visits by big-name acts.

Sports & the Outdoors

BICYCLING Explore Connemara by renting a bike from **John Mannion & Son** (⊠ Railway View ☎ 095/21160).

GOLF On a dramatic stretch of Atlantic coastline, the 18-hole, par-72 course at the **Connemara Golf Club** (⊠ South of Clifden, Ballyconneely ☎ 095/23502) measures 7,174 yards.

Shopping

The Connemara Hamper (⊠ Market St. ☎ 095/21054), a small but well-stocked specialty food shop, is an ideal place to pick up picnic fare, with its excellent Irish farmhouse cheeses, pâtés, smoked Connemara salmon, and Irish handmade chocolates. **Millar's Connemara Tweeds** (⊠ Main St. ☎ 095/21038), an arts-and-crafts gallery, carries a good selection of traditional tweeds and hand knits. The **Station House Courtyard** (⊠ Old Railway Station, Bridge St. ☎ 095/21699) is a cobbled courtyard with crafts studios and designer-wear outlets.

Letterfrack

35 *14 km (9 mi) north of Clifden on N59.*

The 5,000-acre **Connemara National Park** lies southeast of the village of Letterfrack. Its visitor center covers the area's history and ecology, particularly the origins and growth of peat—and presents the depressing statistic that more than 80% of Ireland's peat, 5,000 years in the making, has been destroyed in the last 90 years. You can also get details on the many excellent walks and beaches in the area. The misleadingly named "park" is, in fact, just rocky or wooded wilderness territory, albeit with some helpful trails marked out to aid your exploration. It includes part of the famous **Twelve Bens** mountain range, which are for experienced hill walkers only. An easier hike is the spectacular **Pollrark River Gorge** and **Glanmore Valley.** Ask for advice on a hike suited to your abilities and interests at the visitor center. ☎ 095/41054 *Park free, visitor center €2.50* ⊙ *Park freely accessible; visitor center Apr., May, and Sept.–mid-Oct., daily 10–5:30; June, daily 10–6:30; July and Aug., daily 9:30–6:30.*

Where to Stay & Eat

★ **$$$** ✕▥ **Renvyle House.** A lake at its front door, the Atlantic Ocean at its back door, and the mountains of Connemara as a backdrop form the enthralling setting for this hotel 8 km (5 mi) north of Letterfrack. Once the legendary retreat of that noted Irish man of letters, Oliver St. John Gogarty of Dublin (on whom James Joyce modeled Buck Mulligan in *Ulysses*)—and, as such, a focal point for the Irish literary renaissance of the early 20th century—Renvyle is rustic and informal; it has exposed beams and brickwork, and numerous open turf fires. The main salon, called the Long Room, is one of the most eminently civilized rooms in Ireland—all tranquil beige, endless chairs, and pretty pictures. The comfortable guest rooms, elegantly decorated in a floral style, all have breathtaking views. The softly lighted restaurant's table d'hôte menu is based on traditional Irish fare ($$$$). ⊠ *Renvyle, Co. Galway* ☎ *095/ 43511* 🖷 *095/43515* ⊕ *www.renvyle.com* ⊃ *68 rooms* ⌂ *Restaurant, 9-hole golf course, 2 tennis courts, pool, fishing, horseback riding, bar; no a/c* ☰ *AE, DC, MC, V* ☉ *Closed Jan.–mid-Feb.* ⦿ *BP.*

★ $$$ ✕⊡ **Rosleague Manor.** This pink, creeper-clad, two-story Georgian house occupies 30 lovely acres overlooking an eye-knocking view: a gorgeous lawn backdropped by Ballinakill Bay and the dreamy mountains of Connemara. Inside, the clutter of walking sticks and shooting sticks beneath the grandfather clock in the hall sets the informal, country-house tone. Well-used antiques, four-poster or large brass bedsteads, and drapes that match the William Morris wallpaper decorate the solidly comfortable and impeccably kept bedrooms. The best rooms are at the front on the first floor, overlooking the bay. At dinner in the superb restaurant, baked monkfish with crispy capers and balsamic vinegar is one of the tastiest entrées. ⊠ *Rosleague Bay, Co. Galway* ☎ *095/41101* 🖷 *095/ 41168* ⊕ *www.rosleague.com* ⊃ *20 rooms* ⌂ *Restaurant, tennis court, sauna, horseback riding, bar; no a/c* ☰ *AE, MC, V* ☉ *Closed Nov.–mid-Mar.* ⦿ *BP.*

Nightlife
For traditional music, try the **Bards' Den** (⊠ Main St. ☎ 095/41042).

Shopping
Connemara Handcrafts (⊠ Village center ☎ 095/41058), on the N59, carries an extensive selection of crafts and women's fashions made by the stellar Avoca Handweavers; there's also a quaint coffee shop.

Kylemore Valley

㊱ *Runs for 6½ km (4 mi) between Letterfrack and intersection of N59 and R344.*

One of the more conventionally beautiful stretches of road in Connemara passes through Kylemore Valley, which is between the Twelve Bens to the south and the naturally forested Dorruagh Mountains to the north. Kylemore (the name is derived from Coill Mór, Irish for "big wood") looks "as though some colossal giant had slashed it out with a couple of strokes from his mammoth sword," as artist and author John FitzMaurice Mills has written. **Kylemore Abbey,** one of the most photographed castles in all of Ireland, is visible across a reedy lake with a backdrop of wooded hillside. The vast Gothic Revival, turreted, gray-stone castle was built as a private home between 1861 and 1868 by Mitchell Henry, a member of Parliament for County Galway, and his wife, Margaret, who had fallen in love with the spot during a carriage ride while on their honeymoon. The Henrys spared no expense—the final bill for their house is said to have come to £1.5 million—and employed mostly local laborers, thereby abetting the famine relief effort (this area was among the worst hit in all of Ireland). Adjacent to the house is a spectacular neo-Gothic church, which, sadly, became the burial place for Margaret, who died after contracting "Nile fever" on a trip to Egypt. In 1920, nuns from the

FodorsChoice
★

Irish Abbey of the Nuns of St. Benedict, who fled their abbey in Belgium during World War I, eventually sought refuge in Kylemore, which had been through a number of owners and decades of decline after the Henrys died. Still in residence, the Benedictine nuns run a girls' boarding school here. Three reception rooms and the main hall are open to the public, as are a crafts center and a simple cafeteria. There's also a 6-acre walled Victorian garden; a shuttle bus from the abbey departs every 15 minutes during opening hours for the garden. An exhibition and video explaining the history of the house can be viewed year-round at the abbey, and the grounds are freely accessible most of the year. Ask at the excellent crafts shop for directions to the **Gothic Chapel** (a five-minute walk from the abbey), a tiny replica of Norwich Cathedral built by the Henrys. (Norwich was built by the English Benedictines, in a felicitous anticipation of Kylemore's fate.) ⊠ *About ¾ km (½ mi) back from Kylemore Valley Rd.* ☎ *095/41146* ⊕ *www.kylemoreabbey.com* ⊠ *€11, including shuttle bus to garden* ☉ *Crafts shop, grounds, and cafeteria daily 10–6; exhibition and garden Easter–Nov., daily 9–5:30.*

Fodor's Choice   Beyond Kylemore, N59 travels for some miles along **Killary Harbour,** a
★   narrow fjord (the only one in Ireland) that runs for 16 km (10 mi) between County Mayo's Mweelrea Mountains to the north and County Galway's Dorruagh Mountains to the south. The dark, deep water of the fjord reflects the magnificent steep-sided hills that border it, creating a haunting scene of natural grandeur. The harbor has an extremely safe anchorage, 13 fathoms (78 feet) deep for almost its entire length and sheltered from storms by mountain walls. The rafts floating in Killary Harbour belong to fish-farming consortia that artificially raise salmon and trout in cages beneath the water. This is a matter of some controversy all over the West. Although some people welcome the employment opportunities, others bemoan the visual blight of the rafts. From April through October **Killary Cruises** (⊠ Nancy's Point, 2 km [1 mi] west of Leenane on N59 Clifden Rd. ☎ 091/566–736 ⊕ www.killarycruises.com) runs 1½-hour trips around Killary Harbour in an enclosed catamaran launch with seating for 150 passengers, plus a bar and restaurant.

Leenane

37   *18 km (11 mi) east of Letterfrack on N59.*

Nestled idyllically at the foot of the Maamturk Mountains and overlooking the tranquil waters of Killary Harbour, Leenane is a tiny village noted for its role as the setting for the film *The Field,* which starred Richard Harris. The **Sheep and Wool Centre,** in the center of Leenane, focuses on the traditional industry of North Connemara and West Mayo. More than 20 breeds of sheep graze around the house, and there are demonstrations of carding, spinning, weaving, and the dyeing of wool with natural plant dyes. ☎ *095/42323* ⊕ *www.leenane-connemara.com* ⊠ *€3* ☉ *Apr.–June, Sept., and Oct., daily 9:30–7; July and Aug., daily 9–7.*

Where to Stay & Eat

$$$$ ✕▢ **Delphi Mountain Resort & Spa.** Built entirely from natural materials, chiefly local stone and storm-felled timber, and topped off by a grass roof, the spa blends exquisitely into its stunningly beautiful surroundings. The design may seem futuristic, but in fact the curving corridors are meant to recall traditional Irish ring forts. While natural stone is used at every opportunity, indoors as well as out, the result is surprisingly comfortable; it helps that a massive turf fire, whose aroma penetrates the whole hotel, is lighted in the reception area every morning. Guest rooms continue the organic theme with natural fabrics and modern wood furnishings; all have either a

> ## IMAGE PROBLEM
>
> Martin McDonagh's *Leenane Trilogy*, featuring a cast of tragicomic grotesques, presents an unflattering view of rural Irish life. Although the plays were an international hit for Galway's Druid Theatre Company, it brought a renown that the people of Leenane presumably could have done without.

balcony or patio, and are decorated with contemporary paintings and ceramics. Large windows in the bar and restaurant enable you to make the most of the views of unspoiled hills all around. The Canadian chef, Jeff McCourt, is committed to using organic produce in short, strongly seasonal menus ($$$$) prepared in a contemporary Irish style. While a wide range of body-pampering therapies are offered in the spa, there's no gym: the idea is that you use the great outdoors as your gym, and staff will advise on suitable activities. The mountain air itself is a tonic, and, what's more, it's free. ⊠ *Co. Galway* ☎ *095/42208* 🖷 *095/42303* ⊕ *www.delphiescape.com* ⟿ *14 rooms, 8 suites* ⚘ *Restaurant, spa, fishing, bicycles, hiking, horseback riding, bar* ▤ *AE, MC, V* ⊗ *Closed mid-Dec.–mid-Jan.* ⑂ *BP.*

$$$ **Delphi Lodge.** In the heart of what is arguably Mayo's most spectacular mountain and lake scenery, 5 km (3 mi) east of Leenane off N59, this attractive Georgian sporting lodge heavily stocked with fishing paraphernalia has a lovely lakeside setting. Owners Peter and Jane Mantle are gracious hosts and valuable storehouses of information and stories. Fishing is the main attraction, but guests also come for the peace and quiet, or like England's Prince Charles, a recent visitor, to sketch the scenery. Pine furniture, floral curtains, and wonderfully comfortable beds fill the bright, spacious bedrooms, some with lake views. Don't expect a TV: because of the surrounding mountains, there's no reception. Guests dine together ($$$$) at a long oak table; there's an excellent wine list and a self-service bar. There are also cottages, which require a three-day minimum stay. ⊠ *Co. Galway* ☎ *095/42222* 🖷 *095/42296* ⊕ *www.delphilodge.ie* ⟿ *12 rooms, 5 cottages* ⚘ *Dining room, fishing, billiards, lounge, library; no a/c, no room TVs* ▤ *AE, MC, V* ⊗ *Closed mid-Dec.–mid-Jan.* ⑂ *BP.*

FodorsChoice ★

EN ROUTE You have two options for traveling onward to Westport. The first is to take the direct route on N59. The second is to detour through the **Doolough Valley** between the Mweelrea Mountains (to the west) and the Sheeffry Hills (to the east) and on to Westport via Louisburgh (on the southern shore of Clew Bay). The latter route adds about 24 km (15 mi) to the trip, but devotees of this part of the West claim that it will take you through the region's most impressive, unspoiled stretch of scenery. If you opt for the longer route, turn left onto R335 1½ km (1 mi) beyond Leenane. Just after this turn, you can hear the powerful rush of the Aasleagh Falls. You can park over the bridge, stroll along the river's shore, and soak in the splendor of the surrounding mountains.

Look out as you travel north for the great bulk of 2,500-foot-high **Croagh Patrick**; its size and conical shape make it one of the West's most distinctive landmarks. On clear days a small white building is visible at its summit (it stands on a ½-acre plateau), as is the wide path that ascends to it. The latter is the Pilgrim's Path. Each year about 25,000 people, many of them barefoot, follow the path to pray to St. Patrick in the oratory on its peak. St. Patrick spent the 40 days and nights of Lent here in 441, during the period in which he was converting Ireland to Christianity. The traditional date for the pilgrimage is the last Sunday in July; in the past, the walk was made at night, with pilgrims carrying burning torches, but that practice has been discontinued. The climb involves a gentle uphill slope, but you need to be fit and agile to complete the last half-hour, over scree (small loose rocks with no trail). This is why most climbers carry a stick or staff (traditionally made of ash, and called an ash plant), which helps you to stop sliding backward. These can sometimes be bought in the car park. The hike can be made in about three hours (round-trip) on any fine day and is well worth the effort for the magnificent views of the islands of Clew Bay, the Sheeffry Hills to the south (with the Bens visible behind them), and the peaks of Mayo to the north. The climb starts at Murrisk, a village about 8 km (5 mi) before Westport on the R335 Louisburgh road.

Westport

★ ❸ *32 km (20 mi) north of Leenane on R335.*

By far the most attractive town in County Mayo, Westport is on an inlet of Clew Bay, a wide expanse of sea dotted with islands and framed by mountain ranges. One of the most gentrified and Anglo-Irish heritage towns in Ireland, its Georgian origins are clearly defined by the broad streets skirting the gently flowing river and, particularly, by the lime-fringe central avenue called the Mall. Built as an O'Malley stronghold, the entire town received a face-lift when the Brownes, who came from Sussex in the reign of Elizabeth I, constructed Westport House and much of the modern town, which was laid out by architect James Wyatt when he was employed to finish the grand estate of Westport House. Today Westport's streets radiate from its central **Octagon,** where an old-fashioned farmers' market is held on Thursday mornings; look for work clothes, harnesses, tools, and children's toys for sale. Traditional shops—of ironmongers, drapers, and the like—dot the streets that lead to the Octagon, while a riverside mall is lined with tall lime trees. At Westport's Quay, about 2 km (1 mi) outside town, a large warehouse has been attractively restored as holiday apartments, and there are some good bars and decent restaurants.

The showpiece of the town remains **Westport House and Country Park,** a stately home built on the site of an earlier castle (believed to have been the home of the 16th-century warrior queen, Grace O'Malley) and most famed for its setting right on the shores of a beautiful lake. The house was begun in 1730 to the designs of Richard Castle, added to in 1778, and completed in 1788 by architect James Wyatt for the Marquess of Sligo of the Browne family. The rectangular, three-story house is furnished with late-Georgian and Victorian pieces. Family portraits by Opie and Reynolds, a huge collection of old Irish silver and old Waterford glass, plus an opulent group of paintings—including *The Holy Family* by Rubens—are on display. A word of caution: Westport isn't your usual staid country house. The old dungeons now house video games and the grounds have given way to a small amusement park for children and a children's zoo. In fact, the lake is now littered with swan-shaped "pedaloes," boats that may be fun for families but help destroy the perfect Georgian grace of the setting. If these elements don't sound like a draw, arrive early when it's less likely to be busy. The Farmyard area has garden-plant sales, an indoor soft-play area, a gift shop, and a coffee shop. ⊠ *Off N59 south of Westport turnoff, clearly signposted from Octagon* ☎ *098/25430* ⊕ *www.westporthouse.ie* ✉ *House €9.50; attractions €18, family day-ticket for all attractions €59* ☉ *House and gardens, Mar., Sun.–Fri., 11:30–4; Apr.–June and Sept., Sun.–Fri., 11:30–5. July and Aug., Sun.–Fri., 11:30–6. Grounds and attractions, May, Sun. and holidays 11:30–5; June, Sun–Weds. 11:30–5, July and Aug. Sun.–Fri., 11:30–6.*

Clew Bay is said to have 365 islands, one for every day of the year. The biggest and most interesting to visit is **Clare Island**, at the mouth of the bay. In fine weather the rocky, hilly island, which is 8 km (5 mi) long and 5 km (3 mi) wide, affords beautiful views south toward Connemara, east across Clew Bay, and north to Achill Island. About 150 people live on the island today, but before the 1845–47 famine it had a population of about 1,700. A 15th-century tower overlooking the harbor was once the stronghold of Granuaile, the pirate queen, who ruled the area until her death in 1603. She is buried on the island, in its 12th-century Cistercian abbey. Today most visitors seek out the island for its unusual peace and quiet, golden beaches, and unspoiled landscape. Ferries depart from Roonagh Pier, near Louisburgh, a scenic 19-km (12-mi) drive from Westport on R335 past several long sandy beaches. The crossing takes about 15 minutes. Dolphins often accompany the boats on the trip, and there are large populations of seals under the island's cliffs. Bird-watchers, hikers, cyclists, and sea anglers may want to stay for longer than a day trip; inquire at the Westport TIO or call the **Clare Island Development Office** (☎ 098/25087) for information about accommodations on the island. ☎ *098/25045 O'Malley's Ferries, 098/25212 Pirate Queen boat* ✉ *Ferry €16 round-trip* ☉ *Sailings usually twice daily, May–mid-Sept., weather permitting.*

Where to Stay & Eat

★ **$$–$$$** ✕ **Quay Cottage.** Fishing nets, glass floats, lobster pots, and greenery hang from the high-pitched, exposed-beam roof of this tiny waterside cottage at the entrance to Westport House. It's an informal wine bar and a shellfish restaurant. Rush-seat chairs, polished oak tables, and an open fire in the evenings add to the comfortable, none-too-formal atmosphere. Try the chowder special (a thick vegetable and mussel soup), garlic-butter crab claws, or a half-pound steak fillet, and be sure to sample the homemade brown bread and ice cream. ⊠ *The Quay* ☎ *098/26412* ▤ *AE, MC, V* ☉ *Closed Jan., Sun. and Mon. Nov.–Easter.*

$$$$ ✕▥ **Newport House.** This handsome, riverside Georgian house dominates the village of Newport, 12 km (7 mi) north of Westport on N59. Kieran and Thelma Thompson's grand and elegant private home has spacious public rooms furnished with gilt-frame family portraits, Regency mirrors and chairs, handwoven Donegal carpeting, and crystal chandeliers. A sweeping staircase leads to the bedrooms, which are decorated with pretty chintz drapes and a mix of Victorian antiques and old furniture. Most bedrooms have sitting areas and good views of the gardens. Home-smoked salmon and fresh local seafood are specialties on the traditional four-course set dinner menu; the ice cream is also homemade. ⊠ *Newport, Co. Mayo* ☎ *098/41222* ▤ *098/41613* ⊕ *www.newporthouse. ie* ➬ *19 rooms* ⚐ *Restaurant, fishing, bar; no a/c, no room TVs* ▤ *AE, DC, MC, V* ☉ *Closed mid-Oct.–mid-Mar.* ▯◯▮ *BP.*

★ $$ ✕▥ **Olde Railway Hotel.** When the English novelist William Makepeace Thackeray stayed here in 1842, he called it "one of the prettiest, comfortablist inns in Ireland." You can understand why. Fishing trophies, Victorian plates, framed prints, and watercolors brighten up the lobby and lounge of this unusual, family-run inn. A fascinating mix of Victorian and older antiques decorates the sunny bedrooms, which have double-glaze Georgian sash windows. Delightfully, the rooms overlook either the Carrowbeg River or the pretty gardens. The pretty glass-pane Conservatory Restaurant ($$$$) serves fresh local produce and game specialties and the bar has an excellent, good-value menu. ⊠ *The Mall, Co. Mayo* ☎ *098/ 25166* ▤ *098/25090* ⊕ *www.theolderailwayhotel.com* ➬ *15 rooms* ⚐ *Restaurant, cable TV, fishing, bicycles, bar; no a/c* ▤ *AE, MC, V* ▯◯▮ *BP.*

Nightlife

A good spot to try for traditional music and good pub grub is the **Towers Pub and Restaurant** (⊠ The Quay ☎ 098/26534). In summer there are outdoor tables set up here beside the bay. In Westport's town center try **Matt Molloy's** (⊠ Bridge St. ☎ 098/26655); Matt Malloy is not only the owner but also a member of the musical group the Chieftains. Traditional music is, naturally, the main attraction.

Sports & the Outdoors

BICYCLING Enjoy the spectacular scenery of Clew Bay at a leisurely pace on a rented bike from **J. P. Breheny & Sons** (⊠ Castlebar St. ☎ 098/25020).

FISHING Fishing tackle, bait, and licenses can be obtained at **Hewetson Bros** (⊠ Bridge St. ☎ 098/26018). To book a place for the day on a deep-sea-fishing boat operating out of Westport's Clew Bay, contact **Francis Clarke or Austin Gill** (☎ 098/25481).

GOLF The Fred Hawtree–designed **Westport Golf Club** (⊠ Carrowholly ☎ 098/ 28262), beneath Croagh Patrick, overlooks Clew Bay. The 18-hole, par-73 course has twice been the venue for the Irish Amateur Championship.

Shopping

Carraig Donn (⊠ Bridge St. ☎ 098/26287) carries its own line of knitwear and a good selection of crystal, jewelry, and ceramics. **McCormack's**

(⊠ Bridge St. ☎ 098/25619) has a traditional butcher shop downstairs, but upstairs it's an attractive gallery and café with work by local artists for sale. **O'Reilly/Turpin** (⊠ Bridge St. ☎ 098/28151) sells the best of contemporary Irish design in knitwear, ceramics, and other decorative items. **Satch Kiely** (⊠ Westport Quay ☎ 098/25775) carries fine antique furniture and decorative pieces. **Treasure Trove** (⊠ Bridge St. ☎ 098/25118) has a good stock of antiques and curios, including linen and local memorabilia. **Westport Crystal** (⊠ The Quay ☎ 098/27780) is a factory outlet that sells exclusive stemware and giftware.

Castlebar

39 *18 km (11 mi) east of Westport on N5.*

The administrative capital of Mayo, Castlebar is a tidy little town with an attractive, tree-bordered green. Hatred of landlords ran high in the area, due to the ruthless, battering-ram evictions ordered by the earl of Lucan during the mid-19th-century famine. The disappearance in the 1960s of his high-living successor, the seventh earl, after the violent death in London of his children's nanny, is said to have given the few tenants who remain a perfect pretext for withholding their rents. In 1879 Michael Davitt founded the Land League, which fought for land reform, in the **Imperial Hotel** (⊠ The Green ☎ 094/902–1961); it's worth a visit to take in the splendor of the decor in the Gothic-style dining room, which was used for many historic meetings in the 19th century. At the **Linen Hall Arts Centre** (⊠ Linenhall St. ☎ 094/902–3733), exhibitions and performances are often scheduled.

Turlough

40 *6½ km (4 mi) east of Castlebar on N5.*

Before the opening of the Museum of Country Life, Turlough was chiefly visited for its round tower (freely accessible), which marks the site of an early monastery, traditionally associated with St. Patrick, and the nearby ruins of a 17th-century church. Nowadays, it's one of many Irish villages whose empty streets bear witness to dramatic changes in the rural way of life. Once a thriving hub, with a village school, two pubs, and a busy shop, Turlough now has a population of about 300, one pub with a small shop attached, and no school. Rather than working on the land, most of the locals commute to jobs in nearby Castlebar. To understand the forces that have led to such dramatic changes in Turlough, pay a visit to the **Museum of Country Life,** which focuses on rural Ireland between 1860 and 1960—a way of life that remained unchanged for many years, then suddenly came to an end within living memory. At this highly acclaimed museum, the only branch of the National Museum of Ireland outside Dublin, you're invited to imagine yourself back in a vanished world, before the internal combustion engine, rural electrification, indoor plumbing, television, and increased education transformed people's lives and expectations. For many, this is a journey into a strange place, where water had to be carried from a well, turf had to be brought home from the bog, fires had to be lighted daily for

FodorsChoice ★

heat and cooking, and clothes had to be made painstakingly by hand in the long winter evenings. Among the displayed items are authentic furniture and utensils; hunting, fishing, and agricultural implements; clothing; and objects relating to games, pastimes, religion, and education.

The museum experience starts in Turlough Park House, built in the High Victorian Gothic style in 1865 and set in pretty lakeside gardens. Just three rooms have been restored to illustrate the way the landowners lived. A sensational modern four-story, curved building houses the main exhibit. Cleverly placed windows allow panoramic views of the surrounding park and the distant round tower, allowing you to reflect on the reality beyond the museum's walls. Temporary exhibitions, such as one called "Romanticism and Reality," help illustrate the divide between the dreamy image of old rural life and its actual hardships. The shop sells museum-branded and handcrafted gift items as well as a good selection of books on related topics. A café with indoor and outdoor tables is in the stable yard, and you can take scenic lakeside walks in the park. Crafts demonstrations and workshops take place on Wednesday and Sunday afternoons. ⊠ *Turlough Park* ☎ *01/648–6453 in Dublin* ⊕ *www. museum.ie* ☑ *Free* ☉ *Tues.–Sat. 10–5, Sun. 2–5.*

EN ROUTE As you travel from Turlough northeast to Ballina, you have a choice of two routes. The longer and more scenic is via the tiny, wooded village of Pontoon, skirting the western shore of Lough Conn and passing through the rough bogland of the Glen of Nephin, beneath the dramatic heather-clad slopes of Nephin Mountain (2,653 feet). The shorter route follows N5 and N58 to Foxford, a pretty village with several crafts and antiques shops. A good place for a break is the **Foxford Woolen Mills Visitor Center,** where you can explore the crafts shop and grab a bite at the restaurant. The "Foxford Experience" tells the story of the wool mill, famous for its tweeds and blankets, from the time of the famine in the mid-19th century—when it was founded by the Sisters of Charity to combat poverty—to the present day. ⊠ *Lower Main St., Foxford* ☎ *094/ 925–6756* ☑ *€8* ☉ *Nov.–Apr., Mon.–Sat. 10–6, Sun. 2–6; May–Oct., Mon.–Sat. 10–6, Sun. noon–6; tour every 20 min.*

Ballina

㊶ *34 km (22 mi) northeast of Turlough.*

Ballina's chief attraction is fishing for salmon and trout in the River Moy and nearby Lough Conn. With a population of 7,500, this is the largest town in County Mayo. To some eyes, Ballina's town center may appear rundown, but its unspoiled, old-fashioned shops and pubs contain many treasures. Try the bar food (Mon.–Sat. 11 AM–6 PM) at **Gaughan's** (⊠ O'Rahilly St. ☎ 096/21151), where the classic wooden interior dates from the mid-19th century.

Where to Stay & Eat

$$ **Fodor'sChoice** ★   ✕🛏 **Enniscoe House.** Magnificent and magical, this pink, square Georgian mansion is dramatically sited on the shores of Lough Conn under towering Mount Nephin. However, there's nothing intimidating about its interior, even though its well-worn grandeur is steeped in history. Susan

Kellett is a descendant of the original family who arrived here in the 1660s, and will give you the story behind the many ancestral portraits staring at you from the calico-flocked library walls. Your jaw may drop at the sight of the magisterial main salon—a vast room done in stately house ivories and beiges, swathed in period wallpapers and draperies, set with 18th-century breakfronts, gilded French side tables, Chippendale mahogany chairs, gilt-frame paintings, and enough cozy corners to please even a Jane Austen. A maze of quirky corridors and staircases leads to the guest rooms, which are both charming and characterful, with candy-stripe wallpapers, floral drapes on tall sash windows, and massive beds (some four-posters are so high you need a step ladder to get in). The beauty continues outside, as the demesne's 150 acres are crisscrossed with walks and have more than 3 km (2 mi) of peaceful lakeshore. All paths lead to the 5 acres of Victorian gardens, now under restoration. Here you can find historic farm buildings converted into offices housing independent organizations, including a Mayo genealogy center, an antiques shop, and a tearoom. Meals ($$$$; reserve ahead) include fruits and vegetables grown in the organic garden. There are also four self-catering apartments. The house lies 4½ km (3 mi) south of Crossmolina and 20 km (12½ mi) west of Ballina. All in all, this is a hotel that remains a fabulous destination in itself. Go! ⊠ *Castlehill, near Crossmolina, Co. Mayo* ☎ *096/31112* 🖷 *096/31773* ⊕ *www.enniscoe.com* 🛏 *6 rooms* ♿ *Restaurant, fishing, some pets allowed; no a/c, no room TVs* ▤ *AE, MC, V* ⊗ *Closed Nov.–Mar.* ⦿ *BP.*

Sports & the Outdoors

BICYCLING Head for the coast north of Ballina on a bike from **Gerry's Cycle Center** (⊠ 6 Lord Edward St. ☎ 096/70455).

FISHING Fishing bait, tackle, and licenses can be obtained from **John Walkin** (⊠ Tone St. ☎ 096/22442).

GOLF **Ballina Golf Club** (⊠ Bonniconlon Rd. ☎ 096/21718) is an 18-hole parkland course, built in 1924, 1½ km (1 mi) from the town center; you can rent golf clubs here. The 18-hole **Carne Golf Links** (⊠ Belmullet ☎ 097/82292), at Belmullet Golf Club, 72 km (45 mi) west of Ballina, is one of Ireland's renowned links courses.

Shopping

McGrath's Food and Delicatessen (⊠ O'Rahilly St. ☎ 096/21198) is an old-fashioned grocery, handy for picnic ingredients.

THE WEST ESSENTIALS

To research prices, get advice from other travelers, and book travel arrangements, visit www.fodors.com.

Transportation

If you're traveling extensively by public transportation, be sure to load up on information (the best taxi-for-call companies, rail and bus schedules, etc.) upon arriving at the ticket counter or help desk of the bigger train and bus stations in the area, such as Galway City and Westport.

BY AIR

Aer Arann has two flights a day from London's Luton Airport and four a day from Dublin to Galway Airport (GWY). Aer Arann also flies to Edinburgh, Manchester, Lorient, and Liverpool from Galway. Ryanair flies to Knock daily from London's Stansted Airport and from Gatwick Airport; flying time is 80 minutes. BmiBaby flies to Knock from Manchester daily.

Aer Arann has four flights daily on weekdays and two flights on weekends to the Oileáin Árainn (Aran Islands) from Connemara Airport in Inverin. During July and August planes leave every half hour. The flights call at all three Aran Islands. The journey takes about six minutes and costs about €44 round-trip. The airline will book a B&B for you when you book your flight. Ask about other special offers at the time of booking.

🖬 Carriers **Aer Arann** ☎ 091/593–034. **Aer Lingus** ☎ 01/844–4747. **BmiBaby** ☎ 1890/340122. **Ryanair** ☎ 01/844–4411.

AIRPORTS

The West's most convenient international airport is Shannon, 25 km (16 mi) east of Ennis in the southwest. See Chapter 5, The Southwest. Galway Airport, near Galway City, is used mainly for internal flights, with steadily increasing U.K. traffic. Knock International Airport, at Charlestown—near Knock, in County Mayo—has direct daily service to London's Stansted, Luton, and Gatwick, and to Manchester and Birmingham. A small airport for internal traffic only is at Knockrowen, Castlebar, in County Mayo. Flying time from Dublin is 25 to 30 minutes to all airports. No scheduled flights run from the United States to Galway or Knock; use Shannon Airport. Connemara Airport at Inverin, which is 29 km (18 mi) west of Galway on R336, services the Aran Islands.

🖬 Airport Information **Connemara Airport** ☎ 091/593–034. **Galway Airport** ☎ 091/752–874 ⊕ www.galwayairport.com. **Knock International Airport** ☎ 094/936–7222 ⊕ www.knockairport.com. **Shannon Airport** ☎ 061/471–444 ⊕ www.shannonairport.com.

TRANSFERS From Shannon Airport you can pick up a rental car to drive into the West, or you can take a bus to Limerick, from which there are bus connections into the West. Galway Airport is 6½ km (4 mi) from Galway City. No regular bus service is available from the airport to Galway, but most flight arrivals are taken to Galway Rail Station in the city center by an airline courtesy coach. Inquire when you book. A taxi from the airport to the city center costs about €15. If you're flying to Knock International Airport, you can pick up your rental car at the airport. Otherwise, inquire at the time of booking about transport to your final destination. There's a bus link to Charlestown where you can connect with Bus Éireann's national network. Connemara Airport is 27 km from Galway City, and is accessible by shuttle bus.

BY BOAT & FERRY

A ferry leaves Tarbert for Killimer every hour on the half hour and takes 20 minutes to cross the Shannon Estuary from North County Kerry to

West County Clare; this saves you a 137-km (85-mi) drive through Limerick City. The ferry runs every day of the year except Christmas and costs €15 one-way, €25 round-trip. (Ferries return from Killimer every hour on the hour.)

There are several options for traveling to the Oileáin Árainn (Aran Islands). Aran Ferries runs a boat to the islands from Ros an Mhil (Rossaveal), 32 km (20 mi) west of Galway City, which makes the crossing in 20 minutes and costs about €28 round-trip (or, weather permitting, you can opt for a boat that takes an hour, costing about €20), including the shuttle bus from Galway. If you're heading for Inis Oirr (Inisheer), the smallest island, the shortest crossing is from Doolin in County Clare. Aran Ferries offers service from Doolin Pier, with up to 12 sailings daily, from June through the end of September. The crossing takes about 20 minutes and costs €20 round-trip.

Island Ferries, which has a booking office in the TIO (Travel Information Office) in Galway City, has a one-hour crossing from Ros an Mhil (Rossaveal) for €25 round-trip, with up to five sailings a day in summer, weather permitting. Bicycles are transported free off-season, but there may be a charge in July and August: inquire when booking. There's lively competition between the ferry companies, so shop around for the best deal. Discounts are available for families, students, and groups of four or more. If you want to stay a night or two on the islands, ask about accommodations when booking your ferry, as there are some very good deals. Between June and September, O'Brien Shipping (a subsidiary of Doolin Ferries) sails for the Aran Islands from Galway Docks, a five-minute walk from Eyre Square. The ferries run three times a week in June and September (usually Tuesday, Thursday, and Saturday), daily in July and August. The crossing takes 90 minutes and costs €20 round-trip.

For travel between the Aran Islands, frequent interisland ferries (run by Aran Ferries, Island Ferries, and O'Brien Ferries) are available in summer, but tickets are nontransferable, so ask the captain of your ferry about the interisland schedule if you plan to visit more than one island; otherwise, your trip can become expensive. You can purchase ferry tickets on the island or at the TIO in Galway.

🚢 **Boat & Ferry Information Aran Ferries** ✉ Travel Information Office, Forster St., Eyre Sq., Galway City ☎ 091/568-903 or 091/537-700 ⊕ www.aranislandferries.com. **Doolin Ferries** ✉ Doolin Pier, Co. Clare ☎ 065/707-4455 ⊕ www.doolinferries.com. **Island Ferries** ✉ Kinlay Hostel, Eyre Sq., Galway City ☎ 091/568-903, 091/572-273 evenings ⊕ www.aranislandferries.com. **O'Brien Shipping** ✉ New Docks, Galway City ☎ 091/567-676 ⊕ www.doolinferries.com. **Tarbert-Killimer Ferry** ☎ 065/905-3124 ⊕ www.shannonferries.com.

BY BUS

Bus Éireann runs several expressway buses into the region from Dublin, Cork City, and Limerick City to Ennis, Galway City, Westport, and Ballina, the principal depots in the region. Expect bus rides to last about one hour longer than the time it would take you to travel the distance by car. In July and August, the provincial bus service is augmented by daily services to most resort towns. Outside these months, many coastal towns receive only one or two buses per week. Bus routes are often slow and circuitous, and service can be erratic. A copy of the Bus Éireann timetable (€1.50 from any station) is essential. Citylink operates frequent buses, with up to 17 departures daily, between Galway City and Dublin and Dublin Airport. The trip costs €13 one-way. Citylink also makes five daily trips in each direction between Shannon Airport and Galway City, costing €15 one way.

🚌 Bus Depots **Ballina Station** ☎ 096/71800. **Ennis Station** ☎ 065/682-4177. **Galway City Station** (Ceannt Station) ☎ 091/562-000. **Westport Station** ☎ 098/25711. 🚌 Bus Lines **Bus Éireann** ☎ 01/836-6111 in Dublin, 061/313-333 in Limerick, 021/508-188 in Cork ⊕ www.buseireann.ie. **Citylink** ✉ Unit 1, Forster Ct., Galway City ☎ 091/564-163 ⊕ www.citylink.ie.

BY CAR

A car is the best means of traveling within the West. The 219-km (136-mi) Dublin–Galway trip takes about three hours. From Cork City take N20 through Mallow and N21 to Limerick City, picking up the N18 Ennis–Galway road in Limerick. The 209-km (130-mi) drive from Cork to Galway takes about three hours. From Killarney the shortest and most pleasant route to cover the 193 km (120 mi) to Galway (three hours) is to take N22 to Tralee, then N69 through Listowel to Tarbert and the ferry across the Shannon Estuary to Killimer in County Clare. From there, join N68 in Kilrush, and then pick up N18 in Ennis.

ROAD CONDITIONS The West has good, wide main roads (National Primary Routes) and better-than-average local roads (National Secondary Routes), both known as "N" routes. If you stray off the beaten track on the smaller Regional ("R") or unnumbered routes, particularly in Connemara and County Mayo, you may encounter some hazardous mountain roads. Narrow, steep, and twisty, they are also frequented by untended sheep, cows, and ponies grazing "the long acre" (as the strip of grass beside the road is called) or simply straying in search of greener pastures. If you find a sheep in your path, just sound the horn, and it should scramble away. A good maxim for these roads is: "you never know what's around the next corner." Bear this in mind, and adjust your speed accordingly. Hikers and cyclists constitute an additional hazard on narrow roads.

Within the Connemara Irish-speaking area, signs are in Irish only. The main signs to recognize are Gaillimh (Galway), Ros an Mhil (Rossaveal), An Teach Doite (Maam Cross), and Sraith Salach (Recess).

ROAD MAPS A good map, available through newsagents and TIOs (Travel Information Offices), gives Irish and English names where needed.

TAXIS Within Galway City taxis operate on the meter. Outside the city, agree on the fare in advance. Sample fares include Galway to Moycullen €16, to Salthill €10; Shannon Airport to Galway City €115; Knock Airport to Galway City €108.

Galway Taxis (☎ 091/561–111 ⊕ www.galwaytaxi.com). **Big O Taxis** (☎ 091/585–858 ⊕ www.bigotaxis.com).

BY TRAIN

The region's main rail stations are in Galway City, Westport, and Ballina. For County Clare, travel from Cork City, Killarney, or Dublin's Heuston Station to Limerick City and continue the journey by bus. Trains for Galway, Westport, and Ballina leave from Dublin's Heuston Station. The journey time to Galway is 3 hours; to Ballina, 3¾ hours; and to Westport, 3½ hours.

Rail service within the region is limited. The major destinations of Galway City and Westport/Ballina are on different branch lines. Connections can only be made between Galway and the other two cities by traveling inland for about an hour to Athlone.

🚆 Train Information **Irish Rail–Iarnod Éireann** ⊕ www.irishrail.ie/home. **Ballina Station** ☎ 096/71818. **Galway Station** ☎ 091/564-222. **Heuston Station** ☎ 01/836-6222. **Limerick City Station** ☎ 061/315-555. **Westport Station** ☎ 098/25253.

TRANSPORTATION AROUND THE WEST

A car is helpful in the West, especially from September through June. Although the main cities of the area are easily reached from the rest of Ireland by rail or bus, transport within the region can be sparse. If a rental car is out of the question, one option is to make Galway your base and take day tours (available mid-June through September) west to Connemara and south to the Burren, and a day or overnight trip to the Aran Islands. Of course, it *is* possible to explore the region by local and intercity bus services, but have no illusions that buses run every hour.

Contacts & Resources

CAR RENTAL

If you haven't already booked a rental car at Shannon Airport, try the following rental agencies.

🚗 Agencies **Avis** ⊠ Galway Airport ☎ 091/568-886. **Avis** ⊠ Knock International Airport, Charlestown ☎ 094/936-7707. **Budget** ⊠ Eyre Sq., Galway City ☎ 091/566-376. **Budget** ⊠ Knock International Airport, Charlestown ☎ 090/662-4668. **Casey's Auto Rentals** ⊠ Turlough Rd., Castlebar ☎ 094/902-4618. **Casey's Auto Rentals** ⊠ Knock international Airport, Charlestown ☎ 094/902-1411. **Diplomat Rent A Car** ⊠ Knock International Airport, Charlestown ☎ 094/936-7252. **Euro Mobil** ⊠ Tuam Rd., Galway City ☎ 091/753-037. **Hertz Rent A Car** ⊠ Galway Airport ☎ 091/752-502. **Hertz Rent A Car** ⊠ Knock International Airport, Charlestown ☎ 094/936-7333. **Johnson & Perrot** ⊠ Headford Rd., Galway City ☎ 091/568-886.

EMERGENCIES

For a doctor or dentist in County Clare, contact the Mid-Western Health Board (in County Limerick); in Counties Galway and Mayo, contact the Western Health Board.

🚑 Doctors & Dentists **Mid-Western Health Board** ⊠ Catherine St., Limerick ☎ 061/316-655. **Western Health Board** ⊠ Merlin Park, Galway City ☎ 091/751-131.

🚑 Emergency Services **Ambulance, fire, police** ☎ 999.

🚑 Pharmacies **Matt O'Flaherty** ⊠ 39 Eyre Sq., Galway City ☎ 091/562-927. **O'Donnell's** ⊠ Bridge St., Westport ☎ 098/25163.

INTERNET, MAIL & SHIPPING

Most hotels in the West now offer some form of Internet access. The Internet cafés below also offer printing, photocopying, faxing, and money transfers. Post Offices generally open weekdays 9 AM–5:30 PM and Saturday 9 AM–1 PM. Smaller branches may close between 1 PM and 2 PM.

🔲 Internet Cafés **Neat Surf Technologies** ⊠ 7 Francis St., Galway City ☎ 091/533-976. **Net£access** ⊠ Olde Malt Arcade, Galway City ☎ 091/535-470.
🔲 Post Offices **Ennis GPO** ⊠ Bank Place, Ennis ☎ 065/682-1054. **Galway City GPO** ⊠ 3 Eglinton St., Galway City ☎ 091/563-768. **Westport GPO** ⊠ The Mall, Westport ☎ 098/25219.

TOUR OPTIONS

Galway City's TIO (Travel Information Office) has details of walking tours of Galway, which are organized by request. All TIOs in the West provide lists of suggested cycle tours.

The only full- and half-day guided bus tours in the region start from Galway. Bus Éireann coordinates two full-day tours, one covering Connemara and the other the Burren (each €18). Tours run from early June to mid-October only, with the widest choice available between mid-July and mid-August. Book in advance at the Galway City TIO, Ceannt Railway Station on Eyre Square, or the Salthill TIO, which also serve as departure points.

Lally Tours runs a day tour through Connemara and County Mayo and another to the Burren. It also operates a vintage double-decker bus, departing from Eyre Square, which runs hourly tours of Galway City from 10:30 AM until 4:30 PM from mid-March to October; tickets cost €10.

O'Neachtain Day Tours operates full-day tours of Connemara and the Burren. Tickets, €22 each, can be purchased from the Galway City TIO; tours depart across the street.

Healy Tours offers historical sightseeing tours with professional guides, including Kylemore Abbey and Connemara or the Cliffs of Moher and the Burren. Tickets, €22 each, can be purchased from the Galway and Salthill Tourist Information Offices or on the tour bus.

Burren Walking Holidays organizes two- and three-night guided walking tours of the Burren on weekends between mid-March and September. Walks are graded according to ability, and are mostly on "green roads" (grassy pathways) with great views over the Atlantic. In early summer there are a series of special themed weekends on wildflowers, environmental heritage, and farming traditions. Contact Mary Howard at the Carrigann Hotel in Lisdoonvarna, County Clare.

The Connemara Walking Centre in Clifden, run by leading archeologist Michael Gibbons, organizes everything from daylong mountain treks to weeklong holidays.

Also based in Clifden, Connemara Safari Walking Holidays offers five- and seven-day residential walking holidays starting in either Clifden or

Westport. They specialize in "island-hopping" and will take you to remote islands for some unforgettable walks.

Croagh Patrick Walking Holidays runs weeklong walking holidays between April and September, based in B&B accommodations in the countryside near Westport on Clew Bay. Prices include pickup from Shannon Airport, all transfers to and from walks, and the services of an experienced guide. Contact Gerry Greensmyth in Belclare, Westport, County Mayo.

⛨ Tours **Burren Walking Holidays** ✉ Carrigann Hotel, Lidsoonvarna, Co. Clare ☎ 065/ 707-4036 ⊕ www.gateway-to-the-burren.com. **Bus Éireann** ☎ 091/562-000. **Ceannt Railway Station** ☎ 091/562-000. **Connemara Safari Walking Holidays** ✉ Sky Rd., Clifden, Co. Galway ☎ 095/21071 ⊕ www.walkingconnemara.com. **Connemara Walking Centre** ✉ Island House, Market St., Clifden, Co. Galway ☎ 095/21492 ⊕ www. walkingireland.com. **Healy Tours** ☎ 091/770-066 ⊕ www.healytours.ie. **Lally Tours** ☎ 091/ 562-905 ⊕ www.lallytours.com. **Croagh Patrick Walking Holidays** ✉ Belclare, Westport, Co. Mayo ☎ 098/26090 ⊕ www.walkingguideireland.com. **O'Neachtain Day Tours** ☎ 091/553-188 ⊕ www.oneachtaintours.com. **Salthill TIO** ☎ 091/520-500.

VISITOR INFORMATION

Bord Fáilte provides free information service, tourist literature, and an accommodations booking service at its TIOs (Travel Information Offices). The following offices are open all year, generally weekdays 9–6, daily during the high season: Aran Islands (Inis Mór), Ennis, Galway City, Oughterard, and Westport.

Other TIOs, which operate seasonally, generally weekdays 9–6 and Saturday 9–1, are open as follows: Achill (June–August), Ballina (April–October), Castlebar (May–mid-September), Clifden (March–October), Cliffs of Moher (April–October), Kilkee (May–August), Kilrush (June–August), Salthill (May–September), Thoor Ballylee (April–mid-October).

⛨ Tourist Information The areas covered in this chapter come under two different regional headquarters of tourism: Shannon ⊕ www.shannonregiontourism.ie and West of Ireland ⊕ www.irelandwest.ie. The following come under Shannon: Cliffs of Moher, Ennis, and Kilrush. All the rest are Ireland West. **Oileáin Árainn (Aran Islands)–Inis Mór (Inishmore)** ✉ Co. Galway ☎ 099/61263 🖷 099/61420. **Ballina** ✉ Cathedral Rd., Co. Mayo ☎ 096/974-2604. **Clifden** ✉ Galway Rd., Co. Galway ☎ 095/21163. **Cliffs of Moher** ✉ Co. Clare ☎ 065/708-1171. **Ennis** ✉ Arthur's Row, Town Center, Co. Clare ☎ 065/ 682-8366 ⊕ www.ennis.ie. **Galway City** ✉ Forster St., Eyre Sq., Co. Galway ☎ 091/537- 700 ⊕ www.irelandwest.ie. **Oughterard** ✉ Main St., Co. Galway ☎ 091/552-808. **Salthill** ✉ The Promenade, Co. Galway ☎ 091/520-500. **Thoor Ballylee** ✉ Near Gort, Co. Clare ☎ 091/631-436. **Westport** ✉ The Mall, Co. Mayo ☎ 098/25711 🖷 098/26709.

The Northwest

INCLUDING COUNTIES DONEGAL, LEITRIM, AND SLIGO

Ramelton harbor, County Donegal

WORD OF MOUTH

"County Sligo is chock-full of sightseeing possibilities and is one of Ireland's most underrated, underexplored regions. Just outside Sligo town is Drumcliff, the final resting place of W. B. Yeats. His gravesite is in a churchyard in the shadow of the great Ben Bulben, a flat-topped peak that is one of the most memorable sights in all Ireland. Drumcliff also features a fine 10th-century High Cross and a Round Tower."

—DavidD

www.fodors.com/forums

WELCOME TO THE NORTHWEST

TOP REASONS TO GO

★ **Gaeltacht Country:** Venture to the seaside village of Ard an Ratha to listen to the seductive rhythms of locals conversing in full Irish (Gaelic) flight. Don't worry: everyone has English at the ready for lost visitors.

★ **The Yeats Trail:** From Sligo Town's museums head out to the majestic Ben Bulben peak to follow in the footsteps of the famous brother duo, W. B. Yeats, the great poet, and Jack B. Yeats, one of Ireland's finest 20th-century painters.

★ **Garbo's Shangri-la:** The legendary screen actress was just one of the many notables who enjoyed a stay at Glenveagh Castle.

★ **Hiking the Slieve League cliffs:** To truly humble yourself before ocean, cliff, and sky, hike these fabled headlands, the highest sea cliffs in Europe. The views will set your heart racing and the Atlantic sea winds are sure to blow away the cobwebs.

Greencastle Fishing Port, Inishowen Head, County Donegal

1 Yeats Country: What the poet William Butler Yeats would say about his native **Sligo Town**—a once picturesque spot now overrun with modern shopping malls—can only be imagined but it makes a great jumping-off point for exploring Yeats Country: the lake isle at **Innisfree,** the cairn-crowned **Knocknarea** (a peak often painted by brother Jack), and **Drumcliff,** where W. B. lies buried under the shadow of Ben Bulben.

Hiking in Sligo

Gleann Cholm Cille, County Donegal

2 Around Donegal Bay: **Donegal Town,** with its fine medieval castle and abbey, is the gateway to County Donegal, regarded by many as the runner-up to Kerry as Ireland's most scenic region. This is the ever-shrinking heart of the Donegal Gaeltacht (Irish-speaking region), where the moody hamlet of **Gleann Cholm Cille** and the majestic Slieve League mountains beckon, as does the Belleek china of **Ballyshannon.**

Donegal Castle

3 Northern Donegal: The is the far Northwest, Ireland's back-of-the-beyond. The gateway town is **Letterkenny,** presided over by the 212-foot-high spire of St. Eunan's Cathedral. Westward lies **Glenveagh National Park,** where you'll find the storybook lair and gardens of Glenveagh Castle.

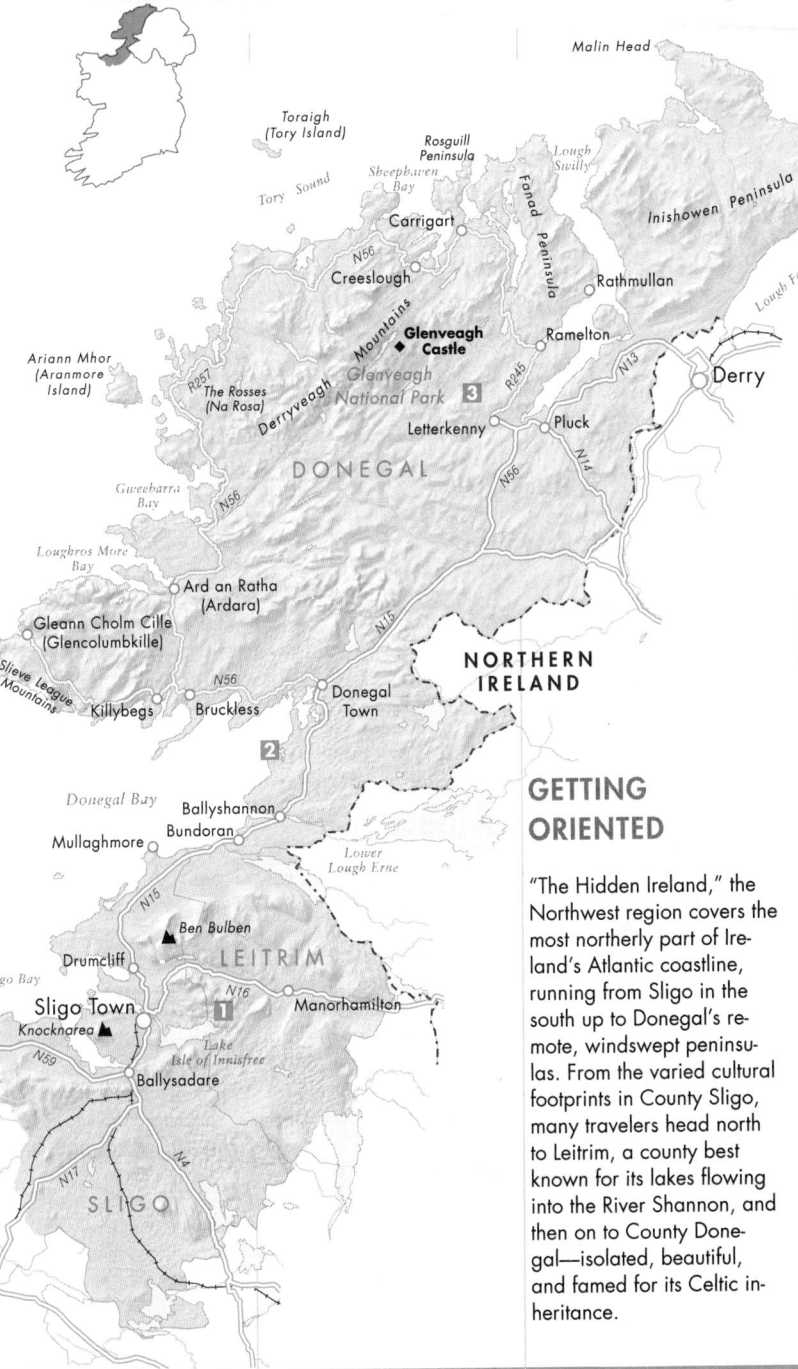

Malin Head

Toraigh
(Tory Island)

Rosguill
Peninsula

Sheephaven
Bay

Tory Sound

Lough
Swilly

Inishowen Peninsula

Carrigart

N56

Creeslough

Fanad Peninsula

Rathmullan

Lough Foyle

Glenveagh
Castle

Ramelton

Derry

Ariann Mhor
(Aranmore
Island)

R257

The Rosses
(Na Rosa)

Derryveagh
Mountains

Glenveagh
National Park **3**

Letterkenny

R245

N13

Pluck

N14

Gweebarra
Bay

N56

D O N E G A L

N56

Loughros More
Bay

Ard an Ratha
(Ardara)

N15

Gleann Cholm Cille
(Glencolumbkille)

Slieve League
Mountains

Killybegs

N56

Bruckless

Donegal
Town

NORTHERN
IRELAND

2

Donegal Bay

Ballyshannon

Bundoran

Mullaghmore

Lower
Lough Erne

N15

Ben Bulben

Drumcliff

L E I T R I M

Sligo Bay

N16

Manorhamilton

Sligo Town

Knocknarea

N59

Lake
Isle of Innisfree

Ballysadare

N17

N4

S L I G O

7

GETTING ORIENTED

"The Hidden Ireland," the Northwest region covers the most northerly part of Ireland's Atlantic coastline, running from Sligo in the south up to Donegal's remote, windswept peninsulas. From the varied cultural footprints in County Sligo, many travelers head north to Leitrim, a county best known for its lakes flowing into the River Shannon, and then on to County Donegal—isolated, beautiful, and famed for its Celtic inheritance.

NORTHWEST PLANNER

Finding a Place to Stay

True, it's the farthest-flung corner of Ireland, but northwest Ireland has a steady stream of arrivals—especially in July and August. Thanks to the area's popularity, good bed-and-breakfasts and small hotels are abundant.

In the two major towns—Sligo Town and Donegal Town—and the small coastal resorts in between, many traditional provincial hotels have been modernized (albeit not always elegantly). Yet most manage to retain some of the charm that comes with older buildings and personalized service.

Away from these areas, your best overnight choice is usually a modest guesthouse that includes bed, breakfast, and an evening meal, though you can also find first-class country-house hotels with a gracious professionalism comparable to properties elsewhere in Ireland.

Consider staying in an Irish-speaking home to get to know members of the area's Gaeltacht population; the local Tourist Information Office (TIO) can be helpful in making a booking with an Irish-speaking family.

Assume that all hotel rooms reviewed in this chapter have air-conditioning, in-room phones and TVs, and private bathrooms unless otherwise noted.

Making the Most of Your Time

In all honesty, there is only one way to fully explore the rural Northwest of Ireland and that's by car. Once here, you can always rent a car at Knock airport or Sligo Town. But if coming from Dublin, many opt to rent from one of the bigger companies at the larger airports. If arriving from Northern Ireland, there are rental agencies aplenty in Derry or Belfast, but be sure to tell your hire company if you are planning to cross the border. Cars are invariably compact—no SUVs—and stick shift is the norm (you will have to specially request an automatic). The roads between the larger towns are fairly well maintained and signposted but come slightly off the beaten track and conditions can vary from bad to dirt track. As long as you're not in a mad rush this can add to the delight of your journey. This is rural Ireland and if the scenery doesn't make this blissfully clear, then the suspension on your rented car certainly will!

Getting Around by Public Transportation

Getting around on bus is easy enough if you plan to only visit the larger towns. Ireland's principal bus company is Bus Éireann. The routes are regular and reliable and you'll find route planners and schedules on their website, www.buseireann.ie. There are also several privately run local bus companies operating in the Northwest, including McGeehans.

As for train travel, Sligo Town is the northernmost direct rail link to Dublin. From Dublin, three trains a day make the three hour and 20 minute journey (prices vary and can be higher on weekends).

If you want to get to Sligo Town by rail from other provincal towns, you're forced to make some inconvenient connections and take roundabout routes. Sadly, the rest of the region has no railway services.

Do You Read Irish?

County Donegal was part of the ancient kingdom of Ulster not conquered by the English until the 17th century. When the English withdrew in the 1920s, they had still not eradicated rural Donegal's Celtic inheritance. It thus shouldn't come as a surprise that it contains Ireland's largest Gaeltacht (Irish-speaking) area. Driving in this part of the country, you may either be frustrated or amused when you come to a crossroads whose signposts show only the Irish place-names, often so unlike the English versions as to be completely incomprehensible. To make things more confusing, some shop and hotel owners have opted to go with the English, not Irish, variant for their establishments' names. All is not lost, however, as maps—and this chapter—generally give both the Irish and the English names, and locals are usually more than happy to help out with directions (in English)—often with a colorful yarn thrown in. So if you're in a hurry, first of all you're in the wrong place, and secondly, you should have started sooner.

How's the Weather?

When it rains, it really pours. Forget about the winter months, when inclement weather and a heavy fog swings in from the Atlantic and settles in until spring, masking much of the beautiful scenery. But in all seasons remember to pack a warm and waterproof coat (especially if you're headed to the coast) and bring a good pair of walking shoes. It's not all doom and gloom: The weather can be glorious in the summer months—just don't bet your house on it.

Feiles & Festivals

In the northwest, each village tends to have its own *féile* (festival) during the summer months and it's often worth making the effort to attend.

Music festivals are tops, from the traditional Irish Sligo Feis Ceoil in mid-April to the Country and Western music extravaganza in Bundoran in June and the jazz and blues weekend feile in Gortahork, Donegal, in April. But being an Irish-speaking stronghold, the emphasis is on Irish traditional music.

Every weekend during summer you are guaranteed a bit of "craic" (fun) with lively sessions in most pubs. Sligo Town, Ard an Ratha (Ardara), and Letterkenny are all hot spots.

There are village festivals dedicated to hill-walking, fishing, poetry, art, and food—few can resist the Mullaghmore Lobster Festival in August.

Dining & Lodging Price Categories (in Euros)				
	$$$$	**$$$**	**$$**	**$**	**¢**
Restaurants	over €29	€22–29	€15–22	€8–15	under €8
Hotels	over €230	€180–230	€130–180	€80–130	under €80

Restaurant prices are for a main course at dinner. Hotel prices are for a standard double room in high season.

Updated by
Allison Morris

GLANCE AT A MAP OF IRELAND THAT HAS scenic roads printed in green and chances are your eye will be drawn to the far-flung peninsulas of Northwest Ireland. At virtually every bend in the roads weaving through counties Donegal, Leitrim, and Sligo, there will be something to justify all those green markings. On an island with no shortage of majestic scenery, the Northwest claims its full share. Cool, clean waters from the roaring Atlantic have carved the terrain into long peninsulas—creating a raw, sensual landscape that makes it seem as if the earth is still under construction.

But what you see *this moment* may not be what you will see an hour hence. Clouds and rain linger over mountains, glens, cliffs, beaches, and bogs, to be chased minutes later by sunshine and rainbows. The air, light, and colors of the countryside change as though viewed under a kaleidoscope. Skies brighten, then darken, calling forth a spectrum of subtle reds and purples from fields of unkempt gorse and heather, and then just as quickly painting the grassy meadows greener than any green you've ever seen. The writer William Butler Yeats and his brother Jack Butler Yeats, a painter, immortalized this splendidly lush and rugged countryside in their work.

Northwest Ireland covers the most northerly part of Ireland's Atlantic coastline, running from Sligo in the south along Donegal's remote, windswept peninsulas to Malin Head in the far north. These maritime landscapes are said to have given their colors to the most famous local product, handwoven tweed, which reflects the browns of the peaty heathland and the purples of the heather. Donegal, a sparsely populated rural county of small farms and fishing boats, shares its inland border with Northern Ireland; the border is partly formed by the River Foyle. Inland from Sligo is Leitrim, a county best known for its numerous lakes and loughs, some of which join up with the River Shannon, on the easterly border of this region.

The area is overwhelmingly rural and underpopulated. That's not to say there isn't a bit of action here. Sligo Town, for instance, has gone through a major renaissance. On a typical weekday, the little winding streets are as busy as those of Galway, and, when it comes to stylish restaurants and trendy people, it seems to be giving Dublin's Temple Bar a run for its money—an amazing feat for a town of only 19,000 souls. Sligo Town pulses not only in the present but also with the charge of history, for it was the childhood home of W. B. and Jack B. Yeats, the place that, more than any other, gave rise to their particular geniuses—or, as Jack B. put it: "Sligo was my school and the sky above it." There are more bright lights in Letterkenny, which has to its credit the longest main street of any town in Ireland. Glenveagh National Park exemplifies the surprising alliance between nature and culture in this part of Ireland: here, perched on the edge of a glorious lake in the midst of 24,000 acres of thrilling wilderness, sits a fairy-tale castle, restored by the great American art connoisseur, Henry McIlhenny. Elsewhere, a few places are blighted by careless development—Bundoran, a beach resort full of so-called "Irish gift shops" and "amusement arcades," is one of the places to pass through rather than visit—but on the whole, Northwest Ireland remains big enough, untamed enough, and grand enough.

Exploring the Northwest

This chapter outlines three autonomous routes through Northwest Ireland. These routes can easily be linked if you want to poke around the area over five or so days. The first journey begins in Sligo Town and covers its immediate environs—all the major sights within a roughly 24-km (15-mi) radius, many of which have strong associations with the Yeatses. The second trip skirts the entirety of Donegal Bay, from Mullaghmore in the south to Gleann Cholm Cille (Glencolumbkille) to the far north and west, before heading inland as far as Ard an Ratha (Ardara). The last route begins at the other end of Donegal, in Letterkenny, and travels to magical Glenveagh National Park. If you decide to explore this chapter from back to front (which makes sense if you're arriving from Northern Ireland), pick it up in Letterkenny.

YEATS COUNTRY: SLIGO TO DRUMCLIFF

Just as James Joyce made Dublin his own through his novels and stories, Sligo and environs are bound to the work of W. B. Yeats (1865–1939), Ireland's first of four Nobel laureates, and, no less, his brother Jack B. (1871–1957), one of Ireland's most important 20th-century painters, whose expressionistic landscapes and portraits are as emotionally fraught as his brother's poems are lyrical and plangent. The brothers intimately knew and eloquently celebrated in their art not only Sligo Town itself but the surrounding countryside with its lakes, farms, woodland, and the dramatic mountains that rise up not far from the center of town. On this route, you will often see glimpses of Ben Bulben Mountain, which looms over the western end of the Dartry range. The areas covered here are the most accessible parts of Northwest Ireland, easily reached from Galway.

Sligo Town

★ *60 km (37 mi) northeast of Ballina, 138 km (86 mi) northeast of Galway, 217 km (135 mi) northwest of Dublin.*

Sligo (population 19,000), the only sizable town in the whole of Northwest Ireland, is the best place to begin a tour of Yeats Country. It retains all the charm of smaller, sleepier villages, even though it's in the throes of an economic boom. Europe's largest videotape factory is just outside of town, it's the center of Ireland's plastics industry, and for the past three years the streets have been ringing with the bite of buzz saws, as apartments, shopping malls, and cinema complexes have been erected behind tasteful, traditional facades. By day Sligo is as lively and crowded as its considerably larger neighbor to the southwest, Galway, with locals, students from the town's college, and tourists bustling past its historic buildings and along its narrow sidewalks and winding streets, and crowding its one-of-a-kind shops, restaurants, and traditional pubs. More than any other town in Northwest Ireland, the Sligo of today has an energy that would surprise anyone who hasn't been there in the last few years.

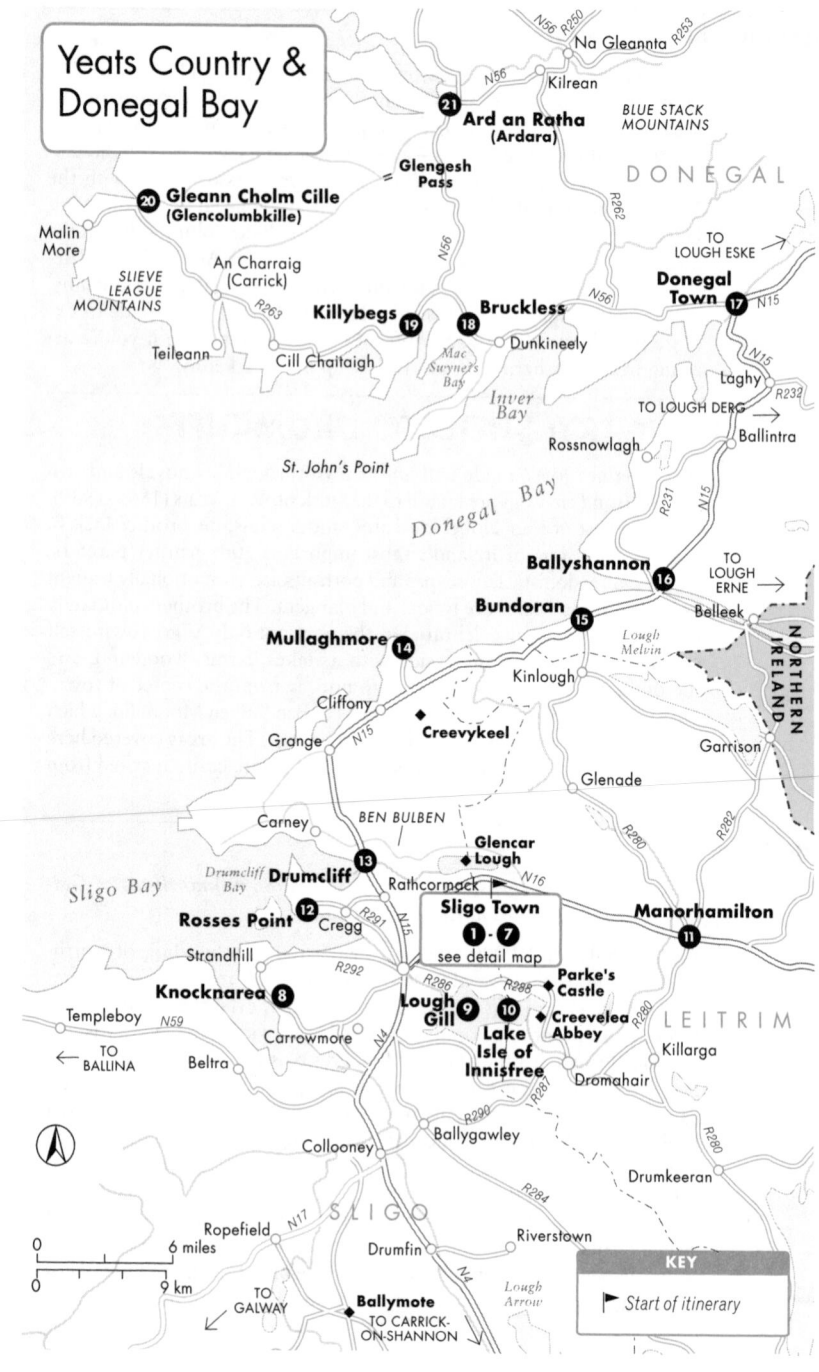

Yeats Country & Donegal Bay

21 Ard an Ratha (Ardara)

Glengesh Pass

20 Gleann Cholm Cille (Glencolumbkille)

Malin More

SLIEVE LEAGUE MOUNTAINS

An Charraig (Carrick)

Teileann

Cill Chaitaigh

19 Killybegs

18 Bruckless

Dunkineely

Mac Suyner's Bay

St. John's Point

BLUE STACK MOUNTAINS

D O N E G A L

TO LOUGH ESKE

17 Donegal Town

Laghy

TO LOUGH DERG

Ballintra

Rossnowlagh

Inver Bay

Donegal Bay

16 Ballyshannon

Belleek

TO LOUGH ERNE

N O R T H E R N   I R E L A N D

15 Bundoran

Lough Melvin

Garrison

Kinlough

14 Mullaghmore

Cliffony

Grange

Creevykeel

Glenade

Glenade

BEN BULBEN

Carney

13 Drumcliff

Drumcliff Bay

Rathcormack

Glencar Lough

Sligo Bay

12 Rosses Point

Cregg

Strandhill

Sligo Town 1 · 7 *see detail map*

Manorhamilton 11

8 Knocknarea

Templeboy

TO BALLINA

Carrowmore

Beltra

Lough Gill 9

10 Lake Isle of Innisfree

Parke's Castle

Creevelea Abbey

Killarga

L E I T R I M

Dromahair

Colooney

Ballygawley

Drumkeeran

Ropefield

TO GALWAY

Drumfin

Riverstown

Lough Arrow

S L I G O

Ballymote

TO CARRICK-ON-SHANNON

0 — 6 miles
0 — 9 km

KEY
▶ *Start of itinerary*

EATING WELL IN NORTHWEST IRELAND

Although Northwest Ireland has not been considered a noted gastronomic center, many visitors make their journeys memorable by stopping off en route at a local pub to enjoy steaming hot soups, stews, and hot meat platters in front of a raging turf fires. In the last few years, Sligo Town has become host to a number of food-related shops worth visiting, and this being farming country, the region has a number of top-notch Farmers' Markets, usually held during the March to October growing season (great for picnic fixings).

Newcomers are serving up well-above-average food in memorable settings, though the majority of restaurants still serve plain and simple fare, such as traditional Irish lamb stew or bacon and cabbage served with generous helpings of potatoes (often prepared in at least two ways on the same plate), washed down with creamy, lip-smacking pints of Guinness. You're likely to find the finest food at the higher-quality country houses—Donegal mountain spring lamb, Glen Bay lobster and crab, Donegal Bay oysters and mussels, Lough Swilly wild salmon, and Guinness cakes—where chefs elegantly specialize in a hybrid Irish-French haute cuisine.

Generally, restaurants in towns stay open year-round, as they do not have to rely solely on the tourist trade. But eateries in remote villages will often close for an extended period during the winter months, usually from November to mid-March. It does tend to vary, but check with the tourist office to avoid disappointment.

Squeezed onto a patch of land between Sligo Bay and Lough Gill, the town is clustered on the south shore between two bridges that span the River Garavogue, just east of where the river opens into the bay. Thanks to the pedestrian zone along the south shore of the river (between the two bridges), you can enjoy vistas of the river while right in the center of town. All along High Street and Church and Charles streets, Sligo has churches of almost every denomination. Presbyterians, Methodists, and even Plymouth Brethren are represented, as well as Anglicans (Church of Ireland) and, of course, Roman Catholics. According to the Irish writer Sean O'Faolain, "The best Protestant stock in all Ireland is in Sligo." The Yeats family was part of that stock.

Sligo was often a battleground in its earlier days. It was attacked by Viking invaders in 807 and, later, by a succession of rival Irish and Anglo-Norman conquerors. In 1642 the British soldiers of Sir Frederick Hamilton fell upon Sligo, killing every visible inhabitant, burning the town, and destroying the interior of the beautiful medieval abbey. Between 1845 and 1849, more than a million inhabitants of Sligo county died in the potato famine or fled to escape it—an event poignantly captured in a letter written by a local father, Owen Larkin, to his son in America in 1850, its words inscribed on a brass plaque down by the river: "I am now I may say alone in the world all my brothers and sisters are dead and children but yourself. We are all ejected out of Lord Ardilaun's ground, the times was so bad and all Ireland in such a state of poverty that no person could pay rent. My only hope now rests with you, as I am without one shilling and I must either beg or go to the poorhouse." Stand there a moment by the river, then turn again to the bustling heart of Sligo, and marvel at humanity's capacity to rise above adversity.

❶ Picturesquely set atop the stone Hyde Bridge, the **Yeats Memorial Building** makes for a suitably imposing address for the Yeats Society, Sligo Art Gallery, and the Tourist Information Centre. The Sligo Arts Gallery lends itself well to the host of rotating exhibitions of contemporary art. In addition, the Yeats International Summer School is conducted here every August. Across the street is Rohan Gillespie's photo-worthy sculpture of the poet, draped in a flowing coat overlaid with excerpts from his work. It was unveiled in 1989 by Michael Yeats, W. B.'s son, in commemoration of the 50th anniversary of his father's death. ✉ *Hyde Bridge* ☎ *071/914–5847 gallery, 074/914–2693 summer school* 🖶 *071/914–7426* ⊕ *www.sligoartgallery.com* ✆ *Free* ☉ *Mon.–Sat. 10–5:30.*

❷ Housed in a beautifully renovated school, built in 1862, the **Model Arts Centre and Niland Gallery**, is one of Ireland's premier arts venues with an extensive calendar devoted to the visual and performing arts. The main attraction is one of Ireland's largest collections of works by 20th-century artists from Ireland and abroad. The gallery displays works by Jack B. Yeats, who said, "I never did a painting without putting a thought of Sligo in it." (Beckett wrote that Yeats painted "desperately immediate images.") Paintings by John Yeats (father of Jack B. and W. B.), who had a considerable reputation as a portraitist, also hang here, as do portraits by Sean Keating and Paul Henry. The center has performance and workshop spaces and hosts literature, music, and film programs. There's also the Atrium café. ✉ *The Mall* ☎ *071/914–1405* ⊕ *www.modelart.ie* ✆ *Free* ☉ *Tues.–Sat. 10–5:30, Sun. 11–4, and during performances.*

❸ A massive stone complex that is still redolent of "auld grandeur" and famed for its medieval tomb sculptures, **Sligo Abbey** is the town's only existing relic of the Middle Ages. Maurice FitzGerald erected the structure for the Dominicans in 1253. After a fire in 1414, it was extensively rebuilt, only to be destroyed again by Cromwell's Puritans under the command of Sir Frederick Hamilton, in 1642. Today the abbey consists of a ruined nave, aisle, transept, and tower. Some fine stonework remains, especially in the 15th-century cloisters. The visitor center is the base for guided tours, which are included with admission. The site is accessible to the disabled, though some parts of the grounds are quite rocky. ✉ *Abbey St.* ☎ *071/914–6406* ⊕ *www.heritageireland.ie* ✆ *€2* ☉ *Apr.–Oct., daily 10–6; Nov.–Jan., Fri.–Sun. 9:30–4:30.*

❹ The **Courthouse,** built in 1878 in the Victorian Gothic style, has a flamboyant, turreted sandstone exterior. Unfortunately the structure is not open to tourists. After it was built, it became a symbol of English power. The Courthouse takes its inspiration from the much larger Law Courts in London. Just north of the Courthouse on the east side of Teeling Street, look for the window designating the law firm Argue and Phibbs, one

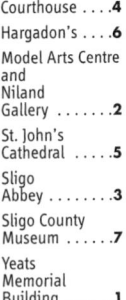

Sligo Town

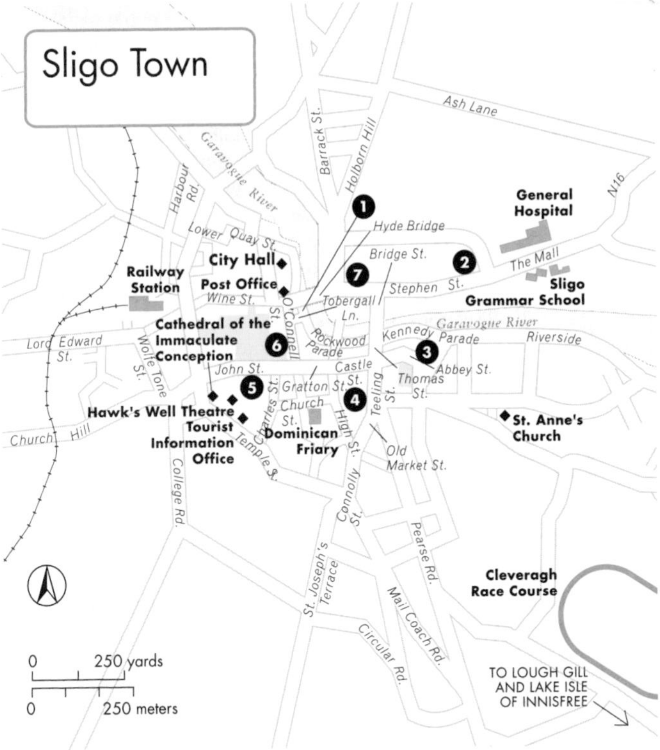

of Sligo's most popular photo-ops. ✉ *Teeling St.* ☎ *No phone* ☾ *Closed to public.*

Designed in 1730 by Richard Castle, who designed Powerscourt and Russborough houses in County Wicklow, little **St. John's Cathedral** (Church of Ireland) has a handsome square tower and fortifications. In the north transept is a memorial to Susan Mary Yeats, mother of W. B. and Jack B. Next door is the larger and newer Roman Catholic Cathedral of the Immaculate Conception (with an entrance on Temple Street), consecrated in 1874. ✉ *John St.* ☎ *No phone.*

⑥ Sligo's most famous pub, **Hargadon's,** is a dark, old-style public house with cozy, private, wood-panel snugs (cubicles); stone-and-wood floors; rust-red interior walls; and a handsome golden-oak and green-painted facade. The pub has been operated by the Hargadon family since 1908; before that it was owned by a local member of the

> **WORD OF MOUTH**
>
> "A terrific place for a pint (or two) is Hargadon's. Talk about an original! Hargadon's is full of character and old-world ambience. After one visit, you'll have a hard time returning to those pre-packaged and sterile Irish-theme pubs." –DavidD

British parliament, who was more interested in debating with his peers in London than pulling pints in Sligo. Hargadon's is justly famous for its bowls of stew and pints of creamy Guinness. ✉ *4 O'Connell St.* ☎ *071/917–0933.*

❼ The showpiece of the **Sligo County Museum** is its Yeats Hall, which houses a comprehensive collection of W. B. Yeats's writings from 1889 to 1936, various editions of his plays and prose, the Nobel Prize medal awarded to him in 1923, and the Irish tricolor (flag) that draped his coffin when he was buried at nearby Drumcliff. The penmanship is dreadful, but Yeats's letters to James Stephens and Oliver St. John Gogarty offer insight into Yeats's obsessive love for Sligo. The museum also has small sections on local society, history, and archaeology. Some artwork by Jack B. Yeats is hung in the adjoining church. ✉ *Stephen St.* ☎ *071/914–1623* ✉ *Free* ☉ *June–Sept., Tues.–Sat. 10–noon and 2–4:50; Oct.–May, Tues.–Sat. 2–4:50.*

Where to Stay & Eat

$–$$ ✕ **Bistro Bianconi.** With blond-wood furniture and white-tile floors, Bianconi lives up to its name in the dining room's design, but it serves Italian food full of color. Peruse the long list of fancy pizzas baked in a wood-burning oven. Cannelloni and ravioli are also popular. ✉ *44 O'-Connell St.* ☎ *071/914–1744* ▭ *MC, V* ☉ *Closed Sun.*

$$$$ ✕▦ **Cromleach Lodge.** Comfort is paramount at this small hotel with fantastic views out over Lough Arrow. Plate-glass windows pepper the modern building, whose low-slung dimensions are topped off with a faux mansard roof. Inside, things are considerably more comfy and stylish: reception areas are dotted with antiques and fine wallpapers, while spacious guest bedrooms are decorated in pastel shades. The restaurant ($$–$$$; reservations required) is notable; Chef Moira Tighe won Irish Chef of the Year award in 2000 (and her staff offers a series of cooking lesson "holidays" in February). Two fetching entrées are fillet of turbot on a julienne of fennel with Pernod cream, and warm salad of marinated lamb fillet with organic lentils. Also delicious is the restaurant's panoramic vista. Staff members lead walks ranging from 20 minutes to two hours long. ✉ *27 km (17 mi) east of Sligo, 8 km (5 mi) east of Ballymote; off N4 at Castlebaldwin, Lough Arrow, Co. Sligo* ☎ *071/916–5155* 🖷 *071/916–5455* ⊕ *www.cromleach.com* ⤶ *11 rooms* ♨ *Restaurant, Wi-Fi, golf privileges, hiking, bar, meeting room; no a/c* ▭ *AE, DC, MC, V* ☉ *Closed Nov.–Jan.* ⏩ *BP, MAP.*

$$–$$$ ✕▦ **Markree Castle.** One of the most beautiful fortress fronts in Ireland
Fodor's Choice greets you on arrival at Markree, Sligo's oldest inhabited castle and the
★ home of the Cooper family for 350 years. Today, Charles and Mary Cooper preside over this lush and lavish 1,000-acre estate. Renovated in 1802, the castle was given the full storybook treatment, with a vast and oak-panel entry hall and skylight atrium. Atop the grand staircase is a glorious stained-glass window depicting the Cooper family tree (their roots are essentially English—having arrived with the bloody troops of Cromwell—but they were also related to the great Irish clan of the O'Briens). Upstairs, guest bedrooms are super-spacious, many adorned with cozy-sumptuous pieces of 19th century–style furniture; bathrooms

are modern. Chandeliered and gilt-limned, the restaurant dining room has ornate Louis XIV plasterwork—ask about the three-course table d'hôte menu (€38) that's occasionally served—and serves food good enough to draw in families for Sunday brunch. ☒ *11 km (7 mi) south of Sligo Town, off N4, Collooney, Co. Sligo* ☎ *071/916–7800* 🖷 *071/916–7840* ⊕ *www.markreecastle.ie* 🛏 *30 rooms* ⚒ *Restaurant, horseback riding, bar; no a/c* ▭ *AE, MC, V* ⦾ *BP, MAP.*

$$ ✕⌷ **Temple House.** Off the beaten path on more than 1,000 acres, this vast Georgian mansion and working organic farm has been in owners Sandy and Deb Perceval's family since 1665. Their son Roderick manages the estate. Georgian and Victorian furniture—mahogany tables and original rugs—adorn the bedrooms. Outside, formal terraced gardens and a lake beckon. Deb prepares the prix-fixe evening meal ($$$$; book by noon) using the farm's own produce. Typical entrées include herbed leg of lamb with roast potatoes and tomato fondue with glazed carrots. High tea is served for children at 6:30 PM; they are not allowed at dinner. ☒ *19 km (12 mi) south of Sligo, off N17, Ballymote, Co. Sligo* ☎ *071/918–3329* 🖷 *071/918–3808* ⊕ *www.templehouse.ie* 🛏 *6 rooms* ⚒ *Restaurant, boating, fishing; no a/c, no room phones, no room TVs* ▭ *AE, MC, V* ⦾ *Closed Dec.–Mar.* ⦿ *BP.*

★ **$** ✕⌷ **Glebe House.** Dorothy and Jeremy Bird run a Georgian guest house and a restaurant ($$$$) with an emphasis on local produce. You might choose from roast rack of Sligo lamb in an herb crust or wild Owenmore salmon with an herb hollandaise from the prix-fixe menu. Indulge in pink grapefruit and gin sorbet or chocolate and Amaretto mousse for dessert. It's a relaxed place, with simple but pleasant guest rooms. ☒ *12 km (7 mi) south of Sligo Town, Coolaney Rd., off N4 at 2nd roundabout, Collooney, Co. Sligo* ☎ *071/916–7787* 🛏 *4 rooms, 1 with bath* ⚒ *Restaurant, fishing, hiking, meeting rooms; no a/c, no room TVs* ▭ *MC, V* ⦿ *BP, MAP.*

★ **$$$** ⌷ **Coopershill.** Seven generations of the O'Hara family have lived in this three-story Georgian farmhouse since it was built in 1774. Beyond the elegant, symmetrical stone facade, with its central Palladian window, an appealing mix of antique bureaus, marble busts, mounted deer heads, and 19th-century paintings fill the large reception rooms, especially the main emerald-hued salon. Spacious, beautifully furnished guest rooms have floral wallpaper, and most have four-poster or canopy beds. Dine by candlelight on meals made with fresh Irish ingredients, accompanied by a wide choice of wines, served from a grand sideboard set with family silver and crystal. Nonguests are welcome to dine only when the lodging is not full. ☒ *Off N4, 17 km (11 mi) southeast of Sligo, Riverstown, Co. Sligo* ☎ *071/916–5108* 🖷 *071/916–5466* ⊕ *www.coopershill.com* 🛏 *8 rooms* ⚒ *Dining room, tennis court, fishing, billiards; no a/c, no room TVs* ▭ *AE, DC, MC, V* ⦾ *Closed Nov.–Mar.* ⦿ *BP.*

Nightlife & the Arts

PUBS A few miles south of town, a popular spot with the locals, the **Thatch pub** (☒ Thatch, Ballysadare ☎ 071/916–7288) has traditional music sessions from Thursday to Sunday. A sizable dance floor at **Toffs** (☒ Kennedy Parade ☎ 071/916–1250) teems with Sligo's younger set moving to a mix of contemporary dance music and older favorites. It stays open later than most places.

THEATER With a jammed-packed calendar year-round, **Hawk's Well Theatre** hosts amateur and professional companies from all over Ireland (and occasionally from Britain) in an eclectic mix of shows. ⊠ *Temple St.* ☎ *071/ 916–1526* ⊕ *www.hawkswell.com/* 🖾 *€15–€25* ⊙ *Box office weekdays 10–6, Sat. 2–6.*

Shopping

Sligo Town has Northwest Ireland's most thriving shopping scene, with lots of food-related, crafts, and hand-knits shops. In addition to stylish sweaters, **Carraig Donn** (⊠ 41 O'Connell St. ☎ 071/914–4158) carries pottery, glassware, linens, and Aran knits for children. The **Cat & the Moon** (⊠ 4 Castle St. ☎ 071/914–3686) specializes in eclectic and stylish Irish-made crafts, jewelry, pottery, ironwork, and scarves. The upscale deli **Cosgrove and Son** (⊠ 32 Market St. ☎ 071/914–2809) sells everything from Parma ham to carrageen moss boiled in milk (a local cure for upset stomachs). Stock up here for a picnic. **Cross Sections** (⊠ 2 Grattan St. ☎ 071/914–2265) sells lovely tableware, glassware, and kitchenware. **Tír na nóg** (⊠ Grattan St. ☎ 071/916–2752), Irish for "Land of the Ever-young," sells organic foods, including local cheeses and honeys, and other health-oriented items. A sister store across the street sells cards and posters.

Knocknarea

❽ *8 km (5 mi) southwest of Sligo Town on R292, Strandhill Rd.*

Knocknarea—the "cairn-heaped grassy hill," as W. B. Yeats called this spot several miles southwest of Sligo Town, rises 1,083 feet high on a promontory that juts into Sligo Bay. The mountain is also memorably depicted in brother Jack B.'s painting *Knocknarea and the Flowing Tide.* A car park on R292 gives pedestrian access (a 45-minute walk) to the summit, where there's a tremendous view of the mountains of counties Donegal and Sligo. At the summit, and visible from a distance, sits a huge cairn—a heaped-stone monument—made with 40,000 tons of rock. The cairn is traditionally associated with Maeve, the 1st-century AD Celtic queen of Connaught who went to war with the men of Ulster in a bid to win the mighty Bull of Cuailgne, and who was subsequently killed while bathing in a lake. The story is told in the *Táin,* the greatest of all the Irish heroic legends. Romantics like to think that Maeve is buried in this massive cairn, although archaeologists suspect that it more likely covers a 3,000-year-old grave. Either way, it's a pleasant climb on a summer day, and nature has installed a handy stream for washing off your boots as you take the lane back down.

Strandhill, a seaside resort with a touch of charm, is 3 km (2 mi) northwest of Knocknarea, off R292. It has a fine, sandy beach and rolling waves favored by surfers. The **Perfect Day Surf Club** (⊠ Esplanade, Strandhill ☎ 071/916–8464) caters to surfing novices and aficionados alike and is approved by the European Surf Federation and Irish Surfing Association. Two hours of instruction plus equipment is €25. **Celtic Sea-**

Continued on page 501

Prepping dishes for Spongeware patterns

A PIECE OF
THE SHAMROCK

With its Belleek porcelains and Waterford crystals, Ireland has always been a treasured island for shoppers. Today, its traditional crafts—centuries old yet very much alive—are enjoying a revival of the fittest.

Remember all those traditional leprechaun figurines with "Made in China" stickers on their bottoms? Fifteen years ago, Aunt Maud was probably resigned to buying one when she wanted to bring a bit of the Emerald Isle home with her. Today, however, Irish traditional crafts are flourishing as never before. In a land where many villages are still redolent of a preindustrial age, "trad" culture has become commerce—big commerce. Claddagh friendship rings, spongeware pottery, heirloom Aran sweaters, Belleek china wedding plates, Carrickmacross lace, and Waterford crystal (so finely cut you'll need to don anti-brilliance eye goggles) are all objects endowed with vibrant personality. If Ireland has never been a country of great artists it has always been one of great *artistry*.

From north to south, an army of indulgent shoppers tour the country joking "Veni, vidi, Visa—I came, I saw, I charged." While the entire country is blooming with craftsworkers, the Northwest region offers some seventh-level shopping, thanks to hand-knit Aran sweaters, fine Parian china, and hand-woven tweeds. Those who want to make browsing—and buying—easy will find the famous multidealer town cooperatives (such as Midleton's Courtyard Crafts or Doolin's Celtic Waves) as tempting as boxes of Godiva chocolates. But, in general, the more interesting craftspeople are found outside the main cities, and intrepid consumers should head for smaller towns where overheads are lower (and the scenery is better). Don't buy the first blackthorn walking stick you see. Take a good look around and visit any number of crafts shops—it's part of the fun and you'll probably end up with a bogwood paperweight and basketweave china tureen as well!

Above: Claddagh ring.
Below: Louis Mulcahey at work on his pottery.
Dingle Peninsula, Southwest Ireland

CHERISHED COLLECTIBLES

WATERFORD CRYSTAL

Founded in 1783, Waterford crystal is noted for its sparkle, clarity, and heft. Thicker glass means that each piece can be wedge-cut on a diamond wheel to dramatic effect (as you can see during the famous factory tour held at the Waterford factory in Southeast Ireland). Waterford artisans apprentice for *eight* years.

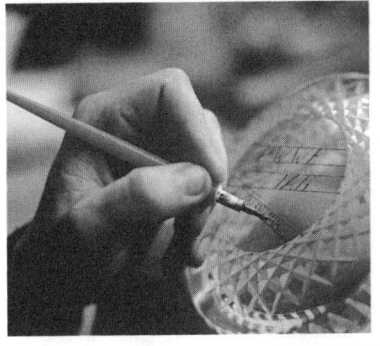

BELLEEK CHINA

China has been made in Belleek, a village just on the border with County Fermanagh, Northern Ireland, since 1857. This local product is a fine-bone china with a delicate green or yellow-on-white design. Americans love it.

TRADITIONAL LACEMAKING

Traditional Irish crochet and lace-making use a fine cotton and date back to the 1840s when they originated in the cottage homes and lace schools of Carrickmacross.

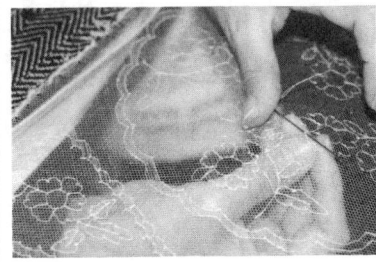

SPONGEWARE POTTERY

One of Ireland's most beautiful collectibles, Irish Spongeware first appeared in 18th-century potteries. With the use of a cut sponge, patterns and images—often "rural" in flavor, like plants and sheep—are applied to the lovely cream-colored surface.

CLADDAGH RINGS

Born in the Claddagh area of Galway during the 17th century, the Claddagh ring incorporates three symbols: a heart (for love), a pair of hands (for friendship), and a crown (for loyalty). Worn on the right hand, with crown and heart facing out, it symbolizes the wearer is still "free"; worn on the left, with symbols tucked under, indicates marriage.

A PIECE OF THE SHAMROCK

7

ARAN: FROM FLEECE TO FASHION

Made of plain, undyed wool and knit with distinctive crisscross patterns, sometime referred to as *bainin* sweaters or "ganseys," the Aran sweater is a combination of folklore and fashion.

Since harsh weather made warmth and protection vital out in the Atlantic Ocean, the women of Aran long ago discovered the solution to this problem in this strong, comfortable, hand-knit sweater. Indeed, these Arans can hold 30 percent of their weight in water before they even start to feel wet. The reason? Traditionally, the wool used was unwashed and retained its water-repellent natural sheep's lanolin.

Not so long ago, these pullovers were worn by every County Donegal fisherman, usually made to a design belonging exclusively to his own family. It's said that a native can tell which family the knitter belongs to from the patterns used in a genuine Aran sweater. Often the patterns used religious symbols and folk motifs, such as the Tree of Life, the Honeycomb (standing for thrift and thought to be lucky), the SeaHorse, the Blackberry—all are patterns in the almost sculptured, deeply knitted work that characterizes the Aran method. Their famous basket stitch represents the fisherman's basket, a hope for a *curragh* (fisherboat) heavy with catch. A colorful belt called a *crios* (pronounced "criss") is handcrafted in

many traditional designs by the Aran women and makes a useful accessory.

Most of the Aran sweaters you'll see throughout Ireland are made far north of the islands themselves, in County Donegal, an area most associated with high-quality, handwoven textiles. The best are painstakingly knitted by hand, a process that can take weeks. As a result, prices are not cheap, and if you think you've found a bargain, check the label before buying—it's more likely a factory copy. Still, the less expensive, lighter-weight, hand-loomed sweaters (knitted on a mechanical loom, not with needles) are less than half the price, and more practical for most lifestyles. But the real McCoy is still coveted: some of the finest examples woven by Inis Meáin are sold at luxury stores like Bergdorf Goodman and Wilkes Bashford. And young Irish designers like Liadain De Buitlear (⊕ www.liadainbuitlear.com) are giving the traditional Aran a newer-than-now spin, highly popular in Dublin boutiques.

Above Left: A large selection of styles and sizes
Above right: A closer look at the knitting

weed Baths (✉ Esplanade, Strandhill ☎ 071/916–8686 ⊕ www.celticseaweedbaths.com) has a one-hour steam-and-seaweed bath treatment for €18.

EN ROUTE

Carrowmore, the largest group of megalithic tombs in the British Isles, is a short drive southeast of Knocknarea (on the minor road back to Sligo Town). The oldest of the 60 passage tombs, dolmens, and other ruins here predate those at Newgrange by roughly 700 years; most are communal tombs dating from 4800 BC. Unfortunately more than 100 have been badly damaged, leaving around 40. A restored cottage houses a small exhibition about the tombs. ✉ *Carrowmore, Co. Sligo* ☎ *071/916–1534* 🎟 *€2* ⊙ *Mar.–Oct., daily 10–5:15.*

> ### YOUR LIFE OR YOUR STONE
>
> The cairn at the top of Knocknarea mount was almost ruined by visitors who took little stones as souvenirs. The Office of Public Works, with a typically Irish solution to an Irish problem, put out the myth that anyone removing a rock would be cursed forevermore. They also declared that a single woman adding a small stone to the cairn would find herself married within the year. Result? The cairn is now back to its former glory.

Lough Gill

★ ❾ *17½ km (11 mi) east of Knocknarea, 1½ km (1 mi) east of Sligo Town on R286.*

Beautiful, gentle Lough Gill means simply "Lake Beauty" in Irish. In fine weather the river-fed lough and its surroundings are serenity itself: sunlight on the meadows all around, lough-side cottages, the gentle sound of water, salmon leaping, a yacht sailing by. To get to the Lough from Sligo Town, take Stephen Street, which turns into N16 (signposted to Manorhamilton and Enniskillen). Turn right almost at once onto R286. Within minutes you can see gorgeous views of the lake so adored by the young W. B. Yeats.

In the 17th century an English Planter (a Protestant colonist settling on Irish lands confiscated from Catholic owners) built the fortified house of **Parke's Castle** on the eastern shore of Lough Gill. He needed the strong fortifications to defend himself against a hostile populace. His relations with the people were made worse by the fact that he obtained his building materials mainly by dismantling a historic fortress on the site that had belonged to the clan leaders the O'Rourkes of Breffni (once the name of the district). The entrance fee includes a short video show on the castle and local history, and a guided tour. In summer, boat tours of the lough leave from here. There's also a snack bar. ✉ *R288,*

> ### LOUD AND CLEAR
>
> Legend has it that when the soldiers of Sir Frederick Hamilton sacked Sligo in 1642, they flung the silver bell of the abbey into the depths of Lough Gill; today it's said that only the "pure" can hear it ring.

Fivemile Bourne, Co. Leitrim ☎ 071/916–4149, 087/270–4032 for appointment ⊕ www.heritageireland.ie ☜ €2.75 ☉ Apr.–Oct., 10–6, last admission at 5:15; Nov.–Apr., by appointment.

A few minutes' walk along a footpath south of Parke's Castle lie the handsome ruins of **Creevelea Abbey.** In fact not an abbey but a friary, Creevelea was founded for the Franciscans in 1508 by a later generation of O'Rourkes. It was the last Franciscan community to be founded before the suppression of the monasteries by England's King Henry VIII. Like many other decrepit abbeys, the place still holds religious significance for the locals, who revere it. One curiosity here is the especially large south transept; notice, too, its endearing little cloisters, with carvings of St. Francis of Assisi. ⊠ *R288, Dromahair, Co. Leitrim.*

Where to Stay & Eat

¢ ✕▦ **Stanford Village Inn.** This stone-front inn is one of the few stops for sustenance near Lough Gill. A hearty meal of traditional, homey food ($–$$), an open fire, and, if your timing is good, an impromptu session of traditional Irish music await you. It has six newly refurbished country rooms. ⊠ *7 km (5 mi) from Parke's Castle, 19 km (12 mi) from Sligo Town, off R288, Dromahair, Co. Leitrim* ☎ *071/916–4140* ☏ *071/916–4770* ⇎ *6 rooms* ☼ *Restaurant, bar; no a/c* ▤ *MC, V* ⦿ *BP.*

Lake Isle of Innisfree

❿ *15 km (9 mi) south of Sligo Town via Dromahair on N4 and R287.*

In 1890 W. B. Yeats was walking through the West End of London when, seeing in a shop window a ball dancing on a jet of water, he was suddenly overcome with nostalgia for the lakes of his Sligo home. It was the moment, and the feeling, that shaped itself into his most famous poem, "The Lake Isle of Innisfree":

I will arise and go now, and go to Innisfree,
And a small cabin build there, of clay and wattles made:
Nine bean-rows will I have there, a hive for the honey-bee,
And live alone in the bee-loud glade.

And I will find some peace there for peace comes dropping slow. . . .

Though there's nothing visually exceptional about Innisfree (pronounced *innish*-free), the "Lake Isle" is a must-see if you're a W. B. Yeats fan. To reach Innisfree from Dromahair, take R287, the minor road that heads back along the south side of Lough Gill, toward Sligo Town. Turn right at a small crossroads, after 4 or 5 km (2 or 3 mi), where signposts point to Innisfree. A little road leads another couple of miles down to the lakeside, where you can see the island just offshore.

Manorhamilton

⓫ *16 km (10 mi) northeast of Dromahair on R280, 25 km (15 mi) east of Sligo Town on N16.*

The small rural town of Manorhamilton was built in the 17th century for the Scottish planter Sir Frederick Hamilton, who had been given the

The Sporting Life

ALONG THE RUGGED COASTS OF SLIGO AND DONEGAL, beaches come in all shapes and sizes. Chief among them is Strandhill, a few miles outside Sligo Town; it's a particularly delightful stretch of fine sand and rolling waves, perfect for surfers. Donegal's seaside resorts, like the family-oriented Bundoran on the west coast and Buncrana in northern Donegal, can get very crowded in summer, and are packed full of amusement arcades. But there are quieter alternatives, like Rossnowlagh (meaning "heavenly cove"), in Donegal Bay, with its pristine shoreline. Water sports from windsurfing to sailing are rife in both counties, and fishing enthusiasts will be in their element, with excellent fishing for salmon, sea, brown, and rainbow trouts in countless lakes, rivers and streams. The Atlantic coast offers unrestricted shore angling. The numerous headlands of the north Donegal coast are perfect settings for invigorating walks, with the fresh Atlantic sea air sure to blow away the cobwebs. See if you can get as far as Malin Head, the most northerly tip of Ireland. The Slieve League cliffs are the highest sea cliffs in Europe, and the view from the top will set your heart racing. Inland, the Blue Stack Mountains in Donegal offer wonderful views of the surrounding area, looming above Sligo Town, with the serene mass of Ben Bulben seeming to glow in the sunset. Both counties are justly famous for their loughs (lakes), from beautiful, gentle Lough Gill, with its tiny island of Innisfree, immortalized in a poem by W. B. Yeats, to the pilgrims' favorite Lough Derg, with its shrines to St. Patrick.

local manor house by Charles I of England (hence the town's name). The manor itself is now an ivy-covered ruin, and there's not much to see of it; the surrounding scenery, however, is spectacular.

EN ROUTE   On your way to Manorhamilton, stop at **Glencar Lough** (⊠ N16, 9 km [5 mi] east of Sligo Town), where there are several waterfalls; a footpath veering off a parking lot leads to one of the highest. The lake is fed by the River Drumcliff and streams at the foot of the Dartry Mountains: "Where the wandering water gushes/From the hills above Glencar/In pools among the rushes/That scarce could bathe a star," as W. B. Yeats put it in his poem "The Stolen Child."

Rosses Point

⑫ *38½ km (24 mi) west of Manorhamilton, 8 km (5 mi) northwest of Sligo Town on R291.*

It's obvious why W. B. and Jack B. Yeats often stayed at Rosses Point during their summer vacations: glorious pink-and-gold summer sunsets over a seemingly endless stretch of sandy beach. Coney Island lies just off Rosses Point. Local lore has it that the captain of the ship *Arathusa* christened Brooklyn's Coney Island after this one, but there's probably more legend than truth to this, as it's widely agreed that New York's

Coney Island was named after the Dutch word *konijn* (wild rabbits, which abounded there during the 17th century).

The popular **County Sligo Golf Club** (✉ Rosses Point ☎ 071/917–7186 ⊕ www.countysligogolfclub.ie) is one of Ireland's grand old venues; it's more than a century old, and has hosted most of the country's major championships. Established in 1894 on land leased from Henry Middleton, an uncle of the famous Yeats brothers, the course offers magnificent views of the sea and Ben Bulben. The **Sligo Yacht Club** (✉ Rosses Point ☎ 071/917–7168 ⊕ www.sligoyachtclub.org), with a fleet of some 25 boats, has sailing and social programs, and regularly hosts races.

Drumcliff

 15 km (9 mi) northeast of Rosses Point, 7 km (4½ mi) north of Sligo Town on N15.

W. B. Yeats lies buried with his wife, Georgie, in an unpretentious grave in the cemetery of Drumcliff's simple Protestant church, where his grandfather was rector for many years. W. B. died on the French Riviera in 1939; it took almost a decade for his body to be brought back to the place that more than any other might be called his soul-land. In the poem "Under Ben Bulben," he spelled out not only where he was to be buried but also what should be written on the tombstone: "Cast a cold eye/On life, on death./Horseman, pass by!" It is easy to see why the majestic Ben Bulben (1,730 feet), with its sawed-off peak (not unlike Yosemite's Half-Dome), made such an impression on the poet: the mountain gazes calmly down upon the small church, as it does on all of the surrounding landscape—and at the same time stands as a sentinel facing the mighty Atlantic.

Drumcliff is where St. Columba, a recluse and missionary who established Christian churches and religious communities in Northwest Ireland, is thought to have founded a monastic settlement around AD 575. The monastery that he founded before sailing off to the Scottish isle of Iona flourished for many centuries, but all that is left of it now is the base of a round tower and a carved high cross (both across N15 from the church) dating from around AD 1000, with scenes from the Old and New Testaments, including Adam and Eve with the serpent, and Cain slaying Abel.

Drumcliff Craft Shop is a good place to buy local crafts, books of W. B. Yeats's poetry, and books about the poet's life. You can also get a snack here. ✉ *Next to Protestant church, Co. Sligo* ☎ *071/914–4956* ☺ *Mon.–Sat. 9:30–6, Sun. noon–6.*

HILLTOP DOINGS

The massive flat-domed plateau of Ben Bulben dominates the surrounding bog land. Dating to 574 when St. Columcille founded a monastery on its peak (these fellows were seriously into inaccessibility), it became a major religious destination until Oliver Cromwell extinguished it. The 1,729-ft climb has superb views but remember it is always windy on top and frequently soggy underfoot.

AROUND DONEGAL BAY

As you drive north to Donegal Town, the glens of the Dartry Mountains (to which Ben Bulben belongs) gloriously roll by to the east. Look across coastal fields for views of the waters of Donegal Bay to the west. In the distant horizon the Donegal hills beckon. This stretch, dotted with numerous prehistoric sites, has become Northwest Ireland's most popular vacation area. There are a few small and unremarkable seashore resorts, and in some places you may find examples of haphazard and fairly tasteless construction that detracts from the scenery. In between these minor resort developments, wide-open spaces are free of traffic. The most intriguing area lies on the north side of the bay—all that rocky indented coastline due west of Donegal Town. Here you enter the heart of away-from-it-all: County Donegal.

Mullaghmore

⓮ *20 km (13 mi) northeast of Lissadell House, 37 km (24 mi) north of Sligo Town off N15.*

In July and August, the picturesque, sleepy fishing village of Mullaghmore becomes congested with tourists. Its main attractions: a 3-km-long (2-mi-long) sandy beach; and the turreted, fairy-tale Classie Bawn—the late Lord Louis Mountbatten's home (he, his grandson, and a local boy were killed when the IRA blew up his boat in the bay in 1979). A short drive along the headland is punctuated by unobstructed views beyond the rocky coastline out over Donegal Bay. When the weather is fair, you can see all the way across to St. John's Point and Drumanoo Head in Donegal.

Creevykeel is one of Ireland's best megalithic court-tombs. There's a burial area and an enclosed open-air court where rituals were performed around 3000 BC. Bronze artifacts found here are now in the National Museum in Dublin. The site (signposted from N15) lies off the road, just beyond the edge of the village of Cliffony. ⊠ *3 km (2 mi) southeast of Mullaghmore off N15.*

Where to Stay & Eat

$ ✕🏨 **Beach Hotel.** If there's a chill in the air, you can warm up at the roaring fires in the restaurant ($–$$$) and residents' lounge of this large harborside Victorian hotel. The exterior of the simple, three-story building wears a dashing coat of red. Inside, nautical accents tout the history of the bay (it seems three galleons of the Spanish Armada went aground here in September 1588). Enjoy wonderful views of the pier and the bay from the hotel bars, or tuck into the de'Cuellar Restaurant's acclaimed seafood menu. Try the favorites: hot crab claws, lobster, and the house seafood platter. Save room for the homemade apple-and-rhubarb crumble. ⊠ *The Harbour, Co. Sligo* ☎ *071/916–6103* 🖷 *071/916–6448* ⊕ *www.beachhotelmullaghmore.com* ⇆ *28 rooms* ⌂ *Restaurant, indoor pool, gym, hair salon, hot tub, sauna, steam room, 2 bars; no a/c* ⊟ *AE, MC, V* ⏏❘ *BP, MAP.*

Bundoran

 17 km (11 mi) northeast of Mullaghmore, 35 km (22 mi) northeast of Sligo Town on N15.

Resting on the south coast of County Donegal, Bundoran is one of Ireland's most popular seaside resorts, a favorite haunt of the Irish from both the north and the south. To avoid souvenir shops and amusement arcades, head north of the center to the handsome beach at **Tullan Strand,** washed by good surfing waves. Between the main beach and Tullan, the Atlantic has sculpted cliff-side rock formations that the locals have christened with whimsical names such as the Fairy Bridges, the Wishing Chair, and the Puffing Hole (which blows wind and water from the waves pounding below).

Ballyshannon

 6 km (4 mi) north of Bundoran, 42 km (26 mi) northeast of Sligo Town on N15.

The former garrison town of Ballyshannon rises gently from the banks of the River Erne and has good views of Donegal Bay and the surrounding mountains. Come in early August, when this quiet village springs to life with a grand festival of folk and traditional music. The town is a hodgepodge of shops, arcades, and hotels. Its triangular central area has several bars and places to grab a snack. The town was also the birthplace of the prolific poet William Allingham.

A few kilometers down the road are several factories where eggshell-thin Irish porcelainware has been made by master craftsmen for generations. It's said that if a newlywed couple receives a piece of this china, their marriage will be blessed with everlasting happiness. The name Belleek has become synonymous with much of Ireland's delicate ivory porcelain figurines and woven china baskets (sometimes painted with shamrocks); **Belleek Pottery Ltd.** is the best known of the producers, in operation since 1857. Their main factories are just down the road from Ballyshannon in Northern Ireland (which is why their prices are quoted in pounds sterling, not euros). Watch the introductory film, take the 30-minute tour, stop by for refreshment in the tearoom, or just head to the on-site shop. A cup-and-saucer set starts at UK£16, a typical basket UK£69, and prices head skyward from there. The factory-museum-store is near the border with Northern Ireland. Company products can also be found in the shops of Donegal and Sligo. ⊠ *6 km (4 mi) east of Ballyshannon, Belleek, Northern Ireland* ☎ *028/6865–8501 in Northern Ireland* ⊕ *www.belleek.ie* 🖾 *UK£4* ☉ *Apr.–June, Sept., and Oct., weekdays 9–6, Sat. 10–6, Sun. 2–6; July and Aug., weekdays 9–8, Sat. 10–6, Sun. 11–6; Nov.–Mar., weekdays 9–5:30.*

The fourth generation (since 1866) of the Daly family handcrafts and paints the elaborate floral and basket-weave designs at **Celtic Weave China.** Because it's a small, personal operation, they can make a single piece of china to your specifications. Prices start at €7, and most pieces cost less than €125. ⊠ *R230, 5 km (3 mi) east of Ballyshannon, Cloghore,*

Co. Donegal ☎ *071/985–1844* ⊕ *www.celticweavechina.ie* ✉ *Free* ⊙ *Weekdays 8–6, Sat. 9–5.*

OFF THE
BEATEN
PATH

LOUGH DERG – From Whitsunday to the Feast of the Assumption (June to mid-August), tens of thousands beat a path to the celebrated lake of Lough Derg, ringed by heather-clad slopes. In the center of the lough, Station Island—known as St. Patrick's Purgatory (the saint is said to have fasted here for 40 days and nights)—is one of Ireland's most popular pilgrimage sites. It's also the most rigorous and austere of such sites in the country. Pilgrims stay on the island for three days without sleeping, and ingest only black tea and dry toast. They walk barefoot around the island, on its flinty stones, to pray at a succession of shrines. The pilgrimage has been followed since time immemorial; during the Middle Ages, devotees from foreign lands flocked here. Nonpilgrims may not visit the island from June to mid-August. To find out how to become a pilgrim, write to the Reverend Prior. To reach the shores of Lough Derg, turn off the main N15 Sligo–Donegal road in the village of Laghy onto the minor R232 Pettigo road, which hauls itself over the Black Gap and descends sharply into the border village of Pettigo, about 21 km (13 mi) from N15. From here, take the Lough Derg access road for 8 km (5 mi). During pilgrim season, buses connect Pettigo with Donegal, Laghey, and Ballybofey. ✉ *Lough Derg Visitor Centre, Main St., Pettigo* ☎ *072/61546.*

Nightlife

7

The biggest and most popular pub, **Seán Óg's** (✉ Market St. ☎ 071/985–8964), has live music on Friday, Saturday, and Sunday evenings.

Donegal Town

17 *21 km (13 mi) north of Ballyshannon, 66 km (41 mi) northeast of Sligo Town on N15.*

The town of Donegal was previously known in Irish as Dun na nGall, "Fort of the Foreigners." The foreigners were Vikings, who set up camp here in the 9th century to facilitate their pillaging and looting. They were driven out by the powerful O'Donnell clan (originally Cinel Conaill), who made it the capital of Tyrconail, their extensive Ulster territories. Donegal was rebuilt in the early 17th century, during the Plantation period, when Protestant colonists were planted on Irish property confiscated from its Catholic owners. The **Diamond**, like that of many other Irish villages, dates from this period. Once a marketplace, it has a 20-foot-tall obelisk monument (1937), which honors the town monks who, before driven out by the English in the 17th century, took the time to copy down a series of Old Irish legends in what they called *The Annals of the Four Masters.*

With a population of about 3,000, Donegal is Northwest Ireland's largest small village—marking the entry into the back-of-the-beyond of the wilds of County Donegal. The town is centered on the triangular Diamond, where three roads converge (N56 to the west, N15 to the south and the northeast) and the mouth of the River Eske pours gently into Donegal Bay. You should have your bearings in five minutes, and seeing the historical sights takes less than an hour; if you stick around any longer, it'll probably be to do some shopping—arguably Donegal's top attraction.

Picturesque **Donegal Castle** was built by clan leader Hugh O'Donnell in the 1470s. More than a century later, this structure was the home of his descendant Hugh Roe O'Donnell, who faced the might of the invading English and was the last clan chief of Tyrconail. In 1602 he died on a trip to Spain while trying to rally reinforcements from his allies. In 1610 its new English owner, Sir Basil Brooke, reconstructed the little castle, adding the fine Jacobean fortified mansion with towers and turrets that can still be seen. Inside there are only a few rooms to see, including the garderobe (the restroom) and a great hall with an exceptional vaulted wood-beam roof. Also of note is the gargantuan sandstone fireplace nicely wrought with minute details. The small enclosed grounds are pleasant. ⊠ *Tirchonaill St., near north corner of Diamond* ☎ *074/972–2405* 🎟 *€4* ⊙ *Apr.–Oct., daily 10–6; Nov.–Mar., Fri.–Sun., 10–4.*

The ruins of the **Franciscan Abbey,** founded in 1474 by Hugh O'Donnell, are a five-minute walk south of town at a spectacular site perched above the Eske River, where it begins to open up into Donegal Bay. The complex was burned to the ground in 1593, razed by the English in 1601, and ransacked again in 1607; the ruins include the choir, south transept, and two sides of the cloisters, between which lie hundreds of graves dating to the 18th century. The abbey was probably where the *Annals of the Four Masters,* which chronicles the whole of Celtic history and mythology of Ireland from earliest times up to the year 1618, was written from 1632 to 1636. The Four Masters were monks who believed (correctly, as it turned out) that Celtic culture was doomed by the English conquest, and they wanted to preserve as much of it as they could. At the National Library in Dublin, you can see copies of the monks' work; the original is kept under lock and key. ⊠ *Off N15, behind Hyland Central Hotel* 🎟 *Free* ⊙ *Freely accessible.*

Where to Stay & Eat

★ ¢–$ ✕ **Blueberry Tea Room.** Proprietors Brian and Ruperta Gallagher serve breakfast, lunch, afternoon tea, and a light evening meal—always using home-grown herbs. Daily specials—Irish lamb stew, pasta dishes, and quiche—are served from 8 AM to 8 PM. Soups, sandwiches, salads, and fruit are on the regular menu, along with homemade desserts, breads, scones, and jams. Upstairs is an Internet café. It's across the street from Donegal Castle. ⊠ *Castle St.* ☎ *074/972–2933* 🍴 *V* ⊙ *Closed Sun.*

★ $$$$ ✕🛏 **Harvey's Point.** Set in a remote and breathtaking location on the shores of Lough Eske at the foot of the Blue Stack Mountains, Harvey's Point offers a spirit-lifting setting. The drive to the hotel is awe-inspiring in itself—no other man-made structure blights the perfect landscape for miles and your surprise is complete when the elegant edifice looms up along the shores of the lake. Reception areas gleam with cherrywoods and polished stone and flaunt great views (along with wild geese and swans clucking for attention from time to time). A major extension, with 42 new guest rooms, was completed in 2005, with huge suites with bathrooms the size of most Irish hotel rooms. The Irish-with-a-French-flair restaurant serves a four-course dinner—a great option is the roast Donegal lamb with crispy sweetbreads. Even if your itinerary prevents you from overnighting, it is well worth dropping in for the Sunday carvery lunch, famous with the locals. ⊠ *6 km (4 mi) northwest of Donegal Town, off N15, Lough Eske, Co. Donegal* ☎ *074/972–2208* 🖷 *074/972–2352* ⊕ *www.harveyspoint.com* ⟿ *75 rooms* ⌂ *Restaurant, bicycles, bar, meeting rooms; no a/c* ⊟ *AE, DC, MC, V* ⟡ *MAP.*

$$$$ ✕⊞ **St. Ernan's House.** A most sweetly situated country house, St. Ernan's sits on its own tiny wooded tidal island in Donegal Bay. Fitted out with a lordly verandah, white stone trim, and a facade that glows in lilac hues, the two-story house was built by a nephew of the duke of Wellington in 1826. Today this forgetaway remains a relaxed, serene lodging, thanks to owner–managers Brian and Carmel O'Dowd. The entry salon is nearly baronial in taste, thanks to its aged, wood panels and elegant fireplace. Guest rooms are neatly refurbished; most of the furnishings are standard-issue antique or traditional chair or sofa stylishly done up in plaid ticking. All fades into insignificance when you drink in the bay views. Dinner is served in the intimate dining room ($$$) and may include fresh homemade tagliatelle with smoked salmon followed by crispy breast of duckling or wild salmon. ⊠ *3 km (2 mi) south of Donegal Town, off R267, St. Ernan's, Co. Donegal* ☎ *074/972–1065* 🖷 *074/972–2098* ⊕ *www.sainternans.com* ⟿ *10 rooms, 2 suites* ⌂ *Restaurant; no a/c* ⊟ *MC, V* ⊙ *Closed Nov.–mid-Apr.* ⟡ *BP.*

FodorsChoice
★

$–$$ ⊞ **Central Hotel.** With its bright white shutters and boldly red facade, this pretty-as-an-Irish-picture inn sits smack on Donegal's central square. While family-run, it is affiliated with the big Irish firm of White's Hotels. Huge picture windows in the back reveal lovely views of Donegal Bay. The efficient staff serves good, filling food in the Captain's Cove restaurant and there's an adjacent and cheaper Carvery. ⊠ *The Diamond, Co. Donegal* ☎ *074/972–1027* 🖷 *074/972–2295* ⊕ *www.whites-hotelsireland.com* ⟿ *112 rooms* ⌂ *2 restaurants, cable TV, in-room data ports, indoor pool, health club, bar, no-smoking rooms; no a/c* ⊟ *AE, DC, MC, V* ⟡ *BP, MAP.*

Nightlife

The **Abbey Hotel** (⊠ The Diamond ☎ 074/972–1014) has music every night in July and August and a disco every Saturday and Sunday night throughout the year. In summer, people pack **McGroarty's Bar** (⊠ The Diamond ☎ 074/972–1049) to hear traditional music Thursday nights and contemporary music on weekends. It's also a good place to stop for a casual bite to eat.

Sports & the Outdoors

Donegal Golf Club (⊠ 8 km [5 mi] from Donegal Town, Murvagh, Laghy, Co. Donegal ☎ 074/973–4054 ⊕ www.donegalgolfclub.ie) is one of Ireland's great 18-hole championship courses.

Shopping

Long the principal marketplace for the region's wool products, Donegal Town has several smaller shops with local hand weaving, knits, and crafts. **Browse a While** (⊠ Main St. ☎ 074/912–2783) is a good place to stop if you're in the mood for some light reading. The shop is stocked with tons of magazines and a small selection of pulp fiction. Explore

Donegal Craft Village (⊠ N15, 1½ km [1 mi] south of town ☎ No phone), a complex of workshops where you can buy pottery, handwoven goods, jewelery, and ceramics from local young craftspeople. You can even watch the items being made Monday to Saturday 9–6, and Sunday 11–6.

The main hand-weaving store in town, **Magee's** (⊠ The Diamond ☎ 074/972–2660) carries renowned private-label tweeds for both men and women (jackets, hats, scarves, suits, and more), as well as pottery, linen, and crystal. **Simple Simon's** (⊠ The Diamond ☎ 074/972–2687), the only fresh food shop here, sells organic vegetables, essential oils, and other whole-earth items, as well as breads and cakes from the kitchen on the premises. They also stock a lot of local Irish cheeses.

EN ROUTE As you travel west on N56, which runs slightly inland from a magnificent shoreline of rocky inlets with great sea views, it's worthwhile turning off the road from time to time to catch a better view of the coast. About 6 km (4 mi) out of Donegal Town, N56 skirts Mountcharles, a bleak hillside village that looks back across the bay.

Bruckless

⑱ *19 km (12 mi) west of Donegal Town on N56.*

Don't be fooled by the round tower in the churchyard at Bruckless—it's 19th-century, not medieval. Soon after Bruckless, N56 turns inland across the bogs toward Ard an Ratha. The road now becomes R263, which runs through attractive heathland and wooded hills down to Killybegs.

Where to Stay & Eat

$ ×⊞ **Castle Murray House Hotel.** Panoramas of distant mountains, the sapphire-blue waters of MacSwyne's Bay, and the long, narrow peninsula, punctuated at its tip by a lighthouse, await you at this hotel 1½ km (1 mi) out on the 10-km-long (6-mi-long) St. John's Point Peninsula. The original house—sorry, it's your basic suburban number and not a "castle" in the least—has been extended and modernized; rooms are basic and contemporary, with individual color schemes. Natives trek here for the white-tablecloth restaurant overlooking the bay ($$$$). Prix-fixe selections might include glazed duck breast with confit of sweet ginger or steamed black sole with brandy cream. Lobster is a specialty. ⊠ *3 km (2 mi) southeast of Bruckless, 1½ km (1 mi) from Dunkineely, off N56, Dunkineely, Co. Donegal* ☎ *074/973–7022* 🖷 *074/973–7330* ⊕ *www.castlemurray.com* ⤴ *10 rooms* ⚴ *Restaurant, bar; no a/c* ▤ *MC, V* ☾ *Hotel closed mid-Jan.–mid-Feb.; restaurant closed Mon. and Tues., Jan.–May* ⎯⎮ *BP.*

Killybegs

⑲ *6 km (4 mi) west of Bruckless on R263, 28 km (17 mi) west of Donegal Town.*

Trawlers from Spain and France are moored in the harbor at Killybegs, one of Ireland's busiest fishing ports. Though it's one of the most industrialized places along this coast, it's not without some charm, thanks to its waterfront location. Killybegs once served as a center for the manufacture of Donegal hand-tufted carpets, examples of which are in the White House and the Vatican. **Killybegs Carpets** (✉ Kilcar Rd. ☎ 074/973–1688) has a factory on the outskirts of the village, and produces high-quality hand-knotted and hand-tufted carpets to order: a square meter costs around €2,000. Visitors are welcome to commission a piece, but examples of the carpets are not sold off the peg.

**EN
ROUTE**
The narrows, climbs, and twists of R263 afford terrific views of Donegal Bay before descending into pretty Cill Chartaigh (Kilcar), a traditional center of tweed making. Signposted by its Irish name, the next village, An Charraig (Carrick), clings to the foot of the **Slieve League Mountains,** whose dramatic, color-streaked ocean cliffs are, at 2,000 feet, the highest in Ireland and among the most spectacular. Slieve League (Sliah Liec, or Mountain of the Pillars) is a ragged, razor-back rise bordered by the River Glen. To see the cliffs, take the little road to the Irish-speaking village of Teileann, 1½ km (1 mi) south from Carrick. Then take the narrow lane (signposted to the Bunglass Cliffs) that climbs steeply to the top of the cliffs. The mountain looks deceptively climbable from the back (the inaccessible point borders the Atlantic), but once the fog rolls in, the footing can be perilous. If you want to take in this thrilling perspective—presuming you're hardy and careful—walk along the difficult coastal path from Teileann.

Where to Stay & Eat

$ ✕☎ **Bay View Hotel.** Across from Killybegs's harbor, the Bay View is the town's most bustling spot. The hotel lobby, in light wood, offers a modern take on classic designs, and the functional but very pleasant bedrooms are decorated in pale colors; many rooms offer bayside views. The Irish table d'hôte menu changes daily, with Bruckless mussels in a white wine and garlic sauce and braised young duckling served with market vegetables and an orange and cherry coulis as potential options ($$$$). The hotel is well placed for seeing the glorious north shore of Donegal Bay. Special rates include golf greens fees for Portnoo (outside Ard an Ratha) and Murvagh (outside Donegal). ✉ *Main St., Co. Donegal* ☎ *074/973–1950* ☎ *074/973–1856* ⊕ *www.bayviewhotel.ie* ➱ *40 rooms* ⚘ *Restaurant, indoor pool, health club, bar; no a/c* ☰ *AE, MC, V* ⬦ *BP, MAP.*

Shopping

The **Harbour Store** (✉ Main St. ☎ 074/973–2122), right on the wharf, has plenty to make both fisherfolk and landlubbers happy, including boots and rain gear, competitively priced sweaters, and unusual bright-yellow or -orange fiberglass-covered gloves (made in Taiwan).

Gleann Cholm Cille (Glencolumbkille)

20 *27 km (17 mi) west of Killybegs on R263, 54 km (27 mi) west of Donegal Town.*

"Back of beyond," at the far end of a stretch of barren moorland, the tiny hamlet of Gleann Cholm Cille clings dramatically to the rockbound harbor of Glen Bay. Known alternatively as Glencolumbkille (pronounced glen-colm-*kill*), it remains the heart of County Donegal's shrinking Gaeltacht region and retains a strong rural Irish flavor, as do its pubs and brightly painted row houses. The name means St. Columba's Glen; the legend goes that St. Columba, the Christian missionary, lived here during the 6th century with a group of followers before many of them moved on to find greater glory by settling Scotland's Isle of Iona. Some 40

prehistoric cairns, scattered around the village, have become connected locally with the St. Columba myths. The **House of St. Columba,** on the cliff top rising north of the village, is a small oratory said to have been used by the saint himself. Inside, stone constructions are thought to have been his bed and chair. Every year on June 9, starting at midnight, local people make a 3-km (2-mi) barefoot procession called "An Turas" (the journey) around 15 medieval crosses and ancient cairns, collectively called the stations of the cross.

★ Walk through the beachfront **Folk Village Museum** to explore rural life. This *clachan,* or tiny village, comprises a mere six cottages, all of which are white-washed, thatched-roofed, and extremely modest in appearance. Three showcase particular years in Irish culture: 1720, 1820, and 1920; pride of place goes to the 1881 schoolhouse and the recreated *sheebeen* (pub). The complex was built after local priest Father McDyer started a cooperative to help combat rural depopulation. You'll also find an interpretive center, nature walk, tea shop (don't dare miss out on the Guinness cakes), and crafts shop selling local handmade products, including, intriguingly, wines made from fuchsias, bluebells, heather, and seaweed. In summer the museum hosts traditional music evenings. Three small cottages, with bare-earth floors, represent the very basic living conditions of the 1720s, 1820s, and 1920s. ⊠ *Near beach* ☎ *074/973–0017* ⊕ *www.glenfolkvillage.com* ⊠ €3 ⊗ *Easter–Sept., Mon.–Sat. 10–6, Sun. noon–6.*

Cliffs surrounding Gleaan Cholm Cille rise up to more than 700 ft, including Glen Head; many cliffs are studded with ancient hermit cells. Also of note is a squat Martello Tower, built by the British in 1804 to protect against an anticipated French invasion that never happened. Another good walk is the 8-km (5-mi) trek to Malinbeg, reached by the coast road running past Doon Point. Look for the ruins of no less than five burial cairns, a ring fort, a second Martello tower, and one of the best beaches in Ireland, famed for its calm waters, dramatic scenery, and lovely golden sand.

Ard an Ratha (Ardara)

★ ㉑ *28 km (17 mi) northeast of Gleann Cholm Cille, 40 km (25 mi) northwest of Donegal Town on N56.*

Dream-Weavers

MOST OF THE ARAN SWEATERS you'll see throughout Ireland are made in County Donegal, the area most associated with high-quality, handwoven tweeds and hand-knit items. Made of plain, undyed wool and knit with distinctive crisscross patterns, Aran sweaters are durable, soft, often weatherproof, and can be astonishingly warm. They once provided essential protection against the wild, stormy Atlantic Ocean. Indeed, these Arans can hold 30% of their weight in water before they even start to feel wet. Not so long ago, these pullovers were worn by every County Donegal fisherman, usually made to a design belonging exclusively to his own family. It's said that a native can tell which family the knitter belongs to from the patterns used in a genuine Aran sweater. Produced for centuries in the fishing communities of north and west Ireland, they are painstakingly knitted by hand, a process that can take weeks. As a result, prices are not cheap, and if you think you've found a bargain, check the label before buying—it's more likely a factory copy. When it comes to Donegal tweed, weavers—inspired by the soft greens, red rusts, and dove grays of the famed Donegal landscape—have been producing it for centuries. In long-gone days, crofters' wives concocted the dyes to give Donegal tweed its distinctive flecks, and then their husbands wove the cloth into tweed. Traditional Donegal tweed was a salt-and-pepper mix, but gradually weavers began adding dyes distilled from yellow gorse, purple blackberries, orange lichen, and green moss. Today most tweed comes from factories. However, there are still about 25 local craftsmen working from their cottages. Chic fashion designers like Armani, Ralph Lauren, and Burberry all use handwoven Donegal tweed—obviously, more fashionable than ever.

At the head of a lovely ocean inlet, the unpretentious, old-fashioned hamlet of Ard an Ratha (Ardara) is built around the L-shape intersection of its two main streets. (If you come from Gleann Cholm Cille, expect a scenic drive full of hairpin curves and steep hills as you cross over Glengesh Pass.) For centuries, great cloth fairs were held on the first of every month; cottage workers in the surrounding countryside still provide Ard an Ratha (and County Donegal) with high-quality, handwoven cloths, and hand knits. Aran sweaters—an area specialty—are durable, soft, and often weatherproof, made of undyed wool knit in distinct crisscross patterns. Ard an Ratha has several stores to choose from.

Where to Stay & Eat

$$$ ✕🛏 **Nesbitt Arms Hotel.** Offering both casual pub grub and more substantial fare, this old-fashioned inn gets understandably busy in summer. Decor harks back to the days when Ard an Ratha was Donegal's foremost weaving and wool center, which explains the wooden loom in the corner of the dining room. And what about the weaver depicted on the menu? He's the grandfather of the owner, Marie Gallagher, who, along with her husband, recently took over the operation. If you want

VOICES OF IRELAND

Eddie Doherty
From War-Child to Weaver

The small village of Ardara is famed for its hand weavers and crafts people who have been producing Donegal tweed for hundreds of years. And there is no finer man to educate you on the ancient method of weaving than Ardara's most famous adopted son, Eddie Doherty.

Eddie owns a small tweed workshop (Front Street, 074/954-1304) and personally weaves beautiful hand-crafted fabric that can be turned into all manner of apparel. A jack-of-all-trades, he is also the landlord of Eddie Doherty's pub in Ardara village—despite never touching a drop of the hard stuff himself.

The sign on the door of the country pub (which serves a first-rate pint, incidentally) says it has been in the family for over a century. However, Eddie was not born and bred in County Donegal but was evacuated to Ardara from Belfast during World War II. The toddler was sent to stay with relatives of his mother along with his older brother to escape German bombing. He stayed on to make Ardara his adopted homeland.

"As it turns out, my aunt was widowed and she became very attached to me, so after the war my brother returned to Belfast and I stayed put—the war split up a lot of families for one reason or another."

Had he not divulged his unusual past over the bar of Eddie Doherty's pub you would never know he wasn't a born and bred Donegal man. His life was typical of young men growing up in the rural countryside in the 1950s.

"I left school at 16 and went to work in a local factory where I learned warping, weaving and all aspects of the trade. I just carried on with it since then, the colors I use reflect the colors in the landscape. I split my time between the bar and the shop, but I'm always on hand to give a demonstration to visitors. If I'm not in the shop there's a sign telling visitors to call at the pub, sure I'm easy found."

"And there's always a warm welcome in Ardara—that's the Donegal way," he smiles.

a quick bite, check out the daily specials in the bar—the beef and Guinness pie is particularly tasty. Upstairs in the dining room, standout dishes include a smoked salmon–and–dill terrine starter, followed by crispy baked duck with black-cherry-and-orange sauce. The hotel also lets simple rooms. ⊠ *Main St.* ☎ *074/954–1103* ▭ *MC, V.*

★ $ ✕▥ **Woodhill House.** The cream-color exterior of John and Nancy Yates's spacious manor house is Victorian, but parts of the interior and the coach house date from the 17th century; there's even a small agricultural museum. High ceilings, marble fireplaces, and stained glass are part of the public spaces. Bedrooms have superb views of the Donegal highlands. The 40-seat restaurant ($$$$) uses local ingredients in dishes on its French-Irish table d'hôte menus: roast duckling with cherry-and-orange sauce, rack of lamb with herbs picked from the 18th-century walled garden, elaborate homemade desserts. Frequent Irish folk music sessions take place in the bar. At the time of this writing, work continued on a new wing with six guest rooms overlooking the gardens. ⊠ *Just outside Ard an Ratha, Donegal Rd., Co. Donegal* ☎ *074/954–1112* 🖷 *074/954– 1516* ⊕ *www.woodhillhouse.com* ⇝ *9 rooms* ⚇ *Restaurant, fishing, horseback riding, bar; no a/c* ⊟ *AE, DC, MC, V* ⊙ *Closed Christmas wk* ⑩ *BP.*

¢–$ 🖫 **Green Gate.** For an alternative to country estates and village hotels, try Frenchman Paul Chatenoud's remote cottage B&B overlooking Ard an Ratha, the Atlantic, and spectacular Donegal scenery—it's one of Ireland's most beautiful little guesthouses. The four spare rooms are in a converted stone outbuilding with a thatched roof. Chatenoud, as charming as his hideaway, eagerly directs you to Donegal's best-kept secrets. To reach the hotel from Ard an Ratha, follow the sign for Donegal and turn right after 200 yards. ⊠ *Ardvally, Co. Donegal* ☎ *074/954–1546* ⊕ *www.thegreengate-ireland.com* ⇝ *4 rooms* ⚇ *No a/c, no room phones, no room TVs* ⊟ *No credit cards* ⑩ *BP.*

FodorśChoice ★

Nightlife

For a small, old-fashioned village, Ard an Ratha has a surprising number of pubs, many of which have traditional music in the evenings. The **Central Bar** (⊠ Main St. ☎ 074/954–1311) has music almost every night in July and August and on weekends the rest of the year. One of the smallest bars in the Republic, **Nancy's Pub** (⊠ Front St. ☎ 074/954–1187) makes you wonder if you've wandered into the owner's sitting room, but it occasionally finds space for a folk group.

Shopping

Many handwoven and locally made knitwear items are on sale in Ard an Ratha. Some stores commission goods directly from knitters, and prices are about as low as anywhere. Handsome, chunky Aran hand-knit sweaters (€80–€130), cardigans (similar prices), and scarves (€25) are all widely available. Stores such as **Campbells Tweed Shop** (⊠ Front St. ☎ 074/954–1128) carry ready-to-wear tweeds—sports jackets can run up to €120. **C. Bonner & Son** (⊠ Front St. ☎ 074/954–1303) stocks factory knitwear from €30 to €120, as well as pottery, tweeds, jewelry, and gifts. There's also a good selection of hand-knit Aran sweaters and cardigans available. **E. Doherty (Ardara) Ltd** (⊠ Front St. ☎ 074/954–1304) sells handwoven tweeds, from scarves for €25 to capes for €195, as well as traditional Irish products, such as glassware and linen, from Ard an Ratha and other parts of the country. At **John Molloy** (⊠ Main St. ☎ 074/954–1133) you will find a factory shop offering high-quality, handwoven Donegal tweed, and hand-knit Aran sweaters.

NORTHERN DONEGAL

Traveling on northern County Donegal's country roads, you've escaped at last from the world's hurry and hassle. There's almost nothing up here but scenery, and plenty of it: broad, island-studded loughs of deep, dark tranquillity; unkempt, windswept, sheep-grazed grasses on mountain slopes; ribbons of luminous greenery following sparkling streams;

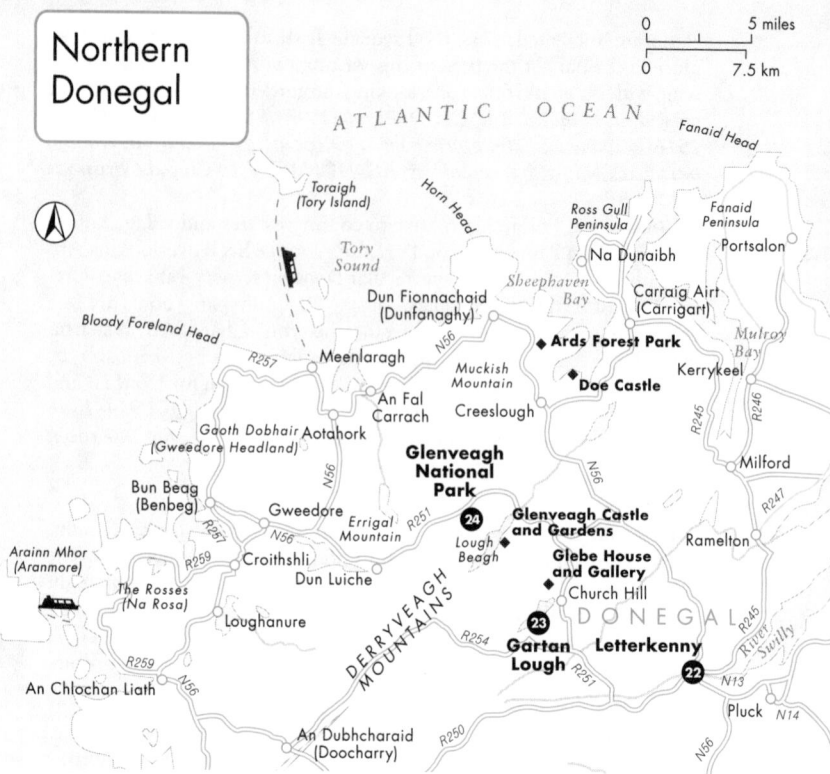

Northern
Donegal

0   5 miles
0   7.5 km

ATLANTIC   OCEAN   Fanaid Head

Toraigh (Tory Island)   Horn Head   Ross Gull Peninsula   Fanaid Peninsula   Portsalon

Tory Sound   Sheephaven Bay   Na Dunaibh   Carraig Airt (Carrigart)

Dun Fionnachaid (Dunfanaghy)   Mulroy Bay

Bloody Foreland Head   R257   Meenlaragh   N56   ♦ Ards Forest Park   Kerrykeel

Muckish Mountain   ♦ Doe Castle

An Fal Carrach   Creeslough   R245   R246

Gaoth Dobhair (Gweedore Headland)   Aotahork   Glenveagh National Park   Milford

Bun Beag (Benbeg)   Gweedore   Errigal Mountain   R251   R247

Arainn Mhor (Aranmore)   R259   Croithshli   Lough Beagh   ㉔ Glenveagh Castle and Gardens   Ramelton

Dun Luiche   ♦ Glebe House and Gallery   Church Hill

The Rosses (Na Rosa)   Loughanure   ♦ DONEGAL

R254   ㉓   Letterkenny   River Swilly

An Chlochan Liath   N56   Gartan Lough   R251   ㉒   N13

Pluck   N14

An Dubhcharaid (Doocharry)   R250   N56

and the mellow hues of wide bog lands, all under shifting and changing cloudscapes. This trip begins in Letterkenny, the largest town in the county (population 6,500), and makes a beeline to the Irish Xanadu of Henry P. McIlhenny's Glenveagh Castle. Just one word of warning—don't be surprised if you find a sheep standing in the middle of a mountain road looking as though you, rather than it, are in the wrong place.

Letterkenny

㉒ *55 km (34 mi) northeast of Ard an Ratha, 51 km (32 mi) northeast of Donegal Town, 35 km (21 mi) west of Derry.*

One of the fastest-growing towns in all of Ireland, Letterkenny, like Donegal to the south, is at the gateway to the far northwest; you're likely to come through here if you're driving west out of Northern Ireland. Letterkenny's claim to fame has been that it has the longest main street in the whole country. None of Letterkenny's shops or pubs are particularly special, but lots of locals bustling around make it an interesting place to get a feel for what it's like to live in a modest-size Irish town. The 212-foot-high spire of **St. Eunan's Cathedral** (⊠ Convent Rd. ☎ No phone) dominates the town, especially when illuminated at night. This striking, ornate neo-Gothic structure was finally finished in 1901, and is the only cathedral in the county. Designed by William Hague of Dublin and built of white Donegal sandstone, the exterior of the building is said to be in perfect classical-rule proportion. Inside, the intricate decorative ceilings and ceramic floor mosaics are the work of an Italian artist, Signor Amici of Rome. The main and side altars are carved from the finest Italian marble, while the great nave arch depicts the lives of St. Eunan and St. Columba in meticulous detail.

Where to Stay & Eat

$$–$$$ ✕⌂ **Mount Errigal Hotel.** One of County Donegal's smartest and most modern hotels, although not at all posh, Mount Errigal Hotel appeals to both business and family travelers. Service is friendly and professional. The clean and comfortable bedrooms are efficiently arranged with light-color wood furnishings. The Strawberry Garden, the hotel's popular and softly lighted restaurant serves contemporary Irish food ($$), while its dazzling Café Renaissance's steel chandeliers, moderne seating, and wood-panel accents will light up any design aficionado's eyes. The bar buzzes with locals seeking a relaxed night out, and folk music, jazz, and dancing are frequently scheduled on weekends. ⊠ *Ballyraine, Co. Donegal* ☎ *074/912–2700* 🖨 *074/912–5085* ⊕ *www.mounterrigal.com* 🛏 *140 rooms, 2 suites* ⚬ *Restaurant, Wi-Fi, indoor pool, gym, health club, 2 bars, meeting rooms; no a/c* ⊟ *AE, DC, MC, V* ⏐⊙⏐ *BP, MAP.*

Gartan Lough

㉓ *21 km (13 mi) northwest of Letterkenny on R251.*

Gartan Lough and the surrounding mountainous country are astonishingly beautiful. St. Columba was supposedly born here in AD 521, and the legendary event is marked by a huge cross at the beginning of a footpath into Glenveagh National Park. (Close to Church Hill village, Gartan Lough is technically within the national park and is administered partly by the park authorities.)

On the northwest shore of Gartan Lough just off R251 is **Glebe House and Gallery,** a sweetly elegant red-brick Regency manor with 25 acres of gardens. For 30 years, Glebe House was the home of the distinguished landscape and portrait artist Derek Hill, who furnished the house in a mix of styles with art from around the world; in 1981 he gave the house and its contents, including his outstanding art collection, to the nation. Highlights include paintings by Renoir and Bonnard, lithographs by Kokoschka, ceramics and etchings by Picasso, and the paintings *Whippet Racing* and *The Ferry, Early Morning* by Jack B. Yeats, as well as Donegal folk art

THE GOOD EARTH

Near Gartan Lough are other dubious "relics" of St. Columba, which are popularly believed to possess magical powers: the Natal Stone, where the saint is thought to have first opened his eyes, and the Stone of Loneliness, where he is said to have slept. The superstitions do rub off—in the First World War, soldiers carried pocketsful of Gartan soil to the trenches as a protective relic.

produced by the Toraigh Islanders. The decoration and furnishings of the house, including original William Morris wallpaper, are also worth a look. ⊠ *Church Hill* ☎ *074/913–7071* 💳 *€2.75* ⊙ *Sat.–Thurs. 11–6:30.*

At the **Colmcille Heritage Centre** you can learn more about St. Columba and his times. The exhibition and interpretation center has medieval manuscripts, stained glass, and displays tracing the decline of the Celtic religion and the rise of Irish Christianity. Audiovisual displays and interactive computer presentations enhance the historical journey. The staff can show you walks in the area. ⊠ *R254, Church Hill* ☎ *074/913–7306* 💳 *€2* ⊙ *May–Sept., Mon.–Sat. 10:30–6:30, Sun. 1–6:30.*

Glenveagh National Park

㉔ *27 km (16 mi) northwest of Letterkenny on R250 and R251.*

Fodor'sChoice
★

Bordered by the Derryveagh Mountains (Derryveagh means "forest of oak and birch"), Glenveagh National Park encompasses 24,000 acres of wilderness—mountain, moorland, lakes, and woods—that has been called the largest and most dramatic tract in the wildest part of Donegal. Within its borders, a thick carpet of russet-color heath and dense woodland rolls down the Derryveagh slopes into the broad open valley of the River Veagh (or Owenbeagh), which opens out into Glenveagh's spine: long and narrow, dark and clear Lough Beagh.

The lands of Glenveagh (pronounced glen-*vay*) have long been recognized as a remote and beautiful region. Between 1857 and 1859, John George Adair, a ruthless gentleman farmer, assembled the estate that now makes up the park. In 1861 he evicted the estate's hundreds of poor tenants without compensation and destroyed their cottages. Nine years later Adair began to build **Glenveagh Castle** on the eastern shore of Lough Veagh, but he soon departed for Texas. He died in 1885 without returning to Ireland, but his widow, Cornelia, moved back to make Glenveagh her home. She created four gardens, covering 27 acres; planted luxuriant rhododendrons; and began the job of making this turret-and-battlement laden 19th-century folly livable. At the end of a dramatic 2-mi-long entryway, perched over the lake waters, this is a true fairytale castle. Like a doll-house Balmoral, its castellated, rectangular keep, battlemented ramparts, and a Round Tower enchantingly conjure up all the Victorian fantasies of a medieval redoubt.

The gardens and castle as they appear today are almost entirely an American invention, the product of the loving attentions of Glenveagh's last owners, including Mr. Kingsley Porter, a venerated professor of medieval art history at Harvard. He, then, passed the property over to U.S. millionaire Henry P. McIlhenny, who bought the estate in 1937 and, beginning in 1947, lived here for part of every year for almost 40 years. An avid art collector and philanthropist (his collection of Degas, Toulouse-Lautrec, and Ingres masterworks now resides at the Philadelphia Museum of Art), McIlhenny decorated every inch of the house himself in faux-baronial fashion and entertained the beau monde (Greta Garbo once slept in the Pink Room) lavishly. The house has been maintained just as it was on his last occupancy in 1983; later that year, he made a gift of the house to the nation. He had sold the government the surrounding land in 1975, which it opened to the public in 1984 as Ireland's third national park.

Beyond the castle, footpaths lead into more remote sections of the park, including the **Derrylahan Nature Trail,** a 1½-km (1-mi) signposted trail where you may suddenly catch sight of a soaring falcon or chance upon a shy red deer. The park is the home of one of Ireland's two largest herds; the other is at Killarney. Guided walks are held from May through October. The visitor center at the park's entrance has a permanent exhibition on the local way of life and on the influence of climate on the park's flora and fauna. Skip the sleep-inducing audiovisual and instead have a bite to eat in the cafeteria, or enjoy your own picnic on the extensive estate grounds, which are free for walkers. A bus runs from the visitor center to the castle. ✉ *R251, Church Hill* ☎ *074/913–7090* ⊕ *www. heritageireland.ie* 🚌 *Shuttle bus* €*2 round-trip, castle tour*€*3* ☉ *Feb.–Nov., daily 10–6:30.*

NORTHWEST ESSENTIALS

To research prices, get advice from other travelers, and book travel arrangements, visit www.fodors.com.

Transportation

If traveling extensively by public transportation, be sure to load up on information (the best taxi-for-call companies, rail and bus schedules, etc.) upon arriving at the ticket counter or help desk of the bigger train and bus stations in the area, such as Sligo Town and Letterkenny.

BY AIR

CARRIERS Aer Arann has flights from Knock International daily to Dublin and four times a week to Liverpool. It also flies twice daily between Sligo and Dublin. BmiBaby flies from Knock to Manchester daily and to Birmingham six days a week. EasyJet has flights from London Gatwick to Knock daily. Ryanair has daily flights to Knock Airport from London Stansted and London Gatwick, and also serves City of Derry Airport daily from London and Dublin. Aer Lingus has flights to Derry from Dublin. British Airways Express flies to City of Derry Airport from Manchester, Glasgow, and Dublin.

🛫 Airlines & Contacts **Aer Arann** ☎ 081/821–0210 or 0800/587–2324 ⊕ www.aerarann. ie. **British Airways City Express** ☎ 0870/850–9850 ⊕ www.britishairways.com. **British Midland Airways (BmiBaby)** ☎ 0870/607–0555 ⊕ www.bmibaby.com. **Ryanair** ☎ 0818/830–3030 ⊕ www.ryanair.com.

AIRPORTS

The principal international air-arrival point to Northwest Ireland is the tiny airport at Charlestown, Knock International Airport, 55 km (34 mi) south of Sligo Town. City of Derry Airport, a few miles over the border, receives flights from Manchester and Glasgow. City of Derry (also called Eglinton) is a particularly convenient airport for reaching northern County Donegal. Donegal Airport, in Carrickfinn, is not far from An Chlochan Liath (Dungloe) and typically receives flights from Dublin. Sligo Airport at Strandhill, 8 km (5 mi) west of Sligo Town, is the other area airport.

🛪 Airport Information **City of Derry Airport** ☎ 028/7181-0784. **Donegal Airport** ☎ 074/954-8232. **Knock International Airport** ☎ 094/936-7222. **Sligo Airport** ☎ 071/916-8280 or 071/916-8318.

TRANSFERS   If you aren't driving, Knock Airport becomes less attractive; there are no easy public transportation links, except the once-a-day (in season) local bus to Charlestown, 11 km (7 mi) away. Nor can you rely on catching a bus at the smaller airports, except at Sligo Airport, where buses run from Sligo Town to meet all flights.

You can get taxis—both cars and minibuses—right outside Knock Airport. The average rate is around €1.50 per kilometer. If you're not flying into Knock, you may have to phone a taxi company. Phone numbers of taxi companies are available from airport information desks and are also displayed beside pay phones inside the airport terminals.

🛪 Taxi Companies **Castle Cabs** ☎ 087/638-8588 or 087/252-7407. **OK Cabs** ☎ 087/639-6666. **Tom Cronnolly** ☎ 087/244-0597.

BY BUS

Bus Éireann can get you from Dublin to Sligo Town in four hours for €16 one-way, €24.50 round-trip. Four buses a day from Dublin are available. Another bus route, six times a day from Dublin (five on Sunday), goes to Letterkenny, in the heart of County Donegal, in 4¼ hours, via a short trip across the Northern Ireland border; it's €16 one-way, €26 round-trip. Other Bus Éireann services connect Sligo Town to towns all over Ireland. Bus Éireann also operates out of Sligo Town and Letterkenny to destinations all over the region, as well as to other parts of Ireland. From Sligo Town, you can reach almost any point in the region for less than €16. McGeehans is one of several local bus companies linking towns and villages in Northwest Ireland.

🛪 Bus Information **Bus Éireann** ☎ 01/836-6111 in Dublin, 071/916-0066 in Sligo Town, 074/912-1309 in Letterkenny. **McGeehans** ☎ 074/954-6150.

BY CAR

Sligo, the largest town in Northwest Ireland, is relatively accessible on the main routes. The N4 travels the 224 km (140 mi) directly from Dublin to Sligo. Allow at least four hours for this journey. The N15 continues from Sligo Town to Donegal Town and proceeds from Donegal Town to Derry City, just over the border in Northern Ireland. The fastest approach for anyone driving up from the west and the southwest is on N17, connecting Sligo to Galway, though the landscape is undistinguished.

ROAD   Roads are not congested, but in some places they are in a poor state of
CONDITIONS   repair (French bus drivers refused to take their buses into County Donegal some summers back, as a gesture of protest about the state of the roads). In the Irish-speaking areas, signposts are written only in the Irish (Gaelic) language, which can be confusing. Make sure that your map lists both English and Irish place names.

BY TRAIN

Sligo Town is the northernmost direct rail link to Dublin. From Dublin, three trains a day make the 3 hour and 20 minute journey for €24 one-way, €33 round-trip (prices are a bit higher on weekends). If you want to get to Sligo Town by rail from other provincial towns, you're forced to make some inconvenient connections and take roundabout routes. The rest of the region has no railway services.

🚹 Train Information **Irish Rail** ☎ 01/836-6222 ⊕ www.irishrail.ie.

Contacts & Resources

CAR RENTAL

You can rent a car in Sligo Town from Hertz. Murray's Europcar rents cars from Knock Airport. A medium-size four-door costs around €65 per day with unlimited mileage (inclusive of insurance and taxes) or around €250 per week. If you're planning to tour mostly northern County Donegal, you may find it more convenient to rent a car in Derry from Ford. If you're planning to drive a rental car across the border to Northern Ireland, inform the company in advance and check the insurance policy.

🚹 Agencies **Avis** ☎ 071/912-8004 operates out of Sligo Airport. **Hertz** ☎ 071/914-4068. **Ford** ☎ 028/7181-2222. **Murray's Europcar** ☎ 094/936-7221 at Knock Airport, 01/614-2800 reservations.

EMERGENCIES

🚹 **Ambulance, fire, police** ☎ 999. **Letterkenny General Hospital** ⊠ High Rd., Letterkenny, Co. Donegal ☎ 074/912-5888. **Sligo General Hospital** ⊠ The Mall, Sligo Town, Co. Sligo ☎ 071/917-1111.

INTERNET, MAIL & SHIPPING

Most hotels will allow guests to use their Internet facilities, but cyber-cafés are thin on the ground in this part of rural Ireland. There's one in Sligo Town, called the **Cygo Internet Café** (⊠ 19 O'Connell St. ☎ 071/914-0082) and its hookup costs about €3.50 for one hour.

Mail service in the Northwest of Ireland is reliable and efficient. The two main post offices in Donegal Town and Sligo Town are open weekdays 9 AM to 5:30 PM, Saturday 9 AM to 1 PM, and closed Sunday and public holidays. Look for the green signs that say "An Post." In rural villages, the opening hours are generally the same but most post offices will close for lunch from 1 to 2.

🚹 Post offices **Donegal Town post office** ⊠ Tirconaill St ☎ 074/972-1024. **Sligo Town post office** ⊠ Lower Knox St. ☎ 071/915-9273.

TOUR OPTIONS

Bus Éireann has budget-priced, guided, one-day bus tours of the Donegal Highlands and to Glenveagh National Park; they start from Bundoran, Sligo Town, Ballyshannon, and Donegal Town. For a friendly, relaxed minibus tour of the area in July and August, call John Houze. He's a knowledgeable guide who leads popular tours (€14 each) to the Lake Isle of Innisfree, the Holy Well, and Parke's Castle; and north of Sligo Town to W. B. Yeats's grave and Glencar Lake and waterfall.

Walking tours of Sligo Town may be arranged in advance for groups, and last about 1½ hours. Depending on the number of people, the charge is approximately €4.

🚶 Bus Tours **Bus Éireann** ☎ 01/836-6111 ⊕ www.buseireann.ie. **John Houze** ☎ 071/914-2747 or 086/193-5045.

🚶 Walking Tours **Sligo Path Guided Walking Tours** ☎ 071/915-0920.

VISITOR INFORMATION

The Tourist Information Office (TIO) in Sligo Town provides a walking map of Sligo, information about bus tours of Yeats Country, and details of boat tours of Lough Gill. It's also the main visitor information center for Northwest Ireland. Open hours are September to mid-March, weekdays 9–5; mid-March to August, weekdays 9–6, Saturday 10–2, and Sunday 11–3. If you're traveling in County Donegal in the north, try the TIO at Letterkenny, about 1½ km (1 mi) south of town. It's open September to May, weekdays 9–5; June to August, Monday–Saturday 9–6 and Sunday noon–3. The offices at Bundoran and An Chlochan Liath (Dungloe) are open only during the summer months (usually the first week in June to the second week in September).

🚶 Tourist Information **Bundoran TIO** ⊠ Main St., Bundoran, Co. Donegal ☎ 071/984-1350 ⊕ www.countydonegal.com. **Co. Donegal TIO** ⊠ N13, Derry Rd., Letterkenny, Co. Donegal ☎ 074/912-1160 ⊕ www.irelandnorthwest.ie. **Co. Sligo TIO** ⊠ Temple and Charles Sts., Sligo Town, Co. Donegal ☎ 071/916-1201 ⊕ www.sligotown.net is a good unofficial guide to Sligo town. **Donegal Town TIO** ⊠ Quay St., Donegal Town, Co. Donegal ☎ 074/972-1148 ⊕ www.donegaltown.ie. **Dungloe TIO** ⊠ Village Center, An Chlochan Liath (Dungloe), Co. Donegal ☎ 074/952-1297 ⊕ www.countydonegal.com.

Northern Ireland

INCLUDING COUNTIES ANTRIM, ARMAGH,
DERRY, DOWN, FERMANAGH, AND TYRONE

Giant's Causeway

WORD OF MOUTH

"Tyrone's Ulster-American Folk Park is history brought to life in a format perfect for vacation time. You get to walk into cottages where the poorest families dined on potatoes around an open fire. Then the tour takes you to the boat yards where you sit in a typical 'coffin-ship,' which brought hundreds of thousands of Irish to the U.S. during the famine. The sound effects are amazing. I have grown up with this story, yet I found myself close to tears."

—AnnaG

www.fodors.com/forums

WELCOME TO NORTHERN IRELAND

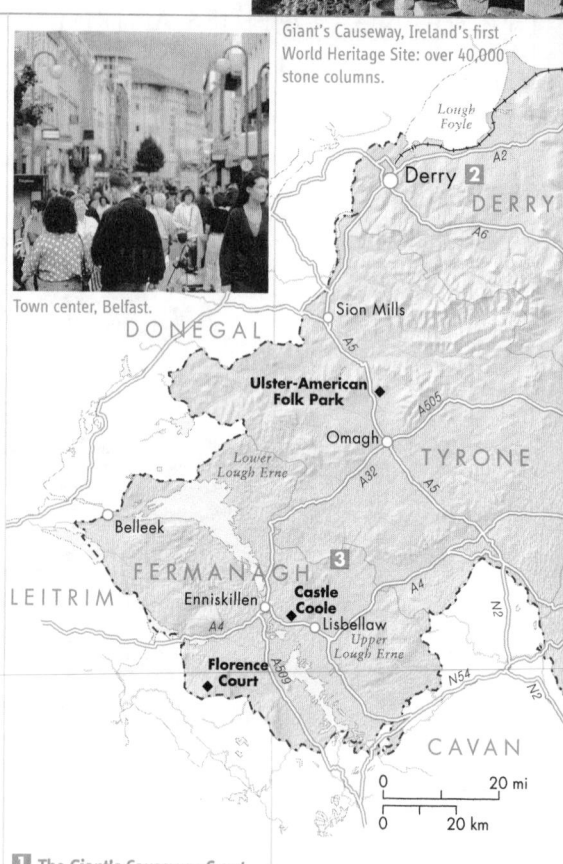

Giant's Causeway, Ireland's first World Heritage Site: over 40,000 stone columns.

Town center, Belfast.

TOP REASONS TO GO

★ **Belfast, Gateway City:** As the locals put it, "despite what you've probably heard, Belfast is not what you expect"—so get ready to love this bustling city that bristles with Victorian shop fronts and hip restaurants.

★ **The Giant's Causeway:** This spectacular remnant of Ireland's volcanic period will steal you away from your 21st-century existence and transport you to a time when the giant Finn Mc-Cool roamed the land.

★ **Nine Glens of Antrim:** Fabled haunt of "the wee folk," the glacier-carved valleys have a beauty that has become synonymous with Irishness. Don't miss Glenariff, dubbed "Little Switzerland" by Thackeray.

★ **Ulster-American Folk Park:** A tale of two countries joined by a common people is told at this impressive open-air museum, which recreates a 19th-century Tyrone village and boasts the Centre for Migration Studies.

1 The Giant's Causeway Coast. North of the famously beautiful **Glens of Antrim**—still considered "gentle" (supernatural) in spirit—this continues up to Northern Ireland's premier attraction, the **Giant's Causeway.** Farther along the North Antrim coast is **Bushmills,** the oldest distillery in the world; **Dunluce Castle,** spectacularly perched over its "Mermaid's Cave"; and the heart-stopping **Carrick-a-Rede** rope bridge.

2 Derry. A walk through Ireland's only walled city provides a unique way to view the layout of the 17th-century inner town, particularly noticeable in the streets and alleys that fan outward from the Diamond, where fine examples of Georgian and Victorian architecture rub shoulders with old-style pubs and museums.

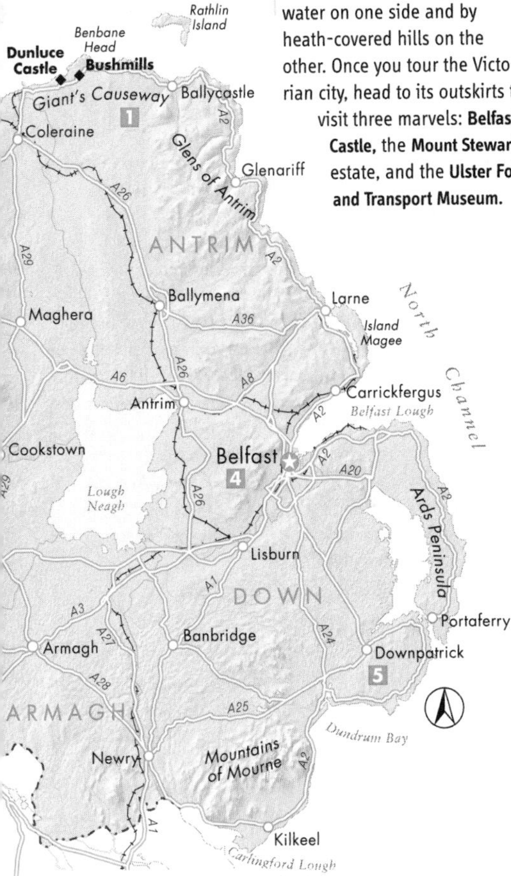

4 Belfast & Environs. **Belfast's** location is striking, nestled on the coast, buffered by green water on one side and by heath-covered hills on the other. Once you tour the Victorian city, head to its outskirts to visit three marvels: **Belfast Castle,** the **Mount Stewart** estate, and the **Ulster Folk and Transport Museum.**

GETTING ORIENTED

With peace—precious peace—abiding, Northern Ireland can finally go about the business of charming visitors full-time. North of the vibrant Victorian city of Belfast, they'll find the ageless wonders of the Causeway Coast while south of the inspiring skyline of Derry lies the Border Counties, where tiny "Ulster" towns dot the scenic landscapes around the Lakes of Fermanagh and Mountains of Mourne.

8

3 The Western Border Counties. The Fermanagh Lakeland is an intricate patchwork quilt of undulating hillsides and some of the most uncongested lakes in Europe. A paradise of open horizons and opportunities for those who love the outdoor life, it is also home to stately homes like **Florence Court** and **Castle Coole,** the **Ulster-American Folk Park,** and the famous porcelain town of **Belleek.**

5 The Eastern Border Counties. South of Belfast past the Ards Peninsula is St. Patrick Country: **Downpatrick,** reputed to be the burial place of the saint; **Armagh's** two St. Patrick cathedrals; and the seaside **Mountains of Mourne.**

Carrick-a-Rede Rope Bridge, Co. Antrim, Northern Ireland

NORTHERN IRELAND PLANNER

Talking About It

While "The Troubles" are now hopefully a thing of the past, Northern Ireland is a political entity that draws its mandate from religion and history—a country where God and politics are tightly interwoven and where ancient quarrels can sometimes still affect the tone of everyday life. So if you find yourself in a pub, it often helps to play a little dumb about facts and events, as the residents seem to be even more willing to explain the history to visitors with no preconceived notions of how things should be. Take any questions of politics gently at first, smell the air of the company you're in, then play the gee-this-is-all-new-to-me card, and things should roll along fine. And certainly stay away from any deep political discussion after four pints of beer! Whatever the differences between North and South, Catholic and Protestant, all locals are keen to dispel the past's dangerous image, and your welcome will be the warmer because of this.

Giant's Causeway

Making the Most of Your Time

Though Northern Ireland may not look that big on paper, tackling a fair share of its many attractions in less than a week isn't possible without exhausting yourself in the process. If your time is limited, choose the eastern half (Belfast, the Antrim Coast, and the Mountains of Mourne) or the western half (Derry and the Border Counties). The cities are small enough to tackle in a day or two. But remember that the rural wonders—the Antrim Coast, the Fermanagh lakes, the Mountains of Mourne—cast their spell easily. You may head out to enjoy them for a day trip and find yourself wishing that you'd factored in more time to explore the endless string of postcard-worthy villages, emerald-green glens, and rugged mountains. And although distances are not great, neither are the roads—you'll spend most of your time traveling smaller roads, not major express highways.

Getting Around

Northern Ireland is small—about half the size of Delaware and less than one-fifth the size of the Republic of Ireland, its neighbor to the south. And because it's so small, one option is to simply base yourself in the two main cities, Belfast and Derry, and make day trips out. However, one of the real glories of Ulster is its endless supply of spectacular rural scenery, so much so that you may find yourself ho-humming at your umpteenth view of emerald green glens. The good news is that bus travel is both quick and fairly priced. The extensive network of the state-owned Ulsterbus (⊕ www.ulsterbus.co.uk) means it's easy to reach many towns. The bad news is that Northern Irish Railways (NIR) is sorely limited, with only three main routes: Belfast–Derry, Belfast–Bangor; and Belfast-Dublin. In the past decade, however, more runs have been scheduled, along with an official merger of the national bus and train system, now officially dubbed Translink (www.translink.co.uk). That noted, in many areas, including the wildly popular Causeway Coast, you'll definitely end up on such bus routes as the Causeway Coast Express if you don't drive a car.

Finding a Place to Stay

Major hotel chains based both in the republic and abroad have invested in Northern Ireland's cities. In Belfast's environs you can also choose from the humblest terraced town houses or farm cottages to the grandest country houses. Dining rooms of country-house lodgings frequently match the standard of top-quality restaurants. All accommodations in the province are inspected and categorized by the Northern Ireland Tourist Board Information Centre, which publishes hostelry names, addresses, and ratings in the free guidebooks *Hotel and Guest House Guide* and *Bed & Breakfast Guide*, also available online. Hundreds of excellent-value specials—single nights to weekend deals, the most intimate bed-and-breakfasts to Belfast's finest hotels—become available in the low season, October to March. Assume that all hotel rooms reviewed in this chapter have air-conditioning, in-room phones and TVs, and private bathrooms unless otherwise indicated.

Feeling Festive in Belfast?

Northern Ireland is a great place for festivals and almost every town has its own theme festival of some sort. The Belfast Festival at Queen's University is one of the biggest with a packed program of arts, music, and literature held in October. Belfast's Cathedral Arts Quarter Festival, held late April–early May, uses established, new, and unusual venues throughout the oldest part of the city center for two weeks of music, theater, and visual arts. Feile an Phobail, the West Belfast Festival, held in early August, is a 10-day schedule of events with a political and international theme. Hillsborough International Oyster Festival, held in September, is three days of good food and entertainment—the highlight is, of course, an oyster-eating competition. For a rundown on many other festivals, contact the Northern Ireland Tourist Board.

How's The Weather?

If the weather is good—and most of the year it isn't—touring Northern Ireland can be a real pleasure. But the place is so green for a reason: lots of rain, which means you should certainly pack your Burberry. Because you're on the coast, even on bright summer days you can feel the chill from the sea, so it's best to travel layered-up and, depending on the meterological situation, peel back a sweater or two. Needless to say, the weather is a little friendlier to tourists May to September.

POUNDS, NOT EUROS

Northern Ireland uses British currency. Euros are rarely accepted. You may sometimes be given bank notes, drawn on Ulster banks. Be sure not to get stuck with a lot of these when you leave, because they're accepted with reluctance, if at all, in the rest of the United Kingdom and will be difficult to change at banks back home.

Dunluce Castle

Dining & Lodging Price Categories (in Pounds Sterling)					
	$$$$	**$$$**	**$$**	**$**	**¢**
Restaurants	over £22	£18–22	£13–18	£7–13	under £7
Hotels	over £160	£115–160	£80–115	£50–80	under £50

Restaurant prices are for a main course at dinner. Hotel prices are for a standard double room in high season.

Updated by
Allison Morris

LEGEND HAS IT THAT A MILLENNIUM ago a seafaring chieftain caught sight of the green shores of Northern Ireland, and offered the land to whichever of his two sons would be first to lay a hand upon it. As the two rivals rowed toward shore in separate boats, one began to draw ahead—whereupon the other drew his sword, cut off his own hand, and hurled it onto the beach—and so, by blood and sacrifice, gained the province. To this day the coat of arms of Northern Ireland bears the severed limb: the celebrated "Red Hand of Ulster."

From this ancient bardic tale to the recent Troubles—lasting from 1969 to 1994—Northern Ireland has had a long and often ferocious history. But all such thoughts vanish in the face of the country's natural beauty, magnificent stately houses, and the warm hospitality of its people. The Six Counties, or Ulster (as Northern Ireland is often called), cover less than 14,245 square km (5,500 square mi). These boundaries contain some of the most unspoiled scenery you could ever hope to find on this earth—the granite Mountains of Mourne; the Giant's Causeway, made of extraordinary volcanic rock; more than 320 km (200 mi) of coastline beaches and hidden coves; and rivers and leaf-sheltered lakes, including Europe's largest freshwater lake, Lough Neagh, that provide fabled fishing grounds. Ancient castles and Palladian-perfect 18th-century houses are as numerous hereabouts as almost anywhere else in Europe, and each has its own tale of heroic feats, dastardly deeds, and lovelorn ghosts. Northern Ireland not only houses this heritage within its native stone, but has also given the world perhaps an even greater legacy: its roster of celebrated descendants. Nearly one in six of the more than 4½ million Irish who journeyed across the Atlantic in search of fortune in the New World came from Ulster, and of this group (and from their family stock), more than a few left their mark in America: Davy Crockett, President Andrew Jackson, General Ulysses S. Grant, President Woodrow Wilson, General Stonewall Jackson, financier Thomas Mellon, merchant J. Paul Getty, writers Edgar Allan Poe and Mark Twain, and astronaut Neil Armstrong.

Present-day Northern Ireland, a province under the rule of the United Kingdom, includes six of the old Ulster's nine counties and retains its sense of separation, both in the vernacular of the landscape and, some would say, in the character of the people. The hardheaded and industrious Scots-Presbyterians, imported to make Ulster a bulwark against Ireland's Catholicism, have had a profound and ineradicable effect on the place. The north has more factories, neater-looking farms, better roads, and—in its cities—more fine, two-story redbrick houses typical of those found in the republic. For all that, the border between north and south is of little consequence if you're just here to see the country.

On the political front, peace reigns in Northern Ireland today. There are no checkpoints anymore—not security-related ones anyway. As far as border issues go (with the Republic of Ireland to the south), the border is there in name only. No one is stopped or questioned, no passports are checked, and there isn't even a sign announcing you are passing into the republic. Visitors—even ones with English accents—are not hassled in any way, and Americans are more than warmly welcomed. Further progress was made toward peace in the summer of 2005 with the IRA's announcement that they were disbanding, and decommissioning their weapons—a historic move.

Only the direst political commentators predict a return to the dark days of conflict. Instead, the "peace dividend" has led to massive investment in places like Belfast, Derry, and Newry. Every year, Derry gets dolled up for its annual Halloween fancy-dress party and Northern Ireland's vivacious spirit truly takes center stage. Everyone realizes that the more tourists that are welcomed, the further the "normalization" process for these embattled people proceeds. As usual, many visitors arrive to view Belfast's "Peace Walls"—built to keep two warring communities apart—but their painted images have changed and are now less of war and more of hope and history. No longer are the Republican heartlands of the Falls and the loyalist Shankill no-go areas, but are now touted as places to witness at first hand human triumph over adversity. Naysayers may remind you that Belfast is no utopia and there is still a way to go—but just come during Feile an Phobail (the West Belfast Festival held in August) and you'll see just how heartedly the city celebrates Northern Ireland's new-found peace.

Exploring Northern Ireland

The city of Belfast is Northern Ireland's main gateway. A naturally lively, friendly city, Belfast has plenty of distinguished hotels and restaurants, fascinating museums, Victorian architecture, and strong maritime connections. It's testimony to the spirit of Belfast that the long years of sectarian violence have not dimmed its vibrancy. Northern Ireland's second city, Derry, is also looking to the future and has an appealing personality of its own. Rows of beautiful Georgian houses are being restored and museums and crafts shops have opened in the small city center, still enclosed by its medieval walls and one of Europe's best-preserved examples of a fortified town.

Along the shores of Northern Ireland's coasts and lakes, green, gentle slopes descend majestically into hazy, dark-blue water against a background of more slopes, more water, and huge, cloud-scattered skies. The Antrim Coast is among the most scenic in all of Ireland: Dunluce Castle, the Giant's Causeway, and the small towns along the excellent roads traversing the east coast give the traveler a choice of rewarding stops. Enniskillen, in County Fermanagh, is bright and bustling, and the surrounding Lough Erne has magnificent lake views, as well as one of Ireland's famous round towers, on Devenish Island. On the other side of Enniskillen stand Castle Coole and Florence Court, two exquisitely graceful mansions built for members of the 18th-century Anglo-Irish nobility. And many will say you'll never forgive yourself if you don't discover the pretty scenery and slow pace of life that is County Down where the beautiful and dark Mountains of Mourne do indeed—just as the song says—sweep down to the sea.

BELFAST

The city of Belfast was a great Victorian success story, an industrial boom town whose prosperity was built on trade—especially linen and shipbuilding. Famously (or infamously), the *Titanic* was built here, giving Belfast, for a time, the nickname "Titanic Town." The key word here, of course, is *was*—linen is no longer a major industry, and shipbuilding is greatly diminished. For two decades, news about Belfast meant news about the Troubles—until the 1994 cease-fire. Since then, Northern Ireland's capital city has benefited from major hotel investment, gentrified quaysides (or strands), a heralded performing arts center, and strenuous efforts on the part of the tourist board to claim a share of the visitors pouring into the Emerald Isle. Although the 1996 bombing of offices at the Canary Wharf in London disrupted the 1994 peace agreement, cease-fire was officially reestablished on July 20, 1997, and this embattled city began its quest for a newfound identity.

Magnificent Victorian structures still line the streets of the city center, but instead of housing linen mills or cigarette factories, they are home to chic new hotels and fashionable bars. Smart restaurants abound, and the people of Belfast, who for years would not venture out of their districts, appear to be making up for lost time. Each area of the city has changed considerably in the new peaceful era, but perhaps none more than the docklands around the Harland and Wolff shipyards, whose historic and enormous cranes, known to the locals as Sampson and Goliath, still dominate the city's skyline. New developments—dubbed Laganside and the Titanic Quarter—are springing up all around the now-deserted shipyards, from luxury hotels to modern office blocks. And in the center of the city, Victoria Square is a gigantic new shopping and residential complex, replete with geodesic dome, floors of glossy shops, and renovated Victorian row houses. In the west of the city, the physical scars of the Troubles are still evident, from the *peace line* that divides Catholic and Protestant West Belfast to the murals on every gable wall. Visitors are discovering that it's safe to venture beyond the city center; indeed, backpackers are becoming a regular sight on the Falls Road, and taxi tours of these once troubled areas are more popular than ever.

Before English and Scottish settlers arrived in the 1600s, Belfast was a tiny village called Béal Feirste ("sandbank ford") belonging to Ulster's ancient O'Neill clan. With the advent of the Plantation period (when settlers arrived in the 1600s), Sir Arthur Chichester, from Devon in southwest England, received the city from the English crown, and his son was made Earl of Donegall. Huguenots fleeing persecution from France settled near here, bringing their valuable linen-work skills. In the 18th century Belfast underwent a phenomenal expansion—its population doubled in size every 10 years, despite an ever present sectarian divide. Although the Anglican gentry despised the Presbyterian artisans—who, in turn, distrusted the native Catholics—Belfast's growth continued at a dizzying speed. Having laid the foundation stone of the city's university in 1845, Queen Victoria returned to Belfast in 1849 (she is recalled in the names of buildings, streets, bars, monuments, and other places around the city), and in the same year, the university opened under the name Queen's College. Nearly 40 years later, in 1888, Victoria granted Belfast its city charter. Today its population is 300,000—one-quarter of Northern Ireland's citizens.

Belfast is a fairly compact city, 167 km (104 mi) north of Dublin. The city center is made up of three roughly contiguous areas that are easy to navigate on foot; from the south end to the north it is about an hour's leisurely walk.

Golden Mile

This arrowhead-shape area extending from Howard Street in the north to Shaftesbury Square at the southern tip, bordered on the west by Great Victoria Street and on the east by Bedford Street and Dublin Road, is a great area from which to begin an exploration of Belfast. Although it doesn't glow quite the way the name suggests, bustling Golden Mile and its immediate environs harbor some of Belfast's most noteworthy historic buildings. In addition, the area is filled with hotels, major civic and office buildings, as well as some restaurants, cafés, and shops. Even if you don't end up staying here, you're likely to pass through it often.

TIMING   You need about 1½ hours to enjoy this route—you can extend this time depending on how long you would like to spend soaking up the atmosphere, and anything else, of places like the Crown Liquor Saloon on your way.

What to See

★ ❹ **City Hall.** Massive, exuberant, Renaissance Revival City Hall dominates Donegall Square. Built between 1898 and 1906 and modeled on St. Paul's Cathedral in London, it was designed by Brumwell Thomas, who was knighted but had to sue to get his fee. It was from a specially built platform on its front steps that American President Bill Clinton made an emotional address to the people during his historic 1995 visit. Before you enter, take a stroll around Donegall Square, to see statues of Queen Victoria; a monument commemorating the *Titanic*, which was built in Belfast; and a column honoring the U.S. Expeditionary Force, which landed in the city on January 26, 1942—the first contingent of the U.S. Army to land in Europe in World War II. Enter under the porte cochere at the front of the building. From the entrance hall (the base of which is a whispering gallery), the view up to the heights of the 173-foot-high Great Dome is a feast for the eyes. With its complicated series of arches and openings, stained-glass windows, Italian-marble inlays, decorative plasterwork, and paintings, this is Belfast's most ornate public space—homage to the might of the British empire. The guided tour gives access to the Council Chamber, Great Hall, and Reception Room, all upstairs. Your guide should have plenty of juicy stories to tell about past events in the Chamber, once dubbed the "bear pit," as Unionist and Nationalist elected councillors verbally battled it out while civil unrest raged in the streets. ⊠ *Donegall Sq., Central District* ☎ *028/9032–0202* ⊕ *www.belfastcity.gov.uk* ☑ *Free* ☉ *Mon.–Thurs. 9–5, Fri. 9–4.30; guided tours June–Sept., weekdays at 11, 2, and 3, Sat. at 2:30; Oct.–May, weekdays at 11 and 2:30, Sat. at 2:30.*

NORTHERN IRELAND THROUGH THE AGES

IRELAND'S ANCIENT HISTORY truly began in the north, when settlers came to the banks of the River Bann 9,000 years ago.

Five thousand years later Bronze Age settlers built the great stone circles idiomatic to Counties Down and Tyrone, and later the Iron Age brought the Celts.

St. Patrick, the son of a Roman official who was forced into slavery in County Antrim, returned to spread Christianity in the 5th century.

Starting with the first Norman incursions in the 12th century, however, the English made greater and greater inroads into Ireland, endeavoring to subdue what they believed was a potential enemy.

Ulster proved the hardest to conquer, but in 1607, in the great exodus known as the Flight of the Earls, many of Ulster's beaten-down Irish nobility fled to France and Spain, never to return to their homeland.

Their abandoned lands were distributed by the English to "the Planters"—staunch Protestants from England and Scotland.

After three centuries of smoldering tensions and religious strife, 1916 saw the Easter Uprising and then, in the parliamentary elections of 1918, an overwhelming Nationalist vote across Ireland for Sinn Féin ("Ourselves Alone"), the party that believed in independence for all of Ireland.

In the five northeastern counties of Ulster, however, only seven seats went to the Nationalists, and 22 to the Unionists, whose objective was to remain an integral part of the United Kingdom.

At 2:10 AM on December 6, 1921, in the British prime minister's residence at 10 Downing Street, Michael Collins—the Republican leader and controversial hero—signed the Anglo-Irish Treaty.

This designated a six-county North to remain in British hands in exchange for complete independence, as the Irish Free State, for Ireland's 26 counties.

Fast-forward to 1968, when, in the spirit of student uprisings occurring in Paris and Washington, and after 40 years of living with an apparently permanent and sectarian Unionist majority, students in Belfast's Queen's University launched a civil rights protest, claiming equal rights in jobs, housing, and opportunity.

The brutality with which these marches were suppressed, triggering riots and counter-riots, led to worldwide revulsion.

The Irish Republican Army (IRA), which had been dormant for decades, took over what was left of the shattered civil rights movement, which once had a smattering of Protestant students among its ranks.

Armed British troops, who had at first been welcomed in the Catholic ghettos as protectors from Protestant paramilitaries, now found themselves shunned by both sides. Britain imposed Direct Rule.

January 30, 1972, came to be known as Bloody Sunday, when British paratroopers opened fire on people participating in a nonviolent protest in Derry against the British policy of internment without trial.

When the smoke cleared, 13 people, all Catholic and unarmed, had been killed. Many rallied in support of the victims, who were accused by the British Army of handling weapons.

In an event known as the Bloody Sunday Justice Campaign, the supporters attained some success when the British government finally admitted the victims were "innocent."

Derry is filled with murals and memorials that serve as constant reminders of the struggle for justice, including one monument carved with the inscription, "Their epitaph is the continuing struggle for democracy."

Decades of guerrilla conflict ensued between the IRA, the UDA/UVF (Protestant/Loyalist paramilitaries), and the British government and continued in a mix of lulls and terrors—apart from the IRA's annual Christmas "truce"—until the summer of 1994, when the "Provos," as they are colloquially known, called for an ongoing cease-fire, confirmed in July 1997.

After two years of intensive and complex talks, an agreement was finally reached between Northern Ireland's political parties in April 1998.

The Good Friday Agreement (so called because it was secured on the Friday before Easter Sunday), also known as the Belfast Agreement, gave the province limited powers and its own parliament.

Put to the people of both the north and south of Ireland in separate referenda, it was endorsed by an overwhelming majority and elections to the parliament were held in June 1998.

But a mere two months later, the province's fragile peace was shattered when a massive car-bomb exploded in the quiet market town of Omagh, County Tyrone.

On August 15, dissident Republicans—a minority within the movement who were, and still are, opposed to the Good Friday Agreement—succeeded in killing 31 people, including unborn twins. It was the single worst atrocity in the history of the Troubles.

Despite this appalling act, the peace process continued and Unionists eventually entered government proceedings with Sinn Féin at the end of 1999.

8

Since then, the assembly—the first democratically elected in the history of Northern Ireland—has been suspended three times.

Political parties are divided into pro-agreement and anti-agreement camps and when fresh elections to the assembly were held in November 2003, it was the anti-agreement Democratic Unionist Party that profited.

Despite these numerous setbacks, Northern Ireland is today enjoying the longest period of peace and stability in its history.

❸ **Crown Liquor Saloon.** Opposite the Europa Hotel on Great Victoria
FodorsChoice Street and now owned by the National Trust (the United Kingdom's of-
★ ficial conservation organization), the Crown is one of Belfast's glories.
Built in 1894, the bar has richly carved woodwork around cozy snugs
(cubicles), leather seats, color tile work, and an abundance of mirrors.
It has been kept immaculate and is still lighted by gas. It has been immaculately preserved, apart from some of the stained glass windows that
were blown out by an IRA bomb after having survived almost a century. They claim to serve the perfect pint of Guinness—so no need to
ask what anyone's drinking—and a great plateful of oysters. When you
settle down in your snug, note the little gunmetal plates used by the Vic-
torians for lighting their matches. ⊠ *46 Great Victoria St., Golden
Mile* ☎ *028/9027–9901* ☽ *Mon.–Sat. 11:30 AM–midnight, Sun. 11:30–10.*

❶ **Europa Hotel.** A landmark in Belfast, the Europa is a monument to the
resilience of the city in the face of the Troubles. The most bombed hotel
in western Europe, it was targeted 11 times by the IRA since the early
1970s and was refurbished every time, and today shows no signs of its
explosive history. Indeed, even with this track history, President Bill Clinton and his wife Hillary chose the hotel for an overnight visit during
their 1995 visit—for 24 hours the phones were answered with "White
House Belfast, can I help you?" The president's room is now called the
Clinton Suite and contains memorabilia from the presidential stay. The
Europa is owned by affable Ulster millionaire and hotel magnate Billy
Hastings. ⊠ *Great Victoria St. at Glengall St., Golden Mile* ☎ *028/
9027–1066* ⊕ *www.hastingshotels.com.*

★ **❷** **Grand Opera House.** The Grand Opera House exemplifies the Victori-
ans' fascination with ornamentation, opulent gilt moldings, and intricate plasterwork. The renowned theater architect Frank Matcham
beautifully designed the building in 1894. In the past five years, the theater has undergone a massive extension program that has almost doubled its size, thanks to a brand new foyer bar, café, and party room.
Contemporary Irish artist Cherith McKinstry's exquisite angel-and-
cherub-laden fresco floats over the auditorium ceiling. You can take a
tour of the opera house, but by far the best way to see and enjoy the
place is to attend a show. The theater regularly hosts musicals, operas,
plays, and concerts. ⊠ *Great Victoria St., Central District* ☎ *028/
9024–1919* ⊕ *www.goh.co.uk* ☒ *£3* ☽ *Tours Sat., hrs vary, so phone
ahead.*

❺ **St. Malachy's Church.** Just inside the doors to St. Malachy's Cathedral is
a memorial to its chief benefactor, Captain Thomas Griffiths. The
church, designed by Thomas Jackson, was built in 1844, and its interior is well worth a viewing. Pay particular attention to its fan-vaulted
ceiling. Although many of the original fixtures and fittings have succumbed
to the ravages of time, this swirling masterpiece of plasterwork survives
intact. Inspiration for the design was taken from the chapel of Henry
VII at Westminster Abbey in London. Note the 150-year-old church organ.
⊠ *Alfred St., Golden Mile* ☎ *028/9032–1713* ☒ *Free.*

❻ **Ulster Hall.** The home of the Ulster Orchestra, and host to occasional rock
concerts (one of the most famous was marked by Led Zeppelin's stage

A GOOD WALK: VICTORIAN BELFAST

MOST OF BELFAST'S landmarks were built during the reign of Queen Victoria. Three decades ago, many of them were considered unappealing—"Victorian Grisly" was the epithet used by more than one critic—but today they are marvelous remnants of an age that considered show, pomp, and circumstance paramount.

Fire up your time machine by starting out in the heart of the city and the focal point of the downtown area: huge Donegall Square, still dominated by the columned and domed **❹ City Hall,** built between 1898 and 1906. Fashioned of Portland stone and modeled after London's St. Paul's Cathedral, the structure is topped by a 173-foot-high dome. Edwardian-style stained glass, ornate plasterwork, and a mural by Belfast artist John Luke gleam forth from all corners of the three main reception rooms.

Facing City Hall is the **❼ Linen Hall Library,** which reposes in an old linen warehouse designed in a noble Late Victorian–Early Edwardian way. Scholars love its Robert Burns collection, journalists its vast repository of documents on The Troubles.

Head up Wellington Place to Great Victoria Street. Here on the strip known as "the Golden Mile" you'll see the **❷ Grand Opera House,** housed in a wonderful Victorian gingerbread building built in 1894 with plenty of fanciful turrets and curlicues. The interior (guided tours offered) is a red-and-gilt extravaganza of brass rails, gilded balconies, stucco elephants, and exotic motifs. Just across the street

is that Victorian showstopper: the **❸ Crown Liquor Saloon,** now owned by the National Trust and entirely lighted by gas lamps. The place positively oozes history, with carved wood, stained glass, and the Distiller's Mirror.

Stroll down Howard Street and make a right turn on Bedford one block to **❻ Ulster Hall,** another 19th-century theater. Its Mulholland organ is a Victorian monument as is the 1903 painted ceiling; the theater interior can be viewed during the day. Two blocks to the west is Alfred Street, presided over by **❺ St. Malachy's Church,** a 19th-century edifice with a famed fan-work ceiling inspired by that of Westminster Abbey.

Head north to Victoria Street and continue six or so blocks until reaching the **❾ Albert Memorial Clock Tower,** Belfast's very own leaning tower, named for Queen Victoria's beloved consort. The reason for the lean is that it was originally built on what was one of the banks of the Farset River (happily, the clock is now stabilized).

Walk one block north to Waring Street, then up Hill Street, and left on Talbot to Lower Donegall Street to find **❽ St. Anne's Cathedral,** a Victorian-era essay in Irish Romanesque. You're now smack-dab in the Cathedral Quarter, dominated with small art galleries and interesting bars, so head off to the John Hewitt pub on Donegall—named after the poet, it's a place where the world is often put to rights.

debut of the song "Stairway to Heaven" in March 1971), Ulster Hall was built as a ballroom in 1862. The hall was the venue for the political rallying of Nationalist politicians, among them Charles Stewart Parnell (1846–91) and Patrick Henry Pearse (1879–1916), before the Irish Republic was formed in 1921. There's also a splendid Mulholland Organ, a Victorian instrument of considerable size. There's no charge for looking around when shows are not going on. ⊠ *Bedford St., Golden Mile* ☎ *028/9032–3900* ⊕ *www. ulsterhall.co.uk.*

> **WHEN IT POURS, IT REIGNS**
>
> Ulster Hall transforms for one week every November—when organic ale is on tap for purists—for the festival hosted by the Campaign for Real Ale. With nightly jazz performances to help the "warm beer" go down easier it's a brilliant and popular attraction.

Central District

Belfast's Central District, immediately north of the Golden Mile, extends from Donegall Square north to St. Anne's Cathedral. It's not geographically the center of the city, but it's the old heart of Belfast. Shoppers note: it also has the highest concentration of retail outlets in town. It's a frenetic place—the equivalent of Dublin's Grafton and Henry streets in one—where both locals *and* visitors shop. Cafés, pubs, offices, and stores of all kinds, from department stores to the Gap and Waterstone's (there's even a Disney store), occupy the redbrick and white-Portland-stone and modern buildings that line its narrow streets. Many of the streets are pedestrian-only, so it's a good place to take a leisurely stroll, browse, and see some sights to boot. It's easy to get waylaid shopping and investigating sights along the river when taking this walk, so give yourself at least two hours to cover the area comfortably.

What to See

❾ Albert Memorial Clock Tower. Tilting a little to one side, not unlike Pisa's more notorious leaning landmark, is the clock tower that was named for Queen Victoria's husband, Prince Albert. The once-dilapidated square on which it stands has undergone a face-lift and a recent restoration has brought the clock itself back to its original glory. The tower itself is not open to the public. ⊠ *Victoria Sq., Central District.*

⓫ Custom House. The 19th-century architect Charles Lanyon designed the Custom House. This building, along with many others in Belfast, including the main building of Queen's University and the unusual Sinclair Seaman's Church, bear the hallmarks of his skill. It's not open to the public, but it's worth circling the house to view the lofty pediment of Brittania, Mercury, and Neptune on the front, carved by acclaimed stonemason Thomas Fitzpatrick. Custom House Square has recently been refurbished for use for open air concerts and performances during the Autumn festival season. ⊠ *Donegall Quay, Central District.*

CLOSE UP

Churches Around the City

BELFAST HAS SO MANY churches you could visit a different one nearly every day of the year and still not make it to all of them.

The oldest house of worship is the Church of Ireland **Knockbreda Parish Church** (⊠ Church Rd. off A24, South Belfast, Belfast ☎ 028/9064–5372). This dark structure was built in 1737 by Richard Cassels, who designed many of Ireland's finest mansions. It quickly became *the* place to be buried–witness the vast 18th-century tombs in the churchyard.

The **First Presbyterian Church** (⊠ Rosemary St., Central District, Belfast) dates from 1783 and has an interesting elliptical interior. It also hosts lunchtime concerts.

The Church of Ireland's **St. George's** (⊠ High St., Central District, Belfast ☎ 028/9023–1275), built in 1816, has a tremendous Georgian portico and pretty box pews.

By the riverfront is one of the most appealing churches, Presbyterian **Sinclair Seamen's Church** (⊠ Corporation Sq. off Donegall Quay, Central District, Belfast ☎ 028/9071–5997). Designed by Charles Lanyon, the architect of Queen's University, it has served the seafaring community since 1857. The pulpit is shaped like a ship's prow; the bell is from HMS *Hood*, sunk in 1916; and even the collection plates are shaped like lifeboats.

The elegant neo-Gothic "twin spires" of **St. Peter's Cathedral** (⊠ St. Peters Sq., West Belfast, Belfast ☎ 028/9032–7573), dominates the skyline of West Belfast. Finding this Roman Catholic cathedral is difficult, but worth the effort. Built in 1866, when the Catholic population was rapidly increasing, St. Peter's acted as a focal point for the community.

★ **High Street.** Off High Street, especially down to Ann Street (parallel to the south), run narrow lanes and alleyways called entries. Though mostly cleaned up and turned into chic shopping lanes, they still hang on to something of their raffish character, and have distinctive pubs with little-altered Victorian interiors. Among the most notable are the Morning Star (Pottinger's Entry off High Street), with its large windows and fine curving bar; White's Tavern (entry off High Street), Belfast's oldest pub, founded in 1630, which, although considerably updated, is still warm and comfortable, with plush seats and a big, open fire; Magennis's Whiskey Café (on May Street), in splendid counterpoint to the Waterfront Hall's space-age style; and McHugh's (in Queen's Square), in what is reckoned to be the city's oldest extant building, dating from 1710.

Lagan Boat Company. Take a guided 75-minute river tour that departs from the dock by the Lagan Lookout Visitor Centre and travels down to Stranmillis and back, with running commentary on the colorful history of the city. A one-hour Titanic tour takes in the shipyard where the famous liner was built as well as harbor sights related to the ship. Each tour costs £6. ⊠ 48 St. John's Close, at Laganbank Rd., Central District ☎ 028/9033–0844 ⊕ www.laganboatcompany.com.

🐾 ❿ **Lagan Lookout Visitor Centre.** At the edge of Lagan Weir, the center delves into the history of the River Lagan and the weir by means of interactive exhibits. It's a good way for children to learn about the river's history and surroundings. At night, the exterior of the building is flooded with blue light, adding to the feel that the riverside developments in Belfast have been inspired by the Southbank in London. The famous shipyard cranes, Samson and Goliath, are visible beyond. ✉ *Lagan Weir, Donegall Quay, Central District* ☎ *028/9031-5444* ⊕ *www.laganside.com* 🎫 *£2* ⊙ *Apr.–Sept., weekdays 11–5, Sat. noon–5, Sun. 2–5; Oct.–Mar., Tues.–Fri. 11–3:30, Sat. 1–4:30, Sun. 2–4:30.*

> ### TUNNEL OF TREASURES
>
> The emergence of public commissioned art along the River Lagan has prompted the Visitor Centre to run special "art trails," lasting from one hour to two-and-a-half hours. Times vary and details are available on the website. During the Cathedral Quarter Arts Festival in late April/ May, exhibitions take place in the Lagan Weir tunnel, which is transformed into a unique viewing gallery.

❼ **Linen Hall Library.** This gray building on Donegall Square's northwest corner is in fact a comfortable private library, founded in 1788 and designed by Charles Lanyon. The library has an unparalleled collection of 80,000 documents relating to the Troubles. One early librarian, Thomas Russell, was hanged in 1803 for supporting an Irish uprising. On the walls are paintings and prints depicting Belfast views and landmarks. Much of this artwork is for sale. It's an ideal hideaway for relaxing with a newspaper and enjoying the library's café. ✉ *17 Donegall Sq. N, Central District* ☎ *028/9032-1707* ⊕ *www.linenhall.com* 🎫 *Free* ⊙ *Weekdays 9:30–5:30, Sat. 9:30–1.*

❽ **St. Anne's Cathedral.** A somber heaviness—a hallmark of the Irish neo-Romanesque style—marks this large edifice, which is basilican in plan and was built at the turn of the 20th century. Lord Carson (1854–1935), who was largely responsible for keeping the six counties inside the United Kingdom, is buried here beneath a suitably austere gray slab. New landscaping around the Anglican cathedral provides a perch to rest your feet in good weather. The guides on duty show you around for no charge. ✉ *Donegall St., Central District* ☎ *028/9032-8332* ⊕ *www. belfastcathedral.com* 🎫 *Free* ⊙ *Daily 10–4.*

NEED A BREAK?

At the start of Royal Avenue, turn left onto Bank Street to find **Kelly's Cellars** (✉ 30–32 Bank St., Central District ☎ 028/9024-6058), a circa-1720 pub with loads of character. Try the two specialties: Ulster fry or champ and sausages. Two centuries ago, Kelly's Cellars was the regular meeting place of a militant Nationalist group, the Society of United Irishmen, whose leader, Wolfe Tone (who was a Protestant), is remembered as the founder of Irish Republicanism. Traditional music and plenty of local banter make the pub particularly lively on weekends.

W5: Whowhatwherewhywhen. Part of the Odyssey complex in Belfast's docks, this science discovery center takes a high-tech, hands-on approach to interpreting science, engineering, and technology for adults and children. Video displays and flashing lights provide a modern feel, and you can do everything from explore the weather to build bridges and robots. ⊠ 2 *Queen's Quay, Central District* ☎ *028/9046–7700* ⊕ *www.w5online.co.uk* 🔲 *£6* ⊙ *Mon.–Sat. 10–6, Sun. noon–6; last admission at 5.*

University Area

At Belfast's southern end, the part of the city around Queen's University is dotted with parks, botanical gardens, and leafy streets with fine, intact, two- and three-story 19th-century buildings. The area evokes an older, more leisurely pace of life. The many pubs and excellent restaurants make this area the hub of the city's nightlife. However, remember that Belfast is a student town and this is the main university area—the pace of life here can be fast (and sometimes a little furious) during school-term weekends.

What to See

★ ⓮ **Botanic Gardens.** In the Victorian heyday, it was not unusual to find 10,000 of Belfast's citizens strolling about here on a Saturday afternoon. These gardens are a glorious haven of grass, trees, flowers, curving walks, and wrought-iron benches laid out in 1827 on land that slopes down to the River Lagan. The curved-iron and glass Palm House is a conservatory marvel designed, in 1839, by Charles Lanyon. The Tropical Ravine House, though not architecturally distinguished, has an outstanding collection of tropical flora, in addition to some indigenous plants (it was famously said that it once held more Killarney ferns than could be found in Killarney itself). Once known as "the Glen," the Ravine House is unusually and exotically built over a faux-ravine that you walk around. ⊠ *Stranmillis Rd., University Area* ☎ *028/9032–4902* 🔲 *Free* ⊙ *Gardens daily dawn–dusk; Palm House and Tropical Ravine House Apr.–Aug., weekdays 10–5, weekends 1–5; Sept.–Mar., weekdays 10–4, weekends 2–4.*

⓭ **Queen's University.** Dominating University Road is Queen's University itself. The main buildings, modeled on Oxford's Magdalen College and designed by the ubiquitous Charles Lanyon, were built in 1849 in the Tudor Revival style. The long, handsome redbrick-and-sandstone facade of the main building features large lead-glass windows, and is topped with three square towers and crenellations galore. University Square, really a terrace, is from the same era. The Seamus Heaney Library is named after the Ulster-born 1997 Nobel prize–winning poet. The Queen's Visitors' Centre hosts a regular program of exhibitions and serves as an information point for visitors and tourists, as well as offering a varied selection of souvenirs and gifts. Guided tours can be arranged by prior reservation. ⊠ *University Rd., University Area* ☎ *028/9033–5252* ⊕ *www.qub.ac.uk* ⊙ *May–Sept., Mon.–Sat. 10–4; Oct.–Apr., weekdays 10–4.*

8

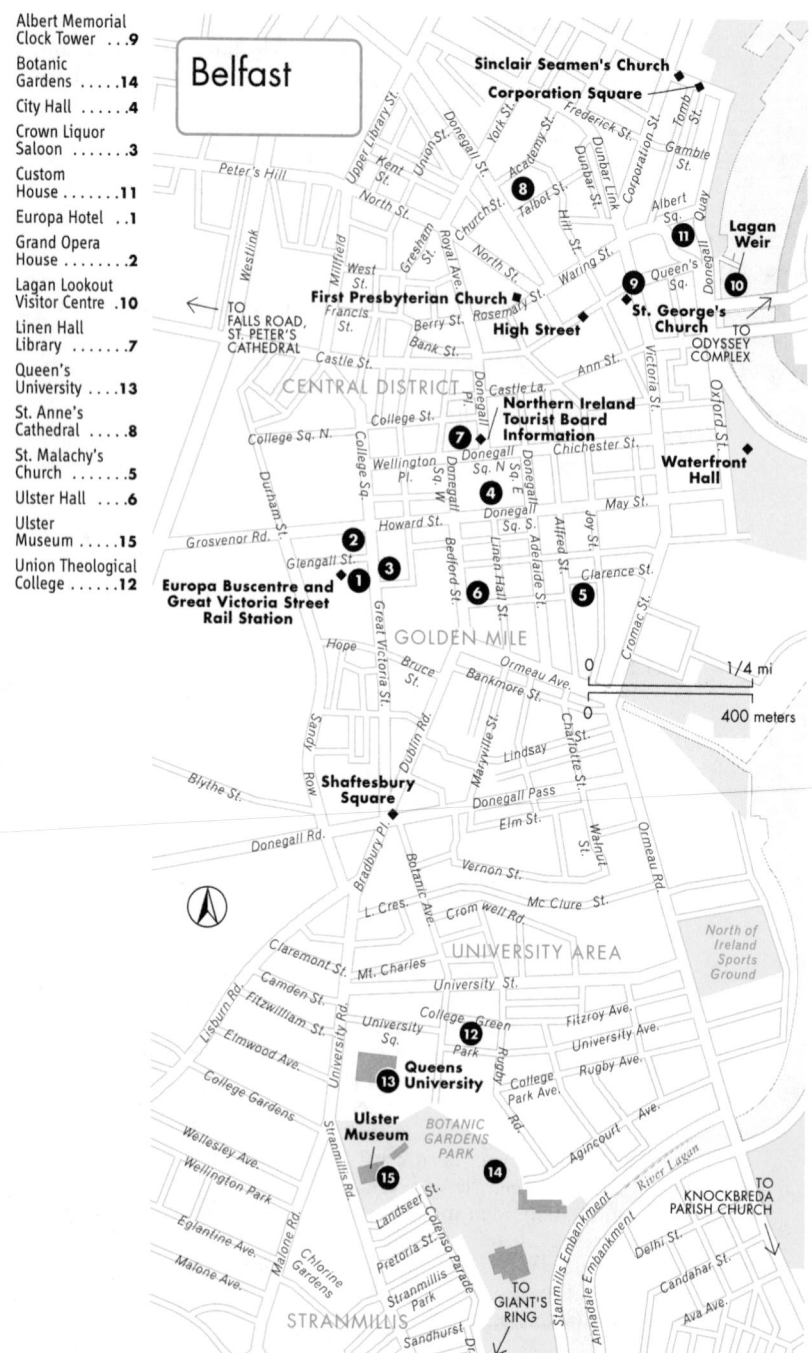

Stranmillis. Once its own village, Stranmillis is now an off-campus quarter—an appealing neighborhood with tree-lined residential streets and a wide choice of ethnic eateries. You can get here via Stranmillis Road (near the Ulster Museum). The "Little Paris" stretch of shops and cafés extends down to the riverside towpath along the Lagan. Malone Road joins the river farther south, close to the out-of-town Giant's Ring (off Ballyleeson Road), a large, Neolithic earthwork focused on a dolmen. To get this far, unless you're a vigorous walker (it's possible to come all the way on the Lagan towpath), you may be happier driving or taking a bus. Ulsterbus 13 passes close to the site, and on the return journey it will take you back to Donegall Square.

⑮ Ulster Museum. Set in a grandly impressive marble edifice at the southwest corner of the Botanic Gardens, the Ulster Museum is about to undergo a major renovation; beginning in fall 2006 it will be shuttered until 2009. The museum's forte is the history and prehistory of Ireland, in particular Northern Ireland, with exhibitions colorfully tracing the rise of Belfast's crafts, trade, and industry; the Nationalist movement; a large natural history section, with its famed skeleton of the extinct Irish giant deer; a trove of jewelry and gold ornaments—as well as a cannon and other armaments—recovered from the Spanish Armada vessel *Girona* and two sister galleons sunk off the Antrim coast in 1588; and a considerable collection of 19th- and 20th-century art. ✉ *Stranmillis Rd., University Area* ☎ *028/9038–3000* ⊕ *www.ulstermuseum.org.uk* ⊘ *Closed for renovations fall 2006–09.*

⑫ Union Theological College. Like Queen's University on the opposite side of the street, the Union Theological College, with its colonnaded, Doric facade, owes the charm of its appearance to architect Charles Lanyon. The building's other claim to fame is that, before the completion of the parliament buildings at Stormont, Northern Ireland's House of Commons was convened in its library, and the college's chapel played host to the Senate. At this writing, the college is finishing a renovation; upon reopening, it will offer tours to visitors. ✉ *108 Botanic Ave., University Area* ☎ *028/9020–5080* ⊕ *www.union.ac.uk* ✉ *Free.*

Belfast Environs

The three sights below are closer to Belfast than others covered in this chapter. However, none of the sites along the Ards Peninsula and the north coast are more than a few hours' drive from Belfast—perfect for day trips.

What to See

★ **⑯ Belfast Castle.** In 1934 this spectacularly baronial castle, built for the Marquis of Donegall in 1865, was passed to Belfast Corporation. Although the castle functions primarily as a restaurant, it also houses the Cave Hill Heritage Centre, which provides information about the castle's history and its natural surroundings in Cave Hill Country Park. Guided tours (by reservation) of the reception rooms built by the Earls of Shaftesbury are sometimes offered on weekends in May and June. The best reason to visit is to take a stroll in the lovely ornamental gardens and then make the ascent to McArt's Fort. This promontory, at the top

Belfast's Wall Murals

IN NORTHERN IRELAND they say the Protestants make the money and the Catholics make the art, and as with all clichés, there is some truth in it. It's a truth that will become clear as you look up at the gable walls of blue-collar areas of Belfast on which the two communities—Catholic and Protestant—have expressed themselves in colorful murals that have given rise to one of the more quirky tours of the city.

Although the wildly romantic Catholic murals often aspire to the levels of Sistine Chapel-lite, those in Protestant areas (like the tough, no-nonsense Shankill and the Newtownards Road) are more workmanlike efforts that sometimes resemble war comics without the humor. It was not always this way.

In Protestant areas, murals were once painted by skilled coachbuilders to mark the July 12 celebrations of the defeat of the Catholic King James by King William at the Battle of the Boyne. As such, they typically depicted William resplendent in freshly laundered scarlet tunic and plumed cap, sitting on a white stallion that has mastered the art of walking on water. On the banks of the Boyne sits a mildly disheveled James, the expression on his face making him look as if he has just eaten an overdose of anchovies. Other popular themes in Protestant areas are the Red Hand of Ulster, symbolizing the founding of the province, and, on Carnmore Street, the 13 Protestant apprentice boys shutting the gates of Derry against King James in 1688, leading to the famous siege.

More recently, though, Protestant murals have taken on a grimmer air, and typical subjects include wall-eyed paramilitaries perpetually standing firm against increasing liberalism, nationalism, and all the other isms that Protestants see eroding their stern, Bible-driven way of life. Nationalist murals, on the other hand, first sprang up in areas like the Falls Road in 1981, when IRA inmates of the Maze prison began a hunger strike in an unsuccessful bid to be recognized by the British government as political prisoners rather than common criminals. Ten died, and the face of the most famous, Bobby Sands, looks down now from a gable wall on the Falls Road alongside the words: "Our revenge will be the laughter of our children."

Since then, themes of freedom from oppression and a rising Nationalist confidence have expressed themselves in murals that romantically and surreally mix and match images from the *Book of Kells*, the Celtic Mist mock-heroic posters of Irish artist Jim Fitzpatrick, assorted phoenixes rising from ashes, and revolutionaries clad in splendidly idiosyncratic sombreros and bandannas from ideological battlegrounds in Mexico and South America. Irish words and phrases that you will see springing up regularly include the much-used slogan "Tiocfaidh ár lá" (pronounced *chuck*y ohr *law* and meaning "Our day will come") and the simple cry "Saoirse" (pronounced *seer*-she), meaning "Freedom."

The murals in both Protestant and Catholic areas are safe to view in daylight and outside the sensitive week of the July 12 marches by Protestant Orangemen. However, the most sensible way to view them would be to take a guided tour with Citybus.

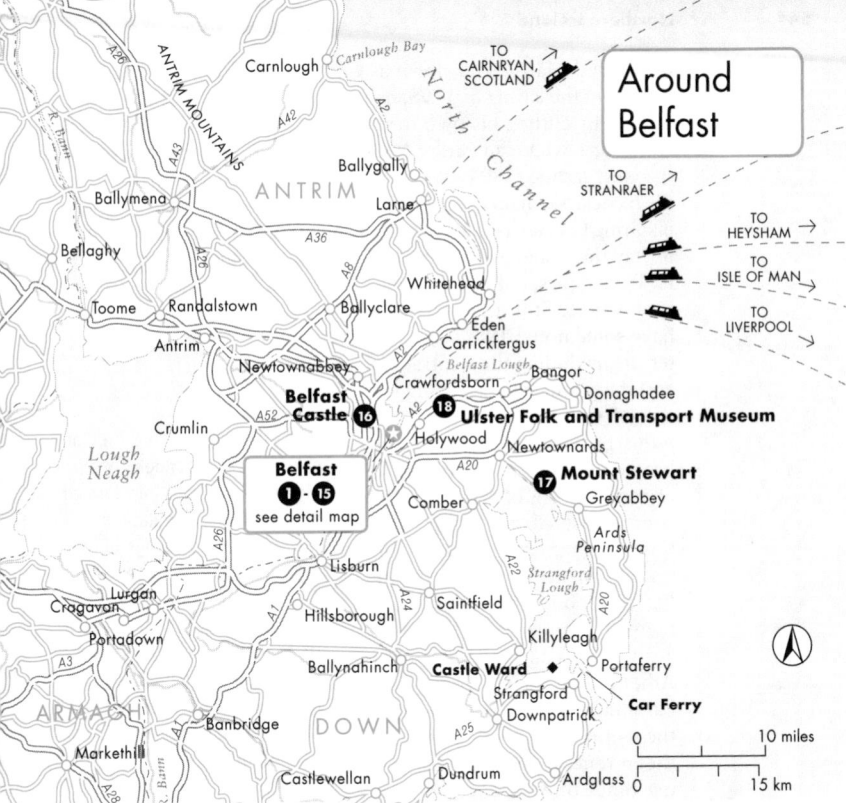

of sheer cliffs 1,200 feet above the city, affords an excellent view across Belfast. Take the path uphill from the parking lot, turn right at the next intersection of pathways, and then keep left as you journey up the sometimes steep hill to the fort. ⊠ *4 km (2½ mi) north of Belfast on Antrim Rd.* ☎ *028/9077–6925* ⊕ *www.belfastcastle.co.uk/* ⊠ *Free* ⊙ *Visitor center daily 9–6.*

Belfast Zoo. Since the mid-1990s great strides have been taken to make this place a more friendly and less repressive environment for the animals. But note that it's on the steep side of Cave Hill and getting around the zoo involves a strenuous uphill walk for even the most energetic (not ideal for anyone with mobility problems)—a pushchair would be advisable for small children. The zoo is noted for its children's farm and underwater views of the resident penguins and sea lions. It's near Belfast Castle—just hop on a pink metrobus (Numbers 1A, 1B, 1C, or 1D) at Donegall Square West, by City Hall. ⊠ *Antrim Rd.* ☎ *028/9077–6277* ⊕ *www.belfastzoo.co.uk* ⊠ *£7* ⊙ *Apr.–Sept., daily 10–5; Oct.–Mar., daily 10–2:30.*

★ ⓱ **Mount Stewart.** The grandest stately house near Belfast, this was the country estate of the Marquesses of Londonderry, whose fame, or infamy, became known around the world thanks to the historical role played by the 2nd Marquess. Known as Castlereagh, this Secretary of Ireland put down the Rising of 1798, helped forge the Act of Union, and killed himself by cutting his own throat. Mount Stewart was constructed in two stages where an earlier house had stood: George Dance designed the west facade (1804–05), and William Vitruvius Morrison designed the Neoclassic main part of the building (1845–49), complete with awe-inspiring Grecian portico facade. The 7th Marchioness, Edith, managed to wave her wand over the interior—after a fashion: Chinese vases, Louis-Philippe tables, and Spanish oak chairs do their worst to clutter up the rooms here. Still, the house does have some noted 18th-century interiors, including the Central Hall and the grand staircase hung with one of George Stubbs's most famous portraits, that of the celebrated racehorse Hambletonian, after he won one of the most prominent contests of the 18th century—this is perhaps the greatest in-situ setting for a painting in Ireland. On the grounds, don't miss the octagonal Temple of the Winds—a copy of a similar structure in Athens—and there's a remarkable bathhouse and pool at the end of the wooded peninsula just before the entrance to the grounds. Opening times often change here—it's prudent to phone ahead or log on to the Web site for the complete schedule. ✉ *Portaferry Rd., Newtownards, Co. Down* ☎ *028/4278–8387* ⊕ *www.nationaltrust.org.uk* 🎫 *£5.45* ⊙ *Gardens Apr. and Oct., daily 10–6; May–Sept., daily 10–8; Nov.–Mar., daily 10–4; house by guided tour Mar.–June and Oct., weekends noon–6; July and Aug., daily noon–6; Sept., Wed.–Mon. noon–6.*

> **THE GREENING OF BELFAST**
>
> It was due to Edith, the 7th Marchioness of Londonderry, that Mount Stewart was transformed into a garden showplace in the 1920s. Taking advantage of the salubrious microclimate of the Ards Peninsula, she created, in short order, a Shamrock Garden, Dodo Garden (note the stone figures that honor her close circle of friends—the "Warlock" is Winston Churchill), and Lady Mairi's Garden, complete with a "Mary, Mary, Quite Contrary" statue surrounded with silverbells and cockleshells.

NEED A BREAK?

Reputed to be the oldest pub in Ireland, **Grace Neill's** (✉ **33 High St., 22 km [13 mi] from Mount Stewart, Donaghadee** ☎ **028/9188–4595**) served its first pint in 1611 and has hosted such luminaries as Peter the Great, Franz Liszt, and John Keats. Behind the original pub, a cubby under the stairs with bar stools, is a larger bar where you can try a simple peppered beef sandwich with a pint of Guinness. Saturday sees jazz, and on Sunday afternoons, there's other music.

⓲ **Ulster Folk and Transport Museum.** Devoted to the province's social history, the excellent Ulster Folk and Transport Museum vividly brings Northern Ireland's past to life. First, the Folk Museum invites you to visit Ballycultra—a typical Ulster town of the early 1900s—which comes alive thanks to costumed guides who practice such regional skills as lace-making, sampler-making, spinning, weaving, wood turning, forgework, printing, open-hearth cooking, carpentry, basket-making, and needle-

Fodor'sChoice ★

work. The setting is evocative: a score of reconstructed buildings moved here from around the region, including a traditional weaver's dwelling, terraces of Victorian town houses, an 18th-century country church, a village flax mill, a farmhouse, and a rural school. Across the main road (by footbridge) is the beautifully designed Transport Museum, where exhibits include locally built airplanes and motorcycles; the iconoclastic car produced by former General Motors whiz kid John De Lorean in his Belfast factory in 1982; and a moving section on the *Titanic*, the Belfast-built luxury liner that sank on her first voyage, in 1912, killing 1,500 of the passengers and crew. A miniature railway runs on Saturday in July and August. The museum is on the 70 acres of Cultra Manor, encircled by a larger park and recreation area. ⊠ *163 Bangor Rd., 16 km (10 mi) northeast of Belfast on A2, Cultra* ☎ *028/9042–8428* ⊕ *www.uftm.org.uk* ☑ *£7* ⊙ *Mar.–June, weekdays 10–5, Sat. 10–6, Sun. 11–6; July–Sept., Mon.–Sat. 10–6, Sun. 11–6; Oct.–Feb., weekdays 10–4, Sat. 10–5, Sun. 11–5.*

Where to Eat

$$$–$$$$ ✕ **Restaurant Michael Deane.** Armed with a Michelin star, a sharp tongue
Fodor'sChoice (usually aimed at rival chefs), and a fabulous way with confit of quail,
★ Michael Deane has become one of Ireland's most buzz-worthy chefs. Journalists like him because of his acerbic soundbites, gourmands love him when they bite into his fois gras and pigeon terrine. Located in one of Belfast's Victorian districts, this is fine dining at its local best. The setting is lavish, although some carp that all the garden treillage, tartan rugs, marble trim, and upholstered taffeta have seen better days. The centerpiece is the actual kitchen where Belfast's power brokers (who usually opt for the Menu Prestige at £65 for nine courses) see their dishes delivered under the watchful gaze of head chef Derek Creagh. Deane's tastes are eclectic—he has worked in Bangkok, and the influence of Thai cooking is revealed in his especially subtle way with spices. Squab is a specialty, served as a kedgeree with cucumber and quail eggs for a starter. As a main dish he serves French squab with local rabbit, roast potato, and parsnip with Madeira. Ravioli of Lobster, Seared Scallops and Clonakilty black pudding, or the Slow Roast Mount Stewart Pheasant are all winners. If you can't fit into this intimately scaled room (only 30 seats, so book early), you can settle for the Brasserie found on the ground floor, where the prices are much gentler and the setting much livelier. ⊠ *36–40 Howard St., Golden Mile* ☎ *028/9033–1134 restaurant, 028/9056–0000 brasserie* ▭ *AE, MC, V* ⊙ *Restaurant closed Sun.–Tues., brasserie closed Sun.*

★ **$$–$$$** ✕ **Aldens.** East Belfast was a gastronomic wilderness until this cool modernist restaurant opened with chef Cath Gradwell at the helm. Now city-center folk regularly make the pilgrimage to take advantage of an opulent menu and wine list at comparably reasonable prices. The set dinner menus Monday to Thursday are particularly good value— £21 for three courses. Lunch is an informal affair—traditional pork and leek sausages with mash and onion gravy—but dinner tarts up with such tasty treats as roast poussin with tabbouleh and broad beans or the grilled quail with wild cranberry compote and baked polenta. With its great atmosphere, gentle prices, perpetually friendly staff, and fine food, it's little wonder that Aldens has scooped several top awards in recent years, including the prestigious Bridgestone accolade. This is a good time-out if visiting the Parliament buildings at Stormont Castle. ✉ *229 Upper Newtownards Rd., East Belfast* ☎ *028/9065–0079* ☰ *AE, DC, MC, V* ☽ *Closed Sun. No lunch Sat.*

★ **$$–$$$** ✕ **Cayenne.** One of Belfast's most exciting restaurants, Cayenne explodes with culinary fireworks. To wit, the duck and shiitake pot stickers with sesame ginger sauce or the salt 'n' chili squid with chili jam and aioli—and let's not forget the hot banana strudel. These are just a few of the creations of celebrity TV chefs Paul and Jeanne Rankin. They travel widely, have several other restaurants, but happily mastermind this Golden Mile spot. The cutting-edge fusion cuisine, always with that Asian twist, comes up winners with such other dishes as coconut-crusted cod, breast of duck with wild rice pancakes, and Donegal wild salmon with hazelnut beurre blanc. A favorite with theatergoers, Cayenne accepts orders until 11:15 on Friday and Saturday evenings. ✉ *Shaftesbury Sq. at Great Victoria St., Golden Mile* ☎ *028/9033–1532* ☰ *AE, DC, MC, V* ☽ *No lunch weekends.*

$–$$$ ✕ **Ginger.** Chef–owner Simon McCance's Asian-influenced Irish classics attracts foodies to this tiny gem just off Great Victoria Street. A short but perfectly balanced menu emphasizes locally sourced seafood and lean meats. Highlights include the lip-smacking roast hoisin duck salad, and fresh peppered swordfish in a creamy bacon and mussel sauce. The wine list is one of the most reasonably priced in Belfast and boasts a mouth-watering Sancerre, exclusive to Ginger. Next door, Ginger Café provides lunchtime sustenance for office workers in the form of fresh salads and tasty sandwiches. One drawback is the lack of a no-smoking area, although pipes and cigars are banned. ✉ *7–8 Hope St., Golden Mile* ☎ *028/9024–4421* ☰ *MC, V* ☽ *Closed Sun. No dinner Mon., no lunch Sat.*

$–$$$ ✕ **Red Panda.** It comes as a surprise to visitors to learn that Belfast has a large Chinese community, a sizable portion of whom seems to favor this bustling spot (making reservations always a good way to go). Both venues—Belfast city center and the one in the Odyssey Arena complex—are large, spacious, and modern with plenty going on to visually tempt the taste buds. A five-course set dinner can include such delights as crispy aromatic duck pancakes or the sizzling King prawns with ginger. More adventurous diners will want to spring for the stir-fried squid with Chinese bok choi. ✉ *60 Great Victoria St., Central District* ☎ *028/9080–8700* ✉ *Odyssey Arena 2, Queen's Quay* ☰ *AE, DC, MC, V* ☽ *No lunch weekends and Sun. dinner.*

$–$$$ ✕ **Zen.** Entrepreneur Eddie Fung has miraculously transformed a red-brick 19th-century Belfast mill into an Asian oasis housing the city's finest Japanese restaurant. Upstairs you traverse a 30-foot-long mirrored catwalk with glass walkway to get to the seating area. Choose between wooden booths, or, if you're prepared to hunker down on the floor, Japanese-style, opt for the traditional dining area. Downstairs, hand-pick your meal at the sushi bar, or choose a discreet table for two under the serene gaze of (reputedly) Ireland's largest Buddha. Zen—meaning "higher place"—opened in 2003 and quickly garnered a reputation for

EATING WELL IN NORTHERN IRELAND

WHEN IT COMES TO FOOD, Northern Ireland is most famed (or notorious) for its Ulster Fry, a fried-up, carbohydrate blowout of a breakfast that is a cardiologist's nightmare. Sausage, bacon, eggs, black pudding, fried soda bread, and potato bread (perhaps a grilled tomato or fried mushrooms) all make a meal that sounds as dangerous to your health as bungee jumping without a rope.

After a night on the Guinness, however, you'll understand why this breakfast is so popular: it makes a great cure for a hangover.

Happily, when you go beyond breakfast, Northern Ireland has witnessed an influx of international influences with restaurants, bistros, wine bars, and—as in Dublin—European-style café-bars, where you can get good food *and* linger over a drink.

The food scene in Belfast is experiencing the same renaissance as the city itself and its best chefs—such as home-grown TV celebrity Michael Deane—are the match for anything else in Ireland. He and others have brought a sophisticated, internationalist approach to cooking.

In most cases, however, restaurants still offer hearty, unpretentious cooking. You're virtually guaranteed to find certain traditional dishes on menus here, such as Guinness and beef pie; champ (creamy, buttery mashed potatoes with scallions); oysters from Strangford Lough; Ardglass herring; and mussels from Dundrum.

But even traditional favorites are getting the nouvelle treatment, thanks to the rise of the gastro pub, bars that now serve up sensational pub grub.

In addition, the delights of ethnic restaurants, including Chinese, Japanese, Indian, Persian, and Thai, are available in Belfast, and even beyond. In the two main cities of Belfast and Derry, Italian food rules the middle-market, but for authenticity, head to Belfast's version of Chinatown. The streets around central Bradbury Square abound with first-rate Chinese restaurants in which, to paraphrase P. J. O'Rourke in *Holidays in Hell,* you'll be offered at least six types of potatoes with your Peking duck.

Throughout Northern Ireland, seafood is a specialty and most restaurants close to the coast often showcase Glenarm Co. Antrim farmed salmon, among the best in the world.

Combating any ill-effects from those Ulster Frys is the growing trend for farmers' markets, where local food suppliers offer up the best in regional, organic foods.

As for the cost of a meal here, by the standards of the republic or the United States, or even the rest of the United Kingdom, restaurant prices are surprisingly moderate, but they're inching higher.

Outside Belfast, particularly in Derry eateries, you can still be guaranteed some true bargains. A service charge of 10% may be indicated on the bill; it's customary to pay this, unless the service was unsatisfactory.

8

authentic fresh sushi and sashimi. Purists may be bemused at the deep-fried prawns but everyone declares them delicious. ⊠ *Behind City Hall, 55–59 Adelaide St., Central District* 028/9023–2244 ☰ AE, MC, V ⊗ No lunch Sat.

$–$$ ⤬ **Nick's Warehouse.** Nick Price has created one of Belfast's most relaxing watering holes in this cool, cozy wine bar with adjacent restaurant. At the busy bar you can get warm salads with a choice of nut oils and tasty casseroles. In the slightly more formal restaurant, top bets include duck with red cabbage and apple compote, and halibut with langoustine and sweet peppers. Finish off your meal with a sampling of the cheese selection. The wine and imported beer lists are impressive. Nick's is on a narrow cobbled street in an increasingly fashionable area. Reservations are essential for the restaurant. ⊠ *35 Hill St., Central District* ☏ *028/9043–9690* ☰ *AE, MC, V* ⊗ *Closed Sun. No lunch Sat. No dinner Mon.*

$–$$ ⤬ **Raj Put.** You won't leave this Indian restaurant feeling as if you've been kissing a flame-thrower: in even the hottest dishes, nuanced flavors shine through. Aromatic spices, nuts, and herbs mingle in the piquant chicken masala. For side dishes, favorites include a tasty *saag aloo* (spicy potatoes and spinach). Wash it all down with cold Indian lager. You can sit in or take away. ⊠ *461 Lisburn Rd., University Area* ☏ *028/9066–2168* ☰ *AE, MC, V.*

$ ⤬ **Whitefort Inn.** Situated beside Casment Park—home ground of the Antrim Gaelic Athletic Club—this lively and impressive bar–restaurant is just the place to catch your breath after taking a black-taxi tour of the nearby political murals. When it opened in 2003, one local newspaper thought it looked more like a Las Vegas hotel foyer than a West Belfast bar, but the opulent decor was at least a sign of the sheer level of investment in this area since the peace process. Stop off for a meal in the upstairs Copper One restaurant or just to enjoy a quick "half" in the downstairs bar. ⊠ *Andersonstown Rd., West Belfast* ☏ *028/9060–2210* ☰ *MC, V.*

¢–$ ⤬ **The Morning Star.** Halfway down a narrow lane is the 19th-century Morning Star, one of the city's most historic pubs, first built as a coaching stop for the Belfast to Dublin post. There's a traditional bar downstairs and a cozy velvet and wood-panel restaurant upstairs. Head chef Seamus McAlister, far from resting on the pub's laurels, is constantly experimenting—he's known for his quirky takes on fresh local ingredients. You might find venison and game in winter, lamb in spring, and in summer grilled haddock with dark rum or roast Antrim pork. Also notable is the steak menu; you'd be hard-pressed to find a larger assortment of aged beef cuts. Sizzling steaks arrive at the table on red-hot cast-iron skillets and are served with a flourish by the friendly staff. ⊠ *17–19 Pottingers Entry, Central District* ☏ *028/9023–5986* ☰ *MC, V* ⊗ *Closed Sun.*

¢–$ ⤬ **The Northern Whig.** Housed in an elegant former newspaper building, the Northern Whig is spacious and stylish. Three 30-foot-high statues of Soviet heroes that once topped Communist Party headquarters in Prague dominate the wood-and-leather interior. In the evenings, one wall slides away so you can watch classic movies, a jazz band, or a DJ playing laid-back blues, soul, or retro. The food is brasserie-style—not astonishing, but good. It's the environment, the thoughtful wine list, and the cocktail bar, which specializes in rare vodkas, that are the main draw. ⊠ 2 Bridge St., Central District ☎ 028/9050–9888 ⊟ MC, V.

★ ¢ ✕ **Deane's Deli.** Half take-out deli, half comfort-food eaterie, this is the latest addition to the Micheal Deane kingdom. Situated close to historic Ulster Hall, this is an all-day affair and, at that, you'll rarely find an empty seat—try the old-fashioned beer-battered fish-and-chips or one of the ever-changing daily specials. Just next door is the gourmand deli, where the shelves groan with homemade cheeses, breads, chocolates, and chutneys, many of which hail from the local farmers' market. They make great take-away sandwiches. ⊠ 44 Bedford St., Central District ☎ 028/ 9024–8800 ⊟ AE, MC, V ⊙ Closed Sun.

★ ¢ ✕ **Long's.** Long's has been serving fish-and-chips in its tiny, completely basic Athol Street premises for more than 80 years. Garbage collectors, millionaires, and every sector in between flocks here for the secret-batter-recipe fish, served with chips, bread, butter, and a mug of tea. ⊠ 39 Athol St., Golden Mile ☎ 028/9032–1848 ⊟ No credit cards ⊙ Closed Sun.

Where to Stay

Central District

★ $$$ ▣ **Malmaison.** The renaissance of Belfast's industrial Laganside district was spearheaded in part by the spiffy 2004 renovation of the historic former McCausland Hotel. The stunning 19th-century former grain warehouse has been transformed with low lighting, bold black-wood paneling, and velvet drapes creating a modern Gothic feel. The bar—dubbed Dracula's living room by one wag—continues the moody but luxurious look, with red crushed velvet chairs and dark suede sofas. Oversize purple Alice in Wonderland–style furniture adds to the slightly surreal aesthetic. Swish bedrooms contain flat-screen TVs and DVD players, and comfortable beds with Irish linens in muted colors. In the restaurant, helmed by inspired chef Alexander Plumb, specialties include steak hand-chosen from the Duke of Buccleuch's estate in the Scottish Highlands and aged for a minimum of 21 days. Situated on the edge of blossoming Laganside, the hotel is five minutes' walk from the heart of Belfast. ⊠ 34–38 Victoria St., Central District, BT1 3GH ☎ 028/9022–0200 🖷 028/9022–0220 ⊕ www.malmaison.com 🛏 62 rooms, 2 suites ⚸ Restaurant, Wi-Fi, bar, meeting rooms ⊟ AE, MC, V.

$$–$$$ ▣ **Belfast Hilton.** This riverside hotel should be able to cater to your every whim with its excellent business and leisure facilities. Earthy colors and bold stripes decorate the beds and windows. Ask for a suite or room with a view of the river. The restaurant serves contemporary cuisine and it has good views of the river and the city. The hotel is beside Waterfront Hall, in an area undergoing urban renewal. ⊠ 4 Lanyon Pl., Central District, BT1 3LP ☎ 028/9027–7000 🖷 028/9027–7277 ⊕ www. hilton.co.uk 🛏 181 rooms, 14 suites ⚸ Restaurant, minibars, cable TV, in-room data ports, indoor pool, hair salon, sauna, bar, business services, meeting rooms, no-smoking floors ⊟ AE, DC, MC, V ⊺⊙⫯ BP.

8

Golden Mile

★ **$$$–$$$$** 🏨 **TENsq.** You don't get much more downtown or contemporary than this fashionable boutique hotel right behind City Hall. The Neoclassical facade of this former post office hides a serene interior that houses a fashionable bar and also the Grill Room, which serves lunch and evening meals. The bedrooms are minimalist-Asian in style—with big, low-lying beds topped with white duvets, soft armchairs to sink into, and fresh flowers brought daily. There are ISDN lines for computers in all rooms, and a common DVD and CD library. ✉ *10 Donegall Sq. S, Golden Mile, BT1 5JD* ☎ *028/9024–1001* 🖷 *028/9024–3210* ⊕ *www.ten-sq.com* ➯ *23 rooms* ♻ *Restaurant, café, in-room data ports, 2 bars, concierge, free parking* ▭ *AE, MC, V* ⊚| *BP, MAP.*

$$–$$$ 🏨 **Holiday Inn Belfast.** Expect outstanding facilities at a reasonable price. Furnishings are modernist blond wood and leather, and rooms are best described as Japan-meets-Sweden: strong, simple colors and sliding wooden screens (a lovely touch) instead of curtains. Superbly located, with only a 10-minute walk to the city center and five minutes to the Golden Mile. ✉ *22 Ormeau Ave., Golden Mile BT2 8HS* ☎ *870/0400–9005* 🖷 *028/9062–6546* ⊕ *www.holiday-inn.co.uk* ➯ *170 rooms* ♻ *Restaurant, indoor pool, health club, hot tub, massage, sauna, steam room, bar; no a/c* ▭ *AE, DC, MC, V* ⊚| *BP, MAP.*

$–$$ 🏨 **Jurys Inn Belfast.** The first Jurys north of the border brings the chain's flat-rate formula—a single price for up to three adults or two adults and two children—to the Golden Mile. Once you get past the forbidding warehouselike exterior, a spacious, marble-tile foyer with warm green and salmon hues awaits. Room decor is pretty standard. Some rooms overlook College Square, the cricket lawn of the 1814 Royal Belfast Academical Institution. The Arches restaurant serves well-prepared hotel food. Tartan fabrics and dark wood decorate the Inn Pub, which serves pub grub all day. ✉ *Fisherwick Pl. at Great Victoria St., Golden Mile, BT2 7AP* ☎ *028/9053–3500* 🖷 *028/9053–3511* ⊕ *www.jurysdoyle.com* ➯ *190 rooms* ♻ *Restaurant, in-room data ports, bar, meeting rooms, no-smoking floors; no a/c* ▭ *AE, DC, MC, V* ⊚| *CP.*

$ 🏨 **Benedict's of Belfast.** Friendly, lively, and convenient, Benedict's stands out on Shaftsbury Square. Rooms on the second floor are bright and colorful, and have wooden floors; rooms on the third floor are darker, with an Asian influence—dark wood and light walls, simple but comfortable. If you don't feel like straying too far from your home base for some nightlife, Benedict's has a buzzing bar and restaurant serving finely done Continental food. They have a "beat the clock" promotion on their menu: a rib-eye steak with champ potatoes and brandy sauce, for instance, is usually £14 but order it up 5:30–7:30 PM and it's only £5.50. ✉ *7–21 Bradbury Pl., Golden Mile, BT7 1RQ* ☎ *028/9059–1999* 🖷 *028/9059–1990* ⊕ *www.benedictshotel.co.uk* ➯ *32 rooms* ♻ *Restaurant, cable TV, in-room data ports, bar; no a/c* ▭ *AE, MC, V* ⊚| *BP.*

Outside the City Center

★ **$$$$** ✕🏨 **Culloden Hotel.** Built in 1876 by the very rich William Robinson and christened in honor of his wife's famed family, this imposingly grand vision in Belfast stone presides over the forested slopes of the Holywood hills and the busy waters of Belfast Lough. Topped off with a storybook turret and crenellated tower, the Scottish Baronial mansion was greatly enlarged in the early 20th century when it was given as a residence to the Bishops of Down, then transformed in the 1960s into a hotel (today, the flagship of the luxe Hastings chain). Inside, Neoclassical salons warmed by lime-green walls, gilded coffered ceilings, 19th-century paintings, stained-glass accents, and overstuffed Louis XV–style chairs make you feel like you're a member of the Robinson family. Antiques and silk-and-velvet fabrics grace guest rooms both in the original section and in a newer wing; all rooms have fine views. At mealtime choose from the posh Mitre restaurant—transformed from the former refectory and now a pleasant room of paneled walls, green-fabric booths, and presided over by a statue of St. Pat—and the Cultra Inn, which serves snacks and full meals. The hotel is close to both the village of Holywood (temptingly filled with boutiques) and the Ulster Folk and Transport Museum. Chances are, however, that you won't want to leave Culloden's lovely 12 acres of grounds. Even those tempted by a quick walk to the nearby Royal Belfast Golf Club may not be able to forgo another afternoon spent at the hotel's Elysium Spa, a glamorous Beverly Hills–type affair. ⊠ *8 km (5 mi) east of Belfast on A2, 142 Bangor Rd., Holywood, Co. Down BT18 0EX* ☎ *028/9042–1066* 🖷 *028/9042–6777* ⊕ *www. hastingshotels.com* ⤴ *79 rooms, 10 suites* ⚹ *2 restaurants, Wi-Fi, tennis court, indoor pool, hair salon, sauna, spa, croquet, squash, bar, laundry service, meeting rooms, no-smoking rooms; no a/c* ⊟ *AE, DC, MC, V* ⦿ *BP, MAP.*

★ **$–$$** ⤬🖰 **The Old Inn.** Set in the village of Crawfordsburn, this 1614 coach inn, reputedly Ireland's oldest, certainly looks the part: it's pure 17th-century England, with a sculpted thatch roof, half doors, and leaded-glass windows. As it was near one of the leading cross-channel ports linking Ireland and England, the coach always stopped here, often bearing visitors with names like Swift, Tennyson, Thackeray, Dickens, and Trollope. More recently, C.S. Lewis and his wife, Joy, "booked" the inn to enjoy a belated honeymoon. You can see why: some of the finest bedrooms have 17th-century-style woodwork, sitting rooms, and faux-Jacobean beds, while public salons offer beam ceilings, roaring log fires, and lots of Ulster "craic" (chat). Repair to the grand 1614 restaurant to tuck into a Finnebrogue venison with sweet potato puree, red-onion marmalade and thyme beurre blanc and also savor the delicious setting of flocked curtains, English wood panels, sculpted portrait medallions, and a soaring coved ceiling. "Pub Fayre" is offered at the Churn Bistro, where the menu is solidly Irish, the staff jovial, and the locals inquisitive. Over the centuries, large portions of the inn were rebuilt, and the East Wing is a completely modern take on Irish Georgian style. ⊠ *16 km (10 mi) east of Belfast on A2, 15 Main St., Crawfordsburn, Co. Down BT19 1JH*

HIDEOUT HISTORY

If you're lucky enough to stay in the oldest parts of The Old Inn, you still may be able to uncover a secret hiding place for contraband, as smugglers, like the famous highwayman Dick Turpin, made this one of their favored homes-away-from-home.

☎ *028/9185–3255* 🖷 *028/9185–2775* ⊕ *www.theoldinn.com* ↵ *32 rooms* ♨ *Restaurant, Wi-Fi, 2 bars; no a/c* ▭ *AE, MC, V* ❄ *BP.*

$$ ▦ **Rayanne House.** Famous both for its food and for its hospitality, this country house run by the devoted Bernadette McClelland is in leafy Holywood, 10 km (6 mi) from Belfast city center. Rooms are airy, each with individual country furnishings and garden views. Breakfast includes an Irish grill and such specialties as prune soufflé on a puree of green figs, and hot Rayanne baked cereal (laced with spices, fruit, whiskey, honey, and cream). The meal is served in an intimate dining room, made even more intimate by family antiques, paintings, and candelabra. Lunch and dinner are available by request 24 hours in advance. ⊠ *8 km (5 mi) east of Belfast on A2, 60 Demesne Rd., Holywood, Co. Down BT18 9EX* ☎ *028/9042–5859* ⊕ *www.rayannehouse.co.uk* ↵ *9 suites* ♨ *Dining room, meeting rooms; no a/c* ▭ *MC, V* ❄ *BP, MAP.*

$ ▦ **Roseleigh House.** This charming Victorian guesthouse on a tree-filled avenue in residential south Belfast is a friendly option. Light-filled, spacious rooms decorated in calming blues with traditional floral bedspreads have modern comforts. Fresh flowers and daily newspapers adorn the coffee table in the residents' drawing room. Although Roseleigh is much renovated, stained-glass windows, elaborate fireplaces, and period cornicing on the ceilings point to the late-Victorian date of the house. Evening meals can be requested with 24 hours' notice and breakfasts are healthy and robust. ⊠ *19 Rosetta Park, Belfast BT6 ODL* ☎ *029/ 9064–4414* ⊕ *www.roseleighhouse.co.uk* ↵ *9 rooms* ♨ *Dining room, lounge; no a/c* ▭ *MC, V* ❄ *BP, MAP.*

University Area

$$ ▦ **Wellington Park Hotel.** Formerly a private residence and currently run by the Mooney family, this modern establishment is among the best in the University Area. The quiet, contemporary bedrooms are well designed, with built-in wood furniture; some have sleeping lofts. There's traditional European food in both the bar and restaurant—though the menu in the restaurant is slightly more expansive and expensive than in the bar. There's live music at the bar Friday and Saturday nights (soul, jazz, and Irish). ⊠ *21 Malone Rd., University Area, BT9 6RU* ☎ *028/9038–1111* 🖷 *028/9066–5410* ⊕ *www.mooneyhotelgroup.com* ↵ *75 rooms* ♨ *Restaurant, bar, laundry service, meeting rooms; no a/c* ▭ *DC, MC, V* ❄ *BP.*

★ **$–$$** ▦ **Ash-Rowan Guest House.** Thomas Andrews, designer of the ill-fated *Titanic,* brought his bride to live in this spacious Victorian home after their wedding, then went off to work 14-hour days at the Harland and Wolff shipyard. Former restaurateurs Sam and Evelyn Hazlett now own, run, and cook for this outstanding B&B on a tranquil residential avenue. Every bedroom has its own style, all with Victorian overtones. Feel free to take advantage of the reading lounge, as well as the books around the house, and the conservatory. Breakfasts and dinners are first-rate. ⊠ *12 Windsor Ave., University Area, BT9 6EE* ☎ *028/9066–1758* 🖷 *028/9066–3227* ↵ *5 rooms* ♨ *Dining room, lounge; no a/c, no smoking* ▭ *MC, V* ☉ *Closed Christmas wk* ❄ *BP, MAP.*

$ ▦ **Dukes Hotel.** Although this distinguished redbrick Victorian building has only 12 rooms, it has big-hotel amenities, including a spacious lobby, extensive exercise facilities, and two restaurants—one Chinese and one that serves healthy, local cuisine (traditionalists won't be disappointed, however, as fried food can be had). The hotel's color scheme is a distinguished, executive-style gray, enlivened with plenty of greenery, and a waterfall splashes down parallel to the stairway. Although not exceptional, the rooms are modern and comfortable, decorated in neutral shades. The lively bar is popular with staff and students from nearby Queen's University. ⊠ *65–67 University St., University Area, BT7 1HL* ☎ *028/9023–6666* 🖷 *028/9023–7177* ⊕ *www.welcome-group. co.uk* 🛏 *12 rooms* ⚙ *2 restaurants, gym, sauna, bar, meeting rooms; no a/c* ⊟ *AE, DC, MC, V* ⦿ *BP.*

$ 🖭 **Madison's.** A gracious hotel run by Botanic Inns, Madison's is in one of Belfast's liveliest spots—surrounded by the shops and cafés of lovely, tree-lined Botanic Avenue. The facade and public areas are decorated in a modish Barcelona-inspired take on Art Nouveau. Modern rooms— in primary yellows, reds, and rich blues—are stylish if sparsely furnished. The downstairs houses a restaurant that serves tasty contemporary cuisine at reasonable prices, and hip Club 33 fills the basement. Staying here you have discounted access to the extensive fitness facilities of Queen's University, including a pool. ⊠ *59 Botanic Ave., University Area, BT7 1JL* ☎ *028/9050–9800* 🖷 *028/9050–9808* ⊕ *www.madisonshotel. com* 🛏 *35 rooms* ⚙ *Restaurant, bar, business services; no a/c* ⊟ *AE, MC, V* ⦿ *BP.*

$ 🖭 **Old Rectory.** Mary and Jerry Callan's well-appointed house was built in 1896 as a rectory. Rooms are decorated in pastels and have good views of the mountains. Enjoy complimentary whiskey each evening in the parlor. Breakfast is hearty but healthy, a rarity in Ulster B&Bs: there's smoked salmon, scrambled eggs, fresh fruit salad, vegetarian sausages, homemade low-sugar jams, wheat bread, and freshly squeezed blended juices. ⊠ *148 Malone Rd., University Area, BT9 5LH* ☎ *028/9066–7882* 🖷 *028/9068–3759* 🛏 *6 rooms* ⚙ *No a/c* ⊟ *No credit cards* ⦿ *BP, MAP.*

¢ 🖭 **All Seasons.** Enjoying a superb location on the fashionable Lisburn Road in the south of the city, this spot has practically on its doorstep some of the city's most stylish boutiques and trendiest bars. Friendly owner Theodore McLaughlin has created a cozy home with a comfortable lounge, spacious dining room, and spotlessly clean rooms. Cranmore Park, a popular venue during the summer for sunbathers, is two minutes away on foot. ⊠ *356 Lisburn Rd., University Area, BT9 6GJ* ☎ *028/9068–2814* ⊕ *www.allseasonsbelfast.com* 🛏 *5 rooms* ⚙ *No a/c* ⊟ *MC, V* ⦿ *BP.*

Nightlife & the Arts

Nightlife

Belfast has dozens of pubs packed with relics of the Victorian and Edwardian periods. Although pubs typically close around 11:30 PM, many city-center–Golden Mile nightclubs stay open until 1 AM.

CENTRAL DISTRICT The **Apartment** (⊠ *2 Donegall Sq. W, Central District* ☎ *028/9050–9777*), beside City Hall, is the city center's trendiest bar, serving drinks and brasserie-style pub grub to Belfast's cool young things. Extensive but

Enjoy Those Tipples

GOING TO THE PUB, short for "public house," is Northern Ireland's favorite national pastime and every village, no matter how small, has at least one, and usually several. In fact, rural pubs are often indistinguishable from the house next door, so it pays to check with the locals for the best place for a pint and a bit of "craic." In Belfast and Derry, ornate Victorian inns sit side by side with new, brash bars playing loud music. In the last five years, dozens of ultramodern bars and nightclubs full of hip, fashionable young things have sprung up, particularly around the university area of Belfast. When it comes to the tipples, northerners are as fanatical as their southern counterparts and virtually every bar stocks a mind-boggling array of locally brewed and imported lagers, ales, stouts, and ciders. Guinness, of course, is the perennial favorite, but don't be surprised when the bartender asks you if you would prefer "normal" or "cold-flow." The latter was introduced in the mid-1990s and serves up a colder pint. Older drinkers, however, remain true to the original "porter" and simply ask for a pint "of the black stuff." Local lagers, like Harp, are popular and, at about £2.20 a pint, are often a good deal cheaper than imported beer. Smooth and creamy Caffrey's ale is delicious, but be warned: it packs quite a punch. Beer comes in two sizes—a "pint" and a "glass" (a half-pint). Then, of course, there's Bushmills whiskey, which makes a great Irish coffee (hot coffee with a shot of whiskey dropped in it, topped with a thick layer of double cream). As a general rule, kids are welcome until 6 PM, as long as they are accompanied by an adult. As a rule, bars that serve food are always more child-friendly.

inexpensive wine and cocktail lists attract a good crowd. **Bittles Bar** (⊠ 70 Upper Church La., Central District ☎ 028/9031–1088), on Victoria Square, serves pub grub. Gilded shamrocks bedeck this interesting triangular-shape Victorian pub on the fringes of the Cathedral Quarter. Paintings of literary characters and local landmarks adorn the walls, while a high, wood-panel ceiling gives an illusion of spaciousness. **Kelly's Cellars** (⊠ 30–32 Bank St., Central District ☎ 028/9024–6058), open since 1720, has blues bands on Saturday night. The **Kremlin** (⊠ 96 Donegall St., Central District ⊕ www.kremlin-belfast.com ☎ 028/9031–9061) nightclub is the city's oldest and most outrageous gay-oriented club. When it opened in a blaze of publicity in 1999, it revolutionized the city's gay scene. And it wears its heart on its sleeve: a massive statue of Lenin above the front door greets customers, and the over-the-top Soviet theme continues inside. Superstar DJs regularly fly in to perform.

Madden's Bar (⊠ Berry St., behind Castle Court, Central District ☎ 028/9024–4114) is a popular pub with traditional tune fests on occasion. At **Magennis' Bar and Whiskey Café** (⊠ 83 May St., Central District ☎ 028/9023–0295) you get two pubs for the price of one: the quiet, 100-year-old bar frequented by older regulars, and the hip café, crowded with younger clientele. The free tapas on Friday evenings pull in the after-work crowd, who pop in for a quick pint and end up staying all night. Live folk music on Sunday afternoons is a great finish to the weekend. Regulars prop up the horseshoe-shape bar in the Victorian showpiece, the **Morning Star** (⊠ 17–19 Pottinger's Entry, Central District ☎ 028/9023–5968), from noon until night. Strike up a conversation with some of the locals and you're guaranteed a bit of craic.

McHugh's (⊠ 29–30 Queen's Sq., Central District ☎ 028/9050–9990), in Belfast's oldest building, dating from 1711, has three floors of bars and restaurants, and live music on weekends. **Pat's Bar** (⊠ 19–22 Prince's Dock St., Central District ☎ 028/9074–4524) has first-rate sessions of traditional music on Saturday nights. The **Rotterdam** (⊠ 54 Pilot St., Central District ☎ 028/9074–6021), which housed convicts bound for Australia until it became a pub in 1820, is filled with fascinating old junk. It hosts traditional Irish music on Monday and Thursday, jazz on Tuesday, and rock on Friday and Saturday. **Union Street** (⊠ 8–14 Union St., Central District ☎ 028/9031–6060) is a gay-friendly bar near the Cathedral Quarter with charming staff and a wide selection of reasonably priced wines and imported beers. Housed in a converted 19th-century shoe factory, this three-story redbrick Victorian is one of the city's few "gastro-pubs," with a more formal upstairs restaurant that's popular with local foodies, and a simpler downstairs spot serving chili-fried whitebait-and-chips that you may wash down with a glass of chilled sauvignon blanc. **White's Tavern** (⊠ 2–12 Winecellar Entry, Central District ☎ 028/9024–3080) claims to be the oldest public house in Belfast. In winter a roaring fire greets you as soon as you enter the bar. Friendly staff serve good pub grub, including the famous "champ," a creamy, buttery, cholesterol-laden concoction of mashed potatoes and spring onions. In 2004 the upstairs restaurant was transformed into the city's newest and coolest nightspot. Downstairs, enjoy the traditional Irish sessions on Friday and Saturday nights.

GOLDEN MILE AREA The glorious Crown Liquor Saloon is far from being the only old pub in the Golden Mile area—most of Belfast's evening life takes place in bars and restaurants here. There are a number of replicated Victorian bars where more locals and fewer visitors gather.

The **Beaten Docket** (⊠ 48 Great Victoria St., Golden Mile ☎ 028/9024–2986), named after a losing betting slip, is a noisy, modern pub that attracts a young crowd. Here they play up-to-the-minute music, but it can get a bit boisterous, so some may prefer a quiet snug (booth) across the road in the famed Crown Liquor Saloon. **Benedict's** (⊠ 7–21 Bradbury Pl., Golden Mile ☎ 028/9059–1999) is a bar, music venue, disco, 150-seat restaurant, and hotel. One of the city's newest additions to the Golden Mile, the faux-Gothic exterior of the hotel belies its modern origins. Straying from the model of the Victorian-style public house, the **Limelight** (⊠ 17 Ormeau Ave., Golden Mile ☎ 028/9032–5968) is a disco-nightclub with cabaret on Tuesday, Friday, and Saturday, and recorded music on other nights. It's extremely popular with students, and books musicians as well as DJs.

Morrisons (⊠ 21 Bedford St., Golden Mile ☎ 028/9032–0030) is a haunt of media types. It has a music lounge upstairs, and hosts discussions for film buffs arranged by local directors in conjunction with the Northern Ireland Film Council. **Robinson's** (✉ 38–40 Great Victoria St., Golden Mile ☏ 028/9024–7447), two doors from the Crown, is a popular pub that draws a young crowd with folk music in its Fibber Magee's bar on Sunday and funk in the trendy BT1 wine and cocktail bar on weekends.

UNIVERSITY AREA The stylish and modern **Bar Twelve** (✉ Crescent Town House, 13 Lower Crescent, University Area ☏ 028/9032–3349) is an excellent venue for some fashionable wine-sipping. On weekend nights, DJs spin 1960s and '70s soul and funk tunes. Settle into the comfortable leather armchairs for a long chat while you work your way through the impressive wine list. The **Botanic Inn** (✉ 23–27 Malone Rd., University Area ☏ 028/9050–9740), known as "the Bot" to its student clientele, is a big, popular disco-pub. The **Chelsea Wine Bar** (✉ 346 Lisburn Rd., University Area ☏ 028/9068–7177) is packed with affluent professionals determined to prove that 30 is where life begins. The contemporary cuisine is reasonably priced. **Cutter's Wharf** (✉ 4 Lockview Rd., University Area ☏ 028/9066–3388), down by the river south of the university, is at its best on summer evenings and during music performances on Sunday after 6. Spacious and light inside, it rarely gets too packed; if seating is limited, try the picnic tables and chairs on the wooden deck outside.

The **Eglantine Inn** (✉ 32–40 Malone Rd., University Area ☏ 028/9038–1994), known as "the Egg," faces the Bot across Malone Road. The **Empire Music Hall** (✉ 42 Botanic Ave., University Area ☏ 028/9032–8110), a deconsecrated church, is the city's leading music venue. Stand-up comedy nights are usually on Tuesday. The **Fly Bar** (✉ 5–6 Lower Crescent, University Area ☏ 028/9050–9750), with its over-the-top interior playing on the fly theme, is a lively spot for a cocktail in the evening.

Lavery's Gin Palace (✉ 12 Bradbury Pl., University Area ☏ 028/9087–1106) mixes old-fashioned beer-drinking downstairs with dancing upstairs. On the increasingly fashionable Lisburn Road, **TaTu** (✉ 701 Lisburn Rd., University Area ☏ 028/9038–0818) is a spacious homage to industrial chic filled with a cool, under-thirty crowd. It serves good casual food.

The **M-Club** (✉ 23 Bradbury Pl., University Area ☏ 028/9023–3131) is Belfast's hottest place for dedicated clubbers, with soap-opera celebrities flown in weekly to mix with the local nighthawks.

The Arts

The **Northern Ireland Arts Council** (☏ 028/9038–5200 ⊕ www.artscouncil-ni.org) produces the bimonthly *Artslink* poster-brochure listing happenings throughout Belfast and the North. It's widely available throughout the city. The **Belfast Festival at Queen's University** (Festival office ✉ 25 College Gardens, University Area ☏ 028/9097–2600 ⊕ www.belfastfestival.com), which lasts for three weeks (usually late October into early November), is the city's major arts festival. The **Promenade Concerts** (☏ 028/9066–8798 ⊕ www.ulster-orchestra.org.uk) are performed in June by the Ulster Orchestra in conjunction with the BBC.

ART GALLERIES **Bell Gallery.** This gallery in Nelson Bell's Victorian home shows many of Ireland's more traditional and representational painters from the

18th to the 21st century. ✉ *13 Adelaide Park, at Malone Rd., South University* ☎ *028/9066–2998* ⊕ *www.bellgallery.com* ⊘ *Mon.–Thurs. 9–5, Fri. 9–3.*

Fenderesky Gallery. Under the same roof as the Crescent Arts Centre, Iranian philosopher Jamshid Mirfenderesky's gallery is one of the few in Ireland exhibiting the work of a stable of modern Irish artists known throughout Europe. ✉ *Crescent Arts Centre, 2 University Rd., University Area* ☎ *028/9023–5245* ⊘ *Tues.–Sat. 11:30–5.*

FILM **Queen's Film Theatre** (✉ 20 University Sq., University Area ☎ 028/9097–1097), Belfast's main art cinema, shows domestic and foreign movies on its two screens. **Movie House Cinema** (✉ 14 Dublin Rd., Golden Mile ☎ 028/9024–5700) has 10 screens of major British and American box-office favorites.

MAJOR VENUES **Crescent Arts Centre.** Watch experimental dance and theater, witness provocative art in the Fenderesky Gallery, and listen to lively jazz concerts: it's all part of the Crescent. You can also take classes in this huge, rambling stone building, a former girls' high school off the campus end of Bradbury Place. ✉ *2–4 University Rd., University Area* ☎ *028/9024–2338* ⊕ *www.crescentarts.org.*

Grand Opera House. Shows from all over the British Isles—and sometimes farther afield—play at this beautifully restored Victorian theater. Though it has no company of its own, there's a constant stream of West End musicals and plays of widely differing kinds, plus occasional operas and ballets. It's worth going to a show if only to enjoy the opera house itself. ✉ *2 Great Victoria St., Golden Mile* ☎ *028/9024–1919* ⊕ *www.goh.co.uk.*

King's Hall. Pop and rock concerts take center stage at this venue that also serves as a conference center. ✉ *484 Lisburn Rd., South University* ☎ *028/9066–5225* ⊕ *www.kingshall.co.uk.*

Lyric Theatre. Set in south Belfast at King's Bridge, on the banks of the Lagan, this is the theater where Hollywood fave Liam Neeson made his stage debut. Traditional and contemporary Irish culture inspires the thoughtful dramas staged here and usually each new production is accompanied by a show, in the upper foyer lobby, of contemporary art by local artists. ✉ *55 Ridgeway St., South University* ☎ *028/9038–1081* ⊕ *www.lyrictheatre.co.uk.*

Odyssey Arena. Built to mark the Millennium and now home to the Belfast Giants—the city's first ice-hockey team (most of whom hail from North America)—the Odyssey complex also features the interactive science and technology center known as W5 (see below), a Sheridan IMAX theater, an indoor bowling alley, and the Odyssey Pavilion complex, replete with bars, restaurants, shops, nightclubs, and the Warner Village Cinemas multiplex. The latter kicks into high gear at night, while more family-oriented activities can be had by day. The center ring is the 10,000-seat Arena, Ireland's biggest indoor venue, which often hosts rock, pop, and classical troupes. Situated on Queen's Island, the Odyssey is close to the old Harland and Wolff shipyard and set along the banks of the River

8

VOICES OF NORTHERN IRELAND

Pearse Elliot
Belfast-born Writer, Director & Actor

Native son of Belfast, Pearse Elliot is now one of the most recognized names in theater and film to have come out of Northern Ireland.

Today he has a hit movie and a running series for BBC, so the fact that he had a "Trouble"-d childhood underlines the future-forward spirit of Belfast, his hometown.

During The Troubles, he grew up in the city's rough Lenadoon district. His working-class West Belfast neighborhood was blighted by poverty and unemployment and some of his school friends and neighbors were killed during the conflict.

But Pearse was not about to let this mar his life. "Raised in the rough Lenadoon district of West Belfast, I grew up in the heart of The Troubles, yet I have nothing but fond memories of my early years. No matter that clouds of black smoke rose like ominous smoke signals from the burning city below, my childhood was spent roaming the fields that lay behind my small family home. Walking my dogs, I didn't see just how violent and restrictive our world could be."

"In my early 20s, I started writing about my experiences and wound up winning the BBC Young Playwright competition—for a script written in longhand on a school notepad. It was a mix of gutsy reality and black humor and must have struck a chord—I was signed up to make a feature film in no time."

He has now three successful films under his belt and in 2004 he wrote a BBCNI sitcom, *Pulling Moves*, about four fast Belfast friends—Wardrobe, Ta, Darragh, and Shay—who try to improve their lot by "flirting with the skirts of legality."

His 2005 movie, *The Mighty Celt*, was about the relationship between a young boy and a racing greyhound, played out against a backdrop of figures who support the IRA stance and others who feel that conflict is inherently bad.

Set in the grim housing estates of Belfast, it stars *X-Files* actress Gillian Anderson and *Full Monty* actor Robert Carlyle—both of whom mastered superb Belfast accents (usually regarded by some critics as so thick as to need subtitles)—and reached number one at the Irish box office.

Not bad for a lad who barely finished high school and has never stepped foot in a university.

Despite this heady success, "Belfast will always be my home," Elliot notes.

"It is who I am. I love the people—in particular, their resilience: the way we have of looking at even the bleakest of situations with a humorous view. People here are grateful for what they have and what they have achieved because we know that it can be so much worse."

Lagan. ✉ *Queen's Quay, Central District* ☎ *028/9045–1055* ⊕ *www. theodyssey.co.uk.*

Old Museum Arts Centre (OMAC). A powerhouse of challenging, avant-garde theater and modern dance, OMAC also has a risk-taking art gallery. ✉ *7 College Sq. N, Central District* ☎ *028/9023–3332* ⊕ *www. oldmuseumartscentre.org.*

Ulster Hall. This, the main home to the Ulster Orchestra, has excellent acoustics and a splendid Victorian organ. The classical music season runs from September through March; most concerts are on Friday. ✉ *Bedford St., Golden Mile* ☎ *028/9032–3900* ⊕ *www.ulster-orchestra. org.uk.*

Waterfront Hall. Everyone in Belfast sings the praises of this striking civic structure. From the looks of it, the hall is an odd marriage of *Close Encounters* modern and Castel Sant'Angelo antique. It houses a major 2,235-seat concert hall (for ballet and classical, rock, and Irish music) and a 500-seat studio space (for modern dance, jazz, and experimental theater). The Terrace Café restaurant and two bars make the hall a convenient place to eat, have a pint, and enjoy the river views before or after your culture fix. ✉ *Lanyon Pl., Central District* ☎ *028/9033–4455* ⊕ *www.waterfront.co.uk.*

Shopping

Belfast's main shopping streets include High Street, Royal Avenue, and several of the smaller streets connecting them. The area is mostly traffic-free (except for buses and delivery vehicles). The long thoroughfare of Donegall Pass, running from Shaftesbury Square at the point of the Golden Mile east to Ormeau Road, is a unique mix of biker shops and antiques arcades. All Belfast is abuzz watching the construction of the £300 million flagship Victoria Square complex, under construction at press time and due to be inaugurated by summer 2007: a host of world-class designers are tipped to set up shop here.

Market & Mall

Castle Court (✉ 10 Royal Ave., Central District ☎ 028/9023–4591) is the city's largest and most varied upscale shopping mall. **Debenhams** (☎ 028/9043–9777) department store can fill many of your shopping needs, from cosmetics to kitchenware. Trendy stores like **Gap** (☎ 028/9023–6444) can be found under Castle Court's glass roof, alongside British clothing chains like **Miss Selfridge** (☎ 028/9023–5008) and **Warehouse** (☎ 02890/43–9606). Boys who like their toys will be in their element in the **Gadget Shop** (☎ 0800/7838343). Plenty of parking makes shopping easy in the mall. If you've an interest in bric-a-brac, visit the enormous, renovated **St. George's Market** (✉ May St., Central District ☎ 028/9043–5704), an indoor market that takes place Friday and Saturday morning. Get there early on Saturday for an award-winning farmers' market, featuring organically grown fruit and vegetables, as well as treats such as homemade cakes and bread.

Occupying an eight-block site in central Belfast, **Victoria Square** (✉ Chichester, Montgomery, Ann streets, and Victoria Square, Central District

8

✉ not established at press time ⊕ www.victoriasquare.com) is changing the Belfast skyline with a Disneylandlike complex of shopping malls and residences, set to begin opening in mid-2007. One of the largest construction projects in Ireland, presided over by a vast geodesic glass dome eight-stories high (replete with viewing platforms over the city), the complex will be a glossy steel-and-glass edifice of hypermodern design. Offering a delightful contrast, however, the complex also incorporates noted Victorian landmarks like the McErvel's Seed Warehouse and the Royal Belfast Ginger Ale Manufactury. Two department stores will be the main shopping anchors: H&M and the House of Fraser. In addition, a slew of other stores, including Virgin Megastore and Lunn's Jewelers will attract shoppers who previously just headed to Castle Court. Restaurants, cafés, and cinemas will round out this "day-out experience."

Specialty Shops

Clark and Dawe (✉ 485 Lisburn Rd., University Area ☎ 028/9066–8228) makes and sells men's and women's suits and shirts. **Craftworks** (✉ Bedford House, 16–22 Bedford St., Golden Mile ☎ 028/9024–4465) stocks crafts by local designers. **Natural Interior** (✉ 51 Dublin Rd., Golden Mile ☎ 028/9024–2656) has Irish-linen throws, trimmed in velvet, by the designer Larissa Watson-Regan. It also stocks her vividly colored wall panels and cushions. **The Church of Ireland Bookshop** (✉ 61/67 Donegall St. ☎ 028/9066–7754) stocks rare books and manuscripts.

Smyth and Gibson (✉ Bedford House, Bedford St., Golden Mile ☎ 028/9023–0388) makes and sells beautiful, luxurious linen and cotton shirts and accessories. Looking for linen souvenirs? **Smyth's Irish Linens** (✉ 65 Royal Ave., Central District ☎ 028/9024–2232) carries a large selection of handkerchiefs, tablecloths, napkins, and other traditional goods. It's opposite Castle Court Mall. **The Steensons** (✉ Bedford House, Bedford St., Golden Mile ☎ 028/9024–8269) sells superb, locally designed jewelry. **Utopia** (✉ Fountain Centre, College St., Central District ☎ 028/9024–1342) stocks intricate silver pendants and earrings made by up-and-coming local jewelry designer Abbie Dixon. Also worth a look are the hand-carved wooden and marble chess sets.

THE GIANT'S CAUSEWAY COAST

Starting in Belfast, stretching for 80 km (50 mi) along Northern Ireland's Atlantic shore, the Causeway Coast holds many of the province's "don't miss" attractions. The man-made brilliance of the castle at Dunluce, the endless string of whitewashed fishing villages along the sea, and the world-famous natural wonder that is the Giant's Causeway are just some of the delights to be discovered here. Once your car or mountain bike (ideal for the Causeway's flat terrain) makes its way past some fair-size towns, you'll enter the splendid Glens area—one of the more "gentle" (an Irish turn-of-phrase for supernatural) places in all Ireland. Here, ageless villages—still inhabited by descendants of the ancient Irish and the Hebridean Scots who hailed from across the narrow Sea of Moyle—are set in peaceful, old-growth forests that have become synonymous with Irishness. But once past the Giant's Causeway you'll find more cosmo-

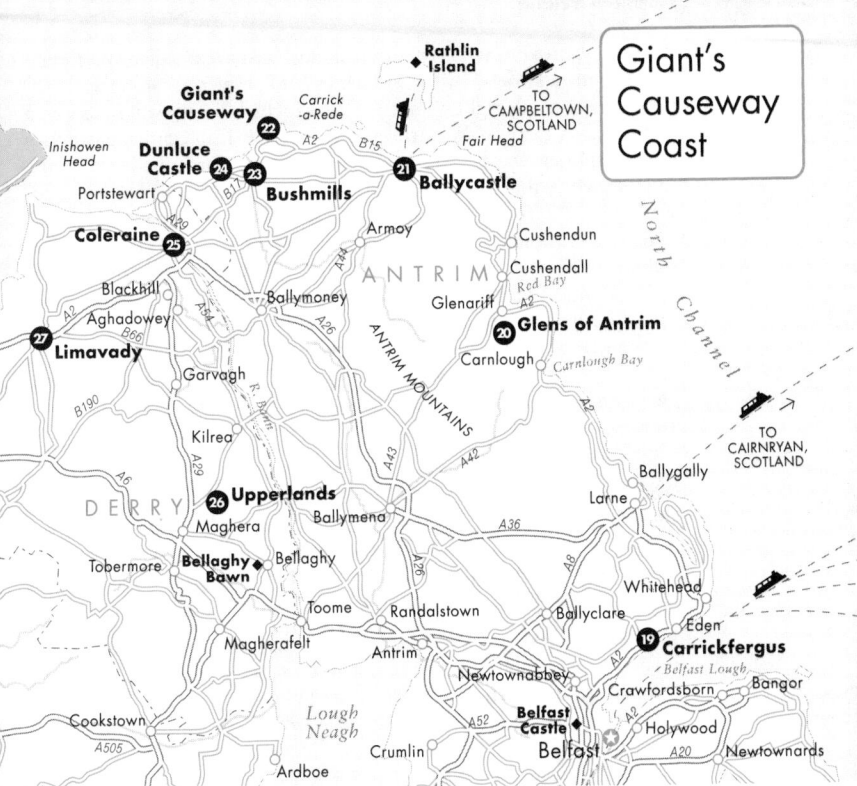

politan pleasures, including Bushmills—the oldest licensed distillery in the world—and the old walled city of Derry.

Carrickfergus

🔞 *16 km (10 mi) northeast of Belfast on A2.*

Carrickfergus, on the shore of Belfast Lough, grew up around its ancient castle. When the town was enclosed by ramparts at the start of the 17th century, it was the only English-speaking town in Northern Ireland. Not surprisingly, this was the loyal port where William of Orange chose to land on his way to fight the Catholic forces at the Battle of the Boyne in 1690. However, the English did have one or two small setbacks, including the improbable victory in 1778 of John Paul Jones, the American naval hero, over the British warship *HMS Drake*. Although a long way from home, this stands as the first naval victory of America's fledgling navy fleet. After this battle, which was waged in Belfast Lough, the inhabitants of Carrickfergus stood on the waterfront and cheered Jones when his ship passed the town castle, demonstrating their support for the American Revolution.

Carrickfergus Castle, one of the first and one of the largest of Irish castles, is still in good shape. It was built atop a rock ledge in 1180 by John de Courcy, provincial Ulster's first Anglo-Norman invader. Apart from being captured briefly by the French in 1760, the castle stood as a bastion of British rule right up until 1928, at which time it still functioned as an English garrison. Walk through the castle's 13th-century gatehouse into the Outer Ward. Continue into the Inner Ward, the heart of the fortress, where the five-story keep stands, a massive, sturdy building with walls almost 8 feet thick. Inside the keep is the Cavalry Regimental Museum, with historic weapons and the vaulted Great Hall. These days Carrickfergus Castle hosts entertaining medieval banquets (inquire at Carrickfergus tourist information office or the Northern Ireland Tourist Board Information Centre). If you're here at the beginning of August, you can enjoy the annual Lughnasa festival, a lively medieval-costume entertainment. ⊠ *Off A2* ☎ *028/9335–1273* ⊕ *www.ehsni.gov.uk/ places/monuments/carrick.shtml* ⌧ *£3* ⊙ *Apr., May, and Sept., Mon.–Sat. 10–6, Sun. 2–6; June–Aug., Mon.–Sat. 10–6, Sun. noon–6; Oct.–Mar., Mon.–Sat. 10–4, Sun. 2–4.*

Old buildings that remain from Carrickfergus's past include St. Nicholas's Church, built by John de Courcy in 1205 (remodeled in 1614) and the handsomely restored North Gate in the town's medieval walls. Dobbins Inn on High Street, which has been a hotel for more than three centuries, is a watering hole that's popular with locals.

The **Andrew Jackson Centre** tells the tale of the U.S. president whose parents emigrated from here in 1765. This thatched cottage just outside of town is a reconstruction of an 18th-century structure thought to resemble their home. ⊠ *2 km (1 mi) northeast of Carrickfergus, Larne Rd., Boneybefore* ☎ *028/9335–8049* ⊕ *www.carrickfergus.org* ⌧ *£1* ⊙ *Apr., May, and Oct., weekdays 10–1 and 2–4, weekends 2–4; June–Sept., weekdays 10–1 and 2–6, weekends 2–6.*

Glens of Antrim

★ ⑳ *Beginning 24 km (15 mi) north of Carrickfergus at Larne.*

Soon after Larne, the coast of County Antrim becomes spectacular—wave upon wave of high green hills that curve down to the hazy sea are dotted with lush glens, or valleys, first carved out by glaciers at the end of the last ice age. Nine wooded river valleys occupy the 86 km (54 mi) between Larne and Ballycastle. A narrow, winding, two-lane road (A2, which splits from the coastal at Cushendall) hugs the slim strip of land between the hills and the sea, bringing you to the magnificent Glens of Antrim running down from the escarpment of the Antrim Plateau to the eastern shore. Until the building of this road in 1834, the Glens were home to isolated farming communities—people who adhered to the romantic, mystical Celtic legends and the everyday use of the Irish language. Steeped in Irish mythology, the Glens were first inhabited by small bands of Irish monks as early as AD 700. Some residents proudly note that Ossian, the greatest of the Celtic poets, is supposedly buried near Glenaan. Given the original remoteness of the area, a great tradition of storytelling still exists.

The Glens are worth several days of serious exploration. Even narrower B-roads curl west off A2, up each of the beautiful glens where trails await hikers. You'll need a full week and a rainproof tent to complete the nine-glen circuit (working from south to north, Glenarm, Glencloy, Glenariff, Glenballyeamon, Glenaan, Glencorp, Glendun, Glenshesk, and Glentasie—Taisie was a princess of Rathlin Island); or you could just head for Glenariff Park, the most accessible of Antrim's glens. Tourist offices in the area, such as the one in Cushendall, sell a *Guide to the Glens.*

> ## WATCH YOUR BACK
>
> In the beautiful Glens of Antrim, locals often talk of "the wee folk," said to reside in and around the "gentle" (i.e., supernatural) places of Lurigethan Mountain and Tiveragh Hill. The fairies inhabiting these places are mischievous creatures who mostly mind their own business, but woe betide anyone rash enough to cut off a fairy thorn.

A little resort made of white limestone, **Carnlough** overlooks a charming harbor that's surrounded by stone walls. The harbor can be reached by crossing over the limestone bridge from Main Street, built especially for the Marquis of Londonderry. The small harbor, once a port of call for fishermen, now shelters pleasure yachts. Carnlough is surrounded on three sides by hills that rise 1,000 feet from the sea. There's a small tourist office inside the post office, which is useful if you need information on exploring the scenic Glens of Antrim and the coast road. ⊠ *24 km (15 mi) north of Larne on A2.*

★ In **Glenariff Forest Park** you can explore the most beautiful and unsettled of Antrim's glens. Glenariff was christened "Little Switzerland" by Thackeray for its spectacular combination of rugged hills and lush vales. The main valley opens onto Red Bay at the village of Glenariff (also known as Waterfoot). Inside the park are picnic facilities and dozens of good hikes. The 5½-km (3½-mi) Waterfall Trail, marked with blue arrows, passes outstanding views of Glenariff River, its waterfalls, and small but swimmable loughs. Escape from the summer crowds by taking one of the longest trails, such as the Scenic Hike. Pick up a detailed trail map at the park visitor center, which also has a small cafeteria. ⊠ *7 km (5 mi) north of Carnlough off A2, 98 Glenariff Rd., Glenariff* ☎ *028/2175–8232* ⊇ *Vehicles £4, pedestrians £2* ☉ *Apr.–Sept., daily 8–8; Oct.–Mar., daily 10–dusk.*

Turnley's Tower—a curious, fortified square tower of red stone, built in 1820 as a curfew tower and jail for "idlers and rioters"—stands in **Cushendall,** at a crossroads in the middle of the village. Another village of the picture-postcard variety, Cushendall is called the capital of the Glens due to having a few more streets than the other villages hereabouts. The road from Waterfoot to Cushendall is barely a mile long and worth the walk or cycle to see the coastal caves (one of whose residents was called the Nun Marry) that line the route. ⊠ *3 km (2 mi) north of Glenariff on A2.*

8

★ Off the main A2 route, the road between Cushendall and Cushendun turns into one of a Tour-de-France hilliness, so cyclists beware. Your reward, however, will be the tiny jewel of a village, **Cushendun**, which was designed by Clough Williams-Ellis, who also designed the famous Italianate village of Portmeirion in Wales. From this part of the coast you can see the Mull of Kintyre on the Scottish mainland. ⊠ *2 km (1½ mi) north of Cushendall on Coast Rd.*

> ### ELIXIR OF YOUTH?
>
> The coastal caves of Cushendall have been used for various purposes, including housing. One of the more colorful residents was a lady called Nun Marry who lived in one cave for 50 years, supplementing her income as one of the region's better potion brew makers. The damp and windy conditions obviously agreed with her—and perhaps a taste of her own brew?—for she lived to the ripe old age of 100.

EN ROUTE The narrow and precipitous Antrim Coast Road cuts off from A2 and heads north from Cushendun past dramatically beautiful Murlough Bay to Fair Head and on to Ballycastle. In this area is Drumnakill, a renowned pagan site; Torr Head, a jutting peninsula; and three state parks that allow for some fabulous hikes, fine hill-walking, and great views of Scotland from Fair Head. Or you can rejoin A2 at Cushendun via B92 (a left turn). After a few miles the road descends—passing ruins of the Franciscans' 16th-century Bonamargy Friary—into Ballycastle.

Where to Stay & Eat

$$$ ✕⌂ **Galgorm Manor.** The manor house itself is photogenic, and the estate grounds—where you may go riding, practice archery, and shoot clay pigeons—cinematic. Full privileges at an 18-hole, par-72 golf course five minutes from the hotel is an added treat. The River Maine (good for brown trout) flows within view of many of the large rooms, which have wood beams hanging on the ceilings above substantial dark-wood beds. Gillies bar is decidedly Irish; the restaurant serves hearty portions of traditional Irish food ($–$$). Galgorm is off A42, 3 km (2 mi) west of Ballymena, 32 km (20 mi) inland of Larne, 40 km (25 mi) north of Belfast. ⊠ *40 km (25 mi) east of Larne on A36, 136 Fenaghy Rd., Ballymena, Co. Antrim BT42 1EA* ☎ *028/2588–1001* 🖷 *028/2588–0080* ⊕ *www.galgorm.com* ⇨ *24 rooms* ⌂ *Restaurant, golf privileges, fishing, archery, horseback riding, bar, meeting rooms; no a/c* 🖃 *AE, MC, V* ⦿*❙ BP, MAP.*

★ **$$** ✕⌂ **Londonderry Arms Hotel.** What awaits at Londonderry Arms are lovely seaside gardens, ivy-clad walls, gorgeous antiques, regional paintings and maps, and lots of fresh flowers. This ivy-covered traditional inn on Carnlough Harbor was built as a coach stop in 1848. In 1921 Sir Winston Churchill inherited it; since 1947 it has been owned and run by the hospitable O'Neill family. Both the original and the newer rooms have Georgian furnishings and luxurious fabrics, and are immaculately kept. The restaurant serves substantial, traditional Irish meals that emphasize fresh, local seafood, simply prepared ($–$$). The hotel has an elevator and is wheelchair accessible. ⊠ *20 Harbour Rd., Carnlough, Co. Antrim BT44 0EU* ☎*028/2888–5255* 🖷*028/2888–5263* ⊕*www.glensofantrim.com* ⇨ *35 rooms* ⌂ *Restaurant, bar, meeting rooms; no a/c* 🖃 *AE, DC, MC, V* ⦿*❙ BP, MAP.*

$$$ ✕🏠 **Ballygally Castle.** A baronial castle, built by a Scottish lord in 1625, rises dramatically beside Ballygally Bay. Attached to it is a modern extension that provides room for facilities but clashes a bit with the original. Bedrooms in the castle have retained beamed ceilings despite comfortable-if-bland furnishings throughout. Ask for a room in a turret—one comes complete with milady's ghost. On Saturday in the dining room, a decent table d'hôte evening meal is served to musical accompaniment; a Sunday bistro meal is available. ✉ *274 Coast Rd., Ballygally, Co. Antrim BT40 2QZ* ☎ *028/2858–1066* 🖷 *028/2858–3681* ⊕ *www.hastingshotels.com* 🛏 *44 rooms* 🍴 *Dining room, bar, babysitting; no a/c* ⊟ *AE, DC, MC, V* ⭐ *BP.*

Ballycastle

㉑ *86 km (54 mi) northeast of Larne, 37½ km (23 mi) north of Carnlough.*

Ballycastle is the main resort at the northern end of the Glens of Antrim. People from the province flock here in summer. The town is shaped like an hourglass—with its strand and dock on one end, its pubs and chippers on the other, and the 1-km (½-mi) Quay Road in between. Beautifully aged shops and pubs line its Castle, Diamond, and Main streets. Every year since 1606, on the last Monday and Tuesday in August, Ballycastle has hosted the **Oul' Lammas Fair,** a modern version of the ancient Celtic harvest festival of Lughnasa (Irish for "August"). Ireland's oldest fair, this is a very popular two-day event at which sheep and wool are still sold alongside the wares of more modern shopping stalls. Treat yourself to the fair's traditional snacks, "dulse" (sun-dried seaweed), and "yellow man" (rock-hard yellow toffee).

From Ballycastle town you have a view of L-shape **Rathlin Island,** where in 1306 the Scottish king Robert the Bruce took shelter in a cave (under the east lighthouse) and, according to the popular legend, was inspired to continue his armed struggle against the English by watching a spider patiently spinning its web. It was on Rathlin in 1898 that Guglielmo Marconi set up the world's first cross-water radio link, from the island's lighthouse to Ballycastle. Bird-watching and hiking are the island's main activities. Unless the sea is extremely rough, a ferryboat makes twice-daily journeys for £9. The trip can take up to 45 minutes; be mindful of the weather to ensure that you can return the same day. ✉ *9½ km (6 mi) from Ballycastle.*

SHOOT THE CHUTE

If you summon up the nerve to cross the famous 60-ft Carrick-a-Rede rope bridge, which sways over a rocky outcrop and the turbulent sea, be mindful that you have to do it again to get back to the mainland.

★ Off the Ballycastle coast you can see the **Carrick-a-Rede** rope bridge, which spans a 60-foot gap between the mainland and Carrick-a-Rede Island. The island's name means "rock in the road" and refers to how it stands in the path of the salmon who follow the coast as they migrate to their home rivers to spawn. For the past 150 years salmon fishermen have set up the rope bridge in spring, taking it down again after the salmon season ends. The bridge is open to the public and has some heart-stopping views of the crashing waves below. ⊠ *8 km (5 mi) west of Bally-castle on B15* ⊡ *Free* ☉ *Mid-Mar.–June and Sept., daily 10–6; July and Aug., daily 9:30–7:30.*

Where to Eat

★ ¢–$$ ✕ **Wysner's.** Head chef Jackie Wysner has won several awards for both this small family restaurant and the eponymous butcher shop next door. Menus vary daily, though the cooking emphasizes fresh local ingredients—from the hills and the sea. Specialties of the upstairs restaurant include North Atlantic salmon (caught nearby at Carrick-a-Rede), fillet of halibut with langoustine, and fillet of beef with mustard-seed cream sauce. A daytime menu is served downstairs in the informal café. ⊠ *16–18 Ann St.* ☎ *028/2076–2372* ▭ *MC, V* ☉ *Closed Sun.*

Giant's Causeway

❷❷ *19⅓ km (12 mi) west of Ballycastle.*

Fodor'sChoice
★

"When the world was moulded and fashioned out of formless chaos, this must have been a bit over—a remnant of chaos," said the great Thackeray about Northern Ireland's premier tourist draw, the Giant's Causeway. Imagine a mass of 37,000 mostly hexagonal pillars of volcanic basalt, clustered like a giant honeycomb and extending hundreds of yards into the sea. Legend has it this "causeway" was created 60 million years ago, when boiling lava, erupting from an underground fissure that stretched from Northern Ireland to the Scottish coast, crystallized as it burst into the sea, and formed according to the same natural principle that structures a honeycomb. As all Ulster folk know, though, the scientific truth is that the columns were created as stepping-stones by the giant Finn McCool in a bid to reach a giantess he'd fallen in love with on the Scottish island of Staffa (where the causeway resurfaces). Unfortunately, the giantess's boyfriend found out, and in the ensuing battle Finn pulled out a huge chunk of earth and flung it toward Scotland. The resulting hole became Lough Neagh, and the sod landed to create the Isle of Man.

To reach the causeway, you can either walk 1½ km (1 mi) down a long, scenic hill or take a minibus from the visitor center. West of the causeway, Port-na-Spania is the spot where the 16th-century Spanish Armada galleon *Girona* went down on the rocks. The ship was carrying an astonishing cargo of gold and jewelry, some of which was recovered in 1967 and is now on display in the Ulster Museum in Belfast. Beyond this, Chimney Point is the name given to one of the causeway structures on which the

> ### KEEP YOUR EYE ON THE ROAD
>
> For excellent—and generally deserted—hiking, check with the staff at the Causeway Centre for tips on a dozen easy hikes in the area, including one that follows the pristine coastline toward the ruined tower of Dunseverick Castle, 5 km (3 mi) away—the impressive landscape along the way is the main reward.

Spanish fired, thinking that it was Dunluce Castle, which is 8 km (5 mi) west.

Arriving by car at the Giant's Causeway, you first reach a cliff-top parking lot beside the modern **Causeway Centre,** a visitor center, which houses displays about the area and a superb audiovisual exhibition explaining the formation of the causeway coast, as well as a crafts shop. The nearby Causeway Hotel is a good place to stop off for lunch after any hunger-inducing walk. Word of warning: dress appropriately by taking a warm jacket and wear sensible walking shoes, as the causeway can be slippery on wet days. Small children will need to be properly supervised. ⊠ *44 Causeway Rd., Bushmills* ☎ *028/2073–1855* ⊕ *www. nationaltrust.org.uk* ⊠ *Visitor center movie £1, guided tours £2, parking £5* ⊙ *Visitor center Mar.–June, Sept., and Oct., daily 10–5; July and Aug., daily 10–6; Nov.–Feb., daily 10–4:30.*

Bushmills

㉓ *3 km (2 mi) west of Giant's Causeway.*

Reputedly the oldest licensed distillery in the world, Bushmills was first granted a charter by King James I in 1608, though historical records refer to a distillery here as early as 1276. Bushmills produces the most famous of Irish whiskeys—its namesake—and what is widely regarded as the best, the rarer black-label version known to aficionados as Black Bush. During the guided tour you will discover the secrets of the special water from St. Columb's Mill, the story behind malted Irish barley, and learn about triple distillation in copper stills and aging (which happens for long years in oak casks).

You begin in the mashing and fermentation room, proceed to the maturing and bottling warehouse, and conclude, yes, with the much anticipated, complimentary shot of *uise beatha,* the "water of life." You can also have a light lunch in the Distillery Kitchen or pick up souvenirs in the distillery gift shop. If you're very lucky you could pick up a bottle of Bushmills Malt 21 Year Old, an extremely rare single Malt Irish whiskey, of which only a very limited number of bottles are available every year. Or if you really have a chubby wallet you could ask about the Bushmill's Malt Artist's Reserve—a mere £300 a bottle. One drop of this elixir and you'll realize that this small distillery is still top of its game four centuries after its founding. Children under 7 are not permitted on the tour. ⊠ *Off A2* ☎ *028/2073–3218* ⊕ *www.bushmills.com* ⊠ *£4*

> **WORD OF MOUTH**
>
> "We spent two nights at Bushmill's, the old Irish Whiskey-owned inn right in the town of Bushmills: wonderful old rooms, cozy atmosphere, superb restaurant, even a room with a 'secret' revolving bookcase. Since it poured rain, we canceled plans to hike the Giant's Causeway and went to Bushmills. I became an 'official taster': Suffice it to say that I have been drinking Irish Whiskey instead of Scotch ever since."
>
> −Patrick

8

⊙ *Tours Apr.–Oct., Mon.–Sat. 9:30–5:30, Sun. noon–5:30; Nov.–Mar., weekdays 10:30–3:30, weekends 1:30–3:30.*

Where to Stay

$$–$$$$ ⊞ **Bushmills Inn.** Owner Roy Bolton oversees this cozy old coach inn. Stripped pine, peat fires, and gaslights warm the public rooms. Some of the bedrooms are quite small, so look before you decide. The livery stables now house the informal restaurant, which serves fresh and hearty food, and the bar. The staff can provide a baby-listening service—you leave the tot in the room with a phone that records any noise, and they alert you to cries. The distillery is a stroll away from the main square and the inn, as is the salmon-filled River Bush. Rooms in the less-expensive Coaching House section are smaller and overlook the road, perfect if you're on a budget. ⊠ *9 Dunluce Rd., Bushmills, Co. Antrim BT57 8QG* ☎ *028/2073–3000 or 028/2073–2339* 🖷 *028/2073–2048* ⊕ *www.bushmills-inn.com* 🗗 *32 rooms* ♨ *Restaurant, Wi-Fi, bar, meeting rooms; no a/c* ⊟ *AE, MC, V* ⑩ *BP.*

¢ ⊞ **Causeway Hotel.** Owned by England's National Trust and flaunting a stunning location overlooking the Atlantic Ocean, this hotel is only a half-mile distant from the celebrated Giant's Causeway. The hotel was founded in the 1840s, then expanded in 1863 by one Mr. Trail (who masterminded the Giant's Causeway Tramway that ran along the coast), and in 1890 it became the first Irish hotel to be completely lit by electricity. Alas and alack, they should bring back some of the candles. Nearly all the historic patina has long disappeared—both the exterior and the interior is largely comprised of white-on-white walls. Granted, the bar is welcoming, the dining room capacious, and the "high tea" a winner, but this spot will always be prized more for its setting than its mise-en-scene. One thing that hasn't changed much is the grub—nouvelle cuisine thankfully never caught on in this part of the world so prepare yourself for what the locals call "a good feed" (featured throughout the day in a myriad of bed and board rates). Other hotels may offer lush facilities but this one gives you the tranquillity and beauty of the glorious Antrim coastline right at your doorstep. ⊠ *40 Causway Rd., Bushmills, Co. Antrim BT57 8SU* ☎ *028/2073–1210 or 028/2073–1226* 🖷 *028/2073–2552* ⊕ *www.giants-causeway-hotel.com* 🗗 *28 rooms* ♨ *Restaurant, Wi-Fi, bar, meeting rooms; no a/c* ⊟ *AE, MC, V* ⑩ *MAP.*

Dunluce Castle

★ ㉔ *3 km (2 mi) west of Bushmills.*

Halfway between Portrush and the Giant's Causeway, dramatically perched on a cliff at land's end, Dunluce Castle is one of the North's most evocative ruins. Even roofless, this shattered bulk conjures up a strength and aura that is quintessentially Antrim. Its long-storied history is filled with marvels, beginning with the fact that it stands on a 100-foot-high basalt rock, which contains the "Mermaid's Cave" (accessible by both land and sea). Originally a 13th-century Norman fortress, it was captured in the 16th century by the local MacDonnell clan chiefs—the so-called "Lords of the Isles." They enlarged the castle, paying for some of the work with their profits from salvaging the

Spanish galleon *Girona*—note the two openings in the old gatehouse wall made for cannon that Sorely Boy MacDonnell rescued from the wreck—and made it an important base for ruling northeastern Ulster. Perhaps they expanded the castle a little too much, for in 1639 faulty construction caused the kitchens (with all the cooks) to plummet into the sea during a storm. Elsewhere on the grounds are the 1630 Manor House and the terraced Earl's Garden. From here, castle dwellers looked on in horror as the *Exmouth*—bound for Quebec—went down after fighting rough seas for three days in 1857. Exhibits at the castle detail this shipwreck, which caused the demise of 240 passengers. ⊠ *Coastal Rd., Portrush* ☎ *028/2073–1938* ⊕ *www.northantrim.com/dunlucecastle. htm* ⊠ *£1.50* ⊙ *Apr., May, and Sept., Mon.–Sat. 10–5:30, Sun. 2–6; June–Aug., Mon.–Sat. 10–6, Sun. noon–6; Oct.–Mar., Mon.–Sat. 10–4, Sun. 2–4.*

Dunluce Center is an entertainment complex with three floors of interactive play zones, shops, and a café near Dunluce Castle. ⊠ *10 Sandhill Dr., Portrush* ☎ *028/7082–4444* ⊕ *www.dunlucecentre.co.uk* ⊠ *£8:50* ⊙ *Easter week, daily 10:30–6:30; Apr. and May, weekends noon–6:30; June, weekdays noon–5, weekends noon–6:30; July and Aug., daily 10:30–6:30; Sept.–Mar., weekends noon–5.*

Where to Eat

★ ¢–$$ ✕ **Ramore Wine Bar.** On Portrush's picturesque harbor, this spot has panoramic views, with daily offerings posted on a blackboard. ⊠ *The Harbor, Portrush* ☎ *028/7082–4313* ☎ *028/7082–3194* ▭ *MC, V.*

Sports & the Outdoors

In a poll of legendary Irish courses, the **Royal Portrush Golf Club** (⊠ Dunluce Rd., Portrush ☎ 028/7082–2311 ⊕ www.royalportrushgolfclub. com) came out tops. The championship Dunluce is a sea of sand hills and curving fairways (£95 on weekdays, £110 on weekends). The valley course is a less-exposed, tamer track (£32.50 on weekdays, £37.50 on weekends). Both are typically open to visitors on weekdays but it's best to call ahead. For more details, see the chapter on Irish Greens. **Portstewart Strand** (⊠ Coastal Rd., Portrush) has some of Ireland's best surfing. It's signposted as "The Strand" on all major junctions in town.

8

Coleraine

㉕ *13 km (8 mi) southwest of Dunluce Castle.*

The 5th-century BC town of Coleraine became the home of the University of Ulster in 1968. The River Bann flows through the town, dividing the county of Antrim from that of Derry. As well as being a fishing town, Coleraine has an important linen industry. Some of Ireland's oldest relics, dating from the first inhabitants of this island (about 7000 BC), were found on Mountsandel, just south of Coleraine. One of the many dolmens in this region is called Slaghtaverty—after an evil dwarf who used his magical harp to mesmerize women. He was buried alive and upside down by the great Finn McCool (maker of the Giant's Causeway), so the sounds of his harp would not escape from the ground.

Where to Stay

$ ☒ **Greenhill House.** A great base for exploring the Antrim coast, this charming Georgian country house is a peaceful retreat run by Elizabeth and James Hegarty. Floral fabrics and antique, carved furnishings decorate pleasant rooms. Breakfasts are substantial. ☒ *13 km (8 mi) south of Coleraine on A29, 24 Greenhill Rd., Aghadowey, Co. Derry BT51 4EU* ☎ *028/7086–8241* 🖷 *028/7086–8365* ⊕ *www.greenhill.house.btinternet. co.uk* �' *6 rooms* ⚘ *Dining room, Wi-Fi; no a/c* ☰ *MC, V* ☾ *Closed Nov.–Feb.* ❖| *BP.*

Upperlands

㉖   *32 km (20 mi) south of Coleraine, 56 km (35 mi) northwest of Belfast.*

The River Bann—rich in eels for roasting and smoking and in salmon for poaching—flows out of Lough Neagh. On its left bank are the towns and fortifications of the 17th-century Planters, built by London's Livery Companies, whose descendants developed the linen industry. Today, virtually all of that rural industrial heritage is gone, with the notable exception of the village of Upperlands. Make sure you tour **William Clark and Sons**, a working linen mill where age-old wooden machinery still beetles (polishes by pounding with hammers) threads for the linen linings of suits for England's Royals. There's also a small linen museum here. ☒ *A29, Upperlands* ☎ *028/7954–7200* ▱ *Free* ☾ *By appointment Mon.–Thurs. 10–4.*

Where to Stay & Eat

$$$ ☒☒ **Ardtara House.** A 19th-century Victorian home, Ardtara was built
Fodor'sChoice by a descendant of the founder of the town's first linen mill. Eight large
★ bedrooms are furnished with antiques, and each has a fireplace—as do some of the marble bathrooms. The terra-cotta-and-pink drawing room, with plaster moldings and a marble fireplace, looks out on the wide front lawn and tennis court. The hotel's restaurant ($$) is in the former snooker room, with dark panels and a wallpaper hunting scene. The terrine of duck appetizer is popular, as is the stellar poached fillet of lamb with buttered Savoy cabbage. ☒ *8 Gorteade Rd., Co. Derry BT46 5SA* ⊕ *www. ardtara.com* ☎ *028/7964–4490* 🖷 *028/7964–5080* �' *8 rooms* ⚘ *Restaurant, tennis court, meeting room; no a/c* ☰ *AE, MC, V* ❖| *BP.*

Limavady

㉗   *21 km (13 mi) west of Coleraine, 27 km (17 mi) east of Derry.*

In 1851, at No. 51 on Limavady's Georgian main street, Jane Ross wrote down the tune played by a traveling fiddler and called it "Londonderry Air," better known now as "Danny Boy." While staying at an inn on Ballyclose Street, William Thackeray (1811–63) wrote his rather lustful poem "Peg of Limavaddy" about a barmaid. Among the many Americans descended from Ulster emigrants was President James Monroe, whose relatives came from the Limavady area.

Where to Stay & Eat

$$$ ☒☒ **Radisson Roe Park Hotel & Golf Resort.** A country estate serves as the model for the deluxe modern resort amid 155 acres on the banks of the

River Roe. The place is relatively large and impersonal, although the lobby is a feast of welcoming ruby-hued carpets and gilt lanterns. Regular guest rooms have simple, clean-line beds in woods and rich earth tones. Suite furnishings move a bit up the ornate scale: canopy beds and velvet armchairs. Green's restaurant is formal and international ($–$$$); the Coach House brasserie is a relaxed place where golfers congregate; and O'Cahan's bar takes its name from a local chieftain besieged on a riverside promontory, whose Irish wolfhound leaped an impossible chasm to bring relief—doubtless an inspiration to golfers flagging at the ninth. ⊠*Roe Park, Co. Derry BT49 9LB* ☎ *028/7772–2222* 🖷 *028/7772–2313* ⊕ *www.radissonroepark.com* ⊃ *118 rooms, 6 suites* ♨ *2 restaurants, Wi-Fi, 18-hole golf course, indoor pool, fitness classes, gym, hair salon, massage, sauna, steam room, fishing, horseback riding, 2 bars, babysitting, meeting rooms; no a/c* ▭ *AE, DC, MC, V* ⦿| *BP, MAP.*

DERRY

If Belfast were the Beethoven of Northern Ireland, Derry would be the Mozart—fey, witty, and a touch surreal. Every Halloween, for example, the entire populace of Derry—the second biggest city in Northern Ireland—turns out in wild homemade costumes, and pubs have been known to refuse a drink to anyone who hasn't made the effort to dress up. Despite the derelict factories along the banks of the River Foyle and a reputation marred by Troubles-related violence, the city has worked hard to move forward. Such efforts show in the quaint, bustling town center, encircled by 20-foot-tall 17th-century walls. The city's winding streets slope down to the Foyle, radiating from the Diamond—Derry's historic center—where St. Columba founded his first monastery in 546. Fine Georgian and Victorian buildings sit side by side with gaily painted Victorian-front shops, cafés, and pubs.

Exploring Derry

Derry's name is a shadow of its history. Those in favor of British rule call the city Londonderry, its old Plantation-period name: the "London" part was tacked on in 1613 after the Flight of the Earls, and the city and county were handed over to the Corporation of London, which represented London's merchants. The corporation brought in a large population of English and Scottish Protestant settlers, built towns for them, and reconstructed Derry within the city walls, which survive almost unchanged to this day. Both before then and after, Derry's sturdy ramparts withstood many fierce attacks—they have never been breached, which explains the city's coy sobriquet, "The Maiden City." The most famous attack was the

THE HIGH AND THE FLIGHTY

Aviation fans, take note: Derry was where Amelia Earhart touched down on May 21, 1932, after her historic solo flight across the Atlantic. Local lore has it that the first man to reach her airplane greeted her in typically unfazed Derry fashion: "Aye, and what do you want, then?"

siege of 1688–89, begun after 13 apprentice boys slammed the city gates in the face of the Catholic king, James II. Inhabitants, who held out for 105 days and were reduced to eating dogs, cats, and laundry starch, nevertheless helped to secure the British throne for the Protestant king, William III. Whatever you choose to call it, Derry is one of Northern Ireland's most underrated towns. Derry, incidentally, has links to Boston that date as far back as the 17th and 18th centuries, when many Derry residents escaped their hardships at home by emigrating to that U.S. city and beyond.

To really experience Derry's history, stroll along the parapet walkway atop the ramparts of the **city walls,** built between 1614 and 1618 and one of the few intact sets of city walls in Europe. Pierced by eight gates (originally four) and as much as 30 feet thick, the gray-stone ramparts are only 1½ km (1 mi) all around. Today most of the life of the town takes place outside of them. You can join one of the guided tours given by the information center, or follow the sites below in a counterclockwise direction.

Walking tours of the city walls leave from the **Tourist Information Centre** and last just under two hours. They depart at 2:30 weekdays year-round, as well as at 11:15 and 3:15 in July and August. ⊠ *44 Foyle St., West Bank* ☎ *028/7126–7284 or 028/7137–7577* 🖷 *028/7137–7992* ⊕ *www.derryvisitor.com* ▱ *Centre free, tour £5* ☉ *Mid-Mar.–June and Oct., weekdays 9–5, Sat. 10–5; July–Sept., weekdays 9–7, Sat. 10–6, Sun. 10–5; Nov.–mid-Mar., weekdays 9–5.*

Thanks to **Open Top Tours,** you can now tour Derry onboard a double-decker bus. Departing from the Tourist Information Centre and Guildhall Monday through Saturday, on the hour from 10 to 4, the bus ride lasts an hour, hits all the sightseeing spots, and has a guide with onboard commentary. ⊠ *6 Pinetrees* ☎ *07740249998* ⊕ *www.opentoptoour.com* ▱ *£9.*

Derry Taxis offers an alternative tour of Derry taking in local murals, monuments, and historic buildings. Find their taxi stands on Foyle and William streets. ☎ *028/ 7126–0247* ⊕ *www.derrytaxitours.com.*

Derry city council meets monthly at **Guildhall,** an ornate Victorian stone and sandstone building dating from 1890. Some of the most beautiful glass creations in Ireland, the hall's stained-glass windows were shattered by two IRA bombs in June 1977 and rebuilt by the Campbell's firm in Belfast, which had installed the original windows in 1890 and still had the plans (now *that's* a filing system). Elsewhere, the eye is delighted by neo-Gothic strutwork, ornate ceilings, baronial wood paneling, a magnificent organ, and the fourth largest clock (modeled on Big Ben) in Ireland. The Guildhall also hosts occasional musical recitals. ⊠ *Guildhall Sq., West Bank* ☎ *028/7137–7335* ▱ *Free* ☉ *Weekdays 8:30–5.*

Tall, brooding, medieval, and magical, a reconstructed granite-stone O'Dohertys Tower contains the **Tower Museum,** which chronicles the history of Derry. The building was constructed in 1615 by the O'Dohertys for their overlords, the O'Donnells, in lieu of tax payments. Highlights of the museum include a small section on the eccentric Bishop Frederick Augustus Hervey (1763–1803), who conducted a lifelong affair

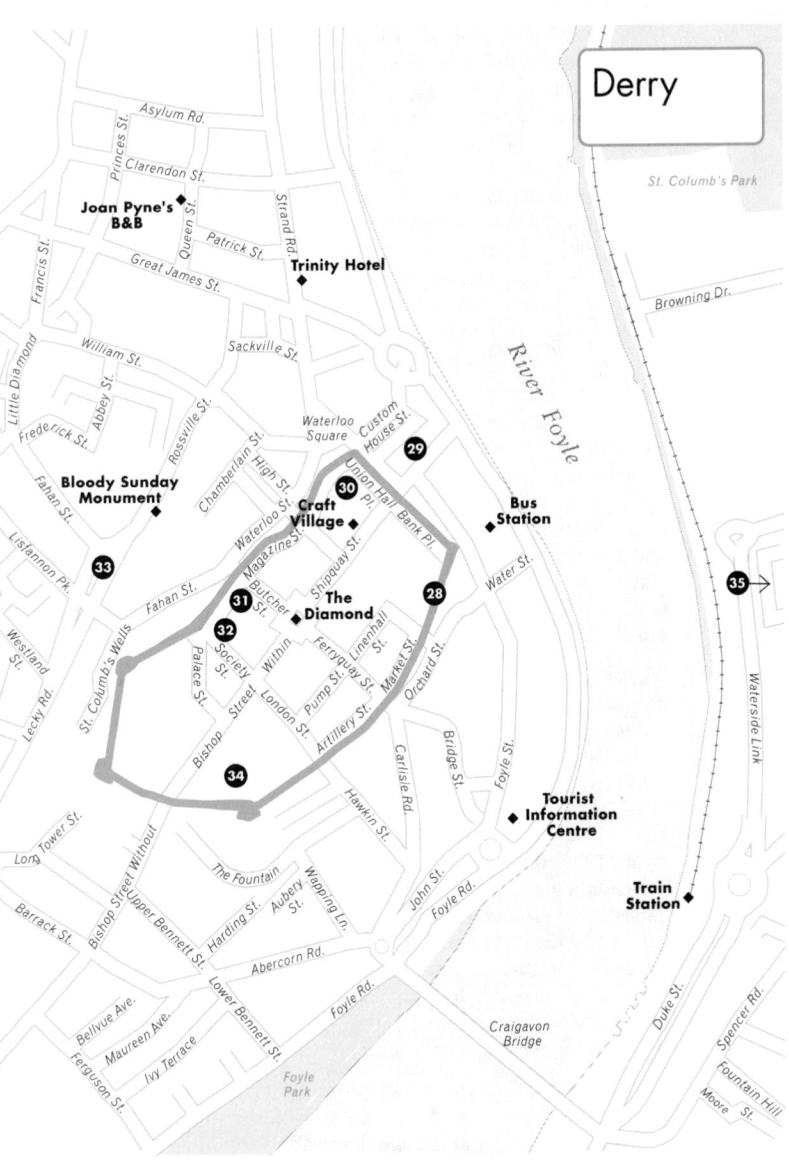

Derry

with the mistress of Frederick William II of Prussia, built the now derelict Downhill Castle above the cliffs outside the city, and allegedly had his curates stage naked sprints along the beach while he horsewhipped them. The winners were awarded the most lucrative parishes in the district. There's excellent information celebrating the life and legacy of St. Columba. The vivid "Story of Derry" exhibition covers the city's history, from its origins as a monastic settlement in an oak grove up to the Troubles, beginning in 1969 after years of institutionalized discrimination in jobs and public housing. (A well-known Derry joke is that the skeleton in the city's coat of arms was actually a Catholic waiting for a house.) The museum underwent a major renovation in 2005, adding an exhibition on the Spanish Armada. ⊠ *Union Hall Pl., West Bank* ☎ *028/7137–2411* 🖾 *£4* ⊗ *Sept.–June, Tues.–Sat. 10–5; July and Aug., Mon.–Sat. 10–5, Sun. 2–5.*

㉛ The "Fifth Province" exhibition at the **Calgach Centre** provides a high-tech tour of the city's history, including its importance in creating the Irish diaspora of 17 million people. Sit in a comfortable armchair for a virtual-reality time-trip through the coming of the Vikings and the Normans, the flight of the Irish nobility from English persecution in 1601, and the famine of 1845–49, when 1½ million emigrated to the United States and a million died of starvation. At this writing the center was under repair, with reopening date uncertain. ⊠ *4–22 Butcher St., West Bank* ☎ *028/7137–3177* 🖾 *£3* ⊗ *Mon.–Fri. 9:30–4.*

㉜ Imposing in its Scottish Baronial fortified grandeur, **Apprentice Boys' Memorial Hall** is a meeting place for the exclusively Protestant organization set up in 1715 to honor 13 apprentice boys who slammed the city gate in the face of the Catholic King James in 1688 and sparked the Siege of Derry, which has been a symbol of Protestant stubbornness ever since. Inside there's an initiation room in which 20,000 have pledged to uphold Protestant values, and a magnificently chaotic museum filled to the brim with furniture, firearms, books, bombs, swords, and sculpture. It's a fascinating glimpse into a mostly closed world. An upstairs bar and dance hall—now used for meetings, initiations, and social events, organized by the Apprentice Boys—has walls lined with 12 banners representing the lost tribes of Israel. (Some Protestants believe the lost tribes of Israel ended up in Northern Ireland and are their forebears.) ⊠ *Society St., West Bank* ☎ *028/7134–6677* 🖾 *Donations accepted* ⊗ *Tours by appointment; open to public 2nd wk of Aug.*

Walker Memorial, a statue of the governor of Derry during the siege, is a symbol of Derry's divided nature. It was blown up by the IRA in 1973, and the story goes that the statue's head rolled down the hill into the Catholic Bogside, where it was captured by a local youth. He ransomed it back to the Protestants for a small fortune, and today it sits on the shoulders of a replica of the original statue beside the Apprentice Boys' Memorial Hall. ⊠ *Apprentice Boys' Memorial Hall, Society St., West Bank.*

㉝ At **Free Derry Corner** is the white gable wall where Catholics defiantly painted the slogan "You are now entering Free Derry" as a declaration of a zone from which police and the British Army were banned until 1972, when the army broke down the barricades. That year, 13 civil rights

A Political ABC

DUP. Right-wing Democratic Unionist Party, founded by firebrand preacher Reverend Ian Paisley in 1971. Now increasingly sidelined.

IRA. Irish Republican Army. Largest group of Republican paramilitaries, responsible for thousands of murders and bombings.

Loyalist. Extreme Unionist.

Nationalist. Anyone supporting a united Ireland.

Northern Ireland Assembly. Regional government, sitting at Stormont.

Orange Order. Protestant organization whose annual July 12 marches celebrate the 1690 victory of Protestant King William of Orange over Catholic King James.

Republican. Extreme Nationalist.

SDLP. Social, Democratic, and Labour Party. Largest and most moderate Nationalist party.

Sinn Féin. Literally "Ourselves Alone," political counterpart of IRA, now firmly installed in democratic Northern Ireland Assembly.

The Troubles. The 1969–97 campaign by Republican and Loyalist terrorists in which 3,636 people were killed.

UDA. Ulster Defence Association. Largest Loyalist paramilitary group, involved in hundreds of murders.

UFF and UVF. Ulster Freedom Fighters and Ulster Volunteer Force, breakaway Loyalist paramilitary groups.

Ulster. Historic name for northern province of Ireland. Now generally used, especially by Protestants, to describe Northern Ireland.

Ulster Unionist Party. Largest and most moderate Unionist party.

Unionist. Anyone supporting continuing union with Great Britain.

8

marchers were shot and killed by British soldiers in an event that rankles Catholics to this day. "Bloody Sunday," as it became known, is commemorated by the mural of a civil rights march. ⊠ *Fahan and Rossville Sts., West Bank.*

34 **St. Columb's Cathedral** was the first Protestant cathedral built in the United Kingdom after the Reformation, and contains the oldest and largest bells in Ireland (dating from the 1620s). It's a treasure house of Derry Protestant emblems, memorials, and relics from the siege of 1688–89. The church was built in 1633 in simple Planter's Gothic style, with an intricate corbeled roof and austere spire. In the vestibule is the 270-pound mortar ball that during the Siege of Derry was fired over the wall with an invitation to surrender sent by King James. Legend has it that when it was read, every man, woman, and child in the city rushed to the walls and shouted, "No surrender!"—a Protestant battle cry to this day. The attached Chapter House Museum has the oldest surviving map of Derry (from 1600) and the Bible owned by Governor George Walker during the siege. Knowledgeable tour guides are on hand. ⊠ *London St. off Bishop St., West Bank* ☎ *028/7126–7313* ⊕ *www.stcolumbscathedral. org* ⊠ *£1* ⊙ *Apr.–Oct., daily 9–5; Nov.–Mar., daily 9–4.*

NEED A BREAK?

Derry is packed with agreeable pubs, but **Badgers** (⊠ 16 Orchard St., West Bank ☎ 028/7136–0763) has the best choice of wholesome food. It's also the watering hole for local media types, artists, writers, and musicians.

㉟ Across the River Foyle from the city walls, the **Workhouse Museum** was built in 1832 as an institution to alleviate poverty but became the end of the road for people who had tried in vain to make their lives better. During the famine years (1845–49), the city was the main emigration port for Northern Ireland, and many families came to Derry hoping to get on a boat. Instead, unable to afford the trip, they ended up applying for aid at the Workhouse, where hard labor earned a bed and food. Many families were separated once inside, and this was often the last time children saw their parents alive. From the beginning to the end of the famine, 1½ million people left Ireland and 1 million died. The museum details life in the Workhouse and has some thoughtful exhibits about famine in general.

Many of the descendants of those who left came back during World War II: thousands of U.S. servicemen arrived in the city in 1942 to turn it into a base for the Battle of the Atlantic. Exhibits on the top two floors of the Workhouse chronicle the story of that battle, from the Yanks' arrival in the January rain (which prompted one of them to ask if the city's barrage balloons were actually there to stop the place from sinking) through the end of the war, when 64 U-boats lined up in the harbor to surrender. By 1946 the city's biggest export was G.I. brides. There's a space for traveling exhibitions that change regularly; call for details. ⊠ 23 Glendermott Rd., East Bank ☎ 028/7131–8328 ☞ Free ☉ July and Aug., Mon.–Thurs. and Sat. 10:30–4:30; Sept.–June, Mon.–Thurs. and Sat. 10–4:30.

EN ROUTE

For a delightfully rustic alternative to driving back to Belfast on A6, drive along the minor road B48, which skirts the foot of the Sperrin Mountains and reaches all the way to Omagh. Or, you may want to head north from Derry to explore the Inishowen Peninsula, the northernmost point of Ireland.

Where to Stay & Eat

$–$$$ ✕ **Thompsons on the River.** Situated on the banks of the Foyle, this spot takes its name from the old Thompsons Mill that once occupied this historic building. Decor is airy and cool while the cuisine is stylish and hot: best bets include caraway-scented roast stuffed loin of pork or the fillets of red mullet in tomato and cumin sauce. Thanks to its popularity, reservations are recommended (and practically essential on weekends). Add in an impressive but not expensive wine list and this adds up to a fine place to chill with great views of the river. ⊠ City Hotel on Queens Quay, Central District ☎ 028/7136–5800 ▭ AE, MC, V.

$–$$ ✕ **The Exchange.** Overdressed twentysomethings lounge by the circular and ultramodern bar in this chic restaurant-cum-wine bar. Since its 2002 opening, it's become *the* place to be seen in Derry, so weekend evenings can be extremely busy. Unfortunately, reservations are not taken so be prepared to wait at the bar—but with a chilled glass of sauvignon blanc from the excellent wine list, it's no hardship. Locally caught seafood is delicious and standouts include the halibut in shrimp sauce and the *Hua Hin* crab cakes flecked with coconut. Service is super-efficient but can feel a touch brisk. ⊠ *Exchange House, Queen's Quay, Central District* ☎ 028/7127–3990 ⊟ AE, MC, V.

$–$$ ✕ **Spice.** It's worth the walk up the hill from town to this cozy restaurant with food that draws heavily on Pan-Asian influences. Main course highlights include crab claws and red Thai curry, served with plain or fried rice or noodles. ⊠ *162–164 Spencer Rd., East Bank* ☎ 028/7134–4875 ⊟ MC, V.

¢–$ ✕ **Fitzroy's.** This popular city center brasserie gives "quare packin'" (Derry-speak for good value for money), with belt-busting portions of old favorites like burgers, steaks, and Caesar salads in the evening. Lunchtimes are busy, with weary shoppers and office staff stopping by for a turkey-stuffing-and-cranberry panini sandwich or a big bowl of homemade leek-and-potato soup. The fully licensed bar stocks a good range of bottled beers and wines. ⊠ *2–4 Bridge St., Central District* ☎ 028/7126–6211 ⊕ *www.fitzroysrestaurant.com* ⊟ MC, V.

$$$ ▣ **Beech Hill.** Journey past a fairy-tale gatehouse among clumps of beech trees, past streams and a duck pond on the grounds at Beech Hill. This grand 1729 country home is very much attuned to the present with a number of conveniences to satisfy the demanding traveler (a trouser press, and tea and coffeemakers in-room). The vast honeymoon suite, with a four-poster bed, overlooks the gardens. Rooms in the old building are decorated in Georgian style; 10 rooms in a modern extension are larger and contemporary. A small museum celebrates the fact that Beech Hill housed a contingent of U.S. Marines during World War II. ⊠ *3 km (2 mi) southeast of town off A6, 32 Ardmore Rd., Beech Hill, BT47 3QP* ☎ 028/7134–9279 🖷 028/7134–5366 ⊕ *www.beech-hill.com* ⤶ *28 rooms, 5 suites* ⌂ *Restaurant, Wi-Fi, tennis court, gym, hot tub, massage, sauna, bar, meeting rooms; no a/c* ⊟ AE, MC, V ⭤ BP, MAP.

$$ ▣ **Tower Hotel.** The only hotel within Derry city's historic walls, this modern and comfortable hotel has more to offer than its unequaled location. Rooms are decorated in vibrant shades of red and blue, with pine furnishings and well-stocked bathrooms. The sleek oak-wood bar, with its low-hanging lights, is a favorite watering hole with locals as well as visiting guests. The bistro-style restaurant has won plenty of kudos, and the location is primo—just check out the view of the Bogside and the "Free Derry" corner from the upper bedrooms and the fourth-floor gym. ⊠ *Butcher St., Central District, BT48 6HL* ☎ 028/7137–1000 🖷 028/7137–1234 ⊕ *www.towerhotelgroup.com* ⤶ *90 rooms, 3 suites* ⌂ *Restaurant, Wi-Fi, gym, sauna, bar, meeting rooms; no a/c* ⊟ AE, DC, MC, V ⭤ BP, MAP.

★ ¢ ▣ **The Merchant's House.** Number 16 Queen Street was originally a Victorian merchant's family town home built to Georgian proportions, then a rectory and bank, before Joan Pyne turned it into the city's grandest B&B. Garnet-color walls, elaborate plasterwork, and a fireplace make the parlor warm and welcoming. Little wonder the guestbook features some prominent names, including the late Hurd Hatfield, star of the movie *The Picture of Dorian Gray.* Joan also owns a similar but smaller building three minutes' walk away called the **Saddler's House.** Charming and cozy, this Victorian jewel of a home (who can resist its faintingly pink

8

living room parlor?) has been lovingly restored and is packed with interesting antiques and family portraits, and is another excellent value for the money. Incidentally, many architecturally interesting homes occupy the neighborhood. ⊠ *16 Queen St., West Bank, BT48 7EQ* ☎ *028/7126–4223* 🖷 *028/7126–6913* ⊕ *www.thesaddlershouse.com* 🛏 *6 rooms in Merchant's House; 7 rooms with shared bath in Saddler's House* ▤ *MC, V* ⍟ *BP.*

Nightlife & the Arts

ART GALLERIES The **Context Gallery** (⊠ 5–7 Artillery St., West Bank ☎ 028/7137–3538) shows works by up-and-coming Irish and international artists. The **McGilloway Gallery** (⊠ 6 Shipquay St., West Bank ☎ 028/7136–6011) stocks a broad selection of representational modern Irish art. Owner Ken McGilloway serves wine on Friday evenings until 9 PM during selected exhibitions. The **Orchard Gallery** (⊠ Orchard St., West Bank ☎ 028/7126–9675) is known across Europe for its political and conceptual art.

PUBS & CLUBS The **Gweedore Bar** (⊠ 59–63 Waterloo St., West Bank ☎ 028/7126–3513) is a favorite for hip-hop and house music. Listen to traditional Irish music at **Peadar O'Donnell's** (⊠ 63 Waterloo St., West Bank ☎ 028/7137–2318). **Sugar Nightclub** (⊠ 33 Shipquay St., West Bank ☎ 028/7126–6017) is the place for disco.

THEATER & The **Playhouse** (⊠ 5–7 Artillery St., West Bank ☎ 028/7126–8027)
OPERA stages traditional and contemporary plays and also holds contemporary music concerts. The catch-all **Millennium Forum Theatre and Conference Centre** (⊠ Newmarket St., West Bank ☎ 028/7126–4455 ⊕ www. millenniumforum.co.uk) presents everything and anything—from comedians to musicians to plays—on stage. The **Verbal Arts Centre** (⊠ Bishop St., Stable La. and Mall Wall, West Bank ☎ 028/7126–6946 ⊕ www. verbalartscentre.co.uk) celebrates literature through performances and classes. It re-creates the great old Irish tradition of fireside tales at regular storytelling events.

Shopping

Shopping in town is generally low-key and unpretentious, but there are some upscale gems of Irish craftsmanship. Stroll up Shipquay Street to find small arts and crafts stores and an indoor shopping center. **Bookworm** (⊠ 18–20 Bishop St., West Bank ☎ 028/7128–2727) is the best bookshop in Ireland, according to writer Nuala O'Faoláin. **Occasions** (⊠ 48 Spencer Rd., East Bank ☎ 028/7132–9595) sells Irish crafts and gifts. Stop at the gift shop **Pauline's Patch** (⊠ 32 Shipquay St., West Bank ☎ 028/7127–9794) for knickknacks. **Thomas the Goldsmith** (⊠ 7 Pump St., West Bank ☎ 028/7137–4549) stocks exquisite work by international jewelry designers. Off Shipquay Street, the **Trip** (⊠ 29 Ferryquay St., West Bank ☎ 028/7137–2382) is a teenage-clothing shop that specializes in knitwear.

THE WESTERN BORDER COUNTIES

While blissfully off the beaten track, this region contains some dazzling sights: the Ulster-American Folk Park; the great stately houses of Cas-

The Sounds of Music

NORTHERN IRELAND HAS A RICH musical culture similar to that of the south of Ireland, with its strong folk roots and an added Scottish influence. Traditional Irish music, originally played at weddings and wakes, can be heard in most country pubs, and in a cluster of bars in the central district of Belfast. Old-style songs—popularly known as *séan nós*, a sort of storytelling with music—are still very popular in the border counties. "Sessions" have become the stuff of legend, and are best described as spontaneous gatherings of musicians, which anyone can join if they have an instrument. They usually feature the *bódhran* (a kind of drum), the tin whistle, the fiddle, and the *uillean* pipes—a fiendishly difficult instrument to master, much like the bagpipes. Unfortunately, today's visitors are more likely to hear a hired band playing traditional music than an authentic session, but the spirit remains. If you're a classical music buff, check out the world-class Ulster Orchestra, based in Belfast's Ulster Hall but also appearing in Derry, Armagh, and Enniskillen. If you love opera, don't miss Castle Ward Opera Festival—set in the spectacular surroundings of Castle Ward estate in Strangford, County Down, the annual event takes place in June. Meanwhile, Belfast's nightclubs groove on all frequencies, from pop hits to techno to hip-hop. Visitors should make like the locals and consult *The Big List*, a free and detailed guide to what's on in every pub and club in the city (which can be picked up at most bars and restaurants).

8

tle Coole and Florence Court; and the pottery town of Belleek. During the worst of the Troubles, the counties of Tyrone, Fermanagh, Armagh, and Down, which border the republic, were known as "bandit country," but now you can enjoy a worry-free trip through the calm countryside and stop in at some very "Ulster" towns, delightfully distinct from the rest of Ireland.

Omagh

55 km (34 mi) south of Derry on A5.

Omagh, the county town of Tyrone, lies close to the Sperrin Mountains, with the River Strule to the north. Playwright Brian Friel was born here. Sadly, it's more known as the scene of the worst atrocity of the Troubles, when an IRA bomb killed 29 people in 1998. The town has two places of worship—a Church of Ireland church and a Catholic double-spire church. North of Omagh the country is pretty and rustic, with small farm villages. Several miles north of Omagh is the big attraction of the region: the excellent **Ulster-American Folk Park** re-creates a Tyrone village of two centuries ago, a log-built American settlement of the same period, and the docks and ships that the emigrants to America would have used. The centerpiece of the park is an old whitewashed cottage, now a museum, which is the ancestral home of Thomas Mellon (1855–1937), the U.S. banker and philanthropist. Another thatched cot-

★

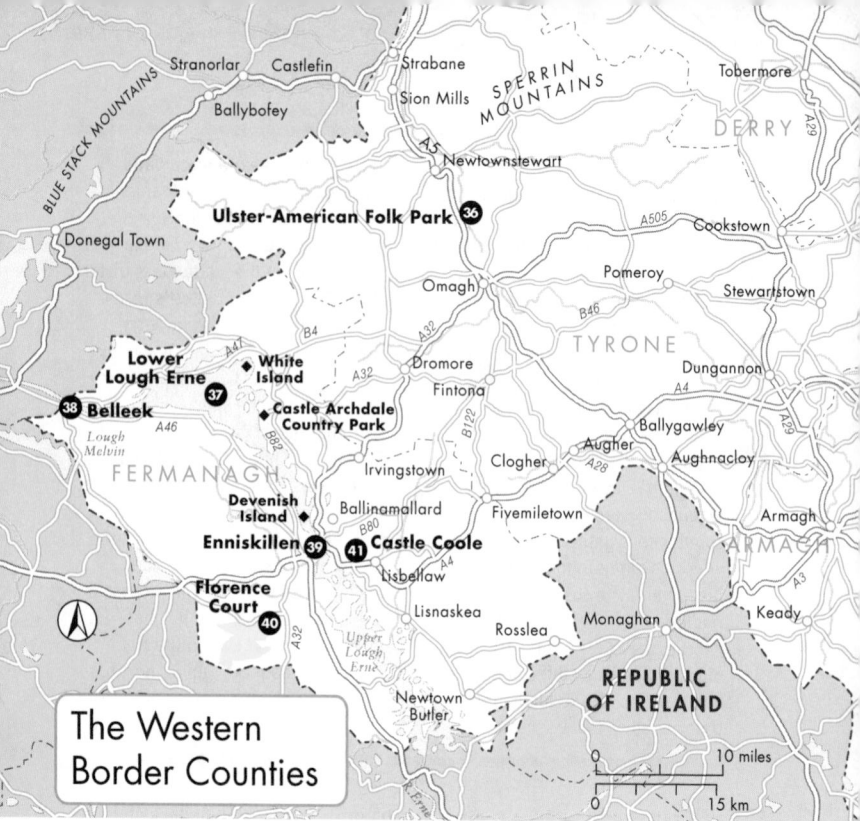

The Western Border Counties

tage is a reconstruction of the boyhood home of Archbishop John Hughes, founder of New York's St. Patrick's Cathedral. There are also full-scale replicas of Irish peasant cottages, Pennsylvania farmhouses, a New York tenement room, immigrant transport ship holders, plus a 19th-century Ulster village, complete with staff dressed in 19th-century costumes. Other exhibitions trace the contribution of the Northern Irish people to American history. The park also has a crafts shop and café. Last admission is 1½ hours before closing. ⊠ *Mellon Rd., 10 km (6 mi) north of town on A5, Castletown, Omagh, Co. Tyrone* ☎ *028/8224–3292* ⊕ *www.folkpark.com* ⊠ *£4.50* ⊘ *Apr.–Sept., Mon.–Sat. 10:30–6, Sun. 11–6:30; Oct.–Mar., weekdays 10:30–5.*

Take A5 north to **Strabane,** the birthplace of the surrealist novelist Brian O'Nolan, alias Flann O'Brien. James Wilson, grandfather of U.S. President Woodrow Wilson, emigrated from here. **Grays Printers Museum** (⊠ 49 Main St., Strabane ☎ 028/7188–4094) is in an 18th-century print shop with original 19th-century presses. John Dunlap (1746–1812), who apprenticed here before emigrating to Philadelphia, founded America's first daily newspaper, the *Philadelphia Packet*, in 1771 and was also the man who printed and distributed the American Declaration of Independence. ⊠ *31 km (19 mi) north of Omagh on A5.*

EN ROUTE

Head east on A505 from Omagh into the pensive landscape of moist heath and peat bog. Left of A505, a few kilometers before Cookstown, Beaghmore is a Bronze Age ceremonial site preserved for millennia beneath a blanket of peat. It has seven stone circles and 12 cairns. A little beyond Wellbrook you come to Cookstown, a Plantation village with a broad main street. From here, head down the back lanes to Lough Neagh, the largest lake in the British Isles, noted for an abundance of eels. On its shore at Ardboe stands a remarkable 10th-century high cross, more than 18 feet tall and carved with intricate biblical scenes.

Wellbrook Beetling Mill is where locally made linen was first "beetled"—pounded with noisy, water-driven hammers to give it a smooth finish. The National Trust keeps the mill in working order. ⊠ *20 Wellbrook Rd., Cookstown, Co. Tyrone* ☎ *028/8674–8210* ⊕ *www.nationaltrust.org.uk* ☜ *£3* ⊙ *Mar.–June and Sept., weekends noon–6; July and Aug., daily noon–6.*

Lower Lough Erne

㊲ *38 km (23 mi) southwest of Omagh off A32.*

If you're driving in the vicinity of Lough Erne, don't rush—take your time and enjoy the panoramas of green wooded hills stretching down to the still waters. **Castle Archdale Country Park,** on the northeast side of Lough Erne, has a lakeside marina and a museum containing a World War II exhibition on the Battle of the Atlantic. ⊠ *Down narrow road about 6½ km (4 mi) from Kesh, off B82, Co. Fermanagh* ☎ *028/ 6862–1588* ☜ *Free* ⊙ *Daily 9–dusk.*

From Castle Archdale, a ferry (£3) runs from June through September, Tuesday through Sunday, taking passengers to see the carved Celtic figures on **White Island.** After you drive 13 km (8 mi) south from Castle Archdale Park to where the B82 joins the A32, a small sign shows the way to catch the little boat that goes to Devenish Island. The boat runs weekends-only April through September; you can also make a reservation with at least 24 hours' notice. On **Devenish Island** you can see Ireland's best example of a round tower, which stands 82 feet tall, and the extensive but ruined 12th-century monastery with a richly carved high cross.

Sports & the Outdoors

Inland cruising on the Erne waterway—777 square km (300 square mi) of lakes and rivers—is a major treat. Upper and Lower Lough Erne are enclosed by some of Ireland's finest scenery and are studded with more than 100 little islands. Out on the lakes and the River Erne, which links them, you have all the solitude you want, but you can find company at waterside hostelries. To hire a boat, contact **Erne Charter Boat Association** (⊠ Belleek Charter Cruising, Erne Gateway Centre, Corry, Co. Fermanagh ☎ 028/6865–8027). Expect to pay at least £400 to hire a four-berth cruiser for two or three nights, available May to September.

8

Beautiful Belleek

CLOSE UP

THE ORIGINS OF BELLEEK CHINA are every bit as romantic as the Belleek blessing plates traditionally given to brides and grooms on their wedding day—that is, if you believe the legends. The story goes that in the mid 1800s, John Caldwell Bloomfield, the man behind the world-famous porcelain, accidentally discovered the raw ingredients necessary to produce china. After inheriting his father's estate in the Fermanagh Lakelands on the shore of the Erne River, he whitewashed his cottage using a flaky white powder dug up in his backyard. A passerby, struck by the luminescent sheen of the freshly painted cottage, commented on the unusual brightness of the walls to the lord of the manor. Bloomfield promptly ordered a survey of the land, which duly uncovered all the minerals needed to make porcelain. The venture was complete when Bloomfield met his business partners—London architect Robert Armstrong and the wealthy Dublin merchant David McBirney. They decided to first produce earthenware, and then porcelain. And the rest, as they say, is history. The delicate, flawless porcelain (Bloomfield declared that any piece with even the slightest blemish should be destroyed) soon attracted the attention of Queen Victoria and many other aristos. Other companies tried to mimic the china's delicate beauty, but genuine Belleek porcelain is recognizable by its seashell designs, basket weaves, and marine themes. The company is now owned by an Irish-born American businessman, Dr. George Moore, and continues to flourish. It has become a favored tradition in Ireland to give a piece of Belleek china at weddings, giving rise to a saying: "If a newly married couple receives a piece of Belleek, their marriage will be blessed with lasting happiness."

Belleek

38 *3 km (2 mi) west of Lower Lough Erne on A47.*

World-famous Belleek Pottery is made in the old town of Belleek on the northwestern edge of Lower Lough Erne, at the border with northwest Ireland. Other porcelainware makers are a few kilometers across the border. On the riverbank stands the visitor center of **Belleek Pottery Ltd.**, producers of Parian china, a fine, eggshell-thin, ivory porcelain shaped into dishes, figurines, vases, and baskets. There's a factory, showroom, exhibition, museum, and café. On tours of the factory you can get up close and talk to craftspeople—there's hardly any noise coming from machinery in the workshops. Everything here is made by hand in the same method used in 1857. The showroom is filled with beautiful but pricey gifts: a cup-and-saucer set costs about £16, and a bowl in a basket-weave style (typical of Belleek) runs £69 and up. For a history of the legend and beauty of this coveted porcelain, see the CloseUp box, "Beautiful Belleek." ☎ *028/6865–8501* ⊕ *www.belleek.ie* ☜ *£4* ⊙ *Apr.–June, Sept., and Oct., weekdays 9–6, Sat. 10–6, Sun. 2–6; July and Aug., weekdays 9–8, Sat. 10–6, Sun. 11–6; Nov.–Mar., weekdays 9–5:30.*

Enniskillen

39 *5 km (3 mi) south of Devenish Island, Lower Lough Erne, on A32.*

Enniskillen is the pleasant, smart-looking capital of County Fermanagh and the only place of any size in the county. The town center is, strikingly, on an island in the River Erne between Lower and Upper Lough Erne. The principal thoroughfares, Townhall and High streets, are crowded with old-style pubs and rows of redbrick Georgian flats. The tall, dark spires of the 19th-century St. Michael's and St. MacArtin's cathedrals, both on Church Street, tower over the leafy town center. Among the several relaxed and welcoming old pubs in Enniskillen's town center, the one with the most appeal is **Blake's of the Hollow** on the main street, a place hardly altered since it opened in 1887. Its name derives from the fact that the heart of the town lies in a slight hollow and the pub's landlord is named William Blake (don't ask, he's not related to the English poet, painter, and engraver). ⊠ *6 Church St., Co. Fermanagh* ☎ *028/6632–2143.*

Enniskillen's main sight is the waterfront **Enniskillen Castle**, one of the best-preserved monuments in the North. Built by the Maguire clan in 1670, this stronghold houses the local history collection of the Fermanagh County Museum and the polished paraphernalia of the Royal Inniskilling Fusiliers Regimental Museum. A Heritage Centre also stands within the curtilage of the castle. ⊠ *Castlebarracks, Co. Fermanagh* ☎ *028/ 6632–5000* ⊕ *www.enniskillencastle.co.uk* ☒ *£2.50* ◷ *May, June, Sept., Mon. and Sat. 2–5, Tues.–Fri. 10–5; July and Aug., Mon. and weekends 2–5, Tues.–Fri. 10–5; Oct.–Apr., Mon. 2–5, Tues.–Fri. 10–5.*

At the Erne riverside, the 16th-century **Water Gate**, between two handsome turrets, protected the town from invading armies. Beyond the West Bridge is **Portora Royal School**, established in 1608 by King James I. On the grounds are some ruins of Portora Castle. Among writers educated here are Samuel Beckett and Oscar Wilde, the pride of the school (until his trial for homosexuality).

Where to Stay

$$ 🏨 **The Manor House Hotel.** On the shores of Lower Lough Erne, this stately 19th-century manor harks back to a more tranquil age. Romantic canopied four-poster beds and traditional floral patterns await guests in the hotel's bedrooms, but be sure to ask for a room at the back so you can savor stunning views of the lakelands. Heavy linen napkins and silver cutlery add the finishing touches to the very good, if slightly formal, manor restaurant, presided over by the ambitious chef Jean-Michel Maquet. Why not take advantage of the excellent golf and fishing facilities and ask the friendly staff to book you a seat on the hotel's boat, the grandly named *Lady of the Lake*, for a cruise of Lough Erne? The idyllic location contributes to the hotel's laid-back relaxing air: sip a cocktail (or two) in the Belleek bar before dinner and you won't fail to unwind. ⊠ *7 mi northwest of Enniskillen, Killadeas, Co. Fermanagh* ☎ *028/6862–2200* ☒ *028/6862–1545* ⊕ *www.manor-house-hotel.com* 🛏 *81 rooms* ♨ *Restaurant, Wi-Fi, 9-hole golf course, tennis court, in-*

8

door pool, health club, hot tub, sauna, boating, fishing, 2 bars; no a/c ☐ *AE, MC, V* ⦿❘ *BP, MAP.*

Florence Court

★ ⓵⓪ *11 km (7 mi) south of Enniskillen on A4 and A32.*

When it comes to Early Irish Georgian houses, there are few as magical as Florence Court. Less known than some showier estates, this three-story Anglo-Irish mansion was built around 1730 for John Cole, father of the first earl of Enniskillen. Topped off about 1760 with its distinctive two flanking colonnaded wings, the central house is adorably adorned with a positive surfeit of Palladian windows, keystones, and balustrades thanks to, as one architectural historian put it, "the vaingloriousness of a provincial hand." Even more impressive is its bucolically baroque setting, as the Cuilcagh Mountains form a wonderful contrast to the shimmering white stone facade. Up to five years ago, the house—victim of a disastrous fire in the 1950s—was barely furnished, but a magnificent National Trust restoration as well as a 1988 legacy left by the last countess of Enniskillen have now returned many family heirlooms to these interiors. Showstoppers in terms of decor are the Rococo plasterwork ceilings in the dining room; the Venetian Room; and the famous staircase, all ascribed to Robert West, one of Dublin's most famous stuccadores (plaster workers). For a peek at the "downstairs" world, check the restored kitchen and other service quarters. ✉ *11 km (7 mi) south of Enniskillen on A4 and A32, Co. Fermanagh* ☎ *028/6634–8249* ⊕ *www.nationaltrust.org.uk* 📧 *£4.25* ☉ *Grounds Oct.–Apr., daily 10–4; May–Sept., daily 10–8; mansion Mar.–May and Sept., weekends noon–6; June, weekdays 1–6, weekends noon–6; July and Aug., daily noon–6.*

Castle Coole

★ ⓵⓵ *3 km (2 mi) east of Enniskillen on A4.*

In the 18th century and through most of the 19th, the Loughs of Erne and their environs were remote places far from Ireland's bustling cities. But it was just this isolated green and watery countryside that attracted the Anglo-Irish gentry, who built grand houses. This "uncommonly perfect" mansion (to quote the eminent architectural historian Desmond Guinness) is on its own landscaped oak woods and gardens at the end of a long tree-lined driveway. Although the Irish architect Richard Johnston made the original drawings in the 1790s, and was responsible for the foundation, the castle was, for all intents and purposes, the work of James Wyatt, commissioned by the first Earl of Belmore (whose family was related to the Counts of Enniskillen, who

> **LISTEN CLOSELY AND YOU SHALL HEAR . . .**
>
> Florence Court's ancestral park is one of Northern Ireland's glories—dotted with noted heirloom trees (including the Florence Court weeping beech), it also has nooks and dells where, legend has it, you can hear the "song of the little people."

built Florence Court). One of the best-known architects of his time, Wyatt was based in London but only visited Ireland once, so Alexander Stewart was drafted as the resident builder-architect who oversaw much of the construction. The designer wasn't the only imported element; in fact, much of Castle Coole came from England, including the main facade, which is clad in Portland stone shipped from Dorset to Ballyshannon and then hauled here by horse and cart. And what a facade it is—in perfect symmetry, white colonnaded wings extend from either side of the mansion's three-story, nine-bay center block, with a Palladian central portico and pediment. It is perhaps the apotheosis of the 18th century's reverence for the Greeks.

Inside, the house is remarkably preserved; most of the lavish plasterwork and original furnishings are in place. On its completion in September 1798, the construction had cost £70,000 and the furnishings another £22,000, compared to the £6 million cost of a restoration in 1995–96, during which anything not in keeping with the original design was removed. The saloon is one of the finest rooms in the house, with a vast expanse of oak flooring, gilded Regency furniture, and gray scagliola pilasters with Corinthian capitals. The present earl of Belmore still lives on the estate and uses one wing of the house. He often attends the public concerts that are held here during the summer months. ✉ *Dublin Rd., A4, Co. Fermanagh* ☎ *028/6632–2690* ⊕ *www. nationaltrust.org.uk* 💷 *Grounds free, mansion £4.50* ⊙ *Grounds Oct.–Apr., daily 10–4; May–Sept. daily 10–8; mansion Mar.–May and Sept., weekends noon–6; June, Wed.–Mon. noon–6; July and Aug., daily noon–6.*

8

THE EASTERN BORDER COUNTIES

Home to St. Patrick's shrines of Armagh and Downpatrick and one of Ireland's best-known ranges—the Mountains of Mourne—Counties Armagh and Down make a fittingly moving finale to any tour of Northern Ireland.

Armagh

42 *74 km (42 mi) east of Castle Coole.*

The spiritual capital of Ireland for 5,000 years, and the seat of both Protestant and Catholic archbishops, Armagh is the most venerated of Irish cities. St. Patrick called it "my sweet hill" and built his stone church on the hill where the Anglican cathedral now stands. On the opposite hill, the twin-spired Catholic cathedral is flanked by two large marble statues of archbishops who look across the land. Despite the pleasing Georgian terraces around the elegant Mall east of the town center, Armagh can seem drab. Having suffered as a trouble spot in the sectarian conflict, though, it's now the scene of some spirited and sympathetic renovation.

The **Astronomy Centre and Planetarium** is undergoing a major one- to three-year refurbishment. It contains models of spacecraft, video shows of the sky, and hands-on computer displays. The Earthorium explores the world from three levels—its interior, surface, and atmosphere. The outdoor 30-acre AstroPark has a model solar system. Since 2004, the 16-inch telescope as well as the Robinson Dome, also known as "the 10-inch dome" for the 1875 Grub telescope it houses, have been closed for renovation but they are now scheduled to reopen in late 2006. ⊠ *College Hill, Co. Armagh* ☎ *028/3752–3689* ⊕ *www.armaghplanet. com* ⊠ *AstroPark and Robinson Dome free; Earthorium £1; special shows and other exhibitions £3* ☉ *Weekdays 2–4:45; check for new schedule after facility reopens.*

The pale limestone, Gothic **St. Patrick's Roman Catholic Cathedral,** the seat of a Roman Catholic archdiocese, rises above a hill to dominate the north end of Armagh. Inside, the rather gloomy interior is enlivened by a magnificent organ whose potential is fully realized at services. Construction of the twin-spire cathedral started in 1840 in the neo-Gothic style, but the Great Famine brought work to a halt until 1854. It was finally completed in 1873. An arcade of statues over the main doorway on the exterior is one of the cathedral's most interesting features. The altar is solid Irish granite and the woodwork is Austrian oak. ⊠ *Hilltop, Co. Armagh* ☎ *028/3752–2638* ⊕ *www.armagharchdiocese.org.*

Near the town center, a squat, battlement tower identifies **St. Patrick's Anglican Cathedral,** in simple, early-19th-century, low-Gothic style. It stands on the site of much older churches and contains several relics of Armagh's long history, including sculpted, pre-Christian idols. Brian Boru, the High King (king of all Ireland) who visited Armagh in 1004—and was received with great ceremony—is buried here. In 1014, at the Battle of Clontarf, he drove the Vikings out of Ireland—but was killed after the battle was won. Inside are memorials and tombs by important 18th-century sculptors such as Roubilliac and Rysbrack. ⊠ *Abbey St., Co. Armagh* ⊕ *www. stpatricks-cathedral.org* ⊠ *Free* ☉ *Tours June–Aug., Mon.–Sat. 11:30 and 2:30.*

Closed until 2007 for a major renovation, **Palace Stables Heritage Centre** presents a diorama of everyday life—upstairs and downstairs—in the 18th-century days of the extremely wealthy Richard Robinson. Baron Rokeby was this man's ancestral title but he was best known as the region's archbishop of the Church of Ireland. He commissioned local architect Francis Johnston, who had designed much of Georgian Dublin, to create a new Armagh out of the slums into which it had degenerated. The archbishop gave the city a clean water supply and a sewer system, then turned the city's racecourse into an elegant mall. He paved and lighted the streets; financed improvements to the Bishop's Palace and the Protestant cathedral; and endowed the public library, the observatory, the Royal School, and the county infirmary. The museum is located past the 13th-century Franciscan friary ruins, in the stables of the former archbishop's demesne. ⊠ *Palace Demesne, Friary Rd., Co. Armagh* ☎ *028/3752–9629* ⊠ *£4.50* ☉ *June–Sept., Mon.–Sat. 10–5, Sun. 1–5.*

Just outside Armagh, **Navan Fort** is Ulster's Camelot—the region's ancient capital. Excavations date evidence of activity going back to 700 BC. The fort has strong associations with figures of Irish history. Legend has it that thousands of years ago this was the site of the palace of

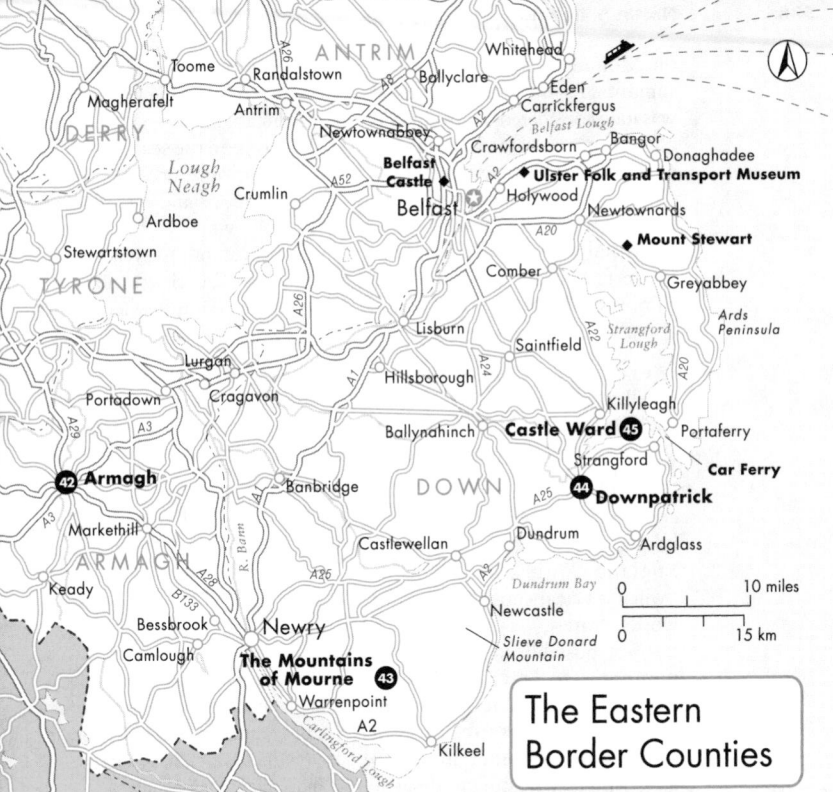

The Eastern
Border Counties

Queen Macha; subsequent tales call it the barracks of the legendary Ulster warrior Cuchulainn and his Red Branch Knights. Remains dating from 94 BC are particularly intriguing: a great conical structure, 120 feet in diameter, was formed from five concentric circles made of 275 wooden posts, with a 276th, about 12 yards high, situated in the center. In a ritual whose meaning is not known, it was filled with brushwood and set on fire. ⊠ *3 km (2 mi) west of Armagh on A28, Co. Armagh* 🖼 *Free.*

OFF THE
BEATEN
PATH

LINEN GREEN – Looking for a bargain? Venture north to Linen Green, an outlet mall where you can purchase clothing, lingerie, shoes, gifts, and furniture. You can buy woven items from well-known producers—such as Paul Costelloe, Ulster Weavers, Foxford, and Anne Storey—at a discount. ⊠ *20 km (12 mi) north of Armagh off A29, Moygashel, Co. Armagh* 🕿 *028/8775-3761* 🌐 *www.linengreen.com* 🕒 *Mon.–Sat. 10–5.*

The Mountains of Mourne

43 *52½ km (32½ mi) southeast of Armagh on A28, 51 km (32 mi) south of Belfast.*

Subjects of a song that is sung on every Irish occasion from baptism to funerals, the Mountains of Mourne must surely qualify as one of Ireland's best-known ranges. According to those lyrics by Percy French, the Mountains of Mourne "sweep down to the sea," from 2,000-foot summits. East of the unprepossessing border town of Newry, this area was long considered ungovernable, its hardy inhabitants living from smuggling contraband into the numerous rocky coves on the seashore. Much of the Mourne range is still inaccessible except on foot. The countryside is gorgeous: high, windswept pasture and moorland threaded with bright streams, bound by a tracery of drystone walls, and dotted with sheep and whitewashed farmhouses snuggled in stands of sycamore. It's the perfect landscape for away-from-it-all walkers, cyclists, and serious climbers. Climbers should inform their hotel when and where they're going before setting off.

The road to the **Silent Valley** reservoir park leads to mountain views and excellent photo-ops. ✉ *6 km (4 mi) north of Kilkeel off B27, right turn, Co. Down* ☎ *028/9074–6581* 🎫 *Vehicles £3, pedestrians £2* ⊙ *June–Aug., daily 10–6:30; Sept.–May, daily 10–4.*

Newcastle, a bracing Victorian cold-water bathing station, is the main center for visitors to the hills. Looming above Newcastle is **Slieve Donard,** its panoramic, 2,805-foot-high summit grandly claiming views into England, Wales, and Scotland "when it's clear enough"—in other words, "rarely," say the pessimists. It's not possible to drive up the mountain so leave your car in Donard car park. It should take roughly three hours to climb to the summit of the mountain and no longer than two hours to descend. Experienced hikers should not find it difficult but if you prefer an easier trek, follow the trails signposted in Tollymore Forest Park. Hiking boots are essential and, as the weather can be unpredictable, it's

> **WORD OF MOUTH**
>
> "If you like hiking, consider the Mountains of Mourne—wonderful scenery and very few other people other than walkers and locals know about their beauty. It is also the area where the Brontë family originated. The Silent Valley drive is wonderful."
>
> —Cambe

advisable to take an extra layer of clothing, even in summer. Covering 1,200 acres and entered through picturesque Gothic gateways, **Tollymore Forest Park** extends up the valley of the River Shimna. Many pretty stone bridges cross over the sparkling waters here. ✉ *Tullybrannigan Rd., Newcastle, Co. Down* ☎ *028/4372–2428* ⊕ *www.forestserviceni.gov.uk* 🎫 *Vehicles £4, pedestrians £2* ⊙ *Daily 10–dusk.*

A huge maze, grown to symbolize the convoluted path to peace, is the latest addition to **Castlewellan Forest Park,** which comprises 1,150 acres of forested hills running between the Mourne Mountains and Slieve Croob. With the maze, lake, secluded arbors, and arboretum, the park makes an excellent introduction to the area. ✉ *Castlewellan, Co. Down* ☎ *028/4377–8664* ⊕ *www.forestserviceni.gov.uk* 🎫 *Vehicles £4, pedestrians free* ⊙ *Daily 10–dusk.*

Where to Stay

$$$$ 🏨 **Slieve Donard Hotel.** A lavish redbrick monument to Victoriana, this turreted hotel stands like a palace on green lawns at one end of Newcastle's 6½-km (4-mi) sandy beach. The traditional furnishings may make you feel as if you're stepping back to the town's turn-of-the-20th-century heyday as an elegant seaside resort (though the rooms have modern comforts). Ask for a room overlooking the water. At the entrance to the grounds, the Percy French gatehouse restaurant serves adequate seafood dishes; there's music Friday and Saturday night. The Royal County Down Golf Club is next door, and the hotel has two exercise rooms. ⊠ *Downs Rd., Newcastle, Co. Down BT33 0AH* ☎ *028/4372–1066* 🖷 *028/4372–1166* ⊕ *www.hastingshotels.com* ⤴ *124 rooms* ♨ *2 restaurants, indoor pool, gym, hair salon, hot tub, spa, steam room, bar, helipad; no a/c* ⊟ *AE, DC, MC, V* ⯒❙ *BP, MAP.*

$$$ 🖼 **Burrendale Hotel & Country Club.** Thanks to the hotel's owners, the Small family, this low-slung modern building, shaded by clumps of beech, is one of the most relaxing establishments on the north's east coast. Staff members are cheery, and bedrooms are decorated in quiet tones. Chefs at the Cottage Kitchen and Vine restaurants are competent (the former is casual, the latter more formal) and clearly aim to please the locals, who like their plates overflowing. ⊠ *51 Castlewellan Rd., Newcastle, Co. Down BT33 0JY* ☎ *028/4372–2599* 🖷 *028/4372–2328* ⊕ *www.burrendale.com* ⤴ *69 rooms* ♨ *2 restaurants, Wi-Fi, indoor pool, gym, hot tub, sauna, steam room, 2 bars, meeting rooms; no a/c* ⊟ *AE, DC, MC, V* ⯒❙ *BP, MAP.*

$$–$$$ 🖼 **Glassdrumman Lodge.** For those who wish to be pampered as well as immersed in the ancient Kingdom of Mourne, Graeme and Joan Hall's eclectically simple and stylish lodge is the place. The outside of the house is less than spectacular, but the busy estate has more than enough drama to compensate, for the family grows their own crops, raises their own farm animals, churns their own butter, and bakes their own bread. Rooms are decorated in bright colors and have large windows with glorious views. ⊠ *Mill Rd., Annalong, Co. Down BT34 4RH* ☎ *028/ 4376–8451* 🖷 *028/4376–7041* ⊕ *www.glassdrummanlodge.com* ⤴ *10 rooms, 2 suites* ♨ *Restaurant, laundry service, business services; no a/c* ⊟ *AE, DC, MC, V* ⯒❙ *BP.*

Sports & the Outdoors

Tollymore Mountain Centre (⊠ Bryansford, Newcastle, Co. Down ☎ 028/ 4372–2158) provides advice on mountain climbing and trails. The **Royal County Down** (⊠ Off A2, Newcastle, Co. Down ☎ 028/4372–3314 ⊕ www.royalcountydown.org) is considered by many golfers to be one of the finest courses in the world. Between April and October, a game on the Championship Links can run up to £115; the Annesley Links top at £35.

Downpatrick

🔢 *21 km (18 mi) east of Newcastle on A2 and A25.*

Downpatrick once was called "Plain and Simple Down" but had its name changed by John de Courcy, a Norman knight who moved to the town in 1176. De Courcy set about promoting St. Patrick, the 5th-century Briton who was captured by the Irish and served as a slave in the Down area before he escaped to France, where he learned about Christianity and bravely returned to try to convert the local chiefs. Although it's not true that Patrick brought a new faith to Ireland—there was already a bishop of Ireland before Patrick got here—he must have been a better missionary than most because he did indeed win influential converts. The clan chief of the Down area gave him land at the village of Saul, near Downpatrick, to build a monastery.

Down Cathedral is one of the disputed burial places of St. Patrick. In the churchyard, a somber slab inscribed "Patric" is supposedly the

> ### A DAY LIKE ANY OTHER
>
> St Patrick's Day—March 17th—is a great time to visit Downpatrick as the whole town turns out in carnival dress for the holiday parade. But why is St. Paddy fêted on March 17th? Legend has it he died on that date, perhaps in 461 AD. Others point to the fact that this date marked one of the great pagan festivals celebrating the onset of spring and the sowing of crops.

saint's tomb, but no one knows where he's actually buried. It might be here, at Saul, or, some scholars argue, more likely at Armagh. The church, which lay ruined from 1538 to 1790 (it reopened in 1818), preserves parts of some of the earlier churches and monasteries that have stood on this site, the oldest of which dates back to the 6th century. Even by then, the cathedral site had long been an important fortified settlement: Down takes its name from the Celtic word "dun," or fort. ⌂ *Hilltop, Co. Down* ⊕ *www.downcathedral.org* ⊠ *Free.*

For some hard facts concerning the patron saint of Ireland, visit the interactive exhibits of **St. Patrick Centre** next to the cathedral; It's housed, together with the Down Museum, inside a former 18th-century jail. The ancient myths and stories of early Christian Ireland are brought to life in this information center. Using cutting-edge exhibition technology, you can explore how St. Patrick's legacy developed in early Christian times and examine the art and metalwork, which was produced during this "Golden Age." Younger children will love the puppet shows detailing the life of the saint and can even paint their own Book of Kells, with quills. The Grove art gallery exhibits jewelry, textiles, and paintings by local artists and craftsmen. If the weather is fine, have lunch on the terrace of the Cathedral Garden restaurant, with its dramatic views of Down Cathedral and the Mountains of Mourne. ⌂ *The Mall, Co. Down* ☎ *028/4461–9000* ⊕ *www.saintpatrickcentre.com* ⊠ *£6* ☉ *Oct.–Mar., Mon.–Sat. 10–5; Apr., May, and Sept., Mon.–Sat. 9:30–5:30, Sun. 1–5:30; June–Aug., Mon.–Sat. 9:30–6, Sun. 10–6.*

Where to Stay & Eat

★ $ ✕⌂ **Dufferin Arms Coaching Inn.** Stewart and Morris Crawford preside over this 1803 inn next to picture-perfect, grandly gracious Killyleagh Castle (reputedly the longest inhabited castle in Ireland and most probably the country's prettiest). Rooms in the low-slung, bright-red building are quaint, lush, and cozy, with four-poster beds. Downstairs, the original stables have been converted into the Kitchen Restaurant ($–$$), which sometimes hosts medieval feasts. It specializes in Irish cooking—

the poached salmon and the roast duck in cherry sauce are two best bets. One of the bars has snugs, another an open fire. Diversions such as pub quizzes and Cajun and jazz music keep things lively. ☒ *10 km (6 mi) north of Downpatrick, 31–33 High St., Killyleagh, Co. Down BT30 9QF* ☎ *028/4482–1134* 🖷 *028/4482–8755* ⊕ *www.dufferincoachinginn. com* 🖙 *6 rooms* ⌂ *Restaurant, 3 bars, meeting rooms, Internet room; no a/c* ▤ *AE, MC, V* ⍩⊙| *BP.*

Castle Ward

★ ④⑤ *11 km (7 mi) northeast of Downpatrick, 3 km (2 mi) west of Strangford village on A25, on southern shore of Strangford Lough, entrance by Ballyculter Lodge.*

With a 500-acre park, an artificial lake, a Neoclassical tempietto, and a vast house in Bath stone magically set on the slopes running down to the "Narrows" of the southern shore of Strangford Lough, Castle Ward must have been some place to call home. About 2 mi from the village of Strangford, off the road to Downpatrick, this regal stately home was designed around 1760 in, rather famously, two differing styles. Bernard Ward, 1st Viscount Bangor, could rarely see eye to eye (gossip had it) with his wife, Lady Anne, and the result was that he decided to make the entrance front and salons elegant exercises in Palladian Neoclassicism, while milady transformed the garden facade and her own rooms using the most fashionable style of the day, Strawberry Hill Gothick. His white-and-beige Music Room is picked out in exquisite plasterwork (note how craftsmen decided to save a little money by taking objects, such as a tricorn hat and basket, and simply covering them in plaster), while her Boudoir has an undulating fan-vaulted ceiling that conjures up the "gothick" medievalisms of King Henry VII's chapel at Westminster. In point of fact, the couple's contretemps were dinner-table hearsay and they actually got along famously and the Gothic style was used to beef up the ancestral image of a "Castle" Ward. Be sure to walk through the park (which has

> ### AN EVENING OF THRILLS
>
> After Castle Ward fell into ruin (one Ward descendant had to resort to selling bread at the gate), the Victorian era ushered in new wealth, restoring the house to a sparkling state, never more so than during summer evenings when it becomes Ireland's Glyndebourne and hosts opera performances in its small private theater.

its own Wildlife Center) to enjoy the wonderful vistas overlooking the waters to the town of Portaferry and the Ards Peninsula. ☒ *1 mi west of Strangford on Downpatrick Rd., A25* ☎ *028/4488–1204* ⊕ *www. nationaltrust.org.uk/main* 🖾 *£5.50* ☉ *July and Aug., daily 1–6; Sept.–June, weekends 1–6, grounds open May, Wed.–Mon., daily 10–8; June–Sept., daily 10–8, Oct.–Apr., daily 10–4.*

NORTHERN IRELAND ESSENTIALS

To research prices, get advice from other travelers, and book travel arrangements, visit www.fodors.com.

Transportation

If traveling extensively by public transportation, be sure to load up on information (the best taxi-for-call companies, rail and bus schedules, etc.) upon arriving at the ticket counter or help desk of the bigger train and bus stations in the area, such as Belfast, Derry, and Armagh.

BY AIR

Scheduled services from the United States and Canada are mostly routed through Dublin, Glasgow, London, or Manchester. Several new routes were introduced to Belfast International to great fanfare in 2005. Zoom offers low-cost direct flights from Toronto, and Continental offers direct service from New York City (out of Newark).

Frequent services to Belfast's two airports are scheduled throughout the day from London Heathrow, London Gatwick, and Luton (all of which have fast coordinated subway or rail connections to central London) and from 17 other U.K. airports. Flights from London take about one hour. Aer Arann flies twice daily from Cork to Belfast on weekdays. British Airways flies to Belfast City Airport and Derry from Manchester and London's Heathrow and Gatwick. British Midlands, through its low-cost carrier BMI Baby, flies from Birmingham, Cardiff, Durham, Manchester and Nottingham to Belfast International. Jet2 flies from Belfast International to Barcelona, Leeds, and Prague. EasyJet flies from Belfast International to several European airports, including Alicante, Amsterdam, Bristol, Edinburgh, Glasgow, Liverpool, Luton, Paris, Rome, and Stansted. Eastern Airways flies from Belfast to Aberdeen. Flybe, also known as British European Airways, flies from Belfast City to Birmingham, Bristol, Edinburgh, Glasgow, Leeds, London Gatwick, Norwich, and Southampton, among others.

🛪 Carriers **Aer Arann** ☎ 081/821-0210 or 0800/587-2324 ⊕ www.aerarann.ie. **Aer Lingus** ☎ 0845/084-4444 ⊕ www.aerlingus.com. **British Airways** ☎ 0845/773-3377 ⊕ www.britishairways.com. **British Midland Airways** ☎ 0870/607-0555 ⊕ www. bmibaby.com. **Continental** ☎ 0845/607-6760 ⊕ www.continental.com/uk. **EasyJet** ☎ 08712442366 ⊕ www.easyjet.com. **Flybe** ☎ 0871/700-0123 ⊕ www.flybe.com. **Jet2** ☎ 0871/226-1737 ⊕ www.jet2.com. **Zoom** ☎ 0870/240-0055 ⊕ www.zoomairlines. com.

AIRPORTS

Belfast International Airport at Aldergove is the north's principal air arrival point, 30½ km (19 mi) north of town. Belfast City Airport is the secondary airport, 6½ km (4 mi) east of the city. It receives flights from U.K. provincial airports, from London's Gatwick and Heathrow, and from Stansted and Luton (both near London). City of Derry Airport is 8 km (5 mi) from Derry and receives flights from Dublin, Glasgow, and Manchester.

⚑ Airport Information **Belfast City Airport** ☎028/9093-9093 ⊕www.belfastcityairport.
com. **Belfast International Airport at Aldergove** ☎028/9448-4848 ⊕ www.bial.co.
uk. **City of Derry Airport** ☎028/7181-0784 ⊕ www.cityofderryairport.com.

TRANSFERS Ulsterbus operates a bus every half hour (one-way £6, round-trip £9)
between Belfast International Airport and Belfast city center, as well as
between Belfast City Airport and the city center (one-way £2). Contact
Translink for information on all buses. From Belfast City Airport, you
can also travel into Belfast by train from Sydenham Halt to Central Station or catch a taxi from the airport to your hotel. If you arrive at the
City of Derry Airport, you may need to call a taxi to get to your destination.

⚑ **Delta Cabs** ☎028/7127-9999. **Eglinton Taxis** ☎028/7181-1231. **Foyle Taxis** ☎028/
7126-3905. **Translink** ☎028/9066-6630 ⊕ www.translink.co.uk.

BY BOAT & FERRY

Norse Merchant Ferries has 11-hour daytime or overnight car ferries
that connect Belfast with the English west-coast port of Liverpool every
day. P&O European Ferries has a one-hour sailing to Larne from Cairnryan, Scotland; infrequent trains take passengers on to Belfast. The *Sea-
Cat* high-speed catamaran sails between Belfast and Troon in Scotland,
between Belfast and Glasgow, and between the Isle of Man and Belfast.
The *StenaLine HSS* fast catamaran sails between Belfast and Stranraer,
Scotland in 1½ hours.

⚑ Boat & Ferry Information **Norse Merchant Ferries** ✉ Victoria Terminal 2, W. Bank
Rd., Belfast ☎028/9077-9090 ⊕ www.norsemerchant.com. **P&O European Ferries**
☎ 0870/242-4777 ⊕ www.poirishsea.com. **SeaCat and Steam Packet Company Services** ☎ 0870/552-3523 ⊕ www.seacat.co.uk. *StenaLine HSS* ☎ 028/9074-7747
⊕ www.stenaline.com.

BY BUS

Northern Ireland's main bus company, Ulsterbus, runs direct service between Dublin and Belfast. Queries about Ulsterbus service, or any other
bus and rail transportation in Northern Ireland, can be answered by the
national central reservation center, Translink. The republic's Bus Éireann runs direct services to Belfast from Dublin. Buses arrive at and depart from Belfast's Europa Buscentre; the ride takes three hours. Buses
to Belfast also run from London and from Birmingham, making the Stranraer ferry crossing.

You can take advantage of frequent and inexpensive Ulsterbus links between all Northern Ireland towns. In Belfast, the Europa Buscentre is
just behind the Europa Hotel. The Laganside Buscentre is around the
corner from Belfast's Albert Clock Tower and about 1 km (½ mi) from
Central Station. Within Belfast the city bus service is comprehensive. All
routes start from Donegall Square, where there's a kiosk with timetables.

⚑ Bus Depot **Europa Central Buscentre** ✉ Great Victoria St., Golden Mile, Belfast
☎028/9066-6630. **Laganside Buscentre** ✉ Oxford St., Central District, Belfast ☎028/
9066-6630.

⚑ Bus Lines **Bus Éireann** ☎ 01/836-6111 in Dublin ⊕ www.buseireann.ie. **Translink**
☎ 028/9066-6630 ⊕ www.translink.co.uk.

FARES If you want to tour the north by bus, contact Translink: a Freedom of Northern Ireland Ticket allows unlimited travel on bus or train (£14 per day, £34 for 3 days, and £50 per week). An Irish Rover bus ticket from Ulsterbus covers Ireland, north and south, and costs £48 for 3 days, £109 for 8, and £156 for 15. An Emerald Card (bus and rail) costs £157 for 8 days and £271 for 15 days.

BY CAR

Many roads from the Irish Republic into Northern Ireland were once closed for security reasons, but all are now reinstated, leaving you with a choice of legitimate crossing points. Army checkpoints at approved frontier posts are rare, and few customs formalities are observed. The fast N1/A1 road connects Belfast to Dublin in 160 km (100 mi) with an average driving time of just over two hours. In general, roads here are in much better shape and signposted more clearly than in the Irish Republic.

PARKING Belfast has many parking garages, as well as street meter-ticket parking. Before parking on the street, check the posted regulations: during rush hours many spots become no-parking.

TRAFFIC Bad rush-hour delays can occur on the West Link in Belfast joining M1 (heading south or west) and M2 (heading east or north). Major roadworks will be underway in Belfast during 2007 and detours may be in place. On the whole, driving is quicker and easier in the north than in areas south of the border.

TAXIS Most taxis operate on the meter; ask for a price for longer journeys. You can order in advance. Most cabs will hold four people but you can prebook a larger taxi that will hold six. Typical fares: Belfast International Airport to Belfast city center is around £25; Belfast City Airport to the city center is around £6; Derry City Airport to Derry city center is around £12. The minimum fare is usually £2.50 and £1.05 per mile thereafter although the larger multi-seater cabs are more expensive.

Value Cabs (⊠ 27 Grosvenor Rd, Belfast ☎ 028/9080–9080 ⊕ www. valuecabs.co.uk). **FonACAB** (⊠ 23a Botanic Ave., Belfast ☎ 028/ 9033–3333 ⊕ www.fonacab.com). **Foyle Taxis** (⊠ 10a Newmarket St., Derry ☎ 028/7126–3905).

BY TRAIN

The Dublin–Belfast Express train, run jointly by Northern Ireland Railways and Iarnród Éireann, travels between the two cities in about two hours. Eight trains (check timetables, as some trains are much slower) run daily in each direction (five on Sunday) between Dublin and Belfast's misnamed Central Station—it's not, in fact, that central. A free shuttle bus service from Belfast Central Station will drop you off at City Hall or Ulsterbus's city-center Europa Buscentre. You can change trains at Central Station for the city-center Great Victoria Street Station, which is adjacent to the Europa Buscentre and the Europa Hotel.

The Dublin–Belfast Express train, run jointly by Northern Ireland Railways and Iarnród Éireann, travels between the two cities in about two hours. Eight trains (check timetables, as some trains are much slower) run daily in each direction (three on Sunday) between Dublin and Belfast's misnamed Central Station—it's not, in fact, that central. A free shuttle bus service from Belfast Central Station will drop you off at City Hall or Ulsterbus's city-center Europa Buscentre. You can change trains at Central Station for the city-center Great Victoria Street Station, which is adjacent to the Europa Buscentre and the Europa Hotel.

Northern Ireland Railways runs only four rail routes from Belfast's Central Station: northwest to Derry via Coleraine and the Causeway Coast; east to Bangor along the shore of Belfast Lough; northeast to Larne (for the P&O European ferry to Scotland) and south to Dublin. There are frequent connections to Central Station from the city-center Great Victoria Street Station and from Botanic Station in the university area. A Freedom of Northern Ireland Ticket allows unlimited travel on trains (£14 per day, £34 for three days, and £50 per week). An Irish Rover train ticket provides five days of rail travel for £109.

🚆 Train Lines **Iarnród Éireann** ☎ 1850/366222 timetables ⊕ www.irishrial.ie/home. **Northern Ireland Railways** ✉ 28 Wellington Pl., Central District, Belfast ☎ 02/ 9066-6630 Translink ⊕ www.translink.co.uk.

🚆 Train Stations **Botanic Station** ✉ Botanic Ave., University Area, Belfast ☎ 028/ 9089-9411. **Central Station** ✉ E. Bridge St., Golden Mile, Belfast ☎ 028/9089-9411.

Contacts & Resources

CAR RENTAL

You can choose among several rental companies, but renting a car won't be cheap. A compact car costs £150–£250 per week (including taxes, insurance, and unlimited mileage). If you're planning to take a rental car across the border into the republic, inform the company and check its insurance procedures. Main rental offices include Avis, Dan Dooley, Europcar, Ford, and Hertz. A £300 security deposit is required at the Ford agency in Derry, and a £500 to £750 security deposit is required by Hertz.

🚗 Agencies **Avis** ✉ Belfast International Airport, Belfast ☎ 028/9442-2333 or 0870/ 606-0100 ✉ Belfast City Airport, Belfast ☎ 0870/606-0100 ✉ Great Victoria St., Belfast ☎ 028/9024-0404. **Budget** ✉ Belfast International Airport, Belfast ☎ 028/ 9442-3332 ✉ Belfast City Airport, Belfast ☎ 028/9045-1111 ✉ 96-102 Great Victoria St., Belfast ☎ 028/9023-0700 ⊕ www.budget.ie. **Dan Dooley** ✉ Belfast International Airport, Belfast ☎ 028/9445-2522 ⊕ www.dooleycarrentals.com. **Europcar** ✉ Belfast International Airport, Belfast ☎ 028/9442-3444 or 0800/068-0303 ✉ Belfast City Airport, Belfast ☎ 028/9045-0904 or 0800/068-0303 ⊕ www.europcar.ie. **Ford** ✉ Desmond Motors, City of Derry Airport, Derry ☎ 028/7181-2222. **Hertz** ✉ Belfast International Airport, Belfast ☎ 028/9442-2533 ✉ Belfast City Airport, Belfast ☎ 028/ 9073-2451.

EMERGENCIES

The general emergency number is 999. Belfast City Hospital and the Royal Victoria Hospital are the two Belfast hospitals with emergency rooms. Altnagelvin Hospital in Derry has an emergency room.

🏥 **Altnagelvin Hospital** ✉ Glenshana Rd., on outskirts of East Derry ☎ 028/7134-5171. **Ambulance, coast guard, fire, police** ☎ 999. **Belfast City Hospital** ✉ Lisburn Rd., University Area, Belfast ☎ 028/9032-9241. **Belfast's main police station** ✉ 6-10 N.

Queen St., Central District, Belfast ☎ 028/9065-0222. **Royal Victoria Hospital** ⊠ Grosvenor Rd., West Belfast, Belfast ☎ 028/9024-0503.

INTERNET CAFÉS AND POST OFFICES

In smaller towns, ask your hotel concierge if there are any Internet cafés nearby. It will typically cost about £1 for 15 minutes surfing-time. Post Office hours are generally weekdays 9–5:30 and Saturday 9–12:30. Smaller post offices still close at 12:30 PM on Wednesday; in larger city center areas post offices also are open 1–6 Sunday.

🖥 Internet Cafés **Revelations** ⊠ 27 Shaftsbury Sq., Belfast ☎ 028/9032-0337 ⊕ www.revelations.co.uk. **Bean-there.com** ⊠ 20 The Diamond, Derry ☎ 028/7128-1303 ⊕ www.bean-there.com.

🖥 Post Offices **Belfast GPO** ⊠ Victoria Sq., Belfast ☎ 028/2459-8466. **Derry GPO** ⊠ 2 Boxland St., Derry ☎ 028/7609-3555.

MEDIA

The Irish News is a mainly Nationalist daily that covers Northern Ireland plus an all-Ireland section with some world news. Despite its name, *Belfast Telegraph* does not cover just Belfast but all of Northern Ireland. With both a morning and afternoon edition, this paper tends to have a slightly more Unionist editorial stance.

MONEY MATTERS

Main banks are open weekdays 9:30–4:30, smaller branches weekdays 10:30–3:30. Changing money outside banking hours is possible at Thomas Cook branches. The branch at Belfast Airport is open daily 6:45 AM–8 PM; the branch at Donegall Place is open from Monday through Wednesday, Friday, and Saturday 9–5:30, Thursday 10–5:30. You can also change bills at Travelex Worldwide Money.

🖥 Currency Exchange **Thomas Cook** ⊠ 11 Donegall Pl., Central District, Belfast ☎ 028/9088-3900 ⊕ www.thomascook.com. **Travelex Worldwide Money** ⊠ Belfast International Airport, Belfast ☎ 028/9444-7500 ⊕ www.travelex.co.uk.

TOUR OPTIONS

BIKE TOURS Irish Cycle Tours organizes four- and eight-day tours of the Mournes, Glens of Antrim, and Causeway Coast, and the Sperrin Mountains and Donegal. The company closed its Belfast office in 2004 and is now based in County Kerry in the republic, hence the southern Irish phone number. Mourne Cycle Tours runs bike tours complete with hotel accommodations (bikes are delivered to the hotel), with rates for a two-night booking costing between £90 and £110.

🖥 Bike Touring **Irish Cycle Tours** ☎ 066/712-8733 in republic ⊕ www.irishcycletours.com. **Mourne Self-Guided Cycling Breaks** ☎ 028/4372-4348 ⊕ www.mournecycletours.com.

BOAT TOURS On the Lower Lough Erne, Erne Tours operates an approximately 90-minute trip (£7) aboard the *Kestrel,* a 63-seat water bus, which leaves Round O Pier at Enniskillen Sunday May and June at 2:30, and daily July and August at 10:30, 2:15, and 4:15. Weekdays the boat stops for a half hour at Devenish Island. In September, tours leave Tuesday, Saturday, and Sunday at 2:30. Mid-May to end of August the company also has a Saturday evening dinner cruise departing at 6:30.

🎣 **Erne Tours** ⊠ Round O Pier, Enniskillen 📞 028/6632-2882, 028/6632-4822 dinner cruise.

BUS TOURS Belfast City Sightseeing runs an open-top bus tour (with shelter in case it rains) through Belfast. The Belfast City Tour (£8) covers the City Hall, Albert Clock, Shipyard, Titanic Quarter, Shankill Road, the peace line, the Falls Road, and past the Grand Opera House on Great Victoria Street. Tours leave Castle Place (opposite McDonalds) daily on the half-hour from 9:30 to 4:30, and tickets are valid all day on a hop-on, hop-off basis. The entire route, without stops, takes about 70 minutes.

Ulsterbus operates half-day or full-day trips June through September from Belfast to the Glens of Antrim, the Giant's Causeway, the Fermanagh lakes, Lough Neagh, the Mountains of Mourne, and the Ards Peninsula. Ulsterbus has also teamed up with the Old Bushmills Distillery to run the Bushmills Bus: an open-top tour bus running from Coleraine (via Bushmills to observe whiskey-making) to the Giant's Causeway and the coastal resorts. Contact Ulsterbus through Translink.

MiniCoach operates day tours of Belfast (£8–£16), and to the Giant's Causeway, Bushmills Distillery, and Carrickfergus.

🎣 **Belfast City Sightseeing** 📞 028/9062-6888 ⊕ www.belfastcitysightseeing.com. **Mini-Coach** ⊠ 22 Donegall Rd., Central District, Belfast 📞 028/9032-4733 ⊕ www.minicoachni.co.uk. **Translink** 📞 028/9066-6630 ⊕ www.translink.co.uk.

TAXI TOURS Belfast City Black Taxi Tours do 75-minute tours in a London-style black taxi of either Loyalist or Nationalist sights. The cost is £25 for up to two people, £30 for three people, and £33 for four people. Black Taxi Tours provide a similar itinerary at £25 per taxi for one or two people and £8 per person after that. The Loyalist tours leave from North Street or Bridge Street and prices can vary depending on pick-up point; the Nationalist Tours, through West Belfast Taxis, pick you up at your hotel.

🎣 **Belfast City Black Taxi Tours** 📞 028/9030-1832 ⊕ www.allirelandtours.com. **Black Taxi Tours** 📞 028/9064-2264 ⊕ www.belfasttours.com. **Nationalist Tours** 📞 028/9031-5777.

WALKING TOURS Belfast Safaris offers tailor-made walking tours of Belfast city with a twist. All of the guides are local and passionate about their neighborhoods. Tours are organized according to each group's specific interests, and can include politics, art, or even soccer. Want to learn Irish or play the tin whistle? It can all be arranged. The Antrim Road trail starts at Duncairn Gardens, the birthplace of the artist John Luke, and finishes at Belfast Castle for a panoramic view of the city. The cost is £8 per person for a standard tour, more for longer, custom routes.

Historical Pub Tours of Belfast walking tours of the city's pubs leave on Tuesday at 7 PM and Saturday at 4 PM. The cost is £5. In Derry, walking tours (£4) are organized through the city's Tourist Information Centre.

🎣 **Belfast Safaris** ⊕ www.belfastsafaris.com 📞 028/9022-2925. **Derry Tourist Information Centre** ⊠ 44 Foyle St., West Bank, Derry 📞 028/7126-7284 or 028/7137-7577 ⊕ www.derryvisitor.com. **Historical Pub Tours of Belfast** ⊠ Depart from Crown Liquor Saloon, 46 Great Victoria St., Golden Mile, Belfast 📞 028/9268-3665.

VISITOR INFORMATION

The Northern Ireland Tourist Board (NTIB) Information Centre in Belfast is the main tourist information center for the whole of the north. The office incorporates the plush, comprehensive Belfast Welcome Centre—the main tourist office for Belfast city, run by the Belfast Visitor and Convention Bureau. It's open October to May, Monday 9:30–5:30, Tuesday to Saturday 9–5:30; and June to September, Monday 9:30–5:30, Tuesday to Saturday 9–5:30, Sunday noon–5. Year-round Tourist Information Offices (TIOs) are listed below by town. June to August many more towns and villages open TIOs.

🏚 NTIB **Northern Ireland Tourist Board Information Centre** ⊠ 47 Donegall Pl., Central District, Belfast BT1 5AU ☎ 028/9024–6609 ⊕ www.discovernorthernireland.com. 🏚 Regional Tourist Information **Armagh** ⊠ 40 English St., Co. Armagh BT6 17BA ☎ 028/3752–1800 ⊕ www.visitarmagh.com. **Ballycastle** ⊠ 7 Mary St., Co. Antrim BT54 6QH ☎ 028/2076–2024 ⊕ www.countyantrim.com/antrim_ballycastle.htm. **Bangor** ⊠ Quay St., Co. Down BT20 5ED ☎ 028/9127–0069 ⊕ www.northdowntourism.com. **Carrickfergus** ⊠ Heritage Plaza, Co. Antrim BT38 7DG ☎ 028/9335–8049 ⊕ www.carrickfergus.org. **Coleraine** ⊠ Railway Rd., Co. Derry BT52 IPE ☎ 028/7034–4723 ⊕ www.colerainebc.gov.uk. **Derry** ⊠ Foyle St., Co. Derry BT48 6AT ☎ 028/7126–7284 or 028/7137–7577 ⊕ www.derryvisitor.com. **Downpatrick** ⊠ 53A Market St., Co. Down BT30 6L2 ☎ 028/4461–2233 ⊕ www.downdc.gov.uk. **Enniskillen** ⊠ Lakeland Visitor Centre, Shore Rd., Co. Fermanagh BT74 7EF ☎ 028/6632–3110 ⊕ www.fermanaghlakelands.com. **Giant's Causeway** ⊠ Visitor Centre, Co. Antrim BT57 8SU ☎ 028/2073–1855 ⊕ www.moyle-council.org. **Killymaddy** ⊠ Ballygally Rd., Dungannon, Co. Tyrone BT70 ITF ☎ 028/8776–7259 ⊕ www.dungannonlife.com. **Larne** ⊠ Narrow Gauge Rd., Co. Antrim BT40 1XB ☎ 028/2826–0088 ⊕ www.larne.gov.uk. **Limavady** ⊠ Connell St., Co. Derry BT49 OHA ☎ 028/7776–0307 ⊕ www.limavady.gov.uk. **Lisburn** ⊠ 53 Lisburn Sq., Co. Antrim BT28 IAG ☎ 028/9266–0038 ⊕ www.visitlisburn.com. **Newcastle** ⊠ Central Promenade, Co. Down BT33 OAA ☎ 028/4372–2222 ⊕ www.downdc.gov.uk. **Newtownards** ⊠ Regent St., Co. Down BT23 4AD ☎ 028/9182–6846 ⊕ www.kingdomsofdown.com. **Newry** ⊠ Town Hall, Bank Parade, Co. Armagh BT35 6HR ☎ 028/3026–8877 ⊕ www.newryandmourne.gov.uk.

Irish Greens

Portstewart, Londonberry, Northern Ireland

WORD OF MOUTH

"For great Irish golf, Ballybunion, Lahinch, Tralee, and Dingle all await, and they are easily reachable from Shannon airport. This is a pilgrimage that no golfer should miss. If I had only two days for golf I would choose Ballybunion and Lahinch. The natural dunes along the sea is links golf at its finest. Not only is the golf great, the west coast of Ireland is the best scenery that the Emerald Isle has to offer. Bring your raingear and a thirst for Guinness."

—39Steps

Updated by
Anto Howard

ASK MOST GOLFERS WHERE TO FIND the golf vacation of a lifetime—breathtaking and diverse courses, lovely settings, history seeping into every shot—and they'll probably say Scotland. Unless, of course, they've been to Ireland. The nation's oldest course dates from 1881, and the Golfing Union of Ireland is the oldest such establishment in the world. It started in 1891: all nine original clubs were in Ulster. Now the number of affiliated golf clubs is 4,002, with more than 200,000 members, and there are still more clubs that haven't joined.

Ireland is one of those remarkable places where mountains and sea often meet. Scraggly coastline and rolling hills of heather dominate the courses here, not the other way around. Real golfers are challenged, rather than deterred, by the vagaries of the elements—the wind, rain, and mist—and the lack of golf carts on courses in rougher terrain. Ireland's ever-beguiling (and often frustrating) courses attract players from around the globe. Tom Watson, winner of five British Opens, lists Ballybunion as his favorite course; so does the legendary writer Herbert Warren Wind—who, from an American viewpoint, put Irish golf on the map when he wrote, "To put it simply, Ballybunion revealed itself to be nothing less than the finest seaside course I have ever seen." And although Ballybunion is generally considered the Emerald Isle's prize jewel, many courses now rival it—from such classics as Portmarnock and Waterville to newer courses such as Mount Juliet, the K Club, and the Old Head of Kinsale.

There's more to Irish golf than its great links courses, though. Druids Glen features prominently alongside the likes of the K Club, Mount Juliet, Carton House, and Fota Island in every debate on the great inland golf courses. And although it's purely a matter of opinion—and, perhaps, your last scorecard—as to which is best, Druids Glen was voted European Golf Course of the Year at the prestigious Hertz International Travel Awards for 2000, and is considered one of the top 20 courses in Ireland by *Golf Digest* magazine. Carton House was home to the last two Irish Opens. In 2006, however, the action moves to the K Club, as the giants of the U.S. and European tours go head to head for the old trophy during golf's greatest match-play competition.

The wonderfully alive, challenging natural terrain is one of the things that makes Irish golf so remarkable. Of the estimated 150 top-quality links courses in the world, 39 of them are in Ireland. Most of these leading courses were designed by celebrated golf architects, such as Tom Morris, James Braid, Harry Colt, and Alister MacKenzie, who capitalized on spectacular landscapes. Others—such as Severiano Ballesteros, with his new course at Killenard in County Laois—will continue in their steps.

- **The Weather Factor.** You see all kinds of weather in Ireland—driving winds, rain, sleet, and sunshine—and you may see it all in one round. There are no rain-checks here. You play unless there's lightning, so pack your sweaters and rain gear, especially if you're planning your trip between fall and spring.

- **The Sunday Bag Factor.** If you don't have a golf bag that's light enough for you to carry for 18 holes, invest in one before your trip. Electric carts are generally available only at the leading venues, so you usually have the option of using a caddy or caddy car (pull cart) or of carrying your own bag. Many courses have caddies but don't guarantee their availability because they're not employed by the course—so you may have to tote your bag yourself. Be prepared with a carryall or a Sunday bag.

- **The Northern Ireland Factor.** Some of the best and most beautiful courses are in Northern Ireland, where the leading venues—like Royal County Down and Royal Portrush—are less remote than in the republic. Remember that this part of the island is under British rule, so all currency is in U.K. pounds, although many clubs and businesses will accept the euro. There are no restrictions when traveling from one part of the country to the other.

- **The Private Club Factor.** Unlike those in America, most private golf clubs in Ireland are happy to let visitors play their courses and use their facilities. It's important to remember, however, that such clubs place members first; guests come second. In some, you'll need a letter of introduction from your club in America to secure your playing privilege. There are often preferred days for visitors; call in advance to be sure that a club can make time for you.

North of Dublin

Carton House Golf Club. This just-outside-of-Dublin estate has quickly become one of the brightest stars in the Irish golfing universe. It's in a majestic 1,100 acre park that was the ancestral home of the earls of Kildare, presided over by an enormous and very grand 18th-century stately house. Two of the biggest names in golf designed the championship courses here. The parkland Mark O'Meara course makes use of the estate's rolling hills, specimen trees, and the River Rye. The highlight comprises the 14th, 15th, and 16th stretch: a pair of classy par-3s wrapped around an heroic par-5. The second 18 holes created by Colin Montgomerie is an inland links-style course, which is flatter and virtually treeless. There's a good mix of long par-4s backed up with tricky short ones. Recessed pot bunkers lie in wait to pick up off-line shots. ⊠ *Maynooth, Co. Kildare* ☎ *01/628–6271* ⊕ *www.carton.ie* 🏌 *36 holes. Yardage: 7,006. Par 72 (O'Meara); 7,301. Par 72. Practice area, caddies, caddy carts, buggies, catering* 🏌 *Fees: Sun.–Wed. €115; Thurs.–Sat. €135* ☺ *Visitors: daily.*

County Louth Golf Club. This course is better known by the name of its hometown, Baltray, and covers 190 acres by the Irish Sea at the mouth of the river Boyne. It's rated as "a hidden gem" among *Golf Digest*'s 100 best courses in the world, and, as such, this wonderful links course surprisingly even manages to keep a relatively low profile at home. Long hitters will love the atypical layout, a par-73 that features five par-5s, but beware the well-protected, undulating greens. ⊠ *Baltray, Drogheda, Co. Louth* ☎ *041/988–1530* ⊕ *www.countylouthgolfclub. com* 🏌 *18 holes. Yardage: 6,936. Par 72. Practice area, caddies (reserve in advance), caddy carts, club rental, catering* 🏌 *Fees: weekdays except Tues. €115; weekends €135* ☺ *Visitors: Mon. and Wed.–Sun.*

Island Golf Club. Talk about exclusive—until 1960, the only way to reach this club was by boat. It was about as remote as you could get and still be only 24 km (15 mi) from Dublin. But things have changed. The Island has opened its doors to reveal a fine links course with holes that force you to navigate between spectacular sand dunes toward small, challenging greens. ⊠ *Corballis, Donabate, Co. Dublin* ☎ *01/843–6205* ⊕ *www.theislandgolfclub.com* ⅄. *18 holes. Yardage: 6,646. Par 71. Practice area, caddies, caddy carts, catering* ⊑ *Fees: €125* ⊙ *Visitors: daily.*

Fodor'sChoice
★ **Portmarnock Golf Club.** The hoo-ha and court battles over Portmarnock's refusal to admit women members often overshadows the club's position as the most famous of Ireland's "Big Four" (Ballybunion, Royal County Down, and Royal Portrush are the others). This links course, on a sandy peninsula north of Dublin, has hosted numerous major championships and Tom Watson often used it as a preparation for the Open. Known for its flat fairways and greens, it provides a fair test for any golfer who can keep it out of the heavy rough. ⊠ *Portmarnock, Co. Dublin* ☎ *01/846–2968* ⊕ *www.portmarnockgolfclub.ie* ⅄. *27 holes. Yardage: 7,150, 3,449. Par 72, 37. Practice area, driving range, caddies (reserve in advance), caddy carts, catering* ⊑ *Fees: weekdays €165; weekends €190* ⊙ *Visitors: Mon., Tues., and Thurs.–Sun.*

Royal Dublin Golf Club. Links courses are usually in remote, even desolate areas, but this captivating one is only 6 km (4 mi) from the center of Dublin. On Bull Island, a bird sanctuary, Royal Dublin is Ireland's third-oldest club. This links course has always been challenging but Martin Hawtree's ongoing redesign is making things even trickier. Watch out for the 5th, the 13th, and the infamous 18th—a par-4 dogleg with plenty of opportunities to shoot out-of-bounds. ⊠ *Dollymount, Dublin 3* ☎ *01/833–6346* ⊕ *www.theroyaldublingolfclub.com* ⅄. *18 holes. Yardage: 6,963. Par 72. Practice area, caddies, caddy carts, club rental, catering* ⊑ *Fees: €150* ⊙ *Visitors: Mon, Tues., Thurs., and Fri.*

St. Margaret's Golf and Country Club. For those tired of getting blown off-course on Dublin's breezy links, this is 18 holes of pure bliss. The broad fairways on this parklands course are a little more forgiving than the likes of Portmarnock but don't be lulled into a false sense of security—there are some real roller coasters along the way (like the awesome 12th). Two lakes and a babbling brook could bring your efforts on this hole to a watery end. ⊠ *St. Margaret's, Co. Dublin* ☎ *01/864–0400* ⊕ *www.stmargaretsgolf.com* ⅄. *18 holes. Yardage: 6, 917. Par 73. Practice area, driving range, caddy carts, club rental, shoe rental, catering* ⊑ *Fees: Mon. €50; Tues.–Thurs. €60; Fri.–Sun. €70* ⊙ *Visitors: daily.*

South of Dublin

Druids Glen Golf Club. The beautiful Druids Glen course, 40 km (25 mi) south of Dublin in County Wicklow, has hosted the Irish Open on four occasions since it opened in 1995 and is known in golfing circles as the "Augusta of Europe." The wonderful landscaping and the extensive use of water in the layout explain the comparisons to the home of *The Masters*. It's essentially an American-style target course incorporating some delightful changes in elevation, and its forbidding, par-3 17th has an island green, like the corresponding hole at TPC Sawgrass. A second course, Druids Heath is a marvelous attempt to combine the best of links, heathland, and parkland golf. ⊠ *Newtownmountkennedy, Co. Wicklow* ☎ *01/287–3600* ⊕ *www.druidsglen.ie* ⅂ *36 holes. Yardage: Glen, 6560. Par 71; Heath 6,833. Par 71. Practice area, caddies, caddy carts, buggies, catering* ⊠ *Fees: €75–€175* ⊙ *Visitors: daily.*

FodorsChoice **The K Club.** "Home to the 2006 Ryder Cup" says all a golfer needs to
★ know about the pedigree of the K Club. It remains Ireland's premier luxury golf resort, with two full championship parkland courses. The Palmer course is named after its designer, the legendary Arnold Palmer, and offers a round of golf in lush, wooded surroundings bordered by the River Liffey. The generous fairways and immaculate greens are offset by formidable length, which makes it one of the most demanding courses in the Dublin vicinity. Additional stress is presented by negotiating the numerous doglegs, water obstacles, and sand bunkers. The Smurfitt course is essentially an "inland links" course. The signature 7th hole wows visitors with its water cascades and man-made rock-quarry feature. The on-site facilities are terrific and include a 95-room resort with three restaurants, a health club, tennis and squash courts, a pool, and massage and other spa treatments. ⊠ *Kildare Country Club, Straffan, Co. Kildare* ☎ *01/627–3333* ⊕ *www.kclub.ie* ⅂ *36 holes. Yardage: Palmer, 7,337. Par 72; Smurfitt 7,277. Par 72. Practice area, driving range, caddies, caddy carts, club rental, shoe rental, catering* ⊠ *Fees: €130–€350* ⊙ *Visitors: daily.*

FodorsChoice **Mount Juliet Golf Course.** Attached to a magisterial country-house hotel,
★ this Jack Nicklaus–designed championship parkland course, 19 km (11 mi) from Kilkenny Town, includes practice greens, a driving range, and, for those who feel a little rusty, a David Leadbetter golf academy. The heavily forested course has eight holes that play over water, including the wonderful 3rd hole—a par 3 over a stream from an elevated tee. The back 9 presents a series of difficult bunker shots. A sporting day out comes to a welcome end in the Hunter's Yard or Rose Garden lodge, which cater to both the thirsty and the hungry. Greens fees are above average, and although visitors are always welcome, a weekday round is best, since it's often crowded with members on weekends. ⊠ *Mount Juliet Estate, Thomastown, Co. Kilkenny* ☎ *056/73000* ⊕ *www.mountjuliet.com* ⅂ *18 holes. Yardage: 7,300. Par 72. Practice area, driving range, caddies, caddy carts, club rental, lessons, catering* ⊠ *Fees: €75–€160* ⊙ *Visitors: daily.*

Powerscourt Golf Club. Set on the most spectacular estate in Ireland (once presided over by the Slazenger family), these two recently built courses are nestled in the foothills of the Wicklow Mountains on the ancient Powerscourt lands, home to a legendary 18th-century stately home and garden. Panoramic views to the sea and Sugarloaf Mountain—and all those 200-year-old trees—give the impression that the course has been here for years. The older East course is a largely parkland course, but some holes have certain links characteristics. The course's tiered greens will test even the best golfers. The more recently built West course is even more challenging and is designed with top-class tournament golf in mind. ✉ *Enniskerry, Co. Wicklow* ☎ *01/204–6033* ⊕ *www. powerscourt.ie* ⅄ *36 holes. Yardage: (East Course) 7,022; (West course) 6,938. Par 72. Practice area, driving range, caddies, caddy carts, catering* ☕ *Fees: €130* ⊙ *Visitors: daily.*

Tulfarris Golf Club. It's a case of "water, water everywhere" as you play through the 18 magnificently designed holes at this scenic County Wicklow club. Thankfully, it's not all in the water traps—the course is on three peninsulas in the idyllic Blessington lakes so you get great views around every corner. Another great aspect of the course is that no two holes are alike and only two are aligned in the same direction. This is definitely a course battling to make its name at the top table of Irish golf. ✉ *Blessington, Co. Wicklow* ☎ *045/867–609* ⊕ *www.tulfarris.com* ⅄ *18 holes. Yardage: 7,116. Par 72. Practice area, caddies, caddy carts, catering* ☕ *Fees: weekdays €80; weekends €100* ⊙ *Visitors: daily.*

Southwest

Adare Manor Golf Course. This parkland stretch is on the ancestral estate of the Earl of Dunraven. Its immediate success was virtually guaranteed by the international profile of its designer, Robert Trent Jones Sr. The grand old man of golf-course architects seemed far more comfortable with the wooded terrain than he was when designing the second links at Ballybunion. As a result, he delivered a course with the potential to host events of the highest caliber. The front 9 is dominated by an artificial 14-acre lake with a $500,000 polyethylene base. It's in play at the 3rd, 5th, 6th, and 7th holes. The dominant hazards on the homeward journey are the River Mague and the majestic trees, which combine to make the par-5 18th one of the most challenging finishing holes imaginable. ✉ *Adare, Co. Limerick* ☎ *061/395–044* ⊕ *www. adaremanor.com* ⅄ *18 holes. Yardage: 7,125. Par 72. Practice area, caddies, caddy carts, catering* ☕ *Fees: €130* ⊙ *Visitors: daily.*

Fodor'sChoice
★

Ballybunion Golf Club. President Bill Clinton will be eternally associated in Irish golfers' minds with this revered course. In fact there's even a brass statue of him teeing in the nearby village, to commemorate his visit there in 1999. On the shore of the Atlantic next to the southern entrance of the Shannon, it has the huge dunes of Lahinch without the blind shots. It's no pushover, but every hole is pleasurable. Watch out for "Mrs. Simpson," a double fairway bunker on the 1st hole, named after the wife of Tom Simpson, the architect who remodeled the course in 1937. (Tom Watson did the same in 1995.) The Cashen Course, which opened in 1985, was designed by Robert Trent Jones Sr. ✉ *Sandhill Rd., Ballybunion, Co. Kerry* ☎ *068/27611* ⊕ *www.ballybuniongolfclub.ie* ⅄ *36 holes. Yardage: 6,542 (Old), 6,477 (Cashen). Par 72, 70. Practice area, driving range, caddies, catering* ☕ *Fees: €150 (Old); €110 (Cashen); €200 (both on same day)* ⊙ *Visitors: weekdays.*

Cork Golf Club. If you know golf-course architecture, you're familiar with the name Alister MacKenzie, who designed Cypress Point in California and Augusta National in Georgia. One of his few designs in Ireland is Cork, better known as Little Island. There's water on this parkland course, but it's not the temperamental ocean; instead, Little Island is in Cork Harbor, a gentle bay of the Irish Sea. The highlight for most is the par-4 6th where a broad fairway narrows toward the green, nestled in former quarry. The course is little known, but it's one of the Emerald Isle's best. ⊠ *Little Island, Co. Cork* ☎ *021/435–3451* ⊕ *www.corkgolfclub. ie* ⚐ *18 holes. Yardage: 6,731. Par 72. Practice area, caddies, caddy carts, club rental, catering* 🖾 *Fees: Mon.–Thurs. €85; Fri.–Sun. €95* ⊘ *Visitors: daily.*

Dooks Golf Club. On the second tier of courses in Ireland's southwest, Dooks doesn't quite measure up to the world-class clubs. It is, nonetheless, a completely worthwhile day of golf if you're touring the area and boasts spectacular scenery including views of the majestic Magillacuddy's Reeks. Built in the old tradition of seaside links, it's shorter and a bit gentler, although the greens are small and tricky. ⊠ *Dooks, Glenbeigh, Co. Kerry* ☎ *066/976–8205* ⊕ *www.dooks.com* ⚐ *18 holes. Yardage: 6,401. Par 71. Caddy carts, club rental, catering* 🖾 *Fees: €70* ⊘ *Visitors: weekdays.*

Heritage Golf and Country Club. Millions of dollars have been spent on developing this recent arrival of the Irish golf scene—and it shows. This 18-hole championship course has second-to-none facilities including a 38,000 square foot clubhouse. A life-size bronze of Seve Ballesteros greets you at the entrance to the course he designed here, which is noted for its mix of challenging doglegs and water traps (including five on-course lakes). Add four demanding par-5s to the mix and the result is a truly world-class parkland course. The development of luxury on-site accommodation has also increased the club's attractiveness to the visiting golfer. ⊠ *Killenard, Co. Laois* ☎ *0502/45040* ⊕ *www.theheritage.com* ⚐ *18 holes. Yardage: 7,319. Par 72. Caddy carts, driving range, practice area, catering* 🖾 *Fees: weekdays, €115; weekends, €130* ⊘ *Visitors: daily.*

Killarney Golf and Fishing Club. Freshwater fishing is the sport here, for this club is among a stunning mixture of mountains, lakes, and forests. There are three courses: Mahony's Point, along the shores of Lough Leane; the Lackabane, on the far side of the road from the main entrance; and the jewel in the crown, water-feature-packed Killeen. Despite the abundance of seaside links, many well-traveled golfers name Killarney their favorite place to play in Ireland. ⊠ *Mahony's Point, Killarney, Co. Kerry* ☎ *064/31034* ⊕ *www.killarney-golf.com* ⚐ *54 holes. Yardage: 6,780 (Mahony's), 7,050 (Lackabane), 7,178 (Killeen). All courses: Par 72. Practice area, caddies, caddy carts, catering* 🖾 *Fees: €100 (Mahony's Point); €80 (Lackabane); €120 (Killeen)* ⊘ *Visitors: Mon.–Sat.*

Old Head Golf Links. Golf doesn't get much more spectacular than this. On a celebrated 215-acre County Cork peninsula, which juts out into the wild Atlantic nearly 300 feet below, you can find an awe-inspiring spectacle that defies comparison. The only golfing stretches that could be likened to it are the 16th and 17th holes at Cypress Point and small, Pacific sections of Pebble Beach, from the 7th to the 10th and the long 18th. Even if your golf is moderate, expect your pulse to race at the stunning views and wildlife. ✉ *Kinsale, Co. Cork* ☎ *021/477–8444* ⊕ *www. oldheadgolflinks.com* 🏌 *18 holes. Yardage: 7,215. Par 72. Practice area, caddies (reserve in advance), caddy carts, catering* 💳 *Fees:* €*275* ⊗ *Visitors: daily.*

Tralee Golf Club. Tralee is what all modern-golf-course architects *wish* they could do in the States: find unspoiled, seaside links and route a course on it that's designed for the modern game. This is an Arnold Palmer–Ed Seay design that opened in 1984, and the location is fantastic—cliffs, craters, dunes, and the gale-blowing ocean. Don't let the flat front nine lull you to sleep—the back 9 can be a ferocious wake-up call. ✉ *West Barrow, Ardfert, Co. Kerry* ☎ *066/713–6379* ⊕ *www.traleegolfclub. com* 🏌 *18 holes. Yardage: 6,975. Par 74. Practice area, putting green, caddies, caddy carts, club hire, catering* 💳 *Fees:* €*160* ⊗ *Visitors: Mon., Tues., and Thurs.–Sat.*

Waterville Golf Links. Here's what you should know about Waterville before you play: the 1st hole of this course is aptly named "Last Easy." At 7,184 yards from the tips, Waterville is the longest course in Ireland or Britain, and it's generally regarded as their toughest test. Now the good news—the scenery is so majestic you may not care that your score is approaching the yardage. Six holes run along the cliffs by the sea, surrounding the other 12, which have a tranquil, if not soft, feel to them. ✉ *Waterville, Co. Kerry* ☎ *066/947–4545* ⊕ *www.watervillegolflinks. ie* 🏌 *18 holes. Yardage: 7,225. Par 74. Practice area, caddies, caddy carts, buggies, catering* 💳 *Fees:* €*150* ⊗ *Visitors: daily.*

West

Carne Golf Links. Clinging to the very northwest tip of County Mayo, this is literally the last golf course before you hit Boston. This Eddie Hackett–designed links ducks and dives among towering sand dunes next to what locals call "the wild Atlantic." From the elevated tees and greens you can see a string of Atlantic islands: Inishkea, Inishglora, and Achill. But don't be distracted by the amazing views—you'll need all your wits about you to beat the constant challenge of the high winds. ✉ *Belmullet, Co. Mayo* ☎ *097/82292* ⊕ *www.carnegolflinks.com* 🏌 *18 holes. Yardage: 6,119. Par 72. Practice area, caddies, caddy carts, buggies, club hire, catering* 💳 *Fees:* €*50* ⊗ *Visitors: daily.*

Doonbeg Golf Club. Despite being held up for a time (due to government legislation to protect a rare local snail), Greg Norman–designed Doonbeg has arrived with a major splash on the Irish links scene. Physically stunning, this tough, unforgiving course stretches along nearly 2 mi of pristine Atlantic beech and dunes. The magnificent par-4 15th—with funnel-shape green surrounded by huge dunes—is at the center of the whole course. Gamblers beware: anything long could easily run off the green and never be seen again. If you make it to the tricky 18th, you'll be rewarded with breathtaking views of the ocean. ✉ *Doonbeg, Co. Clare* ☎ *065/905–5602* ⊕ *www.doonbeggolfclub.com* 🏌 *18 holes. Yardage: 6,885. Par 72. Practice area, caddies, caddy carts, catering* 💳 *Fees: weekdays* €*185; weekends* €*195* ⊗ *Visitors: daily.*

Lahinch Golf Club. There's a real Scottish flavor to this venerable links course. The club was founded by members of Scotland's Black Watch regiment based in Limerick and the first course was designed by Old Tom Morris from St. Andrews in 1892. Then, in the 1920s, design maestro Alister MacKenzie created a wonderfully challenging 18 holes—full of undulating greens, huge bunkers, and maddening blind shots. Poorly thought-out alterations in the 1930s obliterated many of his innovations and it wasn't until 1999 that a four-year project to re-create the MacKenzie magic began. The Castle Course is less of a challenge to the experienced player but it has its moments: awkwardly placed bunkers and water hazards lie in wait. ⊠ *Lahinch, Co. Clare* ☎ *065/708–1003* ⊕ *www. lahinchgolf.com* ⚑ *36 holes. Yardage: 6,735 (Old Course), 5,594 (Castle Course). Par 72, 70. Practice area, caddies, caddy carts, catering* ⊠ *Fees: €135 (Old Course); €50 (Castle)* ⊘ *Visitors: daily.*

Westport Golf Club. Twice this inland course hosted the Irish Amateur Championship. It lies in the shadows of religious history: rising 2,500 feet above Clew Bay, with its hundreds of islands, is Croagh Patrick, a mountain that legend connects with St. Patrick. The mountain is considered sacred, and it attracts multitudes of worshippers to its summit every year. All the prayers might pay off at the 15th, where your drive has to carry the ball over 200 yards of ocean. ⊠ *Westport, Co. Mayo* ☎ *098/28262* ⊕ *www.golfwestport.com* ⚑ *18 holes. Yardage: 6,980. Par 73. Practice area, driving range, caddies, caddy carts, buggies, catering* ⊠ *Fees: Mon.–Thurs. €42; Fri.–Sun. €55* ⊘ *Visitors: daily.*

Northwest

Rosapenna Golf Links. The ghost of Old Tom Morris is alive and kicking on the first of the two courses at this recently revamped, old-school links. In 1891 the legendary Morris spotted the potential of this secluded stretch of Donegal coastline and staked out the original course himself. Long-dead greats such as Harry Vardon and James Braid played here, where the first 10 holes are classic links and the last eight actually play inland and uphill into high meadow. The priceless Atlantic views haven't changed since Morris's day, but the recent addition of the testing and tantalizing Sandy Hills links course has made this place a must-stop for the serious golfer. ⊠ *Downings, Co. Donegal* ☎ *074/915–53016* ⊕ *www.rosapennagolflinks.ie* ⚑ *36 holes. Yardage: Morris: 6,270. Par 70. Sandy Hills: 7,225. Par 72. Practice area, caddies (summer only), caddy carts, club rental, catering* ⊠ *Fees: Morris €50; Sandy Hills €75* ⊘ *Visitors: daily.*

Donegal Golf Club. Recently named by *Golf World* as one of Ireland's top 10 clubs, this is a course that has always rated high in the estimations of local golfers. On the shores of Donegal Bay and approached through a forest, the windswept links are shadowed by the Blue Stack Mountains, with the Atlantic as a backdrop. The greens are large, but the rough is deep and penal, and there's a constant battle against erosion by the sea. The par-3 5th, fittingly called "The Valley of Tears," begins a run of four of the course's biggest challenges, which could have you discreetly hiding your score card by the time you reach the 18th. ⊠ *Murvagh, Laghey, Co. Donegal* ☎ *074/973–4054* ⊕ *www. donegalgolfclub.ie* ⅂ *18 holes. Yardage: 6,753. Par 73. Practice area, caddy carts, buggies, club hire, catering* ▭ *Fees: Mon.–Thurs.* €*55; Fri.–Sun.* €*70* ⊙ *Visitors: daily.*

Enniscrone Golf Club. Enniscrone's setting is a natural for good golf—it's a combination of flatlands, foothills, and the Atlantic. The Dunes is the flagship course here and though it's not overly long on the score-card, persistent winds can add yards to almost every hole. There's also the 9-hole Scurmore course. It's among the small number of clubs in Ireland with electric caddy carts. ⊠ *Enniscrone, Co. Sligo* ☎ *096/ 36297* ⊕ *www.enniscronegolf.com* ⅂ *27 holes. Yardage: 6,948 (The Dunes); 6,734 (Scurmore). Par 73 (The Dunes); Par 72 (Scurmore). Practice area, putting green, caddies (weekends and holidays), caddy carts, buggies, club rental* ▭ *Fees: weekdays* €*55; weekends* €*70* ⊙ *Visitors: weekdays; weekends by appointment.*

Northern Ireland

Ballycastle Golf Club. Pleasure comes first here, with challenge as an afterthought. It's beautiful (five holes wind around the remains of a 13th-century friary), short (less than 6,000 yards), and has an unusual mix of both links and parkland holes. It's also right next to Bushmills, the world's oldest distillery—at nearly 400 years. ⊠ *2 Cushendall Rd., Ballycastle BT54 6QP, Co. Antrim* ☎ *048/2076–2536* ⊕ *www. ballycastlegolfclub.com* ⅂ *18 holes. Yardage: 5,927. Par 71. Practice area, caddy cars, club hire, catering* ▭ *Fees: weekdays £20; weekends £30* ⊙ *Visitors: daily.*

Castlerock Golf Club. Where else in the world can you play a hole called "Leg o' Mutton"? It's a 200-yard par-3 with railway tracks to the right and a burn to the left—just one of several unusual holes at this course, which claims to have the best greens in Ireland. The finish is spectacular: from the elevated 17th tee, where you can see the shores of Scotland, to the majestic 18th, which plays uphill to a plateau green. The club also boasts the equally scenic 9-hole Bann course. ⊠ *65 Circular Rd., Castlerock, Co. Derry* ☎ *048/7084–8314* ⊕ *www.castlerockgc.co. uk* ⅂ *27 holes. Yardage: 6,747; 4,892. Par 73, 67. Practice area, caddies (reserve in advance), caddy cars, catering* ▭ *Fees: weekdays £50; weekends £70* ⊙ *Visitors: Mon.–Thurs.*

Malone Golf Club. Fisherfolk may find the 22-acre lake at the center of this parkland layout distracting because it's filled with trout. The golf, however, is just as well-stocked—with large trees and well-manicured, undulating greens, this is one of the most challenging inland tests in Ireland. Bring your power game—there are only three par-5s, but they're all more than 520 yards. However, for many, the feature hole is the par-3 15th. Water lies to the front and back of the small green and there are bunkers to the right; pinpoint accuracy is a must. ⊠ *240 Upper Malone Rd., Dunmurry, Belfast* ☎ *048/9061–2695* ⊕ *www.malonegolfclub. co.uk* ⅂ *27 holes. Yardage: 6,706, 3,160. Par 72, 36. Practice area, cad-*

dies (summer only), caddy cars, buggies, club hire, catering ✉ *Fees: weekdays £55; weekends £60* ☉ *Visitors: daily.*

Portstewart Golf Club. More than a century old, Portstewart may scare you with its opening hole, generally regarded as the toughest starter in Ireland. Picture a 425-yard par-4 that descends from an elevated tee to a small green tucked between the dunes. The greens are known for uniformity and speed, and seven of the holes have been redesigned to toughen the course. If you want a break from the grand scale of championship links, there's the Old Course and the Riverside, 36 holes of downsize, executive-style golf. ✉ *117 Strand Rd., Portstewart, Co. Derry* ☎ *048/7083–2015* ⊕ *www.portstewartgc.co.uk* ⛳ *54 holes. Yardage: 6,895 (Championship), 4,730 (Old Course), 5,725 (Riverside). Par 72, 64, 68. Practice area, caddies, caddy cars, buggies, catering* ✉ *Fees: weekdays £65 (Championship), £10 (Old Course), £18 (Riverside); weekends, £85 (Championship), £15 (Old Course), £23 (Riverside)* ☉ *Visitors: daily.*

Fodor's Choice
★ **Royal County Down.** Catch it on the right day at the right time and you may think you're on the moon; Royal County Down is a links course with a sea of craterlike bunkers and small dunes. And for better players, every day is the right one. Harry Vardon labeled it the toughest course on the Emerald Isle, and if you can't hit your drive long and straight, you might find it the toughest course in the world. ✉ *Golf Links Rd., Newcastle, Co. Down* ☎ *048/4372–2419* ⊕ *www.royalcountydown. org* ⛳ *36 holes. Yardage: 7,065 (Championship), 4,681 (Annesley). Par 71, 63. Practice area, caddies, caddy cars, catering* ✉ *Fees: weekdays £110–125 (Championship), £30 (Annesley); weekends £140 (Championship), £35 (Annesley)* ☉ *Visitors: Sun.–Tues., Thurs.–Fri. (Championship); daily (Annesley).*

Fodor's Choice
★ **Royal Portrush.** A legend in Irish golfing circles, this course is the only Irish club to have hosted a British Open. The championship Dunluce course is named for the ruins of a nearby castle and is a sea of sand hills and curving fairways. Despite its understated appearance it poses many and varied challenges. "White Rocks," the par-5 5th hole, is quite literally a cliff hanger. It's a wicked dogleg with the green perched on the edge of a cliff. The Valley course is a less-exposed, tamer track. Both are conspicuous for their lack of bunkers. In a poll of Irish golf legends, Dunluce was voted the best in Ireland. ✉ *Dunluce Rd., Portrush, Co. Antrim* ☎ *048/7082–2311* ⊕ *www.royalportrushgolfclub.com* ⛳ *36 holes. Yardage: 6,818 (Dunluce), 6,273 (Valley). Par 72, 71. Practice area, caddies, caddy carts, buggies, catering* ✉ *Dunluce: weekdays £95; weekends £110; Valley: weekdays £32.50; weekends £37.50* ☉ *Visitors: Tues.–Sun.*

9

SMART TRAVEL TIPS

There are planners and there are those who, excuse the pun, fly by the seat of their pants. We happily place ourselves among the planners. Our writers and editors try to anticipate all the issues you may face before and during any journey, and then they do their research. This section is the product of their efforts. Use it to get excited about your trip to Ireland, to inform your travel planning, or to guide you on the road should the seat of your pants start to feel threadbare.

ADDRESSES

We've provided the fullest addresses possible for hotels, restaurants, and sights. Many of Ireland's villages and towns are so tiny they barely have street names, much less house numbers. If you're having trouble finding your destination, ask for directions—you're bound to get a hospitable response.

AIRPORTS

The major gateways to Ireland are Dublin Airport (DUB) on the east coast, 10 km (6 mi) north of the city center, and Shannon Airport (SNN) on the west coast, 25 km (16 mi) west of Limerick. Two airports serve Belfast: Belfast International Airport (BFS) at Aldergrove, 24 km (15 mi) from the city, handles local and U.K. flights, as well as all other international traffic; Belfast City Airport (BHD), 6½ km (4 mi) from the city, handles local and U.K. flights only. In addition, the City of Derry Airport (LDY) receives flights from Dublin and Manchester, Liverpool, East Midlands, and Glasgow in the United Kingdom.

Airports **Airline and Airport Links.com** ⊕ www.airlineandairportlinks.com has links to many of the world's airlines and airports. **Belfast City Airport** ☏ 028/9045-7745 ⊕ www.belfastcityairport.com. **Belfast International Airport at Aldergrove** ☏ 028/9448-4848 ⊕ www.belfastairport.com. **City of Derry Airport** ☏ 028/7181-0784 ⊕ www.cityofderryairport.com. **Dublin Airport** ☏ 01/814-1111 ⊕ www.dublinairport.ie. **Shannon Airport** ☏ 061/712-000 ⊕ www.shannonairport.com.

Airport Security Issues **Transportation Security Agency** ⊕ www.tsa.gov/public has answers for almost every question that might come up.

DUTY-FREE SHOPPING

Duty-free shopping isn't available for people traveling between European Union (EU) countries, and you can no longer buy duty-free goods aboard many international Aer Lingus flights. If you like to shop and you're on one of these flights, stock up on goods at the airport before boarding. For duty-free allowances when entering Ireland from a non-EU country, *see* Customs & Duties.

AIR TRAVEL

From North America and the United Kingdom, Aer Lingus, the national flag carrier, has the most direct flights to Ireland.

Flying into Ireland involves few hassles, although an increase in traffic in the last decade has caused a slight increase in flight delays and time spent waiting for baggage to clear customs. Flights within Ireland tend to be filled with business travelers. The lack of competition on internal routes coupled with the country's relatively small size make train and car travel more affordable options.

Flying time to Ireland is 6½ hours from New York, 7½ hours from Chicago, 10 hours from Los Angeles, and 1 hour from London.

CARRIERS

Aer Lingus operates regularly scheduled flights to Shannon and Dublin from New York's JFK (John F. Kennedy Airport), Boston's Logan, Chicago's O'Hare, and LAX (Los Angeles International Airport). Delta has a daily departure from New York's JFK that flies first to Shannon and then to Dublin. Continental flies daily direct to Dublin and Shannon, departing from Newark Liberty International Airport in New Jersey. With the exception of special offers, the prices of the three airlines tend to be similar.

London to Dublin is one of the world's busiest international air routes. Aer Lingus, British Airways, British Midlands, and CityJet all have several daily flights. Ryanair—famous for its cheap, no-frills service—offers several daily flights from London Gatwick, Luton, and Stansted airports. With such healthy competition, bar-

gains abound. British Airways, British Midlands, and low-cost airline EasyJet offer regularly scheduled flights to Belfast from London Gatwick, Luton, and Stansted airports.

Aer Lingus provides service within Ireland to Dublin, Cork, Galway, Kerry, and Shannon. Aer Arann Express flies from Dublin to Cork, Derry, Donegal, Galway, Knock, and Sligo. British Airways has daily service between Dublin and Derry.

🛫 **Aer Arann Express** ☎ 353/1844-7700 in Republic of Ireland, 0800/587-2324 ⊕ www.aerarannexpress.com. **Aer Lingus** ☎ 800/474-7424 ⊕ www.aerlingus.com. **British Airways** ☎ 800/147-9297 ⊕ www.britishairways.com. **British Midlands** ⊕ www.flybmi.com. **CityJet** ⊕ www.cityjet.com. **Continental Airlines** ☎ 800/523-3273 for U.S. and Mexico reservations, 800/231-0856 for international reservations ⊕ www.continental.com. **Delta Airlines** ☎ 800/221-1212 for U.S. reservations, 800/241-4141 for international reservations ⊕ www.delta.com. **EasyJet** ⊕ www.easyjet.com **Ryanair** ⊕ www.ryanair.com.

CHECK-IN & BOARDING

Double-check your flight times, especially if you made your reservations far in advance. Airlines change their schedules, and alerts may not reach you. Always **bring a government-issued photo ID to the airport** (even when it's not required, a passport is best), and **arrive when you need to and not before.** Check in usually at least an hour before domestic flights and two to three hours for international flights. But many airlines have more stringent advance check-in requirements at some busy airports. The TSA estimates the waiting time for security at most major airports and publishes the information on its Web site. Note that if you aren't at the gate at least 10 minutes before your flight is scheduled to take off (sometimes earlier), you won't be allowed to board.

Don't stand in a line if you don't have to. Buy an e-ticket, check in at an electronic kiosk, or—even better—check in on your airline's Web site before you leave home. If you don't need to check luggage, you could bypass all but the security lines. These days, most domestic airline tickets are electronic; international tickets may be either electronic or paper.

You usually pay a surcharge (generally at least $25) to get a paper ticket, and its sole advantage is that it may be easier to endorse over to another airline if your flight is canceled and the airline with which you booked can't accommodate you on another flight. With an e-ticket, the only thing you receive is an e-mailed receipt citing your itinerary and reservation and ticket numbers. Be sure to carry this with you as you'll need it to get past security. If you lose your receipt, though, you can simply print out another copy or ask the airline to do it for you at check-in.

During busy travel seasons and around holiday periods, if a flight is oversold, the gate agent will usually ask for volunteers and will offer some sort of compensation if you're willing to take a different flight. **Know your rights.** If you're bumped from a flight *involuntarily*, the airline must give you some kind of compensation if an alternate flight can't be found within one hour. If your flight is delayed because of something within the airline's control (so bad weather doesn't count), then the airline has a responsibility to get you to your destination on the same day, even if they have to book you on another airline and in an upgraded class if necessary. Read your airline's Contract of Carriage; it's usually buried somewhere on the airline's Web site.

Be prepared to quickly adjust your plans by programming a few numbers into your cell: your airline, an airport hotel or two, your destination hotel, your car service, and/or your travel agent. Bring snacks and sufficient diversions, and you'll be covered if you get stuck in the airport, on the tarmac, or even in the air during turbulence.

Checking in and boarding an outbound plane tends to be civilized. Security is professional but not overbearing, and airport staffers are usually helpful and patient. In the busy summer season lines can get long, and you should play it safe and arrive a couple hours before your flight.

CUTTING COSTS

Increasingly, airlines are quoting prices for one-way fares. Be sure to read the fine print to see if taxes are included or if there's a booking charge. The least expensive tickets must usually be purchased in advance. Airlines generally allow you to change your return date for a fee; most low-fare tickets, however, are nonrefundable. It's always good to **comparison shop.** Web sites (aka consolidators) and travel agents can have different arrangements with the airlines and offer different prices for exactly the same flight and day. Certain Web sites have tracking features that will e-mail you immediately when good deals are posted. Other people prefer to stick with one or two frequent-flier programs, racking up free trips and accumulating perks that can make trips easier. On some airlines, perks include a special reservations number, early boarding, access to upgrades, and more roomy economy-class seating.

Check early and often. Start looking for cheap fares up to a year in advance, and keep looking until you see something you can live with; you never know when a good deal may pop up. That said, **jump on the good deals.** Waiting even a few minutes might mean paying more. For most people, saving money is more important than flexibility, so the more affordable nonrefundable tickets work. Just remember that you'll pay dearly (often as much as $100) if you must change your travel plans. Check on prices for departures at different times of the day and to and from alternate airports, and look for departures on Tuesday, Wednesday, and Thursday, typically the cheapest days to travel. Remember to **weigh your options,** though. A cheaper flight might have a long layover rather than being nonstop, or landing at a secondary airport might substantially increase your ground transportation costs.

Note that many airline Web sites—and most ads—show prices *without* taxes and surcharges. Don't buy until you know the full price. Government taxes add up quickly. Also **watch those ticketing fees.** Surcharges are usually added when you buy your ticket anywhere but on an airline's own Web site. (By the way, that includes on the phone—even if you call the airline directly—and for paper tickets regardless of how you book).

Look into air passes. Many airlines, singly or in collaboration, offer discount air passes that allow foreigners to travel economically in a particular country or region. These visitor passes usually must be reserved and purchased before you leave home. Information about passes often can be found on most airlines' international Web pages, which tend to be aimed at travelers from outside the carrier's home country. Also, try typing the name of the pass into a search engine, or search for "pass" within the carrier's Web site.

Charter carriers, such as Sceptre Charters, offer flights to Dublin and Shannon from various U.S. cities. Air Transat flies from Canada. Note that in certain seasons, usually fall and winter, their charter deals include mandatory hotel and car-rental packages.

🚺 Charters **Air Transat** ☎ 877/872–6728 ⊕ www. airtransat.com. **Sceptre Charters** ☎ 800/221–0924 ⊕ www.sceptreireland.com.

🚺 Online Consolidators **AirlineConsolidator.com** ⊕ www.airlineconsolidator.com, for international tickets. **Best Fares** ⊕ www.bestfares.com; $59.90 annual membership. **Cheap Tickets** ⊕ www. cheaptickets.com. **Expedia** ⊕ www.expedia.com. **Hotwire** ⊕ www.hotwire.com. **lastminute.com** ⊕ www.lastminute.com specializes in last-minute travel; the main site is for the U.K., but it has a link to a U.S. site. **Luxury Link** ⊕ www.luxurylink.com has auctions (surprisingly good deals) as well as offers at the high-end side of travel. **Orbitz** ⊕ www. orbitz.com. **Onetravel.com** ⊕ www.onetravel.com. **Priceline.com** ⊕ www.priceline.com. **Travelocity** ⊕ www.travelocity.com.

ENJOYING THE FLIGHT

Get the seat you want. Avoid those on the aisle directly across from the lavatories. Most frequent fliers say those are even worse than the seats that don't recline (e. g., those in the back row and those in front of a bulkhead). For more legroom, you can request emergency-aisle seats, but only do so if you're capable of moving the 35- to 60-pound airplane exit door—a

Federal Aviation Administration requirement of passengers in these seats. Seats behind a bulkhead also offer more legroom, but they don't have under-seat storage. Often, you can pick a seat when you buy your ticket on an airline's Web site. But it's not always a guarantee, particularly if the airline changes the plane after you book your ticket; check back before you leave. SeatGuru.com has more information about specific seat configurations, which vary by aircraft.

Fewer airlines are providing free food for passengers in economy class. **Don't go hungry.** If you're scheduled to fly during meal times, verify if your airline offers anything to eat; even when it does, be prepared to pay. If you have dietary concerns, request special meals. These can be vegetarian, low-cholesterol, or kosher, for example. It's a good idea to pack some healthful snacks in your carry-on bag.

Ask the airline about its children's menus, activities, and fares. On some lines infants and toddlers fly for free if they sit on a parent's lap, and older children fly for half price in their own seats. Also inquire about policies involving car seats; having one may limit where you can sit. While you're at it, ask about seatbelt extenders for car seats. And note that you can't count on a flight attendant to automatically produce an extender; you may have to inquire about it again when you board.

HOW TO COMPLAIN

If your baggage goes astray or your flight goes awry, complain right away. Most carriers require that you **file a claim immediately.** The Aviation Consumer Protection Division of the Department of Transportation publishes *Fly-Rights*, which discusses airlines and consumer issues and is available online. You can also find articles and information on mytravelrights.com, the Web site of the nonprofit Consumer Travel Rights Center.

🚺 Airline Complaints **Office of Aviation Enforcement and Proceedings** (Aviation Consumer Protection Division) ☎ 202/366–2220 ⊕ airconsumer.ost. dot.gov. **Federal Aviation Administration Consumer Hotline** ☎ 866/835–5322 ⊕ www.faa.gov.

BIKE TRAVEL

Ireland is a cyclist's paradise. The scenery is phenomenal; the roads are flat—with some gently rising hills—and uncrowded; repair and support services are good; and the distance from one village to the next is rarely more than 16 km (10 mi). Most ferries will transport bikes for free. If there's room, Irish buses and Irish Rail will transport them for a small fee. All that said, foul weather and rough roads in remote areas are all too common, so rain gear and spare parts are musts.

Most bike-rental shops offer 18- to 24-gear mountain bikes with index gears and rear carriers for about €20 per day or €80 per week. A refundable deposit of about €80 is often required. For a fee of €20 or so, you can rent a bike at one location and drop it off at another. Book well in advance for travel between May and September, as demand is high and availability is limited. Raleigh Ireland has dealers all over the country who do repairs and rentals.

If you enjoy bird life and sea vistas, try planning a coastal route, perhaps in the southeast. Between Arklow and Wexford it's predominantly flat, with expanses of sandy beaches. The Hook Peninsula between Wexford and Waterford has a network of small, quiet roads, many of them leading to tranquil fishing villages. If you travel from Waterford to Dungarvan via Dunmore East and Tramore, you'll see a variety of scenery combining cliff-top rides with stretches of beachfront.

In the Midlands, level terrain means a less strenuous ride. The twisting roads are generally in good condition, and there are pleasant picnic spots in the many state-owned forests just off the main roads. Bord Fáilte recommends two long tours: one in the Athlone-Mullingar-Roscommon area and another in the Cavan-Monaghan-Mullingar region. Avoid the major trunk roads that bisect the region.

The scenery is truly spectacular in the southwest around Glengarriff, Killarney, and Dingle. The length of the hills—rather than their steepness—is the challenge here, but without the hills there wouldn't be such great views. A less-strenuous option is the coast of West Cork between Kinsale and Glengarriff. The Beara Peninsula is popular for its varied coastal scenery and relative lack of vehicles. Traffic can be a problem in July and August on the Ring of Kerry, where there's a lack of alternative routes to the one main circuit.

🚲 **Bike Maps Discovery Series** ✉ Ordnance Survey, Phoenix Park, Dublin 8 ☎ 01/820-6439 or 01/820-6443.

🚲 **Bike Tours & Rentals Cycleways** ✉ 185-186 Parnell St., Dublin 1 ☎ 01/873-4748 ⊕ www.cycleways.com. **Irish Cycling Safaris** ✉ Belfield Bike Shop, Belfield House, University College, Dublin 4 ☎ 01/260-0749 ⊕ www.cyclingsafaris.com. **Raleigh Ireland** ✉ Raleigh House, Kylemore Rd., Dublin ☎ 01/626-1333. **VBT (Vermont Biking Tours)** ✉ 614 Monkton Rd., Bristol, VT 05443 ☎ 800/245-3868 ⊕ www.vbt.com.

BOAT & FERRY TRAVEL

TO & FROM IRELAND

The ferry is a convenient way to travel between Ireland and elsewhere in Europe, particularly the United Kingdom. There are six main ferry ports to Ireland; four in the republic at Dublin Port, Dun Laoghaire, Rosslare, and Cork, and two in Northern Ireland at Belfast and Larne. The cost of your trip can vary substantially, so spend time with a travel agent and compare prices carefully. Bear in mind, too, that flying can be cheaper, so look into all types of transportation before booking.

Irish Ferries operates the *Ulysses*, the world's largest car ferry, on its Dublin to Holyhead, Wales, route (3 hrs, 15 min); there's also a swift service (1 hr, 50 min) between these two ports. There are several trips daily. The company also runs between Rosslare and Pembroke, Wales (3 hrs, 45 min), and has service to France. Stena Line sails several times a day between Dublin and Holyhead (3 hrs, 15 min) and has swift service to Dun Laoghaire (1 hr, 40 min). The company also runs a fast craft (1 hr, 45 min) and a superferry (3 hrs, 15 min) between Belfast and Stranraer, Scotland, as well as a fast craft (1 hr, 40 min) and a superferry (3 hrs, 30 min) between Rosslare and Fishguard, Wales. There are several trips daily on both routes.

Norfolk Line offers a Dublin and Belfast to Liverpool service (8 hrs). P&O Irish Sea vessels run between Larne and Troon, Scotland (4 hrs), a couple times a day. The company also sails from Dublin to Liverpool twice daily (7 hrs) with a choice of daytime or overnight sailings. Swansea Cork Ferries travels between Swansea and Cork from mid-March to early November. The crossing takes 10 hours, but easy access by road to both ports makes this longer sea route a good choice for motorists.

WITHIN IRELAND

A 10-minute car ferry crosses the River Suir between Ballyhack in County Wexford and Passage East (near Arthurstown) in County Waterford, introducing you to two pretty fishing villages. The ferry operates continuously during daylight hours and costs €5.70 per car, (€8.25 round-trip)€1.20 for foot passengers. A boat from Tarbert in County Kerry leaves every hour on the half hour for Killimer in County Clare; return ferries leave Killimer every hour on the hour. The 30-minute journey across the Shannon Estuary costs €15 per car, (€25 round-trip), €4 for foot passengers. The scenic Cork Harbor crossing allows those traveling from West Cork or Kinsale to Cobh and the east coast to bypass the city center. The five-minute car ferry runs from Glenbrook (near Ringaskiddy) in the west to Carrigaloe (near Cobh) in the east and operates continuously from 7:15 AM to 12:45 AM daily. It costs €5.50 per car, €1 for foot passengers.

There are regular services to the Aran Islands from Galway City, Rossaveal in County Galway, and Doolin in County Clare. Ferries also sail to Inishbofin off the Galway coast and Arranmore off the Donegal coast, and to Bere, Sherkin, and Cape Clear Islands off the coast of County Cork. Bere has a car ferry, but the other islands are all small enough to explore on foot, so the ferries are for foot passengers and bicycles only. Other islands—the Blaskets and the Skelligs in Kerry, Rathlin in Antrim, and Tory, off

the Donegal coast—can be reached by private arrangements with local boatmen. Some are seasonal, and it's best to check with the nearest Tourist Information Office near the time of your visit, or see www.ireland.ie. In Northern Ireland in County Down a 10-minute ferry will take pedestrians and cars from Strangford to Portaferry on the Ards Peninsula. This ferry runs every half hour. It costs £1.80 for passengers and £8.50 per car.

Boating the Shannon River system is an appealing alternative to traveling overland. In some places bicycles can be rented so you can drop anchor and explore.

FARES & SCHEDULES

You can get schedules and purchase tickets, with a credit card if you like, directly from the ferry lines. You can also pick up tickets at Dublin tourism offices and at any major travel agent in Ireland or the United Kingdom. Payment must be made in the currency of the country of the port of departure. Bad weather can delay or cancel ferry sailings so it's always a good idea to call before departing for the port.
🛈 **Ferry Information Irish Ferries** ☎ 1890/313131 in Ireland, 08705/171717 in U.K., 0143/944694 in France ⊕ www.irishferries.com. **Norfolk Line** ☎ 01/819-2999 in Ireland, 0870/600-4321 in U.K. ⊕ www.norfolkline-ferries.co.uk/en/is-passenger. **P&O Irish Sea** ☎ 1800/409049 in Ireland, 0870/2424777 in U.K. ⊕ www.poirishsea.com. **Stena Line** ☎ 01/204-7777 in Ireland, 028/9074-7747 in Northern Ireland, 08705/707070 in U.K. ⊕ www.stenaline.co.uk. **Swansea Cork Ferries** ☎ 021/483-6000 in Ireland, 01792/456116 in U.K. ⊕ www.swanseacorkferries.com.
🛈 **Boat Travel on the Shannon Ireland Line Cruisers** ✉ Killaloe ☎ 061/375-011. **Riversdale Barge Holidays** ✉ Ballinamore ☎ 078/44122. **Shannon Castle Line** ✉ Williamstown Harbor, Whitegate ☎ 061/927-042. **Silver Line Cruisers** ✉ The Marina, Banagher ☎ 0509/51112 ⊕ www.silverlinecruisers.com. **Waveline Cruisers** ✉ Quigley's Marina, Killinure Point, Glassan ☎ 0902/85711 ⊕ www.waveline.ie.

BUSINESS HOURS

Business hours are 9–5, sometimes later in the larger towns. In smaller towns, stores often close from 1 to 2 for lunch. If a holiday falls on a weekend, most businesses are closed on Monday.

BANKS & OFFICES

Banks are open 10–4 weekdays. In small towns banks may close from 12:30 to 1:30. They remain open until 5 one afternoon per week; the day varies, although it's usually Thursday. Post offices are open weekdays 9–5 and Saturday 9–1; some of the smaller branches close for lunch.

In Northern Ireland bank hours are weekdays 9:30–4:30. Post offices are open weekdays 9–5:30, Saturday 9–1. Some close for an hour at lunch 1–2.

GAS STATIONS

There are some 24-hour gas stations along the highways; otherwise, hours vary from morning rush hour to late evenings.

MUSEUMS & SIGHTS

Museums and sights are generally open Tuesday–Saturday 10–5 and Sunday 2–5.

PHARMACIES

Most pharmacies are open Monday–Saturday 9–5:30 or 6. Larger towns and cities often have 24-hour establishments.

SHOPS

Most shops are open Monday–Saturday 9–5:30 or 6. Once a week—normally Wednesday, Thursday, or Saturday—shops close at 1 PM. These times do *not* apply to Dublin, where stores generally stay open later, and they can vary from region to region, so it's best to check locally. Larger malls usually stay open late once a week—generally until 9 on Thursday or Friday. Convenience stores and gas stations in both Dublin and rural Ireland are generally open until 8 or 9 PM.

Shops in Belfast are open weekdays 9–5:30, with a late closing on Thursday, usually at 9. Elsewhere in Northern Ireland, shops close for the afternoon once a week, usually Wednesday or Thursday. In addition, most smaller shops close for an hour or so at lunch.

BUS TRAVEL

In the Republic of Ireland, long-distance bus services are operated by Bus Éireann, which also provides local service in Cork,

Galway, Limerick, and Waterford. There's only one class, and prices are similar for all seats. Note, though, that outside of the peak season, services are limited; some routes (e.g., Killarney–Dingle) disappear altogether. There's often only one trip a day on express routes, and one a week to some remote villages. Rural bus services shut down at around 7 or 8 PM. To ensure that a bus journey is feasible, buy a copy of Bus Éireann's timetable—€1.50 from any bus terminal—or check online. Many of the destination indicators are in Irish (Gaelic), so make sure you get on the right bus.

Numerous bus companies run between Britain and the Irish Republic, but be ready for long hours on the road and possible delays. All use either the Holyhead–Dublin or Fishguard/Pembroke–Rosslare ferry routes. National Express, a consortium of companies, has services from all major British cities to more than 90 Irish destinations. Buses are cheap but slow: the journey from London to Galway takes around 17 hours.

In Northern Ireland, all buses are operated by the state-owned Ulsterbus. Service is generally good, with particularly useful links to those towns not served by train. Ulsterbus also offers tours. Buses to Belfast run from London and from Birmingham, making the Stranraer–Port of Belfast crossing. Contact National Express.

RESERVATIONS & PAYING

Check with the bus office to see if reservations are accepted for your route; if not, show up early to get a seat. Note: prepaid tickets don't apply to a particular bus time, just a route, so if one vehicle is full you can try another. You can buy tickets online, or at the main tourist offices, at the bus station, or on the bus (though it's cash only for the latter option). A return fare from Dublin to Cork costs €26 and Dublin to Galway return is €17.

You can save money by buying a multiday pass, some of which can be combined with rail service. There are also cost-cutting passes that will give access to travel in both Northern Ireland and the Republic of Ireland. A Freedom of Northern Ireland ticket costs £47 for seven days' unlimited bus and rail travel—a really good deal when you consider that a one-day ticket costs £13. In the Republic, passes include the Irish Explorer Rail and Bus Pass, which gives you eight days' bus travel out of 15 consecutive days for €194. The bus-only Irish Rover Card costs €158 for eight days' travel out of 15 consecutive days across both Northern Ireland and the Republic. The Emerald Card is valid for both bus and rail in Northern Ireland and the Republic, and costs €228 for eight days travel out of 15 consecutive days. Contact Bus Éireann or Ulsterbus for details.

🚍 **Bus Information Bus Éireann** ☎ 01/836-6111 in Republic of Ireland ⊕ www.buseireann.ie. **National Express** ☎ 08705/808-080 in U.K. ⊕ www.nationalexpress.co.uk. **Ulsterbus** ☎ 028/9033-3000 in Northern Ireland ⊕ www.ulsterbus.co.uk.

CAMERAS & PHOTOGRAPHY

Nature has blessed Ireland with spectacular landscapes. In addition to cliffs, hills, and beaches, sunsets along the north and west coasts can be particularly dramatic because of the variable cloud cover and the clarity of light. Take a step outside at dusk during your visit wherever you may be and see if you can catch a sunset. The *Kodak Guide to Shooting Great Travel Pictures* (available at bookstores everywhere) is loaded with tips.

🚍 **Photo Help Kodak Information Center** ⊕ www.kodak.com.

EQUIPMENT PRECAUTIONS

Don't pack film or equipment in checked luggage, where it is much more susceptible to damage. X-ray machines used to view checked luggage are extremely powerful and therefore are likely to ruin your film. Try to ask for hand inspection of film, which becomes clouded after repeated exposure to airport X-ray machines, and keep videotapes and computer disks away from metal detectors. Always keep film, tape, and computer disks out of the sun. Carry an extra supply of batteries, and be prepared to turn on your camera, camcorder, or laptop to prove to airport security personnel that the device is real.

FILM & DEVELOPING

Major brands of film are available throughout Ireland, although there's no 24-hour developing available. Advantix film and developing are available in larger centers. A roll of 36-exposure color film costs €6–€8. Many film processors are also able to make prints from digital cameras or transfer your digital photos to a CD.

VIDEOS

Videotape is widely available. The local tape standard is PAL, and a standard 180-minute cassette costs around €5.

CAR RENTAL

Request car seats and extras such as GPS when you book, and make sure that a confirmed reservation guarantees you a car. Agencies sometimes overbook, particularly for busy weekends and holiday periods. Rates are sometimes—but not always—better if you book in advance or reserve through a rental agency's Web site. There are other reasons to book ahead, though: for popular destinations, during busy times of the year, or to ensure that you get a certain type of car (vans, SUVs, exotic sports cars).

If you're renting a car in the Irish Republic and intend to visit Northern Ireland (or vice versa), make this clear when you get your car, and check that the rental insurance applies when you cross the border.

Renting a car in Ireland is far more expensive than organizing a rental before you leave home. Rates in Dublin for an economy car with a manual transmission and unlimited mileage are from €35 a day and €160 a week to €50 a day and €190 a week, depending on the season. This includes the republic's 12.5% tax on car rentals. Rates in Belfast begin at £25 a day and £130 a week including the 17.5% tax on car rentals in the North.

Both manual and automatic transmissions are readily available, though automatics cost extra. Typical economy car models include Volkswagen Polo, Ford Fiesta, Toyota Yaris, and Nissan Micra. Minivans, luxury cars (Mercedes or Alfa Romeos), and four-wheel-drive vehicles (say, a Jeep

Cherokee) are also options, but the daily rates are high. Argus Rent A Car and Dan Dooley have convenient locations at Dublin, Shannon, Belfast, and Belfast City airports as well as at ferry ports.

Most rental companies require you to be over 24 to rent a car in Ireland (a few will rent to those over 21) and to have had a license for more than a year. Some companies refuse to rent to visitors over 74. Children under 12 years of age aren't allowed to ride in the front seat unless they're in a properly fitted child seat.

CUTTING COSTS

Really weigh your options. Find out if a credit card you carry or organization or frequent-renter program to which you belong has a discount program. And check that such discounts really are the best deal. You can often do better with special weekend or weekly rates offered by a rental agency. (And even if you only want to rent for five or six days, ask if you can get the weekly rate; it may very well be cheaper than the daily rate for that period of time.)

Price local car-rental companies as well as the majors. Also investigate wholesalers, which don't own fleets but rent in bulk from those that do and often offer better rates (note you must usually pay for such rentals before leaving home). Consider adding a car rental onto your air/hotel vacation package; the cost will often be cheaper than if you had rented the car separately on your own.

When traveling abroad, **look for guaranteed exchange rates,** which protect you against a falling dollar. With your rate locked in, you won't pay more, even if the price goes up in the local currency. (Note to self: not the best thing if the dollar is surging rather than plunging.)

Beware of hidden charges. Those great rental rates may not be so great when you add in taxes, surcharges, cancellation penalties, taxes, drop-off charges (if you're planning to pick up the car in one city and leave it in another), and surcharges (for being under or over a certain age, for additional drivers, or for driving over state or country borders or out of a specific radius from your point of rental).

Note that airport rental offices often add supplementary surcharges that you may avoid by renting from an agency whose office is just off airport property. Don't buy the tank of gas that's in the car when you rent it unless you plan to do a lot of driving. Avoid hefty refueling fees by filling the tank at a station well away from the rental agency (those nearby are often more expensive) just before you turn in the car.

🚗 Major Agencies **Alamo** ☎ 800/522-9696 in U.S., 1800/301401 in Ireland, 01/260-3771 in Dublin ⊕ www.alamo.com. **Avis** ☎ 800/331-1084 in U.S., 1890/405060 in Ireland, 01/605-7500 in Dublin ⊕ www.avis.com. **Budget** ☎ 800/472-3325 in U.S., 1850/575767 in Ireland ⊕ www.budget.com. **Dollar** ☎ 800/800-6000 in U.S., 01/670-7890 in Dublin ⊕ www.dollar.com. **Hertz** ☎ 800/654-3001 in U.S., 01/676-7476 in Ireland ⊕ www.hertz.com. **National Car Rental** ☎ 800/227-3876 in U.S., 01/844-4162 in Dublin, 1800/301401 in Ireland ⊕ www.nationalcar.com.

🚗 Local Agencies **Argus** ☎ 01/490-4444 in Dublin, 048/9442-3444 in Belfast ⊕ www.argus-rentacar.com. **Dooley** Car Rentals ☎ 800/331-9301 in U.S., 0800/282189 in U.K., 062/53103 in Ireland ⊕ www.dan-dooley.ie.

🚗 Wholesalers **Auto Europe** ☎ 888/223-5555 ⊕ www.autoeurope.com. **Eurovacations** ☎ 877/471-3876 ⊕ www.eurovacations.com. **Europe by Car** ☎ 212/581-3040 in New York, 800/223-1516 ⊕ www.europebycar.com. **Kemwel** ☎ 877/820-0668 ⊕ www.kemwel.com.

INSURANCE

Everyone who rents a car wonders about whether the insurance that the rental companies offer is worth the expense. No one—not even us—has a simple answer. This is particularly true abroad, where laws are different than at home.

If you own a car, your personal auto insurance may cover a rental to some degree, though not all policies protect you abroad; always read your policy's fine print. If you don't have auto insurance, then seriously consider buying the collision- or loss-damage waiver (CDW or LDW) from the car-rental company, which eliminates your liability for damage to the car. Some credit cards offer CDW coverage, but it's usually supplemental to your own insurance and rarely covers SUVs, minivans, luxury models, and the like. If your coverage is secondary, you may still be liable for loss-of-use costs from the car-rental company. But no credit-card insurance is valid unless you use that card for *all* transations, from reserving to paying the final bill. All companies exclude car rental in some countries, so be sure to find out about the destination to which you are traveling.

Some countries require you to purchase CDW coverage or require car-rental companies to include it in quoted rates. Ask your rental company about issues like these in your destination. In most cases, it's cheaper to add a supplemental CDW plan to your comprehensive travel insurance policy than to purchase it from a rental company. That said, you don't want to pay for a supplement if you're required to buy insurance from the rental company.

Note that you can decline the insurance from the rental company and purchase it through a third-party provider such as Travel Guard (www.travelguard.com)—$9 per day for $35,000 of coverage. That's sometimes just under half the price of the CDW offered by some car-rental companies. Also, Diner's Club offers primary CDW coverage on all rentals reserved and paid for with the card. This means that Diner's Club's company—not your own car insurance—pays in case of an accident. It *doesn't* mean your car-insurance company won't raise your rates once it discovers you had an accident.

SURCHARGES

Drivers between the ages of 24 and 26, and 70 and 74 will probably be subject to an insurance surcharge—if they're allowed to drive a rental car at all. An additional driver will add about €5 a day to your car rental, and a child seat costs about €20 for the rental and will require 24-hour advance notice.

CAR TRAVEL

U.S. driver's licences are recognized in Ireland.

Roads in the Irish Republic are generally good, though four-lane highways, or motorways, are the exception rather than the rule. In addition, many roads twist and wind their way up and down hills and through towns, which can slow you down. On small, rural roads, **watch out for cattle and sheep**; they may be just around the next bend. Reckless drivers are also a problem in the countryside, so remain cautious and alert. Ireland ranks third worst among the original 15 EU countries on road accident frequency and has the highest auto accident fatality rate in Europe.

Road signs in the republic are generally in both Irish (Gaelic) and English; in Dingle, the northwest and Connemara, most are in Irish only, so get a good road map. On the new green signposts distances are in kilometers; on the old white signposts they're in miles, but recent legislation means the green signposts are here to stay. Knowing the name of the next town on your itinerary is more important than knowing the route number: neither the small local signposts nor the local people refer to roads by official numbers. Traffic signs are the same as in the rest of Europe, and roadway markings are standard.

There are no border checkpoints between the republic and Northern Ireland, where the road network is excellent and, outside Belfast, uncrowded. Road signs and traffic regulations conform to the British system.

All ferries on both principal routes to the Irish Republic take cars. Fishguard and Pembroke are relatively easy to reach by road. The car trip to Holyhead, on the other hand, is sometimes difficult: delays on the A55 North Wales coastal road aren't unusual. Car ferries to Belfast leave from the Scottish port of Stranraer and the English city of Liverpool; those to Larne leave from Stranraer and Cairnryan. Speed limits are generally 95 to 100 kph (roughly 60 to 70 mph) on the motorways, 80 kph (50 mph) on other roads, and 50 kph (30 mph) in towns.

EMERGENCY SERVICES

Membership in an emergency car service is a good idea if you're using your own vehicle in Ireland. The Automobile Association of Ireland is a sister organization of its English counterpart and is highly recommended. Note that the AA can only help you or your vehicle if you are a member of the association. If not, contact your car-rental company for assistance. If involved in an accident you should note the details of the vehicle and the driver and witnesses and report the incident to a member of the Garda Síochána (the Irish Police) or the Police Service of Northern Ireland (PSNI) as soon as possible. Since traffic congestion is chronic in Dublin, emergency services are more likely to be dispatched quickly to help you and to clear the road. If your car does break down, if at all possible try to stop it in a well-lighted area near a public phone. If you're on a secondary or minor road, remain in your car with the doors locked after you call for assistance. If you break down on the motorway, you should pull onto the hard shoulder and stay out of your car with the passenger side door open and the other doors locked. This will allow you to jump into the car quickly if you sense any trouble. Make sure you check credentials of anyone who offers assistance—note the license-plate number and color of the assisting vehicle before you step out of the car.

🚗 **Automobile Association of Ireland** ☎ 01/617–9999 in Ireland, 0800/887766 in Northern Ireland, 08457/887766 from cell phone in Northern Ireland ⊕ www.aaireland.ie in Ireland, www.theaa.com in Northern Ireland. **Police** ☎ 999.

GASOLINE

You can find gas stations along most roads. Self-service is the norm. Major credit cards and traveler's checks are usually accepted. Prices are near the lower end for Europe, with unleaded gas priced around €1.10 in Ireland and £0.90 a liter in Northern Ireland—more than three times what gasoline costs in the United States. Prices vary significantly from station to station, so it's worth driving around the block.

ROAD CONDITIONS

Most roads are paved and make for easy travel. Roads are classified as M, N, or R: those designated with an M for "motorway" are double-lane divided highways

with paved shoulders; N, or national, routes are generally undivided highways with shoulders; and R, or regional, roads tend to be narrow and twisty.

Rush hour traffic in Dublin, Cork, Limerick, Belfast, and Galway can be intense. Rush hours in Dublin run 7 AM to 9:30 AM and 5 PM to 7 PM; special events such as football (soccer) games will also tie up traffic in and around the city as will heavy rain.

RULES OF THE ROAD

The Irish, like the British, **drive on the left-hand side of the road.** Safety belts must be worn by the driver and all passengers, and children under 12 must travel in the back unless riding in a car seat. It's compulsory for motorcyclists and their passengers to wear helmets. Speed limits in Ireland are posted in kilometers per hour and in Northern Ireland in miles per hour, so if crossing the border be sure to make the adjustment.

Drunk-driving laws are strict. The legal limit is 80 mg of alcohol per 100 ml of blood. Ireland has a Breathalyzer test, which the police can administer anytime. If you refuse to take it, the odds are you'll be prosecuted anyway. As always, the best advice is **don't drink if you plan to drive.**

Speed cameras and radar are used throughout Ireland. Speeding carries an on-the-spot fine of €80 and if the Gardaí (police) charges you with excessive speeding you could be summoned to court. This carries a much higher fine and you will be summoned within six months (meaning you could be required to return to Ireland).

Note that a continuous white line down the center of the road prohibits passing. Barred markings on the road and flashing yellow beacons indicate a crossing, where pedestrians have right of way. At a junction of two roads of equal importance, the driver to the right has right of way. On a roundabout, vehicles approaching from the right have right of way. Also, remember there are no right turns permitted on a red light. If another motorist flashes their headlights at you they are not warning of a speed trap ahead, they are giving you right of way.

Despite the relatively light traffic, parking in towns can be a problem. Signs with the letter *P* indicate that parking is permitted; a stroke through the *P* warns you to stay away or you'll be liable for a fine of €20–€65; however, if your car gets towed away or clamped, the fine is around €180. In Dublin and Cork, parking lots are your best bet, but check the rate first in Dublin; they vary wildly.

In Northern Ireland there are plenty of parking lots in the towns (usually free except in Belfast), and you should use them. In Belfast, you can't park your car in some parts of the city center, more because of congestion than security problems.

COMPUTERS ON THE ROAD

If you're traveling with a laptop, carry a spare battery and adapter. Most laptops will work at both 120V and 220V, but you will need an adapter so the plug will fit in the socket. In the countryside, a surge protector is a good idea.

Going online is becoming routine in Dublin, thanks, in part, to the Wi-Fi hot spots—which allow you to make a wireless connection from your laptop onto a network—popping up across the city. Nethouse has the most Internet cafés in the country, with nine locations in Dublin and one in Cork. There are also many independent Internet cafés across the country. Prices vary from the low end in Dublin of €2.60 per hour to €5 per hour in smaller cities. There are also new Wi-Fi hot spots in other major cities throughout the country, such as the Insomnia Coffee and Sandwich Bar chain in Galway. Dublin Airport and Dun Laoghaire Harbor have facilities to access wireless connection to the Internet. Hotels in Dublin that offer Wi-Fi access include the Conrad and the Four Seasons. A Wi-Fi connection will cost about €9 for an hour or €22 for unlimited access within a 24-hour period.

CUSTOMS & DUTIES

You're always allowed to bring goods of a certain value back home without having to pay any duty or import tax. There's also a limit on the amount of tobacco and liquor you can bring back duty-free, and some countries have separate limits for perfumes; for exact figures, check with your customs department. The values of so-called "duty-free" goods are included in these amounts. When you shop abroad, save all your receipts as customs inspectors may ask to see them as well as the items you purchased. If the total value of your goods is more than the duty-free limit, then you'll have to pay a tax (most often a flat percentage) on the value of everything beyond that limit.

Duty-free allowances have been abolished for those traveling between countries in the EU. For goods purchased outside the EU, you may import duty-free: (1) 200 cigarettes or 100 cigarillos or 50 cigars or 250 grams of smoking tobacco; (2) 2 liters of wine, and either 1 liter of alcoholic drink over 22% volume or 2 liters of alcoholic drink under 22% volume (sparkling or fortified wine included); (3) 50 grams (60 ml) of perfume and ¼ liter of eau de toilette and (4) other goods (including beer) to a value of €175 per person (€90 per person for travelers under 15 years of age).

Goods that cannot be freely imported to the Irish Republic include firearms, ammunition, explosives, indecent or obscene books and pictures, oral smokeless tobacco products, meat and meat products, poultry and poultry products. Plants and plant products (including shrubs, vegetables, fruit, bulbs, and seeds) can be imported from other countries within the EU only, provided they are eligible under the EU's plant passport scheme. Domestic cats and dogs from outside the United Kingdom and live animals from outside Northern Ireland must be quarantined for six months, unless they are traveling under the EU's Pet Travel Scheme.

🔝 Information in Ireland **Customs and Excise** ✉ Irish Life Building, 2nd fl., Middle Abbey St., Dublin 1 ☎ 01/878-8811 ⊕ www.revenue.ie. **HM Customs and Excise** ✉ Portcullis House, 21 Cowbridge Rd. E, Cardiff CF11 9SS ☎ 0845/010-9000 or 0208/929-0152, 0208/929-6731 or 0208/910-3602 complaints ⊕ www.hmce.gov.uk.

For details of the **Pet Travel Scheme** see ⊕ www.
agriculture.gov.ie ⊕ www.irishanimals.ie.
🔳 **U.S. Information U.S. Customs and Border
Protection** ⊕ www.cbp.gov.

DISCOUNTS & DEALS

Be sure to take advantage of the Irish
state's Heritage Service Heritage Card,
which gives you access to 65 Heritage sites
for €20 (the family pass is €50). Cards
are sold in Ireland at all Heritage Service
sites and online.

Visitor Services (⊠ Office of Public Works,
6 Upper Ely Pl., Dublin 2 ☎ 01/674–6000
🖷 01/661–6764 ⊕ www.heritageireland.
ie).

ELECTRICITY

Consider making a small investment in a
universal adapter, which has several types
of plugs in one lightweight, compact unit.
Most laptops and mobile phone chargers
are dual voltage (i.e., they operate equally
well on 110 and 220 volts) and so require
only an adapter. These days the same is
true more of small appliances such as hair
dryers. Always check labels and manufac-
turer instructions to be sure, though.
Don't use 110-volt outlets marked FOR
SHAVERS ONLY for high-wattage appliances
such as hair dryers.

The current in Ireland is 220 volts, 50 cycles alternating current (AC); wall outlets
take plugs with three prongs.
🔳 **Steve Kropla's Help for World Travelers**
⊕ www.kropla.com has information on electrical
and telephone plugs around the world. **Walkabout
Travel Gear** ⊕ www.walkabouttravelgear.com has a
good discussion about electricity under "adapters."

EMERGENCIES

The police force in the Republic of Ireland
is called the Garda Síochána ("Guardians
of the Peace," in English), usually referred
to as the Gardaí (pronounced gar-dee).
The force is unarmed and is headed by a
government-appointed commissioner, who
is answerable to the Minister for Justice,
who in turn is accountable to the Dáil (the
Irish legislature). Easily identified by their
fluorescent yellow blazers in winter, or, if
weather permits in summer, by a dark blue
shirt and peaked cap, the Gardaí are gen-

erally very helpful. They, and all other
emergency forces, can be contacted
through one phone number: 999. Wherever you are, this number will connect you
with local police, ambulance, and fire services. You can expect a prompt response
to your call. The Garda Síochána Web site
provides contact information for local stations. In Northern Ireland the police force
is called the PSNI. They are distinguished
by their dark blue coats and white shirts.
They can be contacted by dialing 999 in
Northern Ireland.
🔳 **United States Embassies** ⊠ 42 Elgin Rd., Ballsbridge, Dublin 4 ☎ 01/668-8777 ⊠ Queen's
House, 14 Queen St., Golden Mile, Belfast BT1 6EQ
☎ 028/9032-8239.
🔳 **General Emergency Contacts Ambulance, fire,
police** ☎ 999. **An Garda Síochána** ⊕ www.garda.
ie. **Police Service of Northern Ireland** ⊕ www.
psni.police.uk.

HOLIDAYS

Irish national holidays in 2007 are as follows: January 1 (New Year's Day); March
17 (St. Patrick's Day); April 6 (Good Friday); April 8 (Easter Monday); May 1
(May Day); June 7 and August 6 (summer
bank holidays); October 29 (autumn bank
holiday); and December 25–26 (Christmas
and St. Stephen's Day). If you plan to visit
at Easter, remember that theaters and cinemas are closed for the last three days of
the preceding week.

In Northern Ireland the following are holidays: January 1 (New Year's Day); March
17 (St. Patrick's Day); April 6 (Good Friday); April 8 (Easter Monday); May 1
(May Day); May 7 (early May bank holiday); May 28 (spring bank holiday); July
12 (Battle of the Boyne); August 27 (summer bank holiday); and December 25–26
(Christmas and Boxing Day).

IRISH LANGUAGE

In the old days, Ireland's native language
was called Gaelic and some people chuck-
led that it was the world's most perfect
medium for prayers, curses, and lovemak-
ing. These days, Gaelic is called Irish and
no one is joking any longer. In March
2005, legislation was passed to restore the
sovereignty of Irish, originally a Celtic lan-

guage related to Scots Gaelic, Breton, and Welsh, as Ireland's official national language. English is technically the second language of the country but it is, in fact, the everyday tongue of 95% of the population. However, the western coastlands of Ireland are still home to the Gaeltacht (pronounced *gale*-taukt). These Irish-speaking communities are found mainly in sparsely populated rural areas along the western seaboard, on some islands, and in pockets in West Cork and County Waterford. Travelers to these western seaboard regions in Counties Donegal and Galway should note that new laws have mandated Irish as the sole language for signage. In these Gaeltacht areas, English is now outlawed in road signs and official maps. As the Associated Press reported, "Locals concede the switch will confuse foreigners in an area that depends heavily on tourism, but they say it's the price of patriotism."

The Gaeltacht includes some big tourist destinations. For instance, if travelers are in Killarney and now wish to go to Dingle, they will have to follow signposts that say "An Daingean," because that is Dingle in Irish. Other instances include: Oileáin Árainn (Aran Islands); Corca Dhuibhne (Dingle Peninsula); and Arainn Mhor (Aranmore Island). As this changeover affects more than 2,000 other place-names, have an updated or Irish-friendly map if touring these Gaeltacht regions. Don't rely on official Ordnance Survey maps, which can now only print Irish place-names in these areas, even in cases where the English versions remain popular in local parlance (many hotels will retain their English names, such as the Dingle Bay Hotel). Main place-names are given in both Irish and English in this guidebook for the affected regions.

Outside these Gaeltacht areas, Ireland remains officially bilingual in its road signs. "This will allow you to get lost in both Irish and English," as Mr. O'Reilly pointed out on Fodor's Web site. With just 55,000 native Irish speakers in a population of 4 million, a major national debate has sprung up (which you can follow if you

Google Irish Placenames Act 2004) and local councils and tourist authorities have begun to protest the new laws. For now, a good touring map will give both Irish and English names to places within the Gaeltacht. And some basic Irish vocabulary certainly wouldn't hurt: *fir* (men) and *mná* (women) should prove useful when inquiring about public restrooms.

LODGING

You should try to sample from Ireland's vast range of accommodations. In Dublin and other cities, boutique hotels combine luxury with contemporary (and often truly Irish) design. Manors and castles offer a unique combination of luxury and history. Less impressive, but equally charming, are the provincial inns and country hotels with simple but adequate facilities. You can meet a wide cross section of Irish people by hopping from one B&B to the next, or you can keep to yourself for a week or two in a thatched cottage. ITB-approved guesthouses and B&Bs display a green shamrock outside and are usually considered more reputable than those without. Hotels and other accommodations in Northern Ireland are similar to those in the Republic of Ireland.

Fáilte Ireland has a grading system and publishes a list of "approved" hotels, guesthouses, B&Bs, farmhouses, hostels, and campgrounds. For each accommodation, the list gives a maximum charge that can't be exceeded without special authorization. Prices must be displayed in every room; if the hotel oversteps its limit, don't hesitate to complain to the hotel manager and/or Fáilte Ireland.

The lodgings we list are the cream of the crop in each price category. We always list the facilities that are available, but we don't specify whether they cost extra; when pricing accommodations, always ask what's included and what costs extra. Lodgings are assigned price categories based on the range from their least-expensive standard double room at high season (excluding holidays) to the most expensive. Lodgings marked ✕▨ are lodgings whose restaurants warrant a special trip.

Did the resort look as good in real life as it did in the photos? Did you sleep like a baby, or were the walls paper thin? Did you get your money's worth? Rate hotels and write your own reviews in Travel Ratings or start a discussion about your favorite places in Travel Talk on www.fodors.com. Yes, you, too, can be a correspondent!

Most hotels and other lodgings require you to give your credit card details before they will confirm your reservation. If you don't feel comfortable e-mailing this information, ask if you can fax it (some places even prefer faxes). However you book, get confirmation in writing and have a copy of it handy when you check in.

Be sure you understand the hotel's cancellation policy. Some places allow you to cancel without any kind of penalty—even if you prepaid to secure a discounted rate—if you cancel at least 24 hours in advance. Others require you to cancel a week in advance or penalize you for the cost of one night. Small inns and B&Bs are most likely to require you to cancel far in advance. Most hotels allow children under a certain age to stay in their parents' room at no extra charge, but others charge for them as extra adults; find out the cutoff age for discounts.

Assume that hotels operate on the European Plan (**EP**, no meals) unless we specify that they use the Breakfast Plan (**BP**, with full breakfast), Continental Plan (**CP**, continental breakfast), Full American Plan (**FAP**, all meals), Modified American Plan (**MAP**, breakfast and dinner) or are **all-inclusive** (all meals and most activities).

CATEGORY	COST*
$$$$	over €230
$$$	€180–€230
$$	€130–€180
$	€80–€130
¢	under €80

*Republic of Ireland: All prices are in euros and are for two people in a double room, including V.A.T. and a service charge (often applied in larger hotels).

CATEGORY	COST*
$$$$	over £160
$$$	£115–£160
$$	£80–£115
$	£50–£80
¢	under £50

*Northern Ireland: All prices are in pounds sterling and are for two people in a double room, including V.A.T. and a service charge (often applied in larger hotels).

APARTMENT & HOUSE RENTALS

At Home Abroad ☎ 212/421-9165 ⊕ www.athomeabroadinc.com. **Barclay International Group** ☎ 516/364-0064 or 800/845-6636 ⊕ www.barclayweb.com. **Drawbridge to Europe** ☎ 541/482-7778 or 888/268-1148 ⊕ www.drawbridgetoeurope.com. **Homes Away** ☎ 416/920-1873 or 800/374-6637 ⊕ www.homesaway.com. **Hometours International** ☎ 865/690-8484 or 866/367-4668 ⊕ thor.he.net/~hometour/. **Interhome** ☎ 305/940-2299 or 800/882-6864 ⊕ www.interhome.us. **Suzanne B. Cohen & Associations** ☎ 207/622-0743 ⊕ www.villaeurope.com. **Vacation Home Rentals Worldwide** ☎ 201/767-9393 or 800/633-3284 ⊕ www.vhrww.com. **Villanet** ☎ 206/417-3444 or 800/964-1891 ⊕ www.rentavilla.com. **Villas & Apartments Abroad** ☎ 212/213-6435 ⊕ www.vaanyc.com. **Villas of Distinction** ☎ 707/778-1800 or 800/289-0900 ⊕ www.villasofdistinction.com. **Villas International** ☎ 415/499-9490 or 800/221-2260 ⊕ www.villasintl.com. **Wimco** ☎ 800/449-1553 ⊕ www.wimco.com.

Local Agents Days Serviced Apartments ☎ 01/639-1100 ⊕ www.apartments-dublin.com. **Board Fáilte** ☎ 01/602-4000 ⊕ www.failteireland.ie.

BED & BREAKFASTS & GUESTHOUSES

B&Bs are classified by Fáilte Ireland as either town homes, country homes, or farmhouses. Many town-and-country B&Bs now have at least one bedroom with a bathroom, but don't expect this as a matter of course. The Irish farms that offer rooms by the week with partial or full board are more likely to be modern bungalows or undistinguished two-story houses than creeper-clad Georgian mansions. Room and part board—breakfast and an evening meal—starts at €255 per week. Many travelers don't bother booking a B&B in advance. They are so plentiful in rural areas that it's often more fun to leave the decision open, allowing yourself a choice of final destinations for the night. However, if you have discerning taste and enjoy meeting a variety of pleasant characters, check out the places listed by Friendly Homes of Ireland. Long weekends are the exception to this rule where B&Bs tend to be booked up far in advance, so keep an eye to the calendar for local holidays.

To qualify as a guesthouse, establishments must have at least five bedrooms. Some guesthouses are above a bar or restaurant; others are part of a home. As a rule, they're cheaper (some include an optional evening meal) and offer fewer amenities than hotels. But often that's where the differences end. Most have high standards of cleanliness and hospitality, and most have a bathroom, a TV, and a direct-dial phone in each room. Premier Guesthouses are generally small inns, run by the owner, and hard to distinguish from hotels.

🚩 Reservation Services **Bed & Breakfast.com** ☎ 512/322-2710 or 800/462-2632 ⊕ www. bedandbreakfast.com also sends out an online newsletter. **Bed & Breakfast Inns Online** ☎ 615/ 868-1946 ⊕ www.bbonline.com. **BnB Finder.com** ☎ 212/432-7693 or 888/469-6663 ⊕ www. bnbfinder.com.

🚩 Local Services **Bed & Breakfast Association of Northern Ireland** ☎ 28/4461-5542. **Irish Farm Holidays** ☎ 61/400-700 ⊕ www.irishfarmholidays. com. **Town & Country Homes Association** ☎ 71/ 982-2222 ⊕ www.townandcountry.ie. **Premier Guesthouses** ☎ 01/205-2826 ⊕ www. premierguesthouses.com. **Friendly Homes of Ireland** ☎ 01/668-6483 ⊕ www.tourismresources.ie.

CAMPING

An abundance of coastal campsites compensates for the shortage of inland ones. Rates start at about €5 per tent, €8 per caravan (RV) overnight.

🚩 **Irish Caravan and Camping Council** ⌂ Box 4443, Dublin 2 ⊕ www.camping-ireland.ie.

COTTAGES

Vacation cottages, which are usually in clusters, are rented by the week. Although often built in the traditional style, most have central heating and all the other modern conveniences. It's essential to reserve in advance.

🚩 Reservations Services **Irish Cottage Holiday Homes Association** ⊠ Bracken Court, Bracken Rd., Sandyford, Dublin 8 ☎ 01/205-2777 ⊕ www. irishcottageholidays.com. **Northern Ireland Self-Catering Holidays Association** ⊠ 63 Somerton Rd., North Belfast, Belfast BT15 4DD ☎ 28/ 9077-6174 ⊕ www.nischa.com.

CASTLES & MANORS

Some of the most magical experiences on an Irish vacation are stays at some of the country's spectacular castle-hotels, such as Dromoland (Newmarket-on-Fergus), Ashford (Cong), and Castle Leslie (Glaslough). For directories to help you get to know the wide array of manor house and castle accommodations, including a goodly number of private country estates and castles, contact Ireland's Blue Book of Country Houses & Restaurants or Elegant Ireland.

🚩 Reservations Services **Elegant Ireland** ⌂ 15 Harcourt St. Dublin 2, Ireland ☎ 01/475-1632 🖶 01/475-1012 ⊕ www.elegant.ie. **Ireland's Blue Book** ⊠ 8 Mount St. Crescent, Dublin, South City Centre 2 ☎ 01/676-9914 ⊕ www. irelandsbluebook.com.

HOME EXCHANGES

With a direct home exchange, you stay in someone else's home while they stay in yours. Some outfits also deal with vacation homes, so you're not actually staying in someone's full-time residence, just their vacant weekend place.

🚩 Exchange Clubs **HomeLink International** ☎ 813/975-9825 or 800/638-3841 ⊕ www. homelink.org; $80 yearly for Web-only membership; $125 with Web access and two directories. **Home Exchange.com** ☎ 800/877-8723 ⊕ www. homeexchange.com charges; $49.95 yearly for a 1-year online listing; this is a Web-based company with no catalog. **Intervac U.S.** ☎ 800/756-4663 ⊕ www.intervacus.com; $128.88 yearly for a listing, online access, and a catalog; $78.88 without catalog.

HOSTELS

Hostels offer barebones lodging at low, low prices—often in shared dorm rooms with shared baths—to people of all ages, though the primary market is young travelers, especially students. Most hostels serve breakfast; dinner and/or shared cooking facilities may also be available. In some hostels, you aren't allowed to be in your room during the day, and there may be a curfew at night. Nevertheless, hostels provide a sense of community, with public rooms where travelers often gather to share stories. Many hostels are affiliated with Hostelling International (HI), an umbrella group of hostel associations with some 4,500 member properties in more than 70 countries. Other hostels are completely independent and may be nothing more than a really cheap hotel.

Membership in any HI association, open to travelers of all ages, allows you to stay in HI-affiliated hostels at member rates. One-year membership is about $28 for adults; hostels charge about $10–$30 per night. Members have priority if the hostel is full; they're also eligible for discounts around the world, even on rail and bus travel in some countries.

☎ **Hostelling International–USA** ☎ 301/495-1240 ⊕ www.hiusa.org. **Independent Holiday Hostels** ☎ 01/836-4700 ⊕ www.hostels-ireland.com. **Irish Youth Hostel Association** (An Óige) ✉ 67 Mountjoy St., North City Centre, Dublin 7 ☎ 01/830-4555 ⊕ www.irelandyha.org. **Northern Ireland Hostelling International** ✉ 22-32 Donegal Rd., University Area, Belfast BT12 5JN ☎ 28/9032-4733 ⊕ www.hini.org.uk.

HOTELS

Weigh all your options (we can't say this enough). Join "frequent guest" programs. You may get preferential treatment in room choice and/or upgrades in your favorite chains. Check general travel sites and hotel Web sites as not all chains are represented on all travel sites. Always research or inquire about special packages and corporate rates. If you prefer to book by phone, note you can sometimes get a better price if you call the hotel's local toll-free number (if one is available) rather than the central reservations number.

If your destination's high season is December through April and you're trying to book, say, in late April, you might save considerably by changing your dates by a week or two. Note, though, that many properties charge peak-season rates for your entire stay even if your travel dates

straddle peak and nonpeak seasons. High-end chains catering to businesspeople are often busy only on weekdays and often drop rates dramatically on weekends to fill up rooms. **Ask when rates go down.**

Watch out for hidden costs, including resort fees, energy surcharges, and "convenience" fees for such things as unlimited local phone service you won't use and a free newspaper—possibly written in a language you can't read. Always verify whether local hotel taxes are or are not included in the rates you're quoted, so that you'll know the real price of your stay. In some places, taxes can add 20% or more to your bill. If you're traveling overseas **look for price guarantees,** which protect you against a falling dollar. With your rate locked in, you won't pay more, even if the price goes up in the local currency.

Standard features in most hotels include private bath, two twin beds (you can usually ask for a king-size instead), TV (often with VCR), free parking, and no-smoking rooms. There's usually no extra charge for these services. All hotels listed have private bath unless otherwise noted.

☎ Discount Hotel Rooms **Accommodations Express** ☎ 800/444-7666 or 800/277-1064. **Hotels.com** ☎ 800/219-4606 or 800/364-0291 ⊕ www.hotels.com. **Steigenberger Reservation Service** ☎ 800/223-5652 ⊕ www.srs-worldhotels.com. **Turbotrip.com** ☎ 800/473-7829 ⊕ w3.turbotrip.com.

☎ Information & Bookings **Ireland Hotels Federation** ☎ 01/497-6459 ⊕ www.irelandhotels.com. **ITB** ⊕ www.tourismireland.com. **Northern Ireland Hotels Federation** ☎ 28/9035-1110 ⊕ www.nihf.co.uk.

MAIL & SHIPPING

Outside of Dublin and Northern Ireland, postal codes aren't used; what's more important here is the county, so be sure to include it when addressing an envelope.

Letters by standard post take a week to 10 days to reach the United States and Canada, 3 to 5 days to reach the United Kingdom.

OVERNIGHT SERVICES

If your package or letter absolutely has to get there the next day there are several overnight services available in Ireland. The most extensive and inexpensive service is the SDS service offered by the national postal carrier, An Post. Letters and packages can be sent from main post offices to any destination in Ireland. International deliveries can be made to more than 200 destinations. The EMS Courier offers next-day prenoon delivery and it comes with a money-back guarantee for deliveries to Ireland and the United Kingdom. Sending documents to North America will take two working days, parcels three. This courier is available from Dublin, Cork, Galway, Waterford, Limerick, and Shannon. Sending documents by EMS to U.K. cities and New York costs from €17 to €36. A 4.5-kg (2-pound) parcel will cost about €25 to send within Ireland, €62 to the United Kingdom, and €95 to New York. Familiar global carriers such as DHL, Federal Express, and UPS also operate services in Ireland.

🔢 Local Contacts **DHL** ☎ 800/725-725 ⊕ www.dhl.ie. **FedEx** ☎ 800/535-800 ⊕ www.fedex.com/ie. **SDS Courier** ☎ 1890/367-737 ⊕ www.sds.ie. **UPS** ☎ 800/575-757 ⊕ www.ups.com.

POSTAL RATES

Airmail rates to the United States and Canada from the Irish Republic are €0.75 for letters and postcards. Rates are also €0.75 for letters and postcards to Europe. Mail to overseas can be sent economy or airmail. Letters and postcards within the Irish Republic cost €0.45.

Rates from Northern Ireland are 47p for letters and 47p for postcards (not over 10 grams) to the United States and Canada. Letters and postcards to Australia and New Zealand cost 72p. To the rest of the United Kingdom and the Irish Republic, rates are 32p for first-class letters and 23p for second-class.

RECEIVING MAIL

Mail can be held for collection at any post office for free for up to three months. It should be addressed to the recipient "c/o Poste Restante." In Dublin, use the General Post Office. The Irish postal service, known as An Post, has a Web site with a branch locator and loads of other postal information.

🔢 **An Post** ⊕ www.anpost.ie. **General Post Office** ✉ O'Connell St., Dublin 1 ☎ 01/705-8833.

MEALS & MEALTIMES

It wasn't so long ago that people shared jokes about Ireland's stodgy, overcooked, slightly gray food. But in the last decade there have been changes in all aspects of Irish life, including food and drink. The country is going through a culinary renaissance, and Dublin chefs are leading the charge. They're putting nouvelle spins on Irish favorites. And, spurred by a wave of new immigration, ethnic eateries of all types have sprung up in most major towns and cities. No longer, however, will you "enjoy" your favorite tipple in the blue haze of a smoke-filled pub. The Republic of Ireland became the first European country to ban smoking in all pubs and restaurants last year. This does not apply to Northern Ireland.

The restaurants we list are the cream of the crop in each price category. Properties indicated by an ✕⊡ are lodging establishments whose restaurant warrants a special trip.

IRISH SPECIALTIES

A postmodern renaissance in Irish cuisine has led to a pursuit for authenticity. Many of the finer restaurants in Dublin, Cork, and Galway now offer a couple of dishes that are variations on a traditional theme. *Coddle,* a boiled stew of bacon, sausage, and smoked meats, is an old Dublin favorite. A typical Irish breakfast includes fried eggs, rashers (bacon), black and white puddings (black pudding is made with pork, pork blood, cereals, and seasoning; white pudding is similar, but without the blood), sausage, tomatoes, beans, soda bread, and a pot of tea. Lunch might feature a hearty sandwich; dinners usually include meat, potatoes, and two vegetables. Some of the best food is found at family-run bed-and-breakfasts and in inexpensive cafés. Irish smoked salmon—usually served on brown soda bread with plenty of butter—is among the finest in the world, and many a wondrous dish has been created around the humble cockle and mussel, abundant in the clear Atlantic waters. Galway and the west are rapidly becoming famous for their oyster beds. Of course there's the omnipresent potato, too. The Irish have many words for the humble spud, and they've invented plenty of ways to serve it. The best of these is "boxty," a traditional pancake of once- and twice-cooked potatoes: it makes the perfect bed for a beef-and-Guinness stew, or the equally hearty lamb casserole. For more on the delights of the new (and old) Irish cuisine, see the introduction to the Where to Eat section in the Dublin chapter.

MEALTIMES

Breakfast is served from 7 to 10, lunch runs from 12:30 to 2:30, and dinners are usually mid-evening occasions.

Pubs are generally open Monday and Tuesday 10:30 AM–11:30 PM and Thursday–Saturday 10:30 AM–12:30 AM. On Sunday, pubs are open 12:30 PM–11 PM or later on certain Sundays. All pubs close on Christmas Day and Good Friday, but hotel bars are open for guests.

Pubs in Northern Ireland are open 11:30 AM–11 PM Monday–Saturday and 12:30 PM–2:30 PM and 7 PM–10 PM on Sunday (note that Sunday openings are at the owner's or manager's discretion).

Unless otherwise noted, the restaurants listed in this guide are open daily for lunch and dinner.

PAYING

Traveler's checks and credit cards are widely accepted, although it's cash-only at smaller pubs and takeout restaurants. For guidelines on tipping see Tipping below. Note that Dublin and Southeast chapters prices are a few euros higher.

CATEGORY	COST*
$$$$	over €29
$$$	€22–€29
$$	€15–€22
$	€8–€15
¢	under €8

*In Republic of Ireland: all prices are per person for a main course at dinner and are given in euros.

CATEGORY	COST*
$$$$	over £22
$$$	£18–£22
$$	£13–£18
$	£7–£13
¢	under £7

*In Northern Ireland: all prices are per person for a main course at dinner and are given in pounds sterling.

WINES, BEER & SPIRITS

All types of alcoholic beverages are available in Ireland. Beer and wine are sold in shops and supermarkets, and you can get drinks "to go" at some bars, although at inflated prices. Stout (Guinness, Murphy's, Beamish) is the Irish beer; whiskey comes in many brands, the most notable being Bushmills and Jameson, and is smoother and more blended than Scotch.

Was the service stellar or not up to snuff? Did the food give you shivers of delight or leave you cold? Did the prices and portions make you happy or sad? Rate restaurants and write your own reviews in Travel Ratings or start a discussion about your favorite places in Travel Talk on www.fodors.com. Your comments might even appear in our books. Yes, you, too, can be a correspondent!

MONEY MATTERS

A modest hotel in Dublin costs about €130 a night for two; this figure can be reduced to under €90 by staying in a registered guesthouse or inn, and reduced to about €45 by staying in a suburban B&B. Lunch, consisting of a good one-dish plate of bar food at a pub, costs around €8–€12; a sandwich at the same pub costs about €4. In Dublin's better restaurants, dinner will run €25–€40 per person, excluding drinks and tip.

Theater and entertainment in most places are inexpensive—about €18 for a good seat, and double that for a big-name, pop-music concert. For the price of a few drinks and (in Dublin and Killarney) a small entrance fee of about €2, you can spend a memorable evening at a *seisun* (pronounced say-*shoon*) in a music pub. Entrance to most public galleries is free, but stately homes and similar attractions charge anywhere from €4 to a whopping €8 per person.

Just about everything is more expensive in Dublin, so add at least 10% to these sample prices: cup of coffee, €1.80; pint of beer, €4.50; soda, €1.60; and 2-km (1-mi) taxi ride, €6. Travelers from the United Kingdom will find value when visiting Ireland. Due to the exchange rate, Canadians, Australians, New Zealanders, and—to a lesser extent, Americans—will find Ireland a little pricey when they convert costs to their home currency.

Hotels and meals in Northern Ireland are less expensive than in the United Kingdom and the Republic of Ireland. Also, the lower level of taxation makes taxable goods such as gasoline, alcoholic drinks, and tobacco cheaper.

Banks rarely have every foreign currency on hand, and it may take as long as a week to order. If you're planning to exchange funds before leaving home, don't wait until the last minute.

Prices throughout this guide are given for adults. Substantially reduced fees are almost always available for children, students, and senior citizens. For information on taxes, see Taxes.

ATMS & BANKS

Your own bank will probably charge a fee for using ATMs abroad; the foreign bank you use may also charge a fee. Nevertheless, you'll usually get a better rate of exchange via an ATM than you will at a currency-exchange office or even when changing money in a bank. And extracting funds as you need them is a safer option than carrying around a large amount of cash.

ATMs are found in all major towns and are, by far, the easiest way to keep yourself stocked with euros and pounds. Most major banks are connected to Cirrus or PLUS systems; there's a four-digit maximum for your PIN.

CREDIT CARDS

Throughout this guide, the following abbreviations are used: **AE**, American Express; **DC**, Diners Club; **MC**, MasterCard; and **V**, Visa.

It's a good idea to inform your credit-card company before you travel, especially if you're going abroad and don't travel internationally very often. Otherwise, the credit-card company might put a hold on your card owing to unusual activity—not a good thing halfway through your trip. Record all your credit card numbers—as well as the phone numbers to call if your cards are lost or stolen—in a safe place so you're prepared should something go wrong. Both MasterCard and Visa have general numbers you can call (collect if you're abroad) if your card is lost, but you're better off calling the number of your issuing bank since MasterCard and Visa usually just transfer you to your bank; your bank's number is usually printed on your card.

If you plan to use your credit card for cash advances, you'll need to apply for a PIN at least two weeks before your trip. Although it's usually cheaper (and safer) to use a credit card abroad for large purchases (so you can cancel payments or be reimbursed if there's a problem), note that some credit card companies *and* the banks that issue them add substantial percentages to all foreign transactions, whether they're done in a foreign currency or not. Check on these fees before leaving home so that there won't be any surprises when you get the bill.

Before you charge something, ask the merchant whether he or she plans to do a dynamic currency conversion (DCC). In such a transaction the credit-card *processor* (shop, restaurant, or hotel, not Visa or MasterCard) converts the currency and charges you in dollars. In most cases you'll pay the merchant a 3% fee for this service in addition to any credit-card company and issuing-bank foreign-transaction surcharges.

DCC programs are becoming increasingly widespread. Merchants who participate in them are supposed to ask whether you want to be charged in dollars or the local currency, but they don't always do so. And even if they do offer you a choice, they may well avoid mentioning the additional surcharges. The good news is that you *do* have a choice. And if this practice really gets your goat, you can avoid it entirely thanks to American Express; with its cards, DCC simply isn't an option.

Note that when using your credit card, **check that the merchant is putting the transaction through in euros or pounds sterling.** If he or she puts it through in the currency of your home country—a transaction called a dynamic currency conversion—the exchange rate might be less favorable and the service charges higher than if you allow the credit-card company to do the conversion for you. Be sure to ask at the time, and insist on being billed in euros to get the most advantageous rate and avoid the service charge.

☎ Reporting Lost Cards American Express ☎ 800/992-3404 in U.S., 336/393-1111 collect from abroad ⊕ www.americanexpress.com. **Diners Club** ☎ 800/234-6377 in U.S., 303/799-1504 collect from abroad ⊕ www.dinersclub.com. **Discover** ☎ 800/347-2683 in U.S., 801/902-3100 collect from abroad ⊕ www.discovercard.com. **MasterCard** ☎ 800/622-7747 in U.S., 636/722-7111 collect from abroad ⊕ www.mastercard.com. **Visa** ☎ 800/847-2911 in U.S., 410/581-9994 collect from abroad ⊕ www.visa.com.

CURRENCY & EXCHANGE

The Irish Republic is a member of the European Monetary Union (EMU). Euro notes come in denominations of €500, €200, €100, €50, €20, €10, and €5. The euro is divided into 100 cents, and coins are available as €2 and €1 and 50, 20, 10, 5, 2, and 1 cent.

The unit of currency in Northern Ireland is the pound sterling (£), divided into 100 pence (p). The bills (called notes) are 50, 20, 10, and 5 pounds. Coins are £2, £1, 50p, 20p, 10p, 5p, 2p, and 1p. The bank of Northern Ireland prints its own notes, which look different from the English or Scottish Sterling.

Check out today's rates at www.oanda.com.

At this writing, one euro is equal to U.S. $0.81. One pound sterling is equal to U.S. $1.83. Rates fluctuate regularly, though, particularly for the euro, so monitor them closely.

Even if a currency exchange booth has a sign promising no commission, rest assured that there's some kind of huge, hidden fee. (Oh . . . that's right. The sign didn't say no *fee*.) And, in terms of rates, you're almost always better off getting foreign currency through an ATM or exchanging money at a bank.

☎ Exchange Rate Information Yahoo Finance ⊕ http://finance.yahoo.com/currency. **Oanda.com** ⊕ www.oanda.com also allows you to print out a handy table with the current day's conversion rates. **XE.com** ⊕ www.xe.com.

TRAVELER'S CHECKS & CARDS

Some consider this the currency of the cave man, and it's true that fewer establishments accept traveler's checks these days. Nevertheless, they're a cheap and secure way to carry extra money, particularly on trips to urban areas. Both Citibank (under the Visa brand) and American Express issue traveler's checks in the United States, but Amex is better known and more widely accepted; you can also avoid hefty surcharges by cashing Amex checks at Amex offices. Whatever you do, keep track of all the serial numbers in case the checks are lost or stolen.

American Express now offers a stored-value card called a Travelers Cheque Card, which you can use wherever American Express credit cards are accepted, including ATMs. The card can carry a minimum of $300 and a maximum of $2,700, and it's a very safe way to carry your funds. Although you can get replacement funds in 24 hours if your card is lost or stolen, it doesn't really strike us as a very good deal. In addition to a high initial cost ($14.95 to set up the card, plus $5 each time you "reload"), you still have to pay a 2% fee for each purchase in a foreign currency (similar to that of any credit card). Further, each time you use the card in an ATM you pay a transaction fee of $2.50 on top of the 2% transaction fee for the conversion—add it all up and it can be considerably more than you would pay for simply using your own ATM card. Regular traveler's checks are just as secure and cost less.

🔢 **American Express** ☎ 888/412-6945 in U.S., 801/945-9450 collect outside of U.S. to add value or speak to customer service ⊕ www.americanexpress. com.

PACKING

WHAT YOU'LL NEED IN IRELAND

In Ireland you can experience all four seasons in a day. There can be damp chilly stretches even in July and August, the warmest months of the year. Layers are the best way to go. Pack several long- and short-sleeve T-shirts (in winter, some should be thermal or silk), a sweatshirt, a lightweight sweater, a heavyweight sweater, and a hooded, waterproof windbreaker that's large enough to go over several layers if necessary. A portable umbrella is absolutely essential, and the smaller and lighter it is, the better, as you'll want it with you every second. You should bring at least two pairs of walking shoes; footwear can get soaked in minutes and then take hours to dry.

The Irish are generally informal about clothes. In the more expensive hotels and restaurants people dress formally for dinner, and a jacket and tie may be required in bars after 7 PM, but very few places operate a strict dress policy. Old or tattered blue jeans and running shoes are forbidden in certain bars and dance clubs.

If you're used to packing things or stowing dirty clothes in plastic shopping or drawstring bags, bring your own. About the only place you can find them here is in the closets of better hotel rooms (for on-site dry cleaning and laundry). Plastic bags carry a 15-cent government levy and can be sold by supermarkets, but it's illegal to give them away. So most stores use paper bags, or recycle boxes. Also, although salesclerks are good about wrapping crystal and pottery for travel, you can never be too careful with such items; bring along some bubble wrap.

PASSPORTS & VISAS

All U.S. citizens, even infants, need a valid passport to enter Ireland for stays of up to 90 days. Citizens of the United Kingdom, when traveling on flights departing from Great Britain, do not need a passport to enter Ireland but it's advisable to carry some form of photo ID. Passport requirements for Northern Ireland are the same as for the republic.

PASSPORTS

We're always surprised at how few Americans have passports—only 25% at this writing, though the number is expected to grow in coming years, when it becomes impossible to reenter the United States from trips to neighboring Canada or Mexico without one. Remember this: a passport verifies both your identity and nationality—a great reason to have one.

U.S. passports are valid for 10 years. Applications are available online and at post offices as well as passport offices. The cost to apply is $97 for adults, $82 for children under 16; renewals are $67. Allow six weeks to process the paperwork for either a new or renewed passport. For an expediting fee of $60, you can reduce the time to about two weeks. If your trip is less than two weeks away, you can get a passport even more rapidly by going to a passport office with the necessary documentation. Private expediters can get things done in as little as 48 hours but charge hefty fees for their services. Children under 14 must appear in person to apply for or renew a passport; both parents must accompany the child (or send a notarized statement with their permission) and provide proof of their relationship to the child.

Before your trip, make two copies of your passport's data page (one for someone at home and another for you to carry separately). Or scan the page and e-mail it to someone at home and/or yourself.

VISAS

Visas are essentially formal permissions to travel to a country. Visas allow countries to keep track of you and other visitors and to generate revenue (from visa fees). You *always* need a visa to enter a foreign country; however, many countries routinely issue tourist visas on arrival, particularly to U.S. citizens. When your passport is stamped or scanned in the immigration line, you're actually being issued a visa. Sometimes you have to stand in a separate line and pay a small fee to get your stamp before going through immigration, but you can still do this at the airport on arrival. Getting a visa isn't always that easy. Some countries require you to arrange for one in advance of your trip. There's usually—but not always—a fee involved, and said fee may be nominal ($10 or less) or substantial ($100 or more).

If you must apply for a visa in advance, you can usually do it in person or by mail. When you apply by mail, you send your passport to a designated consulate, where your passport will be examined and the visa issued. Expediters—usually the same ones who handle expedited passport applications—can do all the work to obtain your visa for you; however, there's always an additional cost (often more than $50 per visa).

Most visas limit you to a single trip—basically during the actual dates of your planned vacation. Other visas allow you to visit as many times as you wish for a specific period of time. Remember that requirements change, sometimes at the drop of a hat, and the burden is on you to make sure that you have the appropriate visas. Otherwise, you'll be turned away at the airport or, worse, deported after you arrive in the country. No company or travel insurer gives refunds if your travel plans are disrupted because you didn't have the correct visa.

⤤ U.S. Passport Information U.S. Department of State ☎ 877/487-2778 ⊕ http://travel.state.gov/passport

⤤ U.S. Passport & Visa Expediters A. Briggs Passport & Visa Expeditors ☎ 800/806-0581 or 202/464-3000 ⊕ www.abriggs.com. **American Passport Express** ☎ 800/455-5166 or 603/559-9888 ⊕ www.americanpassport.com. **Passport Express** ☎ 800/362-8196 or 401/272-4612 ⊕ www.passportexpress.com. **Travel Document Systems** ☎ 800/874-5100 or 202/638-3800 ⊕ www.traveldocs.com. **Travel the World Visas** ☎ 866/886-8472 or 301/495-7700 ⊕ www.world-visa.com.

PHONES

The good news is that you can now make a direct-dial telephone call from virtually any point on earth. The bad news? You can't always do so cheaply. Calling from a hotel is almost always the most expensive option; hotels usually add huge surcharges to all calls, particularly international ones. In some countries you can phone from call centers or even the post office. Calling cards usually keep costs to a minimum, but only if you purchase them locally. And then there are mobile phones ⇨ *below*, which are sometimes more prevalent—particularly in the developing world—than land lines; as expensive as mobile phone calls can be, they're still usually a much cheaper option than calling from your hotel.

Ireland's telephone system is up to the standards of the United Kingdom and the United States. Direct-dialing is common; local phone numbers have five to eight digits. You can make international calls from most phones, and some cell phones also work here, depending on the carrier.

Do not make calls from your hotel room unless it's absolutely necessary. Practically all hotels add 200% to 300% to the cost.

The country code for Ireland is 353; for Northern Ireland, which is part of the United Kingdom telephone system, it's 44. The local area code for Northern Ireland is 028. However, when dialing Northern Ireland from the republic you can simply dial 048 without using the U.K. country code. When dialing an Irish number from abroad, drop the initial 0 from the local area code. The country code is 1 for the United States and Canada, 61 for Australia, 64 for New Zealand, and 44 for the United Kingdom.

Public pay phones can be found in street booths and in restaurants, hotels, bars, and shops, some of which display a sign saying YOU CAN PHONE FROM HERE. There are at least three models of pay phones; read the instructions or ask for assistance.

CALLING WITHIN IRELAND

If the operator has to connect your call, it will cost at least one-third more than direct dial.

⤤ Directory Information Republic of Ireland ☎ 11811 for directory inquiries in the republic and Northern Ireland, 11818 for U.K. and international numbers, 114 for operator assistance with international calls, 10 for operator assistance for calls in Ireland, Northern Ireland, and U.K. **Northern Ireland and the U.K.** ☎ 192 for directory inquiries in Northern Ireland and U.K., 153 for international directory inquiries, which includes the republic, 155 for the international operator, 100 for operator assistance for calls in U.K. and Northern Ireland.

To make a local call just dial the number direct. Public phones take either coins (€0.25 for a call) or cards, but not both. At coin phones just pick up the receiver and deposit the money before you dial the number. At card phones pick up the receiver, wait until the display tells you to insert the card, then dial. In the republic, €0.25 will buy you a three-minute local call; around €1 is needed for a three-minute long-distance call within the republic. In Northern Ireland, a local call costs 10p.

To make a long-distance call, dial the area code, then the number. The local code for Northern Ireland is 028, unless you're dialing from the republic, in which case you dial 048 or 004428, followed by the eight-digit number.

CALLING OUTSIDE IRELAND

The country code is 1 for the United States. The international prefix from Ireland is 00. For calls to Great Britain (except Northern Ireland), dial 0044 before the exchange code, and drop the initial zero of the local code. For the United States and Canada dial 001, for Australia 0061, and for New Zealand 0064.

🚩 **Access Codes AT&T Direct** ☎ 1800/550-000 from Republic of Ireland, 0500/890-011 from Northern Ireland. **MCI WorldPhone** ☎ 1800/551-001 from Republic of Ireland, 0800/890-222 from Northern Ireland using British Telecom, BT, 0500/890-222 using Cable & Wireless, C&W. **Sprint International Access** ☎ 1800/552-001 from Republic of Ireland, 0800/890-877 from Northern Ireland using BT, 0500/890-877 using C&W.

CALLING CARDS

"Callcards" are sold in post offices and newsagents. These come in denominations of 10, 20, and 50 units and range in price from €10 to €30.

MOBILE PHONES

If you have a multiband phone (some countries use different frequencies than what's used in the United States) and your service provider uses the world-standard GSM network (as do T-Mobile, Cingular, and Verizon), you can probably use your phone abroad. Roaming fees can be steep, though: 99¢ a minute is considered reasonable. And overseas, you normally pay the toll charges for incoming calls. It's almost always cheaper to send a text message than to make a call because text messages have a low set fee (often less than 5¢).

If you just want to make local calls, consider buying a new SIM card (note that your provider may have to unlock your phone for you to use a different SIM card) and a prepaid service plan in the destination. You'll then have a local number and can make local calls at local rates. If your trip is extensive you could also simply buy a new cell phone in your destination as the initial cost will be offset over time.

If you travel internationally frequently, save one of your old mobile phones or buy a cheap one on the Internet; ask your cell phone company to unlock it for you, and take it with you as a travel phone, buying a new SIM card with pay-as-you-go service in each destination.

🚩 **Cellular Abroad** ☎ 800/287-3020 or 310/829-6878 ⊕ www.cellularabroad.com rents cell phones and sells country-specific SIM cards as well as mobile phones that work in many countries. **Mobal** ☎ 888/888-9162 ⊕ www.mobalrental.com rents mobiles and sells GSM phones ($49 or $99) that will operate in 140 countries. Per-call rates vary throughout the world. **Planet Fone** ☎ 888/988-4777 ⊕ www.planetfone.com rents cell phones, but the per-minute rates are expensive.

RESTROOMS

Public restrooms are in short supply in Ireland. They'll be easy enough to find in public places such as airports, train stations, and shopping malls, but if you don't find yourself in one of these locations your best bet is to look for the nearest pub (never more than a few minutes away in Ireland!). Restrooms are often labeled in Irish—Fir (men) and Mná. Pubs are increasingly putting up signs that restrooms are for customers only—but this is difficult to enforce. If it's outside of shopping or pub hours your last option may be the nearest hotel. Most gas stations will have toilets available. Only toilets in hotels or shopping centers will be up to a polished North American standard. Although many toilets look well-worn they are generally clean. Unfortunately, few toilets are heated and an open window is typically used for ventilation, making for uncomfortably cold restrooms in the colder months.

The Bathroom Diaries is a Web site that's flush with unsanitized info on restrooms the world over—each one located, reviewed, and rated.

🚻 Find a Loo **The Bathroom Diaries** ⊕ www.thebathroomdiaries.com

SAFETY

Distribute your cash, credit cards, IDs, and other valuables between a deep front pocket, an inside jacket or vest pocket, and a hidden money pouch. Don't reach for the money pouch once you're in public.

The theft of car radios, mobile phones, cameras, video recorders, and other items of value from cars is common in Dublin and other major cities and towns. Never leave any valuable items on car seats or in the foot space between the back and front seats or in glove compartments. In fact, never leave anything whatsoever in sight in your car—even if you're leaving it for only a short time. You should also think twice about leaving valuables in your car while visiting tourist attractions anywhere in the country.

GOVERNMENT ADVISORIES

As different countries have different worldviews, look at travel advisories from a range of governments to get more of a sense of what's going on out there. And be sure to parse the language carefully. For example, a warning to "avoid all travel" carries more weight than one urging you to "avoid nonessential travel," and both are much stronger than a plea to "exercise caution." A U.S. government travel warning is more permanent (though not necessarily more serious) than a so-called public announcement, which carries an expiration date.

The U.S. Department of State's Web site has more than just travel warnings and advisories. The consular information sheets issued for every country have general safety tips, entry requirements (though be sure to verify these with the country's embassy), and other useful details.

Consider registering online with the state department (https://travelregistration.state.gov/ibrs/), so the government will know to look for you should a crisis occur in the country you're visiting. If you travel frequently also look into the Registered Traveler program of the Transportation Security Administration (TSA; www.tsa.gov). The program, which is still being tested in five U.S. airports, is designed to cut down on gridlock at security checkpoints by allowing prescreened travelers to pass quickly through kiosks that scan an iris and/or a fingerprint. How sci-fi is that?

🚩 General Information & Warnings **U.S. Department of State** ⊕ www.travel.state.gov.

TAXES

When making a purchase, ask for a V.A.T. refund form and find out whether the merchant gives refunds—not all stores do, nor are they required to. Have the form stamped like any customs form by customs officials when you leave the country or, if you're visiting several European Union countries, when you leave the EU. Be ready to show customs officials what you've bought (pack purchases together, in your carry-on luggage); budget extra time for this. After you're through passport control, take the form to a refund-service counter for an on-the-spot refund (which is usually the quickest and easiest option), or mail it to the address on the form (or the envelope with it) after you arrive home. You receive the total refund stated on the form, but the processing time can be long, especially if you request a credit-card adjustment.

Global Refund is a Europe-wide service with 225,000 affiliated stores and more than 700 refund counters at major airports and border crossings. Its refund form, called a Tax Free Check, is the most common across the European continent. The service issues refunds in the form of cash, check, or credit-card adjustment.

When leaving the Irish Republic, U.S. and Canadian visitors get a refund of the value-added tax (V.A.T.), which currently accounts for a hefty 21% of the purchase price of many goods and 13.5% of those that fall outside the luxury category. Apart from clothing, most items of interest to visitors, right down to ordinary toilet soap, are rated at 21%. V.A.T. is not refundable on accommodation, car rental, meals, or any other form of personal services received on vacation.

Many crafts outlets and department stores operate a system called Cashback, which enables U.S. and Canadian visitors to collect V.A.T. rebates in the currency of their choice at Dublin or Shannon Airport on departure. Some stores give you the rebate at the register; with others you claim your refund after you've returned home. Refund forms must be picked up at the time of purchase, and they must be stamped by customs before you leave for home. If a store gives you a refund at the register, you'll also be given papers to have stamped by customs; you'll then put the papers in an envelope (also provided by the store) and mail it before you leave. Most major stores deduct V.A.T. at the time of sale if goods are to be shipped overseas; however, there's a shipping charge.

When leaving Northern Ireland, U.S. and Canadian visitors can also get a refund of the 17.5% V.A.T. by the over-the-counter and the direct-export methods. Most larger stores provide these services on request and will handle the paperwork. For the over-the-counter method, you must spend more than £75 in one store. Ask the store for Form V.A.T. 407 (you must have identification—passports are best), to be given to customs when you leave the country. The refund will be forwarded to you in about eight weeks (minus a small service charge) either in the form of a sterling check or as a credit to your charge card. The direct-export method, where the goods are shipped directly to your home, is more cumbersome. V.A.T. Form 407/1/93 must be certified by customs, police, or a notary public when you get home and then sent back to the store, which will refund your money.

📷 **V.A.T. Refunds Global Refund** ☎ 800/566–9828 ⊕ www.globalrefund.com.

TIME

Dublin is five hours ahead of New York and eight hours ahead of Los Angeles.

TIPPING

In some hotels and restaurants a service charge of around 10%—rising to 15% in plush spots—is added to the bill. If in doubt, ask whether service is included. In places where it's included, tipping isn't necessary unless you have received particularly good service. If there's no service charge, add a minimum of 10% to the total. Taxi drivers or Hackney cabs, who make the trip for a prearranged sum, don't expect tips. There are few porters and plenty of baggage trolleys at airports, so tipping is usually not an issue; if you use a porter, €1 is the minimum. Tip hotel porters at least €1 per suitcase. Hairdressers normally expect about 10% of the total spent. You don't tip in pubs, but for waiter service in a bar, a hotel lounge, or a Dublin lounge bar, leave about €1. It's not customary to tip for concierge service.

TRAIN TRAVEL

The republic's Irish Rail trains are generally reliable, reasonably priced, and comfortable. You can easily reach all the principal towns from Dublin, though services between provincial cities are roundabout. To get to Cork City from Wexford, for example, you have to go via Limerick Junction. It's often quicker, though perhaps less comfortable, to take a bus. Most mainline trains have one standard class. Round-trip tickets are usually cheapest.

Northern Ireland Railways has three main rail routes, all operating out of Belfast's Central Station. These are north to Derry, via Ballymena and Coleraine; east to Bangor along the shores of Belfast Lough; and south to Dublin and the Irish Republic. Note that Eurailpasses aren't valid in Northern Ireland.

You should plan to be at the train station at least 30 minutes before your train departs to ensure you'll get a seat. It's not uncommon on busier routes to find that you have to stand since all seats have been sold and taken.

CUTTING COSTS

To save money, **look into rail passes.** But be aware that if you don't plan to cover many miles, you may come out ahead by buying individual tickets.

Ireland (excluding Northern Ireland) is one of 17 countries in which you can **use Eurailpasses,** which provide unlimited first-class rail travel, in all of the participating countries, for the duration of the pass. If you plan to rack up the miles, get a standard pass. These are available for 15 days ($588), 21 days ($762), one month ($946), two months ($1,338), and three months ($1,654). In addition to standard Eurailpasses, **ask about special rail-pass plans.** Among these are the Eurail Youthpass (for those under age 26), the Eurail Saverpass (which gives a discount for two or more people traveling together), a Eurail Flexipass (which allows a certain number of travel days within a set period), the Euraildrive Pass and the Europass Drive (which combines travel by train and rental car). Whichever pass you choose, you must **purchase your pass before you leave** for Europe.

The Irish Explorer Rail & Bus Pass covers all the state-run and national railways and bus lines throughout the republic. It does not apply to the North or to transportation within cities. An eight-day ticket for use on buses *and* trains during a 15-day period is €203. The Emerald Isle Card offers unlimited bus and train travel anywhere in Ireland and Northern Ireland, valid within cities as well. An 8-day pass gives you eight days of travel over a 15-day period; it costs roughly €228. A pass for 15 days of travel over a 30-day period costs about €340. Irish Rail International provides details on both passes.

In Northern Ireland, the **Freedom of Northern Ireland Pass** entitling you to seven days' unlimited travel on scheduled bus and rail services, April–October, is available from main Northern Ireland Railway stations. It costs £47 for adults (half price for children under 12 and se-

nior citizens). Interrail tickets are also valid in Northern Ireland.

Information & Passes CIE Tours International ☎ 800/243-8687 ⊕ www.cietours.com. **DER Travel Services** ☎ 888/337-7350 ⊕ www.dertravel.com. **Rail Europe** ☎ 800/438-7245 ⊕ www.raileurope.com.

FARES & SCHEDULES

Train schedules are easy to obtain and available in a variety of formats. Irish Rail and Northern Ireland Rail have Web sites that produce a schedule in response to your input of an itinerary. Alternatively you can visit any train station to obtain a printed schedule or call either company's customer service line. Take special note of schedules when traveling on holiday weekends as schedules are usually changed. Both rail services print amended schedules well in advance.

Sample fares? A return ticket from Dublin to Cork will cost around €51; Dublin to Belfast is approximately €46.

Train Information Irish Rail (Iarnrod Éireann) ☎ 01/836-6222 ⊕ www.irishrail.ie is the rail division of CIE. **Northern Ireland Railways** ☎ 028/9089-9411 ⊕ www.translink.co.uk.

Belfast Central Station ⊠ East Bridge St., Belfast BT1 3PB ☎ 028/9089-9400 ⊕ www.translink.co.uk. **Connolly Station** ⊠ Amiens St., Dublin 1 ☎ 01/703-2358 ⊕ www.irishrail.ie. **Galway Station** ⊠ Station Rd., Galway ☎ 091/562-730 ⊕ www.irishrail.ie. **Heuston Station** ⊠ Dublin 8 ☎ 01/703-3299 ⊕ www.irishrail.ie. **Kent Station** ⊠ Lower Glenmuir Rd., Cork ☎ 021/450-6766 ⊕ www.irishrail.ie.

PAYING

Tickets can be purchased online or at the train station. Cash, traveler's checks, and credit-card payments are accepted. You must pay in the local currency. In Dublin, Connolly and Heuston stations have automated ticket machines that take either cash or credit-card payments, offering a convenient way to avoid long lines at ticket windows.

RESERVATIONS

Many travelers assume that rail passes guarantee them seats on the trains they wish to ride. Not so. You need to **book**

seats ahead even if you're using a rail pass. Seat reservations are required on some European trains, particularly high-speed trains, and are a good idea on trains that may be crowded—particularly in summer on popular routes. You'll also need a reservation if you purchase sleeping accommodations.

There's only one class of train travel in Ireland (with the exception of the Enterprise, the express train that travels from Dublin to Belfast, for which you can purchase a First Class or Standard Class ticket and the Dublin to Cork train). In general, specific seat reservations can only be made for trains deemed to be busy (ask when buying your ticket if they're taking reservations for your route). For example, the train traveling from Dublin to Cork on a Friday evening is considered a peak time, thanks to all the students and business travelers heading home for the weekend. On such a route, you would just be able to buy a ticket, not a specific seat designation. At peak hours and for popular routes, it's advisable to arrive early at the station to purchase your ticket (or buy it online) or you may find yourself standing for a significant portion of your journey.

TRAVEL AGENCIES

If you use an agent—brick-and-mortar or virtual—you'll pay a fee for the service. And know that the service you get from some online agents isn't comprehensive. For example Expedia or Travelocity don't search for prices on budget airlines like JetBlue or small foreign carriers. That said, some agents (online or not) *do* have access to fares that are difficult to find otherwise, and the savings can more than make up for any surcharge.

A knowledgeable brick-and-mortar travel agent can be a godsend if you're booking a cruise, a package trip that's not available to you directly, an air pass, or a complicated itinerary including several overseas flights. What's more, travel agents that specialize in a destination may have exclusive access to certain deals and insider information on things such as charter flights. Agents who specialize in types of travelers (senior citizens, gays and lesbians, natur-

ists) or types of trips (cruises, luxury travel, safaris) can also be invaluable.

A top-notch agent planning your trip to Russia will make sure you get the correct visa application and complete it on time; the agent booking your cruise may get you a cabin upgrade or arrange to have a bottle of champagne chilling in your cabin when you embark. And complain about the surcharges all you like, but when things don't work out the way you'd hoped, it's nice to have an agent to put things right.

🛈 Agent Resources **American Society of Travel Agents** ☎ 703/739-2782 ⊕ www.travelsense.org. 🛈 Online Agents **Expedia** ⊕ www.expedia.com. **Onetravel.com** ⊕ www.onetravel.com. **Orbitz** ⊕ www.orbitz.com. **Priceline.com** ⊕ www. priceline.com. **Travelocity** ⊕ www.travelocity.com.

VISITOR INFORMATION

For information on travel in the Irish Republic, contact **Tourism Ireland** (⊕ www. discoverireland.com), the international marketing authority for **Fáilte Ireland** (pronounced *fal*-cha), as the tourist information network in called within the Republic of Ireland. Information on travel in the North is available from the **Northern Ireland Tourist Board** (NITB; ⊕ www. discovernorthernireland.com).

🛈 **Fáilte Ireland** ✉ Baggot St. Bridge, Dublin 2 ☎ 01/602-4000, 1850/230-330 toll-free within Ireland ⊕ www.ireland.ie. **U.K.- Tourism Ireland** ✉ Nation House, 103 Wigmore St., London W1U IQS ☎ 020/7518-0800 ⊕ www.discoverireland.com. **U.S.- Tourism Ireland** ✉ 345 Park Ave., 17th fl., New York, NY 10154 ☎ 212/418-0800 ⊕ www. discoverireland.com. 🛈 **NITB Northern Ireland** ✉ 59 North St., Belfast BT1 1NB ☎ 028/9023-1221. **Canada** ✉ 2 Bloor St. W, Suite 1501, Toronto, Ontario M4W 3E2 ☎ 416/925-6368. **U.K.** ✉ 24 Haymarket, London SW1 4DG ☎ 020/7766-9920, 08701/555-250 info line. **U.S.** ✉ 551 5th Ave., Suite 701, New York, NY 10176 ☎ 212/922-0101 or 800/326-0036.

WEB SITES

We're really proud of our Web site: Fodors.com is a great place to begin any journey. Scan Travel Wire for suggested itineraries, travel deals, restaurant and hotel openings, and other up-to-the-minute info. Check out Booking to research prices and book plane tickets, hotel rooms, rental cars, and vacation packages. Head to Travel Talk for on-the-ground pointers from travelers who frequent our message boards. You can also link to loads of other travel-related resources.

After your trip, be sure to rate the places you visited and share your experiences and travel tips with us and other Fodorites in Travel Ratings and Travel Talk on www. fodors.com.

For lots of entertaining bits—Irish and otherwise—visit ⊕ www.irishabroad.com. Some of the most popular sites are Browse Ireland (⊕ www.browseireland.com) and Heritage Ireland (⊕ www.heritageireland. ie). The Web site ⊕ www.ireland-information.com is dedicated to providing as many free resources and as much free information about Ireland as possible on an array of topics from genealogy to shopping. For a central directory of links to all things Irish, log on to ⊕ www.finditireland.com. Comhaltas Ceoltóirí Eireann is an association that promotes the music, culture, and art of Ireland and its Web site ⊕ www.comhaltas.com has helpful news about the Irish traditional music scene. For listings of all music, film, and theater events, see ⊕ www.entertainment.ie. The site of ⊕ www.ireland-now.com can provide history legend and lore to enhance your visit to Ireland. Keep in mind that many of the leading newspapers of Ireland (⇨ Media) have Web sites, which can be gold mines of timely information. For a weekly newsletter to keep Irish people abroad up-to-date on events at home, log on to ⊕ www.emigrant.ie.

Officially designated Heritage Towns are featured on ⊕ www.heritagetowns.com. For information on arts events of all kinds, try ⊕ www.art.ie, which is affiliated with and has links to the arts councils of both the Irish Republic and Northern Ireland. For more information on counties in the west of Ireland, try ⊕ www.trueireland. com or ⊕ www.irelandwest.ie. A handy regional site is ⊕ www.southeastireland. com. Portions of the Bord Fáilte's eloquent magazine, *Ireland of the Welcomes*, are available online at ⊕ www. irelandofthewelcomes.com. For an eloquent site devoted to some of Ireland's most historic buildings, see ⊕ www.irish-architecture.com, while ⊕ www. castlesireland.com and ⊕ www. celticcastles.com will please the castle lover. Green-thumbers will enjoy ⊕ www. gardensireland.com.

🎵 Currency Conversion **Google** ⊕ www.google. com does currency conversion. Just type in the amount you want to convert and an explanation of how you want it converted (e.g., "14 Swiss francs in dollars"), and then voila. **XE.com** ⊕ www.xe.com is a good currency conversion Web site.

🎵 Time Zones **Timeanddate.com** ⊕ www. timeanddate.com/worldclock can help you figure out the correct time anywhere in the world.

🎵 Weather **Accuweather.com** ⊕ www. accuweather.com is an independent weather-forecasting service with especially good coverage of hurricanes. **Weather.com** ⊕ www.weather.com is the Web site for the Weather Channel.

🎵 Other Resources **CIA World Factbook** ⊕ www. odci.gov/cia/publications/factbook/index.html has profiles of every country in the world. It's a good source if you need some quick facts and figures.

INDEX

PHOTO CREDITS

NOTES

ABOUT OUR WRITERS

For our coverage of Dublin, Anto Howard has checked every fact, burnished every metaphor to the fine gleam of ancient brogues, and has so lovingly described the towns and villages found in the Dublin Environs chapter that even their natives will leave for the pleasure of coming back. Six post-graduate years of living in New York City recently convinced Anto of the charms of his native Ireland and he duly returned to take up residence in Dublin. He has written and edited books and articles about such far-flung places as Costa Rica, Las Vegas, and Russia, and has contributed to such publications as *National Geographic Traveler* and *Esat Online.* Anto (christened Anthony—Dubliners have a habit of abbreviating perfectly good names) is also a playwright, and his shows have been produced in Dublin and in New York.

Alannah Hopkin grew up in London but spent most of her childhood summers on her uncle's farm near Kinsale, where she learned two of the most important things in life: how to ride a horse and how to sail a boat. After graduate studies in Irish literature, she worked as a writer in London—but ancestral voices were calling her home, and she spent more and more time in County Cork, where horses and boats were easier to find. After publishing her first novel, *A Joke Goes A Long Way in the Country,* she made the big leap, and moved to Kinsale for a trial six months—and is still there 20 years later. Another novel was followed by a book on the cult of St. Patrick and an acclaimed guide to the pleasures of County Cork. She has written on travel and the arts for the London *Sunday Times,* contributes regularly to the *Irish Examiner* and the *Irish Times,* and is writing a book on West Cork. She has worked on *Fodor's Ireland* since 1985, and this year she updated the Southwest, West, and Smart Travel Tips chapters.

Updater of our Northwest and Ireland chapters, Allison Morri[s] born city girl. A mother of three—relatively small even by modern-day Irish standards (she comes from a family of nine)—she juggles motherhood rather chaotically with a decade-long career as a journalist. Having worked for several years as a reporter for *The Andersonstown News,* she now acts in a free-lance capacity for a number of leading Northern Ireland daily newspapers. Getting away from city life is facilitated with long weekends on the Northwest coast. With the fire going and a "half" of Guinness in hand, the vocal cords are invariably stretched as the siblings of the extended Morris clan—some more talented than others—get down to some serious singing. It's just as well the nearest neighbor is half a mile away!

Born in "the Kingdom" of Kerry, the urge to roam infected John Daly from an early age. Taking a two-week vacation in New York after university finals that morphed into a decade spent roaming the hinterland of America from Alaska to Texas, the lure of home eventually drew him back across the Atlantic. After stints as owner of a pub in Dublin and a restaurant in Cork, a midlife career U-turn into writing saw him settle in Kinsale. With a large extended family that's never seen him stuck for a bed anywhere from Cashel to Wexford, the task of updating the Midlands and Southeast chapters provided an added bonus of visiting cousins and relations normally encountered only at weddings and christenings. A regular contributor to the *Irish Independent,* the *Irish Examiner* and *Hibernia* magazine, he recently finished his first television project—a documentary on Calcutta's street children that premiered at last year's Galway Film Festival. Drawn inexorably homeward to his native Kerry, he's currently working on the next television production, a behind-the-scenes look at Puck Fair, Ireland's oldest festival.